DEPARTMENT OF COMMERCE
BUREAU OF THE CENSUS
WASHINGTON

ABSTRACT

OF THE

FOURTEENTH CENSUS

OF THE

UNITED STATES

1920

For sale by the Superintendent of Documents, Washington
Cloth, $1.50

WASHINGTON
GOVERNMENT PRINTING OFFICE
1923

REPORTS OF THE FOURTEENTH CENSUS.

POPULATION:

Volume   I.—NUMBER AND DISTRIBUTION OF INHABITANTS.
Volume   II.—GENERAL REPORT AND ANALYTICAL TABLES.
Volume   III.—COMPOSITION AND CHARACTERISTICS OF THE POPULATION, BY STATES.
Volume   IV.—OCCUPATIONS.

AGRICULTURE:

Volume   V.—GENERAL REPORT AND ANALYTICAL TABLES.
Volume   VI.—REPORTS FOR STATES, WITH STATISTICS FOR COUNTIES.
       Part 1.—The Northern States.
       Part 2.—The Southern States.
       Part 3,—The Western States and the Outlying Possessions.
Volume   VII.—IRRIGATION AND DRAINAGE—GENERAL REPORT AND ANALYTICAL TABLES, AND REPORTS FOR STATES, WITH STATISTICS FOR COUNTIES.

MANUFACTURES:

Volume   VIII.—GENERAL REPORT AND ANALYTICAL TABLES.
Volume   IX.—REPORTS FOR STATES, WITH STATISTICS FOR COUNTIES AND PRINCIPAL CITIES.
Volume   X.—REPORTS FOR SELECTED INDUSTRIES.

MINING:

Volume   XI.—MINES AND QUARRIES—GENERAL REPORT AND ANALYTICAL TABLES, AND REPORTS FOR STATES AND SELECTED INDUSTRIES.

ABSTRACT OF THE FOURTEENTH CENSUS.
ABSTRACT OF THE CENSUS OF MANUFACTURES.

(2)

LETTER OF TRANSMITTAL.

—————

DEPARTMENT OF COMMERCE,
BUREAU OF THE CENSUS,
Washington, D. C., December 15, 1922.

SIR:

I transmit herewith the Abstract of the Fourteenth Census.   This volume contains all of the essential statistics collected at the census of 1920 for population, occupations, agriculture, irrigation, drainage, manufactures, and mines and quarries.

Respectfully,

W. M. STEUART,
Director of the Census.

Hon. HERBERT HOOVER,
Secretary of Commerce.

(3)

ORGANIZATION OF THE BUREAU OF THE CENSUS DURING THE FOURTEENTH DECENNIAL CENSUS: 1919–1922.

DIRECTOR:
WILLIAM M. STEUART, : 1921–1922
SAM. L. ROGERS, : : : 1919–1921

ASSISTANT DIRECTOR:
JOSEPH A. HILL, : : : 1921–1922
WILLIAM M. STEUART, : 1919–1921

CHIEF CLERK:
ARTHUR J. HIRSCH, : : : 1921–1922
THOMAS J. FITZGERALD, : 1919–1921

DIVISION OF POPULATION:
WILLIAM C. HUNT, CHIEF STATISTICIAN.

DIVISION OF AGRICULTURE:
WILLIAM L. AUSTIN, CHIEF STATISTICIAN.

DIVISION OF MANUFACTURES:
EUGENE F. HARTLEY, CHIEF STATISTICIAN.

DIVISION OF VITAL STATISTICS:
WILLIAM H. DAVIS, CHIEF STATISTICIAN.

DIVISION OF STATISTICS OF CITIES:
STARKE M. GROGAN, CHIEF STATISTICIAN.

DIVISION OF REVISION AND RESULTS:
JOSEPH A. HILL, CHIEF STATISTICIAN, 1919–1921.

GEOGRAPHER:
CHARLES S. SLOANE.

(1)

GENERAL CONTENTS.

(5)

MAP OF THE UNITED STATES, SHOWING GEOGRAPHIC DIVISIONS.

(6)

PREFACE.

This Abstract summarizes the more important and significant statistics contained in the eleven volumes of the Fourteenth Census Reports and is designed to meet the requirements of those who desire the statistics for the census as a whole in convenient form for ready reference or who may not have access to the complete reports.

The Abstract is divided into seven parts: Population, Occupations, Agriculture, Irrigation, Drainage, Manufactures, and Mines and Quarries. This presentation conforms in general to that of the Fourteenth Census Reports. Each part contains a detailed table of contents and definitions of terms which have been given precise or special significance in census work.

Nearly all the tables presenting statistics by states also give figures for the United States as a whole and for nine groups of states, designated as geographic divisions. The states which constitute the geographic divisions are given below in their respective groupings, and the relation of the several groups can be ascertained by reference to the map on the opposite page.

NEW ENGLAND DIVISION.
Maine.
New Hampshire.
Vermont.
Massachusetts.
Rhode Island.
Connecticut.

MIDDLE ATLANTIC DIVISION.
New York.
New Jersey.
Pennsylvania.

EAST NORTH CENTRAL DIVISION.
Ohio.
Indiana.
Illinois.
Michigan.
Wisconsin.

WEST NORTH CENTRAL DIVISION.
Minnesota.
Iowa.
Missouri.
North Dakota.
South Dakota.
Nebraska.
Kansas.

SOUTH ATLANTIC DIVISION.
Delaware.
Maryland.
District of Columbia.
Virginia.
West Virginia.
North Carolina.
South Carolina.
Georgia.
Florida.

EAST SOUTH CENTRAL DIVISION.
Kentucky.
Tennessee.
Alabama.
Mississippi.

WEST SOUTH CENTRAL DIVISION.
Arkansas.
Louisiana.
Oklahoma.
Texas.

MOUNTAIN DIVISION.
Montana.
Idaho.
Wyoming.
Colorado.
New Mexico.
Arizona.
Utah.
Nevada.

PACIFIC DIVISION.
Washington.
Oregon.
California.

This grouping of the states facilitates the study of social, economic, and industrial phenomena with reference to their geographical aspects. In forming these groups the lines have been based partly on present and partly on historical conditions. The advantage of this geographic order lies chiefly in the ease with which conditions in contiguous states can be compared.

If more detailed information is desired in regard to any subject covered by the census or for any minor civil division (small city or village, township, etc.) not shown in this Abstract, the reader is referred to the Reports of the Fourteenth Census. A list of these reports is printed on page 2.

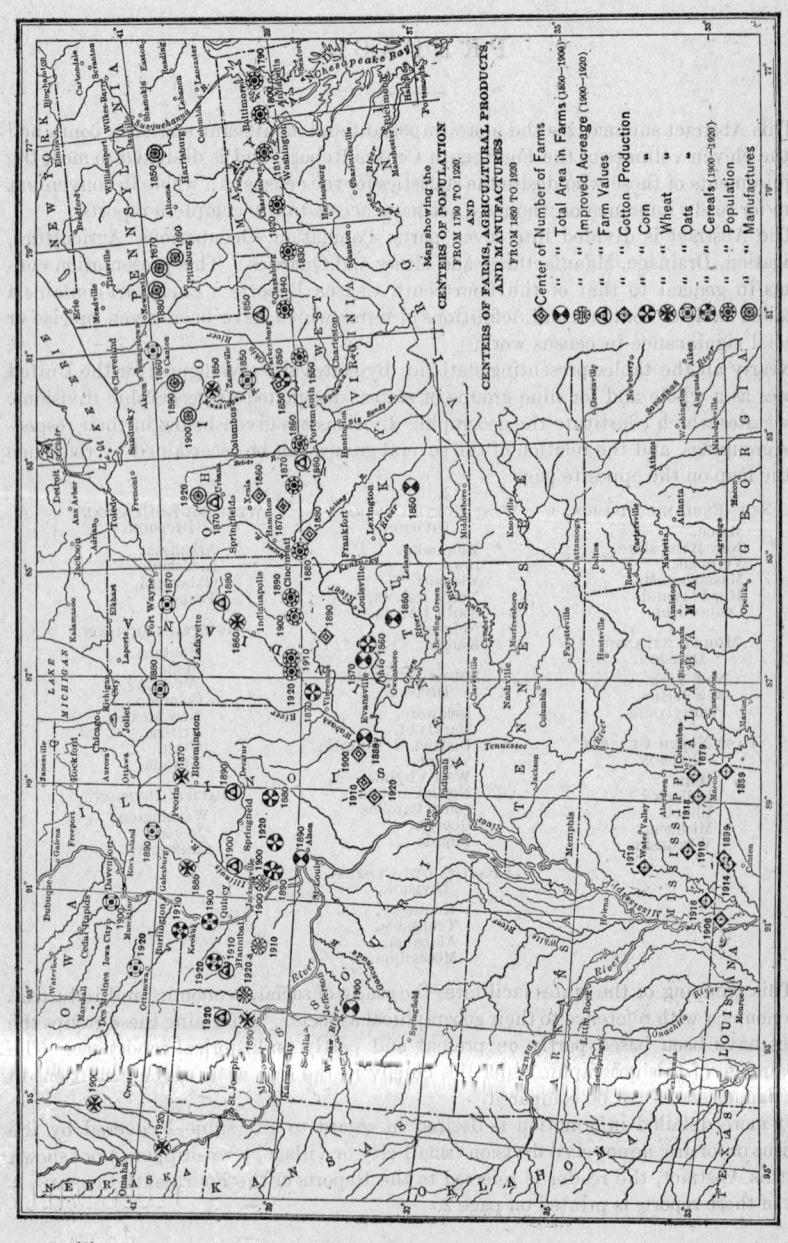

Map showing the
CENTERS OF POPULATION
FROM 1790 TO 1920
AND
CENTERS OF FARMS, AGRICULTURAL PRODUCTS,
AND MANUFACTURES
FROM 1850 TO 1920

Center of Number of Farms
"   " Total Area in Farms (1860-1900)
"   " Improved Acreage (1900-1920)
"   " Farm Values
"   " Corn Production
"   " Cotton Production
"   " Wheat
"   " Oats
"   " Cereals (1900-1920)
"   " Population
"   " Manufactures

NOTE.—The centers for manufactures and for all crops except cotton are based on data for the year preceding the census year indicated on the map; for the centers of cotton production the exact dates are shown on the map.

(8)

POPULATION.

(9)

CONTENTS.

CONTENTS.

CONTENTS. **13**

POPULATION.

DEFINITIONS AND EXPLANATION OF TERMS.

Alien.—According to census classification, any foreign-born person who has taken no step toward becoming an American citizen.

Colored.—Negroes, Indians, Chinese, Japanese, and "all other." "All other" comprises Filipinos, Hindus, Koreans, Hawaiians, Malays, Siamese, Samoans, and Maoris.

Continental United States.—Comprises the 48 states and the District of Columbia.

Country of birth of foreign-born white.—Because of the many political changes which have resulted from the World War, the 1920 statistics on this subject are presented on the basis of the postwar map.

Country of origin of foreign white stock.—Based upon the country of birth of the father of a foreign-born person or the foreign parent or parents of a native. Statistics are presented on the basis of the prewar map.

Dwelling.—A dwelling, for census purposes, is a place in which one or more persons regularly sleep. It need not be a house in the usual sense of the word, but may be a hotel, boarding house, institution, or the like. A boat, a tent, a freight car, or a room in a factory, store, or office building, although occupied by only one person, is also counted as a dwelling, while, on the other hand, an entire apartment house, although containing many families, constitutes but one dwelling.

Family.—The term "family," as used in the census, signifies a group of persons, whether related by blood or not, who live together as one household, usually sharing the same table. One person living alone is counted as a family, and, on the other hand, all the occupants and employees of a hotel, boarding house, or lodging house, if that is their usual place of abode, and all the inmates of an institution, however numerous, are treated as constituting a single family.

Foreign born.—Comprises all persons not born in the United States or any of the outlying possessions or at sea under the United States flag.

Foreign parentage.—Refers to persons having both parents foreign born.

Foreign white stock.—Comprises three classes, namely, foreign-born whites, native whites of foreign parentage, and native whites of mixed parentage.

Illiterate.—The Census Bureau classifies as illiterate any person 10 years of age or over who is unable to write in any language, not necessarily English, regardless of ability to read.

Mixed parentage.—Refers to persons having one parent native and the other foreign born.

Mother tongue.—The language of customary speech in the homes of immigrants prior to immigration.

Native.—Refers to persons born in continental United States, in any of the outlying possessions, or at sea under the United States flag.

Native parentage.—Refers to persons having both parents native.

Outlying possessions.—Alaska, American Samoa, Guam, Hawaii, Panama Canal Zone, Philippine Islands, Porto Rico, and the Virgin Islands of the United States. Detailed statistics regarding the population of the outlying possessions, except the Philippine Islands and the Virgin Islands, have been published in the form of separate bulletins and as sections of Volume III of the Fourteenth Census Reports.

Philippine Islands.—Not enumerated in 1920, a census of the Philippines having been taken by the Philippine government as of December 31, 1918.

School attendance.—The Fourteenth Census inquiry was as to whether the person enumerated had attended school, college, or any kind of educational institution at any time between September 1, 1919, and the census date, January 1, 1920.

Urban and rural.—All incorporated places (and all towns in Massachusetts, Rhode Island, and New Hampshire) having 2,500 inhabitants or more are treated as *urban* and the remainder of the country as *rural.*

Virgin Islands of the United States.—Not enumerated in 1920, a special census having been taken by the Census Bureau as of November 1, 1917.

(14)

NUMBER AND DISTRIBUTION OF INHABITANTS.

TABLE 1.—ACCESSIONS OF TERRITORY: 1790-1920.

ACCESSION.	Gross area (land and water) in square miles.	PER CENT DISTRIBUTION.	
		Aggregate area.	Area of the United States.
Aggregate, 1920	3,743,529	100.0	
Continental United States	3,026,789	80.9	100.0
Territory in 1790 [1]	892,135	23.8	29.5
Louisiana Purchase (1803)	827,987	22.1	27.4
Florida (1819)	58,666	1.6	1.9
By treaty with Spain (1819)	13,435	0.4	0.4
Texas (1845)	389,166	10.4	12.9
Oregon (1846)	286,541	7.7	9.5
Mexican Cession (1848)	529,189	14.1	17.5
Gadsden Purchase (1853)	29,670	0.8	1.0
Outlying possessions	716,740	19.1	
Alaska (1867)	590,884	15.8	
Hawaii (1898)	6,449	0.2	
Philippine Islands (1899)	115,026	3.1	
Porto Rico (1899)	3,435	0.1	
Guam (1899)	210	(2)	
American Samoa (1900)	77	(2)	
Panama Canal Zone (1904)	527	(2)	
Virgin Islands of the United States (1917)	132	(2)	

[1] Includes drainage basin of Red River of the North, not a part of any accession, but in the past sometimes considered a part of the Louisiana Purchase.
[2] Less than one-tenth of 1 per cent.

TABLE 2.—AREA OF THE UNITED STATES AND OUTLYING POSSESSIONS: 1790-1920.

CENSUS YEAR.	Gross area (land and water) in square miles.	Per cent of area in 1920.	AREA OF UNITED STATES EXCLUSIVE OF OUTLYING POSSESSIONS.				Gross area of outlying possessions (square miles).
			Gross area (land and water) in square miles.	Per cent of area in 1920.	Land (square miles).	Water [1] (square miles).	
1920	3,743,529	100.0	3,026,789	100.0	2,973,774	53,015	716,740
1910	3,743,397	100.0	3,026,789	100.0	2,973,890	52,899	716,608
1900	3,742,870	100.0	3,026,789	100.0	2,974,159	52,630	716,081
1890	3,617,673	96.6	3,026,789	100.0	2,973,965	52,824	590,884
1880	3,617,673	96.6	3,026,789	100.0	2,973,965	52,824	590,884
1870	3,617,673	96.6	3,026,789	100.0	2,973,965	52,824	590,884
1860	3,026,789	80.9	3,026,789	100.0	2,973,965	52,824	
1850	2,997,119	80.1	2,997,119	99.0	2,944,337	52,782	
1840	1,792,223	47.9	1,792,223	59.2	1,753,588	38,635	
1830	1,792,223	47.9	1,792,223	59.2	1,753,588	38,635	
1820	1,792,223	47.9	1,792,223	59.2	1,753,588	38,635	
1810	1,720,122	46.0	1,720,122	56.8	1,685,865	34,257	
1800	892,135	23.8	892,135	29.5	867,980	24,155	
1790	892,135	23.8	892,135	29.5	867,980	24,155	

[1] Does not include water surface of oceans, Gulf of Mexico, or Great Lakes, lying within jurisdiction of United States.

TABLE 3.—POPULATION OF THE UNITED STATES AND OUTLYING POSSESSIONS: 1920 AND 1910.

AREA.	Gross area (land and water) in square miles.	POPULATION. 1920	1910
United States, with outlying possessions............	3,743,529	[1] 117,823,165	101,146,530
Continental United States.......................	3,026,789	105,710,620	91,972,266
Outlying possessions...........................	716,740	[1] 12,112,545	9,174,264
Alaska........	590,884	55,036	64,356
American Samoa.............................	77	8,056	[2] 7,251
Guam....	210	13,275	11,806
Hawaii.....	6,449	255,912	191,909
Panama Canal Zone...........................	527	22,858	[2] 62,810
Porto Rico.........	3,435	1,299,809	1,118,012
Military and naval, etc., services abroad [3]........		117,238	55,608
Philippine Islands...........................	115,026	[4] 10,314,310	[5] 7,635,426
Virgin Islands of the United States.............	132	[6] 26,051	[7] 27,086

[1] Revised total; correction in population of Philippine Islands.
[2] Population in 1912.
[3] Comprises military, Red Cross, and consular services abroad, and naval service abroad or in American waters but not on fixed station.
[4] Population Dec. 31, 1918. Revised figures; population given in Vol. I (10,350,640) was taken from preliminary bulletin issued in 1920 by the Philippine Government.
[5] Population in 1903.
[6] Population Nov. 1, 1917.
[7] Population in 1911.

TABLE 4.—POPULATION OF THE UNITED STATES, EXCLUSIVE OF OUTLYING POSSESSIONS: 1790-1920.

CENSUS YEAR.	Population.	INCREASE OVER PRECEDING CENSUS. Number.	Per cent.	Per cent of increase with correction for 1870 and 1880.[1]
1920............	105,710,620	13,738,354	14.9	14.9
1910............	91,972,266	15,977,691	21.0	21.0
1900............	75,994,575	13,046,861	20.7	20.7
1890............	62,947,714	12,791,931	25.5	25.5
1880............	50,155,783	11,597,412	30.1	[1] 26.0
1870............	38,558,371	7,115,050	22.6	[1] 26.6
1860............	31,443,321	8,251,445	35.6	35.6
1850............	23,191,876	6,122,423	35.9	35.9
1840............	17,069,453	4,203,433	32.7	32.7
1830............	12,866,020	3,227,567	33.5	33.5
1820............	9,638,453	2,398,572	33.1	33.1
1810............	7,239,881	1,931,398	36.4	36.4
1800............	5,308,483	1,379,269	35.1	35.1
1790............	3,929,214			

[1] Enumeration of 1870 incomplete in Southern states. Percentages in this column for 1860-1870 and 1870-1880 represent estimated true rates of increase

TABLE 5.—POSITION OF THE CENTER OF POPULATION: 1790–1920.

[The center of population may be said to represent the center of gravity of the population. If the surface of the United States be considered as a rigid level plane without weight, capable of sustaining the population distributed thereon, individuals being assumed to be of equal weight and the plane to be supported, as on a pivotal point, at its center of gravity, the influence of each individual in maintaining the equilibrium of the plane would be directly proportional to his distance from the pivotal point or center of gravity. This is the point referred to by the term "center of population."]

CENSUS YEAR.	LOCATION.		APPROXIMATE LOCATION BY IMPORTANT TOWNS.	MOVEMENT IN MILES DURING PRECEDING DECADE.			
	North latitude.	West longitude.		From point to point in direct line.	Westward.	Northward.	Southward.
	° ′ ″	° ′ ″					
1790....	39 16 30	76 11 12	23 miles east of Baltimore, Md.......	......	......	......	0.5
1800....	39 16 6	76 56 30	18 miles west of Baltimore, Md.......	40.6	40.6	......	
1810....	39 11 30	77 37 12	40 miles northwest by west of Washington, D. C. (in Va.).	36.9	36.5	......	5.3
1820....	39 5 42	78 33 0	16 miles east of Moorefield, W. Va.[1]...	50.5	50.1	......	6.7
1830....	38 57 54	79 16 54	19 miles west-southwest of Moorefield, W. Va.[1]	40.4	39.4	......	9.0
1840....	39 2 0	80 18 0	16 miles south of Clarksburg, W. Va.[1].	55.0	54.8	4.7	......
1850....	38 59 0	81 19 0	23 miles southeast of Parkersburg, W. Va.[1]	54.8	54.7	......	3.5
1860....	39 0 24	82 48 48	20 miles south by east of Chillicothe, Ohio.	80.6	80.6	1.6	......
1870....	39 12 0	83 35 42	48 miles east by north of Cincinnati, Ohio.	44.1	42.1	13.3	......
1880....	39 4 8	84 39 40	8 miles west by south of Cincinnati, Ohio (in Ky.).	58.1	57.4	......	9.1
1890....	39 11 56	85 32 53	20 miles east of Columbus, Ind........	48.6	47.7	9.0	......
1900....	39 9 36	85 48 54	6 miles southeast of Columbus, Ind...	14.6	14.4	......	2.8
1910....	39 10 12	86 32 20	In the city of Bloomington, Ind......	39.0	38.9	0.7	......
1920....	39 10 21	86 43 15	{1.9 miles west of Whitehall, Clay township, Owen County, Ind. 8.3 miles south-southeast of Spencer, Washington township, Owen County, Ind.	9.8	9.8	0.2	......

[1] Present area of West Virginia included in Virginia until 1861; admitted as a separate state in 1863.

75108°—23——2

TABLE 6.—POPULATION OF THE UNITED

	DIVISION AND STATE.	POPULATION.					
		1920	1910	1900	1890 [1]	1880	1870
1	United States.....	105,710,620	91,972,266	75,994,575	62,947,714	50,155,783	38,558,371
	GEOGRAPHIC DIVISIONS:						
2	New England.......	7,400,909	6,552,681	5,592,017	4,700,749	4,010,529	3,487,924
3	Middle Atlantic......	22,261,144	19,315,892	15,454,678	12,706,220	10,496,878	8,810,806
4	East North Central...	21,475,543	18,250,621	15,985,581	13,478,305	11,206,668	9,124,517
5	West North Central..	12,544,249	11,637,921	10,347,423	8,932,112	6,157,443	3,856,594
6	South Atlantic.......	13,990,272	12,194,895	10,443,480	8,857,922	7,597,197	5,853,610
7	East South Central..	8,893,307	8,409,901	7,547,757	6,429,154	5,585,151	4,404,445
8	West South Central..	10,242,224	8,784,534	6,532,290	4,740,983	3,334,220	2,029,965
9	Mountain.............	3,336,101	2,633,517	1,674,657	1,213,935	653,119	315,385
10	Pacific..............	5,566,871	4,192,304	2,416,692	1,888,334	1,114,578	675,125
	NEW ENGLAND:						
11	Maine...............	768,014	742,371	694,466	661,086	648,936	626,915
12	New Hampshire.....	443,083	430,572	411,588	376,530	346,991	318,300
13	Vermont.............	352,428	355,956	343,641	332,422	332,286	330,551
14	Massachusetts.......	3,852,356	3,366,416	2,805,346	2,238,947	1,783,085	1,457,351
15	Rhode Island........	604,397	542,610	428,556	345,506	276,531	217,353
16	Connecticut.........	1,380,631	1,114,756	908,420	746,258	622,700	537,454
	MIDDLE ATLANTIC:						
17	New York...........	10,385,227	9,113,614	7,268,894	6,003,174	5,082,871	4,382,759
18	New Jersey..........	3,155,900	2,537,167	1,883,669	1,444,933	1,131,116	906,096
19	Pennsylvania........	8,720,017	7,665,111	6,302,115	5,258,113	4,282,891	3,521,951
	EAST NORTH CENTRAL:						
20	Ohio................	5,759,394	4,767,121	4,157,545	3,672,329	3,198,062	2,665,260
21	Indiana.............	2,930,390	2,700,876	2,516,462	2,192,404	1,978,301	1,680,637
22	Illinois.............	6,485,280	5,638,591	4,821,550	3,826,352	3,077,871	2,539,891
23	Michigan............	3,668,412	2,810,173	2,420,982	2,093,890	1,636,937	1,184,059
24	Wisconsin...........	2,632,067	2,333,860	2,069,042	1,693,330	1,315,497	1,054,670
	WEST NORTH CENTRAL:						
25	Minnesota...........	2,387,125	2,075,708	1,751,394	1,310,283	780,773	439,706
26	Iowa................	2,404,021	2,224,771	2,231,853	1,912,297	1,624,615	1,194,020
27	Missouri............	3,404,055	3,293,335	3,106,665	2,679,185	2,168,380	1,721,295
28	North Dakota.......	646,872	577,056	319,146	190,983	} 135,177	4 14,181
29	South Dakota.......	636,547	583,888	401,570	348,600		
30	Nebraska............	1,296,372	1,192,214	1,066,300	1,062,656	452,402	122,993
31	Kansas..............	1,769,257	1,690,949	1,470,495	1,428,108	996,096	364,399
	SOUTH ATLANTIC:						
32	Delaware............	223,003	202,322	184,735	168,493	146,608	125,015
33	Maryland...........	1,449,661	1,295,346	1,188,044	1,042,390	934,943	780,894
34	District of Columbia..	437,571	331,069	278,718	230,392	177,624	131,700
35	Virginia............	2,309,187	2,061,612	1,854,184	1,655,980	1,512,565	1,225,163
36	West Virginia.......	1,463,701	1,221,119	958,800	762,794	618,457	442,014
37	North Carolina......	2,559,123	2,206,287	1,893,810	1,617,949	1,399,750	1,071,361
38	South Carolina......	1,683,724	1,515,400	1,340,316	1,151,149	995,577	705,606
39	Georgia.............	2,895,832	2,609,121	2,216,331	1,837,353	1,542,180	1,184,109
40	Florida.............	968,470	752,619	528,542	391,422	269,493	187,748
	EAST SOUTH CENTRAL:						
41	Kentucky...........	2,416,630	2,289,905	2,147,174	1,858,635	1,648,690	1,321,011
42	Tennessee...........	2,337,885	2,184,789	2,020,616	1,767,518	1,542,359	1,258,520
43	Alabama............	2,348,174	2,138,093	1,828,697	1,513,401	1,262,505	996,992
44	Mississippi.........	1,790,618	1,797,114	1,551,270	1,289,600	1,131,597	. 827,922
	WEST SOUTH CENTRAL:						
45	Arkansas...........	1,752,204	1,574,449	1,311,564	1,128,211	802,525	484,471
46	Louisiana...........	1,798,509	1,656,388	1,381,625	1,118,588	939,946	726,915
47	Oklahoma...........	2,028,283	1,657,155	7 790,391	7 258,657		
48	Texas...............	4,663,228	3,896,542	3,048,710	2,235,527	1,591,749	818,579
	MOUNTAIN:						
49	Montana............	548,889	376,053	243,329	142,924	39,159	20,595
50	Idaho..............	431,866	325,594	161,772	88,548	32,610	14,999
51	Wyoming............	194,402	145,965	92,531	62,555	20,789	9,118
52	Colorado...........	939,629	799,024	539,700	413,249	194,327	39,864
53	New Mexico........	360,350	327,301	195,310	160,282	119,565	91,874
54	Arizona.............	334,162	204,354	122,931	88,243	40,440	9,658
55	Utah...............	449,396	373,351	276,749	210,779	143,963	86,786
56	Nevada.............	77,407	81,875	42,335	47,355	62,266	42,491
	PACIFIC:						
57	Washington.........	1,356,621	1,141,990	518,103	357,232	75,116	23,955
58	Oregon.............	783,389	672,765	413,536	317,704	174,768	90,923
59	California..........	3,426,861	2,377,549	1,485,053	1,213,398	864,694	560,247

[1] Includes population (325,464) of Indian Territory and Indian reservations, specially enumerated in 1890, but not included in the general report on population for 1890.
[2] Includes persons (6,100 in 1840 and 5,318 in 1830) on public ships in the service of the United States, not credited to any division or state.
[3] Population of area taken to form state of Missouri in 1821; part of Louisiana territory in 1810.

STATES, BY DIVISIONS AND STATES: 1790–1920.

POPULATION.								
1860	1850	1840	1830	1820	1810	1800	1790	
31,443,321	23,191,876	[2]17,069,453	[2]12,866,020	9,638,453	7,239,881	5,308,483	3,929,214	1
3,135,283	2,728,116	2,234,822	1,954,717	1,660,071	1,471,973	1,233,011	1,009,408	2
7,458,985	5,898,735	4,526,260	3,587,664	2,699,845	2,014,702	1,402,565	958,632	3
6,926,884	4,523,260	2,924,728	1,470,018	792,719	272,324	51,006	....	4
2,169,832	880,335	426,814	140,455	66,586	19,783	....	....	5
5,364,703	4,679,090	3,925,299	3,645,752	3,061,063	2,674,891	2,286,494	1,851,806	6
4,020,991	3,363,271	2,575,445	1,815,969	1,190,489	708,590	335,407	109,368	7
1,747,667	940,251	449,985	246,127	167,680	77,618	....	....	8
174,923	72,927	....	....	....	....	....	....	9
444,053	105,891	....	....	....	....	....	....	10
628,279	583,169	501,793	399,455	298,335	228,705	151,719	96,540	11
326,073	317,976	284,574	269,328	244,161	214,460	183,858	141,885	12
315,098	314,120	291,948	280,652	235,981	217,895	154,465	85,425	13
1,231,066	994,514	737,699	610,408	523,287	472,040	422,845	378,787	14
174,620	147,545	108,830	97,199	83,059	76,931	69,122	68,825	15
460,147	370,792	309,978	297,675	275,248	261,942	251,002	237,946	16
3,880,735	3,097,394	2,428,921	1,918,608	1,372,812	959,049	589,051	340,120	17
672,035	489,555	373,306	320,823	277,575	245,562	211,149	184,139	18
2,906,215	2,311,786	1,724,033	1,348,233	1,049,458	810,091	602,365	434,373	19
2,339,511	1,980,329	1,519,467	937,903	581,434	230,760	45,365	....	20
1,350,428	988,416	685,866	343,031	147,178	24,520	5,641	....	21
1,711,951	851,470	476,183	157,445	55,211	12,282	....	....	22
749,113	397,654	212,267	31,639	8,896	4,762	....	....	23
775,881	305,391	30,945	....	....	....	....	....	24
172,023	6,077	....	....	....	....	....	....	25
674,913	192,214	43,112	....	....	....	....	....	26
1,182,012	682,044	383,702	140,455	66,586	[3]19,783	....	....	27
[5]4,837	....	....	....	....	....	....	....	28 / 29
28,841	....	....	....	....	....	....	....	30
107,206	....	....	....	....	....	....	....	31
112,216	91,532	78,085	76,748	72,749	72,674	64,273	59,096	32
687,049	583,034	470,019	447,040	407,350	380,546	341,548	319,728	33
75,080	51,687	43,712	39,834	33,039	24,023	14,093	....	34
1,596,318	1,421,661	1,239,797	1,211,405	1,065,366	974,600	880,200	747,610	35
								36
992,622	869,039	753,419	737,987	638,829	555,500	478,103	393,751	37
703,708	668,507	594,398	581,185	502,741	415,115	345,591	249,073	38
1,057,286	906,185	691,392	516,823	340,989	252,433	162,686	82,548	39
140,424	87,445	54,477	34,730	....	....	....	....	40
1,155,684	982,405	779,828	687,917	564,317	406,511	220,955	73,677	41
1,109,801	1,002,717	829,210	681,904	422,823	261,727	105,602	35,691	42
964,201	771,623	590,756	309,527	127,901	....	....	....	43
791,305	606,526	375,651	136,621	75,448	40,352	8,850	....	44
435,450	209,897	97,574	30,388	14,273	[6]1,062	....	....	45
708,002	517,762	352,411	215,739	153,407	76,556	....	....	46
								47
604,215	212,592	....	....	....	....	....	....	48
								49
								50
								51
34,277	....	....	....	....	....	....	....	52
93,516	61,547	....	....	....	....	....	....	53
								54
40,273	11,380	....	....	....	....	....	....	55
6,857	....	....	....	....	....	....	....	56
11,594	....	....	....	....	....	....	....	57
52,465	13,294	....	....	....	....	....	....	58
379,994	92,597	....	....	....	....	....	....	59

[4] Population of that part of Dakota territory taken to form North Dakota: 1880, 36,909; 1870, 2,405. Population of part taken to form South Dakota: 1880, 98,268; 1870, 11,776.
[5] Dakota territory.
[6] Population of area taken to form Arkansas territory in 1819; part of Louisiana territory in 1810.
[7] Includes population of Indian Territory, as follows: 1900, 392,060; 1890, 180,182.

TABLE 7.—RANK AND DECENNIAL RATES OF INCREASE IN

[A minus sign (—)

DIVISION AND STATE.	RANK IN POPULATION.													
	1920	1910	1900	1890	1880	1870	1860	1850	1840	1830	1820	1810	1800	1790
1 United States...														
GEOGRAPHIC DIVISIONS:														
2 New England	VII	VII	VII	VII	VI	VI	V	V	V	III	III	III	III	II
3 Middle Atlantic	I	I	II	II	II	II	I	I	I	II	II	II	II	III
4 East North Central	II	II	I	I	I	I	II	III	III	V	V	V	V	.....
5 West North Central	IV	IV	IV	IV	IV	V	VI	VII	VII	VII	VII	VII		
6 South Atlantic	III	III	III	IV	III	III	III	II	II	II	I	I	I	I
7 East South Central	VI	VI	V	V	V	IV	IV	IV	IV	IV	IV	IV	IV	IV
8 West South Central	V	V	VI	VI	VII	VII	VII	VII	VI	VI	VI	VI		
9 Mountain	IX	IX	IX	IX	IX	IX	IX	IX						
10 Pacific	VIII	VIII	VIII	VIII	VIII	VIII	VIII	VIII						
NEW ENGLAND:														
11 Maine	35	34	31	30	27	23	22	16	13	12	12	14	14	11
12 New Hampshire	41	39	37	33	31	31	27	22	22	18	15	16	11	10
13 Vermont	45	42	39	37	32	30	28	23	21	17	16	15	13	12
14 Massachusetts	6	6	7	6	7	7	7	6	8	8	7	5	5	4
15 Rhode Island	38	38	35	36	33	32	29	28	24	23	20	17	16	15
16 Connecticut	29	31	29	29	28	25	24	21	20	16	14	9	8	8
MIDDLE ATLANTIC:														
17 New York	1	1	1	1	1	1	1	1	1	1	1	2	3	5
18 New Jersey	10	11	16	18	19	17	21	19	18	14	13	12	10	9
19 Pennsylvania	2	2	2	2	2	2	2	2	2	2	3	3	2	2
EAST NORTH CENTRAL:														
20 Ohio	4	4	4	4	3	3	3	3	3	4	5	13	18	.....
21 Indiana	11	9	8	8	6	6	6	7	10	13	18	21	21	.....
22 Illinois	3	3	3	3	4	4	4	11	14	20	24	24		
23 Michigan	7	8	9	9	9	13	16	20	23	27	27	25		
24 Wisconsin	13	13	13	14	16	15	15	24	30					
WEST NORTH CENTRAL:														
25 Minnesota	17	19	19	20	26	28	30	36						
26 Iowa	16	15	10	10	10	11	20	27	29					
27 Missouri	9	7	5	5	5	5	8	13	16	21	23	23		
28 North Dakota	36	37	40	42	}³40	³45	³42							
29 South Dakota	37	36	38	35										
30 Nebraska	31	29	27	26	30	36	39							
31 Kansas	24	22	22	19	20	29	33							
SOUTH ATLANTIC:														
32 Delaware	47	47	45	43	38	35	32	30	26	24	22	19	17	16
33 Maryland	28	27	26	27	23	20	19	17	15	11	10	8	7	6
34 District of Columbia	42	43	41	40	36	34	35	33	28	25	25	22	19	.....
35 Virginia	20	20	17	15	14	10	5	4	4	3	2	1	1	1
36 West Virginia	27	28	28	28	29	27								
37 North Carolina	14	16	15	16	15	14	12	10	7	5	4	4	4	3
38 South Carolina	26	26	24	23	21	22	18	14	11	9	8	6	6	7
39 Georgia	12	10	11	12	13	12	11	9	9	10	11	11	12	13
40 Florida	32	33	33	32	34	33	31	31	27	26				
EAST SOUTH CENTRAL:														
41 Kentucky	15	14	12	11	8	8	9	8	6	6	6	7	9	14
42 Tennessee	19	17	14	13	12	9	10	5	5	7	9	10	15	17
43 Alabama	18	18	18	17	17	16	13	12	12	15	19			
44 Mississippi	23	21	20	21	18	18	14	15	17	22	21	20	-20	.....
WEST SOUTH CENTRAL:														
45 Arkansas	25	25	25	24	25	26	25	26	25	28	26	26		
46 Louisiana	22	24	23	25	22	21	17	18	19	19	17	18		
47 Oklahoma	21	23	⁵30	39										
48 Texas	5	5	6	7	11	19	23	25						
MOUNTAIN:														
49 Montana	39	40	47	45	45	43								
50 Idaho	42	45	46	46	46	44								
51 Wyoming	48	48	48	48	47	47								
52 Colorado	33	32	32	31	35	41	38							
53 New Mexico	44	44	44	44	41	37	34	32						
54 Arizona	46	46	47	47	44	46								
55 Utah	40	41	42	41	39	39	37	35						
56 Nevada	49	49	49	49	43	40	41							
PACIFIC:														
57 Washington	30	30	34	34	42	42	40							
58 Oregon	34	35	36	38	37	38	36	34						
59 California	8	12	21	22	24	24	26	29						

¹ In computing the decennial increases from 1820 to 1850, persons on public ships in 1830 and 1840 (see Table 6) were included.
² Less than one-tenth of 1 per cent.
³ Dakota territory.

POPULATION, FOR DIVISIONS AND STATES: 1790-1920.

denotes decrease.]

PER CENT OF INCREASE IN POPULATION.													
1910 to 1920	1900 to 1910	1890 to 1900	1880 to 1890	1870 to 1880	1860 to 1870	1850 to 1860	1840 to 1850	1830 to 1840	1820 to 1830	1810 to 1820	1800 to 1810	1790 to 1800	
14.9	21.0	20.7	25.5	30.1	22.6	35.6	[1] 35.9	[1] 32.7	[1] 33.5	33.1	36.4	35.1	1
12.9	17.2	19.0	17.2	15.0	11.2	14.9	22.1	14.3	17.7	12.8	19.4	22.2	2
15.2	25.0	21.6	21.0	19.1	18.1	26.5	30.3	26.2	32.9	34.0	43.6	46.3	3
17.7	14.2	18.6	20.3	22.8	31.7	53.1	54.7	99.0	85.4	191.1	433.9	......	4
7.8	12.5	15.8	45.1	59.7	77.7	146.5	106.3	203.9	110.9	236.6	......	......	5
14.7	16.8	17.9	16.6	29.8	9.1	14.7	19.2	7.7	19.1	14.4	17.0	23.5	6
5.7	11.4	17.4	15.1	26.8	9.5	19.6	30.6	41.8	52.5	68.0	111.3	206.7	7
16.6	34.5	37.8	42.2	64.3	16.2	85.9	109.0	82.8	46.8	116.0	......	......	8
26.7	57.3	38.0	85.9	107.1	80.3	139.9	......						9
32.8	73.5	28.0	69.4	65.1	52.0	319.3	......						10
3.5	6.9	5.0	1.9	3.5	-0.2	7.7	16.2	25.6	33.9	30.4	50.7	57.2	11
2.9	4.6	9.3	8.5	9.0	-2.4	2.5	11.7	5.7	10.3	13.8	16.6	29.6	12
-1.0	3.6	3.4	(²)	0.5	4.9	0.3	7.6	4.0	18.9	8.3	41.1	80.8	13
14.4	20.0	25.3	25.6	22.4	18.4	23.8	34.8	20.9	16.6	10.9	11.6	11.6	14
11.4	26.6	24.0	24.9	27.2	24.5	18.4	35.6	12.0	17.0	8.0	11.3	0.4	15
23.9	22.7	21.7	19.8	15.9	16.8	24.1	19.6	4.1	8.1	5.1	4.4	5.5	16
14.0	25.4	21.1	18.1	16.0	12.9	25.3	27.5	26.6	39.8	43.1	62.8	73.2	17
24.4	34.7	30.4	27.7	24.8	34.8	37.3	31.1	16.4	15.6	13.0	16.3	14.7	18
13.8	21.6	19.9	22.8	21.6	21.2	25.7	34.1	27.9	28.5	29.5	34.5	38.7	19
20.8	14.7	13.2	14.8	20.0	13.9	18.1	30.3	62.0	61.3	152.0	408.7	......	20
8.5	7.3	14.8	10.8	17.7	24.5	36.6	44.1	99.9	133.1	500.2	334.7	......	21
15.0	16.9	26.0	24.3	21.2	48.4	101.1	78.8	202.4	185.2	349.5	......	......	22
30.5	16.1	15.6	27.9	38.2	58.1	88.4	87.3	570.9	255.7	86.8	......		23
12.8	12.8	22.2	28.7	24.7	35.9	154.1	886.9	......					24
15.0	18.5	33.7	67.8	77.6	155.6	2,730.7	......						25
8.1	-0.3	16.7	17.7	36.1	76.9	251.1	345.8	......					26
3.4	6.0	16.0	23.6	26.0	45.6	73.3	77.8	173.2	110.9	236.6	......		27
{ 12.1	80.8	67.1	}³ 299.2	³ 853.2	³ 193.2	......							{28
9.0	45.4	15.2											29
8.7	11.8	0.3	134.9	267.8	326.5	......							30
4.6	15.0	3.0	43.4	173.4	239.9	......							31
10.2	9.5	9.6	14.9	17.3	11.4	22.6	17.2	1.7	5.5	0.1	13.1	8.8	32
11.9	9.0	14.0	11.5	19.7	13.7	17.8	24.0	5.1	9.7	7.0	11.4	6.8	33
32.2	18.8	21.0	29.7	34.9	75.4	45.3	18.2	9.7	20.6	37.5	70.5	......	34
12.0	11.2	12.0	9.5	23.5	⁴ -23.3	12.3	14.7	2.3	13.7	9.3	10.7	17.7	35
19.9	27.4	25.7	23.3	39.9	......								36
16.0	16.5	17.1	15.6	30.7	7.9	14.2	15.3	2.1	15.5	15.0	16.2	21.4	37
11.1	13.1	16.4	15.6	41.1	0.3	5.3	12.5	2.3	15.6	21.1	20.1	38.8	38
11.0	17.7	20.6	19.1	30.2	12.0	16.7	31.1	33.8	51.6	35.1	55.2	97.1	39
28.7	42.4	35.0	45.2	43.5	33.7	60.6	60.5	56.9	......				40
5.5	6.6	15.5	12.7	24.8	14.3	17.6	26.0	13.4	21.9	38.8	84.0	199.9	41
7.0	8.1	14.3	14.6	22.6	13.4	10.7	20.9	21.6	61.3	61.6	147.8	195.9	42
9.8	16.9	20.8	19.9	26.6	3.4	25.0	30.6	90.9	142.0	......			43
-0.4	15.8	20.3	14.0	36.7	4.6	30.5	61.5	175.0	81.1	87.0	356.0	......	44
11.3	20.0	16.3	40.6	65.6	11.3	107.5	115.1	221.1	112.9	1,244.0	......		45
8.6	19.9	23.5	19.0	29.3	2.7	36.7	46.9	63.4	40.6	100.4	......		46
22.4	109.7	205.6	......										47
19.7	27.8	36.4	40.4	94.5	35.5	184.2	......						48
46.0	54.5	70.3	265.0	90.1	......								49
32.6	101.3	82.7	171.5	117.4	......								50
33.2	57.7	47.9	200.9	128.0	......								51
17.6	48.0	30.6	112.7	387.5	16.3	......							52
10.1	67.6	21.9	34.1	30.1	-1.8	51.9	......						53
63.5	66.2	39.3	118.2	318.7	......								54
20.4	34.9	31.3	46.4	65.9	253.9	......							55
-5.5	93.4	-10.6	-23.9	46.5	519.7	......							56
18.8	120.4	45.0	375.6	213.6	106.6	......							57
16.4	62.7	30.2	81.8	92.2	73.3	294.7	......						58
44.1	60.1	22.4	40.3	54.3	47.4	310.4	......						59

⁴ Decrease due to loss of territory, West Virginia having been detached from Virginia and admitted as a separate state in 1863.
⁵ The territory of Oklahoma in 1900 ranked 38 and Indian Territory 39. In computing the rank for 1900 the population of Indian Territory was included with that of Oklahoma.

TABLE 8.—POPULATION PER SQUARE MILE, BY DIVISIONS AND STATES: 1920, 1910, AND 1900.

DIVISION AND STATE.	Population: 1920	Land area (square miles): 1920	POPULATION PER SQUARE MILE.		
			1920	1910	1900
United States	105,710,620	2,973,774	35.5	30.9	25.6
GEOGRAPHIC DIVISIONS:					
New England	7,400,909	61,976	119.4	105.7	90.2
Middle Atlantic	22,261,144	100,000	222.6	193.2	154.5
East North Central	21,475,543	245,564	87.5	74.3	65.2
West North Central	12,544,249	510,804	24.6	22.8	20.3
South Atlantic	13,990,272	269,071	52.0	45.3	38.8
East South Central	8,893,307	179,509	49.5	46.8	42.0
West South Central	10,242,224	429,746	23.8	20.4	15.2
Mountain	3,336,101	859,009	3.9	3.1	1.9
Pacific	5,566,871	318,095	17.5	13.2	7.6
NEW ENGLAND:					
Maine	768,014	29,895	25.7	24.8	23.2
New Hampshire	443,083	9,031	49.1	47.7	45.6
Vermont	352,428	9,124	38.6	39.0	37.7
Massachusetts	3,852,356	8,039	479.2	418.8	349.0
Rhode Island	604,397	1,067	566.4	508.5	401.6
Connecticut	1,380,631	4,820	286.4	231.3	188.5
MIDDLE ATLANTIC:					
New York	10,385,227	47,654	217.9	191.2	152.5
New Jersey	3,155,900	7,514	420.0	337.7	250.7
Pennsylvania	8,720,017	44,832	194.5	171.0	140.6
EAST NORTH CENTRAL:					
Ohio	5,759,394	40,740	141.4	117.0	102.1
Indiana	2,930,390	36,045	81.3	74.9	70.1
Illinois	6,485,280	56,043	115.7	100.6	86.1
Michigan	3,668,412	57,480	63.8	48.9	42.1
Wisconsin	2,632,067	55,256	47.6	42.2	37.4
WEST NORTH CENTRAL:					
Minnesota	2,387,125	80,858	29.5	25.7	21.7
Iowa	2,404,021	55,586	43.2	40.0	40.2
Missouri	3,404,055	68,727	49.5	47.9	45.2
North Dakota	646,872	70,183	9.2	8.2	4.5
South Dakota	636,547	76,868	8.3	7.6	5.2
Nebraska	1,296,372	76,808	16.9	15.5	13.9
Kansas	1,769,257	81,774	21.6	20.7	18.0
SOUTH ATLANTIC:					
Delaware	223,003	1,965	113.5	103.0	94.0
Maryland	1,449,661	9,941	145.8	130.3	119.5
District of Columbia	437,571	60	7,292.9	5,517.8	4,645.3
Virginia	2,309,187	40,262	57.4	51.2	46.1
West Virginia	1,463,701	24,022	60.9	50.8	39.9
North Carolina	2,559,123	48,740	52.5	45.3	38.9
South Carolina	1,683,724	30,495	55.2	49.7	44.0
Georgia	2,895,832	58,725	49.3	44.4	37.7
Florida	968,470	54,861	17.7	13.7	9.6
EAST SOUTH CENTRAL:					
Kentucky	2,416,630	40,181	60.1	57.0	53.4
Tennessee	2,337,885	41,687	56.1	52.4	48.5
Alabama	2,348,174	51,279	45.8	41.7	35.7
Mississippi	1,790,618	46,362	38.6	38.8	33.5
WEST SOUTH CENTRAL:					
Arkansas	1,752,204	52,525	33.4	30.0	25.0
Louisiana	1,798,509	45,409	39.6	36.5	30.4
Oklahoma [1]	2,028,283	69,414	29.2	23.9	11.4
Texas	4,663,228	262,398	17.8	14.8	11.6
MOUNTAIN:					
Montana	548,889	[2] 146,131	3.8	2.6	1.7
Idaho	431,866	[2] 83,354	5.2	3.9	1.9
Wyoming	194,402	[2] 97,548	2.0	1.5	0.9
Colorado	939,629	103,658	9.1	7.7	5.2
New Mexico	360,350	122,503	2.9	2.7	1.6
Arizona	334,162	113,810	2.9	1.8	1.1
Utah	449,396	82,184	5.5	4.5	3.4
Nevada	77,407	109,821	0.7	0.7	0.4
PACIFIC:					
Washington	1,356,621	66,836	20.3	17.1	7.8
Oregon	783,389	95,607	8.2	7.0	4.3
California	3,426,861	155,652	22.0	15.3	9.5

[1] Includes population of Indian Territory for 1900.
[2] Total land area includes part of Yellowstone National Park, geographically located in Idaho (36 square miles), Montana (198 square miles), and Wyoming (2,948 square miles). Total population of park (165) returned as in Wyoming.

TABLE 9.—AREA AND POPULATION OF COUNTIES: 1920 AND 1910.

COUNTY.	Land area in square miles: 1920.	1920 Total.	1920 Per square mile.	1910	COUNTY.	Land area in square miles: 1920.	1920 Total.	1920 Per square mile.	1910
ALABAMA	51,279	2,348,174	45.8	2,138,093	ALABAMA—Con.				
Autauga	584	18,908	32.4	20,038	Talladega	755	41,005	54.3	37,921
Baldwin	1,595	20,730	13.0	18,178	Tallapoosa	763	29,744	39.0	31,034
Barbour	912	32,067	35.2	32,728	Tuscaloosa	1,346	53,680	39.9	47,559
Bibb	634	23,144	36.5	22,791	Walker	792	50,593	63.9	37,013
Blount	649	25,538	39.3	21,456					
					Washington	1,087	14,279	13.1	14,454
Bullock	610	25,333	41.5	30,196	Wilcox	896	31,080	34.7	33,810
Butler	763	29,531	38.7	29,030	Winston	630	14,378	22.8	12,855
Calhoun	616	47,822	77.6	39,115					
Chambers	612	41,201	67.3	36,056	ARIZONA	113,810	334,162	2.9	204,354
Cherokee	577	20,862	36.2	20,226					
					Apache	11,379	13,196	1.2	9,196
Chilton	713	22,770	31.9	23,187	Cochise	6,170	46,465	7.5	34,591
Choctaw	932	20,753	22.3	18,483	Coconino	18,623	9,982	0.5	8,130
Clarke	1,216	26,409	21.7	30,987	Gila	4,699	25,678	5.5	16,348
Clay	614	22,645	36.9	21,006	Graham	4,630	10,148	2.2	23,999
Cleburne	569	13,360	23.5	13,385					
					Greenlee	1,878	15,362	8.2	......
Coffee	678	30.070	44.4	26,119	Maricopa	8,891	89,576	10.1	34,488
Colbert	618	31,997	51.8	24,802	Mohave	13,390	5,259	0.4	3,773
Conecuh	849	24,593	29.0	21,433	Navajo	9,899	16,077	1.6	11,471
Coosa	655	14,839	22.7	16,634	Pima	9,505	34,680	3.6	22,818
Covington	1,042	38,103	36.6	32,124					
					Pinal	5,380	16,130	3.0	9,045
Crenshaw	618	23,017	37.2	23,313	Santa Cruz	1,229	12,689	10.3	6,766
Cullman	763	33,034	43.3	28,321	Yavapai	8,150	24,016	2.9	15,996
Dale	563	22,711	40.3	21,608	Yuma	9,987	14,904	1.5	7,733
Dallas	957	54,697	57.2	53,401					
Dekalb	786	34,426	43.8	28,261	ARKANSAS	52,525	1,752,204	33.4	1,574,449
Elmore	638	28,085	44.0	28,245	Arkansas	1,000	21,483	21.5	16,103
Escambia	957	22,464	23.5	18,889	Ashley	940	23,410	24.9	25,268
Etowah	539	47,275	87.7	39,109	Baxter	586	10,216	17.4	10,389
Fayette	643	18,365	28.6	16,248	Benton	876	36,253	41.4	33,389
Franklin	647	22,011	34.0	19,369	Boone	608	16,098	26.5	14,318
Geneva	578	29,315	50.7	26,230	Bradley	659	15,970	24.2	14,518
Greene	635	18,133	28.6	22,717	Calhoun	629	11,807	18.8	9,894
Hale	646	24,289	37.6	27,883	Carroll	641	17,786	27.7	16,829
Henry	560	21,547	38.5	20,943	Chicot	607	21,749	35.8	21,987
Houston	579	37,334	64.5	32,414	Clark	882	25,632	29.1	23,686
Jackson	1,140	35,864	31.5	32,918	Clay	654	27,276	41.7	23,690
Jefferson	1,120	310,054	276.8	226,476	Cleburne	596	12,696	21.3	11,903
Lamar	601	18,149	30.2	17,487	Cleveland	603	12,260	20.3	13,481
Lauderdale	694	39,556	57.0	30,936	Columbia	785	27,670	35.2	23,820
Lawrence	700	24,307	34.7	21,984	Conway	563	22,578	40.1	22,729
Lee	608	32,821	54.0	32,867	Craighead	687	37,541	54.6	27,627
Limestone	596	31,341	52.6	26,880	Crawford	593	25,739	43.4	23,942
Lowndes	739	25,406	34.4	31,894	Crittenden	582	29,309	50.4	22,447
Macon	614	23,561	38.4	26,049	Cross	619	18,579	30.0	14,042
Madison	811	51,268	63.2	47,041	Dallas	679	14,424	21.2	12,621
Marengo	966	36,065	37.3	39,923	Desha	747	20,297	27.2	15,274
Marion	743	22,008	29.6	17,495	Drew	847	21,822	25.8	21,960
Marshall	602	32,669	54.3	28,553	Faulkner	651	27,681	42.5	23,708
Mobile	1,226	100,117	81.7	80,854	Franklin	606	19,864	32.0	20,638
Monroe	1,012	28,884	28.5	27,155	Fulton	625	11,182	17.9	12,193
Montgomery	801	80,853	100.9	82,178	Garland	738	25,785	34.9	27,271
Morgan	587	40,196	68.5	33,781	Grant	637	10,710	16.8	9,425
Perry	737	25,373	34.4	31,222	Greene	561	26,105	46.5	23,852
Pickens	875	25,353	29.0	25,055	Hempstead	727	31,602	43.5	28,285
Pike	671	31,631	47.1	30,815	Hot Spring	613	17,784	29.0	15,022
Randolph	590	27,064	45.9	24,659	Howard	602	18,565	30.8	16,898
Russell	655	27,448	41.9	25,937	Independence	762	23,976	31.5	24,776
St. Clair	648	23,383	36.1	20,715	Izard	583	13,871	23.8	14,561
Shelby	819	27,097	33.1	26,949	Jackson	634	25,446	40.1	23,501
Sumter	908	25,569	28.2	28,699	Jefferson	903	60,330	66.8	52,734

TABLE 9.—AREA AND POPULATION OF COUNTIES: 1920 AND 1910—Continued.

COUNTY	Land area in square miles: 1920.	POPULATION 1920 Total.	POPULATION 1920 Per square mile.	1910	COUNTY	Land area in square miles: 1920.	POPULATION 1920 Total.	POPULATION 1920 Per square mile.	1910
ARKANSAS—Con.					CALIFORNIA—Con.				
Johnson	675	21,062	31.2	19,698	Marin	529	27,342	51.7	25,114
Lafayette	525	15,522	29.6	13,741	Mariposa	1,463	2,775	1.9	3,956
Lawrence	592	22,098	37.3	20,001	Mendocino	3,539	24,116	6.8	23,929
Lee	601	28,852	48.0	24,252	Merced	1,995	24,579	12.3	15,148
Lincoln	571	18,774	32.9	15,118	Modoc	3,823	5,425	1.4	6,191
Little River	546	16,301	29.9	13,597	Mono	3,030	960	0.3	2,042
Logan	726	25,866	35.6	26,350	Monterey	3,330	27,980	8.4	24,146
Lonoke	807	33,400	41.4	27,983	Napa	783	20,678	26.4	19,800
Madison	836	14,918	17.8	16,056	Nevada	974	10,850	11.1	14,955
Marion	646	10,154	15.7	10,203	Orange	795	61,375	77.2	34,436
Miller	623	24,021	38.6	19,555	Placer	1,411	18,584	13.2	18,237
Mississippi	792	47,320	59.7	30,468	Plumas	2,593	5,681	2.2	5,259
Monroe	603	21,601	35.8	19,907	Riverside	7,223	50,297	7.0	34,696
Montgomery	784	11,112	14.2	12,455	Sacramento	983	91,029	92.6	67,806
Nevada	620	21,934	35.4	19,344	San Benito	1,392	8,995	6.5	8,041
Newton	846	11,199	13.2	10,612	San Bernardino	20,175	73,401	3.6	56,706
Ouachita	733	20,636	28.2	21,774	San Diego	4,221	112,248	26.6	61,665
Perry	552	9,905	17.9	9,402	San Francisco	42	506,676	12,063.7	416,912
Phillips	692	44,530	64.3	33,535	San Joaquin	1,448	79,905	55.2	50,731
Pike	601	12,397	20.6	12,565	San Luis Obispo	3,334	21,893	6.6	19,383
Poinsett	721	20,848	28.9	12,791	San Mateo	447	36,781	82.3	26,585
Polk	846	16,412	19.4	17,216	Santa Barbara	2,740	41,097	15.0	27,738
Pope	828	27,153	32.8	24,527	Santa Clara	1,328	100,676	75.8	83,539
Prairie	662	17,447	26.4	13,853	Santa Cruz	435	26,269	60.4	26,140
Pulaski	779	109,464	140.5	86,751	Shasta	3,858	13,361	3.5	18,920
Randolph	654	17,713	27.1	18,987	Sierra	923	1,783	1.9	4,098
St. Francis	628	28,385	45.2	22,548	Siskiyou	6,256	18,545	3.0	18,801
Saline	743	16,781	22.6	16,657	Solano	822	40,602	49.4	27,559
Scott	970	13,232	13.6	14,302	Sonoma	1,582	52,090	32.9	48,394
Searcy	673	14,590	21.7	14,825	Stanislaus	1,450	43,557	30.0	22,522
Sebastian	531	56,739	106.9	52,278	Sutter	608	10,115	16.6	6,328
Sevier	572	18,301	32.0	16,616	Tehama	2,925	12,882	4.4	11,401
Sharp	609	11,132	18.3	11,688	Trinity	3,096	2,551	0.8	3,301
Stone	611	8,779	14.4	8,946	Tulare	4,856	59,031	12.2	35,440
Union	1,048	29,691	28.3	30,723	Tuolumne	2,190	7,768	3.5	9,979
Van Buren	730	13,666	18.7	13,509	Ventura	1,858	28,724	15.5	18,347
Washington	955	35,468	37.1	33,889	Yolo	1,014	17,105	16.9	13,926
White	1,037	34,603	33.4	28,574	Yuba	632	10,375	16.4	10,042
Woodruff	577	21,547	37.3	20,049					
Yell	955	25,655	26.9	26,323					
CALIFORNIA	155,652	3,426,861	22.0	2,377,549	COLORADO	103,658	939,629	9.1	799,024
Alameda	732	344,177	470.2	246,131	Adams	1,262	14,430	11.4	8,892
Alpine	776	243	0.3	309	Alamosa	727	5,148	7.1	
Amador	601	7,793	13.0	9,086	Arapahoe	842	13,766	16.3	10,263
Butte	1,698	30,030	17.7	27,301	Archuleta	1,220	3,590	2.9	3,302
Calaveras	1,027	6,183	6.0	9,171	Baca	2,552	8,721	3.4	2,516
Colusa	1,140	9,290	8.1	7,732	Bent	1,524	9,705	6.4	5,043
Contra Costa	714	53,889	75.5	31,674	Boulder	764	31,861	41.7	30,330
Del Norte	1,024	2,759	2.7	2,417	Chaffee	1,083	7,165	7.0	7,622
Eldorado	1,737	6,426	3.7	7,492	Cheyenne	1,777	3,746	2.1	3,687
Fresno	5,950	128,779	21.6	75,657	Clear Creek	390	2,891	7.4	5,001
Glenn	1,337	11,853	8.9	7,172	Conejos	1,252	8,416	6.7	11,285
Humboldt	3,575	37,413	10.5	33,857	Costilla	1,185	5,032	4.2	5,498
Imperial	4,089	43,453	10.6	13,591	Crowley	808	6,383	7.9	
Inyo	9,991	7,031	0.7	6,974	Custer	747	2,172	2.9	1,947
Kern	8,003	54,843	6.9	37,715	Delta	1,201	13,668	11.4	13,688
Kings	1,159	22,031	19.0	16,230	Denver	58	256,491	4,422.3	213,381
Lake	1,238	5,402	4.4	5,526	Dolores	1,043	1,243	1.2	642
Lassen	4,531	8,507	1.9	4,802	Douglas	845	3,517	4.2	3,192
Los Angeles	4,115	936,455	227.6	504,131	Eagle	1,620	3,385	2.1	2,985
Madera	2,112	12,203	5.8	8,368	El Paso	2,121	44,027	20.8	43,321

TABLE **9.**—AREA AND POPULATION OF COUNTIES: 1920 AND 1910—Continued.

COUNTY.	Land area in square miles: 1920.	POPULATION. 1920		1910	COUNTY.	Land area in square miles: 1920.	POPULATION. 1920		1910
		Total.	Per square mile.				Total.	Per square mile.	
COLORADO—Con.					DISTRICT OF COLUMBIA [1]	60	437,571	7,292.9	331,069
Elbert	1,857	6,980	3.8	5,331					
Fremont	1,557	17,883	11.5	18,181	FLORIDA	54,861	968,470	17.7	752,619
Garfield	3,107	9,304	3.0	10,144					
Gilpin	132	1,364	10.3	4,131	Alachua	1,257	31,689	25.2	34,305
Grand	1,866	2,659	1.4	1,862	Baker	593	5,622	9.5	4,805
					Bay	781	11,407	14.6	
Gunnison	3,179	5,590	1.8	5,897	Bradford	539	12,503	23.2	14,090
Hinsdale	971	538	0.6	646	Brevard	1,025	8,505	8.3	4,717
Huerfano	1,500	16,879	11.3	13,320					
Jackson	1,632	1,340	0.8	1,013	Broward	1,212	5,135	4.2	
Jefferson	808	14,400	17.8	14,231	Calhoun	1,089	8,775	8.1	7,465
					Citrus	620	5,220	8.4	6,731
Kiowa	1,798	3,755	2.1	2,899	Clay	615	5,621	9.1	6,116
Kit Carson	2,159	8,915	4.1	7,483	Columbia	792	14,290	18.0	17,689
La Plata	1,851	11,218	6.1	10,812					
Lake	371	6,630	17.9	10,600	Dade	2,019	42,753	21.2	11,933
Larimer	2,629	27,872	10.6	25,270	De Soto	3,754	25,434	6.8	14,200
					Duval	782	113,540	145.2	75,163
Las Animas	4,809	38,975	8.1	33,643	Escambia	657	49,386	75.2	38,029
Lincoln	2,570	8,273	3.2	5,917	Flagler	491	2,442	5.0	
Logan	1,822	18,427	10.1	9,549					
Mesa	3,163	22,281	7.0	22,197	Franklin	541	5,318	9.8	5,201
Mineral	866	779	0.9	1,239	Gadsden	540	23,539	43.6	22,198
					Hamilton	528	9,873	18.7	11,825
Moffat	4,658	5,129	1.1		Hernando	497	4,548	9.2	4,997
Montezuma	2,051	6,260	3.1	5,029	Hillsborough	1,036	88,257	85.2	78,374
Montrose	2,264	11,852	5.2	10,291					
Morgan	1,286	16,124	12.5	9,577	Holmes	473	12,850	27.2	11,557
Otero	1,259	22,623	18.0	20,201	Jackson	939	31,224	33.3	29,821
					Jefferson	585	14,502	24.8	17,210
Ouray	519	2,620	5.0	3,514	Lafayette	1,263	6,242	4.9	6,710
Park	2,242	1,977	0.9	2,492	Lake	1,047	12,744	12.2	9,509
Phillips	688	5,499	8.0	3,179					
Pitkin	1,019	2,707	2.7	4,566	Lee	4,031	9,540	2.4	6,294
Prowers	1,630	13,845	8.5	9,520	Leon	715	18,059	25.3	19,427
					Levy	1,148	9,921	8.6	10,361
Pueblo	2,433	57,638	23.7	52,223	Liberty	823	5,006	6.1	4,700
Rio Blanco	3,223	3,135	1.0	2,332	Madison	719	16,516	23.0	16,919
Rio Grande	898	7,855	8.7	6,563					
Routt	2,309	8,948	3.9	7,561	Manatee	1,337	18,712	14.0	9,550
Saguache	3,133	4,638	1.5	4,160	Marion	1,647	23,968	14.6	26,941
					Monroe	1,100	19,550	17.8	21,563
San Juan	453	1,700	3.8	3,063	Nassau	630	11,340	18.0	10,525
San Miguel	1,288	5,281	4.1	4,700	Okaloosa	956	9,360	9.8	
Sedgwick	531	4,207	7.9	3,061					
Summit	649	1,724	2.7	2,003	Okeechobee	747	2,132	2.9	
					Orange	929	19,890	21.4	19,107
Teller	547	6,696	12.2	14,351	Osceola	1,356	7,195	5.3	5,507
Washington	2,521	11,208	4.4	6,002	Palm Beach	2,538	18,654	7.3	5,577
Weld	4,022	54,059	13.4	39,177	Pasco	767	8,802	11.5	7,502
Yuma	2,367	13,897	5.9	8,499					
					Pinellas	293	28,265	96.5	
CONNECTICUT	4,820	1,380,631	286.4	1,114,756	Polk	1,907	38,661	20.3	24,148
					Putnam	752	14,568	19.4	13,096
Fairfield	631	320,936	508.6	245,322	St. Johns	608	13,061	21.5	13,208
Hartford	729	336,027	460.9	250,182	St. Lucie	1,077	7,886	7.3	4,075
Litchfield	925	76,262	82.4	70,260					
Middlesex	369	47,550	128.9	45,637	Santa Rosa	1,025	13,670	13.3	14,897
					Seminole	321	10,986	34.2	
New Haven	603	415,214	688.6	337,282	Sumter	583	7,851	13.5	6,696
New London	659	104,611	158.7	91,253	Suwannee	692	19,789	28.6	18,603
Tolland	404	27,216	67.4	26,459	Taylor	1,045	11,219	10.7	7,103
Windham	500	52,815	105.6	48,361					
					Volusia	1,123	23,374	20.8	16,510
DELAWARE	1,965	223,003	113.5	202,322	Wakulla	602	5,129	8.5	4,802
					Walton	1,095	12,119	11.1	16,460
Kent	617	31,023	50.3	32,721	Washington	620	11,828	19.1	16,403
New Castle	435	148,239	340.8	123,188					
Sussex	913	43,741	47.9	46,413					

[1] Not divided into counties.

TABLE 9.—AREA AND POPULATION OF COUNTIES: 1920 AND 1910—Continued.

COUNTY.	Land area in square miles: 1920.	POPULATION.			COUNTY.	Land area in square miles: 1920.	POPULATION.		
		1920		1910			1920		1910
		Total.	Per square mile.				Total.	Per square mile.	
GEORGIA	58,725	2,895,832	49.3	2,609,121	GEORGIA—Con.				
Appling	454	10,594	23.3	12,318	Gilmer	440	8,406	19.1	9,237
Atkinson	330	7,656	23.2	....	Glascock	170	4,192	24.7	4,669
Bacon	271	6,460	23.8	....	Glynn	439	19,370	44.1	15,720
Baker	357	8,298	23.2	7,973	Gordon	375	17,736	47.3	15,861
Baldwin	307	19,791	64.5	18,354	Grady	444	20,306	45.7	18,457
Banks	222	11,814	53.2	11,244	Greene	416	18,972	45.6	18,512
Barrow	168	13,188	78.5	....	Gwinnett	440	30,327	68.9	28,824
Bartow	471	24,527	52.1	25,388	Habersham	290	10,730	37.0	10,134
Ben Hill	256	14,599	57.0	11,863	Hall	437	26,822	61.4	25,730
Berrien	500	15,573	31.1	22,772	Hancock	530	18,357	34.6	19,189
Bibb	277	71,304	257.4	56,646	Haralson	284	14,440	50.8	13,514
Bleckley	205	10,532	51.4	....	Harris	501	15,775	31.5	17,886
Brooks	514	24,538	47.7	23,832	Hart	261	17,944	68.8	16,216
Bryan	431	6,343	14.7	6,702	Heard	285	11,126	39.0	11,189
Bulloch	668	26,133	39.1	26,464	Henry	324	20,420	63.0	19,927
Burke	956	30,836	32.3	27,268	Houston	585	21,964	37.5	23,609
Butts	203	12,327	60.7	13,624	Irwin	378	12,670	33.5	10,461
Calhoun	284	10,225	36.0	11,334	Jackson	355	24,654	69.4	30,169
Camden	711	6,969	9.8	7,690	Jasper	321	16,362	51.0	16,552
Campbell	211	11,709	55.5	10,874	Jeff Davis	300	7,322	24.4	6,050
Candler	228	9,228	40.5	....	Jefferson	646	22,602	35.0	21,379
Carroll	492	34,752	70.6	30,855	Jenkins	342	14,328	41.9	11,520
Catoosa	169	6,677	39.5	7,184	Johnson	292	13,546	46.4	12,897
Charlton	881	4,536	5.1	4,722	Jones	377	13,269	35.2	13,103
Chatham	370	100,032	270.4	79,690	Laurens	806	39,605	49.1	35,501
Chattahoochee	218	5,266	24.2	5,586	Lee	326	10,904	33.4	11,679
Chattooga	328	14,312	43.6	13,608	Liberty	936	12,707	13.6	12,924
Cherokee	429	18,569	43.3	16,661	Lincoln	291	9,739	33.5	8,714
Clarke	114	26,111	229.0	23,273	Lowndes	476	26,521	55.7	24,436
Clay	203	7,557	37.2	8,960	Lumpkin	280	5,240	18.7	5,444
Clayton	142	11,159	78.6	10,453	McDuffie	287	11,509	40.1	10,325
Clinch	900	7,984	8.9	8,424	McIntosh	470	5,119	10.9	6,442
Cobb	353	30,437	86.2	28,397	Macon	369	17,667	47.9	15,016
Coffee	632	18,653	29.5	21,953	Madison	284	18,803	66.2	16,851
Colquitt	529	29,332	55.4	19,789	Marion	360	7,604	21.1	9,147
Columbia	350	11,718	33.5	12,328	Meriwether	496	26,168	52.8	25,180
Cook	241	11,180	46.4	....	Miller	253	9,565	37.8	7,986
Coweta	443	29,047	65.6	28,800	Milton	145	6,885	47.5	7,239
Crawford	319	8,893	27.9	8,310	Mitchell	548	25,588	46.7	22,114
Crisp	277	18,914	68.3	16,423	Monroe	584	20,138	34.5	20,450
Dade	186	3,918	21.1	4,139	Montgomery	190	9,167	48.2	19,638
Dawson	216	4,204	19.5	4,686	Morgan	390	20,143	51.6	19,717
Decatur	823	31,785	38.6	29,045	Murray	342	9,490	27.7	9,763
Dekalb	272	44,051	162.0	27,881	Muscogee	235	44,195	188.1	36,227
Dodge	431	22,540	52.3	20,127	Newton	262	21,680	82.7	18,449
Dooly	397	20,522	51.7	20,554	Oconee	172	11,067	64.3	11,104
Dougherty	342	20,063	58.7	16,035	Oglethorpe	504	20,287	40.3	18,680
Douglas	208	10,177	50.4	8,953	Paulding	324	14,025	43.3	14,124
Early	524	18,983	36.2	18,122	Pickens	231	8,222	35.6	9,041
Echols	362	3,313	9.2	3,309	Pierce	517	11,934	23.1	10,749
Effingham	448	9,985	22.3	9,971	Pike	307	21,212	69.1	19,495
Elbert	361	23,905	66.2	24,125	Polk	317	20,357	64.2	20,203
Emanuel	889	25,862	29.1	25,140	Pulaski	258	11,587	44.9	22,835
Evans	287	6,594	23.0	....	Putnam	361	15,151	42.0	13,876
Fannin	401	12,103	30.2	12,574	Quitman	144	3,417	23.7	4,594
Fayette	234	11,396	48.7	10,966	Rabun	377	5,746	15.2	5,562
Floyd	502	39,841	79.4	36,736	Randolph	412	16,721	40.6	18,841
Forsyth	247	11,755	47.6	11,940	Richmond	319	63,692	199.7	58,886
Franklin	279	19,957	71.5	17,894	Rockdale	119	9,521	80.0	8,916
Fulton	185	232,606	1,257.3	177,733	Schley	154	5,243	34.0	5,213

TABLE 9.—AREA AND POPULATION OF COUNTIES: 1920 AND 1910—Continued.

COUNTY	Land area in square miles: 1920	1920 Total	1920 Per square mile	1910
GEORGIA—Con.				
Screven	794	23,552	29.7	20,202
Spalding	209	21,908	104.8	19,741
Stephens	166	11,215	67.6	9,728
Stewart	411	12,089	29.4	13,437
Sumter	456	29,640	65.0	29,092
Talbot	312	11,158	35.8	11,696
Taliaferro	212	8,841	41.7	8,766
Tattnall	466	14,502	31.1	18,569
Taylor	340	11,473	33.7	10,839
Telfair	373	15,291	41.0	13,288
Terrell	322	19,601	60.9	22,003
Thomas	530	33,044	62.3	29,071
Tift	243	14,493	59.6	11,487
Toombs	393	13,897	35.4	11,206
Towns	181	3,937	21.8	3,932
Treutlen	137	7,664	55.9	
Troup	435	36,097	83.0	26,228
Turner	231	12,466	54.0	10,075
Twiggs	314	10,407	33.1	10,736
Union	324	6,455	19.9	6,918
Upson	317	14,786	46.6	12,757
Walker	432	23,370	54.1	18,692
Walton	331	24,216	73.2	25,393
Ware	771	28,361	36.8	22,957
Warren	404	11,828	29.3	11,860
Washington	669	28,147	42.1	28,174
Wayne	788	14,381	18.3	13,069
Webster	302	5,342	17.7	6,151
Wheeler	264	9,817	37.2	
White	245	6,105	24.9	5,110
Whitfield	283	16,897	59.7	15,934
Wilcox	403	15,511	38.5	13,486
Wilkes	458	24,210	52.9	23,441
Wilkinson	472	11,376	24.1	10,078
Worth	651	23,863	36.7	19,147
IDAHO	[1]83,354	431,866	5.2	325,594
Ada	1,154	35,213	30.5	29,088
Adams	1,366	2,966	2.2	
Bannock	1,837	27,532	15.0	19,242
Bear Lake	980	8,783	9.0	7,729
Benewah	786	6,997	8.9	
Bingham	2,184	18,310	8.4	23,306
Blaine	2,797	4,473	1.6	8,387
Boise	1,840	1,822	1.0	5,250
Bonner	1,748	12,957	7.4	13,588
Bonneville	1,904	17,501	9.2	
Boundary	1,276	4,474	3.5	
Butte	2,048	2,940	1.4	
Camas	1,070	1,730	1.6	
Canyon	592	26,932	45.5	25,323
Caribou	1,263	2,191	1.7	
Cassia	2,595	15,659	6.0	7,197
Clark	1,778	1,886	1.1	
Clearwater	2,508	4,993	2.0	
Custer	4,921	3,550	0.7	3,001
Elmore	2,808	5,087	1.8	4,785

COUNTY	Land area in square miles: 1920	1920 Total	1920 Per square mile	1910
IDAHO—Con.				
Franklin	556	8,650	15.6	
Fremont	1,849	10,380	5.6	24,606
Gem	567	6,427	11.3	
Gooding	740	7,548	10.2	
Idaho	8,539	11,749	1.4	12,384
Jefferson	1,094	9,441	8.6	
Jerome	606	5,729	9.5	
Kootenai	1,253	17,878	14.3	22,747
Latah	1,071	18,092	16.9	18,818
Lemhi	4,597	5,164	1.1	4,786
Lewis	470	5,851	12.4	
Lincoln	1,188	3,446	2.9	12,676
Madison	481	9,167	19.1	
Minidoka	756	9,035	12.0	
Nez Perce	851	15,253	17.9	24,860
Oneida	1,209	6,723	5.6	15,170
Owyhee	7,956	4,694	0.6	4,044
Payette	414	7,021	17.0	
Power	1,391	5,105	3.7	
Shoshone	2,597	14,250	5.5	13,963
Teton	463	3,921	8.5	
Twin Falls	1,957	28,398	14.5	13,543
Valley	3,779	2,524	0.7	
Washington	1,479	9,424	6.4	11,101
ILLINOIS	56,043	6,485,280	115.7	5,638,591
Adams	842	62,188	73.9	64,588
Alexander	226	23,980	106.1	22,741
Bond	388	16,045	41.4	17,075
Boone	293	15,322	52.3	15,481
Brown	297	9,336	31.4	10,397
Bureau	881	42,648	48.4	43,975
Calhoun	256	8,245	32.2	8,610
Carroll	453	19,345	42.7	18,035
Cass	371	17,896	48.2	17,372
Champaign	1,043	56,959	54.6	51,829
Christian	700	38,458	54.9	34,594
Clark	493	21,165	42.9	23,517
Clay	462	17,684	38.3	18,661
Clinton	483	22,947	47.5	22,832
Coles	525	35,108	66.9	34,517
Cook	933	3,053,017	3,272.3	2,405,233
Crawford	453	22,771	50.3	26,281
Cumberland	353	12,858	36.4	14,281
De Kalb	638	31,339	49.1	33,457
De Witt	415	19,252	46.4	18,906
Douglas	417	19,604	47.0	19,591
Du Page	345	42,120	122.1	33,432
Edgar	621	25,769	41.5	27,336
Edwards	238	9,431	39.6	10,049
Effingham	511	19,556	38.3	20,055
Fayette	729	26,187	35.9	28,075
Ford	500	16,466	32.9	17,096
Franklin	445	57,293	128.7	25,943
Fulton	884	48,163	54.5	49,549
Gallatin	338	12,856	38.0	14,628

[1] Total land area includes part of Yellowstone National Park (36 square miles); total population of park returned as in Wyoming.

TABLE 9.—AREA AND POPULATION OF COUNTIES: 1920 AND 1910—Continued.

COUNTY.	Land area in square miles: 1920.	POPULATION. 1920 Total.	Per square mile.	1910	COUNTY.	Land area in square miles: 1920.	POPULATION. 1920 Total.	Per square mile.	1910
ILLINOIS—Con.					ILLINOIS—Con.				
Greene	515	22,883	44.4	22,365	Union	403	20,249	50.2	21,856
Grundy	433	18,580	42.9	24,162	Vermilion	921	86,162	93.6	77,996
Hamilton	455	15,920	35.0	18,227	Wabash	220	14,034	63.8	14,913
Hancock	780	28,523	36.6	30,638	Warren	546	21,488	39.4	23,313
Hardin	185	7,533	40.7	7,015					
					Washington	561	18,035	32.1	18,759
Henderson	376	9,770	26.0	9,724	Wayne	733	22,772	31.1	25,697
Henry	824	45,162	54.8	41,736	White	507	20,081	39.6	23,052
Iroquois	1,121	34,841	31.1	35,543	Whiteside	679	36,174	53.3	34,507
Jackson	588	37,091	63.1	35,143					
Jasper	508	16,064	31.6	18,157	Will	844	92,911	110.1	84,371
					Williamson	449	61,092	136.1	45,098
Jefferson	603	28,480	47.2	29,111	Winnebago	529	90,929	171.9	63,153
Jersey	367	12,682	34.6	13,954	Woodford	528	19,340	36.6	20,506
Jo Daviess	623	21,917	35.2	22,657					
Johnson	348	12,022	34.5	14,331					
Kane	527	99,499	188.8	91,862	INDIANA	36,045	2,930,390	81.3	2,700,876
Kankakee	668	44,940	67.3	40,752	Adams	337	20,503	60.8	21,840
Kendall	324	10,074	31.1	10,777	Allen	661	114,303	172.9	93,386
Knox	711	46,727	65.7	46,159	Bartholomew	407	23,887	58.7	24,813
La Salle	1,146	92,925	81.1	90,132	Benton	408	12,206	29.9	12,688
Lake	455	74,285	163.3	55,058	Blackford	168	14,084	83.8	15,820
Lawrence	358	21,380	59.7	22,661	Boone	427	23,575	55.2	24,673
Lee	742	28,004	37.7	27,750	Brown	324	7,019	21.7	7,975
Livingston	1,043	39,070	37.5	40,465	Carroll	377	16,315	43.3	17,970
Logan	617	29,562	47.9	30,216	Cass	416	38,333	92.1	36,368
McDonough	588	27,074	46.0	26,887	Clark	375	29,381	78.3	30,260
McHenry	620	33,164	53.5	32,509	Clay	361	29,447	81.6	32,535
McLean	1,191	70,107	58.9	68,008	Clinton	408	27,737	68.0	26,674
Macon	585	65,175	111.4	54,186	Crawford	303	11,201	37.0	12,057
Macoupin	860	57,274	66.6	50,685	Daviess	433	26,856	62.0	27,747
Madison	737	106,895	145.0	89,847	De Kalb	370	25,600	69.2	25,054
Marion	569	37,497	65.9	35,094	Dearborn	313	20,033	64.0	21,396
Marshall	396	14,760	37.3	15,679	Decatur	378	17,813	47.1	18,793
Mason	555	16,634	30.0	17,377	Delaware	392	56,377	143.8	51,414
Massac	240	13,559	56.5	14,200	Dubois	427	19,915	46.6	19,843
Menard	317	11,694	36.9	12,796	Elkhart	462	56,384	122.0	49,008
Mercer	540	18,800	34.8	19,723	Fayette	216	17,142	79.4	14,415
Monroe	389	12,839	33.0	13,508	Floyd	148	30,661	207.2	30,293
Montgomery	689	41,403	60.1	35,311	Fountain	395	18,823	47.7	20,439
Morgan	576	33,567	58.3	34,420	Franklin	394	14,806	37.6	15,335
Moultrie	338	14,839	43.9	14,630	Fulton	367	16,478	44.9	16,879
Ogle	756	26,830	35.5	27,864	Gibson	486	29,201	60.1	30,137
Peoria	636	111,710	175.6	100,255	Grant	423	51,353	121.4	51,426
Perry	451	22,901	50.8	22,088	Greene	543	36,770	67.7	36,873
Piatt	451	15,714	34.8	16,376	Hamilton	399	24,222	60.7	27,026
Pike	786	26,866	34.2	28,622	Hancock	307	17,210	56.1	19,030
Pope	385	9,625	25.0	11,215	Harrison	486	18,656	38.4	20,232
Pulaski	190	14,629	77.0	15,650	Hendricks	408	20,291	49.7	20,840
Putnam	173	7,579	43.8	7,561	Henry	307	34,682	87.4	29,758
Randolph	587	29,109	49.6	29,120	Howard	297	43,965	148.0	60,177
Richland	357	14,044	39.3	15,970	Huntington	386	31,671	82.0	90,689
Rock Island	424	92,297	217.7	70,404	Jackson	518	24,228	46.8	24,727
St. Clair	663	136,520	205.9	119,870	Jasper	562	13,961	24.8	13,044
Saline	399	38,353	96.1	30,204	Jay	375	23,318	62.2	24,961
Sangamon	876	100,262	114.5	91,024	Jefferson	364	20,709	56.9	20,483
Schuyler	432	13,285	30.8	14,852	Jennings	383	13,280	34.7	14,203
Scott	249	9,489	38.1	10,067	Johnson	322	20,739	64.4	20,394
Shelby	772	29,601	38.3	31,693	Knox	510	46,195	90.6	39,183
Stark	290	9,693	33.4	10,098	Kosciusko	541	27,120	50.1	27,936
Stephenson	559	37,743	67.5	36,821	La Porte	595	50,443	84.8	45,797
Tazewell	647	38,540	59.6	34,027	Lagrange	387	14,009	36.2	15,148

TABLE 9.—AREA AND POPULATION OF COUNTIES: 1920 AND 1910—Continued.

COUNTY.	Land area in square miles: 1920.	1920 Total.	1920 Per square mile.	1910	COUNTY.	Land area in square miles: 1920.	1920 Total.	1920 Per square mile.	1910
INDIANA—Con.					IOWA—Con.				
Lake	492	159,957	325.1	82,864	Buena Vista	571	18,556	32.5	15,981
Lawrence	456	28,228	61.9	30,625	Butler	577	17,845	30.9	17,119
Madison	450	69,151	153.7	65,224	Calhoun	568	17,783	31.3	17,090
Marion	397	348,061	876.7	263,661	Carroll	571	21,549	37.7	20,117
Marshall	441	23,744	53.8	24,175	Cass	564	19,421	34.4	19,047
Martin	339	11,865	35.0	12,950	Cedar	570	17,560	30.8	17,765
Miami	381	28,668	75.2	29,350	Cerro Gordo	567	34,675	61.2	25,011
Monroe	416	24,519	58.9	23,426	Cherokee	573	17,760	31.0	16,741
Montgomery	501	28,490	56.9	29,296	Chickasaw	497	15,431	31.0	15,375
Morgan	406	20,010	49.3	21,182	Clarke	428	10,506	24.5	10,736
Newton	405	10,144	25.0	10,504	Clay	563	15,660	27.8	12,766
Noble	417	22,470	53.9	24,009	Clayton	762	25,032	32.9	25,576
Ohio	85	4,024	47.3	4,329	Clinton	691	43,371	62.8	45,394
Orange	407	16,974	41.7	17,192	Crawford	715	20,614	28.8	20,041
Owen	393	12,760	32.5	14,053	Dallas	589	25,120	42.6	23,628
Parke	447	18,875	42.2	22,214	Davis	501	12,574	25.1	13,315
Perry	384	16,692	43.5	18,078	Decatur	533	16,566	31.1	16,347
Pike	338	18,684	55.3	19,684	Delaware	571	18,183	31.8	17,888
Porter	415	20,256	48.8	20,540	Des Moines	409	35,520	86.8	36,145
Posey	402	19,334	48.1	21,670	Dickinson	376	10,241	27.2	8,137
Pulaski	432	12,385	28.7	13,312	Dubuque	601	58,262	96.9	57,450
Putnam	483	19,880	41.2	20,520	Emmet	393	12,627	32.1	9,816
Randolph	447	26,484	59.2	29,013	Fayette	724	29,251	40.4	27,919
Ripley	448	18,694	41.7	19,452	Floyd	495	18,860	38.1	17,119
Rush	409	19,241	47.0	19,349	Franklin	578	15,807	27.3	14,780
St. Joseph	460	103,304	224.6	84,312	Fremont	507	15,447	30.5	15,623
Scott	190	7,424	39.1	8,323	Greene	574	16,467	28.7	16,023
Shelby	407	25,982	63.8	26,802	Grundy	501	14,420	28.8	13,574
Spencer	403	18,400	45.7	20,676	Guthrie	595	17,596	29.6	17,374
Starke	305	10,278	33.7	10,567	Hamilton	570	19,531	34.3	19,242
Steuben	305	13,360	43.8	14,274	Hancock	570	14,723	25.8	12,731
Sullivan	460	31,630	68.8	32,439	Hardin	569	23,337	41.0	20,921
Switzerland	222	9,311	41.9	9,914	Harrison	691	24,488	35.4	23,162
Tippecanoe	503	42,813	85.1	40,063	Henry	427	18,298	42.9	18,640
Tipton	260	16,152	62.1	17,459	Howard	468	13,705	29.3	12,920
Union	162	6,021	37.2	6,260	Humboldt	431	12,951	30.0	12,182
Vanderburg	233	92,293	396.1	77,438	Ida	430	11,689	27.2	11,296
Vermilion	254	27,625	108.8	18,865	Iowa	583	18,600	31.9	18,409
Vigo	409	100,212	245.0	87,930	Jackson	632	19,931	31.5	21,258
Wabash	425	27,231	64.1	26,926	Jasper	730	27,855	38.2	27,034
Warren	368	9,699	26.4	10,899	Jefferson	431	16,440	38.1	15,951
Warrick	392	19,862	50.7	21,911	Johnson	610	26,462	43.4	25,914
Washington	519	16,645	32.1	17,445	Jones	569	18,607	32.7	19,050
					Keokuk	578	20,983	36.3	21,160
Wayne	411	48,136	117.1	43,757	Kossuth	973	25,082	25.8	21,971
Wells	365	20,509	56.2	22,418					
White	507	17,351	34.2	17,602	Lee	511	39,676	77.6	36,702
Whitley	338	15,660	46.3	16,892	Linn	709	74,004	104.4	60,720
					Louisa	396	12,179	30.8	12,855
					Lucas	432	15,686	36.3	13,462
IOWA	55,586	2,404,021	43.2	2,224,771	Lyon	582	15,431	26.5	14,624
Adair	573	14,259	24.9	14,420	Madison	563	15,020	26.7	15,621
Adams	427	10,521	24.6	10,998	Mahaska	568	26,270	46.3	29,860
Allamakee	639	17,285	27.1	17,328	Marion	563	24,957	44.3	22,995
Appanoose	513	30,535	59.5	28,701	Marshall	572	32,630	57.0	30,279
Audubon	443	12,520	28.3	12,671	Mills	438	15,422	35.2	15,811
Benton	712	24,080	33.8	23,156	Mitchell	463	13,921	30.1	13,435
Black Hawk	565	56,570	100.1	44,865	Monona	686	17,125	25.0	16,633
Boone	569	29,892	52.5	27,626	Monroe	432	23,467	54.3	25,429
Bremer	434	16,728	38.5	15,843	Montgomery	424	17,048	40.2	16,604
Buchanan	567	19,890	35.1	19,748	Muscatine	432	29,042	67.2	29,505

TABLE 9.—AREA AND POPULATION OF COUNTIES: 1920 AND 1910—Continued.

COUNTY.	Land area in square miles: 1920.	POPULATION. 1920 Total.	Per square mile.	1910	COUNTY.	Land area in square miles: 1920.	POPULATION. 1920 Total.	Per square mile.	1910
IOWA—Con.					**KANSAS—Con.**				
O'Brien	569	19,051	33.5	17,262	Geary	390	13,452	34.5	12,681
Osceola	395	10,223	25.9	8,956	Gove	1,080	4,748	4.4	6,044
Page	531	24,137	45.5	24,002	Graham	897	7,624	8.5	8,700
Palo Alto	561	15,486	27.6	13,845	Grant	578	1,087	1.9	1,087
Plymouth	856	23,584	27.6	23,129	Gray	857	4,711	5.5	3,121
Pocahontas	576	15,602	27.1	14,808	Greeley	776	1,028	1.3	1,335
Polk	582	154,029	264.7	110,438	Greenwood	1,158	14,715	12.7	16,060
Pottawattamie	942	61,550	65.3	55,832	Hamilton	984	2,586	2.6	3,360
Poweshiek	580	19,910	34.3	19,589	Harper	799	13,656	17.1	14,748
Ringgold	540	12,919	23.9	12,904	Harvey	540	20,744	38.4	19,200
Sac	574	17,500	30.5	16,555	Haskell	577	1,455	2.5	993
Scott	449	73,952	164.7	60,000	Hodgeman	858	3,734	4.4	2,930
Shelby	589	16,065	27.3	16,552	Jackson	675	15,495	23.0	16,861
Sioux	760	26,458	34.8	25,248	Jefferson	543	14,750	27.2	15,826
Story	567	26,185	46.2	24,083	Jewell	900	16,240	18.0	18,148
Tama	720	21,861	30.4	22,156	Johnson	486	18,314	37.7	18,288
Taylor	534	15,514	29.1	16,312	Kearney	853	2,617	3.1	3,206
Union	427	17,268	40.4	16,616	Kingman	867	12,119	14.0	13,386
Van Buren	477	14,060	29.5	15,020	Kiowa	723	6,164	8.5	6,174
Wapello	428	37,937	88.6	37,743	Labette	643	34,047	53.0	31,423
Warren	570	18,047	31.7	18,194	Lane	715	2,848	4.0	2,603
Washington	559	20,421	36.5	19,925	Leavenworth	440	38,402	87.3	41,207
Wayne	524	15,378	29.3	16,184	Lincoln	721	9,894	13.7	10,142
Webster	714	37,611	52.7	34,629	Linn	613	13,815	22.5	14,735
Winnebago	399	13,489	33.8	11,914	Logan	1,082	3,223	3.0	4,240
Winneshiek	686	22,091	32.2	21,729	Lyon	845	26,154	31.0	24,927
Woodbury	864	92,171	106.7	67,616	McPherson	900	21,845	24.3	21,521
Worth	399	11,630	29.1	9,950	Marion	953	22,923	24.1	22,415
Wright	575	20,348	35.4	17,951	Marshall	905	22,730	25.1	23,880
					Meade	984	5,542	5.6	5,055
KANSAS	81,774	1,769,257	21.6	1,690,949	Miami	602	19,809	32.9	20,030
Allen	508	23,509	46.3	27,640	Mitchell	713	13,886	19.5	14,089
Anderson	577	12,986	22.5	13,829	Montgomery	644	49,645	77.1	49,474
Atchison	412	23,411	56.8	28,107	Morris	696	12,005	17.2	12,397
Barber	1,134	9,739	8.6	9,916	Morton	718	3,177	4.4	1,333
Barton	892	18,422	20.7	17,876	Nemaha	716	18,487	25.8	19,072
Bourbon	656	23,198	35.4	24,007	Neosho	580	24,000	41.4	23,754
Brown	571	20,949	36.7	21,314	Ness	1,079	7,490	6.9	5,883
Butler	1,434	43,842	30.6	23,059	Norton	876	11,423	13.0	11,614
Chase	769	7,144	9.3	7,527	Osage	718	18,621	25.9	19,905
Chautauqua	652	11,598	17.8	11,429	Osborne	894	12,441	13.9	12,827
Cherokee	605	33,609	55.6	38,162	Ottawa	712	10,714	15.0	11,811
Cheyenne	1,008	5,587	5.5	4,248	Pawnee	742	9,323	12.6	8,859
Clark	973	4,989	5.1	4,093	Phillips	887	12,505	14.1	14,150
Clay	638	14,365	22.5	15,251	Pottawatomie	829	16,154	19.5	17,522
Cloud	702	17,714	25.2	18,388	Pratt	720	12,000	17.8	11,156
Coffey	644	14,204	22.1	15,205	Rawlins	1,081	6,700	6.4	6,380
Comanche	788	5,302	6.7	3,281	Reno	1,242	44,423	35.8	37,853
Cowley	1,133	35,155	31.0	31,790	Republic	704	15,855	22.5	17,447
Crawford	605	61,800	102.1	51,178	Rice	707	14,832	21.0	15,106
Decatur	891	8,121	9.1	8,976	Riley	604	20,650	34.2	15,783
Dickinson	838	25,777	30.8	24,361	Rooks	890	9,966	11.2	11,282
Doniphan	378	13,438	35.6	14,422	Rush	719	8,360	11.6	7,826
Douglas	469	23,998	51.2	24,724	Russell	895	10,748	12.0	10,800
Edwards	611	7,057	11.5	7,033	Saline	720	25,103	34.9	20,338
Elk	652	9,034	13.9	10,128	Scott	714	3,121	4.4	3,047
Ellis	901	14,138	15.7	12,170	Sedgwick	994	92,234	92.8	73,095
Ellsworth	724	10,379	14.3	10,444	Seward	643	6,220	9.7	4,091
Finney	1,276	7,674	6.0	6,908	Shawnee	544	69,159	127.1	61,874
Ford	1,082	14,273	13.2	11,393	Sheridan	896	5,484	6.1	5,651
Franklin	585	21,946	37.5	20,884					

TABLE 9.—AREA AND POPULATION OF COUNTIES: 1920 AND 1910—Continued.

COUNTY.	Land area in square miles: 1920.	POPULATION. 1920 Total.	Per square mile.	1910	COUNTY.	Land area in square miles: 1920.	POPULATION. 1920 Total.	Per square mile.	1910
KANSAS—Con.					KENTUCKY—Con.				
Sherman	1,049	5,592	5.3	4,549	Hancock	193	6,945	36.0	8,512
Smith	888	14,985	16.9	15,365	Hardin	606	24,287	40.1	22,696
Stafford	796	11,559	14.5	12,510	Harlan	478	31,546	66.0	10,566
Stanton	685	908	1.3	1,034	Harrison	311	15,798	50.8	16,873
Stevens	729	3,943	5.4	2,453	Hart	430	18,544	43.1	18,173
Sumner	1,179	29,213	24.8	30,654					
Thomas	1,065	5,517	5.2	5,455	Henderson	435	27,609	63.5	29,352
Trego	899	5,880	6.5	5,398	Henry	303	13,411	44.3	13,716
Wabaunsee	795	11,424	14.4	12,721	Hickman	225	10,244	45.5	11,750
Wallace	921	2,424	2.6	2,759	Hopkins	546	34,133	62.5	34,291
					Jackson	333	11,687	35.1	10,734
Washington	902	17,984	19.9	20,229					
Wichita	721	1,856	2.6	2,006	Jefferson	387	286,369	740.0	262,920
Wilson	581	21,157	36.4	19,810	Jessamine	172	12,205	71.0	12,613
Woodson	503	8,984	17.9	9,450	Johnson	268	19,622	73.2	17,482
Wyandotte	143	122,218	854.7	100,068	Kenton	163	73,453	450.6	70,355
					Knott	348	11,655	33.5	10,791
KENTUCKY	40,181	2,416,630	60.1	2,289,905					
					Knox	356	24,172	67.9	22,116
Adair	400	17,289	43.2	16,503	Larue	288	10,004	34.7	10,701
Allen	394	16,761	42.5	14,882	Laurel	447	19,814	44.3	19,872
Anderson	201	9,982	49.7	10,146	Lawrence	422	17,643	41.8	20,067
Ballard	252	12,045	47.8	12,690	Lee	199	11,918	59.9	9,531
Barren	485	25,356	52.3	25,293					
Bath	270	11,996	44.4	13,988	Leslie	373	10,097	27.1	8,976
Bell	384	33,988	88.5	28,447	Letcher	355	24,467	68.9	10,623
Boone	251	9,572	38.1	9,420	Lewis	491	15,829	32.2	16,887
Bourbon	304	18,418	60.6	17,462	Lincoln	338	16,481	48.8	17,897
Boyd	159	29,281	184.2	23,444	Livingston	392	9,732	24.8	10,627
Boyle	186	14,998	80.6	14,668	Logan	643	23,633	36.8	24,977
Bracken	204	10,210	50.0	10,308	Lyon	277	8,795	31.8	9,423
Breathitt	483	20,614	42.7	17,540	McCracken	239	37,246	155.8	35,064
Breckinridge	568	19,652	34.6	21,034	McCreary	406	11,676	28.8	
Bullitt	308	9,328	30.3	9,487	McLean	253	12,502	49.4	13,241
Butler	417	15,197	36.4	15,805	Madison	446	26,284	58.9	26,951
Caldwell	322	13,975	43.4	14,063	Magoffin	302	13,859	45.9	13,654
Calloway	412	20,802	50.5	19,867	Marion	345	15,527	45.0	16,330
Campbell	145	61,868	426.7	59,369	Marshall	327	15,215	46.5	15,771
Carlisle	198	8,231	41.6	9,048	Martin	227	7,654	33.7	7,291
Carroll	132	8,346	63.2	8,110	Mason	227	17,760	78.2	18,611
Carter	413	22,474	54.4	21,966	Meade	301	9,442	31.4	9,783
Casey	379	17,213	45.4	15,479	Menifee	203	5,779	28.5	6,153
Christian	725	35,883	49.5	38,845	Mercer	253	14,795	58.5	14,063
Clark	265	17,901	67.6	17,987	Metcalfe	303	10,075	33.3	10,453
Clay	478	19,795	41.4	17,789	Monroe	441	14,214	32.2	13,663
Clinton	233	8,589	36.9	8,153	Montgomery	198	12,245	61.8	12,868
Crittenden	391	13,120	33.6	13,296	Morgan	365	16,518	45.3	16,259
Cumberland	387	10,648	27.5	9,846	Muhlenberg	472	33,353	70.7	28,598
Daviess	478	40,733	85.2	41,020	Nelson	411	16,137	39.3	16,830
Edmonson	308	10,894	35.4	10,469	Nicholas	208	9,894	47.6	10,601
Elliott	263	8,887	33.8	9,814	Ohio	584	26,473	45.3	27,642
Estill	254	15,569	61.3	12,273	Oldham	180	7,689	42.7	7,248
Fayette	269	54,664	203.2	47,715	Owen	367	12,554	34.2	14,248
Fleming	325	15,614	48.0	16,066	Owsley	216	7,820	36.2	7,979
Floyd	399	27,427	68.7	18,623	Pendleton	279	11,719	42.0	11,985
Franklin	199	19,357	97.3	21,135	Perry	335	26,042	77.7	11,255
Fulton	193	15,197	78.7	14,114	Pike	779	49,477	63.5	31,679
Gallatin	109	4,664	42.8	4,697	Powell	181	6,745	37.3	6,268
Garrard	237	12,503	52.8	11,894	Pulaski	628	34,010	54.2	35,986
Grant	264	10,435	39.5	10,581	Robertson	109	3,871	35.5	4,121
Graves	551	32,483	59.0	33,539	Rockcastle	310	15,406	49.7	14,473
Grayson	497	19,927	40.1	19,958	Rowan	272	9,467	34.8	9,438
Green	279	11,391	40.8	11,871	Russell	329	11,854	36.0	10,861
Greenup	346	20,062	58.0	18,475	Scott	289	15,318	53.0	16,956

TABLE 9.—AREA AND POPULATION OF COUNTIES: 1920 AND 1910—Continued.

COUNTY.	Land area in square miles: 1920.	1920 Total.	Per square mile.	1910
KENTUCKY—Con.				
Shelby	427	18,532	43.4	18,041
Simpson	216	11,150	51.6	11,460
Spencer	186	7,785	41.9	7,567
Taylor	279	12,236	43.9	11,961
Todd	367	15,694	42.8	16,488
Trigg	428	14,208	33.2	14,539
Trimble	154	6,011	39.0	6,512
Union	325	18,040	55.5	19,886
Warren	530	30,858	58.2	30,579
Washington	299	14,773	49.4	13,940
Wayne	478	16,208	33.9	17,518
Webster	344	20,762	60.4	20,974
Whitley	442	27,749	62.8	31,982
Wolfe	230	8,783	38.2	9,864
Woodford	195	11,784	60.4	12,571
LOUISIANA[1]	45,409	1,798,509	39.6	1,656,388
Acadia	647	34,820	53.8	31,847
Allen	663	18,382	27.7	......
Ascension	291	22,155	76.1	23,887
Assumption	484	17,912	37.0	24,128
Avoyelles	847	35,300	41.7	34,102
Beauregard	1,172	20,767	17.7	......
Bienville	848	20,977	24.7	21,776
Bossier	863	22,266	25.8	21,738
Caddo	880	83,265	94.6	58,200
Calcasieu	1,086	32,807	30.2	62,767
Caldwell	531	9,514	17.9	8,593
Cameron	1,501	3,952	2.6	4,288
Catahoula	718	11,074	15.4	10,415
Claiborne	778	27,885	35.8	25,050
Concordia	714	12,466	17.5	14,278
De Soto	872	29,376	33.7	27,689
East Baton Rouge	455	44,513	97.8	34,580
East Carroll	420	11,231	26.7	11,637
East Feliciana	464	17,487	37.7	20,055
Evangeline	964	23,485	24.4	......
Franklin	630	24,100	38.3	11,989
Grant	683	14,403	21.1	15,958
Iberia	589	26,855	45.6	31,262
Iberville	584	26,806	45.9	30,954
Jackson	578	14,486	25.1	13,818
Jefferson	429	21,563	50.3	18,247
Jefferson Davis	729	18,999	26.1	......
La Salle	640	9,856	15.4	9,402
Lafayette	979	30,841	110.5	28,733
Lafourche	994	30,344	30.5	60,111
Lincoln	472	16,962	35.9	18,485
Livingston	662	11,643	17.6	10,627
Madison	650	10,829	16.7	10,676
Morehouse	831	19,311	23.2	18,786
Natchitoches	1,289	38,602	29.9	36,455
Orleans	178	387,219	2,175.4	339,075
Ouachita	642	30,319	47.2	25,830
Plaquemines	1,011	10,194	10.1	12,524
Pointe Coupee	576	24,697	42.9	25,289
Rapides	1,370	59,444	43.4	44,545
LOUISIANA—Con.				
Red River	400	15,301	38.3	11,402
Richland	565	20,860	36.9	15,769
Sabine	1,020	20,713	20.3	19,874
St. Bernard	621	4,968	8.0	5,277
St. Charles	295	8,586	29.1	11,207
St. Helena	420	8,427	20.1	9,172
St James	254	21,228	83.6	23,009
St. John the Baptist	231	11,896	51.5	14,338
St. Landry	681	51,697	75.9	66,661
St. Martin	525	21,990	41.9	23,070
St. Mary	632	30,754	48.7	39,368
St. Tammany	906	20,645	22.8	18,917
Tangipahoa	790	31,440	39.8	29,160
Tensas	632	12,085	19.1	17,060
Terrebonne	1,760	26,974	15.3	28,320
Union	918	19,621	21.4	20,451
Vermilion	1,213	26,482	21.8	26,390
Vernon	1,367	20,493	15.0	17,384
Washington	655	24,164	36.9	18,886
Webster	609	24,707	40.6	19,186
West Baton Rouge	214	11,092	51.8	12,636
West Carroll	366	8,857	24.2	6,249
West Feliciana	352	12,303	35.0	13,449
Winn	969	16,119	16.6	18,357
MAINE	29,895	768,014	25.7	742,371
Androscoggin	459	65,796	143.3	59,822
Aroostook	6,453	81,728	12.7	74,664
Cumberland	853	124,376	145.8	112,014
Franklin	1,789	19,825	11.1	19,119
Hancock	1,522	30,361	19.9	35,575
Kennebec	879	63,844	72.6	62,863
Knox	351	26,245	74.8	28,981
Lincoln	457	15,976	35.0	18,216
Oxford	1,980	37,700	19.0	36,256
Penobscot	3,258	87,684	26.9	85,285
Piscataquis	3,770	20,554	5.5	19,887
Sagadahoc	250	23,021	92.1	18,574
Somerset	3,633	37,171	10.2	36,301
Waldo	724	21,328	29.5	23,383
Washington	2,528	41,709	16.5	42,905
York	989	70,696	71.5	68,526
MARYLAND	9,941	1,449,661	145.8	1,295,346
Allegany	443	69,938	157.9	62,411
Anne Arundel	426	43,408	101.9	39,553
Baltimore	607	74,817	123.3	122,349
Baltimore city	79	733,826	9,288.9	558,485
Calvert	218	9,744	44.7	10,325
Caroline	319	18,652	58.5	19,216
Carroll	447	34,245	76.6	33,934
Cecil	377	23,612	62.6	23,759
Charles	464	17,705	38.2	16,386
Dorchester	576	27,895	48.4	28,669

[1] Divisions of state designated as parishes.

TABLE 9.—AREA AND POPULATION OF COUNTIES: 1920 AND 1910—Continued.

COUNTY.	Land area in square miles: 1920.	POPULATION. 1920 Total.	POPULATION. 1920 Per square mile.	1910	COUNTY.	Land area in square miles: 1920.	POPULATION. 1920 Total.	POPULATION. 1920 Per square mile.	1910
MARYLAND— Con.					MICHIGAN—Con.				
Frederick	663	52,541	79.2	52,673	Gladwin	519	8,827	17.0	8,413
Garrett	685	19,678	28.7	20,105	Gogebic	1,133	33,225	29.3	23,333
Harford	442	29,291	66.3	27,965	Grand Traverse	467	19,518	41.8	23,784
Howard	250	15,826	63.3	16,106	Gratiot	579	33,914	58.6	28,820
Kent	282	15,026	53.3	16,957	Hillsdale	597	28,161	47.2	29,673
Montgomery	521	34,921	67.0	32,089	Houghton	1,019	71,930	70.6	88,098
Prince Georges	482	43,347	89.9	36,147	Huron	854	32,786	38.4	34,758
Queen Annes	365	16,001	43.8	16,839	Ingham	553	81,554	147.5	53,310
St. Marys	371	16,112	43.4	17,030	Ionia	579	33,087	57.1	33,550
Somerset	331	24,602	74.3	26,455	Iosco	570	8,199	14.4	9,753
Talbot	268	18,306	68.3	19,620	Iron	1,200	22,107	18.4	15,164
Washington	459	59,694	130.1	49,617	Isabella	572	22,610	39.5	23,029
Wicomico	371	28,165	75.9	26,815	Jackson	707	72,539	102.6	53,426
Worcester	495	22,309	45.1	21,841	Kalamazoo	562	71,225	126.7	60,427
					Kalkaska	573	5,577	9.7	8,097
MASSACHU- SETTS	8,039	3,852,356	479.2	3,366,416	Kent	860	183,041	212.8	159,145
					Keweenaw	554	6,322	11.4	7,156
Barnstable	409	26,670	65.2	27,542	Lake	579	4,437	7.7	4,939
Berkshire	966	113,033	117.0	105,259	Lapeer	666	25,782	38.7	26,033
Bristol	567	359,005	633.2	318,573	Leelanau	338	9,061	26.8	10,608
Dukes	107	4,372	40.9	4,504					
Essex	497	482,156	970.1	436,477	Lenawee	743	47,767	64.3	47,907
					Livingston	568	17,522	30.8	17,736
Franklin	697	49,361	70.8	43,600	Luce	920	6,149	6.7	4,004
Hampden	636	300,305	472.2	231,369	Mackinac	1,044	8,026	7.7	9,249
Hampshire	585	69,599	119.0	63,327	Macomb	472	38,103	80.7	32,606
Middlesex	832	778,352	935.5	669,915					
Nantucket	51	2,797	54.8	2,962	Manistee	562	20,899	37.2	26,688
					Marquette	1,870	45,786	24.5	46,739
Norfolk	406	219,081	539.6	187,506	Mason	494	19,831	40.1	21,832
Plymouth	675	156,968	232.5	144,337	Mecosta	571	17,765	31.1	19,466
Suffolk	55	835,522	15,191.3	731,388	Menominee	1,056	23,778	22.5	25,648
Worcester	1,556	455,135	292.5	399,657					
					Midland	529	17,237	32.6	14,005
					Missaukee	582	9,004	15.5	10,606
MICHIGAN	57,480	3,668,412	63.8	2,810,173	Monroe	573	37,115	64.8	32,917
					Montcalm	724	30,441	42.0	32,069
Alcona	684	5,912	8.6	5,703	Montmorency	561	4,089	7.3	3,755
Alger	920	9,983	10.9	7,675					
Allegan	833	37,540	45.1	39,819	Muskegon	504	62,362	123.7	40,577
Alpena	584	17,869	30.6	19,965	Newaygo	851	17,378	20.4	19,220
Antrim	475	11,543	24.3	15,692	Oakland	886	90,050	101.6	49,576
					Oceana	543	15,601	28.7	18,379
Arenac	374	9,460	25.3	9,640	Ogemaw	580	7,786	13.4	8,907
Baraga	917	7,662	8.4	6,127					
Barry	556	21,383	38.5	22,633	Ontonagon	1,333	12,428	9.3	8,650
Bay	443	69,548	157.0	68,238	Osceola	577	15,221	26.4	17,889
Benzie	314	6,947	22.1	10,638	Oscoda	576	1,783	3.1	2,027
					Otsego	528	6,043	11.4	6,552
Berrien	569	62,653	110.1	53,622	Ottawa	565	47,660	84.4	45,301
Branch	497	23,997	48.3	25,605					
Calhoun	693	72,918	105.2	56,638	Presque Isle	678	12,131	17.9	11,249
Cass	493	20,395	41.4	20,624	Roscommon	538	2,032	3.8	2,274
Charlevoix	411	15,788	38.4	19,157	Saginaw	828	100,286	121.1	89,290
					St. Clair	710	58,009	81.7	52,341
Cheboygan	725	13,991	19.3	17,872	St. Joseph	503	26,818	53.3	25,499
Chippewa	1,573	24,818	15.8	24,472					
Clare	582	8,250	14.2	9,240	Sanilac	976	31,237	32.0	33,930
Clinton	571	23,110	40.5	23,129	Schoolcraft	1,207	9,977	8.3	8,681
Crawford	575	4,049	7.0	3,934	Shiawassee	557	35,924	64.5	33,246
					Tuscola	827	33,320	40.3	34,913
Delta	1,169	30,909	26.4	30,108					
Dickinson	776	19,456	25.1	20,524	Van Buren	617	30,715	49.8	33,185
Eaton	571	29,377	51.4	30,499	Washtenaw	704	49,520	70.3	44,714
Emmet	485	15,639	32.2	18,561	Wayne	620	1,177,645	1,899.4	531,591
Genesee	655	125,668	191.9	64,555	Wexford	577	18,207	31.6	20,769

TABLE 9.—AREA AND POPULATION OF COUNTIES: 1920 AND 1910—Continued.

COUNTY.	Land area in square miles: 1920.	POPULATION. 1920 Total.	POPULATION. 1920 Per square mile.	1910	COUNTY.	Land area in square miles: 1920.	POPULATION. 1920 Total.	POPULATION. 1920 Per square mile.	1910
MINNESOTA....	80,858	2,387,125	29.5	2,075,708	MINNESOTA—Con.				
Aitkin	1,830	15,043	8.2	10,371	Ramsey	161	244,554	1,519.0	223,675
Anoka	459	15,626	34.0	12,493	Red Lake	432	7,263	16.8	6,564
Becker	1,349	22,851	16.9	18,840	Redwood	881	20,908	23.7	18,425
Beltrami	3,822	27,079	7.1	19,337	Renville	978	23,634	24.2	23,123
Benton	405	14,073	34.7	11,615	Rice	495	28,307	57.2	25,911
Big Stone	491	9,766	19.9	9,367	Rock	492	10,965	22.3	10,222
Blue Earth	762	31,477	41.3	29,337	Roseau	1,670	13,305	8.0	11,338
Brown	612	22,421	36.6	20,134	St. Louis	6,503	206,391	31.7	163,274
Carlton	867	19,391	22.4	17,559	Scott	366	14,245	38.9	14,888
Carver	376	16,946	45.1	17,455	Sherburne	448	9,651	21.5	8,136
Cass	2,104	15,897	7.6	11,620	Sibley	585	15,635	26.7	15,540
Chippewa	591	15,720	26.6	13,458	Stearns	1,362	55,741	40.9	47,733
Chisago	427	14,445	33.8	13,537	Steele	431	18,061	41.9	16,146
Clay	1,043	21,780	20.9	19,640	Stevens	564	9,778	17.3	8,293
Clearwater	1,019	8,569	8.4	6,870	Swift	741	15,093	20.4	12,949
Cook	1,498	1,841	1.2	1,336	Todd	957	26,059	27.2	23,407
Cottonwood	640	14,570	22.8	12,651	Traverse	568	7,943	14.0	8,049
Crow Wing	1,057	24,566	23.2	16,861	Wabasha	541	17,919	33.1	18,554
Dakota	599	28,967	48.4	25,171	Wadena	538	10,699	19.9	8,652
Dodge	440	12,552	28.5	12,094	Waseca	431	14,133	32.8	13,466
Douglas	648	19,039	29.4	17,669	Washington	397	23,761	59.9	26,013
Faribault	719	20,998	29.2	19,949	Watonwan	434	12,457	28.7	11,382
Fillmore	868	25,330	29.2	25,680	Wilkin	745	10,187	13.7	9,063
Freeborn	735	24,692	33.6	22,282	Winona	637	33,653	52.8	33,398
Goodhue	767	30,799	40.2	31,637	Wright	691	28,635	41.5	28,082
Grant	553	9,788	17.7	9,114	Yellow Medicine	749	16,550	22.1	15,406
Hennepin	565	415,419	735.3	333,480					
Houston	570	14,013	24.6	14,297					
Hubbard	958	10,136	10.6	9,831					
Isanti	442	13,278	30.0	12,615	MISSISSIPPI	46,362	1,790,618	38.6	1,797,114
Itasca	2,730	23,876	8.7	17,208	Adams	426	22,183	52.1	25,265
Jackson	702	15,955	22.7	14,491	Alcorn	386	21,369	55.4	18,159
Kanabec	534	9,086	17.0	6,461	Amite	714	18,960	26.6	22,954
Kandiyohi	801	22,060	27.5	18,969	Attala	715	24,831	34.7	28,851
Kittson	1,111	10,638	9.6	9,669	Benton	396	9,851	24.9	10,245
Koochiching	3,141	13,520	4.3	6,431	Bolivar	879	57,669	65.6	48,905
Lac qui Parle	790	15,554	19.7	15,435	Calhoun	579	16,823	29.1	17,726
Lake	2,099	8,251	3.9	8,011	Carroll	624	20,324	32.6	23,139
Le Sueur	466	17,870	38.3	18,609	Chickasaw	501	22,212	44.3	22,846
Lincoln	535	11,268	21.1	9,874	Choctaw	414	12,491	30.2	14,357
Lyon	708	18,837	26.6	15,722	Claiborne	489	13,019	26.6	17,403
McLeod	496	20,444	41.2	18,691	Clarke	675	17,927	26.6	21,630
Mahnomen	572	6,197	10.8	3,249	Clay	408	17,490	42.9	20,203
Marshall	1,788	19,443	10.9	16,338	Coahoma	530	41,511	78.3	34,217
Martin	719	21,085	29.3	17,518	Copiah	769	28,672	37.3	35,914
Meeker	621	18,103	29.2	17,022	Covington	410	14,869	36.3	16,909
Mille Lacs	583	14,180	24.3	10,705	De Soto	475	24,059	51.0	28,100
Morrison	1,143	25,841	22.6	24,053	Forrest	462	21,000	46.0	09,700
Mower	711	25,993	36.6	22,640	Franklin	547	14,156	25.9	15,193
Murray	704	13,631	19.4	11,755	George	475	5,564	11.7	6,599
Nicollet	443	15,036	33.9	14,125	Greene	710	10,430	14.7	6,050
Nobles	722	17,917	24.8	15,210	Grenada	442	13,607	30.8	15,727
Norman	860	14,880	17.3	13,446	Hancock	469	10,380	22.1	11,207
Olmsted	666	28,014	42.1	22,497	Harrison	570	32,855	57.6	34,658
Otter Tail	2,039	50,818	24.9	46,036	Hinds	858	57,110	66.6	63,726
Pennington	607	12,091	19.9	9,376	Holmes	751	34,513	46.0	39,088
Pine	1,413	21,117	14.9	15,878	Humphreys	408	19,192	47.0	....
Pipestone	469	12,050	25.7	9,553	Issaquena	406	7,618	18.8	10,560
Polk	1,979	37,090	18.7	36,001	Itawamba	529	15,647	29.6	14,526
Pope	693	13,631	19.7	12,746	Jackson	710	19,208	27.1	15,451

TABLE **9.**—AREA AND POPULATION OF COUNTIES: 1920 AND 1910—Continued.

COUNTY.	Land area in square miles: 1920.	POPULATION. 1920 Total.	Per square mile.	1910	COUNTY.	Land area in square miles: 1920.	POPULATION. 1920 Total.	Per square mile.	1910
MISSISSIPPI—Con.					MISSOURI—Con.				
Jasper	667	18,508	27.7	18,498	Barton	596	16,879	28.3	16,747
Jefferson	507	15,946	31.5	18,221	Bates	870	23,933	27.5	25,869
Jefferson Davis	404	12,755	31.6	12,860	Benton	745	12,989	17.4	14,881
Jones	696	32,919	47.3	29,885	Bollinger	609	13,909	22.8	14,576
Kemper	752	19,619	26.1	20,348	Boone	688	29,672	43.1	30,533
Lafayette	664	19,243	29.0	21,883	Buchanan	408	93,684	229.6	93,020
Lamar	495	12,869	26.0	11,741	Butler	699	24,106	34.5	20,624
Lauderdale	700	45,897	65.6	46,919	Caldwell	433	13,849	32.0	14,605
Lawrence	418	12,663	30.3	13,080	Callaway	808	23,007	28.5	24,400
Leake	576	16,973	29.5	18,298	Camden	687	10,474	15.2	11,582
Lee	448	29,618	66.1	28,894	Cape Girardeau	580	29,839	51.4	27,621
Leflore	572	37,256	65.1	36,290	Carroll	703	20,480	29.1	23,098
Lincoln	578	24,652	42.7	28,597	Carter	506	7,482	14.8	5,504
Lowndes	499	27,632	55.4	30,703	Cass	721	21,536	29.9	22,973
Madison	725	29,292	40.4	33,505	Cedar	498	13,933	28.0	16,080
Marion	535	17,144	32.0	15,599	Chariton	768	21,769	28.3	23,503
Marshall	689	26,105	37.9	26,796	Christian	553	15,252	27.6	15,832
Monroe	770	32,613	42.4	35,178	Clark	498	11,874	23.8	12,811
Montgomery	398	13,805	34.7	17,706	Clay	402	20,455	50.9	20,302
Neshoba	561	19,303	34.4	17,980	Clinton	423	14,461	34.2	15,297
Newton	568	20,727	36.5	23,085	Cole	389	24,680	63.4	21,957
Noxubee	682	23,710	34.8	28,503	Cooper	558	19,308	34.6	20,311
Oktibbeha	457	16,872	36.9	19,676	Crawford	747	12,355	16.5	13,576
Panola	696	27,845	40.0	31,274	Dade	501	14,173	28.3	15,613
Pearl River	797	15,468	19.4	10,593	Dallas	543	12,033	22.2	13,181
Perry	644	8,987	14.0	7,685	Daviess	564	16,641	29.5	17,605
Pike	407	28,725	70.6	37,272	De Kalb	425	11,694	27.5	12,531
Pontotoc	494	19,962	40.4	19,688	Dent	746	12,318	16.5	13,245
Prentiss	409	17,606	43.0	16,931	Douglas	804	15,436	19.2	16,664
Quitman	395	19,861	50.3	11,593	Dunklin	530	32,773	61.8	30,328
Rankin	791	20,272	25.6	23,944	Franklin	879	28,427	32.3	29,830
Scott	597	16,420	27.5	16,723	Gasconade	514	12,381	24.1	12,847
Sharkey	422	14,190	33.6	15,694	Gentry	490	15,634	31.9	16,820
Simpson	575	18,109	31.5	17,201	Greene	667	68,698	103.0	63,831
Smith	626	16,178	25.8	16,603	Grundy	433	17,554	40.5	16,744
Stone	443	6,528	14.7	....	Harrison	721	19,719	27.3	20,466
Sunflower	674	46,374	68.8	28,787	Henry	744	25,116	33.8	27,242
Tallahatchie	629	35,953	57.2	29,078	Hickory	407	7,033	17.3	8,741
Tate	400	19,636	49.1	19,714	Holt	446	14,084	31.6	14,539
Tippah	446	15,419	34.6	14,631	Howard	468	13,997	29.9	15,653
Tishomingo	428	15,091	35.3	13,067	Howell	915	21,102	23.1	21,065
Tunica	418	20,386	48.8	18,646	Iron	553	9,458	17.1	8,563
Union	412	20,044	48.7	18,997	Jackson	610	367,846	603.0	283,522
Walthall	389	13,455	34.6	....	Jasper	635	75,941	119.6	89,673
					Jefferson	681	26,555	39.0	27,878
Warren	572	33,362	58.3	37,488					
Washington	723	51,092	70.7	48,933	Johnson	831	24,899	30.0	26,297
Wayne	812	15,467	19.0	14,709	Knox	514	10,783	21.0	12,403
Webster	416	12,644	30.4	14,853	Laclede	753	16,857	22.4	17,363
					Lafayette	612	30,006	49.0	30,154
Wilkinson	667	15,319	23.0	18,075	Lawrence	609	24,211	39.8	26,583
Winston	597	18,139	30.4	17,139					
Yalobusha	490	18,738	38.2	21,519	Lewis	504	13,465	26.7	15,514
Yazoo	905	37,149	41.0	46,672	Lincoln	607	15,956	26.3	17,033
					Linn	626	24,778	39.6	25,253
					Livingston	531	18,857	35.5	19,453
MISSOURI	68,727	3,404,055	49.5	3,293,335	McDonald	527	14,690	27.9	13,539
Adair	571	21,404	37.5	22,700	Macon	809	27,518	34.0	30,868
Andrew	428	14,075	32.9	15,282	Madison	499	10,721	21.5	11,273
Atchison	528	13,008	24.6	13,604	Maries	520	9,500	18.3	10,088
Audrain	685	20,589	30.1	21,687	Marion	436	30,226	69.3	30,572
Barry	784	23,473	29.9	23,869	Mercer	453	11,281	24.9	12,335

TABLE 9.—AREA AND POPULATION OF COUNTIES: 1920 AND 1910—Continued.

COUNTY.	Land area in square miles: 1920.	1920 Total.	1920 Per square mile.	1910
MISSOURI—Con.				
Miller	593	15,567	26.3	16,717
Mississippi	413	12,860	31.1	14,557
Moniteau	410	13,532	33.0	14,375
Monroe	666	16,414	24.6	18,304
Montgomery	514	15,233	29.6	15,604
Morgan	614	12,015	19.6	12,863
New Madrid	652	25,180	38.6	19,488
Newton	622	24,886	40.0	27,136
Nodaway	871	27,744	31.9	28,833
Oregon	778	12,889	16.6	14,681
Osage	593	13,559	22.9	14,283
Ozark	746	11,125	14.9	11,926
Pemiscot	456	26,634	58.4	19,559
Perry	462	14,434	31.2	14,898
Pettis	685	35,813	52.3	33,913
Phelps	670	14,941	22.3	15,796
Pike	653	20,345	31.2	22,556
Platte	415	13,996	33.7	14,429
Polk	641	20,351	31.7	21,561
Pulaski	542	10,490	19.4	11,438
Putnam	517	13,115	25.4	14,308
Ralls	481	10,412	21.6	12,913
Randolph	491	27,633	56.3	26,182
Ray	565	20,508	36.3	21,451
Reynolds	828	10,106	12.2	9,592
Ripley	627	12,061	19.2	13,099
St. Charles	535	22,828	42.7	24,695
St. Clair	706	15,341	21.7	16,412
St. Francois	458	31,403	68.6	35,738
St. Louis	487	100,737	206.9	82,417
St. Louis city	61	772,897	12,670.4	687,029
Ste. Genevieve	481	9,809	20.4	10,607
Saline	754	28,826	38.2	29,448
Schuyler	309	8,383	27.1	9,062
Scotland	439	10,700	24.4	11,869
Scott	419	23,409	55.9	22,372
Shannon	992	11,865	12.0	11,443
Shelby	509	13,617	26.8	14,864
Stoddard	815	29,755	36.5	27,807
Stone	510	11,941	23.4	11,559
Sullivan	649	17,781	27.4	18,598
Taney	655	8,178	12.5	9,134
Texas	1,159	20,548	17.7	21,458
Vernon	839	26,069	31.1	28,827
Warren	410	8,490	20.7	9,123
Washington	741	13,803	18.6	13,378
Wayne	775	13,012	16.8	15,181
Webster	585	16,009	30.1	17,377
Worth	265	7,642	28.8	8,007
Wright	677	17,733	26.2	18,315
MONTANA[1]	146,131	548,889	3.8	376,053
Beaverhead	5,657	7,369	1.3	6,446
Big Horn	4,966	7,015	1.4	
Blaine	4,229	9,057	2.1	
Broadwater	1,206	3,239	2.7	3,491
Carbon	2,060	15,279	7.4	13,962
MONTANA—Con.				
Carter	3,375	3,972	1.2	
Cascade	3,411	38,836	11.4	28,833
Chouteau	4,213	11,051	2.6	17,191
Custer	3,741	12,194	3.3	14,123
Dawson	2,359	9,239	3.9	12,725
Deer Lodge	745	15,323	20.6	12,988
Fallon	1,608	4,548	2.8	
Fergus	7,146	28,344	4.0	17,385
Flathead	6,109	21,705	3.6	18,785
Gallatin	2,507	15,864	6.3	14,079
Garfield	4,837	5,368	1.1	
Glacier	2,981	4,178	1.4	
Granite	1,717	4,167	2.4	2,942
Hill	2,892	13,958	4.8	
Jefferson	1,632	5,203	3.2	5,601
Lewis and Clark	3,447	18,660	5.4	21,853
Liberty	1,451	2,416	1.7	
Lincoln	3,624	7,797	2.2	3,638
McCone	2,645	4,747	1.8	
Madison	3,622	7,495	2.1	7,229
Meagher	2,369	2,622	1.1	4,190
Mineral	1,230	2,327	1.9	
Missoula	3,173	24,041	7.6	23,596
Musselshell	2,903	12,030	4.1	
Park	2,661	11,330	4.3	10,731
Phillips	5,178	9,311	1.8	
Pondera	1,658	5,741	3.5	
Powder River	3,337	3,357	1.0	
Powell	2,329	6,909	3.0	5,904
Prairie	1,742	3,684	2.1	
Ravalli	2,391	10,098	4.2	11,666
Richland	2,103	8,989	4.3	
Roosevelt	2,353	10,347	4.4	
Rosebud	4,993	8,002	1.6	7,985
Sanders	2,861	4,903	1.7	3,713
Sheridan	2,686	13,847	5.2	
Silver Bow	726	60,313	83.1	56,848
Stillwater	1,777	7,630	4.3	
Sweet Grass	1,969	4,926	2.5	4,029
Teton	2,044	5,870	2.9	9,546
Toole	1,958	3,724	1.9	
Treasure	960	1,990	2.1	
Valley	5,447	11,542	2.1	13,630
Wheatland	1,411	5,619	4.0	
Wibaux	883	3,113	3.5	
Yellowstone	2,611	29,600	11.3	22,944
NEBRASKA	76,808	1,206,272	16.9	1,192,214
Adams	565	22,621	40.0	20,900
Antelope	872	15,243	17.5	14,003
Arthur	721	1,412	2.0	
Banner	742	1,435	1.9	1,444
Blaine	711	1,778	2.5	1,672
Boone	692	14,146	20.4	13,145
Box Butte	1,076	8,407	7.8	6,131
Boyd	535	8,243	15.4	8,826
Brown	1,235	6,749	5.5	6,083
Buffalo	945	23,787	25.2	21,907

[1] Total land area includes part of Yellowstone National Park (198 square miles); total population of park returned as in Wyoming.

TABLE **9.**—AREA AND POPULATION OF COUNTIES: 1920 AND 1910—Continued.

COUNTY.	Land area in square miles: 1920.	POPULATION.		1910	COUNTY.	Land area in square miles: 1920.	POPULATION.		1910
		1920					1920		
		Total.	Per square mile.				Total.	Per square mile.	
NEBRASKA—Con.					NEBRASKA—Con.				
Burt	475	12,559	26.4	12,726	Platte	673	19,464	28.9	19,006
Butler	583	14,606	25.1	15,403	Polk	430	10,714	24.9	10,521
Cass	538	18,029	33.5	19,786	Redwillow	720	11,434	15.9	11,056
Cedar	735	16,225	22.1	15,191	Richardson	545	18,968	34.8	17,448
Chase	899	4,939	5.5	3,613	Rock	1,004	3,703	3.7	3,627
Cherry	5,979	11,753	2.0	10,414					
Cheyenne	1,194	8,405	7.0	4,551	Saline	573	16,514	28.8	17,866
Clay	579	14,486	25.0	15,729	Sarpy	240	9,370	39.0	9,274
Colfax	405	11,624	28.7	11,610	Saunders	756	20,589	27.2	21,179
Cuming	577	13,769	23.9	13,782	Scotts Bluff	723	20,710	28.6	8,355
					Seward	574	15,867	27.6	15,895
Custer	2,588	26,407	10.2	25,668					
Dakota	253	7,694	30.4	6,564	Sheridan	2,469	9,625	3.9	7,328
Dawes	1,402	10,160	7.2	8,254	Sherman	573	8,877	15.5	8,278
Dawson	985	16,004	16.2	15,961	Sioux	2,055	4,528	2.2	5,599
Deuel	439	3,282	7.5	1,786	Stanton	431	7,756	18.0	7,542
					Thayer	578	13,976	24.2	14,775
Dixon	472	11,815	25.0	11,477					
Dodge	531	23,197	43.7	22,145					
Douglas	331	204,524	617.9	168,546	Thomas	716	1,773	2.5	1,191
Dundy	927	4,869	5.3	4,098	Thurston	387	9,589	24.8	8,704
Fillmore	576	13,671	23.7	14,674	Valley	570	9,823	17.2	9,480
					Washington	380	12,180	32.1	12,738
Franklin	578	10,067	17.4	10,303					
Frontier	975	8,540	8.8	8,572					
Furnas	721	11,657	16.2	12,083	Wayne	450	9,725	21.6	10,397
Gage	862	29,721	34.5	30,325	Webster	578	10,922	18.9	12,008
Garden	1,687	4,572	2.7	3,538	Wheeler	578	2,531	4.4	2,292
					York	575	17,146	29.8	18,721
Garfield	575	3,496	6.1	3,417					
Gosper	464	4,669	10.1	4,933					
Grant	780	1,486	1.9	1,097	NEVADA	109,821	77,407	0.7	81,875
Greeley	571	8,685	15.2	8,047					
Hall	528	23,720	44.9	20,361	Churchill	5,050	4,649	0.9	2,811
					Clark	8,045	4,859	0.6	3,321
Hamilton	538	13,237	24.6	13,459	Douglas	733	1,825	2.5	1,895
Harlan	574	9,220	16.1	9,578	Elko	17,059	8,083	0.5	8,133
Hayes	722	3,327	4.6	3,011	Esmeralda	3,413	2,410	0.7	9,369
Hitchcock	724	6,045	8.3	5,415					
Holt	2,393	17,151	7.2	15,545	Eureka	4,157	1,350	0.3	1,830
					Humboldt	9,804	3,743	0.4	6,825
Hooker	722	1,378	1.9	981	Lander	5,721	1,484	0.3	1,786
Howard	561	10,739	19.1	10,783	Lincoln	10,511	2,287	0.2	3,489
Jefferson	578	16,140	27.9	16,852					
Johnson	374	8,940	23.9	10,187	Lyon	1,509	4,078	2.7	3,568
Kearney	516	8,583	16.6	9,106	Mineral	4,019	1,848	0.5	
					Nye	18,294	6,504	0.4	7,513
Keith	1,068	5,294	5.0	3,692	Ormsby	156	2,453	15.7	3,415
Keyapaha	775	3,594	4.6	3,452					
Kimball	958	4,498	4.7	1,942	Pershing	6,053	2,803	0.5	
Knox	1,114	18,894	17.0	18,358	Storey	251	1,469	5.9	3,045
Lancaster	853	85,902	100.7	73,793	Washoe	6,251	18,627	3.0	17,434
					White Pine	8,795	8,935	1.0	7,441
Lincoln	2,536	23,420	9.2	15,684					
Logan	573	1,596	2.8	1,521					
Loup	576	1,946	3.4	2,188					
McPherson	864	1,692	2.0	2,470	NEW HAMP-				
Madison	576	22,511	39.1	19,101	SHIRE	9,031	443,083	49.1	430,572
Merrick	463	10,763	23.2	10,379	Belknap	397	21,178	53.3	21,309
Morrill	1,417	9,151	6.5	4,584	Carroll	955	15,017	15.7	16,316
Nance	446	8,712	19.5	8,926	Cheshire	728	30,975	42.5	30,659
Nemaha	389	12,547	32.3	13,095	Coos	1,798	36,093	20.1	30,753
Nuckolls	579	13,236	22.9	13,019	Grafton	1,729	40,572	23.5	41,652
Otoe	606	19,494	32.2	19,323	Hillsborough	895	135,512	151.4	126,072
Pawnee	431	9,578	22.2	10,582	Merrimack	932	51,770	55.5	53,335
Perkins	886	3,967	4.5	2,570	Rockingham	691	52,498	76.0	52,188
Phelps	538	9,900	18.4	10,451	Strafford	379	38,546	101.7	38,951
Pierce	577	10,681	18.5	10,122	Sullivan	527	20,922	39.7	19,337

TABLE 9.—AREA AND POPULATION OF COUNTIES: 1920 AND 1910—Continued.

COUNTY.	Land area in square miles: 1920.	1920 Total.	1920 Per square mile.	1910	COUNTY.	Land area in square miles: 1920.	1920 Total.	1920 Per square mile.	1910
NEW JERSEY.	7,514	3,155,900	420.0	2,537,167	NEW YORK—Con.				
Atlantic	569	83,914	147.5	71,894	Cayuga	703	65,221	92.8	67,106
Bergen	237	210,703	889.0	138,002	Chatauqua	1,069	115,348	107.9	105,126
Burlington	815	81,770	100.3	66,565	Chemung	407	65,872	161.8	54,662
Camden	222	190,508	858.1	142,029	Chenango	894	34,969	39.1	35,575
Cape May	265	19,460	73.4	19,745	Clinton	1,049	43,898	41.8	48,230
Cumberland	500	61,348	122.7	55,153	Columbia	644	38,930	60.5	43,658
Essex	127	652,089	5,134.6	512,886	Cortland	503	29,625	58.9	29,249
Gloucester	332	48,224	145.3	37,368	Delaware	1,449	42,774	29.5	45,575
Hudson	43	629,154	14,631.5	537,231	Dutchess	806	91,747	113.8	87,661
Hunterdon	437	32,885	75.3	33,569	Erie	1,034	634,688	613.8	528,985
Mercer	226	159,881	707.4	125,657					
Middlesex	312	162,334	520.3	114,426	Essex	1,836	31,871	17.4	33,458
Monmouth	479	104,925	219.1	94,734	Franklin	1,678	43,541	25.9	45,717
					Fulton	516	44,927	87.1	44,534
Morris	475	82,694	174.1	74,704	Genesee	496	37,976	76.6	37,615
Ocean	637	22,155	34.8	21,318	Greene	643	25,796	40.1	30,214
Passaic	196	259,174	1,322.3	215,902					
Salem	343	36,572	106.6	26,999	Hamilton	1,700	3,970	2.3	4,373
					Herkimer	1,459	64,962	44.5	56,356
Somerset	305	47,991	157.3	38,820	Jefferson	1,274	82,250	64.6	80,382
Sussex	529	24,905	47.1	26,781	Kings	71	2,018,356	28,427.5	1,634,351
Union	103	200,157	1,943.3	140,197	Lewis	1,270	23,704	18.7	24,849
Warren	362	45,057	124.5	43,187					
					Livingston	631	36,830	58.4	38,037
NEW MEXICO.	122,503	360,350	2.9	327,301	Madison	650	39,535	60.8	39,289
					Monroe	663	352,034	531.0	283,212
Bernalillo	1,214	29,855	24.6	23,606	Montgomery	398	57,928	145.5	57,567
Chaves	6,042	12,075	2.0	16,850	Nassau	274	126,120	460.3	83,930
Colfax	3,798	21,550	5.7	16,460					
Curry	1,406	11,236	8.0	11,443	New York	22	2,284,103	103,822.9	2,762,522
De Baca	2,400	3,196	1.3		Niagara	522	118,705	227.4	92,036
					Oneida	1,250	182,833	146.3	154,157
Dona Ana	3,821	16,548	4.3	12,893	Onondaga	781	241,465	309.2	200,298
Eddy	4,245	9,116	2.1	12,400	Ontario	649	52,652	81.1	52,286
Grant	3,981	21,939	5.5	14,813					
Guadalupe	3,031	8,015	2.6	10,927	Orange	834	119,844	143.7	116,001
Hidalgo	3,447	4,338	1.3		Orleans	396	28,619	72.3	32,000
					Oswego	966	71,045	73.5	71,664
Lea	4,378	3,545	0.8		Otsego	1,009	46,200	45.8	47,216
Lincoln	4,779	7,823	1.6	7,822	Putnam	233	10,802	46.4	14,665
Luna	2,976	12,270	4.1	3,913					
McKinley	5,506	13,731	2.5	12,963	Queens	108	469,042	4,343.0	284,041
Mora	2,475	13,915	5.6	12,611	Rensselaer	663	113,129	170.6	122,276
					Richmond	57	116,531	2,044.4	85,969
Otero	6,689	7,902	1.2	7,069	Rockland	183	45,548	248.9	46,873
Quay	2,905	10,444	3.6	14,912	St. Lawrence	2,701	88,121	32.6	89,005
Rio Arriba	5,871	19,552	3.3	16,624					
Roosevelt	2,487	6,548	2.6	12,064	Saratoga	823	60,029	72.9	61,917
San Juan	5,476	8,333	1.5	8,504	Schenectady	206	109,363	530.9	88,235
					Schoharie	642	21,303	33.2	23,855
San Miguel	4,894	22,867	4.7	22,930	Schuyler	336	13,098	39.0	14,004
Sandoval	3,871	8,863	2.3	8,579	Seneca	336	24,705	73.6	26,972
Santa Fe	1,070	15,030	7.6	14,770					
Sierra	3,118	4,619	1.5	5,668	Steuben	1,398	80,627	57.7	83,362
Socorro	15,070	14,061	0.9	14,761	Suffolk	920	110,246	119.8	96,138
					Sullivan	1,002	33,163	33.1	33,808
Taos	2,252	12,773	5.7	12,008	Tioga	520	24,212	46.6	25,624
Torrance	3,369	9,731	2.9	10,119					
Union	5,370	16,680	3.1	11,404	Tompkins	476	35,285	74.1	33,647
Valencia	5,659	13,795	2.4	13,320	Ulster	1,137	74,979	65.9	91,769
					Warren	876	31,673	36.2	32,223
NEW YORK.	47,654	10,385,227	217.9	9,113,614	Washington	837	44,888	53.6	47,778
Albany	527	186,106	353.1	173,666	Wayne	599	48,827	81.5	50,179
Allegany	1,047	36,842	35.2	41,412	Westchester	448	344,436	768.8	283,055
Bronx	41	732,016	17,854.0		Wyoming	601	30,314	50.4	31,880
Broome	705	113,610	161.1	78,809	Yates	343	16,641	48.5	18,642
Cattaraugus	1,343	71,323	53.1	65,919					

TABLE 9.—AREA AND POPULATION OF COUNTIES: 1920 AND 1910—Continued.

COUNTY.	Land area in square miles: 1920.	POPULATION. 1920		1910	COUNTY.	Land area in square miles: 1920.	POPULATION. 1920		1910
		Total.	Per square mile.				Total.	Per square mile.	
NORTH CAROLINA	48,740	2,559,123	52.5	2,206,287	NORTH CAROLINA—Con.				
					Mitchell	213	11,278	52.9	17,245
Alamance	492	32,718	66.5	28,712	Montgomery	498	14,607	29.3	14,967
Alexander	289	12,212	42.3	11,592	Moore	639	21,388	33.5	17,010
Alleghany	234	7,403	31.6	7,745	Nash	586	41,061	70.1	33,727
Anson	556	28,334	51.0	25,465	New Hanover	216	40,620	188.1	32,037
Ashe	427	21,001	49.2	19,074					
					Northampton	504	23,184	46.0	22,323
Avery	238	10,335	43.4	....	Onslow	743	14,703	19.8	14,125
Beaufort	840	31,024	36.9	30,877	Orange	390	17,895	45.9	15,064
Bertie	703	23,993	34.1	23,039	Pamlico	350	9,060	25.9	9,966
Bladen	976	19,761	20.2	18,006	Pasquotank	223	17,670	79.2	16,693
Brunswick	790	14,876	18.8	14,432					
					Pender	815	14,788	18.1	15,471
Buncombe	639	64,148	100.4	49,798	Perquimans	252	11,137	44.2	11,054
Burke	534	23,297	43.6	21,408	Person	391	18,973	48.5	17,356
Cabarrus	390	33,730	86.5	26,240	Pitt	627	45,569	72.7	36,340
Caldwell	471	19,984	42.4	20,579	Polk	251	8,832	35.2	7,640
Camden	220	5,382	24.5	5,640					
					Randolph	803	30,856	38.4	29,491
Carteret	573	15,384	26.8	13,776	Richmond	521	25,567	49.1	19,673
Caswell	402	15,759	39.2	14,858	Robeson	990	54,674	55.2	51,945
Catawba	408	33,839	82.9	27,918	Rockingham	579	44,149	76.3	36,442
Chatham	696	23,814	34.2	22,635	Rowan	489	44,062	90.1	37,521
Cherokee	454	15,242	33.6	14,136					
Chowan	165	10,649	64.5	11,303	Rutherford	544	31,426	57.8	28,385
Clay	220	4,646	21.1	3,909	Sampson	886	36,002	40.6	29,982
Cleveland	496	34,272	69.1	29,494	Scotland	349	15,600	44.7	15,363
Columbus	933	30,124	32.3	28,020	Stanly	416	27,429	65.9	19,909
Craven	660	29,048	44.0	25,594	Stokes	480	20,575	42.9	20,151
Cumberland	670	35,064	52.3	35,284					
Currituck	292	7,268	24.9	7,693	Surry	520	32,464	62.4	29,705
Dare	377	5,115	13.6	4,841	Swain	553	13,224	23.9	10,403
Davidson	569	35,201	61.9	29,404	Transylvania	379	9,303	24.5	7,191
Davie	258	13,578	52.6	13,394	Tyrrell	390	4,849	12.4	5,219
					Union	565	36,029	63.8	33,277
Duplin	790	30,223	38.3	25,442					
Durham	312	42,219	135.3	35,276	Vance	279	22,799	81.7	19,425
Edgecombe	509	37,995	74.6	32,010	Wake	824	75,155	91.2	63,229
Forsyth	376	77,269	205.5	47,311	Warren	425	21,593	50.8	20,266
Franklin	468	26,667	57.0	24,692	Washington	327	11,429	35.0	11,062
					Watauga	303	13,477	44.5	13,556
Gaston	363	51,242	141.2	37,063					
Gates	359	10,537	29.4	10,455	Wayne	571	43,640	76.4	35,698
Graham	298	4,872	16.3	4,749	Wilkes	735	32,644	44.4	30,282
Granville	503	26,846	53.4	25,102	Wilson	373	36,813	98.7	28,269
Greene	252	16,212	64.3	13,083	Yadkin	324	16,391	50.6	15,428
					Yancey	298	15,093	50.6	12,072
Guilford	691	79,272	114.7	60,497					
Halifax	676	43,766	64.7	37,646					
Harnett	588	28,313	48.2	22,174					
Haywood	546	23,496	43.0	21,020					
Henderson	358	18,248	51.0	16,262	NORTH DAKOTA	70,183	646,872	9.2	577,056
Hertford	341	16,294	47.8	15,436	Adams	997	5,593	5.6	5,407
Hoke	417	11,722	28.1	....	Barnes	1,510	18,678	12.4	18,066
Hyde	617	8,386	13.6	8,840	Benson	1,364	13,095	9.6	12,681
Iredell	588	37,956	64.6	34,315	Billings	1,168	3,126	2.7	10,186
Jackson	494	13,396	27.1	12,998	Bottineau	1,681	15,109	9.0	17,295
Johnston	807	48,998	60.7	41,401	Bowman	1,164	4,768	4.1	4,668
Jones	417	9,912	23.8	8,721	Burke	1,113	9,511	8.5	9,064
Lee	261	13,400	51.3	11,376	Burleigh	1,651	15,578	9.4	13,087
Lenoir	390	29,555	75.8	22,769	Cass	1,763	41,477	23.5	33,935
Lincoln	299	17,862	59.7	17,132	Cavalier	1,494	15,555	10.4	15,659
McDowell	443	16,763	37.8	13,538	Dickey	1,142	10,499	9.2	9,839
Macon	513	12,887	25.1	12,191	Divide	1,270	9,637	7.6	6,015
Madison	436	20,083	46.1	20,132	Dunn	2,084	8,828	4.2	5,302
Martin	438	20,828	47.6	17,797	Eddy	651	6,493	10.0	4,800
Mecklenburg	597	80,695	135.2	67,031	Emmons	1,563	11,288	7.2	9,796

TABLE 9.—AREA AND POPULATION OF COUNTIES: 1920 AND 1910—Continued.

COUNTY.	Land area in square miles: 1920.	POPULATION. 1920 Total.	POPULATION. 1920 Per square mile.	1910	COUNTY.	Land area in square miles: 1920.	POPULATION. 1920 Total.	POPULATION. 1920 Per square mile.	1910
NORTH DAKOTA —Con.					**OHIO—Con.**				
Foster...........	644	6,108	9.5	5,313	Delaware........	445	26,013	58.5	27,182
Golden Valley....	1,013	4,832	4.8	....	Erie............	256	39,789	155.4	38,327
Grand Forks.....	1,433	28,795	20.1	27,888	Fairfield.......	495	40,484	81.8	39,201
Grant...........	1,681	9,553	5.7	....	Fayette.........	413	21,518	52.1	21,744
Griggs..........	717	7,402	10.3	6,274	Franklin........	517	283,951	549.2	221,567
Hettinger........	1,132	7,685	6.8	6,557	Fulton..........	405	23,445	57.9	23,914
Kidder..........	1,386	7,798	5.6	5,962	Gallia..........	449	23,311	51.9	25,745
La Moure........	1,147	11,564	10.1	10,724	Geauga..........	416	15,036	36.1	14,670
Logan...........	997	7,723	7.7	6,168	Greene..........	415	31,221	75.2	29,733
McHenry.........	1,888	15,544	8.2	17,627	Guernsey........	518	45,352	87.6	42,716
McIntosh........	1,003	9,010	9.0	7,251					
McKenzie........	2,847	9,544	3.4	5,720	Hamilton........	407	493,678	1,213.0	460,732
McLean..........	2,305	17,266	7.5	14,496	Hancock.........	535	38,394	71.8	37,860
Mercer..........	1,110	8,224	7.4	4,747	Hardin..........	473	29,167	61.7	30,407
Morton..........	1,947	18,714	9.6	25,289	Harrison........	401	19,625	48.9	19,076
					Henry...........	414	23,362	56.4	25,119
Mountrail........	1,914	12,140	6.3	8,491					
Nelson..........	981	10,362	10.6	10,140	Highland........	549	27,610	50.3	28,711
Oliver..........	720	4,425	6.1	3,577	Hocking.........	411	23,291	56.7	23,650
Pembina.........	1,117	15,177	13.6	14,749	Holmes..........	418	16,965	40.6	17,909
Pierce..........	1,055	9,283	8.8	9,740	Huron...........	494	32,424	65.6	34,206
					Jackson.........	404	27,342	67.7	30,791
Ramsey..........	1,205	15,427	12.8	15,199					
Ransom..........	860	11,618	13.5	10,345	Jefferson.......	407	77,580	190.6	65,423
Renville........	899	7,776	8.6	7,840	Knox............	513	29,580	57.7	30,181
Richland........	1,437	20,887	14.5	19,659	Lake............	241	28,667	119.0	22,927
Rolette.........	918	10,061	11.0	9,558	Lawrence........	443	39,540	89.3	39,488
					Licking.........	669	56,426	84.3	55,590
Sargent.........	855	9,655	11.3	9,202					
Sheridan........	996	7,935	8.0	8,103	Logan...........	451	30,104	66.7	30,084
Sioux...........	1,114	3,308	3.0	....	Lorain..........	497	90,612	182.3	76,037
Slope...........	1,223	4,940	4.0	....	Lucas...........	342	275,721	806.2	192,728
Stark...........	1,356	13,542	10.0	12,504	Madison.........	497	19,662	39.6	19,902
					Mahoning........	427	186,310	436.3	116,151
Steele..........	717	7,401	10.3	7,616					
Stutsman........	2,282	24,575	10.8	18,189	Marion..........	409	42,004	102.7	33,971
Towner..........	1,037	8,327	8.0	8,963	Medina..........	435	26,067	59.9	23,598
Traill..........	865	12,210	14.1	12,545	Meigs...........	412	26,189	63.6	25,594
					Mercer..........	450	26,872	59.7	27,536
Walsh...........	1,282	19,078	14.9	19,491	Miami...........	408	48,428	118.7	45,047
Ward............	2,054	28,811	14.0	25,281					
Wells...........	1,293	12,957	10.0	11,814	Monroe..........	448	20,660	46.1	24,244
Williams........	2,138	17,980	8.4	14,234	Montgomery......	455	209,532	460.5	163,763
					Morgan..........	402	14,555	36.2	16,097
					Morrow..........	403	15,570	38.6	16,815
OHIO..........	40,740	5,759,394	141.4	4,767,121	Muskingum.......	664	57,980	87.3	57,488
Adams...........	546	22,403	41.0	24,755	Noble...........	399	17,849	44.7	18,601
Allen...........	406	68,223	168.0	56,580	Ottawa..........	270	22,193	82.2	22,360
Ashland.........	421	24,627	58.5	22,975	Paulding........	413	18,736	45.4	22,730
Ashtabula........	723	65,545	90.7	59,547	Perry...........	399	36,098	90.5	35,396
Athens..........	487	50,430	103.6	47,798	Pickaway........	490	25,788	52.6	26,158
Auglaize........	397	29,527	74.4	31,246	Pike............	428	14,151	33.1	15,723
Belmont.........	530	93,193	175.8	76,856	Portage.........	521	30,209	60.6	30,307
Brown...........	481	22,621	47.0	24,832	Preble..........	410	20,909	55.9	23,834
Butler..........	452	87,025	192.5	70,271	Putnam..........	482	27,751	57.6	29,072
Carroll.........	387	15,942	41.2	15,761	Richland........	503	55,178	109.7	47,667
Champaign.......	421	25,071	59.6	26,351	Ross............	668	41,556	62.2	40,069
Clark...........	407	80,728	198.3	66,435	Sandusky........	413	37,109	89.9	35,171
Clermont........	465	28,291	60.8	29,551	Scioto..........	623	62,550	100.9	48,463
Clinton.........	411	23,036	56.0	23,680	Seneca..........	550	43,176	78.5	42,421
Columbiana......	534	83,131	155.7	76,619	Shelby..........	413	25,923	62.8	24,663
Coshocton.......	558	29,595	53.0	30,121	Stark...........	566	177,218	313.1	122,987
Crawford........	409	36,054	88.2	34,036	Summit..........	408	286,065	701.1	108,253
Cuyahoga........	463	943,495	2,037.8	637,425	Trumbull........	633	83,920	132.6	52,766
Darke...........	586	42,911	73.2	42,933	Tuscarawas......	555	63,578	114.6	57,035
Defiance........	405	24,549	60.6	24,498	Union...........	446	20,918	46.9	21,871

TABLE 9.—AREA AND POPULATION OF COUNTIES: 1920 AND 1910—Continued.

COUNTY.	Land area in square miles: 1920.	POPULATION.			COUNTY.	Land area in square miles: 1920.	POPULATION.		
		1920		1910			1920		1910
		Total.	Per square mile.				Total.	Per square mile.	
OHIO—Con.					OKLAHOMA—Con.				
Van Wert	406	28,210	69.5	29,119	Mayes	676	16,829	24.9	13,596
Vinton	412	12,075	29.3	13,096	Murray	424	13,115	30.9	12,744
Warren	413	25,716	62.3	24,497	Muskogee	814	61,710	75.8	52,743
Washington	630	43,049	68.3	45,422	Noble	734	13,560	18.5	14,945
					Nowata	586	15,899	27.1	14,223
Wayne	557	41,346	74.2	38,058	Okfuskee	623	25,051	40.2	19,995
Williams	411	24,627	59.9	25,198					
Wood	612	44,892	73.4	46,330	Oklahoma	717	116,307	162.2	85,232
Wyandot	406	19,481	48.0	20,760	Okmulgee	697	55,072	79.0	21,115
					Osage	2,277	36,536	16.0	20,101
					Ottawa	477	41,108	86.2	15,713
OKLAHOMA	69,414	2,028,283	29.2	1,657,155	Pawnee	584	19,126	32.8	17,332
Adair	584	13,703	23.5	10,535	Payne	678	30,180	44.5	23,735
Alfalfa	867	16,253	18.7	18,138					
Atoka	997	20,862	20.9	13,808					
Beaver	1,812	14,048	7.7	13,631	Pittsburg	1,370	52,570	38.4	47,650
Beckham	917	18,989	20.7	19,699	Pontotoc	728	30,949	42.5	24,331
Blaine	931	15,875	17.1	17,960	Pottawatomie	793	46,028	58.0	43,595
					Pushmataha	1,430	17,514	12.2	10,118
Bryan	928	40,700	43.9	29,854	Roger Mills	1,135	10,638	9.4	12,861
Caddo	1,289	34,207	26.5	35,685	Rogers	710	17,605	24.8	17,736
Canadian	891	22,288	25.0	23,501					
Carter	831	40,247	48.4	25,358	Seminole	633	23,808	37.6	19,964
Cherokee	791	19,872	25.1	16,778	Sequoyah	693	26,786	38.7	25,005
Choctaw	790	32,144	40.7	21,862	Stephens	897	24,692	27.5	22,252
					Texas	2,065	13,975	6.8	14,249
Cimarron	1,849	3,436	1.9	4,553	Tillman	850	22,433	26.4	18,650
Cleveland	554	19,389	35.0	18,843	Tulsa	585	109,023	186.4	34,995
Coal	525	18,406	35.1	15,817					
Comanche	1,096	26,629	24.3	41,489	Wagoner	545	21,371	39.2	22,086
Cotton	630	16,679	26.5	......	Washington	425	27,002	63.5	17,484
Craig	757	19,160	25.3	17,404	Washita	1,006	22,237	22.1	25,034
					Woods	1,255	15,939	12.7	17,567
Creek	962	62,480	64.9	26,223	Woodward	1,233	14,663	11.9	16,592
Custer	998	18,736	18.8	23,231					
Delaware	794	13,868	17.5	11,469					
Dewey	989	12,434	12.6	14,132					
Ellis	1,218	11,673	9.6	15,375	OREGON	95,607	783,389	8.2	672,765
Garfield	1,061	37,500	35.3	33,050					
					Baker	3,086	17,929	5.8	18,076
Garvin	821	32,445	39.5	26,545	Benton	688	13,744	20.0	10,663
Grady	1,112	33,943	30.5	30,309	Clackamas	1,868	37,698	20.2	29,931
Grant	994	16,072	16.2	18,760	Clatsop	821	23,030	28.1	16,106
Greer	644	15,836	24.6	16,449	Columbia	662	13,960	21.1	10,580
Harmon	548	11,261	20.5	11,328					
Harper	1,033	7,623	7.4	8,189	Coos	1,628	22,257	13.7	17,959
					Crook	2,934	3,424	1.2	9,315
Haskell	615	19,397	31.5	18,875	Curry	1,612	3,025	1.9	2,044
Hughes	790	26,045	33.0	24,040	Deschutes	3,065	9,622	3.1	......
Jackson	778	22,141	28.5	23,737	Douglas	4,991	21,332	4.3	19,674
Jefferson	767	17,664	23.0	17,430					
Johnston	658	20,125	30.6	16,734	Gilliam	1,201	3,960	3.3	3,701
Kay	934	34,907	37.4	26,999	Grant	4,520	5,496	1.2	5,607
					Harney	9,933	3,992	0.4	4,059
Kingfisher	890	15,671	17.6	18,825	Hood River	540	8,315	15.4	8,016
Kiowa	1,062	23,094	21.7	27,526	Jackson	2,794	20,405	7.3	25,756
Latimer	735	13,866	18.9	11,321					
Le Flore	1,614	42,765	26.5	29,127	Jefferson	1,779	3,211	1.8	......
Lincoln	959	33,406	34.8	34,779	Josephine	1,637	7,655	4.7	9,567
Logan	739	27,550	37.3	31,740	Klamath	5,999	11,413	1.9	8,554
					Lake	7,920	3,991	0.5	4,658
Love	496	12,433	25.1	10,236	Lane	4,587	36,166	7.9	33,783
McClain	562	19,326	34.4	15,659					
McCurtain	1,897	37,905	20.0	20,681	Lincoln	1,008	6,084	6.0	5,587
McIntosh	708	26,404	37.3	20,961	Linn	2,258	24,550	10.9	22,662
Major	937	12,426	13.3	15,248	Malheur	9,883	10,907	1.1	8,601
Marshall	419	14,674	35.0	11,619	Marion	1,193	47,187	39.6	39,780

TABLE 9.—AREA AND POPULATION OF COUNTIES: 1920 AND 1910—Continued.

COUNTY.	Land area in square miles: 1920.	POPULATION 1920 Total.	Per square mile.	1910
OREGON—Con.				
Morrow	2,025	5,617	2.8	4,357
Multnomah	434	275,898	635.7	226,261
Polk	709	14,181	20.0	13,469
Sherman	836	3,826	4.6	4,242
Tillamook	1,125	8,810	7.8	6,266
Umatilla	3,203	25,946	8.1	20,309
Union	2,007	16,636	8.3	16,191
Wallowa	3,169	9,778	3.1	8,364
Wasco	2,343	13,648	5.8	16,336
Washington	731	26,376	36.1	21,522
Wheeler	1,704	2,791	1.6	2,484
Yamhill	714	20,529	28.8	18,285
PENNSYLVANIA	44,832	8,720,017	194.5	7,665,111
Adams	528	34,583	65.5	34,319
Allegheny	725	1,185,808	1,635.6	1,018,463
Armstrong	653	75,568	115.7	67,880
Beaver	429	111,621	260.2	78,353
Bedford	1,026	38,277	37.3	38,879
Berks	865	200,854	232.2	183,222
Blair	535	128,334	239.9	108,858
Bradford	1,145	53,166	46.4	54,526
Bucks	608	82,476	135.7	76,530
Butler	790	77,270	97.8	72,689
Cambria	717	197,839	275.9	166,131
Cameron	392	6,297	16.1	7,644
Carbon	406	62,565	154.1	52,846
Centre	1,146	44,304	38.7	43,424
Chester	777	115,120	148.2	109,213
Clarion	601	36,170	60.2	36,638
Clearfield	1,142	103,236	90.4	93,768
Clinton	878	33,555	38.2	31,545
Columbia	479	48,349	100.9	48,467
Crawford	1,038	60,667	58.4	61,565
Cumberland	528	58,578	110.9	54,479
Dauphin	522	153,116	293.3	136,152
Delaware	185	173,084	935.6	117,906
Elk	806	34,981	43.4	35,871
Erie	781	153,536	196.6	115,517
Fayette	796	188,104	236.3	167,449
Forest	424	7,477	17.6	9,435
Franklin	751	62,275	82.9	59,775
Fulton	403	9,617	23.9	9,703
Greene	574	30,804	53.7	28,882
Huntingdon	918	39,848	43.4	38,304
Indiana	820	80,810	97.9	66,210
Jefferson	666	62,104	93.2	63,090
Juniata	392	14,464	36.9	15,013
Lackawanna	451	286,311	634.8	259,570
Lancaster	941	173,797	184.7	167,029
Lawrence	360	85,545	237.6	70,032
Lebanon	360	63,152	175.4	59,565
Lehigh	344	148,101	430.5	118,832
Luzerne	892	390,991	438.3	343,186
Lycoming	1,220	83,100	68.1	80,813
McKean	987	48,934	49.6	47,868
Mercer	700	93,788	134.0	77,699
Mifflin	398	31,439	79.0	27,785
Monroe	623	24,295	39.0	22,941

COUNTY.	Land area in square miles: 1920.	POPULATION 1920 Total.	Per square mile.	1910
PENNSYLVANIA—Con.				
Montgomery	484	199,310	411.8	169,590
Montour	130	14,080	108.3	14,868
Northampton	372	153,506	412.7	127,667
Northumberland	454	122,079	268.9	111,420
Perry	564	22,875	40.6	24,136
Philadelphia	128	1,823,779	14,248.3	1,549,008
Pike	544	6,818	12.5	8,033
Potter	1,071	21,089	19.7	29,729
Schuylkill	777	217,754	280.2	207,894
Snyder	311	17,129	55.1	16,800
Somerset	1,034	82,112	79.4	67,717
Sullivan	458	9,520	20.8	11,293
Susquehanna	824	34,763	42.2	37,746
Tioga	1,142	37,118	32.5	42,829
Union	305	15,850	52.0	16,249
Venango	661	59,184	89.5	56,359
Warren	902	40,024	44.4	39,573
Washington	862	188,992	219.2	143,680
Wayne	739	27,435	37.1	29,236
Westmoreland	1,039	273,568	263.3	231,304
Wyoming	397	14,101	35.5	15,509
York	903	144,521	160.0	136,405
RHODE ISLAND	1,067	604,397	566.4	542,610
Bristol	24	23,113	963.0	17,602
Kent	174	38,269	219.9	36,378
Newport	114	42,893	376.3	39,335
Providence	430	475,190	1,105.1	424,353
Washington	325	24,932	76.7	24,942
SOUTH CAROLINA	30,495	1,683,724	55.2	1,515,400
Abbeville	510	27,139	53.2	34,804
Aiken	1,100	45,574	41.4	41,849
Allendale	435	16,098	37.0	
Anderson	758	76,349	100.7	69,568
Bamberg	375	20,962	55.9	18,544
Barnwell	522	23,081	44.2	34,209
Beaufort	702	22,269	31.7	30,355
Berkeley	1,238	22,558	18.2	23,487
Calhoun	391	18,384	47.0	16,634
Charleston	888	108,450	122.1	88,594
Cherokee	373	27,570	73.9	26,179
Chester	509	33,389	56.4	29,425
Chesterfield	877	31,969	35.2	26,301
Clarendon	704	34,878	49.5	32,188
Colleton	1,126	29,897	26.6	35,390
Darlington	605	39,126	64.7	36,027
Dillon	471	25,278	53.7	22,615
Dorchester	613	19,459	31.7	17,891
Edgefield	524	23,928	45.7	28,281
Fairfield	706	27,159	38.5	29,442
Florence	699	50,406	72.1	35,671
Georgetown	828	21,716	26.2	22,270
Greenville	761	88,498	116.3	68,377
Greenwood	473	35,791	75.7	34,225
Hampton	513	19,550	38.1	25,126

TABLE 9.—AREA AND POPULATION OF COUNTIES: 1920 AND 1910—Continued.

COUNTY.	Land area in square miles: 1920.	POPULATION.		1910	COUNTY.	Land area in square miles: 1920.	POPULATION.		1910
		1920					1920		
		Total.	Per square mile.				Total.	Per square mile.	
SOUTH CARO-LINA—Con.					SOUTH DAKOTA—Con.				
Horry	1,158	32,077	27.7	26,995	Harding	2,682	3,953	1.5	4,228
Jasper	596	9,868	16.6		Hughes	759	5,711	7.5	6,271
Kershaw	673	29,398	43.7	27,094	Hutchinson	817	13,475	16.5	12,319
Lancaster	515	28,628	55.6	26,650	Hyde	866	3,315	3.8	3,307
Laurens	690	42,560	61.7	41,550	Jackson	816	2,472	3.0	
Lee	407	26,827	65.9	25,318	Jerauld	531	6,338	11.9	5,120
Lexington	779	35,676	45.8	32,040	Jones	982	3,004	3.1	
McCormick	379	16,444	43.4		Kingsbury	814	12,802	15.7	12,560
Marion	529	23,721	44.8	20,596	Lake	562	12,257	21.8	10,711
					Lawrence	797	13,029	16.3	19,694
Marlboro	519	33,180	63.9	31,189					
Newberry	601	35,552	59.1	34,586	Lincoln	574	13,893	24.2	12,712
Oconee	650	30,117	46.3	27,337	Lyman	1,643	6,591	4.0	10,848
Orangeburg	1,131	64,907	57.4	55,893	McCook	573	9,990	17.4	9,589
					McPherson	1,157	7,705	6.7	6,791
Pickens	529	28,329	53.6	25,422	Marshall	889	9,596	10.8	8,021
Richland	751	78,122	104.0	55,143					
Saluda	435	22,088	50.8	20,943	Meade	3,491	9,367	2.7	12,640
Spartanburg	765	94,265	123.2	83,465	Mellette	1,303	3,850	3.0	1,700
					Miner	568	8,560	15.1	7,661
Sumter	574	43,040	75.0	38,472	Minnehaha	815	42,490	52.1	29,631
Union	492	30,372	61.7	29,911	Moody	527	9,742	18.5	8,695
Williamsburg	927	38,539	41.6	37,626					
York	651	50,536	77.6	47,718	Pennington	2,792	12,720	4.6	12,453
					Perkins	2,914	7,993	2.7	11,348
					Potter	898	4,382	4.9	4,466
					Roberts	1,111	16,514	14.9	14,897
SOUTH DAKOTA	76,868	636,547	8.3	[1] 583,888	Sanborn	576	7,877	13.7	6,607
					Shannon	964	2,003	2.1	([2])
Aurora	719	7,246	10.1	6,143	Spink	1,511	15,768	10.4	15,981
Beadle	1,250	19,273	15.4	15,776	Stanley	1,521	2,908	1.9	14,975
Bennett	1,173	1,924	1.6	96	Sully	1,058	2,831	2.7	2,462
Bon Homme	573	11,940	20.8	11,061	Todd	1,397	2,784	2.0	2,164
Brookings	791	16,119	20.4	14,178					
					Tripp	1,629	11,970	7.3	8,323
Brown	1,750	29,509	16.9	25,867	Turner	617	14,871	24.1	13,840
Brule	837	7,141	8.5	6,451	Union	452	11,099	24.6	10,676
Buffalo	479	1,715	3.6	1,589	Walworth	742	8,447	11.4	6,488
Butte	2,289	6,819	3.0	4,993					
Campbell	774	5,305	6.9	5,244	Washabaugh	1,071	1,166	1.1	([2])
					Washington	1,157	1,521	1.3	([2])
Charles Mix	1,134	16,256	14.3	14,899	Yankton	523	15,233	29.1	13,135
Clark	974	11,136	11.4	10,901	Ziebach	[1]2,504	3,718	1.5	
Clay	403	9,654	24.0	8,711					
Codington	701	16,549	23.6	14,092					
Corson	2,526	7,249	2.9	2,929	TENNESSEE [3]	41,687	2,337,885	56.1	2,184,789
Custer	1,573	3,907	2.5	4,458	Anderson	342	18,298	53.5	17,717
Davison	432	14,139	32.7	11,625	Bedford	514	21,737	42.3	22,667
Day	1,061	15,194	14.3	14,372	Benton	456	12,046	26.4	12,452
Deuel	632	8,759	13.9	7,768	Bledsoe	391	7,218	18.5	6,329
Dewey	1,907	4,802	2.5	1,145	Blount	571	28,800	50.4	20,809
Douglas	435	6,993	16.1	6,400	Bradley	336	18,652	55.5	16,336
Edmunds	1,158	8,336	7.2	7,654	Campbell	459	28,265	61.6	27,387
Fall River	1,756	6,985	4.0	7,763	Cannon	268	10,241	38.2	10,825
Faulk	1,018	6,442	6.3	6,716	Carroll	619	24,361	39.4	23,971
Grant	691	10,880	15.7	10,303	Carter	353	21,488	60.9	19,838
Gregory	1,032	12,700	12.3	13,061	Cheatham	314	10,039	32.0	10,540
Haakon	1,819	4,596	2.5		Chester	313	9,669	30.9	9,090
Hamlin	520	8,054	15.5	7,475	Claiborne	468	23,286	49.8	23,504
Hand	1,426	8,778	6.2	7,870	Clay	254	9,193	36.2	9,009
Hanson	432	6,202	14.4	6,237	Cocke	427	20,782	48.7	19,399

[1] Includes population of Armstrong and Schnasse Counties (939) and of Sterling County (252), taken to form part of Ziebach County since 1910; of Pine Ridge Indian Reservation (6,607), not returned by counties.
[2] Not returned separately.
[3] Total for 1910 includes population (5,210) of James County, annexed to Hamilton County in 1919.

TABLE 9.—AREA AND POPULATION OF COUNTIES: 1920 AND 1910—Continued.

COUNTY.	Land area in square miles: 1920.	POPULATION.			COUNTY.	Land area in square miles: 1920.	POPULATION.		
		1920		1910			1920		1910
		Total.	Per square mile.				Total.	Per square mile.	
TENNESSEE— Con.					TENNESSEE— Con.				
Coffee	443	17,344	39.2	15,625	Scott	550	13,411	24.4	12,947
Crockett	267	17,438	65.3	16,076	Sequatchie	264	3,632	13.8	4,202
Cumberland	655	10,094	15.4	9,327	Sevier	587	22,384	38.1	22,296
Davidson	511	167,815	328.4	149,478	Shelby	801	223,216	278.7	191,439
De Kalb	311	15,370	49.4	15,434	Smith	296	17,134	57.9	18,548
Decatur	288	10,198	35.4	10,093					
Dickson	549	19,342	35.2	19,955	Stewart	449	14,664	32.7	14,860
Dyer	500	29,983	60.0	27,721	Sullivan	436	36,259	83.2	28,120
Fayette	618	31,499	51.0	30,257	Sumner	558	27,708	49.7	25,621
Fentress	486	10,435	21.5	7,446	Tipton	442	30,258	68.5	29,459
					Trousdale	106	5,996	56.6	5,874
Franklin	575	20,641	35.9	20,491					
Gibson	633	43,388	68.5	41,630	Unicoi	201	10,120	50.3	7,201
Giles	628	30,948	49.3	32,629	Union	235	11,615	49.4	11,414
Grainger	307	13,369	43.5	13,888	Van Buren	293	2,624	9.0	2,784
Greene	613	32,824	53.5	31,083	Warren	423	17,306	40.9	16,534
					Washington	325	34,052	104.8	28,968
Grundy	375	9,753	26.0	8,322					
Hamblen	158	15,056	95.3	13,650	Wayne	749	12,877	17.2	12,062
Hamilton	574	115,954	202.0	89,267	Weakley	580	31,053	53.5	31,929
Hancock	228	10,454	45.9	10,778	White	363	15,701	43.3	15,420
Hardeman	697	22,278	32.0	23,011	Williamson	586	23,409	39.9	24,213
					Wilson	613	26,241	42.8	25,394
Hardin	582	17,291	29.7	17,521					
Hawkins	482	22,918	47.5	23,587					
Haywood	508	25,386	50.0	25,910					
Henderson	536	18,436	34.4	17,030					
Henry	626	27,151	43.4	25,434	TEXAS	262,398	4,663,228	17.8	3,896,542
Hickman	570	16,216	28.4	16,527	Anderson	938	34,318	36.6	29,650
Houston	197	6,212	31.5	6,224	Andrews	1,565	350	0.2	975
Humphreys	451	13,482	29.9	13,908	Angelina	940	22,287	23.7	17,705
Jackson	301	14,955	49.7	15,036	Aransas	240	2,064	8.6	2,106
Jefferson	312	17,677	56.7	17,755	Archer	872	5,254	6.0	6,525
Johnson	294	12,230	41.6	13,191	Armstrong	903	2,816	3.1	2,682
Knox	504	112,926	224.1	94,187	Atascosa	1,358	12,702	9.4	10,004
Lake	122	9,075	74.4	8,704	Austin	728	18,874	25.9	17,699
Lauderdale	456	21,494	47.1	21,105	Bailey	1,030	517	0.5	312
Lawrence	611	23,593	38.6	17,569	Bandera	811	4,001	4.9	4,921
Lewis	286	5,707	20.0	6,033	Bastrop	867	26,649	30.7	25,344
Lincoln	587	25,786	43.9	25,908	Baylor	880	7,027	8.0	8,411
Loudon	219	16,275	74.3	13,612	Bee	856	12,137	14.2	12,090
McMinn	432	25,133	58.2	21,046	Bell	1,083	46,412	42.9	49,186
McNairy	588	18,350	31.2	16,356	Bexar	1,263	202,096	160.0	119,676
Macon	286	14,922	52.2	14,559	Blanco	750	4,063	5.4	4,311
Madison	552	43,824	79.4	39,357	Borden	895	965	1.1	1,386
Marion	504	17,402	34.5	18,820	Bosque	975	18,032	18.5	19,013
Marshall	378	17,375	46.0	16,872	Bowie	873	39,472	45.2	34,827
Maury	582	35,403	60.8	40,456	Brazoria	1,340	20,614	15.4	13,299
Meigs	207	6,077	29.4	6,131	Brazos	597	21,975	36.8	18,919
Monroe	675	22,969	79.8	20,716	Brewster	5,935	4,822	0.8	5,220
Montgomery	516	32,265	62.5	33,672	Briscoe	903	2,018	0.0	0,162
Moore	141	4,491	31.9	4,800	Brooks	974	4,560	4.7	
Morgan	529	13,285	25.1	11,458	Brown	956	21,682	22.7	22,935
Obion	552	28,393	51.4	29,946	Burleson	684	16,855	24.6	18,687
Overton	446	17,617	39.5	15,854	Burnet	974	9,499	9.8	10,755
Perry	487	7,765	15.9	8,815	Caldwell	511	25,160	49.2	24,237
Pickett	162	5,205	32.1	5,087	Calhoun	563	4,700	8.3	3,635
Polk	432	14,243	33.0	14,116	Callahan	854	11,844	13.9	12,973
Putnam	404	22,231	55.0	20,023	Cameron	1,401	36,662	26.2	27,158
Rhea	365	13,812	37.8	15,410	Camp	207	11,103	53.6	9,551
Roane	380	24,624	64.8	22,860	Carson	893	3,078	3.4	2,127
Robertson	455	25,621	56.3	25,466	Cass	951	30,041	31.6	27,587
Rutherford	614	33,059	53.8	33,199	Castro	896	1,948	2.2	1,850

TABLE **9.**—AREA AND POPULATION OF COUNTIES: 1920 AND 1910—Continued.

COUNTY.	Land area in square miles: 1920.	POPULATION.			COUNTY.	Land area in square miles: 1920.	POPULATION.		
		1920		1910			1920		1910
		Total.	Per square mile.				Total.	Per square mile	
TEXAS—Con.					**TEXAS—Con.**				
Chambers........	618	4,162	6.7	4,234	Hall............	901	11,137	12.4	8,279
Cherokee.........	1,049	37,633	35.9	29,038	Hamilton........	833	14,676	17.6	15,315
Childress........	733	10,933	14.9	9,538	Hansford........	882	1,354	1.5	935
Clay.............	1,158	16,864	14.6	17,043	Hardeman.......	761	12,487	16.4	11,213
Cochran.........	869	67	0.1	65	Hardin..........	862	15,983	18.5	12,947
Coke............	931	4,557	4.9	6,412	Harris..........	1,654	186,667	112.9	115,693
Coleman.........	1,290	18,805	14.6	22,618	Harrison........	872	43,565	50.0	37,243
Collin...........	878	49,609	56.5	49,021	Hartley.........	1,507	1,109	0.7	1,298
Collingsworth....	898	9,154	10.2	5,224	Haskell.........	923	14,193	15.4	16,249
Colorado.........	972	19,013	19.6	18,897	Hays...........	623	15,920	25.6	15,518
Comal...........	559	8,824	15.8	8,434	Hemphill........	873	4,280	4.9	3,170
Comanche.......	948	25,748	27.2	27,186	Henderson.......	946	28,327	29.9	20,131
Concho..........	918	5,847	6.4	6,654	Hidalgo.........	1,629	38,110	23.4	13,728
Cooke...........	902	25,667	28.5	26,603	Hill............	966	43,332	44.9	46,760
Coryell..........	1,085	20,601	19.0	21,703	Hockley.........	867	137	0.2	137
Cottle..........	1,012	6,901	6.8	4,396	Hood...........	405	8,759	21.6	10,008
Crane...........	878	37	......	331	Hopkins.........	813	34,791	42.8	31,038
Crockett........	3,215	1,500	0.5	1,296	Houston.........	1,231	28,601	23.2	29,564
Crosby..........	870	6,084	7.0	1,765	Howard.........	891	6,962	7.8	8,881
Culberson........	3,787	912	0.2	....	Hudspeth........	4,621	962	0.2	....
Dallam	1,532	4,528	3.0	4,001	Hunt...........	893	50,350	56.4	48,116
Dallas..........	859	210,551	245.1	135,748	Hutchinson......	879	721	0.8	892
Dawson.........	903	4,309	4.8	2,320	Irion...........	998	1,610	1.6	1,283
De Witt.........	879	27,971	31.8	23,501	Jack............	962	9,863	10.3	11,817
Deaf Smith......	1,549	3,747	2.4	3,942	Jackson.........	893	11,244	12.6	6,471
Delta...........	261	15,887	60.9	14,566	Jasper..........	978	15,569	15.9	14,000
Denton..........	952	35,355	37.1	31,258	Jeff Davis.......	2,263	1,445	0.6	1,678
Dickens.........	881	5,876	6.7	3,092	Jefferson........	920	73,120	79.5	38,182
Dimmit.........	1,360	5,296	3.9	3,460	Jim Hogg........	1,140	1,914	1.7	....
Donley..........	906	8,035	8.9	5,284	Jim Wells........	791	6,587	8.3	....
Duval...........	1,703	8,251	4.8	8,964	Johnson.........	740	37,286	50.4	34,460
Eastland.........	925	58,505	63.2	23,421	Jones...........	922	22,323	24.2	24,299
Ector...........	892	760	0.9	1,178	Karnes..........	692	19,049	27.5	14,942
Edwards.........	1,960	2,283	1.2	3,768	Kaufman........	834	41,276	49.5	35,323
El Paso.........	923	101,877	110.4	52,599	Kendall.........	598	4,779	8.0	4,517
Ellis...........	975	55,700	57.1	53,629	Kent...........	875	3,335	3.8	2,655
Erath...........	1,083	28,385	26.2	32,095	Kerr............	1,142	5,842	5.1	5,505
Falls...........	745	36,217	48.6	35,649	Kimble.........	1,301	3,581	2.8	3,261
Fannin..........	838	48,186	57.5	44,801	King...........	867	655	0.8	810
Fayette..........	968	29,965	31.0	29,796	Kinney.........	1,312	3,746	2.9	3,401
Fisher..........	885	11,009	12.4	12,596	Kleberg.........	698	7,837	11.2	....
Floyd..........	1,011	9,758	9.7	4,638	Knox...........	862	9,240	10.7	9,625
Foard..........	612	4,747	7.8	5,726	La Salle........	1,561	4,821	3.1	4,747
Fort Bend.......	792	22,931	29.0	18,168	Lamar.........	945	55,742	59.0	46,544
Franklin........	289	9,304	32.2	9,331	Lamb..........	1,022	1,175	1.1	540
Freestone........	882	23,264	26.4	20,557	Lampasas.......	740	8,800	11.9	9,532
Frio...........	1,124	9,296	8.3	8,895	Lavaca.........	950	28,964	30.5	26,418
Gaines..........	1,540	1,018	0.7	1,255	Lee............	562	14,014	24.9	13,132
Galveston........	395	53,150	134.6	44,479	Leon...........	1,101	18,286	16.6	16,583
Garza..........	870	4,253	4.9	1,995	Liberty.........	1,160	14,637	12.6	10,686
Gillespie........	1,109	10,015	9.0	9,447	Limestone.......	974	33,283	34.2	34,621
Glasscock.......	866	555	0.6	1,143	Lipscomb.......	888	3,684	4.1	2,634
Goliad.........	799	9,348	11.7	9,909	Live Oak.......	1,116	4,171	3.7	3,442
Gonzales........	1,020	28,438	27.9	28,055	Llano..........	971	5,360	5.5	6,520
Gray...........	899	4,663	5.2	3,405	Loving.........	753	82	0.1	249
Grayson........	942	74,165	78.7	65,996	Lubbock........	868	11,096	12.8	3,624
Gregg..........	312	16,767	53.7	14,140	Lynn..........	864	4,751	5.5	1,713
Grimes.........	812	23,101	28.4	21,205	McCulloch......	1,073	11,020	10.3	13,405
Guadalupe.......	703	27,719	39.4	24,913	McLennan......	1,049	82,921	79.0	73,250
Hale............	1,036	10,104	9.8	7,566	McMullen........	1,302	952	0.7	1,091

TABLE **9.**—AREA AND POPULATION OF COUNTIES: 1920 AND 1910—Continued.

COUNTY.	Land area in square miles: 1920.	1920 Total.	1920 Per square mile.	1910	COUNTY.	Land area in square miles: 1920.	1920 Total.	1920 Per square mile.	1910
TEXAS—Con.					TEXAS—Con.				
Madison	495	11,956	24.2	10,318	Stonewall	852	4,086	4.8	5,320
Marion	391	10,886	27.8	10,472	Sutton	1,521	1,598	1.1	1,569
Martin	904	1,146	1.3	1,549	Swisher	898	4,388	4.9	4,012
Mason	969	4,824	5.0	5,683	Tarrant	903	152,800	169.2	108,572
Matagorda	1,136	16,589	14.6	13,594	Taylor	908	24,081	26.5	26,293
Maverick	1,251	7,418	5.9	5,151	Terrell	2,635	1,595	0.6	1,430
Medina	1,353	11,679	8.6	13,415	Terry	870	2,236	2.6	1,474
Menard	914	3,162	3.5	2,707	Throckmorton	879	3,589	4.1	4,563
Midland	887	2,449	2.8	3,464	Titus	398	18,128	45.5	16,422
Milam	959	38,104	39.7	36,780	Tom Green	1,454	15,210	10.5	17,882
Mills	696	9,019	13.0	9,694	Travis	1,004	57,616	57.4	55,620
Mitchell	885	7,527	8.5	8,956	Trinity	716	13,623	19.0	12,768
Montague	929	22,200	23.9	25,123	Tyler	908	10,415	11.5	10,250
Montgomery	1,017	17,334	17.0	15,679	Upshur	600	22,472	37.5	19,960
Moore	921	571	0.6	561	Upton	1,195	253	0.2	501
Morris	259	10,289	39.7	10,439	Uvalde	1,589	10,769	6.8	11,233
Motley	1,030	4,107	4.0	2,396	Val Verde	3,083	12,706	4.1	8,613
Nacogdoches	1,059	28,457	26.9	27,406	Van Zandt	831	30,784	37.0	25,651
Navarro	1,060	50,624	47.8	47,070	Victoria	890	18,271	20.5	14,990
Newton	889	12,196	13.7	10,850	Walker	791	18,556	23.5	16,061
Nolan	880	10,868	12.4	11,999	Waller	519	10,292	19.8	12,138
Nueces	775	22,807	29.4	21,955	Ward	827	2,615	3.2	2,389
Ochiltree	891	2,331	2.6	1,602	Washington	628	26,624	42.4	25,561
Oldham	1,543	709	0.5	812	Webb	3,219	29,152	9.1	22,503
Orange	363	15,379	42.4	9,528	Wharton	1,112	24,288	21.8	21,123
Palo Pinto	958	23,431	24.5	19,506	Wheeler	895	7,397	8.3	5,258
Panola	842	21,755	25.8	20,424	Wichita	604	72,911	120.7	16,094
Parker	875	23,382	26.7	26,331	Wilbarger	928	15,112	16.3	12,000
Parmer	902	1,699	1.9	1,555	Willacy	1,274	1,033	0.8	
Pecos	4,134	3,857	0.9	2,071	Williamson	1,129	42,934	38.0	42,228
Polk	1,217	16,784	13.8	17,459	Wilson	813	17,289	21.3	17,066
Potter	934	16,710	17.9	12,424	Winkler	844	81	0.1	442
Presidio	3,812	12,202	3.2	5,218	Wise	863	23,363	27.1	26,450
Rains	267	8,099	30.3	6,787	Wood	657	27,707	42.2	23,417
Randall	937	3,675	3.9	3,312	Yoakum	879	504	0.6	602
					Young	875	13,379	15.3	13,657
Reagan	1,071	377	0.4	392	Zapata	1,040	2,929	2.8	3,809
Real	619	1,461	2.4		Zavalla	1,348	3,108	2.3	1,889
Red River	1,039	35,829	34.5	28,564					
Reeves	2,781	4,457	1.6	4,392	UTAH	82,184	449,396	5.5	373,351
Refugio	740	4,050	5.5	2,814					
Roberts	882	1,469	1.7	950	Beaver	2,660	5,139	1.9	4,717
Robertson	872	27,933	32.0	27,454	Box Elder	5,444	18,788	3.5	13,894
Rockwall	149	8,591	57.7	8,072	Cache	1,164	26,992	23.2	23,062
Runnels	1,083	17,074	15.8	20,858	Carbon	1,487	15,489	10.4	8,624
Rusk	983	31,689	32.2	26,946	Daggett	850	400	0.5	
Sabine	589	12,299	20.9	8,582	Davis	275	11,450	41.6	10,191
San Augustine	622	13,737	22.1	11,264	Duchesne	3,266	5,635	2.8	
San Jacinto	602	9,867	16.4	9,542	Emery	4,453	7,411	1.7	6,750
San Patricio	676	11,386	16.8	7,307	Garfield	5,234	4,768	0.9	3,660
San Saba	1,116	10,045	9.0	11,245	Grand	3,692	1,808	0.5	1,595
Schleicher	1,387	1,851	1.3	1,893	Iron	3,256	5,787	1.8	3,933
Scurry	887	9,003	10.1	10,924	Juab	3,401	9,871	2.9	10,702
Shackelford	947	4,960	5.2	4,201	Kane	4,215	2,054	0.5	1,652
Shelby	833	27,464	33.0	26,423	Millard	6,561	9,659	1.5	6,118
Sherman	935	1,473	1.6	1,376	Morgan	626	2,542	4.1	2,467
Smith	920	46,769	50.8	41,746	Piute	763	2,770	3.6	1,734
Somervell	184	3,563	19.4	3,931	Rich	1,031	1,890	1.8	1,883
Starr	1,348	11,089	8.2	13,151	Salt Lake	756	159,282	210.7	131,426
Stephens	925	15,403	16.7	7,980	San Juan	7,761	3,379	0.4	2,377
Sterling	948	1,053	1.1	1,493	Sanpete	1,616	17,505	10.8	16,704

TABLE 9.—AREA AND POPULATION OF COUNTIES: 1920 AND 1910—Continued.

COUNTY.	Land area in square miles: 1920.	POPULATION.			COUNTY.	Land area in square miles: 1920.	POPULATION.		
		1920		1910			1920		1910
		Total.	Per square mile.				Total.	Per square mile.	
UTAH—Con.					VIRGINIA—Con.				
Sevier	1,978	11,281	5.7	9,775	Dinwiddie } Petersburg city	521	48,961	94.0	39,569
Summit	1,870	7,862	4.2	8,200	Elizabeth City	54	25,249	467.6	21,225
Tooele	6,849	7,965	1.2	7,924	Essex	258	8,542	33.1	9,105
Uintah	4,294	8,470	2.0	7,050	Fairfax	417	21,943	52.6	20,536
Utah	2,034	40,792	20.1	37,942					
					Fauquier	666	21,869	32.8	22,526
Wasatch	1,167	4,625	4.0	8,920	Floyd	376	13,115	34.9	14,092
Washington	2,465	6,764	2.7	5,123	Fluvanna	285	8,547	30.0	8,323
Wayne	2,475	2,097	0.8	1,749	Franklin	697	26,283	37.7	26,480
Weber	541	43,463	80.3	35,179	Frederick } Winchester city	435	19,344	44.5	18,651
VERMONT	9,124	352,428	38.6	355,956	Giles	369	11,901	32.3	11,623
Addison	756	18,666	24.7	20,010	Gloucester	223	11,894	53.3	12,477
Bennington	661	21,577	32.6	21,378	Goochland	287	8,863	30.9	9,237
Caledonia	618	25,762	41.7	26,031	Grayson	425	19,816	46.6	19,856
Chittenden	543	43,708	80.5	42,447	Greene	155	6,369	41.1	6,937
Essex	638	7,364	11.5	7,384					
					Greensville	307	11,606	37.8	11,890
Franklin	652	30,026	46.1	29,866	Halifax	814	41,374	50.8	40,044
Grand Isle	83	3,784	45.6	3,761	Hanover	512	18,088	35.3	17,200
Lamoille	436	11,858	27.2	12,585	Henrico } Richmond city	280	190,639	680.9	151,065
Orange	676	17,279	25.6	18,703					
Orleans	688	23,913	34.8	23,337	Henry	444	20,238	45.6	18,459
					Highland	422	4,931	11.7	5,317
Rutland	911	46,213	50.7	48,139	Isle of Wight	314	14,433	46.0	14,929
Washington	719	38,921	54.1	41,702	James City	164	6,138	37.4	6,338
Windham	795	26,373	33.2	26,932	King and Queen	320	9,161	28.6	9,576
Windsor	948	36,984	39.0	33,681	King George	180	5,762	32.0	6,378
					King William	263	8,739	33.2	8,547
VIRGINIA	40,262	2,309,187	57.4	2,061,612	Lancaster	130	9,757	75.1	9,752
					Lee	446	25,293	56.7	23,840
Accomac	502	34,795	69.3	36,650	Loudoun	519	20,577	39.6	21,167
Albemarle } Charlottesville city	751	36,693	48.9	36,636	Louisa	516	17,089	33.1	16,578
Alleghany } Clifton Forge city	458	21,496	46.9	19,921	Lunenburg	430	15,260	35.5	12,780
					Madison	324	9,595	29.6	10,055
					Mathews	94	8,447	89.9	8,922
Amelia	371	9,800	26.4	8,720	Mecklenburg	669	31,208	46.6	28,956
Amherst	470	19,771	42.1	18,932					
Appomattox	342	9,255	27.1	8,904	Middlesex	146	8,157	55.9	8,852
Arlington } Alexandria city	31	34,100	1,100.0	25,560	Montgomery } Radford city	401	23,222	57.9	21,470
					Nansemond } Suffolk city	423	29,322	69.3	26,886
Augusta } Staunton city	1,006	45,294	45.0	43,049	Nelson	473	17,277	36.5	16,821
Bath	545	6,389	11.7	6,538	New Kent	191	4,541	23.8	4,082
Bedford	791	30,669	38.8	29,549	Norfolk } Norfolk city } Portsmouth city	415	227,522	548.2	153,386
Bland	360	5,593	15.5	5,154					
Botetourt	548	16,557	30.2	17,727	Northampton	239	17,852	74.7	16,672
Brunswick	557	21,025	37.7	19,244	Northumberland	205	11,518	56.2	10,777
Buchanan	514	15,441	30.0	12,334	Nottoway	310	14,161	45.7	13,462
Buckingham	584	14,885	25.5	15,204	Orange	359	13,320	37.1	13,486
Campbell } Lynchburg city	557	56,786	101.9	52,537	Page	322	14,770	45.9	14,147
Caroline	529	15,954	30.2	16,596	Patrick	485	16,850	34.7	17,195
Carroll	458	21,283	46.5	21,116	Pittsylvania } Danville city	1,015	78,032	76.9	69,729
Charles City	188	4,793	25.5	5,253	Powhatan	273	6,552	24.0	6,099
Charlotte	496	17,540	35.4	15,785	Prince Edward	356	14,767	41.5	14,266
Chesterfield	468	20,496	43.8	21,299					
Clarke	171	7,165	41.9	7,468	Prince George } Hopewell city	294	14,312	48.7	7,848
Craig	333	4,100	12.3	4,711	Prince William	345	13,660	39.6	12,026
Culpeper	384	13,292	34.6	13,472	Princess Anne	279	13,626	48.8	11,526
Cumberland	293	9,111	31.1	9,195	Pulaski	333	17,111	51.4	17,246
Dickenson	325	13,542	41.7	9,199					

TABLE 9.—AREA AND POPULATION OF COUNTIES: 1920 AND 1910—Continued.

COUNTY.	Land area in square miles: 1920.	1920 Total.	Per square mile.	1910	COUNTY.	Land area in square miles: 1920.	1920 Total.	Per square mile.	1910
VIRGINIA—Con.					WASHINGTON— Con.				
Rappahannock...	274	8,070	29.5	8,044	Snohomish.......	2,064	67,690	32.8	59,209
Richmond.......	204	7,434	36.4	7,415	Spokane.........	1,756	141,289	80.5	139,404
Roanoke.........	305	73,237	240.1	54,497	Stevens.........	2,505	21,605	8.6	25,297
Roanoke city...					Thurston........	709	22,366	31.5	17,581
Rockbridge......	616	24,537	39.8	24,416	Wahkiakum.....	267	3,472	13.0	3,285
BuenaVista city									
					Walla Walla.....	1,265	27,539	21.8	31,931
Rockingham.....	876	35,922	41.0	34,903	Whatcom.......	2,082	50,600	24.3	49,511
Harrisonburg city...					Whitman........	2,108	31,323	14.9	33,280
Russell..........	496	26,786	54.0	23,474	Yakima.........	5,059	63,710	12.6	41,709
Scott...........	543	24,776	45.6	23,814					
Shenandoah......	510	20,808	40.8	20,942	WEST VIRGINIA.	24,022	1,463,701	60.9	1,221,119
Smyth..........	435	22,125	50.9	20,326	Barbour.........	348	18,028	51.8	15,858
Southampton....	604	27,555	45.6	26,302	Berkeley........	325	24,554	75.6	21,999
Spotsylvania.....	413	16,453	39.8	15,809	Boone..........	506	15,319	30.3	10,331
Fredericksburg city...					Braxton.........	517	23,973	46.4	23,023
Stafford.........	274	8,104	29.6	8,070	Brooke..........	89	16,527	185.7	11,098
Surry..........	278	9,305	33.5	9,715	Cabell..........	261	65,746	251.9	46,685
Sussex..........	515	12,834	24.9	13,664	Calhoun........	286	10,268	35.9	11,258
Tazewell........	531	27,840	52.4	24,946	Clay...........	332	11,486	34.6	10,233
Warren.........	216	8,852	41.0	8,589	Doddridge......	317	11,976	37.8	12,672
Warwick. Newport News city...	69	47,013	681.3	26,246	Fayette.........	667	60,377	90.5	51,903
					Gilmer.........	331	10,668	32.2	11,379
					Grant..........	461	8,993	19.5	7,838
Washington...... Bristol city....	604	39,105	64.7	39,077	Greenbrier......	998	26,242	26.3	24,833
Westmoreland...	252	10,240	40.6	9,313	Hampshire......	648	11,713	18.1	11,694
Wise...........	420	46,500	110.7	34,162	Hancock........	83	19,975	240.7	10,465
Wythe..........	479	20,217	42.2	20,372	Hardy..........	574	9,601	16.7	9,163
York...........	136	8,046	59.2	7,757	Harrison........	416	74,793	179.8	48,381
					Jackson........	461	18,658	40.5	20,956
WASHINGTON..	66,836	1,356,621	20.3	1,141,990	Jefferson.......	211	15,729	74.5	15,889
					Kanawha.......	860	119,650	139.1	81,457
Adams..........	1,912	9,623	5.0	10,920	Lewis..........	393	20,455	52.0	18,281
Asotin..........	606	6,539	10.8	5,831	Lincoln........	418	19,378	46.4	20,491
Benton.........	1,671	10,903	6.5	7,937	Logan..........	438	41,006	93.6	14,476
Chelan.........	2,900	20,906	7.2	15,104	McDowell.......	533	68,571	128.7	47,856
Clallam.........	1,726	11,368	6.6	6,755	Marion.........	315	54,571	173.2	42,794
Clarke..........	634	32,805	51.7	26,115	Marshall........	310	33,681	108.6	32,388
Columbia.......	858	6,093	7.1	7,042	Mason..........	475	21,459	45.2	23,019
Cowlitz.........	1,153	11,791	10.2	12,561	Mercer.........	419	49,558	118.3	38,371
Douglas.........	1,787	9,392	5.3	9,227	Mineral........	349	19,849	56.9	16,674
Ferry..........	2,220	5,143	2.3	4,800	Mingo.........	416	26,364	63.4	19,431
Franklin........	1,206	5,877	4.9	5,153	Monongalia.....	358	33,618	93.9	24,334
Garfield........	694	3,875	5.6	4,199	Monroe........	457	13,141	28.8	13,055
Grant..........	2,720	7,771	2.9	8,698	Morgan........	233	8,357	35.9	7,848
Grays Harbor....	1,869	44,745	23.9	35,590	Nicholas........	680	20,717	30.5	17,699
Island. ,,,,,..	208	5,489	26.4	4,704	Ohio...........	107	62,892	587.8	57,572
Jefferson........	1,005	6,557	3.0	8,337	Pendleton.......	699	9,652	13.8	9,349
King...........	2,111	389,273	184.4	284,638	Pleasants.......	132	7,379	55.9	8,074
Kitsap.........	371	33,162	89.4	17,647	Pocahontas.....	904	15,002	16.6	14,740
Kittitas........	2,329	17,737	7.6	18,561	Preston........	660	27,996	43.1	26,341
Klickitat........	1,825	9,268	5.1	10,180	Putnam........	336	17,531	52.2	18,587
Lewis..........	2,369	36,840	15.6	32,127	Raleigh.........	597	42,482	71.2	25,633
Lincoln.........	2,302	15,141	6.6	17,539	Randolph.......	1,036	26,804	25.9	26,028
Mason..........	930	4,919	5.3	5,156	Ritchie.........	453	16,506	36.4	17,875
Okanogan.......	5,221	17,094	3.3	12,887	Roane.........	522	20,129	38.6	21,543
Pacific.........	895	14,891	16.6	12,532	Summers.......	369	19,092	51.7	18,420
Pend Oreille.....	1,361	6,363	4.7	......	Taylor.........	175	18,742	107.1	16,554
Pierce..........	1,701	144,127	84.7	120,812	Tucker.........	405	16,791	41.5	18,675
San Juan........	178	3,605	20.3	3,603	Tyler..........	260	14,186	54.6	16,211
Skagit.........	1,774	33,373	18.8	29,241	Upshur........	351	17,851	50.9	16,629
Skamania.......	1,685	2,357	1.4	2,887	Wayne.........	517	26,012	50.3	24,081

TABLE 9.—AREA AND POPULATION OF COUNTIES: 1920 AND 1910—Continued.

COUNTY.	Land area in square miles: 1920.	POPULATION.			COUNTY.	Land area in square miles: 1920.	POPULATION.		
		1920		1910			1920		1910
		Total.	Per square mile.				Total.	Per square mile.	
WEST VIRGINIA— Con.					WISCONSIN—Con.				
Webster	583	11,562	19.8	9,680	Pepin	236	7,481	31.7	7,577
Wetzel	357	23,069	64.6	23,855	Pierce	563	21,663	38.5	22,079
Wirt	218	7,536	34.6	9,047	Polk	935	26,870	28.7	21,367
Wood	364	42,306	116.2	38,001	Portage	812	33,649	41.4	30,945
Wyoming	502	15,180	30.2	10,392	Price	1,279	18,517	14.5	13,795
					Racine	324	78,961	243.7	57,424
WISCONSIN	55,256	2,632,067	47.6	2,333,860	Richland	590	19,823	33.6	18,809
					Rock	716	66,150	92.4	55,538
Adams	684	9,287	13.6	8,604	Rusk	925	16,403	17.7	11,160
Ashland	1,082	24,538	22.7	21,965	St. Croix	735	26,106	35.5	25,910
Barron	885	34,281	38.7	29,114	Sauk	842	32,548	38.7	32,869
Bayfield	1,503	17,201	11.4	15,987					
Brown	529	61,889	117.0	54,098	Sawyer	1,320	8,243	6.2	6,227
					Shawano	1,158	33,975	29.3	31,884
Buffalo	687	15,615	22.7	16,006	Sheboygan	521	59,913	115.0	54,888
Burnett	860	10,735	12.5	9,026	Taylor	991	18,045	18.2	13,641
Calumet	324	17,228	53.2	16,701	Trempealeau	748	24,506	32.8	22,928
Chippewa	1,039	36,482	35.1	32,103					
Clark	1,218	35,120	28.8	30,074	Vernon	821	29,252	35.6	28,116
					Vilas	934	5,649	6.0	6,019
Columbia	778	30,468	39.2	31,129	Walworth	560	29,327	52.4	29,614
Crawford	579	16,772	29.0	16,288	Washburn	835	11,377	13.6	8,196
Dane	1,202	89,432	74.4	77,435	Washington	431	25,713	59.7	23,784
Dodge	897	49,742	55.5	47,436					
Door	469	19,073	40.7	18,711	Waukesha	549	42,612	77.6	37,100
					Waupaca	759	34,200	45.1	32,782
Douglas	1,337	49,771	37.2	47,422	Waushara	646	16,712	25.9	18,886
Dunn	869	26,970	31.0	25,260	Winnebago	459	63,897	139.2	62,116
Eau Claire	638	35,771	56.1	32,721	Wood	809	34,643	42.8	30,583
Florence	497	3,602	7.2	3,381					
Fond du Lac	726	56,119	77.3	51,610	WYOMING	97,548	194,402	2.0	145,965
Forest	1,017	9,850	9.7	6,782	Albany	4,399	9,283	2.1	11,574
Grant	1,169	39,044	33.4	39,007	Big Horn	3,110	12,105	3.9	8,886
Green	593	21,568	36.4	21,641	Campbell	4,761	5,233	1.1	
Green Lake	360	14,875	41.3	15,491	Carbon	8,007	9,525	1.2	11,282
Iowa	781	21,504	27.5	22,497	Converse	4,133	7,871	1.9	6,294
Iron	792	10,261	13.0	8,306					
Jackson	990	17,746	17.9	17,075	Crook	2,866	5,524	1.9	6,492
Jefferson	552	35,022	63.4	34,306	Fremont	12,261	11,820	1.0	11,822
Juneau	802	19,209	24.0	19,569	Goshen	2,186	8,064	3.7	
Kenosha	282	51,284	181.9	32,929	Hot Springs	2,025	5,164	2.6	
					Johnson	4,164	4,617	1.1	3,453
Kewaunee	337	16,091	47.7	16,784					
La Crosse	481	44,355	92.2	43,996	Laramie	2,678	20,699	7.7	26,127
Lafayette	642	20,002	31.2	20,075	Lincoln	8,945	12,487	1.4	
Langlade	875	21,471	24.5	17,062	Natrona	5,322	14,635	2.7	4,766
Lincoln	902	21,084	23.4	19,064	Niobrara	2,604	6,321	2.4	
Manitowoc	602	51,644	85.8	44,978	Park	5,207	7,298	1.4	4,909
Marathon	1,554	65,259	42.0	55,054	Platte	2,125	7,421	3.5	
Marinette	1,415	34,361	24.3	33,812	Sheridan	2,574	18,182	7.1	16,324
Marquette	457	10,443	22.9	10,741	Sweetwater	10,495	13,640	1.3	11,575
Milwaukee	235	539,449	2,295.5	433,187					
					Uinta	2,094	6,611	3.2	16,982
Monroe	937	28,666	30.6	28,881	Washakie	2,241	3,106	1.4	
Oconto	1,118	27,104	24.2	25,657	Weston	2,403	4,631	1.9	4,960
Oneida	1,183	13,996	11.8	11,433	Yellowstone National Park (part of) [1]	2,948	165	0.1	519
Outagamie	646	55,113	85.3	49,102					
Ozaukee	233	16,335	70.1	17,123					

[1] Geographically located within limits of Idaho, Montana, and Wyoming; total population returned as in Wyoming.

TABLE **10.**—POPULATION OF CITIES HAVING, IN

[Except as explained in footnotes, population shown for each census

	CITY.	POPULATION.					
		1920	1910	1900	1890	1880	1870
	New York, N. Y.[1]	5,620,048	4,766,883	3,437,202	2,507,414	1,911,698	1,478,103
	Bronx borough	732,016	430,980	200,507	88,908	51,980	37,393
1	Brooklyn borough	2,018,356	1,634,351	1,166,582	838,547	599,495	419,921
	Manhattan borough	2,284,103	2,331,542	1,850,093	1,441,216	1,164,673	942,292
	Queens borough	469,042	284,041	152,999	87,050	56,559	45,468
	Richmond borough	116,531	85,969	67,021	51,693	38,991	33,029
2	Chicago, Ill.	2,701,705	2,185,283	1,698,575	1,099,850	503,185	298,977
3	Philadelphia, Pa.	1,823,779	1,549,008	1,293,697	1,046,964	847,170	674,022
4	Detroit, Mich.	993,678	465,766	285,704	205,876	116,340	79,577
5	Cleveland, Ohio	796,841	560,663	381,768	261,353	160,146	92,829
6	St. Louis, Mo.	772,897	687,029	575,238	451,770	350,518	310,864
7	Boston, Mass.[2]	748,060	670,585	560,892	448,477	362,839	250,526
8	Baltimore, Md.	733,826	558,485	508,957	434,439	332,313	267,354
9	Pittsburgh, Pa.[3]	588,343	533,905	451,512	343,904	235,071	139,256
10	Los Angeles, Calif.	576,673	319,198	102,479	50,395	11,183	5,728
11	Buffalo, N. Y.	506,775	423,715	352,387	255,664	155,134	117,714
12	San Francisco, Calif.[4]	506,676	416,912	342,782	298,997	233,959	149,473
13	Milwaukee, Wis.	457,147	373,857	285,315	204,468	115,587	71,440
14	Washington, D. C.[5]	437,571	331,069	278,718	230,392	177,624	109,199
15	Newark, N. J.	414,524	347,469	246,070	181,830	136,508	105,059
16	Cincinnati, Ohio	401,247	363,591	325,902	296,908	255,139	216,239
17	New Orleans, La.	387,219	339,075	287,104	242,039	216,090	191,418
18	Minneapolis, Minn.	380,582	301,408	202,718	164,738	46,887	13,066
19	Kansas City, Mo.	324,410	248,381	163,752	132,716	55,785	32,260
20	Seattle, Wash.	315,312	237,194	80,671	42,837	3,533	1,107
21	Indianapolis, Ind.	314,194	233,650	169,164	105,436	75,056	48,244
22	Jersey City, N. J.	298,103	267,779	206,433	163,003	120,722	82,546
23	Rochester, N. Y.	295,750	218,149	162,608	133,896	89,366	62,386
24	Portland, Oreg.	258,288	207,214	90,426	46,385	17,577	8,293
25	Denver, Colo.	256,491	213,381	133,859	106,713	35,629	4,759
26	Toledo, Ohio	243,164	168,497	131,822	81,434	50,137	31,584
27	Providence, R. I.	237,595	224,326	175,597	132,146	104,857	68,904
28	Columbus, Ohio	237,031	181,511	125,560	88,150	51,647	31,274
29	Louisville, Ky.	234,891	223,928	204,731	161,129	123,758	100,753
30	St. Paul, Minn.	234,698	214,744	163,065	133,156	41,473	20,030
31	Oakland, Calif.	216,261	150,174	66,960	48,682	34,555	10,500
32	Akron, Ohio	208,435	69,067	42,728	27,601	16,512	10,006
33	Atlanta, Ga.	200,616	154,839	89,872	65,533	37,409	21,789
34	Omaha, Nebr.[6]	191,601	124,096	102,555	140,452	30,518	16,083
35	Worcester, Mass.	179,754	145,986	118,421	84,655	58,291	41,105
36	Birmingham, Ala.	178,806	132,685	38,415	26,178	3,086	----------
37	Syracuse, N. Y.	171,717	137,249	108,374	88,143	51,792	43,051
38	Richmond, Va.	171,667	127,628	85,050	81,388	63,600	51,038
39	New Haven, Conn.	162,537	133,605	108,027	81,298	[7]62,882	[7]50,840
40	Memphis, Tenn.	162,351	131,105	102,320	64,495	33,592	40,226
41	San Antonio, Tex.	161,379	96,614	53,321	37,673	20,550	12,256
42	Dallas, Tex.	158,976	92,104	42,638	38,067	10,358	----------
43	Dayton, Ohio	152,559	116,577	85,333	61,220	38,678	30,473
44	Bridgeport, Conn.	143,555	102,054	70,996	48,866	27,643	18,969
45	Houston, Tex.	138,276	78,800	44,633	27,557	16,513	9,382
46	Hartford, Conn.	138,036	98,915	79,850	53,230	42,015	37,180
47	Scranton, Pa.	137,783	129,867	102,026	75,215	45,850	35,092
48	Grand Rapids, Mich.	137,634	112,571	87,565	60,278	32,016	16,507
49	Paterson, N. J.	135,875	125,600	105,171	78,347	51,031	33,579
50	Youngstown, Ohio	132,358	79,066	44,885	33,220	15,435	8,075
51	Springfield, Mass.	129,614	88,926	62,059	44,179	33,340	26,703
52	Des Moines, Iowa	126,468	86,368	62,139	50,093	22,408	12,035
53	New Bedford, Mass.	121,217	96,652	62,442	40,733	26,845	21,320
54	Fall River, Mass.	120,485	119,295	104,863	74,398	48,961	26,766
55	Trenton, N. J.	119,289	96,815	73,307	57,458	29,910	22,874
56	Nashville, Tenn.	118,342	110,364	80,865	76,168	43,350	25,865
57	Salt Lake City, Utah	118,110	92,777	53,531	44,843	20,768	12,854
58	Camden, N. J.	116,309	94,538	75,935	58,313	41,659	20,045
59	Norfolk, Va.	115,777	67,452	46,624	34,871	21,966	19,229
60	Albany, N. Y.	113,344	100,253	94,151	94,923	90,758	69,422
61	Lowell, Mass.	112,759	106,294	94,969	77,696	59,475	40,928
62	Wilmington, Del.	110,168	87,411	76,508	61,431	42,478	30,841
63	Cambridge, Mass.	109,694	104,839	91,886	70,028	52,669	39,634
64	Reading, Pa.	107,784	96,071	78,961	58,661	43,278	33,930
65	Fort Worth, Tex.	106,482	73,312	26,688	23,076	6,663	----------
66	Spokane, Wash.	104,437	104,402	36,848	19,922	----------	----------
67	Kansas City, Kans.	101,177	82,331	51,418	38,316	3,200	----------
68	Yonkers, N. Y.	100,176	79,803	47,931	32,033	18,892	----------

[1] Population shown is for New York and its boroughs as now constituted.

[2] Hyde Park town annexed to Boston city since 1910. Combined population: 1910, 686,092; 1900, 574,136; 1890, 458,670; 1880, 369,927; 1870, 254,662. Hyde Park not returned separately at earlier censuses.

[3] Includes population of Allegheny, as follows: 1900, 129,896; 1890, 105,287; 1880, 78,682; 1870, 53,180; 1860, 28,702; 1850, 21,262; 1840, 10,089; and 1830, 2,801. Allegheny not returned separately at earlier censuses.

[4] Population as reported by state census of 1852; returns for 1850 for San Francisco were destroyed by fire.

1920, 100,000 INHABITANTS OR MORE: 1790–1920.
year does not include that of territory subsequently annexed.]

POPULATION.

1860	1850	1840	1830	1820	1810	1800	1790	No.
1,174,779	696,115	391,114	242,278	152,056	119,734	79,216	49,401	1
23,593	8,032	5,346	3,023	2,782	2,267	1,755	1,781	
279,122	138,882	47,613	20,535	11,187	8,303	5,740	4,495	
813,669	515,547	312,710	202,589	123,706	96,373	60,515	33,131	
32,903	18,593	14,480	9,049	8,246	7,444	6,642	6,159	
25,492	15,061	10,965	7,082	6,135	5,347	4,564	3,835	
109,260	29,963	4,470						2
565,529	121,376	93,665	80,462	63,802	53,722	41,220	28,522	3
45,619	21,019	9,102	2,222	1,422				4
43,417	17,034	6,071	1,076	606				5
160,773	77,860	16,469						6
177,840	136,881	93,383	61,392	43,298	33,787	24,937	18,320	7
212,418	169,054	102,313	80,620	62,738	46,555	26,514	13,503	8
77,923	67,863	31,204	15,369	7,248	4,768	1,565		9
4,385	1,610							10
81,129	42,261	18,213	8,668	2,095				11
56,802	[4] 34,776							12
45,246	20,061	1,712						13
61,122	40,001	23,364	18,826	13,247	8,208			14
71,941	38,894	17,290						15
161,044	115,435	46,338	24,831	9,642	2,540			16
168,675	116,375	102,193	46,082	27,176	17,242			17
2,564								18
4,418								19
								20
18,611	8,091	2,692						21
29,226	6,856	3,072						22
48,204	36,403	20,191	9,207					23
2,874								24
								25
13,766	3,829	1,222						26
50,666	41,513	23,171	16,833	11,767	10,071	7,614	6,380	27
18,554	17,882	6,048	2,435					28
68,033	43,194	21,210	10,341	4,012	1,357	359	200	29
10,401	1,112							30
1,543								31
3,477	3,266							32
9,554	2,572							33
1,883								34
24,960	17,049	7,497	4,173	2,962	2,577	2,411	2,095	35
								36
28,119	22,271							37
37,910	27,570	20,153	16,060	12,067	9,735	5,737	3,761	38
[7] 39,267	[7] 20,345	12,960	10,180	7,147	5,772	4,049		39
22,623	8,841							40
8,235	3,488							41
								42
20,081	10,977	6,067	2,950	1,000	383			43
[7] 13,299	[7] 7,560	3,294						44
4,845	2,396							45
[7] 29,152	[7] 17,966	9,468	7,074	4,726	3,955			46
9,223								47
8,085	2,686							48
19,586								49
2,759	2,802							50
15,199	11,766	10,985	6,784	3,914	2,767	2,312	1,574	51
3,965								52
22,300	16,443	12,087	7,592	3,947	5,651	4,361	3,313	53
14,026	11,524	6,738	4,158	1,594	1,296			54
17,228	6,461	4,035	3,925	3,942	3,002			55
16,988	10,165	6,929	5,566					56
8,236								57
14,358	9,479	3,371						58
14,620	14,326	10,920	9,814	8,478	9,193	6,926	2,959	59
62,367	50,763	33,721	24,209	12,630	10,762	5,349	3,498	60
36,827	33,383	20,796	6,474					61
21,258	13,979	8,367						62
26,060	15,215	8,409	6,072	3,295	2,323	2,453	2,115	63
23,162	15,743	8,410	5,856	4,332	(8)	2,386		64
								65
								66
								67
								68

[5] Population as returned from 1880 to 1920 is for District of Columbia, with which city has been coextensive since 1895.

[6] Omaha and South Omaha cities consolidated since 1910. Combined population: 1910, 150,355; 1900, 128,556; 1890, 148,514. South Omaha not returned separately at earlier censuses.

[7] Population of town, including city; town and city not returned separately.

[8] Not returned separately.

TABLE 11.—POPULATION OF CITIES HAVING, IN 1920, 25,000 INHABITANTS OR MORE, WITH DECENNIAL INCREASE: 1900–1920.

[Except as explained in footnotes, population shown for each census year does not include that of territory subsequently annexed.]

[A minus sign (−) denotes decrease.]

| CITY. | POPULATION. | | | INCREASE. | | | |
| | | | | 1910–1920 | | 1900–1910 | |
	1920	1910	1900	Number.	Per cent.	Number.	Per cent.
ALABAMA.							
Birmingham	178,806	132,685	38,415	46,121	34.8	94,270	245.4
Mobile	60,777	51,521	38,469	9,256	18.0	13,052	33.9
Montgomery	43,464	38,136	30,346	5,328	14.0	7,790	25.7
ARIZONA.							
Phoenix	29,053	11,134	5,544	17,919	160.9	5,590	100.8
ARKANSAS.							
Fort Smith	28,870	23,975	11,587	4,895	20.4	12,388	106.9
Little Rock	65,142	45,941	38,307	19,201	41.8	7,634	19.9
CALIFORNIA.							
Alameda	28,806	23,383	16,464	5,423	23.2	6,919	42.0
Berkeley	56,036	40,434	13,214	15,602	38.6	27,220	206.0
Fresno	45,086	24,892	12,470	20,194	81.1	12,422	99.6
Long Beach	55,593	17,809	2,252	37,784	212.2	15,557	690.8
Los Angeles	576,673	319,198	102,479	257,475	80.7	216,719	211.5
Oakland	216,261	150,174	66,960	66,087	44.0	83,214	124.3
Pasadena	45,354	30,291	9,117	15,063	49.7	21,174	232.2
Sacramento	65,908	44,696	29,282	21,212	47.5	15,414	52.6
San Diego	74,683	39,578	17,700	35,105	88.7	21,878	123.6
San Francisco	506,676	416,912	342,782	89,764	21.5	74,130	21.6
San Jose	39,642	28,946	21,500	10,696	37.0	7,446	34.6
Stockton	40,296	23,253	17,506	17,043	73.3	5,747	32.8
COLORADO.							
Colorado Springs [1]	30,105	29,078	21,085	1,027	3.5	7,993	37.9
Denver	256,491	213,381	133,859	43,110	20.2	79,522	59.4
Pueblo	43,050	[2] 41,747	28,157	1,303	3.1	13,590	48.3
CONNECTICUT.							
Bridgeport	143,555	102,054	70,996	41,501	40.7	31,058	43.7
Hartford	138,036	98,915	79,850	39,121	39.6	19,065	23.9
Meriden	29,867	27,265	24,296	2,602	9.5	2,969	12.2
New Britain	59,316	43,916	25,998	15,400	35.1	17,918	68.9
New Haven	162,537	133,605	108,027	28,932	21.7	25,578	23.7
New London	25,688	19,659	17,548	6,029	30.7	2,111	12.0
Norwalk [3]	27,743	6,954	6,125	20,789	299.0	829	13.5
Stamford	35,096	25,138	15,997	9,958	39.6	9,141	57.1
Waterbury	91,715	73,141	45,859	18,574	25.4	27,282	59.5
DELAWARE.							
Wilmington	110,168	87,411	76,508	22,757	26.0	10,903	14.3
DISTRICT OF COLUMBIA.							
Washington	437,571	331,069	278,718	106,502	32.2	52,351	18.8
FLORIDA.							
Jacksonville	91,558	57,699	28,429	33,859	58.7	29,270	100.0
Miami	29,571	5,471	1,681	24,100	440.5	3,790	225.5
Pensacola	31,035	22,982	17,747	8,053	35.0	5,235	29.5
Tampa	51,608	37,782	15,839	13,826	36.6	21,943	138.5

[1] Colorado City and Colorado Springs city consolidated since 1910. Combined population: 1910, 33,411; 1900, 23,999.

[2] The population in 1910 shown for Pueblo in the Thirteenth Census reports includes the population of certain territory outside the city limits. The population of this area was 2,531 in 1920 and 2,648 in 1910. The combined population of the city of Pueblo and of this outside area was 45,581 in 1920 and 44,395 in 1910. The area in question was not returned separately in 1900.

[3] Norwalk and South Norwalk cities consolidated and made coextensive with Norwalk town since 1910. Population of town: 1910, 24,211; 1900, 19,932.

TABLE 11.—POPULATION OF CITIES HAVING, IN 1920, 25,000 INHABITANTS OR MORE, WITH DECENNIAL INCREASE: 1900-1920—Continued.

[Except as explained in footnotes, population shown for each census year does not include that of territory subsequently annexed.]

[A minus sign (−) denotes decrease.]

| CITY. | POPULATION. | | | INCREASE. | | | |
| | | | | 1910–1920 | | 1900–1910 | |
	1920	1910	1900	Number.	Per cent.	Number.	Per cent.
GEORGIA.							
Atlanta	200,616	154,839	89,872	45,777	29.6	64,967	72.3
Augusta	52,548	41,040	39,441	11,508	28.0	1,599	4.1
Columbus	31,125	20,554	17,614	10,571	51.4	2,940	16.7
Macon	52,995	40,665	23,272	12,330	30.3	17,393	74.7
Savannah	83,252	65,064	54,244	18,188	28.0	10,820	19.9
ILLINOIS.							
Aurora	36,397	29,807	24,147	6,590	22.1	5,660	23.4
Bloomington	28,725	25,768	23,286	2,957	11.5	2,482	10.7
Chicago	2,701,705	2,185,283	1,698,575	516,422	23.6	486,708	28.7
Cicero town	44,995	14,557	16,310	30,438	209.1	−1,753	−10.7
Danville	33,776	27,871	16,354	5,905	21.2	11,517	70.4
Decatur	43,818	31,140	20,754	12,678	40.7	10,386	50.0
East St. Louis	66,767	58,547	29,655	8,220	14.0	28,892	97.4
Elgin	27,454	25,976	22,433	1,478	5.7	3,543	15.8
Evanston	37,234	24,978	19,259	12,256	49.1	5,719	29.7
Joliet	38,442	34,670	29,353	3,772	10.9	5,317	18.1
Moline	30,734	24,199	17,248	6,535	27.0	6,951	40.3
Oak Park village	39,858	19,444		20,414	105.0		
Peoria	76,121	66,950	56,100	9,171	13.7	10,850	19.3
Quincy	35,978	36,587	36,252	−609	−1.7	335	0.9
Rock Island	35,177	24,335	19,493	10,842	44.6	4,842	24.8
Rockford	65,651	45,401	31,051	20,250	44.6	14,350	46.2
Springfield	59,183	51,678	34,159	7,505	14.5	17,519	51.3
INDIANA.							
Anderson	29,767	22,476	20,178	7,291	32.4	2,298	11.4
East Chicago	35,967	19,098	3,411	16,869	88.3	15,687	459.9
Evansville	85,264	69,647	59,007	15,617	22.4	10,640	18.0
Fort Wayne	86,549	63,933	45,115	22,616	35.4	18,818	41.7
Gary	55,378	16,802		38,576	229.6		
Hammond	36,004	20,925	12,376	15,079	72.1	8,549	69.1
Indianapolis	314,194	233,650	169,164	80,544	34.5	64,486	38.1
Kokomo	30,067	17,010	10,609	13,057	76.8	6,401	60.3
Muncie	36,524	24,005	20,942	12,519	52.2	3,063	14.6
Richmond	26,765	22,324	18,226	4,441	19.9	4,098	22.5
South Bend	70,983	53,684	35,999	17,299	32.2	17,685	49.1
Terre Haute	66,083	58,157	36,673	7,926	13.6	21,484	58.6
IOWA.							
Cedar Rapids	45,566	32,811	25,656	12,755	38.9	7,155	27.9
Council Bluffs	36,162	29,292	25,802	6,870	23.5	3,490	13.5
Davenport	56,727	43,028	35,254	13,699	31.8	7,774	22.1
Des Moines	126,468	86,368	62,139	40,100	46.4	24,229	39.0
Dubuque	39,141	38,494	36,297	647	1.7	2,197	6.1
Sioux City	71,227	47,828	33,111	23,399	48.9	14,717	44.4
Waterloo	36,230	26,693	12,580	9,537	35.7	14,113	112.2
KANSAS.							
Kansas City	101,177	82,331	51,418	18,846	22.9	30,913	60.1
Topeka	50,022	43,684	33,608	6,338	14.5	10,076	30.0
Wichita	72,217	52,450	24,671	19,767	37.7	27,779	112.6
KENTUCKY.							
Covington	57,121	53,270	42,938	3,851	7.2	10,332	24.1
Lexington	41,534	35,099	26,369	6,435	18.3	8,730	33.1
Louisville	234,891	223,928	204,731	10,963	4.9	19,197	9.4
Newport	29,317	30,309	28,301	−992	−3.3	2,008	7.1
LOUISIANA.							
New Orleans	387,219	339,075	287,104	48,144	14.2	51,971	18.1
Shreveport	43,874	28,015	16,013	15,859	56.6	12,002	75.0

TABLE 11.—POPULATION OF CITIES HAVING, IN 1920, 25,000 INHABITANTS OR MORE, WITH DECENNIAL INCREASE: 1900–1920—Continued.

[Except as explained in footnotes, population shown for each census year does not include that of territory subsequently annexed.]

[A minus sign (−) denotes decrease.]

CITY.	POPULATION.			INCREASE.			
				1910–1920		1900–1910	
	1920	1910	1900	Number.	Per cent.	Number.	Per cent.
MAINE.							
Bangor	25,978	24,803	21,850	1,175	4.7	2,953	13.5
Lewiston	31,791	26,247	23,761	5,544	21.1	2,486	10.5
Portland	69,272	58,571	50,145	10,701	18.3	8,426	16.8
MARYLAND.							
Baltimore	733,826	558,485	508,957	175,341	31.4	49,528	9.7
Cumberland	29,837	21,839	17,128	7,998	36.6	4,711	27.5
Hagerstown	28,064	16,507	13,591	11,557	70.0	2,916	21.5
MASSACHUSETTS.							
Boston [1]	748,060	670,585	560,892	77,475	11.6	109,693	19.6
Brockton	66,254	56,878	40,063	9,376	16.5	16,815	42.0
Brookline town [2]	37,748	27,792	19,935	9,956	35.8	7,857	39.4
Cambridge	109,694	104,839	91,886	4,855	4.6	12,953	14.1
Chelsea	43,184	32,452	34,072	10,732	33.1	−1,620	−4.8
Chicopee	36,214	25,401	19,167	10,813	42.6	6,234	32.5
Everett	40,120	33,484	24,336	6,636	19.8	9,148	37.6
Fall River	120,485	119,295	104,863	1,190	1.0	14,432	13.8
Fitchburg	41,029	37,826	31,531	3,203	8.5	6,295	20.0
Haverhill	53,884	44,115	37,175	9,769	22.1	6,940	18.7
Holyoke	60,203	57,730	45,712	2,473	4.3	12,018	26.3
Lawrence	94,270	85,892	62,559	8,378	9.8	23,333	37.3
Lowell	112,759	106,294	94,969	6,465	6.1	11,325	11.9
Lynn	99,148	89,336	68,513	9,812	11.0	20,823	30.4
Malden	49,103	44,404	33,664	4,699	10.6	10,740	31.9
Medford	39,038	23,150	18,244	15,888	68.6	4,906	26.9
New Bedford	121,217	96,652	62,442	24,565	25.4	34,210	54.8
Newton	46,054	39,806	33,587	6,248	15.7	6,219	18.5
Pittsfield	41,763	32,121	21,766	9,642	30.0	10,355	47.6
Quincy	47,876	32,642	23,899	15,234	46.7	8,743	36.6
Revere	28,823	18,219	10,395	10,604	58.2	7,824	75.3
Salem	42,529	43,697	35,956	−1,168	−2.7	7,741	21.5
Somerville	93,091	77,236	61,643	15,855	20.5	15,593	25.3
Springfield	129,614	88,926	62,059	40,688	45.8	26,867	43.3
Taunton	37,137	34,259	31,036	2,878	8.4	3,223	10.4
Waltham	30,915	27,834	23,481	3,081	11.1	4,353	18.5
Worcester	179,754	145,986	118,421	33,768	23.1	27,565	23.3
MICHIGAN.							
Battle Creek	36,164	25,267	18,563	10,897	43.1	6,704	36.1
Bay City	47,554	45,166	27,628	2,388	5.3	17,538	63.5
Detroit	993,678	465,766	285,704	527,912	113.3	180,062	63.0
Flint	91,599	38,550	13,103	53,049	137.6	25,447	194.2
Grand Rapids	137,634	112,571	87,565	25,063	22.3	25,006	28.6
Hamtramck village	48,615	3,559		45,056	1,266.0		
Highland Park	46,499	4,120	427	42,379	1,028.6	3,693	864.9
Jackson	48,374	31,433	25,180	16,941	53.9	6,253	24.8
Kalamazoo	48,487	39,437	24,404	9,050	22.9	15,033	61.6
Lansing	57,327	31,229	16,485	26,098	83.6	14,744	89.4
Muskegon	36,570	24,062	20,818	12,508	52.0	3,244	15.6
Pontiac	34,273	14,532	9,769	19,741	135.8	4,763	48.8
Port Huron	25,044	18,863	19,158	7,081	37.5	−295	−1.5
Saginaw	61,903	50,510	42,345	11,000	22.6	8,165	19.3
MINNESOTA.							
Duluth	98,917	78,466	52,969	20,451	26.1	25,497	48.1
Minneapolis	380,582	301,408	202,718	79,174	26.3	98,690	48.7
St. Paul	234,698	214,744	163,065	19,954	9.3	51,679	31.7
MISSOURI.							
Joplin	29,902	32,073	26,023	−2,171	−6.8	6,050	23.2
Kansas City	324,410	248,381	163,752	76,029	30.6	84,629	51.7
St. Joseph	77,939	77,403	102,979	536	0.7	−25,576	−24.8
St. Louis	772,897	687,029	575,238	85,868	12.5	111,791	19.4
Springfield	39,631	35,201	23,267	4,430	12.6	11,934	51.3

[1] Hyde Park town annexed to Boston city since 1910. Combined population: 1910, 686,092; 1900, 574,136.
[2] Unincorporated.

TABLE 11.—POPULATION OF CITIES HAVING, IN 1920, 25,000 INHABITANTS OR MORE, WITH DECENNIAL INCREASE: 1900-1920—Continued.

[Except as explained in footnotes, population shown for each census year does not include that of territory subsequently annexed.]

[A minus sign (−) denotes decrease.]

CITY.	POPULATION.			INCREASE.			
				1910–1920		1900–1910	
	1920	1910	1900	Number.	Per cent.	Number.	Per cent.
MONTANA.							
Butte	41,611	39,165	30,470	2,446	6.2	8,695	28.5
NEBRASKA.							
Lincoln	54,948	43,973	40,169	10,975	25.0	3,804	9.5
Omaha [1]	191,601	124,096	102,555	67,505	54.4	21,541	21.0
NEW HAMPSHIRE.							
Manchester	78,384	70,063	56,987	8,321	11.9	13,076	22.9
Nashua	28,379	26,005	23,898	2,374	9.1	2,107	8.8
NEW JERSEY.							
Atlantic City	50,707	46,150	27,838	4,557	9.9	18,312	65.8
Bayonne	76,754	55,545	32,722	21,209	38.2	22,823	69.7
Camden	116,309	94,538	75,935	21,771	23.0	18,603	24.5
Clifton	26,470						
East Orange	50,710	34,371	21,506	16,339	47.5	12,865	59.8
Elizabeth	95,783	73,409	52,130	22,374	30.5	21,279	40.8
Hoboken	68,166	70,324	59,364	−2,158	−3.1	10,960	18.5
Irvington town	25,480	11,877	5,255	13,603	114.5	6,622	126.0
Jersey City	298,103	267,779	206,433	30,324	11.3	61,346	29.7
Kearny town	26,724	18,659	10,896	8,065	43.2	7,763	71.2
Montclair town	28,810	21,550	13,962	7,260	33.7	7,588	54.3
New Brunswick	32,779	23,388	20,006	9,391	40.2	3,382	16.9
Newark	414,524	347,469	246,070	67,055	19.3	101,399	41.2
Orange	33,268	29,630	24,141	3,638	12.3	5,489	22.7
Passaic	63,841	54,773	27,777	9,068	16.6	26,996	97.2
Paterson	135,875	125,600	105,171	10,275	8.2	20,429	19.4
Perth Amboy	41,707	32,121	17,699	9,586	29.8	14,422	81.5
Plainfield	27,700	20,550	15,369	7,150	34.8	5,181	33.7
Trenton	119,289	96,815	73,307	22,474	23.2	23,508	32.1
West Hoboken town	40,074	35,403	23,094	4,671	13.2	12,309	53.3
West New York town	29,926	13,560	5,267	16,366	120.7	8,293	157.5
NEW YORK.							
Albany	113,344	100,253	94,151	13,091	13.1	6,102	6.5
Amsterdam	33,524	31,267	20,929	2,257	7.2	10,338	49.4
Auburn	36,192	34,668	30,345	1,524	4.4	4,323	14.2
Binghamton	66,800	48,443	39,647	18,357	37.9	8,796	22.2
Buffalo	506,775	423,715	352,387	83,060	19.6	71,328	20.2
Elmira	45,393	37,176	35,672	8,217	22.1	1,504	4.2
Jamestown	38,917	31,297	22,892	7,620	24.3	8,405	36.7
Kingston	26,688	25,908	24,535	780	3.0	1,373	5.6
Mount Vernon	42,726	30,919	21,228	11,807	38.2	9,691	45.7
New Rochelle	36,213	28,867	14,720	7,346	25.4	14,147	96.1
New York	5,620,048	4,766,883	3,437,202	853,165	17.9	1,329,681	38.7
Bronx borough	732,016	430,980	200,507	301,036	69.8	230,473	114.9
Brooklyn borough	2,018,356	1,634,351	1,166,582	384,005	23.5	467,769	40.1
Manhattan borough	2,284,103	2,331,542	1,850,093	−47,439	−2.0	481,449	26.0
Queens borough	469,042	284,041	152,999	185,001	65.1	131,042	85.6
Richmond borough	116,531	85,969	67,021	30,562	35.6	18,948	28.3
Newburgh	30,366	27,805	24,943	2,561	9.2	2,862	11.5
Niagara Falls	50,760	30,445	19,457	20,315	66.7	10,988	56.5
Poughkeepsie	35,000	27,936	24,029	7,064	25.3	3,907	16.3
Rochester	295,750	218,149	162,608	77,601	35.6	55,541	34.2
Rome	26,341	20,497	15,343	5,844	28.5	5,154	33.6
Schenectady	88,723	72,826	31,682	15,897	21.8	41,144	129.9
Syracuse	171,717	137,249	108,374	34,468	25.1	28,875	26.6
Troy	72,013	76,813	60,651	−4,800	−6.2	16,162	26.6
Utica	94,156	74,419	56,383	19,737	26.5	18,036	32.0
Watertown	31,285	26,730	21,696	4,555	17.0	5,034	23.2
Yonkers	100,176	79,803	47,931	20,373	25.5	31,872	66.5
NORTH CAROLINA.							
Asheville	28,504	18,762	14,694	9,742	51.9	4,068	27.7
Charlotte	46,338	34,014	18,091	12,324	36.2	15,923	88.0
Wilmington	33,372	25,748	20,976	7,624	29.6	4,772	22.7
Winston-Salem [2]	48,395	[2] 22,700	[2] 13,650	25,695	113.2	9,050	66.3

[1] Omaha and South Omaha cities consolidated since 1910. Combined population: 1910, 150,355; 1900, 128,556.

[2] Winston city and Salem town consolidated as Winston-Salem since 1910. Figures shown for 1910 and 1900 represent combined population of Winston and Salem.

56   ABSTRACT OF THE CENSUS—POPULATION.

TABLE **11.**--POPULATION OF CITIES HAVING, IN 1920, 25,000 INHABITANTS OR MORE, WITH DECENNIAL INCREASE: 1900-1920—Continued.

[Except as explained in footnotes, population shown for each census year does not include that of territory subsequently annexed.]

[A minus sign (−) denotes decrease.]

| CITY. | POPULATION. | | | INCREASE. | | | |
| | | | | 1910–1920 | | 1900–1910 | |
	1920	1910	1900	Number.	Per cent.	Number.	Per cent.
OHIO.							
Akron	208,435	69,067	42,728	139,368	201.8	26,339	61.6
Canton	87,091	50,217	30,667	36,874	73.4	19,550	63.7
Cincinnati	401,247	363,591	325,902	37,656	10.4	37,689	11.6
Cleveland	796,841	560,663	381,768	236,178	42.1	178,895	46.9
Columbus	237,031	181,511	125,560	55,520	30.6	55,951	44.6
Dayton	152,559	116,577	85,333	35,982	30.9	31,244	36.6
East Cleveland	27,292	9,179	2,757	18,113	197.3	6,422	232.9
Hamilton	39,675	35,279	23,914	4,396	12.5	11,365	47.5
Lakewood	41,732	15,181	3,355	26,551	174.9	11,826	352.5
Lima	41,326	30,508	21,723	10,818	35.5	8,785	40.4
Lorain	37,295	28,883	16,028	8,412	29.1	12,855	80.2
Mansfield	27,824	20,768	17,640	7,056	34.0	3,128	17.7
Marion	27,891	18,232	11,862	9,659	53.0	6,370	53.7
Newark	26,718	25,404	18,157	1,314	5.2	7,247	39.9
Portsmouth	33,011	23,481	17,870	9,530	40.6	5,611	31.4
Springfield	60,840	46,921	38,253	13,919	29.7	8,668	22.7
Steubenville	28,508	22,391	14,349	6,117	27.3	8,042	56.0
Toledo	243,164	168,497	131,822	74,667	44.3	36,675	27.8
Warren	27,050	11,081	8,529	15,969	144.1	2,552	29.9
Youngstown	132,358	79,066	44,885	53,292	67.4	34,181	76.2
Zanesville	29,569	28,026	23,538	1,543	5.5	4,488	19.1
OKLAHOMA.							
Muskogee	30,277	25,278	4,254	4,999	19.8	21,024	494.2
Oklahoma City	91,295	64,205	10,037	27,090	42.2	54,168	539.7
Tulsa	72,075	18,182	1,390	53,893	296.4	16,792	1,208.1
OREGON.							
Portland	258,288	207,214	90,426	51,074	24.6	116,788	129.2
PENNSYLVANIA.							
Allentown	73,502	51,913	35,416	21,589	41.6	16,497	46.6
Altoona	60,331	52,127	38,973	8,204	15.7	13,154	33.8
Bethlehem [1]	50,358	12,837	7,293	37,521	292.3	5,544	76.0
Chester	58,030	38,537	33,988	19,493	50.6	4,549	13.4
Easton	33,813	28,523	25,238	5,290	18.5	3,285	13.0
Erie	93,372	66,525	52,733	26,847	40.4	13,792	26.2
Harrisburg	75,917	64,186	50,167	11,731	18.3	14,019	27.9
Hazleton	32,277	25,452	14,230	6,825	26.8	11,222	78.9
Johnstown	67,327	55,482	35,936	11,845	21.3	19,546	54.4
Lancaster	53,150	47,227	41,459	5,923	12.5	5,768	13.9
McKeesport	46,781	42,694	34,227	4,087	9.6	8,467	24.7
New Castle	44,938	36,280	28,339	8,658	23.9	7,941	28.0
Norristown borough	32,319	27,875	22,265	4,444	15.9	5,610	25.2
Philadelphia	1,823,779	1,549,008	1,293,697	274,771	17.7	255,311	19.7
Pittsburgh	588,343	533,905	[2] 451,512	54,438	10.2	82,393	18.2
Reading	107,784	96,071	78,961	11,713	12.2	17,110	21.7
Scranton	137,783	129,867	102,026	7,916	6.1	27,841	27.3
Wilkes-Barre	73,833	67,105	51,721	6,728	10.0	15,384	29.7
Williamsport	36,198	31,860	28,757	4,338	13.6	3,103	10.8
York	47,512	44,750	33,708	2,762	6.2	11,042	32.8
RHODE ISLAND.							
Cranston	29,407	21,107	13,343	8,300	39.3	7,764	58.2
Newport	30,255	27,149	22,441	3,106	11.4	4,708	21.0
Pawtucket	64,248	51,622	39,231	12,626	24.5	12,391	31.6
Providence	237,595	224,326	175,597	13,269	5.9	48,729	27.8
Woonsocket	43,496	38,125	28,204	5,371	14.1	9,921	35.2
SOUTH CAROLINA.							
Charleston	67,957	58,833	55,807	9,124	15.5	3,026	5.4
Columbia	37,524	26,319	21,108	11,205	42.6	5,211	24.7

[1] South Bethlehem borough and Bethlehem borough consolidated and incorporated as Bethlehem city since 1910. Combined population: 1910, 32,810; 1900, 23,999.
[2] Includes population of Allegheny, 129,896.

TABLE 11.—POPULATION OF CITIES HAVING, IN 1920, 25,000 INHABITANTS OR MORE, WITH DECENNIAL INCREASE: 1900–1920—Continued.

[Except as explained in footnotes, population shown for each census year does not include that of territory subsequently annexed.]

[A minus sign (−) denotes decrease.]

| CITY. | POPULATION. | | | INCREASE. | | | |
| | | | | 1910–1920 | | 1900–1910 | |
	1920	1910	1900	Number.	Per cent.	Number.	Per cent.
SOUTH DAKOTA.							
Sioux Falls	25,202	14,094	10,266	11,108	78.8	3,828	37.3
TENNESSEE.							
Chattanooga	57,895	44,604	30,154	13,291	29.8	14,450	47.9
Knoxville	77,818	36,346	32,637	41,472	114.1	3,709	11.4
Memphis	162,351	131,105	102,320	31,246	23.8	28,785	28.1
Nashville	118,342	110,364	80,865	7,978	7.2	29,499	36.5
TEXAS.							
Austin	34,876	29,860	22,258	5,016	16.8	7,602	34.2
Beaumont	40,422	20,640	9,427	19,782	95.8	11,213	118.9
Dallas	158,976	92,104	42,638	66,872	72.6	49,466	116.0
El Paso	77,560	39,279	15,906	38,281	97.5	23,373	146.9
Fort Worth	106,482	73,312	26,688	33,170	45.2	46,624	174.7
Galveston	44,255	36,981	37,789	7,274	19.7	−808	−2.1
Houston	138,276	78,800	44,633	59,476	75.5	34,167	76.6
San Antonio	161,379	96,614	53,321	64,765	67.0	43,293	81.2
Waco	38,500	26,425	20,686	12,075	45.7	5,739	27.7
Wichita Falls	40,079	8,200	2,480	31,879	388.8	5,720	230.6
UTAH.							
Ogden	32,804	25,580	16,313	7,224	28.2	9,267	56.8
Salt Lake City	118,110	92,777	53,531	25,333	27.3	39,246	73.3
VIRGINIA.							
Lynchburg	30,070	29,494	18,891	576	2.0	10,603	56.1
Newport News	35,596	20,205	19,635	15,391	76.2	570	2.9
Norfolk	115,777	67,452	46,624	48,325	71.6	20,828	44.7
Petersburg	31,012	24,127	21,810	6,885	28.5	2,317	10.6
Portsmouth	54,387	33,190	17,427	21,197	63.9	15,763	90.5
Richmond	171,667	127,628	85,050	44,039	34.5	42,578	50.1
Roanoke	50,842	34,874	21,495	15,968	45.8	13,379	62.2
WASHINGTON.							
Bellingham	25,585	24,298	[1] 11,062	1,287	5.3	13,236	119.7
Everett	27,644	24,814	7,838	2,830	11.4	16,976	216.6
Seattle	315,312	237,194	80,671	78,118	32.9	156,523	194.0
Spokane	104,437	104,402	36,848	35	([2])	67,554	183.3
Tacoma	96,965	83,743	37,714	13,222	15.8	46,029	122.0
WEST VIRGINIA.							
Charleston	39,608	22,996	11,099	16,612	72.2	11,897	107.2
Clarksburg	27,869	9,201	4,050	18,668	202.9	5,151	127.2
Huntington	50,177	31,161	11,923	19,016	61.0	19,238	161.4
Wheeling	56,208	41,641	38,878	14,567	35.0	2,763	7.1
WISCONSIN.							
Green Bay	31,017	25,236	18,684	5,781	22.9	6,552	35.1
Kenosha	40,472	21,371	11,606	19,101	89.4	9,765	84.1
La Crosse	30,421	30,417	28,895	4	([2])	1,522	5.3
Madison	38,378	25,531	19,164	12,847	50.3	6,367	33.2
Milwaukee	457,147	373,857	285,315	83,290	22.3	88,542	31.0
Oshkosh	33,162	33,062	28,284	100	0.3	4,778	16.9
Racine	58,593	38,002	29,102	20,591	54.2	8,900	30.6
Sheboygan	30,955	26,398	22,962	4,557	17.3	3,436	15.0
Superior	39,671	40,384	31,091	−713	−1.8	9,293	29.9

[1] Population of Fairhaven and New Whatcom cities combined.
[2] Less than one-tenth of 1 per cent.

TABLE **12.**—POPULATION OF CITIES AND OTHER INCORPORATED PLACES HAVING, IN 1920, 2,500 INHABITANTS OR MORE, ARRANGED IN GROUPS ACCORDING TO POPULATION: 1920 AND 1910.

GROUP 1.—CITIES AND OTHER INCORPORATED PLACES OF 25,000 OR MORE (287 places).

CITY, TOWN, VILLAGE, OR BOROUGH.	1920	1910	CITY, TOWN, VILLAGE, OR BOROUGH.	1920	1910	CITY, TOWN, VILLAGE, OR BOROUGH.	1920	1910
ALABAMA.			**ILLINOIS—con.**			**MASSACHUSETTS—con.**		
Birmingham...	178,806	132,685	Rock Island....	35,177	24,335	Somerville.....	93,091	77,236
Mobile.........	60,777	51,521	Rockford.......	65,651	45,401	Springfield.....	129,614	88,926
Montgomery...	43,464	38,136	Springfield.....	59,183	51,678	Taunton........	37,137	34,259
ARIZONA.			**INDIANA.**			Waltham.......	30,915	27,834
Phoenix........	29,053	11,134	Anderson......	29,767	22,476	Worcester.....	179,754	145,986
ARKANSAS.			East Chicago...	35,967	19,098	**MICHIGAN.**		
Fort Smith.....	28,870	23,975	Evansville.....	85,264	69,647	Battle Creek....	36,164	25,267
Little Rock....	65,142	45,941	Fort Wayne....	86,549	63,933	Bay City.......	47,554	45,166
CALIFORNIA.			Gary..........	55,378	16,802	Detroit.........	993,678	465,766
Alameda.......	28,806	23,383	Hammond......	36,004	20,925	Flint..........	91,599	38,550
Berkeley.......	56,036	40,434	Indianapolis...	314,194	233,650	Grand Rapids..	137,634	112,571
Fresno........	45,086	24,892	Kokomo........	30,067	17,010	Hamtramck....	48,615	3,559
Long Beach....	55,593	17,809	Muncie........	36,524	24,005	Highland Park..	46,499	4,120
Los Angeles....	576,673	319,198	Richmond......	26,765	22,324	Jackson........	48,374	31,433
Oakland.......	216,261	150,174	South Bend....	70,983	53,684	Kalamazoo....	48,487	39,437
Pasadena.......	45,354	30,291	Terre Haute....	66,083	58,157	Lansing........	57,327	31,229
Sacramento....	65,908	44,696	**IOWA.**			Muskegon......	36,570	24,062
San Diego......	74,683	39,578	Cedar Rapids...	45,566	32,811	Pontiac........	34,273	14,532
San Francisco..	506,676	416,912	Council Bluffs..	36,162	29,292	Port Huron....	25,944	18,863
San Jose.......	39,642	28,946	Davenport.....	56,727	43,028	Saginaw.......	61,903	50,510
Stockton.......	40,296	23,253	Des Moines....	126,468	86,368	**MINNESOTA.**		
COLORADO.			Dubuque.......	39,141	38,494	Duluth........	98,917	78,466
Colorado Spgs..	30,105	29,078	Sioux City.....	71,227	47,828	Minneapolis...	380,582	301,408
Denver.........	256,491	213,381	Waterloo......	36,230	26,693	St. Paul.......	234,698	214,744
Pueblo.........	43,050	¹41,747	**KANSAS.**			**MISSOURI.**		
CONNECTICUT.			Kansas City....	101,177	82,331	Joplin.........	29,902	32,073
Bridgeport.....	143,555	102,054	Topeka........	50,022	43,684	Kansas City....	324,410	248,381
Hartford.......	138,036	98,915	Wichita........	72,217	52,450	St. Joseph.....	77,939	77,403
Meriden........	29,867	27,265	**KENTUCKY.**			St. Louis.......	772,897	687,029
New Britain....	59,316	43,916	Covington......	57,121	53,270	Springfield.....	39,631	35,201
New Haven....	162,537	133,605	Lexington.....	41,534	35,099	**MONTANA.**		
New London....	25,688	19,659	Louisville.....	234,891	223,928	Butte..........	41,611	39,165
Norwalk.......	27,743	6,954	Newport.......	29,317	30,309	**NEBRASKA.**		
Stamford......	35,096	25,138	**LOUISIANA.**			Lincoln........	54,948	43,973
Waterbury.....	91,715	73,141	New Orleans...	387,219	339,075	Omaha........	191,601	124,096
DELAWARE.			Shreveport.....	43,874	28,015	**NEW HAMPSHIRE.**		
Wilmington....	110,168	87,411	**MAINE.**			Manchester.....	78,384	70,063
DISTRICT OF COLUMBIA.			Bangor........	25,978	24,803	Nashua........	28,379	26,005
Washington....	437,571	331,069	Lewiston.......	31,791	26,247	**NEW JERSEY.**		
FLORIDA.			Portland.......	69,272	58,571	Atlantic City...	50,707	46,150
Jacksonville...	91,558	57,699	**MARYLAND.**			Bayonne.......	76,754	55,545
Miami.........	29,571	5,471	Baltimore......	733,826	558,485	Camden.......	116,309	94,538
Pensacola......	31,035	22,982	Cumberland....	29,837	21,839	Clifton........	26,470	
Tampa.........	51,608	37,782	Hagerstown....	28,064	16,507	East Orange....	50,710	34,371
GEORGIA.			**MASSACHUSETTS.**			Elizabeth......	95,783	73,409
Atlanta........	200,616	154,839	Boston........	748,060	670,585	Hoboken.......	68,166	70,324
Augusta........	52,548	41,040	Brockton......	66,254	56,878	Irvington......	25,480	11,877
Columbus......	31,125	20,554	Brookline town	37,748	27,792	Jersey City.....	298,103	267,779
Macon.........	52,995	40,665	Cambridge.....	109,694	104,839	Kearny........	26,724	18,659
Savannah......	83,252	65,064	Chelsea........	43,184	32,452	Montclair......	28,810	21,550
ILLINOIS.			Chicopee......	36,214	25,401	New Brunswick	32,779	23,388
Aurora.........	36,397	29,807	Everett........	40,120	33,484	Newark........	414,524	347,469
Bloomington...	28,725	25,768	Fall River.....	120,485	119,295	Orange........	33,268	29,630
Chicago........	2,701,705	2,185,283	Fitchburg......	41,029	37,826	Passaic........	63,841	54,773
Cicero.........	44,995	14,557	Haverhill......	53,884	44,115	Paterson......	135,875	125,600
Danville.......	33,776	27,871	Holyoke.......	60,203	57,730	Perth Amboy..	41,707	32,121
Decatur........	43,818	31,140	Lawrence......	94,270	85,892	Plainfield......	27,700	20,550
East St. Louis..	66,767	58,547	Lowell........	112,759	106,294	Trenton.......	119,289	96,815
Elgin..........	27,454	25,976	Lynn..........	99,148	89,336	West Hoboken.	40,074	35,403
Evanston.......	37,234	24,978	Malden........	49,103	44,404	West New York	29,926	13,560
Joliet.........	38,442	34,670	Medford.......	39,038	23,150	**NEW YORK.**		
Moline........	30,734	24,199	New Bedford...	121,217	96,652	Albany........	113,344	100,253
Oak Park......	39,858	19,444	Newton........	46,054	39,806	Amsterdam....	33,524	31,267
Peoria........	76,121	66,950	Pittsfield......	41,763	32,121	Auburn........	36,192	34,668
Quincy........	35,978	36,587	Quincy........	47,876	32,642	Binghamton....	66,800	48,443
			Revere........	28,823	18,219	Buffalo........	506,775	423,715
			Salem.........	42,529	43,697			

¹ Corrected figures.

TABLE 12.—POPULATION OF CITIES AND OTHER INCORPORATED PLACES HAVING, IN 1920, 2,500 INHABITANTS OR MORE, ARRANGED IN GROUPS ACCORDING TO POPULATION: 1920 AND 1910—Continued.

GROUP 1.—CITIES AND OTHER INCORPORATED PLACES OF 25,000 OR MORE (287 places)—Continued.

CITY, TOWN, VILLAGE, OR BOROUGH.	1920	1910	CITY, TOWN, VILLAGE, OR BOROUGH.	1920	1910	CITY, TOWN, VILLAGE, OR BOROUGH.	1920	1910
NEW YORK— con.			**OHIO—con.**			**TENNESSEE— con.**		
Elmira	45,393	37,176	Youngstown	132,358	79,066	Memphis	162,351	131,105
Jamestown	38,917	31,297	Zanesville	29,569	28,026	Nashville	118,342	110,364
Kingston	26,688	25,908	**OKLAHOMA.**			**TEXAS.**		
Mount Vernon	42,726	30,919	Muskogee	30,277	25,278	Austin	34,876	29,860
New Rochelle	36,213	28,867	Oklahoma City	91,295	64,205	Beaumont	40,422	20,640
New York	5,620,048	4,766,883	Tulsa	72,075	18,182	Dallas	158,976	92,104
Bronx	732,016	430,980	**OREGON.**			El Paso	77,560	39,279
Brooklyn	2,018,356	1,634,351	Portland	258,288	207,214	Fort Worth	106,482	73,312
Manhattan	2,284,103	2,331,542	**PENNSYLVANIA.**			Galveston	44,255	36,981
Queens	469,042	284,041	Allentown	73,502	51,913	Houston	138,276	78,800
Richmond	116,531	85,969	Altoona	60,331	52,127	San Antonio	161,379	96,614
Newburgh	30,366	27,805	Bethlehem	50,358	12,837	Waco	38,500	26,425
Niagara Falls	50,760	30,445	Chester	58,030	38,537	Wichita Falls	40,079	8,200
Poughkeepsie	35,000	27,936	Easton	33,813	28,523	**UTAH.**		
Rochester	295,750	218,149	Erie	93,372	66,525	Ogden	32,804	25,580
Rome	26,341	20,497	Harrisburg	75,917	64,186	Salt Lake City	118,110	92,777
Schenectady	88,723	72,826	Hazleton	32,277	25,452	**VIRGINIA.**		
Syracuse	171,717	137,249	Johnstown	67,327	55,482	Lynchburg	30,070	29,494
Troy	72,013	76,813	Lancaster	53,150	47,227	Newport News	35,596	20,205
Utica	94,156	74,419	McKeesport	46,781	42,694	Norfolk	115,777	67,452
Watertown	31,285	26,730	New Castle	44,938	36,280	Petersburg	31,012	24,127
Yonkers	100,176	79,803	Norristown	32,319	27,875	Portsmouth	54,387	33,190
NORTH CAROLINA.			Philadelphia	1,823,779	1,549,008	Richmond	171,667	127,628
Asheville	28,504	18,762	Pittsburgh	588,343	533,905	Roanoke	50,842	34,874
Charlotte	46,338	34,014	Reading	107,784	96,071	**WASHINGTON.**		
Wilmington	33,372	25,748	Scranton	137,783	129,867	Bellingham	25,585	24,298
Winston-Salem	48,395	22,700	Wilkes-Barre	73,833	67,105	Everett	27,644	24,814
OHIO.			Williamsport	36,198	31,860	Seattle	315,312	237,194
Akron	208,435	69,067	York	47,512	44,750	Spokane	104,437	104,402
Canton	87,091	50,217	**RHODE ISLAND.**			Tacoma	96,965	83,743
Cincinnati	401,247	363,591	Cranston	29,407	21,107	**WEST VIRGINIA.**		
Cleveland	796,841	560,663	Newport	30,255	27,149	Charleston	39,608	22,996
Columbus	237,031	181,511	Pawtucket	64,248	51,622	Clarksburg	27,869	9,201
Dayton	152,559	116,577	Providence	237,595	224,326	Huntington	50,177	31,161
East Cleveland	27,292	9,179	Woonsocket	43,496	38,125	Wheeling	56,208	41,641
Hamilton	39,675	35,279	**SOUTH CAROLINA.**			**WISCONSIN.**		
Lakewood	41,732	15,181	Charleston	67,957	58,833	Green Bay	31,017	25,236
Lima	41,326	30,508	Columbia	37,524	26,319	Kenosha	40,472	21,371
Lorain	37,295	28,883	**SOUTH DAKOTA.**			La Crosse	30,421	30,417
Mansfield	27,824	20,768	Sioux Falls	25,202	14,094	Madison	38,378	25,531
Marion	27,891	18,232	**TENNESSEE.**			Milwaukee	457,147	373,857
Newark	26,718	25,404	Chattanooga	57,895	44,604	Oshkosh	33,162	33,062
Portsmouth	33,011	23,481	Knoxville	77,818	36,346	Racine	58,593	38,002
Springfield	60,840	46,921				Sheboygan	30,955	26,398
Steubenville	28,508	22,391				Superior	39,671	40,384
Toledo	243,164	168,497						
Warren	27,050	11,081						

GROUP 2.—CITIES AND OTHER INCORPORATED PLACES OF 10,000 TO 25,000 (459 places).

	1920	1910		1920	1910		1920	1910
ALABAMA.			**CALIFORNIA.**			**CONNECTICUT.**		
Anniston	17,734	12,794	Bakersfield	18,638	12,727	Ansonia	17,643	15,152
Bessemer	18,674	10,864	Eureka	12,923	11,845	Bristol	20,620	9,527
Dothan	10,034	7,016	Glendale	13,536	2,746	Danbury	18,943	20,234
Florence	10,529	6,689	Pomona	13,505	10,207	Derby	11,238	8,991
Gadsden	14,737	10,557	Richmond	16,843	6,802	Middletown	13,638	11,851
Selma	15,589	13,649	Riverside	19,341	15,212	Naugatuck	15,051	12,722
Tuscaloosa	11,996	8,407	San Bernardino	18,721	12,779	Norwich	22,304	20,367
ARIZONA.			Santa Ana	15,485	8,429	Torrington	20,623	15,483
Tucson	20,292	13,193	Santa Barbara	19,441	11,659	Willimantic	12,330	11,230
ARKANSAS.			Santa Cruz	10,917	11,146	**FLORIDA.**		
Hot Springs	11,695	14,434	Santa Monica	15,252	7,847	Key West	18,749	19,945
North Little Rock	14,048	11,138	Vallejo	21,107	11,340	St. Petersburg	14,237	4,127
Pine Bluff	19,280	15,102	Venice	10,385	3,119	**GEORGIA.**		
Texarkana	¹8,257	5,655	**COLORADO.**			Albany	11,555	8,190
			Boulder	11,006	9,539	Athens	16,748	14,913
			Greeley	10,958	8,179	Brunswick	14,413	10,182
			Trinidad	10,906	10,204			

¹ Texarkana, Ark., and Texarkana, Tex., based upon combined population (19,737 in 1920), included in places of 10,000 to 25,000.

TABLE 12.—POPULATION OF CITIES AND OTHER INCORPORATED PLACES HAVING, IN 1920, 2,500 INHABITANTS OR MORE, ARRANGED IN GROUPS ACCORDING TO POPULATION: 1920 AND 1910—Continued.

GROUP 2.—CITIES AND OTHER INCORPORATED PLACES OF 10,000 TO 25,000 (459 places)—Continued.

CITY, TOWN, VILLAGE, OR BOROUGH.	1920	1910
GEORGIA—con.		
La Grange	17,038	5,587
Rome	13,252	12,099
Valdosta	10,783	7,656
Waycross	18,068	14,485
IDAHO.		
Boise	21,393	17,358
Pocatello	15,001	9,110
ILLINOIS.		
Alton	24,682	17,528
Belleville	24,823	21,122
Berwyn	14,150	5,841
Blue Island	11,424	8,043
Cairo	15,203	14,548
Canton	10,928	10,453
Centralia	12,491	9,680
Champaign	15,873	12,421
Chicago Heights	19,653	14,525
Forest Park	10,768	6,594
Freeport	19,669	17,567
Galesburg	23,834	22,089
Granite City	14,757	9,903
Herrin	10,986	6,861
Jacksonville	15,713	15,326
Kankakee	16,753	13,986
Kewanee	16,026	9,307
La Salle	13,050	11,537
Lincoln	11,882	10,892
Mattoon	13,552	11,456
Maywood	12,072	8,033
Murphysboro	10,703	7,485
Ottawa	10,816	9,535
Pekin	12,086	9,897
Streator	14,779	14,253
Urbana	10,244	8,245
Waukegan	19,226	16,069
INDIANA.		
Bloomington	11,595	8,838
Clinton	10,962	6,229
Crawfordsville	10,139	9,371
Elkhart	24,277	19,282
Elwood	10,790	11,028
Frankfort	11,585	8,634
Huntington	14,000	10,272
Jeffersonville	10,098	10,412
La Porte	15,158	10,525
Lafayette	22,486	20,081
Logansport	21,626	19,050
Marion	23,747	19,359
Michigan City	19,457	19,027
Mishawaka	15,195	11,886
New Albany	22,992	20,629
New Castle	14,458	9,446
Peru	12,410	10,910
Vincennes	17,160	14,895
Whiting	10,145	6,587
IOWA.		
Boone	10,171	10,347
Burlington	24,057	24,324
Clinton	24,151	25,577
Fort Dodge	19,347	15,543
Fort Madison	12,066	8,900
Iowa City	11,267	10,091
Keokuk	14,423	14,008
Marshalltown	15,731	13,374
Mason City	20,065	11,230
Muscatine	16,068	16,178
Ottumwa	23,003	22,012
KANSAS.		
Arkansas City	11,253	7,508
Atchison	12,630	16,429
Chanute	10,286	9,272
Coffeyville	13,452	12,687
KANSAS—con.		
El Dorado	10,995	3,129
Emporia	11,273	9,058
Fort Scott	10,693	10,463
Hutchinson	23,298	16,364
Independence	11,920	10,480
Lawrence	12,456	12,374
Leavenworth	16,912	19,363
Parsons	16,028	12,463
Pittsburg	18,052	14,755
Salina	15,085	9,688
KENTUCKY.		
Ashland	14,729	8,688
Henderson	12,169	11,452
Owensboro	17,424	16,011
Paducah	24,735	22,760
LOUISIANA.		
Alexandria	17,510	11,213
Baton Rouge	21,782	14,897
Lake Charles	13,088	11,449
Monroe	12,675	10,209
MAINE.		
Auburn	16,985	15,064
Augusta	14,114	13,211
Bath	14,731	9,396
Biddeford	18,008	17,079
Waterville	13,351	11,458
MARYLAND.		
Annapolis	11,214	8,609
Frederick	11,066	10,411
MASSACHUSETTS.		
Adams town	12,967	13,026
Amesbury town	10,036	9,894
Attleboro	19,731	16,215
Arlington town	18,665	11,187
Belmont town	10,749	5,542
Beverly	22,561	18,650
Braintree town	10,580	8,066
Clinton town	12,979	13,075
Danvers town	11,108	9,407
Dedham town	10,792	9,284
Easthampton town	11,261	8,524
Framingham town	17,033	12,948
Gardner town	16,971	14,699
Gloucester	22,947	24,398
Greenfield town	15,462	10,427
Leominster	19,744	17,580
Marlborough	15,028	14,579
Melrose	18,204	15,715
Methuen	15,189	11,448
Milford town	13,471	13,055
Natick town	10,907	9,866
Newburyport	15,618	14,949
North Adams	22,282	22,019
Northampton	21,951	19,431
Northbridge town	10,174	8,807
Norwood town	12,627	8,014
Peabody	19,552	15,721
Plymouth town	13,045	12,141
Saugus town	10,874	8,047
Southbridge town	14,245	12,592
Wakefield town	13,025	11,404
Watertown town	21,457	12,875
Webster town	13,258	11,509
West Springfield town	13,443	9,224
Westfield town	18,604	16,044
MASSACHUSETTS—con.		
Weymouth town	15,057	12,895
Winchester town	10,485	9,309
Winthrop town	15,455	10,132
Woburn	16,574	15,308
MICHIGAN.		
Adrian	11,878	10,763
Alpena	11,101	12,706
Ann Arbor	19,516	14,817
Benton Harbor	12,233	9,185
Escanaba	13,103	13,194
Holland	12,183	10,490
Ironwood	15,739	12,821
Ishpeming	10,500	12,448
Marquette	12,718	11,503
Monroe	11,573	6,893
Owosso	12,575	9,639
Sault Ste. Marie	12,096	12,615
Traverse City	10,925	12,115
Wyandotte	13,851	8,287
MINNESOTA.		
Austin	10,118	6,960
Faribault	11,089	9,001
Hibbing	15,089	8,832
Mankato	12,469	10,365
Rochester	13,722	7,844
St. Cloud	15,873	10,600
Virginia	14,022	10,473
Winona	19,143	18,583
MISSISSIPPI.		
Biloxi	10,937	8,049
Columbus	10,501	8,988
Greenville	11,560	9,610
Hattiesburg	13,270	11,733
Jackson	22,817	21,262
Laurel	13,037	8,465
Meridian	23,399	23,285
Natchez	12,608	11,791
Vicksburg	18,072	20,814
MISSOURI.		
Cape Girardeau	10,252	8,475
Carthage	10,068	9,483
Columbia	10,392	9,662
Hannibal	19,306	18,341
Independence	11,686	9,859
Jefferson City	14,490	11,850
Moberly	12,808	10,923
Sedalia	21,144	17,822
MONTANA.		
Anaconda	11,668	10,134
Billings	15,100	10,031
Great Falls	24,121	13,948
Helena	12,037	12,515
Missoula	12,668	12,869
NEBRASKA.		
Grand Island	13,947	10,326
Hastings	11,647	9,338
North Platte	10,466	4,793
NEVADA.		
Reno	12,016	10,867
NEW HAMPSHIRE.		
Berlin	16,104	11,780
Concord	22,167	21,497
Dover	13,029	13,247
Keene	11,210	10,068
Laconia	10,897	10,183
Portsmouth	13,569	11,269

TABLE 12.—POPULATION OF CITIES AND OTHER INCORPORATED PLACES HAVING, IN 1920, 2,500 INHABITANTS OR MORE, ARRANGED IN GROUPS ACCORDING TO POPULATION: 1920 AND 1910—Continued.

GROUP 2.—CITIES AND OTHER INCORPORATED PLACES OF 10,000 TO 25,000 (459 places)—Continued.

CITY, TOWN, VILLAGE, OR BOROUGH.	1920	1910	CITY, TOWN, VILLAGE, OR BOROUGH.	1920	1910	CITY, TOWN, VILLAGE, OR BOROUGH.	1920	1910
NEW JERSEY.			**NORTH DAKOTA.**			**PENNSYLVANIA —con.**		
Asbury Park...	12,400	10,150	Fargo	21,961	14,331	Du Bois	13,681	12,623
Belleville	15,660	......	Grand Forks...	14,010	12,478	Dunmore	20,250	17,615
Bloomfield	22,019	15,070	Minot	10,476	6,188	Duquesne	19,011	15,727
Bridgeton	14,323	14,209	**OHIO.**			Farrell	15,586	10,190
Englewood	11,627	9,924	Alliance	21,603	15,083	Greensburg	15,033	13,012
Garfield	19,381	10,213	Ashtabula	22,082	18,266	Homestead	20,452	18,713
Gloucester	12,162	9,462	Barberton	18,811	9,410	Jeannette	10,627	8,077
Hackensack	17,667	14,050	Bellaire	15,061	12,946	Lebanon	24,643	19,240
Harrison	15,721	14,498	Bucyrus	10,425	8,122	McKees Rocks	16,713	14,702
Long Branch	13,521	13,298	Cambridge	13,104	11,327	Mahanoy City	15,599	15,936
Millville	14,691	12,451	Chillicothe	15,831	14,508	Meadville	14,568	12,780
Morristown	12,548	12,507	Cleveland Heights	15,236	2,955	Monessen	18,179	11,775
Phillipsburg	16,923	13,903	Coshocton	10,847	9,603	Mount Carmel	17,469	17,532
Rahway	11,042	9,337	Cuyahoga Falls	10,200	4,020	Nanticoke	22,614	18,877
Roosevelt	11,047	5,786	East Liverpool	21,411	20,387	New Kensington	11,987	7,707
Summit	10,174	7,500	East Youngstown	11,237	4,972	North Braddock	14,928	11,824
Union	20,651	21,023	Elyria	20,474	14,825	Oil City	21,274	15,657
West Orange	15,573	10,980	Findlay	17,021	14,858	Old Forge	12,237	11,324
NEW MEXICO.			Fremont	12,468	9,939	Olyphant	10,236	8,505
Albuquerque...	15,157	11,020	Ironton	14,007	13,147	Phoenixville	10,484	10,743
NEW YORK.			Kenmore	12,683	1,561	Pittston	18,497	16,267
Batavia	13,541	11,613	Lancaster	14,706	13,093	Plymouth	16,500	16,996
Beacon	10,996	10,629	Marietta	15,140	12,923	Pottstown	17,431	15,599
Cohoes	22,987	24,709	Martins Ferry	11,634	9,133	Pottsville	21,876	20,236
Corning	15,820	13,730	Massillon	17,428	13,879	Punxsutawney	10,311	9,058
Cortland	13,294	11,504	Middletown	23,594	13,152	Shamokin	21,204	19,588
Dunkirk	19,336	17,221	New Philadelphia	10,718	8,542	Sharon	21,747	15,270
Fulton	13,043	10,480	Niles	13,080	8,361	Shenandoah	24,726	25,774
Geneva	14,648	12,446	Norwood	24,966	16,185	Steelton	13,428	14,246
Glens Falls	16,638	15,243	Piqua	15,044	13,388	Sunbury	15,721	13,770
Gloversville	22,075	20,642	Salem	10,305	8,943	Swissvale	10,908	7,381
Herkimer	10,453	7,520	Sandusky	22,897	19,989	Tamaqua	12,363	9,462
Hornell	15,025	13,617	Tiffin	14,375	11,894	Uniontown	15,692	13,344
Hudson	11,745	11,417	**OKLAHOMA.**			Warren	14,272	11,080
Ilion	10,169	6,588	Ardmore	14,181	8,618	Washington	21,480	18,778
Ithaca	17,004	14,802	Bartlesville	14,417	6,181	West Chester	11,717	11,767
Johnstown	10,908	10,447	Chickasha	10,179	10,320	Wilkensburg	24,403	18,924
Lackawanna	17,918	14,549	Enid	16,576	13,799	Woodlawn	12,495	1,396
Little Falls	13,029	12,273	Guthrie	11,757	11,654	**RHODE ISLAND.**		
Lockport	21,308	17,970	McAlester	12,095	12,954	Bristol town	11,375	8,565
Middletown	18,420	15,313	Okmulgee	17,430	4,176	Central Falls	24,174	22,754
North Tonawanda	15,482	11,955	Sapulpa	11,634	8,283	Cumberland town	10,077	10,107
Ogdensburg	14,609	15,933	Shawnee	15,348	12,474	East Providence town...	21,793	15,808
Olean	20,506	14,743	**OREGON.**			Warwick town	13,481	26,629
Oneida	10,541	8,317	Astoria	14,027	9,599	West Warwick town	15,461	....
Oneonta	11,582	9,491	Eugene	10,593	9,009	**SOUTH CAROLINA.**		
Ossining	10,739	11,480	Salem	17,679	14,094	Anderson	10,570	9,654
Oswego	23,626	23,368	**PENNSYLVANIA.**			Florence	10,968	7,057
Peekskill	15,868	15,245	Ambridge	12,730	5,205	Greenville	23,127	15,741
Plattsburg	10,909	11,138	Beaver Falls	12,802	12,191	Spartanburg	22,638	17,517
Port Chester	16,573	12,809	Berwick	12,181	5,357	**SOUTH DAKOTA.**		
Port Jervis	10,171	9,564	Braddock	20,879	19,357	Aberdeen	14,537	10,753
Rensselaer	10,823	10,711	Bradford	15,525	14,544	**TENNESSEE.**		
Saratoga Springs	13,181	12,693	Bristol	10,273	9,256	Bristol	[1] 8,047	7,148
Tonawanda	10,068	8,290	Butler	23,778	20,728	Jackson	18,860	15,779
Watervliet	16,073	15,074	Canonsburg	10,632	3,891	Johnson City...	12,442	8,502
White Plains	21,031	15,949	Carbondale	18,640	17,040	**TEXAS.**		
NORTH CAROLINA.			Carlisle	10,916	10,303	Abilene	10,274	9,204
Durham	21,719	18,241	Carnegie	11,516	10,009	Amarillo	15,494	9,957
Gastonia	12,871	5,759	Carrick	10,504	6,117	Brownsville	11,791	10,517
Goldsboro	11,296	6,107	Chambersburg	13,171	11,800	Cleburne	12,820	10,364
Greensboro	19,861	15,895	Charleroi	11,516	9,615	Corpus Christi	10,522	8,222
High Point	14,302	9,525	Coatesville	14,515	11,084	Corsicana	11,356	9,749
New Bern	12,198	9,961	Columbia	10,836	11,454			
Raleigh	24,418	19,218	Connellsville	13,804	12,845			
Rocky Mount	12,742	8,051	Dickson City	11,049	9,331			
Salisbury	13,884	7,153	Donora	14,131	8,174			
Wilson	10,612	6,717						

[1] Bristol, Tenn., and Bristol, Va., based upon combined population (14,776 in 1920), included in places of 10,000 to 25,000.

Table 12.—POPULATION OF CITIES AND OTHER INCORPORATED PLACES HAVING, IN 1920, 2,500 INHABITANTS OR MORE, ARRANGED IN GROUPS ACCORDING TO POPULATION: 1920 AND 1910—Continued.

Group 2.—Cities and other Incorporated Places of 10,000 to 25,000 (459 places)—Continued.

CITY, TOWN, VILLAGE, OR BOROUGH.	1920	1910	CITY, TOWN, VILLAGE, OR BOROUGH.	1920	1910	CITY, TOWN, VILLAGE, OR BOROUGH.	1920	1910
TEXAS—con.			VIRGINIA.			WISCONSIN.		
Del Rio	10,589	......	Alexandria	18,060	15,329	Appleton	19,561	16,773
Denison	17,065	13,632	Bristol	²6,729	6,247	Ashland	11,334	11,594
Greenville	12,384	8,850	Charlottesville	10,688	6,765	Beloit	21,284	15,125
Laredo	22,710	14,855	Danville	21,539	19,020	Eau Claire	20,906	18,310
Marshall	14,271	11,452	Staunton	10,623	10,604	Fond du Lac	23,427	18,797
Palestine	11,039	10,482				Janesville	18,293	13,894
Paris	15,040	11,269	WASHINGTON.			Manitowoc	17,563	13,027
Port Arthur	22,251	7,663				Marinette	13,610	14,610
Ranger	16,205	......	Aberdeen	15,337	13,660	Stevens Point	11,371	8,692
San Angelo	10,050	10,321	Hoquiam	10,058	8,171	Waukesha	12,558	8,740
Sherman	15,031	12,412	Vancouver	12,637	9,300	Wausau	18,661	16,560
Temple	11,033	10,993	Walla Walla	15,503	19,364	West Allis	13,745	6,645
Texarkana	¹11,480	9,790	Yakima	18,539	14,082			
Tyler	12,085	10,400				WYOMING.		
UTAH.			WEST VIRGINIA.			Casper	11,447	2,639
			Bluefield	15,282	11,188	Cheyenne	13,829	11,320
Provo	10,303	8,925	Fairmont	17,851	9,711			
VERMONT.			Martinsburg	12,515	10,698			
Barre	10,008	10,734	Morgantown	12,127	9,150			
Burlington	22,779	20,468	Moundsville	10,669	8,918			
Rutland	14,954	13,546	Parkersburg	20,050	17,842			

Group 3.—Cities and other Incorporated Places of 5,000 to 10,000 (721 places).

CITY, TOWN, VILLAGE, OR BOROUGH.	1920	1910	CITY, TOWN, VILLAGE, OR BOROUGH.	1920	1910	CITY, TOWN, VILLAGE, OR BOROUGH.	1920	1910
ALABAMA.			CALIFORNIA—con.			GEORGIA.		
Alabama City	5,432	4,313	San Leandro	5,703	3,471	Americus	9,010	8,063
Albany	7,652	6,118	San Luis			Cordele	6,538	5,883
Fairfield	5,003	......	Obispo	5,895	5,157	Dalton	5,222	5,324
Huntsville	8,018	7,611	San Mateo	5,979	4,384	Decatur	6,150	2,466
Phenix City	5,432	4,555	San Rafael	5,512	5,934	Dublin	7,707	5,795
Sheffield	6,682	4,865	Santa Clara	5,220	4,348	East Point	5,241	3,682
Talladega	6,546	5,854	Santa Rosa	8,758	7,817	Elberton	6,475	6,483
Troy	5,696	4,961	South Pasa-			Fitzgerald	6,870	5,795
ARIZONA.			dena	7,652	4,649	Gainesville	6,272	5,925
Bisbee	9,205	9,019	Visalia	5,753	4,550	Griffin	8,240	7,478
Douglas	9,916	6,437	Watsonville	5,013	4,446	Marietta	6,190	5,949
Globe	7,044	7,083	Whittier	7,997	4,550	Moultrie	6,789	3,349
Miami	6,689	......				Newnan	7,037	5,548
Nogales	5,199	3,514	COLORADO.			Thomasville	8,196	6,727
Prescott	5,010	5,092	Fort Collins	8,755	8,210			
ARKANSAS.			Grand Junction	8,665	7,754	IDAHO.		
Blytheville	6,447	3,849	Longmont	5,848	4,256	Burley	5,408	......
Fayetteville	5,362	4,471	Loveland	5,065	3,651	Caldwell	5,106	3,543
Helena	9,112	8,772	Sterling	6,415	3,044	Coeur d'Alene	6,447	7,291
Jonesboro	9,384	7,123				Idaho Falls	8,064	4,827
Marianna	5,074	4,810	CONNECTICUT.			Lewiston	6,574	6,043
Paragould	6,306	5,248	Greenwich	5,939	3,886	Nampa	7,621	4,205
Van Buren	5,224	3,878	Putnam	7,711	6,637	Twin Falls	8,324	5,258
West Helena	6,226	......	Rockville	7,726	7,977			
CALIFORNIA.			Shelton	9,475	4,807	ILLINOIS.		
Alhambra	9,096	5,021	Southington	5,085	3,714	Beardstown	7,111	6,107
Anaheim	5,526	2,628	Wallingford	9,648	8,690	Belvidere	7,804	7,253
Brawley	5,389	881	Winsted	8,248	7,754	Benton	7,201	2,675
Calexico	6,223	797				Carbondale	6,267	5,411
Chico	9,339	3,750	FLORIDA.			Carlinville	5,212	3,616
El Centro	5,464	1,610	Daytona	5,445	3,082	Charleston	6,615	5,884
Hanford	5,888	4,829	Fernandina	5,457	3,482	Clinton	5,898	5,165
Marysville	5,461	5,430	Gainesville	6,860	6,183	Collinsville	9,753	7,478
Modesto	9,241	4,034	Lakeland	7,062	3,719	De Kalb	7,871	8,102
Monrovia	5,480	3,576	Orlando	9,282	3,894	Dixon	8,191	7,216
Monterey	5,479	4,923	Palatka	5,102	3,779	Duquoin	7,285	5,454
Napa	6,757	5,791	St. Augustine	6,192	5,494	East Moline	8,675	2,665
Ontario	7,280	4,274	Sanford	5,588	3,570	Edwardsville	5,336	5,014
Palo Alto	5,900	4,486	Tallahassee	5,637	5,018	Eldorado	5,004	3,366
Petaluma	6,226	5,880	West Palm			Harrisburg	7,125	5,309
Redlands	9,571	10,449	Beach	8,659	1,743	Harvey	9,216	7,227
			West Tampa	8,463	8,258	Highland Park	6,167	4,209
						Hillsboro	5,074	3,424
						Hoopeston	5,451	4,698

¹ Texarkana, Ark., and Texarkana, Tex., based upon combined population (19,737 in 1920), included in places of 10,000 to 25,000.

² Bristol, Tenn., and Bristol, Va., based upon combined population (14,776 in 1920), included in places of 10,000 to 25,000.

Table 12.—POPULATION OF CITIES AND OTHER INCORPORATED PLACES HAVING, IN 1920, 2,500 INHABITANTS OR MORE, ARRANGED IN GROUPS ACCORDING TO POPULATION: 1920 AND 1910—Continued.

Group 3.—Cities and other Incorporated Places of 5,000 to 10,000 (721 places)—Continued.

CITY, TOWN, VILLAGE, OR BOROUGH.	1920	1910
ILLINOIS—con.		
Johnston City..	7,137	3,248
La Grange......	6,525	5,282
Lawrenceville..	5,080	3,235
Litchfield.....	6,215	5,971
Macomb........	6,714	5,774
Marion........	9,582	7,093
Melrose Park...	7,147	4,806
Metropolis.....	5,055	4,655
Monmouth.....	8,116	9,128
Mount Carmel..	7,456	6,934
Mount Vernon..	9,815	8,007
Normal........	5,143	4,024
North Chicago..	5,839	3,306
Pana..........	6,122	6,055
Paris..........	7,985	7,664
Peru..........	8,869	7,984
Pontiac.......	6,664	6,090
Savanna......	5,237	3,691
Spring Valley..	6,493	7,035
Staunton......	6,027	5,048
Sterling.......	8,182	7,467
Taylorville....	5,806	5,446
W. Frankfort ..	8,478	2,111
W. Hammond..	7,492	4,948
Wilmette......	7,814	4,943
Winnetka.....	6,694	3,168
Woodstock.....	5,523	4,331
Zion..........	5,580	4,789
INDIANA.		
Bedford........	9,076	8,716
Bicknell........	7,635	2,794
Bluffton........	5,391	4,987
Brazil.........	9,293	9,340
Columbus.....	8,990	8,813
Connersville....	9,901	7,738
Goshen........	9,525	8,514
Greensburg.....	5,345	5,420
Hartford City..	6,183	6,187
Kendallville....	5,273	4,981
Lebanon......	6,257	5,474
Linton........	5,856	5,906
Madison.......	6,711	6,934
Mount Vernon..	5,284	5,563
Portland......	5,958	5,130
Princeton.....	7,132	6,448
Rushville......	5,498	4,925
Seymour......	7,348	6,305
Shelbyville....	9,701	9,500
Valparaiso.....	6,518	6,987
Wabash.......	9,872	8,687
Warsaw.......	5,478	4,430
Washington....	8,743	7,854
IOWA.		
Albia..........	5,067	4,969
Ames..........	6,270	4,223
Atlantic.......	5,329	4,560
Cedar Falls.....	6,316	5,012
Centerville....	8,486	6,936
Chariton......	5,175	3,794
Charles City...	7,350	5,892
Cherokee.....	5,824	4,884
Creston.......	8,034	6,924
Fairfield......	5,948	4,970
Grinnell.......	5,362	5,036
Newton.......	6,627	4,616
Oelwein.......	7,455	6,028
Oskaloosa.....	9,427	9,466
Perry.........	5,642	4,630
Red Oak......	5,578	4,830
Shenandoah...	5,255	4,976
Webster City...	5,657	5,208
KANSAS.		
Dodge City.....	5,061	3,214
Iola...........	8,513	9,032
Junction City..	7,533	5,598
Manhattan.....	7,989	5,722
Newton........	9,781	7,862
Ottawa........	9,018	7,650
Pratt..........	5,183	3,302
Rosedale.......	7,674	5,960
Wellington....	7,048	7,034
Winfield.......	7,933	6,700
KENTUCKY.		
Bellevue.......	7,379	6,683
Bowling Green.	9,638	9,173
Danville.......	5,099	5,420
Dayton........	7,646	6,979
Fort Thomas...	5,028	......
Frankfort......	9,805	10,465
Hopkinsville...	9,696	9,419
Madisonville...	5,030	4,966
Mayfield......	6,583	5,916
Maysville.....	6,107	6,141
Middlesborough	8,041	7,305
Paris..........	6,310	5,859
Richmond.....	5,622	5,340
Winchester....	8,333	7,156
LOUISIANA.		
Bogalusa.......	8,245	......
Crowley........	6,108	5,099
Gretna........	7,197	......
Houma........	5,160	5,024
Lafayette......	7,855	6,392
Minden.......	6,105	3,002
Morgan City...	5,429	5,477
New Iberia.....	6,278	7,499
MAINE.		
Belfast.........	5,083	4,618
Brewer........	6,064	5,667
Brunswick....	5,784	5,341
Calais........	6,084	6,116
Gardiner......	5,475	5,311
Old Town.....	6,956	6,317
Rockland......	8,109	8,174
Rumford Falls (Rumford P.O.)	7,016	5,427
Saco..........	6,817	6,583
South Portland	9,254	7,471
Westbrook.....	9,453	8,281
MARYLAND.		
Cambridge.....	7,467	6,407
Frostburg......	6,017	6,028
Salisbury......	7,553	6,690
MASSACHUSETTS.		
Abington town.	5,787	5,455
Agawam town..	5,023	3,501
Amherst town..	5,550	5,112
Andover town..	8,268	7,301
Athol town....	9,792	8,536
Bridgewater town..........	8,438	7,688
Canton town...	5,945	4,797
Chelmsford town..........	5,682	5,010
Concord town..	6,461	6,421
Dartmouth town..........	6,493	4,378
Dracut town...	5,280	3,461
Easton town...	5,041	5,139
MASSACHUSETTS—con.		
Fairhaven town	7,291	5,122
Franklin town .	6,497	5,641
Grafton town...	6,887	5,705
Great Barrington town......	6,315	5,926
Hingham town.	5,604	4,965
Hudson town..	7,607	6,743
Ipswich town..	6,201	5,777
Lexington town	6,350	4,918
Ludlow town...	7,470	4,948
Mansfield town.	6,255	5,183
Marblehead town......	7,324	7,338
Maynard town .	7,086	6,390
Middleborough town......	8,453	8,214
Millbury town..	5,653	4,740
Milton town....	9,382	7,924
Montague town.	7,675	6,866
Needham town.	7,012	5,026
North Andover town......	6,265	5,529
North Attleborough town....	9,238	9,562
Orange town...	5,393	5,282
Palmer town...	9,896	8,610
Reading town..	7,439	5,818
Rockland town	7,544	6,928
South Hadley town.........	5,527	4,894
Spencer town..	5,930	6,740
Stoneham town	7,873	7,090
Stoughton town	6,865	6,316
Swampscott town.........	8,101	6,204
Uxbridge town.	5,384	4,671
Walpole town..	5,446	4,892
Ware town.....	8,525	8,774
Wellesley town.	6,224	5,413
Westborough town.........	5,789	5,446
Whitman town.	7,147	7,292
Winchenden town.........	5,904	5,678
MICHIGAN.		
Albion.........	8,354	5,833
Alma..........	7,542	2,757
Bessemer......	5,482	4,583
Cadillac.......	9,750	8,375
Charlotte......	5,126	4,886
Cheboygan....	5,642	6,859
Coldwater.....	6,114	5,945
Dowagiac.....	5,440	5,088
Grand Haven..	7,205	5,856
Hancock.......	7,527	8,981
Hastings.......	5,132	4,383
Hillsdale......	5,476	5,001
Ionia.........	6,935	5,030
Iron Mountain.	8,251	9,216
Laurium......	6,696	8,537
Ludington.....	8,810	9,132
Manistee......	9,694	12,381
Manistique....	6,380	4,722
Menominee....	8,907	10,507
Midland.......	5,483	2,527
Mount Clemens.	9,488	7,707
Munising......	5,037	2,952
Muskegon Heights......	9,514	1,690
Negaunee.....	7,419	8,460
Niles..........	7,311	5,156

TABLE **12.**—POPULATION OF CITIES AND OTHER INCORPORATED PLACES HAVING, IN 1920, 2,500 INHABITANTS OR MORE, ARRANGED IN GROUPS ACCORDING TO POPULATION: 1920 AND 1910—Continued.

GROUP 3.—CITIES AND OTHER INCORPORATED PLACES OF 5,000 TO 10,000 (721 places)—Continued.

CITY, TOWN, VILLAGE, OR BOROUGH.	1920	1910
MICHIGAN—con.		
Petoskey	5,064	4,778
River Rouge	9,822	4,163
Royal Oak	6,007	1,071
St. Joseph	7,251	5,936
Sturgis	5,995	3,635
Three Rivers	5,209	5,072
Ypsilanti	7,413	6,230
MINNESOTA.		
Albert Lea	8,056	6,192
Bemidji	7,086	5,099
Brainerd	9,591	8,526
Chisholm	9,039	7,684
Cloquet	5,127	7,031
Crookston	6,825	7,559
Eveleth	7,205	7,036
Fergus Falls	7,581	6,887
Little Falls	5,500	6,078
Moorhead	5,720	4,840
New Ulm	6,745	5,648
Owatonna	7,252	5,658
Red Wing	8,637	9,048
South St. Paul	6,860	4,510
Stillwater	7,735	10,198
Willmar	5,892	4,135
MISSISSIPPI.		
Clarksdale	7,552	4,079
Corinth	5,498	5,020
Greenwood	7,793	5,836
Gulfport	8,157	6,386
McComb	7,775	6,237
Pascagoula	6,082	3,379
Tupelo	5,055	3,881
Yazoo City	5,244	6,796
MISSOURI.		
Brookfield	6,304	5,749
Chillicothe	6,772	6,265
Clinton	5,098	4,992
De Soto	5,003	4,721
Fulton	5,595	5,228
Kirksville	7,213	6,347
Maplewood	7,431	4,976
Marshall	5,200	4,869
Mexico	6,013	5,939
Nevada	7,139	7,176
Poplar Bluff	8,042	6,916
St. Charles	8,503	9,437
Trenton	6,951	5,656
University	6,792	2,417
Webb City	7,807	11,817
Webster Groves	9,474	7,080
MONTANA.		
Bozeman	6,183	5,107
Havre	5,429	3,624
Kalispell	5,147	5,549
Lewistown	6,120	2,992
Livingston	6,311	5,359
Miles City	7,937	4,007
NEBRASKA.		
Beatrice	9,664	9,356
Columbus	5,410	5,014
Fairbury	5,454	5,294
Fremont	9,605	8,718
Kearney	7,702	6,202
Nebraska City	6,279	5,488
Norfolk	8,634	6,025
Scottsbluff	6,912	1,746
York	5,388	6,235

CITY, TOWN, VILLAGE, OR BOROUGH.	1920	1910
NEW HAMPSHIRE.		
Claremont town	9,524	7,529
Derry town	5,382	5,123
Franklin	6,318	6,132
Lebanon town	6,162	5,718
Rochester	9,673	8,868
Somersworth	6,688	6,704
NEW JERSEY.		
Boonton	5,372	4,930
Bound Brook	5,906	3,970
Burlington	9,049	8,336
Cliffside Park	5,709	3,394
Collingswood	8,714	4,795
Dover	9,803	7,468
E. Rutherford	5,463	4,275
Fort Lee	5,761	4,472
Guttenberg	6,726	5,647
Haddonfield	5,646	4,142
Hammonton	6,417	5,088
Hawthorne	5,135	3,400
Lodi	8,175	4,138
Madison	5,523	4,658
N. Plainfield	6,916	6,117
Nutley	9,421	6,009
Pennsgrove	6,060	2,118
Pleasantville	5,887	4,390
Princeton	5,917	5,136
Red Bank	9,251	7,398
Ridgefield Park	8,575	(1)
Ridgewood	7,580	5,416
Roselle	5,737	2,725
Roselle Park	5,438	3,138
Rutherford	9,497	7,045
Salem	7,435	6,614
Secaucus	5,423	4,740
Somerville	6,718	5,060
South Amboy	7,897	7,007
South Orange	7,274	6,014
South River	6,596	4,772
Vineland	6,799	5,282
Wallington	5,715	3,448
Westfield	9,063	6,420
Woodbury	5,801	4,642
NEW MEXICO.		
Raton	5,544	4,539
Roswell	7,033	6,172
Santa Fe	7,236	5,072
NEW YORK.		
Canandaigua	7,356	7,217
Depew	5,850	3,921
Endicott	9,500	2,408
Fredonia	6,051	5,285
Freeport	8,599	4,836
Glen Cove	8,664	
Hastings-upon-Hudson	5,526	4,552
Haverstraw	5,226	5,669
Hempstead	6,382	4,964
Hudson Falls	5,761	5,189
Johnson City	8,587	3,775
Lancaster	6,059	4,364
Malone	7,556	6,467
Mamaroneck	6,571	5,699
Massena	5,993	2,951
Mechanicville	8,166	6,634
Medina	6,011	5,683
Newark	6,964	6,227
N. Tarrytown	5,927	5,421
Norwich	8,268	7,422

CITY, TOWN, VILLAGE, OR BOROUGH.	1920	1910
NEW YORK—con.		
Rockville Center	6,262	3,667
Rye	5,308	3,964
Salamanca	9,276	5,792
Saranac Lake	5,174	4,983
Seneca Falls	6,389	6,588
Solvay	7,352	5,139
Tarrytown	5,807	5,600
Walden	5,493	4,004
Waverly	5,270	4,855
Whitehall	5,258	4,917
NORTH CAROLINA.		
Burlington	5,952	4,808
Concord	9,903	8,715
Elizabeth City	8,925	8,412
Fayetteville	8,877	7,045
Greenville	5,772	4,101
Henderson	5,222	4,503
Hickory	5,076	3,716
Kingston	9,771	6,995
Lexington	5,254	4,163
Reidsville	5,333	4,828
Statesville	7,895	4,599
Thomasville	5,676	3,877
Washington	6,314	6,211
NORTH DAKOTA.		
Bismarck	7,122	5,443
Devils Lake	5,140	5,157
Jamestown	6,627	4,358
OHIO.		
Ashland	9,249	6,795
Athens	6,418	5,463
Bellefontaine	9,336	8,238
Bellevue	5,776	5,209
Bowling Green	5,788	5,222
Circleville	7,049	6,744
Conneaut	9,343	8,319
Defiance	8,876	7,327
Delaware	8,756	9,076
Delphos	5,745	5,038
Dennison	5,524	4,008
Dover	8,101	6,621
East Palestine	5,750	3,537
Fostoria	9,987	9,597
Galion	7,374	7,214
Gallipolis	6,070	5,560
Girard	6,556	3,736
Greenville	7,104	6,237
Jackson	5,842	5,468
Kent	7,070	4,488
Kenton	7,690	7,185
Logan	5,493	4,850
Mount Vernon	9,237	9,087
Nelsonville	6,440	6,082
Norwalk	7,379	7,858
Painesville	7,272	5,501
Ravenna	7,219	5,010
St. Bernard	6,312	5,002
St. Marys	5,679	5,732
Shelby	5,578	4,903
Sidney	8,590	6,607
Struthers	5,847	3,370
Troy	7,260	6,122
Uhrichsville	6,428	4,751
Urbana	7,621	7,739
Van Wert	8,100	7,157
Wapakoneta	5,295	5,349

[1] Not returned separately.

TABLE 12.—POPULATION OF CITIES AND OTHER INCORPORATED PLACES HAVING, IN 1920, 2,500 INHABITANTS OR MORE, ARRANGED IN GROUPS ACCORDING TO POPULATION: 1920 AND 1910—Continued.

GROUP 3.—CITIES AND OTHER INCORPORATED PLACES OF 5,000 TO 10,000 (721 places)—Continued.

CITY, TOWN, VILLAGE, OR BOROUGH.	1920	1910	CITY, TOWN, VILLAGE, OR BOROUGH.	1920	1910	CITY, TOWN, VILLAGE, OR BOROUGH.	1920	1910
OHIO—con.			PENNSYLVANIA—con.			SOUTH CAROLINA—con.		
Washington Court House..	7,962	7,277	Kane............	7,283	6,626	Newberry......	5,894	5,028
Wellston........	6,687	6,875	Kingston........	8,952	6,449	Orangeburg....	7,290	5,906
Wellsville......	8,849	7,769	Kittanning.....	7,153	4,311	Rock Hill......	8,809	7,216
West Park.....	8,581	3,179	Knoxville.....	7,201	5,651	Sumter........	9,508	8,109
Wilmington....	5,037	4,491	Lansford.......	9,625	8,321	Union.........	6,141	5,623
Wooster........	8,204	6,136	Larksville......	9,438	9,288	SOUTH DAKOTA.		
Xenia..........	9,110	8,706	Latrobe........	9,484	8,777			
OKLAHOMA.			Lehighton......	6,102	5,316	Huron.........	8,302	5,791
			Lewistown.....	9,849	8,166	Lead..........	5,013	8,392
Ada...........	8,012	4,349	Lock Haven....	8,557	7,772	Mitchell.......	8,478	6,515
Blackwell......	7,174	3,266	Luzerne.......	5,908	5,426	Rapid City.....	5,777	3,854
Cushing........	6,326	1,072	Marcus Hook...	5,324	1,573	Watertown.....	9,400	7,010
Drumright.....	6,460	......	Middletown....	5,920	5,374	Yankton......	5,024	3,787
Durant........	7,340	5,330	Midland........	5,452	1,244	TENNESSEE.		
El Reno.......	7,737	7,872	Millvale........	8,031	7,861			
Henryetta.....	5,889	1,671	Milton.........	8,638	7,460	Clarksville......	8,110	8,548
Hugo..........	6,368	4,582	Minersville....	7,845	7,240	Cleveland......	6,522	5,549
Lawton........	8,930	7,788	Monongahela City..	8,688	7,598	Columbia......	5,526	5,754
Miami.........	6,802	2,907	Mount Oliver...	5,575	4,241	Dyersburg.....	6,444	4,149
Norman........	5,004	3,724	Mount Pleasant	5,862	5,812	Kingsport.....	5,692	......
Pawhuska......	6,414	2,776	Munhall.......	6,418	5,185	Morristown.....	5,875	4,007
Picher........	9,676	......	Nanty-Glo.....	5,028	......	Murfreesboro...	5,367	4,679
Ponca City....	7,051	2,521	New Brighton..	9,361	8,329	TEXAS.		
Vinita.........	5,010	4,082	Northampton..	9,349	8,729			
OREGON.			Palmerton......	7,168	......	Belton........	5,098	4,164
			Parsons........	5,628	4,338	Bonham.......	6,008	4,844
Baker City.....	7,729	6,742	Pitcairn........	5,738	4,975	Brenham......	5,066	4,718
Bend..........	5,415	536	Rankin........	7,301	6,042	Brownwood....	8,223	6,967
Corvallis......	5,752	4,552	Renovo........	5,877	4,621	Bryan........	6,307	4,132
La Grande.....	6,913	4,843	Ridgway......	6,037	5,408	Burkburnett...	5,300	......
Medford.......	5,756	8,840	Rochester......	6,957	5,903	Childress.....	5,003	3,818
Oregon City....	5,686	4,287	St. Clair (Allegheny Co.)...	6,585	5,640	Cisco.........	7,422	2,410
Pendleton.....	7,387	4,460				Denton........	7,626	4,732
The Dalles....	5,807	4,880	St.Clair(Schuylkill Co.)......	6,495	6,455	Eagle Pass....	5,765	3,536
PENNSYLVANIA.			St. Marys......	6,967	6,346	Eastland......	9,368	855
			Sayre.........	8,078	6,426	Ennis........	7,224	5,669
Archbald.......	8,603	7,194	Schuylkill Haven.....	5,437	4,747	Gainesville....	8,648	7,624
Arnold........	6,120	1,818	Scottdale.......	5,768	5,456	Hillsboro.....	6,952	6,115
Ashland.......	6,666	6,855	Sharpsburg....	8,921	8,153	Longview......	5,713	5,155
Ashley........	6,520	5,601	Stroudsburg....	5,278	4,379	McAllen......	5,331	......
Avalon........	5,277	4,317	Summit Hill...	5,499	4,209	McKinney.....	6,677	4,714
Bangor........	5,402	5,369	Swoyersville...	6,876	5,396	Mineral Wells..	7,890	3,950
Bellevue.......	8,198	6,323	Tarentum......	8,925	7,414	Navasota......	5,060	3,284
Blakely........	6,564	5,345	Taylor.........	9,876	9,060	Orange........	9,212	5,527
Bloomsburg....	7,819	7,413	Throop........	6,672	5,133	San Benito....	5,070	......
Clairton.......	6,264	3,326	Titusville.....	8,432	8,533	Sulphur Springs	5,558	5,151
Clearfield......	8,529	6,851	Turtle Creek..	8,138	4,995	Taylor.........	5,965	5,314
Coaldale......	6,336	5,154	Tyrone........	9,084	7,176	Terrell.......	8,349	7,050
Conshohocken..	8,481	7,480	Vandergrift....	9,531	3,876	Vernon.......	5,142	3,195
Coraopolis......	6,162	5,252	Waynesboro....	9,720	7,199	Victoria......	5,957	3,673
Corry.........	7,228	5,991	West Hazleton..	5,854	4,715	Waxahachie..	7,958	6,205
Crafton........	5,954	4,583	West Pittston..	6,968	6,848	Weatherford...	6,203	5,074
Danville.......	6,952	7,517	Wilmerding....	6,441	6,133	Yoakum.......	6,184	4,657
Darby.........	7,922	6,305	Windber.......	9,462	8,013	UTAH.		
Dormont.......	6,455	1,115	Winton........	7,583	5,280			
Dorranceton...	6,334	4,046	RHODE ISLAND.			Brigham......	5,282	3,685
Duryea........	7,776	7,487				Logan.........	9,439	7,522
East Conemaugh..	5,256	5,046	Burrillville town.........	8,606	7,878	VERMONT.		
East Pittsburgh	6,527	5,615	Coventry town.	5,670	5,848	Bennington....	7,230	6,211
Edwardsville...	9,027	8,407	Johnston town.	6,855	5,935	Brattleboro....	7,324	6,517
Ellwood City...	8,958	3,902	Lincoln town...	9,543	9,825	Montpelier.....	7,125	7,856
Etna..........	6,341	5,830	N. Providence town.........	7,697	5,407	St. Albans.....	7,588	6,381
Ford City......	5,605	4,850				St. Johnsbury..	7,164	6,693
Forest City....	6,004	5,749	S. Kingstown town.........	5,181	5,176	Springfield.....	5,283	3,250
Frackville.....	5,590	3,118	Warren town..	7,841	6,585	VIRGINIA.		
Franklin.......	9,970	9,767	Westerly town.	9,952	8,696	Clifton Forge...	6,164	5,748
Freeland.......	6,666	6,197	SOUTH CAROLINA.			Covington......	5,623	4,234
Glassport......	6,959	5,540				Fredericksburg.	5,882	5,874
Greenville.....	8,101	5,909	Chester........	5,557	4,754	Hampton......	6,138	5,505
Hanover.......	8,664	7,057	Gaffney.......	5,065	4,767	Harrisonburg...	5,875	4,879
Huntingdon....	7,051	6,861	Greenwood....	8,703	6,614	Pulaski.......	5,282	4,807
Indiana........	7,043	5,749				South Norfolk..	7,724	......
Jersey Shore...	6,103	5,381				Suffolk.......	9,123	7,008
Johnsonburg...	5,400	4,334				Winchester....	6,883	5,864
Juniata.......	7,660	5,285						

TABLE 12.—POPULATION OF CITIES AND OTHER INCORPORATED PLACES HAVING, IN 1920, 2,500 INHABITANTS OR MORE, ARRANGED IN GROUPS ACCORDING TO POPULATION: 1920 AND 1910—Continued.

GROUP 3.—CITIES AND OTHER INCORPORATED PLACES OF 5,000 TO 10,000 (721 places)—Continued.

CITY, TOWN, VILLAGE, OR BOROUGH.	1920	1910	CITY, TOWN, VILLAGE, OR BOROUGH.	1920	1910	CITY, TOWN, VILLAGE, OR BOROUGH.	1920	1910
WASHINGTON.			WISCONSIN.			WISCONSIN—con.		
Anacortes	5,284	4,168	Antigo	8,451	7,196	South		
Bremerton	8,918	2,993	Baraboo	5,538	6,324	Milwaukee	7,598	6,092
Centralia	7,549	7,311	Beaver Dam	7,992	6,758	Stoughton	5,101	4,761
Olympia	7,795	6,996	Chippewa Falls	9,130	8,893	Two Rivers	7,305	4,850
Port Angeles	5,351	2,286	Cudahy	6,725	3,691	Watertown	9,299	8,829
Puyallup	6,323	4,544	De Pere	5,165	4,477	Wauwatosa	5,818	3,346
Wenatchee	6,324	4,050	Kaukauna	5,951	4,717	Wisconsin		
WEST VIRGINIA.			Marshfield	7,394	5,783	Rapids	7,243	6,521
Elkins	6,788	5,260	Menasha	7,214	6,081	WYOMING.		
Grafton	8,517	7,563	Menominie	5,104	5,036			
Keyser	6,003	3,705	Merrill	8,068	8,689	Laramie	6,301	8,237
Princeton	6,224	3,027	Neenah	7,171	5,734	Rock Springs	6,456	5,778
Weston	5,701	2,213	Portage	5,582	5,440	Sheridan	9,175	8,408
Williamson	6,819	3,561	Rhinelander	6,654	5,637			

GROUP 4.—CITIES AND OTHER INCORPORATED PLACES OF 2,500 TO 5,000 (1,320 places).

	1920	1910		1920	1910		1920	1910
ALABAMA.			ARKANSAS—con.			CALIFORNIA—con.		
Andalusia	4,023	2,480	Stamps	2,564	2,316	South San		
Athens	3,323	1,715	Stuttgart	4,522	2,740	Francisco	4,411	1,989
Attalla	3,462	2,513	Truman	2,598	......	Taft	3,317	......
Brewton	2,682	2,185	Wynne	2,933	2,353	Tulare	3,539	2,758
Brighton	3,665	1,502	CALIFORNIA.			Turlock	3,394	1,573
Carbon Hill	2,666	1,627				Upland	2,912	2,384
Decatur	4,752	4,228	Benicia	2,693	2,360	Ventura	4,342	2,945
Demopolis	2,779	2,417	Burbank	2,913	......	Watts	4,529	1,922
Enterprise	3,013	2,322	Burlingame	4,107	1,565	Woodland	4,147	3,187
Eufaula	4,939	4,259	Coalinga	2,934	4,199	COLORADO.		
Florala	2,633	2,439	Colton	4,282	3,980			
Girard	4,942	4,214	Corona	4,129	3,540	Alamosa	3,171	3,013
Greenville	3,471	3,377	Coronado	3,289	1,477	Brighton	2,715	850
Jasper	3,246	2,509	Daly City	3,779	......	Canon City	4,551	5,162
Lanett	4,976	3,820	Dinuba	3,400	970	Delta	2,623	2,388
Opelika	4,960	4,734	Dunsmuir	2,528	1,719	Durango	4,116	4,686
Ozark	2,518	2,229	East San Diego	4,148	......	Englewood	4,356	2,983
Piedmont	2,645	2,226	Fort Bragg	2,616	2,408	Florence	2,629	2,712
Roanoke	3,841	2,034	Fullerton	4,415	1,725	Fort Morgan	3,818	2,800
Tuscumbia	3,855	3,324	Gilroy	2,862	2,437	La Junta	4,964	4,154
Union Springs	4,125	4,055	Grass Valley	4,006	4,520	Lamar	2,512	2,977
ARIZONA.			Hayward	3,487	2,746	Leadville	4,959	7,508
			Hollister	2,781	2,308	Montrose	3,581	3,254
Clifton	4,163	4,874	Huntington			Rocky Ford	3,746	3,230
Flagstaff	3,186	1,633	Park	4,513	1,299	Salida	4,689	4,425
Glendale	2,737	......	Inglewood	3,286	1,536	Walsenburg	3,565	2,423
Jerome	4,030	2,393	Lindsay	2,576	1,814	CONNECTICUT.		
Mesa	3,036	1,692	Lodi	4,850	2,697			
Winslow	3,730	2,381	Madera	3,444	2,404	Branford	2,619	2,560
Yuma	4,237	2,914	Martinez	3,858	2,115	Danielson	3,130	2,934
ARKANSAS.			Merced	3,974	3,102	Groton	4,236	1,895
			Mill Valley	2,554	2,551	Jewett City	3,196	3,023
Arkadelphia	3,311	2,745	Monterey Park	4,108	......	Stafford Springs	3,383	3,059
Batesville	4,299	3,399	National City	3,116	1,733	DELAWARE.		
Benton	2,933	1,708	Needles	2,807	......			
Brinkley	2,714	1,740	Orange	4,884	2,920	Dover	4,042	3,720
Camden	3,238	3,995	Oroville	3,340	3,859	Milford	2,703	2,603
Clarendon	2,638	2,037	Oxnard	4,417	2,555	New Castle	3,854	3,351
Conway	4,564	2,794	Pacific Grove	2,974	2,384	FLORIDA.		
Crossett	2,707	2,038	Piedmont	4,282	1,719			
De Queen	3,017	2,018	Pittsburg	4,715	2,572	Apalachicola	3,066	3,065
El Dorado	3,887	4,202	Porterville	4,007	2,696	Arcadia	3,479	1,736
Fordyce	2,996	2,794	Red Bluff	3,104	3,530	Bartow	4,203	2,662
Forrest City	3,377	2,484	Redding	2,962	3,572	Bradentown	3,868	1,886
Harrison	3,477	1,602	Redondo Beach	4,913	2,935	De Land	3,324	2,812
Hope	4,790	3,639	Redwood City	4,020	2,442	Fort Myers	3,678	2,463
Malvern	3,864	2,778	Roseville	4,477	2,608	Kissimmee	2,722	2,157
Mena	3,441	3,953	Salinas	4,308	3,736	Lake City	3,341	5,032
Morrillton	3,010	2,424	San Fernando	3,204	......	Live Oak	3,103	3,450
Newport	3,771	3,557	San Gabriel	2,640	......	Ocala	4,914	4,370
Prescott	2,691	2,705	Sanger	2,578	......	Plant City	3,729	2,481
Rogers	3,318	2,820	Santa Maria	3,943	2,260	Quincy	3,118	3,204
Russellville	4,505	2,936	Santa Paula	3,967	2,216	South Jacksonville		
Searcy	2,836	2,331	Sausalito	2,790	2,383	ville	2,775	1,147
Siloam Springs	2,569	2,405	Selma	3,158	1,750			

TABLE 12.—POPULATION OF CITIES AND OTHER INCORPORATED PLACES HAVING, IN 1920, 2,500 INHABITANTS OR MORE, ARRANGED IN GROUPS ACCORDING TO POPULATION: 1920 AND 1910—Continued.

GROUP 4.—CITIES AND OTHER INCORPORATED PLACES OF 2,500 TO 5,000 (1,320 places)—Continued.

CITY, TOWN, VILLAGE, OR BOROUGH.	1920	1910	CITY, TOWN, VILLAGE, OR BOROUGH.	1920	1910	CITY, TOWN, VILLAGE, OR BOROUGH.	1920	1910
GEORGIA.			**ILLINOIS—con.**			**INDIANA—con.**		
Bainbridge	4,792	4,217	Geneva	2,803	2,451	Hobart	3,450	1,753
Barnesville	3,059	3,068	Georgetown	3,061	2,307	Huntingburg	3,261	2,464
Buford	2,500	1,683	Gillespie	4,063	2,241	Jasonville	4,461	3,295
Canton	2,679	2,002	Glen Ellyn	2,851	1,763	Jasper	2,539	2,196
Carrollton	4,363	3,297	Glencoe	3,381	1,899	Lawrenceburg	3,466	3,930
Cartersville	4,350	4,067	Greenville	3,091	3,178	Martinsville	4,895	4,529
Cedartown	4,053	3,551	Harvard	3,294	3,008	Mitchell	3,025	3,438
College Park	3,622	2,173	Havana	3,614	3,525	Monticello	2,536	2,168
Covington	3,203	2,697	Highland	2,902	2,675	Nappanee	2,678	2,260
Cuthbert	3,022	3,210	Hinsdale	4,042	2,451	Noblesville	4,758	5,073
Dawson	3,504	3,827	Jerseyville	3,839	4,113	North Manchester	2,711	2,428
Douglas	3,401	3,550	Lake Forest	3,657	3,349	North Vernon	3,084	2,915
Eastman	2,707	2,355	Lockport	2,684	2,555	Plymouth	4,338	3,838
Eatonton	2,519	2,036	Lyons	2,564	1,483	Rensselaer	2,912	2,393
Fort Valley	3,223	2,697	Madison	4,996	5,046	Rochester	3,720	3,364
Hawkinsville	3,070	3,420	Marseilles	3,391	3,291	Rockport	2,581	2,736
Kirkwood	2,934	1,226	Mendota	3,934	3,806	Salem	2,836	2,283
Manchester	2,776	922	Morris	4,505	4,563	Sullivan	4,489	4,115
Milledgeville	4,619	4,385	Morrison	3,000	2,410	Tell City	4,086	3,369
Monroe	3,211	3,029	Mound City	2,756	2,837	Tipton	4,507	4,075
Pelham	2,640	1,880	Mounds	2,661	1,686	Union City	[1] 3,406	3,209
Porterdale	2,880	......	Mount Olive	3,503	3,501	West Lafayette	3,830	3,867
Quitman	4,393	3,915	Naperville	3,830	3,449	West Terre Haute	4,310	3,083
Sandersville	2,695	2,641	Nokomis	3,405	1,872	Winchester	4,021	4,266
Statesboro	3,807	2,529	Oglesby	4,135	3,104	**IOWA.**		
Tallapoosa	2,719	2,117	Olney	4,491	5,011	Algona	3,724	2,908
Thomaston	2,502	1,645	Park Ridge	3,383	2,009	Anamosa	2,881	2,983
Tifton	3,005	2,381	Paxton	3,033	2,912	Belle Plaine	3,887	3,121
Toccoa	3,567	3,120	Pinckneyville	2,649	2,722	Carroll	4,254	3,546
Vidalia	2,860	1,776	Princeton	4,126	4,131	Clarinda	4,511	3,832
Washington	4,208	3,065	River Forest	4,358	2,456	Clarion	2,826	2,065
Waynesboro	3,311	2,729	Riverside	2,532	1,702	Clear Lake	2,804	2,014
Winder	3,335	2,443	Robinson	3,375	3,863	Colfax	2,504	2,524
IDAHO.			Rochelle	3,310	2,732	Cresco	3,195	2,658
Blackfoot	3,937	2,202	Rock Falls	2,927	2,657	Decorah	4,039	3,592
Kellogg	3,017	1,273	Roodhouse	2,928	2,171	Denison	3,581	3,133
Malad	2,598	1,303	St. Charles	4,099	4,046	Eagle Grove	4,433	3,387
Montpelier	2,984	1,924	Salem	3,457	2,669	Eldora	3,189	1,995
Moscow	3,956	3,670	Sesser	2,841	1,292	Emmetsburg	2,762	2,325
Preston	3,235	2,110	Shelbyville	3,568	3,590	Estherville	4,699	3,404
Rexburg	3,569	1,893	Silvis	2,541	1,163	Glenwood	3,862	4,052
St. Anthony	2,957	1,238	Sparta	3,340	3,081	Hampton	2,992	2,617
Sandpoint	2,876	2,993	Sullivan	2,532	2,621	Harlan	2,831	2,570
Wallace	2,816	3,000	Summit	4,019	949	Independence	3,672	3,517
Weiser	3,154	2,600	Sycamore	3,602	3,926	Indianola	3,628	3,283
ILLINOIS.			Toluca	2,503	2,407	Iowa Falls	3,954	2,797
Abington	2,721	2,464	Tuscola	2,564	2,453	Jefferson	3,416	2,477
Anna	3,019	2,809	Vandalia	3,316	2,974	Knoxville	3,523	3,190
Auburn	2,660	1,814	Venice	3,895	3,718	Le Mars	4,683	4,157
Averyville	3,815	2,668	Virden	4,682	4,000	Manchester	3,111	2,758
Batavia	4,395	4,436	Watseka	2,817	2,476	Maquoketa	3,626	3,570
Benld	3,316	1,912	West Chicago	2,594	2,378	Marion	4,138	4,400
Brookfield	3,589	2,186	Westville	4,241	2,607	Missouri Valley	3,985	3,187
Bushnell	2,716	2,619	Wheaton	4,137	3,423	Mount Pleasant	3,987	3,874
Carmi	2,667	2,833	White Hall	2,954	2,854	Mystic	2,796	2,663
Carterville	3,404	2,971	Wood River	3,476	84	Nevada	2,668	2,138
Chester	2,904	2,747	**INDIANA.**			New Hampton	2,539	2,275
Christopher	3,830	1,825	Alexandria	4,172	5,096	Osage	2,878	2,445
Des Plaines	3,451	2,348	Angola	2,650	2,610	Osceola	2,684	2,416
Downers Grove	3,543	2,601	Attica	3,392	3,335	Pella	3,338	3,021
Effingham	4,024	3,898	Auburn	4,650	3,919	Sac City	2,630	2,201
Elmhurst	4,594	2,360	Aurora	4,299	4,410	Sheldon	3,488	2,941
Fairbury	2,532	2,505	Boonville	4,451	3,934	Spencer	4,599	3,005
Fairfield	2,754	2,479	Columbia City	3,499	3,448	Storm Lake	3,658	2,428
Farmington	2,631	2,421	Crown Point	3,232	2,526	Tama	2,601	2,290
Flora	3,558	2,704	Decatur	4,762	4,471	Valley Junction	3,631	2,573
Frankfort Heights	3,423	......	Dunkirk	2,532	3,031	Vinton	3,381	3,336
Galena	4,742	4,835	Franklin	4,909	4,502	Washington	4,697	4,380
Galva	2,974	2,498	Garrett	4,796	4,149	Waverly	3,352	3,205
Geneseo	3,375	3,199	Gas City	2,870	3,224	Winterset	2,906	2,818
			Greencastle	3,780	3,790			
			Greenfield	4,168	4,448			

[1] Union City, Ind., and Union City, Ohio, based upon combined population (4,940 in 1920), included in places of 2,500 to 5,000.

TABLE 12.—POPULATION OF CITIES AND OTHER INCORPORATED PLACES HAVING, IN 1920, 2,500 INHABITANTS OR MORE, ARRANGED IN GROUPS ACCORDING TO POPULATION: 1920 AND 1910—Continued.

GROUP 4.—CITIES AND OTHER INCORPORATED PLACES OF 2,500 TO 5,000 (1,320 places)—Continued.

CITY, TOWN, VILLAGE, OR BOROUGH.	1920	1910	CITY, TOWN, VILLAGE, OR BOROUGH.	1920	1910	CITY, TOWN, VILLAGE, OR BOROUGH.	1920	1910
KANSAS.			**LOUISIANA—con.**			**MASSACHUSETTS—con.**		
Abilene........	4,895	4,118	Homer.........	3,305	1,855	Medfield town.	3,595	3,466
Anthony.......	2,740	2,669	Jeanerette....	2,512	2,206	Medway town.	2,956	2,696
Augusta........	4,219	1,235	Jennings......	3,824	3,925	Monson town...	4,826	4,758
Baxter Springs.	3,608	1,598	Kentwood....	3,059	3,609	Nantucket town	2,797	2,962
Beloit..........	3,315	3,082	Leesville.....	2,518	2,043	North Brookfield town....	2,610	3,075
Caney..........	3,427	3,597	Mansfield....	2,564	1,799	Oxford town...	3,820	3,361
Cherryvale.....	4,698	4,304	Merryville....	2,963	......	Provincetown town..........	4,246	4,369
Clay Center....	3,715	3,438	Natchitoches..	3,388	2,532	Randolph town	4,756	4,301
Columbus......	3,155	3,064	Oakdale......	4,016	......	Rockport town.	3,878	4,211
Concordia......	4,705	4,415	Opelousas....	4,437	4,623	Scituate town.	2,534	2,482
Council Grove..	2,857	2,545	Patterson.....	2,538	2,998	Seekonk town..	2,898	2,397
Eureka........	2,606	2,333	Plaquemine...	4,632	4,955	Shrewsbury town..........	3,708	1,946
Fredonia.......	3,954	3,040	Rayne........	2,720	2,247	Somerset town.	3,520	2,798
Frontenac.....	3,225	3,396	Ruston.......	3,389	3,377	Sutton town...	2,578	3,078
Galena........	4,712	6,096	Slidell.......	2,958	2,188	Templeton town	4,019	3,756
Garden City...	3,848	3,171	Thibodaux....	3,526	3,824	Tewksbury town..........	4,450	3,750
Girard........	3,161	2,446	Winnfield.....	2,975	2,925	Wareham town.	4,415	4,102
Goodland......	2,664	1,993	**MAINE.**			Warren town...	3,467	4,188
Great Bend....	4,460	4,622	Eastport......	4,494	4,961	West Bridgewater town.	2,908	2,231
Hays..........	3,165	1,961	Ellsworth.....	3,058	3,549	Westford town.	3,170	2,851
Herington.....	4,065	3,273	Fairfield.....	2,747	2,801	Westport town.	3,115	2,928
Hiawatha......	3,222	2,974	Hallowell.....	2,764	2,864	Wilbraham town..........	2,780	2,332
Holton........	2,703	2,842	Madison......	2,729	2,408	Williamstown town..........	3,707	3,708
Horton........	4,009	3,600	Presque Isle...	3,452	2,938	Wilmington town..........	2,581	1,858
Humboldt.....	2,525	2,548	**MARYLAND.**			Wrentham town..........	2,808	1,743
Larned........	3,139	2,911	Brunswick....	3,905	3,721			
Liberal........	3,613	1,716	Chestertown..	2,537	2,735	**MICHIGAN.**		
Lyons.........	2,516	2,071	Crisfield.....	4,116	3,468	Allegan........	3,637	3,419
McPherson....	4,595	3,546	Easton.......	3,442	3,083	Belding........	3,911	4,119
Marysville....	3,048	2,260	Elkton.......	2,660	2,487	Big Rapids....	4,558	4,519
Mulberry.....	2,697	997	Havre de Grace.	4,377	4,212	Birmingham...	3,694	1,607
Neodesha.....	3,943	2,872	Hyattsville...	2,675	1,917	Boyne City....	4,284	5,218
Olathe........	3,268	3,272	Takoma Park..	3,168	1,242	Buchanan.....	3,187	1,831
Osawatomie...	4,772	4,046	Westernport..	3,977	2,702	Caro..........	2,704	2,272
Paola.........	3,238	3,207	Westminster..	3,521	3,295	Crystal Falls...	3,394	3,775
						Durand.......	2,672	2,315
KENTUCKY.			**MASSACHUSETTS.**			Ecorse........	4,394	1,063
Catlettsburg....	4,183	3,520	Acushnet town.	3,075	1,692	Fenton........	2,507	2,331
Central City....	3,108	2,545	Auburn town..	3,891	2,420	Ferndale......	2,640	......
Corbin........	3,406	2,589	Ayer town....	3,052	2,797	Ford..........	4,294	1,689
Cynthiana....	3,857	3,603	Barnstable town	4,836	4,676	Gladstone.....	4,953	4,211
Earlington.....	3,652	3,931	Barre town....	3,357	2,957	Grand Ledge..	3,043	2,893
Elizabethtown.	2,530	1,970	Billerica town.	3,646	2,789	Greenville....	4,304	4,045
Franklin......	3,154	3,063	Blackstone town..........	4,299	5,648	Houghton.....	4,466	5,113
Fulton........	3,415	2,575	Bourne town..	2,530	2,474	Howell........	2,951	2,338
Georgetown..	3,903	4,533	Cohasset town.	2,639	2,585	Iron River....	4,295	2,450
Glasgow......	2,559	2,316	Dalton town..	3,752	3,568	Lapeer........	4,723	3,946
Harlan........	2,647	657	Deerfield town.	2,803	2,209	Marine City....	3,731	3,770
Harrodsburg..	3,765	3,147	Dighton town.	2,574	2,235	Marshall......	4,270	4,236
Hazard........	4,348	537	Dudley town..	3,701	4,267	Mount Pleasant	4,819	3,972
Hickman......	2,633	2,736	East Bridgewater town.	3,486	3,363	Norway.......	4,533	4,974
Highland Park.	3,979	1,977	Falmouth town	3,500	3,144	Onaway......	2,789	2,702
Irvine........	2,705	272	Foxborough town..........	4,136	3,863	Otsego........	3,168	2,812
Jenkins.......	4,707	......	Groveland town	2,650	2,253	Plymouth.....	2,857	1,671
Lebanon......	3,239	3,077	Hadley town..	2,784	1,999	Rochester.....	2,549	1,516
Ludlow.......	4,582	4,163	Hanover town.	2,575	2,326	St. Clair......	3,204	2,633
Morganfield...	2,651	2,725	Hardwick town	3,085	3,524	St. Johns.....	3,925	3,154
Mount Sterling.	3,995	3,932	Harvard town.	2,546	1,034	St. Louis......	3,036	1,940
Nicholasville..	2,786	2,935	Hatfield town.	2,651	1,986	South Haven..	3,829	3,577
Oakdale......	3,198	3,013	Holbrook town.	3,161	2,816	Wakefield.....	4,151	714
Pineville.....	2,908	2,161	Holden town..	2,970	2,147	**MINNESOTA.**		
Princeton.....	3,689	3,015	Holliston town.	2,707	2,711	Alexandria....	3,388	3,001
Providence....	4,151	2,084	Hopedale town.	2,777	2,188	Anoka........	4,287	3,972
Russellville....	3,124	3,111	Kingston town.	2,505	2,445	Aurora.......	2,809	1,919
Shelbyville....	3,760	3,412	Lee town......	4,085	4,106	Blue Earth....	2,568	2,319
Somerset.....	4,672	4,491	Leicester town.	3,635	3,237			
LOUISIANA.			Lenox town...	2,691	3,060			
Abbeville.....	3,461	2,907	Longmeadow town..........	2,618	1,084			
Covington....	2,942	2,601						
De Ridder....	3,535	2,100						
Donaldsonville.	3,745	4,090						
Eunice.......	3,272	1,684						
Franklin......	3,504	3,857						
Hammond....	3,855	2,942						

TABLE 12.—POPULATION OF CITIES AND OTHER INCORPORATED PLACES HAVING, IN 1920, 2,500 INHABITANTS OR MORF, ARRANGED IN GROUPS ACCORDING TO POPULATION: 1920 AND 1910—Continued.

GROUP 4.—CITIES AND OTHER INCORPORATED PLACES OF 2,500 TO 5,000 (1,320 places)—Continued.

CITY, TOWN, VILLAGE, OR BOROUGH.	1920	1910	CITY, TOWN, VILLAGE, OR BOROUGH.	1920	1910	CITY, TOWN, VILLAGE, OR BOROUGH.	1920	1910
MINNESOTA—con.			MISSOURI—con.			NEW JERSEY—con.		
Columbia Hts..	2,968	590	Maryville	4,711	4,762	Freehold	4,768	3,233
Crosby	3,500	......	Monett	4,206	4,177	Glen Ridge	4,620	3,260
Detroit	3,426	2,807	Neosho	3,968	3,661	Hackettstown	2,936	2,715
Ely	4,902	3,572	Richmond	4,409	3,664	Haddon Heights	2,950	1,452
Fairmont	4,630	2,958	Sikeston	3,613	3,327	Haledon	3,435	2,560
Gilbert	3,510	1,700	Slater	3,797	3,238	Hasbrouck Heights	2,895	2,155
Grand Rapids..	2,914	2,230	Warrensburg	4,811	4,689	Highland Park	4,866	1,517
Hastings	4,571	3,983	Washington	3,132	3,670	Hightstown	2,674	1,879
Hutchinson	3,379	2,368	West Plains	3,178	2,914	Keyport	4,415	3,554
International Falls	3,448	1,487				Lambertvijle	4,660	4,657
Lake City	2,846	3,142	MONTANA.			Leonia	2,979	1,486
Litchfield	2,790	2,333	Deer Lodge	3,780	2,570	Little Ferry	2,715	2,541
Luverne	2,782	2,540	Dillon	2,701	1,835	Merchantville	2,749	1,996
Marshall	3,092	2,152	Glendive	3,816	2,428	Metuchen	3,334	2,138
Melrose	2,529	2,591	Red Lodge	4,515	4,860	Milltown	2,573	1,584
Montevideo	4,419	3,056	Whitefish	2,867	1,479	Newton	4,125	4,467
Northfield	4,023	3,265				Ocean City	2,512	1,950
Pipestone	3,325	2,475	NEBRASKA.			Palisades Park	2,633	1,411
St. James	2,673	2,102	Alliance	4,591	3,105	Paulsboro	4,352	2,121
St. Peter	4,335	4,176	Auburn	2,863	2,729	Pitman	3,385	1,950
Sauk Center	2,699	2,154	Aurora	2,962	2,630	Prospect Park	4,292	2,719
Staples	2,570	2,558	Blair	2,702	2,584	Raritan	4,457	3,672
Thief River Falls	4,685	3,714	Broken Bow	2,567	2,260	Rockaway	2,655	1,902
Two Harbors..	4,546	4,990	Chadron	4,412	2,687	Tenafly	3,585	2,756
Waseca	3,908	3,054	Falls City	4,930	3,255	Verona	3,039	1,675
West Minneapolis	3,055	3,022	Gering	2,508	627	Wanaque	2,916	......
West St. Paul.	2,962	2,660	Havelock	3,602	2,680	Washington	3,341	3,567
Worthington	3,481	2,385	Holdrege	3,108	3,030	Westwood	2,597	1,870
			McCook	4,303	3,765	Wharton	2,877	2,983
MISSISSIPPI.			Plattsmouth	4,190	4,287	Wildwood	2,790	898
Aberdeen	4,071	3,708	Schuyler	2,636	2,152			
Amory	2,861	2,122	Sidney	2,852	1,185	NEW MEXICO.		
Bay St. Louis.	3,033	3,388	Superior	2,719	2,106	Clovis	4,904	3,255
Brookhaven	4,706	5,293	University Pl.	4,112	3,200	Deming	3,212	1,864
Canton	3,252	3,929	Wymore	2,592	2,613	Gallup	3,920	2,204
Charleston	3,007	1,834				Las Cruces	3,969	3,836
Columbia	2,826	2,029	NEVADA.			Las Vegas (East Las Vegas P.O.)	4,304	3,755
Grenada	3,402	2,814	Sparks	3,238	2,500	Las Vegas	3,902	3,179
Moss Point	3,340	3,054				Silver City	2,662	3,217
New Albany	2,531	2,032	NEW HAMPSHIRE.			Tucumcari	3,117	2,526
Oklona	3,852	2,584	Conway town	3,102	3,413			
Starkville	2,596	2,698	Exeter town	4,604	4,897	NEW YORK.		
Water Valley	4,315	4,275	Gorham town	2,734	2,155	Albion	4,683	5,016
West Point	4,400	4,864	Haverhill town	3,406	3,498	Amityville	3,265	2,517
Winona	2,572	2,512	Lancaster town	2,819	3,054	Avon	2,585	2,053
			Littleton town	4,239	4,069	Babylon	2,523	2,600
MISSOURI.			Milford town	3,783	3,939	Baldwinsville..	3,685	3,099
Aurora	3,575	4,148	Newmarket town	3,181	3,348	Ballston Spa	4,103	4,138
Bonne Terre	3,815	......	Newport town .	4,109	3,765	Bath	4,795	3,884
Boonville	4,665	4,252	Northumberland town	2,567	2,184	Brockport	2,980	3,579
Butler	2,702	2,894	Pembroke town	2,563	3,062	Bronxville	3,055	1,863
Cameron	3,248	2,980	Peterboro town	2,615	2,277	Canastota	3,995	3,247
Carrollton	3,218	3,452	Walpole town	2,553	2,668	Canton	2,631	2,701
Caruthersville..	4,750	3,655				Carthage	4,320	3,563
Chaffee	3,035	2,082	NEW JERSEY.			Catskill	4,728	5,296
Charleston	3,410	3,144	Audubon	4,740	1,343	Cedarhurst	2,838	......
Clayton	3,028	......	Bergenfield	3,667	1,991	Chatham	2,710	2,251
Dexter	2,635	2,322	Beverly	2,562	2,140	Clyde	2,528	2,695
Eldon	2,636	1,999	Bogota	3,906	1,125	Cooperstown	2,725	2,484
Excelsior Spgs.	4,165	3,900	Bordentown	4,371	4,250	Corinth	2,576	2,166
Farmington	2,685	2,613	Butler	2,886	2,265	Dannemora	2,623	1,146
Festus	3,348	2,556	Caldwell	3,993	2,236	Dansville	4,631	3,938
Fredricktown	3,124	2,632	Cape May	2,999	2,471	Dobbs Ferry	4,401	3,455
Higginsville	2,724	2,628	Carlstadt	4,472	3,807	Dolgeville	3,448	2,685
Kennett	3,622	3,033	Dumont	2,537	1,783	East Aurora	3,703	2,781
Kirkwood	4,422	4,171	Dunellen	3,394	1,990	East Rochester	3,901	2,398
Lebanon	2,848	2,430	East Newark	3,057	3,163	East Syracuse..	4,106	3,274
Lexington	4,695	5,242	Edgewater	3,530	2,655	Ellenville	3,116	3,114
Liberty	3,097	2,980	Egg Harbor	2,622	2,181	Elmira Heights.	4,188	2,732
Louisiana	4,060	4,454	Fairview	4,882	2,441	Fairport	4,626	3,112
Macon	3,549	3,584	Flemington	2,590	2,693			
Marceline	3,760	3,920	Franklin	4,075	......			

TABLE 12.—POPULATION OF CITIES AND OTHER INCORPORATED PLACES HAVING, IN 1920, 2,500 INHABITANTS OR MORE, ARRANGED IN GROUPS ACCORDING TO POPULATION: 1920 AND 1910—Continued.

GROUP 4.—CITIES AND OTHER INCORPORATED PLACES OF 2,500 TO 5,000 (1,320 places)—Continued.

CITY, TOWN, VILLAGE, OR BOROUGH.	1920	1910	CITY, TOWN, VILLAGE, OR BOROUGH.	1920	1910	CITY, TOWN, VILLAGE, OR BOROUGH.	1920	1910
NEW YORK—con.			NORTH CARO-LINA—con.			OHIO—con.		
Falconer	2,742	2,141				Upper		
Fort Edward	3,871	3,762	Morganton	2,867	2,712	Sandusky	3,708	3,779
Fort Plain	2,747	2,762	Mount Airy	4,752	3,844	Wadsworth	4,742	3,073
Frankfort	4,198	3,303	Newton	3,021	2,316	Wauseon	3,035	2,650
Goshen	2,843	3,081	Oxford	3,606	3,018	Willard	3,889	2,950
Gouverneur	4,143	4,128	Roanoke Rapids	3,369	1,670	Willoughby	2,656	2,072
Gowanda	2,673	2,012	Rockingham	2,509	2,155			
Granville	3,024	3,920	Sanford	2,977	2,282	OKLAHOMA.		
Green Island	4,411	4,737	Shelby	3,609	3,127	Altus	4,522	4,821
Greenport	3,122	3,089	Spencer	2,510	1,915	Alva	3,913	3,688
Hamburg	3,185	2,134	Tarboro	4,568	4,129	Anadarko	3,116	3,439
Highland Falls	2,588	2,470	Wadesboro	2,648	2,376	Bristow	3,460	1,667
Hoosick Falls	4,896	5,532				Cardin	2,640	
Irvington	2,701	2,319	NORTH DAKOTA.			Claremore	3,435	2,866
Kenmore	3,160	1,020	Dickinson	4,122	3,678	Cleveland	2,717	1,310
La Salle	3,813	1,299	Grafton	2,512	2,229	Clinton	2,596	2,781
Lawrence	2,861	1,189	Mandan	4,336	3,873	Coalgate	3,009	3,255
Leroy	4,203	3,771	Valley City	4,686	4,606	Collinsville	3,801	1,324
Lowville	3,127	2,940	Wahpeton	3,069	2,467	Commerce	2,555	
Lynbrook	4,371		Williston	4,178	3,124	Duncan	3,463	2,477
Lyons	4,253	4,460				Elk City	2,814	3,165
Mineola	3,016	1,981	OHIO.			Frederick	3,822	3,027
Mohawk	2,919	2,079	Barnesville	4,865	4,233	Hartshorne	3,480	2,963
Mount Kisco	3,944	2,802	Bedford	2,677	1,783	Hobart	2,936	3,845
Mount Morris	3,312	2,782	Berea	2,959	2,609	Holdenville	2,932	2,296
Nyack	4,444	4,619	Bridgeport	3,977	3,974	Hominy	2,875	760
Owego	4,147	4,633	Bryan	4,252	3,641	Idabel	3,067	1,493
Patchogue	4,031	3,824	Byesville	2,775	3,156	Madill	2,717	1,564
Penn Yan	4,517	4,597	Celina	4,226	3,493	Mangum	3,405	3,667
Perry	4,717	4,388	Cheviot	4,108	1,930	Newkirk	2,533	1,992
Pleasantville	3,590	2,207	Clyde	3,099	2,815	Nowata	4,435	3,672
Potsdam	4,039	4,036	Crestline	4,313	3,807	Pauls Valley	3,694	2,689
Sag Harbor	2,993	3,408	Crooksville	3,311	3,028	Perry	3,154	3,133
Saugerties	4,013	3,929	Eaton	3,210	3,187	Poteau	2,679	1,830
Scarsdale	3,506		Elmwood Place	3,991	3,423	Purcell	2,938	2,740
Scotia	4,358	2,957	Euclid	3,363	1,953	Sand Springs	4,076	
Sidney	2,670	2,507	Fairport Harbor	4,211	2,263	Stillwater	4,701	3,444
Silver Creek	3,260	2,512	Franklin	3,071	2,659	Sulphur	3,667	3,684
Southampton	2,891	2,509	Garfield Heights	2,550		Wagoner	3,436	4,018
Spring Valley	3,818	2,353	Geneva	3,081	2,496	Walters	3,032	1,377
Suffern	3,154	2,663	Glouster	3,140	2,527	Waurika	3,204	2,928
Tuckahoe	3,509	2,722	Greenfield	4,344	4,228	Woodward	3,849	2,696
Tupper Lake	2,508	3,067	Hillsboro	4,356	4,296	Wynona	2,749	
Union	3,303	1,544	Hubbard	3,320	1,699	Yale	2,601	685
Walton	3,598	3,103	Lebanon	3,396	2,698			
Wappingers Falls	3,235	3,195	Leetonia	2,688	2,665	OREGON.		
Warsaw	3,622	3,206	Lisbon	3,113	3,084	Albany	4,840	4,275
Waterford	2,637	3,245	Lockland	4,007	3,439	Ashland	4,283	5,020
Waterloo	3,809	3,931	London	4,080	3,530	Dallas	2,701	2,124
Watkins	2,785	2,817	Marysville	3,635	3,576	Grants Pass	3,151	3,897
Wellsville	4,996	4,382	Maumee	3,195	2,307	Hood River	3,195	2,331
Westfield	3,413	2,985	Medina	3,430	2,734	Klamath Falls	4,801	2,758
Whitesboro	3,038	2,375	Miamisburg	4,383	4,271	McMinnville	2,767	2,400
			Middleport	3,772	3,194	Marshfield	4,034	2,980
NORTH CAROLINA.			Mingo Junction	4,616	4,049	Newburg	2,566	2,260
Albemarle	2,691	2,116	Montpelier	3,052	2,759	North Bend	3,268	2,078
Asheboro	2,559	1,865	Napoleon	4,143	4,007	Roseberg	4,381	4,738
Beaufort	2,968	2,483	New Boston	4,817	1,858			
Belmont	2,941	1,176	New Comers-town	3,389	2,943	PENNSYLVANIA.		
Canton	2,584	1,393	New Lexington	3,157	2,559	Aliquippa	2,931	1,743
Dunn	2,805	1,823	Newburgh Heights	2,957	940	Ambler	3,094	2,649
Edenton	2,777	2,789	Oberlin	4,236	4,365	Apollo	3,227	3,006
Hamlet	3,808	2,173	Orrville	4,107	3,101	Aspinwall	3,170	2,592
Hendersonville	3,720	2,818	Pomeroy	4,294	4,023	Athens	4,384	3,796
Kings Mountain	2,800	2,218	Port Clinton	3,928	3,007	Avoca	4,950	4,634
Laurinburg	2,643	2,322	Reading	4,540	3,985	Barnesboro	4,183	3,535
Lenoir	3,718	3,364	Salineville	2,700	2,403	Beaver	4,135	3,456
Lincolnton	3,390	2,413	Sebring	3,541	2,104	Bellefonte	3,996	4,145
Lumberton	2,691	2,230	Shadyside	3,084		Bellwood	2,629	2,277
Monroe	4,084	4,082	Toronto	4,684	4,271	Bentleyville	3,679	1,922
Mooresville	4,315	3,400	Union City	[1]1,534	1,595	Birdsboro	3,299	2,930
Morehead City	2,958	2,039				Blairsville	4,391	3,572
						Boyertown	3,189	2,433

[1] Union City, Ind., and Union City, Ohio, based upon combined population (4,940 in 1920), included in places of 2,500 to 5,000.

TABLE 12.—POPULATION OF CITIES AND OTHER INCORPORATED PLACES HAVING, IN 1920, 2,500 INHABITANTS OR MORE, ARRANGED IN GROUPS ACCORDING TO POPULATION: 1920 AND 1910—Continued.

GROUP 4.—CITIES AND OTHER INCORPORATED PLACES OF 2,500 TO 5,000 (1,320 places)—Continued.

CITY, TOWN, VILLAGE, OR BOROUGH.	1920	1910	CITY, TOWN, VILLAGE, OR BOROUGH.	1920	1910	CITY, TOWN, VILLAGE, OR BOROUGH.	1920	1910
PENNSYLVANIA —continued.			PENNSYLVANIA —continued.			RHODE ISLAND—con.		
Brackenridge...	4,987	3,134	Moosic..........	4,364	3,964	North Kingstown town...	3,397	4,048
Bridgeport.....	4,680	3,860	Morrisville.....	3,639	2,002	North Smithfield town....	3,200	2,699
Bridgeville....	3,092	1,983	Mount Union....	4,744	3,338	Portsmouth town........	2,590	2,681
Brookville.....	3,272	3,003	Narberth.......	3,704	1,790	Scituate town...	3,006	3,493
Brownsville....	2,502	2,324	Nazareth.......	4,288	3,978	Smithfield town	3,199	2,739
Burnham........	2,765	......	New Philadelphia..........	2,537	2,512	Tiverton town..	3,894	4,032
Catasauqua.....	4,714	5,250	North Bellevernon...	2,605	1,522	SOUTH CAROLINA.		
Centerville....	4,793	1,413	North East.....	3,481	2,672	Abbeville.......	4,570	4,459
Clarion........	2,793	2,612	Northampton Heights........	3,791	1,037	Aiken..........	4,103	3,911
Clifton Heights.	3,469	3,155	Northumberland.	4,061	3,517	Batesburg......	2,848	1,995
Clymer.........	2,867	1,753	Oakmont........	4,512	3,436	Beaufort.......	2,831	2,486
College Hill...	2,643	1,787	Osceola........	2,512	2,437	Bennettsville..	3,197	2,646
Collingdale (Darby P.O.).	3,834	1,361	Palmyra........	3,646	......	Camden.........	3,930	3,569
Coplay.........	2,845	2,670	Parkesburg.....	2,543	2,522	Cheraw.........	3,150	2,873
Coudersport....	2,836	3,100	Parnassus......	3,816	2,578	Clinton........	3,767	3,272
Curwensville...	2,973	2,549	Patton.........	3,628	3,907	Darlington.....	4,669	3,789
Dale...........	3,115	2,285	Pen Argyl......	4,096	3,967	Easley.........	3,568	2,983
Derry..........	2,889	2,954	Perkasie.......	3,150	2,779	Eau Claire.....	2,566	1,234
Dowingtown.....	4,024	3,326	Philipsburg....	3,900	3,585	Georgetown.....	4,579	5,530
Doylestown.....	3,837	3,304	Polk...........	2,662	2,066	Hartsville.....	3,624	2,365
Dupont.........	4,576	......	Port Carbon....	2,882	2,678	Lancaster......	3,032	2,098
East Mauch Chunk........	3,868	3,548	Port Vue.......	2,538	1,978	Laurens........	4,629	4,818
East Stroudsburg.......	4,855	3,330	Portage........	4,804	2,954	Marion.........	3,892	3,844
Eddystone......	2,670	1,167	Prospect Park..	2,536	1,655	Summerville....	2,550	2,355
Edgewood.......	3,181	2,596	Quakertown.....	4,391	3,801	Yorkville......	2,731	2,326
Elizabeth......	2,703	2,311	Red Lion.......	4,198	2,092	SOUTH DAKOTA.		
Elizabethtown..	3,319	2,587	Reynoldsville..	4,116	3,189	Brookings......	3,924	2,971
Ellsworth......	2,828	2,084	Royersford.....	3,278	3,073	Madison........	4,144	3,137
Emaus..........	4,370	3,501	Sewickley......	4,955	4,479	Mobridge.......	3,517	1,200
Emporium.......	3,036	2,916	Sharpsville....	4,674	3,634	Pierre.........	3,209	3,656
Ephrata........	3,735	3,192	Shippensburg...	4,372	3,457	Redfield.......	2,755	2,856
Exeter.........	4,176	3,537	Slatington.....	4,014	4,454	Vermilion......	2,590	2,187
Export.........	2,596	......	Somerset.......	3,121	2,612	TENNESSEE.		
Forty Fort.....	3,389	2,353	Souderton......	3,125	1,875	Alcoa..........	3,358	......
Franklin (Conemaugh P.O.)..	2,632	2,102	South Allentown.....	2,549	1,814	Alton Park.....	3,020	......
Freedom........	3,452	3,060	South Brownsville..	4,675	3,943	Athens.........	2,580	2,264
Freeport.......	2,696	2,248	South Fork.....	4,239	4,592	Brownsville....	3,062	2,882
Galeton........	2,969	4,027	South Williamsport.	4,341	3,734	Covington......	3,410	2,990
Gallitzin......	3,586	3,504	Southwest Greensburg..	2,538	2,127	E. Chattanooga.	4,720	......
Gettysburg.....	4,439	4,030	Spangler.......	3,035	2,700	Elizabethton...	2,749	2,478
Gilberton......	4,766	5,401	Spring City....	2,944	2,880	Erwin..........	2,965	1,149
Girardville....	4,482	4,396	Springdale.....	2,929	1,999	Etowah.........	2,516	1,685
Grove City.....	4,944	3,674	Sugar Notch....	2,612	2,439	Fayetteville...	3,629	3,439
Hamburg........	2,764	2,301	Susquehanna Depot.	3,764	3,478	Franklin.......	3,123	2,924
Hellertown.....	3,008	915	Sykesville.....	2,507	1,756	Gallatin.......	2,757	2,399
Hollidaysburg..	4,071	3,734	Towanda........	4,269	4,281	Greeneville....	3,775	1,920
Honesdale......	2,756	2,945	Trafford.......	2,859	1,959	Harriman.......	4,019	3,061
Hummelstown....	2,654	2,128	Union City.....	3,850	3,684	Humboldt.......	3,913	3,446
Ingram.........	2,900	2,037	Verona.........	2,938	2,849	La Follette....	3,056	2,816
Irwin..........	3,235	2,886	Waynesburg.....	3,332	3,545	Lebanon........	4,084	3,659
Jenkintown.....	3,366	2,968	Wellsboro......	3,452	3,183	Lenoir City....	4,210	3,392
Jermyn.........	3,326	3,158	West Homestead.	3,435	3,009	Lewisburg......	2,711	1,830
Kulpmont.......	4,695	......	West Newton....	2,645	2,880	McMinnville....	2,814	2,299
Kutztown.......	2,684	2,360	West Reading...	2,921	2,064	Martin.........	2,837	2,228
Lansdale.......	4,728	3,551	West York......	3,320	2,435	Maryville......	3,739	2,381
Landsdowne.....	4,797	4,066	Westview.......	2,797	1,626	Newport........	2,753	2,003
Leechburg......	3,991	3,624	Williamstown...	2,878	2,904	Paris..........	4,730	3,881
Lewisburg......	3,204	3,081	Wilson.........	3,243	1,108	Pulaski........	2,780	2,928
Lititz.........	3,680	2,082	Wyoming........	3,582	3,010	Rockwood.......	4,652	3,660
Lykens.........	2,880	2,943	RHODE ISLAND.			St. Elmo.......	3,890	2,426
McAdoo.........	4,674	3,389	Barrington town........	3,897	2,452	Shelbyville....	2,912	2,869
McDonald.......	2,751	2,543	East Greenwich town.....	3,290	3,420	Springfield....	3,860	2,085
Manheim........	2,712	2,202				Tracy City.....	2,669	......
Mauch Chunk....	3,666	3,952				Trenton........	2,751	2,402
Mayfield.......	3,832	3,662				Tullahoma.....	3,479	3,049
Mechanicsburg..	4,688	4,469				Union City.....	4,412	4,389
Media..........	4,109	3,562						
Meyersdale.....	3,716	3,741						
Millersburg....	2,936	2,394						
Miners Mills...	4,365	3,159						
Monaca.........	3,838	3,376						

TABLE 12.—POPULATION OF CITIES AND OTHER INCORPORATED PLACES HAVING, IN 1920, 2,500 INHABITANTS OR MORE, ARRANGED IN GROUPS ACCORDING TO POPULATION: 1920 AND 1910—Continued.

GROUP 4.—CITIES AND OTHER INCORPORATED PLACES OF 2,500 TO 5,000 (1,320 places)—Continued.

CITY, TOWN, VILLAGE, OR BOROUGH.	1920	1910
TEXAS.		
Arlington	3,031	1,794
Athens	3,176	2,261
Ballinger	2,767	3,536
Bay City	3,454	3,156
Beeville	3,063	3,269
Big Spring	4,273	4,102
Bowie	3,179	2,874
Cameron	4,298	3,263
Clarksville	3,386	2,065
Coleman	2,868	3,046
Comanche	3,524	2,756
Commerce	3,842	2,818
Cooper	2,563	1,513
Crockett	3,061	3,947
Cuero	3,671	3,109
Dalhart	2,676	2,580
De Leon	3,302	1,015
Desdemona	3,008	....
Dublin	3,229	2,551
Electra	4,744	640
Georgetown	2,871	3,096
Gonzales	3,128	3,139
Gorman	3,200	963
Graham	2,544	1,569
Hearne	2,741	2,352
Henrietta	2,563	2,104
Honey Grove	2,642	2,300
Huntsville	4,689	2,072
Jacksonville	3,723	2,875
Jefferson	2,549	2,515
Kaufman	2,501	1,959
Kingsville	4,770	....
Lockhart	3,731	2,945
Lubbock	4,051	1,938
Lufkin	4,878	2,749
Magnolia Park	4,080	....
Marfa	3,553	....
Marlin	4,310	3,870
Mart	3,105	2,939
Memphis	2,839	1,936
Mercedes	3,414	1,209
Mexia	3,482	2,694
Mission	3,847	....
Mount Pleasant	4,099	3,137
Nacogdoches	3,546	3,369
New Braunfels	3,590	3,165
Pittsburg	2,540	1,916
Plainview	3,989	2,829
Polytechnic	4,338	....
Quanah	3,691	3,127
San Marcos	4,527	4,071
Seguin	3,631	3,116
Smithville	3,204	3,167
Sour Lake	3,032	....
Stamford	3,704	3,902
Stephenville	3,891	2,561
Sweetwater	4,307	4,176
Teague	3,306	3,288
Texas City	2,500	....
Uvalde	3,885	3,998
UTAH.		
American Fork	2,763	2,797
Bingham Canyon	2,676	2,881

CITY, TOWN, VILLAGE, OR BOROUGH.	1920	1910
UTAH—con.		
Eureka	3,608	3,416
Lehi	3,078	2,964
Murray	4,584	4,057
Nephi	2,603	2,759
Park City	3,393	3,439
Payson	3,031	2,397
Richfield	3,262	2,559
Spanish Fork	4,036	3,464
Springville	3,010	3,356
Tooele	3,602	2,753
VERMONT.		
Bellows Falls	4,860	4,883
Newport	4,976	2,548
Proctor	2,692	2,756
Windsor	3,061	1,906
Winooski	4,932	4,520
VIRGINIA.		
Abingdon	2,532	1,757
Bedford	3,243	2,508
Big Stone Gap	3,009	2,590
Buena Vista	3,911	3,245
Cape Charles	2,517	1,948
Farmville	2,586	2,971
Graham	2,752	1,917
Lexington	2,870	2,931
Marion	3,253	2,727
Martinsville	4,075	3,368
Norton	3,068	1,866
Phoebus	3,043	2,394
Pocahontas	2,591	2,452
Radford	4,627	4,202
Salem	4,159	3,849
South Boston	4,338	3,516
Vinton	2,779	1,928
Wytheville	2,947	3,054
WASHINGTON.		
Auburn	3,163	957
Charleston	3,338	1,062
Chehalis	4,558	4,507
Cle Elum	2,661	2,749
Colfax	3,027	2,783
Dayton	2,695	2,389
Ellensburg	3,967	4,209
Hillyard	3,942	3,276
Medical Lake	2,545	1,730
Mount Vernon	3,341	2,381
Pasco	3,362	2,083
Port Townsend	2,847	4,181
Raymond	4,260	2,450
Renton	3,301	2,740
Roslyn	2,673	3,126
Sedro-Woolley	3,389	2,129
Snohomish	2,985	3,244
Toppenish	3,120	1,598
WEST VIRGINIA.		
Beckley	4,149	2,161
Benwood	3,773	4,976
Buckhannon	3,785	2,225
Charles Town	2,527	2,662
Chester	3,283	3,184
Follansbee	3,135	2,031

CITY, TOWN, VILLAGE, OR BOROUGH.	1920	1910
WEST VIRGINIA—con.		
Hinton	3,912	3,656
Logan	2,998	1,640
McMechen	3,356	2,921
Mannington	3,673	2,672
Piedmont	2,835	2,054
Point Pleasant	3,059	2,045
Richwood	4,331	3,061
St. Albans	2,825	1,209
Salem	2,920	2,169
Sistersville	3,238	2,684
South Charleston	3,650	....
Welch	3,232	1,526
Wellsburg	4,918	4,189
WISCONSIN.		
Berlin	4,400	4,636
Burlington	3,626	3,212
Clintonville	3,275	1,747
Delavan	3,016	2,450
Edgerton	2,688	2,513
Fort Atkinson	4,915	3,877
Hartford	4,515	2,982
Hudson	3,014	2,810
Hurley	3,188	....
Jefferson	2,572	2,582
Ladysmith	3,581	2,352
Lake Geneva	2,632	3,079
Mayville	3,011	2,282
Mineral Point	2,569	2,925
Monroe	4,788	4,410
New London	4,667	3,383
North Milwaukee	3,047	1,860
Oconomowoc	3,301	3,054
Oconto	4,920	5,629
Park Falls	2,676	1,972
Platteville	4,353	4,452
Plymouth	3,415	3,094
Port Washington	3,340	3,792
Prairie du Chien	3,537	3,149
Reedsburg	2,997	2,615
Rice Lake	4,457	3,968
Richland Center	3,409	2,652
Ripon	3,929	3,739
Shawano	3,544	2,923
Shorewood	2,650	707
Sparta	4,466	3,973
Stanley	2,577	2,675
Sturgeon Bay	4,553	4,262
Tomah	3,257	3,419
Tomahawk	2,898	2,907
Viroqua	2,574	2,059
Washburn	3,707	3,830
Waupaca	2,839	2,789
Waupun	4,440	3,362
West Bend	3,378	2,462
Whitewater	3,215	3,224
WYOMING.		
Evanston	3,479	2,583
Greybull	2,692	258
Rawlins	3,969	4,256

TABLE 13.—POPULATION OF PRINCIPAL CITIES, TOWNS, AND VILLAGES IN OUTLY-
ING POSSESSIONS: 1920 AND 1910.

[This table shows the population of all cities, towns, or villages having a minimum limit of 1,000 in
Alaska, Hawaii, and Guam and of 2,500 in Porto Rico. American Samoa and the Panama Canal
Zone have no cities, towns, or villages with as many as 1,000 inhabitants. For total population of
each outlying possession, see Table 3.]

ALASKA.

TOWN.	1920	1910	TOWN.	1920	1910
Fairbanks	1,155	3,541	Sitka [1]	1,175	1,039
Juneau	3,058	1,644	Anchorage	1,856	
Ketchikan	2,458	1,613			

[1] Sitka village (population 539 in 1910) and Sitka (native) village (population 500 in 1910) consolidated
and incorporated as a town since 1910.

HAWAII. [1]

CITY.	1920	1910	CITY.	1920	1910
Honolulu district [2]	83,327	52,183	Hilo	10,431	6,745

[1] No other cities and no towns or villages in Hawaii.
[2] Generally considered as Honolulu city.

PORTO RICO.

CITY, TOWN, OR VILLAGE.	1920	1910	CITY, TOWN, OR VILLAGE.	1920	1910
Aguadilla town	8,035	6,135	Lares town	2,693	2,751
Anasco town	2,552	3,064	Manati town [1]	6,147	4,439
Arecibo town	10,039	9,612	Mayaguez town	19,124	16,563
Arroyo town	3,025	3,220	Naguabo tow n	3,691	3,303
Bayamon town	10,411	5,272	Ponce city	41,912	35,005
Cabo Rojo town	4,327	3,847	Rio Piedras town	5,820	3,084
Caguas town	12,149	10,354	Sabana Grande town	2,856	2,636
Carolina town	3,151	3,244	San German town	5,019	4,999
Cataño village	6,602	4,786	San Juan city	71,443	48,716
Cayey town	5,243	4,498	San Lorenzo town	3,662	2,663
Coamo town	4,259	3,869	San Sebastian town	2,611	1,920
Fajardo town	6,571	6,086	Utuado town	3,700	3,208
Guayama town	8,924	8,321	Vega Baja town	3,607	3,082
Gurabo town	2,550	2,230	Vieques town	3,424	3,158
Humacao town	6,183	5,159	Yabucoa town	2,888	2,816
Juncos town	4,263	4,141	Yauco town	7,053	6,589

[1] Part of barrio Bajura Afuero annexed to barrio Pueblo Poniente (comprising part of Manati town)
since 1910.

GUAM.

CITY.	1920
Agana [1]	7,432

[1] Includes population of Anigua (321), Tutujan (56), and Moina (28). No returns for 1910.

TABLE 14.—DISTRIBUTION OF POPULATION IN GROUPS OF CITIES, CLASSIFIED ACCORDING TO SIZE, AND IN RURAL TERRITORY: 1890–1920.

CLASS OF PLACES.	1920	1910	1900	1890
	NUMBER OF PLACES.			
United States:				
Urban territory.............................	[1] 2,787	[1] 2,313	[1] 1,801	[1] 1,417
Places of 1,000,000 or more..............	3	3	3	3
Places of 500,000 to 1,000,000...........	9	5	3	1
Places of 250,000 to 500,000.............	13	11	9	7
Places of 100,000 to 250,000.............	43	31	23	17
Places of 50,000 to 100,000..............	76	59	40	30
Places of 25,000 to 50,000...............	143	119	82	66
Places of 10,000 to 25,000...............	459	367	280	228
Places of 5,000 to 10,000................	721	612	468	339
Places of 2,500 to 5,000.................	1,320	1,106	893	726
Rural territory.............................				
Incorporated places of less than 2,500.......	[2] 12,905	11,832	8,930	[3] 6,490
Other rural territory.......................				
	POPULATION.			
United States......................	105,710,620	91,972,266	75,994,575	62,947,714
Urban territory......................	54,304,603	42,166,120	30,380,433	22,298,359
Places of 1,000,000 or more................	10,145,532	8,501,174	6,429,474	3,662,115
Places of 500,000 to 1,000,000.............	6,223,769	3,010,667	1,645,087	806,343
Places of 250,000 to 500,000..............	4,540,838	3,949,839	2,861,296	2,447,608
Places of 100,000 to 250,000..............	6,519,187	4,840,458	3,272,490	2,781,894
Places of 50,000 to 100,000...............	5,265,747	4,178,915	2,709,338	2,022,822
Places of 25,000 to 50,000................	5,075,041	4,026,045	2,800,627	2,268,786
Places of 10,000 to 25,000................	6,942,742	5,524,434	4,338,250	3,429,247
Places of 5,000 to 10,000.................	4,997,794	4,254,856	3,220,766	2,372,717
Places of 2,500 to 5,000..................	4,593,953	3,879,732	3,103,105	2,506,827
Rural territory......................	51,406,017	49,806,146	45,614,142	40,649,355
Incorporated places of less than 2,500...........	8,969,241	8,169,149	6,301,533	4,757,974
Other rural territory.......................	42,436,776	41,636,997	39,312,609	35,891,381
	PER CENT OF TOTAL POPULATION.			
United States......................	100.0	100.0	100.0	100.0
Urban territory......................	51.4	45.8	40.0	35.4
Places of 1,000,000 or more................	9.6	9.2	8.5	5.8
Places of 500,000 to 1,000,000.............	5.9	3.3	2.2	1.3
Places of 250,000 to 500,000..............	4.3	4.3	3.8	3.9
Places of 100,000 to 250,000..............	6.2	5.3	4.3	4.4
Places of 50,000 to 100,000...............	5.0	4.5	3.6	3.2
Places of 25,000 to 50,000................	4.8	4.4	3.7	3.6
Places of 10,000 to 25,000................	6.6	6.0	5.7	5.4
Places of 5,000 to 10,000.................	4.7	4.6	4.2	3.8
Places of 2,500 to 5,000..................	4.3	4.2	4.1	4.0
Rural territory......................	48.6	54.2	60.0	64.6
Incorporated places of less than 2,500...........	8.5	8.9	8.3	7.6
Other rural territory.......................	40.1	45.3	51.7	57.0

[1] The total number of places of certain classes for the United States as a whole is less than the sum of the numbers shown for the individual states of the country, for the reason that each of three cities lies in two adjoining states, namely, Bristol (Virginia and Tennessee), Texarkana (Arkansas and Texas), and Union City (Indiana and Ohio), and is counted in each state. Moreover, one of those cities, Bristol, lies in two geographic divisions (South Atlantic and East South Central), and is counted in both. Each of these cities consists of two incorporated municipalities, but each is, from the statistical standpoint, one city and should be classed according to its total population. In each case that part of the population living in each state, whatever its number, is credited to the group of cities to which, according to its total population, the city belongs. Classed in this manner, Bristol fell in 1920 and 1910 in the class of cities having 10,000 to 25,000 inhabitants, and in 1900 and 1890 in the 5,000–10,000 class; Texarkana fell, in 1920, 1910, and 1900, in the 10,000–25,000 class, and in 1890 in the 5,000–10,000 class; and Union City fell at each census from 1890 to 1920 in the 2,500–5,000 class.

[2] Includes 48 places not returned separately.

[3] The number of incorporated places can not be exactly determined from the returns of the 1890 census, at which incorporated places were not distinguished from unincorporated ones, and very small places, whether incorporated or not, were not enumerated separately. It has been assumed that those places were incorporated in 1890 which were returned separately in that year and were returned in 1900 as incorporated. (See Reports of the Twelfth Census: 1900, Population, Vol. I, p. lviii.) The figures given for 1890 in this table for incorporated places having fewer than 2,500 inhabitants may, therefore, include the population of some unincorporated places and exclude that of some incorporated places.

Table 15.—URBAN AND RURAL POPULATION, BY DIVISIONS AND STATES: 1920 AND 1910.

DIVISION AND STATE.	POPULATION: 1920			POPULATION: 1910		PER CENT URBAN.	
	Total.	Urban.	Rural.	Urban.	Rural.	1920	1910
United States	105,710,620	54,304,603	51,406,017	42,166,120	49,806,146	51.4	45.8
GEOGRAPHIC DIVISIONS:							
New England........	7,400,909	5,865,073	1,535,836	4,998,082	1,554,599	79.2	76.3
Middle Atlantic......	22,261,144	16,672,595	5,588,549	13,723,373	5,592,519	74.9	71.0
East North Central..	21,475,543	13,049,272	8,426,271	9,617,271	8,633,350	60.8	52.7
West North Central..	12,544,249	4,727,372	7,816,877	3,873,716	7,764,205	37.7	33.3
South Atlantic.......	13,990,272	4,338,792	9,651,480	3,092,153	9,102,742	31.0	25.4
East South Central...	8,893,307	1,994,207	6,899,100	1,574,229	6,835,672	22.4	18.7
West South Central..	10,242,224	2,970,829	7,271,395	1,957,456	6,827,078	29.0	22.3
Mountain.............	3,336,101	1,214,980	2,121,121	947,511	1,686,006	36.4	36.0
Pacific...............	5,566,871	3,471,483	2,095,388	2,382,329	1,809,975	62.4	56.8
NEW ENGLAND:							
Maine................	768,014	299,569	468,445	262,248	480,123	39.0	35.3
New Hampshire.....	443,083	279,761	163,322	255,099	175,473	63.1	59.2
Vermont.............	352,428	109,976	242,452	98,917	257,039	31.2	27.8
Massachusetts........	3,852,356	3,650,248	202,108	3,125,367	241,049	94.8	92.8
Rhode Island........	604,397	589,180	15,217	524,654	17,956	97.5	96.7
Connecticut..........	1,380,631	936,339	444,292	731,797	382,959	67.8	65.6
MIDDLE ATLANTIC:							
New York...........	10,385,227	8,589,844	1,795,383	7,185,494	1,928,120	82.7	78.8
New Jersey..........	3,155,900	2,474,936	680,964	1,907,210	629,957	78.4	75.2
Pennsylvania........	8,720,017	5,607,815	3,112,202	4,630,669	3,034,442	64.3	60.4
EAST NORTH CENTRAL:							
Ohio................	5,759,394	3,677,136	2,082,258	2,665,143	2,101,978	63.8	55.9
Indiana.............	2,930,390	1,482,855	1,447,535	1,143,835	1,557,041	50.6	42.4
Illinois.............	6,485,280	4,403,153	2,082,127	3,476,929	2,161,662	67.9	61.7
Michigan............	3,668,412	2,241,560	1,426,852	1,327,044	1,483,129	61.1	47.2
Wisconsin...........	2,632,067	1,244,568	1,387,499	1,004,320	1,329,540	47.3	43.0
WEST NORTH CENTRAL:							
Minnesota..........	2,387,125	1,051,593	1,335,532	850,294	1,225,414	44.1	41.0
Iowa...............	2,404,021	875,495	1,528,526	680,054	1,544,717	36.4	30.6
Missouri............	3,404,055	1,586,903	1,817,152	1,398,817	1,894,518	46.6	42.5
North Dakota.......	646,872	88,239	558,633	63,236	513,820	13.6	11.0
South Dakota........	636,547	101,872	534,675	76,673	507,215	16.0	13.1
Nebraska............	1,296,372	405,306	891,066	310,852	881,362	31.3	26.1
Kansas..............	1,769,257	617,964	1,151,293	493,790	1,197,159	34.9	29.2
SOUTH ATLANTIC:							
Delaware...........	223,003	120,767	102,236	97,085	105,237	54.2	48.0
Maryland...........	1,449,661	869,422	580,239	658,192	637,154	60.0	50.8
District of Columbia..	437,571	437,571	....	331,069	....	100.0	100.0
Virginia............	2,309,187	673,984	1,635,203	476,529	1,585,083	29.2	23.1
West Virginia.......	1,463,701	369,007	1,094,694	228,242	992,877	25.2	18.7
North Carolina......	2,559,123	490,370	2,068,753	318,474	1,887,813	19.2	14.4
South Carolina......	1,683,724	293,987	1,389,737	224,832	1,290,568	17.5	14.8
Georgia.............	2,895,832	727,859	2,167,973	538,650	2,070,471	25.1	20.6
Florida.............	968,470	355,825	612,645	219,080	533,539	36.7	29.1
EAST SOUTH CENTRAL:							
Kentucky...........	2,416,630	633,543	1,783,087	555,442	1,734,463	26.2	24.3
Tennessee...........	2,337,885	611,226	1,726,659	441,045	1,743,744	26.1	20.2
Alabama............	2,348,174	509,317	1,838,857	370,431	1,767,662	21.7	17.3
Mississippi..........	1,790,618	240,121	1,550,497	207,311	1,589,803	13.4	11.5
WEST SOUTH CENTRAL:							
Arkansas...........	1,752,204	290,497	1,461,707	202,681	1,371,768	16.6	12.9
Louisiana...........	1,798,509	628,163	1,170,346	496,516	1,159,872	34.9	30.0
Oklahoma...........	2,028,283	539,480	1,488,803	320,155	1,337,000	26.6	19.3
Texas..............	4,663,228	1,512,689	3,150,539	938,104	2,958,438	32.4	24.1
MOUNTAIN:							
Montana............	548,889	172,011	376,878	133,420	242,633	31.3	35.5
Idaho..............	431,866	119,037	312,829	69,898	255,696	27.6	21.5
Wyoming...........	194,402	57,348	137,054	43,221	102,744	29.5	29.6
Colorado...........	939,629	453,259	486,370	404,840	394,184	48.2	50.7
New Mexico.........	360,350	64,960	295,390	46,571	280,730	18.0	14.2
Arizona............	334,162	117,527	216,635	63,260	141,094	35.2	31.0
Utah...............	449,396	215,584	233,812	172,934	200,417	48.0	46.3
Nevada.............	77,407	15,254	62,153	13,367	68,508	19.7	16.3
PACIFIC:							
Washington.........	1,356,621	748,735	607,886	605,530	536,460	55.2	53.0
Oregon.............	783,389	391,019	392,370	307,060	365,705	49.9	45.6
California..........	3,426,861	2,331,729	1,095,132	1,469,739	907,810	68.0	61.8

TABLE **16.**—NUMBER AND AGGREGATE POPULATION OF URBAN PLACES OF SPECIFIED SIZES, AND POPULATION OF RURAL DISTRICTS, BY DIVISIONS AND STATES: 1890–1920.

DIVISION AND STATE.	PLACES OF—							
	100,000 or more.		25,000 to 100,000.		10,000 to 25,000.		5,000 to 10,000.	
	Number of places.	Population.	Number of places.	Population.	Number of places.	Population.	Number of places.	Population.
UNITED STATES:								
1920	68	27,429,326	219	10,340,788	1 459	6,942,742	721	4,997,794
1910	50	20,302,138	178	8,204,960	1 367	5,524,434	612	4,254,856
1900	38	14,208,347	122	5,509,965	1 280	4,338,250	1 468	3,220,766
1890	28	9,697,960	96	4,291,608	228	3,429,247	1 339	2,372,717
GEOGRAPHIC DIVISIONS.								
New England:								
1920	11	2,203,306	35	1,699,018	68	1,054,768	85	598,045
1910	8	1,606,984	33	1,601,269	56	851,779	89	628,603
1900	5	1,067,800	25	1,250,258	51	810,334	88	604,527
1890	2	580,623	22	1,026,947	41	647,318	63	448,489
Middle Atlantic:								
1920	15	10,549,599	48	2,353,654	111	1,697,009	158	1,113,921
1910	11	8,599,877	44	2,110,782	91	1,349,807	130	875,771
1900	11	6,465,480	29	1,315,158	67	1,027,611	93	636,600
1890	9	4,446,905	23	1,084,175	52	770,956	75	547,893
East North Central:								
1920	12	6,775,993	61	2,681,461	101	1,543,115	166	1,172,577
1910	10	4,761,966	38	1,553,809	88	1,396,143	154	1,086,197
1900	8	3,403,810	23	935,320	79	1,252,955	130	899,043
1890	6	2,173,891	16	698,122	64	947,440	95	652,288
West North Central:								
1920	7	2,131,833	14	733,831	48	705,677	78	540,654
1910	5	1,575,658	17	801,931	33	455,439	71	498,769
1900	6	1,310,307	12	448,447	22	335,850	59	402,293
1890	5	1,022,832	9	354,998	20	312,545	41	286,188
South Atlantic:								
1920	6	1,769,625	25	1,119,452	1 36	534,462	64	436,404
1910	4	1,172,021	16	712,387	1 27	444,714	58	397,081
1900	2	787,675	9	514,853	27	429,391	1 31	203,328
1890	2	664,831	8	409,189	19	286,374	1 21	145,079
East South Central:								
1920	4	694,390	7	367,926	1 23	343,900	37	247,470
1910	4	598,082	7	289,285	15	220,364	33	229,933
1900	2	307,051	9	348,494	7	98,512	22	154,241
1890	1	161,129	6	264,388	9	147,837	16	111,454
West South Central:								
1920	5	952,332	12	607,225	1 36	515,442	60	399,984
1910	1	339,075	12	636,814	1 27	354,582	33	229,386
1900	1	287,104	6	243,376	1 13	174,907	22	156,377
1890	1	242,039	5	158,255	9	118,479	1 14	94,704
Mountain:								
1920	2	374,601	5	176,623	16	227,902	32	218,948
1910	1	213,381	5	230,995	12	144,593	25	174,020
1900	1	133,859	3	112,158	7	99,787	11	71,664
1890	1	106,713	1	44,843	7	97,218	8	47,185
Pacific:								
1920	6	1,977,647	12	601,598	21	320,467	41	269,791
1910	6	1,435,094	6	267,688	19	307,013	19	135,096
1900	2	445,261	6	341,901	7	108,903	13	92,693
1890	1	298,997	6	250,691	7	101,080	7	39,437
NEW ENGLAND.								
Maine:								
1920			3	127,041	5	77,189	11	76,095
1910			2	84,818	5	81,615	11	74,084
1900			1	50,145	6	96,867	10	66,759
1890			1	36,425	5	77,024	7	48,154
New Hampshire:								
1920			2	106,763	6	86,976	6	43,747
1910			2	96,068	6	78,044	6	40,074
1900			1	56,987	4	67,374	7	53,926
1890			1	44,126	3	49,105	6	42,584
Vermont:								
1920					3	47,741	6	41,714
1910					3	44,748	5	33,658
1900					2	30,139	6	37,572
1890					1	14,590	2	13,706

1 See note 1 to Table 14, p. 74.

TABLE **16.**—NUMBER AND AGGREGATE POPULATION OF URBAN PLACES OF SPECI-FIED SIZES, AND POPULATION OF RURAL DISTRICTS, BY DIVISIONS AND STATES: 1890–1920—Continued.

DIVISION AND STATE.	PLACES OF—		Rural districts— population.	PER CENT OF TOTAL POPULATION LIVING IN—					
	2,500 to 5,000.			Places of—					Rural dis-tricts.
	Num-ber of places.	Popula-tion.		100,000 or more.	25,000 to 100,000.	10,000 to 25,000.	5,000 to 10,000.	2,500 to 5,000.	
UNITED STATES:									
1920	[1]1,320	4,593,953	51,406,017	25.9	9.8	6.6	4.7	4.3	48.6
1910	[1]1,106	3,879,732	49,806,146	22.1	8.9	6.0	4.6	4.2	54.2
1900	[1]893	3,103,105	45,614,142	18.7	7.3	5.7	4.2	4.1	60.0
1890	[1]726	2,506,827	40,649,355	15.4	6.8	5.4	3.8	4.0	64.6
GEOGRAPHIC DIVISIONS.									
New England:									
1920	93	309,936	1,535,836	29.8	23.0	14.3	8.1	4.2	20.8
1910	87	309,447	1,554,599	24.5	24.4	13.0	9.6	4.7	23.7
1900	90	320,508	1,538,590	19.1	22.4	14.5	10.8	5.7	27.5
1890	122	436,522	1,560,850	12.4	21.8	13.8	9.5	9.3	33.2
Middle Atlantic:									
1920	272	958,412	5,588,549	47.4	10.6	7.6	5.0	4.3	25.1
1910	223	787,136	5,592,519	44.5	10.9	7.0	4.5	4.1	29.0
1900	179	631,034	5,378,795	41.8	8.5	6.6	4.1	4.1	34.8
1890	139	483,843	5,372,448	35.0	8.5	6.1	4.3	3.8	42.3
East North Central:									
1920	[1]246	876,126	8,426,271	31.6	12.5	7.2	5.5	4.1	39.2
1910	[1]232	819,156	8,633,350	26.1	8.5	7.6	6.0	4.5	47.3
1900	[1]211	728,847	8,765,606	21.3	5.9	7.8	5.6	4.6	54.8
1890	[1]178	625,440	8,381,124	16.1	5.2	7.0	4.8	4.6	62.2
West North Central:									
1920	175	615,377	7,816,877	17.0	5.8	5.6	4.3	4.9	62.3
1910	156	541,919	7,764,205	13.5	6.9	3.9	4.3	4.7	66.7
1900	132	449,647	7,400,879	12.7	4.3	3.2	3.9	4.3	71.5
1890	98	332,256	6,623,293	11.5	4.0	3.5	3.2	3.7	74.2
South Atlantic:									
1920	142	478,849	9,651,480	12.6	8.0	3.8	3.1	3.4	69.0
1910	105	365,950	9,102,742	9.6	5.8	3.6	3.3	3.0	74.6
1900	84	297,385	8,210,848	7.5	4.9	4.1	1.9	2.8	78.6
1890	68	222,546	7,129,903	7.5	4.6	3.2	1.6	2.5	80.5
East South Central:									
1920	98	340,521	6,899,100	7.8	4.1	3.9	2.8	3.8	77.6
1910	67	236,565	6,835,672	7.1	3.4	2.6	2.7	2.8	81.3
1900	65	222,758	6,416,701	4.1	4.6	1.3	2.0	3.0	85.0
1890	39	132,500	5,611,846	2.5	4.1	2.3	1.7	2.1	87.3
West South Central:									
1920	147	495,846	7,271,395	9.3	5.9	5.0	3.9	4.8	71.0
1910	117	397,599	6,827,078	3.9	7.2	4.0	2.6	4.5	77.7
1900	56	195,433	5,475,093	4.4	3.7	2.7	2.4	3.0	83.8
1890	32	102,522	4,024,984	5.1	3.3	2.5	2.0	2.2	84.9
Mountain:									
1920	62	216,906	2,121,121	11.2	5.3	6.8	6.6	6.5	63.6
1910	54	184,522	1,686,006	8.1	8.8	5.5	6.6	7.0	64.0
1900	38	123,895	1,133,294	8.0	6.7	6.0	4.3	7.4	67.7
1890	18	59,668	858,308	8.8	3.7	8.0	3.9	4.9	70.7
Pacific:									
1920	85	301,980	2,095,388	35.5	10.8	5.8	4.8	5.4	37.6
1910	65	237,438	1,809,975	34.2	6.4	7.3	3.2	5.7	43.2
1900	38	133,598	1,294,336	18.4	14.1	4.5	3.8	5.5	53.6
1890	32	111,530	1,086,599	15.8	13.3	5.4	2.1	5.9	57.5
NEW ENGLAND.									
Maine:									
1920	6	19,244	468,445	....	16.5	10.1	9.9	2.5	61.0
1910	6	21,731	480,123	....	11.4	11.0	10.0	2.9	64.7
1900	5	19,056	461,639	....	7.2	13.9	9.6	2.7	66.5
1890	3	12,178	487,305	....	5.5	11.7	7.3	1.8	73.7
New Hampshire:									
1920	13	42,275	163,322	....	24.1	19.6	9.9	9.5	36.9
1910	12	40,913	175,473	....	22.3	18.1	9.3	9.5	40.8
1900	14	47,982	185,319	....	13.8	16.4	13.1	11.7	45.0
1890	18	56,664	184,051	....	11.7	13.0	11.3	15.0	48.9
Vermont:									
1920	5	20,521	242,452	....	....	13.5	11.8	5.8	68.8
1910	6	20,511	257,039	....	....	12.6	9.5	5.8	72.2
1900	2	8,120	267,810	....	....	8.8	10.9	2.4	77.9
1890	6	22,342	281,784	....	....	4.4	4.1	6.7	84.8

[1] See note 1 to Table 14, p. 74.

TABLE 16.—NUMBER AND AGGREGATE POPULATION OF URBAN PLACES OF SPECI-
FIED SIZES, AND POPULATION OF RURAL DISTRICTS, BY DIVISIONS AND STATES:
1890-1920—Continued.

DIVISION AND STATE.	PLACES OF—							
	100,000 or more.		25,000 to 100,000.		10,000 to 25,000.		5,000 to 10,000.	
	Number of places.	Population.	Number of places.	Population.	Number of places.	Population.	Number of places.	Population.
NEW ENGLAND—con.								
Massachusetts:								
1920	7	1,521,583	20	1,028,383	39	594,111	47	321,312
1910	5	1,146,999	20	1,008,483	30	450,898	49	342,831
1900	3	784,176	17	852,988	27	413,698	46	310,720
1890	1	448,477	15	706,723	21	319,886	35	250,050
Rhode Island:								
1920	1	237,595	4	167,406	6	96,361	8	61,345
1910	1	224,326	4	143,525	4	69,776	9	63,915
1900	1	175,597	2	67,435	5	87,405	7	49,008
1890	1	132,146	1	27,633	4	78,403	8	57,240
Connecticut:								
1920	3	444,128	6	269,425	9	152,390	7	53,832
1910	2	235,659	5	268,375	8	126,698	9	74,041
1900	1	108,027	4	222,703	7	114,851	12	86,542
1890			4	212,040	7	108,310	5	36,755
MIDDLE ATLANTIC.								
New York:								
1920	6	6,807,810	16	755,097	36	540,139	30	200,606
1910	5	5,646,249	16	685,322	30	439,571	25	162,373
1900	4	4,060,571	8	396,462	28	458,937	26	184,029
1890	4	2,711,204	9	442,324	22	346,523	30	221,375
New Jersey:								
1920	5	1,084,100	16	718,899	18	267,130	35	242,399
1910	3	740,848	11	623,079	18	271,936	21	142,066
1900	3	557,674	7	349,073	14	218,271	16	107,651
1890	2	344,833	5	275,530	9	125,899	10	74,334
Pennsylvania:								
1920	4	2,657,689	16	879,658	57	889,740	93	670,916
1910	8	2,212,780	17	802,381	43	638,300	84	571,332
1900	4	1,847,235	14	569,623	25	350,403	51	344,920
1890	3	1,390,868	9	366,321	21	298,534	35	252,184
EAST NORTH CENTRAL.								
Ohio:								
1920	7	2,171,635	14	535,822	29	456,388	44	317,584
1910	5	1,390,839	9	393,371	23	360,984	45	321,860
1900	4	965,052	5	241,866	19	305,089	43	299,714
1890	2	558,261	7	349,709	14	199,186	29	199,869
Indiana:								
1920	1	314,194	11	559,351	19	298,280	23	166,968
1910	1	233,650	4	245,421	20	339,996	26	188,790
1900	1	169,164	4	176,794	14	218,623	23	161,751
1890	1	105,436	3	116,366	10	143,945	18	119,441
Illinois:								
1920	1	2,701,705	16	700,310	27	406,143	47	324,046
1910	1	2,185,283	11	434,395	20	331,285	41	286,079
1900	1	1,698,575	6	216,570	19	319,195	27	182,236
1890	1	1,099,850	2	72,518	19	294,926	15	99,207
Michigan:								
1920	2	1,131,312	12	583,309	14	179,991	32	225,476
1910	2	578,337	7	261,592	15	203,817	24	166,749
1900	1	285,704	4	182,718	14	219,890	22	158,649
1890	1	205,876	3	134,439	11	160,098	18	125,348
Wisconsin:								
1920	1	457,147	8	302,669	12	202,313	20	138,503
1910	1	373,857	7	219,030	10	160,061	18	122,719
1900	1	285,315	4	117,372	13	197,158	15	96,693
1890	1	204,468	1	25,090	10	149,285	15	108,222
WEST NORTH CENTRAL.								
Minnesota:								
1920	2	615,280	1	98,917	8	111,525	16	114,851
1910	2	516,152	1	78,466	5	60,219	16	115,083
1900	2	365,783	1	52,969	3	42,631	11	72,066
1890	2	297,894	1	33,115	2	29,468	6	40,362

TABLE 16.—NUMBER AND AGGREGATE POPULATION OF URBAN PLACES OF SPECIFIED SIZES, AND POPULATION OF RURAL DISTRICTS, BY DIVISIONS AND STATES: 1890–1920—Continued.

DIVISION AND STATE.	PLACES OF—		Rural districts—population.	PER CENT OF TOTAL POPULATION LIVING IN—					
	2,500 to 5,000.			Places of—					Rural districts.
	Number of places.	Population.		100,000 or more.	25,000 to 100,000.	10,000 to 25,000.	5,000 to 10,000.	2,500 to 5,000.	
NEW ENGLAND—con.									
Massachusetts:									
1920	56	184,859	202,108	39.5	26.7	15.4	8.3	4.8	5.2
1910	48	176,156	241,049	34.1	30.0	13.4	10.2	5.2	7.2
1900	57	205,516	238,248	28.0	30.4	14.7	11.1	7.3	8.5
1890	77	278,718	235,093	20.0	31.6	14.3	11.2	12.4	10.5
Rhode Island:									
1920	8	26,473	15,217	39.3	27.7	15.9	10.1	4.4	2.5
1910	7	23,112	17,956	41.3	26.5	12.9	11.8	4.3	3.3
1900	8	28,202	20,909	41.0	15.7	20.4	11.4	6.6	4.9
1890	9	31,180	18,904	38.2	8.0	22.7	16.6	9.0	5.5
Connecticut:									
1920	5	16,564	444,292	32.2	19.5	11.0	3.9	1.2	32.2
1910	8	27,024	382,959	21.1	24.1	11.4	6.6	2.4	34.4
1900	4	11,632	364,665	11.9	24.5	12.6	9.5	1.3	40.1
1890	9	35,440	353,713	....	28.4	14.5	4.9	4.7	47.4
MIDDLE ATLANTIC.									
New York:									
1920	81	286,192	1,795,383	65.6	7.3	5.2	1.9	2.8	17.3
1910	72	251,979	1,928,120	62.0	7.5	4.8	1.8	2.8	21.2
1900	56	198,112	1,970,783	55.9	5.5	6.3	2.5	2.7	27.1
1890	49	178,311	2,103,437	45.2	7.4	5.8	3.7	3.0	35.0
New Jersey:									
1920	47	162,408	680,964	34.4	22.8	8.5	7.7	5.1	21.6
1910	35	129,281	629,957	29.2	24.6	10.7	5.6	5.1	24.8
1900	27	96,493	554,507	29.6	18.5	11.6	5.7	5.1	29.4
1890	16	56,042	568,295	23.9	19.1	8.7	5.1	3.9	39.3
Pennsylvania:									
1920	144	509,812	3,112,202	30.5	10.1	10.2	7.7	5.8	35.7
1910	116	405,876	3,034,442	28.9	10.5	8.3	7.5	5.3	39.6
1900	96	336,429	2,853,505	29.3	9.0	5.6	5.5	5.3	45.3
1890	74	249,490	2,700,716	26.5	7.0	5.7	4.8	4.7	51.4
EAST NORTH CENTRAL.									
Ohio:									
1920	[1] 54	195,707	2,082,258	37.7	9.3	7.9	5.5	3.4	36.2
1910	[1] 57	198,089	2,101,978	29.2	8.3	7.6	6.8	4.2	44.1
1900	[1] 55	186,661	2,159,163	23.2	5.8	7.3	7.2	4.5	51.9
1890	[1] 56	197,365	2,167,939	15.2	9.5	5.4	5.4	5.4	59.0
Indiana:									
1920	[1] 39	144,062	1,447,535	10.7	19.1	10.2	5.7	4.9	49.4
1910	[1] 37	135,978	1,557,041	8.7	9.1	12.6	7.0	5.0	57.6
1900	[1] 38	136,357	1,653,773	6.7	7.0	8.7	6.4	5.4	65.7
1890	[1] 31	104,851	1,602,365	4.8	5.3	6.6	5.4	4.8	73.1
Illinois:									
1920	80	270,949	2,082,127	41.7	10.8	6.3	5.0	4.2	32.1
1910	71	239,887	2,161,662	38.8	7.7	5.9	5.1	4.3	38.3
1900	61	199,792	2,205,182	35.2	4.5	6.6	3.8	4.1	45.7
1890	41	143,671	2,116,180	28.7	1.9	7.7	2.6	3.8	55.3
Michigan:									
1920	33	121,472	1,426,852	30.8	15.9	4.9	6.1	3.3	38.9
1910	31	116,549	1,483,129	20.6	9.3	7.3	5.9	4.1	52.8
1900	30	112,362	1,488,659	11.8	7.5	8.8	6.6	4.6	60.7
1890	30	104,332	1,363,596	9.8	6.4	7.6	6.0	5.0	65.1
Wisconsin:									
1920	41	143,936	1,387,499	17.4	11.5	7.7	5.3	5.5	52.7
1910	37	128,653	1,329,540	16.0	9.4	6.9	5.3	5.5	57.0
1900	28	93,675	1,278,829	13.8	5.7	9.5	4.7	4.5	61.8
1890	21	75,221	1,131,044	12.1	1.5	8.8	6.4	4.4	66.8
WEST NORTH CENTRAL.									
Minnesota:									
1920	32	111,020	1,335,532	25.8	4.1	4.7	4.8	4.7	55.9
1910	24	80,374	1,225,414	24.9	3.8	2.9	5.5	3.9	59.0
1900	20	64,651	1,153,294	20.9	3.0	2.4	4.1	3.7	65.9
1890	12	42,210	867,234	22.7	2.5	2.2	3.1	3.2	66.2

[1] See note 1 to Table 14, p. 74.

TABLE 16.—NUMBER AND AGGREGATE POPULATION OF URBAN PLACES OF SPECIFIED SIZES, AND POPULATION OF RURAL DISTRICTS, BY DIVISIONS AND STATES: 1890-1920—Continued.

DIVISION AND STATE.	PLACES OF—							
	100,000 or more.		25,000 to 100,000.		10,000 to 25,000.		5,000 to 10,000.	
	Number of places.	Population.	Number of places.	Population.	Number of places.	Population.	Number of places.	Population.
WEST NORTH CENTRAL—continued.								
Iowa:								
1920	1	126,468	6	285,053	11	192,629	18	114,802
1910			8	330,091	9	137,107	9	59,402
1900			6	218,259	8	129,096	10	70,618
1890			4	145,082	7	115,234	8	56,582
Missouri:								
1920	2	1,097,307	3	147,472	8	110,146	16	109,337
1910	2	935,410	3	144,677	5	70,753	17	120,938
1900	3	841,969	1	26,023	3	51,278	18	120,291
1890	2	584,486	1	52,324	3	48,775	11	73,573
North Dakota:								
1920					3	46,447	3	18,889
1910					2	26,809	3	16,788
1900							2	17,241
1890							1	5,664
South Dakota:								
1920			1	25,202	1	14,537	6	41,994
1910					2	24,847	4	27,708
1900					1	10,266	1	6,210
1890					1	10,177		
Nebraska:								
1920	1	191,601	1	54,948	3	36,060	9	65,048
1910	1	124,096	2	70,232	1	10,326	9	61,670
1900	1	102,555	2	66,170			7	48,004
1890	1	140,452	1	55,154	3	39,361	5	38,811
Kansas:								
1920	1	101,177	2	122,239	14	194,333	10	75,733
1910			3	178,465	9	125,378	13	97,180
1900			2	85,026	7	102,579	10	67,863
1890			2	69,323	4	69,530	10	71,196
SOUTH ATLANTIC.								
Delaware:								
1920	1	110,168						
1910			1	87,411				
1900			1	76,508				
1890			1	61,431				
Maryland:								
1920	1	733,826	2	57,901	2	22,280	3	21,037
1910	1	558,485			3	48,757	4	27,734
1900	1	508,957			2	30,719	4	28,842
1890	1	434,439			2	22,847	2	15,797
District of Columbia:								
1920	1	437,571						
1910	1	331,069						
1900	1	278,718						
1890	1	230,392						
Virginia:								
1920	2	287,444	5	201,907	[1] 5	67,639	9	58,694
1910	1	127,628	4	165,010	[1] 6	95,532	6	36,764
1900			2	131,674	7	130,306	[1] 6	38,261
1890			2	116,259	6	96,460	[1] 5	29,910
West Virginia:								
1920			4	170,662	6	88,494	6	40,052
1910			2	70,902	4	62,124	6	49,803
1900			1	38,878	3	34,725	4	24,231
1890			1	34,522	1	10,108	3	22,576
North Carolina:								
1920			4	156,609	10	153,903	13	89,970
1910			2	59,762	5	89,283	13	96,184
1900					6	87,447	6	42,181
1890					4	54,526	3	21,346
South Carolina:								
1920			2	105,481	4	67,303	8	56,967
1910			2	85,152	2	33,258	9	60,737
1900			1	55,807	3	44,363	4	22,056
1890			1	54,955	1	15,353	2	14,151
Georgia:								
1920	1	200,616	4	219,920	7	101,857	14	95,937
1910	1	154,839	3	146,769	5	72,233	14	90,403
1900			3	183,557	3	51,131	7	47,757
1890			3	142,022	2	40,049	5	35,967

[1] See note 1 to Table 14, p. 74.

TABLE 16.—NUMBER AND AGGREGATE POPULATION OF URBAN PLACES OF SPECI- FIED SIZES, AND POPULATION OF RURAL DISTRICTS, BY DIVISIONS AND STATES: 1890–1920—Continued.

DIVISION AND STATE.	PLACES OF— 2,500 to 5,000.		Rural districts— population.	PER CENT OF TOTAL POPULATION LIVING IN—					Rural districts.
				Places of—					
	Number of places.	Popula- tion.		100,000 or more.	25,000 to 100,000.	10,000 to 25,000.	5,000 to 10,000.	2,500 to 5,000.	
WEST NORTH CENTRAL— continued.									
Iowa:									
1920	45	156,543	1,528,526	5.3	11.9	8.0	4.8	6.5	63.6
1910	43	153,454	1,544,717	....	14.8	6.2	2.7	6.9	69.4
1900	46	154,413	1,659,467	....	9.8	5.8	3.2	6.9	74.4
1890	27	88,866	1,506,533	....	7.6	6.0	3.0	4.6	78.8
Missouri:									
1920	34	122,641	1,817,152	32.2	4.3	3.2	3.2	3.6	53.4
1910	35	127,039	1,894,518	28.4	4.4	2.1	3.7	3.9	57.5
1900	25	88,543	1,978,561	27.1	0.8	1.7	3.9	2.9	63.7
1890	27	97,808	1,822,219	21.8	2.0	1.8	2.7	3.7	68.0
North Dakota:									
1920	6	22,903	558,633	....	....	7.2	2.9	3.5	86.4
1910	5	19,639	513,820	....	....	4.6	2.9	3.4	89.0
1900	2	6,172	295,733	....	....	....	5.4	1.9	92.7
1890	1	4,979	180,340	....	....	....	3.0	2.6	94.4
South Dakota:									
1920	6	20,139	534,675	....	4.0	2.3	6.6	3.2	84.0
1910	7	24,118	507,215	....	....	4.3	4.7	4.1	86.9
1900	7	24,460	360,634	....	....	2.6	1.5	6.1	89.8
1890	6	18,378	320,045	....	....	....	2.9	....	5.3	91.8
Nebraska:									
1920	17	57,649	891,066	14.8	4.2	2.8	5.0	4.4	68.7
1910	14	44,528	881,362	10.4	5.9	0.9	5.2	3.7	73.9
1900	11	35,973	813,598	9.6	6.2	....	4.5	3.4	76.3
1890	6	17,863	771,015	13.2	5.2	3.7	3.7	1.7	72.6
Kansas:									
1920	35	124,482	1,151,293	5.7	6.9	11.0	4.3	7.0	65.1
1910	28	92,767	1,197,159	....	10.6	7.4	5.7	5.5	70.8
1900	21	75,435	1,139,592	....	5.8	7.0	4.6	5.1	77.5
1890	19	62,152	1,155,907	....	4.9	4.9	5.0	4.4	80.9
SOUTH ATLANTIC.									
Delaware:									
1920	3	10,599	102,236	49.4	....	43.2	....	....	4.8	45.8
1910	3	9,674	105,237	....	43.2	....	....	4.8	52.0
1900	3	9,209	99,018	....	41.4	....	....	5.0	53.6
1890	3	9,636	97,426	....	36.5	....	....	5.7	57.8
Maryland:									
1920	10	34,378	580,239	50.6	4.0	1.5	1.5	2.4	40.0
1910	7	23,216	637,154	43.1	....	3.8	2.1	1.8	49.2
1900	7	22,688	596,838	42.8	....	2.6	2.4	1.9	50.2
1890	7	22,619	546,688	41.7	....	2.2	1.5	2.2	52.4
District of Columbia:									
1920	....	....	....	100.0	....	....	....	....	....
1910	....	....	....	100.0	....	....	....	....	....
1900	....	....	....	100.0	....	....	....	....	....
1890	....	....	....	100.0	....	....	....	....	....
Virginia:									
1920	18	58,300	1,635,203	12.4	8.7	2.9	2.5	2.5	70.8
1910	15	51,595	1,585,083	6.2	8.0	4.6	1.8	2.5	76.9
1900	12	39,826	1,514,117	....	7.1	7.0	2.1	2.1	81.7
1890	12	40,092	1,373,259	....	7.0	5.8	1.8	2.4	82.9
West Virginia:									
1920	19	66,599	1,094,694	....	11.9	6.0	2.7	4.6	74.8
1910	13	42,913	992,877	....	6.0	5.1	4.1	3.5	81.3
1900	8	27,631	833,335	....	4.1	3.6	2.5	2.9	86.9
1890	5	14,359	681,429	....	4.5	1.3	2.9	1.9	89.3
North Carolina:									
1920	28	89,888	2,068,753	....	6.1	6.0	3.5	3.5	80.8
1910	20	73,245	1,887,813	....	2.7	4.0	4.4	3.3	85.6
1900	16	57,162	1,707,020	....	....	4.6	2.2	3.0	90.1
1890	11	39,837	1,502,190	....	....	3.4	1.3	2.5	92.8
South Carolina:									
1920	18	64,236	1,389,737	....	6.3	4.0	3.4	3.8	82.5
1910	12	45,685	1,290,568	....	5.6	2.2	4.0	3.0	85.2
1900	12	49,030	1,169,060	....	4.2	3.3	1.6	3.7	87.2
1890	10	31,724	1,034,966	....	4.8	1.3	1.2	2.8	89.9
Georgia:									
1920	33	109,529	2,167,973	6.9	7.6	3.5	3.3	3.8	74.9
1910	22	74,406	2,070,491	5.9	5.6	2.8	3.5	2.9	79.4
1900	18	63,937	1,869,949	....	8.3	2.3	2.2	2.9	84.4
1890	12	39,434	1,579,881	....	7.7	2.2	2.0	2.1	86.0

TABLE 16.—NUMBER AND AGGREGATE POPULATION OF URBAN PLACES OF SPECIFIED SIZES, AND POPULATION OF RURAL DISTRICTS, BY DIVISIONS AND STATES: 1890–1920—Continued.

DIVISION AND STATE.	PLACES OF—							
	100,000 or more.		25,000 to 100,000.		10,000 to 25,000.		5,000 to 10,000.	
	Number of places.	Population.	Number of places.	Population.	Number of places.	Population.	Number of places.	Population.
SOUTH ATLANTIC—con.								
Florida:								
1920			4	203,772	2	32,986	11	73,747
1910			2	95,481	2	42,927	6	35,456
1900			1	28,429	3	50,700		
1890					3	47,031	1	5,532
EAST SOUTH CENTRAL.								
Kentucky:								
1920	1	234,891	3	127,972	4	69,057	14	100,317
1910	1	223,928	3	118,678	4	60,688	12	84,079
1900	1	204,731	3	97,608	3	42,907	8	56,616
1890	1	161,129	1	37,371	3	59,282	7	50,631
Tennessee:								
1920	2	280,693	2	135,713	[1] 3	39,349	7	43,536
1910	2	241,469	2	80,950	[1] 2	22,927	5	33,479
1900	1	102,320	3	143,656	1	14,511	[1] 3	20,754
1890			3	169,763	2	32,574	[1] 3	16,618
Alabama:								
1920	1	178,806	2	104,241	7	99,293	8	50,461
1910	1	132,685	2	89,657	4	47,864	6	41,695
1900			3	107,230			7	49,462
1890			2	57,254	1	21,883	4	31,627
Mississippi:								
1920					9	136,201	8	53,156
1910					5	88,885	10	70,680
1900					3	41,094	4	27,409
1890					3	34,098	2	12,578
WEST SOUTH CENTRAL.								
Arkansas:								
1920			2	94,012	[1] 4	53,280	8	53,135
1910			1	45,941	[1] 5	70,304	3	21,143
1900			1	38,307	[1] 3	27,997	2	15,523
1890			1	25,874	1	11,311	[1] 4	26,755
Louisiana:								
1920	1	387,219	1	43,874	4	65,055	8	52,377
1910	1	339,075	1	28,015	4	47,768	5	29,491
1900	1	287,104			2	27,282	4	24,571
1890	1	242,039			2	22,457		
Oklahoma: [2]								
1920			3	193,647	9	123,617	15	104,193
1910			2	89,483	6	79,383	6	44,072
1900					2	20,043	1	5,681
1890							1	5,333
Texas:								
1920	4	565,113	6	275,692	[1] 20	273,490	29	190,279
1910			8	473,375	[1] 13	157,127	19	134,680
1900			5	205,069	[1] 7	99,585	15	110,602
1890			4	132,381	6	84,711	[1] 10	62,616
MOUNTAIN.								
Montana:								
1920			1	41,611	5	73,384	6	87,197
1910			1	39,165	5	59,497	3	16,015
1900			1	30,470	2	25,700	1	9,453
1890					2	24,557		
Idaho:								
1920					2	36,394	7	47,544
1910					1	17,358	4	27,702
1900							1	5,957
1890								
Wyoming:								
1920					2	25,276	3	21,932
1910					1	11,320	3	22,423
1900					1	14,087	1	8,207
1890					1	11,690	1	6,388

[1] See note 1 to Table 14, p. 74.
[2] Includes population of Indian Territory for 1900 and 1890.

Table 16.—NUMBER AND AGGREGATE POPULATION OF URBAN PLACES OF SPECIFIED SIZES, AND POPULATION OF RURAL DISTRICTS, BY DIVISIONS AND STATES: 1890–1920—Continued.

DIVISION AND STATE.	PLACES OF— 2,500 to 5,000.		Rural districts— population.	PER CENT OF TOTAL POPULATION LIVING IN—					
				Places of—					Rural districts.
	Number of places.	Population.		100,000 or more.	25,000 to 100,000.	10,000 to 25,000.	5,000 to 10,000.	2,500 to 5,000.	
SOUTH ATLANTIC—con.									
Florida:									
1920	13	45,320	612,645	....	21.0	3.4	7.6	4.7	63.3
1910	13	45,216	533,539	....	12.7	5.7	4.7	6.0	70.9
1900	8	27,902	421,511	....	5.4	9.6	....	5.3	79.7
1890	8	24,795	314,064	....	....	12.0	1.4	6.3	80.2
EAST SOUTH CENTRAL.									
Kentucky:									
1920	29	101,306	1,783,087	9.7	5.3	2.9	4.2	4.2	73.8
1910	20	68,069	1,734,463	9.8	5.2	2.7	3.7	3.0	75.7
1900	19	65,806	1,679,506	9.5	4.5	2.0	2.6	3.1	78.2
1890	14	48,300	1,501,922	8.7	2.0	3.2	2.7	2.6	80.8
Tennessee:									
1920	33	111,935	1,726,659	12.0	5.8	1.7	1.9	4.8	73.9
1910	18	62,220	1,743,744	11.1	3.7	1.0	1.5	2.8	79.8
1900	14	45,398	1,693,977	5.1	7.1	0.7	1.0	2.2	83.8
1890	6	19,439	1,529,124	....	9.6	1.8	0.9	1.1	86.5
Alabama:									
1920	21	76,516	1,838,857	7.6	4.4	4.2	2.1	3.3	78.3
1910	15	58,530	1,767,662	6.2	4.2	2.2	2.0	2.7	82.7
1900	17	60,022	1,611,983	....	5.9	....	2.7	3.3	88.1
1890	12	41,471	1,361,166	....	3.8	1.4	2.1	2.7	89.9
Mississippi:									
1920	15	50,764	1,550,497	....	....	7.6	3.0	2.8	86.6
1910	14	47,746	1,589,803	....	....	4.9	3.9	2.7	88.5
1900	15	51,532	1,431,235	....	....	2.6	1.8	3.3	92.3
1890	7	23,290	1,219,634	....	....	2.6	1.0	1.8	94.6
WEST SOUTH CENTRAL.									
Arkansas:									
1920	27	90,070	1,461,707	....	5.4	3.0	3.0	5.1	83.4
1910	19	65,293	1,371,768	....	2.9	4.5	1.3	4.1	87.1
1900	9	29,906	1,199,831	....	2.9	2.1	1.2	2.3	91.5
1890	3	9,219	1,055,052	....	2.3	1.0	2.4	0.8	93.5
Louisiana:									
1920	24	79,638	1,170,346	21.5	2.4	3.6	2.9	4.4	65.1
1910	15	52,167	1,159,872	20.5	1.7	2.9	1.8	3.1	70.0
1900	8	27,331	1,015,337	20.8	....	2.0	1.8	2.0	73.5
1890	6	19,349	834,743	21.6	....	2.0	....	1.7	74.6
Oklahoma: [1]									
1920	36	118,023	1,488,803	....	9.5	6.1	5.1	5.8	73.4
1910	32	107,217	1,337,000	....	5.4	4.8	2.7	6.5	80.7
1900	10	32,693	731,974	....	....	2.5	0.7	4.1	92.6
1890	1	4,151	249,173	....	....	....	2.1	1.6	96.3
Texas:									
1920	60	208,115	3,150,539	12.1	5.9	5.9	4.1	4.5	67.6
1910	51	172,922	2,958,438	....	12.1	4.0	3.5	4.4	75.9
1900	29	105,503	2,527,951	....	6.7	3.3	3.6	3.5	82.9
1890	22	69,803	1,886,016	....	5.9	3.8	2.8	3.1	84.4
MOUNTAIN.									
Montana:									
1920	5	17,679	376,878	....	7.6	13.8	6.8	3.2	68.7
1910	5	18,743	242,633	....	10.4	15.8	4.3	5.0	64.5
1900	6	18,931	158,775	....	12.5	10.6	3.9	7.8	65.3
1890	4	14,230	104,137	....	....	17.2	....	10.0	72.9
Idaho:									
1920	11	35,099	312,829	....	....	8.4	11.0	8.1	72.4
1910	7	24,838	255,696	....	....	5.3	8.5	7.6	78.5
1900	1	4,046	151,769	....	....	....	3.7	2.5	93.8
1890	....	....	88,548	....	....	....	....	....	100.0
Wyoming:									
1920	3	10,140	137,054	....	....	13.0	11.3	5.2	70.5
1910	3	9,478	102,744	....	....	7.8	15.4	6.5	70.4
1900	1	4,363	65,874	....	....	15.2	8.9	4.7	71.2
1890	1	3,406	41,071	....	....	18.7	10.2	5.4	65.7

[1] Includes population of Indian Territory for 1900 and 1890.

TABLE 16.—NUMBER AND AGGREGATE POPULATION OF URBAN PLACES OF SPECI-
FIED SIZES, AND POPULATION OF RURAL DISTRICTS, BY DIVISIONS AND STATES:
1890–1920—Continued.

DIVISION AND STATE.	PLACES OF—							
	100,000 or more.		25,000 to 100,000.		10,000 to 25,000.		5,000 to 10,000.	
	Number of places.	Population.	Number of places.	Population.	Number of places.	Population.	Number of places.	Population.
MOUNTAIN—continued.								
Colorado:								
1920	1	256,491	2	73,155	3	32,870	5	34,748
1910	1	213,381	2	73,473	1	10,204	7	52,558
1900	1	133,859	1	28,157	3	43,687	2	11,495
1890	1	106,713			3	46,082	3	15,792
New Mexico:								
1920					1	15,157	3	19,813
1910					1	11,020	2	11,244
1900							2	11,841
1890							1	6,185
Arizona:								
1920			1	29,053	1	20,292	6	43,063
1910					2	24,327	4	27,631
1900							2	13,075
1890							1	5,150
Utah:								
1920	1	118,110	1	32,804	1	10,303	2	14,721
1910			2	118,357			2	16,447
1900			1	53,531	1	16,313	2	11,636
1890			1	44,843	1	14,889	1	5,159
Nevada:								
1920					1	12,016		
1910					1	10,867		
1900								
1890							1	8,511
PACIFIC.								
Washington:								
1920	2	419,749	3	150,194	5	72,074	7	47,544
1910	2	341,596	1	83,743	5	96,218	4	31,778
1900			3	155,233	1	10,049	2	14,672
1890			2	78,843	1	19,922		
Oregon:								
1920	1	258,288			3	42,299	8	50,445
1910	1	207,214			1	14,094	5	39,210
1900			1	90,426			2	15,044
1890			1	46,385	1	10,532	2	11,313
California:								
1920	3	1,299,610	9	451,404	13	206,094	26	171,802
1910	3	886,284	5	183,945	13	196,701	10	64,108
1900	2	445,261	2	96,242	6	98,854	9	62,977
1890	1	298,997	3	125,463	5	70,626	5	28,124

TABLE 16.—NUMBER AND AGGREGATE POPULATION OF URBAN PLACES OF SPECI-
FIED SIZES, AND POPULATION OF RURAL DISTRICTS, BY DIVISIONS AND STATES:
1890-1920—Continued.

DIVISION AND STATE.	PLACES OF—		Rural districts— population.	PER CENT OF TOTAL POPULATION LIVING IN—					
	2,500 to 5,000.			Places of—					Rural districts.
	Num-ber of places.	Popula-tion.		100,000 or more.	25,000 to 100,000.	10,000 to 25,000.	5,000 to 10,000.	2,500 to 5,000.	
MOUNTAIN—continued.									
Colorado:									
1920	15	55,995	486,370	27.3	7.8	3.5	3.7	6.0	51.8
1910	16	55,224	394,184	26.7	9.2	1.3	6.6	6.9	49.3
1900	13	43,453	279,049	24.8	5.2	8.1	2.1	8.1	51.7
1890	6	17,318	227,344	25.8		11.2	3.8	4.2	55.0
New Mexico:									
1920	8	29,990	295,390			4.2	5.5	8.3	82.0
1910	7	24,307	280,730			3.4	3.4	7.4	85.8
1900	5	15,540	167,929				6.1	8.0	86.0
1890	1	3,785	150,312				3.9	2.4	93.8
Arizona:									
1920	7	25,119	216,635		8.7	6.1	12.9	7.5	64.8
1910	3	11,302	141,094			11.9	13.5	5.5	69.0
1900	2	6,420	103,436				10.6	5.2	84.1
1890	1	3,152	79,941				5.8	3.6	90.6
Utah:									
1920	12	39,646	233,812	26.3	7.3	2.3	3.3	8.8	52.0
1910	12	38,130	200,417		31.7		4.4	10.2	53.7
1900	8	23,947	171,322		19.3	5.9	4.2	8.7	61.9
1890	3	10,264	135,624		21.3	7.1	2.4	4.9	64.3
Nevada:									
1920	1	3,238	62,153			15.5		4.2	80.3
1910	1	2,500	68,508			13.3		3.1	83.7
1900	2	7,195	35,140					17.0	83.0
1890	2	7,513	31,331				18.0	15.9	66.2
PACIFIC.									
Washington:									
1920	18	59,174	607,886	30.9	11.1	5.3	3.5	4.4	44.8
1910	15	52,195	536,460	29.9	7.3	8.4	2.8	4.6	47.0
1900	9	31,523	306,626		30.0	1.9	2.8	6.1	59.2
1890	7	28,413	230,054		22.1	5.6		8.0	64.4
Oregon:									
1920	11	39,987	392,370	33.0		5.4	6.4	5.1	50.1
1910	11	46,542	365,705	30.8		2.1	5.8	6.9	54.4
1900	8	27,710	280,356		21.9		3.6	6.7	67.8
1890	6	16,863	232,611		14.6	3.3	3.6	5.3	73.2
California:									
1920	56	202,819	1,095,132	37.9	13.2	6.0	5.0	5.9	32.0
1910	39	138,701	907,810	37.3	7.7	8.3	2.7	5.8	38.2
1900	21	74,365	707,354	30.0	6.5	6.7	4.2	5.0	47.6
1890	19	66,254	623,934	24.6	10.3	5.8	2.3	5.5	51.4

TABLE 17.—POPULATION OF URBAN CLASSES AND OF RURAL TERRITORY AS CONSTITUTED IN 1920, WITH INCREASE: 1920 AND 1910.

[The figures for 1920 and 1910 relate to the same individual places but not to the same classification of places, since certain communities passed during the decade from the rural to the urban or from the urban to the rural class and others passed from one urban group to another.]

CLASS OF PLACES.	Number of places in 1920.	POPULATION.		INCREASE: 1910–1920	
		1920	1910	Number.	Per cent.
United States...............	....	105,710,620	91,972,266	13,738,354	14.9
Territory urban in 1920...............	[1] 2,787	54,304,603	43,193,184	11,111,419	25.7
Places having in 1920—					
1,000,000 or more...................	3	10,145,532	8,505,411	1,640,121	19.3
500,000 to 1,000,000.................	9	6,223,769	4,664,460	1,559,309	33.4
250,000 to 500,000..................	13	4,540,838	3,712,128	828,710	22.3
100,000 to 250,000..................	43	6,519,187	5,087,486	1,431,701	28.1
50,000 to 100,000...................	76	5,265,747	3,999,370	1,266,377	31.7
25,000 to 50,000....................	143	5,075,041	3,777,417	1,297,624	34.4
10,000 to 25,000....................	459	6,942,742	5,617,089	1,325,653	23.6
5,000 to 10,000.....................	721	4,997,794	4,051,188	946,606	23.4
2,500 to 5,000......................	1,320	4,593,953	3,778,635	815,318	21.6
25,000 or more......................	287	37,770,114	29,746,272	8,023,842	27.0
100,000 or more.....................	68	27,429,326	21,969,485	5,459,841	24.9
250,000 or more.....................	25	20,910,139	16,881,999	4,028,140	23.9
500,000 or more.....................	12	16,369,301	13,169,871	3,199,430	24.3
1,000,000 or more...................	3	10,145,532	8,505,411	1,640,121	19.3
Territory rural in 1920...............	....	51,406,017	48,779,082	2,626,935	5.4

[1] See note 1 to Table 14, p. 74.

TABLE 18.—AREA AND POPULATION OF CENTRAL CITY, METROPOLITAN DISTRICT, AND ADJACENT TERRITORY, FOR CITIES OF 200,000 INHABITANTS OR MORE: 1920 AND 1910.

[A metropolitan district has as its nucleus a city of 200,000 population or more and includes in addition those suburban areas which lie within approximately 10 miles beyond the municipal limits and in which the density of population is 150 per square mile or more. The adjacent territory is the total suburban territory, regardless of its density of population, which lies within a distance of approximately 10 miles beyond the limits of the central city.]

[Population shown for central cities for each census year does not include that of annexations made subsequently to census date, but total population given for each district for 1920 and 1910 relates to same area.]

DISTRICT.	Area in acres: 1920	POPULATION.		Per cent of increase:[1] 1910–1920
		1920	1910	
Total for 29 metropolitan districts	6,816,110.3	29,238,582	23,045,544	26.9
In central cities (32 cities)	1,518,715.9	22,111,380	17,673,818	25.1
Outside central cities	5,297,394.4	7,127,202	5,371,726	32.7
Cities and adjacent territory	13,369,925.9	30,188,543	23,870,351	26.5
Adjacent territory	11,851,210.0	8,077,163	6,196,533	30.3
AKRON.				
Metropolitan district	113,912.0	285,113	104,320	173.3
In city proper	14,520.0	208,435	69,067	201.8
Outside	99,392.0	76,678	35,253	117.5
City and adjacent territory	348,664.0	305,696	122,915	148.7
Adjacent territory	334,144.0	97,261	53,848	80.6
ATLANTA.				
Metropolitan district	85,266.2	249,226	185,235	34.5
In city proper	16,773.4	200,616	154,839	29.6
Outside	68,492.8	48,610	30,396	59.9
City and adjacent territory	364,723.0	279,235	208,075	34.2
Adjacent territory	347,949.6	78,619	53,236	47.7
BALTIMORE.				
Metropolitan district	244,160.0	787,458	663,810	18.6
In city proper	50,560.0	733,826	558,485	31.4
Outside	193,600.0	53,632	105,325	−49.1
City and adjacent territory	432,448.0	814,395	689,841	18.1
Adjacent territory	381,888.0	80,569	131,356	−38.7
BOSTON.				
Metropolitan district	365,073.3	1,772,254	1,531,138	15.7
In city proper	27,870.0	748,060	670,585	11.6
Outside	337,203.3	1,024,194	860,553	19.0
City and adjacent territory	392,016.6	1,801,320	1,556,671	15.7
Adjacent territory	364,146.6	1,053,260	886,086	18.9
BUFFALO.				
Metropolitan district	140,015.0	602,847	493,290	22.2
In city proper	24,894.3	506,775	423,715	19.6
Outside	115,120.7	96,072	69,575	38.1
City and adjacent territory	306,223.0	623,865	511,147	22.1
Adjacent territory	281,328.7	117,090	87,432	33.9
CHICAGO.				
Metropolitan district	469,569.6	3,178,924	2,455,942	29.4
In city proper	123,382.9	2,701,705	2,185,283	23.6
Outside	346,186.7	477,219	270,659	76.3
City and adjacent territory	594,410.4	3,201,301	2,472,712	29.5
Adjacent territory	471,027.5	499,596	287,429	73.8
CINCINNATI.				
Metropolitan district	211,938.4	606,850	567,876	6.9
In city proper	45,529.6	401,247	363,591	10.4
Outside	166,408.8	205,603	204,285	0.6
City and adjacent territory	527,812.2	681,287	637,156	6.9
Adjacent territory	482,282.6	280,040	273,565	2.4

[1] A minus sign (−) denotes decrease.

TABLE 18.—AREA AND POPULATION OF CENTRAL CITY, METROPOLITAN DISTRICT, AND ADJACENT TERRITORY, FOR CITIES OF 200,000 INHABITANTS OR MORE: 1920 AND 1910—Continued.

[See notes at head of this table, p. 87.]

DISTRICT.	Area in acres: 1920	POPULATION. 1920	POPULATION. 1910	Per cent of increase:[1] 1910–1920
CLEVELAND.				
Metropolitan district	148,846.9	925,720	622,571	48.7
In city proper	36,089.0	796,841	560,663	42.1
Outside	112,757.9	128,879	61,908	108.2
City and adjacent territory	351,584.0	951,579	643,854	47.8
Adjacent territory	315,495.0	154,738	83,191	86.0
COLUMBUS.				
Metropolitan district	80,689.0	260,338	199,146	30.7
In city proper	14,449.0	237,031	181,511	30.6
Outside	66,240.0	23,307	17,635	32.2
City and adjacent territory	347,313.0	284,841	222,521	28.0
Adjacent territory	332,864.0	47,810	41,010	16.6
DENVER.				
Metropolitan district	46,205.0	264,232	219,314	20.5
In city proper	37,085.0	256,491	213,381	20.2
Outside	9,120.0	7,741	5,933	30.5
City and adjacent territory	510,438.4	289,465	240,657	20.3
Adjacent territory	473,353.4	32,974	27,276	20.9
DETROIT.				
Metropolitan district	175,253.8	1,165,153	514,086	126.6
In city proper	49,839.0	993,678	465,766	113.3
Outside	125,414.8	171,475	48,320	254.9
City and adjacent territory	295,906.6	1,181,057	522,740	125.9
Adjacent territory	246,067.6	187,379	56,974	228.9
INDIANAPOLIS.				
Metropolitan district	153,918.9	339,105	254,494	33.2
In city proper	27,893.9	314,194	233,650	34.5
Outside	126,025.0	24,911	20,844	19.5
City and adjacent territory	465,542.4	367,317	283,226	29.7
Adjacent territory	437,648.5	53,123	49,576	7.2
KANSAS CITY (MO. AND KANS.).				
Metropolitan district	264,006.7	477,354	369,276	29.3
In city proper (Kansas City, Mo.)	37,395.0	324,410	248,381	30.6
In city proper (Kansas City, Kans.)	10,138.1	101,177	82,331	22.9
Outside	216,473.6	51,767	38,564	34.2
Cities and adjacent territory	604,077.1	502,242	393,245	27.7
Adjacent territory	556,544.0	76,655	62,533	22.6
LOS ANGELES.				
Metropolitan district	831,605.0	879,008	464,841	89.1
In city proper	234,037.0	576,673	319,198	80.7
Outside	597,568.0	302,335	145,643	107.6
City and adjacent territory	941,870.6	880,050	466,462	88.8
Adjacent territory	707,833.6	300,000	147,264	106.4
LOUISVILLE.				
Metropolitan district	214,126.9	318,159	294,606	8.0
In city proper	14,348.8	234,891	223,928	4.9
Outside	199,778.1	83,268	70,678	17.8
City and adjacent territory	472,505.6	340,985	317,743	7.3
Adjacent territory	458,156.8	106,094	93,815	13.1

[1] A minus sign (−) denotes decrease.

TABLE 18.—AREA AND POPULATION OF CENTRAL CITY, METROPOLITAN DISTRICT, AND ADJACENT TERRITORY, FOR CITIES OF 200,000 INHABITANTS OR MORE: 1920 AND 1910—Continued.

[See notes at head of this table, p. 87.]

DISTRICT.	Area in acres: 1920	POPULATION.		Per cent of increase:[1] 1910–1920
		1920	1910	
MILWAUKEE.				
Metropolitan district	128,287.3	537,737	431,417	24.6
In city proper	16,184.9	457,147	373,857	22.3
Outside	112,102.4	80,590	57,560	40.0
City and adjacent territory	219,519.3	546,822	440,206	24.2
Adjacent territory	203,334.4	89,675	66,349	35.2
MINNEAPOLIS–ST. PAUL.				
Metropolitan district	94,303.0	629,216	526,256	19.6
In city proper (Minneapolis)	31,834.0	380,582	301,408	26.3
In city proper (St. Paul)	33,389.0	234,698	214,744	9.3
Outside	29,080.0	13,936	10,104	37.9
Cities and adjacent territory	638,859.4	679,864	571,707	18.9
Adjacent territory	573,636.4	64,584	55,555	16.3
NEW ORLEANS.				
Metropolitan district	126,240.0	397,915	348,109	14.3
In city proper	113,920.0	387,219	339,075	14.2
Outside	12,320.0	10,696	9,034	18.4
City and adjacent territory	361,625.6	419,679	367,235	14.3
Adjacent territory	247,705.6	32,460	28,160	15.3
NEW YORK.				
Metropolitan district	751,887.3	7,910,415	6,566,859	20.5
In city proper	191,360.0	5,620,048	4,766,883	17.9
Outside	560,527.3	2,290,367	1,799,976	27.2
City and adjacent territory	875,515.2	8,034,349	6,657,946	20.7
Adjacent territory	684,155.2	2,414,301	1,891,063	27.7
PHILADELPHIA.				
Metropolitan district	483,439.4	2,407,234	1,983,306	21.4
In city proper	81,920.0	1,823,779	1,549,008	17.7
Outside	401,519.4	583,455	434,298	34.3
City and adjacent territory	645,329.8	2,428,728	2,004,185	21.2
Adjacent territory	563,409.8	604,949	455,177	32.9
PITTSBURGH.				
Metropolitan district	422,039.9	1,207,504	1,033,052	16.9
In city proper	25,517.2	588,343	533,905	10.2
Outside	396,522.7	619,161	499,147	24.0
City and adjacent territory	499,223.9	1,216,464	1,041,385	16.8
Adjacent territory	473,706.7	628,121	507,480	23.8
PORTLAND, OREG.				
Metropolitan district	160,762.0	299,882	240,005	24.9
In city proper	40,442.0	258,288	207,214	24.6
Outside	120,320.0	41,594	32,791	26.8
City and adjacent territory	440,742.8	329,246	264,303	24.6
Adjacent territory	400,300.8	70,958	57,089	24.3
PROVIDENCE.				
Metropolitan district	126,469.4	444,228	395,972	12.2
In city proper	11,388.0	237,595	224,326	5.9
Outside	115,081.4	206,633	171,646	20.4
City and adjacent territory	271,590.4	551,502	489,772	12.6
Adjacent territory	260,202.4	313,907	265,446	18.3

[1] A minus sign (−) denotes decrease.

TABLE 18.—AREA AND POPULATION OF CENTRAL CITY, METROPOLITAN DISTRICT, AND ADJACENT TERRITORY, FOR CITIES OF 200,000 INHABITANTS OR MORE: 1920 AND 1910—Continued.

[See notes at head of this table, p. 87.]

DISTRICT.	Area in acres: 1920	POPULATION.		Per cent of increase:[1] 1910–1920
		1920	1910	
ROCHESTER.				
Metropolitan district	118,391.8	320,966	248,512	29.2
In city proper	18,891.0	295,750	218,149	35.6
Outside	99,500.8	25,216	30,363	—17.0
City and adjacent territory	338,084.6	342,999	272,741	25.8
Adjacent territory	319,193.6	47,249	54,592	—13.5
ST. LOUIS.				
Metropolitan district	197,757.1	952,012	828,733	14.9
In city proper	39,040.0	772,897	687,029	12.5
Outside	158,717.1	179,115	141,704	26.4
City and adjacent territory	456,257.4	1,014,457	881,925	15.0
Adjacent territory	417,317.4	241,560	194,896	23.9
SAN FRANCISCO-OAKLAND.				
Metropolitan district	286,500.8	891,477	686,873	29.8
In city proper (San Francisco)	26,880.0	506,676	416,912	21.5
In city proper (Oakland)	29,248.0	216,261	150,174	44.0
Outside	230,372.8	168,540	119,787	40.7
Cities and adjacent territory	381,880.0	900,921	692,654	30.1
Adjacent territory	325,752.0	177,984	125,568	41.7
SEATTLE.				
Metropolitan district	145,638.4	357,950	255,622	40.0
In city proper	37,478.4	315,312	237,194	32.9
Outside	108,160.0	42,638	18,428	131.4
City and adjacent territory	381,606.4	383,324	274,997	39.4
Adjacent territory	344,128.0	68,012	37,803	79.9
TOLEDO.				
Metropolitan district	59,661.2	263,717	180,375	46.2
In city proper	18,010.0	243,164	168,497	44.3
Outside	41,651.2	20,553	11,878	73.0
City and adjacent territory	336,890.0	294,248	208,872	40.9
Adjacent territory	318,880.0	51,084	40,375	26.5
WASHINGTON.				
Metropolitan district	170,146.0	506,588	380,508	33.1
In city proper	38,408.4	437,571	331,069	32.2
Outside	131,737.6	69,017	49,439	39.6
City and adjacent territory	567,166.2	540,702	413,458	30.8
Adjacent territory	528,757.8	103,131	82,389	25.2

[1] A minus sign (—) denotes decrease.

TABLE 19.—AREA AND POPULATION OF CENTRAL CITY AND OF ADJACENT TERRI-
TORY, FOR CITIES OF 100,000 TO 200,000 INHABITANTS: 1920 AND 1910.

[The adjacent territory is the total suburban territory lying within a distance of approximately 10 miles beyond the limits of the central city.]

[Population shown for central cities for each census year does not include that of annexations made subsequently to census date, but total population given for each district for 1920 and 1910 relates to same area.]

DISTRICT.	Area in acres: 1920	POPULATION.		Per cent of increase:[1] 1910–1920
		1920	1910	
Total for 29 districts	10,097,292.3	6,698,418	5,312,730	26.1
Total in central cities (30 cities)	469,903.0	4,143,265	3,165,314	30.9
Total outside central cities	9,627,389.3	2,555,153	2,147,416	19.0
ALBANY. (Including Troy and Schenectady.)				
Total in city and outside	418,195.2	382,959	357,467	7.1
In Albany	11,924.1	113,344	100,253	13.1
Outside Albany	406,271.1	269,615	257,214	4.8
BIRMINGHAM.				
Total in city and outside	399,443.2	290,884	208,066	39.8
In city proper	31,346.6	178,806	132,685	34.8
Outside city proper	368,096.6	112,078	75,381	48.7
BRIDGEPORT.				
Total in city and outside	191,130.0	190,043	132,554	43.4
In city proper	9,370.0	143,555	102,054	40.7
Outside city proper	181,760.0	46,488	30,500	52.4
DALLAS.				
Total in city and outside	123,725.0	184,515	112,008	64.7
In city proper	14,605.0	158,976	92,104	72.6
Outside city proper	109,120.0	25,539	19,904	28.3
DAYTON.				
Total in city and outside	347,547.0	210,177	163,646	28.4
In city proper	10,107.0	152,559	116,577	30.9
Outside city proper	337,440.0	57,618	47,069	22.4
DES MOINES.				
Total in city and outside	435,069.2	154,231	111,584	38.2
In city proper	33,597.2	126,468	86,368	46.4
Outside city proper	401,472.0	27,763	25,216	10.1
FALL RIVER-NEW BEDFORD.				
Total in cities and outside	416,404.0	333,130	296,935	12.2
In Fall River	21,723.0	120,485	119,295	1.0
In New Bedford	12,206.0	121,217	96,652	25.4
Outside Fall River and New Bedford	382,475.0	91,428	80,988	12.9
FORT WORTH.				
Total in city and outside	299,280.0	136,691	93,699	45.9
In city proper	10,553.4	106,482	73,312	45.2
Outside city proper	288,726.6	30,209	20,387	48.2
GRAND RAPIDS.				
Total in city and outside	315,360.0	171,204	145,632	17.6
In city proper	11,211.0	137,634	112,571	22.3
Outside city proper	304,149.0	33,570	33,061	1.5
HARTFORD.				
Total in city and outside	320,057.3	300,423	225,024	33.5
In city proper	10,162.9	138,036	98,915	39.6
Outside city proper	309,894.4	162,387	126,109	28.8

[1] A minus sign (−) denotes decrease.

TABLE 19.—AREA AND POPULATION OF CENTRAL CITY AND OF ADJACENT TERRI-
TORY, FOR CITIES OF 100,000 TO 200,000 INHABITANTS: 1920 AND 1910—Continued.

[See notes at head of this table, p. 91.]

DISTRICT.	Area in acres: 1920	POPULATION.		Per cent of increase:[1] 1910–1920
		1920	1910	
HOUSTON.				
Total in city and outside	497,504.0	168,351	103,584	62.5
In city proper	23,338.0	138,276	78,800	75.5
Outside city proper	474,166.0	30,075	24,784	21.3
LOWELL. (Including Lawrence.)				
Total in city and outside	365,108.0	313,206	283,741	10.4
In Lowell	8,308.0	112,759	106,294	6.1
Outside Lowell	356,800.0	200,447	177,447	13.0
MEMPHIS.				
Total in city and outside	454,098.0	214,169	181,143	18.2
In city proper	14,994.0	162,351	131,105	23.8
Outside city proper	439,104.0	51,818	50,038	3.6
NASHVILLE.				
Total in city and outside	347,724.8	169,194	150,902	12.1
In city proper	11,544.0	118,342	110,364	7.2
Outside city proper	336,180.8	50,852	40,538	25.4
NEW HAVEN.				
Total in city and outside	229,696.0	264,829	211,640	25.1
In city proper	11,460.0	162,537	133,605	21.7
Outside city proper	218,236.0	102,292	78,035	31.1
NORFOLK. (Including Portsmouth and Newport News.)				
Total in city and outside	269,689.6	303,278	205,445	47.6
In Norfolk	4,771.8	115,777	67,452	71.6
Outside Norfolk	264,917.8	187,501	137,993	35.9
OMAHA.				
Total in city and outside	373,330.0	249,999	207,829	20.3
In city proper	23,634.0	191,601	124,096	54.4
Outside city proper	349,696.0	58,398	83,733	−30.3
READING.				
Total in city and outside	314,103.5	169,655	153,960	10.2
In city proper	6,090.7	107,784	96,071	12.2
Outside city proper	308,012.8	61,871	57,889	6.9
RICHMOND.				
Total in city and outside	396,224.0	205,807	168,854	21.9
In city proper	15,360.0	171,667	127,628	34.5
Outside city proper	380,864.0	34,140	41,226	−17.2
SALT LAKE CITY.				
Total in city and outside	437,504.0	150,066	119,903	25.2
In city proper	32,704.0	118,110	92,777	27.3
Outside city proper	401,800.0	31,956	27,126	17.8
SAN ANTONIO.				
Total in city and outside	379,366.1	191,160	109,852	74.0
In city proper	22,860.5	161,379	96,614	67.0
Outside city proper	356,505.6	29,781	13,238	125.0
SCRANTON.				
Total in city and outside	331,446.5	347,793	314,998	10.4
In city proper	12,361.7	137,783	129,867	6.1
Outside city proper	319,084.8	210,010	185,131	13.4

[1] A minus sign (−) denotes decrease.

TABLE **19.**—AREA AND POPULATION OF CENTRAL CITY AND OF ADJACENT TERRI-
TORY, FOR CITIES OF 100,000 TO 200,000 INHABITANTS: 1920 AND 1910—Continued.

[See notes at head of this table, p. 91.]

| DISTRICT. | Area in acres: 1920 | POPULATION. | | Per cent of in-crease:[1] 1910-1920 |
		1920	1910	
SPOKANE.				
Total in city and outside	405,600.0	127,492	124,838	2.1
In city proper	24,819.0	104,437	104,402	([2])
Outside city proper	380,781.0	23,055	20,436	12.8
SPRINGFIELD, MASS.				
Total in city and outside	392,003.0	332,762	258,092	28.9
In city proper	20,451.0	129,614	88,926	45.8
Outside city proper	371,552.0	203,148	169,166	20.1
SYRACUSE.				
Total in city and outside	325,401.6	227,562	185,327	22.8
In city proper	11,782.0	171,717	137,249	25.1
Outside city proper	313,619.6	55,845	48,078	16.2
TRENTON.				
Total in city and outside	233,386.0	181,197	143,297	26.4
In city proper	4,490.0	119,289	96,815	23.2
Outside city proper	228,896.0	61,908	46,482	33.2
WILMINGTON.				
Total in city and outside	243,496.7	171,703	134,904	27.3
In city proper	4,495.1	110,168	87,411	26.0
Outside city proper	239,001.6	61,535	47,493	29.6
WORCESTER.				
Total in city and outside	398,953.6	268,551	228,271	17.6
In city proper	23,731.0	179,754	145,986	23.1
Outside city proper	375,222.6	88,797	82,285	7.9
YOUNGSTOWN.				
Total in city and outside	436,446.0	287,387	179,535	60.1
In city proper	15,902.0	132,358	79,066	67.4
Outside city proper	420,544.0	155,029	100,469	54.3

[1] A minus sign (−) denotes decrease.   [2] Less than one-tenth of 1 per cent.

COMPOSITION AND CHARACTERISTICS OF THE POPULATION.

TABLE 20.—COLOR OR RACE, FOR THE UNITED STATES: 1790–1920.

[Figures are given under each class for all census years for which data are available.]

CENSUS YEAR.	Total population.	COLOR OR RACE.							
		White.	Negro.			Indian.	Chinese.	Japanese.	All other.
			Total.	Black.	Mulatto.				
1920	105,710,620	94,820,915	10,463,131	8,802,577	1,660,554	244,437	61,639	111,010	¹ 9,488
1910	91,972,266	81,731,957	9,827,763	7,777,077	2,050,686	265,683	71,531	72,157	² 3,175
1900	75,994,575	66,809,196	8,833,994			237,196	89,863	24,326	....
1890	62,947,714	55,101,258	³ 7,488,676	6,337,980	1,132,060	248,253	107,488	2,039	....
1880	50,155,783	43,402,970	6,580,793			⁴ 66,407	105,465	148	....
1870 ⁵	38,558,371	33,589,377	4,880,009	4,295,960	584,049	⁴ 25,731	63,199	55	....
1870 ⁶	*39,818,449*	*34,337,292*	*5,392,172*			⁴ *25,731*	*63,199*	*55*	
1860	31,443,321	26,922,537	4,441,830	3,853,467	588,363	⁴ 44,021	34,933		
1850	23,191,876	19,553,068	3,638,808	3,233,057	405,751				
1840	17,069,453	14,195,805	2,873,648						
1830	12,866,020	10,537,378	2,328,642						
1820	9,638,453	7,866,797	1,771,656						
1810	7,239,881	5,862,073	1,377,808						
1800	5,308,483	4,306,446	1,002,037						
1790	3,929,214	3,172,006	757,208						

DECADE.	INCREASE,⁷ BY COLOR OR RACE.						
	Total population.	White.	Negro.	Indian.	Chinese.	Japanese.	All other.
1910–1920	13,738,354	13,088,958	635,368	−21,246	−9,892	38,853	6,313
1900–1910	15,977,691	14,922,761	993,769	28,487	−18,332	47,831	3,175
1890–1900	13,046,861	11,707,938	1,345,318	−11,057	−17,625	22,287	....
1880–1890	⁸ 12,466,467	⁹ 11,580,920	⁹ 889,247	⁹ −7,601	⁹ 2,010	1,891	....
1870–1880	11,597,412	9,813,593	1,700,784	⁴ 40,676	42,266	93	....
1870–1880 ⁶	*10,337,334*	*9,065,678*	*1,188,621*	⁴ *40,676*	*42,266*	*93*	
1860–1870 ⁶	*8,375,128*	*7,414,755*	*950,342*	⁴ *−18,290*	*28,266*	*55*	
1860–1870	7,115,050	6,666,840	438,179	⁴ −18,290	28,266	55	
1850–1860	8,251,445	7,369,469	803,022	⁴ 44,021	34,933		
1840–1850	6,122,423	5,357,263	765,160				
1830–1840	4,203,433	3,658,427	545,006				
1820–1830	3,227,567	2,670,581	556,986				
1810–1820	2,398,572	2,004,724	393,848				
1800–1810	1,931,398	1,555,627	375,771				
1790–1800	1,379,269	1,134,440	244,829				

¹ Comprises 5,603 Filipinos, 2,507 Hindus, 1,224 Koreans, 110 Hawaiians, 19 Malays, 17 Siamese, 6 Samoans, and 2 Maoris.
² Comprises 160 Filipinos, 2,545 Hindus, 102 Koreans, and 8 Maoris.
³ Includes 10,000 Negroes enumerated in Indian Territory, not distinguished as black or mulatto.
⁴ Exclusive of Indians in Indian Territory and on Indian reservations, not enumerated at censuses prior to 1890.
⁵ As enumerated.
⁶ Estimated corrected figures. Enumeration in 1870 incomplete.
⁷ A minus sign (−) denotes decrease.
⁸ Figures for 1890 are exclusive of 325,464 persons (117,368 whites, 18,636 Negroes, 189,447 Indians, and 13 Chinese), specially enumerated in Indian Territory and on Indian reservations.
⁹ See note 8.

TABLE 20.—COLOR OR RACE, FOR THE UNITED STATES: 1790-1920—Continued.

CENSUS YEAR.	PER CENT OF TOTAL POPULATION.						PER CENT OF TOTAL NEGRO.		PER CENT OF INCREASE [1] SINCE PRECEDING CENSUS.					
	White.	Negro.	Indian.	Chinese.	Japanese.	All other.	Black.	Mulatto.	White.	Negro.	Indian.	Chinese.	Japanese.	All other.
1920	89.7	9.9	0.2	0.1	0.1	(2)	84.1	15.9	16.0	6.5	−8.0	−13.8	53.8	198.8
1910	88.9	10.7	0.3	0.1	0.1	(2)	79.1	20.9	22.3	11.2	12.0	−20.4	196.6	.....
1900	87.9	11.6	0.3	0.1	(2)	.....			21.2	18.0	−4.5	−16.4	1,093.0	.....
1890	87.5	11.9	0.4	0.2	(2)	.....	84.8	15.2	[3]26.7	[3]13.5	[3]−11.4	[3]1.9	1,277.7	.....
1880 [6]	86.5	13.1	0.1	0.2	(2)	.....			29.2	34.9	[4]158.1	66.9	(5)	.....
1880 [6]									*26.4*	*22.0*	*[4]158.1*	*66.9*	*(5)*	.....
1870 [7]	87.1	12.7	0.1	0.2	(2)		88.0	12.0	24.8	9.9	[4]−41.5	80.9		
1870 [6]	*86.2*	*13.5*	*0.1*	*0.2*	*(2)*				*27.5*	*21.4*	*[4]−41.5*	*80.9*		
1860	85.6	14.1	0.1	0.1			86.8	13.2	37.7	22.1				
1850	84.3	15.7					88.8	11.2	37.7	26.6				
1840	83.2	16.8							34.7	23.4				
1830	81.9	18.1							33.9	31.4				
1820	81.6	18.4							34.2	28.6				
1810	81.0	19.0							36.1	37.5				
1800	81.1	18.9							35.8	32.3				
1790	80.7	19.3												

[1] A minus sign (−) denotes decrease.
[2] Less than one-tenth of 1 per cent.
[3] Figures for 1890 are exclusive of persons specially enumerated in Indian Territory and on Indian reservations.
[4] Exclusive of Indians in Indian Territory and on Indian reservations, not enumerated at censuses prior to 1890.
[5] Per cent not shown, base being less than 100.
[6] Per cent of increase based upon estimated corrected figures. Enumeration in 1870 incomplete.
[7] As enumerated.

TABLE 21.—NATIVITY AND PARENTAGE OF TOTAL POPULATION AND

[Figures are given under each class for all census years for which data are available. The term "native parents foreign born; and "mixed parentage," those

CLASS OF POPULATION AND CENSUS YEAR.	POPULATION.		NATIVE POPULATION.			FOREIGN-BORN POPULATION.		
	Native.	Foreign born.	Native parentage.	Foreign parentage.	Mixed parentage.	Native parentage.	Foreign parentage.	Mixed parentage.
Total:								
1920	91,789,928	13,920,692	68,994,682	15,764,366	7,030,880	(1)	13,832,797	87,895
1910	78,456,380	13,515,886	59,491,427	12,949,181	6,015,772	(1)	13,429,955	85,931
1900	65,653,299	10,341,276	49,956,178	10,650,802	5,046,319	9,458	10,269,085	62,733
1890	53,698,154	9,249,560	----------	----------	----------	----------	----------	----------
1880	43,475,840	6,679,943	----------	----------	----------	----------	----------	----------
1870 [2]	32,991,142	5,567,229	----------	----------	----------	----------	----------	----------
1860	27,304,624	4,138,697	----------	----------	----------	----------	----------	----------
1850	20,947,274	2,244,602	----------	----------	----------	----------	----------	----------
White:								
1920	81,108,161	13,712,754	58,421,957	15,694,539	6,991,665	(1)	13,627,161	85,593
1910	68,386,412	13,345,545	49,488,575	12,916,311	5,981,526	(1)	13,261,666	83,879
1900	56,595,379	10,213,817	40,949,362	10,632,280	5,013,737	8,854	10,143,607	61,356
1890	45,979,391	9,121,867	34,475,716	8,085,019	3,418,656	105,899	8,926,762	89,206
1880	36,843,291	6,559,679	28,568,424	6,363,769	1,911,098	----------	----------	----------
1870 [2]	28,095,665	5,493,712	22,771,397	4,167,098	1,157,170	----------	----------	----------
1860	22,825,784	4,096,753	----------	----------	----------	----------	----------	----------
1850	17,312,533	2,240,535	----------	----------	----------	----------	----------	----------
Negro:								
1920	10,389,328	73,803	10,334,151	25,843	29,334	(1)	72,630	1,173
1910	9,787,424	40,339	9,748,439	14,560	24,425	(1)	38,887	1,452
1900	8,813,658	20,336	8,779,267	9,198	25,193	538	18,690	1,108
Indian:								
1920	238,138	6,299	230,410	2,719	5,009	(1)	6,137	162
1910	262,930	2,753	253,481	1,900	7,549	(1)	2,407	346
1900	234,983	2,213	227,272	1,358	6,353	47	1,937	229
Chinese:								
1920	18,532	43,107	2,391	11,952	4,189	(1)	42,210	897
1910	14,935	56,596	738	12,076	2,121	(1)	56,368	228
1900	9,010	80,853	245	7,762	1,003	12	80,817	24
Japanese:								
1920	29,672	81,338	212	28,948	512	(1)	81,276	62
1910	4,502	67,655	44	4,313	145	(1)	67,629	26
1900	269	24,057	32	204	33	7	24,034	16
All other:								
1920	6,097	3,391	5,561	365	171	(1)	3,383	8
1910	177	2,998	150	21	6	(1)	2,998	-------

[1] In 1920 and 1910 all persons born in foreign territory, both parents being natives of the United
[2] Enumeration in 1870 incomplete.

OF EACH COLOR OR RACE CLASS, FOR THE UNITED STATES: 1850–1920.

parentage" includes those persons having both parents native; "foreign parentage," those having both having one parent native and the other foreign born.]

CLASS OF POPULATION AND CENSUS YEAR.	PER CENT OF TOTAL OF EACH CLASS.							PER CENT OF TOTAL NATIVE OF EACH CLASS.			PER CENT OF TOTAL FOREIGN BORN OF EACH CLASS.	
	Population.		Native population.			Foreign-born population.		Native.			Foreign born.	
	Native.	Foreign born.	Native parentage.	Foreign parentage.	Mixed parentage.	Foreign parentage.	Mixed parentage.	Native parentage.	Foreign parentage.	Mixed parentage.	Foreign parentage.	Mixed parentage.
Total:												
1920	86.8	13.2	65.3	14.9	6.7	13.1	0.1	75.2	17.2	7.7	99.4	0.6
1910	85.3	14.7	64.7	14.1	6.5	14.6	0.1	75.8	16.5	7.7	99.4	0.6
1900	86.4	13.6	65.7	14.0	6.6	13.5	0.1	76.1	16.2	7.7	99.3	0.6
1890	85.3	14.7	....	....	......	....	......	....	....	......	....	......
1880	86.7	13.3	....	....	......	....	......	....	....	......	....	......
1870[2]	85.6	14.4	....	....	......	....	......	....	....	......	....	......
1860	86.8	13.2	....	....	......	....	......	....	....	......	....	......
1850	90.3	9.7	....	....	......	....	......	....	....	......	....	......
White:												
1920	85.5	14.5	61.6	16.6	7.4	14.4	0.1	72.0	19.4	8.6	99.4	0.6
1910	83.7	16.3	60.5	15.8	7.3	16.2	0.1	72.4	18.9	8.7	99.4	0.6
1900	84.7	15.3	61.3	15.9	7.5	15.2	0.1	72.4	18.8	8.9	99.3	0.6
1890	83.4	16.6	62.6	14.7	6.2	16.2	0.2	75.0	17.6	7.4	97.9	1.0
1880	84.9	15.1	65.8	14.7	4.4	....	......	77.5	17.3	5.2	....	......
1870[2]	83.6	16.4	67.8	12.4	3.4	....	......	81.0	14.8	4.1	....	......
1860	84.8	15.2	....	....	......	....	......	....	....	......	....	......
1850	88.5	11.5	....	....	......	....	......	....	....	......	....	......
Negro:												
1920	99.3	0.7	98.8	0.2	0.3	0.7	(3)	99.5	0.2	0.3	98.4	1.6
1910	99.6	0.4	99.2	0.1	0.2	0.4	(3)	99.6	0.1	0.2	96.4	3.6
1900	99.8	0.2	99.4	0.1	0.3	0.2	(3)	99.6	0.1	0.3	91.9	5.4
Indian:												
1920	97.4	2.6	94.3	1.1	2.0	2.5	0.1	96.8	1.1	2.1	97.4	2.6
1910	99.0	1.0	95.4	0.7	2.8	0.9	0.1	96.4	0.7	2.9	87.4	12.6
1900	99.1	0.9	95.8	0.6	2.7	0.8	0.1	96.7	0.6	2.7	87.5	10.3
Chinese:												
1920	30.1	69.9	3.9	19.4	6.8	68.5	1.5	12.9	64.5	22.6	97.9	2.1
1910	20.9	79.1	1.0	16.9	3.0	78.8	0.3	4.9	80.9	14.2	99.6	0.4
1900	10.0	90.0	0.3	8.6	1.1	89.9	(3)	2.7	86.1	11.1	100.0	(3)
Japanese:												
1920	26.7	73.3	0.2	26.1	0.5	73.2	0.1	0.7	97.6	1.7	99.9	.01
1910	6.2	93.8	0.1	6.0	0.2	93.7	(3)	1.0	95.8	3.2	100.0	(3)
1900	1.1	98.9	0.1	0.8	0.1	98.8	0.1	11.9	75.8	12.3	99.9	.01
All other:												
1920	64.3	35.7	58.6	3.8	1.8	35.7	0.1	91.2	6.0	2.8	99.8	0.2
1910	5.6	94.4	4.7	0.7	0.2	94.4	......	84.7	11.9	3.4	100.0	......

States, were classified as American citizens born abroad and were included in the native class.
[3] Less than one-tenth of 1 per cent.

TABLE 22.—COLOR OR RACE, NATIVITY, AND

DIVISION AND STATE.	Total population: 1920	COLOR OR RACE.					
		White.	Negro.	Indian.	Chinese.	Japanese.	All other.
United States	105,710,620	94,820,915	10,463,131	244,437	61,639	111,010	9,488
GEOGRAPHIC DIVISIONS:							
New England	7,400,909	7,316,079	79,051	1,715	3,602	347	115
Middle Atlantic	22,261,144	21,641,840	600,183	5,940	8,812	3,266	1,103
East North Central	21,475,543	20,938,862	514,554	15,695	5,043	927	462
West North Central	12,544,249	12,225,387	278,521	37,263	1,678	1,215	185
South Atlantic	13,990,272	9,648,940	4,325,120	13,673	1,824	360	355
East South Central	8,893,307	6,367,547	2,523,532	1,628	542	35	28
West South Central	10,242,224	8,115,727	2,063,579	60,618	1,534	578	188
Mountain	3,336,101	3,212,899	30,891	76,899	4,339	10,792	371
Pacific	5,566,871	5,353,634	47,790	31,011	34,265	93,490	6,681
NEW ENGLAND:							
Maine	768,014	765,695	1,310	839	161	7	2
New Hampshire	443,083	442,331	621	28	95	8	......
Vermont	352,428	351,817	572	24	11	4	......
Massachusetts	3,852,356	3,803,524	45,466	555	2,544	191	76
Rhode Island	604,397	593,980	10,036	110	225	35	11
Connecticut	1,380,631	1,358,732	21,046	159	566	102	26
MIDDLE ATLANTIC:							
New York	10,385,227	10,172,027	198,483	5,503	5,793	2,686	735
New Jersey	3,155,900	3,037,087	117,132	100	1,190	325	66
Pennsylvania	8,720,017	8,432,726	284,568	337	1,829	255	302
EAST NORTH CENTRAL:							
Ohio	5,759,394	5,571,893	186,187	151	941	130	92
Indiana	2,930,390	2,849,071	80,810	125	283	81	20
Illinois	6,485,280	6,299,333	182,274	194	2,776	472	231
Michigan	3,668,412	3,601,627	60,082	5,614	792	184	113
Wisconsin	2,632,067	2,616,938	5,201	9,611	251	60	6
WEST NORTH CENTRAL:							
Minnesota	2,387,125	2,368,936	8,809	8,761	508	85	26
Iowa	2,404,021	2,384,181	19,005	529	235	29	42
Missouri	3,404,055	3,225,044	178,241	171	412	135	52
North Dakota	646,872	639,954	467	6,254	124	72	1
South Dakota	636,547	619,147	832	16,384	142	38	4
Nebraska	1,296,372	1,279,219	13,242	2,888	189	804	30
Kansas	1,769,257	1,708,906	57,925	2,276	68	52	30
SOUTH ATLANTIC:							
Delaware	223,003	192,615	30,335	2	43	8	......
Maryland	1,449,661	1,204,737	244,479	32	371	29	13
District of Columbia	437,571	326,860	109,966	37	461	103	144
Virginia	2,309,187	1,617,909	690,017	824	278	56	103
West Virginia	1,463,701	1,377,235	86,345	7	98	10	6
North Carolina	2,559,123	1,783,779	763,407	11,824	88	24	1
South Carolina	1,683,724	818,538	864,719	304	93	15	55
Georgia	2,895,832	1,689,114	1,206,365	125	211	9	8
Florida	968,470	638,153	329,487	518	181	106	25
EAST SOUTH CENTRAL:							
Kentucky	2,416,630	2,180,560	235,938	57	62	9	4
Tennessee	2,337,885	1,885,993	451,758	56	57	8	13
Alabama	2,348,174	1,447,032	900,652	405	59	18	8
Mississippi	1,790,618	853,962	935,184	1,105	364	....	3
WEST SOUTH CENTRAL:							
Arkansas	1,752,204	1,279,757	472,220	106	113	5	3
Louisiana	1,798,509	1,096,611	700,257	1,066	387	57	131
Oklahoma	2,028,283	1,821,194	149,408	57,337	261	67	16
Texas	4,663,228	3,918,165	741,694	2,109	773	449	38
MOUNTAIN:							
Montana	548,889	534,260	1,658	10,956	872	1,074	69
Idaho	431,866	425,600	920	3,098	585	1,569	26
Wyoming	194,402	190,146	1,375	1,040	252	1,194	92
Colorado	939,629	924,103	11,318	1,383	291	2,404	70
New Mexico	360,350	334,673	5,733	19,512	171	251	10
Arizona	334,162	291,449	8,005	32,989	1,137	550	32
Utah	449,396	441,901	1,446	2,711	342	2,936	60
Nevada	77,407	70,699	346	4,907	689	754	12
PACIFIC:							
Washington	1,356,621	1,319,777	6,883	9,061	2,363	17,387	1,150
Oregon	783,389	769,146	2,144	4,590	3,090	4,151	268
California	3,426,861	3,264,711	38,763	17,360	28,812	71,952	5,263

PARENTAGE, BY DIVISIONS AND STATES: 1920.

DIVISION AND STATE.	NATIVITY.		WHITE POPULATION BY NATIVITY AND PARENTAGE.				
			Native white.				Foreign-born white.
	Native.	Foreign born.	Total.	Native parentage.	Foreign parentage.	Mixed parentage.	
United States..	91,789,928	13,920,692	81,108,161	58,421,957	15,694,539	6,991,665	13,712,754
GEOGRAPHIC DIVISIONS:							
New England.....	5,514,964	1,885,945	5,445,425	2,803,149	1,906,340	735,936	1,870,654
Middle Atlantic...	17,300,726	4,960,418	16,729,265	9,631,012	5,397,951	1,700,302	4,912,575
East North Central	18,243,402	3,232,141	17,715,583	11,790,370	4,043,692	1,881,521	3,223,279
West North Central	11,168,596	1,375,653	10,853,426	7,475,548	2,126,126	1,251,752	1,371,961
South Atlantic....	13,659,735	330,537	9,333,020	8,779,416	353,643	199,961	315,920
East South Central	8,820,318	72,989	6,295,608	6,092,782	115,484	87,342	71,939
West South Central	9,777,396	464,828	7,656,394	6,959,785	415,799	280,810	459,333
Mountain.........	2,868,481	467,620	2,759,674	2,002,508	451,132	306,034	453,225
Pacific...........	4,436,310	1,130,561	4,319,766	2,887,387	884,372	548,007	1,033,868
NEW ENGLAND:							
Maine............	660,200	107,814	658,346	495,780	86,150	76,416	107,349
New Hampshire...	351,686	91,397	351,098	225,512	81,039	44,547	91,233
Vermont.........	307,870	44,558	307,291	228,325	42,100	36,866	44,526
Massachusetts.....	2,763,808	1,088,548	2,725,990	1,230,773	1,093,258	401,959	1,077,534
Rhode Island.....	429,208	175,189	420,481	173,553	182,660	64,268	173,499
Connecticut.......	1,002,192	378,439	982,219	449,206	421,133	111,880	376,513
MIDDLE ATLANTIC:							
New York........	7,559,852	2,825,375	7,385,915	3,668,266	2,844,083	873,566	2,786,112
New Jersey........	2,413,414	742,486	2,298,474	1,212,675	829,058	256,741	738,613
Pennsylvania......	7,327,460	1,392,557	7,044,876	4,750,071	1,724,810	569,995	1,387,850
EAST NORTH CENTRAL:							
Ohio.............	5,078,942	680,452	4,893,196	3,669,122	838,251	385,823	678,697
Indiana..........	2,779,062	151,328	2,698,203	2,329,544	227,066	141,593	150,868
Illinois..........	5,274,696	1,210,584	5,092,382	3,066,563	1,467,036	558,783	1,206,951
Michigan.........	2,939,120	729,292	2,874,992	1,670,447	775,288	429,257	726,635
Wisconsin........	2,171,582	460,485	2,156,810	1,054,694	736,051	366,065	460,128
WEST NORTH CENTRAL:							
Minnesota........	1,900,330	486,795	1,882,772	827,627	708,126	347,019	486,164
Iowa.............	2,178,027	225,994	2,158,534	1,528,553	376,710	253,271	225,647
Missouri.........	3,217,220	186,835	3,039,018	2,536,936	300,064	202,018	186,026
North Dakota.....	515,009	131,863	508,451	207,966	203,973	96,512	131,503
South Dakota.....	554,013	82,534	536,756	308,598	141,341	86,817	82,391
Nebraska.........	1,145,707	150,665	1,129,567	757,064	231,948	140,555	149,652
Kansas...........	1,658,290	110,967	1,598,328	1,308,804	163,964	125,560	110,578
SOUTH ATLANTIC:							
Delaware.........	203,102	19,901	172,805	139,876	23,288	9,641	19,810
Maryland.........	1,346,482	103,179	1,102,560	893,088	143,203	66,269	102,177
Dist. of Columbia.	408,206	29,365	298,312	239,488	35,129	23,695	28,548
Virginia..........	2,277,482	31,705	1,587,124	1,534,494	30,514	22,116	30,785
West Virginia.....	1,401,596	62,105	1,315,329	1,232,857	56,625	25,847	61,906
North Carolina....	2,551,851	7,272	1,776,680	1,765,203	5,737	5,740	7,099
South Carolina....	1,677,142	6,582	812,137	799,418	7,025	5,694	6,401
Georgia..........	2,879,268	16,564	1,672,928	1,642,697	16,371	13,860	16,186
Florida..........	914,606	53,864	595,145	532,295	35,751	27,099	43,008
EAST SOUTH CENTRAL:							
Kentucky.........	2,385,724	30,906	2,149,780	2,039,134	65,931	44,715	30,780
Tennessee........	2,322,237	15,648	1,870,515	1,832,757	20,423	17,335	15,478
Alabama.........	2,330,147	18,027	1,429,370	1,394,129	19,591	15,650	17,662
Mississippi.......	1,782,210	8,408	845,943	826,762	9,539	9,642	8,019
WEST SOUTH CENTRAL:							
Arkansas.........	1,738,067	14,137	1,265,782	1,226,692	19,030	20,060	13,975
Louisiana.........	1,752,082	46,427	1,051,740	941,724	67,016	43,000	44,871
Oklahoma........	1,987,851	40,432	1,781,226	1,679,107	53,083	49,036	39,968
Texas............	4,299,396	363,832	3,557,646	3,112,262	276,670	168,714	360,519
MOUNTAIN:							
Montana.........	453,298	95,591	440,640	275,803	101,918	62,919	93,620
Idaho............	391,119	40,747	386,705	294,252	47,920	44,533	38,963
Wyoming.........	167,835	26,567	164,891	122,884	25,234	16,773	25,255
Colorado.........	820,491	119,138	807,149	603,041	130,059	74,049	116,954
New Mexico......	330,542	29,808	305,596	273,317	18,865	13,414	29,077
Arizona..........	253,596	80,566	213,350	151,145	39,534	22,671	78,089
Utah.............	390,196	59,200	385,446	245,781	75,901	63,764	56,455
Nevada..........	61,404	16,003	55,897	36,285	11,701	7,911	14,802
PACIFIC:							
Washington.......	1,091,329	265,292	1,069,722	711,706	214,618	143,398	250,055
Oregon..........	675,745	107,644	666,995	497,726	95,827	73,442	102,151
California........	2,669,236	757,625	2,583,049	1,677,955	573,927	331,167	681,662

TABLE 23.—PER CENT DISTRIBUTION OF TOTAL POPULATION BY COLOR OR RACE, NATIVITY, AND PARENTAGE, BY DIVISIONS AND STATES: 1920.

DIVISION AND STATE.	COLOR OR RACE.			NATIVITY.		NATIVE WHITE, BY PARENTAGE.				For-eign-born white.
	White.	Negro.	Ind., Chi., Jap., and all other.	Na-tive.	For-eign born.	Total.	Native parent-age.	For-eign parent-age.	Mixed parent-age.	
United States	89.7	9.9	0.4	86.8	13.2	76.7	55.3	14.8	6.6	13.0
GEOGRAPHIC DIVISIONS:										
New England	98.9	1.1	0.1	74.5	25.5	73.6	37.9	25.8	9.9	25.3
Middle Atlantic	97.2	2.7	0.1	77.7	22.3	75.2	43.3	24.2	7.6	22.1
East North Central	97.5	2.4	0.1	84.9	15.1	82.5	54.9	18.8	8.8	15.0
West North Central	97.5	2.2	0.3	89.0	11.0	86.5	59.6	16.9	10.0	10.9
South Atlantic	69.0	30.9	0.1	97.6	2.4	66.7	62.8	2.5	1.4	2.3
East South Central	71.6	28.4	(1)	99.2	0.8	70.8	68.5	1.3	1.0	0.8
West South Central	79.2	20.1	0.6	95.5	4.5	74.8	68.0	4.1	2.7	4.5
Mountain	96.3	0.9	2.8	86.0	14.0	82.7	60.0	13.5	9.2	13.6
Pacific	96.2	0.9	3.0	79.7	20.3	77.6	51.9	15.9	9.8	18.6
NEW ENGLAND:										
Maine	99.7	0.2	0.1	86.0	14.0	85.7	64.6	11.2	9.9	14.0
New Hampshire	99.8	0.1	(1)	79.4	20.6	79.2	50.9	18.3	10.1	20.6
Vermont	99.8	0.2	(1)	87.4	12.6	87.2	64.8	11.9	10.5	12.6
Massachusetts	98.7	1.2	0.1	71.7	28.3	70.8	31.9	28.4	10.4	28.0
Rhode Island	98.3	1.7	0.1	71.0	29.0	69.6	28.7	30.2	10.6	28.7
Connecticut	98.4	1.5	0.1	72.6	27.4	71.1	32.5	30.5	8.1	27.3
MIDDLE ATLANTIC:										
New York	97.9	1.9	0.1	72.8	27.2	71.1	35.3	27.4	8.4	26.8
New Jersey	96.2	3.7	0.1	76.5	23.5	72.8	38.4	26.3	8.1	23.4
Pennsylvania	96.7	3.3	(1)	84.0	16.0	80.8	54.5	19.8	6.5	15.9
EAST NORTH CENTRAL:										
Ohio	96.7	3.2	(1)	88.2	11.8	85.0	63.7	14.6	6.7	11.8
Indiana	97.2	2.8	(1)	94.8	5.2	92.1	79.5	7.7	4.8	5.1
Illinois	97.1	2.8	0.1	81.3	18.7	78.5	47.3	22.6	8.6	18.6
Michigan	98.2	1.6	0.2	80.1	19.9	78.4	45.5	21.1	11.7	19.8
Wisconsin	99.4	0.2	0.4	82.5	17.5	81.9	40.1	28.0	13.9	17.5
WEST NORTH CENTRAL:										
Minnesota	99.2	0.4	0.4	79.6	20.4	78.9	34.7	29.7	14.5	20.4
Iowa	99.2	0.8	(1)	90.6	9.4	89.8	63.6	15.7	10.5	9.4
Missouri	94.7	5.2	(1)	94.5	5.5	89.3	74.5	8.8	5.9	5.5
North Dakota	98.9	0.1	1.0	79.6	20.4	78.6	32.1	31.5	14.9	20.3
South Dakota	97.3	0.1	2.6	87.0	13.0	84.3	48.5	22.2	13.6	12.9
Nebraska	98.7	1.0	0.3	88.4	11.6	87.1	58.4	17.9	10.8	11.5
Kansas	96.6	3.3	0.1	93.7	6.3	90.3	74.0	9.3	7.1	6.2
SOUTH ATLANTIC:										
Delaware	86.4	13.6	(1)	91.1	8.9	77.5	62.7	10.4	4.3	8.9
Maryland	83.1	16.9	(1)	92.9	7.1	76.1	61.6	9.9	4.6	7.0
District of Columbia	74.7	25.1	0.2	93.3	6.7	68.2	54.7	8.0	5.4	6.5
Virginia	70.1	29.9	0.1	98.6	1.4	68.7	66.5	1.3	1.0	1.3
West Virginia	94.1	5.9	(1)	95.8	4.2	89.9	84.2	3.9	1.8	4.2
North Carolina	69.7	29.8	0.5	99.7	0.3	69.4	69.0	0.2	0.2	0.3
South Carolina	48.6	51.4	(1)	99.6	0.4	48.2	47.5	0.4	0.3	0.4
Georgia	58.3	41.7	(1)	99.4	0.6	57.8	56.7	0.6	0.5	0.6
Florida	65.9	34.0	0.1	94.4	5.6	61.5	55.0	3.7	2.8	4.4
EAST SOUTH CENTRAL:										
Kentucky	90.2	9.8	(1)	98.7	1.3	89.0	84.4	2.7	1.9	1.3
Tennessee	80.7	19.3	(1)	99.3	0.7	80.0	78.4	0.9	0.7	0.7
Alabama	61.6	38.4	(1)	99.2	0.8	60.9	59.4	0.8	0.7	0.8
Mississippi	47.7	52.2	0.1	99.5	0.5	47.2	46.2	0.5	0.5	0.4
WEST SOUTH CENTRAL:										
Arkansas	73.0	27.0	(1)	99.2	0.8	72.2	70.0	1.1	1.1	0.8
Louisiana	61.0	38.9	0.1	97.4	2.6	58.5	52.4	3.7	2.4	2.5
Oklahoma	89.8	7.4	2.8	98.0	2.0	87.8	82.8	2.6	2.4	2.0
Texas	84.0	15.9	0.1	92.2	7.8	76.3	66.7	5.9	3.6	7.7
MOUNTAIN:										
Montana	97.3	0.3	2.4	82.6	17.4	80.3	50.2	18.6	11.5	17.1
Idaho	98.6	0.2	1.2	90.6	9.4	89.5	68.1	11.1	10.3	9.0
Wyoming	97.8	0.7	1.5	86.3	13.7	84.8	63.2	13.0	8.6	13.0
Colorado	98.3	1.2	0.4	87.3	12.7	85.9	64.2	12.8	7.9	12.4
New Mexico	92.9	1.6	5.5	91.7	8.3	84.8	73.0	5.2	3.7	8.1
Arizona	87.2	2.4	10.4	75.9	24.1	63.8	45.2	11.8	6.0	23.4
Utah	98.3	0.3	1.3	86.8	13.2	85.8	54.7	16.9	14.2	12.6
Nevada	91.3	0.4	8.2	79.3	20.7	72.2	46.9	15.1	10.2	19.1
PACIFIC:										
Washington	97.3	0.5	2.2	80.4	19.6	78.9	52.5	15.8	10.6	18.4
Oregon	98.2	0.3	1.5	86.3	13.7	85.1	63.5	12.2	9.4	13.0
California	95.3	1.1	3.6	77.9	22.1	75.4	49.0	16.7	9.7	19.9

[1] Less than one-tenth of 1 per cent.

TABLE 24.—WHITE AND NEGRO POPULATION, WITH PER CENT NEGRO IN TOTAL POPULATION, BY DIVISIONS AND STATES: 1920 AND 1910.

DIVISION AND STATE.	1920			1910			PER CENT NEGRO IN TOTAL POPULATION.	
	Total population.[1]	White.	Negro.	Total population.[1]	White.	Negro.	1920	1910
United States	105,710,620	94,820,915	10,463,131	91,972,266	81,731,957	9,827,763	9.9	10.7
GEOG. DIVISIONS:								
New England	7,400,909	7,316,079	79,051	6,552,681	6,480,514	66,306	1.1	1.0
Middle Atlantic	22,261,144	21,641,840	600,183	19,315,892	18,880,452	417,870	2.7	2.2
E. North Central	21,475,543	20,938,862	514,554	18,250,621	17,927,622	300,836	2.4	1.6
W. North Central	12,544,249	12,225,387	278,521	11,637,921	11,351,621	242,662	2.2	2.1
South Atlantic	13,990,272	9,648,940	4,325,120	12,194,895	8,071,603	4,112,488	30.9	33.7
E. South Central	8,893,307	6,367,547	2,523,532	8,409,901	5,754,326	2,652,513	28.4	31.5
W. South Central	10,242,224	8,115,727	2,063,579	8,784,534	6,721,491	1,984,426	20.1	22.6
Mountain	3,336,101	3,212,899	30,801	2,633,517	2,520,455	21,467	0.9	0.8
Pacific	5,566,871	5,353,634	47,790	4,192,304	4,023,873	29,195	0.9	0.7
NEW ENGLAND:								
Maine	768,014	765,695	1,310	742,371	739,995	1,363	0.2	0.2
New Hampshire	443,083	442,331	621	430,572	429,906	564	0.1	0.1
Vermont	352,428	351,817	572	355,956	354,298	1,621	0.2	0.5
Massachusetts	3,852,356	3,803,524	45,466	3,366,416	3,324,926	38,055	1.2	1.1
Rhode Island	604,397	593,980	10,036	542,610	532,492	9,529	1.7	1.8
Connecticut	1,380,631	1,358,732	21,046	1,114,756	1,098,897	15,174	1.5	1.4
MIDDLE ATLANTIC:								
New York	10,385,227	10,172,027	198,483	9,113,614	8,966,845	134,191	1.9	1.5
New Jersey	3,155,900	3,037,087	117,132	2,537,167	2,445,894	89,760	3.7	3.5
Pennsylvania	8,720,017	8,432,726	284,568	7,665,111	7,467,713	193,919	3.3	2.5
E. NORTH CENTRAL:								
Ohio	5,759,394	5,571,893	186,187	4,767,121	4,654,897	111,452	3.2	2.3
Indiana	2,930,390	2,849,071	80,810	2,700,876	2,639,961	60,320	2.8	2.2
Illinois	6,485,280	6,299,333	182,274	5,638,591	5,526,962	109,049	2.8	1.9
Michigan	3,668,412	3,601,627	60,082	2,810,173	2,785,247	17,115	1.6	0.6
Wisconsin	2,632,067	2,616,938	5,201	2,333,860	2,320,555	2,900	0.2	0.1
W. NORTH CENTRAL:								
Minnesota	2,387,125	2,368,936	8,809	2,075,708	2,059,227	7,084	0.4	0.3
Iowa	2,404,021	2,384,181	19,005	2,224,771	2,209,191	14,973	0.8	0.7
Missouri	3,404,055	3,225,044	178,241	3,293,335	3,134,932	157,452	5.2	4.8
North Dakota	646,872	639,954	467	577,056	569,855	617	0.1	0.1
South Dakota	636,547	619,147	832	583,888	563,771	817	0.1	0.1
Nebraska	1,296,372	1,279,219	13,242	1,192,214	1,180,293	7,689	1.0	0.6
Kansas	1,769,257	1,708,906	57,925	1,690,949	1,634,352	54,030	3.3	3.2
SOUTH ATLANTIC:								
Delaware	223,003	192,615	30,335	202,322	171,102	31,181	13.6	15.4
Maryland	1,449,661	1,204,737	244,479	1,295,346	1,062,639	232,250	16.9	17.9
Dist. of Columbia	437,571	326,860	109,966	331,069	236,128	94,446	25.1	28.5
Virginia	2,309,187	1,617,909	690,017	2,061,612	1,389,809	671,096	29.9	32.6
West Virginia	1,463,701	1,377,235	86,345	1,221,119	1,156,817	64,173	5.9	5.3
North Carolina	2,559,123	1,783,779	763,407	2,206,287	1,500,511	697,843	29.8	31.6
South Carolina	1,683,724	818,538	864,719	1,515,400	679,161	835,843	51.4	55.2
Georgia	2,895,832	1,689,114	1,206,365	2,609,121	1,431,802	1,176,987	41.7	45.1
Florida	968,470	638,153	329,487	752,619	443,634	308,669	34.0	41.0
E. SOUTH CENTRAL:								
Kentucky	2,416,630	2,180,560	235,938	2,289,905	2,027,951	261,656	9.8	11.4
Tennessee	2,337,885	1,885,993	451,758	2,184,789	1,711,432	473,088	19.3	21.7
Alabama	2,348,174	1,447,032	900,652	2,138,093	1,228,832	908,282	38.4	42.5
Mississippi	1,790,618	853,962	935,184	1,797,114	786,111	1,009,487	52.2	56.2
W. SOUTH CENTRAL:								
Arkansas	1,752,204	1,279,757	472,220	1,574,449	1,131,026	442,891	27.0	28.1
Louisiana	1,798,509	1,096,611	700,257	1,656,388	941,086	713,874	38.9	43.1
Oklahoma	2,028,283	1,821,194	149,408	1,657,155	1,444,531	137,612	7.4	8.3
Texas	4,663,228	3,918,165	741,694	3,896,542	3,204,848	690,049	15.9	17.7
MOUNTAIN:								
Montana	548,889	534,260	1,658	376,053	360,580	1,834	0.3	0.5
Idaho	431,866	425,668	920	325,594	319,221	651	0.2	0.2
Wyoming	194,402	190,146	1,375	145,965	140,318	2,235	0.7	1.5
Colorado	939,629	924,103	11,318	799,024	783,415	11,453	1.2	1.4
New Mexico	360,350	334,673	5,733	327,301	304,594	1,628	1.6	0.5
Arizona	334,162	291,449	8,005	204,354	171,468	2,009	2.4	1.0
Utah	449,396	441,901	1,446	373,351	366,583	1,144	0.3	0.3
Nevada	77,407	70,699	346	81,875	74,276	513	0.4	0.6
PACIFIC:								
Washington	1,356,621	1,319,777	6,883	1,141,990	1,109,111	6,058	0.5	0.5
Oregon	783,389	769,146	2,144	672,765	655,090	1,492	0.3	0.2
California	3,426,861	3,264,711	38,763	2,377,549	2,259,672	21,645	1.1	0.9

[1] Includes Indians, Chinese, Japanese, and all other.

TABLE 25.—NEGRO POPULATION, DISTINGUISHED AS BLACK OR MULATTO, WITH PER CENT MULATTO IN TOTAL NEGRO POPULATION, BY DIVISIONS AND STATES: 1920 AND 1910.

DIVISION AND STATE.	1920			1910			PER CENT MULATTO IN TOTAL NEGRO.	
	Total Negro.	Black.	Mulatto.	Total Negro.	Black.	Mulatto.	1920	1910
United States..	10,463,131	8,802,577	1,660,554	9,827,763	7,777,077	2,050,686	15.9	20.9
GEOG. DIVISIONS:								
New England.....	79,051	63,734	15,317	66,306	44,156	22,150	19.4	33.4
Middle Atlantic...	600,183	530,350	69,833	417,870	335,901	81,969	11.6	19.6
E. North Central..	514,554	408,197	106,357	300,836	201,027	99,809	20.7	33.2
W. North Central.	278,521	226,567	51,954	242,662	173,031	69,631	18.7	28.7
South Atlantic....	4,325,120	3,627,737	697,383	4,112,488	3,256,669	855,819	16.1	20.8
E. South Central..	2,523,532	2,143,871	379,661	2,652,513	2,145,458	507,055	15.0	19.1
W. South Central.	2,063,579	1,743,116	320,463	1,984,426	1,586,440	397,986	15.5	20.1
Mountain........	30,801	25,235	5,566	21,467	15,332	6,135	18.1	28.6
Pacific...........	47,790	33,770	14,020	29,195	19,063	10,132	29.3	34.7
NEW ENGLAND:								
Maine...........	1,310	884	426	1,363	737	626	32.5	45.9
New Hampshire..	621	439	182	564	356	208	29.3	36.9
Vermont........	572	327	245	1,621	1,185	436	42.8	26.9
Massachusetts.....	45,466	35,562	9,904	38,055	24,100	13,955	21.8	36.7
Rhode Island.....	10,036	7,919	2,117	9,529	6,350	3,179	21.1	33.4
Connecticut......	21,046	18,603	2,443	15,174	11,428	3,746	11.6	24.7
MIDDLE ATLANTIC:								
New York........	198,483	171,507	26,976	134,191	103,583	30,608	13.6	22.8
New Jersey......	117,132	103,684	13,448	89,760	75,553	14,207	11.5	15.8
Pennsylvania.....	284,568	255,159	29,409	193,919	156,765	37,154	10.3	19.2
E. NORTH CENTRAL:								
Ohio.............	186,187	148,234	37,953	111,452	72,203	39,249	20.4	35.2
Indiana..........	80,810	66,812	13,998	60,320	45,767	14,553	17.3	24.1
Illinois..........	182,274	138,634	43,640	109,049	72,221	36,828	23.9	33.8
Michigan.........	60,082	50,463	9,619	17,115	9,079	8,036	16.0	47.0
Wisconsin........	5,201	4,054	1,147	2,900	1,757	1,143	22.1	39.4
W. NORTH CENTRAL:								
Minnesota	8,809	6,563	2,246	7,084	4,468	2,616	25.5	36.9
Iowa............	19,005	15,555	3,450	14,973	11,329	3,644	18.2	24.3
Missouri.........	178,241	148,339	29,902	157,452	112,762	44,690	16.8	28.4
North Dakota.....	467	355	112	617	460	157	24.0	25.4
South Dakota.....	832	547	285	817	521	296	34.3	36.2
Nebraska........	13,242	9,620	3,622	7,689	5,602	2,087	27.4	27.1
Kansas..........	57,925	45,588	12,337	54,030	37,889	16,141	21.3	29.9
SOUTH ATLANTIC:								
Delaware.........	30,335	27,822	2,513	31,181	27,475	3,706	8.3	11.9
Maryland.........	244,479	213,186	31,293	232,250	189,098	43,152	12.8	18.6
Dist. of Columbia..	109,966	81,502	28,464	94,446	61,494	32,952	25.9	34.9
Virginia..........	690,017	525,846	164,171	671,096	448,186	222,910	23.8	33.2
West Virginia.....	86,345	69,073	17,272	64,173	43,294	20,879	20.0	32.5
North Carolina....	763,407	637,981	125,426	697,843	553,720	144,123	16.4	20.7
South Carolina....	864,719	748,250	116,469	835,843	701,462	134,381	13.5	16.1
Georgia..........	1,206,365	1,037,153	169,212	1,176,987	972,782	204,205	14.0	17.3
Florida..........	329,487	286,924	42,563	308,669	259,158	49,511	12.9	16.0
E. SOUTH CENTRAL:								
Kentucky.........	235,938	194,444	41,494	261,656	195,713	65,943	17.6	25.2
Tennessee........	451,758	368,852	82,906	473,088	354,391	118,697	18.4	25.1
Alabama.........	900,652	767,533	133,119	908,282	756,872	151,410	14.8	16.7
Mississippi.......	935,184	813,042	122,142	1,009,487	838,482	171,005	13.1	16.9
W. SOUTH CENTRAL:								
Arkansas.........	472,220	410,624	61,596	442,891	361,520	81,371	13.0	18.4
Louisiana........	700,257	583,550	116,707	713,874	561,297	152,577	16.7	21.4
Oklahoma........	149,408	122,011	27,397	137,612	98,269	39,343	18.3	28.6
Texas.............	711,604	626,931	114,763	690,049	565,354	124,695	15.5	18.1
MOUNTAIN:								
Montana..........	1,658	1,275	383	1,834	1,223	611	20.1	33.3
Idaho............	920	738	182	651	425	226	19.8	34.7
Wyoming.........	1,375	1,016	359	2,235	1,942	293	26.1	13.1
Colorado.........	11,318	8,568	2,750	11,453	7,815	3,638	24.3	31.8
New Mexico.......	5,733	4,949	784	1,628	1,189	439	13.7	27.0
Arizona..........	8,005	7,314	691	2,009	1,561	448	8.6	22.3
Utah............	1,446	1,117	329	1,144	854	290	22.8	25.3
Nevada..........	346	258	88	513	323	190	25.4	37.0
PACIFIC:								
Washington.......	6,883	3,936	2,947	6,058	4,218	1,840	42.8	30.4
Oregon...........	2,144	1,480	664	1,492	1,058	434	31.0	29.1
California........	38,763	28,354	10,409	21,645	13,787	7,858	26.9	36.3

TABLE 26.—NATIVE AND FOREIGN-BORN POPULATION, WITH PER CENT FOREIGN BORN IN TOTAL POPULATION, BY DIVISIONS AND STATES: 1920 AND 1910.

DIVISION AND STATE.	1920			1910			PER CENT FOREIGN BORN IN TOTAL POPULATION.	
	Total population.	Native.	Foreign born.	Total population.	Native.	Foreign born.	1920	1910
United States..	105,710,620	91,789,928	13,920,692	91,972,266	78,456,380	13,515,886	13.2	14.7
GEOG. DIVISIONS:								
New England.....	7,400,909	5,514,964	1,885,945	6,552,681	4,727,571	1,825,110	25.5	27.9
Middle Atlantic...	22,261,144	17,300,726	4,960,418	19,315,892	14,464,719	4,851,173	22.3	25.1
E. North Central..	21,475,543	18,243,402	3,232,141	18,250,621	15,176,855	3,073,766	15.1	16.8
W. North Central.	12,544,249	11,168,596	1,375,653	11,637,921	10,021,226	1,616,695	11.0	13.9
South Atlantic....	13,990,272	13,659,735	330,537	12,194,895	11,894,901	299,994	2.4	2.5
E. South Central..	8,893,307	8,820,318	72,989	8,409,901	8,322,076	87,825	0.8	1.0
W. South Central.	10,242,224	9,777,396	464,828	8,784,534	8,432,342	352,192	4.5	4.0
Mountain.........	3,336,101	2,868,481	467,620	2,633,517	2,180,195	453,322	14.0	17.2
Pacific...........	5,566,871	4,436,310	1,130,561	4,192,304	3,236,495	955,809	20.3	22.8
NEW ENGLAND:								
Maine............	768,014	660,200	107,814	742,371	631,809	110,562	14.0	14.9
New Hampshire...	443,083	351,686	91,397	430,572	333,905	96,667	20.6	22.5
Vermont..........	352,428	307,870	44,558	355,956	306,035	49,921	12.6	14.0
Massachusetts.....	3,852,356	2,763,808	1,088,548	3,366,416	2,307,171	1,059,245	28.3	31.5
Rhode Island.....	604,397	429,208	175,189	542,610	363,469	179,141	29.0	33.0
Connecticut.......	1,380,631	1,002,192	378,439	1,114,756	785,182	329,574	27.4	29.6
MIDDLE ATLANTIC:								
New York........	10,385,227	7,559,852	2,825,375	9,113,614	6,365,603	2,748,011	27.2	30.2
New Jersey.......	3,155,900	2,413,414	742,486	2,537,167	1,876,379	660,788	23.5	26.0
Pennsylvania.....	8,720,017	7,327,460	1,392,557	7,665,111	6,222,737	1,442,374	16.0	18.8
E. NORTH CENTRAL:								
Ohio.............	5,759,394	5,078,942	680,452	4,767,121	4,168,747	598,374	11.8	12.6
Indiana..........	2,930,390	2,779,062	151,328	2,700,876	2,541,213	159,663	5.2	5.9
Illinois...........	6,485,280	5,274,696	1,210,584	5,638,591	4,433,277	1,205,314	18.7	21.4
Michigan.........	3,668,412	2,939,120	729,292	2,810,173	2,212,623	597,550	19.9	21.3
Wisconsin........	2,632,067	2,171,582	460,485	2,333,860	1,820,995	512,865	17.5	22.0
W. NORTH CENTRAL:								
Minnesota........	2,387,125	1,900,330	486,795	2,075,708	1,532,113	543,595	20.4	26.2
Iowa.............	2,404,021	2,178,027	225,994	2,224,771	1,951,006	273,765	9.4	12.3
Missouri..........	3,404,055	3,217,220	186,835	3,293,335	3,063,556	229,779	5.5	7.0
North Dakota.....	646,872	515,009	131,863	577,056	420,402	156,654	20.4	27.1
South Dakota.....	636,547	554,013	82,534	583,888	483,098	100,790	13.0	17.3
Nebraska.........	1,296,372	1,145,707	150,665	1,192,214	1,015,552	176,662	11.6	14.8
Kansas...........	1,769,257	1,658,290	110,967	1,690,949	1,555,499	135,450	6.3	8.0
SOUTH ATLANTIC:								
Delaware.........	223,003	203,102	19,901	202,322	184,830	17,492	8.9	8.6
Maryland.........	1,449,661	1,346,482	103,179	1,295,346	1,190,402	104,944	7.1	8.1
Dist. of Columbia.	437,571	408,206	29,365	331,069	306,167	24,902	6.7	7.5
Virginia..........	2,309,187	2,277,482	31,705	2,061,612	2,034,555	27,057	1.4	1.3
West Virginia.....	1,463,701	1,401,596	62,105	1,221,119	1,163,901	57,218	4.2	4.7
North Carolina....	2,559,123	2,551,851	7,272	2,206,287	2,200,195	6,092	0.3	0.3
South Carolina....	1,683,724	1,677,142	6,582	1,515,400	1,509,221	6,179	0.4	0.4
Georgia..........	2,895,832	2,879,268	16,564	2,609,121	2,593,644	15,477	0.6	0.6
Florida...........	968,470	914,606	53,864	752,619	711,986	40,633	5.6	5.4
E. SOUTH CENTRAL:								
Kentucky.........	2,416,630	2,385,724	30,906	2,289,905	2,249,743	40,162	1.3	1.8
Tennessee........	2,337,885	2,322,237	15,648	2,184,789	2,166,182	18,607	0.7	0.9
Alabama.........	2,348,174	2,330,147	18,027	2,138,093	2,118,807	19,286	0.8	0.9
Mississippi.......	1,790,618	1,782,210	8,408	1,797,114	1,787,344	9,770	0.5	0.5
W. SOUTH CENTRAL:								
Arkansas.........	1,752,204	1,738,067	14,137	1,574,449	1,557,403	17,046	0.8	1.1
Louisiana........	1,798,509	1,752,082	46,427	1,656,388	1,603,622	52,766	2.6	3.2
Oklahoma........	2,028,283	1,987,851	40,432	1,657,155	1,616,713	40,442	2.0	2.4
Texas............	4,663,228	4,299,396	363,832	3,896,542	3,654,604	241,938	7.8	6.2
MOUNTAIN:								
Montana.........	548,889	453,298	95,591	376,053	281,340	94,713	17.4	25.2
Idaho............	431,866	391,119	40,747	325,594	283,016	42,578	9.4	13.1
Wyoming.........	194,402	167,835	26,567	145,965	116,945	29,020	13.7	19.9
Colorado.........	939,629	820,491	119,138	799,024	669,437	129,587	12.7	16.2
New Mexico.......	360,350	330,542	29,808	327,301	304,155	23,146	8.3	7.1
Arizona..........	334,162	253,596	80,566	204,354	155,589	48,765	24.1	23.9
Utah.............	449,396	390,196	59,200	373,351	307,529	65,822	13.2	17.6
Nevada..........	77,407	61,404	16,003	81,875	62,184	19,691	20.7	24.1
PACIFIC:								
Washington.......	1,356,621	1,091,329	265,292	1,141,990	885,749	256,241	19.6	22.4
Oregon..........	783,389	675,745	107,644	672,765	559,629	113,136	13.7	16.8
California........	3,426,861	2,669,236	757,625	2,377,549	1,791,117	586,432	22.1	24.7

TABLE **27.**—INDIANS, CHINESE, JAPANESE, AND "ALL OTHER," BY DIVISIONS AND STATES: 1920 AND 1910.

DIVISION AND STATE.	INDIAN.		CHINESE.		JAPANESE.		ALL OTHER.[1]	
	1920	1910	1920	1910	1920	1910	1920	1910
United States	244,437	265,683	61,639	71,531	111,010	72,157	9,488	3,175
GEOGRAPHIC DIVISIONS:								
New England	1,715	2,076	3,602	3,499	347	272	115	14
Middle Atlantic	5,940	7,717	8,812	8,189	3,266	1,643	1,103	21
East North Central	15,695	18,255	5,043	3,415	927	482	462	11
West North Central	37,263	41,406	1,678	1,195	1,215	1,000	185	37
South Atlantic	13,673	9,054	1,824	1,582	360	156	355	12
East South Central	1,623	2,612	542	414	35	26	28	10
West South Central	60,618	76,767	1,534	1,303	578	428	188	119
Mountain	76,899	75,338	4,339	5,614	10,792	10,447	371	196
Pacific	31,011	32,458	34,265	46,320	93,490	57,703	6,681	2,755
NEW ENGLAND:								
Maine	839	892	161	108	7	13	2	
New Hampshire	28	34	95	67	8	1		
Vermont	24	26	11	8	4	3		
Massachusetts	555	688	2,544	2,582	191	151	76	14
Rhode Island	110	284	225	272	35	33	11	
Connecticut	159	152	566	462	102	71	26	
MIDDLE ATLANTIC:								
New York	5,503	6,046	5,793	5,266	2,686	1,247	735	19
New Jersey	100	168	1,190	1,139	325	206	66	
Pennsylvania	337	1,503	1,829	1,784	255	190	302	2
EAST NORTH CENTRAL:								
Ohio	151	127	941	569	130	76	92	
Indiana	125	279	283	276	81	38	20	2
Illinois	194	188	2,776	2,103	472	285	231	4
Michigan	5,614	7,519	792	241	184	49	113	2
Wisconsin	9,611	10,142	251	226	60	34	6	3
WEST NORTH CENTRAL:								
Minnesota	8,761	9,053	508	275	85	67	26	2
Iowa	529	471	235	97	29	36	42	3
Missouri	171	313	412	535	135	99	52	4
North Dakota	6,254	6,486	124	39	72	59	1	
South Dakota	16,384	19,137	142	121	38	42	4	
Nebraska	2,888	3,502	189	112	804	590	30	28
Kansas	2,276	2,444	68	16	52	107	30	
SOUTH ATLANTIC:								
Delaware	2	5	43	30	8	4		
Maryland	32	55	371	378	29	24	13	
District of Columbia	37	68	461	369	103	47	144	11
Virginia	824	539	278	154	56	14	103	
West Virginia	7	36	98	90	10	3	6	
North Carolina	11,824	7,851	88	80	24	2	1	
South Carolina	304	331	93	57	15	8	55	
Georgia	125	95	211	233	9	4	8	
Florida	518	74	181	191	106	50	25	1
EAST SOUTH CENTRAL:								
Kentucky	57	234	62	52	9	12	4	
Tennessee	56	216	57	43	8	8	13	2
Alabama	405	909	59	62	18	4	8	4
Mississippi	1,105	1,253	364	257		2	3	4
WEST SOUTH CENTRAL:								
Arkansas	106	460	113	62	5	9	3	1
Louisiana	1,066	780	387	507	57	31	131	110
Oklahoma	57,337	74,825	261	139	67	48	16	
Texas	2,109	702	773	595	449	340	38	8
MOUNTAIN:								
Montana	10,956	10,745	872	1,285	1,074	1,585	69	24
Idaho	3,098	3,488	585	859	1,569	1,363	26	12
Wyoming	1,343	1,486	252	246	1,194	1,596	92	84
Colorado	1,383	1,482	291	373	2,464	2,300	70	1
New Mexico	19,512	20,570	171	248	251	258	10	
Arizona	32,989	29,201	1,137	1,305	550	371	32	
Utah	2,711	3,123	342	371	2,936	2,110	60	20
Nevada	4,907	5,240	689	927	754	864	12	55
PACIFIC:								
Washington	9,061	10,997	2,363	2,709	17,387	12,929	1,150	186
Oregon	4,590	5,090	3,090	7,363	4,151	3,418	268	312
California	17,360	16,371	28,812	36,248	71,952	41,356	5,263	2,257

[1] Comprises Filipinos, Hindus, Koreans, Hawaiians, Malays, Siamese, Samoans, and Maoris, in 1920; Filipinos, Hindus, Koreans, and Maoris, in 1910.

TABLE 28.—PER CENT OF INCREASE, BY COLOR OR RACE, NATIVITY, AND PARENTAGE, BY DIVISIONS AND STATES: 1910-1920.

[Per cent not shown where base is less than 100.   A minus sign (—) denotes decrease.]

DIVISION AND STATE.	COLOR OR RACE.			NATIVITY.		NATIVE WHITE.				Foreign-born white.
	White.	Negro.	Ind., Chi., Jap., and all other.	Native.	Foreign born.	Total.	Native parentage.	Foreign parentage.	Mixed parentage.	
United States	16.0	6.5	3.4	17.0	3.0	18.6	18.1	21.5	16.9	2.8
GEOGRAPHIC DIVISIONS:										
New England	12.9	19.2	−1.4	16.7	3.3	16.7	7.3	30.5	24.3	3.1
Middle Atlantic	14.6	43.6	8.8	19.6	2.3	19.0	13.8	31.2	15.0	1.8
East North Central	16.8	71.0	−0.2	20.2	5.2	19.2	20.9	17.2	13.5	5.1
West North Central	7.7	14.8	−7.6	11.4	−14.9	11.4	14.6	1.1	12.6	−15.0
South Atlantic	19.5	5.2	50.1	14.8	10.2	19.9	19.6	28.9	20.9	8.7
East South Central	10.7	−4.9	−27.2	6.0	−16.9	11.1	11.7	−6.8	−4.1	−17.2
West South Central	20.7	4.0	−20.0	16.0	32.0	20.1	20.7	14.2	16.4	31.7
Mountain	27.5	43.5	0.9	31.6	3.2	32.5	36.5	21.9	23.9	3.7
Pacific	33.0	63.7	18.8	37.1	18.3	36.6	36.9	34.5	38.3	20.0
NEW ENGLAND:										
Maine	3.5	−3.9	−0.4	4.5	−2.5	4.5	0.2	17.3	24.3	−2.5
New Hampshire	2.9	10.1	28.4	5.3	−5.5	5.3	−2.0	19.9	25.4	−5.5
Vermont	−0.7	−64.7		0.6	−10.7	0.9	−0.5	6.6	3.7	−10.7
Massachusetts	14.4	19.5	−2.0	19.8	2.8	19.9	11.5	29.1	24.2	2.5
Rhode Island	11.5	5.3	−35.3	18.1	−2.2	18.6	8.6	26.6	27.6	−2.5
Connecticut	23.6	38.7	24.5	27.6	14.8	27.5	13.5	45.8	30.7	14.5
MIDDLE ATLANTIC:										
New York	13.4	47.9	17.0	18.8	2.8	18.4	13.6	26.9	14.1	2.1
New Jersey	24.2	30.5	11.1	28.6	12.4	28.6	20.1	43.9	27.2	12.2
Pennsylvania	12.9	46.7	−21.7	17.8	−3.5	16.8	12.5	33.2	11.5	−3.5
EAST NORTH CENTRAL:										
Ohio	19.7	67.1	70.2	21.8	13.7	20.6	21.0	24.9	9.3	13.6
Indiana	7.9	34.0	−14.5	9.4	−5.2	8.8	9.4	7.6	1.5	−5.3
Illinois	−14.0	67.1	42.4	19.0	0.4	17.8	17.9	19.1	13.6	0.4
Michigan	29.3	251.0	−14.2	32.8	22.0	31.3	36.4	26.8	21.4	22.0
Wisconsin	12.8	79.3	−4.6	19.3	−10.2	19.3	38.2	1.6	14.2	−10.2
WEST NORTH CENTRAL:										
Minnesota	15.0	24.4	−0.2	24.0	−10.4	24.2	43.9	6.1	26.8	−10.5
Iowa	7.9	26.9	37.6	11.6	−17.4	11.5	17.3	−4.8	7.0	−17.5
Missouri	2.9	13.2	−19.0	5.0	−18.7	4.6	6.2	−3.8	−2.0	−18.7
North Dakota	12.3	−24.3	−2.0	22.5	−15.8	22.9	28.0	13.3	35.6	−15.8
South Dakota	9.8	1.8	−14.2	14.7	−18.1	15.9	25.6	−1.2	16.6	−18.1
Nebraska	8.4	72.2	−7.6	12.8	−14.7	12.5	17.9	−1.2	10.0	−14.9
Kansas	4.6	7.2	−5.5	6.6	−18.1	6.6	8.4	−3.5	2.8	−18.2
SOUTH ATLANTIC:										
Delaware	12.6	−2.7		9.9	13.8	12.4	9.4	32.6	16.1	13.7
Maryland	13.4	5.3	−2.6	13.1	−1.7	15.0	16.4	9.9	7.7	−1.9
District of Columbia	38.4	16.4	50.5	33.3	17.9	40.9	43.7	32.5	27.8	17.2
Virginia	16.4	2.8	78.4	11.9	17.2	16.4	15.8	41.2	35.4	15.6
West Virginia	19.1	34.6	−6.2	20.4	8.5	19.6	18.3	59.9	16.3	8.5
North Carolina	18.9	9.4	50.5	16.0	19.4	18.9	18.8	47.6	15.6	19.5
South Carolina	20.5	3.5	17.9	11.1	6.5	20.7	20.8	22.0	5.9	5.7
Georgia	18.0	2.5	6.3	11.0	7.0	18.1	18.1	23.7	11.4	7.4
Florida	43.8	6.7	162.7	28.5	32.6	45.2	42.3	77.5	72.8	27.1
EAST SOUTH CENTRAL:										
Kentucky	7.5	−9.8	−55.7	6.0	−23.0	8.1	9.4	−13.8	−7.2	−23.2
Tennessee	10.2	−4.5	−50.2	7.2	−15.9	10.5	10.8	−0.7	−2.6	−16.1
Alabama	17.8	−0.8	−49.9	10.0	−6.5	18.1	18.4	10.9	6.1	−6.8
Mississippi	8.6	−7.4	−2.9	−0.3	−13.9	8.9	9.2	4.2	−6.7	−14.6
WEST SOUTH CENTRAL:										
Arkansas	13.2	6.6	−57.1	11.6	−17.1	13.6	13.8	3.5	10.1	−17.4
Louisiana	16.5	−1.9	14.9	9.3	−12.0	18.3	21.3	−2.0	−3.0	−13.3
Oklahoma	26.1	8.6	−23.1	23.0	(1)	26.8	28.1	6.4	11.0	−0.3
Texas	22.3	7.5	104.8	17.6	50.4	20.0	19.6	21.7	25.4	50.2
MOUNTAIN:										
Montana	48.2	−9.6	−4.9	61.1	0.9	63.8	70.1	48.6	64.7	2.2
Idaho	33.3	41.3	−7.8	38.2	−4.3	38.7	44.5	19.6	26.8	−3.6
Wyoming	35.5	−38.5	−15.6	43.5	−8.5	45.7	52.3	27.8	31.5	−6.9
Colorado	18.0	−1.2	1.3	22.6	−8.1	22.9	26.9	13.3	11.0	−7.8
New Mexico	9.9	252.1	−5.4	8.7	28.8	8.4	6.9	30.9	12.5	28.4
Arizona	70.0	298.5	12.4	63.0	65.2	71.2	83.3	51.4	41.2	66.8
Utah	20.5	26.4	7.6	26.9	−10.1	27.1	43.2	2.6	10.8	−10.9
Nevada	−4.8	−32.6	−10.2	−1.3	−18.7	−0.7	2.7	−5.0	−8.3	−17.8
PACIFIC:										
Washington	19.0	13.6	11.7	23.2	3.5	23.3	21.6	22.7	33.2	3.7
Oregon	17.4	43.7	−25.2	20.7	−4.9	20.8	19.4	20.8	31.4	−0.8
California	44.5	79.1	28.2	49.0	29.2	48.2	51.6	42.3	42.4	31.8

[1] Decrease of less than one-tenth of 1 per cent.

TABLE 29.—WHITE POPULATION BY NATIVITY AND

	DIVISION AND STATE.	TOTAL WHITE POPULATION.		TOTAL NATIVE WHITE.		NATIVE WHITE— NATIVE PARENTAGE.	
		1920	1910	1920	1910	1920	1910
1	United States.....	94,820,915	81,731,957	81,108,161	68,386,412	58,421,957	49,488,575
	GEOGRAPHIC DIVISIONS:						
2	New England.......	7,316,079	6,480,514	5,445,425	4,666,128	2,803,149	2,613,419
3	Middle Atlantic.....	21,641,840	18,880,452	16,729,265	14,054,273	9,631,012	8,462,961
4	East North Central.	20,938,862	17,927,622	17,715,583	14,860,402	11,790,370	9,751,968
5	West North Central.	12,225,387	11,351,621	10,853,426	9,738,390	7,475,548	6,523,687
6	South Atlantic......	9,648,940	8,071,603	9,333,020	7,781,048	8,779,416	7,341,205
7	East South Central.	6,367,547	5,754,326	6,295,608	5,667,469	6,092,782	5,452,492
8	West South Central.	8,115,727	6,721,491	7,656,394	6,372,732	6,959,785	5,767,449
9	Mountain..........	3,212,899	2,520,455	2,759,674	2,083,545	2,002,508	1,466,624
10	Pacific.............	5,353,634	4,023,873	4,319,766	3,162,425	2,887,387	2,108,770
	NEW ENGLAND:						
11	Maine.............	765,695	739,995	658,346	629,862	495,780	494,907
12	New Hampshire....	442,331	429,906	351,098	333,348	225,512	230,231
13	Vermont...........	351,817	354,298	307,291	304,437	228,325	229,382
14	Massachusetts.....	3,803,524	3,324,926	2,725,990	2,273,876	1,230,773	1,103,429
15	Rhode Island.......	593,980	532,492	420,481	354,467	173,553	159,821
16	Connecticut........	1,358,732	1,098,897	982,219	770,138	449,206	395,649
	MIDDLE ATLANTIC:						
17	New York..........	10,172,027	8,966,845	7,385,915	6,237,573	3,668,266	3,230,325
18	New Jersey.........	3,037,087	2,445,894	2,298,474	1,787,706	1,212,675	1,009,909
19	Pennsylvania......	8,432,726	7,467,713	7,044,876	6,028,994	4,750,071	4,222,727
	EAST NORTH CENTRAL:						
20	Ohio..............	5,571,893	4,654,897	4,893,196	4,057,652	3,669,122	3,033,259
21	Indiana...........	2,849,071	2,639,961	2,698,203	2,480,639	2,329,544	2,130,088
22	Illinois...........	6,299,333	5,526,962	5,092,382	4,324,402	3,066,563	2,600,555
23	Michigan..........	3,601,627	2,785,247	2,874,992	2,189,723	1,670,447	1,224,841
24	Wisconsin.........	2,616,938	2,320,555	2,156,810	1,807,986	1,054,694	763,225
	WEST NORTH CENTRAL:						
25	Minnesota.........	2,368,936	2,059,227	1,882,772	1,516,217	827,627	575,081
26	Iowa.............	2,384,131	2,209,191	2,158,534	1,935,707	1,528,553	1,303,526
27	Missouri..........	3,225,044	3,134,932	3,039,018	2,906,036	2,536,936	2,387,835
28	North Dakota......	639,954	569,855	508,451	413,697	207,966	162,461
29	South Dakota......	619,147	563,771	536,756	463,143	308,598	245,652
30	Nebraska..........	1,279,219	1,180,293	1,129,567	1,004,428	757,064	642,075
31	Kansas...........	1,708,906	1,634,352	1,598,328	1,499,162	1,308,804	1,207,057
	SOUTH ATLANTIC:						
32	Delaware..........	192,615	171,102	172,805	153,682	139,876	127,809
33	Maryland..........	1,204,737	1,062,639	1,102,560	958,465	893,088	766,627
34	District of Columbia	326,860	236,128	298,312	211,777	239,488	166,711
35	Virginia..........	1,617,909	1,389,809	1,587,124	1,363,181	1,534,494	1,325,238
36	West Virginia......	1,377,235	1,156,817	1,315,329	1,099,745	1,232,857	1,042,107
37	North Carolina.....	1,783,779	1,500,511	1,776,680	1,494,569	1,765,203	1,485,718
38	South Carolina.....	818,538	679,161	812,137	673,107	799,418	661,970
39	Georgia...........	1,689,114	1,431,802	1,672,928	1,416,730	1,642,697	1,391,058
40	Florida...........	638,153	443,634	595,145	409,792	532,295	373,967
	EAST SOUTH CENTRAL:						
41	Kentucky..........	2,180,560	2,027,951	2,149,780	1,987,898	2,039,134	1,863,194
42	Tennessee.........	1,885,993	1,711,432	1,870,515	1,692,973	1,832,757	1,654,606
43	Alabama..........	1,447,032	1,228,832	1,429,370	1,209,876	1,394,129	1,177,459
44	Mississippi........	853,962	786,111	845,943	776,722	826,762	757,233
	WEST SOUTH CENTRAL:						
45	Arkansas..........	1,279,757	1,131,026	1,265,782	1,114,117	1,226,692	1,077,509
46	Louisiana..........	1,096,611	941,086	1,051,740	889,304	941,724	776,587
47	Oklahoma.........	1,821,194	1,444,531	1,781,226	1,404,447	1,679,107	1,310,403
48	Texas............	3,918,165	3,204,848	3,557,646	2,964,864	3,112,262	2,602,950
	MOUNTAIN:						
49	Montana..........	534,260	360,580	440,040	269,936	275,803	162,127
50	Idaho.............	425,668	319,221	386,705	278,794	294,252	200,500
51	Wyoming.........	190,146	140,318	164,891	113,200	122,884	80,696
52	Colorado..........	924,103	783,415	807,149	656,564	603,041	475,136
53	New Mexico.......	334,673	304,594	305,596	281,940	273,317	255,609
54	Arizona...........	291,449	171,468	213,350	124,644	151,145	82,468
55	Utah.............	441,901	366,583	385,446	303,190	245,781	171,663
56	Nevada...........	70,699	74,276	55,897	56,277	36,285	35,326
	PACIFIC:						
57	Washington........	1,319,777	1,109,111	1,069,722	867,914	711,706	585,386
58	Oregon	769,146	655,090	666,995	552,089	497,726	416,851
59	California.........	3,264,711	2,259,672	2,583,049	1,742,422	1,677,955	1,106,533

PARENTAGE, BY DIVISIONS AND STATES: 1920 AND 1910.

NATIVE WHITE— FOREIGN OR MIXED PARENTAGE.		FOREIGN-BORN WHITE.		PER CENT OF TOTAL WHITE POPULATION.						
				Native, native parentage.		Native, foreign or mixed parentage.		Foreign born.		
1920	1910	1920	1910	1920	1910	1920	1910	1920	1910	
22,686,204	18,897,837	13,712,754	13,345,545	61.6	60.5	23.9	23.1	14.5	16.3	1
2,642,276	2,052,709	1,870,654	1,814,386	38.3	40.3	36.1	31.7	25.6	28.0	2
7,098,253	5,591,312	4,912,575	4,826,179	44.5	44.8	32.8	29.6	22.7	25.6	3
5,925,213	5,108,434	3,223,279	3,067,220	56.3	54.4	28.3	28.5	15.4	17.1	4
3,377,878	3,214,703	1,371,961	1,613,231	61.1	57.5	27.6	28.3	11.2	14.2	5
553,604	439,843	315,920	290,555	91.0	91.0	5.7	5.4	3.3	3.6	6
202,826	214,977	71,939	86,857	95.7	94.8	3.2	3.7	1.1	1.5	7
696,609	605,283	459,333	348,759	85.8	85.8	8.6	9.0	5.7	5.2	8
757,166	616,921	453,225	436,910	62.3	58.2	23.6	24.5	14.1	17.3	9
1,432,379	1,053,655	1,033,868	861,448	53.9	52.4	26.8	26.2	19.3	21.4	10
162,566	134,955	107,349	110,133	64.7	66.9	21.2	18.2	14.0	14.9	11
125,586	103,117	91,233	96,558	51.0	53.6	28.4	24.0	20.6	22.5	12
78,966	75,055	44,526	49,861	64.9	64.7	22.4	21.2	12.7	14.1	13
1,495,217	1,170,447	1,077,534	1,051,050	32.4	33.2	39.3	35.2	28.3	31.6	14
246,928	194,646	173,499	178,025	29.2	30.0	41.6	36.6	29.2	33.4	15
533,013	374,489	376,513	328,759	33.1	36.0	39.2	34.1	27.7	29.9	16
3,717,649	3,007,248	2,786,112	2,729,272	36.1	36.0	36.5	33.5	27.4	30.4	17
1,085,799	777,797	738,613	658,188	39.9	41.3	35.8	31.8	24.3	26.9	18
2,294,805	1,806,267	1,387,850	1,438,719	56.3	56.5	27.2	24.2	16.5	19.3	19
1,224,074	1,024,393	678,697	597,245	65.9	65.2	22.0	22.0	12.2	12.8	20
368,659	350,551	150,868	159,322	81.8	80.7	12.9	13.3	5.3	6.0	21
2,025,819	1,723,847	1,206,951	1,202,560	48.7	47.1	32.2	31.2	19.2	21.8	22
1,204,545	964,882	726,635	595,524	46.4	44.0	33.4	34.6	20.2	21.4	23
1,102,116	1,044,761	460,128	512,569	40.3	32.9	42.1	45.0	17.6	22.1	24
1,055,145	941,136	486,164	543,010	34.9	27.9	44.5	45.7	20.5	26.4	25
629,981	632,181	225,647	273,484	64.1	59.0	26.4	28.6	9.5	12.4	26
502,082	518,201	186,026	228,896	78.7	76.2	15.6	16.5	5.8	7.3	27
300,485	251,236	131,503	156,158	32.5	28.5	47.0	44.1	20.5	27.4	28
228,158	217,491	82,391	100,628	49.8	43.6	36.9	38.6	13.3	17.8	29
372,503	362,353	149,652	175,865	59.2	54.4	29.1	30.7	11.7	14.9	30
289,524	292,105	110,578	135,190	76.6	73.9	16.9	17.9	6.5	8.3	31
32,929	25,873	19,810	17,420	72.6	74.7	17.1	15.1	10.3	10.2	32
209,472	191,838	102,177	104,174	74.1	72.1	17.4	18.1	8.5	9.8	33
58,824	45,066	28,548	24,351	73.3	70.6	18.0	19.1	8.7	10.3	34
52,630	37,943	30,785	26,628	94.8	95.4	3.3	2.7	1.9	1.9	35
82,472	57,638	61,906	57,072	89.5	90.1	6.0	5.0	4.5	4.9	36
11,477	8,851	7,099	5,942	99.0	99.0	0.6	0.6	0.4	0.4	37
12,719	11,137	6,401	6,054	97.7	97.5	1.6	1.6	0.8	0.9	38
30,231	25,672	16,186	15,072	97.3	97.2	1.8	1.8	1.0	1.1	39
62,850	35,825	43,008	33,842	83.4	84.3	9.8	8.1	6.7	7.6	40
110,646	124,704	30,780	40,053	93.5	91.9	5.1	6.1	1.4	2.0	41
37,758	38,367	15,478	18,459	97.2	96.7	2.0	2.2	0.8	1.1	42
35,241	32,417	17,662	18,956	96.3	95.8	2.4	2.6	1.2	1.5	43
19,181	19,489	8,019	9,389	96.8	96.3	2.2	2.5	0.9	1.2	44
39,090	36,608	13,975	16,909	95.9	95.3	3.1	3.2	1.1	1.5	45
110,016	112,717	44,871	51,782	85.9	82.5	10.0	12.0	4.1	5.5	46
102,119	94,044	39,968	40,084	92.2	90.7	5.6	6.5	2.2	2.8	47
445,384	361,914	360,519	239,984	79.4	81.2	11.4	11.3	9.2	7.5	48
164,837	106,809	93,620	91,644	51.6	45.0	30.9	29.6	17.5	25.4	49
92,453	75,195	28,963	40,427	69.1	63.8	21.7	23.6	9.2	12.7	50
42,007	32,504	25,255	27,118	64.6	57.5	22.1	23.2	18.3	19.3	51
204,108	181,428	116,954	126,851	65.3	60.6	22.1	23.2	12.7	16.2	52
32,279	26,331	29,077	22,654	81.7	83.9	9.6	8.6	8.7	7.4	53
62,205	42,176	78,099	46,824	51.9	48.1	21.3	24.6	26.8	27.3	54
139,665	131,527	56,455	63,393	55.6	46.8	31.6	35.9	12.8	17.3	55
19,612	20,951	14,802	17,999	51.3	47.6	27.7	28.2	20.9	24.2	56
358,016	282,528	250,055	241,197	53.9	52.8	27.1	25.5	18.9	21.7	57
169,269	135,238	102,151	103,001	64.7	63.6	22.0	20.6	13.3	15.7	58
905,094	635,889	681,662	517,250	51.4	49.0	27.7	28.1	20.9	22.9	59

TABLE 30.—COLOR OR RACE, NATIVITY, AND PARENTAGE,

CITY.	Total population: 1920	COLOR OR RACE.					
		White.	Negro.	Indian.	Chinese.	Japanese.	All other.
Akron, Ohio	208,435	202,718	5,580	4	119	4	10
Albany, N. Y	113,344	112,036	1,239	3	60	4	2
Atlanta, Ga	200,616	137,785	62,796	5	30		
Baltimore, Md	733,826	625,130	108,322	14	328	23	9
Birmingham, Ala	178,806	108,550	70,230	1	22		3
Boston, Mass	748,060	730,485	16,350	34	1,075	76	40
Bridgeport, Conn	143,555	141,220	2,228	3	99	5	
Buffalo, N. Y	506,775	502,042	4,511	97	102	13	10
Cambridge, Mass	109,694	104,250	5,334	9	81	17	3
Camden, N. J	116,309	107,753	8,500	2	53		1
Chicago, Ill	2,701,705	2,589,169	109,458	94	2,353	417	214
Cincinnati, Ohio	401,247	371,097	30,079	6	41	18	6
Cleveland, Ohio	796,841	762,026	34,451	34	275	37	18
Columbus, Ohio	237,031	214,721	22,181	16	92	4	17
Dallas, Tex	158,976	134,888	24,023	4	11	43	7
Dayton, Ohio	152,559	143,495	9,025	2	30	4	3
Denver, Colo	256,491	249,644	6,075	66	212	465	29
Des Moines, Iowa	126,468	120,887	5,512	8	36	2	23
Detroit, Mich	993,678	952,065	40,838	155	438	100	82
Fall River, Mass	120,485	120,114	315	10	45	1	
Fort Worth, Tex	106,482	90,466	15,896	2	86	30	2
Grand Rapids, Mich	137,634	136,472	1,090	25	40	5	2
Hartford, Conn	138,036	133,681	4,199	6	135	5	10
Houston, Tex	138,276	104,268	33,960	8	13	25	2
Indianapolis, Ind	314,194	279,411	34,678	8	82	12	3
Jersey City, N. J	298,103	290,009	8,000	2	85	3	4
Kansas City, Kans	101,177	86,703	14,405	24	5	38	2
Kansas City, Mo	324,410	293,517	30,719	36	45	64	29
Los Angeles, Calif	576,673	546,864	15,579	189	2,062	11,618	361
Louisville, Ky	234,891	194,769	40,087	10	21	3	1
Lowell, Mass	112,759	112,509	170		79		1
Memphis, Tenn	162,351	101,113	61,181	12	34	5	6
Milwaukee, Wis	457,147	454,824	2,229	24	65	2	3
Minneapolis, Minn	380,582	376,365	3,927	37	196	52	5
Nashville, Tenn	118,342	82,703	35,633	3	1	2	
New Bedford, Mass	121,217	116,142	4,998	14	61	1	1
New Haven, Conn	162,537	157,816	4,573	19	103	18	8
New Orleans, La	387,219	285,916	100,930	18	246	39	70
New York, N. Y	5,620,048	5,459,463	152,467	149	5,042	2,312	615
Bronx borough	732,016	726,990	4,803	8	146	66	3
Brooklyn borough	2,018,356	1,984,953	31,912	32	811	250	398
Manhattan borough	2,284,103	2,168,906	109,133	61	3,862	1,931	210
Queens borough	469,042	463,661	5,120	47	160	52	2
Richmond borough	116,531	114,953	1,499	1	63	13	2
Newark, N. J	414,524	397,223	16,977	19	281	14	10
Norfolk, Va	115,777	72,226	43,392	3	117	31	8
Oakland, Calif	216,261	204,004	5,489	36	3,821	2,709	202
Omaha, Nebr	191,601	181,046	10,315	25	126	76	13
Paterson, N. J	135,875	134,254	1,551	2	64	4	
Philadelphia, Pa	1,823,779	1,688,180	134,229	120	869	130	251
Pittsburgh, Pa	588,343	550,261	37,725	17	306	32	2
Portland, Oreg	258,288	252,961	1,556	96	1,846	1,715	114
Providence, R. I	237,595	231,756	5,655	30	135	14	5
Reading, Pa	107,784	106,851	924		6	2	1
Richmond, Va	171,667	117,574	54,041	18	29	5	
Rochester, N. Y	295,750	294,089	1,579	32	42	7	1
St. Louis, Mo	772,897	702,615	69,854	33	328	47	20
St. Paul, Minn	234,698	231,171	3,376	32	96	13	10
Salt Lake City, Utah	118,110	116,791	718	3	188	403	17
San Antonio, Tex	161,379	146,799	14,341	18	193	18	10
San Francisco, Calif	506,676	490,022	2,414	45	7,744	5,358	1,093
Scranton, Pa	137,783	137,214	563		5	1	
Seattle, Wash	315,312	302,580	2,894	106	1,351	7,874	507
Spokane, Wash	104,437	103,380	727	22	139	168	1
Springfield, Mass	129,614	126,799	2,650	14	148		3
Syracuse, N. Y	171,717	170,372	1,260	68	13	2	2
Toledo, Ohio	243,164	237,385	5,691	11	63	14	
Trenton, N. J	119,289	114,902	4,315	6	63	1	2
Washington, D. C	437,571	326,860	109,966	37	461	103	144
Wilmington, Del	110,168	99,382	10,746	2	34	4	
Worcester, Mass	179,754	178,391	1,258	20	80	4	1
Yonkers, N. Y	100,176	98,178	1,940	1	28	29	
Youngstown, Ohio	132,358	125,595	6,662	1	80	2	18

FOR CITIES HAVING 100,000 INHABITANTS OR MORE: 1920.

| CITY | NATIVITY. | | WHITE POPULATION BY NATIVITY AND PARENTAGE. | | | | |
| | | | Native white. | | | | Foreign-born white. |
	Native.	Foreign born.	Total.	Native parentage.	Foreign parentage.	Mixed parentage.	
Akron, Ohio............	170,414	38,021	164,829	125,079	28,345	11,405	37,889
Albany, N. Y...........	95,649	17,695	94,400	56,265	27,034	11,101	17,636
Atlanta, Ga............	195,827	4,789	133,047	124,948	4,815	3,284	4,738
Baltimore, Md.........	649,017	84,809	541,219	378,380	116,749	46,090	83,911
Birmingham, Ala........	172,666	6,140	102,466	92,211	6,677	3,578	6,084
Boston, Mass...........	505,441	242,619	491,566	181,811	238,241	71,514	238,919
Bridgeport, Conn........	96,773	46,782	94,806	36,816	47,094	10,896	46,414
Buffalo, N. Y...........	384,951	121,824	380,512	165,135	154,359	61,018	121,530
Cambridge, Mass........	76,398	33,296	72,146	29,045	32,283	10,818	32,104
Camden, N. J...........	95,955	20,354	87,491	56,249	22,817	8,425	20,262
Chicago, Ill............	1,893,147	808,558	1,783,687	642,871	888,496	252,320	805,482
Cincinnati, Ohio........	358,326	42,921	328,270	206,605	80,311	41,354	42,827
Cleveland, Ohio.........	556,668	240,173	522,488	212,247	246,529	63,712	239,538
Columbus, Ohio.........	220,844	16,187	198,666	159,069	24,202	15,395	16,055
Dallas, Tex............	150,175	8,801	126,158	112,509	8,019	5,630	8,730
Dayton, Ohio...........	139,394	13,165	130,384	100,996	18,887	10,501	13,111
Denver, Colo...........	218,261	38,230	212,024	144,678	43,062	24,284	37,620
Des Moines, Iowa........	115,199	11,269	109,663	84,361	15,266	10,036	11,224
Detroit, Mich..........	702,794	290,884	662,768	313,997	247,035	101,736	289,297
Fall River, Mass........	78,064	42,421	77,783	19,168	45,235	13,380	42,331
Fort Worth, Tex........	98,980	7,502	83,107	75,515	4,526	3,066	7,359
Grand Rapids, Mich.....	109,207	28,427	108,117	56,079	34,779	17,259	28,355
Hartford, Conn........	97,124	40,912	93,014	40,327	41,754	10,933	40,667
Houston, Tex..........	126,188	12,088	92,256	72,433	11,801	8,022	12,012
Indianapolis, Ind.......	297,098	17,096	262,453	219,297	26,579	16,577	16,958
Jersey City, N. J.......	221,809	76,294	214,028	87,083	98,620	28,325	75,981
Kansas City, Kans......	89,456	11,721	75,047	56,575	12,149	6,323	11,656
Kansas City, Mo........	296,827	27,583	266,197	209,134	35,183	21,880	27,320
Los Angeles, Calif......	454,542	122,131	434,807	294,458	86,808	53,541	112,057
Louisville, Ky..........	223,224	11,667	183,148	139,403	27,076	16,669	11,621
Lowell, Mass...........	74,643	38,116	74,469	24,676	37,041	12,752	38,040
Memphis, Tenn.........	156,507	5,844	95,338	82,795	7,671	4,872	5,775
Milwaukee, Wis........	346,987	110,160	344,756	130,845	152,719	61,192	110,068
Minneapolis, Minn......	292,334	88,248	288,333	133,178	108,824	46,331	88,032
Nashville, Tenn........	115,930	2,412	80,316	74,022	3,653	2,641	2,387
New Bedford, Mass......	70,139	51,078	67,453	20,098	36,379	10,976	48,689
New Haven, Conn......	116,413	46,124	112,130	44,401	54,702	13,027	45,686
New Orleans, La........	359,854	27,365	259,924	190,641	41,806	27,477	25,992
New York, N. Y........	3,591,888	2,028,160	3,467,916	1,164,834	1,873,013	430,069	1,991,547
Bronx borough......	464,274	267,742	460,019	132,770	268,380	58,869	266,971
Brooklyn borough...	1,352,168	666,188	1,325,666	456,240	703,417	166,009	659,287
Manhattan borough..	1,333,839	950,264	1,246,826	388,279	720,454	138,093	922,080
Queens borough.....	356,871	112,171	351,985	149,342	147,400	55,243	111,676
Richmond borough..	84,736	31,795	83,420	38,203	33,362	11,855	31,533
Newark, N. J..........	296,975	117,549	280,220	113,413	133,375	33,432	117,003
Norfolk, Va............	108,779	6,998	65,639	57,759	5,207	2,673	6,587
Oakland, Calif.........	166,366	49,895	158,842	90,279	44,061	24,502	45,162
Omaha, Nebr..........	155,956	35,645	145,665	86,525	41,454	17,686	35,381
Paterson, N. J.........	90,633	45,242	89,109	31,824	44,082	13,203	45,145
Philadelphia, Pa........	1,423,035	400,744	1,290,253	698,782	447,071	144,400	397,927
Pittsburgh, Pa.........	467,521	120,792	429,995	216,530	157,581	55,884	120,266
Portland, Oreg........	208,510	49,778	205,847	136,216	41,935	27,696	47,114
Providence, R. I........	167,700	69,895	162,805	63,728	76,048	23,029	68,951
Reading, Pa...........	98,211	9,573	97,298	81,000	11,916	4,382	9,553
Richmond, Va..........	166,954	4,713	112,937	102,956	5,847	4,134	4,637
Rochester, N. Y........	224,339	71,411	222,768	111,976	78,445	32,347	71,321
St. Louis, Mo..........	669,271	103,626	599,376	359,482	157,979	81,915	103,239
St. Paul, Minn.........	182,976	51,722	179,576	77,378	70,190	32,008	51,595
Salt Lake City, Utah....	98,213	19,897	97,347	56,234	23,515	17,598	19,434
San Antonio, Tex.......	124,555	36,824	110,153	76,299	21,061	12,793	36,646
San Francisco, Calif.....	357,481	149,195	349,822	167,179	125,648	56,995	140,200
Scranton, Pa..........	109,196	28,587	108,646	48,715	45,217	14,714	28,568
Seattle, Wash.........	234,336	80,976	228,705	139,701	54,678	34,326	73,875
Spokane, Wash........	87,341	17,096	86,554	57,324	16,566	12,664	16,826
Springfield, Mass......	98,153	31,461	95,549	48,945	32,991	13,613	31,250
Syracuse, N. Y.........	139,334	32,383	138,051	80,072	40,882	17,097	32,321
Toledo, Ohio..........	204,868	38,296	199,240	124,055	51,101	24,084	38,145
Trenton, N. J.........	89,121	30,168	84,829	44,195	32,181	8,453	30,073
Washington, D. C......	408,206	29,365	298,312	239,488	35,129	23,695	28,548
Wilmington, Del........	93,831	16,337	83,103	56,868	19,132	7,103	16,279
Worcester, Mass.......	126,227	53,527	124,973	50,716	56,841	17,416	53,418
Yonkers, N. Y.........	74,380	25,796	72,478	30,059	32,280	10,139	25,700
Youngstown, Ohio......	98,413	33,945	91,761	46,459	34,459	10,843	33,834

TABLE 31.—PER CENT DISTRIBUTION OF TOTAL POPULATION BY COLOR OR RACE, NATIVITY, AND PARENTAGE, FOR CITIES HAVING 100,000 INHABITANTS OR MORE: 1920.

CITY.	COLOR OR RACE.			NATIVITY.		NATIVE WHITE.				Foreign-born white.
	White.	Negro.	Ind., Chi., Jap., and all other.	Native.	Foreign born.	Total.	Native parentage.	Foreign parentage.	Mixed parentage.	
Akron, Ohio	97.3	2.7	0.1	81.8	18.2	79.1	60.0	13.6	5.5	18.2
Albany, N. Y	98.8	1.1	0.1	84.4	15.6	83.3	49.6	23.9	9.8	15.6
Atlanta, Ga	68.7	31.3	(¹)	97.6	2.4	66.3	62.3	2.4	1.6	2.4
Baltimore, Md	85.2	14.8	0.1	88.4	11.6	73.8	51.6	15.9	6.3	11.4
Birmingham, Ala	60.7	39.3	(¹)	96.6	3.4	57.3	51.6	3.7	2.0	3.4
Boston, Mass	97.7	2.2	0.2	67.6	32.4	65.7	24.3	31.8	9.6	31.9
Bridgeport, Conn	98.4	1.6	0.1	67.4	32.6	66.0	25.6	32.8	7.6	32.3
Buffalo, N. Y	99.1	0.9	(¹)	76.0	24.0	75.1	32.6	30.5	12.0	24.0
Cambridge, Mass	95.0	4.9	0.1	69.6	30.4	65.8	26.5	29.4	9.9	29.3
Camden, N. J	92.6	7.3	(¹)	82.5	17.5	75.2	48.4	19.6	7.2	17.4
Chicago, Ill	95.8	4.1	0.1	70.1	29.9	66.0	23.8	32.9	9.3	29.8
Cincinnati, Ohio	92.5	7.5	(¹)	89.3	10.7	81.8	51.5	20.0	10.3	10.7
Cleveland, Ohio	95.6	4.3	(¹)	69.9	30.1	65.6	26.6	30.9	8.0	30.1
Columbus, Ohio	90.6	9.4	0.1	93.2	6.8	83.8	67.1	10.2	6.5	6.8
Dallas, Tex	84.8	15.1	(¹)	94.5	5.5	79.4	70.8	5.0	3.5	5.5
Dayton, Ohio	94.1	5.9	(¹)	91.4	8.6	85.5	66.2	12.4	6.9	8.6
Denver, Colo	97.3	2.4	0.3	85.1	14.9	82.7	56.4	16.8	9.5	14.7
Des Moines, Iowa	95.6	4.4	0.1	91.1	8.9	86.7	66.7	12.1	7.9	8.9
Detroit, Mich	95.8	4.1	0.1	70.7	29.3	66.7	31.6	24.9	10.2	29.1
Fall River, Mass	99.7	0.3	(¹)	64.8	35.2	64.6	15.9	37.5	11.1	35.1
Fort Worth, Tex	85.0	14.9	0.1	93.0	7.0	78.0	70.9	4.3	2.9	6.9
Grand Rapids, Mich	99.2	0.8	0.1	79.3	20.7	78.6	40.7	25.3	12.5	20.6
Hartford, Conn	96.8	3.0	0.1	70.4	29.6	67.4	29.2	30.2	7.9	29.5
Houston, Tex	75.4	24.6	(¹)	91.3	8.7	66.7	52.4	8.5	5.8	8.7
Indianapolis, Ind	88.9	11.0	(¹)	94.6	5.4	83.5	69.8	8.5	5.3	5.4
Jersey City, N. J	97.3	2.7	(¹)	74.4	25.6	71.8	29.2	33.1	9.5	25.5
Kansas City, Kans	85.7	14.2	0.1	88.4	11.6	74.2	55.9	12.0	6.2	11.5
Kansas City, Mo	90.5	9.5	0.1	91.5	8.5	82.1	64.5	10.8	6.7	8.4
Los Angeles, Calif	94.8	2.7	2.5	78.8	21.2	75.4	51.1	15.1	9.3	19.4
Louisville, Ky	82.9	17.1	(¹)	95.0	5.0	78.0	59.3	11.5	7.1	4.9
Lowell, Mass	99.8	0.2	0.1	66.2	33.8	66.0	21.9	32.8	11.3	33.7
Memphis, Tenn	62.3	37.7	(¹)	96.4	3.6	58.7	51.0	4.7	3.0	3.6
Milwaukee, Wis	99.5	0.5	(¹)	75.9	24.1	75.4	28.6	33.4	13.4	24.1
Minneapolis, Minn	98.9	1.0	0.1	76.8	23.2	75.8	35.0	28.6	12.2	23.1
Nashville, Tenn	69.9	30.1	(¹)	98.0	2.0	67.9	62.5	3.1	2.2	2.0
New Bedford, Mass	95.8	4.1	0.1	57.9	42.1	55.6	16.6	30.0	9.1	40.2
New Haven, Conn	97.1	2.8	0.1	71.6	28.4	69.0	27.3	33.7	8.0	28.1
New Orleans, La	73.8	26.1	0.1	92.9	7.1	67.1	49.2	10.8	7.1	6.7
New York, N. Y	97.1	2.7	0.1	63.9	36.1	61.7	20.7	33.3	7.7	35.4
Bronx borough	99.3	0.7	(¹)	63.4	36.6	62.8	18.1	36.7	8.0	36.5
Brooklyn borough	98.3	1.6	0.1	67.0	33.0	65.7	22.6	34.9	8.2	32.7
Manhattan borough	95.0	4.8	0.3	58.4	41.6	54.6	17.0	31.5	6.0	40.4
Queens borough	98.9	1.1	0.1	76.1	23.9	75.0	31.8	31.4	11.8	23.8
Richmond borough	98.6	1.3	0.1	72.7	27.3	71.6	32.8	28.6	10.2	27.1
Newark, N. J	95.8	4.1	0.1	71.6	28.4	67.6	27.4	32.2	8.1	28.2
Norfolk, Va	62.4	37.5	0.1	94.0	6.0	56.7	49.9	4.5	2.3	5.7
Oakland, Calif	94.3	2.5	3.1	76.9	23.1	73.4	41.7	20.4	11.3	20.9
Omaha, Nebr	94.5	5.4	0.1	81.4	18.6	76.0	45.2	21.6	9.2	18.5
Paterson, N. J	98.8	1.1	0.1	66.7	33.3	65.6	23.4	32.4	9.7	33.2
Philadelphia, Pa	92.6	7.4	0.1	78.0	22.0	70.7	38.3	24.5	7.9	21.8
Pittsburgh, Pa	93.5	6.4	0.1	79.5	20.5	73.1	36.8	26.8	9.5	20.4
Portland, Oreg	97.9	0.6	1.5	80.7	19.3	79.7	52.7	16.2	10.7	18.2
Providence, R. I	97.5	2.4	0.1	70.6	29.4	68.5	26.8	32.0	9.7	29.0
Reading, Pa	99.1	0.9	(¹)	91.1	8.9	90.3	75.2	11.1	4.1	8.9
Richmond, Va	68.5	31.5	(¹)	97.3	2.7	65.8	60.0	3.4	2.4	2.7
Rochester, N. Y	99.4	0.5	(¹)	75.9	24.1	75.3	37.9	26.5	10.9	24.1
St. Louis, Mo	90.9	9.0	0.1	86.6	13.4	77.5	46.5	20.4	10.6	13.4
St. Paul, Minn	98.5	1.4	0.1	78.0	22.0	76.5	33.0	29.9	13.6	22.0
Salt Lake City, Utah	99.0	0.6	0.5	83.2	16.8	82.4	47.6	19.9	14.9	16.5
San Antonio, Tex	91.0	8.9	0.1	77.2	22.8	68.3	47.3	13.1	7.9	22.7
San Francisco, Calif	96.7	0.5	2.8	70.6	29.4	60.0	33.0	24.8	11.2	27.7
Scranton, Pa	99.6	0.4	(¹)	79.3	20.7	78.9	35.4	32.8	10.7	20.7
Seattle, Wash	96.0	0.9	3.1	74.3	25.7	72.5	44.8	17.3	10.9	23.4
Spokane, Wash	99.0	0.7	0.3	83.6	16.4	82.9	54.9	15.9	12.1	16.1
Springfield, Mass	97.8	2.0	0.1	75.7	24.3	73.7	37.8	25.5	10.5	24.1
Syracuse, N. Y	99.2	0.7	(¹)	81.1	18.9	80.4	46.6	23.8	10.0	18.8
Toledo, Ohio	97.6	2.3	(¹)	84.3	15.7	81.9	51.0	21.0	9.9	15.7
Trenton, N. J	96.3	3.6	0.1	74.7	25.3	71.1	37.0	27.0	7.1	25.2
Washington, D. C	74.7	25.1	0.2	93.3	6.7	68.2	54.7	8.0	5.4	6.5
Wilmington, Del	90.2	9.8	(¹)	85.2	14.8	75.4	51.6	17.4	6.4	14.8
Worcester, Mass	99.2	0.7	0.1	70.2	29.8	69.5	28.2	31.6	9.7	29.7
Yonkers, N. Y	98.0	1.9	0.1	74.2	25.8	72.4	30.0	32.2	10.1	25.7
Youngstown, Ohio	94.9	5.0	0.1	74.4	25.6	69.3	35.1	26.0	8.2	25.6

¹ Less than one-tenth of 1 per cent.

TABLE 32.—PER CENT OF INCREASE, BY COLOR OR RACE, NATIVITY, AND PARENT-
AGE, FOR CITIES HAVING, IN 1920, 100,000 INHABITANTS OR MORE: 1910–1920.

[Per cent not shown where base is less than 100.   A minus sign (−) denotes decrease.]

CITY.	White.	Negro.	Indian, Chinese, Japanese, and all other.	NATIVE WHITE.				Foreign-born white.
				Total.	Native parentage.	Foreign parentage.	Mixed parentage.	
Akron, Ohio	196.4	749.3		198.8	231.0	153.7	84.0	186.1
Albany, N. Y	13.0	19.5		16.5	26.5	5.5	1.7	−2.9
Atlanta, Ga	34.0	21.0		35.1	35.8	28.8	20.5	7.4
Baltimore, Md	32.1	27.8	7.2	36.6	44.7	20.7	20.7	8.9
Birmingham, Ala	35.1	34.3		37.2	39.1	30.1	10.9	6.7
Boston, Mass	11.4	20.5	−7.5	18.5	15.2	21.9	15.9	−0.7
Bridgeport, Conn	40.3	67.3		47.1	35.6	61.7	32.9	28.3
Buffalo, N. Y	19.0	154.4	66.9	25.4	38.0	16.1	20.3	2.6
Cambridge, Mass	4.2	13.3	−4.3	10.3	13.4	9.5	4.9	−7.2
Camden, N. J	21.9	39.9		20.3	13.4	42.1	19.1	29.2
Chicago, Ill	21.0	148.2	45.0	31.4	44.4	26.0	21.5	3.1
Cincinnati, Ohio	7.9	53.2		14.3	33.3	−9.7	−4.5	−24.6
Cleveland, Ohio	38.1	307.8	25.5	46.7	60.4	43.7	21.7	22.4
Columbus, Ohio	27.3	74.1		30.3	36.1	11.2	11.5	−1.4
Dallas, Tex	82.2	33.3		83.3	88.3	51.2	49.2	67.3
Dayton, Ohio	28.5	86.4		33.2	39.7	12.7	19.4	−5.3
Denver, Colo	20.6	12.0	−12.7	26.1	35.3	8.2	13.5	−3.4
Des Moines, Iowa	44.9	88.1		50.2	56.8	29.0	35.7	8.0
Detroit, Mich	107.0	611.3		118.5	172.8	87.5	80.1	84.8
Fall River, Mass	1.1	−11.3		14.4	20.9	12.0	13.9	−16.8
Fort Worth, Tex	50.9	19.7		49.1	50.6	41.2	27.4	74.8
Grand Rapids, Mich	22.0	63.9		29.4	37.5	17.4	31.2	0.1
Hartford, Conn	37.7	140.6		41.3	30.0	53.0	45.2	30.2
Houston, Tex	90.2	41.9		90.2	94.8	77.0	71.9	90.1
Indianapolis, Ind	31.9	59.0		36.7	45.6	1.5	8.7	−14.2
Jersey City, N. J	10.8	34.2	−41.3	16.3	16.3	18.4	9.9	−2.2
Kansas City, Kans	18.8	55.1		19.8	17.8	30.4	18.9	12.7
Kansas City, Mo	30.6	30.4	26.1	33.5	36.1	26.0	23.6	7.9
Los Angeles, Calif	79.1	105.0	126.2	77.7	73.2	89.9	84.4	85.0
Louisville, Ky	6.2	−1.1		10.4	22.8	−19.0	−12.3	−33.4
Lowell, Mass	6.0	27.8		18.9	19.2	16.8	24.5	−12.5
Memphis, Tenn	28.7	16.7		32.2	38.0	5.9	−0.4	−10.7
Milwaukee, Wis	22.0	127.4		31.9	66.0	13.0	29.0	−1.2
Minneapolis, Minn	26.0	51.5	101.4	35.5	38.5	27.6	48.3	2.4
Nashville, Tenn	12.0	−2.4		13.4	16.2	−13.0	−10.5	−20.2
New Bedford, Mass	24.0	73.2		32.1	7.3	44.9	51.9	14.2
New Haven, Conn	21.4	28.4	48.0	28.6	17.7	38.2	32.2	6.8
New Orleans, La	14.6	13.1	−9.0	17.2	29.3	−8.9	−3.1	−6.1
New York, N. Y	16.9	66.3	35.0	26.5	26.4	29.6	14.8	3.3
Bronx borough	70.4	16.7	4.7	65.6	43.4	90.8	32.3	79.3
Brooklyn borough	23.3	40.5	29.0	27.6	21.5	36.5	11.9	15.4
Manhattan borough	−4.3	80.3	36.9	7.2	12.8	6.1	−0.9	−16.5
Queens borough	65.2	60.1	71.7	74.6	85.3	67.2	68.3	41.2
Richmond borough	35.6	30.1		37.9	35.3	47.7	22.9	29.9
Newark, N. J	17.6	79.2	28.6	23.4	19.7	32.9	4.6	5.7
Norfolk, Va	70.5	73.3		69.2	67.6	82.6	82.2	84.8
Oakland, Calif	43.7	79.7	31.1	51.1	63.6	33.7	44.2	22.6
Omaha, Nebr.[1]	24.9	100.6	−11.4	32.4	40.9	19.8	26.1	1.4
Paterson, N. J	8.3	0.8		13.4	12.1	18.6	1.4	−0.6
Philadelphia, Pa	15.4	58.9	16.3	19.4	19.7	23.7	6.7	4.0
Pittsburgh, Pa	8.3	47.2	30.3	17.0	23.0	13.7	5.6	−14.4
Portland, Oreg	27.1	48.9	−47.7	32.7	30.8	27.5	52.9	7.6
Providence, R. I	6.0	6.4	−52.5	14.4	6.3	22.1	14.9	−9.6
Reading, Pa	12.1	17.4		12.5	8.4	44.9	24.2	8.4
Richmond, Va	45.4	15.6		47.1	48.9	26.1	36.6	13.5
Rochester, N. Y	35.4	79.6		40.8	50.3	38.3	20.0	20.9
St. Louis, Mo	9.4	58.9	−26.3	16.0	33.2	−3.1	−2.4	−17.9
St. Paul, Minn	9.3	7.4		15.9	25.6	1.4	32.4	−8.7
Salt Lake City, Utah	27.7	−2.6	7.4	34.4	47.4	13.6	29.6	2.1
San Antonio, Tex	71.1	33.8		61.1	71.0	44.3	39.5	110.5
San Francisco, Calif	22.5	47.0	−6.7	30.0	44.9	17.1	22.6	7.1
Scranton, Pa	6.1	−0.7		15.4	25.7	11.3	−0.5	−18.6
Seattle, Wash	32.9	26.0	37.7	37.0	32.1	39.9	55.6	21.4
Spokane, Wash	0.3	0.6	−45.7	5.7	5.0	1.6	15.4	−20.7
Springfield, Mass	45.1	79.7		48.4	37.0	62.1	63.9	35.9
Syracuse, N. Y	25.2	12.1		31.1	37.1	25.3	19.7	5.0
Toledo, Ohio	42.5	203.2		48.1	65.1	25.1	29.9	19.1
Trenton, N. J	22.0	67.2		25.0	14.3	45.9	18.2	14.3
Washington, D. C	38.4	16.4	50.5	40.9	43.7	32.5	27.8	17.2
Wilmington, Del	26.9	18.3		28.6	26.6	37.2	23.5	19.0
Worcester, Mass	23.3	1.4		29.9	22.4	36.3	33.4	10.2
Yonkers, N. Y	25.6	25.2		40.5	38.9	43.9	34.8	−3.3
Youngstown, Ohio	62.9	244.1		75.6	81.5	79.5	45.5	36.1

[1] Per cent of increase based upon population, for 1910, of Omaha and South Omaha combined.

TABLE **33.**—WHITE POPULATION BY NATIVITY AND PARENTAGE, FOR

	CITY.	TOTAL WHITE POPULATION.		TOTAL NATIVE WHITE.		NATIVE WHITE— NATIVE PARENTAGE.	
		1920	1910	1920	1910	1920	1910
1	Akron, Ohio............	202,718	68,404	164,829	55,163	125,079	37,793
2	Albany, N. Y............	112,036	99,171	94,400	81,006	56,265	44,473
3	Atlanta, Ga............	137,785	102,861	133,047	98,451	124,948	91,987
4	Baltimore, Md..........	625,130	473,387	541,219	396,344	378,380	261,474
5	Birmingham, Ala.......	108,550	80,369	102,466	74,669	92,211	66,312
6	Boston, Mass...........	730,485	655,696	491,566	414,974	181,811	157,870
7	Bridgeport, Conn.......	141,220	100,650	94,806	64,470	36,816	27,156
8	Buffalo, N. Y..........	502,042	421,809	380,512	303,365	165,135	119,692
9	Cambridge, Mass........	104,250	100,017	72,146	65,409	29,045	25,615
10	Camden, N. J...........	107,753	88,391	87,491	72,709	56,249	49,581
11	Chicago, Ill............	2,589,169	2,139,057	1,783,687	1,357,840	642,871	445,139
12	Cincinnati, Ohio........	371,097	343,919	328,270	287,127	206,605	154,937
13	Cleveland, Ohio........	762,029	551,925	522,488	356,222	212,247	132,314
14	Columbus, Ohio.........	214,721	168,709	198,666	152,424	159,069	116,846
15	Dallas, Tex.............	134,888	74,043	126,158	68,824	112,509	59,746
16	Dayton, Ohio...........	143,495	111,707	130,384	97,860	100,996	72,301
17	Denver, Colo...........	249,644	207,071	212,024	168,130	144,678	106,945
18	Des Moines, Iowa.......	120,887	83,414	109,663	73,019	84,361	53,785
19	Detroit, Mich..........	952,065	459,926	662,768	303,361	313,997	115,106
20	Fall River, Mass.......	120,114	118,857	77,783	67,983	19,168	15,858
21	Fort Worth, Tex........	90,466	59,960	83,107	55,751	75,515	50,139
22	Grand Rapids, Mich....	136,472	111,879	108,117	83,544	56,079	40,777
23	Hartford, Conn.........	133,681	97,078	93,014	65,835	40,327	31,011
24	Houston, Tex...........	104,268	54,832	92,256	48,514	72,433	37,181
25	Indianapolis, Ind......	279,411	211,780	262,453	192,013	219,297	150,593
26	Jersey City, N. J.......	290,009	261,659	214,028	183,962	87,083	74,861
27	Kansas City, Kans......	86,703	72,996	75,047	62,652	56,575	48,021
28	Kansas City, Mo........	293,517	224,677	266,197	199,350	209,134	153,717
29	Los Angeles, Calif......	546,864	305,307	434,807	244,723	294,458	169,967
30	Louisville, Ky..........	194,769	183,390	183,148	165,954	139,403	113,543
31	Lowell, Mass...........	112,509	106,102	74,469	62,645	24,676	20,703
32	Memphis, Tenn.........	101,113	78,590	95,338	72,123	82,795	59,985
33	Milwaukee, Wis........	454,824	372,809	344,756	261,353	130,845	78,823
34	Minneapolis, Minn......	376,365	298,672	288,333	212,734	133,178	96,186
35	Nashville, Tenn........	82,703	73,831	80,316	70,838	74,022	63,687
36	New Bedford, Mass.....	116,142	93,699	67,453	51,074	20,098	18,738
37	New Haven, Conn......	157,816	129,944	112,130	87,160	44,401	37,726
38	New Orleans, La........	288,916	249,403	259,924	221,717	190,641	147,473
39	New York, N. Y........	5,459,463	4,669,162	3,467,916	2,741,459	1,164,834	921,318
40	Bronx borough......	726,990	426,650	460,019	277,715	132,770	92,569
41	Brooklyn borough..	1,984,953	1,610,487	1,325,606	1,039,131	456,240	375,548
42	Manhattan borough.	2,168,906	2,266,578	1,246,826	1,162,559	388,279	344,351
43	Queens borough.....	463,661	280,691	351,985	201,576	149,342	80,607
44	Richmond borough .	114,953	84,756	83,420	60,478	38,203	28,243
45	Newark, N. J...........	397,223	337,742	280,220	227,087	113,413	94,737
46	Norfolk, Va............	72,226	42,353	65,639	38,789	57,759	34,471
47	Oakland, Calif.........	204,004	141,956	158,842	105,134	90,279	55,198
48	Omaha, Nebr.[1]........	181,046	144,941	145,665	110,039	86,525	61,416
49	Paterson, N. J..........	134,254	123,969	89,109	78,571	31,824	28,392
50	Philadelphia, Pa........	1,688,180	1,463,371	1,290,253	1,080,793	698,782	584,008
51	Pittsburgh, Pa.........	550,261	508,008	429,995	367,572	216,530	176,089
52	Portland, Oreg.........	252,961	198,952	205,847	155,172	136,216	104,163
53	Providence, R. I........	231,756	218,623	162,805	142,320	63,728	59,966
54	Reading, Pa............	106,851	95,276	97,298	86,464	81,000	74,714
55	Richmond, Va..........	117,574	80,879	112,937	76,794	102,956	69,130
56	Rochester, N. Y........	294,089	217,205	222,768	158,212	111,976	74,525
57	St. Louis, Mo..........	702,615	642,488	599,376	516,782	359,482	269,836
58	St. Paul, Minn..........	231,171	211,516	179,576	154,992	77,378	61,594
59	Salt Lake City, Utah....	110,761	91,471	97,347	72,436	56,234	38,152
60	San Antonio, Tex.......	146,799	85,001	110,153	68,394	76,200	44,629
61	San Francisco, Calif....	490,022	400,014	349,822	269,140	167,170	115,359
62	Scranton, Pa...........	137,214	129,288	108,646	94,176	48,715	38,745
63	Seattle, Wash..........	302,580	227,753	228,705	166,918	139,701	105,784
64	Spokane, Wash.........	103,380	103,071	86,554	81,851	57,324	54,574
65	Springfield, Mass.......	126,799	87,387	95,549	64,388	48,945	35,732
66	Syracuse, N. Y.........	170,372	136,101	138,051	105,320	80,072	58,408
67	Toledo, Ohio...........	237,385	166,567	199,240	134,530	124,055	75,147
68	Trenton, N. J..........	114,902	94,198	84,829	67,888	44,195	38,679
69	Washington, D. C.......	326,860	236,128	298,312	211,777	239,488	166,711
70	Wilmington, Del........	99,382	78,309	83,103	64,631	56,868	44,937
71	Worcester, Mass........	178,391	144,664	124,973	96,172	50,716	41,421
72	Yonkers, N. Y..........	98,178	78,190	72,478	51,600	30,059	21,640
73	Youngstown, Ohio......	125,595	77,109	91,761	52,249	46,459	25,595

[1] Includes, for 1910, population of South Omaha, consolidated with Omaha since 1910.

CITIES HAVING, IN 1920, 100,000 INHABITANTS OR MORE: 1920 AND 1910.

NATIVE WHITE—FOREIGN OR MIXED PARENTAGE.		FOREIGN-BORN WHITE.		PER CENT OF TOTAL WHITE POPULATION.						
				Native, native parentage.		Native, foreign or mixed parentage.		Foreign born.		
1920	1910	1920	1910	1920	1910	1920	1910	1920	1910	
39,750	17,370	37,889	13,241	61.7	55.2	19.6	25.4	18.7	19.4	1
38,135	36,533	17,636	18,165	50.2	44.8	34.0	36.8	15.7	18.3	2
8,099	6,464	4,738	4,410	90.7	89.4	5.9	6.3	3.4	4.3	3
162,839	134,870	83,911	77,043	60.5	55.2	26.0	28.5	13.4	16.3	4
10,255	8,357	6,084	5,700	84.9	82.5	9.4	10.4	5.6	7.1	5
309,755	257,104	238,919	240,722	24.9	24.1	42.4	39.2	32.7	36.7	6
57,990	37,314	46,414	36,180	26.1	27.0	41.1	37.1	32.9	35.9	7
215,377	183,673	121,530	118,444	32.9	28.4	42.9	43.5	24.2	28.1	8
43,101	39,794	32,104	34,608	27.9	25.6	41.3	39.8	30.8	34.6	9
31,242	23,128	20,262	15,682	52.2	56.1	29.0	26.2	18.8	17.7	10
1,140,816	912,701	805,482	781,217	24.8	20.8	44.1	42.7	31.1	36.5	11
121,665	132,190	42,827	56,792	55.7	45.1	32.8	38.4	11.5	16.5	12
310,241	223,908	239,538	195,703	27.9	24.0	40.7	40.6	31.4	35.5	13
39,597	35,578	16,055	16,285	74.1	69.3	18.4	21.1	7.5	9.7	14
13,649	9,078	8,730	5,219	83.4	80.7	10.1	12.3	6.5	7.0	15
29,388	25,559	13,111	13,847	70.4	64.7	20.5	22.9	9.1	12.4	16
67,346	61,185	37,620	38,941	58.0	51.6	27.0	29.5	15.1	18.8	17
25,302	19,234	11,224	10,395	69.8	64.5	20.9	23.1	9.3	12.5	18
348,771	188,255	289,297	156,565	33.0	25.0	36.6	40.9	30.4	34.0	19
58,615	52,125	42,331	50,874	16.0	13.3	48.8	43.9	35.2	42.8	20
7,592	5,612	7,359	4,209	83.5	83.6	8.4	9.4	8.1	7.0	21
52,038	42,767	28,355	28,335	41.1	36.4	38.1	38.2	20.8	25.3	22
52,687	34,824	40,667	31,243	30.2	31.9	39.4	35.9	30.4	32.2	23
19,823	11,333	12,012	6,318	69.5	67.8	19.0	20.7	11.5	11.5	24
43,156	41,420	16,958	19,767	78.5	71.1	15.4	19.6	6.1	9.3	25
126,945	109,101	75,981	77,697	30.0	28.6	43.8	41.7	26.2	29.7	26
18,472	14,631	11,656	10,344	65.3	65.8	21.3	20.0	13.4	14.2	27
57,063	45,633	27,320	25,327	71.3	68.4	19.4	20.3	9.3	11.3	28
140,349	74,756	112,057	60,584	53.8	55.7	25.7	24.5	20.5	19.8	29
43,745	52,411	11,621	17,436	71.6	61.9	22.5	28.6	6.0	9.5	30
49,793	41,942	38,040	43,457	21.9	19.5	44.3	39.5	33.8	41.0	31
12,543	12,138	5,775	6,467	81.9	76.3	12.4	15.4	5.7	8.2	32
213,911	182,530	110,068	111,456	28.8	21.1	47.0	49.0	24.2	29.9	33
155,155	116,548	88,032	85,938	35.4	32.2	41.2	39.0	23.4	28.8	34
6,294	7,151	2,387	2,993	89.5	86.3	7.6	9.7	2.9	4.1	35
47,355	32,336	48,689	42,625	17.3	20.0	40.8	34.5	41.9	45.5	36
67,729	49,434	45,686	42,784	28.1	29.0	42.9	38.0	28.9	32.9	37
69,283	74,244	25,992	27,686	66.7	59.1	24.2	29.8	9.1	11.1	38
2,303,082	1,820,141	1,991,547	1,927,703	21.3	19.7	42.2	39.0	36.5	41.3	39
327,249	185,146	266,971	148,935	18.3	21.7	45.0	43.4	36.7	34.9	40
869,426	663,583	659,287	571,356	23.0	23.3	43.8	41.2	33.2	35.5	41
858,547	818,208	922,080	1,104,019	17.9	15.2	39.6	36.1	42.5	48.7	42
202,643	120,969	111,676	79,115	32.2	28.7	43.7	43.1	24.1	28.2	43
45,217	32,235	31,533	24,278	33.2	33.3	39.3	38.0	27.4	28.6	44
166,807	132,350	117,003	110,655	28.6	28.1	42.0	39.2	29.5	32.8	45
7,880	4,318	6,587	3,564	80.0	81.4	10.9	10.2	9.1	8.4	46
68,563	49,936	45,162	36,822	44.3	38.9	33.6	35.2	22.1	25.9	47
59,140	48,623	35,381	34,902	47.8	42.4	32.7	33.5	19.5	24.1	48
57,285	50,179	45,145	45,398	23.7	22.9	42.7	40.5	33.6	36.6	49
591,471	496,785	397,927	382,578	41.4	39.9	35.0	33.9	23.6	26.1	50
213,465	191,483	120,266	140,436	39.4	34.7	38.8	37.7	21.9	27.6	51
69,631	51,009	47,114	43,780	53.8	52.4	27.5	25.6	18.6	22.0	52
99,077	82,354	68,951	76,303	27.5	27.4	42.8	37.7	29.8	34.9	53
16,298	11,750	9,553	8,812	75.8	78.4	15.3	12.3	8.9	9.2	54
9,981	7,664	4,637	4,085	87.6	85.5	8.5	9.5	3.9	5.1	55
110,792	83,687	71,321	58,993	38.1	34.3	37.7	38.5	24.3	27.2	56
239,894	246,946	103,239	125,706	51.2	42.0	34.1	38.4	14.7	19.6	57
102,198	93,398	51,595	56,524	33.5	29.1	44.2	44.2	22.3	26.7	58
41,113	34,284	19,434	19,035	48.2	41.7	35.2	37.5	16.6	20.8	59
33,854	23,765	36,646	17,407	52.0	52.0	23.1	27.7	25.0	20.3	60
182,643	153,781	140,200	130,874	34.1	28.8	37.3	38.4	28.6	32.7	61
59,931	55,431	28,568	35,112	35.5	30.0	43.7	42.9	20.8	27.2	62
89,004	61,134	73,875	60,835	46.2	46.4	29.4	26.8	24.4	26.7	63
29,230	27,277	16,826	21,220	55.4	52.9	28.3	26.5	16.3	20.6	64
46,604	28,656	31,250	22,999	38.6	40.9	36.8	32.8	24.6	26.3	65
57,979	46,912	32,321	30,781	47.0	42.9	34.0	34.5	19.0	22.6	66
75,185	59,383	38,145	32,037	52.3	45.1	31.7	35.7	16.1	19.2	67
40,634	29,209	30,073	26,310	38.5	41.1	35.4	31.0	26.2	27.9	68
58,824	45,066	28,548	24,351	73.3	70.6	18.0	19.1	8.7	10.3	69
26,235	19,694	16,279	13,678	57.2	57.4	26.4	25.1	16.4	17.5	70
74,257	54,751	53,418	48,492	28.4	28.6	41.6	37.8	29.9	33.5	71
42,419	29,960	25,700	26,590	30.6	27.7	43.2	38.3	26.2	34.0	72
45,302	26,654	33,834	24,860	37.0	33.2	36.1	34.6	26.9	32.2	73

TABLE 34.—COLOR OR RACE, NATIVITY, AND PARENTAGE, FOR CITIES HAVING FROM 25,000 TO 100,000 INHABITANTS: 1920.

CITY.	All classes: 1920	TOTAL WHITE.		NATIVE WHITE.						FOREIGN-BORN WHITE.		NEGRO.	
				Native parentage.		Foreign parentage.		Mixed parentage.					
		Number.	Per cent.	Number.	Per cent.	Number.	Per cent.	Number.	Per cent.	Number.	Per cent.	Number.	Per cent.
ALABAMA:													
Mobile	60,777	36,854	60.6	29,060	47.8	2,942	4.8	2,846	4.7	2,006	3.3	23,906	39.3
Montgomery	43,464	23,631	54.4	21,145	48.6	996	2.3	729	1.7	761	1.8	19,827	45.6
ARIZONA:													
Phoenix	29,053	27,716	95.4	18,191	62.6	3,063	10.5	2,417	8.3	4,045	13.9	1,075	3.7
ARKANSAS:													
Fort Smith	28,870	25,276	87.6	21,718	75.2	1,289	4.5	1,415	4.9	854	3.0	3,584	12.4
Little Rock	65,142	47,657	73.2	40,851	62.7	2,618	4.0	2,390	3.7	1,798	2.8	17,477	26.8
CALIFORNIA:													
Alameda	28,806	27,839	96.6	12,160	42.2	5,941	20.6	3,861	13.4	5,877	20.4	217	0.8
Berkeley	56,036	54,196	96.7	28,669	51.2	9,381	16.7	6,573	11.7	9,573	17.1	507	0.9
Fresno	45,086	42,820	95.0	23,793	52.8	7,221	16.0	3,254	7.2	8,552	19.0	508	1.1
Long Beach	55,593	55,040	99.0	37,888	68.2	5,603	10.1	4,750	8.5	6,799	12.2	142	0.3
Pasadena	45,354	43,762	96.5	27,966	61.7	4,975	11.0	4,036	8.9	6,785	15.0	1,094	2.4
Sacramento	65,908	62,207	94.4	32,696	49.6	11,510	17.5	7,128	10.8	10,873	16.5	675	1.0
San Diego	74,683	72,555	97.2	41,514	55.6	10,068	13.5	7,678	10.3	13,295	17.8	997	1.3
San Jose	39,642	38,783	97.8	18,011	45.4	8,541	21.5	4,411	11.1	7,820	19.7	191	0.5
Stockton	40,296	37,994	94.3	20,491	50.9	6,419	15.9	4,103	10.2	6,981	17.3	336	0.8
COLORADO:													
Colorado Springs	30,105	29,071	96.6	20,930	69.5	3,020	10.0	2,517	8.4	2,604	8.6	1,009	3.4
Pueblo	43,050	41,535	96.5	23,596	54.8	7,480	17.4	3,066	7.1	7,393	17.2	1,395	3.2
CONNECTICUT:													
Meriden	29,867	29,712	99.5	8,212	27.5	10,643	35.6	2,848	9.9	7,909	26.5	148	0.5
New Britain	59,316	58,993	99.5	11,161	18.8	22,942	38.7	3,660	6.2	21,230	35.8	303	0.5
New London	25,688	25,126	97.8	10,372	40.4	6,580	25.6	2,334	9.1	5,840	22.7	508	2.0
Norwalk	27,743	27,086	97.6	11,611	41.9	7,141	25.7	2,379	8.6	5,955	21.5	631	2.3
Stamford	35,096	34,205	97.5	9,093	25.9	11,656	33.2	2,752	7.8	10,704	30.5	874	2.5
Waterbury	91,715	90,711	98.9	22,122	24.1	31,211	34.0	7,484	8.2	29,894	32.6	951	1.0
FLORIDA:													
Jacksonville	91,558	49,972	54.6	39,960	43.6	3,497	3.8	2,621	2.9	3,894	4.3	41,520	45.3
Miami	29,571	20,269	68.5	14,348	48.5	1,811	6.1	1,547	5.2	2,563	8.7	9,270	31.3
Pensacola	31,035	20,624	66.5	16,304	52.5	1,169	3.8	1,706	5.5	1,445	4.7	10,404	33.5
Tampa	51,608	40,045	77.6	17,542	34.0	8,943	17.3	2,894	5.6	10,666	20.7	11,531	22.3
GEORGIA:													
Augusta	52,548	29,888	56.9	26,883	51.2	1,190	2.3	888	1.7	927	1.8	22,582	43.0
Columbus	31,125	22,028	70.8	20,908	67.2	382	1.2	412	1.3	326	1.0	9,093	29.2
Macon	52,995	29,898	56.4	27,923	52.7	707	1.3	570	1.1	698	1.3	23,093	43.6
Savannah	83,252	44,030	52.9	34,420	41.3	3,736	4.5	2,627	3.2	3,247	3.9	39,179	47.1
ILLINOIS:													
Aurora	36,397	35,765	98.3	16,399	45.1	8,707	23.9	4,183	11.5	6,476	17.8	627	1.7
Bloomington	28,725	27,884	97.1	18,021	62.7	4,470	15.6	2,562	8.9	2,831	9.9	799	2.8
Cicero town	44,995	44,986	100.0	6,470	14.4	18,827	41.8	4,223	9.4	15,466	34.4	4	(1)
Danville	33,776	31,387	92.9	24,329	72.0	3,086	9.1	2,056	6.1	1,916	5.7	2,366	7.0
Decatur	43,818	42,631	97.3	33,254	75.9	4,043	9.2	2,744	6.3	2,590	5.9	1,178	2.7
East St. Louis	66,767	59,304	88.8	38,854	58.2	8,967	13.4	4,701	7.0	6,782	10.2	7,437	11.1
Elgin	27,454	27,333	99.6	12,598	45.9	6,442	23.5	3,238	11.8	5,055	18.4	116	0.4
Evanston	37,234	34,676	93.1	16,723	44.9	7,140	18.9	4,142	11.1	6,771	18.2	2,522	6.8
Joliet	38,442	37,719	98.1	12,693	33.0	12,266	31.9	4,270	11.1	8,490	22.1	701	1.8
Moline	30,734	30,393	98.9	12,793	41.6	7,409	24.1	2,800	9.1	7,391	24.0	338	1.1
Oak Park village	39,858	39,669	99.5	20,206	50.7	8,463	21.2	5,366	13.5	5,634	14.1	169	0.4
Peoria	76,121	73,967	97.2	46,213	60.7	12,381	16.3	7,583	10.0	7,750	10.2	2,130	2.8
Quincy	35,978	34,760	96.6	22,553	62.7	5,930	16.5	3,866	10.7	2,411	6.7	1,210	3.4
Rock Island	35,177	34,416	97.8	17,828	50.7	7,456	21.2	3,780	10.7	5,352	15.2	754	2.1
Rockford	65,651	65,125	99.2	24,141	36.8	17,864	27.2	5,777	8.8	17,343	26.4	490	0.7
Springfield	59,183	56,403	95.3	35,255	59.6	9,915	16.8	4,978	8.4	6,255	10.6	2,769	4.7
INDIANA:													
Anderson	29,767	29,651	99.6	25,484	85.6	1,338	4.5	1,089	3.7	940	3.2	912	3.1
East Chicago	35,967	34,510	95.9	5,054	14.0	12,319	34.7	1,574	4.4	14,663	40.8	1,424	4.0
Evansville	85,264	78,852	92.5	59,270	70.7	9,058	10.6	6,070	7.5	3,149	3.7	6,301	7.5
Fort Wayne	86,549	85,073	98.3	57,675	66.6	12,045	13.0	6,790	10.1	6,634	7.7	1,454	1.7
Gary	55,378	50,044	90.4	16,519	29.8	13,912	25.1	3,153	5.7	16,460	29.7	5,299	9.6
Hammond	36,004	35,836	99.5	14,953	41.5	9,546	26.5	3,219	8.9	8,118	22.5	137	0.4
Kokomo	30,067	29,189	97.1	25,635	85.3	1,352	4.5	1,036	3.4	1,166	3.9	876	2.9
Muncie	36,524	34,460	94.3	30,900	84.6	1,361	3.7	1,379	3.8	820	2.2	2,054	5.6
Richmond	26,765	25,261	94.4	20,272	75.7	2,454	9.2	1,408	5.3	1,127	4.2	1,494	5.6
South Bend	70,983	69,696	98.2	33,915	47.8	16,835	20.7	5,555	7.8	13,391	18.9	1,269	1.8
Terre Haute	66,083	62,422	94.5	48,976	74.1	5,809	8.8	3,970	6.0	3,667	5.5	3,646	5.5

¹ Less than one-tenth of 1 per cent.

TABLE 34.—COLOR OR RACE, NATIVITY, AND PARENTAGE, FOR CITIES HAVING FROM 25,000 TO 100,000 INHABITANTS: 1920—Continued.

CITY.	All classes: 1920	TOTAL WHITE.		NATIVE WHITE.						FOREIGN-BORN WHITE.		NEGRO.	
				Native parentage.		Foreign parentage.		Mixed parentage.					
		Number.	Per cent.	Number.	Per cent.	Number.	Per cent.	Number.	Per cent.	Number.	Per cent.	Number.	Per cent.
IOWA:													
Cedar Rapids	45,566	44,878	98.5	26,667	58.5	7,790	17.1	4,558	10.0	5,863	12.9	677	1.5
Council Bluffs	36,162	35,559	98.3	23,306	64.4	5,119	14.2	3,146	8.7	3,988	11.0	598	1.7
Davenport	56,727	56,029	98.8	29,394	51.8	12,147	21.4	6,844	12.1	7,644	13.5	681	1.2
Dubuque	39,141	39,063	99.8	19,559	50.0	9,268	23.7	6,015	15.4	4,221	10.8	73	0.2
Sioux City	71,227	69,993	98.3	38,751	54.4	13,205	18.5	6,821	9.6	11,216	15.7	1,139	1.6
Waterloo	36,230	35,382	97.7	24,175	66.7	4,594	12.7	3,684	10.2	2,929	8.1	837	2.3
KANSAS:													
Topeka	50,022	45,696	91.4	33,594	67.2	4,820	9.6	3,282	6.6	4,000	8.0	4,272	8.5
Wichita	72,217	68,623	95.0	58,052	80.4	3,702	5.1	3,848	5.3	3,021	4.2	3,545	4.9
KENTUCKY:													
Covington	57,121	54,075	94.7	37,391	65.5	8,590	15.0	5,211	9.1	2,883	5.0	3,040	5.3
Lexington	41,534	29,077	70.0	25,983	62.6	1,367	3.3	927	2.2	800	1.9	12,450	30.0
Newport	29,317	28,453	97.1	17,834	60.8	5,448	18.6	3,078	10.5	2,093	7.1	864	2.9
LOUISIANA:													
Shreveport	43,874	26,368	60.1	22,747	51.8	1,349	3.1	976	2.2	1,296	3.0	17,485	39.9
MAINE:													
Bangor	25,978	25,745	99.1	15,593	60.0	3,684	14.2	2,728	10.5	3,740	14.4	208	0.8
Lewiston	31,791	31,714	99.8	9,606	30.2	8,719	27.4	3,127	9.8	10,262	32.3	54	0.2
Portland	69,272	68,890	99.4	35,969	51.9	12,588	18.2	7,104	10.3	13,229	19.1	300	0.4
MARYLAND:													
Cumberland	29,837	28,402	95.2	23,310	78.1	2,210	7.4	1,719	5.8	1,163	3.9	1,433	4.8
Hagerstown	28,064	26,549	94.6	24,853	88.6	639	2.3	629	2.2	428	1.5	1,509	5.4
MASSACHUSETTS:													
Brockton	66,254	65,635	99.1	24,643	37.2	16,895	25.5	6,973	10.5	17,124	25.8	559	0.8
Brookline town	37,748	37,360	99.0	16,928	44.8	7,492	19.8	3,580	9.5	9,360	24.8	349	0.9
Chelsea	43,184	42,776	99.1	6,910	16.0	15,595	36.1	3,073	7.1	17,198	39.8	373	0.9
Chicopee	36,214	36,196	100.0	6,158	17.0	14,210	39.2	3,646	10.1	12,182	33.6	10	(1)
Everett	40,120	38,977	97.2	11,754	29.3	11,495	28.7	4,649	11.6	11,079	27.6	1,129	2.8
Fitchburg	41,029	40,978	99.9	10,042	24.5	13,427	32.7	4,347	10.6	13,162	32.1	32	0.1
Haverhill	53,884	53,495	99.3	21,573	40.0	12,794	23.7	5,821	10.8	13,307	24.7	361	0.7
Holyoke	60,203	60,031	99.7	10,994	18.3	21,901	36.4	6,881	11.4	20,255	33.6	146	0.2
Lawrence	94,270	93,992	99.7	12,325	13.1	34,605	36.7	7,999	8.5	39,063	41.4	219	0.2
Lynn	99,148	98,267	99.1	33,988	34.3	24,772	25.0	11,589	11.7	27,858	28.1	812	0.8
Malden	49,103	48,557	98.9	15,087	30.7	14,344	29.2	5,021	10.2	14,105	28.7	531	1.1
Medford	39,038	38,487	98.6	15,463	39.6	9,021	23.1	5,449	14.0	8,554	21.9	535	1.4
Newton	46,054	45,475	98.7	20,148	43.7	10,411	22.6	4,737	10.3	10,179	22.1	561	1.2
Pittsfield	41,763	41,329	99.0	18,468	44.2	10,194	24.4	4,456	10.7	8,211	19.7	398	1.0
Quincy	47,876	47,808	99.9	14,845	31.0	14,166	29.6	5,048	10.5	13,749	28.7	27	0.1
Revere	28,823	28,768	99.8	6,892	23.9	9,916	34.4	3,113	10.8	8,847	30.7	48	0.2
Salem	42,529	42,328	99.5	12,736	29.9	13,604	32.0	4,785	11.3	11,203	26.3	130	0.3
Somerville	93,091	92,725	99.6	32,289	34.7	25,157	27.0	11,097	11.9	24,182	26.0	328	0.4
Taunton	37,137	36,787	99.1	12,068	32.5	10,820	29.1	3,901	10.5	9,998	26.9	345	0.9
Waltham	30,915	30,843	99.8	10,676	34.5	8,490	27.5	3,573	11.6	8,104	26.2	43	0.1
MICHIGAN:													
Battle Creek	36,164	35,073	97.0	25,411	70.3	3,072	8.5	3,212	8.9	3,378	9.3	1,055	2.9
Bay City	47,554	47,416	99.7	17,950	37.7	12,480	26.2	8,032	16.9	8,954	18.8	127	0.3
Flint	91,599	89,834	98.1	50,186	54.8	13,729	15.0	10,792	11.8	15,127	16.5	1,701	1.9
Hamtramck village	48,615	46,593	95.8	2,073	4.3	19,423	40.0	2,035	4.2	23,062	47.4	2,022	4.2
Highland Park	46,499	46,055	99.0	19,605	42.2	8,480	18.2	5,309	11.4	12,661	27.2	358	0.8
Jackson	48,374	47,530	98.3	30,658	63.4	6,604	13.7	4,952	10.2	5,316	11.0	810	1.7
Kalamazoo	48,487	47,707	98.4	27,873	57.5	7,686	15.9	4,941	10.2	7,207	14.9	752	1.6
Lansing	57,327	56,602	98.7	38,373	66.9	6,489	11.3	5,755	10.0	5,985	10.4	698	1.2
Muskegon	36,570	36,368	99.4	15,198	41.6	9,608	26.3	4,772	13.0	6,780	18.5	182	0.5
Pontiac	34,273	33,645	98.2	20,031	58.4	4,271	12.5	4,158	12.1	5,185	15.1	619	1.8
Port Huron	25,944	25,439	98.1	9,100	35.1	5,363	20.7	4,630	17.8	6,346	24.5	500	1.9
Saginaw	61,903	61,529	99.4	25,805	41.7	14,593	23.6	9,526	15.4	11,605	18.7	328	0.5
MINNESOTA:													
Duluth	98,917	98,314	99.4	23,931	24.2	32,000	32.4	12,265	12.4	30,118	30.4	495	0.5
MISSOURI:													
Joplin	29,902	29,136	97.4	26,134	87.4	1,054	3.5	1,221	4.1	727	2.4	741	2.5
St. Joseph	77,939	73,712	94.6	53,531	68.7	8,490	10.9	5,268	6.8	6,423	8.2	4,209	5.4
Springfield	39,631	37,962	95.8	33,852	85.4	1,504	3.8	1,633	4.1	973	2.5	1,664	4.2
MONTANA:													
Butte	41,611	41,139	98.9	13,444	32.3	10,789	25.9	5,452	13.1	11,454	27.5	214	0.5
NEBRASKA:													
Lincoln	54,948	54,016	98.3	33,381	60.8	8,899	16.2	4,538	8.3	7,198	13.1	896	1.6
NEW HAMPSHIRE:													
Manchester	78,384	78,306	99.9	18,851	24.0	23,815	30.4	8,124	10.4	27,516	35.1	62	0.1
Nashua	28,379	28,338	99.9	8,799	31.0	7,785	27.4	2,962	10.4	8,792	31.0	31	0.1

1 Less than one-tenth of 1 per cent.

TABLE 34.—COLOR OR RACE, NATIVITY, AND PARENTAGE, FOR CITIES HAVING FROM 25,000 TO 100,000 INHABITANTS: 1920—Continued.

CITY.	All classes: 1920	TOTAL WHITE.		NATIVE WHITE.						FOREIGN-BORN WHITE.		NEGRO.	
				Native parentage.		Foreign parentage.		Mixed parentage.					
		Number.	Per cent.	Number.	Per cent.	Number.	Per cent.	Number.	Per cent.	Number.	Per cent.	Number.	Per cent.
NEW JERSEY:													
Atlantic City	50,707	39,686	78.3	22,087	43.6	7,320	14.4	3,270	6.4	7,009	13.8	10,946	21.6
Bayonne	76,754	76,072	99.1	14,497	18.9	30,107	39.2	5,996	7.8	25,472	33.2	648	0.8
Clifton	26,470	26,408	99.8	4,866	18.4	9,672	36.5	2,259	8.5	9,611	36.3	47	0.2
East Orange	50,710	48,310	95.3	27,455	54.1	8,578	16.9	5,497	10.8	6,780	13.4	2,378	4.7
Elizabeth	95,783	93,770	97.9	25,887	27.0	31,126	32.5	8,542	8.9	28,215	29.5	1,970	2.1
Hoboken	68,166	67,914	99.6	14,473	21.2	23,840	35.0	6,105	9.0	23,496	34.5	204	0.3
Irvington town	25,480	25,372	99.6	9,806	38.5	6,995	27.5	3,063	12.0	5,508	21.6	104	0.4
Kearny town	26,724	26,622	99.6	7,739	29.0	8,111	30.4	2,868	10.7	7,904	29.6	78	0.3
Montclair town	28,810	25,310	87.9	12,671	44.0	5,013	17.4	2,467	8.6	5,159	17.9	3,467	12.0
New Brunswick	32,779	31,634	96.5	11,546	35.2	8,942	27.3	2,211	6.7	8,935	27.3	1,124	3.4
Orange	33,268	29,626	89.1	10,063	30.2	9,425	28.3	3,175	9.5	6,963	20.9	3,621	10.9
Passaic	63,841	63,223	99.0	8,816	13.8	24,837	38.9	3,205	5.0	26,365	41.3	591	0.9
Perth Amboy	41,707	41,189	98.8	6,348	15.2	17,255	41.4	2,668	6.4	14,918	35.8	492	1.2
Plainfield	27,700	25,240	91.1	11,614	41.9	5,812	21.0	2,312	8.3	5,502	19.9	2,445	8.8
West Hoboken town	40,074	40,037	99.9	8,504	21.2	13,508	33.7	3,949	9.9	14,076	35.1	13	(1)
West New York town	29,926	29,829	99.7	7,916	26.5	9,748	32.6	3,237	10.8	8,928	29.8	92	0.3
NEW YORK:													
Amsterdam	33,524	33,371	99.5	10,328	30.8	10,634	31.7	2,602	7.8	9,807	29.3	148	0.4
Auburn	36,192	35,688	98.6	15,819	43.7	8,914	24.6	3,376	9.3	7,579	20.9	491	1.4
Binghamton	66,800	66,140	99.0	40,030	59.9	11,389	17.0	4,353	6.5	10,368	15.5	623	0.9
Elmira	45,393	44,829	98.8	29,047	64.0	7,613	16.8	3,463	7.6	4,706	10.4	555	1.2
Jamestown	38,917	38,720	99.5	13,406	34.4	10,722	27.6	3,177	8.2	11,415	29.3	191	0.5
Kingston	26,688	26,123	97.9	16,149	60.5	4,983	18.7	2,228	8.3	2,763	10.4	563	2.1
Mount Vernon	42,726	41,358	96.8	15,010	35.1	11,815	27.7	4,443	10.4	10,090	23.6	1,345	3.1
New Rochelle	36,213	33,536	92.6	11,730	32.4	9,417	26.0	3,932	10.9	8,457	23.4	2,637	7.3
Newburgh	30,366	29,719	97.9	14,975	49.3	6,825	22.5	2,980	9.8	4,939	16.3	632	2.1
Niagara Falls	50,760	50,237	99.0	13,477	26.6	13,779	27.1	5,095	10.0	17,886	35.2	509	1.0
Poughkeepsie	35,000	34,130	97.5	18,448	52.7	7,334	21.0	2,818	8.1	5,530	15.8	850	2.4
Rome	26,341	26,164	99.3	12,639	48.0	6,213	23.6	2,078	7.9	5,234	19.9	170	0.6
Schenectady	88,723	88,245	99.5	35,897	40.5	23,922	27.0	7,936	8.9	20,490	23.1	388	0.4
Troy	72,013	71,401	99.2	33,082	45.9	18,790	26.1	8,046	11.2	11,483	15.9	579	0.8
Utica	94,156	93,764	99.6	33,751	35.8	27,528	29.2	9,228	9.8	23,257	24.7	354	0.4
Watertown	31,285	31,171	99.6	16,246	51.9	4,640	14.8	4,456	14.2	5,829	18.6	94	0.3
NORTH CAROLINA:													
Asheville	28,504	21,347	74.9	19,984	70.1	431	1.5	377	1.3	555	1.9	7,145	25.1
Charlotte	46,338	31,693	68.4	30,196	65.2	469	1.0	514	1.1	514	1.1	14,641	31.6
Wilmington	33,372	19,896	59.6	18,316	54.9	523	1.6	433	1.3	624	1.9	13,461	40.3
Winston-Salem	48,395	27,649	57.1	26,911	55.6	206	0.4	236	0.5	296	0.6	20,735	42.8
OHIO:													
Canton	87,091	85,767	98.5	53,783	61.8	11,581	13.3	5,723	6.6	14,680	16.9	1,283	1.5
East Cleveland	27,292	27,161	99.5	15,067	55.2	4,963	18.2	3,288	12.0	3,843	14.1	131	0.5
Hamilton	39,675	38,337	96.6	27,201	68.6	5,447	13.7	3,026	7.6	2,663	6.7	1,328	3.3
Lakewood	41,732	41,621	99.7	20,557	49.3	9,153	21.9	4,656	11.2	7,255	17.4	100	0.2
Lima	41,326	40,062	96.9	32,572	78.8	3,080	7.5	2,493	6.0	1,917	4.6	1,243	3.0
Lorain	37,295	36,742	98.5	10,970	29.4	11,165	29.9	2,680	7.2	11,927	32.0	552	1.5
Mansfield	27,824	27,572	99.1	18,952	68.1	3,627	13.0	1,786	6.4	3,207	11.5	249	0.9
Marion	27,891	27,651	99.1	23,549	84.4	1,655	5.9	1,493	5.4	954	3.4	239	0.9
Newark	26,718	26,163	97.9	20,959	78.4	2,211	8.3	1,488	5.6	1,505	5.6	551	2.1
Portsmouth	33,011	31,847	96.5	27,621	83.7	1,989	6.0	1,543	4.7	694	2.1	1,160	3.5
Springfield	60,840	53,799	88.4	43,037	70.7	4,850	8.0	3,155	5.2	2,757	4.5	7,029	11.6
Steubenville	28,508	27,382	96.1	14,282	50.1	5,727	20.1	1,792	6.3	5,581	19.6	1,115	3.9
Warren	27,050	26,342	97.4	16,092	59.5	3,654	13.5	1,919	7.1	4,677	17.3	702	2.6
Zanesville	29,569	28,005	94.7	22,762	77.0	2,367	8.0	1,604	5.4	1,272	4.3	1,559	5.3
OKLAHOMA:													
Muskogee	30,277	22,717	75.0	20,565	67.9	714	2.4	897	3.0	541	1.8	7,195	23.8
Oklahoma City	91,295	82,071	90.8	71,446	78.0	1,228	4.6	3,720	4.1	3,477	3.8	8,241	9.0
Tulsa	72,075	62,901	87.3	55,000	77.0	2,706	3.8	2,510	0.5	2,025	2.8	8,878	12.3

1 Less than one-tenth of 1 per cent.

TABLE 34.—COLOR OR RACE, NATIVITY, AND PARENTAGE, FOR CITIES HAVING FROM 25,000 TO 100,000 INHABITANTS: 1920—Continued.

CITY.	All classes: 1920	TOTAL WHITE.		NATIVE WHITE.						FOREIGN-BORN WHITE.		NEGRO.	
				Native parentage.		Foreign parentage.		Mixed parentage.					
		Number.	Per cent.	Number.	Per cent.	Number.	Per cent.	Number.	Per cent.	Number.	Per cent.	Number.	Per cent.
PENNSYLVANIA:													
Allentown	73,502	73,316	99.7	51,937	70.7	10,147	13.8	2,620	3.6	8,612	11.7	176	0.2
Altoona	60,331	59,431	98.5	43,390	71.9	7,222	12.0	3,507	5.8	5,312	8.8	888	1.5
Bethlehem	50,358	49,992	99.3	26,503	52.6	10,244	20.3	2,302	4.6	10,943	21.7	344	0.7
Chester	58,030	50,827	87.6	25,627	44.2	10,390	17.9	3,518	6.1	11,292	19.5	7,125	12.3
Easton	33,813	33,520	99.1	22,959	67.9	4,570	13.5	1,970	5.8	4,021	11.9	283	0.8
Erie	93,372	92,596	99.2	41,179	44.1	24,656	26.4	9,391	10.1	17,370	18.6	749	0.8
Harrisburg	75,917	70,654	93.1	59,268	78.1	4,661	6.1	2,581	3.4	4,144	5.5	5,248	6.9
Hazleton	32,277	32,247	99.9	11,384	35.3	11,044	34.2	3,796	11.8	6,023	18.7	22	0.1
Johnstown	67,327	65,656	97.5	34,207	50.8	14,799	22.0	4,508	6.7	12,142	18.0	1,650	2.5
Lancaster	53,150	52,227	98.3	42,126	79.3	4,389	8.3	2,998	5.6	2,714	5.1	915	1.7
McKeesport	46,781	45,832	98.0	16,284	34.8	13,914	29.7	3,764	8.0	11,870	25.4	928	2.0
New Castle	44,938	44,061	98.0	22,580	50.2	9,484	21.1	3,304	7.4	8,693	19.3	867	1.9
Norristown borough	32,319	30,801	95.3	19,411	60.1	5,088	15.7	2,005	6.2	4,297	13.3	1,507	4.7
Wilkes-Barre	73,833	73,276	99.2	28,709	38.9	21,424	29.0	8,576	11.6	14,567	19.7	552	0.7
Williamsport	36,198	35,283	97.5	27,432	75.8	3,351	9.3	2,234	6.2	2,266	6.3	914	2.5
York	47,512	46,088	97.0	41,552	87.5	1,834	3.9	1,509	3.2	1,193	2.5	1,416	3.0
RHODE ISLAND:													
Cranston	29,407	29,193	99.3	11,151	37.9	7,794	26.5	2,732	9.3	7,516	25.6	204	0.7
Newport	30,255	28,616	94.6	12,275	40.6	7,173	23.7	3,416	11.3	5,752	19.0	1,607	5.3
Pawtucket	64,248	63,888	99.4	14,780	23.0	19,670	30.6	8,414	13.1	21,024	32.7	332	0.5
Woonsocket	43,496	43,409	99.8	6,760	15.5	14,726	33.9	5,897	13.6	16,026	36.8	70	0.2
SOUTH CAROLINA:													
Charleston	67,957	35,585	52.4	28,262	41.6	3,159	4.6	2,021	3.0	2,143	3.2	32,326	47.6
Columbia	37,524	23,067	61.5	21,605	57.6	513	1.4	405	1.1	544	1.4	14,455	38.5
SOUTH DAKOTA:													
Sioux Falls	25,202	25,079	99.5	14,068	55.8	4,833	19.2	3,217	12.8	2,961	11.7	83	0.3
TENNESSEE:													
Chattanooga	57,895	39,001	67.4	34,911	60.3	1,601	2.8	1,249	2.2	1,240	2.1	18,889	32.6
Knoxville	77,818	66,511	85.5	63,558	81.7	1,071	1.4	1,070	1.4	812	1.0	11,302	14.5
TEXAS:													
Austin	34,876	27,928	80.1	20,905	59.9	2,691	7.7	1,785	5.1	2,547	7.3	6,921	19.8
Beaumont	40,422	27,186	67.3	21,710	53.7	2,065	5.1	1,493	3.7	1,918	4.7	13,210	32.7
El Paso	77,560	75,804	97.7	27,456	35.4	11,248	14.5	3,747	4.8	33,353	43.0	1,330	1.7
Galveston	44,255	34,318	77.5	17,289	39.1	6,158	13.9	3,979	9.0	6,892	15.6	9,888	22.3
Waco	38,500	30,762	79.9	25,897	67.3	1,826	4.7	1,272	3.3	1,767	4.6	7,726	20.1
Wichita Falls	40,079	37,848	94.4	33,856	84.5	1,118	2.8	1,154	2.9	1,720	4.3	2,217	5.5
UTAH:													
Ogden	32,804	32,125	97.9	16,857	51.4	5,769	17.6	4,890	14.9	4,609	14.1	265	0.8
VIRGINIA:													
Lynchburg	30,070	21,740	72.3	20,527	68.3	464	1.5	402	1.3	347	1.2	8,329	27.7
Newport News	35,596	21,466	60.3	16,889	47.4	1,711	4.8	819	2.3	2,047	5.8	14,077	39.5
Petersburg	31,012	17,390	56.1	16,145	52.1	464	1.5	277	0.9	511	1.6	13,608	43.9
Portsmouth	54,387	31,099	57.2	26,744	49.2	1,853	3.4	959	1.8	1,543	2.8	23,245	42.7
Roanoke	50,842	41,499	81.6	39,000	76.7	921	1.8	709	1.4	869	1.7	9,331	18.4
WASHINGTON:													
Bellingham	25,585	25,464	99.5	12,667	49.5	4,272	16.7	3,197	12.5	5,328	20.8	40	0.2
Everett	27,644	27,388	99.1	13,038	47.2	5,270	19.1	3,339	12.1	5,741	20.8	150	0.5
Tacoma	96,965	94,556	97.5	44,657	46.1	18,689	19.3	10,647	11.0	20,563	21.2	898	0.9
WEST VIRGINIA:													
Charleston	39,608	35,082	88.6	31,044	78.4	1,588	4.0	1,096	2.8	1,354	3.4	4,502	11.4
Clarksburg	27,869	26,610	95.5	21,750	78.0	2,129	7.6	794	2.8	1,937	7.0	1,258	4.5
Huntington	50,177	47,286	94.2	44,720	89.1	920	1.8	914	1.8	732	1.5	2,883	5.7
Wheeling	56,208	54,575	97.1	34,059	60.6	9,575	17.0	5,145	9.2	5,796	10.3	1,623	2.9
WISCONSIN:													
Green Bay	31,017	30,907	99.6	14,492	46.7	7,956	25.7	4,894	15.8	3,565	11.5	32	0.1
Kenosha	40,472	40,358	99.7	11,409	28.2	12,270	30.3	3,965	9.8	12,714	31.4	101	0.2
La Crosse	30,421	30,380	99.9	13,192	43.4	8,090	26.6	4,651	15.3	4,447	14.6	39	0.1
Madison	38,378	38,065	99.2	19,145	49.9	8,950	23.3	5,118	13.3	4,852	12.6	259	0.7
Oshkosh	33,162	33,090	99.8	12,456	37.6	10,089	30.4	4,751	14.3	5,794	17.5	39	0.1
Racine	58,593	58,268	99.4	17,211	29.4	17,878	30.5	6,980	11.9	16,199	27.6	294	0.5
Sheboygan	30,955	30,953	100.0	8,205	26.5	10,376	33.5	4,098	13.2	8,274	26.7		
Superior	39,671	39,472	99.5	10,830	27.3	12,437	31.4	5,441	13.7	10,764	27.1	107	0.3

TABLE 35.—COLOR OR RACE, NATIVITY, AND PARENTAGE, FOR URBAN

DIVISION AND STATE.	TOTAL POPULATION.			NATIVE WHITE—NATIVE PARENTAGE.			NATIVE WHITE—FOREIGN OR MIXED PARENTAGE.		
	Urban.	Rural.	Per cent urban	Urban.	Rural.	Per cent urban	Urban.	Rural.	Per cent urban
United States	54,304,603	51,406,017	51.4	24,556,729	33,865,228	42.0	15,706,372	6,979,832	69.2
GEOG. DIVISIONS:									
New England	5,865,073	1,535,836	79.2	1,867,235	935,914	66.6	2,279,995	362,281	86.3
Middle Atlantic	16,672,595	5,588,549	74.9	5,976,653	3,654,359	62.1	5,925,321	1,172,932	83.5
E. North Central	13,049,272	8,426,271	60.8	5,970,956	5,819,414	50.6	4,109,954	1,815,259	69.4
W. North Central	4,727,372	7,816,877	37.7	2,627,908	4,847,640	35.2	1,275,306	2,102,572	37.8
South Atlantic	4,338,792	9,651,480	31.0	2,559,203	6,220,213	29.2	410,397	143,207	74.1
E. South Central	1,994,207	6,899,100	22.4	1,231,225	4,861,557	20.2	142,928	59,898	70.5
W. South Central	2,970,829	7,271,395	29.0	1,904,386	5,055,399	27.4	303,768	392,841	43.6
Mountain	1,214,980	2,121,121	36.4	695,078	1,307,430	34.7	314,358	442,808	41.5
Pacific	3,471,483	2,095,388	62.4	1,724,085	1,163,302	59.7	944,345	488,034	65.9
NEW ENGLAND:									
Maine	299,569	468,445	39.0	153,986	341,794	31.1	85,170	77,396	52.4
New Hampshire	279,761	163,322	63.1	112,873	112,639	50.1	94,901	30,685	75.6
Vermont	109,976	242,452	31.2	59,302	169,023	26.0	32,295	46,671	40.9
Massachusetts	3,650,248	202,108	94.8	1,116,638	114,135	90.7	1,441,872	53,345	96.4
Rhode Island	589,180	15,217	97.5	163,733	9,820	94.3	243,679	3,249	98.7
Connecticut	936,339	444,292	67.8	260,703	188,503	58.0	382,078	150,935	71.7
MIDDLE ATLANTIC:									
New York	8,589,844	1,795,383	82.7	2,487,080	1,181,186	67.8	3,322,640	395,009	89.4
New Jersey	2,474,936	680,964	78.4	837,624	375,051	69.1	915,112	170,687	84.3
Pennsylvania	5,607,815	3,112,202	64.3	2,651,949	2,098,122	55.8	1,687,569	607,236	73.5
E. NORTH CENTRAL:									
Ohio	3,677,136	2,082,258	63.8	1,996,363	1,672,759	54.4	953,098	270,976	77.9
Indiana	1,482,855	1,447,535	50.6	1,043,866	1,285,678	44.8	247,929	120,730	67.3
Illinois	4,403,153	2,082,127	67.9	1,583,665	1,482,898	51.6	1,607,483	418,336	79.3
Michigan	2,241,560	1,426,852	61.1	902,177	768,270	54.0	760,947	443,598	63.2
Wisconsin	1,244,568	1,387,499	47.3	444,885	609,809	42.2	540,497	561,619	49.0
W. NORTH CENTRAL:									
Minnesota	1,051,593	1,335,532	44.1	356,046	471,581	43.0	445,068	610,077	42.2
Iowa	875,495	1,528,526	36.4	552,275	976,278	36.1	217,456	412,525	34.5
Missouri	1,586,903	1,817,152	46.6	949,293	1,587,643	37.4	353,930	148,152	70.5
North Dakota	88,239	558,633	13.6	36,448	171,518	17.5	35,049	265,436	11.7
South Dakota	101,872	534,675	16.0	58,251	250,347	18.9	30,888	197,270	13.5
Nebraska	405,306	891,066	31.3	225,605	531,459	29.8	107,590	264,913	28.9
Kansas	617,964	1,151,293	34.9	449,990	858,814	34.4	85,325	204,199	29.5
SOUTH ATLANTIC:									
Delaware	120,767	102,236	54.2	63,747	76,129	45.6	27,172	5,757	82.5
Maryland	869,422	580,239	60.0	482,491	410,597	54.0	174,279	35,193	83.2
Dist. of Columbia[2]	437,571		100.0	239,488		100.0	58,824		100.0
Virginia	673,984	1,635,203	29.2	413,778	1,120,716	27.0	31,469	21,161	59.8
West Virginia	369,007	1,094,694	25.2	288,802	944,055	23.4	37,869	44,603	45.9
North Carolina	490,370	2,068,753	19.2	324,229	1,440,974	18.4	6,623	4,854	57.7
South Carolina	293,987	1,389,737	17.5	164,425	634,993	20.6	8,717	4,002	68.5
Georgia	727,859	2,167,973	25.1	419,183	1,223,514	25.5	22,987	7,244	76.0
Florida	355,825	612,645	36.7	163,060	369,235	30.6	42,457	20,393	67.6
E. SOUTH CENTRAL:									
Kentucky	633,543	1,783,087	26.2	422,898	1,616,236	20.7	83,610	27,036	75.6
Tennessee	611,226	1,726,659	26.1	402,359	1,430,398	22.0	26,830	10,928	71.1
Alabama	509,317	1,838,857	21.7	278,827	1,115,302	20.0	22,400	12,841	63.6
Mississippi	240,121	1,550,497	13.4	127,141	699,621	15.4	10,088	9,093	52.6
W. SOUTH CENTRAL:									
Arkansas	290,497	1,461,707	16.6	195,777	1,030,915	16.0	15,474	23,616	39.6
Louisiana	628,163	1,170,346	34.9	320,229	621,495	34.0	84,383	25,633	76.7
Oklahoma	539,480	1,488,803	26.6	437,374	1,241,733	26.0	34,780	67,339	34.1
Texas	1,512,689	3,150,539	32.4	951,006	2,161,256	30.6	169,131	276,253	38.0
MOUNTAIN:									
Montana	172,011	376,876	31.3	81,508	194,295	29.6	55,425	109,412	33.6
Idaho	119,037	312,060	27.6	80,213	214,039	27.3	26,213	66,240	28.4
Wyoming	57,348	137,054	29.5	33,705	69,179	27.4	13,744	28,263	32.7
Colorado	453,259	486,370	48.2	276,329	326,712	45.8	100,000	97,270	52.3
New Mexico	64,960	295,390	18.0	48,859	224,458	17.9	8,625	23,654	26.7
Arizona	117,527	216,635	35.2	58,330	92,815	38.6	26,299	35,906	42.3
Utah	215,584	233,812	48.0	108,034	137,747	44.0	73,125	66,540	52.4
Nevada	15,254	62,153	19.7	8,100	28,185	22.3	4,089	15,523	20.8
PACIFIC:									
Washington	748,735	607,886	55.2	373,611	338,095	52.5	206,245	151,771	57.6
Oregon	391,019	392,370	49.9	227,549	270,177	45.7	95,034	74,235	56.1
California	2,331,729	1,095,132	68.0	1,122,925	555,030	66.9	643,066	262,028	71.0

[1] Per cent not shown, base being less than 100.

AND RURAL COMMUNITIES, BY DIVISIONS AND STATES: 1920.

DIVISION AND STATE.	FOREIGN-BORN WHITE.			NEGRO.			INDIAN, CHINESE, JAPANESE, AND ALL OTHER.		
	Urban.	Rural.	Per cent urban.	Urban.	Rural.	Per cent urban.	Urban.	Rural.	Per cent urban
United States....	10,356,983	3,355,771	75.5	3,559,473	6,903,658	34.0	125,046	301,528	29.3
GEOG. DIVISIONS:									
New England........	1,641,728	228,926	87.8	71,416	7,635	90.3	4,699	1,080	81.3
Middle Atlantic......	4,239,681	672,894	86.3	517,432	82,751	86.2	13,508	5,613	70.6
East North Central..	2,511,626	711,653	77.9	448,873	65,681	87.2	7,863	14,264	35.5
West North Central.	607,384	764,577	44.3	212,591	65,930	76.3	4,183	36,158	10.4
South Atlantic......	222,488	93,432	70.4	1,144,371	3,180,749	26.5	2,333	13,879	14.4
East South Central.	48,407	23,532	67.3	571,316	1,952,216	22.6	331	1,897	14.9
West South Central.	220,460	238,873	48.0	535,282	1,528,297	25.9	6,933	55,985	11.0
Mountain...........	181,439	271,786	40.0	16,678	14,123	54.1	7,427	84,974	8.0
Pacific.............	683,770	350,098	66.1	41,514	6,276	86.9	77,769	87,678	47.0
NEW ENGLAND:									
Maine.............	59,152	48,197	55.1	766	544	58.5	495	514	49.1
New Hampshire.....	71,429	19,804	78.3	441	180	71.0	117	14	89.3
Vermont............	18,146	26,380	40.8	220	352	38.5	13	26	(1)
Massachusetts.......	1,045,106	32,428	97.0	43,624	1,842	95.9	3,008	358	89.4
Rhode Island........	171,685	1,814	99.0	9,710	326	96.8	373	8	77.5
Connecticut.........	276,210	100,303	73.4	16,655	4,391	79.1	693	160	81.2
MIDDLE ATLANTIC:									
New York..........	2,585,350	200,762	92.8	185,212	13,271	93.3	9,562	5,155	65.0
New Jersey.........	628,402	110,211	85.1	92,328	24,804	78.8	1,470	211	87.4
Pennsylvania........	1,025,929	361,921	73.9	239,892	44,676	84.3	2,476	247	90.9
EAST NORTH CENTRAL:									
Ohio...............	570,449	108,248	84.1	155,975	30,212	83.8	1,251	63	95.2
Indiana............	118,813	32,055	78.8	71,813	8,997	88.9	434	75	85.3
Illinois.............	1,046,677	160,274	86.7	161,728	20,546	88.7	3,600	73	98.0
Michigan...........	521,554	205,081	71.8	55,006	5,076	91.6	1,876	4,827	28.0
Wisconsin..........	254,133	205,995	55.2	4,351	850	83.7	702	9,226	7.1
WEST NORTH CENTRAL:									
Minnesota..........	241,463	244,701	49.7	8,250	559	93.7	766	8,614	8.2
Iowa...............	90,019	135,628	39.9	15,345	3,660	80.7	400	435	47.9
Missouri...........	148,813	37,213	80.0	134,167	44,074	75.3	700	70	90.9
North Dakota.......	16,161	115,342	12.3	272	195	58.2	309	6,142	4.8
South Dakota......	12,150	70,241	14.7	340	492	40.9	243	16,325	1.5
Nebraska...........	59,346	90,306	39.7	12,121	1,121	91.5	644	3,267	16.5
Kansas.............	39,432	71,146	35.7	42,096	15,829	72.7	1,121	1,305	46.2
SOUTH ATLANTIC:									
Delaware...........	16,815	2,995	84.9	12,992	17,343	42.8	41	12	(1)
Maryland...........	87,740	14,437	85.9	124,509	119,970	50.9	403	42	90.6
Dist. of Columbia² ..	28,548	....	100.0	109,966	....	100.0	745	....	100.0
Virginia............	19,226	11,559	62.5	209,134	480,883	30.3	377	884	29.9
West Virginia.......	19,755	42,151	31.9	22,484	63,861	26.0	97	24	80.2
North Carolina......	4,239	2,860	59.7	155,165	608,242	20.3	114	11,823	1.0
South Carolina......	4,224	2,177	66.0	116,489	748,230	13.5	132	335	28.3
Georgia............	12,432	3,754	76.8	273,036	933,329	22.6	221	132	62.6
Florida............	29,509	13,499	68.6	120,596	208,891	36.6	203	627	24.5
EAST SOUTH CENTRAL:									
Kentucky...........	21,561	9,219	70.0	105,393	130,545	44.7	81	51	61.4
Tennessee..........	11,484	3,994	74.2	170,464	281,294	37.7	89	45	66.4
Alabama...........	11,183	6,479	63.3	196,833	703,819	21.9	74	416	15.1
Mississippi.........	4,179	3,840	52.1	98,626	836,558	10.5	87	1,385	5.9
WEST SOUTH CENTRAL:									
Arkansas...........	5,590	8,385	40.0	73,592	398,628	15.6	64	163	28.2
Louisiana..........	32,609	12,262	72.7	190,413	509,844	27.2	529	1,112	32.2
Oklahoma..........	14,211	25,757	35.6	47,904	101,504	32.1	5,211	52,470	9.0
Texas..............	168,050	192,469	46.6	223,373	518,321	30.1	1,129	2,240	33.5
MOUNTAIN:									
Montana...........	32,763	60,857	35.0	1,270	388	76.6	1,045	11,926	8.1
Idaho.............	11,124	27,839	28.6	645	275	70.1	842	4,436	16.0
Wyoming...........	8,437	16,818	33.4	833	542	60.6	629	2,252	21.8
Colorado...........	59,626	57,328	51.0	9,364	1,954	82.7	1,102	3,106	26.2
New Mexico........	5,665	23,412	19.5	861	4,872	15.0	950	18,994	4.8
Arizona............	28,913	49,189	37.0	2,631	5,374	32.9	1,357	33,351	3.9
Utah...............	32,311	24,144	57.2	1,006	440	69.6	1,108	4,941	18.3
Nevada............	2,603	12,199	17.6	68	278	19.7	394	5,968	6.2
PACIFIC:									
Washington.........	149,686	100,369	59.9	5,782	1,101	84.0	13,411	16,550	44.8
Oregon............	61,508	40,643	60.2	1,844	300	86.0	5,084	7,015	42.0
California..........	472,576	209,086	69.3	33,888	4,875	87.4	59,274	64,113	48.0

² No rural population, as Washington city is coextensive with the District of Columbia.

TABLE 36.—SEX DISTRIBUTION AND RATIO OF MALES TO FEMALES,

[Figures are given under each class for all

CLASS OF POPULATION AND CENSUS YEAR.	Both sexes.	Male.	Female.	PER CENT.[1]		Males to 100 females.[2]
				Male.	Female.	
Total population:						
1920	105,710,620	53,900,431	51,810,189	51.0	49.0	104.0
1910	91,972,266	47,332,277	44,639,989	51.5	48.5	106.0
1900	75,994,575	38,816,448	37,178,127	51.1	48.9	104.4
1890	62,947,714	32,237,101	30,710,613	51.2	48.8	105.0
1880	50,155,783	25,518,820	24,636,963	50.9	49.1	103.6
1870	38,558,371	19,493,565	19,064,806	50.6	49.4	102.2
1860	31,443,321	16,085,204	15,358,117	51.2	48.8	104.7
1850	23,191,876	11,837,660	11,354,216	51.0	49.0	104.3
1840	17,069,453	8,688,532	8,380,921	50.9	49.1	103.7
1830	12,866,020	6,532,489	6,333,531	50.8	49.2	103.1
1820	9,638,453	4,896,605	4,741,848	50.8	49.2	103.3
White:						
1920	94,820,915	48,430,655	46,390,260	51.1	48.9	104.4
1910	81,731,957	42,178,245	39,553,712	51.6	48.4	106.6
1900	66,809,196	34,201,735	32,607,461	51.2	48.8	104.9
1890	55,101,258	28,270,379	26,830,879	51.3	48.7	105.4
1880	43,402,970	22,130,900	21,272,070	51.0	49.0	104.0
1870	33,589,377	17,029,088	16,560,289	50.7	49.3	102.8
1860	26,922,537	13,811,387	13,111,150	51.3	48.7	105.3
1850	19,553,068	10,026,402	9,526,666	51.3	48.7	105.2
1840	14,195,805	7,255,544	6,940,261	51.1	48.9	104.5
1830	10,537,378	5,366,213	5,171,165	50.9	49.1	103.8
1820	7,866,797	3,995,809	3,870,988	50.8	49.2	103.2
1810	5,862,073	2,988,130	2,873,943	51.0	49.0	104.0
1800	4,306,446	2,195,305	2,111,141	51.0	49.0	104.0
1790	3,172,006	1,615,434	1,556,572	50.9	49.1	103.8
Native white—						
1920	81,108,161	40,902,333	40,205,828	50.4	49.6	101.7
1910	68,386,412	34,654,457	33,731,955	50.7	49.3	102.7
1900	56,595,379	28,686,450	27,908,929	50.7	49.3	102.8
1890	45,979,391	23,318,521	22,660,870	50.7	49.3	102.9
1880	36,843,291	18,609,265	18,234,026	50.5	49.5	102.1
1870	28,095,665	14,086,509	14,009,156	50.1	49.9	100.6
1860	22,825,784	11,619,157	11,206,627	50.9	49.1	103.7
1850	17,312,533	8,786,968	8,525,565	50.8	49.2	103.1
Native parentage—						
1920	58,421,957	29,636,781	28,785,176	50.7	49.3	103.0
1910	49,488,575	25,229,218	24,259,357	51.0	49.0	104.0
1900	40,949,362	20,849,847	20,099,515	50.9	49.1	103.7
1890	34,475,716	17,536,950	16,938,766	50.9	49.1	103.5
Foreign or mixed parentage—						
1920	22,686,204	11,265,552	11,420,652	49.7	50.3	98.6
1910	18,897,837	9,425,239	9,472,598	49.9	50.1	99.5
1900	15,646,017	7,836,603	7,809,414	50.1	49.9	100.3
1890	11,503,675	5,781,571	5,722,104	50.3	49.7	101.0
Foreign parentage—						
1920	15,694,539	7,810,531	7,884,008	49.8	50.2	99.1
1910	12,916,311	6,456,793	6,459,518	50.0	50.0	100.0
1900	10,632,280	5,341,350	5,290,930	50.2	49.8	101.0
Mixed parentage—						
1920	6,991,665	3,455,021	3,536,644	49.4	50.6	97.7
1910	5,981,526	2,968,446	3,013,080	49.6	50.4	98.5
1900	5,013,737	2,495,253	2,518,484	49.8	50.2	99.1
Foreign-born white—						
1920	13,712,754	7,528,322	6,184,432	54.9	45.1	121.7
1910	13,345,545	7,523,788	5,821,757	56.4	43.6	129.2
1900	10,213,817	5,515,285	4,698,532	54.0	46.0	117.4
1890	9,121,867	4,951,858	4,170,009	54.3	45.7	118.7
1880	6,559,679	3,521,635	3,038,044	53.7	46.3	115.9
1870	5,493,712	2,942,579	2,551,133	53.6	46.4	115.3
1860	4,000,753	2,192,230	1,904,523	53.5	46.5	115.1
1850	2,240,535	1,239,401	1,001,101	55.3	44.7	123.8

[1] Per cent not shown where base is less than 100.
[2] Ratio not shown where number of females is less than 100.

BY POPULATION CLASSES, FOR THE UNITED STATES: 1790–1920.

census years for which data are available.]

CLASS OF POPULATION AND CENSUS YEAR.	Both sexes.	Male.	Female.	PER CENT.[1]		Males to 100 females.[2]
				Male.	Female.	
Negro:						
1920	10,463,131	5,209,436	5,253,695	49.8	50.2	99.2
1910	9,827,763	4,885,881	4,941,882	49.7	50.3	98.9
1900	8,833,994	4,386,547	4,447,447	49.7	50.3	98.6
1890	7,488,676	3,735,603	3,753,073	49.9	50.1	99.5
1880	6,580,793	3,253,115	3,327,678	49.4	50.6	97.8
1870	4,880,009	2,393,263	2,486,746	49.0	51.0	96.2
1860	4,441,830	2,216,744	2,225,086	49.9	50.1	99.6
1850	3,638,808	1,811,258	1,827,550	49.8	50.2	99.1
1840	2,873,648	1,432,988	1,440,660	49.9	50.1	99.5
1830	2,328,642	1,166,276	1,162,366	50.1	49.9	100.3
1820	1,771,656	900,796	870,860	50.8	49.2	103.4
Black [3]—						
1920	8,802,577	4,444,514	4,358,063	50.5	49.5	102.0
1910	7,777,077	3,922,332	3,854,745	50.4	49.6	101.8
1870	4,295,960	2,115,367	2,180,593	49.2	50.8	97.0
1860	3,853,467	1,936,536	1,916,931	50.3	49.7	101.0
Mulatto [3]—						
1920	1,660,554	764,922	895,632	46.1	53.9	85.4
1910	2,050,686	963,549	1,087,137	47.0	53.0	88.6
1870	584,049	277,896	306,153	47.6	52.4	90.8
1860	588,363	280,208	308,155	47.6	52.4	90.9
Indian:						
1920	244,437	125,068	119,369	51.2	48.8	104.8
1910	265,683	135,133	130,550	50.9	49.1	103.5
1900	237,196	119,484	117,712	50.4	49.6	101.5
1890	248,253	125,719	122,534	50.6	49.4	102.6
1880	66,407	33,985	32,422	51.2	48.8	104.8
1870	25,731	12,534	13,197	48.7	51.3	95.0
1860	44,021	23,924	20,097	54.3	45.7	119.0
Chinese:						
1920	61,639	53,891	7,748	87.4	12.6	695.5
1910	71,531	66,856	4,675	93.5	6.5	1,430.1
1900	89,863	85,341	4,522	95.0	5.0	1,887.2
1890	107,488	103,620	3,868	96.4	3.6	2,678.9
1880	105,465	100,686	4,779	95.5	4.5	2,106.8
1870	63,199	58,633	4,566	92.8	7.2	1,284.1
1860	34,933	33,149	1,784	94.9	5.1	1,858.1
Japanese:						
1920	111,010	72,707	38,303	65.5	34.5	189.8
1910	72,157	63,070	9,087	87.4	12.6	694.1
1900	24,326	23,341	985	96.0	4.0	2,369.6
1890	2,039	1,780	259	87.3	12.7	687.3
1880	148	134	14	90.5	9.5	....
1870	55	47	8	....	....	....
All other:						
1920	9,488	8,674	814	91.4	8.6	1,065.6
1910	3,175	3,092	83	97.4	2.6	....
Filipinos—						
1920	5,603	5,232	371	93.4	6.6	1,410.2
1910	160	144	16	90.0	10.0	....
Hindus—						
1920	2,507	2,409	98	96.1	3.9	....
1910	2,545	2,526	19	99.3	0.7	....
Koreans—						
1920	1,224	923	301	75.4	24.6	306.6
1910	462	419	43	90.7	9.3	....
Maoris—						
1920	2	2	....	....	....	....
1910	8	3	5	....	....	....
Hawaiians—						
1920	110	75	35	68.2	31.8	....
Malays—						
1920	19	17	2	....	....	....
Samoans—						
1920	6	4	2	....	....	....
Siamese—						
1920	17	12	5	....	....	....

[3] Distinction between blacks and mulattos for Negro population not made in 1880 or 1900; distribution by sex for black population (6,337,980) and mulatto population (1,132,060) not made for 1890.

TABLE 37.—SEX DISTRIBUTION AND RATIO OF MALES TO FEMALES, FOR TOTAL,

DIVISION AND STATE.	TOTAL POPULATION.					
	1920		1910		Males to 100 females.	
	Male.	Female.	Male.	Female.	1920	1910
United States	53,900,431	51,810,189	47,332,277	44,639,989	104.0	106.0
GEOGRAPHIC DIVISIONS:						
New England	3,672,591	3,728,318	3,265,114	3,287,567	98.5	99.3
Middle Atlantic	11,206,445	11,054,699	9,813,266	9,502,626	101.4	103.3
East North Central	11,035,041	10,440,502	9,392,839	8,857,782	105.7	106.0
West North Central	6,459,067	6,085,182	6,092,855	5,545,066	106.1	109.9
South Atlantic	7,035,843	6,954,429	6,134,605	6,060,290	101.2	101.2
East South Central	4,471,690	4,421,617	4,245,169	4,164,732	101.1	101.9
West South Central	5,265,829	4,976,395	4,544,505	4,240,029	105.8	107.2
Mountain	1,789,299	1,546,802	1,478,018	1,155,499	115.7	127.9
Pacific	2,964,626	2,602,245	2,365,906	1,826,398	113.9	129.5
NEW ENGLAND:						
Maine	388,752	379,262	377,052	365,319	102.5	103.2
New Hampshire	222,112	220,971	216,290	214,282	100.5	100.9
Vermont	178,854	173,574	182,568	173,388	103.0	105.3
Massachusetts	1,890,014	1,962,342	1,655,248	1,711,168	96.3	96.7
Rhode Island	297,524	306,873	270,314	272,296	97.0	99.3
Connecticut	695,335	685,296	563,642	551,114	101.5	102.3
MIDDLE ATLANTIC:						
New York	5,187,350	5,197,877	4,584,597	4,529,017	99.8	101.2
New Jersey	1,590,075	1,565,825	1,286,463	1,250,704	101.5	102.9
Pennsylvania	4,429,020	4,290,997	3,942,206	3,722,905	103.2	105.9
EAST NORTH CENTRAL:						
Ohio	2,955,980	2,803,414	2,434,758	2,332,363	105.4	104.4
Indiana	1,489,074	1,441,316	1,383,295	1,317,581	103.3	105.0
Illinois	3,304,833	3,180,447	2,911,674	2,726,917	103.9	106.8
Michigan	1,928,436	1,739,976	1,454,534	1,355,639	110.8	107.3
Wisconsin	1,356,718	1,275,349	1,208,578	1,125,282	106.4	107.4
WEST NORTH CENTRAL:						
Minnesota	1,245,537	1,141,588	1,108,511	967,197	109.1	114.6
Iowa	1,229,392	1,174,629	1,148,171	1,076,600	104.7	106.6
Missouri	1,723,319	1,680,736	1,687,813	1,605,522	102.5	105.1
North Dakota	341,673	305,199	317,554	259,502	112.0	122.4
South Dakota	337,120	299,427	317,112	266,776	112.6	118.9
Nebraska	672,805	623,567	627,782	564,432	107.9	111.2
Kansas	909,221	860,036	885,912	805,037	105.7	110.0
SOUTH ATLANTIC:						
Delaware	113,755	109,248	103,435	98,887	104.1	104.6
Maryland	729,455	720,206	644,225	651,121	101.3	98.9
District of Columbia	203,543	234,028	158,050	173,019	87.0	91.3
Virginia	1,168,492	1,140,695	1,035,348	1,026,264	102.4	100.9
West Virginia	763,100	700,601	644,044	577,075	108.9	111.6
North Carolina	1,279,062	1,280,061	1,098,476	1,107,811	99.9	99.2
South Carolina	838,293	845,431	751,842	763,558	99.2	98.5
Georgia	1,444,823	1,451,009	1,305,019	1,304,102	99.6	100.1
Florida	495,320	473,150	394,166	358,453	104.7	110.0
EAST SOUTH CENTRAL:						
Kentucky	1,227,494	1,189,136	1,161,709	1,128,196	103.2	103.0
Tennessee	1,173,967	1,163,918	1,103,491	1,081,298	100.9	102.1
Alabama	1,173,105	1,175,069	1,074,209	1,063,884	99.8	101.0
Mississippi	897,124	893,494	905,760	891,354	100.4	101.6
WEST SOUTH CENTRAL:						
Arkansas	895,228	856,976	810,026	764,423	104.5	106.0
Louisiana	903,335	895,174	835,275	821,113	100.9	101.7
Oklahoma	1,058,044	970,239	881,578	775,577	109.0	113.7
Texas	2,409,222	2,254,006	2,017,626	1,878,916	106.9	107.4
MOUNTAIN:						
Montana	300,011	248,948	226,872	149,181	120.5	152.1
Idaho	233,919	197,947	185,546	140,048	118.2	132.5
Wyoming	110,359	84,043	91,670	54,295	131.3	168.8
Colorado	492,731	446,898	430,697	368,327	110.3	116.9
New Mexico	190,456	169,894	175,245	152,056	112.1	115.3
Arizona	183,602	150,560	118,574	85,780	121.9	138.2
Utah	232,051	217,345	196,863	176,488	106.8	111.5
Nevada	46,240	31,167	52,551	29,324	148.4	179.2
PACIFIC:						
Washington	734,701	621,920	658,663	483,327	118.1	136.3
Oregon	416,334	367,055	384,265	288,500	113.4	133.2
California	1,813,591	1,613,270	1,322,978	1,054,571	112.4	125.5

WHITE, AND NEGRO POPULATION, BY DIVISIONS AND STATES: 1920 AND 1910.

DIVISION AND STATE.	WHITE.				NEGRO.			
	1920		Males to 100 females.		1920		Males to 100 females.	
	Male.	Female.	1920	1910	Male.	Female.	1920	1910
United States ...	48,430,655	46,390,260	104.4	106.6	5,209,436	5,253,695	99.2	98.9
GEOGRAPHIC DIVISIONS:								
New England.......	3,627,911	3,688,168	98.4	99.2	40,155	38,896	103.2	97.8
Middle Atlantic......	10,890,488	10,751,352	101.3	103.4	301,147	299,036	100.7	94.9
East North Central..	10,748,049	10,190,813	105.5	106.0	273,026	241,528	113.0	108.3
West North Central.	6,293,744	5,931,643	106.1	109.9	143,762	134,759	106.7	107.8
South Atlantic......	4,893,290	4,755,650	102.9	103.2	2,133,377	2,191,743	97.3	97.5
East South Central..	3,226,512	3,141,035	102.7	103.6	1,243,795	1,279,737	97.2	98.4
West South Central.	4,203,877	3,911,850	107.5	109.3	1,029,457	1,034,122	99.5	100.4
Mountain...........	1,717,709	1,495,190	114.9	127.4	19,726	11,075	178.1	121.3
Pacific.............	2,829,075	2,524,559	112.1	125.4	24,991	22,799	109.6	120.4
NEW ENGLAND:								
Maine..............	387,455	378,240	102.4	103.2	716	594	120.5	105.6
New Hampshire....	221,667	220,664	100.5	100.9	333	288	115.6	104.3
Vermont...........	178,504	173,313	103.0	104.9	320	252	127.0	261.8
Massachusetts......	1,864,317	1,939,207	96.1	96.6	22,912	22,554	101.6	97.1
Rhode Island.......	292,131	301,849	96.8	99.2	5,096	4,940	103.2	95.1
Connecticut........	683,837	674,895	101.3	102.3	10,778	10,268	105.0	91.0
MIDDLE ATLANTIC:								
New York..........	5,081,010	5,091,017	99.8	101.3	95,418	103,065	92.6	91.3
New Jersey........	1,531,146	1,505,941	101.7	103.1	57,432	59,700	96.2	94.5
Pennsylvania......	4,278,332	4,154,394	103.0	106.1	148,297	136,271	108.8	97.7
EAST NORTH CENTRAL:								
Ohio..............	2,854,664	2,717,229	105.1	104.3	100,160	86,027	116.4	108.5
Indiana...........	1,446,825	1,402,246	103.2	104.9	41,817	38,993	107.2	106.0
Illinois...........	3,207,773	3,091,560	103.8	106.6	93,835	88,439	106.1	109.1
Michigan..........	1,890,265	1,711,362	110.5	107.2	34,249	25,833	132.6	111.1
Wisconsin.........	1,348,522	1,268,416	106.3	107.4	2,965	2,236	132.6	103.7
WEST NORTH CENTRAL:								
Minnesota.........	1,235,728	1,133,208	109.0	114.5	4,851	3,958	122.6	144.2
Iowa.............	1,218,711	1,165,470	104.6	106.5	10,121	8,884	113.9	118.5
Missouri..........	1,631,697	1,593,347	102.4	105.1	90,991	87,250	104.3	104.6
North Dakota......	338,031	301,923	112.0	122.6	276	191	144.5	161.4
South Dakota......	328,197	290,950	112.8	119.5	475	357	133.1	134.1
Nebraska..........	663,230	615,989	107.7	111.0	7,309	5,933	123.2	124.2
Kansas............	878,150	830,756	105.7	110.1	29,739	28,186	105.5	107.3
SOUTH ATLANTIC:								
Delaware..........	98,049	94,566	103.7	104.4	15,655	14,680	106.6	105.5
Maryland..........	605,601	599,136	101.1	99.2	123,453	121,026	102.0	97.7
District of Columbia.	152,031	174,829	87.0	94.9	50,855	59,111	86.0	82.2
Virginia..........	825,133	792,776	104.1	102.8	342,536	347,481	98.6	97.1
West Virginia.....	715,869	661,366	108.2	110.5	47,129	39,216	120.2	132.8
North Carolina.....	899,031	884,748	101.6	101.2	373,965	389,442	96.0	94.8
South Carolina.....	415,823	402,715	103.3	102.4	422,185	442,534	95.4	95.4
Georgia...........	854,109	835,005	102.3	102.4	590,443	615,922	95.9	97.2
Florida...........	327,644	310,509	105.5	110.2	167,156	162,331	103.0	109.5
EAST SOUTH CENTRAL:								
Kentucky..........	1,108,853	1,071,707	103.5	103.2	118,548	117,390	101.0	101.0
Tennessee.........	951,224	934,769	101.8	103.3	222,639	229,119	97.2	97.6
Alabama..........	733,039	713,993	102.7	103.8	439,779	460,873	95.4	97.2
Mississippi.......	433,396	420,566	103.1	104.7	462,829	472,355	98.0	99.2
WEST SOUTH CENTRAL:								
Arkansas..........	658,169	621,588	105.9	107.7	236,895	235,325	100.7	101.7
Louisiana.........	557,498	539,113	103.4	104.3	344,794	355,463	97.0	98.3
Oklahoma.........	952,691	868,503	109.7	114.7	76,294	73,114	104.3	109.5
Texas.............	2,035,519	1,882,646	108.1	109.0	371,474	370,220	100.3	100.0
MOUNTAIN:								
Montana..........	291,592	242,668	120.2	152.2	962	696	138.2	136.3
Idaho.............	230,136	195,532	117.7	131.3	585	335	174.6	157.3
Wyoming..........	107,501	82,645	130.1	165.6	863	512	168.6	223.4
Colorado..........	484,245	439,858	110.1	116.4	5,834	5,484	106.4	105.0
New Mexico........	175,350	159,323	110.1	115.8	4,593	1,140	402.9	120.9
Arizona...........	159,345	132,104	120.6	142.9	5,859	2,146	273.0	110.4
Utah.............	227,232	214,669	105.9	110.1	834	612	136.3	152.5
Nevada...........	42,308	28,391	149.0	181.5	196	150	130.7	105.2
PACIFIC:								
Washington........	711,693	608,084	117.0	134.2	3,957	2,926	135.2	160.9
Oregon............	407,159	361,987	112.5	130.1	1,197	947	126.4	155.0
California.........	1,710,223	1,554,488	110.0	120.1	19,837	18,926	104.8	109.3

TABLE 38.—SEX DISTRIBUTION, 1920, AND RATIO OF MALES TO FEMALES, 1920
DIVISIONS

DIVISION AND STATE.	NATIVE WHITE—NATIVE PARENTAGE.				NATIVE WHITE—FOREIGN PARENTAGE.			
	1920		Males to 100 females.		1920		Males to 100 females.	
	Male.	Female.	1920	1910	Male.	Female.	1920	1910
United States	29,636,781	28,785,176	103.0	104.0	7,810,531	7,884,008	99.1	100.0
GEOGRAPHIC DIVISIONS:								
New England	1,388,963	1,414,186	98.2	98.1	935,127	971,213	96.3	96.3
Middle Atlantic	4,788,608	4,842,404	98.9	98.9	2,658,961	2,738,990	97.1	97.1
East North Central	5,991,476	5,798,894	103.3	102.9	2,016,078	2,027,614	99.4	99.1
West North Central	3,810,076	3,665,472	103.9	106.6	1,076,084	1,050,042	102.5	104.3
South Atlantic	4,433,700	4,345,716	102.0	102.1	176,458	177,185	99.6	98.1
East South Central	3,086,676	3,006,106	102.7	103.5	55,361	60,123	92.1	93.8
West South Central	3,587,989	3,371,796	106.4	108.2	212,320	203,479	104.3	105.8
Mountain	1,055,895	946,613	111.5	119.8	234,201	216,931	108.0	115.2
Pacific	1,493,398	1,393,989	107.1	117.4	445,941	438,431	101.7	108.4
NEW ENGLAND:								
Maine	250,299	245,481	102.0	101.9	43,382	42,768	101.4	101.8
New Hampshire	112,848	112,664	100.2	99.2	40,039	41,000	97.7	96.3
Vermont	115,392	112,933	102.2	102.7	21,184	20,916	101.3	100.2
Massachusetts	601,525	629,248	95.6	95.2	534,966	558,292	95.8	95.9
Rhode Island	86,368	87,185	99.1	99.6	88,657	94,003	94.3	95.6
Connecticut	222,531	226,675	98.2	97.6	206,899	214,234	96.6	96.1
MIDDLE ATLANTIC:								
New York	1,821,141	1,847,125	98.6	98.9	1,395,548	1,448,535	96.3	96.4
New Jersey	605,157	607,518	99.6	98.9	409,035	420,023	97.4	97.4
Pennsylvania	2,362,310	2,387,761	98.9	98.9	854,378	870,432	98.2	98.3
EAST NORTH CENTRAL:								
Ohio	1,860,779	1,808,343	102.9	101.5	413,305	424,946	97.3	96.2
Indiana	1,175,902	1,153,642	101.9	102.8	112,924	114,142	98.9	100.4
Illinois	1,552,087	1,514,476	102.5	103.9	724,616	742,420	97.6	98.5
Michigan	866,769	803,678	107.9	104.2	394,176	381,112	103.4	100.6
Wisconsin	535,939	518,755	103.3	103.2	371,057	364,994	101.7	101.3
WEST NORTH CENTRAL:								
Minnesota	424,834	402,793	105.5	110.2	358,334	349,792	102.4	103.8
Iowa	775,407	753,146	103.0	103.8	189,693	187,017	101.4	102.7
Missouri	1,283,069	1,253,867	102.3	104.2	146,528	153,536	95.4	97.9
North Dakota	108,334	99,632	108.7	121.6	104,728	99,245	105.5	111.5
South Dakota	161,980	146,618	110.5	118.2	74,127	67,214	110.3	111.6
Nebraska	389,049	368,015	105.7	108.5	118,286	113,662	104.1	105.2
Kansas	667,403	641,401	104.1	107.4	84,388	79,576	106.0	107.5
SOUTH ATLANTIC:								
Delaware	70,517	69,359	101.7	102.5	11,479	11,809	97.2	98.0
Maryland	448,287	444,801	100.8	99.0	70,267	72,936	96.3	94.9
District of Columbia	109,872	129,616	84.8	93.4	16,549	18,580	89.1	93.4
Virginia	778,053	756,441	102.9	101.6	16,545	13,969	118.4	110.6
West Virginia	632,425	600,432	105.3	106.3	28,591	28,034	102.0	102.2
North Carolina	888,953	876,250	101.4	101.0	2,932	2,805	104.5	100.4
South Carolina	405,120	394,298	102.7	102.0	3,678	3,347	109.9	95.2
Georgia	828,637	814,060	101.8	101.9	8,522	7,849	108.6	103.6
Florida	271,836	260,459	104.4	107.6	17,895	17,856	100.2	102.7
EAST SOUTH CENTRAL:								
Kentucky	1,039,134	1,000,000	103.9	103.8	30,816	35,115	87.8	90.3
Tennessee	923,544	909,213	101.6	103.0	10,158	10,265	99.0	98.5
Alabama	704,980	689,149	102.3	103.2	9,695	9,896	98.0	100.4
Mississippi	419,018	407,744	102.8	104.2	4,692	4,847	96.8	100.8
WEST SOUTH CENTRAL:								
Arkansas	628,856	597,826	105.2	106.8	10,369	8,661	119.7	118.8
Louisiana	478,415	463,309	103.3	104.2	31,923	35,093	91.0	94.2
Oklahoma	870,888	805,219	108.5	113.1	28,271	24,812	113.9	118.7
Texas	1,607,830	1,505,432	106.7	107.5	141,757	134,913	105.1	105.8
MOUNTAIN:								
Montana	147,662	128,141	115.2	139.6	53,379	48,529	110.0	124.4
Idaho	155,973	138,279	112.8	123.0	25,781	22,139	116.5	123.4
Wyoming	68,042	54,842	124.1	151.8	13,535	11,699	115.7	139.3
Colorado	313,759	289,282	108.5	112.0	65,574	64,485	101.7	105.4
New Mexico	141,937	131,380	108.0	111.1	9,715	9,150	106.2	116.1
Arizona	82,435	68,710	120.0	135.0	20,497	19,037	107.7	122.3
Utah	125,360	120,421	104.1	108.2	39,185	36,716	106.7	105.8
Nevada	20,727	15,558	133.2	161.3	6,535	5,166	126.5	147.2
PACIFIC:								
Washington	374,555	337,151	111.1	124.2	111,145	103,473	107.4	116.4
Oregon	258,647	239,079	108.2	121.6	49,146	46,681	105.3	116.5
California	860,196	817,759	105.2	112.4	285,650	288,277	99.1	103.6

AND 1910, FOR THE WHITE POPULATION BY NATIVITY AND PARENTAGE, BY AND STATES.

DIVISION AND STATE.	NATIVE WHITE—MIXED PARENTAGE.				FOREIGN-BORN WHITE.			
	1920		Males to 100 females.		1920		Males to 100 females.	
	Male.	Female.	1920	1910	Male.	Female.	1920	1910
United States	3,455,021	3,536,644	97.7	98.5	7,528,322	6,184,432	121.7	129.2
GEOGRAPHIC DIVISIONS:								
New England	358,085	377,851	94.8	95.2	945,736	924,918	102.3	104.8
Middle Atlantic	825,353	874,949	94.3	94.9	2,617,566	2,295,009	114.1	120.9
East North Central	931,161	950,360	98.0	97.7	1,809,334	1,413,945	128.0	131.3
West North Central	628,562	623,190	100.9	101.6	779,022	592,939	131.4	141.3
South Atlantic	97,989	101,972	96.1	96.9	185,143	130,777	141.6	146.9
East South Central	42,382	44,960	94.3	95.6	42,093	29,846	141.0	139.2
West South Central	142,791	138,019	103.5	104.2	260,777	198,556	131.3	138.8
Mountain	156,240	149,794	104.3	109.0	271,373	181,852	149.2	189.6
Pacific	272,458	275,549	98.9	104.2	617,278	416,590	148.2	181.9
NEW ENGLAND:								
Maine	37,967	38,449	98.7	101.6	55,807	51,542	108.3	111.1
New Hampshire	21,936	22,611	97.0	96.6	46,844	44,389	105.5	110.4
Vermont	18,217	18,649	97.7	96.5	23,711	20,815	113.9	127.3
Massachusetts	194,507	207,452	93.8	94.0	533,319	544,215	98.0	99.5
Rhode Island	30,942	33,326	92.8	94.1	86,164	87,335	98.7	103.6
Connecticut	54,516	57,364	95.0	95.1	199,891	176,622	113.2	116.7
MIDDLE ATLANTIC:								
New York	421,746	451,820	93.3	94.5	1,442,575	1,343,537	107.4	110.5
New Jersey	125,299	131,442	95.3	95.4	391,655	346,958	112.9	118.2
Pennsylvania	278,308	291,687	95.4	95.4	783,336	604,514	129.6	145.5
EAST NORTH CENTRAL:								
Ohio	189,236	196,587	96.3	95.8	391,344	287,353	136.2	137.8
Indiana	69,819	71,774	97.3	97.7	88,180	62,688	140.7	156.4
Illinois	273,806	284,977	96.1	97.4	657,264	549,687	119.6	127.3
Michigan	215,514	213,743	100.8	99.1	413,806	312,829	132.3	127.4
Wisconsin	182,786	183,279	99.7	98.6	258,740	201,388	128.5	130.8
WEST NORTH CENTRAL:								
Minnesota	173,972	173,047	100.5	100.9	278,588	207,576	134.2	144.0
Iowa	126,546	126,725	99.9	99.2	127,065	98,582	128.9	135.7
Missouri	98,682	103,336	95.5	97.5	103,418	82,608	125.2	135.9
North Dakota	49,583	46,929	105.7	109.1	75,386	56,117	134.3	145.8
South Dakota	44,480	42,337	105.1	108.5	47,610	34,781	136.9	145.8
Nebraska	71,618	68,937	103.9	103.8	84,277	65,375	128.9	136.7
Kansas	63,681	61,879	102.9	104.2	62,678	47,900	130.9	149.9
SOUTH ATLANTIC:								
Delaware	4,684	4,957	94.5	96.9	11,369	8,441	134.7	132.4
Maryland	32,419	33,850	95.8	94.7	54,628	47,549	114.9	108.9
District of Columbia	10,468	13,227	79.1	89.7	15,142	13,406	112.9	113.0
Virginia	11,484	10,632	108.0	104.4	19,051	11,734	162.4	169.0
West Virginia	12,943	12,904	100.3	100.5	41,910	19,996	209.6	261.8
North Carolina	2,805	2,935	95.6	97.0	4,341	2,758	157.4	170.5
South Carolina	2,930	2,764	106.0	99.2	4,095	2,306	177.6	159.3
Georgia	6,946	6,914	100.5	98.9	10,004	6,182	161.8	171.4
Florida	13,310	13,789	96.5	99.7	24,603	18,495	133.7	157.6
EAST SOUTH CENTRAL:								
Kentucky	21,424	23,291	92.0	93.2	17,479	13,301	131.4	117.2
Tennessee	8,501	8,834	96.2	97.2	9,021	6,457	139.7	152.4
Alabama	7,739	7,911	97.8	98.5	10,625	7,037	151.0	165.9
Mississippi	4,718	4,924	95.8	99.9	4,968	3,051	162.8	173.7
WEST SOUTH CENTRAL:								
Arkansas	10,353	9,707	106.7	107.0	8,591	5,384	159.6	168.3
Louisiana	20,352	22,648	89.9	92.3	26,808	18,063	148.4	133.9
Oklahoma	25,601	23,435	109.2	113.4	24,931	15,037	165.8	178.1
Texas	86,485	82,229	105.2	105.0	200,447	160,072	125.2	132.6
MOUNTAIN:								
Montana	32,322	30,597	105.6	116.5	58,229	35,391	164.5	238.4
Idaho	23,505	21,028	111.8	114.0	24,877	14,086	176.6	227.5
Wyoming	8,990	7,783	115.5	130.9	16,934	8,321	203.5	287.2
Colorado	36,693	37,356	98.2	101.1	68,219	48,735	140.0	160.1
New Mexico	6,853	6,561	104.5	113.6	16,845	12,232	137.7	139.6
Arizona	11,756	10,915	107.7	113.7	44,657	33,442	133.5	188.4
Utah	31,812	31,952	99.6	101.1	30,875	25,580	120.7	131.0
Nevada	4,309	3,602	119.6	132.6	10,737	4,065	264.1	331.4
PACIFIC:								
Washington	72,875	70,523	103.3	110.0	153,118	96,937	158.0	199.7
Oregon	37,056	36,386	101.8	108.7	62,310	39,841	156.4	209.9
California	162,527	168,640	96.4	100.7	401,850	279,812	143.6	169.6

TABLE 39.—SEX DISTRIBUTION AND RATIO OF MALES TO FEMALES, FOR TOTAL, OR MORE:

CITY.	TOTAL POPULATION.				Males to 100 females.	
	1920		1910		1920	1910
	Male.	Female.	Male.	Female.		
Akron, Ohio	121,169	87,266	36,604	32,463	138.9	112.8
Albany, N. Y	54,674	58,670	48,270	51,983	93.2	92.9
Atlanta, Ga	96,457	104,159	74,501	80,338	92.6	92.7
Baltimore, Md	361,560	372,266	268,195	290,290	97.1	92.4
Birmingham, Ala	89,015	89,791	67,268	65,417	99.1	102.8
Boston, Mass	368,756	379,304	329,703	340,882	97.2	96.7
Bridgeport, Conn	73,709	69,846	52,549	49,505	105.5	106.1
Buffalo, N. Y	253,654	253,121	212,502	211,213	100.2	100.6
Cambridge, Mass	52,428	57,266	50,161	54,678	91.6	91.7
Camden, N. J	59,212	57,097	47,396	47,142	103.7	100.5
Chicago, Ill	1,369,917	1,331,788	1,125,764	1,059,519	102.9	106.3
Cincinnati, Ohio	194,342	206,905	177,511	186,080	93.9	95.4
Cleveland, Ohio	413,398	383,443	289,262	271,401	107.8	106.6
Columbus, Ohio	118,810	118,221	91,452	90,059	100.5	101.5
Dallas, Tex	79,506	79,470	46,499	45,605	100.0	102.0
Dayton, Ohio	77,114	75,445	58,848	57,729	102.2	101.9
Denver, Colo	131,906	124,585	107,395	105,986	105.9	101.3
Des Moines, Iowa	62,178	64,290	43,135	43,233	96.7	99.8
Detroit, Mich	540,248	453,430	240,354	225,412	119.1	106.6
Fall River, Mass	57,918	62,567	57,627	61,668	92.6	93.4
Fort Worth, Tex	56,366	50,116	39,007	34,305	112.5	113.7
Grand Rapids, Mich	67,516	70,118	55,539	57,032	96.3	97.4
Hartford, Conn	69,106	68,930	49,211	49,704	100.3	99.0
Houston, Tex	69,048	69,228	40,126	38,674	99.7	103.8
Indianapolis, Ind	155,839	158,355	116,069	117,581	98.4	98.7
Jersey City, N. J	150,416	147,687	137,457	130,322	101.8	105.5
Kansas City, Kans	51,798	49,379	42,773	39,558	104.9	108.1
Kansas City, Mo	162,362	162,048	126,414	121,967	100.2	103.6
Los Angeles, Calif	285,175	291,498	162,669	156,529	97.8	103.9
Louisville, Ky	112,159	122,732	108,548	115,380	91.4	94.1
Lowell, Mass	54,271	58,488	51,525	54,769	92.8	94.1
Memphis, Tenn	79,116	83,235	66,270	64,835	95.1	102.2
Milwaukee, Wis	228,614	228,533	189,488	184,369	100.0	102.8
Minneapolis, Minn	189,215	191,367	157,345	144,063	98.9	109.2
Nashville, Tenn	56,004	62,338	52,155	58,209	89.8	89.6
New Bedford, Mass	59,388	61,829	47,731	48,921	96.1	97.6
New Haven, Conn	80,221	82,316	66,695	66,910	97.5	99.7
New Orleans, La	189,026	198,193	163,239	175,836	95.4	92.8
New York, N. Y	2,802,638	2,817,410	2,382,482	2,384,401	99.5	99.9
Bronx borough	364,208	367,808	217,120	213,860	99.0	101.5
Brooklyn borough	1,007,859	1,010,497	809,791	824,560	99.7	98.2
Manhattan borough	1,135,708	1,148,395	1,166,659	1,164,883	98.9	100.2
Queens borough	233,440	235,602	144,205	139,836	99.1	103.1
Richmond borough	61,423	55,108	44,707	41,262	111.5	108.3
Newark, N. J	209,200	205,324	173,389	174,080	101.9	99.6
Norfolk, Va	60,018	55,759	32,867	34,585	107.6	95.0
Oakland, Calif	111,954	104,307	78,222	71,952	107.3	108.7
Omaha, Nebr.[2]	98,954	92,647	79,363	70,992	106.8	111.8
Paterson, N. J	67,248	68,627	62,439	63,161	98.0	98.9
Philadelphia, Pa	907,633	916,146	760,463	788,545	99.1	96.4
Pittsburgh, Pa	296,260	292,083	273,589	260,316	101.4	105.1
Portland, Oreg	132,115	126,173	118,868	88,346	104.7	134.5
Providence, R. I	115,154	122,441	110,288	114,038	94.0	96.7
Reading, Pa	53,198	54,586	47,576	48,495	97.5	98.1
Richmond, Va	80,631	91,036	60,905	66,723	88.6	91.3
Rochester, N. Y	145,494	150,256	108,352	109,797	96.8	98.7
St. Louis, Mo	383,402	389,495	346,068	340,961	98.4	101.5
St. Paul, Minn	117,368	117,330	111,809	102,935	100.0	108.6
Salt Lake City, Utah	58,697	59,413	47,583	45,194	98.8	105.3
San Antonio, Tex	80,782	80,597	47,855	48,749	100.2	98.2
San Francisco, Calif	272,703	233,973	236,901	180,011	116.6	131.6
Scranton, Pa	67,549	70,234	65,591	64,276	96.2	102.0
Seattle, Wash	167,601	147,711	136,773	100,421	113.5	136.2
Spokane, Wash	52,329	52,108	57,513	46,889	100.4	122.7
Springfield, Mass	63,722	65,892	43,221	45,705	96.7	94.6
Syracuse, N. Y	85,935	85,782	68,806	68,443	100.2	100.5
Toledo, Ohio	125,518	117,646	84,691	83,806	106.7	101.1
Trenton, N. J	60,639	58,650	50,231	46,584	103.4	107.8
Washington, D. C	203,543	234,028	158,050	173,019	87.0	91.3
Wilmington, Del	56,180	53,988	43,938	43,473	104.1	101.1
Worcester, Mass	89,586	90,168	73,424	72,562	99.4	101.2
Yonkers, N. Y	49,010	51,166	40,103	39,700	95.8	101.0
Youngstown, Ohio	70,770	61,588	43,649	35,417	114.9	123.2

[1] Ratio not shown, number of females being less than 100.

WHITE, AND NEGRO POPULATION, FOR CITIES HAVING, IN 1920, 100,000 INHABITANTS 1920 AND 1910.

CITY.	WHITE.				NEGRO.			
	1920		Males to 100 females.		1920		Males to 100 females.	
	Male.	Female.	1920	1910	Male.	Female.	1920	1910
Akron, Ohio	117,481	85,237	137.8	112.7	3,554	2,026	175.4	119.0
Albany, N. Y	53,975	58,061	93.0	92.8	635	604	105.1	92.0
Atlanta, Ga	67,435	70,350	95.9	99.2	28,993	33,803	85.8	81.0
Baltimore, Md	308,324	316,806	97.3	93.6	52,889	55,433	95.4	85.5
Birmingham, Ala	54,832	53,718	102.1	107.3	34,160	36,070	94.7	96.3
Boston, Mass	359,403	371,082	96.9	96.4	8,295	8,055	103.0	96.6
Bridgeport, Conn	72,386	68,834	105.2	106.2	1,220	1,008	121.0	97.3
Buffalo, N. Y	250,973	251,069	100.0	100.5	2,522	1,989	126.8	111.1
Cambridge, Mass	49,800	54,450	91.5	91.6	2,535	2,799	90.6	89.8
Camden, N. J	54,856	52,897	103.7	100.8	4,304	4,196	102.6	94.3
Chicago, Ill	1,311,243	1,277,926	102.6	106.1	55,943	53,515	104.5	105.9
Cincinnati, Ohio	179,144	191,953	93.3	95.0	15,145	14,934	101.4	101.8
Cleveland, Ohio	394,337	367,689	107.2	106.5	18,733	15,718	119.2	105.7
Columbus, Ohio	106,905	107,816	99.2	100.6	11,788	10,393	113.4	113.9
Dallas, Tex	67,629	67,259	100.6	104.2	11,828	12,195	97.0	92.9
Dayton, Ohio	72,308	71,187	101.6	101.8	4,776	4,249	112.4	104.6
Denver, Colo	128,221	121,423	105.6	100.8	3,069	3,006	102.1	95.6
Des Moines, Iowa	59,342	61,545	96.4	99.6	2,771	2,741	101.1	103.5
Detroit, Mich	515,989	436,076	118.3	106.6	23,605	17,233	137.0	108.3
Fall River, Mass	57,716	62,398	92.5	93.3	152	163	93.3	96.1
Fort Worth, Tex	48,247	42,219	114.3	115.7	8,010	7,886	101.6	104.3
Grand Rapids, Mich	66,908	69,564	96.2	97.3	555	535	103.7	109.1
Hartford, Conn	66,832	66,849	100.0	99.1	2,137	2,062	103.6	84.1
Houston, Tex	52,621	51,647	101.9	111.2	16,394	17,566	93.3	88.3
Indianapolis, Ind	138,362	141,049	98.1	98.7	17,378	17,300	100.5	98.1
Jersey City, N. J	146,229	143,780	101.7	105.4	4,099	3,901	105.1	102.7
Kansas City, Kans	44,615	42,088	106.0	109.3	7,130	7,275	98.0	99.1
Kansas City, Mo	146,741	146,776	100.0	103.8	15,472	15,247	101.5	101.7
Los Angeles, Calif	268,231	278,633	96.3	101.3	7,389	8,190	90.2	94.0
Louisville, Ky	93,037	101,732	91.5	94.2	19,094	20,993	91.0	93.7
Lowell, Mass	54,098	58,411	92.6	94.0	100	70	(¹)	(¹)
Memphis, Tenn	50,132	50,981	98.3	108.9	28,935	32,246	89.7	92.9
Milwaukee, Wis	227,310	227,514	99.9	102.8	1,233	996	123.8	95.2
Minneapolis, Minn	186,852	189,513	98.6	108.9	2,133	1,794	118.9	137.1
Nashville, Tenn	39,827	42,876	92.9	94.7	16,173	19,460	83.1	80.0
New Bedford, Mass	56,565	59,577	94.9	97.2	2,756	2,242	122.9	106.1
New Haven, Conn	77,822	79,994	97.3	99.7	2,269	2,304	98.5	92.5
New Orleans, La	141,790	144,126	98.4	95.6	46,919	54,101	86.9	84.7
New York, N. Y	2,723,217	2,736,246	99.5	100.0	72,351	80,116	90.3	85.0
Bronx borough	361,748	365,242	99.0	101.6	2,269	2,534	89.5	86.6
Brooklyn borough	991,274	993,679	99.8	98.3	15,197	16,715	90.9	82.2
Manhattan borough	1,078,586	1,090,320	98.9	100.2	51,912	57,221	90.7	86.2
Queens borough	230,998	232,663	99.3	103.3	2,238	2,882	77.7	81.9
Richmond borough	60,611	54,342	111.5	108.6	735	764	96.2	83.1
Newark, N. J	200,348	196,875	101.8	99.8	8,552	8,425	101.5	89.6
Norfolk, Va	38,077	34,149	111.5	97.7	21,794	21,598	100.9	90.4
Oakland, Calif	103,922	100,082	103.8	103.9	3,029	2,460	123.1	112.0
Omaha, Nebr.²	93,151	87,895	106.0	111.1	5,598	4,717	118.7	120.5
Paterson, N. J	66,452	67,802	98.0	98.9	731	820	89.1	85.6
Philadelphia, Pa	839,296	848,884	98.9	96.8	67,132	67,097	100.1	87.6
Pittsburgh, Pa	276,025	274,236	100.7	104.8	19,913	17,812	111.8	108.8
Portland, Oreg	128,430	124,531	103.1	127.4	833	723	115.2	139.1
Providence, R. I	112,150	119,606	93.8	96.6	2,850	2,805	101.6	94.1
Reading, Pa	52,698	54,153	97.3	98.0	491	433	113.4	108.2
Richmond, Va	55,896	61,678	90.6	95.1	24,696	29,345	84.2	85.0
Rochester, N. Y	144,689	149,400	96.8	98.7	744	835	89.1	93.2
St. Louis, Mo	347,665	354,950	97.9	101.3	35,359	34,495	102.5	101.7
St. Paul, Minn	115,427	115,744	99.7	108.0	1,829	1,547	118.2	153.5
Salt Lake City, Utah	57,832	58,949	98.1	104.0	392	326	120.2	143.2
San Antonio, Tex	73,741	73,058	100.9	99.9	6,842	7,499	91.2	84.5
San Francisco, Calif	260,885	229,137	113.9	125.8	1,362	1,052	129.5	166.1
Scranton, Pa	67,243	69,971	96.1	102.0	300	263	114.1	116.4
Seattle, Wash	159,279	143,301	111.1	131.2	1,671	1,223	136.6	154.5
Spokane, Wash	51,706	51,674	100.1	121.6	382	345	110.7	117.8
Springfield, Mass	62,232	64,567	96.4	94.6	1,339	1,311	102.1	83.2
Syracuse, N. Y	85,207	85,165	100.0	100.5	677	583	116.1	106.2
Toledo, Ohio	122,255	115,130	106.2	101.0	3,184	2,507	127.0	99.7
Trenton, N. J	58,330	56,572	103.1	107.4	2,241	2,074	108.1	123.1
Washington, D. C	152,031	174,829	87.0	94.9	50,855	59,111	86.0	82.2
Wilmington, Del	50,574	48,808	103.6	101.9	5,568	5,178	107.5	93.6
Worcester, Mass	88,898	89,493	99.3	101.2	608	650	93.5	84.9
Yonkers, N. Y	48,061	50,117	95.9	101.1	898	1,042	86.2	89.6
Youngstown, Ohio	66,774	58,821	113.5	123.2	3,900	2,762	141.2	124.1

² Includes, for 1910, population of South Omaha, consolidated with Omaha since 1910.

TABLE **40.**—SEX DISTRIBUTION, 1920, AND RATIO OF MALES TO FEMALES, 1920 AND
HAVING, IN 1920, 100,000

CITY.	NATIVE WHITE—NATIVE PARENTAGE.				NATIVE WHITE—FOREIGN PARENTAGE.			
	1920		Males to 100 females.		1920		Males to 100 females.	
	Male.	Female.	1920	1910	Male.	Female.	1920	1910
Akron, Ohio	72,485	52,594	137.8	110.4	14,565	13,780	105.7	94.0
Albany, N. Y	27,226	29,039	93.8	93.3	12,682	14,352	88.4	89.6
Atlanta, Ga	60,913	64,035	95.1	97.8	2,327	2,488	93.5	94.5
Baltimore, Md	185,737	192,643	96.4	92.6	56,318	60,431	93.2	91.6
Birmingham, Ala	46,261	45,950	100.7	105.3	3,307	3,370	98.1	102.8
Boston, Mass	89,898	91,913	97.8	96.1	116,910	121,331	96.4	97.4
Bridgeport, Conn	18,668	18,148	102.9	102.2	23,121	23,973	96.4	94.3
Buffalo, N. Y	82,313	82,822	99.4	100.2	74,705	79,654	93.8	94.1
Cambridge, Mass	13,503	15,542	86.9	88.8	15,879	16,404	96.8	95.6
Camden, N. J	28,376	27,873	101.8	98.6	11,294	11,523	98.0	98.7
Chicago, Ill	322,922	319,949	100.9	103.8	434,412	454,084	95.7	95.9
Cincinnati, Ohio	101,319	105,286	96.2	97.9	36,620	43,691	83.8	85.6
Cleveland, Ohio	107,693	104,554	103.0	101.6	121,995	124,534	98.0	95.6
Columbus, Ohio	78,836	80,233	98.3	99.7	11,644	12,558	92.7	92.2
Dallas, Tex	55,785	56,724	98.3	103.1	4,065	3,954	102.8	98.5
Dayton, Ohio	50,926	50,070	101.7	99.9	8,950	9,937	90.1	88.8
Denver, Colo	75,229	69,449	108.3	100.2	20,675	22,387	92.4	94.9
Des Moines, Iowa	41,163	43,198	95.3	99.1	7,241	8,025	90.2	88.9
Detroit, Mich	170,624	143,373	119.0	105.4	125,202	121,833	102.8	94.9
Fall River, Mass	9,176	9,992	91.8	92.9	21,887	23,348	93.7	95.0
Fort Worth, Tex	39,539	35,976	109.9	110.9	2,415	2,111	114.4	116.8
Grand Rapids, Mich	27,445	28,634	95.8	95.9	16,512	18,267	90.4	88.8
Hartford, Conn	19,843	20,484	96.9	96.9	20,386	21,368	95.4	95.5
Houston, Tex	36,157	36,276	99.7	109.8	5,812	5,989	97.0	99.1
Indianapolis, Ind	108,588	110,709	98.1	97.2	12,600	13,979	90.1	92.1
Jersey City, N. J	44,007	43,076	102.2	102.7	48,116	50,504	95.3	98.0
Kansas City, Kans	28,689	27,886	102.9	104.2	6,040	6,109	98.9	97.0
Kansas City, Mo	103,801	105,333	98.5	102.6	17,202	17,981	95.7	95.6
Los Angeles, Calif	142,121	152,337	93.3	99.8	41,282	45,526	90.7	92.7
Louisville, Ky	67,500	71,903	93.9	96.2	12,002	15,074	79.6	85.7
Lowell, Mass	11,810	12,866	91.8	89.3	17,781	19,260	92.3	93.4
Memphis, Tenn	40,818	41,977	97.2	108.5	3,746	3,925	95.4	95.9
Milwaukee, Wis	65,054	65,791	98.9	98.0	72,222	80,497	89.7	91.1
Minneapolis, Minn	66,416	66,762	99.5	111.4	50,273	58,551	85.9	92.3
Nashville, Tenn	35,652	38,370	92.9	95.2	1,637	2,016	81.2	81.0
New Bedford, Mass	9,687	10,411	93.0	92.7	17,706	18,673	94.8	97.7
New Haven, Conn	21,545	22,856	94.3	94.8	26,492	28,210	93.9	94.6
New Orleans, La	94,570	96,071	98.4	97.6	19,148	22,658	84.5	87.5
New York, N. Y	575,847	588,987	97.8	98.0	919,740	953,273	96.5	96.3
Bronx borough	66,172	66,598	99.4	100.6	131,452	136,928	96.0	95.7
Brooklyn borough	226,063	230,177	98.2	95.4	344,079	359,338	95.8	95.3
Manhattan borough	188,954	199,325	94.8	99.1	355,145	365,309	97.2	96.9
Queens borough	74,416	74,926	99.3	100.6	72,145	75,255	95.9	97.8
Richmond borough	20,242	17,961	112.7	105.3	16,919	16,443	102.9	101.9
Newark, N. J	56,465	56,948	99.2	96.1	65,567	67,808	96.7	94.1
Norfolk, Va	29,524	28,235	104.6	94.5	2,774	2,433	114.0	98.4
Oakland, Calif	45,443	44,836	101.4	99.9	21,154	22,907	92.3	92.2
Omaha, Nebr.[1]	44,332	42,193	105.1	109.3	20,241	21,213	95.4	98.2
Paterson, N. J	15,378	16,446	93.5	94.2	21,539	22,543	95.5	95.1
Philadelphia, Pa	344,382	354,400	97.2	95.1	219,690	227,381	96.6	95.4
Pittsburgh, Pa	107,253	109,277	98.1	99.0	76,444	81,137	94.2	95.2
Portland, Oreg	67,180	69,036	97.3	123.7	20,492	21,443	95.6	107.9
Providence, R. I	30,646	33,082	92.6	93.2	36,516	39,532	92.4	93.3
Reading, Pa	39,371	41,629	94.6	94.1	5,828	6,088	95.7	95.2
Richmond, Va	48,641	54,315	89.6	93.6	2,817	3,030	93.0	94.3
Rochester, N. Y	54,847	57,129	96.0	97.4	37,474	40,971	91.5	90.8
St. Louis, Mo	178,475	181,007	98.6	99.9	74,412	83,567	89.0	91.2
St. Paul, Minn	39,171	38,207	102.5	111.9	33,024	37,166	88.9	97.2
Salt Lake City, Utah	28,191	28,043	100.5	110.4	11,598	11,917	97.3	97.8
San Antonio, Tex	67,090	68,371	98.8	100.0	10,137	10,024	92.8	94.0
San Francisco, Calif	88,737	78,442	113.1	126.9	61,660	64,360	95.5	100.8
Scranton, Pa	23,589	25,126	93.9	96.7	21,543	23,674	91.0	91.8
Seattle, Wash	71,333	68,368	104.3	126.1	27,286	27,392	99.6	105.7
Spokane, Wash	28,322	29,002	97.7	115.3	7,920	8,646	91.6	105.7
Springfield, Mass	23,856	25,089	95.1	92.7	16,054	16,937	94.8	92.4
Syracuse, N. Y	39,807	40,265	98.9	98.3	19,816	21,066	94.1	90.3
Toledo, Ohio	63,758	60,297	105.7	99.0	25,039	26,062	96.1	95.1
Trenton, N. J	21,862	22,333	97.9	98.9	15,991	16,190	98.8	99.5
Washington, D. C	109,872	129,616	84.8	93.4	16,549	18,580	89.1	93.4
Wilmington, Del	28,419	28,449	99.9	98.2	9,353	9,779	95.6	95.8
Worcester, Mass	24,816	25,900	95.8	95.2	27,803	29,038	95.7	94.4
Yonkers, N. Y	14,565	15,494	94.0	95.7	15,577	16,703	93.3	94.6
Youngstown, Ohio	23,755	22,704	104.6	109.6	16,991	17,468	97.3	98.3

[1] Includes, for 1910, population of South Omaha, consolidated with Omaha since 1910.

1910, FOR THE WHITE POPULATION BY NATIVITY AND PARENTAGE, FOR CITIES
INHABITANTS OR MORE.

CITY.	NATIVE WHITE—MIXED PARENTAGE.				FOREIGN-BORN WHITE.			
	1920		Males to 100 females.		1920		Males to 100 females.	
	Male.	Female.	1920	1910	Male.	Female.	1920	1910
Akron, Ohio	5,824	5,581	104.4	97.4	24,607	13,282	185.3	149.9
Albany, N. Y	5,091	6,010	84.7	88.8	8,976	8,660	103.6	98.9
Atlanta, Ga	1,495	1,789	83.6	86.5	2,700	2,038	132.5	150.4
Baltimore, Md	22,235	23,855	93.2	91.5	44,034	39,877	110.4	100.6
Birmingham, Ala	1,765	1,813	97.4	99.1	3,499	2,585	135.4	145.8
Boston, Mass	34,825	36,689	94.9	96.0	117,770	121,149	97.2	95.8
Bridgeport, Conn	5,318	5,578	95.3	98.6	25,279	21,135	119.6	122.3
Buffalo, N. Y	29,207	31,811	91.8	91.9	64,748	56,782	114.0	112.8
Cambridge, Mass	5,199	5,619	92.5	92.7	15,219	16,885	90.1	90.2
Camden, N. J	4,100	4,325	94.8	90.7	11,086	9,176	120.8	116.1
Chicago, Ill	122,145	130,175	93.8	95.6	431,764	373,718	115.5	121.1
Cincinnati, Ohio	19,413	21,941	88.5	91.6	21,792	21,035	103.6	105.9
Cleveland, Ohio	31,574	32,138	98.2	95.4	133,075	106,463	125.0	124.6
Columbus, Ohio	7,312	8,083	90.5	87.8	9,113	6,942	131.3	135.6
Dallas, Tex	2,682	2,948	91.0	88.1	5,097	3,633	140.3	142.2
Dayton, Ohio	5,038	5,463	92.2	89.7	7,394	5,717	129.3	144.0
Denver, Colo	11,421	12,863	88.8	90.4	20,896	16,724	124.9	115.8
Des Moines, Iowa	4,727	5,309	89.0	91.6	6,211	5,013	123.9	123.8
Detroit, Mich	51,068	50,668	100.8	96.5	169,095	120,202	140.7	122.9
Fall River, Mass	6,319	7,061	89.5	93.4	20,334	21,997	92.4	92.1
Fort Worth, Tex	1,555	1,511	102.9	106.3	4,738	2,621	180.8	205.4
Grand Rapids, Mich	7,952	9,307	85.4	84.9	14,999	13,356	112.3	116.4
Hartford, Conn	5,133	5,800	88.5	93.1	21,470	19,197	111.8	106.4
Houston, Tex	3,843	4,179	92.0	97.5	6,809	5,203	130.9	149.8
Indianapolis, Ind	7,815	8,762	89.2	87.8	9,359	7,599	123.2	134.4
Jersey City, N. J	13,894	14,431	96.3	96.5	40,212	35,769	112.4	120.5
Kansas City, Kans	3,036	3,287	92.4	97.4	6,850	4,806	142.5	162.9
Kansas City, Mo	10,361	11,519	89.9	92.0	15,377	11,943	128.8	132.3
Los Angeles, Calif	24,640	28,901	85.3	86.3	60,188	51,869	116.0	121.8
Louisville, Ky	7,653	9,016	84.9	89.4	5,882	5,739	102.5	103.5
Lowell, Mass	6,041	6,711	90.0	91.7	18,466	19,574	94.3	97.3
Memphis, Tenn	2,302	2,570	89.6	92.9	3,266	2,509	130.2	147.4
Milwaukee, Wis	29,331	31,861	92.1	93.7	60,703	49,365	123.0	128.0
Minneapolis, Minn	21,761	24,570	88.6	93.3	48,402	39,630	122.1	132.8
Nashville, Tenn	1,251	1,390	90.0	91.1	1,287	1,100	117.0	111.4
New Bedford, Mass	5,308	5,668	93.6	92.1	23,864	24,825	96.1	99.9
New Haven, Conn	6,253	6,774	92.3	92.9	23,532	22,154	106.2	111.4
New Orleans, La	12,575	14,902	84.4	84.7	15,497	10,495	147.7	112.1
New York, N. Y	207,540	222,529	93.3	93.9	1,020,090	971,457	105.0	105.1
Bronx borough	28,668	30,201	94.9	96.4	135,456	131,515	103.0	109.8
Brooklyn borough	79,605	86,404	92.1	92.2	341,527	317,760	107.5	105.0
Manhattan borough	65,981	72,112	91.5	93.5	468,506	453,574	103.3	103.6
Queens borough	27,305	27,938	97.7	98.3	57,132	54,544	104.7	115.1
Richmond borough	5,981	5,874	101.8	101.7	17,469	14,064	124.2	122.6
Newark, N. J	16,402	17,030	96.3	93.7	61,914	55,089	112.4	110.6
Norfolk, Va	1,340	1,333	100.5	86.2	4,439	2,148	206.7	141.5
Oakland, Calif	11,833	12,669	93.4	91.2	25,492	19,670	129.6	130.6
Omaha, Nebr	8,668	9,018	96.1	101.1	19,910	15,471	128.7	134.5
Paterson, N. J	6,330	6,873	92.1	93.5	23,205	21,940	105.8	107.0
Philadelphia, Pa	69,706	74,694	93.3	91.7	205,518	192,409	106.8	102.9
Pittsburgh, Pa	26,961	28,923	93.2	95.0	65,367	54,899	119.1	128.7
Portland, Oreg	13,414	14,282	93.9	100.0	27,344	19,770	138.3	172.7
Providence, R. I	10,909	12,120	90.0	92.8	34,079	34,872	97.7	103.3
Reading, Pa	2,042	2,340	87.3	91.8	5,457	4,096	133.2	145.8
Richmond, Va	1,905	2,229	85.5	92.3	2,533	2,104	120.4	127.2
Rochester, N. Y	15,376	16,971	90.6	91.4	36,992	34,329	107.8	112.6
St. Louis, Mo	38,512	43,403	88.7	93.2	56,266	46,973	119.8	126.9
St. Paul, Minn	15,229	16,779	90.8	93.2	28,003	23,592	118.7	126.2
Salt Lake City, Utah	8,306	9,292	89.4	95.4	9,737	9,697	100.4	104.0
San Antonio, Tex	6,182	6,611	93.5	94.5	19,494	17,152	113.7	107.7
San Francisco, Calif	27,842	29,153	95.5	101.7	82,918	57,282	144.8	162.4
Scranton, Pa	6,972	7,742	90.1	92.6	15,139	13,429	112.7	127.2
Seattle, Wash	16,881	17,445	96.8	101.2	43,779	30,096	145.5	179.6
Spokane, Wash	6,001	6,663	90.1	102.8	9,463	7,363	128.5	171.5
Springfield, Mass	6,449	7,164	90.0	92.3	15,873	15,377	103.2	100.7
Syracuse, N. Y	8,151	8,946	91.1	90.2	17,433	14,888	117.1	123.2
Toledo, Ohio	11,707	12,377	94.6	92.7	21,751	16,394	132.7	120.2
Trenton, N. J	4,000	4,453	89.8	98.9	16,477	13,596	121.2	132.2
Washington, D. C	10,468	13,227	79.1	89.7	15,142	13,406	112.9	113.0
Wilmington, Del	3,455	3,648	94.7	93.2	9,347	6,932	134.8	127.5
Worcester, Mass	8,405	9,011	93.3	95.6	27,874	25,544	109.1	115.1
Yonkers, N. Y	4,929	5,210	94.6	95.7	12,990	12,710	102.2	113.6
Youngstown, Ohio	5,331	5,512	96.7	96.4	20,697	13,137	157.5	180.6

TABLE 41.—SEX DISTRIBUTION AND RATIO OF MALES TO FEMALES FOR TOTAL, NATIVE WHITE, FOREIGN-BORN WHITE, AND NEGRO POPULATION, FOR CITIES HAVING FROM 25,000 TO 100,000 INHABITANTS: 1920.

CITY.	ALL CLASSES.			NATIVE WHITE.			FOREIGN-BORN WHITE.			NEGRO.		
	Male.	Female.	Males to 100 females	Male.	Female.	Males to 100 females	Male.	Female.	Males to 100 females	Male.	Female.	Males to 100 females. (1)
ALABAMA:												
Mobile	29,149	31,628	92.2	16,845	18,003	93.6	1,190	816	145.8	11,102	12,804	86.7
Montgomery	20,186	23,278	86.7	11,166	11,704	95.4	461	300	153.7	8,553	11,274	75.9
ARIZONA:												
Phoenix	15,175	13,878	109.3	12,191	11,480	106.2	2,284	1,761	129.7	534	541	98.7
ARKANSAS:												
Fort Smith	14,194	14,676	96.7	11,993	12,429	96.5	487	367	132.7	1,708	1,876	91.0
Little Rock	31,750	33,392	95.1	22,429	23,430	95.7	1,024	774	132.3	8,292	9,185	90.3
CALIFORNIA:												
Alameda	14,055	14,751	95.3	10,401	11,561	90.0	3,110	2,767	112.4	103	114	90.4
Berkeley	26,232	29,804	88.0	20,293	24,330	83.4	4,831	4,742	101.9	234	273	85.7
Fresno	23,629	21,457	110.1	17,311	16,957	102.1	4,866	3,686	132.0	242	266	91.0
Long Beach	26,153	29,440	88.8	22,414	25,827	86.8	3,413	3,386	100.8	63	79	.....
Pasadena	19,861	25,493	77.9	16,106	20,871	77.2	2,911	3,874	75.1	485	609	79.6
Sacramento	34,529	31,379	110.0	25,537	25,797	99.0	6,542	4,331	151.1	365	310	117.7
San Diego	36,773	37,910	97.0	28,294	30,966	91.4	7,155	6,140	116.5	488	509	95.9
San Jose	19,342	20,300	95.3	14,506	16,457	88.1	4,265	3,555	120.0	79	112	70.5
Stockton	21,722	18,574	116.9	15,785	15,228	103.7	4,275	2,706	158.0	173	163	106.1
COLORADO:												
Colorado Springs	13,778	16,327	84.4	12,044	14,423	83.5	1,268	1,336	94.9	448	561	79.9
Pueblo	22,057	20,993	105.1	16,997	17,145	99.1	4,238	3,155	134.3	736	659	111.7
CONNECTICUT:												
Meriden	14,959	14,908	100.3	10,742	11,061	97.1	4,114	3,795	108.4	96	52	.....
New Britain	30,859	28,457	108.4	18,859	18,904	99.8	11,792	9,438	124.9	188	115	163.5
New London	12,766	12,922	98.8	9,481	9,805	96.7	2,987	2,853	104.7	245	263	93.2
Norwalk	13,469	14,274	94.4	10,115	11,016	91.8	3,008	2,947	102.1	327	304	107.6
Stamford	17,526	17,570	99.7	11,535	11,966	96.4	5,566	5,138	108.3	408	466	87.6
Waterbury	47,430	44,285	107.1	30,075	30,742	97.8	16,808	13,086	128.4	503	448	112.3
FLORIDA:												
Jacksonville	45,011	46,547	96.7	22,544	23,534	95.8	2,190	1,704	128.5	20,222	21,298	94.9
Miami	14,982	14,589	102.7	8,996	8,710	103.3	1,384	1,179	117.4	4,579	4,691	97.6
Pensacola	15,911	15,124	105.2	9,794	9,385	104.4	1,052	393	267.7	5,059	5,345	94.6
Tampa	25,998	25,610	101.5	14,439	14,940	96.6	5,917	4,749	124.6	5,614	5,917	94.9
GEORGIA:												
Augusta	25,299	27,249	92.8	14,072	14,889	94.5	550	377	145.9	10,610	11,972	88.6
Columbus	14,641	16,484	88.8	10,389	11,313	91.8	210	116	181.0	4,039	5,054	79.9
Macon	25,568	27,427	93.2	14,298	14,902	95.9	399	299	133.4	10,867	12,226	88.9
Savannah	40,511	42,741	94.8	20,057	20,726	96.8	1,855	1,392	133.3	18,566	20,613	90.1
ILLINOIS:												
Aurora	18,121	18,276	99.2	14,239	15,050	94.6	3,557	2,919	121.9	320	307	104.2
Bloomington	13,787	14,938	92.3	11,923	13,130	90.8	1,418	1,413	100.4	420	379	110.8
Cicero town	23,196	21,799	106.4	14,723	14,797	99.5	8,465	7,001	120.9	3	1	.....
Danville	16,825	16,951	99.3	14,595	14,876	98.1	1,034	882	117.2	1,183	1,183	100.0
Decatur	21,721	22,097	98.3	19,728	20,313	97.1	1,390	1,200	115.8	597	581	102.8
East St. Louis	35,065	31,702	110.6	27,066	25,456	106.3	4,069	2,713	150.0	3,908	3,529	110.7
Elgin	12,839	14,615	87.8	10,336	11,942	86.6	2,434	2,621	92.9	64	52	.....
Evanston	17,188	20,046	85.7	12,783	15,121	84.5	3,244	3,527	92.0	1,131	1,391	81.3
Joliet	19,584	18,858	103.8	14,393	14,836	97.0	4,790	3,700	129.5	383	318	120.4
Moline	16,277	14,457	112.6	11,682	11,320	103.2	4,402	2,989	147.3	190	148	128.4
Oak Park village	18,821	21,037	89.5	16,026	18,009	89.0	2,704	2,930	92.3	72	97	.....
Peoria	37,910	38,211	99.2	32,439	33,738	96.1	4,278	3,512	121.8	1,170	960	121.9
Quincy	17,527	18,451	95.0	15,725	16,624	94.6	1,206	1,205	100.1	588	622	94.5
Rock Island	18,011	17,166	104.9	14,654	14,410	101.7	2,945	2,407	122.4	407	347	117.3
Rockford	33,550	32,101	104.5	23,393	24,389	95.9	9,848	7,495	131.4	273	217	125.8
Springfield	28,696	30,487	94.1	23,976	26,172	91.6	3,319	2,936	113.0	1,390	1,379	100.8
INDIANA:												
Anderson	15,149	14,618	103.6	14,119	13,792	102.4	563	377	149.3	463	449	103.1
East Chicago	20,926	15,041	139.1	10,240	9,507	108.8	9,678	4,985	194.1	875	549	159.4
Evansville	41,462	43,802	94.7	36,624	39,083	93.7	1,030	1,000	103.4	3,186	3,208	99.3
Fort Wayne	42,588	43,961	96.9	38,025	40,414	94.1	3,701	2,870	131.1	778	676	115.1
Gary	31,810	23,568	135.0	18,034	15,550	116.0	10,752	5,708	188.4	2,991	2,308	129.6
Hammond	19,359	16,645	116.3	14,406	13,312	108.2	4,830	3,288	146.9	97	40	.....
Kokomo	15,574	14,493	107.5	14,393	13,630	105.6	727	439	165.6	452	424	106.6
Muncie	18,557	17,967	103.3	16,960	16,680	101.7	512	308	166.2	1,075	979	109.8
Richmond	13,416	13,349	100.5	11,934	12,200	97.8	669	458	146.1	804	690	116.5
South Bend	36,214	34,769	104.2	28,057	28,248	99.3	7,427	5,964	124.5	712	557	127.8
Terre Haute	32,853	33,230	98.9	28,895	29,860	96.8	2,117	1,550	136.6	1,828	1,818	100.6
IOWA:												
Cedar Rapids	22,433	23,133	97.0	18,934	20,081	94.3	3,147	2,716	115.9	344	333	103.3
Council Bluffs	18,234	17,928	101.7	15,674	15,897	98.6	2,225	1,763	126.2	332	266	124.8
Davenport	28,656	28,071	102.1	24,206	24,179	100.1	4,055	3,589	113.0	378	303	124.8
Dubuque	18,873	20,268	93.1	16,581	18,261	90.8	2,244	1,977	113.5	43	30	.....
Sioux City	37,568	33,659	111.6	30,252	28,525	106.1	6,607	4,609	143.3	643	496	129.6
Waterloo	18,119	18,111	100.0	15,945	16,508	96.6	1,716	1,213	141.5	448	389	115.2

1 Ratio not shown where number of females is less than 100.

TABLE 41.—SEX DISTRIBUTION AND RATIO OF MALES TO FEMALES FOR TOTAL, NATIVE WHITE, FOREIGN-BORN WHITE, AND NEGRO POPULATION, FOR CITIES HAVING FROM 25,000 TO 100,000 INHABITANTS: 1920—Continued.

CITY.	ALL CLASSES.			NATIVE WHITE.			FOREIGN-BORN WHITE.			NEGRO.		
	Male.	Female.	Males to 100 females	Male.	Female.	Males to 100 females	Male.	Female.	Males to 100 females	Male.	Female.	Males to 100 females. (1)
KANSAS:												
Topeka	23,918	26,104	91.6	19,777	21,919	90.2	2,071	1,929	107.4	2,041	2,231	91.5
Wichita	35,659	36,558	97.5	32,168	33,434	96.2	1,700	1,321	128.7	1,769	1,776	99.6
KENTUCKY:												
Covington	27,461	29,660	92.6	24,538	26,654	92.1	1,433	1,450	98.8	1,484	1,556	95.4
Lexington	20,048	21,486	93.3	13,604	14,673	92.7	493	307	160.6	5,945	6,505	91.4
Newport	14,033	15,284	91.8	12,588	13,772	91.4	1,032	1,061	97.3	413	451	91.6
LOUISIANA:												
Shreveport	21,765	22,109	98.4	12,843	12,229	105.0	727	569	127.8	8,176	9,309	87.8
MAINE:												
Bangor	12,133	13,845	87.6	10,190	11,815	86.2	1,823	1,917	95.1	98	110	89.1
Lewiston	15,356	16,435	93.4	10,424	11,028	94.5	4,884	5,378	90.8	25	29	......
Portland	33,306	35,966	92.6	26,691	28,970	92.1	6,401	6,828	93.7	141	159	88.7
MARYLAND:												
Cumberland	15,155	14,682	103.2	13,602	13,637	99.7	681	482	141.3	870	563	154.5
Hagerstown	13,724	14,340	95.7	12,706	13,415	94.7	275	153	179.7	737	772	95.5
MASSACHUSETTS:												
Brockton	32,809	33,445	98.1	23,693	24,818	95.5	8,795	8,329	105.6	274	285	96.1
Brookline town	15,148	22,600	67.0	12,122	15,878	76.3	2,929	6,431	45.5	65	284	22.9
Chelsea	22,364	20,820	107.4	13,040	12,538	104.0	9,101	8,097	112.4	196	177	110.7
Chicopee	18,437	17,777	103.7	11,994	12,020	99.8	6,427	5,755	111.7	8	2	......
Everett	19,793	20,327	97.4	13,828	14,070	98.3	5,401	5,678	95.1	551	578	95.3
Fitchburg	20,162	20,867	96.6	13,470	14,346	93.9	6,655	6,507	102.3	18	14	......
Haverhill	26,490	27,394	96.7	19,461	20,727	93.9	6,829	6,478	105.4	174	187	93.0
Holyoke	28,901	31,302	92.3	19,171	20,605	93.0	9,622	10,633	90.5	83	63	......
Lawrence	46,881	47,389	98.9	26,841	28,088	95.6	19,839	19,224	103.2	142	77	......
Lynn	48,874	50,274	97.2	34,565	35,784	96.6	13,782	14,076	97.9	404	408	99.0
Malden	23,302	25,801	90.3	16,442	18,010	91.3	6,604	7,501	88.0	241	290	83.1
Medford	18,623	20,415	91.2	14,376	15,557	92.4	3,971	4,583	86.6	261	274	95.3
Newton	20,807	25,247	82.4	16,441	18,855	87.2	4,138	6,041	68.5	211	350	60.3
Pittsfield	20,407	21,356	96.5	15,879	17,239	92.1	4,297	3,914	109.8	195	203	96.1
Quincy	24,205	23,671	102.3	17,041	17,018	100.1	7,115	6,634	107.3	15	12	......
Revere	14,437	14,386	100.4	9,947	9,974	99.7	4,459	4,388	101.6	24	24	......
Salem	20,691	21,838	94.7	15,056	16,069	93.7	5,522	5,681	97.2	57	73	......
Somerville	44,350	48,741	91.0	32,658	35,885	91.0	11,506	12,676	90.8	153	175	87.4
Taunton	18,109	19,028	95.2	13,001	13,788	94.3	4,879	5,119	95.3	224	121	185.1
Waltham	14,626	16,289	89.8	10,838	11,901	91.1	3,743	4,361	85.8	18	25	......
MICHIGAN:												
Battle Creek	17,855	18,309	97.5	15,384	16,311	94.3	1,883	1,495	126.0	560	495	113.1
Bay City	23,890	23,664	101.0	19,200	19,262	99.7	4,611	4,343	106.2	72	55	......
Flint	51,655	39,944	129.3	40,987	33,720	121.6	9,497	5,630	168.7	1,121	580	193.3
Hamtramck village	27,378	21,237	128.9	11,988	11,543	103.9	14,282	8,780	162.7	1,108	914	121.2
Highland Park	25,656	20,843	123.1	17,707	15,687	112.9	7,681	4,980	154.2	193	165	117.0
Jackson	25,227	23,147	109.0	21,795	20,419	106.7	2,897	2,419	119.8	505	305	165.6
Kalamazoo	23,965	24,522	97.7	19,678	20,822	94.5	3,877	3,330	116.4	385	367	104.9
Lansing	30,098	27,229	110.5	26,258	24,359	107.8	3,437	2,548	134.9	377	321	117.4
Muskegon	19,154	17,416	110.0	15,356	14,222	108.0	3,672	3,108	118.1	105	77	......
Pontiac	18,872	15,401	122.5	15,346	13,114	117.0	3,155	2,030	155.4	362	257	140.9
Port Huron	13,039	12,905	101.0	9,587	9,506	100.9	3,178	3,168	100.3	270	230	117.4
Saginaw	31,024	30,879	100.5	24,724	25,200	98.1	6,092	5,513	110.5	179	149	120.1
MINNESOTA:												
Duluth	51,873	47,044	110.3	33,790	34,406	98.2	17,722	12,396	143.0	270	225	120.0
MISSOURI:												
Joplin	14,597	15,305	95.4	13,795	14,614	94.4	418	309	135.3	368	373	98.7
St. Joseph	38,916	39,023	99.7	33,080	34,209	96.7	3,617	2,806	128.9	2,208	2,001	110.3
Springfield	19,003	20,628	92.1	17,643	19,346	91.2	547	426	128.4	811	853	95.1
MONTANA:												
Butte	22,665	18,946	119.6	15,386	14,299	107.6	6,933	4,521	153.4	120	94	......
NEBRASKA:												
Lincoln	26,554	28,394	93.5	22,347	24,471	91.3	3,694	3,504	105.4	484	412	117.5
NEW HAMPSHIRE:												
Manchester	37,583	40,801	92.1	24,295	26,495	91.7	13,241	14,275	92.8	31	31	......
Nashua	14,123	14,256	99.1	9,536	10,010	95.3	4,551	4,241	107.3	26	5	......
NEW JERSEY:												
Atlantic City	24,223	26,484	91.5	15,369	17,308	88.8	3,547	3,462	102.5	5,251	5,695	92.2
Bayonne	39,917	36,837	108.4	25,378	25,222	100.6	14,187	11,285	125.7	320	328	97.6
Clifton	13,319	13,151	101.3	8,331	8,466	98.4	4,954	4,657	106.4	20	27	......
East Orange	23,256	27,454	84.7	19,141	22,389	85.5	3,105	3,675	84.5	988	1,390	71.1
Elizabeth	49,530	46,253	107.1	32,815	32,740	100.2	15,641	12,574	124.4	1,035	935	110.7
Hoboken	35,663	32,503	109.7	22,455	21,963	102.2	13,050	10,446	124.9	112	92	......
Irvington town	12,638	12,842	98.4	9,738	10,126	96.2	2,844	2,664	106.8	52	52	......
Kearny town	13,473	13,251	101.7	9,324	9,394	99.3	4,098	3,806	107.7	34	44	......
Montclair town	13,186	15,624	84.4	9,335	10,816	86.3	2,392	2,767	86.4	1,428	2,039	70.0

1 Ratio not shown where number of females is less than 100.

TABLE 41.—SEX DISTRIBUTION AND RATIO OF MALES TO FEMALES FOR TOTAL, NATIVE WHITE, FOREIGN-BORN WHITE, AND NEGRO POPULATION, FOR CITIES HAVING FROM 25,000 TO 100,000 INHABITANTS: 1920—Continued.

CITY.	ALL CLASSES.			NATIVE WHITE.			FOREIGN-BORN WHITE.			NEGRO.		
	Male.	Female.	Males to 100 females	Male.	Female.	Males to 100 females	Male.	Female.	Males to 100 females	Male.	Female.	Males to 100 females. (1)
NEW JERSEY—Con.												
New Brunswick...	16,278	16,501	98.6	11,149	11,550	96.5	4,546	4,389	103.6	562	562	100.0
Orange	16,191	17,077	94.8	10,981	11,682	94.0	3,483	3,480	100.1	1,706	1,915	89.1
Passaic	31,840	32,001	99.5	18,026	18,832	95.7	13,495	12,870	104.9	292	299	97.7
Perth Amboy	21,817	19,890	109.7	13,248	13,023	101.7	8,285	6,633	124.9	264	228	115.8
Plainfield	13,325	14,375	92.7	9,495	10,243	92.7	2,709	2,793	97.0	1,108	1,337	82.9
West Hoboken town	19,864	20,210	98.3	12,605	13,356	94.4	7,233	6,843	105.7	5	8	......
West New York town	14,993	14,933	100.4	10,245	10,656	96.1	4,695	4,233	110.9	48	44	......
NEW YORK:												
Amsterdam	16,217	17,307	93.7	11,148	12,416	89.8	5,000	4,807	104.0	67	81	......
Auburn	18,211	17,981	101.3	13,683	14,426	94.8	4,222	3,357	125.8	293	198	148.0
Binghamton	32,479	34,321	94.6	26,581	29,191	91.1	5,585	4,783	116.8	283	340	83.2
Elmira	22,748	22,645	100.5	19,867	20,256	98.1	2,557	2,149	119.0	316	239	132.2
Jamestown	19,184	19,733	97.2	13,060	14,245	91.7	6,016	5,399	111.4	106	85	......
Kingston	12,562	14,126	88.9	10,869	12,491	87.0	1,417	1,346	105.3	274	289	94.8
Mount Vernon	20,434	22,292	91.7	14,724	16,544	89.0	5,138	4,952	103.8	549	796	69.0
New Rochelle	17,708	18,505	95.7	12,382	12,697	97.5	4,188	4,269	98.1	1,108	1,529	72.5
Newburgh	14,838	15,528	95.6	11,898	12,882	92.4	2,607	2,332	111.8	319	313	101.9
Niagara Falls	27,113	23,647	114.7	16,487	15,864	103.9	10,320	7,566	136.4	298	211	141.2
Poughkeepsie	16,708	18,292	91.3	13,439	15,161	88.6	2,866	2,664	107.6	384	466	82.4
Rome	13,889	12,452	111.5	10,606	10,324	102.7	3,173	2,061	154.0	103	67	......
Schenectady	44,857	43,866	102.3	33,252	34,503	96.4	11,324	9,166	123.5	193	195	99.0
Troy	33,076	38,937	84.7	27,440	32,478	84.5	5,326	6,157	86.5	277	302	91.7
Utica	45,802	48,354	94.7	33,411	37,096	90.1	12,177	11,080	109.9	178	176	101.1
Watertown	15,170	16,115	94.1	12,225	13,117	93.2	2,880	2,949	97.7	49	45	......
NORTH CAROLINA:												
Asheville	13,304	15,200	87.5	9,886	10,906	90.6	275	280	98.2	3,135	4,010	78.2
Charlotte	22,345	23,993	93.1	15,247	15,932	95.7	284	230	123.5	6,810	7,831	87.0
Wilmington	16,170	17,202	94.0	9,520	9,752	97.6	398	226	176.1	6,241	7,220	86.4
Winston-Salem	24,182	24,213	99.9	13,764	13,589	101.3	177	119	148.7	10,232	10,503	97.4
OHIO:												
Canton	47,188	39,903	118.3	36,332	34,755	104.5	10,057	4,623	217.5	763	520	146.7
East Cleveland	12,849	14,443	89.0	10,932	12,386	88.3	1,874	1,969	95.2	43	88	......
Hamilton	20,371	19,304	105.5	18,059	17,615	102.5	1,513	1,150	131.6	792	536	147.8
Lakewood	20,110	21,622	93.0	16,205	18,161	89.2	3,843	3,412	112.6	52	48	......
Lima	20,700	20,626	100.4	18,943	19,202	98.7	1,085	832	130.4	653	590	110.7
Lorain	20,416	16,879	121.0	12,649	12,166	104.0	7,447	4,480	166.2	319	233	136.9
Mansfield	14,066	13,758	102.2	12,090	12,275	98.5	1,817	1,390	130.7	156	93	......
Marion	13,960	13,931	100.2	13,266	13,431	98.8	563	391	144.0	131	108	121.3
Newark	13,376	13,342	100.3	12,191	12,467	97.8	889	616	144.3	292	259	112.7
Portsmouth	16,385	16,626	98.6	15,352	15,801	97.2	401	293	136.9	628	532	118.0
Springfield	30,503	30,337	100.5	25,327	25,715	98.5	1,512	1,245	121.4	3,653	3,376	108.2
Steubenville	15,035	13,473	111.6	10,915	10,886	100.3	3,504	2,077	168.7	609	506	120.4
Warren	14,282	12,768	111.9	10,793	10,872	99.3	3,056	1,621	188.5	427	275	155.3
Zanesville	14,293	15,276	93.6	12,767	13,966	91.4	720	552	130.4	803	756	106.2
OKLAHOMA:												
Muskogee	14,889	15,388	96.8	10,997	11,179	98.4	342	199	171.9	3,375	3,820	88.4
Oklahoma City	46,640	44,655	104.4	40,177	39,217	102.4	2,162	1,315	164.4	4,151	4,090	101.5
Tulsa	37,639	34,436	109.3	31,868	29,008	109.9	1,240	785	158.0	4,366	4,512	96.8
PENNSYLVANIA:												
Allentown	36,053	37,449	96.3	31,383	33,321	94.2	4,568	4,044	113.0	93	83	......
Altoona	29,814	30,517	97.7	26,268	27,851	94.3	3,070	2,242	136.9	464	424	109.4
Bethlehem	25,928	24,430	106.1	19,323	19,726	98.0	6,396	4,547	140.7	189	155	121.9
Chester	31,554	26,476	119.2	20,446	19,089	107.1	7,140	4,152	172.0	3,900	3,225	120.9
Easton	16,499	17,314	95.3	14,099	15,400	91.6	2,245	1,776	126.4	145	138	105.1
Erie	46,960	46,412	101.2	36,770	36,150	95.6	9,734	7,636	127.5	429	320	134.1
Harrisburg	37,176	38,741	96.0	32,120	34,388	93.4	2,360	1,784	132.3	2,079	2,600	104.3
Hazleton	15,893	16,384	97.0	12,592	13,632	92.4	3,282	2,741	119.7	10	9	......
Johnstown	35,025	32,302	108.4	26,479	27,035	97.9	7,340	4,802	152.9	1,185	465	254.8
Lancaster	25,033	28,117	89.0	23,175	26,338	88.0	1,401	1,313	106.7	452	463	97.6
McKeesport	24,386	22,395	108.9	16,900	17,062	99.1	6,965	4,905	142.0	500	428	116.8
New Castle	22,928	22,010	104.2	17,407	17,961	96.9	5,037	3,656	137.8	474	393	120.6
Norristown borough	15,610	16,709	93.4	12,691	13,813	91.9	2,143	2,154	99.5	766	741	103.4
Wilkes-Barre	36,339	37,494	96.9	28,251	30,458	92.8	7,782	6,785	114.7	301	251	119.9
Williamsport	17,496	18,702	93.6	15,797	17,220	91.7	1,267	999	126.8	431	483	89.2
York	23,061	24,451	94.3	21,699	23,196	93.5	652	541	120.5	705	711	99.2

1 Ratio not shown where number of females is less than 100.

TABLE 41.—SEX DISTRIBUTION AND RATIO OF MALES TO FEMALES FOR TOTAL, NATIVE WHITE, FOREIGN-BORN WHITE, AND NEGRO POPULATION, FOR CITIES HAVING FROM 25,000 TO 100,000 INHABITANTS: 1920—Continued.

CITY.	ALL CLASSES.			NATIVE WHITE.			FOREIGN-BORN WHITE.			NEGRO.		
	Male.	Female.	Males to 100 females	Male.	Female.	Males to 100 females	Male.	Female.	Males to 100 females	Male.	Female.	Males to 100 females (1)
RHODE ISLAND:												
Cranston	14,685	14,722	99.7	10,773	10,904	98.8	3,779	3,737	101.1	125	79	......
Newport	16,488	13,767	119.8	12,995	9,869	131.7	2,709	3,043	89.0	760	847	89.7
Pawtucket	31,158	33,090	94.2	20,653	22,211	93.0	10,302	10,722	96.1	181	151	119.9
Woonsocket	21,191	22,305	95.0	13,126	14,257	92.1	7,997	8,029	99.6	51	19	......
SOUTH CAROLINA:												
Charleston	32,750	35,207	93.0	16,658	16,784	99.2	1,254	889	141.1	14,801	17,525	84.5
Columbia	17,926	19,598	91.5	10,981	11,542	95.1	313	231	135.5	6,630	7,825	84.7
SOUTH DAKOTA:												
Sioux Falls	12,917	12,285	105.1	11,248	10,870	103.5	1,592	1,369	116.3	47	36	......
TENNESSEE:												
Chattanooga	28,978	28,917	100.2	18,711	19,050	98.2	695	545	127.5	9,567	9,322	102.6
Knoxville	37,603	40,215	93.5	31,720	33,979	93.4	446	366	121.9	5,434	5,868	92.6
TEXAS:												
Austin	16,425	18,451	89.0	12,013	13,368	89.9	1,320	1,227	107.6	3,073	3,848	79.9
Beaumont	20,713	19,709	105.1	12,927	12,341	104.7	1,170	748	156.4	6,597	6,613	99.8
El Paso	37,193	40,367	92.1	21,026	21,425	98.1	15,208	18,145	83.8	673	657	102.4
Galveston	23,350	20,905	111.7	13,984	13,442	104.0	4,294	2,598	165.3	5,027	4,861	103.4
Waco	18,692	19,808	94.4	14,078	14,917	94.4	990	777	127.4	3,612	4,114	87.8
Wichita Falls	24,035	16,044	149.8	21,472	14,656	146.5	1,309	411	318.5	1,242	975	127.4
UTAH:												
Ogden	16,491	16,313	101.1	13,728	13,788	99.6	2,308	2,301	100.3	153	112	136.6
VIRGINIA:												
Lynchburg	13,828	16,242	85.1	9,959	11,434	87.1	199	148	134.5	3,670	4,659	78.8
Newport News	20,145	15,451	130.4	11,153	8,266	134.9	1,288	759	169.7	7,654	6,423	119.2
Petersburg	14,599	16,413	88.9	8,118	8,768	92.6	301	210	143.3	6,174	7,434	83.1
Portsmouth	28,002	26,385	106.1	15,438	14,118	109.3	893	650	137.4	11,635	11,610	100.2
Roanoke	25,037	25,805	97.0	20,062	20,568	97.5	509	360	141.4	4,455	4,876	91.4
WASHINGTON:												
Bellingham	13,288	12,297	108.1	10,137	9,999	101.4	3,082	2,246	137.2	21	19	......
Everett	14,624	13,020	112.3	11,054	10,593	104.4	3,404	2,337	145.7	79	71	......
Tacoma	51,601	45,364	113.7	38,024	35,969	105.7	12,042	8,521	141.3	488	410	119.0
WEST VIRGINIA:												
Charleston	19,953	19,655	101.5	16,901	16,827	100.4	796	558	142.7	2,234	2,268	98.5
Clarksburg	14,183	13,686	103.6	12,369	12,304	100.5	1,177	760	154.9	636	622	102.3
Huntington	25,177	25,000	100.7	23,264	23,290	99.9	455	277	164.3	1,450	1,433	101.2
Wheeling	27,436	28,772	95.4	23,401	25,378	92.2	3,192	2,604	122.6	834	789	105.7
WISCONSIN:												
Green Bay	15,109	15,908	95.0	13,189	14,153	93.2	1,872	1,693	110.6	18	14	......
Kenosha	22,258	18,214	122.2	14,225	13,419	106.0	7,962	4,752	167.6	58	43	......
La Crosse	14,502	15,919	91.1	12,255	13,678	89.6	2,227	2,220	100.3	18	21	......
Madison	18,275	20,103	90.9	15,476	17,737	87.3	2,620	2,232	117.4	134	125	107.2
Oshkosh	15,945	17,217	92.6	12,888	14,408	89.5	3,019	2,775	108.8	20	19	......
Racine	31,524	27,069	116.5	21,566	20,503	105.2	9,749	6,450	151.1	180	114	157.9
Sheboygan	15,751	15,204	103.6	11,094	11,585	95.8	4,655	3,619	128.6	......	......	......
Superior	20,980	18,691	112.2	14,494	14,214	102.0	6,374	4,390	145.2	62	45	......

1 Ratio not shown where number of females is less than 100.

134 ABSTRACT OF THE CENSUS—POPULATION.

TABLE 42.—SEX DISTRIBUTION, 1920, WITH RATIO OF MALES TO FEMALES, 1920 AND 1910, FOR URBAN AND RURAL COMMUNITIES, BY DIVISIONS AND STATES.

DIVISION AND STATE.	URBAN.		Males to 100 females.		RURAL.		Males to 100 females.	
	Male: 1920	Female: 1920	1920	1910	Male: 1920	Female: 1920	1920	1910
United States.....	27,203,312	27,101,291	100.4	101.7	26,697,119	24,708,898	108.0	109.8
GEOGRAPHIC DIVISIONS:								
New England........	2,886,507	2,978,566	96.9	97.2	786,084	749,752	104.8	106.5
Middle Atlantic......	8,324,263	8,348,332	99.7	100.6	2,882,182	2,706,367	106.5	110.1
East North Central...	6,648,676	6,400,596	103.9	103.2	4,386,365	4,039,906	108.6	109.3
West North Central..	2,357,197	2,370,175	99.5	104.5	4,101,870	3,715,007	110.4	112.7
South Atlantic.......	2,118,444	2,220,348	95.4	94.1	4,917,399	4,734,081	103.9	103.8
East South Central...	965,075	1,029,132	93.8	94.5	3,506,615	3,392,485	103.4	103.7
West South Central..	1,492,700	1,478,129	101.0	101.2	3,773,129	3,498,266	107.9	109.0
Mountain............	623,658	591,322	105.5	113.3	1,165.641	955,480	122.0	137.0
Pacific..............	1,786,792	1,684,691	106.1	120.2	1,177,834	917,554	128.4	143.0
NEW ENGLAND:								
Maine..............	145,876	153,693	94.9	94.1	242,876	225,569	107.7	108.6
New Hampshire......	137,335	142,426	96.4	96.8	84,777	78,545	107.9	107.2
Vermont............	53,423	56,553	94.5	96.9	125,431	117,021	107.2	108.7
Massachusetts.......	1,788,597	1,861,651	96.1	96.2	101,417	100,691	100.7	103.3
Rhode Island........	289,650	299,530	96.7	98.9	7,874	7,343	107.2	110.5
Connecticut.........	471,626	464,713	101.5	101.4	223,709	220,583	101.4	103.9
MIDDLE ATLANTIC:								
New York...........	4,267,046	4,322,798	98.7	99.5	920.304	875,079	105.2	108.1
New Jersey..........	1,239,359	1,235,577	100.3	101.0	350,716	330,248	106.2	108.8
Pennsylvania........	2,817,858	2,789,957	101.0	102.3	1,611,162	1,501,040	107.3	111.7
EAST NORTH CENTRAL:								
Ohio...............	1,878,047	1,799,089	104.4	102.0	1,077,933	1,004,325	107.3	107.5
Indiana............	746,333	736,522	101.3	102.5	742,741	704,794	105.4	106.8
Illinois............	2,220,242	2,182,911	101.7	104.9	1,084,591	997,536	108.7	109.9
Michigan..........	1,180,219	1,061,341	111.2	103.3	748,217	678,635	110.3	111.0
Wisconsin..........	623,835	620,733	100.5	101.7	732,883	654,616	112.0	111.9
WEST NORTH CENTRAL:								
Minnesota..........	530,580	521,013	101.8	112.5	714,957	620,575	115.2	116.1
Iowa...............	434,666	440.829	98.6	100.4	794,726	733,800	108.3	109.5
Missouri...........	785,397	801,506	98.0	101.3	937,922	879,230	106.7	108.0
North Dakota.......	43,630	44,609	97.8	115.6	298,043	260,590	114.4	123.2
South Dakota.......	51,482	50,390	102.2	113.5	285,638	249,037	114.7	119.7
Nebraska...........	205,612	199,694	103.0	106.3	467,193	423,873	110.2	113.0
Kansas.............	305,830	312,134	98.0	102.1	603,391	547,902	110.1	113.5
SOUTH ATLANTIC:								
Delaware...........	61,338	59,429	103.2	100.4	52,417	49,819	105.2	108.6
Maryland...........	429,119	440,303	97.5	92.7	300,336	279,903	107.3	105.8
District of Columbia..	203,543	234,028	87.0	91.3	(1)	(1)	(1)	(1)
Virginia...........	331,496	342,488	96.8	94.0	836,996	798,207	104.9	103.0
West Virginia.......	185,713	183,294	101.3	104.2	577,387	517,307	111.6	113.4
North Carolina......	238,191	252,179	94.5	91.1	1,040,871	1,027,882	101.3	100.6
South Carolina......	141,107	152,880	92.3	90.2	697,186	692,551	100.7	100.0
Georgia............	351,657	376,202	93.5	92.6	1,093,166	1,074,807	101.7	102.1
Florida............	176,280	179,545	98.2	102.8	319,040	293,605	108.7	113.1
EAST SOUTH CENTRAL:								
Kentucky...........	306,257	327,286	93.6	94.1	921,237	861,850	106.9	106.0
Tennessee..........	295,852	315,374	93.8	95.4	878,115	848,544	103.5	103.8
Alabama...........	248,600	260,717	95.4	95.9	924,505	914,352	101.1	102.1
Mississippi.........	114,366	125,755	90.9	90.9	782,758	767,739	102.0	103.1
WEST SOUTH CENTRAL:								
Arkansas...........	142,931	147,566	96.9	100.4	752,297	709,410	106.0	106.8
Louisiana..........	306,746	321,417	95.4	93.0	596,589	573,757	104.0	105.7
Oklahoma..........	277,035	262,445	105.6	114.6	781,009	707,794	110.3	113.4
Texas.............	765,988	740,701	102.6	101.7	1,643,234	1,507,305	109.0	109.3
MOUNTAIN:								
Montana............	90,171	81,840	110.2	130.9	209,770	107,100	105.5	165.4
Idaho.............	61,488	57,549	106.8	129.5	172,431	140,398	122.8	133.3
Wyoming...........	31,973	25,375	126.0	151.4	78,386	58,668	133.6	176.9
Colorado...........	229,374	223,885	102.5	104.4	263,357	223,013	118.1	131.5
New Mexico........	32,372	32,588	99.3	101.5	158,084	137,306	115.1	117.7
Arizona............	61,790	55,737	110.9	126.0	121,812	94,823	128.5	144.2
Utah..............	108,165	107,419	100.7	106.2	123,886	109,926	112.7	116.4
Nevada............	8,325	6,929	120.1	133.1	37,915	24,238	156.4	190.4
PACIFIC:								
Washington.........	395,447	353,288	111.9	132.4	339,254	268,632	126.3	140.9
Oregon............	200,473	190,546	105.2	131.2	215,861	176,509	122.3	134.9
California..........	1,190,872	1,140,857	104.4	113.6	622,719	472,413	131.8	147.8

¹ No rural population, as Washington city is coextensive with the District of Columbia.

TABLE 43.—DISTRIBUTION BY AGE PERIODS OF THE TOTAL POPULATION, FOR THE UNITED STATES: 1850—1920.

AGE PERIOD.	POPULATION.				
	1920	1910	1900	1890	1880
All ages	105,710,620	91,972,266	75,994,575	[1] 62,622,250	50,155,783
Under 5 years	11,573,230	10,631,364	9,170,628	7,634,693	6,914,516
Under 1 year	2,257,255	2,217,342	1,916,892	1,566,734	1,447,983
5 to 9 years	11,398,075	9,760,632	8,874,123	7,573,998	6,479,660
10 to 14 years	10,641,137	9,107,140	8,080,234	7,033,509	5,715,186
15 to 19 years	9,430,556	9,063,603	7,556,089	6,557,563	5,011,415
20 to 24 years	9,277,021	9,056,984	7,335,016	6,196,676	5,087,772
25 to 29 years	9,086,491	8,180,003	6,529,441	5,227,777	4,080,621
30 to 34 years	8,071,193	6,972,185	5,556,039	4,578,630	3,368,943
35 to 39 years	7,775,281	6,396,100	4,964,781	3,866,161	3,000,419
40 to 44 years	6,345,557	5,261,587	4,247,166	3,185,518	2,468,811
45 to 49 years	5,763,620	4,469,197	3,454,612	2,731,640	2,089,445
50 to 54 years	4,734,873	3,900,791	2,942,829	2,326,262	1,839,883
55 to 59 years	3,549,124	2,786,951	2,211,172	1,672,336	1,271,434
60 to 64 years	2,982,548	2,267,150	1,791,363	1,458,034	1,104,219
65 to 69 years	2,068,475	1,679,503	1,302,926	1,010,110	725,876
70 to 74 years	1,395,036	1,113,728	883,841	701,751	495,442
75 to 79 years	856,560	667,302	519,857	393,062	281,065
80 to 84 years	402,779	321,754	251,512	203,851	146,362
85 to 89 years	156,539	122,818	88,600	75,240	49,835
90 to 94 years	39,980	33,473	23,992	23,645	16,100
95 to 99 years	9,579	7,391	6,266	5,648	4,763
100 years and over	4,267	3,555	3,504	3,981	4,016
Age unknown	148,699	169,055	200,584	162,165	....

AGE PERIOD.	POPULATION—continued.			PER CENT DISTRIBUTION.							
	1870	1860	1850	1920	1910	1900	1890	1880	1870	1860	1850
All ages	38,558,371	31,443,321	23,191,876	100.0	100.0	100.0	100.0	100.0	100.0	100.0	100.0
Under 5 years	5,514,713	4,842,496	3,497,773	10.9	11.6	12.1	12.2	13.8	14.3	15.4	15.1
Under 1 year	1,100,475	934,583	629,446	2.1	2.4	2.5	2.5	2.9	2.9	3.0	2.7
5 to 9 years	4,814,713	4,171,200	3,241,268	10.8	10.6	11.7	12.1	12.9	12.5	13.3	14.0
10 to 14 years	4,786,189	3,720,780	2,890,629	10.1	9.9	10.6	11.2	11.4	12.4	11.8	12.5
15 to 19 years	4,040,588	3,361,495	2,529,792	8.9	9.9	9.9	10.5	10.0	10.5	10.7	10.9
20 to 24 years	3,748,299	{ 5,726,400	{ 4,277,318	8.8	9.8	9.7	9.9	10.1	9.7	{ 18.2	{ 18.4
25 to 29 years	3,075,118			8.6	8.9	8.6	8.3	8.1	8.0		
30 to 34 years	2,562,829	{ 4,021,248	{ 2,825,819	7.6	7.6	7.3	7.3	6.7	6.6	{ 12.8	{ 12.2
35 to 39 years	2,314,976			7.4	7.0	6.5	6.2	6.0	6.0		
40 to 44 years	1,939,712	{ 2,614,330	{ 1,846,660	6.0	5.7	5.6	5.1	4.9	5.0	{ 8.3	{ 8.0
45 to 49 years	1,578,932			5.5	4.9	4.5	4.4	4.2	4.1		
50 to 54 years	1,367,969	{ 1,585,879	{ 1,109,540	4.5	4.2	3.9	3.7	3.7	3.5	{ 5.0	{ 4.8
55 to 59 years	876,552			3.4	3.0	2.9	2.7	2.5	2.3		
60 to 64 years	778,971	{ 888,809	{ 609,926	2.8	2.5	2.4	2.3	2.2	2.0	{ 2.8	{ 2.6
65 to 69 years	484,353			2.0	1.8	1.7	1.6	1.4	1.3		
70 to 74 years	344,358	{ 348,890	{ 257,234	1.3	1.2	1.2	1.1	1.0	0.9	{ 1.1	{ 1.1
75 to 79 years	175,686			0.8	0.7	0.7	0.6	0.6	0.5		
80 to 84 years	{ 129,077	{ 93,552	{ 77,382	0.4	0.3	0.3	0.3	0.3	{ 0.3	0.3	0.3
85 to 89 years				0.1	0.1	0.1	0.1	0.1			
90 to 94 years	{ 16,653	{ 13,778	{ 11,695	[2]	[2]	[2]	[2]	[2]	{ [2]	[2]	0.1
95 to 99 years				[2]	[2]	[2]	[2]	[2]			
100 years and over	3,522	2,953	2,555	[2]	[2]	[2]	[2]	[2]	[2]	[2]	[2]
Age unknown	5,161	51,511	14,285	0.1	0.2	0.3	0.3	......	[2]	0.2	0.1

[1] Exclusive of 325,464 persons specially enumerated in 1890 in Indian Territory and on Indian reservations, for whom statistics of age are not available.

[2] Less than one-tenth of 1 per cent.

TABLE 44.—DISTRIBUTION OF MALES AND FEMALES BY

	SEX AND AGE PERIOD.	POPULATION.				
		1920	1910	1900	1890	1880
	MALES.					
1	All ages............	53,900,431	47,332,277	38,816,448	[1] 32,067,880	25,518,820
2	Under 5 years..........	5,857,461	5,380,596	4,633,612	3,884,869	3,507,709
3	Under 1 year..........	1,141,939	1,123,409	969,257	799,373	734,024
4	5 to 9 years............	5,753,001	4,924,123	4,479,396	3,830,352	3,275,131
5	10 to 14 years...........	5,369,306	4,601,753	4,083,041	3,574,787	2,907,481
6	15 to 19 years...........	4,673,792	4,527,282	3,750,451	3,248,711	2,476,088
7	20 to 24 years...........	4,527,045	4,580,290	3,624,580	3,104,893	2,554,684
8	25 to 29 years...........	4,538,233	4,244,348	3,323,543	2,698,311	2,109,741
9	30 to 34 years...........	4,130,783	3,656,768	2,901,321	2,425,664	1,744,308
10	35 to 39 years...........	4,074,361	3,367,016	2,616,865	2,051,044	1,527,159
11	40 to 44 years...........	3,285,543	2,786,350	2,255,916	1,654,604	1,243,773
12	45 to 49 years...........	3,117,550	2,378,916	1,837,836	1,418,102	1,078,695
13	50 to 54 years...........	2,535,545	2,110,013	1,564,622	1,208,922	966,702
14	55 to 59 years...........	1,880,065	1,488,437	1,145,257	871,663	674,927
15	60 to 64 years...........	1,581,800	1,185,966	917,167	758,710	584,858
16	65 to 69 years...........	1,079,817	863,994	667,669	525,627	379,498
17	70 to 74 years...........	706,301	561,644	449,609	363,642	250,001
18	75 to 79 years...........	419,965	331,280	261,579	199,093	138,601
19	80 to 84 years...........	185,903	153,745	122,273	97,862	67,941
20	85 to 89 years...........	69,272	56,335	40,742	34,063	21,908
21	90 to 94 years...........	16,383	14,553	9,858	9,848	6,351
22	95 to 99 years...........	3,869	3,045	2,417	2,186	1,855
23	100 years and over..........	1,561	1,380	1,271	1,398	1,409
24	Age unknown..........	92,875	114,443	127,423	103,529	....
	FEMALES.					
25	All ages............	51,810,189	44,639,989	37,178,127	[1] 30,554,370	24,636,963
26	Under 5 years..........	5,715,769	5,250,768	4,537,016	3,749,824	3,406,807
27	Under 1 year..........	1,115,316	1,093,933	947,635	767,361	713,959
28	5 to 9 years............	5,645,074	4,836,509	4,394,727	3,743,646	3,204,529
29	10 to 14 years...........	5,271,831	4,505,387	3,997,193	3,458,722	2,807,705
30	15 to 19 years...........	4,756,764	4,536,321	3,805,638	3,308,852	2,535,327
31	20 to 24 years...........	4,749,976	4,476,694	3,710,436	3,091,783	2,533,088
32	25 to 29 years...........	4,548,258	3,935,655	3,205,898	2,529,466	1,970,880
33	30 to 34 years...........	3,940,410	3,315,417	2,654,718	2,152,966	1,624,635
34	35 to 39 years...........	3,700,920	3,029,084	2,347,916	1,815,117	1,473,260
35	40 to 44 years...........	3,060,014	2,475,237	1,991,250	1,530,914	1,225,038
36	45 to 49 years...........	2,646,070	2,090,281	1,616,776	1,313,538	1,010,750
37	50 to 54 years...........	2,199,328	1,790,778	1,378,207	1,117,340	873,181
38	55 to 59 years...........	1,669,059	1,298,514	1,065,915	800,673	596,507
39	60 to 64 years...........	1,400,748	1,081,184	874,196	699,324	519,361
40	65 to 69 years...........	988,658	815,509	635,257	484,483	346,378
41	70 to 74 years...........	688,735	552,084	434,232	338,109	245,441
42	75 to 79 years...........	436,595	336,022	258,278	193,969	142,464
43	80 to 84 years...........	216,876	168,009	129,239	105,989	78,421
44	85 to 89 years...........	87,267	66,483	47,858	41,177	27,927
45	90 to 94 years...........	23,597	18,920	14,134	13,797	9,749
46	95 to 99 years...........	5,710	4,346	3,849	3,462	2,908
47	100 years and over..........	2,706	2,175	2,233	2,583	2,607
48	Age unknown..........	55,824	54,612	73,161	58,636	....

[1] Exclusive of persons (169,221 males and 156,243 females) specially enumerated in 1890 in Indian Territory and on Indian reservations, for whom statistics of age are not available.

AGE PERIODS, FOR THE UNITED STATES: 1850—1920.

POPULATION—continued.			PER CENT DISTRIBUTION.								
1870	1860	1850	1920	1910	1900	1890	1880	1870	1860	1850	
19,493,565	16,085,204	11,837,660	100.0	100.0	100.0	100.0	100.0	100.0	100.0	100.0	1
2,797,257	2,449,547	1,769,460	10.9	11.4	11.9	12.1	13.7	14.3	15.2	14.9	2
557,617	471,804	318,226	2.1	2.4	2.5	2.5	2.9	2.9	2.9	2.7	3
*2,437,442	2,109,545	1,640,407	10.7	10.4	11.5	11.9	12.8	12.5	13.1	13.9	4
2,435,585	1,900,868	1,473,116	10.0	9.7	10.5	11.1	11.4	12.5	11.8	12.4	5
1,989,695	1,650,012	1,237,680	8.7	9.6	9.7	10.1	9.7	10.2	10.3	10.5	6
1,835,946	{2,911,558	{2,194,469	8.4	9.7	9.3	9.7	10.0	9.4	{18.1	{18.5	7
1,515,671			8.4	9.0	8.6	8.4	8.3	7.8			8
1,273,633	{2,129,017	{1,490,135	7.7	7.7	7.5	7.6	6.8	6.5	{13.2	{12.6	9
1,179,366			7.6	7.1	6.7	6.4	6.0	6.1			10
990,021	{1,392,223	{967,573	6.1	5.9	5.8	5.2	4.9	5.1	{8.7	{8.2	11
839,578			5.8	5.0	4.7	4.4	4.2	4.3			12
740,360	{835,350	{575,685	4.7	4.5	4.0	3.8	3.8	3.8	{5.2	{4.9	13
469,495			3.5	3.1	3.0	2.7	2.6	2.4			14
407,491	{455,754	{309,515	2.9	2.5	2.4	2.4	2.3	2.1	{2.8	{2.6	15
250,662			2.0	1.8	1.7	1.6	1.5	1.3			16
173,036	{172,563	{127,460	1.3	1.2	1.2	1.1	1.0	0.9	{1.1	{1.1	17
86,282			0.8	0.7	0.7	0.6	0.5	0.4			18
60,042	43,790	36,727	0.3	0.3	0.3	0.3	0.3	{0.3	0.3	0.3	19
			0.1	0.1	0.1	0.1	0.1				20
6,922	5,854	5,183	(2)	(2)	(2)	(2)	(2)	{(2)	(2)	(2)	21
1,286	1,233	1,077	(2)	(2)	(2)	(2)	(2)		(2)	(2)	22
			(2)	(2)	(2)	(2)	(2)				23
3,795	27,890	9,173	0.2	0.2	0.3	0.3	------	(2)	0.2	0.1	24
19,064,806	15,358,117	11,354,216	100.0	100.0	100.0	100.0	100.0	100.0	100.0	100.0	25
2,717,456	2,392,949	1,728,313	11.0	11.8	12.2	12.3	13.8	14.3	15.6	15.2	26
542,858	462,779	311,220	2.2	2.5	2.5	2.5	2.9	2.8	3.0	2.7	27
2,377,271	2,061,655	1,600,861	10.9	10.8	11.8	12.3	13.0	12.5	13.4	14.1	28
2,350,604	1,819,912	1,417,513	10.2	10.1	10.8	11.3	11.4	12.3	11.8	12.5	29
2,050,893	1,711,483	1,292,112	9.2	10.2	10.2	10.8	10.3	10.8	11.1	11.4	30
1,912,353	{2,814,842	{2,082,849	9.2	10.0	10.0	10.1	10.3	10.0	{18.3	{18.3	31
1,559,447			8.8	8.8	8.6	8.3	8.0	8.2			32
1,289,196	{1,892,231	{1,335,684	7.6	7.4	7.1	7.0	6.6	6.8	{12.3	{11.8	33
1,135,610			7.1	6.8	6.3	5.9	6.0	6.0			34
949,691	{1,222,107	{879,087	5.9	5.5	5.4	5.0	5.0	5.0	{8.0	{7.7	35
739,354			5.1	4.7	4.3	4.3	4.1	3.9			36
627,609	{750,529	{533,855	4.2	4.0	3.7	3.7	3.5	3.3	{4.9	{4.7	37
407,057			3.2	2.9	2.9	2.6	2.4	2.1			38
371,480	{433,055	{300,411	2.7	2.4	2.4	2.3	2.1	1.9	{2.8	{2.6	39
233,691			1.9	1.8	1.7	1.6	1.4	1.2			40
171,322	{176,327	{129,774	1.3	1.2	1.2	1.1	1.0	0.9	{1.1	{1.1	41
89,404			0.8	0.8	0.7	0.6	0.6	0.5			42
{69,035	{49,762	{40,655	0.4	0.4	0.3	0.3	0.3	{0.4	{0.3	{0.4	43
			0.2	0.1	0.1	0.1	0.1				44
9,731	7,924	6,512	(2)	(2)	(2)	(2)	(2)	{0.1	{0.1	{0.1	45
			(2)	(2)	(2)	(2)	(2)				46
2,236	1,720	1,478									47
1,366	23,621	5,112	0.1	0.1	0.2	0.2	------	(2)	0.2	(2)	48

[2] Less than one-tenth of 1 per cent.

TABLE 45.—DISTRIBUTION BY BROAD AGE GROUPS FOR POPULATION CLASSES, BY

CLASS OF POPULATION AND AGE GROUP.	POPULATION.			PER CENT DISTRIBUTION.					
	1920			1920			1910		
	Both sexes.	Male.	Female.	Both sexes.	Male.	Female.	Both sexes.	Male.	Female.
All classes [1]	105,710,620	53,900,431	51,810,189	100.0	100.0	100.0	100.0	100.0	100.0
Under 5 years	11,573,230	5,857,461	5,715,769	10.9	10.9	11.0	11.6	11.4	11.8
5 to 14 years	22,039,212	11,122,307	10,916,905	20.8	20.6	21.1	20.5	20.1	20.9
15 to 24 years	18,707,577	9,200,837	9,506,740	17.7	17.1	18.3	19.7	19.2	20.2
25 to 44 years	31,278,522	16,028,920	15,249,602	29.6	29.7	29.4	29.1	29.7	28.6
25 to 34 years	17,157,684	8,669,016	8,488,668	16.2	16.1	16.4	16.5	16.7	16.2
35 to 44 years	14,120,838	7,359,904	6,760,934	13.4	13.7	13.0	12.7	13.0	12.3
45 to 64 years	17,030,165	9,114,960	7,915,205	16.1	16.9	15.3	14.6	15.1	14.0
45 to 54 years	10,498,493	5,653,095	4,845,398	9.9	10.5	9.4	9.1	9.5	8.7
55 to 64 years	6,531,672	3,461,865	3,069,807	6.2	6.4	5.9	5.5	5.7	5.3
65 years and over	4,933,215	2,483,071	2,450,144	4.7	4.6	4.7	4.3	4.2	4.4
Native white— Native par. [1]	58,421,957	29,636,781	28,785,176	100.0	100.0	100.0	100.0	100.0	100.0
Under 5 years	7,366,530	3,741,194	3,625,336	12.6	12.6	12.6	13.2	13.2	13.3
5 to 14 years	13,433,572	6,803,480	6,630,092	23.0	23.0	23.0	22.6	22.5	22.7
15 to 24 years	10,775,753	5,344,295	5,431,458	18.4	18.0	18.9	19.7	19.4	20.1
25 to 44 years	15,776,025	7,968,863	7,807,162	27.0	26.9	27.1	26.2	26.3	26.0
25 to 34 years	8,860,843	4,421,983	4,438,860	15.2	14.9	15.4	15.1	15.0	15.1
35 to 44 years	6,915,182	3,546,880	3,368,302	11.8	12.0	11.7	11.1	11.3	10.9
45 to 64 years	8,239,032	4,354,663	3,884,369	14.1	14.7	13.5	13.6	14.1	13.2
45 to 54 years	4,989,713	2,649,866	2,339,847	8.5	8.9	8.1	8.1	8.4	7.8
55 to 64 years	3,249,319	1,704,797	1,544,522	5.6	5.8	5.4	5.5	5.6	5.3
65 years and over	2,738,876	1,365,527	1,373,349	4.7	4.6	4.8	4.4	4.3	4.6
Native white— For. par. [1]	15,694,539	7,810,531	7,884,008	100.0	100.0	100.0	100.0	100.0	100.0
Under 5 years	2,124,350	1,072,885	1,051,465	13.5	13.7	13.3	14.1	14.2	14.0
5 to 14 years	3,870,731	1,944,735	1,925,996	24.7	24.9	24.4	22.8	22.9	22.7
15 to 24 years	2,814,123	1,383,857	1,430,266	17.9	17.7	18.1	20.8	20.5	21.1
25 to 44 years	4,094,449	2,017,298	2,077,151	26.1	25.8	26.3	28.4	28.2	28.6
25 to 34 years	2,338,688	1,150,323	1,188,365	14.9	14.7	15.1	15.2	15.0	15.4
35 to 44 years	1,755,761	866,975	888,786	11.2	11.1	11.3	13.2	13.1	13.2
45 to 64 years	2,418,332	1,208,166	1,210,166	15.4	15.5	15.3	12.6	12.8	12.4
45 to 54 years	1,489,610	745,976	743,634	9.5	9.6	9.4	9.2	9.4	9.1
55 to 64 years	928,722	462,190	466,532	5.9	5.9	5.9	3.4	3.5	3.3
65 years and over	364,554	179,375	185,179	2.3	2.3	2.3	1.2	1.3	1.2
Native white— Mixed par. [1]	6,991,665	3,455,021	3,536,644	100.0	100.0	100.0	100.0	100.0	100.0
Under 5 years	838,057	423,778	414,279	12.0	12.3	11.7	14.3	14.6	14.0
5 to 14 years	1,651,018	833,214	817,804	23.6	24.1	23.1	26.9	27.3	26.5
15 to 24 years	1,454,834	715,997	738,837	20.8	20.7	20.9	23.2	23.0	23.4
25 to 44 years	2,059,616	986,381	1,073,235	29.5	28.5	30.3	25.9	25.2	26.5
25 to 34 years	1,175,111	559,355	615,756	16.8	16.2	17.4	15.8	15.2	16.3
35 to 44 years	884,505	427,026	457,479	12.7	12.4	12.9	10.1	10.0	10.2
45 to 64 years	833,541	419,843	413,698	11.9	12.2	11.7	8.1	8.3	8.0
45 to 54 years	558,931	280,968	277,963	8.0	8.1	7.9	5.5	5.6	5.4
55 to 64 years	274,610	138,875	135,735	3.9	4.0	3.8	2.6	2.7	2.5
65 years and over	151,369	74,189	77,180	2.2	2.1	2.2	1.6	1.6	1.6

[1] Totals include persons of unknown age.

SEX, 1920, WITH PERCENTAGES FOR 1920 AND 1910, FOR THE UNITED STATES.

CLASS OF POPULATION AND AGE GROUP.	POPULATION. 1920			PER CENT DISTRIBUTION. 1920			1910		
	Both sexes.	Male.	Female.	Both sexes.	Male.	Female.	Both sexes.	Male.	Female.
Foreign-born white [1]	13,712,754	7,528,322	6,184,432	100.0	100.0	100.0	100.0	100.0	100.0
Under 5 years	44,984	22,857	22,127	0.3	0.3	0.4	0.8	0.7	0.9
5 to 14 years	501,246	252,926	248,320	3.7	3.4	4.0	4.9	4.4	5.6
15 to 24 years	1,454,786	716,258	738,528	10.6	9.5	11.9	15.8	15.6	15.9
25 to 44 years	6,271,742	3,550,778	2,720,964	45.7	47.2	44.0	44.1	45.8	41.9
25 to 34 years	3,105,838	1,738,906	1,366,932	22.6	23.1	22.1	23.7	25.0	22.1
35 to 44 years	3,165,904	1,811,872	1,354,032	23.1	24.1	21.9	20.3	20.8	19.7
45 to 64 years	4,091,505	2,292,387	1,799,118	29.8	30.5	29.1	25.4	25.2	25.7
45 to 54 years	2,467,052	1,395,969	1,071,083	18.0	18.5	17.3	15.5	15.7	15.3
55 to 64 years	1,624,453	896,418	728,035	11.8	11.9	11.8	9.9	9.5	10.5
65 years and over	1,328,227	679,384	648,843	9.7	9.0	10.5	8.9	8.1	9.9
Negro [1]	10,463,131	5,209,436	5,253,695	100.0	100.0	100.0	100.0	100.0	100.0
Under 5 years	1,143,699	568,633	575,066	10.9	10.9	10.9	12.9	12.9	12.8
5 to 14 years	2,503,121	1,247,592	1,255,529	23.9	23.9	23.9	24.4	24.5	24.4
15 to 24 years	2,138,062	1,000,585	1,137,477	20.4	19.2	21.7	21.3	20.3	22.3
25 to 44 years	2,941,236	1,415,444	1,525,792	28.1	27.2	29.0	26.8	26.7	27.0
25 to 34 years	1,607,604	755,931	851,673	15.4	14.5	16.2	15.8	15.4	16.1
35 to 44 years	1,333,632	659,513	674,119	12.7	12.7	12.8	11.1	11.3	10.9
45 to 64 years	1,380,797	789,791	591,006	13.2	15.2	11.2	11.3	12.2	10.4
45 to 54 years	950,699	548,501	402,198	9.1	10.5	7.7	7.2	7.8	6.7
55 to 64 years	430,098	241,290	188,808	4.1	4.6	3.6	4.0	4.4	3.6
65 years and over	332,713	173,881	158,832	3.2	3.3	3.0	3.0	3.1	2.9
Indian [1]	244,437	125,068	119,369	100.0	100.0	100.0	100.0	100.0	100.0
Under 5 years	33,346	16,591	16,755	13.6	13.3	14.0	15.2	14.9	15.5
5 to 14 years	64,339	32,156	32,183	26.3	25.7	27.0	25.6	25.6	25.6
15 to 24 years	45,426	23,123	22,303	18.6	18.5	18.7	18.9	19.1	18.7
25 to 44 years	55,336	28,805	26,531	22.6	23.0	22.2	22.6	22.8	22.5
25 to 34 years	30,011	15,521	14,490	12.3	12.4	12.1	12.6	12.6	12.6
35 to 44 years	25,325	13,284	12,041	10.4	10.6	10.1	10.1	10.2	9.9
45 to 64 years	32,060	17,481	14,579	13.1	14.0	12.2	12.4	12.6	12.2
45 to 54 years	19,534	10,751	8,783	8.0	8.6	7.4	7.2	7.4	7.1
55 to 64 years	12,526	6,730	5,796	5.1	5.4	4.9	5.2	5.2	5.1
65 years and over	13,139	6,512	6,627	5.4	5.2	5.6	4.9	4.5	5.3
Chi., Jap., and all other [1]	182,137	135,272	46,865	100.0	100.0	100.0	100.0	100.0	100.0
Under 5 years	22,264	11,523	10,741	12.2	8.5	22.9	3.3	1.8	17.0
5 to 14 years	15,185	8,204	6,981	8.3	6.1	14.9	3.0	2.0	13.2
15 to 24 years	24,593	16,722	7,871	13.5	12.4	16.8	16.5	16.2	19.9
25 to 44 years	80,118	61,351	18,767	44.0	45.4	40.0	51.1	51.8	43.8
25 to 34 years	39,589	26,997	12,592	21.7	20.0	26.9	30.7	30.6	31.2
35 to 44 years	40,529	34,354	6,175	22.3	25.4	13.2	20.4	21.2	12.6
45 to 64 years	34,898	32,629	2,269	19.2	24.1	4.8	22.6	24.4	5.2
45 to 54 years	22,954	21,064	1,890	12.6	15.6	4.0	15.3	16.5	3.7
55 to 64 years	11,944	11,565	379	6.6	8.5	0.8	7.3	7.9	1.5
65 years and over	4,337	4,203	134	2.4	3.1	0.3	1.6	1.8	0.5

TABLE **46.**—DISTRIBUTION BY AGE PERIODS FOR POPULATION

AGE PERIOD.	ALL CLASSES.			WHITE.		
	Both sexes.	Male.	Female.	Both sexes.	Male.	Female.
All ages	105,710,620	53,900,431	51,810,189	94,820,915	48,430,655	46,390,260
Under 5 years	11,573,230	5,857,461	5,715,769	10,373,921	5,260,714	5,113,207
Under 1 year	2,257,255	1,141,939	1,115,316	2,017,767	1,023,270	994,497
5 to 9 years	11,398,075	5,753,001	5,645,074	10,087,245	5,099,205	4,988,040
10 to 14 years	10,641,137	5,369,306	5,271,831	9,369,322	4,735,150	4,634,172
15 to 19 years	9,430,556	4,673,792	4,756,764	8,314,155	4,141,831	4,172,324
20 to 24 years	9,277,021	4,527,045	4,749,976	8,185,341	4,018,576	4,166,765
25 to 29 years	9,086,491	4,538,233	4,548,258	8,141,690	4,094,301	4,047,389
30 to 34 years	8,071,193	4,130,783	3,940,410	7,338,790	3,776,266	3,562,524
35 to 39 years	7,775,281	4,074,361	3,700,920	6,965,805	3,665,341	3,300,464
40 to 44 years	6,345,557	3,285,543	3,060,014	5,755,547	2,987,412	2,768,135
45 to 49 years	5,763,620	3,117,550	2,646,070	5,188,040	2,779,175	2,408,865
50 to 54 years	4,734,873	2,535,545	2,199,328	4,317,266	2,293,604	2,023,662
55 to 59 years	3,549,124	1,880,065	1,669,059	3,305,671	1,740,661	1,565,010
60 to 64 years	2,982,548	1,581,800	1,400,748	2,771,433	1,461,619	1,309,814
65 to 69 years	2,068,475	1,079,817	988,658	1,924,296	998,779	925,517
70 to 74 years	1,395,036	706,301	688,735	1,298,738	655,916	642,822
75 to 79 years	856,560	419,965	436,595	801,678	391,383	410,295
80 to 84 years	402,779	185,903	216,876	373,066	172,064	201,002
85 to 89 years	156,539	69,272	87,267	143,536	63,308	80,228
90 to 94 years	39,980	16,383	23,597	33,713	13,852	19,861
95 to 99 years	9,579	3,869	5,710	6,831	2,706	4,125
100 years and over	4,267	1,561	2,706	1,168	467	701
Age unknown	148,699	92,875	55,824	123,663	78,325	45,338

AGE PERIOD.	NATIVE WHITE—NATIVE PARENTAGE.			NATIVE WHITE—FOREIGN PARENTAGE.		
	Both sexes.	Male.	Female.	Both sexes.	Male.	Female.
All ages	58,421,957	29,636,781	28,785,176	15,694,539	7,810,531	7,884,008
Under 5 years	7,366,530	3,741,194	3,625,336	2,124,350	1,072,885	1,051,465
Under 1 year	1,453,404	737,923	715,481	396,780	200,361	196,419
5 to 9 years	6,977,863	3,534,092	3,443,771	2,107,263	1,058,518	1,048,745
10 to 14 years	6,455,709	3,269,388	3,186,321	1,763,468	886,217	877,251
15 to 19 years	5,599,046	2,797,477	2,801,569	1,429,368	707,722	721,646
20 to 24 years	5,176,707	2,546,818	2,629,889	1,384,755	676,135	708,620
25 to 29 years	4,764,802	2,367,312	2,397,490	1,286,562	631,349	655,213
30 to 34 years	4,096,041	2,054,671	2,041,370	1,052,126	518,974	533,152
35 to 39 years	3,815,852	1,962,634	1,853,218	924,617	459,056	465,561
40 to 44 years	3,099,330	1,584,246	1,515,084	831,144	407,919	423,225
45 to 49 years	2,753,013	1,463,247	1,289,766	813,043	409,412	403,631
50 to 54 years	2,236,700	1,186,619	1,050,081	676,567	336,564	340,003
55 to 59 years	1,719,190	899,029	820,161	519,246	257,752	261,494
60 to 64 years	1,530,129	805,768	724,361	409,476	204,438	205,038
65 to 69 years	1,126,722	584,783	541,939	208,359	103,405	104,954
70 to 74 years	784,183	395,582	388,601	90,854	44,781	46,073
75 to 79 years	487,797	234,584	253,213	43,198	21,058	22,140
80 to 84 years	225,018	102,493	124,525	16,029	7,333	8,696
85 to 89 years	87,530	37,459	50,071	4,960	2,330	2,632
90 to 94 years	20,159	7,922	12,237	975	440	535
95 to 99 years	3,853	1,475	2,378	240	110	130
100 years and over	614	229	385	37	18	19
Age unknown	92,169	58,759	33,410	8,000	4,215	3,785

CLASSES, BY SEX, FOR THE UNITED STATES: 1920.

AGE PERIOD.	NEGRO.			INDIAN, CHINESE, JAPANESE, AND ALL OTHER.		
	Both sexes.	Male.	Female.	Both sexes.	Male.	Female.
All ages	10,463,131	5,209,436	5,253,695	426,574	260,340	166,234
Under 5 years	1,143,699	568,633	575,066	55,610	28,114	27,496
Under 1 year	227,660	112,660	115,000	11,828	6,009	5,819
5 to 9 years	1,266,207	631,341	634,866	44,623	22,455	22,168
10 to 14 years	1,236,914	616,251	620,663	34,901	17,905	16,996
15 to 19 years	1,083,215	513,416	569,799	33,186	18,545	14,641
20 to 24 years	1,054,847	487,169	567,678	36,833	21,300	15,533
25 to 29 years	909,739	424,352	485,387	35,062	19,580	15,482
30 to 34 years	697,865	331,579	366,286	34,538	22,938	11,600
35 to 39 years	773,931	383,587	390,344	35,545	25,433	10,112
40 to 44 years	559,701	275,926	283,775	30,309	22,205	8,104
45 to 49 years	551,589	320,506	231,083	23,991	17,869	6,122
50 to 54 years	399,110	227,995	171,115	18,497	13,946	4,551
55 to 59 years	229,980	129,153	100,827	13,473	10,251	3,222
60 to 64 years	200,118	112,137	87,981	10,997	8,044	2,953
65 to 69 years	137,035	76,184	60,851	7,144	4,854	2,290
70 to 74 years	91,579	47,411	44,168	4,719	2,974	1,745
75 to 79 years	52,352	27,172	25,180	2,530	1,410	1,120
80 to 84 years	28,122	13,049	15,073	1,591	790	801
85 to 89 years	12,281	5,620	6,661	722	344	378
90 to 94 years	5,847	2,340	3,507	420	191	229
95 to 99 years	2,562	1,087	1,475	186	76	110
100 years and over	2,935	1,018	1,917	164	76	88
Age unknown	23,503	13,510	9,993	1,533	1,040	493

AGE PERIOD	NATIVE WHITE—MIXED PARENTAGE.			FOREIGN-BORN WHITE.		
	Both sexes.	Male.	Female.	Both sexes.	Male.	Female.
All ages	6,991,665	3,455,021	3,536,644	13,712,754	7,528,322	6,184,432
Under 5 years	838,057	423,778	414,279	44,984	22,857	22,127
Under 1 year	163,014	82,649	80,365	4,569	2,337	2,232
5 to 9 years	832,235	420,821	411,414	169,884	85,774	84,110
10 to 14 years	818,783	412,393	406,390	331,362	167,152	164,210
15 to 19 years	757,799	377,362	380,437	527,942	259,270	268,672
20 to 24 years	697,035	338,635	358,400	926,844	456,988	469,856
25 to 29 years	635,963	303,552	332,411	1,454,363	792,088	662,275
30 to 34 years	539,148	255,803	283,345	1,651,475	946,818	704,657
35 to 39 years	487,531	234,974	252,557	1,737,805	1,008,677	729,128
40 to 44 years	396,974	192,052	204,922	1,428,099	803,195	624,904
45 to 49 years	322,309	162,093	160,216	1,299,675	744,423	555,252
50 to 54 years	236,622	118,875	117,747	1,167,377	651,546	515,831
55 to 59 years	158,513	80,091	78,422	908,722	503,789	404,933
60 to 64 years	116,097	58,784	57,313	715,731	392,629	323,102
65 to 69 years	69,989	35,191	34,798	519,226	275,400	243,826
70 to 74 years	42,376	20,821	21,555	381,325	194,732	186,593
75 to 79 years	24,196	11,571	12,625	246,487	124,170	122,317
80 to 84 years	10,084	4,537	5,547	118,935	56,701	62,234
85 to 89 years	3,671	1,615	2,056	47,473	22,004	25,469
90 to 94 years	862	367	495	11,717	5,123	6,594
95 to 99 years	159	72	87	2,579	1,049	1,530
100 years and over	32	15	17	485	205	280
Age unknown	3,230	1,619	1,611	20,264	13,732	6,532

TABLE 47.—PER CENT DISTRIBUTION BY AGE PERIODS FOR PRINCIPAL POPULATION CLASSES, BY SEX, FOR THE UNITED STATES: 1920.

AGE PERIOD.	ALL CLASSES.			WHITE.			NEGRO.		
	Both sexes.	Male.	Female.	Both sexes.	Male.	Female.	Both sexes.	Male.	Female.
All ages	100.0	100.0	100.0	100.0	100.0	100.0	100.0	100.0	100.0
Under 5 years	10.9	10.9	11.0	10.9	10.9	11.0	10.9	10.9	10.9
Under 1 year	2.1	2.1	2.2	2.1	2.1	2.1	2.2	2.2	2.2
5 to 9 years	10.8	10.7	10.9	10.6	10.5	10.8	12.1	12.1	12.1
10 to 14 years	10.1	10.0	10.2	9.9	9.8	10.0	11.8	11.8	11.8
15 to 19 years	8.9	8.7	9.2	8.8	8.6	9.0	10.4	9.9	10.8
20 to 24 years	8.8	8.4	9.2	8.6	8.3	9.0	10.1	9.4	10.8
25 to 29 years	8.6	8.4	8.8	8.6	8.5	8.7	8.7	8.1	9.2
30 to 34 years	7.6	7.7	7.6	7.7	7.8	7.7	6.7	6.4	7.0
35 to 39 years	7.4	7.6	7.1	7.3	7.6	7.1	7.4	7.4	7.4
40 to 44 years	6.0	6.1	5.9	6.1	6.2	6.0	5.3	5.3	5.4
45 to 49 years	5.5	5.8	5.1	5.5	5.7	5.2	5.3	6.2	4.4
50 to 54 years	4.5	4.7	4.2	4.6	4.7	4.4	3.8	4.4	3.3
55 to 59 years	3.4	3.5	3.2	3.5	3.6	3.4	2.2	2.5	1.9
60 to 64 years	2.8	2.9	2.7	2.9	3.0	2.8	1.9	2.2	1.7
65 to 69 years	2.0	2.0	1.9	2.0	2.1	2.0	1.3	1.5	1.2
70 to 74 years	1.3	1.3	1.3	1.4	1.4	1.4	0.9	0.9	0.8
75 to 79 years	0.8	0.8	0.8	0.8	0.8	0.9	0.5	0.5	0.5
80 to 84 years	0.4	0.3	0.4	0.4	0.4	0.4	0.3	0.3	0.3
85 to 89 years	0.1	0.1	0.2	0.2	0.1	0.2	0.1	0.1	0.1
90 to 94 years	(1)	(1)	(1)	(1)	(1)	(1)	0.1	(1)	0.1
95 to 99 years	(1)	(1)	(1)	(1)	(1)	(1)	(1)	(1)	(1)
100 years and over	(1)	(1)	(1)	(1)	(1)	(1)	(1)	(1)	(1)
Age unknown	0.1	0.2	0.1	0.1	0.2	0.1	0.2	0.3	0.2

AGE PERIOD.	NATIVE WHITE.									FOREIGN-BORN WHITE.		
	Native parentage.			Foreign parentage.			Mixed parentage.					
	Both sexes.	Male.	Female.	Both sexes.	Male.	Female.	Both sexes.	Male.	Female.	Both sexes.	Male.	Female.
All ages	100.0	100.0	100.0	100.0	100.0	100.0	100.0	100.0	100.0	100.0	100.0	100.0
Under 5 years	12.6	12.6	12.6	13.5	13.7	13.3	12.0	12.3	11.7	0.3	0.3	0.4
Under 1 year	2.5	2.5	2.5	2.5	2.6	2.5	2.3	2.4	2.3	(1)	(1)	(1)
5 to 9 years	11.9	11.9	12.0	13.4	13.6	13.3	11.9	12.2	11.6	1.2	1.1	1.4
10 to 14 years	11.1	11.0	11.1	11.2	11.3	11.1	11.7	11.9	11.5	2.4	2.2	2.7
15 to 19 years	9.6	9.4	9.7	9.1	9.1	9.2	10.8	10.9	10.8	3.9	3.4	4.3
20 to 24 years	8.9	8.6	9.1	8.8	8.7	9.0	10.0	9.8	10.1	6.8	6.1	7.6
25 to 29 years	8.2	8.0	8.3	8.2	8.1	8.3	9.1	8.8	9.4	10.6	10.5	10.7
30 to 34 years	7.0	6.9	7.1	6.7	6.6	6.8	7.7	7.4	8.0	12.0	12.6	11.4
35 to 39 years	6.5	6.6	6.4	5.9	5.9	5.9	7.0	6.8	7.1	12.7	13.4	11.8
40 to 44 years	5.3	5.3	5.3	5.3	5.2	5.4	5.7	5.6	5.8	10.4	10.7	10.1
45 to 49 years	4.7	4.9	4.5	5.2	5.2	5.1	4.6	4.7	4.5	9.5	9.9	9.0
50 to 54 years	3.8	4.0	3.6	4.3	4.3	4.3	3.4	3.4	3.3	8.5	8.7	8.3
55 to 59 years	2.9	3.0	2.8	3.3	3.3	3.3	2.3	2.3	2.2	6.6	6.7	6.5
60 to 64 years	2.6	2.7	2.6	2.6	2.6	2.6	1.7	1.7	1.6	5.2	5.2	5.2
65 to 69 years	1.9	2.0	1.9	1.3	1.3	1.3	1.0	1.0	1.0	3.8	3.7	3.9
70 to 74 years	1.3	1.3	1.4	0.6	0.6	0.6	0.6	0.6	0.6	2.3	2.6	3.0
75 to 79 years	0.8	0.8	0.9	0.3	0.3	0.3	0.3	0.3	0.4	1.0	1.6	2.0
80 to 84 years	0.4	0.3	0.4	0.1	0.1	0.1	0.1	0.1	0.2	0.9	0.8	1.0
85 to 89 years	0.1	0.1	0.2	(1)	(1)	(1)	0.1	(1)	0.1	0.3	0.3	0.4
90 to 94 years	(1)	(1)	(1)	(1)	(1)	(1)	(1)	(1)	(1)	0.1	0.1	0.1
95 to 99 years	(1)	(1)	(1)	(1)	(1)	(1)	(1)	(1)	(1)	(1)	(1)	(1)
100 years and over	(1)	(1)	(1)	(1)	(1)	(1)	(1)	(1)	(1)	(1)	(1)	(1)
Age unknown	0.2	0.2	0.1	0.1	0.1	(1)	(1)	(1)	(1)	0.1	0.2	0.1

¹Less than one-tenth of 1 per cent.

TABLE 48.—DISTRIBUTION BY AGE PERIODS, FOR INDIAN, CHINESE, AND JAPANESE POPULATION, BY SEX, FOR THE UNITED STATES: 1920.

AGE PERIOD.	NUMBER.								
	Indian.			Chinese.			Japanese.		
	Both sexes.	Male.	Female.	Both sexes.	Male.	Female.	Both sexes.	Male.	Female.
All ages	244,437	125,068	119,369	61,639	53,891	7,748	111,010	72,707	38,303
Under 5 years	33,346	16,591	16,755	2,898	1,480	1,418	19,029	9,853	9,176
Under 1 year	6,416	3,236	3,180	622	299	323	4,704	2,428	2,276
5 to 9 years	34,166	16,931	17,235	2,511	1,370	1,141	7,743	4,048	3,695
10 to 14 years	30,173	15,225	14,948	2,005	1,223	782	2,569	1,379	1,190
15 to 19 years	25,417	12,710	12,707	2,760	2,161	599	4,342	3,081	1,261
20 to 24 years	20,009	10,413	9,596	4,845	4,122	723	9,636	4,535	5,101
25 to 29 years	16,537	8,558	7,979	5,279	4,543	736	11,270	4,600	6,670
30 to 34 years	13,474	6,963	6,511	4,682	4,093	589	15,253	10,819	4,434
35 to 39 years	13,707	7,213	6,494	5,319	4,789	530	15,394	12,369	3,025
40 to 44 years	11,618	6,071	5,547	5,345	4,913	432	12,762	10,670	2,092
45 to 49 years	10,806	5,987	4,819	5,527	5,242	285	7,181	6,184	997
50 to 54 years	8,728	4,764	3,964	6,045	5,850	195	3,515	3,129	386
55 to 59 years	6,573	3,594	2,979	5,594	5,476	118	1,214	1,094	120
60 to 64 years	5,953	3,136	2,817	4,504	4,416	88	489	443	46
65 to 69 years	4,655	2,429	2,226	2,303	2,261	42	151	134	17
70 to 74 years	3,455	1,748	1,707	1,217	1,188	29	31	26	5
75 to 79 years	2,150	1,049	1,101	355	344	11	12	6	6
80 to 84 years	1,457	666	791	129	120	9	2	2	
85 to 89 years	674	298	376	42	40	2	5	5	
90 to 94 years	409	180	229	8	8				
95 to 99 years	179	69	110	7	7				
100 years and over	160	73	87	4	3	1			
Age unknown	791	400	391	260	242	18	412	330	82

AGE PERIOD.	PER CENT DISTRIBUTION.								
All ages	100.0	100.0	100.0	100.0	100.0	100.0	100.0	100.0	100.0
Under 5 years	13.6	13.3	14.0	4.7	2.7	18.3	17.1	13.6	24.0
Under 1 year	2.6	2.6	2.7	1.0	0.6	4.2	4.2	3.3	5.9
5 to 9 years	14.0	13.5	14.4	4.1	2.5	14.7	7.0	5.6	9.6
10 to 14 years	12.3	12.2	12.5	3.3	2.3	10.1	2.3	1.9	3.1
15 to 19 years	10.4	10.2	10.6	4.5	4.0	7.7	3.9	4.2	3.3
20 to 24 years	8.2	8.3	8.0	7.9	7.6	9.3	8.7	6.2	13.3
25 to 29 years	6.8	6.8	6.7	8.6	8.4	9.5	10.2	6.3	17.4
30 to 34 years	5.5	5.6	5.5	7.6	7.6	7.6	13.7	14.9	11.6
35 to 39 years	5.6	5.8	5.4	8.6	8.9	6.8	13.9	17.0	7.9
40 to 44 years	4.8	4.9	4.6	8.7	9.1	5.6	11.5	14.7	5.5
45 to 49 years	4.4	4.8	4.0	9.0	9.7	3.7	6.5	8.5	2.6
50 to 54 years	3.6	3.8	3.3	9.8	10.9	2.5	3.2	4.3	1.0
55 to 59 years	2.7	2.9	2.5	9.1	10.2	1.5	1.1	1.5	0.3
60 to 64 years	2.4	2.5	2.4	7.3	8.2	1.1	0.4	0.6	0.1
65 to 69 years	1.9	1.9	1.9	3.7	4.2	0.5	0.1	0.2	(1)
70 to 74 years	1.4	1.4	1.4	2.0	2.2	0.4	(1)	(1)	(1)
75 to 79 years	0.9	0.8	0.9	0.6	0.6	0.1	(1)	(1)	(1)
80 to 84 years	0.6	0.5	0.7	0.2	0.2	0.1	(1)	(1)	
85 to 89 years	0.3	0.2	0.3	0.1	0.1	(1)	(1)	(1)	
90 to 94 years	0.2	0.1	0.2	(1)	(1)				
95 to 99 years	0.1	0.1	0.1	(1)	(1)				
100 years and over	0.1	0.1	0.1	(1)	(1)	(1)			
Age unknown	0.3	0.3	0.3	0.4	0.4	0.2	0.4	0.5	0.2

[1] Less than one-tenth of 1 per cent.

TABLE 49.—DISTRIBUTION OF POPULATION CLASSES BY BROAD AGE GROUPS, BY DIVISIONS AND STATES: 1920.

AGE.	All classes.	NATIVE WHITE.			Foreign-born white.	Negro.	Indian, Chinese, Japanese, and all other.
		Native parentage.	Foreign parentage.	Mixed parentage.			
UNITED STATES.							
All ages, number	105,710,620	58,421,957	15,694,539	6,991,665	13,712,754	10,463,131	426,574
Under 5 years	11,573,230	7,366,530	2,124,350	838,057	44,984	1,143,699	55,610
5 to 14 years	22,039,212	13,433,572	3,870,731	1,651,018	501,246	2,503,121	79,524
15 to 24 years	18,707,577	10,775,753	2,814,123	1,454,834	1,454,786	2,138,062	70,019
25 to 34 years	17,157,684	8,860,843	2,338,688	1,175,111	3,105,838	1,607,604	69,600
35 to 44 years	14,120,838	6,915,182	1,755,761	884,505	3,165,904	1,333,632	65,854
45 to 54 years	10,498,493	4,989,713	1,489,610	558,931	2,467,052	950,699	42,488
55 to 64 years	6,531,672	3,249,319	928,722	274,610	1,624,453	430,098	24,470
65 years and over	4,933,215	2,738,876	364,554	151,369	1,328,227	332,713	17,476
Age unknown	148,699	92,169	8,000	3,230	20,264	23,503	1,533
All ages, per cent	100.0	100.0	100.0	100.0	100.0	100.0	100.0
Under 5 years	10.9	12.6	13.5	12.0	0.3	10.9	13.0
5 to 14 years	20.8	23.0	24.7	23.6	3.7	23.9	18.6
15 to 24 years	17.7	18.4	17.9	20.8	10.6	20.4	16.4
25 to 34 years	16.2	15.2	14.9	16.8	22.6	15.4	16.3
35 to 44 years	13.4	11.8	11.2	12.7	23.1	12.7	15.4
45 to 54 years	9.9	8.5	9.5	8.0	18.0	9.1	10.0
55 to 64 years	6.2	5.6	5.9	3.9	11.8	4.1	5.7
65 years and over	4.7	4.7	2.3	2.2	9.7	3.2	4.1
GEOGRAPHIC DIVISIONS.							
NEW ENGLAND.							
All ages, number	7,400,909	2,803,149	1,906,340	735,936	1,870,654	79,051	5,779
Under 5 years	753,030	308,941	315,755	114,720	5,857	7,415	342
5 to 14 years	1,352,622	515,042	552,888	205,611	66,278	12,285	518
15 to 24 years	1,208,526	442,503	376,966	162,989	211,661	13,563	844
25 to 34 years	1,215,814	401,035	244,525	108,785	444,957	15,541	971
35 to 44 years	1,044,653	349,050	167,109	69,456	443,935	13,919	1,184
45 to 54 years	846,784	301,768	139,451	41,658	353,565	9,198	1,144
55 to 64 years	540,420	233,146	79,704	21,130	201,818	4,059	563
65 years and over	432,159	247,329	29,336	11,407	141,052	2,835	200
Age unknown	6,901	4,335	606	180	1,531	236	13
All ages, per cent	100.0	100.0	100.0	100.0	100.0	100.0	100.0
Under 5 years	10.2	11.0	16.6	15.6	0.3	9.4	5.9
5 to 14 years	18.3	18.4	29.0	27.9	3.5	15.5	9.0
15 to 24 years	16.3	15.8	19.8	22.1	11.3	17.2	14.6
25 to 34 years	16.4	14.3	12.8	14.8	23.8	19.7	16.8
35 to 44 years	14.1	12.5	8.8	9.4	23.7	17.6	20.5
45 to 54 years	11.4	10.8	7.3	5.7	18.9	11.6	19.8
55 to 64 years	7.3	8.3	4.2	2.9	10.8	5.1	9.7
65 years and over	5.8	8.8	1.5	1.5	7.5	3.6	3.5
MIDDLE ATLANTIC.							
All ages, number	22,261,144	9,631,012	5,397,951	1,700,302	4,912,575	600,183	19,121
Under 5 years	2,354,451	1,130,577	934,255	231,318	9,848	47,306	1,147
5 to 14 years	4,285,734	1,997,195	1,629,979	405,326	163,967	87,216	2,051
15 to 24 years	3,741,583	1,723,828	973,480	338,189	589,178	113,886	3,022
25 to 34 years	3,834,710	1,530,892	641,841	274,615	1,247,586	135,385	4,391
35 to 44 years	3,188,579	1,211,466	451,274	209,249	1,199,299	113,237	4,054
45 to 54 years	2,376,207	906,979	405,039	136,806	860,498	64,206	2,679
55 to 64 years	1,436,850	597,633	255,040	66,741	492,759	23,374	1,303
65 years and over	1,020,881	520,468	104,977	37,417	343,250	14,347	422
Age unknown	22,149	11,974	2,066	641	6,190	1,226	52
All ages, per cent	100.0	100.0	100.0	100.0	100.0	100.0	100.0
Under 5 years	10.6	11.7	17.3	13.6	0.2	7.9	6.0
5 to 14 years	19.3	20.7	30.2	23.8	3.3	14.5	10.7
15 to 24 years	16.8	17.9	18.0	19.9	12.0	19.0	15.8
25 to 34 years	17.2	15.9	11.9	16.2	25.4	22.6	23.0
35 to 44 years	14.3	12.6	8.4	12.3	24.4	18.9	21.2
45 to 54 years	10.7	9.4	7.5	8.0	17.5	10.7	14.0
55 to 64 years	6.5	6.2	4.7	3.9	10.0	3.9	6.8
65 years and over	4.6	5.4	1.9	2.2	7.0	2.4	2.2

TABLE 49.—DISTRIBUTION OF POPULATION CLASSES BY BROAD AGE GROUPS, BY DIVISIONS AND STATES: 1920—Continued.

AGE.	All classes.	NATIVE WHITE. Native parentage.	NATIVE WHITE. Foreign parentage.	NATIVE WHITE. Mixed parentage.	Foreign-born white.	Negro.	Indian, Chinese, Japanese, and all other.
GEOGRAPHIC DIVISONS— Continued.							
EAST NORTH CENTRAL.							
All ages, number	21,475,543	11,790,370	4,043,692	1,881,521	3,223,279	514,554	22,127
Under 5 years	2,220,032	1,491,025	481,147	202,103	6,468	36,991	2,298
5 to 14 years	4,088,944	2,620,804	864,609	421,952	103,999	73,529	4,051
15 to 24 years	3,642,633	2,176,485	679,383	389,472	297,802	95,858	3,633
25 to 34 years	3,684,814	1,851,260	662,802	327,330	722,592	117,266	3,564
35 to 44 years	2,973,734	1,386,250	505,373	252,700	731,736	94,424	3,251
45 to 54 years	2,230,859	1,000,703	441,988	162,351	566,851	56,422	2,544
55 to 64 years	1,479,117	672,022	290,825	80,252	411,566	22,880	1,572
65 years and over	1,132,157	576,871	115,537	44,588	378,063	15,927	1,171
Age unknown	23,253	14,950	2,028	773	4,202	1,257	43
All ages, per cent	100.0	100.0	100.0	100.0	100.0	100.0	100.0
Under 5 years	10.3	12.6	11.9	10.7	0.2	7.2	10.4
5 to 14 years	19.0	22.2	21.4	22.4	3.2	14.3	18.3
15 to 24 years	17.0	18.5	16.8	20.7	9.2	18.6	16.4
25 to 34 years	17.2	15.7	16.4	17.4	22.4	22.8	16.1
35 to 44 years	13.8	11.8	12.5	13.4	22.7	18.4	14.7
45 to 54 years	10.4	8.5	10.9	8.6	17.6	11.0	11.5
55 to 64 years	6.9	5.7	7.2	4.3	12.8	4.4	7.1
65 years and over	5.3	4.9	2.9	2.4	11.7	3.1	5.3
WEST NORTH CENTRAL.							
All ages, number	12,544,249	7,475,548	2,126,126	1,251,752	1,371,961	278,521	40,341
Under 5 years	1,341,412	1,032,060	143,939	137,420	2,826	19,689	5,478
5 to 14 years	2,562,668	1,812,235	354,698	309,971	32,687	43,922	9,155
15 to 24 years	2,246,266	1,398,762	413,015	286,883	91,260	48,994	7,352
25 to 34 years	2,025,311	1,102,643	432,819	216,722	212,344	55,535	5,248
35 to 44 years	1,625,049	814,899	330,075	151,116	275,490	49,029	4,440
45 to 54 years	1,236,684	584,256	251,768	87,343	276,843	32,955	3,519
55 to 64 years	833,928	388,799	147,021	40,134	240,124	15,339	2,511
65 years and over	654,608	328,496	51,442	21,619	238,571	11,989	2,491
Age unknown	18,323	13,398	1,349	544	1,816	1,069	147
All ages, per cent	100.0	100.0	100.0	100.0	100.0	100.0	100.0
Under 5 years	10.7	13.8	6.8	11.0	0.2	7.1	13.6
5 to 14 years	20.4	24.2	16.7	24.8	2.4	15.8	22.7
15 to 24 years	17.9	18.7	19.4	22.9	6.7	17.6	18.2
25 to 34 years	16.1	14.7	20.4	17.3	15.5	19.9	13.0
35 to 44 years	13.0	10.9	15.5	12.1	20.1	17.6	11.0
45 to 54 years	9.9	7.8	11.8	7.0	20.2	11.8	8.7
55 to 64 years	6.6	5.2	6.9	3.2	17.5	5.5	6.2
65 years and over	5.2	4.4	2.4	1.7	17.4	4.3	6.2
SOUTH ATLANTIC.							
All ages, number	13,990,272	8,779,416	353,643	199,961	315,920	4,325,120	16,212
Under 5 years	1,729,369	1,131,305	46,879	20,483	857	527,394	2,451
5 to 14 years	3,381,017	2,119,614	82,634	38,159	11,108	1,125,359	4,143
15 to 24 years	2,706,546	1,667,291	57,954	37,132	36,980	904,219	2,970
25 to 34 years	2,031,209	1,276,735	45,570	33,621	75,576	597,559	2,148
35 to 44 years	1,665,223	1,026,008	37,778	29,025	73,888	496,723	1,801
45 to 54 years	1,200,015	722,053	40,375	21,599	54,908	359,706	1,374
55 to 64 years	700,250	454,622	28,829	12,006	32,989	171,014	790
65 years and over	556,519	371,793	13,443	7,814	28,888	134,072	509
Age unknown	20,124	9,995	181	122	726	9,074	26
All ages, per cent	100.0	100.0	100.0	100.0	100.0	100.0	100.0
Under 5 years	12.4	12.9	13.3	10.2	0.3	12.2	15.1
5 to 14 years	24.2	24.1	23.4	19.1	3.5	26.0	25.6
15 to 24 years	19.3	19.0	16.4	18.6	11.7	20.9	18.3
25 to 34 years	14.5	14.5	12.9	16.8	23.9	13.8	13.2
35 to 44 years	11.9	11.7	10.7	14.5	23.4	11.5	11.1
45 to 54 years	8.6	8.2	11.4	10.8	17.4	8.3	8.5
55 to 64 years	5.0	5.2	8.2	6.0	10.4	4.0	4.9
65 years and over	4.0	4.2	3.8	3.9	9.1	3.1	3.1

Table 49.—DISTRIBUTION OF POPULATION CLASSES BY BROAD AGE GROUPS, BY DIVISIONS AND STATES: 1920—Continued.

AGE.	All classes.	NATIVE WHITE. Native parentage.	NATIVE WHITE. Foreign parentage.	NATIVE WHITE. Mixed parentage.	Foreign-born white.	Negro.	Indian, Chinese, Japanese, and all other.
Geographic Divisions—Continued.							
East South Central.							
All ages, number	8,893,307	6,092,782	115,484	87,342	71,939	2,523,532	2,228
Under 5 years	1,088,134	797,844	6,744	5,450	163	277,670	263
5 to 14 years	2,210,996	1,539,143	14,718	13,054	1,854	641,716	511
15 to 24 years	1,702,626	1,155,331	13,193	15,228	5,724	512,759	391
25 to 34 years	1,252,787	855,340	14,898	16,527	11,843	353,853	326
35 to 44 years	1,034,178	687,673	18,807	16,090	14,372	296,967	269
45 to 54 years	777,838	494,773	22,763	11,616	13,523	234,939	224
55 to 64 years	451,533	306,695	17,275	5,775	10,830	110,817	141
65 years and over	365,167	251,378	6,990	3,554	13,530	89,620	95
Age unknown	10,048	4,605	96	48	100	5,191	8
All ages, per cent	100.0	100.0	100.0	100.0	100.0	100.0	100.0
Under 5 years	12.2	13.1	5.8	6.2	0.2	11.0	11.8
5 to 14 years	24.9	25.3	12.7	14.9	2.6	25.4	22.9
15 to 24 years	19.1	19.0	11.4	17.4	8.0	20.3	17.5
25 to 34 years	14.1	14.0	12.9	18.9	16.5	14.0	14.6
35 to 44 years	11.6	11.3	16.3	18.4	20.0	11.8	12.1
45 to 54 years	8.7	8.1	19.7	13.3	18.8	9.3	10.1
55 to 64 years	5.1	5.0	15.0	6.6	15.1	4.4	6.3
65 years and over	4.1	4.1	6.1	4.1	18.8	3.6	4.3
West South Central.							
All ages, number	10,242,224	6,959,785	415,799	280,810	459,333	2,063,579	62,918
Under 5 years	1,216,509	894,870	49,995	31,669	8,244	222,582	9,149
5 to 14 years	2,519,413	1,782,338	91,638	67,992	49,441	509,573	18,431
15 to 24 years	2,032,527	1,373,627	76,212	57,137	78,560	434,891	12,100
25 to 34 years	1,563,198	1,048,640	63,309	44,912	84,356	314,115	7,866
35 to 44 years	1,223,684	792,807	52,214	37,063	81,344	253,874	6,382
45 to 54 years	847,836	524,564	42,964	23,672	68,837	183,488	4,311
55 to 64 years	469,924	303,812	27,701	11,444	45,990	78,568	2,409
65 years and over	349,353	226,883	11,346	6,694	40,926	61,438	2,066
Age unknown	19,780	12,244	420	227	1,635	5,050	204
All ages, per cent	100.0	100.0	100.0	100.0	100.0	100.0	100.0
Under 5 years	11.9	12.9	12.0	11.3	1.8	10.8	14.5
5 to 14 years	24.6	25.6	22.0	24.2	10.8	24.7	29.3
15 to 24 years	19.8	19.7	18.3	20.3	17.1	21.1	19.2
25 to 34 years	15.3	15.1	15.2	16.0	18.4	15.2	12.5
35 to 44 years	11.9	11.4	12.6	13.2	17.7	12.3	10.1
45 to 54 years	8.3	7.5	10.3	8.4	15.0	8.9	6.9
55 to 64 years	4.6	4.4	6.7	4.1	10.0	3.8	3.8
65 years and over	3.4	3.3	2.7	2.4	8.9	3.0	3.3
Mountain.							
All ages, number	3,336,101	2,002,508	451,132	306,034	453,225	30,801	92,401
Under 5 years	396,814	286,226	54,586	37,805	4,670	1,540	11,987
5 to 14 years	710,354	487,823	96,897	72,857	28,925	3,005	20,847
15 to 24 years	565,353	354,806	76,047	61,867	50,128	6,741	15,764
25 to 34 years	563,184	315,240	77,102	54,228	95,221	8,500	12,893
35 to 44 years	461,032	236,083	65,226	40,203	102,080	5,424	12,016
45 to 54 years	316,063	155,915	46,666	23,324	78,220	3,321	8,617
55 to 64 years	190,964	94,567	25,567	10,872	53,531	1,294	5,133
65 years and over	119,276	60,830	8,743	4,700	39,362	817	4,824
Age unknown	10,061	11,018	298	178	1,088	159	320
All ages, per cent	100.0	100.0	100.0	100.0	100.0	100.0	100.0
Under 5 years	11.9	14.3	12.1	12.4	1.0	5.0	13.0
5 to 14 years	21.3	24.4	21.5	23.8	6.4	9.8	22.6
15 to 24 years	16.9	17.7	16.9	20.2	11.1	21.9	17.1
25 to 34 years	16.9	15.7	17.1	17.7	21.0	27.6	14.0
35 to 44 years	13.8	11.8	14.5	13.1	22.5	17.6	13.0
45 to 54 years	9.5	7.8	10.3	7.6	17.3	10.8	9.3
55 to 64 years	5.7	4.7	5.7	3.6	11.8	4.2	5.6
65 years and over	3.6	3.0	1.9	1.5	8.7	2.7	5.2

TABLE 49.—DISTRIBUTION OF POPULATION CLASSES BY BROAD AGE GROUPS, BY DIVISIONS AND STATES: 1920—Continued.

AGE.	All classes.	NATIVE WHITE.			Foreign-born white.	Negro.	Indian, Chinese, Japanese, and all other.
		Native parentage.	Foreign parentage.	Mixed parentage.			
GEOGRAPHIC DIVISIONS—Continued.							
PACIFIC.							
All ages, number	5,566,871	2,887,387	884,372	548,007	1,033,868	47,790	165,447
Under 5 years	473,479	293,682	91,050	57,089	6,051	3,112	22,495
5 to 14 years	927,464	559,378	182,670	116,096	42,987	6,516	19,817
15 to 24 years	861,517	483,120	147,873	105,937	93,493	7,151	23,943
25 to 34 years	986,657	479,058	155,822	98,371	211,363	9,850	32,193
35 to 44 years	904,706	410,946	127,905	79,603	243,760	10,035	32,457
45 to 54 years	666,207	298,702	98,596	50,562	193,807	6,464	18,076
55 to 64 years	428,686	198,023	56,760	26,256	134,846	2,753	10,048
65 years and over	303,095	154,828	22,740	13,576	104,585	1,668	5,698
Age unknown	15,060	9,650	956	517	2,976	241	720
All ages, per cent	100.0	100.0	100.0	100.0	100.0	100.0	100.0
Under 5 years	8.5	10.2	10.3	10.4	0.6	6.5	13.6
5 to 14 years	16.7	19.4	20.7	21.2	4.2	13.6	12.0
15 to 24 years	15.5	16.7	16.7	19.3	9.0	15.0	14.5
25 to 34 years	17.7	16.6	17.6	18.0	20.4	20.6	19.5
35 to 44 years	16.3	14.2	14.5	14.5	23.6	21.0	19.6
45 to 54 years	12.0	10.3	11.1	9.2	18.7	13.5	10.9
55 to 64 years	7.7	6.9	6.4	4.8	13.0	5.8	6.1
65 years and over	5.4	5.4	2.6	2.5	10.1	3.5	3.4
NEW ENGLAND.							
Maine.							
All ages, number	768,014	435,780	86,150	76,416	107,349	1,310	1,009
Under 5 years	75,140	49,736	11,527	12,826	828	113	110
5 to 14 years	141,632	89,887	23,214	22,981	5,171	199	180
15 to 24 years	124,928	75,964	18,462	16,241	13,874	234	153
25 to 34 years	109,443	66,070	12,181	9,176	21,649	234	133
35 to 44 years	100,362	62,602	7,718	6,173	23,535	189	145
45 to 54 years	88,380	57,182	6,373	4,404	20,141	140	140
55 to 64 years	65,133	45,462	4,350	2,758	12,380	104	79
65 years and over	62,101	48,163	2,283	1,839	9,654	94	68
Age unknown	895	714	42	18	117	3	1
All ages, per cent	100.0	100.0	100.0	100.0	100.0	100.0	100.0
Under 5 years	9.8	10.0	13.4	16.8	0.8	8.6	10.9
5 to 14 years	18.4	18.1	26.9	30.1	4.8	15.2	17.8
15 to 24 years	16.3	15.3	21.4	21.3	12.9	17.9	15.2
25 to 34 years	14.3	13.3	14.1	12.0	20.2	17.9	13.2
35 to 44 years	13.1	12.6	9.0	8.1	21.9	14.4	14.4
45 to 54 years	11.5	11.5	7.4	5.8	18.8	10.7	13.9
55 to 64 years	8.5	9.2	5.0	3.6	11.5	7.9	7.8
65 years and over	8.1	9.7	2.7	2.4	9.0	7.2	6.7
New Hampshire.							
All ages, number	443,083	225,512	81,039	44,547	91,233	621	131
Under 5 years	41,391	21,229	11,997	7,634	456	72	3
5 to 14 years	78,553	38,564	22,616	13,508	3,740	119	6
15 to 24 years	70,597	32,031	18,331	9,524	10,600	84	27
25 to 34 years	65,473	28,520	11,474	5,520	19,826	108	25
35 to 44 years	59,683	28,243	6,955	3,726	20,627	107	25
45 to 54 years	53,174	27,425	5,511	2,403	17,756	51	28
55 to 64 years	38,210	23,188	2,887	1,404	10,681	36	14
65 years and over	35,210	25,775	1,204	805	7,396	29	1
Age unknown	792	537	64	23	151	15	2
All ages, per cent	100.0	100.0	100.0	100.0	100.0	100.0	100.0
Under 5 years	9.3	9.4	14.8	17.1	0.5	11.6	2.3
5 to 14 years	17.7	17.1	27.9	30.3	4.1	19.2	4.6
15 to 24 years	15.9	14.2	22.6	21.4	11.6	13.5	20.6
25 to 34 years	14.8	12.6	14.2	12.4	21.7	17.4	19.1
35 to 44 years	13.5	12.5	8.6	8.4	22.6	17.2	19.1
45 to 54 years	12.0	12.2	6.8	5.4	19.5	8.2	21.4
55 to 64 years	8.6	10.3	3.6	3.2	11.7	5.8	10.7
65 years and over	7.9	11.4	1.5	1.8	8.1	4.7	0.8

TABLE **49.**—DISTRIBUTION OF POPULATION CLASSES BY BROAD AGE GROUPS, BY DIVISIONS AND STATES: 1920—Continued.

AGE.	All classes.	NATIVE WHITE.			Foreign-born white.	Negro.	Indian, Chinese, Japanese, and all other.
		Native parentage.	Foreign parentage.	Mixed parentage.			
NEW ENGLAND—Con.							
Vermont.							
All ages, number......	352,428	228,325	42,100	36,866	44,526	572	39
Under 5 years............	34,544	24,250	5,339	4,358	540	52	5
5 to 14 years.............	65,997	45,158	9,111	8,479	3,123	121	5
15 to 24 years............	56,061	37,889	6,046	7,082	4,954	86	4
25 to 34 years............	48,711	30,424	4,677	5,235	8,299	68	8
35 to 44 years............	46,125	27,320	4,764	4,621	9,304	108	8
45 to 54 years............	41,255	24,375	5,330	3,639	7,849	59	3
55 to 64 years............	29,665	18,239	4,159	2,059	5,161	46	1
65 years and over.........	29,694	20,377	2,651	1,381	5,253	28	4
Age unknown.............	376	293	23	12	43	4	1
All ages, per cent......	100.0	100.0	100.0	100.0	100.0	100.0	(1)
Under 5 years............	9.8	10.6	12.7	11.8	1.2	9.1	(1)
5 to 14 years.............	18.7	19.8	21.6	23.0	7.0	21.2	(1)
15 to 24 years............	15.9	16.6	14.4	19.2	11.1	15.0	(1)
25 to 34 years............	13.8	13.3	11.1	14.2	18.6	11.9	(1)
35 to 44 years............	13.1	12.0	11.3	12.5	20.9	18.9	(1)
45 to 54 years............	11.7	10.7	12.7	9.9	17.6	10.3	(1)
55 to 64 years............	8.4	8.0	9.9	5.6	11.6	8.0	(1)
65 years and over.........	8.4	8.9	6.3	3.7	11.8	4.9	(1)
Massachusetts.							
All ages, number......	3,852,356	1,230,773	1,093,258	401,959	1,077,534	45,466	3,366
Under 5 years............	385,761	141,475	175,207	61,778	2,824	4,308	169
5 to 14 years.............	693,364	226,624	311,661	113,047	34,935	6,857	240
15 to 24 years............	629,875	193,719	219,190	91,009	117,791	7,674	492
25 to 34 years............	653,189	181,055	144,552	61,199	256,567	9,244	572
35 to 44 years............	557,783	153,506	98,730	37,623	258,980	8,181	763
45 to 54 years............	446,856	129,721	81,809	21,579	207,711	5,307	729
55 to 64 years............	275,949	99,663	45,957	10,492	117,262	2,253	322
65 years and over.........	206,447	103,105	15,869	5,157	80,744	1,497	75
Age unknown.............	3,132	1,905	283	75	720	145	4
All ages, per cent......	100.0	100.0	100.0	100.0	100.0	100.0	100.0
Under 5 years............	10.0	11.5	16.0	15.4	0.3	9.5	5.0
5 to 14 years.............	18.0	18.4	28.5	28.1	3.2	15.1	7.1
15 to 24 years............	16.4	15.7	20.0	22.6	10.9	16.9	14.6
25 to 34 years............	17.0	14.7	13.2	15.2	23.8	20.3	17.0
35 to 44 years............	14.5	12.5	9.0	9.4	24.0	18.0	22.7
45 to 54 years............	11.6	10.5	7.5	5.4	19.3	11.7	21.7
55 to 64 years............	7.2	8.1	4.2	2.6	10.9	5.0	9.6
65 years and over.........	5.4	8.4	1.5	1.3	7.5	3.3	2.2
Rhode Island.							
All ages, number......	604,397	173,553	182,660	64,268	173,499	10,036	381
Under 5 years............	62,356	21,055	29,153	10,657	493	997	21
5 to 14 years.............	112,089	33,087	52,408	18,603	6,347	1,599	45
15 to 24 years............	103,993	28,868	37,593	14,898	21,028	1,576	30
25 to 34 years............	98,885	25,120	24,304	9,384	38,255	1,756	66
35 to 44 years............	85,842	21,350	16,639	5,726	40,265	1,790	72
45 to 54 years............	69,073	17,513	13,103	3,067	34,073	1,243	74
55 to 64 years............	41,676	12,966	6,967	1,337	19,746	611	49
65 years and over.........	30,190	13,476	2,456	607	13,176	453	22
Age unknown.............	293	118	37	9	116	11	2
All ages, per cent.....	100.0	100.0	100.0	100.0	100.0	100.0	100.0
Under 5 years............	10.3	12.1	16.0	16.6	0.3	9.9	5.5
5 to 14 years.............	18.5	19.1	28.7	28.9	3.7	15.9	11.8
15 to 24 years............	17.2	16.6	20.6	23.2	12.1	15.7	7.9
25 to 34 years............	16.4	14.5	13.3	14.6	22.0	17.5	17.3
35 to 44 years............	14.2	12.3	9.1	8.9	23.2	17.8	18.9
45 to 54 years............	11.4	10.1	7.2	4.8	19.6	12.4	19.4
55 to 64 years............	6.9	7.5	3.8	2.1	11.4	6.1	12.9
65 years and over.........	5.0	7.8	1.3	0.9	7.6	4.5	5.8

1 Per cent not shown, base being less than 100.

TABLE 49.—DISTRIBUTION OF POPULATION CLASSES BY BROAD AGE GROUPS, BY DIVISIONS AND STATES: 1920—Continued.

AGE.	All classes.	NATIVE WHITE.			Foreign-born white.	Negro.	Indian, Chinese, Japanese, and all other.
		Native parentage.	Foreign parentage.	Mixed parentage.			

NEW ENGLAND—Con.

Connecticut.

All ages, number	1,380,631	449,206	421,133	111,880	376,513	21,046	853
Under 5 years	153,838	51,196	82,532	17,487	716	1,873	34
5 to 14 years	260,987	81,722	133,878	28,993	12,962	3,390	42
15 to 24 years	223,072	74,032	77,344	24,235	43,414	3,909	138
25 to 34 years	240,113	69,846	47,337	18,271	100,361	4,131	167
35 to 44 years	194,858	56,029	32,303	11,587	91,224	3,544	171
45 to 54 years	148,046	45,552	27,325	6,566	66,035	2,398	170
55 to 64 years	89,787	33,628	15,384	3,080	36,588	1,009	98
65 years and over	68,517	36,433	4,873	1,618	24,829	734	30
Age unknown	1,413	768	157	43	384	58	3
All ages, per cent	100.0	100.0	100.0	100.0	100.0	100.0	100.0
Under 5 years	11.1	11.4	19.6	15.6	0.2	8.9	4.0
5 to 14 years	18.9	18.2	31.8	25.9	3.4	16.1	4.9
15 to 24 years	16.2	16.5	18.4	21.7	11.5	18.6	16.2
25 to 34 years	17.4	15.5	11.2	16.3	26.7	19.6	19.6
35 to 44 years	14.1	12.5	7.7	10.4	24.2	16.8	20.0
45 to 54 years	10.7	10.1	6.5	5.9	17.5	11.4	19.9
55 to 64 years	6.5	7.5	3.7	2.8	9.7	4.8	11.5
65 years and over	5.0	8.1	1.2	1.4	6.6	3.5	3.5

MIDDLE ATLANTIC.

New York.

All ages, number	10,385,227	3,668,266	2,844,083	873,566	2,786,112	198,483	14,717
Under 5 years	1,010,290	417,525	455,599	115,374	6,086	14,726	980
5 to 14 years	1,874,569	726,440	826,445	202,210	93,574	24,091	1,809
15 to 24 years	1,742,798	654,345	520,354	173,826	354,756	37,216	2,301
25 to 34 years	1,863,021	606,711	353,466	147,421	700,825	51,177	3,421
35 to 44 years	1,539,172	468,087	253,885	112,139	662,364	39,576	3,121
45 to 54 years	1,148,173	344,434	229,224	71,193	481,830	19,693	1,799
55 to 64 years	702,142	231,032	145,725	33,226	284,030	7,223	906
65 years and over	493,097	213,428	58,154	17,812	198,995	4,366	342
Age unknown	11,965	6,264	1,231	365	3,652	415	38
All ages, per cent	100.0	100.0	100.0	100.0	100.0	100.0	100.0
Under 5 years	9.7	11.4	16.0	13.2	0.2	7.4	6.7
5 to 14 years	18.1	19.8	29.1	23.1	3.4	12.1	12.3
15 to 24 years	16.8	17.8	18.3	19.9	12.7	18.8	15.6
25 to 34 years	17.9	16.5	12.4	16.9	25.2	25.8	23.2
35 to 44 years	14.8	12.8	8.9	12.8	23.8	19.9	21.2
45 to 54 years	11.1	9.4	8.1	8.1	17.3	9.9	12.2
55 to 64 years	6.8	6.3	5.1	3.8	10.2	3.6	6.2
65 years and over	4.7	5.8	2.0	2.0	7.1	2.2	2.3

New Jersey.

All ages, number	3,155,900	1,212,675	829,058	256,741	738,613	117,132	1,681
Under 5 years	338,696	141,675	149,304	36,152	1,350	10,171	44
5 to 14 years	614,194	248,145	255,172	65,781	25,184	19,838	74
15 to 24 years	526,203	215,060	151,204	54,905	83,757	21,052	225
25 to 34 years	550,350	196,119	101,509	41,850	187,740	22,729	403
35 to 44 years	458,374	154,828	69,716	28,810	183,811	20,802	407
45 to 54 years	337,239	115,527	58,003	17,294	132,490	13,579	346
55 to 64 years	194,802	74,687	32,685	7,833	74,091	5,366	140
65 years and over	133,481	65,100	11,243	4,048	49,664	3,391	35
Age unknown	2,561	1,534	222	68	526	204	7
All ages, per cent	100.0	100.0	100.0	100.0	100.0	100.0	100.0
Under 5 years	10.7	11.7	18.0	14.1	0.2	8.7	2.6
5 to 14 years	19.5	20.5	30.8	25.6	3.4	16.9	4.4
15 to 24 years	16.7	17.7	18.2	21.4	11.3	18.0	13.4
25 to 34 years	17.4	16.2	12.2	16.3	25.4	19.4	24.0
35 to 44 years	14.5	12.8	8.4	11.2	24.9	17.8	24.2
45 to 54 years	10.7	9.5	7.0	6.7	17.9	11.6	20.6
55 to 64 years	6.2	6.2	3.9	3.1	10.0	4.6	8.3
65 years and over	4.2	5.4	1.4	1.6	6.7	2.9	2.1

TABLE 49.—DISTRIBUTION OF POPULATION CLASSES BY BROAD AGE GROUPS, BY DIVISIONS AND STATES: 1920—Continued.

AGE.	All classes.	NATIVE WHITE.			Foreign-born white.	Negro.	Indian, Chinese, Japanese, and all other.
		Native parentage.	Foreign parentage.	Mixed parentage.			
MIDDLE ATLANTIC—Con.							
Pennsylvania.							
All ages, number......	8,720,017	4,750,071	1,724,810	569,995	1,387,850	284,568	2,723
Under 5 years............	1,005,465	571,377	329,352	79,792	2,412	22,409	123
5 to 14 years.............	1,796,971	1,022,610	548,362	137,335	45,209	43,287	168
15 to 24 years............	1,472,582	854,423	301,922	109,458	150,665	55,618	496
25 to 34 years............	1,421,339	728,062	186,866	85,344	359,021	61,479	567
35 to 44 years............	1,191,033	588,551	127,673	68,300	353,124	52,859	526
45 to 54 years............	890,795	447,018	117,812	48,319	246,178	30,934	534
55 to 64 years............	539,906	291,914	76,630	25,682	134,638	10,785	257
65 years and over.......	394,303	241,940	35,580	15,557	94,591	6,590	45
Age unknown.............	7,623	4,176	613	208	2,012	607	7
All ages, per cent......	100.0	100.0	100.0	100.0	100.0	100.0	100.0
Under 5 years............	11.5	12.0	19.1	14.0	0.2	7.9	4.5
5 to 14 years.............	20.6	21.5	31.8	24.1	3.3	15.2	6.2
15 to 24 years............	16.9	18.0	17.5	19.2	10.9	19.5	18.2
25 to 34 years............	16.3	15.3	10.8	15.0	25.9	21.6	20.8
35 to 44 years............	13.7	12.4	7.4	12.0	25.4	18.6	19.3
45 to 54 years............	10.2	9.4	6.8	8.5	17.7	10.9	19.6
55 to 64 years............	6.2	6.1	4.4	4.5	9.7	3.8	9.4
65 years and over.......	4.5	5.1	2.1	2.7	6.8	2.3	1.7
EAST NORTH CENTRAL.							
Ohio.							
All ages, number......	5,759,394	3,669,122	838,251	385,823	678,697	186,187	1,314
Under 5 years............	586,136	418,294	117,586	34,743	1,238	14,227	48
5 to 14 years.............	1,057,131	751,431	186,485	68,134	23,499	27,542	40
15 to 24 years............	965,313	672,593	115,946	69,073	72,741	34,711	249
25 to 34 years............	990,126	599,325	110,760	67,630	171,229	40,813	369
35 to 44 hears............	819,078	465,297	97,844	61,632	161,066	32,961	278
45 to 54 years............	614,798	339,485	99,357	45,771	109,416	20,576	193
55 to 64 years............	403,463	225,002	74,584	24,266	70,791	8,710	110
65 years and over.......	319,437	194,932	35,464	14,470	68,250	6,295	26
Age unknown.............	3,912	2,763	225	104	467	352	1
All ages, per cent......	100.0	100.0	100.0	100.0	100.0	100.0	100.0
Under 5 years............	10.2	11.4	14.0	9.0	0.2	7.6	3.7
5 to 14 years.............	18.4	20.5	22.2	17.7	3.5	14.8	3.0
15 to 24 years............	16.8	18.3	13.8	17.9	10.7	18.6	18.9
25 to 34 years............	17.2	16.3	13.2	17.5	25.2	21.9	28.1
35 to 44 years............	14.2	12.7	11.7	16.0	23.7	17.7	21.2
45 to 54 years............	10.7	9.3	11.9	11.9	16.1	11.1	14.7
55 to 64 years............	7.0	6.1	8.9	6.3	10.4	4.7	8.4
65 years and over.......	5.5	5.3	4.2	3.8	10.1	3.4	2.0
Indiana.							
All ages, number......	2,930,390	2,329,544	227,066	141,593	150,868	80,810	509
Under 5 years............	289,195	251,471	22,221	9,339	216	5,922	26
5 to 14 years.............	559,381	483,095	37,954	20,912	4,498	12,901	21
15 to 24 years............	497,329	420,420	26,008	23,275	12,574	14,981	71
25 to 34 years............	459,385	357,509	28,774	24,734	32,063	16,199	106
35 to 44 years............	394,314	290,637	30,902	25,179	33,640	13,833	123
45 to 54 years...........	318,838	227,731	36,528	19,855	25,348	9,274	102
55 to 64 years...........	224,423	160,064	29,998	11,443	18,587	4,293	38
65 years and over.......	183,695	135,730	14,533	6,788	23,472	3,145	18
Age unknown.............	3,830	2,878	148	69	470	262	4
All ages, per cent......	100.0	100.0	100.0	100.0	100.0	100.0	100.0
Under 5 years............	9.9	10.8	9.8	6.6	0.1	7.3	5.1
5 to 14 years.............	19.1	20.7	16.7	14.8	3.0	16.0	4.1
15 to 24 years............	17.0	18.0	11.5	16.4	8.3	18.5	13.9
25 to 34 years............	15.7	15.3	12.7	17.5	21.3	20.0	20.8
35 to 44 years............	13.5	12.5	13.6	17.8	22.3	17.1	24.2
45 to 54 years............	10.9	9.8	16.1	14.0	16.8	11.5	20.0
55 to 64 years............	7.7	6.9	13.2	8.1	12.3	5.3	7.5
65 years and over.......	6.3	5.8	6.4	4.8	15.6	3.9	3.5

TABLE **49.**—DISTRIBUTION OF POPULATION CLASSES BY BROAD AGE GROUPS, BY DIVISIONS AND STATES: 1920—Continued.

AGE.	All classes.	NATIVE WHITE.			Foreign-born white.	Negro.	Indian, Chinese, Japanese, and all other.
		Native parentage.	Foreign parentage.	Mixed parentage.			
EAST NORTH CENTRAL— Continued.							
Illinois.							
All ages, number	6,485,280	3,066,563	1,467,036	558,783	1,206,951	182,274	3,673
Under 5 years	655,073	394,165	183,903	62,919	1,629	12,333	124
5 to 14 years	1,240,594	702,900	346,259	129,769	36,219	25,252	195
15 to 24 years	1,101,668	571,322	265,913	119,508	111,856	32,544	525
25 to 34 years	1,154,990	486,616	246,524	99,919	278,759	42,334	838
35 to 44 years	923,362	357,692	170,212	73,173	285,445	35,933	907
45 to 54 years	679,499	251,694	140,968	43,933	221,558	20,643	703
55 to 64 years	423,523	162,607	84,067	19,424	149,415	7,711	299
65 years and over	297,647	134,267	28,297	9,834	120,145	5,037	67
Age unknown	8,924	5,300	893	304	1,925	487	15
All ages, per cent	100.0	100.0	100.0	100.0	100.0	100.0	100.0
Under 5 years	10.1	12.9	12.5	11.3	0.1	6.8	3.4
5 to 14 years	19.1	22.9	23.6	23.2	3.0	13.9	5.3
15 to 24 years	17.0	18.6	18.1	21.4	9.3	17.9	14.3
25 to 34 years	17.8	15.9	16.8	17.9	23.1	23.2	22.8
35 to 44 years	14.2	11.7	11.6	13.1	23.7	19.7	24.7
45 to 54 years	10.5	8.2	9.6	7.9	18.4	11.3	19.1
55 to 64 years	6.5	5.3	5.7	3.5	12.4	4.2	8.1
65 years and over	4.6	4.4	1.9	1.8	10.0	2.8	1.8
Michigan.							
All ages, number	3,668,412	1,670,447	775,288	429,257	726,635	60,082	6,703
Under 5 years	404,586	234,339	107,586	54,881	2,894	4,141	745
5 to 14 years	694,673	374,635	175,108	107,754	28,746	7,084	1,346
15 to 24 years	611,807	297,181	139,145	89,135	72,505	12,704	1,137
25 to 34 years	656,704	262,829	135,848	69,827	170,458	16,676	1,066
35 to 44 years	501,772	188,424	92,124	49,655	159,988	10,732	849
45 to 54 years	360,950	134,740	67,907	31,435	120,858	5,364	646
55 to 64 years	243,216	92,443	40,394	16,628	91,316	1,954	481
65 years and over	190,972	83,588	16,818	9,790	79,067	1,290	419
Age unknown	3,732	2,268	358	152	803	137	14
All ages, per cent	100.0	100.0	100.0	100.0	100.0	100.0	100.0
Under 5 years	11.0	14.0	13.9	12.8	0.4	6.9	11.1
5 to 14 years	18.9	22.4	22.6	25.1	4.0	11.8	20.1
15 to 24 years	16.7	17.8	17.9	20.8	10.0	21.1	17.0
25 to 34 years	17.9	15.7	17.5	16.3	23.5	27.8	15.9
35 to 44 years	13.7	11.3	11.9	11.6	22.0	17.9	12.7
45 to 54 years	9.8	8.1	8.8	7.3	16.6	8.9	9.6
55 to 64 years	6.6	5.5	5.2	3.9	12.6	3.3	7.2
65 years and over	5.2	5.0	2.2	2.3	10.9	2.1	6.3
Wisconsin.							
All ages, number	2,632,067	1,054,694	736,051	366,065	460,128	5,201	9,928
Under 5 years	285,042	192,756	49,851	40,221	491	368	1,355
5 to 14 years	537,165	308,743	118,803	95,383	11,037	750	2,449
15 to 24 years	466,516	214,969	132,371	88,481	28,126	918	1,651
25 to 34 years	423,609	144,981	140,896	65,220	70,083	1,244	1,185
35 to 44 years	335,208	84,200	114,291	43,061	91,597	965	1,094
45 to 54 years	256,774	47,053	97,228	21,357	89,671	565	900
55 to 64 years	184,492	31,906	61,782	8,491	81,457	212	644
65 years and over	140,406	28,345	20,425	3,706	87,129	160	641
Age unknown	2,855	1,741	404	145	537	19	9
All ages, per cent	100.0	100.0	100.0	100.0	100.0	100.0	100.0
Under 5 years	10.8	18.3	6.8	11.0	0.1	7.1	13.6
5 to 14 years	20.4	29.3	16.1	26.1	2.4	14.4	24.7
15 to 24 years	17.7	20.4	18.0	24.2	6.1	17.7	16.6
25 to 34 years	16.1	13.7	19.1	17.8	15.2	23.9	11.9
35 to 44 years	12.7	8.0	15.5	11.8	19.9	18.6	11.0
45 to 54 years	9.8	4.5	13.2	5.8	19.5	10.9	9.1
55 to 64 years	7.0	3.0	8.4	2.3	17.7	4.1	6.5
65 years and over	5.3	2.7	2.8	1.0	18.9	3.1	6.5

TABLE **49.**—DISTRIBUTION OF POPULATION CLASSES BY BROAD AGE GROUPS, BY DIVISIONS AND STATES: 1920—Continued.

AGE.	All classes.	NATIVE WHITE.			Foreign-born white.	Negro.	Indian, Chinese, Japanese, and all other.
		Native parentage.	Foreign parentage.	Mixed parentage.			
WEST NORTH CENTRAL.							
Minnesota.							
All ages, number	2,387,125	827,627	708,126	347,019	486,164	8,809	9,380
Under 5 years	261,394	160,041	51,576	47,122	748	522	1,385
5 to 14 years	482,560	234,977	131,998	102,679	9,622	1,003	2,281
15 to 24 years	437,528	159,112	159,511	88,131	27,915	1,289	1,570
25 to 34 years	403,424	111,469	153,942	55,646	79,091	2,039	1,237
35 to 44 years	303,893	67,698	99,945	30,204	103,080	2,004	962
45 to 54 years	227,643	42,795	67,427	14,453	100,944	1,211	813
55 to 64 years	157,264	28,140	34,271	6,026	87,821	467	539
65 years and over	110,766	21,812	9,084	2,630	76,418	257	565
Age unknown	2,653	1,583	372	128	525	17	28
All ages, per cent	100.0	100.0	100.0	100.0	100.0	100.0	100.0
Under 5 years	11.0	19.3	7.3	13.6	0.2	5.9	14.8
5 to 14 years	20.2	28.4	18.6	29.6	2.0	11.4	24.3
15 to 24 years	18.3	19.2	22.5	25.4	5.7	14.6	16.7
25 to 34 years	16.9	13.5	21.7	16.0	16.3	23.1	13.2
35 to 44 years	12.7	8.2	14.1	8.7	21.2	22.7	10.3
45 to 54 years	9.5	5.2	9.5	4.2	20.8	13.7	8.7
55 to 64 years	6.6	3.4	4.8	1.7	18.1	5.3	5.7
65 years and over	4.6	2.6	1.3	0.8	15.7	2.9	6.0
Iowa.							
All ages, number	2,404,021	1,528,553	376,710	253,271	225,647	19,005	835
Under 5 years	250,887	208,256	18,207	22,425	379	1,550	70
5 to 14 years	467,780	361,802	43,493	54,499	4,820	3,045	121
15 to 24 years	425,863	290,632	61,126	57,953	12,671	3,304	177
25 to 34 years	385,334	226,884	76,137	47,009	31,360	3,746	198
35 to 44 years	308,278	162,551	68,185	34,439	39,827	3,166	110
45 to 54 years	246,734	119,772	59,716	20,944	43,957	2,250	95
55 to 64 years	171,316	82,348	36,492	10,015	41,352	1,074	35
65 years and over	144,392	73,626	13,082	5,870	51,012	780	22
Age unknown	3,437	2,682	272	117	269	90	7
All ages, per cent	100.0	100.0	100.0	100.0	100.0	100.0	100.0
Under 5 years	10.4	13.6	4.8	8.9	0.2	8.2	8.4
5 to 14 years	19.5	23.7	11.5	21.5	2.1	16.0	14.5
15 to 24 years	17.7	19.0	16.2	22.9	5.6	17.4	21.2
25 to 34 years	16.0	14.8	20.2	18.6	13.9	19.7	23.7
35 to 44 years	12.8	10.6	18.1	13.6	17.7	16.7	13.2
45 to 54 years	10.3	7.8	15.9	8.3	19.5	11.8	11.4
55 to 64 years	7.1	5.4	9.7	4.0	18.3	5.7	4.2
65 years and over	6.0	4.8	3.5	2.3	22.6	4.1	2.6
Missouri.							
All ages, number	3,404,055	2,536,936	300,064	202,018	186,026	178,241	770
Under 5 years	327,909	288,529	16,433	10,646	308	11,956	37
5 to 14 years	673,496	575,020	36,905	29,301	4,601	27,618	51
15 to 24 years	598,886	477,512	35,939	38,859	14,986	31,476	114
25 to 34 years	545,417	390,766	45,557	43,165	29,356	36,417	156
35 to 44 years	465,750	306,089	51,989	38,342	37,099	32,080	151
45 to 54 years	365,590	225,674	57,877	25,241	35,513	21,133	152
55 to 64 years	237,294	147,451	39,937	10,779	29,426	9,620	81
65 years and over	185,502	122,907	15,232	5,562	34,507	7,269	25
Age unknown	4,211	2,988	195	123	230	672	3
All ages, per cent	100.0	100.0	100.0	100.0	100.0	100.0	100.0
Under 5 years	9.6	11.4	5.5	5.3	0.2	6.7	4.8
5 to 14 years	19.8	22.7	12.3	14.5	2.5	15.5	6.6
15 to 24 years	17.6	18.8	12.0	19.2	8.1	17.7	14.8
25 to 34 years	16.0	15.4	15.2	21.4	15.8	20.4	20.3
35 to 44 years	13.7	12.1	17.3	19.0	19.9	18.0	19.6
45 to 54 years	10.7	8.9	19.3	12.5	19.1	11.9	19.7
55 to 64 years	7.0	5.8	13.3	5.3	15.8	5.4	10.5
65 years and over	5.4	4.8	5.1	2.8	18.5	4.1	3.2

TABLE 49.—DISTRIBUTION OF POPULATION CLASSES BY BROAD AGE GROUPS, BY DIVISIONS AND STATES: 1920—Continued.

AGE.	All classes.	NATIVE WHITE.			Foreign-born white.	Negro.	Indian, Chinese, Japanese, and all other.
		Native parentage.	Foreign parentage.	Mixed parentage.			
WEST NORTH CENTRAL— Continued.							
North Dakota.							
All ages, number	646,872	207,966	203,973	96,512	131,503	467	6,451
Under 5 years	90,889	45,085	24,678	19,889	312	20	905
5 to 14 years	160,532	63,012	57,507	34,384	3,926	83	1,620
15 to 24 years	115,994	35,364	46,865	20,417	12,157	49	1,142
25 to 34 years	97,569	25,550	36,500	11,107	23,571	90	751
35 to 44 years	78,012	17,809	21,641	6,534	31,255	108	665
45 to 54 years	51,712	10,734	10,736	2,748	26,921	70	503
55 to 64 years	31,548	5,879	4,730	1,021	19,460	30	428
65 years and over	19,324	3,654	1,188	376	13,691	15	400
Age unknown	1,292	879	128	36	210	2	37
All ages, per cent	100.0	100.0	100.0	100.0	100.0	100.0	100.0
Under 5 years	14.1	21.7	12.1	20.6	0.2	4.3	14.0
5 to 14 years	24.8	30.3	28.2	35.6	3.0	17.8	25.1
15 to 24 years	17.9	17.0	23.0	21.2	9.2	10.5	17.7
25 to 34 years	15.1	12.3	17.9	11.5	17.9	19.3	11.6
35 to 44 years	12.1	8.6	10.6	6.8	23.8	23.1	10.3
45 to 54 years	8.0	5.2	5.3	2.8	20.5	15.0	7.8
55 to 64 years	4.9	2.8	2.3	1.1	14.8	6.4	6.6
65 years and over	3.0	1.8	0.6	0.4	10.4	3.2	6.2
South Dakota.							
All ages, number	636,547	308,598	141,341	86,817	82,391	832	16,568
Under 5 years	79,831	56,213	8,985	12,120	113	70	2,330
5 to 14 years	141,031	85,059	24,698	25,586	1,707	162	3,819
15 to 24 years	116,181	56,050	31,577	20,445	5,229	137	2,743
25 to 34 years	104,564	43,608	32,298	13,790	12,769	149	1,950
35 to 44 years	78,710	29,495	21,976	8,263	17,063	136	1,777
45 to 54 years	53,165	17,715	12,631	3,844	17,384	84	1,507
55 to 64 years	36,082	11,345	6,905	1,892	14,707	54	1,179
65 years and over	25,536	8,040	2,156	839	13,231	35	1,235
Age unknown	1,447	1,073	115	38	188	5	28
All ages, per cent	100.0	100.0	100.0	100.0	100.0	100.0	100.0
Under 5 years	12.5	18.2	6.4	14.0	0.1	8.4	14.1
5 to 14 years	22.2	27.6	17.5	29.5	2.1	19.5	23.1
15 to 24 years	18.3	18.2	22.3	23.5	6.3	16.5	16.6
25 to 34 years	16.4	14.1	22.9	15.9	15.5	17.9	11.8
35 to 44 years	12.4	9.6	15.5	9.5	20.7	16.3	10.7
45 to 54 years	8.4	5.7	8.9	4.4	21.1	10.1	9.1
55 to 64 years	5.7	3.7	4.9	2.2	17.9	6.5	7.1
65 years and over	4.0	2.6	1.5	1.0	16.1	4.2	7.5
Nebraska.							
All ages, number	1,296,372	757,064	231,948	140,555	149,652	13,242	3,911
Under 5 years	143,240	112,252	14,195	15,172	212	878	531
5 to 14 years	272,688	191,875	36,820	37,687	3,762	1,754	790
15 to 24 years	235,867	139,230	49,487	34,439	9,660	2,403	648
25 to 34 years	214,251	110,887	55,000	23,595	21,018	3,099	652
35 to 44 years	163,093	78,795	37,672	15,062	28,282	2,700	582
45 to 54 years	118,405	54,679	22,383	8,154	31,409	1,458	322
55 to 64 years	81,941	37,255	11,774	4,130	28,033	578	171
65 years and over	64,341	30,054	4,436	2,262	27,063	338	188
Age unknown	2,546	2,037	181	54	213	34	27
All ages, per cent	100.0	100.0	100.0	100.0	100.0	100.0	100.0
Under 5 years	11.0	14.8	6.1	10.8	0.1	6.6	13.6
5 to 14 years	21.0	25.3	15.9	26.8	2.5	13.2	20.2
15 to 24 years	18.2	18.4	21.3	24.5	6.5	18.1	16.6
25 to 34 years	16.5	14.6	23.7	16.8	14.0	23.4	16.7
35 to 44 years	12.6	10.4	16.2	10.7	18.9	20.4	14.9
45 to 54 years	9.1	7.2	9.7	5.8	21.0	11.0	8.2
55 to 64 years	6.3	4.9	5.1	2.9	18.7	4.4	4.4
65 years and over	5.0	4.0	1.9	1.6	18.1	2.6	4.8

TABLE **49.**—DISTRIBUTION OF POPULATION CLASSES BY BROAD AGE GROUPS, BY DIVISIONS AND STATES: 1920—Continued.

AGE.	All classes.	NATIVE WHITE.			Foreign-born white.	Negro.	Indian, Chinese, Japanese, and all other.
		Native parentage.	Foreign parentage.	Mixed parentage.			
WEST NORTH CENTRAL— Continued.							
Kansas.							
All ages, number......	1,769,257	1,308,804	163,964	125,560	110,578	57,925	2,426
Under 5 years...........	187,262	161,684	9,865	10,046	754	4,693	220
5 to 14 years.............	364,581	300,490	23,277	25,835	4,249	10,257	473
15 to 24 years.............	315,947	240,862	28,510	26,639	8.642	10,336	958
25 to 34 years.............	274,752	193,479	33,385	22,410	15,179	9,995	304
35 to 44 years.............	227,313	152,462	28,667	18,272	18,884	8,835	193
45 to 54 years.............	173,435	112,887	20,998	11,959	20,715	6,749	127
55 to 64 years.............	118,483	76,381	12,912	6,271	19,325	3,516	78
65 years and over.........	104,747	68,403	6,264	4,080	22,649	3,295	56
Age unknown............	2,737	2,156	86	48	181	249	17
All ages, per cent......	100.0	100.0	100.0	100.0	100.0	100.0	100.0
Under 5 years............	10.6	12.4	6.0	8.0	0.7	8.1	9.1
5 to 14 years.............	20.6	23.0	14.2	20.6	3.8	17.7	19.5
15 to 24 years.............	17.9	18.4	17.4	21.2	7.8	17.8	39.5
25 to 34 years.............	15.5	14.8	20.4	17.8	13.7	17.3	12.5
35 to 44 years.............	12.8	11.6	17.5	14.6	17.1	15.3	8.0
45 to 54 years.............	9.8	8.6	12.8	9.5	18.7	11.7	5 2
55 to 64 years.............	6.7	5.8	7.9	5.0	17.5	6.1	3.2
65 years and over.........	5.9	5.2	3.8	3.2	20.5	5.7	2.3
SOUTH ATLANTIC.							
Delaware.							
All ages, number......	223,003	139,876	23,288	9,641	19,810	30,335	53
Under 5 years............	22,929	14,687	4,150	1,271	44	2,776	1
5 to 14 years.............	41,358	26,320	6,348	2,096	621	5,971	2
15 to 24 years.............	38,528	24,581	3,872	1,750	2,396	5,926	3
25 to 34 years.............	36,291	21,952	2,767	1,534	5,311	4,717	10
35 to 44 years.............	30,403	18,228	1,949	1,251	4,670	4,291	14
45 to 54 years.............	24,055	14,450	2,091	876	3,273	3,347	18
55 to 64 years.............	16,315	10,566	1,524	517	1,905	1,800	3
65 years and over.........	12,402	8,664	580	339	1,522	1,295	2
Age unknown............	722	428	7	7	68	212	....
All ages, per cent......	100.0	100.0	100.0	100.0	100.0	100.0	(¹)
Under 5 years............	10.3	10.5	17.8	13.2	0.2	9.2	(¹)
5 to 14 years.............	18.5	18.8	27.3	21.7	3.1	19.7	(¹)
15 to 24 years.............	17.3	17.6	16.6	18.2	12.1	19.5	(¹)
25 to 34 years.............	16.3	15.7	11.9	15.9	26.8	15.5	(¹)
35 to 44 years.............	13.6	13.0	8.4	13.0	23.6	14.1	(¹)
45 to 54 years.............	10.8	10.3	9.0	9.1	16.5	11.0	(¹)
55 to 64 years.............	7.3	7.6	6.5	5.4	9.6	5.9	(¹)
65 years and over.........	5.6	6.2	2.5	3.5	7.7	4.3	(¹)
Maryland.							
All ages, number......	1,449,661	893,088	143,203	66,269	102,177	244,479	445
Under 5 years............	147,005	101,453	14,768	6,483	140	24,145	16
5 to 14 years.............	283,574	187,167	30,359	12,577	2,935	50,519	17
15 to 24 years.............	263,756	166,941	25,204	12,545	11,421	47,590	55
25 to 34 years.............	234,839	142,532	19,321	11,306	21,312	40,281	87
35 to 44 years.............	196,117	112,814	15,844	10,047	22,560	34,752	100
45 to 54 years.............	154,358	84,755	18,009	7,275	19,147	25,066	106
55 to 64 years.............	96,053	55,340	13,519	3,798	12,857	12,287	52
65 years and over.........	72,468	45,104	6,151	2,225	11,719	9,177	12
Age unknown............	1,491	702	28	10	86	662	....
All ages, per cent......	100.0	100.0	100.0	100.0	100.0	100.0	100.0
Under 5 years............	10.1	11.4	10.3	9.8	0.1	9.9	3.6
5 to 14 years.............	19.6	21.0	21.2	19.0	2.9	20.7	3.8
15 to 24 years.............	18.2	18.7	17.6	18.9	11.2	19.5	12.4
25 to 34 years.............	16.2	16.0	13.5	17.1	20.9	16.5	19.6
35 to 44 years.............	13.5	12.6	11.1	15.2	22.1	14.2	22.5
45 to 54 years.............	10.6	9.5	12.6	11.0	18.7	10.3	23.8
55 to 64 years.............	6.6	6.0	9.4	5.7	12.6	5.0	11.7
65 years and over.........	5.0	4.8	4.3	3.4	11.5	3.8	2.7

¹ Per cent not shown, base being less than 100.

TABLE **49.**—DISTRIBUTION OF POPULATION CLASSES BY BROAD AGE GROUPS, BY DIVISIONS AND STATES: 1920—Continued.

AGE.	All classes.	NATIVE WHITE.			Foreign-born white.	Negro.	Indian, Chinese, Japanese, and all other.
		Native parentage.	Foreign parentage.	Mixed parentage.			
SOUTH ATLANTIC—Con.							
District of Columbia.							
All ages, number	437,571	239,488	35,129	23,695	28,548	109,966	745
Under 5 years	30,436	18,244	2,781	1,555	52	7,774	30
5 to 14 years	59,656	33,760	5,194	3,111	720	16,842	29
15 to 24 years	84,581	48,298	6,022	4,603	3,256	22,253	149
25 to 34 years	89,921	50,352	5,800	5,166	6,574	21,857	172
35 to 44 years	71,164	35,804	5,146	4,044	6,497	19,524	149
45 to 54 years	52,190	25,976	5,442	2,857	5,158	12,639	118
55 to 64 years	27,099	14,207	3,264	1,418	3,095	5,043	72
65 years and over	20,635	11,646	1,434	901	3,073	3,566	15
Age unknown	1,889	1,201	46	40	123	468	11
All ages, per cent	100.0	100.0	100.0	100.0	100.0	100.0	100.0
Under 5 years	7.0	7.6	7.9	6.6	0.2	7.1	4.0
5 to 14 years	13.6	14.1	14.8	13.1	2.5	15.3	3.9
15 to 24 years	19.3	20.2	17.1	19.4	11.4	20.2	20.0
25 to 34 years	20.6	21.0	16.5	21.8	23.0	19.9	23.1
35 to 44 years	16.3	15.0	14.6	17.1	22.8	17.8	20.0
45 to 54 years	11.9	10.8	15.5	12.1	18.1	11.5	15.8
55 to 64 years	6.2	5.9	9.3	6.0	10.8	4.6	9.7
65 years and over	4.7	4.9	4.1	3.8	10.8	3.2	2.0
Virginia.							
All ages, number	2,309,187	1,534,494	30,514	22,116	30,785	690,017	1,261
Under 5 years	277,184	189,591	3,773	2,311	90	81,263	156
5 to 14 years	549,128	364,362	7,209	4,344	1,107	171,862	244
15 to 24 years	446,525	292,508	5,926	4,524	3,808	139,518	241
25 to 34 years	327,948	218,380	4,336	3,463	7,392	94,172	205
35 to 44 years	278,390	180,827	3,285	2,913	7,385	83,813	167
45 to 54 years	206,340	133,649	2,043	2,347	5,428	61,744	129
55 to 64 years	120,626	83,591	1,981	1,311	3,009	30,656	78
65 years and over	100,008	70,122	939	893	2,521	25,493	40
Age unknown	3,038	1,464	22	10	45	1,496	1
All ages, per cent	100.0	100.0	100.0	100.0	100.0	100.0	100.0
Under 5 years	12.0	12.4	12.4	10.4	0.3	11.8	12.4
5 to 14 years	23.8	23.7	23.6	19.6	3.6	24.9	19.3
15 to 24 years	19.3	19.1	19.4	20.5	12.4	20.2	19.1
25 to 34 years	14.2	14.2	14.2	15.7	24.0	13.6	16.3
35 to 44 years	12.1	11.8	10.8	13.2	24.0	12.1	13.2
45 to 54 years	8.9	8.7	10.0	10.6	17.6	8.9	10.2
55 to 64 years	5.2	5.4	6.5	5.9	9.8	4.4	6.2
65 years and over	4.3	4.6	3.1	4.0	8.2	3.7	3.2
West Virginia.							
All ages, number	1,463,701	1,232,857	56,625	25,847	61,906	86,345	121
Under 5 years	195,934	169,766	13,958	3,160	187	8,854	9
5 to 14 years	348,519	306,041	17,891	5,165	2,964	16,451	7
15 to 24 years	271,153	234,934	5,717	4,260	7,738	18,489	15
25 to 34 years	217,406	173,154	4,310	3,705	19,334	16,869	34
35 to 44 years	178,251	140,780	4,318	3,738	16,425	12,967	23
45 to 54 years	122,713	99,007	4,804	2,945	8,323	7,609	25
55 to 64 years	70,799	58,827	3,745	1,716	3,692	2,814	5
65 years and over	56,140	48,310	1,837	1,141	3,028	1,822	2
Age unknown	2,786	2,038	45	17	215	470	1
All ages, per cent	100.0	100.0	100.0	100.0	100.0	100.0	100.0
Under 5 years	13.4	13.8	24.6	12.2	0.3	10.3	7.4
5 to 14 years	23.8	24.8	31.6	20.0	4.8	19.1	5.8
15 to 24 years	18.5	19.1	10.1	16.5	12.5	21.4	12.4
25 to 34 years	14.9	14.0	7.6	14.3	31.2	19.5	28.1
35 to 44 years	12.2	11.4	7.6	14.5	26.5	15.0	19.0
45 to 54 years	8.4	8.0	8.5	11.4	13.4	8.8	20.7
55 to 64 years	4.8	4.8	6.6	6.6	6.0	3.3	4.1
65 years and over	3.8	3.9	3.2	4.4	4.9	2.1	1.7

TABLE **49.**—DISTRIBUTION OF POPULATION CLASSES BY BROAD AGE GROUPS, BY DIVISIONS AND STATES: 1920—Continued.

AGE.	All classes.	NATIVE WHITE.			Foreign-born white.	Negro.	Indian, Chinese, Japanese, and all other.
		Native parentage.	Foreign parentage.	Mixed parentage.			
SOUTH ATLANTIC—Con.							
North Carolina.							
All ages, number	2,559,123	1,765,203	5,737	5,740	7,099	763,407	11,937
Under 5 years	358,808	248,913	694	652	35	106,460	2,054
5 to 14 years	674,499	455,760	1,332	1,191	227	212,451	3,538
15 to 24 years	500,219	333,715	1,015	1,040	810	161,417	2,222
25 to 34 years	339,253	240,101	868	916	1,687	94,309	1,372
35 to 44 years	273,279	191,780	651	731	1,642	77,346	1,129
45 to 54 years	191,441	132,307	618	581	1,283	55,897	755
55 to 64 years	119,699	88,405	348	354	786	29,334	472
65 years and over	98,716	72,580	208	271	616	24,656	385
Age unknown	3,209	1,642	3	4	13	1,537	10
All ages, per cent	100.0	100.0	100.0	100.0	100.0	100.0	100.0
Under 5 years	14.0	14.1	12.1	11.4	0.5	13.9	17.2
5 to 14 years	26.4	25.8	23.2	20.7	3.2	27.8	29.6
15 to 24 years	19.5	18.9	17.7	18.1	11.4	21.1	18.6
25 to 34 years	13.3	13.6	15.1	16.0	23.8	12.4	11.5
35 to 44 years	10.7	10.9	11.3	12.7	23.1	10.1	9.5
45 to 54 years	7.5	7.5	10.8	10.1	18.1	7.3	6.3
55 to 64 years	4.7	5.0	6.1	6.2	11.1	3.8	4.0
65 years and over	3.9	4.1	3.6	4.7	8.7	3.2	3.2
South Carolina.							
All ages, number	1,683,724	799,418	7,025	5,694	6,401	864,719	467
Under 5 years	228,581	109,781	633	565	13	117,526	63
5 to 14 years	458,867	204,726	1,108	1,005	169	251,763	96
15 to 24 years	342,965	154,618	1,308	1,093	820	185,041	85
25 to 34 years	225,339	114,160	1,014	1,022	1,587	107,487	69
35 to 44 years	183,874	91,928	947	834	1,365	88,750	50
45 to 54 years	122,399	58,884	1,027	591	1,115	60,724	58
55 to 64 years	66,988	36,038	682	325	651	29,264	28
65 years and over	53,375	28,792	304	257	668	23,336	18
Age unknown	1,336	491	2	2	13	828	....
All ages, per cent	100.0	100.0	100.0	100.0	100.0	100.0	100.0
Under 5 years	13.6	13.7	9.0	9.9	0.2	13.6	13.5
5 to 14 years	27.3	25.6	15.8	17.7	2.6	29.1	20.6
15 to 24 years	20.4	19.3	18.6	19.2	12.8	21.4	18.2
25 to 34 years	13.4	14.3	14.4	17.9	24.8	12.4	14.8
35 to 44 years	10.9	11.5	13.5	14.6	21.3	10.3	10.7
45 to 54 years	7.3	7.4	14.6	10.4	17.4	7.0	12.4
55 to 64 years	4.0	4.5	9.7	5.7	10.2	3.4	6.0
65 years and over	3.2	3.6	4.3	4.5	10.4	2.7	3.9
Georgia.							
All ages, number	2,895,832	1,642,697	16,371	13,860	16,186	1,206,365	353
Under 5 years	363,229	215,192	1,453	1,183	36	145,332	33
5 to 14 years	747,685	416,892	3,351	2,345	443	324,610	44
15 to 24 years	580,363	316,293	2,951	2,438	1,954	256,681	46
25 to 34 years	411,122	237,663	2,658	2,465	3,743	164,530	63
35 to 44 years	325,977	188,833	2,038	2,209	3,686	129,160	51
45 to 54 years	232,024	125,020	1,994	1,604	2,920	100,417	69
55 to 64 years	130,381	78,581	1,283	975	1,874	47,629	39
65 years and over	102,111	63,099	642	640	1,515	36,207	8
Age unknown	2,940	1,124	1	1	15	1,799	....
All ages, per cent	100.0	100.0	100.0	100.0	100.0	100.0	100.0
Under 5 years	12.5	13.1	9.0	8.5	0.2	12.0	9.3
5 to 14 years	25.8	25.4	20.5	16.9	2.7	26.9	12.5
15 to 24 years	20.0	19.3	18.0	17.6	12.1	21.3	13.0
25 to 34 years	14.2	14.5	16.2	17.8	23.1	13.6	17.8
35 to 44 years	11.3	11.5	12.4	15.9	22.8	10.7	14.4
45 to 54 years	8.0	7.6	12.2	11.6	18.0	8.3	19.5
55 to 64 years	4.5	4.8	7.8	7.0	11.6	3.9	11.0
65 years and over	3.5	3.8	3.9	4.6	9.4	3.0	2.3

TABLE 49.—DISTRIBUTION OF POPULATION CLASSES BY BROAD AGE GROUPS, BY DIVISIONS AND STATES: 1920—Continued.

AGE.	All classes.	NATIVE WHITE.			Foreign-born white.	Negro.	Indian, Chinese, Japanese, and all other.
		Native parentage.	Foreign parentage.	Mixed parentage.			
SOUTH ATLANTIC—Con.							
Florida.							
All ages, number......	968,470	532,295	35,751	27,099	43,008	329,487	830
Under 5 years............	105,263	63,678	4,669	3,303	260	33,264	89
5 to 14 years............	217,731	124,586	9,842	6,325	1,922	74,890	166
15 to 24 years............	178,456	95,403	5,939	4,879	4,777	67,304	154
25 to 34 years............	149,090	78,441	4,496	4,044	8,636	53,337	136
35 to 44 years............	127,768	65,014	3,600	3,258	9,658	46,120	118
45 to 54 years............	94,495	48,005	3,347	2,523	8,261	32,263	96
55 to 64 years............	52,290	30,867	2,483	1,592	5,120	12,187	41
65 years and over........	40,664	25,396	1,348	1,147	4,226	8,520	27
Age unknown............	2,713	905	27	28	148	1,602	3
All ages, per cent......	100.0	100.0	100.0	100.0	100.0	100.0	100.0
Under 5 years............	10.9	12.0	13.1	12.2	0.6	10.1	10.7
5 to 14 years............	22.5	23.4	27.5	23.3	4.5	22.7	20.0
15 to 24 years............	18.4	17.9	16.6	18.0	11.1	20.4	18.6
25 to 34 years............	15.4	14.7	12.6	14.9	20.1	16.2	16.4
35 to 44 years............	13.2	12.2	10.1	12.0	22.5	14.0	14.2
45 to 54 years............	9.8	9.0	9.4	9.3	19.2	9.8	11.6
55 to 64 years............	5.4	5.8	6.9	5.9	11.9	3.7	4.9
65 years and over........	4.2	4.8	3.8	4.2	9.8	2.6	3.3
EAST SOUTH CENTRAL.							
Kentucky.							
All ages, number......	2,416,630	2,039,134	65,931	44,715	30,780	235,938	132
Under 5 years............	291,625	266,945	2,070	2,098	30	20,468	14
5 to 14 years............	558,808	502,132	4,654	5,657	518	45,828	19
15 to 24 years............	445,862	385,852	6,122	7,870	1,883	44,118	17
25 to 34 years............	347,062	286,527	8,532	9,273	4,513	38,186	31
35 to 44 years............	289,810	229,509	11,996	8,974	5,392	33,917	22
45 to 54 years............	225,894	171,182	15,607	6,347	5,625	27,120	13
55 to 64 years............	141,879	107,268	12,303	2,948	5,135	14,213	12
65 years and over........	113,772	88,412	4,586	1,528	7,646	11,596	4
Age unknown............	1,918	1,307	61	20	38	492	....
All ages, per cent......	100.0	100.0	100.0	100.0	100.0	100.0	100.0
Under 5 years............	12.1	13.1	3.1	4.7	0.1	8.7	10.6
5 to 14 years............	23.1	24.6	7.1	12.7	1.7	19.4	14.4
15 to 24 years............	18.4	18.9	9.3	17.6	6.1	18.7	12.9
25 to 34 years............	14.4	14.1	12.9	20.7	14.7	16.2	23.5
35 to 44 years............	12.0	11.3	18.2	20.1	17.5	14.4	16.7
45 to 54 years............	9.3	8.4	23.7	14.2	18.3	11.5	9.8
55 to 64 years............	5.9	5.3	18.7	6.6	16.7	6.0	9.1
65 years and over........	4.7	4.3	7.0	3.4	24.8	4.9	3.0
Tennessee.							
All ages, number......	2,337,885	1,832,757	20,423	17,335	15,478	451,758	134
Under 5 years............	280,739	232,474	1,425	1,135	45	45,653	7
5 to 14 years............	562,821	452,394	3,217	2,668	429	104,103	10
15 to 24 years............	445,443	345,774	2,617	3,000	1,348	92,684	20
25 to 34 years............	335,058	257,983	2,812	3,120	2,581	68,534	28
35 to 44 years............	276,135	210,152	3,278	3,174	3,215	56,285	31
45 to 54 years............	210,131	157,025	3,597	2,290	2,940	44,259	20
55 to 64 years............	124,215	90,384	2,357	1,168	2,238	22,060	8
65 years and over........	101,189	79,371	1,106	769	2,661	17,275	7
Age unknown............	2,154	1,200	14	11	21	905	3
All ages, per cent......	100.0	100.0	100.0	100.0	100.0	100.0	100.0
Under 5 years............	12.0	12.7	7.0	6.5	0.3	10.1	5.2
5 to 14 years............	24.1	24.7	15.8	15.4	2.8	23.0	7.5
15 to 24 years............	19.1	18.9	12.8	17.3	8.7	20.5	14.9
25 to 34 years............	14.3	14.1	13.8	18.0	16.7	15.2	20.9
35 to 44 years............	11.8	11.5	16.1	18.3	20.8	12.5	23.1
45 to 54 years............	9.0	8.6	17.6	13.2	19.0	9.8	14.9
55 to 64 years............	5.3	5.3	11.5	6.7	14.5	4.9	6.0
65 years and over........	4.3	4.3	5.4	4.4	17.2	3.8	5.2

TABLE **49.**—DISTRIBUTION OF POPULATION CLASSES BY BROAD AGE GROUPS, BY DIVISIONS AND STATES: 1920—Continued.

AGE.	All classes.	NATIVE WHITE. Native parentage.	Foreign parentage.	Mixed parentage.	Foreign-born white.	Negro.	Indian, Chinese, Japanese, and all other.
EAST SOUTH CENTRAL— Continued.							
Alabama.							
All ages, number	2,348,174	1,394,129	19,591	15,650	17,662	900,652	490
Under 5 years	299,522	191,569	2,163	1,494	64	104,155	77
5 to 14 years	617,643	368,145	4,749	3,206	640	240,761	142
15 to 24 years	456,268	265,343	3,225	2,850	1,695	183,092	63
25 to 34 years	325,332	196,632	2,617	2,566	3,235	120,211	71
35 to 44 years	261,647	153,641	2,262	2,244	4,100	99,347	53
45 to 54 years	196,974	103,918	2,207	1,679	3,448	85,683	39
55 to 64 years	104,583	63,658	1,621	918	2,416	35,948	22
65 years and over	83,498	50,470	739	685	2,037	29,545	22
Age unknown	2,707	753	8	8	27	1,910	1
All ages, per cent	100.0	100.0	100.0	100.0	100.0	100.0	100.0
Under 5 years	12.8	13.7	11.0	9.5	0.4	11.6	15.7
5 to 14 years	26.3	26.4	24.2	20.5	3.6	26.7	29.0
15 to 24 years	19.4	19.0	16.5	18.2	9.6	20.3	12.9
25 to 34 years	13.9	14.1	13.4	16.4	18.3	13.3	14.5
35 to 44 years	11.1	11.0	11.5	14.3	23.2	11.0	10.8
45 to 54 years	8.4	7.5	11.3	10.7	19.5	9.5	8.0
55 to 64 years	4.5	4.6	8.3	5.9	13.7	4.0	4.5
65 years and over	3.6	3.6	3.8	4.4	11.5	3.3	4.5
Mississippi.							
All ages, number	1,790,618	826,762	9,539	9,642	8,019	935,184	1,472
Under 5 years	216,248	106,856	1,086	723	24	107,394	165
5 to 14 years	471,724	216,472	2,093	1,523	267	251,024	340
15 to 24 years	355,053	158,362	1,229	1,508	798	192,865	291
25 to 34 years	245,335	114,198	937	1,568	1,514	126,922	196
35 to 44 years	206,586	94,371	1,271	1,698	1,665	107,418	163
45 to 54 years	144,839	62,648	1,352	1,300	1,510	77,877	152
55 to 64 years	80,856	39,385	994	741	1,041	38,596	99
65 years and over	66,708	33,125	559	572	1,186	31,204	62
Age unknown	3,269	1,345	13	9	14	1,884	4
All ages, per cent	100.0	100.0	100.0	100.0	100.0	100.0	100.0
Under 5 years	12.1	12.9	11.4	7.5	0.3	11.5	11.2
5 to 14 years	26.3	26.2	22.0	15.8	3.3	26.8	23.1
15 to 24 years	19.8	19.2	12.9	15.6	10.0	20.6	19.8
25 to 34 years	13.7	13.8	9.8	16.3	18.9	13.6	13.3
35 to 44 years	11.5	11.4	13.3	17.6	20.8	11.5	11.1
45 to 54 years	8.1	7.6	14.2	13.5	18.8	8.3	10.3
55 to 64 years	4.5	4.8	10.4	7.7	13.0	4.1	6.7
65 years and over	3.7	4.0	5.9	5.9	14.8	3.3	4.2
WEST SOUTH CENTRAL.							
Arkansas.							
All ages, number	1,752,204	1,226,692	19,030	20,060	13,975	472,220	227
Under 5 years	220,811	166,833	1,118	1,533	36	51,274	17
5 to 14 years	449,959	325,703	3,059	3,889	299	116,977	32
15 to 24 years	335,858	228,787	3,348	3,723	1,024	98,932	44
25 to 34 years	248,877	170,866	3,249	3,247	1,953	69,526	36
35 to 44 years	201,480	135,823	2,825	2,999	2,796	57,001	36
45 to 54 years	150,071	96,103	2,669	2,426	3,088	46,354	31
55 to 64 years	80,772	56,836	1,810	1,347	2,455	18,279	25
65 years and over	62,092	44,801	917	878	2,008	10,092	6
Age unknown	1,684	780	15	18	16	855	....
All ages, per cent	100.0	100.0	100.0	100.0	100.0	100.0	100.0
Under 5 years	12.6	13.6	5.9	7.6	0.3	10.9	7.5
5 to 14 years	25.7	26.6	16.1	19.4	2.1	24.8	14.1
15 to 24 years	19.2	18.7	17.6	18.6	7.3	21.0	19.4
25 to 34 years	14.2	13.9	17.1	16.2	14.0	14.7	15.9
35 to 44 years	11.5	11.1	14.8	15.0	20.0	12.1	15.9
45 to 54 years	8.6	7.8	14.0	12.1	22.1	9.8	13.7
55 to 64 years	4.6	4.6	9.6	6.7	17.6	3.9	11.0
65 years and over	3.5	3.7	4.8	4.4	16.5	2.8	2.6

TABLE 49.—DISTRIBUTION OF POPULATION CLASSES BY BROAD AGE GROUPS, BY DIVISIONS AND STATES: 1920—Continued.

AGE.	All classes.	NATIVE WHITE.			Foreign-born white.	Negro.	Indian, Chinese, Japanese, and all other.
		Native parentage.	Foreign parentage.	Mixed parentage.			
WEST SOUTH CENTRAL—Continued.							
Louisiana.							
All ages, number	1,798,509	941,724	67,016	43,000	44,871	700,257	1,641
Under 5 years	209,213	122,771	5,422	3,366	186	77,296	172
5 to 14 years	442,457	245,775	14,182	6,993	1,259	173,871	377
15 to 24 years	359,592	193,141	9,850	7,067	4,808	144,447	279
25 to 34 years	271,829	142,879	7,153	7,626	8,510	105,433	228
35 to 44 years	221,598	107,067	8,721	7,920	9,558	88,117	215
45 to 54 years	151,922	66,247	10,933	5,773	8,323	60,460	186
55 to 64 years	78,130	35,514	7,427	2,671	5,692	26,718	108
65 years and over	59,443	26,315	3,273	1,541	6,439	21,801	74
Age unknown	4,325	2,015	55	43	96	2,114	2
All ages, per cent	100.0	100.0	100.0	100.0	100.0	100.0	100.0
Under 5 years	11.6	13.0	8.1	7.8	0.4	11.0	10.5
5 to 14 years	24.6	26.1	21.2	16.3	2.8	24.8	23.0
15 to 24 years	20.0	20.5	14.7	16.4	10.7	20.6	17.0
25 to 34 years	15.1	15.2	10.7	17.7	19.0	15.1	13.9
35 to 44 years	12.3	11.4	13.0	18.4	21.3	12.6	13.1
45 to 54 years	8.4	7.0	16.3	13.4	18.5	8.6	11.3
55 to 64 years	4.3	3.8	11.1	6.2	12.7	3.8	6.6
65 years and over	3.3	2.8	4.9	3.6	14.4	3.1	4.5
Oklahoma.							
All ages, number	2,028,283	1,679,107	53,083	49,036	39,968	149,408	57,681
Under 5 years	252,578	219,711	3,844	3,940	303	16,214	8,566
5 to 14 years	509,191	433,952	9,197	9,798	1,516	37,342	17,386
15 to 24 years	392,325	326,276	9,861	9,489	4,406	31,065	11,228
25 to 34 years	304,685	250,413	9,635	8,386	7,087	22,163	7,001
35 to 44 years	238,537	191,143	7,877	7,464	7,934	18,501	5,618
45 to 54 years	167,858	131,112	6,388	5,377	7,780	13,449	3,752
55 to 64 years	95,056	74,105	4,314	2,868	5,782	5,939	2,048
65 years and over	64,772	49,983	1,933	1,684	4,944	4,338	1,890
Age unknown	3,281	2,412	34	30	216	397	192
All ages, per cent	100.0	100.0	100.0	100.0	100.0	100.0	100.0
Under 5 years	12.5	13.1	7.2	8.0	0.8	10.9	14.9
5 to 14 years	25.1	25.8	17.3	20.0	3.8	25.0	30.1
15 to 24 years	19.3	19.4	18.6	19.4	11.0	20.8	19.5
25 to 34 years	15.0	14.9	18.2	17.1	17.7	14.8	12.1
35 to 44 years	11.8	11.4	14.8	15.2	19.9	12.4	9.7
45 to 54 years	8.3	7.8	12.0	11.0	19.5	9.0	6.5
55 to 64 years	4.7	4.4	8.1	5.8	14.5	4.0	3.6
65 years and over	3.2	3.0	3.6	3.4	12.4	2.9	3.3
Texas.							
All ages, number	4,663,228	3,112,262	276,670	168,714	360,519	741,694	3,369
Under 5 years	533,907	385,555	39,611	22,830	7,719	77,798	394
5 to 14 years	1,117,806	776,908	65,200	47,312	46,367	181,383	636
15 to 24 years	944,752	625,423	53,153	36,858	68,322	160,447	549
25 to 34 years	737,807	484,482	43,272	25,653	66,806	116,993	601
35 to 44 years	562,069	358,774	32,791	18,680	61,056	90,255	513
45 to 54 years	377,385	231,102	22,974	10,096	49,646	63,225	342
55 to 64 years	215,966	137,357	14,130	4,558	32,061	27,632	228
65 years and over	163,046	105,624	5,223	2,591	27,235	22,277	96
Age unknown	10,490	7,037	316	136	1,307	1,684	10
All ages, per cent	100.0	100.0	100.0	100.0	100.0	100.0	100.0
Under 5 years	11.4	12.4	14.3	13.5	2.1	10.5	11.7
5 to 14 years	24.0	25.0	23.6	28.0	12.9	24.5	18.9
15 to 24 years	20.3	20.1	19.2	21.8	19.0	21.6	16.3
25 to 34 years	15.8	15.6	15.6	15.2	18.5	15.8	17.8
35 to 44 years	12.1	11.5	11.9	11.1	16.9	12.2	15.2
45 to 54 years	8.1	7.4	8.3	6.0	13.8	8.5	10.2
55 to 64 years	4.6	4.4	5.1	2.7	8.9	3.7	6.8
65 years and over	3.5	3.4	1.9	1.5	7.6	3.0	2.8

TABLE 49.—DISTRIBUTION OF POPULATION CLASSES BY BROAD AGE GROUPS, BY DIVISIONS AND STATES: 1920—Continued.

AGE.	All classes.	NATIVE WHITE.			Foreign-born white.	Negro.	Indian, Chinese, Japanese, and all other.
		Native parentage.	Foreign parentage.	Mixed parentage.			
MOUNTAIN.							
Montana.							
All ages, number	548,889	275,803	101,918	62,919	93,620	1,658	12,971
Under 5 years	67,372	43,402	12,013	9,756	329	109	1,763
5 to 14 years	111,401	64,610	23,478	16,287	4,140	188	2,698
15 to 24 years	82,513	43,238	18,051	12,091	6,883	189	2,061
25 to 34 years	101,877	47,164	20,232	11,038	21,523	297	1,623
35 to 44 years	82,830	35,225	13,493	7,424	24,650	390	1,648
45 to 54 years	52,766	20,745	8,561	3,820	18,026	260	1,354
55 to 64 years	31,385	12,452	4,498	1,758	11,557	137	983
65 years and over	16,808	7,406	1,517	706	6,284	82	813
Age unknown	1,937	1,561	75	39	228	6	28
All ages, per cent	100.0	100.0	100.0	100.0	100.0	100.0	100.0
Under 5 years	12.3	15.7	11.8	15.5	0.4	6.6	13.6
5 to 14 years	20.3	23.4	23.0	25.9	4.4	11.3	20.8
15 to 24 years	15.0	15.7	17.7	19.2	7.4	11.4	15.9
25 to 34 years	18.6	17.1	19.9	17.5	23.0	17.9	12.5
35 to 44 years	15.1	12.8	13.2	11.8	26.3	23.5	12.7
45 to 54 years	9.6	7.5	8.4	6.1	19.3	15.7	10.4
55 to 64 years	5.7	4.5	4.4	2.8	12.3	8.3	7.6
65 years and over	3.1	2.7	1.5	1.1	6.7	4.9	6.3
Idaho.							
All ages, number	431,866	294,252	47,920	44,533	38,963	920	5,278
Under 5 years	54,536	45,372	3,431	4,856	173	55	649
5 to 14 years	97,876	77,452	7,895	10,437	1,179	99	814
15 to 24 years	73,640	52,741	7,881	9,123	3,015	130	750
25 to 34 years	68,987	43,264	9,227	8,122	7,363	219	792
35 to 44 years	57,373	32,698	8,479	6,115	9,018	191	872
45 to 54 years	40,007	21,183	6,483	3,578	8,034	142	587
55 to 64 years	24,269	12,991	3,346	1,620	5,817	51	444
65 years and over	14,839	8,308	1,151	666	4,329	31	354
Age unknown	339	243	27	16	35	2	16
All ages, per cent	100.0	100.0	100.0	100.0	100.0	100.0	100.0
Under 5 years	12.6	15.4	7.2	10.9	0.4	6.0	12.3
5 to 14 years	22.7	26.3	16.5	23.4	3.0	10.8	15.4
15 to 24 years	17.1	17.9	16.4	20.5	7.7	14.1	14.2
25 to 34 years	16.0	14.7	19.3	18.2	18.9	23.8	15.0
35 to 44 years	13.3	11.1	17.7	13.7	23.1	20.8	16.5
45 to 54 years	9.3	7.2	13.5	8.0	20.6	15.4	11.1
55 to 64 years	5.6	4.4	7.0	3.6	14.9	5.5	8.4
65 years and over	3.4	2.8	2.4	1.5	11.1	3.4	6.7
Wyoming.							
All ages, number	194,402	122,884	25,234	16,773	25,255	1,375	2,881
Under 5 years	22,524	16,864	3,176	1,954	105	59	366
5 to 14 years	38,343	27,633	5,541	3,695	1,041	128	305
15 to 24 years	31,946	21,135	4,268	3,353	2,501	261	428
25 to 34 years	39,318	23,697	4,865	3,363	6,538	305	550
35 to 44 years	29,927	16,285	3,529	2,368	6,717	330	698
45 to 54 years	17,049	8,965	2,243	1,226	4,153	185	277
55 to 64 years	9,431	4,937	1,192	593	2,478	65	166
65 years and over	4,989	2,736	409	217	1,507	35	85
Age unknown	875	632	11	4	215	7	6
All ages, per cent	100.0	100.0	100.0	100.0	100.0	100.0	100.0
Under 5 years	11.6	13.7	12.6	11.6	0.4	4.3	12.7
5 to 14 years	19.7	22.5	22.0	22.0	4.1	9.3	10.6
15 to 24 years	16.4	17.2	16.9	20.0	9.9	19.0	14.9
25 to 34 years	20.2	19.3	19.3	20.1	25.9	22.2	19.1
35 to 44 years	15.4	13.3	14.0	14.1	26.6	24.0	24.2
45 to 54 years	8.8	7.3	8.9	7.3	16.4	13.5	9.6
55 to 64 years	4.9	4.0	4.7	3.5	9.8	4.7	5.8
65 years and over	2.6	2.2	1.6	1.3	6.0	2.5	3.0

TABLE 49.—DISTRIBUTION OF POPULATION CLASSES BY BROAD AGE GROUPS, BY DIVISIONS AND STATES: 1920—Continued.

AGE.	All classes.	NATIVE WHITE.			Foreign-born white.	Negro.	Indian, Chinese, Japanese, and all other.
		Native parentage.	Foreign parentage.	Mixed parentage.			
MOUNTAIN—Continued.							
Colorado.							
All ages, number	939,629	603,041	130,059	74,049	116,954	11,318	4,208
Under 5 years	97,058	72,113	15,080	7,904	542	693	726
5 to 14 years	184,300	129,555	31,159	15,894	5,623	1,496	573
15 to 24 years	156,970	104,615	24,060	14,749	11,145	1,818	583
25 to 34 years	153,730	97,044	19,207	13,034	21,542	2,138	765
35 to 44 years	134,428	77,501	17,138	10,241	26,473	2,270	805
45 to 54 years	100,424	56,129	12,298	6,909	23,055	1,632	401
55 to 64 years	64,002	35,107	7,915	3,437	16,672	706	165
65 years and over	41,063	23,862	3,128	1,818	11,694	454	107
Age unknown	7,654	7,115	74	63	208	111	83
All ages, per cent	100.0	100.0	100.0	100.0	100.0	100.0	100.0
Under 5 years	10.3	12.0	11.6	10.7	0.5	6.1	17.3
5 to 14 years	19.6	21.5	24.0	21.5	4.8	13.2	13.6
15 to 24 years	16.7	17.3	18.5	19.9	9.5	16.1	13.9
25 to 34 years	16.4	16.1	14.8	17.6	18.4	18.9	18.2
35 to 44 years	14.3	12.9	13.2	13.8	22.6	20.1	19.1
45 to 54 years	10.7	9.3	9.5	9.3	19.7	14.4	9.5
55 to 64 years	6.8	5.8	6.1	4.6	14.3	6.2	3.9
65 years and over	4.4	4.0	2.4	2.5	10.0	4.0	2.5
New Mexico.							
All ages, number	360,350	273,317	18,865	13,414	29,077	5,733	19,944
Under 5 years	46,399	37,143	4,015	2,030	585	181	2,445
5 to 14 years	87,281	69,402	4,818	3,442	3,693	343	5,583
15 to 24 years	67,259	51,112	2,863	2,457	5,165	1,904	3,758
25 to 34 years	55,915	40,268	2,433	2,012	6,355	2,263	2,584
35 to 44 years	41,308	29,725	1,871	1,557	5,393	594	2,168
45 to 54 years	30,754	22,527	1,487	1,105	3,814	276	1,545
55 to 64 years	18,735	13,875	945	539	2,388	94	894
65 years and over	12,244	8,887	423	266	1,643	73	952
Age unknown	455	378	10	6	41	5	15
All ages, per cent	100.0	100.0	100.0	100.0	100.0	100.0	100.0
Under 5 years	12.9	13.6	21.3	15.1	2.0	3.2	12.3
5 to 14 years	24.2	25.4	25.5	25.7	12.7	6.0	28.0
15 to 24 years	18.7	18.7	15.2	18.3	17.8	33.2	18.8
25 to 34 years	15.5	14.7	12.9	15.0	21.9	39.5	13.0
35 to 44 years	11.5	10.9	9.9	11.6	18.5	10.4	10.9
45 to 54 years	8.5	8.2	7.9	8.2	13.1	4.8	7.7
55 to 64 years	5.2	5.1	5.0	4.0	8.2	1.6	4.5
65 years and over	3.4	3.3	2.2	2.0	5.7	1.3	4.8
Arizona.							
All ages, number	334,162	151,145	39,534	22,671	78,099	8,005	34,708
Under 5 years	40,807	19,165	10,062	3,839	2,698	333	4,710
5 to 14 years	70,567	33,442	10,348	6,227	11,081	566	8,903
15 to 24 years	60,273	26,822	5,550	3,935	15,460	2,194	6,312
25 to 34 years	60,452	26,385	5,033	3,460	18,139	2,868	4,567
35 to 44 years	46,854	20,691	3,938	2,718	14,645	1,220	3,642
45 to 54 years	29,254	12,757	2,658	1,505	8,776	553	3,005
55 to 64 years	14,953	6,914	1,348	670	4,173	162	1,686
65 years and over	9,977	4,317	557	307	2,908	90	1,798
Age unknown	1,025	652	40	10	219	19	85
All ages, per cent	100.0	100.0	100.0	100.0	100.0	100.0	100.0
Under 5 years	12.2	12.7	25.5	16.9	3.5	4.2	13.6
5 to 14 years	21.1	22.1	26.2	27.5	14.2	7.1	25.7
15 to 24 years	18.0	17.7	14.0	17.4	19.8	27.4	18.2
25 to 34 years	18.1	17.5	12.7	15.3	23.2	35.8	13.2
35 to 44 years	14.0	13.7	10.0	12.0	18.8	15.2	10.5
45 to 54 years	8.8	8.4	6.7	6.6	11.2	6.9	8.7
55 to 64 years	4.5	4.6	3.4	3.0	5.3	2.1	4.9
65 years and over	3.0	2.9	1.4	1.4	3.7	1.1	5.2

TABLE 49.—DISTRIBUTION OF POPULATION CLASSES BY BROAD AGE GROUPS, BY DIVISIONS AND STATES: 1920—Continued.

AGE.	All classes.	NATIVE WHITE.			Foreign-born white.	Negro.	Indian, Chinese, Japanese, and all other.
		Native parentage.	Foreign parentage.	Mixed parentage.			
MOUNTAIN—Continued.							
Utah.							
All ages, number	449,396	245,781	75,901	63,764	56,455	1,446	6,049
Under 5 years	61,375	48,052	5,553	6,747	165	95	763
5 to 14 years	108,117	78,371	11,589	15,366	1,805	155	831
15 to 24 years	81,977	49,541	12,043	14,694	4,598	203	898
25 to 34 years	68,502	31,239	14,207	11,710	9,895	342	1,109
35 to 44 years	53,987	18,209	14,440	8,374	11,355	348	1,261
45 to 54 years	36,145	9,789	11,307	4,340	9,844	205	660
55 to 64 years	22,949	6,242	5,497	1,927	8,951	56	276
65 years and over	15,883	4,076	1,212	572	9,761	33	229
Age unknown	461	262	53	34	81	9	22
All ages, per cent	100.0	100.0	100.0	100.0	100.0	100.0	100.0
Under 5 years	13.7	19.6	7.3	10.6	0.3	6.6	12.6
5 to 14 years	24.1	31.9	15.3	24.1	3.2	10.7	13.7
15 to 24 years	18.2	20.2	15.9	23.0	8.1	14.0	14.8
25 to 34 years	15.2	12.7	18.7	18.4	17.5	23.7	18.3
35 to 44 years	12.0	7.4	19.0	13.1	20.1	24.1	20.8
45 to 54 years	8.0	4.0	14.9	6.8	17.4	14.2	10.9
55 to 64 years	5.1	2.5	7.2	3.0	15.9	3.9	4.6
65 years and over	3.5	1.7	1.6	0.9	17.3	2.3	3.8
Nevada.							
All ages, number	77,407	36,285	11,701	7,911	14,802	346	6,362
Under 5 years	6,743	4,115	1,256	719	73	15	565
5 to 14 years	12,469	7,358	2,069	1,509	363	30	1,140
15 to 24 years	10,775	5,602	1,331	1,465	1,361	42	974
25 to 34 years	14,403	6,179	1,898	1,489	3,866	68	903
35 to 44 years	14,325	5,749	2,338	1,406	3,829	81	922
45 to 54 years	9,664	3,820	1,629	841	2,518	68	788
55 to 64 years	5,240	2,049	826	328	1,495	23	519
65 years and over	3,473	1,238	346	148	1,236	19	486
Age unknown	315	175	8	6	61	....	65
All ages, per cent	100.0	100.0	100.0	100.0	100.0	100.0	100.0
Under 5 years	8.7	11.3	10.7	9.1	0.5	4.3	8.9
5 to 14 years	16.1	20.3	17.7	19.1	2.5	8.7	17.9
15 to 24 years	13.9	15.4	11.4	18.5	9.2	12.1	15.3
25 to 34 years	18.6	17.0	16.2	18.8	26.1	19.7	14.2
35 to 44 years	18.5	15.8	20.0	17.8	25.9	23.4	14.5
45 to 54 years	12.5	10.5	13.9	10.6	17.0	19.7	12.4
55 to 64 years	6.8	5.6	7.1	4.1	10.1	6.6	8.2
65 years and over	4.5	3.4	3.0	1.9	8.4	5.5	7.6
PACIFIC.							
Washington.							
All ages, number	1,356,621	711,706	214,618	143,398	250,055	6,883	29,961
Under 5 years	126,434	82,750	20,064	17,594	1,399	399	4,228
5 to 14 years	245,811	149,782	47,532	34,620	9,077	814	3,986
15 to 24 years	217,499	121,305	41,830	29,523	19,287	922	4,632
25 to 34 years	239,867	116,052	40,902	24,461	50,856	1,400	6,196
35 to 44 years	213,392	97,999	28,238	17,921	61,982	1,563	5,689
45 to 54 years	151,215	67,541	19,930	10,700	49,250	1,034	2,760
55 to 64 years	97,405	43,248	11,401	5,590	35,010	111	1,011
65 years and over	60,211	29,642	4,409	2,888	22,139	158	325
Age unknown	4,787	3,387	252	151	727	69	201
All ages, per cent	100.0	100.0	100.0	100.0	100.0	100.0	100.0
Under 5 years	9.3	11.6	9.3	12.3	0.6	5.8	14.1
5 to 14 years	18.1	21.0	22.1	24.1	3.6	11.8	13.3
15 to 24 years	16.0	17.0	19.5	20.6	7.7	13.4	15.5
25 to 34 years	17.7	16.3	19.1	17.1	20.3	20.3	20.7
35 to 44 years	15.7	13.8	13.2	12.5	24.8	22.7	19.0
45 to 54 years	11.1	9.5	9.3	7.5	19.7	15.0	9.2
55 to 64 years	7.2	6.1	5.3	3.9	14.1	6.5	4.5
65 years and over	4.4	4.2	2.1	2.0	8.9	3.5	3.1

TABLE **49.**—DISTRIBUTION OF POPULATION CLASSES BY BROAD AGE GROUPS, BY DIVISIONS AND STATES: 1920—Continued.

AGE.	All classes.	NATIVE WHITE.			Foreign-born white.	Negro.	Indian, Chinese, Japanese, and all other.
		Native parentage.	Foreign parentage.	Mixed parentage.			
PACIFIC—Continued.							
Oregon.							
All ages, number	783,389	497,726	95,827	73,442	102,151	2,144	12,099
Under 5 years	71,318	54,660	7,618	7,215	392	117	1,316
5 to 14 years	142,098	103,265	17,896	15,746	3,231	263	1,697
15 to 24 years	125,924	84,201	17,361	14,416	7,587	268	2,091
25 to 34 years	132,767	79,182	19,028	13,277	18,997	411	1,872
35 to 44 years	118,904	67,674	14,379	10,477	23,955	531	1,888
45 to 54 years	88,391	49,424	10,421	6,745	20,165	343	1,293
55 to 64 years	60,550	33,679	6,327	3,546	15,704	133	1,161
65 years and over	42,583	25,052	2,731	1,979	11,993	71	757
Age unknown	854	589	66	41	127	7	24
All ages, per cent	100.0	100.0	100.0	100.0	100.0	100.0	100.0
Under 5 years	9.1	11.0	7.9	9.8	0.4	5.5	10.9
5 to 14 years	18.1	20.7	18.7	21.4	3.2	12.3	14.0
15 to 24 years	16.1	16.9	18.1	19.6	7.4	12.5	17.3
25 to 34 years	16.9	15.9	19.9	18.1	18.6	19.2	15.5
35 to 44 years	15.2	13.6	15.0	14.3	23.5	24.8	15.6
45 to 54 years	11.3	9.9	10.9	9.2	19.7	16.0	10.7
55 to 64 years	7.7	6.8	6.6	4.8	15.4	6.2	9.6
65 years and over	5.4	5.0	2.8	2.7	11.7	3.3	6.3
California.							
All ages, number	3,426,861	1,677,955	573,927	331,167	681,662	38,763	123,387
Under 5 years	275,727	156,272	63,368	32,280	4,260	2,596	16,951
5 to 14 years	539,555	306,331	117,242	65,730	30,679	5,439	14,134
15 to 24 years	518,094	277,614	88,682	61,998	66,619	5,961	17,220
25 to 34 years	614,023	283,824	95,892	60,633	141,510	8,039	24,125
35 to 44 years	572,410	245,273	85,288	51,205	157,823	7,941	24,880
45 to 54 years	426,601	181,737	68,245	33,117	124,392	5,087	14,023
55 to 64 years	270,731	121,096	38,972	17,120	83,824	2,176	7,543
65 years and over	200,301	100,134	15,600	8,759	70,433	1,359	4,016
Age unknown	9,419	5,674	638	325	2,122	165	495
All ages, per cent	100.0	100.0	100.0	100.0	100.0	100.0	100.0
Under 5 years	8.0	9.3	11.0	9.7	0.6	6.7	13.7
5 to 14 years	15.7	18.3	20.4	19.8	4.5	14.0	11.5
15 to 24 years	15.1	16.5	15.5	18.7	9.8	15.4	14.0
25 to 34 years	17.9	16.9	16.7	18.3	20.8	20.7	19.6
35 to 44 years	16.7	14.6	14.9	15.5	23.2	20.5	20.2
45 to 54 years	12.4	10.8	11.9	10.0	18.2	13.1	11.4
55 to 64 years	7.9	7.2	6.8	5.2	12.3	5.6	6.1
65 years and over	5.8	6.0	2.7	2.6	10.3	3.5	3.3

TABLE 50.—DISTRIBUTION BY BROAD AGE GROUPS, FOR

[By class of population for

CITY AND CLASS OF POPULATION.	All ages.[1]	AGE PERIODS.					
		Under 5 years.	5 to 14 years.	15 to 24 years.	25 to 44 years.	45 to 64 years.	65 years and over.
Alabama.							
BIRMINGHAM—All classes	178,806	16,520	34,133	37,016	63,151	23,401	4,183
Native white—Native parentage	92,211	9,571	18,121	18,427	32,137	11,477	2,399
Foreign parentage	6,677	936	2,068	1,299	1,526	753	93
Mixed parentage	3,578	377	840	820	1,091	401	48
Foreign-born white	6,084	17	236	706	2,815	1,841	462
Negro	70,230	5,617	12,868	15,760	25,566	8,926	1,180
MOBILE—All classes	60,777	5,222	11,064	12,024	20,511	9,663	2,177
MONTGOMERY—All classes	43,464	3,603	7,957	8,932	14,830	6,628	1,489
Arizona.							
PHOENIX—All classes	29,053	2,527	4,739	5,030	10,739	4,888	1,080
Arkansas.							
FORT SMITH—All classes	28,870	2,734	5,845	5,514	9,117	4,509	1,069
LITTLE ROCK—All classes	65,142	5,274	10,786	12,666	23,844	10,053	2,254
California.							
LOS ANGELES—All classes	576,673	38,128	77,207	85,681	214,141	124,600	35,523
Native white—Native parentage	294,458	20,633	42,362	45,965	104,679	60,249	19,841
Foreign parentage	86,808	8,816	16,419	12,871	27,909	17,765	2,914
Mixed parentage	53,541	4,563	9,029	9,525	19,725	8,870	1,752
Foreign-born white	112,057	898	5,920	12,807	48,513	33,109	10,451
Negro	15,579	988	2,155	2,524	6,585	2,801	459
Chinese	2,062	133	236	263	588	748	85
Japanese	11,618	2,048	1,042	1,551	5,904	1,027	15
OAKLAND—All classes	216,261	16,407	32,637	32,877	79,913	42,866	11,206
Native white—Native parentage	90,279	9,156	16,890	15,154	30,222	14,729	3,970
Foreign parentage	44,061	3,705	8,136	7,505	16,259	7,445	961
Mixed parentage	24,502	2,499	4,911	4,751	8,655	3,196	474
Foreign-born white	45,162	128	1,334	3,762	19,831	14,792	5,194
Negro	5,489	296	627	840	2,634	915	170
Chinese	3,821	211	391	429	887	1,469	431
Japanese	2,709	405	325	360	·1,307	306	6
SAN FRANCISCO—All classes	506,676	32,521	65,342	80,663	202,042	101,485	21,732
Native white—Native parentage	167,179	15,283	28,079	33,828	60,506	22,789	4,776
Foreign parentage	125,648	10,303	21,785	20,178	45,766	24,925	2,482
Mixed parentage	56,995	5,092	10,126	11,603	22,037	7,306	740
Foreign-born white	140,200	358	3,750	12,031	66,558	43,500	13,429
Negro	2,414	133	209	356	1,202	427	60
Chinese	7,744	617	905	1,357	2,645	1,958	219
Japanese	5,358	696	450	850	2,789	535	18
ALAMEDA—All classes	28,806	2,434	4,700	4,172	9,945	5,849	1,691
BERKELEY—All classes	56,036	4,056	8,686	9,647	18,534	11,915	3,136
FRESNO—All classes	45,086	3,911	7,418	7,649	16,631	7,624	1,797
LONG BEACH—All classes	55,593	3,251	7,263	7,481	16,786	14,674	6,086
PASADENA—All classes	45,354	2,742	6,040	5,858	13,899	11,870	4,866
SACRAMENTO—All classes	65,908	5,155	9,808	10,406	24,248	13,128	3,134
SAN DIEGO—All classes	74,683	5,108	10,167	10,178	23,788	18,321	6,839
SAN JOSE—All classes	39,642	3,011	6,686	6,246	12,074	8,450	2,898
STOCKTON—All classes	40,296	3,037	5,885	6,018	14,582	8,643	2,103
Colorado.							
DENVER—All classes	256,491	17,651	36,889	41,719	89,373	51,908	12,465
Native white—Native parentage	114,073	12,301	23,009	24,108	48,590	24,373	6,074
Foreign parentage	40,067	2,805	7,082	8,629	14,468	8,163	1,223
Mixed parentage	24,284	2,057	1,590	5,090	9,794	3,546	546
Foreign-born white	37,620	80	935	2,871	11,997	14,440	4,774
Negro	6,075	305	694	969	2,559	1,233	919
COLORADO SPRINGS—All classes	30,105	2,053	4,670	5,057	9,328	6,939	1,944
PUEBLO—All classes	43,050	4,072	8,108	7,115	14,065	7,786	1,767
Connecticut.							
BRIDGEPORT—All classes	143,555	17,010	25,971	24,026	50,179	21,784	4,357
Native white—Native parentage	36,816	4,579	6,361	6,523	12,019	5,538	1,689
Foreign parentage	47,094	10,198	15,161	8,651	8,674	3,971	419
Mixed parentage	10,896	1,951	2,636	2,250	3,055	877	124
Foreign-born white	46,414	106	1,548	6,198	25,387	11,005	2,087
Negro	2,228	175	261	390	991	· 359	38

[1] Includes persons of unknown age.

CITIES HAVING 25,000 INHABITANTS OR MORE: 1920.

cities of 100,000 and over.]

CITY AND CLASS OF POPULATION.	PER CENT OF TOTAL.					
	Under 5 years.	5 to 14 years.	15 to 24 years.	25 to 44 years.	45 to 64 years.	65 years and over.
Alabama.						
BIRMINGHAM—All classes	9.2	19.1	20.7	35.3	13.1	2.3
Native white—Native parentage	10.4	19.7	20.0	34.9	12.4	2.6
Foreign parentage	14.0	31.0	19.5	22.9	11.3	1.4
Mixed parentage	10.5	23.5	22.9	30.5	11.2	1.3
Foreign-born white	0.3	3.9	11.6	46.3	30.3	7.6
Negro	8.0	18.3	22.4	36.4	12.7	1.7
MOBILE—All classes	8.6	18.2	19.8	33.7	15.9	3.6
MONTGOMERY—All classes	8.3	18.3	20.6	34.1	15.2	3.4
Arizona.						
PHOENIX—All classes	8.7	16.3	17.3	37.0	16.8	3.7
Arkansas.						
FORT SMITH—All classes	9.5	20.2	19.1	31.6	15.6	3.7
LITTLE ROCK—All classes	8.1	16.6	19.4	36.6	15.4	3.5
California.						
LOS ANGELES—All classes	6.6	13.4	14.9	37.1	21.6	6.2
Native white—Native parentage	7.0	14.4	15.6	35.5	20.5	6.7
Foreign parentage	10.2	18.9	14.8	32.2	20.5	3.4
Mixed parentage	8.5	16.9	17.8	36.8	16.6	3.3
Foreign-born white	0.8	5.3	11.4	43.3	29.5	9.3
Negro	6.3	13.8	16.2	42.3	18.0	2.9
Chinese	6.5	11.4	12.8	28.5	36.3	4.1
Japanese	17.6	9.0	13.3	50.8	8.8	0.1
OAKLAND—All classes	7.6	15.1	15.2	37.0	19.8	5.2
Native white—Native parentage	10.1	18.7	16.8	33.5	16.3	4.4
Foreign parentage	8.4	18.5	17.0	36.9	16.9	2.2
Mixed parentage	10.2	20.0	19.4	35.3	13.0	1.9
Foreign-born white	0.3	3.0	8.3	43.9	32.8	11.5
Negro	5.4	11.4	15.3	48.0	16.7	3.1
Chinese	5.5	10.2	11.2	23.2	38.4	11.3
Japanese	15.0	12.0	13.3	48.2	11.3	0.2
SAN FRANCISCO—All classes	6.4	12.9	15.9	39.9	20.0	4.3
Native white—Native parentage	9.1	16.8	20.2	36.2	13.6	2.9
Foreign parentage	8.2	17.3	16.1	36.4	19.8	2.0
Mixed parentage	8.9	17.8	20.4	38.7	12.8	1.3
Foreign-born white	0.3	2.7	8.6	47.5	31.0	9.6
Negro	5.5	8.7	14.7	49.8	17.7	2.5
Chinese	8.0	11.7	17.5	34.2	25.3	2.8
Japanese	13.0	8.4	15.9	52.1	10.0	0.3
ALAMEDA—All classes	8.4	16.3	14.5	34.5	20.3	5.9
BERKELEY—All classes	7.2	15.5	17.2	33.1	21.3	5.6
FRESNO—All classes	8.7	16.5	17.0	36.9	16.9	4.0
LONG BEACH—All classes	5.8	13.1	13.5	30.2	26.4	10.9
PASADENA—All classes	6.0	13.3	12.9	30.6	26.2	10.7
SACRAMENTO—All classes	7.8	14.9	15.8	36.8	19.9	4.8
SAN DIEGO—All classes	6.8	13.6	13.6	31.9	24.5	9.2
SAN JOSE—All classes	7.6	16.9	15.8	30.5	21.3	7.3
STOCKTON—All classes	7.5	14.6	14.9	36.2	21.4	5.2
Colorado.						
DENVER—All classes	6.9	14.4	16.3	34.8	20.2	4.9
Native white—Native parentage	8.5	15.9	16.7	33.6	16.8	4.2
Foreign parentage	6.6	17.8	20.0	33.6	19.0	2.8
Mixed parentage	8.5	18.6	20.8	35.1	14.6	2.2
Foreign-born white	0.2	2.5	7.6	39.6	38.4	11.6
Negro	5.0	11.4	16.0	42.1	20.3	3.6
COLORADO SPRINGS—All classes	6.8	15.5	16.8	31.0	23.0	6.5
PUEBLO—All classes	9.5	18.8	16.5	32.7	18.1	4.1
Connecticut.						
BRIDGEPORT—All classes	11.8	18.1	16.7	35.0	15.2	3.0
Native white—Native parentage	12.4	17.3	17.7	32.6	15.0	4.6
Foreign parentage	21.7	32.2	18.4	18.4	8.4	0.9
Mixed parentage	17.9	24.2	20.6	28.0	8.0	1.1
Foreign-born white	0.2	3.3	13.4	54.7	23.7	4.5
Negro	7.9	11.7	17.5	44.5	16.1	1.7

TABLE **50.**—DISTRIBUTION BY BROAD AGE GROUPS, FOR

[By class of population for

CITY AND CLASS OF POPULATION.	All ages.[1]	AGE PERIODS.					
		Under 5 years.	5 to 14 years.	15 to 24 years.	25 to 44 years.	45 to 64 years.	65 years and over.
Connecticut—Continued.							
HARTFORD—All classes	138,036	14,253	23,067	23,976	47,967	23,370	5,331
Native white—Native parentage	40,327	4,322	6,352	7,436	12,980	6,716	2,488
Foreign parentage	41,754	7,879	12,116	7,951	8,757	4,554	476
Mixed parentage	10,933	1,602	2,475	2,441	3,308	975	132
Foreign-born white	40,667	70	1,443	5,155	21,391	10,473	2,118
Negro	4,199	378	678	955	1,477	595	115
NEW HAVEN—All classes	162,537	17,940	31,004	27,266	51,555	27,540	6,944
Native white—Native parentage	44,401	5,242	7,815	8,019	13,131	7,198	2,822
Foreign parentage	54,702	10,195	17,594	10,286	10,382	5,625	598
Mixed parentage	13,027	1,988	3,288	2,755	3,649	1,158	176
Foreign-born white	45,686	76	1,623	5,449	22,600	12,691	3,181
Negro	4,573	430	680	738	1,725	824	163
MERIDEN—All classes	29,867	3,172	5,553	5,122	9,025	5,375	1,590
NEW BRITAIN—All classes	59,316	8,142	12,060	9,795	19,642	7,998	1,667
NEW LONDON—All classes	25,688	2,571	4,391	4,481	8,109	4,785	1,347
NORWALK—All classes	27,743	2,596	5,057	4,390	8,367	5,537	1,746
STAMFORD—All classes	35,096	4,196	7,086	5,523	11,387	5,518	1,307
WATERBURY—All classes	91,715	10,430	17,564	16,113	31,575	13,311	2,669
Delaware.							
WILMINGTON—All classes	110,168	11,541	18,522	19,814	36,675	18,718	4,671
Native white—Native parentage	56,868	6,261	9,662	10,931	18,375	8,981	2,592
Foreign parentage	19,132	3,590	5,385	3,343	3,758	2,665	386
Mixed parentage	7,103	977	1,586	1,329	2,085	914	205
Foreign-born white	16,279	33	455	2,056	8,416	4,135	1,119
Negro	10,746	679	1,432	2,153	4,023	2,007	368
District of Columbia.							
WASHINGTON—All classes	437,571	30,436	59,656	84,581	161,085	79,289	20,635
Native white—Native parentage	239,488	18,244	33,760	48,298	86,156	40,183	11,646
Foreign parentage	35,129	2,781	5,194	6,022	10,946	8,706	1,434
Mixed parentage	23,695	1,555	3,111	4,603	9,210	4,275	901
Foreign-born white	28,548	52	720	3,256	13,071	8,253	3,073
Negro	109,966	7,774	16,842	22,253	41,381	17,682	3,596
Florida.							
JACKSONVILLE—All classes	91,558	7,990	15,614	17,484	34,555	12,832	2,470
MIAMI—All classes	29,571	2,918	4,669	5,168	10,924	4,768	1,019
PENSACOLA—All classes	31,035	2,896	5,794	6,520	10,324	4,441	974
TAMPA—All classes	51,608	5,115	10,733	9,734	17,384	7,185	1,352
Georgia.							
ATLANTA—All classes	200,616	17,134	34,541	42,172	72,162	28,183	6,331
Native white—Native parentage	124,948	11,789	22,108	25,683	44,059	17,109	4,167
Foreign parentage	4,815	479	1,224	884	1,333	785	110
Mixed parentage	3,284	306	578	540	1,208	531	121
Foreign-born white	4,738	15	156	579	2,210	1,418	358
Negro	62,796	4,544	10,470	14,483	23,344	8,326	1,571
AUGUSTA—All classes	52,548	4,263	8,944	10,769	18,367	8,324	1,771
COLUMBUS—All classes	31,125	2,671	6,116	7,214	9,737	4,280	1,103
MACON—All classes	52,995	4,342	9,576	11,438	18,409	7,467	1,715
SAVANNAH—All classes	83,252	6,994	14,080	17,831	30,532	11,495	2,212
Illinois.							
CHICAGO—All classes	2,701,705	272,455	481,271	448,688	971,263	438,055	85,195
Native white—Native parentage	642,871	96,138	139,293	111,974	201,423	75,394	16,237
Foreign parentage	888,496	132,441	236,862	178,055	245,384	87,362	7,804
Mixed parentage	252,320	36,304	68,336	56,515	70,745	18,361	1,893
Foreign-born white	805,482	1,060	24,390	81,929	399,536	240,038	57,250
Negro	109,458	6,404	12,222	19,772	52,716	16,066	1,959
AURORA—All classes	36,397	3,420	6,008	5,858	12,077	7,061	1,941
BLOOMINGTON—All classes	28,725	2,255	4,458	4,853	9,168	5,928	2,009
CICERO TOWN—All classes	44,995	5,618	10,452	7,817	15,301	5,013	757
DANVILLE—All classes	33,776	2,999	5,823	5,766	10,979	6,285	1,907
DECATUR—All classes	43,818	3,827	7,499	8,266	13,889	8,100	2,209
EAST ST. LOUIS—All classes	66,767	6,591	12,523	12,184	23,214	10,387	1,825
ELGIN—All classes	27,454	1,735	3,738	4,773	8,854	6,285	1,939

[1] Includes persons of unknown age.

CITIES HAVING 25,000 INHABITANTS OR MORE: 1920—Continued.

cities of 100,000 and over.]

CITY AND CLASS OF POPULATION.	PER CENT OF TOTAL.					
	Under 5 years.	5 to 14 years.	15 to 24 years.	25 to 44 years.	45 to 64 years.	65 years and over.
Connecticut—Continued.						
HARTFORD—All classes	10.3	16.7	17.4	34.7	16.9	3.9
Native white—Native parentage	10.7	15.8	18.4	32.2	16.7	6.2
Foreign parentage	18.9	29.0	19.0	21.0	10.9	1.1
Mixed parentage	14.7	22.6	22.3	30.3	8.9	1.2
Foreign-born white	0.2	3.5	12.7	52.6	25.8	5.2
Negro	9.0	16.1	22.7	35.2	14.2	2.7
NEW HAVEN—All classes	11.0	19.1	16.8	31.7	16.9	4.3
Native white—Native parentage	11.8	17.6	18.1	29.6	16.2	6.4
Foreign parentage	18.6	32.2	18.8	19.0	10.3	1.1
Mixed parentage	15.3	25.2	21.1	28.0	8.9	1.4
Foreign-born white	0.2	3.6	11.9	49.5	27.8	7.0
Negro	9.4	14.9	16.1	37.7	18.0	3.6
MERIDEN—All classes	10.6	18.6	17.1	30.2	18.0	5.3
NEW BRITAIN—All classes	13.7	20.3	16.5	33.1	13.5	2.8
NEW LONDON—All classes	10.0	17.1	17.4	31.6	18.6	5.2
NORWALK—All classes	9.4	18.2	15.8	30.2	20.0	6.3
STAMFORD—All classes	12.0	20.2	15.7	32.4	15.7	3.7
WATERBURY—All classes	11.4	19.2	17.6	34.4	14.5	2.9
Delaware.						
WILMINGTON—All classes	10.5	16.8	18.0	33.3	17.0	4.2
Native white—Native parentage	11.0	17.0	19.2	32.3	15.8	4.6
Foreign parentage	18.8	28.1	17.5	19.6	13.9	2.0
Mixed parentage	13.8	22.3	18.7	29.4	12.9	2.9
Foreign-born white	0.2	2.8	12.6	51.7	25.4	6.9
Negro	6.3	13.3	20.0	37.4	18.7	3.4
District of Columbia.						
WASHINGTON—All classes	7.0	13.6	19.3	36.8	18.1	4.7
Native white—Native parentage	7.6	14.1	20.2	36.0	16.8	4.9
Foreign parentage	7.9	14.8	17.1	31.2	24.8	4.1
Mixed parentage	6.6	13.1	19.4	38.9	18.0	3.8
Foreign-born white	0.2	2.5	11.4	45.8	28.9	10.8
Negro	7.1	15.3	20.2	37.6	16.1	3.2
Florida.						
JACKSONVILLE—All classes	8.7	17.1	19.1	37.7	14.0	2.7
MIAMI—All classes	9.9	15.8	17.5	36.9	16.1	3.4
PENSACOLA—All classes	9.3	18.7	21.0	33.3	14.3	3.1
TAMPA—All classes	9.9	20.8	18.9	33.7	13.9	2.6
Georgia.						
ATLANTA—All classes	8.5	17.2	21.0	36.0	14.0	3.2
Native white—Native parentage	9.4	17.7	20.6	35.3	13.7	3.3
Foreign parentage	9.9	25.4	18.4	27.7	16.3	2.3
Mixed parentage	9.3	17.6	16.4	36.8	16.2	3.7
Foreign-born white	0.3	3.3	12.2	46.6	29.9	7.6
Negro	7.2	16.7	23.1	37.2	13.3	2.5
AUGUSTA—All classes	8.1	17.0	20.5	35.0	15.8	3.4
COLUMBUS—All classes	8.6	19.6	23.2	31.3	13.8	3.5
MACON—All classes	8.2	18.1	21.6	34.7	14.1	3.2
SAVANNAH—All classes	8.4	16.9	21.4	36.7	13.8	2.7
Illinois.						
CHICAGO—All classes	10.1	17.8	16.6	36.0	16.2	3.2
Native white—Native parentage	15.0	21.7	17.4	31.3	11.7	2.5
Foreign parentage	14.9	26.7	20.0	27.6	9.8	0.9
Mixed parentage	14.4	27.1	22.4	28.0	7.3	0.8
Foreign-born white	0.1	3.0	10.2	49.6	29.8	7.1
Negro	5.9	11.2	18.1	48.2	14.7	1.8
AURORA—All classes	9.4	16.5	16.1	33.2	19.4	5.3
BLOOMINGTON—All classes	7.9	15.5	16.9	31.9	20.6	7.0
CICERO TOWN—All classes	12.5	23.2	17.4	34.0	11.1	1.7
DANVILLE—All classes	8.9	17.2	17.1	32.5	18.6	5.6
DECATUR—All classes	8.7	17.1	18.9	31.7	18.5	5.0
EAST ST. LOUIS—All classes	9.9	18.8	18.2	34.8	15.6	2.7
ELGIN—All classes	6.3	13.6	17.4	32.3	22.9	7.1

TABLE **50.**—DISTRIBUTION BY BROAD AGE GROUPS, FOR

[By class of population for

CITY AND CLASS OF POPULATION.	All ages.[1]	AGE PERIODS.					
		Under 5 years.	5 to 14 years.	15 to 24 years.	25 to 44 years.	45 to 64 years.	65 years and over.
Illinois—Continued.							
EVANSTON—All classes	37,234	3,402	6,184	5,997	12,870	7,009	1,705
JOLIET—All classes	38,442	3,898	7,219	6,917	12,405	6,450	1,528
MOLINE—All classes	30,734	2,554	4,925	5,272	11,365	5,249	1,333
OAK PARK VILLAGE—All classes	39,858	3,255	6,635	6,015	13,948	8,009	1,868
PEORIA—All classes	76,121	5,666	11,424	12,956	26,768	15,401	3,812
QUINCY—All classes	35,978	2,617	5,493	6,148	11,233	7,871	2,575
ROCK ISLAND—All classes	35,177	2,914	5,483	5,972	12,473	6,623	1,611
ROCKFORD—All classes	65,651	5,876	10,229	11,909	22,890	11,400	3,184
SPRINGFIELD—All classes	59,183	4,925	10,457	10,194	19,399	11,074	3,088
Indiana.							
INDIANAPOLIS—All classes	314,194	25,504	47,826	55,410	110,923	58,812	14,513
Native white—Native parentage	219,297	20,400	36,848	41,717	75,043	35,536	8,784
Foreign parentage	26,579	1,570	3,071	3,200	8,703	8,660	1,352
Mixed parentage	16,577	1,037	2,306	2,897	6,585	3,210	530
Foreign-born white	16,958	16	369	1,247	6,789	5,674	2,813
Negro	34,678	2,480	5,230	6,332	13,763	5,691	1,031
ANDERSON—All classes	29,767	2,691	5,050	5,678	9,393	5,499	1,439
EAST CHICAGO—All classes	35,967	5,585	7,414	5,142	13,424	3,712	338
EVANSVILLE—All classes	85,264	7,136	14,648	15,692	27,661	15,818	4,261
FORT WAYNE—All classes	86,549	7,720	13,914	16,355	29,078	15,337	4,095
GARY—All classes	55,378	7,295	10,504	8,687	22,644	5,584	582
HAMMOND—All classes	36,004	4,414	7,496	6,041	12,506	4,712	780
KOKOMO—All classes	30,067	3,080	5,032	5,638	9,646	5,189	1,474
MUNCIE—All classes	36,524	3,175	6,307	6,665	11,576	6,856	1,876
RICHMOND—All classes	26,765	2,154	4,290	4,406	8,512	5,567	1,812
SOUTH BEND—All classes	70,983	7,753	14,261	12,480	22,832	10,931	2,643
TERRE HAUTE—All classes	66,083	5,469	11,218	11,852	21,838	12,494	3,163
Iowa.							
DES MOINES—All classes	126,468	11,170	20,362	23,197	43,825	21,853	5,858
Native white—Native parentage	84,361	8,804	15,179	16,415	27,369	12,873	3,577
Foreign parentage	15,266	1,131	2,321	2,608	5,851	2,916	421
Mixed parentage	10,036	735	1,722	2,183	3,755	1,378	257
Foreign-born white	11,224	28	320	960	4,713	3,736	1,450
Negro	5,512	472	818	1,009	2,112	931	153
CEDAR RAPIDS—All classes	45,566	3,910	7,389	8,111	15,417	8,372	2,325
COUNCIL BLUFFS—All classes	36,162	3,400	6,394	6,510	11,478	6,378	1,819
DAVENPORT—All classes	56,727	4,481	8,964	9,635	19,570	10,883	3,088
DUBUQUE—All classes	39,141	3,613	6,476	6,887	12,099	7,745	2,293
SIOUX CITY—All classes	71,227	6,769	11,204	13,598	25,616	11,884	2,587
WATERLOO—All classes	36,230	3,406	6,222	6,359	12,438	6,109	1,636
Kansas.							
KANSAS CITY—All classes	101,177	10,194	18,628	18,042	33,336	16,867	3,992
Native white—Native parentage	56,575	6,445	11,367	10,921	17,265	8,286	2,229
Foreign parentage	12,149	2,018	2,989	1,969	3,053	1,844	271
Mixed parentage	6,323	499	1,211	1,378	2,165	934	134
Foreign-born white	11,656	110	643	1,327	5,474	3,234	858
Negro	14,405	1,120	2,412	2,439	5,342	2,553	500
TOPEKA—All classes	50,022	4,412	8,109	8,735	15,668	9,614	3,358
WICHITA—All classes	72,217	6,171	12,148	13,052	24,474	12,410	3,801
Kentucky.							
LOUISVILLE—All classes	234,891	18,071	38,187	41,060	79,172	45,700	11,281
Native white—Native parentage	139,403	14,371	28,824	28,449	44,545	18,552	4,542
Foreign parentage	27,076	618	1,818	2,732	8,573	11,485	1,818
Mixed parentage	16,669	721	2,145	3,194	7,003	3,227	366
Foreign-born white	11,621	8	167	534	3,169	4,676	3,052
Negro	40,087	2,353	5,182	7,043	16,161	7,754	1,502
COVINGTON—All classes	57,121	4,883	9,648	9,866	18,815	10,949	2,936
LEXINGTON—All classes	41,534	2,915	6,179	6,856	14,376	8,807	2,346
NEWPORT—All classes	29,317	2,532	4,853	5,155	9,591	5,690	1,486

[1] Includes persons of unknown age.

CITIES HAVING 25,000 INHABITANTS OR MORE: 1920—Continued.

cities of 100,000 and over.]

CITY AND CLASS OF POPULATION.	PER CENT OF TOTAL.					
	Under 5 years.	5 to 14 years.	15 to 24 years.	25 to 44 years.	45 to 64 years.	65 years and over.
Illinois—Continued.						
EVANSTON—All classes	9.1	16.6	16.1	34.6	18.8	4.6
JOLIET—All classes	10.1	18.8	18.0	32.3	16.8	4.0
MOLINE—All classes	8.3	16.0	17.2	37.0	17.1	4.3
OAK PARK VILLAGE—All classes	8.2	16.6	15.1	35.0	20.1	4.7
PEORIA—All classes	7.4	15.0	17.0	35.2	20.2	5.0
QUINCY—All classes	7.3	15.3	17.1	31.2	21.9	7.2
ROCK ISLAND—All classes	8.3	15.6	17.0	35.5	18.8	4.6
ROCKFORD—All classes	9.0	15.6	18.1	34.9	17.4	4.8
SPRINGFIELD—All classes	8.3	17.7	17.2	32.8	18.7	5.2
Indiana.						
INDIANAPOLIS—All classes	8.1	15.2	17.6	35.3	18.7	4.6
Native white—Native parentage	9.3	16.8	19.0	34.2	16.2	4.0
Foreign parentage	5.9	11.6	12.0	32.7	32.6	5.1
Mixed parentage	6.3	13.9	17.5	39.7	19.4	3.2
Foreign-born white	0.1	2.2	7.4	40.0	33.5	16.6
Negro	7.2	15.1	18.3	39.7	16.4	3.0
ANDERSON—All classes	9.0	17.0	19.1	31.6	18.5	4.8
EAST CHICAGO—All classes	15.5	20.6	14.3	37.3	10.3	0.9
EVANSVILLE—All classes	8.4	17.2	18.4	32.4	18.6	5.0
FORT WAYNE—All classes	8.9	16.1	18.9	33.6	17.7	4.7
GARY—All classes	13.2	19.0	15.7	40.9	10.1	1.1
HAMMOND—All classes	12.3	20.8	16.8	34.7	13.1	2.2
KOKOMO—All classes	10.2	16.7	18.8	32.1	17.3	4.9
MUNCIE—All classes	8.7	17.3	18.2	31.7	18.8	5.1
RICHMOND—All classes	8.0	16.0	16.5	31.8	20.8	6.8
SOUTH BEND—All classes	10.9	20.1	17.6	32.2	15.4	3.7
TERRE HAUTE—All classes	8.3	17.0	17.9	33.0	18.9	4.8
Iowa.						
DES MOINES—All classes	8.8	16.1	18.3	34.7	17.3	4.6
Native white—Native parentage	10.4	18.0	19.5	32.4	15.3	4.2
Foreign parentage	7.4	15.2	17.1	38.3	19.1	2.8
Mixed parentage	7.3	17.2	21.8	37.4	13.7	2.6
Foreign-born white	0.2	2.9	8.6	42.0	33.3	12.9
Negro	8.6	14.8	18.3	38.3	16.9	2.8
CEDAR RAPIDS—All classes	8.6	16.2	17.8	33.8	18.4	5.1
COUNCIL BLUFFS—All classes	9.4	17.7	18.0	31.7	17.6	5.0
DAVENPORT—All classes	7.9	15.8	17.0	34.5	19.2	5.4
DUBUQUE—All classes	9.2	16.5	17.6	30.9	19.8	5.9
SIOUX CITY—All classes	9.5	15.7	19.1	36.0	16.0	3.6
WATERLOO—All classes	9.4	17.2	17.6	34.3	16.9	4.5
Kansas.						
KANSAS CITY—All classes	10.1	18.4	17.8	32.9	16.7	3.9
Native white—Native parentage	11.4	20.1	19.3	30.5	14.6	3.9
Foreign parentage	16.6	24.6	16.2	25.1	15.2	2.2
Mixed parentage	7.9	19.2	21.8	34.2	14.8	2.1
Foreign-born white	0.9	5.5	11.4	47.0	27.7	7.4
Negro	7.8	16.7	16.9	37.1	17.7	3.5
TOPEKA—All classes	8.8	16.2	17.5	31.3	19.2	6.7
WICHITA—All classes	8.5	16.8	18.1	33.9	17.2	5.3
Kentucky.						
LOUISVILLE—All classes	7.7	16.2	17.9	33.8	19.5	4.8
Native white—Native parentage	10.3	20.7	20.4	32.0	13.3	3.3
Foreign parentage	2.3	6.7	10.1	31.7	42.4	6.7
Mixed parentage	4.3	12.9	19.2	42.0	19.4	2.2
Foreign-born white	0.1	1.4	4.6	27.3	40.2	26.3
Negro	5.9	12.9	17.6	40.3	19.3	3.7
COVINGTON—All classes	8.5	16.9	17.3	32.9	19.2	5.1
LEXINGTON—All classes	7.0	14.9	16.5	34.6	21.2	5.6
NEWPORT—All classes	8.6	16.6	17.6	32.7	19.4	5.1

TABLE **50.**—DISTRIBUTION BY BROAD AGE GROUPS, FOR

[By class of population for

CITY AND CLASS OF POPULATION.	All ages.[1]	AGE PERIODS.					
		Under 5 years.	5 to 14 years.	15 to 24 years.	25 to 44 years.	45 to 64 years.	65 years and over.
Louisiana.							
NEW ORLEANS—All classes	387,219	32,383	70,341	77,494	130,099	61,792	14,329
Native white—Native parentage	190,641	20,923	42,593	44,301	59,224	19,407	3,887
Foreign parentage	41,806	1,813	5,305	5,235	11,845	14,974	2,593
Mixed parentage	27,477	1,729	3,850	4,553	10,905	5,535	864
Foreign-born white	25,992	99	749	2,948	10,291	7,682	4,182
Negro	100,930	7,798	17,811	20,412	37,677	14,080	2,791
SHREVEPORT—All classes	43,874	3,436	7,293	9,231	16,598	5,728	1,249
Maine.							
BANGOR—All classes	25,978	1,962	4,146	4,140	7,937	5,789	1,982
LEWISTON—All classes	31,791	3,000	5,867	6,180	9,474	5,583	1,633
PORTLAND—All classes	69,272	6,126	10,906	11,161	22,253	14,337	4,406
Maryland.							
BALTIMORE—All classes	733,826	69,356	126,386	134,368	242,926	128,409	32,230
Native white—Native parentage	378,380	43,157	73,307	73,057	120,218	54,074	14,498
Foreign parentage	116,749	12,808	26,151	21,442	27,928	23,910	4,492
Mixed parentage	46,090	4,907	8,974	8,744	14,989	7,184	1,286
Foreign-born white	83,911	109	2,407	9,875	36,752	25,837	8,914
Negro	108,322	8,366	15,540	21,204	42,874	17,266	3,031
CUMBERLAND—All classes	29,837	2,867	5,457	5,762	9,271	4,628	1,293
HAGERSTOWN—All classes	28,064	2,983	5,285	4,946	8,804	4,565	1,354
Massachusetts.							
BOSTON—All classes	748,060	70,846	127,023	124,740	250,055	140,690	33,100
Native white—Native parentage	181,811	22,049	33,155	30,765	52,983	30,387	11,387
Foreign parentage	238,241	36,423	66,631	49,849	53,912	27,671	3,649
Mixed parentage	71,514	10,565	18,633	16,003	19,235	6,185	853
Foreign-born white	238,919	536	6,648	25,274	116,281	73,204	16,708
Negro	16,350	1,212	1,860	2,680	7,146	2,864	482
CAMBRIDGE—All classes	109,694	10,673	19,032	18,855	35,271	20,422	5,408
Native white—Native parentage	29,045	3,538	5,080	5,100	8,099	5,033	2,178
Foreign parentage	32,283	4,970	9,068	6,916	7,219	3,600	509
Mixed parentage	10,818	1,521	2,882	2,580	2,807	899	129
Foreign-born white	32,104	103	1,064	3,367	15,136	9,994	2,430
Negro	5,334	535	935	862	1,968	870	159
FALL RIVER—All classes	120,485	13,640	25,413	21,872	34,290	20,429	4,814
Native white—Native parentage	19,168	3,467	5,144	3,405	3,890	2,314	943
Foreign parentage	45,235	7,508	14,011	9,860	9,825	3,647	377
Mixed parentage	13,380	2,523	4,637	3,239	2,357	557	67
Foreign-born white	42,331	101	1,577	5,324	18,079	13,821	3,416
Negro	315	40	44	37	117	66	9
LOWELL—All classes	112,759	11,766	20,198	19,324	35,671	20,743	4,998
Native white—Native parentage	24,676	3,769	5,246	3,831	6,275	3,871	1,655
Foreign parentage	37,041	5,626	9,892	8,266	8,992	3,782	476
Mixed parentage	12,752	2,243	3,912	2,861	2,786	810	140
Foreign-born white	38,040	114	1,119	4,326	17,527	12,208	2,724
Negro	170	12	26	31	60	38	3
NEW BEDFORD—All classes	121,217	12,977	22,402	21,811	39,475	19,788	4,741
Native white—Native parentage	20,098	2,468	3,713	2,999	5,370	3,820	1,722
Foreign parentage	36,379	7,192	11,730	7,977	6,947	2,291	240
Mixed parentage	10,976	2,355	3,744	2,369	1,964	464	78
Foreign-born white	48,689	215	2,389	7,636	23,280	12,591	2,566
Negro	4,998	747	823	813	1,887	595	132
SPRINGFIELD—All classes	1?0,614	1?,??0	20,984	21,385	45,948	22,618	5,731
Native white—Native parentage	48,945	5,111	8,088	6,1??	15,751	8,350	3,093
Foreign parentage	32,991	5,222	8,272	6,605	8,475	4,006	6??
Mixed parentage	13,613	1,971	3,215	3,016	4,073	1,1?5	1??
Foreign-born white	31,250	62	1,014	3,607	16,450	8,224	1,874
Negro	2,650	177	392	476	1,118	406	79
WORCESTER—All classes	179,754	19,139	31,818	29,605	59,802	31,077	8,207
Native white—Native parentage	50,716	6,607	9,683	8,426	14,092	8,370	3,470
Foreign parentage	56,841	9,589	15,617	11,448	13,538	5,928	710
Mixed parentage	17,416	2,708	4,684	3,898	4,665	1,279	181
Foreign-born white	53,418	122	1,621	5,582	27,049	15,230	3,790
Negro	1,258	109	202	240	421	231	53
BROCKTON—All classes	66,254	6,102	11,275	10,534	22,060	12,992	3,264
BROOKLINE TOWN—All classes	37,748	2,504	4,654	5,626	13,306	8,981	2,636
CHELSEA—All classes	43,184	5,088	9,084	7,688	13,157	6,325	1,782

[1] Includes persons of unknown age.

CITIES HAVING 25,000 INHABITANTS OR MORE: 1920—Continued.

cities of 100,000 and over.]

CITY AND CLASS OF POPULATION.	PER CENT OF TOTAL.					
	Under 5 years.	5 to 14 years.	15 to 24 years.	25 to 44 years.	45 to 64 years.	65 years and over.
Louisiana.						
NEW ORLEANS—All classes	8.4	18.2	20.0	33.6	16.0	3.7
Native white—Native parentage	11.0	22.3	23.2	31.1	10.2	2.0
Foreign parentage	4.3	12.7	12.5	28.3	35.8	6.2
Mixed parentage	6.3	14.0	16.6	39.7	20.1	3.1
Foreign-born white	0.4	2.9	11.3	39.6	29.6	16.1
Negro	7.7	17.6	20.2	37.3	14.0	2.8
SHREVEPORT—All classes	7.8	16.6	21.0	37.8	13.1	2.8
Maine.						
BANGOR—All classes	7.6	16.0	15.9	30.6	22.3	7.6
LEWISTON—All classes	9.4	18.5	19.4	29.8	17.6	5.1
PORTLAND—All classes	8.8	15.7	16.1	32.1	20.7	6.4
Maryland.						
BALTIMORE—All classes	9.5	17.2	18.3	33.1	17.5	4.4
Native white—Native parentage	11.4	19.4	19.3	31.8	14.3	3.8
Foreign parentage	11.0	22.4	18.4	23.9	20.5	3.8
Mixed parentage	10.6	19.5	19.0	32.5	15.6	2.8
Foreign-born white	0.1	2.9	11.8	43.8	30.8	10.6
Negro	7.7	14.3	19.6	39.6	15.9	2.8
CUMBERLAND—All classes	9.6	18.3	19.3	31.1	15.5	4.3
HAGERSTOWN—All classes	10.6	18.8	17.6	31.4	16.3	4.8
Massachusetts.						
BOSTON—All classes	9.5	17.0	16.7	33.4	18.8	4.4
Native white—Native parentage	12.1	18.2	16.9	29.1	16.7	6.3
Foreign parentage	15.3	28.0	20.9	22.6	11.6	1.5
Mixed parentage	14.8	26.1	22.4	26.9	8.6	1.2
Foreign-born white	0.2	2.8	10.6	48.7	30.6	7.0
Negro	7.4	11.4	16.4	43.7	17.5	2.9
CAMBRIDGE—All classes	9.7	17.4	17.2	32.2	18.6	4.9
Native white—Native parentage	12.2	17.5	17.6	27.9	17.3	7.5
Foreign parentage	15.4	28.1	21.4	22.4	11.2	1.6
Mixed parentage	14.1	26.6	23.8	25.9	8.3	1.2
Foreign-born white	0.3	3.3	10.5	47.1	31.1	7.6
Negro	10.0	17.5	16.2	36.9	16.3	3.0
FALL RIVER—All classes	11.3	21.1	18.2	28.5	17.0	4.0
Native white—Native parentage	18.1	26.8	17.8	20.3	12.1	4.9
Foreign parentage	16.6	31.0	21.8	21.7	8.1	0.8
Mixed parentage	18.9	34.7	24.2	17.6	4.2	0.5
Foreign-born white	0.2	3.7	12.6	42.7	32.6	8.1
Negro	12.7	14.0	11.7	37.1	21.0	2.9
LOWELL—All classes	10.4	17.9	17.1	31.6	18.4	4.4
Native white—Native parentage	15.3	21.3	15.5	25.4	15.7	6.7
Foreign parentage	15.2	26.7	22.3	24.3	10.2	1.3
Mixed parentage	17.6	30.7	22.4	21.8	6.4	1.1
Foreign-born white	0.3	2.9	11.4	46.1	32.1	7.2
Negro	7.1	15.3	18.2	35.3	22.4	1.8
NEW BEDFORD—All classes	10.7	18.5	18.0	32.6	16.3	3.9
Native white—Native parentage	12.3	18.5	14.9	26.7	19.0	8.6
Foreign parentage	19.8	32.2	21.9	19.1	6.3	0.7
Mixed parentage	21.5	34.1	21.6	17.9	4.2	0.7
Foreign-born white	0.4	4.9	15.7	47.8	25.9	5.3
Negro	14.9	16.5	16.3	37.8	11.9	2.6
SPRINGFIELD—All classes	9.9	16.2	16.5	35.4	17.5	4.4
Native white—Native parentage	11.1	16.5	16.7	32.2	17.1	6.3
Foreign parentage	15.8	25.1	18.4	25.7	13.3	1.6
Mixed parentage	14.5	23.6	22.2	29.9	8.8	1.0
Foreign-born white	0.2	3.2	11.5	52.6	26.3	6.0
Negro	6.7	14.8	18.0	42.2	15.3	3.0
WORCESTER—All classes	10.6	17.7	16.5	33.3	17.3	4.6
Native white—Native parentage	13.0	19.1	16.6	27.8	16.5	6.8
Foreign parentage	16.9	27.5	20.1	23.8	10.4	1.2
Mixed parentage	15.5	26.9	22.4	26.8	7.3	1.0
Foreign-born white	0.2	3.0	10.4	50.6	28.5	7.1
Negro	8.7	16.1	19.1	33.5	18.4	4.2
BROCKTON—All classes	9.2	17.0	15.9	33.3	19.6	4.9
BROOKLINE TOWN—All classes	6.6	12.3	14.9	35.2	23.8	7.0
CHELSEA—All classes	11.8	21.0	17.8	30.5	14.6	4.1

TABLE 50.—DISTRIBUTION BY BROAD AGE GROUPS, FOR

[By class of population for

CITY AND CLASS OF POPULATION.	All ages.[1]	AGE PERIODS.					
		Under 5 years.	5 to 14 years.	15 to 24 years.	25 to 44 years.	45 to 64 years.	65 years and over.
Massachusetts—Continued.							
CHICOPEE—All classes	36,214	5,203	7,933	6,168	11,088	4,818	993
EVERETT—All classes	40,120	4,397	7,777	6,897	12,134	7,186	1,723
FITCHBURG—All classes	41,029	4,500	7,821	7,063	12,876	6,919	1,826
HAVERHILL—All classes	53,884	5,039	8,888	8,978	17,438	10,439	3,046
HOLYOKE—All classes	60,203	6,215	11,315	11,131	19,209	9,987	2,320
LAWRENCE—All classes	94,270	10,526	18,054	16,211	30,587	15,571	3,289
LYNN—All classes	99,148	9,085	16,440	15,758	33,122	19,388	5,328
MALDEN—All classes	49,103	4,692	9,329	8,428	14,655	9,452	2,541
MEDFORD—All classes	39,038	4,098	6,793	6,276	12,893	7,059	1,916
NEWTON—All classes	46,054	3,925	7,944	7,324	14,363	9,582	2,899
PITTSFIELD—All classes	41,763	4,345	7,442	6,796	13,764	7,459	1,904
QUINCY—All classes	47,876	5,358	9,045	7,566	16,028	8,021	1,852
REVERE—All classes	28,823	3,355	6,366	4,859	9,027	4,282	907
SALEM—All classes	42,529	4,378	8,030	7,097	12,848	7,813	2,341
SOMERVILLE—All classes	93,091	9,084	15,557	15,083	29,988	18,172	5,203
TAUNTON—All classes	37,137	3,905	6,782	5,978	11,054	7,213	2,199
WALTHAM—All classes	30,915	2,741	5,180	5,421	9,828	5,992	1,744
Michigan.							
DETROIT—All classes	993,678	112,117	156,947	179,614	391,688	127,744	24,708
Native white—Native parentage	313,997	43,970	55,731	64,346	113,611	30,245	5,784
Foreign parentage	247,035	47,475	58,858	44,567	69,754	23,475	2,801
Mixed parentage	101,736	16,526	24,255	21,643	30,697	7,731	844
Foreign-born white	289,297	1,632	13,973	39,679	156,811	62,047	14,861
Negro	40,838	2,482	4,094	9,191	20,448	4,105	415
GRAND RAPIDS—All classes	137,634	13,696	24,424	23,370	44,011	24,658	7,311
Native white—Native parentage	56,079	7,605	11,549	9,747	16,183	8,248	2,653
Foreign parentage	34,779	3,737	7,490	7,181	11,033	4,634	681
Mixed parentage	17,259	2,208	4,339	3,846	4,788	1,768	301
Foreign-born white	28,355	50	891	2,426	11,534	9,796	3,621
Negro	1,090	95	146	155	438	200	55
BATTLE CREEK—All classes	36,164	2,906	5,284	6,292	12,506	7,121	2,003
BAY CITY—All classes	47,554	5,106	9,710	8,574	13,523	7,852	2,772
FLINT—All classes	91,599	9,548	13,536	19,747	33,316	12,452	2,727
HAMTRAMCK VILLAGE—All classes	48,615	10,129	10,724	6,454	18,457	2,606	230
HIGHLAND PARK—All classes	46,499	4,743	6,451	8,168	19,871	6,079	1,155
JACKSON—All classes	48,374	4,533	7,436	8,559	16,737	8,580	2,507
KALAMAZOO—All classes	48,487	4,497	7,712	8,368	15,556	9,398	2,865
LANSING—All classes	57,327	5,692	8,640	11,090	19,582	9,682	2,471
MUSKEGON—All classes	36,570	3,820	6,069	7,076	11,654	6,029	1,814
PONTIAC—All classes	34,273	3,160	4,968	6,703	12,191	5,709	1,478
PORT HURON—All classes	25,944	2,609	4,686	4,442	7,685	5,055	1,424
SAGINAW—All classes	61,903	6,156	11,490	10,837	19,183	10,928	3,240
Minnesota.							
MINNEAPOLIS—All classes	380,582	35,585	58,410	66,844	138,333	65,398	15,623
Native white—Native parentage	133,178	19,362	26,673	24,521	40,814	16,607	4,979
Foreign parentage	108,824	9,835	18,639	23,930	40,713	14,137	1,508
Mixed parentage	46,331	5,947	10,607	10,757	14,552	3,897	546
Foreign-born white	88,032	208	2,060	7,015	40,197	30,000	8,475
Negro	3,927	217	403	568	1,924	700	112
ST. PAUL—All classes	234,698	21,967	38,490	42,541	81,447	40,274	9,606
Native white—Native parentage	77,378	12,966	18,079	14,710	22,067	7,334	1,942
Foreign parentage	70,190	4,819	11,144	15,618	26,964	10,601	1,016
Mixed parentage	32,008	3,879	7,615	7,803	9,943	2,484	273
Foreign-born white	51,595	96	1,263	3,910	20,860	19,135	6,286
Negro	3,376	196	373	480	1,545	687	86
DULUTH—All classes	98,017	10,113	17,607	18,079	34,492	15,619	2,866
Missouri.							
KANSAS CITY—All classes	324,410	24,000	45,494	56,173	124,170	59,776	13,730
Native white—Native parentage	209,134	17,869	32,201	38,681	77,179	34,376	8,009
Foreign parentage	35,183	2,915	5,766	5,335	12,074	7,983	1,074
Mixed parentage	21,880	1,611	3,157	4,076	8,972	3,524	518
Foreign-born white	27,320	134	1,051	2,833	11,492	8,750	3,011
Negro	30,719	1,462	3,307	5,210	14,673	5,114	739
ST. LOUIS—All classes	772,897	58,703	122,554	137,595	276,898	144,270	32,122
Native white—Native parentage	359,482	39,563	76,398	78,382	117,719	39,007	8,014
Foreign parentage	157,979	10,308	24,418	20,123	52,004	47,349	5,709
Mixed parentage	81,915	4,585	11,901	17,306	35,353	11,621	1,108
Foreign-born white	103,239	85	2,573	9,642	40,437	34,857	15,542
Negro	69,854	4,143	9,244	12,100	31,222	11,269	1,732

[1] Includes persons of unknown age.

CITIES HAVING 25,000 INHABITANTS OR MORE: 1920—Continued.

cities of 100,000 and over.]

CITY AND CLASS OF POPULATION.	PER CENT OF TOTAL.					
	Under 5 years.	5 to 14 years.	15 to 24 years.	25 to 44 years.	45 to 64 years.	65 years and over.
Massachusetts—Continued.						
CHICOPEE—All classes	14.4	21.9	17.0	30.6	13.3	2.7
EVERETT—All classes	11.0	19.4	17.2	30.2	17.9	4.3
FITCHBURG—All classes	11.0	19.1	17.2	31.4	16.9	4.5
HAVERHILL—All classes	9.4	16.5	16.7	32.4	19.4	5.7
HOLYOKE—All classes	10.3	18.8	18.5	31.9	16.6	3.9
LAWRENCE—All classes	11.2	19.2	17.2	32.4	16.5	3.5
LYNN—All classes	9.2	16.6	15.9	33.4	19.6	5.4
MALDEN—All classes	9.6	19.0	17.2	29.8	19.2	5.2
MEDFORD—All classes	10.5	17.4	16.1	33.0	18.1	4.9
NEWTON—All classes	8.5	17.2	15.9	31.2	20.8	6.3
PITTSFIELD—All classes	10.4	17.8	16.3	33.0	17.9	4.6
QUINCY—All classes	11.2	18.9	15.8	33.5	16.8	3.9
REVERE—All classes	11.6	22.1	16.9	31.3	14.9	3.1
SALEM—All classes	10.3	18.9	16.7	30.2	18.4	5.5
SOMERVILLE—All classes	9.8	16.7	16.2	32.2	19.5	5.6
TAUNTON—All classes	10.5	18.3	16.1	29.8	19.4	5.9
WALTHAM—All classes	8.9	16.8	17.5	31.8	19.4	5.6
Michigan.						
DETROIT—All classes	11.3	15.8	18.1	39.4	12.9	2.5
Native white—Native parentage	14.0	17.7	20.5	36.2	9.6	1.8
Foreign parentage	19.2	23.8	18.0	28.2	9.5	1.1
Mixed parentage	16.2	23.8	21.3	30.2	7.6	0.8
Foreign-born white	0.6	4.8	13.7	54.2	21.4	5.1
Negro	6.1	10.0	22.5	50.1	10.1	1.0
GRAND RAPIDS—All classes	10.0	17.7	17.0	32.0	17.9	5.3
Native white—Native parentage	13.6	20.6	17.4	28.9	14.7	4.7
Foreign parentage	10.7	21.5	20.6	31.7	13.3	2.0
Mixed parentage	12.8	25.1	22.3	27.7	10.2	1.7
Foreign-born white	0.2	3.1	8.6	40.7	34.5	12.8
Negro	8.7	13.4	14.2	40.2	18.3	5.0
BATTLE CREEK—All classes	8.0	14.6	17.4	34.6	19.7	5.5
BAY CITY—All classes	10.7	20.4	18.0	28.4	16.5	5.8
FLINT—All classes	10.4	14.8	21.6	36.4	13.6	3.0
HAMTRAMCK VILLAGE—All classes	20.8	22.1	13.3	38.0	5.4	0.5
HIGHLAND PARK—All classes	10.2	13.9	17.6	42.7	13.1	2.5
JACKSON—All classes	9.4	15.4	17.7	34.6	17.7	5.2
KALAMAZOO—All classes	9.3	15.9	17.3	32.1	19.4	5.9
LANSING—All classes	9.9	15.1	19.3	34.2	16.9	4.3
MUSKEGON—All classes	10.4	16.6	19.3	31.9	16.5	5.0
PONTIAC—All classes	9.2	14.5	19.6	35.6	16.7	4.3
PORT HURON—All classes	10.1	18.1	17.1	29.6	19.5	5.5
SAGINAW—All classes	9.9	18.6	17.5	31.0	17.7	5.2
Minnesota.						
MINNEAPOLIS—All classes	9.4	15.3	17.6	36.3	17.2	4.1
Native white—Native parentage	14.5	20.0	18.4	30.6	12.5	3.7
Foreign parentage	9.0	17.1	22.0	37.4	13.0	1.4
Mixed parentage	12.8	22.9	23.2	31.4	8.4	1.2
Foreign-born white	0.2	2.3	8.0	45.7	34.1	9.6
Negro	5.5	10.3	14.5	49.0	17.8	2.9
ST. PAUL—All classes	9.4	16.4	18.1	34.7	17.2	4.1
Native white—Native parentage	16.8	23.4	19.0	28.5	9.5	2.5
Foreign parentage	6.9	15.9	22.3	38.4	15.1	1.4
Mixed parentage	12.1	23.8	24.4	31.1	7.8	0.9
Foreign-born white	0.2	2.4	7.6	40.4	37.1	12.2
Negro	5.8	11.0	14.2	45.8	20.3	2.5
DULUTH—All classes	10.2	17.8	18.3	34.9	15.8	2.9
Missouri.						
KANSAS CITY—All classes	7.4	14.0	17.3	38.4	18.4	4.2
Native white—Native parentage	8.5	15.4	18.5	36.9	16.4	4.0
Foreign parentage	8.3	16.4	15.2	34.3	22.7	3.1
Mixed parentage	7.4	14.4	18.6	41.0	16.1	2.4
Foreign-born white	0.5	3.8	10.4	42.1	32.0	11.0
Negro	4.8	10.8	17.0	47.8	16.6	2.4
ST. LOUIS—All classes	7.6	15.9	17.8	35.8	18.7	4.2
Native white—Native parentage	11.0	21.3	21.8	32.7	10.9	2.2
Foreign parentage	6.5	14.2	12.7	32.9	30.0	3.6
Mixed parentage	5.6	14.5	21.1	43.2	14.2	1.4
Foreign-born white	0.1	2.5	9.3	39.2	33.8	15.1
Negro	5.9	13.2	17.3	44.7	16.1	2.5

TABLE **50.**—DISTRIBUTION BY BROAD AGE GROUPS, FOR

[By class of population for

CITY AND CLASS OF POPULATION.	All ages.[1]	AGE PERIODS.					
		Under 5 years.	5 to 14 years.	15 to 24 years.	25 to 44 years.	45 to 64 years.	65 years and over.
Missouri—Continued.							
JOPLIN—All classes	29,902	2,544	5,716	5,189	9,745	5,288	1,408
ST. JOSEPH—All classes	77,939	6,378	12,530	14,144	25,719	15,132	3,797
SPRINGFIELD—All classes	39,631	3,411	7,152	7,319	12,378	7,126	2,043
Montana.							
BUTTE—All classes	41,611	3,515	6,659	6,431	15,944	7,254	924
Nebraska.							
OMAHA—All classes	191,601	16,518	31,695	34,415	68,213	32,488	7,275
Native white—Native parentage	86,525	9,419	16,292	16,303	28,866	12,060	2,755
Foreign parentage	41,454	4,479	8,917	8,518	13,640	5,219	642
Mixed parentage	17,686	1,905	4,032	4,042	5,629	1,849	221
Foreign-born white	35,381	43	1,073	3,669	15,300	11,771	3,434
Negro	10,315	652	1,364	1,846	4,666	1,553	210
LINCOLN—All classes	54,948	5,051	9,447	9,805	17,531	9,878	3,079
New Hampshire.							
MANCHESTER—All classes	78,384	8,196	14,670	14,011	24,101	13,733	3,568
NASHUA—All classes	28,379	2,844	5,073	4,971	8,914	5,016	1,504
New Jersey.							
CAMDEN—All classes	116,309	12,959	21,939	20,260	37,728	18,975	4,273
Native white—Native parentage	56,249	6,543	11,079	10,216	17,179	8,789	2,380
Foreign parentage	22,817	4,436	6,625	4,221	4,612	2,557	359
Mixed parentage	8,425	1,175	2,004	1,748	2,307	1,020	167
Foreign-born white	20,262	54	766	2,570	10,511	5,181	1,147
Negro	8,500	750	1,513	1,499	3,100	1,401	219
JERSEY CITY—All classes	298,103	33,375	57,752	52,780	97,320	47,390	9,383
Native white—Native parentage	87,083	12,986	20,962	18,502	23,894	8,693	2,003
Foreign parentage	98,620	15,941	26,477	18,704	23,839	12,405	1,231
Mixed parentage	28,325	3,639	6,981	6,664	8,464	2,312	260
Foreign-born white	75,981	131	2,058	7,504	37,914	22,614	5,731
Negro	8,000	677	1,272	1,396	3,162	1,334	156
NEWARK—All classes	414,524	44,559	80,135	72,265	138,286	65,778	13,294
Native white—Native parentage	113,413	13,824	23,182	21,874	35,785	14,760	3,899
Foreign parentage	133,375	24,221	41,915	25,041	26,703	13,824	1,636
Mixed parentage	33,432	4,783	8,281	7,175	9,681	3,123	382
Foreign-born white	117,003	258	4,059	15,006	58,903	31,627	7,094
Negro	16,977	1,467	2,688	3,131	7,081	2,324	271
PATERSON—All classes	135,875	12,855	25,377	24,779	43,846	23,582	5,379
Native white—Native parentage	31,824	4,323	6,673	6,200	8,998	4,383	1,223
Foreign parentage	44,082	6,547	13,280	9,523	10,057	4,175	490
Mixed parentage	13,203	1,789	3,460	3,358	3,393	1,047	151
Foreign-born white	45,145	69	1,740	5,397	20,755	13,704	3,464
Negro	1,551	127	223	290	605	253	51
TRENTON—All classes	119,289	13,027	22,637	20,430	39,203	19,521	4,423
Native white—Native parentage	44,195	4,626	7,881	7,967	13,992	7,461	2,254
Foreign parentage	32,181	6,715	10,602	5,866	5,585	3,047	364
Mixed parentage	8,453	1,257	2,280	1,789	2,205	774	147
Foreign-born white	30,073	44	1,177	3,924	15,754	7,610	1,548
Negro	4,315	385	697	875	1,628	609	107
ATLANTIC CITY—All classes	50,707	3,751	7,947	7,598	18,845	10,343	2,135
BAYONNE—All classes	76,754	11,193	17,287	13,083	24,319	9,306	1,546
CLIFTON—All classes	26,470	3,309	5,058	4,527	8,553	3,562	655
EAST ORANGE—All classes	50,710	4,066	7,667	7,402	18,734	10,173	2,735
ELIZABETH—All classes	95,783	11,684	19,146	15,663	32,200	14,038	2,870
HOBOKEN—All classes	68,166	6,897	12,772	12,197	22,760	11,352	2,151
IRVINGTON TOWN—All classes	25,480	2,453	4,736	4,199	8,828	4,285	975
KEARNY TOWN—All classes	26,724	2,853	5,252	4,743	8,554	4,230	1,087
MONTCLAIR TOWN—All classes	28,810	2,579	5,205	4,443	9,752	5,446	1,373
NEW BRUNSWICK—All classes	32,779	3,919	6,350	5,319	10,893	4,984	1,292
ORANGE—All classes	33,268	3,623	6,593	5,736	10,383	5,564	1,348
PASSAIC—All classes	63,841	8,647	13,898	11,090	20,905	7,943	1,344
PERTH AMBOY—All classes	41,707	6,264	9,621	6,795	13,165	4,981	843
PLAINFIELD—All classes	27,700	2,833	4,967	4,323	9,334	4,831	1,347
WEST HOBOKEN TOWN—All classes	40,074	3,710	7,688	7,175	13,352	6,842	1,288
WEST NEW YORK TOWN—All classes	29,926	3,468	5,974	5,416	10,463	4,014	581

[1] Includes persons of unknown age.

CITIES HAVING 25,000 INHABITANTS OR MORE: 1920—Continued.

cities of 100,000 and over.]

CITY AND CLASS OF POPULATION.	PER CENT OF TOTAL.					
	Under 5 years.	5 to 14 years.	15 to 24 years.	25 to 44 years.	45 to 64 years.	65 years and over.
Missouri—Continued.						
JOPLIN—All classes	8.5	19.1	17.4	32.6	17.7	4.7
ST. JOSEPH—All classes	8.2	16.1	18.1	33.0	19.4	4.9
SPRINGFIELD—All classes	8.6	18.0	18.5	31.2	18.0	5.2
Montana.						
BUTTE—All classes	8.4	16.0	15.5	38.3	17.4	2.2
Nebraska.						
OMAHA—All classes	8.6	16.5	18.0	35.6	17.0	3.8
Native white—Native parentage	10.9	18.8	18.8	33.4	13.9	3.2
Foreign parentage	10.8	21.5	20.5	32.9	12.6	1.5
Mixed parentage	10.8	22.8	22.9	31.8	10.5	1.2
Foreign-born white	0.1	3.0	10.4	43.2	33.3	9.7
Negro	6.3	13.2	17.9	45.2	15.1	2.0
LINCOLN—All classes	9.2	17.2	17.8	31.9	18.0	5.6
New Hampshire.						
MANCHESTER—All classes	10.5	18.7	17.9	30.7	17.5	4.6
NASHUA—All classes	10.0	17.9	17.5	31.4	17.7	5.3
New Jersey.						
CAMDEN—All classes	11.1	18.9	17.4	32.4	16.3	3.7
Native white—Native parentage	11.6	19.7	18.2	30.5	15.6	4.2
Foreign parentage	19.4	29.0	18.5	20.2	11.2	1.6
Mixed parentage	13.9	23.8	20.7	27.4	12.1	2.0
Foreign-born white	0.3	3.8	12.7	51.9	25.6	5.7
Negro	8.8	17.8	17.6	36.5	16.5	2.6
JERSEY CITY—All classes	11.2	19.4	17.7	32.6	15.9	3.1
Native white—Native parentage	14.9	24.1	21.2	27.4	10.0	2.3
Foreign parentage	16.2	26.8	19.0	24.2	12.6	1.2
Mixed parentage	12.8	24.6	23.5	29.9	8.2	0.9
Foreign-born white	0.2	2.7	9.9	49.9	29.8	7.5
Negro	8.5	15.9	17.4	39.5	16.7	1.9
NEWARK—All classes	10.7	19.3	17.4	33.4	15.9	3.2
Native white—Native parentage	12.2	20.4	19.3	31.6	13.0	3.4
Foreign parentage	18.2	31.4	18.8	20.0	10.4	1.2
Mixed parentage	14.3	24.8	21.5	29.0	9.3	1.1
Foreign-born white	0.2	3.5	12.8	50.3	27.0	6.1
Negro	8.6	15.8	18.4	41.7	13.7	1.6
PATERSON—All classes	9.5	18.7	18.2	32.3	17.4	4.0
Native white—Native parentage	13.6	21.0	19.5	28.3	13.8	3.8
Foreign parentage	14.9	30.1	21.6	22.8	9.5	1.1
Mixed parentage	13.5	26.2	25.4	25.7	7.9	1.1
Foreign-born white	0.2	3.9	12.0	46.0	30.4	7.7
Negro	8.2	14.4	18.7	39.0	16.3	3.3
TRENTON—All classes	10.9	19.0	17.1	32.9	16.4	3.7
Native white—Native parentage	10.5	17.8	18.0	31.7	16.9	5.1
Foreign parentage	20.9	32.9	18.2	17.4	9.5	1.1
Mixed parentage	14.9	27.0	21.2	26.1	9.2	1.7
Foreign-born white	0.1	3.9	13.0	52.4	25.3	5.1
Negro	8.9	16.2	20.3	37.7	14.1	2.5
ATLANTIC CITY—All classes	7.4	15.7	15.0	37.2	20.4	4.2
BAYONNE—All classes	14.6	22.5	17.0	31.7	12.1	2.0
CLIFTON—All classes	12.5	22.1	17.1	32.3	13.5	2.5
EAST ORANGE—All classes	7.9	15.1	14.6	36.9	20.0	5.4
ELIZABETH—All classes	12.2	20.0	16.4	33.7	14.7	3.0
HOBOKEN—All classes	10.1	18.7	17.9	33.4	16.7	3.2
IRVINGTON TOWN—All classes	9.6	18.6	16.5	34.6	16.8	3.8
KEARNY TOWN—All classes	10.7	19.7	17.7	32.0	15.8	4.1
MONTCLAIR TOWN—All classes	9.0	18.1	15.4	33.8	18.9	4.8
NEW BRUNSWICK—All classes	12.0	19.4	16.2	33.2	15.2	3.9
ORANGE—All classes	10.9	19.8	17.2	31.2	16.7	4.1
PASSAIC—All classes	13.5	21.8	17.4	32.7	12.4	2.1
PERTH AMBOY—All classes	15.0	23.1	16.3	31.6	11.9	2.0
PLAINFIELD—All classes	10.2	17.9	15.6	33.7	17.4	4.9
WEST HOBOKEN TOWN—All classes	9.3	19.2	17.9	33.3	17.1	3.2
WEST NEW YORK TOWN—All classes	11.6	20.0	18.1	35.0	13.4	1.9

TABLE 50.—DISTRIBUTION BY BROAD AGE GROUPS, FOR

[By class of population for

CITY AND CLASS OF POPULATION.	All ages.[1]	AGE PERIODS.					
		Under 5 years.	5 to 14 years.	15 to 44 years.	25 to 44 years.	45 to 64 years.	65 years and over.
New York.							
ALBANY—All classes	113,344	8,734	16,656	18,221	39,749	23,370	6,540
Native white—Native parentage..	56,265	5,280	10,085	10,962	18,945	8,485	2,458
Foreign parentage.	27,034	2,554	4,186	3,320	8,225	7,517	1,223
Mixed parentage...	11,101	798	1,717	2,068	4,337	1,878	295
Foreign-born white	17,636	18	518	1,662	7,684	5,239	2,508
Negro	1,239	81	145	201	531	227	54
BUFFALO—All classes	506,775	52,092	90,078	86,421	170,969	87,625	19,190
Native white—Native parentage..	165,135	23,000	35,446	31,111	53,550	17,914	3,902
Foreign parentage	154,359	20,220	35,398	30,089	39,920	24,843	3,822
Mixed parentage...	61,018	8,238	14,567	12,459	18,726	6,383	624
Foreign-born white	121,530	344	4,177	11,831	56,479	37,849	10,760
Negro	4,511	277	466	878	2,212	593	76
NEW YORK CITY—All classes	5,620,048	560,869	1,031,357	999,418	1,942,755	901,613	176,231
Native white—Native parentage..	1,164,834	156,797	245,198	229,346	360,125	136,264	33,603
Foreign parentage..	1,873,013	321,764	595,754	373,145	380,744	179,482	21,302
Mixed parentage...	430,069	66,894	106,688	89,965	123,724	37,885	4,710
Foreign-born white	1,991,547	3,947	66,434	276,731	1,000,197	527,172	114,131
Negro	152,467	11,147	16,794	29,091	73,414	19,279	2,423
Bronx borough—All classes	732,016	76,856	142,075	132,175	253,881	106,692	19,879
Native white—Native parentage..	132,770	21,555	32,200	26,704	38,588	11,170	2,383
Foreign parentage	268,380	43,964	85,122	56,701	58,318	21,856	2,330
Mixed parentage...	58,869	10,556	15,864	12,211	15,930	3,900	386
Foreign-born white	266,971	362	7,887	35,740	139,189	68,994	14,627
Negro	4,803	408	983	795	1,756	706	150
Brooklyn borough—All classes	2,018,356	213,651	394,990	367,067	657,567	317,358	66,066
Native white—Native parentage..	456,240	63,438	99,513	92,935	134,487	51,491	13,658
Foreign parentage	703,417	119,782	228,626	140,657	136,895	68,487	8,656
Mixed parentage...	166,009	26,574	40,832	34,048	47,033	15,351	2,104
Foreign-born white	659,287	1,229	21,949	92,994	324,692	177,025	40,919
Negro	31,912	2,595	4,039	6,042	13,798	4,642	720
Manhattan borough—All classes	2,284,103	210,089	379,484	401,043	837,339	382,073	70,165
Native white—Native parentage..	388,279	42,468	65,098	73,181	135,300	56,985	12,943
Foreign parentage.	720,454	136,556	237,598	141,312	132,904	63,729	7,704
Mixed parentage...	138,093	21,245	32,410	28,627	40,661	13,440	1,623
Foreign-born white	922,080	2,013	32,930	136,200	469,509	233,995	46,488
Negro	109,133	7,548	10,735	21,050	55,319	12,915	1,364
Queens borough—All classes	469,042	48,279	91,271	79,635	157,634	76,625	15,115
Native white—Native parentage..	149,342	24,510	39,435	28,884	41,154	12,122	2,997
Foreign parentage	147,400	16,217	33,924	28,614	45,445	21,102	2,040
Mixed parentage...	55,243	6,912	14,450	12,390	16,854	4,169	447
Foreign-born white	111,676	193	2,615	8,815	52,097	38,338	9,486
Negro	5,120	430	823	896	1,980	821	139
Richmond borough—All classes	116,531	11,994	23,537	19,498	36,334	18,865	5,006
Native white—Native parentage.	38,203	4,826	8,952	7,642	10,596	4,496	1,622
Foreign parentage.	33,362	5,245	10,184	5,861	7,182	4,308	572
Mixed parentage...	11,855	1,607	3,132	2,689	3,246	1,025	150
Foreign-born white	31,533	150	1,053	2,982	14,710	8,820	2,611
Negro	1,499	166	214	308	561	195	50
ROCHESTER—All classes	295,750	29,300	49,565	47,983	101,079	54,011	13,484
Native white—Native parentage..	111,976	13,286	21,447	20,651	36,930	15,189	4,280
Foreign parentage	78,445	11,949	17,824	11,549	19,989	14,656	2,443
Mixed parentage...	32,347	3,724	6,968	6,600	10,668	3,879	494
Foreign-born white	71,321	227	3,135	8,895	32,757	20,009	6,214
Negro	1,579	113	183	265	703	260	53
SYRACUSE—All classes	171,717	16,275	27,409	28,048	58,850	32,839	8,222
Native white—Native parentage.	80,072	8,631	13,976	14,490	26,851	12,472	3,607
Foreign parentage.	40,882	5,626	8,875	6,476	10,330	8,398	1,168
Mixed parentage...	17,097	1,864	3,380	3,423	5,783	2,349	293
Foreign-born white	32,001	69	1,009	3,436	15,309	9,381	3,104
Negro	1,260	74	150	211	610	231	49
YONKERS—All classes	100,176	10,524	20,718	16,921	32,313	16,750	3,205
Native white—Native parentage..	30,059	4,003	7,030	5,388	8,709	3,887	1,024
Foreign parentage	32,280	4,981	9,831	6,543	6,921	3,616	382
Mixed parentage...	10,139	1,353	2,766	2,254	2,744	888	131
Foreign-born white	25,700	39	741	2,383	13,166	7,641	1,709
Negro	1,940	145	345	342	766	302	39
AMSTERDAM—All classes	33,524	3,551	6,516	5,201	10,905	5,868	1,469
AUBURN—All classes	36,192	3,310	6,018	5,608	11,985	6,939	2,300
BINGHAMTON—All classes	66,800	6,403	9,943	10,566	22,116	13,614	4,081
ELMIRA—All classes	45,393	3,838	6,471	8,443	14,537	9,279	2,784
JAMESTOWN—All classes	38,917	3,379	6,418	6,797	12,312	7,651	2,326
KINGSTON—All classes	26,688	1,956	4,352	4,488	7,953	6,055	1,868
MOUNT VERNON—All classes	42,726	4,114	8,172	6,835	13,809	7,775	2,010

[1] Includes persons of unknown age.

CITIES HAVING 25,000 INHABITANTS OR MORE: 1920—Continued.

cities of 100,000 and over.]

CITY AND CLASS OF POPULATION.	PER CENT OF TOTAL.					
	Under 5 years.	5 to 14 years.	15 to 24 years.	25 to 44 years.	45 to 64 years.	65 years and over.
New York.						
ALBANY—All classes	7.7	14.7	16.1	35.1	20.6	5.8
Native white—Native parentage	9.4	17.9	19.5	33.7	15.1	4.4
Foreign parentage	9.4	15.5	12.3	30.4	27.8	4.5
Mixed parentage	7.2	15.5	18.6	39.1	16.9	2.7
Foreign-born white	0.1	2.9	9.4	43.6	29.7	14.2
Negro	6.5	11.7	16.2	42.9	18.3	4.4
BUFFALO—All classes	10.3	17.8	17.1	33.7	17.3	3.8
Native white—Native parentage	13.9	21.5	18.8	32.4	10.8	2.4
Foreign parentage	13.1	22.9	19.5	25.9	16.1	2.5
Mixed parentage	13.5	23.9	20.4	30.7	10.5	1.0
Foreign-born white	0.3	3.4	9.7	46.5	31.1	8.9
Negro	6.1	10.3	19.5	49.0	13.1	1.7
NEW YORK CITY—All classes	10.0	18.4	17.8	34.6	16.0	3.1
Native white—Native parentage	13.5	21.1	19.7	30.9	11.7	2.9
Foreign parentage	17.2	31.8	19.9	20.3	9.6	1.1
Mixed parentage	15.6	24.8	20.9	28.8	8.8	1.1
Foreign-born white	0.2	3.3	13.9	50.2	26.5	5.7
Negro	7.3	11.0	19.1	48.2	12.6	1.6
Bronx borough—All classes	10.5	19.4	18.1	34.7	14.6	2.7
Native white—Native parentage	16.2	24.3	20.1	29.1	8.4	1.8
Foreign parentage	16.4	31.7	21.1	21.7	8.1	0.9
Mixed parentage	17.9	26.9	20.7	27.1	6.6	0.7
Foreign-born white	0.1	3.0	13.4	52.1	25.8	5.5
Negro	8.5	20.5	16.6	36.6	14.7	3.1
Brooklyn borough—All classes	10.6	19.6	18.2	32.6	15.7	3.3
Native white—Native parentage	13.9	21.8	20.4	29.5	11.3	3.0
Foreign parentage	17.0	32.5	20.0	19.5	9.7	1.2
Mixed parentage	16.0	24.6	20.5	28.3	9.2	1.3
Foreign-born white	0.2	3.3	14.1	49.2	26.9	6.2
Negro	8.1	12.7	18.9	43.2	14.5	2.3
Manhattan borough—All classes	9.2	16.6	17.6	36.7	16.7	3.1
Native white—Native parentage	10.9	16.8	18.8	34.8	14.7	3.3
Foreign parentage	19.0	33.0	19.6	18.4	8.8	1.1
Mixed parentage	15.4	23.5	20.7	29.4	9.7	1.2
Foreign-born white	0.2	3.6	14.8	50.9	25.4	5.0
Negro	6.9	9.8	19.3	50.7	11.8	1.2
Queens borough—All classes	10.3	19.5	17.0	33.6	16.3	3.2
Native white—Native parentage	16.4	26.4	19.3	27.6	8.1	2.0
Foreign parentage	11.0	23.0	19.4	30.8	14.3	1.4
Mixed parentage	12.5	26.2	22.4	30.5	7.5	0.8
Foreign-born white	0.2	2.3	7.9	46.7	34.3	8.5
Negro	8.4	16.1	17.5	38.7	16.0	2.7
Richmond borough—All classes	10.3	20.2	16.7	31.2	16.2	4.3
Native white—Native parentage	12.6	23.4	20.0	27.7	11.8	4.2
Foreign parentage	15.7	30.5	17.6	21.5	12.9	1.7
Mixed parentage	13.6	26.4	22.7	27.4	8.6	1.3
Foreign-born white	0.5	3.3	9.5	46.6	28.0	8.3
Negro	11.1	14.3	20.5	37.4	13.0	3.3
ROCHESTER—All classes	9.9	16.8	16.2	34.2	18.3	4.6
Native white—Native parentage	11.9	19.2	18.4	33.0	13.6	3.8
Foreign parentage	15.2	22.7	14.7	25.5	18.7	3.1
Mixed parentage	11.5	21.5	20.4	33.0	12.0	1.5
Foreign-born white	0.3	4.4	12.5	45.9	28.1	8.7
Negro	7.2	11.6	16.8	44.5	16.5	3.4
SYRACUSE—All classes	9.5	16.0	16.3	34.3	19.1	4.8
Native white—Native parentage	10.8	17.5	18.1	33.5	15.6	4.5
Foreign parentage	13.8	21.7	15.8	25.3	20.5	2.9
Mixed parentage	10.9	19.8	20.0	33.8	13.7	1.7
Foreign-born white	0.2	3.1	10.6	47.4	29.0	9.6
Negro	5.9	12.1	16.7	43.0	18.3	3.9
YONKERS—All classes	10.5	20.7	16.9	32.3	16.3	3.3
Native white—Native parentage	13.3	23.4	17.9	29.0	12.9	3.4
Foreign parentage	15.4	30.5	20.3	21.4	11.2	1.2
Mixed parentage	13.3	27.3	22.2	27.1	8.8	1.3
Foreign-born white	0.2	2.9	9.3	51.2	29.7	6.6
Negro	7.5	17.8	17.6	39.5	15.6	2.0
AMSTERDAM—All classes	10.6	19.4	15.5	32.5	17.5	4.4
AUBURN—All classes	9.1	16.6	15.5	33.1	19.2	6.4
BINGHAMTON—All classes	9.6	14.9	15.8	33.1	20.4	6.1
ELMIRA—All classes	8.5	14.3	18.6	32.0	20.4	6.1
JAMESTOWN—All classes	8.7	16.5	17.5	31.6	19.7	6.0
KINGSTON—All classes	7.3	16.3	16.8	29.8	22.7	7.0
MOUNT VERNON—All classes	9.6	19.1	16.0	32.3	18.2	4.7

TABLE 50.—DISTRIBUTION BY BROAD AGE GROUPS, FOR

[By class of population for

CITY AND CLASS OF POPULATION.	All ages.[1]	AGE PERIODS.					
		Under 5 years.	5 to 14 years.	15 to 24 years.	25 to 44 years.	45 to 64 years.	65 years and over.
New York—Continued.							
NEW ROCHELLE—All classes	36,213	3,370	6,983	6,067	11,888	6,317	1,273
NEWBURGH—All classes	30,366	2,503	4,919	5,141	9,630	6,348	1,805
NIAGARA FALLS—All classes	50,760	6,206	9,493	8,067	18,206	7,461	1,267
POUGHKEEPSIE—All classes	35,000	3,273	5,828	5,629	11,055	6,953	2,224
ROME—All classes	26,341	2,800	5,034	4,412	8,052	4,546	1,491
SCHENECTADY—All classes	88,723	8,693	16,419	14,347	30,639	15,192	3,352
TROY—All classes	72,013	5,348	11,009	12,112	23,458	15,738	4,249
UTICA—All classes	94,156	9,529	16,785	14,759	31,129	17,185	4,759
WATERTOWN—All classes	31,285	2,716	5,070	5,137	9,828	6,513	2,012
North Carolina.							
ASHEVILLE—All classes	28,504	2,892	5,621	5,446	9,559	4,046	902
CHARLOTTE—All classes	46,338	5,053	9,105	9,849	15,147	5,693	1,311
WILMINGTON—All classes	33,372	3,431	6,496	7,048	10,692	4,474	1,140
WINSTON-SALEM—All classes	48,395	4,812	8,661	13,895	14,848	5,127	973
Ohio.							
AKRON—All classes	208,435	20,879	27,961	48,873	82,071	23,971	4,491
Native white—Native parentage	125,079	12,684	16,763	34,788	46,022	12,291	2,406
Foreign parentage	28,345	6,461	7,067	4,401	6,909	3,027	468
Mixed parentage	11,405	1,341	1,847	2,546	4,113	1,366	190
Foreign-born white	37,889	86	1,735	5,751	22,225	6,684	1,364
Negro	5,580	306	547	1,356	2,733	573	59
CINCINNATI—All classes	401,247	30,736	61,728	65,998	137,857	83,067	21,521
Native white—Native parentage	206,605	23,735	43,850	41,354	67,632	24,081	5,770
Foreign parentage	80,311	3,012	7,359	8,403	25,867	30,615	5,012
Mixed parentage	41,354	1,963	5,462	8,033	17,621	7,374	879
Foreign-born white	42,827	26	898	3,002	13,999	15,760	9,094
Negro	30,079	1,995	4,157	5,193	12,705	5,219	766
CLEVELAND—All classes	796,841	88,433	146,675	133,892	290,543	113,620	23,154
Native white—Native parentage	212,247	28,507	42,247	39,423	72,275	24,217	5,281
Foreign parentage	246,529	46,792	74,500	44,149	57,274	21,262	2,510
Mixed parentage	63,712	10,298	16,934	13,602	17,239	5,060	563
Foreign-born white	239,538	453	8,842	29,639	127,336	58,790	14,356
Negro	34,451	2,371	4,140	7,011	16,237	4,206	440
COLUMBUS—All classes	237,031	19,315	35,687	41,480	83,799	44,984	11,344
Native white—Native parentage	159,069	14,999	26,851	29,870	54,601	25,750	6,680
Foreign parentage	24,202	1,693	3,170	3,136	7,397	7,402	1,397
Mixed parentage	15,395	953	2,153	2,784	5,796	3,165	534
Foreign-born white	16,055	26	486	1,651	6,633	5,055	2,188
Negro	22,181	1,638	3,022	4,011	9,315	3,582	542
DAYTON—All classes	152,559	14,024	24,136	26,232	53,057	27,919	7,073
Native white—Native parentage	100,996	10,796	17,967	19,335	34,326	14,500	3,985
Foreign parentage	18,887	1,794	2,963	2,176	5,166	5,874	909
Mixed parentage	10,501	709	1,570	1,808	3,987	2,102	322
Foreign-born white	13,111	21	427	1,278	5,785	3,994	1,599
Negro	9,025	704	1,206	1,627	3,775	1,439	258
TOLEDO—All classes	243,164	22,739	39,550	42,825	85,790	,951	10,183
Native white—Native parentage	124,055	14,123	23,003	24,425	41,461	,953	4,024
Foreign parentage	51,101	5,594	9,902	8,913	16,067	9,334	1,284
Mixed parentage	24,084	2,605	4,815	4,836	8,186	3,170	468
Foreign-born white	38,145	68	1,195	3,570	17,317	11,669	4,294
Negro	5,691	346	635	1,069	2,712	800	112
YOUNGSTOWN—All classes	132,358	16,477	24,500	22,052	48,412	17,506	3,297
Native white—Native parentage	46,459	6,432	9,434	8,741	15,347	5,253	1,187
Foreign parentage	34,459	7,899	10,384	5,414	7,379	3,093	285
Mixed parentage	10,843	1,647	2,296	2,419	3,177	882	119
Foreign-born white	33,834	52	1,266	4,076	19,281	7,508	1,627
Negro	6,662	443	818	1,382	3,169	755	78
CANTON—All classes	87,091	8,904	13,845	15,473	32,115	13,550	3,183
EAST CLEVELAND—All classes	27,268	2,770	3,917	4,262	10,000	4,823	1,189
HAMILTON—All classes	39,675	3,672	6,155	7,190	12,569	7,352	1,925
LAKEWOOD—All classes	41,732	4,251	7,314	5,844	16,158	6,123	1,107
LIMA—All classes	41,326	4,144	7,242	7,319	13,319	7,442	1,848
LORAIN—All classes	37,295	4,784	8,173	5,649	12,855	5,013	807
MANSFIELD—All classes	27,824	2,498	4,305	4,761	9,152	5,364	1,684
MARION—All classes	27,891	2,796	4,930	4,798	8,798	5,116	1,447
NEWARK—All classes	26,718	2,240	4,364	4,403	8,549	5,520	1,633
PORTSMOUTH—All classes	33,011	3,492	5,843	6,468	10,664	5,169	1,355
SPRINGFIELD—All classes	60,840	5,476	10,260	10,279	19,723	11,479	3,565
STEUBENVILLE—All classes	28,508	3,337	5,317	4,710	9,947	4,182	1,007
WARREN—All classes	27,050	3,021	4,211	4,791	9,748	4,171	1,094
ZANESVILLE—All classes	29,569	2,731	4,922	4,690	9,193	6,104	1,910

[1] Includes persons of unknown age.

CITIES HAVING 25,000 INHABITANTS OR MORE: 1920—Continued.

cities of 100,000 and over.]

CITY AND CLASS OF POPULATION.	PER CENT OF TOTAL.					
	Under 5 years.	5 to 14 years.	15 to 24 years.	25 to 44 years.	45 to 64 years.	65 years and over.
New York—Continued.						
NEW ROCHELLE—All classes	9.3	19.3	16.8	32.8	17.4	3.5
NEWBURGH—All classes	8.2	16.2	16.9	31.7	20.9	5.9
NIAGARA FALLS—All classes	12.2	18.7	15.9	35.9	14.7	2.5
POUGHKEEPSIE—All classes	9.4	16.7	16.1	31.6	19.9	6.4
ROME—All classes	10.6	19.1	16.7	30.6	17.3	5.7
SCHENECTADY—All classes	9.8	18.5	16.2	34.5	17.1	3.8
TROY—All classes	7.4	15.3	16.8	32.6	21.9	5.9
UTICA—All classes	10.1	17.8	15.7	33.1	18.3	5.1
WATERTOWN—All classes	8.7	16.2	16.4	31.4	20.8	6.4
North Carolina.						
ASHEVILLE—All classes	10.1	19.7	19.1	33.5	14.2	3.2
CHARLOTTE—All classes	10.9	19.6	21.3	32.7	12.3	2.8
WILMINGTON—All classes	10.3	19.5	21.1	32.0	13.4	3.4
WINSTON-SALEM—All classes	9.9	17.9	28.7	30.7	10.6	2.0
Ohio.						
AKRON—All classes	10.0	13.4	23.4	39.4	11.5	2.2
Native white—Native parentage	10.1	13.4	27.8	36.8	9.8	1.9
Foreign parentage	22.8	24.9	15.5	24.4	10.7	1.7
Mixed parentage	11.8	16.2	22.3	36.1	12.0	1.7
Foreign-born white	0.2	4.6	15.2	58.7	17.6	3.6
Negro	5.5	9.8	24.3	49.0	10.3	1.1
CINCINNATI—All classes	7.7	15.4	16.4	34.4	20.7	5.4
Native white—Native parentage	11.5	21.2	20.0	32.7	11.7	2.8
Foreign parentage	3.8	9.2	10.5	32.2	38.1	6.2
Mixed parentage	4.7	13.2	19.4	42.6	17.8	2.1
Foreign-born white	0.1	2.1	7.0	32.7	36.8	21.2
Negro	6.6	13.8	17.3	42.2	17.4	2.5
CLEVELAND—All classes	11.1	18.4	16.8	36.5	14.3	2.9
Native white—Native parentage	13.4	19.9	18.6	34.1	11.4	2.5
Foreign parentage	19.0	30.2	17.9	23.2	8.6	1.0
Mixed parentage	16.2	26.6	21.3	27.1	7.9	0.9
Foreign-born white	0.2	3.7	12.4	53.2	24.5	6.0
Negro	6.9	12.0	20.4	47.1	12.2	1.3
COLUMBUS—All classes	8.1	15.1	17.5	35.4	19.0	4.8
Native white—Native parentage	9.4	16.9	18.8	34.3	16.2	4.2
Foreign parentage	7.0	13.1	13.0	30.6	30.6	5.8
Mixed parentage	6.2	14.0	18.1	37.6	20.6	3.5
Foreign-born white	0.2	3.0	10.3	41.3	31.5	13.6
Negro	7.4	13.6	18.1	42.0	16.1	2.4
DAYTON—All classes	9.2	15.8	17.2	34.8	18.3	4.6
Native white—Native parentage	10.7	17.8	19.1	34.0	14.4	3.9
Foreign parentage	9.5	15.7	11.5	27.4	31.1	4.8
Mixed parentage	6.8	15.0	17.2	38.0	20.0	3.1
Foreign-born white	0.2	3.3	9.7	44.1	30.5	12.2
Negro	7.8	13.4	18.0	41.8	15.9	2.9
TOLEDO—All classes	9.4	16.3	17.6	35.3	17.3	4.2
Native white—Native parentage	11.4	18.5	19.7	33.4	13.7	3.3
Foreign parentage	10.9	19.4	17.4	31.4	18.3	2.5
Mixed parentage	10.8	20.0	20.1	34.0	13.2	1.9
Foreign-born white	0.2	3.1	9.4	45.4	30.6	11.3
Negro	6.1	11.2	18.8	47.7	14.1	2.0
YOUNGSTOWN—All classes	12.4	18.5	16.7	36.6	13.2	2.5
Native white—Native parentage	13.8	20.3	18.8	33.0	11.3	2.6
Foreign parentage	22.9	30.1	15.7	21.4	9.0	0.8
Mixed parentage	15.2	23.9	22.3	29.3	8.1	1.1
Foreign-born white	0.2	3.7	12.0	57.0	22.2	4.8
Negro	6.6	12.3	20.7	47.6	11.3	1.2
CANTON—All classes	10.2	15.9	17.8	36.9	15.6	3.7
EAST CLEVELAND—All classes	8.7	14.4	15.6	39.2	17.7	4.4
HAMILTON—All classes	9.3	17.0	18.7	31.7	18.5	4.9
LAKEWOOD—All classes	10.2	17.5	14.0	38.7	16.1	3.4
LIMA—All classes	10.0	17.5	17.7	32.2	18.0	4.5
LORAIN—All classes	12.8	21.9	15.1	34.5	13.4	2.2
MANSFIELD—All classes	9.0	15.5	17.1	32.9	19.3	6.1
MARION—All classes	10.0	17.7	17.2	31.5	18.3	5.2
NEWARK—All classes	8.4	16.3	16.5	32.0	20.7	6.1
PORTSMOUTH—All classes	10.6	17.7	19.6	32.3	15.7	4.1
SPRINGFIELD—All classes	9.0	16.9	16.9	32.4	18.9	5.9
STEUBENVILLE—All classes	11.7	18.7	16.5	34.9	14.7	3.5
WARREN—All classes	11.2	15.6	17.7	36.0	15.4	4.0
ZANESVILLE—All classes	9.2	16.6	15.9	31.1	20.6	6.5

TABLE 50.—DISTRIBUTION BY BROAD AGE GROUPS, FOR

[By class of population for

CITY AND CLASS OF POPULATION.	All ages.[1]	AGE PERIODS.					
		Under 5 years.	5 to 14 years.	15 to 24 years.	25 to 44 years.	45 to 64 years.	65 years and over.
Oklahoma.							
MUSKOGEE—All classes	30,277	2,760	5,850	5,716	10,340	4,513	1,017
OKLAHOMA CITY—All classes	91,295	7,468	14,882	18,639	33,409	13,757	3,016
TULSA—All classes	72,075	6,384	11,746	14,745	28,502	9,017	1,507
Oregon.							
PORTLAND—All classes	258,288	19,970	39,397	40,518	95,628	50,387	12,140
Native white—Native parentage	136,216	13,056	24,110	22,805	47,085	23,009	6,039
Foreign parentage	41,935	3,580	7,698	7,438	15,239	6,997	951
Mixed parentage	27,696	2,688	5,380	5,434	9,982	3,638	555
Foreign-born white	47,114	194	1,721	4,154	21,178	15,435	4,353
Negro	1,556	82	169	176	732	353	40
Pennsylvania.							
PHILADELPHIA—All classes	1,823,779	178,669	321,197	313,992	608,889	323,044	76,449
Native white—Native parentage	698,782	81,548	136,168	125,702	219,347	105,082	30,229
Foreign parentage	447,071	69,001	121,961	83,360	97,887	64,247	10,458
Mixed parentage	144,400	17,722	32,164	28,958	43,427	18,656	3,392
Foreign-born white	397,927	557	12,839	50,020	188,978	115,374	29,859
Negro	134,229	9,769	17,998	25,701	58,714	19,269	2,488
PITTSBURGH—All classes	588,343	62,006	110,383	102,045	197,840	95,779	19,709
Native white—Native parentage	216,530	28,862	46,840	40,511	67,727	26,787	5,477
Foreign parentage	157,581	23,357	41,610	30,298	38,330	20,357	3,556
Mixed parentage	55,884	6,875	13,285	11,910	16,387	6,416	986
Foreign-born white	120,266	168	2,972	12,317	59,246	36,375	9,092
Negro	37,725	2,732	5,660	6,956	15,981	5,740	595
READING—All classes	107,784	10,123	19,502	17,871	34,102	20,539	5,600
Native white—Native parentage	81,000	7,268	14,475	13,972	25,582	15,350	4,318
Foreign parentage	11,916	2,293	3,717	1,842	2,056	1,721	282
Mixed parentage	4,382	467	827	664	1,399	837	188
Foreign-born white	9,553	13	315	1,228	4,705	2,501	786
Negro	924	82	168	163	356	127	26
SCRANTON—All classes	137,783	15,289	29,813	25,057	41,607	21,569	4,342
Native white—Native parentage	48,715	7,255	12,581	9,852	12,789	5,037	1,147
Foreign parentage	45,217	6,084	12,449	9,121	11,270	5,674	611
Mixed parentage	14,714	1,878	3,969	3,697	3,993	1,042	128
Foreign-born white	28,568	36	729	2,303	13,316	9,699	2,449
Negro	563	36	85	83	238	113	7
ALLENTOWN—All classes	73,502	7,826	13,852	12,205	24,007	12,156	3,414
ALTOONA—All classes	60,331	6,368	11,363	10,635	19,186	10,163	2,583
BETHLEHEM—All classes	50,358	6,608	9,572	8,260	16,768	7,314	1,810
CHESTER—All classes	58,030	6,767	9,311	10,778	20,695	8,618	1,807
EASTON—All classes	33,813	3,204	5,673	5,462	11,046	6,512	1,871
ERIE—All classes	93,372	10,615	17,692	15,814	30,311	14,976	3,938
HARRISBURG—All classes	75,917	6,232	11,916	12,854	26,189	14,759	3,817
HAZLETON—All classes	32,277	3,951	7,529	6,227	8,666	4,829	1,054
JOHNSTOWN—All classes	67,327	8,742	14,293	11,680	21,268	9,298	2,031
LANCASTER—All classes	53,150	4,863	8,693	9,078	16,195	10,717	3,580
MCKEESPORT—All classes	46,781	5,763	9,872	8,337	14,698	6,785	1,268
NEW CASTLE—All classes	44,938	5,437	9,087	7,392	14,504	6,783	1,658
NORRISTOWN BOROUGH—All classes	32,319	2,991	5,147	5,021	10,242	6,768	2,138
WILKES-BARRE—All classes	73,833	8,402	15,421	13,431	22,086	11,818	2,637
WILLIAMSPORT—All classes	36,198	3,103	5,743	6,572	11,087	7,456	2,208
YORK—All classes	47,512	4,295	8,232	8,562	14,377	9,180	2,856
Rhode Island.							
PROVIDENCE—All classes	237,505	23,449	42,618	39,037	76,081	45,195	11,083
Native white—Native parentage	67,778	7,243	11,703	10,240	18,631	11,399	4,463
Foreign parentage	76,048	12,110	20,007	14,940	16,033	9,133	1,143
Mixed parentage	23,029	3,393	6,021	5,187	6,072	1,934	218
Foreign-born white	68,951	103	1,995	7,817	32,339	21,655	5,010
Negro	5,655	532	874	844	2,135	1,029	236
CRANSTON—All classes	29,407	2,905	5,353	4,356	9,259	5,687	1,820
NEWPORT—All classes	30,255	2,541	4,646	7,064	9,159	5,399	1,432
PAWTUCKET—All classes	64,248	6,480	11,359	11,644	20,414	11,533	2,799
WOONSOCKET—All classes	43,496	4,760	8,521	8,653	12,887	7,040	1,624
South Carolina.							
CHARLESTON—All classes	67,957	6,275	12,474	14,115	23,022	9,594	2,142
COLUMBIA—All classes	37,524	3,252	6,522	8,175	13,486	4,873	1,154

[1] Includes persons of unknown age.

CITIES HAVING 25,000 INHABITANTS OR MORE: 1920—Continued.

cities of 100,000 and over.]

CITY AND CLASS OF POPULATION.	PER CENT OF TOTAL.					
	Under 5 years.	5 to 14 years.	15 to 24 years.	25 to 44 years.	45 to 64 years.	65 years and over.
Oklahoma.						
MUSKOGEE—All classes	9.1	19.3	18.9	34.2	14.9	3.4
OKLAHOMA CITY—All classes	8.2	16.3	20.4	36.6	15.1	3.3
TULSA—All classes	8.9	16.3	20.5	39.5	12.5	2.1
Oregon.						
PORTLAND—All classes	7.7	15.3	15.7	37.0	19.5	4.7
Native white—Native parentage	9.6	17.7	16.7	34.6	16.9	4.4
Foreign parentage	8.5	18.4	17.7	36.3	16.7	2.3
Mixed parentage	9.7	19.4	19.6	36.0	13.1	2.0
Foreign-born white	0.4	3.7	8.8	45.0	32.8	9.2
Negro	5.3	10.9	11.3	47.0	22.7	2.6
Pennsylvania.						
PHILADELPHIA—All classes	9.8	17.6	17.2	33.4	17.7	4.2
Native white—Native parentage	11.7	19.5	18.0	31.4	15.0	4.3
Foreign parentage	15.4	27.3	18.6	21.9	14.4	2.3
Mixed parentage	12.3	22.3	20.1	30.1	12.9	2.3
Foreign-born white	0.1	3.2	12.6	47.5	29.0	7.5
Negro	7.3	13.4	19.1	43.7	14.4	1.9
PITTSBURGH—All classes	10.5	18.8	17.3	33.6	16.3	3.3
Native white—Native parentage	13.3	21.6	18.7	31.3	12.4	2.5
Foreign parentage	14.8	26.4	19.2	24.3	12.9	2.3
Mixed parentage	12.3	23.8	21.3	29.3	11.5	1.8
Foreign-born white	0.1	2.5	10.2	49.3	30.2	7.6
Negro	7.2	15.0	18.4	42.4	15.2	1.6
READING—All classes	9.4	18.1	16.6	31.6	19.1	5.2
Native white—Native parentage	9.0	17.9	17.2	31.6	19.0	5.3
Foreign parentage	19.2	31.2	15.5	17.3	14.4	2.4
Mixed parentage	10.7	18.9	15.2	31.9	19.1	4.3
Foreign-born white	0.1	3.3	12.9	49.3	26.2	8.2
Negro	8.9	18.2	17.6	38.5	13.7	2.8
SCRANTON—All classes	11.1	21.6	18.2	30.2	15.7	3.2
Native white—Native parentage	14.9	25.8	20.2	26.3	10.3	2.4
Foreign parentage	13.5	27.5	20.2	24.9	12.5	1.4
Mixed parentage	12.8	27.0	25.1	27.1	7.1	0.9
Foreign-born white	0.1	2.6	8.1	46.6	34.0	8.6
Negro	6.4	15.1	14.7	42.3	20.1	1.2
ALLENTOWN—All classes	10.6	18.8	16.6	32.7	16.5	4.6
ALTOONA—All classes	10.6	18.8	17.6	31.8	16.8	4.3
BETHLEHEM—All classes	13.1	19.0	16.4	33.3	14.5	3.6
CHESTER—All classes	11.7	16.0	18.6	35.7	14.9	3.1
EASTON—All classes	9.5	16.8	16.2	32.7	19.3	5.5
ERIE—All classes	11.4	18.9	16.9	32.5	16.0	4.2
HARRISBURG—All classes	8.2	15.7	16.9	34.5	19.4	5.0
HAZLETON—All classes	12.2	23.3	19.3	26.8	15.0	3.3
JOHNSTOWN—All classes	13.0	21.2	17.3	31.6	13.8	3.0
LANCASTER—All classes	9.1	16.4	17.1	30.5	20.2	6.7
MCKEESPORT—All classes	12.3	21.1	17.8	31.4	14.5	2.7
NEW CASTLE—All classes	12.1	20.2	16.4	32.3	15.1	3.7
NORRISTOWN BOROUGH—All classes	9.3	15.9	15.5	31.7	20.9	6.6
WILKES-BARRE—All classes	11.4	20.9	18.2	29.9	16.0	3.6
WILLIAMSPORT—All classes	8.6	15.9	18.2	30.6	20.6	6.1
YORK—All classes	9.0	17.3	18.0	30.3	19.3	6.0
Rhode Island.						
PROVIDENCE—All classes	9.9	17.9	16.4	32.0	19.0	4.7
Native white—Native parentage	11.4	18.4	16.1	29.2	17.9	7.0
Foreign parentage	16.0	28.9	19.6	21.9	12.0	1.5
Mixed parentage	14.7	26.1	22.5	27.2	8.4	0.9
Foreign-born white	0.1	2.9	11.3	46.9	31.4	7.3
Negro	9.4	15.5	14.9	37.8	18.2	4.2
CRANSTON—All classes	9.9	18.2	14.8	31.5	19.3	6.2
NEWPORT—All classes	8.4	15.4	23.3	30.3	17.8	4.7
PAWTUCKET—All classes	10.1	17.7	18.1	31.8	18.0	4.4
WOONSOCKET—All classes	10.9	19.6	19.9	29.6	16.2	3.7
South Carolina.						
CHARLESTON—All classes	9.2	18.4	20.8	33.9	14.1	3.2
COLUMBIA—All classes	8.7	17.4	21.8	35.9	13.0	3.1

TABLE **50.**—DISTRIBUTION BY BROAD AGE GROUPS, FOR

[By class of population for

CITY AND CLASS OF POPULATION.	All ages.[1]	AGE PERIODS.					
		Under 5 years.	5 to 14 years.	15 to 24 years.	25 to 44 years.	45 to 64 years.	65 years and over.
South Dakota.							
Sioux Falls—All classes	25,202	2,426	4,090	4,688	8,632	4,085	1,054
Tennessee.							
Memphis—All classes	162,351	12,060	25,358	31,564	61,716	25,630	5,427
Native white—Native parentage	82,795	7,416	14,468	16,405	29,785	11,737	2,672
Foreign parentage	7,671	662	1,398	987	2,300	2,040	274
Mixed parentage	4,872	336	662	848	2,040	859	121
Foreign-born white	5,775	13	164	586	2,458	1,797	746
Negro	61,181	3,630	8,666	12,733	25,102	9,185	1,611
Nashville—All classes	118,342	9,630	21,139	23,578	38,123	20,685	5,076
Native white—Native parentage	74,022	6,917	14,491	15,180	23,095	11,421	2,888
Foreign parentage	3,653	160	393	404	1,181	1,320	194
Mixed parentage	2,641	124	337	511	1,050	514	104
Foreign-born white	2,387	4	67	234	789	836	457
Negro	35,633	2,424	5,850	7,248	12,005	6,594	1,433
Chattanooga—All classes	57,895	4,487	9,590	12,446	21,091	8,510	1,717
Knoxville—All classes	77,818	7,786	15,347	16,063	24,364	11,567	2,540
Texas.							
Dallas—All classes	158,976	12,800	24,975	33,361	60,230	22,243	4,983
Native white—Native parentage	112,509	9,874	18,633	24,354	41,368	14,597	3,443
Foreign parentage	8,019	800	1,425	1,502	2,742	1,352	195
Mixed parentage	5,630	551	927	1,138	2,153	714	142
Foreign-born white	8,730	115	531	1,199	3,795	2,357	693
Negro	24,023	1,458	3,454	5,150	10,140	3,215	510
Fort Worth—All classes	106,482	8,544	16,673	22,501	40,731	14,570	3,019
Native white—Native parentage	75,515	6,438	12,547	16,027	27,884	10,065	2,203
Foreign parentage	4,526	643	706	767	1,462	815	125
Mixed parentage	3,066	271	559	603	1,156	405	67
Foreign-born white	7,359	177	622	1,485	3,305	1,401	351
Negro	15,896	1,009	2,235	3,610	6,872	1,840	269
Houston—All classes	138,276	11,062	23,446	27,871	51,181	20,351	4,172
Native white—Native parentage	72,433	6,871	13,711	14,846	25,500	9,453	1,976
Foreign parentage	11,801	1,224	2,243	2,108	3,737	2,178	304
Mixed parentage	8,022	703	1,453	1,639	3,054	1,031	137
Foreign-born white	12,012	192	809	1,758	5,090	3,148	1,002
Negro	33,960	2,067	5,225	7,514	13,773	4,539	752
San Antonio—All classes	161,379	14,805	30,232	33,804	53,179	23,484	5,503
Native white—Native parentage	76,299	8,102	15,666	16,581	24,353	9,254	2,206
Foreign parentage	21,061	3,277	4,471	3,490	5,665	3,687	447
Mixed parentage	12,793	1,765	3,020	2,721	3,887	1,242	148
Foreign-born white	36,646	675	4,743	7,820	13,468	7,506	2,306
Negro	14,341	965	2,311	3,168	5,708	1,727	392
Austin—All classes	34,876	2,454	6,377	6,706	10,894	5,985	2,376
Beaumont—All classes	40,422	3,872	7,701	8,401	14,498	4,936	983
El Paso—All classes	77,560	8,343	15,572	14,864	25,872	10,817	2,053
Galveston—All classes	44,255	3,562	7,113	8,547	16,201	7,123	1,616
Waco—All classes	38,500	3,361	7,666	7,516	12,734	5,736	1,343
Wichita Falls—All classes	40,079	3,366	5,833	8,066	15,115	4,210	637
Utah.							
Salt Lake City—All classes	118,110	12,805	23,532	21,227	37,223	18,416	4,712
Native white—Native parentage	56,234	8,897	14,870	10,978	14,816	5,308	1,258
Foreign parentage	23,515	1,711	3,769	4,275	8,875	4,506	357
Mixed parentage	17,598	2,035	1,166	4,040	5,600	1,585	159
Foreign-born white	19,434	60	677	1,757	7,283	6,776	2,897
Negro	718	39	66	91	359	142	23
Ogden—All classes	32,804	3,874	6,992	6,093	9,822	4,817	1,185

[1] Includes persons of unknown age.

CITIES HAVING 25,000 INHABITANTS OR MORE: 1920—Continued.

cities of 100,000 and over.]

CITY AND CLASS OF POPULATION.	PER CENT OF TOTAL.					
	Under 5 years.	5 to 14 years.	15 to 24 years.	25 to 44 years.	45 to 64 years.	65 years and over.
South Dakota.						
SIOUX FALLS—All classes................	9.6	16.2	18.6	34.3	16.2	4.2
Tennessee.						
NEMPHIS—All classes...................	7.4	15.6	19.4	38.0	15.8	8.3
Native white—Native parentage........	9.0	17.5	19.8	36.0	14.2	3.2
Foreign parentage........	8.6	18.2	12.9	30.0	26.6	3.6
Mixed parentage.........	6.9	13.6	17.4	41.9	17.6	2.5
Foreign-born white..................	0.2	2.8	10.1	42.6	31.1	12.9
Negro...................	5.9	14.2	20.8	41.0	15.0	2.6
NASHVILLE—All classes................	8.1	17.9	19.9	32.2	17.5	4.3
Native white—Native parentage........	9.3	19.6	20.5	31.2	15.4	3.9
Foreign parentage........	4.4	10.8	11.1	32.3	36.1	5.3
Mixed parentage.........	4.7	12.8	19.3	39.8	19.5	3.9
Foreign-born white..................	0.2	2.8	9.8	33.1	35.0	19.1
Negro...................	6.8	16.4	20.3	33.7	18.5	4.0
CHATTANOOGA—All classes..............	7.8	16.6	21.5	36.4	14.7	3.0
KNOXVILLE—All classes................	10.0	19.7	20.6	31.3	14.9	3.3
Texas.						
DALLAS—All classes.....................	8.1	15.7	21.0	37.9	14.0	3.1
Native white—Native parentage..	8.8	16.6	21.6	36.8	13.0	3.1
Foreign parentage........	10.0	17.8	18.7	34.2	16.9	2.4
Mixed parentage.........	9.8	16.5	20.2	38.2	12.7	2.5
Foreign-born white..................	1.3	6.1	13.7	43.5	27.0	7.9
Negro...................	6.1	14.4	21.4	42.2	13.4	2.1
FORT WORTH—All classes..............	8.0	15.7	21.1	38.3	13.7	2.8
Native white—Native parentage........	8.5	16.6	21.2	36.9	13.3	2.9
Foreign parentage........	14.2	15.6	16.9	32.3	18.0	2.8
Mixed parentage.........	8.8	18.2	19.7	37.7	13.2	2.2
Foreign-born white..................	2.4	8.5	20.2	44.9	19.0	4.8
Negro...................	6.3	14.1	22.7	43.2	11.6	1.7
HOUSTON—All classes	8.0	17.0	20.2	37.0	14.7	3.0
Native white—Native parentage........	9.5	18.9	20.5	35.2	13.1	2.7
Foreign parentage........	10.4	19.0	17.9	31.7	18.5	2.6
Mixed parentage.........	8.8	18.1	20.4	38.1	12.9	1.7
Foreign-born white..................	1.6	6.7	14.6	42.4	26.2	8.3
Negro...................	6.1	15.4	22.1	40.6	13.4	2.2
SAN ANTONIO—All classes..............	9.2	18.7	20.9	33.0	14.6	3.4
Native white—Native parentage........	10.6	20.5	21.7	31.9	12.1	2.9
Foreign parentage........	15.6	21.2	16.6	26.9	17.5	2.1
Mixed parentage.........	13.8	23.6	21.3	30.4	9.7	1.2
Foreign-born white..................	1.8	12.9	21.3	36.8	20.5	6.3
Negro...................	6.7	16.1	22.1	39.8	12.0	2.7
AUSTIN—All classes....................	7.0	18.3	19.2	31.2	17.2	6.8
BEAUMONT—All classes.................	9.6	19.1	20.8	35.9	12.2	2.4
EL PASO—All classes...................	10.8	20.1	19.2	33.4	13.9	2.6
GALVESTON—All classes................	8.0	16.1	19.3	36.6	16.1	3.7
WACO—All classes.....................	8.7	19.9	19.5	33.1	14.9	3.5
WICHITA FALLS—All classes.............	8.4	14.6	20.1	37.7	10.5	1.6
Utah.						
SALT LAKE CITY—All classes...........	10.8	19.9	18.0	31.5	15.6	4.0
Native white—Native parentage........	15.8	26.4	19.5	26.3	9.4	2.2
Foreign parentage........	7.3	16.0	18.2	37.7	19.2	1.5
Mixed parentage.........	11.6	23.7	23.0	31.8	9.0	0.9
Foreign-born white..................	0.3	3.2	9.0	37.5	34.9	14.9
Negro...................	5.4	9.2	12.7	49.0	19.8	3.2
OGDEN—All classes....................	11.8	21.3	18.6	29.9	14.7	3.6

Table **50.**—DISTRIBUTION BY BROAD AGE GROUPS, FOR

[By class of population for

CITY AND CLASS OF POPULATION.	All ages.[1]	AGE PERIODS.					
		Under 5 years.	5 to 14 years.	15 to 24 years.	25 to 44 years.	45 to 64 years.	65 years and over.
Virginia.							
Norfolk—All classes	115,777	9,664	18,375	24,321	43,452	16,941	2,985
Native white—Native parentage	57,759	5,298	9,766	11,806	20,554	8,498	1,821
Foreign parentage	5,207	765	1,370	1,096	1,297	608	69
Mixed parentage	2,673	313	492	501	867	432	66
Foreign-born white	6,587	12	202	1,001	3,651	1,434	286
Negro	43,392	3,271	6,541	9,893	17,003	5,923	743
Richmond—All classes	171,667	15,569	29,579	34,858	57,806	26,603	6,643
Native white—Native parentage	102,956	10,083	18,627	20,986	33,496	15,319	4,170
Foreign parentage	5,847	538	1,154	819	1,591	1,447	288
Mixed parentage	4,134	347	708	759	1,350	789	179
Foreign-born white	4,637	13	140	494	2,106	1,363	504
Negro	54,041	4,587	8,943	11,788	19,244	7,674	1,501
Lynchburg—All classes	30,070	2,828	5,727	6,377	9,393	4,573	1,094
Newport News—All classes	35,596	3,001	5,415	8,665	13,262	4,260	603
Petersburg—All classes	31,012	2,999	5,722	6,557	9,929	4,405	1,176
Portsmouth—All classes	54,387	5,397	9,848	11,812	18,257	7,609	1,443
Roanoke—All classes	50,842	5,610	9,903	10,401	16,401	6,982	1,451
Washington.							
Seattle—All classes	315,312	24,198	44,300	49,191	125,556	59,225	11,542
Native white—Native parentage	139,701	13,441	23,494	23,482	50,525	23,012	5,108
Foreign parentage	54,678	4,920	9,928	10,245	20,008	8,385	1,063
Mixed parentage	34,326	3,842	6,900	7,063	11,897	3,988	549
Foreign-born white	73,875	531	2,895	6,415	36,894	22,128	4,671
Negro	2,894	130	259	371	1,465	574	72
Spokane—All classes	104,437	8,402	17,676	17,102	35,276	21,084	4,803
Native white—Native parentage	57,324	5,844	11,426	10,140	18,085	9,367	2,399
Foreign parentage	16,566	1,088	2,718	2,927	5,868	3,509	441
Mixed parentage	12,664	1,282	2,800	2,708	4,062	1,560	249
Foreign-born white	16,826	110	599	1,205	6,846	6,389	1,665
Negro	727	50	99	97	277	171	32
Bellingham—All classes	25,585	2,232	4,476	4,384	7,957	5,110	1,390
Everett—All classes	27,644	2,411	4,812	4,719	9,271	5,257	1,141
Tacoma—All classes	96,965	8,025	15,684	15,631	33,191	18,327	4,107
West Virginia.							
Charleston—All classes	39,608	3,974	7,206	7,851	13,796	5,528	1,173
Clarksburg—All classes	27,869	3,225	5,454	5,400	9,214	3,656	831
Huntington—All classes	50,177	5,347	9,688	9,974	16,164	7,316	1,570
Wheeling—All classes	56,208	5,234	10,102	9,623	18,240	10,236	2,654
Wisconsin.							
Milwaukee—All classes	457,147	45,889	81,235	81,833	156,030	73,913	17,807
Native white—Native parentage	130,845	23,971	34,054	27,164	35,946	7,827	1,638
Foreign parentage	152,719	14,227	27,797	29,989	52,293	25,419	2,924
Mixed parentage	61,192	7,413	15,538	14,707	19,024	4,211	281
Foreign-born white	110,068	125	3,571	9,598	47,631	36,124	12,924
Negro	2,229	142	266	361	1,096	312	40
Green Bay—All classes	31,017	3,171	6,119	6,067	9,269	4,864	1,467
Kenosha—All classes	40,472	4,737	7,637	7,475	14,424	5,092	1,021
La Crosse—All classes	30,421	2,693	5,273	5,598	9,111	5,836	1,889
Madison—All classes	38,378	3,403	6,155	6,996	13,169	6,888	1,690
Oshkosh—All classes	33,162	2,926	6,182	5,753	9,431	6,591	2,245
Racine—All classes	58,593	6,113	9,783	11,110	20,537	8,852	2,143
Sheboygan—All classes	30,955	3,340	6,065	5,312	9,273	5,431	1,526
Superior—All classes	39,671	1,047	7,932	7,251	12,692	6,450	1,023

[1] Includes persons of unknown age.

CITIES HAVING 25,000 INHABITANTS OR MORE: 1920—Continued.

cities of 100,000 and over.]

CITY AND CLASS OF POPULATION.	PER CENT OF TOTAL.					
	Under 5 years.	5 to 14 years.	15 to 24 years.	25 to 44 years.	45 to 64 years.	65 years and over.
Virginia.						
Norfolk—All classes	8.3	15.9	21.0	37.5	14.6	2.6
Native white—Native parentage	9.2	16.9	20.4	35.6	14.7	3.2
Foreign parentage	14.7	26.3	21.0	24.9	11.7	1.3
Mixed parentage	11.7	18.4	18.7	32.4	16.2	2.5
Foreign-born white	0.2	3.1	15.2	55.4	21.8	4.3
Negro	7.5	15.1	22.8	39.2	13.6	1.7
Richmond—All classes	9.1	17.2	20.3	33.7	15.5	3.9
Native white—Native parentage	9.8	18.1	20.4	32.5	14.9	4.1
Foreign parentage	9.2	19.7	14.0	27.2	24.7	4.9
Mixed parentage	8.4	17.1	18.4	32.7	19.1	4.3
Foreign-born white	0.3	3.0	10.7	45.4	29.4	10.9
Negro	8.5	16.5	21.8	35.6	14.2	2.8
Lynchburg—All classes	9.4	19.0	21.2	31.2	15.2	3.6
Newport News—All classes	8.4	15.2	24.3	37.3	12.0	1.7
Petersburg—All classes	9.7	18.5	21.1	32.0	14.2	3.8
Portsmouth—All classes	9.9	18.1	21.7	33.6	14.0	2.7
Roanoke—All classes	11.0	19.5	20.5	32.3	13.7	2.9
Washington.						
Seattle—All classes	7.7	14.0	15.6	39.8	18.8	3.7
Native white—Native parentage	9.6	16.8	16.8	36.2	16.5	3.7
Foreign parentage	9.0	18.2	18.7	36.6	15.3	1.9
Mixed parentage	11.2	20.1	20.6	34.7	11.6	1.6
Foreign-born white	0.7	3.9	8.7	49.9	30.0	6.3
Negro	4.5	8.9	12.8	50.6	19.8	2.5
Spokane—All classes	8.0	16.9	16.4	33.8	20.2	4.6
Native white—Native parentage	10.2	19.9	17.7	31.5	16.3	4.2
Foreign parentage	6.6	16.4	17.7	35.4	21.2	2.7
Mixed parentage	10.1	22.1	21.4	32.1	12.3	2.0
Foreign-born white	0.7	3.6	7.2	40.7	38.0	9.9
Negro	6.9	13.6	13.3	38.1	23.5	4.4
Bellingham—All classes	8.7	17.5	17.1	31.1	20.0	5.4
Everett—All classes	8.7	17.4	17.1	33.5	19.0	4.1
Tacoma—All classes	8.3	16.2	16.1	34.2	18.9	4.2
West Virginia.						
Charleston—All classes	10.0	18.2	19.8	34.8	14.0	3.0
Clarksburg—All classes	11.6	19.6	19.4	33.1	13.1	3.0
Huntington—All classes	10.7	19.3	19.9	32.2	14.6	3.1
Wheeling—All classes	9.3	18.0	17.1	32.5	18.2	4.7
Wisconsin.						
Milwaukee—All classes	10.0	17.8	17.9	34.1	16.2	3.9
Native white—Native parentage	18.3	26.0	20.8	27.5	6.0	1.3
Foreign parentage	9.3	18.2	19.6	34.2	16.6	1.9
Mixed parentage	12.1	25.4	24.0	31.1	6.9	0.5
Foreign-born white	0.1	3.2	8.7	43.3	32.8	11.7
Negro	6.4	11.9	16.2	49.2	14.0	1.8
Green Bay—All classes	10.2	19.7	19.6	29.9	15.7	4.7
Kenosha—All classes	11.7	18.9	18.5	35.6	12.6	2.5
La Crosse—All classes	8.9	17.3	18.4	29.9	19.2	6.2
Madison—All classes	8.9	16.0	18.2	34.3	17.9	4.4
Oshkosh—All classes	8.8	18.6	17.3	28.4	19.9	6.8
Racine—All classes	10.4	16.7	19.0	35.1	15.1	3.7
Sheboygan—All classes	10.8	19.6	17.2	30.0	17.5	4.9
Superior—All classes	10.7	20.0	18.3	32.0	16.3	2.6

TABLE **51.**—DISTRIBUTION BY BROAD AGE GROUPS FOR POPULATION CLASSES, IN URBAN AND RURAL COMMUNITIES, BY DIVISIONS AND STATES: 1920.

AGE PERIOD.	All classes.	NATIVE WHITE.		Foreign-born white.	Negro.
		Native parentage.	Foreign or mixed parentage.		
UNITED STATES.					
URBAN POPULATION.					
All ages, number	54,304,603	24,556,729	15,706,372	10,356,983	3,559,473
Under 5 years	5,275,751	2,791,238	2,174,535	29,504	268,069
Under 1 year	1,031,950	554,000	414,579	3,072	57,332
5 to 9 years	5,050,276	2,534,608	2,096,478	120,016	291,762
10 to 14 years	4,664,312	2,333,029	1,790,012	245,035	291,094
15 to 19 years	4,445,963	2,210,680	1,503,354	413,728	310,522
20 to 44 years	23,203,269	9,985,517	5,689,320	5,700,938	1,762,692
45 years and over	11,566,197	4,639,820	2,444,682	3,832,747	621,935
Age unknown	98,835	61,837	7,991	15,015	13,399
All ages, per cent	100.0	100.0	100.0	100.0	100.0
Under 5 years	9.7	11.4	13.8	0.3	7.5
5 to 9 years	9.3	10.3	13.3	1.2	8.2
10 to 14 years	8.6	9.5	11.4	2.4	8.2
15 to 19 years	8.2	9.0	9.6	4.0	8.7
20 to 44 years	42.7	40.7	36.2	55.0	49.5
45 years and over	21.3	18.9	15.6	37.0	17.5
RURAL POPULATION.					
All ages, number	51,406,017	33,865,228	6,979,832	3,355,771	6,903,658
Under 5 years	6,297,479	4,575,292	787,872	15,480	875,630
Under 1 year	1,225,305	899,404	145,215	1,497	170,328
5 to 9 years	6,347,799	4,443,255	843,020	49,868	974,445
10 to 14 years	5,976,825	4,122,680	792,239	86,327	945,820
15 to 19 years	4,984,593	3,388,366	683,813	114,214	772,693
20 to 44 years	17,352,274	10,967,215	2,546,535	1,497,648	2,233,391
45 years and over	10,397,183	6,338,088	1,323,114	1,586,985	1,091,575
Age unknown	49,864	30,332	3,239	5,249	10,104
All ages, per cent	100.0	100.0	100.0	100.0	100.0
Under 5 years	12.3	13.5	11.3	0.5	12.7
5 to 9 years	12.3	13.1	12.1	1.5	14.1
10 to 14 years	11.6	12.2	11.4	2.6	13.7
15 to 19 years	9.7	10.0	9.8	3.4	11.2
20 to 44 years	33.8	32.4	36.5	44.6	32.4
45 years and over	20.2	18.7	19.0	47.3	15.8
GEOGRAPHIC DIVISIONS.					
NEW ENGLAND.					
URBAN POPULATION.					
All ages, number	5,865,073	1,867,235	2,279,995	1,641,728	71,416
Under 5 years	599,209	214,016	373,681	4,627	6,662
Under 1 year	117,487	42,803	72,609	466	1,560
5 to 9 years	552,726	178,469	350,245	18,210	5,615
10 to 14 years	508,127	161,638	302,862	38,329	5,161
15 to 19 years	467,410	147,388	250,271	64,423	5,113
20 to 44 years	2,360,791	676,298	735,592	912,265	34,317
45 years and over	1,371,484	486,278	266,685	602,576	14,349
Age unknown	5,326	3,148	659	1,298	208
All ages, per cent	100.0	100.0	100.0	100.0	100.0
Under 5 years	10.2	11.5	16.4	0.3	9.3
5 to 9 years	9.4	9.6	15.4	1.1	7.9
10 to 14 years	8.7	8.7	13.3	2.3	7.2
15 to 19 years	8.0	7.9	11.0	3.9	7.2
20 to 44 years	40.3	36.2	32.3	55.6	48.1
45 years and over	23.4	26.0	11.7	36.7	20.1
RURAL POPULATION.					
All ages, number	1,535,836	935,914	762,981	228,926	7,675
Under 5 years	153,821	94,925	56,794	1,230	753
Under 1 year	29,441	18,542	10,589	128	156
5 to 9 years	149,164	88,754	55,998	3,559	750
10 to 14 years	142,605	86,181	49,394	6,180	759
15 to 19 years	121,728	74,057	38,110	8,841	632
20 to 44 years	519,064	294,845	105,857	115,024	2,961
45 years and over	447,879	295,965	56,001	93,859	1,752
Age unknown	1,575	1,187	127	233	28
All ages, per cent	100.0	100.0	100.0	100.0	100.0
Under 5 years	10.0	10.1	15.7	0.5	9.9
5 to 9 years	9.7	9.5	15.5	1.6	9.8
10 to 14 years	9.3	9.2	13.6	2.7	9.9
15 to 19 years	7.9	7.9	10.5	3.9	8.3
20 to 44 years	33.8	31.5	29.2	50.2	38.8
45 years and over	29.2	31.6	15.5	41.0	22.9

TABLE 51.—DISTRIBUTION BY BROAD AGE GROUPS FOR POPULATION CLASSES, IN URBAN AND RURAL COMMUNITIES, BY DIVISIONS AND STATES: 1920—Continued.

AGE PERIOD.	All classes.	NATIVE WHITE.		Foreign-born white.	Negro.
		Native parentage.	Foreign or mixed parentage.		
GEOGRAPHIC DIVISIONS—Con.					
MIDDLE ATLANTIC.					
URBAN POPULATION.					
All ages, number	**16,672,595**	**5,976,653**	**5,925,321**	**4,239,681**	**517,432**
Under 5 years	1,725,761	715,015	962,724	8,285	39,187
Under 1 year	334,848	141,066	183,829	1,011	8,820
5 to 9 years	1,626,893	628,045	920,163	41,627	36,612
10 to 14 years	1,478,189	580,170	765,365	98,091	34,203
15 to 19 years	1,346,881	535,667	591,433	182,275	36,951
20 to 44 years	7,031,300	2,387,444	1,889,056	2,462,567	283,868
45 years and over	3,446,332	1,121,584	794,321	1,441,688	85,550
Age unknown	17,239	8,728	2,259	5,148	1,061
All ages, per cent	100.0	100.0	100.0	100.0	100.0
Under 5 years	10.4	12.0	16.2	0.2	7.6
5 to 9 years	9.8	10.5	15.5	1.0	7.1
10 to 14 years	8.9	9.7	12.9	2.3	6.6
15 to 19 years	8.1	9.0	10.0	4.3	7.1
20 to 44 years	42.2	39.9	31.9	58.1	54.9
45 years and over	20.7	18.8	13.4	34.0	16.5
RURAL POPULATION.					
All ages, number	**5,588,549**	**3,654,359**	**1,172,932**	**672,894**	**82,751**
Under 5 years	628,690	415,562	202,849	1,563	8,119
Under 1 year	119,496	79,568	37,913	211	1,686
5 to 9 years	613,446	400,715	196,021	7,844	8,234
10 to 14 years	567,206	388,265	153,756	16,405	8,167
15 to 19 years	468,716	331,848	105,953	22,766	7,604
20 to 44 years	1,917,975	1,211,227	302,206	368,455	34,085
45 years and over	1,387,606	903,496	211,699	254,819	16,377
Age unknown	4,910	3,246	448	1,042	165
All ages, per cent	100.0	100.0	100.0	100.0	100.0
Under 5 years	11.2	11.4	17.3	0.2	9.8
5 to 9 years	11.0	11.0	16.7	1.2	10.0
10 to 14 years	10.1	10.6	13.1	2.4	9.9
15 to 19 years	8.4	9.1	9.0	3.4	9.2
20 to 44 years	34.3	33.1	25.8	54.8	41.2
45 years and over	24.8	24.7	18.0	37.9	19.8
EAST NORTH CENTRAL.					
URBAN POPULATION.					
All ages, number	**13,049,272**	**5,970,956**	**4,109,954**	**2,511,626**	**448,873**
Under 5 years	1,300,667	732,861	531,051	5,398	30,972
Under 1 year	249,053	143,498	97,994	613	6,868
5 to 9 years	1,205,077	640,783	505,860	27,218	30,912
10 to 14 years	1,076,614	567,441	422,012	57,396	29,537
15 to 19 years	1,032,583	539,149	371,163	89,943	31,947
20 to 44 years	5,668,681	2,439,325	1,603,027	1,376,421	245,383
45 years and over	2,748,482	1,040,877	674,770	951,834	78,988
Age unknown	17,168	10,520	2,071	3,416	1,134
All ages, per cent	100.0	100.0	100.0	100.0	100.0
Under 5 years	10.0	12.3	12.9	0.2	6.9
5 to 9 years	9.2	10.7	12.3	1.1	6.9
10 to 14 years	8.3	9.5	10.3	2.3	6.6
15 to 19 years	7.9	9.0	9.0	3.6	7.1
20 to 44 years	43.4	40.9	39.0	54.8	54.7
45 years and over	21.1	17.4	16.4	37.9	17.6
RURAL POPULATION.					
All ages, number	**8,426,271**	**5,819,414**	**1,815,259**	**711,653**	**65,681**
Under 5 years	919,365	758,164	152,199	1,070	6,019
Under 1 year	171,720	143,657	26,348	112	1,216
5 to 9 years	919,648	727,238	178,168	5,803	6,522
10 to 14 years	887,605	685,342	180,521	13,582	6,558
15 to 19 years	760,473	573,652	161,654	17,942	5,967
20 to 44 years	2,839,444	1,861,869	681,216	267,824	24,251
45 years and over	2,093,651	1,208,719	460,771	404,646	16,241
Age unknown	6,085	4,430	730	786	123
All ages, per cent	100.0	100.0	100.0	100.0	100.0
Under 5 years	10.9	13.0	8.4	0.2	9.2
5 to 9 years	10.9	12.5	9.8	0.8	9.9
10 to 14 years	10.5	11.8	9.9	1.9	10.0
15 to 19 years	9.0	9.9	8.9	2.5	9.1
20 to 44 years	33.7	32.0	37.5	37.6	36.9
45 years and over	24.8	20.8	25.4	56.9	24.7

TABLE 51.—DISTRIBUTION BY BROAD AGE GROUPS FOR POPULATION CLASSES, IN URBAN AND RURAL COMMUNITIES, BY DIVISIONS AND STATES: 1920—Continued.

AGE PERIOD.	All classes.	NATIVE WHITE.		Foreign-born white.	Negro.
		Native parentage.	Foreign or mixed parentage.		
GEOGRAPHIC DIVISIONS—Con.					
WEST NORTH CENTRAL.					
URBAN POPULATION.					
All ages, number	4,727,372	2,627,908	1,275,306	607,384	212,591
Under 5 years	416,519	299,418	101,632	1,518	13,698
Under 1 year	79,083	57,509	18,479	144	2,888
5 to 9 years	407,764	277,542	109,462	5,748	14,827
10 to 14 years	389,343	255,493	107,158	10,966	15,476
15 to 19 years	392,994	245,276	112,493	18,395	16,053
20 to 44 years	2,022,980	1,058,709	581,120	273,512	107,708
45 years and over	1,087,683	484,034	262,577	296,320	43,993
Age unknown	10,089	7,436	864	925	836
All ages, per cent	100.0	100.0	100.0	100.0	100.0
Under 5 years	8.8	11.4	8.0	0.2	6.4
5 to 9 years	8.6	10.6	8.6	0.9	7.0
10 to 14 years	8.2	9.7	8.4	1.8	7.3
15 to 19 years	8.3	9.3	8.8	3.0	7.6
20 to 44 years	42.8	40.3	45.6	45.0	50.7
45 years and over	23.0	18.4	20.6	48.8	20.7
RURAL POPULATION.					
All ages, number	7,816,877	4,847,640	2,102,572	764,577	65,930
Under 5 years	924,893	732,642	179,727	1,308	5,991
Under 1 year	174,509	141,288	30,948	122	1,160
5 to 9 years	905,333	674,669	214,099	5,064	6,728
10 to 14 years	860,228	604,531	233,950	10,909	6,891
15 to 19 years	751,432	492,869	231,960	17,153	6,280
20 to 44 years	2,729,220	1,519,450	905,057	270,034	23,517
45 years and over	1,637,537	817,517	336,750	459,218	16,290
Age unknown	8,234	5,962	1,029	891	233
All ages, per cent	100.0	100.0	100.0	100.0	100.0
Under 5 years	11.8	15.1	8.5	0.2	9.1
5 to 9 years	11.6	13.9	10.2	0.7	10.2
10 to 14 years	11.0	12.5	11.1	1.4	10.5
15 to 19 years	9.6	10.2	11.0	2.2	9.5
20 to 44 years	34.9	31.3	43.0	35.3	35.7
45 years and over	20.9	16.9	16.0	60.1	24.7
SOUTH ATLANTIC.					
URBAN POPULATION.					
All ages, number	4,338,792	2,559,203	410,397	222,488	1,144,371
Under 5 years	409,261	269,940	45,613	516	93,077
Under 1 year	85,335	56,633	8,965	56	19,650
5 to 9 years	403,101	253,189	45,409	2,193	102,243
10 to 14 years	386,467	239,072	41,075	4,769	101,492
15 to 19 years	393,552	237,734	35,575	9,562	110,569
20 to 44 years	1,900,941	1,088,602	150,184	119,417	541,524
45 years and over	834,393	465,302	92,300	85,472	190,566
Age unknown	11,077	5,364	241	559	4,900
All ages, per cent	100.0	100.0	100.0	100.0	100.0
Under 5 years	9.4	10.5	11.1	0.2	8.1
5 to 9 years	9.3	9.9	11.1	1.0	8.9
10 to 14 years	8.9	9.3	10.0	2.1	8.9
15 to 19 years	9.1	9.3	8.7	4.3	9.7
20 to 44 years	43.8	42.5	36.6	53.7	47.3
45 years and over	19.2	18.2	22.5	38.4	16.7
RURAL POPULATION.					
All ages, number	9,651,480	6,220,213	143,207	93,432	3,100,740
Under 5 years	1,320,108	861,365	21,745	611	424,717
Under 1 year	260,930	172,743	4,088	38	83,567
5 to 9 years	1,344,355	847,190	19,684	1,485	473,789
10 to 14 years	1,247,094	780,163	14,625	2,661	447,835
15 to 19 years	1,015,559	637,941	11,642	3,589	361,004
20 to 44 years	3,092,926	2,005,757	43,679	53,876	985,404
45 years and over	1,622,391	1,083,166	31,766	31,313	474,226
Age unknown	9,047	4,631	62	167	4,174
All ages, per cent	100.0	100.0	100.0	100.0	100.0
Under 5 years	13.7	13.8	15.2	0.4	13.7
5 to 9 years	13.9	13.6	13.7	1.6	14.9
10 to 14 years	12.9	12.5	10.2	2.8	14.1
15 to 19 years	10.5	10.3	8.1	3.8	11.3
20 to 44 years	32.0	32.2	30.5	57.7	31.0
45 years and over	16.8	17.4	22.2	33.5	14.9

TABLE 51.—DISTRIBUTION BY BROAD AGE GROUPS FOR POPULATION CLASSES, IN URBAN AND RURAL COMMUNITIES, BY DIVISIONS AND STATES: 1920—Continued.

| AGE PERIOD. | All classes. | NATIVE WHITE. | | Foreign-born white. | Negro. |
		Native parentage.	Foreign or mixed parentage.		
GEOGRAPHIC DIVISIONS—Con.					
EAST SOUTH CENTRAL.					
URBAN POPULATION.					
All ages, number	1,994,207	1,231,225	142,928	48,407	571,316
Under 5 years	176,132	126,894	7,395	90	41,730
Under 1 year	36,405	26,205	1,357	14	8,826
5 to 9 years	185,992	126,817	8,707	358	50,101
10 to 14 years	186,064	124,070	9,308	822	51,853
15 to 19 years	183,794	119,137	9,422	1,492	53,730
20 to 44 years	855,442	511,980	59,547	19,589	264,154
45 years and over	402,697	220,362	48,437	25,986	107,813
Age unknown	4,086	1,965	112	70	1,935
All ages, per cent	100.0	100.0	100.0	100.0	100.0
Under 5 years	8.8	10.3	5.2	0.2	7.3
5 to 9 years	9.3	10.3	6.1	0.7	8.8
10 to 14 years	9.3	10.1	6.5	1.7	9.1
15 to 19 years	9.2	9.7	6.6	3.1	9.4
20 to 44 years	42.9	41.6	41.7	40.5	46.2
45 years and over	20.2	17.9	33.9	53.7	18.9
RURAL POPULATION.					
All ages, number	6,899,100	4,861,557	59,898	23,532	1,952,216
Under 5 years	912,002	670,950	4,799	73	235,940
Under 1 year	185,216	138,134	887	7	46,130
5 to 9 years	941,952	665,409	5,041	207	271,047
10 to 14 years	896,988	622,847	4,716	467	268,715
15 to 19 years	727,593	506,464	4,083	685	216,187
20 to 44 years	2,222,762	1,560,763	21,691	10,173	629,508
45 years and over	1,191,841	832,484	19,536	11,897	327,563
Age unknown	5,962	2,640	32	30	3,256
All ages, per cent	100.0	100.0	100.0	100.0	100.0
Under 5 years	13.2	13.8	8.0	0.3	12.1
5 to 9 years	13.7	13.7	8.4	0.9	13.9
10 to 14 years	13.0	12.8	7.9	2.0	13.8
15 to 19 years	10.5	10.4	6.8	2.9	11.1
20 to 44 years	32.2	32.1	36.2	43.2	32.2
45 years and over	17.3	17.1	32.6	50.6	16.8
WEST SOUTH CENTRAL.					
URBAN POPULATION.					
All ages, number	2,970,829	1,904,386	303,768	220,460	535,282
Under 5 years	270,209	194,302	32,258	3,788	39,086
Under 1 year	55,150	39,062	7,561	389	7,978
5 to 9 years	285,215	197,048	29,951	9,733	47,652
10 to 14 years	280,816	190,605	26,793	12,860	49,743
15 to 19 years	279,964	185,027	25,336	16,368	52,525
20 to 44 years	1,311,812	824,664	121,566	107,018	255,917
45 years and over	531,228	305,183	67,536	69,966	87,405
Age unknown	11,585	7,557	328	727	2,954
All ages, per cent	100.0	100.0	100.0	100.0	100.0
Under 5 years	9.1	10.2	10.6	1.7	7.3
5 to 9 years	9.6	10.3	9.9	4.4	8.9
10 to 14 years	9.5	10.0	8.8	5.8	9.3
15 to 19 years	9.4	9.7	8.3	7.4	9.8
20 to 44 years	44.2	43.3	40.0	48.5	47.8
45 years and over	17.9	16.0	22.2	31.7	16.3
RURAL POPULATION.					
All ages, number	7,271,395	5,055,399	392,841	238,873	1,528,297
Under 5 years	946,300	700,568	49,406	4,456	183,496
Under 1 year	188,247	139,122	10,769	401	36,207
5 to 9 years	1,000,964	721,116	53,333	11,303	206,325
10 to 14 years	952,418	673,569	49,553	15,545	205,853
15 to 19 years	790,087	547,836	44,006	18,338	173,857
20 to 44 years	2,437,546	1,657,547	139,939	102,536	520,581
45 years and over	1,135,885	750,076	56,285	85,787	236,089
Age unknown	8,195	4,687	319	908	2,096
All ages, per cent	100.0	100.0	100.0	100.0	100.0
Under 5 years	13.0	13.9	12.6	1.9	12.0
5 to 9 years	13.8	14.3	13.6	4.7	13.5
10 to 14 years	13.1	13.3	12.6	6.5	13.5
15 to 19 years	10.9	10.8	11.2	7.7	11.4
20 to 44 years	33.5	32.8	35.6	42.9	34.1
45 years and over	15.6	14.8	14.3	35.9	15.4

TABLE **51.**—DISTRIBUTION BY BROAD AGE GROUPS FOR POPULATION CLASSES, IN URBAN AND RURAL COMMUNITIES, BY DIVISIONS AND STATES: 1920—Continued.

| AGE PERIOD. | All classes. | NATIVE WHITE. | | Foreign-born white. | Negro. |
		Native parentage.	Foreign or mixed parentage.		
GEOGRAPHIC DIVISIONS—Con.					
MOUNTAIN.					
URBAN POPULATION.					
All ages, number	1, 214, 980	695, 078	314, 358	181, 439	16, 678
Under 5 years	116, 560	82, 217	31, 431	1, 302	1, 030
Under 1 year	23, 101	16, 306	6, 332	106	218
5 to 9 years	114, 284	76, 649	32, 589	3, 594	990
10 to 14 years	107, 558	69, 445	31, 367	5, 206	1, 016
15 to 19 years	100, 008	61, 486	29, 796	7, 146	1, 074
20 to 44 years	511, 946	276, 897	135, 491	87, 660	8, 502
45 years and over	254, 358	119, 157	53, 421	76, 021	3, 915
Age unknown	10, 266	9, 227	263	510	151
All ages, per cent	100. 0	100. 0	100. 0	100. 0	100. 0
Under 5 years	9. 6	11. 8	10. 0	0. 7	6. 2
5 to 9 years	9. 4	11. 0	10. 4	2. 0	5. 9
10 to 14 years	8. 9	10. 0	10. 0	2. 9	6. 1
15 to 19 years	8. 2	8. 8	9. 5	3. 9	6. 4
20 to 44 years	42. 1	39. 8	43. 1	48. 3	51. 0
45 years and over	20. 9	17. 1	17. 0	41. 9	23. 5
RURAL POPULATION.					
All ages, number	2, 121, 121	1, 307, 430	442, 808	271, 786	14, 123
Under 5 years	280, 254	204, 009	60, 960	3, 368	510
Under 1 year	55, 048	40, 205	12, 386	307	112
5 to 9 years	260, 540	183, 631	56, 842	8, 657	530
10 to 14 years	227, 972	158, 098	48, 956	11, 468	469
15 to 19 years	185, 196	123, 311	40, 063	13, 229	659
20 to 44 years	792, 419	444, 435	169, 323	139, 394	10, 430
45 years and over	371, 945	192, 155	66, 451	95, 092	1, 517
Age unknown	2, 795	1, 791	213	578	8
All ages, per cent	100. 0	100. 0	100. 0	100. 0	100. 0
Under 5 years	13. 2	15. 6	13. 8	1. 2	3. 6
5 to 9 years	12. 3	14. 0	12. 8	3. 2	3. 8
10 to 14 years	10. 7	12. 1	11. 1	4. 2	3. 3
15 to 19 years	8. 7	9. 4	9. 0	4. 9	4. 7
20 to 44 years	37. 4	34. 0	38. 2	51. 3	73. 9
45 years and over	17. 5	14. 7	15. 0	35. 0	10. 7
PACIFIC.					
URBAN POPULATION.					
All ages, number	3, 471, 483	1, 724, 085	944, 345	683, 770	41, 514
Under 5 years	261, 433	156, 575	88, 750	3, 980	2, 627
Under 1 year	51, 488	30, 918	17, 453	273	524
5 to 9 years	269, 224	156, 066	94, 092	11, 335	2, 810
10 to 14 years	251, 134	145, 095	84, 072	16, 596	2, 613
15 to 19 years	248, 777	139, 816	77, 865	24, 124	2, 560
20 to 44 years	1, 539, 376	721, 598	413, 737	342, 489	21, 319
45 years and over	889, 540	397, 043	184, 635	282, 884	9, 365
Age unknown	11, 999	7, 892	1, 194	2, 362	220
All ages, per cent	100. 0	100. 0	100. 0	100. 0	100. 0
Under 5 years	7. 5	9. 1	9. 4	0. 6	6. 3
5 to 9 years	7. 8	9. 1	10. 0	1. 7	6. 8
10 to 14 years	7. 2	8. 4	8. 9	2. 4	6. 3
15 to 19 years	7. 2	8. 1	8. 2	3. 5	6. 2
20 to 44 years	44. 3	41. 9	43. 8	50. 1	51. 4
45 years and over	25. 6	23. 0	19. 6	41. 4	22. 6
RURAL POPULATION.					
All ages, number	2, 095, 388	1, 163, 302	488, 034	350, 098	6, 276
Under 5 years	212, 046	137, 107	59, 389	2, 071	485
Under 1 year	40, 698	26, 145	11, 287	171	94
5 to 9 years	212, 007	134, 533	63, 854	5, 946	520
10 to 14 years	194, 709	123, 684	60, 700	9, 110	573
15 to 19 years	163, 809	100, 388	46, 342	11, 671	368
20 to 44 years	800, 918	411, 322	177, 567	170, 332	2, 654
45 years and over	508, 448	254, 510	83, 855	150, 354	1, 520
Age unknown	3, 061	1, 758	279	614	21
All ages, per cent	100. 0	100. 0	100. 0	100. 0	100. 0
Under 5 years	10. 1	11. 8	12. 2	0. 6	7. 7
5 to 9 years	10. 1	11. 6	13. 1	1. 7	8. 3
10 to 14 years	9. 3	10. 6	11. 6	2. 6	9. 1
15 to 19 years	7. 8	8. 6	9. 5	3. 3	8. 0
20 to 44 years	38. 2	35. 4	36. 4	48. 7	42. 3
45 years and over	24. 3	21. 9	17. 2	42. 9	24. 2

TABLE 51.—DISTRIBUTION BY BROAD AGE GROUPS FOR POPULATION CLASSES, IN URBAN AND RURAL COMMUNITIES, BY DIVISIONS AND STATES: 1920—Continued.

AGE PERIOD.	All classes.	NATIVE WHITE.		Foreign-born white.	Negro.
		Native parentage.	Foreign or mixed parentage.		
NEW ENGLAND.					
Maine.					
URBAN POPULATION.					
All ages, number.............	299,569	153,986	85,170	59,152	766
Under 5 years...................	27,469	14,454	12,505	397	64
Under 1 year.................	5,481	2,907	2,510	35	20
5 to 9 years...................	26,135	12,678	12,328	1,023	59
10 to 14 years.................	25,232	12,007	11,421	1,733	42
15 to 19 years.................	24,979	11,441	10,304	3,141	62
20 to 44 years.................	115,544	56,950	28,105	29,971	331
45 years and over.............	79,819	46,183	10,466	22,811	208
Age unknown..................	391	273	41	76	....
All ages, per cent.............	100.0	100.0	100.0	100.0	100.0
Under 5 years.................	9.2	9.4	14.7	0.7	8.4
5 to 9 years...................	8.7	8.2	14.5	1.7	7.7
10 to 14 years.................	8.4	7.8	13.4	2.9	5.5
15 to 19 years.................	8.3	7.4	12.1	5.3	8.1
20 to 44 years.................	38.6	37.0	33.0	50.7	43.2
45 years and over.............	26.6	30.0	12.3	38.6	27.2
RURAL POPULATION.					
All ages, number.............	468,445	341,794	77,396	48,197	544
Under 5 years.................	47,671	35,282	11,848	431	49
Under 1 year.................	9,219	6,884	2,268	39	12
5 to 9 years...................	45,506	32,860	11,629	913	47
10 to 14 years.................	44,759	32,342	10,817	1,502	51
15 to 19 years.................	38,881	27,769	8,637	2,388	41
20 to 44 years.................	155,329	108,476	22,905	23,558	223
45 years and over.............	135,795	104,624	11,541	19,364	130
Age unknown..................	504	441	19	41	3
All ages, per cent.............	100.0	100.0	100.0	100.0	100.0
Under 5 years.................	10.2	10.3	15.3	0.9	9.0
5 to 9 years...................	9.7	9.6	15.0	1.9	8.6
10 to 14 years.................	9.6	9.5	14.0	3.1	9.4
15 to 19 years.................	8.3	8.1	11.2	5.0	7.5
20 to 44 years.................	33.2	31.7	29.6	48.9	41.0
45 years and over.............	29.0	30.6	14.9	40.2	23.9
New Hampshire.					
URBAN POPULATION.					
All ages, number.............	279,761	112,873	94,901	71,429	441
Under 5 years...................	26,967	11,151	15,384	378	51
Under 1 year.................	5,152	2,154	2,954	33	9
5 to 9 years...................	25,666	10,136	14,415	1,078	35
10 to 14 years.................	24,775	9,564	13,141	2,030	38
15 to 19 years.................	23,171	8,425	11,545	3,169	23
20 to 44 years.................	107,210	38,232	30,904	37,813	201
45 years and over.............	71,435	35,010	9,447	26,861	78
Age unknown..................	537	355	65	100	15
All ages, per cent.............	100.0	100.0	100.0	100.0	100.0
Under 5 years.................	9.6	9.9	16.2	0.5	11.6
5 to 9 years...................	9.2	9.0	15.2	1.5	7.9
10 to 14 years.................	8.9	8.5	13.8	2.8	8.6
15 to 19 years.................	8.3	7.5	12.2	4.4	5.2
20 to 44 years.................	38.3	33.9	32.6	52.9	45.6
45 years and over.............	25.5	31.0	10.0	37.6	17.7
RURAL POPULATION.					
All ages, number.............	163,322	112,639	30,685	19,804	180
Under 5 years.................	14,424	10,078	4,247	78	21
Under 1 year.................	2,768	1,989	764	11	4
5 to 9 years...................	14,096	9,471	4,372	227	24
10 to 14 years.................	14,016	9,393	4,196	405	22
15 to 19 years.................	11,981	7,812	3,473	681	13
20 to 44 years.................	53,391	34,325	9,608	9,390	62
45 years and over.............	55,159	41,378	4,767	8,972	38
Age unknown..................	255	182	22	51	....
All ages, per cent.............	100.0	100.0	100.0	100.0	100.0
Under 5 years.................	8.8	8.9	13.8	0.4	11.7
5 to 9 years...................	8.6	8.4	14.2	1.1	13.3
10 to 14 years.................	8.6	8.3	13.7	2.0	12.2
15 to 19 years.................	7.3	6.9	11.3	3.4	7.2
20 to 44 years.................	32.7	30.5	31.3	47.4	34.4
45 years and over.............	33.8	36.7	15.5	45.3	21.1

TABLE 51.—DISTRIBUTION BY BROAD AGE GROUPS FOR POPULATION CLASSES, IN URBAN AND RURAL COMMUNITIES, BY DIVISIONS AND STATES: 1920—Continued.

AGE PERIOD.	All classes.	NATIVE WHITE.		Foreign-born white.	Negro.
		Native parentage.	Foreign or mixed parentage.		
NEW ENGLAND—Continued.					
Vermont.					
URBAN POPULATION.					
All ages, number............	109,976	59,302	32,295	18,146	220
Under 5 years................	10,352	6,234	4,013	89	16
Under 1 year..............	1,946	1,188	743	10	5
5 to 9 years.................	9,779	5,627	3,854	276	22
10 to 14 years...............	9,483	5,499	3,449	516	19
15 to 19 years...............	9,308	5,388	3,153	752	15
20 to 44 years...............	42,386	22,158	10,940	9,186	93
45 years and over...........	28,522	14,290	6,868	7,308	53
Age unknown................	146	106	18	19	2
All ages, per cent...........	100.0	100.0	100.0	100.0	100.0
Under 5 years................	9.4	10.5	12.4	0.5	7.3
5 to 9 years.................	8.9	9.5	11.9	1.5	10.0
10 to 14 years...............	8.6	9.3	10.7	2.8	8.6
15 to 19 years...............	8.5	9.1	9.8	4.1	6.8
20 to 44 years...............	38.5	37.4	33.9	50.6	42.3
45 years and over...........	25.9	24.1	21.3	40.3	24.1
RURAL POPULATION.					
All ages, number............	242,452	169,023	46,671	26,380	352
Under 5 years................	24,192	18,016	5,684	451	36
Under 1 year..............	4,628	3,487	1,092	44	5
5 to 9 years.................	23,633	17,236	5,341	1,009	44
10 to 14 years...............	23,102	16,796	4,946	1,322	36
15 to 19 years...............	20,200	14,728	4,029	1,405	36
20 to 44 years...............	79,003	53,359	14,303	11,214	118
45 years and over...........	72,092	48,701	12,351	10,955	80
Age unknown................	230	187	17	24	2
All ages, per cent...........	100.0	100.0	100.0	100.0	100.0
Under 5 years................	10.0	10.7	12.2	1.7	10.2
5 to 9 years.................	9.7	10.2	11.4	3.8	12.5
10 to 14 years...............	9.5	9.9	10.6	5.0	10.2
15 to 19 years...............	8.3	8.7	8.6	5.3	10.2
20 to 44 years...............	32.6	31.6	30.6	42.5	33.5
45 years and over...........	29.7	28.8	26.5	41.5	22.7
Massachusetts.					
URBAN POPULATION.					
All ages, number............	3,650,248	1,116,638	1,441,872	1,045,106	43,624
Under 5 years................	367,497	131,199	229,337	2,746	4,086
Under 1 year..............	71,535	25,900	44,385	294	923
5 to 9 years.................	341,269	108,826	218,158	10,809	3,371
10 to 14 years...............	315,061	97,587	191,142	23,135	3,128
15 to 19 years...............	286,656	86,181	158,364	38,910	3,064
20 to 44 years...............	1,473,077	399,913	472,491	577,933	21,206
45 years and over...........	863,671	291,097	172,038	390,871	8,635
Age unknown................	3,017	1,835	342	702	134
All ages, per cent...........	100.0	100.0	100.0	100.0	100.0
Under 5 years................	10.1	11.7	15.9	0.3	9.4
5 to 9 years.................	9.3	9.7	15.1	1.0	7.7
10 to 14 years...............	8.6	8.7	13.3	2.2	7.2
15 to 19 years...............	7.9	7.7	11.0	3.7	7.0
20 to 44 years...............	40.4	35.8	32.8	55.3	48.6
45 years and over...........	23.7	26.1	11.9	37.4	19.8
RURAL POPULATION.					
All ages, number............	202,108	114,135	53,345	32,428	1,842
Under 5 years................	18,264	10,276	7,648	78	222
Under 1 year..............	3,356	1,940	1,362	5	42
5 to 9 years.................	18,337	10,001	8,011	379	184
10 to 14 years...............	18,477	10,210	7,357	662	174
15 to 19 years...............	15,475	8,420	5,951	948	115
20 to 44 years...............	65,639	33,766	15,497	15,547	704
45 years and over...........	65,581	41,392	8,825	14,846	422
Age unknown................	115	70	16	18	11
All ages, per cent...........	100.0	100.0	100.0	100.0	100.0
Under 5 years................	9.0	9.0	14.3	0.2	12.1
5 to 9 years.................	9.2	8.8	15.0	1.0	10.0
10 to 14 years...............	9.1	8.9	13.9	2.0	9.4
15 to 19 years...............	7.7	7.4	11.2	2.9	6.8
20 to 44 years...............	32.5	29.6	29.1	47.9	38.2
45 years and over...........	32.4	36.3	16.5	45.8	22.9

TABLE **51.**—DISTRIBUTION BY BROAD AGE GROUPS FOR POPULATION CLASSES, IN URBAN AND RURAL COMMUNITIES, BY DIVISIONS AND STATES: 1920—Continued.

AGE PERIOD.	All classes.	NATIVE WHITE.		Foreign-born white.	Negro.
		Native parentage.	Foreign or mixed parentage.		
NEW ENGLAND—Continued.					
Rhode Island.					
URBAN POPULATION.					
All ages, number	589,180	163,733	243,679	171,685	9,710
Under 5 years	61,054	20,266	39,319	486	964
Under 1 year	12,457	4,302	7,887	35	232
5 to 9 years	56,881	16,704	37,384	1,957	817
10 to 14 years	52,504	14,777	32,653	4,328	723
15 to 19 years	50,440	14,257	27,753	7,717	705
20 to 44 years	231,913	57,201	79,434	90,856	4,264
45 years and over	136,125	40,429	27,093	66,228	2,231
Age unknown	263	99	43	113	6
All ages, per cent	100.0	100.0	100.0	100.0	100.0
Under 5 years	10.4	12.4	16.1	0.3	9.9
5 to 9 years	9.6	10.2	15.3	1.1	8.4
10 to 14 years	8.9	9.0	13.4	2.5	7.4
15 to 19 years	8.6	8.7	11.4	4.5	7.3
20 to 44 years	39.4	34.9	32.6	52.9	43.9
45 years and over	23.1	24.7	11.1	38.6	23.0
RURAL POPULATION.					
All ages, number	15,217	9,820	3,249	1,814	326
Under 5 years	1,302	789	471	7	33
Under 1 year	289	170	111		7
5 to 9 years	1,372	821	502	17	30
10 to 14 years	1,332	785	472	45	29
15 to 19 years	1,215	746	373	69	27
20 to 44 years	5,152	3,134	984	906	126
45 years and over	4,814	3,526	444	767	76
Age unknown	30	19	3	3	5
All ages, per cent	100.0	100.0	100.0	100.0	100.0
Under 5 years	8.6	8.0	14.5	0.4	10.1
5 to 9 years	9.0	8.4	15.5	0.9	9.2
10 to 14 years	8.8	8.0	14.5	2.5	8.9
15 to 19 years	8.0	7.6	11.5	3.8	8.3
20 to 44 years	33.9	31.9	30.3	49.9	38.7
45 years and over	31.6	35.9	13.7	42.3	23.3
Connecticut.					
URBAN POPULATION.					
All ages, number	936,339	260,703	382,078	276,210	16,655
Under 5 years	105,870	30,712	73,123	531	1,481
Under 1 year	20,916	6,352	14,150	59	371
5 to 9 years	92,996	24,498	64,106	3,067	1,311
10 to 14 years	81,072	22,204	51,056	6,587	1,211
15 to 19 years	72,856	21,696	39,152	10,734	1,244
20 to 44 years	390,661	101,844	113,718	166,506	8,222
45 years and over	191,912	59,269	40,773	88,497	3,135
Age unknown	972	480	150	288	51
All ages, per cent	100.0	100.0	100.0	100.0	100.0
Under 5 years	11.3	11.8	19.1	0.2	8.9
5 to 9 years	9.9	9.4	16.8	1.1	7.9
10 to 14 years	8.7	8.5	13.4	2.4	7.3
15 to 19 years	7.8	8.3	10.2	3.9	7.5
20 to 44 years	41.7	39.1	29.8	60.3	49.4
45 years and over	20.5	22.7	10.7	32.0	18.8
RURAL POPULATION.					
All ages, number	444,292	188,503	150,935	100,303	4,391
Under 5 years	47,968	20,484	26,896	185	392
Under 1 year	9,181	4,072	4,992	29	86
5 to 9 years	46,000	18,365	26,143	1,064	421
10 to 14 years	40,919	16,655	21,566	2,244	447
15 to 19 years	33,976	14,582	15,647	3,350	390
20 to 44 years	160,550	61,785	42,560	54,409	1,728
45 years and over	114,438	56,344	18,073	38,955	1,006
Age unknown	441	288	50	96	7
All ages, per cent	100.0	100.0	100.0	100.0	100.0
Under 5 years	10.8	10.9	17.8	0.2	8.9
5 to 9 years	10.4	9.7	17.3	1.1	9.6
10 to 14 years	9.2	8.8	14.3	2.2	10.2
15 to 19 years	7.6	7.7	10.4	3.3	8.9
20 to 44 years	36.1	32.8	28.2	54.2	39.4
45 years and over	25.8	29.9	12.0	38.8	22.0

TABLE 51.—DISTRIBUTION BY BROAD AGE GROUPS FOR POPULATION CLASSES, IN URBAN AND RURAL COMMUNITIES, BY DIVISIONS AND STATES: 1920—Continued.

AGE PERIOD.	All classes.	NATIVE WHITE.		Foreign-born white.	Negro.
		Native parentage.	Foreign or mixed parentage.		
MIDDLE ATLANTIC.					
New York.					
URBAN POPULATION.					
All ages, number	**8,589,844**	**2,487,080**	**3,322,640**	**2,585,350**	**185,212**
Under 5 years	845,868	299,026	527,450	5,476	13,512
Under 1 year	163,238	59,046	100,277	673	3,154
5 to 9 years	804,584	256,704	510,527	25,796	11,218
10 to 14 years	740,395	237,284	431,280	61,129	10,423
15 to 19 years	680,737	220,856	330,053	117,422	12,027
20 to 44 years	3,712,075	1,016,757	1,077,991	1,501,734	109,410
45 years and over	1,795,661	451,223	443,913	870,353	28,224
Age unknown	10,524	5,230	1,426	3,440	398
All ages, per cent	100.0	100.0	100.0	100.0	100.0
Under 5 years	9.8	12.0	15.9	0.2	7.3
5 to 9 years	9.4	10.3	15.4	1.0	6.1
10 to 14 years	8.6	9.5	13.0	2.4	5.6
15 to 19 years	7.9	8.9	9.9	4.5	6.5
20 to 44 years	43.2	40.9	32.4	58.1	59.1
45 years and over	20.9	18.1	13.4	33.7	15.2
RURAL POPULATION.					
All ages, number	**1,795,383**	**1,181,186**	**395,009**	**200,762**	**13,271**
Under 5 years	164,422	118,499	43,523	610	1,214
Under 1 year	30,625	22,273	7,932	60	245
5 to 9 years	167,567	117,105	46,446	2,175	1,236
10 to 14 years	162,023	115,347	40,402	4,474	1,214
15 to 19 years	136,962	99,068	30,456	5,829	1,102
20 to 44 years	615,217	392,462	122,591	92,960	5,430
45 years and over	547,751	337,671	111,421	94,502	3,058
Age unknown	1,441	1,034	170	212	17
All ages, per cent	100.0	100.0	100.0	100.0	100.0
Under 5 years	9.2	10.0	11.0	0.3	9.1
5 to 9 years	9.3	9.9	11.8	1.1	9.3
10 to 14 years	9.0	9.8	10.2	2.2	9.1
15 to 19 years	7.6	8.4	7.7	2.9	8.3
20 to 44 years	34.3	33.2	31.0	46.3	40.9
45 years and over	30.5	28.6	28.2	47.1	23.0
New Jersey.					
URBAN POPULATION.					
All ages, number	**2,474,936**	**837,624**	**915,112**	**628,402**	**92,328**
Under 5 years	268,200	102,302	157,167	1,151	7,542
Under 1 year	51,661	19,965	29,915	144	1,627
5 to 9 years	252,872	90,518	148,396	6,268	7,651
10 to 14 years	226,324	82,841	121,392	14,997	7,066
15 to 19 years	199,910	74,884	93,019	24,838	7,125
20 to 44 years	1,027,887	326,442	288,035	366,915	45,646
45 years and over	498,135	159,837	106,871	213,817	17,145
Age unknown	1,608	800	232	416	153
All ages, per cent	100.0	100.0	100.0	100.0	100.0
Under 5 years	10.8	12.2	17.2	0.2	8.2
5 to 9 years	10.2	10.8	16.2	1.0	8.3
10 to 14 years	9.1	9.9	13.3	2.4	7.7
15 to 19 years	8.1	8.9	10.2	4.0	7.7
20 to 44 years	41.5	39.0	31.5	58.4	49.4
45 years and over	20.1	19.1	11.7	34.0	18.6
RURAL POPULATION.					
All ages, number	**680,001**	**375,051**	**170,687**	**110,211**	**24,804**
Under 5 years	70,406	39,373	20,929	199	2,629
Under 1 year	13,003	7,416	5,037	27	522
5 to 9 years	70,086	38,044	28,231	1,180	2,609
10 to 14 years	64,912	36,742	22,934	2,723	2,512
15 to 19 years	55,251	32,437	16,400	4,160	2,245
20 to 44 years	251,879	132,244	50,540	59,395	9,567
45 years and over	167,387	95,477	24,235	42,428	5,191
Age unknown	953	734	58	110	51
All ages, per cent	100.0	100.0	100.0	100.0	100.0
Under 5 years	10.4	10.5	16.6	0.2	10.6
5 to 9 years	10.3	10.1	16.5	1.1	10.5
10 to 14 years	9.5	9.8	13.4	2.5	10.1
15 to 19 years	8.1	8.6	9.6	3.8	9.1
20 to 44 years	37.0	35.3	29.6	53.9	38.6
45 years and over	24.6	25.5	14.2	38.5	20.9

TABLE 51.—DISTRIBUTION BY BROAD AGE GROUPS FOR POPULATION CLASSES, IN URBAN AND RURAL COMMUNITIES, BY DIVISIONS AND STATES: 1920—Continued.

AGE PERIOD.	All classes.	NATIVE WHITE.		Foreign-born white.	Negro.
		Native parentage.	Foreign or mixed parentage.		
MIDDLE ATLANTIC—Continued.					
Pennsylvania.					
URBAN POPULATION.					
All ages, number	5, 607, 815	2, 651, 949	1, 687, 569	1, 025, 929	239, 892
Under 5 years	611, 693	313, 687	278, 107	1, 658	18, 133
Under 1 year	119, 949	62, 055	53, 637	194	4, 039
5 to 9 years	569, 437	280, 823	261, 240	9, 563	17, 743
10 to 14 years	511, 470	260, 045	212, 693	21, 965	16, 714
15 to 19 years	466, 234	239, 927	168, 361	40, 015	17, 799
20 to 44 years	2, 291, 338	1, 044, 245	523, 030	593, 918	128, 812
45 years and over	1, 152, 536	510, 524	243, 537	357, 518	40, 181
Age unknown	5, 107	2, 698	601	1, 292	510
All ages, per cent	100.0	100.0	100.0	100.0	100.0
Under 5 years	10.9	11.8	16.5	0.2	7.6
5 to 9 years	10.2	10.6	15.5	0.9	7.4
10 to 14 years	9.1	9.8	12.6	2.1	7.0
15 to 19 years	8.3	9.0	10.0	3.9	7.4
20 to 44 years	40.9	39.4	31.0	57.9	53.7
45 years and over	20.6	19.3	14.4	34.8	16.7
RURAL POPULATION					
All ages, number	3, 112, 202	2, 098, 122	607, 236	361, 921	44, 676
Under 5 years	393, 772	257, 690	131, 037	754	4, 276
Under 1 year	75, 868	49, 879	24, 944	124	919
5 to 9 years	375, 793	245, 566	121, 344	4, 473	4, 389
10 to 14 years	340, 271	236, 176	90, 420	9, 208	4, 441
15 to 19 years	276, 503	200, 343	59, 097	12, 777	4, 257
20 to 44 years	1, 050, 879	686, 521	129, 075	216, 100	19, 088
45 years and over	672, 468	470, 348	76, 043	117, 889	8, 128
Age unknown	2, 516	1, 478	220	720	97
All ages, per cent	100.0	100.0	100.0	100.0	100.0
Under 5 years	12.7	12.3	21.6	0.2	9.6
5 to 9 years	12.1	11.7	20.0	1.2	9.8
10 to 14 years	10.9	11.3	14.9	2.5	9.9
15 to 19 years	8.9	9.5	9.7	3.5	9.5
20 to 44 years	33.8	32.7	21.3	59.7	42.7
45 years and over	21.6	22.4	12.5	32.6	18.2
EAST NORTH CENTRAL.					
Ohio.					
URBAN POPULATION.					
All ages, number	3, 677, 136	1, 996, 363	953, 098	570, 449	155, 975
Under 5 years	362, 776	223, 983	126, 379	1, 017	11, 357
Under 1 year	69, 757	43, 569	23, 627	114	2, 437
5 to 9 years	328, 985	197, 530	113, 962	6, 415	11, 062
10 to 14 years	295, 619	180, 791	90, 949	13, 361	10, 500
15 to 19 years	284, 023	176, 996	74, 420	21, 449	11, 106
20 to 44 years	1, 615, 018	853, 298	348, 466	328, 873	83, 575
45 years and over	787, 933	361, 905	198, 665	198, 971	28, 074
Age unknown	2, 782	1, 860	257	363	301
All ages, per cent	100.0	100.0	100.0	100.0	100.0
Under 5 years	9.9	11.2	13.3	0.2	7.3
5 to 9 years	8.9	9.9	12.0	1.1	7.1
10 to 14 years	8.0	9.1	9.5	2.3	6.7
15 to 19 years	7.7	8.9	7.8	3.8	7.1
20 to 44 years	43.9	42.7	36.6	57.7	53.6
45 years and over	21.4	18.1	20.8	34.9	18.0
RURAL POPULATION.					
All ages, number	2, 082, 258	1, 672, 759	270, 976	108, 248	30, 212
Under 5 years	223, 360	194, 311	25, 950	221	2, 870
Under 1 year	42, 185	37, 029	4, 542	27	585
5 to 9 years	219, 817	189, 038	26, 670	1, 120	2, 986
10 to 14 years	212, 710	184, 072	23, 038	2, 603	2, 994
15 to 19 years	180, 631	156, 498	17, 702	3, 636	2, 791
20 to 44 years	694, 845	550, 423	82, 297	51, 078	11, 013
45 years and over	549, 765	397, 514	95, 247	49, 486	7, 507
Age unknown	1, 130	903	72	104	51
All ages, per cent	100.0	100.0	100.0	100.0	100.0
Under 5 years	10.7	11.6	9.6	0.2	9.5
5 to 9 years	10.6	11.3	9.8	1.0	9.9
10 to 14 years	10.2	11.0	8.5	2.4	9.9
15 to 19 years	8.7	9.4	6.5	3.4	9.2
20 to 44 years	33.4	32.9	30.4	47.2	36.5
45 years and over	26.4	23.8	35.1	45.7	24.8

TABLE 51.—DISTRIBUTION BY BROAD AGE GROUPS FOR POPULATION CLASSES, IN URBAN AND RURAL COMMUNITIES, BY DIVISIONS AND STATES: 1920—Continued.

AGE PERIOD.	All classes.	NATIVE WHITE.		Foreign-born white.	Negro.
		Native parentage.	Foreign or mixed parentage.		
East North Central—Con.					
Indiana.					
URBAN POPULATION.					
All ages, number	1,482,855	1,043,866	247,929	118,813	71,813
Under 5 years	138,979	107,530	26,088	183	5,160
Under 1 year	27,392	21,182	5,066	18	1,122
5 to 9 years	133,419	101,611	24,972	1,190	5,640
10 to 14 years	123,845	95,755	20,136	2,534	5,417
15 to 19 years	122,255	95,300	17,352	3,911	5,679
20 to 44 years	616,074	424,784	92,214	63,525	35,295
45 years and over	345,364	216,826	66,998	47,028	14,376
Age unknown	2,919	2,060	169	442	246
All ages, per cent	100.0	100.0	100.0	100.0	100.0
Under 5 years	9.4	10.3	10.5	0.2	7.2
5 to 9 years	9.0	9.7	10.1	1.0	7.9
10 to 14 years	8.4	9.2	8.1	2.1	7.5
15 to 19 years	8.2	9.1	7.0	3.3	7.9
20 to 44 years	41.5	40.7	37.2	53.5	49.1
45 years and over	23.3	20.8	27.0	39.6	20.0
RURAL POPULATION.					
All ages, number	1,447,535	1,285,678	120,730	32,055	8,997
Under 5 years	150,216	143,941	5,472	33	762
Under 1 year	27,964	26,865	947	5	145
5 to 9 years	151,562	143,868	6,578	223	887
10 to 14 years	150,555	141,861	7,180	551	957
15 to 19 years	131,949	123,259	7,004	777	903
20 to 44 years	480,750	425,223	42,302	10,064	3,136
45 years and over	381,592	306,708	52,147	20,379	2,336
Age unknown	911	818	47	28	16
All ages, per cent	100.0	100.0	100.0	100.0	100.0
Under 5 years	10.4	11.2	4.5	0.1	8.5
5 to 9 years	10.5	11.2	5.4	0.7	9.9
10 to 14 years	10.4	11.0	5.9	1.7	10.6
15 to 19 years	9.1	9.6	5.8	2.4	10.0
20 to 44 years	33.2	33.1	35.0	31.4	34.9
45 years and over	26.4	23.9	43.2	63.6	26.0
Illinois.					
URBAN POPULATION.					
All ages, number	4,403,153	1,583,665	1,607,483	1,046,677	161,728
Under 5 years	430,985	203,160	215,777	1,417	10,507
Under 1 year	80,944	39,052	39,256	187	2,429
5 to 9 years	418,100	180,762	217,604	8,971	10,648
10 to 14 years	375,807	158,729	183,921	22,590	10,488
15 to 19 years	345,332	141,778	155,441	36,801	11,176
20 to 44 years	1,910,401	626,257	620,743	571,423	89,894
45 years and over	915,366	268,984	212,977	403,785	28,572
Age unknown	7,162	3,995	1,020	1,690	443
All ages, per cent	100.0	100.0	100.0	100.0	100.0
Under 5 years	9.8	12.8	13.4	0.1	6.5
5 to 9 years	9.5	11.4	13.5	0.9	6.6
10 to 14 years	8.5	10.0	11.4	2.2	6.5
15 to 19 years	7.8	9.0	9.7	3.5	6.9
20 to 44 years	43.4	39.5	38.6	54.6	55.6
45 years and over	20.8	17.0	13.2	38.6	17.7
RURAL POPULATION.					
All ages, number	2,092,127	1,482,898	418,336	160,274	20,546
Under 5 years	224,088	191,005	31,045	212	1,826
Under 1 year	42,107	36,220	5,506	17	364
5 to 9 years	227,164	186,656	37,048	1,072	2,088
10 to 14 years	219,523	176,753	37,455	9,786	2,020
15 to 19 years	195,220	153,738	35,260	4,422	1,707
20 to 44 years	729,067	493,857	163,805	63,414	7,948
45 years and over	485,303	279,584	113,546	87,333	4,819
Age unknown	1,762	1,305	177	235	44
All ages, per cent	100.0	100.0	100.0	100.0	100.0
Under 5 years	10.8	12.9	7.4	0.1	8.9
5 to 9 years	10.9	12.6	8.9	0.9	10.2
10 to 14 years	10.5	11.9	9.0	2.1	9.9
15 to 19 years	9.4	10.4	8.4	2.8	8.7
20 to 44 years	35.0	33.3	39.2	39.6	38.7
45 years and over	23.3	18.9	27.1	54.5	23.5

TABLE **51.**—DISTRIBUTION BY BROAD AGE GROUPS FOR POPULATION CLASSES, IN URBAN AND RURAL COMMUNITIES, BY DIVISIONS AND STATES: 1920—Continued.

| AGE PERIOD. | All classes. | NATIVE WHITE. | | Foreign-born white. | Negro. |
		Native parentage.	Foreign or mixed parentage.		
EAST NORTH CENTRAL—Con.					
Michigan.					
URBAN POPULATION.					
All ages, number	2, 241, 560	902, 177	760, 947	521, 554	55, 006
Under 5 years	243, 978	122, 594	115, 116	2, 477	3, 652
Under 1 year	47, 482	24, 912	21, 463	254	821
5 to 9 years	206, 625	97, 570	97, 189	8, 501	3, 258
10 to 14 years	173, 395	80, 140	76, 352	13, 977	2, 847
15 to 19 years	174, 338	78, 795	71, 448	20, 263	3, 704
20 to 44 years	1, 014, 018	375, 710	302, 688	300, 379	34, 188
45 years and over	426, 537	145, 770	97, 814	175, 364	7, 227
Age unknown	2, 669	1, 598	340	593	130
All ages, per cent	100. 0	100. 0	100. 0	100. 0	100. 0
Under 5 years	10. 9	13. 6	15. 1	0. 5	6. 6
5 to 9 years	9. 2	10. 8	12. 8	1. 6	5. 9
10 to 14 years	7. 7	8. 9	10. 0	2. 7	5. 2
15 to 19 years	7. 8	8. 7	9. 4	3. 9	6. 7
20 to 44 years	45. 2	41. 6	39. 8	57. 6	62. 2
45 years and over	19. 0	16. 2	12. 9	33. 6	13. 1
RURAL POPULATION.					
All ages, number	1, 426, 852	768, 270	443, 598	205, 081	5, 076
Under 5 years	160, 608	111, 745	47, 351	417	489
Under 1 year	29, 804	21, 379	8, 159	37	102
5 to 9 years	161, 595	103, 521	54, 931	2, 012	490
10 to 14 years	153, 058	93, 404	54, 390	4, 256	489
15 to 19 years	121, 176	70, 411	44, 841	5, 120	392
20 to 44 years	460, 751	223, 518	156, 757	77, 189	1, 828
45 years and over	368, 601	165, 001	85, 158	115, 877	1, 381
Age unknown	1, 063	670	170	210	7
All ages, per cent	100. 0	100. 0	100. 0	100. 0	100. 0
Under 5 years	11. 3	14. 5	10. 7	0. 2	9. 6
5 to 9 years	11. 3	13. 5	12. 4	1. 0	9. 7
10 to 14 years	10. 7	12. 2	12. 3	2. 1	9. 6
15 to 19 years	8. 5	9. 2	10. 1	2. 5	7. 7
20 to 44 years	32. 3	29. 1	35. 3	37. 6	36. 0
45 years and over	25. 8	21. 5	19. 2	56. 5	27. 2
Wisconsin.					
URBAN POPULATION.					
All ages, number	1, 244, 568	444, 885	540, 497	254, 133	4, 351
Under 5 years	123, 949	75, 594	47, 691	304	296
Under 1 year	23, 478	14, 783	8, 582	40	59
5 to 9 years	117, 948	63, 310	52, 133	2, 141	304
10 to 14 years	107, 948	52, 026	50, 654	4, 934	285
15 to 19 years	106, 635	46, 280	52, 502	7, 519	282
20 to 44 years	513, 170	159, 276	238, 916	112, 221	2, 431
45 years and over	273, 282	47, 392	98, 316	126, 686	739
Age unknown	1, 636	1, 007	285	328	14
All ages, per cent	100. 0	100. 0	100. 0	100. 0	100. 0
Under 5 years	10. 0	17. 0	8. 8	0. 1	6. 8
5 to 9 years	9. 5	14. 2	9. 6	0. 8	7. 0
10 to 14 years	8. 7	11. 7	9. 4	1. 9	6. 6
15 to 19 years	8. 6	10. 4	9. 7	3. 0	6. 5
20 to 44 years	41. 2	35. 8	44. 2	44. 2	55. 9
45 years and over	22. 0	10. 7	18. 2	49. 9	17. 0
RURAL POPULATION.					
All ages, number	1, 387, 499	609, 809	561, 619	205, 995	850
Under 5 years	161, 093	117, 162	42, 381	187	72
Under 1 year	29, 660	22, 164	7, 194	26	20
5 to 9 years	159, 510	104, 155	52, 941	1, 076	71
10 to 14 years	151, 759	89, 252	58, 458	2, 886	90
15 to 19 years	131, 497	69, 746	56, 847	3, 987	88
20 to 44 years	474, 031	168, 848	236, 055	66, 079	326
45 years and over	308, 390	59, 912	114, 673	131, 571	198
Age unknown	1, 219	734	264	209	5
All ages, per cent	100. 0	100. 0	100. 0	100. 0	100. 0
Under 5 years	11. 6	19. 2	7. 5	0. 1	8. 5
5 to 9 years	11. 5	17. 1	9. 4	0. 5	8. 4
10 to 14 years	10. 9	14. 6	10. 4	1. 4	10. 6
15 to 19 years	9. 5	11. 4	10. 1	1. 9	10. 4
20 to 44 years	34. 2	27. 7	42. 0	32. 1	38. 4
45 years and over	22. 2	9. 8	20. 4	63. 9	23. 3

TABLE 51.—DISTRIBUTION BY BROAD AGE GROUPS FOR POPULATION CLASSES, IN URBAN AND RURAL COMMUNITIES, BY DIVISIONS AND STATES: 1920—Continued.

AGE PERIOD.	All classes.	NATIVE WHITE. Native parentage.	NATIVE WHITE. Foreign or mixed parentage.	Foreign-born white.	Negro.
WEST NORTH CENTRAL.					
Minnesota.					
URBAN POPULATION.					
All ages, number	1,051,593	356,046	445,068	241,463	8,250
Under 5 years	102,693	57,517	44,194	453	479
Under 1 year	19,325	11,244	7,941	30	100
5 to 9 years	94,802	45,909	46,461	1,922	455
10 to 14 years	84,696	36,136	44,399	3,693	439
15 to 19 years	85,620	32,271	46,582	6,277	448
20 to 44 years	459,309	133,088	204,694	116,499	4,622
45 years and over	222,690	49,970	58,440	112,305	1,792
Age unknown	1,783	1,155	298	314	15
All ages, per cent	100.0	100.0	100.0	100.0	100.0
Under 5 years	9.8	16.2	9.9	0.2	5.8
5 to 9 years	9.0	12.9	10.4	0.8	5.5
10 to 14 years	8.1	10.1	10.0	1.5	5.3
15 to 19 years	8.1	9.1	10.5	2.6	5.4
20 to 44 years	43.7	37.4	46.0	48.2	56.0
45 years and over	21.2	14.0	13.1	46.5	21.7
RURAL POPULATION.					
All ages, number	1,335,532	471,581	610,077	244,701	559
Under 5 years	158,701	102,524	54,504	295	43
Under 1 year	29,766	20,184	9,251	31	13
5 to 9 years	153,797	83,919	67,329	1,264	56
10 to 14 years	149,265	69,013	76,488	2,743	53
15 to 19 years	133,989	52,776	76,175	4,243	48
20 to 44 years	465,927	120,144	259,928	83,067	214
45 years and over	272,983	42,777	75,451	152,878	143
Age unknown	870	428	202	211	2
All ages, per cent	100.0	100.0	100.0	100.0	100.0
Under 5 years	11.9	21.7	8.9	0.1	7.7
5 to 9 years	11.5	17.8	11.0	0.5	10.0
10 to 14 years	11.2	14.6	12.5	1.1	9.5
15 to 19 years	10.0	11.2	12.5	1.7	8.6
20 to 44 years	34.9	25.5	42.6	33.9	38.3
45 years and over	20.4	9.1	12.4	62.5	25.6
Iowa.					
URBAN POPULATION.					
All ages, number	875,495	552,275	217,456	90,019	15,345
Under 5 years	76,668	62,201	12,996	217	1,233
Under 1 year	14,534	11,875	2,365	26	259
5 to 9 years	73,609	57,418	14,255	707	1,214
10 to 14 years	71,045	53,547	14,852	1,481	1,158
15 to 19 years	72,758	52,156	17,166	2,222	1,180
20 to 44 years	358,505	215,359	100,791	34,777	7,340
45 years and over	221,324	110,356	57,248	50,483	3,158
Age unknown	1,586	1,238	148	132	62
All ages, per cent	100.0	100.0	100.0	100.0	100.0
Under 5 years	8.8	11.3	6.0	0.2	8.0
5 to 9 years	8.4	10.4	6.6	0.8	7.9
10 to 14 years	8.1	9.7	6.8	1.6	7.5
15 to 19 years	8.3	9.4	7.9	2.5	7.7
20 to 44 years	40.9	39.0	46.4	38.6	47.8
45 years and over	25.3	20.0	26.3	56.1	20.6
RURAL POPULATION.					
All ages, number	1,528,526	976,278	412,525	135,628	3,660
Under 5 years	174,219	146,055	27,636	162	317
Under 1 year	32,632	27,735	4,820	19	53
5 to 9 years	166,370	132,000	32,560	809	339
10 to 14 years	156,756	118,290	36,325	1,823	334
15 to 19 years	142,223	99,796	39,577	2,529	338
20 to 44 years	545,989	312,756	187,360	44,331	1,358
45 years and over	341,118	165,390	88,871	85,838	946
Age unknown	1,851	1,444	241	137	28
All ages, per cent	100.0	100.0	100.0	100.0	100.0
Under 5 years	11.4	15.0	6.7	0.1	8.7
5 to 9 years	10.9	13.6	7.9	0.6	9.3
10 to 14 years	10.3	12.1	8.8	1.3	9.1
15 to 19 years	9.3	10.2	9.6	1.9	9.2
20 to 44 years	35.7	32.0	45.4	32.7	37.1
45 years and over	22.3	16.9	21.5	63.3	25.8

TABLE 51.—DISTRIBUTION BY BROAD AGE GROUPS FOR POPULATION CLASSES, IN URBAN AND RURAL COMMUNITIES, BY DIVISIONS AND STATES: 1920—Continued.

| AGE PERIOD. | All classes. | NATIVE WHITE. | | Foreign-born white. | Negro. |
		Native parentage.	Foreign or mixed parentage.		
WEST NORTH CENTRAL—Con.					
Missouri.					
URBAN POPULATION.					
All ages, number	1,586,903	949,293	353,930	148,813	134,167
Under 5 years	124,352	94,514	21,766	266	7,772
Under 1 year	23,540	17,913	3,944	37	1,640
5 to 9 years	128,454	93,915	24,653	1,164	8,701
10 to 14 years	128,665	91,501	24,919	2,843	9,385
15 to 19 years	130,977	90,495	24,943	5,513	9,990
20 to 44 years	700,620	404,902	158,850	65,863	70,663
45 years and over	371,186	172,246	98,587	72,986	27,120
Age unknown	2,649	1,720	212	178	536
All ages, per cent	100.0	100.0	100.0	100.0	100.0
Under 5 years	7.8	10.0	6.1	0.2	5.8
5 to 9 years	8.1	9.9	7.0	0.8	6.5
10 to 14 years	8.1	9.6	7.0	1.9	7.0
15 to 19 years	8.3	9.5	7.0	3.7	7.4
20 to 44 years	44.2	42.7	44.9	44.3	52.7
45 years and over	23.4	18.1	27.9	49.0	20.2
RURAL POPULATION.					
All ages, number	1,817,152	1,587,643	148,152	37,213	44,074
Under 5 years	203,557	194,015	5,313	42	4,184
Under 1 year	39,143	37,468	832	6	837
5 to 9 years	209,921	197,565	7,468	160	4,723
10 to 14 years	206,456	192,039	9,166	434	4,809
15 to 19 years	176,186	161,515	9,735	611	4,312
20 to 44 years	602,270	517,455	60,323	9,454	15,008
45 years and over	417,200	323,786	56,041	26,460	10,902
Age unknown	1,562	1,268	106	52	136
All ages, per cent	100.0	100.0	100.0	100.0	100.0
Under 5 years	11.2	12.2	3.6	0.1	9.5
5 to 9 years	11.6	12.4	5.0	0.4	10.7
10 to 14 years	11.4	12.1	6.2	1.2	10.9
15 to 19 years	9.7	10.2	6.6	1.6	9.8
20 to 44 years	33.1	32.6	40.7	25.4	34.1
45 years and over	23.0	20.4	37.8	71.1	24.7
North Dakota.					
URBAN POPULATION.					
All ages, number	88,239	36,448	35,049	16,161	272
Under 5 years	9,713	5,988	3,644	56	12
Under 1 year	1,819	1,169	641	4	3
5 to 9 years	9,125	4,931	3,981	187	16
10 to 14 years	8,038	3,876	3,818	270	12
15 to 19 years	7,812	3,270	3,964	523	9
20 to 44 years	37,290	13,412	16,008	7,583	163
45 years and over	15,710	4,514	3,591	7,493	60
Age unknown	551	457	43	49	
All ages, per cent	100.0	100.0	100.0	100.0	100.0
Under 5 years	11.0	16.4	10.4	0.3	4.4
5 to 9 years	10.3	13.5	11.4	1.2	5.9
10 to 14 years	9.1	10.6	10.9	1.7	4.4
15 to 19 years	8.9	9.0	11.3	3.2	3.3
20 to 44 years	42.3	36.8	45.7	46.9	59.9
45 years and over	17.8	12.4	10.2	46.4	22.1
RURAL POPULATION.					
All ages, number	558,633	171,518	265,436	115,342	195
Under 5 years	81,176	39,097	40,923	256	8
Under 1 year	14,781	7,437	7,176	15	2
5 to 9 years	76,648	31,258	43,505	1,053	26
10 to 14 years	66,721	22,947	40,587	2,416	29
15 to 19 years	53,642	16,191	32,463	4,402	15
20 to 44 years	192,831	45,850	90,629	54,475	60
45 years and over	86,874	15,753	17,208	52,579	55
Age unknown	741	422	121	161	2
All ages, per cent	100.0	100.0	100.0	100.0	100.0
Under 5 years	14.5	22.8	15.4	0.2	4.1
5 to 9 years	13.7	18.2	16.4	0.9	13.3
10 to 14 years	11.9	13.4	15.3	2.1	14.9
15 to 19 years	9.6	9.4	12.2	3.8	7.7
20 to 44 years	34.5	26.7	34.1	47.2	30.8
45 years and over	15.6	9.2	3.5	45.6	28.2

TABLE 51.—DISTRIBUTION BY BROAD AGE GROUPS FOR POPULATION CLASSES, IN URBAN AND RURAL COMMUNITIES, BY DIVISIONS AND STATES: 1920—Continued.

| AGE PERIOD. | All classes. | NATIVE WHITE. | | Foreign-born white. | Negro. |
		Native parentage.	Foreign or mixed parentage.		
WEST NORTH CENTRAL—Con.					
South Dakota.					
URBAN POPULATION.					
All ages, number............	101,872	58,251	30,888	12,150	340
Under 5 years..................	10,014	7,770	2,157	30	19
Under 1 year..................	1,809	1,407	384	2	6
5 to 9 years..................	9,402	6,846	2,438	76	27
10 to 14 years................	8,688	5,930	2,549	164	31
15 to 19 years................	8,921	5,527	3,061	293	30
20 to 44 years................	43,084	22,658	14,980	5,159	168
45 years and over............	21,046	8,907	5,666	6,367	61
Age unknown..................	717	613	37	61	4
All ages, per cent..........	100.0	100.0	100.0	100.0	100.0
Under 5 years................	9.8	13.3	7.0	0.2	5.6
5 to 9 years................	9.2	11.8	7.9	0.6	7.9
10 to 14 years..............	8.5	10.2	8.3	1.3	9.1
15 to 19 years..............	8.8	9.5	9.9	2.4	8.8
20 to 44 years..............	42.3	38.9	48.5	42.5	49.4
45 years and over...........	20.7	15.3	18.3	52.4	17.9
RURAL POPULATION.					
All ages, number............	534,675	250,347	197,270	70,241	492
Under 5 years................	69,817	48,443	18,948	83	51
Under 1 year................	13,135	9,412	3,282	13	12
5 to 9 years................	65,119	40,456	22,096	421	57
10 to 14 years..............	57,822	31,827	23,201	1,046	47
15 to 19 years..............	50,555	24,128	23,243	1,735	33
20 to 44 years..............	196,895	76,840	87,065	27,874	191
45 years and over...........	93,737	28,193	22,601	38,955	112
Age unknown.................	730	460	116	127	1
All ages, per cent..........	100.0	100.0	100.0	100.0	100.0
Under 5 years................	13.1	19.4	9.6	0.1	10.4
5 to 9 years................	12.2	16.2	11.2	0.6	11.6
10 to 14 years..............	10.8	12.7	11.8	1.5	9.6
15 to 19 years..............	9.5	9.6	11.8	2.5	6.7
20 to 44 years..............	36.8	30.7	44.1	39.7	38.8
45 years and over...........	17.5	11.3	11.5	55.5	22.8
Nebraska.					
URBAN POPULATION.					
All ages, number............	405,306	225,605	107,590	59,346	12,121
Under 5 years................	36,509	25,115	10,462	97	786
Under 1 year................	6,835	4,754	1,894	12	162
5 to 9 years................	36,352	23,590	11,229	701	800
10 to 14 years..............	33,997	21,432	10,323	1,428	796
15 to 19 years..............	33,369	20,069	10,229	2,212	833
20 to 44 years..............	173,951	91,764	48,079	26,974	6,719
45 years and over...........	89,649	42,396	17,190	27,815	2,155
Age unknown.................	1,479	1,239	78	119	32
All ages, per cent..........	100.0	100.0	100.0	100.0	100.0
Under 5 years................	9.0	11.1	9.7	0.2	6.5
5 to 9 years................	9.0	10.5	10.4	1.2	6.6
10 to 14 years..............	8.4	9.5	9.6	2.4	6.6
15 to 19 years..............	8.2	8.9	9.5	3.7	6.9
20 to 44 years..............	42.9	40.7	44.7	45.5	55.4
45 years and over...........	22.1	18.8	16.0	46.9	17.8
RURAL POPULATION.					
All ages, number............	891,066	531,459	264,913	90,306	1,121
Under 5 years................	106,731	87,137	18,905	115	92
Under 1 year................	19,979	16,777	3,087	5	19
5 to 9 years................	104,228	79,842	24,373	530	75
10 to 14 years..............	98,111	68,011	28,332	1,103	83
15 to 19 years..............	85,683	53,208	30,423	1,665	107
20 to 44 years..............	320,208	163,871	126,524	28,109	543
45 years and over...........	175,038	79,592	35,949	58,690	219
Age unknown.................	1,067	798	157	94	2
All ages, per cent..........	100.0	100.0	100.0	100.0	100.0
Under 5 years................	12.0	16.4	7.1	0.1	8.2
5 to 9 years................	11.7	14.8	9.2	0.6	6.7
10 to 14 years..............	11.0	12.8	10.8	1.2	7.4
15 to 19 years..............	9.6	10.0	11.5	1.8	9.5
20 to 44 years..............	35.9	30.8	47.8	31.1	48.4
45 years and over...........	19.6	15.0	13.6	65.0	19.5

TABLE 51.—DISTRIBUTION BY BROAD AGE GROUPS FOR POPULATION CLASSES, IN URBAN AND RURAL COMMUNITIES, BY DIVISIONS AND STATES: 1920—Continued.

AGE PERIOD.	All classes.	NATIVE WHITE.		Foreign-born white.	Negro.
		Native parentage.	Foreign or mixed parentage.		
WEST NORTH CENTRAL—Con.					
Kansas.					
URBAN POPULATION.					
All ages, number	617,964	449,990	85,325	39,432	42,096
Under 5 years	56,570	46,313	6,413	399	3,397
Under 1 year	11,221	9,147	1,310	33	718
5 to 9 years	56,020	44,933	6,445	991	3,614
10 to 14 years	54,214	43,071	6,298	1,087	3,655
15 to 19 years	53,537	41,488	6,548	1,355	3,563
20 to 44 years	250,221	177,526	37,718	16,657	18,033
45 years and over	146,078	95,645	21,855	18,871	9,647
Age unknown	1,324	1,014	48	72	187
All ages, per cent	100.0	100.0	100.0	100.0	100.0
Under 5 years	9.2	10.3	7.5	1.0	8.1
5 to 9 years	9.1	10.0	7.6	2.5	8.6
10 to 14 years	8.8	9.6	7.4	2.8	8.7
15 to 19 years	8.7	9.2	7.7	3.4	8.5
20 to 44 years	40.5	39.5	44.2	42.2	42.8
45 years and over	23.6	21.3	25.6	47.9	22.9
RURAL POPULATION.					
All ages, number	1,151,293	858,814	204,199	71,146	15,829
Under 5 years	130,692	115,371	13,498	355	1,296
Under 1 year	25,073	22,279	2,500	33	224
5 to 9 years	129,250	110,021	16,768	827	1,452
10 to 14 years	125,097	102,465	19,601	1,344	1,536
15 to 19 years	109,154	85,255	20,389	1,969	1,427
20 to 44 years	405,100	282,534	93,228	22,724	6,143
45 years and over	250,587	162,026	40,629	43,818	3,913
Age unknown	1,413	1,142	86	109	62
All ages, per cent	100.0	100.0	100.0	100.0	100.0
Under 5 years	11.4	13.4	6.6	0.5	8.2
5 to 9 years	11.2	12.8	8.2	1.2	9.2
10 to 14 years	10.9	11.9	9.6	1.9	9.7
15 to 19 years	9.5	9.9	10.0	2.8	9.0
20 to 44 years	35.2	32.9	45.7	31.9	38.8
45 years and over	21.8	18.9	19.9	61.6	24.7
SOUTH ATLANTIC.					
Delaware.					
URBAN POPULATION.					
All ages, number	120,767	63,747	27,172	16,815	12,992
Under 5 years	12,503	6,888	4,711	33	870
Under 1 year	2,606	1,459	961	4	182
5 to 9 years	10,652	5,512	4,055	177	906
10 to 14 years	9,675	5,347	3,102	303	923
15 to 19 years	9,388	5,326	2,414	596	1,051
20 to 44 years	51,725	26,899	8,424	10,191	6,192
45 years and over	26,587	13,704	4,452	5,450	2,963
Age unknown	237	71	14	65	87
All ages, per cent	100.0	100.0	100.0	100.0	100.0
Under 5 years	10.4	10.8	17.3	0.2	6.7
5 to 9 years	8.8	8.6	14.9	1.1	7.0
10 to 14 years	8.0	8.4	11.4	1.8	7.1
15 to 19 years	7.8	8.4	8.9	3.5	8.1
20 to 44 years	42.8	42.2	31.0	60.6	47.7
45 years and over	22.0	21.5	16.4	32.4	22.8
RURAL POPULATION.					
All ages, number	102,236	76,129	5,757	2,995	17,343
Under 5 years	10,426	7,799	710	11	1,906
Under 1 year	2,068	1,538	119	1	410
5 to 9 years	10,492	7,714	675	48	2,055
10 to 14 years	10,539	7,747	612	93	2,087
15 to 19 years	9,184	6,749	467	126	1,842
20 to 44 years	34,925	25,787	1,818	1,464	5,849
45 years and over	26,185	19,976	1,475	1,250	3,479
Age unknown	485	357		3	125
All ages, per cent	100.0	100.0	100.0	100.0	100.0
Under 5 years	10.2	10.2	12.3	0.4	11.0
5 to 9 years	10.3	10.1	11.7	1.6	11.8
10 to 14 years	10.3	10.2	10.6	3.1	12.0
15 to 19 years	9.0	8.9	8.1	4.2	10.6
40 to 44 years	34.2	33.9	31.6	48.9	33.7
45 years and over	25.6	26.2	25.6	41.7	20.1

TABLE 51.—DISTRIBUTION BY BROAD AGE GROUPS FOR POPULATION CLASSES, IN URBAN AND RURAL COMMUNITIES, BY DIVISIONS AND STATES: 1920—Continued.

AGE PERIOD.	All classes.	NATIVE WHITE.		Foreign-born white.	Negro.
		Native parentage.	Foreign or mixed parentage.		
SOUTH ATLANTIC—Continued.					
Maryland.					
URBAN POPULATION.					
All ages, number...............	869,422	482,491	174,279	87,740	124,509
Under 5 years..................	82,386	54,019	18,534	116	9,706
Under 1 year................	17,462	11,476	3,696	23	2,266
5 to 9 years...................	77,195	48,308	18,574	747	9,560
10 to 14 years.................	74,056	45,233	18,107	1,761	8,951
15 to 19 years.................	74,976	44,949	15,916	3,954	10,143
20 to 44 years.................	368,925	199,642	62,442	44,616	62,016
45 years and over..............	190,919	89,926	40,679	36,484	23,671
Age unknown...................	965	414	27	62	462
All ages, per cent.............	100.0	100.0	100.0	100.0	100.0
Under 5 years..................	9.5	11.2	10.6	0.1	7.8
5 to 9 years...................	8.9	10.0	10.7	0.9	7.7
10 to 14 years.................	8.5	9.4	10.4	2.0	7.2
15 to 19 years.................	8.6	9.3	9.1	4.5	8.1
20 to 44 years.................	42.4	41.4	35.8	50.9	49.8
45 years and over..............	22.0	18.6	23.3	41.6	19.0
RURAL POPULATION.					
All ages, number...............	580,239	410,597	35,193	14,437	119,970
Under 5 years..................	64,619	47,434	2,717	24	14,439
Under 1 year................	12,437	9,092	487	7	2,850
5 to 9 years...................	66,508	47,343	3,078	135	15,949
10 to 14 years.................	65,815	46,283	3,177	292	16,059
15 to 19 years.................	56,021	39,457	2,963	448	13,150
20 to 44 years.................	194,790	138,239	12,946	6,275	37,314
45 years and over..............	131,960	91,553	10,298	7,239	22,859
Age unknown...................	526	288	14	24	200
All ages, per cent.............	100.0	100.0	100.0	100.0	100.0
Under 5 years..................	11.1	11.6	7.7	0.2	12.0
5 to 9 years...................	11.5	11.5	8.7	0.9	13.3
10 to 14 years.................	11.3	11.3	9.0	2.0	13.4
15 to 19 years.................	9.7	9.6	8.4	3.1	11.0
20 to 44 years.................	33.6	33.7	36.8	43.5	31.1
45 years and over..............	22.7	22.3	29.3	50.1	19.1
District of Columbia.					
URBAN POPULATION. [1]					
All ages, number...............	437,571	239,488	58,824	28,548	109,966
Under 5 years..................	30,436	18,244	4,336	52	7,774
Under 1 year................	6,586	4,024	950	3	1,599
5 to 9 years...................	29,840	16,890	4,320	204	8,410
10 to 14 years.................	29,816	16,870	3,985	516	8,432
15 to 19 years.................	33,526	18,668	4,072	1,045	9,703
20 to 44 years.................	212,140	115,786	26,709	15,282	53,931
45 years and over..............	99,924	51,829	15,316	11,326	21,248
Age unknown...................	1,889	1,201	86	123	468
All ages, per cent.............	100.0	100.0	100.0	100.0	100.0
Under 5 years..................	7.0	7.6	7.4	0.2	7.1
Under 1 year................	1.5	1.7	1.6	(2)	1.5
5 to 9 years...................	6.8	7.1	7.3	0.7	7.6
10 to 14 years.................	6.8	7.0	6.7	1.8	7.7
15 to 19 years.................	7.7	7.8	6.9	3.7	8.8
20 to 44 years.................	48.5	48.3	45.4	53.5	49.0
45 years and over..............	22.8	21.6	26.0	39.7	19.3

[1] No rural population, as Washington city is coextensive with the District of Columbia.
[2] Less than one-tenth of 1 per cent.

TABLE 51.—DISTRIBUTION BY BROAD AGE GROUPS FOR POPULATION CLASSES, IN URBAN AND RURAL COMMUNITIES, BY DIVISIONS AND STATES: 1920—Continued.

AGE PERIOD.	All classes.	NATIVE WHITE.		Foreign-born white.	Negro.
		Native parentage.	Foreign or mixed parentage.		
SOUTH ATLANTIC—Continued.					
Virginia.					
URBAN POPULATION.					
All ages, number	673,984	413,778	31,469	19,226	209,134
Under 5 years	63,963	42,384	3,589	46	17,930
Under 1 year	13,678	9,025	681	6	3,963
5 to 9 years	62,558	40,442	3,593	203	18,310
10 to 14 years	59,255	38,009	3,237	425	17,573
15 to 19 years	62,987	39,062	2,898	820	20,184
20 to 44 years	299,189	176,575	11,552	11,283	99,575
45 years and over	124,271	76,591	6,574	6,412	34,580
Age unknown	1,761	715	26	37	982
All ages, per cent	100.0	100.0	100.0	100.0	100.0
Under 5 years	9.5	10.2	11.4	0.2	8.6
5 to 9 years	9.3	9.8	11.4	1.1	8.8
10 to 14 years	8.8	9.2	10.3	2.2	8.4
15 to 19 years	9.3	9.4	9.2	4.3	9.7
20 to 44 years	44.4	42.7	36.7	58.7	47.6
45 years and over	18.4	18.5	20.9	33.4	16.5
RURAL POPULATION.					
All ages, number	1,635,203	1,120,716	21,161	11,559	480,883
Under 5 years	213,221	147,207	2,495	44	63,333
Under 1 year	41,979	29,144	453	3	12,354
5 to 9 years	220,577	147,900	2,594	167	69,787
10 to 14 years	206,738	138,011	2,129	312	66,192
15 to 19 years	171,373	115,646	2,384	520	52,731
20 to 44 years	51,314	360,432	7,613	5,962	145,013
45 years and over	302,703	210,771	3,940	4,546	83,313
Age unknown	1,277	749	6	8	514
All ages, per cent	100.0	100.0	100.0	100.0	100.0
Under 5 years	13.0	13.1	11.8	0.4	13.2
5 to 9 years	13.5	13.2	12.3	1.4	14.5
10 to 14 years	12.6	12.3	10.1	2.7	13.8
15 to 19 years	10.5	10.3	11.3	4.5	11.0
20 to 44 years	31.8	32.2	36.0	51.6	30.2
45 years and over	18.5	18.8	18.6	39.3	17.3
West Virginia.					
URBAN POPULATION.					
All ages, number	369,007	288,802	37,869	19,755	22,484
Under 5 years	39,120	32,704	4,613	55	1,742
Under 1 year	7,570	6,351	848	1	370
5 to 9 years	36,712	30,401	4,373	223	1,713
10 to 14 years	34,031	28,170	3,584	473	1,801
15 to 19 years	33,300	27,555	2,891	776	2,070
20 to 44 years	155,001	119,804	12,801	11,264	11,083
45 years and over	69,033	48,773	9,565	6,852	3,815
Age unknown	1,810	1,395	42	112	260
All ages, per cent	100.0	100.0	100.0	100.0	100.0
Under 5 years	10.6	11.3	12.2	0.3	7.7
5 to 9 years	9.9	10.5	11.5	1.1	7.6
10 to 14 years	9.2	9.8	9.5	2.4	8.0
15 to 19 years	9.0	9.5	7.6	3.9	9.2
20 to 44 years	42.0	41.5	33.8	57.0	49.3
45 years and over	18.7	16.9	25.3	34.7	17.0
RURAL POPULATION.					
All ages, number	1,094,694	944,055	44,603	42,151	63,861
Under 5 years	156,814	137,062	12,505	132	7,112
Under 1 year	30,948	26,947	2,437	14	1,549
5 to 9 years	147,660	130,019	9,830	817	6,992
10 to 14 years	130,116	117,451	5,269	1,451	5,945
15 to 19 years	108,011	97,577	2,705	1,781	5,947
20 to 44 years	370,498	303,932	7,651	29,676	29,225
45 years and over	180,619	157,371	6,623	8,191	8,430
Age unknown	976	643	20	103	210
All ages, per cent	100.0	100.0	100.0	100.0	100.0
Under 5 years	14.3	14.5	28.0	0.3	11.1
5 to 9 years	13.5	13.8	22.0	1.9	10.9
10 to 14 years	11.9	12.4	11.8	3.4	9.3
15 to 19 years	9.9	10.3	6.1	4.2	9.3
20 to 44 years	33.8	32.2	17.2	70.4	45.8
45 years and over	16.5	16.7	14.8	19.4	13.2

TABLE **51.**—DISTRIBUTION BY BROAD AGE GROUPS FOR POPULATION CLASSES, IN URBAN AND RURAL COMMUNITIES, BY DIVISIONS AND STATES: 1920—Continued.

AGE PERIOD.	All classes.	NATIVE WHITE. Native parentage.	Foreign or mixed parentage.	Foreign-born white.	Negro.
SOUTH ATLANTIC—Continued.					
North Carolina.					
URBAN POPULATION.					
All ages, number	490,370	324,229	6,623	4,239	155,165
Under 5 years	53,828	38,064	771	15	14,965
Under 1 year	11,346	8,017	143	2	3,180
5 to 9 years	52,875	36,056	773	35	16,007
10 to 14 years	48,983	32,837	686	73	15,384
15 to 19 years	49,633	31,891	613	157	16,967
20 to 44 years	205,627	133,058	2,483	2,419	67,599
45 years and over	78,372	51,827	1,292	1,529	23,703
Age unknown	1,052	496	5	11	540
All ages, per cent	100.0	100.0	100.0	100.0	100.0
Under 5 years	11.0	11.7	11.6	0.4	9.6
5 to 9 years	10.8	11.1	11.7	0.8	10.3
10 to 14 years	10.0	10.1	10.4	1.7	9.9
15 to 19 years	10.1	9.8	9.3	3.7	10.9
20 to 44 years	41.9	41.0	37.5	57.1	43.6
45 years and over	16.0	16.0	19.5	36.1	15.3
RURAL POPULATION.					
All ages, number	2,068,753	1,440,974	4,854	2,860	608,242
Under 5 years	304,980	210,849	575	20	91,495
Under 1 year	60,712	42,459	101	3	17,707
5 to 9 years	302,767	204,802	582	48	95,398
10 to 14 years	269,874	182,065	482	71	85,662
15 to 19 years	218,565	147,242	396	100	69,641
20 to 44 years	638,926	453,405	1,729	1,463	178,865
45 years and over	331,484	241,465	1,088	1,156	86,184
Age unknown	2,157	1,146	2	2	997
All ages, per cent	100.0	100.0	100.0	100.0	100.0
Under 5 years	14.7	14.6	11.8	0.7	15.0
5 to 9 years	14.6	14.2	12.0	1.7	15.7
10 to 14 years	13.0	12.6	9.9	2.5	14.1
15 to 19 years	10.6	10.2	8.2	3.5	11.4
20 to 44 years	30.9	31.5	35.6	51.2	29.4
45 years and over	16.0	16.8	22.4	40.4	14.2
South Carolina.					
URBAN POPULATION.					
All ages, number	293,987	164,425	8,717	4,224	116,489
Under 5 years	29,424	18,446	827	7	10,130
Under 1 year	6,063	3,904	152		2,000
5 to 9 years	29,949	17,277	764	38	11,860
10 to 14 years	29,548	16,660	730	84	12,068
15 to 19 years	28,529	15,583	645	137	12,156
20 to 44 years	127,115	69,331	3,379	2,221	52,137
45 years and over	48,753	26,906	2,369	1,725	17,706
Age unknown	669	222	3	12	432
All ages, per cent	100.0	100.0	100.0	100.0	100.0
Under 5 years	10.0	11.2	9.5	0.2	8.7
5 to 9 years	10.2	10.5	8.8	0.9	10.2
10 to 14 years	10.1	10.1	8.4	2.0	10.4
15 to 19 years	9.7	9.5	7.4	3.2	10.4
20 to 44 years	43.2	42.2	38.8	52.6	44.8
45 years and over	16.6	16.4	27.2	40.8	15.2
RURAL POPULATION.					
All ages, number	1,389,737	634,993	4,002	2,177	748,230
Under 5 years	199,157	91,335	371	6	107,396
Under 1 year	39,295	18,046	65		20,271
5 to 9 years	205,878	89,060	348	93	116,405
10 to 14 years	193,492	81,729	271	24	111,430
15 to 19 years	154,232	66,139	466	75	87,521
20 to 44 years	442,302	209,653	1,728	1,339	229,461
45 years and over	194,009	96,808	817	709	95,618
Age unknown	667	269	1	1	396
All ages, per cent	100.0	100.0	100.0	100.0	100.0
Under 5 years	14.3	14.4	9.3	0.3	14.4
5 to 9 years	14.8	14.0	8.7	1.1	15.6
10 to 14 years	13.9	12.9	6.8	1.1	14.9
15 to 19 years	11.1	10.4	11.6	3.4	11.7
20 to 44 years	31.8	33.0	43.2	61.5	30.7
45 years and over	14.0	15.2	20.4	32.6	12.8

TABLE 51.—DISTRIBUTION BY BROAD AGE GROUPS FOR POPULATION CLASSES, IN URBAN AND RURAL COMMUNITIES, BY DIVISIONS AND STATES: 1920—Continued.

| AGE PERIOD. | All classes. | NATIVE WHITE. | | Foreign-born white. | Negro. |
		Native parentage.	Foreign or mixed parentage.		
SOUTH ATLANTIC—Continued.					
Georgia.					
URBAN POPULATION.					
All ages, number..............	727,859	419,183	22,987	12,432	273,036
Under 5 years.................	65,377	42,848	2,110	31	20,373
Under 1 year.................	13,627	9,098	396	2	4,128
5 to 9 years..................	69,625	42,505	2,397	108	24,606
10 to 14 years................	69,049	41,134	2,164	257	25,486
15 to 19 years................	70,087	40,608	1,915	534	27,026
20 to 44 years................	326,332	180,188	9,042	6,508	130,500
45 years and over.............	126,282	71,480	5,357	4,982	44,372
Age unknown..................	1,107	420	2	12	673
All ages, per cent............	100.0	100.0	100.0	100.0	100.0
Under 5 years.................	9.0	10.2	9.2	0.2	7.5
5 to 9 years..................	9.6	10.1	10.4	0.9	9.0
10 to 14 years................	9.5	9.8	9.4	2.1	9.3
15 to 19 years................	9.6	9.7	8.3	4.3	9.9
20 to 44 years................	44.8	43.0	39.3	52.3	47.8
45 years and over.............	17.3	17.1	23.3	40.1	16.3
RURAL POPULATION.					
All ages, number..............	2,167,973	1,223,514	7,244	3,754	933,329
Under 5 years.................	297,852	172,344	526	5	124,959
Under 1 year.................	59,343	35,345	100	....	23,894
5 to 9 years..................	312,748	171,878	544	14	140,300
10 to 14 years................	296,263	161,375	591	64	134,218
15 to 19 years................	237,462	128,733	556	126	108,030
20 to 44 years................	683,581	393,260	3,246	2,215	284,815
45 years and over.............	338,234	195,220	1,781	1,327	139,881
Age unknown..................	1,833	704	....	3	1,126
All ages, per cent............	100.0	100.0	100.0	100.0	100.0
Under 5 years.................	13.7	14.1	7.3	0.1	13.4
5 to 9 years..................	14.4	14.0	7.5	0.4	15.0
10 to 14 years................	13.7	13.2	8.2	1.7	14.4
15 to 19 years................	11.0	10.5	7.7	3.4	11.6
20 to 44 years................	31.5	32.1	44.8	59.0	30.5
45 years and over.............	15.6	16.0	24.6	35.3	15.0
Florida.					
URBAN POPULATION.					
All ages, number..............	355,825	163,060	42,457	29,509	120,596
Under 5 years.................	32,224	16,343	6,122	161	9,587
Under 1 year.................	6,397	3,279	1,138	15	1,962
5 to 9 years..................	33,695	15,798	6,560	458	10,871
10 to 14 years................	32,054	14,812	5,480	877	10,874
15 to 19 years................	31,126	14,092	4,211	1,543	11,269
20 to 44 years................	154,887	67,319	13,352	15,633	58,491
45 years and over.............	70,252	34,266	6,696	10,712	18,508
Age unknown..................	1,587	430	36	125	996
All ages, per cent............	100.0	100.0	100.0	100.0	100.0
Under 5 years.................	9.1	10.0	14.4	0.5	8.0
5 to 9 years..................	9.5	9.7	15.5	1.6	9.0
10 to 14 years................	9.0	9.1	12.9	3.0	9.0
15 to 19 years................	8.7	8.6	9.9	5.2	9.3
20 to 44 years................	43.5	41.3	31.4	53.0	48.5
45 years and over.............	19.7	21.0	15.8	36.3	15.3
RURAL POPULATION.					
All ages, number..............	612,645	369,235	20,393	13,499	208,891
Under 5 years.................	73,039	47,335	1,850	99	23,677
Under 1 year.................	14,148	9,272	326	10	4,532
5 to 9 years..................	77,725	48,474	2,033	233	26,903
10 to 14 years................	74,257	45,502	2,094	354	26,242
15 to 19 years................	60,711	36,398	1,705	413	22,139
20 to 44 years................	208,590	121,049	6,948	5,482	74,862
45 years and over.............	117,197	70,002	5,744	6,895	34,462
Age unknown..................	1,126	475	19	23	606
All ages, per cent............	100.0	100.0	100.0	100.0	100.0
Under 5 years.................	11.9	12.8	9.1	0.7	11.3
5 to 9 years..................	12.7	13.1	10.0	1.7	12.9
10 to 14 years................	12.1	12.3	10.3	2.6	12.6
15 to 19 years................	9.9	9.9	8.4	3.1	10.6
20 to 44 years................	34.0	32.8	34.1	40.6	35.9
45 years and over.............	19.1	19.0	28.2	51.1	16.5

TABLE 51.—DISTRIBUTION BY BROAD AGE GROUPS FOR POPULATION CLASSES, IN URBAN AND RURAL COMMUNITIES, BY DIVISIONS AND STATES: 1920—Continued.

AGE PERIOD.	All classes.	NATIVE WHITE.		Foreign-born white.	Negro.
		Native parentage.	Foreign or mixed parentage.		
EAST SOUTH CENTRAL.					
Kentucky.					
URBAN POPULATION.					
All ages, number............	633,543	422,898	83,610	21,561	105,393
Under 5 years...............	53,007	43,667	2,540	16	6,778
Under 1 year............	10,577	8,780	460	3	1,333
5 to 9 years...............	54,783	43,867	3,198	83	7,634
10 to 14 years............	54,770	42,395	3,999	236	8,134
15 to 19 years............	54,016	40,451	4,721	404	8,437
20 to 44 years............	264,845	172,969	36,219	6,742	48,870
45 years and over.........	151,330	79,093	32,866	14,054	25,297
Age unknown.............	792	456	67	26	243
All ages, per cent.........	100.0	100.0	100.0	100.0	100.0
Under 5 years............	8.4	10.3	3.0	0.1	6.4
5 to 9 years.............	8.6	10.4	3.8	0.4	7.2
10 to 14 years...........	8.6	10.0	4.8	1.1	7.7
15 to 19 years...........	8.5	9.6	5.6	1.9	8.0
20 to 44 years...........	41.8	40.9	43.3	31.3	46.4
45 years and over........	23.9	18.7	39.3	65.2	24.0
RURAL POPULATION.					
All ages, number...........	1,783,087	1,616,236	27,036	9,219	130,545
Under 5 years..............	238,618	223,278	1,628	14	13,690
Under 1 year............	47,628	44,618	307	2	2,701
5 to 9 years...............	232,788	215,866	1,672	64	15,179
10 to 14 years............	216,467	200,004	1,442	135	14,881
15 to 19 years............	181,808	167,076	1,401	171	13,155
20 to 44 years............	582,065	521,392	10,426	4,471	45,759
45 years and over.........	330,215	287,769	10,453	4,352	27,632
Age unknown.............	1,126	851	14	12	249
All ages, per cent.........	100.0	100.0	100.0	100.0	100.0
Under 5 years............	13.4	13.8	6.0	0.2	10.5
5 to 9 years.............	13.1	13.4	6.2	0.7	11.6
10 to 14 years...........	12.1	12.4	5.3	1.5	11.4
15 to 19 years...........	10.2	10.3	5.2	1.9	10.1
20 to 44 years...........	32.6	32.3	38.6	48.5	35.1
45 years and over........	18.5	17.8	38.7	47.2	21.2
Tennessee.					
URBAN POPULATION.					
All ages, number............	611,226	402,359	26,830	11,484	170,464
Under 5 years..............	53,526	40,182	1,756	34	11,550
Under 1 year............	10,931	8,218	320	4	2,388
5 to 9 years...............	55,799	39,821	1,988	106	13,883
10 to 14 years............	56,358	39,461	2,062	226	14,608
15 to 19 years............	57,942	39,478	1,961	490	16,010
20 to 44 years............	266,185	168,549	11,324	5,174	81,083
45 years and over.........	120,323	74,316	7,719	5,436	32,830
Age unknown.............	1,093	552	20	18	500
All ages, per cent.........	100.0	100.0	100.0	100.0	100.0
Under 5 years............	8.8	10.0	6.5	0.3	6.8
5 to 9 years.............	9.1	9.9	7.4	0.9	8.1
10 to 14 years...........	9.2	9.8	7.7	2.0	8.6
15 to 19 years...........	9.5	9.8	7.3	4.3	9.4
20 to 44 years...........	43.5	41.9	42.2	45.1	47.6
45 years and over........	19.7	18.5	28.8	47.3	19.3
RURAL POPULATION.					
All ages, number...........	1,726,659	1,430,398	10,928	3,994	281,294
Under 5 years..............	227,213	192,292	804	11	34,103
Under 1 year............	45,790	38,993	142	2	6,653
5 to 9 years...............	230,585	191,836	919	30	37,796
10 to 14 years............	220,079	181,276	916	67	37,816
15 to 19 years............	180,429	147,928	769	92	31,635
20 to 44 years............	552,080	457,954	3,947	1,388	88,775
45 years and over.........	315,212	258,464	3,568	2,403	50,764
Age unknown.............	1,061	648	5	3	405
All ages, per cent.........	100.0	100.0	100.0	100.0	100.0
Under 5 years............	13.2	13.4	7.4	0.3	12.1
5 to 9 years.............	13.4	13.4	8.4	0.8	13.4
10 to 14 years...........	12.7	12.7	8.4	1.7	13.4
15 to 19 years...........	10.4	10.3	7.0	2.3	11.2
20 to 44 years...........	32.0	32.0	36.1	34.8	31.6
45 years and over........	18.3	18.1	32.7	60.2	18.0

TABLE 51.—DISTRIBUTION BY BROAD AGE GROUPS FOR POPULATION CLASSES, IN URBAN AND RURAL COMMUNITIES, BY DIVISIONS AND STATES: 1920—Continued.

| AGE PERIOD. | All classes. | NATIVE WHITE. | | Foreign-born white. | Negro. |
		Native parentage.	Foreign or mixed parentage.		
EAST SOUTH CENTRAL—Con.					
Alabama.					
URBAN POPULATION.					
All ages, number	509,317	278,827	22,400	11,183	196,833
Under 5 years	48,688	30,358	2,238	36	16,052
Under 1 year	10,588	6,586	418	6	3,578
5 to 9 years	51,938	29,864	2,560	137	19,377
10 to 14 years	50,309	28,538	2,331	284	19,156
15 to 19 years	48,396	26,525	1,999	474	19,395
20 to 44 years	222,259	118,486	8,276	5,649	89,807
45 years and over	86,853	44,816	4,985	4,587	32,439
Age unknown	874	240	11	16	607
All ages, per cent	100.0	100.0	100.0	100.0	100.0
Under 5 years	9.6	10.9	10.0	0.3	8.2
5 to 9 years	10.2	10.7	11.4	1.2	9.8
10 to 14 years	9.9	10.2	10.4	2.5	9.7
15 to 19 years	9.5	9.5	8.9	4.2	9.9
20 to 44 years	43.6	42.5	36.9	50.5	45.6
45 years and over	17.1	16.1	22.3	41.0	16.5
RURAL POPULATION.					
All ages, number	1,838,857	1,115,302	12,841	6,479	703,819
Under 5 years	250,834	161,211	1,419	28	88,103
Under 1 year	51,962	34,450	254	3	17,240
5 to 9 years	266,293	161,483	1,545	68	103,116
10 to 14 years	249,103	148,260	1,519	151	99,112
15 to 19 years	196,597	117,505	1,238	223	77,603
20 to 44 years	575,995	353,100	4,251	2,684	215,845
45 years and over	298,202	173,230	2,864	3,314	118,737
Age unknown	1,833	513	5	11	1,303
All ages, per cent	100.0	100.0	100.0	100.0	100.0
Under 5 years	13.6	14.5	11.1	0.4	12.5
5 to 9 years	14.5	14.5	12.0	1.0	14.7
10 to 14 years	13.5	13.3	11.8	2.3	14.1
15 to 19 years	10.7	10.5	9.6	3.4	11.0
20 to 44 years	31.3	31.7	33.1	41.4	30.7
45 years and over	16.2	15.5	22.3	51.1	16.9
Mississippi.					
URBAN POPULATION.					
All ages, number	240,121	127,141	10,088	4,179	98,626
Under 5 years	20,911	12,687	861	4	7,350
Under 1 year	4,309	2,621	159	1	1,527
5 to 9 years	23,472	13,265	961	32	9,207
10 to 14 years	24,627	13,676	916	76	9,955
15 to 19 years	23,440	12,683	741	124	9,888
20 to 44 years	102,153	51,976	3,728	2,024	44,394
45 years and over	44,191	22,137	2,867	1,909	17,247
Age unknown	1,327	717	14	10	585
All ages, per cent	100.0	100.0	100.0	100.0	100.0
Under 5 years	8.7	10.0	8.5	0.1	7.5
5 to 9 years	9.8	10.4	9.5	0.8	9.3
10 to 14 years	10.3	10.8	9.1	1.8	10.1
15 to 19 years	9.8	10.0	7.3	3.0	10.0
20 to 44 years	42.5	40.9	37.0	48.4	45.0
45 years and over	18.4	17.4	28.4	45.7	17.5
RURAL POPULATION.					
All ages, number	1,550,497	699,621	9,093	3,840	836,558
Under 5 years	195,337	94,169	948	20	100,044
Under 1 year	39,836	20,073	184		19,536
5 to 9 years	212,286	96,224	905	45	114,956
10 to 14 years	211,339	93,307	839	114	116,906
15 to 19 years	168,759	73,955	675	199	93,794
20 to 44 years	512,622	228,317	3,067	1,630	279,129
45 years and over	248,212	113,021	2,651	1,828	130,430
Age unknown	1,942	628	8	4	1,299
All ages, per cent	100.0	100.0	100.0	100.0	100.0
Under 5 years	12.6	13.5	10.4	0.5	12.0
5 to 9 years	13.7	13.8	10.0	1.2	13.7
10 to 14 years	13.6	13.3	9.2	3.0	14.0
15 to 19 years	10.9	10.6	7.4	5.2	11.2
20 to 44 years	33.1	32.6	33.7	42.4	33.4
45 years and over	16.0	16.2	29.2	47.6	15.6

TABLE 51.—DISTRIBUTION BY BROAD AGE GROUPS FOR POPULATION CLASSES, IN URBAN AND RURAL COMMUNITIES, BY DIVISIONS AND STATES: 1920—Continued.

| AGE PERIOD. | All classes. | NATIVE WHITE. | | Foreign-born white. | Negro. |
		Native parentage.	Foreign or mixed parentage.		
WEST SOUTH CENTRAL.					
Arkansas.					
URBAN POPULATION.					
All ages, number	290,497	195,777	15,474	5,590	73,592
Under 5 years	26,624	20,540	868	9	5,202
Under 1 year	5,440	4,213	155		1,072
5 to 9 years	28,356	20,747	1,032	29	6,545
10 to 14 years	28,383	20,197	1,205	59	6,915
15 to 19 years	27,091	18,341	1,315	119	7,311
20 to 44 years	123,830	80,125	6,896	2,283	34,503
45 years and over	55,490	35,502	4,137	3,086	12,744
Age unknown	723	325	21	5	372
All ages, per cent	100.0	100.0	100.0	100.0	100.0
Under 5 years	9.2	10.5	5.6	0.2	7.1
5 to 9 years	9.8	10.6	6.7	0.5	8.9
10 to 14 years	9.8	10.3	7.8	1.1	9.4
15 to 19 years	9.3	9.4	8.5	2.1	9.9
20 to 44 years	42.6	40.9	44.6	40.8	46.9
45 years and over	19.1	18.1	26.7	55.2	17.3
RURAL POPULATION.					
All ages, number	1,461,707	1,030,915	23,616	8,385	398,628
Under 5 years	194,187	146,293	1,783	27	46,072
Under 1 year	40,304	30,634	331	3	9,334
5 to 9 years	200,132	146,802	2,243	76	50,998
10 to 14 years	193,088	137,957	2,468	135	52,519
15 to 19 years	156,761	109,251	2,240	259	44,997
20 to 44 years	478,533	327,759	8,940	3,112	138,648
45 years and over	238,045	162,398	5,930	4,765	64,911
Age unknown	961	455	12	11	483
All ages, per cent	100.0	100.0	100.0	100.0	100.0
Under 5 years	13.3	14.2	7.5	0.3	11.6
5 to 9 years	13.7	14.2	9.5	0.9	12.8
10 to 14 years	13.2	13.4	10.5	1.6	13.2
15 to 19 years	10.7	10.6	9.5	3.1	11.3
20 to 44 years	32.7	31.8	37.9	37.1	34.8
45 years and over	16.3	15.8	25.1	56.8	16.3
Louisiana.					
URBAN POPULATION.					
All ages, number	628,163	320,229	84,383	32,609	190,413
Under 5 years	54,841	34,652	5,156	112	14,882
Under 1 year	10,857	6,861	970	8	3,010
5 to 9 years	60,481	35,737	6,444	317	17,945
10 to 14 years	61,272	35,468	6,509	602	18,671
15 to 19 years	60,352	34,191	6,121	1,250	18,773
20 to 44 years	273,106	136,496	32,806	15,454	88,117
45 years and over	115,584	42,709	27,256	14,802	30,639
Age unknown	2,527	976	91	72	1,386
All ages, per cent	100.0	100.0	100.0	100.0	100.0
Under 5 years	8.7	10.8	6.1	0.3	7.8
5 to 9 years	9.6	11.2	7.6	1.0	9.4
10 to 14 years	9.8	11.1	7.7	1.8	9.8
15 to 19 years	9.6	10.7	7.3	3.8	9.9
20 to 44 years	43.5	42.6	38.9	47.4	46.3
45 years and over	18.4	13.3	32.3	45.4	16.1
RURAL POPULATION.					
All ages, number	1,170,346	621,495	25,633	12,262	509,844
Under 5 years	154,372	88,119	3,632	74	62,414
Under 1 year	29,403	16,935	671	10	11,756
5 to 9 years	162,749	89,583	4,269	124	68,654
10 to 14 years	157,955	85,057	3,950	216	68,601
15 to 19 years	127,953	67,764	2,007	137	56,729
20 to 44 years	391,608	204,636	6,523	5,735	174,378
45 years and over	173,911	85,367	4,362	5,652	78,340
Age unknown	1,798	1,039	7	24	728
All ages, per cent	100.0	100.0	100.0	100.0	100.0
Under 5 years	13.2	14.2	14.2	0.6	12.2
5 to 9 years	13.9	14.4	16.7	1.0	13.5
10 to 14 years	13.5	13.7	15.4	1.8	13.5
15 to 19 years	10.9	10.9	11.3	3.6	11.1
20 to 44 years	33.5	32.9	25.4	46.8	34.2
45 years and over	14.9	13.7	17.0	46.1	15.4

TABLE 51.—DISTRIBUTION BY BROAD AGE GROUPS FOR POPULATION CLASSES, IN URBAN AND RURAL COMMUNITIES, BY DIVISIONS AND STATES: 1920—Continued.

		NATIVE WHITE.			
AGE PERIOD.	All classes.	Native parentage.	Foreign or mixed parentage.	Foreign-born white.	Negro.
WEST SOUTH CENTRAL—Con.					
Oklahoma.					
URBAN POPULATION.					
All ages, number	539,480	437,374	34,780	14,211	47,904
Under 5 years	51,816	44,935	2,275	133	3,830
Under 1 year	10,401	9,033	472	11	754
5 to 9 years	52,933	45,176	2,312	242	4,473
10 to 14 years	51,003	43,243	2,258	277	4,491
15 to 19 years	49,871	41,402	2,470	490	4,875
20 to 44 years	238,113	189,736	16,570	7,353	22,590
45 years and over	94,427	71,823	8,865	5,663	7,479
Age unknown	1,317	1,059	30	53	166
All ages, per cent	100.0	100.0	100.0	100.0	100.0
Under 5 years	9.6	10.3	6.5	0.9	8.0
5 to 9 years	9.8	10.3	6.6	1.7	9.3
10 to 14 years	9.5	9.9	6.5	1.9	9.4
15 to 19 years	9.2	9.5	7.1	3.4	10.2
20 to 44 years	44.1	43.4	47.6	51.7	47.2
45 years and over	17.5	16.4	25.5	39.8	15.6
RURAL POPULATION.					
All ages, number	1,488,803	1,241,733	67,339	25,757	101,504
Under 5 years	200,762	174,776	5,509	170	12,384
Under 1 year	39,102	34,165	976	17	2,312
5 to 9 years	208,821	178,881	6,955	403	14,185
10 to 14 years	196,434	166,652	7,470	594	14,193
15 to 19 years	159,464	133,822	7,286	1,011	11,643
20 to 44 years	488,099	402,872	26,386	10,573	32,621
45 years and over	233,259	183,377	13,699	12,843	16,247
Age unknown	1,964	1,353	34	163	231
All ages, per cent	100.0	100.0	100.0	100.0	100.0
Under 5 years	13.5	14.1	8.2	0.7	12.2
5 to 9 years	14.0	14.4	10.3	1.6	14.0
10 to 14 years	13.2	13.4	11.1	2.3	14.0
15 to 19 years	10.7	10.8	10.8	3.9	11.5
20 to 44 years	32.8	32.4	39.2	41.0	32.1
45 years and over	15.7	14.8	20.3	49.9	16.0
Texas.					
URBAN POPULATION.					
All ages, number	1,512,689	951,006	169,131	168,050	223,373
Under 5 years	136,928	94,175	23,959	3,534	15,172
Under 1 year	28,452	18,955	5,964	370	3,142
5 to 9 years	143,445	95,388	20,163	9,145	18,689
10 to 14 years	140,158	91,697	16,821	11,922	19,666
15 to 19 years	142,650	91,093	15,430	14,509	21,566
20 to 44 years	676,763	418,307	65,294	81,928	110,707
45 years and over	265,727	155,149	27,278	46,415	36,543
Age unknown	7,018	5,197	186	597	1,030
All ages, per cent	100.0	100.0	100.0	100.0	100.0
Under 5 years	9.1	9.9	14.2	2.1	6.8
5 to 9 years	9.5	10.0	11.9	5.4	8.4
10 to 14 years	9.3	9.6	9.9	7.1	8.8
15 to 19 years	9.4	9.6	9.1	8.6	9.7
20 to 44 years	44.7	44.0	38.6	48.8	49.6
45 years and over	17.6	16.3	16.1	27.6	16.4
RURAL POPULATION.					
All ages, number	3,150,539	2,161,256	276,253	192,469	518,321
Under 5 years	396,979	291,380	38,482	4,185	62,626
Under 1 year	79,438	57,388	8,791	371	12,805
5 to 9 years	429,262	305,900	39,866	10,700	72,488
10 to 14 years	404,941	283,923	35,662	14,600	70,540
15 to 19 years	345,909	236,999	31,593	16,631	60,488
20 to 44 years	1,079,306	722,280	98,090	83,116	174,934
45 years and over	490,670	318,934	32,294	62,527	76,591
Age unknown	3,472	1,840	266	710	654
All ages, per cent	100.0	100.0	100.0	100.0	100.0
Under 5 years	12.6	13.5	13.9	2.2	12.1
5 to 9 years	13.6	14.2	14.4	5.6	14.0
10 to 14 years	12.9	13.1	12.9	7.6	13.6
15 to 19 years	11.0	11.0	11.4	8.6	11.7
20 to 44 years	34.3	33.4	35.5	43.2	33.8
45 years and over	15.6	14.8	11.7	32.5	14.8

75108°—22——14

TABLE 51.—DISTRIBUTION BY BROAD AGE GROUPS FOR POPULATION CLASSES, IN URBAN AND RURAL COMMUNITIES, BY DIVISIONS AND STATES: 1920—Continued.

AGE PERIOD.	All classes.	NATIVE WHITE.		Foreign-born white.	Negro.
		Native parentage.	Foreign or mixed parentage.		
MOUNTAIN.					
Montana.					
URBAN POPULATION.					
All ages, number	172,011	81,508	55,425	32,763	1,270
Under 5 years	16,835	10,661	5,974	98	85
Under 1 year	3,228	2,088	1,100	3	16
5 to 9 years	15,846	9,185	6,133	410	73
10 to 14 years	14,244	7,629	5,880	626	76
15 to 19 years	13,364	6,746	5,649	864	59
20 to 44 years	77,016	33,693	24,306	17,940	620
45 years and over	33,177	12,334	7,418	12,690	352
Age unknown	1,469	1,260	65	135	⋅5
All ages, per cent	100.0	100.0	100.0	100.0	100.0
Under 5 years	9.8	13.1	10.8	0.3	6.7
5 to 9 years	9.2	11.3	11.1	1.3	5.7
10 to 14 years	8.3	9.4	10.6	1.9	6.0
15 to 19 years	7.8	8.3	10.2	2.6	4.6
20 to 44 years	44.8	41.3	43.9	54.8	48.8
45 years and over	19.3	15.1	13.4	38.7	27.7
RURAL POPULATION.					
All ages, number	376,878	194,295	109,412	60,857	388
Under 5 years	50,477	32,741	15,795	231	24
Under 1 year	9,518	6,304	2,868	21	8
5 to 9 years	44,228	26,579	15,040	1,152	26
10 to 14 years	37,083	21,217	12,712	1,952	13
15 to 19 years	28,664	15,724	9,944	1,966	23
20 to 44 years	148,176	69,464	42,430	32,286	174
45 years and over	67,782	28,269	13,442	23,177	127
Age unknown	468	301	49	93	1
All ages, per cent	100.0	100.0	100.0	100.0	100.0
Under 5 years	13.4	16.9	14.4	0.4	6.2
5 to 9 years	11.7	13.7	13.7	1.9	6.7
10 to 14 years	9.8	10.9	11.6	3.2	3.4
15 to 19 years	7.6	8.1	9.1	3.2	5.9
20 to 44 years	39.3	35.8	38.8	53.1	44.8
45 years and over	18.0	14.5	12.3	38.1	32.7
Idaho.					
URBAN POPULATION.					
All ages, number	119,037	80,213	26,213	11,124	645
Under 5 years	12,634	10,450	2,030	55	40
Under 1 year	2,472	2,058	388	3	8
5 to 9 years	12,272	9,823	2,273	117	31
10 to 14 years	11,368	8,787	2,306	221	31
15 to 19 years	10,508	7,751	2,364	332	33
20 to 44 years	48,382	30,410	12,071	5,102	353
45 years and over	23,753	12,902	5,156	5,284	155
Age unknown	120	90	13	13	2
All ages, per cent	100.0	100.0	100.0	100.0	100.0
Under 5 years	10.6	13.0	7.7	0.5	6.2
5 to 9 years	10.3	12.2	8.7	1.1	4.8
10 to 14 years	9.5	11.0	8.8	2.0	4.8
15 to 19 years	8.8	9.7	9.0	3.0	5.1
20 to 44 years	40.6	37.9	46.0	45.9	54.7
45 years and over	20.0	16.1	19.7	47.5	24.0
RURAL POPULATION.					
All ages, number	312,829	214,039	66,240	27,839	275
Under 5 years	41,902	34,922	6,257	118	15
Under 1 year	8,098	6,787	1,173	9	4
5 to 9 years	39,007	31,456	6,827	294	20
10 to 14 years	33,290	27,386	6,926	547	17
15 to 19 years	27,811	20,532	6,137	808	19
20 to 44 years	113,299	70,010	28,375	13,154	135
45 years and over	55,362	29,580	11,685	12,896	69
Age unknown	219	153	30	9?	....
All ages, per cent	100.0	100.0	100.0	100.0	100.0
Under 5 years	13.4	16.3	9.4	0.4	5.5
5 to 9 years	12.5	14.7	10.3	1.1	7.3
10 to 14 years	11.3	12.8	10.5	2.0	6.2
15 to 19 years	8.9	9.6	9.3	2.9	6.9
20 to 44 years	36.2	32.7	42.8	47.3	49.1
45 years and over	17.7	13.8	17.6	46.3	25.1

TABLE 51.—DISTRIBUTION BY BROAD AGE GROUPS FOR POPULATION CLASSES, IN URBAN AND RURAL COMMUNITIES, BY DIVISIONS AND STATES: 1920—Continued.

AGE PERIOD.	All classes.	NATIVE WHITE.		Foreign-born white.	Negro.
		Native parentage.	Foreign or mixed parentage.		
MOUNTAIN—Continued.					
Wyoming.					
URBAN POPULATION.					
All ages, number	57,348	33,705	13,744	8,437	833
Under 5 years	5,653	4,051	1,480	37	50
Under 1 year	1,133	826	284	3	8
5 to 9 years	5,248	3,581	1,495	123	41
10 to 14 years	4,450	2,911	1,305	192	39
15 to 19 years	4,146	2,543	1,247	289	46
20 to 44 years	28,036	15,906	6,459	4,801	472
45 years and over	9,485	4,422	1,753	2,971	178
Age unknown	330	291	5	24	7
All ages, per cent	100.0	100.0	100.0	100.0	100.0
Under 5 years	9.9	12.0	10.8	0.4	6.0
5 to 9 years	9.2	10.6	10.9	1.5	4.9
10 to 14 years	7.8	8.6	9.5	2.3	4.7
15 to 19 years	7.2	7.5	9.1	3.4	5.5
20 to 44 years	48.9	47.2	47.0	56.9	56.7
45 years and over	16.5	13.1	12.8	35.2	21.4
RURAL POPULATION.					
All ages, number	137,054	89,179	28,263	16,818	542
Under 5 years	16,871	12,813	3,650	68	9
Under 1 year	3,085	2,367	632	6	2
5 to 9 years	15,637	11,668	3,515	265	24
10 to 14 years	13,008	9,473	2,921	461	24
15 to 19 years	10,634	7,516	2,369	552	46
20 to 44 years	58,375	35,152	11,671	10,114	332
45 years and over	21,984	12,216	4,127	5,167	107
Age unknown	545	341	10	191	
All ages, per cent	100.0	100.0	100.0	100.0	100.0
Under 5 years	12.3	14.4	12.9	0.4	1.7
5 to 9 years	11.4	13.1	12.4	1.6	4.4
10 to 14 years	9.5	10.6	10.3	2.7	4.4
15 to 19 years	7.8	8.4	8.4	3.3	8.5
20 to 44 years	42.6	39.4	41.3	60.1	61.3
45 years and over	16.0	13.7	14.6	30.7	19.7
Colorado.					
URBAN POPULATION.					
All ages, number	453,259	276,329	106,838	59,626	9,364
Under 5 years	35,718	25,895	8,967	225	537
Under 1 year	6,966	5,104	1,711	13	110
5 to 9 years	37,008	25,258	10,340	810	544
10 to 14 years	36,633	24,264	10,491	1,252	599
15 to 19 years	35,466	22,663	10,190	1,884	684
20 to 44 years	189,604	112,580	45,346	26,540	4,576
45 years and over	111,723	58,989	21,413	28,772	2,313
Age unknown	7,107	6,680	91	143	111
All ages, per cent	100.0	100.0	100.0	100.0	100.0
Under 5 years	7.9	9.4	8.4	0.4	5.7
5 to 9 years	8.2	9.1	9.7	1.4	5.8
10 to 14 years	8.1	8.8	9.8	2.1	6.4
15 to 19 years	7.8	8.2	9.5	3.2	7.3
20 to 44 years	41.8	40.7	42.4	44.5	48.9
45 years and over	24.6	21.3	20.0	48.3	24.7
RURAL POPULATION.					
All ages, number	486,370	326,712	97,270	57,328	1,954
Under 5 years	61,340	46,218	14,017	317	156
Under 1 year	12,278	9,184	2,875	38	29
5 to 9 years	58,078	42,239	14,052	1,317	172
10 to 14 years	52,581	37,794	12,170	2,244	181
15 to 19 years	43,166	30,349	9,658	2,821	164
20 to 44 years	176,892	113,568	33,235	27,915	802
45 years and over	93,766	56,109	14,092	22,649	479
Age unknown	547	435	46	65	
All ages, per cent	100.0	100.0	100.0	100.0	100.0
Under 5 years	12.6	14.1	14.4	0.6	8.0
5 to 9 years	11.9	12.9	14.4	2.3	8.8
10 to 14 years	10.8	11.6	12.5	3.9	9.3
15 to 19 years	8.9	9.3	9.9	4.9	8.4
20 to 44 years	36.4	34.8	34.2	48.7	41.0
45 years and over	19.3	17.2	14.5	39.5	24.5

TABLE 51.—DISTRIBUTION BY BROAD AGE GROUPS FOR POPULATION CLASSES, IN URBAN AND RURAL COMMUNITIES, BY DIVISIONS AND STATES: 1920—Continued.

AGE PERIOD.	All classes.	NATIVE WHITE.		Foreign-born white.	Negro.
		Native parentage.	Foreign or mixed parentage.		
MOUNTAIN—Continued.					
New Mexico.					
URBAN POPULATION.					
All ages, number	64,960	48,859	8,625	5,665	861
Under 5 years	6,732	5,589	989	71	59
Under 1 year	1,352	1,119	210	5	14
5 to 9 years	7,153	5,714	1,009	192	74
10 to 14 years	6,917	5,344	888	257	71
15 to 19 years	5,940	4,576	769	315	65
20 to 44 years	26,115	19,358	3,491	2,720	406
45 years and over	11,977	8,172	1,474	2,098	184
Age unknown	126	106	5	12	2
All ages, per cent	100.0	100.0	100.0	100.0	100.0
Under 5 years	10.4	11.4	11.5	1.3	6.9
5 to 9 years	11.0	11.7	11.7	3.4	8.6
10 to 14 years	10.6	10.9	10.3	4.5	8.2
15 to 19 years	9.1	9.4	8.9	5.6	7.5
20 to 44 years	40.2	3C.6	40.5	48.0	47.2
45 years and over	18.4	16.7	17.1	37.0	21.4
RURAL POPULATION.					
All ages, number	295,390	224,458	23,654	23,412	4,872
Under 5 years	39,667	31,554	5,056	514	122
Under 1 year	8,077	6,384	1,242	25	31
5 to 9 years	39,203	31,101	3,691	1,514	116
10 to 14 years	34,008	27,243	2,672	1,730	82
15 to 19 years	28,720	22,626	2,039	1,923	169
20 to 44 years	103,707	74,545	6,894	11,955	4,121
45 years and over	49,756	37,117	3,291	5,747	259
Age unknown	329	272	11	29	3
All ages, per cent	100.0	100.0	100.0	100.0	100.0
Under 5 years	13.4	14.1	21.4	2.2	2.5
5 to 9 years	13.3	13.9	15.6	6.5	2.4
10 to 14 years	11.5	12.1	11.3	7.4	1.7
15 to 19 years	9.7	10.1	8.6	8.2	3.5
20 to 44 years	35.1	33.2	29.1	51.1	84.6
45 years and over	16.8	16.5	13.9	24.5	5.3
Arizona.					
URBAN POPULATION.					
All ages, number	117,527	58,330	26,299	28,910	2,631
Under 5 years	12,559	6,352	5,147	715	200
Under 1 year	2,786	1,287	1,347	73	48
5 to 9 years	11,629	5,876	3,887	1,601	177
10 to 14 years	10,202	5,122	2,984	1,893	148
15 to 19 years	9,400	4,671	2,240	2,263	144
20 to 44 years	52,828	26,079	9,011	15,665	1,455
45 years and over	20,190	9,689	3,001	6,648	488
Age unknown	719	541	29	125	19
All ages, per cent	100.0	100.0	100.0	100.0	100.0
Under 5 years	10.7	10.9	19.6	2.5	7.6
5 to 9 years	9.9	10.1	14.8	5.5	6.7
10 to 14 years	8.7	8.8	11.3	6.5	5.6
15 to 19 years	8.0	8.0	8.5	7.8	5.5
20 to 44 years	44.9	44.7	34.3	54.2	55.3
45 years and over	17.2	16.6	11.4	23.0	18.5
RURAL POPULATION.					
All ages, number	216,635	92,815	35,906	49,189	5,374
Under 5 years	28,248	12,813	9,751	1,983	133
Under 1 year	5,766	2,535	2,271	397	27
5 to 9 years	26,265	11,866	5,780	3,747	126
10 to 14 years	22,471	10,578	3,924	3,840	115
15 to 19 years	19,035	8,455	2,714	4,219	164
20 to 44 years	86,316	34,693	10,669	26,097	4,489
45 years and over	33,994	14,299	4,044	9,209	317
Age unknown	306	111	21	94	
All ages, per cent	100.0	100.0	100.0	100.0	100.0
Under 5 years	13.0	13.8	24.4	4.0	2.5
5 to 9 years	12.1	12.8	16.1	7.6	2.3
10 to 14 years	10.4	11.4	10.9	7.8	2.1
15 to 19 years	8.8	9.1	7.6	8.6	3.6
20 to 44 years	39.8	37.4	29.7	53.1	83.5
45 years and over	15.7	15.4	11.3	18.7	5.9

TABLE 51.—DISTRIBUTION BY BROAD AGE GROUPS FOR POPULATION CLASSES, IN URBAN AND RURAL COMMUNITIES, BY DIVISIONS AND STATES: 1920—Continued.

| AGE PERIOD. | All classes. | NATIVE WHITE. | | Foreign-born white. | Negro. |
		Native parentage.	Foreign or mixed parentage.		
MOUNTAIN—Continued.					
Utah.					
URBAN POPULATION.					
All ages, number	215,584	108,034	73,125	32,311	1,006
Under 5 years	25,287	18,507	6,512	91	58
Under 1 year	4,972	3,692	1,239	6	14
5 to 9 years	23,931	16,470	7,041	319	49
10 to 14 years	22,650	14,723	7,145	716	49
15 to 19 years	20,173	11,911	7,037	1,125	41
20 to 44 years	82,964	35,312	32,979	13,489	581
45 years and over	40,301	10,949	12,362	16,526	223
Age unknown	278	162	49	45	5
All ages, per cent	100.0	100.0	100.0	100.0	100.0
Under 5 years	11.7	17.1	8.9	0.3	5.8
5 to 9 years	11.1	15.2	9.6	1.0	4.9
10 to 14 years	10.5	13.6	9.8	2.2	4.9
15 to 19 years	9.4	11.0	9.6	3.5	4.1
20 to 44 years	38.5	32.7	45.1	41.7	57.8
45 years and over	18.7	10.1	16.9	51.1	22.2
RURAL POPULATION.					
All ages, number	233,812	137,747	66,540	24,144	440
Under 5 years	36,088	29,545	5,788	74	37
Under 1 year	7,094	5,935	1,014	6	8
5 to 9 years	32,560	25,508	6,334	247	29
10 to 14 years	28,976	21,670	6,435	523	28
15 to 19 years	23,200	15,947	6,206	666	26
20 to 44 years	78,129	35,819	29,246	10,568	245
45 years and over	34,676	9,158	12,493	12,030	71
Age unknown	183	100	38	36	4
All ages, per cent	100.0	100.0	100.0	100.0	100.0
Under 5 years	15.4	21.4	8.7	0.3	8.4
5 to 9 years	13.9	18.5	9.5	1.0	6.6
10 to 14 years	12.4	15.7	9.7	2.2	6.4
15 to 19 years	9.9	11.6	9.3	2.8	5.9
20 to 44 years	33.4	26.0	44.0	43.8	55.7
45 years and over	14.8	6.6	18.8	49.8	16.1
Nevada.					
URBAN POPULATION.					
All ages, number	15,254	8,100	4,089	2,603	68
Under 5 years	1,082	712	332	10	1
Under 1 year	192	132	53		
5 to 9 years	1,197	742	411	22	1
10 to 14 years	1,094	665	368	49	3
15 to 19 years	1,011	625	300	74	2
20 to 44 years	7,001	3,559	1,828	1,403	39
45 years and over	3,752	1,700	844	1,032	22
Age unknown	117	97	6	13	
All ages, per cent	100.0	100.0	100.0	100.0	
Under 5 years	7.1	8.8	8.1	0.4	(1)
5 to 9 years	7.8	9.2	10.1	0.8	(1)
10 to 14 years	7.2	8.2	9.0	1.9	(1)
15 to 19 years	6.6	7.7	7.3	2.8	(1)
20 to 44 years	45.9	43.9	44.7	53.9	(1)
45 years and over	24.6	21.0	20.6	39.6	(1)
RURAL POPULATION.					
All ages, number	62,153	28,185	15,523	12,199	278
Under 5 years	5,661	3,403	1,643	63	14
Under 1 year	1,132	709	311	5	3
5 to 9 years	5,562	3,214	1,603	121	17
10 to 14 years	4,616	2,737	1,196	171	9
15 to 19 years	3,966	2,162	996	274	18
20 to 44 years	27,525	11,184	6,803	7,305	132
45 years and over	14,625	5,407	3,274	4,217	88
Age unknown	198	78	8	48	
All ages, per cent	100.0	100.0	100.0	100.0	100.0
Under 5 years	9.1	12.1	10.6	0.5	5.0
5 to 9 years	8.9	11.4	10.3	1.0	6.1
10 to 14 years	7.4	9.7	7.7	1.4	3.2
15 to 19 years	6.4	7.7	6.4	2.2	6.5
20 to 44 years	44.3	39.7	43.8	59.9	47.5
45 years and over	23.5	19.2	21.1	34.6	31.7

[1] Per cent not shown, base being less than 100.

TABLE 51.—DISTRIBUTION BY BROAD AGE GROUPS FOR POPULATION CLASSES, IN URBAN AND RURAL COMMUNITIES, BY DIVISIONS AND STATES: 1920—Continued.

AGE PERIOD.	All classes.	NATIVE WHITE.		Foreign-born white.	Negro.
		Native parentage.	Foreign or mixed parentage.		

PACIFIC.

Washington.

URBAN POPULATION.

AGE PERIOD.	All classes.	Native parentage.	Foreign or mixed parentage.	Foreign-born white.	Negro.
All ages, number	748,735	373,611	206,245	149,686	5,782
Under 5 years	61,644	38,640	20,000	956	328
Under 1 year	12,338	7,783	3,938	87	62
5 to 9 years	62,330	37,083	21,741	2,424	334
10 to 14 years	56,343	32,692	19,891	3,087	297
15 to 19 years	55,876	30,736	19,563	4,534	296
20 to 44 years	336,962	156,717	91,590	77,782	3,045
45 years and over	171,469	74,763	33,132	60,280	1,416
Age unknown	4,111	2,980	328	623	66
All ages, per cent	100.0	100.0	100.0	100.0	100.0
Under 5 years	8.2	10.3	9.7	0.6	5.7
5 to 9 years	8.3	9.9	10.5	1.6	5.8
10 to 14 years	7.5	8.8	9.6	2.1	5.1
15 to 19 years	7.5	8.2	9.5	3.0	5.1
20 to 44 years	45.0	41.9	44.4	52.0	52.7
45 years and over	22.9	20.0	16.1	40.3	24.5

RURAL POPULATION.

AGE PERIOD.	All classes.	Native parentage.	Foreign or mixed parentage.	Foreign-born white.	Negro.
All ages, number	607,886	338,095	151,771	100,369	1,101
Under 5 years	64,790	44,110	17,658	443	71
Under 1 year	12,331	8,542	3,199	41	13
5 to 9 years	65,928	42,077	20,679	1,351	86
10 to 14 years	61,210	37,930	19,841	2,215	97
15 to 19 years	50,609	30,280	16,319	2,804	87
20 to 44 years	227,311	117,623	55,403	47,005	457
45 years and over	137,362	65,668	21,796	46,447	300
Age unknown	676	407	75	104	3
All ages, per cent	100.0	100.0	100.0	100.0	100.0
Under 5 years	10.7	13.0	11.6	0.4	6.4
5 to 9 years	10.8	12.4	13.6	1.3	7.8
10 to 14 years	10.1	11.2	13.1	2.2	8.8
15 to 19 years	8.3	9.0	10.8	2.8	7.9
20 to 44 years	37.4	34.8	36.5	46.8	41.5
45 years and over	22.6	19.4	14.4	46.3	27.2

Oregon.

URBAN POPULATION.

AGE PERIOD.	All classes.	Native parentage.	Foreign or mixed parentage.	Foreign-born white.	Negro.
All ages, number	391,019	227,549	95,034	61,508	1,844
Under 5 years	30,660	21,649	8,186	251	96
Under 1 year	5,830	4,181	1,486	18	17
5 to 9 years	32,210	21,730	9,371	724	115
10 to 14 years	30,023	20,059	8,329	1,380	95
15 to 19 years	29,334	18,837	8,146	2,019	93
20 to 44 years	171,503	94,514	43,428	30,250	975
45 years and over	96,790	50,447	17,499	26,788	463
Age unknown	499	313	75	96	7
All ages, per cent	100.0	100.0	100.0	100.0	100.0
Under 5 years	7.8	9.5	8.6	0.4	5.2
5 to 9 years	8.2	9.5	9.9	1.2	6.2
10 to 14 years	7.7	8.8	8.8	2.2	5.2
15 to 19 years	7.5	8.3	8.6	3.3	5.0
20 to 44 years	43.9	41.5	45.7	49.2	52.9
45 years and over	24.8	22.2	18.4	43.6	25.1

RURAL POPULATION.

AGE PERIOD.	All classes.	Native parentage.	Foreign or mixed parentage.	Foreign-born white.	Negro.
All ages, number	392,370	270,177	74,235	40,643	300
Under 5 years	40,659	33,011	6,647	141	21
Under 1 year	7,767	6,370	1,172	17	9
5 to 9 years	40,874	31,898	7,984	363	19
10 to 14 years	38,991	29,578	7,958	764	61
15 to 19 years	33,441	24,377	7,274	949	25
20 to 44 years	143,317	93,329	30,090	17,321	117
45 years and over	94,734	57,708	14,250	21,074	84
Age unknown	355	276	32	31	
All ages, per cent	100.0	100.0	100.0	100.0	100.0
Under 5 years	10.4	12.2	9.0	0.3	7.0
5 to 9 years	10.4	11.8	10.8	0.9	6.3
10 to 14 years	9.9	10.9	10.7	1.9	11.3
15 to 19 years	8.5	9.0	9.8	2.3	8.3
20 to 44 years	36.5	34.5	40.5	42.6	39.0
45 years and over	24.1	21.4	19.2	51.9	28.0

TABLE 51.—DISTRIBUTION BY BROAD AGE GROUPS FOR POPULATION CLASSES, IN URBAN AND RURAL COMMUNITIES, BY DIVISIONS AND STATES: 1920—Continued.

AGE PERIOD.	All classes.	NATIVE WHITE.		Foreign-born white.	Negro.
		Native parentage.	Foreign or mixed parentage.		
PACIFIC—Continued.					
California.					
URBAN POPULATION.					
All ages, number	2,331,729	1,122,925	643,066	472,576	33,888
Under 5 years	169,129	96,286	60,564	2,773	2,203
Under 1 year	33,320	18,954	12,029	168	445
5 to 9 years	174,684	97,253	62,980	8,187	2,361
10 to 14 years	164,768	92,344	55,852	12,129	2,221
15 to 19 years	163,567	90,243	50,156	17,571	2,171
20 to 44 years	1,030,911	470,367	278,719	234,457	17,299
45 years and over	621,281	271,833	134,004	195,816	7,486
Age unknown	7,389	4,599	791	1,643	147
All ages, per cent	100.0	100.0	100.0	100.0	100.0
Under 5 years	7.3	8.6	9.4	0.6	6.5
5 to 9 years	7.5	8.7	9.8	1.7	7.0
10 to 14 years	7.1	8.2	8.7	2.6	6.6
15 to 19 years	7.0	8.0	7.8	3.7	6.4
20 to 44 years	44.2	41.9	43.3	49.6	51.0
45 years and over	26.6	24.2	20.8	41.4	22.1
RURAL POPULATION.					
All ages, number	1,095,132	555,030	262,028	209,086	4,875
Under 5 years	106,598	59,986	35,084	1,487	393
Under 1 year	20,600	11,230	6,916	113	72
5 to 9 years	105,595	60,558	35,171	4,232	415
10 to 14 years	94,508	56,176	28,969	6,131	442
15 to 19 years	79,759	45,731	22,749	7,918	391
20 to 44 years	430,290	200,370	92,074	106,006	2,080
45 years and over	276,352	131,134	47,809	82,833	1,136
Age unknown	2,030	1,075	172	479	18
All ages, per cent	100.0	100.0	100.0	100.0	100.0
Under 5 years	9.7	10.8	13.4	0.7	8.1
5 to 9 years	9.6	10.9	13.4	2.0	8.5
10 to 14 years	8.6	10.1	11.1	2.9	9.1
15 to 19 years	7.3	8.2	8.7	3.8	8.0
20 to 44 years	39.3	36.1	35.1	50.7	42.7
45 years and over	25.2	23.6	18.2	39.6	23.3

TABLE 52.—MARITAL CONDITION OF THE POPULATION 15 YEARS OF

CLASS OF POPULATION AND CENSUS YEAR.	Total.[1]	MALES.						
		Single.		Married.		Widowed.		Di-vorced.
		Number.	Per cent.	Number.	Per cent.	Number.	Per cent.	
All classes:								
1920	36,920,663	12,967,565	35.1	21,849,266	59.2	1,758,308	4.8	235,284
1910	32,425,805	12,550,129	38.7	18,092,600	55.8	1,471,390	4.5	156,162
1900	25,620,399	10,297,940	40.2	13,955,650	54.5	1,177,976	4.6	84,230
1890 [2]	20,777,872	8,655,711	41.7	11,205,205	53.9	815,437	3.9	49,100
White:								
1920	33,335,586	11,782,665	35.3	19,698,113	59.1	1,549,164	4.6	207,663
1910	29,158,125	11,360,282	39.0	16,253,940	55.7	1,274,388	4.4	135,203
1900	22,808,628	9,173,430	40.2	12,455,858	54.6	1,020,387	4.5	72,761
1890	18,534,187	7,732,832	41.7	9,992,910	53.9	721,971	3.9	43,829
Negro:								
1920	3,393,211	1,104,877	32.6	2,050,407	60.4	200,734	5.9	26,689
1910	3,059,312	1,083,472	35.4	1,749,228	57.2	189,970	6.2	20,146
1900	2,633,008	1,033,285	39.2	1,422,886	54.0	151,233	5.7	11,026
1890	2,119,721	842,764	39.8	1,175,513	55.5	91,683	4.3	5,212
Indian:								
1920	76,321	26,450	34.7	43,095	56.5	5,711	7.5	680
1910	80,383	27,391	34.1	46,154	57.4	5,319	6.6	679
1900	72,076	24,323	33.7	41,067	57.0	4,974	6.9	418
1890	19,911	7,990	40.1	9,863	49.5	1,241	6.2	45
Chinese:								
1920	49,818	23,096	46.4	24,782	49.7	1,355	2.7	66
1910	64,394	34,330	53.3	26,449	41.1	1,139	1.8	45
1900	83,633	48,997	58.6	31,794	38.0	1,310	1.6	19
1890	102,322	70,625	69.0	26,720	26.1	530	0.5	13
Japanese:								
1920	57,427	24,423	42.5	31,250	54.4	1,118	1.9	154
1910	60,536	42,688	70.5	15,918	26.3	495	0.8	86
1900	23,054	17,905	77.7	4,045	17.5	72	0.3	6
1890	1,731	1,500	86.7	199	11.5	12	0.7	1
All other:								
1920	8,300	6,054	72.9	1,619	19.5	226	2.7	32
1910	3,055	1,966	64.4	911	29.8	79	2.6	3
Native white:								
1920	26,083,047	9,927,618	38.1	14,795,171	56.7	1,111,115	4.3	175,713
1910	22,018,232	9,091,366	41.3	11,821,805	53.7	889,662	4.0	112,144
1900	17,551,269	7,627,637	43.5	9,100,302	51.8	693,949	4.0	59,415
1890	13,953,598	6,262,921	44.9	7,142,105	51.2	483,646	3.5	34,722
Native white—Native parentage:								
1920	19,092,107	6,776,518	35.5	11,244,289	58.9	874,821	4.6	134,789
1910	16,233,095	6,185,324	38.1	9,144,099	56.3	728,883	4.5	87,456
1900	13,088,058	5,195,263	39.7	7,193,922	55.0	587,894	4.5	47,993
1890	10,880,185	4,359,200	40.1	6,030,295	55.4	432,260	4.0	30,182
Native white—Foreign or mixed parentage:								
1920	6,990,940	3,151,100	45.1	3,550,882	50.8	236,294	3.4	40,924
1910	5,785,137	2,906,042	50.2	2,677,706	46.3	160,779	2.8	24,688
1900	4,463,211	2,432,374	54.5	1,906,380	42.7	106,055	2.4	11,422
1890	3,073,413	1,903,721	61.9	1,111,810	36.2	51,386	1.7	4,540
Native white—Foreign parentage: [4]								
1920	4,792,911	2,141,310	44.7	2,445,291	51.0	171,612	3.6	26,197
1910	4,059,778	1,989,127	49.0	1,926,075	47.4	117,046	2.9	16,471
Native white—Mixed parentage: [4]								
1920	2,198,029	1,009,790	45.9	1,105,591	50.3	64,682	2.9	14,727
1910	1,775,359	916,915	53.1	751,631	43.6	43,733	2.5	8,217
Foreign-born white:								
1920	7,252,539	1,855,047	25.6	4,902,942	67.5	438,049	6.0	31,950
1910	7,139,893	2,268,916	31.8	4,432,135	62.1	384,726	5.4	23,059
1900	5,257,359	1,545,793	29.4	3,355,556	63.8	326,438	6.2	13,346
1890	4,580,589	1,469,911	32.1	2,850,805	62.2	238,325	5.2	9,107

[1] Total includes persons whose marital condition was not reported.
[2] Figures for 1890 are exclusive of 325,464 persons (169,221 males and 156,243 females) specially enumerated in Indian Territory and on Indian reservations, for whom statistics of marital condition are not available.

AGE AND OVER, BY CLASSES, FOR THE UNITED STATES: 1890 TO 1920.

CLASS OF POPULATION AND CENSUS YEAR.	Total.[1]	FEMALES.							
		Single.		Married.		Widowed.		Di- vorced.
		Number.	Per cent.	Number.	Per cent.	Number.	Per cent.	
All classes:								
1920	35,177,515	9,616,902	27.3	21,318,933	60.6	3,917,625	11.1	273,304
1910	30,047,325	8,933,170	29.7	17,684,687	58.9	3,176,228	10.6	185,068
1900	24,249,191	7,566,530	31.2	13,810,057	57.0	2,717,715	11.2	114,647
1890[2]	19,602,178	6,233,316	31.8	11,124,785	56.8	2,154,598	11.0	71,883
White:								
1920	31,654,841	8,772,732	27.7	19,210,238	60.7	3,399,662	10.7	228,565
1910	26,857,337	8,091,249	30.1	15,852,011	59.0	2,705,990	10.1	150,801
1900	21,483,052	6,747,306	31.4	12,319,767	57.3	2,291,872	10.7	91,737
1890	17,404,915	5,575,143	32.0	9,924,785	57.0	1,831,772	10.5	61,125
Negro:								
1920	3,423,100	825,258	24.1	2,039,181	59.6	507,961	14.8	43,871
1910	3,103,344	823,996	26.6	1,775,949	57.2	459,831	14.8	33,286
1900	2,690,583	803,683	29.9	1,443,817	53.7	414,107	15.4	22,033
1890	2,175,550	652,314	30.0	1,187,434	54.6	320,194	14.7	10,688
Indian:								
1920	70,431	16,238	23.1	43,923	62.4	9,217	13.1	826
1910	76,982	16,324	21.2	49,095	63.8	10,071	13.1	959
1900	71,497	14,350	20.1	43,906	61.4	11,458	16.0	870
1890	18,412	4,717	25.6	10,543	57.3	2,541	13.8	67
Chinese:								
1920	4,407	962	21.8	3,046	69.1	371	8.4	15
1910	2,955	680	23.0	2,016	68.2	229	7.7	5
1900	3,204	778	24.3	2,157	67.3	259	8.1	3
1890	3,074	993	32.3	1,951	63.5	85	2.8	3
Japanese:								
1920	24,242	1,604	6.6	22,193	91.5	388	1.6	23
1910	6,648	908	13.7	5,581	84.0	96	1.4	17
1900	855	413	48.3	410	48.0	19	2.2	4
1890	227	149	65.6	72	31.7	6	2.6	
All other:								
1920	494	108	21.9	352	71.3	26	5.3	4
1910	59	13	(3)	35	(3)	11	(3)	
Native white:								
1920	25,740,856	7,936,933	30.8	15,086,735	58.6	2,480,407	9.6	200,909
1910	21,411,031	7,097,139	33.1	12,228,008	57.1	1,905,878	8.9	130,259
1900	17,037,720	5,878,706	34.5	9,464,321	55.5	1,589,287	9.3	79,219
1890	13,594,996	4,787,906	35.2	7,489,739	55.1	1,256,918	9.2	52,146
Native white—Native parentage:								
1920	18,529,748	5,268,490	28.4	11,195,865	60.4	1,885,000	10.2	152,743
1910	15,523,900	4,644,122	29.9	9,219,385	59.4	1,523,560	9.8	100,053
1900	12,561,813	3,893,417	31.0	7,251,375	57.7	1,332,334	10.6	62,585
1890	10,530,675	3,226,180	30.6	6,132,027	58.2	1,120,959	10.6	44,284
Native white—Foreign or mixed parentage:								
1920	7,211,108	2,668,443	37.0	3,890,870	54.0	595,407	8.3	48,166
1910	5,887,131	2,453,017	41.7	3,008,623	51.1	382,318	6.5	30,206
1900	4,475,907	1,985,289	44.4	2,212,946	49.4	256,953	5.7	16,634
1890	3,064,321	1,561,726	51.0	1,357,712	44.3	135,959	4.4	7,862
Native white—Foreign parentage:[4]								
1920	4,906,547	1,791,271	36.5	2,648,054	54.0	431,821	8.8	29,535
1910	4,092,572	1,660,120	40.6	2,128,165	52.0	276,348	6.8	18,987
Native white—Mixed parentage:[4]								
1920	2,304,561	877,172	38.1	1,242,816	53.9	163,586	7.1	18,631
1910	1,794,559	792,897	44.2	880,458	49.1	105,970	5.9	11,219
Foreign born white:								
1920	5,913,985	835,799	14.1	4,123,503	69.7	919,255	15.5	27,656
1910	5,446,306	994,110	18.3	3,624,003	66.5	800,112	14.7	20,542
1900	4,445,332	868,600	19.5	2,855,446	64.2	702,585	15.8	12,518
1890	3,809,919	787,237	20.7	2,435,046	63.9	574,854	15.1	8,979

[3] Per cent not shown, base being less than 100.　　[4] Not reported separately in 1900 or 1890.

TABLE 53.—MARITAL CONDITION OF THE POPULATION 15 TO 34 YEARS OF AGE, BY STATES:

CLASS OF POPULATION AND AGE.	Total.	Single.		Married.		Widowed or divorced.	Marital condition not reported.
		Number.	Per cent.	Number.	Per cent.		
All classes : [1]							
15 years	925,679	923,997	99.8	1,600	0.2	82	
16 years	976,834	973,468	99.7	3,222	0.3	144	
17 years	926,033	918,068	99.1	7,699	0.8	266	
18 years	938,646	909,332	96.9	24,944	2.7	770	3,600
19 years	906,600	842,905	93.0	58,909	6.5	1,327	3,459
20 years	843,501	732,213	86.8	105,369	12.5	2,426	3,493
21 years	920,779	719,816	78.2	193,663	21.0	4,168	3,132
22 years	918,849	648,916	70.6	260,530	28.4	6,267	3,136
23 years	911,705	574,761	63.0	326,245	35.8	7,906	2,793
24 years	932,211	524,917	56.3	394,511	42.3	10,024	2,759
25 years	932,333	462,811	49.6	454,791	48.8	12,210	2,521
26 years	915,495	403,477	44.1	495,955	54.2	13,435	2,628
27 years	910,809	349,753	38.4	543,508	59.7	15,079	2,469
28 years	943,654	326,869	34.6	596,913	63.3	17,402	2,470
29 years	835,942	246,811	29.5	570,957	68.3	16,200	1,974
30 years	956,567	277,588	29.0	654,280	68.4	22,244	2,455
31 years	724,643	178,698	24.7	528,367	72.9	16,015	1,563
32 years	826,738	201,562	24.4	602,328	72.9	21,073	1,775
33 years	795,555	171,147	21.5	602,059	75.7	20,738	1,611
34 years	827,280	166,874	20.2	636,323	76.9	22,464	1,619
Native white—Native parentage:							
15 years	561,320	560,321	99.8	955	0.2	44	
16 years	588,313	586,290	99.7	1,935	0.3	88	
17 years	554,815	549,577	99.1	5,083	0.9	155	
18 years	555,858	536,783	96.6	16,670	3.0	400	2,005
19 years	537,171	494,744	92.1	39,749	7.4	773	1,905
20 years	489,567	417,792	85.3	68,577	14.0	1,320	1,878
21 years	538,528	410,990	76.3	123,437	22.9	2,354	1,747
22 years	513,123	349,503	68.1	158,545	30.9	3,460	1,615
23 years	501,825	301,383	60.1	194,715	38.8	4,344	1,383
24 years	503,775	267,588	53.1	229,306	45.5	5,533	1,348
25 years	490,375	225,827	46.1	256,950	52.4	6,440	1,158
26 years	482,989	194,082	40.2	280,357	58.0	7,430	1,120
27 years	478,647	165,413	34.6	303,826	63.5	8,366	1,042
28 years	483,036	148,406	30.7	324,209	67.1	9,400	1,021
29 years	432,265	111,139	25.7	311,487	72.1	8,899	740
30 years	465,522	118,151	25.4	335,288	72.0	11,111	972
31 years	377,883	80,526	21.3	287,816	76.2	8,857	684
32 years	407,537	85,766	21.0	309,923	76.0	11,172	676
33 years	395,788	72,745	18.4	311,543	78.7	10,955	545
34 years	407,941	70,257	17.2	325,397	79.8	11,699	588
Native white—Foreign or mixed parentage:							
15 years	217,665	217,364	99.9	280	0.1	21	
16 years	229,349	228,875	99.8	458	0.2	16	
17 years	216,114	215,387	99.7	692	0.3	35	
18 years	213,207	210,572	98.8	1,804	0.8	73	758
19 years	208,749	202,904	97.2	4,970	2.4	89	786
20 years	196,971	184,813	93.8	11,162	5.7	216	780
21 years	207,208	182,598	88.1	23,580	11.4	392	638
22 years	204,611	167,729	82.0	35,648	17.4	611	623
23 years	204,073	152,776	74.9	49,777	24.4	968	552
24 years	201,907	136,943	67.8	63,098	31.3	1,287	579
25 years	195,074	117,884	60.4	75,087	38.5	1,675	428
26 years	195,292	105,080	53.8	87,747	44.9	2,061	404
27 years	190,438	89,070	47.0	98,052	51.5	2,467	340
28 years	183,714	77,645	42.3	102,991	50.1	2,757	321
29 years	170,383	62,154	36.5	103,158	61.7	2,772	259
30 years	174,244	61,120	35.1	109,431	62.8	3,427	206
31 years	147,332	44,661	30.3	99,633	67.6	2,864	174
32 years	154,506	47,290	30.6	103,519	67.0	3,477	220
33 years	146,913	40,538	27.6	102,633	69.9	3,532	210
34 years	151,782	39,467	26.0	108,229	71.3	3,920	166

[1] Includes Indians, Chinese, Japanese, and "all other."

SEX AND SINGLE YEARS, FOR PRINCIPAL POPULATION CLASSES, FOR THE UNITED 1920.

CLASS OF POPULATION AND AGE.	FEMALES.						
	Total.	Single.		Married.		Widowed or divorced.	Marital condition not reported.
		Number	Per cent.	Number.	Per cent.		
All classes: [1]							
15 years	935,766	922,433	98.6	12,834	1.4	499	....
16 years	996,124	953,230	95.7	41,626	4.2	1,268	....
17 years	929,140	835,418	89.9	90,930	9.8	2,792	....
18 years	971,400	776,931	80.0	186,645	19.2	5,554	2,270
19 years	924,334	649,638	70.3	264,507	28.6	8,143	2,046
20 years	937,601	562,965	60.0	360,112	38.4	12,385	2,139
21 years	900,933	473,019	52.5	412,235	45.8	14,020	1,659
22 years	968,431	434,966	44.9	512,587	52.9	19,141	1,737
23 years	969,884	371,616	38.3	574,133	59.2	22,726	1,409
24 years	973,127	321,485	33.0	624,630	64.2	25,724	1,288
25 years	990,861	287,842	29.0	672,240	67.8	29,541	1,238
26 years	937,840	236,899	25.3	669,638	71.4	30,197	1,106
27 years	880,836	194,201	22.0	655,125	74.4	30,610	900
28 years	942,759	190,285	20.2	715,183	75.9	36,375	916
29 years	795,962	139,058	17.5	624,315	78.4	31,907	682
30 years	995,298	184,062	18.5	762,156	76.6	48,033	1,047
31 years	681,985	98,967	14.5	552,979	81.1	29,517	522
32 years	812,005	119,743	14.7	651,391	80.2	40,202	669
33 years	726,524	92,550	12.7	597,208	82.2	36,197	569
34 years	724,598	92,797	12.8	592,120	81.7	39,132	549
Native white—Native parentage:							
15 years	559,798	551,027	98.4	8,510	1.5	261	....
16 years	590,463	562,188	95.2	27,626	4.7	649	....
17 years	550,013	489,199	88.9	59,341	10.8	1,473	....
18 years	564,828	445,196	78.8	115,692	20.5	2,807	1,133
19 years	536,467	369,500	68.9	161,755	30.2	4,186	1,026
20 years	525,985	309,914	58.9	208,865	39.7	6,101	1,105
21 years	519,006	264,414	50.9	246,513	47.5	7,198	881
22 years	531,617	232,847	43.8	288,518	54.3	9,391	861
23 years	529,576	198,526	37.5	319,125	60.3	11,272	653
24 years	523,705	169,507	32.4	340,999	65.1	12,590	609
25 years	520,612	149,038	28.6	357,374	68.6	13,623	577
26 years	497,852	123,932	24.9	358,724	72.1	14,671	525
27 years	468,010	101,771	21.7	350,877	75.0	14,953	409
28 years	489,720	97,416	19.9	374,411	76.5	17,464	429
29 years	421,296	72,085	17.1	333,308	79.1	15,573	330
30 years	496,868	92,739	18.7	382,686	77.0	20,948	495
31 years	370,659	52,498	14.2	302,778	81.7	15,108	275
32 years	417,667	60,739	14.5	337,139	80.7	19,448	341
33 years	379,666	47,497	12.5	314,051	82.7	17,823	295
34 years	376,510	47,063	12.5	310,314	82.4	18,858	275
Native white—Foreign or mixed parentage:							
15 years	220,423	219,497	99.6	888	0.4	38	....
16 years	232,488	229,379	98.7	3,030	1.3	79	....
17 years	218,133	209,695	96.1	8,284	3.8	154	....
18 years	219,883	198,133	90.1	20,764	9.4	386	600
19 years	211,156	174,766	82.8	35,185	16.7	649	556
20 years	210,426	156,584	74.4	52,237	24.8	1,101	504
21 years	206,871	137,618	66.5	67,277	32.5	1,552	424
22 years	216,525	127,931	59.1	86,029	39.7	2,129	436
23 years	218,119	111,928	51.3	102,944	47.2	2,882	365
24 years	215,079	97,466	45.3	113,871	52.9	3,428	314
25 years	215,597	86,974	40.3	124,248	57.6	4,101	274
26 years	206,900	72,874	35.2	129,129	62.4	4,619	278
27 years	194,823	60,294	30.9	129,405	66.4	4,858	266
28 years	197,546	57,207	29.0	134,493	68.1	5,627	219
29 years	172,758	42,872	24.8	124,402	72.0	5,338	146
30 years	199,441	53,561	26.9	138,662	69.5	7,025	193
31 years	150,793	30,869	20.5	114,439	75.9	5,386	99
32 years	166,805	36,829	22.1	123,109	73.8	6,732	135
33 years	149,646	29,035	19.4	114,382	76.4	6,120	109
34 years	149,812	29,285	19.5	113,525	75.8	6,903	99

CLASS OF POPULATION AND AGE.	MALES.						
	Total.	Single.		Married.		Widowed or divorced.	Marital condition not reported.
		Number.	Per cent.	Number.	Per cent.		
Foreign-born white:							
15 years	40,280	40,168	99.7	107	0.3	5	
16 years	49,626	49,395	99.5	221	0.4	10	
17 years	51,561	51,239	99.4	296	0.6	26	
18 years	58,338	57,244	98.1	777	1.3	39	278
19 years	59,465	57,281	96.3	1,857	3.1	49	278
20 years	64,817	59,370	91.6	4,956	7.6	128	363
21 years	70,754	60,874	86.0	9,414	13.3	148	318
22 years	91,271	72,257	79.2	18,248	20.0	312	454
23 years	104,781	73,390	70.0	30,452	29.1	466	473
24 years	125,365	78,977	63.0	45,225	36.1	671	492
25 years	143,142	81,468	56.9	60,169	42.0	949	556
26 years	148,325	75,457	50.9	70,912	47.8	1,161	795
27 years	155,695	69,705	44.8	83,768	53.8	1,434	788
28 years	182,549	75,756	41.5	104,010	57.0	1,988	795
29 years	162,377	56,399	34.7	103,321	63.6	1,948	709
30 years	214,137	73,176	34.2	137,022	64.0	3,084	855
31 years	147,226	41,967	28.5	102,538	69.6	2,159	562
32 years	196,045	53,746	27.4	138,310	70.6	3,345	644
33 years	191,445	46,366	24.2	140,989	73.6	3,435	655
34 years	197,965	45,121	22.8	148,476	75.0	3,704	664
Negro:							
15 years	103,063	102,805	99.7	246	0.2	12	
16 years	106,028	105,415	99.4	584	0.6	29	
17 years	100,059	98,441	98.4	1,568	1.6	50	
18 years	107,218	100,882	94.1	5,560	5.2	255	521
19 years	97,048	84,100	86.7	12,085	12.5	409	454
20 years	87,789	66,456	75.7	20,164	23.0	736	433
21 years	100,001	61,911	61.9	36,459	36.5	1,249	382
22 years	105,414	56,167	53.3	47,008	44.6	1,847	392
23 years	96,854	44,293	45.7	50,145	51.8	2,077	339
24 years	97,111	38,768	39.9	55,577	57.2	2,472	294
25 years	99,348	35,011	35.2	60,946	61.3	3,057	334
26 years	85,079	26,695	31.4	55,392	65.1	2,720	272
27 years	82,241	23,105	28.1	56,154	68.3	2,722	260
28 years	90,327	23,126	25.6	63,752	70.6	3,159	290
29 years	67,357	15,476	23.0	49,151	73.0	2,506	224
30 years	97,320	22,822	23.5	69,737	71.7	4,457	304
31 years	48,377	10,063	20.8	36,136	74.7	2,058	120
32 years	63,499	12,782	20.1	47,571	74.9	2,953	193
33 years	57,278	10,052	17.5	44,349	77.4	2,710	167
34 years	65,105	10,469	16.1	51,448	79.0	3,022	166

SEX AND SINGLE YEARS, FOR PRINCIPAL POPULATION CLASSES, FOR THE UNITED 1920—Continued.

CLASS OF POPULATION AND AGE.	FEMALES.						
	Total.	Single.		Married.		Widowed or divorced.	Marital condition not reported.
		Number.	Per cent.	Number.	Per cent.		
Foreign-born white:							
15 years	41,619	41,018	98.6	571	1.4	30	....
16 years	51,145	49,122	96.0	1,978	3.9	45	....
17 years	52,539	47,446	90.3	4,999	9.5	94	....
18 years	61,266	48,963	79.9	11,944	19.5	207	152
19 years	62,103	42,691	68.7	18,985	30.6	287	140
20 years	75,045	42,018	56.0	32,215	42.9	613	199
21 years	71,502	33,591	47.0	37,168	52.0	618	125
22 years	97,729	37,032	37.9	59,429	60.8	1,110	158
23 years	106,253	32,011	30.1	72,670	68.4	1,418	154
24 years	119,327	29,485	24.7	87,867	73.6	1,834	141
25 years	132,177	28,210	21.3	101,402	76.7	2,398	167
26 years	128,464	22,858	17.8	102,947	80.1	2,517	142
27 years	125,148	18,623	14.9	103,626	82.8	2,796	103
28 years	151,251	21,702	14.3	125,765	83.1	3,668	116
29 years	125,235	14,890	11.9	106,795	85.3	3,444	106
30 years	177,443	21,807	12.3	149,838	84.4	5,659	139
31 years	107,181	10,275	9.6	93,471	87.2	3,357	78
32 years	151,187	14,697	9.7	130,952	86.6	5,426	112
33 years	134,973	10,840	8.0	118,951	88.1	5,090	92
34 years	133,873	11,438	8.5	116,823	87.3	5,526	86
Negro:							
15 years	111,019	108,090	97.4	2,762	2.5	167	....
16 years	118,984	109,730	92.2	8,773	7.4	481	....
17 years	105,728	86,765	82.1	17,908	16.9	1,055	....
18 years	122,224	82,448	67.5	37,299	30.5	2,111	366
19 years	111,844	61,136	54.7	47,427	42.4	2,968	313
20 years	122,832	53,137	43.3	64,890	52.8	4,486	319
21 years	100,918	36,603	36.3	59,520	59.0	4,576	219
22 years	119,352	36,421	30.5	76,245	63.9	6,416	270
23 years	112,864	28,662	25.4	76,927	68.2	7,047	228
24 years	111,712	24,588	22.0	79,158	70.9	7,751	215
25 years	118,865	23,217	19.5	86,147	72.5	9,285	216
26 years	101,375	16,937	16.7	76,022	75.0	8,259	157
27 years	89,849	13,294	14.8	68,544	76.3	7,895	116
28 years	101,068	13,751	13.6	77,694	76.9	9,472	151
29 years	74,230	9,081	12.2	57,605	77.6	7,451	93
30 years	117,909	15,716	13.3	87,777	74.4	14,206	210
31 years	51,431	5,245	10.2	40,547	78.8	5,571	68
32 years	73,974	7,339	9.9	58,057	78.5	8,499	79
33 years	60,435	5,103	8.4	48,199	79.8	7,064	69
34 years	62,537	4,951	7.9	49,756	79.6	7,743	87

TABLE 54.—MARITAL CONDITION OF THE TOTAL POPULATION, BY SEX AND STATES:

CLASS OF POPULATION AND AGE PERIOD.	MALES: 1920					
	Single.		Married.		Widowed or divorced.	
	Number.	Per cent.	Number.	Per cent.	Number.	Per cent.
All classes [1]	29,944,007	55.6	21,852,439	40.5	1,993,745	3.7
Under 15 years of age	16,976,442	100.0	3,173	([2])	153	([2])
15 years and over	12,967,565	35.1	21,849,266	59.2	1,993,592	5.4
15 to 19 years	4,567,770	97.7	96,374	2.1	2,589	0.1
20 to 24 years	3,200,623	70.7	1,280,318	28.3	30,791	0.7
25 to 34 years	2,785,590	32.1	5,685,481	65.6	176,860	2.0
35 to 44 years	1,188,586	16.1	5,873,308	79.8	284,292	3.9
45 to 54 years	677,420	12.0	4,580,056	81.0	386,138	6.8
55 to 64 years	337,592	9.8	2,697,429	77.9	420,836	12.2
65 years and over	182,211	7.3	1,607,187	64.7	687,162	27.7
Age unknown	27,773	29.9	29,113	31.3	4,924	5.3
Native white—Native parentage	17,319,288	58.4	11,246,113	37.9	1,009,690	3.4
Under 15 years of age	10,542,770	100.0	1,824	([2])	80	([2])
15 years and over	6,776,518	35.5	11,244,289	58.9	1,009,610	5.3
15 to 19 years	2,727,715	97.5	64,392	2.3	1,460	0.1
20 to 24 years	1,747,256	68.6	774,580	30.4	17,011	0.7
25 to 34 years	1,272,312	28.8	3,046,796	68.9	94,329	2.1
35 to 44 years	491,663	13.9	2,909,069	82.0	140,745	4.0
45 to 54 years	280,785	10.6	2,184,378	82.4	180,708	6.8
55 to 64 years	149,315	8.8	1,347,772	79.1	204,812	12.0
65 years and over	91,915	6.7	902,207	66.1	367,953	26.9
Age unknown	15,557	26.5	15,095	25.7	2,592	4.4
Native white—Foreign parentage	5,158,428	66.0	2,445,770	31.3	197,832	2.5
Under 15 years of age	3,017,118	100.0	479	([2])	23	([2])
15 years and over	2,141,310	44.7	2,445,291	51.0	197,809	4.1
15 to 19 years	701,637	99.1	4,896	0.7	151	([2])
20 to 24 years	551,884	81.6	119,851	17.7	2,107	0.3
25 to 34 years	467,578	40.6	662,155	57.6	18,579	1.6
35 to 44 years	196,345	22.6	639,164	73.7	30,428	3.5
45 to 54 years	135,804	18.2	561,888	75.3	47,427	6.4
55 to 64 years	65,414	14.2	342,016	74.0	54,225	11.7
65 years and over	20,572	11.5	113,895	63.5	44,595	24.9
Age unknown	2,076	49.3	1,426	33.8	297	7.0
Native white—Mixed parentage	2,266,533	65.6	1,105,830	32.0	79,419	2.3
Under 15 years of age	1,256,743	100.0	239	([2])	10	([2])
15 years and over	1,009,790	45.9	1,105,591	50.3	79,409	3.6
15 to 19 years	373,465	99.0	3,308	0.9	83	([2])
20 to 24 years	272,975	80.6	63,414	18.7	1,367	0.4
25 to 34 years	217,840	38.9	330,365	59.1	10,373	1.9
35 to 44 years	83,115	19.5	328,223	76.9	15,306	3.6
45 to 54 years	39,916	14.2	223,551	79.6	17,242	6.1
55 to 64 years	15,448	11.1	107,353	77.3	15,917	11.5
65 years and over	6,238	8.4	48,819	65.8	18,997	25.6
Age unknown	793	49.0	558	34.5	124	7.7
Foreign-born white	2,130,562	28.3	4,903,186	65.1	470,023	6.2
Under 15 years of age	275,515	99.9	244	0.1	24	([2])
15 years and over	1,855,047	25.6	4,902,942	67.6	469,999	6.5
15 to 19 years	255,327	98.5	3,258	1.3	129	([2])
20 to 24 years	344,868	75.5	108,295	23.7	1,725	0.4
25 to 34 years	619,161	35.6	1,089,515	62.7	23,207	1.3
35 to 44 years	317,080	17.5	1,436,395	79.3	53,228	2.9
45 to 54 years	170,915	12.2	1,137,747	81.5	84,084	6.0
55 to 64 years	89,194	10.0	700,795	78.2	104,611	11.7
65 years and over	52,979	7.3	422,265	62.2	202,153	29.8
Age unknown	5,523	40.0	4,672	34.0	862	6.3
Negro	2,920,711	56.1	2,050,782	39.4	227,439	4.4
Under 15 years of age	1,815,834	100.0	375	([2])	16	([2])
15 years and over	1,104,877	32.6	2,050,407	60.4	227,423	6.7
15 to 19 years	491,643	95.8	20,043	3.9	755	0.1
20 to 24 years	267,595	54.9	209,353	43.0	8,381	1.7
25 to 34 years	189,601	25.1	534,636	70.7	29,364	3.9
35 to 44 years	87,260	13.2	527,996	80.1	42,864	6.5
45 to 54 years	42,948	7.8	449,997	82.0	54,619	10.0
55 to 64 years	13,967	5.8	187,471	77.7	39,376	16.3
65 years and over	8,444	4.9	113,864	65.5	51,054	29.4
Age unknown	3,419	25.3	7,047	52.2	1,010	7.5

[1] Includes Indians, Chinese, Japanese, and "all other."

AGE PERIODS, FOR PRINCIPAL POPULATION CLASSES, FOR THE UNITED 1920 AND 1910.

CLASS OF POPULATION AND AGE PERIOD.	FEMALES: 1920					
	Single.		Married.		Widowed or divorced.	
	Number.	Per cent.	Number.	Per cent.	Number.	Per cent.
All classes [1]	26,243,696	50.7	21,324,487	41.2	4,191,255	8.1
Under 15 years of age	16,626,794	100.0	5,554	[2]	326	[2]
15 years and over	9,616,902	27.3	21,318,933	60.6	4,190,929	11.9
15 to 19 years	4,137,650	87.0	596,542	12.5	18,256	0.4
20 to 24 years	2,164,051	45.6	2,483,697	52.3	93,996	2.0
25 to 34 years	1,636,404	19.3	6,492,355	76.5	351,711	4.1
35 to 44 years	767,882	11.4	5,426,434	80.3	560,520	8.3
45 to 54 years	464,838	9.6	3,587,794	74.0	787,620	16.3
55 to 64 years	257,029	8.4	1,878,478	61.2	929,813	30.3
65 years and over	173,442	7.1	830,160	33.9	1,440,230	58.8
Age unknown	15,606	28.0	23,473	42.0	8,783	15.7
Native white—Native parentage	15,520,296	53.9	11,199,314	38.9	2,037,916	7.1
Under 15 years of age	10,251,806	100.0	3,449	[2]	173	[2]
15 years and over	5,268,490	28.4	11,195,865	60.4	2,037,743	11.0
15 to 19 years	2,417,110	86.3	372,924	13.3	9,376	0.3
20 to 24 years	1,175,208	44.7	1,404,020	53.4	46,552	1.8
25 to 34 years	844,778	19.0	3,421,662	77.1	168,469	3.8
35 to 44 years	367,563	10.9	2,747,693	81.6	250,249	7.4
45 to 54 years	215,435	9.2	1,780,111	76.1	341,835	14.6
55 to 64 years	130,330	8.4	975,239	63.1	436,631	28.3
65 years and over	108,365	7.9	480,833	35.0	780,608	56.8
Age unknown	9,701	29.0	13,383	40.1	4,023	12.0
Native white—Foreign parentage	4,768,233	60.5	2,648,525	33.6	461,384	5.9
Under 15 years of age	2,976,962	100.0	471	[2]	28	[2]
15 years and over	1,791,271	36.5	2,648,054	54.0	461,356	9.4
15 to 19 years	674,765	93.5	45,336	6.3	747	0.1
20 to 24 years	417,140	58.9	283,156	40.0	6,869	1.0
25 to 34 years	327,577	27.6	823,381	69.3	36,170	3.0
35 to 44 years	166,760	18.8	656,869	73.9	64,442	7.3
45 to 54 years	120,476	16.2	509,685	68.5	112,858	15.2
55 to 64 years	63,214	13.5	264,796	56.8	138,020	29.6
65 years and over	19,654	10.6	63,422	34.2	101,787	55.0
Age unknown	1,685	44.5	1,409	37.2	463	12.2
Native white—Mixed parentage	2,109,026	59.6	1,243,035	35.1	182,227	5.2
Under 15 years of age	1,231,854	100.0	219	[2]	10	[2]
15 years and over	877,172	38.1	1,242,816	53.9	182,217	7.9
15 to 19 years	356,705	93.8	22,815	6.0	559	0.1
20 to 24 years	214,387	59.8	139,202	38.8	4,223	1.2
25 to 34 years	172,223	28.0	422,413	68.6	20,539	3.3
35 to 44 years	75,498	16.5	348,933	76.3	32,754	7.2
45 to 54 years	36,024	13.0	200,886	72.3	40,860	14.7
55 to 64 years	14,698	10.8	81,568	60.1	39,345	29.0
65 years and over	6,928	9.0	26,391	34.2	43,743	56.7
Age unknown	709	44.0	608	37.7	194	12.0
Foreign-born white	1,105,893	17.9	4,123,806	66.7	946,961	15.3
Under 15 years of age	270,094	99.9	303	0.1	50	[2]
15 years and over	835,799	14.1	4,123,503	69.7	946,911	16.0
15 to 19 years	229,240	85.3	38,477	14.3	663	0.2
20 to 24 years	174,137	37.1	289,349	61.6	5,593	1.2
25 to 34 years	175,340	12.8	1,150,570	84.2	39,881	2.9
35 to 44 years	110,355	8.2	1,148,448	84.8	93,912	6.9
45 to 54 years	72,875	6.8	822,439	76.8	174,596	16.3
55 to 64 years	40,600	5.6	457,165	62.8	229,243	31.5
65 years and over	31,726	4.9	213,713	32.9	401,812	61.9
Age unknown	1,526	23.4	3,342	51.2	1,211	18.5
Negro	2,654,719	50.5	2,040,252	38.8	551,895	10.5
Under 15 years of age	1,829,461	99.9	1,071	0.1	63	[2]
15 years and over	825,258	24.1	2,039,181	59.6	551,832	16.1
15 to 19 years	448,169	78.7	114,169	20.0	6,782	1.2
20 to 24 years	179,411	31.6	356,740	62.8	30,276	5.3
25 to 34 years	114,634	13.5	650,348	76.4	85,445	10.0
35 to 44 years	46,996	7.0	508,417	75.4	117,767	17.5
45 to 54 years	19,683	4.9	266,087	66.2	115,747	28.8
55 to 64 years	7,973	4.2	95,665	50.7	84,682	44.9
65 years and over	6,516	4.1	43,271	27.2	108,343	68.2
Age unknown	1,876	18.8	4,484	44.9	2,790	27.9

[2] Less than one-tenth of 1 per cent.

TABLE 54.—MARITAL CONDITION OF THE TOTAL POPULATION, BY SEX
STATES:

CLASS OF POPULATION AND AGE PERIOD.	MALES: 1910					
	Single.		Married.		Widowed or divorced.	
	Number.	Per cent.	Number.	Per cent.	Number.	Per cent.
All classes [1]	27,455,607	58.0	18,093,498	38.2	1,627,648	3.4
Under 15 years of age	14,905,478	100.0	898	(²)	96	(²)
15 years and over	12,550,129	38.7	18,092,600	55.8	1,627,552	5.0
15 to 19 years	4,448,067	98.3	51,877	1.1	1,457	(²)
20 to 24 years	3,432,161	74.9	1,100,093	24.0	25,547	0.6
25 to 34 years	2,767,957	35.0	4,964,769	62.8	145,002	1.8
35 to 44 years	1,026,502	16.7	4,873,153	79.2	241,389	3.9
45 to 54 years	499,751	11.1	3,658,931	81.5	322,724	7.2
55 to 64 years	222,950	8.3	2,112,699	79.0	334,095	12.5
65 years and over	123,322	6.2	1,303,768	65.6	552,133	27.8
Age unknown	29,419	25.7	27,310	23.9	5,205	4.5
Native white—Native parentage	15,180,989	60.2	9,144,513	36.2	816,383	3.2
Under 15 years of age	8,995,665	100.0	414	(²)	44	(²)
15 years and over	6,185,324	38.1	9,144,099	56.3	816,339	5.0
15 to 19 years	2,504,473	98.1	33,818	1.3	706	(²)
20 to 24 years	1,691,385	72.5	618,300	26.5	12,633	0.5
25 to 34 years	1,181,751	31.2	2,524,551	66.6	72,167	1.9
35 to 44 years	415,192	14.5	2,319,342	81.3	114,435	4.0
45 to 54 years	209,014	9.8	1,757,732	82.8	152,575	7.2
55 to 64 years	106,387	7.5	1,144,917	80.4	170,767	12.0
65 years and over	61,042	5.6	733,401	67.3	290,510	26.7
Age unknown	16,080	23.4	12,038	17.5	2,546	3.7
Native white—Foreign parentage	4,386,006	67.9	1,926,201	29.8	133,527	2.1
Under 15 years of age	2,396,879	100.0	126	(²)	10	(²)
15 years and over	1,989,127	49.0	1,926,075	47.4	133,517	3.3
15 to 19 years	712,993	99.1	2,232	0.3	72	(²)
20 to 24 years	510,431	84.0	93,069	15.3	1,288	0.2
25 to 34 years	431,080	44.4	525,379	54.1	12,998	1.3
35 to 44 years	200,710	23.7	615,593	72.7	29,613	3.5
45 to 54 years	95,687	15.8	467,794	77.3	40,872	6.8
55 to 64 years	28,226	12.6	168,991	75.3	27,117	12.1
65 years and over	8,151	10.0	51,654	63.6	21,289	26.2
Age unknown	1,849	45.1	1,363	33.3	268	6.5
Native white—Mixed parentage	2,159,944	72.8	751,684	25.3	51,955	1.8
Under 15 years of age	1,243,029	100.0	53	(²)	5	(²)
15 years and over	916,915	53.1	751,631	43.6	51,950	3.0
15 to 19 years	372,412	99.1	1,403	0.4	54	(²)
20 to 24 years	259,143	84.5	45,468	14.8	834	0.3
25 to 34 years	193,630	43.0	249,097	55.3	6,893	1.5
35 to 44 years	58,968	19.9	226,624	76.4	10,823	3.6
45 to 54 years	21,215	12.7	134,539	80.4	11,503	6.9
55 to 64 years	7,556	9.5	62,277	78.5	9,404	11.9
65 years and over	3,297	7.0	31,730	66.9	12,341	26.0
Age unknown	694	45.0	493	32.0	98	6.4
Foreign-born white	2,652,619	35.3	4,432,298	58.9	407,814	5.4
Under 15 years of age	383,703	99.9	163	(²)	29	(²)
15 years and over	2,268,916	31.8	4,432,135	62.1	407,785	5.7
15 to 19 years	346,672	98.6	2,851	0.8	78	(²)
20 to 24 years	661,481	80.3	156,222	19.0	1,607	0.2
25 to 34 years	738,979	39.3	1,115,745	59.4	17,191	0.9
35 to 44 years	269,854	17.3	1,246,128	79.7	43,482	2.8
45 to 54 years	137,594	11.6	970,464	82.1	72,309	6.1
55 to 64 years	64,807	9.1	557,016	78.2	89,100	12.5
65 years and over	47,299	7.1	070,107	62.5	183,161	30.2
Age unknown	6,300	32.0	4,510	90.4	002	4.0
Negro	2,909,902	59.6	1,749,359	35.8	210,124	4.3
Under 15 years of age	1,826,430	100.0	131	(²)	8	(²)
15 years and over	1,083,472	35.4	1,749,228	57.2	210,116	6.9
15 to 19 years	492,153	96.9	11,064	2.2	520	0.1
20 to 24 years	287,994	59.7	182,110	37.8	8,969	1.9
25 to 34 years	189,196	25.1	527,149	69.9	34,669	4.6
35 to 44 years	67,203	12.2	439,901	80.0	41,602	7.6
45 to 54 years	25,869	6.8	308,831	81.4	43,922	11.6
55 to 64 years	10,792	5.0	168,881	78.1	36,141	16.7
65 years and over	6,285	4.1	102,670	67.3	42,890	28.1
Age unknown	3,980	23.3	8,622	50.5	1,403	8.2

[1] Includes Indians, Chinese, Japanese, and "all other."

AND AGE PERIODS, FOR PRINCIPAL POPULATION CLASSES, FOR THE UNITED 1920 AND 1910—Con.

CLASS OF POPULATION AND AGE PERIOD.	FEMALES: 1910					
	Single.		Married.		Widowed or divorced.	
	Number.	Per cent.	Number.	Per cent.	Number.	Per cent.
All classes [1]	23,522,121	52.7	17,688,169	39.6	3,361,527	7.5
Under 15 years of age	14,588,951	100.0	3,482	(²)	231	(²)
15 years and over	8,933,170	29.7	17,684,687	58.9	3,361,296	11.2
15 to 19 years	3,986,764	87.9	513,239	11.3	13,911	0.3
20 to 24 years	2,163,683	48.3	2,225,362	49.7	75,724	1.7
25 to 34 years	1,516,726	20.9	5,443,894	75.1	281,589	3.9
35 to 44 years	628,516	11.4	4,410,310	80.1	461,165	8.4
45 to 54 years	331,573	8.5	2,904,043	74.8	642,320	16.6
55 to 64 years	167,991	7.1	1,479,454	62.2	729,652	30.7
65 years and over	124,223	6.3	687,335	35.0	1,147,461	58.4
Age unknown	14,694	26.9	21,050	38.5	9,474	17.3
Native white—Native parentage	13,377,257	55.1	9,221,615	38.0	1,623,705	6.7
Under 15 years of age	8,733,135	100.0	2,230	(²)	92	(²)
15 years and over	4,644,122	29.9	9,219,385	59.4	1,623,613	10.5
15 to 19 years	2,199,856	86.7	318,334	12.5	6,345	0.3
20 to 24 years	1,094,534	46.6	1,226,851	51.8	32,753	1.4
25 to 34 years	713,194	19.5	2,823,023	77.1	121,953	3.3
35 to 44 years	284,455	10.8	2,163,079	81.9	192,085	7.3
45 to 54 years	162,006	8.5	1,455,951	76.7	279,908	14.7
55 to 64 years	99,801	7.7	833,750	64.5	358,250	27.7
65 years and over	82,137	7.4	398,184	35.8	628,809	56.6
Age unknown	8,139	28.3	10,213	35.5	3,510	12.2
Native white—Foreign parentage	4,026,839	62.3	2,128,379	32.9	295,348	4.6
Under 15 years of age	2,366,719	100.0	214	(²)	13	(²)
15 years and over	1,660,120	40.6	2,128,165	52.0	295,335	7.2
15 to 19 years	689,242	94.2	37,924	5.2	458	0.1
20 to 24 years	392,180	62.0	234,717	37.1	4,135	0.7
25 to 34 years	307,391	31.0	656,285	66.2	26,662	2.7
35 to 44 years	159,071	18.7	630,802	74.0	62,334	7.3
45 to 54 years	80,946	13.8	412,518	70.3	93,318	15.9
55 to 64 years	22,630	10.6	127,197	59.3	64,393	30.0
65 years and over	7,087	9.0	27,550	35.2	43,622	55.7
Age unknown	1,573	45.1	1,172	33.6	413	11.8
Native white—Mixed parentage	2,011,313	66.8	880,548	29.2	117,204	3.9
Under 15 years of age	1,218,416	100.0	90	(²)	15	(²)
15 years and over	792,897	44.2	880,458	49.1	117,189	6.5
15 to 19 years	359,049	94.7	17,871	4.7	344	0.1
20 to 24 years	209,787	64.3	112,560	34.5	2,742	0.8
25 to 34 years	146,786	29.9	329,398	67.0	14,753	3.0
35 to 44 years	47,959	15.6	237,076	76.9	23,027	7.5
45 to 54 years	18,202	11.1	119,341	73.1	25,709	15.7
55 to 64 years	6,732	8.8	46,857	61.4	22,629	29.7
65 years and over	3,812	7.9	16,876	34.8	27,806	57.3
Age unknown	570	41.4	479	34.8	179	13.0
Foreign-born white	1,369,303	23.5	3,624,215	62.3	820,700	14.1
Under 15 years of age	375,193	99.9	212	0.1	46	(²)
15 years and over	994,110	18.3	3,624,003	66.5	820,654	15.1
15 to 19 years	277,841	86.3	42,049	13.1	466	0.1
20 to 24 years	272,178	44.9	329,016	54.3	3,960	0.7
25 to 34 years	231,734	18.0	1,025,086	79.5	31,269	2.4
35 to 44 years	98,440	8.6	965,486	84.1	83,451	7.3
45 to 54 years	54,634	6.1	687,718	77.4	145,798	16.4
55 to 64 years	31,728	5.2	372,214	61.1	204,571	33.6
65 years and over	25,790	4.5	199,737	34.7	349,669	60.7
Age unknown	1,765	27.1	2,697	41.5	1,470	22.6
Negro	2,661,778	53.9	1,776,643	36.0	493,179	10.0
Under 15 years of age	1,837,782	100.0	694	(²)	62	(²)
15 years and over	823,996	26.6	1,775,949	57.2	493,117	15.9
15 to 19 years	448,515	81.2	94,087	17.0	6,134	1.1
20 to 24 years	191,396	34.9	323,773	59.0	31,652	5.8
25 to 34 years	115,682	14.5	592,547	74.5	85,801	10.8
35 to 44 years	38,105	7.1	401,069	74.4	98,887	18.4
45 to 54 years	15,537	4.7	220,800	66.4	95,853	28.8
55 to 64 years	6,946	3.9	95,023	52.8	77,547	43.1
65 years and over	5,243	3.7	42,404	29.9	93,421	66.0
Age unknown	2,572	18.4	6,246	44.7	3,822	27.4

² Less than one-tenth of 1 per cent.

TABLE 55.—MARITAL CONDITION OF THE POPULATION 15 YEARS OF AGE AND OVER,

DIVISION OR STATE AND CLASS OF POPULATION.	MALES 15 YEARS OF AGE AND OVER.							
	Total.[1]	Single.		Married.		Widowed.		Di-vorced.
		Number.	Per cent.	Number.	Per cent.	Number.	Per cent.	
UNITED STATES.								
All classes[2]	36,920,663	12,967,565	35.1	21,849,266	59.2	1,758,308	4.8	235,284
Native white—Native parentage	19,092,107	6,776,518	35.5	11,244,289	58.9	874,821	4.6	134,789
Native white—Foreign or mixed par.	6,990,940	3,151,100	45.1	3,550,882	50.8	236,294	3.4	40,924
Foreign-born white	7,252,539	1,855,047	25.6	4,902,942	67.6	438,049	6.0	31,950
Negro	3,393,211	1,104,877	32.6	2,050,407	60.4	200,734	5.9	26,689
GEOGRAPHIC DIVISIONS.								
NEW ENGLAND.								
All classes[2]	2,614,119	935,919	35.8	1,522,214	58.2	137,307	5.3	14,408
Native white—Native parentage	972,911	331,847	34.1	569,103	58.5	60,870	6.3	8,897
Native white—Foreign or mixed par.	696,851	374,281	53.7	297,366	42.7	21,697	3.1	2,691
Foreign-born white	909,765	216,041	23.7	636,924	70.0	53,046	5.8	2,596
Negro	30,498	11,870	38.9	16,732	54.9	1,591	5.2	215
MIDDLE ATLANTIC.								
All classes[2]	7,863,502	2,788,863	35.5	4,658,707	59.2	368,584	4.7	23,737
Native white—Native parentage	3,210,550	1,175,331	36.6	1,852,452	57.7	159,676	5.0	13,922
Native white—Foreign or mixed par.	1,873,841	914,692	48.8	884,508	47.2	66,587	3.6	4,680
Foreign-born white	2,530,225	605,712	23.9	1,780,343	70.4	130,220	5.1	4,216
Negro	235,674	85,397	36.2	136,401	57.9	11,815	5.0	887
EAST NORTH CENTRAL.								
All classes[2]	7,844,734	2,704,777	34.5	4,692,684	59.8	368,357	4.7	61,984
Native white—Native parentage	3,908,456	1,396,227	35.7	2,290,648	58.6	175,973	4.5	36,429
Native white—Foreign or mixed par.	1,953,028	806,506	41.3	1,064,703	54.5	65,850	3.4	13,030
Foreign-born white	1,753,645	419,937	23.9	1,207,092	68.8	112,897	6.4	9,551
Negro	218,760	76,969	35.2	125,254	57.3	13,075	6.0	2,887
WEST NORTH CENTRAL.								
All classes[2]	4,480,690	1,632,528	36.4	2,596,866	58.0	206,467	4.6	31,535
Native white—Native parentage	2,367,289	874,598	36.9	1,364,601	57.6	100,946	4.3	19,004
Native white—Foreign or mixed par.	1,225,560	535,668	43.7	646,061	52.7	34,764	2.8	6,412
Foreign-born white	761,080	178,443	23.4	514,637	67.6	61,796	8.1	4,242
Negro	112,538	38,637	34.3	63,551	56.5	8,169	7.3	1,752
SOUTH ATLANTIC.								
All classes[2]	4,459,049	1,538,338	34.5	2,686,520	60.2	207,103	4.6	16,262
Native white—Native parentage	2,783,077	972,859	35.0	1,678,260	60.3	116,616	4.2	9,290
Native white—Foreign or mixed par.	179,697	74,986	41.7	95,611	53.2	7,948	4.4	943
Foreign-born white	179,095	54,376	30.4	113,468	63.4	10,063	5.6	594
Negro	1,311,264	433,651	33.1	795,982	60.7	72,281	5.5	5,415
EAST SOUTH CENTRAL.								
All classes[2]	2,799,332	894,179	31.9	1,742,015	62.2	142,301	5.1	15,260
Native white—Native parentage	1,896,799	621,430	32.8	1,180,367	62.2	84,210	4.4	7,611
Native white—Foreign or mixed par.	77,824	26,448	34.0	46,791	60.1	3,956	5.1	541
Foreign-born white	41,062	9,531	23.2	27,538	67.1	3,694	9.0	213
Negro	782,663	236,391	30.2	486,794	62.2	50,380	6.4	6,887
WEST SOUTH CENTRAL.								
All classes[2]	3,375,273	1,145,995	34.0	2,027,272	60.1	166,000	4.9	22,863
Native white—Native parentage	2,227,731	771,816	34.6	1,336,835	60.0	97,489	4.4	12,251
Native white—Foreign or mixed par.	233,688	92,425	39.6	129,959	55.6	9,335	4.0	1,522
Foreign-born white	231,050	70,114	30.3	141,822	61.4	16,643	7.2	1,043
Negro	664,084	204,818	30.8	408,050	61.4	41,453	6.2	7,904
MOUNTAIN.								
All classes[2]	1,228,847	467,345	38.0	683,164	55.6	50,171	4.6	13,432
Native white—Native parentage	663,674	249,428	37.6	370,161	55.8	29,378	4.4	7,811
Native white—Foreign or mixed par.	258,172	106,906	41.4	139,250	53.9	8,821	3.4	2,824
Foreign-born white	254,224	88,352	34.8	147,673	58.1	14,852	5.8	2,231
Negro	17,457	9,724	55.7	6,611	37.9	756	4.3	277
PACIFIC.								
All classes[2]	2,255,117	859,621	38.1	1,239,824	55.0	106,015	4.7	35,803
Native white—Native parentage	1,061,620	382,982	36.1	601,862	56.7	49,663	4.7	19,514
Native white—Foreign or mixed par.	492,279	219,188	44.5	246,633	50.1	17,336	3.5	8,281
Foreign-born white	592,393	212,541	35.9	333,445	56.3	34,838	5.9	7,264
Negro	20,273	7,420	36.6	11,032	54.4	1,214	6.0	465

[1] Total includes persons whose marital condition was not reported.

BY SEX, FOR PRINCIPAL POPULATION CLASSES, BY DIVISIONS AND STATES: 1920.

DIVISION OR STATE AND CLASS OF POPULATION.	Total.[1]	FEMALES 15 YEARS OF AGE AND OVER.						Divorced.
		Single.		Married.		Widowed.		
		Number.	Per cent.	Number.	Per cent.	Number.	Per cent.	
UNITED STATES.								
All classes [2]	35,177,515	9,616,902	27.3	21,318,933	60.6	3,917,625	11.1	273.304
Native white—Native parentage	18,529,748	5,268,490	28.4	11,195,865	60.4	1,885,000	10.2	152,743
Native white—Foreign or mixed par.	7,211,108	2,668,443	37.0	3,890,870	54.0	595,407	8.3	48,166
Foreign-born white	5,913,985	835,799	14.1	4,123,503	69.7	919,255	15.5	27,656
Negro	3,423,100	825,258	24.1	2,039,181	59.6	507,961	14.8	43,871
GEOGRAPHIC DIVISIONS.								
NEW ENGLAND.								
All classes [2]	2,681,138	860,653	32.1	1,485,377	55.4	315,093	11.8	17,441
Native white—Native parentage	1,006,255	320,837	31.9	534,679	53.1	139,246	13.8	10,339
Native white—Foreign or mixed par.	756,451	371,256	49.1	331,003	43.8	50,003	6.6	3,548
Foreign-born white	888,754	160,504	18.1	603,268	67.9	120,992	13.6	3,258
Negro	28,853	7,833	27.1	15,954	55.3	4,732	16.4	287
MIDDLE ATLANTIC.								
All classes [2]	7,757,457	2,310,805	29.8	4,518,248	58.2	888,739	11.5	29,367
Native white—Native parentage	3,292,690	1,057,617	32.1	1,852,408	56.3	361,294	11.0	17,108
Native white—Foreign or mixed par.	2,023,534	844,769	41.7	987,130	48.8	182,908	9.0	6,134
Foreign-born white	2,208,535	348,395	15.8	1,541,876	69.8	310,281	14.0	4,919
Negro	229,987	59,219	25.7	135,197	58.8	34,007	14.8	1,190
EAST NORTH CENTRAL.								
All classes [2]	7,321,833	1,916,579	26.2	4,545,175	62.1	785,038	10.7	65,090
Native white—Native parentage	3,770,085	1,068,181	28.3	2,292,058	60.8	365,386	9.7	38,786
Native white—Foreign or mixed par.	2,002,374	665,130	33.2	1,156,234	57.7	163,530	8.2	15,289
Foreign-born white	1,359,167	148,405	10.9	974,174	71.7	226,814	16.7	7,998
Negro	185,274	33,781	18.2	119,604	64.6	28,657	15.5	2,931
WEST NORTH CENTRAL.								
All classes [2]	4,159,479	1,150,373	27.7	2,555,896	61.4	411,472	9.9	34,727
Native white—Native parentage	2,263,964	656,392	29.0	1,379,396	60.9	202,817	9.0	21,270
Native white—Foreign or mixed par.	1,206,290	414,657	34.4	702,907	58.3	79,244	6.6	7,790
Foreign-born white	575,368	56,197	9.8	404,122	70.2	110,643	19.2	3,466
Negro	102,372	20,548	20.1	62,061	60.6	17,465	17.1	2,062
SOUTH ATLANTIC.								
All classes [2]	4,420,837	1,222,561	27.7	2,654,236	60.0	513,797	11.6	23,110
Native white—Native parentage	2,745,420	783,803	28.5	1,669,800	60.8	275,545	10.0	12,149
Native white—Foreign or mixed par.	185,752	63,953	34.4	98,424	53.0	22,188	11.9	1,055
Foreign-born white	124,860	17,911	14.3	86,322	69.1	20,054	16.1	422
Negro	1,361,103	355,986	26.2	797,273	58.6	195,668	14.4	9,465
EAST SOUTH CENTRAL.								
All classes [2]	2,794,845	706,269	25.3	1,725,179	61.7	334,697	12.0	24,914
Native white—Native parentage	1,858,996	484,438	26.1	1,174,207	63.2	187,356	10.1	10,955
Native white—Foreign or mixed par.	85,036	25,804	30.3	46,344	54.5	12,180	14.3	646
Foreign-born white	28,860	3,654	12.7	17,907	62.0	7,119	24.7	133
Negro	821,483	192,268	23.4	486,417	59.2	127,985	15.6	13,176
WEST SOUTH CENTRAL.								
All classes [2]	3,131,029	766,117	24.5	1,988,774	63.5	339,238	10.8	31,236
Native white—Native parentage	2,054,846	515,544	25.1	1,331,436	64.8	189,767	9.2	14,517
Native white—Foreign or mixed par.	221,627	65,938	29.8	130,912	59.1	22,805	10.3	1,700
Foreign-born white	170,598	29,519	17.3	109,951	64.5	30,011	17.6	826
Negro	667,340	151,058	22.6	406,214	60.9	94,624	14.2	13,980
MOUNTAIN.								
All classes [2]	1,000,086	233,864	23.4	654,476	65.4	98,277	9.8	11,510
Native white—Native parentage	564,785	143,474	25.4	364,567	64.5	48,411	8.6	6,902
Native white—Foreign or mixed par.	236,849	65,753	27.8	150,620	63.6	17,526	7.4	2,748
Foreign-born white	165,406	18,424	11.1	117,521	71.1	27,816	16.8	1,417
Negro	8,799	1,383	15.7	5,645	64.2	1,513	17.2	236
PACIFIC.								
All classes [2]	1,910,811	449,681	23.5	1,191,572	62.4	231,274	12.1	35,909
Native white—Native parentage	972,707	238,204	24.5	597,314	61.4	115,178	11.8	20,717
Native white—Foreign or mixed par.	493,195	151,183	30.7	287,296	58.3	45,023	9.1	9,256
Foreign-born white	392,437	52,790	13.5	268,362	68.4	65,525	16.7	5,217
Negro	17,889	3,182	17.8	10,816	60.5	3,310	18.5	544

[2] Includes Indians, Chinese, Japanese, and "all other."

Table 55.—MARITAL CONDITION OF THE POPULATION 15 YEARS OF AGE AND OVER,

DIVISION OR STATE AND CLASS OF POPULATION.	Total.¹	Single. Number.	Per cent.	Married. Number.	Per cent.	Widowed. Number.	Per cent.	Divorced.
NEW ENGLAND.								
Maine.								
All classes ²	279,478	92,085	32.9	166,171	59.5	18,123	6.5	2,628
Native white—Native parentage	179,623	54,944	30.6	109,474	60.9	12,836	7.1	2,067
Native white—Foreign or mixed par.	46,064	22,558	49.0	21,441	46.5	1,738	3.8	271
Foreign-born white	52,806	14,186	26.9	34,758	65.8	3,471	6.6	282
Negro	553	239	43.2	260	47.0	44	8.0	6
New Hampshire.								
All classes ²	161,931	54,688	33.8	94,791	58.5	10,324	6.4	1,762
Native white—Native parentage	82,833	25,066	30.3	49,895	60.2	6,367	7.7	1,315
Native white—Foreign or mixed par.	33,987	17,782	52.3	14,851	43.7	1,072	3.2	216
Foreign-born white	44,759	11,683	26.1	29,871	66.7	2,871	6.4	226
Negro	247	109	44.1	120	48.6	13	5.3	5
Vermont.								
All classes ²	127,905	41,894	32.8	76,310	59.7	8,372	6.5	1,171
Native white—Native parentage	80,228	26,598	33.2	47,252	58.9	5,441	6.8	816
Native white—Foreign or mixed par.	25,581	9,936	38.8	14,093	55.1	1,316	5.1	224
Foreign-born white	21,840	5,237	24.0	14,850	68.0	1,602	7.3	126
Negro	233	108	46.4	110	47.2	11	4.7	4
Massachusetts.								
All classes ²	1,347,788	496,697	36.9	775,687	57.6	67,582	5.0	5,825
Native white—Native parentage	415,663	147,344	35.4	239,979	57.7	24,154	5.8	3,115
Native white—Foreign or mixed par.	397,634	218,689	55.0	165,229	41.6	12,101	3.0	1,291
Foreign-born white	514,524	122,621	23.8	359,609	69.9	30,467	5.9	1,297
Negro	17,383	6,834	39.3	9,540	54.9	824	4.7	117
Rhode Island.								
All classes ²	210,543	77,269	36.7	121,208	57.6	10,711	5.1	1,226
Native white—Native parentage	59,048	22,327	37.8	32,616	55.2	3,493	5.9	576
Native white—Foreign or mixed par.	64,634	35,266	54.6	27,110	41.9	1,910	3.0	315
Foreign-born white	82,765	18,051	21.8	59,304	71.7	5,054	6.1	300
Negro	3,833	1,538	40.1	2,018	52.6	240	6.3	35
Connecticut.								
All classes ²	486,474	173,286	35.6	288,047	59.2	22,195	4.6	1,796
Native white—Native parentage	155,516	55,568	35.7	89,887	57.8	8,579	5.5	1,008
Native white—Foreign or mixed par.	128,951	70,050	54.3	54,642	42.4	3,560	2.8	374
Foreign-born white	193,071	44,263	22.9	138,532	71.8	9,581	5.0	365
Negro	8,249	3,042	36.9	4,684	56.8	459	5.6	48
MIDDLE ATLANTIC.								
New York.								
All classes ²	3,732,828	1,350,088	36.2	2,183,536	58.5	173,113	4.6	10,166
Native white—Native parentage	1,243,486	476,643	38.3	693,545	55.8	62,274	5.0	5,267
Native white—Foreign or mixed par.	1,010,836	497,467	49.2	473,009	46.8	35,949	3.6	2,332
Foreign-born white	1,392,276	342,291	24.6	969,247	69.6	71,243	5.1	2,301
Negro	76,684	28,031	36.6	44,240	57.7	3,423	4.5	241
New Jersey.								
All classes ²	1,110,387	382,481	34.4	672,749	60.6	50,577	4.6	2,593
Native white—Native parentage	408,141	148,187	36.3	237,697	58.2	20,116	4.9	1,329
Native white—Foreign or mixed par.	279,796	138,056	49.3	132,022	47.2	8,685	3.1	581
Foreign-born white	378,336	81,386	21.5	276,550	73.1	19,260	5.1	531
Negro	42,680	14,047	32.9	25,882	60.6	2,487	5.8	152
Pennsylvania.								
All classes ²	3,020,287	1,056,294	35.0	1,802,422	59.7	144,894	4.8	10,978
Native white—Native parentage	1,558,923	550,501	35.3	921,210	59.1	77,286	5.0	7,326
Native white—Foreign or mixed par.	583,209	279,169	47.9	279,477	47.9	21,953	3.8	1,767
Foreign-born white	759,613	182,035	24.0	534,546	70.4	39,717	5.2	1,384
Negro	116,310	43,319	37.2	66,279	57.0	5,905	5.1	494

¹ Total includes persons whose marital condition was not reported.

BY SEX, FOR PRINCIPAL POPULATION CLASSES, BY DIVISIONS AND STATES: 1920—Con.

DIVISION OR STATE AND CLASS OF POPULATION.	Total.[1]	FEMALES 15 YEARS OF AGE AND OVER.							
		Single.		Married.		Widowed.		Divorced
		Number.	Per cent.	Number.	Per cent.	Number.	Per cent.	

NEW ENGLAND.

Maine.

All classes [2]	271,764	72,159	26.6	162,623	59.8	34,017	12.5	2,685
Native white—Native parentage	176,534	44,308	25.1	105,396	59.7	24,543	13.9	2,102
Native white—Foreign or mixed par.	45,954	19,191	41.8	23,188	50.5	3,232	7.0	309
Foreign-born white	48,544	8,440	17.4	33,639	69.3	6,142	12.7	262
Negro	445	150	33.7	228	51.2	60	13.5	7

New Hampshire.

All classes [2]	161,208	46,292	28.7	92,353	57.3	20,431	12.7	1,845
Native white—Native parentage	82,886	21,655	26.1	46,867	56.5	12,901	15.6	1,317
Native white—Foreign or mixed par.	35,844	16,771	46.8	16,667	46.5	2,062	5.8	273
Foreign-born white	42,278	7,810	18.5	28,701	67.9	5,451	12.9	247
Negro	183	51	27.9	108	59.0	15	8.2	8

Vermont.

All classes [2]	123,982	32,397	26.1	74,505	60.1	15,989	12.9	1,014
Native white—Native parentage	78,689	21,274	27.0	46,303	58.8	10,328	13.1	740
Native white—Foreign or mixed par.	26,098	8,381	32.1	14,758	56.5	2,763	10.6	186
Foreign-born white	19,023	2,691	14.1	13,353	70.2	2,871	15.1	85
Negro	166	49	29.5	88	53.0	26	15.7	3

Massachusetts.

All classes [2]	1,425,443	490,170	34.4	758,897	53.2	167,253	11.7	8,000
Native white—Native parentage	447,011	159,021	35.6	220,932	49.4	62,399	14.0	4,188
Native white—Foreign or mixed par.	435,890	223,523	51.3	182,000	41.8	28,267	6.5	1,831
Foreign-born white	525,251	102,768	19.6	346,595	66.0	73,705	14.0	1,833
Negro	16,918	4,743	28.0	9,159	54.1	2,838	16.8	145

Rhode Island.

All classes [2]	219,409	74,098	33.8	118,772	54.1	24,577	11.2	1,834
Native white—Native parentage	60,363	21,125	35.0	30,374	50.3	7,975	13.2	852
Native white—Foreign or mixed par.	71,493	36,290	50.8	30,269	42.3	4,444	6.2	461
Foreign-born white	83,894	15,683	18.7	56,189	67.0	11,501	13.7	465
Negro	3,607	988	27.4	1,913	53.0	645	17.9	55

Connecticut.

All classes [2]	479,332	145,537	30.4	278,227	58.0	52,826	11.0	2,063
Native white—Native parentage	160,772	53,454	33.2	84,807	52.7	21,100	13.1	1,140
Native white—Foreign or mixed par.	141,172	67,100	47.5	64,121	45.4	9,235	6.5	488
Foreign-born white	169,764	23,112	13.6	124,791	73.5	21,322	12.6	366
Negro	7,534	1,852	24.6	4,458	59.2	1,148	15.2	69

MIDDLE ATLANTIC.

New York.

All classes [2]	3,767,540	1,164,525	30.9	2,134,604	56.7	448,670	11.9	13,562
Native white—Native parentage	1,280,815	430,885	33.6	692,314	54.1	148,557	11.6	6,756
Native white—Foreign or mixed par.	1,107,185	471,119	42.6	528,974	47.8	102,266	9.2	3,218
Foreign-born white	1,294,176	237,901	18.4	866,376	66.9	184,663	14.3	3,148
Negro	82,982	23,895	28.8	45,512	54.8	12,973	15.6	426

New Jersey.

All classes [2]	1,092,623	311,293	28.5	653,587	59.8	123,076	11.3	3,297
Native white—Native parentage	414,714	132,014	31.8	233,470	56.3	46,896	11.3	1,746
Native white—Foreign or mixed par.	299,594	124,973	41.7	149,351	49.9	24,143	8.1	758
Foreign-born white	333,743	43,047	12.9	244,684	73.3	45,102	13.5	572
Negro	44,443	11,227	25.3	26,001	58.5	6,920	15.6	220

Pennsylvania.

All classes [2]	2,897,294	834,987	28.8	1,730,057	59.7	316,993	10.9	12,508
Native white—Native parentage	1,597,161	494,718	31.0	926,624	58.0	165,841	10.4	8,606
Native white—Foreign or mixed par.	616,755	248,677	40.3	308,805	50.1	56,499	9.2	2,158
Foreign-born white	580,616	67,447	11.6	430,816	74.2	80,516	13.9	1,199
Negro	102,562	24,097	23.5	63,684	62.1	14,114	13.8	544

[2] Includes Indians, Chinese, Japanese, and "all other."

232230 ABSTRACT OF THE CENSUS—POPULATION.

TABLE 55.—MARITAL CONDITION OF THE POPULATION 15 YEARS OF AGE AND OVER,

DIVISION OR STATE AND CLASS OF POPULATION.	Total.¹	MALES 15 YEARS OF AGE AND OVER.						Di-vorced.
		Single.		Married.		Widowed.		
		Number.	Per cent.	Number.	Per cent.	Num-ber.	Per cent.	
EAST NORTH CENTRAL.								
Ohio.								
All classes ²	2,125,426	712,996	33.5	1,290,796	60.7	101,596	4.8	17,225
Native white—Native parentage	1,268,641	440,316	34.7	757,095	59.7	58,127	4.6	11,404
Native white—Foreign or mixed par.	397,260	146,946	37.0	229,927	57.9	17,123	4.3	2,949
Foreign-born white	378,869	96,344	25.4	258,117	68.1	21,974	5.8	1,822
Negro	79,550	28,759	36.2	45,216	56.8	4,347	5.5	1,043
Indiana.								
All classes ²	1,059,899	327,582	30.9	663,577	62.6	55,549	5.2	10,339
Native white—Native parentage	803,900	254,275	31.6	499,292	62.1	40,107	5.0	8,123
Native white—Foreign or mixed par.	137,136	42,303	30.8	86,707	63.2	6,750	4.9	1,150
Foreign-born white	85,873	20,057	23.4	58,536	68.2	6,363	7.4	533
Negro	32,583	10,730	32.9	18,878	57.9	2,314	7.1	530
Illinois.								
All classes ²	2,347,493	830,251	35.4	1,387,092	59.1	107,204	4.6	16,587
Native white—Native parentage	996,562	369,740	37.1	571,628	57.4	43,763	4.4	8,527
Native white—Foreign or mixed par.	634,072	282,943	44.6	326,692	51.5	19,204	3.0	3,879
Foreign-born white	638,304	150,113	23.5	443,998	69.6	39,065	6.1	3,256
Negro	75,490	25,741	34.1	43,552	57.7	5,091	6.7	918
Michigan.								
All classes ²	1,371,116	474,065	34.6	820,071	59.8	62,418	4.6	12,358
Native white—Native parentage	557,291	196,421	35.2	327,860	58.8	25,329	4.5	6,630
Native white—Foreign or mixed par.	384,411	164,553	42.8	204,809	53.3	11,664	3.0	2,979
Foreign-born white	397,779	100,966	25.4	269,723	67.8	24,034	6.0	2,378
Negro	28,742	10,787	37.5	16,350	56.9	1,197	4.2	350
Wisconsin.								
All classes ²	940,800	359,883	38.3	531,148	56.5	41,590	4.4	5,475
Native white—Native parentage	282,062	135,475	48.0	134,773	47.8	8,647	3.1	1,745
Native white—Foreign or mixed par.	400,149	169,761	42.4	216,568	54.1	11,109	2.8	2,073
Foreign-born white	252,820	52,457	20.7	176,718	69.9	21,461	8.5	1,562
Negro	2,395	952	39.7	1,258	52.5	126	5.3	46
WEST NORTH CENTRAL.								
Minnesota.								
All classes ²	868,738	365,880	42.1	460,829	53.0	35,687	4.1	4,134
Native white—Native parentage	224,526	104,553	46.6	110,741	49.3	6,913	3.1	1,393
Native white—Foreign or mixed par.	363,582	187,785	51.6	166,374	45.8	7,383	2.0	1,313
Foreign-born white	273,395	70,918	25.9	179,690	65.7	20,943	7.7	1,322
Negro	4,120	1,543	37.5	2,248	54.6	238	5.8	79
Iowa.								
All classes ²	865,407	303,626	35.1	512,060	59.2	40,763	4.7	6,944
Native white—Native parentage	486,568	179,795	37.0	280,521	57.7	20,471	4.2	4,434
Native white—Foreign or mixed par.	246,076	94,801	38.5	141,523	57.5	7,910	3.2	1,512
Foreign-born white	124,427	26,141	21.0	85,345	68.6	11,805	9.5	836
Negro	7,861	2,649	33.7	4,459	56.7	556	7.1	160
Missouri.								
All classes ²	1,216,243	400,977	33.4	733,960	60.3	62,703	5.2	9,895
Native white—Native parentage	845,074	292,126	34.6	503,955	59.6	39,871	4.7	6,659
Native white—Foreign or mixed par.	198,064	67,276	34.0	120,127	60.7	8,715	4.4	1,611
Foreign-born white	100,946	21,962	21.8	69,323	68.7	8,814	8.7	638
Negro	71,577	24,609	34.4	40,331	56.3	5,375	7.5	978
North Dakota.								
All classes ²	214,001	87,934	41.1	116,254	54.3	7,765	3.6	815
Native white—Native parentage	53,088	23,175	43.7	27,469	51.7	1,649	3.1	298
Native white—Foreign or mixed par.	85,283	45,542	53.4	37,535	44.0	1,599	1.9	208
Foreign-born white	73,266	18,406	25.1	49,901	68.1	4,364	6.0	289
Negro	224	109	48.7	88	39.3	16	7.1	5

¹ Total includes persons whose marital condition was not reported.

BY SEX, FOR PRINCIPAL POPULATION CLASSES, BY DIVISIONS AND STATES: 1920—Con.

DIVISION OR STATE AND CLASS OF POPULATION.	FEMALES 15 YEARS OF AGE AND OVER.							
	Total.[1]	Single.		Married.		Widowed.		Di-vorced
		Number.	Per cent.	Number.	Per cent.	Num-ber.	Per cent.	
EAST NORTH CENTRAL.								
Ohio.								
All classes [2]	1,990,701	507,550	25.5	1,241,451	62.4	221,755	11.1	18,466
Native white—Native parentage	1,230,756	337,908	27.5	756,513	61.5	122,797	10.0	12,560
Native white—Foreign or mixed par.	419,866	128,219	30.5	242,606	57.8	45,389	10.8	3,412
Foreign-born white	275,091	29,102	10.6	199,510	72.5	44,740	16.3	1,546
Negro	64,868	12,287	18.9	42,745	65.9	8,823	13.6	946
Indiana.								
All classes [2]	1,021,915	244,659	23.9	650,187	63.6	114,244	11.2	10,723
Native white—Native parentage	791,078	196,246	24.8	503,009	63.6	81,498	10.3	8,664
Native white—Foreign or mixed par.	141,097	37,206	26.4	86,285	61.2	16,213	11.5	1,203
Foreign-born white	60,281	5,714	9.5	42,614	70.7	11,526	19.1	286
Negro	29,404	5,477	18.6	18,254	62.1	4,995	17.0	568
Illinois.								
All classes [2]	2,242,120	617,873	27.6	1,353,118	60.3	247,985	11.1	19,275
Native white—Native parentage	972,936	292,277	30.0	573,176	58.9	95,809	9.8	9,844
Native white—Foreign or mixed par.	668,897	246,452	36.8	364,441	54.5	51,736	7.7	5,211
Foreign-born white	530,799	66,445	12.5	372,439	70.2	87,916	16.6	3,108
Negro	69,199	12,629	18.3	42,872	62.0	12,498	18.1	1,109
Michigan.								
All classes [2]	1,198,037	285,297	23.8	782,648	65.3	118,412	9.9	10,768
Native white—Native parentage	504,182	130,517	25.9	319,367	63.3	48,105	9.5	5,789
Native white—Foreign or mixed par.	374,805	120,550	32.2	226,386	60.4	24,725	6.6	2,894
Foreign-born white	297,216	30,798	10.4	221,204	74.4	43,181	14.5	1,806
Negro	20,115	3,056	15.2	14,622	72.7	2,144	10.7	265
Wisconsin.								
All classes [2]	869,060	261,200	30.1	517,771	59.6	82,642	9.5	5,858
Native white—Native parentage	271,133	111,233	41.0	139,993	51.6	17,177	6.3	1,929
Native white—Foreign or mixed par.	397,709	132,703	33.4	236,516	59.5	25,467	6.4	2,569
Foreign-born white	195,780	16,346	8.3	138,407	70.7	39,451	20.2	1,252
Negro	1,688	332	19.7	1,111	65.8	197	11.7	43
WEST NORTH CENTRAL.								
Minnesota.								
All classes [2]	774,433	248,592	32.1	450,785	58.2	68,945	8.9	4,843
Native white—Native parentage	208,083	82,353	39.6	109,161	52.5	14,557	7.0	1,588
Native white—Foreign or mixed par.	358,188	145,048	40.5	193,538	54.0	17,158	4.8	1,892
Foreign-born white	202,399	20,160	10.0	144,330	71.3	36,385	18.0	1,250
Negro	3,164	537	17.0	2,063	65.2	492	15.5	66
Iowa.								
All classes [2]	819,947	224,706	27.4	505,294	61.6	81,118	9.9	7,510
Native white—Native parentage	471,927	140,133	29.7	284,197	60.2	41,780	8.9	4,875
Native white—Foreign or mixed par.	245,281	75,019	30.6	151,068	61.6	17,097	7.0	1,884
Foreign-born white	96,021	8,363	8.7	65,639	68.4	21,290	22.2	581
Negro	6,549	1,162	17.7	4,279	65.3	923	14.1	169
Missouri.								
All classes [2]	1,186,407	308,051	26.0	724,886	61.1	139,774	11.8	11,639
Native white—Native parentage	828,313	223,770	27.0	511,735	61.8	83,346	10.1	8,012
Native white—Foreign or mixed par.	210,733	60,522	28.7	123,177	58.5	24,876	11.8	1,888
Foreign-born white	80,171	9,771	12.2	50,142	62.5	19,547	24.4	560
Negro	67,090	13,966	20.8	39,772	59.3	11,991	17.9	1,176
North Dakota.								
All classes [2]	181,450	54,685	30.1	113,843	62.7	11,618	6.4	735
Native white—Native parentage	46,781	16,182	34.6	27,726	59.3	2,423	5.2	261
Native white—Foreign or mixed par.	78,744	32,525	41.3	43,326	55.0	2,400	3.0	239
Foreign-born white	53,999	5,548	10.3	41,525	76.9	6,586	12.2	226
Negro	140	31	22.1	85	60.7	22	15.7	2

[2] Includes Indians, Chinese, Japanese, and "all other."

TABLE 55.—MARITAL CONDITION OF THE POPULATION 15 YEARS OF AGE AND OVER,

DIVISION OR STATE AND CLASS OF POPULATION.	Total.[1]	MALES 15 YEARS OF AGE AND OVER.						
		Single.		Married.		Widowed.		Di-vorced.
		Number.	Per cent.	Number.	Per cent.	Num-ber.	Per cent.	
WEST NORTH CENTRAL—Con.								
South Dakota.								
All classes [2]	224,873	89,284	39.7	123,995	55.1	9,000	4.0	1,272
Native white—Native parentage	90,071	37,715	41.9	47,859	53.1	3,157	3.5	630
Native white—Foreign or mixed par..	82,442	38,668	46.9	41,212	50.0	1,896	2.3	322
Foreign-born white	46,678	11,190	24.0	31,392	67.3	3,603	7.7	257
Negro	365	155	42.5	180	49.3	20	5.5	7
Nebraska.								
All classes [2]	461,298	169,428	36.7	267,199	57.9	19,715	4.3	3,231
Native white—Native parentage	234,558	89,731	38.3	132,633	56.5	9,188	3.9	1,913
Native white—Foreign or mixed par..	136,935	59,218	43.2	73,224	53.5	3,407	2.5	717
Foreign-born white	82,226	17,521	21.3	57,247	69.6	6,735	8.2	487
Negro	5,982	2,272	38.0	3,255	54.4	342	5.7	98
Kansas.								
All classes [2]	630,130	210,101	33.3	382,569	60.7	30,744	4.9	5,244
Native white—Native parentage	433,404	147,503	34.0	261,445	60.3	19,697	4.5	3,677
Native white—Foreign or mixed par..	113,178	42,378	37.4	66,066	58.4	3,854	3.4	723
Foreign-born white	60,142	12,305	20.5	41,739	69.4	5,532	9.2	413
Negro	22,409	7,300	32.6	12,990	58.0	1,622	7.2	425
SOUTH ATLANTIC.								
Delaware.								
All classes [2]	81,611	27,815	34.1	48,850	59.9	4,264	5.2	307
Native white—Native parentage	49,936	16,232	32.5	30,706	61.5	2,518	5.0	203
Native white—Foreign or mixed par..	9,229	4,144	44.9	4,681	50.7	354	3.8	43
Foreign-born white	11,038	3,084	27.9	7,296	66.1	623	5.6	20
Negro	11,359	4,318	38.0	6,157	54.2	768	6.8	41
Maryland.								
All classes [2]	512,513	184,547	36.0	297,995	58.1	26,771	5.2	2,440
Native white—Native parentage	302,244	111,585	36.9	174,318	57.7	14,374	4.8	1,516
Native white—Foreign or mixed par..	70,277	29,004	41.3	37,522	53.4	3,348	4.8	347
Foreign-born white	53,048	12,445	23.5	36,865	69.5	3,528	6.7	151
Negro	86,565	31,320	36.2	49,116	56.7	5,511	6.4	426
District of Columbia.								
All classes [2]	159,013	60,976	38.3	88,698	55.8	7,616	4.8	884
Native white—Native parentage	84,034	33,483	39.8	46,061	54.8	3,459	4.1	494
Native white—Foreign or mixed par..	20,697	8,942	43.2	10,750	51.9	866	4.2	114
Foreign-born white	14,741	4,854	32.9	8,823	59.9	897	6.1	64
Negro	38,916	13,354	34.3	22,801	58.6	2,387	6.1	208
Virginia.								
All classes [2]	751,890	275,096	36.6	437,986	58.3	34,381	4.6	2,940
Native white—Native parentage	496,665	181,627	36.6	292,051	58.8	20,483	4.1	1,645
Native white—Foreign or mixed par..	19,095	9,207	48.2	9,080	47.6	694	3.6	92
Foreign-born white	18,450	6,169	33.4	11,222	60.8	932	5.1	77
Negro	217,056	77,781	35.8	125,347	57.7	12,252	5.6	1,124
West Virginia.								
All classes [2]	487,684	172,948	35.5	291,096	59.7	19,674	4.0	2,401
Native white—Native parentage	391,183	135,576	34.7	236,873	60.6	15,743	4.0	1,929
Native white—Foreign or mixed par..	21,334	7,841	36.8	12,344	57.9	994	4.7	116
Foreign-born white	40,346	15,744	39.0	22,925	56.8	1,379	3.4	75
Negro	34,727	13,730	39.5	18,920	54.5	1,556	4.5	313
North Carolina.								
All classes [2]	756,631	257,881	34.1	463,809	61.3	31,539	4.2	1,322
Native white—Native parentage	530,510	180,779	34.1	326,878	61.6	20,709	3.9	817
Native white—Foreign or mixed par..	3,788	1,520	40.1	2,113	55.8	136	3.6	4
Foreign-born white	4,215	1,276	30.3	2,678	63.5	227	5.4	13
Negro	214,825	73,172	34.1	130,114	60.6	10,357	4.8	482

[1] Total includes persons whose marital condition was not reported.

BY SEX, FOR PRINCIPAL POPULATION CLASSES, BY DIVISIONS AND STATES: 1920—Con.

DIVISION OR STATE AND CLASS OF POPULATION.	Total.[1]	FEMALES 15 YEARS OF AGE AND OVER.						
		Single.		Married.		Widowed.		Di-vorced.
		Number.	Per cent.	Number.	Per cent.	Number.	Per cent.	
WEST NORTH CENTRAL—Con.								
South Dakota.								
All classes [2]	190,812	53,858	28.2	121,408	63.6	13,862	7.3	1,128
Native white—Native parentage	77,255	24,379	31.6	47,389	61.3	4,626	6.0	574
Native white—Foreign or mixed par.	74,327	25,371	34.1	45,430	61.1	3,056	4.1	314
Foreign-born white	33,893	3,033	8.9	25,052	73.9	5,535	16.3	184
Negro	235	52	22.1	146	62.1	33	14.0	3
Nebraska.								
All classes [2]	419,146	113,867	27.2	263,890	63.0	37,298	8.9	3,368
Native white—Native parentage	218,379	63,061	28.9	135,106	61.9	17,802	8.2	1,993
Native white—Foreign or mixed par.	131,694	44,462	33.8	79,330	60.2	6,876	5.2	842
Foreign-born white	63,452	5,433	8.6	45,623	71.9	11,886	18.7	397
Negro	4,628	719	15.5	3,125	67.5	663	14.3	116
Kansas.								
All classes [2]	587,284	146,614	25.0	375,790	64.0	58,857	10.0	5,504
Native white—Native parentage	413,226	106,514	25.8	264,082	63.9	38,283	9.3	3,967
Native white—Foreign or mixed par.	107,323	31,710	29.5	67,038	62.5	7,781	7.3	731
Foreign-born white	45,433	3,889	8.6	31,811	70.0	9,414	20.7	268
Negro	20,566	4,081	19.8	12,591	61.2	3,341	16.2	530
SOUTH ATLANTIC.								
Delaware.								
All classes [2]	77,105	19,962	25.9	47,469	61.6	9,094	11.8	358
Native white—Native parentage	48,933	12,693	25.9	30,292	61.9	5,529	11.3	255
Native white—Foreign or mixed par.	9,835	3,522	35.8	5,219	53.1	1,046	10.6	46
Foreign-born white	8,107	989	12.2	5,959	73.5	1,141	14.1	16
Negro	10,229	2,758	27.0	5,998	58.6	1,378	13.5	41
Maryland.								
All classes [2]	506,569	147,204	29.1	294,043	58.0	62,087	12.3	2,700
Native white—Native parentage	302,224	92,994	30.8	174,908	57.9	32,303	10.7	1,698
Native white—Foreign or mixed par.	75,008	25,862	34.5	39,635	52.8	9,097	12.1	374
Foreign-born white	46,054	6,572	14.3	30,757	66.8	8,546	18.6	154
Negro	83,250	21,767	26.1	48,723	58.5	12,138	14.6	474
District of Columbia.								
All classes [2]	188,466	70,330	37.3	88,602	47.0	27,761	14.7	1,381
Native white—Native parentage	103,450	43,236	41.8	46,059	44.5	13,094	12.7	832
Native white—Foreign or mixed par.	25,486	10,846	42.6	11,201	43.9	3,253	12.8	166
Foreign-born white	13,035	2,985	22.9	7,618	58.4	2,360	18.1	51
Negro	46,434	13,244	28.5	23,686	51.0	9,051	19.5	332
Virginia.								
All classes [2]	730,985	211,140	28.9	432,557	59.2	82,483	11.3	3,898
Native white—Native parentage	483,876	142,878	29.5	290,007	59.9	48,405	10.0	2,162
Native white—Foreign or mixed par.	15,898	5,402	34.0	8,650	54.4	1,757	11.1	72
Foreign-born white	11,138	1,419	12.7	8,201	73.6	1,469	13.2	31
Negro	219,836	61,380	27.9	125,550	57.1	30,828	14.0	1,631
West Virginia.								
All classes [2]	431,564	110,169	25.5	280,811	65.1	36,995	8.6	2,635
Native white—Native parentage	365,867	96,526	26.4	236,389	64.6	29,944	8.2	2,208
Native white—Foreign or mixed par.	20,964	6,501	31.0	11,960	57.1	2,370	11.3	110
Foreign-born white	18,409	1,641	8.9	14,801	80.4	1,891	10.3	44
Negro	26,313	5,500	20.9	17,652	67.1	2,789	10.6	273
North Carolina.								
All classes [2]	769,185	225,149	29.3	460,742	59.9	79,118	10.3	2,325
Native white—Native parentage	530,020	154,074	29.1	324,426	61.2	49,075	9.3	1,284
Native white—Foreign or mixed par.	3,820	1,331	34.8	2,040	53.4	431	11.3	12
Foreign-born white	2,622	492	18.8	1,734	66.1	376	14.3	6
Negro	229,671	68,505	29.8	130,537	56.8	28,963	12.6	1,009

[2] Includes Indians, Chinese, Japanese, and "all other."

TABLE 55.—MARITAL CONDITION OF THE POPULATION 15 YEARS OF AGE AND OVER,

DIVISION OR STATE AND CLASS OF POPULATION.	Total.[1]	MALES 15 YEARS OF AGE AND OVER.						Di-vorced.
		Single.		Married.		Widowed.		
		Number.	Per cent.	Number.	Per cent.	Num-ber.	Per cent.	
SOUTH ATLANTIC—Con.								
South Carolina.								
All classes [2]	492,228	168,536	34.2	300,701	61.1	21,413	4.4	597
Native white—Native parentage	245,109	87,531	35.7	147,070	60.0	9,930	4.1	224
Native white—Foreign or mixed par..	4,973	2,318	46.6	2,443	49.1	190	3.8	15
Foreign-born white	4,005	1,469	36.7	2,297	57.4	223	5.6	3
Negro	237,928	77,126	32.4	148,780	62.5	11,062	4.6	355
Georgia.								
All classes [2]	884,801	283,338	32.0	554,356	62.7	42,314	4.8	3,242
Native white—Native parentage	507,019	168,787	33.3	315,461	62.2	20,631	4.1	1,472
Native white—Foreign or mixed par..	11,275	4,667	41.4	6,077	53.9	462	4.1	60
Foreign-born white	9,750	3,085	31.6	5,996	61.5	602	6.2	44
Negro	356,516	106,681	29.9	226,716	63.6	20,604	5.8	1,665
Florida.								
All classes [2]	332,678	107,201	32.2	203,029	61.0	19,131	5.8	2,096
Native white—Native parentage	176,377	57,259	32.5	108,842	61.7	8,769	5.0	990
Nativ e white—Foreign or mixed par..	19,029	7,343	38.6	10,601	55.7	904	4.8	152
Foreign-born white	23,502	6,250	26.6	15,366	65.4	1,652	7.0	147
Negro	113,372	36,169	31.9	68,031	60.0	7,784	6.9	801
EAST SOUTH CENTRAL.								
Kentucky.								
All classes [2]	795,502	260,277	32.7	487,561	61.3	41,289	5.2	5,138
Native white—Native parentage	647,596	212,840	32.9	399,878	61.7	30,502	4.7	3,359
Native white—Foreign or mixed par..	45,091	14,834	32.9	27,536	61.1	2,319	5.1	359
Foreign-born white	17,201	4,061	23.6	11,208	65.2	1,802	10.5	102
Negro	85,538	28,509	33.3	48,898	57.2	6,664	7.8	1,318
Tennessee.								
All classes [2]	745,280	235,742	31.6	465,672	62.5	38,823	5.2	3,971
Native white—Native parentage	574,476	183,397	31.9	361,427	62.9	26,603	4.6	2,346
Native white—Foreign or mixed par..	14,346	4,930	34.4	8,588	59.9	733	5.1	84
Foreign-born white	8,771	1,951	22.2	5,990	68.3	764	8.7	46
Negro	147,594	45,423	30.8	89,625	60.7	10,714	7.3	1,495
Alabama.								
All classes [2]	710,229	226,392	31.9	444,168	62.5	34,420	4.8	3,486
Native white—Native parentage	420,614	138,013	32.8	263,870	62.7	16,737	4.0	1,321
Native white—Foreign or mixed par..	11,637	4,365	37.5	6,658	57.2	526	4.5	70
Foreign-born white	10,262	2,394	23.3	7,057	68.8	746	7.3	47
Negro	267,539	81,556	30.5	166,488	62.2	16,398	6.1	2,043
Mississippi.								
All classes [2]	548,321	171,768	31.3	344,614	62.8	27,769	5.1	2,665
Native white—Native parentage	254,113	87,180	34.3	155,192	61.1	10,368	4.1	585
Native white—Foreign or mixed par..	6,750	2,319	34.4	4,009	59.4	378	5.6	28
Foreign-born white	4,828	1,125	23.3	3,283	68.0	382	7.9	18
Negro	281,992	80,903	28.7	181,783	64.5	16,604	5.9	2,031
WEST SOUTH CENTRAL.								
Arkansas.								
All classes [2]	555,957	171,241	30.8	349,040	62.8	30,594	5.5	3,954
Native white—Native parentage	378,943	120,066	31.7	237,262	62.6	18,922	5.0	1,952
Native white—Foreign or mixed par..	15,876	5,640	35.5	9,269	58.4	810	5.1	128
Foreign-born white	8,433	2,047	24.3	5,516	65.4	788	9.3	56
Negro	152,569	43,422	28.5	96,929	63.5	10,069	6.6	1,818

[1] Total includes persons whose marital condition was not reported.

BY SEX, FOR PRINCIPAL POPULATION CLASSES, BY DIVISIONS AND STATES: 1920—Con.

DIVISION OR STATE AND CLASS OF POPULATION.	Total.[1]	FEMALES 15 YEARS OF AGE AND OVER.						Divorced.
		Single.		Married.		Widowed.		
		Number.	Per cent.	Number.	Per cent.	Number.	Per cent.	
SOUTH ATLANTIC—Con.								
South Carolina.								
All classes [2]	504,048	143,457	28.5	298,648	59.2	59,865	11.9	1,325
Native white—Native parentage	239,802	69,293	28.9	145,679	60.7	24,135	10.1	366
Native white—Foreign or mixed par.	4,435	1,514	34.1	2,255	50.8	645	14.5	18
Foreign-born white	2,214	319	14.4	1,468	66.3	419	18.9	3
Negro	257,502	72,308	28.1	149,187	57.9	34,653	13.5	938
Georgia.								
All classes [2]	900,117	225,856	25.1	551,522	61.3	115,829	12.9	5,926
Native white—Native parentage	503,594	133,336	26.5	313,576	62.3	53,941	10.7	2,296
Native white—Foreign or mixed par.	10,624	3,457	32.5	5,636	53.0	1,477	13.9	51
Foreign-born white	5,957	976	16.4	3,932	66.0	1,033	17.3	11
Negro	379,907	88,081	23.2	228,351	60.1	59,376	15.6	3,568
Florida.								
All classes [2]	312,798	69,294	22.2	199,842	63.9	40,565	13.0	2,562
Native white—Native parentage	167,654	38,773	23.1	108,464	64.7	19,119	11.4	1,048
Native white—Foreign or mixed par.	19,682	5,518	28.0	11,828	60.1	2,112	10.7	206
Foreign-born white	17,324	2,518	14.5	11,852	68.4	2,819	16.3	106
Negro	107,961	22,443	20.8	67,589	62.6	16,492	15.3	1,199
EAST SOUTH CENTRAL.								
Kentucky.								
All classes [2]	770,695	195,055	25.3	481,060	62.4	87,378	11.3	6,392
Native white—Native parentage	622,461	158,644	25.5	397,984	63.9	60,896	9.8	4,286
Native white—Foreign or mixed par.	51,076	15,661	30.7	27,570	54.0	7,401	14.5	414
Foreign-born white	13,031	1,671	12.8	7,148	54.9	4,123	31.6	70
Negro	84,104	19,073	22.7	48,345	57.5	14,955	17.8	1,621
Tennessee.								
All classes [2]	749,045	190,536	25.4	461,883	61.7	89,285	11.9	6,676
Native white—Native parentage	573,413	149,811	26.1	359,211	62.6	60,144	10.5	3,802
Native white—Foreign or mixed par.	14,967	4,479	29.9	8,213	54.9	2,161	14.4	105
Foreign-born white	6,233	821	13.2	3,996	64.1	1,379	22.1	30
Negro	154,408	35,418	22.9	90,448	58.6	25,599	16.6	2,739
Alabama.								
All classes [2]	720,780	182,268	25.3	440,207	61.1	90,369	12.5	6,649
Native white—Native parentage	413,801	107,431	26.0	262,307	63.4	41,570	10.0	1,942
Native white—Foreign or mixed par.	11,992	3,689	30.8	6,637	55.3	1,561	13.0	90
Foreign-born white	6,696	799	11.9	4,765	71.2	1,092	16.3	27
Negro	288,197	70,327	24.4	166,443	57.8	46,129	16.0	4,590
Mississippi.								
All classes [2]	554,325	138,410	25.0	342,029	61.7	67,665	12.2	5,197
Native white—Native parentage	249,321	68,552	27.5	154,705	62.1	24,746	9.9	925
Native white—Foreign or mixed par.	7,001	1,975	28.2	3,924	56.0	1,057	15.1	37
Foreign-born white	2,900	363	12.5	1,998	68.9	525	18.1	6
Negro	294,774	67,450	22.9	181,181	61.5	41,302	14.0	4,226
WEST SOUTH CENTRAL.								
Arkansas.								
All classes [2]	525,477	116,084	22.1	344,325	65.5	58,954	11.2	5,370
Native white—Native parentage	355,213	80,679	22.7	236,299	66.5	35,521	10.0	2,266
Native white—Foreign or mixed par.	13,615	3,592	26.4	8,419	61.8	1,472	10.8	103
Foreign-born white	5,207	668	12.8	3,461	66.5	1,025	19.7	41
Negro	151,400	31,135	20.6	96,121	63.5	20,931	13.8	2,958

[2] Includes Indians, Chinese, Japanese, and "all other."

TABLE 55.—MARITAL CONDITION OF THE POPULATION 15 YEARS OF AGE AND OVER,

DIVISION OR STATE AND CLASS OF POPULATION.	Total.[1]	MALES 15 YEARS OF AGE AND OVER.							
		Single.		Married.		Widowed.		Divorced
		Number.	Per cent.	Number.	Per cent.	Number.	Per cent.	
WEST SOUTH CENTRAL—Con.								
Louisiana.								
All classes [2]	575,500	201,248	35.0	342,062	59.4	27,170	4.7	2,519
Native white—Native parentage	291,492	110,679	38.0	167,042	57.3	11,320	3.9	912
Native white—Foreign or mixed par..	37,377	13,518	36.2	21,583	57.7	1,985	5.3	215
Foreign-born white	26,075	7,746	29.7	16,240	62.3	1,825	7.0	80
Negro	219,800	68,948	31.4	136,856	62.3	11,991	5.5	1,311
Oklahoma.								
All classes [2]	671,835	219,012	32.6	412,202	61.4	32,252	4.8	5,423
Native white—Native parentage	541,866	177,539	32.8	333,801	61.6	24,253	4.5	3,987
Native white—Foreign or mixed par..	40,426	13,988	34.6	24,178	59.8	1,777	4.4	389
Foreign-born white	23,978	6,457	26.9	15,316	63.9	1,704	7.1	200
Negro	49,426	15,383	31.1	29,557	59.8	3,561	7.2	712
Texas.								
All classes [2]	1,571,981	554,494	35.3	923,968	58.8	75,984	4.8	10,967
Native white—Native parentage	1,015,430	363,532	35.8	598,730	59.0	42,994	4.2	5,400
Native white—Foreign or mixed par..	140,009	59,279	42.3	74,929	53.5	4,763	3.4	790
Foreign-born white	172,564	53,864	31.2	104,750	60.7	12,326	7.1	707
Negro	242,289	77,065	31.8	144,708	59.7	15,832	6.5	4,063
MOUNTAIN.								
Montana.								
All classes [2]	209,491	84,007	40.1	113,159	54.0	8,590	4.1	2,324
Native white—Native parentage	93,001	35,440	38.1	51,745	55.6	3,642	3.9	1,138
Native white—Foreign or mixed par..	54,646	25,869	47.3	26,431	48.4	1,689	3.1	535
Foreign-born white	55,950	20,616	36.8	31,617	56.5	2,921	5.2	555
Negro	810	347	42.8	393	48.5	43	5.3	26
Idaho.								
All classes [2]	156,167	59,795	38.3	87,969	56.3	6,409	4.1	1,667
Native white—Native parentage	93,290	35,911	38.5	52,591	56.4	3,611	3.9	1,001
Native white—Foreign or mixed par..	35,729	13,855	38.8	20,313	56.9	1,174	3.3	354
Foreign-born white	24,167	8,853	36.6	13,433	55.6	1,490	6.2	289
Negro	500	235	47.0	226	45.2	31	6.2	6
Wyoming.								
All classes [2]	79,366	33,171	41.8	41,408	52.2	3,180	4.0	966
Native white—Native parentage	45,379	18,222	40.2	24,370	53.7	1,791	3.9	589
Native white—Foreign or mixed par..	15,198	6,811	44.8	7,628	50.2	508	3.3	216
Foreign-born white	16,379	6,987	42.7	8,295	50.6	795	4.9	129
Negro	762	371	48.7	328	43.0	37	4.9	23
Colorado.								
All classes [2]	350,813	123,473	35.2	200,800	57.2	17,592	5.0	4,378
Native white—Native parentage	211,929	73,778	34.8	120,913	57.1	10,163	4.8	2,876
Native white—Foreign or mixed par..	67,096	28,272	42.1	35,351	52.7	2,566	3.8	834
Foreign-born white	65,052	19,090	29.3	40,802	62.7	4,416	6.8	573
Negro	4,744	1,570	33.1	2,665	56.2	349	7.4	88
New Mexico								
All classes [2]	123,167	45,425	36.9	68,973	56.0	7,500	6.9	944
Native white—Native parentage	88,189	31,190	35.4	50,832	57.6	5,347	6.1	669
Native white—Foreign or mixed par..	9,484	3,911	41.2	4,945	52.1	522	5.5	96
Foreign-born white	14,684	4,741	32.3	8,783	59.8	1,016	6.9	92
Negro	4,324	3,188	73.7	974	22.5	108	2.5	52

[1] Total includes persons whose marital condition was not reported.

BY SEX, FOR PRINCIPAL POPULATION CLASSES, BY DIVISIONS AND STATES: 1920—Con.

DIVISION OR STATE AND CLASS OF POPULATION.	Total.[1]	FEMALES 15 YEARS OF AGE AND OVER.						
		Single.		Married.		Widowed.		Divorced.
		Number.	Per cent.	Number.	Per cent.	Number.	Per cent.	

WEST SOUTH CENTRAL—Con.

Louisiana.

All classes [2]	571,339	155,276	27.2	338,897	59.3	71,278	12.5	4,416
Native white—Native parentage	281,686	84,454	30.0	168,859	59.9	26,455	9.4	1,247
Native white—Foreign or mixed par.	42,676	12,893	30.2	21,660	50.8	7,799	18.3	250
Foreign-born white	17,351	2,519	14.5	10,740	61.9	3,984	23.0	49
Negro	229,290	55,308	24.1	137,442	59.9	33,003	14.4	2,869

Oklahoma.

All classes [2]	594,679	132,818	22.3	402,863	67.7	51,984	8.7	5,886
Native white—Native parentage	483,578	108,852	22.5	330,520	68.3	39,026	8.1	4,307
Native white—Foreign or mixed par.	34,914	8,672	24.8	23,104	66.2	2,768	7.9	327
Foreign-born white	14,171	1,221	8.6	10,626	75.0	2,189	15.4	103
Negro	46,426	10,246	22.1	29,013	62.5	6,096	13.1	945

Texas.

All classes [2]	1,439,534	361,939	25.1	902,689	62.7	157,022	10.9	15,564
Native white—Native parentage	934,369	241,559	25.9	595,758	63.8	88,765	9.5	6,697
Native white—Foreign or mixed par.	130,422	40,781	31.3	77,729	59.6	10,766	8.3	1,020
Foreign-born white	133,869	25,111	18.8	85,124	63.6	22,813	17.0	633
Negro	240,224	54,369	22.6	143,638	59.8	34,594	14.4	7,208

MOUNTAIN.

Montana.

All classes [2]	160,625	37,036	23.1	108,119	67.3	13,388	8.3	1,821
Native white—Native parentage	74,790	18,415	24.6	50,029	56.9	5,285	7.1	884
Native white—Foreign or mixed par.	48,657	14,670	30.1	30,508	62.7	2,931	6.0	502
Foreign-born white	33,201	3,293	9.9	24,805	74.7	4,712	14.2	357
Negro	551	86	15.6	347	63.0	100	18.1	18

Idaho.

All classes [2]	123,287	28,124	22.8	84,554	68.6	9,391	7.6	1,146
Native white—Native parentage	78,138	19,619	25.1	52,351	67.0	5,354	6.9	770
Native white—Foreign or mixed par.	30,105	7,179	23.8	20,948	69.6	1,729	5.7	237
Foreign-born white	13,444	1,122	8.3	10,092	75.1	2,100	15.6	122
Negro	266	35	13.2	189	71.1	35	13.2	7

Wyoming.

All classes [2]	54,169	11,120	20.5	38,172	70.5	4,089	7.5	660
Native white—Native parentage	33,008	7,258	22.0	23,042	69.8	2,221	6.7	414
Native white—Foreign or mixed par.	12,443	3,105	25.0	8,388	67.4	784	6.3	154
Foreign-born white	7,730	622	8.0	6,010	77.7	977	12.6	78
Negro	426	68	16.0	279	65.5	68	16.0	11

Colorado.

All classes [2]	307,458	73,098	23.8	195,193	63.5	34,186	11.1	4,058
Native white—Native parentage	189,444	46,366	24.5	120,254	63.5	19,306	10.2	2,697
Native white—Foreign or mixed par.	66,975	20,823	31.1	39,208	58.5	6,034	9.0	859
Foreign-born white	45,737	5,034	11.0	32,402	70.8	7,903	17.3	368
Negro	4,385	783	17.9	2,577	58.8	876	20.0	134

New Mexico.

All classes [2]	103,503	24,993	24.1	66,577	64.3	10,832	10.5	942
Native white—Native parentage	78,583	19,515	24.8	50,508	64.3	7,728	9.8	724
Native white—Foreign or mixed par.	8,490	2,482	29.2	5,127	60.4	781	9.2	89
Foreign-born white	10,115	1,450	14.3	7,055	69.7	1,528	15.1	58
Negro	885	117	13.2	648	73.2	104	11.8	11

[2] Includes Indians, Chinese, Japanese, and "all other."

238   ABSTRACT OF THE CENSUS—POPULATION.

Table 55.—MARITAL CONDITION OF THE POPULATION 15 YEARS OF AGE AND OVER,

DIVISION OR STATE AND CLASS OF POPULATION.	Total.[1]	MALES 15 YEARS OF AGE AND OVER.							
		Single.		Married.		Widowed.		Divorced.
		Number.	Per cent.	Number.	Per cent.	Number.	Per cent.	
Mountain—Con.								
Arizona.								
All classes [2]	127,117	51,329	40.4	67,735	53.3	6,182	4.9	1,166
Native white—Native parentage	55,598	21,802	39.2	30,217	54.3	2,505	4.5	666
Native white—Foreign or mixed par..	16,903	7,592	44.9	8,371	49.5	710	4.2	200
Foreign-born white	37,579	14,529	38.7	20,882	55.6	1,810	4.8	183
Negro	5,436	3,688	67.8	1,532	28.2	149	2.7	65
Utah.								
All classes [2]	146,262	53,294	36.4	86,397	59.1	5,078	3.5	1,246
Native white—Native parentage	61,418	26,627	43.4	32,489	52.9	1,662	2.7	525
Native white—Foreign or mixed par..	51,081	16,858	33.0	32,438	63.5	1,340	2.6	407
Foreign-born white	29,897	8,029	26.9	19,531	65.3	1,969	6.6	288
Negro	704	254	36.1	404	57.4	29	4.1	15
Nevada.								
All classes [2]	36,464	16,851	46.2	16,723	45.9	1,560	4.3	741
Native white—Native parentage	14,870	6,458	43.4	7,004	47.1	657	4.4	407
Native white—Foreign or mixed par..	8,035	3,738	46.5	3,773	47.0	312	3.9	182
Foreign-born white	10,516	5,507	52.4	4,330	41.2	435	4.1	122
Negro	177	71	40.1	89	50.3	10	5.6	2
Pacific.								
Washington.								
All classes [2]	546,019	212,021	38.8	298,950	54.8	23,915	4.4	8,602
Native white—Native parentage	256,979	92,597	36.0	146,956	57.2	11,063	4.3	4,562
Native white—Foreign or mixed par..	122,994	57,120	46.4	59,938	48.7	3,877	3.2	1,894
Foreign-born white	147,839	54,736	37.0	82,441	55.8	8,303	5.6	1,975
Negro	3,339	1,357	40.6	1,623	48.6	218	6.5	103
Oregon.								
All classes [2]	308,126	112,181	36.4	175,423	56.9	14,474	4.7	5,633
Native white—Native parentage	178,671	62,377	34.9	104,035	58.2	8,451	4.7	3,555
Native white—Foreign or mixed par..	61,479	25,872	42.1	32,476	52.8	2,014	3.3	1,073
Foreign-born white	60,507	20,639	34.1	35,093	58.0	3,738	6.2	944
Negro	1,011	393	38.9	534	52.8	50	4.9	27
California.								
All classes [2]	1,400,972	535,419	38.2	765,451	54.6	67,626	4.8	21,568
Native white—Native parentage	625,970	228,008	36.4	350,871	56.1	30,149	4.8	11,397
Native white—Foreign or mixed par..	307,806	136,196	44.2	154,219	50.1	11,445	3.7	5,314
Foreign-born white	384,047	137,166	35.7	215,911	56.2	22,797	5.9	4,345
Negro	15,923	5,670	35.6	8,875	55.7	946	5.9	335

[1] Total includes persons whose marital condition was not reported.

BY SEX, FOR PRINCIPAL POPULATION CLASSES, BY DIVISIONS AND STATES: 1920—Con.

DIVISION OR STATE AND CLASS OF POPULATION.	FEMALES 15 YEARS OF AGE AND OVER.							
	Total.[1]	Single.		Married.		Widowed.		Di-vorced.
		Number.	Per cent.	Number.	Per cent.	Num-ber.	Per cent.	
MOUNTAIN—Con.								
Arizona.								
All classes [2]	95,671	20,170	21.1	63,685	66.6	10,808	11.3	852
Native white—Native parentage	42,940	9,805	22.8	28,758	67.0	3,820	8.9	486
Native white—Foreign or mixed par.	14,826	3,943	26.6	9,465	63.8	1,229	8.3	167
Foreign-born white	26,741	4,395	16.4	18,030	67.4	4,158	15.5	115
Negro	1,670	218	13.1	1,160	69.5	253	15.1	38
Utah.								
All classes [2]	133,642	35,127	26.3	83,713	62.6	13,168	9.9	1,531
Native white—Native parentage	57,940	20,246	34.9	33,200	57.3	3,797	6.6	657
Native white—Foreign or mixed par.	49,329	12,257	24.8	32,970	66.8	3,494	7.1	583
Foreign-born white	24,588	2,233	9.1	16,293	66.3	5,752	23.4	273
Negro	492	51	10.4	368	74.8	60	12.2	13
Nevada.								
All classes [2]	21,731	4,196	19.3	14,463	66.6	2,415	11.1	500
Native white—Native parentage	9,942	2,250	22.6	6,425	64.6	900	9.1	270
Native white—Foreign or mixed par.	6,024	1,294	21.5	4,006	66.5	544	9.0	157
Foreign-born white	3,850	275	7.1	2,834	73.6	686	17.8	46
Negro	124	25	20.2	77	62.1	17	13.7	4
PACIFIC.								
Washington.								
All classes [2]	438,357	100,343	22.9	287,871	65.7	41,889	9.6	7,816
Native white—Native parentage	222,195	52,529	23.6	144,170	64.9	20,905	9.4	4,327
Native white—Foreign or mixed par.	115,212	36,171	31.4	69,321	60.2	7,658	6.6	1,987
Foreign-born white	91,740	10,519	11.5	67,306	73.4	12,461	13.6	1,370
Negro	2,331	339	14.5	1,545	66.3	357	15.3	81
Oregon.								
All classes [2]	261,847	60,142	23.0	170,069	64.9	26,514	10.1	4,988
Native white—Native parentage	161,130	37,160	23.1	104,569	64.9	15,972	9.9	3,340
Native white—Foreign or mixed par.	59,315	17,826	30.1	36,061	60.8	4,373	7.4	1,041
Foreign-born white	38,021	4,486	11.8	27,190	71.5	5,763	15.2	559
Negro	753	112	14.9	511	67.9	99	13.1	30
California.								
All classes [2]	1,210,607	289,196	23.9	733,632	60.6	162,871	13.5	23,105
Native white—Native parentage	589,382	148,515	25.2	348,575	59.1	78,301	13.3	13,050
Native white—Foreign or mixed par.	318,668	97,186	30.5	181,914	57.1	32,992	10.4	6,228
Foreign-born white	262,676	37,785	14.4	173,866	66.2	47,301	18.0	3,288
Negro	14,805	2,731	18.4	8,760	59.2	2,854	19.3	433

[2] Includes Indians, Chinese, Japanese, and "all other."

TABLE 56.—MARITAL CONDITION OF THE POPULATION 15 YEARS OF AGE AND
INHABITANTS

CITY AND CLASS OF POPULATION.	MALES 15 YEARS OF AGE AND OVER.							
	Total.[1]	Single.		Married.		Widowed.		Di-vorced.
		Number.	Per cent.	Number.	Per cent.	Number.	Per cent.	
Akron, Ohio.								
All classes [2]	96,896	43,839	45.2	49,237	50.8	2,790	2.9	924
Native white—Native parentage	57,897	28,340	48.9	27,347	47.2	1,503	2.6	643
Native white—Foreign or mixed par.	12,062	5,392	44.7	6,180	51.2	352	2.9	128
Foreign-born white	23,694	8,535	36.0	14,178	59.8	822	3.5	129
Negro	3,111	1,496	48.1	1,479	47.5	110	3.5	24
Albany, N. Y.								
All classes [2]	41,837	16,205	38.7	23,036	55.1	2,381	5.7	159
Native white—Native parentage	19,438	8,253	42.5	10,216	52.6	851	4.4	90
Native white—Foreign or mixed par.	13,098	5,564	42.5	6,746	51.5	736	5.6	37
Foreign-born white	8,714	2,141	24.6	5,787	66.4	757	8.7	17
Negro	528	211	40.0	265	50.2	36	6.8	15
Atlanta, Ga.								
All classes [2]	70,780	23,090	32.6	43,670	61.7	3,667	5.2	302
Native white—Native parentage	43,894	14,994	34.2	26,820	61.1	1,827	4.2	225
Native white—Foreign or mixed par.	2,535	974	38.4	1,458	57.5	88	3.5	12
Foreign-born white	2,610	654	25.1	1,798	68.9	141	5.4	12
Negro	21,715	6,450	29.7	13,587	62.6	1,610	7.4	53
Baltimore, Md.								
All classes [2]	263,826	93,869	35.6	154,589	58.6	13,695	5.2	1,551
Native white—Native parentage	127,296	48,027	37.7	72,405	56.9	5,939	4.7	867
Native white—Foreign or mixed par.	51,931	21,668	41.7	27,536	53.0	2,420	4.7	286
Foreign-born white	42,748	9,592	22.4	30,320	70.9	2,696	6.3	122
Negro	41,516	14,412	34.7	24,174	58.2	2,631	6.3	276
Birmingham, Ala.								
All classes [2]	63,975	20,760	32.5	39,373	61.5	3,221	5.0	531
Native white—Native parentage	32,385	11,235	34.7	19,687	60.8	1,226	3.8	207
Native white—Foreign or mixed par.	2,927	1,327	45.3	1,493	51.0	82	2.8	22
Foreign-born white	3,379	821	24.3	2,348	69.5	188	5.6	14
Negro	25,262	7,371	29.2	15,831	62.7	1,723	6.8	288
Boston, Mass.								
All classes [2]	269,269	111,245	41.3	142,521	52.9	13,085	4.9	1,358
Native white—Native parentage	62,015	26,679	43.0	30,720	49.5	3,307	5.3	591
Native white—Foreign or mixed par.	85,302	50,000	58.6	32,041	37.6	2,857	3.3	314
Foreign-born white	114,209	31,488	27.6	75,587	66.2	6,557	5.7	390
Negro	6,771	2,665	39.4	3,625	53.5	354	5.2	63
Bridgeport, Conn.								
All classes [2]	52,131	18,539	35.6	31,280	60.0	1,921	3.7	193
Native white—Native parentage	13,227	5,077	38.4	7,409	56.0	574	4.3	85
Native white—Foreign or mixed par.	13,359	7,041	52.7	5,856	43.8	358	2.7	53
Foreign-born white	24,436	5,973	24.4	17,407	71.2	944	3.9	51
Negro	1,009	395	39.1	562	55.7	44	4.4	4
Buffalo, N. Y.								
All classes [2]	182,359	65,935	36.2	107,583	59.0	7,816	4.3	569
Native white—Native parentage	52,015	21,978	41.5	28,764	54.3	1,825	3.4	226
Native white—Foreign or mixed par.	64,647	29,560	45.7	32,632	50.5	2,115	2.7	186
Foreign-born white	62,490	13,455	21.5	44,503	72.0	2,780	6.1	144
Negro	2,132	879	41.2	1,145	53.7	82	3.8	11
Cambridge, Mass.								
All classes [2]	37,510	14,735	39.3	20,836	55.5	1,817	4.8	96
Native white—Native parentage	9,231	3,752	40.6	4,943	53.5	482	5.2	45
Native white—Foreign or mixed par.	11,763	6,777	57.6	4,605	39.1	348	3.0	24
Foreign-born white	14,654	3,586	24.5	10,134	69.2	901	6.1	25
Negro	1,775	572	32.2	1,115	62.8	86	4.8	2

[1] Total includes persons whose marital condition was not reported.

OVER, BY SEX, FOR PRINCIPAL POPULATION CLASSES, FOR CITIES HAVING 100,000 OR MORE: 1920.

CITY AND CLASS OF POPULATION.	Total.[1]	FEMALES 15 YEARS OF AGE AND OVER.						Divorced.
		Single.		Married.		Widowed.		
		Number.	Per cent.	Number.	Per cent.	Number.	Per cent.	
Akron, Ohio.								
All classes [2]	62,699	13,946	22.2	42,734	68.2	5,284	8.4	705
Native white—Native parentage	37,735	9,327	24.7	24,975	66.2	2,922	7.7	491
Native white—Foreign or mixed par.	10,972	3,120	28.4	6,771	61.7	955	8.7	121
Foreign-born white	12,374	1,245	10.1	9,788	79.1	1,267	10.2	70
Negro	1,616	254	15.7	1,199	74.2	140	8.7	23
Albany, N. Y.								
All classes [2]	46,117	16,839	36.5	22,530	48.9	6,514	14.1	178
Native white—Native parentage	21,462	8,871	41.3	9,983	46.5	2,481	11.6	102
Native white—Foreign or mixed par.	15,782	6,340	40.2	7,286	46.2	2,083	13.2	53
Foreign-born white	8,386	1,494	17.8	5,007	59.7	1,853	22.1	21
Negro	485	134	27.6	252	52.0	97	20.0	2
Atlanta, Ga.								
All classes [2]	78,161	19,390	24.8	44,425	56.8	13,760	17.6	551
Native white—Native parentage	47,157	12,831	27.2	27,149	57.6	6,765	14.3	392
Native white—Foreign or mixed par.	2,977	961	32.3	1,615	54.2	383	12.9	16
Foreign-born white	1,957	300	15.3	1,328	67.9	323	16.5	5
Negro	26,067	5,296	20.3	14,333	55.0	6,288	24.1	138
Baltimore, Md.								
All classes [2]	274,258	82,603	30.1	152,688	55.7	37,035	13.5	1,854
Native white—Native parentage	134,620	45,021	33.4	73,045	54.3	15,458	11.5	1,066
Native white—Foreign or mixed par.	58,068	20,866	35.9	29,725	51.2	7,148	12.3	315
Foreign-born white	38,647	5,605	14.5	25,690	66.5	7,204	18.6	136
Negro	42,900	11,105	25.9	24,213	56.4	7,224	16.8	337
Birmingham, Ala.								
All classes [2]	64,178	14,670	22.9	39,049	60.8	9,421	14.7	971
Native white—Native parentage	32,134	8,357	26.0	19,583	60.9	3,849	12.0	325
Native white—Foreign or mixed par.	3,107	1,089	35.0	1,670	53.7	315	10.1	29
Foreign-born white	2,452	288	11.7	1,776	72.4	369	15.0	13
Negro	26,483	4,935	18.6	16,020	60.5	4,887	18.5	604
Boston, Mass.								
All classes [2]	280,922	105,906	37.7	137,853	49.1	35,055	12.5	1,694
Native white—Native parentage	64,592	28,031	43.4	26,840	41.6	8,762	13.6	751
Native white—Foreign or mixed par.	92,201	49,862	54.1	34,927	37.9	6,939	7.5	417
Foreign-born white	117,526	26,310	22.4	72,526	61.7	18,090	15.4	471
Negro	6,507	1,679	25.8	3,496	53.7	1,257	19.3	54
Bridgeport, Conn.								
All classes [2]	48,443	13,452	27.8	29,741	61.4	4,915	10.1	238
Native white—Native parentage	12,649	4,102	32.4	6,958	55.0	1,438	11.4	120
Native white—Foreign or mixed par.	14,685	6,705	45.7	6,936	47.2	958	6.5	51
Foreign-born white	20,324	2,503	12.3	15,332	75.4	2,402	11.8	58
Negro	783	142	18.1	514	65.6	116	14.8	9
Buffalo, N. Y.								
All classes [2]	182,246	56,519	31.0	104,353	57.3	20,395	11.2	703
Native white—Native parentage	53,744	20,493	38.1	28,323	52.7	4,535	8.4	307
Native white—Foreign or mixed par.	72,307	28,208	39.0	37,223	51.5	6,542	9.0	240
Foreign-born white	54,519	7,504	13.8	37,678	69.1	9,106	16.7	139
Negro	1,636	300	18.3	1,105	67.5	210	12.8	17
Cambridge, Mass								
All classes [2]	42,473	16,258	38.3	20,658	48.6	5,308	12.5	215
Native white—Native parentage	11,196	4,925	44.0	4,606	41.1	1,561	13.9	94
Native white—Foreign or mixed par.	12,897	7,125	55.2	4,782	37.1	915	7.1	58
Foreign-born white	16,283	3,608	22.2	10,123	62.2	2,497	15.3	45
Negro	2,089	596	28.5	1,139	54.5	333	15.9	18

[2] Includes Indians, Chinese, Japanese, and "all other."

TABLE 56.—MARITAL CONDITION OF THE POPULATION 15 YEARS OF AGE AND INHABITANTS OR

CITY AND CLASS OF POPULATION.	Total.[1]	MALES 15 YEARS OF AGE AND OVER.						
		Single.		Married.		Widowed.		Di-vorced.
		Number.	Per cent.	Number.	Per cent.	Number.	Per cent.	
Camden, N. J.								
All classes [2]	41,826	13,465	32.2	26,070	62.3	2,110	5.0	121
Native white—Native parentage	19,548	6,429	32.9	11,986	61.3	1,026	5.2	81
Native white—Foreign or mixed par..	8,353	3,622	43.4	4,378	52.4	328	3.9	22
Foreign-born white	10,668	2,392	22.4	7,715	72.3	531	5.0	12
Negro	3,206	999	31.2	1,965	61.3	223	7.0	6
Chicago, Ill.								
All classes [2]	991,179	362,178	36.5	578,949	58.4	40,023	4.0	6,609
Native white—Native parentage	204,635	83,009	40.6	110,751	54.1	7,505	3.7	2,177
Native white—Foreign or mixed par..	317,969	162,186	51.0	145,481	45.8	7,507	2.4	1,936
Foreign-born white	419,005	99,374	23.7	294,380	70.3	22,000	5.3	2,036
Negro	46,977	16,166	34.4	27,284	58.1	2,949	6.3	454
Cincinnati, Ohio.								
All classes [2]	147,890	53,414	36.1	85,551	57.8	7,652	5.2	1,111
Native white—Native parentage	67,276	27,922	41.5	36,217	53.8	2,526	3.8	546
Native white—Foreign or mixed par..	47,056	17,351	36.9	27,037	57.5	2,280	4.8	353
Foreign-born white	21,339	4,179	19.6	14,890	69.8	2,135	10.0	95
Negro	12,170	3,940	32.4	7,384	60.7	709	5.8	115
Cleveland, Ohio.								
All classes [2]	295,411	103,595	35.1	178,661	60.5	10,657	3.6	2,097
Native white—Native parentage	72,312	27,778	38.4	41,200	57.0	2,449	3.4	771
Native white—Foreign or mixed par..	78,818	38,710	49.1	37,589	47.7	1,881	2.4	550
Foreign-born white	128,440	31,414	24.5	90,540	70.5	5,699	4.4	626
Negro	15,527	5,526	35.6	9,194	59.2	622	4.0	147
Columbus, Ohio.								
All classes [2]	91,110	31,670	34.8	53,970	59.2	4,109	4.5	1,212
Native white—Native parentage	57,708	20,452	35.4	34,048	59.0	2,296	4.0	815
Native white—Foreign or mixed par..	14,948	5,373	35.9	8,686	58.1	707	4.7	174
Foreign-born white	8,826	2,451	27.8	5,686	64.4	609	6.9	67
Negro	9,519	3,337	35.1	5,503	57.8	493	5.2	156
Dallas, Tex.								
All classes [2]	60,629	21,006	34.6	35,500	58.6	3,206	5.3	834
Native white—Native parentage	41,423	14,710	35.5	24,314	58.7	1,889	4.6	480
Native white—Foreign or mixed par..	4,872	1,915	39.3	2,729	56.0	165	3.4	56
Foreign-born white	4,774	1,441	30.2	2,974	62.3	280	5.9	45
Negro	9,514	2,918	30.7	5,460	57.4	871	9.2	253
Dayton, Ohio.								
All classes [2]	57,906	18,392	31.8	35,939	62.1	2,663	4.6	821
Native white—Native parentage	36,385	12,172	33.5	22,141	60.9	1,453	4.0	549
Native white—Foreign or mixed par..	10,461	3,309	31.6	6,560	62.7	478	4.6	108
Foreign-born white	7,168	1,594	22.2	4,983	69.5	514	7.2	65
Negro	3,865	1,302	33.7	2,245	58.1	217	5.6	98
Denver, Colo.								
All classes [2]	104,850	37,498	35.8	55,768	53.2	5,749	5.5	1,884
Native white—Native parentage	57,708	20,349	35.2	29,291	50.7	3,037	5.3	1,250
Native white—Foreign or mixed par..	22,570	?	42.?	12,207	51.8	915	?	?91
Foreign-born white	20,384	5,911	29.0	12,625	61.9	1,601	7.5	221
Negro	2,599	882	33.9	1,432	55.1	174	6.7	49
Des Moines, Iowa.								
All classes [2]	46,487	14,810	31.9	28,543	61.4	2,149	4.6	847
Native white—Native parentage	29,240	9,347	32.0	17,975	61.5	1,269	4.3	560
Native white—Foreign or mixed par..	9,010	3,334	37.0	5,204	57.8	300	3.3	144
Foreign-born white	6,020	1,430	23.8	4,047	67.2	443	7.4	84
Negro	2,154	660	30.6	1,294	60.1	137	6.4	58

[1] Total includes persons whose marital condition was not reported.

OVER, BY SEX, FOR PRINCIPAL POPULATION CLASSES, FOR CITIES HAVING 100,000
MORE: 1920—Continued.

CITY AND CLASS OF POPULATION.	FEMALES 15 YEARS OF AGE AND OVER.							
	Total.[1]	Single.		Married.		Widowed.		Di-vorced.
		Number.	Per cent.	Number.	Per cent.	Number.	Per cent.	
Camden, N. J.								
All classes [2]	39,535	9,614	24.3	25,128	63.6	4,621	11.7	148
Native white—Native parenatge	19,079	5,081	26.6	11,623	60.9	2,271	11.9	96
Native white—Foreign or mixed par.	8,649	2,989	34.6	4,865	56.2	768	8.9	26
Foreign-born white	8,774	910	10.4	6,737	76.8	1,102	12.6	17
Negro	3,031	633	20.9	1,902	62.8	480	15.8	9
Chicago, Ill.								
All classes [2]	956,800	274,924	28.7	560,645	58.6	110,299	11.5	8,938
Native white—Native parentage	202,805	71,470	35.2	106,190	52.4	21,536	10.6	2,972
Native white—Foreign or mixed par.	348,904	146,955	42.1	173,778	49.8	24,434	7.0	3,034
Foreign-born white	361,027	48,732	13.5	253,443	70.2	56,012	15.5	2,252
Negro	43,855	7,719	17.6	27,084	61.8	8,306	18.9	680
Cincinnati, Ohio.								
All classes [2]	160,893	50,874	31.6	84,733	52.7	23,772	14.8	1,442
Native white—Native parentage	71,744	26,307	36.7	37,532	52.3	7,108	9.9	762
Native white—Foreign or mixed par.	56,813	19,237	33.9	28,511	50.2	8,622	15.2	422
Foreign-born white	20,564	3,032	14.7	11,294	54.9	6,120	29.8	108
Negro	11,757	2,293	19.5	7,388	62.8	1,920	16.3	150
Cleveland, Ohio.								
All classes [2]	266,322	68,142	25.6	168,144	63.1	27,421	10.3	2,433
Native white—Native parentage	69,181	22,214	32.1	39,398	56.9	6,563	9.5	955
Native white—Foreign or mixed par.	82,899	32,383	39.1	44,073	53.2	5,689	6.9	693
Foreign-born white	101,803	11,520	11.3	75,960	74.6	13,630	13.4	637
Negro	12,413	2,017	16.2	8,696	70.1	1,539	12.4	147
Columbus, Ohio.								
All classes [2]	90,919	25,537	28.1	52,357	57.6	11,372	12.5	1,611
Native white—Native parentage	59,511	17,890	30.1	33,896	57.0	6,540	11.0	1,158
Native white—Foreign or mixed par.	16,680	5,099	30.6	9,068	54.4	2,278	13.7	230
Foreign-born white	6,717	986	14.7	4,220	62.8	1,453	21.6	55
Negro	8,002	1,559	19.5	5,167	64.6	1,101	13.8	168
Dallas, Tex.								
All classes [2]	60,572	15,341	25.3	35,146	58.0	8,710	14.4	1,346
Native white—Native parentage	42,579	11,759	27.6	24,354	57.2	5,641	13.2	810
Native white—Foreign or mixed par.	5,074	1,518	29.9	2,902	57.2	582	11.5	71
Foreign-born white	3,310	541	16.3	2,202	66.5	536	16.2	26
Negro	9,597	1,520	15.8	5,679	59.2	1,951	20.3	439
Dayton, Ohio.								
All classes [2]	56,493	13,930	24.7	34,904	61.8	6,794	12.0	830
Native white—Native parentage	35,848	9,443	26.3	22,044	61.5	3,755	10.5	583
Native white—Foreign or mixed par.	11,891	3,381	28.4	6,844	57.6	1,529	12.9	129
Foreign-born white	5,495	567	10.3	3,825	69.6	1,062	19.3	39
Negro	3,250	534	16.4	2,187	67.3	448	13.8	79
Denver, Colo.								
All classes [2]	97,101	25,586	26.3	54,996	56.6	13,791	14.2	2,039
Native white—Native parentage	51,640	13,939	27.0	28,920	56.0	6,865	13.3	1,264
Native white—Foreign or mixed par.	26,659	9,023	33.8	14,201	53.3	2,942	11.0	475
Foreign-born white	16,221	2,188	13.5	10,366	63.9	3,456	21.3	207
Negro	2,477	422	17.0	1,428	57.7	525	21.2	93
Des Moines, Iowa.								
All classes [2]	48,449	13,699	28.3	28,263	58.3	5,301	10.9	1,074
Native white—Native parentage	31,138	9,047	29.1	18,017	57.9	3,245	10.4	755
Native white—Foreign or mixed par.	10,383	3,585	34.5	5,704	54.9	899	8.7	177
Foreign-born white	4,856	693	14.3	3,205	66.0	872	18.0	71
Negro	2,068	373	18.0	1,336	64.6	284	13.7	70

[2]Includes Indians, Chinese, Japanese, and "all other."

TABLE 56.—MARITAL CONDITION OF THE POPULATION 15 YEARS OF AGE AND
INHABITANTS OR

CITY AND CLASS OF POPULATION.	Total.[1]	MALES 15 YEARS OF AGE AND OVER.							Di-vorced.
		Single.		Married.		Widowed.			
		Number.	Per cent.	Number.	Per cent.	Number.	Per cent.		
Detroit, Mich.									
All classes [2]	404,761	158,372	39.1	228,912	56.6	13,534	3.3		3,506
Native white—Native parentage	120,241	50,355	41.9	64,533	53.7	3,730	3.1		1,471
Native white—Foreign or mixed par..	102,277	48,636	47.6	50,186	49.1	2,517	2.5		868
Foreign-born white	161,229	51,208	31.8	102,323	63.5	6,553	4.1		957
Negro	20,397	7,804	38.3	11,637	57.1	727	3.6		204
Fall River, Mass.									
All classes [2]	38,430	13,932	36.3	22,352	58.2	2,024	5.3		104
Native white—Native parentage	4,887	2,058	42.1	2,544	52.1	264	5.4		21
Native white—Foreign or mixed par..	13,888	7,941	57.2	5,522	39.8	383	2.8		39
Foreign-born white	19,497	3,877	19.9	14,192	72.8	1,369	7.0		44
Negro	108	33	30.6	67	62.0	8	7.4		....
Fort Worth, Tex.									
All classes [2]	43,869	16,364	37.3	24,651	56.2	2,106	4.8		537
Native white—Native parentage	30,123	11,115	36.9	17,132	56.9	1,357	4.5		369
Native white—Foreign or mixed par..	2,888	1,185	41.0	1,526	52.8	130	4.5		32
Foreign-born white	4,307	1,844	42.8	2,161	50.2	267	6.2		20
Negro	6,447	2,167	33.6	3,789	58.8	.344	5.3		116
Grand Rapids, Mich.									
All classes [2]	48,657	15,194	31.2	30,580	62.8	2,273	4.7		565
Native white—Native parentage	17,994	5,610	31.2	11,249	62.5	811	4.5		303
Native white—Foreign or mixed par..	15,632	6,708	42.9	8,374	53.6	391	2.5		148
Foreign-born white	14,533	2,688	18.5	10,677	73.5	1,050	7.2		105
Negro	446	149	33.4	270	60.5	19	4.3		8
Hartford, Conn.									
All classes [2]	50,418	19,010	37.7	29,145	57.8	2,051	4.1		185
Native white—Native parentage	14,479	5,586	38.6	8,139	56.2	647	4.5		97
Native white—Foreign or mixed par..	13,440	7,307	54.4	5,725	42.6	363	2.7		37
Foreign-born white	20,746	5,486	26.4	14,256	68.7	957	4.6		38
Negro	1,618	557	34.4	967	59.8	82	5.1		12
Houston, Tex.									
All classes [2]	51,962	17,216	33.1	31,174	60.0	2,618	5.0		893
Native white—Native parentage	25,892	9,247	35.7	15,287	59.0	1,006	3.9		323
Native white—Foreign or mixed par..	6,828	2,616	38.3	3,873	56.7	257	3.8		77
Foreign-born white	6,295	1,599	25.4	4,220	67.0	423	6.7		48
Negro	12,918	3,741	29.0	7,783	60.2	931	7.2		443
Indianapolis, Ind.									
All classes [2]	119,176	35,814	30.0	74,730	62.7	6,204	5.2		1,555
Native white—Native parentage	79,885	24,676	30.9	49,750	62.3	3,687	4.6		1,093
Native white—Foreign or mixed par..	16,430	5,214	31.7	10,213	62.2	787	4.8		187
Foreign-born white	9,149	1,817	19.9	6,435	70.3	754	8.2		76
Negro	13,615	4,048	29.7	8,299	61.0	974	7.2		198
Jersey City, N. J.									
All classes [2]	104,710	39,446	37.7	60,368	57.7	4,604	4.4		159
Native white—Native parentage	26,903	12,115	45.0	13,668	50.8	1,036	3.9		58
Native white—Foreign or mixed par..	35,461	18,021	50.8	16,143	45.5	1,197	3.4		48
Foreign-born white	39,121	8,203	21.0	28,601	73.1	2,216	5.7		44
Negro	3,139	1,051	33.5	1,923	61.3	153	4.9		9
Kansas City, Kans.									
All classes [2]	37,376	11,624	31.1	23,371	62.5	1,797	4.8		549
Native white—Native parentage	19,725	6,116	31.0	12,378	62.8	901	4.6		312
Native white—Foreign or mixed par..	5,705	2,281	40.0	3,178	55.7	190	3.3		55
Foreign-born white	6,465	1,743	27.0	4,318	66.8	354	5.5		43
Negro	5,431	1,447	26.6	3,484	64.2	352	6.5		139

[1] Total includes persons whose marital condition was not reported.

OVER, BY SEX, FOR PRINCIPAL POPULATION CLASSES, FOR CITIES HAVING 100,000 MORE: 1920—Continued.

CITY AND CLASS OF POPULATION.	Total.[1]	FEMALES 15 YEARS OF AGE AND OVER.						Divorced.
		Single.		Married.		Widowed.		
		Number.	Per cent.	Number.	Per cent.	Number.	Per cent.	
Detroit, Mich.								
All classes [2]	319,853	78,746	24.6	209,219	65.4	28,489	8.9	3,188
Native white—Native parentage	94,055	26,786	28.5	58,703	62.4	7,193	7.6	1,305
Native white—Foreign or mixed par.	99,380	34,498	34.7	57,453	57.8	6,463	6.5	915
Foreign-born white	112,463	15,433	13.7	82,713	73.5	13,444	12.0	797
Negro	13,865	2,004	14.5	10,294	74.2	1,381	10.0	170
Fall River, Mass.								
All classes [2]	43,002	15,885	36.9	22,376	52.0	4,579	10.6	144
Native white—Native parentage	5,670	2,592	45.7	2,403	42.4	637	11.2	36
Native white—Foreign or mixed par.	16,048	9,033	56.3	6,200	38.6	751	4.7	55
Foreign-born white	21,156	4,231	20.0	13,703	64.8	3,164	15.0	51
Negro	123	27	22.0	68	55.3	26	21.1	2
Fort Worth, Tex.								
All classes [2]	37,396	8,674	23.2	23,253	62.2	4,700	12.6	628
Native white—Native parentage	26,407	6,414	24.3	16,386	62.1	3,112	11.8	391
Native white—Foreign or mixed par.	2,525	680	26.9	1,536	60.8	277	11.0	21
Foreign-born white	2,253	347	15.4	1,560	69.2	325	14.4	11
Negro	6,205	1,233	19.9	3,765	60.7	986	15.9	205
Grand Rapids, Mich.								
All classes [2]	50,857	14,426	28.4	30,200	59.4	5,495	10.8	692
Native white—Native parentage	18,931	5,645	29.8	10,767	56.9	2,132	11.3	366
Native white—Foreign or mixed par.	18,632	7,168	38.5	10,015	53.8	1,229	6.6	207
Foreign-born white	12,881	1,535	11.9	9,157	71.1	2,072	16.1	107
Negro	403	72	17.9	257	63.8	62	15.4	12
Hartford, Conn.								
All classes [2]	50,298	16,727	33.3	27,885	55.4	5,440	10.8	237
Native white—Native parentage	15,174	5,740	37.8	7,397	48.7	1,924	12.7	110
Native white—Foreign or mixed par.	15,175	7,310	48.2	6,703	44.2	1,088	7.2	71
Foreign-born white	18,408	3,304	17.9	12,838	69.7	2,219	12.1	44
Negro	1,525	365	23.9	941	61.7	207	13.6	12
Houston, Tex.								
All classes [2]	51,806	11,903	23.0	31,211	60.2	7,271	14.0	1,398
Native white—Native parentage	25,959	6,791	26.2	15,470	59.6	3,193	12.3	501
Native white—Foreign or mixed par.	7,372	2,008	27.2	4,373	59.3	881	12.0	109
Foreign-born white	4,716	625	13.3	3,200	67.9	843	17.9	47
Negro	13,750	2,479	18.0	8,160	59.3	2,353	17.1	741
Indianapolis, Ind.								
All classes [2]	121,688	29,217	24.0	73,583	60.5	16,048	13.2	1,894
Native white—Native parentage	82,164	20,547	25.0	50,023	60.9	9,441	11.5	1,368
Native white—Foreign or mixed par.	18,742	5,465	29.2	10,625	56.7	2,392	12.8	234
Foreign-born white	7,424	869	11.7	4,690	63.2	1,768	23.8	56
Negro	13,353	2,334	17.5	8,243	61.7	2,446	18.3	236
Jersey City, N. J.								
All classes [2]	102,266	31,309	30.6	58,551	57.3	12,067	11.8	228
Native white—Native parentage	26,232	10,557	40.2	13,173	50.2	2,401	9.2	77
Native white—Foreign or mixed par.	38,446	16,386	42.6	18,396	47.8	3,525	9.2	85
Foreign-born white	34,671	3,782	10.9	25,120	72.5	5,693	16.4	48
Negro	2,912	583	20.0	1,859	63.8	448	15.4	17
Kansas City, Kans.								
All classes [2]	34,979	7,556	21.6	22,749	65.0	4,116	11.8	541
Native white—Native parentage	19,038	4,392	23.1	12,376	65.0	1,948	10.2	310
Native white—Foreign or mixed par.	6,050	1,895	31.3	3,534	58.4	553	9.1	65
Foreign-born white	4,438	390	8.8	3,341	75.3	678	15.3	27
Negro	5,442	875	16.1	3,493	64.2	936	17.2	138

[2] Includes Indians, Chinese, Japanese, and "all other."

TABLE 56.—MARITAL CONDITION OF THE POPULATION 15 YEARS OF AGE AND
INHABITANTS OR

CITY AND CLASS OF POPULATION.	Total.[1]	MALES 15 YEARS OF AGE AND OVER.						Divorced.
		Single.		Married.		Widowed.		
		Number.	Per cent.	Number.	Per cent.	Number.	Per cent.	
Kansas City, Mo.								
All classes [2]	127,472	42,613	33.4	76,423	60.0	6,265	4.9	1,957
Native white—Native parentage	78,673	26,468	33.6	47,262	60.1	3,532	4.5	1,281
Native white—Foreign or mixed par..	20,724	7,794	37.6	11,824	57.1	813	3.9	275
Foreign-born white	14,769	3,821	25.9	9,857	66.7	922	6.2	148
Negro	13,175	4,452	33.8	7,433	56.4	995	7.6	253
Los Angeles, Calif.								
All classes [2]	227,455	77,225	34.0	134,206	59.0	11,263	5.0	4,309
Native white—Native parentage	110,657	35,800	32.4	66,472	60.1	5,609	5.1	2,558
Native white—Foreign or mixed par..	46,551	18,528	39.8	25,255	54.3	1,805	3.9	912
Foreign-born white	56,736	17,997	31.7	34,531	60.9	3,348	5.9	708
Negro	5,880	1,758	29.9	3,635	61.8	367	6.2	112
Louisville, Ky.								
All classes [2]	84,139	28,853	34.3	49,480	58.8	4,643	5.5	1,085
Native white—Native parentage	45,877	17,137	37.4	26,287	57.3	1,905	4.2	505
Native white—Foreign or mixed par..	16,988	5,684	33.5	10,226	60.2	876	5.2	185
Foreign-born white	5,796	873	15.1	4,174	72.0	701	12.1	43
Negro	15,451	5,147	33.3	8,779	56.8	1,160	7.5	352
Lowell, Mass.								
All classes [2]	38,583	14,375	37.3	21,865	56.7	2,164	5.6	118
Native white—Native parentage	7,344	2,762	37.6	4,070	55.4	453	6.2	51
Native white—Foreign or mixed par..	13,229	7,392	55.9	5,381	40.7	414	3.1	27
Foreign-born white	17,859	4,161	23.3	12,332	69.1	1,290	7.2	39
Negro	79	31	......	42	......	5	.....	1
Memphis, Tenn.								
All classes [2]	60,664	20,116	33.2	36,147	59.6	3,524	5.8	647
Native white—Native parentage	29,920	10,563	35.3	17,612	58.9	1,284	4.3	304
Native white—Foreign or mixed par..	4,495	1,713	38.1	2,548	56.7	186	4.1	40
Foreign-born white	3,180	797	25.1	2,125	66.8	228	7.2	23
Negro	23,022	7,024	30.5	13,840	60.1	1,821	7.9	280
Milwaukee, Wis.								
All classes [2]	165,115	60,154	36.4	97,368	59.0	6,061	3.7	1,248
Native white—Native parentage	35,915	16,546	46.1	18,133	50.5	768	2.1	325
Native white—Foreign or mixed par..	69,272	30,316	43.8	36,774	53.1	1,622	•2.3	504
Foreign-born white	58,834	12,878	21.9	41,851	71.1	3,626	6.2	396
Negro	1,034	382	36.9	584	56.5	43	4.2	23
Minneapolis, Minn.								
All classes [2]	142,005	53,594	37.7	81,740	57.6	5,290	3.7	998
Native white—Native parentage	43,222	16,380	37.9	24,934	57.7	1,436	3.3	384
Native white—Foreign or mixed par..	49,504	23,567	47.6	24,383	49.3	1,086	2.2	307
Foreign-born white	47,235	12,871	27.2	31,301	66.3	2,652	5.6	280
Negro	1,835	668	36.4	1,025	55.9	113	6.2	27
Nashville, Tenn.								
All classes [2]	40,559	12,817	31.6	24,815	61.2	2,460	6.1	419
Native white—Native parentage	24,872	8,309	33.4	15,000	61.1	1,102	4.7	178
Native white—Foreign or mixed par..	2,363	900	38.1	1,328	56.2	120	5.0	8
Foreign-born white	1,241	273	22.0	863	69.5	100	8.1	4
Negro	12,080	3,333	27.6	7,420	61.4	1,075	8.9	230
New Bedford, Mass.								
All classes [2]	41,993	14,606	34.8	25,286	60.2	1,896	4.5	184
Native white—Native parentage	6,638	2,183	32.9	3,967	59.8	414	6.2	64
Native white—Foreign or mixed par..	10,679	6,125	57.4	4,263	39.9	242	2.3	44
Foreign-born white	22,593	5,335	23.6	16,003	70.8	1,184	5.2	66
Negro	2,016	935	46.4	1,016	50.4	55	2.7	9

[1] Total includes persons whose marital condition was not reported.

OVER, BY SEX, FOR PRINCIPAL POPULATION CLASSES, FOR CITIES HAVING 100,000 MORE: 1920—Continued.

CITY AND CLASS OF POPULATION.	Total.[1]	FEMALES 15 YEARS OF AGE AND OVER.						
		Single.		Married.		Widowed.		Di-vorced.
		Number.	Per cent.	Number.	Per cent.	Number.	Per cent.	
Kansas City, Mo.								
All classes [2]	127,444	32,351	25.4	75,256	59.1	17,082	13.4	2,632
Native white—Native parentage	80,391	21,185	26.4	47,398	59.0	9,895	12.3	1,835
Native white—Foreign or mixed par.	22,890	7,001	30.6	12,958	56.6	2,574	11.2	342
Foreign-born white	11,366	1,592	14.0	7,467	65.7	2,187	19.2	107
Negro	12,775	2,567	20.1	7,420	58.1	2,423	19.0	348
Los Angeles, Calif.								
All classes [2]	233,883	57,226	24.5	132,890	56.8	37,612	16.1	5,946
Native white—Native parentage	120,806	30,536	25.3	66,613	55.1	19,882	16.5	3,677
Native white—Foreign or mixed par.	54,971	16,597	30.2	29,959	54.5	7,017	12.8	1,346
Foreign-born white	48,503	8,646	17.8	29,806	61.5	9,283	19.1	716
Negro	6,556	1,186	18.1	3,800	58.0	1,364	20.8	201
Louisville, Ky.								
All classes [2]	94,544	28,102	29.7	49,685	52.6	15,196	16.1	1,497
Native white—Native parentage	50,331	16,611	33.0	26,861	53.4	6,090	12.1	731
Native white—Foreign or mixed par.	21,455	6,980	32.5	10,903	50.8	3,340	15.6	224
Foreign-born white	5,650	723	12.8	2,935	51.9	1,956	34.6	31
Negro	17,101	3,786	22.1	8,983	52.5	3,809	22.3	510
Lowell, Mass.								
All classes [2]	42,212	15,892	37.6	21,353	50.6	4,779	11.3	163
Native white—Native parentage	8,317	3,246	39.0	3,840	46.2	1,145	13.8	76
Native white—Foreign or mixed par.	14,891	8,351	56.1	5,602	37.6	890	6.0	43
Foreign-born white	18,948	4,279	22.6	11,876	62.7	2,739	14.5	44
Negro	53	16	......	32	......	5	......	......
Memphis, Tenn.								
All classes [2]	64,269	15,397	24.0	36,279	56.4	11,370	17.7	1,131
Native white—Native parentage	30,991	8,507	27.4	17,596	56.8	4,432	14.3	416
Native white—Foreign or mixed par.	4,990	1,452	29.1	2,678	53.7	807	16.2	49
Foreign-born white	2,418	348	14.4	1,525	63.1	528	21.8	14
Negro	25,863	5,088	19.7	14,475	56.0	5,603	21.7	652
Milwaukee, Wis.								
All classes [2]	164,908	51,986	31.5	94,036	57.0	17,053	10.3	1,666
Native white—Native parentage	36,905	16,809	45.5	17,603	47.7	2,018	5.5	425
Native white—Foreign or mixed par.	79,664	29,893	37.5	43,124	54.1	5,773	7.2	810
Foreign-born white	47,538	5,155	10.8	32,760	68.9	9,159	19.3	413
Negro	787	125	15.9	541	68.7	101	12.8	18
Minneapolis, Minn.								
All classes [2]	144,582	47,369	32.8	80,173	55.5	15,062	10.4	1,657
Native white—Native parentage	43,921	15,765	35.9	22,965	52.3	4,492	10.2	614
Native white—Foreign or mixed par.	60,623	25,391	41.9	30,471	50.3	3,941	6.5	637
Foreign-born white	38,529	5,948	15.4	25,770	66.9	6,385	16.6	378
Negro	1,472	256	17.4	943	64.1	241	16.4	27
Nashville, Tenn.								
All classes [2]	47,014	12,922	27.5	25,151	53.5	8,049	17.1	865
Native white—Native parentage	27,742	8,326	30.0	15,284	55.1	3,740	13.5	382
Native white—Foreign or mixed par.	2,917	1,018	34.9	1,413	48.4	475	16.3	10
Foreign-born white	1,075	171	15.9	612	56.9	281	26.1	8
Negro	15,279	3,406	22.3	7,842	51.3	3,553	23.3	465
New Bedford, Mass.								
All classes [2]	43,845	14,025	32.0	24,592	56.1	4,903	11.2	298
Native white—Native parentage	7,279	2,394	32.9	3,619	49.7	1,150	15.8	109
Native white—Foreign or mixed par.	11,655	6,138	52.7	4,923	42.2	524	4.5	60
Foreign-born white	23,492	5,210	22.2	15,157	64.5	3,006	12.8	110
Negro	1,412	280	19.8	890	63.0	222	15.7	19

[2] Includes Indians, Chinese, Japanese, and "all other."

TABLE 56.—MARITAL CONDITION OF THE POPULATION 15 YEARS OF AGE AND INHABITANTS OR

CITY AND CLASS OF POPULATION.	Total.[1]	MALES 15 YEARS OF AGE AND OVER.						Divorced.
		Single.		Married.		Widowed.		
		Number.	Per cent.	Number.	Per cent.	Number.	Per cent.	
New Haven, Conn.								
All classes [2]	55,681	19,972	35.9	32,838	59.0	2,431	4.4	154
Native white—Native parentage	15,049	5,639	37.5	8,513	56.6	707	4.7	60
Native white—Foreign or mixed par..	16,098	8,761	54.4	6,742	41.9	457	2.8	44
Foreign-born white	22,680	4,924	21.7	16,497	72.7	1,157	5.1	41
Negro	1,730	582	33.6	1,031	59.6	107	6.2	9
New Orleans, La.								
All classes [2]	137,980	55,317	40.1	74,758	54.2	6,540	4.7	765
Native white—Native parentage	62,740	29,755	47.4	30,187	48.1	2,153	3.4	345
Native white—Foreign or mixed par..	25,399	8,657	34.1	15,108	59.5	1,434	5.6	163
Foreign-born white	15,082	5,274	35.0	8,482	56.2	1,134	7.5	46
Negro	34,472	11,466	33.3	20,874	60.6	1,809	5.2	211
New York, N. Y.								
All classes [2]	2,001,025	761,471	38.1	1,143,643	57.2	78,999	3.9	4,303
Native white—Native parentage	373,679	170,877	45.7	183,128	49.0	14,229	3.8	1,433
Native white—Foreign or mixed par..	577,054	315,691	54.7	241,324	41.8	17,441	3.0	1,152
Foreign-born white	984,648	249,327	25.3	682,608	69.3	44,826	4.6	1,560
Negro	59,012	21,269	36.0	34,474	58.4	2,431	4.1	152
BRONX BOROUGH.								
All classes [2]	253,000	88,672	35.0	154,407	61.0	8,731	3.5	316
Native white—Native parentage	38,754	17,419	44.9	19,801	51.1	1,259	3.2	78
Native white—Foreign or mixed par..	81,198	43,694	53.8	35,217	43.4	1,899	2.3	93
Foreign-born white	131,302	26,988	20.6	98,332	74.9	5,465	4.2	141
Negro	1,573	486	30.9	979	62.2	103	6.5	3
BROOKLYN BOROUGH.								
All classes [2]	702,374	261,257	37.2	409,005	58.2	28,300	4.0	1,175
Native white—Native parentage	144,478	65,825	45.6	71,788	49.7	5,741	4.0	380
Native white—Foreign or mixed par..	214,573	115,344	53.8	91,331	42.6	6,864	3.2	352
Foreign-born white	329,966	75,011	22.7	238,289	72.2	15,157	4.6	402
Negro	12,008	4,228	35.2	7,145	59.5	529	4.4	41
MANHATTAN BOROUGH.								
All classes [2]	839,400	339,436	40.4	455,693	54.3	33,185	4.0	2,538
Native white—Native parentage	134,966	63,418	47.0	62,368	46.2	5,418	4.0	881
Native white—Foreign or mixed par..	205,533	123,123	59.9	75,102	36.5	6,356	3.1	612
Foreign-born white	450,850	133,843	29.7	291,771	64.7	19,667	4.4	938
Negro	43,204	15,813	36.6	24,991	57.8	1,693	3.9	102
QUEENS BOROUGH.								
All classes [2]	162,947	54,050	33.2	101,540	62.3	6,825	4.2	210
Native white—Native parentage	42,285	17,693	41.8	23,102	54.6	1,299	3.1	72
Native white—Foreign or mixed par..	63,134	27,166	43.0	33,955	53.8	1,853	2.9	73
Foreign-born white	55,678	8,591	15.4	43,326	77.8	3,588	6.4	62
Negro	1,663	508	30.5	1,068	64.2	80	4.8	3
RICHMOND BOROUGH.								
All classes [2]	43,304	18,056	41.7	22,998	53.1	1,958	4.5	64
Native white—Native parentage	13,196	6,522	49.4	6,069	46.0	512	3.9	22
Native white—Foreign or mixed par..	12,616	6,304	50.4	5,719	45.3	469	3.7	22
Foreign-born white	16,852	4,001	29.0	10,890	64.6	949	5.6	17
Negro	564	234	41.5	291	51.6	26	4.0	3
Newark, N. J.								
All classes [2]	146,406	52,786	36.1	87,249	59.6	5,662	3.9	385
Native white—Native parentage	37,771	15,554	41.2	20,526	54.3	1,458	3.9	159
Native white—Foreign or mixed par..	42,132	21,868	51.9	18,777	44.6	1,275	3.0	110
Foreign-born white	59,730	13,209	22.1	43,731	73.2	2,597	4.3	72
Negro	6,483	2,017	31.1	4,070	62.8	327	5.0	44

[1] Total includes persons whose marital condition was not reported.

OVER, BY SEX, FOR PRINCIPAL POPULATION CLASSES, FOR CITIES HAVING 100,000 MORE: 1920—Continued.

CITY AND CLASS OF POPULATION.	Total.[1]	FEMALES 15 YEARS OF AGE AND OVER.						Divorced.
		Single.		Married.		Widowed.		
		Number.	Per cent.	Number.	Per cent.	Number.	Per cent.	
New Haven, Conn.								
All classes [2]	57,912	18,620	32.1	32,171	55.6	6,676	11.5	270
Native white—Native parentage	16,295	6,001	36.8	8,026	49.3	2,072	12.7	119
Native white—Foreign or mixed par.	18,566	8,954	48.2	8,114	43.7	1,357	7.3	80
Foreign-born white	21,307	3,275	15.4	15,018	70.5	2,919	13.7	58
Negro	1,733	389	22.4	1,005	58.0	326	18.8	13
New Orleans, La.								
All classes [2]	146,515	45,296	30.9	74,831	51.1	24,842	17.0	1,168
Native white—Native parentage	64,385	24,333	37.8	32,189	50.0	7,247	11.3	457
Native white—Foreign or mixed par.	31,187	9,158	29.4	15,384	49.3	6,401	20.5	197
Foreign-born white	10,062	1,719	17.1	5,308	52.8	2,966	29.5	34
Negro	40,849	10,079	24.7	21,931	53.7	8,223	20.1	479
New York, N. Y.								
All classes [2]	2,026,797	667,484	32.9	1,115,670	55.0	232,991	11.5	6,775
Native white—Native parentage	389,160	161,207	41.4	183,567	47.2	41,100	10.6	2,239
Native white—Foreign or mixed par.	634,928	299,539	47.2	278,650	43.9	53,839	8.5	1,805
Foreign-born white	936,518	187,510	20.0	617,211	65.9	127,783	13.6	2,416
Negro	65,514	19,032	29.0	35,795	54.6	10,238	15.6	315
BRONX BOROUGH.								
All classes [2]	260,085	81,513	31.3	152,172	58.5	25,289	9.7	464
Native white—Native parentage	40,261	16,920	42.0	19,948	49.5	3,175	7.9	83
Native white—Foreign or mixed par.	90,545	42,933	47.4	41,431	45.8	5,824	6.4	157
Foreign-born white	127,420	21,053	16.5	89,827	70.5	16,013	12.6	219
Negro	1,839	601	32.7	954	51.9	275	15.0	5
BROOKLYN BOROUGH.								
All classes [2]	707,341	224,395	31.7	399,517	56.5	80,071	11.3	1,768
Native white—Native parentage	148,811	61,061	41.0	71,406	48.0	15,420	10.4	540
Native white—Foreign or mixed par.	239,039	109,745	45.9	107,236	44.9	20,939	8.8	576
Foreign-born white	306,143	49,731	16.2	213,615	69.8	41,603	13.6	579
Negro	13,270	3,835	28.9	7,212	54.3	2,103	15.8	73
MANHATTAN BOROUGH.								
All classes [2]	855,130	301,870	35.3	441,585	51.6	106,236	12.4	4,180
Native white—Native parentage	145,747	62,357	42.8	63,204	43.4	18,287	12.5	1,490
Native white—Foreign or mixed par.	224,905	116,857	52.0	86,001	38.2	20,873	9.3	950
Foreign-born white	436,287	108,763	24.9	265,819	60.9	59,634	13.7	1,517
Negro	47,646	13,739	28.8	26,194	55.0	7,419	15.6	223
QUEENS BOROUGH.								
All classes [2]	166,545	47,861	28.7	100,679	60.5	17,478	10.5	289
Native white—Native parentage	43,112	16,497	38.3	23,270	54.0	3,181	7.4	95
Native white—Foreign or mixed par.	68,006	24,846	36.5	37,788	55.6	5,185	7.6	108
Foreign-born white	53,190	5,845	11.0	38,465	72.3	8,726	16.4	76
Negro	2,204	660	29.9	1,137	51.6	386	17.5	10
RICHMOND BOROUGH.								
All classes [2]	37,696	11,845	31.4	21,717	57.6	3,917	10.4	74
Native white—Native parentage	11,229	4,372	38.9	5,739	51.1	1,037	9.2	31
Native white—Foreign or mixed par.	12,433	5,158	41.5	6,194	49.8	1,018	8.2	14
Foreign-born white	13,478	2,118	15.7	9,485	70.4	1,807	13.4	25
Negro	555	197	35.5	298	53.7	55	9.9	4
Newark, N. J.								
All classes [2]	143,424	42,791	29.8	84,071	58.6	15,939	11.1	425
Native white—Native parentage	38,636	14,380	37.2	19,948	51.6	4,082	10.6	180
Native white—Foreign or mixed par.	45,475	20,012	44.0	21,513	47.3	3,744	8.2	132
Foreign-born white	52,956	7,061	13.3	38,524	72.7	7,219	13.6	81
Negro	6,339	1,334	21.0	4,075	64.3	891	14.1	32

[2] Includes Indians, Chinese, Japanese, and "all other."

TABLE 56.—MARITAL CONDITION OF THE POPULATION 15 YEARS OF AGE AND
INHABITANTS OR

CITY AND CLASS OF POPULATION.	MALES 15 YEARS OF AGE AND OVER.							
	Total.[1]	Single.		Married.		Widowed.		Divorced.
		Number.	Per cent.	Number.	Per cent.	Number.	Per cent.	
Norfolk, Va.								
All classes[2]	46,183	17,685	38.3	26,087	56.5	2,046	4.4	337
Native white—Native parentage	21,951	8,192	37.3	12,781	58.2	805	3.7	166
Native white—Foreign or mixed par.	2,660	1,318	49.5	1,222	45.9	96	3.6	22
Foreign-born white	4,331	1,908	44.1	2,239	51.7	160	3.7	17
Negro	17,098	6,191	36.2	9,779	57.2	984	5.8	132
Oakland, Calif.								
All classes[2]	87,404	31,516	36.1	49,773	56.9	4,239	4.8	1,670
Native white—Native parentage	32,328	11,630	36.0	18,487	57.2	1,381	4.3	746
Native white—Foreign or mixed par.	23,465	9,865	42.0	12,321	52.5	752	3.2	497
Foreign-born white	24,752	7,228	29.2	15,486	62.6	1,615	6.5	347
Negro	2,591	1,102	42.5	1,275	49.2	138	5.3	71
Omaha, Nebr.								
All classes[2]	74,872	28,312	37.8	41,749	55.8	3,376	4.5	952
Native white—Native parentage	31,634	11,904	37.6	17,551	55.5	1,336	4.2	485
Native white—Foreign or mixed par.	19,147	9,110	47.6	9,203	48.1	548	2.9	244
Foreign-born white	19,325	5,532	28.6	12,347	63.9	1,229	6.4	147
Negro	4,580	1,651	36.0	2,583	56.4	259	5.7	76
Paterson, N. J.								
All classes[2]	48,038	17,323	36.1	28,306	58.9	2,267	4.7	115
Native white—Native parentage	9,836	4,008	40.7	5,353	54.4	440	4.5	31
Native white—Foreign or mixed par.	15,297	8,289	54.2	6,501	42.5	460	3.0	38
Foreign-born white	22,281	4,820	21.6	16,071	72.1	1,335	6.0	42
Negro	560	165	29.5	358	63.9	32	5.7	4
Philadelphia, Pa.								
All classes[2]	656,839	236,089	35.9	383,769	58.4	33,459	5.1	2,266
Native white—Native parentage	235,095	90,958	38.7	130,341	55.4	12,023	5.1	1,176
Native white—Foreign or mixed par.	168,062	79,031	47.0	81,151	48.3	7,178	4.3	516
Foreign-born white	198,831	46,923	23.6	139,541	70.2	11,572	5.8	431
Negro	53,715	18,535	34.5	32,261	60.1	2,670	5.0	142
Pittsburgh, Pa.								
All classes[2]	209,688	78,921	37.6	120,158	57.3	9,308	4.4	886
Native white—Native parentage	69,243	28,344	40.9	37,622	54.3	2,644	3.8	451
Native white—Foreign or mixed par.	60,561	29,741	49.1	28,362	46.8	2,129	3.5	233
Foreign-born white	63,767	15,081	23.7	44,699	70.1	3,745	5.9	147
Negro	15,812	5,583	35.3	9,350	59.1	788	5.0	54
Portland, Oreg.								
All classes[2]	102,381	35,711	34.9	59,738	58.3	4,260	4.2	2,596
Native white—Native parentage	48,782	15,765	32.3	29,477	60.4	2,026	4.2	1,486
Native white—Foreign or mixed par.	24,000	9,831	41.0	12,883	53.7	696	2.9	578
Foreign-born white	26,402	8,688	32.9	15,716	59.5	1,458	5.5	508
Negro	708	251	35.5	400	56.5	34	4.8	19
Providence, R. I.								
All classes[2]	82,186	30,159	36.7	47,392	57.7	4,047	4.9	563
Native white—Native parentage	21,094	7,973	37.8	11,661	55.3	1,215	5.8	238
Native white—Foreign or mixed par.	25,781	14,000	54.3	10,823	42.0	791	3.1	157
Foreign-born white	33,004	7,307	22.1	23,049	71.6	1,898	5.8	149
Negro	2,169	841	38.8	1,172	54.0	137	6.3	19
Reading, Pa.								
All classes[2]	38,335	11,936	31.1	23,933	62.4	2,160	5.6	276
Native white—Native parentage	28,456	8,862	31.1	17,708	62.2	1,632	5.7	237
Native white—Foreign or mixed par.	4,218	1,617	38.3	2,363	56.0	205	4.9	29
Foreign-born white	5,282	1,299	24.6	3,659	69.3	305	5.8	10
Negro	370	152	41.1	200	54.1	18	4.9	

[1] Total includes persons whose marital condition was not reported.

OVER, BY SEX, FOR PRINCIPAL POPULATION CLASSES, FOR CITIES HAVING 100,000 MORE: 1920—Continued.

CITY AND CLASS OF POPULATION.	Total.[1]	FEMALES 15 YEARS OF AGE AND OVER.							
		Single.		Married.		Widowed.		Divorced.
		Number.	Per cent.	Number.	Per cent.	Number.	Per cent.	
Norfolk, Va.								
All classes [2]	41,555	10,393	25.0	25,306	60.9	5,414	13.0	425
Native white—Native parentage	20,744	5,363	25.9	12,741	61.4	2,407	11.6	222
Native white—Foreign or mixed par.	2,280	791	34.7	1,250	54.8	224	9.8	14
Foreign-born white	2,042	260	12.7	1,556	76.2	219	10.7	6
Negro	16,482	3,978	24.1	9,753	59.2	2,564	15.6	183
Oakland, Calif.								
All classes [2]	79,813	18,919	23.7	47,873	60.0	11,208	14.0	1,744
Native white—Native parentage	31,905	8,377	26.3	18,255	57.2	4,390	13.8	857
Native white—Foreign or mixed par.	25,847	7,708	29.8	15,009	58.1	2,554	9.9	556
Foreign-born white	18,948	2,339	12.3	12,477	65.8	3,836	20.2	276
Negro	1,975	315	15.9	1,230	62.3	373	18.9	54
Omaha, Nebr.								
All classes [2]	68,516	19,030	27.8	40,719	59.4	7,512	11.0	1,072
Native white—Native parentage	29,180	8,680	29.7	16,896	57.9	2,923	10.0	557
Native white—Foreign or mixed par.	20,660	7,913	38.3	10,962	53.1	1,488	7.2	266
Foreign-born white	14,940	1,880	12.6	10,319	69.1	2,559	17.1	155
Negro	3,719	555	14.9	2,527	67.9	542	14.6	94
Paterson, N. J.								
All classes [2]	49,605	16,053	32.4	27,887	56.2	5,494	11.1	153
Native white—Native parentage	10,992	4,193	38.1	5,466	49.7	1,275	11.6	54
Native white—Foreign or mixed par.	16,912	8,410	49.7	7,357	43.5	1,100	6.5	37
Foreign-born white	21,055	3,275	15.6	14,711	69.9	3,006	14.3	58
Negro	641	173	27.0	351	54.8	112	17.5	4
Philadelphia, Pa.								
All classes [2]	667,074	205,963	30.9	373,687	56.0	83,850	12.6	2,799
Native white—Native parentage	245,971	86,181	35.0	128,726	52.3	29,308	11.9	1,474
Native white—Foreign or mixed par.	182,561	76,115	41.7	87,178	47.8	18,408	10.1	663
Foreign-born white	185,700	30,878	16.6	125,730	67.7	28,397	15.3	453
Negro	52,747	12,770	24.2	31,992	60.7	7,722	14.6	209
Pittsburgh, Pa.								
All classes [2]	206,266	64,636	31.3	115,400	55.9	24,925	12.1	1,130
Native white—Native parentage	71,585	26,444	36.9	37,326	52.1	7,219	10.1	530
Native white—Foreign or mixed par.	67,777	28,262	41.7	32,218	47.5	6,909	10.2	330
Foreign-born white	53,359	7,274	13.6	36,907	69.2	8,962	16.8	177
Negro	13,521	2,651	19.6	8,931	66.1	1,834	13.6	93
Portland, Oreg.								
All classes [2]	96,540	23,974	24.8	58,553	60.7	11,037	11.4	2,931
Native white—Native parentage	50,268	12,463	24.8	30,132	59.9	5,793	11.5	1,853
Native white—Foreign or mixed par.	26,285	8,536	32.5	14,919	56.8	2,155	8.2	669
Foreign-born white	18,797	2,826	15.0	12,600	67.0	2,978	15.8	383
Negro	597	76	12.7	414	69.3	80	13.4	26
Providence, R. I.								
All classes [2]	89,342	31,389	35.1	46,225	51.7	10,807	12.1	889
Native white—Native parentage	23,688	9,037	38.2	10,946	46.2	3,326	14.0	369
Native white—Foreign or mixed par.	29,705	15,334	51.6	11,960	40.3	2,141	7.2	259
Foreign-born white	33,849	6,462	19.1	22,213	65.6	4,944	14.6	220
Negro	2,080	554	26.6	1,094	52.6	390	18.8	41
Reading, Pa.								
All classes [2]	39,824	11,147	28.0	23,648	59.4	4,646	11.7	357
Native white—Native parentage	30,801	8,822	28.6	18,053	58.6	3,592	11.7	316
Native white—Foreign or mixed par.	4,776	1,767	37.0	2,477	51.9	493	10.3	34
Foreign-born white	3,943	487	12.4	2,920	74.1	527	13.4	6
Negro	304	71	23.4	198	65.1	34	11.2	1

[2] Includes Indians, Chinese, Japanese, and "all other."

TABLE 56.—MARITAL CONDITION OF THE POPULATION 15 YEARS OF AGE AND
INHABITANTS OR

CITY AND CLASS OF POPULATION.	MALES 15 YEARS OF AGE AND OVER.							
	Total.[1]	Single.		Married.		Widowed.		Di-vorced.
		Num-ber.	Per cent.	Num-ber.	Per cent.	Num-ber.	Per cent.	
Richmond, Va.								
All classes [2]	58,541	20,323	34.7	34,860	59.5	2,722	4.6	290
Native white—Native parentage	34,488	12,634	36.6	20,227	58.6	1,383	4.0	131
Native white—Foreign or mixed par.	3,323	1,245	37.5	1,902	57.2	159	4.8	15
Foreign-born white	2,457	565	23.0	1,718	69.9	153	6.2	15
Negro	18,238	5,867	32.2	10,992	60.3	1,026	5.6	129
Rochester, N. Y.								
All classes [2]	105,777	36,954	34.9	63,681	60.2	4,643	4.4	327
Native white—Native parentage	37,315	14,451	38.7	21,133	56.6	1,491	4.0	159
Native white—Foreign or mixed par.	32,518	13,797	42.4	17,323	53.3	1,280	3.9	90
Foreign-born white	35,284	8,481	24.0	24,816	70.3	1,848	5.2	76
Negro	605	202	33.4	377	62.3	24	4.0	2
St. Louis, Mo.								
All classes [2]	292,198	106,790	36.5	168,509	57.7	13,879	4.7	2,545
Native white—Native parentage	119,751	50,356	42.1	63,812	53.3	4,163	3.5	1,169
Native white—Foreign or mixed par.	88,240	33,291	37.7	50,551	57.3	3,520	4.0	767
Foreign-born white	54,962	12,952	23.6	37,306	67.9	4,319	7.9	298
Negro	28,887	10,012	34.7	16,678	57.7	1,868	6.5	290
St. Paul, Minn.								
All classes [2]	86,946	33,992	39.1	48,640	55.9	3,463	4.0	610
Native white—Native parentage	23,443	10,017	42.7	12,420	53.0	675	2.9	179
Native white—Foreign or mixed par.	34,483	16,701	48.4	16,733	48.5	787	2.3	226
Foreign-born white	27,359	6,654	24.3	18,572	67.9	1,915	7.0	169
Negro	1,561	569	36.5	868	55.6	85	5.4	35
Salt Lake City, Utah.								
All classes [2]	40,485	13,769	34.0	24,640	60.9	1,416	3.5	519
Native white—Native parentage	16,293	6,150	37.7	9,378	57.6	472	2.9	230
Native white—Foreign or mixed par.	14,055	5,017	35.7	8,528	60.7	339	2.4	154
Foreign-born white	9,384	2,296	24.5	6,333	67.5	580	6.2	122
Negro	340	119	35.0	193	56.8	16	4.7	11
San Antonio, Tex.								
All classes [2]	58,356	21,213	36.4	33,665	57.7	2,782	4.8	601
Native white—Native parentage	25,952	10,078	38.8	14,582	56.2	967	3.7	281
Native white—Foreign or mixed par.	10,225	4,153	40.6	5,586	54.6	383	3.7	93
Foreign-born white	16,770	5,370	32.0	10,133	60.4	1,151	6.9	84
Negro	5,232	1,559	29.8	3,243	62.0	280	5.4	142
San Francisco, Calif.								
All classes [2]	223,704	97,940	43.8	105,865	47.3	9,607	4.3	4,297
Native white—Native parentage	66,898	30,500	45.6	29,325	43.8	2,324	3.5	1,739
Native white—Foreign or mixed par.	65,712	31,953	48.6	29,861	45.4	2,360	3.6	1,400
Foreign-born white	80,880	31,107	38.5	41,431	51.2	4,741	5.9	1,118
Negro	1,181	554	46.9	514	43.5	44	3.7	24
Scranton, Pa.								
All classes [2]	45,189	16,861	37.3	26,386	58.4	1,753	3.9	96
Native white—Native parentage	13,730	5,786	42.1	7,423	54.1	450	3.3	40
Native white—Foreign or mixed par.	16,455	8,209	49.9	7,746	47.1	438	2.7	34
Foreign-born white	14,756	2,704	18.7	11,085	75.1	853	5.8	20
Negro	242	99	40.5	130	53.7	12	5.0	2
Seattle, Wash.								
All classes [2]	133,208	52,453	39.4	72,673	54.6	5,157	3.9	2,633
Native white—Native parentage	52,937	18,723	35.4	30,718	58.0	2,102	4.0	1,287
Native white—Foreign or mixed par.	31,223	13,935	44.6	15,740	50.4	887	2.8	605
Foreign-born white	42,086	16,828	40.0	22,511	53.5	1,966	4.7	675
Negro	1,472	570	38.7	739	50.2	105	7.1	52

[1] Total includes persons whose marital condition was not reported.

OVER, BY SEX, FOR PRINCIPAL POPULATION CLASSES, FOR CITIES HAVING 100,000 MORE: 1920—Continued.

CITY AND CLASS OF POPULATION.	Total.[1]	FEMALES 15 YEARS OF AGE AND OVER.						Divorced.
		Single.		Married.		Widowed.		
		Number.	Per cent.	Number.	Per cent.	Number.	Per cent.	
Richmond, Va.								
All classes [2]	67,978	21,703	31.9	35,171	51.7	10,263	15.1	543
Native white—Native parentage	39,758	13,536	34.0	20,587	51.8	5,294	13.3	273
Native white—Foreign or mixed par.	3,911	1,359	34.7	1,960	50.1	560	14.3	26
Foreign-born white	2,027	344	17.0	1,285	63.4	391	19.3	6
Negro	22,273	6,461	29.0	11,335	50.9	4,016	18.0	238
Rochester, N. Y.								
All classes [2]	111,108	34,939	31.4	62,523	56.3	13,068	11.8	418
Native white—Native parentage	39,928	14,697	36.8	20,846	52.2	4,114	10.3	212
Native white—Foreign or mixed par.	37,809	14,687	38.8	19,159	50.7	3,800	10.1	120
Foreign-born white	32,675	5,369	16.4	22,115	67.7	5,056	15.5	78
Negro	678	174	25.7	398	58.7	97	14.3	8
St. Louis, Mo.								
All classes [2]	299,442	88,346	29.5	165,846	55.4	41,477	13.9	3,444
Native white—Native parentage	123,770	44,238	35.7	65,681	53.1	11,975	9.7	1,730
Native white—Foreign or mixed par.	102,442	32,748	32.0	55,370	54.1	13,216	12.9	1,024
Foreign-born white	45,619	6,000	13.2	28,131	61.7	11,120	24.4	318
Negro	27,580	5,355	19.4	16,644	60.3	5,162	18.7	370
St. Paul, Minn.								
All classes [2]	87,295	29,317	33.6	47,815	54.8	9,276	10.6	797
Native white—Native parentage	22,890	9,077	39.7	11,623	50.8	1,877	8.2	264
Native white—Foreign or mixed par.	40,258	16,891	42.0	20,313	50.5	2,716	6.7	315
Foreign-born white	22,877	3,150	13.8	15,043	65.8	4,478	19.6	189
Negro	1,246	194	15.6	818	65.7	204	16.4	29
Salt Lake City, Utah.								
All classes [2]	41,288	11,144	27.0	24,381	59.1	4,915	11.9	791
Native white—Native parentage	16,174	5,382	33.3	8,953	55.4	1,485	9.2	330
Native white—Foreign or mixed par.	15,377	4,523	29.4	9,322	60.6	1,213	7.9	311
Foreign-born white	9,363	1,200	12.8	5,828	62.2	2,169	23.2	141
Negro	273	30	11.0	187	68.5	47	17.2	9
San Antonio, Tex.								
All classes [2]	57,986	15,718	27.1	32,539	56.1	8,644	14.9	1,016
Native white—Native parentage	26,579	7,865	29.6	15,032	56.6	3,188	12.0	456
Native white—Foreign or mixed par.	11,096	3,315	29.9	6,202	55.9	1,391	12.5	183
Foreign-born white	14,458	3,364	23.3	8,010	55.4	2,971	20.5	89
Negro	5,833	1,171	20.1	3,282	56.3	1,090	18.7	288
San Francisco, Calif.								
All classes [2]	185,109	52,442	28.3	100,816	54.5	26,177	14.1	5,332
Native white—Native parentage	56,919	18,152	31.9	29,313	51.5	6,945	12.2	2,366
Native white—Foreign or mixed par.	69,625	24,214	34.8	35,719	51.3	7,666	11.0	1,926
Foreign-born white	55,212	9,456	17.1	33,441	60.6	11,235	20.3	986
Negro	891	194	21.8	493	55.3	167	18.7	35
Scranton, Pa.								
All classes [2]	47,492	16,386	34.5	25,807	54.3	5,098	10.7	126
Native white—Native parentage	15,149	6,256	41.3	7,533	49.7	1,274	8.4	62
Native white—Foreign or mixed par.	19,096	8,759	45.9	8,799	46.1	1,466	7.7	49
Foreign-born white	13,047	1,326	10.2	9,353	71.7	2,326	17.8	14
Negro	200	45	22.5	122	61.0	32	16.0	1
Seattle, Wash.								
All classes [2]	113,606	27,975	24.6	70,054	61.7	12,331	10.9	3,150
Native white—Native parentage	49,829	12,647	25.4	29,925	60.1	5,616	11.3	1,602
Native white—Foreign or mixed par.	32,191	10,491	32.6	18,284	56.8	2,547	7.9	845
Foreign-born white	28,363	4,490	15.8	19,230	67.8	3,958	14.0	654
Negro	1,033	149	14.4	695	67.3	148	14.3	41

[2] Includes Indians, Chinese, Japanese, and " all other."

TABLE 56.—MARITAL CONDITION OF THE POPULATION 15 YEARS OF AGE AND
INHABITANTS OR

CITY AND CLASS OF POPULATION.	Total.[1]	MALES 15 YEARS OF AGE AND OVER.						
		Single.		Married.		Widowed.		Di-vorced.
		Num-ber.	Per cent.	Num-ber.	Per cent.	Num-ber.	Per cent.	
Spokane, Wash.								
All classes[2]	39,145	13,447	34.4	23,457	59.9	1,628	4.2	578
Native white—Native parentage	19,642	6,615	33.7	11,924	60.7	763	3.9	326
Native white—Foreign or mixed par.	9,879	4,004	40.5	5,432	55.0	291	2.9	144
Foreign-born white	9,107	2,657	29.2	5,788	63.6	558	6.1	95
Negro	302	95	31.5	180	59.6	15	5.0	12
Springfield, Mass.								
All classes[2]	46,723	16,209	34.7	28,213	60.4	2,019	4.3	257
Native white—Native parentage	17,098	5,677	33.2	10,447	61.1	823	4.8	136
Native white—Foreign or mixed par.	13,097	6,269	47.9	6,353	48.5	396	3.0	72
Foreign-born white	15,337	3,833	25.0	10,708	69.8	750	4.9	43
Negro	1,046	367	35.1	623	59.6	50	4.8	6
Syracuse, N. Y.								
All classes[2]	63,998	22,276	34.8	38,504	60.2	2,888	4.5	270
Native white—Native parentage	28,489	10,229	35.9	16,859	59.2	1,213	4.3	171
Native white—Foreign or mixed par.	18,026	7,638	42.4	9,631	53.4	672	3.7	62
Foreign-born white	16,880	4,146	24.6	11,711	69.4	969	5.7	34
Negro	566	243	42.9	286	50.5	34	6.0	3
Toledo, Ohio.								
All classes[2]	94,177	32,833	34.9	56,200	59.7	4,086	4.3	985
Native white—Native parentage	45,044	16,437	36.5	26,196	58.2	1,798	4.0	589
Native white—Foreign or mixed par.	25,256	10,300	40.8	13,857	54.9	860	3.4	229
Foreign-born white	21,105	5,049	23.9	14,582	69.1	1,315	6.2	122
Negro	2,694	1,002	37.2	1,535	57.0	110	4.1	45
Trenton, N. J.								
All classes[2]	42,852	14,879	34.7	25,766	60.1	2,028	4.7	113
Native white—Native parentage	15,579	5,726	36.8	8,935	57.4	834	5.4	62
Native white—Foreign or mixed par.	9,584	4,972	51.9	4,247	44.3	332	3.5	31
Foreign-born white	15,890	3,533	22.2	11,533	72.6	769	4.8	20
Negro	1,731	611	35.3	1,021	59.0	92	5.3	
Washington, D. C.								
All classes[2]	159,013	60,976	38.3	88,698	55.8	7,616	4.8	884
Native white—Native parentage	84,034	33,483	39.8	46,061	54.8	3,459	4.1	494
Native white—Foreign or mixed par.	20,697	8,942	43.2	10,750	51.9	866	4.2	114
Foreign-born white	14,741	4,854	32.9	8,823	59.9	897	6.1	64
Negro	38,916	13,354	34.3	22,801	58.6	2,387	6.1	208
Wilmington, Del.								
All classes[2]	41,374	15,038	36.3	24,027	58.1	2,050	5.0	201
Native white—Native parentage	20,614	7,336	35.6	12,143	58.9	978	4.7	128
Native white—Foreign or mixed par.	7,081	3,329	47.0	3,455	48.8	260	3.7	34
Foreign-born white	9,103	2,533	27.8	6,050	66.5	486	5.3	19
Negro	4,540	1,813	39.9	2,372	52.2	325	7.2	20
Worcester, Mass.								
All classes[2]	63,974	24,151	37.8	36,858	57.6	2,712	4.2	188
Native white—Native parentage	16,635	5,985	36.0	9,636	57.9	883	5.3	97
Native white—Foreign or mixed par.	19,802	11,033	55.7	8,233	41.6	480	2.4	40
Foreign-born white	26,997	6,928	25.7	18,686	69.2	1,319	4.9	49
Negro	468	174	37.2	266	56.8	26	5.6	2
Yonkers, N. Y.								
All classes[2]	33,237	11,765	35.4	20,109	60.5	1,300	3.9	44
Native white—Native parentage	8,956	3,499	39.1	5,100	56.9	351	0.7	20
Native white—Foreign or mixed par.	10,991	5,710	52.0	4,964	45.2	298	2.7	12
Foreign-born white	12,598	2,328	18.5	9,605	76.2	647	5.1	11
Negro	647	207	32.0	416	64.3	23	3.6	1
Youngstown, Ohio.								
All classes[2]	50,133	17,804	35.5	30,218	60.3	1,742	3.5	286
Native white—Native parentage	15,797	5,492	34.8	9,581	60.7	555	3.5	144
Native white—Foreign or mixed par.	10,936	5,199	47.5	5,390	49.3	291	2.7	53
Foreign-born white	20,039	5,720	28.5	13,475	67.2	751	3.7	65
Negro	3,268	1,335	40.9	1,739	53.2	143	4.4	24

[1] Total includes persons whose marital condition was not reported.

OVER, BY SEX, FOR PRINCIPAL POPULATION CLASSES, FOR CITIES HAVING 100,000 MORE: 1920—Continued.

CITY AND CLASS OF POPULATION.	Total.[1]	FEMALES 15 YEARS OF AGE AND OVER.							
		Single.		Married.		Widowed.		Di-vorced.
		Number.	Per cent.	Number.	Per cent.	Number.	Per cent.	
Spokane, Wash.								
All classes[2]	39,214	10,437	26.6	23,444	59.8	4,430	11.3	884
Native white—Native parentage	20,412	5,680	27.8	12,016	58.9	2,203	10.8	500
Native white—Foreign or mixed par.	11,463	3,726	32.5	6,507	56.8	992	8.7	235
Foreign-born white	7,010	983	14.0	4,695	67.0	1,190	17.0	139
Negro	276	41	14.9	182	65.9	44	15.9	9
Springfield, Mass.								
All classes[2]	49,027	15,623	31.9	27,349	55.8	5,681	11.6	352
Native white—Native parentage	18,318	6,012	32.8	9,674	52.8	2,418	13.2	204
Native white—Foreign or mixed par.	14,827	6,553	44.2	7,112	48.0	1,070	7.2	85
Foreign-born white	14,837	2,776	18.7	9,969	67.2	2,032	13.7	56
Negro	1,035	279	27.0	588	56.8	160	15.5	7
Syracuse, N. Y.								
All classes[2]	64,035	18,580	29.0	37,461	58.5	7,646	11.9	318
Native white—Native parentage	28,976	9,177	31.7	16,300	56.3	3,277	11.3	210
Native white—Foreign or mixed par.	20,208	7,424	36.7	10,710	53.0	1,996	9.9	69
Foreign-born white	14,364	1,869	13.0	10,153	70.7	2,297	16.0	36
Negro	467	106	22.7	283	60.6	75	16.1	3
Toledo, Ohio.								
All classes[2]	86,698	22,212	25.6	53,870	62.1	9,463	10.9	1,110
Native white—Native parentage	41,885	11,672	27.9	25,485	60.8	4,014	9.6	694
Native white—Foreign or mixed par.	27,013	8,586	31.8	15,765	58.4	2,396	8.9	256
Foreign-born white	15,777	1,613	10.2	11,203	71.0	2,816	17.8	133
Negro	2,016	340	16.9	1,412	70.0	237	11.8	26
Trenton, N. J.								
All classes[2]	40,773	11,634	28.5	24,342	59.7	4,642	11.4	122
Native white—Native parentage	16,109	5,224	32.4	8,839	54.9	1,946	12.1	79
Native white—Foreign or mixed par.	10,196	4,460	43.7	4,823	47.3	889	8.7	21
Foreign-born white	12,962	1,579	12.2	9,746	75.2	1,615	12.5	14
Negro	1,502	370	24.6	933	62.1	190	12.6	8
Washington, D. C.								
All classes[2]	188,466	70,330	37.3	88,602	47.0	27,761	14.7	1,381
Native white—Native parentage	103,450	43,236	41.8	46,059	44.5	13,094	12.7	832
Native white—Foreign or mixed par.	25,486	10,846	42.6	11,201	43.9	3,253	12.8	166
Foreign-born white	13,035	2,985	22.9	7,618	58.4	2,360	18.1	51
Negro	46,434	13,244	28.5	23,686	51.0	9,051	19.5	332
Wilmington, Del.								
All classes[2]	38,731	10,684	27.6	23,019	59.4	4,759	12.3	250
Native white—Native parentage	20,331	5,858	28.8	11,943	58.7	2,353	11.6	169
Native white—Foreign or mixed par.	7,616	2,875	37.7	3,890	51.1	808	10.6	42
Foreign-born white	6,688	798	11.9	4,916	73.5	957	14.3	15
Negro	4,095	1,153	28.2	2,269	55.4	641	15.7	24
Worcester, Mass.								
All classes[2]	64,823	22,299	34.4	35,426	54.7	6,761	10.4	302
Native white—Native parentage	17,791	6,557	36.9	8,781	49.4	2,287	12.9	149
Native white—Foreign or mixed par.	21,857	11,465	52.5	9,079	41.5	1,221	5.6	84
Foreign-born white	24,678	4,145	16.8	17,287	70.1	3,171	12.8	65
Negro	479	129	26.9	265	55.3	81	16.9	4
Yonkers, N. Y.								
All classes[2]	35,697	11,807	33.1	19,935	55.8	3,876	10.9	57
Native white—Native parentage	10,070	3,878	38.5	5,175	51.4	984	9.8	23
Native white—Foreign or mixed par.	12,497	5,922	47.4	5,574	44.6	976	7.8	20
Foreign-born white	12,322	1,784	14.5	8,771	71.2	1,749	14.2	12
Negro	803	222	27.6	411	51.2	167	20.8	2
Youngstown, Ohio.								
All classes[2]	41,248	10,124	24.5	26,984	65.4	3,801	9.2	316
Native white—Native parentage	14,796	4,308	29.1	9,023	61.0	1,298	8.8	155
Native white—Foreign or mixed par.	11,840	4,289	36.2	6,667	56.3	795	6.7	84
Foreign-born white	12,477	1,190	9.5	9,730	78.0	1,498	12.0	54
Negro	2,133	336	15.8	1,563	73.3	210	9.8	23

[2] Includes Indians, Chinese, Japanese, and "all other."

TABLE 57.—MARITAL CONDITION OF THE POPULATION 15 YEARS OF AGE AND

CITY.	Total.[1]	Single.	Married. Number.	Married. Per cent.	Widowed.	Divorced.
			MALES 15 YEARS OF AGE AND OVER.			
ALABAMA:						
Mobile	21,169	7,064	12,673	59.9	1,136	276
Montgomery	14,584	4,809	8,814	60.4	807	142
ARIZONA:						
Phoenix	11,550	4,213	6,504	56.3	636	171
ARKANSAS:						
Fort Smith	9,940	3,115	6,199	62.4	497	67
Little Rock	23,781	7,801	14,219	59.8	1,300	377
CALIFORNIA:						
Alameda	10,440	3,250	6,646	63.7	422	117
Berkeley	19,810	6,860	12,021	60.7	765	154
Fresno	17,943	6,580	10,356	57.7	713	216
Long Beach	20,927	5,322	14,204	67.9	1,162	223
Pasadena	15,388	4,351	10,049	65.3	835	130
Sacramento	27,083	10,411	14,972	55.3	1,224	445
San Diego	29,130	9,594	16,976	58.3	1,860	563
San Jose	14,501	4,924	8,390	57.9	767	244
Stockton	17,182	6,733	9,036	52.6	741	315
COLORADO:						
Colorado Springs	10,425	3,189	6,607	63.4	474	127
Pueblo	15,969	5,434	9,415	59.0	817	180
CONNECTICUT:						
Meriden	10,469	3,788	6,134	58.6	476	35
New Britain	20,588	7,575	12,160	59.1	787	48
New London	9,314	3,371	5,474	58.8	435	29
Norwalk	9,668	3,162	5,934	61.4	493	51
Stamford	11,873	4,022	7,363	62.0	442	21
Waterbury	33,207	12,956	18,914	57.0	1,220	85
FLORIDA:						
Jacksonville	33,405	9,921	21,216	63.5	1,975	239
Miami	11,203	3,521	6,986	62.4	497	152
Pensacola	11,607	4,066	6,711	57.8	647	68
Tampa	18,035	6,424	10,506	58.3	912	151
GEORGIA:						
Augusta	18,750	6,081	11,386	60.7	1,146	88
Columbus	10,406	3,406	6,291	60.5	640	68
Macon	18,685	5,878	11,820	63.3	867	98
Savannah	30,440	10,388	18,373	60.4	1,516	144
ILLINOIS:						
Aurora	13,392	4,388	8,328	62.2	571	85
Bloomington	10,452	3,342	6,445	61.7	534	106
Cicero town	15,096	5,084	9,537	63.2	416	33
Danville	12,360	3,695	7,743	62.6	681	231
Decatur	16,061	4,958	10,126	63.0	769	202
East St. Louis	25,427	8,830	15,010	59.0	1,278	271
Elgin	10,091	3,514	5,997	59.4	419	77
Evanston	12,397	3,807	8,040	64.9	480	57
Joliet	14,001	5,411	7,902	56.4	585	100
Moline	12,539	4,781	7,068	56.4	532	146
Oak Park village	13,749	4,026	9,104	66.2	533	49
Peoria	29,458	10,268	17,023	57.8	1,587	529
Quincy	13,452	4,790	7,749	57.6	743	148
Rock Island	13,822	4,862	8,136	58.9	660	153
Rockford	25,504	9,360	14,695	57.6	1,053	267
Springfield	21,068	7,190	12,457	59.1	1,130	257
INDIANA:						
Anderson	11,231	3,575	7,018	62.5	500	128
East Chicago	14,406	5,320	8,454	58.7	379	68
Evansville	30,538	10,036	18,411	60.3	1,788	270
Fort Wayne	31,914	10,786	19,294	60.5	1,346	462
Gary	22,893	9,125	12,979	56.7	600	151
Hammond	10,466	4,611	8,058	60.7	447	134
Kokomo	11,520	3,456	7,096	63.5	629	142
Muncie	13,797	3,937	8,817	60.0	702	325
Richmond	10,203	3,169	6,272	61.5	661	131
South Bend	25,231	8,418	15,454	61.3	1,027	200
Terre Haute	24,625	7,860	15,194	61.7	1,195	360
IOWA:						
Cedar Rapids	16,781	5,281	10,496	62.5	781	213
Council Bluffs	13,245	4,327	7,978	60.2	695	147
Davenport	21,866	7,658	12,806	58.6	1,016	297
Dubuque	13,823	5,284	7,761	56.1	662	99
Sioux City	28,524	11,590	15,301	53.6	1,195	419
Waterloo	13,320	4,088	8,495	63.8	551	168

[1] Total includes persons whose marital condition was not reported.

OVER, BY SEX, FOR CITIES HAVING FROM 25,000 TO 100,000 INHABITANTS: 1920.

CITY.	FEMALES 15 YEARS OF AGE AND OVER.					
	Total.[1]	Single.	Married.		Widowed.	Di-vorced.
			Number.	Per cent.		
ALABAMA:						
Mobile	23,322	6,085	12,690	54.4	4,083	445
Montgomery	17,320	4,527	9,048	52.2	3,364	378
ARIZONA:						
Phoenix	10,237	2,396	6,293	61.5	1,355	183
ARKANSAS:						
Fort Smith	10,351	2,599	6,160	59.5	1,415	131
Little Rock	25,301	6,263	14,434	57.0	3,912	621
CALIFORNIA:						
Alameda	11,232	2,690	6,631	59.0	1,699	201
Berkeley	23,484	7,302	12,256	52.2	3,552	364
Fresno	15,814	3,813	9,927	62.8	1,780	276
Long Beach	24,152	5,346	14,419	59.7	4,025	349
Pasadena	21,184	6,719	10,336	48.8	3,798	298
Sacramento	23,862	5,591	14,419	60.4	3,286	550
San Diego	30,278	7,086	17,341	57.3	5,140	672
San Jose	15,444	4,313	8,410	54.5	2,332	342
Stockton	14,192	3,157	8,800	62.0	1,795	335
COLORADO:						
Colorado Springs	12,957	3,950	6,832	52.7	1,941	212
Pueblo	14,901	3,499	9,364	62.8	1,831	188
CONNECTICUT:						
Meriden	10,673	3,426	5,954	55.8	1,248	33
New Britain	18,526	5,484	11,367	61.4	1,640	28
New London	9,412	2,742	5,412	57.5	1,204	53
Norwalk	10,422	3,018	5,934	56.9	1,368	79
Stamford	11,941	3,440	7,244	60.7	1,211	40
Waterbury	30,514	9,946	17,615	57.7	2,841	95
FLORIDA:						
Jacksonville	34,549	7,242	21,581	62.5	5,357	346
Miami	10,781	2,306	6,938	64.4	1,337	184
Pensacola	10,738	2,486	6,552	61.0	1,585	86
Tampa	17,725	4,051	10,621	59.9	2,752	281
GEORGIA:						
Augusta	20,591	5,156	11,422	55.5	3,776	205
Columbus	11,932	3,076	6,483	54.3	2,237	132
Macon	20,392	4,618	11,853	58.1	3,731	177
Savannah	31,738	8,155	18,552	58.5	4,831	191
ILLINOIS:						
Aurora	13,577	3,772	8,118	59.8	1,532	145
Bloomington	11,560	3,376	6,430	55.6	1,602	133
Cicero town	13,829	3,569	9,158	66.2	1,046	47
Danville	12,594	2,987	7,696	61.1	1,668	237
Decatur	16,431	4,205	10,052	61.2	1,979	194
East St. Louis	22,226	5,063	14,378	64.7	2,496	287
Elgin	11,890	4,052	6,116	51.4	1,466	168
Evanston	15,251	5,433	7,977	52.3	1,696	115
Joliet	13,324	4,192	7,563	56.8	1,447	114
Moline	10,716	2,706	6,804	63.5	1,078	121
Oak Park village	16,219	5,233	9,057	55.8	1,789	117
Peoria	29,573	8,565	16,625	56.2	3,773	566
Quincy	14,416	4,470	7,673	53.2	2,058	188
Rock Island	12,958	3,336	8,024	61.9	1,425	165
Rockford	24,042	6,991	14,373	59.8	2,346	295
Springfield	22,733	7,191	12,306	54.1	2,902	311
INDIANA:						
Anderson	10,795	2,510	6,911	64.0	1,182	191
East Chicago	8,562	1,502	6,523	76.2	480	39
Evansville	32,942	9,565	18,374	55.8	4,619	362
Fort Wayne	33,001	10,181	18,830	57.1	3,501	473
Gary	14,686	2,506	11,092	75.5	981	97
Hammond	10,826	2,410	7,464	68.9	835	115
Kokomo	10,426	2,006	7,109	68.2	1,181	127
Muncie	13,245	2,758	8,745	66.0	1,393	346
Richmond	10,118	2,473	6,127	60.6	1,382	132
South Bend	23,738	6,199	14,918	62.8	2,337	235
Terre Haute	24,771	6,361	14,933	60.3	3,017	450
IOWA:						
Cedar Rapids	17,486	4,834	10,359	59.2	1,993	291
Council Bluffs	13,123	3,509	7,868	60.0	1,446	183
Davenport	21,416	6,141	12,456	58.2	2,482	302
Dubuque	15,229	5,618	7,736	50.8	1,759	106
Sioux City	24,730	7,308	14,694	59.4	2,319	399
Waterloo	13,282	3,388	8,276	62.3	1,349	264

TABLE 57.—MARITAL CONDITION OF THE POPULATION 15 YEARS OF AGE AND OVER,

CITY.	MALES 15 YEARS OF AGE AND OVER.					
	Total.[1]	Single.	Married.		Widowed.	Divorced.
			Number.	Per cent.		
KANSAS:						
Topeka	17,725	5,117	11,403	64.3	932	232
Wichita	26,437	7,644	17,015	64.4	1,373	307
KENTUCKY:						
Covington	20,183	7,032	11,979	59.4	1,007	153
Lexington	15,536	5,353	9,067	58.4	899	186
Newport	10,373	3,509	6,243	60.2	507	109
LOUISIANA:						
Shreveport	16,589	5,630	9,811	59.1	893	126
MAINE:						
Bangor	9,144	3,218	5,328	58.3	508	75
Lewiston	10,949	4,208	6,024	55.0	632	56
Portland	24,806	8,286	14,985	60.4	1,343	181
MARYLAND:						
Cumberland	10,946	4,191	6,104	55.8	520	76
Hagerstown	9,658	2,969	6,109	63.3	506	69
MASSACHUSETTS:						
Brockton	24,023	8,276	14,340	59.7	1,166	208
Brookline town	11,682	4,091	6,998	59.9	543	38
Chelsea	15,255	5,698	8,677	56.9	806	63
Chicopee	11,881	4,182	7,182	60.4	489	15
Everett	13,719	4,727	8,347	60.8	601	37
Fitchburg	14,078	4,982	8,407	59.7	619	53
Haverhill	19,368	6,685	11,478	59.3	1,009	176
Holyoke	20,159	7,773	11,326	56.2	995	49
Lawrence	32,557	11,783	19,068	58.6	1,601	84
Lynn	36,136	12,899	21,015	58.2	1,873	343
Malden	16,303	5,622	9,802	60.1	829	47
Medford	13,120	4,083	8,447	64.4	552	35
Newton	14,765	5,202	8,945	60.6	582	28
Pittsfield	14,501	4,983	8,764	60.4	671	51
Quincy	16,905	5,988	10,152	60.1	700	49
Revere	9,499	3,270	5,843	61.5	354	23
Salem	14,507	5,612	8,087	55.7	753	46
Somerville	32,205	10,869	19,724	61.2	1,502	100
Taunton	12,767	4,779	7,291	57.1	633	52
Waltham	10,512	4,072	5,911	56.2	486	39
MICHIGAN:						
Battle Creek	13,788	3,839	8,901	64.6	744	286
Bay City	16,335	5,556	9,824	60.1	825	123
Flint	40,091	15,466	22,320	55.7	1,521	604
Hamtramck village	16,789	5,785	10,551	62.8	367	41
Highland Park	20,012	7,999	11,225	56.1	557	218
Jackson	19,196	6,200	11,563	60.2	988	433
Kalamazoo	17,887	5,480	11,149	62.3	881	344
Lansing	22,832	7,230	14,204	62.2	1,012	313
Muskegon	14,153	5,209	8,157	57.6	648	110
Pontiac	14,764	5,699	8,250	55.9	534	171
Port Huron	9,381	2,839	6,018	64.2	447	58
Saginaw	22,073	7,015	13,839	62.7	970	170
MINNESOTA:						
Duluth	37,924	16,180	19,988	52.7	1,455	226
MISSOURI:						
Joplin	10,430	2,940	6,700	64.2	578	191
St. Joseph	29,512	9,736	17,579	59.6	1,631	399
Springfield	13,774	3,757	9,113	66.2	721	127
MONTANA:						
Butte	17,616	7,444	8,691	49.3	624	213
NEBRASKA:						
Lincoln	19,274	6,026	12,267	63.6	843	189
NEW HAMPSHIRE:						
Manchester	26,121	9,203	15,401	58.6	1,079	147
Nashua	10,239	3,717	5,937	58.0	508	56
NEW JERSEY:						
Atlantic City	18,346	5,942	11,277	61.5	1,020	89
Bayonne	25,665	9,307	15,371	59.9	933	35
Clifton	8,763	2,718	5,709	65.1	325	11
East Orange	17,450	4,978	11,810	67.7	586	29
Elizabeth	33,955	12,257	20,267	59.7	1,347	38
Hoboken	25,764	10,909	13,623	52.9	1,113	81
Irvington town	9,050	2,685	5,976	66.0	362	15
Kearny town	9,388	3,275	5,566	59.3	536	8
Montclair town	9,263	2,840	6,004	64.8	368	21
New Brunswick	11,125	3,719	6,784	61.0	557	20
Orange	11,043	4,163	6,350	57.5	504	15

[1] Total includes persons whose marital condition was not reported.

BY SEX, FOR CITIES HAVING FROM 25,000 TO 100,000 INHABITANTS: 1920—Continued.

CITY.	FEMALES 15 YEARS OF AGE AND OVER.					
	Total.[1]	Single.	Married.		Widowed.	Di-vorced.
			Number.	Per cent.		
KANSAS:						
Topeka	19,776	5,439	11,392	57.6	2,570	365
Wichita	27,461	6,856	16,918	61.6	3,150	474
KENTUCKY:						
Covington	22,407	6,989	12,007	53.6	3,176	223
Lexington	16,904	4,724	9,070	53.7	2,846	244
Newport	11,559	3,475	6,305	54.5	1,598	174
LOUISIANA:						
Shreveport	16,556	3,839	9,590	57.9	2,799	302
MAINE:						
Bangor	10,726	3,657	5,432	50.6	1,488	142
Lewiston	11,975	4,520	5,953	49.7	1,400	94
Portland	27,434	8,762	14,754	53.8	3,556	352
MARYLAND:						
Cumberland	10,567	3,300	5,926	56.1	1,198	79
Hagerstown	10,138	2,853	6,065	59.8	1,148	70
MASSACHUSETTS:						
Brockton	24,854	7,616	14,205	57.2	2,721	287
Brookline town	18,908	8,965	7,173	37.9	2,581	163
Chelsea	13,757	4,441	7,898	57.4	1,352	58
Chicopee	11,197	3,459	6,840	61.1	875	18
Everett	14,227	4,172	8,383	58.9	1,597	71
Fitchburg	14,630	4,993	8,110	55.4	1,438	76
Haverhill	20,589	6,426	11,343	55.1	2,534	269
Holyoke	22,514	8,964	11,178	49.6	2,318	45
Lawrence	33,133	11,286	18,310	55.3	3,406	106
Lynn	37,487	11,644	20,718	55.3	4,663	449
Malden	18,779	6,569	9,782	52.1	2,317	108
Medford	15,027	4,660	8,578	57.1	1,716	68
Newton	19,420	8,103	9,017	46.4	2,229	60
Pittsfield	15,475	5,231	8,464	54.7	1,702	71
Quincy	16,568	4,794	9,913	59.8	1,779	74
Revere	9,603	2,715	5,868	61.1	959	48
Salem	15,614	5,917	7,861	50.3	1,769	61
Somerville	36,245	11,789	19,741	54.5	4,532	174
Taunton	13,683	4,796	7,157	52.3	1,654	67
Waltham	12,482	5,172	5,838	46.8	1,390	76
MICHIGAN:						
Battle Creek	14,186	3,304	8,829	62.2	1,702	336
Bay City	16,403	4,796	9,706	59.2	1,751	150
Flint	28,424	6,256	19,552	68.8	2,176	416
Hamtramck village	10,973	1,515	8,999	82.0	403	43
Highland Park	15,293	3,439	10,333	67.6	1,362	152
Jackson	17,209	3,893	10,928	63.5	2,080	306
Kalamazoo	18,391	4,777	11,079	60.2	2,120	401
Lansing	20,163	4,250	13,534	67.1	2,019	311
Muskegon	12,528	3,274	7,850	62.7	1,278	114
Pontiac	11,381	2,653	7,560	66.4	1,034	111
Port Huron	9,268	2,313	5,828	62.9	1,039	78
Saginaw	22,184	5,969	13,516	60.9	2,409	237
MINNESOTA:						
Duluth	33,273	10,994	19,235	57.8	2,715	290
MISSOURI:						
Joplin	11,212	2,497	6,710	59.8	1,743	247
St. Joseph	29,519	7,824	17,450	59.1	3,600	557
Springfield	15,294	3,918	9,145	59.8	1,974	219
MONTANA:						
Butte	13,821	3,497	8,185	59.2	1,836	207
NEBRASKA:						
Lincoln	21,176	6,249	12,234	57.8	2,407	269
NEW HAMPSHIRE:						
Manchester	29,397	10,678	15,073	51.3	3,310	222
Nashua	10,223	3,338	5,645	55.2	1,143	78
NEW JERSEY:						
Atlantic City	20,663	5,792	11,359	55.0	3,325	169
Bayonne	22,609	6,184	14,416	63.8	1,954	33
Clifton	8,540	2,225	5,541	64.9	750	24
East Orange	21,587	6,891	11,910	55.2	2,659	69
Elizabeth	30,998	8,759	19,129	61.7	3,027	61
Hoboken	22,733	6,832	12,996	57.2	2,769	120
Irvington town	9,241	2,348	5,930	64.2	926	24
Kearny town	9,231	2,912	5,435	58.9	862	18
Montclair town	11,763	4,177	6,133	52.1	1,381	49
New Brunswick	11,385	3,347	6,678	58.7	1,307	26
Orange	12,009	4,155	6,324	52.7	1,492	31

TABLE 57.—MARITAL CONDITION OF THE POPULATION 15 YEARS OF AGE AND OVER,

CITY.	MALES 15 YEARS OF AGE AND OVER.					
	Total.[1]	Single.	Married.		Widowed.	Divorced.
			Number.	Per cent.		
NEW JERSEY—Con.						
Passaic	20,626	6,589	13,309	64.5	665	27
Perth Amboy	13,759	4,516	8,680	63.1	454	18
Plainfield	9,355	2,876	6,054	64.7	383	28
West Hoboken town	14,255	5,004	8,644	60.6	573	19
West New York town	10,243	3,123	6,696	65.4	393	25
NEW YORK:						
Amsterdam	11,281	3,636	7,098	62.9	502	30
Auburn	13,508	4,636	8,074	59.8	706	65
Binghamton	24,309	8,143	14,827	60.8	1,222	138
Elmira	17,587	6,366	10,256	58.3	838	87
Jamestown	14,220	4,523	8,902	62.6	682	82
Kingston	9,433	3,321	5,517	58.5	565	28
Mount Vernon	14,150	4,750	8,752	61.9	605	25
New Rochelle	12,452	4,602	7,305	58.7	443	36
Newburgh	11,135	3,879	6,507	58.4	684	29
Niagara Falls	19,226	7,048	11,406	59.3	673	44
Poughkeepsie	12,207	3,980	7,471	61.2	677	38
Rome	9,849	3,962	5,271	53.5	588	26
Schenectady	32,299	10,748	20,031	62.0	1,372	112
Troy	24,861	9,750	13,556	54.5	1,473	56
Utica	32,707	11,247	19,673	60.1	1,643	140
Watertown	11,243	3,362	7,122	63.3	696	61
NORTH CAROLINA:						
Asheville	9,123	2,902	5,748	63.0	404	43
Charlotte	15,352	5,089	9,498	61.9	718	16
Wilmington	11,384	4,059	6,747	59.3	508	25
Winston-Salem	17,572	7,151	9,682	55.1	685	40
OHIO:						
Canton	35,630	13,007	20,951	58.8	1,331	325
East Cleveland	9,722	2,686	6,667	68.6	304	49
Hamilton	15,160	5,404	8,831	58.3	758	159
Lakewood	14,320	3,559	10,238	71.5	451	54
Lima	14,904	4,406	9,587	64.3	693	209
Lorain	13,881	4,929	8,382	60.4	444	117
Mansfield	10,596	3,326	6,629	62.6	481	135
Marion	10,095	2,886	6,602	65.4	492	114
Newark	9,994	3,031	6,258	62.6	544	151
Portsmouth	11,782	3,881	7,223	61.3	534	127
Springfield	22,664	7,319	13,875	61.2	1,252	186
Steubenville	10,598	3,911	6,170	58.2	439	62
Warren	10,621	3,568	6,591	62.1	382	71
Zanesville	10,486	3,128	6,685	63.8	557	114
OKLAHOMA:						
Muskogee	10,640	3,045	6,899	64.8	547	129
Oklahoma City	35,478	11,799	21,305	60.1	1,703	629
Tulsa	28,524	10,012	16,778	58.8	1,245	445
PENNSYLVANIA:						
Allentown	25,253	7,377	16,521	65.4	1,213	124
Altoona	20,979	6,929	13,001	62.0	932	101
Bethlehem	17,802	5,616	11,372	63.9	727	71
Chester	23,580	9,273	13,130	55.7	1,042	67
Easton	12,075	3,859	7,547	62.5	595	58
Erie	32,853	11,239	19,881	60.5	1,484	219
Harrisburg	28,122	8,545	17,829	63.4	1,459	235
Hazleton	10,130	3,778	5,891	58.2	435	11
Johnstown	23,407	8,542	13,859	59.2	886	116
Lancaster	18,301	5,745	11,329	61.9	1,072	141
McKeesport	16,562	5,907	10,032	60.6	549	44
New Castle	15,735	5,110	9,846	62.6	652	89
Norristown borough	11,507	4,005	6,575	57.1	624	00
Wilkes-Barre	24,465	9,124	14,165	57.9	1,070	50
Williamsport	13,095	4,209	8,018	61.2	797	59
York	16,848	5,010	10,639	63.1	990	194
RHODE ISLAND:						
Cranston	10,462	3,379	6,445	61.6	556	78
Newport	12,796	6,600	5,632	44.0	481	65
Pawtucket	22,349	8,089	13,022	58.3	1,135	85
Woonsocket	14,630	5,528	8,281	56.6	754	40
SOUTH CAROLINA:						
Charleston	23,411	8,322	13,829	59.1	1,178	43
Columbia	13,175	5,021	7,490	56.9	605	46
SOUTH DAKOTA:						
Sioux Falls	9,566	3,420	5,606	58.6	371	89

[1] Total includes persons whose marital condition was not reported.

MARITAL CONDITION. 261

BY SEX, FOR CITIES HAVING FROM 25,000 TO 100,000 INHABITANTS: 1920—Continued.

CITY.	FEMALES 15 YEARS OF AGE AND OVER.					
	Total.[1]	Single.	Married.		Widowed.	Di-vorced.
			Number.	Per cent.		
NEW JERSEY—Con.						
Passaic	20,670	6,129	12,718	61.5	1,745	56
Perth Amboy	12,063	3,054	7,981	66.2	963	29
Plainfield	10,545	3,200	6,026	57.1	1,263	44
West Hoboken town	14,421	4,307	8,461	58.7	1,614	22
West New York town	10,241	2,639	6,624	64.7	939	35
NEW YORK:						
Amsterdam	12,176	3,653	6,994	57.4	1,452	62
Auburn	13,356	3,932	7,541	56.5	1,781	80
Binghamton	26,055	7,411	14,851	57.0	3,530	240
Elmira	17,497	5,148	9,970	57.0	2,232	111
Jamestown	14,900	4,232	8,841	59.3	1,706	106
Kingston	10,947	3,818	5,478	50.0	1,601	43
Mount Vernon	16,260	5,362	8,825	54.2	2,041	49
New Rochelle	13,408	4,471	7,359	54.9	1,537	29
Newburgh	11,809	3,755	6,447	54.6	1,543	25
Niagara Falls	15,835	4,144	10,311	65.1	1,303	53
Poughkeepsie	13,692	4,227	7,391	54.0	1,961	76
Rome	8,658	2,708	4,918	56.8	1,007	23
Schenectady	31,312	8,280	19,384	61.9	3,485	137
Troy	30,795	12,561	13,634	44.3	4,493	78
Utica	35,135	11,099	19,385	55.2	4,433	209
Watertown	12,256	3,324	7,101	57.9	1,727	100
NORTH CAROLINA:						
Asheville	10,868	3,293	5,920	54.5	1,530	78
Charlotte	16,828	4,940	9,519	56.6	2,308	39
Wilmington	12,061	3,284	6,764	56.1	1,921	69
Winston-Salem	17,350	5,615	9,555	55.1	2,074	95
OHIO:						
Canton	28,712	6,837	18,764	65.4	2,728	374
East Cleveland	11,283	3,171	6,708	59.5	1,265	123
Hamilton	14,088	3,768	8,477	60.2	1,670	167
Lakewood	15,847	4,053	9,976	63.0	1,700	111
Lima	15,036	3,669	9,476	63.0	1,637	250
Lorain	10,457	2,145	7,489	71.6	749	73
Mansfield	10,425	2,641	6,327	60.7	1,279	169
Marion	10,070	2,242	6,566	65.2	1,128	132
Newark	10,120	2,467	6,143	60.7	1,325	183
Portsmouth	11,894	3,277	7,098	59.7	1,377	131
Springfield	22,440	5,732	13,644	60.8	2,835	204
Steubenville	9,256	2,434	5,690	61.5	1,026	95
Warren	9,197	2,182	6,007	65.3	937	69
Zanesville	11,430	3,036	6,640	58.1	1,561	186
OKLAHOMA:						
Muskogee	11,027	2,541	6,853	62.1	1,394	234
Oklahoma City	33,467	8,200	20,594	61.5	3,862	782
Tulsa	25,421	6,333	16,059	63.2	2,486	532
PENNSYLVANIA:						
Allentown	26,571	7,197	16,302	61.4	2,878	179
Altoona	21,621	6,320	12,782	59.1	2,385	122
Bethlehem	16,376	4,129	10,588	64.7	1,572	79
Chester	18,372	4,600	11,689	63.6	2,002	63
Easton	12,861	3,609	7,465	58.0	1,695	84
Erie	32,212	9,249	19,215	59.7	3,491	235
Harrisburg	29,647	8,032	17,658	59.6	3,638	295
Hazleton	10,667	3,733	5,740	53.8	1,144	29
Johnstown	20,885	6,044	12,716	60.9	2,020	102
Lancaster	21,293	6,993	11,322	53.2	2,774	195
McKeesport	14,584	4,025	9,097	62.4	1,377	70
New Castle	14,679	3,572	9,404	64.1	1,596	95
Norristown borough	12,674	4,277	6,705	52.9	1,588	87
Wilkes-Barre	25,545	8,742	13,740	53.8	2,960	60
Williamsport	14,257	4,407	7,877	55.3	1,865	100
York	18,137	5,157	10,595	58.4	2,101	281
RHODE ISLAND:						
Cranston	10,687	3,047	6,222	58.2	1,258	143
Newport	10,272	3,383	5,521	53.7	1,266	91
Pawtucket	24,060	8,511	12,804	53.2	2,585	146
Woonsocket	15,585	6,082	8,030	51.5	1,391	61
SOUTH CAROLINA:						
Charleston	25,797	7,318	13,809	53.5	4,559	76
Columbia	14,575	4,408	7,690	52.8	2,345	119
SOUTH DAKOTA:						
Sioux Falls	9,120	2,750	5,408	59.3	820	121

TABLE 57.—MARITAL CONDITION OF THE POPULATION 15 YEARS OF AGE AND OVER,

CITY.	MALES 15 YEARS OF AGE AND OVER.					
	Total.[1]	Single.	Married.		Widowed.	Divorced.
			Number.	Per cent.		
TENNESSEE:						
Chattanooga	21,901	7,593	12,946	59.1	1,123	236
Knoxville	26,205	8,092	16,779	64.0	1,126	167
TEXAS:						
Austin	12,071	4,323	6,705	55.5	903	114
Beaumont	14,942	5,085	8,930	59.8	713	207
El Paso	25,349	8,767	15,054	59.4	1,274	227
Galveston	18,147	7,317	9,282	51.1	995	400
Waco	13,178	4,005	8,352	63.4	652	141
Wichita Falls	19,376	6,963	9,374	48.4	708	228
UTAH:						
Ogden	10,959	3,453	7,030	64.1	380	91
VIRGINIA:						
Lynchburg	9,604	3,466	5,648	58.8	447	38
Newport News	16,015	7,277	8,023	50.1	491	69
Petersburg	10,273	3,555	6,171	60.1	510	33
Portsmouth	20,424	7,634	11,656	57.1	1,025	98
Roanoke	17,281	5,763	10,826	62.6	592	80
WASHINGTON:						
Bellingham	9,893	3,506	5,707	57.7	511	158
Everett	10,925	3,990	6,280	57.5	442	196
Tacoma	39,793	14,373	21,914	55.1	1,645	623
WEST VIRGINIA:						
Charleston	14,347	5,005	8,630	60.2	477	202
Clarksburg	9,875	3,350	6,076	61.5	353	56
Huntington	17,601	5,786	10,934	62.1	668	182
Wheeling	19,893	7,080	11,793	59.3	910	75
WISCONSIN:						
Green Bay	10,479	3,726	6,114	58.3	508	107
Kenosha	16,142	6,782	8,732	54.1	469	128
La Crosse	10,571	3,785	6,207	58.7	498	76
Madison	13,492	4,675	8,180	60.6	506	80
Oshkosh	11,416	3,822	6,898	60.4	588	94
Racine	23,523	9,536	12,871	54.7	853	172
Sheboygan	10,964	3,763	6,672	60.9	446	48
Superior	14,882	6,166	7,889	53.0	611	132

[1] Total includes persons whose marital condition was not reported.

BY SEX, FOR CITIES HAVING FROM 25,000 TO 100,000 INHABITANTS: 1920—Continued.

CITY.	Total.[1]	Single.	Married.		Widowed.	Divorced.
			Number.	Per cent.		
TENNESSEE:						
Chattanooga	21,917	5,516	12,901	58.9	3,190	299
Knoxville	28,480	7,697	16,808	59.0	3,617	333
TEXAS:						
Austin	13,974	4,373	6,865	49.1	2,464	254
Beaumont	13,907	2,982	8,895	64.0	1,674	355
El Paso	28,296	7,667	15,600	55.1	4,727	282
Galveston	15,433	3,871	8,856	57.4	2,268	419
Waco	14,295	3,593	8,256	57.8	2,117	305
Wichita Falls	11,504	2,290	7,942	69.0	925	128
UTAH:						
Ogden	10,979	2,783	6,894	62.8	1,131	166
VIRGINIA:						
Lynchburg	11,911	4,193	5,796	48.7	1,824	89
Newport News	11,165	2,521	7,488	67.1	1,079	70
Petersburg	12,018	3,675	6,380	53.1	1,900	55
Portsmouth	18,718	4,500	11,419	61.0	2,697	97
Roanoke	18,048	5,174	10,683	59.2	2,057	116
WASHINGTON:						
Bellingham	8,984	2,278	5,605	62.4	983	114
Everett	9,496	2,218	6,148	64.7	945	178
Tacoma	33,463	7,939	21,248	63.5	3,518	653
WEST VIRGINIA:						
Charleston	14,081	3,832	8,511	60.4	1,474	249
Clarksburg	9,315	2,440	5,970	64.1	828	60
Huntington	17,541	4,599	10,880	62.0	1,809	239
Wheeling	20,979	6,589	11,712	55.8	2,518	143
WISCONSIN:						
Green Bay	11,248	3,945	6,054	53.8	1,109	132
Kenosha	11,956	3,228	7,695	64.4	923	97
La Crosse	11,884	4,162	6,187	52.1	1,401	129
Madison	15,328	5,413	8,060	52.6	1,677	140
Oshkosh	12,638	4,149	6,893	54.5	1,443	137
Racine	19,174	5,543	11,783	61.5	1,683	143
Sheboygan	10,586	3,085	6,427	60.7	1,000	55
Superior	12,610	3,856	7,661	60.8	957	117

FEMALES 15 YEARS OF AGE AND OVER.

[1] Total includes persons whose marital condition was not reported.

TABLE 58.—MARITAL CONDITION OF THE URBAN AND RURAL POPULATION 15 YEARS

CLASSES, FOR THE

CLASS OF POPULATION AND AGE PERIOD.	MALES 15 YEARS OF AGE AND OVER.							
	Total.[1]	Single.		Married.		Widowed.		Divorced.
		Number.	Per cent.	Number.	Per cent.	Number.	Per cent.	
ALL CLASSES.[2]								
Urban communities:								
15 years and over	19, 695, 500	6, 982, 294	35. 5	11, 605, 237	58. 9	897, 500	4. 6	142, 778
15 to 19 years	2, 130, 053	2, 090, 406	98. 1	35, 608	1. 7	635	(³)	336
20 to 24 years	2, 421, 604	1, 774, 284	73. 3	625, 517	25. 8	8, 608	0. 4	5, 682
25 to 34 years	5, 057, 251	1, 730, 334	34. 2	3, 210, 968	63. 5	68, 504	1. 4	33, 841
35 to 44 years	4, 178, 866	729, 697	17. 5	3, 272, 922	78. 3	124, 618	3. 0	42, 727
45 to 64 years	4, 763, 789	559, 406	11. 7	3, 758, 311	78. 9	385, 855	8. 1	51, 853
65 years and over	1, 081, 828	80, 260	7. 4	684, 452	63. 3	307, 066	28. 4	7, 771
Age unknown	62, 109	17, 907	28. 8	17, 459	28. 1	2, 214	3. 6	568
Rural communities:								
15 years and over	17, 225, 163	5, 985, 271	34. 7	10, 244, 029	59. 5	860, 808	5. 0	92, 506
15 to 19 years	2, 543, 739	2, 477, 364	97. 4	60, 766	2. 4	1, 195	(³)	423
20 to 24 years	2, 105, 441	1, 426, 339	67. 7	654, 801	31. 1	11, 903	0. 6	4, 598
25 to 34 years	3, 611, 765	1, 055, 256	29. 2	2, 474, 513	68. 5	57, 420	1. 6	17, 095
35 to 44 years	3, 181, 038	458, 889	14. 4	2, 600, 386	81. 7	96, 082	3. 0	20, 865
45 to 64 years	4, 351, 171	455, 606	10. 5	3, 519, 174	80. 9	330, 708	7. 6	38, 558
65 years and over	1, 401, 243	101, 951	7. 3	922, 735	65. 9	361, 590	25. 8	10, 735
Age unknown	30, 766	9, 866	32. 1	11, 654	37. 9	1, 910	6. 2	232
NATIVE WHITE—NATIVE PARENTAGE.								
Urban communities:								
15 years and over	8, 350, 138	3, 025, 709	36. 2	4, 846, 805	58. 0	363, 354	4. 4	77, 523
15 to 19 years	1, 060, 228	1, 036, 261	97. 7	22, 023	2. 1	307	(³)	201
20 to 24 years	1, 163, 280	819, 028	70. 4	333, 529	28. 7	4, 137	0. 4	3, 338
25 to 34 years	2, 150, 465	673, 505	31. 3	1, 422, 891	66. 2	29, 876	1. 4	19, 595
35 to 44 years	1, 636, 491	258, 770	15. 8	1, 301, 932	79. 6	49, 573	3. 0	23, 233
45 to 64 years	1, 816, 138	195, 452	10. 8	1, 445, 336	79. 6	145, 698	8. 0	26, 612
65 years and over	483, 243	33, 294	6. 9	312, 004	64. 6	132, 745	27. 5	4, 238
Age unknown	40, 293	9, 399	23. 3	9, 090	22. 6	1, 018	2. 5	306
Rural communities:								
15 years and over	10, 741, 969	3, 750, 809	34. 9	6, 397, 484	59. 6	511, 467	4. 8	57, 266
15 to 19 years	1, 737, 249	1, 691, 454	97. 4	42, 369	2. 4	683	(³)	269
20 to 24 years	1, 383, 538	928, 228	67. 1	441, 051	31. 9	6, 728	0. 5	2, 808
25 to 34 years	2, 271, 518	598, 807	26. 4	1, 623, 905	71. 5	34, 042	1. 5	10, 816
35 to 44 years	1, 910, 389	232, 893	12. 2	1, 607, 137	84. 1	54, 956	2. 9	12, 983
45 to 64 years	2, 538, 525	234, 648	9. 2	2, 086, 814	82. 2	189, 753	7. 5	23, 457
65 years and over	882, 284	58, 621	6. 6	590, 203	66. 9	224, 182	25. 4	6, 788
Age unknown	18, 466	6, 158	33. 3	6, 005	32. 5	1, 123	6. 1	145
NATIVE WHITE—FOREIGN PARENTAGE.								
Urban communities:								
15 years and over	3, 233, 948	1, 493, 560	46. 2	1, 601, 951	49. 5	114, 275	3. 5	18, 729
15 to 19 years	502, 152	497, 758	99. 1	3, 575	0. 7	84	(³)	25
20 to 24 years	485, 955	394, 421	81. 2	88, 426	18. 2	1, 035	0. 2	522
25 to 34 years	797, 721	325, 818	40. 8	456, 818	57. 3	9, 516	1. 2	4, 274
35 to 44 years	568, 535	132, 504	23. 3	413, 736	72. 8	16, 200	2. 8	5, 464
45 to 64 years	773, 174	129, 741	16. 8	573, 594	74. 2	61, 360	7. 9	7, 661
65 years and over	103, 488	11, 802	11. 4	64, 900	62. 7	25, 923	25. 0	741
Age unknown	2, 923	1, 516	51. 9	902	30. 9	157	5. 4	42
Rural communities:								
15 years and over	1, 558, 963	647, 730	41. 6	810, 010	51. 1	57, 337	3. 7	7, 468
15 to 19 years	205, 570	203, 879	99. 2	1, 321	0. 6	32	(³)	10
20 to 24 years	190, 180	157, 463	82. 8	31, 425	16. 5	387	0. 2	163
25 to 34 years	352, 602	141, 760	40. 2	205, 337	58. 2	3, 686	1. 0	1, 103
35 to 44 years	298, 440	63, 841	21. 4	225, 428	75. 5	7, 092	2. 4	1, 672
45 to 64 years	434, 992	71, 477	16. 4	330, 310	75. 9	28, 824	6. 6	3, 807
65 years and over	75, 887	8, 770	11. 6	48, 995	64. 6	17, 232	22. 7	699
Age unknown	1, 292	560	43. 3	524	40. 6	84	6. 5	14

[1] Total includes persons whose marital condition was not reported.

OF AGE AND OVER, BY SEX AND AGE PERIODS, FOR PRINCIPAL POPULATION
UNITED STATES: 1920.

CLASS OF POPULATION AND AGE PERIOD.	Total.[1]	FEMALES 15 YEARS OF AGE AND OVER.						Di-vorced.
		Single.		Married.		Widowed.		
		Number.	Per cent.	Number.	Per cent.	Number.	Per cent.	
ALL CLASSES.[2]								
Urban communities:								
15 years and over	19,618,764	5,698,673	29.0	11,310,188	57.6	2,395,622	12.2	186,181
15 to 19 years	2,315,910	2,064,740	89.2	241,588	10.4	4,381	0.2	3,056
20 to 24 years	2,680,496	1,350,388	50.4	1,276,092	47.6	31,859	1.2	17,879
25 to 34 years	4,988,362	1,137,218	22.8	3,621,083	72.6	166,820	3.3	58,522
35 to 44 years	3,876,690	543,587	14.0	2,953,031	76.2	322,241	8.3	54,218
45 to 64 years	4,463,857	493,192	11.0	2,843,001	63.7	1,075,477	24.1	47,220
65 years and over	1,256,723	99,414	7.9	360,534	28.7	789,581	62.8	4,808
Age unknown	36,726	10,134	27.6	14,859	40.5	5,263	14.3	478
Rural communities:								
15 years and over	15,558,751	3,918,229	25.2	10,008,745	64.3	1,522,003	9.8	87,123
15 to 19 years	2,440,854	2,072,910	84.9	354,954	14.5	7,858	0.3	2,961
20 to 24 years	2,069,480	813,663	39.3	1,207,605	58.4	33,555	1.6	10,703
25 to 34 years	3,500,306	499,186	14.3	2,871,272	82.0	103,460	3.0	22,909
35 to 44 years	2,884,244	224,295	7.8	2,473,403	85.8	163,252	5.7	20,809
45 to 64 years	3,451,348	228,675	6.6	2,623,271	76.0	569,943	16.5	24,793
65 years and over	1,193,421	74,028	6.2	469,626	39.4	641,040	53.7	4,801
Age unknown	19,098	5,472	28.7	8,614	45.1	2,895	15.2	147
NATIVE WHITE—NATIVE PARENTAGE.								
Urban communities:								
15 years and over	8,547,716	2,654,151	31.1	4,801,681	56.2	976,781	11.4	101,304
15 to 19 years	1,150,452	1,013,637	88.1	132,184	11.5	1,953	0.2	1,826
20 to 24 years	1,264,443	635,128	50.2	603,563	47.7	13,621	1.1	10,409
25 to 34 years	2,185,811	520,786	23.8	1,561,682	71.4	68,995	3.2	32,417
35 to 44 years	1,585,027	226,433	14.3	1,204,587	76.0	123,562	7.8	29,031
45 to 64 years	1,752,571	199,193	11.4	1,122,339	64.0	404,388	23.1	24,650
65 years and over	587,868	53,079	9.0	168,976	28.7	362,042	61.6	2,725
Age unknown	21,544	5,895	27.4	8,350	38.8	2,220	10.3	246
Rural communities:								
15 years and over	9,982,032	2,614,339	26.2	6,394,184	64.1	908,219	9.1	51,439
15 to 19 years	1,651,117	1,403,473	85.0	240,740	14.6	3,925	0.2	1,672
20 to 24 years	1,365,446	540,080	39.6	800,457	58.6	16,564	1.2	5,958
25 to 34 years	2,253,049	323,992	14.4	1,859,980	82.6	53,900	2.4	13,157
35 to 44 years	1,783,275	141,130	7.9	1,543,106	86.5	85,505	4.8	12,151
45 to 64 years	2,131,798	146,572	6.9	1,633,011	76.6	334,196	15.7	15,232
65 years and over	785,481	55,286	7.0	311,857	39.7	412,657	52.5	3,184
Age unknown	11,866	3,806	32.1	5,033	42.4	1,472	12.4	85
NATIVE WHITE—FOREIGN PARENTAGE.								
Urban communities:								
15 years and over	3,544,449	1,394,008	39.3	1,786,049	50.4	336,269	9.5	23,873
15 to 19 years	535,170	502,373	93.9	31,650	5.9	331	0.1	203
20 to 24 years	540,520	329,697	61.0	204,493	37.8	3,526	0.7	1,713
25 to 34 years	862,859	263,589	30.5	569,472	66.0	21,459	2.5	7,433
35 to 44 years	622,518	135,299	21.7	434,200	69.7	45,481	7.3	7,025
45 to 64 years	854,808	146,879	17.2	507,645	59.4	192,515	22.5	6,993
65 years and over	125,740	14,860	11.8	37,613	29.9	72,639	57.8	459
Age unknown	2,834	1,311	46.3	976	34.4	318	11.2	47
Rural communities:								
15 years and over	1,362,098	397,263	29.2	862,005	63.3	95,552	7.0	5,662
15 to 19 years	186,476	172,392	92.4	13,686	7.3	159	0.1	54
20 to 24 years	168,100	87,443	52.0	78,663	46.8	1,238	0.7	392
25 to 34 years	325,506	63,988	19.7	253,909	78.0	5,903	1.8	1,375
35 to 44 years	266,268	31,461	11.8	222,669	83.6	10,496	3.9	1,440
45 to 64 years	355,358	36,811	10.4	266,836	75.1	49,201	13.8	2,169
65 years and over	59,439	4,794	8.1	25,809	43.4	28,460	47.9	229
Age unknown	951	374	39.3	433	45.5	95	10.0	3

[2] Includes Indians, Chinese, Japanese, and "all other."   [3] Less than one-tenth of 1 per cent.

TABLE 58.—MARITAL CONDITION OF THE URBAN AND RURAL POPULATION 15 YEARS
CLASSES, FOR THE UNITED

CLASS OF POPULATION AND AGE PERIOD.	Total.[1]	MALES 15 YEARS OF AGE AND OVER.						
		Single.		Married.		Widowed.		Divorced.
		Number.	Per cent.	Number.	Per cent.	Number.	Per cent.	
NATIVE WHITE—MIXED PARENTAGE.								
Urban communities:								
15 years and over	1,344,599	627,809	46.7	667,821	49.7	37,299	2.8	9,954
15 to 19 years	225,898	223,468	98.9	2,112	0.9	40	([2])	13
20 to 24 years	214,472	171,984	80.2	41,072	19.2	521	0.2	423
25 to 34 years	359,263	143,237	39.9	208,452	58.0	4,497	1.3	2,649
35 to 44 years	265,935	53,616	20.2	201,777	75.9	7,038	2.6	3,302
45 to 64 years	242,174	31,905	13.2	190,457	78.6	16,415	6.8	3,190
65 years and over	35,793	3,052	8.5	23,607	66.0	8,733	24.4	351
Age unknown	1,064	547	51.4	344	32.3	55	5.2	26
Rural communities:								
15 years and over	853,430	381,981	44.8	437,770	51.3	27,383	3.2	4,773
15 to 19 years	151,464	149,997	99.0	1,196	0.8	23	([2])	7
20 to 24 years	124,163	100,991	81.3	22,342	18.0	263	0.2	160
25 to 34 years	200,092	74,603	37.3	121,913	60.9	2,348	1.2	879
35 to 44 years	161,091	29,499	18.3	126,446	78.5	3,755	2.3	1,211
45 to 64 years	177,669	23,459	13.2	140,447	79.0	11,504	6.5	2,050
65 years and over	38,396	3,186	8.3	25,212	65.7	9,452	24.6	461
Age unknown	555	246	44.3	214	38.6	38	6.8	5
FOREIGN-BORN WHITE.								
Urban communities:								
15 years and over	5,362,678	1,355,757	25.3	3,667,834	68.4	298,225	5.6	22,413
15 to 19 years	197,865	195,113	98.6	2,250	1.1	73	([2])	18
20 to 24 years	360,275	270,300	75.0	87,031	24.2	1,025	0.3	318
25 to 34 years	1,378,523	471,065	34.2	883,278	64.1	14,916	1.1	3,320
35 to 44 years	1,379,788	223,156	16.2	1,112,177	80.6	33,865	2.5	6,415
45 to 64 years	1,625,196	163,955	10.1	1,323,147	81.4	124,332	7.7	10,248
65 years and over	411,122	28,017	6.8	256,622	62.4	123,489	30.0	2,003
Age unknown	9,909	4,151	41.9	3,329	33.6	525	5.3	91
Rural communities:								
15 years and over	1,889,861	499,290	26.4	1,235,108	65.4	139,824	7.4	9,537
15 to 19 years	61,405	60,214	98.1	1,008	1.6	33	0.1	5
20 to 24 years	96,713	74,568	77.1	21,264	22.0	306	0.3	76
25 to 34 years	360,383	148,096	41.1	206,237	57.2	4,237	1.2	734
35 to 44 years	432,084	93,924	21.7	324,218	75.0	11,125	2.6	1,823
45 to 64 years	667,191	96,154	14.4	515,395	77.2	49,123	7.4	4,992
65 years and over	268,262	24,962	9.3	165,643	61.7	74,774	27.9	1,887
Age unknown	3,823	1,372	35.9	1,343	35.1	226	5.9	20
NEGRO.								
Urban communities:								
15 years and over	1,325,398	441,845	33.3	782,776	59.1	82,518	6.2	13,928
15 to 19 years	138,893	132,913	95.7	5,550	4.0	131	0.1	78
20 to 24 years	189,209	111,451	58.9	74,299	39.3	1,872	1.0	1,073
25 to 34 years	352,012	105,975	30.1	231,454	65.8	9,576	2.7	3,943
35 to 44 years	307,200	54,511	17.7	230,159	74.9	17,591	5.7	4,230
45 to 64 years	285,246	31,803	11.1	211,700	74.2	37,091	13.0	4,068
65 years and over	45,421	3,148	6.9	25,912	57.0	15,806	34.8	435
Age unknown	7,417	2,044	27.6	3,702	49.9	451	6.1	101
Rural communities:								
15 years and over	2,067,812	663,032	32.1	1,267,631	61.3	118,216	5.7	12,761
15 to 19 years	374,523	358,730	95.8	14,493	3.9	414	0.1	132
20 to 24 years	297,960	156,144	52.4	135,061	45.3	4,105	1.4	1,331
25 to 34 years	403,919	83,626	20.7	303,182	75.1	12,456	3.1	3,389
35 to 44 years	352,313	32,749	9.3	297,837	84.5	18,046	5.1	2,997
45 to 64 years	504,545	25,112	5.0	425,768	84.4	48,820	9.7	4,016
65 years and over	128,460	5,296	4.1	87,952	68.5	33,964	26.4	849
Age unknown	6,093	1,375	22.6	3,345	54.9	411	6.7	47

[1] Total includes persons whose marital condition was not reported.

OF AGE AND OVER, BY SEX AND AGE PERIODS, FOR PRINCIPAL POPULATION STATES: 1920—Continued.

CLASS OF POPULATION AND AGE PERIOD.	Total.[1]	FEMALES 15 YEARS OF AGE AND OVER.						Divorced.
		Single.		Married.		Widowed.		
		Number.	Per cent.	Number.	Per cent.	Number.	Per cent.	
NATIVE WHITE—MIXED PARENTAGE.								
Urban communities:								
15 years and over	1,522,351	614,734	40.4	775,296	50.9	116,124	7.6	14,712
15 to 19 years	240,134	225,658	94.0	13,884	5.8	206	0.1	171
20 to 24 years	244,324	152,501	62.4	88,431	36.2	1,692	0.7	1,337
25 to 34 years	421,661	133,494	31.7	271,963	64.5	10,813	2.6	4,992
35 to 44 years	305,557	59,512	19.5	220,453	72.1	20,845	6.8	4,556
45 to 64 years	264,436	38,390	14.5	167,009	63.2	55,424	21.0	3,425
65 years and over	45,069	4,642	10.3	13,152	29.2	27,008	59.9	213
Age unknown	1,170	537	45.9	404	34.5	136	11.6	18
Rural communities:								
15 years and over	782,210	262,438	33.6	467,520	59.8	47,462	6.1	3,919
15 to 19 years	140,303	131,047	93.4	8,931	6.4	107	0.1	75
20 to 24 years	114,076	61,886	54.2	50,771	44.5	873	0.8	321
25 to 34 years	194,095	38,729	20.0	150,450	77.5	3,692	1.9	1,042
35 to 44 years	151,922	15,986	10.5	128,480	84.6	6,300	4.1	1,053
45 to 64 years	149,262	12,332	8.3	115,445	77.3	20,092	13.5	1,264
65 years and over	32,111	2,286	7.1	13,239	41.2	16,359	50.9	163
Age unknown	441	172	39.0	204	46.3	39	8.8	1
FOREIGN-BORN WHITE.								
Urban communities:								
15 years and over	4,599,750	715,989	15.6	3,140,910	68.3	714,477	15.5	22,627
15 to 19 years	215,863	187,587	86.9	27,557	12.8	341	0.2	130
20 to 24 years	399,282	156,097	39.1	237,899	59.6	3,649	0.9	975
25 to 34 years	1,121,251	156,558	14.0	930,009	82.9	28,766	2.6	4,939
35 to 44 years	1,061,819	95,494	9.0	885,660	83.4	72,657	6.8	6,953
45 to 64 years	1,353,515	94,476	7.0	926,690	68.5	322,347	23.8	8,427
65 years and over	442,914	24,433	5.5	130,570	29.5	285,852	64.5	1,125
Age unknown	5,106	1,344	26.3	2,525	49.5	865	16.9	48
Rural communities:								
15 years and over	1,314,235	119,810	9.1	982,593	74.8	204,778	15.6	5,029
15 to 19 years	52,809	41,653	78.9	10,920	20.7	158	0.3	34
20 to 24 years	70,574	18,040	25.6	51,450	72.9	816	1.2	153
25 to 34 years	245,681	18,782	7.6	220,561	89.8	5,515	2.2	631
35 to 44 years	292,213	14,861	5.1	262,788	89.9	13,185	4.5	1,117
45 to 64 years	445,603	18,999	4.3	352,914	79.2	70,695	15.9	2,370
65 years and over	205,929	7,293	3.5	83,143	40.4	114,123	55.4	712
Age unknown	1,426	182	12.8	817	57.3	286	20.1	12
NEGRO.								
Urban communities:								
15 years and over	1,383,150	315,842	22.8	790,160	57.1	250,844	18.1	23,523
15 to 19 years	171,629	133,250	77.6	35,902	20.9	1,544	0.9	717
20 to 24 years	227,792	76,027	33.4	138,579	60.8	9,325	4.1	3,426
25 to 34 years	388,894	62,352	16.0	280,736	72.2	36,616	9.4	8,666
35 to 44 years	297,585	26,659	9.0	204,411	68.7	59,462	20.0	6,617
45 to 64 years	236,447	14,153	6.0	117,854	49.8	100,321	42.4	3,697
65 years and over	54,821	2,380	4.3	10,121	18.5	41,856	76.4	282
Age unknown	5,982	1,021	17.1	2,557	42.7	1,720	28.8	118
Rural communities:								
15 years and over	2,039,950	509,416	25.0	1,249,021	61.2	257,117	12.6	20,348
15 to 19 years	398,170	314,919	79.1	78,267	19.7	3,436	0.9	1,085
20 to 24 years	339,886	103,384	30.4	218,161	64.2	13,761	4.0	3,764
25 to 34 years	462,779	52,282	11.3	369,612	79.9	33,675	7.3	6,488
35 to 44 years	376,534	20,337	5.4	304,006	80.7	46,808	12.4	4,880
45 to 64 years	354,559	13,503	3.8	243,898	68.8	92,797	26.2	3,614
65 years and over	104,011	4,136	4.0	33,150	31.9	65,730	63.2	475
Age unknown	4,011	855	21.3	1,927	48.0	910	22.7	42

[2] Less than one-tenth of 1 per cent.

Table **59.**—MARITAL CONDITION OF THE POPULATION 15 YEARS OF AGE AND OVER,

DIVISION AND STATE.	Total.[1]	MALES 15 YEARS OF AGE AND OVER IN URBAN COMMUNITIES.				Wid-owed.	Di-vorced.
		Single.		Married.			
		Number.	Per cent.	Number.	Per cent.		
United States	**19,695,500**	**6,982,294**	**35.5**	**11,605,237**	**58.9**	**897,500**	**142,778**
GEOGRAPHIC DIVISIONS:							
New England	2,054,291	750,699	36.5	1,190,432	57.9	100,421	9,367
Middle Atlantic	5,898,539	2,123,743	36.0	3,477,612	59.0	260,241	17,314
East North Central	4,850,190	1,688,675	34.8	2,899,924	59.8	207,757	42,994
West North Central	1,748,935	610,816	34.9	1,033,921	59.1	81,866	17,391
South Atlantic	1,524,487	533,894	35.0	905,081	59.4	73,532	7,869
East South Central	693,466	227,629	32.8	421,205	60.7	37,000	6,210
West South Central	1,076,509	373,082	34.7	632,595	58.8	53,140	11,403
Mountain	454,705	162,623	35.8	259,683	57.1	20,185	5,899
Pacific	1,394,378	511,133	36.7	784,784	56.3	63,358	24,331
NEW ENGLAND:							
Maine	106,535	35,997	33.8	63,589	59.7	5,942	790
New Hampshire	98,661	34,087	34.5	58,161	59.0	5,409	778
Vermont	38,624	12,944	33.5	23,229	60.1	2,147	247
Massachusetts	1,274,710	471,984	37.0	732,693	57.5	62,787	5,328
Rhode Island	204,743	75,279	36.8	117,910	57.6	10,275	1,158
Connecticut	331,018	120,408	36.4	194,850	58.9	13,861	1,066
MIDDLE ATLANTIC:							
New York	3,064,023	1,129,339	36.9	1,781,059	58.1	131,233	7,903
New Jersey	864,141	298,552	34.5	524,809	60.7	37,473	1,934
Pennsylvania	1,970,375	695,852	35.3	1,171,744	59.5	91,535	7,477
EAST NORTH CENTRAL:							
Ohio	1,382,423	474,754	34.3	834,398	60.4	59,241	12,419
Indiana	548,104	170,664	31.1	341,776	62.4	27,074	6,668
Illinois	1,605,045	567,662	35.4	951,743	59.3	68,781	12,254
Michigan	866,165	311,884	36.0	510,086	58.9	34,305	8,488
Wisconsin	448,453	163,711	36.5	261,921	58.4	18,356	3,165
WEST NORTH CENTRAL:							
Minnesota	388,910	153,455	39.5	216,611	55.7	15,280	2,342
Iowa	323,711	108,232	33.4	194,631	60.1	16,154	4,008
Missouri	593,785	203,353	34.2	353,232	59.5	29,686	6,242
North Dakota	30,227	11,243	37.2	17,503	57.9	1,079	138
South Dakota	37,367	13,483	36.1	21,725	58.1	1,522	311
Nebraska	152,331	54,053	35.5	88,915	58.4	7,010	1,673
Kansas	222,604	66,997	30.1	141,304	63.5	11,135	2,677
SOUTH ATLANTIC:							
Delaware	45,135	16,246	36.0	26,369	58.4	2,250	210
Maryland	312,579	111,753	35.8	182,692	58.4	16,047	1,801
District of Columbia	159,013	60,976	38.3	88,698	55.8	7,616	884
Virginia	239,818	87,057	36.3	140,088	58.4	10,726	1,291
West Virginia	130,909	45,321	34.6	78,817	60.2	5,010	904
North Carolina	161,110	56,414	35.0	97,117	60.3	6,866	346
South Carolina	97,184	34,049	35.0	58,171	59.9	4,598	195
Georgia	250,999	81,516	32.5	154,507	61.6	13,255	1,264
Florida	127,740	40,562	31.8	78,622	61.5	7,164	974
EAST SOUTH CENTRAL:							
Kentucky	225,254	75,549	33.5	134,917	59.9	12,113	2,377
Tennessee	213,519	68,589	32.1	131,092	61.4	11,561	1,896
Alabama	174,087	56,459	32.4	106,883	61.4	9,071	1,460
Mississippi	80,606	27,032	33.5	48,313	59.9	4,255	477
WEST SOUTH CENTRAL:							
Arkansas	101,631	31,801	31.3	62,829	61.8	5,595	1,158
Louisiana	219,222	82,733	37.7	123,661	56.4	10,325	1,325
Oklahoma	199,091	64,394	32.3	121,627	61.1	9,471	2,738
Texas	556,565	194,154	34.9	324,478	58.3	27,749	6,182
MOUNTAIN:							
Montana	66,845	25,657	38.4	36,888	55.2	2,481	798
Idaho	43,244	15,298	35.4	25,610	59.2	1,710	507
Wyoming	24,207	9,667	39.9	13,073	54.0	992	296
Colorado	174,946	59,858	34.2	99,202	56.7	9,015	2,679
New Mexico	22,126	7,613	34.4	13,082	59.1	1,201	175
Arizona	44,687	16,997	38.0	24,774	55.4	2,035	489
Utah	72,019	25,016	34.7	43,583	60.5	2,481	775
Nevada	6,631	2,517	38.0	3,465	52.3	264	150
PACIFIC:							
Washington	304,844	114,888	37.7	169,880	55.7	12,596	5,463
Oregon	153,906	53,755	34.9	90,014	58.5	6,604	3,364
California	935,628	342,490	36.6	524,890	56.1	44,158	15,504

[1] Total includes persons whose marital condition was not reported.

BY SEX, FOR URBAN AND RURAL COMMUNITIES, BY DIVISIONS AND STATES: 1920.

DIVISION AND STATE.	MALES 15 YEARS OF AGE AND OVER IN RURAL COMMUNITIES.						
	Total.[1]	Single.		Married.		Wid-owed.	Di-vorced.
		Number.	Per cent.	Number.	Per cent.		
United States	17,225,163	5,985,271	34.7	10,244,029	59.5	860,808	92,506
GEOGRAPHIC DIVISIONS:							
New England	559,828	185,220	33.1	331,782	59.3	36,886	5,041
Middle Atlantic	1,964,963	665,120	33.8	1,181,095	60.1	108,343	6,423
East North Central	2,994,544	1,016,102	33.9	1,792,760	59.9	160,600	18,990
West North Central	2,731,755	1,021,712	37.4	1,562,945	57.2	124,601	14,144
South Atlantic	2,934,562	1,004,444	34.2	1,781,439	60.7	133,571	8,393
East South Central	2,105,866	666,550	31.7	1,320,810	62.7	105,301	9,050
West South Central	2,298,764	772,913	33.6	1,394,677	60.7	112,860	11,460
Mountain	774,142	304,722	39.4	423,481	54.7	35,989	7,533
Pacific	860,739	348,488	40.5	455,040	52.9	42,657	11,472
NEW ENGLAND:							
Maine	172,943	56,088	32.4	102,582	59.3	12,181	1,838
New Hampshire	63,270	20,601	32.6	36,630	57.9	4,915	984
Vermont	89,281	28,950	32.4	53,081	59.5	6,225	924
Massachusetts	73,078	24,713	33.8	42,994	58.8	4,795	497
Rhode Island	5,800	1,990	34.3	3,298	56.9	436	68
Connecticut	155,456	52,878	34.0	93,197	60.0	8,334	730
MIDDLE ATLANTIC:							
New York	668,805	220,749	33.0	402,477	60.2	41,880	2,263
New Jersey	246,246	83,929	34.1	147,940	60.1	13,104	659
Pennsylvania	1,049,912	360,442	34.3	630,678	60.1	53,359	3,501
EAST NORTH CENTRAL:							
Ohio	743,003	238,242	32.1	456,398	61.4	42,355	4,806
Indiana	511,765	156,918	30.7	321,801	62.9	28,475	3,671
Illinois	742,448	262,589	35.4	435,349	58.6	38,423	4,333
Michigan	504,951	162,181	32.1	309,985	61.4	28,113	3,870
Wisconsin	492,347	196,172	39.8	269,227	54.7	23,234	2,310
WEST NORTH CENTRAL:							
Minnesota	479,828	212,425	44.3	244,218	50.9	20,407	1,792
Iowa	541,696	195,394	36.1	317,429	58.6	24,609	2,936
Missouri	622,458	202,922	32.6	380,728	61.2	33,107	3,653
North Dakota	183,774	76,691	41.7	98,751	53.7	6,686	677
South Dakota	187,506	75,801	40.4	102,270	54.5	7,478	961
Nebraska	308,967	115,375	37.3	178,284	57.7	12,705	1,558
Kansas	407,526	143,104	35.1	241,265	59.2	19,609	2,567
SOUTH ATLANTIC:							
Delaware	36,476	11,569	31.7	22,481	61.6	2,014	97
Maryland	199,934	72,794	36.4	115,303	57.7	10,724	639
District of Columbia[2]							
Virginia	512,072	188,039	36.7	297,898	58.2	23,655	1,649
West Virginia	356,775	127,627	35.8	212,279	59.8	14,664	1,530
North Carolina	595,521	201,467	33.8	366,692	61.6	24,673	976
South Carolina	395,044	134,487	34.0	242,530	61.4	16,815	402
Georgia	633,802	201,822	31.8	399,849	63.1	29,059	1,978
Florida	204,938	66,639	32.5	124,407	60.7	11,967	1,122
EAST SOUTH CENTRAL:							
Kentucky	570,248	184,728	32.4	352,644	61.8	29,176	2,761
Tennessee	531,761	167,153	31.4	334,580	62.9	27,262	2,075
Alabama	536,142	169,933	31.7	337,285	62.9	25,349	2,026
Mississippi	467,715	144,736	30.9	296,301	63.4	23,514	2,188
WEST SOUTH CENTRAL:							
Arkansas	454,326	139,440	30.7	286,211	63.0	24,999	2,796
Louisiana	356,278	118,515	33.3	218,401	61.3	16,845	1,194
Oklahoma	472,744	154,618	32.7	290,575	61.5	22,781	2,685
Texas	1,015,416	360,340	35.5	599,490	59.0	48,235	4,785
MOUNTAIN:							
Montana	142,646	58,350	40.9	76,271	53.5	6,109	1,526
Idaho	112,923	44,497	39.4	62,353	55.2	4,693	1,130
Wyoming	55,159	23,504	42.6	28,335	51.4	2,188	670
Colorado	175,867	63,615	36.2	101,598	57.8	8,577	1,699
New Mexico	101,041	37,812	37.4	55,891	55.3	6,382	769
Arizona	82,430	34,332	41.6	42,961	52.1	4,147	677
Utah	74,243	28,278	38.1	42,814	57.7	2,597	471
Nevada	29,833	14,334	48.0	13,258	44.4	1,296	591
PACIFIC:							
Washington	241,175	97,133	40.3	129,070	53.5	11,319	3,119
Oregon	154,220	58,426	37.9	85,409	55.4	7,870	2,269
California	465,344	192,929	41.5	240,561	51.7	23,468	6,064

[2] No rural population, as Washington city is coextensive with the District of Columbia.

TABLE 59.—MARITAL CONDITION OF THE POPULATION 15 YEARS OF AGE AND OVER,

DIVISION AND STATE.	Total.[1]	Single.		Married.		Widowed.	Divorced.
		Number.	Per cent.	Number.	Per cent.		
United States	19,618,764	5,698,673	29.0	11,310,188	57.6	2,395,622	186,181
GEOGRAPHIC DIVISIONS:							
New England	2,150,720	724,710	33.7	1,161,799	54.0	248,940	13,244
Middle Atlantic	5,943,213	1,841,879	31.0	3,375,215	56.8	694,367	23,600
East North Central	4,616,724	1,250,489	27.1	2,788,524	60.4	521,642	49,774
West North Central	1,764,811	509,932	28.9	1,018,588	57.7	210,277	23,112
South Atlantic	1,615,476	468,838	29.0	902,001	55.8	229,890	12,135
East South Central	752,553	199,413	26.5	422,147	56.1	119,250	10,878
West South Central	1,058,080	271,074	25.6	622,030	58.8	145,555	17,060
Mountain	421,873	109,002	25.8	253,863	60.2	50,881	6,874
Pacific	1,295,314	323,336	25.0	766,021	59.1	174,820	29,504
NEW ENGLAND:							
Maine	114,198	35,633	31.2	62,856	55.0	14,383	1,205
New Hampshire	103,692	33,035	31.9	56,986	55.0	12,383	1,062
Vermont	41,738	13,014	31.2	22,832	54.7	5,508	347
Massachusetts	1,351,711	469,131	34.7	716,537	53.0	157,454	7,515
Rhode Island	213,998	72,628	33.9	115,600	54.0	23,881	1,773
Connecticut	325,383	101,269	31.1	186,988	57.5	35,331	1,342
MIDDLE ATLANTIC:							
New York	3,134,974	1,008,204	32.2	1,739,194	55.5	370,713	11,548
New Jersey	863,399	252,421	29.2	509,747	59.0	97,577	2,659
Pennsylvania	1,944,840	581,254	29.9	1,126,274	57.9	226,077	9,393
EAST NORTH CENTRAL:							
Ohio	1,307,333	343,072	26.2	796,572	60.9	152,435	14,510
Indiana	538,508	131,718	24.5	332,152	61.7	65,671	7,519
Illinois	1,573,216	445,771	28.3	926,435	58.9	182,738	15,512
Michigan	751,397	188,462	25.1	479,594	63.8	74,515	8,226
Wisconsin	446,270	141,466	31.7	253,771	56.9	46,283	4,007
WEST NORTH CENTRAL:							
Minnesota	380,492	126,099	33.1	211,945	55.7	38,215	3,489
Iowa	330,462	94,640	28.6	191,835	58.1	38,611	4,865
Missouri	611,647	169,524	27.7	348,930	57.0	83,788	8,534
North Dakota	31,136	10,903	35.0	17,131	55.0	2,678	253
South Dakota	36,401	11,288	31.0	21,219	58.3	3,345	421
Nebraska	146,117	40,792	27.9	87,239	59.7	15,821	2,016
Kansas	228,556	56,686	24.8	140,289	61.4	27,819	3,534
SOUTH ATLANTIC:							
Delaware	42,802	11,755	27.5	25,358	59.2	5,405	263
Maryland	323,206	97,069	30.0	180,641	55.9	43,109	2,152
District of Columbia	188,466	70,330	37.3	88,602	47.0	27,761	1,381
Virginia	248,390	72,430	29.2	139,104	56.0	34,469	1,951
West Virginia	128,235	35,714	27.9	76,978	60.0	13,684	1,249
North Carolina	173,574	51,989	30.0	97,034	55.9	23,467	772
South Carolina	107,882	31,769	29.4	58,856	54.6	16,669	429
Georgia	272,809	68,486	25.1	156,145	57.2	45,469	2,459
Florida	130,112	29,296	22.5	79,283	60.9	19,857	1,479
EAST SOUTH CENTRAL:							
Kentucky	245,729	69,887	28.4	134,361	54.7	37,827	3,413
Tennessee	232,024	60,248	26.0	131,793	56.8	36,329	3,455
Alabama	184,295	44,823	24.3	106,780	57.9	29,786	2,728
Mississippi	90,505	24,455	27.0	49,213	54.4	15,308	1,282
WEST SOUTH CENTRAL:							
Arkansas	105,503	24,747	23.5	63,043	59.8	15,494	2,015
Louisiana	232,347	68,192	29.3	123,842	53.3	37,153	2,333
Oklahoma	184,637	43,313	23.5	117,990	63.9	19,650	3,379
Texas	535,593	134,822	25.2	317,155	59.2	73,258	9,333
MOUNTAIN:							
Montana	58,181	15,620	26.8	35,418	60.9	6,085	555
Idaho	39,519	10,032	25.4	24,956	63.1	3,919	588
Wyoming	17,790	3,784	21.3	12,069	67.8	1,641	264
Colorado	168,954	43,906	26.0	98,366	58.2	22,834	3,058
New Mexico	22,032	6,207	28.2	12,816	58.2	2,720	248
Arizona	38,450	8,977	23.3	24,021	62.5	4,899	480
Utah	71,697	19,338	27.0	43,005	60.0	8,134	1,154
Nevada	5,250	1,138	21.7	3,212	61.2	646	184
PACIFIC:							
Washington	263,574	64,294	24.4	164,865	62.5	28,073	6,016
Oregon	144,220	35,748	24.8	88,214	61.2	16,406	3,776
California	887,520	223,294	25.2	512,942	57.8	130,341	19,712

[1] Total includes persons whose marital condition was not reported.

BY SEX, FOR URBAN AND RURAL COMMUNITIES, BY DIVISIONS AND STATES: 1920—Con.

DIVISION AND STATE.	Total.[1]	FEMALES 15 YEARS OF AGE AND OVER IN RURAL COMMUNITIES.				Widowed.	Divorced.
		Single.		Married.			
		Number.	Per cent.	Number.	Per cent.		
United States	15,558,751	3,918,229	25.2	10,008,745	64.3	1,522,003	87,123
GEOGRAPHIC DIVISIONS:							
New England	530,418	135,943	25.6	323,578	61.0	66,153	4,197
Middle Atlantic	1,814,244	468,926	25.8	1,143,033	63.0	194,372	5,767
East North Central	2,705,109	666,090	24.6	1,756,651	64.9	263,396	15,316
West North Central	2,394,668	640,441	26.7	1,537,308	64.2	201,195	11,615
South Atlantic	2,805,361	753,723	26.9	1,752,235	62.5	283,907	10,975
East South Central	2,042,292	506,856	24.8	1,303,032	63.8	215,447	14,036
West South Central	2,072,949	495,043	23.9	1,366,744	65.9	193,683	14,176
Mountain	578,213	124,862	21.6	400,613	69.3	47,396	4,636
Pacific	615,497	126,345	20.5	425,551	69.1	56,454	6,405
NEW ENGLAND:							
Maine	157,566	36,526	23.2	99,767	63.3	19,634	1,480
New Hampshire	57,516	13,257	23.0	35,367	61.5	8,048	783
Vermont	82,244	19,383	23.6	51,673	62.8	10,481	667
Massachusetts	73,732	21,039	28.5	42,360	57.5	9,799	485
Rhode Island	5,411	1,470	27.2	3,172	58.6	696	61
Connecticut	153,949	44,268	28.8	91,239	59.3	17,495	721
MIDDLE ATLANTIC:							
New York	632,566	156,321	24.7	395,410	62.5	77,957	2,014
New Jersey	229,224	58,872	25.7	143,840	62.8	25,499	638
Pennsylvania	952,454	253,733	26.6	603,783	63.4	90,916	3,115
EAST NORTH CENTRAL:							
Ohio	683,368	164,478	24.1	444,879	65.1	69,320	3,956
Indiana	483,407	112,941	23.4	318,035	65.8	48,573	3,204
Illinois	668,904	172,102	25.7	426,683	63.8	65,247	3,763
Michigan	446,640	96,835	21.7	303,054	67.9	43,897	2,542
Wisconsin	422,790	119,734	28.3	264,000	62.4	36,359	1,851
WEST NORTH CENTRAL:							
Minnesota	393,941	122,493	31.1	238,840	60.6	30,730	1,354
Iowa	489,485	130,066	26.6	313,459	64.0	42,507	2,645
Missouri	574,760	138,527	24.1	375,956	65.4	55,986	3,105
North Dakota	150,314	43,782	29.1	96,712	64.3	8,940	482
South Dakota	154,411	42,570	27.6	100,189	64.9	10,517	707
Nebraska	273,029	73,075	26.8	176,651	64.7	21,477	1,352
Kansas	358,728	89,928	25.1	235,501	65.6	31,038	1,970
SOUTH ATLANTIC:							
Delaware	34,303	8,207	23.9	22,111	64.5	3,689	95
Maryland	183,363	50,135	27.3	113,402	61.8	18,978	548
District of Columbia [2]							
Virginia	482,595	138,710	28.7	293,453	60.8	48,014	1,947
West Virginia	303,329	74,455	24.5	203,833	67.2	23,311	1,386
North Carolina	595,611	173,160	29.1	363,708	61.1	55,651	1,553
South Carolina	396,166	111,688	28.2	239,792	60.5	43,196	896
Georgia	627,308	157,370	25.1	395,377	63.0	70,360	3,467
Florida	182,686	39,998	21.9	120,559	66.0	20,708	1,083
EAST SOUTH CENTRAL:							
Kentucky	524,966	125,168	23.8	346,699	66.0	49,551	2,979
Tennessee	517,021	130,288	25.2	330,090	63.8	52,956	3,221
Alabama	536,485	137,445	25.6	333,427	62.2	60,583	3,921
Mississippi	463,820	113,955	24.6	292,816	63.1	52,357	3,915
WEST SOUTH CENTRAL:							
Arkansas	419,974	91,337	21.7	281,282	67.0	43,460	3,355
Louisiana	338,992	87,084	25.7	215,055	63.4	34,125	2,083
Oklahoma	410,042	89,505	21.8	284,873	69.5	32,334	2,507
Texas	903,941	227,117	25.1	585,534	64.8	83,764	6,231
MOUNTAIN:							
Montana	102,444	21,416	20.9	72,701	71.0	7,300	923
Idaho	83,768	18,092	21.6	59,598	71.1	5,472	558
Wyoming	36,379	7,336	20.2	26,103	71.8	2,448	396
Colorado	138,504	29,192	21.1	96,827	69.9	11,352	1,000
New Mexico	81,471	18,786	23.1	53,761	66.0	8,112	694
Arizona	57,221	11,193	19.6	39,664	69.3	5,909	372
Utah	61,945	15,789	25.5	40,708	65.7	5,034	377
Nevada	16,481	3,058	18.6	11,251	68.3	1,769	316
PACIFIC:							
Washington	174,783	36,049	20.6	123,006	70.4	13,816	1,800
Oregon	117,627	24,394	20.7	81,855	69.6	10,108	1,212
California	323,087	65,902	20.4	220,690	68.3	32,530	3,393

[2] No rural population, as Washington city is coextensive with the District of Columbia.

TABLE 60.—NUMBER AND PER CENT NATIVE AND FOREIGN BORN IN THE TOTAL POPU-LATION, WITH CLASSIFICATION OF NATIVE ACCORDING TO WHETHER BORN IN STATE OF RESIDENCE OR ELSEWHERE, FOR THE UNITED STATES: 1850-1920.

CENSUS YEAR.	Total population.	NATIVE POPULATION.						
		Total.		With state of birth reported.				
				Born in state of residence.		Born in other states.		
		Number.	Per cent of total population.	Number.	Per cent of total population.	Number.	Per cent of total population.	Per cent of native population.
1920	105,710,620	91,789,928	86.8	71,071,013	67.2	20,274,450	19.2	22.1
1910	91,972,266	78,456,380	85.3	61,185,305	66.5	16,910,114	18.4	21.6
1900	75,994,575	65,653,299	86.4	51,901,722	68.3	13,501,045	17.8	20.6
1890	[1] 62,622,250	53,372,703	85.2	41,871,611	66.9	11,094,108	17.7	20.8
1880	50,155,783	43,475,840	86.7	33,882,734	67.6	9,592,764	19.1	22.1
1870	38,558,371	32,991,142	85.6	25,321,340	65.7	7,657,320	19.9	23.2
1860	[2] 27,489,561	[2] 23,353,386	85.0	17,527,069	63.8	5,774,434	21.0	24.7
1850	[2] 19,987,563	[2] 17,742,961	88.8	13,457,049	67.3	4,251,250	21.3	24.0

CENSUS YEAR.	NATIVE POPULATION—continued.			FOREIGN-BORN POPULATION.	
	State of birth not reported.	Born in outlying posses-sions cr at sea.	Amer-ican citizens born abroad.	Number.	Per cent of total population.
1920	313,582	38,873	92,010	13,920,692	13.2
1910	285,685	8,925	66,351	13,515,886	14.7
1900	180,458	5,175	64,899	10,341,276	13.6
1890	396,652	1,785	8,547	9,249,547	14.8
1880		342		6,679,943	13.3
1870	12,262	220		5,567,229	14.4
1860	49,265	2,618		[2] 4,136,175	15.0
1850	34,662			[2] 2,244,602	11.2

[1] Exclusive of population of Indian Territory and Indian reservations, specially enumerated in 1890, with a native population of 325,451 and a foreign population of 13, not distributed by state of birth. These areas were not enumerated prior to 1890.
[2] White and free colored population only.

TABLE **61.**—TOTAL POPULATION AND TOTAL WHITE POPULATION DISTRIBUTED AS BORN IN DIVISION OF RESIDENCE, IN OTHER DIVISIONS, OR IN FOREIGN COUNTRIES, BY GEOGRAPHIC DIVISIONS, 1920, WITH PERCENTAGES FOR 1920 AND 1910.

DIVISION OF RESIDENCE.	Total.	BORN IN THE UNITED STATES AND WITH STATE OF BIRTH REPORTED.		FOREIGN BORN.	BORN IN THE UNITED STATES AND WITH STATE OF BIRTH REPORTED.				FOREIGN BORN.	
		Born in division of residence.	Born in other divisions.		Born in division of residence.		Born in other divisions.			
					1920	1910	1920	1910	1920	1910
	TOTAL POPULATION: **1920**				PER CENT OF TOTAL POPULATION.					
United States	1 105,710,620	77,906,515	13,438,948	13,920,692	73.7	72.6	12.7	12.3	13.2	14.7
New England	7,400,909	5,040,243	449,015	1,885,945	68.1	66.2	6.1	5.5	25.5	27.9
Middle Atlantic	22,261,144	15,949,575	1,264,649	4,960,418	71.6	69.7	5.7	4.9	22.3	25.1
East North Central	21,475,543	15,796,227	2,367,738	3,232,141	73.6	73.4	11.0	9.3	15.1	16.8
West North Central	12,544,249	8,893,937	2,216,017	1,375,653	70.9	65.4	17.7	20.2	11.0	13.9
South Atlantic	13,990,272	12,718,854	909,047	330,537	90.9	92.6	6.5	4.7	2.4	2.5
East South Central	8,893,307	8,190,448	612,977	72,989	92.1	91.5	6.9	7.3	0.8	1.0
West South Central	10,242,224	7,658,879	2,066,629	464,828	74.8	72.3	20.2	23.3	4.5	4.0
Mountain	3,336,101	1,520,606	1,315,787	467,620	45.6	41.8	39.4	40.2	14.0	17.2
Pacific	5,566,871	2,137,746	2,237,089	1,130,561	38.4	35.8	40.2	40.3	20.3	22.8
	WHITE POPULATION: **1920**				PER CENT OF WHITE POPULATION.					
United States	2 94,820,915	68,601,740	12,119,885	13,712,754	72.3	70.6	12.8	12.7	14.5	16.3
New England	7,316,079	5,003,487	417,067	1,870,654	68.4	66.4	5.7	5.2	25.6	28.0
Middle Atlantic	21,641,840	15,714,467	936,794	4,912,575	72.6	70.3	4.3	3.9	22.7	25.6
East North Central	20,938,862	15,606,106	2,035,589	3,223,279	74.5	73.9	9.7	8.7	15.4	17.1
West North Central	12,225,387	8,699,489	2,099,261	1,371,961	71.2	65.3	17.2	20.0	11.2	14.2
South Atlantic	9,648,940	8,487,281	824,645	315,920	88.0	89.8	8.5	6.5	3.3	3.6
East South Central	6,367,547	5,791,383	495,062	71,939	91.0	90.3	7.8	8.0	1.1	1.5
West South Central	8,115,727	5,791,839	1,823,403	459,333	71.4	67.9	22.5	26.5	5.7	5.2
Mountain	3,212,899	1,442,878	1,287,952	453,225	44.9	40.7	40.1	41.2	14.1	17.3
Pacific	5,353,634	2,064,810	2,200,112	1,033,868	38.6	36.1	41.1	41.5	19.3	21.4

1 Includes persons born in the United States, state of birth not reported; persons born in outlying possessions, or at sea under United States flag; and American citizens born abroad. The combined number of these classes in the United States in 1920 was 444,465, or four-tenths of 1 per cent of the total population.
2 Includes white persons born in the United States, state of birth not reported; white persons born in outlying possessions, or at sea under United States flag; and white American citizens born abroad. The combined number of these classes in the United States in 1920 was 386,536, or four-tenths of 1 per cent of the total white population.

75108°—23——18

TABLE 62.—TOTAL POPULATION DISTRIBUTED AS BORN IN STATE OF RESIDENCE, IN OTHER STATES, OR IN FOREIGN COUNTRIES, BY STATES, 1920, WITH PERCENTAGES FOR 1920 AND 1910.

[For geographic divisions, see Table 61.]

STATE OF RESIDENCE.	TOTAL POPULATION: 1920				PER CENT OF TOTAL POPULATION.					
	Total.[1]	Born in the United States and with state of birth reported.		Foreign born.	Born in the United States and with state of birth reported.				Foreign born.	
		Born in state of residence.	Born in other states.		Born in state of residence.		Born in other states.			
					1920	1910	1920	1910	1920	1910
United States	105,710,620	71,071,013	20,274,450	13,920,692	67.2	66.5	19.2	18.4	13.2	14.7
NEW ENGLAND:										
Maine	768,014	598,345	58,475	107,814	77.9	78.0	7.6	6.7	14.0	14.9
New Hampshire	443,083	257,074	91,950	91,397	58.0	57.7	20.8	19.2	20.6	22.5
Vermont	352,428	250,538	54,748	44,558	71.1	70.4	15.5	14.7	12.6	14.0
Massachusetts	3,852,356	2,265,287	487,242	1,088,548	58.8	55.3	12.6	12.9	28.3	31.5
Rhode Island	604,397	324,792	102,790	175,189	53.7	49.2	17.0	17.5	29.0	33.0
Connecticut	1,380,631	756,212	241,805	378,439	54.8	54.5	17.5	15.7	27.4	29.6
MIDDLE ATLANTIC:										
New York	10,385,227	6,634,469	865,523	2,825,375	63.9	62.0	8.3	7.5	27.2	30.2
New Jersey	3,155,900	1,693,459	711,531	742,486	53.7	53.0	22.5	20.7	23.5	26.0
Pennsylvania	8,720,017	6,564,988	744,254	1,392,557	75.3	73.6	8.5	7.4	16.0	18.8
EAST NORTH CENTRAL:										
Ohio	5,759,394	4,079,758	983,017	680,452	70.8	74.4	17.1	12.7	11.8	12.6
Indiana	2,930,390	2,209,448	561,058	151,328	75.4	75.2	19.1	18.6	5.2	5.9
Illinois	6,485,280	4,090,918	1,156,685	1,210,584	63.1	60.4	17.8	17.7	18.7	21.4
Michigan	3,668,412	2,223,333	697,365	729,292	60.6	62.7	19.0	15.5	19.9	21.3
Wisconsin	2,632,067	1,852,574	309,809	460,485	70.4	66.8	11.8	11.0	17.5	22.0
WEST NORTH CENTRAL:										
Minnesota	2,387,125	1,392,176	499,584	486,795	58.3	54.0	20.9	19.4	20.4	26.2
Iowa	2,404,021	1,624,606	543,565	225,994	67.6	63.7	22.6	23.6	9.4	12.3
Missouri	3,404,055	2,382,282	821,375	186,835	70.0	67.5	24.1	25.0	5.5	7.0
North Dakota	646,872	304,679	204,092	131,863	47.1	34.3	31.6	37.6	20.4	27.1
South Dakota	636,547	303,260	247,194	82,534	47.6	38.6	38.8	43.6	13.0	17.3
Nebraska	1,296,372	735,442	402,676	150,665	56.7	50.0	31.1	34.7	11.6	14.8
Kansas	1,769,257	967,838	681,185	110,967	54.7	48.7	38.5	42.8	6.3	8.0
SOUTH ATLANTIC:										
Delaware	223,003	142,963	59,045	19,901	64.1	67.8	26.5	23.4	8.9	8.6
Maryland	1,449,661	1,107,290	236,134	103,179	76.4	79.2	16.3	12.5	7.1	8.1
District of Columbia	437,571	160,109	244,222	29,365	36.6	42.1	55.8	49.7	6.7	7.5
Virginia	2,309,187	1,978,940	293,493	31,705	85.7	89.4	12.7	9.2	1.4	1.3
West Virginia	1,463,701	1,113,343	283,552	62,105	76.1	76.2	19.4	18.8	4.2	4.7
North Carolina	2,559,123	2,391,258	157,996	7,272	93.4	94.7	6.2	4.9	0.3	0.3
South Carolina	1,683,724	1,565,791	109,369	6,582	93.0	94.4	6.5	5.1	0.4	0.4
Georgia	2,895,832	2,595,423	279,246	150,665	89.6	90.6	9.6	8.5	0.6	0.6
Florida	968,470	560,103	349,624	53,864	57.8	61.5	36.1	32.5	5.6	5.4
EAST SOUTH CENTRAL:										
Kentucky	2,416,630	2,134,989	247,732	30,906	88.3	88.7	10.3	9.4	1.3	1.8
Tennessee	2,337,885	1,994,580	322,329	15,648	85.3	85.7	13.8	13.1	0.7	0.9
Alabama	2,348,174	2,055,273	269,981	18,027	87.5	86.9	11.5	12.0	0.8	0.9
Mississippi	1,790,618	1,595,136	183,405	8,408	89.1	87.0	10.2	12.2	0.5	0.5
WEST SOUTH CENTRAL:										
Arkansas	1,752,204	1,196,930	533,148	14,137	68.3	67.1	30.4	31.4	0.8	1.1
Louisiana	1,798,509	1,522,615	223,013	46,427	84.7	84.9	12.4	11.5	2.6	3.2
Oklahoma	2,020,000	810,020	1,155,880	40,432	40.4	31.1	57.0	65.9	2.0	2.4
Texas	4,663,228	3,306,311	968,382	363,832	70.9	70.1	20.8	23.3	7.8	6.2
MOUNTAIN:										
Montana	548,889	172,818	274,877	95,591	31.5	26.4	50.1	47.3	17.4	25.2
Idaho	431,866	148,028	240,313	40,747	34.3	27.7	55.6	58.4	9.4	13.1
Wyoming	194,402	48,982	116,830	26,567	25.2	21.8	60.1	57.7	13.7	19.9
Colorado	939,629	317,506	492,079	119,138	33.8	29.2	52.4	53.8	12.7	16.2
New Mexico	360,350	209,234	119,877	29,808	58.1	56.4	33.3	36.0	8.3	7.1
Arizona	334,162	109,776	137,573	80,566	32.9	38.6	41.2	36.6	24.1	23.9
Utah	449,396	314,006	73,999	59,200	69.9	65.1	16.5	16.2	13.2	17.6
Nevada	77,407	24,761	35,734	16,003	32.0	26.4	46.2	48.5	20.7	24.1
PACIFIC:										
Washington	1,356,621	410,175	662,451	265,292	30.2	23.0	48.8	53.3	19.6	22.4
Oregon	783,389	295,723	374,327	107,644	37.7	33.5	47.8	49.0	13.7	16.8
California	3,426,861	1,268,243	1,363,951	757,625	37.0	38.0	39.8	36.3	22.1	24.7

[1] Includes persons born in the United States, state of birth not reported; persons born in outlying possessions, or at sea under United States flag; and American citizens born abroad. The combined number of these classes in the United States in 1920 was 444,465, or four-tenths of 1 per cent of the total population.

TABLE 63.—WHITE POPULATION DISTRIBUTED AS BORN IN STATE OF RESIDENCE, IN OTHER STATES, OR IN FOREIGN COUNTRIES, BY STATES, 1920, WITH PERCENTAGES FOR 1920 AND 1910.

[For geographic divisions, see Table 61.]

STATE OF RESIDENCE.	WHITE POPULATION: 1920				PER CENT OF WHITE POPULATION.					
	Total.[1]	Born in the United States and with state of birth reported.		Foreign born.	Born in the United States and with state of birth reported.				Foreign born.	
		Born in state of residence.	Born in other states.		Born in state of residence.		Born in other states.			
					1920	1910	1920	1910	1920	1910
United States......	94,820,915	62,524,789	18,196,836	13,712,754	65.9	64.6	19.2	18.7	14.5	16.3
NEW ENGLAND:										
Maine................	765,695	596,893	58,109	107,349	78.0	78.0	7.6	6.7	14.0	14.9
New Hampshire......	442,331	256,800	91,656	91,233	58.1	57.8	20.7	19.1	20.6	22.5
Vermont.............	351,817	250,196	54,519	44,526	71.1	70.6	15.5	14.4	12.7	14.1
Massachusetts........	3,803,524	2,246,606	468,631	1,077,534	59.1	55.5	12.3	12.5	28.3	31.6
Rhode Island........	593,980	320,269	98,665	173,499	53.9	49.4	16.6	16.9	29.2	33.4
Connecticut.........	1,358,732	748,187	230,023	376,513	55.1	54.6	16.9	15.2	27.7	29.9
MIDDLE ATLANTIC:										
New York...........	10,172,027	6,566,130	765,945	2,786,112	64.6	62.4	7.5	6.9	27.4	30.4
New Jersey.........	3,037,087	1,650,564	640,091	738,613	54.3	53.4	21.1	19.4	24.3	26.9
Pennsylvania........	8,432,726	6,464,194	564,337	1,387,850	76.7	74.4	6.7	6.2	16.5	19.3
EAST NORTH CENTRAL:										
Ohio................	5,571,893	4,012,837	865,637	678,697	72.0	74.9	15.5	12.0	12.2	12.8
Indiana.............	2,849,071	2,181,795	508,423	150,868	76.6	76.0	17.8	17.7	5.3	6.0
Illinois.............	6,299,333	4,046,455	1,020,859	1,206,951	64.2	61.0	16.2	16.8	19.2	21.8
Michigan............	3,601,627	2,207,704	650,259	726,635	61.3	62.7	18.1	15.4	20.2	21.4
Wisconsin...........	2,616,938	1,842,264	305,462	460,128	70.4	66.7	11.7	11.0	17.6	22.1
WEST NORTH CENTRAL:										
Minnesota...........	2,368,936	1,382,057	492,350	486,164	58.3	54.0	20.8	19.3	20.5	26.4
Iowa................	2,384,181	1,618,130	530,884	225,647	67.9	63.9	22.3	23.3	9.5	12.4
Missouri............	3,225,044	2,280,498	746,767	186,026	70.7	67.4	23.2	24.8	5.8	7.3
North Dakota........	639,954	298,954	203,361	131,503	46.7	33.8	31.8	37.9	20.5	27.4
South Dakota........	619,147	288,924	244,501	82,391	46.7	37.2	39.5	44.5	13.3	17.8
Nebraska...........	1,279,219	731,066	391,329	149,652	57.1	50.1	30.6	34.5	11.7	14.9
Kansas.............	1,708,906	942,997	646,932	110,578	55.2	48.9	37.9	42.3	6.5	8.3
SOUTH ATLANTIC:										
Delaware.	192,615	122,524	49,445	19,810	63.6	66.9	25.7	22.7	10.3	10.2
Maryland............	1,204,737	910,534	189,777	102,177	75.6	77.6	15.8	12.4	8.5	9.8
District of Columbia...	326,860	113,486	181,813	28,548	34.7	41.9	55.6	47.2	8.7	10.3
Virginia.............	1,617,909	1,360,807	223,106	30,785	84.1	87.7	13.8	10.2	1.9	1.9
West Virginia........	1,377,235	1,079,987	231,288	61,906	78.4	78.1	16.8	16.7	4.5	4.9
North Carolina.......	1,783,779	1,665,379	109,612	7,099	94.5	6.1	5.0	0.4	0.4	0.4
South Carolina.......	818,538	718,524	92,445	6,401	87.8	89.8	11.3	9.3	0.8	0.9
Georgia.............	1,689,114	1,471,937	198,469	16,186	87.1	88.5	11.7	10.2	1.0	1.1
Florida.............	638,153	342,353	250,440	43,008	53.6	59.6	39.2	32.3	6.7	7.6
EAST SOUTH CENTRAL:										
Kentucky............	2,180,560	1,933,612	213,855	30,780	88.7	88.6	9.8	9.3	1.4	2.0
Tennessee...........	1,885,993	1,628,768	238,751	15,478	86.4	86.5	12.7	12.2	0.8	1.1
Alabama.............	1,447,032	1,213,217	213,626	17,662	83.8	82.8	14.8	15.5	1.2	1.5
Mississippi..........	853,962	732,695	111,921	8,019	85.8	84.3	13.1	14.3	0.9	1.2
WEST SOUTH CENTRAL:										
Arkansas............	1,279,757	885,648	375,105	13,975	69.2	67.2	29.3	30.9	1.1	1.5
Louisiana...........	1,096,611	887,092	160,368	44,871	80.9	81.0	14.6	13.0	4.1	5.5
Oklahoma...........	1,821,194	702,130	1,068,052	39,968	38.6	27.9	58.6	68.8	2.2	2.8
Texas..............	3,918,165	2,650,041	886,806	360,519	67.6	66.4	22.6	25.8	9.2	7.5
MOUNTAIN:										
Montana............	534,260	162,852	272,356	93,620	30.5	24.9	51.0	48.5	17.5	25.4
Idaho...............	425,668	145,087	238,917	38,963	34.1	27.3	56.1	59.2	9.2	12.7
Wyoming...........	190,146	47,507	115,432	25,255	25.0	21.5	60.7	58.6	13.3	19.3
Colorado............	924,103	313,547	482,961	116,954	33.9	29.4	52.3	53.7	12.7	16.2
New Mexico..........	334,673	189,989	114,398	29,077	56.8	53.9	34.2	38.2	8.7	7.4
Arizona.............	291,449	79,576	129,858	78,099	27.3	29.4	44.6	42.2	26.8	27.3
Utah...............	441,901	310,819	72,498	56,455	70.3	65.6	16.4	16.1	12.8	17.3
Nevada.............	70,699	19,962	35,071	14,802	28.2	22.6	49.6	52.2	20.9	24.2
PACIFIC:										
Washington..........	1,319,777	396,184	656,453	250,055	30.0	22.6	49.7	54.3	18.9	21.7
Oregon.............	769,146	290,378	371,416	102,151	37.8	33.6	48.3	50.0	13.3	15.7
California...........	3,264,711	1,216,634	1,333,857	681,662	37.3	38.6	40.9	37.5	20.9	22.9

[1] Includes white persons born in the United States, state of birth not reported; white persons born in outlying possessions, or at sea under United States flag; and white American citizens born abroad. The combined number of these classes in the United States in 1920 was 386,536, or four-tenths of 1 per cent of the total white population.

TABLE 64.—NATIVE POPULATION OF EACH DIVISION AND

	DIVISION OR STATE OF RESIDENCE.	Total native population.	POPULATION BORN IN—				
			United States.	Geographic division.			
				New England.	Middle Atlantic.	East North Central.	West North Central.
1	United States..	91,789,928	91,659,045	5,660,113	18,019,528	19,062,140	11,320,725
	GEOG. DIVISIONS:						
2	New England.....	5,514,964	5,500,369	5,040,243	309,699	48,580	17,479
3	Middle Atlantic...	17,300,726	17,271,642	256,717	15,949,575	280,091	74,523
4	E. North Central..	18,243,402	18,223,214	104,048	755,098	15,796,227	483,254
5	W. North Central.	11,168,596	11,157,842	53,641	253,532	1,303,163	8,893,937
6	South Atlantic....	13,659,735	13,654,338	51,487	277,206	183,878	52,642
7	E. South Central..	8,820,318	8,819,018	6,146	28,167	141,767	35,149
8	W. South Central.	9,777,396	9,771,813	14,133	75,377	309,966	545,431
9	Mountain........	2,868,481	2,858,988	25,956	99,717	320,857	534,497
10	Pacific...........	4,436,310	4,401,821	107,742	271,157	677,611	683,813
	NEW ENGLAND:						
11	Maine...........	660,200	657,872	640,819	7,467	2,844	1,800
12	New Hampshire..	351,686	350,275	333,598	9,826	2,389	978
13	Vermont.........	307,870	305,785	277,301	22,382	2,543	1,169
14	Massachusetts....	2,763,808	2,757,341	2,556,337	121,323	27,412	9,047
15	Rhode Island.....	429,208	428,283	397,113	19,614	3,151	1,210
16	Connecticut......	1,002,192	1,000,813	835,075	129,087	10,241	3,275
	MIDDLE ATLANTIC:						
17	New York........	7,559,852	7,537,778	171,798	6,966,472	127,139	39,928
18	New Jersey.......	2,413,414	2,410,562	47,960	2,205,801	31,254	9,544
19	Pennsylvania.....	7,327,460	7,323,302	36,959	6,777,302	121,698	25,051
	E. NORTH CENTRAL:						
20	Ohio.............	5,078,942	5,075,425	22,908	307,619	4,284,374	45,966
21	Indiana..........	2,779,062	2,777,975	5,750	47,654	2,487,484	39,946
22	Illinois..........	5,274,696	5,270,360	33,764	168,595	4,489,408	248,895
23	Michigan.........	2,939,120	2,929,513	29,235	184,454	2,550,920	52,358
24	Wisconsin........	2,171,582	2,169,941	12,391	46,776	1,984,041	96,089
	W. NORTH CENTRAL:						
25	Minnesota........	1,900,330	1,897,151	17,149	43,612	231,445	1,570,441
26	Iowa.............	2,178,027	2,176,305	9,976	57,068	269,615	1,774,038
27	Missouri.........	3,217,220	3,215,650	8,754	48,276	307,772	2,547,230
28	North Dakota.....	515,009	513,573	2,289	8,885	58,521	428,812
29	South Dakota.....	554,013	553,234	2,978	12,416	74,393	445,731
30	Nebraska.........	1,145,707	1,144,761	6,043	34,323	134,582	913,467
31	Kansas...........	1,658,290	1,657,168	6,452	48,952	226,835	1,214,218
	SOUTH ATLANTIC:						
32	Delaware.........	203,102	202,987	1,547	25,666	1,748	677
33	Maryland........	1,346,482	1,345,664	8,223	70,847	15,291	5,727
34	Dist. of Columbia.	408,206	407,070	12,908	43,389	23,263	11,211
35	Virginia.........	2,277,482	2,276,564	7,069	35,416	19,748	7,692
36	West Virginia....	1,401,596	1,401,322	1,866	45,893	59,594	3,919
37	North Carolina...	2,551,851	2,551,563	2,727	8,581	5,735	2,921
38	South Carolina....	1,677,142	1,676,867	1,732	5,303	3,279	1,625
39	Georgia..........	2,879,268	2,878,774	3,627	11,638	12,094	4,883
40	Florida..........	914,606	913,527	11,788	30,473	43,126	13,987
	E. SOUTH CENTRAL:						
41	Kentucky.........	2,385,724	2,385,348	2,037	10,233	86,829	11,897
42	Tennessee........	2,322,237	2,321,874	1,836	8,697	28,086	12,195
43	Alabama.........	2,330,147	2,329,815	1,599	6,788	16,737	5,698
44	Mississippi.......	1,782,210	1,781,981	674	2,449	10,115	5,359
	W. SOUTH CENTRAL:						
45	Arkansas.........	1,738,067	1,737,736	1,469	6,966	63,478	82,733
46	Louisiana........	1,752,082	1,751,110	2,196	7,800	16,282	12,830
47	Oklahoma........	1,987,851	1,986,951	3,089	27,331	137,435	336,370
48	Texas............	4,299,396	4,290,016	7,379	33,280	92,771	113,498
	MOUNTAIN:						
49	Montana.........	453,298	451,155	5,286	17,302	77,801	190,007
50	Idaho............	391,119	389,653	2,669	10,189	43,532	75,276
51	Wyoming.........	167,835	167,518	1,592	7,012	22,848	54,577
52	Colorado.........	820,491	819,323	10,033	42,362	119,949	209,791
53	New Mexico......	330,542	329,993	1,074	4,971	15,599	21,931
54	Arizona..........	253,596	251,537	2,534	8,594	21,948	22,808
55	Utah............	390,196	388,644	1,586	6,089	13,333	16,059
56	Nevada..........	61,404	61,165	1,182	3,198	5,847	5,788
	PACIFIC:						
57	Washington......	1,091,329	1,081,468	20,414	54,513	193,179	218,842
58	Oregon...........	675,745	672,829	8,546	27,065	99,429	123,312
59	California........	2,669,236	2,647,524	78,782	189,579	385,003	341,659

EACH STATE, BY DIVISION AND STATE OF BIRTH: 1920.

POPULATION BORN IN—							Born at sea under United States flag.	American citizens born abroad.	
Geographic division—Continued.					United States, state not reported.	Outlying possessions.			
South Atlantic.	East South Central.	West South Central.	Mountain.	Pacific.					
14,377,095	10,368,842	8,339,585	1,870,479	2,326,956	313,582	38,020	853	92,010	1
48,362	7,238	4,933	5,082	7,642	11,111	874	151	13,570	2
527,279	61,582	26,368	15,758	22,331	57,418	12,569	142	16,373	3
319,430	567,909	75,423	33,788	28,788	59,249	1,512	149	18,527	4
102,843	237,367	172,815	64,676	27,980	47,888	906	88	9,760	5
12,718,854	290,907	35,488	8,186	9,253	26,437	2,120	55	3,222	6
298,930	8,190,448	96,156	3,631	3,031	15,593	340	11	949	7
227,893	842,330	7,658,879	35,572	15,927	46,305	845	48	4,690	8
50,276	69,402	140,824	1,520,606	74,258	22,595	861	40	8,592	9
83,228	101,659	128,699	183,180	2,137,746	26,986	17,993	169	16,327	10
1,926	417	296	427	824	1,052	46	26	2,256	11
1,076	219	167	373	398	1,251	12	13	1,386	12
769	245	184	334	359	499	13	7	2,065	13
24,703	4,033	2,985	2,378	4,311	4,812	559	73	5,835	14
4,818	593	350	250	483	701	64	12	849	15
15,070	1,731	951	1,320	1,267	2,796	180	20	1,179	16
136,223	22,273	14,433	8,046	13,680	37,786	10,906	86	11,082	17
92,746	8,536	3,721	2,157	3,271	5,572	694	29	2,129	18
298,310	30,773	8,214	5,555	5,380	14,060	969	27	3,162	19
184,843	190,857	14,229	6,328	5,651	12,650	369	33	3,115	20
30,844	144,629	8,503	3,079	2,617	7,469	92	15	980	21
61,240	181,749	39,652	13,867	10,433	22,757	610	41	3,685	22
37,183	43,377	10,070	6,482	6,619	8,815	359	40	9,208	23
5,320	7,297	2,969	4,032	3,468	7,558	82	20	1,539	24
6,477	6,495	3,827	7,033	5,281	5,391	126	21	3,032	25
15,985	17,684	9,944	9,359	4,502	8,134	201	10	1,511	26
40,250	151,506	81,522	11,886	6,461	11,993	242	27	1,301	27
2,479	1,758	973	3,552	1,502	4,802	19	9	1,408	28
3,246	2,925	2,284	4,862	1,619	2,780	37	5	737	29
10,732	11,397	10,280	13,736	3,558	6,643	93	7	846	30
23,674	45,602	63,985	14,248	5,057	8,145	188	9	925	31
171,192	624	211	148	195	979	26	2	87	32
1,232,304	5,571	2,682	1,015	1,764	2,240	278	9	531	33
294,823	10,630	4,509	1,598	2,000	2,739	610	14	512	34
2,159,718	34,841	4,765	1,613	1,571	4,131	389	7	522	35
1,241,205	40,868	1,796	874	880	4,427	54	3	217	36
2,508,454	17,253	2,521	553	509	2,309	81	1	206	37
1,649,891	10,664	2,054	260	352	1,707	136	------	139	38
2,733,998	98,339	8,575	748	767	4,105	231	7	256	39
727,269	72,117	8,375	1,377	1,215	3,800	315	12	752	40
44,559	2,217,352	7,691	1,085	1,038	2,627	97	6	273	41
97,070	2,139,173	27,444	1,392	1,016	4,965	68	1	294	42
130,017	2,147,326	15,879	648	562	4,561	100	3	229	43
27,284	1,686,597	45,142	506	415	3,440	75	1	153	44
48,648	231,698	1,290,915	2,372	1,799	7,658	46	8	277	45
21,660	103,636	1,578,947	1,005	1,272	5,482	406	10	556	46
48,185	162,490	1,242,950	12,148	5,111	11,842	84	6	810	47
109,400	344,506	3,546,067	20,047	7,745	21,323	309	24	3,047	48
6,552	7,148	6,548	187,118	11,673	3,460	123	4	2,016	49
7,078	7,158	9,205	206,584	26,650	1,312	92	4	1,370	50
3,100	3,011	4,745	66,809	2,118	1,706	55	5	257	51
16,363	24,065	35,651	344,520	6,851	9,738	183	14	971	52
5,962	12,022	47,894	218,001	1,657	882	43	2	504	53
6,980	11,631	32,566	127,683	12,605	4,188	171	4	1,884	54
3,221	3,348	2,871	337,292	4,206	639	113	5	1,434	55
1,020	1,019	1,344	32,599	8,498	670	81	2	156	56
23,147	21,702	19,672	50,585	470,572	8,842	3,527	37	6,297	57
10,030	12,861	14,281	28,357	346,134	2,814	944	14	1,958	58
50,051	67,096	94,746	104,238	1,321,040	15,330	13,522	118	8,072	59

TABLE 64.—NATIVE POPULATION OF EACH DIVISION AND EACH

	DIVISION OR STATE OF RESIDENCE.	POPULATION BORN IN—								
		New England division.						Middle Atlantic division.		
		Maine.	New Hampshire.	Vermont.	Massachusetts.	Rhode Island.	Connecticut.	New York.	New Jersey.	Pennsylvania.
1	**United States.**	807,012	391,862	406,955	2,693,737	417,677	942,870	8,086,198	2,025,396	7,907,934
	GEOG. DIVISIONS:									
2	New England....	723,464	357,113	331,726	2,430,731	378,810	818,399	236,838	31,481	41,380
3	Middle Atlantic..	19,424	10,451	28,554	109,081	17,669	71,538	7,098,213	1,889,792	6,961,570
4	E. North Central.	12,171	6,226	14,143	47,642	5,846	18,020	319,016	34,076	402,006
5	W. North Central	11,058	4,095	10,612	18,479	2,562	6,835	116,737	12,043	124,752
6	South Atlantic...	7,166	3,406	4,290	23,258	4,164	9,203	84,853	25,537	166,816
7	E. South Central.	769	423	549	2,684	680	1,041	11,910	2,046	14,211
8	W. South Central	2,190	979	1,583	6,090	1,294	1,997	30,980	4,547	39,850
9	Mountain........	5,796	1,840	3,743	9,988	1,250	3,339	45,221	6,405	48,091
10	Pacific..........	24,974	7,329	11,755	45,784	5,402	12,498	142,430	19,469	109,258
	NEW ENGLAND:									
11	Maine...........	598,345	12,428	3,194	23,820	1,499	1,533	4,938	910	1,619
12	New Hampshire.	17,056	257,074	20,859	35,071	1,677	1,861	7,786	912	1,128
13	Vermont.........	2,530	10,417	250,538	11,328	738	1,750	20,655	645	1,082
14	Massachusetts...	93,931	69,052	45,778	2,265,287	38,821	43,468	91,177	11,565	18,581
15	Rhode Island....	4,887	3,736	3,031	47,092	324,792	13,575	13,011	2,848	3,755
16	Connecticut......	6,715	4,406	8,326	48,133	11,283	756,212	99,271	14,601	15,215
	MIDDLE ATLANTIC:									
17	New York.......	12,231	6,481	23,216	70,911	10,797	48,162	6,634,469	115,901	216,102
18	New Jersey......	3,664	2,345	2,766	20,520	3,765	14,900	331,862	1,693,459	180,480
19	Pennsylvania....	3,529	1,625	2,572	17,650	3,107	8,476	131,882	80,432	6,564,988
	E. NORTH CENTRAL:									
20	Ohio.............	2,111	1,217	2,209	10,954	1,372	5,045	76,141	10,043	221,435
21	Indiana..........	624	371	665	2,639	431	1,020	14,668	2,633	30,353
22	Illinois..........	3,647	2,224	4,524	16,205	1,867	5,297	84,669	10,990	72,936
23	Michigan.........	3,263	1,579	3,816	13,836	1,657	5,084	113,576	8,243	62,635
24	Wisconsin........	2,526	833	2,929	4,008	519	1,574	29,962	2,167	14,647
	W. NORTH CENTRAL:									
25	Minnesota........	5,320	1,285	2,961	5,425	587	1,571	26,999	2,068	14,545
26	Iowa............	1,468	931	2,589	3,162	480	1,346	25,092	2,496	29,480
27	Missouri.........	1,127	582	1,034	4,054	496	1,461	21,704	2,857	23,715
28	North Dakota....	567	179	487	711	111	234	4,755	370	3,760
29	South Dakota....	656	225	767	866	121	343	6,840	507	5,069
30	Nebraska........	897	434	1,282	2,037	423	970	15,104	1,731	17,488
31	Kansas..........	1,023	459	1,492	2,224	344	910	16,243	2,014	30,695
	SOUTH ATLANTIC:									
32	Delaware........	163	87	121	686	104	386	3,753	3,535	18,378
33	Maryland........	1,230	376	519	3,897	691	1,510	15,432	5,771	49,644
34	Dist. of Columbia.	1,603	881	1,052	6,370	1,000	2,002	18,719	4,351	20,319
35	Virginia.........	947	461	480	3,291	616	1,274	13,710	4,294	17,412
36	West Virginia....	241	93	320	742	120	350	4,254	1,273	40,366
37	North Carolina...	348	219	274	1,099	343	444	3,865	944	3,772
38	South Carolina...	232	105	116	768	212	299	2,977	603	1,723
39	Georgia..........	440	214	297	1,677	369	630	6,225	1,236	4,177
40	Florida..........	1,962	970	1,111	4,728	709	2,308	15,918	3,530	11,025
	E. SOUTH CENTRAL:									
41	Kentucky........	198	95	147	1,035	233	329	3,961	685	5,587
42	Tennessee........	239	161	218	744	143	331	3,833	668	4,196
43	Alabama.........	195	124	132	672	184	292	2,914	504	3,370
44	Mississippi......	137	43	52	233	120	89	1,202	189	1,058
	W. SOUTH CENTRAL:									
45	Arkansas........	226	98	162	566	222	195	2,969	419	3,578
46	Louisiana........	306	87	146	1,111	224	322	4,387	656	2,757
47	Oklahoma........	526	223	498	1,140	303	399	8,187	1,092	18,052
48	Texas...........	1,122	571	777	3,273	545	1,081	15,437	2,380	15,463
	MOUNTAIN:									
49	Montana.........	1,626	385	790	1,851	197	437	7,616	996	8,000
50	Idaho...........	799	202	453	837	125	253	4,477	464	5,248
51	Wyoming........	306	126	272	634	84	170	2,845	331	3,836
52	Colorado........	1,800	693	1,482	3,954	486	1,618	19,515	2,792	20,055
53	New Mexico.....	190	98	124	433	66	163	2,300	412	2,259
54	Arizona.........	462	175	277	1,109	149	362	3,877	738	3,979
55	Utah............	304	83	220	682	93	204	2,900	436	2,753
56	Nevada.........	309	78	125	488	50	132	1,691	236	1,271
	PACIFIC:									
57	Washington......	6,583	1,428	2,325	7,236	717	2,125	27,150	2,827	24,536
58	Oregon..........	2,446	597	1,245	3,028	339	891	13,204	1,335	12,526
59	California.......	15,945	5,304	8,185	35,520	4,346	9,482	102,076	15,307	72,196

STATE, BY DIVISION AND STATE OF BIRTH: 1920—Continued.

	POPULATION BORN IN—									
	East North Central division.					West North Central division.				
Ohio.	Indiana.	Illinois.	Michigan.	Wisconsin.	Minnesota.	Iowa.	Missouri.	North Dakota.	South Dakota.	
5,223,474	3,060,703	5,606,383	2,711,479	2,460,101	1,817,102	2,544,207	3,518,892	405,379	432,691	1
12,900	4,356	13,107	12,629	5,588	4,342	3,933	4,099	633	685	2
130,948	28,334	61,997	39,909	18,903	11,077	17,198	24,947	2,076	2,298	3
4,478,681	2,543,780	4,383,472	2,396,605	1,993,689	81,468	130,290	164,999	12,008	13,564	4
195,591	187,381	602,687	75,136	242,368	1,532,921	2,033,032	2,659,388	343,489	364,930	5
94,925	27,115	33,458	18,482	9,898	6,361	11,764	17,661	1,625	1,720	6
55,876	45,768	29,252	7,011	3,860	2,572	4,891	20,543	419	745	7
61,978	74,532	142,034	16,889	14,533	9,365	58,652	311,888	1,817	3,890	8
58,179	50,841	120,763	37,878	53,196	54,136	118,033	141,792	19,565	19,299	9
134,396	98,596	219,613	106,940	118,066	114,860	166,414	173,575	23,747	25,560	10
584	286	723	787	464	857	263	258	80	66	11
518	174	605	686	406	282	236	162	48	50	12
595	194	694	543	517	235	337	156	64	92	13
6,978	2,390	7,399	7,894	2,751	2,075	2,045	2,381	279	307	14
896	329	797	739	390	277	260	253	62	38	15
3,329	983	2,889	1,980	1,060	616	792	889	100	132	16
43,692	12,248	34,248	25,247	11,704	6,818	9,337	12,265	1,254	1,461	17
11,376	3,735	9,153	4,571	2,419	1,403	2,146	3,371	235	235	18
75,880	12,351	18,596	10,091	4,780	2,856	5,715	9,311	587	602	19
4,079,758	94,662	45,337	54,886	9,731	4,890	10,691	16,336	964	962	20
135,070	2,209,448	108,662	26,838	7,466	2,762	8,864	15,004	1,024	761	21
105,008	152,246	4,090,918	54,622	86,614	19,336	72,989	110,645	2,706	4,113	22
143,520	74,937	71,826	2,223,333	37,304	10,162	11,532	16,251	2,192	2,149	23
15,325	12,487	66,729	36,926	1,852,574	44,318	26,214	6,763	5,122	5,579	24
15,679	12,692	59,999	30,038	113,037	1,392,176	105,853	9,594	26,278	20,177	25
44,238	33,033	145,050	9,557	37,737	24,400	1,624,606	58,711	3,474	14,293	26
48,629	53,587	184,795	9,446	11,315	5,347	56,302	2,382,282	1,109	2,066	27
4,385	6,802	15,838	5,104	26,392	71,197	27,631	4,176	304,679	15,517	28
6,037	6,335	29,435	5,460	27,126	29,770	71,463	8,351	6,293	303,260	29
22,477	20,622	68,002	7,132	16,349	6,220	92,115	39,603	987	7,639	30
54,146	54,310	99,568	8,399	10,412	3,811	55,062	156,671	669	1,978	31
607	276	403	319	143	85	146	242	39	31	32
6,290	2,189	3,768	1,918	1,126	857	1,168	1,913	194	178	33
8,046	4,234	5,999	2,813	2,171	1,578	2,744	3,490	259	374	34
7,614	3,434	4,125	2,849	1,726	1,062	1,552	2,594	390	295	35
51,279	3,890	2,566	1,325	534	296	759	1,506	79	84	36
2,093	1,169	1,302	795	376	179	379	832	58	86	37
1,025	716	831	440	267	148	306	587	193	76	38
4,197	2,740	2,959	1,479	719	546	1,253	1,875	65	156	39
13,774	8,467	11,505	6,544	2,836	1,610	3,457	4,622	348	440	40
40,225	31,918	11,975	1,782	929	531	1,132	7,553	149	138	41
8,486	7,705	8,385	2,408	1,102	674	1,549	7,665	127	369	42
5,157	3,742	4,885	1,828	1,125	582	1,217	2,592	99	136	43
2,008	2,403	4,007	993	704	785	993	2,733	44	102	44
8,522	16,176	34,361	2,642	1,777	1,009	6,431	62,623	200	426	45
3,868	3,408	6,158	1,765	1,083	745	2,259	6,995	119	138	46
29,725	35,432	61,574	5,173	5,531	3,437	34,004	178,934	659	1,556	47
19,863	19,516	39,941	7,309	6,142	4,174	15,958	63,336	839	1,770	48
9,128	9,859	22,739	12,570	23,505	33,517	27,666	22,366	15,059	9,726	49
6,786	6,044	15,520	5,732	9,450	8,592	17,779	20,242	2,236	2,554	50
3,975	3,813	9,801	1,996	3,263	2,228	13,903	11,429	613	2,884	51
26,026	20,974	51,432	10,184	11,333	6,145	45,253	62,799	947	2,754	52
3,370	3,289	6,296	1,532	1,112	561	3,428	9,837	140	257	53
4,955	4,032	7,680	3,099	2,182	1,413	4,087	9,074	259	578	54
2,718	2,029	5,315	1,751	1,520	1,173	4,348	4,236	200	379	55
1,221	801	1,980	1,014	831	507	1,569	1,809	111	167	56
28,629	23,000	52,549	38,130	50,871	57,944	49,254	41,815	12,032	10,136	57
16,970	14,347	29,462	16,698	21,952	20,961	30,609	26,932	4,954	5,262	58
88,797	61,249	137,602	52,112	45,243	35,955	86,551	104,828	6,761	10,162	59

TABLE 64.—NATIVE POPULATION OF EACH DIVISION AND EACH

	DIVISION OR STATE OF RESIDENCE.	POPULATION BORN IN—								
		West North Central div.—Con.		South Atlantic division.						
		Nebraska.	Kansas.	Delaware.	Maryland.	Dist. of Columbia.	Virginia.	West Virginia.	North Carolina.	South Carolina.
1	United States..	1,066,914	1,535,540	207,804	1,416,193	226,066	2,661,359	1,378,424	2,835,102	1,870,809
	GEOG. DIVISIONS:									
2	New England....	1,666	2,121	1,786	7,904	3,226	15,066	1,468	6,710	3,588
3	Middle Atlantic..	6,775	10,152	42,193	123,474	18,936	157,729	40,358	49,131	35,839
4	E. North Central	30,963	49,962	3,324	34,286	6,053	73,889	107,215	27,007	14,188
5	W. North Central	846,992	1,113,185	1,259	11,593	2,390	38,846	18,530	13,297	3,934
6	South Atlantic...	4,910	8,601	156,160	1,216,372	187,413	2,260,003	1,161,734	2,633,514	1,759,367
7	E. South Central.	1,509	4,470	287	3,372	997	51,067	12,948	45,628	21,200
8	W. South Central	23,612	136,207	477	4,747	1,351	30,407	13,972	36,668	26,451
9	Mountain........	80,575	101,097	742	4,478	1,451	13,015	8,616	9,294	2,676
10	Pacific..........	69,912	109,745	1,576	9,967	4,249	21,337	13,583	13,853	3,566
	NEW ENGLAND:									
11	Maine..........	139	137	86	765	132	330	105	150	85
12	New Hampshire.	92	108	45	216	96	304	68	104	55
13	Vermont........	133	152	21	142	46	265	68	75	46
14	Massachusetts...	815	1,145	728	3,841	1,798	7,800	626	3,832	2,188
15	Rhode Island....	174	146	128	934	351	1,860	170	512	287
16	Connecticut......	313	433	778	2,006	803	4,507	431	2,037	927
	MIDDLE ATLANTIC:									
17	New York.......	3,880	4,913	3,216	20,206	7,573	44,986	4,093	17,803	17,050
18	New Jersey......	842	1,312	9,876	19,058	3,473	29,919	2,115	10,451	5,385
19	Pennsylvania....	2,053	3,927	29,101	84,210	7,890	82,824	34,150	20,877	13,404
	E. NORTH CENTRAL:									
20	Ohio............	3,803	8,320	937	14,869	1,934	39,582	88,573	11,598	6,339
21	Indiana.........	3,422	8,109	374	2,934	437	10,359	5,513	6,273	948
22	Illinois.........	14,908	24,198	905	9,819	2,346	15,907	7,448	5,463	3,868
23	Michigan........	3,987	6,085	899	5,512	1,043	6,801	4,865	3,312	2,797
24	Wisconsin.......	4,843	3,250	209	1,152	293	1,240	816	361	236
	W. NORTH CENTRAL:									
25	Minnesota.......	10,957	5,406	179	1,244	398	1,772	1,073	579	272
26	Iowa...........	29,784	18,770	241	2,350	313	5,796	3,063	2,122	314
27	Missouri........	16,412	83,712	363	3,519	820	17,245	5,121	5,476	1,535
28	North Dakota...	3,899	1,713	42	330	68	829	530	460	98
29	South Dakota....	22,309	4,285	51	393	99	937	540	320	633
30	Nebraska........	735,442	31,461	162	1,387	235	4,462	1,959	1,195	235
31	Kansas	28,189	967,838	221	2,370	457	7,805	6,244	3,145	847
	SOUTH ATLANTIC:									
32	Delaware........	52	82	142,963	22,400	400	3,236	356	676	310
33	Maryland........	539	878	9,641	1,107,290	15,868	62,984	18,688	10,252	3,538
34	Dist. of Columbia	961	1,805	1,016	48,936	160,109	63,006	4,331	8,025	4,258
35	Virginia........	766	1,033	1,330	17,857	8,332	1,978,940	19,610	113,151	11,502
36	West Virginia...	354	841	157	13,240	640	95,818	1,113,343	13,636	1,544
37	North Carolina...	674	713	273	2,065	520	37,233	1,735	2,391,258	62,323
38	South Carolina...	114	201	97	889	326	4,522	395	50,040	1,565,791
39	Georgia.........	355	633	157	1,631	673	7,592	735	29,118	75,171
40	Florida.........	1,095	2,415	526	2,064	545	6,672	2,541	17,358	34,930
	E. SOUTH CENTRAL:									
41	Kentucky........	397	1,997	67	1,048	264	20,444	10,453	5,685	1,304
42	Tennessee.......	498	1,313	118	968	324	21,955	1,663	27,745	5,384
43	Alabama........	362	710	73	808	211	5,206	627	6,660	9,809
44	Mississippi......	252	450	29	548	198	3,462	205	5,539	4,703
	W. SOUTH CENTRAL:									
45	Arkansas........	2,130	9,914	33	534	162	4,729	1,598	11,128	9,312
46	Louisiana.......	746	1,828	60	846	233	3,262	630	2,907	2,575
47	Oklahoma.......	14,852	100,926	150	1,137	343	8,270	6,841	7,667	3,442
48	Texas..........	5,001	21,527	234	2,230	613	14,146	4,900	11,066	11,122
	MOUNTAIN:									
49	Montana.........	10,631	9,302	97	718	205	2,028	1,132	1,515	306
50	Idaho..........	10,591	13,282	58	397	182	2,157	1,329	2,028	184
51	Wyoming........	16,445	7,075	67	337	69	778	720	585	141
52	Colorado........	36,848	55,045	331	1,765	495	4,126	3,421	2,518	637
53	New Mexico.....	1,220	6,488	45	349	137	1,299	591	997	522
54	Arizona........	1,701	5,696	59	500	191	1,491	810	940	602
55	Utah..........	2,489	3,234	59	271	127	840	465	573	225
56	Nevada.........	650	975	26	141	45	296	148	138	59
	PACIFIC:									
57	Washington......	20,092	27,569	305	1,944	1,138	6,410	4,548	5,729	655
58	Oregon..........	15,303	19,291	129	928	455	2,831	1,905	2,382	323
59	California.......	34,517	62,885	1,142	7,095	2,656	12,096	7,130	5,742	2,588

STATE, BY DIVISION AND STATE OF BIRTH: 1920—Continued.

			POPULATION BORN IN—							
South Atlantic div.—Con.		East South Central division.				West South Central division.				
Georgia.	Florida.	Kentucky.	Tennessee.	Alabama.	Mississippi.	Arkansas.	Louisiana.	Oklahoma.	Texas.	
3,128,986	652,352	2,930,790	2,743,221	2,607,273	2,087,558	1,640,814	1,782,749	1,050,159	3,865,863	1
6,322	2,292	2,783	1,818	1,828	809	508	1,975	429	2,021	2
42,854	16,765	21,182	14,502	20,298	5,600	3,113	8,594	2,606	12,055	3
44,961	8,507	362,348	111,262	56,654	37,645	19,043	20,664	13,517	22,199	4
10,625	2,369	108,026	81,749	15,655	31,937	58,492	11,521	63,994	38,808	5
2,750,751	593,540	59,964	77,117	137,475	16,351	6,605	9,420	3,748	15,715	6
147,843	15,588	2,190,839	2,139,095	2,164,357	1,696,157	26,797	42,240	4,581	22,538	7
105,318	8,502	113,092	258,212	191,943	279,083	1,478,900	1,669,062	899,405	3,611,512	8
8,325	1,679	28,869	22,621	8,867	9,045	20,983	5,217	34,985	79,639	9
11,987	3,110	43,687	36,845	10,196	10,931	26,373	14,056	26,894	61,376	10
136	137	160	104	91	62	42	60	45	149	11
101	87	100	46	47	26	27	38	18	84	12
54	52	90	73	54	28	22	44	30	88	13
2,804	1,086	1,638	1,048	888	459	275	1,423	204	1,083	14
387	189	218	160	119	96	53	87	30	180	15
2,840	741	577	387	629	138	89	323	102	437	16
14,583	6,713	8,992	5,944	4,723	2,614	1,482	5,430	1,114	6,407	17
9,261	3,208	2,724	1,740	3,385	687	534	1,126	344	1,717	18
19,010	6,844	9,466	6,818	12,190	2,299	1,097	2,038	1,148	3,931	19
17,910	3,101	134,471	27,653	23,166	5,567	2,739	3,010	4,175	4,305	20
3,312	694	114,575	21,772	5,070	3,212	2,660	1,429	1,964	2,450	21
13,177	2,307	91,021	48,402	18,469	23,857	10,463	13,446	5,068	10,675	22
9,802	2,152	18,181	12,124	9,316	3,756	2,645	2,205	1,591	3,629	23
760	253	4,100	1,311	633	1,253	536	574	719	1,140	24
691	269	3,635	1,517	702	641	764	556	964	1,543	25
1,470	316	8,706	4,921	1,275	2,782	2,259	941	4,056	2,688	26
5,319	852	63,332	57,250	9,114	21,810	38,531	6,969	18,329	17,693	27
79	43	948	333	86	391	185	71	321	396	28
194	79	1,398	891	165	471	549	94	882	759	29
640	457	5,299	3,141	1,347	1,610	2,057	824	3,962	3,437	30
2,232	353	24,708	13,696	2,966	4,232	14,147	2,066	35,480	12,292	31
465	386	178	160	232	54	28	50	33	100	32
2,988	1,055	1,979	1,707	1,181	704	434	764	301	1,183	33
3,984	1,158	3,484	3,221	2,258	1,667	656	1,101	392	2,360	34
6,901	2,095	10,367	18,675	4,451	1,348	778	1,064	550	2,373	35
2,306	521	27,921	6,148	5,968	831	378	281	546	591	36
11,173	1,874	2,158	11,069	2,797	1,229	613	513	233	1,162	37
24,981	2,850	1,085	5,757	2,951	871	425	562	190	877	38
2,595,423	23,498	4,727	22,040	66,998	4,574	1,673	2,062	701	4,139	39
102,530	560,103	8,065	8,340	50,639	5,073	1,620	3,023	802	2,930	40
4,586	708	2,134,989	71,535	8,211	2,617	2,239	1,761	1,050	2,641	41
37,495	1,419	43,272	1,994,580	38,037	63,284	13,538	3,885	1,636	8,385	42
95,283	11,340	7,087	49,846	2,055,273	35,120	3,193	5,101	1,020	6,565	43
10,479	2,121	5,491	23,134	62,836	1,595,136	7,827	31,493	875	4,947	44
20,392	760	23,878	75,335	33,953	98,532	1,196,930	40,241	19,891	33,853	45
8,661	2,486	5,488	6,890	20,469	70,789	19,829	1,522,615	1,793	34,710	46
19,393	942	39,104	60,126	34,277	28,983	174,106	12,977	819,229	236,638	47
56,872	4,314	44,622	115,861	103,244	80,779	88,035	93,229	58,492	3,306,311	48
463	88	3,877	2,158	337	776	1,278	286	2,570	2,414	49
627	116	2,846	3,455	376	481	2,958	216	3,593	2,438	50
318	85	1,516	915	358	222	936	184	1,559	2,066	51
2,556	514	11,314	7,143	2,726	2,882	6,433	1,570	14,295	13,353	52
1,749	273	3,586	4,133	2,299	2,004	4,256	1,151	7,551	34,936	53
1,983	404	3,946	3,373	2,189	2,123	4,284	1,442	4,573	22,267	54
502	159	1,303	1,113	475	457	571	249	617	1,434	55
127	40	481	331	107	100	267	119	227	731	56
1,825	593	9,885	8,032	1,730	2,055	5,675	1,257	5,773	6,967	57
834	243	5,406	5,580	810	1,065	3,735	696	4,626	5,224	58
9,328	2,274	28,396	23,233	7,656	7,811	16,963	12,103	16,495	49,185	59

TABLE **64.**—NATIVE POPULATION OF EACH DIVISION AND EACH

DIVISION OR STATE OF RESIDENCE.	POPULATION BORN IN— Mountain division.							
	Montana.	Idaho.	Wyoming.	Colorado.	New Mexico.	Arizona.	Utah.	Nevada.
1 United States..	240,513	210,106	81,540	473,372	268,492	139,386	408,838	48,232
GEOG. DIVISIONS:								
2 New England. ...	769	242	255	2,477	463	214	323	339
3 Middle Atlantic...	2,234	900	1,471	6,573	1,692	848	1,546	494
4 E. North Central..	6,228	3,666	2,131	14,324	2,987	1,404	2,455	593
5 W. North Central.	12,737	5,634	6,398	30,557	4,059	1,451	3,007	833
6 South Atlantic....	1,090	676	542	2,877	879	657	1,234	231
7 E. South Central..	467	251	168	1,452	501	412	249	131
8 W. South Central.	1,876	1,741	1,143	11,083	13,410	3,642	2,218	459
9 Mountain.........	184,514	164,713	62,351	352,966	235,886	115,045	375,576	29,555
10 Pacific............	30,598	32,283	7,081	51,063	8,615	15,713	22,230	15,597
NEW ENGLAND:								
11 Maine.............	107	34	23	152	29	24	27	31
12 New Hampshire..	60	15	13	95	49	11	15	115
13 Vermont..........	68	20	41	115	47	9	21	13
14 Massachusetts.....	367	126	125	1,076	237	111	190	146
15 Rhode Island.....	41	13	8	129	20	8	19	12
16 Connecticut.......	126	34	45	910	81	51	51	22
MIDDLE ATLANTIC:								
17 New York........	1,178	474	442	3,405	917	457	897	276
18 New Jersey.......	290	131	153	963	164	126	229	101
19 Pennsylvania.....	766	295	876	2,205	611	265	420	117
E. NORTH CENTRAL:								
20 Ohio.............	843	396	431	2,774	1,040	305	446	93
21 Indiana...........	546	203	213	1,427	234	185	212	59
22 Illinois...........	1,968	2,074	852	6,280	938	471	1,058	226
23 Michigan.........	1,446	529	385	2,505	626	312	517	162
24 Wisconsin........	1,425	464	250	1,338	149	131	222	53
W. NORTH CENTRAL:								
25 Minnesota........	3,680	556	434	1,624	192	100	348	99
26 Iowa..............	1,519	1,853	798	3,805	443	182	612	147
27 Missouri..........	1,043	800	677	6,810	1,173	404	799	180
28 North Dakota.....	2,604	224	121	349	51	20	53	130
29 South Dakota....	1,786	310	1,298	1,112	107	62	131	56
30 Nebraska.........	1,218	911	2,474	8,002	286	135	624	86
31 Kansas...........	887	980	596	8,855	1,807	548	440	135
SOUTH ATLANTIC:								
32 Delaware.........	26	10	14	67	5	9	15	2
33 Maryland.........	154	69	73	394	101	62	121	41
34 Dist. of Columbia.	219	117	106	544	131	105	313	63
35 Virginia..........	214	117	92	430	222	108	400	30
36 West Virginia.....	91	58	87	321	151	66	92	8
37 North Carolina....	65	85	39	187	44	67	51	15
38 South Carolina....	34	32	15	81	22	42	24	10
39 Georgia...........	88	73	43	290	57	99	78	20
40 Florida...........	199	115	73	563	146	99	140	42
E. SOUTH CENTRAL:								
41 Kentucky.........	162	62	70	403	150	136	83	19
42 Tennessee.........	146	81	50	642	207	91	87	88
43 Alabama..........	72	26	27	280	90	82	54	17
44 Mississippi........	87	82	21	127	54	103	25	7
W. SOUTH CENTRAL:								
45 Arkansas.........	213	242	116	1,108	406	154	96	37
46 Louisiana.........	92	51	30	423	150	149	63	47
47 Oklahoma.........	800	907	486	4,937	3,549	866	453	141
48 Texas.............	762	541	511	4,615	9,305	2,173	1,606	234
MOUNTAIN:								
49 Montana..........	172,818	3,604	2,631	4,121	326	189	2,631	798
50 Idaho.............	5,101	148,028	3,182	6,427	448	465	41,837	1,096
51 Wyoming.........	2,443	1,737	48,982	7,202	697	161	5,410	177
52 Colorado..........	1,443	1,436	3,491	317,506	16,212	756	3,294	382
53 New Mexico.......	154	163	130	5,673	209,234	2,118	482	47
54 Arizona...........	720	733	290	4,019	7,850	109,776	3,723	572
55 Utah.............	1,374	8,324	3,322	6,321	967	1,256	314,006	1,722
56 Nevada...........	461	688	323	1,697	152	324	4,193	24,761
PACIFIC:								
57 Washington.......	16,816	15,308	2,243	9,965	743	715	3,696	1,099
58 Oregon...........	4,850	9,513	1,461	6,714	531	573	3,578	1,137
59 California.........	8,932	7,462	3,377	34,384	7,341	14,425	14,956	13,361

STATE, BY DIVISION AND STATE OF BIRTH: 1920—Continued.

					POPULATION BORN IN—						
Pacific division.			Outlying possessions.								
Washington.	Oregon.	California.	Alaska.	American Samoa.	Guam.	Hawaii.	Panama Canal Zone.	Philippine Islands.	Porto Rico.	Virgin Islands of the U. S.	
517,036	400,453	1,409,467	4,155	37	115	10,551	1,052	8,302	11,811	1,997	1
1,147	610	5,885	58	......	4	250	41	173	274	74	2
4,636	2,390	15,305	145	1	10	376	392	1,316	8,512	1,817	3
8,389	4,370	16,029	189	2	1	254	120	509	414	23	4
9,540	5,837	12,603	153	3	1	166	47	367	160	9	5
2,844	1,172	5,237	122	5	9	218	179	673	878	36	6
728	422	1,881	17	......	......	33	44	58	182	6	7
2,910	2,567	10,450	69	......	4	109	70	264	317	12	8
24,383	17,560	32,315	186	13	1	270	14	285	90	2	9
462,459	365,525	1,309,762	3,216	13	85	8,875	145	4,657	984	18	10
101	74	649	9	......	......	10	4	8	13	2	11
68	33	297	1	......	......	4	1	2	3	1	12
67	46	246	4	......	1	4	1	......	2	1	13
608	327	3,376	33	......	3	192	18	119	163	31	14
81	28	374	1	......	......	13	2	22	24	2	15
222	102	943	10	......	......	27	15	22	69	37	16
2,527	1,280	9,873	83	1	6	248	282	858	7,719	1,709	17
666	311	2,294	14	......	3	59	62	134	360	62	18
1,443	799	3,138	48	......	1	69	48	324	433	46	19
1,490	913	3,248	48	......	......	39	42	109	124	7	20
697	456	1,464	12	......	......	14	12	34	19	1	21
2,612	1,392	6,429	50	......	......	107	28	275	142	8	22
1,938	1,061	3,620	63	1	......	79	34	77	98	7	23
1,652	548	1,268	16	1	1	15	4	14	31	......	24
2,649	932	1,700	42	......	......	19	8	41	13	3	25
1,478	943	2,081	20	......	......	61	7	72	38	3	26
1,595	1,097	3,769	34	2	......	27	14	101	63	1	27
704	346	452	7	......	......	2	3	3	4	......	28
656	404	559	16	......	......	8	......	6	7	......	29
1,039	956	1,563	18	1	1	19	2	41	10	1	30
1,419	1,159	2,479	16	......	......	30	13	103	25	1	31
61	23	111	......	......	......	2	4	7	13	......	32
674	180	910	21	1	1	29	24	67	127	8	33
434	244	1,322	17	......	3	58	57	318	148	9	34
518	195	858	13	3	2	42	19	140	163	7	35
396	152	332	5	......	......	7	9	10	23	......	36
185	74	250	8	......	1	6	10	12	38	6	37
103	44	205	3	......	......	8	9	60	55	1	38
153	79	535	28	......	......	40	15	34	111	3	39
320	181	714	27	1	2	26	32	25	200	2	40
267	149	622	4	......	......	18	14	29	32	......	41
235	161	620	4	......	......	8	15	13	28	......	42
132	71	359	6	......	......	4	9	8	70	3	43
94	41	280	3	......	......	3	6	8	52	3	44
386	280	1,133	11	......	......	9	2	13	11	......	45
205	117	950	10	......	......	20	40	110	217	9	46
1,177	1,173	2,761	15	......	4	23	9	27	5	1	47
1,142	997	5,606	33	......	......	57	19	114	84	2	48
6,635	2,630	2,408	43	......	......	21	2	50	7	......	49
13,432	9,970	3,248	33	2	......	30	4	10	13	......	50
641	588	889	10	1	......	6	......	35	2	1	51
1,579	1,316	3,956	29	2	1	39	1	81	30	......	52
201	217	1,239	8	......	......	10	......	20	5	......	53
891	1,159	10,555	26	1	......	51	7	55	31	......	54
624	901	2,681	15	7	......	66	......	22	2	1	55
380	779	7,339	22	......	......	47	......	12	......	......	56
410,175	39,587	20,810	1,928	......	4	464	24	1,071	34	2	57
29,702	295,723	20,709	592	......	1	129	16	189	15	2	58
22,582	30,215	1,268,243	696	13	80	8,282	105	3,397	935	14	59

Table **65.**—TOTAL POPULATION DISTRIBUTED AS BORN IN STATE OF RESIDENCE, IN OTHER STATES, OR IN FOREIGN COUNTRIES, 1920, WITH PERCENTAGES FOR 1920 AND 1910, FOR CITIES HAVING, IN 1920, 50,000 INHABITANTS OR MORE.

CITY OF RESIDENCE AND CLASS OF POPULATION.	POPULATION: 1920				PER CENT OF TOTAL POPULATION.					
	Total.1	Born in the United States and with state of birth reported.		Foreign born.	Born in state of residence.		Born in other states.		Foreign born.	
		Born in state of residence.	Born in other states.		1920	1910	1920	1910	1920	1910
ALABAMA:										
Birmingham	178,806	127,325	44,514	6,140	71.2	64.3	24.9	30.9	3.4	4.3
Mobile	60,777	44,779	13,455	2,157	73.7	77.2	22.1	17.6	3.5	4.5
ARKANSAS:										
Little Rock	65,142	36,616	23,991	1,815	56.2	52.5	36.8	40.2	2.8	4.3
CALIFORNIA:										
Berkeley	56,036	24,117	20,614	10,506	43.0	43.9	36.8	33.7	18.7	21.4
Long Beach	55,593	6,863	41,234	7,100	12.3		74.2		12.8	
Los Angeles	576,673	116,116	333,157	122,131	20.1	20.0	57.8	58.6	21.2	20.7
Oakland	216,261	94,214	67,884	49,895	43.6	42.6	31.4	28.8	23.1	27.2
Sacramento	65,908	32,638	19,782	12,988	49.5	47.1	30.0	27.6	19.7	24.7
San Diego	74,683	14,868	44,821	14,088	19.9	20.2	60.0	58.5	18.9	19.8
San Francisco	506,676	227,510	122,241	149,195	44.9	43.5	24.1	20.9	29.4	34.1
COLORADO:										
Denver	256,491	74,236	136,658	38,230	28.9	25.7	53.3	54.6	14.9	18.6
CONNECTICUT:										
Bridgeport	143,555	66,872	29,455	46,782	46.6	46.8	20.5	17.5	32.6	35.5
Hartford	138,036	69,574	27,329	40,912	50.4	50.8	19.8	17.2	29.6	31.7
New Britain	59,316	32,007	5,904	21,340	54.0	49.6	10.0	9.2	36.0	41.1
New Haven	162,537	91,049	24,842	46,124	56.0	53.6	15.3	13.9	28.4	32.2
Waterbury	91,715	48,737	12,904	29,974	53.1	52.0	14.1	13.0	32.7	34.9
DELAWARE:										
Wilmington	110,168	59,370	34,049	16,337	53.9	56.3	30.9	27.8	14.8	15.7
DISTRICT OF COLUMBIA:										
Washington	437,571	160,109	244,222	29,365	36.6	42.1	55.8	49.7	6.7	7.5
FLORIDA:										
Jacksonville	91,558	39,412	47,136	4,144	43.0	41.2	51.5	53.1	4.5	4.7
Tampa	51,608	25,579	14,367	11,352	49.6	43.6	27.8	27.1	22.0	28.6
GEORGIA:										
Atlanta	200,616	152,879	42,113	4,789	76.2	76.5	21.0	20.3	2.4	2.9
Augusta	52,548	36,275	15,035	999	69.0	71.4	28.6	26.0	1.9	2.3
Macon	52,995	46,092	6,050	703	87.0	88.3	11.4	9.5	1.3	1.7
Savannah	83,252	54,318	25,242	3,336	65.2	64.4	30.3	30.1	4.0	5.3
ILLINOIS:										
Chicago	2,701,705	1,389,075	493,308	808,558	51.4	46.6	18.3	17.0	29.9	35.8
East St. Louis	66,767	36,814	22,814	6,798	55.1	51.0	34.2	32.5	10.2	16.1
Peoria	76,121	52,456	15,515	7,821	68.9	64.6	20.4	21.9	10.3	13.2
Rockford	65,651	34,135	13,893	17,373	52.0	49.6	21.2	19.6	26.5	30.5
Springfield	59,183	42,119	10,534	6,268	71.2	66.4	17.8	19.6	10.6	13.4
INDIANA:										
Evansville	85,264	56,547	25,300	3,164	66.3	64.7	29.7	28.7	3.7	6.4
Fort Wayne	86,549	59,684	19,917	6,657	69.0	66.7	23.0	21.6	7.7	11.3
Gary	55,378	15,390	23,309	16,510	27.8		42.1		29.8	
Indianapolis	314,194	203,314	91,802	17,096	64.7	63.9	29.2	27.2	5.4	8.5
South Bend	70,983	42,369	14,924	13,415	59.7	53.8	21.0	20.9	18.9	25.0
Terre Haute	66,083	43,726	18,153	3,683	66.2	63.1	27.5	29.6	5.6	6.6
IOWA:										
Davenport	56,727	31,866	16,866	7,663	56.2	56.4	29.7	23.8	13.5	18.8
Des Moines	126,468	75,268	38,875	11,269	59.5	56.3	30.7	30.8	8.9	12.1
Sioux City	71,227	32,735	26,676	11,250	46.0	42.9	37.5	34.3	15.8	21.9
KANSAS:										
Kansas City	101,177	39,959	48,959	11,721	39.5	36.7	48.4	49.6	11.6	12.6
Topeka	50,022	26,803	18,706	4,035	53.6	45.5	37.4	44.4	8.1	9.5
Wichita	72,217	29,883	38,285	3,044	41.4	36.0	53.0	57.3	4.2	5.5
KENTUCKY:										
Covington	57,121	41,726	12,412	2,894	73.0	71.2	21.7	21.3	5.1	7.4
Louisville	234,891	181,096	41,536	11,667	77.1	75.3	17.7	16.7	5.0	7.8

1 Includes persons born in the United States, state of birth not reported; persons born in outlying possessions, or at sea under United States flag; and American citizens born abroad.

TABLE 65.—TOTAL POPULATION DISTRIBUTED AS BORN IN STATE OF RESIDENCE, IN OTHER STATES, OR IN FOREIGN COUNTRIES, 1920, WITH PERCENTAGES FOR 1920 AND 1910, FOR CITIES HAVING, IN 1920, 50,000 INHABITANTS OR MORE—Continued.

CITY OF RESIDENCE AND CLASS OF POPULATION.	POPULATION: 1920			PER CENT OF TOTAL POPULATION.					
	Total.[1]	Born in the United States and with state of birth reported.		Foreign born.	Born in state of residence.		Born in other states.		Foreign born.
		Born in state of residence.	Born in other states.		1920	1910	1920	1910	1920	1910
LOUISIANA:										
New Orleans........	387,219	310,086	47,908	27,365	80.1	79.7	12.4	11.2	7.1	8.4
MAINE:										
Portland............	69,272	46,815	8,877	13,346	67.6	67.3	12.8	11.4	19.3	20.7
MARYLAND:										
Baltimore...........	733,826	533,190	114,635	84,809	72.7	73.8	15.6	12.1	11.6	13.9
MASSACHUSETTS:										
Boston..............	748,060	420,345	82,086	242,619	56.2	51.7	11.0	11.6	32.4	36.3
Brockton...........	66,254	42,027	6,908	17,191	63.4	60.9	10.4	11.5	25.9	27.2
Cambridge..........	109,694	62,856	13,220	33,296	57.3	54.3	12.1	11.6	30.4	33.7
Fall River..........	120,485	70,674	7,228	42,421	58.7	50.1	6.0	7.1	35.2	42.7
Haverhill...........	53,884	29,408	11,024	13,335	54.6	52.1	20.5	22.2	24.7	25.4
Holyoke............	60,203	33,425	6,406	20,280	55.5	48.5	10.6	10.9	33.7	40.3
Lawrence...........	94,270	47,645	7,127	39,201	50.5	42.8	7.6	8.7	41.6	48.3
Lowell..............	112,759	62,333	11,998	38,116	55.3	48.0	10.6	10.8	33.8	40.9
Lynn...............	99,148	56,760	14,035	28,138	57.2	53.0	14.2	15.7	28.4	30.9
New Bedford........	121,217	60,584	9,309	51,078	50.0	45.9	7.7	8.7	42.1	45.2
Somerville..........	93,091	55,916	12,695	24,254	60.1	56.8	13.6	15.8	26.1	27.0
Springfield.........	129,614	65,817	31,948	31,461	50.8	50.2	24.6	23.4	24.3	26.0
Worcester...........	179,754	104,571	21,213	53,527	58.2	54.4	11.8	12.1	29.8	33.3
MICHIGAN:										
Detroit.............	993,678	445,883	251,862	290,884	44.9	52.7	25.3	13.0	29.3	33.8
Flint...............	91,599	52,930	22,671	15,213	57.8	62.2	24.8	19.8	16.6	17.5
Grand Rapids.......	137,634	89,229	19,398	28,427	64.8	60.1	14.1	14.1	20.7	25.2
Lansing..	57,327	39,814	11,009	6,042	69.5	67.6	19.2	19.0	10.5	12.8
Saginaw............	61,903	41,798	8,126	11,655	67.5	63.3	13.1	12.9	18.8	23.2
MINNESOTA:										
Duluth.............	98,917	43,512	24,737	30,196	44.0	35.6	25.0	24.5	30.5	39.1
Minneapolis.........	380,582	185,521	105,051	88,248	48.7	43.4	27.6	26.9	23.2	28.6
St. Paul............	234,698	127,905	54,117	51,722	54.5	50.0	23.1	23.4	22.0	26.4
MISSOURI:										
Kansas City........	324,410	• 146,667	147,633	27,583	45.2	42.9	45.5	44.5	8.5	10.3
St. Joseph..........	77,939	46,306	24,351	6,438	59.4	54.0	31.2	34.3	8.3	10.5
St. Louis...........	772,897	472,971	193,568	103,626	61.2	57.9	25.0	23.3	13.4	18.4
NEBRASKA:										
Lincoln.............	54,948	26,261	20,899	7,235	47.8	40.0	38.0	42.5	13.2	16.4
Omaha..............	191,601	78,104	75,353	35,645	40.8	36.3	39.3	41.1	18.6	21.9
NEW HAMPSHIRE:										
Manchester..........	78,384	40,525	9,970	27,537	51.7	43.7	12.7	13.0	35.1	42.4
NEW JERSEY:										
Atlantic City........	50,707	16,700	26,273	7,509	32.9	34.3	51.8	50.5	14.8	14.7
Bayonne............	76,754	37,529	13,625	25,514	48.9	43.6	17.8	19.3	33.2	37.0
Camden............	116,309	57,835	37,885	20,354	49.7	50.5	32.6	32.6	17.5	16.7
East Orange........	50,710	23,213	20,411	6,890	45.8	43.3	40.3	39.6	13.6	16.7
Elizabeth...........	95,783	51,021	16,250	28,276	53.3	50.5	17.0	16.9	29.5	32.6
Hoboken............	68,166	31,431	13,073	23,543	46.1	41.3	19.2	19.1	34.5	39.4
Jersey City.........	298,103	158,671	62,583	76,294	53.2	49.1	21.0	21.6	25.6	29.1
Newark.............	414,524	226,357	69,177	117,549	54.6	52.8	16.7	14.9	28.4	31.9
Passaic.............	63,841	28,714	8,656	26,396	45.0	34.3	13.6	13.5	41.3	52.0
Paterson...........	135,875	76,008	14,504	45,242	55.9	50.5	13.6	13.3	33.3	36.2
Trenton............	119,289	70,802	18,045	30,168	59.4	58.1	15.1	14.4	25.3	27.2

[1] Includes persons born in the United States, state of birth not reported; persons born in outlying possessions, or at sea under United States flag; and American citizens born abroad.

TABLE **65.**—TOTAL POPULATION DISTRIBUTED AS BORN IN STATE OF RESIDENCE, IN OTHER STATES, OR IN FOREIGN COUNTRIES, 1920, WITH PERCENTAGES FOR 1920 AND 1910, FOR CITIES HAVING, IN 1920, 50,000 INHABITANTS OR MORE—Continued.

| | POPULATION: **1920** | | | | PER CENT OF TOTAL POPULATION. | | | | | |
| CITY OF RESIDENCE AND CLASS OF POPULATION. | Total.[1] | Born in the United States and with state of birth reported. | | Foreign born. | Born in state of residence. | | Born in other states. | | Foreign born. | |
		Born in state of residence.	Born in other states.		1920	1910	1920	1910	1920	1910
NEW YORK:										
Albany	113,344	87,779	7,643	17,695	77.4	75.9	6.7	5.8	15.6	18.2
Binghamton	66,800	40,502	14,942	10,401	60.6	64.2	22.4	19.0	15.6	15.3
Buffalo	506,775	337,601	45,443	121,824	66.6	64.2	9.0	7.4	24.0	28.0
New York	5,620,048	3,107,563	447,800	2,028,160	55.3	51.2	8.0	7.6	36.1	40.8
Bronx boro	732,016	426,041	33,402	267,742	58.2	58.2	4.6	6.9	36.6	34.7
Brooklyn boro	2,018,356	1,217,615	127,687	666,188	60.3	57.9	6.3	6.8	33.0	35.2
Manhattan boro	2,284,103	1,071,382	241,470	950,264	46.9	43.1	10.6	8.4	41.6	47.9
Queens boro	469,042	321,367	32,376	112,171	68.5	65.6	6.9	6.3	23.9	27.9
Richmond boro	116,531	71,158	12,865	31,795	61.1	61.1	11.0	10.3	27.3	28.4
Niagara Falls	50,760	25,572	6,818	17,948	50.4	49.2	13.4	10.5	35.4	39.8
Rochester	295,750	200,479	22,219	71,411	67.8	65.6	7.5	6.8	24.1	27.1
Schenectady	88,723	60,517	7,447	20,564	68.2	65.5	8.4	8.8	23.2	25.7
Syracuse	171,717	126,485	12,249	32,383	73.7	71.4	7.1	5.8	18.9	22.5
Troy	72,013	56,215	4,056	11,525	78.1	74.3	5.6	5.3	16.0	20.1
Utica	94,156	66,013	4,704	23,291	70.1	67.0	5.0	4.2	24.7	28.6
Yonkers	100,176	64,036	10,102	25,796	63.9	56.8	10.1	9.6	25.8	33.5
OHIO:										
Akron	208,435	88,010	81,686	38,021	42.2	63.8	39.2	16.8	18.2	19.2
Canton	87,091	55,441	16,828	14,729	63.7	68.4	19.3	14.2	16.9	17.2
Cincinnati	401,247	265,910	91,599	42,921	66.3	65.3	22.8	18.6	10.7	15.6
Cleveland	796,841	413,127	140,812	240,173	51.8	52.8	17.7	11.9	30.1	35.0
Columbus	237,031	172,973	46,055	16,187	73.0	74.4	19.4	15.9	6.8	9.0
Dayton	152,559	106,381	32,667	13,165	69.7	73.0	21.4	14.9	8.6	11.9
Springfield	60,840	46,796	10,943	2,772	76.9	76.7	18.0	16.2	4.6	6.8
Toledo	243,164	149,599	54,372	38,296	61.5	62.1	22.4	18.5	15.7	19.1
Youngstown	132,358	62,992	35,074	33,945	47.6	48.2	26.5	20.0	25.6	31.5
OKLAHOMA:										
Oklahoma City	91,295	24,255	63,048	3,565	26.6	13.9	69.1	80.3	3.9	5.2
Tulsa	72,075	14,775	54,260	2,066	20.5		75.3		2.9	
OREGON:										
Portland	258,288	76,607	130,190	49,778	29.7	24.4	50.4	50.6	19.3	24.3
PENNSYLVANIA:										
Allentown	73,502	61,444	3,390	8,622	83.6	84.0	4.6	4.0	11.7	12.0
Altoona	60,331	52,229	2,734	5,326	86.6	85.7	4.5	4.2	8.8	10.0
Bethlehem	50,358	36,035	3,295	10,975	71.6		6.5		21.8	
Chester	58,030	31,489	15,044	11,389	54.3		25.9		19.6	
Erie	93,372	63,435	12,284	17,396	67.9	66.2	13.2	11.0	18.6	22.5
Harrisburg	75,917	64,344	7,178	4,190	84.8	85.0	9.5	8.4	5.5	6.5
Johnstown	67,327	51,332	3,794	12,172	76.2	67.8	5.6	4.5	18.1	27.6
Lancaster	53,150	47,934	2,368	2,718	90.2	89.3	4.5	3.8	5.1	6.8
Philadelphia	1,823,779	1,165,137	252,244	400,744	63.9	63.4	13.8	11.6	22.0	24.8
Pittsburgh	588,343	392,205	73,955	120,792	66.7	62.3	12.6	10.9	20.5	26.4
Reading	107,784	94,527	3,579	9,573	87.7	87.8	3.3	3.0	8.9	9.2
Scranton	137,783	102,229	6,823	28,587	74.2	66.8	5.0	6.0	20.7	27.0
Wilkes-Barre	73,833	55,879	3,262	14,580	75.7	70.9	4.4	5.0	19.7	24.0
RHODE ISLAND:										
Pawtucket	64,248	31,986	10,994	21,138	49.8	47.5	17.1	17.4	32.9	34.8
Providence	237,595	127,301	39,837	69,895	53.6	47.6	16.8	17.8	29.4	34.3
SOUTH CAROLINA:										
Charleston	67,557	50,350	7,010	9,901	85.7	89.7	10.8	6.0	2.2	1.2

[1] Includes persons born in the United States, state of birth not reported; persons born in outlying possessions, or at sea under United States flag; and American citizens born abroad.

TABLE 65.—TOTAL POPULATION DISTRIBUTED AS BORN IN STATE OF RESIDENCE, IN OTHER STATES, OR IN FOREIGN COUNTRIES, 1920, WITH PERCENTAGES FOR 1920 AND 1910, FOR CITIES HAVING, IN 1920, 50,000 INHABITANTS OR MORE—Continued.

CITY OF RESIDENCE AND CLASS OF POPULATION.	POPULATION: 1920				PER CENT OF TOTAL POPULATION.					
	Total.[1]	Born in the United States and with state of birth reported.		Foreign born.	Born in state of residence.		Born in other states.		Foreign born.	
		Born in state of residence.	Born in other states.		1920	1910	1920	1910	1920	1910
TENNESSEE:										
Chattanooga	57,895	29,665	26,751	1,253	51.2	49.4	46.2	46.7	2.2	3.0
Knoxville	77,818	63,598	13,123	821	81.7	75.3	16.9	22.2	1.1	2.2
Memphis	162,351	74,943	78,863	5,844	46.2	47.5	48.6	46.2	3.6	5.0
Nashville	118,342	98,495	17,131	2,412	83.2	83.3	14.5	13.8	2.0	2.7
TEXAS:										
Dallas	158,976	97,061	51,479	8,801	61.1	57.1	32.4	36.6	5.5	5.7
El Paso	77,560	22,503	20,893	33,655	29.0	31.5	26.9	30.2	43.4	36.9
Fort Worth	106,482	63,521	33,352	7,502	59.7	57.7	31.3	35.2	7.0	5.8
Houston	138,276	85,954	39,551	12,088	62.2	63.2	28.6	28.0	8.7	8.1
San Antonio	161,379	93,323	30,160	36,824	57.8	60.1	18.7	21.1	22.8	18.1
UTAH:										
Salt Lake City	118,110	66,848	30,693	19,897	56.6	49.9	26.0	28.0	16.8	21.1
VIRGINIA:										
Norfolk	115,777	66,463	41,998	6,998	57.4	64.4	36.3	30.0	6.0	5.4
Portsmouth	54,387	33,383	19,276	1,582	61.4	67.6	35.4	28.9	2.9	3.5
Richmond	171,667	140,474	24,920	4,713	81.8	86.3	14.5	10.3	2.7	3.2
Roanoke	50,842	42,380	7,514	878	83.4	84.9	14.8	12.8	1.7	2.2
WASHINGTON:										
Seattle	315,312	72,161	156,576	80,976	22.9	16.1	49.7	53.8	25.7	28.4
Spokane	104,437	26,408	59,944	17,096	25.3	16.2	57.4	61.2	16.4	20.9
Tacoma	96,965	26,984	45,078	21,705	27.8	21.0	46.5	49.1	22.4	26.9
WEST VIRGINIA:										
Huntington	50,177	30,494	18,532	735	60.8	56.3	36.9	40.3	1.5	1.7
Wheeling	56,208	36,349	13,799	5,808	64.7	61.7	24.5	24.9	10.3	13.0
WISCONSIN:										
Milwaukee	457,147	296,480	48,821	110,160	64.9	60.4	10.7	9.5	24.1	29.8
Racine	58,593	32,193	10,066	16,215	54.9	53.9	17.2	13.0	27.7	32.9

[1] Includes persons born in the United States, state of birth not reported; persons born in outlying possessions, or at sea under United States flag; and American citizens born abroad.

TABLE 66.—NATIVE POPULATION, BY DIVISION AND STATE OF BIRTH,

	CITY OF RESIDENCE.	Total native population.	United States.	New England.	Middle Atlantic.	East North Central.	West North Central.
				POPULATION BORN IN—			
					Geographic division.		
1	Akron, Ohio	170,414	170,248	2,125	29,493	98,004	2,991
2	Albany, N. Y	95,649	95,537	3,081	89,701	1,109	287
3	Atlanta, Ga	195,827	195,721	1,009	3,415	3,845	1,312
4	Baltimore, Md	649,017	648,571	4,850	33,117	7,199	2,309
5	Birmingham, Ala	172,666	172,595	396	2,143	3,985	1,322
6	Boston, Mass	505,441	504,278	461,228	20,797	5,642	1,891
7	Bridgeport, Conn	96,773	96,630	73,643	18,969	1,164	359
8	Buffalo, N. Y	384,951	383,788	4,798	356,331	12,764	2,233
9	Cambridge, Mass	76,398	76,178	68,979	3,075	1,109	400
10	Camden, N. J	95,955	95,903	981	84,630	984	254
11	Chicago, Ill	1,893,147	1,890,676	19,170	89,496	1,563,938	81,711
12	Cincinnati, Ohio	358,326	358,153	1,440	7,865	284,334	3,257
13	Cleveland, Ohio	556,668	555,980	5,938	62,029	437,328	6,627
14	Columbus, Ohio	220,844	220,670	1,114	9,404	180,939	2,425
15	Dallas, Tex	150,175	150,060	634	2,795	7,311	7,767
16	Dayton, Ohio	139,394	139,291	813	4,995	115,623	1,538
17	Denver, Colo	218,261	217,847	4,758	18,997	40,614	44,830
18	Des Moines, Iowa	115,199	115,029	892	4,058	15,816	87,722
19	Detroit, Mich	702,794	699,649	13,638	71,776	532,710	18,580
20	Fall River, Mass	78,064	77,943	75,514	1,486	400	102
21	Fort Worth, Tex	98,980	98,893	387	1,929	4,823	5,714
22	Grand Rapids, Mich	109,207	109,006	1,001	5,361	98,738	1,645
23	Hartford, Conn	97,124	97,015	80,741	10,592	1,209	372
24	Houston, Tex	126,188	126,049	611	2,757	6,435	5,445
25	Indianapolis, Ind	297,098	296,897	1,365	6,589	234,452	6,085
26	Jersey City, N. J	221,809	221,596	3,847	207,190	2,016	626
27	Kansas City, Kans	89,456	89,404	325	2,362	9,016	63,883
28	Kansas City, Mo	296,827	296,478	2,336	11,411	39,284	201,227
29	Los Angeles, Calif	454,542	452,086	16,957	50,548	105,277	76,558
30	Louisville, Ky	223,224	223,133	497	2,613	20,712	2,391
31	Lowell, Mass	74,643	74,403	70,971	2,137	619	150
32	Memphis, Tenn	156,507	156,434	365	1,860	7,192	4,167
33	Milwaukee, Wis	346,987	346,772	2,026	8,537	320,338	9,446
34	Minneapolis, Minn	292,334	291,611	5,900	12,031	50,734	213,873
35	Nashville, Tenn	115,930	115,889	172	860	2,695	913
36	New Bedford, Mass	70,139	69,950	66,827	1,811	459	108
37	New Haven, Conn	116,413	116,241	97,923	13,007	1,282	499
38	New Orleans, La	359,854	359,201	1,136	4,691	5,859	3,177
39	New York, N. Y	3,591,888	3,577,362	90,478	3,250,161	55,739	18,883
40	Bronx borough	464,274	463,718	8,402	439,454	4,091	1,211
41	Brooklyn borough	1,352,168	1,348,952	29,260	1,265,255	14,674	4,811
42	Manhattan borough	1,333,839	1,323,788	43,270	1,133,726	31,394	11,112
43	Queens borough	356,871	356,371	7,123	334,456	4,198	1,315
44	Richmond borough	84,736	84,533	2,423	77,270	1,382	434
45	Newark, N. J	296,975	296,742	7,715	268,024	3,741	946
46	Norfolk, Va	108,779	108,634	1,297	4,793	2,148	728
47	Oakland, Calif	166,366	162,741	5,269	10,541	17,515	13,852
48	Omaha, Nebr	155,956	155,765	1,670	6,936	19,390	112,953
49	Paterson, N. J	90,633	90,588	1,513	86,894	622	172
50	Philadelphia, Pa	1,423,035	1,421,474	16,065	1,240,485	16,425	5,850
51	Pittsburgh, Pa	467,551	467,188	2,501	401,466	19,780	2,760
52	Portland, Oreg	208,510	207,504	3,862	11,584	37,632	39,122
53	Providence, R. I	167,700	167,429	154,322	8,105	1,258	488
54	Reading, Pa	98,211	98,184	355	95,872	541	217
55	Richmond, Va	166,954	166,852	706	4,073	1,751	611
56	Rochester, N. Y	224,339	223,879	3,969	209,270	5,487	1,146
57	St. Louis, Mo	660,971	668,809	3,258	14,657	91,103	484,646
58	St. Paul, Minn	182,976	182,660	2,366	6,330	26,922	141,296
59	Salt Lake City, Utah	98,213	97,816	824	3,180	6,664	7,210
60	San Antonio, Tex	124,555	124,006	718	3,009	6,253	5,359
61	San Francisco, Calif	357,481	352,973	9,900	24,907	29,067	22,559
62	Scranton, Pa	109,196	109,153	598	106,527	782	222
63	Seattle, Wash	234,336	230,929	6,663	16,147	47,452	47,441
64	Spokane, Wash	87,341	86,711	1,660	4,817	18,092	21,394
65	Springfield, Mass	98,153	97,909	81,954	11,199	1,456	495
66	Syracuse, N. Y	139,334	139,085	2,641	130,739	2,837	814
67	Toledo, Ohio	204,868	204,611	1,613	12,644	177,304	3,156
68	Trenton, N. J	89,121	89,045	1,039	82,880	876	206
69	Washington, D. C	408,206	407,070	12,908	43,389	23,263	11,211
70	Wilmington, Del	93,831	93,771	1,047	15,844	985	331
71	Worcester, Mass	126,227	125,976	117,465	5,626	1,137	382
72	Yonkers, N. Y	74,380	74,254	2,581	67,709	1,324	402
73	Youngstown, Ohio	98,413	98,317	643	22,927	65,601	804

FOR CITIES HAVING 100,000 INHABITANTS OR MORE: 1920.

| | POPULATION BORN IN— | | | | | | Born at sea under U.S. flag. | American citizens born abroad. | |
| Geographic division—Continued. | | | | | United States, state not reported. | Outlying possessions. | | | |
South Atlantic.	East South Central.	West South Central.	Mountain.	Pacific.					
22,594	12,347	1,288	417	437	552	26	3	137	1
832	158	73	65	116	115	22	.....	90	2
168,257	14,902	1,857	172	223	729	32	2	72	3
594,803	2,967	1,352	439	789	746	166	6	274	4
19,009	142,098	2,593	152	141	756	21	1	49	5
9,151	1,277	797	563	1,085	1,847	186	15	962	6
1,643	185	113	128	123	303	33	1	109	7
3,713	1,794	586	339	486	744	74	4	1,085	8
1,909	217	104	102	181	102	24	1	195	9
8,406	225	110	66	64	183	8	.....	44	10
30,132	65,702	20,618	5,748	5,868	8,293	465	13	1,993	11
11,332	47,265	1,332	324	360	644	34	1	138	12
18,916	18,336	2,455	1,253	1,057	2,041	58	7	623	13
16,312	7,477	723	340	294	1,642	51	1	122	14
5,397	16,483	107,015	676	462	1,520	15	2	98	15
4,456	10,733	506	186	198	243	27	1	75	16
5,230	7,609	7,219	79,332	2,305	6,953	70	4	340	17
1,554	1,715	1,209	754	423	886	49	.....	121	18
23,512	27,391	5,393	2,207	2,538	1,904	198	14	2,933	19
235	42	40	19	64	41	42	1	78	20
3,344	9,931	69,636	679	430	2,020	13	.....	74	21
597	589	281	209	206	379	11	2	188	22
3,303	286	125	138	137	112	24	4	81	23
3,656	8,072	97,680	458	391	544	13	.....	126	24
5,996	38,209	1,538	454	428	1,781	24	1	176	25
6,208	697	288	121	261	342	83	2	128	26
1,726	4,821	5,789	739	257	486	10	.....	42	27
5,772	13,199	16,638	3,038	1,395	2,178	63	7	279	28
12,669	16,467	23,193	24,415	123,189	2,813	692	16	1,748	29
3,974	190,749	1,283	177	236	501	28	2	61	30
226	71	43	39	75	72	2	.....	238	31
5,980	122,308	11,461	240	233	2,628	10	1	62	32
1,557	1,594	737	510	556	1,471	15	2	198	33
1,873	2,027	1,140	1,577	1,417	1,039	30	7	686	34
2,866	106,575	1,413	66	66	263	12	.....	29	35
442	66	37	28	115	57	25	5	159	36
2,498	205	130	152	195	350	22	3	147	37
5,770	21,963	314,381	300	717	1,207	286	7	360	38
102,066	14,256	10,289	4,312	9,179	21,999	10,307	47	4,172	39
4,148	729	539	280	589	4,275	226	4	326	40
22,646	2,954	2,499	1,161	2,042	3,650	2,045	20	1,151	41
69,073	9,506	6,503	2,441	5,827	10,936	7,809	17	2,225	42
4,535	763	530	300	523	2,628	145	4	351	43
1,664	304	218	130	198	510	82	2	119	44
12,066	2,010	395	275	362	1,208	50	3	180	45
97,060	1,501	602	121	211	173	93	.....	52	46
2,703	2,937	4,269	6,562	98,450	643	3,159	16	450	47
2,238	3,847	3,682	2,017	724	2,308	32	1	158	48
1,055	101	39	37	79	76	7	.....	38	49
126,918	5,778	2,811	1,248	1,801	4,093	698	10	853	50
29,553	7,922	1,214	427	537	1,028	46	4	313	51
3,099	3,595	3,884	9,293	94,726	707	330	7	669	52
2,339	181	116	124	205	291	19	6	246	53
914	98	31	34	44	78	7	1	19	54
155,889	1,690	414	139	121	1,458	15	2	85	55
1,593	505	226	201	301	1,181	21	2	437	56
8,387	46,428	15,161	1,651	1,248	2,270	104	10	348	57
1,298	1,428	822	863	797	638	36	1	279	58
1,301	1,336	1,140	73,969	1,917	275	61	2	334	59
2,657	6,433	97,689	798	567	523	66	3	480	60
5,616	5,490	6,320	10,844	235,048	3,222	3,525	26	957	61
633	79	54	91	66	101	3	1	39	62
4,515	4,563	4,061	12,236	85,659	2,192	1,724	10	1,673	63
1,385	1,425	1,233	6,616	29,730	359	31	1	598	64
2,024	223	132	130	152	144	7	1	236	65
995	260	153	142	150	351	12	2	235	66
3,308	4,420	861	318	347	640	9	5	243	67
3,433	195	88	54	76	198	18	3	55	68
294,823	10,630	4,509	1,598	2,000	2,739	610	14	512	69
74,436	445	132	82	117	352	16	2	42	70
768	119	74	95	118	192	15	2	234	71
1,501	229	101	112	179	116	15	2	109	72
4,731	2,687	387	132	154	251	17	1	78	73

TABLE 66.—NATIVE POPULATION, BY DIVISION AND STATE OF BIRTH,

	CITY OF RESIDENCE.	POPULATION BORN IN—								
		New England division.						Middle Atlantic division.		
		Maine.	New Hampshire.	Vermont.	Massachusetts.	Rhode Island.	Connecticut.	New York.	New Jersey.	Pennsylvania.
1	Akron, Ohio	208	106	182	1,102	122	405	5,630	900	22,963
2	Albany, N. Y	146	116	833	1,377	112	497	87,779	694	1,228
3	Atlanta, Ga	111	68	63	498	73	196	1,913	349	1,153
4	Baltimore, Md	627	192	290	2,382	391	968	9,508	3,322	20,287
5	Birmingham, Ala	35	23	49	183	31	75	850	160	1,133
6	Boston, Mass	18,681	8,470	4,702	420,345	4,590	4,440	14,626	2,104	4,067
7	Bridgeport, Conn	605	408	541	4,465	752	66,872	14,077	2,312	2,580
8	Buffalo, N. Y	409	214	572	2,287	276	1,040	337,601	1,731	16,999
9	Cambridge, Mass	2,774	1,346	758	62,856	608	637	2,068	340	667
10	Camden, N. J	99	43	53	499	90	197	2,481	57,835	24,314
11	Chicago, Ill	1,973	1,026	2,041	10,087	1,059	2,984	52,105	5,820	31,571
12	Cincinnati, Ohio	125	73	101	794	92	255	3,830	575	3,460
13	Cleveland, Ohio	439	251	448	3,000	368	1,432	23,243	2,263	36,523
14	Columbus, Ohio	105	70	130	507	56	246	2,832	542	6,030
15	Dallas, Tex	94	53	58	286	47	96	1,544	221	1,030
16	Dayton, Ohio	70	31	31	404	54	223	1,807	279	2,909
17	Denver, Colo	771	281	606	2,096	239	765	9,844	1,434	7,719
18	Des Moines, Iowa	143	57	183	337	49	123	1,799	218	2,041
19	Detroit, Mich	1,072	657	1,159	6,968	978	2,804	37,083	3,764	30,929
20	Fall River, Mass	730	501	273	70,674	2,789	547	981	213	292
21	Fort Worth, Tex	67	23	50	155	28	64	994	100	835
22	Grand Rapids, Mich	91	69	163	491	51	136	3,745	309	1,307
23	Hartford, Conn	966	672	1,704	7,083	742	69,574	7,952	1,280	1,360
24	Houston, Tex	84	44	60	288	44	91	1,411	197	1,149
25	Indianapolis, Ind	148	70	109	672	108	258	2,829	511	3,249
26	Jersey City, N. J	236	141	195	1,719	295	1,261	42,542	158,671	5,977
27	Kansas City, Kans	49	22	55	141	12	46	912	124	1,326
28	Kansas City, Mo	335	151	272	1,043	132	403	5,641	663	5,101
29	Los Angeles, Calif	2,763	1,199	1,770	7,873	981	2,371	26,958	4,133	19,457
30	Louisville, Ky	38	26	34	273	28	98	1,264	176	1,173
31	Lowell, Mass	2,554	3,714	1,420	62,333	523	427	1,652	179	306
32	Memphis, Tenn	35	19	31	181	36	63	1,034	149	677
33	Milwaukee, Wis	243	116	248	984	109	326	5,083	556	2,898
34	Minneapolis, Minn	1,910	431	921	1,905	199	534	7,353	706	3,972
35	Nashville, Tenn	15	15	27	81	6	28	434	79	347
36	New Bedford, Mass	825	629	384	60,584	2,856	1,549	1,265	202	344
37	New Haven, Conn	709	391	746	4,392	636	91,049	9,735	1,516	1,756
38	New Orleans, La	213	50	75	493	92	213	2,871	457	1,363
39	New York, N. Y	7,151	2,974	5,060	40,429	7,102	27,762	3,107,563	79,735	62,863
40	Bronx borough	499	209	454	3,676	735	2,829	426,041	7,685	5,728
41	Brooklyn borough	2,438	948	1,401	12,904	2,082	9,487	1,217,615	27,800	19,840
42	Manhattan borough	3,359	1,502	2,651	19,678	3,556	12,524	1,071,382	32,006	30,338
43	Queens borough	522	234	411	3,131	554	2,271	321,367	7,913	5,176
44	Richmond borough	333	81	143	1,040	175	651	71,158	4,331	1,781
45	Newark, N. J	388	430	366	3,102	752	2,677	32,127	226,357	9,540
46	Norfolk, Va	166	66	54	646	111	254	2,414	561	1,818
47	Oakland, Calif	1,125	280	446	2,558	279	581	6,312	996	3,233
48	Omaha, Nebr	228	92	264	692	113	281	3,503	445	2,988
49	Paterson, N. J	51	60	52	581	177	592	8,808	76,008	2,078
50	Philadelphia, Pa	1,350	634	844	8,019	1,598	3,620	33,521	41,827	1,165,137
51	Pittsburgh, Pa	219	109	178	1,315	153	527	7,735	1,526	392,205
52	Portland, Oreg	929	247	494	1,550	186	456	5,922	664	4,998
53	Providence, R. I	2,048	1,281	1,131	17,751	127,301	4,810	5,611	1,024	1,470
54	Reading, Pa	27	14	17	157	35	105	835	510	94,527
55	Richmond, Va	71	48	82	309	67	129	1,708	580	1,785
56	Rochester, N. Y	310	211	454	1,953	225	816	200,479	1,106	7,685
57	St. Louis, Mo	310	154	200	1,700	211	557	7,719	1,127	5,811
58	St. Paul, Minn	701	157	347	997	96	200	6,087	551	2,081
59	Salt Lake City, Utah	137	35	104	401	51	96	1,640	222	1,318
60	San Antonio, Tex	91	44	74	358	37	114	1,545	231	1,233
61	San Francisco, Calif	1,578	472	576	5,571	557	1,146	15,957	1,970	6,980
62	Scranton, Pa	48	32	30	291	36	161	3,285	1,013	102,229
63	Seattle, Wash	1,894	381	619	2,857	249	663	8,503	1,015	6,629
64	Spokane, Wash	421	149	225	638	59	168	2,603	199	2,015
65	Springfield, Mass	1,428	1,861	4,691	65,817	929	7,228	9,198	869	1,132
66	Syracuse, N. Y	193	156	370	1,248	158	516	126,485	786	3,468
67	Toledo, Ohio	138	105	198	732	108	332	5,810	550	6,284
68	Trenton, N. J	71	56	57	452	55	348	3,522	70,802	8,556
69	Washington, D. C	1,603	881	1,052	6,370	1,000	2,002	18,719	4,351	20,319
70	Wilmington, Del	86	48	67	531	78	237	2,208	2,268	11,368
71	Worcester, Mass	2,721	2,423	2,817	104,571	1,846	3,087	4,165	531	930
72	Yonkers, N. Y	117	83	156	1,046	164	1,015	64,036	2,174	1,499
73	Youngstown, Ohio	46	33	53	330	39	142	2,680	363	19,884

FOR CITIES HAVING 100,000 INHABITANTS OR MORE: 1920—Continued.

	POPULATION BORN IN—									
	East North Central division.				West North Central division.					
Ohio.	Indiana.	Illinois.	Michigan.	Wisconsin.	Minnesota.	Iowa.	Missouri.	North Dakota.	South Dakota.	
88,010	4,345	3,114	1,870	665	313	643	1,200	52	44	1
392	95	311	212	99	38	67	84	4	11	2
1,368	852	955	455	215	152	256	610	14	44	3
2,982	1,014	1,851	842	510	333	422	975	47	49	4
1,563	875	1,023	334	190	111	239	681	14	18	5
1,606	551	1,742	1,279	464	386	422	581	49	60	6
358	114	393	200	99	54	79	119	9	8	7
5,133	1,085	2,340	3,289	917	405	489	750	63	65	8
355	131	273	239	111	95	95	101	5	13	9
415	122	216	145	86	46	49	90	5	8	10
42,676	46,399	1,389,075	36,308	49,480	10,596	26,893	28,081	1,037	1,607	11
265,910	13,414	3,044	1,372	594	289	575	1,687	37	41	12
413,127	6,379	6,853	8,969	2,000	1,040	1,309	2,541	143	144	13
172,973	3,748	2,349	1,422	447	249	522	847	45	64	14
1,574	1,421	3,261	635	420	259	934	4,837	38	71	15
106,381	6,201	1,683	1,042	316	138	324	617	27	21	16
9,334	6,538	16,637	4,110	3,995	1,897	10,725	13,951	251	700	17
3,262	2,529	7,619	867	1,539	1,431	75,268	6,651	177	479	18
40,280	17,555	22,284	445,883	6,708	3,042	3,258	8,446	469	454	19
76	17	73	180	54	25	22	25	....	1	20
1,181	951	2,079	339	273	204	791	3,170	27	45	21
3,090	2,487	2,721	89,229	1,211	254	512	376	56	90	22
444	121	326	212	106	83	100	96	11	14	23
1,482	1,291	2,660	559	443	247	1,007	2,651	42	77	24
16,258	203,314	12,037	1,976	867	376	1,295	2,703	69	79	25
738	214	669	251	144	102	118	265	14	10	26
1,985	1,890	4,304	428	499	264	2,330	20,234	34	78	27
8,658	7,098	18,766	2,259	2,503	1,469	10,361	146,667	169	416	28
25,511	17,329	38,064	13,657	10,716	8,252	19,968	24,104	1,135	1,874	29
3,401	14,522	2,036	491	262	141	305	1,507	19	31	30
98	32	116	313	60	48	30	29	14	1	31
1,594	1,983	2,767	559	289	227	471	2,890	27	36	32
2,816	2,133	19,610	8,299	296,480	3,192	2,643	1,821	417	333	33
4,197	3,023	10,948	5,491	27,075	185,521	14,488	2,910	4,457	3,420	34
874	809	709	220	83	45	121	581	2	11	35
73	30	80	220	56	29	21	22	4	6	36
410	138	374	232	128	104	111	133	10	16	37
1,581	967	2,112	739	460	228	556	1,857	36	39	38
20,189	5,900	18,223	7,194	4,233	2,949	3,865	7,582	382	370	39
1,580	304	1,416	542	249	195	243	475	31	18	40
5,267	1,495	4,868	1,895	1,149	743	1,013	1,900	105	87	41
11,244	3,426	10,246	4,083	2,395	1,718	2,242	4,550	197	227	42
1,577	498	1,289	501	333	220	281	502	30	24	43
521	177	404	173	107	73	86	155	19	14	44
1,315	461	1,058	599	308	152	223	322	29	15	45
767	397	450	395	139	127	145	269	26	18	46
3,825	2,358	6,251	2,758	2,323	1,885	3,437	4,232	204	365	47
3,377	2,596	9,520	1,463	2,434	1,574	19,958	7,815	172	1,064	48
199	60	183	135	45	23	41	50	5	11	49
6,812	2,020	4,473	2,033	1,087	767	1,181	2,539	118	133	50
13,662	1,918	2,403	1,203	594	299	632	1,137	44	48	51
6,452	4,809	10,752	7,103	8,516	8,294	9,678	7,387	1,571	1,708	52
399	128	336	267	128	108	107	125	21	15	53
263	64	124	53	37	33	42	93	8	3	54
733	260	374	257	127	73	119	206	40	31	55
1,822	497	1,182	1,588	398	197	286	318	30	36	56
9,536	10,160	66,186	2,556	2,665	1,303	4,718	472,971	190	201	57
2,208	1,401	5,920	2,436	14,957	127,905	6,779	1,729	1,980	1,373	58
1,397	1,018	2,617	872	760	610	1,908	1,911	99	158	59
1,456	1,285	2,406	629	477	311	790	2,789	64	79	60
6,455	3,737	10,786	4,134	3,955	3,438	5,219	7,179	465	595	61
292	75	208	141	66	27	50	77	2	5	62
7,536	5,251	13,337	9,908	11,420	14,663	10,471	7,980	2,476	2,040	63
2,498	2,099	5,273	2,973	5,249	6,649	5,373	3,613	1,377	827	64
419	131	370	388	148	123	125	119	14	23	65
887	298	643	776	233	162	222	190	24	36	66
149,599	7,322	3,442	16,049	892	325	643	1,340	63	81	67
430	122	195	75	54	37	51	48	15	10	68
8,046	4,234	5,999	2,813	2,171	1,578	2,744	3,490	259	374	69
343	148	250	165	79	40	68	143	3	12	70
298	121	321	278	119	115	88	77	31	10	71
424	111	494	187	108	53	112	150	2	10	72
62,992	855	954	605	195	106	183	302	14	14	73

TABLE 66.—NATIVE POPULATION, BY DIVISION AND STATE OF BIRTH,

	CITY OF RESIDENCE	West North Central div.—Con.		South Atlantic division.					
		Ne-braska.	Kansas.	Dela-ware.	Mary-land.	District of Col-umbia.	Virginia.	West Vir-ginia.	North Caro-lina.
1	Akron, Ohio	243	496	63	1,874	167	2,792	13,527	1,307
2	Albany, N. Y	45	38	26	159	88	299	24	64
3	Atlanta, Ga	92	144	42	483	201	1,827	167	3,030
4	Baltimore, Md	171	312	1,902	533,190	4,771	38,464	3,342	7,466
5	Birmingham, Ala	82	177	14	257	48	1,219	160	1,126
6	Boston, Mass	155	238	194	1,272	601	3,176	142	1,490
7	Bridgeport, Conn	39	51	52	231	113	614	68	219
8	Buffalo, N. Y	183	278	120	765	227	829	347	326
9	Cambridge, Mass	36	55	22	189	134	672	30	487
10	Camden, N. J	27	29	2,159	2,466	212	1,663	113	704
11	Chicago, Ill	5,651	7,846	478	4,560	1,510	5,533	1,975	1,964
12	Cincinnati, Ohio	191	437	46	750	212	2,535	2,027	1,245
13	Cleveland, Ohio	572	878	174	1,915	460	3,710	3,450	1,439
14	Columbus, Ohio	206	492	56	745	151	5,123	5,227	2,111
15	Dallas, Tex	335	1,293	15	260	83	895	231	729
16	Dayton, Ohio	129	282	27	678	85	1,515	813	352
17	Denver, Colo	7,197	10,109	167	830	305	1,210	813	522
18	Des Moines, Iowa	1,904	1,812	20	173	56	647	243	155
19	Detroit, Mich	1,047	1,864	354	2,811	624	3,740	2,330	2,037
20	Fall River, Mass	16	13	7	33	14	49	5	23
21	Fort Worth, Tex	253	1,224	20	105	19	579	202	362
22	Grand Rapids, Mich	121	236	13	167	31	148	58	52
23	Hartford, Conn	29	39	56	203	107	648	39	243
24	Houston, Tex	391	1,030	10	218	44	611	157	442
25	Indianapolis, Ind	462	1,101	39	586	153	1,465	660	1,140
26	Jersey City, N. J	51	66	218	802	274	1,791	81	656
27	Kansas City, Kans	984	39,959	13	176	33	464	208	207
28	Kansas City, Mo	4,373	37,772	71	736	215	1,774	783	680
29	Los Angeles, Calif	7,228	13,997	323	1,769	691	2,734	1,645	1,113
30	Louisville, Ky	92	296	23	295	88	1,160	340	493
31	Lowell, Mass	12	16	12	38	21	83	11	14
32	Memphis, Tenn	140	376	33	219	76	1,123	142	936
33	Milwaukee, Wis	560	480	52	351	72	266	132	82
34	Minneapolis, Minn	1,782	1,295	57	384	133	505	248	152
35	Nashville, Tenn	40	113	11	109	21	556	85	405
36	New Bedford, Mass	5	21	14	73	26	134	17	71
37	New Haven, Conn	56	69	185	388	144	707	52	514
38	New Orleans, La	147	314	45	521	105	1,153	153	505
39	New York, N. Y	1,557	2,178	2,112	14,336	5,521	33,261	1,803	13,668
40	Bronx borough	115	134	150	935	261	1,355	73	434
41	Brooklyn borough	434	529	647	3,850	1,261	7,545	456	4,139
42	Manhattan borough	865	1,313	1,039	8,298	3,598	22,455	1,080	8,386
43	Queens borough	114	144	181	925	312	1,369	129	477
44	Richmond borough	29	58	95	328	89	537	65	232
45	Newark, N. J	97	108	314	1,268	358	3,974	219	1,496
46	Norfolk, Va	47	96	198	2,289	498	66,463	558	23,657
47	Oakland, Calif	1,488	2,241	63	437	183	653	233	282
48	Omaha, Nebr	78,104	4,266	32	370	104	559	227	176
49	Paterson, N. J	20	22	39	170	20	383	29	242
50	Philadelphia, Pa	442	670	17,255	31,368	4,287	37,892	1,704	11,704
51	Pittsburgh, Pa	192	408	230	4,505	1,083	11,128	5,660	2,144
52	Portland, Oreg	4,747	5,737	63	458	260	791	484	452
53	Providence, R. I	58	54	54	434	176	956	73	275
54	Reading, Pa	16	22	154	327	46	219	43	45
55	Richmond, Va	79	63	118	1,670	425	140,474	988	8,648
56	Rochester, N. Y	108	171	52	363	131	516	105	151
57	St. Louis, Mo	1,296	3,967	107	1,119	370	2,152	683	802
58	St. Paul, Minn	850	680	21	262	114	341	140	110
59	Salt Lake City, Utah	1,094	1,430	32	157	93	302	153	203
60	San Antonio, Tex	286	1,040	16	197	72	512	226	330
61	San Francisco, Calif	2,319	3,344	146	1,201	418	1,308	516	531
62	Scranton, Pa	26	35	44	189	34	182	41	58
63	Seattle, Wash	4,307	5,504	110	621	427	1,169	638	620
64	Spokane, Wash	1,633	1,922	18	186	44	464	197	268
65	Springfield, Mass	33	58	23	205	107	528	58	251
66	Syracuse, N. Y	92	88	50	288	75	235	56	94
67	Toledo, Ohio	236	468	48	480	92	768	845	320
68	Trenton, N. J	17	28	314	573	77	888	104	331
69	Washington, D. C	961	1,805	1,016	48,936	160,109	63,006	4,331	8,025
70	Wilmington, Del	23	42	59,370	11,157	314	2,101	169	391
71	Worcester, Mass	30	31	34	92	39	215	25	124
72	Yonkers, N. Y	23	52	41	252	102	645	28	225
73	Youngstown, Ohio	60	125	55	689	85	1,319	1,081	398

FOR CITIES HAVING 100,000 INHABITANTS OR MORE: 1920—Continued.

	POPULATION BORN IN—										
South Atlantic div.—Con.			East South Central division.				West South Central division.				
South Carolina.	Georgia.	Forida.	Kentucky.	Tennessee.	Alabama.	Mississippi.	Arkansas.	Louisiana.	Oklahoma.	Texas.	
418	1,909	537	5,458	3,470	2,840	579	251	370	218	449	1
57	82	33	74	42	20	22	9	31	4	29	2
7,994	152,879	1,634	1,481	4,052	8,306	1,063	351	561	97	848	3
2,800	2,139	729	1,015	831	726	395	172	505	110	565	4
1,777	13,557	851	1,939	7,053	127,325	5,781	483	1,064	127	919	5
903	1,009	364	487	333	307	150	73	362	65	297	6
102	128	116	82	43	41	19	14	38	12	49	7
405	506	188	717	520	312	245	86	210	62	228	8
161	153	61	100	48	47	22	15	32	16	41	9
233	611	245	72	58	72	23	15	20	13	62	10
2,306	10,211	1,595	20,610	18,088	12,761	14,243	3,529	10,231	1,283	5,575	11
1,116	3,066	335	37,486	4,818	4,216	745	215	581	122	414	12
1,837	5,202	729	5,449	5,061	6,152	1,674	541	581	524	809	13
798	1,954	147	4,693	1,407	1,146	231	131	154	193	245	14
496	2,487	201	3,221	6,342	3,511	3,409	3,627	4,077	2,250	97,061	15
250	621	115	8,028	1,678	832	195	105	122	71	208	16
254	859	270	3,582	2,076	1,061	890	1,400	722	1,590	3,507	17
53	170	37	813	430	313	159	243	106	432	428	18
2,302	7,984	1,330	10,644	7,305	6,854	2,588	1,380	1,430	648	1,935	19
33	62	9	20	11	9	2	9	13	1	17	20
268	1,635	154	1,962	3,788	2,249	1,932	2,330	1,691	2,094	63,521	21
25	74	29	286	166	86	51	57	53	49	122	22
124	1,760	123	70	61	134	21	11	44	11	59	23
404	1,434	336	1,324	1,988	2,407	2,353	1,396	9,526	804	85,954	24
322	1,457	174	28,127	8,023	1,035	1,024	399	364	219	556	25
788	1,064	534	222	167	265	43	28	119	18	123	26
173	407	45	1,648	1,363	574	1,236	1,991	683	1,574	1,541	27
347	993	173	6,502	3,670	1,289	1,738	4,626	1,908	4,120	5,984	28
673	3,094	627	7,098	5,226	2,193	1,950	3,257	4,251	2,486	13,199	29
309	1,095	171	181,096	7,431	1,613	609	329	389	122	443	30
9	19	19	29	19	16	7	3	30	1	9	31
624	2,499	328	4,302	74,943	5,871	37,192	7,244	2,432	265	1,520	32
67	438	97	741	438	192	223	111	232	73	321	33
92	218	84	1,052	529	245	201	240	214	219	467	34
337	1,176	166	5,081	98,495	2,179	820	404	269	111	629	35
38	46	23	25	14	15	12	1	18	1	17	36
157	230	121	81	55	57	12	17	36	14	63	37
557	1,764	967	1,682	1,838	4,599	13,844	702	310,086	172	3,421	38
14,172	11,775	5,418	5,537	3,748	3,247	1,724	890	4,161	541	4,697	39
388	367	185	283	202	134	110	53	229	30	227	40
2,115	1,721	912	1,244	786	579	345	201	962	141	1,195	41
11,085	9,059	4,073	3,508	2,501	2,354	1,143	549	2,689	313	2,952	42
468	503	171	342	201	125	95	57	203	42	228	43
116	125	77	160	58	55	31	30	78	15	95	44
812	2,954	671	291	170	1,444	105	43	139	36	177	45
1,808	1,156	433	407	536	376	182	91	190	54	267	46
198	492	162	1,273	819	419	426	514	1,265	369	2,121	47
93	330	347	1,188	868	1,014	777	659	501	916	1,606	48
84	63	25	53	25	15	8	2	10	3	24	49
8,200	10,356	4,152	1,726	1,399	2,101	552	281	858	202	1,470	50
1,187	2,990	626	2,045	1,506	3,856	515	167	319	121	607	51
138	331	122	1,567	1,263	346	419	805	348	1,023	1,708	52
143	147	81	74	48	44	15	16	42	6	52	53
24	30	26	40	34	17	7	10	2	1	18	54
2,396	902	268	565	606	377	142	70	105	37	202	55
81	130	64	257	113	88	47	31	75	28	92	56
616	2,169	369	12,818	15,400	4,787	13,423	6,781	3,448	1,059	3,873	57
71	189	50	669	378	212	169	165	152	144	361	58
90	198	73	555	467	187	127	216	130	206	588	59
230	889	185	1,516	2,025	1,376	1,516	1,346	2,179	841	93,323	60
326	842	328	2,580	1,547	743	620	917	1,575	656	3,172	61
40	32	13	27	24	15	13	16	7	5	26	62
177	553	200	2,116	1,352	526	569	953	464	760	1,884	63
46	129	33	630	568	121	106	332	90	352	459	64
248	519	85	81	58	69	15	8	55	12	57	65
63	84	50	129	68	43	20	26	39	11	80	66
160	498	97	2,269	1,388	474	289	224	189	134	314	67
264	721	161	63	47	62	23	12	34	10	32	68
4,258	3,984	1,158	3,484	3,221	2,258	1,667	656	1,101	392	2,360	69
240	381	313	105	114	191	35	15	32	13	72	70
140	72	27	43	32	27	17	7	28	6	33	71
77	85	46	105	57	45	22	19	33	3	46	72
252	734	118	686	497	1,318	186	63	90	79	155	73

TABLE 66.—NATIVE POPULATION, BY DIVISION AND STATE OF BIRTH.

	CITY OF RESIDENCE.	POPULATION BORN IN—							
		Mountain division.							
		Montana.	Idaho.	Wyoming.	Colorado.	New Mexico.	Arizona.	Utah.	Nevada.
1	Akron, Ohio	79	22	18	213	32	26	24	3
2	Albany, N. Y	10	3	2	33	4	4	6	3
3	Atlanta, Ga	25	10	11	73	14	9	27	3
4	Baltimore, Md	63	23	33	186	30	26	63	15
5	Birmingham, Ala	7	1	8	81	16	19	14	6
6	Boston, Mass	90	33	23	249	49	24	59	36
7	Bridgeport, Conn	22	3	4	73	9	9	7	1
8	Buffalo, N. Y	46	24	29	143	35	15	38	9
9	Cambridge, Mass	16	7	5	49	9	2	11	3
10	Camden, N. J	11	3	6	19	4	4	16	3
11	Chicago, Ill	850	609	279	2,786	326	223	559	116
12	Cincinnati, Ohio	26	26	13	164	33	21	34	7
13	Cleveland, Ohio	130	81	57	543	283	44	96	19
14	Columbus, Ohio	60	24	22	149	24	24	31	6
15	Dallas, Tex	51	34	21	300	148	57	48	17
16	Dayton, Ohio	18	5	9	87	41	9	16	1
17	Denver, Colo	486	258	1,307	74,236	1,881	163	880	121
18	Des Moines, Iowa	122	78	76	376	33	23	35	11
19	Detroit, Mich	426	133	123	963	220	104	184	54
20	Fall River, Mass	8	....	....	6	1	1	2	1
21	Fort Worth, Tex	33	29	37	287	141	89	40	23
22	Grand Rapids, Mich	46	13	13	89	18	7	18	5
23	Hartford, Conn	17	5	4	92	3	4	6	7
24	Houston, Tex	33	24	32	219	57	39	43	11
25	Indianapolis, Ind	59	20	14	257	31	21	39	13
26	Jersey City, N. J	17	8	8	52	10	4	14	8
27	Kansas City, Kans	69	41	34	418	107	36	28	6
28	Kansas City, Mo	200	126	128	1,929	276	95	239	45
29	Los Angeles, Calif	1,726	966	687	8,979	2,294	5,021	3,793	949
30	Louisville, Ky	16	9	14	85	15	16	15	7
31	Lowell, Mass	7	....	1	14	4	4	6	3
32	Memphis, Tenn	32	9	11	117	16	30	21	4
33	Milwaukee, Wis	108	51	29	222	18	21	53	8
34	Minneapolis, Minn	787	117	68	408	38	21	110	28
35	Nashville, Tenn	8	4	3	32	3	2	12	2
36	New Bedford, Mass	6	1	....	12	2	....	6	1
37	New Haven, Conn	13	6	8	106	5	5	8	1
38	New Orleans, La	33	21	8	122	47	34	28	7
39	New York, N. Y	553	237	179	1,833	496	274	574	166
40	Bronx borough	36	19	9	117	54	13	26	6
41	Brooklyn borough	134	55	45	444	192	83	160	48
42	Manhattan borough	335	131	106	1,094	182	143	348	102
43	Queens borough	30	19	11	135	46	20	32	7
44	Richmond borough	18	13	8	43	22	15	8	3
45	Newark, N. J	40	20	20	106	27	16	25	21
46	Norfolk, Va	14	8	15	32	20	15	17	
47	Oakland, Calif	629	407	212	1,774	204	423	1,276	1,637
48	Omaha, Nebr	189	116	356	1,021	70	31	218	16
49	Paterson, N. J	6	....	....	13	10	....	4	4
50	Philadelphia, Pa	178	59	129	520	144	78	111	29
51	Pittsburgh, Pa	54	25	46	204	32	22	33	11
52	Portland, Oreg	1,846	2,422	470	2,532	158	171	1,353	341
53	Providence, R. I	18	5	5	66	7	5	12	6
54	Reading, Pa	2	....	13	10	4	2	2	1
55	Richmond, Va	8	14	4	29	13	9	61	1
56	Rochester, N. Y	31	10	9	99	15	7	13	8
57	St. Louis, Mo	170	97	95	915	147	73	150	27
58	St. Paul, Minn	430	40	38	250	20	9	60	16
59	Salt Lake City, Utah	698	2,174	837	2,572	153	193	66,848	494
60	San Antonio, Tex	45	27	51	268	209	119	65	14
61	San Francisco, Calif	1,062	664	294	3,078	385	748	1,788	2,825
62	Scranton, Pa	22	4	11	39	3	1	9	2
63	Seattle, Wash	4,795	1,917	534	3,148	168	183	1,147	344
64	Spokane, Wash	2,309	2,749	162	813	56	44	374	109
65	Springfield, Mass	30	7	9	49	14	5	6	10
66	Syracuse, N. Y	22	8	10	78	9	6	6	3
67	Toledo, Ohio	44	22	18	145	44	13	27	5
68	Trenton, N. J	6	6	7	22	4	5	3	1
69	Washington, D. C	219	117	106	544	131	105	313	63
70	Wilmington, Del	10	6	10	39	4	4	8	1
71	Worcester, Mass	18	2	6	36	5	.10	11	7
72	Yonkers, N. Y	15	5	2	53	10	....	25	2
73	Youngstown, Ohio	7	4	15	79	12	5	8	2

FOR CITIES HAVING 100,000 INHABITANTS OR MORE: 1920—Continued.

| | POPULATION BORN IN— | | | | | | | | | | |
| Pacific division. | | | Outlying possessions. | | | | | | | | |
Wash-ington.	Oregon.	California.	Alaska.	Ameri-can Samoa.	Guam.	Hawaii.	Pana-ma Canal Zone.	Philip-pine Islands.	Porto Rico.	Virgin Islands of the U. S.	
120	90	227	1			2		3	20		1
23	9	84				3		3	16		2
45	22	156	7			4	2		19		3
260	71	458	11			9	14	35	91	6	4
34	17	90	1				1		19		5
149	62	874	12			35	7	48	67	17	6
20	6	97				3	4	1	25		7
115	47	324	2		1	2	3	8	56	2	8
28	28	125	3			6	2	3	5	5	9
15	8	41					1	3	4		10
1,289	662	3,917	30			69	14	236	110	6	11
59	56	245	4			5	4	9	12		12
219	150	688	6			4	6	16	26		13
87	35	172	10			6	4	24	7		14
76	67	319				7		7	1		15
32	20	146	5			2	5	6	9		16
474	385	1,446	10	1	1	13		32	13		17
121	87	215	4			10	1	32	2		18
588	347	1,603	19	1		50	15	48	59	6	19
4	8	52				40			2		20
84	41	305	1			3	1	6	2	1	21
52	48	106	2					6	2	1	22
21	11	105				1	2	2	4	15	23
60	56	275	3			1	3	3	3		24
105	54	269	4			4	2	9	5		25
85	18	158	1			1	6	7	56	12	26
83	37	137	2				4	2	2		27
327	221	847	14			15	1	27	6		28
3,626	3,447	116,116	65	1	1	265	12	308	39	1	29
44	24	168	1			7	5	10	5		30
7	3	65			1		1				31
36	16	181				3		3	4		32
205	75	276	1			6		2	6		33
656	219	542	9			7	1	10	2	1	34
10	13	43					5	1	6		35
14	1	100			1	17		5	2		36
35	17	143	1			4		4	11	2	37
109	48	560	5			13	25	59	177	7	38
1,603	762	6,814	52		3	186	246	773	7,364	1,683	39
121	51	417	6			11	5	4	157	43	40
404	164	1,474	15		1	59	51	495	1,287	137	41
954	483	4,390	26		2	106	178	257	5,772	1,468	42
83	48	392	2			7	10	9	86	31	43
41	16	141	3			3	2	8	62	4	44
49	37	276	1			9	6	11	22	1	45
52	17	142	4	2		7	2	11	66	1	46
1,794	2,442	94,214	64	2	19	2,792	11	170	101		47
174	134	416	7	1	1			20	2	1	48
5	6	68							7		49
532	122	1,147	15		1	38	14	282	319	29	50
119	53	365	1			4	5	12	18	6	51
11,171	76,607	6,948	131		1	80	6	101	9	2	52
31	12	162				6	1	2	9	1	53
11	20	13				1			6		54
40	18	63				10	1	2	2		55
58	30	213	1		2	6		1	11		56
228	123	897	3	2		7	4	38	49	1	57
392	139	266	10			4	3	17	1	1	58
294	362	1,261	9	3		31		16	1	1	59
63	51	453	9			8	2	41	6		60
3,396	4,142	227,510	173	1	17	1,576	25	1,249	474	10	61
22	11	33	2					1			62
72,161	6,143	7,355	948		1	203	16	537	18	1	63
26,408	2,078	1,244	15			11		4	1		64
24	10	118	1			2	1	2		1	65
32	16	102	2			2	1	3	4		66
84	56	207	1			2	5		1		67
15	4	57	1						10	3	68
434	244	1,322	17		3	58	57	318	148	9	69
35	8	74				1	2	4	9		70
16	15	87				11		2	2		71
35	13	131							13	2	72
29	23	102				2		4	7	4	73

TABLE **67.**—URBAN AND RURAL POPULATION DISTRIBUTED AS BORN IN DIVISION OF RESIDENCE, IN OTHER DIVISIONS, ·OR IN FOREIGN COUNTRIES, BY DIVISIONS: 1920.

DIVISION OF RESIDENCE.	Total.[1]	BORN IN THE UNITED STATES AND WITH STATE OF BIRTH REPORTED.				FOREIGN BORN.	
		Born in division of residence.		Born in other divisions.			
		Number.	Per cent.	Number.	Per cent.	Number.	Per cent.
		URBAN POPULATION.					
United States	54,304,603	35,851,517	66.0	7,659,466	14.1	10,500,942	19.3
New England	5,865,073	3,840,324	65.5	350,465	6.0	1,656,120	28.2
Middle Atlantic	16,672,595	11,296,845	67.8	1,021,833	6.1	4,286,036	25.7
East North Central	13,049,272	8,748,990	67.0	1,724,922	13.2	2,519,937	19.3
West North Central	4,727,372	3,027,059	64.0	1,057,539	22.4	609,942	12.9
South Atlantic	4,338,792	3,591,011	82.8	495,608	11.4	233,879	5.4
East South Central	1,994,207	1,652,530	82.9	282,780	14.2	49,015	2.5
West South Central	2,970,829	1,983,912	66.8	735,344	24.8	223,424	7.5
Mountain	1,214,980	495,879	40.8	515,027	42.4	186,147	15.3
Pacific	3,471,483	1,214,967	35.0	1,475,948	42.5	736,442	21.2
		RURAL POPULATION.					
United States	51,406,017	42,054,998	81.8	5,779,482	11.2	3,419,750	6.7
New England	1,535,836	1,199,919	78.1	98,550	6.4	229,825	15.0
Middle Atlantic	5,588,549	4,652,730	83.3	242,816	4.3	674,382	12.1
East North Central	8,426,271	7,047,237	83.6	642,816	7.6	712,204	8.5
West North Central	7,816,877	5,866,878	75.1	1,158,478	14.8	765,711	9.8
South Atlantic	9,651,480	9,127,843	94.6	413,439	4.3	96,658	1.0
East South Central	6,899,100	6,537,918	94.8	330,197	4.8	23,974	0.3
West South Central	7,271,395	5,674,967	78.0	1,331,285	18.3	241,404	3.3
Mountain	2,121,121	1,024,727	48.3	800,760	37.8	281,473	13.3
Pacific	2,095,388	922,779	44.0	761,141	36.3	394,119	18.8

[1] Includes persons born in the United States, state of birth not reported; persons born in outlying possessions, or at sea under United States flag; and American citizens born abroad. The combined number of these classes in the United States in 1920 was as follows: Urban, 292,678, or five-tenths of 1 per cent of the total urban population; rural, 151,787, or three-tenths of 1 per cent of the total rural population.

TABLE 68.—URBAN AND RURAL POPULATION DISTRIBUTED AS BORN IN STATE OF RESIDENCE, IN OTHER STATES, OR IN FOREIGN COUNTRIES, BY STATES: 1920.

	URBAN POPULATION.					
		Born in the United States and with state of birth reported.				Foreign born.	
STATE OF RESIDENCE.	Total.[1]	Born in state of residence.		Born in other states.			
		Number.	Per cent.	Number.	Per cent.	Number.	Per cent.
United States..........	54,304,603	32,069,159	59.1	11,441,824	21.1	10,500,942	19.3
NEW ENGLAND:							
Maine.....................	299,569	212,774	71.0	25,842	8.6	59,465	19.9
New Hampshire..........	279,761	151,449	54.1	54,959	19.6	71,574	25.6
Vermont...................	109,976	71,552	65.1	19,488	17.7	18,167	16.5
Massachusetts.............	3,650,248	2,127,910	58.3	456,106	12.5	1,055,640	28.9
Rhode Island.............	589,180	314,329	53.4	99,981	17.0	173,365	29.4
Connecticut...............	936,339	497,114	53.1	159,285	17.0	277,909	29.7
MIDDLE ATLANTIC:							
New York.................	8,589,844	5,184,387	60.4	732,058	8.5	2,623,903	30.5
New Jersey...............	2,474,936	1,291,367	52.2	545,556	22.0	631,873	25.5
Pennsylvania..............	5,607,815	3,999,609	71.3	565,701	10.1	1,030,260	18.4
EAST NORTH CENTRAL:							
Ohio.....................	3,677,136	2,338,945	63.6	755,100	20.5	572,098	15.6
Indiana...................	1,482,855	989,915	66.8	367,231	24.8	119,251	8.0
Illinois....................	4,403,153	2,479,409	56.3	853,121	19.4	1,050,200	23.9
Michigan..................	2,241,560	1,226,386	54.7	478,704	21.4	523,978	23.4
Wisconsin.................	1,244,568	825,597	66.3	159,504	12.8	254,410	20.4
WEST NORTH CENTRAL:							
Minnesota.................	1,051,593	547,090	52.0	257,136	24.5	242,008	23.0
Iowa......................	875,495	526,048	60.1	253,652	29.0	90,285	10.3
Missouri...................	1,586,903	955,444	60.2	472,308	29.8	149,551	9.4
North Dakota.............	88,239	33,817	38.3	36,702	41.6	16,308	18.5
South Dakota.............	101,872	38,174	37.5	50,026	49.1	12,236	12.0
Nebraska..................	405,306	182,037	44.9	159,077	39.2	59,905	14.8
Kansas....................	617,964	284,421	46.0	288,666	46.7	39,649	6.4
SOUTH ATLANTIC:							
Delaware..................	120,767	67,094	55.6	36,374	30.1	16,878	14.0
Maryland..................	869,422	629,929	72.5	148,716	17.1	88,678	10.2
District of Columbia......	437,571	160,109	36.6	244,222	55.8	29,365	6.7
Virginia...................	673,984	507,678	75.3	143,510	21.3	20,018	3.0
West Virginia.............	369,007	243,184	65.9	103,347	28.0	19,864	5.4
North Carolina............	490,370	415,393	84.7	69,614	14.2	4,373	0.9
South Carolina............	293,987	251,737	85.6	37,444	12.7	4,356	1.5
Georgia...................	727,859	570,610	78.4	141,738	19.5	12,733	1.7
Florida....................	355,825	167,119	47.0	148,801	41.8	37,614	10.6
EAST SOUTH CENTRAL:							
Kentucky..................	633,543	490,485	77.4	119,508	18.9	21,667	3.4
Tennessee.................	611,226	423,544	69.3	172,175	28.2	11,621	1.9
Alabama...................	509,317	386,118	75.8	109,275	21.5	11,431	2.2
Mississippi................	240,121	182,995	76.2	51,210	21.3	4,296	1.8
WEST SOUTH CENTRAL:							
Arkansas..................	290,497	168,408	58.0	112,214	38.6	5,647	1.9
Louisiana.................	628,163	492,772	78.4	98,113	15.6	34,093	5.4
Oklahoma.................	539,480	158,470	29.4	361,039	66.9	14,449	2.7
Texas.....................	1,512,689	920,524	60.9	407,716	27.0	169,235	11.2
MOUNTAIN:							
Montana..................	172,011	54,086	31.4	81,613	47.4	33,482	19.5
Idaho.....................	119,037	35,414	29.8	70,875	59.5	11,801	9.9
Wyoming.................	57,348	13,232	23.1	34,259	59.7	8,966	15.6
Colorado..................	453,259	136,508	30.1	247,029	54.5	60,483	13.3
New Mexico...............	64,960	28,885	44.5	29,988	46.2	5,754	8.9
Arizona...................	117,527	29,070	24.7	56,632	48.2	29,704	25.3
Utah......................	215,584	133,995	62.2	47,279	21.9	33,152	15.4
Nevada...................	15,254	4,232	27.7	7,809	51.2	2,805	18.4
PACIFIC:							
Washington...............	748,735	192,405	25.7	384,119	51.3	159,291	21.3
Oregon....................	391,019	123,250	31.5	199,430	51.0	65,073	16.6
California.................	2,331,729	804,139	34.5	987,572	42.4	512,078	22.0

[1] Includes persons born in the United States, state of birth not reported; persons born in outlying possessions, or at sea under United States flag; and American citizens born abroad. The combined number of these classes in the United States in 1920 was as follows: Urban, 292,678, or five-tenths of 1 per cent of the total urban population; rural, 151,787, or three-tenths of 1 per cent of the total rural population.

TABLE 68.—URBAN AND RURAL POPULATION DISTRIBUTED AS BORN IN STATE OF RESIDENCE, IN OTHER STATES, OR IN FOREIGN COUNTRIES, BY STATES: 1920—Continued.

STATE OF RESIDENCE.	RURAL POPULATION.						
	Total.[1]	Born in the United States and with state of birth reported.				Foreign born.	
		Born in state of residence.		Born in other states.			
		Number.	Per cent.	Number.	Per cent.	Number.	Per cent.
United States.........	51,406,017	39,001,854	75.9	8,832,626	17.2	3,419,750	6.7
NEW ENGLAND:							
Maine..............	468,445	385,571	82.3	32,633	7.0	48,349	10.3
New Hampshire.........	163,322	105,625	64.7	36,991	22.6	19,823	12.1
Vermont.............	242,452	178,986	73.8	35,260	14.5	26,391	10.9
Massachusetts...........	202,108	137,377	68.0	31,136	15.4	32,908	16.3
Rhode Island...........	15,217	10,463	68.8	2,809	18.5	1,824	12.0
Connecticut...........	444,292	259,098	58.3	82,520	18.6	100,530	22.6
MIDDLE ATLANTIC:							
New York............	1,795,383	1,450,082	80.8	133,465	7.4	201,472	11.2
New Jersey...........	680,964	402,092	59.0	165,975	24.4	110,613	16.2
Pennsylvania..........	3,112,202	2,565,379	82.4	178,553	5.7	362,297	11.6
EAST NORTH CENTRAL:							
Ohio...............	2,082,258	1,740,813	83.6	227,917	10.9	108,354	5.2
Indiana.............	1,447,535	1,219,533	84.2	193,827	13.4	32,077	2.2
Illinois.............	2,082,127	1,611,509	77.4	303,564	14.6	160,384	7.7
Michigan............	1,426,852	996,947	69.9	218,661	15.3	205,314	14.4
Wisconsin............	1,387,499	1,026,977	74.0	150,305	10.8	206,075	14.9
WEST NORTH CENTRAL:							
Minnesota...........	1,335,532	845,086	63.3	242,448	18.2	244,787	18.3
Iowa...............	1,528,526	1,098,558	71.9	289,913	19.0	135,709	8.9
Missouri............	1,817,152	1,426,838	78.5	349,067	19.2	37,284	2.1
North Dakota..........	558,633	270,862	48.5	167,390	30.0	115,555	20.7
South Dakota..........	534,675	265,086	49.6	197,168	36.9	70,298	13.1
Nebraska............	891,066	553,405	62.1	243,599	27.3	90,760	10.2
Kansas.............	1,151,293	683,417	59.4	392,519	34.1	71,318	6.2
SOUTH ATLANTIC:							
Delaware............	102,236	75,869	74.2	22,671	22.2	3,023	3.0
Maryland...........	580,239	477,361	82.3	87,418	15.1	14,501	2.5
District of Columbia [2].....							
Virginia............	1,635,203	1,471,262	90.0	149,983	9.2	11,687	0.7
West Virginia..........	1,094,694	870,159	79.5	180,205	16.5	42,241	3.9
North Carolina.........	2,068,753	1,975,865	95.5	88,382	4.3	2,899	0.1
South Carolina.........	1,389,737	1,314,054	94.6	71,925	5.2	2,226	0.2
Georgia.............	2,167,973	2,024,813	93.4	137,508	6.3	3,831	0.2
Florida.............	612,645	392,984	64.1	200,823	32.8	16,250	2.7
EAST SOUTH CENTRAL:							
Kentucky............	1,783,087	1,644,504	92.2	128,224	7.2	9,239	0.5
Tennessee............	1,726,659	1,571,036	91.0	150,154	8.7	4,027	0.2
Alabama............	1,838,857	1,669,155	90.8	160,706	8.7	6,596	0.4
Mississippi...........	1,550,497	1,412,141	91.1	132,195	8.5	4,112	0.3
WEST SOUTH CENTRAL:							
Arkansas............	1,461,707	1,028,522	70.4	420,934	28.8	8,490	0.6
Louisiana...........	1,170,346	1,029,843	88.0	124,900	10.7	12,334	1.1
Oklahoma...........	1,488,803	660,759	44.4	794,841	53.4	25,983	1.7
Texas..............	3,150,539	2,385,787	75.7	560,666	17.8	194,597	6.2
MOUNTAIN:							
Montana............	376,878	118,732	31.5	193,264	51.3	69,100	18.3
Idaho..............	313,328	112,614	36.0	169,438	54.2	28,946	9.3
Wyoming............	137,054	35,750	26.1	82,571	60.2	17,601	12.8
Colorado............	486,370	180,998	37.2	245,050	50.4	58,655	12.1
New Mexico..........	295,390	180,349	61.1	89,889	30.4	24,054	8.1
Arizona............	216,635	80,706	37.3	80,941	37.4	50,862	23.5
Utah...............	233,812	180,011	77.0	26,720	11.4	26,048	11.1
Nevada.............	62,153	20,529	33.0	27,925	44.9	13,198	21.2
PACIFIC:							
Washington...........	607,886	217,770	35.8	278,332	45.8	106,001	17.4
Oregon.............	392,370	172,473	44.0	174,862	44.6	42,571	10.8
California...........	1,095,132	464,104	42.4	376,379	34.4	245,547	22.4

[1] Includes persons born in the United States, state of birth not reported; persons born in outlying possessions, or at sea under United States flag; and American citizens born abroad. The combined number of these classes in the United States in 1920 was as follows: Urban, 292,678, or five-tenths of 1 per cent of the total urban population; rural, 151,787, or three-tenths of 1 per cent of the total rural population.

[2] No rural population, as Washington city is coextensive with the District of Columbia.

TABLE 69.—COUNTRY OF BIRTH OF FOREIGN-BORN POPULATION, BY SEX, FOR THE UNITED STATES: 1920.

COUNTRY OF BIRTH.	NUMBER.			PER CENT.		Males to 100 females.	PER CENT DISTRIBUTION.		
	Total.	Male.	Female.	Male.	Female.		Total.	Male.	Female.
Total foreign born............	13,920,692	7,675,435	6,245,257	55.1	44.9	122.9	100.0	100.0	100.0
Europe.................	11,882,053	6,570,781	5,311,272	55.3	44.7	123.7	85.4	85.6	85.0
Northwestern Europe.........	3,830,094	1,979,591	1,850,503	51.7	48.3	107.0	27.5	25.8	29.6
England..................	813,853	425,664	388,189	52.3	47.7	109.7	5.8	5.5	6.2
Scotland..................	254,570	133,956	120,614	52.6	47.4	111.1	1.8	1.7	1.9
Wales....................	67,066	36,184	30,882	54.0	46.0	117.2	0.5	0.5	0.5
Ireland..................	1,037,234	455,571	581,663	43.9	56.1	78.3	7.5	5.9	9.3
Norway..................	363,863	202,758	161,105	55.7	44.3	125.9	2.6	2.6	2.6
Sweden..................	625,585	344,938	280,647	55.1	44.9	122.9	4.5	4.5	4.5
Denmark.................	189,154	114,063	75,091	60.3	39.7	151.9	1.4	1.5	1.2
Netherlands..............	131,766	75,510	56,256	57.3	42.7	134.2	0.9	1.0	0.9
Belgium..................	62,687	35,971	26,716	57.4	42.6	134.6	0.5	0.5	0.4
Luxemburg...............	12,585	7,671	4,914	61.0	39.0	156.1	0.1	0.1	0.1
Switzerland..............	118,659	67,830	50,829	57.2	42.8	133.4	0.9	0.9	0.8
France...................	153,072	79,475	73,597	51.9	48.1	108.0	1.1	1.0	1.2
Alsace-Lorraine.......	*34,321*	*19,197*	*15,124*	*55.9*	*44.1*	*126.9*	*0.2*	*0.3*	*0.2*
Central Europe.............	4,330,874	2,389,053	1,941,821	55.2	44.8	123.0	31.1	31.1	31.1
Germany.................	1,686,108	891,293	794,815	52.9	47.1	112.1	12.1	11.6	12.7
Poland..................	1,139,979	646,388	493,591	56.7	43.3	131.0	8.2	8.4	7.9
Czechoslovakia............	362,438	196,253	166,185	54.1	45.9	118.1	2.6	2.6	2.7
Austria..................	575,627	323,453	252,174	56.2	43.8	128.3	4.1	4.2	4.0
Hungary.................	397,283	216,914	180,369	54.6	45.4	120.3	2.9	2.8	2.9
Jugo-Slavia...............	169,439	114,752	54,687	67.7	32.3	209.8	1.2	1.5	0.9
Eastern Europe.............	1,803,971	1,013,471	790,500	56.2	43.8	128.2	13.0	13.2	12.7
Russia..................	1,400,495	774,017	626,478	55.3	44.7	123.6	10.1	10.1	10.0
Lithuania................	135,068	82,866	52,202	61.4	38.6	158.7	1.0	1.1	0.8
Finland..................	149,824	85,287	64,537	56.9	43.1	132.2	1.1	1.1	1.0
Rumania.................	102,823	58,135	44,688	56.5	43.5	130.1	0.7	0.8	0.7
Bulgaria.................	10,477	9,508	969	90.8	9.2	981.2	0.1	0.1	(1)
Turkey in Europe.........	5,284	3,658	1,626	69.2	30.8	225.0	(1)	(1)	(1)
Southern Europe.............	1,911,213	1,185,001	726,212	62.0	38.0	163.2	13.7	15.4	11.6
Greece..................	175,976	143,606	32,370	81.6	18.4	443.6	1.3	1.9	0.5
Albania..................	5,608	4,905	703	87.5	12.5	697.7	(1)	0.1	(1)
Italy....................	1,610,113	958,277	651,836	59.5	40.5	147.0	11.6	12.5	10.4
Spain...................	49,535	36,667	12,868	74.0	26.0	284.9	0.4	0.5	0.2
Portugal.................	69,981	41,546	28,435	59.4	40.6	146.1	0.5	0.5	0.5
Other Europe [2].............	5,901	3,665	2,236	62.1	37.9	163.9	(1)	(1)	(1)
Asia.....................	237,950	172,460	65,490	72.5	27.5	263.3	1.7	2.2	1.0
Armenia...................	36,628	25,352	11,276	69.2	30.8	224.8	0.3	0.3	0.2
Palestine.................	3,203	2,062	1,141	64.4	35.6	180.7	(1)	(1)	(1)
Syria....................	51,901	31,241	20,660	60.2	39.8	151.2	0.4	0.4	0.3
Turkey in Asia...........	11,019	8,042	2,977	73.0	27.0	270.1	0.1	0.1	(1)
China....................	43,560	40,754	2,806	93.6	6.4	1,452.4	0.3	0.5	(1)
Japan....................	81,502	57,304	24,198	70.3	29.7	236.8	0.6	0.7	0.4
India....................	4,901	3,774	1,127	77.0	23.0	334.9	(1)	(1)	(1)
Other Asia...............	5,236	3,931	1,305	75.1	24.9	301.2	(1)	0.1	(1)
America.................	1,727,017	890,917	836,100	51.6	48.4	106.6	12.4	11.6	13.4
Canada and Newfoundland....	1,138,174	556,837	581,337	48.9	51.1	95.8	8.2	7.3	9.3
Canada—French..........	307,786	157,748	150,038	51.3	48.7	105.1	2.2	2.1	2.4
Canada—Other...........	817,139	392,931	424,208	48.1	51.9	92.6	5.9	5.1	6.8
Newfoundland...........	13,249	6,158	7,091	46.5	53.5	86.8	0.1	0.1	0.1
West Indies [3].............	78,962	43,263	35,699	54.8	45.2	121.2	0.6	0.6	0.6
Cuba...................	14,872	8,341	6,531	56.1	43.9	127.7	0.1	0.1	0.1
Other West Indies [3].......	64,090	34,922	29,168	54.5	45.5	119.7	0.5	0.5	0.5
Mexico....................	486,418	276,526	209,892	56.8	43.2	131.7	3.5	3.6	3.4
Central and South America...	23,463	14,291	9,172	60.9	39.1	155.8	0.2	0.2	0.1
Central America..........	4,912	2,849	2,063	58.0	42.0	138.1	(1)	(1)	(1)
South America...........	18,551	11,442	7,109	61.7	38.3	161.0	0.1	0.1	0.1
All other..............	73,672	41,277	32,395	56.0	44.0	127.4	0.5	0.5	0.5
Africa....................	5,781	3,433	2,348	59.4	40.6	146.2	(1)	(1)	(1)
Australia.................	10,914	6,019	4,895	55.1	44.9	123.0	0.1	0.1	0.1
Atlantic Islands...........	44,340	24,523	19,817	55.3	44.7	123.7	0.3	0.3	0.3
Pacific Islands [3]...........	3,712	2,050	1,662	55.2	44.8	123.3	(1)	(1)	(1)
Country not specified........	3,589	2,320	1,269	64.6	35.4	182.8	(1)	(1)	(1)
Born at sea...............	5,336	2,932	2,404	54.9	45.1	122.0	(1)	(1)	(1)

[1] Less than one-tenth of 1 per cent.
[2] Comprises Danzig, Fiume, Saar Basin, and "Europe, not specified."
[3] Except possessions of the United States.

TABLE 70.—COUNTRY OF BIRTH OF FOREIGN-BORN POPU-

1920

COUNTRY OF BIRTH. (POSTWAR BOUNDARIES.)	Both sexes.			Male.	Female.	Males to 100 females.
	Number.	Per cent of total foreign-born population.	Per cent of total population.			
Total foreign born	13,920,692	100.0	13.2	7,675,435	6,245,257	122.9
Europe	11,882,053	85.4	11.2	6,570,781	5,311,272	123.7
Northwestern Europe	3,830,094	27.5	3.6	1,979,591	1,850,503	107.0
England	813,853	5.8	0.8	425,664	388,189	109.7
Scotland	254,570	1.8	0.2	133,956	120,614	111.1
Wales	67,066	0.5	0.1	36,184	30,882	117.2
Ireland	1,037,234	7.5	1.0	455,571	581,663	78.3
Norway	363,863	2.6	0.3	202,758	161,105	125.9
Sweden	625,585	4.5	0.6	344,938	280,647	122.9
Denmark	189,154	1.4	0.2	114,063	75,091	151.9
Netherlands	131,766	0.9	0.1	75,510	56,256	134.2
Belgium	62,687	0.5	0.1	35,971	26,716	134.6
Luxemburg	12,585	0.1	(1)	7,671	4,914	156.1
Switzerland	118,659	0.9	0.1	67,830	50,829	133.4
France	153,072	1.1	0.1	79,475	73,597	108.0
Central Europe	4,330,874	31.1	4.1	2,389,053	1,941,821	123.0
Germany	1,686,108	12.1	1.6	891,293	794,815	112.1
Poland	1,139,979	8.2	1.1	646,388	493,591	131.0
Czechoslovakia	362,438	2.6	0.3	196,253	166,185	118.1
Austria	575,627	4.1	0.5	323,453	252,174	128.3
Hungary	397,283	2.9	0.4	216,914	180,369	120.3
Jugo-Slavia	169,439	1.2	0.2	114,752	54,687	209.8
Eastern Europe	1,803,971	13.0	1.7	1,013,471	790,500	128.2
Russia	1,400,495	10.1	1.3	774,017	626,478	123.6
Lithuania	135,068	1.0	0.1	82,866	52,202	158.7
Finland	149,824	1.1	0.1	85,287	64,537	132.2
Rumania	102,823	0.7	0.1	58,135	44,688	130.1
Bulgaria	10,477	0.1	(1)	9,508	969	981.2
Turkey in Europe	5,284	(1)	(1)	3,658	1,626	225.0
Southern Europe	1,911,213	13.7	1.8	1,185,001	726,212	163.2
Greece	175,976	1.3	0.2	143,606	32,370	443.6
Albania	5,608	(1)	(1)	4,905	703	697.7
Italy	1,610,113	11.6	1.5	958,277	651,836	147.0
Spain	49,535	0.4	(1)	36,667	12,868	284.9
Portugal	69,981	0.5	0.1	41,546	28,435	146.1
Other Europe	4 5,901	(1)	(1)	3,665	2,236	163.9
Asia	237,950	1.7	0.2	172,460	65,490	263.3
Armenia	36,628	0.3	(1)	25,352	11,276	224.8
Palestine	3,203	(1)	(1)	2,062	1,141	180.7
Syria	51,901	0.4	(1)	31,241	20,660	151.2
Turkey in Asia	11,019	0.1	(1)	8,042	2,977	270.1
China	43,560	0.3	(1)	40,754	2,806	1,452.4
Japan	81,502	0.6	0.1	57,304	24,198	236.8
India	4,901	(1)	(1)	3,774	1,127	334.9
Other Asia	5,236	(1)	(1)	3,931	1,305	301.2
America	1,727,017	12.4	1.6	890,917	836,100	106.6
Canada—French	307,786	2.2	0.3	157,748	150,038	105.1
Canada—Other	817,139	5.9	0.8	392,931	424,208	92.6
Newfoundland	13,249	0.1	(1)	6,158	7,091	86.8
West Indies 5	78,962	0.6	0.1	43,263	35,699	121.2
Mexico	486,418	3.5	0.5	276,526	209,892	131.7
Central and South America	23,463	0.2	(1)	14,291	9,172	155.8
All other 6	73,672	0.5	0.1	41,277	32,395	127.4

1 Less than one-tenth of 1 per cent.
2 Persons reported in 1910 as of Polish mother tongue born in Germany (98,182 males; 91,914 females), Austria (199,485 males; 129,933 females), and Russia (270,363 males; 148,007 females) have been deducted from the respective countries and combined as Poland for comparison with number reported in 1920 as born in Poland.

LATION, BY SEX, FOR THE UNITED STATES: 1920 AND 1910.

COUNTRY OF BIRTH. (PREWAR BOUNDARIES.)	1910					
	Both sexes.			Male.	Female.	Males to 100 females.
	Number.	Per cent of total foreign-born population.	Per cent of total population.			
Total foreign born	13,515,886	100.0	14.7	7,667,748	5,848,138	131.1
Europe	11,791,841	87.2	12.8	6,702,997	5,088,844	131.7
Northwestern Europe	4,239,067	31.4	4.6	2,226,393	2,012,674	110.6
England	877,719	6.5	1.0	477,320	400,399	119.2
Scotland	261,076	1.9	0.3	144,659	116,417	124.3
Wales	82,488	0.6	0.1	45,397	37,091	122.4
Ireland	1,352,251	10.0	1.5	611,556	740,695	82.6
Norway	403,877	3.0	0.4	230,156	173,721	132.5
Sweden	665,207	4.9	0.7	369,953	295,254	125.3
Denmark	181,649	1.3	0.2	109,120	72,529	150.5
Netherlands	120,063	0.9	0.1	68,363	51,700	132.2
Belgium	49,400	0.4	0.1	29,895	19,505	153.3
Luxemburg	3,071	(1)	(1)	1,963	1,108	177.2
Switzerland	124,848	0.9	0.1	72,726	52,122	139.5
France	117,418	0.9	0.1	65,285	52,133	125.2
Central Europe	4,600,298	34.0	5.0	2,636,069	1,964,229	134.2
Germany	[2]2,311,237	17.1	2.5	1,239,593	1,071,644	115.7
Poland	[2]937,884	6.9	1.0	568,030	369,854	153.6
Austria	[2]845,555	6.3	0.9	513,970	331,585	155.0
Hungary	495,609	3.7	0.5	305,543	190,066	160.8
Serbia	4,639	(1)	(1)	3,837	802	478.4
Montenegro	5,374	(1)	(1)	5,096	278	1,833.1
Eastern Europe	1,423,743	10.5	1.5	811,796	611,947	132.7
Russia	[2]1,184,412	8.8	1.3	656,856	527,556	124.5
Finland	129,680	1.0	0.1	79,098	50,582	156.4
Rumania	65,923	0.5	0.1	36,521	29,402	124.2
Bulgaria	11,498	0.1	(1)	10,797	701	1,540.2
Turkey in Europe [3]	32,230	0.2	(1)	28,524	3,706	769.7
Southern Europe	1,525,875	11.3	1.7	1,026,951	498,924	205.8
Greece	101,282	0.7	0.1	93,447	7,835	1,192.7
(3)						
Italy	1,343,125	9.9	1.5	880,904	462,221	190.6
Spain	22,108	0.2	(1)	16,785	5,323	315.3
Portugal	59,360	0.4	0.1	35,815	23,545	152.1
Europe, not specified	2,858	(1)	(1)	1,788	1,070	167.1
Asia	191,484	1.4	0.2	162,050	29,434	550.6
Turkey in Asia	59,729	0.4	0.1	40,467	19,262	210.1
China	56,756	0.4	0.1	54,968	1,788	3,074.3
Japan	67,744	0.5	0.1	60,758	6,986	869.7
India	4,664	(1)	(1)	3,779	885	427.0
Other Asia	2,591	(1)	(1)	2,078	513	405.1
America	1,489,231	11.0	1.6	777,596	711,635	109.3
Canada—French	385,083	2.8	0.4	201,164	183,919	109.4
Canada—Other	819,554	6.1	0.9	404,792	414,762	97.6
Newfoundland	5,080	(1)	(1)	2,525	2,555	98.8
West Indies [5]	47,635	0.4	0.1	26,764	20,871	128.2
Mexico	221,915	1.6	0.2	136,677	85,238	160.3
Central and South America	9,964	0.1	(1)	5,674	4,290	132.3
All other [6]	43,330	0.3	(1)	25,105	18,225	137.8

[3] Albania included with Turkey in Europe in 1910.
[4] Comprises Danzig (2,049), Fiume (384), Saar Basin (263), and "Europe, not specified" (3,205).
[5] Except possessions of the United States.
[6] Africa, Australia, Atlantic Islands, Pacific Islands except possessions of the United States, "country not specified," and born at sea.

TABLE 71.—COUNTRY OF BIRTH OF FOREIGN-BORN

[Figures for each census year relate to

	COUNTRY OF BIRTH.	NUMBER.					
		1920	1910	1900	1890	1880	1870
1	Total foreign born	13,920,692	13,515,886	10,341,276	9,249,560	6,679,943	5,567,229
2	Europe	11,882,053	11,791,841	8,871,780	8,020,608	5,744,311	4,936,618
3	Northwestern Europe	3,830,094	4,239,067	4,202,683	4,380,752	3,494,484	3,124,638
4	England	813,853	877,719	840,513	909,092	664,160	555,046
5	Scotland	254,570	261,076	233,524	242,231	170,136	140,835
6	Wales	67,066	82,488	93,586	100,079	83,302	74,533
7	Ireland	1,037,234	1,352,251	1,615,459	1,871,509	1,854,571	1,855,827
8	Norway	363,863	403,877	336,388	322,665	181,729	114,246
9	Sweden	625,585	665,207	582,014	478,041	194,337	97,332
10	Denmark	189,154	181,649	153,690	132,543	64,196	30,107
11	Netherlands	131,766	120,063	94,931	81,828	58,090	46,802
12	Belgium	62,687	49,400	29,757	22,639	15,535	12,553
13	Luxemburg	12,585	3,071	3,031	2,882	12,836	5,802
14	Switzerland	118,659	124,848	115,593	104,069	88,621	75,153
15	France	153,072	117,418	104,197	113,174	106,971	116,402
16	Central and Eastern Europe	6,134,845	6,024,041	4,136,646	3,420,629	2,187,776	1,784,449
17	Germany	1,686,108	[2]2,311,237	2,663,418	2,784,894	1,966,742	1,690,533
18	Poland	1,139,979	[2]937,884	383,407	147,440	48,557	14,436
19	Czechoslovakia	362,438					
20	Austria	575,627	[2]845,555	432,798	241,377	124,024	70,797
21	Hungary	397,283	495,609	145,714	62,435	11,526	3,737
22	Jugo-Slavia	169,439					
23	Serbia		4,639				
24	Montenegro		5,374				
25	Russia	1,400,495	} [2]1,184,412	423,726	} 182,644	35,722	4,644
26	Lithuania	135,068					
27	Finland	149,824	129,680	62,641			
28	Rumania	102,823	65,923	15,032			
29	Bulgaria	10,477	11,498				
30	Turkey in Europe	5,284	[2]32,230	[4]9,910	[4]1,839	[4]1,205	[4]302
31	Southern Europe	1,911,213	1,525,875	530,200	206,648	58,265	25,853
32	Greece	175,976	101,282	8,515	1,887	776	390
33	Albania	5,608	(3)				
34	Italy	1,610,113	1,343,125	484,027	182,580	44,230	17,157
35	Spain	49,535	22,108	7,050	6,185	5,121	3,764
36	Portugal	69,981	59,360	30,608	15,996	8,138	4,542
37	Other Europe [5]	5,901	2,858	2,251	12,579	3,786	1,678
38	Asia	237,950	191,484	120,248	113,396	107,630	64,565
39	Armenia	36,628	} 59,729	(4)	(4)	(4)	(4)
40	Palestine	3,203					
41	Syria	51,901					
42	Turkey in Asia	11,019					
43	China	43,560	56,756	81,534	106,701	104,468	63,042
44	Japan	81,502	67,744	24,788	2,292	401	73
45	India	4,901	4,664	2,031	2,143	1,707	586
46	Other Asia	5,236	2,591	11,895	2,260	1,054	864
47	America	1,727,017	1,489,231	1,317,380	1,088,245	807,230	551,335
48	Canada—French [6]	307,786	385,083	395,126	302,496	} 717,157	493,464
49	Canada—Other [6]	817,139	819,554	784,796	678,442		
50	Newfoundland	13,249	5,090				
51	Cuba	14,872	15,133	11,081	} 23,256	6,917	5,319
52	Other West Indies	[7]64,090	[7]32,502	[7]14,304		9,484	6,051
53	Mexico	486,418	221,915	103,393	77,853	68,399	42,435
54	Central America	4,912	1,736	3,897	1,192	707	301
55	South America	18,551	8,228	4,733	5,006	4,566	3,565
56	All other [8]	73,672	43,330	31,868	27,311	20,772	14,711

[1] Less than one-tenth of 1 per cent.
[2] See note 2, Table 70.
[3] Albania included with Turkey in Europe in 1910.
[4] Turkey in Asia included with Turkey in Europe prior to 1910.
[5] Includes "Europe, not specified" at each census, and Danzig, Fiume, and Saar Basin in 1920.

POPULATION, FOR THE UNITED STATES: 1850-1920.

countries as constituted in that year.]

NUMBER—continued.		PER CENT DISTRIBUTION.								
1860	1850	1920	1910	1900	1890	1880	1870	1860	1850	
4,138,697	2,244,602	100.0	100.0	100.0	100.0	100.0	100.0	100.0	100.0	1
3,805,701	2,031,867	85.4	87.2	85.8	86.7	86.0	88.7	92.0	90.5	2
2,472,211	1,437,475	27.3	31.4	40.6	47.4	52.3	56.1	59.7	64.0	3
433,494	278,675	5.8	6.5	8.1	9.5	9.9	10.0	10.5	12.4	4
108,518	70,550	1.8	1.9	2.3	2.6	2.5	2.5	2.6	3.1	5
45,763	29,868	0.5	0.6	0.9	1.1	1.2	1.3	1.1	1.3	6
1,611,304	961,719	7.5	10.0	15.6	20.2	27.8	33.3	38.9	42.8	7
43,995	12,678	2.6	3.0	3.3	3.5	2.7	2.1	1.1	0.6	8
18,625	3,559	4.5	4.9	5.6	5.2	2.9	1.7	0.5	0.2	9
9,962	1,838	1.4	1.3	1.5	1.4	1.0	0.5	0.2	0.1	10
28,281	8,848	0.9	0.9	0.9	0.9	0.9	0.8	0.7	0.4	11
9,072	1,313	0.5	0.4	0.3	0.2	0.2	0.2	0.2	0.1	12
		0.1	(1)	(1)	(1)	0.2	0.1			13
53,327	13,358	0.9	0.9	1.1	1.1	1.3	1.3	1.3	0.6	14
109,870	54,069	1.1	0.9	1.0	1.2	1.6	2.1	2.7	2.4	15
1,311,722	586,240	44.1	44.6	40.0	37.0	32.8	32.1	31.7	26.1	16
1,276,075	583,774	12.1	17.1	25.8	30.1	29.4	30.4	30.8	26.0	17
7,298		8.2	6.9	3.7	1.6	0.7	0.3	0.2		18
		2.6								19
25,061	946	4.1	6.3	4.2	2.6	1.9	1.3	0.6	(1)	20
		2.9	3.7	1.4	0.7	0.2	0.1			21
		1.2								22
			(1)							23
			(1)							24
		10.1	8.8	4.1						25
3,160	1,414	1.0			2.0	0.5	0.1	0.1	0.1	26
		1.1	1.0	0.6	0.6					27
		0.7	0.5	0.1						28
		0.1	0.1							29
128[4]	106[4]	(1)	0.2	0.1	(1)	(1)	(1)	(1)	(1)	30
20,365	8,152	13.7	11.3	5.1	2.2	0.9	0.5	0.5	0.4	31
328	86	1.3	0.7	0.1	(1)	(1)	(1)	(1)	(1)	32
		(1)								33
11,677	3,679	11.6	9.9	4.7	2.0	0.7	0.3	0.3	0.2	34
4,244	3,113	0.4	0.2	0.1	0.1	0.1	0.1	0.1	0.1	35
4,116	1,274	0.5	0.4	0.3	0.2	9.1	0.1	0.1	0.1	36
1,403		(1)	(1)	(1)	0.1	0.1	(1)	(1)		37
36,796	1,135	1.7	1.4	1.2	1.2	1.6	1.2	0.9	0.1	38
		0.3								39
(4)	(4)	(1)	0.4							40
		0.4								41
		0.1								42
35,565	758	0.3	0.4	0.8	1.2	1.6	1.1	0.9	(1)	43
		0.6	0.5	0.2	(1)	(1)	(1)			44
		(1)	(1)		(1)	(1)	(1)			45
1,231	377	(1)	(1)	0.1	(1)	(1)	(1)	(1)	(1)	46
288,285	168,484	12.4	11.0	12.7	11.8	12.1	9.9	7.0	7.5	47
		2.2	2.8	3.8	3.3					48
249,970	147,711	5.9	6.1	7.6	7.3	10.7	8.9	6.0	6.6	49
		0.1	(1)							50
7,353	5,772	0.1	0.1	0.1	0.3	0.1	0.1	0.2	0.3	51
		0.5	0.2	0.1		0.1	0.1			52
27,466	13,317	3.5	1.6	1.0	0.8	1.0	0.8	0.7	0.6	53
233	141	(1)	(1)	(1)	(1)	(1)	(1)	(1)	(1)	54
3,263	1,543	0.1	0.1	(1)	0.1	0.1	0.1	0.1	0.1	55
7,915	43,116	0.5	0.3	0.3	0.3	0.3	0.3	0.2	1.9	56

6 Newfoundland included with Canada prior to 1910.
7 Except possessions of the United States.
8 Africa, Australia, Atlantic Islands, Pacific Islands except possessions of the United States, "country not specified," and born at sea.

TABLE 72.—INCREASE IN FOREIGN-BORN POPULATION BY

[The increases and decreases for each decade have been based on the numbers of persons reported, at the
in which the censuses were taken. The increases and decreases for the decade 1910-1920 are, therefore,
place within that decade.]

[Per cent not shown where base is less than 100.

	COUNTRY OF BIRTH.	1910-1920		1900-1910		1890-1900	
		Number.	Per cent.	Number.	Per cent.	Number.	Per cent.
1	Total foreign born...........	404,806	3.0	3,174,610	30.7	1,091,716	11.8
2	Europe.................	90,212	0.8	2,920,061	32.9	851,172	10.6
	Countries with unchanged boundaries since 1910:						
3	England..................	-63,866	-7.3	37,206	4.4	-68,579	-7.5
4	Scotland.................	-6,506	-2.5	27,552	11.8	-8,707	-3.6
5	Wales...................	-15,422	-18.7	-11,098	-11.9	-6,493	-6.5
6	Ireland..................	-315,017	-23.3	-263,208	-16.3	-256,050	-13.7
7	Norway..................	-40,014	-9.9	67,489	20.1	13,723	4.3
8	Sweden..................	-39,622	-6.0	83,193	14.3	103,973	21.7
9	Netherlands.............	11,703	9.7	25,132	26.5	13,103	16.0
10	Luxemburg..............	9,514	309.8	40	1.3	149	5.2
11	Switzerland.............	-6,189	-5.0	9,255	8.0	11,524	11.1
12	Finland.................	20,144	15.5	67,039	107.0	(1)	....
13	Spain...................	27,427	124.1	15,058	213.6	865	14.0
14	Portugal................	10,621	17.9	28,752	93.9	14,612	91.3
	Countries with changed boundaries since 1910:						
15	Denmark................	7,505	4.1	27,959	18.2	21,147	16.0
16	Belgium................	13,287	26.9	19,643	66.0	7,118	31.4
17	France..................	35,654	30.4	13,221	12.7	-8,977	-7.9
18	Germany................	2 -625,120	-27.0	2 -352,181	-13.2	-121,476	-4.4
19	Austria.................	2 -269,928	-31.9	2 412,757	95.4	191,421	79.3
20	Hungary................	-98,326	-19.8	349,895	240.1	83,279	133.4
21	Russia and Lithuania....	2 351,151	29.6	2 760,686	179.5	1 303,723	166.3
22	Rumania................	36,900	56.0	50,891	338.6	15,032	....
23	Bulgaria................	-1,021	-8.9	11,498			
24	Turkey in Europe........	-26,946	-83.6	3 22,320	225.2	3 8,071	438.9
25	Greece..................	74,694	73.7	92,767	1,089.5	6,628	351.2
26	Italy...................	266,988	19.9	859,098	177.5	301,447	165.1
	Countries organized since 1910:						
27	Poland.................	2 202,095	21.5	2 554,477	144.6	235,967	160.0
28	Czechoslovakia..........	362,438					
29	Jugo-Slavia.............	159,426					
30	Albania.................	3 5,608		(3)			
31	Other Europe 4..........	3,043	106.5	10,620	471.8	-10,328	-82.1
32	Asia....................	46,466	24.3	71,236	59.2	6,852	6.0
33	Armenia................						
34	Palestine...............	43,022	72.0	3 59,729	....	(3)	....
35	Syria...................						
36	Turkey in Asia..........						
37	China..................	-13,196	-23.3	-24,778	-30.4	-25,167	-23.6
38	Japan..................	13,758	20.3	42,956	173.3	22,496	981.5
39	India..................	237	5.1	2,633	129.6	-112	-5.2
40	Other Asia.............	2,645	102.1	-9,304	-78.2	9,635	426.3
41	America................	237,786	16.0	171,851	13.0	229,135	21.1
42	Canada—French 5.......	-77,297	-20.1	-10,043	-2.5	92,630	30.6
43	Canada—Other 9........	2,415	-0.3	34,758	4.4	106,354	15.7
44	Newfoundland 9.........	8,169	160.8	5,080	....		
45	West Indies 6..........	31,327	65.8	22,200	87 ?	2,179	9.4
46	Mexico.................	264,503	119.2	118,522	114.6	25,540	32.8
47	Central and South America....	13,499	135.5	1,334	15.5	2,432	39.2
48	All other 7............	30,342	70.0	11,462	36.0	4,557	16.7

1 Finland included with Russia prior to 1900.
2 See note 2, Table 70.
3 Albania included with Turkey in Europe in 1910. Turkey in Asia included with Turkey in Europe
prior to 1910.
4 Includes "Europe, not specified" at each census, and Danzig, Fiume, and Saar Basin in 1920.

COUNTRY OF BIRTH, FOR THE UNITED STATES: 1850–1920.

beginning and end of the decade, as having been born in the specified countries as constituted in the years affected, in the case of certain countries, by the changes in the boundaries of those countries which took

A minus sign (−) denotes decrease.]

	1880–1890		1870–1880		1860–1870		1850–1860		
	Number.	Per cent.	Number.	Per cent.	Number.	Per cent.	Number.	Per cent.	
	2,569,617	38.5	1,112,714	20.0	1,428,532	34.5	1,894,095	84.4	1
	2,276,297	39.6	807,693	16.4	1,130,917	29.7	1,773,834	87.3	2
	244,932	36.9	109,114	19.7	121,552	28.0	154,819	55.6	3
	72,095	42.4	29,301	20.8	32,317	29.8	37,968	53.8	4
	16,777	20.1	8,769	11.8	28,770	62.9	15,895	53.2	5
	16,938	0.9	−1,256	−0.1	244,523	15.2	649,585	67.5	6
	140,936	77.6	67,483	59.1	70,251	159.7	31,317	247.0	7
	283,704	146.0	97,005	99.7	78,707	422.6	15,066	423.3	8
	23,738	40.9	11,288	24.1	18,521	65.5	18,433	187.2	9
	−9,954	−77.5	7,034	121.2	5,802				10
	15,448	17.4	13,468	17.9	21,826	40.9	39,969	299.2	11
	(1)		(1)		(1)		(1)		12
	1,064	20.8	1,357	36.1	−480	−11.3	1,131	36.3	13
	7,858	96.6	3,596	79.2	426	10.3	2,842	223.1	14
	68,347	106.5	34,089	113.2	20,145	202.2	8,124	442.0	15
	7,104	45.7	2,982	23.8	3,481	38.4	7,759	590.9	16
	6,203	5.8	−9,431	−8.1	6,532	5.9	55,801	103.2	17
	818,152	41.6	276,209	16.3	414,458	32.5	692,301	118.6	18
	117,353	94.6	53,227	75.2	45,736	182.5	24,115	2,549.2	19
	50,909	441.7	7,789	208.4	3,737				20
	[1] 146,922	411.3	[1] 31,078	669.2	[1] 1,484	47.0	[1] 1,746	123.5	21
									22
									23
	[3] 634	52.6	[3] 903	299.0	[3] 174	135.9	[3] 22	20.8	24
	1,111	143.2	386	99.0	62	18.9	242		25
	138,350	312.8	27,073	157.8	5,480	46.9	7,998	217.4	26
	98,883	203.6	34,121	236.4	7,138	97.8	7,298		27
									28
									29
									30
	8,793	232.3	2,108	125.6	275	19.6	1,403		31
	5,766	5.4	43,065	66.7	27,769	75.5	35,661	3,141.9	32
									33
	(3)		(3)		(3)		(3)		34
									35
	2,233	2.1	41,426	65.7	27,477	77.3	34,807	4,592.0	36,37
	1,891	471.6	328		73				38
	436	25.5	1,121	191.3	586				39
	1,206	114.4	190	22.0	−367	−29.8	854	226.5	40
	281,015	34.8	255,895	46.4	263,050	91.2	119,801	71.1	41
	263,781	36.8	223,693	45.3	243,494	97.4	102,259	69.2	42,43,44
	6,855	41.8	4,831	41.8	4,217	57.4	1,581	27.4	45
	9,454	13.8	25,964	61.2	14,969	54.5	14,149	106.2	46
	925	17.5	1,407	36.4	370	10.6	1,812	107.6	47
	6,539	31.5	6,061	41.2	6,796	85.9	−35,201	−81.6	48

[5] Newfoundland included with Canada prior to 1910.
[6] Except possessions of the United States.
[7] Africa, Australia, Atlantic Islands, Pacific Islands except possessions of the United States, "country not specified," and born at sea.

TABLE 73.—COUNTRY OF BIRTH OF FOREIGN-BORN

#	DIVISION AND STATE OF RESIDENCE.	Total foreign born: 1920	England.	Scotland.	Wales.	Ireland.	Norway.	Sweden.	Denmark.	Netherlands.	Belgium.
1	United States...	13,920,692	813,853	254,570	67,066	1,037,234	363,863	625,585	189,154	131,766	62,687
	GEOGRAPHIC DIVS.:										
2	New England.....	1,885,945	147,320	47,501	2,999	267,429	8,564	67,286	8,458	2,912	4,411
3	Middle Atlantic...	4,960,418	273,140	83,885	29,185	472,319	35,362	83,547	22,991	27,847	12,478
4	E. North Central..	3,232,141	163,994	51,650	15,226	135,147	82,137	165,388	43,018	59,863	29,706
5	W. North Central.	1,375,653	53,551	17,196	5,693	49,858	166,280	187,629	61,748	24,399	7,159
6	South Atlantic....	330,537	24,416	7,456	1,773	20,145	2,259	4,418	2,123	1,459	1,547
7	E. South Central...	72,989	6,085	2,093	455	5,934	450	1,514	531	322	235
8	W. South Central..	464,828	13,373	3,711	763	8,330	2,691	6,320	2,580	1,106	1,180
9	Mountain..........	467,620	44,588	12,986	4,907	19,634	17,400	32,232	17,023	5,252	1,608
10	Pacific............	1,130,561	87,386	28,092	6,065	58,438	48,720	77,251	30,682	8,606	4,363
	NEW ENGLAND:										
11	Maine.............	107,814	5,153	2,171	137	5,748	581	2,026	1,065	50	51
12	New Hampshire...	91,397	4,368	1,823	51	7,908	427	1,886	204	177	478
13	Vermont..........	44,558	2,197	1,854	549	2,884	106	1,123	155	32	15
14	Massachusetts....	1,088,548	87,085	28,474	1,367	183,172	5,491	38,012	3,629	2,071	2,497
15	Rhode Island......	175,189	25,791	5,692	245	22,253	545	6,542	365	138	968
16	Connecticut......	378,439	22,726	7,487	650	45,464	1,414	17,697	3,040	444	402
	MIDDLE ATLANTIC:										
17	New York........	2,825,375	135,541	37,656	6,763	284,747	27,573	53,025	14,222	13,772	5,300
18	New Jersey........	742,486	46,861	17,781	1,255	65,971	5,343	10,675	5,704	12,737	2,483
19	Pennsylvania......	1,392,557	90,738	28,448	21,167	121,601	2,446	19,847	3,065	1,338	4,695
	E. NORTH CENTRAL:										
20	Ohio.............	680,452	43,172	12,148	7,772	29,262	1,487	7,266	2,353	2,529	1,902
21	Indiana...........	151,328	8,528	3,707	1,106	7,271	544	4,942	969	2,018	2,530
22	Illinois...........	1,210,584	54,272	19,598	3,444	74,274	27,785	105,577	17,098	14,344	11,329
23	Michigan..........	729,292	47,185	13,175	1,154	16,531	6,888	24,707	7,178	33,499	10,501
24	Wisconsin.........	460,485	10,837	3,022	1,750	7,809	45,433	22,896	15,420	7,473	3,444
	W. NORTH CENTRAL:										
25	Minnesota........	486,795	10,964	3,298	854	10,289	90,188	112,117	16,904	5,380	2,056
26	Iowa.............	225,994	13,038	3,967	1,753	10,686	17,344	22,493	18,020	12,471	1,232
27	Missouri..........	186,835	10,407	2,969	903	15,022	610	4,741	1,688	906	1,113
28	North Dakota.....	131,863	2,289	1,229	120	1,660	38,190	10,543	4,552	903	456
29	South Dakota.....	82,534	2,944	832	346	1,954	16,813	8,573	5,983	3,218	251
30	Nebraska..........	150,665	6,006	1,695	547	5,422	2,165	18,825	12,338	846	551
31	Kansas...........	110,967	7,903	2,576	1,170	4,825	970	10,337	2,263	675	1,500
	SOUTH ATLANTIC:										
32	Delaware.........	19,901	1,497	411	44	2,895	65	316	77	37	24
33	Maryland.........	103,179	5,113	1,692	499	6,580	536	630	382	314	135
34	Dist. Columbia....	29,365	3,001	793	106	4,320	219	481	237	127	76
35	Virginia..........	31,705	3,776	1,327	163	1,732	491	664	459	335	122
36	West Virginia.....	62,105	3,435	998	704	1,459	51	326	121	66	938
37	North Carolina....	7,272	969	446	25	301	70	170	69	115	16
38	South Carolina....	6,582	493	190	10	442	85	133	76	30	61
39	Georgia..........	16,564	1,610	530	86	1,112	132	299	127	78	45
40	Florida..........	53,864	4,522	1,069	136	1,304	610	1,399	575	357	130
	E. SOUTH CENTRAL:										
41	Kentucky.........	30,906	1,865	520	149	3,422	75	214	89	150	90
42	Tennessee........	15,648	1,670	454	143	1,291	63	305	138	58	36
43	Alabama..........	18,027	1,951	975	145	809	215	748	191	83	73
44	Mississippi.......	8,408	599	144	18	412	97	247	113	31	36
	W. SOUTH CENTRAL:										
45	Arkansas.........	14,137	1,141	316	90	676	99	331	180	116	94
46	Louisiana........	46,427	1,841	447	76	2,000	555	522	331	260	350
47	Oklahoma........	40,452	2,007	1,120	319	1,321	297	931	561	176	289
48	Texas...........	363,802	7,704	1,828	278	4,333	1,740	4,506	1,508	554	447
	MOUNTAIN:										
49	Montana.........	95,591	8,160	3,279	879	7,260	9,962	7,179	2,990	1,675	672
50	Idaho...........	40,747	4,451	1,228	575	1,410	2,482	5,112	2,240	439	123
51	Wyoming.........	26,567	2,507	1,439	297	956	651	2,042	936	130	130
52	Colorado........	119,138	9,588	3,357	1,482	6,191	1,525	10,112	2,823	853	430
53	New Mexico......	29,808	889	440	78	434	128	310	115	70	76
54	Arizona..........	80,566	2,883	595	192	1,206	337	859	398	69	60
55	Utah.............	59,200	14,839	2,310	1,304	1,207	2,109	6,073	6,970	1,980	90
56	Nevada..........	16,003	1,271	338	100	970	206	545	551	36	27
	PACIFIC:										
57	Washington......	265,292	20,821	7,886	2,040	8,927	30,305	34,793	8,359	3,097	1,439
58	Oregon..........	107,644	7,953	3,609	592	4,203	6,955	10,532	3,602	917	722
59	California........	757,625	58,612	16,597	3,433	45,308	11,460	31,926	18,721	4,592	2,202

POPULATION, BY DIVISIONS AND STATES: 1920.

NORTHWESTERN EUROPE—continued.			CENTRAL EUROPE.						EASTERN EUROPE.				
Luxemburg.	Switzerland.	France.	Germany.	Poland.	Czechoslovakia.	Austria.	Hungary.	Jugo-Slavia.	Russia.	Lithuania.	Finland.	Rumania.	
12,585	118,659	153,072	1,686,108	1,139,979	362,438	575,627	397,283	169,439	1,400,495	135,068	149,824	102,823	1
114	3,763	13,252	51,129	131,378	9,653	23,081	15,187	2,405	147,371	35,361	19,543	3,128	2
1,017	30,093	55,250	508,227	515,708	123,863	310,844	190,224	48,087	763,894	48,594	17,431	55,910	3
5,093	30,379	29,637	592,058	402,259	143,743	145,275	149,592	72,343	236,022	44,307	46,576	29,338	4
4,846	15,838	11,443	293,035	38,262	50,906	37,504	17,640	18,189	110,767	2,098	31,635	6,950	5
87	2,348	4,119	40,898	25,432	6,620	12,077	10,696	3,581	48,362	3,245	1,281	2,163	6
31	2,176	2,191	16,652	2,590	617	2,023	1,829	766	7,408	76	219	441	7
127	3,433	8,086	47,217	7,206	15,438	9,195	1,664	1,267	14,652	219	455	663	8
372	6,695	4,968	33,652	4,675	5,295	13,070	3,234	10,771	26,690	280	7,718	1,053	9
898	23,934	24,126	103,240	12,469	6,303	22,558	7,217	12,030	45,329	888	24,966	3,177	10
6	62	344	932	1,717	410	305	72	143	3,763	1,032	1,393	67	11
5	72	288	1,714	3,997	75	389	66	120	3,467	1,017	1,558	25	12
2	187	197	630	1,726	108	283	264	56	1,333	67	476	19	13
33	1,368	7,125	22,113	69,157	2,238	8,098	1,387	950	92,034	20,789	14,570	1,445	14
14	211	1,971	3,126	8,158	264	1,307	176	146	8,055	794	320	370	15
54	1,863	3,327	22,614	46,623	6,558	12,699	13,222	990	38,719	11,662	1,226	1,202	16
564	15,053	32,252	295,651	247,519	38,247	151,172	78,374	8,547	529,243	12,121	12,504	40,116	17
167	8,165	10,168	92,382	90,419	16,747	36,917	40,470	3,313	73,527	6,246	2,109	4,564	18
286	6,875	12,830	120,194	177,770	68,869	122,755	71,380	36,227	161,124	30,227	2,818	11,230	19
273	9,656	8,067	111,893	67,579	42,121	48,073	73,181	30,377	43,690	4,095	6,406	13,068	20
101	2,334	3,247	37,377	17,791	3,941	9,100	9,351	4,471	7,673	1,445	237	2,731	21
3,211	7,837	12,006	205,491	162,405	66,709	46,457	34,437	19,285	117,899	30,358	3,080	6,238	22
477	2,755	4,175	86,047	103,926	11,161	22,004	22,607	9,426	45,313	5,475	30,096	6,331	23
1,031	7,797	2,142	151,250	50,558	19,811	19,641	10,016	8,784	21,447	2,934	6,757	970	24
1,782	2,720	1,806	74,634	18,537	12,626	11,550	4,277	10,697	16,100	741	29,108	2,385	25
1,630	2,871	2,125	70,642	2,028	9,150	4,334	747	1,603	7,319	687	107	297	26
140	4,934	3,831	55,776	7,636	4,971	8,676	8,080	2,327	18,769	417	98	1,647	27
229	506	350	11,960	2,236	2,056	2,059	2,519	199	29,617	32	1,108	1,811	28
480	761	337	15,674	792	2,819	1,151	585	470	11,193	14	1,085	154	29
301	1,808	858	40,969	4,615	15,818	4,551	810	738	15,719	139	73	371	30
284	2,238	2,136	23,380	2,418	3,466	5,183	622	2,155	12,050	68	56	285	31
5	76	198	1,632	3,847	122	615	226	27	2,244	90	52	110	32
22	509	818	22,032	12,061	3,553	3,620	1,947	359	24,791	2,206	175	537	33
13	358	688	3,382	716	122	525	219	43	5,181	38	104	86	34
7	239	455	2,802	1,103	897	921	1,293	127	5,421	71	240	165	35
6	545	633	3,798	5,799	1,549	5,115	6,260	2,802	3,911	717	289	625	36
2	72	136	703	210	20	149	66	29	932	29	15	31	37
1	31	78	1,079	351	45	206	56	22	1,187	9	53	26	38
7	161	376	1,936	917	123	401	246	84	3,452	72	42	111	39
24	357	737	3,534	428	189	525	383	88	1,243	13	311	472	40
12	1,315	984	11,137	1,037	240	906	1,084	354	2,736	56	50	192	41
3	616	333	2,159	841	82	398	326	37	2,262	3	33	93	42
8	174	616	2,427	394	232	583	372	155	1,582	12	74	120	43
8	71	258	929	318	63	136	47	220	828	5	62	36	44
8	736	387	3,979	529	492	636	108	117	662	27	18	62	45
9	378	4,193	5,147	377	302	725	305	312	1,928	23	147	93	46
52	629	962	7,029	1,253	1,825	1,393	311	218	5,005	132	101	65	47
58	1,690	2,544	31,062	5,047	12,819	6,441	940	620	7,057	37	189	443	48
153	1,151	888	7,873	1,219	1,895	3,298	935	3,782	5,203	80	3,577	344	49
60	1,347	482	4,143	287	420	781	233	460	1,458	9	989	104	50
18	302	364	2,292	544	518	1,183	349	1,189	1,482	33	856	71	51
91	1,510	1,420	11,992	1,867	1,953	5,722	1,157	2,109	16,669	115	879	394	52
6	148	377	1,178	153	113	423	131	535	254	8	49	8	53
22	293	394	1,516	261	148	486	210	1,167	816	16	407	51	54
18	1,566	434	3,589	240	163	987	179	836	684	12	779	69	55
4	378	609	1,069	104	85	190	40	693	124	7	182	12	56
315	3,671	2,452	22,315	3,906	1,792	6,494	1,056	3,565	11,125	527	11,863	422	57
140	4,166	1,273	13,740	1,480	1,132	2,798	909	1,186	6,979	101	6,050	352	58
443	16,097	20,401	67,185	7,083	3,379	13,266	5,252	7,279	27,225	260	7,053	2,403	59

TABLE 73.—COUNTRY OF BIRTH OF FOREIGN-BORN

	DIVISION AND STATE OF RESIDENCE.	EASTERN EUROPE— continued.		SOUTHERN EUROPE.						ASIA.			
		Bulgaria.	Turkey in Europe.	Greece.	Albania.	Italy.	Spain.	Portugal.	Other Europe.[1]	Armenia.	Palestine.	Syria.	Turkey in Asia.
1	United States	10,477	5,284	175,976	5,608	1,610,113	49,535	69,981	5,901	36,628	3,203	51,901	11,019
	GEOGRAPHIC DIVS.:												
2	New England	214	631	32,186	2,819	238,508	2,864	40,302	209	11,964	271	11,181	2,267
3	Middle Atlantic	1,336	2,534	44,531	1,156	925,222	16,921	3,090	1,412	10,806	1,489	15,501	4,335
4	E. North Central	5,806	1,035	45,135	1,019	203,181	3,022	360	2,211	6,157	662	9,726	2,098
5	W. North Central	1,095	124	11,236	262	34,488	776	59	465	717	142	3,406	322
6	South Atlantic	161	203	11,450	19	40,267	6,547	714	355	402	143	4,064	456
7	E. South Central	51	50	2,014	23	8,584	215	29	89	61	77	1,501	93
8	W. South Central	241	101	3,484	12	27,724	2,522	199	336	148	156	3,436	206
9	Mountain	821	72	9,483	143	28,498	4,563	334	106	362	73	1,324	190
10	Pacific	752	534	16,457	155	103,641	12,105	24,894	718	6,011	190	1,762	1,052
	NEW ENGLAND:												
11	Maine	5	66	1,228	403	2,797	33	153	10	142	10	627	43
12	New Hampshire	8		5,280	118	2,074	20	142	2	276	7	523	60
13	Vermont	3		167	6	4,067	661	29	4	55	1	228	5
14	Massachusetts	120	451	20,441	1,947	117,007	824	29,191	100	8,640	180	7,128	1,672
15	Rhode Island	45	45	1,219	142	32,241	89	8,999	11	1,850	14	1,285	262
16	Connecticut	33	69	3,851	203	80,322	1,237	1,788	82	1,001	59	1,390	225
	MIDDLE ATLANTIC:												
17	New York	614	2,050	26,117	415	545,173	12,722	1,484	842	5,599	1,061	8,127	3,200
18	New Jersey	66	195	4,521	54	157,285	2,002	687	170	2,275	160	2,062	440
19	Pennsylvania	656	289	13,893	687	222,764	2,197	919	400	2,932	268	5,312	695
	E. NORTH CENTRAL:												
20	Ohio	2,535	569	13,540	432	60,658	1,281	149	351	906	185	3,680	637
21	Indiana	431	70	4,182	74	6,712	467	14	75	134	26	717	158
22	Illinois	940	181	16,465	151	94,407	754	110	524	1,715	232	1,149	502
23	Michigan	1,692	179	7,115	261	30,216	446	70	813	2,498	176	3,648	663
24	Wisconsin	208	36	3,833	101	11,188	74	17	448	904	43	532	138
	W. NORTH CENTRAL:												
25	Minnesota	456	30	2,391	41	7,432	36	9	149	174	25	818	100
26	Iowa	269	18	2,884	7	4,956	41	15	78	101	22	512	51
27	Missouri	145	44	3,022	202	14,609	435	12	76	181	63	848	83
28	North Dakota	31	17	420		176	6	2	25	75	5	289	21
29	South Dakota	97	5	375	1	413	5	4	27	18	1	265	12
30	Nebraska	61	4	1,504	9	3,547	38	6	53	138	14	415	28
31	Kansas	36	6	640	2	3,355	215	11	57	30	12	259	27
	SOUTH ATLANTIC:												
32	Delaware		3	286		4,136	142	19	7	6	10	2	6
33	Maryland	18	19	964	1	9,543	226	63	79	43	15	72	39
34	Dist. Columbia	5	72	1,207	8	3,764	111	14	17	63	19	211	62
35	Virginia	17	32	1,797	4	2,435	266	307	82	164	23	550	77
36	West Virginia	98	23	3,186	2	14,147	1,543	17	71	41	20	1,235	157
37	North Carolina	1	17	551		453	16	14	7	10	22	592	23
38	South Carolina	1	10	578		344	19	7	10	6	2	396	5
39	Georgia	5	21	1,473	1	700	125	45	60	28	16	473	49
40	Florida	16	6	1,408	3	4,745	4,099	228	22	41	16	533	38
	E. SOUTH CENTRAL:												
41	Kentucky	28	22	401	1	1,932	68	8	30	20	16	309	22
42	Tennessee	5	5	491	22	2,079	14	7	16	18	30	127	20
43	Alabama	18	22	915		2,732	71	7	33	22	16	482	39
44	Mississippi		1	207		1,841	62	7	10	1	15	583	12
	W. SOUTH CENTRAL:												
45	Arkansas	17	1	277	1	1,314	22	4	10	7	16	213	10
46	Louisiana	49	14	610	2	16,264	1,293	112	74	27	15	954	61
47	Oklahoma	105	11	620	1	2,122	120	13	40	15	20	691	21
48	Texas	70	75	1,977	8	8,024	1,001	70	203	99	105	1,578	114
	MOUNTAIN:												
49	Montana	264	28	1,465	38	3,842	68	31	13	140	8	192	62
50	Idaho	39	5	716	42	1,323	1,417	39	6	13	1	49	15
51	Wyoming	72	2	1,236	5	1,948	139	29	4	62	4	82	25
52	Colorado	349	12	1,802	11	12,580	297	33	43	46	41	289	30
53	New Mexico	18	2	288		1,678	199	19	8	2	2	198	5
54	Arizona	28	10	329	6	1,261	1,013	30	8	8	8	327	15
55	Utah	30	12	3,029	41	3,225	250	4	19	80	5	174	18
56	Nevada	21	1	618		2,641	1,180	149	5	11	4	13	20
	PACIFIC:												
57	Washington	267	229	4,215	93	10,813	412	160	75	259	18	318	288
58	Oregon	214	41	1,928	13	4,324	553	125	34	63	5	185	56
59	California	271	264	10,314	49	88,504	11,140	24,609	609	5,689	167	1,259	708

[1] Comprises Danzig, Fiume, Saar Basin, and "Europe, not specified."

POPULATION, BY DIVISIONS AND STATES: 1920—Continued.

ASIA—continued.				AMERICA.						ALL OTHER.						
				Canada.		Newfoundland	West Indies[2]	Mexico.	Central and So. America.							
China.	Japan.	India.	Other Asia.	French.	Other.					Africa.	Australia.	Atlantic Islands.	Pacific Islands[2]	Country not specified.	Born at sea.	
43,560	81,502	4,901	5,236	307,786	817,139	13,249	78,962	486,418	23,463	5,781	10,914	44,340	3,712	3,589	5,336	1
2,594	315	332	550	240,385	235,871	8,201	5,400	224	1,805	490	537	32,715	176	305	384	2
6,909	2,868	954	1,154	17,045	121,255	2,775	44,596	5,237	11,092	2,156	2,238	1,759	471	660	1,020	3
3,481	784	482	1,598	29,267	224,625	831	2,630	7,181	2,061	873	1,428	299	284	1,521	1,633	4
1,250	966	190	207	10,459	70,246	181	616	22,787	763	315	557	43	134	270	951	5
1,313	304	163	89	813	12,228	230	21,256	641	1,025	315	283	231	104	85	171	6
366	29	46	32	179	3,022	32	686	570	265	98	82	15	21	29	92	7
1,056	406	130	105	590	8,178	100	1,799	261,478	1,550	248	317	68	81	225	256	8
3,149	8,499	167	233	3,482	30,615	196	323	98,484	485	346	624	159	356	212	218	9
23,442	67,331	2,437	1,268	5,566	111,099	703	1,656	89,816	4,417	940	4,848	9,051	2,085	282	611	10
104	8	29	7	35,580	38,840	215	139	9	19	21	23	19	4	12	40	11
63	8	5	2	38,277	14,035	182	52	10	31	12	21	45	4	14	11	12
6	4	6	1	14,181	10,704	67	15	7	43	8	5	4	5	3	10	13
1,807	170	202	107	108,691	154,787	7,168	4,176	146	1,156	317	340	28,294	103	62	216	14
162	29	34	38	28,887	7,595	233	218	8	240	43	43	3,950	23	8	25	15
452	96	56	395	14,769	9,910	336	800	44	316	89	105	403	37	206	82	16
4,559	2,393	624	744	15,560	97,244	1,810	38,288	2,999	8,645	1,528	1,384	1,168	320	260	483	17
941	274	158	190	772	9,624	477	3,141	420	1,133	293	334	437	95	106	170	18
1,409	201	172	220	713	14,387	488	3,167	1,818	1,314	335	520	154	56	294	367	19
640	121	109	185	1,277	23,393	148	865	952	481	174	233	55	39	190	297	20
205	58	21	128	406	4,741	44	145	686	89	44	78	7	26	43	133	21
1,929	402	155	881	4,032	34,741	311	913	4,032	842	371	608	207	114	287	495	22
524	161	152	349	18,635	147,267	245	592	1,333	475	225	400	23	81	128	314	23
183	42	45	55	4,917	14,483	83	115	178	174	59	109	7	24	873	394	24
364	61	51	45	6,796	27,066	56	102	248	125	92	107	16	29	67	266	25
187	20	32	33	401	8,543	35	96	2,650	113	35	101	9	39	36	166	26
310	109	38	31	299	6,263	38	247	3,411	222	94	140	8	23	41	180	27
97	67	5	18	1,533	14,210	20	9	29	39	10	35	......	2	23	75	28
98	24	14	24	508	3,954	3	25	68	27	20	24	......	9	12	72	29
140	642	25	30	351	5,429	20	64	2,611	73	31	80	5	12	71	99	30
54	43	25	26	571	4,781	9	73	13,770	164	33	70	5	20	20	93	31
32	8	2	1	23	430	8	61	52	19	12	12	2	5	......	7	32
283	23	24	15	117	1,777	61	737	87	215	57	62	32	36	11	49	33
345	97	23	11	147	1,579	18	365	73	186	54	25	17	7	13	17	34
211	53	33	14	106	1,841	32	399	80	156	54	45	58	20	15	24	35
61	10	2	10	54	927	6	108	80	52	9	33	5	2	31	28	36
64	19	12	8	15	648	7	89	30	47	21	14	2	8	2	5	37
63	10	15	11	24	247	1	103	17	20	10	5	9	1	1	3	38
147	11	14	8	50	915	22	223	55	69	40	28	11	8	9	11	39
107	73	38	11	277	3,864	75	19,171	167	261	58	59	95	17	3	27	40
42	6	12	12	50	853	13	80	138	38	10	38	2	11	13	54	41
39	13	18	5	47	941	9	85	176	62	28	15	3	4	9	16	42
36	10	8	10	52	852	3	405	146	117	39	21	10	6	4	12	43
249	......	8	5	30	376	7	116	110	48	21	8	......	......	3	10	44
66	5	3	6	58	835	20	43	280	25	32	27	7	7	1	26	45
260	47	57	12	157	1,029	16	1,225	2,487	1,142	61	63	20	10	5	40	46
169	56	10	42	126	2,363	11	59	6,884	72	30	54	2	13	20	51	47
561	298	60	45	249	3,951	53	472	251,827	311	125	173	39	51	199	139	48
641	896	14	39	2,211	12,489	63	43	236	72	50	81	5	39	66	41	49
489	1,180	18	23	476	4,485	59	14	1,215	26	44	57	23	72	41	27	50
191	1,029	12	67	92	1,348	4	21	1,801	29	15	17	8	14	12	10	51
208	1,762	44	33	418	7,224	39	114	11,037	185	56	112	9	40	22	63	52
124	198	3	8	42	696	3	38	20,272	26	26	14	5	4	2	5	53
720	427	27	31	90	1,874	16	76	61,580	78	28	81	1	26	65	22	54
247	2,358	40	24	45	1,426	4	10	1,166	32	117	222	4	138	2	40	55
529	649	9	8	108	1,073	8	7	1,177	37	15	40	104	23	2	10	56
1,727	12,971	206	201	2,581	40,598	318	258	450	322	133	612	46	246	126	180	57
2,151	3,169	134	35	679	13,121	49	92	595	123	73	215	48	161	13	54	58
19,564	51,191	2,097	1,032	2,306	57,380	336	1,306	88,771	3,972	734	4,021	8,957	1,678	143	377	59

[2] Except possessions of the United States.

TABLE 74.—PER CENT DISTRIBUTION OF FOREIGN-BORN

DIVISION AND STATE OF RESIDENCE.	PER CENT OF TOTAL FOREIGN BORN IN SPECIFIED DIVISION OR STATE.														
	Northwestern Europe.												Central Europe.		
	England.	Scotland.	Wales.	Ireland.	Norway.	Sweden.	Denmark.	Netherlands.	Belgium.	Luxemburg.	Switzerland.	France.	Germany.	Poland.	Czechoslovakia.
1 United States	5.8	1.8	0.5	7.5	2.6	4.5	1.4	0.9	0.5	0.1	0.9	1.1	12.1	8.2	2.6
GEOGRAPHIC DIVISIONS:															
2 New England	7.8	2.5	0.2	14.2	0.5	3.6	0.4	0.2	0.2	(1)	0.2	0.7	2.7	7.0	0.5
3 Middle Atlantic	5.5	1.7	0.6	9.5	0.7	1.7	0.5	0.6	0.3	(1)	0.6	1.1	10.2	10.4	2.5
4 East North Central	5.1	1.6	0.5	4.2	2.5	5.1	1.3	1.9	0.9	0.2	0.9	0.9	18.3	12.4	4.4
5 West North Central	3.9	1.3	0.4	3.6	12.1	13.6	4.5	1.8	0.5	0.4	1.2	0.8	21.3	2.8	3.7
6 South Atlantic	7.4	2.3	0.5	6.1	0.7	1.3	0.6	0.4	0.5	(1)	0.7	1.2	12.4	7.7	2.0
7 East South Central	8.3	2.9	0.6	8.1	0.6	2.1	0.7	0.4	0.3	(1)	3.0	3.0	22.8	3.5	0.8
8 West South Central	2.9	0.8	0.2	1.8	0.6	1.4	0.6	0.2	0.3	(1)	0.7	1.7	10.2	1.6	3.3
9 Mountain	9.5	2.8	1.0	4.2	3.7	6.9	3.6	1.1	0.3	0.1	1.4	1.1	7.2	1.0	1.1
10 Pacific	7.7	2.5	0.5	5.2	4.3	6.8	2.7	0.8	0.4	0.1	2.1	2.1	9.1	1.1	0.6
NEW ENGLAND:															
11 Maine	4.8	2.0	0.1	5.3	0.5	1.9	1.0	(1)	(1)	(1)	0.1	0.3	0.9	1.6	0.4
12 New Hampshire	4.8	2.0	0.1	8.7	0.5	2.1	0.2	0.2	0.5	(1)	0.1	0.3	1.9	4.4	0.1
13 Vermont	4.9	4.2	1.2	6.5	0.2	2.5	0.3	0.1	(1)	(1)	0.4	0.4	1.4	3.9	0.2
14 Massachusetts	8.0	2.6	0.1	16.8	0.5	3.5	0.3	0.2	0.2	(1)	0.1	0.7	2.0	6.4	0.2
15 Rhode Island	14.7	3.2	0.1	12.7	0.3	3.7	0.2	0.1	0.6	(1)	0.1	1.1	1.8	4.7	0.2
16 Connecticut	6.0	2.0	0.2	12.0	0.4	4.7	0.8	0.1	0.1	(1)	0.5	0.9	6.0	12.3	1.7
MIDDLE ATLANTIC:															
17 New York	4.8	1.3	0.2	10.1	1.0	1.9	0.5	0.5	0.2	(1)	0.5	1.1	10.5	8.8	1.4
18 New Jersey	6.3	2.4	0.2	8.9	0.7	1.4	0.8	1.7	0.3	(1)	1.1	1.4	12.4	12.2	2.3
19 Pennsylvania	6.5	2.0	1.5	8.7	0.2	1.4	0.2	0.1	0.3	(1)	0.5	0.9	8.6	12.8	4.9
EAST NORTH CENTRAL:															
20 Ohio	6.3	1.8	1.1	4.3	0.2	1.1	0.3	0.4	0.3	(1)	1.4	1.2	16.4	9.9	6.2
21 Indiana	5.6	2.4	0.7	4.8	0.4	3.3	0.6	1.3	1.7	0.1	1.5	2.1	24.7	11.8	2.6
22 Illinois	4.5	1.6	0.3	6.1	2.3	8.7	1.4	1.2	0.9	0.3	0.6	1.0	17.0	13.4	5.5
23 Michigan	6.5	1.8	0.2	2.3	0.9	3.4	1.0	4.6	1.4	0.1	0.4	0.6	11.8	14.3	1.5
24 Wisconsin	2.4	0.7	0.4	1.7	9.9	5.0	3.3	1.6	0.7	0.2	1.7	0.5	32.8	11.0	4.3
WEST NORTH CENTRAL:															
25 Minnesota	2.3	0.8	0.2	2.1	18.5	23.0	3.5	1.1	0.4	0.4	0.6	0.4	15.3	3.8	2.6
26 Iowa	5.8	1.8	0.8	4.7	7.7	10.0	8.0	5.5	0.5	0.7	1.3	0.9	31.3	0.9	4.0
27 Missouri	5.6	1.6	0.5	8.0	0.3	2.5	0.9	0.5	0.6	0.1	2.6	2.1	29.9	4.1	2.7
28 North Dakota	1.7	0.9	0.1	1.3	29.0	8.0	3.5	0.7	0.3	0.2	0.4	0.3	9.1	1.7	1.6
29 South Dakota	3.6	1.0	0.4	2.4	20.4	10.4	7.2	3.9	0.3	0.6	0.9	0.4	19.0	1.0	3.4
30 Nebraska	4.0	1.1	0.4	3.6	1.4	12.5	8.2	0.6	0.4	0.2	1.2	0.6	27.2	3.1	10.5
31 Kansas	7.1	2.3	1.1	4.3	0.9	9.3	2.0	0.6	1.4	0.3	2.0	1.9	21.1	2.2	3.1
SOUTH ATLANTIC:															
32 Delaware	7.5	2.1	0.2	14.5	0.3	1.6	0.4	0.2	0.1	(1)	0.4	1.0	8.2	19.3	0.6
33 Maryland	5.0	1.6	0.5	6.4	0.5	0.6	0.4	0.3	0.1	(1)	0.5	0.8	21.4	11.7	3.4
34 District of Columbia	10.2	2.7	0.4	14.7	0.7	1.6	0.8	0.4	0.3	(1)	1.2	2.3	11.5	2.4	0.4
35 Virginia	11.9	4.2	0.5	5.5	1.5	2.1	1.4	1.1	0.4	(1)	0.8	1.4	8.8	3.5	2.8
36 West Virginia	5.5	1.6	1.1	2.3	0.1	0.5	0.2	0.1	1.5	(1)	0.9	1.0	6.1	9.3	2.5
37 North Carolina	13.3	6.1	0.3	4.1	1.0	2.3	0.9	1.6	0.2	(1)	0.1	1.9	9.7	2.9	0.3
38 South Carolina	7.5	2.9	0.2	6.7	1.3	2.0	1.2	0.5	0.9	(1)	0.5	1.2	16.4	5.3	0.7
39 Georgia	9.7	3.2	0.5	6.7	0.8	1.8	0.8	0.5	0.3	(1)	1.0	2.3	11.7	5.5	0.7
40 Florida	8.4	2.0	0.3	2.4	1.1	2.6	1.1	0.7	0.2	(1)	0.7	1.4	6.6	0.8	0.4
EAST SOUTH CENTRAL:															
41 Kentucky	6.0	1.7	0.5	11.1	0.2	0.7	0.3	0.5	0.3	(1)	4.3	3.2	36.0	3.4	0.8
42 Tennessee	10.7	2.9	0.9	8.3	0.4	1.9	0.9	0.4	0.2	(1)	3.9	2.1	13.8	5.4	0.5
43 Alabama	10.8	5.4	0.8	4.5	1.2	4.1	1.1	0.5	0.4	(1)	1.0	3.4	13.5	2.2	1.3
44 Mississippi	7.1	1.7	0.2	4.9	1.2	2.9	1.3	0.4	0.4	0.1	0.8	3.1	11.0	3.8	0.7
WEST SOUTH CENTRAL:															
45 Arkansas	8.1	2.2	0.6	4.8	0.7	2.0	1.0	0.8	0.7	0.1	5.2	2.7	28.1	3.7	3.5
46 Louisiana	4.0	1.0	0.2	1.0	1.0	1.1	0.7	0.6	0.8	(1)	0.8	9.0	11.1	0.3	0.7
47 Oklahoma	6.6	2.8	0.8	3.3	0.7	2.3	1.4	0.4	0.7	0.1	1.6	2.4	17.4	3.1	4.5
48 Texas	2.1	0.5	0.1	1.2	0.5	1.2	0.4	0.2	0.1	(1)	0.5	0.7	8.5	1.4	3.5
MOUNTAIN:															
49 Montana	8.5	3.4	0.9	7.6	10.4	7.5	3.1	1.8	0.7	0.2	1.2	0.9	8.2	1.3	2.0
50 Idaho	10.9	3.0	1.4	3.5	6.1	12.5	5.5	1.1	0.3	0.1	3.3	1.2	10.2	0.7	1.0
51 Wyoming	9.4	5.4	1.1	3.6	2.5	7.7	3.5	0.5	0.5	0.1	1.1	1.4	8.6	2.0	1.9
52 Colorado	8.0	2.8	1.2	5.2	1.3	8.5	2.4	0.7	0.4	0.1	1.3	1.2	10.1	1.6	1.6
53 New Mexico	3.0	1.5	0.3	1.5	0.4	1.0	0.4	0.2	0.3	(1)	0.5	1.3	4.0	0.5	0.4
54 Arizona	3.6	0.7	0.2	1.5	0.4	1.1	0.5	0.1	0.1	(1)	0.4	0.5	1.9	0.3	0.2
55 Utah	25.1	3.9	2.2	2.0	3.6	10.3	11.8	3.3	0.2	(1)	2.6	0.7	6.1	0.4	0.3
56 Nevada	7.9	2.1	0.6	6.1	1.3	3.4	3.4	0.2	0.2	(1)	2.4	3.8	6.7	0.6	0.5
PACIFIC:															
57 Washington	7.8	3.0	0.8	3.4	11.4	13.1	3.2	1.2	0.5	0.1	1.4	0.9	8.4	1.5	0.7
58 Oregon	7.4	3.4	0.5	3.9	6.5	9.8	3.3	0.9	0.7	0.1	3.9	1.2	12.8	1.4	1.1
59 California	7.7	2.2	0.5	6.0	1.5	4.2	2.5	0.6	0.3	0.1	2.1	2.7	8.9	0.9	0.4

1 Less than one-tenth of 1 per cent.

POPULATION BY COUNTRY OF BIRTH, BY DIVISIONS AND STATES: 1920.

PER CENT OF TOTAL FOREIGN BORN IN SPECIFIED DIVISION OR STATE—continued.

Central Europe—Con.			Eastern Europe					Southern Europe				Asia				America						No.
Austria	Hungary	Jugo-Slavia	Russia	Lithuania	Finland	Rumania	Bulgaria, Turkey in Europe	Greece	Italy	Spain	Portugal	Armenia	Syria	China	Japan	Canada—French	Canada—Other	Newfoundland	West Indies[2]	Mexico	Central and So. America	
4.1	2.9	1.2	10.1	1.0	1.1	0.7	0.1	1.3	11.6	0.4	0.5	0.3	0.4	0.3	0.6	2.2	5.9	0.1	0.6	3.5	0.2	1
1.2	0.8	0.1	7.8	1.9	1.0	0.2	(1)	1.7	12.6	0.2	2.1	0.6	0.6	0.1	(1)	12.7	12.5	0.4	0.3	(1)	0.1	2
6.3	3.8	1.0	15.4	1.0	0.4	1.1	0.1	0.9	18.7	0.3	0.1	0.2	0.3	0.1	0.1	0.3	2.4	0.1	0.9	0.1	0.2	3
4.5	4.6	2.2	7.3	1.4	1.4	0.9	0.2	1.4	6.3	0.1	(1)	0.2	0.3	0.1	(1)	0.9	6.9	(1)	0.1	0.2	0.1	4
2.7	1.3	1.3	8.1	0.2	2.3	0.5	0.1	0.8	2.5	0.1	(1)	0.1	0.2	0.1	0.1	0.8	5.1	(1)	(1)	1.7	0.1	5
3.7	3.2	1.1	14.6	1.0	0.4	0.7	0.1	3.5	12.2	2.0	0.2	0.1	1.2	0.4	0.1	0.2	3.7	0.1	6.4	0.2	0.3	6
2.8	2.5	1.0	10.1	0.1	0.3	0.6	0.1	2.8	11.8	0.3	(1)	0.1	2.1	0.5	(1)	0.2	4.1	(1)	0.9	0.8	0.4	7
2.0	0.4	0.3	3.2	(1)	0.1	0.1	0.1	0.7	6.0	0.5	(1)	(1)	0.7	0.2	0.1	0.1	1.8	(1)	0.4	56.3	0.3	8
2.8	0.7	2.3	5.7	0.1	1.7	0.2	0.2	2.0	6.1	1.0	0.1	0.1	0.3	0.7	1.8	0.7	6.5	(1)	0.1	21.1	0.1	9
2.0	0.6	1.1	4.0	0.1	2.2	0.3	0.1	1.5	9.2	1.1	2.2	0.5	0.2	2.1	6.9	0.5	9.8	0.1	0.1	7.9	0.4	10
0.3	0.1	0.1	3.5	1.0	1.3	0.1	0.1	1.1	2.6	(1)	0.1	0.1	0.6	0.1	(1)	33.0	36.0	0.2	0.1	(1)	(1)	11
0.4	0.1	0.1	3.8	1.1	1.7	(1)	(1)	5.8	2.3	(1)	0.2	0.3	0.6	0.1	(1)	41.9	15.4	0.2	0.1	(1)	0.1	12
0.6	0.6	0.1	3.0	0.2	1.1	(1)	(1)	0.4	9.1	1.5	0.1	0.1	0.5	(1)	(1)	31.8	24.0	0.2	(1)	(1)	0.1	13
0.7	0.1	0.1	8.5	1.9	1.3	0.1	0.1	1.9	10.7	0.1	2.7	0.8	0.7	0.2	(1)	10.0	14.2	0.7	0.4	(1)	0.1	14
0.7	0.1	0.1	4.6	0.5	0.2	0.2	0.1	0.7	18.4	0.1	5.1	1.1	0.7	0.1	(1)	16.5	4.3	0.1	0.1	(1)	0.1	15
3.4	3.5	0.3	10.2	3.1	0.3	0.3	(1)	1.0	21.2	0.3	0.5	0.3	0.4	0.1	(1)	3.9	2.6	0.1	0.2	(1)	0.1	16
5.4	2.8	0.3	18.7	0.4	0.4	1.4	0.1	0.9	19.3	0.5	0.1	0.2	0.3	0.2	0.1	0.6	3.4	0.1	1.4	0.1	0.3	17
5.0	5.5	0.4	9.9	0.8	0.3	0.6	(1)	0.6	21.2	0.3	0.1	0.3	0.3	0.1	(1)	0.1	1.3	0.1	0.4	0.1	0.2	18
8.8	5.1	2.6	11.6	2.2	0.2	0.8	0.1	1.0	16.0	0.2	0.1	0.2	0.4	0.1	(1)	0.1	1.0	(1)	0.2	0.1	0.1	19
7.1	10.8	4.5	6.4	0.6	0.9	1.9	0.5	2.0	8.9	0.2	(1)	0.1	0.5	0.1	(1)	0.2	3.4	(1)	0.1	0.1	0.1	20
6.0	6.2	3.0	5.1	1.6	0.2	1.8	0.3	2.8	4.4	0.3	(1)	0.1	0.5	0.1	(1)	0.3	3.1	(1)	0.1	0.5	0.1	21
3.8	2.8	1.6	9.7	2.5	0.3	0.5	0.1	1.4	7.8	0.1	(1)	0.1	0.1	0.2	(1)	0.3	2.9	(1)	0.1	0.3	0.1	22
3.0	3.1	1.3	6.2	0.8	4.1	0.9	0.3	1.0	4.1	(1)	(1)	0.3	0.5	0.1	(1)	2.6	20.2	(1)	0.1	0.2	0.1	23
4.3	2.2	1.9	4.7	0.6	1.5	0.2	0.1	0.8	2.4	(1)	(1)	0.2	0.1	(1)	(1)	1.1	3.1	(1)	(1)	(1)	(1)	24
2.4	0.9	2.2	3.3	0.2	6.0	0.5	0.1	0.5	1.5	(1)	(1)	(1)	0.2	0.1	(1)	1.4	5.6	(1)	(1)	0.1	(1)	25
1.9	0.3	0.7	3.2	0.3	(1)	0.1	0.1	1.3	2.2	(1)	(1)	(1)	0.2	0.1	(1)	0.2	3.8	(1)	(1)	1.2	0.1	26
4.6	4.3	1.2	10.0	0.2	0.1	0.9	0.1	1.6	7.8	0.2	(1)	0.1	0.5	0.2	0.1	0.2	3.4	(1)	0.1	1.8	0.1	27
1.6	1.9	0.2	22.5	(1)	0.8	1.4	(1)	0.3	0.1	(1)	(1)	0.1	0.2	0.1	0.1	1.2	10.8	(1)	(1)	(1)	(1)	28
1.4	0.7	0.6	13.6	(1)	1.3	0.2	0.1	0.5	0.5	(1)	(1)	0.1	0.3	0.1	(1)	0.6	4.8	(1)	(1)	0.1	(1)	29
3.0	0.5	0.5	10.4	0.1	(1)	0.2	(1)	1.0	2.4	(1)	(1)	0.1	0.3	0.1	0.4	0.2	3.6	(1)	(1)	1.7	(1)	30
4.7	0.6	1.9	10.9	0.1	0.1	0.3	(1)	0.6	3.0	0.2	(1)	(1)	0.2	(1)	(1)	0.5	4.3	(1)	0.1	12.4	0.1	31
3.1	1.1	0.1	11.3	0.5	0.3	0.6	(1)	1.4	20.8	0.7	0.1	(1)	(1)	0.2	(1)	0.1	2.2	(1)	0.3	0.3	0.1	32
3.5	1.9	0.3	24.0	2.1	0.2	0.5	(1)	0.9	9.2	0.2	0.1	(1)	0.1	0.3	(1)	0.1	1.7	0.1	0.7	0.1	0.2	33
1.8	0.7	0.1	17.6	0.1	0.4	0.3	0.3	4.1	12.8	0.4	(1)	0.2	0.7	1.2	0.3	0.5	5.4	0.1	1.2	0.2	0.6	34
2.9	4.1	0.4	17.1	0.2	0.8	0.5	0.2	5.7	7.7	0.8	1.0	0.5	1.7	0.7	0.2	0.3	5.8	0.1	1.3	0.3	0.5	35
8.2	10.1	4.5	6.3	1.2	0.5	1.0	0.2	5.1	22.8	2.5	(1)	0.1	2.0	0.1	(1)	0.1	1.5	(1)	0.2	0.1	0.1	36
2.0	0.9	0.4	12.8	0.4	0.2	0.4	0.2	7.6	6.2	0.2	0.2	0.1	8.1	0.9	0.3	0.2	8.9	0.1	1.2	0.4	0.6	37
3.1	0.9	0.3	18.0	0.1	0.8	0.4	0.2	8.8	5.3	0.3	0.1	0.1	6.0	1.0	0.2	0.4	3.8	(1)	1.6	0.3	0.3	38
2.4	1.5	0.5	20.8	0.4	0.3	0.7	0.2	8.9	4.2	0.8	0.3	0.2	2.9	0.9	0.1	0.3	5.5	0.1	1.3	0.3	0.4	39
1.0	0.7	0.2	2.3	(1)	0.6	0.9	(1)	2.6	8.8	7.6	0.4	0.1	1.0	0.2	0.1	0.5	7.2	0.1	35.6	0.3	0.5	40
2.9	3.5	1.1	8.9	0.2	0.2	0.6	0.2	1.3	6.3	0.2	(1)	0.1	1.0	0.1	(1)	0.2	2.8	(1)	0.3	0.4	0.1	41
2.5	2.1	0.2	14.5	(1)	0.2	0.6	0.1	3.1	13.3	0.1	(1)	0.1	0.8	0.2	0.1	0.3	6.0	0.1	0.5	1.1	0.4	42
3.2	2.1	0.9	8.8	0.1	0.4	0.7	0.2	5.1	15.2	0.4	(1)	0.1	2.7	0.2	0.1	0.3	4.7	(1)	2.2	0.8	0.6	43
1.6	0.6	2.6	9.8	0.1	0.7	0.4	(1)	2.5	21.9	0.7	0.1	(1)	6.9	3.0	....	0.4	4.5	0.1	1.4	1.3	0.6	44
4.5	0.8	0.8	4.7	0.2	0.1	0.4	0.1	2.0	9.3	0.2	(1)	(1)	1.5	0.5	(1)	0.4	5.9	0.1	0.3	2.0	0.2	45
1.6	0.7	0.7	4.2	(1)	0.3	0.2	0.1	1.3	35.0	2.8	0.2	0.1	2.1	0.6	0.1	0.3	2.2	(1)	2.6	5.4	2.5	46
3.4	0.8	0.5	12.4	0.3	0.2	0.2	0.3	1.5	5.2	0.3	(1)	(1)	1.7	0.4	0.1	0.3	5.8	(1)	0.1	17.0	0.2	47
1.8	0.3	0.2	1.9	(1)	0.1	0.1	(1)	0.5	2.2	0.3	(1)	(1)	0.4	0.2	0.1	(1)	1.1	(1)	(1)	69.2	0.1	48
3.5	1.0	4.0	5.4	0.1	3.7	0.4	0.3	1.5	4.0	0.1	(1)	0.1	0.2	0.7	0.9	2.3	13.1	0.1	(1)	0.2	0.1	49
1.9	0.6	1.1	3.6	(1)	2.4	0.3	0.1	1.8	3.2	3.5	0.1	(1)	0.1	1.2	2.9	1.2	11.0	0.1	(1)	3.0	0.1	50
4.5	1.3	4.5	5.6	0.1	3.2	0.3	0.3	4.7	7.3	0.5	0.1	0.2	0.3	0.7	3.9	0.3	5.1	(1)	0.1	6.8	0.1	51
4.8	1.0	1.8	14.0	0.1	0.7	0.3	0.3	1.5	10.6	0.2	(1)	0.1	0.2	0.2	1.5	0.4	6.1	(1)	0.1	9.3	0.2	52
1.4	0.4	1.8	0.9	(1)	0.2	(1)	0.1	1.0	5.6	0.7	0.1	(1)	0.4	0.7	0.1	0.7	2.3	(1)	0.1	68.0	0.1	53
0.6	0.3	1.4	1.0	(1)	0.5	0.1	0.1	0.4	1.6	1.3	(1)	0.1	0.4	0.9	0.5	0.1	2.3	(1)	0.1	76.4	0.1	54
1.7	0.3	1.4	1.2	(1)	1.3	0.1	0.1	5.1	5.4	0.4	(1)	0.1	0.3	0.4	4.0	0.7	2.4	(1)	(1)	2.0	0.1	55
1.2	0.2	4.3	0.8	(1)	1.1	0.1	0.1	3.9	16.5	7.4	0.9	0.1	3.3	4.1	0.7	0.7	6.7	(1)	(1)	7.4	0.2	56
2.4	0.4	1.3	4.2	0.2	4.5	0.2	0.2	1.6	4.1	0.2	0.1	0.1	0.1	0.7	4.9	1.0	15.3	0.1	(1)	0.2	0.1	57
2.6	0.8	1.1	6.5	0.1	5.6	0.3	0.2	1.8	4.0	0.5	0.1	0.1	0.2	2.0	2.9	0.6	12.2	(1)	0.1	0.6	0.1	58
1.8	0.7	1.0	3.6	(1)	0.9	0.3	0.1	1.4	11.7	1.5	3.2	0.8	0.2	2.6	6.8	0.3	7.6	(1)	0.2	11.7	0.5	59

2 Except possessions of the United States.

TABLE 75.—COUNTRY OF BIRTH OF FOREIGN-BORN POPULATION,

	CITY.	Total foreign born: 1920	NORTHWESTERN EUROPE.								
			England.	Scotland.	Wales.	Ireland.	Norway.	Sweden.	Denmark.	Netherlands.	Belgium.
1	Akron, Ohio	38,021	2,605	729	341	863	145	725	205	166	51
2	Albany, N.Y.	17,695	1,057	315	27	3,139	32	127	75	308	16
3	Atlanta, Ga	4,789	478	143	22	208	21	85	29	17	9
4	Baltimore, Md.	84,309	3,195	736	196	5,074	421	417	245	193	80
5	Birmingham, Ala.	6,140	753	445	64	230	19	92	31	13	20
6	Boston, Mass.	242,619	12,540	5,079	279	57,011	1,875	6,780	935	691	580
7	Bridgeport, Conn.	46,782	3,492	843	54	4,300	178	1,783	403	69	41
8	Buffalo, N.Y.	121,824	6,712	1,984	212	7,264	325	1,143	308	435	73
9	Cambridge, Mass.	33,296	1,608	822	62	8,448	185	1,106	92	20	28
10	Camden, N.J.	20,354	1,690	359	99	1,420	205	198	65	28	24
11	Chicago, Ill.	808,558	26,438	9,910	1,584	56,786	20,481	58,563	11,268	8,843	3,079
12	Cincinnati, Ohio	42,921	1,636	414	135	3,887	36	115	96	314	36
13	Cleveland, Ohio	240,173	11,101	3,418	1,161	9,478	596	2,286	620	1,039	102
14	Columbus, Ohio	16,187	1,111	281	438	1,286	35	132	47	53	69
15	Dallas, Tex.	8,801	663	159	21	328	74	169	97	28	25
16	Dayton, Ohio	13,165	573	183	29	682	29	66	23	55	12
17	Denver, Colo	38,230	3,557	1,090	430	3,221	536	3,953	922	416	60
18	Des Moines, Iowa	11,269	1,266	338	205	643	393	1,853	528	113	35
19	Detroit, Mich.	290,884	17,195	6,933	548	7,004	861	2,659	1,505	1,861	6,219
20	Fall River, Mass.	42,421	7,971	600	60	3,201	30	63	33	6	27
21	Fort Worth, Tex.	7,502	326	111	12	300	63	174	30	11	10
22	Grand Rapids, Mich.	28,427	868	214	20	628	165	883	201	11,422	47
23	Hartford, Conn.	40,912	2,051	937	28	6,116	100	2,315	619	35	17
24	Houston, Tex.	12,088	737	173	22	373	59	159	115	56	20
25	Indianapolis, Ind.	17,096	1,193	445	48	2,414	51	182	234	149	22
26	Jersey City, N.J.	76,294	3,505	1,460	131	12,451	1,211	1,076	392	274	171
27	Kansas City, Kans.	11,721	530	127	88	766	51	625	196	26	153
28	Kansas City, Mo.	27,583	1,926	658	136	2,584	183	1,899	437	107	402
29	Los Angeles, Calif.	122,131	11,485	2,802	657	4,932	1,669	4,998	2,003	797	405
30	Louisville, Ky.	11,667	502	155	22	1,576	27	68	38	36	22
31	Lowell, Mass.	38,116	3,616	916	28	7,454	68	523	38	17	197
32	Memphis, Tenn.	5,844	476	130	11	455	16	117	52	15	12
33	Milwaukee, Wis.	110,160	1,970	589	252	1,447	1,852	863	732	528	109
34	Minneapolis, Minn.	88,248	2,964	1,141	232	2,066	16,389	26,515	2,531	407	112
35	Nashville, Tenn.	2,412	230	50	2	288	11	13	15	5	6
36	New Bedford, Mass.	51,078	9,757	541	44	2,027	71	263	55	15	128
37	New Haven, Conn.	46,124	1,957	858	69	7,219	161	1,266	246	43	119
38	New Orleans, La.	27,365	1,227	286	33	1,534	458	317	227	149	101
39	New York, N.Y.	2,028,160	71,613	21,545	1,510	203,450	24,500	33,703	9,092	4,750	3,467
40	Bronx borough.	267,742	8,639	2,511	137	18,679	974	3,108	797	471	234
41	Brooklyn borough.	666,188	25,067	7,534	421	53,660	17,505	15,488	4,201	1,672	726
42	Manhattan borough.	950,264	29,925	8,687	783	116,749	3,595	11,841	2,942	2,164	2,132
43	Queens borough.	112,171	6,065	2,060	107	10,618	844	2,373	795	329	284
44	Richmond borough.	31,795	1,917	753	62	3,744	1,582	893	357	114	91
45	Newark, N.J.	117,549	5,397	2,170	116	8,840	179	833	374	272	72
46	Norfolk, Va.	6,998	512	160	20	338	193	218	93	118	26
47	Oakland, Calif.	49,895	4,539	1,700	766	3,656	1,163	2,663	1,764	309	126
48	Omaha, Nebr.	35,645	1,465	565	61	1,904	388	3,708	2,875	126	263
49	Paterson, N.J.	45,242	3,665	1,861	32	3,200	25	121	69	3,604	815
50	Philadelphia, Pa.	400,744	30,886	8,425	973	64,590	1,255	2,651	1,131	480	517
51	Pittsburgh, Pa.	120,792	7,381	2,758	1,512	13,989	100	1,049	104	90	107
52	Portland, Oreg.	49,778	4,021	1,809	274	1,969	2,915	5,060	1,365	365	293
53	Providence, R.I.	69,895	8,747	1,735	89	11,900	291	2,709	146	64	141
54	Reading, Pa.	9,573	334	83	53	233	16	25	9	17	3
55	Richmond, Va.	4,713	498	191	20	264	21	42	27	17	17
56	Rochester, N.Y.	71,411	5,930	1,142	09	4,005	07	117	174	1,891	414
57	St. Louis, Mo.	100,020	6,001	1,000	151	0,911	167	808	413	401	363
58	St. Paul, Minn.	51,722	1,937	712	73	3,053	3,818	9,912	1,364	256	78
59	Salt Lake City, Utah.	19,897	5,526	977	416	574	870	2,258	1,611	874	18
60	San Antonio, Tex.	36,824	796	138	9	509	53	94	82	59	70
61	San Francisco, Calif.	149,195	10,119	3,569	445	18,257	3,121	6,468	3,389	788	548
62	Scranton, Pa.	28,587	2,313	480	2,714	3,365	3	78	21	9	13
63	Seattle, Wash.	80,976	7,807	3,195	673	3,455	9,119	10,253	2,228	525	541
64	Spokane, Wash.	17,096	1,613	570	134	717	1,533	2,580	477	183	55
65	Springfield, Mass.	31,461	1,952	1,309	32	5,600	92	1,221	84	38	34
66	Syracuse, N.Y.	32,383	2,321	467	93	3,814	45	166	73	61	22
67	Toledo, Ohio	38,296	1,820	365	78	1,513	92	273	177	77	130
68	Trenton, N.J.	30,168	2,775	511	35	1,871	15	85	58	20	18
69	Washington, D.C.	29,365	3,001	793	106	4,320	219	481	237	127	76
70	Wilmington, Del.	16,337	1,032	276	27	2,435	48	223	45	15	14
71	Worcester, Mass.	53,527	3,345	936	36	9,048	334	7,751	227	69	27
72	Yonkers, N.Y.	25,796	1,798	1,259	64	4,140	137	362	95	104	23
73	Youngstown, Ohio.	33,945	2,537	1,024	1,103	1,578	51	769	47	45	12

FOR CITIES HAVING 100,000 INHABITANTS OR MORE: 1920.

NORTHWESTERN EUROPE—con.			CENTRAL EUROPE.						EASTERN EUROPE.				
Luxemburg.	Switzerland.	France.	Germany.	Poland.	Czecho-slovakia.	Austria.	Hungary.	Jugo-Slavia.	Russia.	Lithuania.	Finland.	Rumania.	
4	411	566	2,867	1,420	463	5,344	6,989	1,537	3,056	230	82	569	1
16	60	158	3,068	1,414	97	338	87	24	2,277	161	18	60	2
1	41	124	431	479	42	79	102	9	1,207	42	13	32	3
7	296	570	17,461	11,109	2,985	2,896	1,393	251	23,202	2,038	114	459	4
....	35	186	458	93	14	134	47	15	706	6	3	29	5
11	358	1,271	5,915	7,650	256	1,530	360	135	38,021	4,127	562	673	6
6	137	224	1,979	3,061	2,227	2,697	6,230	193	5,395	698	86	234	7
39	593	2,039	20,898	31,406	514	2,945	2,736	361	6,557	80	163	581	8
....	22	129	418	1,486	27	111	38	7	1,759	1,346	50	81	9
10	90	178	2,320	4,172	85	690	197	172	2,158	183	107	80	10
1,967	3,452	4,569	112,288	137,611	50,392	30,491	26,106	9,693	102,095	18,923	1,577	5,137	11
24	603	1,281	17,833	1,220	300	1,526	2,873	763	4,198	89	13	687	12
68	1,216	1,201	26,476	35,024	23,907	15,228	29,724	15,898	21,502	2,776	1,122	4,377	13
4	354	273	4,098	287	100	713	878	172	1,848	29	64	132	14
4	165	155	1,175	357	217	248	56	28	939	2	8	100	15
5	127	231	4,119	674	195	602	1,921	411	1,124	250	14	176	16
21	509	541	4,664	812	301	1,390	487	238	5,333	34	110	277	17
9	75	116	1,104	325	62	232	50	31	1,389	42	11	88	18
80	889	1,741	30,238	56,624	3,351	10,674	13,564	3,702	27,278	2,653	1,785	4,668	19
....	6	124	135	2,525	13	260	7	19	1,661	1	27	28	20
....	39	64	459	126	120	192	18	41	613	2	1	36	21
10	53	87	2,433	4,269	110	534	155	6	1,046	1,120	102	66	22
10	101	215	1,820	4,880	179	919	272	83	7,654	1,260	80	347	23
3	101	174	1,619	284	164	479	89	22	1,096	4	13	111	24
5	231	332	5,097	378	58	568	313	558	1,309	19	30	701	25
17	486	785	11,113	12,145	400	3,772	1,258	69	7,016	218	787	301	26
5	80	77	1,171	958	383	961	106	1,419	1,076	53	4	18	27
16	352	423	3,958	944	161	749	335	168	3,848	32	35	191	28
92	1,303	2,685	10,563	2,205	826	2,089	1,706	1,453	9,691	84	530	927	29
7	620	384	4,748	343	34	246	99	17	1,413	10	6	57	30
1	5	90	133	2,298	3	65	19	155	916	787	30	17	31
1	65	117	798	290	15	159	82	10	993	....	10	35	32
164	931	565	39,771	23,060	4,497	5,906	4,803	4,164	7,105	398	147	633	33
163	336	354	6,439	4,789	1,828	2,222	571	163	6,222	186	1,120	1,484	34
1	90	73	286	185	12	67	130	10	493	....	4	32	35
....	49	438	463	2,902	181	186	49	21	1,022	48	13	17	36
....	120	226	2,770	3,009	100	675	421	26	8,080	721	91	198	37
3	242	2,833	3,418	230	55	484	81	78	1,348	6	85	71	38
302	9,233	23,085	194,155	145,679	26,437	126,739	64,393	5,271	479,800	7,475	10,240	38,139	39
33	1,255	2,122	29,719	19,008	1,878	23,638	10,644	332	87,345	465	1,309	8,519	40
51	1,765	3,808	56,778	51,928	2,639	31,981	8,795	1,088	189,421	4,985	3,219	12,109	41
158	4,802	14,411	70,837	64,514	18,681	65,603	40,644	3,350	193,778	1,521	4,885	16,714	42
56	1,172	2,243	32,446	7,778	2,958	4,678	3,555	353	7,627	485	455	734	43
4	239	441	4,375	2,451	281	839	755	148	1,629	19	372	63	44
15	613	1,087	14,041	13,702	2,158	7,897	4,278	269	19,968	1,549	80	1,307	45
2	18	60	325	194	15	74	44	17	1,878	20	99	51	46
14	631	1,457	4,662	503	170	986	388	866	1,062	23	390	96	47
19	219	171	4,270	2,374	4,305	1,610	534	351	3,825	89	26	288	48
10	1,363	1,100	3,509	5,736	211	754	616	46	4,400	367	13	53	49
47	1,889	3,886	39,766	31,112	2,240	13,387	11,513	1,099	95,744	4,392	727	5,645	50
52	816	1,661	16,028	15,537	3,607	10,072	4,323	3,784	13,837	2,242	109	1,493	51
44	1,283	529	5,384	909	330	1,599	519	472	5,161	57	1,394	258	52
5	83	389	1,392	2,289	91	719	98	33	5,610	659	83	287	53
2	45	69	1,448	2,542	238	684	135	71	843	54	....	13	54
....	32	89	641	140	32	128	42	2	1,054	8	2	39	55
15	467	757	10,735	4,590	70	1,536	398	177	6,871	766	38	146	56
70	2,105	1,873	30,089	5,224	3,479	5,587	6,637	1,686	13,067	292	39	1,200	57
264	522	330	8,724	2,555	1,797	2,429	1,792	334	4,228	224	97	559	58
10	610	133	2,033	132	48	213	93	56	430	1	75	47	59
6	140	477	2,564	249	108	311	68	25	732	3	6	75	60
97	2,806	6,909	18,514	2,152	757	3,694	1,390	1,320	5,752	60	1,810	765	61
....	140	112	2,612	3,267	117	2,863	888	52	3,415	1,948	9	42	62
59	542	717	4,827	881	302	1,412	350	654	3,349	155	2,256	150	63
22	211	179	1,992	154	100	288	89	113	508	15	157	68	64
3	87	179	1,152	2,442	111	410	115	22	3,852	110	180	52	65
10	238	318	4,751	4,571	155	868	145	67	2,791	43	30	52	66
24	735	594	8,476	10,283	349	1,063	3,041	136	2,069	53	31	272	67
9	74	174	2,388	4,423	1,599	1,010	4,042	501	2,710	105	11	395	68
13	358	688	3,382	716	122	525	219	43	5,181	38	104	86	69
5	52	140	1,150	3,742	34	473	162	25	1,982	77	46	101	70
1	17	119	467	3,632	15	189	25	23	4,778	4,220	2,175	53	71
4	111	228	2,102	2,568	736	2,917	1,162	98	1,987	31	65	57	72
10	120	131	1,469	2,601	2,096	3,160	2,684	2,579	2,214	115	22	1,375	73

TABLE 75.—COUNTRY OF BIRTH OF FOREIGN-BORN POPULATION,

CITY.	EASTERN EUROPE—con.		SOUTHERN EUROPE.						ASIA.			
	Bulgaria.	Turkey in Europe.	Greece.	Albania.	Italy.	Spain.	Portugal.	Other Europe.[1]	Armenia.	Palestine.	Syria.	Turkey in Asia.
1 Akron, Ohio	390	15	1,939	135	3,614	281	14	11	146	17	451	139
2 Albany, N. Y.	8	38	190	30	3,403	20	1	11	21	1	84	16
3 Atlanta, Ga.	....	17	434	....	98	19	4	48	9	5	103	30
4 Baltimore, Md.	16	14	695	1	7,911	150	57	49	30	12	15	19
5 Birmingham, Ala.	4	2	441	....	1,653	10	....	7	14	13	272	2
6 Boston, Mass.	19	102	3,054	292	38,179	326	1,159	20	1,472	86	1,756	238
7 Bridgeport, Conn.	9	13	802	50	8,789	384	188	1	195	11	82	68
8 Buffalo, N. Y.	47	56	574	37	16,411	144	17	151	62	30	311	55
9 Cambridge, Mass.	2	13	352	20	2,730	39	1,957	....	401	....	59	22
10 Camden, N. J.	6	5	77	....	4,994	8	9	11	52	2	38	1
11 Chicago, Ill.	385	101	11,546	27	59,215	380	41	249	1,028	206	478	392
12 Cincinnati, Ohio	55	186	312	5	2,717	39	10	35	34	17	265	16
13 Cleveland, Ohio	332	66	1,605	39	18,288	162	15	133	426	74	787	80
14 Columbus, Ohio	29	2	415	3	2,290	16	3	4	14	5	62	11
15 Dallas, Tex.	11	5	274	....	583	37	....	7	7	12	46	11
16 Dayton, Ohio	19	63	355	12	514	9	....	8	9	1	79	11
17 Denver, Colo.	78	1	768	4	2,872	85	10	20	22	21	44	19
18 Des Moines, Iowa	4	2	230	....	1,177	2	1	3	12	11	61	2
19 Detroit, Mich.	883	82	4,628	156	16,205	262	48	574	1,361	122	1,877	421
20 Fall River, Mass.	....	2	149	....	945	9	5,675	....	5	4	582	4
21 Forth Worth, Tex.	8	19	240	....	156	49	....	1	....	3	28	8
22 Grand Rapids, Mich.	7	2	60	1	525	5	3	19	50	5	301	11
23 Hartford, Conn.	4	16	321	2	7,101	24	167	4	297	20	21	45
24 Houston, Tex.	5	2	177	....	1,290	25	8	6	16	12	173	26
25 Indianapolis, Ind.	110	15	564	13	754	24	2	9	30	9	149	77
26 Jersey City, N. J.	16	14	357	5	14,855	228	22	11	107	11	19	25
27 Kansas City, Kans.	11	3	273	....	104	14	....	4	2	1	2	8
28 Kansas City, Mo.	31	2	570	1	3,318	47	2	17	17	8	153	22
29 Los Angeles, Calif.	59	70	1,036	4	7,931	811	144	88	452	44	346	166
30 Louisville, Ky.	....	1	81	....	535	17	2	19	7	5	123	2
31 Lowell, Mass.	7	8	3,733	7	431	9	1,669	8	357	....	93	63
32 Memphis, Tenn.	....	....	280	....	1,273	4	4	6	1	10	12	3
33 Milwaukee, Wis.	53	14	1,815	44	4,023	43	7	239	134	21	133	73
34 Minneapolis, Minn.	83	5	873	1	766	17	1	11	52	16	240	26
35 Nashville, Tenn.	....	....	97	1	91	4	....	5	4	6	39	2
36 New Bedford, Mass.	13	4	588	280	631	37	7,609	1	14	8	300	31
37 New Haven, Conn.	6	5	314	2	15,084	35	154	5	138	10	46	24
38 New Orleans, La.	2	6	432	2	7,633	1,150	99	60	18	5	129	25
39 New York, N. Y.	308	1,754	21,455	103	390,832	11,140	1,088	425	3,779	913	4,485	2,715
40 Bronx borough	34	102	957	....	39,519	259	39	54	419	113	102	154
41 Brooklyn borough	63	125	2,700	8	138,245	2,922	505	107	746	351	3,405	468
42 Manhattan borough	201	1,507	17,209	91	184,546	7,638	457	218	2,168	423	923	2,039
43 Queens borough	8	14	401	3	19,794	157	45	35	421	22	42	37
44 Richmond borough	2	6	188	1	8,728	164	42	11	25	4	13	17
45 Newark, N. J.	4	17	1,039	....	27,465	555	408	22	179	48	94	35
46 Norfolk, Va.	3	17	667	2	515	196	199	20	16	8	120	14
47 Oakland, Calif.	6	12	928	2	5,094	499	4,286	12	49	5	75	11
48 Omaha, Nebr.	36	3	423	3	3,108	19	1	14	112	2	185	14
49 Paterson, N. J.	1	7	283	1	11,566	60	....	4	344	6	752	70
50 Philadelphia, Pa.	47	81	1,814	260	63,723	648	252	55	1,393	118	426	202
51 Pittsburgh, Pa.	49	17	1,363	24	15,371	54	4	65	42	42	706	32
52 Portland, Oreg.	113	6	896	3	2,847	74	14	15	28	5	134	23
53 Providence, R. I.	17	20	432	4	19,239	32	1,823	2	1,234	7	265	138
54 Reading, Pa.	....	1	579	....	1,810	34	2	1	5	3	1	10
55 Richmond, Va.	....	8	208	....	555	5	9	5	92	9	143	8
56 Rochester, N. Y.	22	30	410	7	19,468	36	141	11	46	23	121	143
57 St. Louis, Mo.	08	35	2,010	102	0,067	241	7	20	122	20	460	41
58 St. Paul, Minn	10	7	354	1	1,685	7	1	11	62	4	363	25
59 Salt Lake City, Utah	1	4	548	5	496	50	....	15	13	2	94	5
60 San Antonio, Tex.	4	3	145	....	575	170	7	11	10	2	136	4
61 San Francisco, Calif.	92	40	3,205	26	23,924	2,503	826	383	234	35	216	124
62 Scranton, Pa.	1	....	161	....	3,433	2	....	7	5	11	205	2
63 Seattle, Wash.	62	184	1,400	72	3,094	168	23	28	74	3	114	206
64 Spokane, Wash.	32	1	107	....	922	7	....	4	12	2	26	1
65 Springfield, Mass.	7	12	939	14	4,491	15	52	1	237	4	380	68
66 Syracuse, N. Y.	26	26	433	8	6,756	20	3	95	116	17	122	19
67 Toledo, Ohio	683	98	682	2	850	18	1	18	99	14	432	58
68 Trenton, N. J.	....	4	127	1	6,617	14	18	19	27	10	65	14
69 Washington, D. C.	5	72	1,207	8	3,764	111	14	17	63	19	211	62
70 Wilmington, Del.	....	3	267	....	3,444	96	18	7	5	4	1	5
71 Worcester, Mass.	3	62	720	461	4,296	7	32	2	1,225	1	688	158
72 Yonkers, N. Y.	2	2	121	....	4,507	25	7	....	77	....	62	13
73 Youngstown, Ohio	117	36	1,297	13	5,538	83	....	11	9	13	277	21

[1] Comprises Danzig, Fiume, Saar Basin, and "Europe, not specified."

FOR CITIES HAVING 100,000 INHABITANTS OR MORE: 1920—Continued.

China.	Japan.	India.	Other Asia.	Canada. French.	Canada. Other.	Newfoundland.	West Indies.[2]	Mexico.	Central and So. America.	Africa.	Australia.	Atlantic Islands.	Pacific Islands.[2]	Country not specified.	Born at sea.	
81	4	10	16	76	1,075	21	55	85	31	23	12	.....	2	3	7	1
34	4	7	2	244	600	12	34	6	29	6	10	2	2	.....	6	2
22	.....	2	4	17	266	10	41	9	13	12	9	1	2	.....	.....	3
253	20	12	12	75	1,087	28	633	55	164	46	31	25	21	2	38	4
13	.....	4	3	5	197	1	42	33	7	10	7	2	.....	1	4	5
743	67	48	18	1,743	40,868	2,799	1,955	60	254	84	75	494	25	7	37	6
86	5	5	8	398	1,072	42	86	3	30	25	17	69	3	2	9	7
70	12	17	22	177	15,739	61	130	65	93	53	44	9	11	22	36	8
61	15	12	14	949	6,959	472	922	3	51	9	20	360	6	.....	3	9
43	.....	2	1	23	223	199	52	.....	30	9	8	9	10	1	11	10
1,647	346	126	815	2,432	23,960	194	773	1,224	617	292	360	32	75	136	228	11
30	13	7	4	27	810	4	96	19	42	14	17	4	5	16	43	12
186	32	13	55	282	8,442	71	252	111	149	50	73	9	11	59	51	13
65	5	5	18	45	643	4	58	13	33	8	10	7	1	5	9	14
9	38	6	1	17	358	6	22	2,295	10	12	9	1	1	.....	5	15
14	5	3	2	20	437	2	26	35	15	5	6	2	.....	6	6	16
147	397	18	12	129	2,983	26	71	1,418	67	25	49	7	15	8	12	17
31	1	5	9	18	572	1	16	158	21	3	12	2	2	.....	5	18
268	84	86	104	3,678	56,024	137	422	725	257	112	173	13	36	26	88	19
40	2	8	1	10,734	862	17	15	6	109	12	8	6,428	.....	.....	7	20
68	25	4	1	16	240	2	8	3,831	12	5	10	.....	2	15	3	21
33	5	1	12	91	2,767	8	19	20	12	10	7	2	1	1	10	22
122	7	7	86	857	1,532	61	65	4	27	13	10	46	8	1	6	23
4	22	3	4	22	336	5	53	3,953	28	8	14	1	6	5	11	24
63	12	5	10	36	726	6	41	29	18	6	18	3	8	7	15	25
71	2	7	6	51	914	54	278	32	92	23	14	21	7	1	13	26
4	33	1	5	14	272	4	16	2,043	10	6	9	.....	1	3	5	27
30	54	7	13	57	1,591	13	45	1,920	49	15	30	3	4	6	14	28
1,272	8,536	101	111	554	13,223	75	287	21,653	385	135	403	42	212	36	53	29
17	3	5	3	19	282	9	22	9	19	7	18	.....	4	11	17	30
59	.....	2	5	10,180	3,610	30	17	4	18	10	9	402	1	2	6	31
30	4	6	1	21	255	.....	30	18	8	6	4	2	.....	2	5	32
36	2	7	18	223	1,839	26	39	66	51	14	37	4	8	623	82	33
134	39	15	10	1,016	6,455	6	39	50	43	28	30	2	8	4	44	34
.....	2	.....	1	3	102	.....	14	6	18	7	2	.....	.....	.....	5	35
47	.....	11	1	9,833	1,171	27	203	2	209	26	5	11,729	1	1	6	36
76	15	14	4	399	990	37	279	4	56	8	15	5	5	5	11	37
162	35	50	3	70	545	12	1,136	1,306	1,072	48	44	18	8	1	28	38
4,001	2,073	413	498	1,757	23,825	1,404	36,480	2,572	7,777	1,238	1,041	961	229	108	208	39
104	45	14	35	164	2,094	90	944	75	309	93	84	62	10	25	25	40
702	220	87	164	442	7,740	827	8,140	486	1,739	402	304	220	57	39	73	41
3,007	1,750	283	286	893	11,631	324	26,472	1,913	5,448	674	557	630	146	27	87	42
129	43	20	6	199	1,618	108	618	68	162	55	75	36	12	11	17	43
59	15	9	7	59	742	55	306	30	119	14	21	13	4	6	6	44
227	12	15	26	108	1,244	45	366	43	149	23	62	75	5	40	26	45
83	30	5	4	23	315	10	125	17	71	8	13	33	3	2	4	46
2,605	1,931	48	24	177	3,623	16	168	1,033	321	59	391	348	201	15	22	47
92	66	6	7	65	1,179	17	32	746	19	10	10	3	1	26	10	48
41	4	5	16	45	281	3	31	10	49	23	23	36	1	3	7	49
709	105	66	118	209	4,035	243	2,181	485	667	140	184	96	25	22	85	50
215	20	11	8	45	1,488	94	230	28	99	32	41	3	5	12	41	51
1,244	1,345	54	11	285	6,173	33	48	104	47	37	115	9	70	7	28	52
98	12	11	20	3,436	3,621	84	126	7	131	20	23	1,510	10	1	12	53
5	2	1	2	4	57	.....	21	101	7	1	2	.....	.....	4	3	54
24	7	2	5	7	221	7	50	4	12	10	7	2	3	.....	4	55
30	7	10	3	188	9,338	28	50	11	50	19	16	15	3	5	15	56
243	35	18	8	93	1,871	14	145	439	114	53	49	3	9	15	75	57
63	8	13	12	587	3,330	14	30	70	17	20	17	4	4	7	29	58
120	326	8	2	25	731	2	7	217	13	43	102	3	48	1	59	59
117	12	7	1	51	349	1	67	28,477	51	6	24	2	2	6	10	60
4,497	4,198	103	149	346	6,757	80	372	3,810	1,848	194	1,634	201	557	29	82	61
6	1	1	.....	11	201	3	18	14	11	15	6	.....	1	3	8	62
921	6,016	49	106	630	13,257	176	131	122	126	50	321	9	122	21	41	63
121	134	11	3	144	3,701	12	8	12	18	14	18	2	11	1	14	64
105	2	5	3	3,719	2,087	56	94	7	41	15	9	8	4	.....	9	65
10	2	5	.....	357	3,142	6	39	10	26	6	12	4	9	4	9	66
37	16	4	4	392	2,822	15	59	243	30	11	10	5	4	17	21	67
40	1	1	8	57	204	6	38	20	28	6	3	1	1	1	6	68
345	97	23	11	147	1,579	18	365	73	186	54	25	17	7	13	17	69
23	4	.....	1	17	208	1	37	44	19	9	9	1	5	.....	5	70
61	4	3	8	4,292	3,851	53	41	1	33	7	4	11	4	.....	12	71
26	20	12	91	45	532	13	85	14	47	9	17	11	6	2	2	72
53	1	19	11	16	504	1	52	66	24	12	6	.....	2	13	8	73

[2] Except possessions of the United States.

TABLE 76.—PER CENT DISTRIBUTION OF FOREIGN-BORN POPULATION BY

	CITY.	PER CENT OF TOTAL FOREIGN BORN IN SPECIFIED CITY. Northwestern Europe.												Central Europe.		
		England.	Scotland.	Wales.	Ireland.	Norway.	Sweden.	Denmark.	Netherlands.	Belgium.	Luxemburg.	Switzerland.	France.	Germany.	Poland.	Czecho-slovakia.
1	Akron, Ohio	6.9	1.9	0.9	2.3	0.4	1.9	0.5	0.4	0.1	(1)	1.1	1.5	7.5	3.7	1.2
2	Albany, N. Y	6.0	1.8	0.2	17.7	0.2	0.7	0.4	1.7	0.1	0.1	0.3	0.9	17.3	8.0	0.5
3	Atlanta, Ga	10.0	3.0	0.5	4.3	0.4	1.8	0.6	0.4	0.2	(1)	0.9	2.6	9.0	10.0	0.9
4	Baltimore, Md	3.8	0.9	0.2	6.0	0.5	0.5	0.3	0.2	0.1	(1)	0.3	0.7	20.6	13.1	3.5
5	Birmingham, Ala	12.3	7.2	1.0	3.7	0.3	1.5	0.5	0.2	0.3	....	0.6	3.0	7.5	1.5	0.2
6	Boston, Mass	5.2	2.1	0.1	23.5	0.8	2.8	0.4	0.3	0.2	(1)	0.1	0.5	2.4	3.2	0.1
7	Bridgeport, Conn	7.5	1.8	0.1	9.2	0.4	3.8	0.9	0.1	0.1	(1)	0.3	0.5	4.2	6.5	4.8
8	Buffalo, N. Y	5.5	1.6	0.2	6.0	0.3	0.9	0.3	0.4	0.1	(1)	0.5	1.7	17.2	25.8	0.4
9	Cambridge, Mass	4.8	2.5	0.2	25.4	0.6	3.3	0.3	0.1	0.1		0.1	0.4	1.3	4.5	0.1
10	Camden, N. J	8.3	1.8	0.5	7.0	1.0	1.0	0.3	0.1	0.1	(1)	0.4	0.9	11.4	20.5	0.4
11	Chicago, Ill	3.3	1.2	0.2	7.0	2.5	7.2	1.4	1.1	0.4	0.2	0.4	0.6	13.9	17.0	6.2
12	Cincinnati, Ohio	3.8	1.0	0.3	9.1	0.1	0.3	0.2	0.7	0.1	0.1	1.4	3.0	41.5	2.8	0.7
13	Cleveland, Ohio	4.6	1.4	0.5	3.9	0.2	1.0	0.3	0.4	(1)	0.1	0.5	0.5	11.0	14.6	10.0
14	Columbus, Ohio	6.9	1.7	2.7	7.9	0.2	0.8	0.3	0.3	0.4	(1)	2.2	1.7	25.3	1.8	0.6
15	Dallas, Tex	7.5	1.8	0.2	3.7	0.8	1.9	1.1	0.3	0.3	(1)	1.9	1.8	13.4	4.1	2.5
16	Dayton, Ohio	4.4	1.4	0.2	5.2	0.2	0.5	0.2	0.4	0.1	(1)	1.0	1.8	31.3	5.1	1.5
17	Denver, Colo	9.3	2.9	1.1	8.4	1.4	10.3	2.4	1.1	0.2	0.1	1.3	1.4	12.2	2.1	0.8
18	Des Moines, Iowa	11.2	3.0	1.8	5.7	3.5	16.4	4.7	1.0	0.3	0.1	0.7	1.0	9.8	2.9	0.6
19	Detroit, Mich	5.9	2.4	0.2	2.4	0.3	0.9	0.5	0.6	2.1	(1)	0.3	0.6	10.4	19.5	1.2
20	Fall River, Mass	18.8	1.4	0.1	7.5	0.1	0.1	0.1	(1)	0.1		(1)	0.3	0.3	6.0	(1)
21	Fort Worth, Tex	4.3	1.5	0.2	4.0	0.8	2.3	0.4	0.1	0.1		0.5	0.9	6.1	1.7	1.6
22	Grand Rapids, Mich	3.1	0.8	0.1	2.2	0.6	3.1	0.7	40.2	0.2	(1)	0.2	0.3	8.6	15.0	0.4
23	Hartford, Conn	5.0	2.3	0.1	14.9	0.2	5.7	1.5	0.1	(1)	(1)	0.2	0.5	4.4	11.9	0.4
24	Houston, Tex	6.1	1.4	0.2	3.1	0.5	1.3	1.0	0.5	0.2	(1)	0.8	1.4	13.4	2.3	1.4
25	Indianapolis, Ind	7.0	2.6	0.3	14.1	0.3	1.1	1.4	0.9	0.1	(1)	1.4	1.9	29.8	2.2	0.3
26	Jersey City, N. J	4.6	1.9	0.2	16.3	1.6	1.4	0.5	0.4	0.2	(1)	0.6	1.0	14.6	15.9	0.5
27	Kansas City, Kans	4.5	1.1	0.8	6.5	0.4	5.3	1.7	0.2	1.3	(1)	0.7	0.7	10.0	8.2	3.3
28	Kansas City, Mo	7.0	2.4	0.5	9.4	0.7	6.9	1.6	0.4	1.5	0.1	1.3	1.5	14.3	3.4	0.6
29	Los Angeles, Calif	9.4	2.3	0.5	4.0	1.4	4.1	1.6	0.7	0.3	0.1	1.1	2.2	8.6	1.8	0.7
30	Louisville, Ky	4.3	1.3	0.2	13.5	0.2	0.6	0.3	0.3	0.2	0.1	5.3	3.3	40.7	2.9	0.3
31	Lowell, Mass	9.5	2.4	0.1	19.6	0.2	1.4	0.1	(1)	0.5	(1)	(1)	0.1	3.0	6.0	(1)
32	Memphis, Tenn	8.1	2.2	0.2	7.8	0.3	2.0	0.9	0.3	0.2	(1)	1.1	2.0	13.7	5.0	0.3
33	Milwaukee, Wis	1.8	0.5	0.2	1.3	1.7	0.8	0.7	0.5	0.1	0.1	0.8	0.5	36.1	20.9	4.1
34	Minneapolis, Minn	3.4	1.3	0.3	2.3	18.6	30.0	2.9	0.5	0.1	0.2	0.4	0.4	7.3	5.4	2.1
35	Nashville, Tenn	9.5	2.1	0.1	11.9	0.5	0.5	0.6	0.2	0.2	(1)	3.7	3.0	11.9	7.7	0.5
36	New Bedford, Mass	19.1	1.1	0.1	4.0	0.1	0.5	0.1	(1)	0.1		0.1	0.9	9.5	7.0	0.4
37	New Haven, Conn	4.2	1.9	0.1	15.7	0.3	2.7	0.5	0.1	0.3	....	0.3	0.5	6.0	6.5	0.2
38	New Orleans, La	4.5	1.0	0.1	5.6	1.7	1.2	0.8	0.5	0.4	(1)	0.9	10.4	12.5	0.8	0.2
39	New York, N. Y	3.5	1.1	0.1	10.0	1.2	1.7	0.4	0.2	0.2	(1)	0.5	1.1	9.6	7.2	1.3
40	Bronx borough	3.2	0.9	0.1	7.0	0.4	1.2	0.3	0.2	0.1	(1)	0.5	0.8	11.1	7.1	0.7
41	Brooklyn borough	3.8	1.1	0.1	8.1	2.6	2.3	0.6	0.3	0.1	(1)	0.3	0.6	8.5	7.8	0.4
42	Manhattan borough	3.1	0.9	0.1	12.3	0.4	1.2	0.3	0.2	0.2	(1)	0.5	1.5	7.5	6.8	2.0
43	Queens borough	5.4	1.8	0.1	9.5	0.8	2.1	0.7	0.3	0.3	(1)	1.0	2.0	28.9	6.9	2.6
44	Richmond borough	6.0	2.4	0.2	11.8	5.0	2.8	1.1	0.4	0.3	(1)	0.8	1.4	13.8	7.7	0.9
45	Newark, N. J	4.6	1.8	0.1	7.5	0.2	0.7	0.3	0.2	0.1	(1)	0.5	0.9	11.9	11.7	1.8
46	Norfolk, Va	7.3	2.3	0.3	4.8	2.8	3.1	1.3	1.7	0.4	(1)	0.3	0.9	4.6	2.8	0.2
47	Oakland, Calif	9.1	3.4	1.5	7.3	2.3	5.3	3.5	0.6	0.3	(1)	1.3	2.9	9.3	1.0	0.3
48	Omaha, Nebr	4.1	1.6	0.2	5.3	1.1	10.4	8.1	0.4	0.7	0.1	0.6	0.5	12.0	6.7	12.1
49	Paterson, N. J	8.1	4.1	0.1	7.1	0.1	0.3	0.2	8.0	1.8	(1)	3.0	2.4	7.8	12.7	0.5
50	Philadelphia, Pa	7.7	2.1	0.2	16.1	0.3	0.7	0.3	0.1	0.1	(1)	0.5	1.0	9.9	7.8	0.6
51	Pittsburgh, Pa	6.1	2.3	1.3	11.6	0.1	0.9	0.1	0.1	0.1	(1)	0.7	1.4	13.3	12.9	3.0
52	Portland, Oreg	8.1	3.6	0.6	4.0	5.9	10.2	2.7	0.7	0.6	0.1	2.6	1.1	10.8	1.8	0.7
53	Providence, R. I	12.5	2.5	0.1	17.0	0.4	3.9	0.2	0.1	0.2	(1)	0.1	0.6	2.0	3.3	0.1
54	Reading, Pa	3.5	0.9	0.6	2.4	0.2	0.3	0.1	0.2	(1)	(1)	0.5	0.7	15.1	26.6	2.5
55	Richmond, Va	10.6	4.1	0.4	5.6	0.4	0.9	0.6	0.4	0.4		0.7	1.9	13.6	3.0	0.7
56	Rochester, N. Y	8.4	1.6	0.1	6.1	0.1	0.6	0.2	2.6	0.6	(1)	0.7	1.1	15.0	6.4	0.1
57	St. Louis, Mo	3.8	1.0	0.1	8.9	0.2	0.9	0.4	0.4	0.4	0.1	2.0	1.8	26.0	5.0	3.4
58	St. Paul, Minn	3.7	1.4	0.1	5.9	7.4	19.2	2.6	0.5	0.2	0.5	1.0	0.6	16.9	4.9	3.5
59	Salt Lake City, Utah	27.8	4.9	2.1	2.9	4.4	11.3	8.1	4.4	0.1	0.1	3.1	0.7	10.2	0.7	0.2
60	San Antonio, Tex	2.2	0.4	(1)	1.4	0.1	0.3	0.2	0.2	0.2	(1)	0.4	1.3	7.0	0.7	0.3
61	San Francisco, Calif	6.8	2.4	0.3	12.2	2.1	4.3	2.3	0.5	0.4	0.1	1.9	4.6	12.4	1.4	0.5
62	Scranton, Pa	8.1	1.7	9.5	11.8	(1)	0.3	0.1	(1)		....	0.5	0.4	9.1	11.4	0.4
63	Seattle, Wash	9.6	3.9	0.8	4.3	11.3	12.7	2.8	0.6	0.7	0.1	0.7	0.9	6.0	1.1	0.4
64	Spokane, Wash	9.4	3.3	0.8	4.2	9.0	15.1	2.8	1.1	0.3	0.1	1.2	1.0	11.7	0.9	0.6
65	Springfield, Mass	6.2	4.2	0.1	17.8	0.3	3.9	0.3	0.1	0.1	(1)	0.3	0.6	3.7	7.8	0.4
66	Syracuse, N. Y	7.2	1.4	0.3	11.8	0.1	0.5	0.2	0.2	0.1	(1)	0.7	1.0	14.7	14.1	0.5
67	Toledo, Ohio	4.8	1.0	0.2	4.0	0.2	0.7	0.5	0.2	0.3	0.1	1.9	1.6	22.1	26.9	0.9
68	Trenton, N. J	9.2	1.7	0.1	6.2	(1)	0.3	0.2	0.1	0.1	(1)	0.2	0.6	7.9	14.7	5.3
69	Washington, D. C	10.2	2.7	0.4	14.7	0.7	1.6	0.8	0.4	0.3	(1)	1.2	2.3	11.5	2.4	0.4
70	Wilmington, Del	6.3	1.7	0.2	14.9	0.3	1.4	0.3	0.1	0.1	(1)	0.3	0.9	7.0	22.9	0.2
71	Worcester, Mass	6.2	1.7	0.1	16.9	0.6	14.5	0.4	0.1	0.1	(1)	(1)	0.6	0.9	6.8	0.1
72	Yonkers, N. Y	7.0	4.9	0.2	16.0	0.5	1.4	0.4	0.4	0.1	(1)	0.4	0.9	8.1	10.0	2.9
73	Youngstown, Ohio	7.5	3.0	3.2	4.6	0.2	2.3	0.1	0.1	(1)	(1)	0.4	0.4	4.3	7.7	6.2

1 Less than one-tenth of 1 per cent.

COUNTRY OF BIRTH, FOR CITIES HAVING 100,000 INHABITANTS OR MORE: 1920.

PER CENT OF TOTAL FOREIGN BORN IN SPECIFIED CITY—continued.

Central Europe—Con.			Eastern Europe.					Southern Europe.				Asia.				America.						
Austria	Hungary	Jugo-Slavia	Russia	Lithuania	Finland	Rumania	Bulg., Turkey in Eu.	Greece	Italy	Spain	Portugal	Armenia	Syria	China	Japan	Canada French	Canada Other	Newfoundland	West Indies[2]	Mexico	Central and So. America	
14.1	18.4	4.0	8.0	0.6	0.2	1.5	1.1	5.1	9.5	0.7	(1)	0.4	1.2	0.2	(1)	0.2	2.8	0.1	0.1	0.2	0.1	1
1.9	0.5	0.1	12.9	0.9	0.1	0.3	0.3	1.1	19.2	0.1	(1)	0.1	0.5	0.2	(1)	1.4	3.4	0.1	0.2	(1)	0.2	4
1.6	2.1	0.2	25.2	0.9	0.3	0.7	0.4	9.1	2.0	0.4	0.1	0.2	2.2	0.5	....	0.4	5.6	0.2	0.9	0.2	0.3	2
3.4	1.6	0.3	27.4	2.4	0.1	0.5	(1)	0.8	9.3	0.2	0.1	(1)	(1)	0.3	(1)	0.1	1.3	(1)	0.7	0.1	0.2	8
2.2	0.8	0.2	11.5	0.1	(1)	0.5	0.1	7.2	26.9	0.2	....	0.2	4.4	0.2	(1)	0.1	3.2	(1)	0.7	0.5	0.1	9
0.6	0.1	0.1	15.7	1.7	0.2	0.3	(1)	1.3	15.7	0.1	0.5	0.6	0.7	0.3	(1)	0.7	16.8	1.2	0.8	(1)	0.1	6
5.8	13.3	0.4	11.5	1.5	0.2	0.5	(1)	1.7	18.8	0.8	0.4	0.4	0.2	0.2	(1)	0.9	2.3	0.1	0.2	(1)	0.1	7
2.4	2.2	0.3	5.4	0.1	0.1	0.5	0.1	0.5	13.5	0.1	(1)	0.1	0.3	0.1	(1)	0.1	12.9	0.1	0.1	0.1	0.1	8
0.3	0.1	(1)	5.3	4.0	0.2	0.2	(1)	1.1	8.2	0.1	5.9	1.2	0.2	0.2	0.2	2.9	20.9	1.4	2.8	(1)	0.2	9
3.4	1.0	0.8	10.6	0.9	0.5	0.4	0.1	0.4	24.5	(1)	(1)	0.3	0.2	0.2	....	0.1	1.1	1.0	0.3	....	0.1	10
3.8	3.2	1.2	12.6	2.3	0.2	0.6	0.1	1.4	7.3	(1)	(1)	0.1	0.1	0.2	(1)	0.3	3.0	(1)	0.1	0.2	0.1	11
3.6	6.7	1.8	9.8	0.2	(1)	1.6	0.6	0.7	6.3	0.1	(1)	0.1	0.6	0.1	(1)	0.1	1.9	(1)	0.2	(1)	0.1	12
6.3	12.4	6.6	9.0	1.2	0.5	1.8	0.2	0.7	7.6	0.1	(1)	0.2	0.3	0.1	(1)	0.1	3.5	(1)	0.1	(1)	0.1	13
4.4	5.4	1.1	11.4	0.2	0.4	0.8	0.2	2.6	14.1	0.1	(1)	0.1	0.4	0.4	(1)	0.3	4.0	(1)	0.4	0.1	0.2	14
2.8	0.6	0.3	10.7	(1)	0.1	1.1	0.2	3.1	6.6	0.4	....	0.1	0.5	0.1	0.4	0.2	4.1	0.1	0.2	26.1	0.1	15
4.6	14.6	3.1	8.5	1.9	0.1	1.3	0.6	2.7	3.9	0.1	....	0.1	0.6	0.1	(1)	0.2	3.3	(1)	0.2	0.3	0.1	16
3.6	1.3	0.6	13.9	0.1	0.3	0.7	0.2	2.0	7.5	0.2	(1)	0.1	0.1	0.4	1.0	0.3	7.8	0.1	0.2	3.7	0.2	17
2.1	0.4	0.3	12.3	0.4	0.1	0.8	0.1	2.0	10.4	(1)	(1)	0.1	0.5	0.3	(1)	0.2	5.1	(1)	0.1	1.4	0.2	18
3.7	4.7	1.3	9.4	0.9	0.6	1.6	0.3	1.6	5.6	0.1	(1)	0.5	0.6	0.1	(1)	1.3	19.3	(1)	0.1	0.2	0.1	19
0.6	(1)	(1)	3.9	(1)	0.1	0.1	(1)	0.4	2.2	(1)	13.4	(1)	1.4	0.1	25.3	2.0	(1)	(1)	(1)	(1)	0.3	20
2.6	0.2	0.5	8.2	(1)	(1)	0.5	0.4	3.2	2.1	0.7	....	0.4	0.9	0.3	0.2	0.2	3.2	(1)	0.1	51.1	0.2	21
1.9	0.5	(1)	3.7	3.9	0.4	0.2	(1)	0.2	1.8	(1)	(1)	0.2	1.1	0.1	(1)	0.3	9.7	(1)	0.1	(1)	0.2	22
2.2	0.7	0.2	18.7	3.1	0.2	0.8	(1)	0.8	17.4	0.1	0.4	0.7	0.1	0.3	(1)	2.1	3.7	0.1	0.2	(1)	0.1	23
4.0	0.7	0.2	9.1	(1)	0.1	0.9	0.1	1.5	10.7	0.2	0.1	0.1	1.4	(1)	0.2	0.2	2.8	(1)	0.4	32.7	0.2	24
3.3	1.8	3.3	7.7	0.1	0.2	4.1	0.7	3.3	4.4	0.1	(1)	0.2	0.9	0.4	0.1	0.2	4.2	(1)	0.2	0.2	0.1	25
4.9	1.6	0.1	9.2	0.3	1.0	0.4	(1)	0.5	19.5	0.3	(1)	0.1	(1)	0.1	(1)	0.1	1.2	0.1	0.4	(1)	0.1	26
8.2	0.9	12.1	9.2	0.5	(1)	0.2	0.1	2.3	0.9	0.1	....	(1)	(1)	0.1	0.3	0.1	2.3	(1)	0.1	17.4	0.1	27
2.7	1.2	0.6	14.0	0.1	0.1	0.7	0.1	2.1	12.0	0.2	(1)	0.1	0.6	0.1	0.2	0.2	5.8	(1)	0.2	7.0	0.2	28
1.7	1.4	1.2	7.9	0.1	0.4	0.8	0.1	0.8	6.5	0.7	0.1	0.4	0.3	1.0	7.0	0.5	10.8	0.1	0.2	17.7	0.3	29
2.1	0.8	0.1	12.1	0.1	0.1	0.5	(1)	0.7	4.6	0.1	(1)	0.1	1.1	0.1	(1)	0.2	2.4	0.1	0.2	0.1	0.2	30
0.2	(1)	0.4	2.4	2.1	0.1	(1)	0.1	9.8	1.1	(1)	4.4	0.9	0.2	0.2	....	26.7	9.5	0.1	(1)	(1)	(1)	31
2.7	1.4	0.2	17.0	....	0.2	0.6	....	4.8	21.8	0.1	0.1	(1)	0.2	0.5	0.1	0.4	4.4	....	0.5	0.3	0.1	32
5.4	4.4	3.8	6.4	0.4	0.1	0.6	0.1	1.6	3.7	(1)	(1)	0.1	0.1	(1)	(1)	0.2	1.7	(1)	(1)	0.1	(1)	33
2.5	0.6	0.2	7.1	0.2	1.3	1.7	0.1	1.0	0.9	(1)	(1)	0.1	0.3	0.2	(1)	1.2	7.3	(1)	(1)	0.1	(1)	34
2.8	5.4	0.4	20.4	....	0.2	1.3	....	4.0	3.8	0.2	....	0.2	1.6	....	0.1	0.1	4.2	....	0.6	0.2	0.7	35
0.4	0.1	(1)	2.0	0.1	(1)	(1)	(1)	1.2	1.2	0.1	14.9	(1)	0.6	0.1	....	19.3	2.3	0.1	0.4	(1)	0.4	36
1.5	0.9	0.1	17.5	1.6	0.2	0.4	(1)	0.7	32.7	0.1	0.3	0.3	0.1	0.2	(1)	0.9	2.1	0.1	0.6	(1)	0.1	37
1.8	0.3	0.3	4.9	(1)	0.3	0.3	(1)	1.6	27.9	4.2	0.4	0.1	0.5	0.6	0.1	0.3	2.0	(1)	4.2	4.8	3.9	38
6.2	3.2	0.2	23.7	0.4	0.5	1.9	0.1	1.1	19.3	0.5	0.1	0.2	0.2	0.2	0.1	0.1	1.2	0.1	1.8	0.1	0.4	39
8.8	4.0	0.1	32.6	0.2	0.5	3.2	0.1	0.4	14.8	0.1	(1)	0.2	(1)	(1)	0.1	0.1	0.8	(1)	0.4	(1)	0.1	40
4.8	1.3	0.2	28.4	0.7	0.5	1.8	(1)	0.4	20.8	0.4	0.1	0.1	0.5	0.1	(1)	0.1	1.2	0.1	1.2	0.1	0.3	41
6.9	4.3	0.4	20.4	0.2	0.5	1.8	0.2	1.8	19.4	0.8	(1)	0.2	0.1	0.3	0.2	0.1	1.2	(1)	2.8	0.2	0.6	42
4.2	3.2	0.3	6.8	0.4	0.4	0.7	(1)	0.4	17.6	0.1	(1)	0.4	(1)	0.1	(1)	0.2	1.4	0.1	0.6	0.1	0.3	43
2.6	2.4	0.5	5.1	0.1	1.2	0.2	(1)	0.6	27.5	0.5	0.1	0.1	(1)	0.2	(1)	0.2	2.3	0.2	1.0	0.1	0.4	44
6.7	3.6	0.2	17.0	1.3	0.1	1.1	(1)	0.9	23.4	0.5	0.3	0.2	0.1	0.2	(1)	0.1	1.1	(1)	0.3	(1)	0.1	45
1.1	0.6	0.2	26.8	0.3	1.4	0.7	0.3	9.5	7.4	2.8	2.8	0.2	1.7	1.2	0.4	0.3	4.5	0.1	1.8	0.2	1.0	46
2.0	0.8	1.7	2.1	(1)	0.8	0.2	1.9	10.2	1.0	8.6	0.1	0.2	5.2	3.9	0.4	7.3	(1)	0.3	2.1	0.6		47
4.5	1.5	1.0	10.7	0.2	0.1	0.8	0.1	1.2	8.7	0.1	(1)	0.3	0.5	0.3	0.2	0.2	3.3	(1)	0.1	2.1	0.1	48
1.7	1.4	0.1	9.7	0.8	(1)	0.1	(1)	0.6	25.6	0.1	....	0.8	1.7	0.1	(1)	0.1	0.6	(1)	0.1	(1)	0.1	49
3.3	2.9	0.3	23.9	1.1	0.2	1.4	(1)	0.5	15.9	0.2	0.1	0.3	0.1	0.2	(1)	0.1	1.0	0.1	0.5	0.1	0.2	50
8.3	3.6	3.1	11.5	1.9	0.1	1.2	0.1	1.1	12.7	(1)	(1)	0.1	0.6	0.2	(1)	0.1	1.2	0.1	0.2	(1)	0.1	51
3.2	1.0	0.9	10.4	0.1	2.8	0.5	0.2	1.8	5.7	0.1	(1)	0.1	0.3	2.5	2.7	0.6	12.4	0.1	0.1	0.2	0.1	52
1.0	0.1	(1)	8.0	0.9	0.1	0.4	0.1	0.6	27.5	(1)	2.6	1.8	0.4	0.1	(1)	4.9	5.2	0.1	0.2	(1)	0.2	53
7.1	1.4	0.7	8.8	0.6	....	0.1	(1)	6.0	18.9	0.4	(1)	(1)	(1)	0.1	(1)	0.6	....	0.2	1.1	0.1		54
2.7	0.9	(1)	22.4	0.2	(1)	0.8	0.2	4.4	11.8	0.1	0.2	2.0	3.0	0.5	0.1	0.4	7.0	0.1	1.1	0.1	0.3	55
2.2	0.6	0.2	9.6	1.1	0.1	0.2	0.1	0.6	27.3	0.1	0.2	(1)	0.2	0.3	13.1	(1)	0.1	(1)	0.1			56
5.4	6.4	1.6	12.6	0.3	(1)	1.2	0.1	2.0	8.7	0.3	(1)	0.1	9.5	0.2	(1)	0.1	1.8	0.1	0.1	0.4	0.1	57
4.7	3.5	0.6	8.2	0.4	0.2	1.1	0.1	0.7	3.3	(1)	0.1	0.5	0.1	1.1	6.4	(1)	0.1	0.1	(1)			58
1.1	0.5	0.3	2.2	(1)	0.4	0.2	(1)	2.8	2.5	0.3	....	0.1	0.5	0.6	1.6	0.1	3.7	(1)	(1)	1.1	0.1	59
0.8	0.2	0.1	2.0	(1)	(1)	0.2	(1)	0.4	1.6	0.5	(1)	(1)	0.4	0.3	(1)	0.1	0.9	(1)	0.2	77.3	0.1	60
2.5	0.9	0.9	3.9	(1)	1.2	0.5	0.1	2.1	16.0	1.7	0.6	0.2	0.1	3.0	2.8	0.2	4.5	0.1	0.2	2.6	1.2	61
10.0	3.1	0.2	11.9	6.8	(1)	0.1	(1)	0.6	12.0	(1)	(1)	0.7	(1)	(1)	0.7	(1)	0.1	(1)	(1)			62
1.7	0.4	0.8	4.1	0.2	2.8	0.2	0.3	1.7	3.8	0.2	(1)	0.1	0.1	1.1	7.4	0.8	16.4	0.2	0.2	0.2	0.3	63
1.7	0.5	0.7	3.0	0.1	0.9	0.4	0.2	0.6	5.4	(1)	....	0.1	0.2	0.7	0.8	8.8	21.6	0.1	0.1	0.1	0.4	64
1.3	0.4	0.1	12.2	0.3	0.6	0.2	0.1	3.0	14.3	(1)	0.2	0.8	1.2	0.3	(1)	11.8	6.6	0.2	0.3	(1)	0.1	65
2.7	0.4	0.2	8.6	0.1	0.1	0.2	0.2	1.3	20.9	0.1	(1)	0.4	0.4	(1)	(1)	1.1	9.7	(1)	0.1	(1)	0.1	66
2.8	7.9	0.4	5.4	0.1	0.1	0.7	2.0	1.8	2.2	(1)	(1)	0.3	1.1	0.1	(1)	1.0	7.4	(1)	0.2	0.6	0.1	67
3.3	13.4	1.7	9.0	0.3	0.1	1.3	(1)	0.4	21.9	(1)	0.1	0.1	0.2	0.2	(1)	0.2	0.7	(1)	0.1	0.1	0.1	68
1.8	0.7	0.1	17.6	0.1	0.4	0.3	0.3	4.1	12.8	0.4	(1)	0.2	0.7	1.2	0.3	0.5	5.4	0.1	1.2	0.2	0.6	69
2.9	1.0	0.2	12.1	0.5	0.3	0.6	(1)	1.6	21.1	0.6	0.1	(1)	(1)	0.1	(1)	0.1	1.3	(1)	0.2	0.3	0.1	70
0.4	(1)	(1)	8.9	7.9	4.1	0.1	0.1	1.3	8.0	(1)	0.1	2.3	1.3	0.1	(1)	8.0	7.2	0.1	0.1	(1)	0.1	71
11.3	4.5	0.4	7.7	0.1	0.3	0.2	(1)	0.5	17.5	0.1	(1)	0.3	0.2	0.1	0.1	0.2	2.1	0.1	0.3	0.1	0.2	72
9.3	7.9	7.6	6.5	0.3	0.1	4.1	0.5	3.8	16.3	0.2	....	(1)	0.8	0.2	(1)	0.1	1.5	(1)	0.2	0.2	0.1	73

[2] Except possessions of the United States.

TABLE 77.—COUNTRY OF BIRTH OF THE FOREIGN-BORN POPULATION IN URBAN AND RURAL COMMUNITIES, FOR THE UNITED STATES: 1920.

COUNTRY OF BIRTH.	NUMBER.			PER CENT.		PER CENT DISTRIBUTION OF FOREIGN BORN.		
	Total.	Urban.	Rural.	Urban.	Rural.	Total.	Urban.	Rural.
Total population	105,710,620	54,304,603	51,406,017	51.4	48.6			
Total foreign born	13,920,692	10,500,942	3,419,750	75.4	24.6	100.0	100.0	100.0
Europe	11,882,053	9,102,938	2,779,115	76.6	23.4	85.4	86.7	81.3
Northwestern Europe	3,830,094	2,737,407	1,092,687	71.5	28.5	27.5	26.1	32.0
England	813,853	620,676	193,177	76.3	23.7	5.8	5.9	5.6
Scotland	254,570	195,614	58,956	76.8	23.2	1.8	1.9	1.7
Wales	67,066	47,716	19,350	71.1	28.9	0.5	0.5	0.6
Ireland	1,037,234	900,947	136,287	86.9	13.1	7.5	8.6	4.0
Norway	363,863	171,698	192,165	47.2	52.8	2.6	1.6	5.6
Sweden	625,585	394,700	230,885	63.1	36.9	4.5	3.8	6.8
Denmark	189,154	101,016	88,138	53.4	46.6	1.4	1.0	2.6
Netherlands	131,766	74,424	57,342	56.5	43.5	0.9	0.7	1.7
Belgium	62,687	41,710	20,977	66.5	33.5	0.5	0.4	0.6
Luxemburg	12,585	7,213	5,372	57.3	42.7	0.1	0.1	0.2
Switzerland	118,659	67,731	50,928	57.1	42.9	0.9	0.6	1.5
France	153,072	113,962	39,110	74.4	25.6	1.1	1.1	1.1
Central Europe	4,330,874	3,207,139	1,123,735	74.1	25.9	31.1	30.5	32.9
Germany	1,686,108	1,137,961	548,147	67.5	32.5	12.1	10.8	16.0
Poland	1,139,979	961,813	178,166	84.4	15.6	8.2	9.2	5.2
Czechoslovakia	362,438	240,453	121,985	66.3	33.7	2.6	2.3	3.6
Austria	575,627	431,670	143,957	75.0	25.0	4.1	4.1	4.2
Hungary	397,283	317,737	79,546	80.0	20.0	2.9	3.0	2.3
Jugo-Slavia	169,439	117,505	51,934	69.3	30.7	1.2	1.1	1.5
Eastern Europe	1,803,971	1,545,926	258,045	85.7	14.8	13.0	14.7	7.5
Russia	1,400,495	1,241,157	159,338	88.6	11.4	10.1	11.8	4.7
Lithuania	135,068	118,634	16,434	87.8	12.2	1.0	1.1	0.5
Finland	149,824	79,974	69,850	53.4	46.6	1.1	0.8	2.0
Rumania	102,823	93,456	9,367	90.9	9.1	0.7	0.9	0.3
Bulgaria	10,477	7,879	2,598	75.2	24.8	0.1	0.1	0.1
Turkey in Europe	5,284	4,826	458	91.3	8.7	(1)	(1)	(1)
Southern Europe	1,911,213	1,607,943	303,270	84.1	15.9	13.7	15.3	8.9
Greece	175,976	154,052	21,924	87.5	12.5	1.3	1.5	0.6
Albania	5,608	5,156	452	91.9	8.1	(1)	(1)	(1)
Italy	1,610,113	1,359,250	250,863	84.4	15.6	11.6	12.9	7.3
Spain	49,535	36,363	13,172	73.4	26.6	0.4	0.3	0.4
Portugal	69,981	53,122	16,859	75.9	24.1	0.5	0.5	0.5
Other Europe [2]	5,901	4,523	1,378	76.6	23.4	(1)	(1)	(1)
Asia	237,950	170,690	67,260	71.7	28.3	1.7	1.6	2.0
Armenia	36,628	30,307	6,321	82.7	17.3	0.3	0.3	0.2
Palestine	3,203	2,914	289	91.0	9.0	(1)	(1)	(1)
Syria	51,901	45,321	6,580	87.3	12.7	0.4	0.4	0.2
Turkey in Asia	11,019	9,854	1,165	89.4	10.6	0.1	0.1	(1)
China	43,560	34,635	8,925	79.5	20.5	0.3	0.3	0.3
Japan	81,502	40,751	40,751	50.0	50.0	0.6	0.4	1.2
India	4,901	2,693	2,208	54.9	45.1	(1)	(1)	0.1
Other Asia	5,236	4,215	1,021	80.5	19.5	(1)	(1)	(1)
America	1,727,017	1,170,024	556,993	67.7	32.3	12.4	11.1	16.3
Canada—French	307,786	243,750	64,036	79.2	20.8	2.2	2.3	1.9
Canada—Other	817,139	591,812	225,327	72.4	27.6	5.9	5.6	6.6
Newfoundland	13,249	12,037	1,212	90.9	9.1	0.1	0.1	(1)
West Indies [3]	78,962	72,742	6,220	92.1	7.9	0.6	0.7	0.2
Mexico	486,418	229,179	257,239	47.1	52.9	3.5	2.2	7.5
Central and South America	23,463	20,504	2,959	87.4	12.6	0.2	0.2	0.1
All other [4]	73,672	57,290	16,382	77.8	22.2	0.5	0.5	0.5

[1] Less than one-tenth of 1 per cent.
[2] Comprises Danzig, Fiume, Saar Basin, and " Europe, not specified."
[3] Except possessions of the United States.
[4] Africa, Australia, Atlantic Islands, Pacific Islands except possessions of the United States, "country not specified," and born at sea.

TABLE 78.—FOREIGN-BORN POPULATION, BY SEX, RACE, AND YEAR OF IMMIGRATION, FOR THE UNITED STATES: 1920.

YEAR OF IMMIGRATION.	ALL CLASSES.		WHITE.		NEGRO.		INDIAN.		CHINESE.		JAPANESE.		All other.
	Number.	Per cent.	Number.	Per cent.	Number.	Per cent.	Number.	Per cent.	Number.	Per cent.	Number.	Per cent.	
BOTH SEXES.													
Total......	13,920,692	100.0	13,712,754	100.0	73,803	100.0	6,299	100.0	43,107	100.0	81,338	100.0	3,391
1919............	214,123	1.5	201,280	1.5	5,938	8.0	644	10.2	1,141	2.6	5,027	6.2	93
1918............	85,570	0.6	76,929	0.6	3,628	4.9	429	6.8	584	1.4	3,953	4.9	47
1917............	116,222	0.8	106,059	0.8	4,537	6.1	435	6.9	952	2.2	4,120	5.1	119
1916............	177,184	1.3	167,675	1.2	3,698	5.0	558	8.9	973	2.3	4,177	5.1	103
1915............	203,098	1.5	193,684	1.4	3,213	4.4	374	5.9	1,299	3.0	4,396	5.4	132
1914............	449,876	3.2	440,707	3.2	3,791	5.1	306	4.9	1,166	2.7	3,755	4.6	151
1911–1913......	1,604,890	11.5	1,585,146	11.6	8,687	11.8	497	7.9	2,508	5.8	7,497	9.2	555
1906–1910......	2,229,868	16.0	2,194,371	16.0	10,779	14.6	563	8.9	4,616	10.7	18,175	22.3	1,364
1901–1905......	1,814,264	13.0	1,790,180	13.1	6,194	8.4	321	5.1	2,639	6.1	14,526	17.9	404
1900 or earlier..	5,761,237	41.4	5,717,465	41.7	10,105	13.7	837	13.3	22,678	52.6	10,040	12.3	112
Not reported...	1,264,360	9.1	1,239,258	9.0	13,233	17.9	1,335	21.2	4,551	10.6	5,672	7.0	311
MALE.													
Total......	7,675,435	100.0	7,528,322	100.0	42,641	100.0	3,539	100.0	40,573	100.0	57,213	100.0	3,147
1919............	119,892	1.6	112,592	1.5	3,521	8.3	405	11.4	937	2.3	2,349	4.1	88
1918............	47,320	0.6	42,723	0.6	1,953	4.6	237	6.7	460	1.1	1,908	3.3	39
1917............	62,559	0.8	56,825	0.8	2,490	5.8	245	6.9	841	2.1	2,069	3.6	89
1916............	96,056	1.3	90,676	1.2	2,004	4.7	305	8.6	859	2.1	2,123	3.7	89
1915............	112,226	1.5	106,752	1.4	1,725	4.0	211	6.0	1,167	2.9	2,256	3.9	115
1914............	256,216	3.3	250,808	3.3	2,136	5.0	181	5.1	1,052	2.6	1,904	3.3	135
1911–1913......	933,333	12.2	921,758	12.2	4,796	11.2	295	8.3	2,222	5.5	3,733	6.5	529
1906–1910......	1,288,152	16.8	1,261,115	16.8	6,326	14.8	331	9.4	4,269	10.5	14,783	25.8	1,328
1901–1905......	1,057,498	13.8	1,037,662	13.8	3,883	9.1	178	5.0	2,492	6.1	12,914	22.6	369
1900 or earlier..	3,168,590	41.3	3,130,503	41.6	6,208	14.6	479	13.5	22,075	54.5	9,224	16.1	101
Not reported...	533,593	7.0	516,908	6.9	7,599	17.8	672	19.0	4,199	10.3	3,950	6.9	265
FEMALE.													
Total......	6,245,257	100.0	6,184,432	100.0	31,162	100.0	2,760	100.0	2,534	100.0	24,125	100.0	244
1919............	94,231	1.5	88,688	1.4	2,417	7.8	239	8.7	204	8.1	2,678	11.1	5
1918............	38,250	0.6	34,206	0.6	1,675	5.4	192	7.0	124	4.9	2,045	8.5	8
1917............	53,663	0.9	49,234	0.8	2,047	6.6	190	6.9	111	4.4	2,051	8.5	30
1916............	81,128	1.3	76,999	1.2	1,694	5.4	253	9.2	114	4.5	2,054	8.5	14
1915............	90,872	1.5	86,932	1.4	1,488	4.8	163	5.9	132	5.2	2,140	8.9	17
1914............	193,660	3.1	189,899	3.1	1,655	5.3	125	4.5	114	4.5	1,851	7.7	16
1911–1913......	671,557	10.8	663,388	10.7	3,891	12.5	202	7.3	286	11.3	3,764	15.6	26
1906–1910......	941,716	15.1	933,256	15.1	4,453	14.3	232	8.4	347	13.7	3,392	14.1	36
1901–1905......	756,766	12.1	752,518	12.2	2,311	7.4	143	5.2	147	5.8	1,612	6.7	35
1900 or earlier..	2,592,647	41.5	2,586,962	41.8	3,897	12.5	358	13.0	603	23.8	816	3.4	11
Not reported...	730,767	11.7	722,350	11.7	5,634	18.1	663	24.0	352	13.9	1,722	7.1	46

TABLE **79.**—FOREIGN-BORN POPULATION BY YEAR

	DIVISION AND STATE.	Total foreign born: 1920	YEAR OF IMMIGRATION.						
			1919	1918	1917	1916	1915	1914	1911–1913
1	United States	13,920,692	214,123	85,570	116,222	177,184	203,098	449,876	1,604,890
	GEOGRAPHIC DIVISIONS:								
2	New England	1,885,945	29,877	9,160	16,766	29,248	31,142	59,020	214,966
3	Middle Atlantic	4,960,418	56,703	17,745	30,605	48,535	65,547	178,633	657,352
4	East North Central	3,232,141	27,055	8,818	13,569	25,994	34,008	106,821	412,127
5	West North Central	1,375,653	8,498	4,189	5,817	9,730	10,649	24,390	85,656
6	South Atlantic	330,537	5,916	2,566	3,040	5,209	5,218	12,452	38,856
7	East South Central	72,989	647	288	247	421	509	1,486	4,726
8	West South Central	464,828	33,994	16,082	16,358	20,225	18,850	20,112	45,929
9	Mountain	467,620	17,661	9,099	11,180	14,747	13,062	15,159	42,897
10	Pacific	1,130,561	33,772	17,623	18,640	23,075	24,113	31,803	102,381
	NEW ENGLAND:								
11	Maine	107,814	3,842	1,147	1,385	2,019	1,950	2,887	8,289
12	New Hampshire	91,397	2,262	660	956	1,637	1,523	2,435	8,227
13	Vermont	44,558	2,065	586	752	1,077	996	1,260	3,909
14	Massachusetts	1,088,548	15,424	4,863	9,390	17,164	18,520	33,726	123,795
15	Rhode Island	175,189	2,670	742	1,700	2,720	2,580	4,829	17,743
16	Connecticut	378,439	3,614	1,162	2,583	4,631	5,573	13,883	53,003
	MIDDLE ATLANTIC:								
17	New York	2,825,375	42,568	12,748	21,380	31,089	39,678	101,615	352,344
18	New Jersey	742,486	5,827	2,048	3,673	6,528	8,891	26,316	99,215
19	Pennsylvania	1,392,557	8,308	2,949	5,552	10,918	16,978	50,702	205,793
	EAST NORTH CENTRAL:								
20	Ohio	680,452	4,999	1,591	3,154	6,304	8,252	30,191	110,368
21	Indiana	151,328	833	274	512	1,089	1,426	4,574	17,392
22	Illinois	1,210,584	6,157	2,707	4,140	7,311	11,249	36,540	143,818
23	Michigan	729,292	13,695	3,787	4,910	9,503	10,712	26,542	103,385
24	Wisconsin	460,485	1,371	459	853	1,787	2,369	8,974	37,164
	WEST NORTH CENTRAL:								
25	Minnesota	486,795	2,481	765	1,435	3,157	3,755	9,125	31,853
26	Iowa	225,994	1,421	512	845	1,399	1,701	4,042	13,758
27	Missouri	186,835	1,144	656	776	1,097	1,374	3,837	13,440
28	North Dakota	131,863	442	161	249	729	849	2,111	6,503
29	South Dakota	82,534	400	122	135	357	509	1,136	3,923
30	Nebraska	150,665	749	458	640	924	1,061	2,325	10,124
31	Kansas	110,967	1,861	1,515	1,737	2,067	1,400	1,814	6,055
	SOUTH ATLANTIC:								
32	Delaware	19,901	174	66	106	204	279	816	3,130
33	Maryland	103,179	684	298	444	640	917	3,357	11,206
34	District of Columbia	29,365	489	179	233	342	376	752	2,467
35	Virginia	31,705	655	366	411	559	539	995	3,013
36	West Virginia	62,105	626	334	607	1,975	1,643	4,123	11,897
37	North Carolina	7,272	160	33	54	75	84	212	686
38	South Carolina	6,582	74	28	33	65	67	186	618
39	Georgia	16,564	228	87	90	171	184	436	1,469
40	Florida	53,864	2,826	1,175	1,062	1,178	1,129	1,575	4,370
	EAST SOUTH CENTRAL:								
41	Kentucky	30,906	177	93	70	130	163	614	2,011
42	Tennessee	15,648	206	63	54	98	112	323	947
43	Alabama	18,027	190	100	96	124	154	379	1,225
44	Mississippi	8,408	74	32	27	69	80	170	543
	WEST SOUTH CENTRAL:								
45	Arkansas	14,137	84	28	47	85	68	172	663
46	Louisiana	46,427	1,099	474	426	324	389	648	1,701
47	Oklahoma	40,432	1,516	748	648	687	562	665	2,178
48	Texas	363,832	31,295	14,832	15,237	19,129	17,831	18,627	41,387
	MOUNTAIN:								
49	Montana	95,591	842	342	576	1,454	1,276	2,780	8,692
50	Idaho	40,717	715	571	480	562	509	935	2,943
51	Wyoming	26,567	578	333	378	536	498	924	3,255
52	Colorado	119,138	1,694	1,383	1,810	2,038	1,649	2,720	10,895
53	New Mexico	29,808	1,729	1,078	1,738	2,230	2,143	1,706	3,349
54	Arizona	80,566	10,879	4,566	5,299	6,720	5,559	3,928	7,333
55	Utah	59,200	793	589	635	858	985	1,655	4,972
56	Nevada	16,003	431	237	264	349	354	511	1,458
	PACIFIC:								
57	Washington	265,292	6,803	2,962	2,836	3,931	4,018	6,658	21,165
58	Oregon	107,644	2,224	690	860	991	1,246	2,590	8,895
59	California	757,625	24,745	13,971	14,944	18,153	18,849	22,555	72,321

OF IMMIGRATION, BY DIVISIONS AND STATES: 1920.

YEAR OF IMMIGRATION—con.				PER CENT OF TOTAL ARRIVING IN—											
1906–1910	1901–1905	1900 or earlier.	Year not reported.	1919	1918	1917	1916	1915	1914	1911–1913	1906–1910	1901–1905	1900 or earlier.	Year not reported.	
2,229,863	1,814,264	5,761,237	1,264,360	1.5	0.6	0.8	1.3	1.5	3.2	11.5	16.0	13.0	41.4	9.1	1
304,735	250,235	832,443	108,353	1.6	0.5	0.9	1.6	1.7	3.1	11.4	16.2	13.3	44.1	5.7	2
919,629	789,504	1,849,913	346,252	1.1	0.4	0.6	1.0	1.3	3.6	13.3	18.5	15.9	37.3	7.0	3
511,268	379,564	1,389,247	323,670	0.8	0.3	0.4	0.8	1.1	3.3	12.8	15.8	11.7	43.0	10.0	4
142,247	131,868	775,031	177,578	0.6	0.3	0.4	0.7	0.8	1.8	6.2	10.3	9.6	56.3	12.9	5
53,817	42,176	118,650	42,637	1.8	0.8	0.9	1.6	1.6	3.8	11.8	16.3	12.8	35.9	12.9	6
8,171	6,685	34,423	15,386	0.9	0.4	0.3	0.6	0.7	2.0	6.5	11.2	9.2	47.2	21.1	7
50,287	31,854	131,588	79,549	7.3	3.5	3.5	4.4	4.1	4.3	9.9	10.8	6.9	28.3	17.1	8
67,312	48,394	177,378	50,731	3.8	1.9	2.4	3.2	2.8	3.2	9.2	14.4	10.3	37.9	10.8	9
172,402	133,984	452,564	120,204	3.0	1.6	1.6	2.0	2.1	2.8	9.1	15.2	11.9	40.0	10.6	10
13,359	11,687	48,103	13,146	3.6	1.1	1.3	1.9	1.8	2.7	7.7	12.4	10.8	44.6	12.2	11
11,825	8,850	41,964	11,058	2.5	0.7	1.0	1.8	1.7	2.7	9.0	12.9	9.7	45.9	12.1	12
5,723	4,665	19,122	4,403	4.6	1.3	1.7	2.4	2.2	2.8	8.8	12.8	10.5	42.9	9.9	13
177,219	144,993	499,067	44,387	1.4	0.4	0.9	1.6	1.7	3.1	11.4	16.3	13.3	45.8	4.1	14
27,577	23,463	79,195	11,970	1.5	0.4	1.0	1.6	1.5	2.8	10.1	15.7	13.4	45.2	6.8	15
69,032	56,577	144,992	23,389	1.0	0.3	0.7	1.2	1.5	3.7	14.0	18.2	15.0	38.3	6.2	16
519,916	448,411	1,058,145	197,481	1.5	0.5	0.8	1.1	1.4	3.6	12.5	18.4	15.9	37.5	7.0	17
139,734	115,086	286,803	48,365	0.8	0.3	0.5	0.9	1.2	3.5	13.4	18.8	15.5	38.6	6.5	18
259,979	226,007	504,965	100,406	0.6	0.2	0.4	0.8	1.2	3.6	14.8	18.7	16.2	36.3	7.2	19
124,243	91,414	248,824	51,112	0.7	0.2	0.5	0.9	1.2	4.4	16.2	18.3	13.4	36.6	7.5	20
22,622	15,438	60,829	26,339	0.6	0.2	0.3	0.7	0.9	3.0	11.5	14.9	10.2	40.2	17.4	21
203,726	156,792	517,963	120,181	0.5	0.2	0.3	0.6	0.9	3.0	11.9	16.8	13.0	42.8	9.9	22
110,051	74,020	295,883	76,804	1.9	0.5	0.7	1.3	1.5	3.6	14.2	15.1	10.1	40.6	10.5	23
50,626	41,900	265,748	49,234	0.3	0.1	0.2	0.4	0.5	1.9	8.1	11.0	9.1	57.7	10.7	24
52,035	52,276	287,015	42,898	0.5	0.2	0.3	0.6	0.8	1.9	6.5	10.7	10.7	59.0	8.8	25
18,633	14,794	136,092	32,797	0.6	0.2	0.4	0.6	0.8	1.8	6.1	8.2	6.5	60.2	14.5	26
23,870	19,883	92,092	28,666	0.6	0.4	0.4	0.6	0.7	2.1	7.2	12.8	10.6	49.3	15.3	27
15,978	19,526	65,523	19,792	0.3	0.1	0.2	0.6	0.6	1.6	4.9	12.1	14.8	49.7	15.0	28
8,137	7,485	47,777	12,553	0.5	0.1	0.2	0.4	0.6	1.4	4.8	9.9	9.1	57.9	15.2	29
14,359	10,436	86,623	22,966	0.5	0.3	0.4	0.6	0.7	1.5	6.7	9.5	6.9	57.5	15.2	30
9,235	7,468	59,909	17,906	1.7	1.4	1.6	1.9	1.3	1.6	5.5	8.3	6.7	54.0	16.1	31
3,447	2,622	6,607	2,450	0.9	0.3	0.5	1.0	1.4	4.1	15.7	17.3	13.2	33.2	12.3	32
15,451	14,709	48,693	6,780	0.7	0.3	0.4	0.6	0.9	3.3	10.9	15.0	14.3	47.2	6.6	33
4,338	3,505	11,567	5,117	1.7	0.6	0.8	1.2	1.3	2.6	8.4	14.8	11.9	39.4	17.4	34
4,892	3,873	10,487	5,915	2.1	1.2	1.3	1.8	1.7	3.1	9.5	15.4	12.2	33.1	18.7	35
13,138	7,995	12,238	7,529	1.0	0.5	1.0	3.2	2.6	6.6	19.2	21.2	12.9	19.7	12.1	36
975	768	2,365	1,860	2.2	0.5	0.7	1.0	1.2	2.9	9.4	13.4	10.6	32.5	25.6	37
894	656	2,438	1,523	1.1	0.4	0.5	1.0	1.0	2.8	9.4	13.6	10.0	37.0	23.1	38
2,594	2,006	6,456	2,843	1.4	0.5	0.5	1.0	1.1	2.6	8.9	15.7	12.1	39.0	17.2	39
8,088	6,042	17,799	8,620	5.2	2.2	2.0	2.2	2.1	2.9	8.1	15.0	11.2	33.0	16.0	40
2,948	2,149	16,962	5,589	0.6	0.3	0.2	0.4	0.5	2.0	6.5	9.5	7.0	54.9	18.1	41
1,822	1,551	6,915	3,557	1.3	0.4	0.3	0.6	0.7	2.1	6.1	11.6	9.9	44.2	22.7	42
2,306	1,915	7,022	4,516	1.1	0.6	0.5	0.7	0.9	2.1	6.8	12.8	10.6	39.0	25.1	43
1,095	1,070	3,524	1,724	0.9	0.4	0.3	0.8	1.0	2.0	6.5	13.0	12.7	41.9	20.5	44
1,325	1,266	6,754	3,645	0.6	0.2	0.3	0.6	0.5	1.2	4.7	9.4	9.0	47.8	25.8	45
4,171	4,957	19,395	12,843	2.4	1.0	0.9	0.7	0.8	1.4	3.7	9.0	10.7	41.8	27.7	46
3,843	3,043	17,476	9,066	3.7	1.9	1.6	1.7	1.4	1.6	5.4	9.5	7.5	43.2	22.4	47
40,948	22,588	87,963	53,995	8.6	4.1	4.2	5.3	4.9	5.1	11.4	11.3	6.2	24.2	14.8	48
15,091	11,376	38,870	14,292	0.9	0.4	0.6	1.5	1.3	2.9	9.1	15.8	11.9	40.7	15.0	49
5,421	4,122	20,253	4,147	1.8	1.4	1.2	1.4	1.5	2.3	7.2	13.3	10.1	49.7	10.2	50
4,764	3,128	8,550	3,623	2.2	1.3	1.4	2.0	1.9	3.5	12.3	17.9	11.8	32.2	13.6	51
16,623	13,765	54,712	11,849	1.4	1.2	1.5	1.7	1.4	2.3	9.1	14.0	11.6	45.9	9.9	52
4,044	2,400	6,512	2,879	5.8	3.6	5.8	7.5	7.2	5.7	11.2	13.6	8.1	21.8	9.7	53
9,903	5,677	12,777	7,925	13.5	5.7	6.6	8.3	6.9	4.9	9.1	12.3	7.0	15.9	9.8	54
8,799	6,039	30,007	3,868	1.3	1.0	1.1	1.4	1.7	2.8	8.4	14.9	10.2	50.7	6.5	55
2,667	1,887	5,697	2,148	2.7	1.5	1.6	2.2	2.2	3.2	9.1	16.7	11.8	35.6	13.4	56
41,213	33,081	111,633	30,992	2.6	1.1	1.1	1.5	1.5	2.5	8.0	15.5	12.5	42.1	11.7	57
16,736	12,605	52,641	8,166	2.1	0.6	0.8	0.9	1.2	2.4	8.3	15.5	11.7	48.9	7.6	58
114,453	88,298	288,290	81,046	3.3	1.8	2.0	2.4	2.5	3.0	9.5	15.1	11.7	38.1	10.7	59

Table 80.—FOREIGN-BORN MALE POPULATION BY YEAR OF IMMIGRATION, BY DIVISIONS AND STATES: 1920.

DIVISION AND STATE.	Total foreign-born males: 1920	YEAR OF IMMIGRATION.						
		1918–1919	1916–1917	1911–1915	1906–1910	1901–1905	1900 or earlier.	Year not reported.
United States....	7,675,435	167,212	158,615	1,301,775	1,288,152	1,057,498	3,168,590	533,593
GEOGRAPHIC DIVISIONS:								
New England.......	956,111	19,192	22,224	164,243	161,596	133,173	415,262	40,421
Middle Atlantic.....	2,647,050	41,870	40,854	500,267	506,043	446,285	976,960	134,771
East North Central..	1,816,081	19,944	22,768	335,702	309,365	228,596	769,016	130,690
West North Central..	781,943	7,143	9,011	74,446	87,313	80,719	450,535	72,776
South Atlantic......	194,364	4,883	5,526	36,522	32,911	25,810	67,610	21,102
East South Central..	42,968	513	415	4,431	5,221	4,391	20,592	7,405
West South Central..	264,915	30,945	19,593	45,690	28,777	18,613	79,548	41,749
Mountain............	282,660	15,435	14,813	43,854	43,882	31,634	107,732	25,310
Pacific...............	689,343	27,287	23,411	96,620	113,044	88,277	281,335	59,369
NEW ENGLAND:								
Maine...............	56,098	2,632	1,708	7,458	7,289	6,386	25,744	4,881
New Hampshire.....	46,973	1,714	1,354	6,857	6,538	4,716	21,551	4,243
Vermont............	23,733	1,359	957	3,418	3,175	2,670	10,349	1,805
Massachusetts......	540,428	9,337	12,350	92,695	92,064	75,331	242,259	16,392
Rhode Island........	87,450	1,649	2,100	13,205	14,353	12,322	39,637	4,184
Connecticut........	201,429	2,501	3,755	40,610	38,177	31,748	75,722	8,916
MIDDLE ATLANTIC:								
New York...........	1,465,875	31,794	25,940	259,827	275,624	247,426	550,806	74,458
New Jersey..........	394,144	4,072	5,356	74,709	77,271	65,005	150,420	17,311
Pennsylvania.......	787,031	6,004	9,558	165,731	153,148	133,854	275,734	43,002
EAST NORTH CENTRAL:								
Ohio................	392,668	3,695	5,990	93,679	76,556	55,283	135,588	21,877
Indiana.............	88,576	613	1,137	15,361	14,952	10,059	35,688	10,766
Illinois.............	660,269	4,391	6,062	108,511	118,063	92,694	282,175	48,373
Michigan............	415,539	10,277	7,988	88,221	68,427	44,902	165,517	30,207
Wisconsin...........	259,029	968	1,591	29,930	31,367	25,658	150,048	19,467
WEST NORTH CENTRAL:								
Minnesota..........	279,099	1,652	2,542	28,119	32,514	32,058	165,642	16,572
Iowa...............	127,369	1,075	1,371	12,387	11,886	9,122	77,643	13,885
Missouri............	104,079	969	1,059	10,754	14,164	12,249	52,958	11,926
North Dakota.......	75,641	301	495	5,740	9,348	11,678	40,657	7,422
South Dakota.......	47,728	288	305	3,585	5,124	4,636	28,543	5,247
Nebraska...........	85,072	735	1,015	8,352	8,782	6,438	50,356	9,394
Kansas..............	62,955	2,123	2,224	5,509	5,495	4,538	34,736	8,330
SOUTH ATLANTIC:								
Delaware............	11,443	146	184	2,631	2,070	1,649	3,661	1,102
Maryland...........	55,486	544	653	9,207	8,510	8,327	25,384	2,861
District of Columbia.	15,799	287	312	2,109	2,466	2,034	6,274	2,317
Virginia.............	19,870	725	727	3,158	3,125	2,496	6,729	2,910
West Virginia.	42,084	585	2,064	12,688	9,039	5,568	7,774	4,366
North Carolina......	4,483	92	84	654	629	512	1,555	957
South Carolina......	4,243	54	62	656	630	454	1,565	822
Georgia.............	10,334	147	172	1,373	1,705	1,309	4,085	1,543
Florida.............	30,622	2,303	1,268	4,046	4,737	3,461	10,583	4,224
EAST SOUTH CENTRAL:								
Kentucky...........	17,578	147	131	2,004	2,019	1,445	9,448	2,384
Tennessee..........	9,159	143	93	826	1,096	980	4,245	1,776
Alabama............	10,911	156	135	1,120	1,443	1,273	4,501	2,283
Mississippi..........	5,320	67	56	481	663	693	2,398	962
WEST SOUTH CENTRAL:								
Arkansas............	8,728	67	83	601	869	813	4,411	1,884
Louisiana...........	28,120	992	483	1,724	2,451	2,974	11,937	7,559
Oklahoma...........	25,322	1,624	878	2,168	2,422	1,955	11,136	5,139
Texas...............	202,745	28,262	18,149	41,197	23,035	12,871	52,064	27,167
MOUNTAIN:								
Montana............	59,818	638	1,176	8,264	10,197	7,665	25,012	6,866
Idaho...............	20,200	776	706	3,102	3,739	2,818	12,946	2,206
Wyoming...........	18,065	612	613	3,312	3,511	2,007	5,600	2,110
Colorado............	69,798	1,776	2,246	9,294	10,007	8,602	32,078	5,494
New Mexico.........	17,375	1,651	2,159	4,086	2,512	1,484	4,174	1,309
Arizona.............	46,403	8,766	6,589	9,341	5,944	3,458	8,072	4,233
Utah................	33,087	737	869	4,642	5,579	3,763	15,662	1,835
Nevada.............	11,821	479	455	1,813	2,093	1,536	4,188	1,257
PACIFIC:								
Washington.........	164,158	5,107	4,021	20,386	27,856	21,801	70,930	14,057
Oregon.............	66,798	1,568	1,084	7,958	11,117	8,264	32,809	3,998
California...........	458,387	20,612	18,306	68,276	74,071	58,212	177,596	41,314

TABLE 81.—FOREIGN-BORN FEMALE POPULATION BY YEAR OF IMMIGRATION, BY DIVISIONS AND STATES: 1920.

DIVISION AND STATE.	Total foreign-born females: 1920	YEAR OF IMMIGRATION.						
		1918–1919	1916–1917	1911–1915	1906–1910	1901–1905	1900 or earlier.	Year not reported.
United States.........	6,245,257	132,481	134,791	956,089	941,716	756,766	2,592,647	730,767
GEOGRAPHIC DIVISIONS:								
New England.........	929,834	19,845	23,790	140,885	143,139	117,062	417,181	67,932
Middle Atlantic..........	2,313,368	32,578	38,286	401,265	413,586	343,219	872,953	211,481
East North Central.......	1,416,060	15,929	16,795	217,254	201,903	150,968	620,231	192,980
West North Central......	593,710	5,544	6,536	46,249	54,934	51,149	324,496	104,802
South Atlantic..........	136,173	3,599	2,723	20,004	20,906	16,366	51,040	21,535
East South Central.......	30,021	422	253	2,290	2,950	2,294	13,831	7,981
West South Central.......	199,913	19,131	16,990	39,201	21,510	13,241	52,040	37,800
Mountain.................	184,960	11,325	11,114	27,264	23,430	16,760	69,646	25,421
Pacific..................	441,218	24,108	18,304	61,677	59,358	45,707	171,229	60,835
NEW ENGLAND:								
Maine....................	51,716	2,357	1,696	5,668	6,070	5,301	22,359	8,265
New Hampshire..........	44,424	1,208	1,239	5,328	5,287	4,134	20,413	6,815
Vermont.................	20,825	1,292	872	2,747	2,548	1,995	8,773	2,598
Massachusetts...........	548,120	10,950	14,204	83,346	85,155	69,662	256,808	27,995
Rhode Island............	87,739	1,763	2,320	11,947	13,224	11,141	39,558	7,786
Connecticut.............	177,010	2,275	3,459	31,849	30,855	24,829	69,270	14,473
MIDDLE ATLANTIC:								
New York................	1,359,500	23,522	26,529	233,810	244,292	200,985	507,339	123,023
New Jersey..............	348,342	3,803	4,845	59,713	62,463	50,081	136,383	31,054
Pennsylvania...........	605,526	5,253	6,912	107,742	106,831	92,153	229,231	57,404
EAST NORTH CENTRAL:								
Ohio....................	287,784	2,895	3,468	55,132	47,687	36,131	113,236	29,235
Indiana.................	62,752	494	464	8,031	7,670	5,379	25,141	15,573
Illinois.................	550,315	4,473	5,389	83,096	85,663	64,098	235,788	71,808
Michigan................	313,753	7,205	6,425	52,418	41,624	29,118	130,366	46,597
Wisconsin...............	201,456	862	1,049	18,577	19,259	16,242	115,700	29,767
WEST NORTH CENTRAL:								
Minnesota...............	207,696	1,594	2,050	16,614	19,521	20,218	121,373	26,326
Iowa....................	98,625	858	873	7,114	6,747	5,672	58,449	18,912
Missouri................	82,756	831	814	7,897	9,706	7,634	39,134	16,740
North Dakota...........	56,222	302	483	3,723	6,630	7,848	24,866	12,370
South Dakota...........	34,806	234	187	1,983	3,013	2,849	19,234	7,306
Nebraska...............	65,593	472	549	5,158	5,577	3,998	36,267	13,572
Kansas.................	48,012	1,253	1,580	3,760	3,740	2,930	25,173	9,576
SOUTH ATLANTIC:								
Delaware................	8,458	94	126	1,594	1,377	973	2,946	1,348
Maryland...............	47,693	438	431	6,273	6,941	6,382	23,309	3,919
District of Columbia......	13,566	381	263	1,486	1,872	1,471	5,293	2,800
Virginia.................	11,835	296	243	1,389	1,767	1,377	3,758	3,005
West Virginia...........	20,021	375	518	4,975	4,099	2,427	4,464	3,163
North Carolina..........	2,789	101	45	328	346	256	810	903
South Carolina..........	2,339	48	36	215	264	202	873	701
Georgia.................	6,230	168	89	716	889	697	2,371	1,300
Florida.................	23,242	1,698	972	3,028	3,351	2,581	7,216	4,396
EAST SOUTH CENTRAL:								
Kentucky...............	13,328	123	69	784	929	704	7,514	3,205
Tennessee...............	6,489	126	59	556	726	571	2,670	1,781
Alabama................	7,116	134	85	638	863	642	2,521	2,233
Mississippi.............	3,088	39	40	312	432	377	1,126	762
WEST SOUTH CENTRAL:								
Arkansas................	5,409	45	49	302	456	453	2,343	1,761
Louisiana...............	18,307	581	267	1,014	1,720	1,983	7,458	5,284
Oklahoma...............	15,110	640	457	1,237	1,421	1,088	6,340	3,927
Texas...................	161,087	17,865	16,217	36,648	17,913	9,717	35,899	26,828
MOUNTAIN:								
Montana................	35,773	546	854	4,484	4,894	3,711	13,858	7,426
Idaho...................	14,454	510	336	1,374	1,682	1,304	7,307	1,941
Wyoming...............	8,502	299	301	1,365	1,253	821	2,950	1,513
Colorado................	49,340	1,301	1,602	5,970	6,316	5,162	22,634	6,355
New Mexico.............	12,433	1,156	1,809	3,112	1,532	916	2,338	1,570
Arizona.................	34,163	6,679	5,430	7,479	3,959	2,219	4,705	3,692
Utah...................	26,113	645	624	2,970	3,220	2,276	14,345	2,033
Nevada.................	4,182	189	158	510	574	351	1,509	891
PACIFIC:								
Washington.............	101,134	4,658	2,746	11,455	13,357	11,280	40,703	16,935
Oregon.................	40,846	1,346	767	4,773	5,619	4,341	19,832	4,168
California...............	299,238	18,104	14,791	45,449	40,382	30,086	110,694	39,732

TABLE 82.—FOREIGN-BORN POPULATION BY YEAR OF IMMIGRATION,

	CITY.	Total foreign born: 1920	YEAR OF IMMIGRATION.						
			1919	1918	1917	1916	1915	1914	1911–1913
1	Akron, Ohio	38,021	569	209	380	840	835	3,240	10,612
2	Albany, N. Y	17,695	95	51	70	110	217	509	1,961
3	Atlanta, Ga	4,789	102	10	27	42	44	118	375
4	Baltimore, Md	84,809	528	235	333	523	769	2,900	9,692
5	Birmingham, Ala	6,140	51	17	31	42	73	146	496
6	Boston, Mass	242,619	2,977	966	1,708	2,774	3,834	7,894	27,733
7	Bridgeport, Conn	46,782	434	220	361	637	713	2,222	7,155
8	Buffalo, N. Y	121,824	1,050	549	701	1,051	1,383	3,886	15,582
9	Cambridge, Mass	33,296	626	218	383	650	646	1,157	4,025
10	Camden, N. J	20,354	191	50	97	176	318	841	3,420
11	Chicago, Ill	808,558	3,988	1,737	2,775	4,876	8,238	27,928	106,717
12	Cincinnati, Ohio	42,921	178	55	107	175	275	973	3,029
13	Cleveland, Ohio	240,173	1,604	490	963	1,786	3,143	11,188	42,884
14	Columbus, Ohio	16,187	100	29	49	137	182	497	1,691
15	Dallas, Tex	8,801	454	259	184	200	166	281	680
16	Dayton, Ohio	13,165	94	29	59	88	113	469	1,920
17	Denver, Colo	38,230	400	300	293	429	364	714	2,559
18	Des Moines, Iowa	11,269	93	30	46	91	111	242	964
19	Detroit, Mich	290,884	8,884	2,461	3,136	5,921	6,660	15,703	58,568
20	Fall River, Mass	42,421	308	175	358	739	818	822	3,872
21	Fort Worth, Tex	7,502	1,079	558	407	349	270	209	526
22	Grand Rapids, Mich	28,427	114	42	93	167	216	633	2,823
23	Hartford, Conn	40,912	394	105	374	592	680	1,678	6,479
24	Houston, Tex	12,088	774	444	384	380	288	328	1,035
25	Indianapolis, Ind	17,096	87	15	44	130	146	465	1,486
26	Jersey City, N. J	76,294	450	154	268	631	869	2,518	9,603
27	Kansas City, Kans	11,721	297	303	424	420	273	437	1,615
28	Kansas City, Mo	27,583	411	267	318	384	431	634	2,135
29	Los Angeles, Calif	122,131	5,909	2,965	3,000	3,166	3,213	3,714	11,630
30	Louisville, Ky	11,667	44	10	8	21	33	122	379
31	Lowell, Mass	38,116	484	197	490	807	840	1,118	3,814
32	Memphis, Tenn	5,844	47	24	12	31	63	120	435
33	Milwaukee, Wis	110,160	308	119	303	556	750	3,659	14,208
34	Minneapolis, Minn	88,248	756	236	401	1,010	1,236	2,518	7,759
35	Nashville, Tenn	2,412	28	1	11	24	9	76	130
36	New Bedford, Mass	51,078	1,513	515	1,501	2,092	1,743	1,927	6,612
37	New Haven, Conn	46,124	292	95	256	482	704	1,383	5,687
38	New Orleans, La	27,365	716	340	345	236	232	398	924
39	New York, N. Y	2,028,160	34,005	9,631	16,900	24,012	30,584	77,416	256,196
40	Bronx borough	267,742	1,282	466	1,048	1,738	2,813	7,795	27,313
41	Brooklyn borough	666,188	8,946	2,531	4,631	6,231	8,414	22,274	75,051
42	Manhattan borough	950,264	21,126	6,314	10,630	14,989	17,982	44,025	141,429
43	Queens borough	112,171	794	178	355	707	949	2,457	9,117
44	Richmond borough	31,795	1,857	142	236	347	426	865	3,286
45	Newark, N. J	117,549	1,006	383	649	1,059	1,422	4,089	15,819
46	Norfolk, Va	6,998	297	179	232	249	168	283	787
47	Oakland, Calif	49,895	820	413	546	695	889	1,220	4,189
48	Omaha, Nebr	35,645	211	123	183	342	449	1,100	4,031
49	Paterson, N. J	45,242	324	93	281	554	535	1,378	5,108
50	Philadelphia, Pa	400,744	2,665	1,036	1,727	3,152	4,577	14,684	52,040
51	Pittsburgh, Pa	120,792	603	180	404	788	1,229	3,781	15,468
52	Portland, Oreg	49,778	1,205	412	452	445	619	1,337	4,678
53	Providence, R. I	69,895	606	224	491	760	904	1,948	7,176
54	Reading, Pa	9,573	55	20	49	202	145	310	1,445
55	Richmond, Va	4,713	50	7	29	53	70	122	434
56	Rochester, N. Y	71,411	948	301	419	828	981	2,726	10,399
57	St. Louis, Mo	103,626	452	195	309	523	729	2,585	9,070
58	St. Paul, Minn	51,722	342	89	218	337	539	1,410	4,048
59	Salt Lake City, Utah	19,897	263	184	204	230	335	487	1,549
60	San Antonio, Tex	36,824	4,763	1,462	1,673	2,054	2,021	1,988	3,981
61	San Francisco, Calif	149,195	3,553	1,733	1,850	2,216	3,147	4,116	13,991
62	Scranton, Pa	28,587	90	49	70	93	189	646	2,536
63	Seattle, Wash	80,976	3,061	1,531	1,343	1,675	1,717	2,388	6,986
64	Spokane, Wash	17,096	454	136	141	260	165	338	994
65	Springfield, Mass	31,461	420	139	218	486	460	1,074	4,159
66	Syracuse, N. Y	32,383	295	126	179	332	432	1,048	4,155
67	Toledo, Ohio	38,296	341	86	149	287	373	1,609	5,430
68	Trenton, N. J	30,168	213	84	130	248	393	1,391	5,114
69	Washington, D. C	29,365	489	179	233	342	376	752	2,467
70	Wilmington, Del	16,337	120	55	85	187	241	705	2,743
71	Worcester, Mass	53,527	434	211	344	951	774	1,651	7,176
72	Yonkers, N. Y	25,796	205	82	111	206	244	745	2,825
73	Youngstown, Ohio	33,945	198	64	216	466	494	2,040	7,289

FOR CITIES HAVING 100,000 INHABITANTS OR MORE: 1920.

YEAR OF IMMIGRATION—con.				PER CENT OF TOTAL ARRIVING IN—											
1906–1910	1901–1905	1900 or earlier.	Year not reported.	1919	1918	1917	1916	1915	1914	1911–1913	1906–1910	1901–1905	1900 or earlier.	Year not reported.	
8,410	4,160	6,967	1,799	1.5	0.5	1.0	2.2	2.2	8.5	27.9	22.1	10.9	18.3	4.7	1
2,814	2,175	9,165	528	0.5	0.3	0.4	0.6	1.2	2.9	11.1	15.9	12.3	51.8	3.0	2
746	677	1,890	758	2.1	0.2	0.6	0.9	0.9	2.5	7.8	15.6	14.1	39.5	15.8	3
13,278	12,979	40,870	2,702	0.6	0.3	0.4	0.6	0.9	3.4	11.4	15.7	15.3	48.2	3.2	4
857	647	2,200	1,580	0.8	0.3	0.5	0.7	1.2	2.4	8.1	14.0	10.5	35.8	25.7	5
39,614	33,202	106,342	15,575	1.2	0.4	0.7	1.1	1.6	3.3	11.4	16.3	13.7	43.8	6.4	6
8,918	6,897	14,070	5,155	0.9	0.5	0.8	1.4	1.5	4.7	15.3	19.1	14.7	30.1	11.0	7
16,736	13,512	50,253	17,121	0.9	0.5	0.6	0.9	1.1	3.2	12.8	13.7	11.1	41.3	14.1	8
5,340	4,420	15,500	331	1.9	0.7	1.2	2.0	1.9	3.5	12.1	16.0	13.3	46.6	1.0	9
3,696	2,744	6,721	2,100	0.9	0.2	0.5	0.9	1.6	4.1	16.8	18.2	13.5	33.0	10.3	10
148,603	111,372	327,286	65,038	0.5	0.2	0.3	0.6	1.0	3.5	13.2	18.4	13.8	40.5	8.0	11
5,512	4,281	24,939	3,397	0.4	0.1	0.2	0.4	0.6	2.3	7.1	12.8	10.0	58.1	7.9	12
49,162	37,910	78,171	12,872	0.7	0.2	0.4	0.7	1.3	4.7	17.9	20.5	15.8	32.5	5.4	13
2,110	1,680	6,679	3,033	0.6	0.2	0.3	0.8	1.1	3.1	10.4	13.0	10.4	41.3	18.7	14
903	719	2,900	2,055	5.2	2.9	2.1	2.3	1.9	3.2	7.7	10.3	8.2	33.0	23.3	15
2,344	1,609	5,621	819	0.7	0.2	0.4	0.7	0.9	3.6	14.6	17.8	12.2	42.7	6.2	16
4,894	4,427	21,984	1,866	1.0	0.8	0.8	1.1	1.0	1.9	6.7	12.8	11.6	57.5	4.9	17
1,390	1,229	5,393	1,680	0.8	0.3	0.4	0.8	1.0	2.1	8.6	12.3	10.9	47.9	14.9	18
56,096	33,068	77,754	22,633	3.1	0.8	1.1	2.0	2.3	5.4	20.1	19.3	11.4	26.7	7.8	19
6,009	5,769	21,917	1,634	0.7	0.4	0.8	1.7	1.9	1.9	9.1	14.2	13.6	51.7	3.9	20
552	315	1,292	1,945	14.4	7.4	5.4	4.7	3.6	2.8	7.0	7.4	4.2	17.2	25.9	21
3,807	2,928	13,941	3,663	0.4	0.1	0.3	0.6	0.8	2.2	9.9	13.4	10.3	49.0	12.9	22
8,051	5,952	15,634	973	1.0	0.3	0.9	1.4	1.7	4.1	15.8	19.7	14.5	38.2	2.4	23
1,212	980	4,020	2,243	6.4	3.7	3.2	3.1	2.4	2.7	8.6	10.0	8.1	33.3	18.6	24
2,058	1,486	7,896	3,283	0.5	0.1	0.3	0.8	0.9	2.7	8.7	12.0	8.7	46.2	19.2	25
13,755	11,199	34,091	2,756	0.6	0.2	0.4	0.8	1.1	3.3	12.6	18.0	14.7	44.7	3.6	26
1,849	1,217	4,006	880	2.5	2.6	3.6	3.6	2.3	3.7	13.8	15.8	10.4	34.2	7.5	27
3,524	2,972	11,331	5,176	1.5	1.0	1.2	1.4	1.6	2.3	7.7	12.8	10.8	41.1	18.8	28
19,327	14,748	44,092	10,367	4.8	2.4	2.5	2.6	2.6	3.0	9.5	15.8	12.1	36.1	8.5	29
833	713	7,081	2,423	0.4	0.1	0.1	0.2	0.3	1.0	3.2	7.1	6.1	60.7	20.8	30
5,527	4,381	19,913	545	1.3	0.5	1.3	2.1	2.2	2.9	10.0	14.5	11.5	52.2	1.4	31
755	722	2,280	1,355	0.8	0.4	0.2	0.5	1.1	2.1	7.4	12.9	12.4	39.0	23.2	32
17,317	12,071	52,884	7,985	0.3	0.1	0.3	0.5	0.7	3.3	12.9	15.7	11.0	48.0	7.2	33
12,727	12,068	43,855	5,682	0.9	0.3	0.5	1.1	1.4	2.9	8.8	14.4	13.7	49.7	6.4	34
295	202	1,159	477	1.2	(¹)	0.5	1.0	0.4	3.2	5.4	12.2	8.4	48.1	19.8	35
8,987	6,622	18,835	731	3.0	1.0	2.9	4.1	3.4	3.8	12.9	17.6	13.0	36.9	1.4	36
8,416	7,581	18,058	3,170	0.6	0.2	0.6	1.0	1.5	3.0	12.3	18.2	16.4	39.2	6.9	37
2,116	2,192	10,811	9,055	2.6	1.2	1.3	0.9	0.8	1.5	3.4	7.7	8.0	39.5	33.1	38
393,860	348,602	726,634	110,320	1.7	0.5	0.8	1.2	1.5	3.8	12.6	19.4	17.2	35.8	5.4	39
52,765	51,314	103,865	17,343	0.5	0.2	0.4	0.6	1.1	2.9	10.2	19.7	19.2	38.8	6.5	40
126,475	119,701	254,710	37,224	1.3	0.4	0.7	0.9	1.3	3.3	11.3	19.0	18.0	38.2	5.6	41
193,909	158,334	297,007	44,519	2.2	0.7	1.1	1.6	1.9	4.6	14.9	20.4	16.7	31.3	4.7	42
16,111	15,039	58,165	8,299	0.7	0.2	0.3	0.6	0.8	2.2	8.1	14.4	13.4	51.9	7.4	43
4,600	4,214	12,887	2,935	5.8	0.4	0.7	1.1	1.3	2.7	10.3	14.5	13.3	40.5	9.2	44
22,532	19,042	43,884	7,664	0.9	0.3	0.6	0.9	1.2	3.5	13.5	19.2	16.2	37.3	6.5	45
1,219	846	1,963	775	4.2	2.6	3.3	3.6	2.4	4.0	11.2	17.4	12.1	28.1	11.1	46
7,812	6,108	23,558	3,645	1.6	0.8	1.1	1.4	1.8	2.4	8.4	15.7	12.2	47.2	7.3	47
5,765	3,912	15,180	4,349	0.6	0.3	0.5	1.0	1.3	3.1	11.3	16.2	11.0	42.6	12.2	48
7,694	6,797	19,750	2,728	0.7	0.2	0.6	1.2	1.2	3.0	11.3	17.0	15.0	43.7	6.0	49
73,974	63,995	158,448	24,446	0.7	0.3	0.4	0.8	1.1	3.7	13.0	18.5	16.0	39.5	6.1	50
20,078	19,713	52,305	6,243	0.5	0.1	0.3	0.7	1.0	3.1	12.8	16.6	16.3	43.3	5.2	51
9,148	6,428	22,849	2,205	2.4	0.8	0.9	0.9	1.2	2.7	9.4	18.4	12.9	45.9	4.4	52
11,343	10,237	31,522	4,684	0.9	0.3	0.7	1.1	1.3	2.8	10.3	16.2	14.6	45.1	6.7	53
1,819	1,558	3,300	670	0.6	0.2	0.5	2.1	1.5	3.2	15.1	19.0	16.3	34.5	7.0	54
691	638	1,737	882	1.1	0.1	0.6	1.1	1.5	2.6	9.2	14.7	13.5	36.9	18.7	55
13,405	8,805	25,188	7,411	1.3	0.4	0.6	1.2	1.4	3.8	14.6	18.8	12.3	35.3	10.4	56
16,389	13,534	49,603	10,237	0.4	0.2	0.3	0.5	0.7	2.5	8.8	15.8	13.1	47.9	9.9	57
6,405	5,610	28,219	4,505	0.7	0.2	0.4	0.7	1.0	2.7	7.8	12.4	10.8	54.6	8.7	58
3,115	2,222	10,536	764	1.3	0.9	1.0	1.2	1.7	2.4	7.8	15.7	11.2	53.0	3.8	59
3,825	2,004	6,698	6,355	12.9	4.0	4.5	5.6	5.5	5.4	10.8	10.4	5.4	18.2	17.3	60
23,251	18,548	60,765	16,025	2.4	1.2	1.2	1.5	2.1	2.8	9.4	15.6	12.4	40.7	10.7	61
4,260	3,795	13,315	3,544	0.3	0.2	0.2	0.3	0.7	2.3	8.9	14.9	13.3	46.6	12.4	62
13,016	10,040	28,204	11,015	3.8	1.9	1.7	2.1	2.1	2.9	8.6	16.1	12.4	34.8	13.6	63
2,499	2,003	9,099	1,007	2.7	0.8	0.8	1.5	1.0	2.0	5.8	14.6	11.7	53.2	5.9	64
5,721	4,465	13,253	1,066	1.3	0.4	0.7	1.5	1.5	3.4	13.2	18.2	14.2	42.1	3.4	65
5,584	4,100	13,969	2,163	0.9	0.4	0.6	1.0	1.3	3.2	12.8	17.2	12.7	43.1	6.7	66
5,545	4,462	17,859	2,155	0.9	0.2	0.4	0.7	1.0	4.2	14.2	14.5	11.7	46.6	5.6	67
6,693	4,961	9,844	1,097	0.7	0.3	0.4	0.8	1.3	4.6	17.0	22.2	16.4	32.6	3.6	68
4,338	3,505	11,567	5,117	1.7	0.6	0.8	1.2	1.3	2.6	8.4	14.8	11.9	39.4	17.4	69
2,911	2,259	5,424	1,607	0.7	0.3	0.5	1.1	1.5	4.3	16.8	17.8	13.8	33.2	9.8	70
9,177	7,240	23,355	2,214	0.8	0.4	0.6	1.8	1.4	3.1	13.4	17.1	13.5	43.6	4.1	71
4,747	3,902	11,926	803	0.8	0.3	0.4	0.8	0.9	2.9	11.0	18.4	15.1	46.2	3.1	72
7,117	4,849	9,082	2,130	0.6	0.2	0.6	1.4	1.5	6.0	21.5	21.0	14.3	26.8	6.3	73

¹ Less than one-tenth of 1 per cent.

TABLE 83.—FOREIGN-BORN MALE POPULATION BY YEAR OF IMMIGRATION, FOR CITIES HAVING 100,000 INHABITANTS OR MORE: 1920.

CITY.	Total foreign-born males: 1920	YEAR OF IMMIGRATION.						
		1918-1919	1916-1917	1911-1915	1906-1910	1901-1905	1900 or earlier.	Year not reported.
Akron, Ohio	24,731	491	896	10,105	5,672	2,669	4,016	882
Albany, N. Y	9,022	56	79	1,471	1,570	1,298	4,374	174
Atlanta, Ga	2,741	47	37	308	447	420	1,128	354
Baltimore, Md	44,805	409	499	7,779	7,148	7,235	20,708	1,027
Birmingham, Ala	3,545	36	46	424	498	431	1,309	801
Boston, Mass	120,122	1,767	2,018	20,956	20,719	17,521	51,481	5,660
Bridgeport, Conn	25,598	373	595	5,899	5,138	3,998	7,703	1,892
Buffalo, N. Y	64,938	817	921	12,529	10,105	8,090	27,077	5,399
Cambridge, Mass	15,837	382	439	2,890	2,733	2,170	7,096	127
Camden, N. J	11,162	115	155	2,687	2,237	1,619	3,607	742
Chicago, Ill	434,307	2,871	3,960	79,494	84,251	64,804	173,801	25,126
Cincinnati, Ohio	21,855	119	169	2,365	3,031	2,472	12,570	1,129
Cleveland, Ohio	133,508	1,061	1,445	33,933	28,741	22,161	41,284	4,883
Columbus, Ohio	9,221	76	121	1,533	1,340	1,090	3,627	1,434
Dallas, Tex	5,153	519	238	708	587	461	1,739	901
Dayton, Ohio	7,438	68	95	1,502	1,453	1,001	2,980	330
Denver, Colo	21,420	398	438	2,244	2,934	2,613	11,965	828
Des Moines, Iowa	6,252	73	86	762	820	727	3,056	728
Detroit, Mich	170,150	6,825	5,034	51,415	35,386	20,348	42,037	9,105
Fall River, Mass	20,408	239	484	2,704	2,949	2,902	10,581	549
Fort Worth, Tex	4,851	1,210	484	685	377	204	856	1,035
Grand Rapids, Mich	15,047	73	123	2,127	2,191	1,737	7,464	1,332
Hartford, Conn	21,683	241	449	4,922	4,441	3,299	7,973	358
Houston, Tex	6,861	708	439	973	737	601	2,432	971
Indianapolis, Ind	9,470	50	107	1,362	1,331	940	4,429	1,251
Jersey City, N. J	40,423	295	489	7,452	7,732	6,320	17,328	807
Kansas City, Kans	6,911	378	485	1,442	1,169	788	2,291	358
Kansas City, Mo	15,584	390	414	1,904	2,165	1,849	6,615	2,247
Los Angeles, Calif	67,312	4,379	3,200	10,283	11,037	8,979	24,746	4,688
Louisville, Ky	5,921	23	13	327	474	443	3,764	877
Lowell, Mass	18,532	319	622	3,041	2,811	2,187	9,337	215
Memphis, Tenn	3,324	34	27	363	460	438	1,348	654
Milwaukee, Wis	60,776	214	504	11,136	10,587	7,453	27,692	3,190
Minneapolis, Minn	48,596	501	744	6,765	7,615	7,087	23,943	1,941
Nashville, Tenn	1,305	10	19	127	179	122	646	202
New Bedford, Mass	25,474	1,104	1,744	5,251	4,552	3,349	9,225	249
New Haven, Conn	23,828	186	347	4,108	4,446	4,216	9,369	1,156
New Orleans, La	16,671	655	362	986	1,296	1,399	6,424	5,549
New York, N. Y	1,041,723	26,006	20,169	186,303	203,566	189,407	374,914	41,358
Bronx borough	135,865	749	1,272	18,974	26,942	27,769	54,553	5,606
Brooklyn borough	345,597	7,417	5,448	54,313	65,565	66,180	132,495	14,179
Manhattan borough	485,229	16,341	12,651	103,843	99,841	84,655	150,421	17,477
Queens borough	57,412	432	463	6,460	8,620	8,360	30,171	2,906
Richmond borough	17,620	1,067	335	2,713	2,598	2,443	7,274	1,190
Newark, N. J	62,319	858	947	11,769	12,267	10,763	23,097	2,618
Norfolk, Va	4,822	403	404	919	829	563	1,306	398
Oakland, Calif	29,252	640	751	3,801	4,872	3,850	13,796	1,542
Omaha, Nebr	20,122	195	328	3,457	3,514	2,420	8,388	1,820
Paterson, N. J	23,268	183	390	3,750	4,114	3,748	10,305	778
Philadelphia, Pa	207,699	1,892	2,650	39,096	39,735	35,163	80,085	9,078
Pittsburgh, Pa	65,783	374	591	11,976	11,586	11,296	27,505	2,455
Portland, Oreg	29,529	783	496	3,882	5,782	4,026	13,634	926
Providence, R. I	34,829	390	560	5,331	5,952	5,412	15,491	1,693
Reading, Pa	5,475	45	129	1,132	1,079	972	1,841	277
Richmond, Va	2,596	26	40	392	389	377	1,004	368
Rochester, N. Y	37,051	575	527	7,409	7,580	5,175	13,180	2,605
St. Louis, Mo	56,606	322	454	6,999	9,075	8,914	27,207	3,645
St. Paul, Minn	28,093	161	395	6,665	7,991	3,395	15,196	1,510
Salt Lake City, Utah	10,112	218	209	1,253	1,682	1,229	5,124	397
San Antonio, Tex	19,639	4,224	1,852	4,031	2,020	1,062	3,729	2,721
San Francisco, Calif	89,905	2,930	2,372	12,893	14,927	11,910	36,006	8,867
Scranton, Pa	15,153	66	81	1,944	2,441	2,202	7,043	1,376
Seattle, Wash	48,725	2,360	1,699	6,809	8,774	6,738	17,594	4,751
Spokane, Wash	9,683	265	211	867	1,515	1,150	5,289	386
Springfield, Mass	16,049	265	357	3,161	3,084	2,418	6,384	380
Syracuse, N. Y	17,473	208	259	3,338	3,295	2,401	7,005	907
Toledo, Ohio	21,857	286	269	4,923	3,473	2,690	9,321	895
Trenton, N. J	16,556	131	174	3,855	3,846	2,940	5,158	452
Washington, D. C	15,799	287	312	2,109	2,466	2,034	6,274	2,317
Wilmington, Del	9,396	102	165	2,296	1,763	1,407	2,941	722
Worcester, Mass	27,961	326	741	5,400	5,080	3,903	11,700	811
Yonkers, N. Y	13,048	120	152	1,951	2,469	2,124	5,946	286
Youngstown, Ohio	20,793	139	437	6,493	4,619	2,998	5,211	896

TABLE 84.—FOREIGN-BORN FEMALE POPULATION BY YEAR OF IMMIGRATION, FOR CITIES HAVING 100,000 INHABITANTS OR MORE: 1920.

CITY.	Total foreign-born females: 1920	YEAR OF IMMIGRATION.						
		1918–1919	1916–1917	1911–1915	1906–1910	1901–1905	1900 or earlier.	Year not reported.
Akron, Ohio	13,290	287	324	4,582	2,738	1,491	2,951	917
Albany, N. Y	8,673	90	101	1,216	1,244	877	4,791	354
Atlanta, Ga	2,048	65	32	229	299	257	762	404
Baltimore, Md	40,004	354	357	5,582	6,130	5,744	20,162	1,675
Birmingham, Ala	2,595	32	27	291	359	216	891	779
Boston, Mass	122,497	2,176	2,464	18,505	18,895	15,681	54,861	9,915
Bridgeport, Conn	21,184	281	403	4,191	3,780	2,899	6,367	3,263
Buffalo, N. Y	56,886	782	831	8,322	6,631	5,422	23,176	11,722
Cambridge, Mass	17,459	462	594	2,938	2,607	2,250	8,404	204
Camden N. J	9,192	126	118	1,892	1,459	1,125	3,114	1,358
Chicago, Ill	374,251	2,854	3,691	63,389	64,352	46,568	153,485	39,912
Cincinnati, Ohio	21,066	114	113	1,912	2,481	1,809	12,369	2,268
Cleveland, Ohio	106,665	1,033	1,304	23,282	20,421	15,749	36,887	7,989
Columbus, Ohio	6,966	53	65	837	770	590	3,052	1,599
Dallas, Tex	3,648	194	146	419	316	258	1,161	1,154
Dayton, Ohio	5,727	55	52	1,000	891	608	2,632	489
Denver, Colo	16,810	302	284	1,393	1,960	1,814	10,019	1,038
Des Moines, Iowa	5,017	50	51	555	570	502	2,337	952
Detroit, Mich	120,734	4,520	4,023	29,516	20,710	12,720	35,717	13,528
Fall River, Mass	22,013	244	613	2,808	3,060	2,867	11,336	1,085
Fort Worth, Tex	2,651	427	272	320	175	111	436	910
Grand Rapids, Mich	13,380	83	137	1,545	1,616	1,191	6,477	2,331
Hartford, Conn	19,229	258	517	3,915	3,610	2,653	7,661	615
Houston, Tex	5,227	510	325	678	475	379	1,588	1,272
Indianapolis, Ind	7,626	52	67	735	727	546	3,467	2,032
Jersey City, N. J	35,871	309	410	5,538	6,023	4,879	16,763	1,949
Kansas City, Kans	4,810	222	359	883	680	429	1,715	522
Kansas City, Mo	11,999	288	288	1,296	1,359	1,123	4,716	2,929
Los Angeles, Calif	54,819	4,495	2,966	8,274	8,290	5,769	19,346	5,679
Louisville, Ky	5,746	31	16	207	359	270	3,317	1,546
Lowell, Mass	19,584	362	675	2,731	2,716	2,194	10,576	330
Memphis, Tenn	2,520	37	16	255	295	284	932	701
Milwaukee, Wis	49,384	213	355	7,481	6,730	4,618	25,192	4,795
Minneapolis, Minn	39,652	491	667	4,748	5,112	4,981	19,912	3,741
Nashville, Tenn	1,107	19	16	88	116	80	513	275
New Bedford, Mass	25,604	924	1,849	5,031	4,435	3,273	9,610	482
New Haven, Conn	22,296	201	391	3,666	3,970	3,365	8,689	2,014
New Orleans, La	10,694	401	219	568	820	793	4,387	3,506
New York, N. Y	986,437	17,630	20,743	177,893	190,294	159,195	351,720	68,962
Bronx borough	131,877	999	1,514	18,947	25,823	23,545	49,312	11,737
Brooklyn borough	320,591	4,060	5,414	51,426	60,910	53,521	122,215	23,045
Manhattan borough	465,035	11,099	12,968	99,593	94,068	73,679	146,586	27,042
Queens borough	54,759	540	599	6,063	7,491	6,679	27,994	5,393
Richmond borough	14,175	932	248	1,864	2,002	1,771	5,613	1,745
Newark, N. J	55,230	531	761	9,561	10,265	8,279	20,787	5,046
Norfolk, Va	2,176	73	77	319	390	283	657	377
Oakland, Calif	20,643	593	490	2,497	2,940	2,258	9,762	2,103
Omaha, Nebr	15,523	139	197	2,123	2,251	1,492	6,792	2,529
Paterson, N. J	21,974	234	445	3,271	3,580	3,049	9,445	1,950
Philadelphia, Pa	193,045	1,809	2,229	32,205	34,239	28,832	78,363	15,368
Pittsburgh, Pa	55,009	409	601	8,502	8,492	8,417	24,800	3,788
Portland, Oreg	20,249	834	401	2,752	3,366	2,402	9,215	1,279
Providence, R. I	35,066	440	691	4,697	5,391	4,825	16,031	2,991
Reading, Pa	4,098	30	122	768	740	586	1,459	393
Richmond, Va	2,117	31	42	234	302	261	733	514
Rochester, N. Y	34,360	674	720	6,697	5,825	3,630	12,008	4,806
St. Louis, Mo	47,020	325	378	5,385	6,814	5,320	22,206	6,592
St. Paul, Minn	23,629	230	260	2,312	2,524	2,215	13,093	2,995
Salt Lake City, Utah	9,785	229	233	1,118	1,433	993	5,412	367
San Antonio, Tex	17,185	2,001	1,875	3,959	1,805	942	2,969	3,634
San Francisco, Calif	59,290	2,356	1,694	8,361	8,324	6,638	24,759	7,158
Scranton, Pa	13,434	73	82	1,427	1,819	1,593	6,272	2,168
Seattle, Wash	32,251	2,232	1,319	4,282	4,242	3,302	10,610	6,264
Spokane, Wash	7,413	325	190	630	984	853	3,810	621
Springfield, Mass	15,412	294	347	2,532	2,637	2,047	6,869	686
Syracuse, N. Y	14,910	213	252	2,297	2,289	1,699	6,904	1,256
Toledo, Ohio	16,439	141	167	2,489	2,072	1,772	8,538	1,260
Trenton, N. J	13,612	166	204	3,043	2,847	2,021	4,686	645
Washington, D. C	13,566	381	263	1,486	1,872	1,471	5,293	2,800
Wilmington, Del	6,941	73	107	1,393	1,148	852	2,483	885
Worcester, Mass	25,566	319	554	4,201	4,097	3,337	11,655	1,403
Yonkers, N. Y	12,748	167	165	1,863	2,278	1,778	5,980	517
Youngstown, Ohio	13,152	123	245	3,330	2,498	1,851	3,871	1,234

TABLE 85.—FOREIGN-BORN POPULATION BY YEAR OF IMMIGRATION, FOR CITIES HAVING FROM 25,000 TO 100,000 INHABITANTS: 1920.

CITY.	Total foreign born: 1920	YEAR OF IMMIGRATION.					
		1916–1919	1911–1915	1906–1910	1901–1905	1900 or earlier.	Year not reported.
ALABAMA:							
Mobile	2,157	134	141	225	197	724	736
Montgomery	771	26	93	106	83	334	129
ARIZONA:							
Phoenix	4,146	909	615	524	333	1,323	442
ARKANSAS:							
Fort Smith	855	7	50	72	84	461	181
Little Rock	1,815	19	94	161	76	749	716
CALIFORNIA:							
Alameda	6,353	317	724	879	743	3,166	524
Berkeley	10,506	850	1,235	1,393	1,295	5,105	628
Fresno	9,715	851	1,550	1,696	1,266	2,931	1,421
Long Beach	7,100	1,049	607	700	506	3,415	823
Pasadena	7,169	614	804	806	611	3,283	1,051
Sacramento	12,988	931	1,780	2,023	1,628	5,134	1,492
San Diego	14,088	1,429	1,834	1,537	1,223	6,278	1,787
San Jose	8,274	252	888	967	991	3,631	1,545
Stockton	8,341	525	1,001	1,136	934	3,534	1,211
COLORADO:							
Colorado Springs	2,639	92	136	169	215	1,539	488
Pueblo	7,489	1,097	952	854	871	2,222	1,493
CONNECTICUT:							
Meriden	7,916	203	1,099	1,198	908	3,846	662
New Britain	21,340	659	5,610	4,843	3,345	6,603	280
New London	5,935	246	1,016	988	941	2,606	138
Norwalk	6,008	123	861	1,080	904	2,471	569
Stamford	10,764	438	2,056	2,272	1,749	3,425	824
Waterbury	29,974	1,420	7,415	5,340	4,231	9,980	1,588
FLORIDA:							
Jacksonville	4,144	226	468	632	550	1,427	841
Miami	7,398	2,361	1,599	1,170	575	1,157	536
Pensacola	1,499	55	105	148	125	550	516
Tampa	11,352	974	1,633	2,492	2,052	3,292	909
GEORGIA:							
Augusta	999	23	115	109	95	360	297
Columbus	333	11	47	60	42	155	18
Macon	703	17	97	116	120	248	105
Savannah	3,336	165	413	520	355	1,600	283
ILLINOIS:							
Aurora	6,482	71	1,035	1,057	667	3,110	542
Bloomington	2,841	26	215	229	162	1,670	539
Cicero town	15,471	157	2,666	3,346	2,694	5,836	772
Danville	1,926	22	118	180	152	1,191	263
Decatur	2,595	28	301	303	264	1,400	299
East St. Louis	6,798	115	1,370	1,330	1,018	1,971	994
Elgin	5,061	35	245	361	233	2,505	1,682
Evanston	6,811	146	1,219	1,009	778	2,938	721
Joliet	8,522	170	1,419	1,372	1,143	3,737	681
Moline	7,398	280	1,206	1,225	820	2,538	329
Oak Park village	5,648	99	360	496	437	3,417	839
Peoria	7,821	113	696	808	652	4,112	1,435
Quincy	2,417	9	53	80	81	1,747	447
Rock Island	5,365	125	655	745	516	2,764	560
Rockford	17,373	618	2,898	2,776	1,998	7,159	1,924
Springfield	6,268	71	522	839	846	2,886	1,104
INDIANA:							
Anderson	946	18	126	124	70	405	203
East Chicago	14,701	368	4,738	3,619	2,003	2,183	1,790
Evansville	3,161	32	107	127	125	2,241	532
Fort Wayne	6,657	165	880	664	523	3,865	560
Gary	16,510	772	4,583	3,961	2,226	2,317	2,651
Hammond	8,136	73	1,831	1,746	1,240	2,612	634
Kokomo	1,170	24	212	181	112	532	109
Muncie	828	24	63	66	51	366	258
Richmond	1,135	25	155	131	93	558	173
South Bend	13,415	174	2,116	2,675	1,785	4,591	2,074
Terre Haute	3,683	35	339	497	411	1,767	634
IOWA:							
Cedar Rapids	5,873	125	934	744	507	2,820	743
Council Bluffs	4,002	131	399	411	247	1,772	1,042
Davenport	7,663	169	455	474	455	4,380	1,730
Dubuque	4,224	61	283	195	185	2,971	529
Sioux City	11,250	348	2,097	1,913	1,211	5,063	618
Waterloo	2,938	75	486	303	189	1,139	746
KANSAS:							
Topeka	4,035	432	591	404	189	1,878	541
Wichita	3,044	435	333	277	169	1,151	679

TABLE 85.—FOREIGN-BORN POPULATION BY YEAR OF IMMIGRATION, FOR CITIES HAVING FROM 25,000 TO 100,000 INHABITANTS: 1920—Continued.

CITY.	Total foreign born: 1920	YEAR OF IMMIGRATION.					
		1916–1919	1911–1915	1906–1910	1901–1905	1900 or earlier.	Year not reported.
KENTUCKY:							
Covington	2,894	18	85	118	134	2,182	357
Lexington	817	27	92	98	74	343	183
Newport	2,094	18	131	170	175	1,422	178
LOUISIANA:							
Shreveport	1,316	56	139	170	154	428	369
MAINE:							
Bangor	3,839	177	333	388	435	1,668	838
Lewiston	10,277	1,006	1,511	1,472	1,039	4,583	666
Portland	13,346	644	1,878	1,949	1,692	6,122	1,061
MARYLAND:							
Cumberland	1,168	13	108	110	106	336	495
Hagerstown	435	11	55	60	48	202	59
MASSACHUSETTS:							
Brockton	17,191	651	2,701	2,987	2,477	7,896	479
Brookline town	9,502	631	1,531	1,369	1,027	4,756	188
Chelsea	17,286	394	3,939	3,813	3,121	5,055	964
Chicopee	12,190	450	2,215	2,551	1,754	4,907	313
Everett	11,227	374	1,265	1,758	1,469	6,212	149
Fitchburg	13,180	805	2,078	2,012	1,616	5,377	1,292
Haverhill	13,335	580	2,243	2,212	1,719	6,152	429
Holyoke	20,280	912	2,957	3,215	2,501	10,223	472
Lawrence	39,201	1,709	8,297	8,147	5,318	14,859	871
Lynn	28,138	1,307	4,597	4,920	4,172	12,824	318
Malden	14,158	441	1,794	2,422	2,200	7,242	59
Medford	8,598	279	938	1,142	1,123	5,043	73
Newton	10,296	496	1,559	1,453	1,245	5,381	162
Pittsfield	8,247	239	1,645	1,436	994	3,224	709
Quincy	13,776	578	2,322	2,297	2,016	6,207	356
Revere	8,857	168	930	1,501	1,506	4,012	740
Salem	11,258	372	1,559	1,696	1,601	5,819	211
Somerville	24,254	1,117	3,072	3,268	3,115	13,497	185
Taunton	10,185	638	1,666	1,465	1,274	4,708	434
Waltham	8,126	455	1,204	1,232	962	4,135	138
MICHIGAN:							
Battle Creek	3,427	144	614	455	252	1,289	673
Bay City	8,956	107	486	619	588	6,291	865
Flint	15,213	1,227	3,788	2,623	1,341	4,535	1,699
Hamtramck village	23,099	451	11,326	6,291	2,706	2,051	274
Highland Park	12,721	1,264	3,662	2,275	1,232	2,917	1,371
Jackson	5,379	149	995	797	520	2,141	777
Kalamazoo	7,232	129	1,099	998	742	2,505	1,759
Lansing	6,042	205	1,220	784	429	2,061	1,343
Muskegon	6,791	132	754	657	543	3,805	900
Pontiac	5,228	396	900	528	234	1,185	1,985
Port Huron	6,368	458	805	530	486	3,748	341
Saginaw	11,655	263	1,201	1,195	849	5,828	2,319
MINNESOTA:							
Duluth	30,196	809	3,864	4,755	4,573	13,601	2,594
MISSOURI:							
Joplin	734	4	43	61	60	461	105
St. Joseph	6,438	227	787	864	505	2,780	1,275
Springfield	977	10	51	36	38	535	307
MONTANA:							
Butte	11,634	394	1,448	1,715	1,332	4,584	2,161
NEBRASKA:							
Lincoln	7,235	169	1,224	1,274	796	2,914	858
NEW HAMPSHIRE:							
Manchester	27,537	1,692	4,367	4,507	2,850	12,253	1,868
Nashua	8,821	607	1,687	1,248	769	3,361	1,149
NEW JERSEY:							
Atlantic City	7,509	247	1,090	1,190	1,148	3,247	587
Bayonne	25,514	682	6,162	5,824	4,489	7,963	394
Clifton	9,634	235	1,950	2.200	1,600	3,418	231
East Orange	6,890	173	694	839	786	3,359	1,039
Elizabeth	28,276	660	6,514	6,073	4,511	9,100	1,418
Hoboken	23,543	962	4,182	4,184	3,696	9,878	641
Irvington town	5,520	40	503	731	688	2,693	865
Kearny town	7,925	222	1,363	1,639	1,047	3,439	215
Montclair town	5,575	347	880	869	664	2,192	623
New Brunswick	8,969	323	2,127	2,009	1,586	2,098	826
Orange	7,039	173	923	918	1,164	3,413	448
Passaic	26,396	340	6,856	6,594	4,589	6,949	1,068
Perth Amboy	15,046	285	3,181	3,285	2,566	4,529	1,200
Plainfield	5,559	216	971	1,050	840	2,084	398
West Hoboken town	14,097	368	2,114	2,535	2,322	6,555	203
West New York town	8,933	173	1,429	1,619	1,416	3,570	726

TABLE 85.—FOREIGN-BORN POPULATION BY YEAR OF IMMIGRATION, FOR CITIES HAVING FROM 25,000 TO 100,000 INHABITANTS: 1920—Continued.

CITY.	Total foreign born: 1920	YEAR OF IMMIGRATION.					
		1916–1919	1911–1915	1906–1910	1901–1905	1900 or earlier.	Year not reported.
NEW YORK:							
Amsterdam	9,808	140	1,913	2,229	1,558	3,226	742
Auburn	7,607	285	1,775	1,595	998	2,741	213
Binghamton	10,401	107	2,440	2,152	1,373	2,674	1,655
Elmira	4,735	81	527	510	415	2,152	1,050
Jamestown	11,427	330	1,596	1,601	1,586	5,395	919
Kingston	2,769	33	180	261	330	1,393	572
Mount Vernon	10,171	284	1,333	1,595	1,818	4,877	264
New Rochelle	8,666	369	1,092	1,469	1,393	3,947	396
Newburgh	4,957	93	585	731	613	2,260	675
Niagara Falls	17,948	1,344	4,725	3,006	2,280	4,318	2,275
Poughkeepsie	5,556	148	833	889	738	2,113	835
Rome	5,240	262	1,409	1,147	691	1,530	201
Schenectady	20,564	543	3,679	3,882	3,659	7,625	1,176
Troy	11,525	124	938	1,221	1,036	6,132	2,074
Utica	23,291	529	4,655	4,955	3,799	9,015	338
Watertown	5,844	269	654	824	773	2,661	663
NORTH CAROLINA:							
Asheville	561	18	29	56	67	237	154
Charlotte	522	29	63	55	70	155	150
Wilmington	647	31	95	83	45	199	194
Winston-Salem	317	19	48	63	44	94	49
OHIO:							
Canton	14,729	1,185	4,939	2,509	1,676	3,476	944
East Cleveland	3,847	120	414	488	416	2,283	126
Hamilton	2,667	30	331	306	234	1,487	279
Lakewood	7,263	113	1,549	1,374	944	2,859	424
Lima	1,933	46	318	211	169	776	413
Lorain	11,941	346	3,393	2,867	2,152	2,867	316
Mansfield	3,209	77	690	751	429	951	311
Marion	955	24	132	110	64	483	142
Newark	1,508	26	341	270	162	569	140
Portsmouth	698	17	63	53	35	379	151
Springfield	2,772	61	367	267	165	1,528	384
Steubenville	5,593	227	1,571	1,315	866	1,232	382
Warren	4,687	260	1,725	1,059	468	1,036	139
Zanesville	1,273	6	209	162	150	612	134
OKLAHOMA:							
Muskogee	556	37	29	38	66	249	137
Oklahoma City	3,565	534	380	389	292	1,422	548
Tulsa	2,066	118	228	264	198	645	613
PENNSYLVANIA:							
Allentown	8,622	97	2,273	2,028	1,517	2,288	419
Altoona	5,326	162	1,007	976	911	2,077	193
Bethlehem	10,975	614	3,345	2,592	1,683	2,051	690
Chester	11,389	565	3,801	2,366	1,326	2,789	542
Easton	4,040	127	971	781	615	1,258	288
Erie	17,396	387	3,163	2,859	1,954	6,662	2,371
Harrisburg	4,190	100	674	730	550	1,263	873
Hazleton	6,026	75	580	731	981	3,352	307
Johnstown	12,172	175	2,970	2,687	2,310	3,746	284
Lancaster	2,718	56	275	296	231	1,497	363
McKeesport	11,887	203	2,389	2,121	1,915	4,367	892
New Castle	8,703	230	2,090	1,755	1,383	2,697	548
Norristown borough	4,337	90	558	660	759	1,727	543
Wilkes-Barre	14,580	80	2,187	2,287	2,065	6,969	992
Williamsport	2,272	47	308	256	216	971	474
York	1,200	22	117	87	131	629	214
RHODE ISLAND:							
Cranston	7,551	175	1,018	1,091	1,112	3,462	693
Newport	5,916	159	635	677	695	3,180	570
Pawtucket	21,138	1,075	3,165	3,288	2,476	9,656	1,478
Woonsocket	16,082	1,350	2,215	2,514	1,663	6,620	1,720
SOUTH CAROLINA:							
Charleston	2,234	77	256	244	190	965	502
Columbia	547	19	65	88	75	199	101
SOUTH DAKOTA:							
Sioux Falls	2,977	62	212	290	212	1,333	868
TENNESSEE:							
Chattanooga	1,253	18	129	171	151	615	169
Knoxville	821	14	61	98	74	409	165

TABLE 85.—FOREIGN-BORN POPULATION BY YEAR OF IMMIGRATION, FOR CITIES HAVING FROM 25,000 TO 100,000 INHABITANTS: 1920—Continued.

CITY.	Total foreign born: 1920	YEAR OF IMMIGRATION.					
		1916–1919	1911–1915	1906–1910	1901–1905	1900 or earlier.	Year not reported.
TEXAS:							
Austin	2,562	203	175	147	118	1,015	904
Beaumont	1,949	216	187	274	270	819	183
El Paso	33,655	9,781	12,777	4,197	2,337	3,701	862
Galveston	7,030	1,024	963	836	603	2,391	1,213
Waco	1,788	101	185	186	138	654	524
Wichita Falls	1,726	516	154	135	122	315	484
UTAH:							
Ogden	4,925	253	597	666	502	2,359	548
VIRGINIA:							
Lynchburg	354	8	39	43	37	157	70
Newport News	2,218	153	299	357	281	647	481
Petersburg	520	16	86	*113	72	162	71
Portsmouth	1,582	65	255	307	212	682	61
Roanoke	878	26	105	95	89	413	150
WASHINGTON:							
Bellingham	5,378	264	596	714	615	2,342	847
Everett	5,822	342	597	826	671	2,772	614
Tacoma	21,705	1,103	2,406	3,379	2,641	9,399	2,777
WEST VIRGINIA:							
Charleston	1,382	40	124	159	176	449	434
Clarksburg	1,943	71	349	324	287	587	325
Huntington	735	23	94	101	61	269	187
Wheeling	5,808	149	906	730	529	2,605	889
WISCONSIN:							
Green Bay	3,568	17	112	203	200	2,432	604
Kenosha	12,725	272	3,353	2,890	1,796	3,346	1,068
La Crosse	4,449	23	143	170	205	3,577	331
Madison	4,888	127	639	651	518	2,486	467
Oshkosh	5,796	16	247	371	404	3,822	936
Racine	16,215	476	3,472	2,870	1,895	6,524	978
Sheboygan	8,275	51	1,640	1,274	837	3,687	786
Superior	10,788	212	1,133	1,499	1,576	4,904	1,464

TABLE 86.—FOREIGN-BORN POPULATION AND FOREIGN-BORN WHITE POPULATION OF URBAN AND RURAL COMMUNITIES, BY SEX AND YEAR OF IMMIGRATION, FOR THE UNITED STATES: 1920.

CLASS OF POPULATION AND YEAR OF IMMIGRATION.	BOTH SEXES.		MALE.		FEMALE.	
	Urban.	Rural.	Urban.	Rural.	Urban.	Rural.
Foreign-born population	10,500,942	3,419,750	5,660,719	2,014,716	4,840,223	1,405,034
1919	152,493	61,630	83,498	36,394	68,995	25,236
1918	57,363	28,207	31,060	16,260	26,303	11,947
1917	84,364	31,858	44,313	18,246	40,051	13,612
1916	131,386	45,798	69,663	26,393	61,723	19,405
1915	154,813	48,285	83,432	28,794	71,381	19,491
1914	364,541	85,335	203,799	52,417	160,742	32,918
1911–1913	1,303,789	301,101	746,998	186,335	556,791	114,766
1906–1910	1,787,112	442,756	1,012,374	275,778	774,738	166,978
1901–1905	1,443,128	371,136	825,715	231,783	617,413	139,353
1900 or earlier	4,175,275	1,585,962	2,217,610	950,980	1,957,665	634,982
Not reported	846,678	417,682	342,257	191,336	504,421	226,346
Per cent of total	100.0	100.0	100.0	100.0	100.0	100.0
1919	1.5	1.8	1.5	1.8	1.4	1.8
1918	0.5	0.8	0.5	0.8	0.5	0.9
1917	0.8	0.9	0.8	0.9	0.8	1.0
1916	1.3	1.3	1.2	1.3	1.3	1.4
1915	1.5	1.4	1.5	1.4	1.5	1.4
1914	3.5	2.5	3.6	2.6	3.3	2.3
1911–1913	12.4	8.8	13.2	9.2	11.5	8.2
1906–1910	17.0	12.9	17.9	13.7	16.0	11.9
1901–1905	13.7	10.9	14.6	11.5	12.8	9.9
1900 or earlier	39.8	46.4	39.2	47.2	40.4	45.2
Not reported	8.1	12.2	6.0	9.5	10.4	16.1

TABLE 86.—FOREIGN-BORN POPULATION AND FOREIGN-BORN WHITE POPULATION OF URBAN AND RURAL COMMUNITIES, BY SEX AND YEAR OF IMMIGRATION, FOR THE UNITED STATES: 1920—Continued.

CLASS OF POPULATION AND YEAR OF IMMIGRATION.	BOTH SEXES.		MALE.		FEMALE.	
	Urban.	Rural.	Urban.	Rural.	Urban.	Rural.
Foreign-born white population............	10,356,983	3,355,771	5,560,396	1,967,926	4,796,587	1,387,845
1919........................	143,212	58,068	78,054	34,538	65,158	23,530
1918........................	51,329	25,600	27,760	14,963	23,569	10,637
1917........................	77,132	28,927	40,164	16,661	36,968	12,266
1916........................	124,881	42,794	65,915	24,761	58,966	18,033
1915........................	148,457	45,227	79,639	27,113	68,818	18,114
1914........................	358,160	82,547	199,986	50,822	158,174	31,725
1911–1913...................	1,289,714	295,432	738,584	183,174	551,130	112,258
1906–1910...................	1,763,726	430,645	995,348	265,767	768,378	164,878
1901–1905...................	1,428,308	361,872	814,106	223,556	614,202	138,316
1900 or earlier.............	4,144,032	1,573,433	2,190,978	939,525	1,953,054	633,908
Not reported...............	828,032	411,226	329,862	187,046	498,170	224,180
Per cent of total........	100.0	100.0	100.0	100.0	100.0	100.0
1919........................	1.4	1.7	1.4	1.8	1.4	1.7
1918........................	0.5	0.8	0.5	0.8	0.5	0.8
1917........................	0.7	0.9	0.7	0.8	0.8	0.9
1916........................	1.2	1.3	1.2	1.3	1.2	1.3
1915........................	1.4	1.3	1.4	1.4	1.4	1.3
1914........................	3.5	2.5	3.6	2.6	3.3	2.3
1911–1913...................	12.5	8.8	13.3	9.3	11.5	8.1
1906–1910...................	17.0	12.8	17.9	13.5	16.0	11.9
1901–1905...................	13.8	10.8	14.6	11.4	12.8	10.0
1900 or earlier.............	40.0	46.9	39.4	47.7	40.7	45.7
Not reported...............	8.0	12.3	5.9	9.5	10.4	16.2

TABLE 87.—FOREIGN-BORN POPULATION OF URBAN AND RURAL

		URBAN COMMUNITIES.								
DIVISION AND STATE.	Total foreign born: 1920	Year of immigration.					Per cent of total arriving in—			
		1916–1919	1911–1915	1901–1910	1900 or earlier.	Year not reported.	1911–1919	1901–1910	1900 or earlier.	Year not reported.
United States.	10,500,942	425,606	1,823,143	3,230,240	4,175,275	846,678	21.4	30.8	39.8	8.1
GEOG. DIVISIONS:										
New England.....	1,656,120	72,623	274,037	493,620	728,764	87,076	20.9	29.8	44.0	5.3
Middle Atlantic...	4,286,036	139,376	781,885	1,488,126	1,599,005	277,644	21.5	34.7	37.3	6.5
E. North Central..	2,519,937	66,229	486,560	744,964	992,962	229,222	21.9	29.6	39.4	9.1
W. North Central.	609,942	17,417	71,980	143,654	300,903	75,988	14.7	23.6	49.3	12.5
South Atlantic....	233,879	10,874	35,435	68,227	93,116	26,227	19.8	29.2	39.8	11.2
E. South Central.	49,015	987	3,886	9,543	24,356	10,243	9.9	19.5	49.7	20.9
W. South Central.	223,424	42,304	44,506	39,067	56,798	40,749	38.9	17.5	25.4	18.2
Mountain.........	186,147	15,201	24,318	44,313	81,564	20,751	21.2	23.8	43.8	11.1
Pacific...........	736,442	60,595	100,536	198,726	297,807	78,778	21.9	27.0	40.4	10.7
NEW ENGLAND:										
Maine...........	59,465	4,419	7,642	13,868	27,135	6,401	20.3	23.3	45.6	10.8
New Hampshire...	71,574	4,253	10,184	16,977	32,176	7,984	20.2	23.7	45.0	11.2
Vermont........	18,167	873	2,478	4,974	8,200	1,642	18.4	27.4	45.1	9.0
Massachusetts...	1,055,640	45,893	171,973	313,764	481,651	42,359	20.6	29.7	45.6	4.0
Rhode Island.....	173,365	7,778	24,924	50,575	78,352	11,736	18.9	29.2	45.2	6.8
Connecticut......	277,909	9,407	56,836	93,462	101,250	16,954	23.8	33.6	36.4	6.1
MIDDLE ATLANTIC:										
New York........	2,623,903	102,036	468,153	917,761	966,917	169,036	21.7	35.0	36.9	6.4
New Jersey......	631,873	15,692	117,065	218,256	242,751	38,109	21.0	34.5	38.4	6.0
Pennsylvania.....	1,030,260	21,648	196,667	352,109	389,337	70,499	21.2	34.2	37.8	6.8
E. NORTH CENTRAL:										
Ohio.............	572,098	14,361	131,608	184,365	203,519	38,245	25.5	32.2	35.6	6.7
Indiana..........	119,251	2,387	21,268	32,988	43,576	19,032	19.8	27.7	36.5	16.0
Illinois..........	1,050,200	18,034	175,935	325,579	435,448	95,204	18.5	31.0	41.5	9.1
Michigan.........	523,978	28,287	122,361	143,088	177,439	52,803	28.8	27.3	33.9	10.1
Wisconsin........	254,410	3,160	35,388	58,944	132,980	23,938	15.2	23.2	52.3	9.4
W. NORTH CENTRAL:										
Minnesota........	242,008	5,393	29,777	62,654	122,633	21,551	14.5	25.9	50.7	8.9
Iowa.............	90,285	2,404	9,608	15,059	49,304	13,910	13.3	16.7	54.6	15.4
Missouri.........	149,551	3,247	16,932	39,238	70,215	19,919	13.5	26.2	47.0	13.3
North Dakota.....	16,308	253	1,300	3,474	7,593	3,688	9.5	21.3	46.6	22.6
South Dakota.....	12,236	192	903	2,322	5,984	2,835	8.9	19.0	48.9	23.2
Nebraska........	59,905	1,656	8,592	14,224	27,522	7,911	17.1	23.7	45.9	13.2
Kansas..........	39,649	4,272	4,868	6,683	17,652	6,174	23.1	16.9	44.5	15.6
SOUTH ATLANTIC:										
Delaware.........	16,878	454	3,851	5,331	5,566	1,676	25.5	31.6	33.0	9.9
Maryland........	88,678	1,680	13,762	27,054	42,290	3,892	17.4	30.5	47.7	4.4
Dist. of Columbia..	29,365	1,243	3,595	7,843	11,567	5,117	16.5	26.7	39.4	17.4
Virginia.........	20,018	1,524	2,975	5,694	6,689	3,136	22.5	28.4	33.4	15.7
West Virginia....	19,864	683	3,592	5,655	6,803	3,131	21.5	28.5	34.2	15.8
North Carolina...	4,373	171	567	1,119	1,351	1,165	16.9	25.6	30.9	26.6
South Carolina...	4,356	134	555	1,027	1,666	974	15.8	23.6	38.2	22.4
Georgia..........	12,733	469	1,522	3,548	5,170	2,024	15.6	27.9	40.6	15.9
Florida..........	37,614	4,516	5,016	10,956	12,014	5,112	25.3	29.1	31.9	13.6
E. SOUTH CENTRAL:										
Kentucky........	21,667	206	1,230	3,062	13,210	3,959	6.6	14.1	61.0	18.3
Tennessee........	11,621	340	1,113	2,697	5,003	2,468	12.5	23.2	43.1	21.2
Alabama.........	11,431	351	1,167	2,677	4,257	2,979	13.3	23.4	37.2	26.1
Mississippi......	4,296	90	376	1,107	1,886	837	10.8	25.8	43.9	19.5
W. SOUTH CENTRAL:										
Arkansas.........	5,647	52	293	891	2,644	1,767	6.1	15.8	46.8	31.3
Louisiana........	61,030	1,325	2,008	5,580	13,682	10,637	11.4	17.2	40.1	31.2
Oklahoma........	14,449	1,675	1,420	2,576	5,405	3,373	21.4	17.8	37.4	23.3
Texas...........	169,235	38,748	40,728	29,720	35,067	24,972	47.0	17.6	20.7	14.8
MOUNTAIN:										
Montana.........	33,482	1,091	3,802	8,462	13,998	6,129	14.6	25.3	41.8	18.3
Idaho...........	11,801	647	1,249	2,513	6,010	1,382	16.1	21.3	50.9	11.7
Wyoming........	8,966	717	1,339	2,458	3,181	1,271	22.9	27.4	35.5	14.2
Colorado.........	60,483	3,062	6,114	14,082	31,643	5,552	15.2	23.3	52.3	9.2
New Mexico.......	5,754	775	937	1,135	2,037	870	29.8	19.7	35.4	15.1
Arizona..........	29,704	7,438	6,657	6,643	6,015	2,951	47.5	22.4	20.2	9.9
Utah............	33,152	1,332	3,909	8,324	17,694	1,893	15.8	25.1	53.4	5.7
Nevada..........	2,805	139	281	696	986	703	15.0	24.8	35.2	25.1
PACIFIC:										
Washington......	159,291	11,543	19,761	44,406	63,637	19,944	19.7	27.9	40.0	12.5
Oregon..........	65,073	3,103	8,214	19,331	30,314	4,111	17.4	29.7	46.6	6.3
California........	512,078	45,949	72,561	134,989	203,856	54,723	23.1	26.4	39.8	10.7

COMMUNITIES BY YEAR OF IMMIGRATION, BY DIVISIONS AND STATES: 1920.

DIVISION AND STATE.	Total foreign born: 1920	Year of immigration.					Per cent of total arriving in—			
		1916–1919	1911–1915	1901–1910	1900 or earlier.	Year not reported.	1911–1919	1901–1910	1900 or earlier.	Year not reported.
RURAL COMMUNITIES.										
United States..	3,419,750	167,493	434,721	813,892	1,585,962	417,682	17.6	23.8	46.4	12.2
GEOG. DIVISIONS:										
New England.....	229,825	12,428	31,091	61,350	103,679	21,277	18.9	26.7	45.1	9.3
Middle Atlantic...	674,382	14,212	119,647	221,007	250,908	68,608	19.8	32.8	37.2	10.2
E. North Central..	712,204	9,207	66,396	145,868	396,285	94,448	10.6	20.5	55.6	13.3
W. North Central.	765,711	10,817	48,715	130,461	474,128	101,590	7.8	17.0	61.9	13.3
South Atlantic....	96,658	5,857	21,091	27,766	25,534	16,410	27.9	28.7	26.4	17.0
E. South Central..	23,974	616	2,835	5,313	10,067	5,143	14.4	22.2	42.0	21.5
W. South Central.	241,404	44,355	40,385	43,074	74,790	38,800	35.1	17.8	31.0	16.1
Mountain........	281,473	37,486	46,800	71,393	95,814	29,980	29.9	25.4	34.0	10.7
Pacific............	394,119	32,515	57,761	107,660	154,757	41,426	22.9	27.3	39.3	10.5
NEW ENGLAND:										
Maine............	48,349	3,974	5,484	11,178	20,968	6,745	19.6	23.1	43.4	14.0
New Hampshire..	19,823	1,262	2,001	3,698	9,788	3,074	16.5	18.7	49.4	15.5
Vermont..........	26,391	3,607	3,687	5,414	10,922	2,761	27.6	20.5	41.4	10.5
Massachusetts.....	32,908	948	4,068	8,448	17,416	2,028	15.2	25.7	52.9	6.2
Rhode Island......	1,824	54	228	465	843	234	15.5	25.5	46.2	12.8
Connecticut......	100,530	2,583	15,623	32,147	43,742	6,435	18.1	32.0	43.5	6.4
MIDDLE ATLANTIC:										
New York........	201,472	5,749	25,484	50,566	91,228	28,445	15.5	25.1	45.3	14.1
New Jersey.......	110,613	2,384	17,357	36,564	44,052	10,256	17.8	33.1	39.8	9.3
Pennsylvania.....	362,297	6,079	76,806	133,877	115,628	29,907	22.9	37.0	31.9	8.3
E. NORTH CENTRAL:										
Ohio.............	108,354	1,687	17,203	31,292	45,305	12,867	17.4	28.9	41.8	11.9
Indiana..........	32,077	321	2,124	5,072	17,253	7,307	7.6	15.8	53.8	22.8
Illinois...........	160,384	2,281	15,672	34,939	82,515	24,977	11.2	21.8	51.4	15.6
Michigan.........	205,314	3,608	18,278	40,983	118,444	24,001	10.7	20.0	57.7	11.7
Wisconsin........	206,075	1,310	13,119	33,582	132,768	25,296	7.0	16.3	64.4	12.3
W. NORTH CENTRAL:										
Minnesota........	244,787	2,445	14,956	41,657	164,382	21,347	7.1	17.0	67.2	8.7
Iowa.............	135,709	1,773	9,893	18,368	86,788	18,887	8.6	13.5	64.0	13.9
Missouri.........	37,284	426	1,719	4,515	21,877	8,747	5.8	12.1	58.7	23.5
North Dakota.....	115,555	1,328	8,163	32,030	57,930	16,104	8.2	27.7	50.1	13.9
South Dakota.....	70,298	822	4,665	13,300	41,793	9,718	7.8	18.9	59.5	13.8
Nebraska.........	90,760	1,115	4,918	10,571	59,101	15,055	6.6	11.6	65.1	16.6
Kansas..........	71,318	2,908	4,401	10,020	42,257	11,732	10.2	14.0	59.3	16.5
SOUTH ATLANTIC:										
Delaware.........	3,023	96	374	738	1,041	774	15.5	24.4	34.4	25.6
Maryland.........	14,501	386	1,718	3,106	6,403	2,888	14.5	21.4	44.2	19.9
Dist. of Columbia[1].										
Virginia..........	11,687	467	1,572	3,071	3,798	2,779	17.4	26.3	32.5	23.8
West Virginia.....	42,241	2,859	14,071	15,478	5,435	4,398	40.1	36.6	12.9	10.4
North Carolina....	2,899	151	415	624	1,014	695	19.5	21.5	35.0	24.0
South Carolina....	2,226	66	316	523	772	549	17.2	23.5	34.7	24.7
Georgia..........	3,831	107	567	1,052	1,286	819	17.6	27.5	33.6	21.4
Florida..........	16,250	1,725	2,058	3,174	5,785	3,508	23.3	19.5	35.6	21.6
E. SOUTH CENTRAL:										
Kentucky........	9,239	264	1,558	2,035	3,752	1,630	19.7	22.0	40.6	17.6
Tennessee........	4,027	81	269	676	1,912	1,089	8.7	16.8	47.5	27.0
Alabama.........	6,596	159	591	1,544	2,765	1,537	11.4	23.4	41.9	23.3
Mississippi.......	4,112	112	417	1,058	1,638	887	12.9	25.7	39.8	21.6
W. SOUTH CENTRAL:										
Arkansas.........	8,490	192	610	1,700	4,110	1,878	9.4	20.0	48.4	22.1
Louisiana........	12,334	494	673	3,248	5,713	2,206	9.5	26.3	46.3	17.9
Oklahoma........	25,983	1,924	1,985	4,310	12,071	5,693	15.0	16.6	46.5	21.9
Texas............	194,597	41,745	37,117	33,816	52,896	29,023	40.5	17.4	27.2	14.9
MOUNTAIN:										
Montana.........	62,109	2,123	8,946	18,005	24,872	8,163	17.8	29.0	40.0	13.1
Idaho...........	28,946	1,681	3,227	7,030	14,243	2,765	17.0	24.3	49.2	9.6
Wyoming........	17,601	1,108	3,338	5,434	5,369	2,352	25.3	30.9	30.5	13.4
Colorado........	58,655	3,863	9,120	16,306	23,069	6,297	22.1	27.8	39.3	10.7
New Mexico.......	24,054	6,000	6,261	5,309	4,475	2,009	51.0	22.1	18.6	8.4
Arizona..........	50,862	20,026	10,163	8,937	6,762	4,974	59.4	17.6	13.3	9.8
Utah............	26,048	1,543	3,703	6,514	12,313	1,975	20.1	25.0	47.3	7.6
Nevada..........	13,198	1,142	2,042	3,858	4,711	1,445	24.1	29.2	35.7	10.9
PACIFIC:										
Washington......	106,001	4,989	12,080	29,888	47,996	11,048	16.1	28.2	45.3	10.4
Oregon..........	42,571	1,662	4,517	10,010	22,327	4,055	14.5	23.5	52.4	9.5
California........	245,547	25,864	41,164	67,762	84,434	26,323	27.3	27.6	34.4	10.7

[1]No rural population, as Washington city is coextensive with the District of Columbia.

TABLE 88.—CITIZENSHIP OF EACH CLASS OF THE POPULATION OF THE

CENSUS YEAR, SEX, AGE, AND COLOR OR RACE.	Total.	Native.	FOREIGN BORN—NUMBER.				
			Total.	Natural-ized.	Having first papers.	Alien.	Citizen-ship not re-ported.
1920							
Both sexes, all ages	105,710,620	91,789,928	13,920,692	6,493,088	1,223,490	5,398,605	805,509
White	94,820,915	81,108,161	13,712,754	6,479,159	1,219,057	5,223,715	790,823
Negro	10,463,131	10,389,328	73,803	10,724	3,496	48,930	10,653
Indian	244,437	238,138	6,299	665	59	4,946	629
Chinese	61,639	18,532	43,107	1,834	430	39,436	1,407
Japanese	111,010	29,672	81,338	572	270	78,740	1,756
All other	9,488	6,097	3,391	134	178	2,838	241
Males, all ages	53,900,431	46,224,996	7,675,435	3,451,609	1,137,911	2,688,929	396,986
White	48,430,655	40,902,333	7,528,322	3,443,968	1,133,727	2,562,917	387,710
Negro	5,209,436	5,166,795	42,641	5,579	3,294	27,653	6,115
Indian	125,068	121,529	3,539	213	51	2,900	375
Chinese	53,891	13,318	40,573	1,342	423	37,514	1,294
Japanese	72,707	15,494	57,213	399	239	55,296	1,279
All other	8,674	5,527	3,147	108	177	2,649	213
Females, all ages	51,810,189	45,564,932	6,245,257	3,041,479	85,579	2,709,676	408,523
White	46,390,260	40,205,828	6,184,432	3,035,191	85,330	2,660,798	403,113
Negro	5,253,695	5,222,533	31,162	5,145	202	21,277	4,538
Indian	119,369	116,609	2,760	452	8	2,046	254
Chinese	7,748	5,214	2,534	492	7	1,922	113
Japanese	38,303	14,178	24,125	173	31	23,444	477
All other	814	570	244	26	1	189	28
Both sexes, 21 years and over	60,886,520	48,200,127	12,686,393	6,221,705	1,198,588	4,522,359	743,741
White	55,113,461	42,614,741	12,498,720	6,208,697	1,194,276	4,364,909	730,838
Negro	5,522,475	5,458,063	64,412	10,104	3,422	41,586	9,300
Indian	116,486	112,044	4,442	603	56	3,297	486
Chinese	50,625	10,131	40,494	1,637	407	37,149	1,301
Japanese	75,727	658	75,069	541	254	72,679	1,595
All other	7,746	4,490	3,256	123	173	2,739	221
Males, 21 years and over	31,403,370	24,339,776	7,063,594	3,322,104	1,120,833	2,253,691	366,966
White	28,442,400	21,513,948	6,928,452	3,314,910	1,116,744	2,138,237	358,561
Negro	2,792,006	2,753,772	38,234	5,316	3,238	24,165	5,515
Indian	61,229	58,670	2,559	187	49	2,026	297
Chinese	46,979	8,694	38,285	1,199	402	35,470	1,214
Japanese	53,411	412	52,999	390	228	51,207	1,174
All other	7,345	4,280	3,065	102	172	2,586	205
Females, 21 years and over	29,483,150	23,860,351	5,622,799	2,899,601	77,755	2,268,668	376,775
White	26,671,061	21,100,793	5,570,268	2,893,787	77,532	2,226,672	372,277
Negro	2,730,469	2,704,291	26,178	4,788	184	17,421	3,785
Indian	55,257	53,374	1,883	416	7	1,271	189
Chinese	3,646	1,437	2,209	438	5	1,679	87
Japanese	22,316	246	22,070	151	26	21,472	421
All other	401	210	191	21	1	153	16
1910							
Males, 21 years and over	26,999,151	20,218,937	6,780,214	3,040,302	572,421	2,370,398	797,093
White	24,357,514	17,710,697	6,646,817	3,034,117	570,772	2,266,535	775,393
Negro	2,458,873	2,437,725	21,148	4,186	749	11,642	4,571
Indian	62,967	61,742	1,225	191	10	406	618
Chinese	60,421	8,463	51,958	1,368	483	43,710	7,097
Japanese	56,630	209	56,429	420	387	46,860	8,760
All other	2,728	101	2,627	20	20	2,245	352
1900							
Males, 21 years and over	21,134,299	16,124,013	5,010,286	2,849,981	412,790	1,001,595	745,920
White	18,918,697	14,014,427	4,904,270	2,845,473	411,898	914,917	731,982
Negro	2,060,302	2,049,958	10,344	3,334	373	3,630	3,007
Indian	57,077	56,071	1,006	138	33	378	457
Chinese	81,018	3,520	77,498	895	373	68,927	7,303
Japanese	17,205	37	17,168	141	113	13,743	3,171
1890 [1]							
Males, 21 years and over	16,940,311	12,591,852	4,348,459	2,545,753	236,061	1,189,452	377,193

[1] Exclusive of population of Indian Territory and Indian reservations, specially enumerated in 1890 but not distributed by age.

UNITED STATES FOR WHICH FIGURES ARE AVAILABLE: 1890–1920.

CENSUS YEAR, SEX, AGE, AND COLOR OR RACE.	FOREIGN BORN—PER CENT.				CITIZENS, NATIVE OR NATURALIZED.	
	Naturalized.	Having first papers.	Alien.	Citizenship not reported.	Number.	Per cent of total of specified class.
1920						
Both sexes, all ages..........	46.6	8.8	38.8	5.8	98,283,016	93.0
White......................	47.2	8.9	38.1	5.8	87,587,320	92.4
Negro......................	14.5	4.7	66.3	14.4	10,400,052	99.4
Indian.....................	10.6	0.9	78.5	10.0	238,803	97.7
Chinese....................	4.3	1.0	91.5	3.3	20,366	33.0
Japanese...................	0.7	0.3	96.8	2.2	30,244	27.2
All other..................	4.0	5.2	83.7	7.1	6,231	65.7
Males, all ages...................	45.0	14.8	35.0	5.2	49,676,605	92.2
White......................	45.7	15.1	34.0	5.2	44,346,301	91.6
Negro......................	13.1	7.7	64.9	14.3	5,172,374	99.3
Indian.....................	6.0	1.4	81.9	10.6	121,742	97.3
Chinese....................	3.3	1.0	92.5	3.2	14,660	27.2
Japanese...................	0.7	0.4	96.6	2.2	15,893	21.9
All other..................	3.4	5.6	84.2	6.8	5,635	65.0
Females, all ages.................	48.7	1.4	43.4	6.5	48,606,411	93.8
White......................	49.1	1.4	43.0	6.5	43,241,019	93.2
Negro......................	16.5	0.6	68.3	14.6	5,227,678	99.5
Indian.....................	16.4	0.3	74.1	9.2	117,061	98.1
Chinese....................	19.4	0.3	75.8	4.5	5,706	73.6
Japanese...................	0.7	0.1	97.2	2.0	14,351	37.5
All other..................	10.7	0.4	77.5	11.5	596	73.2
Both sexes, 21 years and over..	49.0	9.4	35.6	5.9	54,421,832	89.4
White......................	49.7	9.6	34.9	5.8	48,823,438	88.6
Negro......................	15.7	5.3	64.6	14.4	5,468,167	99.0
Indian.....................	13.6	1.3	74.2	10.9	112,647	96.7
Chinese....................	4.0	1.0	91.7	3.2	11,768	23.2
Japanese...................	0.7	0.3	96.8	2.1	1,199	1.6
All other..................	3.8	5.3	84.1	6.8	4,613	59.6
Males, 21 years and over............	47.0	15.9	31.9	5.2	27,661,880	88.1
White......................	47.8	16.1	30.9	5.2	24,828,858	87.3
Negro......................	13.9	8.5	63.2	14.4	2,759,088	98.8
Indian.....................	7.3	1.9	79.2	11.6	58,857	96.1
Chinese....................	3.1	1.1	92.6	3.2	9,893	21.1
Japanese...................	0.7	0.4	96.6	2.2	802	1.5
All other..................	3.3	5.6	84.4	6.7	4,382	59.7
Females, 21 years and over..........	51.6	1.4	40.3	6.7	26,759,952	90.8
White......................	52.0	1.4	40.0	6.7	23,994,580	90.0
Negro......................	18.3	0.7	66.5	14.5	2,709,079	99.2
Indian.....................	22.1	0.4	67.5	10.0	53,790	97.3
Chinese....................	19.8	0.2	76.0	3.9	1,875	51.4
Japanese...................	0.7	0.1	97.3	1.9	397	1.8
All other..................	11.0	0.5	80.1	8.4	231	57.6
1910						
Males, 21 years and over..........	44.8	8.4	35.0	11.8	23,259,239	86.1
White......................	45.6	8.6	34.1	11.7	20,744,814	85.2
Negro......................	19.8	3.5	55.1	21.6	2,441,911	99.3
Indian.....................	15.6	0.8	33.1	50.4	61,933	98.4
Chinese....................	2.6	0.9	82.2	14.2	9,831	16.3
Japanese...................	0.7	0.7	83.0	15.5	629	1.1
All other..................	0.8	0.8	85.1	13.3	121	4.4
1900						
Males, 21 years and over..........	56.9	8.2	20.0	14.9	18,973,994	89.8
White......................	58.0	8.4	18.7	14.9	16,859,900	89.1
Negro......................	32.2	3.6	35.1	29.1	2,053,292	99.7
Indian.....................	13.7	3.3	37.6	45.4	56,209	98.5
Chinese....................	1.2	0.5	88.9	9.4	4,415	5.4
Japanese...................	0.8	0.7	80.1	18.5	178	1.0
1890 [1]						
Males, 21 years and over..........	58.5	5.4	27.4	8.7	15,137,605	89.4

TABLE 89.—CITIZENSHIP OF FOREIGN-BORN WHITE POPULATION,

	COUNTRY OF BIRTH.	FOREIGN-BORN WHITE POPULATION.					
		Total.	Naturalized.		Having first papers.	Alien.	Citizenship not reported.
			Number.	Per cent.			
1	All countries	13,712,754	6,479,159	47.2	1,219,057	5,223,715	790,823
	EUROPE.						
	Northwestern Europe:						
2	England	812,828	512,670	63.1	56,331	175,447	68,380
3	Scotland	254,567	154,931	60.9	20,268	58,824	20,544
4	Wales	67,066	48,897	72.9	3,264	8,271	6,634
5	Ireland	1,037,233	681,362	65.7	52,707	206,959	96,205
6	Norway	363,862	244,743	67.3	32,386	63,035	23,698
7	Sweden	625,580	431,556	69.0	53,007	105,445	35,572
8	Denmark	189,154	130,826	69.2	16,862	28,987	12,479
9	Netherlands	131,766	73,773	56.0	13,465	36,550	7,978
10	Belgium	62,686	30,740	49.0	8,255	19,635	4,056
11	Luxemburg	12,585	9,124	72.5	969	1,507	985
12	Switzerland	118,659	76,957	64.9	8,756	22,635	10,311
13	France	152,890	86,740	56.7	11,205	41,229	13,716
	Central Europe:						
14	Germany	1,686,102	1,227,713	72.8	116,479	210,922	130,988
15	Poland	1,139,978	319,383	28.0	148,420	638,707	33,468
16	Czechoslovakia	362,436	165,997	45.8	49,244	132,176	15,019
17	Austria	575,625	216,968	37.7	67,913	262,690	28,054
18	Hungary	397,282	115,736	29.1	54,002	212,429	15,115
19	Jugo-Slavia	169,437	42,686	25.2	28,892	92,971	4,888
	Eastern Europe:						
20	Russia	1,400,489	562,930	40.2	139,149	644,966	53,444
21	Lithuania	135,068	34,627	25.6	16,890	80,428	3,123
22	Finland	149,824	61,902	41.3	18,797	63,000	6,125
23	Rumania	102,823	42,225	41.1	12,694	43,932	3,952
24	Bulgaria	10,477	1,268	12.1	1,716	7,023	470
25	Turkey in Europe	5,284	1,070	20.2	665	3,349	200
	Southern Europe:						
26	Greece	175,972	29,479	16.8	21,451	117,295	7,747
27	Albania	5,608	413	7.4	517	4,551	127
28	Italy	1,610,109	452,753	28.1	163,499	941,602	52,255
29	Spain	49,247	4,881	9.9	2,428	39,623	2,315
30	Portugal	67,453	11,049	16.4	2,481	51,590	2,333
31	Other Europe[1]	5,901	2,835	48.0	675	1,821	570
	ASIA.						
32	Armenia	36,626	10,574	28.9	4,630	20,125	1,297
33	Palestine	3,202	1,201	37.5	358	1,433	210
34	Syria	51,900	15,001	28.9	6,023	28,119	2,757
35	Turkey in Asia	11,014	2,768	25.1	1,148	6,511	587
36	Other Asia	7,708	2,815	36.5	838	3,379	676
	AMERICA.						
37	Canada—French	307,786	138,019	44.8	23,777	129,975	16,015
38	Canada—Other	810,092	469,284	57.9	48,937	215,582	76,289
39	Newfoundland	13,242	6,271	47.4	1,234	4,624	1,113
40	Mexico	478,383	22,732	4.8	2,989	433,028	19,634
41	West Indies[2]	26,369	7,419	28.1	1,737	11,061	3,567
42	Central and South America	20,929	5,046	24.1	1,232	12,412	2,200
	OTHER COUNTRIES.						
43	Africa	5,222	2,276	43.6	405	2,087	454
44	Australia	10,801	5,345	49.5	916	3,415	1,125
45	Atlantic Islands	38,984	8,138	20.9	1,312	28,353	1,181
46	Pacific Islands[2]	3,643	1,824	50.1	287	1,123	409
47	All other	8,862	4,212	47.5	352	1,578	2,720

[1] Comprises Danzig, Fiume, Saar Basin, and "Europe, not specified."

BY SEX AND COUNTRY OF BIRTH, FOR THE UNITED STATES: 1920.

	FOREIGN-BORN WHITE MALES.					FOREIGN-BORN WHITE FEMALES.						
Total.	Naturalized.		Having first papers.	Alien.	Citizenship not reported.	Total.	Naturalized.		Having first papers.	Alien.	Citizenship not reported.	
	Number.	Per cent.					Number.	Per cent.				
7,528,322	3,443,968	45.7	1,133,727	2,562,917	387,710	6,184,432	3,035,191	49.1	85,330	2,660,798	403,113	1
425,038	265,820	62.5	51,297	73,377	34,544	387,790	246,850	63.7	5,034	102,070	33,836	2
133,955	82,425	61.5	18,464	22,827	10,239	120,612	72,506	60.1	1,804	35,997	10,305	3
36,184	26,152	72.3	3,009	3,574	3,449	30,882	22,745	73.7	255	4,697	3,185	4
455,571	327,146	71.8	44,287	50,286	33,852	581,662	354,216	60.9	8,420	156,673	62,353	5
202,757	134,659	66.4	29,551	27,167	11,380	161,105	110,084	68.3	2,835	35,868	12,318	6
344,933	236,614	68.6	48,173	42,369	17,777	280,647	194,942	69.5	4,834	63,076	17,795	7
114,063	78,030	68.4	15,671	13,175	7,187	75,091	52,796	70.3	1,191	15,812	5,292	8
75,510	41,383	54.8	12,567	17,216	4,344	56,256	32,390	57.6	898	19,334	3,634	9
35,970	17,604	48.9	7,759	8,344	2,263	26,716	13,136	49.2	496	11,291	1,793	10
7,671	5,543	72.3	895	695	538	4,914	3,581	72.9	74	812	447	11
67,830	43,332	63.9	7,983	11,194	5,321	50,829	33,625	66.2	773	11,441	4,990	12
79,351	45,875	57.8	10,010	16,945	6,521	73,539	40,865	55.6	1,195	24,284	7,195	13
891,289	646,579	72.5	102,322	83,576	58,812	794,813	581,134	73.1	14,157	127,346	72,176	14
646,387	176,197	27.3	141,320	311,785	17,085	493,591	143,186	29.0	7,100	326,922	16,383	15
196,251	85,444	43.5	46,110	57,565	7,132	166,185	80,553	48.5	3,134	74,611	7,887	16
323,451	115,481	35.7	64,227	129,355	14,388	252,174	101,487	40.2	3,686	133,335	13,666	17
216,914	59,695	27.5	50,950	99,018	7,251	180,368	56,041	31.1	3,052	113,411	7,864	18
114,750	25,064	21.8	27,952	58,470	3,264	54,687	17,622	32.2	940	34,501	1,624	19
774,013	310,284	40.1	130,870	305,841	27,018	626,476	252,646	40.3	8,279	339,125	26,426	20
82,866	20,891	25.2	16,304	43,869	1,802	52,202	13,736	26.3	586	36,559	1,321	21
85,287	33,065	38.8	17,661	31,449	3,112	64,537	28,837	44.7	1,136	31,551	3,013	22
58,135	23,169	39.9	11,948	21,045	1,973	44,688	19,056	42.6	746	22,907	1,979	23
9,508	994	10.5	1,696	6,395	423	969	274	28.3	20	628	47	24
3,658	711	19.4	640	2,173	134	1,626	359	22.1	25	1,176	66	25
143,602	23,786	16.6	21,080	92,381	6,355	32,370	5,693	17.6	371	24,914	1,392	26
4,905	335	6.8	513	3,950	107	703	78	11.1	4	601	20	27
958,274	275,609	28.8	157,159	495,885	29,621	651,835	177,144	27.2	6,340	445,717	22,634	28
36,434	3,021	8.3	2,355	29,428	1,630	12,813	1,860	14.5	73	10,195	685	29
39,372	6,319	16.0	2,337	29,332	1,384	28,081	4,730	16.8	144	22,258	949	30
3,665	1,560	42.6	631	1,172	302	2,236	1,275	57.0	44	649	268	31
25,351	6,948	27.4	4,472	13,055	876	11,275	3,626	32.2	158	7,070	421	32
2,061	729	35.4	341	863	128	1,141	472	41.4	17	570	82	33
31,240	9,312	29.8	5,733	14,648	1,547	20,660	5,689	27.5	290	13,471	1,210	34
8,039	1,868	23.2	1,108	4,689	374	2,975	900	30.3	40	1,822	213	35
5,082	1,642	32.3	803	2,193	444	2,626	1,173	44.7	35	1,186	232	36
157,748	68,802	43.6	22,447	58,909	7,590	150,038	69,217	46.1	1,330	71,066	8,425	37
389,609	212,579	54.6	43,972	94,586	38,472	420,483	256,705	61.1	4,965	120,996	37,817	38
6,154	2,868	46.6	1,143	1,659	484	7,088	3,403	48.0	91	2,965	629	39
271,564	8,527	3.1	2,658	248,519	11,860	206,819	14,205	6.9	331	184,509	7,774	40
14,133	3,822	27.0	1,119	7,431	1,761	12,236	3,597	29.4	113	6,920	1,606	41
12,624	2,592	20.5	1,131	7,575	1,326	8,305	2,454	29.5	101	4,838	912	42
2,981	1,228	41.2	373	1,114	266	2,241	1,048	46.8	32	973	188	43
5,935	2,613	44.0	837	1,814	671	4,866	2,732	56.1	79	1,601	454	44
21,005	4,597	21.9	1,246	14,508	654	17,979	3,541	19.7	66	13,845	527	45
1,993	911	45.7	272	570	240	1,650	913	55.3	15	553	169	46
5,209	2,143	41.1	331	926	1,809	3,653	2,069	56.6	21	652	911	47

² Except possessions of the United States.

TABLE **90.**—CITIZENSHIP OF FOREIGN-BORN WHITE MALES 21 YEARS OF AGE

COUNTRY OF BIRTH (postwar boundaries).	Foreign-born white males 21 years of age and over.	Naturalized.		Having first papers.	Alien.	Citizenship not reported.
		Number.	Per cent.			
All countries...................	6,928,452	3,314,910	47.8	1,116,744	2,138,237	358,561
EUROPE.						
Northwestern Europe:						
England.....................	392,116	253,937	64.8	50,338	55,148	32,693
Scotland....................	122,568	77,903	63.6	18,125	16,942	9,598
Wales.......................	34,806	25,591	73.5	2,967	2,885	3,363
Ireland.....................	448,573	324,100	72.3	43,995	47,181	33,297
Norway.....................	195,101	131,322	67.3	29,223	23,640	10,916
Sweden.....................	334,849	232,761	69.5	47,632	37,257	17,199
Denmark....................	109,754	76,412	69.6	15,447	10,978	6,917
Netherlands................	67,901	39,462	58.1	12,304	12,135	4,000
Belgium and Luxemburg..........	39,295	21,722	55.3	8,504	6,515	2,554
Switzerland.................	65,656	42,623	64.9	7,915	9,934	5,184
France......................	73,937	44,421	60.1	9,811	13,567	6,138
Central Europe:						
Germany....................	873,231	639,843	73.3	101,473	74,277	57,638
Poland.....................	602,918	168,354	27.9	139,759	279,386	15,419
Czechoslovakia..............	182,913	81,705	44.7	45,520	49,119	6,569
Austria.....................	300,899	109,615	36.4	63,446	114,712	13,126
Hungary....................	196,093	55,188	28.1	50,215	84,406	6,284
Jugo-Slavia.................	107,974	23,140	21.4	27,687	54,134	3,013
Eastern Europe:						
Russia......................	682,208	284,320	41.7	127,879	246,604	23,405
Lithuania...................	79,308	20,254	25.5	16,186	41,194	1,674
Finland.....................	80,407	31,550	39.2	17,466	28,511	2,880
Rumania....................	52,979	21,602	40.8	11,718	17,949	1,710
Bulgaria and Turkey in Europe...	12,530	1,605	12.8	2,310	8,083	532
Southern Europe:						
Greece......................	135,207	23,093	17.1	20,736	85,459	5,919
Italy¹......................	858,111	259,547	30.2	154,330	418,583	25,651
Spain......................	31,540	2,814	8.9	2,285	25,061	1,380
Portugal....................	33,837	5,854	17.3	2,274	24,527	1,182
Other Europe²..............	7,916	1,814	22.9	1,112	4,610	380
ASIA.						
Armenia....................	23,746	6,664	28.1	4,419	11,851	812
Palestine...................	1,703	610	35.8	327	655	111
Syria.......................	28,478	8,821	31.0	5,610	12,683	1,364
Turkey in Asia..............	7,383	1,719	23.3	1,090	4,250	324
Other Asia.................	4,453	1,488	33.4	779	1,810	376
AMERICA.						
Canada—French.............	141,514	66,579	47.0	21,997	46,094	6,844
Canada—Other and Newfoundland....	355,093	205,794	58.0	44,257	69,690	35,352
Mexico.....................	189,974	6,363	3.3	2,506	172,127	8,978
West Indies³...............	11,690	3,461	29.6	1,088	5,673	1,468
Central and South America.........	9,215	2,147	23.3	1,038	5,052	978
All other...................	32,576	10,712	32.9	2,976	15,555	3,333

¹ Poland included with Germany, Austria, and Russia in 1910.
² Comprises Albania, Danzig, Fiume, Saar Basin, and " Europe, not specified."

AND OVER, BY COUNTRY OF BIRTH, FOR THE UNITED STATES: 1920 AND 1910.

COUNTRY OF BIRTH (prewar boundaries).	1910					
	Foreign-born white males 21 years of age and over.	Naturalized.		Having first papers.	Alien.	Citizenship not reported.
		Number.	Per cent.			
All countries	6,646,817	3,034,117	45.6	570,772	2,266,535	775,393
EUROPE.						
Northwestern Europe:						
England	437,152	259,571	59.4	29,959	82,358	65,264
Scotland	133,116	75,161	56.5	10,340	28,600	19,015
Wales	43,054	29,772	69.2	1,986	4,438	6,858
Ireland	597,860	405,590	67.8	34,383	82,230	75,657
Norway	213,042	121,651	57.1	32,324	34,478	24,589
Sweden	349,022	219,057	62.8	40,248	52,041	37,676
Denmark	102,398	63,068	61.6	12,938	14,107	12,285
Netherlands	59,752	33,922	56.8	6,410	11,706	7,714
Belgium and Luxemburg	27,619	11,869	43.0	3,976	8,691	3,083
Switzerland	69,241	42,760	61.8	6,604	10,338	9,539
France	59,661	29,613	49.6	4,852	16,605	8,591
Central Europe:						
Germany[1]	1,278,667	889,007	69.5	92,030	127,103	170,527
Austria[1]	609,347	149,914	24.6	58,636	349,341	51,456
Hungary	255,844	36,610	14.3	25,756	174,518	18,960
Serbia	3,332	298	8.9	218	2,584	232
Montenegro	4,520	120	2.7	260	3,862	278
Eastern Europe:						
Russia[1]	737,120	192,264	26.1	95,562	385,970	63,324
Finland	70,716	21,669	30.6	11,279	32,458	5,310
Rumania	27,835	8,014	28.8	4,929	12,569	2,323
Bulgaria and Turkey in Europe	32,460	1,877	5.8	1,895	26,187	2,501
Southern Europe:						
Greece	74,975	4,946	6.6	4,550	58,208	7,271
Italy	712,812	126,523	17.7	55,522	468,442	62,325
Spain	14,170	2,318	16.4	824	9,213	1,815
Portugal	28,693	7,141	24.9	1,113	18,444	1,995
Europe, not specified	1,586	564	35.6	102	521	399
ASIA.						
Turkey in Asia	32,691	6,940	21.2	3,363	19,413	2,975
Other Asia	2,558	855	33.4	290	965	448
AMERICA.						
Canada—French	170,987	76,367	44.7	6,745	68,807	19,068
Canada—Other and Newfoundland	362,372	195,395	53.9	19,405	81,911	65,661
Mexico	102,009	10,932	10.7	2,358	67,930	20,789
West Indies[3]	9,671	2,961	30.6	611	4,271	1,828
Central and South America	3,315	1,152	34.8	272	1,240	651
All other	19,220	6,216	32.3	1,032	6,986	4,986

[3] Except possessions of the United States.

TABLE 91.—CITIZENSHIP OF FOREIGN-BORN AND FOREIGN-BORN

DIVISION AND STATE.	FOREIGN-BORN POPULATION.								
	Total.	Naturalized.		Having first papers.		Alien.		Citizenship not reported.	
		Number.	Per cent.	Number.	Per cent.	Number.	Per cent.	Number.	Per cent.
United States.....	13,920,692	6,493,088	46.6	1,223,490	8.8	5,398,605	38.8	805,509	5.8
GEOGRAPHIC DIVISIONS:									
New England........	1,885,945	788,403	41.8	141,726	7.5	884,984	46.9	70,832	3.8
Middle Atlantic......	4,960,418	2,134,347	43.0	413,125	8.3	2,162,891	43.6	250,055	5.0
East North Central..	3,232,141	1,643,240	50.8	392,887	12.2	995,148	30.8	200,866	6.2
West North Central..	1,375,653	901,448	65.5	109,998	8.0	252,010	18.3	112,197	8.2
South Atlantic.......	330,537	139,923	42.3	23,202	7.0	139,506	42.2	27,906	8.4
East South Central...	72,989	39,992	54.8	4,124	5.7	17,533	24.0	11,340	15.5
West South Central..	464,828	121,441	26.1	15,338	3.3	291,133	62.6	36,916	7.9
Mountain...........	467,620	221,914	47.5	32,998	7.1	186,904	40.0	25,804	5.5
Pacific..............	1,130,561	502,380	44.4	90,092	8.0	468,496	41.4	69,593	6.2
NEW ENGLAND:									
Maine..............	107,814	42,768	39.7	6,947	6.4	50,579	46.9	7,520	7.0
New Hampshire.....	91,397	38,147	41.7	5,156	5.6	41,661	45.6	6,433	7.0
Vermont...........	44,558	21,086	47.3	2,295	5.2	19,065	42.8	2,112	4.7
Massachusetts.......	1,088,548	459,321	42.2	82,119	7.5	518,365	47.6	28,743	2.6
Rhode Island........	175,189	82,276	47.0	15,325	8.7	69,903	39.9	7,685	4.4
Connecticut........	378,439	144,805	38.3	29,884	7.9	185,411	49.0	18,339	4.8
MIDDLE ATLANTIC:									
New York..........	2,825,375	1,216,185	43.0	241,335	8.5	1,220,801	43.2	147,054	5.2
New Jersey.........	742,486	320,935	43.2	65,384	8.8	321,897	43.4	34,270	4.6
Pennsylvania.......	1,392,557	597,227	42.9	106,406	7.6	620,193	44.5	68,731	4.9
EAST NORTH CENTRAL:									
Ohio..............	680,452	307,527	45.2	81,607	12.0	257,738	37.9	33,580	4.9
Indiana............	151,328	66,351	43.8	25,263	16.7	42,423	28.0	17,291	11.4
Illinois............	1,210,584	667,056	55.1	136,450	11.3	329,506	27.2	77,572	6.4
Michigan...........	729,292	345,709	47.4	93,011	12.8	250,350	34.3	40,222	5.5
Wisconsin..........	460,485	256,597	55.7	56,556	12.3	115,131	25.0	32,201	7.0
WEST NORTH CENTRAL:									
Minnesota..........	486,795	328,421	67.5	44,710	9.2	85,585	17.6	28,079	5.8
Iowa..............	225,994	156,593	69.3	12,228	5.4	36,128	16.0	21,045	9.3
Missouri...........	186,835	108,063	57.8	15,027	8.0	45,522	24.4	18,223	9.8
North Dakota.......	131,863	96,680	73.3	7,144	5.4	17,990	13.6	10,049	7.6
South Dakota.......	82,534	56,990	69.1	6,906	8.4	9,598	11.6	9,040	11.0
Nebraska...........	150,665	92,243	61.2	15,273	10.1	28,365	18.8	14,784	9.8
Kansas............	110,967	62,458	56.3	8,710	7.8	28,822	26.0	10,977	9.9
SOUTH ATLANTIC:									
Delaware..........	19,901	8,405	42.2	1,635	8.2	8,264	41.5	1,597	8.0
Maryland..........	103,179	52,016	50.4	9,700	9.4	37,249	36.1	4,214	4.1
District of Columbia.	29,365	15,626	53.2	2,204	7.5	7,952	27.1	3,583	12.2
Virginia...........	31,705	15,181	47.9	2,555	8.1	10,198	32.2	3,771	11.9
West Virginia.......	62,105	15,122	24.3	3,275	5.3	38,490	62.0	5,218	8.4
North Carolina......	7,272	3,453	47.5	301	4.1	2,201	30.3	1,317	18.1
South Carolina......	6,582	3,243	49.3	451	6.9	1,847	28.1	1,041	15.8
Georgia...........	16,564	8,912	53.8	1,097	6.6	4,734	28.6	1,821	11.0
Florida............	53,864	17,965	33.4	1,984	3.7	28,571	53.0	5,344	9.9
EAST SOUTH CENTRAL:									
Kentucky..........	30,906	18,972	61.4	1,694	5.5	6,024	19.5	4,216	13.6
Tennessee..........	15,648	8,101	51.8	822	5.3	4,118	26.3	2,607	16.7
Alabama...........	18,027	9,059	50.3	1,224	6.8	4,637	25.7	3,107	17.2
Mississippi.........	8,408	3,860	45.9	384	4.6	2,754	32.8	1,410	16.8
WEST SOUTH CENTRAL:									
Arkansas..........	14,137	7,841	55.5	826	5.8	2,916	20.6	2,554	18.1
Louisiana..........	46,427	15,920	34.3	2,307	5.0	21,982	47.3	6,218	13.4
Oklahoma..........	40,422	20,145	49.8	1,971	4.9	12,565	31.1	5,751	14.2
Texas.............	363,832	77,535	21.3	10,234	2.8	253,670	69.7	22,393	6.2
MOUNTAIN:									
Montana............	95,591	60,181	63.0	9,340	9.8	19,066	19.9	7,004	7.3
Idaho.............	40,747	24,982	61.3	3,347	8.2	9,953	24.4	2,465	6.0
Wyoming..........	26,567	12,654	47.6	2,537	9.5	9,391	35.3	1,985	7.5
Colorado...........	119,138	64,738	54.3	9,481	8.0	38,961	32.7	5,958	5.0
New Mexico........	29,808	6,352	21.3	831	2.8	21,092	70.8	1,533	5.1
Arizona...........	80,566	11,960	14.8	1,964	2.4	63,437	78.7	3,205	4.0
Utah..............	59,200	34,601	58.4	4,069	6.9	18,178	30.7	2,352	4.0
Nevada............	16,003	6,446	40.3	1,429	8.9	6,826	42.7	1,302	8.1
PACIFIC:									
Washington.........	265,292	140,426	52.9	30,296	11.4	78,516	29.6	16,054	6.1
Oregon............	107,644	57,726	53.6	12,219	11.4	33,092	30.7	4,607	4.3
California.........	757,625	304,228	40.2	47,577	6.3	356,888	47.1	48,932	6.5

WHITE POPULATION, BY DIVISIONS AND STATES: 1920.

DIVISION AND STATE.	Total.	FOREIGN-BORN WHITE POPULATION.							
		Naturalized.		Having first papers.		Alien.		Citizenship not reported.	
		Number.	Per cent.	Number.	Per cent.	Number.	Per cent.	Number.	Per cent.
United States	13,712,754	6,479,159	47.2	1,219,057	8.9	5,223,715	38.1	790,823	5.8
GEOGRAPHIC DIVISIONS:									
New England	1,870,654	786,429	42.0	140,811	7.5	873,456	46.7	69,958	3.7
Middle Atlantic	4,912,575	2,129,416	43.3	411,046	8.4	2,128,166	43.3	243,947	5.0
East North Central	3,223,279	1,641,238	50.9	392,466	12.2	990,000	30.7	199,575	6.2
West North Central	1,371,961	900,871	65.7	109,904	8.0	249,478	18.2	111,708	8.1
South Atlantic	315,920	138,249	43.8	22,934	7.3	128,507	40.7	26,230	8.3
East South Central	71,939	39,788	55.3	4,082	5.7	16,968	23.6	11,101	15.4
West South Central	459,333	120,903	26.3	15,235	3.3	287,115	62.5	36,080	7.9
Mountain	453,225	221,327	48.8	32,894	7.3	173,832	38.4	25,172	5.6
Pacific	1,033,868	500,938	48.5	89,685	8.7	376,193	36.4	67,052	6.5
NEW ENGLAND:									
Maine	107,349	42,662	39.7	6,925	6.5	50,291	46.8	7,471	7.0
New Hampshire	91,233	38,131	41.8	5,151	5.6	41,527	45.5	6,424	7.0
Vermont	44,526	21,077	47.3	2,292	5.1	19,047	42.8	2,110	4.7
Massachusetts	1,077,534	457,889	42.5	81,414	7.6	510,025	47.3	28,206	2.6
Rhode Island	173,499	82,070	47.3	15,212	8.8	68,643	39.6	7,574	4.4
Connecticut	376,513	144,600	38.4	29,817	7.9	183,923	48.8	18,173	4.8
MIDDLE ATLANTIC:									
New York	2,786,112	1,212,638	43.5	239,591	8.6	1,191,604	42.8	142,279	5.1
New Jersey	738,613	320,374	43.4	65,246	8.8	319,308	43.2	33,685	4.6
Pennsylvania	1,387,850	596,404	43.0	106,209	7.7	617,254	44.5	67,983	4.9
EAST NORTH CENTRAL:									
Ohio	678,697	307,078	45.2	81,527	12.0	256,769	37.8	33,323	4.9
Indiana	150,868	66,273	43.9	25,226	16.7	42,163	27.9	17,206	11.4
Illinois	1,206,951	666,460	55.2	136,346	11.3	327,119	27.1	77,026	6.4
Michigan	726,635	344,909	47.5	92,830	12.8	249,044	34.3	39,852	5.5
Wisconsin	460,128	256,518	55.7	56,537	12.3	114,905	25.0	32,168	7.0
WEST NORTH CENTRAL:									
Minnesota	486,164	328,278	67.5	44,688	9.2	85,181	17.5	28,017	5.8
Iowa	225,647	156,551	69.4	12,224	5.4	35,875	15.9	20,997	9.3
Missouri	186,026	107,942	58.0	15,006	8.1	44,960	24.2	18,118	9.7
North Dakota	131,503	96,568	73.4	7,135	5.4	17,823	13.6	9,977	7.6
South Dakota	82,391	56,955	69.1	6,901	8.4	9,508	11.5	9,027	11.0
Nebraska	149,652	92,170	61.6	15,231	10.2	27,558	18.4	14,663	9.8
Kansas	110,578	62,407	56.4	8,689	7.9	28,573	25.8	10,909	9.9
SOUTH ATLANTIC:									
Delaware	19,810	8,388	42.3	1,632	8.2	8,222	41.5	1,568	7.9
Maryland	102,177	51,837	50.7	9,649	9.4	36,577	35.8	4,114	4.0
District of Columbia	28,548	15,507	54.3	2,186	7.7	7,427	26.0	3,428	12.0
Virginia	30,785	15,038	48.8	2,499	8.1	9,658	31.4	3,590	11.7
West Virginia	61,906	15,080	24.4	3,272	5.3	38,389	62.0	5,165	8.3
North Carolina	7,099	3,420	48.2	298	4.2	2,104	29.6	1,277	18.0
South Carolina	6,401	3,223	50.4	448	7.0	1,735	27.1	995	15.5
Georgia	16,186	8,846	54.7	1,083	6.7	4,506	27.8	1,751	10.8
Florida	43,008	16,910	39.3	1,867	4.3	19,889	46.2	4,342	10.1
EAST SOUTH CENTRAL:									
Kentucky	30,780	18,942	61.5	1,689	5.5	5,957	19.4	4,192	13.6
Tennessee	15,478	8,054	52.0	817	5.3	4,042	26.1	2,565	16.6
Alabama	17,662	8,990	50.9	1,203	6.8	4,471	25.3	2,998	17.0
Mississippi	8,019	3,802	47.4	373	4.7	2,498	31.2	1,346	16.8
WEST SOUTH CENTRAL:									
Arkansas	13,975	7,809	55.9	824	5.9	2,845	20.4	2,497	17.9
Louisiana	44,871	15,783	35.2	2,274	5.1	20,855	46.5	5,959	13.3
Oklahoma	39,968	20,064	50.2	1,957	4.9	12,259	30.7	5,688	14.2
Texas	360,519	77,247	21.4	10,180	2.8	251,156	69.7	21,936	6.1
MOUNTAIN:									
Montana	93,620	60,015	64.1	9,318	10.0	17,491	18.7	6,796	7.3
Idaho	38,963	24,959	64.1	3,340	8.6	8,218	21.1	2,446	6.3
Wyoming	25,255	12,630	50.0	2,530	10.0	8,135	32.2	1,960	7.8
Colorado	116,954	64,666	55.3	9,457	8.1	36,991	31.6	5,840	5.0
New Mexico	29,077	6,294	21.6	821	2.8	20,476	70.4	1,486	5.1
Arizona	78,099	11,757	15.1	1,953	2.5	61,339	78.5	3,050	3.9
Utah	56,455	34,576	61.2	4,048	7.2	15,517	27.5	2,314	4.1
Nevada	14,802	6,430	43.4	1,427	9.6	5,665	38.3	1,280	8.6
PACIFIC:									
Washington	250,055	140,166	56.1	30,191	12.1	63,981	25.6	15,717	6.3
Oregon	102,151	57,627	56.4	12,159	11.9	27,823	27.2	4,542	4.4
California	681,662	303,145	44.5	47,335	6.9	284,389	41.7	46,793	6.9

TABLE 92.—CITIZENSHIP OF FOREIGN-BORN WHITE

DIVISION AND STATE.	Total.	FOREIGN-BORN WHITE MALES.							
		Naturalized.		Having first papers.		Alien.		Citizenship not reported.	
		Number.	Per cent.	Number.	Per cent.	Number.	Per cent.	Number.	Per cent.
United States.....	7,528,322	3,443,968	45.7	1,133,727	15.1	2,562,917	34.0	387,710	5.2
GEOGRAPHIC DIVISIONS:									
New England........	945,736	381,815	40.4	131,196	13.9	403,482	42.7	29,243	3.1
Middle Atlantic......	2,617,566	1,115,431	42.6	380,474	14.5	1,016,419	38.8	105,242	4.0
East North Central...	1,809,334	874,857	48.4	367,160	20.3	468,362	25.9	98,955	5.5
West North Central..	779,022	496,624	63.7	101,622	13.0	121,676	15.6	59,100	7.6
South Atlantic.......	185,143	76,007	41.1	21,311	11.5	72,980	39.4	14,845	8.0
East South Central..	42,093	22,744	54.0	3,764	8.9	9,419	22.4	6,166	14.6
West South Central..	260,777	67,539	25.9	13,879	5.3	158,577	60.8	20,782	8.0
Mountain.............	271,373	125,014	46.1	30,899	11.4	100,107	36.9	15,353	5.7
Pacific..............	617,278	283,937	46.0	83,422	13.5	211,895	34.3	38,024	6.2
NEW ENGLAND:									
Maine...............	55,807	19,013	34.1	6,688	12.0	26,645	47.7	3,461	6.2
New Hampshire......	46,844	18,080	38.6	4,930	10.5	21,060	45.0	2,774	5.9
Vermont.............	23,711	10,189	43.0	2,155	9.1	10,341	43.6	1,026	4.3
Massachusetts........	533,319	221,087	41.5	75,186	14.1	225,897	42.4	11,149	2.1
Rhode Island.........	86,164	40,045	46.5	13,818	16.0	29,180	33.9	3,121	3.6
Connecticut..........	199,891	73,401	36.7	28,419	14.2	90,359	45.2	7,712	3.9
MIDDLE ATLANTIC:									
New York............	1,442,575	632,112	43.8	218,599	15.2	533,084	37.0	58,780	4.1
New Jersey...........	391,655	165,859	42.3	61,641	15.7	150,530	38.4	13,625	3.5
Pennsylvania........	783,336	317,460	40.5	100,234	12.8	332,805	42.5	32,837	4.2
EAST NORTH CENTRAL:									
Ohio................	391,344	163,227	41.7	77,674	19.8	133,363	34.1	17,080	4.4
Indiana.............	88,180	36,131	41.0	23,767	27.0	19,266	21.8	9,016	10.2
Illinois.............	657,264	354,892	54.0	127,218	19.4	137,944	21.0	37,210	5.7
Michigan............	413,806	182,236	44.0	87,779	21.2	123,684	29.9	20,107	4.9
Wisconsin...........	258,740	138,371	53.5	50,722	19.6	54,105	20.9	15,542	6.0
WEST NORTH CENTRAL:									
Minnesota...........	278,588	181,733	65.2	41,197	14.8	41,503	14.9	14,155	5.1
Iowa................	127,065	85,777	67.5	11,339	8.9	18,851	14.8	11,098	8.7
Missouri............	103,418	59,177	57.2	13,930	13.5	21,100	20.4	9,211	8.9
North Dakota........	75,386	54,090	71.8	6,668	8.8	9,114	12.1	5,514	7.3
South Dakota........	47,610	31,915	67.0	6,422	13.5	4,165	8.7	5,108	10.7
Nebraska............	84,277	50,171	59.5	14,052	16.7	12,245	14.5	7,809	9.3
Kansas..............	62,678	33,761	53.9	8,014	12.8	14,698	23.5	6,205	9.9
SOUTH ATLANTIC:									
Delaware............	11,369	4,498	39.6	1,559	13.7	4,547	40.0	765	6.7
Maryland............	54,628	27,088	49.6	8,926	16.3	16,619	30.4	1,995	3.7
District of Columbia..	15,142	8,179	54.0	1,838	12.1	3,376	22.3	1,749	11.6
Virginia.............	19,051	8,862	46.5	2,376	12.5	5,653	29.7	2,160	11.3
West Virginia........	41,910	8,760	20.9	3,157	7.5	26,731	63.8	3,262	7.8
North Carolina.......	4,341	1,981	45.6	288	6.6	1,294	29.8	778	17.9
South Carolina.......	4,095	2,017	49.3	425	10.4	1,039	25.4	614	15.0
Georgia.............	10,004	5,275	52.7	997	10.0	2,677	26.8	1,055	10.5
Florida.............	24,603	9,347	38.0	1,745	7.1	11,044	44.9	2,467	10.0
EAST SOUTH CENTRAL:									
Kentucky............	17,479	10,490	60.0	1,522	8.7	3,395	19.4	2,072	11.9
Tennessee...........	9,021	4,592	50.9	751	8.3	2,182	24.2	1,496	16.6
Alabama.............	10,625	5,274	49.6	1,139	10.7	2,455	23.1	1,757	16.5
Mississippi..........	4,968	2,388	48.1	352	7.1	1,387	27.9	841	16.9
WEST SOUTH CENTRAL:									
Arkansas............	8,591	4,707	54.8	759	8.8	1,565	18.2	1,560	18.2
Louisiana...........	26,808	9,607	35.8	2,185	8.2	12,145	45.3	2,871	10.7
Oklahoma............	24,301	11,559	40.4	1,809	7.0	7,817	31.4	3,740	13.0
Texas...............	200,447	41,666	20.0	9,126	4.6	137,050	60.4	10,605	8.0
MOUNTAIN:									
Montana.............	58,229	35,631	61.2	8,815	15.1	9,613	16.5	4,170	7.2
Idaho...............	24,877	14,715	59.2	3,184	12.8	5,357	21.5	1,621	6.5
Wyoming............	16,934	7,582	44.8	2,450	14.5	5,532	32.7	1,370	8.1
Colorado............	68,219	35,804	52.5	8,791	12.9	20,225	29.6	3,399	5.0
New Mexico..........	16,845	3,557	21.1	765	4.5	11,663	69.2	860	5.1
Arizona.............	44,657	6,462	14.5	1,854	4.2	34,463	77.2	1,878	4.2
Utah................	30,875	17,038	55.2	3,639	11.8	8,935	28.9	1,263	4.1
Nevada.............	10,737	4,225	39.3	1,401	13.0	4,319	40.2	792	7.4
PACIFIC:									
Washington..........	153,118	80,164	52.4	28,626	18.7	35,376	23.1	8,952	5.8
Oregon.............	62,310	32,902	52.8	11,367	18.2	15,247	24.5	2,794	4.5
California...........	401,850	170,871	42.5	43,429	10.8	161,272	40.1	26,278	6.5

MALES AND FEMALES, BY DIVISIONS AND STATES: 1920.

DIVISION AND STATE.	Total.	FOREIGN-BORN WHITE FEMALES.							
		Naturalized.		Having first papers.		Alien.		Citizenship not reported.	
		Number.	Per cent.	Number.	Per cent.	Number.	Per cent.	Number.	Per cent.
United States.....	6,184,432	3,035,191	49.1	85,330	1.4	2,660,798	43.0	403,113	6.5
GEOGRAPHIC DIVISIONS:									
New England........	924,918	404,614	43.7	9,615	1.0	469,974	50.8	40,715	4.4
Middle Atlantic......	2,295,009	1,013,985	44.2	30,572	1.3	1,111,747	48.4	138,705	6.0
East North Central...	1,413,945	766,381	54.2	25,306	1.8	521,638	36.9	100,620	7.1
West North Central..	592,939	404,247	68.2	8,282	1.4	127,802	21.6	52,608	8.9
South Atlantic.......	130,777	62,242	47.6	1,623	1.2	55,527	42.5	11,385	8.7
East South Central...	29,846	17,044	57.1	318	1.1	7,549	25.3	4,935	16.5
West South Central..	198,556	53,364	26.9	1,356	0.7	128,538	64.7	15,298	7.7
Mountain.............	181,852	96,313	53.0	1,995	1.1	73,725	40.5	9,819	5.4
Pacific..............	416,590	217,001	52.1	6,263	1.5	164,298	39.4	29,028	7.0
NEW ENGLAND:									
Maine...............	51,542	23,649	45.9	237	0.5	23,646	45.9	4,010	7.8
New Hampshire......	44,389	20,051	45.2	221	0.5	20,467	46.1	3,650	8.2
Vermont.............	20,815	10,888	52.3	137	0.7	8,706	41.8	1,084	5.2
Massachusetts.......	544,215	236,802	43.5	6,228	1.1	284,128	52.2	17,057	3.1
Rhode Island........	87,335	42,025	48.1	1,394	1.6	39,463	45.2	4,453	5.1
Connecticut.........	176,622	71,199	40.3	1,398	0.8	93,564	53.0	10,461	5.9
MIDDLE ATLANTIC:									
New York...........	1,343,537	580,526	43.2	20,992	1.6	658,520	49.0	83,499	6.2
New Jersey.........	346,958	154,515	44.5	3,605	1.0	168,778	48.6	20,060	5.8
Pennsylvania........	604,514	278,944	46.1	5,975	1.0	284,449	47.1	35,146	5.8
EAST NORTH CENTRAL:									
Ohio................	287,353	143,851	50.1	3,853	1.3	123,406	42.9	16,243	5.7
Indiana.............	62,688	30,142	48.1	1,459	2.3	22,897	36.5	8,190	13.1
Illinois.............	549,687	311,568	56.7	9,128	1.7	189,175	34.4	39,816	7.2
Michigan............	312,829	162,673	52.0	5,051	1.6	125,360	40.1	19,745	6.3
Wisconsin...........	201,388	118,147	58.7	5,815	2.9	60,800	30.2	16,626	8.3
WEST NORTH CENTRAL:									
Minnesota...........	207,576	146,545	70.6	3,491	1.7	43,678	21.0	13,862	6.7
Iowa................	98,582	70,774	71.8	885	0.9	17,024	17.3	9,899	10.0
Missouri............	82,608	48,765	59.0	1,076	1.3	23,860	28.9	8,907	10.8
North Dakota.......	56,117	42,478	75.7	467	0.8	8,709	15.5	4,463	8.0
South Dakota.......	34,781	25,040	72.0	479	1.4	5,343	15.4	3,919	11.3
Nebraska............	65,375	41,999	64.2	1,209	1.8	15,313	23.4	6,854	10.5
Kansas..............	47,900	28,646	59.8	675	1.4	13,875	29.0	4,704	9.8
SOUTH ATLANTIC:									
Delaware............	8,441	3,890	46.1	73	0.9	3,675	43.5	803	9.5
Maryland............	47,549	24,749	52.0	723	1.5	19,958	42.0	2,119	4.5
District of Columbia..	13,406	7,328	54.7	348	2.6	4,051	30.2	1,679	12.5
Virginia............	11,734	6,176	52.6	123	1.0	4,005	34.1	1,430	12.2
West Virginia.......	19,996	6,320	31.6	115	0.6	11,658	58.3	1,903	9.5
North Carolina......	2,758	1,439	52.2	10	0.4	810	29.4	499	18.1
South Carolina......	2,306	1,206	52.3	23	1.0	696	30.2	381	16.5
Georgia.............	6,182	3,571	57.8	86	1.4	1,829	29.6	696	11.3
Florida.............	18,405	7,563	41.1	122	0.7	8,845	48.1	1,875	10.2
EAST SOUTH CENTRAL:									
Kentucky............	13,301	8,452	63.5	167	1.3	2,562	19.3	2,120	15.9
Tennessee...........	6,457	3,462	53.6	66	1.0	1,860	28.8	1,069	16.6
Alabama.............	7,037	3,716	52.8	64	0.9	2,016	28.6	1,241	17.6
Mississippi.........	3,051	1,414	46.3	21	0.7	1,111	36.4	505	16.6
WEST SOUTH CENTRAL:									
Arkansas............	5,384	3,102	57.6	65	1.2	1,280	23.8	937	17.4
Louisiana...........	18,063	6,176	34.2	89	0.5	8,710	48.2	3,088	17.1
Oklahoma...........	15,037	8,505	56.6	148	1.0	4,442	29.5	1,942	12.9
Texas...............	160,072	35,581	22.2	1,054	0.7	114,106	71.3	9,331	5.8
MOUNTAIN:									
Montana.............	35,391	24,384	68.9	503	1.4	7,878	22.3	2,626	7.4
Idaho...............	14,086	10,244	72.7	156	1.1	2,861	20.3	825	5.9
Wyoming............	8,321	5,048	60.7	80	1.0	2,603	31.3	590	7.1
Colorado............	48,735	28,862	59.2	666	1.4	16,766	34.4	2,441	5.0
New Mexico.........	12,232	2,737	22.4	56	0.5	8,813	72.0	626	5.1
Arizona.............	33,442	5,295	15.8	99	0.3	26,876	80.4	1,172	3.5
Utah................	25,580	17,538	68.6	409	1.6	6,582	25.7	1,051	4.1
Nevada.............	4,065	2,205	54.2	26	0.6	1,346	33.1	488	12.0
PACIFIC:									
Washington..........	96,937	60,002	61.9	1,565	1.6	28,605	29.5	6,765	7.0
Oregon.............	39,841	24,725	62.1	792	2.0	12,576	31.6	1,748	4.4
California..........	279,812	132,274	47.3	3,906	1.4	123,117	44.0	20,515	7.3

TABLE 93.—CITIZENSHIP OF FOREIGN-BORN WHITE MALES AND FEMALES

[No inquiry as to the citizenship

DIVISION AND STATE.	FOREIGN-BORN WHITE MALES 21 YEARS OF AGE AND OVER—NUMBER: 1920				
	Total.	Naturalized.	Having first papers.	Alien.	Citizenship not reported.
United States............	6,928,452	3,314,910	1,116,744	2,138,237	358,561
GEOGRAPHIC DIVISIONS:					
New England...............	866,042	367,478	128,790	343,403	26,371
Middle Atlantic............	2,406,975	1,065,420	374,400	871,495	95,660
East North Central.........	1,687,728	843,952	362,436	388,827	92,513
West North Central.........	738,673	483,504	100,226	98,487	56,456
South Atlantic.............	170,407	72,664	20,816	63,077	13,850
East South Central.........	39,697	22,056	3,683	8,079	5,879
West South Central........	208,431	64,503	13,516	111,736	18,676
Mountain..................	241,321	119,979	30,452	76,754	14,136
Pacific....................	569,178	275,354	82,425	176,379	35,020
NEW ENGLAND:					
Maine.....................	49,355	18,028	6,553	21,676	3,098
New Hampshire.............	42,432	17,395	4,839	17,724	2,474
Vermont...................	20,462	9,540	2,106	7,886	930
Massachusetts.............	491,107	213,477	73,725	193,844	10,061
Rhode Island..............	78,118	38,212	13,521	23,562	2,823
Connecticut...............	184,568	70,826	28,046	78,711	6,985
MIDDLE ATLANTIC:					
New York..................	1,318,883	604,256	214,958	446,859	52,810
New Jersey................	360,902	158,727	60,708	129,137	12,330
Pennsylvania..............	727,190	302,437	98,734	295,499	30,520
EAST NORTH CENTRAL:					
Ohio......................	363,504	156,820	76,524	114,287	15,873
Indiana...................	82,908	34,871	23,563	15,980	8,494
Illinois..................	613,797	341,910	125,752	111,349	34,786
Michigan..................	381,868	175,631	86,460	101,206	18,511
Wisconsin.................	245,711	134,720	50,137	46,005	14,849
WEST NORTH CENTRAL:					
Minnesota.................	266,856	177,355	40,727	35,245	13,529
Iowa......................	121,392	84,160	11,109	15,384	10,739
Missouri..................	97,345	57,561	13,765	17,240	8,779
North Dakota..............	70,043	51,350	6,558	7,017	5,118
South Dakota..............	45,340	31,030	6,318	3,103	4,889
Nebraska..................	79,821	49,012	13,868	9,490	7,451
Kansas....................	57,876	33,036	7,881	11,008	5,951
SOUTH ATLANTIC:					
Delaware..................	10,614	4,329	1,539	4,033	713
Maryland..................	50,363	26,077	8,720	13,720	1,846
District of Columbia......	14,042	7,786	1,775	2,842	1,639
Virginia..................	17,431	8,356	2,294	4,792	1,989
West Virginia.............	38,471	8,315	3,105	23,996	3,055
North Carolina............	4,035	1,886	285	1,124	740
South Carolina............	3,850	1,924	417	921	588
Georgia...................	9,319	5,023	958	2,340	998
Florida...................	22,282	8,968	1,723	9,309	2,282
EAST SOUTH CENTRAL:					
Kentucky..................	16,827	10,273	1,472	3,060	2,022
Tennessee.................	8,428	4,430	739	1,821	1,438
Alabama...................	9,814	5,031	1,125	2,030	1,628
Mississippi...............	4,628	2,322	347	1,168	791
WEST SOUTH CENTRAL:					
Arkansas..................	8,166	4,593	753	1,319	1,501
Louisiana.................	24,848	9,350	2,121	10,708	2,669
Oklahoma..................	22,817	11,720	1,777	6,233	3,568
Texas.....................	152,600	39,321	8,865	93,476	10,938
MOUNTAIN:					
Montana...................	54,250	34,009	8,714	7,636	3,891
Idaho.....................	23,366	14,186	3,156	4,489	1,535
Wyoming...................	15,796	7,289	2,427	4,791	1,289
Colorado..................	62,089	34,630	8,648	15,696	3,115
New Mexico................	13,244	3,381	750	8,390	723
Arizona...................	33,582	5,986	1,801	24,147	1,648
Utah......................	28,791	16,377	3,563	7,664	1,187
Nevada....................	10,203	4,121	1,393	3,941	748
PACIFIC:					
Washington................	143,258	77,156	28,308	29,572	8,222
Oregon....................	58,580	31,899	11,255	12,800	2,626
California................	367,340	166,299	42,862	134,007	24,172

21 YEARS OF AGE AND OVER, BY DIVISIONS AND STATES: 1920 AND 1910.

of females was made in 1910.]

DIVISION AND STATE.	FOREIGN-BORN WHITE MALES 21 YEARS OF AGE AND OVER—NUMBER: 1910				
	Total.	Naturalized.	Having first papers.	Alien.	Citizenship not reported.
United States............	6,646,817	3,034,117	570,772	2,266,535	775,393
GEOGRAPHIC DIVISIONS:					
New England................	796,847	323,994	48,508	366,161	58,184
Middle Atlantic.............	2,272,271	879,348	202,012	965,101	225,810
East North Central..........	1,573,343	812,489	148,254	426,278	186,322
West North Central..........	869,408	510,918	76,934	144,177	137,379
South Atlantic..............	150,665	61,134	8,997	57,127	23,407
East South Central..........	46,308	25,955	2,220	8,647	9,486
West South Central..........	171,940	70,765	10,071	52,853	38,251
Mountain...................	257,537	113,670	23,219	85,619	35,029
Pacific.....................	508,498	235,844	50,557	160,572	61,525
NEW ENGLAND:					
Maine......................	48,464	14,994	1,490	23,672	8,308
New Hampshire.............	41,956	16,415	1,421	19,377	4,743
Vermont...................	23,759	10,811	1,164	9,652	2,132
Massachusetts..............	453,601	189,126	30,016	212,033	22,426
Rhode Island...............	75,899	32,040	5,314	31,996	6,549
Connecticut................	153,168	60,608	9,103	69,431	14,026
MIDDLE ATLANTIC:					
New York..................	1,221,013	502,083	131,085	475,259	112,586
New Jersey.................	309,648	128,438	24,511	122,076	34,623
Pennsylvania...............	741,610	248,827	46,416	367,766	78,601
EAST NORTH CENTRAL:					
Ohio.......................	308,478	142,465	17,509	113,856	34,648
Indiana....................	88,927	42,533	13,320	18,354	14,720
Illinois....................	604,524	317,339	43,482	174,581	69,122
Michigan..................	302,177	167,304	26,235	76,550	32,088
Wisconsin.................	269,237	142,848	47,708	42,937	35,744
WEST NORTH CENTRAL:					
Minnesota.................	298,282	179,187	26,222	58,132	34,741
Iowa......................	146,880	90,573	6,654	20,275	29,378
Missouri...................	121,404	65,612	10,117	25,835	19,840
North Dakota..............	79,721	46,636	9,824	10,965	12,296
South Dakota..............	54,528	32,495	8,020	4,376	9,637
Nebraska..................	94,345	57,270	9,924	12,347	14,804
Kansas....................	74,248	39,145	6,173	12,247	16,683
SOUTH ATLANTIC:					
Delaware..................	8,776	3,707	658	3,189	1,222
Maryland..................	47,973	24,256	3,278	13,573	6,866
District of Columbia........	11,738	6,474	1,058	2,304	1,902
Virginia...................	14,882	6,411	859	4,693	2,919
West Virginia..............	34,687	7,263	1,358	22,545	3,521
North Carolina.............	3,296	1,439	194	827	836
South Carolina.............	3,355	1,602	184	739	830
Georgia...................	8,513	4,023	625	1,846	2,019
Florida....................	17,445	5,959	783	7,411	3,292
EAST SOUTH CENTRAL:					
Kentucky..................	20,440	13,225	815	2,754	3,646
Tennessee.................	10,112	5,444	464	1,867	2,337
Alabama..................	10,521	4,841	684	2,793	2,203
Mississippi................	5,235	2,445	257	1,233	1,300
WEST SOUTH CENTRAL:					
Arkansas..................	9,718	5,284	595	1,388	2,451
Louisiana..................	26,519	10,024	1,166	9,151	6,178
Oklahoma.................	23,551	12,074	1,477	4,449	5,551
Texas.....................	112,152	43,383	6,833	37,865	24,071
MOUNTAIN:					
Montana..................	59,313	27,635	6,749	16,937	7,992
Idaho.....................	25,844	12,817	2,478	6,215	4,334
Wyoming.................	18,263	6,837	1,937	8,125	1,364
Colorado..................	70,514	35,245	6,536	19,615	9,118
New Mexico...............	12,502	4,267	709	6,048	1,178
Arizona...................	25,682	5,912	1,113	14,574	4,083
Utah......................	32,652	15,351	2,415	9,626	5,260
Nevada...................	12,767	5,606	1,282	4,479	1,400
PACIFIC:					
Washington................	147,224	68,895	15,258	43,202	19,869
Oregon....................	63,909	29,675	7,591	17,430	9,213
California..................	297,365	137,274	27,708	99,940	32,443

TABLE 93.—CITIZENSHIP OF FOREIGN-BORN WHITE MALES AND FEMALES

[No inquiry as to the citizenship

DIVISION AND STATE.	FOREIGN-BORN WHITE MALES 21 YEARS OF AGE AND OVER—PER CENT.							
	Naturalized.		Having first papers.		Alien.		Citizenship not reported.	
	1920	*1910	1920	1910	1920	1910	1920	1910
United States	47.8	45.6	16.1	8.6	30.9	34.1	5.2	11.7
GEOGRAPHIC DIVISIONS:								
New England	42.4	40.7	14.9	6.1	39.7	46.0	3.0	7.3
Middle Atlantic	44.3	38.7	15.6	8.9	36.2	42.5	4.0	9.9
East North Central	50.0	51.6	21.5	9.4	23.0	27.1	5.5	11.8
West North Central	65.5	58.8	13.6	8.8	13.3	16.6	7.6	15.8
South Atlantic	42.6	40.6	12.2	6.0	37.0	37.9	8.1	15.5
East South Central	55.6	56.0	9.3	4.8	20.4	18.7	14.8	20.5
West South Central	30.9	41.2	6.5	5.9	53.6	30.7	9.0	22.2
Mountain	49.7	44.1	12.6	9.0	31.8	33.2	5.9	13.6
Pacific	48.4	46.4	14.5	9.9	31.0	31.6	6.2	12.1
NEW ENGLAND:								
Maine	36.5	30.9	13.3	3.1	43.9	48.8	6.3	17.1
New Hampshire	41.0	39.1	11.4	3.4	41.8	46.2	5.8	11.3
Vermont	46.6	45.5	10.3	4.9	38.5	40.6	4.5	9.0
Massachusetts	43.5	41.7	15.0	6.6	39.5	46.7	2.0	4.9
Rhode Island	48.9	42.2	17.3	7.0	30.2	42.2	3.6	8.6
Connecticut	38.4	39.6	15.2	5.9	42.6	45.3	3.8	9.2
MIDDLE ATLANTIC:								
New York	45.8	41.1	16.3	10.7	33.9	38.9	4.0	9.2
New Jersey	44.0	41.5	16.8	7.9	35.8	39.4	3.4	11.2
Pennsylvania	41.6	33.6	13.6	6.3	40.6	49.6	4.2	10.6
EAST NORTH CENTRAL:								
Ohio	43.1	46.2	21.1	5.7	31.4	36.9	4.4	11.2
Indiana	42.1	47.8	28.4	15.0	19.3	20.6	10.2	16.6
Illinois	55.7	52.5	20.5	7.2	18.1	28.9	5.7	11.4
Michigan	46.0	55.4	22.6	8.7	26.5	25.3	4.8	10.6
Wisconsin	54.8	53.1	20.4	17.7	18.7	15.9	6.0	13.3
WEST NORTH CENTRAL:								
Minnesota	66.5	60.1	15.3	8.8	13.2	19.5	5.1	11.6
Iowa	69.3	61.7	9.2	4.5	12.7	13.8	8.8	20.0
Missouri	59.1	54.0	14.1	8.3	17.7	21.3	9.0	16.3
North Dakota	73.3	58.5	9.4	12.3	10.0	13.8	7.3	15.4
South Dakota	68.4	59.6	13.9	14.7	6.8	8.0	10.8	17.7
Nebraska	61.4	60.7	17.4	10.5	11.9	13.1	9.3	15.7
Kansas	57.1	52.7	13.6	8.3	19.0	16.5	10.3	22.5
SOUTH ATLANTIC:								
Delaware	40.8	42.2	14.5	7.5	38.0	36.3	6.7	13.9
Maryland	51.8	50.6	17.3	6.8	27.2	28.3	3.7	14.3
District of Columbia	55.4	55.2	12.6	9.0	20.2	19.6	11.7	16.2
Virginia	47.9	43.1	13.2	5.8	27.5	31.5	11.4	19.6
West Virginia	21.6	20.9	8.1	3.9	62.4	65.0	7.9	10.2
North Carolina	46.7	43.7	7.1	5.9	27.9	25.1	18.3	25.4
South Carolina	50.0	47.7	10.8	5.5	23.9	22.0	15.3	24.7
Georgia	53.9	47.3	10.3	7.3	25.1	21.7	10.7	23.7
Florida	40.2	34.2	7.7	4.5	41.8	42.5	10.2	18.9
EAST SOUTH CENTRAL:								
Kentucky	61.1	64.7	8.7	4.0	18.2	13.5	12.0	17.8
Tennessee	52.6	53.8	8.8	4.6	21.6	18.5	17.1	23.1
Alabama	51.3	46.0	11.5	6.5	20.7	26.5	16.6	20.9
Mississippi	50.2	46.7	7.5	4.9	25.2	23.6	17.1	24.8
WEST SOUTH CENTRAL:								
Arkansas	56.2	54.4	9.2	6.1	16.2	14.3	18.4	25.2
Louisiana	57.6	57.8	8.5	4.4	43.1	34.9	10.7	23.3
Oklahoma	49.3	51.3	7.8	6.3	27.3	18.9	15.6	23.6
Texas	25.8	38.7	5.8	6.1	61.3	33.8	7.2	21.5
MOUNTAIN:								
Montana	62.7	46.6	16.1	11.4	14.1	28.6	7.2	13.5
Idaho	60.7	49.6	13.5	9.6	19.2	24.0	6.6	16.8
Wyoming	46.1	37.4	15.4	10.6	30.3	44.5	8.2	7.5
Colorado	55.8	50.0	13.9	9.3	25.3	27.8	5.0	12.9
New Mexico	25.5	34.1	5.7	5.7	63.3	48.4	5.5	11.8
Arizona	17.8	23.0	5.4	4.3	71.9	56.7	4.9	15.9
Utah	56.9	47.0	12.4	7.4	26.6	29.5	4.1	16.1
Nevada	40.4	43.9	13.7	10.0	38.6	35.1	7.3	11.0
PACIFIC:								
Washington	53.9	46.8	19.8	10.4	20.6	29.3	5.7	13.5
Oregon	54.5	46.4	19.2	11.9	21.9	27.3	4.5	14.4
California	45.3	46.2	11.7	9.3	36.5	33.6	6.6	10.9

21 YEARS OF AGE AND OVER, BY DIVISIONS AND STATES: 1920 AND 1910—Continued.

of females was made in 1910.]

DIVISION AND STATE.	Total.	FOREIGN-BORN WHITE FEMALES 21 YEARS OF AGE AND OVER: 1920							
		Naturalized.		Having first papers.		Alien.		Citizenship not reported.	
		Number.	Per cent.	Number.	Per cent.	Number.	Per cent.	Number.	Per cent.
United States.....	5,570,268	2,893,787	52.0	77,532	1.4	2,226,672	40.0	372,277	6.7
GEOGRAPHIC DIVISIONS:									
New England........	839,249	388,049	46.2	8,521	1.0	405,170	48.3	37,509	4.5
Middle Atlantic......	2,070,777	959,199	46.3	27,691	1.3	956,162	46.2	127,725	6.2
East North Central..	1,290,847	732,715	56.8	23,179	1.8	441,004	34.2	93,949	7.3
West North Central..	553,121	390,628	70.6	7,572	1.4	105,135	19.0	49,786	9.0
South Atlantic.......	116,808	58,759	50.3	1,461	1.3	46,150	39.5	10,438	8.9
East South Central...	27,545	16,279	59.1	297	1.1	6,283	22.8	4,686	17.0
West South Central..	148,789	49,755	33.4	1,219	0.8	84,503	56.8	13,312	8.9
Mountain...........	152,687	90,885	59.5	1,790	1.2	51,321	33.6	8,691	5.7
Pacific...............	370,445	207,518	56.0	5,802	1.6	130,944	35.3	26,181	7.1
NEW ENGLAND:									
Maine...............	44,974	22,451	49.9	189	0.4	18,751	41.7	3,583	8.0
New Hampshire.....	39,617	19,226	48.5	201	0.5	16,874	42.6	3,316	8.4
Vermont...........	17,770	10,285	57.9	117	0.7	6,377	35.9	991	5.6
Massachusetts........	497,806	227,939	45.8	5,555	1.1	248,507	49.9	15,805	3.2
Rhode Island........	78,748	39,963	50.7	1,232	1.6	33,445	42.5	4,108	5.2
Connecticut..........	160,334	68,185	42.5	1,227	0.8	81,216	50.7	9,706	6.1
MIDDLE ATLANTIC:									
New York..........	1,209,614	549,557	45.4	19,140	1.6	564,261	46.6	76,656	6.3
New Jersey.........	314,320	146,789	46.7	3,185	1.0	145,890	46.4	18,456	5.9
Pennsylvania........	546,843	262,853	48.1	5,366	1.0	246,011	45.0	32,613	6.0
EAST NORTH CENTRAL:									
Ohio...............	259,019	136,715	52.8	3,350	1.3	104,001	40.2	14,953	5.8
Indiana.............	57,465	28,696	49.9	1,353	2.4	19,682	34.3	7,734	13.5
Illinois.............	504,131	297,536	59.0	8,386	1.7	161,042	31.9	37,167	7.4
Michigan............	281,352	155,327	55.2	4,553	1.6	103,343	36.7	18,129	6.4
Wisconsin...........	188,880	114,441	60.6	5,537	2.9	52,936	28.0	15,966	8.5
WEST NORTH CENTRAL:									
Minnesota...........	195,726	142,035	72.6	3,211	1.6	37,404	19.1	13,076	6.7
Iowa...............	93,087	69,111	74.2	781	0.8	13,686	14.7	9,509	10.2
Missouri............	76,206	46,887	61.5	993	1.3	19,853	26.1	8,473	11.1
North Dakota.......	51,004	39,837	78.1	407	0.8	6,702	13.1	4,058	8.0
South Dakota.......	32,687	24,134	73.8	433	1.3	4,397	13.5	3,723	11.4
Nebraska...........	61,078	40,771	66.8	1,119	1.8	12,705	20.8	6,483	10.6
Kansas.............	43,333	27,853	64.3	628	1.4	10,388	24.0	4,464	10.3
SOUTH ATLANTIC:									
Delaware............	7,631	3,698	48.5	67	0.9	3,131	41.0	735	9.6
Maryland...........	43,261	23,687	54.8	647	1.5	16,914	39.1	2,013	4.7
District of Columbia..	12,334	6,926	56.2	324	2.6	3,491	28.3	1,593	12.9
Virginia.............	10,420	5,701	54.7	108	1.0	3,327	31.9	1,284	12.3
West Virginia........	16,994	5,826	34.3	100	0.6	9,386	55.2	1,682	9.9
North Carolina.......	2,453	1,349	55.0	10	0.4	648	26.4	446	18.2
South Carolina.......	2,091	1,138	54.4	21	1.0	583	27.9	349	16.7
Georgia.............	5,536	3,293	59.5	73	1.3	1,533	27.7	637	11.5
Florida.............	16,088	7,141	44.4	111	0.7	7,137	44.4	1,699	10.6
EAST SOUTH CENTRAL:									
Kentucky............	12,661	8,220	64.9	159	1.3	2,212	17.5	2,070	16.3
Tennessee...........	5,891	3,278	55.6	62	1.1	1,535	26.1	1,016	17.2
Alabama............	6,291	3,472	55.2	59	0.9	1,639	26.1	1,121	17.8
Mississippi..........	2,702	1,309	48.4	17	0.6	897	33.2	479	17.7
WEST SOUTH CENTRAL:									
Arkansas............	5,000	2,976	59.5	64	1.3	1,066	21.3	894	17.9
Louisiana...........	16,380	5,846	35.7	82	0.5	7,586	46.3	2,866	17.5
Oklahoma...........	13,291	8,133	61.2	124	0.9	3,266	24.6	1,768	13.3
Texas..............	114,118	32,800	28.7	949	0.8	72,585	63.6	7,784	6.8
MOUNTAIN:									
Montana............	31,459	22,618	71.9	479	1.5	5,990	19.0	2,372	7.5
Idaho..............	12,804	9,708	75.8	139	1.1	2,217	17.3	740	5.8
Wyoming...........	7,261	4,719	65.0	72	1.0	1,965	27.1	505	7.0
Colorado...........	42,928	27,688	64.5	603	1.4	12,446	29.0	2,191	5.1
New Mexico.........	8,689	2,500	28.8	45	0.5	5,642	64.9	502	5.8
Arizona............	22,391	4,722	21.1	79	0.4	16,638	74.3	952	4.3
Utah...............	23,463	16,815	71.7	348	1.5	5,320	22.7	980	4.2
Nevada.............	3,692	2,115	57.3	25	0.7	1,103	29.9	449	12.2
PACIFIC:									
Washington.........	87,177	56,761	65.1	1,443	1.7	22,954	26.3	6,019	6.9
Oregon.............	36,227	23,581	65.1	726	2.0	10,326	28.5	1,594	4.4
California...........	247,041	127,176	51.5	3,633	1.5	97,664	39.5	18,568	7.5

TABLE **94.**—CITIZENSHIP OF FOREIGN-BORN AND FOREIGN-BORN WHITE

FOREIGN-BORN POPULATION.

CITY.	Total.	Naturalized.		Having first papers.		Alien.		Citizenship not reported.	
		Number.	Per cent.	Number.	Per cent.	Number.	Per cent.	Number.	Per cent.
Akron, Ohio	38,021	11,004	28.9	5,331	14.0	20,538	54.0	1,148	3.0
Albany, N. Y	17,695	10,526	59.5	1,018	5.8	5,802	32.8	349	2.0
Atlanta, Ga	4,789	2,719	56.8	302	6.3	1,311	27.4	457	9.5
Baltimore, Md	84,809	42,527	50.1	8,530	10.1	32,448	38.3	1,304	1.5
Birmingham, Ala	6,140	2,981	48.6	444	7.2	1,553	25.3	1,162	18.9
Boston, Mass	242,619	106,992	44.1	21,300	8.8	104,077	42.9	10,250	4.2
Bridgeport, Conn	46,782	16,733	35.8	4,984	10.7	21,485	45.9	3,580	7.7
Buffalo, N. Y	121,824	63,304	52.0	12,903	10.6	38,039	31.2	7,578	6.2
Cambridge, Mass	33,296	14,156	42.5	2,385	7.2	16,568	49.8	187	0.6
Camden, N. J	20,354	7,762	38.1	2,457	12.1	8,857	43.5	1,278	6.3
Chicago, Ill	808,558	425,817	52.7	101,289	12.5	239,841	29.7	41,611	5.1
Cincinnati, Ohio	42,921	28,323	66.0	2,680	6.2	9,831	22.9	2,087	4.9
Cleveland, Ohio	240,173	101,805	42.4	38,993	16.2	91,564	38.1	7,811	3.3
Columbus, Ohio	16,187	8,856	54.7	1,069	6.6	4,460	27.6	1,802	11.1
Dallas, Tex	8,801	3,544	40.3	590	6.7	3,687	41.9	980	11.1
Dayton, Ohio	13,165	6,936	52.7	1,185	9.0	4,667	35.5	377	2.9
Denver, Colo	38,230	23,918	62.6	3,263	8.5	9,937	26.0	1,112	2.9
Des Moines, Iowa	11,269	7,135	63.3	702	6.2	2,418	21.5	1,014	9.0
Detroit, Mich	290,884	104,915	36.1	47,770	16.4	127,196	43.7	11,003	3.8
Fall River, Mass	42,421	15,346	36.2	1,804	4.3	24,501	57.8	770	1.8
Fort Worth, Tex	7,502	1,816	24.2	229	3.1	4,254	56.7	1,203	16.0
Grand Rapids, Mich	28,427	15,277	53.7	3,479	12.2	7,604	26.7	2,067	7.3
Hartford, Conn	40,912	17,028	41.6	3,375	8.2	19,979	48.8	530	1.3
Houston, Tex	12,088	4,932	40.8	735	6.1	5,475	45.3	946	7.8
Indianapolis, Ind	17,096	8,517	49.8	2,066	12.1	4,403	25.8	2,110	12.3
Jersey City, N. J	76,294	36,785	48.2	6,624	8.7	31,007	40.6	1,878	2.5
Kansas City, Kans	11,721	4,225	36.0	1,640	14.0	5,474	46.7	382	3.3
Kansas City, Mo	27,583	14,614	53.0	1,940	7.0	7,931	28.8	3,098	11.2
Los Angeles, Calif	122,131	49,542	40.6	7,851	6.4	58,514	47.9	6,224	5.1
Louisville, Ky	11,667	7,824	67.1	572	4.9	1,567	13.4	1,704	14.6
Lowell, Mass	38,116	15,168	39.8	2,116	5.6	20,529	53.9	303	0.8
Memphis, Tenn	5,844	2,524	43.2	387	6.6	1,924	32.9	1,009	17.3
Milwaukee, Wis	110,160	55,026	50.0	14,291	13.0	36,293	32.9	4,550	4.1
Minneapolis, Minn	88,248	54,149	61.4	10,651	12.1	19,819	22.5	3,629	4.1
Nashville, Tenn	2,412	1,441	59.7	134	5.6	502	20.8	335	13.9
New Bedford, Mass	51,078	16,517	32.3	2,750	5.4	31,419	61.5	392	0.8
New Haven, Conn	46,124	18,500	40.1	3,725	8.1	20,793	45.1	3,106	6.7
New Orleans, La	27,365	10,233	37.4	1,621	5.9	12,024	43.9	3,487	12.7
New York, N. Y	2,028,160	810,086	39.9	180,404	8.9	938,235	46.3	99,435	4.9
Bronx borough	267,742	130,219	48.6	24,490	9.1	98,700	36.9	14,333	5.4
Brooklyn borough	666,188	281,476	42.3	61,142	9.2	290,239	43.6	33,331	5.0
Manhattan borough	950,264	319,915	33.7	82,358	8.7	504,294	53.1	43,697	4.6
Queens borough	112,171	63,608	56.7	9,193	8.2	33,123	29.5	6,247	5.6
Richmond borough	31,795	14,868	46.8	3,221	10.1	11,879	37.4	1,827	5.7
Newark, N. J	117,549	48,441	41.2	9,164	7.8	54,237	46.1	5,707	4.9
Norfolk, Va	6,998	3,090	44.2	917	13.1	2,566	36.7	425	6.1
Oakland, Calif	49,895	23,506	47.1	4,452	8.9	20,037	40.2	1,900	3.8
Omaha, Nebr	35,645	18,130	50.9	5,146	14.4	9,503	26.7	2,866	8.0
Paterson, N. J	45,242	21,825	48.2	2,956	6.5	18,612	41.1	1,849	4.1
Philadelphia, Pa	400,744	190,206	47.5	32,586	8.1	159,115	39.7	18,837	4.7
Pittsburgh, Pa	120,792	62,524	51.8	8,984	7.4	44,502	36.8	4,782	4.0
Portland, Oreg	49,778	25,029	50.3	6,335	12.7	17,538	35.2	876	1.8
Providence, R. I	69,895	32,783	46.9	6,376	9.1	28,055	40.1	2,681	3.8
Reading, Pa	9,573	3,474	36.3	1,445	15.1	4,177	43.6	477	5.0
Richmond, Va	4,713	2,302	48.8	401	8.5	1,446	30.7	564	12.0
Rochester, N. Y	71,411	36,881	51.6	6,199	8.7	24,660	34.4	3,731	5.2
St. Louis, Mo	100,090	50,000	50.0	10,000	9.7	30,000	27.0	0,090	0.2
St. Paul, Minn	51,722	33,399	64.6	5,651	10.9	10,195	19.7	2,477	4.8
Salt Lake City, Utah	19,897	12,320	61.9	1,552	7.8	5,659	28.4	366	1.8
San Antonio, Tex	36,824	6,409	17.4	925	2.5	27,156	73.7	2,334	6.3
San Francisco, Calif	149,195	70,171	47.0	12,100	8.1	56,010	37.5	10,914	7.3
Scranton, Pa	28,587	15,163	53.0	1,103	3.9	10,186	35.6	2,135	7.5
Seattle, Wash	80,976	37,745	46.6	9,941	12.3	28,395	35.1	4,895	6.0
Spokane, Wash	17,096	10,718	62.7	1,716	10.0	4,311	25.2	351	2.1
Springfield, Mass	31,461	13,321	42.3	3,577	11.4	13,879	44.1	684	2.2
Syracuse, N. Y	32,383	16,405	50.7	2,208	6.8	12,769	39.4	1,001	3.1
Toledo, Ohio	38,296	20,598	53.8	4,292	11.2	12,117	31.6	1,289	3.4
Trenton, N. J	30,168	11,847	39.3	3,555	11.8	13,738	45.5	1,028	3.4
Washington, D. C.	29,365	15,626	53.2	2,204	7.5	7,952	27.1	3,583	12.2
Wilmington, Del	16,337	6,764	41.4	1,399	8.6	7,040	43.1	1,134	6.9
Worcester, Mass	53,527	22,616	42.3	4,997	9.3	23,747	44.4	2,167	4.0
Yonkers, N. Y	25,796	13,749	53.3	2,209	8.6	9,190	35.6	648	2.5
Youngstown, Ohio	33,945	11,830	34.9	2,760	8.1	18,323	54.0	1,032	3.0

POPULATION, FOR CITIES HAVING 100,000 INHABITANTS OR MORE: 1920.

CITY.	Total.	FOREIGN-BORN WHITE POPULATION.							
		Naturalized.		Having first papers.		Alien.		Citizenship not reported.	
		Number.	Per cent.	Number.	Per cent.	Number.	Per cent.	Number.	Per cent.
Akron, Ohio	37,889	10,988	29.0	5,325	14.1	20,446	54.0	1,130	3.0
Albany, N. Y	17,636	10,518	59.6	1,018	5.8	5,757	32.6	343	1.9
Atlanta, Ga	4,738	2,716	57.3	300	6.3	1,278	27.0	444	9.4
Baltimore, Md	83,911	42,372	50.5	8,481	10.1	31,828	37.9	1,230	1.5
Birmingham, Ala	6,084	2,969	48.8	440	7.2	1,530	25.1	1,145	18.8
Boston, Mass	238,919	106,449	44.6	20,936	8.8	101,659	42.5	9,875	4.1
Bridgeport, Conn	46,414	16,689	36.0	4,980	10.7	21,196	45.7	3,549	7.6
Buffalo, N.Y	121,530	63,224	52.0	12,890	10.6	37,903	31.2	7,513	6.2
Cambridge, Mass	32,104	13,974	43.5	2,290	7.1	15,666	48.8	174	0.5
Camden, N. J	20,262	7,749	38.2	2,451	12.1	8,802	43.4	1,260	6.2
Chicago, Ill	805,482	425,327	52.8	101,203	12.6	237,792	29.5	41,160	5.1
Cincinnati, Ohio	42,827	28,293	66.1	2,678	6.3	9,779	22.8	2,077	4.8
Cleveland, Ohio	239,538	101,626	42.4	38,955	16.3	91,241	38.1	7,716	3.2
Columbus, Ohio	16,055	8,833	55.0	1,067	6.6	4,385	27.3	1,770	11.0
Dallas, Tex	8,730	3,533	40.5	590	6.8	3,642	41.7	965	11.1
Dayton, Ohio	13,111	6,922	52.8	1,183	9.0	4,639	35.4	367	2.8
Denver, Colo	37,620	23,885	63.5	3,255	8.7	9,435	25.1	1,045	2.8
Des Moines, Iowa	11,224	7,131	63.5	702	6.3	2,382	21.2	1,009	9.0
Detroit, Mich	289,297	104,478	36.1	47,637	16.5	126,408	43.7	10,774	3.7
Fall River, Mass	42,331	15,340	36.2	1,802	4.3	24,420	57.7	769	1.8
Fort Worth, Tex	7,359	1,802	24.5	229	3.1	4,141	56.3	1,187	16.1
Grand Rapids, Mich	28,355	15,258	53.8	3,477	12.3	7,562	26.7	2,058	7.3
Hartford, Conn	40,667	17,009	41.8	3,366	8.3	19,773	48.6	519	1.3
Houston, Tex	12,012	4,914	40.9	730	6.1	5,438	45.3	930	7.7
Indianapolis, Ind	16,958	8,495	50.1	2,059	12.1	4,316	25.5	2,088	12.3
Jersey City, N. J	75,981	36,710	48.3	6,614	8.7	30,812	40.6	1,845	2.4
Kansas City, Kans	11,656	4,219	36.2	1,635	14.0	5,426	46.6	376	3.2
Kansas City, Mo	27,320	14,594	53.4	1,932	7.1	7,739	28.3	3,055	11.2
Los Angeles, Calif	112,057	49,370	44.1	7,832	7.0	48,769	43.5	6,086	5.4
Louisville, Ky	11,621	7,814	67.2	570	4.9	1,542	13.3	1,695	14.6
Lowell, Mass	38,040	15,159	39.9	2,114	5.6	20,466	53.8	301	0.8
Memphis, Tenn	5,775	2,512	43.5	384	6.6	1,882	32.6	997	17.3
Milwaukee, Wis	110,068	55,008	50.0	14,283	13.0	36,232	32.9	4,545	4.1
Minneapolis, Minn	88,032	54,120	61.5	10,644	12.1	19,662	22.3	3,606	4.1
Nashville, Tenn	2,387	1,432	60.0	134	5.6	497	20.8	324	13.6
New Bedford, Mass	48,689	16,297	33.5	2,651	5.4	29,369	60.3	372	0.8
New Haven, Conn	45,686	18,451	40.4	3,707	8.1	20,480	44.8	3,048	6.7
New Orleans, La	25,992	10,132	39.0	1,591	6.1	11,007	42.3	3,262	12.6
New York, N. Y	1,991,547	807,022	40.5	178,788	9.0	910,655	45.7	95,082	4.8
Bronx borough	266,971	130,134	48.7	24,461	9.2	98,214	36.8	14,162	5.3
Brooklyn borough	659,287	280,790	42.6	60,807	9.2	285,360	43.3	32,330	4.9
Manhattan borough	922,080	317,730	34.5	81,135	8.8	482,577	52.3	40,638	4.4
Queens borough	111,676	63,526	56.9	9,168	8.2	32,813	29.4	6,169	5.5
Richmond borough	31,533	14,842	47.1	3,217	10.2	11,691	37.1	1,783	5.7
Newark, N. J	117,003	48,368	41.3	9,150	7.8	53,869	46.0	5,616	4.8
Norfolk, Va	6,587	3,035	46.1	884	13.4	2,290	34.8	378	5.7
Oakland, Calif	45,162	23,412	51.8	4,424	9.8	15,561	34.5	1,765	3.9
Omaha, Nebr	35,381	18,099	51.2	5,139	14.5	9,314	26.3	2,829	8.0
Paterson, N. J	45,145	21,813	48.3	2,953	6.5	18,548	41.1	1,831	4.1
Philadelphia, Pa	397,927	189,710	47.7	32,459	8.2	157,356	39.5	18,402	4.6
Pittsburgh, Pa	120,266	62,435	51.9	8,966	7.5	44,147	36.7	4,718	3.9
Portland, Oreg	47,114	24,978	53.0	6,313	13.4	14,961	31.8	862	1.8
Providence, R. I	68,951	32,701	47.4	6,333	9.2	27,287	39.6	2,630	3.8
Reading, Pa	9,553	3,469	36.3	1,444	15.1	4,165	43.6	475	5.0
Richmond, Va	4,637	2,287	49.3	395	8.5	1,411	30.4	544	11.7
Rochester, N. Y	71,321	36,863	51.7	6,190	8.7	24,547	34.4	3,721	5.2
St. Louis, Mo	103,239	58,544	56.7	10,018	9.7	28,326	27.4	6,351	6.2
St. Paul, Minn	51,595	33,368	64.7	5,648	10.9	10,114	19.6	2,465	4.8
Salt Lake City, Utah	19,434	12,309	63.3	1,548	8.0	5,214	26.8	363	1.9
San Antonio, Tex	36,646	6,389	17.4	924	2.5	27,039	73.8	2,294	6.3
San Francisco, Calif	140,200	69,929	49.9	12,047	8.6	47,526	33.9	10,698	7.6
Scranton, Pa	28,568	15,158	53.1	1,102	3.9	10,177	35.6	2,131	7.5
Seattle, Wash	73,875	37,651	51.0	9,895	13.4	21,527	29.1	4,802	6.5
Spokane, Wash	16,826	10,708	63.6	1,716	10.2	4,051	24.1	351	2.1
Springfield, Mass	31,250	13,299	42.6	3,564	11.4	13,711	43.9	676	2.2
Syracuse, N. Y	32,321	16,385	50.7	2,206	6.8	12,739	39.4	991	3.1
Toledo, Ohio	38,145	20,542	53.9	4,282	11.2	12,053	31.6	1,268	3.3
Trenton, N. J	30,073	11,839	39.4	3,552	11.8	13,662	45.4	1,020	3.4
Washington, D. C	28,548	15,507	54.3	2,186	7.7	7,427	26.0	3,428	12.0
Wilmington, Del	16,279	6,756	41.5	1,399	8.6	7,011	43.1	1,113	6.8
Worcester, Mass	53,418	22,593	42.3	4,992	9.3	23,670	44.3	2,163	4.0
Yonkers, N. Y	25,700	13,735	53.4	2,199	8.6	9,128	35.6	638	2.5
Youngstown, Ohio	33,834	11,816	34.9	2,754	8.1	18,250	53.9	1,014	3.0

TABLE 95.—CITIZENSHIP OF FOREIGN-BORN WHITE MALES AND

CITY.	Total.	FOREIGN-BORN WHITE MALES.							
		Naturalized.		Having first papers.		Alien.		Citizenship not reported.	
		Number.	Per cent.	Number.	Per cent.	Number.	Per cent.	Number.	Per cent.
Akron, Ohio	24,607	6,279	25.5	5,138	20.9	12,499	50.8	691	2.8
Albany, N. Y	8,976	5,271	58.7	918	10.2	2,655	29.6	132	1.5
Atlanta, Ga	2,700	1,502	55.6	263	9.7	683	25.3	252	9.3
Baltimore, Md	44,034	21,781	49.5	7,803	17.7	13,988	31.8	462	1.0
Birmingham, Ala	3,499	1,641	46.9	419	12.0	768	21.9	671	19.2
Boston, Mass	117,770	53,114	45.1	19,028	16.2	41,919	35.6	3,709	3.1
Bridgeport, Conn	25,279	8,691	34.4	4,793	19.0	10,280	40.7	1,515	6.0
Buffalo, N. Y	64,748	32,362	50.0	12,099	18.7	17,089	26.4	3,198	4.9
Cambridge, Mass	15,219	6,686	43.9	2,142	14.1	6,325	41.6	66	0.4
Camden, N. J	11,086	3,970	35.8	2,370	21.4	4,227	38.1	519	4.7
Chicago, Ill	431,764	223,433	51.7	94,681	21.9	95,053	22.0	18,597	4.3
Cincinnati, Ohio	21,792	14,387	66.0	2,384	10.9	4,244	19.5	777	3.6
Cleveland, Ohio	133,075	53,075	39.9	37,202	28.0	39,338	29.6	3,460	2.6
Columbus, Ohio	9,113	4,698	51.6	956	10.5	2,553	28.0	906	9.9
Dallas, Tex	5,097	1,979	38.8	539	10.6	2,057	40.4	522	10.2
Dayton, Ohio	7,394	3,653	49.4	1,087	14.7	2,467	33.4	187	2.5
Denver, Colo	20,896	12,622	60.4	2,950	14.1	4,762	22.8	562	2.7
Des Moines, Iowa	6,211	3,832	61.7	647	10.4	1,197	19.3	535	8.6
Detroit, Mich	169,095	55,379	32.8	45,248	26.8	63,204	37.4	5,264	3.1
Fall River, Mass	20,334	7,428	36.5	1,659	8.2	10,974	54.0	273	1.3
Fort Worth, Tex	4,738	1,053	22.2	211	4.5	2,779	58.7	695	14.7
Grand Rapids, Mich	14,999	7,880	52.5	3,253	21.7	2,959	19.7	907	6.0
Hartford, Conn	21,470	8,715	40.6	3,167	14.8	9,353	43.6	235	1.1
Houston, Tex	6,809	2,745	40.3	689	10.1	2,891	42.5	484	7.1
Indianapolis, Ind	9,359	4,440	47.4	1,866	19.9	2,089	22.3	964	10.3
Jersey City, N. J	40,212	18,839	46.8	6,265	15.6	14,478	36.0	630	1.6
Kansas City, Kans	6,850	2,234	32.6	1,541	22.5	2,870	41.9	205	3.0
Kansas City, Mo	15,377	8,020	52.2	1,797	11.7	4,021	26.1	1,539	10.0
Los Angeles, Calif	60,188	25,406	42.2	6,994	11.6	24,713	41.1	3,075	5.1
Louisville, Ky	5,882	4,057	69.0	500	8.5	636	10.8	689	11.7
Lowell, Mass	18,466	7,266	39.3	1,945	10.5	9,130	49.4	125	0.7
Memphis, Tenn	3,266	1,398	42.8	345	10.6	999	30.6	524	16.0
Milwaukee, Wis	60,703	28,465	46.9	12,663	20.9	17,513	28.9	2,062	3.4
Minneapolis, Minn	48,402	29,124	60.2	9,655	19.9	8,064	16.7	1,559	3.2
Nashville, Tenn	1,287	773	60.1	125	9.7	231	17.9	158	12.3
New Bedford, Mass	23,864	8,034	33.7	2,408	10.1	13,275	55.6	147	0.6
New Haven, Conn	23,532	9,459	40.2	3,500	14.9	9,422	40.0	1,151	4.9
New Orleans, La	15,497	6,065	39.1	1,533	9.9	6,596	42.6	1,303	8.4
New York, N. Y	1,020,090	424,748	41.6	162,533	15.9	395,912	38.8	36,897	3.6
Bronx borough	135,456	68,185	50.3	22,632	16.7	39,278	29.0	5,361	4.0
Brooklyn borough	341,527	147,373	43.2	56,203	16.5	125,103	36.6	12,848	3.8
Manhattan borough	468,506	168,534	36.0	72,228	15.4	212,342	45.3	15,402	3.3
Queens borough	57,132	32,423	56.8	8,442	14.8	13,750	24.1	2,517	4.4
Richmond borough	17,469	8,233	47.1	3,028	17.3	5,439	31.1	769	4.4
Newark, N. J	61,914	25,156	40.6	8,614	13.9	25,980	42.0	2,164	3.5
Norfolk, Va	4,439	1,831	41.2	863	19.4	1,525	34.4	220	5.0
Oakland, Calif	25,492	12,517	49.1	4,058	15.9	8,008	31.4	909	3.6
Omaha, Nebr	19,910	9,762	49.0	4,795	24.1	4,015	20.2	1,338	6.7
Paterson, N. J	23,205	11,241	48.4	2,693	11.6	8,651	37.3	620	2.7
Philadelphia, Pa	205,518	98,085	47.7	30,176	14.7	70,226	34.2	7,031	3.4
Pittsburgh, Pa	65,367	32,571	49.8	8,397	12.8	22,438	34.3	1,961	3.0
Portland, Oreg	27,344	13,590	49.7	5,827	21.3	7,503	27.4	424	1.6
Providence, R. I	34,079	15,888	46.6	5,701	16.7	11,451	33.6	1,039	3.0
Reading, Pa	5,457	1,934	35.4	1,375	25.2	1,933	35.4	215	3.9
Richmond, Va	2,533	1,230	48.6	355	14.0	663	26.2	285	11.3
Rochester, N. Y	36,992	18,811	50.9	5,707	15.4	10,891	29.4	1,583	4.3
St. Louis, Mo	56,266	31,513	56.0	9,047	16.6	12,695	22.4	2,776	4.9
St. Paul, Minn	28,005	17,500	62.6	5,099	18.2	4,192	15.0	1,127	4.0
Salt Lake City, Utah	9,737	5,792	59.5	1,312	13.5	2,451	25.2	182	1.9
San Antonio, Tex	19,494	3,273	16.8	668	3.4	14,491	74.3	1,062	5.4
San Francisco, Calif	82,918	40,746	49.1	11,007	13.3	25,610	30.9	5,555	6.7
Scranton, Pa	15,139	7,811	51.6	1,030	6.8	5,414	35.8	884	5.8
Seattle, Wash	43,779	20,908	47.8	9,295	21.2	11,171	25.5	2,405	5.5
Spokane, Wash	9,463	5,757	60.8	1,575	16.6	1,974	20.9	157	1.7
Springfield, Mass	15,873	6,452	40.6	3,278	20.7	5,902	37.2	241	1.5
Syracuse, N. Y	17,433	8,130	46.6	2,046	11.7	6,770	38.8	487	2.8
Toledo, Ohio	21,751	10,741	49.4	4,017	18.5	6,414	29.5	574	2.6
Trenton, N. J	16,477	6,230	37.8	3,367	20.4	6,414	38.9	466	2.8
Washington, D. C	15,142	8,179	54.0	1,838	12.1	3,376	22.3	1,749	11.6
Wilmington, Del	9,347	3,621	38.7	1,335	14.3	3,875	41.5	516	5.5
Worcester, Mass	27,874	11,274	40.4	4,713	16.9	11,134	39.9	753	2.7
Yonkers, N. Y	12,990	6,921	53.3	1,813	14.0	3,991	30.7	265	2.0
Youngstown, Ohio	20,697	6,381	30.8	2,635	12.7	11,175	54.0	506	2.4

FEMALES, FOR CITIES HAVING 100,000 INHABITANTS OR MORE: 1920.

CITY.	Total.	FOREIGN-BORN WHITE FEMALES.							
		Naturalized.		Having first papers.		Alien.		Citizenship not reported.	
		Number.	Per cent.	Number.	Per cent.	Number.	Per cent.	Number.	Per cent.
Akron, Ohio	13,282	4,709	35.5	187	1.4	7,947	59.8	439	3.3
Albany, N. Y	8,660	5,247	60.6	100	1.2	3,102	35.8	211	2.4
Atlanta, Ga	2,038	1,214	59.6	37	1.8	595	29.2	192	9.4
Baltimore, Md	39,877	20,591	51.6	678	1.7	17,840	44.7	768	1.9
Birmingham, Ala	2,585	1,328	51.4	21	0.8	762	29.5	474	18.3
Boston, Mass	121,149	53,335	44.0	1,908	1.6	59,740	49.3	6,166	5.1
Bridgeport, Conn	21,135	7,998	37.8	187	0.9	10,916	51.6	2,034	9.6
Buffalo, N. Y	56,782	30,862	54.4	791	1.4	20,814	36.7	4,315	7.6
Cambridge, Mass	16,885	7,288	43.2	148	0.9	9,341	55.3	108	0.6
Camden, N. J	9,176	3,779	41.2	81	0.9	4,575	49.9	741	8.1
Chicago, Ill	373,718	201,894	54.0	6,522	1 7	142,739	38.2	22,563	6.0
Cincinnati, Ohio	21,035	13,906	66.1	294	1.4	5,535	26.3	1,300	6.2
Cleveland, Ohio	106,463	48,551	45.6	1,753	1.6	51,903	48.8	4,256	4.0
Columbus, Ohio	6,942	4,135	59.6	111	1.6	1,832	26.4	864	12.4
Dallas, Tex	3,633	1,554	42.8	51	1.4	1,585	43.6	443	12.2
Dayton, Ohio	5,717	3,269	57.2	96	1.7	2,172	38.0	180	3.1
Denver, Colo	16,724	11,263	67.3	305	1.8	4,673	27.9	483	2.9
Des Moines, Iowa	5,013	3,299	65.8	55	1.1	1,185	23.6	474	9.5
Detroit, Mich	120,202	49,099	40.8	2,389	2.0	63,204	52.6	5,510	4.6
Fall River, Mass	21,997	7,912	36.0	143	0.7	13,446	61.1	496	2.3
Fort Worth, Tex	2,621	749	28.6	18	0.7	1,362	52.0	492	18.8
Grand Rapids, Mich	13,356	7,378	55.2	224	1.7	4,603	34.5	1,151	8.6
Hartford, Conn	19,197	8,294	43.2	199	1.0	10,420	54.3	284	1.5
Houston, Tex	5,203	2,169	41.7	41	0.8	2,547	49.0	446	8.6
Indianapolis, Ind	7,599	4,055	53.4	193	2.5	2,227	29.3	1,124	14.8
Jersey City, N. J	35,769	17,871	50.0	349	1.0	16,334	45.7	1,215	3.4
Kansas City, Kans	4,806	1,985	41.3	94	2.0	2,556	53.2	171	3.6
Kansas City, Mo	11,943	6,574	55.0	135	1.1	3,718	31.1	1,516	12.7
Los Angeles, Calif	51,869	23,964	46.2	838	1.6	24,056	46.4	3,011	5.8
Louisville, Ky	5,739	3,757	65.5	70	1.2	906	15.8	1,006	17.5
Lowell, Mass	19,574	7,893	40.3	169	0.9	11,336	57.9	176	0.9
Memphis, Tenn	2,509	1,114	44.4	39	1.6	883	35.2	473	18.9
Milwaukee, Wis	49,365	26,543	53.8	1,620	3.3	18,719	37.9	2,483	5.0
Minneapolis, Minn	39,630	24,996	63.1	989	2.5	11,598	29.3	2,047	5.2
Nashville, Tenn	1,100	659	59.9	9	0.8	266	24.2	166	15.1
New Bedford, Mass	24,825	8,263	33.3	243	1.0	16,094	64.8	225	0.9
New Haven, Conn	22,154	8,992	40.6	207	0.9	11,058	49.9	1,897	8.6
New Orleans, La	10,495	4,067	38.8	58	0.6	4,411	42.0	1,959	18.7
New York, N. Y	971,457	382,274	39.4	16,255	1.7	514,743	53.0	58,185	6.0
Bronx borough	131,515	61,949	47.1	1,829	1.4	58,936	44.8	8,801	6.7
Brooklyn borough	317,760	133,417	42.0	4,604	1.4	160,257	50.4	19,482	6.1
Manhattan borough	453,574	149,196	32.9	8,907	2.0	270,235	59.6	25,236	5.6
Queens borough	54,544	31,103	57.0	726	1.3	19,063	34.9	3,652	6.7
Richmond borough	14,064	6,609	47.0	189	1.3	6,252	44.5	1,014	7.2
Newark, N. J	55,089	23,212	42.1	536	1.0	27,889	50.6	3,452	6.3
Norfolk, Va	2,148	1,204	56.1	21	1.0	765	35.6	158	7.4
Oakland, Calif	19,670	10,895	55.4	366	1.9	7,553	38.4	856	4.4
Omaha, Nebr	15,471	8,337	53.9	344	2.2	5,299	34.3	1,491	9.6
Paterson, N. J	21,940	10,572	48.2	260	1.2	9,897	45.1	1,211	5.5
Philadelphia, Pa	192,409	91,625	47.6	2,283	1.2	87,130	45.3	11,371	5.9
Pittsburgh, Pa	54,899	29,864	54.4	569	1.0	21,709	39.5	2,757	5.0
Portland, Oreg	19,770	11,388	57.6	486	2.5	7,458	37.7	438	2.2
Providence, R. I	34,872	16,813	48.2	632	1.8	15,836	45.4	1,591	4.6
Reading, Pa	4,096	1,535	37.5	69	1.7	2,232	54.5	260	6.3
Richmond, Va	2,104	1,057	50.2	40	1.9	748	35.6	259	12.3
Rochester, N. Y	34,329	18,052	52.6	483	1.4	13,656	39.8	2,138	6.2
St. Louis, Mo	46,973	27,026	57.5	671	1.4	15,701	33.4	3,575	7.6
St. Paul, Minn	23,592	15,772	66.9	560	2.4	5,922	25.1	1,338	5.7
Salt Lake City, Utah	9,697	6,517	67.2	236	2.4	2,763	28.5	181	1.9
San Antonio, Tex	17,152	3,116	18.2	256	1.5	12,548	73.2	1,232	7.2
San Francisco, Calif	57,282	29,183	50.9	1,040	1.8	21,916	38.3	5,143	9.0
Scranton, Pa	13,429	7,347	54.7	72	0.5	4,763	35.5	1,247	9.3
Seattle, Wash	30,096	16,743	55.6	600	2.0	10,356	34.4	2,397	8.0
Spokane, Wash	7,363	4,951	67.2	141	1.9	2,077	28.2	194	2.6
Springfield, Mass	15,377	6,847	44.5	286	1.9	7,809	50.8	435	2.8
Syracuse, N. Y	14,888	8,255	55.4	160	1.1	5,969	40.1	504	3.4
Toledo, Ohio	16,394	9,801	59.8	265	1.6	5,634	34.4	694	4.2
Trenton, N. J	13,596	5,609	41.3	185	1.4	7,248	53.3	554	4.1
Washington, D. C	13,406	7,328	54.7	348	2.6	4,051	30.2	1,679	12.5
Wilmington, Del	6,932	3,135	45.2	64	0.9	3,136	45.2	597	8.6
Worcester, Mass	25,544	11,319	44.3	279	1.1	12,536	49.1	1,410	5.5
Yonkers, N. Y	12,710	6,814	53.6	386	3.0	5,137	40.4	373	2.9
Youngstown, Ohio	13,137	5,435	41.4	119	0.9	7,075	53.9	508	3.9

TABLE **96.**—CITIZENSHIP OF FOREIGN-BORN WHITE MALES AND FEMALES
OR MORE:

[No inquiry as to the citizenship

CITY.	FOREIGN-BORN WHITE MALES 21 YEARS OF AGE AND OVER—NUMBER.					
	Total.		Naturalized.		Having first papers.	
	1920	1910	1920	1910	1920	1910
1 Akron, Ohio	22,642	7,051	5,951	2,459	5,034	317
2 Albany, N. Y	8,392	8,192	5,083	4,827	904	462
3 Atlanta, Ga	2,476	2,287	1,396	1,011	257	193
4 Baltimore, Md	40,496	33,638	20,944	16,643	7,634	2,664
5 Birmingham, Ala	3,199	2,944	1,564	1,179	416	186
6 Boston, Mass	109,209	103,160	51,418	47,791	18,637	10,438
7 Bridgeport, Conn	23,292	17,114	8,342	6,563	4,728	1,038
8 Buffalo, N. Y	60,068	56,337	31,184	29,409	11,966	4,319
9 Cambridge, Mass	14,000	14,636	6,512	7,162	2,108	1,189
10 Camden, N. J	10,177	7,397	3,764	3,041	2,330	486
11 Chicago, Ill	401,965	379,850	214,854	190,693	93,682	31,585
12 Cincinnati, Ohio	20,588	26,723	14,036	17,253	2,336	1,733
13 Cleveland, Ohio	122,646	94,431	50,535	40,482	36,724	7,826
14 Columbus, Ohio	8,402	8,487	4,489	4,453	914	414
15 Dallas, Tex	4,484	2,811	1,909	1,504	535	134
16 Dayton, Ohio	6,863	7,303	3,520	3,451	1,070	396
17 Denver, Colo	19,728	19,204	12,300	10,959	2,912	2,102
18 Des Moines, Iowa	5,836	5,231	3,711	2,807	637	280
19 Detroit, Mich	153,144	75,323	52,557	32,891	44,464	7,271
20 Fall River, Mass	18,377	20,181	7,205	8,368	1,627	732
21 Fort Worth, Tex	3,892	2,541	1,002	963	209	97
22 Grand Rapids, Mich	13,948	13,689	7,637	7,758	3,225	1,016
23 Hartford, Conn	19,759	13,975	8,381	6,294	3,122	1,112
24 Houston, Tex	5,878	3,466	2,626	1,754	679	239
25 Indianapolis, Ind	8,860	10,407	4,305	6,088	1,857	1,189
26 Jersey City, N. J	37,665	37,707	18,198	16,556	6,174	3,067
27 Kansas City, Kans	6,190	5,710	2,160	2,427	1,519	642
28 Kansas City, Mo	14,096	13,052	7,706	6,953	1,777	890
29 Los Angeles, Calif	53,626	29,576	24,605	14,097	6,890	2,730
30 Louisville, Ky	5,679	8,334	3,967	5,704	492	380
31 Lowell, Mass	17,119	18,191	7,090	7,028	1,912	427
32 Memphis, Tenn	3,024	3,403	1,343	1,664	337	197
33 Milwaukee, Wis	56,586	56,101	27,448	26,155	12,454	9,887
34 Minneapolis, Minn	45,854	45,159	28,261	23,462	9,531	5,427
35 Nashville, Tenn	1,185	1,435	738	951	124	80
36 New Bedford, Mass	20,980	17,151	7,571	5,441	2,337	788
37 New Haven, Conn	21,594	19,194	9,107	8,628	3,439	1,426
38 New Orleans, La	14,304	13,486	5,905	6,138	1,473	595
39 New York, N. Y	927,742	828,793	405,009	318,091	159,824	106,525
40 Bronx borough	124,230	68,676	65,022	33,188	22,286	8,848
41 Brooklyn borough	309,815	248,544	140,340	109,100	55,157	34,260
42 Manhattan borough	423,541	461,246	160,174	148,847	71,039	58,661
43 Queens borough	53,942	38,350	31,524	21,019	8,355	3,848
44 Richmond borough	16,214	11,977	7,949	5,937	2,987	908
45 Newark, N. J	56,524	49,674	24,026	21,427	8,486	4,982
46 Norfolk, Va	4,059	1,820	1,702	931	837	151
47 Oakland, Calif	23,907	19,334	12,190	10,237	3,984	2,004
48 Omaha, Nebr.[1]	18,520	18,165	9,320	9,035	4,755	2,766
49 Paterson, N. J	21,102	20,182	10,708	9,817	2,629	1,387
50 Philadelphia, Pa	188,025	167,072	92,819	69,415	29,628	15,533
51 Pittsburgh, Pa	61,394	70,148	31,217	28,797	8,283	5,355
52 Portland, Oreg	25,409	25,230	13,094	11,251	5,764	3,058
53 Providence, R. I	31,410	32,863	15,217	12,988	5,573	2,815
54 Reading, Pa	5,009	4,528	1,861	1,430	1,362	214
55 Richmond, Va	2,348	2,040	1,175	943	348	123
56 Rochester, N. Y	33,316	27,067	17,681	13,003	5,603	9,017
57 St. Louis, Mo	52,701	63,440	30,562	33,081	9,278	7,040
58 St. Paul, Minn	26,163	30,046	17,043	17,071	5,009	2,586
59 Salt Lake City, Utah	8,947	8,675	5,528	4,335	1,283	958
60 San Antonio, Tex	14,810	7,354	3,056	3,114	644	272
61 San Francisco, Calif	78,211	75,768	39,677	36,375	10,885	10,681
62 Scranton, Pa	14,247	17,461	7,546	7,930	1,023	964
63 Seattle, Wash	40,727	36,097	20,075	16,438	9,186	3,068
64 Spokane, Wash	8,837	12,389	5,555	5,495	1,563	1,374
65 Springfield, Mass	14,674	9,942	6,206	4,182	3,196	792
66 Syracuse, N. Y	16,213	14,944	7,853	7,036	2,002	862
67 Toledo, Ohio	20,281	15,826	10,383	8,752	3,944	724
68 Trenton, N. J	15,075	12,938	5,951	5,253	3,316	943
69 Washington, D. C	14,042	11,738	7,786	6,474	1,775	1,058
70 Wilmington, Del	8,777	6,754	3,488	2,872	1,318	520
71 Worcester, Mass	25,911	22,816	10,892	9,126	4,637	1,514
72 Yonkers, N. Y	12,176	12,295	6,649	5,629	1,767	1,110
73 Youngstown, Ohio	19,282	14,027	6,106	4,268	2,600	661

[1] Includes population of South Omaha for 1910.

21 YEARS OF AGE AND OVER, FOR CITIES HAVING, IN 1920, 100,000 INHABITANTS 1920 and 1910.
of females was made in 1910.]

FOREIGN-BORN WHITE MALES 21 YEARS OF AGE AND OVER—NUMBER.				FOREIGN-BORN WHITE MALES 21 YEARS OF AGE AND OVER—PER CENT.								
Alien.		Citizenship not reported.		Naturalized.		Having first papers.		Alien.		Citizenship not reported.		
1920	1910	1920	1910	1920	1910	1920	1910	1920	1910	1920	1910	
11,028	3,198	629	1,077	26.3	34.9	22.2	4.5	48.7	45.4	2.8	15.3	1
2,291	1,661	114	1,242	60.6	58.9	10.8	5.6	27.3	20.3	1.4	15.2	2
588	565	235	518	56.4	44.2	10.4	8.4	23.7	24.7	9.5	22.6	3
11,494	9,559	424	4,772	51.7	49.5	18.9	7.9	28.4	28.4	1.0	14.2	4
603	839	616	740	48.9	40.0	13.0	6.3	18.8	28.5	19.3	25.1	5
35,815	40,516	3,339	4,415	47.1	46.3	17.1	10.1	32.8	39.3	3.1	4.3	6
8,844	8,136	1,378	1,377	35.8	38.3	20.3	6.1	38.0	47.5	5.9	8.0	7
13,996	16,255	2,922	6,354	51.9	52.2	19.9	7.7	23.3	28.9	4.9	11.3	8
5,323	5,866	57	419	46.5	48.9	15.1	8.1	38.0	40.1	0.4	2.9	9
3,610	2,952	473	918	37.0	41.1	22.9	6.6	35.5	39.9	4.6	12.4	10
76,266	124,553	17,163	33,019	53.5	50.2	23.3	8.3	19.0	32.8	4.3	8.7	11
3,474	6,250	742	1,487	68.2	64.6	11.3	6.5	16.9	23.4	3.6	5.6	12
32,349	40,221	3,038	5,902	41.2	42.9	29.9	8.3	26.4	42.6	2.5	6.3	13
2,160	2,349	839	1,271	53.4	52.5	10.9	4.9	25.7	27.7	10.0	15.0	14
1,591	463	449	710	42.6	53.5	11.9	4.8	35.5	16.5	10.0	25.3	15
2,098	2,964	175	492	51.3	47.3	15.6	5.4	30.6	40.6	2.5	6.7	16
3,980	3,801	536	2,342	62.3	57.1	14.8	10.9	20.2	19.8	2.7	12.2	17
980	893	508	1,251	63.6	53.7	10.9	5.4	16.8	17.1	8.7	23.9	18
51,490	28,733	4,633	6,428	34.3	43.7	29.0	9.7	33.6	38.1	3.0	8.5	19
9,309	10,594	236	487	39.2	41.5	8.9	3.6	50.7	52.5	1.3	2.4	20
2,075	849	606	632	25.7	37.9	5.4	3.8	53.3	33.4	15.6	24.9	21
2,227	3,301	859	1,614	54.8	56.7	23.1	7.4	16.0	24.1	6.2	11.8	22
8,036	5,751	220	818	42.4	45.0	15.8	8.0	40.7	41.2	1.1	5.9	23
2,131	746	442	727	44.7	50.6	11.6	6.9	36.3	21.5	7.5	21.0	24
1,782	1,795	916	1,335	48.6	58.5	21.0	11.4	20.1	17.2	10.3	12.8	25
12,734	14,404	559	3,680	48.3	43.9	16.4	8.1	33.8	38.2	1.5	9.8	26
2,321	1,734	190	907	34.9	42.5	24.5	11.2	37.5	30.4	3.1	15.9	27
3,191	2,564	1,422	2,645	54.7	53.3	12.6	6.8	22.6	19.6	10.1	20.3	28
19,328	8,662	2,803	4,087	45.9	47.7	12.8	9.2	36.0	29.3	5.2	13.8	29
543	1,152	677	1,098	69.9	68.4	8.7	4.6	9.6	13.8	11.9	13.2	30
8,014	9,897	103	839	41.4	38.6	11.2	2.3	46.8	54.4	0.6	4.6	31
839	808	505	734	44.4	48.9	11.1	5.8	27.7	23.7	16.7	21.6	32
14,731	14,435	1,953	5,624	48.5	46.6	22.0	17.6	26.0	25.7	3.5	10.0	33
6,590	10,305	1,472	5,965	61.6	52.0	20.8	12.0	14.4	22.8	3.2	13.2	34
174	170	149	234	62.3	66.3	10.5	5.6	14.7	11.8	12.6	16.3	35
10,946	10,084	126	838	36.1	31.7	11.1	4.6	52.2	58.8	0.6	4.9	36
7,998	7,693	1,050	1,447	42.2	45.0	15.9	7.4	37.0	40.1	4.9	7.5	37
5,740	3,703	1,186	3,050	41.3	45.5	10.3	4.4	40.1	27.5	8.3	22.6	38
330,184	339,473	32,725	64,704	43.7	38.4	17.2	12.9	35.6	41.0	3.5	7.8	39
32,232	20,970	4,690	5,670	52.3	48.3	17.9	12.9	25.9	30.5	3.8	8.3	40
102,756	90,521	11,562	14,663	45.3	43.9	17.8	13.8	33.2	36.4	3.7	5.9	41
178,861	212,777	13,467	40,961	37.8	32.3	16.8	12.7	42.2	46.1	3.2	8.9	42
11,758	11,089	2,305	2,394	58.4	54.8	15.5	10.0	21.8	28.9	4.3	6.2	43
4,577	4,116	701	1,016	49.0	49.6	18.4	7.6	28.2	34.4	4.3	8.5	44
22,102	19,204	1,910	4,061	42.5	43.1	15.0	10.0	39.1	38.7	3.4	8.2	45
1,317	565	203	173	41.9	51.2	20.6	8.3	32.4	31.0	5.0	9.5	46
6,902	5,968	831	1,125	51.0	52.9	16.7	10.4	28.9	30.9	3.5	5.8	47
3,209	4,170	1,236	2,194	50.3	49.7	25.7	15.2	17.3	23.0	6.7	12.1	48
7,197	6,029	568	2,949	50.7	48.6	12.5	6.9	34.1	29.9	2.7	14.6	49
59,133	63,156	6,445	18,968	49.4	41.5	15.8	9.3	31.4	37.8	3.4	11.4	50
20,072	28,439	1,822	7,557	50.8	41.1	13.5	7.6	32.7	40.5	3.0	10.8	51
6,162	7,097	389	3,824	51.5	44.6	22.7	12.1	24.3	28.1	1.5	15.2	52
9,662	14,910	958	2,150	48.4	39.5	17.7	8.6	30.8	45.4	3.0	6.5	53
1,583	2,675	203	209	37.2	31.6	27.2	4.7	31.6	59.1	4.1	4.6	54
563	503	262	471	50.0	46.2	14.8	6.0	24.0	24.7	11.2	23.1	55
8,558	8,361	1,474	2,756	53.1	48.0	16.8	10.9	25.7	30.9	4.4	10.2	56
10,303	15,918	2,608	7,392	58.0	52.1	17.5	11.1	19.5	25.1	4.9	11.7	57
3,332	5,576	1,069	3,815	64.4	58.8	18.9	8.9	12.6	19.2	4.0	13.1	58
1,963	1,990	173	1,392	61.8	50.0	14.3	11.0	21.9	22.9	1.9	16.0	59
10,226	2,223	884	1,745	20.6	42.3	4.3	3.7	69.0	30.2	6.0	23.7	60
22,488	21,872	5,161	6,840	50.7	48.0	13.9	14.1	28.8	28.9	6.6	9.0	61
4,843	6,801	835	1,766	53.0	45.4	7.2	5.5	34.0	38.9	5.9	10.1	62
9,333	11,474	2,133	5,117	49.3	45.5	22.6	8.5	22.9	31.8	5.2	14.2	63
1,576	3,451	143	2,069	62.9	44.4	17.7	11.1	17.8	27.9	1.6	16.7	64
5,058	4,520	214	448	42.3	42.1	21.8	8.0	34.5	45.5	1.5	4.5	65
5,899	4,715	459	2,331	48.4	47.1	12.3	5.8	36.4	31.6	2.8	15.6	66
5,416	4,308	538	2,042	51.2	55.3	19.4	4.6	26.7	27.2	2.7	12.9	67
5,374	5,736	434	1,006	39.5	40.6	22.0	7.3	35.6	44.3	2.9	7.8	68
2,842	2,304	1,639	1,902	55.4	55.2	12.6	9.0	20.2	19.6	11.7	16.2	69
3,487	2,671	484	691	39.7	42.5	15.0	7.7	39.7	39.5	5.5	10.2	70
9,698	11,184	684	992	42.0	40.0	17.9	6.6	37.4	49.0	2.6	4.3	71
3,518	5,060	242	496	54.6	45.8	14.5	9.0	28.9	41.2	2.0	4.0	72
10,098	7,543	478	1,555	31.7	30.4	13.5	4.7	52.4	53.8	2.5	11.1	73

TABLE **96.**—CITIZENSHIP OF FOREIGN-BORN WHITE MALES AND FEMALES 21 YEARS OF AGE AND OVER, FOR CITIES HAVING, IN 1920, 100,000 INHABITANTS OR MORE: 1920 AND 1910—Continued.

[No inquiry as to the citizenship of females was made in 1910.]

CITY.	Total.	Naturalized. Number.	Per cent.	Having first papers. Number.	Per cent.	Alien. Number.	Per cent.	Citizenship not reported. Number.	Per cent.
		FOREIGN-BORN WHITE FEMALES 21 YEARS OF AGE AND OVER: **1920**							
Akron, Ohio	11,270	4,343	38.5	154	1.4	6,399	56.8	374	3.3
Albany, N. Y	7,956	5,025	63.2	89	1.1	2,653	33.3	189	2.4
Atlanta, Ga	1,796	1,100	61.2	33	1.8	495	27.6	168	9.4
Baltimore, Md	36,151	19,663	54.5	605	1.7	15,123	41.8	730	2.0
Birmingham, Ala	2,271	1,227	54.0	19	0.8	606	26.7	419	18.5
Boston, Mass	111,827	51,404	46.0	1,723	1.5	52,954	47.4	5,746	5.1
Bridgeport, Conn	19,016	7,544	39.7	169	0.9	9,444	49.7	1,859	9.8
Buffalo, N. Y	51,648	29,391	56.9	730	1.4	17,537	34.0	3,990	7.7
Cambridge, Mass	15,490	7,058	45.6	134	0.9	8,200	52.9	98	0.6
Camden, N. J	8,203	3,537	43.1	76	0.9	3,912	47.7	678	8.3
Chicago, Ill	341,838	192,341	56.3	6,000	1.8	122,551	35.9	20,946	6.1
Cincinnati, Ohio	19,761	13,511	68.4	266	1.3	4,720	23.9	1,264	6.4
Cleveland, Ohio	95,147	45,650	48.0	1,543	1.6	44,185	46.4	3,769	4.0
Columbus, Ohio	6,324	3,931	62.2	107	1.7	1,496	23.7	790	12.5
Dallas, Tex	3,011	1,455	48.3	45	1.5	1,149	38.2	362	12.0
Dayton, Ohio	5,197	3,115	59.9	85	1.6	1,835	35.3	162	3.1
Denver, Colo	15,554	10,948	70.4	286	1.8	3,860	24.8	460	3.0
Des Moines, Iowa	4,605	3,143	68.3	53	1.2	967	21.0	442	9.6
Detroit, Mich	104,366	45,864	43.9	2,121	2.0	51,569	49.4	4,812	4.6
Fall River, Mass	19,768	7,654	38.7	128	0.6	11,555	58.5	431	2.2
Fort Worth, Tex	1,976	698	35.3	18	0.9	876	44.3	384	19.4
Grand Rapids, Mich	12,233	7,111	58.1	207	1.7	3,830	31.3	1,085	8.9
Hartford, Conn	17,262	7,904	45.8	171	1.0	8,923	51.7	264	1.5
Houston, Tex	4,245	2,020	47.6	33	0.8	1,805	42.5	387	9.1
Indianapolis, Ind	7,140	3,905	54.7	185	2.6	1,967	27.5	1,083	15.2
Jersey City, N. J	33,012	17,146	51.9	318	1.0	14,433	43.7	1,115	3.4
Kansas City, Kans	4,144	1,896	45.8	91	2.2	2,002	48.3	155	3.7
Kansas City, Mo	10,632	6,186	58.2	125	1.2	2,931	27.6	1,390	13.1
Los Angeles, Calif	45,084	22,943	50.9	768	1.7	18,728	41.5	2,645	5.9
Louisville, Ky	5,503	3,656	66.4	66	1.2	797	14.5	984	17.9
Lowell, Mass	17,904	7,628	42.6	151	0.8	9,979	55.7	146	0.8
Memphis, Tenn	2,270	1,053	46.4	38	1.7	733	32.3	446	19.6
Milwaukee, Wis	45,098	25,481	56.5	1,500	3.3	15,781	35.0	2,336	5.2
Minneapolis, Minn	36,881	23,972	65.0	905	2.5	10,100	27.4	1,904	5.2
Nashville, Tenn	1,012	626	61.9	7	0.7	218	21.5	161	15.9
New Bedford, Mass	21,506	7,706	35.8	202	0.9	13,392	62.3	206	1.0
New Haven, Conn	20,040	8,603	42.9	175	0.9	9,485	47.3	1,777	8.9
New Orleans, La	9,510	3,876	40.8	52	0.5	3,781	39.8	1,801	18.9
New York, N. Y	870,140	360,255	41.4	14,838	1.7	441,892	50.8	53,155	6.1
Bronx borough	118,863	58,287	49.0	1,628	1.4	50,947	42.9	8,001	6.7
Brooklyn borough	283,451	125,779	44.4	4,076	1.4	135,643	47.9	17,953	6.3
Manhattan borough	403,879	139,873	34.6	8,260	2.0	232,933	57.7	22,813	5.6
Queens borough	51,070	30,015	58.8	692	1.4	16,923	33.1	3,440	6.7
Richmond borough	12,877	6,301	48.9	182	1.4	5,446	42.3	948	7.4
Newark, N. J	49,435	22,019	44.5	473	1.0	23,797	48.1	3,146	6.4
Norfolk, Va	1,887	1,097	58.1	18	1.0	628	33.3	144	7.6
Oakland, Calif	18,046	10,467	58.0	339	1.9	6,455	35.8	785	4.3
Omaha, Nebr	14,065	7,890	56.1	319	2.3	4,464	31.7	1,392	9.9
Paterson, N. J	19,644	9,992	50.9	226	1.2	8,285	42.2	1,141	5.8
Philadelphia, Pa	173,623	85,864	49.5	2,031	1.2	75,007	43.2	10,721	6.2
Pittsburgh, Pa	50,513	28,382	56.2	513	1.0	19,083	37.8	2,535	5.0
Portland, Oreg	17,724	10,782	60.8	444	2.5	6,105	34.4	393	2.2
Providence, R. I	32,031	16,051	50.1	564	1.8	13,941	43.5	1,475	4.6
Reading, Pa	3,684	1,429	38.8	61	1.7	1,955	53.1	239	6.5
Richmond, Va	1,904	995	51.7	34	1.8	651	34.0	201	12.1
Rochester, N. Y	30,352	16,835	55.5	441	1.5	11,081	36.5	1,995	6.6
St. Louis, Mo	43,015	25,868	60.1	614	1.4	13,154	30.6	3,379	7.9
St. Paul, Minn	21,861	15,172	69.4	518	2.4	4,917	22.5	1,254	5.7
Salt Lake City, Utah	8,867	6,234	70.3	199	2.2	2,267	25.6	167	1.9
San Antonio, Tex	12,299	2,873	23.4	248	2.0	8,162	66.4	1,016	8.3
San Francisco, Calif	52,656	28,099	53.4	1,000	1.9	18,732	35.6	4,825	9.2
Scranton, Pa	12,440	7,051	56.7	67	0.5	4,141	33.3	1,181	9.5
Seattle, Wash	26,813	15,757	58.8	564	2.1	8,399	31.3	2,093	7.8
Spokane, Wash	6,646	4,692	70.6	136	2.0	1,651	24.8	167	2.5
Springfield, Mass	14,050	6,559	46.7	241	1.7	6,843	48.7	407	2.9
Syracuse, N. Y	13,580	7,921	58.3	143	1.1	5,059	37.3	457	3.4
Toledo, Ohio	15,030	9,451	62.9	223	1.5	4,709	31.3	647	4.3
Trenton, N. J	12,016	5,274	43.9	139	1.2	6,094	50.7	509	4.2
Washington, D. C	12,334	6,926	56.2	324	2.6	3,491	28.3	1,593	12.9
Wilmington, Del	6,296	2,982	47.4	58	0.9	2,707	43.0	549	8.7
Worcester, Mass	23,478	10,899	46.4	253	1.1	11,000	46.9	1,326	5.6
Yonkers, N. Y	11,786	6,513	55.3	347	2.9	4,580	38.9	346	2.9
Youngstown, Ohio	11,661	5,113	43.8	102	0.9	5,985	51.3	461	4.0

TABLE 97.—CITIZENSHIP OF FOREIGN-BORN WHITE POPULATION AND OF FOREIGN-BORN WHITE MALES AND FEMALES 21 YEARS OF AGE AND OVER, FOR CITIES HAVING FROM 25,000 TO 100,000 INHABITANTS: 1920.

CITY.	FOREIGN-BORN WHITE POPULATION.						FOREIGN-BORN WHITE POPULATION 21 YEARS OF AGE AND OVER.					
	Total.	Naturalized.		Having first papers.	Alien.	Citizenship not reported.	Total.		Number naturalized.		Per cent naturalized.	
		Number.	Per cent.				Male.	Female.	Male.	Female.	Male.	Female.
ALABAMA:												
Mobile	2,006	1,001	49.9	124	535	346	1,102	719	579	359	52.5	49.9
Montgomery	761	486	63.9	41	158	76	420	269	265	185	63.1	68.8
ARIZONA:												
Phoenix	4,045	1,197	29.6	137	2,369	342	1,957	1,391	621	521	31.7	37.5
ARKANSAS:												
Fort Smith	854	513	60.1	53	131	157	468	344	274	225	58.5	65.4
Little Rock	1,798	1,000	55.6	118	287	393	989	732	539	437	54.5	59.7
CALIFORNIA:												
Alameda	5,877	3,585	61.0	553	1,553	186	2,894	2,568	1,812	1,667	62.6	64.9
Berkeley	9,573	5,669	59.2	848	2,774	282	4,466	4,371	2,786	2,694	62.4	61.6
Fresno	8,552	3,253	38.0	396	4,348	555	4,267	3,095	1,774	1,354	41.6	43.7
Long Beach	6,799	4,009	59.0	318	2,133	339	3,085	3,032	1,954	1,936	63.3	63.9
Pasadena	6,785	3,523	51.9	419	2,303	540	2,836	3,594	1,537	1,886	58.0	52.5
Sacramento	10,873	5,560	51.1	668	3,997	648	6,122	3,934	3,077	2,287	50.3	58.1
San Diego	13,295	6,908	52.0	655	4,966	766	6,489	5,395	3,618	3,051	55.8	56.6
San Jose	7,820	3,214	41.1	341	3,177	1,088	3,973	3,226	1,745	1,381	43.9	42.8
Stockton	6,981	3,023	43.3	372	2,544	1,042	4,038	2,471	1,726	1,215	42.7	49.2
COLORADO:												
Colorado Springs	2,604	1,777	68.2	174	477	176	1,218	1,274	849	883	69.7	69.3
Pueblo	7,393	3,030	41.0	527	3,127	709	3,780	2,660	1,566	1,363	41.4	51.2
CONNECTICUT:												
Meriden	7,909	3,692	46.7	1,006	2,610	601	3,792	3,530	1,834	1,755	48.4	49.7
New Britain	21,230	7,494	35.3	1,695	11,836	205	10,973	8,540	3,821	3,366	34.8	39.4
New London	5,840	2,442	41.8	378	2,919	101	2,742	2,591	1,139	1,209	41.5	46.7
Norwalk	5,955	2,473	41.5	465	2,439	578	2,778	2,671	1,177	1,197	42.4	44.8
Stamford	10,704	3,734	34.9	1,091	5,267	612	5,017	4,575	1,790	1,743	35.7	38.1
Waterbury	29,894	10,279	34.4	2,026	16,430	1,159	15,520	11,739	5,092	4,782	32.8	40.7
FLORIDA:												
Jacksonville	3,894	2,117	54.4	334	1,087	356	2,042	1,510	1,105	891	54.1	59.0
Miami	2,563	1,254	48.9	205	824	280	1,220	1,041	628	563	51.5	54.1
Pensacola	1,445	693	48.0	100	334	318	1,017	362	467	208	45.9	57.5
Tampa	10,666	1,811	17.0	161	8,351	343	5,130	3,928	884	785	17.2	20.0
GEORGIA:												
Augusta	927	427	46.1	43	199	258	516	349	250	151	48.4	43.3
Columbus	326	185	56.7	19	109	13	198	102	105	65	53.0	63.7
Macon	698	393	56.3	55	188	62	361	258	201	159	55.7	61.6
Savannah	3,247	1,880	57.9	189	1,031	147	1,729	1,257	1,010	772	58.4	61.4
ILLINOIS:												
Aurora	6,476	4,061	62.7	648	1,467	300	3,404	2,717	2,084	1,857	61.2	68.3
Bloomington	2,831	2,010	71.0	126	415	280	1,350	1,328	984	989	72.9	74.5
Cicero town	15,466	8,548	55.3	2,554	3,930	434	7,893	6,430	4,341	3,852	55.0	59.9
Danville	1,916	1,420	74.1	121	248	127	1,006	834	719	675	71.5	80.9
Decatur	2,590	1,762	68.0	180	532	116	1,282	1,062	880	815	68.6	76.7
East St. Louis	6,782	2,821	41.6	1,055	2,318	588	3,807	2,426	1,533	1,147	40.3	47.3
Elgin	5,055	3,144	62.2	206	565	1,140	2,341	2,510	1,471	1,589	62.8	63.3
Evanston	6,771	3,855	56.9	706	1,885	325	3,056	3,286	1,864	1,850	61.0	56.3
Joliet	8,490	4,668	55.0	823	2,605	394	4,495	3,440	2,420	2,093	53.8	60.8
Moline	7,391	5,167	69.9	855	1,123	246	4,160	2,707	2,835	2,067	68.1	76.4
Oak Park village	5,634	3,986	70.7	293	816	539	2,632	2,803	2,024	1,879	76.9	67.0
Peoria	7,790	5,036	64.6	533	1,250	971	4,096	3,322	2,656	2,231	64.8	67.2
Quincy	2,411	1,968	81.6	54	122	267	1,193	1,184	982	968	82.3	81.8
Rock Island	5,352	3,788	70.8	482	767	315	2,748	2,204	1,939	1,658	70.6	75.2
Rockford	17,343	9,608	55.4	2,087	4,797	851	9,210	6,824	5,122	4,144	55.6	60.7
Springfield	6,255	4,029	64.4	430	1,252	544	3,091	2,647	2,017	1,779	65.3	67.2
INDIANA:												
Anderson	940	451	48.0	106	227	156	539	350	246	185	45.6	52.9
East Chicago	14,663	3,667	25.0	4,187	6,024	785	9,034	4,360	2,042	1,357	22.6	31.1
Evansville	3,145	2,213	70.4	224	394	314	1,581	1,462	1,141	1,024	72.2	70.0
Fort Wayne	6,634	3,982	60.0	894	1,375	383	3,586	2,711	2,038	1,837	56.8	67.8
Gary	16,460	4,153	25.2	3,322	7,667	1,318	10,005	4,960	2,340	1,544	23.4	31.1
Hammond	8,118	2,965	36.5	2,052	2,562	539	4,539	2,970	1,550	1,275	34.1	42.9
Kokomo	1,166	619	53.1	149	356	42	681	393	347	249	51.0	63.4
Muncie	820	434	52.9	74	156	156	500	292	252	175	50.4	59.9
Richmond	1,127	659	58.5	114	244	110	642	430	360	268	56.1	62.3
South Bend	13,391	4,809	35.9	2,949	4,378	1,255	6,780	5,292	2,455	2,065	36.2	39.0
Terre Haute	3,667	1,892	51.6	623	760	392	2,010	1,410	1,017	804	50.6	57.0

TABLE 97.—CITIZENSHIP OF FOREIGN-BORN WHITE POPULATION AND OF FOREIGN-BORN WHITE MALES AND FEMALES 21 YEARS OF AGE AND OVER, FOR CITIES HAVING FROM 25,000 TO 100,000 INHABITANTS: 1920—Continued.

CITY.	FOREIGN-BORN WHITE POPULATION.						FOREIGN-BORN WHITE POPULATION 21 YEARS OF AGE AND OVER.					
	Total.	Naturalized.		Having first papers.	Alien.	Citizenship not reported.	Total.		Number naturalized.		Per cent naturalized.	
		Number.	Per cent.				Male.	Female.	Male.	Female.	Male.	Female.
IOWA:												
Cedar Rapids	5,863	3,656	62.4	511	1,296	400	2,906	2,474	1,832	1,689	63.0	68.3
Council Bluffs	3,988	2,448	61.4	183	747	610	2,117	1,648	1,258	1,113	59.4	67.5
Davenport	7,644	5,469	71.5	457	941	777	3,915	3,419	2,786	2,563	71.2	75.0
Dubuque	4,221	3,149	74.6	217	487	368	2,194	1,914	1,663	1,457	75.8	76.1
Sioux City	11,216	6,336	56.5	1,105	3,300	475	6,210	4,177	3,395	2,663	54.7	63.8
Waterloo	2,929	1,630	55.7	238	711	350	1,605	1,122	851	719	53.0	64.1
KANSAS:												
Topeka	4,000	2,105	52.6	325	1,309	261	1,814	1,668	991	1,041	54.6	62.4
Wichita	3,021	1,508	49.9	107	988	418	1,494	1,158	793	657	53.1	56.7
KENTUCKY:												
Covington	2,883	2,248	78.0	128	281	226	1,401	1,428	1,148	1,075	81.9	75.3
Lexington	800	436	54.5	46	153	165	473	292	258	166	54.5	56.8
Newport	2,093	1,626	77.7	108	297	62	968	1,007	791	776	81.7	77.1
LOUISIANA:												
Shreveport	1,296	542	41.8	46	452	256	687	495	313	202	45.6	40.8
MAINE:												
Bangor	3,740	1,472	39.4	242	1,548	478	1,670	1,741	627	785	37.5	45.1
Lewiston	10,262	3,681	35.9	624	5,518	439	4,144	4,496	1,703	1,783	41.1	39.7
Portland	13,229	6,285	47.5	932	5,278	734	5,834	6,198	2,782	3,207	47.7	51.7
MARYLAND:												
Cumberland	1,163	493	42.4	57	248	365	642	452	275	202	42.8	44.7
Hagerstown	428	247	57.7	32	105	44	270	147	146	97	54.1	66.0
MASSACHUSETTS:												
Brockton	17,124	8,397	49.0	1,443	7,045	239	8,194	7,651	3,986	4,072	48.6	53.2
Brookline town	9,360	4,133	44.2	456	4,664	107	2,799	6,186	1,813	2,244	64.8	36.3
Chelsea	17,198	5,966	34.7	1,801	8,830	601	8,046	6,942	2,918	2,613	36.3	37.6
Chicopee	12,182	3,635	29.8	1,061	7,328	158	5,982	5,267	1,746	1,734	29.2	32.9
Everett	11,079	6,079	54.9	917	4,031	52	4,984	5,214	2,757	3,096	55.3	59.4
Fitchburg	13,162	4,797	36.4	927	6,764	674	6,054	5,802	2,249	2,370	37.1	40.8
Haverhill	13,307	5,762	43.3	923	6,476	146	6,314	5,958	2,611	2,953	41.4	49.6
Holyoke	20,255	8,244	40.7	1,292	10,420	299	8,905	9,698	3,887	4,033	43.6	41.6
Lawrence	39,063	13,714	35.1	2,449	22,496	404	18,020	17,156	6,591	6,566	36.6	38.3
Lynn	27,858	13,485	48.4	2,224	11,985	164	12,694	12,825	6,146	6,796	48.4	53.0
Malden	14,105	6,964	49.4	1,524	5,603	14	5,982	6,799	3,144	3,578	52.6	52.6
Medford	8,554	5,310	62.1	754	2,471	19	3,675	4,274	2,328	2,779	63.3	65.0
Newton	10,179	4,782	47.0	731	4,583	83	3,886	5,666	2,065	2,572	53.1	45.4
Pittsfield	8,211	3,460	42.1	556	3,831	364	3,940	3,515	1,659	1,654	42.1	47.1
Quincy	13,749	6,974	50.7	2,010	4,562	203	6,524	6,044	3,243	3,384	49.7	56.0
Revere	8,847	4,121	46.6	681	3,503	542	4,134	4,047	2,009	1,980	48.6	48.9
Salem	11,203	5,191	46.3	854	5,063	95	5,113	5,229	2,375	2,611	46.5	49.9
Somerville	24,182	12,515	51.8	2,516	8,988	163	10,776	11,828	5,642	6,563	52.4	55.5
Taunton	9,998	3,309	33.1	428	5,622	639	4,428	4,620	1,513	1,661	34.2	36.0
Waltham	8,104	3,872	47.8	569	3,594	69	3,404	4,009	1,668	2,081	49.0	51.9
MICHIGAN:												
Battle Creek	3,378	1,720	50.9	254	1,085	319	1,766	1,346	847	806	48.0	59.9
Bay City	8,954	6,370	71.1	760	1,564	260	4,379	4,073	3,161	2,994	72.2	73.5
Flint	15,127	5,984	39.6	2,042	6,222	879	8,625	4,775	3,159	2,464	36.6	51.6
Hamtramck vil	23,062	2,607	11.3	4,820	15,431	204	13,130	7,576	1,449	962	11.0	12.7
Highland Park	12,661	4,725	37.3	2,310	4,999	627	6,975	4,277	2,498	1,952	35.8	45.6
Jackson	5,316	2,465	46.4	637	1,863	351	2,733	2,221	1,201	1,194	43.9	53.8
Kalamazoo	7,207	3,304	45.8	570	2,274	059	3,551	2,001	1,600	1,072	45.2	52.7
Lansing	5,085	2,800	46.8	851	1,624	710	2,100	2,981	1,355	1,015	40.0	37.0
Muskegon	6,780	4,147	61.2	838	1,311	484	3,485	2,926	2,072	1,975	59.5	67.5
Pontiac	5,185	2,017	38.9	467	1,749	952	2,875	1,769	963	924	33.5	52.2
Port Huron	6,346	3,960	62.4	496	1,845	45	2,835	2,830	1,794	1,982	63.3	70.0
Saginaw	11,605	6,602	56.9	987	3,003	1,013	5,571	5,001	3,291	3,129	59.1	62.6
MINNESOTA:												
Duluth	30,118	17,425	57.9	4,332	7,137	1,224	16,825	11,337	9,414	7,298	56.0	64.4
MISSOURI:												
Joplin	727	552	75.9	30	79	66	405	294	299	236	73.8	80.3
St. Joseph	6,423	3,467	54.0	570	1,850	536	3,388	2,557	1,817	1,544	53.6	60.4
Springfield	973	640	65.8	40	89	204	528	409	346	283	65.5	69.2
MONTANA:												
Butte	11,454	6,974	60.9	1,257	2,450	773	6,644	4,221	3,873	2,873	58.3	68.1
NEBRASKA:												
Lincoln	7,198	3,066	42.6	1,087	2,405	640	3,209	3,002	1,470	1,433	45.8	47.7
NEW HAMPSHIRE:												
Manchester	27,516	10,930	39.7	1,904	13,499	1,183	11,807	12,552	4,960	5,452	42.0	43.4
Nashua	8,792	2,959	33.7	409	4,508	916	4,089	3,727	1,376	1,458	33.7	39.1

CITIZENSHIP. 359

TABLE 97.—CITIZENSHIP OF FOREIGN-BORN WHITE POPULATION AND OF FOREIGN-BORN WHITE MALES AND FEMALES 21 YEARS OF AGE AND OVER, FOR CITIES HAVING FROM 25,000 TO 100,000 INHABITANTS: 1920—Continued.

CITY.	FOREIGN-BORN WHITE POPULATION.					FOREIGN-BORN WHITE POPULATION 21 YEARS OF AGE AND OVER.					
	Total.	Naturalized.		Having first papers.	Alien.	Citizenship not reported.	Total.		Number naturalized.		Per cent naturalized.	
		Number.	Per cent.				Male.	Female.	Male.	Female.	Male.	Female.
NEW JERSEY:												
Atlantic City.....	7,009	3,974	56.7	493	2,185	357	3,292	3,202	1,903	1,877	57.8	58.6
Bayonne.........	25,472	9,590	37.6	3,190	12,377	315	13,117	10,139	4,843	4,187	36.9	41.3
Clifton...........	9,611	3,957	41.2	776	4,726	152	4,510	4,136	1,948	1,789	43.2	43.3
East Orange.....	6,780	3,836	56.6	416	1,911	617	2,936	3,492	1,846	1,890	62.9	54.1
Elizabeth........	28,215	11,161	39.6	3,145	12,790	1,119	14,586	11,389	5,610	5,042	38.5	44.3
Hoboken.........	23,496	10,520	44.8	2,488	10,159	329	11,991	9,440	5,310	4,712	44.3	49.9
Irvington town..	5,508	3,081	55.9	542	1,291	594	2,698	2,503	1,496	1,505	55.4	60.1
Kearny town....	7,904	3,980	50.4	836	2,760	328	3,722	3,407	1,984	1,755	53.3	51.5
Montclair town..	5,159	2,428	47.1	279	2,094	358	2,203	2,546	1,195	1,154	54.2	45.3
New Brunswick..	8,935	3,228	36.1	1,005	3,982	720	4,098	3,899	1,570	1,458	38.3	37.4
Orange..........	6,963	3,501	50.3	514	2,427	521	3,258	3,251	1,741	1,659	53.4	51.0
Passaic..........	26,365	8,189	31.1	1,768	15,803	605	12,382	11,411	4,006	3,560	32.4	31.2
Perth Amboy....	14,918	5,757	38.6	1,839	6,492	830	7,700	5,967	2,926	2,461	38.0	41.2
Plainfield........	5,502	2,457	44.7	548	2,235	262	2,509	2,537	1,180	1,198	47.0	47.2
West Hoboken...	14,076	6,865	48.8	1,053	6,015	143	6,649	6,201	3,386	3,183	50.9	51.3
West New York..	8,928	4,106	46.0	1,067	3,403	352	4,352	3,809	2,062	1,846	47.4	48.5
NEW YORK:												
Amsterdam......	9,807	3,969	40.5	776	4,564	498	4,669	4,422	1,949	1,853	41.7	41.9
Auburn..........	7,579	3,420	45.1	774	3,235	150	3,944	3,034	1,747	1,532	44.3	50.5
Binghamton.....	10,368	4,281	41.3	888	4,736	463	5,262	4,391	2,064	2,058	39.2	46.9
Elmira...........	4,706	2,761	58.7	164	1,217	564	2,311	1,981	1,376	1,255	59.5	63.4
Jamestown.......	11,415	7,214	63.2	575	3,119	507	5,590	4,944	3,645	3,294	65.2	66.6
Kingston.........	2,763	1,637	59.2	144	660	322	1,344	1,271	820	783	61.0	61.6
Mount Vernon...	10,090	5,492	54.4	1,092	3,228	278	4,711	4,531	2,803	2,447	59.5	54.0
New Rochelle....	8,457	4,786	56.6	841	2,577	253	3,867	3,925	2,435	2,145	63.0	54.6
Newburgh.......	4,939	2,718	55.0	585	1,223	413	2,437	2,143	1,327	1,269	54.5	59.2
Niagara Falls....	17,886	6,326	35.4	1,470	8,775	1,315	9,278	6,475	3,128	2,724	33.7	42.1
Poughkeepsie....	5,530	2,822	51.0	464	1,736	508	2,646	2,430	1,376	1,315	52.0	54.1
Rome............	5,234	1,896	36.2	562	2,619	157	2,900	1,792	1,026	771	35.4	43.0
Schenectady.....	20,490	10,218	49.9	1,341	8,324	607	10,499	8,267	5,218	4,437	49.7	53.7
Troy.............	11,483	7,132	62.1	401	2,497	1,453	5,058	5,813	3,294	3,653	65.1	62.8
Utica............	23,257	9,932	42.7	1,494	11,607	224	11,174	9,984	4,970	4,556	44.5	45.6
Watertown.......	5,829	2,937	50.4	479	2,132	281	2,634	2,645	1,249	1,540	47.4	58.2
N ORTH CAROLINA:												
Asheville........	555	285	51.4	15	188	67	261	258	153	125	58.6	48.4
Charlotte..·.....	514	268	52.1	21	117	108	256	207	131	121	51.2	58.5
Wilmington......	624	303	48.6	44	158	119	371	198	182	103	49.1	52.0
Winston-Salem..	296	138	46.6	23	108	27	167	102	75	58	44.9	56.9
OHIO:												
Canton..........	14,680	5,249	35.8	1,588	7,247	596	9,416	4,069	2,892	2,028	30.7	49.8
East Cleveland...	3,843	2,678	69.7	336	777	52	1,777	1,826	1,288	1,318	72.5	72.2
Hamilton........	2,663	1,782	69.9	193	572	116	1,448	1,083	953	799	65.8	73.8
Lakewood.......	7,255	3,572	49.2	1,127	2,349	207	3,624	3,140	1,739	1,723	48.0	54.9
Lima............	1,917	1,014	52.9	118	537	248	1,012	769	516	454	51.0	59.0
Lorain..........	11,927	3,841	32.2	2,069	5,839	178	6,900	3,930	1,990	1,626	28.8	41.4
Mansfield........	3,207	1,479	46.1	326	1,243	159	1,633	1,167	721	635	44.2	54.4
Marion..........	954	547	57.3	65	249	93	536	361	299	232	55.8	64.3
Newark..........	1,505	719	47.8	142	532	112	821	558	379	311	46.2	55.7
Portsmouth......	694	448	64.6	21	117	108	385	276	248	190	64.4	68.8
Springfield.......	2,757	1,766	64.1	90	684	217	1,420	1,174	880	830	62.0	70.7
Steubenville.....	5,581	1,706	30.6	315	3,199	361	3,235	1,794	908	696	28.1	38.8
Warren..........	4,677	1,321	28.2	395	2,900	61	2,846	1,409	670	588	23.5	41.7
Zanesville........	1,272	726	57.1	87	407	52	697	523	358	352	51.4	67.3
OKLAHOMA:												
Muskogee........	541	275	50.8	35	134	97	330	186	153	115	46.4	61.8
Oklahoma City...	3,477	1,656	47.6	215	1,305	301	1,975	1,130	926	668	46.9	59.1
Tulsa............	2,025	935	46.2	172	510	408	1,163	718	517	378	44.5	52.6

TABLE 97.—CITIZENSHIP OF FOREIGN-BORN WHITE POPULATION AND OF FOREIGN-BORN WHITE MALES AND FEMALES 21 YEARS OF AGE AND OVER, FOR CITIES HAVING FROM 25,000 TO 100,000 INHABITANTS: 1920—Continued.

CITY.	FOREIGN-BORN WHITE POPULATION.					FOREIGN-BORN WHITE POPULATION 21 YEARS OF AGE AND OVER.					
	Total.	Naturalized.		Having first papers.	Alien.	Citizenship not reported.	Total.		Number naturalized.		Per cent naturalized.	
		Number.	Per cent.				Male.	Female.	Male.	Female.	Male.	Female.
PENNSYLVANIA:												
Allentown	8,612	2,765	32.1	717	4,839	291	4,286	3,711	1,403	1,198	32.7	32.3
Altoona	5,312	2,943	55.4	506	1,792	71	2,825	2,009	1,546	1,248	54.7	62.1
Bethlehem	10,943	2,515	23.0	779	7,446	203	5,920	4,060	1,292	1,078	21.8	26.6
Chester	11,292	3,387	30.0	1,236	6,304	365	6,629	3,716	1,791	1,461	27.0	39.3
Easton	4,021	1,332	33.1	267	2,305	117	2,031	1,556	695	590	34.2	37.9
Erie	17,370	7,771	44.7	1,390	6,892	1,317	9,010	6,903	4,014	3,388	44.6	49.1
Harrisburg	4,144	1,905	46.0	302	1,467	470	2,144	1,561	986	780	46.0	50.0
Hazleton	6,023	3,406	56.5	449	2,011	157	3,105	2,543	1,771	1,496	57.0	58.8
Johnstown	12,142	4,200	34.6	1,377	6,360	205	6,848	4,314	2,125	1,832	31.0	42.5
Lancaster	2,714	1,737	64.0	196	628	153	1,316	1,232	836	844	63.5	68.5
McKeesport	11,870	5,283	44.5	787	5,205	595	6,537	4,493	2,654	2,356	40.6	52.4
New Castle	8,693	3,213	37.0	604	4,562	314	4,672	3,243	1,626	1,428	34.8	44.0
Norristown boro.	4,297	1,475	34.3	240	1,942	640	1,958	1,936	749	657	38.3	33.9
Wilkes-Barre	14,567	8,095	55.6	810	5,000	662	7,353	6,313	4,022	3,806	54.7	60.3
Williamsport	2,266	1,330	58.7	119	549	268	1,181	909	706	569	59.8	62.6
York	1,193	732	61.4	61	289	111	611	507	384	320	62.8	63.1
RHODE ISLAND:												
Cranston	7,516	3,766	50.1	817	2,265	668	3,455	3,413	1,759	1,844	50.9	54.0
Newport	5,752	4,025	70.0	310	1,103	314	2,531	2,905	1,861	1,991	73.5	68.5
Pawtucket	21,024	11,297	53.7	1,632	7,289	806	9,348	9,655	5,168	5,510	55.3	57.1
Woonsocket	16,026	6,078	37.9	1,695	7,454	799	6,924	6,837	2,852	2,893	41.2	42.3
SOUTH CAROLINA:												
Charleston	2,143	1,134	52.9	182	522	305	1,179	817	619	469	52.5	57.4
Columbia	544	274	50.4	24	186	60	291	203	144	110	49.5	54.2
SOUTH DAKOTA:												
Sioux Falls	2,961	1,845	62.3	180	339	597	1,524	1,281	934	853	61.3	66.6
TENNESSEE:												
Chattanooga	1,240	864	69.7	62	232	82	642	487	448	360	69.8	73.9
Knoxville	812	492	60.6	41	176	103	413	339	244	220	59.1	64.9
TEXAS:												
Austin	2,547	942	37.0	78	835	692	1,188	1,105	463	460	39.6	41.6
Beaumont	1,918	790	41.2	192	839	97	1,083	655	438	306	40.4	46.7
El Paso	33,353	2,788	8.4	329	30,073	163	9,840	11,745	1,074	1,299	10.9	11.1
Galveston	6,892	3,171	46.0	757	2,361	603	3,876	2,229	1,825	1,177	47.1	52.8
Waco	1,767	812	46.0	95	623	237	892	666	414	334	46.4	50.2
Wichita Falls	1,720	497	28.9	45	879	299	1,133	330	331	152	29.2	46.1
UTAH:												
Ogden	4,609	2,795	60.6	339	1,206	269	2,092	2,067	1,285	1,384	61.4	67.0
VIRGINIA:												
Lynchburg	347	210	60.5	20	78	39	188	129	108	87	57.4	67.4
Newport News	2,047	1,170	57.2	160	439	278	1,196	651	665	405	55.6	62.2
Petersburg	511	250	48.9	22	191	48	279	185	137	97	49.1	52.4
Portsmouth	1,543	953	61.8	109	454	27	794	574	504	376	63.5	65.5
Roanoke	869	457	52.6	75	233	104	469	337	248	193	52.9	57.3
WASHINGTON:												
Bellingham	5,328	3,175	59.6	617	1,244	292	2,833	1,994	1,671	1,361	59.0	68.3
Everett	5,741	3,461	60.3	707	1,334	239	3,169	2,109	1,866	1,454	58.9	68.9
Tacoma	20,563	11,846	57.6	2,515	4,792	1,410	11,270	7,807	6,259	5,151	55.5	66.0
WEST VIRGINIA:												
Charleston	1,354	799	59.0	63	274	218	736	486	438	310	59.5	63.8
Clarksburg	1,937	689	35.6	120	829	299	1,076	651	390	231	36.8	38.4
Huntington	732	374	51.1	46	186	126	429	351	245	116	56.1	39.0
Wheeling	5,196	2,854	49.2	236	2,004	702	3,028	2,386	1,446	1,321	47.8	55.4
WISCONSIN:												
Green Bay	3,565	2,214	62.1	405	560	386	1,801	1,640	1,130	1,043	62.7	63.6
Kenosha	12,714	5,426	42.7	2,903	4,030	355	7,399	4,129	3,006	2,085	40.6	50.5
La Crosse	4,447	2,788	62.7	514	856	289	2,180	2,175	1,380	1,379	63.3	63.4
Madison	4,852	2,902	59.8	585	1,093	272	2,469	2,080	1,481	1,328	60.0	63.8
Oshkosh	5,794	3,664	63.2	589	1,047	494	2,891	2,631	1,863	1,704	64.4	64.8
Racine	16,199	7,792	48.1	2,555	5,264	588	9,078	5,818	4,204	3,246	46.3	55.8
Sheboygan	8,274	3,637	44.0	1,334	2,834	469	4,210	3,172	1,852	1,665	44.0	52.5
Superior	10,764	6,452	59.9	1,259	2,234	819	6,053	4,031	3,567	2,602	58.9	64.5

TABLE 98.—CITIZENSHIP OF FOREIGN-BORN WHITE POPULATION OF URBAN AND RURAL COMMUNITIES, FOR ALL AGES AND FOR PERSONS 21 YEARS OF AGE AND OVER, BY SEX, FOR THE UNITED STATES: 1920 AND 1910.

[No inquiry as to the citizenship of females in 1910.]

CLASS OF COMMUNITY, CENSUS YEAR, SEX, AND AGE.	Total white.	Native white.	FOREIGN-BORN WHITE.		
			Total.	Naturalized.	
				Number.	Per cent.
URBAN COMMUNITIES.					
1920					
Both sexes, all ages	50,620,084	40,263,101	10,356,983	4,765,313	46.0
Male	25,373,627	19,813,231	5,560,396	2,491,155	44.8
Female	25,246,457	20,449,870	4,796,587	2,274,158	47.4
Both sexes, 21 years and over	31,525,050	22,088,194	9,436,856	4,555,054	48.3
Male	15,911,506	10,796,213	5,115,293	2,392,492	46.8
Female	15,613,544	11,291,981	4,321,563	2,162,562	50.0
1910					
Males 21 years and over	12,311,144	7,776,505	4,534,639	2,016,008	44.5
RURAL COMMUNITIES.					
1920					
Both sexes, all ages	44,200,831	40,845,060	3,355,771	1,713,846	51.1
Male	23,057,028	21,089,102	1,967,926	952,813	48.4
Female	21,143,803	19,755,958	1,387,845	761,033	54.8
Both sexes, 21 years and over	23,588,411	20,526,547	3,061,864	1,653,643	54.0
Male	12,530,894	10,717,735	1,813,159	922,418	50.9
Female	11,057,517	9,808,812	1,248,705	731,225	58.6
1910					
Males 21 years and over	12,046,370	9,934,192	2,112,178	1,018,109	48.2

CLASS OF COMMUNITY, CENSUS YEAR, SEX, AND AGE.	FOREIGN-BORN WHITE—continued.					
	Having first papers.		Alien.		Citizenship not reported.	
	Number.	Per cent.	Number.	Per cent.	Number.	Per cent.
URBAN COMMUNITIES.						
1920						
Both sexes, all ages	974,473	9.4	4,090,296	39.5	526,901	5.1
Male	903,634	16.3	1,927,890	34.7	237,717	4.3
Female	70,839	1.5	2,162,406	45.1	289,184	6.0
Both sexes, 21 years and over	954,041	10.1	3,443,807	36.5	483,954	5.1
Male	889,813	17.4	1,615,135	31.6	217,853	4.3
Female	64,228	1.5	1,828,672	42.3	266,101	6.2
1910						
Males 21 years and over	406,373	9.0	1,642,943	36.2	469,315	10.3
RURAL COMMUNITIES.						
1920						
Both sexes, all ages	244,584	7.3	1,133,419	33.8	263,922	7.9
Male	230,093	11.7	635,027	32.3	149,993	7.6
Female	14,491	1.0	498,392	35.9	113,929	8.2
Both sexes, 21 years and over	240,235	7.8	921,102	30.1	246,884	8.1
Male	226,931	12.5	523,102	28.9	140,708	7.8
Female	13,304	1.1	398,000	31.9	106,176	8.5
1910						
Males 21 years and over	164,399	7.8	623,592	29.5	306,078	14.5

TABLE 99.—CITIZENSHIP OF FOREIGN-BORN WHITE POPULATION 21 YEARS OF AGE
UNITED

COUNTRY OF BIRTH.	FOREIGN-BORN WHITE POPULATION 21 YEARS OF AGE AND OVER IN URBAN COMMUNITIES.					
	Total.	Naturalized.		Having first papers.	Alien.	Citizenship not reported.
		Number.	Per cent.			
All countries............	9,436,856	4,555,054	48.3	954,041	3,443,807	483,954
EUROPE.						
Northwestern Europe:						
England.....................	564,447	366,561	64.9	43,474	112,278	42,134
Scotland.....................	177,148	119,963	62.1	15,938	38,469	12,678
Wales........................	45,604	34,361	75.3	2,243	5,072	3,928
Ireland......................	887,302	586,404	66.1	46,844	179,861	74,193
Norway.......................	163,013	192,623	63.0	17,157	33,279	9,954
Sweden.......................	381,737	257,421	67.4	35,692	69,267	19,357
Denmark......................	96,460	65,953	68.4	9,575	15,047	5,885
Netherlands..................	66,756	40,138	60.1	7,739	15,949	3,830
Belgium......................	35,945	17,981	50.0	5,596	10,213	2,155
Luxemburg....................	6,972	5,132	73.6	609	777	454
Switzerland..................	65,370	43,532	66.6	4,933	11,785	5,120
France.......................	104,701	61,389	58.6	7,993	26,584	8,735
Central Europe:						
Germany......................	1,113,368	821,760	73.8	79,658	136,763	75,187
Poland.......................	883,085	250,816	28.4	128,135	482,041	22,093
Czechoslovakia...............	222,663	103,011	46.3	34,685	77,712	7,255
Austria......................	395,441	157,016	39.7	52,385	169,476	16,564
Hungary......................	283,140	88,255	31.2	43,585	141,762	9,538
Jugo-Slavia..................	108,098	26,688	24.7	21,619	57,097	2,694
Eastern Europe:						
Russia.......................	1,073,131	443,798	41.4	122,196	470,183	36,954
Lithuania....................	112,112	28,638	25.5	15,037	66,111	2,326
Finland......................	74,810	25,935	34.7	10,788	35,014	3,073
Rumania......................	83,857	35,972	42.9	11,323	33,525	3,037
Bulgaria.....................	7,484	864	11.5	1,276	5,026	318
Turkey in Europe.............	4,180	845	20.2	606	2,584	145
Southern Europe:						
Greece.......................	140,805	25,171	17.9	18,754	90,996	5,884
Albania......................	4,666	330	7.1	463	3,772	101
Italy........................	1,187,788	355,634	29.9	136,740	660,564	34,850
Spain........................	30,527	3,504	11.5	1,786	23,895	1,342
Portugal.....................	41,929	6,644	15.8	1,829	32,305	1,151
Other Europe [1].............	4,124	2,052	49.8	515	1,193	364
ASIA.						
Armenia......................	27,834	8,196	29.4	3,877	14,898	863
Palestine....................	2,299	861	37.6	321	969	139
Syria........................	40,544	11,738	29.0	5,253	21,648	1,905
Turkey in Asia...............	8,704	2,154	24.7	1,033	5,122	395
Other Asia...................	5,365	1,975	36.8	708	2,302	380
AMERICA.						
Canada—French................	218,124	104,787	48.0	19,324	83,770	10,243
Canada—Other.................	526,755	318,725	60.5	37,257	126,708	44,075
Newfoundland.................	11,151	5,505	49.4	138	3,655	852
Mexico.......................	153,055	9,222	6.0	1,473	135,519	6,821
West Indies [2]..............	19,838	5,844	29.5	1,097	10,478	2,419
Central and South America....	12,612	3,276	26.0	961	7,038	1,337
OTHER COUNTRIES.						
Africa.......................	2,919	1,367	46.8	323	992	237
Australia....................	7,624	3,840	50.4	740	2,324	720
Atlantic Islands.............	25,839	5,256	20.3	923	19,080	580
Pacific Islands [2]..........	2,377	1,225	51.5	198	708	246
All other....................	5,182	2,592	50.0	242	806	1,542

[1] Comprises Danzig, Fiume, Saar Basin, and "Europe, not specified."

AND OVER IN URBAN AND RURAL COMMUNITIES, BY COUNTRY OF BIRTH, FOR THE STATES: 1920.

COUNTRY OF BIRTH.	FOREIGN-BORN WHITE POPULATION 21 YEARS OF AGE AND OVER IN RURAL COMMUNITIES.					
	Total.	Naturalized.		Having first papers.	Alien.	Citizenship not reported.
		Number.	Per cent.			
All countries	3,061,864	1,653,643	54.0	240,235	921,102	246,884
EUROPE.						
Northwestern Europe:						
England	180,951	121,078	66.9	11,364	26,171	22,338
Scotland	54,386	35,609	65.5	3,811	8,374	6,592
Wales	18,631	13,399	71.9	956	1,755	2,521
Ireland	134,375	88,517	65.9	5,420	19,705	20,733
Norway	185,872	135,409	72.9	14,750	22,944	12,769
Sweden	223,812	166,271	74.3	16,534	26,029	14,978
Denmark	84,338	61,586	73.0	6,977	9,702	6,073
Netherlands	50,421	29,783	59.1	5,343	11,829	3,466
Belgium	18,397	10,009	54.4	2,432	4,565	1,391
Luxemburg	5,209	3,813	73.2	354	533	509
Switzerland	49,022	31,976	65.2	3,726	8,430	4,890
France	36,195	21,341	59.0	2,919	7,839	4,096
Central Europe:						
Germany	535,516	391,691	73.1	35,537	54,992	53,296
Poland	164,965	51,819	31.4	17,963	87,370	7,813
Czechoslovakia	112,667	55,324	49.1	13,667	37,101	6,575
Austria	132,720	47,644	35.9	14,350	62,127	8,599
Hungary	70,652	17,928	25.4	9,275	39,999	3,450
Jugo-Slavia	47,858	12,128	25.3	6,904	27,122	1,704
Eastern Europe:						
Russia	138,206	65,763	47.6	12,334	51,265	8,844
Lithuania	15,530	4,595	29.6	1,693	8,725	517
Finland	65,205	32,938	50.5	7,725	22,056	2,486
Rumania	8,260	2,908	35.2	1,013	3,940	399
Bulgaria	2,480	303	12.2	421	1,634	122
Turkey in Europe	421	123	29.2	49	221	28
Southern Europe:						
Greece	20,710	2,958	14.3	2,290	14,357	1,105
Albania	424	40	9.4	44	328	12
Italy	221,145	64,079	29.0	22,946	124,363	9,757
Spain	10,909	946	8.7	561	8,821	581
Portugal	14,647	3,421	23.4	565	9,844	817
Other Europe [1]	1,275	671	52.6	132	307	165
ASIA.						
Armenia	5,692	1,817	31.9	686	2,879	310
Palestine	249	112	45.0	22	89	26
Syria	6,031	2,319	38.5	619	2,603	490
Turkey in Asia	1,059	314	29.7	92	564	89
Other Asia	1,186	543	45.8	103	367	173
AMERICA.						
Canada—French	56,052	28,194	50.3	3,852	19,803	4,203
Canada—Other	200,585	129,778	64.7	10,458	35,549	24,800
Newfoundland	1,109	569	51.3	75	295	170
Mexico	166,662	8,402	5.0	1,273	149,603	7,384
West Indies [2]	1,821	837	46.0	98	522	364
Central and South America	1,934	774	40.0	162	739	259
OTHER COUNTRIES.						
Africa	679	379	55.8	54	151	95
Australia	2,098	1,159	55.2	158	491	290
Atlantic Islands	7,718	2,475	32.1	348	4,418	477
Pacific Islands [2]	820	496	60.5	76	146	102
All other	2,970	1,405	47.3	104	435	1,026

[2] Except possessions of the United States.

TABLE 100.—CITIZENSHIP OF FOREIGN-BORN WHITE POPULATION 21 YEARS OF AGE STATES:

DIVISION AND STATE.	FOREIGN-BORN WHITE POPULATION 21 YEARS OF AGE AND OVER IN URBAN COMMUNITIES.									
	Naturalized.		Having first papers.		Alien.		Citizenship not reported.		Per cent naturalized.	
	Male.	Female.	Male.	Female.	Male.	Female.	Male.	Female.	Male.	Female.
United States....	2,392,492	2,162,562	889,813	64,228	1,615,135	1,828,672	217,853	266,101	46.8	50.0
GEOGRAPHIC DIVISIONS:										
New England.......	326,289	341,133	115,745	7,967	293,684	362,022	20,103	31,349	43.2	45.9
Middle Atlantic.....	922,933	833,789	328,348	25,351	726,960	841,663	72,220	107,398	45.0	46.1
East North Central..	625,408	553,920	300,367	18,771	318,319	367,778	58,897	65,360	48.0	55.1
West North Central..	188,267	161,404	53,075	4,355	54,286	61,103	21,218	22,156	59.4	64.8
South Atlantic......	54,193	46,482	15,828	1,282	36,288	34,137	7,734	6,990	47.5	52.3
East South Central..	15,180	12,227	2,457	230	4,268	4,165	3,502	3,283	59.7	61.4
West South Central..	30,714	23,654	6,957	672	51,582	43,458	8,745	7,438	31.3	31.4
Mountain...........	49,791	44,040	11,887	1,011	25,366	21,316	4,980	3,948	54.1	62.6
Pacific.............	179,717	145,913	55,149	4,589	104,382	93,030	20,454	18,179	50.0	55.8
NEW ENGLAND:										
Maine..............	10,607	12,412	3,738	130	10,147	11,414	1,359	2,199	41.0	47.5
New Hampshire.....	13,708	14,815	3,909	174	12,907	14,058	1,627	2,612	42.6	46.8
Vermont...........	4,488	4,669	1,002	66	2,704	2,580	313	489	52.8	59.8
Massachusetts......	207,383	220,515	71,884	5,453	187,105	241,770	9,455	15,157	43.6	45.7
Rhode Island.......	37,788	39,514	13,462	1,226	23,281	33,175	2,745	4,020	48.9	50.7
Connecticut........	52,315	49,208	21,750	918	57,540	59,025	4,604	6,872	38.4	42.4
MIDDLE ATLANTIC:										
New York..........	551,997	500,083	203,544	18,337	418,250	536,492	44,591	68,847	45.3	44.5
New Jersey.........	134,841	124,825	51,730	2,744	110,940	125,940	8,923	14,306	44.0	46.6
Pennsylvania.......	236,095	208,881	73,074	4,270	197,770	179,231	18,706	24,245	44.9	50.1
EAST NORTH CENTRAL:										
Ohio..............	129,792	114,882	66,238	3,002	97,355	89,907	10,228	11,162	42.7	52.5
Indiana............	25,611	21,171	20,458	1,129	13,923	16,722	5,674	5,371	39.0	47.7
Illinois............	287,889	255,823	115,505	7,893	97,963	148,155	25,176	29,419	54.7	58.0
Michigan..........	111,775	99,756	69,360	3,458	81,218	81,589	11,486	12,220	40.8	50.6
Wisconsin.........	70,341	62,288	28,866	3,289	27,860	31,405	6,333	7,188	52.8	59.8
WEST NORTH CENTRAL:										
Minnesota.........	77,819	65,939	24,876	2,118	19,539	23,940	6,434	6,699	60.5	66.8
Iowa..............	30,977	27,023	4,729	418	7,567	6,369	3,785	3,929	65.8	71.6
Missouri...........	44,263	36,920	12,079	830	14,905	17,544	5,220	5,961	57.9	60.3
North Dakota......	5,577	5,010	729	94	896	914	887	860	68.9	72.8
South Dakota......	3,956	3,494	795	108	528	683	984	947	63.2	66.8
Nebraska..........	15,870	13,905	6,912	537	5,489	6,973	2,305	2,395	51.9	58.4
Kansas............	9,805	9,113	2,955	250	5,362	4,680	1,603	1,365	49.7	59.1
SOUTH ATLANTIC:										
Delaware..........	3,577	3,060	1,352	58	3,629	2,788	515	576	39.4	47.2
Maryland.........	21,950	20,509	7,822	610	11,996	15,428	790	1,116	51.6	54.5
District of Columbia.	7,786	6,926	1,775	324	2,842	3,491	1,639	1,593	55.4	56.2
Virginia...........	5,222	3,732	1,687	89	2,992	2,039	1,009	695	47.9	56.9
West Virginia......	4,545	3,526	1,035	42	4,365	2,429	1,140	969	41.0	50.6
North Carolina.....	1,106	844	204	4	643	395	411	297	46.8	54.8
South Carolina.....	1,159	837	286	16	613	439	321	253	48.7	54.2
Georgia...........	3,708	2,722	666	65	1,713	1,299	695	488	54.7	59.5
Florida............	5,140	4,326	1,001	74	7,495	5,829	1,214	1,003	34.6	38.5
EAST SOUTH CENTRAL:										
Kentucky..........	7,568	6,758	892	129	1,211	1,452	1,192	1,516	62.9	68.6
Tennessee.........	3,142	2,499	608	54	1,353	1,200	919	769	52.2	55.3
Alabama..........	3,134	2,223	715	39	1,200	1,075	1,031	727	51.5	54.7
Mississippi........	1,336	747	242	8	504	438	360	271	54.7	51.0
WEST SOUTH CENTRAL:										
Arkansas..........	1,790	1,330	278	31	459	385	609	470	56.9	60.0
Louisiana..........	7,347	4,803	1,704	65	7,079	4,983	1,727	2,259	41.1	00.7
Oklahoma.........	3,703	2,632	747	58	2,489	1,040	1,668	000	11.0	50.8
Texas.............	17,884	14,889	4,228	518	41,555	36,842	5,100	4,010	26.0	26.5
MOUNTAIN:										
Montana..........	11,120	8,431	2,964	187	2,915	2,517	1,276	1,134	60.8	68.7
Idaho.............	3,773	3,071	629	54	1,280	801	423	270	61.8	73.2
Wyoming..........	2,576	1,915	703	24	1,335	638	366	168	51.7	69.8
Colorado..........	18,318	16,444	4,264	416	6,772	6,288	1,332	1,144	59.7	67.7
New Mexico........	1,109	908	203	19	1,118	945	239	191	41.6	44.0
Arizona...........	2,845	2,472	871	47	8,090	6,451	648	421	22.8	26.3
Utah.............	9,376	10,324	2,047	259	3,435	3,438	458	448	61.2	71.4
Nevada...........	674	475	206	5	421	238	238	172	43.8	53.4
PACIFIC:										
Washington........	43,641	34,520	17,225	1,021	17,215	15,394	4,598	3,866	52.8	63.0
Oregon............	17,641	14,246	7,031	508	7,793	7,340	1,188	883	52.4	62.0
California..........	118,435	97,147	30,893	3,060	79,374	70,296	14,668	13,430	48.7	52.8

AND OVER IN URBAN AND RURAL COMMUNITIES, BY SEX, BY DIVISIONS AND 1920.

DIVISION AND STATE.	FOREIGN-BORN WHITE POPULATION 21 YEARS OF AGE AND OVER IN RURAL COMMUNITIES.									
	Naturalized.		Having first papers.		Alien.		Citizenship not reported.		Per cent aturalized.	
	Male.	Female.	Male.	Female.	Male.	Female.	Male.	Female.	Male.	Female.
United States	922,418	731,225	226,931	13,304	523,102	398,000	140,708	106,176	50.9	58.6
GEOGRAPHIC DIVISIONS:										
New England	41,189	46,916	13,045	554	49,719	43,148	6,268	6,160	37.4	48.5
Middle Atlantic	142,487	125,410	46,052	2,340	144,535	114,499	23,440	20,327	40.0	47.8
East North Central	218,544	178,795	62,069	4,408	70,508	73,226	33,616	28,589	56.8	62.7
West North Central	295,237	229,224	47,151	3,217	44,201	44,032	35,238	27,630	70.0	75.4
South Atlantic	18,471	12,277	4,988	179	26,789	12,013	6,116	3,448	32.8	44.0
East South Central	6,876	4,052	1,226	67	3,811	2,118	2,377	1,403	48.1	53.0
West South Central	33,789	26,101	6,559	547	60,154	41,045	9,931	5,874	30.6	35.5
Mountain	70,188	46,845	18,565	779	51,388	30,005	9,156	4,743	47.0	56.9
Pacific	95,637	61,605	27,276	1,213	71,997	37,914	14,566	8,002	45.7	56.7
NEW ENGLAND:										
Maine	7,421	10,039	2,815	59	11,529	7,337	1,739	1,384	31.6	53.3
New Hampshire	3,687	4,411	930	27	4,817	2,816	847	704	35.9	55.4
Vermont	5,052	5,616	1,104	51	5,182	3,797	617	502	42.3	56.4
Massachusetts	6,094	7,424	1,841	102	6,739	6,737	606	648	39.9	49.8
Rhode Island	424	449	59	6	281	270	78	88	50.4	55.2
Connecticut	18,511	18,977	6,296	309	21,171	22,191	2,381	2,834	38.3	42.8
MIDDLE ATLANTIC:										
New York	52,259	49,474	11,414	803	28,609	27,769	8,219	7,809	52.0	57.6
New Jersey	23,886	21,964	8,978	441	18,197	19,950	3,407	4,150	43.9	47.2
Pennsylvania	66,342	53,972	25,660	1,096	97,729	66,780	11,814	8,368	32.9	41.4
EAST NORTH CENTRAL:										
Ohio	27,028	21,833	10,286	348	16,932	14,094	5,645	3,791	45.1	54.5
Indiana	9,260	7,525	3,105	224	2,057	2,960	2,820	2,363	53.7	57.6
Illinois	54,021	41,713	10,247	493	13,386	12,887	9,610	7,748	61.9	66.4
Michigan	63,856	55,571	17,100	1,095	19,988	21,754	7,025	5,909	59.1	65.9
Wisconsin	64,379	52,153	21,331	2,248	18,145	21,531	8,516	8,778	57.3	61.6
WEST NORTH CENTRAL:										
Minnesota	99,536	76,096	15,851	1,093	15,706	13,464	7,095	6,377	72.0	78.4
Iowa	53,183	42,088	6,380	363	7,817	7,317	6,954	5,580	71.5	76.0
Missouri	13,298	9,967	1,686	163	2,335	2,309	3,559	2,512	63.7	66.7
North Dakota	45,773	34,827	5,829	313	6,121	5,788	4,231	3,198	73.9	78.9
South Dakota	27,074	20,640	5,523	325	2,575	3,714	3,905	2,776	69.3	75.2
Nebraska	33,142	26,866	6,956	582	4,001	5,732	5,146	4,088	67.3	72.1
Kansas	23,231	18,740	4,926	378	5,646	5,708	4,348	3,099	60.9	67.1
SOUTH ATLANTIC:										
Delaware	752	638	187	9	404	343	198	159	48.8	55.5
Maryland	4,127	3,178	898	37	1,724	1,486	1,056	897	52.9	56.8
District of Columbia [1]										
Virginia	3,134	1,969	607	19	1,288	987	980	589	48.1	50.9
West Virginia	3,770	2,300	2,070	58	19,631	6,957	1,915	713	13.8	22.9
North Carolina	780	505	81	6	481	253	329	149	46.7	55.3
South Carolina	765	301	131	5	308	144	267	96	52.0	55.1
Georgia	1,315	571	292	8	627	234	303	149	51.8	59.4
Florida	3,828	2,815	722	37	1,814	1,308	1,068	696	51.5	58.0
EAST SOUTH CENTRAL:										
Kentucky	2,705	1,462	580	30	1,849	760	830	554	45.4	52.1
Tennessee	1,288	779	131	8	468	335	519	247	53.5	56.9
Alabama	1,897	1,249	410	20	830	564	597	394	50.8	56.1
Mississippi	986	562	105	9	664	459	431	208	45.1	45.4
WEST SOUTH CENTRAL:										
Arkansas	2,813	1,646	475	33	860	681	892	424	55.8	59.1
Louisiana	2,003	1,043	417	17	3,629	2,603	942	607	28.7	24.4
Oklahoma	7,536	5,501	1,030	66	3,744	2,018	2,259	1,069	51.7	63.6
Texas	21,437	17,911	4,637	431	51,921	35,743	5,838	3,774	25.6	31.0
MOUNTAIN:										
Montana	22,889	14,187	5,750	292	4,721	3,473	2,615	1,238	63.6	73.9
Idaho	10,413	6,637	2,527	85	3,209	1,416	1,112	470	60.3	77.1
Wyoming	4,713	2,804	1,724	48	3,456	1,327	923	337	43.6	62.1
Colorado	16,312	11,244	4,384	187	8,924	6,158	1,783	1,047	51.9	60.3
New Mexico	2,272	1,592	547	26	7,272	4,697	484	311	21.5	24.0
Arizona	3,141	2,250	930	32	16,057	10,101	1,000	531	14.9	17.3
Utah	7,001	6,491	1,516	89	4,229	1,882	729	532	52.0	72.2
Nevada	3,447	1,640	1,187	20	3,520	865	510	277	39.8	58.5
PACIFIC:										
Washington	33,515	22,241	11,083	422	12,357	7,560	3,624	2,153	55.3	68.7
Oregon	14,258	9,335	4,224	218	5,007	2,986	1,438	711	57.2	70.5
California	47,864	30,029	11,969	573	54,633	27,368	9,504	5,138	38.6	47.6

1 No rural population, as Washington city is coextensive with the District of Columbia.

TABLE 101.—COUNTRY OF ORIGIN OF THE FOREIGN WHITE STOCK

[Figures for 1920 relate to countries as

COUNTRY OF ORIGIN.	TOTAL FOREIGN WHITE STOCK.		Foreign-born white.[1]	NATIVE WHITE OF FOREIGN OR MIXED PARENTAGE.			
	Number.	Per cent distribution.		Total.	Both parents foreign.	Father foreign.	Mother foreign.
Total: 1920	36,398,958	100.0	13,712,754	22,686,204	15,694,539	4,539,776	2,451,889
Northwestern Europe:							
England	2,307,112	6.3	824,088	1,483,024	574,499	571,560	336,965
Scotland	731,239	2.0	310,092	421,147	178,638	153,917	88,592
Wales	230,380	0.6	66,962	163,418	78,114	54,889	30,415
Ireland	4,136,395	11.4	1,164,707	2,971,688	1,966,968	573,021	431,699
Norway	1,023,225	2.8	362,051	661,174	437,623	143,314	80,237
Sweden	1,457,382	4.0	632,656	824,726	599,744	144,382	80,600
Denmark	467,525	1.3	191,496	276,029	170,702	73,915	31,412
Netherlands	362,318	1.0	134,229	228,089	142,547	57,301	28,241
Belgium	122,686	0.3	63,234	59,452	37,525	15,420	6,507
Luxemburg	43,109	0.1	12,837	30,272	16,263	10,847	3,162
Switzerland	327,797	0.9	117,270	210,527	103,452	75,315	31,760
France	333,678	0.9	124,727	208,951	90,073	86,549	32,329
Central and Eastern Europe:							
Germany	7,259,992	19.9	1,915,864	5,344,128	3,397,370	1,367,805	578,953
Austria	3,129,798	8.6	1,445,141	1,684,657	1,435,524	171,678	77,455
Hungary	1,110,905	3.1	598,170	512,735	472,521	29,510	10,704
Russia	3,871,109	10.6	2,020,646	1,850,463	1,671,949	135,098	43,416
Finland	296,276	0.8	150,770	145,506	130,083	9,765	5,658
Rumania	134,318	0.4	85,255	49,063	43,683	3,820	1,560
Bulgaria, Serbia, and Montenegro	43,703	0.1	32,681	11,022	9,696	1,191	135
Turkey in Europe	23,268	0.1	18,907	4,361	3,948	372	41
Southern Europe:							
Greece	212,342	0.6	166,786	45,556	36,990	8,287	279
Italy	3,336,941	9.2	1,615,180	1,721,761	1,556,065	146,304	19,392
Spain	77,947	0.2	52,686	25,261	14,973	7,972	2,316
Portugal	134,794	0.4	67,948	66,846	52,794	11,673	2,379
Europe, not specified	10,998	(2)	3,342	7,656	5,019	1,900	737
Asia:							
Turkey in Asia	164,480	0.5	100,843	63,637	57,915	4,827	895
All other countries	10,735	(2)	5,139	5,596	1,791	2,343	1,462
America:							
Canada—French	848,309	2.3	302,675	545,634	326,435	129,203	89,996
Canada—Other	1,755,519	4.8	558,775	1,196,744	343,595	467,206	385,943
Newfoundland	25,448	0.1	12,320	13,128	7,163	2,780	3,185
West Indies[3]	45,496	0.1	21,909	23,587	9,987	9,005	4,595
Mexico	725,332	2.0	473,287	252,045	178,309	45,720	28,016
Central and South America	19,487	0.1	11,782	7,705	1,424	3,595	2,686
All other	116,458	0.3	48,299	68,159	38,700	19,292	10,167
Of mixed foreign parentage	1,502,457	4.1		1,502,457	1,502,457		
Total: 1900	25,859,834	100.0	10,213,817	15,646,017	10,632,280	3,346,652	1,667,085
Northwestern Europe:							
England	2,173,741	8.4	839,830	1,333,911	565,461	494,929	273,521
Scotland	594,297	2.3	233,473	360,824	163,991	129,735	67,098
Wales	253,045	1.0	93,560	159,485	86,899	47,498	25,088
Ireland	4,826,904	18.7	1,615,232	3,211,672	2,244,241	605,987	361,444
Norway	788,758	3.1	336,379	452,379	349,220	67,649	35,510
Sweden	1,082,388	4.2	581,986	500,402	414,772	55,479	30,151
Denmark	310,127	1.2	153,644	156,483	115,173	29,514	11,796
Switzerland	257,426	1.0	115,581	141,845	74,951	48,806	18,088
France	268,292	1.0	104,031	164,261	71,263	72,110	20,888
Central, Eastern, and Southern Europe:							
Germany	8,111,406	51.4	2,516,118	5,800,010	5,700,700	1,100,000	107,151
Austria	895,500	3.5	491,259	404,241	344,070	42,295	17,876
Hungary	218,447	0.8	145,709	72,738	66,713	4,895	1,130
Russia	955,918	3.7	578,072	377,846	356,249	17,719	3,878
Italy	727,844	2.8	483,963	243,881	218,750	22,442	2,689
All other:							
Canada—French	830,335	3.2	394,461	435,874	265,947	106,833	63,094
Canada—Other	1,637,603	6.3	778,399	859,204	260,471	317,988	280,745
All other countries	871,604	3.4	454,825	416,779	268,251	101,893	46,635
Of mixed for. parentage	1,056,152	4.1		1,056,152	1,056,152		

[1] For 1920, according to birthplace of father; for 1910, 1900, and 1890, according to birthplace of person.
[2] Less than one-tenth of 1 per cent.
[3] Except possessions of the United States.
[4] The report for 1890 classified the foreign born by country of birth without distinction as to color or race. For the purposes of this table it is assumed that, with the exception of "Canada—Other" (see note 6), the number reported for each specified country represented white persons only. The number for "All other

BY NATIVITY AND PARENTAGE, FOR THE UNITED STATES: 1890-1920.

constituted prior to the World War.]

COUNTRY OF ORIGIN.	TOTAL FOREIGN WHITE STOCK.		Foreign-born white.[1]	NATIVE WHITE OF FOREIGN OR MIXED PARENTAGE.			
	Number.	Per cent distribution.		Total.	Both parents foreign.	Father foreign.	Mother foreign.
Total: 1910	32,243,382	100.0	13,345,545	18,897,837	12,916,311	3,923,845	2,057,681
Northwestern Europe:							
England	2,322,442	7.2	876,455	1,445,987	592,285	546,215	307,487
Scotland	659,663	2.0	261,034	398,629	175.391	145,227	78.011
Wales	248,947	0.8	82,479	166,468	84.934	52,555	28.979
Ireland	4,504,360	14.0	1,352,155	3,152,205	2,141,577	603,013	407,615
Norway	979,099	3.0	403,858	575.241	410,951	106,805	57,485
Sweden	1,364,215	4.2	665,183	699,032	546,788	97.504	54,740
Denmark	400,064	1.2	181,621	218,443	147.648	49,721	21,074
Netherlands	293,574	0.9	120,053	173.521	116,331	38,199	18,991
Belgium	89,264	0.3	49,397	39,867	26,448	9,802	3,617
Luxemburg	6,945	(²)	3,068	3,877	2,381	1,244	252
Switzerland	301,650	0.9	124,834	176.816	90,669	61,244	24,903
France	292,389	0.9	117,236	175,153	78.937	73,085	23,131
Central and Eastern Europe:							
Germany	8,282,618	25.7	2,501,181	5,781,437	3,911,847	1,337,651	531,939
Austria	2,001,559	6.2	1,174,924	826,635	709,070	80,595	36,970
Hungary	700,227	2.2	495,600	204,627	191,059	10,106	3,462
Russia	2,541,649	7.9	1,602,752	938,897	873,055	51,856	13,986
Finland	211,026	0.7	129,669	81,357	76,261	3,319	1,777
Rumania	87,721	0.3	65,920	21,801	20,707	821	273
Bulgaria, Serbia, and Montenegro	22,685	0.1	21,451	1,234	948	239	47
Turkey in Europe	35,314	0.1	32,221	3,093	2,560	423	110
Southern Europe:							
Greece	109,665	0.3	101,264	8,401	5,524	2,400	477
Italy	2,098,360	6.5	1,343,070	755,290	695,187	52,947	7,156
Spain	33,134	0.1	21,977	11,157	4,387	5,364	1,406
Portugal	111,122	0.3	57,623	53,499	41,680	10,359	1,460
Europe, not specified	7,576	(²)	2,853	4,723	2,926	1,281	516
Asia:							
Turkey in Asia	78,631	0.2	59,702	18,929	17,480	1,255	194
All other countries	7,264	(²)	4,612	2,652	517	1,329	806
America:							
Canada—French	932,238	2.9	385,083	547,155	330,976	133.999	82,180
Canada—Other	1,822,377	5.7	810.987	1,011.390	307,291	387,617	316,482
Newfoundland	8,635	(²)	5,076	3.559	1,836	853	870
West Indies[3]	41,842	0.1	23,169	18.673	8,681	6,743	3,249
Mexico	382,002	1.2	219,802	162,200	107,866	34,995	19,339
Central and South America	13,510	(²)	9,069	4,441	807	2,050	1,584
All other	74,523	0.2	40,167	34.356	14.214	13,029	7,113
Of mixed foreign parentage	1,177,092	3.7	....	1,177,092	1,177,092	....	....
Total: 1890	20,625,542	100.0	[4]9,121,867	11,503,675	8,085,019	2,378,729	1,039,927
Northwestern Europe:							
England	1,977,595	9.6	909,092	1,068,503	488,661	386,711	193,131
Scotland	519,252	2.5	242,231	277,021	134,243	97,661	45,117
Wales	225,582	1.1	100,079	125,503	75.375	34,863	15,265
Ireland	4,795,681	23.3	1,871,509	2,924,172	2,164,397	502,155	257,620
Norway	606,316	2.9	322,665	283,651	238,679	29,883	15,089
Sweden	730,569	3.5	478,041	252,528	217,217	23,810	11,501
Denmark	216,995	1.1	132,543	84,452	66,196	13,677	4,579
Switzerland	(⁵)	......	(⁵)	(⁵)	......	......	......
France	258,919	1.3	113,174	145,745	68,572	61,187	15,986
Central, Eastern, and Southern Europe:							
Germany	6,857,229	33.2	2,784,894	4,072,335	3,006,342	827,823	238,170
Austria	341,549	1.7	241,377	100,172	90,195	6,744	3,233
Hungary	77,121	0.4	62,435	14,686	13,048	1,390	248
Russia	258,583	1.3	182,644	75,939	69,802	4,962	1,175
Italy	249,544	1.2	182,580	66,964	54,742	11,096	1,126
All other:							
Canada—French	526,934	2.6	302,496	224,438	157,104	42,356	24,978
Canada—Other	1,255,629	6.1	[6]673,000	582,629	183,602	227,144	171,883
All other countries	1,013,774	4.9	523,107	490,667	342,574	107,267	40,826
Of mixed for. parentage	714,270	3.5	....	714,270	714,270	......	......

countries" has been obtained by deducting the sum of the items for the specified countries from the United States total, which represents foreign-born white only.

[5] Switzerland included in "All other countries" in tabulation by birthplace of parents. Number of persons born in Switzerland, 104,069, also included in "All other countries" in this table.

[6] Partly estimated; total reported for "Canada—Other" was 678,442, of whom eight-tenths of 1 per cent were estimated to be nonwhites, this proportion being based upon returns of later censuses.

TABLE **102.**—COUNTRY OF ORIGIN OF THE FOREIGN WHITE STOCK

[Figures for 1920 relate to countries as

	COUNTRY OF ORIGIN.	TOTAL FOREIGN WHITE STOCK.		FOREIGN-BORN WHITE.[1]		NATIVE WHITE OF FOREIGN OR MIXED PARENTAGE. Total.	
		1920	1910	1920	1910	1920	1910
1	Total..................	36,398,958	32,243,382	13,712,754	13,345,545	22,686,204	18,897,837
	Northwestern Europe:						
2	England..................	2,307,112	2,322,442	824,088	876,455	1,483,024	1,445,987
3	Scotland.................	731,239	659,663	310,092	261,034	421,147	398,629
4	Wales....................	230,380	248,947	66,962	82,479	163,418	166,468
5	Ireland..................	4,136,395	4,504,360	1,164,707	1,352,155	2,971,688	3,152,205
6	Norway..................	1,023,225	979,099	362,051	403,858	661,174	575,241
7	Sweden..................	1,457,382	1,364,215	632,656	665,183	824,726	699,032
8	Denmark.................	467,525	400,064	191,496	181,621	276,029	218,443
9	Netherlands.............	362,318	293,574	134,229	120,053	228,089	173,521
10	Belgium.................	122,686	89,264	63,234	49,397	59,452	39,867
11	Luxemburg..............	43,109	6,945	12,837	3,068	30,272	3,877
12	Switzerland.............	327,797	301,650	117,270	124,834	210,527	176,816
13	France..................	333,678	292,389	124,727	117,236	208,951	175,153
	Central and Eastern Europe:						
14	Germany................	7,259,992	8,282,618	1,915,864	2,501,181	5,344,128	5,781,437
15	Austria.................	3,129,798	2,001,559	1,445,141	1,174,924	1,684,657	826,635
16	Hungary................	1,110,905	700,227	598,170	495,600	512,735	204,627
17	Russia..................	3,871,109	2,541,649	2,020,646	1,602,752	1,850,463	938,897
18	Finland.................	296,276	211,026	150,770	129,669	145,506	81,357
19	Rumania................	134,318	87,721	85,255	65,920	49,063	21,801
20	Bulgaria, Serbia, and Montenegro.	43,703	22,685	32,681	21,451	11,022	1,234
21	Turkey in Europe.........	23,268	35,314	18,907	32,221	4,361	3,093
	Southern Europe:						
22	Greece..................	212,342	109,665	166,786	101,264	45,556	8,401
23	Italy...................	3,336,941	2,098,360	1,615,180	1,343,070	1,721,761	755,290
24	Spain...................	77,947	33,134	52,686	21,977	25,261	11,157
25	Portugal................	134,794	111,122	67,948	57,623	66,846	53,499
26	Europe, not specified.........	10,998	7,576	3,342	2,853	7,656	4,723
	Asia:						
27	Turkey in Asia...........	164,480	78,631	100,843	59,702	63,637	18,929
28	All other countries........	10,735	7,264	5,139	4,612	5,596	2,652
	America:						
29	Canada—French..........	848,309	932,238	302,675	385,083	545,634	547,155
30	Canada—Other..........	1,755,519	1,822,377	558,775	810,987	1,196,744	1,011,390
31	Newfoundland...........	25,448	8,635	12,320	5,076	13,128	3,559
32	West Indies[3]............	45,496	41,842	21,909	23,169	23,587	18,673
33	Mexico.................	725,332	382,002	473,287	219,802	252,045	162,200
34	Central and South America.	19,487	13,510	11,782	9,069	7,705	4,441
35	All other..................	116,458	74,523	48,299	40,167	68,159	34,356
36	Of mixed foreign parentage....	1,502,457	1,177,092	....	....	1,502,457	1,177,092

[1] For 1920, according to birthplace of father; for 1910, according to birthplace of person.

BY NATIVITY AND PARENTAGE, FOR THE UNITED STATES: 1920 AND 1910.
constituted prior to the World War.]

| NATIVE WHITE OF FOREIGN OR MIXED PARENTAGE—continued. | | | | INCREASE[2] IN FOREIGN WHITE STOCK: 1910-1920 | | | | | | |
| Foreign parentage. | | Mixed parentage. | | Total. | | Foreign-born white.[1] | | Native white of foreign or mixed parentage. | | |
1920	1910	1920	1910	Number.	Per cent.	Number.	Per cent.	Number.	Per cent.	
15,694,539	12,916,311	6,991,665	5,981,526	4,155,576	12.9	367,209	2.8	3,788,367	20.0	1
574,499	592,285	908,525	853,702	−15,330	−0.7	−52,367	−6.0	37,037	2.6	2
178,638	175,391	242,509	223,238	71,576	10.9	49,058	18.8	22,518	5.6	3
78,114	84,934	85,304	81,534	−18,567	−7.5	−15,517	−18.8	−3,050	−1.8	4
1,966,968	2,141,577	1,004,720	1,010,628	−367,965	−8.2	−187,448	−13.9	−180,517	−5.7	5
437,623	410,951	223,551	164,290	44,126	4.5	−41,807	−10.4	85,933	14.9	6
599,744	546,788	224,982	152,244	93,167	6.8	−32,527	−4.9	125,694	18.0	7
170,702	147,648	105,327	70,795	67,461	16.9	9,875	5.4	57,586	26.4	8
142,547	116,331	85,542	57,190	68,744	23.4	14,176	11.8	54,568	31.4	9
37,525	26,448	21,927	13,419	33,422	37.4	13,837	28.0	19,585	49.1	10
16,263	2,381	14,009	1,496	36,164	520.7	9,769	318.4	26,395	680.8	11
103,452	90,669	107,075	86,147	26,147	8.7	−7,564	−6.1	33,711	19.1	12
90,073	78,937	118,878	96,216	41,289	14.1	7,491	6.4	33,798	19.3	13
3,397,370	3,911,847	1,946,758	1,869,590	−1,022,626	−12.3	−585,317	−23.4	−437,309	−7.6	14
1,435,524	709,070	249,133	117,565	1,128,239	56.4	270,217	23.0	858,022	103.8	15
472,521	191,059	40,214	13,568	410,678	58.6	102,570	20.7	308,108	150.6	16
1,671,949	873,055	178,514	65,842	1,329,460	52.3	417,894	26.1	911,566	97.1	17
130,083	76,261	15,423	5,096	85,250	40.4	21,101	16.3	64,149	78.8	18
43,683	20,707	5,380	1,094	46,597	53.1	19,335	29.3	27,262	125.0	19
9,696	948	1,326	286	21,018	92.7	11,230	52.4	9,788	793.2	20
3,948	2,560	413	533	−12,046	−34.1	−13,314	−41.3	1,268	41.0	21
36,990	5,524	8,566	2,877	102,677	93.6	65,522	64.7	37,155	442.3	22
1,556,065	695,187	165,696	60,103	1,238,581	59.0	272,110	20.3	966,471	128.0	23
14,973	4,387	10,288	6,770	44,813	135.2	30,709	139.7	14,104	126.4	24
52,794	41,680	14,052	11,819	23,672	21.3	10,325	17.9	13,347	24.9	25
5,019	2,926	2,637	1,797	3,422	45.2	489	17.1	2,933	62.1	26
57,915	17,480	5,722	1,449	85,849	109.2	41,141	68.9	44,708	236.2	27
1,791	517	3,805	2,135	3,471	47.8	527	11.4	2,944	111.0	28
326,435	330,976	219,199	216,179	−83,929	−9.0	−82,408	−21.4	−1,521	−0.3	29
343,595	307,291	853,149	704,099	−66,858	−3.7	−252,212	−31.1	185,354	18.3	30
7,163	1,836	5,965	1,723	16,813	194.7	7,244	142.7	9,569	268.9	31
9,987	8,681	13,600	9,992	3,654	8.7	−1,260	−5.4	4,914	26.3	32
178,309	107,866	73,736	54,334	343,330	89.9	253,485	115.3	89,845	55.4	33
1,424	807	6,281	3,634	5,977	44.2	2,713	29.9	3,264	73.5	34
38,700	14,214	29,459	20,142	41,935	56.3	8,132	20.2	33,803	98.4	35
1,502,457	1,177,092	....	....	325,365	27.6	....	....	325,365	27.6	36

[2] A minus sign (−) denotes decrease.   [3] Except possessions of the United States.

75108°—23——24

TABLE 103.—PER CENT DISTRIBUTION OF THE FOREIGN WHITE STOCK BY COUNTRY PARENTAGE CLASSES FOR COUNTRIES

[Figures for 1920 relate to countries as

COUNTRY OF ORIGIN.	Total foreign white stock.		Foreign-born white.[1]		Native white of foreign or mixed parentage.							
					Total.		Both parents foreign.		Father foreign.		Mother foreign.	
	1920	1910	1920	1910	1920	1910	1920	1910	1920	1910	1920	1910
Total...............	100.0	100.0	100.0	100.0	100.0	100.0	100.0	100.0	100.0	100.0	100.0	100.0
Northwestern Europe:												
England...............	6.3	7.2	6.0	6.6	6.5	7.7	3.7	4.6	12.6	13.9	13.7	14.9
Scotland...............	2.0	2.0	2.3	2.0	1.9	2.1	1.1	1.4	3.4	3.7	3.6	3.8
Wales..............	0.6	0.8	0.5	0.6	0.7	0.9	0.5	0.7	1.2	1.3	1.2	1.4
Ireland..............	11.4	14.0	8.5	10.1	13.1	16.7	12.5	16.6	12.6	15.4	17.6	19.8
Norway...............	2.8	3.0	2.6	3.0	2.9	3.0	2.8	3.2	3.2	2.7	3.3	2.8
Sweden..............	4.0	4.2	4.6	5.0	3.6	3.7	3.8	4.2	3.2	2.5	3.3	2.7
Denmark............	1.3	1.2	1.4	1.4	1.2	1.2	1.1	1.1	1.6	1.3	1.3	1.0
Netherlands..........	1.0	0.9	1.0	0.9	1.0	0.9	0.9	0.9	1.3	1.0	1.2	0.9
Belgium..............	0.3	0.3	0.5	0.4	0.3	0.2	0.2	0.2	0.3	0.2	0.3	0.2
Luxemburg...........	0.1	(²)	0.1	(²)	0.1	(²)	0.1	(²)	0.2	(²)	0.1	(²)
Switzerland...........	0.9	0.9	0.9	0.9	0.9	0.9	0.7	0.7	1.7	1.6	1.3	1.2
France...............	0.9	0.9	0.9	0.9	0.9	0.9	0.6	0.6	1.9	1.9	1.3	1.1
Central and Eastern Europe:												
Germany...............	19.9	25.7	14.0	18.7	23.6	30.6	21.6	30.3	30.1	34.1	23.6	25.9
Austria...............	8.6	6.2	10.5	8.8	7.4	4.4	9.1	5.5	3.8	2.1	3.2	1.8
Hungary...............	3.1	2.2	4.4	3.7	2.3	1.1	3.0	1.5	0.7	0.3	0.4	0.2
Russia...............	10.6	7.9	14.7	12.0	8.2	5.0	10.7	6.8	3.0	1.3	1.8	0.7
Finland...............	0.8	0.7	1.1	1.0	0.6	0.4	0.8	0.6	0.2	0.1	0.2	0.1
Rumania...............	0.4	0.3	0.6	0.5	0.2	0.1	0.3	0.2	0.1	(²)	0.1	(²)
Bulgaria, Serbia, and Montenegro..............	0.1	0.1	0.2	0.2	(²)	(²)	0.1	(²)	(²)	(²)	(²)	(²)
Turkey in Europe......	0.1	0.1	0.1	0.2	(²)	(²)	(²)	(²)	(²)	(²)	(²)	(²)
Southern Europe:												
Greece...............	0.6	0.3	1.2	0.8	0.2	(²)	0.2	(²)	0.2	0.1	(²)	(²)
Italy................	9.2	6.5	11.8	10.1	7.6	4.0	9.9	5.4	3.2	1.3	0.8	0.3
Spain...............	0.2	0.1	0.4	0.2	0.1	0.1	0.1	(²)	0.2	0.1	0.1	0.1
Portugal.............	0.4	0.3	0.5	0.4	0.3	0.3	0.3	0.3	0.3	0.3	0.1	0.1
Europe, not specified.......	(²)	(²)	(²)	(²)	(²)	(²)	(²)	(²)	(²)	(²)	(²)	(²)
Asia:												
Turkey in Asia.........	0.5	0.2	0.7	0.4	0.3	0.1	0.4	0.1	0.1	(²)	(²)	(²)
All other countries.....	(²)	(²)	(²)	(²)	(²)	(²)	(²)	(²)	0.1	(²)	0.1	(²)
America:												
Canada—French.......	2.3	2.9	2.2	2.9	2.4	2.9	2.1	2.6	2.8	3.4	3.7	4.0
Canada—Other.........	4.8	5.7	4.1	6.1	5.3	5.4	2.2	2.4	10.3	9.9	15.7	15.4
Newfoundland..........	0.1	(²)	0.1	(²)	0.1	(²)	(²)	(²)	0.1	(²)	0.1	(²)
West Indies[3]...........	0.1	0.1	0.2	0.2	0.1	0.1	0.1	0.1	0.2	0.2	0.2	0.2
Mexico................	2.0	1.2	3.5	1.6	1.1	0.9	1.1	0.8	1.0	0.9	1.1	0.9
Central and South America..............	0.1	(²)	0.1	0.1	(²)	(²)	(²)	(²)	0.1	0.1	0.1	0.1
All other..................	0.3	0.2	0.4	0.3	0.3	0.2	0.2	0.1	0.4	0.3	0.4	0.3
Of mixed foreign parentage.	4.1	3.7	....	....	6.6	6.2	9.6	9.1	....	....	....	....

[1] For 1920, according to birthplace of father; for 1910, according to birthplace of person.

OF ORIGIN FOR NATIVITY AND PARENTAGE CLASSES, AND BY NATIVITY AND OF ORIGIN, FOR THE UNITED STATES: 1920 AND 1910.

constituted prior to the World War.]

COUNTRY OF ORIGIN.	PER CENT DISTRIBUTION BY NATIVITY AND PARENTAGE CLASSES.									
	Foreign-born white.[1]		Native white of foreign or mixed parentage.							
			Total.		Both parents foreign.		Father foreign.		Mother foreign.	
	1920	1910	1920	1910	1920	1910	1920	1910	1920	1910
Total	37.7	41.4	62.3	58.6	43.1	40.1	12.5	12.2	6.7	6.4
Northwestern Europe:										
England	35.7	37.7	64.3	62.3	24.9	25.5	24.8	23.5	14.6	13.2
Scotland	42.4	39.6	57.6	60.4	24.4	26.6	21.0	22.0	12.1	11.8
Wales	29.1	33.1	70.9	66.9	33.9	34.1	23.8	21.1	13.2	11.6
Ireland	28.2	30.0	71.8	70.0	47.6	47.5	13.9	13.4	10.4	9.0
Norway	35.4	41.2	64.6	58.8	42.8	42.0	14.0	10.9	7.8	5.9
Sweden	43.4	48.8	56.6	51.2	41.2	40.1	9.9	7.1	5.5	4.0
Denmark	41.0	45.4	59.0	54.6	36.5	36.9	15.8	12.4	6.7	5.3
Netherlands	37.0	40.9	63.0	59.1	39.3	39.6	15.8	13.0	7.8	6.5
Belgium	51.5	55.3	48.5	44.7	30.6	29.6	12.6	11.0	5.3	4.1
Luxemburg	29.8	44.2	70.2	55.8	37.7	34.3	25.2	17.9	7.3	3.6
Switzerland	35.8	41.4	64.2	58.6	31.6	30.1	23.0	20.3	9.7	8.3
France	37.4	40.1	62.6	59.9	27.0	27.0	25.9	25.0	9.7	7.9
Central and Eastern Europe:										
Germany	26.4	30.2	73.6	69.8	46.8	47.2	18.8	16.2	8.0	6.4
Austria	46.2	58.7	53.8	41.3	45.9	35.4	5.5	4.0	2.5	1.8
Hungary	53.8	70.8	46.2	29.2	42.5	27.3	2.7	1.4	1.0	0.5
Russia	52.2	63.1	47.8	36.9	43.2	34.3	3.5	2.0	1.1	0.6
Finland	50.9	61.4	49.1	38.6	43.9	36.1	3.3	1.6	1.9	0.8
Rumania	63.5	75.1	36.5	24.9	32.5	23.6	2.8	0.9	1.2	0.3
Bulgaria, Serbia, and Montenegro	74.8	94.6	25.2	5.4	22.2	4.2	2.7	1.1	0.3	0.2
Turkey in Europe	81.3	91.2	18.7	8.8	17.0	7.2	1.6	1.2	0.2	0.3
Southern Europe:										
Greece	78.5	92.3	21.5	7.7	17.4	5.0	3.9	2.2	0.1	0.4
Italy	48.4	64.0	51.6	36.0	46.6	33.1	4.4	2.5	0.6	0.3
Spain	67.6	66.3	32.4	33.7	19.2	13.2	10.2	16.2	3.0	4.2
Portugal	50.4	51.9	49.6	48.1	39.2	37.5	8.7	9.3	1.8	1.3
Europe, not specified	30.4	37.7	69.6	62.3	45.6	38.6	17.3	16.9	6.7	6.8
Asia:										
Turkey in Asia	61.3	75.9	38.7	24.1	35.2	22.2	2.9	1.6	0.5	0.2
All other countries	47.9	63.5	52.1	36.5	16.7	7.1	21.8	18.3	13.6	11.1
America:										
Canada—French	35.7	41.3	64.3	58.7	38.5	35.5	15.2	14.4	10.6	8.8
Canada—Other	31.8	44.5	68.2	55.5	19.6	16.9	26.6	21.3	22.0	17.4
Newfoundland	48.4	58.8	51.6	41.2	28.1	21.3	10.9	9.9	12.5	10.1
West Indies [3]	48.2	55.4	51.8	44.6	22.0	20.7	19.8	16.1	10.1	7.8
Mexico	65.3	57.5	34.7	42.5	24.6	28.2	6.3	9.2	3.9	5.1
Central and South America	60.5	67.1	39.5	32.9	7.3	6.0	18.4	15.2	13.8	11.7
All other	41.5	53.9	58.5	46.1	33.2	19.1	16.6	17.5	8.7	9.5
Of mixed foreign parentage			100.0	100.0	100.0	100.0				

[2] Less than one-tenth of 1 per cent.   [3] Except possessions of the United States.

TABLE **104.**—COUNTRY OF ORIGIN OF THE FOREIGN

[Figures relate to countries as

DIVISION AND STATE.	Total foreign white stock.	NORTHWESTERN EUROPE.						
		England.	Scotland.	Wales.	Ireland.	Norway.	Sweden.	Denmark.
United States	36,398,958	2,307,112	731,239	230,380	4,136,395	1,023,225	1,457,382	467,525
GEOGRAPHIC DIVISIONS:								
New England	4,512,930	324,095	111,369	7,264	925,051	15,551	138,102	17,097
Middle Atlantic	12,010,828	700,177	214,891	95,586	1,724,888	61,118	170,736	44,468
East North Central	9,148,492	514,407	157,105	55,323	657,662	235,795	382,816	102,847
West North Central	4,749,839	218,740	72,941	23,966	314,177	542,339	497,264	167,079
South Atlantic	869,524	72,408	24,898	6,251	102,689	5,198	10,139	4,606
East South Central	274,765	22,328	8,170	1,976	41,229	1,214	3,768	1,424
West South Central	1,155,942	52,985	15,531	3,166	55,250	7,519	19,020	7,183
Mountain	1,210,391	166,553	44,778	18,313	86,710	48,005	79,887	55,078
Pacific	2,466,247	235,419	81,556	18,535	228,739	106,486	155,650	67,743
NEW ENGLAND:								
Maine	269,915	13,544	6,041	448	24,216	1,221	4,668	2,411
New Hampshire	216,819	11,230	4,951	122	27,891	887	3,826	404
Vermont	123,492	6,880	5,097	1,464	16,428	228	2,377	345
Massachusetts	2,572,751	185,546	65,536	3,122	610,696	9,663	75,927	7,021
Rhode Island	420,427	52,942	12,444	549	79,640	973	13,571	659
Connecticut	909,526	53,953	17,300	1,559	166,180	2,579	37,733	6,257
MIDDLE ATLANTIC:								
New York	6,503,761	317,179	94,021	19,703	983,036	46,220	99,069	25,516
New Jersey	1,824,412	120,811	42,071	3,946	248,652	10,104	21,690	12,277
Pennsylvania	3,682,655	262,187	78,799	71,937	493,200	4,794	49,977	6,675
EAST NORTH CENTRAL:								
Ohio	1,902,771	131,502	35,034	29,574	151,698	3,181	16,505	5,399
Indiana	519,527	32,121	11,412	3,631	44,952	1,541	12,685	2,638
Illinois	3,232,770	159,304	55,872	10,861	301,924	66,088	235,329	37,004
Michigan	1,931,180	144,733	42,084	3,739	94,201	17,325	61,377	17,668
Wisconsin	1,562,244	46,747	12,703	7,518	61,887	147,660	56,920	40,138
WEST NORTH CENTRAL:								
Minnesota	1,541,309	36,873	14,860	3,730	65,869	280,982	280,077	44,487
Iowa	855,628	56,786	17,725	7,170	75,924	62,568	63,788	47,252
Missouri	688,108	41,598	11,983	3,769	82,213	1,925	13,339	4,733
North Dakota	431,988	8,913	5,352	606	11,336	127,561	28,606	12,728
South Dakota	310,549	12,601	3,885	1,653	14,619	58,866	24,128	16,975
Nebraska	522,155	26,438	7,864	2,507	32,151	7,092	55,057	33,956
Kansas	400,102	35,531	11,272	4,531	32,065	3,345	32,269	6,948
SOUTH ATLANTIC:								
Delaware	52,739	4,541	1,117	205	12,211	110	702	137
Maryland	311,649	15,645	6,483	1,904	33,533	1,076	1,491	851
District of Columbia	87,372	9,085	2,759	511	19,727	725	1,346	610
Virginia	83,415	10,588	3,751	555	9,385	1,008	1,405	855
West Virginia	144,378	10,887	3,460	2,239	11,107	134	822	268
North Carolina	18,576	2,829	1,305	89	1,545	156	376	135
South Carolina	19,120	1,677	725	42	2,675	179	276	190
Georgia	46,417	5,043	1,947	269	6,607	331	774	308
Florida	105,858	12,113	3,351	437	5,899	1,479	2,947	1,252
EAST SOUTH CENTRAL:								
Kentucky	141,426	7,864	2,241	679	23,595	191	578	282
Tennessee	53,236	5,758	1,827	693	8,846	194	806	363
Alabama	52,903	6,301	3,363	536	5,283	561	1,634	468
Mississippi	27,200	2,405	739	68	3,505	268	750	311
WEST SOUTH CENTRAL:								
Arkansas	53,065	5,256	1,585	387	5,053	300	1,016	510
Louisiana	154,887	6,818	1,783	259	14,104	964	1,297	839
Oklahoma	142,087	13,032	4,676	1,419	11,878	1,095	3,329	1,790
Texas	805,003	27,070	7,487	1,101	24,215	5,160	13,378	4,044
MOUNTAIN:								
Montana	258,457	22,809	9,175	2,515	28,448	27,824	16,841	7,456
Idaho	131,416	22,883	5,418	3,083	7,327	7,061	13,062	9,132
Wyoming	67,262	9,061	4,134	1,106	4,942	1,664	4,884	2,730
Colorado	321,062	32,150	11,257	4,672	28,370	4,111	24,384	6,850
New Mexico	61,356	3,034	1,386	257	2,466	380	839	332
Arizona	140,304	8,094	2,113	601	5,450	809	2,035	1,227
Utah	196,120	64,209	10,123	5,716	5,634	5,738	16,762	25,966
Nevada	34,414	4,313	1,172	363	4,073	418	1,080	1,385
PACIFIC:								
Washington	608,071	56,178	22,572	6,111	39,607	65,613	68,075	18,913
Oregon	271,420	25,525	10,965	2,024	18,355	16,120	22,004	8,703
California	1,586,756	153,716	48,019	10,400	170,777	24,753	65,571	40,127

WHITE STOCK, BY DIVISIONS AND STATES: 1920.

constituted prior to the World War.]

DIVISION AND STATE.	NORTHWESTERN EUROPE—continued.					CENTRAL AND EASTERN EUROPE.		
	Netherlands.	Belgium.	Luxemburg.	Switzerland.	France.	Germany.	Austria.	Hungary.
United States.........	362,318	122,686	43,109	327,797	333,678	7,259,992	3,129,798	1,110,905
GEOGRAPHIC DIVISIONS:								
New England............	5,993	6,389	203	7,629	21,887	162,381	194,105	41,962
Middle Atlantic..........	67,725	21,504	2,165	65,418	95,216	1,871,619	1,411,112	553,644
East North Central......	175,721	61,295	16,863	100,011	73,202	2,789,953	958,258	388,690
West North Central.....	72,080	16,477	19,764	56,819	34,437	1,407,203	292,995	58,228
South Atlantic...........	3,428	2,672	208	6,435	10,320	195,706	56,970	24,672
East South Central......	1,389	542	84	7,509	6,912	96,191	7,440	4,334
West South Central.....	3,458	2,818	411	11,364	29,362	246,190	80,831	5,234
Mountain................	12,610	3,128	1,155	19,091	12,247	135,662	53,502	17,439
Pacific..................	19,914	7,861	2,256	53,521	50,095	355,087	74,585	16,702
NEW ENGLAND:								
Maine...................	128	90	8	154	757	2,889	1,348	1,145
New Hampshire.........	300	648	5	171	546	4,464	7,718	201
Vermont................	103	54	2	266	539	2,146	2,699	634
Massachusetts..........	4,176	3,441	72	2,814	11,391	71,568	94,521	4,332
Rhode Island...........	272	1,415	25	415	2,531	9,622	15,035	584
Connecticut............	1,014	741	91	3,809	6,123	71,692	72,784	35,066
MIDDLE ATLANTIC:								
New York...............	32,841	7,830	1,200	30,743	52,822	1,029,448	614,102	156,895
New Jersey.............	30,892	4,144	325	16,333	16,471	303,194	193,591	98,086
Pennsylvania...........	3,992	9,530	640	18,342	25,923	538,977	603,419	298,663
EAST NORTH CENTRAL:								
Ohio....................	8,055	3,883	1,146	35,235	20,274	572,756	246,890	183,466
Indiana.................	6,458	4,997	388	10,438	10,052	225,661	36,948	24,622
Illinois.................	37,759	19,696	9,111	22,524	25,377	865,311	424,054	98,191
Michigan...............	98,705	18,581	1,350	8,913	12,092	413,284	132,336	53,845
Wisconsin..............	24,744	14,138	4,868	22,901	5,407	712,941	118,030	28,566
WEST NORTH CENTRAL:								
Minnesota..............	15,007	4,882	7,100	9,368	4,920	365,933	87,214	24,116
Iowa...................	35,587	2,987	6,919	10,798	6,464	314,491	42,100	3,951
Missouri...............	3,550	2,582	411	16,944	11,607	298,177	36,941	16,000
North Dakota...........	2,790	839	800	1,841	1,134	57,477	15,634	6,096
South Dakota...........	9,074	711	2,040	2,592	1,128	76,263	14,054	1,782
Nebraska...............	3,355	1,147	1,319	6,236	2,786	180,572	68,804	2,196
Kansas.................	2,717	3,329	1,175	9,040	6,398	114,290	28,248	4,087
SOUTH ATLANTIC:								
Delaware...............	90	38	6	156	496	6,393	4,919	539
Maryland...............	843	230	60	1,172	2,009	110,119	23,228	4,071
District of Columbia.....	366	127	33	835	1,447	16,178	1,570	435
Virginia................	628	208	25	682	1,275	12,957	4,417	3,561
West Virginia...........	237	1,577	9	1,981	1,506	20,929	18,797	14,469
North Carolina..........	182	36	2	218	357	2,902	397	132
South Carolina..........	78	98	3	63	338	4,861	785	103
Georgia................	235	120	12	437	1,083	8,547	1,254	586
Florida.................	769	238	58	891	1,809	12,820	1,603	776
EAST SOUTH CENTRAL:								
Kentucky...............	749	237	40	4,473	2,858	70,217	3,010	2,219
Tennessee..............	278	82	14	2,112	1,218	11,063	1,295	767
Alabama................	262	152	13	628	1,686	10,099	1,924	1,216
Mississippi.............	100	71	17	296	1,150	4,812	1,211	132
WEST SOUTH CENTRAL:								
Arkansas...............	423	207	20	2,049	1,556	18,751	3,264	505
Louisiana..............	586	967	16	1,225	16,524	30,699	3,221	849
Oklahoma..............	849	624	202	2,597	3,170	37,521	10,268	1,036
Texas..................	1,600	1,020	173	5,493	8,112	159,219	64,078	2,844
MOUNTAIN:								
Montana................	3,937	1,214	492	2,924	2,130	33,845	15,505	6,439
Idaho..................	1,194	259	210	4,326	1,325	17,855	3,033	744
Wyoming...............	390	240	61	953	822	8,944	5,923	1,303
Colorado...............	2,553	901	278	3,999	3,918	49,323	21,252	5,755
New Mexico............	250	154	24	447	877	5,086	1,815	709
Arizona................	273	165	50	788	1,083	6,399	2,069	1,038
Utah...................	3,913	151	32	4,749	1,037	10,567	2,975	1,066
Nevada................	100	44	8	905	1,055	3,643	930	385
PACIFIC:								
Washington............	7,517	2,590	840	8,898	6,073	82,790	23,564	4,142
Oregon................	2,568	1,531	395	9,921	3,216	51,224	9,904	2,260
California..............	9,829	3,740	1,021	34,702	40,806	221,073	41,117	10,300

TABLE **104.**—COUNTRY OF ORIGIN OF THE FOREIGN

[Figures relate to countries as

DIVISION AND STATE.	CENTRAL AND EASTERN EUROPE—con.					SOUTHERN EUROPE.				Europe, not specified.
	Russia.	Finland.	Rumania.	Bulgaria, Serbia, and Montenegro.	Turkey in Europe.	Greece.	Italy.	Spain.	Portugal.	
United States...	3,871,109	296,276	134,318	43,703	23,268	212,342	3,336,941	77,947	134,794	10,998
GEOG. DIVISIONS:										
New England	470,118	35,253	4,307	649	4,460	43,404	494,798	4,124	67,304	258
Middle Atlantic	1,908,800	26,796	77,876	8,342	9,979	50,878	1,939,300	22,515	4,228	2,073
East North Central	838,762	103,097	33,570	19,179	5,070	53,309	406,075	4,656	1,024	2,963
West North Central	301,845	68,761	8,466	4,501	733	13,206	70,558	1,481	173	1,510
South Atlantic	131,635	1,995	3,144	1,369	427	14,630	81,326	11,388	765	741
East South Central	18,276	403	656	191	94	2,779	19,849	806	62	494
West South Central	40,568	724	991	705	185	4,595	74,446	6,049	469	1,715
Mountain	60,950	14,843	1,144	4,150	555	10,807	56,525	6,893	639	228
Pacific	100,155	44,404	4,164	4,617	1,765	18,734	194,064	20,035	60,130	1,016
NEW ENGLAND:										
Maine	10,983	2,435	76	23	525	1,624	5,589	114	292	17
New Hampshire	9,143	3,038	28	23	311	6,647	3,922	48	184	10
Vermont	4,554	884	18	3	6	236	7,704	1,032	68	6
Massachusetts	274,600	26,173	1,893	409	2,958	28,230	238,178	1,341	49,215	112
Rhode Island	20,429	581	541	74	283	1,622	70,665	164	15,387	20
Connecticut	150,409	2,142	1,751	117	377	5,045	168,740	1,425	2,158	93
MIDDLE ATLANTIC:										
New York	1,168,518	18,158	58,886	1,727	7,662	28,830	1,124,433	16,872	2,268	1,015
New Jersey	227,963	3,524	5,302	386	396	5,848	344,468	2,719	863	287
Pennsylvania	512,319	5,114	13,688	6,229	1,921	16,200	470,399	2,924	1,097	771
E. NORTH CENTRAL:										
Ohio	150,074	12,764	12,928	7,749	2,125	14,624	119,501	1,607	374	532
Indiana	29,526	402	3,562	1,856	841	4,235	12,703	793	46	256
Illinois	391,415	4,885	8,901	3,885	991	21,589	195,804	1,448	459	1,127
Michigan	185,816	70,365	7,270	4,501	784	8,178	55,877	663	114	790
Wisconsin	81,931	14,681	909	1,188	329	4,683	22,190	145	31	258
W. NORTH CENTRAL:										
Minnesota	42,526	61,640	3,523	2,255	164	2,794	14,806	108	21	329
Iowa	16,465	164	412	791	72	3,341	9,689	119	34	317
Missouri	44,945	198	2,136	664	375	3,681	31,141	786	44	396
North Dakota	84,132	3,306	1,650	86	32	440	338	17	8	78
South Dakota	35,500	3,235	169	212	40	383	827	22	9	71
Nebraska	37,525	112	478	330	38	1,748	6,725	68	21	147
Kansas	40,752	106	98	163	12	819	7,032	361	36	172
SOUTH ATLANTIC:										
Delaware	8,919	60	181	2	1	377	8,319	169	21	13
Maryland	69,306	252	699	197	29	1,288	19,720	332	54	145
Dist. of Columbia	11,481	151	140	24	98	1,724	7,500	224	38	68
Virginia	12,662	347	258	58	45	2,277	5,505	391	192	166
West Virginia	12,256	455	722	958	135	3,541	26,808	2,129	18	104
North Carolina	2,520	29	56	29	20	734	998	53	29	22
South Carolina	2,881	78	31	8	19	770	776	66	14	30
Georgia	8,676	68	202	33	54	2,026	1,391	262	62	138
Florida	2,934	555	855	60	26	1,893	10,309	7,762	337	55
E. SOUTH CENTRAL:										
Kentucky	6,536	77	253	75	23	544	4,180	120	15	210
Tennessee	5,986	64	149	21	29	704	4,867	79	15	77
Alabama	3,645	123	197	65	40	1,255	6,457	264	17	140
Mississippi	2,109	139	57	30	2	276	4,345	343	15	67
W. SOUTH CENTRAL:										
Arkansas	1,905	29	83	33	3	405	2,977	72	14	32
Louisiana	1,807	226	115	141	30	813	40,403	3,127	225	369
Oklahoma	16,501	127	86	160	21	812	4,755	293	30	171
Texas	17,805	352	692	365	125	2,565	20,311	2,557	200	1,143
MOUNTAIN:										
Montana	13,013	7,155	320	1,193	263	1,413	6,535	123	47	34
Idaho	3,642	1,954	73	167	56	826	2,493	2,046	69	17
Wyoming	3,237	1,669	86	596	82	1,288	2,657	201	62	10
Colorado	36,675	1,675	482	653	51	2,078	28,527	629	71	114
New Mexico	672	69	13	129	14	328	3,471	399	57	15
Arizona	1,856	636	74	642	20	413	2,334	1,578	62	17
Utah	1,528	1,417	88	361	64	3,667	6,024	377	25	13
Nevada	327	268	8	409	5	694	4,484	1,540	246	8
PACIFIC:										
Washington	26,430	21,053	473	1,074	1,087	4,092	18,754	723	469	114
Oregon	14,745	11,398	372	480	244	2,011	7,550	888	335	53
California	58,980	11,953	3,319	3,063	434	12,631	167,760	18,424	59,326	849

WHITE STOCK, BY DIVISIONS AND STATES: 1920—Continued.

constituted prior to the World War.]

DIVISION AND STATE.	ASIA.		AMERICA.							Of mixed foreign parentage.
	Turkey in Asia.	All other.	Canada—French.	Canada—Other.	New foundland.	West Indies.[1]	Mexico.	Central and South America.	All other countries.	
United States.	164,480	10,735	848,309	1,755,519	25,448	45,496	725,332	19,487	116,458	1,502,457
GEOG. DIVISIONS:										
New England....	41,112	1,206	620,157	510,069	16,017	2,358	281	1,030	58,357	158,590
Middle Atlantic..	48,127	2,713	53,726	234,110	5,170	16,600	5,437	8,219	7,787	477,885
E. North Central.	28,127	2,631	102,655	490,220	1,625	1,656	7,966	1,529	8,354	366,076
W. North Central.	8,572	745	42,027	192,348	419	680	26,485	734	3,611	208,475
South Atlantic...	9,226	391	2,047	24,356	351	20,538	797	898	1,594	35,306
E. South Central.	3,490	129	508	7,271	69	482	756	254	570	13,116
W. South Central.	7,934	442	2,141	22,803	176	1,544	410,009	1,331	1,725	37,068
Mountain........	3,328	429	10,014	69,132	386	371	146,353	371	3,323	65,792
Pacific..........	14,564	2,049	15,034	205,210	1,235	1,267	127,248	5,121	31,137	140,149
NEW ENGLAND:										
Maine..........	1,555	46	86,110	93,947	406	124	12	31	222	6,716
New Hampshire..	1,417	17	90,246	32,642	336	51	9	40	152	5,191
Vermont........	554	19	39,419	25,949	124	21	10	22	81	3,520
Massachusetts....	27,954	478	287,897	318,502	14,007	1,406	178	679	50,198	98,517
Rhode Island.....	5,352	95	75,658	16,846	517	236	12	91	6,608	14,569
Connecticut......	4,280	551	40,827	22,183	627	520	60	167	1,096	30,077
MIDDLE ATLANTIC:										
New York.......	25,233	1,604	49,730	185,474	3,211	12,834	3,134	6,437	4,322	272,788
New Jersey......	7,652	534	2,004	19,246	989	1,894	462	862	1,357	75,069
Pennsylvania....	15,242	575	1,992	29,390	970	1,872	1,841	920	2,108	130,028
E. NORTH CENTRAL:										
Ohio............	8,748	369	4,030	46,456	329	566	1,019	374	1,570	72,434
Indiana.........	1,837	257	1,763	12,511	97	89	740	86	568	18,815
Illinois..........	5,210	1,260	14,322	74,437	615	570	4,592	629	2,768	126,458
Michigan........	10,127	621	62,206	314,844	438	303	1,387	285	1,453	84,925
Wisconsin.......	2,205	124	20,334	41,972	146	128	228	155	1,995	63,444
W. NORTH CENTRAL:										
Minnesota.......	1,926	173	26,430	67,064	148	93	333	106	829	70,623
Iowa............	1,180	137	2,032	29,169	54	151	3,093	118	691	33,089
Missouri........	2,110	130	1,272	16,738	81	296	3,815	177	883	32,468
North Dakota....	835	44	5,774	33,013	34	6	35	16	219	20,212
South Dakota....	646	72	2,126	12,948	17	17	92	37	179	13,576
Nebraska........	1,231	95	1,401	17,153	63	60	2,890	87	370	20,133
Kansas..........	644	94	2,992	16,263	22	57	16,227	193	440	18,374
SOUTH ATLANTIC:										
Delaware........	43	6	42	860	9	43	61	6	38	1,909
Maryland........	272	52	339	3,639	98	396	100	206	408	11,402
Dist. of Columbia.	624	55	467	3,747	44	191	71	170	197	4,604
Virginia.........	1,608	86	296	3,749	59	140	108	141	236	3,791
West Virginia....	2,553	13	137	1,949	5	25	81	31	127	3,909
North Carolina...	1,097	42	43	1,276	6	71	33	45	85	727
South Carolina...	788	14	63	584	9	67	11	32	32	754
Georgia..........	1,085	43	165	1,912	25	156	88	52	109	2,317
Florida..........	1,156	80	495	6,640	96	19,449	244	215	362	5,893
E. SOUTH CENTRAL:										
Kentucky........	791	41	150	2,160	27	51	172	47	235	6,486
Tennessee........	350	22	149	2,153	18	70	245	86	136	2,700
Alabama........	1,111	29	138	1,967	12	279	185	90	125	2,638
Mississippi.......	1,238	37	71	991	12	82	154	31	74	1,292
W. SOUTH CENTRAL:										
Arkansas........	478	23	213	2,360	21	40	366	38	166	2,867
Louisiana........	2,175	100	424	2,571	33	1,018	3,139	896	277	8,338
Oklahoma........	1,661	83	700	7,685	33	94	8,330	56	289	6,714
Texas..........	3,620	236	804	10,187	89	392	398,174	341	993	19,149
MOUNTAIN:										
Montana........	633	61	6,041	25,194	134	40	264	50	401	13,989
Idaho..........	148	54	1,376	11,036	110	21	1,271	20	602	8,523
Wyoming........	244	25	297	3,593	7	28	2,025	34	126	3,738
Colorado........	713	135	1,404	17,043	75	163	14,533	93	461	15,714
New Mexico......	454	38	163	1,664	8	30	34,083	15	75	1,603
Arizona.........	634	54	279	4,056	29	53	91,514	81	268	3,510
Utah...........	447	48	211	4,138	12	19	1,311	34	1,065	16,633
Nevada.........	55	14	243	2,408	11	17	1,352	44	325	2,082
PACIFIC:										
Washington......	1,213	371	7,175	73,205	539	145	507	296	1,488	35,380
Oregon..........	505	141	1,977	27,359	112	109	655	109	813	16,849
California........	12,846	1,537	5,882	104,646	584	1,013	126,086	4,716	28,836	87,920

[1] Except possessions of the United States.

TABLE 105.—PER CENT DISTRIBUTION OF THE FOREIGN WHITE

PER CENT WHICH SPECIFIED COUNTRY OF ORIGIN CONTRIBUTED TO TOTAL FOREIGN WHITE STOCK IN SPECIFIED DIVISION OR STATE.

	DIVISION AND STATE.	England.	Scotland.	Wales.	Ireland.	Norway.	Sweden.	Denmark.	Netherlands.	Belgium.	Luxemburg.	Switzerland.	France.	Germany.	Austria.	Hungary.
		Northwestern Europe.												Central and Eastern Europe.		
1	United States	6.3	2.0	0.6	11.4	2.8	4.0	1.3	1.0	0.3	0.1	0.9	0.9	19.9	8.6	3.1
	GEOGRAPHIC DIVISIONS:															
2	New England	7.2	2.5	0.2	20.5	0.3	3.1	0.4	0.1	0.1	(1)	0.2	0.5	3.6	4.3	0.9
3	Middle Atlantic	5.8	1.8	0.8	14.4	0.5	1.4	0.4	0.6	0.2	(1)	0.5	0.8	15.6	11.7	4.6
4	East North Central	5.6	1.7	0.6	7.2	2.6	4.2	1.1	1.9	0.7	0.2	1.1	0.8	30.5	10.5	4.2
5	West North Central	4.6	1.5	0.5	6.6	11.4	10.5	3.5	1.5	0.3	0.4	1.2	0.7	29.6	6.2	1.2
6	South Atlantic	8.3	2.9	0.7	11.8	0.6	1.2	0.5	0.4	0.3	(1)	0.7	1.2	22.5	6.6	2.8
7	East South Central	8.1	3.0	0.7	15.0	0.4	1.4	0.5	0.5	0.2	(1)	2.7	2.5	35.0	2.7	1.6
8	West South Central	4.6	1.3	0.3	4.8	0.7	1.6	0.6	0.3	0.2	(1)	1.0	2.5	21.3	7.0	0.5
9	Mountain	13.8	3.7	1.5	7.2	4.0	6.6	4.6	1.0	0.3	0.1	1.6	1.0	11.2	4.4	1.4
10	Pacific	9.5	3.3	0.8	9.3	4.3	6.3	2.7	0.8	0.3	0.1	2.2	2.0	14.4	3.0	0.7
	NEW ENGLAND:															
11	Maine	5.0	2.2	0.2	9.0	0.5	1.7	0.9	(1)	(1)	(1)	0.1	0.3	1.1	0.5	0.4
12	New Hampshire	5.2	2.3	0.1	12.9	0.4	1.8	0.2	0.1	0.3	(1)	0.1	0.3	2.1	3.6	0.1
13	Vermont	5.6	4.1	1.2	13.3	0.2	1.9	0.3	0.1	(1)	(1)	0.2	0.4	1.7	2.2	0.5
14	Massachusetts	7.2	2.5	0.1	23.7	0.4	3.0	0.3	0.2	0.1	(1)	0.1	0.4	2.8	3.7	0.2
15	Rhode Island	12.6	3.0	0.1	18.9	0.2	3.2	0.2	0.1	0.3	(1)	0.1	0.6	2.3	3.6	0.1
16	Connecticut	5.9	1.9	0.2	18.3	0.3	4.1	0.7	0.1	0.1	(1)	0.4	0.7	7.9	8.0	3.9
	MIDDLE ATLANTIC:															
17	New York	4.9	1.4	0.3	15.1	0.7	1.5	0.4	0.5	0.1	(1)	0.5	0.8	15.8	9.4	2.4
18	New Jersey	6.6	2.3	0.2	13.6	0.6	1.2	0.7	1.7	0.2	(1)	0.9	0.9	16.6	10.6	5.4
19	Pennsylvania	7.1	2.1	2.0	13.4	0.1	1.4	0.2	0.1	0.3	(1)	0.5	0.7	14.6	16.4	8.1
	EAST NORTH CENTRAL:															
20	Ohio	6.9	1.8	1.6	8.0	0.2	0.9	0.3	0.4	0.2	0.1	1.9	1.1	30.1	13.0	9.6
21	Indiana	6.2	2.2	0.7	8.7	0.3	2.4	0.5	1.2	1.0	0.1	2.0	1.9	43.4	7.1	4.7
22	Illinois	4.9	1.7	0.3	9.4	2.0	7.3	1.1	1.2	0.6	0.3	0.7	0.8	26.8	13.1	3.0
23	Michigan	7.5	2.2	0.2	4.9	0.9	3.2	0.9	5.1	1.0	0.1	0.5	0.6	21.4	6.9	2.8
24	Wisconsin	3.0	0.8	0.5	4.0	9.5	3.6	2.6	1.6	0.9	0.3	1.5	0.3	45.6	7.6	1.8
	WEST NORTH CENTRAL:															
25	Minnesota	2.4	1.0	0.2	4.3	18.2	18.2	2.9	1.0	0.3	0.5	0.6	0.3	23.7	5.7	1.6
26	Iowa	6.6	2.1	0.8	8.9	7.3	7.5	5.5	4.2	0.3	0.8	1.3	0.8	36.8	4.9	0.5
27	Missouri	6.0	1.7	0.5	11.9	0.3	1.9	0.7	0.5	0.4	0.1	2.5	1.7	43.3	5.4	2.3
28	North Dakota	2.1	1.2	0.1	2.6	29.5	6.6	2.9	0.6	0.2	0.2	0.4	0.3	13.3	3.6	1.4
29	South Dakota	4.1	1.3	0.5	4.7	19.0	7.8	5.5	2.9	0.2	0.7	0.8	0.4	24.6	4.5	0.6
30	Nebraska	5.1	1.5	0.5	6.2	1.4	10.5	6.5	0.6	0.2	0.3	1.2	0.5	34.6	13.2	0.4
31	Kansas	8.9	2.8	1.1	8.0	0.8	8.1	1.7	0.7	0.8	0.3	2.3	1.6	28.6	7.1	1.0
	SOUTH ATLANTIC:															
32	Delaware	8.6	2.1	0.4	23.2	0.2	1.3	0.3	0.2	0.1	(1)	0.3	0.9	12.1	9.3	1.0
33	Maryland	5.0	2.1	0.6	10.8	0.3	0.5	0.3	0.3	0.1	(1)	0.4	0.6	35.3	7.5	1.3
34	District of Columbia	10.4	3.2	0.6	22.6	0.8	1.5	0.7	0.4	0.1	(1)	1.0	1.7	18.5	1.8	0.5
35	Virginia	12.7	4.5	0.7	11.3	1.2	1.7	1.0	0.8	0.2	(1)	0.8	1.5	15.5	5.3	4.3
36	West Virginia	7.5	2.4	1.6	7.7	0.1	0.6	0.2	0.2	1.1	(1)	1.1	1.0	14.5	13.0	10.0
37	North Carolina	15.2	7.0	0.5	8.3	0.8	2.0	0.7	1.0	0.2	(1)	1.2	1.9	15.6	2.1	0.7
38	South Carolina	8.8	3.8	0.2	14.0	0.9	1.4	1.0	0.4	0.5	(1)	0.3	1.8	25.4	4.1	0.5
39	Georgia	10.9	4.2	0.6	14.2	0.7	1.7	0.7	0.5	0.3	(1)	0.9	2.3	18.4	2.7	1.3
40	Florida	11.4	3.2	0.4	5.6	1.4	2.8	1.2	0.7	0.2	0.1	0.8	1.7	12.1	1.5	0.7
	EAST SOUTH CENTRAL:															
41	Kentucky	5.6	1.6	0.5	16.7	0.1	0.4	0.2	0.5	0.2	(1)	3.2	2.0	49.6	2.1	1.6
42	Tennessee	10.8	3.4	1.3	16.6	0.4	1.5	0.7	0.5	0.2	(1)	4.0	2.3	20.8	2.4	1.4
43	Alabama	11.9	6.4	1.0	10.0	1.1	3.1	0.9	0.5	0.3	(1)	1.2	3.2	19.1	3.6	2.3
44	Mississippi	8.8	2.7	0.3	12.9	1.0	2.8	1.1	0.4	0.3	0.1	1.1	4.2	17.7	4.5	0.5
	WEST SOUTH CENTRAL:															
45	Arkansas	9.9	3.0	0.7	9.5	0.6	1.9	1.0	1.0	0.8	0.4	3.9	2.9	35.3	6.9	1.0
46	Louisiana	4.4	1.2	0.2	9.1	0.6	0.8	0.5	0.4	0.6	(1)	0.8	10.7	19.8	2.1	0.5
47	Oklahoma	9.2	3.3	1.0	8.4	0.8	2.3	1.3	0.6	0.4	0.1	1.8	2.2	26.4	7.2	0.7
48	Texas	3.5	0.9	0.1	3.0	0.6	1.7	0.5	0.2	0.1	(1)	0.7	1.0	19.8	8.0	0.4
	MOUNTAIN:															
49	Montana	8.8	3.5	1.0	11.0	10.8	6.5	2.9	1.5	0.5	0.2	1.1	0.8	13.1	6.0	2.5
50	Idaho	17.4	4.1	2.3	5.6	5.4	9.9	6.9	0.9	0.2	0.2	3.3	1.0	13.6	2.3	0.6
51	Wyoming	13.5	6.1	1.6	7.3	2.5	7.3	4.1	0.6	0.4	0.1	1.4	1.2	13.3	8.8	1.9
52	Colorado	10.0	3.5	1.5	8.8	1.3	7.6	2.1	0.8	0.3	0.1	1.2	1.2	15.4	6.6	1.8
53	New Mexico	4.9	2.3	0.4	4.0	0.6	1.4	0.5	0.4	0.3	(1)	0.7	1.4	8.3	3.0	1.2
54	Arizona	5.8	1.5	0.4	3.9	0.6	1.5	0.9	0.2	0.1	(1)	0.6	0.8	4.6	1.5	0.7
55	Utah	32.7	5.2	2.9	2.9	2.9	8.5	13.2	2.0	0.1	(1)	2.4	0.5	5.4	1.5	0.5
56	Nevada	12.5	3.4	1.1	11.8	1.2	3.1	4.0	0.3	0.1	(1)	2.6	3.1	10.6	2.7	1.1
	PACIFIC:															
57	Washington	9.2	3.7	1.0	6.5	10.8	11.2	3.1	1.2	0.4	0.1	1.5	1.0	13.6	3.9	0.7
58	Oregon	9.4	4.0	0.7	6.8	5.9	8.1	3.2	0.9	0.6	0.1	3.7	1.2	18.9	3.6	0.8
59	California	9.7	3.0	0.7	10.8	1.6	4.1	2.5	0.6	0.2	0.1	2.2	2.6	13.9	2.6	0.6

1 Less than one-tenth of 1 per cent.

STOCK BY COUNTRY OF ORIGIN, BY DIVISIONS AND STATES: 1920.

PER CENT WHICH SPECIFIED COUNTRY OF ORIGIN CONTRIBUTED TO TOTAL FOREIGN WHITE STOCK IN SPECIFIED DIVISION OR STATE—continued.

Central and Eastern Europe—Con.					Southern Europe.				Europe, not specified.	Asia.		America.						All other countries.	Of mixed foreign parentage.	
Russia.	Finland.	Rumania.	Bulgaria, Serbia, and Montenegro.	Turkey in Europe.	Greece.	Italy.	Spain.	Portugal.		Turkey in Asia.	All other.	French (Canada).	Other (Canada).	Newfoundland.	West Indies.[2]	Mexico.	Central and South America.			
10.6	0.8	0.4	0.1	0.1	0.6	9.2	0.2	0.4	(¹)	0.5	(¹)	2.3	4.8	0.1	0.1	2.0	0.1	0.3	4.1	1
10.4	0.8	0.1	(¹)	0.1	1.0	11.0	0.1	1.5	(¹)	0.9	(¹)	13.7	11.3	0.4	0.1	(¹)	(¹)	1.3	3.5	2
15.9	0.2	0.6	0.1	0.1	0.4	16.1	0.2	(¹)	(¹)	0.4	(¹)	0.4	1.9	(¹)	0.1	(¹)	0.1	0.1	4.0	3
9.2	1.1	0.4	0.2	0.1	0.6	4.4	0.1	(¹)	(¹)	0.3	(¹)	1.1	5.4	(¹)	(¹)	0.1	(¹)	0.1	4.0	4
6.4	1.4	0.2	0.1	(¹)	0.3	1.5	(¹)	(¹)	(¹)	0.2	(¹)	0.9	4.0	(¹)	(¹)	0.6	(¹)	0.1	4.4	5
15.1	0.2	0.4	0.2	(¹)	1.7	9.4	1.3	0.1	0.1	1.1	(¹)	0.2	2.8	(¹)	2.4	0.1	0.1	0.2	4.1	6
6.7	0.1	0.2	0.1	(¹)	1.0	7.2	0.3	(¹)	0.2	1.3	(¹)	0.2	2.6	(¹)	0.2	0.3	0.1	0.2	4.8	7
3.5	0.1	0.1	0.1	(¹)	0.4	6.4	0.5	(¹)	0.1	0.7	(¹)	0.2	2.0	(¹)	0.1	35.5	0.1	0.1	3.2	8
5.0	1.2	0.1	0.3	(¹)	0.9	4.7	0.6	0.1	(¹)	0.3	(¹)	0.8	5.7	(¹)	(¹)	12.1	(¹)	0.3	5.4	9
4.1	1.8	0.2	0.2	0.1	0.8	7.9	0.8	2.4	(¹)	0.6	0.1	0.6	8.3	0.1	0.1	5.2	0.2	1.3	5.7	10
4.1	0.9	(¹)	(¹)	0.2	0.6	2.1	(¹)	0.1	(¹)	0.6	(¹)	31.9	34.8	0.2	(¹)	(¹)	(¹)	0.1	2.5	11
4.2	1.4	(¹)	(¹)	0.1	3.1	1.8	(¹)	0.1	(¹)	0.7	(¹)	41.6	15.1	0.2	(¹)	(¹)	(¹)	0.1	2.4	12
3.7	0.7	(¹)	(¹)	(¹)	0.2	6.2	0.8	0.1	(¹)	0.4	(¹)	31.9	21.0	0.1	(¹)	(¹)	(¹)	0.1	2.9	13
10.7	1.0	0.1	(¹)	0.1	1.1	9.3	0.1	1.9	(¹)	1.1	(¹)	11.2	12.4	0.5	0.1	(¹)	(¹)	2.0	3.8	14
4.9	0.1	0.1	(¹)	0.1	0.4	16.8	(¹)	3.7	(¹)	1.3	(¹)	18.0	4.0	0.1	0.1	(¹)	(¹)	1.6	3.5	15
16.5	0.2	0.2	(¹)	(¹)	0.6	18.6	0.2	0.2	(¹)	0.5	0.1	4.5	2.4	0.1	0.1	(¹)	(¹)	0.1	3.3	16
18.0	0.3	0.9	(¹)	0.1	0.4	17.3	0.3	(¹)	(¹)	0.4	(¹)	0.8	2.9	(¹)	0.2	(¹)	0.1	0.1	4.2	17
12.5	0.2	0.3	(¹)	0.1	0.3	18.9	0.1	(¹)	(¹)	0.4	(¹)	0.1	1.1	(¹)	0.1	(¹)	(¹)	0.1	4.1	18
13.9	0.1	0.4	0.2	0.1	0.4	12.8	0.1	(¹)	(¹)	0.4	(¹)	0.1	0.8	(¹)	0.1	(¹)	(¹)	0.1	3.5	19
7.9	0.7	0.7	0.4	0.1	0.8	6.3	0.1	(¹)	(¹)	0.5	(¹)	0.2	2.4	(¹)	(¹)	0.1	(¹)	0.1	3.8	20
5.7	0.1	0.7	0.4	0.2	0.8	2.4	0.2	(¹)	(¹)	0.4	(¹)	0.3	2.4	(¹)	(¹)	0.1	(¹)	0.1	3.6	21
12.1	0.2	0.3	0.1	(¹)	0.7	6.1	(¹)	(¹)	(¹)	0.2	(¹)	0.4	2.3	(¹)	(¹)	0.1	(¹)	0.1	3.9	22
9.6	3.6	0.4	0.2	(¹)	0.4	2.9	(¹)	(¹)	(¹)	0.5	(¹)	3.2	16.3	(¹)	(¹)	0.1	(¹)	0.1	4.4	23
5.2	0.9	0.1	0.1	(¹)	0.3	1.4	(¹)	(¹)	(¹)	0.1	(¹)	1.3	2.7	(¹)	(¹)	0.1	(¹)	0.1	4.1	24
2.8	4.0	0.2	0.1	(¹)	0.2	1.0	(¹)	(¹)	(¹)	0.1	(¹)	1.7	4.4	(¹)	(¹)	(¹)	(¹)	0.1	4.6	25
1.9	(¹)	(¹)	0.1	(¹)	0.4	1.1	(¹)	(¹)	(¹)	0.1	(¹)	0.2	3.4	(¹)	(¹)	0.4	(¹)	0.1	3.9	26
6.5	(¹)	0.3	0.1	0.1	0.5	4.5	0.1	(¹)	0.1	0.3	(¹)	0.2	2.4	(¹)	(¹)	0.6	(¹)	0.1	4.7	27
19.5	0.8	0.4	(¹)	(¹)	0.1	0.1	(¹)	(¹)	(¹)	0.2	(¹)	1.3	7.6	(¹)	(¹)	(¹)	(¹)	0.1	4.7	28
11.4	1.0	0.1	0.1	0.1	0.1	0.3	(¹)	(¹)	(¹)	0.2	(¹)	0.7	4.2	(¹)	(¹)	(¹)	(¹)	0.1	4.4	29
7.2	(¹)	0.1	0.1	(¹)	0.3	1.3	(¹)	(¹)	(¹)	0.2	(¹)	0.3	3.3	(¹)	(¹)	0.6	(¹)	0.1	3.9	30
10.2	(¹)	(¹)	(¹)	(¹)	0.2	1.8	0.1	(¹)	(¹)	0.2	(¹)	0.7	4.1	(¹)	(¹)	4.1	(¹)	0.1	4.6	31
16.9	0.1	0.3	(¹)	(¹)	0.7	15.8	0.3	(¹)	(¹)	0.1	(¹)	0.1	1.6	(¹)	0.1	0.1	(¹)	0.1	3.6	32
22.2	0.1	0.2	0.1	(¹)	0.4	6.3	0.1	(¹)	(¹)	0.1	(¹)	0.1	1.2	(¹)	0.1	(¹)	0.1	0.1	3.7	33
13.1	0.2	0.2	(¹)	0.1	2.0	8.6	0.3	(¹)	0.1	0.7	0.1	0.5	4.3	0.1	0.2	0.1	0.2	0.2	5.3	34
15.2	0.4	0.3	0.1	0.1	2.7	6.6	0.5	0.2	0.2	1.9	0.1	0.4	4.5	0.1	0.2	0.1	0.2	0.3	4.5	35
8.5	0.3	0.5	0.7	0.1	2.5	18.6	1.5	(¹)	0.1	1.8	(¹)	0.1	1.3	(¹)	(¹)	0.1	(¹)	0.1	2.7	36
13.6	0.2	0.3	0.2	0.1	4.0	5.4	0.3	0.2	0.1	5.9	0.2	0.2	6.9	(¹)	0.4	0.2	0.2	0.5	3.9	37
15.1	0.4	0.2	(¹)	0.1	4.0	4.1	0.3	0.1	0.2	4.1	0.1	0.3	3.1	(¹)	0.4	0.1	0.2	0.2	3.9	38
18.7	0.1	0.4	0.1	0.1	4.4	3.0	0.6	0.1	0.3	2.3	0.1	0.4	4.1	0.1	0.3	0.2	0.1	0.2	5.0	39
2.8	0.5	0.8	0.1	(¹)	1.8	9.7	7.3	0.3	0.1	1.1	0.1	0.5	6.3	0.1	18.4	0.2	0.2	0.3	5.6	40
4.6	0.1	0.2	0.1	(¹)	0.4	3.0	0.1	(¹)	0.1	0.6	(¹)	0.1	1.5	(¹)	(¹)	0.1	(¹)	0.2	4.6	41
11.2	0.1	0.3	(¹)	0.1	1.3	9.1	0.1	(¹)	0.1	0.6	(¹)	0.3	4.0	(¹)	0.1	0.5	0.2	0.3	5.1	42
6.9	0.2	0.4	0.1	0.1	2.4	12.2	0.5	(¹)	0.3	2.1	0.1	0.3	3.7	(¹)	0.5	0.3	0.2	0.2	5.0	43
7.8	0.5	0.2	0.1	(¹)	1.0	16.0	1.3	0.1	0.2	4.6	0.1	0.3	3.6	(¹)	0.3	0.6	0.1	0.3	4.8	44
3.7	(¹)	0.2	0.1	(¹)	0.8	5.6	0.1	(¹)	0.1	0.9	(¹)	0.4	4.4	(¹)	0.1	0.7	0.1	0.3	5.4	45
2.8	0.1	0.1	0.1	(¹)	0.5	30.0	2.0	0.1	0.2	1.4	0.1	0.3	1.7	(¹)	0.7	2.0	0.6	0.2	5.4	46
11.6	0.1	0.1	0.1	(¹)	0.6	3.3	0.2	(¹)	0.1	1.2	0.1	0.5	5.4	(¹)	0.1	5.9	(¹)	0.2	4.7	47
2.2	(¹)	0.1	(¹)	(¹)	0.3	2.5	0.3	(¹)	0.1	0.4	(¹)	0.1	1.3	(¹)	(¹)	49.4	(¹)	0.1	2.4	48
5.0	2.8	0.1	0.5	0.1	0.5	2.5	(¹)	(¹)	(¹)	0.2	(¹)	2.3	9.7	0.1	(¹)	0.1	(¹)	0.2	5.4	49
2.8	1.5	0.1	0.1	(¹)	0.6	1.9	1.6	0.1	(¹)	0.1	(¹)	1.0	8.4	0.1	(¹)	1.0	(¹)	0.5	6.5	50
4.8	2.5	0.1	0.9	0.1	2.1	4.0	0.3	0.1	(¹)	0.4	(¹)	0.4	5.3	(¹)	0.1	3.0	0.1	0.2	5.6	51
11.4	0.5	0.2	0.2	(¹)	0.6	8.9	0.2	(¹)	(¹)	0.2	(¹)	0.4	5.3	(¹)	0.1	4.5	(¹)	0.1	4.9	52
1.1	0.1	(¹)	0.2	(¹)	0.5	5.7	0.7	0.1	(¹)	0.7	0.1	0.3	2.7	(¹)	(¹)	55.5	(¹)	0.1	2.6	53
1.3	0.5	0.1	0.5	(¹)	0.3	1.7	1.1	(¹)	(¹)	0.5	(¹)	0.2	2.9	(¹)	(¹)	65.2	0.1	0.2	2.5	54
0.8	0.7	(¹)	0.2	(¹)	1.9	3.1	0.2	(¹)	(¹)	0.2	(¹)	0.1	2.1	(¹)	(¹)	0.7	(¹)	0.5	8.5	55
1.0	0.8	(¹)	1.2	(¹)	2.0	13.0	4.5	0.7	(¹)	0.2	(¹)	0.7	7.0	(¹)	(¹)	3.9	0.1	0.9	6.0	56
4.3	3.5	0.1	0.2	0.2	0.7	3.1	0.1	0.1	(¹)	0.2	0.1	1.2	12.0	0.1	(¹)	0.1	(¹)	0.2	5.8	57
5.4	4.2	0.1	0.2	0.1	0.7	2.8	0.3	0.1	0.1	0.2	0.1	0.7	10.1	(¹)	(¹)	0.2	(¹)	0.3	6.2	58
3.7	0.8	0.2	0.2	(¹)	0.8	10.6	1.2	3.7	0.1	0.8	0.1	0.4	6.6	(¹)	0.1	7.9	0.3	1.8	5.5	59

[2] Except possessions of the United States.

TABLE **106.**—COUNTRY OF ORIGIN OF THE FOREIGN WHITE

[Figures relate to countries as

CITY.	Total foreign white stock: 1920	NORTHWESTERN EUROPE.						
		England.	Scotland.	Wales.	Ireland.	Norway.	Sweden.	Denmark.
Akron, Ohio	77,639	6,282	1,721	1,229	4,279	312	1,572	417
Albany, N. Y	55,771	3,205	1,072	132	15,254	56	247	174
Atlanta, Ga	12,837	1,354	516	67	1,194	50	236	74
Baltimore, Md	246,750	8,604	2,520	669	24,711	802	936	510
Birmingham, Ala	16,339	2,063	1,332	235	1,255	56	232	63
Boston, Mass	548,674	24,590	11,639	553	174,883	2,975	12,027	1,678
Bridgeport, Conn	104,404	7,178	1,726	132	16,124	294	3,437	774
Buffalo, N. Y	336,907	17,178	5,339	633	32,195	621	2,464	577
Cambridge, Mass	75,205	3,693	1,801	128	26,066	288	2,050	179
Camden, N. J	51,504	4,820	952	234	5,997	413	406	135
Chicago, Ill	1,946,298	60,998	25,173	4,354	199,956	44,961	121,326	22,615
Cincinnati, Ohio	164,492	5,709	1,509	619	20,566	93	257	227
Cleveland, Ohio	549,779	26,146	7,718	3,428	35,305	1,053	4,410	1,273
Columbus, Ohio	55,652	4,035	1,091	2,059	7,974	105	343	110
Dallas, Tex	22,379	2,085	598	88	1,949	219	460	248
Dayton, Ohio	42,499	1,910	567	166	4,294	75	171	60
Denver, Colo	104,966	10,780	3,640	1,290	13,751	1,331	8,910	1,982
Des Moines, Iowa	36,526	4,345	1,319	853	4,126	1,231	5,210	1,159
Detroit, Mich	638,068	39,131	16,587	1,534	32,412	2,241	6,379	2,954
Fall River, Mass	100,946	17,514	1,366	140	12,493	63	138	59
Fort Worth, Tex	14,951	1,107	392	54	1,431	146	407	82
Grand Rapids, Mich	80,393	3,320	855	75	3,571	392	2,280	621
Hartford, Conn	93,354	4,517	1,994	113	20,930	161	4,390	1,292
Houston, Tex	31,835	2,508	596	91	2,110	171	482	307
Indianapolis, Ind	60,114	3,769	1,405	265	11,123	145	484	603
Jersey City, N. J	202,926	9,184	3,693	402	46,644	2,292	2,212	790
Kansas City, Kans	30,128	1,862	517	271	3,731	120	1,588	472
Kansas City, Mo	84,383	6,649	2,383	590	13,633	574	5,068	1,020
Los Angeles, Calif	252,406	28,324	8,291	2,043	20,948	3,876	10,462	4,091
Louisville, Ky	55,366	1,995	632	85	9,496	52	187	115
Lowell, Mass	87,833	7,129	1,994	57	23,595	144	1,093	54
Memphis, Tenn	18,318	1,421	473	53	2,947	50	316	140
Milwaukee, Wis	323,979	6,005	1,931	876	10,038	5,112	2,175	1,997
Minneapolis, Minn	243,187	8,521	3,668	871	13,614	41,237	61,514	5,717
Nashville, Tenn	8,681	765	260	18	2,025	24	44	37
New Bedford, Mass	96,044	16,060	1,106	95	6,858	106	519	110
New Haven, Conn	113,415	4,633	1,874	143	24,862	276	2,744	498
New Orleans, La	95,275	4,060	1,048	96	11,091	685	696	507
New York, N. Y	4,294,629	136,605	47,103	3,777	616,627	40,544	57,750	14,914
Bronx borough	594,220	14,904	5,657	351	67,429	1,803	6,133	1,416
Brooklyn borough	1,528,713	53,764	17,816	1,207	199,709	29,392	28,450	7,075
Manhattan borough	1,780,627	48,639	16,881	1,717	293,627	4,884	16,802	4,170
Queens borough	314,319	14,683	5,102	354	41,945	1,728	4,828	1,608
Richmond borough	76,750	4,615	1,647	148	13,917	2,737	1,537	645
Newark, N. J	283,810	13,128	4,965	348	33,219	323	1,559	784
Norfolk, Va	14,467	1,152	388	59	1,349	259	337	134
Oakland, Calif	113,725	12,029	4,362	1,750	13,500	2,523	5,495	3,764
Omaha, Nebr	94,521	4,542	1,790	300	9,579	1,057	9,282	6,423
Paterson, N. J	102,430	9,165	4,251	90	11,886	52	268	104
Philadelphia, Pa	989,398	75,273	19,473	3,669	222,246	2,231	5,115	2,272
Pittsburgh, Pa	333,731	20,216	7,465	4,913	53,749	216	2,439	249
Portland, Oreg	116,745	11,015	4,813	864	8,872	6,309	10,114	3,081
Providence, R. I	168,028	18,595	4,044	177	41,551	468	5,187	250
Reading, Pa	25,851	1,074	233	241	1,419	30	57	27
Richmond, Va	14,618	1,600	674	82	1,744	42	109	66
Rochester, N. Y	182,113	14,421	3,145	268	19,877	179	933	366
St. Louis, Mo	343,133	13,119	3,624	624	44,405	427	2,307	1,128
St. Paul, Minn	153,793	5,126	2,174	291	15,048	10,499	24,581	4,283
Salt Lake City, Utah	60,547	10,930	3,493	1,670	2,720	2,056	5,461	4,633
San Antonio, Tex	70,500	2,405	527	43	2,309	150	309	193
San Francisco, Calif	322,843	23,132	8,592	1,204	63,299	5,397	11,407	6,278
Scranton, Pa	88,499	6,584	1,228	8,991	17,368	13	214	48
Seattle, Wash	162,879	18,175	7,807	1,835	13,370	17,628	18,855	4,656
Spokane, Wash	46,056	4,600	1,830	458	4,043	3,780	5,395	1,095
Springfield, Mass	77,854	4,751	2,885	102	19,351	154	2,491	185
Syracuse, N. Y	90,300	6,664	1,424	344	17,334	84	330	169
Toledo, Ohio	113,330	5,986	1,337	332	8,201	237	634	387
Trenton, N. J	70,707	6,826	1,178	124	7,746	28	185	142
Washington, D. C	87,372	9,085	2,759	511	19,727	725	1,346	610
Wilmington, Del	42,514	2,992	780	142	9,999	89	485	73
Worcester, Mass	127,675	7,175	2,094	110	31,365	544	15,856	446
Yonkers, N. Y	68,119	4,554	2,601	176	15,442	333	753	209
Youngstown, Ohio	79,136	6,881	2,577	3,708	7,338	115	1,884	99

STOCK, FOR CITIES HAVING 100,000 INHABITANTS OR MORE: 1920.

constituted prior to the World War.]

CITY.	NORTHWESTERN EUROPE—continued.					CENTRAL AND EASTERN EUROPE.		
	Nether-lands.	Bel-gium.	Luxem-burg.	Switzer-land.	France.	Germany.	Austria.	Hun-gary.
Akron, Ohio	281	134	10	1,212	1,041	12,988	10,688	10,957
Albany, N. Y	754	40	59	179	367	13,663	2,260	152
Atlanta, Ga	44	28	2	145	316	2,038	356	236
Baltimore, Md	541	135	24	677	1,386	87,498	20,079	2,618
Birmingham, Ala	38	40		149	453	1,987	386	129
Boston, Mass	1,313	797	18	669	2,100	18,814	8,691	900
Bridgeport, Conn	132	73	10	289	504	6,374	9,658	15,875
Buffalo, N. Y	1,226	217	116	1,696	3,279	114,250	37,295	5,697
Cambridge, Mass	56	36		53	238	1,382	1,242	90
Camden, N. J	86	49	18	261	417	9,319	5,562	496
Chicago, Ill	22,136	4,975	5,080	7,766	9,142	421,443	316,295	70,209
Cincinnati, Ohio	1,213	96	69	1,717	2,234	93,460	4,363	5,395
Cleveland, Ohio	2,778	184	188	3,380	2,048	102,441	124,900	75,666
Columbus, Ohio	163	115	11	1,120	786	20,748	1,795	1,574
Dallas, Tex	100	59	8	431	520	4,831	1,019	114
Dayton, Ohio	189	44	27	373	585	20,194	1,974	3,589
Denver, Colo	1,084	153	69	1,220	1,408	17,889	4,157	1,208
Des Moines, Iowa	467	79	10	334	407	5,734	934	119
Detroit, Mich	4,230	9,350	251	2,508	4,604	148,747	58,378	25,746
Fall River, Mass	19	33		14	172	491	4,420	26
Fort Worth, Tex	37	14	1	108	236	2,082	803	31
Grand Rapids, Mich	30,846	110	16	171	337	12,241	4,257	278
Hartford, Conn	98	27	28	210	410	5,929	6,182	698
Houston, Tex	151	66	9	285	826	7,939	1,611	218
Indianapolis, Ind	433	61	27	786	1,029	25,249	2,164	611
Jersey City, N. J	563	322	25	1,031	1,573	37,385	21,091	2,664
Kansas City, Kans	122	289	9	299	301	5,651	3,818	2,664
Kansas City, Mo	354	786	48	1,145	1,309	18,134	2,613	794
Los Angeles, Calif	1,807	703	250	2,925	6,222	38,522	8,080	3,246
Louisville, Ky	247	93	9	2,172	1,047	29,379	842	188
Lowell, Mass	38	223	1	9	154	561	2,434	40
Memphis, Tenn	72	18	2	225	472	3,767	463	194
Milwaukee, Wis	2,026	388	888	2,219	998	187,933	27,813	12,200
Minneapolis, Minn	974	312	591	1,182	1,189	33,955	13,119	3,101
Nashville, Tenn	42	14	5	284	203	1,830	222	321
New Bedford, Mass	21	213		78	543	1,185	4,038	84
New Haven, Conn	124	207	3	265	432	9,075	3,962	910
New Orleans, La	346	217	6	796	11,213	22,192	1,724	185
New York, N. Y	9,552	4,342	486	16,063	33,957	584,838	431,397	123,175
Bronx borough	1,146	341	40	2,361	2,965	88,614	66,050	20,380
Brooklyn borough	3,519	1,042	115	3,824	7,255	191,637	119,098	19,967
Manhattan borough	3,837	2,402	219	6,905	19,217	180,079	215,789	73,927
Queens borough	851	457	101	2,452	3,729	111,182	25,802	7,022
Richmond borough	199	100	11	521	791	13,326	4,658	1,879
Newark, N. J	658	133	26	1,364	1,779	49,341	34,423	9,054
Norfolk, Va	169	33	4	49	167	1,492	310	100
Oakland, Calif	627	217	39	1,490	2,982	15,098	3,420	765
Omaha, Nebr	344	402	63	586	522	16,748	16,798	1,384
Paterson, N. J	9,448	1,376	16	2,680	1,303	9,821	4,023	1,308
Philadelphia, Pa	1,190	999	89	3,984	6,862	149,310	63,317	22,883
Pittsburgh, Pa	312	226	107	2,513	2,931	75,815	44,152	17,162
Portland, Oreg	956	593	137	3,045	1,309	19,723	4,568	1,086
Providence, R. I	119	192	6	149	604	4,162	4,088	226
Reading, Pa	36	9	6	142	154	7,138	4,702	838
Richmond, Va	55	30		93	236	3,470	461	99
Rochester, N. Y	4,677	624	31	1,186	1,657	45,537	7,533	770
St. Louis, Mo	1,473	806	136	6,538	4,995	149,331	24,174	12,183
St. Paul, Minn	679	196	904	1,535	770	38,273	12,554	3,731
Salt Lake City, Utah	1,525	31	19	1,431	352	5,477	599	196
San Antonio, Tex	134	146	15	436	1,076	11,638	1,114	135
San Francisco, Calif	1,452	836	148	5,298	11,806	53,924	9,983	2,591
Scranton, Pa	41	30	3	398	305	12,131	10,033	2,186
Seattle, Wash	1,143	906	112	1,352	1,812	17,686	4,301	926
Spokane, Wash	407	128	96	576	491	7,902	991	231
Springfield, Mass	92	49	2	188	309	3,424	3,189	214
Syracuse, N. Y	200	56	18	660	720	19,693	6,491	327
Toledo, Ohio	335	254	155	2,295	1,187	43,578	10,347	5,800
Trenton, N. J	70	31	19	169	310	8,870	7,250	11,576
Washington, D. C	366	127	33	835	1,447	16,178	1,570	435
Wilmington, Del	47	17	6	109	327	4,656	4,447	315
Worcester, Mass	131	49	2	37	218	1,692	3,463	67
Yonkers, N. Y	268	42	4	232	483	6,874	11,040	3,811
Youngstown, Ohio	104	31	30	408	315	6,866	11,816	10,725

TABLE 106.—COUNTRY OF ORIGIN OF THE FOREIGN WHITE STOCK.

[Figures relate to countries as

CITY.	Russia.	Finland.	Rumania.	Bulgaria, Serbia, and Montenegro.	Turkey in Europe.	Greece.	Italy.	Spain.	Portugal.	Europe, not specified.
	CENTRAL AND EASTERN EUROPE—con.					SOUTHERN EUROPE.				
Akron, Ohio	6,815	107	757	1,491	261	2,041	6,366	306	17	21
Albany, N. Y	6,361	22	89	8	79	226	6,506	30	3	12
Atlanta, Ga	3,495	23	57	1	34	605	219	41	6	84
Baltimore, Md	64,719	150	616	162	16	950	16,489	221	44	79
Birmingham, Ala	1,609	7	54	15	6	625	3,776	25		27
Boston, Mass	86,206	937	917	28	477	3,881	77,105	513	2,063	29
Bridgeport, Conn	14,630	125	376	35	69	1,053	17,586	415	40	8
Buffalo, N. Y	35,190	254	363	105	104	688	34,955	222	57	64
Cambridge, Mass	7,198	88	106	5	42	520	5,432	63	3,530	1
Camden, N. J	8,707	210	136	22	15	87	9,688	20	26	29
Chicago, Ill	319,566	2,301	7,420	1,807	401	15,539	124,184	716	95	525
Cincinnati, Ohio	9,456	22	771	171	236	376	5,691	80	12	54
Cleveland, Ohio	76,886	1,675	4,112	949	147	1,896	35,687	215	32	73
Columbus, Ohio	3,708	92	161	99	48	496	4,601	26	6	17
Dallas, Texas	2,181	7	169	44	9	365	1,534	86	2	22
Dayton, Ohio	3,520	21	166	60	257	266	943	30	2	23
Denver, Colo	11,864	191	388	146	16	880	7,135	216	25	68
Des Moines, Iowa	3,241	20	149	40	14	272	2,369	12	1	19
Detroit, Mich	103,661	3,269	5,550	2,794	421	5,246	29,047	366	76	554
Fall River, Mass	4,980	50	57	19	2	189	2,088	11	10,207	3
Fort Worth, Tex	1,237	1	37	44	50	282	390	76	1	26
Grand Rapids, Mich	8,544	180	85	8	3	64	1,097	18	5	18
Hartford, Conn	20,776	114	538	8	18	388	14,307	33	155	2
Houston, Tex	2,247	30	178	14	3	251	3,370	128	24	45
Indianapolis, Ind	3,095	41	894	359	211	521	1,578	50	7	15
Jersey City, N. J	25,321	1,338	517	33	17	470	33,767	316	37	13
Kansas City, Kans	2,902	10	35	109	5	326	294	30		20
Kansas City, Mo	8,598	62	306	120	5	752	7,804	93	4	70
Los Angeles, Calif	20,209	731	1,358	445	174	1,267	15,415	1,581	414	158
Louisville, Ky	3,381	15	68	8	1	104	1,243	36	8	140
Lowell, Mass	5,479	48	18	144	21	5,512	825	10	2,671	8
Memphis, Tenn	2,423	18	49			394	2,952	24	10	35
Milwaukee, Wis	29,748	275	665	318	195	2,268	7,843	77	5	48
Minneapolis, Minn	14,167	2,325	2,450	165	37	1,074	1,577	41	5	26
Nashville, Tenn	1,179	6	52	9	1	143	266	12		25
New Bedford, Mass	4,895	23	19	13	331	825	1,227	53	10,967	
New Haven, Conn	20,470	153	329	11	7	434	34,558	55	115	10
New Orleans, La	2,897	110	107	27	13	547	21,818	2,602	175	304
New York, N. Y	985,702	14,542	56,702	1,022	6,770	23,204	802,946	14,659	1,617	700
Bronx borough	178,699	2,235	12,771	67	137	1,263	83,645	472	52	96
Brooklyn borough	415,574	4,913	19,233	218	225	3,457	299,813	4,300	844	195
Manhattan borough	363,509	6,059	23,538	679	6,380	17,704	356,106	9,352	590	330
Queens borough	22,946	752	1,043	42	23	546	45,199	309	77	63
Richmond borough	4,974	583	117	16	5	234	18,183	226	54	16
Newark, N. J	49,704	133	2,152	36	9	1,416	63,589	626	465	36
Norfolk, Va	4,084	117	70	8	26	850	1,131	229	76	33
Oakland, Calif	2,437	663	158	244	12	1,130	9,940	853	11,338	27
Omaha, Nebr	8,601	39	388	189	29	485	5,836	29	1	18
Paterson, N. J	16,261	19	70	17	18	390	22,936	77	3	8
Philadelphia, Pa	205,730	1,057	7,981	275	468	2,208	136,793	1,062	235	126
Pittsburgh, Pa	44,426	160	2,203	553	44	1,754	32,595	74	2	77
Portland, Oreg	10,352	2,244	257	283	185	886	5,142	137	59	29
Providence, R. I	13,537	134	451	34	21	645	42,018	65	3,067	6
Reading, Pa	4,188		12	7	11	715	3,598	37	2	3
Richmond, Va	2,514	3	65	3	6	261	1,282	24	32	20
Rochester, N. Y	18,185	58	204	64	133	433	36,731	56	211	24
St. Louis, Mo	30,922	78	1,480	491	339	2,333	18,104	640	10	311
St. Paul, Minn	9,795	172	711	78	6	428	3,515	14	1	22
Salt Lake City, Utah	927	127	64	21	14	675	970	93	4	5
San Antonio, Tex	1,705	13	132	18	2	203	1,368	355	15	85
San Francisco, Calif	12,068	2,711	1,098	604	89	3,868	45,599	4,208	2,141	494
Scranton, Pa	16,752	15	81	1		209	7,680	16		8
Seattle, Wash	6,552	3,437	173	333	878	1,155	5,475	299	59	33
Spokane, Wash	1,262	256	101	83	5	120	1,814	23	3	9
Springfield, Mass	9,879	295	80	28	39	1,245	8,706	26	34	1
Syracuse, N. Y	9,879	58	76	40	33	532	13,681	34	4	4
Toledo, Ohio	14,561	35	436	897	117	807	1,536	32	7	23
Trenton, N. J	9,472	12	292	12	4	162	13,657	19	4	
Washington, D. C	11,481	151	140	24	98	1,724	7,500	224	38	68
Wilmington, Del	8,276	53	163	2	1	348	6,967	105	20	12
Worcester, Mass	20,751	3,787	97	4	657	811	8,769	11	44	2
Yonkers, N. Y	6,029	120	85	7	3	179	9,892	41	12	2
Youngstown, Ohio	5,755	50	1,559	487	93	1,471	11,877	92	1	8

FOR CITIES HAVING 100,000 INHABITANTS OR MORE: 1920—Continued.
constituted prior to the World War.]

CITY.	ASIA.		AMERICA.						All other countries.	Of mixed foreign parentage.
	Turkey in Asia.	All other.	Canada—French.	Canada—Other.	Newfoundland.	West Indies.[1]	Mexico.	Central and South America.		
Akron, Ohio	1,151	22	188	1,893	43	23	98	19	66	2,831
Albany, N. Y	253	11	781	1,459	20	31	10	11	39	2,206
Atlanta, Ga	294	15	39	549	4	36	18	6	28	627
Baltimore, Md	108	33	218	2,032	52	279	61	127	219	8,465
Birmingham, Ala	549	9	24	461	2	20	40	20	38	614
Boston, Mass	5,470	105	3,933	73,434	5,470	371	45	163	856	25,024
Bridgeport, Conn	535	19	1,170	2,307	72	65	8	18	76	3,217
Buffalo, N. Y	720	45	376	25,118	99	102	80	44	225	15,313
Cambridge, Mass	758	28	2,459	12,835	880	87	5	32	666	3,168
Camden, N. J	134	8	62	495	411	44	1	22	44	2,178
Chicago, Ill	2,794	1,071	7,248	45,455	359	393	1,310	442	995	77,248
Cincinnati, Ohio	508	20	106	1,729	18	74	28	37	227	7,349
Cleveland, Ohio	1,950	91	718	13,683	143	136	114	101	266	19,987
Columbus, Ohio	163	36	184	1,360	5	40	13	33	70	2,465
Dallas, Tex	138	19	66	763	8	32	2,902	24	30	1,249
Dayton, Ohio	183	7	78	839	5	16	24	10	65	1,766
Denver, Colo	139	30	444	6,224	39	97	1,783	40	196	6,173
Des Moines, Iowa	124	17	74	1,737	3	22	195	8	35	1,847
Detroit, Mich	5,496	203	9,301	88,956	197	175	733	114	382	26,475
Fall River, Mass	973	13	28,368	2,135	32	15	1	18	11,639	3,198
Fort Worth, Tex	67	22	34	550	3	13	4,559	12	41	575
Grand Rapids, Mich	665	26	360	7,041	10	16	14	8	33	2,828
Hartford, Conn	582	86	2,477	3,165	95	50	9	14	109	3,449
Houston, Tex	401	5	73	836	7	41	5,211	30	45	1,526
Indianapolis, Ind	497	35	129	1,635	17	32	30	29	75	2,710
Jersey City, N. J	234	10	159	1,925	98	165	26	53	108	8,448
Kansas City, Kans	22	12	78	830	3	3	2,371	3	35	1,326
Kansas City, Mo	393	37	278	3,921	20	46	2,105	28	116	4,525
Los Angeles, Calif	1,483	197	1,305	20,585	124	244	31,173	403	890	14,460
Louisville, Ky	279	9	54	665	18	8	6	13	87	2,684
Lowell, Mass	867	8	23,699	7,233	54	12	1	10	684	3,003
Memphis, Tenn	36	1	43	589	5	28	17	9	19	1,053
Milwaukee, Wis	497	29	1,021	4,208	43	49	43	45	766	13,237
Minneapolis, Minn	519	45	3,842	14,515	18	35	60	20	165	12,536
Nashville, Tenn	82	8	27	241		8	15	34	11	468
New Bedford, Mass	509	7	22,888	2,436	47	38	3	81	17,911	2,755
New Haven, Conn	331	35	1,249	2,143	62	77	6	38	57	3,267
New Orleans, La	362	59	173	1,258	25	855	1,550	796	213	6,522
New York, N. Y	15,342	998	3,476	37,873	2,461	11,483	2,651	5,778	2,691	182,882
Bronx borough	980	56	389	3,625	175	581	78	149	276	28,884
Brooklyn borough	6,839	334	1,074	13,826	1,553	3,720	537	1,306	918	65,964
Manhattan borough	6,883	523	1,443	15,777	480	6,430	1,933	4,082	1,187	68,547
Queens borough	581	57	439	3,396	174	582	71	146	251	15,778
Richmond borough	59	28	131	1,249	79	170	32	95	59	3,709
Newark, N. J	483	67	318	2,355	99	183	65	117	203	10,650
Norfolk, Va	250	14	58	638	17	31	24	56	48	705
Oakland, Calif	232	86	425	7,173	31	80	1,472	332	1,563	7,468
Omaha, Nebr	557	11	208	3,082	47	26	774	26	64	4,291
Paterson, N. J	1,812	19	112	476	2	20	13	12	56	4,318
Philadelphia, Pa	3,040	250	501	6,938	497	1,326	474	502	516	40,506
Pittsburgh, Pa	1,520	29	83	2,680	162	32	26	53	145	14,648
Portland, Oreg	317	74	783	11,252	68	49	116	42	341	7,644
Providence, R. I	2,468	47	9,677	7,488	185	136	4	48	1,817	6,362
Reading, Pa	20	1	14	97	1	16	101	6	12	904
Richmond, Va	492	16	29	412	5	23	7	16	33	614
Rochester, N. Y	556	30	494	16,042	50	31	7	28	58	7,514
St. Louis, Mo	1,203	47	369	4,265	32	139	526	90	287	16,131
St. Paul, Minn	666	35	2,567	7,191	32	31	90	22	153	8,974
Salt Lake City, Utah	196	21	90	1,710	6	14	265	10	310	5,427
San Antonio, Tex	298	20	111	779	7	62	42,437	43	79	2,138
San Francisco, Calif	749	246	767	11,852	145	245	5,180	2,005	2,613	20,814
Scranton, Pa	450	7	24	431	2	9	3	9	48	3,181
Seattle, Wash	551	167	1,480	20,474	310	60	131	128	497	10,123
Spokane, Wash	63	19	410	6,732	26	14	15	9	118	2,951
Springfield, Mass	1,124	14	11,060	4,891	97	50	12	35	51	2,801
Syracuse, N. Y	412	13	1,099	6,509	22	34	8	20	64	3,264
Toledo, Ohio	1,003	21	1,364	5,845	40	38	233	28	111	5,131
Trenton, N. J	165	16	99	390	14	15	19	24	29	1,778
Washington, D. C	624	55	467	3,747	44	191	71	170	197	4,604
Wilmington, Del	27	4	31	402	1	27	53	4	32	1,502
Worcester, Mass	3,582	18	13,708	8,616	84	39	4	15	61	3,366
Yonkers, N. Y	219	142	150	1,136	30	89	19	51	47	3,044
Youngstown, Ohio	557	12	30	987	8	19	70	29	45	3,089

[1] Except possessions of the United States.

TABLE 107.—PER CENT DISTRIBUTION OF THE FOREIGN WHITE STOCK BY

	CITY.	NORTHWESTERN EUROPE.													CENTRAL AND EASTERN EUROPE.	
		England.	Scotland.	Wales.	Ireland.	Norway.	Sweden.	Denmark.	Netherlands.	Belgium.	Luxemburg.	Switzerland.	France.	Germany.	Austria.	Hungary.
1	Akron, Ohio	8.1	2.2	1.6	5.5	0.4	2.0	0.5	0.4	0.2	(1)	1.6	1.3	16.7	13.8	14.1
2	Albany, N.Y.	5.7	1.9	0.2	27.4	0.1	0.4	0.3	1.4	0.1	0.1	0.3	0.7	24.5	4.1	0.3
3	Atlanta, Ga.	10.5	4.0	0.5	9.3	0.4	1.8	0.6	0.3	0.2	(1)	1.1	2.5	15.9	2.8	1.8
4	Baltimore, Md.	3.5	1.0	0.3	10.0	0.3	0.4	0.2	0.2	0.1	(1)	0.3	0.6	35.5	8.1	1.1
5	Birmingham, Ala.	12.6	8.2	1.4	7.7	0.3	1.4	0.4	0.2	0.2	....	0.9	2.8	12.2	2.4	0.8
6	Boston, Mass.	4.5	2.1	0.1	31.9	0.5	2.2	0.3	0.2	0.1	(1)	0.1	0.4	3.4	1.6	0.2
7	Bridgeport, Conn.	6.9	1.7	0.1	15.4	0.3	3.3	0.7	0.1	0.1	(1)	0.3	0.5	6.1	9.3	15.2
8	Buffalo, N.Y.	5.1	1.6	0.2	9.6	0.2	0.7	0.2	0.4	0.1	(1)	0.5	1.0	33.9	11.1	1.7
9	Cambridge, Mass.	4.9	2.4	0.2	34.7	0.4	2.7	0.2	0.1	(1)	....	0.1	0.3	1.8	1.7	0.1
10	Camden, N.J.	9.4	1.8	0.5	11.6	0.8	0.8	0.3	0.2	0.1	(1)	0.5	0.8	18.1	10.8	1.0
11	Chicago, Ill.	3.1	1.3	0.2	10.3	2.3	6.2	1.2	1.1	0.3	0.3	0.4	0.5	21.7	16.3	3.6
12	Cincinnati, Ohio	3.5	0.9	0.4	12.5	0.1	0.2	0.1	0.7	0.1	(1)	1.0	1.4	56.8	2.7	3.3
13	Cleveland, Ohio	4.8	1.4	0.6	6.4	0.2	0.8	0.2	0.5	(1)	(1)	0.6	0.4	18.6	22.7	13.8
14	Columbus, Ohio	7.3	2.0	3.7	14.3	0.2	0.6	0.2	0.3	0.2	(1)	2.0	1.4	37.3	3.2	2.8
15	Dallas, Tex.	9.3	2.7	0.4	8.7	1.0	2.1	1.1	0.4	0.3	(1)	1.9	2.3	21.6	4.6	0.5
16	Dayton, Ohio	4.5	1.3	0.4	10.1	0.2	0.4	0.1	0.4	0.1	0.1	0.9	1.4	47.5	4.6	8.4
17	Denver, Colo.	10.3	3.5	1.2	13.1	1.3	8.5	1.9	1.0	0.1	0.1	1.2	1.3	17.0	4.0	1.2
18	Des Moines, Iowa	11.9	3.6	2.3	11.3	3.4	14.3	3.2	1.3	0.2	(1)	0.9	1.1	15.7	2.6	0.3
19	Detroit, Mich.	6.1	2.6	0.2	5.1	0.4	1.0	0.5	0.7	1.5	(1)	0.4	0.7	23.3	9.1	4.0
20	Fall River, Mass.	17.3	1.4	0.1	12.4	0.1	0.1	0.1	(1)	(1)	....	(1)	0.2	0.5	4.4	(1)
21	Fort Worth, Tex.	7.4	2.6	0.4	9.6	1.0	2.7	0.5	0.2	0.1	(1)	0.7	1.6	13.9	5.4	0.2
22	Grand Rapids, Mich.	4.1	1.1	0.1	4.4	0.5	2.8	0.8	38.4	0.1	(1)	0.2	0.4	15.2	5.3	0.3
23	Hartford, Conn.	4.8	2.1	0.1	22.4	0.2	4.7	1.4	0.1	(1)	(1)	0.2	0.4	6.4	6.6	0.7
24	Houston, Tex.	7.9	1.9	0.3	6.6	0.5	1.5	1.0	0.5	0.2	(1)	0.9	2.6	24.9	5.1	0.7
25	Indianapolis, Ind.	6.3	2.3	0.4	18.5	0.2	0.8	1.0	0.7	0.1	(1)	1.3	1.7	42.0	3.6	1.0
26	Jersey City, N.J.	4.5	1.8	0.2	23.0	1.1	1.1	0.4	0.3	0.2	(1)	0.5	0.8	18.4	10.4	1.3
27	Kansas City, Kans.	6.2	1.7	0.9	12.4	0.4	5.3	1.6	0.4	1.0	(1)	1.0	1.0	18.8	12.7	8.8
28	Kansas City, Mo.	7.9	2.8	0.7	16.2	0.7	6.0	1.2	0.4	0.9	0.1	1.4	1.6	21.5	3.1	0.9
29	Los Angeles, Calif.	11.2	3.3	0.8	8.3	1.5	4.1	1.6	0.7	0.3	0.1	1.2	2.5	15.3	3.2	1.3
30	Louisville, Ky.	3.6	1.1	0.2	17.2	0.1	0.3	0.2	0.4	0.2	(1)	3.9	1.9	53.1	1.5	0.3
31	Lowell, Mass.	8.1	2.3	0.1	26.9	0.2	1.2	0.1	(1)	0.3	(1)	(1)	0.2	0.6	2.8	(1)
32	Memphis, Tenn.	7.8	2.6	0.3	16.1	0.3	1.7	0.8	0.4	0.1	(1)	1.2	2.6	20.6	2.5	1.1
33	Milwaukee, Wis.	1.9	0.6	0.3	3.1	1.6	0.7	0.6	0.6	0.1	0.3	0.7	0.3	58.0	8.6	3.8
34	Minneapolis, Minn.	3.5	1.5	0.4	5.6	17.0	25.3	2.4	0.4	0.1	0.2	0.5	0.5	14.0	5.4	1.3
35	Nashville, Tenn.	8.8	3.0	0.2	23.3	0.3	0.5	0.4	0.5	0.2	0.1	3.3	2.3	21.1	2.6	3.7
36	New Bedford, Mass.	16.7	1.2	0.1	7.1	0.1	0.5	0.1	(1)	0.2	(1)	0.1	0.6	1.2	4.2	0.1
37	New Haven, Conn.	4.1	1.7	0.1	21.9	0.2	2.4	0.4	0.1	0.2	(1)	0.4	0.4	8.0	3.5	0.8
38	New Orleans, La.	4.3	1.1	0.1	11.6	0.7	0.7	0.5	0.4	0.2	(1)	0.8	11.8	23.3	1.8	0.2
39	New York, N.Y.	3.2	1.1	0.1	14.4	0.9	1.3	0.3	0.2	0.1	(1)	0.4	0.8	13.6	10.0	2.9
40	Bronx borough	2.5	1.0	0.1	11.3	0.3	1.0	0.2	0.2	0.1	(1)	0.4	0.5	14.9	11.1	3.4
41	Brooklyn borough	3.5	1.2	0.1	13.1	1.9	1.9	0.5	0.2	0.1	(1)	0.3	0.5	12.5	7.8	1.3
42	Manhattan borough	2.7	0.9	0.1	16.5	0.3	0.9	0.2	0.2	0.1	(1)	0.4	1.1	10.1	12.1	4.2
43	Queens borough	4.7	1.6	0.1	13.3	0.5	1.5	0.5	0.3	0.1	(1)	0.8	1.2	35.4	8.2	2.2
44	Richmond borough	6.0	2.1	0.2	18.1	3.6	2.0	0.8	0.3	0.1	(1)	0.7	1.0	17.4	6.1	2.4
45	Newark, N.J.	4.6	1.7	0.1	11.7	0.1	0.5	0.3	0.2	(1)	(1)	0.5	0.6	17.4	12.1	3.2
46	Norfolk, Va.	8.0	2.7	0.4	9.3	1.8	2.3	0.9	1.2	0.2	(1)	0.3	1.2	10.3	2.1	0.7
47	Oakland, Calif.	10.6	3.8	1.5	11.9	2.2	4.8	3.3	0.6	0.2	(1)	1.3	2.6	13.3	3.0	0.7
48	Omaha, Nebr.	4.8	1.9	0.3	10.1	1.1	9.8	6.8	0.4	0.4	0.1	0.6	0.6	17.7	17.8	1.5
49	Paterson, N.J.	8.9	4.2	0.1	11.6	0.1	0.3	0.1	9.2	1.3	(1)	2.6	1.3	9.6	3.9	1.3
50	Philadelphia, Pa.	7.6	2.0	0.4	22.5	0.2	0.5	0.2	0.1	0.1	(1)	0.4	0.7	15.1	6.4	2.3
51	Pittsburgh, Pa.	6.1	2.2	1.5	16.1	0.1	0.7	0.1	0.1	0.1	(1)	0.8	0.9	22.7	13.2	5.1
52	Portland, Oreg.	9.4	4.1	0.7	7.6	5.4	8.7	2.6	0.8	0.5	0.1	2.6	1.1	16.9	3.9	0.9
53	Providence, R.I.	11.1	2.4	0.1	24.7	0.3	3.1	0.1	0.1	0.1	(1)	0.1	0.4	2.5	2.4	0.1
54	Reading, Pa.	4.2	0.9	0.9	5.5	0.1	0.2	0.1	0.1	(1)	(1)	0.5	0.6	27.6	18.2	3.2
55	Richmond, Va.	10.9	4.6	0.6	11.9	0.3	0.7	0.5	0.4	0.2	....	0.6	1.6	23.7	3.2	0.7
56	Rochester, N.Y.	7.9	1.7	0.1	10.9	0.1	0.5	0.2	2.0	0.0	(1)	0.7	0.9	25.0	4.1	0.4
57	St. Louis, Mo.	3.8	1.1	0.2	12.9	0.1	0.7	0.2	0.4	0.9	(1)	1.0	1.5	10.5	1.0	3.0
58	St. Paul, Minn.	3.3	1.4	0.2	9.8	6.8	15.8	2.1	0.4	0.1	0.6	1.0	0.5	24.9	8.2	2.4
59	Salt Lake City, Utah	32.9	5.8	2.8	4.5	3.4	9.0	7.7	2.5	0.1	(1)	2.4	0.6	9.0	1.0	0.3
60	San Antonio, Tex.	3.4	0.7	0.1	3.3	0.2	0.4	0.3	0.2	0.2	(1)	0.6	1.5	16.5	1.6	0.2
61	San Francisco, Calif.	7.2	2.7	0.4	19.6	1.7	3.5	1.9	0.4	0.3	(1)	1.6	3.7	16.7	3.1	0.8
62	Scranton, Pa.	7.4	1.4	10.2	19.6	(1)	0.2	0.1	(1)	(1)	(1)	0.4	0.3	13.7	11.3	2.5
63	Seattle, Wash.	11.2	4.8	1.1	8.2	10.8	11.6	2.9	0.7	0.6	0.1	0.8	1.1	10.9	2.6	0.6
64	Spokane, Wash.	10.0	4.0	1.0	8.8	8.2	11.7	2.4	0.9	0.3	0.2	1.3	1.1	17.2	2.2	0.5
65	Springfield, Mass.	6.1	3.7	0.1	24.9	0.2	3.2	0.2	0.1	0.1	(1)	0.2	0.4	4.4	4.1	0.3
66	Syracuse, N.Y.	7.4	1.6	0.4	19.2	0.1	0.4	0.2	0.2	0.1	(1)	0.7	0.8	21.8	7.2	0.4
67	Toledo, Ohio	5.3	1.2	0.3	7.2	0.2	0.6	0.3	0.3	0.2	0.1	2.0	1.0	38.5	9.1	5.1
68	Trenton, N.J.	9.7	1.7	0.2	11.0	(1)	0.3	0.2	0.1	(1)	(1)	0.2	0.4	12.5	10.3	16.4
69	Washington, D.C.	10.4	3.2	0.6	22.6	0.8	1.5	0.7	0.4	0.1	(1)	1.0	1.7	18.5	1.8	0.5
70	Wilmington, Del.	7.0	1.8	0.3	23.5	0.2	1.1	0.2	0.1	0.1	(1)	0.3	0.8	11.0	10.5	0.7
71	Worcester, Mass.	5.6	1.6	0.1	24.6	0.4	12.4	0.3	0.1	(1)	(1)	(1)	0.2	1.3	2.7	0.1
72	Yonkers, N.Y.	6.7	3.8	0.3	22.7	0.5	1.1	0.3	0.4	0.1	(1)	0.3	0.7	10.1	16.2	5.6
73	Youngstown, Ohio	8.7	3.3	4.7	9.3	0.1	2.4	0.1	0.1	(1)	(1)	0.5	0.4	8.7	14.9	13.6

¹ Less than one-tenth of 1 per cent.

COUNTRY OF ORIGIN, FOR CITIES HAVING 100,000 INHABITANTS OR MORE: 1920.

Russia	Finland	Rumania	Bulgaria, Serbia, and Montenegro	Turkey in Europe	Greece	Italy	Spain	Portugal	Europe, not specified	Turkey in Asia	All other	French	Other	Newfoundland	West Indies.[2]	Mexico	Central and South America	All other countries	Of mixed foreign parentage	
8.8	0.1	1.0	1.9	0.3	2.6	8.2	0.4	(1)	(1)	1.5	(1)	0.2	2.4	0.1	(1)	0.1	(1)	0.1	3.6	1
11.4	(1)	0.2	(1)	0.1	0.4	11.7	0.1	(1)	(1)	0.5	(1)	1.4	2.6	(1)	0.1	(1)	(1)	0.1	4.0	2
27.2	0.2	0.4	(1)	0.3	4.7	1.7	0.3	(1)	0.7	2.3	0.1	0.3	4.3	(1)	0.3	0.1	(1)	0.2	4.9	3
26.2	0.1	0.2	0.1	(1)	0.4	6.7	0.1	(1)	(1)	(1)	(1)	0.1	0.8	(1)	0.1	(1)	0.1	0.1	3.4	4
9.8	(1)	0.3	0.1	(1)	3.8	23.1	0.2	....	0.2	3.4	0.1	0.1	2.8	(1)	0.1	0.2	0.1	0.2	3.8	5
15.7	0.2	0.2	(1)	0.1	0.7	14.1	0.1	0.4	(1)	1.0	(1)	0.7	13.4	1.0	0.1	(1)	(1)	0.2	4.6	6
14.0	0.1	0.4	(1)	0.1	1.0	16.8	0.4	(1)	(1)	0.5	(1)	1.1	2.2	0.1	0.1	(1)	(1)	0.1	3.1	7
10.4	0.1	0.1	(1)	(1)	0.2	10.4	0.1	(1)	(1)	0.2	(1)	0.1	7.5	(1)	0.1	(1)	(1)	0.1	4.5	8
9.6	0.1	0.1	(1)	0.1	0.7	7.2	0.1	4.7	(1)	1.0	(1)	3.3	17.1	1.2	0.1	(1)	(1)	0.9	4.2	9
16.9	0.4	0.3	(1)	(1)	0.2	18.8	(1)	0.1	0.1	0.3	(1)	0.1	1.0	0.8	0.1	(1)	(1)	0.1	4.2	10
16.4	0.1	0.4	0.1	(1)	0.8	6.4	(1)	(1)	(1)	0.1	0.1	0.4	2.3	(1)	(1)	0.1	(1)	0.1	4.0	11
5.7	(1)	0.5	0.1	0.1	0.2	3.5	(1)	(1)	(1)	0.3	(1)	0.1	1.1	(1)	(1)	(1)	(1)	0.1	4.5	12
14.0	0.3	0.7	0.2	(1)	0.3	6.5	(1)	(1)	(1)	0.4	(1)	0.1	2.5	(1)	(1)	(1)	(1)	(1)	3.6	13
6.7	0.2	0.3	0.2	0.1	0.9	8.3	(1)	(1)	(1)	0.3	0.1	0.3	2.4	(1)	0.1	(1)	0.1	0.1	4.4	14
9.7	(1)	0.8	0.2	(1)	1.6	6.9	0.4	(1)	0.1	0.6	0.1	0.3	3.4	(1)	0.1	13.0	(1)	0.1	5.6	15
8.3	(1)	0.4	0.1	0.6	0.6	2.2	0.1	(1)	0.1	0.4	(1)	0.2	2.0	(1)	(1)	0.1	(1)	0.2	4.2	16
11.3	0.2	0.4	0.1	(1)	0.8	6.8	0.2	(1)	0.1	0.1	(1)	0.4	5.9	(1)	0.1	1.7	(1)	0.2	5.9	17
8.9	0.1	0.4	0.1	(1)	0.7	6.5	(1)	(1)	0.1	0.3	(1)	0.2	4.8	(1)	0.1	0.5	(1)	0.1	5.1	18
16.2	0.5	0.9	0.4	0.1	0.8	4.6	0.1	(1)	0.1	0.9	(1)	1.5	13.9	(1)	(1)	0.1	(1)	0.1	4.1	19
4.9	(1)	0.1	(1)	(1)	0.2	2.1	(1)	10.1	(1)	1.0	(1)	28.1	2.1	(1)	(1)	(1)	(1)	11.5	3.2	20
8.3	(1)	0.2	0.3	0.3	1.9	2.6	0.5	(1)	0.2	0.4	0.1	0.2	3.7	(1)	0.1	30.5	0.1	0.3	3.8	21
10.6	0.2	0.1	(1)	(1)	0.1	1.4	(1)	(1)	(1)	0.8	(1)	0.4	8.8	(1)	(1)	(1)	(1)	(1)	3.5	22
22.3	0.1	0.6	(1)	(1)	0.4	15.3	(1)	0.2	(1)	0.6	0.1	2.7	3.4	0.1	0.1	(1)	(1)	0.1	3.7	23
7.1	0.1	0.6	(1)	(1)	0.8	10.6	0.4	0.1	0.1	1.3	(1)	0.2	2.6	(1)	0.1	16.4	(1)	0.1	4.8	24
5.1	0.1	1.5	0.6	0.4	0.9	2.6	0.1	(1)	(1)	0.8	0.1	0.2	2.7	(1)	0.1	(1)	(1)	0.1	4.5	25
12.5	0.7	0.3	(1)	(1)	0.2	16.6	0.2	(1)	(1)	0.1	(1)	0.1	0.9	(1)	0.1	(1)	(1)	0.1	4.2	26
9.6	(1)	0.1	0.4	(1)	1.1	1.0	0.1	....	0.1	0.1	(1)	0.3	2.8	(1)	(1)	7.9	(1)	0.1	4.4	27
10.2	0.1	0.4	0.1	(1)	0.9	9.2	0.1	(1)	0.1	0.5	(1)	0.3	4.6	(1)	0.1	2.5	(1)	0.1	5.4	28
8.0	0.3	0.5	0.2	0.1	0.5	6.1	0.6	0.2	0.1	0.6	0.1	0.5	8.2	(1)	0.1	12.4	0.2	0.4	5.7	29
6.1	(1)	0.1	(1)	(1)	0.2	2.2	0.1	(1)	0.3	0.5	(1)	0.1	1.2	(1)	(1)	(1)	(1)	0.2	4.8	30
6.2	0.1	(1)	0.2	(1)	6.3	0.9	(1)	3.0	(1)	1.0	(1)	27.0	8.2	0.1	(1)	(1)	(1)	0.8	3.4	31
13.2	0.1	0.3	....	....	2.2	16.1	0.1	0.1	0.2	0.2	(1)	0.2	3.2	(1)	0.2	0.1	(1)	0.1	5.7	32
9.2	0.1	0.2	0.1	0.1	0.7	2.4	(1)	(1)	(1)	0.2	(1)	0.3	1.3	(1)	(1)	(1)	(1)	0.2	4.1	33
5.8	1.0	1.0	0.1	(1)	0.4	0.6	(1)	(1)	(1)	0.2	(1)	1.6	6.0	(1)	(1)	(1)	(1)	0.1	5.2	34
13.6	0.1	0.6	0.1	(1)	1.6	3.1	0.1	....	0.3	0.9	0.1	0.3	2.8	....	0.1	0.2	0.4	0.1	5.4	35
5.1	(1)	(1)	(1)	0.3	0.9	1.3	0.1	11.4	....	0.5	(1)	23.8	2.5	(1)	(1)	(1)	0.1	18.6	2.9	36
18.0	0.1	0.3	(1)	(1)	0.4	30.5	(1)	0.1	(1)	0.3	(1)	1.1	1.9	0.1	0.1	(1)	(1)	0.1	2.9	37
3.0	0.1	0.1	(1)	(1)	0.6	22.9	2.7	0.2	0.3	0.4	0.1	0.2	1.3	(1)	0.9	1.6	0.8	0.2	6.8	38
23.0	0.3	1.3	(1)	0.2	0.5	18.7	0.3	(1)	(1)	0.4	(1)	0.1	0.9	0.1	0.3	0.1	0.1	0.1	4.3	39
30.1	0.4	2.1	(1)	(1)	0.2	14.1	0.1	(1)	(1)	0.2	(1)	0.1	0.6	(1)	0.1	(1)	(1)	0.1	4.9	40
27.2	0.3	1.3	(1)	(1)	0	19.6	0.3	0.1	(1)	0.4	(1)	0.1	0.9	0.1	0.2	(1)	(1)	0.1	4.3	41
20.4	0.3	1.3	(1)	0.4	1.0	20.0	0.5	(1)	(1)	0.4	(1)	0.1	0.9	(1)	0.4	0.1	0.2	0.1	3.8	42
7.3	0.2	0.3	(1)	(1)	0.2	14.4	0.1	(1)	(1)	0.2	(1)	0.1	1.1	0.1	0.2	(1)	(1)	0.1	5.0	43
6.5	0.8	0.2	(1)	(1)	0.3	23.7	0.3	0.1	(1)	0.1	(1)	0.2	1.6	0.1	0.2	(1)	0.1	0.1	4.8	44
17.5	(1)	0.8	(1)	(1)	0.5	22.4	0.2	0.2	(1)	0.2	(1)	0.1	0.8	(1)	0.1	(1)	(1)	0.1	3.8	45
28.2	0.8	0.5	0.1	0.2	5.9	7.8	1.6	0.5	0.2	1.7	0.1	0.4	4.4	0.1	0.2	0.2	0.4	0.3	4.9	46
2.1	0.6	0.1	0.2	(1)	1.0	8.7	0.8	10.0	(1)	0.2	0.1	0.4	6.3	(1)	0.1	1.3	0.3	1.4	6.6	47
9.1	(1)	0.4	0.2	(1)	0.5	6.2	(1)	(1)	(1)	0.6	(1)	0.2	3.3	(1)	0.1	0.8	(1)	0.1	4.5	48
15.9	(1)	0.1	(1)	(1)	0.4	22.4	0.1	(1)	(1)	1.8	(1)	0.1	0.5	(1)	(1)	0.1	(1)	0.1	4.2	49
20.8	0.1	0.8	(1)	(1)	0.2	13.8	0.1	(1)	(1)	0.3	(1)	0.1	0.7	0.1	0.1	(1)	0.1	0.1	4.1	50
13.3	(1)	0.7	0.2	(1)	0.5	9.8	(1)	(1)	(1)	0.5	(1)	0.1	0.8	(1)	(1)	0.1	(1)	(1)	4.4	51
8.9	1.9	0.2	0.2	0.2	0.8	4.4	0.1	0.1	(1)	0.3	0.1	0.7	9.6	0.1	(1)	0.1	(1)	0.3	6.5	52
8.1	0.1	0.3	(1)	(1)	0.4	25.0	(1)	1.8	(1)	1.5	(1)	5.8	4.5	0.1	0.1	(1)	(1)	1.1	3.8	53
16.2	....	(1)	(1)	(1)	2.8	13.9	0.1	(1)	(1)	0.1	(1)	0.1	0.4	(1)	0.1	0.4	(1)	(1)	3.5	54
17.2	(1)	0.4	(1)	(1)	1.8	8.8	0.2	0.2	0.1	3.4	0.1	0.2	2.8	(1)	0.2	(1)	0.1	0.2	4.2	55
10.0	(1)	0.1	(1)	0.1	0.2	20.2	(1)	0.1	(1)	0.3	(1)	0.3	8.8	(1)	(1)	(1)	(1)	0.1	4.1	56
9.0	(1)	0.4	0.1	0.1	0.7	5.3	0.2	(1)	0.1	0.4	(1)	0.1	1.2	(1)	0.2	(1)	(1)	0.1	4.7	57
6.4	0.1	0.5	0.1	(1)	0.3	2.3	(1)	(1)	(1)	0.4	(1)	1.7	4.7	(1)	(1)	0.1	(1)	0.1	5.8	58
1.5	0.2	0.1	(1)	(1)	1.1	1.6	0.2	(1)	(1)	0.3	(1)	0.1	2.8	(1)	0.4	(1)	(1)	0.5	9.0	59
2.4	(1)	0.2	(1)	(1)	0.3	1.9	0.5	(1)	0.1	0.4	(1)	0.2	1.1	(1)	0.1	60.2	0.1	0.1	3.0	60
3.7	0.8	0.3	0.2	(1)	1.2	14.1	1.3	0.7	0.2	0.2	0.1	0.2	3.7	(1)	0.1	1.6	0.6	0.8	6.4	61
18.9	(1)	0.1	(1)	....	0.2	8.7	(1)	....	(1)	0.5	(1)	(1)	0.5	(1)	(1)	(1)	(1)	0.1	3.6	62
4.0	2.1	0.1	0.2	0.5	0.7	3.4	0.2	(1)	(1)	0.3	0.1	0.9	12.6	0.2	(1)	0.1	0.1	0.3	6.2	63
2.7	0.6	0.2	0.2	(1)	0.3	3.9	(1)	(1)	(1)	0.1	(1)	0.9	14.6	0.1	0.1	(1)	(1)	0.3	6.4	64
12.7	0.4	0.1	(1)	0.1	1.6	11.2	(1)	(1)	(1)	1.4	(1)	14.2	6.3	0.1	0.1	(1)	(1)	0.1	3.6	65
10.9	0.1	0.1	(1)	(1)	0.6	15.2	(1)	(1)	(1)	0.5	(1)	1.2	7.2	(1)	(1)	(1)	(1)	0.1	3.6	66
12.8	0.1	0.4	0.8	0.1	0.7	1.4	(1)	(1)	(1)	0.9	(1)	1.2	5.2	(1)	(1)	0.2	(1)	0.1	4.5	67
13.4	(1)	0.4	(1)	(1)	0.2	19.3	(1)	(1)	....	0.2	(1)	0.1	0.6	(1)	(1)	(1)	(1)	(1)	2.5	68
13.1	0.2	0.2	(1)	0.1	2.0	8.6	0.3	(1)	0.1	0.7	0.1	0.5	4.3	0.1	0.2	0.1	0.2	0.2	5.3	69
19.5	0.1	0.4	(1)	(1)	0.8	16.4	0.2	(1)	(1)	0.1	(1)	0.1	0.9	(1)	0.1	0.1	(1)	0.1	3.5	70
16.3	3.0	0.1	(1)	0.5	0.6	6.9	(1)	(1)	(1)	2.8	(1)	10.7	6.7	0.1	(1)	(1)	(1)	(1)	2.6	71
8.9	0.2	0.1	(1)	(1)	0.3	14.5	0.1	(1)	(1)	0.3	0.2	0.2	1.7	(1)	0.1	(1)	0.1	0.1	4.5	72
7.3	0.1	2.0	0.6	0.1	1.9	15.0	0.1	(1)	(1)	0.7	(1)	(1)	1.2	(1)	0.1	(1)	(1)	0.1	3.9	73

[2] Except possessions of the United States.

TABLE 108.—COUNTRY OF ORIGIN OF THE FOREIGN WHITE STOCK, BY NATIVITY AND

Figures relate to countries as

COUNTRY OF ORIGIN.	TOTAL FOREIGN WHITE STOCK.			FOREIGN-BORN WHITE— BIRTHPLACE OF FATHER.		
	Urban.	Rural.	Per cent urban.	Urban.	Rural.	Per cent urban.
Total	26,063,355	10,335,603	71.6	10,356,983	3,355,771	75.5
Northwestern Europe:						
England	1,606,558	700,554	69.6	613,953	210,135	74.5
Scotland	522,101	209,138	71.4	232,818	77,274	75.1
Wales	156,270	74,110	67.8	47,596	19,366	71.1
Ireland	3,433,904	702,491	83.0	998,126	166,581	85.7
Norway	399,113	624,112	39.0	170,376	191,675	47.1
Sweden	862,417	594,965	59.2	399,176	233,480	63.1
Denmark	225,150	242,375	48.2	102,228	89,268	53.4
Netherlands	194,557	167,761	53.7	76,456	57,773	57.0
Belgium	73,783	48,903	60.1	41,977	21,257	66.4
Luxemburg	21,518	21,591	49.9	7,334	5,503	57.1
Switzerland	172,448	155,349	52.6	66,539	50,731	56.7
France	234,382	99,296	70.2	92,056	32,671	73.8
Central and Eastern Europe:						
Germany	4,676,494	2,583,498	64.4	1,312,751	603,113	68.5
Austria	2,296,573	833,225	73.4	1,107,052	338,089	76.6
Hungary	811,680	299,225	73.1	453,601	144,569	75.8
Russia	3,317,285	553,824	85.7	1,783,530	237,116	88.3
Finland	141,358	154,918	47.7	80,269	70,501	53.2
Rumania	126,076	8,242	93.9	80,214	5,041	94.1
Bulgaria, Serbia, and Montenegro	30,654	13,049	70.1	23,256	9,425	71.2
Turkey in Europe	21,397	1,871	92.0	17,266	1,641	91.3
Southern Europe:						
Greece	187,234	25,108	88.2	145,907	20,879	87.5
Italy	2,819,980	516,961	84.5	1,365,564	249,616	84.5
Spain	57,416	20,531	73.7	39,139	13,547	74.3
Portugal	96,643	38,151	71.7	51,140	16,808	75.3
Europe, not specified	7,749	3,249	70.5	2,543	799	76.1
Asia:						
Turkey in Asia	139,587	24,893	84.9	86,859	13,984	86.1
All other countries	8,402	2,333	78.2	4,344	795	84.5
America:						
Canada—French	651,468	196,841	76.8	240,119	62,556	79.3
Canada—Other	1,184,087	571,432	67.4	411,920	146,855	73.7
Newfoundland	23,060	2,388	90.6	11,188	1,132	90.8
West Indies[2]	41,349	4,147	90.9	20,281	1,628	92.6
Mexico	323,682	401,650	44.6	222,997	250,290	47.1
Central and South America	16,577	2,910	85.1	10,744	1,038	91.2
All other	84,718	31,740	72.7	37,664	10,635	78.0
Of mixed foreign parentage	1,097,685	404,772	73.1			

[1] Less than one-tenth of 1 per cent.

PARENTAGE, IN URBAN AND RURAL COMMUNITIES, FOR THE UNITED STATES: 1920.
constituted prior to the World War.]

COUNTRY OF ORIGIN.	NATIVE WHITE OF FOREIGN OR MIXED PARENTAGE.			PER CENT DISTRIBUTION OF FOREIGN WHITE STOCK.					
				Total.		Foreign-born white—Birth-place of father.		Native white of foreign or mixed parentage.	
	Urban.	Rural.	Per cent urban.	Urban.	Rural.	Urban.	Rural.	Urban.	Rural.
Total..................	15,706,372	6,979,832	69.2	100.0	100.0	100.0	100.0	100.0	100.0
Northwestern Europe:									
England.................	992,605	490,419	66.9	6.2	6.8	5.9	6.3	6.3	7.0
Scotland...............	289,283	131,864	68.7	2.0	2.0	2.2	2.3	1.8	1.9
Wales.................	108,674	54,744	66.5	0.6	0.7	0.5	0.6	0.7	0.8
Ireland................	2,435,778	535,910	82.0	13.2	6.8	9.6	5.0	15.5	7.7
Norway................	228,737	432,437	34.6	1.5	6.0	1.6	5.7	1.5	6.2
Sweden...............	463,241	361,485	56.2	3.3	5.8	3.9	7.0	2.9	5.2
Denmark..............	122,922	153,107	44.5	0.9	2.3	1.0	2.7	0.8	2.2
Netherlands..........	118,101	109,988	51.8	0.7	1.6	0.7	1.7	0.8	1.6
Belgium..............	31,806	27,646	53.5	0.3	0.5	0.4	0.6	0.2	0.4
Luxemburg...........	14,184	16,088	46.9	0.1	0.2	0.1	0.2	0.1	0.2
Switzerland...........	105,909	104,618	50.3	0.7	1.5	0.6	1.5	0.7	1.5
France................	142,326	66,625	68.1	0.9	1.0	0.9	1.0	0.9	1.0
Central and Eastern Europe:									
Germany..............	3,363,743	1,980,385	62.9	17.9	25.0	12.7	18.0	21.4	28.4
Austria...............	1,189,521	495,136	70.6	8.8	8.1	10.7	10.1	7.6	7.1
Hungary..............	358,079	154,656	69.8	3.1	2.9	4.4	4.3	2.3	2.2
Russia................	1,533,755	316,708	82.9	12.7	5.4	17.2	7.1	9.8	4.5
Finland...............	61,089	84,417	42.0	0.5	1.5	0.8	2.1	0.4	1.2
Rumania..............	45,862	3,201	93.5	0.5	0.1	0.8	0.2	0.3	(¹)
Bulgaria, Serbia, and Montenegro.........	7,398	3,624	67.1	0.1	0.1	0.2	0.3	(¹)	0.1
Turkey in Europe.........	4,131	230	94.7	0.1	(¹)	0.2	(¹)	(¹)	(¹)
Southern Europe:									
Greece................	41,327	4,229	90.7	0.7	0.2	1.4	0.6	0.3	0.1
Italy.................	1,454,416	267,345	84.5	10.8	5.0	13.2	7.4	9.3	3.8
Spain................	18,277	6,984	72.4	0.2	0.2	0.4	0.4	0.1	0.1
Portugal..............	45,503	21,343	68.1	0.4	0.4	0.5	0.5	0.3	0.3
Europe, not specified..........	5,206	2,450	68.0	(¹)	(¹)	(¹)	(¹)	(¹)	(¹)
Asia:									
Turkey in Asia.............	52,728	10,909	82.9	0.5	0.2	0.8	0.4	0.3	0.2
All other countries.........	4,058	1,538	72.5	(¹)	(¹)	(¹)	(¹)	(¹)	(¹)
America:									
Canada—French..........	411,349	134,285	75.4	2.5	1.9	2.3	1.9	2.6	1.9
Canada—Other...........	772,167	424,577	64.5	4.5	5.5	4.0	4.4	4.9	6.1
Newfoundland...........	11,872	1,256	90.4	0.1	(¹)	0.1	(¹)	0.1	(¹)
West Indies²...............	21,068	2,519	89.3	0.2	(¹)	0.2	(¹)	0.1	(¹)
Mexico...............	100,685	151,360	39.9	1.2	3.9	2.2	7.5	0.6	2.2
Central and South Amer.ca.	5,833	1,872	75.7	0.1	(¹)	0.1	(¹)	(¹)	(¹)
All other.................	47,054	21,105	69.0	0.3	0.3	0.4	0.3	0.3	0.3
Of mixed foreign parentage.....	1,097,685	404,772	73.1	4.2	3.9	......	......	7.0	5.8

² Except possessions of the United States.

75108°—23——25

TABLE 109.—MOTHER TONGUE OF THE FOREIGN WHITE STOCK BY

[Figures for 1910 have been revised by deducting from the total for each mother tongue, as shown

	MOTHER TONGUE.	TOTAL FOREIGN WHITE STOCK.		FOREIGN-BORN WHITE.	
		1920	1910	1920	1910
1	All mother tongues...............	36,398,958	32,243,382	13,712,754	13,345,545
2	English and Celtic [1].....................	9,729,365	9,930,861	3,007,932	3,363,792
3	Germanic.........................	8,622,500	9,000,139	2,449,364	2,910,857
4	Scandinavian......................	2,972,796	2,781,402	1,194,933	1,272,150
5	Latin and Greek...................	6,036,001	4,185,932	2,990,954	2,385,388
6	Slavic and Lettic.................	5,270,581	3,194,647	2,460,332	1,831,666
7	Unclassified......................	2,956,321	2,261,563	1,602,073	1,465,420
8	Unknown or mixed mother tongue.........	811,394	888,838	7,166	116,272
9	English and Celtic [1].....................	9,729,365	9,930,861	3,007,932	3,363,792
	Germanic:				
10	German......	8,164,111	8,646,402	2,267,128	2,759,032
11	Dutch and Frisian.................	370,499	311,015	136,540	126,045
12	Flemish......	87,890	42,722	45,696	25,780
	Scandinavian:				
13	Swedish......	1,485,062	1,394,410	643,203	683,218
14	Norwegian.................	1,020,788	976,827	362,199	402,587
15	Danish [2]......	466,946	410,165	189,531	186,345
	Latin and Greek:				
16	Italian [3]......	3,365,864	2,135,393	1,624,998	1,365,110
17	French......	1,290,110	1,288,897	466,956	528,842
18	Spanish [4]......	850,848	444,132	556,111	258,131
19	Portuguese......	215,728	139,221	105,895	72,649
20	Rumanian......	91,683	49,588	62,336	42,277
21	Greek......	221,768	128,701	174,658	118,379
	Slavic and Lettic:				
22	Polish......	2,436,895	1,684,108	1,077,392	943,781
23	Czech......	622,796	531,193	234,564	228,738
24	Slovak......	619,866	281,707	274,948	166,474
25	Russian [5]......	731,949	91,341	392,049	57,926
26	Ruthenian......	95,458	34,837	55,672	25,131
27	Slovenian......	208,552	181,594	102,744	123,631
	Serbo-Croatian—				
28	Croatian......	140,559	92,260	83,063	74,036
29	Dalmatian......	3,119	5,372	2,112	4,344
30	Serbian......	52,208	26,483	36,471	23,403
31	Montenegrin......	4,535	3,949	4,198	3,886
32	Bulgarian......	14,420	19,183	12,853	18,341
33	Slavic, not specified [6]......	3,624	34,799	2,039	21,012
34	Lithuanian and Lettish.................	336,600	207,821	182,227	140,963
	Unclassified:				
35	Yiddish and Hebrew.................	2,043,613	1,664,142	1,091,820	1,051,767
36	Magyar......	473,538	315,283	268,112	229,094
37	Finnish [7]......	265,472	197,515	133,567	120,086
38	Armenian......	52,840	29,690	37,647	23,938
39	Syrian and Arabic......	104,139	46,495	57,557	32,868
40	Turkish......	8,505	5,310	6,627	4,709
41	Albanian......	6,426	2,358	5,515	2,312
42	All other [8]......	1,788	770	1,228	646
43	Unknown......	20,336	297,918	7,166	116,272
44	Of mixed mother tongue.................	791,058	590,920		

[1] Includes persons reporting Irish, Scotch, or Welsh.
[2] Includes Icelandic (5,634 in 1920; 5,105 in 1910)
[3] Includes Romansh and Friulian (2,206 in 1920; 3,183 in 1910)
[4] Includes Basque (327 in 1920; 656 in 1910).
[5] Probably includes a considerable proportion of Hebrews erroneously reported as Russian in mother tongue.

NATIVITY AND PARENTAGE, FOR THE UNITED STATES: 1920 AND 1910.

in 1910, the number of native whites of mixed mother tongue who were included in that total.]

NATIVE WHITE OF FOREIGN OR MIXED PARENTAGE.								
Total.		Both parents foreign.		Father foreign.		Mother foreign.		
1920	1910	1920	1910	1920	1910	1920	1910	
22,686,204	18,897,837	15,694,539	12,916,311	4,539,776	3,923,845	2,451,889	2,057,681	1
6,721,433	6,567,069	3,585,586	3,706,885	1,845,808	1,727,987	1,290,039	1,132,197	2
6,173,136	6,089,282	3,976,338	4,113,643	1,535,215	1,412,238	661,583	563,401	3
1,777,863	1,509,252	1,224,919	1,120,801	360,891	254,807	192,053	133,644	4
3,045,047	1,800,544	2,383,187	1,329,954	473,995	330,049	187,865	140,541	5
2,810,249	1,362,981	2,474,746	1,207,827	245,232	111,357	90,271	43,797	6
1,354,248	796,143	1,252,219	754,828	73,980	31,337	28,049	9,978	7
804,228	772,566	797,544	682,373	4,655	56,070	2,029	34,123	8
6,721,433	6,567,069	3,585,586	3,706,885	1,845,808	1,727,987	1,290,039	1,132,197	9
5,896,983	5,887,370	3,801,349	3,976,902	1,466,770	1,368,278	628,864	542,190	10
233,959	184,970	146,371	124,382	58,825	40,523	28,763	20,065	11
42,194	16,942	28,618	12,359	9,620	3,437	3,956	1,146	12
841,859	711,192	616,225	558,230	144,699	97,906	80,935	55,056	13
658,589	574,240	436,365	410,364	142,448	106,531	79,776	57,345	14
277,415	223,820	172,329	152,207	73,744	50,370	31,342	21,243	15
1,740,866	770,283	1,571,605	707,710	149,444	55,153	19,817	7,420	16
823,154	760,055	455,918	435,671	236,788	215,510	130,448	108,874	17
294,737	186,001	203,175	119,991	58,958	44,215	32,604	21,795	18
109,833	66,572	87,788	52,562	18,137	12,180	3,908	1,830	19
29,347	7,311	26,236	6,727	2,300	443	811	141	20
47,110	10,322	38,465	7,293	8,368	2,548	277	481	21
1,359,503	740,327	1,208,425	666,535	115,952	56,455	35,126	17,337	22
388,232	302,455	291,005	237,283	60,757	41,724	36,470	23,448	23
344,918	115,233	319,040	110,749	20,346	3,482	5,532	1,002	24
339,900	33,415	303,090	30,467	27,644	2,366	9,166	582	25
39,786	9,706	37,850	9,468	1,589	200	347	38	26
105,808	57,963	96,509	54,810	7,488	2,659	1,811	494	27
57,496	18,224	54,330	17,557	2,780	583	386	84	28
1,007	1,028	902	877	103	145	2	6	29
15,737	3,080	14,742	2,771	888	259	107	50	30
337	63	288	58	41	5	8	....	31
1,567	842	1,104	644	441	154	22	44	32
1,585	13,787	1,539	13,117	27	499	19	171	33
154,373	66,858	145,922	63,491	7,176	2,826	1,275	541	34
951,793	612,375	884,591	584,301	49,707	21,748	17,495	6,326	35
205,426	86,189	189,969	79,630	10,708	4,927	4,749	1,632	36
131,905	77,429	118,191	72,189	8,681	3,404	5,033	1,836	37
15,193	5,752	14,047	5,312	1,063	410	83	30	38
46,582	13,627	42,724	12,799	3,270	704	588	124	39
1,878	601	1,538	477	305	100	35	24	40
911	46	761	37	137	9	13	....	41
560	124	398	83	109	35	53	6	42
13,170	181,646	6,486	91,453	4,655	56,070	2,029	34,123	43
791,058	590,920	791,058	590,920	....	....	....	....	44

[6] Practically all Wendish in 1920; 395 reported as Wendish in 1910.
[7] Includes Lappish and Esthonian (1,390 in 1920; 2,533 in 1910).
[8] Comprises Persian (1,159 in 1920; 592 in 1910), Gypsy (173 in 1920; 156 in 1910), Georgian (65 in 1920; 14 in 1910), Kurdish (122 in 1920; 8 in 1910), and Egyptian (269 in 1920).

TABLE 110.—INCREASE IN THE FOREIGN WHITE STOCK, BY MOTHER TONGUE,

[Per cent not shown where base is less than 100.

	MOTHER TONGUE.	INCREASE: 1910–1920.			
		Total foreign white stock.		Foreign-born white.	
		Number.	Per cent.	Number.	Per cent.
1	**All mother tongues**................	4,155,576	12.9	367,209	2.8
2	English and Celtic..................	−201,496	−2.0	−355,860	−10.6
3	Germanic..........................	−377,639	−4.2	−461,493	−15.9
4	Scandinavian......................	191,394	6.9	−77,217	−6.1
5	Latin and Greek...................	1,850,069	44.2	605,566	25.4
6	Slavic and Lettic..................	2,075,934	65.0	628,666	34.3
7	Unclassified.......................	694,758	30.7	136,653	9.3
8	Unknown or mixed mother tongue...........	−77,444	−8.7	−109,106	−93.8
9	English and Celtic.................	−201,496	−2.0	−355,860	−10.6
	Germanic:				
10	German.......................	−482,291	−5.6	−491,904	−17.8
11	Dutch and Frisian............	59,484	19.1	10,495	8.3
12	Flemish......................	45,168	105.7	19,916	77.3
	Scandinavian:				
13	Swedish......................	90,652	6.5	−40,015	−5.9
14	Norwegian....................	43,961	4.5	−40,388	−10.0
15	Danish.......................	56,781	13.8	3,186	1.7
	Latin and Greek:				
16	Italian.......................	1,230,471	57.6	259,888	19.0
17	French.......................	1,213	0.1	−61,886	−11.7
18	Spanish......................	406,716	91.6	297,980	115.4
19	Portuguese...................	76,507	55.0	33,246	45.8
20	Rumanian....................	42,095	84.9	20,059	47.4
21	Greek........................	93,067	72.3	56,279	47.5
	Slavic and Lettic:				
22	Polish.......................	752,787	44.7	133,611	14.2
23	Czech........................	91,603	17.2	5,826	2.5
24	Slovak.......................	338,159	120.0	108,474	65.2
25	Russian[1]...................	640,608	701.3	334,123	576.8
26	Ruthenian....................	60,621	174.0	30,541	121.5
27	Slovenian....................	26,958	14.8	−20,887	−16.9
	Serbo-Croatian—				
28	Croatian.................	48,299	52.4	9,027	12.2
29	Dalmatian...............	−2,253	−41.9	−2,232	−51.4
30	Serbian..................	25,725	97.1	13,068	55.8
31	Montenegrin.............	586	14.8	312	8.0
32	Bulgarian....................	−4,763	−24.8	−5,488	−29.9
33	Slavic, not specified.........	−31,175	−89.6	−18,973	−90.3
34	Lithuanian and Lettish.......	128,779	62.0	41,264	29.3
	Unclassified:				
35	Yiddish and Hebrew..........	379,471	22.8	40,053	3.8
36	Magyar.......................	158,255	50.2	39,018	17.0
37	Finnish......................	67,957	34.4	13,481	11.2
38	Armenian....................	23,150	78.0	13,709	57.3
39	Syrian and Arabic...........	57,644	124.0	24,689	75.1
40	Turkish......................	3,195	60.2	1,918	40.7
41	Albanian.....................	4,068	172.5	3,203	138.5
42	All other....................	1,018	132.2	582	90.1
43	Unknown......................	−277,582	−93.2	−109,106	−93.8
44	Of mixed mother tongue..........	200,138	33.9		

[1] It is probable that a considerable proportion of the persons returned as Russian in mother tongue were in reality Hebrews. The increase between 1910 and 1920 is, therefore, probably exaggerated.

FOR NATIVITY AND PARENTAGE CLASSES, FOR THE UNITED STATES: 1910-1920.
A minus sign (−) denotes decrease.]

INCREASE: 1910-1920—continued.								
Native white of foreign or mixed parentage								
Total.		Both parents foreign.		Father foreign.		Mother foreign.		
Number.	Per cent.	Number.	Per cent.	Number.	Per cent.	Number.	Per cent.	
3,788,367	20.0	2,778,228	21.5	615,931	15.7	394,208	19.2	1
154,364	2.4	−121,299	−3.3	117,821	6.8	157,842	13.9	2
83,854	1.4	−137,305	−3.3	122,977	8.7	98,182	17.4	3
268,611	17.8	104,118	9.3	106,084	41.6	58,409	43.7	4
1,244,503	69.1	1,053,233	79.2	143,946	43.6	47,324	33.7	5
1,447,268	106.2	1,266,919	104.9	133,875	120.2	46,474	106.1	6
558,105	70.1	497,391	65.9	42,643	136.1	18,071	181.1	7
31,662	4.1	115,171	16.9	−51,415	−91.7	−32,094	−94.1	8
154,364	2.4	−121,299	−3.3	117,821	6.8	157,842	13.9	9
9,613	0.2	−175,553	−4.4	98,492	7.2	86,674	16.0	10
48,989	26.5	21,989	17.7	18,302	45.2	8,698	43.3	11
25,252	149.0	16,259	131.6	6,183	179.9	2,810	245.2	12
130,667	18.4	57,995	10.4	46,793	47.8	25,879	47.0	13
84,349	14.7	26,001	6.3	35,917	33.7	22,431	39.1	14
53,595	23.9	20,122	13.2	23,374	46.4	10,099	47.5	15
970,583	126.0	863,895	122.1	94,291	171.0	12,397	167.1	16
63,099	8.3	20,247	4.6	21,278	9.9	21,574	19.8	17
108,736	58.5	83,184	69.3	14,743	33.3	10,809	49.6	18
43,261	65.0	35,226	67.0	5,957	48.9	2,078	113.6	19
22,036	301.4	19,509	290.0	1,857	419.2	670	475.2	20
36,788	356.4	31,172	427.4	5,820	228.4	−204	−42.4	21
619,176	83.6	541,890	81.3	59,497	105.4	17,789	102.6	22
85,777	28.4	53,722	22.6	19,033	45.6	13,022	55.5	23
229,685	199.3	208,291	188.1	16,864	484.3	4,530	452.1	24
306,485	917.2	272,623	894.8	25,278	1,068.4	8,584	1,474.9	25
30,080	309.9	28,382	299.8	1,389	694.5	309	....	26
47,845	82.5	41,699	76.1	4,829	181.6	1,317	266.6	27
39,272	215.5	36,773	209.4	2,197	376.8	302	....	28
−21	−2.0	25	2.9	−42	−29.0	−4	....	29
12,657	410.9	11,971	432.0	629	242.9	57	....	30
274	....	230	....	36	....	8	....	31
725	86.1	460	71.4	287	186.4	−22	....	32
−12,202	−88.5	−11,578	−88.3	−472	−94.6	−152	−88.9	33
87,515	130.9	82,431	129.8	4,350	153.9	734	135.7	34
339,418	55.4	300,290	51.4	27,959	128.6	11,169	176.6	35
119,237	138.3	110,339	138.6	5,781	117.3	3,117	191.0	36
54,476	70.4	46,002	63.7	5,277	155.0	3,197	174.1	37
9,441	164.1	8,735	164.4	653	159.3	53	....	38
32,955	241.8	29,925	233.8	2,566	364.5	464	374.2	39
1,277	212.5	1,061	222.4	205	205.0	11	....	40
865	....	724	....	128	....	13	....	41
436	351.6	315	....	74	....	47	....	42
−168,476	−92.7	−84,967	−92.9	−51,415	−91.7	−32,094	−94.1	43
200,138	33.9	200,138	33.9	....	....	....	....	44

TABLE 111.—PER CENT DISTRIBUTION OF THE FOREIGN WHITE STOCK BY MOTHER
PARENTAGE CLASSES FOR MOTHER TONGUES,

MOTHER TONGUE.	Total foreign white stock.		Foreign-born white.		Native white of foreign or mixed parentage.							
					Total.		Both parents foreign.		Father foreign.		Mother foreign.	
	1920	1910	1920	1910	1920	1910	1920	1910	1920	1910	1920	1910
All mother tongues	100.0	100.0	100.0	100.0	100.0	100.0	100.0	100.0	100.0	100.0	100.0	100.0
English and Celtic	26.7	30.8	21.9	25.2	29.6	34.8	22.8	28.7	40.7	44.0	52.6	55.0
Germanic	23.7	27.9	17.9	21.8	27.2	32.2	25.3	31.8	33.8	36.0	27.0	27.4
Scandinavian	8.2	8.6	8.7	9.5	7.8	8.0	7.8	8.7	7.9	6.5	7.8	6.5
Latin and Greek	16.6	13.0	21.8	17.9	13.4	9.5	15.2	10.3	10.4	8.4	7.7	6.8
Slavic and Lettic	14.5	9.9	17.9	13.7	12.4	7.2	15.8	9.4	5.4	2.8	3.7	2.1
Unclassified	8.1	7.0	11.7	11.0	6.0	4.2	8.0	5.8	1.6	0.8	1.1	0.5
Unknown or mixed mother tongue	2.2	2.8	0.1	0.9	3.5	4.1	5.1	5.3	0.1	1.4	0.1	1.7
English and Celtic	26.7	30.8	21.9	25.2	29.6	34.8	22.8	28.7	40.7	44.0	52.6	55.0
Germanic:												
German	22.4	26.8	16.5	20.7	26.0	31.2	24.2	30.8	32.3	34.9	25.6	26.3
Dutch and Frisian	1.0	1.0	1.0	0.9	1.0	1.0	0.9	1.0	1.3	1.0	1.2	1.0
Flemish	0.2	0.1	0.3	0.2	0.2	0.1	0.2	0.1	0.2	0.1	0.2	0.1
Scandinavian:												
Swedish	4.1	4.3	4.7	5.1	3.7	3.8	3.9	4.3	3.2	2.5	3.3	2.7
Norwegian	2.8	3.0	2.6	3.0	2.9	3.0	2.8	3.2	3.1	2.7	3.3	2.8
Danish	1.3	1.3	1.4	1.4	1.2	1.2	1.1	1.2	1.6	1.3	1.3	1.0
Latin and Greek:												
Italian	9.2	6.6	11.9	10.2	7.7	4.1	10.0	5.5	3.3	1.4	0.8	0.4
French	3.5	4.0	3.4	4.0	3.6	4.0	2.9	3.4	5.2	5.5	5.3	5.3
Spanish	2.3	1.4	4.1	1.9	1.3	1.0	1.3	0.9	1.3	1.1	1.3	1.1
Portuguese	0.6	0.4	0.8	0.5	0.5	0.4	0.6	0.4	0.4	0.3	0.2	0.1
Rumanian	0.3	0.2	0.5	0.3	0.1	(1)	0.2	0.1	0.1	(1)	(1)	(1)
Greek	0.6	0.4	1.3	0.9	0.2	0.1	0.2	0.1	0.2	0.1	(1)	(1)
Slavic and Lettic:												
Polish	6.7	5.2	7.9	7.1	6.0	3.9	7.7	5.2	2.6	1.4	1.4	0.8
Czech	1.7	1.6	1.7	1.7	1.7	1.6	1.9	1.8	1.3	1.1	1.5	1.1
Slovak	1.7	0.9	2.0	1.2	1.5	0.6	2.0	0.9	0.4	0.1	0.2	(1)
Russian [2]	2.0	0.3	2.9	0.4	1.5	0.2	1.9	0.2	0.6	0.1	0.4	(1)
Ruthenian	0.3	0.1	0.4	0.2	0.2	0.1	0.2	0.1	(1)	(1)	(1)	(1)
Slovenian	0.6	0.6	0.7	0.9	0.5	0.3	0.6	0.4	0.2	0.1	0.1	(1)
Serbo-Croatian:												
Croatian	0.4	0.3	0.6	0.6	0.3	0.1	0.3	0.1	0.1	(1)	(1)	(1)
Dalmatian	(1)	(1)	(1)	(1)	(1)	(1)	(1)	(1)	(1)	(1)	(1)	(1)
Serbian	0.1	0.1	0.3	0.2	0.1	(1)	0.1	(1)	(1)	(1)	(1)	(1)
Montenegrin	(1)	(1)	(1)	(1)	(1)	(1)	(1)	(1)	(1)	(1)	(1)	....
Bulgarian	(1)	0.1	0.1	0.1	(1)	(1)	(1)	(1)	(1)	(1)	(1)	(1)
Slavic, not specified	(1)	0.1	(1)	0.2	(1)	0.1	(1)	0.1	(1)	(1)	(1)	(1)
Lithuanian and Lettish	0.9	0.6	1.3	1.1	0.7	0.4	0.9	0.5	0.2	0.1	0.1	(1)
Unclassified:												
Yiddish and Hebrew	5.6	5.2	8.0	7.9	4.2	3.2	5.6	4.5	1.1	0.6	0.7	0.3
Magyar	1.3	1.0	2.0	1.7	0.9	0.5	1.2	0.6	0.2	0.1	0.2	0.1
Finnish	0.7	0.6	1.0	0.9	0.6	0.4	0.8	0.6	0.2	0.1	0.2	0.1
Armenian	0.1	0.1	0.3	0.2	0.1	(1)	0.1	(1)	(1)	(1)	(1)	(1)
Syrian and Arabic	0.3	0.1	0.4	0.2	0.2	0.1	0.3	0.1	0.1	(1)	(1)	(1)
Turkish	(1)	(1)	(1)	(1)	(1)	(1)	(1)	(1)	(1)	(1)	(1)	(1)
Albanian	(1)	(1)	(1)	(1)	(1)	(1)	(1)	(1)	(1)	(1)	(1)	....
All other	(1)	(1)	(1)	(1)	(1)	(1)	(1)	(1)	(1)	(1)	(1)	(1)
Unknown	0.1	0.9	0.1	0.0	0.1	1.0	(1)	0.7	0.1	1.4	0.1	1.7
Of mixed mother tongue	2.2	1.8	....	....	3.5	3.1	5.0	4.6	....	....	....	....

[1] Less than one-tenth of 1 per cent.

TONGUE FOR NATIVITY AND PARENTAGE CLASSES, AND BY NATIVITY AND FOR THE UNITED STATES: 1920 AND 1910.

MOTHER TONGUE.	Foreign-born white.		Native white of foreign or mixed parentage.							
			Total.		Both parents foreign.		Father foreign.		Mother foreign.	
	1920	1910	1920	1910	1920	1910	1920	1910	1920	1910
All mother tongues	37.7	41.4	62.3	58.6	43.1	40.1	12.5	12.2	6.7	6.4
English and Celtic	30.9	33.9	69.1	66.1	36.9	37.3	19.0	17.4	13.3	11.4
Germanic	28.4	32.3	71.6	67.7	46.1	45.7	17.8	15.7	7.7	6.3
Scandinavian	40.2	45.7	59.8	54.3	41.2	40.3	12.1	9.2	6.5	4.8
Latin and Greek	49.6	57.0	50.4	43.0	39.5	31.8	7.9	7.9	3.1	3.4
Slavic and Lettic	46.7	57.3	53.3	42.7	47.0	37.8	4.7	3.5	1.7	1.4
Unclassified	54.2	64.8	45.8	35.2	42.4	33.4	2.5	1.4	0.9	0.4
Unknown or mixed mother tongue	0.9	13.1	99.1	86.9	98.3	76.8	0.6	6.3	0.3	3.8
English and Celtic	30.9	33.9	69.1	66.1	36.9	37.3	19.0	17.4	13.3	11.4
Germanic:										
German	27.8	31.9	72.2	68.1	46.6	46.0	18.0	15.8	7.7	6.3
Dutch and Frisian	36.9	40.5	63.1	59.5	39.5	40.0	15.9	13.0	7.8	6.5
Flemish	52.0	60.3	48.0	39.7	32.6	28.9	10.9	8.0	4.5	2.7
Scandinavian:										
Swedish	43.3	49.0	56.7	51.0	41.5	40.0	9.7	7.0	5.4	3.9
Norwegian	35.5	41.2	64.5	58.8	42.7	42.0	14.0	10.9	7.8	5.9
Danish	40.6	45.4	59.4	54.6	36.9	37.1	15.8	12.3	6.7	5.2
Latin and Greek:										
Italian	48.3	63.9	51.7	36.1	46.7	33.1	4.4	2.6	0.6	0.3
French	36.2	41.0	63.8	59.0	35.3	33.8	18.4	16.7	10.1	8.4
Spanish	65.4	58.1	34.6	41.9	23.9	27.0	6.9	10.0	3.8	4.9
Portuguese	49.1	52.2	50.9	47.8	40.7	37.8	8.4	8.7	1.8	1.3
Rumanian	68.0	85.3	32.0	14.7	28.6	13.6	2.5	0.9	0.9	0.3
Greek	78.8	92.0	21.2	8.0	17.3	5.7	3.8	2.0	0.1	0.4
Slavic and Lettic:										
Polish	44.2	56.0	55.8	44.0	49.6	39.6	4.8	3.4	1.4	1.0
Czech	37.7	43.1	62.3	56.9	46.7	44.7	9.8	7.9	5.9	4.4
Slovak	44.4	59.1	55.6	40.9	51.5	39.3	3.3	1.2	0.9	0.4
Russian [2]	53.6	63.4	46.4	36.6	41.4	33.4	3.8	2.6	1.3	0.6
Ruthenian	58.3	72.1	41.7	27.9	39.7	27.2	1.7	0.6	0.4	0.1
Slovenian	49.3	68.1	50.7	31.9	46.3	30.2	3.6	1.5	0.9	0.3
Serbo-Croatian:										
Croatian	59.1	80.2	40.9	19.8	38.7	19.0	2.0	0.6	0.3	0.1
Dalmatian	67.7	80.9	32.3	19.1	28.9	16.3	3.3	2.7	0.1	0.1
Serbian	69.9	88.4	30.1	11.6	28.2	10.5	1.7	1.0	0.2	0.2
Montenegrin	92.6	98.4	7.4	1.6	6.4	1.5	0.9	0.1	0.2	
Bulgarian	89.1	95.6	10.9	4.4	7.7	3.4	3.1	0.8	0.2	0.2
Slavic, not specified	56.3	60.4	43.7	39.6	42.5	37.7	0.7	1.4	0.5	0.5
Lithuanian and Lettish	54.1	67.8	45.9	32.2	43.4	30.6	2.1	1.4	0.4	0.3
Unclassified:										
Yiddish and Hebrew	53.4	63.2	46.6	36.8	43.3	35.1	2.4	1.3	0.9	0.4
Magyar	56.6	72.7	43.4	27.3	40.1	25.3	2.3	1.6	1.0	0.5
Finnish	50.3	60.8	49.7	39.2	44.5	36.5	3.3	1.7	1.9	0.9
Armenian	71.2	80.6	28.8	19.4	26.6	17.9	2.0	1.4	0.2	0.1
Syrian and Arabic	55.3	70.7	44.7	29.3	41.0	27.5	3.1	1.5	0.6	0.3
Turkish	77.9	88.7	22.1	11.3	18.1	9.0	3.6	1.9	0.4	0.5
Albanian	85.8	98.0	14.2	2.0	11.8	1.6	2.1	0.4	0.2	
All other	68.7	83.9	31.3	16.1	22.3	10.8	6.1	4.5	3.0	0.8
Unknown	35.2	39.0	64.8	61.0	31.9	30.7	22.9	18.8	10.0	11.5
Of mixed mother tongue			100.0	100.0	100.0	100.0				

[2] See footnote to Table 109, p. 386.

TABLE 112.—MOTHER TONGUE OF THE FOREIGN

DIVISION AND STATE.	All mother tongues: 1920	English and Celtic.	Germanic.			Scandinavian.		
			German.	Dutch and Frisian.	Flemish.	Swedish.	Norwegian.	Danish.
United States	36,398,958	9,729,365	8,164,111	370,499	87,890	1,485,062	1,020,788	466,946
GEOGRAPHIC DIVISIONS:								
New England	4,512,930	1,981,954	185,564	6,045	3,971	142,307	15,274	16,703
Middle Atlantic	12,010,828	3,145,076	2,111,589	69,729	11,913	174,199	60,399	43,673
East North Central	9,148,492	1,984,717	2,896,993	178,484	49,570	389,506	235,434	102,565
West North Central	4,749,839	871,419	1,716,113	73,240	12,041	500,194	542,150	168,131
South Atlantic	869,524	251,295	205,640	3,839	1,497	10,202	5,090	4,513
East South Central	274,765	86,454	106,659	1,732	247	3,732	1,196	1,379
West South Central	1,155,942	162,499	277,264	4,318	1,652	18,836	7,311	7,087
Mountain	1,210,391	413,455	205,994	12,817	2,130	81,791	47,896	55,149
Pacific	2,466,247	832,496	458,295	20,295	4,869	164,295	106,038	67,746
NEW ENGLAND:								
Maine	269,915	142,531	3,005	130	37	4,720	1,156	2,427
New Hampshire	216,819	79,632	4,996	293	605	3,828	883	373
Vermont	123,492	57,656	2,526	153	22	2,395	218	338
Massachusetts	2,572,751	1,257,891	76,341	4,169	2,269	78,937	9,475	6,670
Rhode Island	420,427	171,486	10,663	276	566	13,823	975	616
Connecticut	909,526	272,758	88,033	1,024	472	38,604	2,567	6,279
MIDDLE ATLANTIC:								
New York	6,503,761	1,696,377	1,134,050	33,188	4,160	101,365	45,787	24,912
New Jersey	1,824,412	460,197	355,235	31,785	2,440	22,394	9,994	12,277
Pennsylvania	3,682,655	988,502	622,304	4,756	5,313	50,440	4,618	6,484
EAST NORTH CENTRAL:								
Ohio	1,902,771	419,481	652,728	8,329	1,771	16,422	3,065	5,227
Indiana	519,527	110,818	223,894	6,749	3,889	12,565	1,513	2,559
Illinois	3,232,770	643,522	904,730	38,341	15,925	235,075	66,077	36,995
Michigan	1,931,180	629,660	396,602	100,295	16,856	66,807	17,055	17,591
Wisconsin	1,562,244	181,236	719,039	24,770	11,129	58,637	147,724	40,193
WEST NORTH CENTRAL:								
Minnesota	1,541,309	200,677	395,682	15,160	3,754	283,815	281,046	44,600
Iowa	855,628	197,624	341,301	35,787	2,280	63,461	62,513	47,970
Missouri	688,108	166,426	335,471	3,769	1,735	13,206	1,826	4,605
North Dakota	431,983	62,559	142,826	2,936	668	28,371	127,532	12,750
South Dakota	310,549	48,489	115,672	9,039	582	24,116	58,946	17,015
Nebraska	522,155	90,636	216,148	3,382	920	55,010	7,014	34,260
Kansas	400,102	105,008	169,013	3,167	2,102	32,215	3,273	6,931
SOUTH ATLANTIC:								
Delaware	52,739	19,783	6,120	96	15	703	113	147
Maryland	311,649	65,176	110,684	955	107	1,501	1,054	827
District of Columbia	87,372	38,473	17,495	403	51	1,311	719	574
Virginia	83,415	30,039	14,416	647	85	1,406	987	838
West Virginia	144,378	31,180	24,885	326	928	829	128	263
North Carolina	18,576	7,598	3,145	198	26	369	148	141
South Carolina	19,120	6,126	5,068	109	66	270	178	195
Georgia	46,417	16,864	9,435	292	64	763	314	306
Florida	105,858	36,056	14,392	813	155	3,050	1,449	1,222
EAST SOUTH CENTRAL:								
Kentucky	141,426	38,956	76,036	902	124	548	187	270
Tennessee	53,236	20,318	13,686	350	22	802	192	372
Alabama	52,903	18,792	11,715	337	60	1,645	553	445
Mississippi	27,200	8,388	5,222	143	41	737	264	292
WEST SOUTH CENTRAL:								
Arkansas	53,065	15,920	21,328	578	126	975	288	499
Louisiana	154,887	28,406	32,203	750	544	1,266	953	808
Oklahoma	142,087	41,580	52,530	1,090	350	3,273	1,067	1,703
Texas	805,903	76,856	171,107	1,061	632	13,322	5,003	4,007
MOUNTAIN:								
Montana	258,457	93,539	50,142	3,999	945	17,158	27,793	7,441
Idaho	131,416	53,316	26,259	1,224	196	13,432	7,023	9,142
Wyoming	67,262	24,568	12,519	389	121	4,885	1,638	2,709
Colorado	321,062	100,189	82,195	2,587	576	24,898	4,061	6,878
New Mexico	61,356	9,519	5,984	284	97	853	363	327
Arizona	140,304	21,960	7,697	283	93	2,168	787	1,161
Utah	196,120	96,969	16,772	3,955	72	17,218	5,819	26,066
Nevada	34,414	13,395	4,426	96	30	1,179	412	1,425
PACIFIC:								
Washington	608,071	213,638	110,690	7,499	1,773	72,864	65,405	18,782
Oregon	271,420	90,501	74,531	2,711	1,161	23,609	16,119	8,665
California	1,586,756	528,357	273,074	10,085	1,935	67,822	24,514	40,299

WHITE STOCK, BY DIVISIONS AND STATES: 1920.

DIVISION AND STATE.	Italian.	French.	Spanish.	Portuguese.	Rumanian.	Greek.	Polish.	Czech.	Slovak.
					FOREIGN WHITE STOCK—continued.				
			Latin and Greek.				Slavic and Lettic.		
United States	3,365,864	1,290,110	850,848	215,728	91,683	221,768	2,436,895	622,796	619,866
GEOGRAPHIC DIVISIONS:									
New England	494,924	651,788	5,417	124,252	2,265	44,710	275,342	8,306	25,834
Middle Atlantic	1,943,798	181,048	47,081	4,722	41,248	55,497	992,522	82,289	391,285
East North Central	411,536	204,149	14,775	1,897	35,443	54,895	969,902	266,313	159,310
West North Central	72,035	89,274	28,584	299	5,445	13,428	94,078	167,477	13,006
South Atlantic	81,408	15,504	27,396	878	2,328	15,217	56,045	13,611	9,600
East South Central	19,929	9,443	1,813	98	515	2,893	3,444	934	1,252
West South Central	74,660	36,511	418,064	505	623	4,824	17,470	57,959	2,404
Mountain	60,474	26,282	153,704	905	908	10,967	9,035	10,911	9,664
Pacific	207,100	76,111	154,014	82,172	2,908	19,337	19,057	14,996	7,511
NEW ENGLAND:									
Maine	5,574	87,356	171	309	27	1,704	2,706	66	1,232
New Hampshire	3,902	91,246	87	237	41	6,850	9,205	97	59
Vermont	8,085	40,304	1,046	68	12	241	3,722	155	323
Massachusetts	237,858	303,821	2,169	99,096	834	29,044	145,822	3,648	2,732
Rhode Island	70,699	79,801	228	22,022	389	1,623	16,578	258	284
Connecticut	168,806	49,260	1,716	2,520	962	5,248	97,309	4,082	21,204
MIDDLE ATLANTIC:									
New York	1,124,162	119,622	36,373	2,559	28,552	31,230	403,969	52,730	46,209
New Jersey	344,765	24,103	4,524	953	3,480	6,203	176,342	9,720	48,857
Pennsylvania	474,871	37,323	6,184	1,210	9,216	18,064	412,211	19,839	296,219
EAST NORTH CENTRAL:									
Ohio	121,511	32,578	3,277	457	16,576	15,376	138,106	59,206	78,982
Indiana	12,862	14,806	1,744	49	4,071	4,388	46,251	3,666	11,750
Illinois	196,925	49,124	6,860	1,220	4,998	22,006	382,101	140,011	44,010
Michigan	57,475	77,572	2,400	121	9,229	8,360	251,381	17,005	12,776
Wisconsin	22,763	30,069	494	50	569	4,765	152,063	46,425	11,792
WEST NORTH CENTRAL:									
Minnesota	15,306	33,630	516	27	2,253	2,812	49,490	35,394	6,478
Iowa	9,812	10,653	3,263	77	324	3,408	3,082	32,859	1,880
Missouri	31,500	17,350	4,825	91	1,814	3,751	15,603	13,746	2,531
North Dakota	341	7,267	60	5	365	508	4,751	8,491	333
South Dakota	1,007	3,660	135	9	120	408	1,861	10,982	221
Nebraska	6,730	5,114	3,011	34	514	1,747	14,720	54,024	281
Kansas	7,339	11,600	16,774	56	55	794	4,571	11,981	1,282
SOUTH ATLANTIC:									
Delaware	8,325	626	256	22	117	387	9,194	217	165
Maryland	19,692	2,788	729	87	420	1,355	29,129	9,752	1,398
District of Columbia	7,561	2,342	562	43	88	1,814	946	343	72
Virginia	5,506	1,919	649	226	152	2,366	1,752	1,548	1,670
West Virginia	27,033	2,544	2,298	18	823	3,699	12,663	918	5,901
North Carolina	830	664	129	31	27	765	298	52	94
South Carolina	769	446	127	21	20	802	585	116	19
Georgia	1,410	1,458	520	77	149	2,080	782	241	83
Florida	10,282	2,717	22,126	353	532	1,949	696	424	198
EAST SOUTH CENTRAL:									
Kentucky	4,194	4,107	337	21	278	583	1,307	266	373
Tennessee	4,873	1,846	375	44	83	719	966	248	90
Alabama	6,507	2,094	558	18	116	1,308	611	255	648
Mississippi	4,355	1,396	543	15	38	283	560	165	141
WEST SOUTH CENTRAL:									
Arkansas	3,019	2,299	460	17	67	415	1,292	1,006	769
Louisiana	46,394	18,950	7,603	224	92	849	605	689	337
Oklahoma	4,863	4,592	8,658	30	45	823	2,530	6,335	465
Texas	20,384	10,670	401,343	234	419	2,737	13,043	49,929	833
MOUNTAIN:									
Montana	6,927	8,968	432	43	374	1,472	2,923	4,389	2,264
Idaho	2,653	3,301	3,303	120	61	835	390	1,305	150
Wyoming	3,632	1,321	2,257	69	62	1,407	1,663	1,007	1,075
Colorado	30,145	6,658	15,313	79	258	2,109	3,024	2,957	5,322
New Mexico	3,637	1,272	34,497	59	8	334	246	297	244
Arizona	2,385	1,622	93,278	67	55	431	441	391	154
Utah	6,167	1,769	1,658	30	84	3,682	256	393	864
Nevada	4,928	1,371	2,966	438	6	697	92	172	91
PACIFIC:									
Washington	19,205	15,330	2,216	524	324	4,375	7,805	4,329	4,220
Oregon	7,689	6,481	1,715	416	253	2,069	2,190	2,897	598
California	180,206	54,300	150,083	81,232	2,331	12,893	9,062	7,770	2,693

TABLE 112.—MOTHER TONGUE OF THE FOREIGN WHITE

| DIVISION AND STATE. | FOREIGN WHITE STOCK—continued. | | | | | | | Unclassified. |
| | Slavic and Lettic—Continued. | | | | | | | |
	Russian.[1]	Ruthenian.	Slovenian.	Serbo-Croatian.	Bulgarian.	Slavic, not specified.	Lithuanian and Lettish.	Yiddish and Hebrew.
United States	731,949	95,458	208,552	200,421	14,420	3,624	336,600	2,043,613
GEOGRAPHIC DIVISIONS:								
New England	67,745	5,728	4,014	1,646	189	604	75,185	211,232
Middle Atlantic	411,516	72,461	72,176	66,346	1,759	2,693	134,410	1,339,275
East North Central	107,786	13,146	81,029	79,956	8,290	169	108,678	289,880
West North Central	49,687	2,228	19,184	22,150	1,594	9	5,107	69,678
South Atlantic	29,591	1,067	4,323	4,416	228	23	8,060	71,109
East South Central	6,053	48	942	629	83		216	10,656
West South Central	11,380	211	1,804	1,072	289	117	1,192	13,338
Mountain	13,104	209	12,452	12,421	1,080	7	873	11,350
Pacific	35,087	360	12,628	11,785	908	2	2,879	27,095
NEW ENGLAND:								
Maine	2,241	27	30	61	3		2,185	4,954
New Hampshire	2,886	203	18	72	11	1	2,364	2,036
Vermont	1,245	107	73	82	4		194	1,308
Massachusetts	32,617	1,296	614	796	95		44,064	141,228
Rhode Island	4,122	1,306	22	142	43		1,333	12,257
Connecticut	24,634	2,789	3,257	493	33	603	25,045	49,449
MIDDLE ATLANTIC:								
New York	255,265	17,055	15,025	8,143	655	7	27,096	1,013,289
New Jersey	48,613	8,092	6,894	1,720	99	18	15,884	119,018
Pennsylvania	107,638	47,314	50,257	56,483	1,005	2,668	91,430	206,968
EAST NORTH CENTRAL:								
Ohio	31,318	6,213	39,012	25,595	3,418	18	10,532	57,039
Indiana	5,977	223	3,939	7,846	1,098		3,741	6,672
Illinois	38,750	2,891	21,595	24,844	1,352	110	74,805	167,806
Michigan	23,630	3,337	6,808	14,818	2,067	3	12,022	40,687
Wisconsin	8,111	482	9,675	6,853	355	38	7,578	17,676
WEST NORTH CENTRAL:								
Minnesota	8,562	715	13,803	9,003	621	4	1,031	24,572
Iowa	5,145	53	649	3,526	323	3	1,613	7,399
Missouri	10,530	711	1,021	3,814	262	1	890	27,984
North Dakota	11,365	682	101	177	154		132	1,668
South Dakota	3,416	18	341	464	129		74	728
Nebraska	4,973	20	334	1,608	60		1,093	6,210
Kansas	5,696	29	2,935	3,558	45	1	274	1,117
SOUTH ATLANTIC:								
Delaware	1,909	307	106	21			267	2,521
Maryland	10,074	356	536	375	34	23	5,074	41,057
District of Columbia	3,422	11	50	44	5		76	7,385
Virginia	3,546	27	376	94	20		150	8,670
West Virginia	3,937	332	3,043	3,661	126		2,282	1,871
North Carolina	821	2	42	37	6		38	1,468
South Carolina	1,144	7	19	14			19	1,572
Georgia	3,524	14	77	100	7		63	4,867
Florida	1,214	11	74	70	30		91	1,698
EAST SOUTH CENTRAL								
Kentucky	2,328	42	207	354	33		137	3,668
Tennessee	1,662	4	71	34	13		28	3,790
Alabama	1,269	2	206	174	36		32	2,251
Mississippi	794		458	67	1		19	947
WEST SOUTH CENTRAL:								
Arkansas	677	3	125	95	28		77	749
Louisiana	2,242	1	694	188	53		45	1,840
Oklahoma	3,371	157	326	171	124	1	840	1,414
Texas	5,090	50	659	618	84	116	230	9,325
MOUNTAIN:								
Montana	3,521	83	3,622	4,839	407		258	607
Idaho	734	12	281	507	53	7	49	146
Wyoming	554	36	1,297	946	136		77	516
Colorado	6,052	64	5,246	1,831	366		322	8,702
New Mexico	277	2	453	767	34		21	130
Arizona	1,201	5	381	1,788	35		65	378
Utah	621	6	846	1,013	34		70	777
Nevada	144	1	326	730	15		11	94
PACIFIC:								
Washington	6,976	222	3,445	4,174	314		1,408	3,584
Oregon	3,676	71	975	1,223	302		497	2,700
California	24,435	67	8,208	6,388	292	2	974	20,811

[1] See footnote to Table 109, p. 386.

STOCK, BY DIVISIONS AND STATES: 1920—Continued.

DIVISION AND STATE.	FOREIGN WHITE STOCK—continued.								
	Unclassified—Continued.							Un-known.	Of mixed mother tongue.
	Magyar.	Finnish.	Armenian.	Syrian and Arabic.	Turkish.	Albanian.	All other.		
United States	473,538	265,472	52,840	104,139	8,505	6,426	1,788	20,336	791,058
GEOGRAPHIC DIVISIONS:									
New England........	23,418	31,051	18,603	20,846	1,841	3,261	217	735	61,959
Middle Atlantic......	232,426	22,565	14,121	29,785	3,663	1,414	524	4,639	244,987
East North Central...	177,461	95,842	7,558	20,117	1,467	1,070	591	5,547	194,416
West North Central..	10,538	65,683	821	7,409	209	298	139	3,127	125,064
South Atlantic.......	14,798	1,792	548	8,221	254	29	45	1,302	19,655
East South Central...	2,446	335	85	3,292	89	26	15	865	7,265
West South Central..	2,265	589	213	7,589	103	12	45	1,655	22,081
Mountain.............	3,280	12,575	405	2,706	190	158	48	765	36,686
Pacific..............	6,906	35,040	10,486	4,174	689	158	164	1,701	78,945
NEW ENGLAND:									
Maine...............	64	2,365	230	1,308	24	451	1	46	2,774
New Hampshire......	64	3,010	428	912	57	131	....	28	2,264
Vermont............	388	822	63	486	....	6	....	9	1,441
Massachusetts.......	1,606	23,120	13,204	13,270	1,334	2,354	38	354	35,985
Rhode Island........	203	325	2,950	2,203	265	127	....	44	4,798
Connecticut.........	21,093	1,409	1,728	2,667	161	192	178	254	14,697
MIDDLE ATLANTIC:									
New York...........	93,606	15,362	7,054	14,752	2,891	496	309	2,117	145,394
New Jersey..........	59,190	2,690	3,519	3,871	326	168	72	777	40,192
Pennsylvania........	79,630	4,513	3,548	11,162	446	750	143	1,745	59,401
EAST NORTH CENTRAL:									
Ohio................	97,962	12,491	1,028	7,159	506	456	103	1,505	35,324
Indiana.............	15,357	377	163	1,512	98	85	80	689	10,096
Illinois.............	29,041	4,233	2,210	3,064	308	124	283	1,548	71,886
Michigan............	27,763	65,936	3,175	7,195	465	274	99	904	40,812
Wisconsin...........	7,338	12,805	982	1,187	90	131	26	901	36,298
WEST NORTH CENTRAL:									
Minnesota..........	2,823	58,705	213	1,649	50	27	13	602	48,276
Iowa...............	743	138	118	1,026	46	7	89	549	17,907
Missouri............	4,414	134	233	1,782	61	216	17	948	16,841
North Dakota.......	705	3,398	42	731	15	....	2	204	12,849
South Dakota.......	501	3,184	30	624	8	5	4	194	8,567
Nebraska...........	853	64	154	1,025	14	40	6	288	11,868
Kansas.............	499	60	31	572	15	3	8	342	8,756
SOUTH ATLANTIC:									
Delaware...........	361	57	8	17	2	....	5	44	828
Maryland...........	1,686	243	55	164	18	2	4	237	6,057
District of Columbia..	283	127	75	502	21	2	8	244	2,320
Virginia............	2,156	352	232	1,277	54	3	3	165	2,084
West Virginia.......	9,420	423	62	2,372	108	5	4	173	2,123
North Carolina.....	92	18	12	1,072	3	....	17	67	366
South Carolina......	69	64	6	793	2	....	....	40	454
Georgia............	334	61	29	1,016	35	5	....	93	1,354
Florida............	397	447	69	1,008	11	12	4	239	4,039
EAST SOUTH CENTRAL:									
Kentucky..........	1,542	59	31	704	25	2	5	304	3,496
Tennessee..........	505	32	20	279	4	24	4	207	1,573
Alabama...........	340	108	32	1,056	51	....	1	253	1,430
Mississippi.........	59	136	2	1,253	9	....	5	101	766
WEST SOUTH CENTRAL:									
Arkansas...........	119	15	6	461	....	....	3	167	1,482
Louisiana..........	638	187	39	2,096	60	2	6	421	5,702
Oklahoma..........	422	109	30	1,628	7	2	20	242	3,264
Texas..............	1,086	278	138	3,404	36	8	16	825	11,633
MOUNTAIN:									
Montana...........	704	6,736	144	430	62	34	23	144	8,034
Idaho.............	178	1,590	12	123	4	45	2	87	4,876
Wyoming...........	495	1,689	58	147	34	10	3	33	1,909
Colorado...........	1,344	1,061	43	612	27	13	13	309	7,808
New Mexico........	164	65	2	461	1	....	....	24	934
Arizona............	156	502	19	622	7	6	6	58	2,102
Utah..............	187	802	117	284	38	50	....	82	9,919
Nevada............	52	130	10	27	17	....	1	28	1,104
PACIFIC:									
Washington........	759	15,925	279	602	149	88	23	388	20,756
Oregon............	588	9,738	95	375	32	15	9	222	9,297
California..........	5,559	9,377	10,112	3,197	508	55	132	1,091	48,892

TABLE 113.—PER CENT DISTRIBUTION OF THE FOREIGN WHITE

| | DIVISION AND STATE. | PER CENT OF TOTAL FOREIGN WHITE STOCK IN SPECIFIED DIVISION OR STATE. | | | | | | | | | | | | |
| | | | Germanic. | | | Scandinavian. | | | Latin and Greek. | | | | | |
		English and Celtic	German.	Dutch and Frisian.	Flemish.	Swedish.	Norwegian.	Danish.	Italian.	French.	Spanish.	Portuguese.	Rumanian.	Greek.
1	United States	26.7	22.4	1.0	0.2	4.1	2.8	1.3	9.2	3.5	2.3	0.6	0.3	0.6
	GEOGRAPHIC DIVISIONS:													
2	New England	43.9	4.1	0.1	0.1	3.2	0.3	0.4	11.0	14.4	0.1	2.8	0.1	1.0
3	Middle Atlantic	26.2	17.6	0.6	0.1	1.5	0.5	0.4	16.2	1.5	0.4	(1)	0.3	0.5
4	East North Central	21.7	31.7	2.0	0.5	4.3	2.6	1.1	4.5	2.2	0.2	(1)	0.4	0.6
5	West North Central	18.3	36.1	1.5	0.3	10.5	11.4	3.5	1.5	1.9	0.6	(1)	0.1	0.3
6	South Atlantic	28.9	23.6	0.4	0.2	1.2	0.6	0.5	9.4	1.8	3.2	0.1	0.3	1.8
7	East South Central	31.5	38.8	0.6	0.1	1.4	0.4	0.5	7.3	3.4	0.7	(1)	0.2	1.1
8	West South Central	14.1	24.0	0.4	0.1	1.6	0.6	0.6	6.5	3.2	36.2	(1)	0.1	0.4
9	Mountain	34.2	17.0	1.1	0.2	6.8	4.0	4.6	5.0	2.2	12.7	0.1	0.1	0.9
10	Pacific	33.8	18.6	0.8	0.2	6.7	4.3	2.7	8.4	3.1	6.2	3.3	0.1	0.8
	NEW ENGLAND:													
11	Maine	52.8	1.1	(1)	(1)	1.7	0.4	0.9	2.1	32.4	0.1	0.1	(1)	0.6
12	New Hampshire	36.7	2.3	0.1	0.3	1.8	0.4	0.2	1.8	42.1	(1)	0.1	(1)	3.2
13	Vermont	46.7	2.0	0.1	(1)	1.9	0.2	0.3	6.5	32.6	0.8	0.1	(1)	0.2
14	Massachusetts	48.9	3.0	0.2	0.1	3.1	0.4	0.3	9.2	11.8	0.1	3.9	(1)	1.1
15	Rhode Island	40.8	2.5	0.1	0.1	3.3	0.2	0.1	16.8	19.0	0.1	5.2	0.1	0.4
16	Connecticut	30.0	9.7	0.1	0.1	4.2	0.3	0.7	18.6	5.4	0.2	0.3	0.1	0.6
	MIDDLE ATLANTIC:													
17	New York	26.1	17.4	0.5	0.1	1.6	0.7	0.4	17.3	1.8	0.6	(1)	0.4	0.5
18	New Jersey	25.2	19.5	1.7	0.1	1.2	0.5	0.7	18.9	1.3	0.2	0.1	0.2	0.3
19	Pennsylvania	26.8	16.9	0.1	0.1	1.4	0.1	0.2	12.9	1.0	0.2	(1)	0.3	0.5
	EAST NORTH CENTRAL:													
20	Ohio	22.0	34.3	0.4	0.1	0.9	0.2	0.3	6.4	1.7	0.2	(1)	0.9	0.8
21	Indiana	21.3	43.1	1.3	0.7	2.4	0.3	0.5	2.5	2.8	0.3	(1)	0.8	0.8
22	Illinois	19.9	28.0	1.2	0.5	7.3	2.0	1.1	6.1	1.5	0.2	(1)	0.2	0.7
23	Michigan	32.6	20.5	5.2	0.9	3.5	0.9	0.9	3.0	4.0	0.1	(1)	0.5	0.4
24	Wisconsin	11.6	46.0	1.6	0.7	3.8	9.5	2.6	1.5	1.9	(1)	(1)	(1)	0.3
	WEST NORTH CENTRAL:													
25	Minnesota	13.0	25.7	1.0	0.2	18.4	18.2	2.9	1.0	2.2	(1)	(1)	0.1	0.2
26	Iowa	23.1	39.9	4.2	0.3	7.4	7.3	5.6	1.1	1.2	0.4	(1)	(1)	0.4
27	Missouri	24.2	48.8	0.5	0.3	1.9	0.3	0.7	4.6	2.5	0.7	(1)	0.3	0.5
28	North Dakota	14.5	33.1	0.7	0.2	6.6	29.5	3.0	0.1	1.7	(1)	(1)	0.1	0.1
29	South Dakota	15.6	37.2	2.9	0.2	7.8	19.0	5.5	0.3	1.2	(1)	(1)	(1)	0.1
30	Nebraska	17.4	41.4	0.6	0.2	10.5	1.3	6.6	1.3	1.0	0.6	(1)	0.1	0.3
31	Kansas	26.2	42.2	0.8	0.5	8.1	0.8	1.7	1.8	2.9	4.2	(1)	0.1	0.2
	SOUTH ATLANTIC:													
32	Delaware	37.5	11.6	0.2	(1)	1.3	0.2	0.3	15.8	1.2	0.5	(1)	0.2	0.7
33	Maryland	20.9	35.5	0.3	(1)	0.5	0.3	0.3	6.3	0.9	0.2	(1)	0.1	0.4
34	District of Columbia	44.0	20.0	0.5	0.1	1.5	0.8	0.7	8.7	2.7	0.6	(1)	0.1	2.1
35	Virginia	36.0	17.3	0.8	0.1	1.7	1.2	1.0	6.6	2.3	0.8	0.3	0.2	2.8
36	West Virginia	21.6	17.2	0.2	0.6	0.6	0.1	0.2	18.7	1.8	1.6	(1)	0.6	2.6
37	North Carolina	40.9	16.9	1.1	0.1	2.0	0.8	0.8	4.5	3.6	0.7	0.2	0.1	4.1
38	South Carolina	32.0	26.5	0.6	0.3	1.4	0.9	1.0	4.0	2.3	0.7	0.1	0.1	4.2
39	Georgia	36.3	20.3	0.6	0.1	1.6	0.7	0.7	3.0	3.1	1.1	0.2	0.3	4.5
40	Florida	34.1	13.6	0.8	0.1	2.9	1.4	1.2	9.7	2.6	20.9	0.3	0.5	1.8
	EAST SOUTH CENTRAL:													
41	Kentucky	27.5	53.8	0.6	0.1	0.4	0.1	0.2	3.0	2.9	0.2	(1)	0.2	0.4
42	Tennessee	38.2	25.7	0.7	(1)	1.5	0.4	0.7	9.2	3.5	0.7	0.1	0.2	1.4
43	Alabama	35.5	22.1	0.6	0.1	3.1	1.0	0.8	12.3	4.0	1.1	(1)	0.2	2.5
44	Mississippi	30.8	19.2	0.5	0.2	2.7	1.0	1.1	16.0	5.1	2.0	0.1	0.1	1.0
	WEST SOUTH CENTRAL:													
45	Arkansas	30.0	40.2	1.1	0.2	1.8	0.5	0.9	5.7	4.3	2.9	(1)	0.1	0.8
46	Louisiana	18.3	13.3	0.4	0.2	1.8	0.5	0.9	30.7	4.3	2.9	0.1	0.1	0.8
47	Oklahoma	29.3	37.0	0.7	0.2	2.3	0.8	1.2	3.4	3.2	6.1	(1)	(1)	0.6
48	Texas	9.5	21.2	0.2	0.1	1.7	0.6	0.5	2.5	1.3	49.8	(1)	0.1	0.3
	MOUNTAIN:													
49	Montana	36.2	19.4	1.5	0.4	6.6	10.8	2.9	2.7	3.5	0.2	(1)	0.1	0.6
50	Idaho	40.6	20.0	0.9	0.1	10.2	5.3	7.0	2.0	2.5	2.5	0.1	(1)	0.6
51	Wyoming	36.5	18.6	0.6	0.2	7.3	2.4	4.0	5.4	2.0	3.4	0.1	0.1	2.1
52	Colorado	31.2	25.6	0.8	0.2	7.8	1.3	2.1	9.4	2.1	4.8	(1)	0.1	0.7
53	New Mexico	15.5	9.8	0.5	0.2	1.4	0.6	0.5	5.9	2.1	56.2	0.1	(1)	0.5
54	Arizona	15.7	5.5	0.2	0.1	1.5	0.6	0.8	1.7	1.2	66.5	(1)	(1)	0.3
55	Utah	49.4	8.6	2.0	(1)	8.8	3.0	13.3	3.1	0.9	0.8	(1)	(1)	1.9
56	Nevada	38.9	12.9	0.3	0.1	3.4	1.2	4.1	14.3	4.0	8.6	1.3	(1)	2.0
	PACIFIC:													
57	Washington	35.1	18.2	1.2	0.3	12.0	10.8	3.1	3.2	2.5	0.4	0.1	0.1	0.7
58	Oregon	33.3	27.5	1.0	0.4	8.7	5.9	3.2	2.8	2.4	0.6	0.2	0.1	0.8
59	California	33.3	17.2	0.6	0.1	4.3	1.5	2.5	11.4	3.4	9.5	5.1	0.1	0.8

¹ Less than one-tenth of 1 per cent.

STOCK BY MOTHER TONGUE, BY DIVISIONS AND STATES: 1920.

PER CENT OF TOTAL FOREIGN WHITE STOCK IN SPECIFIED DIVISION OR STATE—continued.

	Slavic and Lettic.										Unclassified.										
Polish.	Czech.	Slovak.	Russian.²	Ruthenian.	Slovenian.	Serbo-Croatian.	Bulgarian.	Slavic, not specified.	Lithuanian and Lettish.	Yiddish and Hebrew.	Magyar.	Finnish.	Armenian.	Syrian and Arabic.	Turkish.	Albanian.	All other.	Unknown.	Of mixed mother tongue.	
6.7	**1.7**	**1.7**	**2.0**	**0.3**	**0.6**	**0.6**	**(¹)**	**(¹)**	**0.9**	**5.6**	**1.3**	**0.7**	**0.1**	**0.3**	**(¹)**	**(¹)**	**(¹)**	**0.1**	**2.2**	**1**
6.1	0.2	0.6	1.5	0.1	0.1	(¹)	(¹)	(¹)	1.7	4.7	0.5	0.7	0.4	0.5	(¹)	0.1	(¹)	(¹)	1.4	2
8.3	0.7	3.3	3.4	0.6	0.6	0.6	(¹)	(¹)	1.1	11.2	1.9	0.2	0.1	0.2	(¹)	(¹)	(¹)	(¹)	2.0	3
10.6	2.9	1.7	1.2	0.1	0.9	0.9	0.1	(¹)	1.2	3.2	1.9	1.0	0.1	0.2	(¹)	(¹)	(¹)	0.1	2.1	4
2.0	3.5	0.3	1.0	(¹)	0.4	0.5	(¹)	(¹)	0.1	1.5	0.2	1.4	(¹)	0.2	(¹)	(¹)	(¹)	0.1	2.6	5
6.4	1.6	1.1	3.4	0.1	0.5	0.5	(¹)	(¹)	0.9	8.2	1.7	0.2	0.1	0.9	(¹)	(¹)	(¹)	0.1	2.3	6
1.3	0.3	0.5	2.2	(¹)	0.3	0.2	(¹)	....	0.1	3.9	0.9	0.1	(¹)	1.2	(¹)	(¹)	(¹)	0.3	2.6	7
1.5	5.0	0.2	1.0	(¹)	0.2	0.1	(¹)	(¹)	0.1	1.2	0.2	0.1	(¹)	0.7	(¹)	(¹)	(¹)	0.1	1.9	8
0.7	0.9	0.8	1.1	(¹)	1.0	1.0	0.1	(¹)	0.1	0.9	0.3	1.0	(¹)	0.2	(¹)	(¹)	(¹)	0.1	3.0	9
0.8	0.6	0.3	1.4	(¹)	0.5	0.5	(¹)	(¹)	0.1	1.1	0.3	1.4	0.4	0.2	(¹)	(¹)	(¹)	0.1	3.2	10
1.0	(¹)	0.5	0.8	(¹)	(¹)	(¹)	(¹)	....	0.8	1.8	(¹)	0.9	0.1	0.5	(¹)	0.2	(¹)	(¹)	1.0	11
4.2	(¹)	(¹)	1.3	0.1	(¹)	(¹)	(¹)	(¹)	1.1	0.9	(¹)	1.4	0.2	0.4	(¹)	0.1	....	(¹)	1.0	12
3.0	0.1	0.3	1.0	0.1	0.1	0.1	(¹)	....	0.2	1.1	0.3	0.7	0.1	0.4	....	(¹)	....	(¹)	1.2	13
5.7	0.1	0.1	1.3	0.1	(¹)	(¹)	(¹)	....	1.7	5.5	0.1	0.9	0.5	0.5	0.1	0.1	(¹)	(¹)	1.4	14
3.9	0.1	0.1	1.0	0.3	(¹)	(¹)	(¹)	....	0.3	2.9	(¹)	0.1	0.7	0.5	0.1	(¹)	(¹)	(¹)	1.1	15
10.7	0.4	2.3	2.7	0.3	0.4	0.1	(¹)	0.1	2.8	5.4	2.3	0.2	0.2	0.3	(¹)	(¹)	(¹)	(¹)	1.6	16
6.2	0.8	0.7	3.9	0.3	0.2	0.1	(¹)	(¹)	0.4	15.6	1.4	0.2	0.1	0.2	(¹)	(¹)	(¹)	(¹)	2.2	17
9.7	0.5	2.7	2.7	0.4	0.4	0.1	(¹)	(¹)	0.9	6.5	3.2	0.1	0.2	0.2	(¹)	(¹)	(¹)	(¹)	2.2	18
11.2	0.5	8.0	2.9	1.3	1.4	1.5	(¹)	0.1	2.5	5.6	2.2	0.1	0.1	0.3	(¹)	(¹)	(¹)	(¹)	1.6	19
7.3	3.1	4.2	1.6	0.3	2.1	1.3	0.2	(¹)	0.6	3.0	5.1	0.7	0.1	0.4	(¹)	(¹)	(¹)	0.1	1.9	20
8.9	0.7	2.3	1.2	(¹)	0.8	1.5	0.2	....	0.7	1.3	3.0	0.1	(¹)	0.3	(¹)	(¹)	(¹)	0.1	1.9	21
11.8	4.3	1.4	1.2	0.1	0.7	0.8	(¹)	(¹)	2.3	5.2	0.9	0.1	0.1	0.1	(¹)	(¹)	(¹)	(¹)	2.2	22
13.0	0.9	0.7	1.2	0.2	0.4	0.8	0.1	(¹)	0.6	2.1	1.4	3.4	0.2	0.4	(¹)	(¹)	(¹)	(¹)	2.1	23
9.7	3.0	0.8	0.5	(¹)	0.6	0.4	(¹)	(¹)	0.5	1.1	0.5	0.8	0.1	0.1	(¹)	(¹)	(¹)	0.1	2.3	24
3.2	2.3	0.4	0.6	(¹)	0.9	0.6	(¹)	(¹)	0.1	1.6	0.2	3.8	(¹)	0.1	(¹)	(¹)	(¹)	0.1	3.1	25
0.4	3.8	0.2	0.6	(¹)	0.1	0.4	(¹)	(¹)	0.2	0.9	0.1	(¹)	(¹)	0.1	(¹)	(¹)	(¹)	0.1	2.1	26
2.3	2.0	0.4	1.5	0.1	0.1	0.6	(¹)	(¹)	0.1	4.1	0.6	(¹)	(¹)	0.3	(¹)	(¹)	(¹)	0.1	2.4	27
1.1	2.0	0.1	2.6	0.2	(¹)	(¹)	(¹)	....	(¹)	0.4	0.2	0.8	(¹)	0.2	(¹)	....	(¹)	0.1	3.0	28
0.6	3.5	0.1	1.1	(¹)	0.1	0.1	(¹)	....	(¹)	0.2	0.2	1.0	(¹)	0.2	(¹)	(¹)	(¹)	0.1	2.8	29
2.8	10.3	0.1	1.0	(¹)	0.1	0.3	(¹)	....	0.2	1.2	0.2	(¹)	(¹)	0.2	(¹)	(¹)	(¹)	0.1	2.3	30
1.1	3.0	0.3	1.4	(¹)	0.7	0.9	(¹)	(¹)	0.1	0.3	0.1	(¹)	(¹)	0.1	(¹)	(¹)	(¹)	0.1	2.2	31
17.4	0.4	0.3	3.6	0.6	0.2	(¹)	....	....	0.5	4.8	0.7	0.1	(¹)	(¹)	(¹)	....	(¹)	0.1	1.6	32
9.3	3.1	0.4	3.2	0.1	0.2	0.1	(¹)	(¹)	1.6	13.2	0.5	0.1	(¹)	0.1	(¹)	(¹)	(¹)	0.1	1.9	33
1.1	0.4	0.1	3.9	(¹)	0.1	0.1	(¹)	....	0.1	8.5	0.3	0.1	0.1	0.6	(¹)	(¹)	(¹)	0.1	2.7	34
2.1	1.9	2.0	4.3	(¹)	0.5	0.1	(¹)	....	0.2	10.4	2.6	0.4	0.3	1.5	0.1	(¹)	(¹)	0.2	2.5	35
8.8	0.6	4.1	2.7	0.2	2.1	2.5	0.1	....	1.6	1.3	6.5	0.3	(¹)	1.6	0.1	(¹)	(¹)	0.1	1.5	36
1.6	0.3	0.5	4.4	(¹)	0.2	0.2	(¹)	....	0.2	7.9	0.5	0.1	0.1	5.8	(¹)	....	0.1	0.4	2.0	37
3.1	0.6	0.1	6.0	(¹)	0.1	0.1	....	....	0.1	8.2	0.4	0.3	(¹)	4.1	(¹)	....	(¹)	0.2	2.4	38
1.7	0.5	0.2	7.6	(¹)	0.2	0.2	(¹)	....	0.1	10.5	0.7	0.1	0.1	2.2	0.1	(¹)	....	0.2	2.9	39
0.7	0.4	0.2	1.1	(¹)	0.1	0.1	(¹)	....	0.1	1.6	0.4	0.4	0.1	1.0	(¹)	(¹)	(¹)	0.2	3.8	40
0.9	0.2	0.3	1.6	(¹)	0.1	0.3	(¹)	....	0.1	2.6	1.1	(¹)	(¹)	0.5	(¹)	(¹)	(¹)	0.2	2.5	41
1.8	0.5	0.2	3.1	(¹)	0.1	0.1	(¹)	....	0.1	7.1	0.9	0.1	(¹)	0.5	(¹)	(¹)	(¹)	0.4	3.0	42
1.2	0.5	1.2	2.4	(¹)	0.4	0.3	0.1	....	0.1	4.3	0.6	0.2	0.1	2.0	0.1	(¹)	(¹)	0.5	2.7	43
2.1	0.6	0.5	2.9	....	1.7	0.2	(¹)	....	0.1	3.5	0.2	0.5	(¹)	4.6	(¹)	(¹)	(¹)	0.4	2.8	44
2.4	1.9	1.4	1.3	(¹)	0.2	0.2	0.1	....	0.1	1.4	0.2	(¹)	(¹)	0.9	....	(¹)	(¹)	0.3	2.8	45
0.4	0.4	0.2	1.4	(¹)	0.4	0.1	(¹)	....	(¹)	1.2	0.4	0.1	(¹)	1.4	(¹)	(¹)	(¹)	0.3	3.7	46
1.8	4.5	0.3	2.4	0.1	0.2	0.1	0.1	(¹)	0.6	1.0	0.3	0.1	(¹)	1.1	(¹)	(¹)	(¹)	0.2	2.3	47
1.6	6.2	0.1	0.6	(¹)	0.1	0.1	(¹)	(¹)	(¹)	1.2	0.1	(¹)	(¹)	0.4	(¹)	(¹)	(¹)	0.1	1.4	48
1.1	1.7	0.9	1.4	(¹)	1.4	1.9	0.2	....	0.1	0.2	0.3	2.6	0.1	0.2	(¹)	(¹)	(¹)	0.1	3.1	49
0.3	1.0	0.1	0.6	(¹)	0.2	0.4	(¹)	(¹)	(¹)	0.1	0.1	1.2	(¹)	0.1	(¹)	(¹)	(¹)	0.1	3.7	50
2.5	1.5	1.6	0.8	0.1	1.9	1.4	0.2	....	0.1	0.8	0.7	2.5	0.1	0.2	0.1	(¹)	(¹)	(¹)	2.8	51
0.9	0.9	1.7	1.9	(¹)	1.6	0.6	0.1	....	0.1	2.7	0.4	0.3	(¹)	0.2	(¹)	(¹)	(¹)	(¹)	2.4	52
0.4	0.5	0.4	0.5	(¹)	0.7	1.3	0.1	....	(¹)	0.2	0.3	0.1	(¹)	0.8	(¹)	....	....	(¹)	1.5	53
0.3	0.3	0.1	0.9	(¹)	0.3	1.3	(¹)	....	(¹)	0.3	0.1	0.4	(¹)	0.4	(¹)	(¹)	(¹)	(¹)	1.5	54
0.1	0.2	0.2	0.3	(¹)	0.4	0.5	(¹)	....	(¹)	0.4	0.1	0.4	0.1	0.1	(¹)	(¹)	(¹)	(¹)	5.1	55
0.3	0.5	0.3	0.4	(¹)	0.9	2.1	(¹)	....	(¹)	0.3	0.2	0.4	(¹)	0.1	(¹)	....	(¹)	0.1	3.2	56
1.3	0.7	0.7	1.1	(¹)	0.6	0.7	0.1	....	0.2	0.6	0.1	2.6	(¹)	0.1	(¹)	(¹)	(¹)	0.1	3.4	57
0.8	1.1	0.2	1.4	(¹)	0.4	0.5	0.1	....	0.2	1.0	0.2	3.6	(¹)	0.1	(¹)	(¹)	(¹)	0.1	3.4	58
0.6	0.5	0.2	1.5	(¹)	0.5	0.4	(¹)	(¹)	0.1	1.3	0.4	0.6	0.6	0.2	(¹)	(¹)	(¹)	0.1	3.1	59

² See footnote to Table 109, p. 386.

TABLE **114.**—MOTHER TONGUE OF THE FOREIGN WHITE STOCK,

CITY.	All mother tongues: 1920	English and Celtic.	Germanic.			Scandinavian.		
			German.	Dutch and Frisian.	Flemish.	Swedish.	Norwegian.	Danish.
Akron, Ohio	77,639	16,243	19,794	292	54	1,588	308	417
Albany, N. Y	55,771	22,358	14,037	728	22	236	52	157
Atlanta, Ga	12,837	3,945	2,363	44	13	231	48	73
Baltimore, Md	246,750	40,909	86,836	496	74	934	795	499
Birmingham, Ala	16,339	5,650	2,452	41	18	233	56	67
Boston, Mass	548,674	306,817	20,538	1,201	575	12,235	2,925	1,596
Bridgeport, Conn	104,404	28,728	7,784	133	37	3,492	303	767
Buffalo, N. Y	336,907	86,517	93,943	1,206	75	2,458	598	564
Cambridge, Mass	75,205	47,742	1,474	48	13	2,068	284	179
Camden, N. J	51,504	13,597	9,655	84	19	489	398	128
Chicago, Ill	1,946,298	357,370	431,340	21,896	3,649	121,386	45,029	22,561
Cincinnati, Ohio	164,492	31,910	102,225	1,096	27	260	84	201
Cleveland, Ohio	549,779	93,110	120,744	2,770	87	4,453	1,000	1,232
Columbus, Ohio	55,652	17,431	22,939	181	59	306	103	112
Dallas, Tex	22,379	5,912	5,418	106	17	469	204	240
Dayton, Ohio	42,499	8,370	21,781	171	17	163	71	50
Denver, Colo	104,966	38,372	23,048	1,041	69	8,950	1,316	1,955
Des Moines, Iowa	36,526	13,185	6,303	458	27	5,197	1,247	1,153
Detroit, Mich	638,068	190,553	126,421	4,131	8,971	6,324	2,175	2,858
Fall River, Mass	100,946	35,774	613	23	14	138	55	52
Fort Worth, Tex	14,951	3,859	2,178	47	4	409	140	80
Grand Rapids, Mich	80,393	15,731	9,904	30,887	73	2,325	377	603
Hartford, Conn	93,354	32,091	7,331	99	17	4,439	164	1,310
Houston, Tex	31,835	6,579	8,634	139	44	476	160	304
Indianapolis, Ind	60,114	19,148	26,609	417	27	465	144	611
Jersey City, N. J	202,926	64,836	40,797	576	211	2,535	2,255	770
Kansas City, Kans	30,128	7,650	7,407	122	260	1,588	116	466
Kansas City, Mo	84,383	28,978	21,309	343	671	5,104	552	1,017
Los Angeles, Calif	252,406	86,594	44,822	1,822	316	10,637	3,849	4,039
Louisville, Ky	55,366	13,535	32,158	345	38	180	56	111
Lowell, Mass	87,833	42,229	500	29	188	1,078	148	48
Memphis, Tenn	18,318	5,724	4,273	54	4	323	52	152
Milwaukee, Wis	323,979	24,801	163,344	2,016	205	2,165	5,114	1,918
Minneapolis, Minn	243,187	44,020	35,082	980	166	61,535	41,309	5,715
Nashville, Tenn	8,681	3,533	2,244	50	2	38	26	39
New Bedford, Mass	96,044	27,891	1,373	31	72	521	113	63
New Haven, Conn	113,415	34,976	10,188	113	162	2,777	275	498
New Orleans, La	95,275	19,768	23,234	354	92	648	678	483
New York, N. Y	4,294,629	897,452	690,789	9,432	2,082	60,017	40,220	14,545
Bronx borough	594,220	98,803	111,627	1,076	127	6,976	1,706	1,382
Brooklyn borough	1,528,713	307,895	215,054	3,568	556	29,217	29,332	6,968
Manhattan borough	1,780,627	397,846	227,489	3,739	1,045	17,163	4,765	4,021
Queens borough	314,319	70,082	121,900	828	286	5,018	1,697	1,542
Richmond borough	76,750	22,826	14,719	221	68	1,643	2,720	632
Newark, N. J	283,810	57,071	57,500	638	66	1,578	301	748
Norfolk, Va	14,467	3,946	1,612	166	19	342	255	127
Oakland, Calif	113,725	42,380	17,553	611	98	5,600	2,478	3,774
Omaha, Nebr	94,521	20,536	17,781	328	382	9,279	1,064	6,437
Paterson, N. J	102,430	27,542	14,313	9,918	799	261	54	110
Philadelphia, Pa	989,398	345,119	173,835	1,172	453	5,288	2,152	2,205
Pittsburgh, Pa	333,731	94,916	83,227	294	113	2,430	207	239
Portland, Oreg	116,745	40,000	30,538	1,008	393	10,522	6,325	3,043
Providence, R. I	168,028	75,810	4,743	129	84	5,254	475	241
Reading, Pa	25,851	3,227	7,282	48	2	56	30	23
Richmond, Va	14,618	4,800	3,693	49	8	108	44	65
Rochester, N. Y	182,113	57,739	47,282	4,648	509	888	169	356
St. Louis, Mo	343,133	70,626	168,872	1,406	431	2,090	604	1,050
St. Paul, Minn	153,793	31,810	47,972	660	92	24,060	10,540	2,014
Salt Lake City, Utah	60,547	31,872	7,175	1,541	11	5,457	2,098	4,674
San Antonio, Tex	70,500	6,553	12,470	134	95	293	137	179
San Francisco, Calif	322,843	118,055	62,468	1,446	427	12,099	5,339	6,178
Scranton, Pa	88,499	36,192	12,265	49	15	201	9	45
Seattle, Wash	162,879	67,300	20,814	1,129	626	19,660	17,620	4,578
Spokane, Wash	46,056	19,144	9,371	391	81	5,384	3,798	1,068
Springfield, Mass	77,854	33,417	3,851	103	17	2,620	152	170
Syracuse, N. Y	90,300	33,859	20,874	187	19	313	82	151
Toledo, Ohio	113,330	23,259	39,713	310	117	631	219	367
Trenton, N. J	70,707	16,981	9,810	71	12	190	24	136
Washington, D. C	87,372	38,473	17,495	403	51	1,311	719	574
Wilmington, Del	42,514	14,964	4,246	57	7	487	89	80
Worcester, Mass	127,675	51,291	1,697	127	36	16,814	524	436
Yonkers, N. Y	68,119	25,322	8,202	269	12	820	324	197
Youngstown, Ohio	79,136	23,412	9,354	108	6	1,891	103	92

FOR CITIES HAVING 100,000 INHABITANTS OR MORE: 1920.

| CITY. | FOREIGN WHITE STOCK—continued. | | | | | | | | |
| | Latin and Greek. | | | | | | Slavic and Lettic. | | |
	Italian.	French.	Spanish.	Portuguese.	Rumanian.	Greek.	Polish.	Czech.	Slovak.
Akron, Ohio	6,416	1,574	430	21	1,705	1,999	2,787	365	4,328
Albany, N.Y	6,480	1,232	71	3	51	280	3,218	116	45
Atlanta, Ga	217	421	150	6	53	610	226	81	17
Baltimore, Md	16,458	1,883	489	73	324	984	26,900	8,694	783
Birmingham, Ala	3,771	521	74		26	641	96	38	67
Boston, Mass	77,005	6,707	800	2,637	390	4,104	11,451	710	188
Bridgeport, Conn	17,602	1,800	456	50	294	1,086	7,095	592	8,843
Buffalo, N.Y	34,923	5,612	363	72	254	740	83,344	478	964
Cambridge, Mass	5,426	2,772	90	4,155	27	516	2,725	28	16
Camden, N.J	9,685	596	60	28	49	93	9,287	67	354
Chicago, Ill	124,457	20,075	2,703	181	3,229	15,755	318,338	106,428	25,720
Cincinnati, Ohio	5,737	3,736	256	15	654	485	1,041	320	96
Cleveland, Ohio	35,627	3,589	459	49	3,894	1,864	65,841	43,997	28,224
Columbus, Ohio	4,592	1,227	108	10	146	513	371	178	241
Dallas, Tex	1,540	744	3,017	3	138	366	255	503	35
Dayton, Ohio	919	893	69	2	212	427	1,318	233	346
Denver, Colo	7,321	2,270	2,091	32	148	890	1,264	704	508
Des Moines, Iowa	2,368	591	207	10	93	288	272	296	110
Detroit, Mich	29,056	15,165	1,301	89	6,979	5,216	128,648	4,519	3,601
Fall River, Mass	2,088	28,671	20	21,997	36	194	5,604	21	
Fort Worth, Tex	390	302	4,649		38	338	373	415	9
Grand Rapids, Mich	1,099	746	44	3	49	66	11,872	225	46
Hartford, Conn	14,290	3,032	81	210	140	418	7,559	187	149
Houston, Tex	3,364	989	5,371	26	75	261	617	489	32
Indianapolis, Ind	1,625	1,436	240	7	865	503	577	229	155
Jersey City, N.J	33,805	2,171	434	41	335	500	27,766	306	1,779
Kansas City, Kans	288	461	2,420	2	23	326	1,979	148	510
Kansas City, Mo	7,815	1,986	2,252	7	159	758	1,285	476	54
Los Angeles, Calif	15,691	8,953	33,540	492	898	1,340	2,516	1,776	402
Louisville, Ky	1,259	1,635	54	8	126	107	326	60	6
Lowell, Mass	818	23,982	14	3,340	7	5,524	4,757	19	4
Memphis, Tenn	2,958	587	58	9	25	397	332	63	10
Milwaukee, Wis	7,898	2,501	175	19	314	2,308	70,238	6,745	3,215
Minneapolis, Minn	1,593	5,416	129	4	1,170	1,066	10,689	2,417	2,829
Nashville, Tenn	261	278	36	30	30	145	199	25	15
New Bedford, Mass	1,215	23,789	76	29,269	17	828	5,722	347	12
New Haven, Conn	34,505	1,844	107	115	190	442	6,343	148	198
New Orleans, La	21,812	12,793	5,341	176	70	560	370	165	225
New York, N.Y	803,048	48,534	32,658	1,845	26,948	25,014	161,310	43,839	19,425
Bronx borough	83,741	4,569	908	70	7,307	1,435	19,067	3,482	1,460
Brooklyn borough	299,845	10,855	7,198	910	8,697	3,680	65,387	3,101	3,284
Manhattan borough	355,997	26,559	23,521	721	10,042	19,074	54,782	28,601	13,061
Queens borough	45,292	5,434	615	93	808	577	17,217	8,330	1,033
Richmond borough	18,173	1,117	416	51	94	248	4,857	325	587
Newark, N.J	63,526	2,806	784	484	754	1,439	24,706	1,213	5,220
Norfolk, Va	1,129	264	306	100	41	883	169	31	7
Oakland, Calif	10,135	4,041	2,720	12,260	124	1,149	615	522	142
Omaha, Nebr	5,831	905	816	6	440	491	5,766	11,416	125
Paterson, N.J	22,896	1,862	116	3	34	416	4,294	169	196
Philadelphia, Pa	136,801	9,518	2,452	272	3,910	2,355	62,634	1,971	4,687
Pittsburgh, Pa	32,579	4,114	147	7	657	1,824	34,903	3,563	12,363
Portland, Oreg	5,176	2,666	378	77	187	907	1,283	892	361
Providence, R.I	42,044	10,576	114	4,883	178	654	4,393	131	26
Reading, Pa	3,608	232	156	2	4	737	6,474	31	1,306
Richmond, Va	1,279	357	34	35	36	280	192	54	53
Rochester, N.Y	36,649	2,586	129	207	148	449	8,231	196	103
St. Louis, Mo	18,505	7,685	1,211	56	1,153	2,441	11,295	9,723	1,304
St. Paul, Minn	3,638	3,717	123	2	495	424	5,874	4,576	169
Salt Lake City, Utah	1,022	684	355	7	65	685	152	136	18
San Antonio, Tex	1,412	1,532	42,984	19	70	213	632	287	21
San Francisco, Calif	46,809	14,464	11,559	2,490	809	3,907	2,880	1,470	590
Scranton, Pa	7,664	383	33		38	428	12,397	183	2,218
Seattle, Wash	5,526	3,845	1,284	63	128	1,277	1,426	876	343
Spokane, Wash	1,857	1,073	47	4	53	117	243	295	36
Springfield, Mass	8,721	11,579	75	50	49	1,299	4,819	280	42
Syracuse, N.Y	13,678	2,028	69	7	53	496	8,321	74	377
Toledo, Ohio	1,550	3,197	319	11	294	877	26,380	607	592
Trenton, N.J	13,656	471	67	6	396	189	9,554	157	4,451
Washington, D.C	7,561	2,342	562	43	88	1,814	946	343	72
Wilmington, Del	6,971	433	175	21	102	353	8,839	60	75
Worcester, Mass	8,769	14,085	32	65	33	864	7,134	31	16
Yonkers, N.Y	9,879	745	109	11	45	190	6,282	284	4,411
Youngstown, Ohio	11,935	468	177	18	1,384	1,561	4,080	203	8,256

TABLE 114.—MOTHER TONGUE OF THE FOREIGN WHITE STOCK, FOR

	FOREIGN WHITE STOCK—continued.							Unclassified.
	Slavic and Lettic—Continued.							
CITY.	Russian.[1]	Ruthenian.	Slovenian.	Serbo-Croatian.	Bulgarian.	Slavic, not specified.	Lithuanian and Lettish.	Yiddish and Hebrew.
Akron, Ohio	2,661	161	985	2,897	503		693	2,554
Albany, N. Y	2,074	7	28	9	13		313	2,843
Atlanta, Ga	1,379	4	4	9			21	2,073
Baltimore, Md	8,665	230	274	309	31	23	4,672	39,333
Birmingham, Ala	544		13	24	4		5	1,054
Boston, Mass	12,571	236	140	101	11		9,413	60,042
Bridgeport, Conn	3,911	262	804	55	6	603	1,550	6,255
Buffalo, N. Y	2,522	961	339	518	55		211	9,705
Cambridge, Mass	739	1	3	4	2		2,548	2,492
Camden, N. J	921	133	37	284	19		496	3,569
Chicago, Ill	28,199	2,051	7,417	13,316	496	110	44,065	159,518
Cincinnati, Ohio	2,841	3	107	269	104	5	106	6,898
Cleveland, Ohio	14,145	4,000	24,804	6,433	422	10	6,685	30,383
Columbus, Ohio	923	2	218	209	78		121	2,762
Dallas, Tex	709	1		34	11		4	1,666
Dayton, Ohio	489	6	304	292	80		577	1,746
Denver, Colo	2,276	20	652	226	76		103	7,627
Des Moines, Iowa	583		16	135	4		269	2,518
Detroit, Mich	13,414	1,750	1,557	6,050	1,147	1	5,475	34,727
Fall River, Mass	746	229		30			1	2,790
Fort Worth, Tex	474	1	12	40	16		5	734
Grand Rapids, Mich	472	84	16	6	11		2,520	659
Hartford, Conn	3,031	228	26	110	2		2,228	13,623
Houston, Tex	524	4	17	44	7		29	2,119
Indianapolis, Ind	816	1	871	248	277		60	2,282
Jersey City, N. J	5,984	387	341	21	21		584	8,989
Kansas City, Kans	1,104	24	508	3,210	12		209	356
Kansas City, Mo	2,868	12	106	289	31		41	5,162
Los Angeles, Calif	8,812	33	1,270	1,346	68	1	271	10,540
Louisville, Ky	1,299	3	6	8			23	2,005
Lowell, Mass	295	3	5	150	1		1,477	1,496
Memphis, Tenn	769		28	12			21	1,497
Milwaukee, Wis	2,060	74	4,170	2,717	157	20	683	11,265
Minneapolis, Minn	3,363	391	471	145	162		253	12,372
Nashville, Tenn	253		14	10				841
New Bedford, Mass	304	10	5	17	15		90	2,355
New Haven, Conn	3,666	166	99	13	7		1,525	12,233
New Orleans, La	1,532	4	1	263	52	2	15	1,258
New York, N. Y	221,153	9,706	10,571	4,037	215	1	16,409	946,139
Bronx borough	48,903	299	1,816	193	30		650	165,416
Brooklyn borough	68,145	1,611	2,279	500	37		11,757	391,267
Manhattan borough	96,497	7,268	5,515	2,886	142	1	2,188	377,945
Queens borough	5,897	300	729	291	4		1,720	10,142
Richmond borough	1,711	228	232	167	2		94	1,369
Newark, N. J	8,865	953	875	194	1		3,372	39,863
Norfolk, Va	1,052	2	9	13	2		38	3,092
Oakland, Calif	1,114	1	1,017	657	7		105	1,139
Omaha, Nebr	1,310	13	216	1,087	37		898	5,406
Paterson, N. J	2,316	94	95	31	1		780	11,709
Philadelphia, Pa	42,826	3,675	1,879	1,092	37		11,467	143,514
Pittsburgh, Pa	7,286	2,017	2,874	8,211	47	4	6,150	22,752
Portland, Oreg	2,335	32	401	665	194		242	2,441
Providence, R. I	2,602	55	11	25	12		1,056	9,821
Reading, Pa	448	97	107	40			226	1,298
Richmond, Va	899	1	2	3	1		12	1,684
Rochester, N. Y	3,105	904	73	139	58		1,508	11,447
St. Louis, Mo	6,275	977	518	2,016	203		640	20,420
St. Paul, Minn	1,119	19	131	194	28	4	139	7,493
Salt Lake City, Utah	377	4	83	52	1		4	566
San Antonio, Tex	659	9	10	24	3		32	963
San Francisco, Calif	5,871	20	2,054	895	99		252	5,598
Scranton, Pa	2,741	564	401	26	1		6,180	3,397
Seattle, Wash	3,061	35	583	741	72		388	2,465
Spokane, Wash	458	5	29	139	43		32	385
Springfield, Mass	1,493	25	33	27	8		217	6,238
Syracuse, N. Y	1,663	206	37	50	94		90	5,453
Toledo, Ohio	762	30	129	153	770		73	4,275
Trenton, N. J	1,168	156	292	10			259	4,563
Washington, D. C	3,422	11	50	44	5		76	7,385
Wilmington, Del	1,642	297	51	20			227	2,318
Worcester, Mass	1,117	9	6	19	1		8,349	7,702
Yonkers, N. Y	3,551	319	688	45	2		252	2,807
Youngstown, Ohio	2,214	860	1,008	3,580	182		346	2,694

[1] See footnote to Table 109, p. 386.

CITIES HAVING 100,000 INHABITANTS OR MORE: 1920—Continued.

CITY.	Magyar.	Finnish.	Armenian.	Syrian and Arabic.	Turkish.	Albanian.	All other.	Unknown.	Of mixed mother tongue.
				FOREIGN WHITE STOCK—continued. Unclassified—Continued.					
Akron, Ohio	5,733	93	163	883	150	138	10	78	1,616
Albany, N. Y	89	16	37	202	13	32	1	16	992
Atlanta, Ga	140	19	11	284	21			19	355
Baltimore, Md	1,001	143	37	53	11	1	4	172	4,660
Birmingham, Ala	63	5	16	537				32	291
Boston, Mass	426	717	2,097	3,150	161	349	8	83	9,290
Bridgeport, Conn	9,443	92	315	161	38	38	21	49	1,739
Buffalo, N. Y	3,289	212	77	627	42	48	6	40	6,144
Cambridge, Mass	43	58	647	81	21	29		5	939
Camden, N. J	205	129	68	60	5			22	967
Chicago, Ill	19,405	1,849	1,310	1,672	198	30	254	592	45,699
Cincinnati, Ohio	1,362	19	51	432	15	2	3	130	4,002
Cleveland, Ohio	42,134	1,597	455	1,440	57	36	45	270	9,923
Columbus, Ohio	1,231	80	25	136	3	2	9	111	1,225
Dallas, Tex	51	9	12	124	1		1	50	739
Dayton, Ohio	2,763	16	14	164	7	12		25	962
Denver, Colo	514	140	25	74	12	5	10	127	3,100
Des Moines, Iowa	50	10	8	120	2			36	970
Detroit, Mich	16,240	3,179	1,692	3,858	274	173	54	351	12,119
Fall River, Mass	10	45	10	971	4			5	805
Fort Worth, Tex	18	2	1	57	1		1	40	318
Grand Rapids, Mich	206	149	75	594	6	1	1	51	1,492
Hartford, Conn	361	78	489	62	30	2	23	8	1,536
Houston, Tex	119	20	7	350	7		2	93	933
Indianapolis, Ind	420	42	63	315	30	12	4	173	1,442
Jersey City, N. J	1,504	1,045	155	62	22	4	2	24	4,664
Kansas City, Kans	121	4	2	7	9		4	25	767
Kansas City, Mo	313	38	21	358	16	1	3	86	2,272
Los Angeles, Calif	1,827	570	962	692	132	2	23	167	8,003
Louisville, Ky	70	6	11	261	1			149	1,520
Lowell, Mass	13	49	510	310	56	6		4	773
Memphis, Tenn	123	3	1	17	1			67	758
Milwaukee, Wis	2,736	234	139	312	44	45	2	278	6,067
Minneapolis, Minn	329	2,220	66	442	7		6	144	8,696
Nashville, Tenn	215	5	1	77		1		59	254
New Bedford, Mass	32	8	17	478	26	319		15	1,014
New Haven, Conn	677	110	220	108	11	2	2	25	1,670
New Orleans, La	111	96	25	343	21	2	5	301	4,479
New York, N. Y	76,575	12,204	4,700	7,760	2,320	108	232	1,126	104,215
Bronx borough	13,190	1,451	644	134	106	2	24	236	17,390
Brooklyn borough	11,037	3,960	897	5,554	290	20	84	301	35,427
Manhattan borough	46,910	5,724	2,648	1,970	1,889	85	102	407	40,024
Queens borough	4,197	592	477	78	25	1	15	149	8,950
Richmond borough	1,241	477	34	24	10		7	33	2,424
Newark, N. J	4,883	93	264	184	11		9	114	5,295
Norfolk, Va	63	125	18	214	9	1		15	417
Oakland, Calif	433	522	73	164	7	3	2	72	4,207
Omaha, Nebr	613	21	118	426	2	35	5	71	2,660
Paterson, N. J	567	13	499	1,252	58	1	3	10	2,018
Philadelphia, Pa	8,060	894	1,907	914	187	298	70	355	17,399
Pittsburgh, Pa	4,925	150	55	1,406	18	30	3	151	6,069
Portland, Oreg	298	1,846	27	260	22	2	8	96	4,120
Providence, R. I	95	68	1,921	449	133	5		23	2,017
Reading, Pa	67		5	1				3	341
Richmond, Va	42	2	155	334	7			22	367
Rochester, N. Y	359	54	72	245	278	10	2	35	3,203
St. Louis, Mo	3,203	49	169	987	36	206	14	274	8,763
St. Paul, Minn	1,079	113	83	572	5	1	2	111	5,072
Salt Lake City, Utah	84	65	18	169	8	9		20	3,135
San Antonio, Tex	60	4	9	275	4		2	78	1,337
San Francisco, Calif	1,528	2,016	297	773	59	30	19	99	12,243
Scranton, Pa	1,449	16	20	426	2			9	1,147
Seattle, Wash	245	2,548	94	194	107	61	15	82	5,693
Spokane, Wash	98	204	14	49				23	1,615
Springfield, Mass	113	161	338	696	54	14	5	14	1,174
Syracuse, N. Y	200	49	158	236	14	25		39	1,398
Toledo, Ohio	5,470	31	105	874	43	1	1	56	2,114
Trenton, N. J	7,044	6	37	100	12	2	4	18	867
Washington, D. C	283	127	75	502	21	2	8	244	2,320
Wilmington, Del	238	55	6	10	1		5	37	648
Worcester, Mass	29	2,927	2,012	1,448	141	596	9	14	1,342
Yonkers, N. Y	1,330	48	98	153	1		50	24	1,649
Youngstown, Ohio	3,584	38	17	522	3	18	2	24	996

TABLE 115.—PER CENT DISTRIBUTION OF THE FOREIGN WHITE STOCK BY

PER CENT OF TOTAL FOREIGN WHITE STOCK IN SPECIFIED CITY.

CITY.	English and Celtic.	Germanic.			Scandinavian.			Latin and Greek.					
		German.	Dutch and Frisian.	Flemish.	Swedish.	Norwegian.	Danish.	Italian.	French.	Spanish.	Portuguese.	Rumanian.	Greek.
1 Akron, Ohio	20.9	25.5	0.4	0.1	2.0	0.4	0.5	8.3	2.0	0.6	(1)	2.2	2.6
2 Albany, N. Y	40.1	25.2	1.3	(1)	0.4	0.1	0.3	11.6	2.2	0.1	(1)	0.1	0.5
3 Atlanta, Ga	30.7	18.4	0.3	0.1	1.8	0.4	0.6	1.7	3.3	1.2	(1)	0.4	4.8
4 Baltimore, Md	16.6	35.2	0.2	(1)	0.4	0.3	0.2	6.7	0.8	0.2	(1)	0.1	0.4
5 Birmingham, Ala	34.6	15.0	0.3	0.1	1.4	0.3	0.4	23.1	3.2	0.5	.....	0.2	3.9
6 Boston, Mass	55.9	3.7	0.2	0.1	2.2	0.5	0.3	14.0	1.2	0.1	0.5	0.1	0.7
7 Bridgeport, Conn	27.5	7.5	0.1	(1)	3.3	0.3	0.7	16.9	1.7	0.4	(1)	0.3	1.0
8 Buffalo, N. Y	25.7	27.9	0.4	(1)	0.7	0.2	0.2	10.4	1.7	0.1	(1)	0.1	0.2
9 Cambridge, Mass	63.5	2.0	0.1	(1)	2.7	0.4	0.2	7.2	3.7	0.1	5.5	(1)	0.7
10 Camden, N. J	26.4	18.7	0.2	(1)	0.9	0.8	0.2	18.8	1.2	0.1	0.1	0.1	0.2
11 Chicago, Ill	18.4	22.2	1.1	0.2	6.2	2.3	1.2	6.4	1.0	0.1	(1)	0.2	0.8
12 Cincinnati, Ohio	19.4	62.1	0.7	(1)	0.2	0.1	0.1	3.5	2.3	0.2	(1)	0.4	0.3
13 Cleveland, Ohio	16.9	22.0	0.5	(1)	0.8	0.2	0.2	6.5	0.7	0.1	(1)	0.7	0.3
14 Columbus, Ohio	31.3	41.2	0.3	0.1	0.5	0.2	0.2	8.3	2.2	0.2	(1)	0.3	0.9
15 Dallas, Tex	26.4	24.2	0.5	0.1	2.1	0.9	1.1	6.9	3.3	13.5	(1)	0.6	1.6
16 Dayton, Ohio	19.7	51.3	0.4	(1)	0.4	0.2	0.1	2.2	2.1	0.2	(1)	0.5	1.0
17 Denver, Colo	36.6	22.0	1.0	0.1	8.5	1.3	1.9	7.0	2.2	2.0	(1)	0.1	0.8
18 Des Moines, Iowa	36.1	17.3	1.3	0.1	14.2	3.4	3.2	6.5	1.6	0.6	(1)	0.3	0.8
19 Detroit, Mich	29.9	19.8	0.6	1.4	1.0	0.3	0.4	4.6	2.4	0.2	(1)	1.1	0.8
20 Fall River, Mass	35.4	0.6	(1)	0.1	0.1	0.1	0.1	2.1	28.4	(1)	21.8	(1)	0.2
21 Fort Worth, Tex	25.8	14.6	0.3	(1)	2.7	0.9	0.5	2.6	2.0	31.1	.....	0.3	2.3
22 Grand Rapids, Mich	19.6	12.3	38.4	0.1	2.9	0.5	0.8	1.4	0.9	0.1	(1)	0.1	0.1
23 Hartford, Conn	34.4	7.9	0.1	(1)	4.8	0.2	1.4	15.3	3.2	0.1	0.2	0.1	0.4
24 Houston, Tex	20.7	27.1	0.4	0.1	1.5	0.5	1.0	10.6	3.1	16.9	0.1	0.2	0.8
25 Indianapolis, Ind	31.9	44.3	0.7	(1)	0.8	0.2	1.0	2.7	2.4	0.4	(1)	1.4	0.8
26 Jersey City, N. J	32.0	20.1	0.3	0.1	1.2	1.1	0.4	16.7	1.1	0.2	(1)	0.2	0.2
27 Kansas City, Kans	25.4	24.6	0.4	0.9	5.3	0.4	1.5	1.0	1.5	8.0	(1)	0.1	1.1
28 Kansas City, Mo	34.3	25.3	0.4	0.8	6.0	0.7	1.2	9.3	2.4	2.7	(1)	0.2	0.9
29 Los Angeles, Calif	34.3	17.8	0.7	0.1	4.2	1.5	1.6	6.2	3.5	13.3	0.2	0.4	0.5
30 Louisville, Ky	24.4	58.1	0.6	0.1	0.3	0.1	0.2	2.3	3.0	0.1	(1)	0.2	0.2
31 Lowell, Mass	48.1	0.6	(1)	0.2	1.2	0.2	0.1	0.9	27.3	(1)	3.8	(1)	6.3
32 Memphis, Tenn	31.2	23.3	0.3	(1)	1.8	0.3	0.8	16.1	3.2	0.3	(1)	0.1	2.2
33 Milwaukee, Wis	7.7	50.4	0.6	0.1	0.7	1.6	0.6	2.4	0.8	0.1	(1)	0.1	0.7
34 Minneapolis, Minn	18.1	14.4	0.4	0.1	25.3	17.0	2.4	0.7	2.2	0.1	(1)	0.5	0.4
35 Nashville, Tenn	40.7	25.8	0.6	(1)	0.4	0.3	0.4	3.0	3.2	0.4	(1)	0.3	1.7
36 New Bedford, Mass	29.0	1.4	(1)	0.1	0.5	0.1	0.1	1.3	24.8	0.1	30.5	(1)	0.9
37 New Haven, Conn	30.8	9.0	0.1	0.1	2.4	0.2	0.4	30.4	1.6	0.1	0.1	0.2	0.4
38 New Orleans, La	20.7	24.4	0.4	0.1	0.7	0.7	0.5	22.9	13.4	5.6	0.2	0.1	0.6
39 New York, N. Y	20.9	16.1	0.2	(1)	1.4	0.9	0.3	18.7	1.1	0.8	(1)	0.6	0.6
40 Bronx borough	16.6	18.8	0.2	(1)	1.2	0.3	0.2	14.1	0.8	0.2	(1)	1.2	0.2
41 Brooklyn borough	20.1	14.1	0.2	(1)	1.9	1.9	0.5	19.6	0.7	0.5	0.1	0.6	0.2
42 Manhattan borough	22.3	12.8	0.2	0.1	1.0	0.3	0.2	20.0	1.5	1.3	(1)	0.6	1.1
43 Queens borough	22.3	38.8	0.3	0.1	1.6	0.5	0.5	14.4	1.7	0.2	(1)	0.3	0.2
44 Richmond borough	29.7	19.2	0.3	0.1	2.1	3.5	0.8	23.7	1.5	0.5	0.1	0.1	0.3
45 Newark, N. J	20.1	20.3	0.2	(1)	0.6	0.1	0.3	22.4	1.0	0.3	0.2	0.3	0.5
46 Norfolk, Va	27.3	11.1	1.1	0.1	2.4	1.8	0.9	7.8	1.8	2.1	0.7	0.3	6.1
47 Oakland, Calif	37.3	15.4	0.5	0.1	4.9	2.2	3.3	8.9	3.6	2.4	10.8	0.1	1.0
48 Omaha, Nebr	21.7	18.8	0.3	0.4	9.8	1.1	6.8	6.2	1.0	0.9	(1)	0.5	0.5
49 Paterson, N. J	26.9	14.0	9.7	0.8	0.3	0.1	0.1	22.4	1.8	0.1	(1)	(1)	0.4
50 Philadelphia, Pa	34.9	17.6	0.1	(1)	0.5	0.2	0.2	13.8	1.0	0.2	(1)	0.4	0.2
51 Pittsburgh, Pa	28.4	24.9	0.1	(1)	0.7	0.1	0.1	9.8	1.2	(1)	(1)	0.2	0.5
52 Portland, Oreg	34.3	26.2	0.9	0.3	9.0	5.4	2.6	4.4	2.3	0.3	0.1	0.2	0.8
53 Providence, R. I	45.1	2.8	0.1	(1)	3.1	0.3	0.1	25.0	6.3	0.1	2.9	0.1	0.4
54 Reading, Pa	12.5	28.2	0.2	(1)	0.2	0.1	0.1	14.0	0.9	0.6	(1)	(1)	2.9
55 Richmond, Va	32.8	25.3	0.3	0.1	0.7	0.3	0.4	8.7	2.4	0.2	0.2	0.2	1.0
56 Rochester, N. Y	31.7	26.0	2.5	0.3	0.5	0.1	0.2	20.1	1.4	0.1	(1)	0.1	0.2
57 St. Louis, Mo	20.6	49.2	0.4	0.1	0.6	0.1	0.6	3.4	2.2	0.4	(1)	0.3	0.7
58 St. Paul, Minn	20.7	31.2	0.4	0.1	15.8	6.9	2.2	2.4	2.4	0.1	(1)	0.3	0.3
59 Salt Lake City, Utah	52.6	11.9	2.5	(1)	9.0	3.5	7.7	1.7	1.1	0.6	(1)	0.1	1.1
60 San Antonio, Tex	9.3	17.7	0.2	0.1	0.4	0.2	0.3	2.0	2.2	61.0	(1)	0.1	0.3
61 San Francisco, Calif	36.6	19.3	0.4	0.1	3.7	1.7	1.9	14.5	4.5	3.6	0.8	0.3	1.2
62 Scranton, Pa	40.9	13.9	0.1	(1)	0.2	(1)	0.1	8.7	0.4	(1)	.....	0.1	0.5
63 Seattle, Wash	41.3	12.8	0.7	0.4	12.1	10.8	2.8	3.4	2.4	0.8	(1)	0.1	0.8
64 Spokane, Wash	41.6	20.3	0.8	0.2	11.7	8.2	2.3	4.0	2.3	0.1	(1)	0.1	0.3
65 Springfield, Mass	42.9	4.9	0.1	(1)	3.4	0.2	0.2	11.2	14.9	0.1	0.1	0.1	1.7
66 Syracuse, N. Y	37.5	23.1	0.2	(1)	0.3	0.1	0.2	15.1	2.2	0.1	(1)	0.1	0.5
67 Toledo, Ohio	20.5	35.0	0.3	0.1	0.6	0.2	0.3	1.4	2.8	0.3	(1)	0.3	0.8
68 Trenton, N. J	24.0	13.9	0.1	(1)	0.3	(1)	0.2	19.3	0.7	0.1	(1)	0.6	0.3
69 Washington, D. C	44.0	20.0	0.5	0.1	1.5	0.8	0.7	8.7	2.7	0.6	(1)	0.1	2.1
70 Wilmington, Del	35.2	10.0	0.1	(1)	1.1	0.2	0.2	16.4	1.0	0.4	(1)	0.2	0.8
71 Worcester, Mass	40.2	1.3	0.1	(1)	13.2	0.4	0.3	6.9	11.0	(1)	0.1	(1)	0.7
72 Yonkers, N. Y	37.2	12.0	0.4	(1)	1.2	0.5	0.3	14.5	1.1	0.2	(1)	0.1	0.3
73 Youngstown, Ohio	29.6	11.8	0.1	(1)	2.4	0.1	0.1	15.1	0.6	0.2	(1)	1.7	2.0

¹ Less than one-tenth of 1 per cent.

MOTHER TONGUE, FOR CITIES HAVING 100,000 INHABITANTS OR MORE : 1920.

PER CENT OF TOTAL FOREIGN WHITE STOCK IN SPECIFIED CITY—continued.

Polish.	Czech.	Slovak.	Russian.[2]	Ruthenian.	Slovenian.	Serbo-Croatian.	Bulgarian.	Slavic, not specified.	Lithuanian and Lettish.	Yiddish and Hebrew.	Magyar.	Finnish.	Armenian.	Syrian and Arabic.	Turkish.	Albanian.	All other.	Unknown.	Of mixed mother tongue.	
3.6	0.5	5.6	3.4	0.2	1.3	3.7	0.6	....	0.9	3.3	7.4	0.1	0.2	1.1	0.2	0.2	(1)	0.1	2.1	1
5.8	0.2	0.1	3.7	(1)	0.1	(1)	(1)	....	0.6	5.1	0.2	(1)	0.1	0.4	(1)	0.1	(1)	(1)	1.8	2
1.8	0.6	0.1	10.7	(1)	(1)	0.1		....	0.2	16.1	1.1	0.1	0.1	2.2	0.2			0.1	2.8	3
10.9	3.5	0.3	3.5	0.1	0.1	0.1	(1)	(1)	1.9	15.9	0.4	0.1	(1)	(1)	(1)	(1)	(1)	0.1	1.9	4
0.6	0.2	0.4	3.3	....	0.1	0.1	(1)		(1)	6.5	0.4	(1)	0.1	3.3	....			0.2	1.8	5
2.1	0.1	(1)	2.3	(1)	(1)	(1)	(1)	....	1.7	10.9	0.1	0.1	0.4	0.6	(1)	(1)	(1)	(1)	1.7	6
6.8	0.6	8.5	3.7	0.3	0.8	0.1	(1)	0.6	1.5	6.0	9.0	0.1	0.3	0.2	(1)	0.1	(1)	(1)	1.7	7
24.7	0.1	0.3	0.7	0.3	0.1	0.2	(1)	....	0.1	2.9	1.0	0.1	(1)	0.2	(1)	(1)	(1)	(1)	1.8	8
3.6	(1)	(1)	1.0	(1)	(1)	(1)	(1)	....	3.4	3.3	0.1	0.1	0.9	0.1	(1)	(1)	....	(1)	1.3	9
18.0	0.1	0.7	1.8	0.3	0.1	0.6	(1)	....	1.0	6.9	0.4	0.3	0.1	0.1	(1)		(1)	(1)	1.9	10
16.4	5.5	1.3	1.4	0.1	0.4	0.7	(1)	(1)	2.3	8.2	1.0	0.1	0.1	0.1	(1)		(1)	(1)	2.3	11
0.6	0.2	0.1	1.7	(1)	0.1	0.2	0.1	(1)	0.1	4.2	0.8	(1)	(1)	0.3	(1)	(1)	(1)	0.1	2.4	12
12.0	8.0	5.1	2.6	0.7	4.5	1.2	0.1	(1)	1.2	5.5	7.7	0.3	0.1	0.3	(1)	(1)	(1)	(1)	1.8	13
0.7	0.3	0.4	1.7	(1)	0.4	0.4	0.1	....	0.2	5.0	2.2	0.1	(1)	0.2	(1)	(1)	(1)	0.2	2.2	14
1.1	2.2	0.2	3.2	(1)	....	(1)	(1)	....	(1)	7.4	0.2	(1)	0.1	0.6	(1)		(1)	0.2	3.3	15
3.1	0.5	0.8	1.2	(1)	0.7	0.7	0.2	....	1.4	4.1	6.5	(1)	(1)	0.4	(1)		....	0.1	2.3	16
1.2	0.7	0.5	2.2	(1)	0.6	0.2	0.1	....	0.1	7.3	0.5	0.1	0.1	0.1	(1)		(1)	0.1	3.0	17
0.7	0.8	0.3	1.6	....	(1)	0.4	(1)	....	0.7	6.9	0.1	(1)	(1)	0.3	(1)		....	0.1	2.7	18
20.2	0.7	0.6	2.1	0.3	0.2	0.9	0.2	(1)	0.9	5.4	2.5	0.5	0.3	0.6	(1)	(1)	(1)	0.1	1.9	19
5.6	(1)		0.7	0.2	....	(1)		....	(1)	2.8	(1)	(1)	(1)	1.0	(1)		(1)	0.3	0.8	20
2.5	2.8	0.1	3.2	(1)	0.1	0.3	0.1	....	(1)	4.9	0.1	0.1	(1)	0.4	(1)		(1)	0.3	2.1	21
14.8	0.3	0.1	0.6	0.1	(1)	(1)	(1)	....	3.1	0.8	0.3	0.2	0.1	0.7	(1)	(1)	(1)	0.1	1.9	22
8.1	0.2	0.2	3.2	0.2	(1)	0.1	(1)	....	2.4	14.6	0.4	0.1	0.5	0.1	(1)		(1)	0.3	1.6	23
1.9	1.5	0.1	1.6	(1)	0.1	0.1	(1)	....	0.1	6.7	0.4	0.1	(1)	1.1	(1)		(1)	0.3	2.9	24
1.0	0.4	0.3	1.4	(1)	1.4	0.4	0.5	....	0.1	3.8	0.7	0.1	0.1	0.5	(1)	(1)	(1)	0.3	2.4	25
13.7	0.2	0.9	2.9	0.2	0.2	(1)	(1)	....	0.3	4.4	0.7	0.5	0.1	(1)	(1)		(1)	(1)	2.3	26
6.6	0.5	1.7	3.7	0.1	1.7	10.7	(1)	....	0.7	1.2	0.4	(1)	(1)	(1)	(1)		(1)	0.1	2.5	27
1.5	0.6	0.1	3.4	(1)	0.1	0.3	(1)	....	0.1	6.1	0.4	(1)	(1)	0.4	(1)		(1)	0.1	2.7	28
1.0	0.7	0.2	3.5	(1)	0.5	0.5	(1)	(1)	0.1	4.2	0.7	0.2	0.4	0.3	0.1		(1)	0.1	3.2	29
0.6	0.1	(1)	2.3	(1)	(1)	(1)		....	(1)	3.6	0.1	(1)	(1)	0.5	(1)		....	0.3	2.7	30
5.4	(1)	(1)	0.3	(1)	(1)	0.2	(1)	....	1.7	1.7	(1)	0.1	0.6	0.4	0.1		(1)	(1)	0.9	31
1.8	0.3	0.1	4.2	....	0.2	0.1		....	0.1	8.2	0.7	(1)	(1)	0.1	(1)		....	0.4	4.1	32
21.7	2.1	1.0	0.6	(1)	1.3	0.8	(1)	(1)	0.2	3.5	0.8	0.1	(1)	0.1	(1)		....	0.1	1.9	33
4.4	1.0	1.2	1.4	0.2	0.2	0.1	0.1	....	0.1	5.1	0.1	0.9	(1)	0.2	(1)		(1)	0.1	3.6	34
2.3	0.3	0.2	2.9	....	0.2	0.1		....		9.7	2.5	0.1	(1)	0.9	....		(1)	0.7	2.9	35
6.0	0.4	(1)	0.3	(1)	(1)	(1)	(1)	....	0.1	2.5	(1)	(1)	(1)	0.5	(1)	0.3	....	(1)	1.1	36
5.6	0.1	0.2	3.2	0.1	0.1	(1)	(1)	....	1.3	10.8	0.6	0.1	0.2	0.1	(1)		(1)	(1)	1.5	37
0.4	0.2	0.2	1.6	(1)	0.3	0.1	(1)	....	(1)	1.3	0.1	0.1	(1)	0.4	(1)		(1)	0.3	4.7	38
3.8	1.0	0.5	5.1	0.2	0.2	0.1	(1)	(1)	0.4	22.0	1.8	0.3	0.1	0.2	0.2	0.1	(1)	(1)	2.4	39
3.2	0.6	0.2	8.2	0.1	0.3	(1)	(1)	....	0.1	27.8	2.2	0.2	0.1	(1)	(1)		(1)	(1)	2.9	40
4.3	0.2	0.2	4.5	0.1	0.1	(1)	(1)	....	0.8	25.6	0.7	0.3	0.1	0.4	(1)		(1)	(1)	2.3	41
3.1	1.6	0.7	5.4	0.4	0.3	0.2	(1)	(1)	0.1	21.2	2.6	0.3	0.1	0.1	0.1	(1)	(1)	(1)	2.2	42
5.5	2.7	0.3	1.9	0.1	0.2	0.1	(1)	....	0.5	3.2	1.3	0.2	0.2	(1)	(1)		(1)	(1)	2.8	43
6.3	0.4	0.8	2.2	0.3	0.3	0.2	(1)	....	0.1	1.8	1.6	0.6	(1)	(1)	(1)		....	(1)	3.2	44
8.7	0.4	1.8	3.1	0.3	0.3	0.1	(1)	....	1.2	14.0	1.7	(1)	0.1	0.1	(1)		(1)	(1)	1.9	45
1.2	0.2	(1)	7.3	(1)	0.1	0.1	(1)	....	0.3	21.4	0.4	0.9	0.1	1.5	0.1	(1)	....	0.1	2.9	46
0.5	0.5	0.1	1.0	(1)	0.9	0.6	(1)	....	0.1	1.0	0.4	0.5	0.1	0.1	(1)	(1)	(1)	0.1	3.7	47
6.1	12.1	0.1	1.4	(1)	0.2	1.2	(1)	....	1.0	5.7	0.6	(1)	0.1	0.5	(1)	(1)	(1)	0.1	2.8	48
4.2	0.2	0.2	2.3	0.1	0.1	(1)	(1)	....	0.8	11.4	0.6	(1)	0.5	1.2	0.1	(1)	(1)	(1)	2.0	49
6.3	0.2	0.5	4.3	0.4	0.2	0.1	(1)	....	1.2	14.5	0.8	0.1	0.2	0.1	(1)	(1)	(1)	(1)	1.8	50
10.5	1.1	3.7	2.2	0.6	0.9	2.5	(1)	(1)	1.8	6.8	1.5	(1)	(1)	0.4	(1)	(1)	(1)	(1)	1.8	51
1.1	0.8	0.3	2.0	(1)	0.3	0.6	0.2	....	0.2	2.1	0.3	1.6	(1)	0.2	(1)	(1)	(1)	0.1	3.5	52
2.6	0.1	(1)	1.5	(1)	(1)	(1)	(1)	....	0.6	5.8	0.1	(1)	1.1	0.3	0.1	(1)		....	1.2	53
25.0	0.1	5.1	1.7	0.4	0.4	0.2		....	0.9	5.0	0.3	....	(1)	(1)	(1)		(1)	(1)	1.3	54
1.3	0.4	0.4	6.1	(1)	(1)	(1)	(1)	....	0.1	11.5	0.3	(1)	1.1	2.3	(1)		(1)	0.2	2.5	55
4.5	0.1	0.1	1.9	0.5	(1)	0.1	(1)	....	0.8	6.3	0.2	(1)	0.1	0.1	0.2	(1)	(1)	(1)	1.8	56
3.3	2.8	0.4	1.8	0.1	0.2	0.7	0.1	....	0.2	6.0	0.9	(1)	(1)	0.3	(1)	0.1	(1)	0.1	2.6	57
3.8	3.0	0.1	0.7	(1)	0.1	0.1	(1)	(1)	0.1	4.9	0.7	0.1	0.1	0.4	(1)	(1)	(1)	0.1	3.3	58
0.3	0.2	(1)	0.6	(1)	0.1	0.1	(1)	....	(1)	0.9	0.1	0.1	(1)	0.3	(1)		(1)	(1)	5.2	59
0.9	0.4	(1)	0.9	(1)	(1)	(1)	(1)	....	(1)	1.4	0.1	(1)	(1)	0.4	(1)		(1)	0.1	1.9	60
0.9	0.5	0.2	1.8	(1)	0.6	0.3	(1)	....	0.1	1.7	0.5	0.6	0.1	0.2	(1)	....	(1)	0.1	3.8	61
14.0	0.2	2.5	3.1	0.6	0.5	(1)	(1)	....	7.0	3.8	1.6	(1)	(1)	0.5	(1)		....	(1)	1.3	62
0.9	0.5	0.2	1.9	(1)	0.4	0.5	(1)	....	0.2	1.5	0.2	1.6	0.1	0.1	0.1	(1)		0.1	3.5	63
0.5	0.6	0.1	1.0	(1)	0.1	0.3	0.1	....	0.1	0.8	0.2	0.4	(1)	0.1	....		(1)	3.5	64
6.2	0.4	0.1	1.9	(1)	(1)	(1)	(1)	....	0.3	8.0	0.1	0.2	0.4	0.9	0.1	(1)		(1)	1.5	65
9.2	0.1	0.4	1.8	0.2	(1)	0.1	0.1	....	0.1	6.0	0.2	0.1	0.2	0.3	(1)		(1)	(1)	1.5	66
23.3	0.5	0.5	0.7	(1)	0.1	0.1	0.7	....	0.1	3.8	4.8	(1)	0.1	0.8	(1)	(1)	(1)	(1)	1.9	67
13.5	0.2	6.3	1.7	0.2	0.4	(1)		....	0.4	6.5	10.0	(1)	0.1	0.1	(1)		(1)	(1)	1.2	68
1.1	0.4	0.1	3.9	(1)	0.1	0.1	(1)	....	0.1	8.5	0.3	0.1	0.1	0.6	(1)	(1)	(1)	(1)	2.7	69
20.8	0.1	0.2	3.9	0.7	0.1	(1)		....	0.5	5.5	0.6	0.1	(1)	(1)	(1)		(1)	0.1	1.5	70
5.6	(1)	(1)	0.9	(1)	(1)	0.1		....	6.5	6.0	(1)	2.3	1.6	1.1	0.1	0.5	(1)	(1)	1.1	71
9.2	0.4	6.5	5.2	0.5	1.0	0.1	(1)	....	0.4	4.1	2.0	0.1	0.1	0.2	(1)		0.1	(1)	2.4	72
5.2	0.3	10.4	2.8	1.1	1.3	4.5	0.2	....	0.4	3.4	4.5	(1)	(1)	0.7	(1)		(1)	(1)	1.3	73

[2] See footnote to Table 109, p. 386.

TABLE 116.—SCHOOL ATTENDANCE OF POPULATION 5 TO 20 YEARS OF AGE, FOR PRINCIPAL POPULATION CLASSES, BY SEX, 1850–1920, AND BY SEX AND SINGLE YEARS, 1920 AND 1910, FOR THE UNITED STATES.

[Because of variations from census to census in the manner of presenting statistics of school attendance, it is impossible to give comparative figures for any specified age group. The school-attendance percentages are, however, based on the population 5 to 20 years of age, inclusive, for the reason that the numbers of persons attending school at ages above and below these limits are insignificant. For all classes and for the white and Negro population in 1860 and 1850 the number 5 to 20 years of age has been calculated by adding estimates for age 20 to the numbers returned as in the 5–19 group; and for the Negro population In 1890 and 1880 the number in the 5–20 group was estimated on the assumption that the proportion which this group formed of the total at all ages was the same for the Negro population as for the total colored population (Negroes, Indians, Chinese, Japanese, and other nonwhites).]

CLASS OF POPULATION AND CENSUS YEAR.	TOTAL POPULATION OF SPECIFIED CLASS, 5 TO 20 YEARS OF AGE, INCLUSIVE.			TOTAL PERSONS ATTENDING SCHOOL.					
				Both sexes.		Male.		Female.	
	Both sexes.	Male.	Female.	Number.	Per cent.	Number.	Per cent.	Number.	Per cent.
All classes:									
1920	33,250,870	16,639,600	16,611,270	21,763,275	65.5	10,886,703	65.4	10,876,572	65.5
1910	29,785,997	14,952,530	14,833,467	18,009,891	60.5	9,037,655	60.4	8,972,236	60.5
1900	26,041,940	13,048,537	12,993,403	13,367,147	51.3	6,668,823	51.1	6,698,324	51.6
1890	22,447,392	11,242,700	11,204,692	11,674,878	52.0	5,954,142	53.0	5,720,736	51.1
1880	18,319,830	9,180,762	9,139,068	9,951,608	54.3	5,123,507	55.8	4,828,101	52.8
1870	14,507,658	7,253,307	7,254,351	6,596,466	45.5	3,416,153	47.1	3,180,313	43.8
1860	11,980,728	6,029,870	5,950,858	5,692,954	47.5	2,978,292	49.4	2,714,662	45.6
1850	9,204,908	4,629,874	4,575,034	4,089,507	44.4	2,160,296	46.7	1,929,211	42.2
White:									
1920	29,333,533	14,727,541	14,605,992	19,644,508	67.0	9,870,374	67.0	9,774,134	66.9
1910	25,992,293	13,092,081	12,900,212	16,279,292	62.6	8,220,847	62.8	8,058,445	62.5
1900	22,441,947	11,271,583	11,170,364	12,231,004	54.5	6,137,874	54.5	6,093,130	54.5
1890	19,250,565	9,655,372	9,595,193	10,667,171	55.4	5,464,413	56.6	5,202,758	54.2
1880	15,618,617	7,838,446	7,780,171	9,095,485	58.2	4,690,093	59.8	4,405,392	56.6
1870	12,528,178	6,274,555	6,253,623	6,414,740	51.2	3,326,797	53.0	3,087,943	49.4
1860	10,099,266	5,086,975	5,012,291	5,660,325	56.0	2,961,698	58.2	2,698,627	53.8
1850	7,681,163	3,868,917	3,812,246	4,063,046	52.9	2,146,432	55.5	1,916,614	50.3
Negro:									
1920	3,796,957	1,848,797	1,948,160	2,049,791	54.0	979,246	53.0	1,070,545	55.0
1910	3,677,860	1,797,688	1,880,172	1,670,650	45.4	783,869	43.6	886,781	47.2
1900	3,499,187	1,721,758	1,777,429	1,096,734	31.3	509,984	29.6	586,750	33.0
1890	3,126,497	1,560,122	1,566,375	999,324	32.0	484,969	31.1	514,355	32.8
1880	2,633,683	1,301,039	1,332,644	856,014	32.5	433,375	33.3	422,639	31.7
1870	1,958,237	963,965	994,272	180,372	9.2	88,594	9.2	91,778	9.2
1860	1,859,370	929,994	929,376	32,629	1.8	16,594	1.8	16,035	1.7
1850	1,524,829	761,229	763,600	26,461	1.7	13,864	1.8	12,597	1.6
Native white— Native par.:									
1920	20,048,170	10,090,524	9,957,646	13,655,361	68.1	6,846,934	67.9	6,808,427	68.4
1910	17,246,081	8,691,250	8,554,831	11,110,583	64.4	5,611,901	64.6	5,498,682	64.3
1900	14,876,715	7,506,903	7,369,812	8,244,687	55.4	4,141,997	55.2	4,102,690	55.7
1890	12,604,550	6,341,747	6,262,803	7,204,755	57.2	3,695,420	58.3	3,509,335	56.0
Native white— For. or mix. par.:									
1920	8,116,313	4,060,004	4,056,309	5,434,720	67.0	2,733,322	67.3	2,701,398	66.6
1910	7,157,099	3,575,800	3,581,299	4,517,203	63.1	2,270,706	63.5	2,246,497	62.7
1900	6,372,199	3,180,232	3,191,967	3,605,128	56.6	1,801,303	56.6	1,803,825	56.5
1890	5,313,470	2,648,167	2,665,303	2,948,534	55.5	1,500,893	56.7	1,447,641	54.3
Foreign-born white:									
1920	1,169,050	577,013	592,037	554,427	47.4	290,118	50.3	264,309	44.6
1910	1,589,113	825,031	764,082	651,506	41.0	338,240	41.0	313,266	41.0
1900	1,193,033	584,448	608,585	381,189	32.0	194,574	33.3	186,615	30.7
1890	1,332,545	665,458	667,087	513,882	38.6	268,100	40.3	245,782	36.0

TABLE 116.—SCHOOL ATTENDANCE OF POPULATION 5 TO 20 YEARS OF AGE, FOR PRINCIPAL POPULATION CLASSES, BY SEX, 1850–1920, AND BY SEX AND SINGLE YEARS, 1920 AND 1910, FOR THE UNITED STATES—Continued.

AGE AND CENSUS YEAR.	NUMBER AND PER CENT OF TOTAL AT SPECIFIED AGE ATTENDING SCHOOL.													
	All classes.		White.				Negro.				Indian, Chinese, Japanese, and all other.			
	Both sexes.		Male.		Female.		Male.		Female.		Male.		Female.	
	Number.	Per cent.	Number.	Per cent.	Number.	Per cent.	Number.	Per cent.	Number.	Per cent.	Number.	Per cent.	Number.	Per cent.
5 years:														
1920.....	441,411	18.8	202,686	19.2	207,736	20.2	14,122	11.2	15.638	12.3	638	12.7	591	11.9
1910.....	346,673	17.0	159,467	17.8	161,229	18.4	11,774	9.3	13,286	10.3	446	10.6	471	11.6
6 years:														
1920.....	1,480,714	63.3	683,070	65.5	680,447	66.5	54,306	41.7	58,921	44.1	1,924	38.9	2,046	41.4
1910.....	1,059,353	52.1	490,944	55.2	487,723	55.8	37,051	28.5	41,073	30.9	1,249	30.1	1,313	31.3
7 years:														
1920.....	1,905,404	83.3	874,634	85.6	859,058	85.9	81,807	64.0	84,650	65.9	2,687	61.0	2,568	60.1
1910.....	1,464,730	75.0	677,023	79.0	663,813	79.2	58,270	46.3	61,834	49.2	1,844	46.7	1,946	50.2
8 years:														
1920.....	2,010,894	88.5	915,061	90.5	901,117	90.7	93,447	72.1	95,296	73.3	2,998	67.9	2,975	68.3
1910.....	1,586,572	82.7	724,680	86.5	711,404	86.6	70,609	56.5	75,577	59.3	2,156	56.0	2,146	56.7
9 years:														
1920.....	1,944,314	90.4	889,955	92.1	869,151	92.1	89,558	76.4	90,287	77.7	2,714	73.8	2,649	73.4
1910.....	1,567,665	86.2	719,310	89.4	699,450	89.4	71,232	63.7	73,308	65.4	2,212	64.3	2,153	63.6
10 years:														
1920.....	2,077,965	93.0	940,070	94.8	921,080	94.9	105,328	79.1	105,560	80.9	2,991	74.8	2,936	75.4
1910.....	1,681,342	90.0	761,994	92.9	745,176	93.3	83,575	68.0	85,580	71.5	2,572	68.5	2,445	68.2
11 years:														
1920.....	1,970,255	93.9	898,983	95.3	887,392	95.4	88,166	81.0	90,668	83.2	2,595	80.7	2,451	80.7
1910.....	1,555,301	91.2	708,698	93.6	700,644	93.8	68,730	70.8	72,993	74.5	2,247	74.6	1,989	72.6
12 years:														
1920.....	2,082,749	93.2	940,739	95.0	914,973	95.1	108,801	79.0	112,367	82.1	3,043	77.5	2,826	77.2
1910.....	1,716,310	89.8	773,524	92.7	754,321	93.2	88,619	67.5	94,648	72.8	2,656	70.8	2,542	73.3
13 years:														
1920.....	1,877,429	92.5	850,181	94.3	837,042	94.3	88,592	77.3	96,516	81.3	2,552	79.2	2,546	80.5
1910.....	1,574,253	88.8	714,102	91.7	703,744	91.8	71,574	64.9	80,242	71.9	2,435	73.9	2,156	74.7
14 years:														
1920.....	1,766,784	86.3	802,209	88.4	777,753	88.0	85,701	70.2	96,060	76.5	2,661	75.1	2,400	74.0
1910.....	1,501,456	81.2	685,670	84.1	664,734	84.0	66,988	57.4	79,046	67.0	2,721	72.3	2,297	71.5
15 years:														
1920.....	1,357,345	72.9	603,158	73.6	614,289	74.7	60,524	58.7	75,070	67.6	2,266	67.6	2,038	70.1
1910.....	1,175,009	68.3	530,808	70.1	528,099	70.4	49,221	48.3	62,639	59.3	2,302	66.0	1,940	67.2
16 years:														
1920.....	1,001,701	50.8	424,156	48.9	467,659	53.5	44,260	41.7	61,785	51.9	2,017	57.3	1,824	59.9
1910.....	943,511	50.6	415,308	51.0	431,179	52.7	38,600	36.2	54,455	46.3	2,173	57.2	1,796	58.2
17 years:														
1920.....	642,360	34.6	269,335	32.7	307,326	37.4	26,105	26.1	36,610	34.6	1,660	47.6	1,324	48.6
1910.....	629,866	35.3	279,588	35.1	288,301	37.0	24,727	24.7	34,363	33.1	1,633	47.3	1,254	47.3
18 years:														
1920.....	413,619	21.7	175,296	21.2	196,272	23.2	15,842	14.8	23,906	19.6	1,343	33.4	960	30.0
1910.....	434,864	22.6	191,480	22.9	199,331	23.4	16,613	15.3	24,894	20.2	1,594	34.3	952	29.6
19 years:														
1920.....	252,680	13.8	117,226	14.6	113,112	14.0	8,631	8.9	11,984	10.7	1,154	27.7	573	20.7
1910.....	254,421	14.4	121,347	15.3	110,169	14.3	8,964	9.9	12,146	11.9	1,203	25.0	592	21.4
20 years:														
1920.....	148,352	8.3	73,643	9.8	63,719	7.9	3,876	4.4	5,885	4.8	836	19.2	393	11.9
1910.....	155,551	8.4	77,656	9.7	64,496	7.8	5,040	5.4	7,088	5.8	904	16.7	367	11.2

TABLE 117.—SCHOOL ATTENDANCE, BY SEX AND AGE PERIODS, FOR

[Per cent not shown

CENSUS YEAR, CLASS OF POPULATION, AND SEX.	Total number of persons attending school.	PERSONS 7 TO 13 YEARS OF AGE.			PERSONS 14 AND 15 YEARS OF AGE.		
		Total number.	Attending school. Number.	Per cent.	Total number.	Attending school. Number.	Per cent.
1920							
All classes	21,763,275	15,306,793	13,869,010	90.6	3,907,710	3,124,129	79.9
Male	10,886,703	7,723,238	6,984,902	90.4	1,958,976	1,556,519	79.5
Female	10,876,572	7,583,555	6,884,108	90.8	1,948,734	1,567,610	80.4
White	19,644,508	13,515,118	12,499,436	92.5	3,432,889	2,797,409	81.5
Male	9,870,374	6,827,330	6,309,623	92.4	1,726,962	1,405,367	81.4
Female	9,774,134	6,687,788	6,189,813	92.6	1,705,927	1,392,042	81.6
Negro	2,049,791	1,738,822	1,331,043	76.5	461,778	317,355	68.7
Male	979,246	869,045	655,699	75.5	225,122	146,225	65.0
Female	1,070,545	869,777	675,344	77.6	236,656	171,130	72.3
Indian	51,865	44,256	31,054	70.2	11,216	7,851	70.0
Male	25,902	22,203	15,543	70.0	5,658	3,920	69.3
Female	25,963	22,053	15,511	70.3	5,558	3,931	70.7
Chinese	6,081	2,944	2,609	88.6	842	703	83.5
Male	4,045	1,712	1,502	87.7	587	479	81.6
Female	2,036	1,232	1,107	89.9	255	224	87.8
Japanese	9,942	5,429	4,672	86.1	924	765	82.8
Male	6,221	2,834	2,438	86.0	617	505	81.8
Female	3,721	2,595	2,234	86.1	307	260	84.7
All other	1,088	224	196	87.5	61	46	......
Male	915	114	97	85.1	30	23	......
Female	173	110	99	90.0	31	23	......
Native white	19,090,081	13,136,967	12,181,396	92.7	3,272,950	2,690,787	82.2
Male	9,580,256	6,636,501	6,148,896	92.7	1,647,491	1,351,089	82.0
Female	9,509,825	6,500,466	6,032,500	92.8	1,625,459	1,339,698	82.4
Native parentage	13,655,361	9,315,013	8,584,679	92.2	2,363,691	1,982,664	83.9
Male	6,846,934	4,713,879	4,338,518	92.0	1,193,040	994,541	83.4
Female	6,808,427	4,601,134	4,246,161	92.3	1,170,651	988,123	84.4
Foreign parentage	3,697,784	2,664,732	2,505,236	94.0	598,719	453,603	75.8
Male	1,863,285	1,338,859	1,259,560	94.1	299,293	229,744	76.8
Female	1,834,499	1,325,873	1,245,676	94.0	299,426	223,859	74.8
Mixed parentage	1,736,936	1,157,222	1,091,481	94.3	310,540	254,520	82.0
Male	870,037	583,763	550,818	94.4	155,158	126,804	81.7
Female	866,899	573,459	540,663	94.3	155,382	127,716	82.2
Foreign-born white	554,427	378,151	318,040	84.1	159,939	106,622	66.7
Male	290,118	190,829	160,727	84.2	79,471	54,278	68.3
Female	264,309	187,322	157,313	84.0	80,468	52,344	65.0
1910							
All classes	18,009,891	12,950,418	11,146,173	86.1	3,569,347	2,676,465	75.0
Male	9,037,655	6,539,326	5,608,062	85.8	1,798,449	1,337,710	74.4
Female	8,972,236	6,411,092	5,538,111	86.4	1,770,898	1,338,755	75.6
White	16,279,292	11,252,886	10,057,883	89.4	3,113,894	2,409,311	77.4
Male	8,220,847	5,690,176	5,079,331	89.3	1,572,638	1,216,478	77.4
Female	8,058,445	5,562,710	4,978,552	89.5	1,541,256	1,192,833	77.4
Negro	1,670,650	1,648,753	1,056,791	64.1	442,103	257,894	58.3
Male	783,869	824,097	512,609	62.2	218,560	116,209	53.2
Female	886,781	824,656	544,182	66.0	223,543	141,685	63.4
Indian	53,458	46,034	29,415	63.9	12,246	8,596	70.2
Male	27,843	23,469	14,885	63.4	6,347	4,488	70.7
Female	25,615	22,565	14,530	64.4	5,899	4,108	69.6
Chinese	3,887	1,840	1,418	77.1	918	556	60.6
Male	2,977	1,109	874	78.8	777	461	59.3
Female	910	731	544	74.4	141	95	67.4
Japanese	2,512	882	647	73.4	170	109	60.0
Male	2,030	462	351	76.0	111	69	61.0
Female	176	420	296	70.5	59	34	......
All other	92	23	19	......	16	6	......
Male	83	13	12	......	16	6	......
Female	9	10	7	......			
Native white	15,627,786	10,773,631	9,640,513	89.5	2,963,982	2,321,048	78.3
Male	7,882,607	5,448,095	4,867,727	89.3	1,497,805	1,170,305	78.1
Female	7,745,179	5,325,536	4,772,786	89.6	1,466,177	1,150,743	78.5
Native parentage	11,110,583	7,647,477	6,744,539	88.2	2,071,568	1,664,279	80.3
Male	5,611,901	3,875,729	3,409,430	88.0	1,051,381	838,613	79.8
Female	5,498,682	3,771,748	3,335,109	88.4	1,020,187	825,666	80.9
Foreign parentage	2,867,327	2,015,386	1,864,944	92.5	584,765	414,773	70.9
Male	1,444,938	1,012,837	938,745	92.7	292,290	210,475	72.0
Female	1,422,389	1,002,549	926,199	92.4	292,475	204,298	69.9
Mixed parentage	1,649,876	1,110,768	1,031,030	92.8	307,649	241,996	78.7
Male	825,768	559,529	519,552	92.9	154,134	121,217	78.6
Female	824,108	551,239	511,478	92.8	153,515	120,779	78.7
Foreign-born white	651,506	479,255	417,370	87.1	149,912	88,263	58.9
Male	338,240	242,081	211,604	87.4	74,833	46,173	61.7
Female	313,266	237,174	205,766	86.8	75,079	42,090	56.1

POPULATION CLASSES, FOR THE UNITED STATES: 1920 AND 1910.

where base is less than 100.]

CENSUS YEAR, CLASS OF POPULATION, AND SEX.	PERSONS 16 AND 17 YEARS OF AGE.			PERSONS 18 TO 20 YEARS OF AGE.			OTHERS ATTENDING SCHOOL.	
	Total number.	Attending school.		Total number.	Attending school.		Under 7 years of age.	21 years of age and over.
		Number.	Per cent.		Number.	Per cent.		
1920								
All classes	3,828,131	1,644,061	42.9	5,522,082	814,651	14.8	1,966,635	344,789
Male	1,902,867	767,533	40.3	2,688,747	397,847	14.8	978,621	201,281
Female	1,925,264	876,528	45.5	2,833,335	416,804	14.7	988,014	143,508
White	3,384,559	1,468,476	43.4	4,851,302	739,268	15.2	1,815,677	324,242
Male	1,689,778	693,491	41.0	2,384,143	366,165	15.4	906,290	189,438
Female	1,694,781	774,985	45.7	2,467,159	373,103	15.1	909,387	134,804
Negro	430,799	168,760	39.2	648,955	70,124	10.8	145,571	16,938
Male	206,087	70,365	34.1	292,055	28,349	9.7	69,672	8,936
Female	224,712	98,395	43.8	356,900	41,775	11.7	75,899	8,002
Indian	10,167	5,320	52.3	14,769	3,346	22.7	3,464	830
Male	5,041	2,536	50.3	7,358	1,755	23.9	1,647	501
Female	5,126	2,784	54.3	7,411	1,591	21.5	1,817	329
Chinese	959	555	57.9	2,235	708	31.7	555	951
Male	726	398	54.8	1,812	562	31.0	301	803
Female	233	157	67.4	423	146	34.5	254	148
Japanese	1,538	890	57.9	3,906	997	25.5	1,334	1,284
Male	1,152	696	60.4	2,518	819	32.5	693	1,070
Female	386	194	50.3	1,388	178	12.8	641	214
All other	109	60	55.0	915	208	22.7	34	544
Male	83	47	......	861	197	22.9	18	533
Female	26	13	......	54	11	......	16	11
Native white	3,179,688	1,420,296	44.7	4,470,268	712,478	15.9	1,797,722	287,402
Male	1,588,591	668,716	42.1	2,201,523	350,519	15.9	897,151	163,885
Female	1,591,097	751,580	47.2	2,268,745	361,959	16.0	900,571	123,517
Native parentage	2,283,604	1,111,569	48.7	3,209,876	562,322	17.5	1,201,706	212,421
Male	1,143,128	522,656	45.7	1,582,596	273,761	17.3	599,140	118,318
Female	1,140,476	588,913	51.6	1,627,280	288,561	17.7	602,566	94,103
Foreign parentage	585,970	179,726	30.7	824,353	84,290	10.2	428,784	46,145
Male	290,421	86,436	29.8	403,530	44,462	11.0	214,490	28,593
Female	295,549	93,290	31.6	420,823	39,828	9.5	214,294	17,552
Mixed parentage	310,114	129,001	41.6	436,039	65,866	15.1	167,232	28,836
Male	155,042	59,624	38.5	215,397	32,296	15.0	83,521	16,974
Female	155,072	69,377	44.7	220,642	33,570	15.2	83,711	11,862
Foreign-born white	204,871	48,180	23.5	381,034	26,790	7.0	17,955	36,840
Male	101,187	24,775	24.5	182,620	15,646	8.6	9,139	25,553
Female	103,684	23,405	22.6	198,414	11,144	5.6	8,816	11,287
1910								
All classes	3,650,951	1,573,377	43.1	5,546,049	844,836	15.2	1,455,784	313,256
Male	1,825,895	762,029	41.7	2,738,284	424,801	15.5	725,816	179,237
Female	1,825,056	811,348	44.5	2,807,765	420,035	15.0	729,968	134,019
White	3,209,712	1,414,376	44.1	4,881,708	764,479	15.7	1,345,467	287,776
Male	1,611,778	694,896	43.1	2,431,769	390,483	16.1	673,546	166,113
Female	1,597,934	719,480	45.0	2,449,939	373,996	15.3	671,921	121,663
Negro	428,250	152,145	35.5	640,236	74,745	11.7	106,684	22,391
Male	206,864	63,327	30.6	291,654	30,617	10.5	50,503	10,604
Female	221,386	88,818	40.1	348,582	44,128	12.7	56,181	11,787
Indian	11,292	6,188	54.8	17,143	4,500	26.2	3,306	1,453
Male	5,765	3,235	56.1	8,661	2,683	31.0	1,590	962
Female	5,527	2,953	53.4	8,482	1,817	21.4	1,716	491
Chinese	1,258	540	42.9	2,701	628	23.3	185	560
Male	1,109	461	41.6	2,432	563	23.1	94	524
Female	149	79	53.0	269	65	24.2	91	36
Japanese	395	120	30.4	3,993	461	11.5	142	1,040
Male	336	103	30.7	3,504	432	12.3	83	999
Female	59	17	......	489	29	5.9	59	41
All other	44	8	......	268	23	8.6	....	36
Male	43	7	......	264	23	8.7	....	35
Female	1	1	......	4	......	......	....	1
Native white	2,990,669	1,376,133	46.0	4,243,662	734,855	17.3	1,303,075	252,162
Male	1,502,091	674,701	44.9	2,085,449	373,719	17.9	652,012	144,143
Female	1,488,578	701,432	47.1	2,158,213	361,136	16.7	651,063	108,019
Native parentage	2,073,951	1,060,244	51.1	2,988,189	586,708	19.6	862,610	192,203
Male	1,044,605	520,842	49.9	1,472,212	301,536	20.5	431,091	110,389
Female	1,029,346	539,402	52.4	1,515,977	285,172	18.8	431,519	81,814
Foreign parentage	604,606	183,963	30.4	825,406	81,648	9.9	285,767	36,232
Male	301,181	90,939	30.2	402,392	40,762	10.1	143,503	20,514
Female	303,425	93,024	30.7	423,014	40,886	9.7	142,264	15,718
Mixed parentage	312,112	131,926	42.3	430,067	66,499	15.5	154,698	23,727
Male	156,305	62,920	40.3	210,845	31,421	14.9	77,418	13,240
Female	155,807	69,006	44.3	219,222	35,078	16.0	77,280	10,487
Foreign-born white	219,043	38,243	17.5	638,046	29,624	4.6	42,392	35,614
Male	109,687	20,195	18.4	346,320	16,764	4.8	21,534	21,970
Female	109,356	18,048	16.5	291,726	12,860	4.4	20,858	13,644

TABLE 118.—SCHOOL ATTENDANCE, BY BROAD AGE GROUPS, BY DIVISIONS AND STATES: 1920 AND 1910.

DIVISION AND STATE.	TOTAL NUMBER OF PERSONS ATTENDING SCHOOL.		PERSONS 7 TO 20 YEARS OF AGE ATTENDING SCHOOL.				PERSONS UNDER 7 YEARS OF AGE ATTENDING SCHOOL.		PERSONS 21 YEARS OF AGE AND OVER ATTENDING SCHOOL.	
			1920		1910					
	1920	1910	Number.	Per cent.	Number.	Per cent.	1920	1910	1920	1910
United States..	21,763,275	18,009,891	19,451,851	68.1	16,240,851	63.2	1,966,635	1,455,784	344,789	313,256
GEOG. DIVISIONS:										
New England.....	1,424,088	1,222,228	1,223,623	69.2	1,051,485	65.3	174,175	149,077	26,290	21,666
Middle Atlantic...	4,260,677	3,531,373	3,746,560	67.8	3,131,190	62.9	447,445	339,656	66,672	60,527
E. North Central..	4,236,641	3,576,003	3,728,706	69.7	3,197,292	65.7	427,749	315,207	80,186	63,504
W. North Central..	2,741,410	2,530,591	2,420,929	71.3	2,271,448	68.4	270,428	209,562	50,053	49,581
South Atlantic....	3,080,686	2,418,444	2,818,406	65.2	2,226,901	58.4	225,573	154,223	36,707	37,320
E. South Central..	2,018,295	1,730,191	1,858,659	65.9	1,589,551	59.6	141,808	114,264	17,828	26,376
W. South Central..	2,247,456	1,795,100	2,097,596	64.4	1,673,480	59.4	125,955	94,808	23,905	26,812
Mountain..........	732,593	505,191	656,638	73.3	460,193	67.3	63,174	35,122	12,781	9,876
Pacific............	1,021,429	700,770	900,734	73.4	639,311	66.9	90,328	43,865	30,367	17,594
NEW ENGLAND:										
Maine.............	154,163	140,831	134,299	71.1	122,218	67.3	17,622	16,257	2,242	2,356
New Hampshire...	81,850	77,550	73,063	69.9	68,048	65.4	7,298	8,374	1,489	1,128
Vermont..........	68,745	70,531	62,544	71.6	62,064	70.4	5,254	7,549	947	918
Massachusetts....	741,029	630,119	633,124	69.8	539,615	65.7	91,931	78,259	15,974	12,245
Rhode Island......	110,838	96,242	95,499	63.8	83,312	60.4	13,822	10,877	1,517	2,053
Connecticut.......	267,463	206,955	225,094	68.1	176,228	63.5	38,248	27,761	4,121	2,966
MIDDLE ATLANTIC:										
New York........	1,900,039	1,650,863	1,656,905	67.3	1,452,179	63.4	206,238	166,968	36,896	31,716
New Jersey........	613,575	469,272	525,979	66.9	405,496	61.6	80,202	56,840	7,394	6,936
Pennsylvania......	1,747,063	1,411,238	1,563,676	68.6	1,273,515	62.7	161,005	115,848	22,382	21,875
E. NORTH CENTRAL:										
Ohio.............	1,125,097	898,088	989,417	71.3	810,136	66.2	107,461	72,575	28,219	15,377
Indiana..........	572,310	529,742	515,237	69.1	482,597	66.7	48,998	36,416	8,075	10,729
Illinois...........	1,251,189	1,064,346	1,108,216	68.4	955,869	63.6	120,945	88,269	22,028	20,208
Michigan..........	723,639	568,926	626,165	70.1	500,305	67.6	85,894	59,416	11,580	9,205
Wisconsin.........	564,406	514,901	489,671	69.5	448,385	65.8	64,451	58,531	10,284	7,985
W. NORTH CENTRAL:										
Minnesota.........	510,238	462,867	451,096	70.1	417,496	69.2	47,778	35,728	11,364	9,643
Iowa.............	526,864	499,272	454,078	72.4	434,117	69.1	62,457	54,961	10,329	10,194
Missouri..........	699,809	665,972	624,395	69.2	608,226	65.9	65,014	46,280	10,400	11,466
North Dakota....	161,221	121,649	146,289	73.9	110,459	65.7	12,162	8,793	2,770	2,397
South Dakota.....	146,956	126,903	131,943	72.8	115,592	68.0	12,691	8,840	2,322	2,471
Nebraska..........	298,619	275,829	256,961	71.7	242,625	69.8	36,565	27,671	5,093	5,533
Kansas...........	397,703	378,099	356,167	73.7	342,933	71.6	33,761	27,289	7,775	7,877
SOUTH ATLANTIC:										
Delaware..........	41,713	36,330	37,759	69.0	33,362	61.8	3,391	2,409	563	559
Maryland..........	270,968	234,628	246,056	64.6	213,622	59.2	20,730	16,967	4,182	4,039
Dist. of Columbia..	70,886	54,688	58,005	64.5	47,662	64.4	6,704	4,726	6,177	2,300
Virginia...........	495,674	401,696	460,037	64.8	381,532	59.1	29,746	14,868	5,891	5,296
West Virginia.....	324,747	267,411	297,044	67.9	244,996	67.0	24,439	18,519	3,264	3,896
North Carolina....	626,981	495,196	576,239	68.6	455,109	63.1	44,817	32,032	5,925	8,055
South Carolina....	427,962	300,359	393,077	68.2	277,210	53.4	31,070	18,663	3,815	4,486
Georgia...........	624,776	494,781	570,386	59.8	452,234	53.1	49,264	36,007	5,126	6,540
Florida...........	196,979	133,355	179,803	64.1	121,174	54.1	15,412	10,032	1,764	2,149
E. SOUTH CENTRAL:										
Kentucky.........	524,342	473,481	480,526	67.0	437,863	62.7	39,203	28,520	4,613	7,098
Tennessee.........	528,993	451,190	488,543	67.4	417,862	61.3	35,533	26,094	4,917	7,234
Alabama..........	527,595	396,845	499,888	64.6	371,850	53.7	23,270	18,641	4,437	6,354
Mississippi........	437,365	408,675	389,702	64.7	361,976	61.0	43,802	41,009	3,861	5,690
W. SOUTH CENTRAL:										
Arkansas..........	410,853	333,795	375,115	65.8	304,909	60.2	31,911	23,450	3,827	5,436
Louisiana.........	356,690	257,097	327,540	57.0	235,264	44.4	25,884	18,194	3,066	3,639
Oklahoma.........	487,013	394,201	444,047	68.0	361,376	69.6	37,546	27,689	5,220	5,136
Texas.............	992,900	810,077	950,688	64.8	771,931	61.2	30,614	25,545	11,598	12,601
MOUNTAIN:										
Montana..........	115,367	62,755	102,621	75.5	56,976	65.8	10,975	4,638	1,771	1,141
Idaho............	104,456	68,603	95,027	77.7	63,613	71.3	7,976	3,798	1,453	1,192
Wyoming..........	38,827	23,745	34,387	72.4	21,475	65.0	3,793	1,842	647	428
Colorado..........	198,060	153,412	175,745	73.2	138,467	69.2	18,176	11,642	4,139	3,303
New Mexico.......	83,370	66,717	75,119	68.5	60,704	62.7	7,171	5,201	1,080	812
Arizona...........	60,688	31,346	54,387	60.8	28,753	55.0	5,271	2,092	1,030	501
Utah.............	118,934	88,056	107,908	79.3	80,725	72.5	8,615	5,052	2,411	2,279
Nevada...........	12,891	10,557	11,444	73.4	9,480	63.6	1,197	857	250	220
PACIFIC:										
Washington.......	265,051	201,695	238,012	74.1	185,795	68.1	19,568	11,329	7,471	4,571
Oregon...........	157,552	121,409	141,613	75.4	111,597	68.2	10,778	6,590	5,161	3,222
California........	598,826	377,666	521,109	72.6	341,919	65.8	59,982	25,946	17,735	9,801

TABLE 119.—SCHOOL ATTENDANCE OF POPULATION 7 TO 20 YEARS OF AGE, BY SEX, BY DIVISIONS AND STATES: 1920 AND 1910.

DIVISION AND STATE.	MALES 7 TO 20 YEARS OF AGE ATTENDING SCHOOL.				FEMALES 7 TO 20 YEARS OF AGE ATTENDING SCHOOL.			
	1920		1910		1920		1910	
	Number.	Per cent.	Number.	Per cent.	Number.	Per cent.	Number.	Per cent.
United States	9,706,801	68.0	8,132,602	63.0	9,745,050	68.2	8,108,249	63.3
GEOGRAPHIC DIVISIONS:								
New England	608,434	69.3	523,899	65.2	615,189	69.1	527,586	65.4
Middle Atlantic	1,879,234	68.4	1,566,531	63.2	1,867,326	67.2	1,564,659	62.5
East North Central	1,869,629	69.6	1,610,601	65.7	1,859,077	69.8	1,586,691	65.6
West North Central	1,208,596	71.0	1,144,488	68.2	1,212,333	71.7	1,126,960	68.7
South Atlantic	1,395,324	64.8	1,101,477	57.9	1,423,082	65.5	1,125,424	58.8
East South Central	925,257	65.9	793,545	59.5	933,402	66.0	796,006	59.8
West South Central	1,040,793	63.9	839,147	59.4	1,056,803	64.8	834,333	59.5
Mountain	328,957	72.6	232,644	66.2	327,681	73.9	227,549	68.4
Pacific	450,577	72.6	320,270	64.9	450,157	74.2	319,041	68.9
NEW ENGLAND:								
Maine	66,239	70.2	60,941	66.7	68,060	72.0	61,277	67.9
New Hampshire	36,128	69.5	33,805	64.4	36,935	70.2	34,243	66.4
Vermont	31,266	70.8	31,030	68.9	31,278	72.5	31,034	71.9
Massachusetts	314,927	70.1	267,791	65.8	318,197	69.4	271,824	65.6
Rhode Island	47,336	63.4	42,589	61.2	48,163	64.1	40,723	59.5
Connecticut	112,538	68.6	87,743	63.4	112,556	67.6	88,485	63.5
MIDDLE ATLANTIC:								
New York	832,157	68.2	723,463	64.2	824,748	66.4	728,716	62.7
New Jersey	263,928	67.5	203,327	62.3	262,051	66.3	202,169	60.9
Pennsylvania	783,149	68.9	639,741	62.5	780,527	68.3	633,774	62.8
EAST NORTH CENTRAL:								
Ohio	494,519	71.0	409,085	66.5	494,898	71.7	401,051	66.0
Indiana	259,245	69.2	243,500	66.6	255,992	69.1	239,097	66.8
Illinois	557,008	68.8	480,526	64.0	551,208	68.0	475,343	63.3
Michigan	314,630	69.5	251,550	67.2	311,535	70.6	248,755	68.1
Wisconsin	244,227	69.0	225,940	65.7	245,444	69.9	222,445	66.0
WEST NORTH CENTRAL:								
Minnesota	225,043	69.7	210,343	69.0	226,053	70.6	207,153	69.5
Iowa	226,167	71.8	218,044	68.6	227,911	72.9	216,073	69.5
Missouri	312,866	69.6	305,552	66.3	311,529	68.9	302,674	65.6
North Dakota	73,083	73.6	56,380	65.0	73,206	74.2	54,079	66.4
South Dakota	66,151	71.8	59,038	67.4	65,792	73.8	56,554	68.7
Nebraska	128,304	71.0	122,544	69.5	128,657	72.5	120,081	70.1
Kansas	176,982	73.0	172,587	70.9	179,185	74.3	170,346	72.4
SOUTH ATLANTIC:								
Delaware	18,957	69.4	17,144	62.2	18,802	68.5	16,218	61.3
Maryland	124,602	64.9	107,311	59.9	121,454	64.2	106,311	58.5
District of Columbia	28,720	67.3	23,135	65.0	29,285	61.9	24,527	64.0
Virginia	226,508	63.3	188,141	58.2	233,529	66.3	193,391	60.0
West Virginia	148,588	67.3	124,686	66.3	148,456	68.5	120,310	67.8
North Carolina	286,398	68.5	227,744	63.2	289,841	68.7	227,365	63.0
South Carolina	193,276	68.0	134,767	52.5	199,801	68.3	142,443	54.4
Georgia	279,458	59.4	219,420	52.3	290,928	60.3	232,814	54.0
Florida	88,817	64.1	59,129	53.0	90,986	64.0	62,045	55.1
EAST SOUTH CENTRAL:								
Kentucky	239,915	66.4	220,640	62.8	240,611	67.6	217,223	62.6
Tennessee	244,777	67.6	209,798	61.2	243,766	67.2	208,064	61.5
Alabama	248,315	65.0	184,397	53.6	251,573	64.2	187,453	53.9
Mississippi	192,250	64.5	178,710	60.6	197,452	64.9	183,266	61.4
WEST SOUTH CENTRAL:								
Arkansas	187,438	66.1	152,402	60.2	187,677	65.6	152,507	60.2
Louisiana	159,544	56.5	114,896	43.9	168,002	57.6	120,368	44.9
Oklahoma	222,124	68.1	185,149	70.0	222,123	69.0	176,227	69.2
Texas	471,687	64.0	386,700	61.0	479,001	65.6	385,231	61.5
MOUNTAIN:								
Montana	51,244	74.6	28,409	62.8	51,377	76.5	28,567	69.0
Idaho	47,975	76.8	32,616	70.1	47,052	78.7	30,997	72.6
Wyoming	17,274	70.1	10,813	60.7	17,113	74.9	10,662	70.0
Colorado	87,277	72.4	69,139	68.2	88,468	74.1	69,328	70.2
New Mexico	37,662	68.5	31,391	63.8	37,457	68.4	29,313	61.5
Arizona	27,363	60.3	14,633	54.1	27,024	61.3	14,120	56.0
Utah	54,429	79.8	40,858	72.7	53,479	78.8	39,867	72.4
Nevada	5,733	71.0	4,785	59.8	5,711	75.9	4,695	68.1
PACIFIC:								
Washington	118,386	73.1	93,199	66.1	119,626	75.0	92,596	70.2
Oregon	70,622	75.0	56,570	66.8	70,991	75.9	55,027	69.6
California	261,569	71.8	170,501	63.8	259,540	73.4	171,418	68.0

TABLE 120.—SCHOOL ATTENDANCE OF POPULATION 7 TO 20 YEARS

DIVISION AND STATE.	PERSONS 7 TO 13 YEARS OF AGE ATTENDING SCHOOL.				PERSONS 14 AND 15 YEARS OF AGE ATTENDING SCHOOL.			
	1920		1910		1920		1910	
	Number.	Per cent.	Number.	Per cent.	Number.	Per cent.	Number.	Per cent.
United States	13,869,010	90.6	11,146,173	86.1	3,124,129	79.9	2,676,465	75.0
GEOGRAPHIC DIVISIONS:								
New England	898,605	95.3	751,547	95.2	179,963	75.3	163,585	73.6
Middle Atlantic	2,805,986	94.3	2,269,431	93.0	582,517	79.3	496,046	73.5
East North Central	2,693,634	95.1	2,239,718	93.5	598,227	82.5	528,507	77.9
West North Central	1,679,682	93.9	1,512,644	91.5	401,680	85.3	386,893	83.6
South Atlantic	1,997,008	85.6	1,508,993	75.6	452,330	75.4	360,081	67.1
East South Central	1,283,921	83.6	1,043,420	75.0	307,840	77.5	265,274	70.4
West South Central	1,447,653	82.5	1,106,205	74.7	351,732	76.9	286,521	72.8
Mountain	452,896	91.8	302,970	86.4	104,983	86.7	76,661	83.4
Pacific	609,625	94.1	411,245	91.2	144,857	89.2	112,897	85.3
NEW ENGLAND:								
Maine	93,615	94.2	83,590	92.3	21,967	83.7	20,350	78.6
New Hampshire	51,544	93.4	48,314	94.9	12,312	86.6	10,991	75.5
Vermont	43,336	93.9	42,700	95.7	10,577	86.2	10,613	85.1
Massachusetts	464,752	96.1	385,813	96.0	90,290	73.9	82,672	73.5
Rhode Island	74,872	95.6	61,436	93.9	11,827	59.0	11,968	62.5
Connecticut	170,486	94.7	129,694	95.6	32,990	74.9	26,991	71.6
MIDDLE ATLANTIC:								
New York	1,226,918	93.9	1,032,247	93.7	265,353	81.5	240,687	78.7
New Jersey	404,928	94.9	300,367	92.6	74,841	71.8	62,658	69.9
Pennsylvania	1,174,140	94.5	936,817	92.3	242,323	79.6	192,701	69.0
EAST NORTH CENTRAL:								
Ohio	703,560	96.0	560,731	94.1	162,380	87.8	133,706	79.0
Indiana	369,713	94.9	335,541	93.3	82,964	80.2	78,746	77.2
Illinois	815,080	94.7	678,407	92.5	171,810	79.0	156,528	75.4
Michigan	453,652	94.9	345,005	94.1	103,747	86.6	85,713	84.5
Wisconsin	351,629	94.5	320,034	93.7	77,326	77.8	73,814	75.4
WEST NORTH CENTRAL:								
Minnesota	314,905	93.9	279,592	93.0	76,759	86.2	74,209	88.4
Iowa	309,744	95.0	291,643	93.2	74,732	85.8	72,278	81.8
Missouri	440,394	93.4	408,655	90.1	103,959	82.1	102,823	78.4
North Dakota	102,876	92.1	75,340	86.1	23,489	87.3	17,760	79.9
South Dakota	91,322	93.5	76,479	87.7	21,411	86.7	19,286	84.1
Nebraska	178,910	93.9	160,389	92.9	42,315	86.0	41,546	86.5
Kansas	241,531	94.5	220,546	92.3	59,015	87.9	58,991	88.8
SOUTH ATLANTIC:								
Delaware	27,336	95.2	22,977	87.0	5,997	80.7	5,841	73.9
Maryland	182,147	92.6	157,223	86.4	38,525	73.6	32,278	63.6
District of Columbia	38,962	93.5	31,101	90.4	9,530	83.2	8,271	84.1
Virginia	324,292	84.8	254,237	74.5	73,671	75.5	64,373	70.1
West Virginia	213,053	89.1	166,925	87.8	48,331	82.3	39,863	79.7
North Carolina	400,846	87.0	291,608	76.5	91,619	77.4	73,078	71.8
South Carolina	274,429	87.1	184,535	67.6	64,264	78.0	45,005	61.9
Georgia	409,754	79.1	318,189	70.5	90,718	67.7	71,843	59.3
Florida	126,189	83.2	82,198	70.5	29,675	78.6	19,529	64.2
EAST SOUTH CENTRAL:								
Kentucky	342,974	88.5	293,068	81.3	78,178	77.6	73,107	73.6
Tennessee	333,118	85.3	269,064	77.2	80,780	79.4	70,524	73.2
Alabama	344,699	80.4	243,275	66.3	83,417	77.5	61,866	63.5
Mississippi	263,130	80.1	238,013	75.4	65,465	75.2	59,777	71.1
WEST SOUTH CENTRAL:								
Arkansas	256,263	82.0	195,383	74.2	62,632	77.0	50,816	71.7
Louisiana	234,249	75.9	165,194	59.8	50,700	67.6	38,200	59.5
Oklahoma	301,666	88.8	189,028	85.1	76,766	85.8	61,933	86.3
Texas	632,476	83.7	510,100	76.8	161,644	79.1	135,390	76.7
MOUNTAIN:								
Montana	71,513	92.8	37,919	87.1	16,058	89.1	9,669	83.9
Idaho	65,102	95.5	40,606	87.4	15,342	91.6	10,901	89.3
Wyoming	24,554	92.8	14,406	88.8	5,294	86.2	3,389	84.3
Colorado	121,353	93.9	90,911	90.9	28,076	86.2	23,136	85.0
New Mexico	52,829	87.4	39,696	77.2	12,002	80.4	9,763	74.6
Arizona	38,179	78.8	19,483	71.8	8,663	73.8	4,832	70.0
Utah	71,611	95.5	53,644	91.6	17,719	93.7	13,408	88.8
Nevada	7,755	90.5	6,305	87.9	1,829	88.8	1,563	82.6
PACIFIC:								
Washington	162,750	94.7	120,345	91.1	38,442	88.6	32,555	87.0
Oregon	94,312	94.7	70,141	90.3	23,224	90.6	19,924	87.7
California	352,563	93.7	220,759	91.6	83,191	89.1	60,418	83.6

OF AGE, BY AGE PERIODS, BY DIVISIONS AND STATES: 1920 AND 1910.

DIVISION AND STATE.	PERSONS 16 AND 17 YEARS OF AGE ATTENDING SCHOOL.				PERSONS 18 TO 20 YEARS OF AGE ATTENDING SCHOOL			
	1920		1910		1920		1910	
	Number.	Per cent.	Number.	Per cent.	Number.	Per cent.	Number.	Per cent.
United States	1,644,061	42.9	1,573,377	43.1	814,651	14.8	844,836	15.2
GEOGRAPHIC DIVISIONS:								
New England	92,749	39.0	85,293	36.8	52,306	15.0	51,060	13.9
Middle Atlantic	240,079	32.3	240,434	33.4	117,978	11.0	125,279	10.9
East North Central	293,581	40.4	284,439	40.0	143,264	13.4	144,628	13.3
West North Central	224,014	48.1	243,032	51.1	115,553	17.3	128,879	17.7
South Atlantic	249,134	43.7	229,240	43.8	119,934	14.6	128,587	16.9
East South Central	181,363	48.3	178,509	47.8	85,535	16.8	102,348	19.6
West South Central	208,180	48.1	187,674	48.9	90,031	14.7	93,080	16.7
Mountain	65,231	57.0	51,831	55.7	33,528	20.0	28,731	19.3
Pacific	89,730	55.4	72,925	52.3	56,522	22.1	42,244	18.1
NEW ENGLAND:								
Maine	12,082	46.5	11,807	45.4	6,635	17.8	6,471	16.5
New Hampshire	5,979	41.7	5,646	37.1	3,228	15.5	3,097	13.2
Vermont	5,611	46.0	5,813	46.3	3,020	18.1	2,938	15.9
Massachusetts	49,260	40.6	43,519	37.3	28,822	16.0	27,611	14.5
Rhode Island	5,527	26.3	5,889	28.4	3,273	10.8	4,019	12.3
Connecticut	14,290	33.0	12,619	31.3	7,328	11.6	6,924	10.8
MIDDLE ATLANTIC:								
New York	107,688	32.6	116,077	34.7	56,946	11.4	63,168	11.5
New Jersey	31,016	29.9	28,917	30.7	15,194	10.0	13,554	9.0
Pennsylvania	101,375	32.8	95,440	32.9	45,838	10.8	48,557	10.8
EAST NORTH CENTRAL:								
Ohio	82,659	44.4	76,376	42.4	40,818	14.4	39,323	14.1
Indiana	41,405	39.9	43,997	42.1	21,155	14.2	24,313	15.4
Illinois	81,699	37.1	80,928	36.8	39,627	12.3	40,006	11.7
Michigan	47,055	39.4	47,279	43.7	21,711	12.3	22,308	13.6
Wisconsin	40,763	42.2	35,859	36.2	19,953	14.6	18,678	13.1
WEST NORTH CENTRAL:								
Minnesota	38,055	42.5	42,443	48.8	21,377	16.6	21,252	16.1
Iowa	45,078	51.4	45,618	50.5	24,524	19.4	24,578	17.9
Missouri	54,963	43.9	63,730	47.5	25,079	14.1	33,018	16.2
North Dakota	13,417	53.4	11,089	49.4	6,507	19.0	6,270	17.4
South Dakota	12,757	52.6	12,979	55.1	6,453	18.6	6,848	18.8
Nebraska	23,830	49.7	26,461	52.9	11,906	16.9	14,229	18.5
Kansas	35,914	54.4	40,712	59.5	19,707	20.8	22,684	21.6
SOUTH ATLANTIC:								
Delaware	2,968	39.1	3,090	39.8	1,458	13.2	1,454	12.2
Maryland	16,812	31.7	16,690	32.1	8,572	10.9	7,431	9.8
District of Columbia	5,566	44.8	5,277	47.6	3,947	16.2	3,013	16.2
Virginia	41,769	44.3	41,057	46.5	20,305	15.0	21,865	17.5
West Virginia	24,599	42.3	24,316	48.4	11,061	13.6	13,892	18.4
North Carolina	54,942	50.1	53,737	54.1	28,832	19.1	36,686	26.4
South Carolina	36,318	49.2	30,380	42.8	18,066	17.2	17,290	16.9
Georgia	49,133	39.7	42,271	37.3	20,781	11.7	19,931	12.1
Florida	17,027	45.5	12,422	40.9	6,912	12.8	7,025	15.0
EAST SOUTH CENTRAL:								
Kentucky	40,983	42.5	46,482	46.9	18,391	13.8	25,206	18.1
Tennessee	49,669	50.7	49,076	50.2	24,976	18.6	29,198	21.0
Alabama	49,559	48.8	41,866	44.0	22,213	16.3	24,843	18.8
Mississippi	41,152	51.7	41,085	50.5	19,955	18.6	23,101	20.5
WEST SOUTH CENTRAL:								
Arkansas	38,423	50.8	36,652	51.8	17,797	17.7	22,058	21.7
Louisiana	28,053	36.8	21,343	30.0	11,508	10.7	10,365	10.0
Oklahoma	46,088	54.2	42,400	60.1	19,774	16.8	21,495	20.8
Texas	95,616	48.8	87,279	51.0	40,952	14.2	39,162	15.7
MOUNTAIN:								
Montana	10,036	58.3	6,106	53.0	5,014	21.2	3,282	16.4
Idaho	9,741	62.3	8,010	66.7	4,842	22.3	4,096	22.1
Wyoming	3,047	52.6	2,372	54.9	1,492	16.4	1,308	15.5
Colorado	16,997	53.2	15,526	54.7	9,319	20.2	8,894	20.0
New Mexico	6,885	50.6	6,995	53.7	3,403	16.4	4,250	22.0
Arizona	4,874	45.3	2,900	43.8	2,671	14.4	1,538	13.3
Utah	12,456	71.4	8,894	58.4	6,122	24.7	4,779	21.3
Nevada	1,195	61.4	1,028	53.0	665	22.0	584	15.0
PACIFIC:								
Washington	23,105	54.5	21,034	53.7	13,715	21.5	11,861	18.5
Oregon	14,931	59.7	13,693	57.1	9,146	24.4	7,839	19.9
California	51,694	54.7	38,198	50.1	33,661	21.9	22,544	17.3

TABLE 121.—SCHOOL ATTENDANCE OF POPULATION 7 TO 20 YEARS OF AGE, FOR

[Per cent not shown

	DIVISION AND STATE.	ALL CLASSES.				NATIVE WHITE—NATIVE PARENTAGE.			
		1920		1910		1920		1910	
		Number.	Per cent.	Number.	Per cent.	Number.	Per cent.	Number.	Per cent.
1	United States...	19,451,851	68.1	16,240,851	63.2	12,241,234	71.3	10,055,770	68.0
	GEOGRAPHIC DIVISIONS:								
2	New England	1,223,623	69.2	1,051,485	65.3	489,081	73.2	445,343	71.8
3	Middle Atlantic	3,746,560	67.8	3,131,190	62.9	1,818,582	69.9	1,625,956	67.8
4	East North Central	3,728,706	69.7	3,197,292	65.7	2,434,054	72.1	2,027,808	70.0
5	West North Central	2,420,929	71.3	2,271,448	68.4	1,696,658	74.0	1,441,569	71.5
6	South Atlantic	2,818,406	65.2	2,226,901	58.4	1,855,629	68.9	1,468,802	64.6
7	East South Central	1,858,659	65.9	1,589,551	59.6	1,369,090	70.4	1,131,194	65.2
8	West South Central	2,097,596	64.4	1,673,480	59.4	1,565,028	69.1	1,235,891	65.6
9	Mountain	656,638	73.3	460,193	67.3	460,004	76.8	298,535	71.2
10	Pacific	900,734	73.4	639,311	66.9	553,108	76.0	380,672	70.6
	NEW ENGLAND:								
11	Maine	134,299	71.1	122,218	67.3	86,387	73.3	81,554	70.7
12	New Hampshire	73,063	69.9	68,048	65.4	36,391	72.8	35,297	71.9
13	Vermont	62,544	71.6	62,064	70.4	43,449	72.8	43,261	72.9
14	Massachusetts	633,124	69.8	539,615	65.7	217,865	75.1	189,613	73.1
15	Rhode Island	95,499	63.8	83,312	60.4	29,858	68.6	27,054	69.3
16	Connecticut	225,094	68.1	176,228	63.5	75,131	70.1	68,564	69.9
	MIDDLE ATLANTIC:								
17	New York	1,656,905	67.3	1,452,179	63.4	665,970	69.7	619,070	69.1
18	New Jersey	525,979	66.9	405,496	61.6	224,392	69.5	188,413	67.1
19	Pennsylvania	1,563,676	68.6	1,273,515	62.7	928,220	70.0	818,473	67.0
	EAST NORTH CENTRAL:								
20	Ohio	989,417	71.3	810,136	66.2	717,654	72.4	607,631	69.8
21	Indiana	515,237	69.1	482,597	66.7	449,571	70.0	421,491	68.3
22	Illinois	1,108,216	68.4	955,869	63.6	650,122	72.1	545,474	69.5
23	Michigan	626,165	70.1	500,305	67.6	341,313	73.0	248,051	72.4
24	Wisconsin	489,671	69.5	448,385	65.8	275,394	73.7	205,161	73.1
	WEST NORTH CENTRAL:								
25	Minnesota	451,096	70.1	417,496	69.2	211,607	75.6	144,057	75.4
26	Iowa	454,078	72.4	434,117	69.1	347,895	75.0	296,204	72.5
27	Missouri	624,395	69.2	608,226	65.9	534,214	70.8	505,627	68.5
28	North Dakota	146,289	73.9	110,459	65.7	55,305	78.7	34,166	71.1
29	South Dakota	131,943	72.8	115,592	68.0	77,199	77.0	53,997	71.9
30	Nebraska	256,961	71.7	242,625	69.8	177,652	75.1	143,755	73.2
31	Kansas	356,167	73.7	342,933	71.6	292,786	75.5	263,763	73.4
	SOUTH ATLANTIC:								
32	Delaware	37,759	69.0	33,362	61.8	24,748	70.3	22,462	64.4
33	Maryland	246,056	64.6	213,622	59.2	166,109	66.9	143,102	62.8
34	District of Columbia	58,005	64.5	47,662	64.4	33,491	66.1	26,914	67.1
35	Virginia	460,037	64.8	381,532	59.1	317,087	67.5	261,753	64.3
36	West Virginia	297,044	67.9	244,996	67.0	263,542	68.2	225,257	68.9
37	North Carolina	576,239	68.6	455,109	63.1	399,852	70.8	316,067	66.8
38	South Carolina	393,077	68.2	277,210	53.4	187,841	73.3	130,390	61.9
39	Georgia	570,386	59.8	452,234	53.1	352,408	66.9	272,317	62.1
40	Florida	179,803	64.1	121,174	54.1	110,551	70.4	70,540	61.8
	EAST SOUTH CENTRAL:								
41	Kentucky	480,526	67.0	437,863	62.7	431,095	67.6	380,683	64.1
42	Tennessee	488,543	67.4	417,862	61.3	406,847	70.7	336,860	64.9
43	Alabama	499,888	64.6	371,850	53.7	325,116	71.2	235,970	62.5
44	Mississippi	389,702	64.7	361,976	61.0	206,032	75.4	177,601	72.0
	WEST SOUTH CENTRAL:								
45	Arkansas	375,115	65.0	304,309	60.2	283,477	70.1	224,305	64.6
46	Louisiana	327,546	57.0	235,264	44.4	205,661	65.4	150,002	56.9
47	Oklahoma	444,247	68.6	361,376	69.6	379,331	69.3	292,864	70.4
48	Texas	950,688	64.8	771,931	61.2	696,559	69.7	568,720	66.5
	MOUNTAIN:								
49	Montana	102,621	75.5	56,976	65.8	59,404	78.3	28,191	69.0
50	Idaho	95,027	77.7	63,613	71.3	74,526	79.6	44,826	73.0
51	Wyoming	34,387	72.4	21,475	65.0	24,776	74.3	13,974	68.1
52	Colorado	175,745	73.2	138,467	69.2	124,402	75.3	91,252	71.3
53	New Mexico	75,119	68.5	60,704	62.7	61,868	71.6	52,456	66.9
54	Arizona	54,387	60.8	28,753	55.0	30,947	74.1	14,582	68.8
55	Utah	107,908	79.3	80,725	72.5	77,103	82.5	47,856	77.8
56	Nevada	11,444	73.4	9,480	63.6	6,978	77.4	5,398	72.2
	PACIFIC:								
57	Washington	238,012	74.1	185,795	68.1	144,865	76.1	108,709	71.1
58	Oregon	141,613	75.4	111,597	68.2	102,108	76.8	77,769	70.7
59	California	521,109	72.6	341,919	65.8	306,135	75.7	194,194	70.3

PRINCIPAL POPULATION CLASSES, BY DIVISIONS AND STATES: 1920 AND 1910.
where base is less than 100.]

NATIVE WHITE—FOREIGN OR MIXED PARENTAGE.				FOREIGN-BORN WHITE.				NEGRO.				
1920		1910		1920		1910		1920		1910		
Number.	Per cent.	Number.	Per cent.	Number.	Per cent.	Number.	Per cent.	Number.	Per cent.	Number.	Per cent.	
4,763,722	69.2	4,016,779	64.9	49?,632	44.5	573,500	38.6	1,887,282	57.5	1,541,575	48.8	1
653,535	70.4	507,030	68.6	69,351	45.1	89,145	37.9	11,167	66.8	9,461	65.3	2
1,669,634	70.1	1,193,976	65.2	179,409	43.3	257,783	39.0	77,076	61.6	51,124	57.6	3
1,112,836	68.2	1,016,626	62.5	111,095	48.2	107,194	39.3	67,374	63.5	41,742	61.3	4
642,546	67.6	738,217	66.5	34,657	46.6	47,872	40.5	39,737	63.6	35,152	58.7	5
102,119	68.3	71,973	60.3	12,101	45.0	11,797	34.5	845,820	58.4	672,549	48.6	6
25,740	66.8	29,800	60.0	2,105	47.8	2,607	39.1	461,566	55.5	425,687	48.7	7
117,437	56.5	106,784	54.1	24,771	28.5	12,881	26.4	375,356	55.5	300,143	45.5	8
157,950	73.1	135,219	69.1	23,342	46.3	15,521	38.2	2,867	60.1	2,373	61.3	9
281,926	73.7	217,154	67.5	42,801	51.9	28,700	41.2	6,319	70.3	3,344	61.0	10
42,329	71.9	33,912	68.4	5,255	45.5	6,378	39.6	176	63.3	213	62.5	11
32,396	70.3	27,606	68.9	4,176	50.0	5,061	34.3	93	69.4	74	55.6	12
16,002	72.2	15,646	70.5	2,989	56.2	3,033	47.1	101	68.2	120	51.1	13
371,485	70.8	294,097	69.4	37,111	44.8	50,254	38.9	6,420	68.9	5,410	66.1	14
58,227	65.9	45,731	64.6	6,038	38.6	9,150	35.2	1,338	63.3	1,320	62.6	15
133,096	70.5	90,038	67.6	13,782	46.0	15,269	35.7	3,039	64.3	2,324	66.9	16
861,480	70.5	652,280	67.1	106,552	43.5	165,321	42.0	21,267	58.9	14,159	55.6	17
258,658	68.9	174,856	64.5	25,389	42.0	30,235	35.2	17,471	64.4	11,938	58.7	18
549,496	70.1	366,840	62.5	47,468	43.7	62,227	34.5	38,338	61.8	25,027	58.4	19
219,026	72.4	162,724	61.3	27,064	50.7	23,481	38.9	25,618	65.0	16,242	62.2	20
49,507	66.6	47,541	59.5	4,536	45.5	4,350	36.9	11,604	63.2	9,136	62.5	21
396,667	66.5	353,182	61.2	38,170	44.8	43,466	37.2	23,008	63.4	13,617	58.9	22
248,259	69.8	226,244	66.4	29,130	50.5	22,217	44.2	6,445	58.4	2,375	63.9	23
199,377	65.9	226,935	62.5	12,195	50.0	13,680	41.0	699	65.5	372	62.8	24
226,365	67.1	255,505	68.6	10,656	48.5	15,010	41.9	969	68.2	741	65.7	25
98,050	66.1	130,013	64.8	5,111	49.0	5,569	35.7	2,897	67.5	2,269	63.4	26
60,911	63.8	74,230	58.0	5,106	43.0	6,767	39.1	24,118	60.7	21,531	55.3	27
85,302	73.6	66,157	68.0	4,637	47.4	8,677	42.4	67		56		28
49,634	68.9	55,002	67.7	1,899	46.0	3,213	40.2	131	63.6	117	67.2	29
73,016	66.5	92,636	67.4	4,062	49.1	4,595	41.4	1,630	63.4	874	61.1	30
49,268	68.2	64,674	68.9	3,186	39.9	4,041	41.1	9,925	69.8	9,564	65.6	31
6,855	69.9	4,784	61.0	656	45.0	567	30.2	5,498	66.5	5,544	59.0	32
36,711	64.8	29,698	55.4	3,429	41.7	4,288	37.6	39,789	58.5	36,503	53.8	33
8,030	68.7	6,606	67.8	1,062	51.5	960	49.1	15,375	60.4	13,147	59.5	34
10,310	67.2	7,183	65.7	1,235	45.2	1,204	42.1	131,284	59.1	111,337	49.5	35
16,844	73.8	8,501	64.6	2,731	45.4	2,054	24.8	13,922	61.4	9,169	53.5	36
2,302	72.6	1,926	72.3	256	46.0	274	40.1	171,379	64.2	135,297	56.0	37
1,981	65.1	1,755	63.5	190	44.1	195	36.4	203,028	64.1	144,803	47.5	38
5,333	71.5	4,392	65.3	591	46.9	639	41.9	212,041	50.7	174,871	43.3	39
13,753	70.5	7,128	60.2	1,951	47.1	1,616	31.7	53,504	53.6	41,878	45.0	40
9,704	61.0	14,377	55.7	583	47.4	701	37.5	39,133	62.7	42,081	55.0	41
5,787	72.4	6,224	65.5	575	53.0	767	45.9	75,324	53.9	73,980	48.8	42
7,083	70.2	6,104	63.0	708	49.1	815	41.1	166,943	54.6	128,850	42.6	43
3,166	69.9	3,095	65.8	239	37.0	324	28.5	180,166	55.8	180,776	52.7	44
6,574	66.4	6,734	62.6	308	41.7	481	34.9	84,729	54.7	73,287	49.9	45
16,906	61.3	13,671	52.6	1,247	37.6	1,522	27.9	103,598	45.4	99,992	29.9	46
18,895	69.9	20,398	70.5	1,139	34.3	1,391	43.1	30,387	61.6	29,208	65.1	47
75,062	52.4	65,981	50.2	22,077	27.8	9,487	24.4	156,642	64.2	127,656	54.4	48
37,003	75.0	24,693	70.3	4,024	56.6	2,400	33.9	171	70.4	176	62.2	49
18,607	74.5	17,334	72.5	1,217	48.8	1,004	34.8	97	65.1	47		50
8,237	71.7	6,332	67.4	962	48.4	745	31.4	114	52.1	132	49.6	51
44,156	72.5	40,073	69.7	5,309	49.0	5,248	45.6	1,524	68.0	1,452	63.3	52
6,330	66.1	5,243	64.2	2,690	45.2	1,076	33.0	298	44.4	200	60.2	53
12,322	67.9	7,985	59.6	6,709	38.5	2,580	35.7	490	49.5	234	61.1	54
28,070	75.1	30,416	69.9	2,101	54.1	2,228	44.0	145	67.8	105	57.7	55
3,225	75.7	3,143	69.2	330	41.8	240	19.2	28		27		56
79,843	73.9	65,874	69.3	9,285	55.2	8,700	44.0	785	70.7	498	57.7	57
33,669	74.4	29,163	67.6	3,686	55.6	3,018	37.2	254	72.2	95	52.8	58
168,414	73.5	122,117	66.5	29,830	50.5	16,982	40.6	5,280	70.2	2,751	62.0	59

TABLE 122.—SCHOOL ATTENDANCE OF POPULATION 7 TO 13 YEARS OF AGE, FOR

[Per cent not shown

	DIVISION AND STATE.	ALL CLASSES.				NATIVE WHITE—NATIVE PARENTAGE.			
		1920		1910		1920		1910	
		Number.	Per cent.	Number.	Per cent.	Number.	Per cent.	Number.	Per cent.
1	United States....	13,869,010	90.6	11,146,173	86.1	8,584,679	92.2	6,744,539	88.2
	GEOGRAPHIC DIVISIONS:								
2	New England.......	898,605	95.3	751,547	95.2	341,324	95.2	297,192	95.2
3	Middle Atlantic....	2,805,986	94.3	2,269,431	93.0	1,313,475	94.7	1,135,936	93.3
4	East North Central.	2,693,634	95.1	2,239,718	93.5	1,729,506	95.4	1,391,070	93.6
5	West North Central.	1,679,682	93.9	1,512,644	91.5	1,184,836	94.3	958,914	91.7
6	South Atlantic.....	1,997,008	85.6	1,508,993	75.6	1,304,485	89.2	977,037	82.1
7	East South Central.	1,283,921	83.6	1,043,420	75.0	944,921	88.5	736,762	80.9
8	West South Central.	1,447,653	82.5	1,106.205	74.7	1,077,986	87.0	808,729	81.1
9	Mountain..........	452,896	91.8	302,970	86.4	317,320	93.9	196,158	88.1
10	Pacific.............	609,625	94.1	411,245	91.2	370,826	94.8	242,741	91.5
	NEW ENGLAND:								
11	Maine.............	93,615	94.2	83,590	92.3	59,314	94.3	53,725	92.7
12	New Hampshire....	51,544	93.4	48,314	94.9	25,305	93.5	23,428	94.8
13	Vermont...........	43,336	93.9	42,700	95.7	29,686	94.0	29,250	95.9
14	Massachusetts......	464,752	96.1	385,813	96.0	151,889	96.5	125,693	96.2
15	Rhode Island......	74,872	95.6	61,436	93.9	22,110	96.1	18,148	94.7
16	Connecticut........	170,486	94.7	129,694	95.6	53,020	94.1	46,948	95.3
	MIDDLE ATLANTIC:								
17	New York.........	1,226,918	93.9	1,032,247	93.7	473,682	93.9	420,711	93.5
18	New Jersey........	404,928	94.9	300,367	92.6	164,326	95.4	133,409	93.0
19	Pennsylvania.......	1,174,140	94.5	936,817	92.3	675,467	95.0	581,816	93.2
	EAST NORTH CENTRAL:								
20	Ohio..............	703,560	96.0	560,731	94.1	501,839	96.1	413,055	94.3
21	Indiana...........	369,713	94.9	335,541	93.3	320,233	95.1	291,719	93.5
22	Illinois...........	815,080	94.7	678,407	92.5	463,333	95.1	373,597	92.6
23	Michigan..........	453,652	94.9	345,005	94.1	244,696	95.3	168,498	94.4
24	Wisconsin..........	351,629	94.5	320,034	93.7	199,405	94.5	144,201	93.9
	WEST NORTH CENTRAL:								
25	Minnesota.........	314,905	93.9	279.592	93.0	150,740	94.1	97,156	93.0
26	Iowa.............	309,744	95.0	291,643	93.2	238,772	95.2	198,977	93.2
27	Missouri..........	440,394	93.4	408,655	90.1	376,204	93.6	337,924	90.3
28	North Dakota......	102,876	92.1	75,340	86.1	39,780	93.0	23,387	88.0
29	South Dakota......	91,322	93.5	76,479	87.7	54,802	94.1	35,978	88.8
30	Nebraska..........	178,910	93.9	160,389	92.9	125,030	93.9	94,895	92.9
31	Kansas............	241,531	94.5	220,546	92.3	199,508	94.9	170,597	92.4
	SOUTH ATLANTIC:								
32	Delaware..........	27,336	95.2	22,977	87.0	17,512	95.5	15,133	88.2
33	Maryland..........	182,147	92.6	157,223	86.4	121,786	94.2	103,721	89.2
34	District of Columbia	38,962	93.5	31,101	90.4	22,062	93.6	17,436	91.5
35	Virginia...........	324,292	84.8	254,237	74.5	222,093	87.7	171,795	79.9
36	West Virginia.....	213,053	89.1	166,925	87.8	187,561	89.1	152,685	88.2
37	North Carolina....	400,846	87.0	291,608	76.5	278,799	89.5	200,597	80.6
38	South Carolina.....	274,429	87.1	184,535	67.6	130,660	93.0	84,968	77.9
39	Georgia...........	409,754	79.1	318,189	70.5	247,712	85.9	184,636	79.7
40	Florida............	126,189	83.2	82,198	70.5	76,300	88.2	46,066	77.1
	EAST SOUTH CENTRAL:								
41	Kentucky..........	342,974	88.5	293,068	81.3	308,311	88.7	254,869	81.6
42	Tennessee.........	333,118	85.3	269,064	77.2	277,342	88.4	216,179	80.5
43	Alabama...........	344,699	80.4	243,275	66.3	223,138	87.5	152,372	76.2
44	Mississippi........	263,130	80.1	238,013	75.4	136,130	90.0	113,342	87.3
	WEST SOUTH CENTRAL:								
45	Arkansas..........	230,211	82.0	195,283	71.9	194,970	80.2	143,553	70.1
46	Louisiana..........	260,301	75.9	165,294	58.8	146,771	85.7	103,524	73.3
47	Oklahoma.........	304,665	85.8	235,528	86.1	261,744	86.5	191,343	87.0
48	Texas.............	652,476	83.7	510,100	76.8	474,598	88.0	370,309	81.4
	MOUNTAIN:								
49	Montana...........	71,513	92.8	37,919	87.1	41,468	93.5	18,650	88.2
50	Idaho.............	65,102	95.5	40,606	87.4	51,536	95.9	29,073	87.6
51	Wyoming..........	24,554	92.8	14,406	88.8	17,722	93.1	9,320	89.2
52	Colorado..........	121,353	93.9	90,911	90.9	85,123	94.1	59,009	90.7
53	New Mexico.......	52,829	87.4	39,696	77.2	43,259	90.0	34,151	81.3
54	Arizona...........	38,179	78.8	19,483	71.8	21,434	92.8	9,772	85.5
55	Utah..............	71,611	95.5	53,644	91.6	52,021	96.0	32,546	91.9
56	Nevada............	7,755	90.5	6,305	87.9	4,757	93.3	3,637	91.4
	PACIFIC:								
57	Washington........	162,750	94.7	120,345	91.1	99,306	95.1	69,757	91.3
58	Oregon............	94,312	94.7	70,141	90.3	68,455	94.8	48,863	90.0
59	California.........	352,563	93.7	220,759	91.6	203,065	94.7	124,121	92.2

PRINCIPAL POPULATION CLASSES, BY DIVISIONS AND STATES: 1920 AND 1910.
where base is less than 100.]

NATIVE WHITE—FOREIGN OR MIXED PARENTAGE.				FOREIGN-BORN WHITE.				NEGRO.				
1920		1910		1920		1910		1920		1910		
Number.	Per cent.	Number.	Per cent.	Number.	Per cent.	Number.	Per cent.	Number.	Per cent.	Number.	Per cent.	
3,596,717	94.1	2,895,974	92.6	318,040	84.1	417,370	87.1	1,331,043	76.5	1,056,791	64.1	1
504,143	95.8	384,594	95.8	44,727	90.1	62,794	92.2	8,079	95.1	6,672	94.7	2
1,323,749	94.4	907,992	93.4	110,784	88.8	187,273	90.0	56,685	93.4	37,217	89.7	3
840,339	95.0	734,462	93.8	72,659	90.5	82,694	89.4	48,791	94.7	28,832	90.6	4
441,521	94.0	492,073	92.3	21,097	85.7	33,584	84.1	27,669	89.7	23,179	83.7	5
77,736	93.6	52,788	87.8	7,316	87.9	8,948	78.7	605,539	77.8	469,114	64.0	6
17,997	92.0	20,295	90.0	1,137	82.1	1,803	74.2	319,750	71.6	284,395	62.5	7
84,135	76.1	73,565	72.1	17,256	47.5	9,078	45.9	258,306	72.5	203,599	58.5	8
110,020	93.3	89,085	90.0	15,814	74.6	11,107	78.9	1,927	91.5	1,576	87.8	9
197,077	94.5	141,120	92.4	27,250	86.2	20,089	87.4	4,297	93.9	2,207	91.0	10
30,639	94.7	24,998	92.3	3,414	89.9	4,630	87.7	122	93.1	133	92.4	11
23,702	94.0	21,074	95.5	2,458	88.1	3,756	92.6	74	....	51	....	12
11,548	94.4	11,194	96.0	2,026	88.4	2,161	92.2	74	....	91	....	13
284,578	96.4	222,095	96.4	23,549	90.1	34,072	92.8	4,598	95.9	3,832	95.8	14
47,477	96.0	35,385	94.2	4,272	90.1	6,932	90.6	981	92.2	931	92.5	15
106,199	95.3	69,848	96.2	9,008	91.2	11,243	93.3	2,230	95.0	1,634	93.8	16
673,873	94.4	485,444	94.5	62,690	88.8	115,079	92.0	15,534	93.1	10,131	91.3	17
210,496	95.1	135,073	93.0	17,104	89.2	23,224	89.1	12,952	94.1	8,634	89.6	18
439,380	94.2	287,475	91.8	30,990	88.4	48,970	85.9	28,199	93.2	18,452	88.8	19
166,213	96.2	118,070	94.4	16,950	92.3	18,373	89.8	18,538	95.8	11,208	91.8	20
37,777	94.0	33,950	92.9	3,099	89.3	3,401	87.7	8,595	94.2	6,413	92.7	21
310,016	94.5	261,272	93.2	25,165	90.3	34,133	88.9	16,443	93.7	9,351	87.3	22
183,595	95.0	157,772	94.3	19,886	90.3	16,141	90.7	4,717	95.2	1,620	93.7	23
142,738	94.9	163,398	93.9	7,559	88.9	10,646	88.9	498	95.0	240	91.3	24
155,990	94.1	170,345	93.3	6,439	88.6	10,287	89.6	660	95.5	456	92.7	25
65,582	94.7	86,997	93.7	3,267	88.0	4,024	86.0	2,046	95.0	1,612	92.4	26
44,245	94.3	51,107	92.4	3,060	88.7	5,215	86.4	16,857	86.8	14,363	80.4	27
59,903	92.4	45,308	87.3	2,521	86.8	5,760	74.0	47	....	33	....	28
33,233	93.8	36,431	88.9	1,105	85.9	2,097	77.6	95	85.6	74	....	29
49,819	94.3	61,213	93.4	2,508	86.5	3,280	88.3	1,143	92.0	604	90.8	30
32,749	94.5	40,672	93.1	2,197	71.3	2,921	82.7	6,821	94.5	6,037	88.8	31
5,476	95.4	3,554	89.3	425	92.2	457	83.7	3,922	94.2	3,830	81.1	32
28,737	95.6	23,360	87.8	2,016	91.9	3,397	83.0	29,600	84.0	26,733	76.4	33
5,451	94.1	4,260	91.8	503	94.0	642	89.2	10,924	93.0	8,743	87.7	34
7,520	92.7	4,922	87.3	695	87.3	874	78.3	93,907	78.1	76,608	64.2	35
13,444	90.2	6,179	89.4	1,942	83.2	1,598	72.5	10,103	88.6	6,456	81.2	36
1,548	89.1	1,244	89.1	133	78.2	182	70.5	118,612	81.8	88,618	68.6	37
1,412	95.0	1,176	86.7	103	83.1	135	77.6	142,232	82.3	98,216	60.4	38
3,769	94.8	2,950	90.1	286	89.7	436	81.8	157,977	70.2	130,157	60.3	39
10,379	92.1	5,143	81.2	1,213	87.4	1,227	70.8	38,262	73.1	29,753	61.0	40
6,831	93.9	10,103	93.2	311.	81.0	486	87.7	27,514	85.9	27,599	74.9	41
3,910	94.0	3,935	89.1	289	90.3	509	82.2	51,569	71.1	48,423	64.7	42
5,027	89.7	4,231	85.3	411	85.4	591	75.8	116,093	69.2	86,004	53.4	43
2,229	88.0	2,026	86.8	126	63.0	217	45.5	124,574	71.5	122,369	67.0	44
4,480	90.9	4,490	86.5	167	78.4	326	60.1	56,726	69.9	46,946	61.8	45
12,860	85.6	9,945	75.0	702	76.1	1,094	53.8	73,821	61.0	50,577	40.7	46
12,275	91.9	13,204	89.9	688	63.9	928	79.7	20,336	77.8	18,932	80.2	47
54,520	70.6	45,926	66.6	15,699	46.0	6,730	42.0	107,423	84.0	87,084	70.2	48
25,966	94.0	16,640	90.1	2,634	84.9	1,639	80.5	112	90.3	102	84.3	49
12,409	95.4	10,606	88.7	696	81.4	664	81.7	66	....	25	....	50
5,935	93.4	4,268	89.5	647	82.2	551	82.0	70	....	91	90.1	51
31,419	95.1	26,884	92.5	3,592	83.7	3,833	86.1	999	93.2	974	89.6	52
4,749	85.7	3,507	80.6	2,035	75.5	773	61.3	213	85.9	126	79.2	53
9,295	83.7	5,683	78.1	4,820	61.3	1,926	66.4	355	90.6	166	86.9	54
17,989	95.8	19,404	93.1	1,196	89.0	1,563	88.8	95	94.1	70	....	55
2,258	93.1	2,093	93.1	194	72.7	158	83.6	17	....	22	....	56
55,048	95.2	42,902	92.3	5,790	89.2	6,142	88.7	552	94.5	328	85.0	57
22,606	95.6	18,311	91.8	2,148	89.9	2,094	87.7	175	93.6	66	....	58
119,423	94.1	79,907	92.6	19,312	85.0	11,853	86.7	3,570	93.8	1,813	92.4	59

TABLE 123.—SCHOOL ATTENDANCE OF POPULATION 7 TO 20 YEARS OF AGE, FOR OR MORE:

[Per cent not shown

CITY.	ALL CLASSES.				NATIVE WHITE—NATIVE PARENTAGE.			
	1920		1910		1920		1910	
	Number.	Per cent.	Number.	Per cent.	Number.	Per cent.	Number.	Per cent.
1 Akron, Ohio	24,908	58.1	9,357	57.4	15,631	55.0	5,794	60.0
2 Albany, N.Y	15,540	66.2	13,792	61.7	9,693	67.2	8,296	65.5
3 Atlanta, Ga	31,082	62.1	22,259	55.5	20,267	64.5	14,186	59.3
4 Baltimore, Md	109,932	62.9	75,469	52.7	63,925	64.7	41,567	54.6
5 Birmingham, Ala	30,570	64.6	19,582	56.9	16,875	68.8	10,866	61.2
6 Boston, Mass	117,768	69.6	105,128	66.8	31,373	73.5	27,184	72.2
7 Bridgeport, Conn	20,928	63.8	14,728	58.7	5,533	65.3	4,517	66.0
8 Buffalo, N.Y	77,337	65.4	68,215	60.7	31,239	69.8	24,972	66.2
9 Cambridge, Mass	18,139	70.8	17,459	68.5	5,110	75.7	4,624	74.9
10 Camden, N.J	18,058	63.2	13,549	56.9	9,298	63.7	7,672	59.3
11 Chicago, Ill	403,532	65.5	323,994	58.5	119,441	71.2	80,854	67.6
12 Cincinnati, Ohio	59,327	69.4	52,107	58.9	41,544	71.6	32,343	62.8
13 Cleveland, Ohio	130,726	70.8	84,581	60.2	39,444	73.4	25,137	69.9
14 Columbus, Ohio	35,682	70.1	25,891	62.4	26,897	71.3	19,239	64.9
15 Dallas, Tex	24,092	64.2	13,141	56.7	18,179	65.5	9,210	58.7
16 Dayton, Ohio	22,697	69.1	16,300	61.0	17,145	70.1	11,990	63.8
17 Denver, Colo	37,322	71.1	32,254	66.1	23,231	73.7	17,776	68.4
18 Des Moines, Iowa	20,991	72.8	13,411	64.5	15,561	73.6	9,198	66.8
19 Detroit, Mich	133,263	64.8	64,545	56.4	48,428	66.3	19,983	65.0
20 Fall River, Mass	21,214	64.0	20,839	61.9	4,603	75.8	3,487	74.4
21 Fort Worth, Tex	15,184	60.3	10,213	55.6	11,818	63.5	7,641	58.3
22 Grand Rapids, Mich	22,874	69.9	17,707	62.9	10,847	74.1	6,850	67.1
23 Hartford, Conn	21,260	69.1	15,623	67.1	6,204	70.8	5,285	72.8
24 Houston, Tex	21,324	62.6	10,690	54.1	12,639	65.6	5,724	57.2
25 Indianapolis, Ind	42,839	62.8	32,538	61.0	32,950	63.2	23,835	62.7
26 Jersey City, N.J	48,180	64.3	43,971	60.4	17,886	66.1	16,844	65.8
27 Kansas City, Kans	16,789	67.4	13,086	61.4	10,420	67.8	8,464	63.7
28 Kansas City, Mo	43,350	66.1	32,231	59.8	30,878	67.3	21,918	61.5
29 Los Angeles, Calif	76,552	71.5	41,977	64.7	43,176	73.7	24,499	67.3
30 Louisville, Ky	34,836	64.4	33,606	58.9	26,022	66.2	22,061	61.2
31 Lowell, Mass	18,351	68.4	16,067	60.4	4,845	78.1	3,558	73.0
32 Memphis, Tenn	23,408	62.5	16,276	53.6	13,693	66.6	9,230	61.4
33 Milwaukee, Wis	77,249	71.5	58,631	57.4	31,570	76.9	19,242	67.6
34 Minneapolis, Minn	56,248	70.0	45,990	64.7	25,236	75.1	16,931	70.7
35 Nashville, Tenn	20,162	65.8	17,959	59.9	13,803	67.5	11,379	62.9
36 New Bedford, Mass	18,197	61.2	14,058	56.4	3,249	72.1	2,696	68.5
37 New Haven, Conn	26,689	67.6	22,085	65.5	7,190	67.9	7,222	72.9
38 New Orleans, La	61,200	60.9	49,845	54.2	37,363	62.6	30,681	59.0
39 New York, N.Y	887,939	65.1	766,240	61.6	210,824	66.0	192,121	67.3
40 Bronx borough	123,388	66.6	74,956	64.6	27,174	67.3	22,748	68.8
41 Brooklyn borough	337,151	64.8	279,822	63.9	85,021	64.8	82,742	67.3
42 Manhattan borough	330,008	64.4	342,159	58.3	57,875	65.2	58,943	64.4
43 Queens borough	77,654	65.9	53,009	66.3	33,170	69.3	20,768	72.1
44 Richmond borough	19,738	66.6	16,294	69.9	7,584	67.0	6,920	74.8
45 Newark, N.J	66,924	64.7	56,376	62.2	20,133	65.7	18,706	66.7
46 Norfolk, Va	16,634	61.4	9,671	58.3	8,775	63.8	5,716	64.9
47 Oakland, Calif	32,335	74.0	21,141	66.2	16,901	77.3	9,436	72.0
48 Omaha, Nebr.[1]	29,750	68.3	22,832	62.2	15,292	70.5	10,274	65.8
49 Paterson, N.J	21,437	61.8	19,714	58.2	5,821	65.1	5,262	63.0
50 Philadelphia, Pa	281,665	66.2	220,394	57.7	120,936	68.3	97,815	61.3
51 Pittsburgh, Pa	99,183	68.9	79,889	58.6	42,952	72.0	33,118	64.4
52 Portland, Oreg	39,801	74.5	24,889	61.1	24,272	76.5	13,828	64.2
53 Providence, R.I	37,151	66.6	32,604	60.8	10,792	71.9	9,819	69.0
54 Reading, Pa	17,500	68.0	13,223	55.1	13,326	67.6	10,917	56.5
55 Richmond, Va	26,711	62.7	17,469	52.6	17,344	65.3	10,830	57.7
56 Rochester, N.Y	43,038	67.0	31,145	60.4	19,388	69.1	13,771	66.3
57 St. Louis, Mo	109,601	62.7	95,109	55.9	68,067	64.5	52,968	60.1
58 St. Paul, Minn	35,002	67.6	34,506	62.3	16,326	74.7	11,955	69.0
59 Salt Lake City, Utah	17,694	70.1	10,251	60.0	14,832	80.7	8,075	74.0
60 San Antonio, Tex	25,226	58.5	15,026	56.1	11,105	65.2	8,156	62.0
61 San Francisco, Calif	64,062	68.0	47,245	58.9	28,740	70.6	17,832	62.0
62 Scranton, Pa	25,737	66.6	21,237	58.1	10,995	70.1	8,250	65.6
63 Seattle, Wash	43,196	71.3	29,724	64.3	22,937	74.0	15,245	68.4
64 Spokane, Wash	18,683	77.1	14,495	64.2	11,865	78.5	8,634	66.3
65 Springfield, Mass	19,400	70.0	13,958	67.3	7,798	72.6	5,825	72.4
66 Syracuse, N.Y	25,898	70.7	19,521	61.1	13,864	73.5	9,920	66.0
67 Toledo, Ohio	36,228	66.8	25,956	61.4	21,764	69.7	13,734	66.9
68 Trenton, N.J	19,441	67.1	14,978	60.6	7,222	68.6	6,679	65.0
69 Washington, D.C	58,005	64.5	47,662	64.4	33,491	66.1	26,914	67.1
70 Wilmington, Del	16,213	65.2	12,597	58.3	8,843	65.7	7,203	61.4
71 Worcester, Mass	28,517	69.0	22,789	64.2	8,995	74.0	7,112	71.8
72 Yonkers, N.Y	18,965	72.9	13,990	65.4	6,674	77.1	4,843	74.0
73 Youngstown, Ohio	21,737	71.8	10,353	55.2	8,866	73.4	4,168	62.9

[1] Includes population of South Omaha for 1910.

PRINCIPAL POPULATION CLASSES, FOR CITIES HAVING, IN 1920, 100,000 INHABITANTS 1920 AND 1910.
where base is less than 100.]

NATIVE WHITE—FOREIGN OR MIXED PARENTAGE.				FOREIGN-BORN WHITE.				NEGRO.				
1920		1910		1920		1910		1920		1910		
Number.	Per cent.	Number.	Per cent.	Number.	Per cent.	Number.	Per cent.	Number.	Per cent.	Number.	Per cent.	
6,860	70.4	2,946	58.4	1,924	51.1	527	36.3	492	51.0	90	57.7	1
5,071	67.0	4,798	59.7	627	50.4	582	39.9	143	64.4	116	56.3	2
1,637	73.5	1,210	65.8	225	52.0	247	44.8	8,952	56.0	6,615	48.1	3
29,720	64.8	20,554	53.5	2,855	40.8	3,546	37.9	13,422	58.4	9,790	50.6	4
2,530	69.4	1,749	62.0	272	47.0	284	41.6	10,893	58.8	6,683	50.7	5
76,600	71.6	63,960	70.9	7,907	47.0	12,430	45.6	1,799	67.4	1,517	66.2	6
13,626	67.9	8,488	65.5	1,533	39.3	1,573	31.1	233	59.9	150	62.8	7
41,303	65.0	38,421	61.0	4,350	47.7	4,633	40.4	416	57.7	183	63.5	8
10,902	71.5	10,525	71.6	1,197	49.5	1,495	43.1	921	76.1	813	71.5	9
6,742	66.3	4,451	57.8	790	44.4	613	34.0	1,228	60.9	810	60.2	10
246,546	66.6	208,076	60.7	26,193	44.2	31,049	36.5	11,140	59.6	3,926	57.9	11
12,684	66.5	15,849	55.1	1,312	54.7	1,762	40.8	3,785	64.3	2,151	57.3	12
76,869	74.2	48,514	61.9	10,484	50.6	10,025	40.8	3,914	60.9	893	59.4	13
5,265	69.4	4,686	58.6	652	51.3	538	41.1	2,860	66.3	1,421	55.6	14
2,188	66.7	1,623	59.1	452	43.1	179	41.8	3,267	59.7	2,128	49.5	15
3,988	70.5	3,296	58.7	509	51.1	490	36.2	1,052	60.9	524	55.7	16
12,312	69.6	12,415	66.1	1,029	47.7	1,425	48.2	689	65.3	601	61.6	17
4,195	73.1	3,506	62.8	424	57.8	353	42.3	801	67.1	354	57.7	18
67,003	69.0	37,244	57.4	14,087	49.3	6,704	37.7	3,699	53.5	609	57.7	19
15,029	65.1	13,906	66.6	1,549	39.1	3,408	42.5	33	......	36	......	20
1,088	62.5	950	59.3	283	23.7	98	23.1	1,994	54.8	1,523	47.0	21
10,893	69.0	9,600	63.3	992	47.7	1,200	44.9	131	68.2	56	53.3	22
12,745	72.8	8,271	71.0	1,670	47.9	1,771	44.8	633	62.9	293	72.2	23
3,204	63.1	1,717	54.3	567	36.0	175	32.1	4,910	60.4	3,072	50.8	24
4,855	63.5	5,477	58.5	411	45.2	458	33.4	4,619	61.9	2,765	60.1	25
27,110	65.9	23,559	62.5	2,082	41.2	2,810	33.8	1,101	64.8	758	63.9	26
3,528	69.2	2,930	61.0	536	48.5	264	26.6	2,299	69.2	1,424	64.1	27
8,301	68.2	7,097	60.4	1,121	47.4	975	43.6	3,039	58.8	2,236	52.0	28
23,663	73.6	13,319	66.0	6,419	55.0	2,892	48.0	2,185	71.6	1,029	62.6	29
3,851	58.7	6,178	55.6	207	48.8	344	36.4	4,755	61.4	5,023	56.4	30
12,289	69.1	10,559	66.7	1,191	42.7	1,938	32.9	24	......	11	......	31
1,889	71.4	1,724	61.8	207	45.1	264	37.7	7,619	55.4	5,053	42.7	32
40,880	69.8	35,393	55.9	4,543	56.3	3,921	38.2	249	65.0	73	53.7	33
28,250	68.4	25,895	65.0	2,370	48.9	2,900	42.0	366	65.7	257	67.6	34
769	68.3	1,023	64.7	111	61.0	157	56.5	5,478	61.8	5,400	53.9	35
12,134	65.8	8,213	63.8	2,156	37.4	2,785	37.1	657	64.8	361	60.2	36
17,026	70.5	11,954	69.1	1,909	49.3	2,435	41.7	562	63.3	469	67.1	37
7,998	60.9	7,727	52.6	846	42.3	852	38.9	14,971	58.3	10,571	45.7	38
585,024	70.3	431,656	68.0	76,975	41.5	133,503	43.4	14,609	56.3	8,770	54.4	39
85,598	71.1	44,527	68.2	9,750	42.2	7,175	42.4	847	69.4	500	61.4	40
223,210	69.9	155,744	68.4	25,407	40.1	38,555	46.6	3,474	57.4	2,731	59.6	41
224,037	71.4	194,142	67.7	38,286	42.3	84,015	42.4	9,373	54.5	4,933	50.7	42
41,107	65.7	29,057	67.0	2,633	41.9	2,753	39.1	734	64.4	425	60.4	43
11,072	69.9	8,186	72.3	899	41.8	1,005	41.2	181	54.8	181	63.1	44
40,267	68.8	29,676	66.0	4,238	40.2	6,775	43.4	2,271	60.8	1,210	62.3	45
1,643	69.3	976	71.7	230	37.6	220	48.1	5,980	57.8	2,757	46.3	46
12,516	73.3	9,846	65.3	1,575	53.5	1,163	45.8	618	69.1	299	60.6	47
11,863	68.9	10,791	62.9	1,338	49.9	1,269	41.5	1,246	63.6	488	57.3	48
13,671	64.5	11,931	61.6	1,728	41.0	2,328	40.0	215	61.6	190	55.9	49
129,870	69.5	93,855	60.0	15,075	43.1	20,035	39.8	15,728	59.7	8,646	54.7	50
47,310	69.3	38,071	59.8	3,670	45.9	5,539	34.4	5,239	66.0	3,150	60.6	51
12,991	74.8	9,266	62.1	2,057	56.8	1,591	41.0	162	71.7	57	52.8	52
23,544	68.6	18,242	65.8	2,049	38.9	3,812	36.2	754	65.9	698	63.6	53
3,696	73.9	1,859	54.8	336	41.2	346	30.6	142	67.3	101	56.7	54
1,742	72.2	1,063	58.6	178	49.2	207	48.1	7,440	56.2	5,369	44.0	55
19,936	66.4	14,424	60.6	3,530	49.0	2,909	41.9	174	64.0	98	58.0	56
30,043	62.4	32,938	53.2	2,960	40.5	4,573	38.9	8,517	62.5	4,598	55.0	57
17,738	64.0	20,443	61.4	1,519	49.4	1,807	42.2	395	71.9	299	63.3	58
7,977	72.1	7,362	66.1	788	52.3	776	44.1	61	......	57	57.0	59
5,470	57.6	4,242	55.2	3,438	41.6	1,074	38.6	2,110	59.5	1,417	48.7	60
29,753	70.0	25,033	61.0	3,954	46.4	3,352	39.7	197	61.0	108	46.6	61
13,908	66.1	11,646	57.9	756	41.9	1,259	34.1	78	68.4	82	59.4	62
16,229	71.4	12,093	66.0	2,892	55.3	1,992	42.7	268	70.2	151	56.3	63
5,988	76.6	5,117	65.5	714	62.5	655	41.5	94	72.9	79	64.2	64
10,052	71.8	6,664	70.6	1,169	49.1	1,226	42.1	377	67.9	237	72.5	65
10,711	70.8	8,302	62.2	1,168	48.9	1,182	34.9	142	58.2	116	59.8	66
12,600	65.2	10,878	58.5	1,303	48.8	1,141	40.2	559	56.4	197	61.0	67
10,383	71.1	6,728	65.1	1,199	41.8	1,292	35.7	637	67.2	279	59.9	68
8,030	68.7	6,606	67.8	1,062	51.5	960	49.1	15,375	60.4	13,147	59.5	69
5,601	69.6	3,687	59.6	485	42.9	420	27.5	1,282	57.2	1,286	59.4	70
17,537	69.9	13,331	66.8	1,782	47.2	2,170	40.3	192	65.3	172	65.4	71
11,163	73.2	7,921	72.5	800	48.8	1,049	29.1	322	68.4	176	57.0	72
10,702	75.4	5,096	58.0	1,455	52.9	906	30.4	712	57.4	183	48.8	73

TABLE 124.—SCHOOL ATTENDANCE OF POPULATION 7 TO 13 YEARS OF AGE, FOR
OR MORE:

[Per cent not shown

	CITY.	ALL CLASSES.				NATIVE WHITE—NATIVE PARENTAGE.			
		1920		1910		1920		1910	
		Number.	Per cent.	Number.	Per cent.	Number.	Per cent.	Number.	Per cent.
1	Akron, Ohio	18,109	96.3	6,664	94.4	11,051	96.7	4,055	94.4
2	Albany, N. Y	10,835	92.6	9,483	91.0	6,584	92.6	5,641	91.1
3	Atlanta, Ga	22,271	92.5	15,459	84.0	14,352	93.9	9,729	87.0
4	Baltimore, Md	84,194	96.1	57,574	85.2	48,589	96.6	31,070	85.5
5	Birmingham, Ala	21,606	90.5	13,681	82.2	11,544	91.7	7,310	83.7
6	Boston, Mass	83,821	94.7	74,483	95.7	21,642	94.9	18,136	95.4
7	Bridgeport, Conn	16,106	90.6	11,290	96.0	3,923	89.9	3,234	95.9
8	Buffalo, N. Y	57,324	92.3	48,793	91.3	22,882	94.0	17,130	92.8
9	Cambridge, Mass	12,889	97.2	12,483	97.5	3,443	97.9	3,010	96.9
10	Camden, N. J	14,318	94.4	10,393	89.5	7,272	94.9	5,789	90.2
11	Chicago, Ill	310,269	93.9	240,844	93.1	88,747	94.2	56,460	93.5
12	Cincinnati, Ohio	42,067	97.2	37,423	95.8	29,709	97.3	23,369	96.0
13	Cleveland, Ohio	97,487	96.2	63,607	95.7	28,193	96.6	17,745	96.6
14	Columbus, Ohio	23,720	95.9	17,356	94.3	17,765	96.0	12,786	94.8
15	Dallas, Tex	16,215	93.3	8,776	82.1	12,128	94.2	6,096	82.5
16	Dayton, Ohio	16,103	96.8	11,545	94.9	12,052	97.1	8,380	95.0
17	Denver, Colo	25,196	96.5	21,194	93.1	15,592	96.7	11,390	92.4
18	Des Moines, Iowa	13,674	96.7	8,914	92.1	10,187	96.8	6,081	92.2
19	Detroit, Mich	99,755	94.7	48,623	92.0	35,371	95.4	14,294	94.1
20	Fall River, Mass	17,506	97.8	16,221	96.4	3,537	98.7	2,583	98.0
21	Fort Worth, Tex	10,393	88.6	7,042	80.5	8,045	91.1	5,263	82.8
22	Grand Rapids, Mich	16,132	95.7	12,187	92.3	7,596	96.1	4,464	90.5
23	Hartford, Conn	15,353	96.9	11,008	97.1	4,200	97.2	3,405	96.3
24	Houston, Tex	14,922	90.2	7,316	79.9	8,688	91.0	3,795	79.4
25	Indianapolis, Ind	31,220	94.4	23,596	95.7	23,923	94.5	17,242	95.8
26	Jersey City, N. J	37,911	94.8	33,199	90.9	13,719	95.4	12,519	91.2
27	Kansas City, Kans	12,479	96.8	9,130	91.0	7,746	97.3	5,925	91.2
28	Kansas City, Mo	29,791	94.4	21,489	92.0	21,132	94.9	14,449	92.1
29	Los Angeles, Calif	51,115	95.0	26,734	93.6	28,306	95.4	15,217	93.7
30	Louisville, Ky	25,713	95.6	24,286	93.4	19,398	95.8	16,159	93.7
31	Lowell, Mass	13,590	97.0	11,769	95.4	3,529	98.0	2,366	95.7
32	Memphis, Tenn	16,447	92.2	11,015	82.6	9,507	93.8	6,105	88.0
33	Milwaukee, Wis	54,250	96.9	44,007	92.1	22,404	97.3	13,439	92.9
34	Minneapolis, Minn	37,631	94.0	28,936	93.7	16,948	94.4	10,191	93.1
35	Nashville, Tenn	14,013	94.5	11,822	86.2	9,603	95.3	7,574	88.4
36	New Bedford, Mass	14,945	95.9	11,147	94.2	2,470	96.2	1,874	96.3
37	New Haven, Conn	20,282	94.6	16,376	97.3	4,970	92.6	4,945	96.8
38	New Orleans, La	45,435	91.6	36,710	82.7	27,813	92.9	22,569	86.2
39	New York, N. Y	675,796	93.7	563,332	94.5	157,560	93.3	137,586	94.2
40	Bronx borough	92,616	93.1	55,012	94.8	20,166	92.2	16,545	94.5
41	Brooklyn borough	259,505	93.5	207,390	94.8	64,167	93.0	59,434	94.5
42	Manhattan borough	247,853	94.0	249,359	93.8	41,506	93.2	41,313	92.8
43	Queens borough	60,456	94.9	39,654	96.2	25,940	95.3	15,357	96.2
44	Richmond borough	15,366	92.9	11,917	96.3	5,781	92.9	4,937	96.3
45	Newark, N. J	52,380	94.2	42,217	95.0	15,169	94.6	13,521	94.9
46	Norfolk, Va	11,919	93.2	6,722	85.3	6,272	93.6	3,859	89.6
47	Oakland, Calif	21,914	96.0	13,729	94.2	11,371	96.8	6,065	94.4
48	Omaha, Nebr.[1]	20,957	95.3	15,395	92.4	10,636	94.9	6,720	92.6
49	Paterson, N. J	16,910	94.8	15,541	94.0	4,421	95.7	3,985	92.8
50	Philadelphia, Pa	210,282	94.0	168,485	92.1	89,216	94.4	71,942	92.9
51	Pittsburgh, Pa	72,200	94.5	59,128	91.0	30,753	95.2	23,534	91.6
52	Portland, Oreg	26,804	97.5	15,375	90.3	16,377	97.9	8,392	90.0
53	Providence, R. I	28,554	95.7	23,913	94.1	7,824	96.2	6,630	94.9
54	Reading, Pa	12,951	95.5	10,455	93.0	9,635	95.5	8,570	94.4
55	Richmond, Va	19,166	93.2	12,438	82.0	12,273	94.7	7,600	86.9
56	Rochester, N. Y	32,021	94.6	22,170	95.2	13,960	95.0	9,375	95.3
57	St. Louis, Mo	81,959	94.8	70,222	91.7	50,954	95.0	39,027	92.1
58	St. Paul, Minn	25,148	95.0	22,835	94.1	11,536	95.5	7,676	92.9
59	Salt Lake City, Utah	15,683	96.7	10,000	92.5	9,932	96.0	5,399	93.4
60	San Antonio, Tex	17,904	83.7	10,410	80.0	6,000	90.0	5,677	83.4
61	San Francisco, Calif	42,293	92.2	31,134	91.2	18,137	92.5	11,872	91.2
62	Scranton, Pa	19,234	93.1	16,053	90.0	8,058	92.9	5,922	91.7
63	Seattle, Wash	28,688	93.9	18,556	91.0	15,334	94.6	9,447	91.4
64	Spokane, Wash	12,229	98.0	9,239	88.8	7,835	98.1	5,456	88.3
65	Springfield, Mass	13,999	95.9	9,437	96.7	5,377	95.7	3,696	96.0
66	Syracuse, N. Y	18,269	96.4	13,440	97.1	9,389	96.6	6,376	90.4
67	Toledo, Ohio	26,220	96.3	18,906	94.6	15,364	97.1	9,589	95.7
68	Trenton, N. J	15,143	97.6	10,822	94.6	5,261	97.8	4,501	95.2
69	Washington, D. C	38,962	93.5	31,101	90.4	22,062	93.6	17,436	91.5
70	Wilmington, Del	12,261	96.0	8,977	89.2	6,472	96.6	4,932	90.1
71	Worcester, Mass	20,873	95.1	16,292	95.1	6,367	96.2	4,676	95.6
72	Yonkers, N. Y	13,949	97.1	10,059	96.5	4,714	97.2	3,322	96.4
73	Youngstown, Ohio	16,001	96.8	7,657	86.3	6,265	97.3	2,987	87.3

[1] Includes population of South Omaha for 1910.

PRINCIPAL POPULATION CLASSES, FOR CITIES HAVING, IN 1920, 100,000 INHABITANTS
1920 AND 1910.
where base is less than 100.]

NATIVE WHITE—FOREIGN OR MIXED PARENTAGE.				FOREIGN-BORN WHITE.				NEGRO.				
1920		1910		1920		1910		1920		1910		
Number.	Per cent.	Number.	Per cent.	Number.	Per cent.	Number.	Per cent.	Number.	Per cent.	Number.	Per cent.	
5,391	96.0	2,135	95.3	1,312	94.4	409	91.1	355	94.7	65	......	1
3,783	92.7	3,324	91.0	370	91.1	427	87.7	94	......	91	......	2
1,195	95.9	796	90.6	105	91.3	171	83.4	6,618	89.1	4,762	77.5	3
23,712	96.3	16,522	86.4	1,675	93.0	2,822	82.8	10,215	93.7	7,155	82.4	4
1,797	87.5	1,261	87.3	160	88.4	211	82.1	8,105	89.5	4,899	78.9	5
56,464	95.1	47,373	96.4	4,409	88.6	7,899	92.5	1,253	95.1	1,053	96.3	6
10,989	91.2	6,761	96.5	1,021	86.7	1,182	94.0	170	95.5	113	91.9	7
31,320	91.6	28,251	90.8	2,804	88.0	3,279	87.4	302	94.7	129	93.5	8
8,072	97.5	7,890	98.1	733	90.9	1,030	95.0	638	96.7	551	97.9	9
5,547	94.7	3,531	89.1	556	92.5	492	85.9	943	89.6	579	88.0	10
196,671	94.1	157,513	93.5	16,946	90.6	24,156	89.5	7,798	92.2	2,680	91.8	11
8,887	97.1	11,258	96.0	671	97.2	1,317	91.5	2,799	96.2	1,479	94.1	12
60,122	96.4	37,323	95.8	6,375	92.8	7,912	93.2	2,792	96.2	620	95.5	13
3,591	95.9	3,161	93.7	327	91.1	411	88.0	2,034	96.6	992	93.1	14
1,514	92.4	1,060	84.7	292	73.6	126	82.9	2,278	92.4	1,493	79.2	15
2,939	95.9	2,412	96.1	299	92.6	385	89.3	811	98.1	368	92.0	16
8,503	96.8	8,332	94.2	613	89.6	1,042	94.2	463	95.7	410	92.3	17
2,711	96.6	2,320	92.7	226	91.9	262	85.3	548	97.0	251	92.6	18
51,973	95.1	28,791	91.6	9,632	90.4	5,092	88.4	2,758	95.5	441	93.2	19
12,824	97.6	11,419	96.0	1,120	96.0	2,188	93.9	25	......	30	......	20
749	85.3	623	82.6	198	45.8	73	54.9	1,401	88.3	1,083	72.1	21
7,820	96.0	6,771	93.5	619	89.2	912	92.3	90	......	39	......	22
9,704	97.3	6,237	97.9	995	92.7	1,172	96.1	451	96.2	194	95.6	23
2,366	90.0	1,169	80.7	402	67.3	120	66.7	3,463	92.2	2,232	81.1	24
3,541	94.2	3,953	95.7	244	87.8	347	90.8	3,510	94.0	2,052	95.2	25
21,926	94.8	17,983	91.2	1,420	89.0	2,144	87.0	845	95.6	553	91.9	26
2,699	97.1	2,067	92.0	405	86.2	211	83.1	1,623	96.8	924	89.6	27
5,863	94.1	4,786	92.8	677	85.6	720	89.6	2,110	93.3	1,532	89.2	28
16,728	95.5	8,717	93.3	4,000	91.0	2,003	90.3	1,411	94.3	689	95.4	29
2,766	96.0	4,449	94.8	103	88.8	235	89.4	3,446	94.5	3,443	91.0	30
9,311	97.3	8,053	95.9	727	87.8	1,343	92.1	21	......	7	......	31
1,363	93.7	1,124	95.5	116	89.9	185	77.4	5,461	89.3	3,598	73.4	32
29,043	96.9	27,355	92.2	2,610	93.6	3,168	88.1	188	97.4	44	......	33
19,072	94.1	16,582	94.3	1,326	87.9	2,007	92.1	272	95.4	154	93.3	34
510	96.0	652	92.6	46	......	94	83.2	3,853	92.3	3,502	81.0	35
10,328	96.9	6,977	95.2	1,621	90.4	2,031	89.5	525	94.3	264	94.6	36
13,735	95.6	9,308	97.1	1,146	92.1	1,800	96.2	430	93.9	323	93.9	37
5,996	91.6	5,599	84.7	480	86.3	627	78.8	11,127	88.6	7,904	73.2	38
463,215	94.5	327,186	95.2	43,941	88.2	92,220	92.6	10,763	92.9	6,225	91.9	39
66,500	93.8	33,103	95.3	5,265	88.6	5,002	92.5	673	94.1	358	94.0	40
178,226	94.2	118,177	95.4	14,498	88.3	27,802	93.1	2,597	91.7	1,946	92.0	41
177,345	94.9	147,795	94.7	21,919	88.5	56,675	92.4	6,807	93.1	3,504	91.4	42
32,318	95.2	21,977	96.6	1,652	85.7	2,020	93.6	536	93.1	294	93.0	43
8,826	94.0	6,134	96.8	607	78.8	721	92.7	150	94.3	123	93.9	44
32,746	94.5	22,811	95.6	2,688	89.2	5,017	93.1	1,770	95.0	860	93.7	45
1,248	94.4	676	92.3	135	93.8	154	86.5	4,261	92.3	2,033	76.4	46
8,850	96.0	6,397	94.6	866	91.1	850	92.5	427	96.8	196	92.5	47
8,656	96.0	7,372	93.0	760	91.7	947	87.5	895	95.6	354	91.5	48
11,113	94.9	9,568	94.9	1,220	90.2	1,829	92.6	156	95.7	158	92.4	49
100,824	94.2	74,300	92.2	8,588	88.5	15,642	89.1	11,616	92.8	6,573	89.2	50
35,582	94.2	29,147	91.3	2,046	90.1	4,133	86.5	3,813	95.3	2,310	89.4	51
8,953	97.5	5,740	91.7	1,181	92.4	1,136	87.5	113	94.2	39	......	52
18,825	96.1	14,028	94.5	1,331	89.0	2,739	90.6	564	95.8	493	94.6	53
2,993	96.3	1,522	88.1	204	86.8	287	81.3	119	95.2	76	......	54
1,253	95.6	750	90.3	88	86.3	152	92.7	5,549	89.7	3,936	72.5	55
15,714	94.9	10,621	95.7	2,216	90.8	2,098	92.1	126	97.7	75	......	56
23,046	94.9	24,392	92.2	1,758	91.4	3,599	87.7	6,193	93.8	3,183	88.2	57
12,474	94.7	13,673	95.0	875	92.8	1,301	92.5	253	98.8	185	93.4	58
5,278	95.7	4,841	94.2	417	90.1	560	89.6	44	......	34	......	59
4,046	78.5	3,056	78.9	2,453	68.6	782	66.2	1,497	89.9	1,045	79.0	60
20,945	93.1	16,490	92.4	2,311	84.4	2,329	88.9	135	91.8	68	......	61
10,620	93.5	9,088	89.8	498	89.4	977	82.1	58	......	66	......	62
10,945	93.9	7,565	91.6	1,798	90.2	1,356	86.5	182	96.8	110	86.6	63
3,925	98.1	3,269	90.4	389	95.3	461	83.5	66	......	49	......	64
7,589	96.6	4,804	97.4	690	89.8	780	95.1	273	96.8	153	99.4	65
8,070	96.8	6,104	92.3	702	90.8	869	87.5	98	90.7	90	......	66
9,589	95.5	8,250	93.8	848	92.4	926	91.1	419	94.2	138	95.2	67
8,582	97.8	5,124	95.0	842	93.6	1,020	90.5	458	97.0	177	92.7	68
5,451	94.1	4,260	91.8	503	94.0	642	89.2	10,924	93.0	8,743	87.7	69
4,508	95.6	2,792	88.7	318	92.4	342	83.0	962	94.6	910	87.9	70
13,263	95.0	10,018	95.1	1,103	90.1	1,468	93.2	132	96.4	128	96.2	71
8,507	97.5	5,858	97.1	495	89.0	741	92.7	229	96.6	137	96.5	72
8,262	97.0	3,799	87.1	937	93.8	716	80.2	537	93.9	155	79.9	73

TABLE 125.—SCHOOL ATTENDANCE, BY SEX AND AGE PERIODS, FOR CITIES HAVING 25,000 INHABITANTS OR MORE: 1920.

CITY.	TOTAL.			7 TO 13 YEARS OF AGE.		14 AND 15 YEARS OF AGE.		16 AND 17 YEARS OF AGE.		18 to 20 years of age.	Under 7 years of age.	21 years of age and over.
	Both sexes.	Male.	Female.	Number.	Per cent.	Number.	Per cent.	Number.	Per cent.			
ALABAMA:												
Birmingham	32,089	15,387	16,702	21,606	90.5	4,911	81.5	2,728	43.1	1,325	1,091	428
Mobile	11,495	5,395	6,100	7,415	95.2	1,644	82.2	812	38.4	270	1,262	92
Montgomery	8,053	3,722	4,331	5,129	91.7	1,256	82.8	799	49.2	432	350	87
ARIZONA:												
Phoenix	5,130	2,524	2,606	3,050	93.5	712	85.7	477	53.1	271	514	106
ARKANSAS:												
Fort Smith	5,501	2,601	2,900	3,525	86.0	813	80.2	484	43.1	244	377	58
Little Rock	11,546	5,489	6,057	7,096	93.5	1,754	84.1	1,017	47.7	601	798	280
CALIFORNIA:												
Alameda	5,495	2,737	2,758	3,212	96.5	742	92.3	491	60.7	333	510	207
Berkeley	12,501	6,188	6,313	5,786	94.9	1,530	93.0	1,209	69.7	1,363	1,063	1,550
Fresno	8,099	4,013	4,086	4,893	95.3	1,180	89.8	712	50.2	460	698	156
Long Beach	8,951	4,331	4,620	4,784	94.0	1,282	89.1	958	67.5	684	956	287
Los Angeles	92,045	45,622	46,423	51,115	95.0	12,422	90.4	7,785	54.0	5,230	11,485	4,008
Oakland	37,672	18,719	18,953	21,914	96.0	5,130	91.6	3,155	55.0	2,136	3,927	1,410
Pasadena	7,674	3,845	3,829	4,009	95.0	1,091	92.4	799	70.2	600	870	305
Sacramento	11,061	5,419	5,642	6,472	95.4	1,525	90.7	1,030	55.5	586	1,250	198
San Diego	11,948	5,941	6,007	6,515	93.4	1,599	89.6	1,023	56.7	705	1,429	677
San Francisco	73,039	38,213	34,826	42,293	92.2	9,909	88.2	6,600	50.7	5,260	6,264	2,713
San Jose	7,995	3,846	4,149	4,553	96.1	1,179	92.9	741	59.9	583	723	216
Stockton	6,509	3,234	3,275	3,968	96.5	879	91.2	558	51.9	297	675	132
COLORADO:												
Colorado Springs	6,055	2,891	3,164	3,191	95.7	912	90.6	655	64.6	542	484	271
Denver	44,198	21,747	22,451	25,196	96.5	5,822	83.7	3,732	51.1	2,572	5,085	1,791
Pueblo	8,797	4,236	4,561	5,384	94.9	1,154	81.8	652	45.3	343	1,075	189
CONNECTICUT:												
Bridgeport	25,032	12,587	12,445	16,106	90.6	3,098	74.7	1,162	27.5	562	3,726	378
Hartford	25,531	12,784	12,747	15,353	96.9	3,298	80.9	1,679	40.3	930	3,785	486
Meriden	5,662	3,033	2,629	3,490	91.7	861	77.1	306	30.5	142	762	101
New Britain	12,179	6,153	6,026	8,034	97.5	1,382	71.8	516	28.4	303	1,798	146
New Haven	32,715	16,393	16,322	20,282	94.6	3,668	70.8	1,733	33.7	1,006	5,354	672
New London	4,911	2,401	2,510	2,943	97.6	667	86.6	341	42.5	179	667	114
Norwalk	4,894	2,446	2,448	3,210	91.0	647	71.4	222	26.1	93	633	89
Stamford	7,696	3,874	3,822	4,762	96.9	937	83.8	409	37.0	193	1,303	92
Waterbury	18,463	9,311	9,152	11,500	94.3	2,305	79.9	1,042	34.8	537	2,789	290
DELAWARE:												
Wilmington	18,090	8,964	9,126	12,261	96.0	2,249	72.2	998	29.6	705	1,525	352
DIST. OF COLUMBIA:												
Washington	70,886	35,788	35,098	38,962	93.5	9,530	83.2	5,566	44.8	3,947	6,704	6,177
FLORIDA:												
Jacksonville	16,123	7,672	8,451	10,228	94.5	2,268	83.4	1,259	43.1	557	1,555	256
Miami	4,656	2,323	2,333	2,813	88.5	650	86.7	352	42.1	159	609	73
Pensacola	5,685	2,667	3,018	3,863	94.6	793	80.8	398	35.2	150	441	40
Tampa	10,534	5,252	5,282	7,149	94.2	1,447	79.4	667	33.8	304	877	90
GEORGIA:												
Atlanta	34,203	16,486	17,717	22,271	92.5	4,676	73.6	2,603	37.4	1,532	2,445	676
Augusta	9,190	4,366	4,824	5,616	90.7	1,228	71.2	764	41.9	417	1,016	149
Columbus	5,960	2,793	3,167	3,927	90.0	729	67.9	422	31.0	190	628	64
Macon	9,502	4,491	5,011	6,284	92.4	1,278	71.8	697	36.9	433	685	125
Savannah	14,257	6,604	7,653	9,331	93.8	1,907	74.3	994	35.7	520	1,342	163
ILLINOIS:												
Aurora	6,166	3,117	3,049	3,950	95.7	805	76.7	424	37.6	182	655	150
Bloomington	4,971	2,345	2,626	3,030	95.3	724	83.2	387	42.8	325	343	162
Chicago	466,053	235,455	230,598	310,269	93.9	57,275	72.6	23,621	29.1	12,367	51,327	11,194
Cicero town	9,057	4,673	4,384	6,945	96.6	897	57.2	210	13.1	71	861	73
Danville	5,989	2,961	3,028	3,951	96.2	902	78.9	420	36.8	204	433	79
Decatur	8,048	3,959	4,089	5,123	97.8	1,053	75.4	596	37.6	404	679	193
East St. Louis	12,374	6,102	6,272	8,424	97.1	1,000	76.7	662	28.5	280	1,274	151
Elgin	4,681	2,020	2,661	3,100	95.6	607	70.6	465	40.0	170	517	60
Evanston	7,269	3,564	3,705	3,858	91.4	970	85.8	627	56.2	569	863	382
Joliet	7,441	3,729	3,712	4,804	96.1	1,030	80.3	493	36.8	259	700	155
Moline	5,313	2,665	2,648	3,137	92.6	722	82.4	401	40.3	209	715	129
Oak Park village	7,662	3,990	3,672	4,422	95.2	1,079	90.5	726	61.1	548	639	248
Peoria	12,349	5,985	6,364	7,609	95.5	1,813	81.0	909	38.2	507	1,272	239
Quincy	5,855	2,919	2,936	3,799	96.9	767	72.2	421	34.9	285	419	164
Rock Island	5,701	2,844	2,857	3,636	94.5	825	81.4	402	38.6	197	518	123
Rockford	10,970	5,504	5,466	6,700	95.5	1,794	93.3	826	39.0	422	960	268
Springfield	11,000	5,344	5,656	7,090	97.2	1,714	85.4	703	34.0	365	957	171

TABLE 125.—SCHOOL ATTENDANCE, BY SEX AND AGE PERIODS, FOR CITIES HAVING 25,000 INHABITANTS OR MORE: 1920—Continued.

CITY.	TOTAL.			7 TO 13 YEARS OF AGE.		14 AND 15 YEARS OF AGE.		16 AND 17 YEARS OF AGE.		18 to 20 years of age.	Under 7 years of age.	21 years of age and over.
	Both sexes.	Male.	Female.	Number.	Per cent.	Number.	Per cent.	Number.	Per cent.			
INDIANA:												
Anderson	5,173	2,641	2,532	3,258	94.7	821	87.2	388	35.8	206	417	83
East Chicago	6,253	3,202	3,051	4,612	93.3	610	67.7	197	21.7	73	713	48
Evansville	15,739	7,774	7,965	9,901	96.7	2,257	85.1	801	26.6	425	2,089	266
Fort Wayne	14,219	6,973	7,246	8,876	93.9	1,833	70.7	877	30.0	575	1,728	330
Gary	9,659	4,847	4,812	6,556	95.3	1,096	83.9	406	32.1	167	1,289	145
Hammond	6,987	3,528	3,459	4,801	95.2	863	74.8	285	25.3	111	861	66
Indianapolis	48,065	23,945	24,120	31,220	94.4	6,628	75.0	3,214	32.9	1,777	4,145	1,081
Kokomo	5,013	2,463	2,550	3,385	97.0	674	75.4	336	33.5	143	407	68
Muncie	6,355	3,163	3,192	4,192	94.6	865	76.1	396	29.7	218	602	82
Richmond	4,726	2,354	2,372	2,862	96.8	689	86.0	330	40.3	213	532	100
South Bend	13,654	6,799	6,855	9,092	93.5	1,814	77.0	690	27.9	339	1,491	228
Terre Haute	12,562	6,108	6,454	7,526	95.6	1,891	86.5	874	38.5	678	1,319	274
IOWA:												
Cedar Rapids	8,776	4,220	4,556	4,858	95.3	1,305	91.6	723	47.6	456	1,207	227
Council Bluffs	7,131	3,547	3,584	4,190	94.5	1,001	90.4	567	44.9	264	975	134
Davenport	11,141	5,704	5,437	6,096	96.3	1,466	89.1	734	42.6	471	1,329	1,045
Des Moines	25,212	12,446	12,766	13,674	96.7	3,513	91.3	2,223	54.0	1,581	3,364	857
Dubuque	6,835	3,400	3,435	4,109	92.0	884	73.1	424	31.1	274	1,026	118
Sioux City	12,633	6,264	6,369	7,356	95.4	1,669	88.9	998	46.2	672	1,626	312
Waterloo	7,165	3,494	3,671	4,028	95.3	994	92.0	562	51.6	343	1,070	168
KANSAS:												
Kansas City	19,320	9,548	9,772	12,479	96.8	2,632	79.7	1,117	32.8	561	2,106	425
Topeka	8,715	4,188	4,527	5,151	92.5	1,300	85.4	800	48.3	482	700	282
Wichita	13,397	6,558	6,839	8,040	94.8	1,933	89.2	1,249	53.7	791	972	412
KENTUCKY:												
Covington	10,034	4,940	5,094	6,537	97.2	1,400	77.3	679	36.5	350	957	111
Lexington	6,881	3,312	3,569	4,111	95.4	1,010	88.2	590	48.4	404	569	197
Louisville	38,935	19,086	19,849	25,713	95.6	5,585	78.4	2,354	30.5	1,184	3,391	708
Newport	4,751	2,330	2,421	3,263	96.4	639	71.2	284	30.0	141	361	63
LOUISIANA:												
New Orleans	68,989	33,533	35,456	45,435	91.6	9,499	70.3	4,223	30.3	2,043	6,904	885
Shreveport	7,257	3,285	3,972	4,597	89.6	1,126	79.4	642	44.0	312	477	103
MAINE:												
Bangor	5,312	2,556	2,756	2,862	96.6	689	89.7	521	66.1	387	717	136
Lewiston	6,129	3,100	3,029	3,983	96.3	817	80.9	338	26.2	221	635	135
Portland	12,849	6,305	6,544	7,261	95.1	1,727	88.4	1,155	55.9	726	1,612	368
MARYLAND:												
Baltimore	122,726	61,491	61,235	84,194	96.1	15,755	68.8	6,404	25.8	3,579	10,485	2,309
Cumberland	5,068	2,516	2,552	3,463	91.9	810	77.4	327	27.6	120	317	31
Hagerstown	5,071	2,459	2,612	3,476	95.7	737	82.7	266	28.1	128	430	34
MASSACHUSETTS:												
Boston	143,679	72,306	71,373	83,821	94.7	18,751	83.4	9,774	43.2	5,422	21,119	4,792
Brockton	11,864	5,969	5,895	7,605	95.9	1,516	76.0	770	40.1	497	1,218	258
Brookline town	6,602	3,224	3,378	3,156	95.9	842	93.1	684	75.5	681	856	383
Cambridge	22,075	11,198	10,877	12,889	97.2	2,782	80.3	1,463	42.1	1,005	3,197	739
Chelsea	8,993	4,548	4,445	5,976	96.6	1,195	78.5	568	38.8	288	848	118
Chicopee	7,229	3,606	3,623	5,158	95.2	668	51.7	242	20.3	130	987	44
Everett	8,154	4,111	4,043	5,230	96.6	1,105	82.0	636	47.6	299	756	128
Fall River	24,929	12,450	12,479	17,506	97.8	2,031	45.4	960	21.6	717	3,440	275
Fitchburg	7,575	3,683	3,892	5,148	93.5	861	59.1	442	33.2	251	770	103
Haverhill	9,274	4,653	4,621	5,945	96.1	1,159	68.8	560	34.7	304	1,181	125
Holyoke	12,290	6,134	6,156	7,559	95.2	1,320	63.2	813	38.4	550	1,754	294
Lawrence	17,103	8,620	8,483	11,838	94.7	1,673	53.4	769	25.2	503	2,013	307
Lowell	21,921	10,697	11,224	13,590	97.0	2,651	73.0	1,325	36.2	785	3,224	346
Lynn	17,470	8,634	8,836	11,164	96.5	2,368	83.2	1,206	42.7	634	1,805	293
Malden	10,136	4,987	5,149	6,339	98.0	1,425	87.0	874	52.6	474	803	221
Medford	7,409	3,694	3,715	4,626	97.8	977	85.3	625	52.9	388	630	163
New Bedford	20,800	10,240	10,560	14,945	95.9	1,886	48.4	770	19.6	596	2,314	289
Newton	10,001	4,967	5,034	5,497	98.1	1,274	88.2	969	65.1	696	1,288	277
Pittsfield	7,260	3,625	3,635	4,693	92.5	978	73.7	496	36.5	222	743	128
Quincy	9,390	4,741	4,649	6,099	97.4	1,219	81.5	696	48.2	379	812	185
Revere	6,477	3,263	3,214	4,306	96.7	782	76.1	380	37.5	155	780	74
Salem	8,737	4,338	4,399	5,466	96.9	1,008	70.8	506	36.2	294	1,320	143
Somerville	16,753	8,189	8,564	10,319	94.9	2,263	82.5	1,337	47.5	832	1,634	368
Springfield	23,689	11,849	11,840	13,929	95.9	2,839	77.8	1,660	44.9	972	3,653	636
Taunton	6,833	3,410	3,423	4,661	97.6	737	62.9	403	35.1	265	659	108
Waltham	5,750	2,910	2,840	3,394	92.7	735	78.9	461	43.4	273	737	150
Worcester	33,548	16,813	16,735	20,873	95.1	4,049	74.3	2,303	41.7	1,292	4,197	834

TABLE 125.—SCHOOL ATTENDANCE, BY SEX AND AGE PERIODS, FOR CITIES HAVING 25,000 INHABITANTS OR MORE: 1920—Continued.

CITY.	TOTAL.			7 TO 13 YEARS OF AGE.		14 AND 15 YEARS OF AGE.		16 AND 17 YEARS OF AGE.		18 to 20 years of age.	Under 7 years of age.	21 years of age and over.
	Both sexes.	Male.	Female.	Number.	Per cent.	Number.	Per cent.	Number.	Per cent.			
MICHIGAN:												
Battle Creek	6,091	2,974	3,117	3,412	94.6	887	89.0	519	47.9	311	796	166
Bay City	10,322	5,243	5,079	6,664	97.0	1,481	82.6	659	35.9	330	1,049	139
Detroit	156,082	79,072	77,010	99,755	94.7	20,983	88.2	8,485	31.9	4,040	19,881	2,938
Flint	13,841	6,903	6,938	8,699	95.2	1,848	85.9	809	30.8	363	1,915	207
Grand Rapids	27,296	13,532	13,764	16,132	95.7	3,909	89.7	1,869	41.3	964	3,858	564
Hamtramck village	8,405	4,355	4,050	6,229	93.7	763	80.8	193	18.6	70	1,003	147
Highland Park	7,290	3,734	3,556	4,177	96.6	933	93.4	553	50.0	284	1,097	246
Jackson	7,959	3,978	3,981	4,898	96.2	1,124	89.6	562	39.5	269	972	134
Kalamazoo	8,437	4,170	4,267	5,048	93.9	1,208	87.2	605	40.9	390	1,003	183
Lansing	10,135	5,352	4,783	5,614	95.1	1,633	92.1	873	45.7	421	1,297	297
Muskegon	6,610	3,372	3,238	4,042	95.7	915	84.7	381	29.2	179	959	134
Pontiac	5,154	2,582	2,572	3,208	95.3	680	84.3	380	39.4	164	660	62
Port Huron	4,854	2,419	2,435	3,022	95.1	732	87.6	363	39.3	190	494	53
Saginaw	11,732	5,833	5,899	7,697	96.2	1,806	89.5	760	34.8	305	1,036	128
MINNESOTA:												
Duluth	18,966	9,409	9,557	11,532	93.5	2,551	90.2	1,271	38.2	740	2,381	491
Minneapolis	67,799	34,272	33,527	37,631	94.0	9,050	90.6	5,572	50.9	3,995	8,100	3,451
St. Paul	42,870	21,646	21,224	25,148	95.0	5,862	87.8	3,002	40.1	1,980	5,473	1,405
MISSOURI:												
Joplin	6,017	2,953	3,064	3,834	96.5	918	84.1	505	44.3	226	482	52
Kansas City	51,121	25,337	25,784	29,791	94.4	7,121	83.3	4,113	44.9	2,325	6,293	1,478
St. Joseph	13,522	6,556	6,966	8,462	95.5	1,973	87.0	1,217	46.8	560	1,056	254
St. Louis	128,207	64,432	63,775	81,959	94.8	16,527	71.9	7,115	28.3	4,000	15,868	2,738
Springfield	7,899	3,765	4,134	4,804	95.6	1,225	88.7	679	49.9	406	607	178
MONTANA:												
Butte	7,370	3,608	3,762	4,378	94.4	1,064	87.7	675	55.5	333	743	177
NEBRASKA:												
Lincoln	12,004	5,979	6,025	6,240	94.6	1,570	94.2	1,025	60.2	879	1,615	675
Omaha	35,707	17,584	18,123	20,957	95.3	4,777	86.5	2,559	44.1	1,457	5,118	839
NEW HAMPSHIRE:												
Manchester	15,636	7,680	7,956	9,755	94.7	2,336	90.1	1,085	40.8	643	1,517	300
Nashua	5,633	2,752	2,881	3,405	97.2	800	91.0	365	39.1	232	709	122
NEW JERSEY:												
Atlantic City	8,650	4,305	4,345	5,338	95.2	1,194	84.3	622	44.1	320	1,065	111
Bayonne	16,790	8,376	8,414	11,259	95.8	2,130	79.1	658	26.7	337	2,212	194
Camden	19,966	9,967	9,999	14,318	94.4	2,604	70.2	797	20.2	339	1,707	201
Clifton	5,859	2,920	2,939	3,971	97.2	540	56.5	189	20.7	83	1,041	35
East Orange	9,184	4,560	4,624	5,212	96.5	1,239	88.8	798	56.3	496	1,203	236
Elizabeth	18,088	9,240	8,848	12,626	96.3	2,072	69.6	859	27.8	360	1,916	255
Hoboken	12,532	6,234	6,298	8,549	95.3	1,364	63.2	499	21.6	356	1,597	167
Irvington town	4,739	2,355	2,384	3,186	96.0	619	75.0	201	25.3	87	574	72
Jersey City	54,779	27,440	27,339	37,911	94.8	6,892	69.9	2,281	22.7	1,096	5,934	665
Kearny town	5,280	2,757	2,523	3,502	96.3	622	67.8	226	23.4	97	782	51
Montclair town	6,406	3,199	3,207	3,538	97.0	827	92.1	564	66.0	410	856	211
New Brunswick	6,475	3,264	3,211	4,249	96.5	749	78.2	301	33.9	151	941	84
Newark	79,347	40,080	39,267	52,380	94.2	9,421	70.1	3,387	25.1	1,736	11,389	1,034
Orange	6,588	3,313	3,275	4,191	92.0	866	73.6	322	28.2	166	948	95
Passaic	12,448	6,288	6,160	8,711	90.8	1,282	61.8	513	25.1	238	1,563	141
Paterson	25,274	12,708	12,566	16,910	94.8	3,003	63.0	1,012	20.7	512	3,553	284
Perth Amboy	9,205	4,728	4,477	6,293	96.7	846	60.1	295	21.6	116	1,577	78
Plainfield	5,451	2,729	2,722	3,329	96.8	662	85.8	363	44.2	179	838	80
Trenton	23,354	11,519	11,835	15,143	97.6	2,494	66.0	1,211	31.0	593	3,752	161
West Hoboken town	7,514	3,744	3,770	5,097	93.6	1,035	71.0	316	22.1	140	852	74
West New York town	5,798	2,944	2,854	4,076	98.0	663	63.0	165	16.5	48	813	33
NEW YORK:												
Albany	18,451	5,601	6,100	10,876	97.6	7,540	87.9	1,011	30.1	951	2,384	574
Amsterdam	5,944	2,910	3,034	4,123	92.2	639	69.0	238	23.0	112	744	83
Auburn	6,627	3,468	3,159	3,945	94.5	883	84.7	387	37.1	222	689	501
Binghamton	10,773	5,393	5,380	6,638	96.7	1,405	87.4	657	36.2	394	1,495	184
Buffalo	89,071	44,917	44,154	57,324	92.3	12,276	78.6	4,961	30.9	2,776	9,732	2,002
Elmira	7,865	4,342	3,523	4,120	92.8	1,028	86.9	713	48.1	787	794	423
Jamestown	7,298	3,675	3,623	4,308	97.0	1,055	84.9	454	34.9	315	997	169
Kingston	4,622	2,283	2,339	2,867	94.0	717	83.4	301	32.6	200	404	133
Mount Vernon	9,203	4,730	4,473	5,557	97.3	1,265	87.9	599	47.0	377	1,221	184
New Rochelle	7,896	4,032	3,864	4,760	96.7	818	81.5	487	44.7	273	1,221	117
New York	1,017,738	514,033	503,705	675,796	93.7	138,102	78.1	49,106	27.0	24,935	109,523	20,276
Bronx boro	139,337	71,258	68,079	92,616	93.1	19,818	81.5	7,547	30.9	3,407	13,741	2,208
Brooklyn boro	383,757	193,228	190,529	259,505	93.5	51,812	77.1	17,423	25.0	8,411	41,431	5,175
Manhattan boro	382,882	192,932	189,950	247,853	94.0	51,568	78.7	19,533	28.5	11,054	41,573	11,301
Queens boro	88,994	44,947	44,047	60,456	94.9	11,842	75.0	3,725	23.8	1,631	10,014	1,326
Richmond boro	22,768	11,668	11,100	15,366	92.9	3,062	79.0	878	24.4	432	2,764	266

TABLE 125.—SCHOOL ATTENDANCE, BY SEX AND AGE PERIODS, FOR CITIES HAVING 25,000 INHABITANTS OR MORE: 1920—Continued.

CITY.	TOTAL.			7 TO 13 YEARS OF AGE.		14 AND 15 YEARS OF AGE.		16 AND 17 YEARS OF AGE.		18 to 20 years of age.	Under 7 years of age.	21 years of age and over.
	Both sexes.	Male.	Female.	Number.	Per cent.	Number.	Per cent.	Number.	Per cent.			
NEW YORK—Con.												
Newburgh	5,083	2,522	2,561	3,296	95.3	748	83.2	258	27.1	145	579	57
Niagara Falls	9,226	4,724	4,502	6,053	94.7	1,232	87.9	462	32.3	173	1,194	112
Poughkeepsie	6,012	2,979	3,033	3,695	93.4	865	83.3	389	35.8	188	765	110
Rochester	51,980	26,219	25,761	32,021	94.6	6,600	79.7	2,715	31.8	1,702	7,517	1,425
Rome	5,643	2,932	2,711	3,285	95.6	741	84.5	372	43.3	326	809	110
Schenectady	18,328	9,238	9,090	11,119	97.3	2,446	90.3	1,256	46.1	727	2,338	442
Syracuse	30,859	15,339	15,520	18,269	96.4	4,005	83.9	2,099	41.7	1,525	4,090	871
Troy	12,276	6,121	6,155	7,301	95.0	1,823	85.7	950	39.9	552	1,393	257
Utica	17,610	8,745	8,865	11,301	97.4	2,246	80.9	851	31.3	467	2,534	211
Watertown	5,591	2,735	2,856	3,345	95.0	812	87.6	376	38.9	186	763	109
Yonkers	22,877	11,593	11,284	13,949	97.1	2,938	86.7	1,290	39.4	788	3,584	328
NORTH CAROLINA:												
Asheville	5,501	2,608	2,893	3,494	90.8	793	81.1	476	47.1	244	423	71
Charlotte	9,153	4,272	4,881	6,029	95.2	1,218	76.1	642	39.7	411	719	134
Wilmington	6,012	2,785	3,227	3,938	87.9	849	73.4	407	36.1	219	539	60
Winston-Salem	8,274	3,984	4,290	5,550	94.5	1,075	66.7	578	27.0	347	622	102
OHIO:												
Akron	29,582	14,791	14,791	18,109	96.3	3,843	90.3	1,863	35.2	1,093	4,008	666
Canton	13,212	6,563	6,649	8,643	91.5	1,837	80.4	919	37.0	394	1,188	231
Cincinnati	68,464	34,204	34,260	42,067	97.2	9,989	90.2	4,585	39.3	2,686	7,177	1,960
Cleveland	150,880	75,536	75,344	97,487	96.2	20,305	88.8	8,601	37.3	4,333	17,591	2,563
Columbus	40,801	20,358	20,443	23,720	95.9	6,037	88.9	3,566	51.0	2,359	3,578	1,541
Dayton	26,511	13,433	13,078	16,103	96.8	3,671	89.3	1,842	43.1	1,081	3,121	693
East Cleveland	4,947	2,432	2,515	2,650	97.5	689	94.8	468	64.8	341	630	169
Hamilton	6,821	3,367	3,454	4,364	94.0	1,086	87.2	462	34.7	242	579	88
Lakewood	8,231	4,109	4,122	4,835	96.8	1,125	93.0	633	58.1	422	1,056	160
Lima	7,772	3,857	3,915	4,868	98.1	1,157	87.3	602	44.9	283	728	134
Lorain	8,041	3,999	4,042	5,478	98.4	1,073	91.9	512	45.3	203	711	64
Mansfield	4,561	2,268	2,293	2,884	97.1	661	84.2	322	38.5	150	458	86
Marion	5,215	2,571	2,644	3,295	96.8	769	88.2	408	45.9	172	507	64
Newark	4,755	2,379	2,376	2,872	97.7	778	88.1	377	44.4	187	472	69
Portsmouth	5,931	2,859	3,072	3,769	96.3	896	85.5	400	34.9	192	627	47
Springfield	10,820	5,323	5,497	6,886	97.0	1,627	90.5	812	45.3	347	972	176
Steubenville	5,195	2,629	2,566	3,458	95.0	695	83.0	359	40.1	141	488	54
Toledo	42,558	21,189	21,369	26,220	96.3	5,536	83.9	2,717	36.0	1,455	5,568	762
Warren	4,599	2,352	2,247	2,720	96.6	645	93.9	359	49.5	178	628	69
Youngstown	24,516	12,227	12,289	16,001	96.8	3,360	89.4	1,617	42.6	759	2,515	264
Zanesville	5,104	2,501	2,603	3,292	96.1	771	88.1	378	40.3	158	423	82
OKLAHOMA:												
Muskogee	6,887	3,295	3,592	3,972	96.2	960	89.3	684	62.1	426	544	301
Oklahoma City	16,679	8,167	8,512	9,669	92.8	2,308	85.7	1,519	49.5	926	1,830	427
Tulsa	12,798	6,296	6,502	7,755	95.2	1,756	87.4	1,139	52.6	603	1,397	148
OREGON:												
Portland	45,290	22,591	22,699	26,804	97.5	6,244	91.1	4,039	56.1	2,714	3,416	2,073
PENNSYLVANIA:												
Allentown	13,197	6,590	6,607	8,996	93.3	1,723	74.9	644	27.5	372	1,277	185
Altoona	11,919	5,896	6,023	7,725	97.4	1,696	89.0	873	43.8	462	1,018	145
Bethlehem	8,842	4,500	4,342	6,097	94.1	1,156	79.7	467	29.3	195	829	98
Chester	8,346	4,142	4,204	5,763	93.3	1,099	75.6	425	24.0	177	789	93
Easton	5,766	2,892	2,874	3,577	93.7	878	87.7	407	38.6	216	607	81
Erie	17,385	8,490	8,895	11,155	91.4	2,494	86.2	1,369	43.2	654	1,234	479
Harrisburg	13,008	6,447	6,561	7,995	96.0	2,134	93.9	1,061	45.3	571	1,022	225
Hazleton	7,224	3,609	3,615	5,049	95.6	969	72.9	368	26.9	175	580	83
Johnstown	13,991	7,026	6,965	9,526	97.2	1,887	81.5	784	32.4	329	1,329	136
Lancaster	9,064	4,569	4,495	5,856	97.1	1,289	80.5	611	33.7	329	838	141
McKeesport	9,350	4,594	4,756	6,303	91.7	1,282	78.0	538	31.8	287	780	160
New Castle	9,242	4,640	4,602	6,063	97.6	1,231	86.6	599	40.6	273	916	160
Norristown borough	5,036	2,494	2,542	3,457	96.2	649	71.2	290	29.7	131	458	51
Philadelphia	318,545	160,311	158,234	210,282	94.0	46,224	84.6	17,455	30.1	7,704	31,418	5,462
Pittsburgh	113,274	57,417	55,857	72,200	94.5	16,016	85.5	7,271	36.8	3,696	11,359	2,732
Reading	19,473	9,797	9,676	12,951	95.5	3,042	85.7	1,042	29.5	465	1,731	242
Scranton	28,911	14,304	14,607	19,234	93.1	4,123	80.0	1,652	29.9	728	2,840	334
Wilkes-Barre	15,927	8,026	7,901	10,282	95.9	2,370	85.6	1,086	38.5	555	1,435	199
Williamsport	6,196	3,040	3,156	3,823	95.6	979	87.2	490	38.3	256	540	108
York	8,553	4,281	4,272	5,592	96.7	1,246	82.0	570	32.9	258	770	117
RHODE ISLAND:												
Cranston	5,447	2,833	2,614	3,522	95.2	659	70.4	330	36.3	194	665	77
Newport	5,070	2,536	2,534	3,046	92.7	702	83.7	367	23.1	205	646	104
Pawtucket	11,608	5,754	5,854	7,662	96.3	1,144	52.5	541	23.2	312	1,779	170
Providence	43,337	21,571	21,766	28,554	95.7	4,824	65.0	2,359	31.8	1,414	5,510	676
Woonsocket	8,110	3,964	4,146	5,712	96.0	752	46.6	300	16.6	212	1,026	108

TABLE 125.—SCHOOL ATTENDANCE, BY SEX AND AGE PERIODS, FOR CITIES HAVING 25,000 INHABITANTS OR MORE: 1920—Continued.

CITY.	TOTAL.			7 TO 13 YEARS OF AGE.		14 AND 15 YEARS OF AGE.		16 AND 17 YEARS OF AGE.		18 to 20 years of age.	Under 7 years of age.	21 years of age and over.
	Both sexes.	Male.	Female.	Number.	Per cent.	Number.	Per cent.	Number.	Per cent.			
SOUTH CAROLINA:												
Charleston........	12,218	5,983	6,235	7,991	91.3	1,679	77.0	851	37.4	440	1,045	212
Columbia.........	6,753	3,141	3,612	4,284	92.8	980	81.9	680	52.1	374	317	118
SOUTH DAKOTA:												
Sioux Falls........	4,729	2,361	2,368	2,708	94.9	685	91.0	427	55.5	293	502	114
TENNESSEE:												
Chattanooga......	10,125	4,998	5,127	6,354	94.3	1,483	82.5	848	42.4	574	729	137
Knoxville.........	15,228	7,412	7,816	10,099	94.5	2,125	78.3	1,050	33.9	579	1,112	263
Memphis..........	25,619	12,045	13,574	16,447	92.2	3,788	78.0	2,131	39.4	1,042	1,778	433
Nashville.........	21,785	10,549	11,236	14,013	94.5	3,335	80.8	1,744	40.1	1,070	1,207	416
TEXAS:												
Austin............	7,836	3,781	4,055	4,306	93.9	1,188	89.7	913	68.1	715	279	435
Beaumont.........	7,703	3,701	4,002	5,135	95.2	1,174	82.4	621	44.1	302	405	66
Dallas............	25,556	12,457	13,099	16,215	93.3	3,988	83.0	2,466	46.2	1,423	902	562
El Paso...........	14,150	6,903	7,247	9,374	87.0	2,251	77.1	1,067	38.4	609	615	234
Fort Worth.......	16,089	7,745	8,344	10,393	88.6	2,490	79.6	1,495	41.6	806	488	417
Galveston.........	6,964	3,369	3,595	4,591	91.4	1,075	80.3	602	40.0	273	271	152
Houston..........	22,512	10,851	11,661	14,922	90.2	3,565	79.3	1,940	40.4	897	748	440
San Antonio......	26,506	13,120	13,386	17,904	83.7	4,152	73.4	2,070	36.1	1,100	773	507
Waco.............	7,892	3,813	4,079	4,996	92.2	1,245	84.3	761	51.8	502	199	189
Wichita Falls.....	5,142	2,588	2,554	3,508	87.5	808	79.7	427	37.1	189	154	56
UTAH:												
Ogden............	7,805	3,978	3,827	4,660	94.7	1,175	93.9	870	70.8	356	605	139
Salt Lake City....	26,888	13,412	13,476	15,685	95.7	3,929	92.6	2,552	63.9	1,528	2,346	848
VIRGINIA:												
Lynchburg........	5,604	2,673	2,931	3,748	92.5	806	74.1	445	36.7	277	240	88
Newport News....	5,142	2,451	2,691	3,445	91.7	735	75.9	387	33.5	226	300	49
Norfolk...........	18,382	8,815	9,567	11,919	93.2	2,542	77.7	1,415	38.4	758	1,472	276
Petersburg........	5,098	2,339	2,759	3,556	88.5	745	75.0	410	33.8	182	147	58
Portsmouth.......	10,039	4,795	5,244	6,564	95.7	1,428	80.2	743	38.9	379	798	127
Richmond.........	29,833	14,261	15,572	19,166	93.2	4,075	74.8	2,212	35.4	1,258	2,367	755
Roanoke..........	9,984	4,844	5,140	6,528	94.9	1,334	81.1	838	45.7	471	633	180
WASHINGTON:												
Bellingham........	5,060	2,453	2,607	2,969	95.8	775	90.5	495	57.8	304	335	182
Everett...........	5,264	2,646	2,618	3,223	95.5	870	90.0	491	51.6	238	328	114
Seattle...........	50,554	25,418	25,136	28,688	93.9	6,742	87.7	4,496	55.2	3,270	4,410	2,948
Spokane..........	21,013	10,348	10,665	12,229	98.0	2,983	92.3	2,040	61.3	1,431	1,463	867
Tacoma...........	16,625	8,128	8,497	10,247	93.8	2,478	86.5	1,396	48.8	833	1,181	490
WEST VIRGINIA:												
Charleston........	7,406	3,638	3,768	4,607	92.6	1,056	81.3	574	43.3	403	627	139
Clarksburg........	5,299	2,618	2,681	3,351	88.9	807	85.9	449	42.8	219	418	55
Huntington.......	9,594	4,743	4,851	6,276	92.9	1,401	80.5	725	37.7	409	633	150
Wheeling..........	10,005	4,921	5,084	6,573	93.6	1,461	79.9	709	36.0	340	766	156
WISCONSIN:												
Green Bay........	6,689	3,295	3,394	3,888	90.1	1,069	87.9	682	56.5	271	639	140
Kenosha..........	7,848	3,873	3,975	4,803	93.6	991	85.0	487	43.6	235	1,257	75
La Crosse.........	6,510	3,109	3,401	3,492	95.1	904	91.4	660	60.4	399	815	240
Madison..........	8,670	4,315	4,355	4,142	97.6	1,068	95.4	853	71.1	719	1,039	849
Milwaukee........	92,161	46,018	46,143	54,250	96.9	12,327	87.7	7,253	50.8	3,419	12,650	2,262
Oshkosh..........	7,159	3,546	3,613	4,137	95.7	982	83.4	611	53.2	335	925	169
Racine............	10,870	5,411	5,459	6,308	94.5	1,542	91.0	875	49.4	292	1,681	172
Sheboygan........	7,082	3,631	3,451	4,055	96.4	850	87.5	588	53.0	229	1,181	179
Superior..........	9,114	4,422	4,692	5,220	93.9	1,251	92.3	867	62.6	396	1,172	208

TABLE 126.—SCHOOL ATTENDANCE OF THE URBAN AND RURAL POPULATION 7 TO 20 YEARS OF AGE, BY DIVISIONS AND STATES: 1920 AND 1910.

DIVISION AND STATE.	PERSONS 7 TO 20 YEARS OF AGE ATTENDING SCHOOL.							
	Urban communities.				Rural communities.			
	1920		1910		1920		1910	
	Number.	Per cent.	Number.	Per cent.	Number.	Per cent.	Number.	Per cent.
United States	8,823,040	67.9	6,541,837	61.6	10,623,811	68.3	9,698,954	64.3
GEOGRAPHIC DIVISIONS:								
New England	957,469	68.7	795,567	64.4	266,154	71.1	255,918	68.2
Middle Atlantic	2,713,760	67.0	2,142,935	61.0	1,032,800	70.0	988,255	67.3
East North Central	2,066,136	68.3	1,484,196	61.4	1,662,570	71.6	1,713,096	69.8
West North Central	773,309	69.8	614,719	63.5	1,647,620	72.1	1,656,729	70.5
South Atlantic	716,011	64.9	462,008	56.5	2,102,395	65.3	1,764,893	58.9
East South Central	342,913	66.0	242,574	58.2	1,515,746	65.9	1,346,977	59.9
West South Central	521,410	65.8	316,592	59.5	1,576,186	63.9	1,356,888	59.4
Mountain	219,292	74.1	156,027	68.1	437,346	72.8	304,166	66.8
Pacific	517,740	72.7	327,279	65.3	382,994	74.4	312,032	68.6
NEW ENGLAND:								
Maine	49,882	70.3	40,800	64.0	84,417	71.6	81,418	69.1
New Hampshire	47,530	70.0	40,638	62.6	25,533	69.7	27,410	70.0
Vermont	18,739	70.9	16,832	68.4	43,805	72.0	45,232	71.2
Massachusetts	597,753	69.6	500,578	65.5	35,371	74.1	39,037	69.5
Rhode Island	92,983	63.6	80,699	60.2	2,516	69.7	2,613	64.9
Connecticut	150,582	67.6	116,020	63.2	74,512	69.1	60,208	63.9
MIDDLE ATLANTIC:								
New York	1,355,633	66.5	1,134,811	62.1	301,272	71.2	317,368	68.8
New Jersey	407,766	66.4	302,135	60.7	118,213	68.9	103,361	64.4
Pennsylvania	950,361	67.9	705,989	59.6	613,315	69.7	567,526	67.0
EAST NORTH CENTRAL:								
Ohio	581,025	69.8	400,367	61.6	408,392	73.7	409,769	71.4
Indiana	231,211	66.2	172,045	61.7	284,026	71.8	310,552	69.8
Illinois	693,177	66.9	529,882	60.2	415,039	71.0	425,987	68.4
Michigan	340,523	67.5	208,785	62.8	285,642	73.4	291,520	71.6
Wisconsin	220,200	72.1	173,117	63.0	269,471	67.4	275,268	67.8
WEST NORTH CENTRAL:								
Minnesota	171,948	70.3	139,267	65.2	279,148	70.0	278,229	71.4
Iowa	146,091	71.9	111,401	65.3	307,987	72.6	322,716	70.5
Missouri	240,826	66.1	205,898	59.5	383,569	71.4	402,328	69.8
North Dakota	17,298	75.3	10,790	67.1	128,991	73.7	99,669	65.5
South Dakota	18,913	75.3	12,992	68.9	113,030	72.4	102,600	67.9
Nebraska	68,771	71.6	51,733	66.4	188,190	71.8	190,892	70.8
Kansas	109,462	72.0	82,638	66.0	246,705	74.5	260,295	73.6
SOUTH ATLANTIC:								
Delaware	17,923	65.8	14,076	58.8	19,836	72.1	19,286	64.1
Maryland	133,997	63.7	91,326	53.7	112,059	65.6	122,296	64.1
District of Columbia	58,005	64.5	47,662	64.4	(1)		(1)	
Virginia	110,409	63.8	72,237	56.5	349,628	65.1	309,295	59.7
West Virginia	65,212	68.2	36,404	61.4	231,832	67.8	208,592	68.1
North Carolina	90,682	64.7	52,352	56.2	485,557	69.4	402,757	64.1
South Carolina	55,017	67.1	35,660	54.6	338,060	68.4	241,550	53.3
Georgia	124,540	63.5	80,872	55.1	445,846	58.9	371,362	52.7
Florida	60,226	67.2	31,419	54.4	119,577	62.6	89,755	53.9
EAST SOUTH CENTRAL:								
Kentucky	101,640	66.6	86,417	60.0	378,886	67.1	351,446	63.4
Tennessee	105,537	66.2	66,873	57.8	383,006	67.8	350,989	62.0
Alabama	91,955	65.7	54,921	54.9	407,933	64.3	316,929	53.6
Mississippi	43,781	65.1	34,363	60.5	345,921	64.7	327,613	61.0
WEST SOUTH CENTRAL:								
Arkansas	55,093	70.7	34,021	63.2	320,022	65.1	270,888	59.8
Louisiana	106,145	62.3	74,669	54.0	221,401	54.8	160,595	41.0
Oklahoma	101,575	71.0	53,461	64.8	342,672	67.9	307,915	70.5
Texas	258,597	64.6	154,441	60.0	692,091	64.9	617,490	61.5
MOUNTAIN:								
Montana	29,673	75.0	20,235	68.2	72,948	75.7	36,741	64.5
Idaho	24,162	77.3	11,383	68.7	70,865	77.8	52,230	71.9
Wyoming	8,777	69.8	6,238	64.8	25,610	73.4	15,237	65.1
Colorado	74,124	72.7	64,878	68.3	101,621	73.6	73,589	70.0
New Mexico	13,268	72.3	8,660	68.6	61,851	67.7	52,044	61.8
Arizona	19,251	67.6	8,950	59.8	35,136	57.6	19,803	53.1
Utah	47,696	78.4	33,978	70.7	60,212	80.1	46,747	74.0
Nevada	2,341	77.5	1,705	67.7	9,103	72.4	7,775	62.8
PACIFIC:								
Washington	117,188	72.7	86,642	66.0	120,824	75.4	99,153	70.0
Oregon	63,720	75.1	41,513	64.5	77,893	75.7	70,084	70.5
California	336,832	72.2	199,124	65.1	184,277	73.3	142,795	66.8

[1] No rural population, as Washington city is coextensive with the District of Columbia.

TABLE 127.—SCHOOL ATTENDANCE OF THE URBAN AND RURAL POPULATION 7 TO 13 YEARS OF AGE, BY DIVISIONS AND STATES: 1920 AND 1910.

DIVISION AND STATE.	PERSONS 7 TO 13 YEARS OF AGE ATTENDING SCHOOL.							
	Urban communities.				Rural communities.			
	1920		1910		1920		1910	
	Number.	Per cent.	Number.	Per cent.	Number.	Per cent.	Number.	Per cent.
United States	6,369,136	94.4	4,627,889	91.8	7,499,874	87.6	6,518,284	82.4
GEOGRAPHIC DIVISIONS:								
New England	706,766	95.7	572,266	95.5	191,839	93.9	179,281	94.2
Middle Atlantic	2,035,434	94.4	1,573,356	93.3	770,552	94.0	696,075	92.3
East North Central	1,498,779	95.3	1,061,080	93.5	1,194,855	94.8	1,178,638	93.4
West North Central	527,554	94.9	408,493	92.6	1,152,128	93.5	1,104,151	91.1
South Atlantic	511,057	93.1	324,424	83.4	1,485,951	83.2	1,184,569	73.7
East South Central	240,895	92.4	166,098	84.8	1,043,026	81.8	877,322	73.4
West South Central	358,054	90.2	214,344	82.7	1,089,599	80.2	891,861	73.0
Mountain	146,465	94.5	101,381	91.1	306,431	90.6	201,589	84.3
Pacific	344,132	94.6	206,447	92.3	265,493	93.5	204,798	90.2
NEW ENGLAND:								
Maine	34,331	95.4	28,116	92.2	59,284	93.6	55,474	92.3
New Hampshire	33,402	94.5	29,231	94.8	18,142	91.6	19,083	95.1
Vermont	12,833	95.5	11,540	96.9	30,503	93.2	31,160	95.3
Massachusetts	439,441	96.1	358,349	96.0	25,311	96.4	27,464	95.8
Rhode Island	73,044	95.6	59,596	93.9	1,828	95.5	1,840	92.9
Connecticut	113,715	94.9	85,434	96.0	56,771	94.3	44,260	94.7
MIDDLE ATLANTIC:								
New York	1,012,643	94.1	819,053	94.1	214,275	92.9	213,194	92.4
New Jersey	315,302	94.9	225,565	92.7	89,626	95.0	74,802	92.2
Pennsylvania	707,489	94.6	528,738	92.4	466,651	94.3	408,079	92.2
EAST NORTH CENTRAL:								
Ohio	415,238	96.3	284,708	94.3	288,322	95.6	276,023	93.9
Indiana	168,821	94.8	122,683	93.1	200,892	95.0	212,858	93.5
Illinois	518,670	94.6	385,043	92.8	296,410	94.9	293,364	92.1
Michigan	246,405	95.3	145,545	93.7	207,247	94.5	199,460	94.4
Wisconsin	149,645	96.0	123,101	94.0	201,984	93.4	196,933	93.4
WEST NORTH CENTRAL:								
Minnesota	117,099	94.5	90,452	93.7	197,806	93.5	189,140	92.6
Iowa	96,250	95.5	74,144	93.0	213,494	94.8	217,499	93.0
Missouri	170,851	94.6	143,327	91.6	269,543	92.6	265,328	89.3
North Dakota	11,310	94.9	6,560	89.7	91,566	91.8	68,780	85.8
South Dakota	11,942	94.9	7,907	91.9	79,380	93.3	68,572	87.2
Nebraska	46,667	95.2	33,108	93.7	132,243	93.4	127,281	92.7
Kansas	73,435	95.4	52,995	91.3	168,096	94.2	167,551	92.6
SOUTH ATLANTIC:								
Delaware	13,483	96.0	10,003	89.4	13,853	94.5	12,974	85.2
Maryland	100,346	95.7	69,152	85.7	81,801	89.0	88,071	86.9
District of Columbia	38,962	93.5	31,101	90.4	(1)		(1)	
Virginia	78,594	92.7	49,679	82.2	245,698	82.5	204,558	72.9
West Virginia	45,786	93.6	25,509	91.0	167,267	87.9	141,416	87.2
North Carolina	64,408	91.9	35,990	80.5	336,438	86.1	255,618	76.0
South Carolina	38,252	92.3	24,308	77.9	236,177	86.3	160,227	66.2
Georgia	88,642	91.2	56,770	80.5	321,112	76.3	261,419	68.6
Florida	42,584	92.7	21,912	78.5	83,605	79.1	60,286	68.0
EAST SOUTH CENTRAL:								
Kentucky	72,541	94.4	60,341	90.6	270,433	87.1	232,727	79.1
Tennessee	73,423	93.6	44,535	84.2	259,695	83.2	224,529	76.0
Alabama	64,726	90.3	37,656	77.5	279,973	78.4	205,619	64.6
Mississippi	30,205	89.2	23,566	84.8	232,925	79.1	214,447	74.5
WEST SOUTH CENTRAL:								
Arkansas	37,222	93.7	22,200	87.0	219,041	80.3	173,117	72.8
Louisiana	76,564	89.4	53,685	79.6	157,685	76.8	111,509	62.2
Oklahoma	68,235	93.9	35,153	87.8	236,430	83.7	200,375	85.8
Texas	176,033	88.4	103,240	81.7	476,443	82.1	406,860	75.7
MOUNTAIN:								
Montana	19,807	94.8	13,118	90.4	51,706	92.1	24,801	85.5
Idaho	15,741	95.4	6,921	89.0	49,361	95.5	33,685	87.1
Wyoming	6,128	92.8	4,054	91.1	18,426	92.8	10,352	87.9
Colorado	49,614	95.5	41,798	92.6	71,739	92.9	49,113	89.5
New Mexico	9,152	92.9	5,758	88.7	43,677	86.4	33,938	75.6
Arizona	13,351	88.6	6,211	82.2	24,828	74.3	13,272	67.7
Utah	31,188	95.8	22,485	92.8	40,423	95.3	31,159	90.8
Nevada	1,484	93.3	1,036	90.0	6,271	89.8	5,269	87.5
PACIFIC:								
Washington	78,470	95.0	54,773	91.7	84,280	94.5	65,572	90.5
Oregon	41,888	96.1	25,311	90.9	52,424	93.7	44,830	90.0
California	223,774	94.3	126,363	92.8	128,789	92.7	94,396	90.0

[1] No rural population, as Washington city is coextensive with the District of Columbia.

TABLE 128.—NUMBER AND PER CENT ILLITERATE IN POPULATION 10 YEARS OF AGE AND OVER, BY SEX, FOR POPULATION CLASSES, FOR THE UNITED STATES: 1870–1920.

[Figures are given under each class for all census years for which data are available.]

CENSUS YEAR AND CLASS OF POPULATION	POPULATION 10 YEARS OF AGE AND OVER			MALES 10 YEARS OF AGE AND OVER			FEMALES 10 YEARS OF AGE AND OVER		
	Total number.	Illiterate Number.	Per cent.	Total number.	Illiterate Number.	Per cent.	Total number.	Illiterate Number.	Per cent.
1920									
All classes	82,739,315	4,931,905	6.0	42,289,969	2,540,209	6.0	40,449,346	2,391,696	5.9
White	74,359,749	3,006,312	4.0	38,070,736	1,551,529	4.1	36,289,013	1,454,783	4.0
Colored [1]	8,379,566	1,925,593	23.0	4,219,233	988,680	23.4	4,160,333	936,913	22.5
Negro	8,053,225	1,842,161	22.9	4,009,462	942,368	23.5	4,043,763	899,793	22.3
Native white	60,861,863	1,242,572	2.0	30,651,045	684,707	2.2	30,210,818	557,865	1.8
Native parentage	44,077,564	1,109,875	2.5	22,361,495	614,612	2.7	21,716,069	495,263	2.3
Foreign or mixed par	16,784,299	132,697	0.8	8,289,550	70,095	0.8	8,494,749	62,602	0.7
Foreign parentage	11,462,926	98,076	0.9	5,679,128	50,442	0.9	5,783,798	47,634	0.8
Mixed parentage	5,321,373	34,621	0.7	2,610,422	19,653	0.8	2,710,951	14,968	0.6
Foreign-born white	13,497,886	1,763,740	13.1	7,419,691	866,822	11.7	6,078,195	896,918	14.8
1910									
All classes	71,580,270	5,516,163	7.7	37,027,558	2,814,950	7.6	34,552,712	2,701,213	7.8
White	63,933,870	3,184,633	5.0	33,164,229	1,662,505	5.0	30,769,641	1,522,128	4.9
Colored [1]	7,646,400	2,331,530	30.5	3,863,329	1,152,445	29.8	3,783,071	1,179,085	31.2
Negro	7,317,922	2,227,731	30.4	3,637,386	1,096,000	30.1	3,680,536	1,131,731	30.7
Native white	50,989,341	1,534,272	3.0	25,843,033	796,055	3.1	25,146,308	738,217	2.9
Native parentage	37,081,278	1,378,884	3.7	18,933,751	715,926	3.8	18,147,527	662,958	3.7
Foreign or mixed par	13,908,063	155,388	1.1	6,909,282	80,129	1.2	6,998,781	75,259	1.1
Foreign parentage	9,602,968	117,336	1.2	4,788,825	59,246	1.2	4,814,143	58,090	1.2
Mixed parentage	4,305,095	38,052	0.9	2,120,457	20,883	1.0	2,184,638	17,169	0.8
Foreign-born white	12,944,529	1,650,361	12.7	7,321,196	866,450	11.8	5,623,333	783,911	13.9
1900									
All classes	57,949,824	6,180,069	10.7	29,703,440	3,011,224	10.1	28,246,384	3,168,845	11.2
White	51,250,918	3,200,746	6.2	26,327,931	1,567,153	6.0	24,922,987	1,633,593	6.6
Colored [1]	6,698,906	2,979,323	44.5	3,375,509	1,444,071	42.8	3,323,397	1,535,252	46.2
Negro	6,415,581	2,853,194	44.5	3,181,650	1,371,432	43.1	3,233,931	1,481,762	45.8
Native white	41,236,662	1,913,611	4.6	20,912,940	955,517	4.6	20,323,722	958,094	4.7
Native parentage	30,310,261	1,734,764	5.7	15,452,855	862,175	5.6	14,857,406	872,589	5.9
Foreign or mixed par	10,926,401	178,847	1.6	5,460,085	93,342	1.7	5,466,316	85,505	1.6
Foreign-born white	10,014,256	1,287,135	12.9	5,414,991	611,636	11.3	4,599,265	675,499	14.7
1890 [2]									
All classes	47,413,559	6,324,702	13.3	24,352,659	3,008,222	12.4	23,060,900	3,316,480	14.4
White	41,931,074	3,212,574	7.7	21,578,245	1,517,722	7.0	20,352,829	1,694,852	8.3
Colored [1]	5,482,485	3,112,128	56.8	2,774,414	1,490,500	53.7	2,708,071	1,621,628	59.9
Negro	5,328,972	3,042,668	57.1	2,646,171	1,438,923	54.4	2,682,801	1,603,745	59.8
Native white	33,144,187	2,065,003	6.2	16,796,497	978,408	5.8	16,347,690	1,036,595	6.6
Native parentage	25,375,766	1,890,723	7.5	12,901,102	888,415	6.9	12,474,664	1,002,308	8.0
Foreign or mixed par	7,768,421	174,280	2.2	3,895,395	89,993	2.3	3,873,026	84,287	2.2
Foreign-born white	8,786,887	1,147,571	13.1	4,781,748	539,314	11.3	4,005,139	608,257	15.2
1880									
All classes	36,761,607	6,239,958	17.0	18,735,980	2,966,421	15.8	18,025,627	3,273,537	18.2
White	32,160,400	3,019,080	9.4	16,425,250	1,410,805	8.6	15,735,150	1,608,275	10.2
Colored [1]	4,601,207	3,220,878	70.0	2,310,730	1,555,616	67.3	2,290,477	1,665,262	72.7
Native white	25,785,789	2,255,460	8.7						
Foreign-born white	6,374,611	763,620	12.0						
1870									
All classes	28,228,945	5,658,144	20.0	14,258,866	2,603,888	18.3	13,970,079	3,054,256	21.9
White	24,717,870	2,851,911	11.5	12,526,487	1,250,970	10.0	12,191,383	1,600,941	13.1
Colored [1]	3,511,075	2,806,233	79.9	1,732,379	1,352,918	78.1	1,778,696	1,453,315	81.7
Negro	3,428,757	2,789,689	81.4	1,664,656	1,342,347	80.6	1,764,101	1,447,342	82.0

[1] Persons of Negro descent, Indians, Chinese, Japanese, and "all other."
[2] Exclusive of persons in Indian Territory and on Indian reservations, areas specially enumerated in 1890, but for which illiteracy statistics are not available.

TABLE 129.—NUMBER AND PER CENT ILLITERATE IN POPULATION 10 YEARS OF
UNITED

[Per cent not shown

CLASS OF POPULATION AND SEX.	ILLITERATE POPULATION.							
	10 years of age and over: 1920 [1]		10 to 14 years of age.		15 to 19 years of age.		20 to 24 years of age.	
	Number.	Per cent.	Number.	Per cent.	Number.	Per cent.	Number.	Per cent.
All classes	4,931,905	6.0	246,360	2.3	283,316	3.0	392,853	4.2
Male	2,540,209	6.0	141,576	2.6	171,489	3.7	203,773	4.5
Female	2,391,696	5.9	104,784	2.0	111,827	2.4	189,080	4.0
White	3,006,312	4.0	100,643	1.1	125,495	1.5	207,649	2.5
Male	1,551,529	4.1	57,150	1.2	74,455	1.8	103,958	2.6
Female	1,454,783	4.0	43,493	0.9	51,040	1.2	103,691	2.5
Negro	1,842,161	22.9	140,892	11.4	152,998	14.1	179,124	17.0
Male	942,368	23.5	81,944	13.3	94,455	18.4	96,895	19.9
Female	899,793	22.3	58,948	9.5	58,543	10.3	82,229	14.5
Indian	61,730	34.9	4,751	15.7	4,373	17.2	4,211	21.0
Male	30,010	32.8	2,427	15.9	2,247	17.7	2,054	19.7
Female	31,720	37.2	2,324	15.5	2,126	16.7	2,157	22.5
Chinese	11,262	20.0	40	2.0	145	5.3	545	11.2
Male	10,064	19.7	28	2.3	132	6.1	427	10.4
Female	1,198	23.1	12	1.5	13	2.2	118	16.3
Japanese	9,276	11.0	29	1.1	292	6.7	1,226	12.7
Male	5,145	8.7	22	1.6	189	6.1	360	7.9
Female	4,131	16.2	7	0.6	103	8.2	866	17.0
All other	1,164	13.0	5	3.2	13	1.9	98	4.2
Male	1,093	13.0	5		11	1.9	79	3.5
Female	71	12.5			2		19	16.8
Native white	1,242,572	2.0	85,856	0.9	97,013	1.2	98,938	1.4
Male	684,707	2.2	49,650	1.1	60,731	1.6	57,040	1.6
Female	557,865	1.8	36,206	0.8	36,282	0.9	41,898	1.1
Native parentage	1,109,875	2.5	71,845	1.1	83,303	1.5	86,669	1.7
Male	614,612	2.7	42,349	1.3	53,406	1.9	50,891	2.0
Female	495,263	2.3	29,496	0.9	29,897	1.1	35,778	1.4
Foreign parentage	98,076	0.9	10,032	0.6	9,934	0.7	9,207	0.7
Male	50,442	0.9	5,181	0.6	5,132	0.7	4,396	0.7
Female	47,634	0.8	4,851	0.6	4,802	0.7	4,811	0.7
Mixed parentage	34,621	0.7	3,979	0.5	3,776	0.5	3,062	0.4
Male	19,653	0.8	2,120	0.5	2,193	0.6	1,753	0.5
Female	14,968	0.6	1,859	0.5	1,583	0.4	1,309	0.4
Foreign-born white	1,763,740	13.1	14,787	4.5	28,482	5.4	108,711	11.7
Male	866,822	11.7	7,500	4.5	13,724	5.3	46,918	10.3
Female	896,918	14.8	7,287	4.4	14,758	5.5	61,793	13.2

[1] Includes persons of unknown age.

AGE AND OVER, BY AGE PERIODS, FOR POPULATION CLASSES, BY SEX, FOR THE STATES: 1920.

where base is less than 100.]

CLASS OF POPULATION AND SEX.	ILLITERATE POPULATION.									
	25 to 34 years of age.		35 to 44 years of age.		45 to 54 years of age.		55 to 64 years of age.		65 years of age and over	
	Number.	Per cent.	Number.	Per cent.	Number.	Per cent.	Number.	Per cent.	Number.	Per cent.
All classes	961,200	5.6	988,961	7.0	857,776	8.2	594,573	9.1	591,385	12.0
Male	486,217	5.6	509,107	6.9	453,950	8.0	292,511	8.4	273,000	11.0
Female	474,983	5.6	479,854	7.1	403,826	8.3	302,062	9.8	318,385	13.0
White	660,706	4.3	662,629	5.2	518,918	5.5	370,421	6.1	352,525	7.7
Male	336,106	4.3	355,103	5.3	279,937	5.5	181,988	5.7	158,298	6.9
Female	324,600	4.3	307,526	5.1	238,981	5.4	188,433	6.6	194,227	8.5
Negro	287,063	17.9	310,538	23.3	323,924	34.1	212,682	49.4	227,310	68.3
Male	143,515	19.0	144,961	22.0	164,954	30.1	103,407	42.9	108,473	62.4
Female	143,548	16.9	165,577	24.6	158,970	39.5	109,275	57.9	118,837	74.8
Indian	8,769	29.2	10,212	40.3	10,644	54.5	8,328	66.5	10,043	76.4
Male	4,078	26.3	4,803	36.2	5,297	49.3	4,131	61.4	4,792	73.6
Female	4,691	32.4	5,409	44.9	5,347	60.9	4,197	72.4	5,251	79.2
Chinese	1,543	15.5	2,106	19.7	2,595	22.4	2,789	27.6	1,432	35.2
Male	1,174	13.6	1,781	18.4	2,400	21.6	2,680	27.1	1,380	34.8
Female	369	27.8	325	33.8	195	40.6	109	52.9	52	
Japanese	2,779	10.5	3,082	10.9	1,487	13.9	299	17.6	38	18.9
Male	1,029	6.7	2,078	9.0	1,156	12.4	254	16.5	27	15.6
Female	1,750	15.8	1,004	19.6	331	23.9	45	27.1	11	
All other	340	11.0	394	23.1	208	30.3	54	37.8	37	
Male	315	10.7	381	23.6	206	31.3	51	37.5	30	
Female	25	15.3	13		2		3		7	
Native white	190,913	1.5	201,739	2.1	202,196	2.9	177,515	4.0	185,133	5.7
Male	108,587	1.8	112,982	2.3	113,275	3.1	92,008	4.0	88,662	5.5
Female	82,326	1.3	88,757	1.9	88,921	2.6	85,507	4.0	96,471	5.9
Native parentage	168,484	1.9	182,269	2.6	183,398	3.7	160,362	4.9	170,603	6.2
Male	97,189	2.2	102,180	2.9	102,506	3.9	82,986	4.9	81,498	6.0
Female	71,295	1.6	80,089	2.4	80,892	3.5	77,376	5.0	89,105	6.5
Foreign parentage	17,124	0.7	14,317	0.8	13,763	0.9	12,965	1.4	10,472	2.9
Male	8,407	0.7	7,778	0.9	7,754	1.0	6,680	1.4	4,980	2.8
Female	8,717	0.7	6,539	0.7	6,009	0.8	6,285	1.3	5,492	3.0
Mixed parentage	5,305	0.5	5,153	0.6	5,035	0.9	4,188	1.5	4,058	2.7
Male	2,991	0.5	3,024	0.7	3,015	1.1	2,342	1.7	2,184	2.9
Female	2,314	0.4	2,129	0.5	2,020	0.7	1,846	1.4	1,874	2.4
Foreign-born white	469,793	15.1	460,890	14.6	316,722	12.8	192,906	11.9	167,392	12.6
Male	227,519	13.1	242,121	13.4	166,662	11.9	89,980	10.0	69,636	10.2
Female	242,274	17.7	218,769	16.2	150,060	14.0	102,926	14.1	97,756	15.1

TABLE **130.**—NUMBER AND PER CENT ILLITERATE IN POPULATION 10 YEARS OF UNITED STATES:

CLASS OF POPULATION AND AGE PERIOD.	1920						1910					
	Both sexes.		Male.		Female.		Both sexes.		Male.		Female.	
	Number.	Per cent.	Number.	Per cent.	Number.	Per cent.	Number.	Per cent.	Number.	Per cent.	Number.	Per cent.
All classes....	**4,931,905**	**6.0**	**2,540,209**	**6.0**	**2,391,696**	**5.9**	**5,516,163**	**7.7**	**2,814,950**	**7.6**	**2,701,213**	**7.8**
10–14 yrs..	246,360	2.3	141,576	2.6	104,784	2.0	370,136	4.1	211,763	4.6	158,373	3.5
15–19 yrs..	283,316	3.0	171,489	3.7	111,827	2.4	448,414	4.9	262,770	5.8	185,644	4.1
20–24 yrs..	392,853	4.2	203,773	4.5	189,080	4.0	622,073	6.9	343,450	7.5	278,623	6.2
25–34 yrs..	961,200	5.6	486,217	5.6	474,983	5.6	1,102,384	7.3	597,657	7.6	504,727	7.0
35–44 yrs..	988,961	7.0	509,107	6.9	479,854	7.1	940,510	8.1	466,287	7.6	474,223	8.6
45–54 yrs..	857,776	8.2	453,950	8.0	403,826	8.3	829,153	9.9	389,608	8.7	439,545	11.3
55–64 yrs..	594,573	9.1	292,511	8.4	302,062	9.8	607,754	12.0	283,076	10.6	324,678	13.6
65 yrs.and over....	591,385	12.0	273,000	11.0	318,385	13.0	573,799	14.5	248,875	12.5	324,924	16.5
Unknown	15,481	10.4	8,586	9.2	6,895	12.4	21,940	13.0	11,464	10.0	10,476	19.2
White........	**3,006,312**	**4.0**	**1,551,529**	**4.1**	**1,454,783**	**4.0**	**3,184,633**	**5.0**	**1,662,505**	**5.0**	**1,522,128**	**4.9**
10–14 yrs..	100,643	1.1	57,150	1.2	43,493	0.9	144,675	1.8	82,569	2.1	62,106	1.6
15–19 yrs..	125,495	1.5	74,455	1.8	51,040	1.2	226,432	2.8	132,616	3.3	93,816	2.4
20–24 yrs..	207,649	2.5	103,958	2.6	103,691	2.5	367,669	4.6	211,861	5.2	155,808	4.0
25–34 yrs..	660,706	4.3	336,106	4.3	324,600	4.3	702,962	5.2	493,285	5.7	299,677	4.7
35–44 yrs..	662,629	5.2	355,103	5.3	307,526	5.1	569,403	5.4	303,719	5.5	265,684	5.4
45–54 yrs..	518,918	5.5	279,937	5.5	238,981	5.4	477,080	6.3	232,165	5.7	244,915	6.9
55–64 yrs..	370,421	6.1	181,988	5.7	188,433	6.6	344,877	7.4	155,476	6.4	189,401	8.6
65 yrs.and over....	352,525	7.7	158,298	6.9	194,227	8.5	342,420	9.4	135,102	7.4	207,318	11.4
Unknown	7,326	5.9	4,534	5.8	2,792	6.2	9,115	6.8	5,712	6.1	3,403	8.5
Negro........	**1,842,161**	**22.9**	**942,368**	**23.5**	**899,793**	**22.3**	**2,227,731**	**30.4**	**1,096,000**	**30.1**	**1,131,731**	**30.7**
10–14 yrs..	140,892	11.4	81,944	13.3	58,948	9.5	218,555	18.9	125,616	21.7	92,939	16.1
15–19 yrs..	152,998	14.1	94,455	18.4	58,543	10.3	214,860	20.3	126,459	24.9	88,401	16.0
20–24 yrs..	179,124	17.0	96,895	19.9	82,229	14.5	245,860	23.9	126,970	26.3	118,890	21.7
25–34 yrs..	287,063	17.9	143,515	19.0	143,548	16.9	380,742	24.6	183,993	24.4	196,749	24.7
35–44 yrs..	310,538	23.3	144,961	22.0	165,577	24.6	351,858	32.3	152,132	27.7	199,726	37.1
45–54 yrs..	323,924	34.1	164,954	30.1	158,970	39.5	334,930	47.0	147,542	38.9	187,388	56.3
55–64 yrs..	212,682	49.4	103,407	42.9	109,275	57.9	249,584	63.0	120,046	55.5	129,538	72.0
65 yrs.and over....	227,310	68.3	108,473	62.4	118,837	74.8	219,255	74.5	107,877	70.7	111,378	78.6
Unknown	7,630	32.5	3,764	27.9	3,866	38.7	12,087	38.9	5,365	31.4	6,722	48.1
Ind., Chi., Jap., and all other....	**83,432**	**25.6**	**46,312**	**22.1**	**37,120**	**31.8**	**103,799**	**31.6**	**56,445**	**25.0**	**47,354**	**46.2**
10–14 yrs..	4,825	13.8	2,482	13.9	2,343	13.8	6,906	20.6	3,578	20.4	3,328	20.9
15–19 yrs..	4,823	14.5	2,579	13.9	2,244	15.3	7,122	20.5	3,695	18.3	3,427	23.5
20–24 yrs..	6,080	16.5	2,920	13.7	3,160	20.3	8,544	21.5	4,619	17.0	3,925	31.2
25–34yrs..	13,431	19.3	6,596	15.5	6,835	25.2	18,680	23.8	10,379	18.0	8,301	40.1
35–44 yrs..	15,794	24.0	9,043	19.0	6,751	37.1	19,249	33.9	10,436	24.8	8,813	60.0
45–54 yrs..	14,934	35.1	9,059	28.5	5,875	55.0	17,143	41.2	9,901	31.0	7,242	74.4
55–64 yrs..	11,470	46.9	7,116	38.9	4,354	70.5	13,293	54.4	7,554	42.9	5,739	83.7
65 yrs.and over....	11,550	66.1	6,229	58.1	5,321	78.7	12,124	78.7	5,896	69.6	6,228	90.0
Unknown	525	34.2	288	27.7	237	48.1	738	19.5	387	11.9	351	65.5

AGE AND OVER, BY AGE PERIODS, FOR POPULATION CLASSES, BY SEX, FOR THE 1920 AND 1910.

CLASS OF POPULATION AND AGE PERIOD.	1920						1910					
	Both sexes.		Male.		Female.		Both sexes.		Male.		Female.	
	Number.	Per cent.	Number.	Per cent.	Number.	Per cent.	Number.	Per cent.	Number.	Per cent.	Number.	Per cent.
Native white.	1,242,572	2.0	684,707	2.2	557,865	1.8	1,534,272	3.0	796,055	3.1	738,217	2.9
10-14 yrs..	85,856	0.9	49,650	1.1	36,206	0.8	131,991	1.7	76,359	2.0	55,632	1.5
15-19 yrs..	97,013	1.2	60,731	1.6	36,282	0.9	140,323	1.9	85,510	2.3	54,813	1.5
20-24 yrs..	98,938	1.4	57,040	1.6	41,898	1.1	148,541	2.3	84,586	2.6	63,955	1.9
25-34 yrs..	190,913	1.5	108,587	1.8	82,326	1.3	247,774	2.4	136,583	2.6	111,191	2.2
35-44 yrs..	201,739	2.1	112,982	2.3	88,757	1.9	235,489	3.0	120,488	3.0	115,001	3.0
45-54 yrs..	202,196	2.9	113,275	3.1	88,921	2.6	248,900	4.5	122,110	4.2	126,790	4.8
55-64 yrs..	177,515	4.0	92,008	4.0	85,507	4.0	197,955	6.0	95,273	5.5	102,682	6.5
65 yrs.and over....	185,133	5.7	88,662	5.5	96,471	5.9	179,219	7.3	73,035	6.0	106,184	8.6
Unknown	3,269	3.2	1,772	2.7	1,497	3.9	4,080	3.8	2,111	2.8	1,969	5.9
Native par.	1,109,875	2.5	614,612	2.7	495,263	2.3	1,378,884	3.7	715,926	3.8	662,958	3.7
10-14 yrs..	71,845	1.1	42,349	1.3	29,496	0.9	117,973	2.2	69,087	2.6	48,886	1.9
15-19 yrs..	83,303	1.5	53,406	1.9	29,897	1.1	121,878	2.4	75,394	3.0	46,484	1.8
20-24 yrs..	86,669	1.7	50,891	2.0	35,778	1.4	130,991	2.8	75,193	3.2	55,798	2.4
25-34 yrs..	168,484	1.9	97,189	2.2	71,295	1.6	220,797	3.0	121,983	3.2	98,814	2.7
35-44 yrs..	182,269	2.6	102,180	2.9	80,089	2.4	210,694	3.8	107,355	3.8	103,339	3.9
45-54yrs..	183,398	3.7	102,506	3.9	80,892	3.5	224,421	5.6	109,758	5.2	114,663	6.0
55-64 yrs..	160,362	4.9	82,986	4.9	77,376	5.0	181,363	6.7	87,500	6.1	93,863	7.3
65 yrs.and over....	170,603	6.2	81,498	6.0	89,105	6.5	167,099	7.6	67,752	6.2	99,347	8.9
Unknown	2,942	3.2	1,607	2.7	1,335	4.0	3,668	3.8	1,904	2.8	1,764	6.1
For. or mix. par.....	132,697	0.8	70,095	0.8	62,602	0.7	155,388	1.1	80,129	1.2	75,259	1.1
10-14 yrs..	14,011	0.5	7,301	0.6	6,710	0.5	14,018	0.6	7,272	0.6	6,746	0.6
15-19 yrs..	13,710	0.6	7,325	0.7	6,385	0.6	18,445	0.8	10,116	0.9	8,329	0.7
20-24 yrs..	12,269	0.6	6,149	0.6	6,120	0.6	17,550	0.9	9,393	1.0	8,157	0.9
25-34 yrs..	22,429	0.6	11,398	0.7	11,031	0.6	26,977	0.9	14,600	1.0	12,377	0.8
35-44 yrs..	19,470	0.7	10,802	0.8	8,668	0.6	24,795	1.1	13,133	1.1	11,662	1.0
45-54 yrs..	18,798	0.9	10,769	1.0	8,029	0.8	24,479	1.6	12,352	1.6	12,127	1.6
55-64 yrs..	17,153	1.4	9,022	1.5	8,131	1.4	16,592	2.8	7,773	2.6	8,819	3.0
65 yrs.and over....	14,530	2.8	7,164	2.8	7,366	2.8	12,120	4.7	5,283	4.1	6,837	5.4
Unknown	327	2.9	165	2.8	162	3.0	412	3.9	207	3.7	205	4.2
Foreign-born white.......	1,763,740	13.1	866,822	11.7	896,918	14.8	1,650,361	12.7	866,450	11.8	783,911	13.9
10-14 yrs..	14,787	4.5	7,500	4.5	7,287	4.4	12,684	3.5	6,210	3.4	6,474	3.7
15-19 yrs..	28,482	5.4	13,724	5.3	14,758	5.5	86,109	12.8	47,106	13.4	39,003	12.1
20-24 yrs..	108,711	11.7	46,918	10.3	61,793	13.2	219,128	15.3	127,275	15.4	91,853	15.1
25-34 yrs..	469,793	15.1	227,519	13.1	242,274	17.7	455,188	14.4	266,702	14.2	188,486	14.6
35-44 yrs..	460,890	14.6	242,121	13.4	218,769	16.2	333,914	12.3	183,231	11.7	150,683	13.1
45-54 yrs..	316,722	12.8	166,662	11.9	150,060	14.0	228,180	11.0	110,055	9.3	118,125	13.3
55-64 yrs..	192,906	11.9	89,980	10.0	102,926	14.1	146,922	11.1	60,203	8.5	86,719	14.2
65 yrs.and over ...	167,392	12.6	69,636	10.2	97,756	15.1	163,201	13.8	62,067	10.2	101,134	17.5
Unknown	4,057	20.0	2,762	20.1	1,295	19.8	5,035	19.2	3,601	18.3	1,434	22.0

TABLE 131.—NUMBER AND PER CENT ILLITERATE IN POPULATION 10 YEARS OF AGE AND OVER, FOR PRINCIPAL POPULATION CLASSES, BY DIVISIONS AND STATES: 1920.

DIVISION AND STATE.	ALL CLASSES: 1920		NATIVE WHITE.				FOREIGN-BORN WHITE.		NEGRO.	
			Native parentage.		Foreign or mixed parentage.					
	Number.	Per cent.	Number.	Per cent.	Number.	Per cent.	Number.	Per cent.	Number.	Per cent.
United States..	4,931,905	6.0	1,109,875	2.5	132,697	0.8	1,763,740	13.1	1,842,161	22.9
GEOG. DIVISIONS:										
New England.....	289,700	4.9	13,185	0.6	13,759	0.8	257,207	14.0	4,607	7.1
Middle Atlantic..	865,382	4.9	52,924	0.7	24,048	0.5	760,010	15.7	25,587	5.0
E. North Central.	495,470	2.9	88,793	1.0	28,390	0.6	342,832	10.8	32,052	7.3
W. North Central	193,221	2.0	59,954	1.1	14,678	0.5	86,760	6.4	24,887	10.5
South Atlantic...	1,212,942	11.5	352,907	5.4	3,878	0.9	39,757	12.8	812,842	25.2
E. South Central.	845,459	12.7	299,025	6.6	2,626	1.5	6,457	9.1	536,583	27.9
W. South Central	773,637	10.0	199,408	3.9	35,021	6.6	128,725	29.9	402,233	25.3
Mountain.........	132,659	5.2	35,163	2.4	5,697	1.0	55,422	12.7	1,457	5.3
Pacific...........	123,435	2.7	8,516	0.4	4,600	0.4	86,570	8.6	1,913	4.6
NEW ENGLAND:										
Maine...........	20,240	3.3	5,106	1.3	3,290	2.9	11,604	11.1	64	5.9
New Hampshire..	15,788	4.4	1,023	0.6	950	1.1	13,746	15.4	33	6.7
Vermont.........	8,488	3.0	1,904	1.1	1,709	2.8	4,837	11.3	28	6.2
Massachusetts....	146,607	4.7	2,926	0.3	4,854	0.5	135,720	12.8	2,565	6.8
Rhode Island....	31,312	6.5	694	0.5	1,561	0.9	28,169	16.5	839	10.2
Connecticut......	67,265	6.2	1,532	0.4	1,395	0.4	63,131	17.0	1,078	6.2
MIDDLE ATLANTIC:										
New York........	425,022	5.1	16,150	0.6	12,256	0.5	389,603	14.2	5,032	2.9
New Jersey.......	127,661	5.1	6,797	0.7	2,899	0.4	111,595	15.3	5,910	6.1
Pennsylvania.....	312,699	4.6	29,977	0.8	8,893	0.6	258,812	18.9	14,645	6.1
E. NORTH CENTRAL:										
Ohio.............	131,006	2.8	28,535	1.0	5,191	0.6	84,387	12.6	12,715	8.1
Indiana..........	52,034	2.2	24,981	1.4	2,948	1.0	17,555	11.8	6,476	9.5
Illinois..........	173,987	3.4	24,437	1.1	6,470	0.4	131,996	11.0	10,476	6.7
Michigan.........	88,046	3.0	7,580	0.6	6,592	0.7	70,535	9.9	2,203	4.2
Wisconsin........	50,397	2.4	3,260	0.5	7,189	0.8	38,359	8.4	182	4.1
W. NORTH CENTRAL:										
Minnesota.......	34,487	1.8	1,988	0.4	3,967	0.5	26,242	5.4	241	3.1
Iowa............	20,680	1.1	5,921	0.5	2,354	0.4	11,004	4.9	1,283	8.1
Missouri.........	83,403	3.0	43,031	2.2	4,035	0.9	17,669	9.6	18,528	12.1
North Dakota....	9,937	2.1	335	0.3	972	0.5	7,238	5.6	16	4.0
South Dakota....	8,109	1.7	660	0.3	830	0.5	3,848	4.7	35	5.2
Nebraska........	13,784	1.4	2,184	0.4	1,176	0.4	9,468	6.4	556	4.8
Kansas..........	22,821	1.6	5,835	0.6	1,344	0.5	11,291	10.5	4,228	8.8
SOUTH ATLANTIC:										
Delaware.........	10,508	5.9	2,295	2.0	132	0.6	3,373	17.3	4,700	19.1
Maryland........	64,434	5.6	13,884	2.0	1,484	0.9	13,575	13.4	35,404	18.2
Dist. of Columbia.	10,509	2.8	564	0.3	76	0.2	1,728	6.1	8,053	8.6
Virginia.........	195,159	11.2	70,081	6.1	394	1.0	2,150	7.1	122,322	23.5
West Virginia....	69,413	6.4	43,573	4.8	751	1.5	14,548	24.0	10,513	15.3
North Carolina...	241,603	13.1	104,673	8.2	171	1.9	474	6.8	133,674	24.5
South Carolina...	220,667	18.1	38,639	6.6	103	1.0	391	6.2	181,422	29.3
Georgia..........	328,838	15.3	66,537	5.5	259	1.1	861	5.4	261,115	29.1
Florida..........	71,811	9.6	12,661	3.1	508	1.1	2,657	6.3	55,639	21.5
E. SOUTH CENTRAL:										
Kentucky........	155,014	8.4	110,902	7.3	1,304	1.3	2,244	7.3	40,548	21.0
Tennessee........	182,629	10.3	101,317	7.4	492	1.5	1,263	8.3	79,532	22.4
Alabama.........	278,082	16.1	64,925	6.4	469	1.7	1,893	10.9	210,690	31.3
Mississippi.......	229,734	17.2	21,881	3.6	361	2.3	1,057	13.3	205,912	20.3
W. SOUTH CENTRAL:										
Arkansas.........	121,837	8.4	40,753	4.6	658	2.0	1,145	8.3	79,245	21.8
Louisiana........	299,092	21.9	78,818	11.4	3,139	3.5	9,707	21.9	206,730	38.5
Oklahoma........	56,864	3.8	29,413	2.4	1,005	1.2	5,456	14.0	14,205	12.4
Texas............	295,844	8.3	50,424	2.2	30,219	9.4	112,417	33.8	102,053	17.8
MOUNTAIN:										
Montana.........	9,544	2.3	669	0.3	398	0.3	5,178	5.6	87	6.0
Idaho...........	4,924	1.5	654	0.3	260	0.3	2,501	6.5	44	5.4
Wyoming........	3,149	2.1	320	0.4	101	0.3	2,233	9.0	66	5.3
Colorado.........	24,208	3.2	7,655	1.7	969	0.6	14,224	12.4	619	6.2
New Mexico......	41,637	15.6	23,757	11.9	1,762	8.2	7,250	27.1	228	4.3
Arizona..........	39,131	15.3	1,454	1.3	1,779	4.6	19,291	27.5	338	4.6
Utah............	6,264	1.9	535	0.3	390	0.3	3,504	6.3	59	4.6
Nevada..........	3,802	5.9	119	0.4	38	0.2	1,241	8.5	16	5.1
PACIFIC:										
Washington......	18,526	1.7	1,628	0.3	751	0.3	11,630	4.7	245	4.0
Oregon..........	9,317	1.5	1,529	0.4	461	0.3	5,172	5.1	89	4.7
California........	95,592	3.3	5,359	0.4	3,388	0.5	69,768	10.5	1,579	4.7

TABLE 132.—NUMBER AND PER CENT ILLITERATE IN POPULATION 21 YEARS OF AGE AND OVER, FOR PRINCIPAL POPULATION CLASSES, BY DIVISIONS AND STATES: 1920.

DIVISION AND STATE.	ALL CLASSES: 1920		NATIVE WHITE.				FOREIGN-BORN WHITE.		NEGRO.	
			Native parentage.		Foreign or mixed parentage.					
	Number.	Per cent.	Number.	Per cent.	Number.	Per cent.	Number.	Per cent.	Number.	Per cent.
United States..	4,333,111	7.1	938,311	3.0	102,358	0.9	1,707,145	13.7	1,512,987	27.4
GEOG. DIVISIONS:										
New England....	280,826	6.1	11,058	0.6	11,805	1.1	252,584	14.8	4,466	8.5
Middle Atlantic...	843,582	6.3	47,443	0.9	19,664	0.6	749,227	16.7	24,531	6.0
E. North Central.	480,238	3.7	81,372	1.3	25,360	0.8	339,165	11.4	31,084	8.7
W. North Central	180,616	2.5	53,246	1.4	12,722	0.6	84,598	6.5	23,550	12.5
South Atlantic...	1,006,764	14.0	297,595	6.6	3,273	1.1	38,785	13.5	664,235	31.5
E. South Central.	700,098	15.5	252,934	8.4	2,391	1.6	6,249	9.3	438,003	34.1
W. South Central.	611,363	11.7	157,177	4.6	19,330	5.2	104,076	29.1	323,869	30.5
Mountain.........	113,384	6.0	30,136	3.0	4,077	1.2	49,959	12.7	1,386	5.8
Pacific...........	116,240	3.2	7,350	0.4	3,736	0.4	82,502	8.8	1,863	5.4
NEW ENGLAND:										
Maine...........	18,572	3.9	4,156	1.3	2,886	4.1	11,302	12.0	60	6.8
New Hampshire..	15,257	5.4	897	0.6	858	1.6	13,437	16.4	30	7.7
Vermont.........	8,152	3.8	1,715	1.3	1,627	3.8	4,772	12.5	28	8.2
Massachusetts....	142,750	5.9	2,469	0.3	3,930	0.6	133,330	13.5	2,491	8.2
Rhode Island.....	30,319	8.2	633	0.6	1,339	1.3	27,480	17.5	820	12.5
Connecticut......	65,776	7.8	1,188	0.4	1,165	0.6	62,263	18.1	1,037	7.5
MIDDLE ATLANTIC:										
New York.......	415,359	6.4	14,497	0.7	10,270	0.6	383,862	15.2	4,815	3.4
New Jersey......	124,358	6.6	6,073	0.9	2,285	0.5	109,893	16.3	5,668	7.5
Pennsylvania.....	303,865	6.0	26,873	1.0	7,109	0.8	255,472	20.1	14,048	7.3
E. NORTH CENTRAL:										
Ohio.............	126,645	3.6	26,100	1.2	4,644	0.7	83,415	13.4	12,316	9.7
Indiana..........	50,147	2.8	23,545	1.8	2,803	1.1	17,393	12.4	6,336	11.7
Illinois..........	169,127	4.3	22,362	1.4	5,547	0.5	130,474	11.7	10,146	7.9
Michigan.........	85,613	3.9	6,798	0.8	5,875	0.9	69,759	10.5	2,111	4.9
Wisconsin........	48,706	3.2	2,567	0.6	6,491	1.0	38,124	8.8	175	4.8
W. NORTH CENTRAL:										
Minnesota........	32,869	2.4	1,406	0.4	3,305	0.6	26,047	5.6	234	3.5
Iowa............	19,444	1.4	5,267	0.7	2,065	0.5	10,749	5.0	1,249	9.9
Missouri.........	77,348	3.8	38,780	2.8	3,834	1.0	17,269	10.0	17,333	14.3
North Dakota....	9,373	2.9	258	0.3	717	0.6	7,126	5.9	16	4.8
South Dakota.....	7,640	2.2	520	0.4	671	0.5	3,795	4.9	35	6.7
Nebraska.........	12,972	1.8	1,832	0.5	965	0.4	9,253	6.6	538	5.7
Kansas...........	20,970	2.0	5,183	0.7	1,165	0.6	10,359	10.2	4,145	11.2
SOUTH ATLANTIC:										
Delaware.........	10,088	7.4	2,190	2.6	110	0.7	3,327	18.2	4,453	24.6
Maryland.........	58,877	6.8	12,533	2.5	1,318	1.1	13,398	14.3	31,544	22.2
Dist. of Columbia.	10,190	3.3	521	0.3	64	0.2	1,699	6.4	7,823	10.7
Virginia.........	162,376	13.5	56,917	7.1	318	1.1	2,086	7.5	102,884	29.3
West Virginia....	61,468	8.2	37,099	6.1	619	1.7	14,062	25.4	9,662	18.9
North Carolina...	204,492	16.9	90,642	10.7	155	2.4	453	7.0	111,109	32.4
South Carolina ...	179,482	23.0	32,894	8.5	94	1.2	385	6.5	146,027	38.7
Georgia..........	261,294	18.4	54,339	6.7	241	1.3	839	5.6	205,819	35.8
Florida..........	58,497	10.9	10,460	3.7	354	1.1	2,536	6.6	44,914	24.8
E. SOUTH CENTRAL:										
Kentucky........	136,235	10.6	94,829	9.2	1,263	1.4	2,202	7.5	37,926	26.4
Tennessee........	153,163	12.6	85,527	9.2	459	1.8	1,240	8.7	65,913	26.9
Alabama.........	228,565	20.0	55,004	8.3	379	1.9	1,825	11.3	171,283	38.8
Mississippi.......	182,135	20.8	17,574	4.4	290	2.4	982	13.4	162,881	35.9
W. SOUTH CENTRAL:										
Arkansas.........	99,413	11.5	33,403	5.7	584	2.3	1,088	8.3	64,309	26.5
Louisiana........	229,980	24.9	61,049	13.5	1,819	2.6	9,328	22.6	157,294	43.8
Oklahoma........	48,076	4.7	24,096	2.9	834	1.3	4,854	13.4	12,491	16.4
Texas...........	233,894	9.6	38,629	2.5	16,093	7.5	88,806	33.3	89,775	23.4
MOUNTAIN:										
Montana.........	9,071	2.8	550	0.4	303	0.4	5,104	6.0	84	6.7
Idaho...........	4,510	1.9	545	0.4	220	0.4	2,377	6.6	41	5.9
Wyoming........	2,940	2.5	269	0.4	77	0.3	2,120	9.2	65	6.1
Colorado........	22,080	3.9	6,671	2.0	769	0.7	13,427	12.8	599	7.4
New Mexico......	34,952	18.9	20,396	15.2	1,211	8.3	6,275	28.6	213	4.4
Arizona.........	30,636	16.3	1,197	1.4	1,159	4.5	16,057	28.7	316	4.8
Utah............	5,679	2.5	410	0.5	309	0.4	3,413	6.5	55	5.0
Nevada..........	3,516	6.7	98	0.5	29	0.2	1,186	8.5	13	4.7
PACIFIC:										
Washington......	17,777	2.1	1,394	0.3	575	0.3	11,494	5.0	241	4.6
Oregon..........	8,905	1.8	1,303	0.5	400	0.4	5,097	5.4	89	5.5
California........	89,558	3.9	4,653	0.4	2,761	0.5	65,911	10.7	1,533	5.6

TABLE 133.—PER CENT ILLITERATE IN POPULATION 10 YEARS OF AGE AND OVER, BY SEX AND PRINCIPAL POPULATION CLASSES, BY DIVISIONS AND STATES: 1920 AND 1910.

DIVISION AND STATE.	ALL CLASSES.						NATIVE WHITE.				FOREIGN-BORN WHITE.		NEGRO.	
	Both sexes.		Male.		Female.		Native parentage.		Foreign or mixed parentage.					
	1920	1910	1920	1910	1920	1910	1920	1910	1920	1910	1920	1910	1920	1910
United States	6.0	7.7	6.0	7.6	5.9	7.8	2.5	3.7	0.8	1.1	13.1	12.7	22.9	30.4
GEOGRAPHIC DIVISIONS:														
New England	4.9	5.3	4.8	5.3	5.0	5.2	0.6	0.7	0.8	1.3	14.0	13.8	7.1	7.8
Middle Atlantic	4.9	5.7	4.7	5.6	5.1	5.7	0.7	1.2	0.5	0.8	15.7	15.8	5.0	7.9
East North Central	2.9	3.4	3.0	3.5	2.8	3.3	1.0	1.7	0.6	0.9	10.8	10.1	7.3	11.0
West North Central	2.0	2.9	2.0	2.9	1.9	2.9	1.1	1.7	0.5	0.7	6.4	7.6	10.5	14.9
South Atlantic	11.5	16.0	12.1	16.0	11.0	16.1	5.4	8.0	0.9	1.2	12.8	13.5	25.2	32.5
East South Central	12.7	17.4	13.3	17.4	12.0	17.3	6.6	9.6	1.5	1.7	9.1	9.7	27.9	34.8
West South Central	10.0	13.2	10.0	12.7	10.0	13.8	3.9	5.6	6.6	7.7	29.9	25.6	25.3	33.1
Mountain	5.2	6.9	4.7	6.3	5.7	7.5	2.4	3.6	1.0	1.2	12.7	12.5	5.3	8.0
Pacific	2.7	3.0	2.8	3.3	2.5	2.5	0.4	0.4	0.4	0.5	8.6	8.0	4.6	6.3
NEW ENGLAND:														
Maine	3.3	4.1	3.9	4.9	2.5	3.2	1.3	1.4	2.9	4.5	11.1	13.7	5.9	8.0
New Hampshire	4.4	4.6	4.5	5.2	4.2	4.1	0.6	0.8	1.1	2.1	15.4	14.5	6.7	10.6
Vermont	3.0	3.7	3.6	4.4	2.4	3.1	1.1	1.2	2.8	4.0	11.3	13.1	6.2	4.8
Massachusetts	4.7	5.2	4.5	5.0	4.9	5.3	0.3	0.4	0.5	0.7	12.8	12.7	6.8	8.1
Rhode Island	6.5	7.7	6.0	7.4	7.0	8.0	0.5	0.7	0.9	1.8	16.5	17.3	10.2	9.5
Connecticut	6.2	6.0	5.8	5.7	6.6	6.3	0.4	0.5	0.4	0.8	17.0	15.4	6.2	6.3
MIDDLE ATLANTIC:														
New York	5.1	5.5	4.5	5.0	5.6	5.9	0.6	0.8	0.5	0.7	14.2	13.7	2.9	5.0
New Jersey	5.1	5.6	4.9	5.5	5.3	5.7	0.7	1.1	0.4	0.7	15.3	14.7	6.1	9.9
Pennsylvania	4.6	5.9	4.7	6.4	4.5	5.4	0.8	1.4	0.6	1.1	18.9	20.1	6.1	9.1
EAST NORTH CENTRAL:														
Ohio	2.8	3.2	3.0	3.5	2.6	3.0	1.0	1.7	0.6	0.9	12.6	11.5	8.1	11.1
Indiana	2.2	3.1	2.4	3.2	2.0	2.9	1.4	2.2	1.0	1.4	11.8	11.7	9.5	13.7
Illinois	3.4	3.7	3.3	3.7	3.4	3.8	1.1	1.7	0.4	0.6	11.0	10.1	6.7	10.5
Michigan	3.0	3.3	3.1	3.6	2.9	3.1	0.6	1.0	0.7	1.2	9.9	9.3	4.2	5.7
Wisconsin	2.4	3.2	2.5	3.1	2.4	3.2	0.5	0.6	0.8	1.0	8.4	8.7	4.1	4.5
WEST NORTH CENTRAL:														
Minnesota	1.8	3.0	1.8	2.9	1.9	3.1	0.4	0.4	0.5	0.6	5.4	7.6	3.1	3.4
Iowa	1.1	1.7	1.2	1.7	1.0	1.7	0.5	0.9	0.4	0.6	4.9	6.3	8.1	10.3
Missouri	3.0	4.3	3.3	4.4	2.8	4.2	2.2	3.4	0.9	1.2	9.6	10.1	12.1	17.4
North Dakota	2.1	3.1	1.9	2.8	2.4	3.5	0.3	0.3	0.5	0.7	5.6	6.3	4.0	4.8
South Dakota	1.7	2.9	1.5	2.5	1.9	3.3	0.4	0.3	0.5	0.4	4.7	5.0	5.2	5.5
Nebraska	1.4	1.9	1.3	1.9	1.4	2.0	0.4	0.6	0.4	0.5	6.4	7.1	4.8	7.2
Kansas	1.6	2.2	1.7	2.3	1.6	2.1	0.6	0.8	0.5	0.8	10.5	10.5	8.8	12.0
SOUTH ATLANTIC:														
Delaware	5.9	8.1	6.2	8.4	5.5	7.8	2.0	3.3	0.6	0.9	17.3	19.8	19.1	25.6
Maryland	5.6	7.2	5.7	7.2	5.4	7.1	2.0	3.0	0.9	1.0	13.4	11.9	18.2	23.4
District of Columbia	2.8	4.9	2.5	4.1	3.0	5.7	0.3	0.6	0.2	0.4	6.1	8.2	8.6	13.5
Virginia	11.2	15.2	12.1	15.7	10.2	14.6	6.1	8.2	1.0	1.2	7.1	9.2	23.5	30.0
West Virginia	6.4	8.3	7.2	8.8	5.6	7.7	4.8	6.7	1.5	2.0	24.0	23.9	15.3	20.3
North Carolina	13.1	18.5	13.7	18.2	12.5	18.7	8.2	12.3	1.9	3.0	6.8	8.3	24.5	31.9
South Carolina	18.1	25.7	18.3	25.0	17.9	26.3	6.6	10.5	1.0	1.4	6.2	6.8	29.3	38.7
Georgia	15.3	20.7	16.2	20.9	14.4	20.5	5.5	8.0	1.1	1.6	5.4	6.0	29.1	36.5
Florida	9.6	13.8	9.6	13.2	9.5	14.4	3.1	5.2	1.1	2.2	6.3	10.5	21.5	25.5
EAST SOUTH CENTRAL:														
Kentucky	8.4	12.1	9.3	12.6	7.6	11.6	7.3	10.7	1.3	1.5	7.3	8.3	21.0	27.6
Tennessee	10.3	13.6	11.2	13.8	9.5	13.4	7.4	9.9	1.5	1.8	8.3	8.3	22.4	27.3
Alabama	16.1	22.9	16.4	22.5	15.8	23.3	6.4	10.1	1.7	2.3	10.9	11.3	31.3	40.1
Mississippi	17.2	22.4	18.1	22.4	16.3	22.5	3.6	5.3	2.3	2.2	13.3	15.1	29.3	35.6
WEST SOUTH CENTRAL:														
Arkansas	9.4	12.6	9.6	12.1	9.1	13.1	4.6	7.1	2.0	2.8	8.3	8.9	21.8	26.4
Louisiana	21.9	29.0	21.6	28.0	22.2	30.1	11.4	15.0	3.5	3.6	21.9	24.0	38.5	48.4
Oklahoma	6.0	5.6	4.1	5.5	3.4	5.8	2.4	3.5	1.2	1.3	14.0	9.8	12.4	17.7
Texas	8.7	9.9	8.5	9.8	8.2	10.1	3.9	3.3	9.4	11.6	33.8	30.0	17.8	24.6
MOUNTAIN:														
Montana	2.3	4.8	2.3	5.2	2.3	4.0	0.3	0.3	0.3	0.4	5.0	0.1	6.0	7.0
Idaho	1.5	2.2	1.7	2.6	1.3	1.6	0.3	0.4	0.3	0.3	6.5	6.9	5.4	6.4
Wyoming	2.1	3.3	2.5	3.7	1.5	2.5	0.4	0.3	0.3	0.4	9.0	9.7	5.3	5.0
Colorado	3.2	3.7	2.9	3.6	3.6	3.8	1.7	2.0	0.6	0.5	12.4	11.3	6.2	8.6
New Mexico	15.6	20.2	12.7	15.9	18.9	25.4	11.9	15.5	8.2	8.9	27.1	31.0	4.3	14.2
Arizona	15.3	20.9	13.9	19.2	17.1	23.5	1.3	2.3	4.6	8.4	27.5	31.5	4.6	7.2
Utah	1.9	2.5	2.1	2.7	1.6	2.2	0.3	0.4	0.3	0.4	6.3	5.9	4.6	4.8
Nevada	5.9	6.7	5.8	6.1	6.2	8.0	0.4	0.4	0.2	0.5	8.5	7.6	5.1	5.5
PACIFIC:														
Washington	1.7	2.0	1.7	2.1	1.6	1.8	0.3	0.3	0.3	0.3	4.7	4.8	4.0	4.3
Oregon	1.5	1.9	1.6	2.2	1.3	1.4	0.4	0.4	0.3	0.4	5.1	6.1	4.7	3.4
California	3.3	3.7	3.5	4.2	3.1	3.1	0.4	0.5	0.5	0.6	10.5	10.0	4.7	7.1

TABLE 134.—PER CENT ILLITERATE IN POPULATION 21 YEARS OF AGE AND OVER, BY SEX AND PRINCIPAL POPULATION CLASSES, BY DIVISIONS AND STATES: 1920 AND 1910.

DIVISION AND STATE.	ALL CLASSES.						NATIVE WHITE.				FOREIGN-BORN WHITE.		NEGRO.	
	Both sexes.		Male.		Female.		Native parentage.		Foreign or mixed parentage.					
	1920	1910	1920	1910	1920	1910	1920	1910	1920	1910	1920	1910	1920	1910
United States.......	7.1	8.9	7.0	8.4	7.3	9.4	3.0	4.3	0.9	1.3	13.7	12.9	27.4	35.7
GEOGRAPHIC DIVISIONS:														
New England..........	6.1	6.3	6.0	6.3	6.2	6.3	0.6	0.8	1.1	1.8	14.8	14.3	8.5	9.4
Middle Atlantic........	6.3	6.9	5.9	6.8	6.6	7.0	0.9	1.5	0.6	1.1	16.7	16.4	6.0	9.4
East North Central.....	3.7	4.3	3.7	4.3	3.6	4.2	1.3	2.2	0.8	1.2	11.4	10.3	8.7	13.6
West North Central....	2.5	3.7	2.5	3.5	2.5	3.9	1.4	2.2	0.6	0.9	6.5	7.7	12.5	18.3
South Atlantic........	14.0	18.6	14.0	17.6	13.9	19.6	6.6	9.3	1.1	1.4	13.5	13.6	31.5	39.1
East South Central.....	15.5	20.4	15.7	19.4	15.2	21.4	8.4	11.3	1.6	1.9	9.3	9.4	34.1	41.4
West South Central....	11.7	15.0	11.3	13.7	12.1	16.5	4.6	6.4	5.2	6.4	29.1	24.4	30.5	38.5
Mountain..............	6.0	7.7	5.4	6.9	6.8	8.9	3.0	4.3	1.0	1.3	12.7	12.2	5.8	9.1
Pacific................	3.2	3.4	3.3	3.7	3.0	3.1	0.4	0.5	0.4	0.6	8.8	7.9	5.4	7.3
NEW ENGLAND:														
Maine.................	3.9	4.7	4.7	5.5	3.1	3.8	1.3	1.5	4.1	6.3	12.0	14.5	6.8	10.3
New Hampshire........	5.4	5.5	5.6	6.2	5.2	4.8	0.6	0.9	1.6	3.1	16.4	15.4	7.7	13.3
Vermont..............	3.8	4.6	4.5	5.3	3.0	3.8	1.3	1.5	3.8	5.3	12.5	14.1	8.2	5.0
Massachusetts.........	5.9	6.2	5.7	6.1	6.1	6.3	0.3	0.4	0.6	1.0	13.5	13.1	8.2	9.7
Rhode Island..........	8.2	9.2	7.6	8.8	8.8	9.6	0.6	0.9	1.3	2.4	17.5	18.1	12.5	11.4
Connecticut...........	7.8	7.2	7.4	6.8	8.4	7.5	0.4	0.6	0.6	1.1	18.1	16.0	7.5	7.8
MIDDLE ATLANTIC:														
New York.............	6.4	6.6	5.7	6.0	7.1	7.2	0.7	1.1	0.6	0.9	15.2	14.3	3.4	5.8
New Jersey...........	6.6	6.7	6.3	6.6	6.9	6.8	0.9	1.4	0.5	0.8	16.3	14.8	7.5	11.9
Pennsylvania.........	6.0	7.3	6.2	7.8	5.9	6.8	1.0	1.8	0.8	1.4	20.1	20.8	7.3	11.0
EAST NORTH CENTRAL:														
Ohio..................	3.6	4.0	3.8	4.2	3.3	3.8	1.2	2.2	0.7	1.1	13.4	11.8	9.7	13.9
Indiana...............	2.8	3.9	3.0	4.1	2.6	3.8	1.8	3.0	1.1	1.7	12.4	11.8	11.7	17.5
Illinois...............	4.3	4.7	4.1	4.6	4.4	4.8	1.4	2.2	0.5	0.8	11.7	10.3	7.9	12.4
Michigan.............	3.9	4.2	3.9	4.4	3.8	4.0	0.8	1.3	0.9	1.6	10.5	9.6	4.9	6.9
Wisconsin.............	3.2	4.2	3.2	4.0	3.2	4.4	0.6	0.9	1.0	1.3	8.8	8.9	4.8	5.3
WEST NORTH CENTRAL:														
Minnesota.............	2.4	4.0	2.2	3.7	2.6	4.4	0.4	0.5	0.6	0.9	5.6	7.7	3.5	3.9
Iowa.................	1.4	2.2	1.4	2.1	1.3	2.2	0.7	1.2	0.5	0.8	5.0	6.3	9.9	12.8
Missouri..............	3.8	5.4	4.0	5.3	3.6	5.5	2.8	4.3	1.0	1.4	10.0	10.2	14.3	21.1
North Dakota.........	2.9	3.7	2.5	3.1	3.5	4.5	0.3	0.4	0.6	0.6	5.9	6.2	4.8	5.3
South Dakota.........	2.2	3.7	1.9	3.1	2.6	4.6	0.4	0.4	0.5	0.5	4.9	5.0	6.7	6.8
Nebraska.............	1.8	2.5	1.7	2.4	1.9	2.7	0.5	0.8	0.4	0.7	6.6	7.1	5.7	8.5
Kansas...............	2.0	2.8	2.1	2.9	2.0	2.8	0.7	1.1	0.6	1.0	10.2	10.3	11.2	15.9
SOUTH ATLANTIC:														
Delaware.............	7.4	10.0	7.7	10.1	7.0	9.8	2.6	4.2	0.7	1.0	18.2	19.7	24.6	32.9
Maryland.............	6.8	8.7	6.9	8.5	6.7	8.9	2.5	3.7	1.1	1.1	14.3	12.3	22.2	28.6
District of Columbia....	3.3	6.0	3.0	4.9	3.6	7.0	0.3	0.7	0.2	0.5	6.4	8.3	10.7	16.8
Virginia..............	13.5	17.9	14.1	17.7	12.7	18.0	7.1	9.4	1.1	1.5	7.5	9.3	29.3	37.1
West Virginia.........	8.2	10.2	8.9	10.4	7.3	10.0	6.1	8.4	1.7	2.3	25.4	23.9	18.9	24.2
North Carolina........	16.9	22.6	17.0	21.3	16.8	24.0	10.7	15.0	2.4	4.0	7.0	8.1	32.4	40.4
South Carolina........	23.0	29.6	22.3	27.1	23.8	32.0	8.5	11.4	1.2	1.4	6.5	6.5	38.7	46.9
Georgia..............	18.4	24.1	18.4	22.8	18.4	25.5	6.7	9.2	1.3	1.8	5.6	5.9	35.8	43.8
Florida...............	10.9	15.5	10.6	14.0	11.3	17.3	3.7	5.7	1.1	1.9	6.6	10.5	24.8	28.8
EAST SOUTH CENTRAL:														
Kentucky.............	10.6	14.5	11.3	14.5	9.8	14.6	9.2	12.8	1.4	1.7	7.5	8.2	26.4	34.7
Tennessee............	12.6	16.3	13.2	15.7	12.0	17.0	9.2	11.9	1.8	2.1	8.7	8.2	26.9	33.3
Alabama.............	20.0	26.2	19.5	24.2	20.5	28.2	8.3	11.5	1.9	2.7	11.3	11.1	38.8	46.4
Mississippi...........	20.8	26.8	20.9	25.3	20.7	28.4	4.4	6.2	2.4	2.3	13.4	13.6	35.9	43.2
WEST SOUTH CENTRAL:														
Arkansas.............	11.5	15.1	11.1	13.5	11.8	16.9	5.7	8.5	2.3	3.2	8.3	8.2	26.5	32.0
Louisiana.............	24.9	31.1	23.6	28.6	26.2	33.7	13.5	16.8	2.6	2.7	22.6	23.2	43.8	52.2
Oklahoma............	4.7	6.9	4.9	6.4	4.5	7.6	2.9	4.2	1.3	1.6	13.4	9.7	16.4	22.7
Texas................	9.6	11.6	9.6	10.9	9.7	12.4	2.5	3.7	7.5	10.0	33.3	28.8	23.4	31.4
MOUNTAIN:														
Montana.............	2.8	5.5	2.7	5.7	2.9	5.1	0.4	0.4	0.4	0.5	6.0	9.2	6.7	8.0
Idaho................	1.9	2.7	2.1	3.1	1.6	2.2	0.4	0.4	0.4	0.4	6.6	6.6	5.9	6.8
Wyoming.............	2.5	3.8	2.9	4.1	1.9	3.2	0.4	0.4	0.3	0.3	9.2	9.5	6.1	5.3
Colorado.............	3.9	4.4	3.5	4.2	4.4	4.7	2.0	2.4	0.7	0.6	12.8	11.3	7.4	10.0
New Mexico..........	18.9	23.4	14.7	17.6	24.1	30.8	15.2	18.8	8.3	9.0	28.6	31.2	4.4	15.9
Arizona..............	16.3	21.9	14.5	19.5	18.8	25.8	1.4	2.4	4.5	7.9	28.7	31.4	4.8	8.4
Utah.................	2.5	3.1	2.8	3.3	2.2	2.9	0.5	0.7	0.4	0.4	6.5	5.9	5.0	5.3
Nevada..............	6.7	6.8	6.4	6.0	7.3	8.7	0.5	0.3	0.2	0.5	8.5	7.0	4.7	6.0
PACIFIC:														
Washington...........	2.1	2.3	2.1	2.4	2.1	2.2	.0.3	0.3	0.3	0.3	5.0	4.7	4.6	4.8
Oregon..............	1.8	2.2	2.0	2.5	1.6	1.8	0.5	0.5	0.4	0.5	5.4	5.9	5.5	3.7
California.............	3.9	4.3	4.0	4.6	3.6	3.7	0.4	0.6	0.5	0.7	10.7	9.8	5.6	8.4

TABLE 135.—NUMBER AND PER CENT ILLITERATE IN POPULATION 10 TO 15 YEARS OF AGE, INCLUSIVE, FOR PRINCIPAL POPULATION CLASSES, BY DIVISIONS AND STATES: 1920.

[Per cent not shown where base is less than 100.

| DIVISION AND STATE. | ALL CLASSES: 1920 | | NATIVE WHITE. | | | | FOREIGN-BORN WHITE. | | NEGRO. | |
| | | | Native parentage. | | Foreign or mixed parentage. | | | | | |
	Number.	Per cent.	Number.	Per cent.	Number.	Per cent.	Number.	Per cent.	Number.	Per cent.
United States	292,467	2.3	85,485	1.1	16,632	0.6	18,183	4.4	166,416	11.5
GEOGRAPHIC DIVISIONS:										
New England	2,472	0.3	1,012	0.3	914	0.2	515	0.9	30	0.4
Middle Atlantic	6,448	0.3	2,566	0.2	2,146	0.2	1,466	1.0	252	0.5
East North Central	5,587	0.2	3,393	0.2	1,404	0.2	538	0.6	196	0.5
West North Central	5,662	0.4	3,207	0.3	944	0.2	603	2.2	654	2.5
South Atlantic	97,032	5.1	26,147	2.2	289	0.4	147	1.6	70,112	10.9
East South Central	77,670	6.1	23,508	2.7	130	0.8	51	3.1	53,839	14.3
West South Central	86,336	6.0	23,037	2.3	9,527	10.6	11,724	34.1	41,288	13.7
Mountain	8,932	2.3	2,032	0.8	856	0.9	2,145	10.7	24	1.3
Pacific	2,328	0.4	583	0.2	422	0.3	994	3.2	21	0.6
NEW ENGLAND:										
Maine	628	0.8	432	0.8	147	0.6	47	1.2	1	0.9
New Hampshire	131	0.3	66	0.3	39	0.2	25	0.8	1	......
Vermont	109	0.3	67	0.3	30	0.3	12	0.5	......	......
Massachusetts	977	0.2	221	0.2	482	0.2	255	0.8	19	0.5
Rhode Island	204	0.3	31	0.2	93	0.2	76	1.4	4	0.5
Connecticut	423	0.3	195	0.4	123	0.1	100	0.9	5	0.3
MIDDLE ATLANTIC:										
New York	2,530	0.2	778	0.2	972	0.2	718	0.9	50	0.4
New Jersey	911	0.3	283	0.2	306	0.2	260	1.2	58	0.5
Pennsylvania	3,007	0.3	1,505	0.3	868	0.2	488	1.3	144	0.6
EAST NORTH CENTRAL:										
Ohio	1,621	0.3	1,155	0.3	269	0.2	122	0.6	75	0.5
Indiana	743	0.2	620	0.2	69	0.2	19	0.5	35	0.5
Illinois	1,657	0.2	923	0.2	425	0.2	232	0.7	77	0.5
Michigan	811	0.2	340	0.2	325	0.2	110	0.5	8	0.2
Wisconsin	755	0.2	355	0.2	316	0.2	55	0.6	1	0.2
WEST NORTH CENTRAL:										
Minnesota	814	0.3	315	0.3	358	0.2	42	0.5	1	0.2
Iowa	518	0.2	330	0.2	137	0.2	42	1.0	9	0.5
Missouri	2,738	0.7	1,949	0.6	84	0.2	96	2.3	609	3.6
North Dakota	246	0.3	42	0.1	120	0.2	19	0.6	......	......
South Dakota	250	0.3	75	0.2	81	0.3	15	1.0	......	......
Nebraska	319	0.2	165	0.2	84	0.2	58	1.8	3	0.3
Kansas	777	0.4	331	0.2	80	0.3	331	11.1	32	0.5
SOUTH ATLANTIC:										
Delaware	125	0.5	41	0.3	10	0.2	6	1.2	68	1.9
Maryland	2,444	1.5	558	0.5	60	0.2	24	0.9	1,802	6.1
District of Columbia	78	0.2	16	0.1	6	0.1	4	0.6	52	0.5
Virginia	16,976	5.4	7,010	3.4	50	0.8	18	1.9	9,867	10.0
West Virginia	3,506	1.8	3,161	1.9	78	0.8	61	2.7	206	2.3
North Carolina	15,711	4.2	5,645	2.2	10	0.7	4	2.1	9,830	8.3
South Carolina	15,909	6.1	1,999	1.7	2	0.2	2	1.3	13,884	9.6
Georgia	35,263	8.3	6,531	2.8	8	0.2	6	1.4	28,713	15.4
Florida	7,020	5.7	1,186	1.7	65	0.7	22	1.4	5,690	13.2
EAST SOUTH CENTRAL:										
Kentucky	8,767	2.8	7,617	2.7	21	0.3	13	2.8	1,116	4.1
Tennessee	16,482	5.1	8,356	3.2	13	0.4	4	1.0	8,109	13.2
Alabama	26,649	7.6	4,981	2.4	47	1.0	15	2.8	21,590	15.6
Mississippi	25,772	9.3	2,554	2.0	49	2.4	19	8.1	23,024	15.5
WEST SOUTH CENTRAL:										
Arkansas	13,463	5.2	4,459	2.4	38	0.9	10	4.0	8,954	12.8
Louisiana	36,066	14.1	8,925	6.3	763	6.2	104	9.9	26,355	25.6
Oklahoma	5,777	1.8	3,309	1.3	109	0.9	101	17.3	1,063	4.8
Texas	31,375	4.9	6,344	1.4	8,617	14.0	11,409	25.7	4,910	4.6
MOUNTAIN:										
Montana	228	0.4	69	0.2	57	0.3	23	0.8	2	1.9
Idaho	197	0.4	63	0.1	21	0.2	42	4.4	1	......
Wyoming	58	0.3	22	0.2	9	0.2	20	2.5	......	......
Colorado	854	0.8	381	0.5	97	0.4	289	6.8	10	1.1
New Mexico	2,820	5.9	1,328	3.5	272	6.5	368	15.5	5	2.6
Arizona	4,394	11.5	96	0.5	348	4.4	1,365	19.9	2	0.6
Utah	272	0.4	61	0.1	45	0.3	22	1.4	2	......
Nevada	109	1.6	12	0.3	7	0.4	16	5.9	2	......
PACIFIC:										
Washington	293	0.2	122	0.1	80	0.2	24	0.4	1	0.2
Oregon	189	0.2	121	0.2	36	0.2	14	0.5	......	......
California	1,846	0.6	340	0.2	306	0.3	956	4.3	20	0.6

TABLE 136.—NUMBER AND PER CENT ILLITERATE IN POPULATION 16 TO 20 YEARS OF AGE, INCLUSIVE, FOR PRINCIPAL POPULATION CLASSES, BY DIVISIONS AND STATES: 1920.

[Per cent not shown where base is less than 100.]

DIVISION AND STATE.	ALL CLASSES: 1920 Number.	ALL CLASSES: 1920 Per cent.	NATIVE WHITE. Native parentage. Number.	NATIVE WHITE. Native parentage. Per cent.	NATIVE WHITE. Foreign or mixed parentage. Number.	NATIVE WHITE. Foreign or mixed parentage. Per cent.	FOREIGN-BORN WHITE. Number.	FOREIGN-BORN WHITE. Per cent.	NEGRO. Number.	NEGRO. Per cent.
United States	306,327	3.3	86,079	1.6	13,707	0.6	38,412	6.6	162,758	15.1
GEOGRAPHIC DIVISIONS:										
New England	6,402	1.1	1,115	0.5	1,040	0.4	4,108	5.0	111	1.8
Middle Atlantic	15,352	0.8	2,915	0.3	2,238	0.3	9,317	4.1	804	1.6
East North Central	9,645	0.5	4,028	0.4	1,626	0.3	3,129	2.7	772	1.9
West North Central	6,943	0.6	3,501	0.5	1,012	0.3	1,559	4.0	683	3.0
South Atlantic	109,146	7.9	29,165	3.4	316	0.7	825	5.6	78,495	16.8
East South Central	67,691	7.6	22,583	3.7	105	0.8	157	6.7	44,741	16.9
West South Central	75,938	7.3	19,194	2.7	6,164	9.0	12,925	33.6	37,076	16.6
Mountain	10,343	3.7	2,995	1.7	764	1.1	3,318	15.0	47	2.3
Pacific	4,867	1.2	583	0.2	442	0.4	3,074	7.7	29	0.9
NEW ENGLAND:										
Maine	1,040	1.6	518	1.3	257	1.4	255	4.1	3	2.9
New Hampshire	400	1.1	60	0.4	53	0.4	284	6.4	2	
Vermont	227	0.8	122	0.6	52	0.8	53	2.4		
Massachusetts	2,880	1.0	236	0.3	442	0.3	2,135	4.8	55	1.7
Rhode Island	789	1.5	30	0.2	129	0.5	613	7.1	15	2.0
Connecticut	1,066	1.0	149	0.4	107	0.2	768	4.9	36	2.1
MIDDLE ATLANTIC:										
New York	7,133	0.9	875	0.3	1,014	0.3	5,023	3.6	167	1.1
New Jersey	2,392	0.9	441	0.4	308	0.3	1,442	4.5	184	1.9
Pennsylvania	5,827	0.8	1,599	0.4	916	0.4	2,852	4.9	453	1.9
EAST NORTH CENTRAL:										
Ohio	2,740	0.6	1,280	0.4	278	0.3	850	3.1	324	2.1
Indiana	1,144	0.5	816	0.4	76	0.3	143	2.8	105	1.5
Illinois	3,203	0.6	1,152	0.4	498	0.3	1,290	2.9	253	1.8
Michigan	1,622	0.5	442	0.3	392	0.3	666	2.4	84	1.7
Wisconsin	936	0.4	338	0.3	382	0.4	180	1.5	6	1.5
WEST NORTH CENTRAL:										
Minnesota	804	0.4	267	0.3	304	0.2	153	1.3	6	1.1
Iowa	718	0.3	324	0.2	152	0.3	213	4.1	25	1.6
Missouri	3,317	1.1	2,302	0.9	117	0.3	304	4.6	586	4.0
North Dakota	318	0.5	35	0.2	135	0.4	93	1.7		
South Dakota	219	0.4	65	0.2	78	0.3	38	1.7		
Nebraska	493	0.4	187	0.3	127	0.3	157	3.8	15	1.5
Kansas	1,074	0.7	321	0.3	99	0.4	601	15.7	51	1.0
SOUTH ATLANTIC:										
Delaware	295	1.6	64	0.5	12	0.4	40	5.1	179	6.2
Maryland	3,113	2.4	793	0.9	106	0.6	153	3.2	2,058	8.8
District of Columbia	241	0.7	27	0.1	6	0.1	25	2.0	178	1.7
Virginia	15,807	6.9	6,154	4.1	26	0.5	46	3.0	9,571	13.5
West Virginia	4,439	3.2	3,313	2.7	54	1.0	425	14.5	645	7.5
North Carolina	21,400	8.2	8,386	4.8	6	0.6	17	5.6	12,735	15.2
South Carolina	25,276	14.1	3,746	4.7	7	0.6	4	1.7	21,511	21.9
Georgia	32,281	10.7	5,667	3.5	10	0.4	16	2.1	26,583	19.8
Florida	6,294	6.9	1,015	2.1	89	1.6	99	4.6	5,035	14.7
EAST SOUTH CENTRAL:										
Kentucky	10,012	4.4	8,456	4.2	20	0.3	29	4.5	1,506	7.0
Tennessee	12,984	5.6	7,434	4.1	20	0.7	19	3.3	5,510	11.6
Alabama	22,868	9.6	4,940	3.6	43	1.4	53	7.1	17,817	18.9
Mississippi	21,827	11.7	1,753	2.1	22	1.6	56	15.9	19,908	19.6
WEST SOUTH CENTRAL:										
Arkansas	8,961	5.1	2,891	2.4	36	1.0	47	11.2	5,982	11.7
Louisiana	32,846	17.9	8,844	9.0	557	6.4	275	14.0	23,081	31.1
Oklahoma	3,556	1.8	2,008	1.2	62	0.6	418	22.6	651	4.0
Texas	30,575	6.3	5,451	1.7	5,509	11.8	12,185	35.6	7,362	9.0
MOUNTAIN:										
Montana	245	0.6	50	0.2	38	0.3	51	1.7	1	
Idaho	217	0.6	46	0.2	19	0.2	82	6.5	2	
Wyoming	151	1.0	29	0.3	15	0.4	93	10.2	1	0.9
Colorado	1,274	1.6	603	1.2	103	0.5	508	10.2	10	1.2
New Mexico	3,865	11.2	2,033	7.7	279	10.1	607	24.4	10	2.8
Arizona	4,101	14.0	161	1.2	272	5.5	1,869	25.8	20	4.0
Utah	313	0.7	64	0.2	36	0.3	69	3.6	2	
Nevada	177	3.6	9	0.3	2	0.2	39	9.3	1	
PACIFIC:										
Washington	456	0.4	112	0.2	96	0.3	112	1.4	3	0.8
Oregon	223	0.4	105	0.2	25	0.2	61	1.9		
California	4,188	1.7	366	0.3	321	0.4	2,901	10.1	26	1.0

TABLE 137.—NUMBER AND PER CENT ILLITERATE IN POPULATION 10 YEARS OF AGE AND OVER, FOR PRINCIPAL POPULATION CLASSES, FOR CITIES HAVING 100,000 INHABITANTS OR MORE: 1920.

CITY.	ALL CLASSES: 1920		NATIVE WHITE.				FOREIGN-BORN WHITE.		NEGRO.	
			Native parentage.		Foreign or mixed parentage.					
	Number.	Per cent.	Number.	Per cent.	Number.	Per cent.	Number.	Per cent.	Number.	Per cent.
Akron, Ohio	5,958	3.5	161	0.2	71	0.3	5,425	14.6	272	5.5
Albany, N.Y	2,918	3.0	144	0.3	130	0.4	2,582	14.8	41	3.8
Atlanta, Ga	11,031	6.6	1,321	1.3	18	0.3	223	4.8	9,465	17.8
Baltimore, Md	26,248	4.4	1,929	0.6	802	0.6	11,622	14.0	11,822	12.9
Birmingham, Ala	12,200	8.4	530	0.7	55	0.7	936	15.6	10,674	18.4
Boston, Mass	24,524	4.0	176	0.1	341	0.2	23,407	9.9	317	2.2
Bridgeport, Conn	7,743	6.9	39	0.1	78	0.2	7,411	16.2	172	9.0
Buffalo, N.Y	17,095	4.2	270	0.2	517	0.3	16,180	13.5	111	2.8
Cambridge, Mass	2,736	3.1	24	0.1	48	0.2	2,547	8.1	108	2.5
Camden, N.J	4,544	5.0	244	0.6	124	0.6	3,510	17.6	654	9.4
Chicago, Ill	99,133	4.6	700	0.1	1,719	0.2	92,473	11.6	3,764	3.9
Cincinnati, Ohio	6,741	2.0	715	0.4	340	0.3	2,843	6.7	2,841	10.9
Cleveland, Ohio	33,164	5.3	219	0.1	405	0.2	30,946	13.1	1,563	5.2
Columbus, Ohio	5,664	2.8	1,826	1.4	444	1.3	1,788	11.3	1,584	8.4
Dallas, Tex	4,252	3.2	435	0.5	94	0.9	1,375	16.4	2,348	11.3
Dayton, Ohio	2,360	1.9	324	0.4	115	0.5	1,202	9.3	717	9.4
Denver, Colo	4,240	1.9	379	0.3	242	0.4	3,328	8.9	222	4.1
Des Moines, Iowa	1,395	1.3	259	0.4	50	0.2	800	7.2	282	6.1
Detroit, Mich	29,954	3.8	481	0.2	593	0.3	27,389	9.7	1,417	3.9
Fall River, Mass	11,178	11.9	50	0.4	459	1.2	10,632	25.5	27	11.0
Fort Worth, Tex	3,509	3.9	303	0.5	90	1.5	2,062	30.1	1,034	7.5
Grand Rapids, Mich	3,683	3.3	95	0.2	79	0.2	3,491	12.4	17	1.9
Hartford, Conn	5,662	5.1	49	0.1	43	0.1	5,286	13.2	266	7.6
Houston, Tex	6,217	5.4	244	0.4	225	1.4	2,592	22.6	3,152	10.8
Indianapolis, Ind	5,463	2.1	1,432	0.8	163	0.4	1,390	8.3	2,458	8.3
Jersey City, N.J	10,089	4.3	104	0.2	263	0.3	9,431	12.5	260	3.9
Kansas City, Kans	3,008	3.7	390	0.9	91	0.7	1,561	13.9	964	8.0
Kansas City, Mo	5,573	2.0	563	0.3	203	0.4	3,077	11.5	1,696	6.1
Los Angeles, Calif	10,203	2.0	474	0.2	333	0.3	7,887	7.3	575	4.3
Louisville, Ky	7,946	4.0	1,470	1.3	358	0.9	869	7.5	5,245	14.9
Lowell, Mass	6,231	6.9	32	0.2	213	0.6	5,960	15.9	6	4.2
Memphis, Tenn	9,280	6.7	378	0.6	45	0.4	534	9.4	8,310	15.6
Milwaukee, Wis	10,950	3.0	77	0.1	377	0.2	10,429	9.6	60	3.1
Minneapolis, Minn	3,844	1.2	104	0.1	213	0.2	3,379	3.9	122	3.5
Nashville, Tenn	7,054	7.2	1,246	2.1	45	0.8	175	7.4	5,588	18.4
New Bedford, Mass	11,631	12.1	47	0.3	270	0.9	10,330	21.7	954	25.2
New Haven, Conn	8,046	6.3	46	0.1	96	0.2	7,738	17.2	149	4.0
New Orleans, La	19,010	5.9	1,375	0.9	764	1.2	3,672	13.9	13,234	15.7
New York, N.Y	281,121	6.2	2,261	0.3	4,291	0.3	270,788	13.8	2,756	2.1
Bronx borough	26,202	4.5	132	0.1	330	0.2	25,020	9.7	63	1.6
Brooklyn borough	98,038	6.1	694	0.2	1,552	0.3	94,737	14.5	791	2.9
Manhattan borough	140,810	7.5	1,209	0.4	1,886	0.3	135,958	14.9	1,723	1.8
Queens borough	12,383	3.3	170	0.2	422	0.3	11,597	10.5	146	3.4
Richmond borough	3,688	4.0	56	0.2	101	0.3	3,476	11.2	33	2.7
Newark, N.J	19,721	6.0	224	0.3	315	0.3	18,403	15.9	626	4.5
Norfolk, Va	6,111	6.3	569	1.2	28	0.5	392	6.0	5,111	13.9
Oakland, Calif	4,638	2.5	115	0.2	192	0.3	3,489	7.8	121	2.5
Omaha, Nebr	4,011	2.5	151	0.2	85	0.2	3,334	9.5	408	4.5
Paterson, N.J	6,903	6.3	125	0.5	158	0.4	6,544	14.7	49	3.7
Philadelphia, Pa	58,631	4.0	1,514	0.3	1,250	0.3	50,379	12.8	5,316	4.6
Pittsburgh, Pa	20,297	4.3	361	0.2	524	0.3	17,712	14.9	1,661	5.2
Portland, Oreg	3,654	1.7	187	0.2	127	0.2	2,701	5.8	69	5.0
Providence, R.I	11,417	5.9	113	0.2	308	0.4	10,434	15.3	530	11.4
Reading, Pa	3,043	3.5	515	0.8	79	0.7	2,417	25.6	30	4.0
Richmond, Va	7,931	5.6	848	1.0	50	0.6	359	7.8	6,665	14.9
Rochester, N.Y	10,871	4.5	137	0.2	165	0.2	10,531	15.0	26	1.9
St. Louis, Mo	17,654	2.7	1,268	0.5	906	0.5	10,327	10.1	4,996	8.2
St. Paul, Minn	3,046	1.6	77	0.1	174	0.2	2,717	5.7	67	2.2
Salt Lake City, Utah	970	1.0	69	0.2	79	0.2	770	4.0	20	3.1
San Antonio, Tex	14,955	11.4	1,301	2.2	1,521	6.2	11,233	33.1	875	7.1
San Francisco, Calif	8,520	1.9	312	0.2	251	0.2	6,585	4.8	68	3.1
Scranton, Pa	6,941	6.5	72	0.2	242	0.6	6,614	23.4	11	2.3
Seattle, Wash	4,061	1.5	149	0.1	104	0.1	2,608	3.6	49	1.9
Spokane, Wash	687	0.8	49	0.1	24	0.1	550	3.3	20	3.2
Springfield, Mass	3,939	3.7	101	0.3	175	0.5	3,536	11.5	118	5.2
Syracuse, N.Y	5,607	4.0	212	0.3	186	0.4	5,158	16.2	40	3.6
Toledo, Ohio	4,897	2.5	368	0.4	244	0.4	4,002	10.6	254	5.0
Trenton, N.J	6,500	6.9	141	0.4	85	0.3	5,995	20.2	245	6.9
Washington, D.C	10,509	2.8	564	0.3	76	0.2	1,728	6.1	8,053	8.6
Wilmington, Del	4,907	5.5	249	0.5	96	0.5	3,083	19.2	1,473	15.7
Worcester, Mass	6,779	4.7	68	0.2	169	0.3	6,507	12.3	27	2.6
Yonkers, N.Y	4,309	5.5	26	0.1	55	0.2	4,162	16.4	56	3.5
Youngstown, Ohio	5,815	5.7	68	0.2	89	0.3	5,332	16.0	316	5.5

Table 138.—NUMBER AND PER CENT ILLITERATE IN POPULATION 21 YEARS OF AGE AND OVER, FOR PRINCIPAL POPULATION CLASSES, FOR CITIES HAVING 100,000 INHABITANTS OR MORE: 1920.

CITY.	ALL CLASSES: 1920		NATIVE WHITE.				FOREIGN-BORN WHITE.		NEGRO.	
			Native parentage.		Foreign or mixed parentage.					
	Number.	Per cent.	Number.	Per cent.	Number.	Per cent.	Number.	Per cent.	Number.	Per cent.
Akron, Ohio	5,840	4.2	143	0.2	63	0.3	5,343	15.8	264	6.3
Albany, N. Y	2,854	3.7	130	0.4	123	0.5	2,541	15.5	40	4.4
Atlanta, Ga	10,162	8.0	1,162	1.5	15	0.3	218	5.1	8,763	21.8
Baltimore, Md	25,394	5.5	1,799	0.8	711	0.8	11,478	15.0	11,336	15.4
Birmingham, Ala	11,276	10.4	480	0.9	30	0.6	901	16.5	9,860	22.7
Boston, Mass	24,190	5.0	145	0.1	259	0.2	23,199	10.5	309	2.6
Bridgeport, Conn	7,557	8.6	29	0.1	59	0.3	7,257	17.2	170	10.6
Buffalo, N. Y	16,727	5.3	234	0.3	425	0.4	15,949	14.3	103	3.0
Cambridge, Mass	2,689	3.9	23	0.1	33	0.2	2,520	8.5	104	3.1
Camden, N. J	4,376	6.3	215	0.7	84	0.6	3,433	18.7	633	11.7
Chicago, Ill	97,547	5.7	586	0.2	1,302	0.2	91,511	12.3	3,678	4.5
Cincinnati, Ohio	6,581	2.4	670	0.6	323	0.3	2,818	7.0	2,768	13.0
Cleveland, Ohio	32,711	6.7	191	0.2	295	0.2	30,678	14.1	1,517	6.1
Columbus, Ohio	4,927	3.1	1,344	1.3	306	1.1	1,737	11.8	1,519	9.7
Dallas, Tex	3,889	3.8	383	0.5	71	0.8	1,201	16.0	2,234	13.6
Dayton, Ohio	2,291	2.3	310	0.5	108	0.5	1,173	9.7	698	11.0
Denver, Colo	4,076	2.3	334	0.3	219	0.5	3,239	9.2	216	4.7
Des Moines, Iowa	1,347	1.6	244	0.5	38	0.2	781	7.5	280	7.6
Detroit, Mich	29,326	4.6	407	0.2	482	0.3	27,009	10.5	1,358	4.4
Fall River, Mass	10,777	15.8	47	0.6	377	1.8	10,316	27.0	27	12.7
Fort Worth, Tex	3,013	4.3	282	0.6	55	1.2	1,700	29.0	956	8.8
Grand Rapids, Mich	3,633	4.2	79	0.3	70	0.3	3,466	13.2	17	2.2
Hartford, Conn	5,572	6.3	40	0.2	35	0.2	5,229	14.1	252	9.4
Houston. Tex	5,641	6.4	197	0.5	169	1.4	2,266	22.4	3,005	13.2
Indianapolis, Ind	5,309	2.5	1,338	1.0	160	0.5	1,374	8.6	2,417	10.2
Jersey City, N. J	9,892	5.6	87	0.2	216	0.4	9,305	13.2	255	4.8
Kansas City, Kans	2,873	4.6	364	1.1	77	0.8	1,480	14.3	950	10.0
Kansas City, Mo	5,295	2.4	510	0.4	178	0.5	2,915	11.8	1,661	7.1
Los Angeles, Calif	9,684	2.3	414	0.2	265	0.3	7,552	7.7	568	5.1
Louisville, Ky	7,747	5.0	1,386	1.7	354	1.0	860	7.7	5,143	17.8
Lowell, Mass	6,001	8.6	25	0.2	181	0.9	5,770	16.5	6	5.0
Memphis, Tenn	8,732	8.1	331	0.6	37	0.4	528	10.0	7,823	18.6
Milwaukee, Wis	10,852	3.8	61	0.1	337	0.3	10,387	10.2	60	3.6
Minneapolis, Minn	3,772	1.5	84	0.1	185	0.2	3,358	4.1	120	3.9
Nashville, Tenn	6,677	9.0	1,135	2.6	45	0.9	171	7.8	5,326	22.9
New Bedford, Mass	11,064	15.0	44	0.4	235	1.5	9,834	23.1	923	30.4
New Haven, Conn	7,933	8.1	39	0.1	76	0.3	7,656	18.4	145	4.7
New Orleans, La	17,752	7.4	1,214	1.2	654	1.3	3,503	14.7	12,317	19.3
New York, N. Y	275,078	7.9	1,753	0.3	3,044	0.3	266,663	14.8	2,621	2.3
Bronx borough	25,822	5.9	102	0.2	224	0.2	25,381	10.4	59	2.0
Brooklyn borough	96,022	8.0	534	0.2	1,176	0.3	93,298	15.7	757	3.4
Manhattan borough	137,537	9.3	943	0.4	1,242	0.4	133,101	16.1	1,630	2.0
Queens borough	12,092	4.3	132	0.2	327	0.3	11,448	10.9	143	4.2
Richmond borough	3,605	5.2	42	0.2	75	0.4	3,435	11.8	32	3.3
Newark, N. J	19,254	7.7	182	0.3	247	0.4	18,084	17.1	592	5.3
Norfolk, Va	5,708	7.6	537	1.5	24	0.6	375	6.3	4,761	16.7
Oakland, Calif	4,490	3.0	97	0.2	163	0.4	3,408	8.1	117	2.8
Omaha, Nebr	3,890	3.1	129	0.2	63	0.2	3,273	10.0	393	5.3
Paterson, N. J	6,737	8.1	111	0.6	139	0.6	6,417	15.7	46	4.4
Philadelphia, Pa	57,269	5.0	1,327	0.3	1,028	0.4	49,607	13.7	5,136	5.4
Pittsburgh, Pa	19,991	5.6	314	0.3	451	0.4	17,571	15.7	1,616	6.2
Portland, Oreg	3,588	2.0	168	0.2	112	0.3	2,674	6.2	69	5.7
Providence, R. I	11,168	7.5	93	0.2	251	0.6	10,274	16.2	518	13.7
Reading, Pa	2,953	4.4	485	1.0	72	1.0	2,364	27.2	30	5.0
Richmond, Va	7,452	6.9	754	1.2	46	0.7	354	8.3	6,291	18.3
Rochester, N. Y	10,623	5.6	110	0.2	139	0.2	10,338	16.2	25	2.2
St. Louis, Mo	17,120	3.3	1,094	0.6	888	0.5	10,182	10.6	4,880	9.7
St. Paul, Minn	2,985	2.0	64	0.2	141	0.2	2,702	5.6	67	2.6
Salt Lake City, Utah	900	1.3	50	0.2	54	0.2	750	4.2	20	3.5
San Antonio, Tex	12,504	12.8	949	2.2	971	5.5	9,728	35.9	831	8.8
San Francisco, Calif	8,260	2.3	271	0.3	210	0.2	6,461	4.9	66	3.4
Scranton, Pa	6,832	8.8	63	0.3	213	0.8	6,543	24.5	11	2.8
Seattle, Wash	3,914	1.8	123	0.1	79	0.1	2,568	3.8	49	2.1
Spokane, Wash	671	1.0	41	0.1	20	0.1	547	3.5	20	3.8
Springfield, Mass	3,884	4.6	88	0.3	162	0.7	3,507	12.2	118	6.4
Syracuse, N. Y	5,400	4.8	130	0.3	133	0.4	5,093	17.1	35	3.8
Toledo, Ohio	4,773	3.0	338	0.5	217	0.5	3,947	11.2	243	5.7
Trenton, N. J	6,365	8.8	130	0.5	68	0.5	5,900	21.8	233	8.3
Washington, D. C	10,190	3.3	521	0.3	64	0.2	1,699	6.4	7,823	10.7
Wilmington, Del	4,756	6.8	230	0.7	78	0.7	3,039	20.2	1,403	18.6
Worcester, Mass	6,669	5.9	60	0.2	142	0.4	6,434	13.0	26	3.2
Yonkers, N. Y	4,245	7.2	20	0.1	40	0.2	4,121	17.2	55	4.4
Youngstown, Ohio	5,726	7.2	61	0.2	70	0.4	5,281	17.1	305	6.4

TABLE **139.**—PER CENT ILLITERATE IN POPULATION 10 YEARS OF AGE AND OVER, BY SEX AND PRINCIPAL POPULATION CLASSES, FOR CITIES HAVING, IN 1920, 100,000 INHABITANTS OR MORE: 1920 AND 1910.

CITY.	ALL CLASSES.						NATIVE WHITE.				FOREIGN-BORN WHITE.		NEGRO.	
	Both sexes.		Male.		Female.		Native parentage.		Foreign or mixed parentage.					
	1920	1910	1920	1910	1920	1910	1920	1910	1920	1910	1920	1910	1920	1910
Akron, Ohio	3.5	3.0	3.6	3.3	3.3	2.6	0.2	0.4	0.3	0.4	14.6	11.6	5.5	8.9
Albany, N. Y.	3.0	3.2	3.1	3.3	2.9	3.2	0.3	0.3	0.4	0.5	14.8	13.8	3.8	4.2
Atlanta, Ga.	6.6	8.6	6.1	7.1	7.1	10.0	1.3	2.1	0.3	0.5	4.8	5.9	17.8	20.9
Baltimore, Md.	4.4	4.4	4.1	3.9	4.7	5.0	0.6	0.6	0.6	0.6	14.0	12.0	12.9	13.2
Birmingham, Ala.	8.4	10.4	8.3	9.5	8.5	11.5	0.7	1.2	0.7	0.7	15.6	15.1	18.4	22.1
Boston, Mass.	4.0	4.4	3.6	3.7	4.4	5.1	0.1	0.1	0.2	0.2	9.9	10.0	2.2	3.5
Bridgeport, Conn.	6.9	5.4	6.7	4.7	7.1	6.1	0.1	0.2	0.2	0.4	16.2	12.1	9.0	5.2
Buffalo, N. Y.	4.2	3.7	4.2	3.5	4.2	4.0	0.2	0.2	0.3	0.5	13.5	10.3	2.8	4.1
Cambridge, Mass.	3.1	3.0	2.9	2.6	3.2	3.4	0.1	0.1	0.2	0.2	8.1	6.6	2.5	5.6
Camden, N. J.	5.0	4.4	5.0	4.4	4.9	4.4	0.6	0.6	0.6	0.7	17.6	14.7	9.4	14.0
Chicago, Ill.	4.6	4.5	4.2	4.2	4.9	4.8	0.1	0.2	0.2	0.3	11.6	10.0	3.9	4.0
Cincinnati, Ohio	2.0	3.1	1.9	2.8	2.1	3.4	0.4	1.0	0.3	0.5	6.7	9.6	10.9	14.3
Cleveland, Ohio	5.3	4.6	5.1	4.4	5.5	4.9	0.1	0.2	0.2	0.3	13.1	10.5	5.2	4.1
Columbus, Ohio	2.8	2.9	3.1	3.0	2.6	2.8	1.4	1.3	1.3	0.9	11.3	12.6	8.4	8.7
Dallas, Tex.	3.2	4.0	3.3	3.4	3.1	4.6	0.5	0.7	0.9	0.4	16.4	6.1	11.3	15.4
Dayton, Ohio	1.9	2.3	1.9	2.3	1.8	2.3	0.4	0.5	0.5	0.5	9.3	10.6	9.4	9.5
Denver, Colo.	1.9	2.1	1.7	1.8	2.1	2.4	0.3	0.2	0.3	0.3	8.9	8.1	4.1	6.0
Des Moines, Iowa	1.3	2.0	1.4	1.8	1.3	2.1	0.4	0.6	0.2	0.5	7.2	8.4	6.1	8.8
Detroit, Mich.	3.8	5.0	3.6	5.4	4.0	4.5	0.2	0.2	0.3	0.5	9.7	11.7	3.9	3.5
Fall River, Mass.	11.9	13.2	11.4	12.2	12.4	14.2	0.4	0.9	1.2	2.0	25.5	23.5	11.0	8.1
Fort Worth, Tex.	3.9	3.8	4.4	3.9	3.4	3.8	0.5	0.7	1.5	1.0	30.1	15.6	7.5	12.0
Grand Rapids, Mich.	3.3	2.5	3.2	2.3	3.5	2.7	0.2	0.2	0.2	0.3	12.4	7.6	1.9	4.8
Hartford, Conn.	5.1	5.0	4.6	4.2	5.6	5.8	0.1	0.2	0.1	0.3	13.2	12.6	7.6	4.8
Houston, Tex.	5.4	6.4	4.9	5.2	5.8	7.6	0.4	0.6	1.4	1.2	22.6	8.9	10.8	16.4
Indianapolis, Ind.	2.1	3.0	2.0	3.0	2.1	3.0	0.8	0.9	0.4	0.5	8.3	11.3	8.3	12.4
Jersey City, N. J.	4.3	5.6	4.1	5.7	4.6	5.4	0.2	0.2	0.2	0.4	12.5	14.5	3.9	4.9
Kansas City, Kans.	3.7	3.9	3.4	3.8	4.0	4.0	0.9	0.5	0.7	0.7	13.9	15.4	8.0	10.0
Kansas City, Mo.	2.0	2.3	2.0	2.0	2.0	2.7	0.3	0.4	0.4	0.4	11.5	8.9	6.1	9.6
Los Angeles, Calif.	2.0	1.9	1.9	1.8	2.2	2.0	0.2	0.2	0.3	0.4	7.3	7.0	4.3	6.0
Louisville, Ky.	4.0	5.3	3.9	4.8	4.1	5.8	1.3	1.3	0.9	1.0	7.5	9.5	14.9	18.7
Lowell, Mass.	6.9	6.0	6.6	6.0	7.1	6.0	0.2	0.3	0.6	0.7	15.9	11.7	4.2	2.7
Memphis, Tenn.	6.7	8.0	6.0	6.5	7.4	9.6	0.6	0.5	0.4	0.3	9.4	9.9	15.6	17.6
Milwaukee, Wis.	3.0	3.6	2.9	3.6	3.1	3.5	0.1	0.1	0.2	0.3	9.6	9.5	3.1	2.9
Minneapolis, Minn.	1.2	2.4	1.1	2.3	1.4	2.6	0.1	0.1	0.2	0.2	3.9	6.8	3.5	2.9
Nashville, Tenn.	7.2	8.8	6.9	7.8	7.4	9.6	2.1	1.8	0.8	0.5	7.4	7.0	18.4	22.0
New Bedford, Mass.	12.1	12.1	11.4	12.0	12.7	12.3	0.3	0.6	0.9	1.6	21.7	20.8	25.2	23.7
New Haven, Conn.	6.3	7.0	5.6	6.2	7.0	7.8	0.1	0.2	0.2	0.4	17.2	17.4	4.0	4.5
New Orleans, La.	5.9	6.9	5.1	5.5	6.8	8.1	0.9	1.0	1.2	1.2	13.9	12.9	15.7	18.3
New York, N. Y.	6.2	6.7	5.1	5.3	7.3	8.0	0.3	0.2	0.3	0.4	13.8	13.2	2.1	3.6
Bronx borough	4.5	4.0	3.3	3.7	5.7	4.4	0.1	0.2	0.2	0.2	9.7	9.1	1.6	5.3
Brooklyn borough	6.1	6.1	5.0	4.9	7.2	7.2	0.2	0.2	0.3	0.4	14.5	13.6	2.9	4.2
Manhattan borough	7.5	8.0	6.2	6.1	8.8	9.8	0.4	0.2	0.3	0.4	14.9	13.8	1.8	3.2
Queens borough	3.3	3.8	3.0	3.8	3.6	3.8	0.2	0.3	0.3	0.3	10.5	10.1	3.4	5.1
Richmond borough	4.0	3.9	3.6	4.0	4.4	3.9	0.2	0.3	0.3	0.5	11.2	10.4	2.7	6.4
Newark, N. J.	6.0	6.0	5.4	5.0	6.7	7.0	0.3	0.3	0.3	0.6	15.9	14.2	4.5	7.5
Norfolk, Va.	6.3	9.0	5.8	7.6	6.9	10.2	1.2	1.3	0.5	0.4	6.0	12.5	13.9	19.7
Oakland, Calif.	2.5	3.0	2.7	3.0	2.4	3.1	0.2	0.2	0.3	0.6	7.8	8.3	2.5	3.3
Omaha, Nebr [1]	2.5	3.1	2.5	3.4	2.5	2.8	0.2	0.2	0.2	0.3	9.5	9.9	4.5	6.5
Paterson, N. J.	6.3	6.9	5.4	5.8	7.1	7.9	0.5	0.9	0.4	0.7	14.7	14.5	3.7	11.3
Philadelphia, Pa.	4.0	4.6	3.6	3.9	4.3	5.2	0.3	0.5	0.3	0.6	12.8	12.9	4.6	7.8
Pittsburgh, Pa.	4.3	6.2	4.3	7.1	4.3	5.3	0.2	0.3	0.3	0.6	14.9	17.5	5.2	6.6
Portland, Oreg.	1.7	1.2	1.9	1.2	1.5	1.1	0.2	0.1	0.2	0.2	5.8	3.9	5.0	1.9
Providence, R. I.	5.9	7.7	5.2	7.1	6.6	8.4	0.2	0.3	0.4	1.0	15.3	17.6	11.4	9.7
Reading, Pa.	3.5	3.0	3.5	3.1	3.4	3.0	0.8	1.1	0.7	1.0	25.6	18.8	4.0	3.4
Richmond, Va.	5.6	8.2	5.2	7.4	6.0	9.0	1.0	1.3	0.6	0.6	7.8	7.1	14.9	19.6
Rochester, N. Y.	4.5	3.9	4.3	3.9	4.8	3.7	0.2	0.2	0.2	0.3	15.0	11.5	1.9	1.4
St. Louis, Mo.	2.7	3.7	2.5	3.4	2.9	4.0	0.5	0.6	0.5	0.6	10.1	11.4	8.2	12.4
St. Paul, Minn.	1.6	2.1	1.4	1.8	1.8	2.4	0.1	0.1	0.2	0.2	5.3	6.3	2.2	2.0
Salt Lake City, Utah	1.0	1.6	1.0	1.7	1.0	1.4	0.2	0.3	0.2	0.3	4.0	4.4	3.1	1.0
San Antonio, Tex.	11.4	0.1	11.6	8.5	11.1	11.7	2.2	2.7	6.2	7.3	33.1	27.0	7.1	13.2
San Francisco, Calif.	1.9	2.1	1.8	1.8	2.1	2.5	0.2	0.2	0.2	0.2	4.8	4.7	3.1	5.1
Scranton, Pa.	6.5	8.9	6.7	9.7	6.3	8.0	0.2	0.6	0.6	1.2	23.4	24.3	2.3	3.3
Seattle, Wash.	1.5	1.1	1.6	1.2	1.5	0.8	0.1	0.1	0.1	0.1	3.6	3.1	1.9	2.7
Spokane, Wash.	0.8	1.3	0.7	1.6	0.9	0.9	0.1	0.1	0.1	0.1	3.3	4.4	3.2	2.4
Springfield, Mass.	3.7	4.5	3.4	4.3	4.0	4.7	0.3	0.3	0.5	0.8	11.5	13.5	5.2	4.6
Syracuse, N. Y.	4.0	4.9	4.0	5.6	4.0	4.2	0.3	0.4	0.4	0.5	16.2	17.3	3.6	5.1
Toledo, Ohio	2.5	2.8	2.6	2.7	2.3	2.8	0.4	0.8	0.4	0.6	10.6	9.6	5.0	4.3
Trenton, N. J.	6.9	5.9	6.7	5.9	7.1	5.9	0.4	0.9	0.3	1.0	20.2	15.3	6.9	17.7
Washington, D. C.	2.8	4.9	2.5	4.1	3.0	5.7	0.3	0.6	0.2	0.4	6.1	8.2	8.6	13.5
Wilmington, Del.	5.5	6.6	5.5	6.7	5.5	6.5	0.5	0.6	0.5	0.7	19.2	21.8	15.7	18.7
Worcester, Mass.	4.7	5.0	4.3	5.0	5.1	5.1	0.2	0.2	0.3	0.6	12.3	12.0	2.6	3.5
Yonkers, N. Y.	5.5	8.4	5.0	8.9	5.9	8.0	0.1	0.2	0.2	0.4	16.4	19.7	3.5	7.0
Youngstown, Ohio	5.7	7.1	6.2	7.7	5.1	6.4	0.2	0.3	0.3	0.5	16.0	17.8	5.5	5.8

[1] Includes South Omaha for 1910.

TABLE 140.—PER CENT ILLITERATE IN POPULATION 21 YEARS OF AGE AND OVER, BY SEX AND PRINCIPAL POPULATION CLASSES, FOR CITIES HAVING, IN 1920, 100,000 INHABITANTS OR MORE: 1920 AND 1910.

[Per cent not shown where base is less than 100.]

CITY	ALL CLASSES.						NATIVE WHITE.				FOREIGN-BORN WHITE.		NEGRO.	
	Both sexes.		Male.		Female.		Native parentage.		Foreign or mixed parentage.					
	1920	1910	1920	1910	1920	1910	1920	1910	1920	1910	1920	1910	1920	1910
Akron, Ohio	4.2	3.6	4.3	3.9	4.1	3.2	0.2	0.5	0.3	0.5	15.8	11.8	6.3	11.7
Albany, N. Y	3.7	3.8	3.8	3.8	3.6	3.8	0.4	0.4	0.5	0.6	15.5	13.7	4.4	4.8
Atlanta, Ga	8.0	10.4	7.2	8.1	8.9	12.4	1.5	2.3	0.3	0.6	5.1	6.2	21.8	25.7
Baltimore, Md	5.5	5.5	5.0	4.7	5.9	6.2	0.8	0.7	0.8	0.7	15.0	12.5	15.4	15.8
Birmingham, Ala	10.4	12.4	10.0	10.7	10.9	14.3	0.9	1.3	0.6	0.4	16.5	14.9	22.7	26.1
Boston, Mass	5.0	5.4	4.6	4.5	5.5	6.2	0.1	0.1	0.2	0.3	10.5	10.4	2.6	4.1
Bridgeport, Conn	8.6	6.3	8.2	5.5	9.0	7.2	0.1	0.3	0.3	0.5	17.2	12.4	10.6	6.2
Buffalo, N. Y	5.3	4.7	5.3	4.4	5.3	5.1	0.3	0.3	0.4	0.6	14.3	10.7	3.0	4.8
Cambridge, Mass	3.9	3.7	3.7	3.2	4.0	4.1	0.1	0.2	0.2	0.3	8.5	6.9	3.1	7.2
Camden, N. J	6.3	5.2	6.2	5.1	6.3	5.2	0.7	0.8	0.6	0.7	18.7	14.5	11.7	17.0
Chicago, Ill	5.7	5.5	5.2	5.1	6.3	6.0	0.2	0.2	0.2	0.3	12.3	10.2	4.5	4.6
Cincinnati, Ohio	2.4	3.9	2.3	3.5	2.5	4.2	0.6	1.4	0.3	0.6	7.0	9.6	13.0	17.0
Cleveland, Ohio	6.7	5.7	6.3	5.3	7.1	6.2	0.2	0.2	0.2	0.3	14.1	11.0	6.1	4.8
Columbus, Ohio	3.1	3.3	3.3	3.4	2.9	3.3	1.3	1.4	1.1	0.9	11.8	12.5	9.7	10.3
Dallas, Tex	3.8	4.7	3.7	3.8	3.8	5.8	0.5	0.7	0.8	0.4	16.0	6.0	13.6	18.3
Dayton, Ohio	2.3	2.8	2.3	2.8	2.2	2.8	0.5	0.7	0.5	0.6	9.7	10.9	11.0	11.4
Denver, Colo	2.3	2.6	2.0	2.2	2.5	3.0	0.3	0.3	0.5	0.3	9.2	8.2	4.7	7.1
Des Moines, Iowa	1.6	2.4	1.7	2.2	1.6	2.6	0.5	0.7	0.2	0.6	7.5	8.8	7.6	10.5
Detroit, Mich	4.6	6.1	4.3	6.5	5.0	5.6	0.2	0.3	0.3	0.6	10.5	12.1	4.4	4.1
Fall River, Mass	15.8	16.6	15.2	15.6	16.3	17.6	0.6	1.1	1.8	3.2	27.0	24.9	12.7	9.2
Fort Worth, Tex	4.3	4.5	4.7	4.4	3.8	4.7	0.6	0.7	1.2	0.9	29.0	15.3	8.8	14.3
Grand Rapids, Mich	4.2	3.0	4.0	2.7	4.4	3.3	0.3	0.2	0.3	0.3	13.2	7.6	2.2	5.2
Hartford, Conn	6.3	6.0	5.7	5.0	7.0	7.1	0.2	0.3	0.2	0.4	14.1	13.4	9.4	5.9
Houston, Tex	6.4	7.7	5.7	5.9	7.0	9.6	0.5	0.7	1.4	1.3	22.4	9.0	13.2	20.0
Indianapolis, Ind	2.5	3.6	2.5	3.5	2.6	3.7	1.0	1.2	0.5	0.6	8.6	11.1	10.2	15.2
Jersey City, N. J	5.6	6.7	5.2	6.8	5.9	6.6	0.2	0.3	0.4	0.5	13.2	14.3	4.8	5.7
Kansas City, Kans	4.6	4.8	4.2	4.6	5.1	5.1	1.1	0.6	0.8	1.0	14.3	15.1	10.0	12.7
Kansas City, Mo	2.4	2.8	2.3	2.3	2.4	3.3	0.4	0.5	0.5	0.4	11.8	9.1	7.1	11.3
Los Angeles, Calif	2.3	2.1	2.1	2.0	2.5	2.3	0.2	0.3	0.3	0.4	7.7	6.9	5.1	7.3
Louisville, Ky	5.0	6.7	4.8	5.9	5.2	7.4	1.7	1.7	1.0	1.1	7.7	9.4	17.8	22.8
Lowell, Mass	8.6	7.2	8.3	7.2	8.9	7.2	0.2	0.3	0.9	1.0	16.5	12.3	5.0	....
Memphis, Tenn	8.1	9.3	7.0	7.1	9.1	11.7	0.6	0.6	0.4	0.2	10.0	9.6	18.6	20.4
Milwaukee, Wis	3.8	4.6	3.6	4.6	4.0	4.6	0.1	0.2	0.3	0.3	10.2	9.7	3.6	3.2
Minneapolis, Minn	1.5	2.9	1.3	2.6	1.7	3.2	0.1	0.1	0.2	0.3	4.1	6.9	3.9	3.3
Nashville, Tenn	9.0	11.0	8.5	9.4	9.5	12.4	2.6	2.1	0.9	0.6	7.8	7.3	22.9	27.9
New Bedford, Mass	15.0	14.6	14.2	14.5	15.8	14.8	0.4	0.7	1.5	2.7	23.1	22.2	30.4	27.4
New Haven, Conn	8.1	8.5	7.2	7.5	9.0	9.6	0.1	0.2	0.3	0.4	18.4	18.3	4.7	5.4
New Orleans, La	7.4	8.4	6.2	6.5	8.5	10.1	1.2	1.2	1.3	1.2	14.7	13.1	19.3	21.7
New York, N. Y	7.9	8.1	6.5	6.4	9.4	9.8	0.3	0.2	0.3	0.4	14.8	14.0	2.3	4.2
Bronx borough	5.9	5.0	4.2	4.5	7.5	5.5	0.2	0.2	0.2	0.3	10.4	9.2	2.0	6.4
Brooklyn borough	8.0	7.5	6.5	6.0	9.5	9.0	0.2	0.2	0.3	0.5	15.7	14.3	3.4	4.9
Manhattan borough	9.3	9.5	7.7	7.2	10.9	11.9	0.4	0.2	0.4	0.4	16.1	14.9	2.0	3.6
Queens borough	4.3	4.8	3.9	4.7	4.6	4.9	0.2	0.4	0.3	0.4	10.9	10.1	4.2	6.3
Richmond borough	5.2	4.9	4.6	4.9	5.8	4.9	0.2	0.4	0.4	0.4	11.8	10.5	3.3	8.4
Newark, N. J	7.7	7.3	6.9	6.0	8.6	8.7	0.3	0.4	0.4	0.7	17.1	14.9	5.3	8.9
Norfolk, Va	7.6	10.4	6.7	8.6	8.6	12.3	1.5	1.6	0.6	0.5	6.3	13.1	16.7	22.6
Oakland, Calif	3.0	3.6	3.1	3.5	2.9	3.7	0.2	0.2	0.4	0.6	8.1	8.5	2.8	3.8
Omaha, Nebr [1]	3.1	3.8	3.1	4.0	3.2	3.5	0.2	0.3	0.2	0.4	10.0	9.8	5.3	7.4
Paterson, N. J	8.1	8.5	7.0	7.0	9.2	10.0	0.6	1.2	0.6	0.9	15.7	15.0	4.4	13.6
Philadelphia, Pa	5.0	5.6	4.5	4.7	5.4	6.3	0.3	0.6	0.4	0.8	13.7	13.4	5.4	9.1
Pittsburgh, Pa	5.6	7.6	5.5	8.5	5.6	6.6	0.3	0.4	0.4	0.7	15.7	17.8	6.2	8.0
Portland, Oreg	2.0	1.3	2.3	1.3	1.8	1.3	0.2	0.1	0.3	0.2	6.2	3.9	5.7	2.1
Providence, R. I	7.5	9.1	6.6	8.3	8.3	8.9	0.2	0.4	0.6	1.3	16.2	18.2	13.7	11.5
Reading, Pa	4.4	3.7	4.4	3.7	4.3	3.6	1.0	1.4	1.0	1.2	27.2	19.1	5.0	4.1
Richmond, Va	6.9	9.9	6.3	8.6	7.5	11.1	1.2	1.5	0.7	0.6	8.3	7.3	18.3	23.6
Rochester, N. Y	5.6	4.4	5.3	4.5	5.8	4.3	0.2	0.3	0.3	0.4	16.2	11.6	2.2	1.7
St. Louis, Mo	3.3	4.5	3.0	4.1	3.7	5.0	0.6	0.7	0.5	0.7	10.6	11.5	9.7	14.6
St. Paul, Minn	2.0	2.6	1.7	2.2	2.2	3.2	0.2	0.3	0.3	0.3	5.6	6.4	2.6	2.7
Salt Lake City, Utah	1.3	1.9	1.3	2.0	1.3	1.8	0.2	0.3	0.2	0.3	4.2	4.4	3.5	5.1
San Antonio, Tex	12.8	11.5	13.3	9.4	12.3	13.6	2.2	3.0	5.5	7.0	35.9	27.3	8.8	16.5
San Francisco, Calif	2.3	2.4	2.0	2.0	2.5	2.9	0.3	0.2	0.2	0.2	4.9	4.6	3.4	5.6
Scranton, Pa	8.8	11.2	9.1	12.2	8.6	10.2	0.3	0.8	0.8	1.4	24.5	24.7	2.8	4.0
Seattle, Wash	1.8	1.2	1.8	1.4	1.7	1.0	0.1	0.1	0.1	0.1	3.8	3.1	2.1	2.9
Spokane, Wash	1.0	1.5	0.9	1.8	1.1	1.1	0.1	0.1	0.1	0.1	3.5	4.2	3.8	2.9
Springfield, Mass	4.6	5.5	4.2	5.2	5.0	5.7	0.3	0.3	0.7	1.1	12.2	14.4	6.4	5.8
Syracuse, N. Y	4.8	5.6	4.8	6.3	4.8	4.8	0.3	0.4	0.4	0.5	17.1	17.2	3.8	5.6
Toledo, Ohio	3.0	3.5	3.1	3.4	2.9	3.6	0.5	1.0	0.5	0.8	11.2	10.0	5.7	5.1
Trenton, N. J	8.8	7.1	8.5	7.0	9.1	7.1	0.5	1.1	0.5	1.2	21.8	15.7	8.3	12.3
Washington, D. C	3.3	6.0	3.0	4.9	3.6	7.0	0.3	0.7	0.2	0.5	6.4	8.3	10.7	16.8
Wilmington, Del	6.8	7.9	6.7	8.0	6.9	7.9	0.7	0.8	0.7	0.8	20.2	21.7	18.6	23.2
Worcester, Mass	5.9	6.1	5.5	6.0	6.4	6.2	0.2	0.3	0.4	0.8	13.0	12.3	3.2	4.2
Yonkers, N. Y	7.2	10.0	6.6	10.6	7.7	9.5	0.1	0.3	0.2	0.5	17.2	19.7	4.4	8.3
Youngstown, Ohio	7.2	8.6	7.6	9.0	6.7	8.1	0.2	0.4	0.4	0.6	17.1	18.4	6.4	6.8

[1] Includes South Omaha for 1910.

TABLE **141.**—NUMBER AND PER CENT ILLITERATE IN POPULATION 10 YEARS OF AGE AND OVER, FOR PRINCIPAL POPULATION CLASSES, FOR CITIES HAVING FROM 25,000 TO 100,000 INHABITANTS: 1920.

[Per cent not shown where base is less than 100.]

CITY.	ALL CLASSES: 1920		NATIVE WHITE.		FOREIGN-BORN WHITE.		NEGRO.	
	Number.	Per cent.	Number.	Per cent.	Number.	Per cent.	Number.	Per cent.
ALABAMA:								
Mobile	4,502	9.0	166	0.6	67	3.4	4,267	21.2
Montgomery	4,554	12.7	81	0.4	33	4.4	4,440	26.8
ARIZONA:								
Phoenix	810	3.4	131	0.7	637	16.6	25	2.7
ARKANSAS:								
Fort Smith	793	3.4	268	1.4	56	6.6	468	15.5
Little Rock	2,421	4.4	792	2.1	49	2.7	1,580	10.5
CALIFORNIA:								
Alameda	319	1.3	23	0.1	251	4.3	14	8.4
Berkeley	497	1.0	26	0.1	397	4.2	8	1.9
Fresno	1,749	4.7	65	0.2	1,429	17.2	19	4.5
Long Beach	266	0.5	44	0.1	176	2.7	6	4.7
Pasadena	232	0.6	37	0.1	137	2.1	45	4.9
Sacramento	1,296	2.3	57	0.1	985	9.2	24	4.0
San Diego	1,008	1.6	127	0.3	792	6.1	48	5.6
San Jose	1,653	5.0	126	0.5	1,430	18.5	16	10.0
Stockton	911	2.7	93	0.4	671	9.8	22	7.6
COLORADO:								
Colorado Springs	248	1.0	60	0.3	130	5.0	56	6.5
Pueblo	1,886	5.4	358	1.4	1,396	19.7	118	9.9
CONNECTICUT:								
Meriden	1,083	4.5	23	0.1	1,059	13.5		
New Britain	4,226	9.5	37	0.2	4,146	19.8	43	16.6
New London	1,098	5.3	20	0.1	1,057	18.3	19	4.4
Norwalk	980	4.4	42	0.3	917	15.6	19	3.6
Stamford	2,024	7.5	28	0.2	1,958	18.6	33	4.7
Waterbury	5,426	7.5	63	0.2	5,326	18.1	34	4.2
FLORIDA:								
Jacksonville	4,125	5.5	221	0.6	140	3.7	3,758	10.8
Miami	821	3.4	17	0.1	55	2.2	748	10.2
Pensacola	1,858	7.4	266	1.8	81	5.7	1,511	17.3
Tampa	2,188	5.3	184	0.9	1,055	10.1	943	9.6
GEORGIA:								
Augusta	4,948	11.3	556	2.4	67	7.3	4,305	22.2
Columbus	2,506	9.9	860	4.9	13	4.0	1,633	21.6
Macon	4,942	11.2	379	1.6	41	6.0	4,520	23.1
Savannah	7,402	10.7	257	0.8	184	5.7	6,953	20.7
ILLINOIS:								
Aurora	548	1.8	58	0.3	455	7.1	35	6.7
Bloomington	365	1.5	82	0.4	205	7.3	69	10.4
Cicero town	1,625	4.8	30	0.2	1,592	10.4		
Danville	769	2.8	333	1.4	188	9.9	244	12.5
Decatur	422	1.2	190	0.6	139	5.4	90	9.1
East St. Louis	2,052	3.8	431	1.1	840	12.5	775	12.8
Elgin	156	0.7	49	0.3	103	2.1	4	3.9
Evanston	613	2.0	32	0.1	489	7.3	86	4.0
Joliet	1,120	3.6	68	0.3	1,006	12.0	46	7.6
Moline	406	1.6	45	0.4	349	4.8	12	4.1
Oak Park village	161	0.5	17	0.1	126	2.2	8	5.1
Peoria	1,194	1.8	231	0.4	791	10.2	161	8.5
Quincy	516	1.7	191	0.7	156	6.5	165	15.2
Rock Island	503	1.7	60	0.3	410	7.7	32	5.0
Rockford	1,771	3.3	117	0.3	1,635	9.5	14	3.4
Springfield	1,280	2.6	239	0.6	791	12.8	239	10.2
INDIANA:								
Anderson	528	2.2	347	1.5	101	10.9	80	10.7
East Chicago	3,359	12.9	90	0.3	3,268	22.6	57	4.7
Evansville	1,852	2.0	968	1.4	160	5.0	804	14.6
Fort Wayne	1,629	2.3	1,066	1.7	446	6.8	110	8.8
Gary	3,126	7.5	59	0.3	2,694	16.6	371	8.2
Hammond	1,771	6.4	59	0.3	1,700	21.2	7	5.4
Kokomo	453	1.9	276	1.2	138	12.0	39	5.4
Muncie	797	2.6	511	1.8	73	9.0	213	12.3
Richmond	330	1.5	148	0.7	95	8.5	85	6.8
South Bend	1,978	3.6	214	0.5	1,721	13.0	39	3.6
Terre Haute	1,038	1.9	481	1.0	305	8.4	251	8.2
IOWA:								
Cedar Rapids	573	1.5	91	0.3	439	7.6	42	7.6
Council Bluffs	444	1.5	81	0.3	314	8.0	49	9.5
Davenport	510	1.1	97	0.2	364	4.8	48	8.5
Dubuque	419	1.3	88	0.3	331	7.9		
Sioux City	1,089	1.9	99	0.2	955	8.6	25	2.5
Waterloo	358	1.2	74	0.3	234	8.1	48	7.0

TABLE 141.—NUMBER AND PER CENT ILLITERATE IN POPULATION 10 YEARS OF AGE AND OVER, FOR PRINCIPAL POPULATION CLASSES, FOR CITIES HAVING FROM 25,000 TO 100,000 INHABITANTS: 1920—Continued.

[Per cent not shown where base is less than 100.]

CITY.	ALL CLASSES: 1920 Number.	Per cent.	NATIVE WHITE. Number.	Per cent.	FOREIGN-BORN WHITE. Number.	Per cent.	NEGRO. Number.	Per cent.
KANSAS:								
Topeka	915	2.2	141	0.4	489	12.7	278	7.7
Wichita	595	1.0	125	0.2	342	11.8	127	4.4
KENTUCKY:								
Covington	756	1.6	277	0.7	67	2.3	412	15.5
Lexington	3,207	9.0	698	2.9	60	7.6	2,449	22.6
Newport	446	1.8	188	0.9	157	7.5	101	14.0
LOUISIANA:								
Shreveport	3,638	9.9	62	0.3	196	15.4	3,373	22.6
MAINE:								
Bangor	241	1.1	69	0.4	170	4.6	1	0.6
Lewiston	1,326	5.1	263	1.7	1,059	10.6	1	......
Portland	1,568	2.7	120	0.3	1,423	11.0	18	7.0
MARYLAND:								
Cumberland	550	2.3	293	1.3	169	14.7	88	7.2
Hagerstown	676	3.0	401	2.0	49	11.4	224	17.6
MASSACHUSETTS:								
Brockton	1,469	2.7	71	0.2	1,380	8.2	10	2.2
Brookline town	80	0.2	15	0.1	61	0.7	3	0.9
Chelsea	3,088	9.3	40	0.3	3,023	17.8	16	5.2
Chicopee	1,780	6.7	71	0.5	1,709	14.2	......	...
Everett	604	1.9	18	0.1	572	5.2	13	1.4
Fitchburg	1,529	4.7	83	0.4	1,444	11.2	2	......
Haverhill	1,382	3.1	95	0.3	1,269	9.6	11	3.5
Holyoke	2,487	5.2	109	0.4	2,372	11.9	4	3.4
Lawrence	7,105	9.6	113	0.3	6,952	18.1	31	15.7
Lynn	1,989	2.4	82	0.2	1,850	6.7	35	5.5
Malden	753	1.9	14	0.1	728	5.2	10	2.4
Medford	320	1.0	25	0.1	286	3.4	8	2.0
Newton	730	1.9	15	0.1	702	7.0	9	1.9
Pittsfield	1,222	3.7	62	0.2	1,153	14.2	2	0.6
Quincy	1,146	3.0	21	0.1	1,121	8.3	......	
Revere	1,263	5.7	16	0.1	1,246	14.2		
Salem	1,788	5.3	72	0.3	1,708	15.4	3	2.9
Somerville	1,311	1.7	80	0.2	1,218	5.1	8	3.0
Taunton	2,746	9.2	127	0.6	2,492	25.3	124	44.4
Waltham	1,150	4.5	510	2.9	624	7.8	9	......
MICHIGAN:								
Battle Creek	345	1.1	65	0.2	255	7.7	16	1.7
Bay City	1,367	3.6	326	1.1	1,039	11.7	1	0.9
Flint	1,466	2.0	196	0.3	1,161	7.9	103	6.8
Hamtramck village	6,231	19.9	60	0.8	6,100	27.1	71	4.4
Highland Park	567	1.5	35	0.1	516	4.2	11	3.5
Jackson	809	2.0	130	0.4	639	12.2	29	4.0
Kalamazoo	1,092	2.7	253	0.8	804	11.3	26	4.4
Lansing	599	1.3	102	0.3	478	8.1	19	3.3
Muskegon	533	1.8	73	0.3	452	6.7	......	
Pontiac	497	1.8	69	0.3	397	7.9	28	5.2
Port Huron	390	1.9	84	0.6	263	4.3	42	10.3
Saginaw	1,282	2.6	199	0.5	1,069	9.3	7	2.5
MINNESOTA:								
Duluth	1,923	2.4	112	0.2	1,787	6.0	8	1.8
MISSOURI:								
Joplin	380	1.5	297	1.3	26	3.6	47	7.0
St. Joseph	2,270	3.5	873	1.6	873	13.8	520	14.3
Springfield	615	1.9	396	1.3	31	3.2	187	13.3
MONTANA:								
Butte	772	2.2	39	0.2	680	6.0	10	5.2
NEBRASKA:								
Lincoln	1,098	2.4	122	0.3	938	13.4	37	4.7
NEW HAMPSHIRE:								
Manchester	4,071	6.5	195	0.5	3,869	14.3	1	......
Nashua	1,957	8.5	104	0.7	1,843	21.4	1	......
NEW JERSEY:								
Atlantic City	973	2.3	79	0.3	550	7.9	335	3.4
Bayonne	6,588	11.7	76	0.3	6,471	25.7	33	6.2
Clifton	1,125	5.6	27	0.3	1,096	11.5	......	
East Orange	277	0.6	28	0.1	160	2.4	86	4.3
Elizabeth	4,688	6.4	140	0.3	4,377	15.7	157	9.7
Hoboken	2,607	4.8	92	0.3	2,503	10.8	6	3.6
Irvington town	300	1.5	36	0.2	259	4.7	4	......
Kearny town	486	2.3	21	0.2	459	5.9	3	......
Montclair town	782	3.3	24	0.2	705	13.9	50	1.7
New Brunswick	1,200	4.7	56	0.4	1,090	12.4	54	5.8

TABLE 141.—NUMBER AND PER CENT ILLITERATE IN POPULATION 10 YEARS OF AGE AND OVER, FOR PRINCIPAL POPULATION CLASSES, FOR CITIES HAVING FROM 25,000 TO 100,000 INHABITANTS: 1920—Continued.

[Per cent not shown where base is less than 100.]

CITY.	ALL CLASSES: 1920		NATIVE WHITE.		FOREIGN-BORN WHITE.		NEGRO.	
	Number.	Per cent.	Number.	Per cent.	Number.	Per cent.	Number.	Per cent.
NEW JERSEY—Con.								
Orange	1,103	4.2	18	0.1	982	14.2	93	3.1
Passaic	5,513	11.6	56	0.3	5,418	20.8	28	5.5
Perth Amboy	1,589	5.3	34	0.2	1,543	10.5	9	2.5
Plainfield	1,007	4.5	42	0.3	834	15.3	130	6.3
West Hoboken town	1,033	3.2	14	0.1	1,011	7.3		
West New York town	891	3.8	31	0.2	860	9.8		
NEW YORK:								
Amsterdam	2,011	7.6	80	0.5	1,929	19.8	1	0.9
Auburn	1,401	4.7	56	0.3	1,327	17.7	17	4.3
Binghamton	1,703	3.1	152	0.3	1,511	14.7	34	6.1
Elmira	822	2.2	58	0.2	726	15.6	34	7.0
Jamestown	1,581	4.9	46	0.2	1,523	13.5	12	7.3
Kingston	477	2.1	120	0.6	320	11.6	37	7.9
Mount Vernon	1,564	4.5	29	0.1	1,488	14.9	40	3.5
New Rochelle	1,171	4.0	29	0.2	1,016	12.2	122	5.4
Newburgh	1,109	4.4	98	0.5	935	19.1	67	12.2
Niagara Falls	2,935	7.5	52	0.2	2,869	16.5	11	2.5
Poughkeepsie	1,059	3.7	100	0.4	907	16.6	41	5.8
Rome	1,881	9.0	558	3.6	1,301	25.3	22	15.7
Schenectady	3,549	5.0	169	0.3	3,350	16.5	18	5.5
Troy	1,611	2.6	158	0.3	1,413	12.4	25	4.9
Utica	4,832	6.4	175	0.3	4,627	20.1	15	4.9
Watertown	756	2.9	178	0.9	568	9.9	4	
NORTH CAROLINA:								
Asheville	1,285	5.7	393	2.4	15	2.7	876	15.2
Charlotte	3,172	8.7	509	2.1	31	6.2	2,632	22.2
Wilmington	2,374	9.0	246	1.6	14	2.3	2,111	19.6
Winston-Salem	4,308	11.0	1,036	4.8	15	5.1	3,256	18.8
OHIO:								
Canton	2,824	4.0	193	0.4	2,554	17.7	73	6.5
East Cleveland	120	0.5	16	0.1	102	2.7	2	1.6
Hamilton	718	2.2	311	1.1	285	10.8	121	10.5
Lakewood	536	1.6	21	0.1	512	7.1	2	
Lima	470	1.4	145	0.5	281	14.9	37	3.6
Lorain	1,029	3.7	18	0.1	993	8.4	18	3.9
Mansfield	263	1.1	39	0.2	208	6.6	16	7.5
Marion	253	1.1	156	0.7	83	8.8	13	6.2
Newark	301	1.4	112	0.6	133	9.0	54	12.0
Portsmouth	741	2.8	562	2.3	52	7.5	127	12.9
Springfield	1,009	2.0	259	0.6	240	8.8	509	8.7
Steubenville	1,404	6.3	60	0.4	1,291	23.5	53	5.7
Warren	1,530	7.0	30	0.2	1,433	31.2	66	10.8
Zanesville	400	1.6	199	0.9	113	8.9	88	7.0
OKLAHOMA:								
Muskogee	634	2.6	88	0.5	50	9.4	487	8.3
Oklahoma City	1,144	1.5	271	0.4	434	12.9	409	5.8
Tulsa	654	1.1	138	0.3	64	3.2	441	6.1
PENNSYLVANIA:								
Allentown	1,256	2.2	153	0.3	1,099	12.9	4	2.8
Altoona	1,043	2.2	195	0.5	801	15.3	44	6.2
Bethlehem	1,331	3.5	131	0.5	1,175	10.9	25	8.5
Chester	3,120	6.8	169	0.6	2,385	21.4	547	8.9
Easton	1,118	4.1	160	0.7	951	24.1	5	2.1
Erie	3,906	5.3	195	0.3	3,683	21.5	18	2.8
Harrisburg	1,538	2.4	276	0.5	879	21.5	381	8.5
Hazleton	1,809	7.4	138	0.7	1,668	27.9	1	
Johnstown	1,971	3.0	188	0.6	1,600	10.0	112	7.8
Lancaster	609	1.4	303	0.7	244	8.7	72	9.6
McKeesport	2,168	6.1	60	0.3	2,057	17.5	51	6.6
New Castle	2,170	6.3	106	0.4	2,000	23.4	61	8.3
Norristown borough	1,507	5.6	250	1.2	1,159	27.3	96	7.7
Wilkes-Barre	3,492	6.1	189	0.4	3,284	22.7	19	3.8
Williamsport	580	1.9	145	0.5	378	16.8	57	7.4
York	712	1.8	474	1.3	137	11.6	99	8.4
RHODE ISLAND:								
Cranston	1,528	6.5	173	1.1	1,333	17.9	21	10.8
Newport	543	2.1	38	0.2	411	7.2	93	6.8
Pawtucket	2,324	4.5	165	0.5	2,141	10.3	15	5.5
Woonsocket	3,086	9.0	306	1.6	2,758	17.7	16	
SOUTH CAROLINA:								
Charleston	5,073	9.2	226	0.8	71	3.3	4,770	18.0
Columbia	3,558	11.4	732	4.0	51	9.5	2,775	22.8

TABLE **141.**—NUMBER AND PER CENT ILLITERATE IN POPULATION 10 YEARS OF AGE AND OVER, FOR PRINCIPAL POPULATION CLASSES, FOR CITIES HAVING FROM 25,000 TO 100,000 INHABITANTS: 1920—Continued.

[Per cent not shown where base is less than 100.]

CITY.	ALL CLASSES: 1920		NATIVE WHITE.		FOREIGN-BORN WHITE.		NEGRO.	
	Number.	Per cent.	Number.	Per cent.	Number.	Per cent.	Number.	Per cent.
SOUTH DAKOTA:								
Sioux Falls	164	0.8	29	0.2	130	4.4	2	......
TENNESSEE:								
Chattanooga	2,849	5.9	554	1.8	64	5.2	2,231	13.8
Knoxville	3,918	6.3	2,582	5.0	35	4.4	1,301	13.7
TEXAS:								
Austin	1,670	5.7	369	1.8	471	19.1	830	14.1
Beaumont	2,843	8.7	265	1.3	400	21.3	2,173	19.8
El Paso	5,202	8.5	299	1.0	4,759	16.0	31	2.7
Galveston	1,974	5.3	202	0.9	914	13.6	843	9.7
Waco	1,343	4.3	161	0.7	347	20.2	835	12.9
Wichita Falls	533	1.6	58	0.2	368	22.2	104	5.2
UTAH:								
Ogden	403	1.6	51	0.3	194	4.3	1	0.4
VIRGINIA:								
Lynchburg	1,776	7.3	369	2.1	9	2.6	1,398	20.7
Newport News	1,842	6.2	62	0.4	42	2.1	1,734	14.6
Petersburg	3,002	12.0	443	3.3	59	11.6	2,498	22.5
Portsmouth	4,326	9.8	177	0.8	81	5.3	4,066	21.3
Roanoke	1,886	4.7	565	1.8	49	5.7	1,272	16.9
WASHINGTON:								
Bellingham	230	1.1	28	0.2	199	3.8	2	......
Everett	273	1.2	40	0.2	212	3.8	3	......
Tacoma	1,405	1.7	127	0.2	1,183	5.8	34	2.6
WEST VIRGINIA:								4.3
Charleston	947	3.0	504	1.9	161	12.1	282	7.3
Clarksburg	632	2.9	238	1.3	313	16.5	81	7.6
Huntington	1,662	4.2	1,336	3.6	27	3.7	296	11.9
Wheeling	1,141	2.5	206	0.5	836	14.6	94	6.7
WISCONSIN:								
Green Bay	845	3.4	402	1.9	441	12.4		......
Kenosha	1,526	4.9	33	0.2	1,490	11.9	3	......
La Crosse	432	1.7	40	0.2	391	8.8		......
Madison	840	2.6	33	0.1	786	16.3	12	5.6
Oshkosh	514	1.9	60	0.3	454	7.9		......
Racine	1,115	2.4	35	0.1	1,056	6.6	21	7.8
Sheboygan	835	3.4	56	0.3	779	9.6		......
Superior	686	2.2	75	0.4	605	5.7	1	1.0

TABLE 142.—NUMBER AND PER CENT ILLITERATE IN THE URBAN AND RURAL
BY DIVISIONS

DIVISION AND STATE.	ILLITERATES IN URBAN POPULATION 10 YEARS OF AGE AND OVER: 1920									
	All classes.		Native white.				Foreign-born white.		Negro.	
			Native parentage.		Foreign or mixed parentage.					
	Number.	Per cent.	Number.	Per cent.	Number.	Per cent.	Number.	Per cent.	Number.	Per cent.
United States..	1,955,112	4.4	155,493	0.8	55,620	0.5	1,327,520	13.0	402,170	13.4
GEOG. DIVISIONS:										
New England.....	245,299	5.2	4,880	0.3	9,054	0.6	226,504	14.0	4,057	6.9
Middle Atlantic...	691,226	5.2	19,420	0.4	15,361	0.4	634,749	15.1	19,643	4.4
E. North Central..	351,628	3.3	30,787	0.7	12,848	0.4	280,567	11.3	26,308	6.8
W. North Central.	79,415	2.0	12,917	0.6	4,846	0.5	45,303	7.5	15,907	8.6
South Atlantic....	227,055	6.4	37,271	1.8	1,949	0.6	24,690	11.2	162,827	17.2
E. South Central..	126,354	7.7	22,409	2.3	1,003	0.8	4,026	8.4	98,864	20.6
W. South Central.	146,820	6.1	19,307	1.3	6,819	2.8	47,788	23.1	72,397	16.1
Mountain.........	25,395	2.6	4,957	0.9	1,473	0.6	17,096	9.7	701	4.8
Pacific...........	61,920	2.1	3,545	0.3	2,267	0.3	46,797	7.0	1,466	4.1
NEW ENGLAND:										
Maine............	8,731	3.5	596	0.5	939	1.6	7,095	12.3	33	5.1
New Hampshire..	12,061	5.3	472	0.5	661	1.0	10,865	15.5	27	7.6
Vermont.........	3,515	3.9	426	0.9	662	2.7	2,415	13.6	9	4.9
Massachusetts...	144,584	4.8	2,489	0.3	4,556	0.5	131,672	12.8	2,328	6.4
Rhode Island.....	30,603	6.5	510	0.4	1,494	0.9	27,743	16.4	808	10.2
Connecticut......	48,805	6.6	387	0.2	742	0.3	46,714	17.1	852	6.1
MIDDLE ATLANTIC:										
New York........	383,309	5.5	7,028	0.4	8,030	0.4	362,795	14.2	4,172	2.6
New Jersey......	102,897	5.3	2,465	0.4	1,991	0.3	93,899	15.1	4,125	5.4
Pennsylvania....	205,020	4.6	9,927	0.5	5,340	0.5	178,055	17.5	11,346	5.6
E. NORTH CENTRAL:										
Ohio.............	94,871	3.2	10,025	0.6	2,885	0.4	71,527	12.7	10,263	7.7
Indiana..........	31,856	2.6	9,462	1.1	1,435	0.7	15,220	13.0	5,669	9.3
Illinois..........	138,868	3.9	7,509	0.6	3,779	0.3	118,686	11.5	8,299	5.9
Michigan.........	60,440	3.4	3,081	0.5	2,714	0.5	52,497	10.3	1,923	4.0
Wisconsin........	25,593	2.6	710	0.2	2,035	0.5	22,637	9.0	154	4.1
W. NORTH CENTRAL:										
Minnesota.......	15,838	1.9	1,136	0.4	1,530	0.4	12,872	5.4	217	3.0
Iowa.............	10,097	1.4	2,421	0.6	882	0.5	5,833	6.5	906	7.0
Missouri.........	34,563	2.6	6,702	0.8	1,632	0.5	14,803	10.0	11,294	9.6
North Dakota....	1,021	1.5	81	0.3	98	0.4	795	5.0	12	4.9
South Dakota....	923	1.1	79	0.2	64	0.2	731	6.1	11	3.7
Nebraska.........	6,716	2.0	497	0.3	238	0.3	5,419	9.3	489	4.6
Kansas...........	10,257	2.0	2,001	0.6	402	0.6	4,850	12.7	2,978	8.5
SOUTH ATLANTIC:										
Delaware........	5,579	5.7	366	0.7	105	0.6	3,183	19.2	1,919	17.1
Maryland........	30,993	4.4	3,400	0.9	920	0.7	12,170	14.0	14,424	13.7
Dist. of Columbia.	10,509	2.8	564	0.3	76	0.2	1,728	6.1	8,053	8.6
Virginia..........	38,621	7.1	7,099	2.1	140	0.6	1,226	6.5	30,117	17.4
West Virginia....	9,258	3.2	3,973	1.8	204	0.7	3,008	15.4	2,051	10.8
North Carolina...	35,671	9.3	10,009	4.0	34	0.7	268	6.4	25,345	20.4
South Carolina....	24,157	10.3	3,546	2.8	27	0.4	249	6.0	20,321	21.5
Georgia...........	56,585	9.5	7,459	2.2	91	0.5	674	5.5	48,322	21.2
Florida...........	15,682	5.4	855	0.7	352	1.2	2,184	7.6	12,275	12.3
E. SOUTH CENTRAL:										
Kentucky........	26,748	5.1	7,537	2.2	604	0.8	1,398	6.5	17,200	18.9
Tennessee........	35,074	7.0	9,021	2.8	152	0.7	873	7.7	25,011	17.2
Alabama.........	42,318	10.4	4,272	2.0	126	0.7	1,290	11.7	36,621	22.7
Mississippi.......	22,214	11.3	1,579	1.6	121	1.5	465	11.2	20,032	24.4
W. SOUTH CENTRAL:										
Arkansas.........	11,604	4.9	2,652	1.7	87	0.6	290	5.2	8,571	13.9
Louisiana.........	46,569	9.1	5,479	2.2	1,020	1.4	5,175	16.1	34,770	22.1
Oklahoma........	8,314	1.9	2,847	0.8	173	0.6	1,690	12.2	3,419	8.6
Texas............	80,333	6.5	8,329	1.1	5,539	4.4	40,633	26.2	25,637	13.5
MOUNTAIN:										
Montana.........	2,266	1.6	111	0.2	81	0.2	1,011	5.6	44	4.0
Idaho............	1,333	1.4	173	0.3	56	0.3	902	8.2	18	8.1
Wyoming.........	958	2.1	69	0.3	32	0.3	677	8.2	50	4.0
Colorado.........	8,743	2.3	1,595	0.7	420	0.5	6,171	10.5	457	5.5
New Mexico......	3,616	7.1	2,389	6.4	237	3.6	899	16.6	44	6.0
Arizona..........	6,072	6.5	365	0.8	473	2.7	4,975	18.7	75	3.3
Utah.............	2,168	1.3	240	0.3	171	0.3	1,531	4.8	23	2.6
Nevada..........	239	1.8	12	0.2	3	0.1	129	5.0	4	(1)
PACIFIC:										
Washington......	9,177	1.5	654	0.2	387	0.2	6,575	4.5	162	3.2
Oregon..........	5,001	1.5	666	0.4	217	0.3	3,182	5.3	76	4.7
California........	47,742	2.4	2,225	0.2	1,663	0.3	37,040	8.0	1,228	4.2

1 Per cent not shown, base being less than 100.

POPULATION 10 YEARS OF AGE AND OVER, FOR PRINCIPAL POPULATION CLASSES, AND STATES: 1920.

DIVISION AND STATE.	ILLITERATES IN RURAL POPULATION 10 YEARS OF AGE AND OVER: 1920									
	All classes.		Native white.				Foreign-born white.		Negro.	
			Native parentage.		Foreign or mixed parentage.					
	Number.	Per cent.	Number.	Per cent.	Number.	Per cent.	Number.	Per cent.	Number.	Per cent.
United States..	2,976,793	7.7	954,382	3.8	77,077	1.4	436,220	13.3	1,439,991	28.5
GEOG. DIVISIONS:										
New England....	44,401	3.6	8,305	1.1	4,705	1.9	30,703	13.7	550	9.0
Middle Atlantic..	174,156	4.0	33,504	1.2	8,687	1.1	125,261	18.9	5,944	9.0
E. North Central.	143,842	2.2	58,006	1.3	15,542	1.0	62,265	8.8	5,744	10.8
W. North Central.	113,806	1.9	47,037	1.4	9,832	0.6	41,457	5.5	8,980	16.9
South Atlantic...	985,887	14.1	315,636	7.0	1,929	1.9	15,067	16.4	650,015	28.6
E. South Central..	719,105	14.3	276,616	7.8	1,623	3.2	2,431	10.5	437,719	30.3
W.South Central .	626,817	11.8	180,101	5.0	28,202	9.7	80,937	36.3	329,836	29.0
Mountain........	107,264	6.8	30,206	3.3	4,224	1.3	38,326	14.8	756	5.8
Pacific..........	61,515	3.7	4,971	0.6	2,333	0.6	39,773	11.6	447	8.5
NEW ENGLAND:										
Maine...........	11,509	3.1	4,510	1.6	2,351	4.4	4,509	9.6	31	6.9
New Hampshire..	3,727	2.8	551	0.6	289	1.3	2,881	14.8	6	4.4
Vermont........	4,973	2.6	1,478	1.1	1,047	2.9	2,422	9.7	19	7.0
Massachusetts....	5,023	3.0	437	0.5	298	0.8	4,048	12.6	237	16.5
Rhode Island....	709	5.7	184	2.2	67	2.9	426	23.8	31	11.8
Connecticut.....	18,460	5.3	1,145	0.8	653	0.7	16,417	16.6	226	6.3
MIDDLE ATLANTIC:										
New York........	41,713	2.9	9,122	1.0	4,226	1.4	26,808	13.5	860	7.9
New Jersey.......	24,764	4.6	4,332	1.5	908	0.8	17,696	16.3	1,785	9.1
Pennsylvania.....	107,679	4.6	20,050	1.3	3,553	1.0	80,757	22.6	3,299	9.2
E. NORTH CENTRAL:										
Ohio.............	36,135	2.2	18,510	1.4	2,306	1.1	12,860	12.0	2,452	10.1
Indiana..........	20,178	1.8	15,519	1.6	1,513	1.4	2,335	7.3	807	11.0
Illinois..........	35,119	2.2	16,928	1.5	2,691	0.8	13,310	8.4	2,177	13.1
Michigan.........	27,606	2.5	4,499	0.8	3,878	1.1	18,038	8.9	280	6.8
Wisconsin........	24,804	2.3	2,550	0.7	5,154	1.1	15,722	7.7	28	4.0
W. NORTH CENTRAL:										
Minnesota........	18,649	1.8	852	0.3	2,437	0.5	13,370	5.5	24	5.2
Iowa............	10,583	0.9	3,500	0.5	1,472	0.4	5,171	3.8	377	12.5
Missouri.........	48,840	3.5	36,329	3.0	2,403	1.8	2,866	7.7	7,234	20.6
North Dakota....	8,916	2.2	254	0.3	874	0.5	6,443	5.7	4	2.5
South Dakota....	7,186	1.8	581	0.4	766	0.5	3,117	4.5	24	6.3
Nebraska.........	7,068	1.0	1,687	0.5	938	0.4	4,049	4.5	67	7.0
Kansas..........	12,564	1.4	3,834	0.6	942	0.5	6,441	9.2	1,250	9.6
SOUTH ATLANTIC:										
Delaware........	4,929	6.1	1,929	3.2	27	0.6	190	6.5	2,781	20.8
Maryland........	33,441	7.4	10,484	3.3	564	1.9	1,405	9.8	20,980	23.4
Dist. of Columbia[2]										
Virginia..........	156,538	13.0	62,982	7.6	254	1.6	924	8.1	92,205	26.5
West Virginia....	60,155	7.6	39,600	5.8	547	2.5	11,540	28.0	8,462	17.0
North Carolina...	205,932	14.1	94,664	9.2	137	3.7	206	7.4	108,329	25.7
South Carolina...	196,510	20.0	35,093	7.7	76	2.3	142	6.6	161,101	30.7
Georgia..........	272,253	17.5	59,078	6.7	168	2.7	187	5.0	212,793	31.9
Florida..........	56,129	12.2	11,806	4.3	156	0.9	473	3.6	43,364	27.4
E. SOUTH CENTRAL:										
Kentucky........	128,266	9.8	103,365	8.8	700	2.9	846	9.3	23,348	23.0
Tennessee........	147,555	11.6	92,296	8.8	340	3.7	390	9.9	54,521	26.0
Alabama.........	235,764	17.8	60,653	7.7	343	3.5	603	9.4	174,069	34.0
Mississippi.......	207,520	18.2	20,302	4.0	240	3.3	592	15.7	185,781	29.9
W. SOUTH CENTRAL:										
Arkansas........	110,233	10.3	38,101	5.2	571	2.9	855	10.3	70,674	23.4
Louisiana........	252,523	29.6	73,339	16.5	2,119	12.0	4,532	37.6	171,960	45.4
Oklahoma........	48,550	4.5	26,566	3.0	832	1.5	3,766	15.0	10,786	14.4
Texas...........	215,511	9.3	42,095	2.7	24,680	12.5	71,784	40.4	76,416	19.9
MOUNTAIN:										
Montana.........	7,278	2.6	555	0.4	317	0.4	3,367	5.7	43	12.7
Idaho...........	3,591	1.5	481	0.3	204	0.4	1,598	5.8	26	10.8
Wyoming........	2,191	2.1	251	0.4	69	0.3	1,556	9.4	30	5.9
Colorado.........	15,465	4.2	6,060	2.5	549	0.8	8,053	14.5	162	10.0
New Mexico......	38,021	17.6	21,368	13.2	1,525	10.2	6,351	29.7	184	4.0
Arizona..........	33,059	20.4	1,089	1.6	1,306	6.1	14,316	32.9	263	5.1
Utah............	4,096	2.5	295	0.4	219	0.4	1,973	8.3	36	9.6
Nevada..........	3,563	7.0	107	0.5	35	0.3	1,112	9.3	12	4.9
PACIFIC:										
Washington......	9,349	2.0	974	0.4	364	0.3	5,055	5.1	83	8.8
Oregon..........	4,316	1.4	863	0.4	244	0.4	1,990	5.0	13	5.0
California........	47,850	5.4	3,134	0.7	1,725	0.9	32,728	16.1	351	8.6

[2] No rural population, as Washington city is coextensive with the District of Columbia.

TABLE 143.—NUMBER AND PER CENT ILLITERATE IN THE URBAN AND RURAL BY DIVISIONS

DIVISION AND STATE.	ILLITERATES IN URBAN POPULATION 21 YEARS OF AGE AND OVER: 1920									
	All classes.		Native white.				Foreign-born white.		Negro.	
			Native parentage.		Foreign or mixed parentage.					
	Number.	Per cent.	Number.	Per cent.	Number.	Per cent.	Number.	Per cent.	Number.	Per cent.
United States..	1,867,441	5.5	136,199	1.0	45,179	0.6	1,300,030	13.8	372,295	16.0
GEOG. DIVISIONS:										
New England....	238,911	6.6	4,180	0.4	7,595	0.8	222,418	14.8	3,934	8.2
Middle Atlantic..	675,689	6.6	17,003	0.5	12,244	0.5	625,567	16.2	18,889	5.2
E. North Central.	342,763	4.2	27,667	0.8	11,048	0.5	277,434	12.0	25,537	8.1
W. North Central.	75,446	2.5	11,345	0.8	4,134	0.5	44,045	7.8	15,503	10.4
South Atlantic...	207,662	7.8	32,492	2.2	1,627	0.7	24,240	11.9	149,002	21.0
E. South Central..	115,739	9.5	19,784	2.8	917	0.9	3,942	8.7	91,045	25.2
W. South Central.	129,057	7.2	16,322	1.5	4,634	2.5	41,367	23.9	66,259	19.8
Mountain........	23,299	3.1	4,374	1.1	1,146	0.6	15,977	9.8	685	5.6
Pacific...........	58,875	2.5	3,032	0.3	1,834	0.3	45,040	7.2	1,441	4.8
NEW ENGLAND:										
Maine...........	8,382	4.4	528	0.5	822	2.2	6,933	13.3	31	5.9
New Hampshire..	11,688	6.7	402	0.6	594	1.6	10,632	16.7	25	8.7
Vermont.........	3,417	4.9	375	1.1	635	3.7	2,395	14.7	9	6.2
Massachusetts....	137,870	6.0	2,090	0.3	3,663	0.6	129,333	13.5	2,257	7.7
Rhode Island.....	29,631	8.3	452	0.5	1,276	1.3	27,068	17.4	789	12.4
Connecticut......	47,923	8.4	333	0.2	605	0.4	46,057	18.3	823	7.4
MIDDLE ATLANTIC:										
New York........	374,939	7.0	6,026	0.4	6,307	0.4	357,382	15.3	3,982	3.0
New Jersey.......	100,603	6.8	2,209	0.5	1,577	0.4	92,443	16.1	3,975	6.5
Pennsylvania.....	200,147	6.0	8,768	0.6	4,360	0.6	175,742	18.7	10,932	6.6
E. NORTH CENTRAL:										
Ohio.............	92,201	3.9	8,941	0.8	2,471	0.5	70,676	13.5	9,950	9.1
Indiana..........	30,812	3.3	8,786	1.4	1,327	0.9	15,078	13.7	5,555	11.4
Illinois..........	135,621	4.9	6,654	0.8	3,000	0.4	117,342	12.1	8,040	6.9
Michigan.........	58,975	4.2	2,711	0.5	2,366	0.6	51,845	11.0	1,844	4.6
Wisconsin........	25,154	3.3	575	0.3	1,884	0.6	22,493	9.5	148	4.8
W. NORTH CENTRAL:										
Minnesota........	14,991	2.3	742	0.4	1,194	0.5	12,765	5.6	211	3.3
Iowa.............	9,514	1.7	2,121	0.7	767	0.5	5,681	6.7	892	8.7
Missouri..........	33,186	3.2	6,120	1.1	1,517	0.6	14,450	10.5	10,974	11.4
North Dakota.....	947	1.8	55	0.3	66	0.4	784	5.2	12	5.4
South Dakota....	884	1.4	62	0.2	55	0.3	720	6.3	11	4.8
Nebraska.........	6,468	2.5	435	0.3	181	0.3	5,307	9.8	473	5.4
Kansas...........	9,456	2.4	1,810	0.7	354	0.6	4,338	12.3	2,930	10.8
SOUTH ATLANTIC:										
Delaware.........	5,405	7.1	339	0.9	87	0.7	3,138	20.2	1,835	20.4
Maryland.........	29,849	5.5	3,159	1.1	821	0.8	12,015	15.0	13,778	16.5
Dist. of Columbia.	10,190	3.3	521	0.3	64	0.2	1,699	6.4	7,823	10.7
Virginia..........	35,339	8.6	6,252	2.5	117	0.7	1,197	6.9	27,737	21.2
West Virginia.....	8,669	4.0	3,582	2.2	176	0.8	2,942	16.3	1,949	13.3
North Carolina...	31,581	11.5	8,586	4.8	28	0.8	259	6.6	22,694	25.8
South Carolina...	21,475	12.6	3,043	3.3	23	0.4	245	6.2	18,151	26.9
Georgia..........	50,629	11.5	6,259	2.6	84	0.6	660	5.8	43,588	25.8
Florida..........	14,525	6.6	751	0.8	227	1.2	2,085	8.0	11,447	15.2
E. SOUTH CENTRAL:										
Kentucky........	25,541	6.3	6,893	2.8	593	0.9	1,386	6.7	16,660	23.0
Tennessee........	32,251	8.6	7,903	3.4	141	0.8	860	8.2	23,330	21.1
Alabama.........	38,429	12.8	3,724	2.4	89	0.7	1,241	12.2	33,366	28.2
Mississippi.......	19,518	13.7	1,264	1.7	94	1.5	455	11.6	17,689	29.5
W. SOUTH CENTRAL:										
Arkansas.........	10,677	0.1	2,295	2.0	80	0.7	282	5.3	8,017	17.4
Louisiana........	41,000	11.0	4,753	2.7	845	1.4	5,065	16.9	30,913	26.6
Oklahoma........	7,641	2.4	2,551	1.0	140	8.0	1,487	11.5	3,282	11.3
Texas............	69,050	7.5	6,723	1.2	3,563	4.0	34,533	27.6	24,047	10.8
MOUNTAIN:										
Montana.........	2,198	2.0	95	0.2	59	0.2	1,789	5.9	44	4.5
Idaho............	1,251	1.8	151	0.4	45	0.3	863	8.4	17	3.4
Wyoming.........	888	2.4	59	0.3	21	0.3	632	8.2	36	5.6
Colorado.........	8,218	2.7	1,411	0.8	362	0.6	5,901	10.7	446	6.5
New Mexico......	3,219	8.7	2,147	8.0	182	3.8	802	16.9	43	7.4
Arizona..........	5,277	7.4	315	0.9	350	3.0	4,372	20.0	73	3.8
Utah.............	2,015	1.7	185	0.4	125	0.3	1,492	5.0	23	2.9
Nevada..........	233	2.2	11	0.2	2	0.1	126	5.2	3	(1)
PACIFIC:										
Washington......	8,799	1.8	533	0.2	280	0.2	6,496	4.7	159	3.6
Oregon..........	4,820	1.8	558	0.4	185	0.3	3,150	5.6	76	5.3
California........	45,256	2.8	1,941	0.3	1,369	0.3	35,394	8.3	1,206	4.9

[1] Per cent not shown, base being less than 100.

POPULATION 21 YEARS OF AGE AND OVER, FOR PRINCIPAL POPULATION CLASSES, AND STATES: 1920.

DIVISION AND STATE.	ILLITERATES IN RURAL POPULATION 21 YEARS OF AGE AND OVER: 1920									
	All classes.		Native white.				Foreign-born white.		Negro.	
			Native parentage.		Foreign or mixed parentage.					
	Number.	Per cent.	Number.	Per cent.	Number.	Per cent.	Number.	Per cent.	Number.	Per cent.
United States..	**2,465,670**	**9.1**	**802,112**	**4.8**	**57,179**	**1.5**	**407,115**	**13.3**	**1,140,692**	**35.7**
GEOG. DIVISIONS:										
New England....	41,915	4.4	6,878	1.2	4,210	2.7	30,166	14.6	532	11.5
Middle Atlantic..	167,893	5.2	30,440	1.5	7,420	1.5	123,660	20.0	5,642	11.5
E. North Central.	137,475	2.9	53,705	1.8	14,312	1.3	61,731	9.2	5,547	14.0
W. North Central	105,170	2.5	41,901	1.9	8,588	0.7	40,553	5.6	8,047	20.6
South Atlantic...	799,102	17.6	265,103	8.9	1,646	2.2	14,545	17.3	515,233	36.8
E. South Central.	584,359	17.7	233,150	10.1	1,474	3.6	2,307	10.5	346,958	37.6
W. South Central.	482,306	14.0	140,855	6.1	14,696	7.8	62,709	34.1	257,610	35.4
Mountain.........	90,085	8.0	25,762	4.2	2,931	1.3	33,982	14.7	701	6.1
Pacific...........	57,365	4.5	4,318	0.7	1,902	0.7	37,462	11.8	422	10.3
NEW ENGLAND:										
Maine...........	10,190	3.6	3,628	1.7	2,064	6.3	4,369	10.3	29	8.3
New Hampshire..	3,569	3.3	495	0.7	264	1.9	2,805	15.4	5	(¹)
Vermont.........	4,735	3.2	1,340	1.3	992	3.8	2,377	10.8	19	9.7
Massachusetts....	4,880	3.8	379	0.5	267	1.1	3,997	13.2	234	21.1
Rhode Island.....	688	7.0	181	2.8	63	4.6	412	24.9	31	15.1
Connecticut.....	17,853	6.6	855	0.7	560	1.0	16,206	17.5	214	8.0
MIDDLE ATLANTIC:										
New York.......	40,420	3.5	8,471	1.2	3,963	1.7	26,480	14.2	833	10.1
New Jersey.......	23,755	5.8	3,864	1.7	708	1.0	17,450	17.3	1,693	11.8
Pennsylvania.....	103,718	6.2	18,105	1.6	2,749	1.4	79,730	24.0	3,116	11.8
E. NORTH CENTRAL:										
Ohio.............	34,444	2.8	17,159	1.9	2,173	1.2	12,739	12.7	2,366	13.1
Indiana..........	19,335	2.3	14,759	2.1	1,476	1.6	2,315	7.6	781	14.6
Illinois..........	33,506	2.8	15,708	2.1	2,547	0.9	13,132	8.7	2,106	16.9
Michigan.........	26,638	3.3	4,087	1.1	3,509	1.5	17,914	9.3	267	8.5
Wisconsin........	23,552	3.1	1,992	0.9	4,607	1.4	15,631	7.9	27	5.2
W. NORTH CENTRAL:										
Minnesota........	17,878	2.5	664	0.4	2,111	0.7	13,282	5.6	23	6.6
Iowa.............	9,930	1.2	3,146	0.7	1,298	0.5	5,068	3.9	357	15.7
Missouri.........	44,162	4.5	32,660	4.0	2,317	2.0	2,819	7.9	6,359	25.1
North Dakota....	8,426	3.1	203	0.3	651	0.6	6,342	6.0	4	3.5
South Dakota....	6,756	2.4	458	0.5	616	0.6	3,075	4.6	24	8.2
Nebraska.........	6,504	1.4	1,397	0.6	784	0.5	3,946	4.6	65	8.7
Kansas...........	11,514	1.8	3,373	0.8	811	0.6	6,021	9.1	1,215	12.3
SOUTH ATLANTIC:										
Delaware.........	4,683	7.8	1,851	4.1	23	0.7	189	7.0	2,618	28.6
Maryland.........	29,028	9.1	9,374	4.2	497	2.2	1,383	10.3	17,766	30.5
Dist. of Columbia²	....	....	....	....	......	....	....	....	....	....
Virginia..........	127,037	16.0	50,665	9.2	201	1.8	889	8.6	75,147	34.1
West Virginia.....	52,799	9.9	33,517	7.5	443	3.2	11,120	29.7	7,713	21.1
North Carolina...	172,911	18.5	82,056	12.2	127	4.6	194	7.5	88,415	34.7
South Carolina...	158,007	25.9	29,851	10.1	71	2.9	140	6.9	127,876	41.3
Georgia..........	210,665	21.4	48,080	8.5	157	3.2	179	5.1	162,231	39.9
Florida..........	43,972	13.9	9,709	5.2	127	1.0	451	3.7	33,467	31.7
E. SOUTH CENTRAL:										
Kentucky........	110,694	12.5	87,936	11.2	670	3.3	816	9.3	21,266	29.8
Tennessee........	120,912	14.4	77,624	11.2	318	4.3	380	10.1	42,583	31.6
Alabama.........	190,136	22.5	51,280	10.1	290	4.2	584	9.8	137,917	42.8
Mississippi.......	162,617	22.2	16,310	4.9	196	3.5	527	15.4	145,192	36.9
W. SOUTH CENTRAL:										
Arkansas.........	88,736	12.8	31,108	6.6	504	3.5	806	10.3	56,292	28.7
Louisiana........	188,291	34.5	56,296	20.1	974	9.3	4,263	37.9	126,381	52.0
Oklahoma........	40,435	5.8	21,545	3.8	688	1.8	3,367	14.5	9,209	19.5
Texas............	164,844	10.9	31,906	3.2	12,530	10.0	54,273	38.3	65,728	27.3
MOUNTAIN:										
Montana.........	6,873	3.2	455	0.5	244	0.4	3,315	6.0	40	13.7
Idaho...........	3,259	2.0	394	0.4	175	0.4	1,514	5.9	24	12.2
Wyoming........	2,052	2.6	210	0.5	56	0.4	1,488	9.7	29	6.9
Colorado........	13,862	5.3	5,260	3.2	407	0.9	7,526	15.0	153	12.2
New Mexico......	31,733	21.4	18,249	16.9	1,029	10.5	5,473	31.8	170	4.0
Arizona.........	25,359	21.8	882	1.9	809	5.7	11,685	34.2	243	5.2
Utah............	3,664	3.4	225	0.5	184	0.5	1,921	8.5	32	10.3
Nevada..........	3,283	7.9	87	0.5	27	0.3	1,060	9.2	10	4.6
PACIFIC:										
Washington......	8,978	2.5	861	0.5	295	0.4	4,998	5.4	82	10.9
Oregon..........	4,085	1.8	745	0.5	215	0.5	1,947	5.1	13	6.6
California........	44,302	6.4	2,712	0.8	1,392	1.0	30,517	16.3	327	10.4

² No rural population, as Washington city is coextensive with the District of Columbia.

TABLE **144.**—NUMBER AND PER CENT UNABLE TO SPEAK ENGLISH, FOR POPULATION CLASSES, BY SEX, IN POPULATION 10 YEARS OF AGE AND OVER, 1890-1920, AND IN POPULATION 21 YEARS OF AGE AND OVER, 1920 AND 1910, FOR THE UNITED STATES.

[Figures are given under each class for all census years for which data are available.]

CENSUS YEAR AND CLASS OF POPULATION.	BOTH SEXES.			MALE.			FEMALE.		
	Total number.	Unable to speak English.		Total number.	Unable to speak English.		Total number.	Unable to speak English.	
		Number.	Per cent.		Number.	Per cent.		Number.	Per cent.
POPULATION 10 YEARS OF AGE AND OVER.									
1920									
Foreign-born white	13,497,886	1,488,948	11.0	7,419,691	680,033	9.2	6,078,195	808,915	13.3
Negro	8,053,225	14,644	0.2	4,009,462	7,207	0.2	4,043,763	7,437	0.2
Indian	176,925	36,752	20.8	91,546	17,469	19.1	85,379	19,283	22.6
Chinese	56,230	10,020	17.8	51,041	8,903	17.4	5,189	1,117	21.5
Japanese	84,238	19,068	22.6	58,806	8,709	14.8	25,432	10,359	40.7
All other [1]	8,948	982	11.0	8,378	916	10.9	570	66	11.6
1910									
Foreign-born white	12,944,529	2,953,011	22.8	7,321,196	1,683,949	23.0	5,623,333	1,269,062	22.6
Negro	7,317,922	22,110	0.3	3,637,386	10,870	0.3	3,680,536	11,240	0.3
Indian	188,758	59,055	31.3	96,582	26,705	27.7	92,176	32,350	35.1
Chinese	68,924	28,370	41.2	65,479	26,632	40.7	3,445	1,738	50.4
Japanese	67,661	26,564	39.3	60,809	22,848	37.6	6,852	3,716	54.2
All other [2]	3,135	2,097	66.9	3,073	2,077	67.6	62	20	([3])
1900									
Native white— Foreign or mixed par.	10,926,401	65,008	0.6	5,460,085	28,164	0.5	5,466,316	36,844	0.7
Foreign-born white	10,014,256	1,217,280	12.2	5,414,991	563,982	10.4	4,599,265	653,298	14.2
Indian	171,552	72,583	42.3	86,504	32,309	37.3	85,048	40,274	47.4
Chinese	87,682	33,498	38.2	84,141	31,191	37.1	3,541	2,307	65.2
Japanese	24,091	14,843	61.6	23,214	14,448	62.2	877	395	45.0
1890									
Native white— Native parentage	25,375,766	168,149	0.7	12,901,102	75,874	0.6	12,474,664	92,275	0.7
Foreign or mixed par.	7,768,421	69,876	0.9	3,895,395	30,659	0.8	3,873,026	39,217	1.0
Foreign-born white	8,786,887	1,371,044	15.6	4,781,748	666,496	13.9	4,005,139	704,548	17.6
Colored	5,482,485	109,427	2.0	2,774,414	85,860	3.1	2,708,071	23,567	0.9
POPULATION 21 YEARS OF AGE AND OVER.									
1920									
Foreign-born white	12,498,720	1,399,759	11.2	6,928,452	637,830	9.2	5,570,268	761,929	13.7
Negro	5,522,475	10,223	0.2	2,792,006	4,989	0.2	2,730,469	5,234	0.2
Indian	116,486	29,023	24.9	61,229	13,662	22.3	55,257	15,361	27.8
Chinese	50,625	9,629	19.0	46,979	8,565	18.2	3,646	1,064	29.2
Japanese	75,727	17,624	23.3	53,411	7,942	14.9	22,316	9,682	43.4
All other [1]	7,746	938	12.1	7,345	875	11.9	401	63	15.7
Foreign born—									
Negro	64,412	2,509	3.9	38,234	1,459	3.8	26,178	1,050	4.0
Indian	4,442	2,769	62.3	2,559	1,495	58.4	1,883	1,274	67.7
Chinese	40,494	8,873	21.9	38,285	7,981	20.8	2,209	892	40.4
Japanese	75,069	17,600	23.4	52,999	7,940	15.0	22,070	9,660	43.8
1910									
Foreign-born white	11,653,925	2,565,612	22.0	6,646,817	1,462,134	22.0	5,007,108	1,103,478	22.0
Negro	4,886,615	13,870	0.3	2,458,873	6,768	0.3	2,427,742	7,102	0.3
Indian	123,136	47,411	38.5	62,967	21,118	33.5	60,169	26,293	43.7
Chinese	62,902	26,338	41.9	60,421	24,816	41.1	2,481	1,522	61.3
Japanese	62,710	24,882	39.7	56,638	21,484	37.9	6,072	3,398	56.0
All other [2]	2,792	1,877	67.2	2,738	1,858	67.9	54	19	([3])

[1] Comprises Filipinos, Hindus, Koreans, Hawaiians, Malays, Siamese, Samoans, and Maoris.
[2] Comprises Filipinos, Hindus, Koreans, and Maoris.
[3] Per cent not shown, base being less than 100.

TABLE 145.—NUMBER AND PER CENT UNABLE TO SPEAK ENGLISH, BY SEX AND AGE PERIODS, IN THE FOREIGN-BORN WHITE POPULATION 10 YEARS OF AGE AND OVER, FOR THE UNITED STATES: 1920 AND 1910.

CENSUS YEAR AND AGE PERIOD.	FOREIGN-BORN WHITE POPULATION 10 YEARS OF AGE AND OVER.								
	Both sexes.			Male.			Female.		
	Total number.	Unable to speak English.		Total number.	Unable to speak English.		Total number.	Unable to speak English.	
		Number.	Per cent.		Number.	Per cent.		Number.	Per cent.
1920									
Total, 10 years and over	13,497,886	1,488,948	11.0	7,419,691	680,033	9.2	6,078,195	808,915	13.3
10 to 14 years	331,362	28,149	8.5	167,152	14,163	8.5	164,210	13,986	8.5
15 to 19 years	527,942	43,711	8.3	259,270	20,651	8.0	268,672	23,060	8.6
20 to 24 years	926,844	119,092	12.8	456,988	48,971	10.7	469,856	70,121	14.9
25 to 29 years	1,454,363	203,676	14.0	792,088	85,814	10.8	662,275	117,862	17.8
30 to 34 years	1,651,475	210,593	12.8	946,818	97,449	10.3	704,657	113,144	16.1
35 to 39 years	1,737,805	207,035	11.9	1,008,677	101,796	10.1	729,128	105,239	14.4
40 to 44 years	1,428,099	154,877	10.8	803,195	75,745	9.4	624,904	79,132	12.7
45 to 49 years	1,299,675	132,442	10.2	744,423	67,487	9.1	555,252	64,955	11.7
50 to 54 years	1,167,377	107,053	9.2	651,546	50,538	7.8	515,831	56,515	11.0
55 to 59 years	908,722	78,121	8.6	503,789	33,907	6.7	404,933	44,214	10.9
60 to 64 years	715,731	69,639	9.7	392,629	29,257	7.5	323,102	40,382	12.5
65 years and over	1,328,227	129,445	9.7	679,384	50,847	7.5	648,843	78,598	12.1
Age unknown	20,264	5,115	25.2	13,732	3,408	24.8	6,532	1,707	26.1
1910									
Total, 10 years and over	12,944,529	2,953,011	22.8	7,321,196	1,683,949	23.0	5,623,333	1,269,062	22.6
10 to 14 years	358,330	56,405	15.7	181,303	28,307	15.6	177,027	28,098	15.9
15 to 19 years	673,761	227,649	33.8	351,754	130,930	37.2	322,007	96,719	30.0
20 to 24 years	1,430,381	497,511	34.8	823,920	310,276	37.7	606,461	187,235	30.9
25 to 29 years	1,662,696	511,695	30.8	990,576	324,067	32.7	672,120	187,628	27.9
30 to 34 years	1,505,715	391,254	26.0	888,668	244,551	27.5	617,047	146,703	23.8
35 to 39 years	1,408,093	301,273	21.4	812,007	180,579	22.2	596,086	120,694	20.2
40 to 44 years	1,303,475	237,525	18.2	751,519	136,638	18.2	551,956	100,887	18.3
45 to 49 years	1,146,360	179,383	15.6	656,455	92,570	14.1	489,905	86,813	17.7
50 to 54 years	925,055	145,482	15.7	526,256	68,781	13.1	398,799	76,701	19.2
55 to 59 years	693,520	100,696	14.5	380,110	42,303	11.1	313,410	58,393	18.6
60 to 64 years	627,583	91,792	14.6	331,914	37,069	11.2	295,669	54,723	18.5
65 years and over	1,183,349	201,709	17.0	607,008	78,903	13.0	576,341	122,806	21.3
Age unknown	26,211	10,637	40.6	19,706	8,975	45.5	6,505	1,662	25.5

TABLE 146.—NUMBER AND PER CENT UNABLE TO SPEAK ENGLISH IN THE FOREIGN-BORN WHITE POPULATION 10 YEARS OF AGE AND OVER, BY DIVISIONS AND STATES: 1920 AND 1910.

DIVISION AND STATE.	FOREIGN-BORN WHITE POPULATION 10 YEARS OF AGE AND OVER.						INCREASE (+) OR DECREASE (−) IN NUMBER UNABLE TO SPEAK ENGLISH: 1910–1920
	1920			1910			
	Total number.	Unable to speak English.		Total number.	Unable to speak English.		
		Number.	Per cent.		Number.	Per cent.	
United States......	13,497,886	1,488,948	11.0	12,944,529	2,953,011	22.8	−1,464,063
GEOGRAPHIC DIVISIONS:							
New England.........	1,843,028	180,851	9.8	1,757,244	326,890	18.6	−146,039
Middle Atlantic......	4,853,256	525,849	10.8	4,661,990	1,217,698	26.1	−691,849
East North Central....	3,183,790	328,981	10.3	2,985,823	693,961	23.2	−364,980
West North Central...	1,358,323	85,259	6.3	1,579,694	274,620	17.4	−189,361
South Atlantic........	311,385	32,042	10.3	280,387	71,389	25.5	−39,347
East South Central....	71,211	2,363	3.3	84,893	9,983	11.8	−7,620
West South Central....	430,053	181,799	42.3	330,431	148,028	44.8	+33,771
Mountain.............	436,304	71,096	16.3	423,068	96,637	22.8	−25,541
Pacific..............	1,010,536	80,708	8.0	840,999	113,805	13.5	−33,097
NEW ENGLAND:							
Maine................	104,585	10,333	9.9	105,336	19,589	18.6	−9,256
New Hampshire.......	89,472	11,339	12.7	92,976	26,783	28.8	−15,444
Vermont.............	42,701	3,065	7.2	47,654	8,342	17.5	−5,277
Massachusetts........	1,063,572	96,426	9.1	1,020,594	171,014	16.8	−74,588
Rhode Island........	171,032	21,620	12.6	171,904	36,961	21.5	−15,341
Connecticut.........	371,666	38,068	10.2	318,780	64,201	20.1	−26,133
MIDDLE ATLANTIC:							
New York............	2,752,055	290,200	10.5	2,634,578	597,012	22.7	−306,812
New Jersey..........	729,799	73,409	10.1	636,848	153,861	24.2	−80,452
Pennsylvania........	1,371,402	162,240	11.8	1,390,564	466,825	33.6	−304,585
EAST NORTH CENTRAL:							
Ohio.................	669,924	81,161	12.1	579,274	163,722	28.3	−82,561
Indiana.............	149,239	13,269	8.9	155,596	40,731	26.2	−27,462
Illinois.............	1,194,979	121,965	10.2	1,168,559	266,557	22.8	−144,592
Michigan............	713,228	68,105	9.5	579,803	102,286	17.6	−34,181
Wisconsin...........	456,420	44,481	9.7	502,591	120,665	24.0	−76,184
WEST NORTH CENTRAL:							
Minnesota...........	482,230	28,311	5.9	533,915	89,850	16.8	−61,539
Iowa................	223,752	9,559	4.3	269,246	37,169	13.8	−27,610
Missouri............	184,394	11,126	6.0	223,578	37,747	16.9	−26,621
North Dakota........	129,951	10,189	7.8	150,451	33,491	22.3	−23,302
South Dakota........	81,781	4,861	5.9	98,334	18,486	18.8	−13,625
Nebraska...........	148,209	9,186	6.2	172,497	29,519	17.1	−20,333
Kansas..............	108,006	12,027	11.1	131,673	28,358	21.5	−16,331
SOUTH ATLANTIC:							
Delaware............	19,541	2,733	14.0	16,940	4,824	28.5	−2,091
Maryland............	101,155	7,765	7.7	100,951	17,544	17.4	−9,779
District of Columbia...	28,292	779	2.8	23,755	1,349	5.7	−570
Virginia.............	30,325	1,135	3.7	25,639	3,983	15.5	−2,848
West Virginia........	60,679	11,121	18.3	54,646	27,461	50.3	−16,340
North Carolina.......	6,981	190	2.7	5,734	779	13.6	−589
South Carolina.......	6,327	116	1.8	5,911	447	7.6	−331
Georgia.............	16,028	285	1.8	14,656	953	6.5	−668
Florida.............	42,057	7,918	18.8	32,155	14,049	43.7	−6,131
EAST SOUTH CENTRAL:							
Kentucky............	30,603	688	2.2	39,571	3,816	9.6	−3,128
Tennessee...........	15,297	506	3.3	17,985	1,648	9.2	−1,142
Alabama.............	17,393	724	4.2	18,291	3,028	16.6	−2,304
Mississippi...........	7,918	445	5.6	9,046	1,491	16.5	−1,046
WEST SOUTH CENTRAL:							
Arkansas............	13,834	697	5.0	16,454	2,741	16.7	−2,044
Louisiana...........	44,244	3,656	8.3	50,333	11,547	22.9	−7,864
Oklahoma...........	39,020	5,362	13.7	39,064	7,075	20.4	−2,013
Texas...............	332,955	172,057	51.7	224,580	125,765	56.0	+46,009
MOUNTAIN:							
Montana.............	91,729	3,098	3.4	89,456	13,718	15.3	−10,620
Idaho...............	38,379	1,956	5.1	39,619	5,805	14.7	−3,849
Wyoming............	24,762	2,003	8.1	26,381	5,970	22.6	−3,967
Colorado............	114,285	10,650	9.3	123,026	22,610	18.4	−11,960
New Mexico..........	26,786	13,225	49.4	21,235	11,776	55.5	+1,449
Arizona.............	70,053	36,352	51.9	43,724	25,072	57.3	+11,280
Utah................	55,724	2,303	4.1	61,840	8,129	13.1	−5,826
Nevada..............	14,586	1,509	10.3	17,787	3,557	20.0	−2,048
PACIFIC:							
Washington..........	244,881	7,796	3.2	234,928	25,568	10.9	−17,772
Oregon..............	100,672	3,342	3.3	100,759	13,531	13.4	−10,189
California..........	664,983	69,570	10.5	505,312	74,706	14.8	−5,136

TABLE 147.—NUMBER AND PER CENT UNABLE TO SPEAK ENGLISH IN THE FOREIGN-BORN WHITE POPULATION 10 YEARS OF AGE AND OVER, BY SEX, BY DIVISIONS AND STATES: 1920.

DIVISION AND STATE.	FOREIGN-BORN WHITE MALES 10 YEARS OF AGE AND OVER.			FOREIGN-BORN WHITE FEMALES 10 YEARS OF AGE AND OVER.			INCREASE (+) OR DECREASE (−) IN NUMBER UNABLE TO SPEAK ENGLISH: 1910–1920	
	Total number.	Unable to speak English.		Total number.	Unable to speak English.		Males.	Females.
		Number.	Per cent.		Number.	Per cent.		
United States..	7,419,691	680,033	9.2	6,078,195	808,915	13.3	−1,003,916	−460,147
GEOG. DIVISIONS:								
New England.....	931,845	70,213	7.5	911,183	110,638	12.1	−94,716	−51,323
Middle Atlantic...	2,587,798	231,273	8.9	2,265,458	294,576	13.0	−464,026	−227,823
E. North Central..	1,789,466	152,312	8.5	1,394,324	176,669	12.7	−244,963	−120,017
W. North Central.	772,147	35,467	4.6	586,176	49,792	8.5	−112,189	−77,172
South Atlantic....	182,846	17,777	9.7	128,539	14,265	11.1	−30,101	−9,246
E. South Central..	41,729	1,110	2.7	29,482	1,253	4.3	−4,818	−2,802
W. South Central.	245,597	93,160	37.9	184,456	88,639	48.1	+14,068	+19,703
Mountain.........	262,733	37,261	14.2	173,571	33,835	19.5	−30,539	+4,998
Pacific...........	605,530	41,460	6.8	405,006	39,248	9.7	−36,632	+3,535
NEW ENGLAND:								
Maine...........	54,398	3,486	6.4	50,187	6,847	13.6	−5,454	−3,802
New Hampshire..	45,952	4,350	9.5	43,520	6,989	16.1	−9,062	−6,382
Vermont.........	22,806	1,348	5.9	19,895	1,717	8.6	−3,473	−1,804
Massachusetts.....	526,272	37,556	7.1	537,300	58,870	11.0	−48,227	−26,361
Rhode Island.....	84,933	7,993	9.4	86,099	13,627	15.8	−9,348	−5,993
Connecticut.......	197,484	15,480	7.8	174,182	22,588	13.0	−19,152	−6,981
MIDDLE ATLANTIC:								
New York........	1,425,461	123,304	8.7	1,326,594	166,896	12.6	−182,110	−124,702
New Jersey.......	387,251	31,661	8.2	342,548	41,748	12.2	−54,705	−25,747
Pennsylvania.....	775,086	76,308	9.8	596,316	85,932	14.4	−227,211	−77,374
E. NORTH CENTRAL:								
Ohio.............	386,901	41,785	10.8	283,023	39,376	13.9	−61,408	−21,153
Indiana...........	87,396	6,517	7.5	61,843	6,752	10.9	−21,717	−5,745
Illinois..........	651,256	53,389	8.2	543,723	68,576	12.6	−95,303	−49,289
Michigan.........	407,057	32,432	8.0	306,171	35,673	11.7	−25,525	−8,656
Wisconsin........	256,856	18,189	7.1	199,564	26,292	13.2	−41,010	−35,174
W. NORTH CENTRAL:								
Minnesota........	276,630	10,900	3.9	205,600	17,411	8.5	−35,095	−26,444
Iowa.............	126,109	4,239	3.4	97,643	5,320	5.4	−16,482	−11,128
Missouri..........	102,587	5,065	4.9	81,807	6,061	7.4	−17,305	−9,316
North Dakota.....	74,633	3,532	4.7	55,318	6,657	12.0	−12,430	−10,872
South Dakota.....	47,289	1,768	3.7	34,492	3,093	9.0	−7,143	−6,482
Nebraska.........	83,542	3,873	4.6	64,667	5,313	8.2	−12,129	−8,204
Kansas...........	61,357	6,090	9.9	46,649	5,937	12.7	−11,605	−4,726
SOUTH ATLANTIC:								
Delaware.........	11,230	1,429	12.7	8,311	1,304	15.7	−1,751	−340
Maryland.........	54,102	3,396	6.3	47,053	4,369	9.3	−5,810	−3,969
Dist. of Columbia.	15,022	329	2.2	13,270	450	3.4	−381	−189
Virginia..........	18,812	588	3.1	11,513	547	4.8	−2,238	−610
West Virginia.....	41,295	7,655	18.5	19,384	3,466	17.9	−14,436	−1,904
North Carolina....	4,287	87	2.0	2,694	103	3.8	−422	−167
South Carolina....	4,063	67	1.6	2,264	49	2.2	−220	−111
Georgia...........	9,923	141	1.4	6,105	144	2.4	−444	−224
Florida...........	24,112	4,085	16.9	17,945	3,833	21.4	−4,399	−1,732
E. SOUTH CENTRAL:								
Kentucky.........	17,401	347	2.0	13,202	341	2.6	−1,930	−1,198
Tennessee........	8,928	230	2.6	6,369	276	4.3	−712	−430
Alabama.........	10,484	319	3.0	6,909	405	5.9	−1,528	−776
Mississippi.......	4,916	214	4.4	3,002	231	7.7	−648	−398
W. SOUTH CENTRAL:								
Arkansas.........	8,528	303	3.6	5,306	394	7.4	−1,230	−814
Louisiana.........	26,417	1,656	6.3	17,767	2,027	11.4	−4,393	−3,471
Oklahoma........	24,412	3,348	13.7	14,608	2,014	13.8	−1,750	−863
Texas............	186,180	87,853	47.2	146,775	84,204	57.4	+21,441	+24,851
MOUNTAIN:								
Montana..........	57,287	1,384	2.4	34,442	1,714	5.0	−9,684	−936
Idaho............	24,565	1,191	4.8	13,814	765	5.5	−3,557	−292
Wyoming.........	16,700	1,301	7.8	8,062	702	8.7	−3,620	−347
Colorado.........	66,869	4,982	7.5	47,416	5,668	12.0	−9,658	−2,302
New Mexico......	15,685	7,024	44.8	11,101	6,201	55.9	−662	+2,111
Arizona..........	40,476	19,009	47.0	29,577	17,343	58.6	+3,307	+7,973
Utah............	30,516	1,342	4.4	25,208	961	3.8	−4,646	−1,180
Nevada..........	10,635	1,028	9.7	3,951	481	12.2	−2,019	−29
PACIFIC:								
Washington.......	150,510	3,772	2.5	94,371	4,024	4.3	−14,683	−3,089
Oregon...........	61,575	1,769	2.9	39,097	1,573	4.0	−8,749	−1,440
California........	393,445	35,919	9.1	271,538	33,651	12.4	−13,200	+8,064

TABLE 148.—NUMBER AND PER CENT UNABLE TO SPEAK ENGLISH IN THE FOREIGN-BORN WHITE POPULATION 21 YEARS OF AGE AND OVER, BY SEX, BY DIVISIONS AND STATES: 1920.

DIVISION AND STATE.	FOREIGN-BORN WHITE POPULATION 21 YEARS OF AGE AND OVER.								
	Both sexes.			Male.			Female.		
	Total number.	Unable to speak English.		Total number.	Unable to speak English.		Total number.	Unable to speak English.	
		Number.	Per cent.		Number.	Per cent.		Number.	Per cent.
United States.....	12,498,720	1,399,759	11.2	6,928,452	637,830	9.2	5,570,268	761,929	13.7
GEOGRAPHIC DIVISIONS:									
New England........	1,705,291	173,515	10.2	866,042	67,350	7.8	839,249	106,165	12.7
Middle Atlantic......	4,477,752	513,768	11.5	2,406,975	226,306	9.4	2,070,777	287,462	13.9
East North Central...	2,978,575	323,675	10.9	1,687,728	149,946	8.9	1,290,847	173,729	13.5
West North Central..	1,291,794	82,212	6.4	738,673	33,964	4.6	553,121	48,248	8.7
South Atlantic.......	287,215	30,504	10.6	170,407	16,881	9.9	116,808	13,623	11.7
East South Central..	67,242	2,216	3.3	39,697	1,043	2.6	27,545	1,173	4.3
West South Central..	357,220	140,308	39.3	208,431	72,655	34.9	148,789	67,653	45.5
Mountain............	394,008	59,736	15.2	241,321	31,717	13.1	152,687	28,019	18.4
Pacific..............	939,623	73,825	7.9	569,178	37,968	6.7	370,445	35,857	9.7
NEW ENGLAND:									
Maine...............	94,329	9,190	9.7	49,355	3,013	6.1	44,974	6,177	13.7
New Hampshire.....	82,049	10,723	13.1	42,432	4,097	9.7	39,617	6,626	16.7
Vermont............	38,232	2,761	7.2	20,462	1,181	5.8	17,770	1,580	8.9
Massachusetts.......	988,913	93,150	9.4	491,107	36,448	7.4	497,806	56,702	11.4
Rhode Island........	156,866	20,648	13.2	78,118	7,601	9.7	78,748	13,047	16.6
Connecticut.........	344,902	37,043	10.7	184,568	15,010	8.1	160,334	22,033	13.7
MIDDLE ATLANTIC:									
New York...........	2,528,497	282,902	11.2	1,318,883	120,426	9.1	1,209,614	162,476	13.4
New Jersey.........	675,222	71,587	10.6	360,902	30,962	8.6	314,320	40,625	12.9
Pennsylvania.......	1,274,033	159,279	12.5	727,190	74,918	10.3	546,843	84,361	15.4
EAST NORTH CENTRAL:									
Ohio................	622,523	79,813	12.8	363,504	41,136	11.3	259,019	38,677	14.9
Indiana.............	140,373	13,064	9.3	82,908	6,405	7.7	57,465	6,659	11.6
Illinois.............	1,117,928	119,788	10.7	613,797	52,462	8.5	504,131	67,326	13.4
Michigan...........	663,160	66,873	10.1	381,808	31,915	8.4	281,352	34,958	12.4
Wisconsin..........	434,591	44,137	10.2	245,711	18,028	7.3	188,880	26,109	13.8
WEST NORTH CENTRAL:									
Minnesota..........	462,582	28,024	6.1	266,856	10,749	4.0	195,726	17,275	8.8
Iowa...............	214,479	9,210	4.3	121,392	4,066	3.3	93,087	5,144	5.5
Missouri............	173,551	10,668	6.1	97,345	4,857	5.0	76,206	5,811	7.6
North Dakota.......	121,047	10,021	8.3	70,043	3,467	4.9	51,004	6,554	12.8
South Dakota.......	78,027	4,771	6.1	45,340	1,722	3.8	32,687	3,049	9.3
Nebraska...........	140,899	8,941	6.3	79,821	3,749	4.7	61,078	5,192	8.5
Kansas.............	101,209	10,577	10.5	57,876	5,354	9.3	43,333	5,223	12.1
SOUTH ATLANTIC:									
Delaware...........	18,245	2,665	14.6	10,614	1,398	13.2	7,631	1,267	16.6
Maryland...........	93,624	7,623	8.1	50,363	3,328	6.6	43,261	4,295	9.9
District of Columbia .	26,376	740	2.8	14,042	311	2.2	12,334	429	3.5
Virginia............	27,851	1,081	3.9	17,431	556	3.2	10,420	525	5.0
West Virginia.......	55,465	10,506	18.9	38,471	7,195	18.7	16,994	3,311	19.5
North Carolina......	6,488	170	2.6	4,035	80	2.0	2,453	90	3.7
South Carolina......	5,941	113	1.9	3,850	65	1.7	2,091	48	2.3
Georgia.............	14,855	269	1.8	9,319	136	1.5	5,536	133	2.4
Florida.............	38,370	7,337	19.1	22,282	3,812	17.1	16,088	3,525	21.9
EAST SOUTH CENTRAL:									
Kentucky...........	29,488	643	2.2	16,827	327	1.9	12,661	316	2.5
Tennessee..........	14,319	479	3.3	8,428	218	2.6	5,891	261	4.4
Alabama...........	16,105	694	4.3	9,814	306	3.1	6,291	388	6.2
Mississippi.........	7,330	400	5.5	4,628	192	4.1	2,702	208	7.7
WEST SOUTH CENTRAL:									
Arkansas...........	13,166	650	4.9	8,166	273	3.3	5,000	377	7.5
Louisiana...........	41,230	7,414	8.3	24,848	1,534	6.2	16,380	1,880	11.5
Oklahoma...........	36,108	4,616	12.8	22,817	2,806	12.7	13,291	1,790	12.9
Texas..............	266,718	131,628	49.4	152,600	67,952	44.5	114,118	60,676	55.8
MOUNTAIN:									
Montana............	85,709	3,020	3.5	54,250	1,342	2.5	31,459	1,678	5.3
Idaho..............	36,170	1,761	4.9	23,366	1,055	4.5	12,804	706	5.5
Wyoming...........	23,057	1,870	8.1	15,796	1,218	7.7	7,261	652	9.0
Colorado...........	105,017	9,555	9.1	62,089	4,445	7.2	42,928	5,110	11.9
New Mexico........	21,933	10,630	48.5	13,244	5,736	43.3	8,689	4,894	56.3
Arizona............	55,973	29,357	52.4	33,582	15,704	46.8	22,391	13,653	61.0
Utah...............	52,254	2,170	4.2	28,791	1,277	4.4	23,463	893	3.8
Nevada.............	13,895	1,373	9.9	10,203	940	9.2	3,692	433	11.7
PACIFIC:									
Washington.........	230,435	7,602	3.3	143,258	3,669	2.6	87,177	3,933	4.5
Oregon.............	94,807	3,209	3.4	58,580	1,689	2.9	36,227	1,520	4.2
California..........	614,381	63,014	10.3	367,340	32,610	8.9	247,041	30,404	12.3

Table 149.—NUMBER UNABLE TO SPEAK ENGLISH IN THE FOREIGN-BORN WHITE POPULATION 10 YEARS OF AGE AND OVER AND 21 YEARS OF AGE AND OVER, BY SEX, WITH PERCENTAGES FOR BOTH SEXES COMBINED, FOR CITIES HAVING 100,000 INHABITANTS OR MORE: 1920.

CITY.	FOREIGN-BORN WHITE POPULATION 10 YEARS OF AGE AND OVER.					FOREIGN-BORN WHITE POPULATION 21 YEARS OF AGE AND OVER.				
	Total number.	Unable to speak English.				Total number.	Unable to speak English.			
		Both sexes.		Male.	Female.		Both sexes.		Male.	Female.
		Number.	Per cent.				Number.	Per cent.		
Akron, Ohio	37,213	4,354	11.7	2,607	1,747	33,912	4,229	12.5	2,536	1,693
Albany, N.Y	17,471	1,669	9.6	777	892	16,348	1,617	9.9	755	862
Atlanta, Ga	4,676	90	1.9	36	54	4,272	85	2.0	34	51
Baltimore, Md	83,083	6,768	8.1	2,834	3,934	76,647	6,654	8.7	2,787	3,867
Birmingham, Ala	5,997	320	5.3	133	187	5,470	307	5.6	129	178
Boston, Mass	236,320	14,069	6.0	5,662	8,407	221,036	13,758	6.2	5,553	8,205
Bridgeport, Conn	45,795	5,980	13.1	2,746	3,234	42,308	5,853	13.8	2,682	3,171
Buffalo, N.Y	119,685	17,157	14.3	8,250	8,907	111,716	16,879	15.1	8,162	8,717
Cambridge, Mass	31,624	1,482	4.7	524	958	29,490	1,435	4.9	511	924
Camden, N.J	19,955	2,832	14.2	1,310	1,522	18,380	2,754	15.0	1,284	1,470
Chicago, Ill	797,618	89,092	11.2	38,612	50,480	743,803	87,699	11.8	38,020	49,679
Cincinnati, Ohio	42,564	1,768	4.2	773	995	40,349	1,739	4.3	756	983
Cleveland, Ohio	236,244	35,390	15.0	16,319	19,071	217,793	35,001	16.1	16,189	18,812
Columbus, Ohio	15,891	1,087	6.8	579	508	14,726	1,058	7.2	563	495
Dallas, Tex	8,394	1,660	19.8	991	669	7,495	1,329	17.7	811	518
Dayton, Ohio	12,960	1,363	10.5	722	641	12,060	1,338	11.1	710	628
Denver, Colo	37,203	1,808	4.9	740	1,068	35,282	1,699	4.8	692	1,007
Des Moines, Iowa	11,110	619	5.6	306	313	10,441	584	5.6	286	298
Detroit, Mich	282,257	33,007	11.7	17,101	15,906	257,510	32,318	12.6	16,827	15,491
Fall River, Mass	41,736	8,441	20.2	2,978	5,463	38,145	8,114	21.3	5,211	2,903
Fort Worth, Tex	6,860	2,443	35.6	1,562	881	5,868	1,989	33.9	1,306	683
Grand Rapids, Mich	28,065	2,084	7.4	845	1,239	26,181	2,062	7.9	836	1,226
Hartford, Conn	40,176	3,192	7.9	1,370	1,822	37,021	3,122	8.4	1,350	1,772
Houston, Tex	11,459	1,827	15.9	880	947	10,123	1,466	14.5	715	751
Indianapolis, Ind	16,818	617	3.7	313	304	16,000	610	3.8	308	302
Jersey City, N.J	75,232	6,249	8.3	2,876	3,373	70,677	6,114	8.7	2,820	3,294
Kansas City, Kans	11,253	1,387	12.3	709	678	10,334	1,224	11.8	645	579
Kansas City, Mo	26,810	2,216	8.3	1,040	1,176	24,728	2,008	8.1	945	1,063
Los Angeles, Calif	108,684	10,619	9.8	4,722	5,897	98,710	9,492	9.6	4,238	5,254
Louisville, Ky	11,569	180	1.6	59	121	11,182	166	1.5	56	110
Lowell, Mass	37,549	6,141	16.4	2,426	3,715	35,023	5,806	16.6	2,332	3,474
Memphis, Tenn	5,704	174	3.1	62	112	5,294	168	3.2	59	109
Milwaukee, Wis	108,934	17,074	15.7	7,162	9,912	101,684	16,969	16.7	7,118	9,851
Minneapolis, Minn	87,083	1,952	2.2	636	1,316	82,735	1,915	2.3	617	1,298
Nashville, Tenn	2,365	29	1.2	11	18	2,197	26	1.2	9	17
New Bedford, Mass	47,636	9,983	21.0	4,020	5,963	42,486	9,277	21.8	3,776	5,501
New Haven, Conn	45,101	5,234	11.6	1,938	3,296	41,634	5,119	12.3	1,887	3,232
New Orleans, La	25,632	1,510	5.9	626	884	23,814	1,401	5.9	584	817
New York, N.Y	1,968,535	208,125	10.6	86,536	121,589	1,797,882	202,651	11.3	84,342	118,309
Bronx borough	264,475	17,633	6.7	6,678	10,955	243,093	17,203	7.1	6,517	10,686
Brooklyn borough	651,941	71,335	10.9	29,463	41,872	593,266	69,507	11.7	28,654	40,853
Manhattan borough	910,438	109,288	12.0	46,121	63,167	827,420	106,258	12.8	44,978	61,280
Queens borough	110,736	6,815	6.2	2,863	3,952	105,012	6,687	6.4	2,809	3,878
Richmond borough	30,945	3,054	9.9	1,411	1,643	29,091	2,996	10.3	1,384	1,612
Newark, N.J	115,609	11,222	9.7	5,111	6,111	105,959	10,880	10.3	4,950	5,930
Norfolk, Va	6,511	199	3.1	112	87	5,946	186	3.1	103	83
Oakland, Calif	44,575	1,383	3.1	567	816	41,953	1,334	3.2	539	795
Omaha, Nebr	35,017	2,132	6.1	938	1,194	32,585	2,049	6.3	894	1,155
Paterson, N.J	44,564	4,230	9.5	1,729	2,501	40,746	4,090	10.0	1,683	2,407
Philadelphia, Pa	393,747	31,742	8.1	13,324	18,418	361,648	31,138	8.6	13,092	18,046
Pittsburgh, Pa	119,182	10,324	8.7	4,938	5,386	111,907	10,180	9.1	4,879	5,301
Portland, Oreg	46,338	1,220	2.6	539	681	43,133	1,188	2.8	524	664
Providence, R.I	68,278	7,416	10.9	2,713	4,703	63,441	7,259	11.4	2,663	4,596
Reading, Pa	9,449	1,407	14.9	601	806	8,693	1,361	15.7	581	780
Richmond, Va	4,576	97	2.1	31	66	4,252	95	2.2	30	65
Rochester, N.Y	70,085	6,362	9.1	2,447	3,915	63,668	6,165	9.7	2,366	3,799
St. Louis, Mo	102,490	5,658	5.5	2,391	3,267	95,716	5,549	5.8	2,351	3,198
St. Paul, Minn	51,086	1,693	3.3	589	1,104	48,314	1,674	3.5	583	1,091
Salt Lake City, Utah	19,182	595	3.1	306	289	17,814	553	3.1	285	268
San Antonio, Tex	33,977	16,466	48.5	8,274	8,192	27,109	13,580	50.1	7,001	6,579
San Francisco, Calif	138,475	7,116	5.1	3,245	3,871	130,867	6,790	5.2	3,080	3,710
Scranton, Pa	28,321	2,462	8.7	1,045	1,417	26,687	2,428	9.1	1,034	1,394
Seattle, Wash	71,988	1,985	2.8	1,017	968	67,540	1,918	2.8	989	929
Spokane, Wash	16,488	317	1.9	124	193	15,483	315	2.0	123	192
Springfield, Mass	30,857	2,185	7.1	820	1,365	28,724	2,121	7.4	799	1,322
Syracuse, N.Y	31,936	2,832	8.9	1,310	1,522	29,793	2,781	9.3	1,294	1,487
Toledo, Ohio	37,667	5,300	14.1	2,702	2,598	35,311	5,215	14.8	2,652	2,563
Trenton, N.J	29,676	3,697	12.5	1,672	2,025	27,091	3,601	13.3	1,638	1,963
Washington, D.C	28,292	779	2.8	329	450	26,376	740	2.8	311	429
Wilmington, Del	16,075	2,459	15.3	1,255	1,204	15,073	2,404	15.9	1,236	1,168
Worcester, Mass	52,821	3,318	6.3	1,230	2,088	49,389	3,249	6.6	1,196	2,053
Yonkers, N.Y	25,439	2,581	10.1	1,111	1,470	23,962	2,529	10.6	1,099	1,430
Youngstown, Ohio	33,343	5,073	15.2	3,108	1,965	30,943	4,987	16.1	3,063	1,924

TABLE 150.—NUMBER UNABLE TO SPEAK ENGLISH IN THE FOREIGN-BORN WHITE POPULATION 10 YEARS OF AGE AND OVER, BY SEX, WITH PERCENTAGES FOR BOTH SEXES COMBINED, FOR CITIES HAVING FROM 25,000 TO 100,000 INHABITANTS: 1920.

CITY.	Total number.	Both sexes: Number.	Both sexes: Per cent.	Male.	Female.	CITY.	Total number.	Both sexes: Number.	Both sexes: Per cent.	Male.	Female.
ALABAMA:						IOWA:					
Mobile	1,973	27	1.4	10	17	Cedar Rapids	5,784	594	10.3	265	329
Montgomery	744	20	2.7	7	13	Council Bluffs	3,944	206	5.2	131	75
ARIZONA:						Davenport	7,574	243	3.2	146	97
Phoenix	3,838	1,355	35.3	673	682	Dubuque	4,193	170	4.1	77	93
ARKANSAS:						Sioux City	11,119	638	5.7	359	279
Fort Smith	848	29	3.4	11	18	Waterloo	2,886	140	4.9	71	69
Little Rock	1,788	23	1.3	12	11	KANSAS:					
CALIFORNIA:						Topeka	3,846	518	13.5	263	255
Alameda	5,781	115	2.0	51	64	Wichita	2,891	539	18.6	324	215
Berkeley	9,434	194	2.1	96	98	KENTUCKY:					
Fresno	8,319	918	11.0	353	565	Covington	2,878	25	0.9	15	10
Long Beach	6,581	306	4.6	153	153	Lexington	791	8	1.0	3	5
Pasadena	6,622	197	3.0	72	125	Newport	2,082	37	1.8	15	22
Sacramento	10,705	705	6.6	314	391	LOUISIANA:					
San Diego	12,918	1,110	8.6	441	669	Shreveport	1,275	48	3.8	19	29
San Jose	7,728	771	10.0	299	472	MAINE:					
Stockton	6,874	521	7.6	240	281	Bangor	3,688	88	2.4	48	40
COLORADO:						Lewiston	9,974	2,614	26.2	688	1,926
Colorado Spgs	2,586	61	2.4	28	33	Portland	12,995	262	2.0	94	168
Pueblo	7,073	1,137	16.1	566	571	MARYLAND:					
CONNECTICUT:						Cumberland	1,153	139	12.1	91	48
Meriden	7,846	656	8.4	291	365	Hagerstown	428	9	2.1	5	4
New Britain	20,982	3,721	17.7	1,444	2,277	MASSACHUSETTS:					
New London	5,770	427	7.4	117	310	Brockton	16,917	688	4.1	257	431
Norwalk	5,891	550	9.3	207	343	Brookline town	9,307	8	0.1	3	5
Stamford	10,554	802	7.6	257	545	Chelsea	16,980	2,423	14.3	1,093	1,330
Waterbury	29,432	2,606	8.9	1,131	1,475	Chicopee	12,025	2,557	21.3	946	1,611
FLORIDA:						Everett	10,952	509	4.6	212	297
Jacksonville	3,825	87	2.3	50	37	Fitchburg	12,900	1,459	11.3	502	957
Miami	2,492	8	0.3	1	7	Haverhill	13,165	785	6.0	264	521
Pensacola	1,428	15	1.1	9	6	Holyoke	19,973	2,083	10.4	765	1,318
Tampa	10,413	5,293	50.8	2,650	2,643	Lawrence	38,463	6,723	17.5	2,676	4,047
GEORGIA:						Lynn	27,544	1,309	4.8	588	721
Augusta	920	21	2.3	9	12	Malden	13,968	327	2.3	97	230
Columbus	323	1	0.3		1	Medford	8,456	157	1.9	50	107
Macon	686	7	1.0	4	3	Newton	10,073	272	2.7	68	204
Savannah	3,215	35	1.1	9	26	Pittsfield	8,094	790	9.8	346	444
ILLINOIS:						Quincy	13,532	914	6.8	378	536
Aurora	6,427	245	3.8	84	161	Revere	8,761	567	6.5	154	413
Bloomington	2,818	137	4.9	56	81	Salem	11,062	1,412	12.8	502	910
Cicero town	15,360	3,226	21.0	1,267	1,959	Somerville	23,835	582	2.4	230	352
Danville	1,904	46	2.4	19	27	Taunton	9,832	1,734	17.6	752	982
Decatur	2,555	80	3.1	36	44	Waltham	8,024	262	3.3	94	168
East St. Louis	6,711	678	10.1	365	313	MICHIGAN:					
Elgin	5,021	160	3.2	71	89	Battle Creek	3,331	144	4.3	92	52
Evanston	6,704	219	3.3	79	140	Bay City	8,895	409	4.6	159	250
Joliet	8,408	1,222	14.5	624	598	Flint	14,709	949	6.5	518	431
Moline	7,305	263	3.6	128	135	Hamtramck vil	22,471	6,843	30.5	3,260	3,583
Oak Park vil	5,604	70	1.2	30	40	Highland Park	12,266	357	2.9	126	231
Peoria	7,734	357	4.0	206	191	Jackson	5,256	315	6.0	148	167
Quincy	2,407	70	0.0	29	41	Kalamazoo	7,118	610	8.7	307	312
Rock Island	5,296	170	3.2	73	97	Lansing	5,070	467	8.0	289	178
Rockford	17,160	1,514	8.8	709	805	Muskegon	6,742	314	4.7	150	164
Springfield	6,188	223	3.6	98	125	Pontiac	5,052	441	8.7	363	78
INDIANA:						Port Huron	6,166	123	2.0	65	58
Anderson	929	82	8.8	44	38	Saginaw	11,435	530	4.6	172	358
East Chicago	14,440	2,906	20.1	1,487	1,419	MINNESOTA:					
Evansville	3,106	29	0.9	9	20	Duluth	29,807	1,366	4.6	711	655
Fort Wayne	6,573	282	4.3	147	135	MISSOURI:					
Gary	16,198	1,377	8.5	729	648	Joplin	722	6	0.8		6
Hammond	8,032	1,085	13.5	556	529	St. Joseph	6,333	888	14.0	506	382
Kokomo	1,149	52	4.5	38	14	Springfield	967	49	5.1	25	24
Muncie	813	36	4.4	24	12	MONTANA:					
Richmond	1,122	25	2.2	10	15	Butte	11,301	232	2.1	98	134
South Bend	13,222	2,237	16.9	992	1,245	NEBRASKA:					
Terre Haute	3,636	177	4.9	110	67	Lincoln	7,015	617	8.8	206	411

TABLE 150.—NUMBER UNABLE TO SPEAK ENGLISH IN THE FOREIGN-BORN WHITE POPULATION 10 YEARS OF AGE AND OVER, BY SEX, WITH PERCENTAGES FOR BOTH SEXES COMBINED, FOR CITIES HAVING FROM 25,000 TO 100,000 INHABITANTS: 1920—Continued.

CITY.	FOREIGN-BORN WHITE POPULATION 10 YEARS OF AGE AND OVER.				CITY.	FOREIGN-BORN WHITE POPULATION 10 YEARS OF AGE AND OVER.			
	Total number.	Unable to speak English.				Total number.	Unable to speak English.		
		Both sexes.		Male.	Female.			Both sexes.		Male.	Female.
		Number.	Per cent.					Number.	Per cent.		
NEW HAMPSHIRE:						PENNSYLVANIA:					
Manchester.....	27,060	4,509	16.7	1,431	3,078	Allentown......	8,505	1,263	14.9	490	773
Nashua..........	8,598	1,890	22.0	792	1,098	Altoona.........	5,228	636	12.2	269	367
NEW JERSEY:						Bethlehem.....	10,795	2,686	24.9	1,482	1,204
Atlantic City...	6,928	330	4.8	164	166	Chester.........	11,133	1,784	16.0	1,096	688
Bayonne........	25,199	3,152	12.5	1,432	1,720	Easton.........	3,944	487	12.3	216	271
Clifton.........	9,502	1,744	18.4	589	1,155	Erie...........	17,103	2,716	15.9	1,440	1,276
East Orange.....	6,714	214	3.2	92	122	Harrisburg.....	4,093	430	10.5	184	246
Elizabeth.......	27,873	2,914	10.5	1,391	1,523	Hazleton.......	5,971	474	7.9	137	337
Hoboken........	23,215	1,287	5.5	488	799	Johnstown......	12,013	1,416	11.8	682	734
Irvington town.	5,465	129	2.4	52	77	Lancaster......	2,692	127	4.7	53	74
Kearny town...	7,800	166	2.1	62	104	McKeesport....	11,769	1,848	15.7	1,072	776
Montclair town.	5,078	684	13.5	345	339	New Castle.....	8,551	1,437	16.8	652	785
New Brunswick	8,794	762	8.7	230	532	Norristown boro	4,250	840	19.8	389	451
Orange.........	6,894	504	7.3	148	356	Wilkes-Barre...	14,460	2,037	14.1	902	1,135
Passaic.........	26,089	5,479	21.0	2,136	3,343	Williamsport...	2,244	337	15.0	176	161
Perth Amboy..	14,759	1,690	11.5	710	980	York...........	1,182	58	4.9	29	29
Plainfield.......	5,438	454	8.3	165	289	RHODE ISLAND:					
West Hoboken town.........	13,936	1,386	9.9	543	843	Cranston.......	7,437	667	9.0	198	469
						Newport.......	5,708	59	1.0	22	37
West New York town.........	8,805	631	7.2	203	428	Pawtucket.....	20,723	1,892	9.1	871	1,021
NEW YORK:						Woonsocket....	15,619	3,287	21.0	1,111	2,176
Amsterdam.....	9,732	1,653	17.0	590	1,063	SOUTH CAROLINA:					
Auburn........	7,485	1,002	13.4	402	600	Charleston......	2,125	22	1.0	14	8
Binghamton....	10,271	2,100	20.4	962	1,138	Columbia......	538	16	3.0	12	4
Elmira.........	4,657	253	5.4	109	144	SOUTH DAKOTA:					
Jamestown.....	11,299	827	7.3	286	541	Sioux Falls.....	2,928	171	5.8	80	91
Kingston.......	2,748	92	3.3	26	66	TENNESSEE:					
Mount Vernon..	9,957	980	9.8	344	636	Chattanooga....	1,230	17	1.4	6	11
New Rochelle..	8,347	283	3.4	105	178	Knoxville......	803	11	1.4	3	8
Newburgh......	4,898	394	8.0	183	211	TEXAS:					
Niagara Falls...	17,370	2,751	15.8	1,502	1,249	Austin.........	2,470	334	13.5	138	196
Poughkeepsie...	5,466	617	11.3	278	339	Beaumont......	1,875	310	16.5	189	121
Rome..........	5,152	993	19.3	522	471	El Paso........	29,736	18,292	61.5	7,137	11,155
Schenectady....	20,250	2,655	13.1	962	1,693	Galveston......	6,711	1,141	17.0	723	418
Troy..........	11,404	308	2.7	117	191	Waco..........	1,716	268	15.6	138	130
Utica..........	23,000	4,090	17.8	1,590	2,500	Wichita Falls..	1,661	458	27.6	376	82
Watertown.....	5,725	208	3.6	113	95	UTAH:					
NORTH CAROLINA:						Ogden..........	4,517	130	2.9	70	60
Asheville.......	549	15	2.7	6	9	VIRGINIA:					
Charlotte.......	503	3	0.6	1	2	Lynchburg.....	344	3	0.9	2	1
Wilmington....	608	7	1.2	5	2	Newport News.	2,018	25	1.2	10	15
Winston-Salem.	293	4	1.4	3	1	Petersburg.....	508	10	2.0	4	6
OHIO:						Portsmouth....	1,520	37	2.4	12	25
Canton.........	14,437	2,506	17.4	1,899	607	Roanoke......	861	9	1.0	4	5
East Cleveland.	3,804	18	0.5	4	14	WASHINGTON:					
Hamilton.......	2,639	157	5.9	82	75	Bellingham.....	5,173	110	2.1	42	68
Lakewood......	7,196	1,000	13.9	426	574	Everett........	5,618	51	0.9	18	33
Lima..........	1,889	80	4.2	40	40	Tacoma........	20,234	791	3.9	424	367
Lorain.........	11,770	1,100	9.3	606	494	WEST VIRGINIA:					
Mansfield.......	3,154	198	6.3	95	103	Charleston.....	1,336	47	3.5	18	29
Marion........	948	75	7.9	44	31	Clarksburg.....	1,901	280	14.7	148	132
Newark........	1,485	162	10.9	97	65	Huntington....	724	15	2.1	6	9
Portsmouth....	692	23	3.3	14	9	Wheeling.......	5,736	552	9.6	306	246
Springfield.....	2,731	157	5.7	86	71	WISCONSIN:					
Steubenville....	5,488	1,077	19.6	663	414	Green Bay.....	3,554	182	5.1	55	127
Warren........	4,593	1,068	23.3	771	297	Kenosha........	12,523	869	6.9	387	482
Zanesville......	1,266	161	12.7	105	56	La Crosse.......	4,434	172	3.9	59	113
OKLAHOMA:						Madison........	4,814	444	9.2	224	220
						Oshkosh........	5,764	273	4.7	98	175
Muskogee......	533	32	6.0	18	14	Racine.........	15,982	1,057	6.6	552	505
Oklahoma City.	3,354	511	15.2	301	210	Sheboygan......	8,105	1,652	20.4	773	879
Tulsa..........	1,988	47	2.4	25	22	Superior.......	10,650	441	4.1	219	222

ABSTRACT OF THE CENSUS—POPULATION.

TABLE 151.—NUMBER AND PER CENT UNABLE TO SPEAK ENGLISH IN THE URBAN AND RURAL FOREIGN-BORN WHITE POPULATION 10 YEARS OF AGE AND OVER, BY SEX, BY DIVISIONS AND STATES: 1920.

DIVISION AND STATE.	FOREIGN-BORN WHITE MALES 10 YEARS OF AGE AND OVER UNABLE TO SPEAK ENGLISH.				FOREIGN-BORN WHITE FEMALES 10 YEARS OF AGE AND OVER UNABLE TO SPEAK ENGLISH.			
	In urban communities.		In rural communities.		In urban communities.		In rural communities.	
	Number.	Per cent.	Number.	Per cent.	Number.	Per cent.	Number.	Per cent.
United States.........	482,570	8.8	197,463	10.2	607,224	12.9	201,691	14.9
GEOGRAPHIC DIVISIONS:								
New England............	63,574	7.8	6,639	5.6	101,209	12.6	9,429	9.0
Middle Atlantic..........	198,032	9.0	33,241	8.8	257,484	13.0	37,092	13.1
East North Central.......	129,521	9.3	22,791	5.6	145,741	13.3	30,928	10.3
West North Central......	15,117	4.5	20,350	4.6	18,254	6.8	31,538	9.9
South Atlantic...........	9,997	8.2	7,780	12.9	10,834	11.1	3,431	11.0
East South Central.......	537	2.0	573	3.8	739	3.5	514	6.2
West South Central.......	35,779	31.3	57,381	43.7	39,096	42.2	49,543	54.0
Mountain................	9,262	9.4	27,999	17.1	10,585	13.6	23,250	24.3
Pacific..................	20,751	5.4	20,709	9.3	23,282	8.2	15,966	13.4
NEW ENGLAND:								
Maine....................	2,168	7.6	1,318	5.1	5,154	17.6	1,693	8.1
New Hampshire...........	3,271	9.4	1,079	9.8	6,089	17.4	900	10.6
Vermont.................	738	8.0	610	4.5	888	10.4	829	7.3
Massachusetts...........	36,889	7.2	667	4.1	57,627	11.1	1,243	7.9
Rhode Island............	7,931	9.4	62	6.8	13,518	15.9	109	12.5
Connecticut.............	12,577	8.6	2,903	5.6	17,933	14.2	4,655	9.8
MIDDLE ATLANTIC:								
New York................	117,337	8.9	5,967	5.6	159,401	12.9	7,495	8.2
New Jersey..............	26,786	8.2	4,875	8.3	36,229	12.4	5,519	11.0
Pennsylvania............	53,909	9.6	22,399	10.5	61,854	13.6	24,078	16.9
EAST NORTH CENTRAL:								
Ohio....................	36,255	11.2	5,530	8.7	34,329	14.3	5,047	11.7
Indiana.................	5,674	8.2	843	4.7	5,753	12.0	999	7.3
Illinois................	48,950	8.8	4,439	4.8	62,958	13.2	5,618	8.4
Michigan................	26,658	9.1	5,774	5.1	26,707	12.3	8,966	10.1
Wisconsin...............	11,984	8.5	6,205	5.3	15,994	14.4	10,298	11.7
WEST NORTH CENTRAL:								
Minnesota...............	4,019	3.0	6,881	4.8	6,078	5.8	11,333	11.2
Iowa....................	2,032	4.1	2,207	2.9	1,962	4.9	3,358	5.8
Missouri................	4,123	5.1	942	4.4	4,994	7.5	1,067	6.9
North Dakota............	188	2.2	3,344	5.1	300	4.1	6,357	13.3
South Dakota............	293	4.5	1,475	3.6	313	5.7	2,780	9.6
Nebraska................	1,656	5.1	2,217	4.4	2,141	8.3	3,172	8.2
Kansas..................	2,806	13.3	3,284	8.2	2,466	14.6	3,471	11.7
SOUTH ATLANTIC:								
Delaware................	1,302	13.6	127	7.6	1,253	17.8	51	4.0
Maryland................	3,045	6.7	351	4.2	4,041	9.8	328	5.5
District of Columbia......	329	2.2	(1)	....	450	3.4	(1)	....
Virginia................	325	2.8	263	3.7	301	4.2	246	5.8
West Virginia...........	1,193	10.1	6,462	21.9	943	12.2	2,523	21.6
North Carolina..........	39	1.6	48	2.7	43	2.6	60	5.9
South Carolina..........	49	2.0	18	1.2	28	1.7	21	3.5
Georgia.................	81	1.1	60	2.2	120	2.4	24	2.3
Florida.................	3,634	22.4	451	5.7	3,655	28.8	178	3.4
EAST SOUTH CENTRAL:								
Kentucky................	114	1.0	233	3.8	194	1.9	147	4.9
Tennessee...............	154	2.4	76	3.0	182	3.7	94	6.5
Alabama.................	183	2.8	136	3.4	257	5.7	148	6.1
Mississippi.............	86	3.4	128	5.4	106	6.6	125	8.9
WEST SOUTH CENTRAL:								
Arkansas................	40	1.4	257	4.9	87	3.7	307	10.3
Louisiana...............	909	4.2	847	11.4	1,113	8.5	911	19.7
Oklahoma................	1,212	13.9	2,136	13.6	636	12.1	1,278	14.5
Texas...................	33,712	40.5	54,141	52.6	37,260	51.7	46,944	62.9
MOUNTAIN:								
Montana.................	352	1.8	1,032	2.7	442	3.4	1,272	6.0
Idaho...................	375	5.8	816	4.5	244	5.4	521	5.6
Wyoming.................	399	7.6	902	7.9	221	7.3	481	9.6
Colorado................	1,824	5.6	3,158	9.2	2,271	8.7	3,397	16.0
New Mexico..............	590	19.6	6,434	50.7	638	26.6	5,563	63.9
Arizona.................	5,124	35.1	13,885	53.6	6,206	51.7	11,137	63.4
Utah....................	489	3.0	853	6.0	466	3.0	495	5.1
Nevada..................	109	6.7	919	10.2	97	10.2	384	12.8
PACIFIC:								
Washington..............	2,105	2.4	1,667	2.6	2,085	3.5	1,939	5.5
Oregon..................	847	2.4	922	3.5	890	3.6	683	4.8
California..............	17,799	6.8	18,120	13.6	20,307	10.1	13,344	19.0

[1] No rural population, as Washington city is coextensive with the District of Columbia.

TABLE 152.—DWELLINGS AND FAMILIES, 1920, WITH NUMBER OF PERSONS TO A DWELLING AND TO A FAMILY, 1920 AND 1910, BY DIVISIONS AND STATES.

DIVISION AND STATE.	1920			PERSONS TO A DWELLING.[1]		PERSONS TO A FAMILY.[1]	
	Population.	Dwellings.	Families.	1920	1910	1920	1910
United States.........	105,710,620	20,697,204	24,351,676	5.1	5.2	4.3	4.5
GEOGRAPHIC DIVISIONS:							
New England.............	7,400,909	1,255,964	1,703,812	5.9	6.0	4.3	4.5
Middle Atlantic..........	22,261,144	3,566,549	5,085,080	6.2	6.2	4.4	4.6
East North Central.......	21,475,543	4,385,541	5,143,913	4.9	4.9	4.2	4.3
West North Central.......	12,544,249	2,716,968	2,957,849	4.6	4.8	4.2	4.5
South Atlantic............	13,990,272	2,781,684	2,991,628	5.0	5.0	4.7	4.8
East South Central.......	8,893,307	1,867,167	1,977,381	4.8	4.9	4.5	4.7
West South Central.......	10,242,224	2,110,879	2,242,810	4.9	4.9	4.6	4.8
Mountain.................	3,336,101	743,775	803,853	4.5	4.5	4.2	4.3
Pacific...................	5,566,871	1,268,677	1,445,350	4.4	4.7	3.9	4.3
NEW ENGLAND:							
Maine....................	768,014	162,304	186,106	4.7	4.7	4.1	4.2
New Hampshire........ ..	443,083	92,184	108,334	4.8	4.8	4.1	4.2
Vermont.................	352,428	77,158	85,804	4.6	4.6	4.1	4.2
Massachusetts............	3,852,356	597,052	874,798	6.5	6.6	4.4	4.6
Rhode Island.............	604,397	98,861	137,160	6.1	6.8	4.4	4.6
Connecticut..............	1,380,631	228,405	311,610	6.0	6.1	4.4	4.5
MIDDLE ATLANTIC:							
New York................	10,385,227	1,325,114	2,441,125	7.8	7.7	4.3	4.5
New Jersey...............	3,155,900	515,211	721,841	6.1	6.2	4.4	4.5
Pennsylvania.............	8,720,017	1,726,224	1,922,114	5.1	5.1	4.5	4.7
EAST NORTH CENTRAL:							
Ohio....................	5,759,394	1,216,542	1,414,068	4.7	4.7	4.1	4.2
Indiana..................	2,930,390	696,466	737,707	4.2	4.3	4.0	4.1
Illinois..................	6,485,280	1,190,414	1,534,077	5.4	5.6	4.2	4.5
Michigan.................	3,668,412	755,931	862,745	4.9	4.5	4.3	4.3
Wisconsin................	2,632,067	526,188	595,316	5.0	5.0	4.4	4.7
WEST NORTH CENTRAL:							
Minnesota................	2,387,125	469,652	526,026	5.1	5.5	4.5	5.0
Iowa....................	2,404,021	559,188	586,070	4.3	4.5	4.1	4.3
Missouri.................	3,404,055	717,256	829,043	4.7	4.9	4.1	4.4
North Dakota............	646,872	129,905	134,881	5.0	4.9	4.8	4.8
South Dakota............	636,547	136,512	142,793	4.7	4.6	4.5	4.5
Nebraska................	1,296,372	288,390	303,436	4.5	4.6	4.3	4.5
Kansas..................	1,769,257	416,065	435,600	4.3	4.4	4.1	4.3
SOUTH ATLANTIC:							
Delaware................	223,003	47,868	52,070	4.7	4.7	4.3	4.5
Maryland................	1,449,661	288,261	324,742	5.0	5.1	4.5	4.7
District of Columbia......	437,571	72,175	96,194	6.1	5.7	4.5	4.6
Virginia.................	2,309,187	450,229	483,363	5.1	5.1	4.8	4.9
West Virginia............	1,463,701	293,002	310,098	5.0	5.1	4.7	4.9
North Carolina...........	2,559,123	495,269	513,377	5.2	5.1	5.0	5.0
South Carolina...........	1,683,724	330,500	349,126	5.1	5.0	4.8	4.8
Georgia.................	2,895,832	586,509	628,525	4.9	4.9	4.6	4.7
Florida..................	968,470	217,871	234,133	4.4	4.5	4.1	4.4
EAST SOUTH CENTRAL:							
Kentucky................	2,416,630	510,981	546,306	4.7	4.9	4.4	4.6
Tennessee...............	2,337,885	488,392	519,108	4.8	4.9	4.5	4.7
Alabama.................	2,348,174	480,392	508,769	4.9	4.8	4.6	4.7
Mississippi..............	1,790,618	387,402	403,198	4.6	4.8	4.4	4.7
WEST SOUTH CENTRAL:							
Arkansas................	1,752,204	375,316	390,960	4.7	4.8	4.5	4.7
Louisiana................	1,798,509	370,377	389,913	4.9	5.0	4.6	4.8
Oklahoma...............	2,028,283	418,557	444,524	4.8	4.8	4.6	4.7
Texas...................	4,663,228	946,629	1,017,413	4.9	5.0	4.6	4.9
MOUNTAIN:							
Montana.................	548,889	130,670	139,912	4.2	4.5	3.9	4.3
Idaho...................	431,866	95,299	100,500	4.5	4.5	4.3	4.4
Wyoming................	194,402	44,710	48,476	4.3	4.7	4.0	4.5
Colorado................	939,629	211,103	230,843	4.5	4.3	4.1	4.1
New Mexico.............	360,350	78,024	83,706	4.6	4.3	4.3	4.1
Arizona.................	334,162	73,673	80,208	4.5	4.5	4.2	4.3
Utah....................	449,396	89,587	98,346	5.0	5.1	4.6	4.8
Nevada..................	77,407	20,709	21,862	3.7	3.6	3.5	3.5
PACIFIC:							
Washington..............	1,356,621	304,735	342,228	4.5	4.8	4.0	4.5
Oregon..................	783,389	185,081	202,890	4.2	4.6	3.9	4.4
California................	3,426,861	778,861	900,232	4.4	4.6	3.8	4.2

[1] Persons to a dwelling: 5.3 in 1900, 5.5 in 1890, and 5.6 in 1880. Persons to a family: 4.7 in 1900, 4.9 in 1890, and 5.0 in 1880.

TABLE 153.—DWELLINGS AND FAMILIES, 1920, WITH NUMBER OF PERSONS TO A DWELLING AND TO A FAMILY, 1920 AND 1910, FOR CITIES HAVING, IN 1920, 100,000 INHABITANTS OR MORE.

CITY.	1920			PERSONS TO A DWELLING.		PERSONS TO A FAMILY.	
	Population.	Dwellings.	Families.	1920	1910	1920	1910
Akron, Ohio	208,435	32,030	44,195	6.5	5.0	4.7	4.4
Albany, N. Y	113,344	18,402	28,097	6.2	6.5	4.0	4.2
Atlanta, Ga	200,616	38,098	49,523	5.3	5.1	4.1	4.3
Baltimore, Md	733,826	136,324	166,857	5.4	5.5	4.4	4.7
Birmingham, Ala	178,806	35,100	43,040	5.1	4.9	4.2	4.3
Boston, Mass	748,060	79,597	164,785	9.4	9.1	4.5	4.8
Bridgeport, Conn	143,555	22,328	31,994	6.4	6.8	4.5	4.7
Buffalo, N. Y	506,775	73,880	116,201	6.9	6.8	4.4	4.6
Cambridge, Mass	109,694	15,113	25,293	7.3	7.2	4.3	4.6
Camden, N. J	116,309	24,921	26,645	4.7	4.7	4.4	4.4
Chicago, Ill	2,701,705	335,777	623,912	8.0	8.9	4.3	4.6
Cincinnati, Ohio	401,247	62,885	106,239	6.4	7.3	3.8	4.2
Cleveland, Ohio	796,841	116,545	182,692	6.8	6.2	4.4	4.5
Columbus, Ohio	237,031	51,663	58,913	4.6	4.6	4.0	4.3
Dallas, Tex	158,976	30,860	36,754	5.2	5.0	4.3	4.5
Dayton, Ohio	152,559	33,918	38,138	4.5	4.4	4.0	4.1
Denver, Colo	256,491	50,636	61,916	5.1	4.8	4.1	4.2
Des Moines, Iowa	126,468	27,127	31,644	4.7	4.6	4.0	4.2
Detroit, Mich	993,678	153,206	218,973	6.5	5.6	4.5	4.6
Fall River, Mass	120,485	13,807	26,399	8.7	10.9	4.6	4.9
Forth Worth, Tex	106,482	19,679	25,052	5.4	5.0	4.3	4.5
Grand Rapids, Mich	137,634	29,157	33,703	4.7	4.8	4.1	4.2
Hartford, Conn	138,036	16,495	30,813	8.4	8.6	4.5	4.5
Houston, Tex	138,276	28,452	33,932	4.9	5.0	4.1	4.6
Indianapolis, Ind	314,194	71,648	81,256	4.4	4.4	3.9	4.0
Jersey City, N. J	298,103	31,145	67,288	9.6	9.6	4.4	4.7
Kansas City, Kans	101,177	22,641	25,009	4.5	4.5	4.0	4.2
Kansas City, Mo	324,410	61,321	82,056	5.3	5.2	4.0	4.2
Los Angeles. Calif	576,673	125,004	159,476	4.6	4.6	3.6	4.1
Louisville, Ky	234,891	47,449	60,490	5.0	5.4	3.9	4.3
Lowell, Mass	112,759	17,488	25,034	6.4	7.1	4.5	4.8
Memphis, Tenn	162,351	35,295	42,369	4.6	4.9	3.8	4.2
Milwaukee, Wis	457,147	66,915	106,101	6.8	6.2	4.3	4.6
Minneapolis, Minn	380,582	65,568	91,843	5.8	6.4	4.1	4.8
Nashville, Tenn	118,342	24,992	30,220	4.7	5.0	3.9	4.2
New Bedford, Mass	121,217	14,961	26,858	8.1	8.4	4.5	4.6
New Haven, Conn	162,537	22,536	36,257	7.2	7.6	4.5	4.6
New Orleans, La	387,219	76,969	85,188	5.0	5.0	4.5	4.6
New York, N. Y	5,620,048	365,963	1,278,341	15.4	15.6	4.4	4.7
Bronx borough	732,016	33,985	166,260	21.5	15.0	4.4	4.6
Brooklyn borough	2,018,356	173,847	453,587	11.6	11.1	4.4	4.6
Manhattan borough	2,284,103	75,534	525,154	30.2	30.9	4.3	4.7
Queens borough	469,042	64,323	109,559	7.3	7.1	4.3	4.6
Richmond borough	116,531	18,274	23,781	6.4	6.1	4.9	4.9
Newark, N. J	414,524	41,535	93,274	10.0	9.0	4.4	4.5
Norfolk, Va	115,777	19,934	26,732	5.8	5.6	4.3	4.4
Oakland, Calif	216,261	47,297	55,793	4.6	4.7	3.9	4.1
Omaha, Nebr	191,601	37,997	44,499	5.0	1 5.3	4.3	1 4.8
Paterson, N. J	135,875	18,769	32,186	7.2	7.9	4.2	4.5
Philadelphia, Pa	1,823,779	352,944	402,946	5.2	5.2	4.5	4.7
Pittsburgh, Pa	588,343	93,890	130,274	6.3	6.1	4.5	4.8
Portland, Oreg	258,288	54,664	67,045	4.7	5.5	3.9	4.9
Providence, R. I	237,595	35,634	54,726	6.7	7.8	4.3	4.6
Reading, Pa	107,784	22,759	25,202	4.7	4.6	4.3	4.4
Richmond, Va	171,667	30,753	39,191	5.6	5.7	4.4	4.7
Rochester, N. Y	295,750	56,502	68,247	5.2	5.6	4.3	4.7
St. Louis, Mo	772,897	118,102	190,640	6.5	6.5	4.1	4.4
St. Paul, Minn	234,698	42,462	54,409	5.5	6.6	4.3	5.2
Salt Lake City, Utah	118,110	23,685	28,216	5.0	5.2	4.2	4.6
San Antonio, Tex	161,379	00,901	36,405	5.3	4.9	4.4	4.6
San Francisco, Calif	506,676	90,132	123,349	5.6	6.4	4.1	4.8
Scranton, Pa	137,783	23,952	29,768	5.8	5.9	4.6	4.9
Seattle, Wash	315,312	60,516	80,048	5.2	5.4	3.9	4.6
Spokane, Wash	104,437	22,389	27,178	4.7	5.1	3.8	4.6
Springfield, Mass	129,614	18,945	30,361	6.8	6.7	4.3	4.5
Syracuse, N. Y	171,717	28,725	41,558	6.0	5.9	4.1	4.4
Toledo, Ohio	243,164	49,501	57,951	4.9	4.7	4.2	4.2
Trenton, N. J	119,289	22,373	25,319	5.3	5.4	4.7	4.9
Washington, D. C	437,571	72,175	96,194	6.1	5.7	4.5	4.6
Wilmington, Del	110,168	20,876	24,488	5.3	5.1	4.5	4.7
Worcester, Mass	179,754	19,337	39,230	9.3	9.7	4.6	4.7
Yonkers, N. Y	100,176	10,302	22,126	9.7	10.2	4.5	4.9
Youngstown, Ohio	132,358	24,007	28,699	5.5	5.5	4.6	4.9

1 Based on figures including South Omaha in 1910.

TABLE 154.—DWELLINGS AND FAMILIES AND NUMBER OF PERSONS TO A DWELLING AND TO A FAMILY, FOR CITIES HAVING FROM 25,000 TO 100,000 INHABITANTS: 1920.

CITY.	Population.	Dwellings.	Families.	Persons to a dwelling.	Persons to a family.	CITY.	Population.	Dwellings.	Families.	Persons to a dwelling.	Persons to a family.
ALABAMA:						KENTUCKY:					
Mobile	60,777	12,350	15,148	4.9	4.0	Covington	57,121	11,100	14,809	5.1	3.9
Montgomery	43,464	9,437	11,568	4.6	3.8	Lexington	41,534	9,500	10,720	4.4	3.9
ARIZONA:						Newport	29,317	5,621	7,792	5.2	3.8
Phoenix	29,053	5,867	7,354	5.0	4.0	LOUISIANA:					
ARKANSAS:						Shreveport	43,874	9,175	10,618	4.8	4.1
Fort Smith	28,870	5,916	6,872	4.9	4.2	MAINE:					
Little Rock	65,142	13,156	15,059	5.0	4.3	Bangor	25,978	5,234	6,145	5.0	4.2
CALIFORNIA:						Lewiston	31,791	3,676	6,750	8.6	4.7
Alameda	28,806	7,191	7,886	4.0	3.7	Portland	69,272	11,036	16,801	6.3	4.1
Berkeley	56,036	12,936	15,159	4.3	3.7	MARYLAND:					
Fresno	45,086	9,493	11,234	4.7	4.0	Cumberland	29,837	5,894	6,433	5.1	4.6
Long Beach	55,593	12,758	17,169	4.4	3.2	Hagerstown	28,064	5,991	6,609	4.7	4.2
Pasadena	45,354	11,712	12,657	3.9	3.6	MASSACHUSETTS:					
Sacramento	65,908	13,779	17,263	4.8	3.8	Brockton	66,254	10,388	16,084	6.4	4.1
San Diego	74,683	18,532	22,723	4.0	3.3	Brookline town	37,748	5,036	8,603	7.5	4.4
San Jose	39,642	9,391	10,669	4.2	3.7	Chelsea	43,184	4,403	8,833	9.8	4.9
Stockton	40,296	8,470	9,981	4.8	4.0	Chicopee	36,214	4,625	7,004	7.8	5.2
COLORADO:						Everett	40,120	6,870	9,187	5.8	4.4
Colorado Springs	30,105	7,680	8,332	3.9	3.6	Fitchburg	41,029	6,180	9,273	6.6	4.4
Pueblo	43,050	8,956	10,484	4.8	4.1	Haverhill	53,884	9,165	12,814	5.9	4.2
CONNECTICUT:						Holyoke	60,203	5,706	12,948	10.6	4.6
Meriden	29,867	4,412	6,955	6.8	4.3	Lawrence	94,270	12,700	19,715	7.4	4.8
New Britain	59,316	6,109	12,072	9.7	4.9	Lynn	99,148	14,841	23,308	6.7	4.3
New London	25,688	4,730	5,937	5.4	4.3	Malden	49,103	8,495	11,238	5.8	4.4
Norwalk	27,743	5,139	6,791	5.4	4.1	Medford	39,038	7,632	9,351	5.1	4.2
Stamford	35,096	4,656	7,839	7.5	4.5	Newton	46,054	8,944	10,189	5.1	4.5
Waterbury	91,715	11,583	19,124	7.9	4.8	Pittsfield	41,763	7,693	9,499	5.4	4.4
FLORIDA:						Quincy	47,876	9,483	11,146	5.0	4.3
Jacksonville	91,558	19,571	23,265	4.7	3.9	Revere	28,823	3,942	6,375	7.3	4.5
Miami	29,571	6,696	7,497	4.4	3.9	Salem	42,529	5,902	9,353	7.2	4.5
Pensacola	31,035	6,353	7,448	4.9	4.2	Somerville	93,091	15,112	22,653	6.2	4.1
Tampa	51,608	10,492	12,137	4.9	4.3	Taunton	37,137	5,989	8,062	6.2	4.6
GEORGIA:						Waltham	30,915	5,681	6,566	5.4	4.7
Augusta	52,548	11,988	13,966	4.4	3.8	MICHIGAN:					
Columbus	31,125	6,224	7,245	5.0	4.3	Battle Creek	36,164	8,240	9,347	4.4	3.9
Macon	52,995	11,299	13,730	4.7	3.9	Bay City	47,554	10,466	11,002	4.5	4.3
Savannah	83,252	16,999	21,267	4.9	3.9	Flint	91,599	16,228	19,570	5.6	4.7
ILLINOIS:						Hamtramck vil	48,615	5,702	9,117	8.5	5.3
Aurora	36,397	7,920	8,973	4.6	4.1	Highland Park	46,499	8,051	10,401	5.8	4.5
Bloomington	28,725	6,829	7,451	4.2	3.9	Jackson	48,374	10,565	11,851	4.6	4.1
Cicero town	44,995	6,463	9,770	7.0	4.6	Kalamazoo	48,487	10,467	11,754	4.6	4.1
Danville	33,776	7,947	8,907	4.3	3.8	Lansing	57,327	12,089	13,811	4.7	4.2
Decatur	43,818	9,768	10,874	4.5	4.0	Muskegon	36,570	7,397	8,696	4.9	4.2
East St. Louis	66,767	14,081	15,768	4.7	4.2	Pontiac	34,273	6,295	7,090	5.4	4.8
Elgin	27,454	5,776	6,490	4.8	4.2	Port Huron	25,944	5,918	6,407	4.4	4.0
Evanston	37,234	6,411	8,472	5.8	4.4	Saginaw	61,903	14,035	14,906	4.4	4.2
Joliet	38,442	6,865	8,654	5.6	4.4	MINNESOTA:					
Moline	30,734	6,535	7,564	4.7	4.1	Duluth	98,917	17,320	21,294	5.7	4.6
Oak Park vil	39,858	8,112	9,737	4.9	4.1	MISSOURI:					
Peoria	76,121	16,743	19,397	4.5	3.9	Joplin	29,902	7,414	8,012	4.0	3.7
Quincy	35,978	8,445	9,378	4.3	3.8	St. Joseph	77,939	17,359	19,189	4.5	4.1
Rock Island	35,177	7,910	8,824	4.4	4.0	Springfield	39,631	9,578	10,412	4.1	3.8
Rockford	65,651	12,668	16,027	5.2	4.1	MONTANA:					
Springfield	59,183	13,006	14,255	4.6	4.2	Butte	41,611	8,287	10,098	5.0	4.1
INDIANA:						NEBRASKA:					
Anderson	29,767	6,827	7,523	4.4	4.0	Lincoln	54,948	12,241	13,812	4.5	4.0
East Chicago	35,967	5,100	7,080	7.1	5.1	NEW HAMPSHIRE:					
Evansville	85,264	19,072	20,648	4.5	4.1	Manchester	78,384	10,657	17,415	7.4	4.5
Fort Wayne	86,549	18,879	20,406	4.6	4.2	Nashua	28,379	5,111	6,305	5.6	4.5
Gary	55,378	8,284	12,022	6.7	4.6	NEW JERSEY:					
Hammond	36,004	6,910	7,983	5.2	4.5	Atlantic City	50,707	9,807	12,468	5.2	4.1
Kokomo	30,067	6,368	7,505	4.3	4.0	Bayonne	76,754	8,299	15,513	9.2	4.9
Muncie	36,524	8,645	9,529	4.2	3.8	Clifton	26,470	4,036	5,800	6.6	4.6
Richmond	26,765	6,506	7,055	4.1	3.8	East Orange	50,710	8,277	12,416	6.1	4.1
South Bend	70,983	14,626	16,113	4.9	4.4	Elizabeth	95,783	13,408	20,641	7.1	4.6
Terre Haute	66,083	15,476	16,745	4.3	3.9	Hoboken	68,166	4,617	15,877	14.8	4.3
IOWA:						Irvington town	25,480	3,889	6,098	6.6	4.2
Cedar Rapids	45,566	10,645	11,612	4.3	3.9	Kearny town	26,724	3,811	5,706	7.0	4.7
Council Bluffs	36,162	8,278	8,789	4.4	4.1	Montclair town	28,810	4,989	6,294	5.8	4.6
Davenport	56,727	12,042	14,388	4.7	3.9	New Brunswick	32,779	5,128	7,404	6.4	4.4
Dubuque	39,141	8,173	9,314	4.8	4.2	Orange	33,268	4,842	7,289	6.9	4.6
Sioux City	71,227	14,014	16,234	5.1	4.4	Passaic	63,841	6,380	13,393	10.0	4.8
Waterloo	36,230	8,348	9,071	4.3	4.0	Perth Amboy	41,707	5,475	8,605	7.6	4.8
KANSAS:						Plainfield	27,700	5,282	6,375	5.2	4.3
Topeka	50,022	12,021	13,039	4.2	3.8	West Hoboken	40,074	4,234	10,131	9.5	4.0
Wichita	72,217	15,846	18,596	4.6	3.9	West New York	29,926	3,063	7,410	9.8	4.0

TABLE 154.—DWELLINGS AND FAMILIES AND NUMBER OF PERSONS TO A DWELLING AND TO A FAMILY, FOR CITIES HAVING FROM 25,000 TO 100,000 INHABITANTS: 1920—Con.

CITY.	Population.	Dwellings.	Families.	Persons to a dwelling.	Persons to a family.
NEW YORK:					
Amsterdam.....	33,524	5,013	7,726	6.7	4.3
Auburn.........	36,192	7,263	8,719	5.0	4.2
Binghamton.....	66,800	10,421	16,000	6.4	4.2
Elmira.........	45,393	9,209	11,357	4.9	4.0
Jamestown......	38,917	7,926	10,206	4.9	3.8
Kingston.......	26,688	5,233	6,701	5.1	4.0
Mount Vernon...	42,726	5,856	9,715	7.3	4.4
New Rochelle...	36,213	5,491	7,725	6.6	4.7
Newburgh.......	30,366	4,944	7,647	6.1	4.0
Niagara Falls....	50,760	8,307	10,857	6.1	4.7
Poughkeepsie....	35,000	5,583	8,732	6.3	4.0
Rome..........	26,341	4,486	5,416	5.9	4.9
Schenectady....	88,723	13,782	20,657	6.4	4.3
Troy..........	72,013	11,554	17,895	6.2	4.0
Utica..........	94,156	13,969	21,657	6.7	4.3
Watertown......	31,285	6,610	7,835	4.7	4.0
NORTH CAROLINA:					
Asheville.......	28,504	5,575	6,477	5.1	4.4
Charlotte......	46,338	9,641	10,720	4.8	4.3
Wilmington....	33,372	7,012	7,847	4.8	4.3
Winston-Salem..	48,395	8,542	9,895	5.7	4.9
OHIO:					
Canton.........	87,091	17,506	20,496	5.0	4.2
East Cleveland..	27,292	5,611	7,122	4.9	3.8
Hamilton.......	39,675	8,570	9,706	4.6	4.1
Lakewood......	41,732	8,534	10,537	4.9	4.0
Lima..........	41,326	9,638	10,659	4.3	3.9
Lorain.........	37,295	6,562	8,004	5.7	4.7
Mansfield......	27,824	6,230	7,215	4.5	3.9
Marion........	27,891	6,798	7,231	4.1	3.9
Newark........	26,718	6,928	7,322	3.9	3.6
Portsmouth....	33,011	6,961	7,967	4.7	4.1
Springfield.....	60,840	14,242	15,484	4.3	3.9
Steubenville....	28,508	5,736	6,516	5.0	4.4
Warren........	27,050	5,670	6,561	4.8	4.1
Zanesville......	29,569	7,356	7,958	4.0	3.7
OKLAHOMA:					
Muskogee......	30,277	6,506	7,414	4.7	4.1
Oklahoma City..	91,295	17,285	21,346	5.3	4.3
Tulsa..........	72,075	13,559	16,910	5.3	4.3
PENNSYLVANIA:					
Allentown......	73,502	15,316	17,298	4.8	4.2
Altoona........	60,331	12,482	13,740	4.8	4.4
Bethlehem.....	50,358	10,190	11,265	4.9	4.5
Chester........	58,030	10,894	12,259	5.3	4.7
Easton........	33,813	7,263	8,257	4.4	4.1
Erie..........	93,372	17,387	21,425	5.4	4.4
Harrisburg.....	75,917	16,935	19,158	4.5	4.0
Hazleton.......	32,277	6,320	6,584	5.1	4.9
Johnstown.....	67,327	12,444	13,858	5.4	4.9
Lancaster......	53,150	12,002	12,844	4.4	4.1
McKeesport.....	46,781	7,781	9,916	6.0	4.7

CITY.	Population.	Dwellings.	Families.	Persons to a dwelling.	Persons to a family.
PENNSYLVANIA— Continued.					
New Castle......	44,938	9,181	10,397	4.9	4.3
Norristown boro.	32,319	5,931	6,624	5.4	4.9
Wilkes-Barre....	73,833	13,464	15,378	5.5	4.8
Williamsport....	36,198	8,079	8,927	4.5	4.1
York..........	47,512	10,886	11,692	4.4	4.1
RHODE ISLAND:					
Cranston.......	29,407	5,311	6,360	5.5	4.6
Newport.......	30,255	4,895	6,440	6.2	4.7
Pawtucket......	64,248	10,609	14,675	6.1	4.4
Woonsocket.....	43,496	5,341	9,080	8.1	4.8
SOUTH CAROLINA:					
Charleston......	67,957	11,714	17,824	5.8	3.8
Columbia.......	37,524	6,704	8,151	5.6	4.6
SOUTH DAKOTA:					
Sioux Falls......	25,202	5,176	6,208	4.9	4.1
TENNESSEE:					
Chattanooga.....	57,895	11,458	14,621	5.1	4.0
Knoxville......	77,818	15,494	17,474	5.0	4.5
TEXAS:					
Austin.........	34,876	7,392	7,925	4.7	4.4
Beaumont......	40,422	7,867	9,495	5.1	4.3
El Paso........	77,560	11,158	18,159	7.0	4.3
Galveston......	44,255	9,273	10,588	4.8	4.2
Waco..........	38,500	8,011	9,374	4.8	4.1
Wichita Falls....	40,079	6,595	7,878	6.1	5.1
UTAH:					
Ogden.........	32,804	6,483	7,803	5.1	4.2
VIRGINIA:					
Lynchburg.....	30,070	5,878	6,558	5.1	4.6
Newport News..	35,596	6,012	7,835	5.9	4.5
Petersburg.....	31,012	6,832	7,540	4.5	4.1
Portsmouth....	54,387	11,210	12,568	4.9	4.3
Roanoke.......	50,842	9,090	11,260	5.6	4.5
WASHINGTON:					
Bellingham.....	25,585	6,009	6,640	4.3	3.9
Everett........	27,644	6,149	7,169	4.5	3.9
Tacoma........	96,965	21,512	24,662	4.5	3.9
WEST VIRGINIA:					
Charleston......	39,608	7,725	9,069	5.1	4.4
Clarksburg.....	27,869	5,604	6,453	5.0	4.3
Huntington....	50,177	9,864	11,350	5.1	4.4
Wheeling......	56,208	11,226	13,919	5.0	4.0
WISCONSIN:					
Green Bay.....	31,017	6,020	6,914	5.2	4.5
Kenosha.......	40,472	6,350	8,098	6.4	5.0
La Crosse......	30,421	6,866	7,526	4.4	4.0
Madison.......	38,378	7,515	9,413	5.1	4.1
Oshkosh.......	33,162	7,523	8,027	4.4	4.1
Racine........	58,593	10,439	12,799	5.6	4.6
Sheboygan.....	30,955	5,823	7,215	5.3	4.3
Superior.......	39,671	7,347	8,692	5.4	4.6

TABLE 155.—DWELLINGS AND FAMILIES FOR URBAN AND RURAL COMMUNITIES, 1920, WITH NUMBER OF PERSONS TO A DWELLING AND TO A FAMILY, 1920 AND 1910, BY DIVISIONS AND STATES.

DIVISION, STATE, AND CLASS OF COMMUNITY.	1920			PERSONS TO A DWELLING.		PERSONS TO A FAMILY.	
	Population.	Dwellings.	Families.	1920	1910	1920	1910
United States:							
Urban	54,304,603	9,484,550	12,803,047	5.7	5.9	4.2	4.5
Rural	51,406,017	11,212,654	11,548,629	4.6	4.7	4.5	4.6
GEOGRAPHIC DIVISIONS.							
NEW ENGLAND:							
Urban	5,865,073	903,949	1,325,076	6.5	6.7	4.4	4.6
Rural	1,535,836	352,015	378,736	4.4	4.4	4.1	4.1
MIDDLE ATLANTIC:							
Urban	16,672,595	2,332,383	3,788,850	7.1	7.3	4.4	4.6
Rural	5,588,549	1,234,166	1,296,230	4.5	4.6	4.3	4.4
EAST NORTH CENTRAL:							
Urban	13,049,272	2,406,316	3,119,157	5.4	5.4	4.2	4.3
Rural	8,426,271	1,979,225	2,024,756	4.3	4.4	4.2	4.3
WEST NORTH CENTRAL:							
Urban	4,727,372	959,775	1,164,089	4.9	5.1	4.1	4.4
Rural	7,816,877	1,757,193	1,793,760	4.4	4.6	4.4	4.5
SOUTH ATLANTIC:							
Urban	4,338,792	846,647	1,006,440	5.1	5.1	4.3	4.5
Rural	9,651,480	1,935,037	1,985,188	5.0	5.0	4.9	4.9
EAST SOUTH CENTRAL:							
Urban	1,994,207	422,751	496,765	4.7	4.8	4.0	4.2
Rural	6,899,100	1,444,416	1,480,616	4.8	4.9	4.7	4.8
WEST SOUTH CENTRAL:							
Urban	2,970,829	606,625	695,135	4.9	4.9	4.3	4.5
Rural	7,271,395	1,504,254	1,547,675	4.8	5.0	4.7	4.9
MOUNTAIN:							
Urban	1,214,980	254,491	295,327	4.8	4.8	4.1	4.4
Rural	2,121,121	489,284	508,526	4.3	4.3	4.2	4.2
PACIFIC:							
Urban	3,471,483	751,613	912,208	4.6	5.0	3.8	4.4
Rural	2,095,388	517,064	533,142	4.1	4.3	3.9	4.2
NEW ENGLAND.							
MAINE:							
Urban	299,569	53,647	70,672	5.6	5.5	4.2	4.4
Rural	468,445	108,657	115,434	4.3	4.3	4.1	4.1
NEW HAMPSHIRE:							
Urban	279,761	51,456	65,051	5.4	5.6	4.3	4.5
Rural	163,322	40,728	43,283	4.0	4.1	3.8	3.8
VERMONT:							
Urban	109,976	20,722	25,994	5.3	5.5	4.2	4.4
Rural	242,452	56,436	59,810	4.3	4.3	4.1	4.1
MASSACHUSETTS:							
Urban	3,650,248	547,896	822,425	6.7	6.9	4.4	4.6
Rural	202,108	49,156	52,373	4.1	4.3	3.9	4.0
RHODE ISLAND:							
Urban	589,180	95,027	133,118	6.2	7.0	4.4	4.6
Rural	15,217	3,834	4,042	4.0	4.2	3.8	3.9
CONNECTICUT:							
Urban	936,339	135,201	207,816	6.9	7.2	4.5	4.6
Rural	444,292	93,204	103,794	4.8	4.8	4.3	4.3
MIDDLE ATLANTIC.							
NEW YORK:							
Urban	8,589,844	889,174	1,983,762	9.7	9.9	4.3	4.6
Rural	1,795,383	435,940	457,363	4.1	4.2	3.9	4.0
NEW JERSEY:							
Urban	2,474,936	366,650	562,334	6.8	7.0	4.4	4.6
Rural	680,964	148,561	159,507	4.6	4.7	4.3	4.4
PENNSYLVANIA:							
Urban	5,607,815	1,076,559	1,242,754	5.2	5.2	4.5	4.7
Rural	3,112,202	649,665	679,360	4.8	4.9	4.6	4.7
EAST NORTH CENTRAL.							
OHIO:							
Urban	3,677,136	714,734	898,839	5.1	5.0	4.1	4.2
Rural	2,082,258	501,808	515,229	4.1	4.2	4.0	4.2
INDIANA:							
Urban	1,482,855	338,981	373,802	4.4	4.4	4.0	4.1
Rural	1,447,535	357,485	363,905	4.0	4.2	4.0	4.2
ILLINOIS:							
Urban	4,403,153	706,812	1,040,938	6.2	6.6	4.2	4.5
Rural	2,082,127	483,602	493,139	4.3	4.5	4.2	4.4

TABLE 155.—DWELLINGS AND FAMILIES FOR URBAN AND RURAL COMMUNITIES, 1920, WITH NUMBER OF PERSONS TO A DWELLING AND TO A FAMILY, 1920 AND 1910, BY DIVISIONS AND STATES—Continued.

DIVISION, STATE, AND CLASS OF COMMUNITY.	1920			PERSONS TO A DWELLING.		PERSONS TO A FAMILY.	
	Population.	Dwellings.	Families.	1920	1910	1920	1910
EAST NORTH CENTRAL—Con.							
MICHIGAN:							
Urban	2,241,560	416,154	515,020	5.4	4.9	4.4	4.4
Rural	1,426,852	339,777	347,725	4.2	4.3	4.1	4.2
WISCONSIN:							
Urban	1,244,568	229,635	290,558	5.4	5.3	4.3	4.5
Rural	1,387,499	296,553	304,758	4.7	4.9	4.6	4.8
WEST NORTH CENTRAL.							
MINNESOTA:							
Urban	1,051,593	191,734	241,261	5.5	6.1	4.4	5.0
Rural	1,335,532	277,918	284,765	4.8	5.1	4.7	5.0
IOWA:							
Urban	875,495	202,124	222,669	4.3	4.4	3.9	4.2
Rural	1,528,526	357,064	363,401	4.3	4.5	4.2	4.4
MISSOURI:							
Urban	1,586,903	295,055	398,030	5.4	5.4	4.0	4.3
Rural	1,817,152	422,201	431,013	4.3	4.5	4.2	4.5
NORTH DAKOTA:							
Urban	88,239	16,575	19,413	5.3	5.6	4.5	5.1
Rural	558,633	113,330	115,468	4.9	4.8	4.8	4.7
SOUTH DAKOTA:							
Urban	101,872	21,200	24,348	4.8	5.0	4.2	4.5
Rural	534,675	115,312	118,445	4.6	4.5	4.5	4.4
NEBRASKA:							
Urban	405,306	86,761	97,810	4.7	4.8	4.1	4.5
Rural	891,066	201,629	205,626	4.4	4.5	4.3	4.5
KANSAS:							
Urban	617,964	146,326	160,558	4.2	4.3	3.8	4.0
Rural	1,151,293	269,739	275,042	4.3	4.4	4.2	4.4
SOUTH ATLANTIC.							
DELAWARE:							
Urban	120,767	23,655	27,314	5.1	5.0	4.4	4.6
Rural	102,236	24,213	24,756	4.2	4.5	4.1	4.4
MARYLAND:							
Urban	869,422	165,383	198,198	5.3	5.3	4.4	4.6
Rural	580,239	122,878	126,544	4.7	4.9	4.6	4.8
DISTRICT OF COLUMBIA:							
Urban	437,571	72,175	96,194	6.1	5.7	4.5	4.6
Rural [1]							
VIRGINIA:							
Urban	673,984	127,674	152,826	5.3	5.3	4.4	4.6
Rural	1,635,203	322,555	330,537	5.1	5.1	4.9	5.0
WEST VIRGINIA:							
Urban	369,007	74,472	85,483	5.0	5.1	4.3	4.6
Rural	1,094,694	218,530	224,615	5.0	5.1	4.9	5.0
NORTH CAROLINA:							
Urban	490,370	98,136	107,915	5.0	4.9	4.5	4.6
Rural	2,068,753	397,133	405,462	5.2	5.2	5.1	5.1
SOUTH CAROLINA:							
Urban	293,987	57,309	69,825	5.1	5.2	4.2	4.3
Rural	1,389,737	273,191	279,301	5.1	5.0	5.0	4.9
GEORGIA:							
Urban	727,859	150,141	179,410	4.8	4.8	4.1	4.2
Rural	2,167,973	436,368	449,115	5.0	4.9	4.8	4.9
FLORIDA:							
Urban	955,895	77,700	89,075	4.6	4.6	4.0	4.3
Rural	612,645	140,169	144,858	4.4	4.5	4.2	4.4
EAST SOUTH CENTRAL.							
KENTUCKY:							
Urban	633,543	134,688	161,733	4.7	5.0	3.9	4.2
Rural	1,783,087	376,293	384,573	4.7	4.8	4.6	4.8
TENNESSEE:							
Urban	611,226	129,488	151,637	4.7	4.9	4.0	4.3
Rural	1,726,659	358,904	367,471	4.8	4.9	4.7	4.9
ALABAMA:							
Urban	509,317	104,695	123,392	4.9	4.7	4.1	4.2
Rural	1,838,857	375,697	385,377	4.9	4.9	4.8	4.8
MISSISSIPPI:							
Urban	240,121	53,880	60,003	4.5	4.6	4.0	4.2
Rural	1,550,497	333,522	343,195	4.6	4.8	4.5	4.7

[1] No rural population, as Washington city is coextensive with the District of Columbia.

TABLE 155.—DWELLINGS AND FAMILIES FOR URBAN AND RURAL COMMUNITIES, 1920, WITH NUMBER OF PERSONS TO A DWELLING AND TO A FAMILY, 1920 AND 1910, BY DIVISIONS AND STATES—Continued.

DIVISION, STATE, AND CLASS OF COMMUNITY.	1920			PERSONS TO A DWELLING.		PERSONS TO A FAMILY.	
	Population.	Dwellings.	Families.	1920	1910	1920	1910
WEST SOUTH CENTRAL.							
ARKANSAS:							
Urban	290,497	63,603	71,001	4.6	4.6	4.1	4.4
Rural	1,461,707	311,713	319,959	4.7	4.8	4.6	4.8
LOUISIANA:							
Urban	628,163	128,684	141,294	4.9	4.9	4.4	4.6
Rural	1,170,346	241,693	248,619	4.8	5.0	4.7	4.9
OKLAHOMA:							
Urban	539,480	111,317	128,357	4.8	4.9	4.2	4.5
Rural	1,488,803	307,240	316,167	4.8	4.8	4.7	4.8
TEXAS:							
Urban	1,512,689	303,021	354,483	5.0	4.9	4.3	4.6
Rural	3,150,539	643,608	662,930	4.9	5.0	4.8	5.0
MOUNTAIN.							
MONTANA:							
Urban	172,011	36,135	42,525	4.8	5.1	4.0	4.6
Rural	376,878	94,535	97,387	4.0	4.3	3.9	4.2
IDAHO:							
Urban	119,037	25,386	28,416	4.7	5.0	4.2	4.7
Rural	312,829	69,913	72,084	4.5	4.4	4.3	4.4
WYOMING:							
Urban	57,348	11,588	13,652	4.9	5.4	4.2	5.0
Rural	137,054	33,122	34,824	4.1	4.5	3.9	4.4
COLORADO:							
Urban	453,259	95,904	112,380	4.7	4.6	4.0	4.2
Rural	486,370	115,199	118,463	4.2	4.1	4.1	4.1
NEW MEXICO:							
Urban	64,960	13,911	15,858	4.7	4.5	4.1	4.2
Rural	295,390	64,113	67,848	4.6	4.3	4.4	4.1
ARIZONA:							
Urban	117,527	24,964	28,814	4.7	4.6	4.1	4.3
Rural	216,635	48,709	51,394	4.4	4.4	4.2	4.3
UTAH:							
Urban	215,584	43,262	49,931	5.0	5.1	4.3	4.7
Rural	233,812	46,325	48,415	5.0	5.1	4.8	5.0
NEVADA:							
Urban	15,254	3,341	3,751	4.6	4.7	4.1	4.3
Rural	62,153	17,368	18,111	3.6	3.4	3.4	3.3
PACIFIC.							
WASHINGTON:							
Urban	748,735	156,661	190,272	4.8	5.2	3.9	4.6
Rural	607,886	148,074	151,956	4.1	4.4	4.0	4.3
OREGON:							
Urban	391,019	86,224	101,728	4.5	5.2	3.8	4.7
Rural	392,370	98,857	101,162	4.0	4.2	3.9	4.2
CALIFORNIA:							
Urban	2,331,729	508,728	620,208	4.6	4.9	3.8	4.2
Rural	1,095,132	270,133	280,024	4.1	4.3	3.9	4.2

75108°—23——30

TABLE **156.**—DISTRIBUTION OF HOMES ACCORDING TO PROPRIETORSHIP AND ENCUMBRANCE, FOR THE UNITED STATES: 1890–1920.

[In compiling this table the unknown items as to proprietorship and encumbrance have been distributed in the same proportions as the known items.]

CENSUS YEAR.	HOMES.				
	Total.	Rented.	Owned.		
			Total.	Free.	Encumbered.
1920	24,351,676	13,236,709	11,114,967	6,862,520	4,252,447
1910	20,255,555	10,982,380	9,273,175	6,236,074	3,037,101
1900	16,187,715	8,719,060	7,468,655	5,127,935	2,340,720
1890	12,690,152	6,623,735	6,066,417	4,369,527	1,696,890

CENSUS YEAR.	PER CENT OF TOTAL HOMES.				PER CENT OF OWNED HOMES.	
	Rented.	Owned.			Free.	Encumbered.
		Total.	Free.	Encumbered.		
1920	54.4	45.6	28.2	17.5	61.7	38.3
1910	54.2	45.8	30.8	15.0	67.2	32.8
1900	53.9	46.1	31.7	14.5	68.7	31.3
1890	52.2	47.8	34.4	13.4	72.0	28.0

TABLE 157.—PER CENT DISTRIBUTION OF HOMES ACCORDING TO PROPRIETORSHIP AND ENCUMBRANCE, BY DIVISIONS AND STATES: 1920 AND 1910.

[In computing the percentages in this table the numbers representing the unknown items as to proprietorship and encumbrance have been distributed in the same proportions as the known items.]

DIVISION AND STATE.	1920 Per cent of all homes.				1920 Per cent of owned homes.		1910 Per cent of all homes				1910 Per cent of owned homes.	
	Rented.	Owned.	Owned free.	Owned encumbered	Free.	Encumbered	Rented.	Owned.	Owned free.	Owned encumbered	Free.	Encumbered
United States	54.4	45.6	28.2	17.5	61.7	38.3	54.2	45.8	30.8	15.0	67.2	32.8
GEOGRAPHIC DIVISIONS:												
New England	60.2	39.8	20.4	19.5	51.1	48.9	60.3	39.7	23.2	16.5	58.5	41.5
Middle Atlantic	62.8	37.2	19.0	18.2	51.2	48.8	64.5	35.5	20.2	15.3	56.8	43.2
East North Central	47.7	52.3	30.6	21.7	58.5	41.5	47.2	52.8	33.8	19.0	64.0	36.0
West North Central	43.6	56.4	33.9	22.5	60.1	39.9	41.8	58.2	37.3	20.8	64.2	35.8
South Atlantic	58.0	42.0	32.0	10.0	76.2	23.8	59.1	40.9	32.8	8.2	80.0	20.0
East South Central	57.3	42.7	33.0	9.7	77.2	22.8	57.7	42.3	33.4	8.9	78.9	21.1
West South Central	57.8	42.2	29.5	12.6	70.0	30.0	57.1	42.9	32.3	10.6	75.3	24.7
Mountain	44.8	55.2	35.5	19.7	64.4	35.6	41.5	58.5	47.1	11.4	80.5	19.5
Pacific	52.1	47.9	28.4	19.4	59.4	40.6	47.0	53.0	35.1	18.0	66.1	33.9
NEW ENGLAND:												
Maine	40.4	59.6	45.0	14.5	75.6	24.4	37.7	62.3	47.6	14.7	76.4	23.6
New Hampshire	50.2	49.8	35.1	14.7	70.4	29.6	49.0	51.0	38.1	12.9	74.7	25.3
Vermont	42.5	57.5	35.1	22.4	61.0	39.0	41.6	58.4	34.9	23.5	59.8	40.2
Massachusetts	65.2	34.8	14.8	20.1	42.4	57.6	66.9	33.1	16.9	16.2	51.1	48.9
Rhode Island	68.9	31.1	15.0	16.1	48.2	51.8	71.7	28.3	15.6	12.7	55.0	45.0
Connecticut	62.4	37.6	14.6	23.0	38.7	61.3	62.8	37.2	17.8	19.5	47.7	52.3
MIDDLE ATLANTIC:												
New York	69.3	30.7	14.5	16.2	47.3	52.7	69.1	30.9	16.4	14.4	53.2	46.8
New Jersey	61.7	38.3	14.5	23.7	38.0	62.0	65.0	35.0	15.4	19.5	44.1	55.9
Pennsylvania	54.8	45.2	26.5	18.7	58.7	41.3	58.5	41.5	26.5	15.0	63.8	36.2
EAST NORTH CENTRAL:												
Ohio	48.4	51.6	31.7	19.9	61.4	38.6	48.8	51.2	34.6	16.6	67.6	32.4
Indiana	45.2	54.8	34.8	20.0	63.6	36.4	45.3	54.7	36.3	18.3	66.4	33.6
Illinois	56.2	43.8	25.4	18.4	58.0	42.0	56.0	44.0	28.0	16.1	63.5	36.5
Michigan	41.1	58.9	32.3	26.6	54.9	45.1	38.4	61.6	37.8	23.7	61.5	38.5
Wisconsin	36.4	63.6	34.1	29.6	53.5	46.5	35.6	64.4	37.9	26.5	58.8	41.2
WEST NORTH CENTRAL:												
Minnesota	39.3	60.7	36.1	24.6	59.4	40.6	38.3	61.7	40.2	21.5	65.2	34.8
Iowa	41.9	58.1	36.7	21.4	63.2	36.8	41.6	58.4	38.0	20.4	65.0	35.0
Missouri	50.5	49.5	28.9	20.7	58.3	41.7	49.1	50.9	30.3	20.6	59.6	40.4
North Dakota	34.7	65.3	30.2	35.1	46.2	53.8	24.9	75.1	45.4	29.7	60.4	39.6
South Dakota	38.5	61.5	35.2	26.3	57.3	42.7	32.1	67.9	47.5	20.4	69.9	30.1
Nebraska	42.6	57.4	34.9	22.4	60.9	39.1	41.0	59.0	40.4	18.6	68.5	31.5
Kansas	43.1	56.9	37.0	19.9	65.0	35.0	40.9	59.1	39.1	20.0	66.1	33.9
SOUTH ATLANTIC:												
Delaware	55.3	44.7	25.1	19.6	56.1	43.9	59.4	40.6	24.8	15.7	61.2	38.8
Maryland	50.1	49.9	30.3	19.5	60.9	39.1	56.1	43.9	29.7	14.2	67.7	32.3
District of Columbia	69.7	30.3	13.5	16.8	44.6	55.4	74.8	25.2	14.6	10.6	58.0	42.0
Virginia	48.9	51.1	40.6	10.5	79.4	20.6	48.8	51.2	42.3	8.9	82.7	17.3
West Virginia	53.2	46.8	37.7	9.1	80.6	19.4	50.8	49.2	41.6	7.5	84.7	15.3
North Carolina	52.6	47.4	39.3	8.1	82.9	17.1	53.0	47.0	38.6	8.3	82.2	17.8
South Carolina	67.8	32.2	25.3	6.9	78.6	21.4	69.4	30.6	24.0	6.6	78.6	21.4
Georgia	69.1	30.9	24.2	6.7	78.2	21.8	69.6	30.4	25.1	5.3	82.6	17.4
Florida	57.5	42.5	32.7	9.7	77.1	22.9	56.3	43.7	36.9	6.7	84.6	15.4
EAST SOUTH CENTRAL:												
Kentucky	48.4	51.6	40.1	11.5	77.8	22.2	48.6	51.4	41.4	10.0	80.6	19.4
Tennessee	52.3	47.7	37.6	10.1	78.8	21.2	53.3	46.7	38.8	7.9	83.0	17.0
Alabama	65.0	35.0	26.3	8.7	75.0	25.0	65.1	34.9	26.6	8.3	76.2	23.8
Mississippi	66.0	34.0	25.9	8.1	76.3	23.7	66.0	34.0	24.5	9.5	72.1	27.9
WEST SOUTH CENTRAL:												
Arkansas	54.9	45.1	32.4	12.7	71.9	28.1	53.6	46.4	36.9	9.5	79.5	20.5
Louisiana	66.3	33.7	26.7	6.9	79.4	20.6	68.0	32.0	26.6	5.4	83.2	16.8
Oklahoma	54.5	45.5	27.0	18.5	59.4	40.6	54.6	45.4	30.4	15.0	67.0	33.0
Texas	57.2	42.8	30.6	12.2	71.4	28.6	54.9	45.1	33.7	11.4	74.8	25.2
MOUNTAIN:												
Montana	39.5	60.5	33.4	27.1	55.2	44.8	40.7	59.3	49.1	10.2	82.7	17.3
Idaho	39.1	60.9	32.6	28.3	53.5	46.5	32.7	67.3	49.6	17.7	73.7	26.3
Wyoming	48.1	51.9	32.4	19.6	62.3	37.7	45.9	54.1	44.1	10.0	81.5	18.5
Colorado	48.4	51.6	32.1	19.5	62.2	37.8	48.7	51.3	37.3	14.0	72.7	27.3
New Mexico	40.6	59.4	49.0	10.4	82.5	17.5	29.7	70.3	66.3	4.0	94.4	5.6
Arizona	57.2	42.8	32.5	10.3	75.9	24.1	51.1	48.9	41.8	7.2	85.4	14.6
Utah	40.0	60.0	41.3	18.7	68.8	31.2	35.4	64.6	51.4	13.1	79.6	20.4
Nevada	52.4	47.6	39.8	7.8	83.6	16.4	46.7	53.3	48.9	4.3	91.9	8.1
PACIFIC:												
Washington	45.3	54.7	32.6	22.2	59.5	40.5	42.9	57.1	39.1	17.9	68.6	31.4
Oregon	45.2	54.8	34.2	20.6	62.4	37.6	40.3	59.7	42.2	17.5	70.6	29.4
California	56.3	43.7	25.6	18.1	58.5	41.5	50.6	49.4	31.3	18.1	63.4	36.6

TABLE 158.—NUMBER OF HOMES, DISTRIBUTED ACCORDING TO PROPRIETORSHIP

DIVISION AND STATE.	Total homes.	Rented.	1920 Owned.				Tenure unknown.
			Total.	Free.	Encumbered.	Unknown.	
United States	24,351,676	12,943,598	10,866,960	6,522,119	4,059,593	285,248	541,118
GEOGRAPHIC DIVISIONS:							
New England	1,703,812	1,010,586	668,324	335,753	322,064	10,507	24,902
Middle Atlantic	5,085,080	3,144,533	1,864,123	934,703	892,787	36,633	76,424
East North Central	5,143,913	2,407,639	2,644,052	1,510,174	1,069,927	63,951	92,222
West North Central	2,957,849	1,257,816	1,626,771	952,049	631,238	43,484	73,262
South Atlantic	2,991,628	1,684,936	1,221,214	896,122	281,864	43,228	85,478
East South Central	1,977,381	1,101,352	823,131	617,367	181,669	24,095	52,898
West South Central	2,242,810	1,252,703	913,378	613,789	262,404	37,185	76,729
Mountain	803,853	349,755	431,039	269,907	149,458	11,674	23,059
Pacific	1,445,350	734,278	674,928	392,255	268,182	14,491	36,144
NEW ENGLAND:							
Maine	186,106	73,860	108,829	80,540	25,979	2,310	3,417
New Hampshire	108,334	53,159	52,778	36,195	15,193	1,390	2,397
Vermont	85,804	35,706	48,370	29,029	18,571	770	1,728
Massachusetts	874,798	564,097	301,245	126,312	171,741	3,192	9,456
Rhode Island	137,160	92,800	41,921	19,889	21,352	680	2,439
Connecticut	311,610	190,964	115,181	43,788	69,228	2,165	5,465
MIDDLE ATLANTIC:							
New York	2,441,125	1,670,088	738,738	342,452	381,776	14,510	32,299
New Jersey	721,841	438,911	271,914	101,598	165,844	4,472	11,016
Pennsylvania	1,922,114	1,035,534	853,471	490,653	345,167	17,651	33,109
EAST NORTH CENTRAL:							
Ohio	1,414,068	673,858	719,097	432,804	271,872	14,421	21,113
Indiana	737,707	326,192	395,402	243,851	139,796	11,755	16,113
Illinois	1,534,077	846,071	658,260	370,221	268,446	19,593	29,746
Michigan	862,745	349,054	499,471	268,287	220,467	10,717	14,220
Wisconsin	595,316	212,464	371,822	195,011	169,346	7,465	11,030
WEST NORTH CENTRAL:							
Minnesota	526,026	202,222	312,367	181,253	123,786	7,328	11,437
Iowa	586,070	239,880	332,567	205,115	119,289	8,163	13,623
Missouri	829,043	409,068	401,667	229,129	163,824	8,714	18,308
North Dakota	134,881	45,050	84,904	37,268	43,375	4,261	4,927
South Dakota	142,793	53,099	84,712	46,438	34,621	3,653	4,982
Nebraska	303,436	125,713	169,098	99,715	63,973	5,410	8,625
Kansas	435,600	182,784	241,456	153,131	82,370	5,955	11,360
SOUTH ATLANTIC:							
Delaware	52,070	28,287	22,829	12,358	9,672	799	954
Maryland	324,742	160,219	159,262	94,695	60,857	3,710	5,261
District of Columbia	96,194	65,654	28,503	12,354	15,375	774	2,037
Virginia	483,363	231,563	242,062	187,547	48,614	5,901	9,738
West Virginia	310,098	160,528	141,362	109,732	26,477	5,153	8,208
North Carolina	513,377	261,303	235,842	186,460	38,498	10,884	16,232
South Carolina	349,126	227,657	108,179	80,911	21,977	5,291	13,290
Georgia	628,525	421,047	188,185	141,899	39,546	6,740	19,293
Florida	234,133	128,678	94,990	70,166	20,848	3,976	10,465
EAST SOUTH CENTRAL:							
Kentucky	546,306	258,643	275,993	209,239	59,846	6,908	11,670
Tennessee	519,108	264,982	241,875	186,199	50,056	5,620	12,251
Alabama	508,769	319,756	172,363	124,456	41,445	6,462	16,650
Mississippi	403,198	257,971	132,900	97,473	30,322	5,105	12,327
WEST SOUTH CENTRAL:							
Arkansas	390,960	208,491	171,253	119,279	46,727	5,247	11,216
Louisiana	389,913	248,802	126,410	94,420	24,515	7,475	14,701
Oklahoma	444,524	231,813	193,840	109,001	74,586	10,253	18,871
Texas	1,017,413	563,597	421,875	291,089	116,576	14,210	31,941
MOUNTAIN:							
Montana	139,912	53,362	81,840	43,776	35,559	2,505	4,710
Idaho	100,060	38,013	59,208	30,974	26,957	1,277	3,279
Wyoming	48,476	22,271	24,060	14,107	8,579	1,314	2,145
Colorado	230,843	109,501	116,781	71,155	43,244	2,382	4,561
New Mexico	83,706	32,907	48,152	38,593	8,208	1,351	2,047
Arizona	80,208	44,163	33,075	24,605	7,797	673	2,870
Utah	98,346	38,598	57,985	38,842	17,582	1,561	1,763
Nevada	21,862	10,940	9,938	7,795	1,532	611	984
PACIFIC:							
Washington	342,228	151,513	183,322	106,729	72,655	3,938	7,393
Oregon	202,890	89,588	108,772	66,491	40,054	2,227	4,530
California	900,232	493,177	382,834	219,035	155,473	8,326	24,221

AND ENCUMBRANCE, BY DIVISIONS AND STATES: 1920 AND 1910.

DIVISION AND STATE.	Total homes.	Rented.	Owned.				Tenure unknown.
			Total.	Free.	Encumbered.	Unknown.	
United States	20,255,555	10,697,895	9,083,711	5,984,284	2,931,695	167,732	473,949
GEOGRAPHIC DIVISIONS:							
New England	1,464,942	870,210	574,590	332,124	236,025	6,441	20,142
Middle Atlantic	4,235,675	2,672,232	1,475,393	825,620	627,696	22,077	88,050
East North Central	4,214,820	1,950,268	2,187,573	1,380,040	777,892	29,641	76,979
West North Central	2,592,069	1,053,539	1,474,343	928,712	523,329	22,302	64,187
South Atlantic	2,539,270	1,451,523	1,017,823	793,024	197,122	27,677	69,924
East South Central	1,796,832	1,008,776	746,057	574,722	154,070	17,265	41,999
West South Central	1,827,105	1,010,563	762,702	554,998	184,095	23,609	53,840
Mountain	614,656	242,311	346,796	272,080	65,806	8,910	25,549
Pacific	970,186	438,473	498,434	322,964	165,660	9,810	33,279
NEW ENGLAND:							
Maine	177,960	65,523	109,298	82,262	25,481	1,555	3,139
New Hampshire	103,156	49,549	52,052	38,344	13,017	691	1,555
Vermont	85,178	35,112	49,489	29,332	19,807	350	577
Massachusetts	734,013	484,932	240,445	121,681	116,492	2,272	8,636
Rhode Island	117,976	83,134	32,849	17,790	14,503	556	1,993
Connecticut	246,659	151,960	90,457	42,715	46,725	1,017	4,242
MIDDLE ATLANTIC:							
New York	2,046,845	1,387,900	622,125	327,186	287,294	7,645	36,820
New Jersey	558,202	355,076	191,177	82,790	104,966	3,421	11,949
Pennsylvania	1,630,628	929,256	662,091	415,644	235,436	11,011	39,281
EAST NORTH CENTRAL:							
Ohio	1,138,165	545,519	574,085	383,346	183,683	7,056	18,561
Indiana	654,891	290,727	352,295	230,099	116,515	5,681	11,869
Illinois	1,264,717	693,083	545,999	340,677	195,713	9,609	25,635
Michigan	657,418	247,152	398,616	241,966	152,441	4,209	11,650
Wisconsin	499,629	173,787	316,578	183,952	129,540	3,086	9,264
WEST NORTH CENTRAL:							
Minnesota	416,452	154,340	251,092	160,913	86,913	3,266	11,020
Iowa	512,515	208,344	292,951	186,763	101,962	4,226	11,220
Missouri	749,812	358,514	374,461	219,577	149,878	5,006	16,837
North Dakota	120,910	28,123	87,641	51,364	34,437	1,840	5,146
South Dakota	131,060	40,302	86,539	58,789	25,633	2,117	4,219
Nebraska	265,549	106,099	153,155	103,165	47,780	2,210	6,295
Kansas	395,771	157,817	228,504	148,141	76,726	3,637	9,450
SOUTH ATLANTIC:							
Delaware	44,951	25,951	17,794	10,501	6,646	647	1,206
Maryland	274,824	149,201	117,297	77,814	37,202	2,281	8,326
District of Columbia	71,339	51,607	17,375	9,918	7,178	279	2,357
Virginia	419,452	198,860	211,322	171,476	35,636	4,210	9,270
West Virginia	248,480	123,068	120,583	100,076	17,784	2,723	4,829
North Carolina	440,334	227,239	203,552	162,914	35,074	5,564	9,543
South Carolina	315,204	210,904	93,757	70,912	19,419	3,426	10,543
Georgia	553,264	373,887	164,116	130,896	27,588	5,632	15,261
Florida	171,422	90,806	72,027	58,517	10,595	2,915	8,589
EAST SOUTH CENTRAL:							
Kentucky	494,788	235,433	251,059	198,329	47,659	5,071	8,296
Tennessee	462,553	240,515	213,125	172,779	35,238	5,108	8,913
Alabama	454,767	285,722	154,716	114,719	36,125	3,872	14,329
Mississippi	384,724	247,106	127,157	88,895	35,048	3,214	10,461
WEST SOUTH CENTRAL:							
Arkansas	333,368	173,251	151,002	116,947	30,085	3,970	9,115
Louisiana	344,144	225,433	106,953	85,230	17,322	4,401	11,758
Oklahoma	351,167	186,109	154,571	99,390	49,764	5,417	10,487
Texas	798,426	425,770	350,176	253,431	86,924	9,821	22,480
MOUNTAIN:							
Montana	86,602	32,511	48,757	38,680	8,118	1,959	5,334
Idaho	73,669	22,035	47,045	33,577	12,155	1,313	4,589
Wyoming	32,092	14,159	16,961	13,556	3,081	324	972
Colorado	194,467	90,929	96,728	68,528	25,653	2,547	6,810
New Mexico	78,883	22,704	54,537	50,632	2,996	909	1,642
Arizona	47,927	23,408	22,712	18,846	3,217	649	1,807
Utah	77,339	26,144	48,131	37,732	9,639	760	3,064
Nevada	23,677	10,421	11,925	10,529	947	449	1,331
PACIFIC:							
Washington	254,692	104,471	140,367	94,215	43,163	2,989	9,854
Oregon	151,858	58,279	87,688	60,500	25,270	1,918	5,891
California	563,636	275,723	270,379	168,249	97,227	4,903	17,534

Table 159.—NUMBER OF HOMES, DISTRIBUTED ACCORDING TO PROPRIETORSHIP
1920 AND

CITY.	Total homes.	Rented.	Owned.				Tenure un-known.
			Total.	Free.	Encum-bered.	Un-known.	
Akron, Ohio	44,195	24,081	19,504	6,703	12,376	425	610
Albany, N. Y	28,097	19,673	7,911	4,359	3,324	228	513
Atlanta, Ga	49,523	36,787	12,076	6,159	5,676	241	660
Baltimore, Md	166,857	88,595	76,298	40,730	34,900	668	1,964
Birmingham, Ala	43,040	29,700	11,632	6,481	4,821	330	1,708
Boston, Mass	164,785	132,658	30,132	9,998	19,609	525	1,995
Bridgeport, Conn	31,994	23,311	7,612	1,639	5,792	181	1,071
Buffalo, N. Y	116,201	70,572	44,297	17,168	26,744	385	1,332
Cambridge, Mass	25,293	20,790	4,454	1,774	2,668	12	49
Camden, N. J	26,645	15,591	10,628	3,492	7,038	98	426
Chicago, Ill	623,912	447,407	165,866	58,382	102,719	4,765	10,639
Cincinnati, Ohio	106,239	75,092	30,266	17,040	12,935	291	881
Cleveland, Ohio	182,692	117,374	63,502	25,777	37,075	650	1,816
Columbus, Ohio	58,913	36,895	21,258	9,936	11,177	145	760
Dallas, Tex	36,754	22,696	13,280	7,058	6,026	196	778
Dayton, Ohio	38,138	21,997	15,889	6,526	9,196	167	252
Denver, Colo	61,916	37,768	23,436	13,325	9,930	181	712
Des Moines, Iowa	31,644	15,123	15,810	7,674	7,823	313	711
Detroit, Mich	218,973	133,253	82,679	31,506	49,509	1,664	3,041
Fall River, Mass	26,399	21,099	5,165	1,927	3,202	36	135
Fort Worth, Tex	25,052	14,566	8,974	4,644	3,923	407	1,512
Grand Rapids, Mich	33,703	16,522	16,661	7,655	8,239	767	520
Hartford, Conn	30,813	24,277	6,372	1,155	5,137	80	164
Houston, Tex	33,932	22,136	11,518	7,460	3,962	96	278
Indianapolis, Ind	81,256	51,874	27,356	11,479	15,220	657	2,026
Jersey City, N. J	67,288	53,045	13,040	4,585	8,066	389	1,203
Kansas City, Kans	25,009	12,901	11,706	6,300	5,281	125	402
Kansas City, Mo	82,056	52,407	27,879	10,069	17,317	493	1,770
Los Angeles, Calif	159,476	102,077	54,278	28,360	25,361	557	3,121
Louisville, Ky	60,490	41,797	17,714	11,356	5,899	459	979
Lowell, Mass	25,034	18,468	6,513	3,032	3,462	19	53
Memphis, Tenn	42,369	29,281	11,925	6,833	4,389	703	1,163
Milwaukee, Wis	106,101	67,853	37,382	14,994	22,031	357	866
Minneapolis, Minn	91,843	53,527	37,090	16,606	19,924	560	1,226
Nashville, Tenn	30,220	20,225	9,470	6,757	2,618	95	525
New Bedford, Mass	26,858	19,105	7,651	2,936	4,678	37	102
New Haven, Conn	36,257	25,859	9,563	2,550	6,814	199	835
New Orleans, La	85,188	63,373	19,003	12,446	5,352	1,205	2,812
New York, N. Y	1,278,341	1,105,900	160,707	33,358	123,865	3,484	11,734
Bronx borough	166,260	151,789	13,591	2,839	10,391	361	880
Brooklyn borough	453,587	362,292	86,818	16,191	69,104	1,523	4,477
Manhattan borough	525,154	510,183	10,768	3,813	6,075	880	4,203
Queens borough	109,559	68,322	39,589	6,980	32,094	515	1,648
Richmond borough	23,781	13,314	9,941	3,535	6,201	205	526
Newark, N. J	93,274	73,517	18,600	4,931	13,286	383	1,157
Norfolk, Va	26,732	20,451	6,171	3,338	2,740	93	110
Oakland, Calif	55,793	31,776	22,966	12,087	10,538	341	1,051
Omaha, Nebr	44,499	22,453	21,028	9,677	10,874	477	1,018
Paterson, N. J	32,186	23,075	8,729	3,333	5,280	116	382
Philadelphia, Pa	402,946	239,698	156,354	45,802	107,974	2,578	6,894
Pittsburgh, Pa	130,274	91,934	36,363	19,151	16,500	712	1,977
Portland, Oreg	67,045	36,911	29,752	15,998	13,552	202	382
Providence, R. I	54,726	41,119	12,641	5,203	7,315	123	966
Reading, Pa	25,202	13,291	11,603	5,379	5,963	261	308
Richmond, Va	39,191	28,492	9,958	6,444	3,345	169	741
Rochester, N. Y	68,247	38,532	28,535	8,678	19,501	356	1,180
St. Louis, Mo	190,640	143,106	44,700	24,202	19,666	832	2,834
St. Paul, Minn	54,409	28,843	24,623	13,723	10,606	294	943
Salt Lake City, Utah	28,216	15,445	12,308	6,138	5,808	362	463
San Antonio, Tex	36,405	22,076	13,588	9,070	3,983	633	941
San Francisco, Calif	123,349	87,754	33,159	19,252	13,100	807	2,436
Scranton, Pa	29,768	18,871	10,371	7,021	3,286	64	526
Seattle, Wash	80,048	42,219	36,420	17,543	18,010	867	1,409
Spokane, Wash	27,178	14,980	12,083	6,862	5,154	67	115
Springfield, Mass	30,361	21,713	8,411	1,907	6,442	62	237
Syracuse, N. Y	41,558	25,446	15,563	5,233	10,053	277	549
Toledo, Ohio	57,951	29,009	28,295	13,844	14,182	269	647
Trenton, N. J	25,319	15,566	9,583	2,550	6,960	73	170
Washington, D. C	96,194	65,654	28,503	12,354	15,375	774	2,037
Wilmington, Del	24,488	14,839	9,192	3,360	5,683	149	457
Worcester, Mass	39,230	28,061	10,749	1,966	8,674	109	420
Yonkers, N. Y	22,126	16,788	5,161	1,244	3,890	27	177
Youngstown, Ohio	28,699	14,821	13,561	6,096	7,319	146	317

AND ENCUMBRANCE, FOR CITIES HAVING, IN 1920, 100,000 INHABITANTS OR MORE: 1910.

CITY.	Total homes.	Rented.	Owned.				Tenure unknown.
			Total.	Free.	Encumbered.	Unknown.	
Akron, Ohio	15,851	7,687	7,824	4,158	3,577	89	340
Albany, N. Y	24,069	17,189	6,338	4,347	1,885	106	542
Atlanta, Ga	35,813	26,213	8,580	5,553	2,947	80	1,020
Baltimore, Md	118,851	75,381	38,400	26,795	11,006	599	5,070
Birmingham, Ala	31,050	21,115	8,910	5,475	3,303	132	1,025
Boston, Mass	139,700	114,312	23,496	10,540	12,731	225	1,892
Bridgeport, Conn	21,689	16,504	4,671	1,531	3,055	85	514
Buffalo, N. Y	91,328	58,745	30,592	14,277	16,033	282	1,991
Cambridge, Mass	22,765	18,378	4,282	2,187	2,064	31	105
Camden, N. J	21,482	14,750	6,087	2,583	3,356	148	645
Chicago, Ill	473,141	342,472	121,447	55,025	64,981	1,441	9,222
Cincinnati, Ohio	87,541	66,153	19,965	12,983	6,801	181	1,423
Cleveland, Ohio	124,822	80,005	43,473	21,701	21,526	246	1,344
Columbus, Ohio	42,645	26,787	14,862	7,468	7,184	210	996
Dallas, Tex	20,516	12,641	7,123	4,733	2,307	83	752
Dayton, Ohio	28,370	17,244	10,596	5,425	5,071	100	530
Denver, Colo	51,339	31,342	17,774	10,732	6,779	263	2,223
Des Moines, Iowa	20,599	10,894	9,123	5,138	3,762	223	582
Detroit, Mich	100,356	57,831	40,471	20,752	19,501	218	2,054
Fall River, Mass	24,378	19,926	4,317	1,881	2,411	25	135
Fort Worth, Tex	16,295	10,202	5,412	3,240	1,967	205	681
Grand Rapids, Mich	26,925	13,690	12,599	6,184	6,230	185	636
Hartford, Conn	21,925	16,879	4,632	1,380	3,200	52	414
Houston, Tex	17,040	11,235	5,132	3,783	1,227	122	673
Indianapolis, Ind	58,645	38,702	19,036	9,829	8,985	222	907
Jersey City, N. J	56,790	44,394	11,209	4,899	6,104	206	1,187
Kansas City, Kans	19,677	10,381	8,872	4,580	4,131	161	424
Kansas City, Mo	59,296	36,537	20,711	8,595	11,870	246	2,048
Los Angeles, Calif	78,678	42,202	34,159	17,249	16,671	239	2,317
Louisville, Ky	52,155	37,621	13,603	10,232	3,251	120	931
Lowell, Mass	21,932	16,761	4,848	2,689	2,132	27	323
Memphis, Tenn	31,154	22,363	7,541	4,906	2,441	194	1,250
Milwaukee, Wis	80,566	50,352	28,824	12,875	15,720	229	1,390
Minneapolis, Minn	63,241	36,195	24,539	13,571	10,515	453	2,507
Nashville, Tenn	26,077	17,868	7,879	5,797	1,972	110	330
New Bedford, Mass	20,820	15,190	5,144	2,543	2,547	54	486
New Haven, Conn	29,271	21,394	7,326	2,792	4,467	67	551
New Orleans, La	73,377	54,113	16,273	12,615	3,058	600	2,991
New York, N. Y	1,020,827	884,616	117,740	34,951	81,007	1,782	18,471
Bronx borough	93,897	80,114	12,071	2,654	9,267	150	1,712
Brooklyn borough	353,666	284,739	63,842	17,335	45,954	553	5,085
Manhattan borough	493,545	468,927	14,103	5,356	7,909	838	10,515
Queens borough	62,001	40,020	21,176	6,410	14,601	165	805
Richmond borough	17,718	10,816	6,548	3,196	3,276	76	354
Newark, N. J	77,039	60,473	15,119	4,979	9,999	141	1,447
Norfolk, Va	15,498	12,024	3,056	2,232	762	62	418
Oakland, Calif	36,723	19,263	16,870	9,683	7,084	103	590
Omaha, Nebr[1]	31,604	17,778	12,590	7,231	5,142	217	1,236
Paterson, N. J	27,978	20,714	6,538	2,695	3,770	73	726
Philadelphia, Pa	327,263	229,354	83,262	35,950	46,312	1,000	14,647
Pittsburgh, Pa	110,457	77,288	29,983	16,052	13,445	486	3,186
Portland, Oreg	42,029	21,495	18,509	11,089	7,131	289	2,025
Providence, R. I	49,129	38,276	10,071	4,795	5,107	169	782
Reading, Pa	21,809	12,865	8,418	4,408	3,974	36	526
Richmond, Va	26,914	19,801	6,255	4,609	1,318	328	858
Rochester, N. Y	46,787	26,525	19,321	7,876	11,306	139	941
St. Louis, Mo	155,555	113,515	37,761	22,178	15,197	386	4,279
St. Paul, Minn	41,548	23,826	16,665	10,910	5,621	134	1,057
Salt Lake City, Utah	20,283	10,500	8,623	4,806	3,694	123	1,160
San Antonio, Tex	21,096	12,080	8,315	6,031	1,990	294	701
San Francisco, Calif	86,414	55,946	27,500	16,329	10,996	175	2,968
Scranton, Pa	26,312	16,116	9,711	5,524	3,935	252	485
Seattle, Wash	51,042	27,245	22,167	13,464	8,508	195	1,630
Spokane, Wash	22,676	10,610	11,165	5,869	5,112	184	901
Springfield, Mass	19,968	14,009	5,821	2,064	3,711	46	138
Syracuse, N. Y	31,551	18,547	12,202	4,873	7,225	104	802
Toledo, Ohio	39,677	21,609	17,170	9,622	7,438	110	898
Trenton, N. J	19,678	13,274	6,019	2,083	3,839	97	385
Washington, D. C	71,339	51,607	17,375	9,918	7,178	279	2,357
Wilmington, Del	18,637	12,567	5,500	2,348	2,948	204	570
Worcester, Mass	30,743	23,057	7,431	2,196	5,162	73	255
Yonkers, N. Y	16,219	12,239	3,764	1,132	2,583	49	216
Youngstown, Ohio	16,228	9,272	6,372	3,665	2,430	277	584

[1] Includes South Omaha for 1910.

TABLE 160.—PER CENT DISTRIBUTION OF HOMES ACCORDING TO PROPRIETORSHIP AND ENCUMBRANCE, FOR CITIES HAVING, IN 1920, 100,000 INHABITANTS OR MORE: 1920 AND 1910.

[In computing the percentages in this table the numbers representing the unknown items as to proprietorship and encumbrance have been distributed in the same proportions as the known items.]

	1920						1910					
	Per cent of all homes.				Per cent of owned homes.		Per cent of all homes.				Per cent of owned homes.	
CITY.	Rented.	Owned.	Owned free.	Owned encumbered.	Free.	Encumbered.	Rented.	Owned.	Owned free.	Owned encumbered.	Free.	Encumbered.
Akron, Ohio	55.3	44.7	15.7	29.0	35.1	64.9	49.6	50.4	27.1	23.3	53.8	46.2
Albany, N. Y	71.3	28.7	16.3	12.4	56.7	43.3	73.1	26.9	18.8	8.1	69.8	30.2
Atlanta, Ga	75.3	24.7	12.9	11.9	52.0	48.0	75.3	24.7	16.1	8.6	65.3	34.7
Baltimore, Md	53.7	46.3	24.9	21.4	53.9	46.1	66.3	33.7	23.9	9.8	70.9	29.1
Birmingham, Ala	71.9	28.1	16.1	12.0	57.3	42.7	70.3	29.7	18.5	11.2	62.4	37.6
Boston, Mass	81.5	18.5	6.3	12.3	33.8	66.2	82.9	17.1	7.7	9.3	45.3	54.7
Bridgeport, Conn	75.4	24.6	5.4	19.2	22.1	77.9	77.9	22.1	7.4	14.7	33.4	66.6
Buffalo, N. Y	61.4	38.6	15.1	23.5	39.1	60.9	65.8	34.2	16.1	18.1	47.1	52.9
Cambridge, Mass	82.4	17.6	7.0	10.6	39.9	60.1	81.1	18.9	9.7	9.2	51.4	48.6
Camden, N. J	59.5	40.5	13.4	27.1	33.2	66.8	70.8	29.2	12.7	16.5	43.5	56.5
Chicago, Ill	73.0	27.0	9.8	17.2	36.2	63.8	73.8	26.2	12.0	14.2	45.9	54.1
Cincinnati, Ohio	71.3	28.7	16.3	12.4	56.8	43.2	76.8	23.2	15.2	8.0	65.6	34.4
Cleveland, Ohio	64.9	35.1	14.4	20.7	41.0	59.0	64.8	35.2	17.7	17.5	50.2	49.8
Columbus, Ohio	63.4	36.6	17.2	19.4	47.1	52.9	64.3	35.7	18.2	17.5	51.0	49.0
Dallas, Tex	63.1	36.9	19.9	17.0	53.9	46.1	64.0	36.0	24.2	11.8	67.2	32.8
Dayton, Ohio	58.1	41.9	17.4	24.5	41.5	58.5	61.9	38.1	19.7	18.4	51.7	48.3
Denver, Colo	61.7	38.3	21.9	16.4	57.3	42.7	63.8	36.2	22.2	14.0	61.3	38.7
Des Moines, Iowa	48.9	51.1	25.3	25.8	49.5	50.5	54.4	45.6	26.3	19.3	57.7	42.3
Detroit, Mich	61.7	38.3	14.9	23.4	38.9	61.1	58.8	41.2	21.2	19.9	51.6	48.4
Fall River, Mass	80.3	19.7	7.4	12.3	37.6	62.4	82.2	17.8	7.8	10.0	43.8	56.2
Fort Worth, Tex	61.9	38.1	20.7	17.5	54.2	45.8	65.3	34.7	21.6	13.1	62.2	37.8
Grand Rapids, Mich	49.8	50.2	24.2	26.0	48.2	51.8	52.1	47.9	23.9	24.1	49.8	50.2
Hartford, Conn	79.2	20.8	3.8	17.0	18.4	81.6	78.5	21.5	6.5	15.0	30.1	69.9
Houston, Tex	65.8	34.2	22.4	11.9	65.3	34.7	68.6	31.4	23.7	7.7	75.5	24.5
Indianapolis, Ind	65.5	34.5	14.8	19.7	43.0	57.0	67.0	33.0	17.2	15.7	52.2	47.8
Jersey City, N. J	80.3	19.7	7.2	12.6	36.2	63.8	79.8	20.2	9.0	11.2	44.5	55.5
Kansas City, Kans	52.4	47.6	25.9	21.7	54.4	45.6	53.9	46.1	24.2	21.9	52.6	47.4
Kansas City, Mo	65.3	34.7	12.8	22.0	36.8	63.2	63.8	36.2	15.2	21.0	42.0	58.0
Los Angeles, Calif	65.3	34.7	18.3	16.4	52.8	47.2	55.3	44.7	22.7	22.0	50.9	49.1
Louisville, Ky	70.2	29.8	19.6	10.2	65.8	34.2	73.4	26.6	20.2	6.4	75.9	24.1
Lowell, Mass	73.9	26.1	12.2	13.9	46.7	53.3	77.6	22.4	12.5	9.9	55.8	44.2
Memphis, Tenn	71.1	28.9	17.6	11.3	60.9	39.1	74.8	25.2	16.3	8.9	64.6	35.4
Milwaukee, Wis	64.5	35.5	14.4	21.1	40.5	59.5	63.6	36.4	16.4	20.0	45.0	55.0
Minneapolis, Minn	59.1	40.9	18.6	22.3	45.5	54.5	59.6	40.4	22.8	17.6	56.3	43.7
Nashville, Tenn	68.1	31.9	23.0	8.9	72.1	27.9	69.4	30.6	22.8	7.8	74.6	25.4
New Bedford, Mass	71.4	28.6	11.0	17.6	38.6	61.4	74.7	25.3	12.6	12.7	50.0	50.0
New Haven, Conn	73.0	27.0	7.4	19.6	27.2	72.8	74.5	25.5	9.8	15.7	38.5	61.5
New Orleans, La	76.9	23.1	16.1	6.9	69.9	30.1	76.9	23.1	18.6	4.5	80.5	19.5
New York, N. Y	87.3	12.7	2.7	10.0	21.3	78.7	88.3	11.7	3.5	8.2	30.2	69.8
Bronx borough	91.8	8.2	1.8	6.5	21.5	78.5	86.9	13.1	2.9	10.2	22.3	77.7
Brooklyn borough	80.7	19.3	3.7	15.7	19.0	81.0	81.7	18.3	5.0	13.3	27.4	72.6
Manhattan borough	97.9	2.1	0.8	1.3	38.6	61.4	97.1	2.9	1.2	1.7	40.4	59.6
Queens borough	63.3	36.7	6.6	30.1	17.9	82.1	65.4	34.6	10.6	24.0	30.5	69.5
Richmond borough	57.3	42.7	15.5	27.2	36.3	63.7	62.3	37.7	18.6	19.1	49.4	50.6
Newark, N. J	79.8	20.2	5.5	14.7	27.1	72.9	80.0	20.0	6.6	13.4	33.2	66.8
Norfolk, Va	70.0	30.0	12.7	10.4	54.9	45.1	79.7	20.3	15.1	5.2	74.6	25.4
Oakland, Calif	50.0	42.0	22.4	19.5	53.4	46.6	53.3	46.7	27.0	19.7	57.7	42.3
Omaha, Nebr[1]	51.6	48.4	22.8	25.6	47.1	52.9	58.0	41.5	21.0	17.0	49.1	50.9
Paterson, N. J	72.6	27.4	10.6	16.8	38.7	61.3	76.0	24.0	10.0	14.0	41.7	58.3
Philadelphia, Pa	60.5	39.5	11.8	27.7	29.8	70.2	73.4	26.6	11.6	15.0	43.7	56.3
Pittsburgh, Pa	71.7	28.3	15.2	13.1	53.7	46.3	72.0	28.0	15.2	12.7	54.4	45.6
Portland, Oreg	55.4	44.6	24.2	20.5	54.1	45.9	53.7	46.3	28.2	18.1	60.9	39.1
Providence, R. I	76.5	23.5	9.8	13.7	41.6	58.4	79.2	20.8	10.1	10.7	48.4	51.6
Reading, Pa	53.4	46.6	22.1	24.5	47.4	52.6	60.4	39.6	20.8	18.8	52.6	47.4
Richmond, Va	74.1	25.9	17.0	8.8	65.8	34.2	76.0	24.0	18.7	5.3	77.8	22.2
Rochester, N. Y	57.5	42.5	13.1	29.4	30.8	69.2	57.9	42.1	17.3	24.8	41.1	58.9
St. Louis, Mo	76.2	23.8	13.1	10.7	55.2	44.8	75.0	25.0	14.8	10.1	59.3	40.7
St. Paul, Minn	53.9	46.1	26.0	20.1	56.4	43.6	58.8	41.2	27.2	14.0	66.0	34.0
Salt Lake City, Utah	55.7	44.3	22.8	21.6	51.4	48.6	54.9	45.1	25.5	19.6	56.5	43.5

[1] Based on figures including South Omaha in 1910.

TABLE **160.**—PER CENT DISTRIBUTION OF HOMES ACCORDING TO PROPRIETORSHIP AND ENCUMBRANCE, FOR CITIES HAVING, IN 1920, 100,000 INHABITANTS OR MORE: 1920 AND 1910—Continued.

[In computing the percentages in this table the numbers representing the unknown items as to proprietorship and encumbrance have been distributed in the same proportions as the known items.]

	1920						1910					
	Per cent of all homes.				Per cent of owned homes.		Per cent of all homes.				Per cent of owned homes.	
CITY.	Rented.	Owned.	Owned free.	Owned encumbered.	Free.	Encumbered.	Rented.	Owned.	Owned free.	Owned encumbered.	Free.	Encumbered.
San Antonio, Tex	62.2	37.8	26.2	11.5	69.5	30.5	59.2	40.8	30.7	10.1	75.2	24.8
San Francisco, Calif	72.6	27.4	16.3	11.1	59.5	40.5	67.0	33.0	19.7	13.3	59.8	40.2
Scranton, Pa	64.5	35.5	24.2	11.3	68.1	31.9	62.4	37.6	22.0	15.6	58.4	41.6
Seattle, Wash	53.7	46.3	22.9	23.5	49.3	50.7	55.1	44.9	27.5	17.4	61.3	38.7
Spokane, Wash	55.4	44.6	25.5	19.2	57.1	42.9	48.7	51.3	27.4	23.9	53.4	46.6
Springfield, Mass	72.1	27.9	6.4	21.5	22.8	77.2	70.6	29.4	10.5	18.9	35.7	64.3
Syracuse, N.Y	62.1	37.9	13.0	25.0	34.2	65.8	60.3	39.7	16.0	23.7	40.3	59.7
Toledo, Ohio	50.6	49.4	24.4	25.0	49.4	50.6	55.7	44.3	25.0	19.3	56.4	43.6
Trenton, N.J	61.9	38.1	10.2	27.9	26.8	73.2	68.8	31.2	11.0	20.2	35.2	64.8
Washington, D.C	69.7	30.3	13.5	16.8	44.6	55.4	74.8	25.2	14.6	10.6	58.0	42.0
Wilmington, Del	61.7	38.3	14.2	24.0	37.2	62.8	69.6	30.4	13.5	16.9	44.3	55.7
Worcester, Mass	72.3	27.7	5.1	22.6	18.5	81.5	75.6	24.4	7.3	17.1	29.8	70.2
Yonkers, N.Y	76.5	23.5	5.7	17.8	24.2	75.8	76.5	23.5	7.2	16.4	30.5	69.5
Youngstown, Ohio	52.2	47.8	21.7	26.1	45.4	54.6	59.3	40.7	24.5	16.2	60.1	39.9

TABLE **161.**—NUMBER OF HOMES, DISTRIBUTED ACCORDING TO PROPRIETORSHIP AND ENCUMBRANCE, FOR CITIES HAVING FROM 25,000 TO 100,000 INHABITANTS: 1920.

CITY.	Total homes: 1920	Rented.	OWNED.				Tenure unknown.
			Total.	Free.	Encumbered.	Unknown.	
ALABAMA:							
Mobile	15,148	10,797	4,088	3,013	972	103	263
Montgomery	11,568	8,846	2,488	1,759	712	17	234
ARIZONA:							
Phoenix	7,354	4,556	2,621	1,384	1,220	17	177
ARKANSAS:							
Fort Smith	6,872	3,758	2,901	1,597	1,250	54	213
Little Rock	15,059	8,658	5,985	3,589	2,323	73	416
CALIFORNIA:							
Alameda	7,886	3,852	3,969	2,201	1,746	22	65
Berkeley	15,159	8,324	6,663	3,564	3,044	55	172
Fresno	11,234	5,776	5,239	2,602	2,576	61	219
Long Beach	17,169	11,016	5,898	3,420	2,452	26	255
Pasadena	12,657	6,415	5,979	3,867	2,076	36	263
Sacramento	17,263	11,012	5,819	3,258	2,515	46	432
San Diego	22,723	14,280	7,820	4,941	2,774	105	623
San Jose	10,669	5,264	5,168	3,532	1,519	117	237
Stockton	9,981	5,922	3,862	2,213	1,607	42	197
COLORADO:							
Colorado Springs	8,332	4,299	3,871	2,518	1,319	34	162
Pueblo	10,484	5,505	4,764	2,980	1,750	34	215
CONNECTICUT:							
Meriden	6,955	4,460	2,353	802	1,479	72	142
New Britain	12,072	8,516	3,458	433	2,972	53	98
New London	5,937	3,972	1,918	790	1,100	28	47
Norwalk	6,791	3,799	2,836	1,109	1,704	23	156
Stamford	7,839	5,554	2,092	452	1,583	57	193
Waterbury	19,124	13,044	5,731	1,128	4,469	134	349
FLORIDA:							
Jacksonville	23,265	17,142	5,443	3,283	2,041	119	680
Miami	7,497	4,422	2,803	1,425	1,318	60	272
Pensacola	7,448	4,914	2,211	1,361	812	38	323
Tampa	12,137	8,636	2,990	2,056	841	93	511
GEORGIA:							
Augusta	13,966	10,694	2,866	2,265	471	130	406
Columbus	7,245	5,875	1,288	1,013	265	10	82
Macon	13,730	10,165	3,373	2,249	1,079	45	192
Savannah	21,267	17,953	3,209	2,199	960	50	105

TABLE **161.**—NUMBER OF HOMES, DISTRIBUTED ACCORDING TO PROPRIETORSHIP AND ENCUMBRANCE, FOR CITIES HAVING FROM 25,000 TO 100,000 INHABITANTS: 1920—Con.

CITY.	Total homes: 1920	Rented.	OWNED.				Tenure un-known.
			Total.	Free.	Encum-bered.	Un-known.	
ILLINOIS:							
Aurora	8,973	3,873	4,933	2,803	2,095	35	167
Bloomington	7,451	3,665	3,680	2,653	937	90	106
Cicero town	9,770	4,623	5,061	1,405	3,624	32	86
Danville	8,907	4,550	4,231	1,927	2,273	31	126
Decatur	10,874	5,386	5,403	3,098	2,131	174	85
East St. Louis	15,768	11,150	4,531	2,119	2,400	12	87
Elgin	6,490	2,837	3,557	2,481	1,002	74	96
Evanston	8,472	4,946	3,334	1,578	1,678	78	192
Joliet	8,654	4,674	3,888	2,314	1,444	130	92
Moline	7,564	3,678	3,783	1,785	1,972	26	103
Oak Park village	9,737	3,598	6,027	1,974	3,978	75	112
Peoria	19,397	10,357	8,648	4,486	4,052	110	392
Quincy	9,378	5,249	3,915	2,722	1,138	55	214
Rock Island	8,824	4,313	4,336	2,347	1,926	63	175
Rockford	16,027	8,072	7,583	3,579	3,829	175	372
Springfield	14,255	7,525	6,504	4,031	2,398	75	226
INDIANA:							
Anderson	7,523	3,570	3,832	1,733	1,811	288	121
East Chicago	7,080	4,284	2,699	984	1,690	25	97
Evansville	20,648	12,138	8,098	5,388	2,639	71	412
Fort Wayne	20,406	9,670	10,452	5,028	5,277	147	284
Gary	12,022	7,572	4,187	1,382	2,684	121	263
Hammond	7,983	3,848	4,020	1,520	2,424	76	115
Kokomo	7,505	4,019	3,434	1,867	1,535	32	52
Muncie	9,529	5,051	4,373	1,930	2,390	53	105
Richmond	7,055	4,029	2,934	1,853	1,047	34	92
South Bend	16,113	7,729	8,099	3,961	4,046	92	285
Terre Haute	16,745	9,433	7,063	3,131	3,816	116	249
IOWA:							
Cedar Rapids	11,612	5,204	6,236	3,142	3,043	51	172
Council Bluffs	8,789	3,423	5,193	2,656	2,386	151	173
Davenport	14,388	7,532	6,616	3,704	2,765	147	240
Dubuque	9,314	4,990	4,079	2,869	1,121	89	245
Sioux City	16,234	8,952	7,030	3,514	3,407	109	252
Waterloo	9,071	4,583	4,312	2,115	2,149	48	176
KANSAS:							
Topeka	13,039	6,038	6,636	4,058	2,460	118	365
Wichita	18,596	9,664	8,620	4,849	3,639	132	312
KENTUCKY:							
Covington	14,809	9,200	5,513	2,911	2,554	48	96
Lexington	10,720	7,014	3,456	2,488	853	115	250
Newport	7,792	4,823	2,909	1,561	1,338	10	60
LOUISIANA:							
Shreveport	10,618	7,048	3,339	2,235	1,027	77	231
MAINE:							
Bangor	6,145	3,144	2,887	2,081	782	24	114
Lewiston	6,750	4,790	1,896	1,285	589	22	64
Portland	16,801	11,812	4,822	3,002	1,789	31	167
MARYLAND:							
Cumberland	6,433	3,860	2,474	1,482	966	26	99
Hagerstown	6,609	4,448	2,083	1,095	886	102	78
MASSACHUSETTS:							
Brockton	16,084	10,451	5,498	1,595	3,856	47	135
Brookline town	8,603	6,266	2,227	967	1,217	43	110
Chelsea	8,833	6,781	1,975	432	1,531	12	77
Chicopee	7,004	4,391	2,457	718	1,689	50	156
Everett	9,187	6,088	3,089	779	2,305	5	10
Fitchburg	9,273	5,827	3,171	1,117	1,940	114	275
Haverhill	12,814	8,084	4,598	1,900	2,633	65	132
Holyoke	12,948	10,262	2,537	692	1,800	45	149
Lawrence	19,715	15,146	3,941	1,405	2,495	41	328
Lynn	23,308	16,531	6,517	2,343	4,068	106	260
Malden	11,238	7,162	4,061	1,417	2,639	5	15
Medford	9,351	5,400	3,948	1,001	2,911	6	3
Newton	10,189	4,864	5,309	2,299	2,997	13	10
Pittsfield	9,499	6,172	3,133	1,211	1,888	34	194
Quincy	11,146	5,786	5,209	1,411	3,761	37	151
Revere	6,375	4,138	2,140	581	1,526	33	97
Salem	9,353	6,327	2,890	1,183	1,678	29	136
Somerville	22,653	16,450	6,154	2,044	4,097	13	49
Taunton	8,062	4,591	3,418	1,745	1,655	18	53
Waltham	6,566	4,439	2,121	865	1,255	1	6
MICHIGAN:							
Battle Creek	9,347	4,090	5,111	2,183	2,708	220	146
Bay City	11,002	3,570	7,304	5,159	2,115	30	128
Flint	19,570	8,565	10,786	3,464	7,176	146	219
Hamtramck village	9,117	5,002	4,043	476	3,524	43	72

TABLE 161.—NUMBER OF HOMES, DISTRIBUTED ACCORDING TO PROPRIETORSHIP AND ENCUMBRANCE, FOR CITIES HAVING FROM 25,000 TO 100,000 INHABITANTS: 1920—Con.

CITY.	Total homes: 1920	Rented.	OWNED.				Tenure un-known.
			Total.	Free.	Encum-bered.	Un-known.	
MICHIGAN—Con.							
Highland Park	10,401	5,137	5,131	1,211	3,887	33	133
Jackson	11,851	4,510	7,195	3,212	3,912	71	146
Kalamazoo	11,754	5,268	6,339	3,040	3,230	69	147
Lansing	13,811	5,324	8,176	2,566	5,362	248	311
Muskegon	8,696	3,766	4,750	3,212	1,370	168	180
Pontiac	7,090	2,719	4,156	1,712	2,389	55	215
Port Huron	6,407	2,667	3,675	2,264	1,351	60	65
Saginaw	14,906	4,731	9,980	6,464	3,370	146	195
MINNESOTA:							
Duluth	21,294	11,085	9,841	4,632	5,060	149	368
MISSOURI:							
Joplin	8,012	4,243	3,681	2,149	1,393	139	88
St. Joseph	19,189	11,510	7,420	4,135	3,224	61	259
Springfield	10,412	5,158	5,022	2,928	2,034	60	232
MONTANA:							
Butte	10,098	5,731	4,118	2,667	1,206	245	249
NEBRASKA:							
Lincoln	13,812	6,717	6,840	3,887	2,728	225	255
NEW HAMPSHIRE:							
Manchester	17,415	12,445	4,657	2,344	2,222	91	313
Nashua	6,305	4,378	1,778	1,036	634	108	149
NEW JERSEY:							
Atlantic City	12,468	9,931	2,130	624	1,453	53	407
Bayonne	15,513	11,014	4,362	981	3,360	21	137
Clifton	5,800	2,851	2,904	526	2,374	4	45
East Orange	12,416	7,573	4,608	1,117	3,355	136	235
Elizabeth	20,641	13,382	7,006	2,324	4,596	86	253
Hoboken	15,877	14,335	1,400	503	830	67	142
Irvington town	6,098	3,394	2,595	490	2,086	19	109
Kearny town	5,706	3,323	2,302	548	1,736	18	81
Montclair town	6,294	3,273	2,857	923	1,835	99	164
New Brunswick	7,404	4,706	2,611	925	1,553	133	87
Orange	7,289	4,939	2,198	836	1,307	55	152
Passaic	13,393	10,110	3,114	791	2,300	23	169
Perth Amboy	8,605	5,828	2,680	846	1,751	83	97
Plainfield	6,375	3,735	2,519	800	1,691	28	121
West Hoboken town	10,131	8,288	1,723	591	1,108	24	120
West New York town	7,410	5,878	1,495	396	1,088	11	37
NEW YORK:							
Amsterdam	7,726	5,328	2,307	1,201	1,055	51	91
Auburn	8,719	4,746	3,874	2,010	1,834	30	99
Binghamton	16,000	9,650	6,110	2,911	3,145	54	240
Elmira	11,357	6,133	4,999	2,963	1,785	251	225
Jamestown	10,206	5,163	4,920	2,221	2,566	133	123
Kingston	6,701	3,894	2,728	1,662	953	113	79
Mount Vernon	9,715	6,423	3,217	881	2,314	22	75
New Rochelle	7,725	4,710	2,929	830	2,058	41	86
Newburgh	7,647	5,173	2,369	1,082	1,266	21	105
Niagara Falls	10,857	6,531	4,087	1,441	2,566	80	239
Poughkeepsie	8,732	5,989	2,489	1,162	1,309	18	254
Rome	5,416	2,748	2,622	1,490	1,123	9	46
Schenectady	20,657	12,832	7,584	2,580	4,860	144	241
Troy	17,895	12,666	4,734	2,868	1,737	129	495
Utica	21,657	13,904	7,637	3,480	4,103	54	116
Watertown	7,835	4,539	3,212	1,784	1,401	27	84
NORTH CAROLINA:							
Asheville	6,477	3,785	2,411	1,788	522	101	281
Charlotte	10,720	7,057	3,320	2,087	1,008	225	343
Wilmington	7,847	4,889	2,600	1,395	765	440	358
Winston-Salem	9,895	6,709	2,948	1,701	1,207	40	238
OHIO:							
Canton	20,496	9,284	10,883	4,702	5,888	293	329
East Cleveland	7,122	3,793	3,268	1,008	2,249	11	61
Hamilton	9,706	4,871	4,547	2,223	2,174	150	288
Lakewood	10,537	4,442	5,984	2,264	3,594	126	111
Lima	10,659	5,475	5,017	1,887	2,972	158	167
Lorain	8,004	3,687	4,050	2,225	1,801	24	267
Mansfield	7,215	3,080	4,046	2,443	1,558	45	89
Marion	7,231	3,238	3,924	1,920	1,986	18	69
Newark	7,322	3,569	3,681	2,102	1,510	69	72
Portsmouth	7,967	4,238	3,578	1,748	1,664	166	151
Springfield	15,484	8,392	6,798	3,292	3,363	143	294
Steubenville	6,516	3,864	2,414	1,424	935	55	238
Warren	6,561	2,917	3,566	1,575	1,936	55	78
Zanesville	7,958	4,362	3,556	2,331	1,200	25	40

TABLE 161.—NUMBER OF HOMES, DISTRIBUTED ACCORDING TO PROPRIETORSHIP AND ENCUMBRANCE, FOR CITIES HAVING FROM 25,000 TO 100,000 INHABITANTS: 1920—Con.

CITY.	Total homes: 1920	Rented.	OWNED.				Tenure unknown.
			Total.	Free.	Encumbered.	Unknown.	
OKLAHOMA:							
Muskogee	7,414	4,140	3,023	1,710	1,190	123	251
Oklahoma City	21,346	12,645	8,184	3,296	4,804	84	517
Tulsa	16,910	10,197	5,959	3,115	2,628	216	754
PENNSYLVANIA:							
Allentown	17,298	9,877	7,168	3,452	3,583	133	253
Altoona	13,740	7,318	6,341	3,352	2,964	25	81
Bethlehem	11,265	6,850	4,182	1,886	2,052	244	233
Chester	12,259	7,658	4,338	1,535	2,680	123	263
Easton	8,257	4,942	3,181	1,735	1,418	28	134
Erie	21,425	11,583	9,566	4,741	4,725	100	276
Harrisburg	19,158	11,800	7,029	3,410	3,270	349	329
Hazleton	6,584	4,202	2,222	1,202	805	215	160
Johnstown	13,858	8,737	5,038	3,277	1,725	36	83
Lancaster	12,844	7,666	5,062	2,698	2,336	28	116
McKeesport	9,916	5,784	3,921	1,898	1,896	127	211
New Castle	10,397	5,007	5,244	2,608	2,573	63	146
Norristown borough	6,624	3,103	3,403	1,493	1,880	30	118
Wilkes-Barre	15,378	10,169	4,871	3,079	1,586	206	338
Williamsport	8,927	5,534	3,277	2,188	1,024	65	116
York	11,692	6,783	4,769	3,053	1,671	45	140
RHODE ISLAND:							
Cranston	6,360	3,349	2,944	1,058	1,841	45	67
Newport	6,440	3,979	2,315	811	1,426	78	146
Pawtucket	14,675	10,227	4,123	1,507	2,588	28	325
Woonsocket	9,080	6,960	1,981	683	1,272	26	139
SOUTH CAROLINA:							
Charleston	17,824	13,721	3,602	2,334	1,012	256	501
Columbia	8,151	6,169	1,862	1,353	470	39	120
SOUTH DAKOTA:							
Sioux Falls	6,208	3,217	2,822	1,617	1,110	95	169
TENNESSEE:							
Chattanooga	14,621	11,210	3,120	2,003	1,095	22	291
Knoxville	17,474	10,035	7,067	4,604	2,375	88	372
TEXAS:							
Austin	7,925	4,346	3,456	2,466	913	77	123
Beaumont	9,495	6,252	3,114	1,822	1,234	58	129
El Paso	18,159	13,958	3,770	2,218	1,494	58	431
Galveston	10,588	7,364	2,988	2,415	534	39	236
Waco	9,374	5,841	3,311	2,214	975	122	222
Wichita Falls	7,878	4,096	3,181	1,812	1,303	66	601
UTAH:							
Ogden	7,803	3,839	3,851	2,425	1,398	28	113
VIRGINIA:							
Lynchburg	6,558	4,028	2,410	1,815	562	33	120
Newport News	7,835	5,566	2,182	1,115	974	93	87
Petersburg	7,540	5,343	1,968	1,469	322	177	229
Portsmouth	12,568	8,672	3,870	2,247	1,598	25	26
Roanoke	11,260	6,006	5,082	2,963	2,062	57	172
WASHINGTON:							
Bellingham	6,640	2,932	3,559	2,298	1,216	45	149
Everett	7,169	3,547	3,502	1,974	1,498	30	120
Tacoma	24,662	10,656	13,525	7,491	5,882	152	481
WEST VIRGINIA:							
Charleston	9,069	5,665	3,080	1,966	1,005	109	324
Clarksburg	6,453	3,596	2,696	1,586	1,048	62	161
Huntington	11,350	6,317	4,750	2,510	2,105	135	283
Wheeling	13,919	8,505	5,113	3,576	1,400	137	301
WISCONSIN:							
Green Bay	6,914	3,097	3,712	2,075	1,598	39	105
Kenosha	8,680	2,657	4,303	1,572	2,667	64	138
La Crosse	7,530	3,688	3,729	2,554	1,017	158	109
Madison	9,413	5,351	3,939	1,707	2,000	152	123
Madison	8,027	3,047	4,839	2,993	1,782	64	141
Oshkosh	8,027	3,047	4,839	2,993	1,782	64	141
Racine	12,799	5,617	6,984	2,442	4,514	28	198
Sheboygan	7,215	3,198	3,940	2,209	1,702	29	77
Superior	8,692	4,710	3,822	2,343	1,351	128	160

OCCUPATIONS.

(477)

CONTENTS.

(478)

CONTENTS. **479**

MARITAL CONDITION OF OCCUPIED WOMEN.

[For statistics showing the marital condition of gainful workers in cities of 25,000 to 100,000 inhabitants, see Table 23, p. 524.]

OCCUPATIONS.

DEFINITIONS AND EXPLANATION OF TERMS.

Scope of inquiry.—The questions concerning occupations called for a statement of the "trade, profession, or particular kind of work done" by each person engaged in gainful labor, and for a statement of the "industry, business, or establishment in which at work." Although the enumerators were instructed to return an occupation for every person engaged in gainful labor, the occupation returns for children under 10 years of age have not been compiled. The term "gainful workers," therefore, includes all workers except women doing housework in their own homes and children working at home merely on general housework, on chores, or at odd times on other work.

The statistics as here presented relate to continental United States only, comprising the 48 states and the District of Columbia.

Classification.—The classification is occupational rather than industrial. The occupations are grouped, however, under 9 large industry or service units. Since the occupation classification used at the Fourteenth Census differs somewhat from that of the Thirteenth Census, a few occupations are here presented under different general divisions from those under which they were presented in 1910. Such transfers have changed slightly for 1910 the total number of persons in certain general divisions of occupations. Also, in 1920, occasionally an occupational designation was classified under a different occupation group from that under which it was classified in 1910. Because of these changes a moderate increase or decrease from 1910 to 1920 in the number of workers in an occupation may be apparent only and due to a difference in classification. The occupations appreciably affected by transfers of designation are confined mainly to manufacturing and transportation pursuits.

Causes of decrease.—The change in the census date from April 15 in 1910 to January 1 in 1920 doubtless had a pronounced effect on the number of workers returned as pursuing those occupations which are seasonal or largely seasonal. A comparison with the 1910 statistics for the respective agricultural pursuits indicates strongly that, especially in the case of farm laborers, the marked decrease from 1910 to 1920 probably was due in large part to an underenumeration in 1920, because in most sections of the United States agricultural work, especially the work of field laborers, is at or near its lowest ebb in January. In some measure, the decrease in farm laborers is believed to be apparent only and due to an overenumeration in 1910, especially of children engaged in this occupation. The large increase from 1910 to 1920 in the number of laborers and semiskilled operatives in fruit and vegetable canning, etc., probably resulted to a considerable extent from changing the census date to a time nearer the latest harvest season for fruits and vegetables.

The World War brought about drastic and rapid changes in many of our industries. To meet war needs new industries sprang into existence and some existing industries, because not needed to further the war efforts of the Nation, rapidly declined in importance. Along with these industrial changes went corresponding changes in the occupational activities of the people, the number of workers declining rapidly in some occupations and increasing rapidly in others. Large numbers of workers were drawn from the fields to the factories, and from factories producing nonessentials or luxuries to those producing munitions or essentials. The readjustment to a peace-time basis was only partially completed at the date of the census. Hence it is believed that many of the changes from 1910 to 1920 in the number of workers in the respective occupations may properly be ascribed in large part to the changes brought about by the World War.

Foreign parentage.—Refers to persons having both parents foreign born.

Mixed parentage.—Refers to persons having one parent native and the other foreign born.

Native.—Refers to persons born in continental United States, in any of the outlying possessions, or at sea under the United States flag.

Native parentage.—Refers to persons having both parents native.

(480)

TABLE 1.—NUMBER AND PROPORTION OF PERSONS GAINFULLY OCCUPIED, BY SEX, FOR THE UNITED STATES: 1880–1920.

SEX AND CENSUS YEAR.	Total population.	Population 10 years of age and over.	PERSONS 10 YEARS OF AGE AND OVER ENGAGED IN GAINFUL OCCUPATIONS.		
			Number.	Per cent of total population.	Per cent of population 10 years of age and over.
BOTH SEXES.					
1920	105,710,620	82,739,315	41,614,248	39.4	50.3
1910	91,972,266	71,580,270	38,167,336	41.5	53.3
1900	75,994,575	57,949,824	29,073,233	38.3	50.2
1890 [1]	62,622,250	47,413,559	[2] 23,318,183	37.2	49.2
1880	50,155,783	36,761,607	17,392,099	34.7	47.3
MALE.					
1920	53,900,431	42,289,969	33,064,737	61.3	78.2
1910	47,332,277	37,027,558	30,091,564	63.6	81.3
1900	38,816,448	29,703,440	23,753,836	61.2	80.0
1890 [1]	32,067,880	24,352,659	[2] 19,312,651	60.2	79.3
1880	25,518,820	18,735,980	14,744,942	57.8	78.7
FEMALE.					
1920	51,810,189	40,449,346	8,549,511	16.5	21.1
1910	44,639,989	34,552,712	8,075,772	18.1	23.4
1900	37,178,127	28,246,384	5,319,397	14.3	18.8
1890 [1]	30,554,370	23,060,900	[2] 4,005,532	13.1	17.4
1880	24,636,963	18,025,627	2,647,157	10.7	14.7

[1] Figures for 1890 are exclusive of persons in Indian Territory and on Indian reservations, area specially enumerated at that census, but for which occupation statistics are not available.
[2] Corrected figures; for explanation, see Occupation Report for 1900, pp. LXVI–LXXIII.

TABLE 2.—NUMBER AND PER CENT DISTRIBUTION, BY SEX, OF THE PERSONS IN EACH GENERAL DIVISION OF OCCUPATIONS, FOR THE UNITED STATES: 1920 AND 1910.

CENSUS YEAR AND GENERAL DIVISION OF OCCUPATIONS.	Total.	MALE.		FEMALE.	
		Number.	Per cent.	Number.	Per cent.
1920					
All occupations	41,614,248	33,064,737	79.5	8,549,511	20.5
Agriculture, forestry, and animal husbandry	10,953,158	9,869,030	90.1	1,084,128	9.9
Extraction of minerals	1,090,223	1,087,359	99.7	2,864	0.3
Manufacturing and mechanical industries	12,818,524	10,888,183	84.9	1,930,341	15.1
Transportation	3,063,582	2,850,528	93.0	213,054	7.0
Trade	4,242,979	3,575,187	84.3	667,792	15.7
Public service (not elsewhere classified)	770,460	748,666	97.2	21,794	2.8
Professional service	2,143,889	1,127,391	52.6	1,016,498	47.4
Domestic and personal service	3,404,892	1,217,968	35.8	2,186,924	64.2
Clerical occupations	3,126,541	1,700,425	54.4	1,426,116	45.6
1910					
All occupations	38,167,336	30,091,564	78.8	8,075,772	21.2
Agriculture, forestry, and animal husbandry	[1] 12,659,082	[1] 10,851,581	85.7	1,807,501	14.3
Extraction of minerals	[1] 965,169	[1] 964,075	99.9	1,094	0.1
Manufacturing and mechanical industries	[1] 10,628,731	[1] 8,808,161	82.9	[1] 1,820,570	17.1
Transportation	[1] 2,637,420	[1] 2,530,795	96.0	[1] 106,625	4.0
Trade	3,614,670	3,146,582	87.1	468,088	12.9
Public service (not elsewhere classified)	459,291	445,733	97.0	13,558	3.0
Professional service	[1] 1,693,361	[1] 959,470	56.7	[1] 733,891	43.3
Domestic and personal service	[1] 3,772,559	[1] 1,241,338	32.9	[1] 2,531,221	67.1
Clerical occupations	1,737,053	1,143,829	65.8	593,224	34.2

[1] Figures corrected to conform to 1920 classification.

75108°—22——31

TABLE 3.—TOTAL PERSONS 10 YEARS OF AGE AND OVER ENGAGED IN GAINFUL OCCU-
PATIONS, DISTRIBUTED BY SEX AND GENERAL DIVISIONS OF OCCUPATIONS, FOR
THE UNITED STATES: 1920 AND 1910.

SEX AND GENERAL DIVISION OF OCCUPATIONS.	1920		1910	
	Number.	Per cent distribu- tion.	Number.	Per cent distribu- tion.
BOTH SEXES.				
All occupations...............................	41,614,248	100.0	38,167,336	100.0
Agriculture, forestry, and animal husbandry.....	10,953,158	26.3	¹ 12,659,082	33.2
Extraction of minerals...........................	1,090,223	2.6	¹ 965,169	2.5
Manufacturing and mechanical industries.........	12,818,524	30.8	¹ 10,628,731	27.8
Transportation.................................	3,063,582	7.4	¹ 2,637,420	6.9
Trade...	4,242,979	10.2	3,614,670	9.5
Public service (not elsewhere classified)...........	770,460	1.9	459,291	1.2
Professional service............................	2,143,889	5.2	¹ 1,693,361	4.4
Domestic and personal service....................	3,404,892	8.2	¹ 3,772,559	9.9
Clerical occupations............................	3,126,541	7.5	1,737,053	4.6
MALE.				
All occupations...............................	33,064,737	100.0	30,091,564	100.0
Agriculture, forestry, and animal husbandry.....	9,869,030	29.8	¹ 10,851,581	36.1
Extraction of minerals...........................	1,087,359	3.3	¹ 964,075	3.2
Manufacturing and mechanical industries.........	10,888,183	32.9	¹ 8,808,161	29.3
Transportation.................................	2,850,528	8.6	¹ 2,530,795	8.4
Trade...	3,575,187	10.8	3,146,582	10.5
Public service (not elsewhere classified)...........	748,666	2.3	445,733	1.5
Professional service............................	1,127,391	3.4	¹ 959,470	3.2
Domestic and personal service....................	1,217,968	3.7	¹ 1,241,338	4.1
Clerical occupations............................	1,700,425	5.1	1,143,829	3.8
FEMALE.				
All occupations...............................	8,549,511	100.0	8,075,772	100.0
Agriculture, forestry, and animal husbandry......	1,084,128	12.7	1,807,501	22.4
Extraction of minerals...........................	2,864	(²)	1,094	(²)
Manufacturing and mechanical industries.........	1,930,341	22.6	¹ 1,820,570	22.5
Transportation.................................	213,054	2.5	¹ 106,625	1.3
Trade...	667,792	7.8	468,088	5.8
Public service (not elsewhere classified)...........	21,794	0.3	13,558	0.2
Professional service............................	1,016,498	11.9	¹ 733,891	9.1
Domestic and personal service....................	2,186,924	25.6	¹ 2,531,221	31.3
Clerical occupations............................	1,426,116	16.7	593,224	7.3

¹ Figures corrected to conform to 1920 classification.   ² Less than one-tenth of 1 per cent.

TABLE 4.—TOTAL PERSONS 10 YEARS OF AGE AND OVER ENGAGED IN EACH SPECIFIED OCCUPATION, CLASSIFIED BY SEX, FOR THE UNITED STATES: 1920 AND 1910.

[The figures for 1910 for certain of the division totals and also for certain individual occupations have been corrected to conform to the classification for 1920.]

OCCUPATION.	1920			1910		
	Total.	Male.	Female.	Total.	Male.	Female.
All occupations	41,614,248	33,064,737	8,549,511	38,167,336	30,091,564	8,075,772
Agriculture, forestry, and animal husbandry	10,953,158	9,869,030	1,084,128	12,659,082	10,851,581	1,807,501
Dairy farmers, farmers, and stock raisers	6,201,261	5,947,425	253,836	5,979,340	5,717,384	261,956
Dairy farmers	118,813	114,867	3,946	61,816	59,240	2,576
Farmers, general farms	6,004,580	5,757,327	247,253	5,864,492	5,606,789	257,703
Farmers, turpentine farms	309	309	....	511	508	3
Stock raisers	77,559	74,922	2,637	52,521	50,847	1,674
Dairy farm, farm, and stock farm laborers	4,041,627	3,248,712	792,915	6,069,321	4,551,247	1,518,074
Dairy farm laborers	63,367	60,770	2,597	35,014	32,237	2,777
Farm laborers (home farm)[1]	1,850,119	1,273,477	576,642	3,310,534	2,133,949	1,176,585
Farm laborers (working out)[1]	2,055,276	1,843,307	211,969	2,636,966	2,299,444	337,522
Farm laborers (turpentine farm)	16,099	15,790	309	27,557	27,241	316
Stock herders, drovers, and feeders	56,766	55,368	1,398	59,250	58,376	874
Dairy farm, farm, garden, orchard, etc., foremen	93,048	78,708	14,340	51,195	43,419	7,776
Dairy farm foremen	2,479	2,339	140	1,086	1,001	85
Farm foremen, general farms	79,018	65,251	13,767	41,521	34,017	7,504
Farm foremen, turpentine farms	724	724	....	899	898	1
Farm foremen, stock farms	4,894	4,800	94	3,604	3,593	11
Garden and greenhouse foremen	1,874	1,698	176	1,311	1,223	88
Orchard, nursery, etc., foremen	4,059	3,896	163	2,774	2,687	87
Fishermen and oystermen	52,836	52,457	379	68,275	67,799	476
Foresters, forest rangers, and timber cruisers	3,653	3,651	2	4,332	4,332	....
Gardeners, florists, fruit growers, and nurserymen	169,399	160,116	9,283	139,255	131,421	7,834
Florists	8,345	7,407	938	9,028	7,977	1,051
Fruit growers	55,402	52,208	3,194	43,531	41,255	2,276
Gardeners	98,591	93,523	5,068	79,894	75,481	4,413
Landscape gardeners	4,402	4,377	25	3,792	3,777	15
Nurserymen	2,659	2,601	58	3,010	2,931	79
Garden, greenhouse, orchard, and nursery laborers	137,010	127,589	9,421	133,927	126,453	7,474
Cranberry bog laborers	241	236	5	1,384	1,316	68
Garden laborers	81,532	75,234	6,298	81,314	76,372	4,942
Greenhouse laborers	16,239	15,075	1,164	17,757	16,796	961
Orchard and nursery laborers	38,998	37,044	1,954	33,472	31,969	1,503
Lumbermen, raftsmen, and woodchoppers	205,315	205,036	279	161,268	161,191	77
Foremen and overseers	6,090	6,090	....	4,798	4,798	....
Inspectors, scalers, and surveyors	2,344	2,344	....	2,110	2,109	1
Teamsters and haulers	17,106	17,106	....	15,038	15,038	....
Other lumbermen, raftsmen, and woodchoppers	179,775	179,496	279	139,322	139,246	76
Owners and managers of log and timber camps	8,410	8,397	13	7,931	7,927	4
Managers and officials	2,095	2,090	5	1,725	1,725	....
Owners and proprietors	6,315	6,307	8	6,206	6,202	4
Other agricultural and animal husbandry pursuits	40,599	36,939	3,660	44,238	40,408	3,830
Apiarists	2,893	2,759	134	2,145	2,020	125
Corn shellers, hay balers, grain threshers, etc.	9,646	9,642	4	5,617	5,617	....
Ditchers (farm)[1]	5,379	5,379	....	15,198	15,198	....
Irrigators and ditch tenders	2,600	2,597	3	2,883	2,874	9
Poultry raisers	14,116	11,792	2,324	12,151	8,921	3,230
Poultry yard laborers	4,599	3,587	1,012	3,233	2,856	377
Other and not specified pursuits	1,366	1,183	183	3,011	2,922	89

[1] Decrease, 1910 to 1920, probably due mainly to change of census date from Apr. 15 in 1910 to Jan. 1 in 1920.

TABLE 4.—TOTAL PERSONS 10 YEARS OF AGE AND OVER ENGAGED IN EACH SPECIFIED OCCUPATION, CLASSIFIED BY SEX, FOR THE UNITED STATES: 1920 AND 1910—Con.

[The figures for 1910 for certain of the division totals and also for certain individual occupations have been corrected to conform to the classification for 1920.]

OCCUPATION.	1920			1910		
	Total.	Male.	Female.	Total.	Male.	Female.
Extraction of minerals	1,090,223	1,087,359	2,864	965,169	964,075	1,094
Foremen, overseers, and inspectors	36,931	36,923	8	23,338	23,328	10
Foremen and overseers	27,945	27,939	6	22,142	22,133	9
Inspectors	8,986	8,984	2	1,196	1,195	1
Operators, officials, and managers	34,325	34,143	182	25,234	25,127	107
Managers	14,469	14,446	23	9,798	9,786	12
Officials	2,522	2,481	41	1,149	1,140	9
Operators	17,334	17,216	118	14,287	14,201	86
Coal mine operatives	733,936	732,441	1,495	613,924	613,519	405
Copper mine operatives	36,054	35,918	136	39,270	39,251	19
Gold and silver mine operatives	32,700	32,666	34	55,436	55,397	39
Iron mine operatives	38,704	38,605	99	49,948	49,909	39
Operatives in other and not specified mines	41,389	41,282	107	47,252	47,169	83
Lead and zinc mine operatives	20,798	20,749	49	19,486	19,471	15
Other specified mine operatives	11,320	11,271	49	7,945	7,891	54
Not specified mine operatives	9,271	9,262	9	19,821	19,807	14
Quarry operatives	45,162	45,084	78	80,840	80,795	45
Oil, gas, and salt well operatives	91,022	90,297	725	29,927	29,580	347
Oil and gas well operatives	85,550	85,303	247	25,562	25,548	14
Salt well and works operatives	5,472	4,994	478	4,365	4,032	333
Manufacturing and mechanical industries	12,818,524	10,888,183	1,930,341	[1]10,628,731	[1]8,808,161	[1]1,820,570
Apprentices to building and hand trades	73,953	73,897	56	[2]	[2]	[2]
Blacksmiths' apprentices	2,661	2,659	2	[3]2,816	[3]2,814	[3]2
Boiler makers' apprentices	2,005	2,005		[2]	[2]	[2]
Cabinetmakers' apprentices	1,020	1,020		[2]	[2]	[2]
Carpenters' apprentices	4,805	4,797	8	[3]6,069	[3]6,061	[3]8
Coopers' apprentices	365	365		[2]	[2]	[2]
Electricians' apprentices	9,562	9,557	5	[3]2,661	[3]2,660	[3]1
Machinists' apprentices [4]	39,463	39,448	15	[2]	[2]	[2]
Masons' apprentices	1,434	1,434		[3]2,503	[3]2,501	[3]2
Painters', glaziers', and varnishers' apprentices	1,616	1,598	18	[3]2,662	[3]2,653	[3]9
Paper hangers' apprentices	172	165	7	444	440	4
Plasterers' apprentices	398	398		[3]669	[3]669	
Plumbers' apprentices	7,386	7,386		[3]9,903	[3]9,899	[3]4
Roofers' and slaters' apprentices	250	250		304	302	2
Tinsmiths' and coppersmiths' apprentices	2,816	2,815	1	[2]	[2]	[2]
Apprentices to dressmakers and milliners	4,326	17	4,309	12,011	31	11,980
Dressmakers' apprentices	2,715	4	2,711	5,996	7	5,989
Milliners' apprentices	1,611	13	1,598	6,015	24	5,991
Apprentices, other	65,898	60,532	5,366	[2]	[2]	[2]
Architects', designers', and draftsmen's apprentices	3,777	3,479	298	1,153	1,110	43
Jewelers', watchmakers', goldsmiths', and silversmiths' apprentices	2,633	2,247	386	[3]1,839	[3]1,770	[3]69
Printers' and bookbinders' apprentices	11,603	10,366	1,237	[3]12,395	[3]11,454	[3]941
Other apprentices	47,885	44,440	3,445	[2]	[2]	[2]
Bakers	97,940	93,347	4,600	89,531	84,752	1,779
Blacksmiths, forgemen, and hammermen	221,421	221,416	5	240,174	240,143	31
Blacksmiths	195,255	195,251	4	232,988	232,957	31
Forgemen, hammermen, and welders	26,166	26,165	1	7,186	7,186	

[1] Totals include figures for occupations (total, 91,339; male, 88,770; female, 2,569) omitted in detail because not comparable with 1920 figures.
[2] Comparable figures for 1910 not available.
[3] Figures for 1910 approximate only.
[4] Many of the "Machinists' apprentices" probably are machine tenders.

TABLE 4.—TOTAL PERSONS 10 YEARS OF AGE AND OVER ENGAGED IN EACH SPECIFIED OCCUPATION, CLASSIFIED BY SEX, FOR THE UNITED STATES: 1920 AND 1910—Con.

[The figures for 1910 for certain of the division totals and also for certain individual occupations have been corrected to conform to the classification for 1920.]

OCCUPATION.	1920			1910		
	Total.	Male.	Female.	Total.	Male.	Female.
Manufacturing and mechanical industries—Continued.						
Boiler makers	74,088	74,088		44,761	44,761	
Brick and stone masons	131,264	131,257	7	[1] 169,402	[1] 169,387	[1] 15
Builders and building contractors	90,109	90,030	79	174,422	173,573	849
Cabinetmakers	45,511	45,503	8	41,892	41,884	8
Carpenters	887,379	887,208	171	817,120	817,082	38
Compositors, linotypers, and typesetters	140,165	128,859	11,306	127,589	113,538	14,051
Coopers	19,066	19,061	5	25,299	25,292	7
Dressmakers and seamstresses (not in factory)	235,855	336	235,519	449,342	1,582	447,760
Dyers	15,109	14,978	131	14,050	13,396	654
Electricians	212,964	212,945	19	[2] 120,241	[2] 120,155	[2] 86
Electrotypers, stereotypers, and lithographers	13,716	13,530	186	12,506	11,929	577
Electrotypers and stereotypers	5,494	5,484	10	4,368	4,268	100
Lithographers	8,222	8,046	176	8,138	7,661	477
Engineers (stationary), cranemen, hoistmen, etc.	279,984	279,940	44	([3])	([3])	([3])
Engineers (stationary)	242,096	242,064	32	231,041	231,031	10
Cranemen, derrickmen, hoistmen, etc.	37,888	37,876	12	([3])	([3])	([3])
Engravers	15,053	14,492	561	13,967	13,429	538
Filers, grinders, buffers, and polishers (metal)	59,785	57,315	2,470	49,525	46,679	2,846
Buffers and polishers	30,511	28,484	2,027	30,496	28,191	2,305
Filers	10,959	10,893	66	10,236	10,069	167
Grinders	18,315	17,938	377	8,793	8,419	374
Firemen (except locomotive and fire department)	143,875	143,862	13	111,248	111,248	
Foremen and overseers (manufacturing)	307,413	277,242	30,171	175,098	155,358	19,740
Furnacemen, smeltermen, heaters, pourers, etc.	40,806	40,800	6	36,251	36,226	25
Furnacemen and smeltermen	18,201	18,197	4	19,735	19,719	16
Heaters	16,470	16,468	2	10,120	10,111	9
Ladlers and pourers	1,020	1,020		679	679	
Puddlers	5,115	5,115		5,717	5,717	
Glass blowers	9,144	9,055	89	15,564	15,474	90
Jewelers, watchmakers, goldsmiths, and silversmiths	39,592	37,914	1,678	32,574	30,037	2,537
Goldsmiths and silversmiths	4,828	4,771	57	5,757	5,553	204
Jewelers and lapidaries (factory)	8,757	7,701	1,056	10,631	8,783	1,848
Jewelers and watchmakers (not in factory)	26,007	25,442	565	16,186	15,701	485
Laborers (n. o. s.[4]):						
Building, general, and not specified laborers	623,203	608,075	15,128	869,478	853,679	15,799
Chemical and allied industries	74,289	70,994	3,295	41,741	39,711	2,030
Fertilizer factories	12,943	12,808	135	9,847	9,757	90
Paint and varnish factories	4,841	4,677	164	2,959	2,842	117
Powder, cartridge, dynamite, fuse, and fireworks factories	8,467	7,821	646	4,277	3,947	330
Soap factories	4,715	4,346	369	3,433	3,173	260
Other chemical factories	43,323	41,342	1,981	21,225	19,992	1,233
Cigar and tobacco factories	35,157	21,295	13,862	16,392	11,436	4,956

[1] The 1910 figures include cement finishers; these numbered 7,621 in 1920.
[2] Figures for 1910 estimated.
[3] In 1910 most of the "Cranemen, derrickmen, hoistmen, etc.," were classified with the semiskilled operatives of the respective industries.
[4] Not otherwise specified.

TABLE 4.—TOTAL PERSONS 10 YEARS OF AGE AND OVER ENGAGED IN EACH SPECIFIED OCCUPATION, CLASSIFIED BY SEX, FOR THE UNITED STATES: 1920 AND 1910—Con.

[The figures for 1910 for certain of the division totals and also for certain individual occupations have been corrected to conform to the classification for 1920.]

OCCUPATION.	1920			1910		
	Total.	Male.	Female.	Total.	Male.	Female.
Manufacturing and mechanical industries—Continued.						
Laborers (n. o. s.[1])—Continued.						
Clay, glass, and stone industries	124,544	120,215	4,329	154,826	152,438	2,388
Brick, tile, and terra cotta factories	48,636	48,099	537	77,954	77,333	621
Glass factories	28,937	26,461	2,476	24,634	23,686	948
Lime, cement, and artificial stone factories	30,051	29,884	167	36,083	35,931	152
Marble and stone yards	5,084	5,061	23	6,915	6,847	68
Potteries	11,836	10,710	1,126	9,240	8,641	599
Clothing industries	12,776	6,414	6,362	10,240	5,424	4,816
Corset factories	771	194	577	834	286	548
Glove factories	1,757	899	858	870	446	424
Hat factories (felt)	989	825	164	1,759	1,541	218
Shirt, collar, and cuff factories	2,708	1,317	1,391	2,184	821	1,363
Suit, coat, cloak, and overall factories	3,984	2,219	1,765	2,920	1,651	1,269
Other clothing factories	2,567	960	1,607	1,673	679	994
Food industries	159,535	143,397	16,138	82,015	75,691	6,324
Bakeries	8,315	6,869	1,446	4,510	3,755	755
Butter, cheese, and condensed milk factories	15,190	14,174	1,016	4,816	4,688	128
Candy factories	6,584	4,398	2,186	2,978	1,845	1,133
Fish curing and packing	6,300	5,261	1,039	4,870	4,637	233
Flour and grain mills	18,121	17,983	138	9,243	9,152	91
Fruit and vegetable canning, etc	13,058	9,743	3,315	4,670	3,683	987
Slaughter and packing houses	59,548	55,436	4,112	33,903	32,471	1,432
Sugar factories and refineries	15,733	15,414	319	8,755	8,647	108
Other food factories	16,686	14,119	2,567	8,270	6,813	1,457
Harness and saddle industries	1,885	1,727	158	1,298	1,210	88
Helpers in building and hand trades	63,519	63,412	107	66,303	66,222	81
Iron and steel industries	729,613	717,022	12,591	482,941	476,801	6,140
Agricultural implement factories	11,409	11,292	117	11,067	10,953	114
Automobile factories	83,341	80,874	2,467	15,783	15,644	139
Blast furnaces and steel rolling mills [2]	258,830	256,548	2,282	202,392	201,030	1,362
Car and railroad shops	53,643	53,280	363	48,342	48,114	228
Ship and boat building	69,196	68,917	279	11,983	11,975	8
Wagon and carriage factories	9,817	9,594	223	12,391	12,232	159
Other iron and steel factories [3]	179,607	173,734	5,873	138,059	134,295	3,764
Not specified metal industries	63,770	62,783	987	42,924	42,558	366
Other metal industries	67,887	62,771	5,116	44,773	42,134	2,639
Brass mills	18,485	17,614	871	10,885	10,606	279
Clock and watch factories	3,108	1,929	1,179	1,879	1,262	617
Copper factories	10,963	10,908	55	11,586	11,532	54
Gold and silver factories	2,272	2,061	211	1,277	1,101	176
Jewelry factories	1,421	1,255	166	668	528	140
Lead and zinc factories	8,927	8,859	68	7,945	7,871	74
Tinware, enamelware, etc., factories	17,605	15,436	2,169	7,587	6,709	878
Other metal factories	5,106	4,709	397	2,946	2,525	421
Lumber and furniture industries	320,613	309,874	10,739	317,244	313,228	4,016
Furniture factories	35,272	32,600	2,672	23,618	23,089	529
Piano and organ factories	5,321	4,596	725	4,459	4,099	360
Saw and planing mills	245,683	241,334	4,349	260,142	258,361	1,781
Other wood-working factories	34,337	31,344	2,993	29,025	27,679	1,346
Paper and pulp mills	52,263	49,786	2,477	31,388	29,959	1,429
Printing and publishing	11,436	8,886	2,550	7,041	5,217	1,824
Blank book, envelope, tag, paper bag, etc., factories	3,455	2,646	809	1,557	1,096	461
Printing, publishing, and engraving	7,981	6,240	1,741	5,484	4,121	1,363
Shoe factories	19,210	14,194	5,016	10,277	7,952	2,325
Tanneries	27,480	26,703	777	20,798	20,491	307

[1] Not otherwise specified.
[2] Includes tinplate mills.
[3] Includes iron foundries.
[4] Includes box factories (wood).

TABLE 4.—TOTAL PERSONS 10 YEARS OF AGE AND OVER ENGAGED IN EACH SPECIFIED OCCUPATION, CLASSIFIED BY SEX, FOR THE UNITED STATES: 1920 AND 1910—Con.

[The figures for 1910 for certain of the division totals and also for certain individual occupations have been corrected to conform to the classification for 1920.]

OCCUPATION.	1920			1910		
	Total.	Male.	Female.	Total.	Male.	Female.
Manufacturing and mechanical industries—Continued.						
Laborers (n. o. s.[1])—Continued.						
Textile industries—						
Carpet mills	3,953	3,378	575	3,769	3,437	332
Cotton mills	76,315	59,646	16,669	37,804	32,037	5,767
Knitting mills	11,943	6,603	5,340	7,804	4,264	3,540
Lace and embroidery mills	944	677	267	705	468	237
Silk mills	10,080	7,350	2,730	3,798	2,686	1,112
Textile dyeing, finishing, and printing mills	10,605	9,885	720	9,958	9,362	596
Woolen and worsted mills	22,227	18,238	3,989	12,290	10,245	2,045
Other textile mills	17,243	14,564	2,679	11,018	8,608	2,410
Hemp and jute mills	1,254	1,110	144	1,462	1,295	167
Linen mills	458	364	94	738	479	259
Rope and cordage factories	4,268	3,805	463	3,797	3,131	666
Sail, awning, and tent factories	283	237	46	264	234	30
Not specified textile mills	10,980	9,048	1,932	4,757	3,469	1,288
Other industries	463,891	426,398	37,493	246,677	229,517	17,160
Broom and brush factories	2,800	2,407	393	1,565	1,340	225
Button factories	1,407	1,093	314	1,105	790	315
Charcoal and coke works	9,384	9,352	32	11,446	11,431	15
Electric light and power plants	15,417	15,255	162	8,176	8,011	165
Electrical supply factories	26,789	23,562	3,227	11,434	10,053	1,381
Gas works	18,845	18,787	58	16,549	16,534	15
Leather belt, leather case, etc., factories	3,578	3,274	304	1,908	1,757	151
Liquor and beverage industries	10,530	10,295	235	18,857	18,294	563
Paper box factories	3,384	2,401	983	1,403	791	612
Petroleum refineries	31,795	31,566	229	11,215	11,151	64
Rubber factories	51,467	47,515	3,952	13,546	12,224	1,322
Straw factories	577	513	64	413	319	94
Trunk factories	2,486	2,269	217	985	909	76
Turpentine distilleries	9,731	9,605	126	6,405	6,354	51
Other miscellaneous industries	84,337	77,583	6,754	32,237	29,836	2,401
Other not specified industries	191,364	170,921	20,443	109,433	99,723	9,710
Loom fixers	15,961	15,958	3	13,254	13,254	
Machinists, millwrights, and toolmakers	894,662	894,654	8	488,049	487,956	93
Machinists	801,901	801,896	5	461,344	461,271	73
Millwrights	37,669	37,669		17,442	17,442	
Toolmakers and die setters and sinkers	55,092	55,089	3	9,263	9,243	20
Managers and superintendents (manufacturing)	201,721	196,771	4,950	104,210	102,748	1,462
Manufacturers and officials	231,615	223,289	8,326	256,591	251,892	4,699
Manfacturers	183,386	178,441	4,945	235,107	230,809	4,298
Officials	48,229	44,848	3,381	21,484	21,083	401
Mechanics (n. o. s.[1])	281,741	281,690	51	([2])	([2])	([2])
Gunsmiths, locksmiths, and bellhangers	4,645	4,638	7	3,251	3,248	3
Wheelwrights	3,727	3,727		3,732	3,732	
Other mechanics	273,369	273,325	44	([2])	([2])	([2])
Millers (grain, flour, feed, etc.)	23,272	23,265	7	23,152	23,093	59
Milliners and millinery dealers	73,255	3,657	69,598	127,906	5,459	122,447
Molders, founders, and casters (metal)	123,681	123,668	13	120,900	120,783	117
Brass molders, founders, and casters	7,238	7,238		6,512	6,509	3
Iron molders, founders, and casters	114,031	114,022	9	112,122	112.070	52
Other molders, founders, and casters	2,412	2,408	4	2,266	2,204	62
Oilers of machinery	24,612	24,568	44	14,013	13,990	23
Painters, glaziers, varnishers, enamelers, etc.	323,032	319,697	3,335	337,355	334,814	2,541
Enamelers, lacquerers, and japanners	4,137	3,168	969	2,999	1,968	1,031
Painters, glaziers, and varnishers (building)	248,497	248,394	103	273,441	273,060	381
Painters, glaziers, and varnishers (factory)	70,398	68,135	2,263	60,915	59,786	1,129

[1] Not otherwise specified.   [2] Comparable figures for 1910 not available.

TABLE 4.—TOTAL PERSONS 10 YEARS OF AGE AND OVER ENGAGED IN EACH SPECIFIED OCCUPATION, CLASSIFIED BY SEX, FOR THE UNITED STATES: 1920 AND 1910—Con.

[The figures for 1910 for certain of the division totals and also for certain individual occupations have been corrected to conform to the classification for 1920.]

OCCUPATION.	1920			1910		
	Total.	Male.	Female.	Total.	Male.	Female.
Manufacturing and mechanical industries—Continued.						
Paper hangers	18,746	18,338	408	25,577	24,780	797
Pattern and model makers	27,720	27,663	57	23,559	23,006	553
Plasterers and cement finishers	45,876	45,870	6	[1] 47,682	[1] 47,676	[1] 6
Cement finishers	7,621	7,621		(1)	(1)	(1)
Plasterers	38,255	38,249	6	47,682	47,676	6
Plumbers and gas and steam fitters	206,718	206,715	3	148,304	148,304	
Pressmen and plate printers (printing)	18,683	18,683		20,084	19,892	192
Rollers and roll hands (metal)	25,061	25,061		18,407	18,384	23
Roofers and slaters	11,378	11,378		14,078	14,078	
Sawyers	33,809	33,800	9	43,276	43,257	19
Semiskilled operatives (n. o. s.[2]):						
Chemical and allied industries	50,341	32,072	18,269	30,705	17,158	13,547
Fertilizer factories	1,407	1,352	55	635	622	13
Paint and varnish factories	5,521	4,686	835	3,920	3,292	628
Powder, cartridge, dynamite, fuse, and fireworks factories	7,379	4,811	2,568	5,263	2,858	2,405
Soap factories	6,288	3,239	3,049	4,443	2,516	1,927
Other chemical factories	29,746	17,984	11,762	16,444	7,870	8,574
Cigar and tobacco factories	145,222	61,262	83,960	151,801	79,956	71,845
Clay, glass, and stone industries	85,434	72,269	13,165	88,691	79,230	9,461
Brick, tile, and terra cotta factories	9,987	9,357	630	13,407	12,649	758
Glass factories	44,831	37,636	7,195	41,877	37,927	3,950
Lime, cement, and artificial stone factories	7,633	7,426	207	8,609	8,480	129
Marble and stone yards	5,546	5,478	68	8,539	8,389	150
Potteries	17,437	12,372	5,065	16,259	11,785	4,474
Clothing industries	409,361	143,718	265,643	386,136	148,866	237,270
Corset factories	12,642	1,115	11,527	13,073	1,375	11,698
Glove factories	23,357	6,584	16,773	19,339	5,353	13,986
Hat factories (felt)	21,178	14,716	6,462	33,020	22,702	10,318
Shirt, collar, and cuff factories	52,377	10,361	42,016	60,169	13,311	46,858
Suit, coat, cloak, and overall factories	143,872	79,357	64,515	138,042	75,444	62,598
Other clothing factories	155,935	31,585	124,350	122,493	30,681	91,812
Food industries	188,895	116,493	72,402	105,283	68,683	36,600
Bakeries	20,441	8,858	11,583	8,938	3,008	5,930
Butter, cheese, and condensed milk factories	18,841	16,096	2,745	11,598	11,065	533
Candy factories	52,281	20,913	31,368	30,943	13,608	17,335
Fish curing and packing	7,586	4,363	3,223	2,776	1,786	990
Flour and grain mills	8,112	7,524	588	3,992	3,750	242
Fruit and vegetable canning, etc	10,204	3,898	6,306	5,290	2,127	3,163
Slaughter and packing houses	49,991	41,906	8,085	25,897	23,492	2,405
Sugar factories and refineries	3,806	3,144	662	1,871	1,655	216
Other food factories	17,633	9,791	7,842	13,978	8,192	5,786
Harness and saddle industries	18,135	17,573	562	22,650	21,958	692
Iron and steel industries	689,980	632,161	57,819	369,040	345,483	23,557
Agricultural implement factories	7,702	7,136	586	4,866	4,494	372
Automobile factories	101,164	108,376	12,788	21,091	20,243	848
Blast furnaces and steel rolling mills [3]	93,627	89,526	4,101	70,273	67,889	2,384
Car and railroad shops	97,979	97,003	976	47,783	47,406	377
Ship and boat building	97,666	97,175	491	14,530	14,464	66
Wagon and carriage factories	9,430	8,749	681	22,339	21,255	1,084
Other iron and steel factories [4]	245,450	209,112	36,338	154,720	138,677	16,043
Not specified metal industries	16,942	15,084	1,858	33,438	31,055	2,383
Other metal industries	91,291	60,844	30,447	69,815	48,956	20,859
Brass mills	17,482	13,576	3,906	16,885	14,350	2,535
Clock and watch factories	18,244	10,043	8,201	15,628	9,252	6,376
Copper factories	2,986	2,834	152	1,968	1,915	53
Gold and silver factories	6,239	4,432	1,807	5,831	4,141	1,690

[1] Cement finishers were included with "Brick and stone masons" in 1910.
[2] Not otherwise specified.
[3] Includes tinplate mills.
[4] Includes iron foundries.

TABLE 4.—TOTAL PERSONS 10 YEARS OF AGE AND OVER ENGAGED IN EACH SPECIFIED OCCUPATION, CLASSIFIED BY SEX, FOR THE UNITED STATES: 1920 AND 1910—Con.

[The figures for 1910 for certain of the division totals and also for certain individual occupations have been corrected to conform to the classification for 1920.]

OCCUPATION.	1920			1910		
	Total.	Male.	Female.	Total.	Male.	Female.
Manufacturing and mechanical industries—Continued.						
Semiskilled operatives (n. o. s.[1])—Contd.						
Other metal industries—Continued.						
Jewelry factories	15,083	8,946	6,137	10,834	6,334	4,500
Lead and zinc factories	2,464	2,186	278	1,915	1,652	263
Tinware, enamelware, etc., factories	19,356	12,167	7,189	10,611	6,674	3,937
Other metal factories	9,437	6,660	2,777	6,143	4,638	1,505
Lumber and furniture industries	168,719	150,079	18,640	168,271	154,324	13,947
Furniture factories	55,717	48,906	6,811	44,640	40,936	3,704
Piano and organ factories	19,852	16,949	2,903	18,953	17,400	1,553
Saw and planing mills [2]	57,320	54,016	3,304	66,060	63,684	2,376
Other woodworking factories	35,830	30,208	5,622	38,618	32,304	6,314
Paper and pulp mills	54,669	41,321	13,348	36,383	25,803	10,580
Printing and publishing	80,403	39,281	41,122	68,790	32,851	35,939
Blank book, envelope, tag, paper bag, etc., factories	13,694	5,117	8,577	10,032	3,422	6,610
Printing, publishing, and engraving	66,709	34,164	32,545	58,758	29,429	29,329
Shoe factories	206,225	132,813	73,412	181,010	121,744	59,266
Tanneries	32,226	28,598	3,628	33,652	31,746	1,906
Textile industries:						
Carpet mills	23,387	13,003	10,384	37,347	17,655	19,692
Cotton mills	302,454	153,269	149,185	280,149	139,483	140,666
Knitting mills	107,604	26,922	80,682	87,866	22,528	65,338
Lace and embroidery mills	19,083	6,086	12,997	16,027	4,336	11,691
Silk mills	115,721	42,953	72,768	79,379	29,019	50,360
Textile dyeing, finishing, and printing mills	17,736	12,154	5,582	16,371	11,168	5,203
Woolen and worsted mills	126,418	64,703	61,715	105,186	53,130	52,056
Other textile mills	79,994	34,944	45,050	67,228	26,287	40,941
Hemp and jute mills	4,168	1,951	2,217	4,621	2,007	2,614
Linen mills	2,574	860	1,714	1,984	703	1,281
Rope and cordage factories	8,454	4,714	3,740	6,517	3,022	3,495
Sail, awning, and tent factories	3,543	2,538	1,005	3,365	2,324	1,041
Not specified textile mills	61,255	24,881	36,374	50,741	18,231	32,510
Other industries	622,662	410,256	212,406	346,430	222,111	124,319
Broom and brush factories	12,606	10,219	2,387	11,163	9,037	2,126
Building and hand trades	7,003	6,983	20	11,733	10,212	1,521
Button factories	12,977	7,768	5,209	11,461	6,682	4,779
Charcoal and coke works	1,722	1,692	30	1,634	1,618	16
Electric light and power plants	15,949	15,610	339	8,880	8,704	176
Electrical supply factories	64,841	37,452	27,389	24,677	13,636	11,041
Gas works	9,462	9,294	168	5,732	5,689	43
Leather belt, leather case, etc., factories	17,189	12,809	4,380	11,553	8,473	3,080
Liquor and beverage industries	15,655	14,960	695	31,503	29,664	1,839
Paper box factories	20,452	7,077	13,375	17,917	4,862	13,055
Petroleum refineries	8,891	8,229	662	1,739	1,669	70
Rubber factories	86,204	67,370	18,834	31,593	21,170	10,423
Straw factories	14,102	7,751	6,351	5,915	1,945	3,970
Trunk factories	5,456	4,644	812	4,944	4,381	563
Turpentine distilleries	1,138	1,130	8	1,449	1,441	8
Other miscellaneous industries	121,968	75,772	46,196	71,050	41,244	29,806
Other not specified industries	207,047	121,496	85,551	93,487	51,684	41,803
Shoemakers and cobblers (not in factory)	78,859	78,599	260	69,570	68,788	782
Skilled occupations (n. o. s.[1])	19,395	19,326	69	16,808	16,560	248
Annealers and temperers (metal)	2,913	2,910	3	1,901	1,894	7
Piano and organ tuners	7,047	7,007	40	6,633	6,528	105
Wood carvers	3,025	3,008	17	5,368	5,308	60
Other skilled occupations	6,410	6,401	9	2,906	2,830	76
Stonecutters	22,099	22,096	3	35,731	35,726	5
Structural iron workers (building)	18,836	18,836		11,427	11,427	
Tailors and tailoresses	192,232	160,404	31,828	204,608	163,795	40,813

[1] Not otherwise specified.   [2] Includes box factories (wood).

TABLE 4.—TOTAL PERSONS 10 YEARS OF AGE AND OVER ENGAGED IN EACH SPECIFIED OCCUPATION, CLASSIFIED BY SEX, FOR THE UNITED STATES: 1920 AND 1910—Con.

[The figures for 1910 for certain of the division totals and also for certain individual occupations have been corrected to conform to the classification for 1920.]

OCCUPATION.	1920			1910		
	Total.	Male.	Female.	Total.	Male.	Female.
Manufacturing and mechanical industries—Continued.						
Tinsmiths and coppersmiths............	74,968	74,957	11	59,833	59,809	24
Coppersmiths.........................	5,233	5,232	1	3,410	3,410	....
Tinsmiths and sheet metal workers......	69,735	69,725	10	56,423	56,399	24
Upholsterers...........................	29,605	27,338	2,267	20,221	18,928	1,293
Transportation....................	3,063,582	2,850,528	213,054	2,637,420	2,530,795	106,625
Water transportation (selected occupations):						
Boatmen, canal men, and lock keepers...	6,319	6,286	33	5,304	5,289	15
Captains, masters, mates, and pilots.....	26,320	26,318	2	24,242	24,242	....
Longshoremen and stevedores..........	85,928	85,605	323	62,857	62,813	44
Sailors and deck hands................	54,832	54,800	32	46,510	46,498	12
Road and street transportation (selected occupations):						
Carriage and hack drivers..............	9,057	8,966	91	35,376	35,339	37
Chauffeurs............................	285,045	284,096	949	45,785	45,752	33
Draymen, teamsters, and expressmen [1]..	411,132	410,484	648	408,469	408,396	73
Foremen of livery and transfer companies.	3,808	3,866	2	6,606	6,606	....
Garage keepers and managers...........	42,151	41,944	207	5,279	5,256	23
Hostlers and stable hands..............	18,976	18,973	3	63,388	63,382	6
Laborers (garage, road, and street).......	158,482	158,204	278	194,882	194,876	6
Garage...............................	31,450	31,339	111	4,468	4,462	6
Road and street building and repairing.	115,836	115,673	163	180,468	180,468	....
Street cleaning......................	11,196	11,192	4	9,946	9,946	....
Livery stable keepers and managers.....	11,240	11,168	72	34,795	34,612	183
Proprietors and managers of transfer companies.....................	23,497	23,231	266	15,598	15,368	230
Railroad transportation (selected occupations):						
Baggagemen and freight agents..........	16,819	16,789	30	17,033	17,028	5
Baggagemen.........................	11,878	11,875	3	12,273	12,273	....
Freight agents.......................	4,941	4,914	27	4,760	4,755	5
Boiler washers and engine hostlers.......	25,305	25,271	34	10,409	10,409	....
Brakemen.............................	114,107	114,107	....	92,572	92,572	....
Conductors (steam railroad).............	74,539	74,539	....	65,604	65,604	....
Conductors (street railroad).............	63,760	63,507	253	56,932	56,932	....
Foremen and overseers..................	79,294	79,216	78	69,933	69,693	240
Steam railroad.......................	73,046	72,980	66	65,260	65,038	222
Street railroad.......................	6,248	6,236	12	4,673	4,655	18
Laborers...............................	495,713	488,659	7,054	570,975	567,522	3,453
Steam railroad.......................	470,199	463,613	6,586	543,168	539,920	3,248
Street railroad.......................	25,514	25,046	468	27,807	27,602	205
Locomotive engineers [2].................	109,899	109,899	....	96,229	96,229	....
Locomotive firemen [2]..................	91,345	91,345	....	76,381	76,381	....
Motormen.............................	66,519	66,499	20	58,705	58,705	....
Steam railroad.......................	3,560	3,560	....	2,487	2,487	....
Street railroad.......................	62,959	62,939	20	56,218	56,218	....
Officials and superintendents...........	35,881	35,830	51	22,238	22,236	2
Steam railroad.......................	32,426	32,385	41	19,805	19,803	2
Street railroad.......................	3,455	3,445	10	2,433	2,433	....

[1] Teamsters in agriculture, forestry, and the extraction of minerals are classified with the other workers in those industries, respectively; and drivers for bakeries and laundries are classified with deliverymen in trade.

[2] Probably at each census some stationary engineers are included with locomotive engineers, and some other firemen with locomotive firemen.

TABLE 4.—TOTAL PERSONS 10 YEARS OF AGE AND OVER ENGAGED IN EACH SPECIFIED OCCUPATION, CLASSIFIED BY SEX, FOR THE UNITED STATES: 1920 AND 1910—Con.

[The figures for 1910 for certain of the division totals and also for certain individual occupations have been corrected to conform to the classification for 1920.]

OCCUPATION.	1920			1910		
	Total.	Male.	Female.	Total.	Male.	Female.
Transportation—Continued.						
Railroad transportation (selected occ.)—Continued.						
Switchmen, flagmen, and yardmen	111,565	111,000	565	85,147	85,095	52
Switchmen and flagmen (steam railroad)	101,917	101,359	558	73,419	73,367	52
Switchmen and flagmen (street railroad)	2,500	2,496	4	2,153	2,153	
Yardmen (steam railroad)	7,148	7,145	3	9,575	9,575	
Ticket and station agents	26,585	24,324	2,261	24,138	22,930	1,208
Express, post, telegraph, and telephone (selected occupations):						
Agents (express companies)	5,293	5,193	100	5,875	5,804	71
Express messengers and railway mail clerks	25,005	24,996	9	22,021	22,018	3
Express messengers	9,138	9,129	9	6,781	6,778	3
Railway mail clerks	15,867	15,867		15,240	15,240	
Mail carriers	91,451	90,131	1,320	80,678	79,667	1,011
Telegraph and telephone linemen	37,917	37,905	12	28,350	28,347	3
Telegraph messengers	9,403	8,969	434	9,152	9,074	78
Telegraph operators	79,434	62,574	16,860	69,953	61,734	8,219
Telephone operators	190,160	11,781	178,379	97,893	9,631	88,262
Other transportation pursuits:						
Foremen and overseers (n. o. s.[1])	25,995	25,958	37	14,738	14,333	405
Road and street building and repairing	9,558	9,557	1	7,064	7,064	
Telegraph and telephone	6,822	6,797	25	3,843	3,439	404
Water transportation	3,488	3,488		3,016	3,016	
Other transportation[2]	6,127	6,116	11	815	814	1
Inspectors	50,233	49,848	385	33,237	32,962	275
Steam railroad	42,721	42,675	46	27,661	27,525	136
Street railroad	3,451	3,445	6	2,268	2,265	3
Telegraph and telephone	2,821	2,491	330	2,619	2,485	134
Other transportation	1,240	1,237	3	689	687	2
Laborers (n. o. s.[1])	33,432	33,229	203	26,555	26,300	255
Express companies	9,089	9,067	22	3,010	2,979	31
Pipe-lines	7,369	7,362	7	2,605	2,605	
Telegraph and telephone	5,088	5,011	77	5,312	5,251	61
Water transportation	5,966	5,963	3	14,267	14,177	90
Other transportation	5,920	5,826	94	1,361	1,288	73
Proprietors, officials, and managers (n. o. s.[1])	18,957	18,384	573	14,839	13,411	1,428
Telegraph and telephone	11,603	11,059	544	10,089	8,680	1,409
Other transportation	7,354	7,325	29	4,750	4,731	19
Other occupations (semiskilled)	48,124	46,634	1,490	38,742	37,749	993
Road and street building and repairing	4,435	4,331	104	5,076	4,726	350
Steam railroad	28,621	27,916	705	24,424	24,125	299
Street railroad	9,259	9,088	171	5,187	5,147	40
Telegraph and telephone	1,831	1,410	421	1,213	992	221
Water transportation	1,774	1,753	21	1,945	1,905	40
Other transportation	2,204	2,136	68	897	854	43
Trade	4,242,979	3,575,187	667,792	3,614,670	3,146,582	468,088
Bankers, brokers, and money lenders	161,613	156,309	5,304	105,804	103,170	2,634
Bankers and bank officials	82,375	78,149	4,226	56,059	54,387	1,672
Commercial brokers and commission men	27,552	27,358	194	24,009	23,690	319
Loan brokers and loan company officials	4,385	4,255	130	2,111	1,989	122
Pawnbrokers	1,088	1,066	22	1,232	1,191	41
Stockbrokers	29,609	29,233	376	13,729	13,522	207
Brokers not specified and promoters	16,604	16,248	356	8,664	8,391	273

[1] Not otherwise specified.
[2] Marked increase, 1910 to 1920, probably due mainly to increase in garage and pipe-line foremen, here included.

TABLE 4.—TOTAL PERSONS 10 YEARS OF AGE AND OVER ENGAGED IN EACH SPECIFIED OCCUPATION, CLASSIFIED BY SEX, FOR THE UNITED STATES: 1920 AND 1910—Con.

[The figures for 1910 for certain of the division totals and also for certain individual occupations have been corrected to conform to the classification for 1920.]

OCCUPATION.	1920			1910		
	Total.	Male.	Female.	Total.	Male.	Female.
Trade—Continued.						
Clerks in stores [1]	413,918	243,521	170,397	387,183	275,589	111,594
Commercial travelers	179,320	176,514	2,806	163,620	161,027	2,593
Decorators, drapers, and window dressers	8,853	7,698	1,155	5,341	4,902	439
Deliverymen [2]	170,235	170,039	196	229,619	229,469	150
Bakeries and laundries [2]	20,888	20,858	30	24,030	24,012	18
Stores [2]	149,347	149,181	166	205,589	205,457	132
Floorwalkers, foremen, and overseers	26,437	22,367	4,070	20,724	17,649	3,075
Floorwalkers and foremen in stores	20,604	16,565	4,039	17,946	14,900	3,046
Foremen (warehouses, stockyards, etc.)	5,833	5,802	31	2,778	2,749	29
Inspectors, gaugers, and samplers	13,714	12,683	1,031	13,446	11,685	1,761
Insurance agents and officials	134,978	129,589	5,389	97,964	95,302	2,662
Insurance agents	119,918	114,835	5,083	88,463	85,926	2,537
Officials of insurance companies	15,060	14,754	306	9,501	9,376	125
Laborers in coal and lumber yards, warehouses, etc	125,609	124,713	896	81,123	80,450	673
Coal yards	25,192	25,157	35	16,663	16,655	8
Elevators	11,312	11,244	68	6,346	6,335	11
Lumberyards	43,351	43,297	54	43,398	43,389	9
Stockyards	22,888	22,859	29	5,998	5,991	7
Warehouses	22,866	22,156	710	8,718	8,080	638
Laborers, porters, and helpers in stores	125,007	116,602	8,405	102,333	98,169	4,164
Newsboys	27,961	27,635	326	29,708	29,435	273
Proprietors, officials, and managers (n.o.s.) [3]	34,776	33,715	1,061	22,362	21,352	1,010
Employment office keepers	3,026	2,357	669	2,260	1,540	720
Proprietors, etc., elevators	8,858	8,836	22	5,118	5,105	13
Proprietors, etc., warehouses	6,353	6,310	43	4,393	4,368	25
Other proprietors, officials, and managers	16,539	16,212	327	10,591	10,339	252
Real estate agents and officials	149,135	139,927	9,208	125,862	122,935	2,927
Retail dealers [4]	1,328,275	1,249,295	78,980	1,195,029	1,127,926	67,103
Agricultural implements and wagons	7,789	7,760	29	8,518	8,410	108
Art stores and artists' materials	2,646	1,989	657	2,370	1,955	415
Automobiles and accessories	28,768	28,626	142	4,597	4,545	52
Bicycles	2,221	2,200	21	1,532	1,486	46
Books	3,035	2,600	435	3,118	2,796	322
Boots and shoes	22,544	21,781	763	19,346	18,470	876
Butchers and meat dealers	122,105	120,940	1,165	124,048	122,757	1,291
Buyers and shippers of grain	7,305	7,288	17	11,535	11,454	81
Buyers and shippers of live stock	30,464	30,433	31	32,516	32,346	170
Buyers and shippers of other farm produce	10,540	10,507	33	6,864	6,806	58
Candy and confectionery	40,091	32,368	7,723	29,538	21,601	7,937
Cigars and tobacco	19,141	18,031	1,110	17,728	16,375	1,353
Carpets and rugs	1,132	1,116	16	1,238	1,152	86
Clothing and men's furnishings	46,653	43,440	3,213	35,273	34,229	1,044
Coal and wood	26,556	26,057	499	24,466	23,942	524
Coffee and tea	5,044	4,766	278	5,351	5,112	239
Crockery, glassware, and queensware	1,618	1,505	113	2,508	2,298	210
Curios, antiques, and novelties	3,353	2,593	760	2,735	2,377	358
Delicatessen stores	4,333	3,565	768	3,031	2,313	718
Department stores	11,752	10,800	952	8,970	8,564	406
Drugs and medicines, including druggists and pharmacists	80,187	70,005	3,162	67,575	65,414	2,161
Dry goods, fancy goods, and notions	63,909	56,158	7,751	65,093	57,321	7,069
Five and ten cent and variety stores	5,968	4,899	1,069	4,331	3,294	1,037
Florists (dealers) [5]	5,746	4,784	962	2,934	2,527	407
Flour and feed	9,309	9,212	97	9,469	9,363	106
Fruit	23,385	22,185	1,200	19,000	18,228	772
Furniture	26,013	25,337	676	22,209	21,739	470
Furs	4,789	4,434	355	2,280	2,043	237
Gas fixtures and electrical supplies	4,420	4,335	85	1,526	1,497	29
General stores	80,026	76,317	3,709	88,059	84,734	3,325

[1] Many of the "Clerks in stores" probably are "Salesmen and saleswomen."
[2] Decrease, 1910 to 1920, probably due mainly to substitution of motor for horse-drawn delivery wagons.
[3] Not otherwise specified.
[4] Includes, also, managers and superintendents of retail stores.
[5] Growers of flowers are shown under "Agriculture," p. 483.

TABLE 4.—TOTAL PERSONS 10 YEARS OF AGE AND OVER ENGAGED IN EACH SPECIFIED OCCUPATION, CLASSIFIED BY SEX, FOR THE UNITED STATES: 1920 AND 1910—Con.

[The figures for 1910 for certain of the division totals and also for certain individual occupations have been corrected to conform to the classification for 1920.]

OCCUPATION.	1920			1910		
	Total.	Male.	Female.	Total.	Male.	Female.
Trade—Continued.						
Retail dealers[1]—Continued.						
Groceries	239,236	216,059	23,177	195,432	176,993	18,439
Hardware, stoves, and cutlery	41,144	40,453	691	39,663	38,980	683
Harness and saddlery	2,706	2,685	21	7,541	7,484	57
Hucksters and peddlers	50,402	48,493	1,909	80,415	76,630	3,785
Ice	8,203	8,166	37	7,361	7,220	141
Jewelry	21,433	20,652	781	29,962	29,403	559
Junk	22,749	22,596	153	15,219	15,079	140
Leather and hides	4,350	4,307	43	2,475	2,436	39
Lumber	27,687	27,589	98	27,250	26,997	253
Milk	13,104	12,509	595	14,694	13,851	843
Music and musical instruments	7,909	7,360	549	5,222	4,963	259
Newsdealers	8,474	7,808	666	7,075	6,534	541
Oil, paint, and wall paper	6,577	6,298	279	6,818	6,596	222
Opticians	12,632	11,743	889	6,284	5,954	330
Produce and provisions	34,473	32,873	1,600	29,639	28,358	1,281
Rags	2,024	1,985	39	1,975	1,805	170
Stationery	5,951	5,260	691	5,823	5,136	687
Other specified retail dealers	52,681	49,955	2,726	38,612	36,866	1,746
Not specified retail dealers	65,728	59,483	6,245	45,621	41,493	4,128
Salesmen and saleswomen	1,177,494	816,352	361,142	921,130	663,410	257,720
Auctioneers	5,048	5,045	3	3,990	3,985	5
Demonstrators	4,823	1,639	3,184	4,380	1,250	3,130
Sales agents	41,841	40,207	1,634	35,522	31,424	4,098
Salesmen and saleswomen (stores)	1,125,782	769,461	356,321	877,238	626,751	250,487
Undertakers	24,469	23,342	1,127	20,734	19,921	813
Wholesale dealers, importers, and exporters	73,574	72,780	794	51,048	50,123	925
Other pursuits (semiskilled)	67,611	52,106	15,505	41,640	34,068	7,572
Fruit graders and packers	8,074	4,988	3,086	4,715	2,677	2,038
Meat cutters	22,884	22,804	80	15,405	15,378	27
Packers, wholesale and retail trade	19,701	13,603	6,098	13,401	10,392	3,009
Other occupations	16,952	10,711	6,241	8,119	5,621	2,498
Public service (not elsewhere classified)	770,460	748,666	21,794	459,291	445,733	13,558
Firemen (fire department)	50,771	50,771		35,606	35,606	
Guards, watchmen, and doorkeepers	115,553	115,154	399	78,271	78,168	103
Laborers (public service)	106,915	105,385	1,530	67,234	66,505	729
Garbage men and scavengers	5,481	5,475	6	4,227	4,227	
Other laborers	101,434	99,910	1,524	63,007	62,278	729
Marshals, sheriffs, detectives, etc	32,214	30,968	1,246	23,599	23,219	380
Detectives	11,955	11,562	393	6,349	6,162	187
Marshals and constables	6,897	6,880	17	9,073	9,071	2
Probation and truant officers	2,679	1,899	780	1,043	855	188
Sheriffs	10,683	10,627	56	7,134	7,131	3
Officials and inspectors (city and county)	55,597	50,748	4,849	52,254	49,668	2,586
Officials and inspectors (city)	33,505	31,918	1,587	33,210	32,199	1,011
Officials and inspectors (county)	22,092	18,830	3,262	19,044	17,469	1,575
Officials and inspectors (state and United States)	80,334	67,944	12,390	52,926	43,389	9,537
Officials and inspectors (state)	9,126	8,596	530	7,202	6,662	540
Postmasters	31,935	20,727	11,208	27,849	19,127	8,722
Other United States officials	39,273	38,621	652	17,875	17,600	275
Policemen	82,120	81,884	236	61,980	61,980	
Soldiers, sailors, and marines[2]	225,503	225,503		77,153	77,153	
Other pursuits	21,453	20,309	1,144	10,268	10,045	223
Life-savers	2,287	2,285	2	2,158	2,158	
Lighthouse keepers	1,463	1,442	21	1,593	1,552	41
Other occupations	17,703	16,582	1,121	6,517	6,335	182

[1] Includes, also, managers and superintendents of retail stores.
[2] Includes only those resident in continental United States at the date of the enumeration.

TABLE 4.—TOTAL PERSONS 10 YEARS OF AGE AND OVER ENGAGED IN EACH SPECIFIED OCCUPATION, CLASSIFIED BY SEX, FOR THE UNITED STATES: 1920 AND 1910—Con.

[The figures for 1910 for certain of the division totals and also for certain individual occupations have been corrected to conform to the classification for 1920.]

OCCUPATION.	1920			1910		
	Total.	Male.	Female.	Total.	Male.	Female.
Professional service	2,143,889	1,127,391	1,016,498	1,693,361	959,470	733,891
Actors and showmen	48,172	33,818	14,354	48,393	35,293	13,100
Actors	28,361	15,124	13,237	28,297	16,305	11,992
Showmen	19,811	18,694	1,117	[1] 20,096	[1] 18,988	[1] 1,108
Architects	18,185	18,048	137	16,613	16,311	302
Artists, sculptors, and teachers of art	35,402	20,785	14,617	34,104	18,675	15,429
Authors, editors, and reporters	40,865	32,129	8,736	38,750	32,511	6,239
Authors	6,668	3,662	3,006	4,368	2,310	2,058
Editors and reporters	34,197	28,467	5,730	34,382	30,201	4,181
Chemists, assayers, and metallurgists	32,941	31,227	1,714	16,273	15,694	579
Clergymen	127,270	125,483	1,787	118,018	117,333	685
College presidents and professors [2]	33,407	23,332	10,075	15,668	12,710	2,958
Dentists	56,152	54,323	1,829	39,997	38,743	1,254
Designers, draftsmen, and inventors	70,651	62,987	7,664	47,449	44,437	3,012
Designers	15,410	9,758	5,652	11,788	9,211	2,577
Draftsmen	52,865	50,880	1,985	33,314	32,923	391
Inventors	2,376	2,349	27	2,347	2,303	44
Lawyers, judges, and justices	122,519	120,781	1,738	114,704	114,146	558
Musicians and teachers of music	130,265	57,587	72,678	139,310	54,832	84,478
Osteopaths	5,030	3,367	1,663	(3)	(3)	(3)
Photographers	34,259	27,140	7,119	31,775	26,811	4,964
Physicians and surgeons	144,977	137,758	7,219	[3] 151,132	[3] 142,117	[3] 9,015
Teachers	761,766	122,525	639,241	599,237	121,210	478,027
Teachers (athletics, dancing, etc.)	9,711	5,677	4,034	3,931	2,768	1,163
Teachers (school)	752,055	116,848	635,207	595,306	118,442	476,864
Technical engineers	136,121	136,080	41	88,755	88,744	11
Civil engineers and surveyors	64,660	64,642	18	52,033	52,028	5
Electrical engineers	27,077	27,065	12	[4] 15,278	[4] 15,272	[4] 6
Mechanical engineers [5]	37,689	37,678	11	14,514	14,514	
Mining engineers	6,695	6,695		6,930	6,930	
Trained nurses	149,128	5,464	143,664	82,327	5,819	76,508
Veterinary surgeons	13,494	13,493	1	11,652	11,652	
Other professional pursuits	35,018	15,745	19,273	15,677	7,585	8,092
Aeronauts	1,312	1,304	8	(1)	(1)	(1)
Librarians	15,297	1,795	13,502	7,423	1,594	5,829
Other occupations	18,409	12,646	5,763	8,254	5,991	2,263
Semiprofessional pursuits	116,555	70,626	45,929	64,926	44,532	20,394
Abstracters, notaries, and justices of peace	10,071	8,588	1,483	7,445	6,660	785
Fortune tellers, hypnotists, spiritualists, etc	928	230	698	1,600	380	1,220
Healers (except osteopaths and physicians and surgeons)	14,774	6,872	7,902	6,834	2,162	4,672
Keepers of charitable and penal institutions	12,884	7,953	4,931	7,491	5,246	2,245
Keepers of pleasure resorts, race tracks, etc	3,360	3,163	197	2,929	2,706	223
Officials of lodges, societies, etc	11,736	9,574	2,162	8,215	6,245	1,970
Religious, charity, and welfare workers	41,078	14,151	26,927	15,970	7,081	8,889
Theatrical owners, managers, and officials	18,395	17,130	1,257	11,322	11,027	295
Turfmen and sportsmen	1,826	1,005	1	2,744	2,743	1
Other occupations	1,503	1,132	371	976	282	34

[1] Aeronauts were included with "Showmen" in 1910.
[2] Probably includes some teachers in schools below collegiate rank.
[3] Osteopaths were included with "Physicians and surgeons" in 1910.
[4] Figures for 1910 estimated.
[5] Includes, also, all technical engineers not elsewhere classified.

TABLE 4.—TOTAL PERSONS 10 YEARS OF AGE AND OVER ENGAGED IN EACH SPECIFIED OCCUPATION, CLASSIFIED BY SEX, FOR THE UNITED STATES: 1920 AND 1910—Con.

[The figures for 1910 for certain of the division totals and also for certain individual occupations have been corrected to conform to the classification for 1920.]

OCCUPATION.	1920			1910		
	Total.	Male.	Female.	Total.	Male.	Female.
Professional service—Continued.						
Attendants and helpers (professional service)	31,712	14,693	17,019	(1)	(1)	(1)
Dentists' assistants and apprentices	6,708	1,768	4,940	2,048	544	1,504
Librarians' assistants and attendants	2,279	1,067	1,212	3,299	507	2,792
Physicians' and surgeons' attendants	7,051	641	6,410	4,140	689	3,451
Stage hands and circus helpers	5,803	5,377	426	6,836	6,444	392
Theater ushers	5,221	2,868	2,353	2,278	2,131	147
Other attendants and helpers	4,650	2,972	1,678	(1)	(1)	(1)
Domestic and personal service	3,404,892	1,217,968	2,186,924	3,772,559	1,241,338	2,531,221
Barbers, hairdressers, and manicurists	216,211	182,965	33,246	195,275	172,977	22,298
Billiard room, dance hall, skating rink, etc., keepers	24,897	24,655	242	16,761	15,943	818
Billiard and pool room keepers	22,140	22,067	73	13,859	13,700	159
Dance hall, skating rink, etc., keepers	2,757	2,588	169	2,902	2,243	659
Boarding and lodging house keepers	133,392	18,652	114,740	165,452	23,052	142,400
Bootblacks	15,175	15,142	33	14,020	14,000	20
Charwomen and cleaners	36,803	11,848	24,955	34,034	7,195	26,839
Elevator tenders	40,713	33,376	7,337	25,035	25,010	25
Hotel keepers and managers	55,583	41,449	14,134	64,504	50,269	14,235
Housekeepers and stewards	221,612	17,262	204,350	189,273	15,940	173,333
Janitors and sextons	178,628	149,590	29,038	113,081	91,629	21,452
Laborers (domestic and professional service)	32,893	31,224	1,669	53,480	50,265	3,215
Launderers and laundresses (not in laundry)	396,756	10,882	385,874	533,697	13,693	520,004
Laundry operatives [2]	120,715	39,968	80,747	112,264	35,909	76,355
Foremen and overseers	3,611	2,076	1,535	3,071	1,674	1,397
Laborers	13,107	6,570	6,537	8,786	5,432	3,354
Other operatives [2]	103,997	31,322	72,675	100,407	28,803	71,604
Laundry owners, officials, and managers [2]	13,692	12,239	1,453	18,043	17,057	986
Managers and officials	4,665	4,081	584	2,602	2,362	240
Owners and proprietors [2]	9,027	8,158	869	15,441	14,695	746
Midwives and nurses (not trained)	156,769	19,338	137,431	133,043	15,926	117,117
Midwives	4,773		4,773	6,205		6,205
Nurses (not trained)	151,996	19,338	132,658	126,838	15,926	110,912
Porters (except in stores)	88,168	87,683	485	84,128	84,055	73
Porters, domestic and professional service	43,208	42,929	279	54,612	54,560	52
Porters, steam railroad	22,513	22,486	27	17,298	17,297	1
Other porters (except in stores)	22,447	22,268	179	12,218	12,198	20
Restaurant, café, and lunch room keepers	87,987	72,343	15,644	60,832	50,316	10,516
Servants	1,270,946	258,813	1,012,133	1,572,225	262,676	1,309,549
Bell boys, chore boys, etc	17,231	16,472	759	18,329	17,667	662
Butlers	10,690	10,689	1	13,168	13,168	
Chambermaids	29,302	250	29,052	39,789	187	39,602
Coachmen and footmen	2,427	2,427		25,667	25,667	
Cooks	398,475	129,857	268,618	450,440	117,004	333,436
Ladies' maids, valets, etc	5,791	1,268	4,523	} 24,222	2,436	21,786
Nurse maids	11,890	11	11,879			
Other servants	795,140	97,839	697,301	1,000,610	86,547	914,063
Waiters	228,985	112,064	116,921	188,293	102,495	85,798
Other pursuits	84,967	78,475	6,492	199,119	192,931	6,188
Bartenders	26,085	25,976	109	101,234	100,984	250
Bathhouse keepers and attendants	2,858	2,032	826	4,595	3,125	1,470
Cemetery keepers	5,540	5,496	44	4,842	4,811	31
Cleaners and renovators (clothing, etc.)	21,667	17,094	4,573	14,860	12,215	2,645
Hunters, trappers, and guides	7,332	7,288	44	3,887	3,840	47
Saloon keepers	17,835	17,312	523	68,215	66,724	1,491
Umbrella menders and scissors grinders	917	899	18	1,053	1,016	37
Other occupations	2,733	2,378	355	433	216	217

[1] Comparable figures for 1910 not available.
[2] Some of the owners of hand laundries probably are included with laundry operatives.

TABLE 4.—TOTAL PERSONS 10 YEARS OF AGE AND OVER ENGAGED IN EACH SPECIFIED OCCUPATION, CLASSIFIED BY SEX, FOR THE UNITED STATES: 1920 AND 1910—Con.

[The figures for 1910 for certain of the division totals and also for certain individual occupations have been corrected to conform to the classification for 1920.]

OCCUPATION.	1920			1910		
	Total.	Male.	Female.	Total.	Male.	Female.
Clerical occupations	3,126,541	1,700,425	1,426,116	1,737,053	1,143,829	593,224
Agents, canvassers, and collectors	175,772	159,941	15,831	105,127	96,325	8,802
Agents	130,338	121,428	8,910	50,785	48,495	2,290
Canvassers	14,705	10,514	4,191	18,595	13,980	4,615
Collectors	30,729	27,999	2,730	35,747	33,850	1,897
Bookkeepers, cashiers, and accountants	734,688	375,564	359,124	486,700	299,545	187,155
Accountants and auditors	118,451	105,073	13,378	39,239	35,653	3,586
Bookkeepers and cashiers	616,237	270,491	345,746	447,461	263,892	183,569
Clerks (except clerks in stores)	1,487,905	1,015,742	472,163	720,498	597,833	122,665
Shipping clerks	123,684	118,944	4,740	80,353	78,192	2,161
Weighers	16,229	14,730	1,499	11,564	10,984	580
Other clerks	1,347,992	882,068	465,924	628,581	508,657	119,924
Messenger, bundle, and office boys and girls [1]	113,022	98,768	14,254	108,035	96,748	11,287
Bundle and cash boys and girls	6,973	2,506	4,467	10,866	4,274	6,592
Messenger, errand, and office boys and girls [1]	106,049	96,262	9,787	97,169	92,474	4,695
Stenographers and typists	615,154	50,410	564,744	316,693	53,378	263,315

[1] Except telegraph messengers.

TABLE 5.—NUMBER AND PROPORTION OF PERSONS 10 YEARS OF AGE AND OVER ENGAGED IN GAINFUL OCCUPATIONS, BY DIVISIONS AND STATES: 1920 AND 1910.

DIVISION AND STATE.	POPULATION 10 YEARS OF AGE AND OVER: **1920**			POPULATION 10 YEARS OF AGE AND OVER: **1910**		
	Total number.	Engaged in gainful occupations.		Total number.	Engaged in gainful occupations.	
		Number.	Per cent.		Number.	Per cent.
United States................	82,739,315	41,614,248	50.3	71,580,270	38,167,336	53.3
GEOGRAPHIC DIVISIONS:						
New England................	5,945,989	3,234,392	54.4	5,330,914	2,914,680	54.7
Middle Atlantic.............	17,666,354	9,240,216	52.3	15,446,515	8,208,885	53.1
East North Central..........	17,130,786	8,515,849	49.7	14,568,949	7,257,953	49.8
West North Central.........	9,889,740	4,587,996	46.4	9,097,311	4,449,043	48.9
South Atlantic..............	10,513,447	5,339,999	50.8	9,012,826	5,187,729	57.6
East South Central.........	6,677,229	3,310,844	49.6	6,178,578	3,599,695	58.3
West South Central.........	7,739,536	3,716,248	48.0	6,394,043	3,507,081	54.8
Mountain...................	2,564,463	1,254,994	48.9	2,054,249	1,107,937	53.9
Pacific....................	4,611,771	2,413,710	52.3	3,496,885	1,934,333	55.3
NEW ENGLAND:						
Maine......................	621,233	309,858	49.9	603,893	305,457	50.6
New Hampshire.............	361,930	192,827	53.3	354,118	191,703	54.1
Vermont...................	284,472	138,484	48.7	289,128	144,089	49.8
Massachusetts.............	3,106,769	1,728,318	55.6	2,742,684	1,531,068	55.8
Rhode Island..............	483,788	275,000	56.8	440,065	251,901	57.2
Connecticut...............	1,087,797	589,905	54.2	901,026	490,462	54.4
MIDDLE ATLANTIC:						
New York..................	8,402,786	4,503,204	53.6	7,410,819	4,003,844	54.0
New Jersey................	2,494,246	1,310,653	52.5	2,027,946	1,074,360	53.0
Pennsylvania..............	6,769,322	3,426,359	50.6	6,007,750	3,130,681	52.1
EAST NORTH CENTRAL:						
Ohio......................	4,624,456	2,301,516	49.8	3,848,747	1,919,055	49.9
Indiana...................	2,356,214	1,117,032	47.4	2,160,405	1,036,710	48.0
Illinois..................	5,184,943	2,627,738	50.7	4,493,734	2,296,778	51.1
Michigan..................	2,895,606	1,474,014	50.9	2,236,252	1,112,998	49.8
Wisconsin.................	2,069,567	995,549	48.1	1,829,811	892,412	48.8
WEST NORTH CENTRAL:						
Minnesota.................	1,877,132	907,013	48.3	1,628,635	835,452	51.3
Iowa......................	1,913,155	858,698	44.9	1,760,286	826,313	46.9
Missouri..................	2,737,771	1,317,160	48.1	2,594,600	1,288,336	49.7
North Dakota..............	470,210	207,082	44.0	424,730	217,418	51.2
South Dakota..............	482,195	216,571	44.9	443,466	219,077	49.4
Nebraska..................	1,012,552	457,081	45.1	924,032	441,114	47.7
Kansas....................	1,396,725	624,391	44.7	1,321,562	621,333	47.0
SOUTH ATLANTIC:						
Delaware..................	178,930	91,224	51.0	163,080	85,863	52.7
Maryland..................	1,158,953	603,478	52.1	1,023,950	541,164	52.9
District of Columbia......	377,295	236,027	62.6	279,088	157,965	56.6
Virginia..................	1,748,868	833,576	47.7	1,536,297	795,568	51.8
West Virginia.............	1,083,395	491,116	45.3	903,822	448,490	49.6
North Carolina............	1,844,673	895,852	48.6	1,578,595	947,839	60.0
South Carolina............	1,219,316	674,257	55.3	1,078,161	728,627	67.6
Georgia...................	2,150,230	1,129,157	52.5	1,885,111	1,160,126	61.5
Florida...................	751,787	385,312	51.3	564,722	322,087	57.0
EAST SOUTH CENTRAL:						
Kentucky..................	1,837,434	851,122	46.3	1,722,644	866,980	50.3
Tennessee.................	1,770,762	830,096	46.9	1,621,179	855,546	52.8
Alabama...................	1,730,421	908,216	52.5	1,541,575	997,524	64.7
Mississippi...............	1,338,612	721,410	53.9	1,293,180	879,645	68.0
WEST SOUTH CENTRAL:						
Arkansas..................	1,302,905	634,564	48.7	1,134,087	672,403	59.3
Louisiana.................	1,366,066	681,233	49.9	1,213,576	679,183	56.0
Oklahoma..................	1,513,951	681,428	45.0	1,197,476	598,629	50.0
Texas.....................	3,556,614	1,719,023	48.3	2,848,904	1,556,866	54.6
MOUNTAIN:						
Montana...................	421,443	214,183	50.8	303,551	178,747	58.9
Idaho.....................	326,051	153,459	47.1	249,018	131,088	52.6
Wyoming...................	150,993	81,536	54.0	117,585	73,606	62.6
Colorado..................	747,485	366,457	49.0	640,846	338,724	52.9
New Mexico................	267,595	122,031	45.6	240,990	121,497	50.4
Arizona...................	255,461	130,579	51.1	157,659	87,825	55.7
Utah......................	331,530	149,201	45.0	274,778	131,540	47.9
Nevada....................	63,905	37,548	58.8	69,822	44,910	64.3
PACIFIC:						
Washington................	1,101,929	578,667	52.5	933,556	521,501	55.9
Oregon....................	638,987	322,283	50.4	555,631	305,164	54.9
California................	2,870,855	1,512,760	52.7	2,007,698	1,107,668	55.2

TABLE 6.—NUMBER AND PROPORTION OF MALES 10 YEARS OF AGE AND OVER
ENGAGED IN GAINFUL OCCUPATIONS, BY DIVISIONS AND STATES: 1920 AND 1910.

DIVISION AND STATE.	MALES 10 YEARS OF AGE AND OVER: 1920			MALES 10 YEARS OF AGE AND OVER: 1910		
	Total number.	Engaged in gainful occupations.		Total number.	Engaged in gainful occupations.	
		Number.	Per cent.		Number.	Per cent.
United States........................	42,289,969	33,064,737	78.2	37,027,558	30,091,564	81.3
GEOGRAPHIC DIVISIONS:						
New England........................	2,940,130	2,363,377	80.4	2,649,897	2,139,529	80.7
Middle Atlantic....................	8,890,489	7,122,699	80.1	7,863,584	6,380,198	81.1
East North Central................	8,837,101	6,951,808	78.7	7,529,768	5,975,363	79.4
West North Central................	5,112,443	3,815,681	74.6	4,807,164	3,758,603	78.2
South Atlantic.....................	5,282,930	4,096,041	77.5	4,528,942	3,797,257	83.8
East South Central................	3,348,984	2,608,411	77.9	3,116,286	2,659,090	85.3
West South Central................	3,999,088	3,049,275	76.2	3,334,078	2,760,782	82.8
Mountain..........................	1,398,659	1,077,774	77.1	1,185,047	967,924	81.7
Pacific............................	2,480,145	1,979,671	79.8	2,012,792	1,652,818	82.1
NEW ENGLAND:						
Maine.............................	314,575	245,013	77.9	307,375	242,175	78.8
New Hampshire....................	181,286	143,525	79.2	178,151	143,363	80.5
Vermont...........................	144,525	111,585	77.2	148,686	115,781	77.9
Massachusetts.....................	1,514,904	1,225,163	80.9	1,340,517	1,086,767	81.1
Rhode Island......................	237,116	194,438	82.0	219,221	180,962	82.5
Connecticut.......................	547,724	443,653	81.0	455,947	370,481	81.3
MIDDLE ATLANTIC:						
New York..........................	4,186,818	3,367,909	80.4	3,727,218	3,020,158	81.0
New Jersey........................	1,256,332	1,014,663	80.8	1,029,649	834,795	81.1
Pennsylvania......................	3,447,339	2,740,127	79.5	3,106,717	2,525,245	81.3
EAST NORTH CENTRAL:						
Ohio..............................	2,382,040	1,891,546	79.4	1,970,027	1,572,343	79.8
Indiana...........................	1,198,722	931,647	77.7	1,108,767	880,979	79.5
Illinois..........................	2,647,505	2,086,800	78.8	2,333,230	1,865,422	80.0
Michigan..........................	1,536,629	1,228,631	80.0	1,163,835	926,815	79.6
Wisconsin.........................	1,072,205	813,184	75.8	953,909	729,804	76.5
WEST NORTH CENTRAL:						
Minnesota.........................	986,877	742,947	75.3	882,046	689,847	78.2
Iowa..............................	980,360	717,377	73.2	912,728	694,799	76.1
Missouri..........................	1,385,747	1,072,545	77.4	1,334,851	1,076,772	80.7
North Dakota......................	251,989	178,754	70.9	240,658	188,372	78.3
South Dakota......................	258,683	186,885	72.2	245,991	190,363	77.4
Nebraska..........................	528,290	385,292	72.9	491,706	377,811	76.8
Kansas............................	720,497	531,881	73.8	699,184	540,639	77.3
SOUTH ATLANTIC:						
Delaware..........................	91,802	73,122	79.7	83,787	68,317	81.5
Maryland..........................	582,933	466,257	80.0	507,421	410,884	81.0
District of Columbia..............	173,574	143,401	82.6	131,983	105,044	79.6
Virginia..........................	886,493	677,366	76.4	770,504	626,868	81.4
West Virginia.....................	570,617	433,677	76.0	483,221	394,390	81.6
North Carolina....................	917,883	693,155	75.5	781,434	674,849	86.4
South Carolina....................	604,224	468,601	77.6	531,692	460,794	86.7
Georgia...........................	1,069,254	840,412	78.6	939,791	807,185	85.9
Florida...........................	386,150	300,050	77.7	299,109	248,926	83.2
EAST SOUTH CENTRAL:						
Kentucky..........................	933,175	719,629	77.1	874,306	719,369	82.3
Tennessee.........................	885,952	677,988	76.5	817,174	682,248	83.5
Alabama...........................	861,344	684,348	79.5	773,415	683,194	88.3
Mississippi:......................	668,513	526,446	78.7	651,391	574,279	88.2
WEST SOUTH CENTRAL:						
Arkansas..........................	667,972	518,754	77.7	588,133	510,410	86.8
Louisiana.........................	684,958	528,507	77.2	612,534	501,574	81.9
Oklahoma..........................	707,753	586,834	73.6	648,116	520,376	80.3
Texas.............................	1,848,405	1,415,180	76.6	1,485,295	1,228,422	82.7
MOUNTAIN:						
Montana...........................	235,586	185,905	78.9	190,500	159,896	84.0
Idaho.............................	179,948	135,950	75.5	146,783	118,050	80.4
Wyoming...........................	88,316	72,134	81.7	77,260	67,593	87.5
Colorado..........................	395,632	303,870	76.8	350,684	285,083	81.3
New Mexico........................	143,826	107,090	74.5	131,828	106,418	80.7
Arizona...........................	143,651	112,193	78.1	94,812	77,236	81.5
Utah..............................	172,295	127,418	74.0	147,009	113,113	76.9
Nevada............................	39,405	33,214	84.3	46,408	40,535	87.3
PACIFIC:						
Washington........................	605,288	485,767	80.3	552,586	455,375	82.4
Oregon............................	343,059	267,791	78.1	324,717	264,691	81.5
California........................	1,531,798	1,226,113	80.0	1,135,489	932,752	82.1

TABLE 7.—NUMBER AND PROPORTION OF FEMALES 10 YEARS OF AGE AND OVER ENGAGED IN GAINFUL OCCUPATIONS, BY DIVISIONS AND STATES: 1920 AND 1910.

DIVISION AND STATE.	FEMALES 10 YEARS OF AGE AND OVER: 1920			FEMALES 10 YEARS OF AGE AND OVER: 1910		
	Total number.	Engaged in gainful occupations.		Total number.	Engaged in gainful occupations.	
		Number.	Per cent.		Number.	Per cent.
United States	40,449,346	8,549,511	21.1	34,552,712	8,075,772	23.4
GEOGRAPHIC DIVISIONS:						
New England	3,005,859	871,015	29.0	2,681,017	775,151	28.9
Middle Atlantic	8,775,865	2,117,517	24.1	7,582,931	1,828,687	24.1
East North Central	8,293,685	1,564,041	18.9	7,039,181	1,282,590	18.2
West North Central	4,777,297	772,315	16.2	4,290,147	690,440	16.1
South Atlantic	5,230,517	1,243,958	23.8	4,483,884	1,390,472	31.0
East South Central	3,328,245	702,433	21.1	3,062,292	940,605	30.7
West South Central	3,740,448	666,973	17.8	3,059,965	746,299	24.4
Mountain	1,165,804	177,220	15.2	869,202	140,013	16.1
Pacific	2,131,626	434,039	20.4	1,484,093	281,515	19.0
NEW ENGLAND:						
Maine	306,658	64,845	21.1	296,518	63,282	21.3
New Hampshire	180,644	49,302	27.3	175,967	48,340	27.5
Vermont	139,947	26,899	19.2	140,442	28,308	20.2
Massachusetts	1,591,865	503,155	31.6	1,402,167	444,301	31.7
Rhode Island	246,672	80,562	32.7	220,844	70,939	32.1
Connecticut	540,073	146,252	27.1	445,079	119,981	27.0
MIDDLE ATLANTIC:						
New York	4,215,968	1,135,295	26.9	3,683,601	983,686	26.7
New Jersey	1,237,914	295,990	23.9	998,297	239,565	24.0
Pennsylvania	3,321,983	686,232	20.7	2,901,033	605,436	20.9
EAST NORTH CENTRAL:						
Ohio	2,242,416	409,970	18.3	1,878,720	346,712	18.5
Indiana	1,157,492	185,385	16.0	1,051,638	155,731	14.8
Illinois	2,537,438	540,938	21.3	2,160,504	431,356	20.0
Michigan	1,358,977	245,383	18.1	1,072,417	186,183	17.4
Wisconsin	997,362	182,365	18.3	875,902	162,608	18.6
WEST NORTH CENTRAL:						
Minnesota	890,255	164,066	18.4	746,589	145,605	19.5
Iowa	932,795	141,321	15.2	847,558	131,514	15.5
Missouri	1,352,024	244,615	18.1	1,259,749	211,564	16.8
North Dakota	218,221	28,328	13.0	184,072	29,046	15.8
South Dakota	223,512	29,686	13.3	197,475	28,714	14.5
Nebraska	484,262	71,789	14.8	432,326	63,303	14.6
Kansas	676,228	92,510	13.7	622,378	80,694	13.0
SOUTH ATLANTIC:						
Delaware	87,128	18,102	20.8	79,293	17,546	22.1
Maryland	576,020	137,221	23.8	516,529	130,280	25.2
District of Columbia	203,721	92,626	45.5	147,105	52,921	36.0
Virginia	862,375	156,210	18.1	765,793	168,700	22.0
West Virginia	512,778	57,439	11.2	420,601	54,100	12.9
North Carolina	926,790	202,697	21.9	797,161	272,990	34.2
South Carolina	615,092	205,656	33.4	546,469	267,833	49.0
Georgia	1,080,976	288,745	26.7	945,320	352,941	37.3
Florida	365,637	85,262	23.3	265,613	73,161	27.5
EAST SOUTH CENTRAL:						
Kentucky	904,259	131,493	14.5	848,338	147,611	17.4
Tennessee	884,810	152,108	17.2	804,005	173,298	21.6
Alabama	869,077	223,868	25.8	768,160	314,330	40.9
Mississippi	670,099	194,964	29.1	641,789	305,366	47.6
WEST SOUTH CENTRAL:						
Arkansas	634,933	115,810	18.2	545,954	161,993	29.7
Louisiana	681,108	152,726	22.4	601,042	177,609	29.6
Oklahoma	716,198	94,594	13.2	549,360	78,253	14.2
Texas	1,708,209	303,843	17.8	1,363,609	328,444	24.1
MOUNTAIN:						
Montana	185,857	28,278	15.2	113,288	18,851	16.6
Idaho	146,103	17,509	12.0	102,235	13,038	12.8
Wyoming	62,677	9,402	15.0	40,325	6,013	14.9
Colorado	351,853	62,587	17.8	290,162	53,641	18.5
New Mexico	123,769	14,941	12.1	109,162	15,079	13.8
Arizona	111,810	18,386	16.4	62,847	10,589	16.8
Utah	159,235	21,783	13.7	127,769	18,427	14.4
Nevada	24,500	4,334	17.7	23,414	4,375	18.7
PACIFIC:						
Washington	496,641	92,900	18.7	380,970	66,126	17.4
Oregon	295,928	54,492	18.4	230,914	40,473	17.5
California	1,339,057	286,647	21.4	872,209	174,916	20.1

TABLE 8.—NUMBER OF PERSONS 10 YEARS OF AGE AND OVER IN EACH GENERAL DIVISION OF OCCUPATIONS, BY DIVISIONS AND STATES: 1920.

DIVISION AND STATE.	Total persons occupied.	Agriculture, forestry, and animal husbandry.	Extraction of minerals.	Manufacturing and mechanical industries.	Transportation.	Trade.	Public service (not elsewhere classified).	Professional service.	Domestic and personal service.	Clerical occupations.
U. S.	41,614,248	10,953,158	1,090,223	12,818,524	3,063,582	4,242,979	770,460	2,143,889	3,404,892	3,126,541
GEOG. DIVS.:										
New England.	3,234,392	255,580	4,853	1,632,267	215,191	329,470	66,320	175,286	260,441	294,984
Mid. Atlantic.	9,240,216	660,240	343,916	3,812,388	799,229	1,074,964	188,695	523,989	835,019	1,001,776
E. N. Central.	8,515,849	1,633,790	216,238	3,171,064	628,947	943,646	128,335	445,099	614,823	733,907
W. N. Central	4,587,996	1,689,253	74,141	962,321	358,829	528,362	61,375	276,287	342,405	295,023
S. Atlantic...	5,339,999	2,177,438	134,221	1,202,668	324,221	395,864	122,451	211,044	493,084	279,008
E. S. Central.	3,310,844	1,805,142	104,999	523,407	170,665	213,568	36,058	107,134	250,497	99,374
W. S. Central.	3,716,248	1,808,084	83,069	588,383	247,665	319,709	73,123	154,074	284,856	157,285
Mountain....	1,254,994	427,158	93,064	227,431	111,517	123,730	30,918	76,369	96,450	68,357
Pacific.......	2,413,710	496,473	35,722	698,595	207,318	313,666	63,185	174,607	227,317	196,827
NEW ENGLAND:										
Maine........	309,858	77,304	748	120,248	22,640	27,539	5,456	16,624	24,057	15,242
N. Hampshire	192,827	30,426	406	99,323	12,351	14,661	2,940	9,356	14,064	9,300
Vermont.....	138,484	44,260	1,899	44,672	9,278	10,967	1,851	7,621	11,630	6,306
Massachusetts	1,728,318	57,555	1,198	887,898	121,899	193,719	37,776	98,763	149,060	180,450
Rhode Island.	275,000	8,354	160	161,920	15,904	26,554	8,452	12,081	19,207	22,368
Connecticut..	589,905	37,681	442	318,206	33,119	56,030	9,845	30,841	42,423	61,318
MID. ATLANTIC:										
New York....	4,503,204	314,774	7,549	1,757,108	403,574	591,334	100,374	288,764	472,961	566,766
New Jersey...	1,310,653	61,153	3,935	628,575	111,115	144,593	34,624	70,119	104,913	151,626
Pennsylvania.	3,426,359	284,313	332,432	1,426,705	284,540	339,037	53,697	165,106	257,145	283,384
E. N. CENTRAL:										
Ohio.........	2,301,516	360,655	59,573	959,382	173,581	246,235	32,254	117,470	161,737	190,629
Indiana......	1,117,032	294,006	33,322	377,446	83,968	114,535	14,340	56,833	73,299	69,283
Illinois.......	2,627,738	380,705	90,644	876,000	220,361	347,804	51,227	146,641	215,211	299,145
Michigan.....	1,474,014	290,374	28,798	618,425	90,394	144,044	19,953	72,119	96,141	113,766
Wisconsin....	995,549	308,050	3,901	339,811	60,643	91,028	10,561	52,036	68,435	61,084
W. N. CENTRAL:										
Minnesota....	907,013	307,876	14,994	204,002	70,492	104,431	11,774	55,482	70,120	67,842
Iowa.........	858,698	327,124	14,196	176,522	67,315	101,886	9,533	55,991	59,505	46,626
Missouri.....	1,317,160	396,863	21,516	330,883	101,589	158,893	18,456	69,191	114,085	105,384
N. Dakota....	207,082	119,886	1,298	19,187	12,462	18,952	1,694	13,018	13,166	7,419
S. Dakota....	216,571	117,277	1,437	26,282	12,830	21,983	2,013	13,782	13,253	7,714
Nebraska.....	457,081	187,115	388	83,901	36,608	54,863	5,663	30,135	31,239	27,169
Kansas.......	624,391	233,112	20,312	121,544	57,233	67,354	12,242	38,688	41,037	32,869
SO. ATLANTIC:										
Delaware.....	91,224	17,694	70	34,649	7,945	8,080	1,530	4,235	8,696	8,325
Maryland.....	603,478	95,881	6,637	207,415	55,939	66,107	21,782	29,704	67,234	52,870
Dist.Columbia	236,027	947	79	44,505	16,745	22,782	16,070	19,289	42,579	73,031
Virginia......	833,576	301,707	16,205	196,142	63,617	65,101	31,851	34,342	84,603	40,008
W. Virginia..	491,116	125,592	103,151	117,031	37,557	35,109	4,341	22,521	27,053	18,761
N. Carolina..	895,852	477,686	1,990	211,022	36,337	52,895	8,965	29,677	56,649	20,631
S. Carolina...	674,257	420,635	624	109,544	21,932	33,730	10,607	17,856	47,220	12,109
Georgia.......	1,129,157	613,357	2,466	181,633	54,751	76,532	19,582	35,937	106,896	38,003
Florida.......	385,312	123,939	2,999	100,727	29,398	35,528	7,814	17,483	52,154	15,270
E. S. CENTRAL:										
Kentucky....	851,122	393,749	51,471	147,034	49,806	64,848	16,620	31,929	60,761	34,904
Tennessee....	830,096	400,134	17,630	150,703	51,450	67,429	7,683	30,626	73,470	30,971
Alabama.....	908,216	504,645	35,639	150,711	42,085	50,089	6,775	25,398	70,812	22,062
Mississippi...	721,410	506,614	259	74,959	27,324	31,202	4,980	19,181	45,454	11,437
W. S. CENTRAL:										
Arkansas.....	634,564	408,651	5,556	76,334	28,725	38,463	8,073	20,418	34,723	13,621
Louisiana.....	681,233	290,936	7,669	139,144	50,924	54,028	10,365	23,436	72,670	32,061
Oklahoma....	681,428	314,657	38,349	104,785	43,547	64,711	8,968	34,275	42,398	29,738
Texas........	1,719,023	793,840	31,495	268,120	124,469	162,507	45,717	75,945	135,065	81,865
MOUNTAIN:										
Montana.....	214,188	66,000	16,718	32,629	18,520	10,108	2,900	12,634	15,667	10,494
Idaho........	153,459	72,860	5,132	24,900	11,900	12,832	1,649	8,882	9,000	6,131
Wyoming....	81,536	26,045	8,790	15,364	9,857	6,151	1,588	4,161	6,000	3,530
Colorado.....	366,457	100,153	23,382	73,924	32,210	45,730	6,984	24,963	33,018	26,093
New Mexico..	122,031	55,033	7,310	16,118	10,982	8,133	6,411	6,164	8,382	3,498
Arizona......	130,579	36,199	15,437	24,055	11,589	11,314	8,353	7,205	10,175	6,252
Utah.........	149,201	43,259	10,117	33,594	12,429	16,543	2,468	9,997	10,171	10,623
Nevada......	37,548	8,589	6,178	7,182	4,319	2,829	595	2,373	3,747	1,736
PACIFIC:										
Washington..	578,667	131,526	8,821	179,539	53,396	67,345	12,944	36,332	47,224	41,540
Oregon.......	322,283	92,000	2,203	88,425	29,074	36,922	4,662	21,863	25,252	21,882
California....	1,512,760	272,947	24,698	430,631	124,848	209,399	45,579	116,412	154,841	133,405

TABLE 9.—NUMBER OF MALES 10 YEARS OF AGE AND OVER IN EACH GENERAL DIVISION OF OCCUPATIONS, BY DIVISIONS AND STATES: 1920.

DIVISION AND STATE.	Total males occupied.	Agriculture, forestry, and animal husbandry.	Extraction of minerals.	Manufacturing and mechanical industries.	Transportation.	Trade.	Public service (not elsewhere classified).	Professional service.	Domestic and personal service.	Clerical occupations.
U. S.	33,064,737	9,869,030	1,087,359	10,888,183	2,850,528	3,575,187	748,666	1,127,391	1,217,968	1,700,425
GEOG. DIVS:										
New England	2,363,377	247,478	4,843	1,253,096	198,556	274,306	65,022	87,538	92,175	140,363
Mid. Atlantic.	7,122,699	639,254	343,032	3,126,524	741,491	900,307	185,584	294,824	340,120	551,563
E. N. Central.	6,951,808	1,587,033	215,637	2,799,796	577,811	781,712	124,802	237,951	235,962	391,104
W. N. Central	3,815,681	1,642,663	73,995	849,681	332,124	450,368	57,581	124,742	128,032	156,495
South Atlantic	4,096,041	1,797,738	133,843	1,012,013	308,651	340,787	119,639	110,521	117,631	155,218
E. S. Central.	2,608,411	1,494,091	104,792	454,116	162,267	185,276	34,552	55,462	57,184	60,671
W. S. Central.	3,049,275	1,567,024	82,740	543,527	232,309	277,152	70,896	81,596	94,998	99,033
Mountain	1,077,774	413,355	92,851	210,636	105,500	105,644	29,374	39,420	41,522	39,472
Pacific	1,979,671	480,394	35,626	638,794	191,819	259,635	61,216	95,337	110,344	106,506
NEW ENGLAND:										
Maine	245,013	75,203	745	97,295	21,402	23,171	5,188	7,212	7,359	7,438
N. Hampshire	143,525	29,390	404	74,373	11,649	12,203	2,821	4,272	4,248	4,165
Vermont	111,585	43,052	1,898	38,257	8,650	9,358	1,685	3,131	2,624	2,930
Massachusetts	1,225,163	55,759	1,195	668,645	111,350	160,831	37,232	50,626	54,294	85,231
Rhode Island.	194,438	8,084	160	116,670	14,710	22,126	8,383	6,248	7,270	10,787
Connecticut	443,653	35,990	441	257,856	30,795	46,617	9,713	16,049	16,380	29,812
MID. ATLANTIC:										
New York	3,367,909	305,505	7,435	1,406,004	370,154	505,254	98,691	162,195	209,493	303,178
New Jersey	1,014,663	59,200	3,922	516,750	104,616	124,213	34,257	41,913	42,334	87,458
Pennsylvania	2,740,127	274,549	331,675	1,203,770	266,721	270,840	52,636	90,716	88,293	160,927
E. N. CENTRAL:										
Ohio	1,891,546	349,997	59,359	857,307	160,339	202,635	31,522	66,016	60,839	103,532
Indiana	931,647	286,552	33,276	331,848	77,925	95,511	13,851	30,586	25,732	36,366
Illinois	2,086,800	371,237	90,528	753,458	201,205	290,437	50,041	80,988	89,807	159,099
Michigan	1,228,631	281,562	28,582	562,838	82,530	119,309	19,303	36,863	36,882	60,762
Wisconsin	813,184	297,685	3,892	294,345	55,812	73,820	10,085	23,498	22,702	31,340
W. N. CENTRAL:										
Minnesota	742,947	298,258	14,975	180,607	64,977	87,761	11,220	24,307	25,482	35,360
Iowa	717,377	319,831	14,176	158,173	62,685	86,956	8,774	23,097	21,208	22,477
Missouri	1,072,545	383,195	21,468	280,280	94,113	135,441	17,727	37,110	43,960	59,251
N. Dakota	178,754	116,457	1,296	17,849	11,510	16,772	1,408	4,907	4,260	4,295
S. Dakota	186,885	114,259	1,433	24,287	12,041	18,997	1,683	5,505	4,812	3,868
Nebraska	385,292	183,030	387	76,782	33,796	47,117	5,235	12,733	12,402	13,810
Kansas	531,881	227,633	20,260	111,703	53,002	57,324	11,534	17,083	15,908	17,434
S. ATLANTIC:										
Delaware	73,122	17,161	69	30,853	7,526	6,607	1,493	2,580	2,318	4,515
Maryland	466,257	92,745	6,630	171,220	52,951	54,323	21,400	16,971	18,696	31,321
Dist. Columbia	143,401	928	79	38,789	14,833	18,558	15,640	12,294	12,402	29,878
Virginia	677,366	283,102	16,181	167,771	61,397	56,960	31,321	16,510	20,339	23,785
West Virginia	433,677	119,703	102,856	108,031	36,115	29,844	4,128	12,435	8,645	11,920
N. Carolina	693,155	397,214	1,986	164,367	34,803	46,913	8,619	13,461	13,022	12,770
S. Carolina	468,601	293,644	621	88,515	20,926	29,805	10,382	8,209	8,884	7,615
Georgia	840,412	484,330	2,459	152,663	51,781	67,403	19,164	17,908	20,773	23,931
Florida	300,050	108,911	2,962	89,804	28,319	30,374	7,492	10,153	12,552	9,483
E. S. CENTRAL:										
Kentucky	719,629	374,428	51,384	121,498	46,972	55,034	16,087	17,344	16,534	20,348
Tennessee	677,988	363,798	17,590	128,118	48,734	59,514	7,395	16,132	18,091	18,616
Alabama	684,348	381,890	35,564	135,608	40,407	43,561	6,426	13,169	13,467	14,256
Mississippi	526,446	373,975	254	68,892	26,154	27,167	4,644	8,817	9,092	7,451
W. S. CENTRAL:										
Arkansas	518,754	342,341	5,551	72,109	27,288	33,809	7,754	11,357	10,010	8,535
Louisiana	528,507	238,325	7,581	124,707	48,874	46,116	10,033	12,297	18,943	21,631
Oklahoma	586,834	292,496	38,190	99,303	39,671	56,206	8,406	17,902	17,776	16,884
Texas	1,415,180	693,862	31,418	247,408	116,476	141,021	44,703	40,040	48,269	51,983
MOUNTAIN:										
Montana	185,905	82,772	16,691	30,962	17,957	16,427	2,588	5,926	6,603	5,979
Idaho	135,950	71,543	5,129	23,253	10,552	11,875	1,427	4,489	4,270	3,412
Wyoming	72,134	25,221	8,767	14,922	9,516	5,345	1,433	2,044	2,785	2,101
Colorado	303,870	96,925	23,357	67,677	29,900	39,070	6,538	12,547	13,492	14,364
New Mexico	107,090	53,204	7,302	14,142	10,664	7,142	6,353	3,056	3,069	2,158
Arizona	112,193	32,917	15,339	21,840	11,276	9,798	8,223	4,229	4,575	3,996
Utah	127,418	42,372	10,096	30,917	11,484	13,528	2,285	5,668	4,713	6,355
Nevada	33,214	8,401	6,170	6,923	4,151	2,459	527	1,461	2,015	1,107
PACIFIC:										
Washington	485,767	127,720	8,809	168,566	49,834	55,727	12,471	19,235	21,227	22,178
Oregon	267,791	89,692	2,197	81,215	26,826	30,477	4,362	11,201	10,685	11,136
California	1,226,113	262,982	24,620	389,013	115,159	173,431	44,383	64,901	78,432	73,192

TABLE 10.—NUMBER OF FEMALES 10 YEARS OF AGE AND OVER IN EACH GENERAL DIVISION OF OCCUPATIONS, BY DIVISIONS AND STATES: 1920.

DIVISION AND STATE.	Total females occupied.	Agriculture, forestry, and animal husbandry.	Extraction of minerals.	Manufacturing and mechanical industries.	Transportation.	Trade.	Public service (not elsewhere classified).	Professional service.	Domestic and personal service.	Clerical occupations.
United States.	**8,549,511**	**1,084,128**	**2,864**	**1,930,341**	**213,054**	**667,792**	**21,794**	**1,016,498**	**2,186,924**	**1,426,116**
GEOGRAPHIC DIVS.:										
New England....	871,015	8,102	10	379,171	16,635	55,164	1,298	87,748	168,266	154,621
Middle Atlantic..	2,117,517	20,986	884	685,864	57,738	174,657	3,111	229,165	494,899	450,213
E. N. Central.....	1,564,041	46,757	601	371,268	51,136	161,934	3,533	207,148	378,861	342,803
W. N. Central....	772,315	46,590	146	112,640	26,705	77,994	3,794	151,545	214,373	138,528
South Atlantic...	1,243,958	379,700	378	190,655	15,570	55,077	2,812	100,523	375,453	123,790
E. S. Central.....	702,433	311,051	207	69,291	8,398	28,292	1,506	51,672	193,313	38,703
W. S. Central.....	666,973	241,060	329	44,856	15,356	42,557	2,227	72,478	189,858	58,252
Mountain.........	177,220	13,803	213	16,795	6,017	18,086	1,544	36,949	54,928	28,885
Pacific............	434,039	16,079	96	59,801	15,499	54,031	1,969	79,270	116,973	90,321
NEW ENGLAND:										
Maine.............	64,845	2,101	3	22,953	1,238	4,368	268	9,412	16,698	7,804
New Hampshire..	49,302	1,036	2	24,950	702	2,458	119	5,084	9,816	5,135
Vermont..........	26,899	1,208	1	6,415	628	1,609	166	4,490	9,006	3,376
Massachusetts....	503,155	1,796	3	219,253	10,549	32,888	544	48,137	94,766	95,219
Rhode Island.....	80,562	270	.....	45,250	1,194	4,428	69	5,833	11,937	11,581
Connecticut......	146,252	1,691	1	60,350	2,324	9,413	132	14,792	26,043	31,506
MIDDLE ATLANTIC:										
New York........	1,135,295	9,269	114	351,104	33,420	86,080	1,683	126,569	263,468	263,588
New Jersey.......	295,990	1,953	13	111,825	6,499	20,380	367	28,206	62,579	64,168
Pennsylvania.....	686,232	9,764	757	222,935	17,819	68,197	1,061	74,390	168,852	122,457
E. N. CENTRAL:										
Ohio..............	409,970	10,658	214	102,075	13,242	43,600	732	51,454	100,898	87,097
Indiana...........	185,385	7,454	46	45,598	6,043	19,024	489	26,247	47,567	32,917
Illinois...........	540,938	9,468	116	122,542	19,156	57,367	1,186	65,653	125,404	140,046
Michigan..........	245,383	8,812	216	55,587	7,864	24,735	650	35,256	59,259	53,004
Wisconsin........	182,365	10,365	9	45,466	4,831	17,208	476	28,538	45,733	29,739
W. N. CENTRAL:										
Minnesota........	164,066	9,618	19	23,395	5,515	16,670	554	31,175	44,638	32,482
Iowa.............	141,321	7,293	20	18,349	4,630	14,930	759	32,894	38,297	24,149
Missouri..........	244,615	13,668	48	50,603	7,776	23,452	729	32,081	70,125	46,133
North Dakota.....	28,328	3,429	2	1,338	952	2,180	286	8,111	8,906	3,124
South Dakota.....	29,686	3,018	4	1,995	789	2,986	330	8,277	8,441	3,846
Nebraska.........	71,789	4,085	1	7,119	2,812	7,746	428	17,402	18,837	13,359
Kansas...........	92,510	5,479	52	9,841	4,231	10,030	708	21,605	25,129	15,435
SOUTH ATLANTIC:										
Delaware.........	18,102	533	1	3,796	419	1,473	37	1,655	6,378	3,810
Maryland.........	137,221	3,136	7	36,195	2,988	11,784	291	12,733	48,538	21,549
Dist. of Columbia.	92,626	19	.....	5,716	1,912	4,224	430	6,995	30,177	43,153
Virginia..........	156,210	18,605	24	28,371	2,220	8,141	530	17,832	64,264	16,223
West Virginia....	57,439	5,889	295	9,000	1,442	5,265	213	10,086	18,408	6,841
North Carolina...	202,697	80,472	4	46,655	1,534	5,982	346	16,216	43,627	7,861
South Carolina...	205,656	126,991	3	21,029	1,006	3,925	225	9,647	38,336	4,494
Georgia..........	288,745	129,027	7	28,970	2,970	9,129	418	18,029	86,123	14,072
Florida...........	85,262	15,028	37	10,923	1,079	5,154	322	7,330	39,602	5,787
E. S. CENTRAL:										
Kentucky.........	131,493	19,321	87	25,536	2,834	9,814	533	14,585	44,227	14,556
Tennessee........	152,108	36,336	40	22,585	2,716	7,915	288	14,494	55,379	12,355
Alabama..........	223,868	122,795	75	15,103	1,678	6,528	349	12,229	57,345	7,806
Mississippi.......	194,964	132,639	5	6,067	1,170	4,035	336	10,364	36,362	3,986
W. S. CENTRAL:										
Arkansas.........	115,810	66,310	5	4,225	1,437	4,654	319	9,061	24,713	5,086
Louisiana.........	152,726	52,611	88	14,437	2,050	7,912	332	11,139	53,727	10,430
Oklahoma........	94,594	22,161	159	5,482	3,876	8,505	562	16,373	24,622	12,854
Texas............	303,843	99,978	77	20,712	7,993	21,486	1,014	35,905	86,796	29,882
MOUNTAIN:										
Montana..........	28,278	2,240	27	1,667	966	2,771	312	6,708	9,064	4,515
Idaho............	17,509	1,917	3	1,312	656	1,957	222	4,393	4,930	2,719
Wyoming.........	9,402	824	20	410	341	806	125	2,107	3,305	1,429
Colorado..........	62,587	3,228	25	6,247	2,310	6,000	146	12,416	19,020	11,770
New Mexico......	14,941	1,829	8	1,976	318	991	58	3,108	5,049	1,340
Arizona..........	18,386	3,282	98	2,215	313	1,516	130	2,976	5,600	2,256
Utah.............	21,783	887	21	2,677	945	3,015	183	4,329	5,458	4,268
Nevada...........	4,334	188	8	259	168	370	68	912	1,732	629
PACIFIC:										
Washington......	92,900	3,806	12	10,973	3,562	11,618	473	17,097	25,997	19,362
Oregon...........	54,492	2,308	6	7,210	2,248	6,445	300	10,662	14,567	10,746
California........	286,647	9,965	78	41,618	9,689	35,968	1,196	51,511	76,409	60,213

Table 11.—NUMBER AND PROPORTION OF MALES AND FEMALES 10 YEARS OF AGE AND OVER ENGAGED IN GAINFUL OCCUPATIONS, FOR CITIES HAVING 100,000 INHABITANTS OR MORE: 1920.

CITY.	MALES 10 YEARS OF AGE AND OVER: 1920			FEMALES 10 YEARS OF AGE AND OVER: 1920		
	Total number.	Number.	Per ct.	Total number.	Number.	Per ct.
Akron, Ohio	103,031	92,082	89.4	68,905	16,021	23.3
Albany, N. Y	46,041	37,822	82.1	50,281	14,500	28.8
Atlanta, Ga	79,041	66,702	84.4	86,959	32,250	37.1
Baltimore, Md	294,302	245,122	83.3	305,676	92,632	30.3
Birmingham, Ala	72,092	59,070	81.9	72,646	20,082	27.6
Boston, Mass	300,039	245,905	82.0	311,500	104,302	33.5
Bridgeport, Conn	58,051	48,369	83.3	54,316	15,527	28.6
Buffalo, N. Y	203,531	165,362	81.2	203,548	49,981	24.6
Cambridge, Mass	42,155	34,025	80.7	47,174	15,984	33.9
Camden, N. J	46,944	39,336	83.8	44,706	10,758	24.1
Chicago, Ill	1,102,656	919,899	83.4	1,068,365	311,535	29.2
Cincinnati, Ohio	162,909	134,925	82.8	176,032	50,383	28.6
Cleveland, Ohio	329,276	273,715	83.1	300,180	73,531	24.5
Columbus, Ohio	99,943	80,726	80.8	99,621	25,479	25.6
Dallas, Tex	66,624	55,719	83.6	66,867	21,772	32.6
Dayton, Ohio	63,600	53,529	84.2	62,228	15,030	24.2
Denver, Colo	113,951	90,084	79.1	106,598	29,006	27.2
Des Moines, Iowa	51,417	41,301	80.3	53,507	15,350	28.7
Detroit, Mich	439,265	381,300	86.8	354,051	83,814	23.7
Fall River, Mass	44,454	36,094	81.2	49,102	20,404	41.6
Fort Worth, Tex	47,845	40,013	83.6	41,573	10,702	25.7
Grand Rapids, Mich	54,336	43,985	81.0	56,816	15,071	26.5
Hartford, Conn	55,870	46,347	83.0	55,886	17,599	31.5
Houston, Tex	57,597	48,749	84.6	57,791	17,181	29.7
Indianapolis, Ind	130,692	110,137	84.3	133,357	36,221	27.2
Jersey City, N. J	118,314	97,738	82.6	116,025	29,895	25.8
Kansas City, Kans	41,774	34,757	83.2	39,480	9,222	23.4
Kansas City, Mo	138,556	116,858	84.3	138,498	40,322	29.1
Los Angeles, Calif	245,887	197,700	80.4	253,007	68,400	27.0
Louisville, Ky	93,550	78,067	83.4	104,336	34,186	32.8
Lowell, Mass	43,330	35,771	82.6	47,179	18,248	38.7
Memphis, Tenn	66,724	56,428	84.6	70,895	24,143	34.1
Milwaukee, Wis	183,863	153,419	83.4	184,139	51,344	27.9
Minneapolis, Minn	155,633	127,549	82.0	158,379	46,740	29.5
Nashville, Tenn	45,915	37,325	81.3	52,505	17,929	34.1
New Bedford, Mass	47,100	39,796	84.5	49,241	20,773	42.2
New Haven, Conn	62,886	51,037	81.2	65,177	18,955	29.1
New Orleans, La	155,239	128,422	82.7	164,663	49,761	30.2
New York, N. Y	2,249,314	1,839,685	81.8	2,273,375	691,727	30.4
Bronx borough	287,667	230,546	80.1	293,845	77,658	26.4
Brooklyn borough	797,701	646,774	81.1	802,601	215,139	26.8
Manhattan borough	929,796	773,448	83.2	945,490	342,518	36.2
Queens borough	185,084	151,040	81.6	188,338	46,792	24.8
Richmond borough	49,066	37,877	77.2	43,101	9,620	22.3
Newark, N. J	165,297	136,095	82.3	162,137	42,235	26.0
Norfolk, Va	50,602	43,733	86.4	46,091	14,627	31.7
Oakland, Calif	95,211	78,354	82.3	87,640	20,119	23.0
Omaha, Nebr	82,314	67,869	82.5	76,240	21,066	27.6
Paterson, N. J	54,299	44,996	82.9	55,944	18,883	33.8
Philadelphia, Pa	733,672	603,237	82.2	743,994	215,763	29.0
Pittsburgh, Pa	236,075	191,989	81.3	232,498	57,759	24.8
Portland, Oreg	111,545	92,102	82.6	106,016	28,506	26.9
Providence, R. I	92,230	75,875	82.3	99,730	33,430	33.5
Reading, Pa	43,085	35,939	83.4	44,683	13,624	30.5
Richmond, Va	65,384	53,184	81.3	75,420	26,641	35.3
Rochester, N. Y	117,103	96,463	82.4	122,513	37,641	30.7
St. Louis, Mo	322,795	272,659	84.5	330,369	99,791	30.2
St. Paul, Minn	95,967	78,702	82.0	96,312	28,118	29.2
Salt Lake City, Utah	46,101	35,814	77.7	46,995	10,08o	21.5
San Antonio, Tex	65,747	52,740	80.2	65,615	16,807	25.6
San Francisco, Calif	239,479	204,734	85.5	201,085	60,932	30.3
Scranton, Pa	52,137	41,453	79.5	54,775	13,334	24.3
Seattle, Wash	143,387	120,600	84.1	123,974	33,176	26.8
Spokane, Wash	43,379	34,737	80.1	43,538	11,121	25.5
Springfield, Mass	51,633	42,954	83.2	54,047	17,301	32.0
Syracuse, N. Y	70,599	58,546	82.9	70,680	18,759	26.5
Toledo, Ohio	103,603	86,846	83.8	96,193	23,283	24.2
Trenton, N. J	48,053	38,854	80.9	46,061	11,834	25.7
Washington, D. C	173,574	143,401	82.6	203,721	92,626	45.5
Wilmington, Del	45,640	38,552	84.5	43,223	11,767	27.2
Worcester, Mass	71,444	57,885	81.0	72,281	21,008	29.1
Yonkers, N. Y	38,218	30,187	79.0	40,521	11,218	27.7
Youngstown, Ohio	55,569	46,611	83.9	46,656	8,652	18.5

TABLE 12.—NUMBER OF PERSONS 10 YEARS OF AGE AND OVER IN EACH GENERAL DIVISION OF OCCUPATIONS, FOR CITIES HAVING 100,000 INHABITANTS OR MORE: 1920.

CITY.	Total persons occupied.	Agriculture, forestry, and animal husbandry.	Extraction of minerals.	Manufacturing and mechanical industries.	Transportation.	Trade.	Public service (not elsewhere classified.)	Professional service.	Domestic and personal service.	Clerical occupations.
Akron, Ohio	108,103	295	112	71,255	4,045	9,591	976	4,194	7,011	10,624
Albany, N.Y.	52,322	360	15	17,429	7,389	7,468	1,453	3,973	6,093	8,142
Atlanta, Ga.	98,952	604	45	27,459	10,415	16,511	2,415	5,843	21,430	14,230
Baltimore, Md.	337,754	1,509	245	143,080	34,212	47,434	9,929	18,023	43,767	39,555
Birmingham, Ala.	79,152	494	3,003	27,700	8,799	11,243	1,213	4,546	14,916	7,238
Boston, Mass.	350,207	1,978	100	129,474	34,988	52,716	11,120	23,182	46,214	50,435
Bridgeport, Conn.	63,896	224	13	38,506	3,234	6,185	1,202	2,960	3,928	7,644
Buffalo, N.Y.	215,343	567	129	98,625	22,701	28,512	5,700	13,018	18,311	28,275
Cambridge, Mass.	50,009	249	5	21,262	4,453	6,085	1,300	3,794	5,633	7,228
Camden, N.J.	50,094	119	5	29,454	4,144	4,916	1,203	1,763	3,546	4,944
Chicago, Ill.	1,231,434	3,396	601	489,001	110,521	206,975	23,110	71,191	116,102	210,537
Cincinnati, Ohio	185,308	1,404	119	81,232	16,284	26,412	3,287	10,884	22,683	23,003
Cleveland, Ohio	347,246	1,040	299	183,862	25,374	43,451	5,969	17,107	27,144	43,000
Columbus, Ohio	106,205	480	229	42,598	11,586	16,006	3,801	7,303	11,433	12,769
Dallas, Tex.	77,491	676	387	19,327	7,659	16,993	1,470	5,034	12,193	13,752
Dayton, Ohio	68,559	284	26	36,169	3,862	8,861	1,103	4,020	6,140	8,094
Denver, Colo.	119,090	3,250	2,025	33,600	12,724	23,246	1,966	10,167	15,473	16,639
Des Moines, Iowa	56,651	794	1,590	15,857	5,477	11,567	1,127	4,718	6,436	9,085
Detroit, Mich.	465,114	1,208	397	261,709	28,608	53,045	7,647	21,764	34,286	56,450
Fall River, Mass.	56,498	224	45	40,408	2,676	4,956	971	2,200	2,448	2,570
Fort Worth, Tex.	50,715	616	981	17,144	5,886	8,645	828	2,835	7,564	6,216
Grand Rapids, Mich.	59,056	373	86	29,360	4,325	9,114	857	3,587	4,864	6,490
Hartford, Conn.	63,946	449	11	28,763	3,632	9,123	1,214	3,828	6,038	10,888
Houston, Tex.	65,930	598	671	19,902	7,747	10,558	1,091	4,104	11,700	9,559
Indianapolis, Ind.	146,358	708	124	63,900	13,963	22,512	2,429	8,520	15,721	18,481
Jersey City, N.J.	127,633	169	16	51,971	20,115	15,429	3,223	5,611	8,525	22,574
Kansas City, Kans.	43,979	264	44	20,565	6,484	5,299	893	1,881	3,653	4,906
Kansas City, Mo.	157,180	1,304	419	45,720	17,707	31,788	3,094	10,681	21,392	25,075
Los Angeles, Calif.	266,100	10,028	2,047	84,175	22,792	49,569	5,398	29,288	32,467	30,336
Louisville, Ky.	112,253	512	156	44,626	10,781	16,899	2,805	6,129	16,657	13,688
Lowell, Mass.	54,019	273	19	36,402	2,595	5,155	1,058	2,140	2,997	3,380
Memphis, Tenn.	80,571	1,355	22	22,746	9,866	15,023	1,432	4,404	17,168	8,555
Milwaukee, Wis.	204,763	731	116	106,371	14,685	25,808	3,287	11,509	15,860	26,336
Minneapolis, Minn.	174,289	2,330	152	60,235	17,781	32,796	3,319	13,202	18,113	26,361
Nashville, Tenn.	55,254	372	142	17,818	6,305	9,111	1,103	3,170	11,521	5,712
New Bedford, Mass.	60,569	419	15	43,625	2,574	4,905	1,193	1,801	3,255	2,782
New Haven, Conn.	69,992	386	23	32,410	5,667	8,858	1,191	4,791	6,889	9,777
New Orleans, La.	178,183	1,969	123	56,951	25,340	25,870	6,270	9,165	31,498	20,997
New York, N.Y.	2,531,412	7,109	600	952,312	241,378	392,397	60,875	168,037	306,290	402,414
Bronx borough	308,204	960	34	120,214	24,547	54,754	7,471	19,810	20,403	60,011
Brooklyn borough	861,913	1,501	141	349,251	85,640	134,207	24,165	47,964	64,618	154,426
Manhattan borough	1,115,966	1,598	388	380,255	107,220	173,192	19,017	85,386	203,924	144,986
Queens borough	197,832	2,414	24	83,565	18,249	25,513	6,757	11,479	13,381	36,450
Richmond borough	47,497	636	13	19,027	5,722	4,731	3,465	3,398	3,964	6,541
Newark, N.J.	178,330	340	20	93,626	12,493	22,964	4,194	8,876	13,404	22,413
Norfolk, Va.	58,360	331	40	16,538	9,495	8,512	2,811	2,953	11,569	6,111
Oakland, Calif.	98,473	1,632	478	38,740	9,567	15,681	1,861	7,639	11,223	11,652
Omaha, Nebr.	88,935	1,133	43	30,928	8,649	15,823	2,357	5,946	9,433	14,623
Paterson, N.J.	63,879	123	11	40,913	3,563	6,531	1,020	2,771	3,350	5,597
Philadelphia, Pa.	819,000	3,594	483	388,696	66,218	110,579	22,068	42,977	84,424	99,961
Pittsburgh, Pa.	249,748	550	686	100,223	25,145	37,529	5,712	14,912	28,693	36,298
Portland, Oreg.	120,608	4,393	332	43,344	12,294	20,524	2,231	9,671	12,814	15,005
Providence, R.I.	109,305	397	12	58,052	7,765	13,524	1,960	5,852	10,058	11,685
Reading, Pa.	49,563	101	49	31,450	3,634	4,795	687	2,008	3,145	3,694
Richmond, Va.	79,825	309	51	30,892	7,798	12,059	1,341	4,157	13,753	9,465
Rochester, N.Y.	134,104	914	20	72,410	8,538	15,456	2,531	8,122	9,743	16,370
St. Louis, Mo.	372,450	1,560	1,009	151,473	33,553	57,207	7,483	19,364	47,015	53,786
St. Paul, Minn.	106,820	982	82	37,227	11,634	18,328	2,371	7,295	10,684	18,217
Salt Lake City, Utah	45,899	1,518	310	12,825	5,054	8,374	1,287	4,431	4,942	6,531
San Antonio, Tex.	69,547	2,401	343	17,101	9,598	12,186	6,071	4,765	10,331	6,861
San Francisco, Calif.	265,666	3,699	1,229	82,045	26,708	43,320	10,070	29,010	35,557	37,729
Scranton, Pa.	54,787	118	11,417	17,639	5,411	6,551	996	3,163	3,080	6,007
Seattle, Wash.	153,776	4,882	1,301	56,752	16,147	25,379	3,370	12,032	16,899	17,014
Spokane, Wash.	45,858	2,685	529	12,513	5,076	9,265	719	3,953	5,372	5,746
Springfield, Mass.	60,255	295	5	28,180	4,478	8,374	1,464	3,803	5,984	7,672
Syracuse, N.Y.	77,305	398	34	36,346	6,859	10,557	1,496	5,201	7,217	9,167
Toledo, Ohio	110,129	551	86	53,236	11,393	14,652	1,751	5,733	9,346	13,381
Trenton, N.J.	50,688	146	7	29,252	4,144	5,196	906	2,417	3,933	4,687
Washington, D.C.	236,027	947	79	44,505	16,745	22,782	16,070	19,289	42,579	73,031
Wilmington, Del.	50,319	193	56	24,515	5,023	5,272	756	2,662	5,247	6,595
Worcester, Mass.	78,893	533	5	42,631	5,020	8,876	1,439	5,057	6,474	8,858
Yonkers, N.Y.	41,405	382	12	18,751	2,762	4,957	1,043	3,465	3,702	6,331
Youngstown, Ohio	55,263	151	52	29,516	4,667	6,838	936	2,915	4,266	5,922

TABLE 13.—NUMBER AND PROPORTION OF PERSONS 10 YEARS OF AGE AND OVER ENGAGED IN GAINFUL OCCUPATIONS, BY SEX, FOR CITIES HAVING FROM 25,000 TO 100,000 INHABITANTS: 1920.

CITY.	PERSONS 10 YEARS OF AGE AND OVER: 1920.								
	Both sexes.			Male.			Female.		
	Total number.	Engaged in gainful occupations.		Total number.	Engaged in gainful occupations.		Total number.	Engaged in gainful occupations.	
		Number.	Per cent.		Number.	Per cent.		Number.	Per cent.
Alameda, Calif	24,013	11,698	48.7	11,632	9,273	79.7	12,381	2,425	19.6
Allentown, Pa	58,306	31,398	53.9	28,450	23,466	82.5	29,856	7,932	26.6
Altoona, Pa	48,025	24,098	50.2	23,667	19,193	81.1	24,358	4,905	20.1
Amsterdam, N. Y	26,404	15,718	59.5	12,711	10,404	81.9	13,693	5,314	38.8
Anderson, Ind	24,522	13,140	53.6	12,525	10,186	81.3	11,997	2,954	24.6
Asheville, N. C	22,669	11,408	50.3	10,440	7,934	76.0	12,229	3,474	28.4
Atlantic City, N. J	42,992	23,900	55.6	20,354	16,514	81.1	22,638	7,386	32.6
Auburn, N. Y	29,801	16,446	55.2	14,926	12,119	81.2	14,875	4,327	29.1
Augusta, Ga	43,810	26,264	59.9	20,915	17,378	83.1	22,895	8,886	38.8
Aurora, Ill	29,854	15,823	53.0	14,835	12,116	81.7	15,019	3,707	24.7
Austin, Tex	29,416	13,077	44.5	13,719	9,018	65.7	15,697	4,059	25.9
Bangor, Me	21,996	10,566	48.0	10,149	7,521	74.1	11,847	3,045	25.7
Battle Creek, Mich	30,511	16,916	55.4	15,023	12,625	84.0	15,488	4,291	27.7
Bay City, Mich	37,565	18,933	50.4	18,831	14,705	78.1	18,734	4,228	22.6
Bayonne, N. J	56,109	29,239	52.1	29,471	23,898	81.1	26,638	5,341	20.1
Beaumont, Tex	32,602	18,279	56.1	16,812	14,029	83.4	15,790	4,250	26.9
Bellingham, Wash	21,056	10,678	50.7	10,976	8,704	79.3	10,080	1,974	19.6
Berkeley, Calif	47,668	22,092	46.3	21,963	16,248	74.0	25,705	5,844	22.7
Bethlehem, Pa	38,438	20,194	52.5	19,912	16,326	82.0	18,526	3,868	20.9
Binghamton, N. Y	55,089	30,412	55.2	26,751	21,060	78.7	28,338	9,352	33.0
Bloomington, Ill	24,298	12,123	49.9	11,550	9,138	79.1	12,748	2,985	23.4
Brockton, Mass	54,318	32,593	60.0	26,751	22,466	84.0	27,567	10,127	36.7
Brookline town, Mass	32,932	17,378	52.8	12,800	9,833	76.8	20,132	7,545	37.5
Butte, Mont	34,722	19,362	55.8	19,251	15,851	82.3	15,471	3,511	22.7
Canton, Ohio	70,686	39,759	56.2	38,739	33,172	85.6	31,947	6,587	20.6
Cedar Rapids, Iowa	37,851	19,766	52.2	18,483	14,954	80.9	19,368	4,812	24.8
Charleston, S. C	55,253	32,218	58.3	26,407	21,671	82.1	28,846	10,547	36.6
Charleston, W. Va	31,928	16,890	52.9	16,076	13,032	81.1	15,852	3,858	24.3
Charlotte, N. C	36,503	21,233	58.2	17,419	14,430	82.8	19,084	6,803	35.6
Chattanooga, Tenn	48,661	28,596	58.8	24,320	20,459	84.1	24,341	8,137	33.4
Chelsea, Mass	33,249	17,773	53.5	17,382	13,698	78.8	15,867	4,075	25.7
Chester, Pa	46,032	26,947	58.5	25,557	22,242	87.0	20,475	4,705	23.0
Chicopee, Mass	26,685	15,453	57.9	13,678	11,200	81.9	13,007	4,253	32.7
Cicero town, Ill	33,616	18,677	55.6	17,485	14,423	82.5	16,131	4,254	26.4
Clarksburg, W. Va	21,743	10,919	50.2	11,147	8,922	80.0	10,596	1,997	18.8
Clifton, N. J	20,024	11,178	55.8	10,131	8,302	81.9	9,893	2,876	29.1
Colorado Springs, Colo	25,793	11,814	45.8	11,610	8,369	72.1	14,183	3,445	24.3
Columbia, S. C	31,088	16,176	52.0	14,784	11,095	75.0	16,304	5,081	31.2
Columbus, Ga	25,350	15,408	60.8	11,801	9,756	82.7	13,549	5,652	41.7
Council Bluffs, Iowa	29,392	15,043	51.2	14,785	11,644	78.8	14,607	3,399	23.3
Covington, Ky	47,370	25,701	54.3	22,568	18,770	83.2	24,802	6,931	27.9
Cranston, R. I	23,682	11,677	49.3	11,771	8,720	74.1	11,911	2,957	24.8
Cumberland, Md	24,225	12,631	52.1	12,287	10,045	81.8	11,938	2,586	21.7
Danville, Ill	27,876	14,411	51.7	13,838	11,124	80.4	14,038	3,287	23.4
Davenport, Iowa	47,775	24,663	51.6	24,097	18,842	78.2	23,678	5,821	24.6
Decatur, Ill	36,253	18,595	51.3	17,909	14,515	81.0	18,344	4,080	22.2
Dubuque, Iowa	32,125	16,898	52.6	15,328	12,390	80.8	16,797	4,508	26.8
Duluth, Minn	79,392	45,002	56.7	42,017	34,968	83.2	37,375	10,034	26.8
East Chicago, Ind	26,031	14,944	57.4	15,998	13,689	85.6	10,033	1,255	12.5
East Cleveland, Ohio	22,884	11,572	50.6	10,614	8,766	82.6	12,270	2,806	22.9
East Orange, N. J	42,773	21,215	49.6	19,265	15,459	80.2	23,508	5,756	24.5
East St. Louis, Ill	53,660	29,747	55.4	28,409	23,860	84.0	25,251	5,887	23.3
Easton, Pa	27,574	14,555	52.8	13,388	10,984	82.0	14,186	3,571	25.2
El Paso, Tex	61,237	29,523	48.2	29,041	22,475	77.4	32,196	7,048	21.9
Elgin, Ill	23,895	11,949	50.0	11,031	7,891	71.5	12,864	4,058	31.5

TABLE **13.**—NUMBER AND PROPORTION OF PERSONS 10 YEARS OF AGE AND OVER ENGAGED IN GAINFUL OCCUPATIONS, BY SEX, FOR CITIES HAVING FROM 25,000 TO 100,000 INHABITANTS: 1920—Continued.

	PERSONS 10 YEARS OF AGE AND OVER: 1920.								
	Both sexes.			Male.			Female.		
CITY.	Total number.	Engaged in gainful occupations.		Total number.	Engaged in gainful occupations.		Total number.	Engaged in gainful occupations.	
		Number.	Per cent.		Number.	Per cent.		Number.	Per cent.
Elizabeth, N. J	73,577	40,186	54.6	38,341	31,986	83.4	35,236	8,200	23.3
Elmira, N. Y	38,215	20,090	52.6	19,152	15,143	79.1	19,063	4,947	26.0
Erie, Pa	73,539	37,396	50.9	37,050	29,752	80.3	36,489	7,644	20.9
Evanston, Ill	30,560	16,012	52.4	13,822	10,879	78.7	16,738	5,133	30.7
Evansville, Ind	70,677	37,811	53.5	34,107	27,932	81.9	36,570	9,879	27.0
Everett, Mass	31,691	16,401	51.8	15,555	12,523	80.5	16,136	3,878	24.0
Everett, Wash	22,759	12,153	53.4	12,124	10,015	82.6	10,635	2,138	20.1
Fitchburg, Mass	32,453	18,886	58.2	15,906	13,215	83.1	16,547	5,671	34.3
Flint, Mich	74,519	45,054	60.5	43,102	38,047	88.3	31,417	7,007	22.3
Fort Smith, Ark	23,168	11,602	50.1	11,318	8,960	79.2	11,850	2,642	22.3
Fort Wayne, Ind	71,645	39,813	55.6	35,149	29,494	83.9	36,496	10,319	28.3
Fresno, Calif	37,290	20,131	54.0	19,669	16,085	81.8	17,621	4,046	23.0
Galveston, Tex	37,151	21,762	58.6	19,863	16,967	85.4	17,288	4,795	27.7
Gary, Ind	41,792	23,974	57.4	25,028	21,559	86.1	16,764	2,415	14.4
Green Bay, Wis	24,770	12,289	49.6	11,984	9,134	76.2	12,786	3,155	24.7
Hagerstown, Md	22,227	11,456	51.5	10,819	8,914	82.4	11,408	2,542	22.3
Hamilton, Ohio	32,542	17,397	53.5	16,798	14,085	83.8	15,744	3,312	21.0
Hammond, Ind	27,499	14,629	53.2	14,992	12,408	82.8	12,507	2,221	17.8
Hamtramck village, Mich	31,373	17,762	56.6	18,640	16,183	86.8	12,733	1,579	12.4
Harrisburg, Pa	63,812	33,329	52.2	31,139	25,484	81.8	32,673	7,845	24.0
Haverhill, Mass	44,341	26,919	60.7	21,584	18,065	83.7	22,757	8,854	38.9
Hazleton, Pa	24,446	12,254	50.1	11,945	9,243	77.4	12,501	3,011	24.1
Highland Park, Mich	38,116	22,421	58.8	21,390	18,987	88.8	16,726	3,434	20.5
Hoboken, N. J	54,520	31,366	57.5	28,649	24,264	84.7	25,871	7,102	27.5
Holyoke, Mass	48,166	28,632	59.4	22,883	18,464	80.7	25,283	10,168	40.2
Huntington, W. Va	39,901	19,801	49.6	19,974	15,733	78.8	19,927	4,068	20.4
Irvington town, N. J	20,576	10,383	50.5	10,182	8,329	81.8	10,394	2,054	19.8
Jackson, Mich	39,841	22,437	56.3	20,877	17,815	85.3	18,964	4,622	24.4
Jacksonville, Fla	75,391	44,802	59.4	36,954	31,492	85.2	38,437	13,310	34.6
Jamestown, N. Y	32,354	17,728	54.8	15,870	12,969	81.7	16,484	4,759	28.9
Johnstown, Pa	50,867	25,954	51.0	26,678	21,614	81.0	24,189	4,340	17.9
Joliet, Ill	30,776	15,965	51.9	15,720	12,537	79.8	15,056	3,428	22.8
Joplin, Mo	24,580	11,852	48.2	11,889	9,146	76.9	12,691	2,706	21.3
Kalamazoo, Mich	40,015	21,365	53.4	19,755	15,639	79.2	20,260	5,726	28.3
Kearny town, N. J	21,163	11,484	54.3	10,707	8,605	80.4	10,456	2,879	27.5
Kenosha, Wis	31,445	18,318	58.3	17,762	15,146	85.3	13,683	3,172	23.2
Kingston, N. Y	22,630	11,977	52.9	10,537	8,494	80.6	12,093	3,483	28.8
Knoxville, Tenn	62,171	32,596	52.4	29,863	23,728	79.5	32,308	8,868	27.4
Kokomo, Ind	24,359	12,794	52.5	12,675	10,583	83.5	11,684	2,211	18.9
La Crosse, Wis	25,001	12,635	50.5	11,812	9,099	77.0	13,189	3,536	26.8
Lakewood, Ohio	33,558	16,550	49.3	16,002	12,949	80.9	17,556	3,601	20.5
Lancaster, Pa	43,918	24,309	55.4	20,413	16,824	82.4	23,505	7,485	31.8
Lansing, Mich	47,274	26,170	55.4	25,081	21,046	83.9	22,193	5,124	23.1
Lawrence, Mass	71,106	46,996	63.4	36,772	30,775	83.7	37,334	16,221	43.4
Lewiston, Me	25,902	15,322	59.4	12,343	9,919	79.7	13,459	5,480	40.7
Lexington, Ky	35,506	19,975	56.3	17,050	13,475	79.0	18,456	6,500	35.2
Lima, Ohio	33,434	17,106	51.2	16,637	13,430	80.7	16,797	3,676	21.9
Lincoln, Nebr	44,974	22,483	50.0	21,488	16,281	75.8	23,486	6,202	26.4
Little Rock, Ark	54,551	29,249	53.6	26,467	20,850	78.8	28,084	8,399	29.9
Long Beach, Calif	48,818	18,735	38.4	22,782	14,409	63.2	26,036	4,326	16.6
Lorain, Ohio	27,942	14,320	51.2	15,651	12,787	81.7	12,291	1,533	12.5
Lynchburg, Va	24,354	14,054	57.7	10,977	8,760	79.8	13,377	5,294	39.6
Lynn, Mass	81,526	48,032	58.9	39,998	33,403	83.5	41,528	14,629	35.2
McKeesport, Pa	35,798	18,026	50.4	18,895	15,191	80.4	16,903	2,835	16.8
Macon, Ga	43,986	26,357	59.9	21,113	17,541	83.1	22,873	8,816	38.5

TABLE 13.—NUMBER AND PROPORTION OF PERSONS 10 YEARS OF AGE AND OVER ENGAGED IN GAINFUL OCCUPATIONS, BY SEX, FOR CITIES HAVING FROM 25,000 TO 100,000 INHABITANTS: 1920—Continued.

	PERSONS 10 YEARS OF AGE AND OVER: 1920.							
CITY.	Both sexes.			Male.			Female.		
	Total number.	Engaged in gainful occupations.		Total number.	Engaged in gainful occupations.		Total number.	Engaged in gainful occupations.	
		Number.	Per cent.		Number.	Per cent.		Number.	Per cent.
Madison, Wis	31,720	16,469	51.9	14,892	11,559	77.6	16,828	4,910	29.2
Malden, Mass	39,683	20,621	52.0	18,610	14,643	78.7	21,073	5,978	28.4
Manchester, N. H	62,678	37,550	59.9	29,628	23,794	80.3	33,050	13,756	41.6
Mansfield, Ohio	23,079	12,449	53.9	11,637	9,817	84.4	11,442	2,632	23.0
Marion, Ohio	22,554	11,309	50.1	11,257	9,171	81.5	11,297	2,138	18.9
Medford, Mass	31,348	16,109	51.4	14,705	11,904	81.0	16,643	4,205	25.3
Meriden, Conn	23,897	13,081	54.7	11,976	9,680	80.8	11,921	3,401	28.5
Miami, Fla	24,102	14,293	59.3	12,276	10,229	83.3	11,826	4,064	34.4
Mobile, Ala	49,980	28,354	56.7	23,838	19,816	83.1	26,142	8,538	32.7
Moline, Ill	25,593	14,232	55.6	13,692	11,582	84.6	11,901	2,650	22.3
Montclair town, N. J	23,528	11,625	49.4	10,523	7,996	76.0	13,005	3,629	27.9
Montgomery, Ala	35,926	20,862	58.1	16,428	13,242	80.6	19,498	7,620	39.1
Mount Vernon, N. Y	34,396	17,578	51.1	16,195	12,617	77.9	18,201	4,961	27.3
Muncie, Ind	30,188	16,150	53.5	15,361	12,737	82.9	14,827	3,413	23.0
Muskegon, Mich	29,563	16,455	55.7	15,587	13,080	83.9	13,976	3,375	24.1
Muskogee, Okla	24,546	12,181	49.6	12,027	9,352	77.8	12,519	2,829	22.6
Nashua, N. H	22,889	13,261	57.9	11,379	9,314	81.9	11,510	3,947	34.3
New Britain, Conn	44,447	25,255	56.8	23,209	19,310	83.2	21,238	5,945	28.0
New Brunswick, N. J	25,432	13,877	54.6	12,612	10,170	80.6	12,820	3,707	28.9
New Castle, Pa	34,520	17,263	50.0	17,781	14,414	81.1	16,739	2,849	17.0
New London, Conn	20,893	10,740	51.4	10,374	8,384	80.8	10,519	2,356	22.4
New Rochelle, N. Y	29,145	15,586	53.5	14,108	11,226	79.6	15,037	4,360	29.0
Newark, Ohio	22,261	11,452	51.4	11,102	9,088	81.9	11,159	2,364	21.2
Newburgh, N. Y	25,373	13,705	54.0	12,349	10,143	82.1	13,024	3,562	27.3
Newport, Ky	24,334	13,265	54.5	11,542	9,698	84.0	12,792	3,567	27.9
Newport, R. I	25,340	14,744	58.2	13,919	11,872	85.3	11,421	2,872	25.1
Newport News, Va	29,774	18,447	62.0	17,246	15,190	88.1	12,528	3,257	26.0
Newton, Mass	38,138	19,385	50.8	16,745	12,814	76.5	21,393	6,571	30.7
Niagara Falls, N. Y	39,194	21,819	55.7	21,351	17,931	84.0	17,843	3,888	21.8
Norristown borough, Pa	26,717	13,480	50.5	12,787	9,657	75.5	13,930	3,823	27.4
Norwalk, Conn	22,505	12,296	54.6	10,890	8,857	81.3	11,615	3,439	29.6
Oak Park village, Ill	33,286	16,377	49.2	15,439	11,951	77.4	17,847	4,426	24.8
Ogden, Utah	25,398	11,789	46.4	12,739	9,529	74.8	12,659	2,260	17.9
Oklahoma City, Okla	76,348	43,261	56.7	39,108	32,204	82.3	37,240	11,057	29.7
Orange, N. J	26,214	14,021	53.5	12,622	9,972	79.0	13,592	4,049	29.8
Oshkosh, Wis	27,137	13,648	50.3	12,953	10,005	77.2	14,184	3,643	25.7
Pasadena, Calif	39,593	17,588	44.4	16,916	11,720	69.3	22,677	5,868	25.9
Passaic, N. J	47,607	27,312	57.4	23,749	19,330	81.4	23,858	7,982	33.5
Pawtucket, R. I	51,961	31,020	59.7	25,036	21,163	84.5	26,925	9,857	36.6
Pensacola, Fla	25,113	14,185	56.5	12,928	10,821	83.7	12,185	3,364	27.6
Peoria, Ill	64,831	35,412	54.6	32,273	26,828	83.1	32,558	8,584	26.4
Perth Amboy, N. J	30,086	16,006	53.2	15,879	12,876	81.1	14,207	3,130	22.0
Petersburg, Va	25,073	14,455	57.7	11,584	9,453	81.6	13,489	5,002	37.1
Phoenix, Ariz	23,984	12,744	53.1	12,629	10,126	80.2	11,355	2,618	23.1
Pittsfield, Mass	33,453	18,516	55.3	16,193	13,198	81.5	17,260	5,318	30.8
Plainfield, N. J	22,192	11,765	53.0	10,517	8,518	81.0	11,675	3,247	27.8
Pontiac, Mich	28,397	15,744	55.4	15,906	13,156	82.7	12,491	2,588	20.7
Port Huron, Mich	20,897	10,334	49.5	10,500	8,421	80.2	10,397	1,913	18.4
Portland, Me	57,428	30,292	52.7	27,335	22,113	80.9	30,093	8,179	27.2
Portsmouth, Ohio	26,421	13,902	52.6	13,095	10,847	82.8	13,326	3,055	22.9
Portsmouth, Va	43,998	24,794	56.4	22,710	19,341	85.2	21,288	5,453	25.6
Poughkeepsie, N. Y	28,718	15,271	53.2	13,612	10,940	80.4	15,106	4,331	28.7
Pueblo, Colo	34,698	17,580	50.7	17,865	14,048	78.6	16,833	3,532	21.0
Quincy, Ill	30,720	16,010	52.1	14,878	11,965	80.4	15,842	4,045	25.5
Quincy, Mass	37,763	19,681	52.1	19,076	15,573	81.6	18,687	4,108	22.0

TABLE **13.**—NUMBER AND PROPORTION OF PERSONS 10 YEARS OF AGE AND OVER
ENGAGED IN GAINFUL OCCUPATIONS, BY SEX, FOR CITIES HAVING FROM 25,000 TO
100,000 INHABITANTS: 1920—Continued.

CITY.	PERSONS 10 YEARS OF AGE AND OVER: 1920.								
	Both sexes.			Male.			Female.		
	Total number.	Engaged in gainful occupations.		Total number.	Engaged in gainful occupations.		Total number.	Engaged in gainful occupations.	
		Number.	Per cent.		Number.	Per cent.		Number.	Per cent.
Racine, Wis.............	47,245	27,561	58.3	25,799	22,166	85.9	21,446	5,395	25.2
Revere, Mass.............	22,095	11,020	49.9	10,981	8,611	78.4	11,114	2,409	21.7
Richmond, Ind..........	22,387	11,890	53.1	11,232	9,271	82.5	11,155	2,619	23.5
Roanoke, Va.............	39,966	20,423	51.1	19,543	15,783	80.8	20,423	4,640	22.7
Rock Island, Ill..........	29,478	16,060	54.5	15,139	12,666	83.7	14,339	3,394	23.7
Rockford, Ill.............	54,459	30,391	55.8	27,920	23,212	83.1	26,539	7,179	27.1
Rome, N. Y.............	20,874	10,897	52.2	11,079	8,487	76.6	9,795	2,410	24.6
Sacramento, Calif........	55,708	30,954	55.6	29,365	24,419	83.2	26,343	6,535	24.8
Saginaw, Mich...........	49,748	25,681	51.6	24,782	20,073	81.0	24,966	5,608	22.5
St. Joseph, Mo...........	65,160	35,642	54.7	32,538	26,572	81.7	32,622	9,070	27.8
Salem, Mass.............	34,020	19,061	56.0	16,473	13,329	80.9	17,547	5,732	32.7
San Diego, Calif..........	64,291	31,037	48.3	31,544	23,398	74.2	32,747	7,639	23.3
San Jose, Calif..........	33,303	16,000	48.0	16,162	12,135	75.1	17,141	3,865	22.5
Savannah, Ga...........	69,139	41,866	60.6	33,676	28,986	86.1	35,463	12,880	36.3
Schenectady, N. Y.......	71,434	37,491	52.5	36,170	29,164	80.6	35,264	8,327	23.6
Sheboygan, Wis..........	24,479	13,008	53.1	12,490	10,207	81.7	11,989	2,801	23.4
Shreveport, La..........	36,844	21,802	59.2	18,319	15,459	84.4	18,525	6,343	34.2
Sioux City, Iowa.........	58,469	33,334	57.0	31,096	25,859	83.2	27,373	7,475	27.3
Sioux Falls, S. Dak......	20,630	10,675	51.7	10,522	8,007	76.1	10,108	2,668	26.4
Somerville, Mass.........	75,995	40,038	52.7	35,903	29,126	81.1	40,092	10,912	27.2
South Bend, Ind.........	55,601	29,979	53.9	28,480	23,305	81.8	27,121	6,674	24.6
Springfield, Ill..........	48,955	26,060	53.2	23,594	19,167	81.2	25,361	6,893	27.2
Springfield, Mo..........	32,695	15,917	48.7	15,526	12,124	78.1	17,169	3,793	22.1
Springfield, Ohio.........	50,080	26,417	52.7	25,079	20,636	82.3	25,001	5,781	23.1
Stamford, Conn..........	27,058	14,400	53.2	13,443	10,893	81.0	13,615	3,507	25.8
Steubenville, Ohio.......	22,299	11,741	52.7	11,822	9,766	82.6	10,477	1,975	18.9
Stockton, Calif..........	34,172	17,236	50.4	18,583	13,998	75.3	15,589	3,238	20.8
Superior, Wis............	31,276	16,517	52.8	16,687	13,498	80.9	14,589	3,019	20.7
Tacoma, Wash...........	80,721	43,471	53.9	43,426	35,229	81.1	37,295	8,242	22.1
Tampa, Fla..............	41,014	24,419	59.5	20,677	16,659	80.6	20,337	7,760	38.2
Taunton, Mass..........	29,711	15,843	53.3	14,415	11,301	78.4	15,296	4,542	29.7
Terre Haute, Ind.........	55,134	28,696	52.0	27,431	22,441	81.8	27,703	6,255	22.6
Topeka, Kans............	41,438	21,082	50.9	19,651	15,517	79.0	21,787	5,565	25.5
Troy, N. Y..............	61,207	34,307	56.1	27,599	22,270	80.7	33,608	12,037	35.8
Tulsa, Okla..............	59,499	34,223	57.5	31,303	26,359	84.2	28,196	7,864	27.9
Utica, N. Y.............	75,683	41,472	54.8	36,650	29,199	79.7	39,033	12,273	31.4
Waco, Tex..............	31,367	15,432	49.2	15,135	11,651	77.0	16,232	3,781	23.3
Waltham, Mass..........	25,561	14,636	57.3	11,917	9,549	80.1	13,644	5,087	37.3
Warren, Ohio............	21,748	11,831	54.4	11,622	9,813	84.4	10,126	2,018	19.9
Waterbury, Conn........	71,921	40,955	56.9	37,363	31,078	83.2	34,558	9,877	28.6
Waterloo, Iowa..........	29,556	15,278	51.7	14,765	11,867	80.4	14,791	3,411	23.1
Watertown, N. Y........	25,976	13,790	53.1	12,451	10,146	81.5	13,525	3,644	26.9
West Hoboken town, N. J.	32,525	17,286	53.1	16,179	13,126	81.1	16,346	4,160	25.4
West New York town, N.J.	20,007	10,561	53.9	11,641	9,709	83.4	11,666	2,852	24.4
Wheeling, W. Va.........	41,867	23,719	50.6	22,341	17,932	80.1	22,526	5,267	22.4
Wichita, Kans...........	59,737	29,870	50.0	29,386	22,862	77.8	30,351	7,008	23.1
Wichita Falls, Tex.......	33,587	20,234	60.2	20,718	17,344	83.7	12,869	2,890	22.5
Wilkes-Barre, Pa.........	57,506	29,062	50.5	28,276	22,271	78.8	29,230	6,791	23.2
Williamsport, Pa.........	30,237	16,181	53.5	14,500	11,983	82.6	15,737	4,198	26.7
Wilmington, N. C........	26,525	15,311	57.7	12,820	10,861	84.7	13,705	4,450	32.5
Winston-Salem, N. C.....	39,003	26,220	67.2	19,550	16,761	85.7	19,453	9,459	48.6
Woonsocket, R. I........	34,379	20,743	60.3	16,626	13,770	82.8	17,753	6,973	39.3
York, Pa................	39,072	21,522	55.1	18,847	15,590	82.7	20,225	5,932	29.3
Zanesville, Ohio.........	24,364	12,339	50.6	11,726	9,554	81.5	12,638	2,785	22.0

TABLE 14.—NUMBER AND PROPORTION OF PERSONS 10 YEARS OF AGE AND OVER ENGAGED IN GAINFUL OCCUPATIONS, BY SEX AND POPULATION CLASSES, FOR THE UNITED STATES: 1920 AND 1910.

SEX AND CLASS OF POPULATION.	POPULATION 10 YEARS OF AGE AND OVER.					
	1920			1910		
	Total number.	Engaged in gainful occupations.		Total number.	Engaged in gainful occupations.	
		Number.	Per cent.		Number.	Per cent.
BOTH SEXES.						
All classes	82,739,315	41,614,248	50.3	71,580,270	38,167,336	53.3
Native white—Native parentage	44,077,564	20,521,997	46.6	37,081,278	17,954,464	48.4
Native white—Foreign or mixed parentage	16,784,299	8,347,466	49.7	13,908,063	7,008,090	50.4
Foreign-born white	13,497,886	7,746,460	57.4	12,944,529	7,811,502	60.3
Negro	8,053,225	4,824,151	59.9	7,317,922	5,192,535	71.0
Indian, Chinese, Japanese, and all other	326,341	174,174	53.4	328,478	200,745	61.1
Indian	176,925	63,326	35.8	188,758	73,916	39.2
Chinese	56,230	45,614	81.1	68,924	} 1 123,811	90.6
Japanese	84,238	57,903	68.7	67,661		
All other	8,948	7,331	81.9	3,135	3,018	96.3
MALE.						
All classes	42,289,969	33,064,737	78.2	37,027,558	30,091,564	81.3
Native white—Native parentage	22,361,495	16,788,668	75.1	18,933,751	14,855,825	78.5
Native white—Foreign or mixed parentage	8,289,550	6,237,012	75.2	6,909,282	5,285,811	76.5
Foreign-born white	7,419,691	6,627,997	89.3	7,321,196	6,588,711	90.0
Negro	4,009,462	3,252,862	81.1	3,637,386	3,178,554	87.4
Indian, Chinese, Japanese, and all other	209,771	158,198	75.4	225,943	182,663	80.8
Indian	91,546	53,478	58.4	96,582	59,206	61.3
Chinese	51,041	44,882	87.9	65,479	} 1 120,460	95.4
Japanese	58,806	52,614	89.5	60,809		
All other	8,378	7,224	86.2	3,073	2,997	97.5
FEMALE.						
All classes	40,449,346	8,549,511	21.1	34,552,712	8,075,772	23.4
Native white—Native parentage	21,716,069	3,733,329	17.2	18,147,527	3,098,639	17.1
Native white—Foreign or mixed parentage	8,494,749	2,110,454	24.8	6,998,781	1,722,279	24.6
Foreign-born white	6,078,195	1,118,463	18.4	5,623,333	1,222,791	21.7
Negro	4,043,763	1,571,289	38.9	3,680,536	2,013,981	54.7
Indian, Chinese, Japanese, and all other	116,570	15,976	13.7	102,535	18,082	17.6
Indian	85,379	9,848	11.5	92,176	14,710	16.0
Chinese	5,189	732	14.1	3,445	} 1 3,351	32.5
Japanese	25,432	5,289	20.8	6,852		
All other	570	107	18.8	62	21	33.9

1 Separate occupation figures for Chinese and Japanese not available for 1910.

TABLE 15.—PER CENT DISTRIBUTION, BY CLASS OF POPULATION, OF THE POPULA-
TION 10 YEARS OF AGE AND OVER AND OF PERSONS ENGAGED IN GAINFUL OCCU-
PATIONS, FOR BOTH SEXES AND FOR EACH SEX SEPARATELY, FOR THE UNITED
STATES: 1920 AND 1910.

SEX AND CLASS OF POPULATION.	PER CENT DISTRIBUTION OF—			
	Population 10 years of age and over.		Persons engaged in gainful occupations.	
	1920	1910	1920	1910
BOTH SEXES.				
All classes.....................	100.0	100.0	100.0	100.0
Native white—Native parentage..............	53.3	51.8	49.3	47.0
Native white—Foreign or mixed parentage...........	20.2	19.4	20.1	18.4
Foreign-born white.................	16.3	18.1	18.6	20.5
Negro........................	9.7	10.2	11.6	13.6
Indian, Chinese, Japanese, and all other.............	0.4	0.5	0.4	0.5
Indian....................	0.2	0.3	0.2	0.2
Chinese...................	0.1	0.1	0.1	} 1 0.3
Japanese...................	0.1	0.1	0.1	
All other....................	(2)	(2)	(2)	(2)
MALE.				
All classes.....................	100.0	100.0	100.0	100.0
Native white—Native parentage..............	52.9	51.1	50.8	49.4
Native white—Foreign or mixed parentage...........	19.6	18.7	18.9	17.6
Foreign-born white.................	17.5	19.8	20.0	21.9
Negro........................	9.5	9.8	9.8	10.6
Indian, Chinese, Japanese, and all other.............	0.5	0.6	0.5	0.6
Indian....................	0.2	0.3	0.2	0.2
Chinese...................	0.1	0.2	0.1	} 1 0.4
Japanese...................	0.1	0.2	0.2	
All other....................	(2)	(2)	(2)	(2)
FEMALE.				
All classes.....................	100.0	100.0	100.0	100.0
Native white—Native parentage..............	53.7	52.5	43.7	38.4
Native white—Foreign or mixed parentage...........	21.0	20.3	24.7	21.3
Foreign-born white.................	15.0	16.3	13.1	15.1
Negro........................	10.0	10.7	18.4	24.9
Indian, Chinese, Japanese, and all other.............	0.3	0.3	0.2	0.2
Indian....................	0.2	0.3	0.1	0.2
Chinese...................	(2)	(2)	(2)	} (2)
Japanese...................	0.1	(2)	0.1	
All other....................	(2)	(2)	(2)	(2)

1 Separate occupation figures for Chinese and Japanese not available for 1910.
2 Less than one-tenth of 1 per cent.

TABLE 16.—DISTRIBUTION, BY GENERAL DIVISIONS OF OCCUPATIONS, OF GAINFUL WORKERS 10 YEARS OF AGE AND OVER IN EACH PRINCIPAL CLASS OF THE POPULATION, FOR THE UNITED STATES: 1920.

SEX AND GENERAL DIVISION OF OCCUPATIONS.	ALL CLASSES.		NATIVE WHITE— NATIVE PARENTAGE.		NATIVE WHITE— FOREIGN OR MIXED PARENTAGE.	
	Number.	Per cent distribution.	Number.	Per cent distribution.	Number.	Per cent distribution.
BOTH SEXES.						
All occupations	41,614,248	100.0	20,521,997	100.0	8,347,466	100.0
Agriculture, forestry, and animal husbandry	10,953,158	26.3	6,391,480	31.1	1,374,777	16.5
Extraction of minerals	1,090,223	2.6	487,314	2.4	150,620	1.8
Manufacturing and mechanical industries	12,818,524	30.8	5,384,332	26.2	2,890,495	34.6
Transportation	3,063,582	7.4	1,562,409	7.6	633,170	7.6
Trade	4,242,979	10.2	2,194,827	10.7	1,033,446	12.4
Public service (not elsewhere classified)	770,460	1.9	404,627	2.0	185,839	2.2
Professional service	2,143,889	5.2	1,339,408	6.5	489,682	5.9
Domestic and personal service	3,404,892	8.2	1,016,293	5.0	510,637	6.1
Clerical occupations	3,126,541	7.5	1,741,307	8.5	1,078,800	12.9
MALE.						
All occupations	33,064,737	100.0	16,788,668	100.0	6,237,012	100.0
Agriculture, forestry, and animal husbandry	9,869,030	29.8	6,014,204	35.8	1,324,701	21.2
Extraction of minerals	1,087,359	3.3	486,156	2.9	150,062	2.4
Manufacturing and mechanical industries	10,888,183	32.9	4,612,035	27.5	2,256,179	36.2
Transportation	2,850,528	8.6	1,435,331	8.5	561,740	9.0
Trade	3,575,187	10.8	1,842,439	11.0	819,470	13.1
Public service (not elsewhere classified)	748,666	2.3	389,717	2.3	180,977	2.9
Professional service	1,127,391	3.4	684,064	4.1	238,762	3.8
Domestic and personal service	1,217,968	3.7	365,638	2.2	170,296	2.7
Clerical occupations	1,700,425	5.1	959,084	5.7	534,825	8.6
FEMALE.						
All occupations	8,549,511	100.0	3,733,329	100.0	2,110,454	100.0
Agriculture, forestry, and animal husbandry	1,084,128	12.7	377,276	10.1	50,076	2.4
Extraction of minerals	2,864	(1)	1,158	(1)	558	(1)
Manufacturing and mechanical industries	1,930,341	22.6	772,297	20.7	634,316	30.1
Transportation	213,054	2.5	127,078	3.4	71,430	3.4
Trade	667,792	7.8	352,388	9.4	213,976	10.1
Public service (not elsewhere classified)	21,794	0.3	14,910	0.4	4,862	0.2
Professional service	1,016,498	11.9	655,344	17.6	250,920	11.9
Domestic and personal service	2,186,924	25.6	650,655	17.4	340,341	16.1
Clerical occupations	1,426,116	16.7	782,223	21.0	543,975	25.8

[1] Less than one-tenth of 1 per cent.

TABLE **16.**—DISTRIBUTION, BY GENERAL DIVISIONS OF OCCUPATIONS, OF GAINFUL WORKERS 10 YEARS OF AGE AND OVER IN EACH PRINCIPAL CLASS OF THE POPULATION, FOR THE UNITED STATES: 1920—Continued.

SEX AND GENERAL DIVISION OF OCCUPATIONS.	FOREIGN-BORN WHITE.		NEGRO.		INDIAN, CHINESE, JAPANESE, AND ALL OTHER.	
	Number.	Per cent distribution.	Number.	Per cent distribution.	Number.	Per cent distribution.
BOTH SEXES.						
All occupations	7,746,460	100.0	4,824,151	100.0	174,174	100.0
Agriculture, forestry, and animal husbandry	931,561	12.0	2,178,888	45.2	76,452	43.9
Extraction of minerals	377,138	4.9	73,229	1.5	1,922	1.1
Manufacturing and mechanical industries	3,634,249	46.9	886,810	18.4	22,638	13.0
Transportation	547,613	7.1	312,421	6.5	7,969	4.6
Trade	860,530	11.1	140,467	2.9	13,709	7.9
Public service (not elsewhere classified)	127,280	1.6	50,552	1.0	2,162	1.2
Professional service	231,719	3.0	80,183	1.7	2,897	1.7
Domestic and personal service	769,193	9.9	1,064,590	22.1	44,179	25.4
Clerical occupations	267,177	3.4	37,011	0.8	2,246	1.3
MALE.						
All occupations	6,627,997	100.0	3,252,862	100.0	158,198	100.0
Agriculture, forestry, and animal husbandry	891,900	13.5	1,566,627	48.2	71,598	45.3
Extraction of minerals	376,342	5.7	72,892	2.2	1,907	1.2
Manufacturing and mechanical industries	3,219,697	48.6	781,827	24.0	18,445	11.7
Transportation	536,675	8.1	308,896	9.5	7,886	5.0
Trade	770,881	11.6	129,309	4.0	13,088	8.3
Public service (not elsewhere classified)	126,240	1.9	49,586	1.5	2,146	1.4
Professional service	161,162	2.4	41,056	1.3	2,347	1.5
Domestic and personal service	369,232	5.6	273,959	8.4	38,843	24.6
Clerical occupations	175,868	2.7	28,710	0.9	1,938	1.2
FEMALE.						
All occupations	1,118,463	100.0	1,571,289	100.0	15,976	100.0
Agriculture, forestry, and animal husbandry	39,661	3.5	612,261	39.0	4,854	30.4
Extraction of minerals	796	0.1	337	(1)	15	0.1
Manufacturing and mechanical industries	414,552	37.1	104,983	6.7	4,193	26.2
Transportation	10,938	1.0	3,525	0.2	83	0.5
Trade	89,649	8.0	11,158	0.7	621	3.9
Public service (not elsewhere classified)	1,040	0.1	966	0.1	16	0.1
Professional service	70,557	6.3	39,127	2.5	550	3.4
Domestic and personal service	399,961	35.8	790,631	50.3	5,336	33.4
Clerical occupations	91,309	8.2	8,301	0.5	308	1.9

¹ Less than one-tenth of 1 per cent.

TABLE 17.—NUMBER AND PER CENT DISTRIBUTION, BY CLASS OF POPULATION, OF THE POPULATION 10 YEARS OF AGE AND OVER AND OF PERSONS ENGAGED IN GAINFUL OCCUPATIONS, BY GEOGRAPHIC DIVISIONS: 1920.

DIVISION AND CLASS OF POPULATION.	POPULATION 10 YEARS OF AGE AND OVER: 1920		PERSONS ENGAGED IN GAINFUL OCCUPATIONS: 1920	
	Number.	Per cent distribution.	Number.	Per cent distribution.
United States	**82,739,315**	**100.0**	**41,614,248**	**100.0**
Native white—Native parentage	44,077,564	53.3	20,521,997	49.3
Native white—Foreign or mixed parentage	16,784,299	20.2	8,347,466	20.1
Foreign-born white	13,497,886	16.3	7,746,460	18.6
Negro	8,053,225	9.7	4,824,151	11.6
Indian	176,925	0.2	63,326	0.2
Chinese	56,230	0.1	45,614	0.1
Japanese	84,238	0.1	57,903	0.1
All other	8,948	(1)	7,331	(1)
New England	**5,945,989**	**100.0**	**3,234,392**	**100.0**
Native white—Native parentage	2,226,985	37.5	1,128,260	34.9
Native white—Foreign or mixed parentage	1,805,558	30.4	966,703	29.9
Foreign-born white	1,843,028	31.0	1,092,626	33.8
Negro	65,271	1.1	42,872	1.3
Indian	1,368	(1)	747	(1)
Chinese	3,357	0.1	2,885	0.1
Japanese	320	(1)	232	(1)
All other	102	(1)	67	(1)
Middle Atlantic	**17,666,354**	**100.0**	**9,240,216**	**100.0**
Native white—Native parentage	7,471,675	42.3	3,677,057	39.8
Native white—Foreign or mixed parentage	4,816,496	27.3	2,403,301	26.0
Foreign-born white	4,853,256	27.5	2,807,920	30.4
Negro	508,031	2.9	339,213	3.7
Indian	4,589	(1)	2,289	(1)
Chinese	8,321	(1)	7,296	0.1
Japanese	2,930	(1)	2,222	(1)
All other	1,056	(1)	918	(1)
East North Central	**17,130,786**	**100.0**	**8,515,849**	**100.0**
Native white—Native parentage	8,931,324	52.1	4,152,202	48.8
Native white—Foreign or mixed parentage	4,557,935	26.6	2,279,261	26.8
Foreign-born white	3,183,790	18.6	1,795,800	21.1
Negro	440,129	2.6	278,826	3.3
Indian	11,582	0.1	5,051	0.1
Chinese	4,764	(1)	3,892	(1)
Japanese	826	(1)	570	(1)
All other	436	(1)	247	(1)
West North Central	**9,889,740**	**100.0**	**4,587,996**	**100.0**
Native white—Native parentage	5,491,277	55.5	2,409,784	52.5
Native white—Foreign or mixed parentage	2,772,958	28.0	1,310,182	28.6
Foreign-born white	1,358,323	13.7	712,271	15.5
Negro	237,277	2.4	146,432	3.2
Indian	27,175	0.3	7,160	0.2
Chinese	1,560	(1)	1,323	(1)
Japanese	996	(1)	748	(1)
All other	174	(1)	96	(1)
South Atlantic	**10,513,447**	**100.0**	**5,339,999**	**100.0**
Native white—Native parentage	6,547,732	62.3	3,036,727	56.9
Native white—Foreign or mixed parentage	421,149	4.0	211,964	4.0
Foreign-born white	311,385	3.0	189,450	3.5
Negro	3,221,694	30.6	1,895,830	35.5
Indian	9,139	0.1	4,081	0.1
Chinese	1,687	(1)	1,430	(1)
Japanese	317	(1)	237	(1)
All other	344	(1)	280	(1)

[1] Less than one-tenth of 1 per cent.

TABLE 17.—NUMBER AND PER CENT DISTRIBUTION, BY CLASS OF POPULATION, OF THE POPULATION 10 YEARS OF AGE AND OVER AND OF PERSONS ENGAGED IN GAINFUL OCCUPATIONS, BY GEOGRAPHIC DIVISIONS: 1920—Continued.

DIVISION AND CLASS OF POPULATION.	POPULATION 10 YEARS OF AGE AND OVER: 1920		PERSONS ENGAGED IN GAINFUL OCCUPATIONS: 1920	
	Number.	Per cent distribution.	Number.	Per cent distribution.
East South Central	6,677,229	100.0	3,310,844	100.0
Native white—Native parentage	4,502,712	67.4	2,012,783	60.8
Native white—Foreign or mixed parentage	176,884	2.6	89,206	2.7
Foreign-born white	71,211	1.1	41,260	1.2
Negro	1,924,714	28.8	1,166,447	35.2
Indian	1,176	(1)	679	(1)
Chinese	478	(1)	427	(1)
Japanese	26	(1)	19	(1)
All other	28	(1)	23	(1)
West South Central	7,739,536	100.0	3,716,248	100.0
Native white—Native parentage	5,146,751	66.5	2,301,042	61.9
Native white—Foreign or mixed parentage	531,661	6.9	252,273	6.8
Foreign-born white	430,053	5.6	241,498	6.5
Negro	1,587,020	20.5	906,867	24.4
Indian	42,050	0.5	12,917	0.3
Chinese	1,415	(1)	1,257	(1)
Japanese	426	(1)	274	(1)
All other	160	(1)	120	(1)
Mountain	2,564,463	100.0	1,254,994	100.0
Native white—Native parentage	1,456,002	56.8	670,056	53.4
Native white—Foreign or mixed parentage	575,344	22.4	275,371	21.9
Foreign-born white	436,304	17.0	257,468	20.5
Negro	27,741	1.1	20,478	1.6
Indian	56,103	2.2	21,600	1.7
Chinese	4,046	0.2	3,365	0.3
Japanese	8,589	0.3	6,371	0.5
All other	334	(1)	285	(1)
Pacific	4,611,771	100.0	2,413,710	100.0
Native white—Native parentage	2,303,106	49.9	1,134,086	47.0
Native white—Foreign or mixed parentage	1,126,314	24.4	559,205	23.2
Foreign-born white	1,010,536	21.9	608,167	25.2
Negro	41,348	0.9	27,186	1.1
Indian	23,743	0.5	8,802	0.4
Chinese	30,602	0.7	23,739	1.0
Japanese	69,808	1.5	47,230	2.0
All other	6,314	0.1	5,295	0.2

[1] Less than one-tenth of 1 per cent.

TABLE 18.—PER CENT DISTRIBUTION, BY CLASS OF POPULATION, OF PERSONS 10 YEARS OF AGE AND OVER ENGAGED IN GAINFUL OCCUPATIONS, BY DIVISIONS AND STATES: 1920.

DIVISION AND STATE.	PER CENT OF ALL PERSONS OCCUPIED.				
	Native white— native parentage.	Native white— foreign or mixed parentage.	Foreign-born white.	Negro.	Indian, Chinese, Japanese, and all other.
United States....................	49.3	20.1	18.6	11.6	0.4
GEOGRAPHIC DIVISIONS:					
New England........................	34.9	29.9	33.8	1.3	0.1
Middle Atlantic....................	39.8	26.0	30.4	3.7	0.1
East North Central.................	48.8	26.8	21.1	3.3	0.1
West North Central.................	52.5	28.6	15.5	3.2	0.2
South Atlantic.....................	56.9	4.0	3.5	35.5	0.1
East South Central.................	60.8	2.7	1.2	35.2	(1)
West South Central.................	61.9	6.8	6.5	24.4	0.4
Mountain...........................	53.4	21.9	20.5	1.6	2.5
Pacific............................	47.0	23.2	25.2	1.1	3.5
NEW ENGLAND:					
Maine..............................	62.5	17.5	19.7	0.2	0.2
New Hampshire......................	47.9	23.4	28.5	0.2	0.1
Vermont............................	61.7	21.4	16.7	0.2	(1)
Massachusetts......................	29.1	32.6	36.7	1.4	0.1
Rhode Island.......................	26.1	34.9	36.9	1.9	0.1
Connecticut........................	30.9	30.2	36.8	2.0	0.1
MIDDLE ATLANTIC:					
New York...........................	32.3	29.3	35.4	2.7	0.2
New Jersey.........................	35.6	27.7	31.9	4.7	0.1
Pennsylvania.......................	51.2	21.0	23.2	4.5	0.1
EAST NORTH CENTRAL:					
Ohio...............................	58.9	19.9	16.9	4.3	(1)
Indiana............................	75.1	13.6	7.5	3.8	(1)
Illinois...........................	40.5	29.8	25.8	3.8	0.1
Michigan...........................	40.4	29.5	27.6	2.3	0.2
Wisconsin..........................	29.9	45.4	24.1	0.3	0.3
WEST NORTH CENTRAL:					
Minnesota..........................	25.9	44.3	29.0	0.6	0.3
Iowa...............................	56.6	29.7	12.5	1.1	(1)
Missouri...........................	67.2	17.6	7.8	7.3	(1)
North Dakota.......................	25.2	40.7	33.3	0.1	0.7
South Dakota.......................	40.8	38.2	19.5	0.2	1.3
Nebraska...........................	51.2	30.8	16.0	1.6	0.3
Kansas.............................	68.7	18.2	8.7	4.3	0.1
SOUTH ATLANTIC:					
Delaware...........................	59.0	11.9	12.7	16.4	(1)
Maryland...........................	56.0	14.1	9.4	20.4	0.1
District of Columbia...............	52.6	12.7	7.1	27.3	0.2
Virginia...........................	61.9	2.5	2.3	33.3	0.1
West Virginia......................	79.4	4.6	8.2	7.8	(1)
North Carolina.....................	65.2	0.5	0.5	33.4	0.4
South Carolina.....................	42.1	0.8	0.6	56.4	(1)
Georgia............................	50.2	1.1	0.9	47.8	(1)
Florida............................	46.7	5.3	6.8	41.2	0.1
EAST SOUTH CENTRAL:					
Kentucky...........................	78.0	6.4	2.0	13.6	(1)
Tennessee..........................	71.9	1.9	1.1	25.1	(1)
Alabama............................	52.2	1.4	1.1	45.3	(1)
Mississippi........................	38.4	1.0	0.7	59.7	0.1
WEST SOUTH CENTRAL:					
Arkansas...........................	63.2	2.6	1.4	32.8	(1)
Louisiana..........................	44.7	6.2	3.9	45.1	0.1
Oklahoma...........................	80.0	6.0	3.4	8.8	1.7
Texas..............................	61.1	8.9	10.6	19.3	0.1
MOUNTAIN:					
Montana............................	44.0	27.3	26.5	0.5	1.7
Idaho..............................	59.1	23.7	15.4	0.4	1.4
Wyoming............................	57.0	19.8	20.3	1.1	1.8
Colorado...........................	59.8	20.1	17.9	1.7	0.5
New Mexico.........................	70.6	8.3	12.1	3.7	5.2
Arizona............................	43.3	13.4	30.5	4.6	8.2
Utah...............................	41.1	36.4	20.0	0.6	1.9
Nevada.............................	41.1	22.9	28.2	0.7	7.1
PACIFIC:					
Washington.........................	47.0	23.6	26.2	0.7	2.4
Oregon.............................	57.9	21.2	18.7	0.4	1.8
California.........................	44.6	23.4	26.2	1.4	4.3

1 Less than one-tenth of 1 per cent.

TABLE 19.—NUMBER AND PROPORTION OF MALES IN EACH PRINCIPAL CLASS OF BY DIVISIONS

DIVISION AND STATE.	NATIVE WHITE—NATIVE PARENTAGE.			NATIVE WHITE—FOREIGN OR MIXED PARENTAGE.		
	Total number.	Engaged in gainful occupations.		Total number.	Engaged in gainful occupations.	
		Number.	Per cent.		Number.	Per cent.
United States.........	22,361,495	16,788,668	75.1	8,289,550	6,237,012	75.2
GEOGRAPHIC DIVISIONS:						
New England.............	1,097,722	846,384	77.1	872,977	631,391	72.3
Middle Atlantic............	3,698,009	2,837,935	76.7	2,334,928	1,695,788	72.6
East North Central........	4,542,747	3,394,523	74.7	2,256,877	1,752,481	77.7
West North Central.......	2,802,396	1,999,029	71.3	1,398,065	1,058,283	75.7
South Atlantic............	3,300,670	2,506,843	75.9	207,704	160,195	77.1
East South Central.......	2,277,389	1,733,971	76.1	84,800	69,923	82.5
West South Central......	2,666,690	1,983,571	74.4	272,145	209,801	77.1
Mountain.................	778,816	572,282	73.5	298,736	227,990	76.3
Pacific...................	1,197,056	914,130	76.4	563,318	431,160	76.5
NEW ENGLAND:						
Maine......	202,059	155,549	77.0	57,050	39,503	69.2
New Hampshire.........	92,298	71,624	77.6	42,655	29,855	70.0
Vermont...............	91,546	68,492	74.8	29,881	22,754	76.1
Massachusetts.............	470,024	362,009	77.0	496,984	361,091	72.7
Rhode Island............	66,862	52,364	78.3	80,830	60,560	74.9
Connecticut...............	174,933	136,346	77.9	165,577	117,628	71.0
MIDDLE ATLANTIC:						
New York..............	1,420,955	1,089,675	76.7	1,248,316	909,796	72.9
New Jersey.............	468,209	361,806	77.3	352,045	256,334	72.8
Pennsylvania...........	1,808,845	1,386,454	76.6	734,567	529,658	72.1
EAST NORTH CENTRAL:						
Ohio....	1,453,254	1,111,862	76.5	454,617	355,650	78.2
Indiana...................	924,318	701,576	75.9	150,922	122,381	81.1
Illinois...................	1,166,289	859,683	73.7	745,420	572,885	76.9
Michigan.................	645,382	488,328	75.7	450,586	343,168	76.2
Wisconsin................	353,504	233,074	65.9	455,332	358,397	78.7
WEST NORTH CENTRAL:						
Minnesota................	277,714	185,722	66.9	424,575	313,325	73.8
Iowa.....................	573,087	400,726	69.9	272,080	210,577	77.4
Missouri.................	988,780	735,567	74.4	215,252	180,069	83.7
North Dakota............	66,826	43,462	65.0	107,748	69,862	64.8
South Dakota............	109,294	74,584	68.2	95,496	70,377	73.7
Nebraska.................	279,823	194,708	69.6	156,706	117,184	74.8
Kansas...................	506,872	364,260	71.9	126,208	96,889	76.8
SOUTH ATLANTIC:						
Delaware.................	56,554	44,325	78.4	11,074	8,109	73.2
Maryland................	348,488	272,067	78.1	80,971	63,781	78.8
District of Columbia......	92,275	75,509	81.8	22,667	18,553	81.9
Virginia.................	586,495	442,214	75.4	21,785	17,128	78.6
West Virginia............	464,947	344,096	74.0	25,779	18,650	72.3
North Carolina...........	639,875	479,863	75.0	4,385	3,348	76.4
South Carolina...........	294,945	225,052	76.3	5,494	4,541	82.7
Georgia..................	610,262	469,354	76.9	12,635	10,158	80.4
Florida..................	206,829	154,363	74.6	22,914	15,927	69.5
EAST SOUTH CENTRAL:						
Kentucky................	770,836	583,762	75.7	47,751	41,591	87.1
Tennessee...............	687,222	517,557	75.3	15,866	12,245	77.2
Alabama.................	510,436	397,956	78.0	13,545	10,060	74.3
Mississippi..............	308,895	234,696	75.9	7,638	6,027	78.9
WEST SOUTH CENTRAL:						
Arkansas................	459,178	348,777	76.0	17,790	14,287	80.6
Louisiana................	352,112	260,434	74.0	43,110	33,416	77.6
Oklahoma...............	648,851	474,157	73.1	45,356	35,606	78.5
Texas...................	1,206,549	900,203	74.6	166,529	126,492	76.0
MOUNTAIN:						
Montana.................	107,617	81,145	75.4	64,114	48,228	75.2
Idaho....	111,728	79,321	71.0	40,459	31,916	78.9
Wyoming................	51,790	40,670	78.5	17,302	13,734	79.4
Colorado................	243,116	181,508	74.7	78,425	57,528	73.4
New Mexico.............	104,620	76,071	72.7	11,285	8,459	75.0
Arizona.................	63,601	48,933	76.9	20,360	14,802	72.7
Utah....................	79,714	51,272	64.3	57,969	45,989	79.3
Nevada..................	16,630	13,362	80.3	8,822	7,334	83.1
PACIFIC:						
Washington..............	292,575	224,895	76.9	143,047	107,839	75.4
Oregon..................	203,787	153,619	75.4	69,756	53,574	76.8
California...............	700,694	535,616	76.4	350,515	269,747	77.0

THE POPULATION 10 YEARS OF AGE AND OVER ENGAGED IN GAINFUL OCCUPATIONS, AND STATES: 1920.

DIVISION AND STATE.	FOREIGN-BORN WHITE.			NEGRO.		
	Total number.	Engaged in gainful occupations.		Total number.	Engaged in gainful occupations.	
		Number.	Per cent.		Number.	Per cent.
United States	7,419,691	6,627,997	89.3	4,009,462	3,252,862	81.1
GEOGRAPHIC DIVISIONS:						
New England	931,845	853,144	91.6	33,379	28,780	86.2
Middle Atlantic	2,587,798	2,354,559	91.0	256,057	222,328	86.8
East North Central	1,789,466	1,589,630	88.8	236,246	206,118	87.2
West North Central	772,147	645,046	83.5	123,472	104,548	84.7
South Atlantic	182,846	165,656	90.6	1,584,869	1,258,209	79.4
East South Central	41,729	36,790	88.2	943,946	766,741	81.2
West South Central	245,597	212,745	86.6	791,529	629,967	79.6
Mountain	262,733	233,954	89.0	18,178	16,846	92.7
Pacific	605,530	536,473	88.6	21,786	19,325	88.7
NEW ENGLAND:						
Maine	54,398	49,063	90.2	600	520	86.7
New Hampshire	45,952	41,714	90.8	275	234	85.1
Vermont	22,806	20,080	88.0	267	239	89.5
Massachusetts	526,272	483,397	91.9	18,989	16,345	86.1
Rhode Island	84,933	77,659	91.4	4,214	3,606	85.6
Connecticut	197,484	181,231	91.8	9,034	7,836	86.7
MIDDLE ATLANTIC:						
New York	1,425,461	1,287,071	90.3	82,115	72,671	88.5
New Jersey	387,251	355,166	91.7	47,376	40,014	84.5
Pennsylvania	775,086	712,322	91.9	126,566	109,643	86.6
EAST NORTH CENTRAL:						
Ohio	386,901	348,421	90.1	86,147	74,622	86.6
Indiana	87,396	76,707	87.8	35,674	30,620	85.8
Illinois	651,256	580,837	89.2	81,431	70,905	87.1
Michigan	407,057	367,026	90.2	30,413	27,661	91.0
Wisconsin	256,856	216,639	84.3	2,581	2,310	89.5
WEST NORTH CENTRAL:						
Minnesota	276,630	237,632	85.9	4,339	4,038	93.1
Iowa	126,109	98,445	78.1	8,578	7,346	85.6
Missouri	102,587	89,547	87.3	78,532	66,832	85.1
North Dakota	74,633	63,759	85.4	243	243	100.0
South Dakota	47,289	38,876	82.2	407	358	88.0
Nebraska	83,542	66,674	79.8	6,441	5,576	86.6
Kansas	61,357	50,113	81.7	24,932	20,155	80.8
SOUTH ATLANTIC:						
Delaware	11,230	10,307	91.8	12,895	10,342	80.2
Maryland	54,102	48,410	89.5	98,988	81,654	82.5
District of Columbia	15,022	12,929	86.1	42,979	35,865	83.4
Virginia	18,812	17,302	92.0	258,723	200,136	77.4
West Virginia	41,295	38,567	93.4	38,499	32,279	83.8
North Carolina	4,287	3,998	93.3	265,258	203,035	76.5
South Carolina	4,063	3,717	91.5	299,487	235,116	78.5
Georgia	9,923	9,036	91.1	436,182	351,626	80.6
Florida	24,112	21,390	88.7	131,858	108,156	82.0
EAST SOUTH CENTRAL:						
Kentucky	17,401	15,115	86.9	97,102	79,094	81.5
Tennessee	8,928	7,688	86.1	173,840	140,414	80.8
Alabama	10,484	9,505	90.7	326,672	266,651	81.6
Mississippi	4,916	4,482	91.2	346,332	280,582	81.0
WEST SOUTH CENTRAL:						
Arkansas	8,528	7,711	90.4	182,403	147,846	81.1
Louisiana	26,477	23,801	89.9	262,983	210,162	79.9
Oklahoma	24,412	21,766	89.2	58,823	44,582	75.8
Texas	186,180	159,467	85.7	287,320	227,377	79.1
MOUNTAIN:						
Montana	57,287	52,160	91.1	848	800	94.3
Idaho	24,565	22,199	90.4	526	461	87.6
Wyoming	16,700	15,562	93.2	806	705	87.5
Colorado	66,869	58,766	87.9	5,116	4,379	85.6
New Mexico	15,685	13,618	86.8	4,399	4,260	96.8
Arizona	40,476	34,827	86.0	5,550	5,345	96.3
Utah	30,516	26,783	87.8	750	716	95.5
Nevada	10,635	10,039	94.4	183	180	98.4
PACIFIC:						
Washington	150,510	136,812	90.9	3,525	3,223	91.4
Oregon	61,575	54,160	88.0	1,080	1,037	96.0
California	393,445	345,501	87.8	17,181	15,065	87.7

TABLE 20.—NUMBER AND PROPORTION OF FEMALES IN EACH PRINCIPAL CLASS OF
BY DIVISIONS

DIVISION AND STATE.	NATIVE WHITE—NATIVE PARENTAGE.			NATIVE WHITE—FOREIGN OR MIXED PARENTAGE.		
	Total number.	Engaged in gainful occupations.		Total number.	Engaged in gainful occupations.	
		Number.	Per cent.		Number.	Per cent.
United States	21,716,069	3,733,329	17.2	8,494,749	2,110,454	24.8
GEOGRAPHIC DIVISIONS:						
New England	1,129,263	281,876	25.0	932,581	335,312	36.0
Middle Atlantic	3,773,666	839,122	22.2	2,481,568	707,513	28.5
East North Central	4,388,577	757,679	17.3	2,301,058	526,780	22.9
West North Central	2,688,881	410,755	15.3	1,374,893	251,899	18.3
South Atlantic	3,247,062	529,884	16.3	213,445	51,769	24.3
East South Central	2,225,323	278,812	12.5	92,084	19,283	20.9
West South Central	2,480,061	317,471	12.8	259,516	42,472	16.4
Mountain	677,186	97,774	14.4	276,608	47,381	17.1
Pacific	1,106,050	219,956	19.9	562,996	128,045	22.7
NEW ENGLAND:						
Maine	198,447	37,980	19.1	57,206	14,742	25.8
New Hampshire	92,378	20,674	22.4	44,513	15,300	34.4
Vermont	89,666	16,892	18.8	30,193	6,891	22.8
Massachusetts	500,447	141,049	28.2	535,079	202,331	37.8
Rhode Island	68,111	19,405	28.5	88,422	35,460	40.1
Connecticut	180,214	45,876	25.5	177,168	60,588	34.2
MIDDLE ATLANTIC:						
New York	1,455,977	366,593	25.2	1,341,387	409,574	30.5
New Jersey	474,229	104,330	22.0	371,671	107,353	28.9
Pennsylvania	1,843,460	368,199	20.0	768,510	190,586	24.8
EAST NORTH CENTRAL:						
Ohio	1,411,006	242,885	17.2	476,496	102,534	21.5
Indiana	908,276	137,596	15.1	154,627	29,142	18.8
Illinois	1,138,691	205,266	18.0	778,925	210,372	27.0
Michigan	589,635	107,082	18.2	439,372	90,934	20.7
Wisconsin	340,969	64,850	19.0	451,638	93,798	20.8
WEST NORTH CENTRAL:						
Minnesota	260,044	48,840	18.8	418,082	88,602	21.2
Iowa	557,184	85,364	15.3	270,454	44,368	16.4
Missouri	968,147	149,986	15.5	227,630	51,456	22.6
North Dakota	59,866	8,709	14.5	100,684	14,375	14.3
South Dakota	95,789	13,711	14.3	87,023	12,376	14.2
Nebraska	262,557	39,378	15.0	150,828	23,817	15.8
Kansas	485,294	64,767	13.3	120,192	16,905	14.1
SOUTH ATALNTIC:						
Delaware	55,409	9,504	17.2	11,704	2,773	23.7
Maryland	347,496	66,097	19.0	85,598	21,113	24.7
District of Columbia	112,079	48,595	43.4	27,501	11,535	41.9
Virginia	570,066	73,780	12.9	18,574	3,543	19.1
West Virginia	437,724	45,921	10.5	25,372	3,933	15.5
North Carolina	635,557	104,260	16.4	4,391	814	18.5
South Carolina	288,355	58,848	20.4	4,915	1,008	20.5
Georgia	602,860	97,400	16.2	12,019	2,525	21.0
Florida	197,516	25,479	12.9	23,371	4,525	19.4
EAST SOUTH CENTRAL:						
Kentucky	741,620	80,486	10.9	53,857	12,621	23.4
Tennessee	681,404	79,668	11.7	16,425	3,159	19.2
Alabama	500,777	76,024	15.2	13,934	2,257	16.2
Mississippi	301,522	42,634	14.1	7,868	1,246	15.8
WEST SOUTH CENTRAL:						
Arkansas	433,132	52,150	12.0	15,444	2,432	15.7
Louisiana	341,571	44,147	12.9	47,975	8,505	17.7
Oklahoma	586,488	70,843	12.1	39,712	5,525	13.9
Texas	1,118,870	130,001	13.4	156,385	26,010	16.6
MOUNTAIN:						
Montana	89,020	13,109	14.7	57,781	10,090	17.9
Idaho	95,873	11,311	11.8	34,607	4,525	13.1
Wyoming	38,981	5,805	14.9	14,565	2,381	16.3
Colorado	220,315	37,648	17.1	78,307	16,183	20.7
New Mexico	94,739	10,101	10.7	10,249	1,672	16.3
Arizona	50,637	7,637	15.1	18,277	2,738	15.0
Utah	76,037	10,096	13.3	56,021	8,292	14.8
Nevada	11,584	2,067	17.8	6,801	1,261	18.5
PACIFIC:						
Washington	257,221	47,248	18.4	134,891	28,721	21.3
Oregon	185,651	32,876	17.7	67,325	14,768	21.9
California	663,178	139,832	21.1	360,780	84,556	23.4

THE POPULATION 10 YEARS OF AGE AND OVER ENGAGED IN GAINFUL OCCUPATIONS, AND STATES: 1920.

DIVISION AND STATE.	FOREIGN-BORN WHITE.			NEGRO.		
	Total number.	Engaged in gainful occupations.		Total number.	Engaged in gainful occupations.	
		Number.	Per cent.		Number.	Per cent.
United States	6,078,195	1,118,463	18.4	4,043,763	1,571,289	38.9
GEOGRAPHIC DIVISIONS:						
New England	911,183	239,482	26.3	31,892	14,092	44.2
Middle Atlantic	2,265,458	453,361	20.0	251,974	116,885	46.4
East North Central	1,394,324	206,170	14.8	203,883	72,7C8	35.7
West North Central	586,176	67,225	11.5	113,805	41,884	36.8
South Atlantic	128,539	23,794	18.5	1,636,825	637,621	39.0
East South Central	29,482	4,470	15.2	980,768	399,706	40.8
West South Central	184,456	28,753	15.6	795,491	276,900	34.8
Mountain	173,571	23,514	13.5	9,563	3,632	38.0
Pacific	405,006	71,694	17.7	19,562	7,861	40.2
NEW ENGLAND:						
Maine	50,187	11,857	23.6	491	178	36.3
New Hampshire	43,520	13,246	30.4	215	73	34.0
Vermont	19,895	3,044	15.3	187	69	36.9
Massachusetts	537,300	151,510	28.2	18,614	8,159	43.8
Rhode Island	86,099	23,934	27.8	3,978	1,745	43.9
Connecticut	174,182	35,891	20.6	8,407	3,868	46.0
MIDDLE ATLANTIC:						
New York	1,326,594	309,297	23.3	89,188	49,294	55.3
New Jersey	342,548	62,527	18.3	49,325	21,738	44.1
Pennsylvania	596,316	81,537	13.7	113,461	45,853	40.4
EAST NORTH CENTRAL:						
Ohio	283,023	39,948	14.1	71,765	24,571	34.2
Indiana	61,843	6,953	11.2	32,687	11,676	35.7
Illinois	543,723	96,058	17.7	75,774	29,161	38.5
Michigan	306,171	40,400	13.2	21,780	6,687	30.7
Wisconsin	199,564	22,811	11.4	1,877	613	32.7
WEST NORTH CENTRAL:						
Minnesota	205,600	25,174	12.2	3,437	1,257	36.6
Iowa	97,643	9,278	9.5	7,324	2,299	31.4
Missouri	81,807	13,428	16.4	74,329	29,713	40.0
North Dakota	55,318	5,132	9.3	162	45	27.8
South Dakota	34,492	3,363	9.8	271	94	34.7
Nebraska	64,667	6,664	10.3	5,048	1,876	37.2
Kansas	46,649	4,186	9.0	23,234	6,600	28.4
SOUTH ATLANTIC:						
Delaware	8,311	1,239	14.9	11,703	4,586	39.2
Maryland	47,053	8,471	18.0	95,837	41,525	43.3
District of Columbia	13,270	3,889	29.3	50,803	28,588	56.3
Virginia	11,513	1,647	14.3	261,934	77,204	29.5
West Virginia	19,384	1,582	8.2	30,287	6,001	19.8
North Carolina	2,694	548	20.3	280,284	96,309	34.4
South Carolina	2,264	378	16.7	319,441	145,399	45.5
Georgia	6,105	1,202	19.7	459,945	187,603	40.8
Florida	17,945	4,838	27.0	126,591	50,406	39.8
EAST SOUTH CENTRAL:						
Kentucky	13,202	1,952	14.8	95,555	36,419	38.1
Tennessee	6,369	1,060	16.6	180,586	68,217	37.8
Alabama	6,909	913	13.2	347,332	144,650	41.6
Mississippi	3,002	545	18.2	357,295	150,420	42.1
WEST SOUTH CENTRAL:						
Arkansas	5,306	949	17.9	181,000	60,273	33.3
Louisiana	17,767	2,758	15.5	273,379	97,267	35.6
Oklahoma	14,608	1,649	11.3	55,713	15,414	27.7
Texas	146,775	23,397	15.9	285,399	103,946	36.4
MOUNTAIN:						
Montana	34,442	4,491	13.0	602	206	34.2
Idaho	13,814	1,505	10.9	288	80	27.8
Wyoming	8,062	964	12.0	445	207	46.5
Colorado	47,416	6,742	14.2	4,793	1,928	40.2
New Mexico	11,101	1,196	10.8	963	303	31.5
Arizona	29,577	4,935	16.7	1,819	677	37.2
Utah	25,208	3,119	12.4	523	155	29.6
Nevada	3,951	562	14.2	130	76	58.5
PACIFIC:						
Washington	94,371	14,861	15.7	2,539	924	36.4
Oregon	39,097	6,205	15.9	813	317	39.0
California	271,538	50,628	18.6	16,210	6,620	40.8

TABLE 21.—NUMBER AND PROPORTION OF MALES IN EACH PRINCIPAL CLASS OF THE
FOR CITIES HAVING 100,000

CITY.	NATIVE WHITE—NATIVE PARENTAGE.			NATIVE WHITE—FOREIGN OR MIXED PARENTAGE.		
	Total number.	Engaged in gainful occupations.		Total number.	Engaged in gainful occupations.	
		Number.	Per ct.		Number.	Per ct.
Akron, Ohio	61,665	55,253	89.6	13,727	11,112	80.9
Albany, N. Y	22,039	17,310	78.5	14,486	12,099	83.5
Atlanta, Ga	49,234	40,813	82.9	2,944	2,258	76.7
Baltimore, Md	144,834	118,114	81.6	60,550	47,592	78.6
Birmingham, Ala	36,750	29,406	80.0	3,634	2,581	71.0
Boston, Mass	69,905	54,241	77.6	105,469	76,809	72.8
Bridgeport, Conn	14,715	12,015	81.7	17,203	12,218	71.0
Buffalo, N. Y	61,095	47,356	77.5	76,234	58,610	76.9
Cambridge, Mass	10,452	7,932	75.9	14,638	10,582	72.3
Camden, N. J	22,194	18,339	82.6	10,226	7,760	75.9
Chicago, Ill	235,238	186,661	79.3	387,158	294,493	76.1
Cincinnati, Ohio	77,781	61,586	79.2	50,273	43,260	86.1
Cleveland, Ohio	82,061	65,924	80.3	98,982	71,790	72.5
Columbus, Ohio	64,288	50,582	78.7	16,313	13,351	81.8
Dallas, Tex	45,918	37,662	82.0	5,421	4,488	82.8
Dayton, Ohio	40,662	33,540	82.5	11,471	9,678	84.4
Denver, Colo	63,205	48,097	76.1	26,720	20,715	77.5
Des Moines, Iowa	32,886	25,897	78.7	9,976	7,912	79.3
Detroit, Mich	132,321	112,771	85.2	119,414	94,987	79.5
Fall River, Mass	5,981	4,295	71.8	18,270	13,402	73.4
Fort Worth, Tex	33,129	27,152	82.0	3,178	2,621	82.5
Grand Rapids, Mich	20,506	16,184	78.9	18,462	14,029	76.0
Hartford, Conn	15,961	13,026	81.6	16,748	12,160	72.6
Houston, Tex	29,226	23,989	82.1	7,683	6,362	82.8
Indianapolis, Ind	88,725	73,716	83.1	17,740	15,129	85.3
Jersey City, N. J	31,809	24,864	78.2	43,120	32,995	76.5
Kansas City, Kans	22,431	18,208	81.2	6,626	5,235	79.0
Kansas City, Mo	86,408	71,914	83.2	22,904	18,780	82.0
Los Angeles, Calif	120,848	94,961	78.6	52,326	40,194	76.8
Louisville, Ky	52,888	42,669	80.7	18,086	15,674	86.7
Lowell, Mass	8,457	6,501	76.9	16,484	12,237	74.2
Memphis, Tenn	33,371	27,557	82.6	5,007	3,835	76.6
Milwaukee, Wis	43,155	32,562	75.5	79,411	65,495	82.5
Minneapolis, Minn	49,119	37,965	77.3	56,466	44,018	78.0
Nashville, Tenn	28,548	22,813	79.9	2,569	2,064	80.3
New Bedford, Mass	7,491	5,973	79.7	14,026	10,261	73.2
New Haven, Conn	16,886	13,405	79.4	20,757	14,716	70.9
New Orleans, La	73,237	58,747	80.2	27,697	23,054	83.2
New York, N. Y	431,721	337,737	78.2	739,645	522,012	70.6
Bronx borough	46,513	34,733	74.7	104,967	72,454	69.0
Brooklyn borough	168,274	132,139	78.5	277,280	194,361	70.1
Manhattan borough	150,296	120,745	80.3	266,385	184,867	69.4
Queens borough	51,330	38,661	75.3	75,107	59,030	78.6
Richmond borough	15,308	11,459	74.9	15,906	11,300	71.0
Newark, N. J	43,270	34,185	79.0	53,441	38,781	72.6
Norfolk, Va	24,305	20,427	84.0	3,095	2,288	73.9
Oakland, Calif	36,322	28,845	79.4	26,566	20,841	78.4
Omaha, Nebr	35,314	28,585	80.9	22,167	17,195	77.6
Paterson, N. J	11,430	8,942	78.2	19,275	14,372	74.6
Philadelphia, Pa	267,537	213,304	79.7	203,786	153,963	75.6
Pittsburgh, Pa	80,273	62,532	77.9	73,507	54,701	74.4
Portland, Oreg	54,254	43,789	80.7	27,025	21,202	78.5
Providence, R. I	23,829	18,701	78.5	32,168	23,901	74.3
Reading, Pa	32,042	26,585	83.0	5,224	3,987	76.3
Richmond, Va	38,880	30,985	79.7	3,762	2,980	79.2
Rochester, N. Y	42,309	33,469	79.1	37,723	29,802	79.0
St. Louis, Mo	138,574	111,379	80.4	96,834	83,036	85.8
St. Paul, Minn	27,361	20,669	75.5	39,099	31,436	80.4
Salt Lake City, Utah	19,695	13,922	70.7	16,023	12,719	79.4
San Antonio, Tex	29,791	23,119	77.6	11,825	9,235	78.1
San Francisco, Calif	73,607	61,147	83.1	73,279	59,684	81.4
Scranton, Pa	16,627	12,344	74.0	20,246	15,066	74.4
Seattle, Wash	58,266	46,949	80.6	33,110	27,851	78.8
Spokane, Wash	22,296	17,352	77.8	11,243	8,598	76.5
Springfield, Mass	18,998	15,319	80.6	15,659	12,007	76.7
Syracuse, N. Y	31,868	25,639	80.5	20,838	16,543	79.4
Toledo, Ohio	50,443	41,636	82.5	28,744	23,186	80.7
Trenton, N. J	17,360	13,815	79.6	12,443	8,769	70.5
Washington, D. C	92,275	75,509	81.8	22,667	18,553	81.9
Wilmington, Del	22,905	19,304	84.3	8,571	6,328	73.8
Worcester, Mass	18,783	14,676	78.1	24,500	17,597	71.8
Yonkers, N. Y	10,693	7,832	73.2	13,898	9,813	70.6
Youngstown, Ohio	17,947	14,467	80.6	13,627	9,769	71.7

POPULATION 10 YEARS OF AGE AND OVER ENGAGED IN GAINFUL OCCUPATIONS, INHABITANTS OR MORE: 1920.

CITY.	FOREIGN-BORN WHITE.			NEGRO.		
	Total number.	Engaged in gainful occupations.		Total number.	Engaged in gainful occupations.	
		Number.	Per ct.		Number.	Per ct.
Akron, Ohio	24, 264	22, 593	93. 1	3, 242	2, 996	92. 4
Albany, N. Y	8, 893	7, 873	88. 5	562	490	87. 2
Atlanta, Ga	2, 667	2, 458	92. 2	24, 169	21, 148	87. 5
Baltimore, Md	43, 613	39, 245	90. 0	44, 967	39, 870	88. 7
Birmingham, Ala	3, 459	3, 119	90. 2	28, 227	23, 941	84. 8
Boston, Mass	116, 473	107, 602	92. 4	7, 201	6, 360	88. 3
Bridgeport, Conn	24, 967	23, 082	92. 5	1, 064	960	90. 2
Buffalo, N. Y	63, 806	57, 231	89. 7	2, 245	2, 037	90. 7
Cambridge, Mass	14, 980	13, 817	92. 2	1, 998	1, 637	81. 9
Camden, N. J	10, 927	10, 110	92. 5	3, 546	3, 078	86. 8
Chicago, Ill	427, 820	391, 494	91. 5	49, 811	45, 123	90. 6
Cincinnati, Ohio	21, 669	18, 436	85. 1	13, 136	11, 605	88. 3
Cleveland, Ohio	131, 385	120, 698	91. 9	16, 529	15, 010	90. 8
Columbus, Ohio	9, 021	7, 875	87. 3	10, 210	8, 839	86. 6
Dallas, Tex	4, 926	4, 443	90. 2	10, 313	9, 094	88. 2
Dayton, Ohio	7, 312	6, 577	89. 9	4, 127	3, 712	89. 9
Denver, Colo	20, 688	18, 475	89. 3	2, 764	2, 371	85. 8
Des Moines, Iowa	6, 148	5, 415	88. 1	2, 343	2, 028	86. 6
Detroit, Mich	165, 550	153, 205	92. 5	21, 349	19, 808	92. 8
Fall River, Mass	20, 036	18, 242	91. 0	117	110	94. 0
Fort Worth, Tex	4, 472	4, 104	91. 8	6, 960	6, 035	86. 7
Grand Rapids, Mich	14, 842	13, 303	89. 6	474	422	89. 0
Hartford, Conn	21, 243	19, 480	91. 7	1, 782	1, 563	87. 7
Houston, Tex	6, 529	5, 835	89. 4	14, 129	12, 538	88. 7
Indianapolis, Ind	9, 270	8, 165	88. 1	14, 859	13, 033	87. 7
Jersey City, N. J	39, 859	36, 755	92. 2	3, 440	3, 042	88. 4
Kansas City, Kans	6, 656	6, 138	92. 2	6, 008	5, 129	85. 4
Kansas City, Mo	15, 119	13, 609	90. 0	13, 989	12, 449	89. 0
Los Angeles, Calif	58, 491	50, 036	85. 5	6, 356	5, 543	87. 2
Louisville, Ky	5, 859	4, 948	84. 5	16, 689	14, 749	88. 4
Lowell, Mass	18, 233	16, 889	92. 6	84	81	(1)
Memphis, Tenn	3, 235	2, 888	89. 3	25, 064	22, 105	88. 2
Milwaukee, Wis	60, 139	54, 322	90. 3	1, 096	988	90. 1
Minneapolis, Minn	47, 913	43, 604	91. 0	1, 920	1, 773	92. 3
Nashville, Tenn	1, 276	1, 082	84. 8	13, 518	11, 365	84. 1
New Bedford, Mass	23, 337	21, 561	92. 4	2, 179	1, 942	89. 1
New Haven, Conn	23, 243	21, 177	91. 1	1, 875	1, 640	87. 5
New Orleans, La	15, 307	13, 660	89. 2	38, 706	32, 695	84. 5
New York, N. Y	1, 008, 582	917, 249	90. 9	62, 614	56, 516	90. 3
Bronx borough	134, 214	121, 802	90. 8	1, 794	1, 404	78. 3
Brooklyn borough	337, 893	307, 567	91. 0	12, 895	11, 423	88. 6
Manhattan borough	462, 684	421, 796	91. 2	45, 485	41, 551	91. 4
Queens borough	56, 624	51, 581	91. 1	1, 831	1, 589	86. 8
Richmond borough	17, 167	14, 503	84. 5	609	549	90. 1
Newark, N. J	61, 197	56, 544	92. 4	7, 096	6, 314	89. 0
Norfolk, Va	4, 398	4, 156	94. 5	18, 660	16, 720	89. 6
Oakland, Calif	25, 195	22, 405	88. 9	2, 724	2, 435	89. 4
Omaha, Nebr	19, 712	17, 648	89. 5	4, 932	4, 285	86. 9
Paterson, N. J	22, 910	21, 095	92. 1	619	523	84. 5
Philadelphia, Pa	203, 406	184, 101	90. 5	57, 796	50, 809	87. 9
Pittsburgh, Pa	64, 807	59, 414	91. 7	17, 176	15, 071	87. 7
Portland, Oreg	26, 967	24, 101	89. 4	748	721	96. 4
Providence, R. I	33, 711	31, 069	92. 2	2, 379	2, 071	87. 1
Reading, Pa	5, 404	4, 986	92. 3	406	371	91. 4
Richmond, Va	2, 502	2, 247	89. 8	20, 203	16, 946	83. 9
Rochester, N. Y	36, 373	32, 545	89. 5	642	590	91. 9
St. Louis, Mo	55, 885	50, 026	89. 5	31, 140	27, 880	89. 5
St. Paul, Minn	27, 768	25, 020	90. 1	1, 638	1, 491	91. 0
Salt Lake City, Utah	9, 604	8, 477	88. 3	358	308	86. 0
San Antonio, Tex	18, 141	15, 308	84. 4	5, 808	4, 911	84. 6
San Francisco, Calif	82, 046	74, 675	91. 0	1, 239	1, 197	96. 6
Scranton, Pa	15, 002	13, 785	91. 9	256	253	98. 8
Seattle, Wash	42, 832	39, 693	92. 7	1, 535	1, 420	92. 5
Spokane, Wash	9, 292	8, 294	89. 3	327	286	87. 5
Springfield, Mass	15, 681	14, 512	92. 5	1, 149	989	86. 1
Syracuse, N. Y	17, 247	15, 789	91. 5	607	539	88. 8
Toledo, Ohio	21, 488	19, 423	90. 4	2, 850	2, 531	88. 8
Trenton, N. J	16, 297	14, 681	90. 1	1, 885	1, 525	80. 9
Washington, D. C	15, 022	12, 929	86. 1	42, 979	35, 865	83. 4
Wilmington, Del	9, 240	8, 547	92. 5	4, 888	4, 345	88. 9
Worcester, Mass	27, 574	25, 075	90. 9	514	483	94. 0
Yonkers, N. Y	12, 851	11, 891	92. 5	729	610	83. 7
Youngstown, Ohio	20, 460	19, 088	93. 3	3, 441	3, 198	92. 9

[1] Per cent not shown, base being less than 100.

TABLE 22.—NUMBER AND PROPORTION OF FEMALES IN EACH PRINCIPAL CLASS OF TIONS, FOR CITIES HAVING 100,000

CITY.	NATIVE WHITE—NATIVE PARENTAGE.			NATIVE WHITE—FOREIGN OR MIXED PARENTAGE.		
	Total number.	Engaged in gainful occupations.		Total number.	Engaged in gainful occupations.	
		Number.	Per ct.		Number.	Per ct.
Akron, Ohio	41,600	10,603	25.5	12,611	2,889	22.9
Albany, N. Y	24,039	7,345	30.6	17,144	5,330	31.1
Atlanta, Ga	52,621	14,372	27.3	3,409	784	23.0
Baltimore, Md	152,473	40,287	26.4	66,786	17,949	26.9
Birmingham, Ala	36,589	7,005	19.1	3,784	717	18.9
Boston, Mass	72,388	25,381	35.1	112,192	42,780	38.1
Bridgeport, Conn	14,181	4,329	30.5	18,458	6,377	34.5
Buffalo, N. Y	61,954	17,040	27.5	83,936	23,416	27.9
Cambridge, Mass	12,416	3,962	31.9	15,784	6,446	40.8
Camden, N. J	21,729	5,324	24.5	10,548	2,740	26.0
Chicago, Ill	233,490	74,603	32.0	417,687	141,532	33.9
Cincinnati, Ohio	82,159	23,601	28.7	60,110	16,843	28.0
Cleveland, Ohio	78,984	22,605	28.6	102,846	28,112	27.3
Columbus, Ohio	65,990	16,561	25.1	18,002	4,489	24.9
Dallas, Tex	47,208	13,703	29.0	5,628	1,422	25.3
Dayton, Ohio	40,093	9,585	23.9	12,945	3,033	23.4
Denver, Colo	57,490	15,749	27.4	29,803	8,771	29.4
Des Moines, Iowa	34,853	10,046	28.8	11,404	3,512	30.8
Detroit, Mich	105,996	28,243	26.6	116,430	31,275	26.9
Fall River, Mass	6,846	2,321	33.9	20,423	9,776	47.9
Fort Worth, Tex	29,563	6,603	22.3	2,813	582	20.7
Grand Rapids, Mich	21,605	6,023	27.9	21,529	6,638	30.8
Hartford, Conn	16,718	5,561	33.3	18,518	6,801	36.7
Houston, Tex	29,419	7,013	23.8	8,276	1,674	20.2
Indianapolis, Ind	91,017	23,959	26.3	20,094	5,174	25.7
Jersey City, N. J	31,244	9,132	29.2	46,174	14,444	31.3
Kansas City, Kans	21,827	4,937	22.6	6,978	1,822	26.1
Kansas City, Mo	88,123	25,002	28.4	25,010	6,908	27.6
Los Angeles, Calif	131,423	35,668	27.1	61,021	17,060	28.0
Louisville, Ky	57,548	15,999	27.8	22,573	5,995	26.6
Lowell, Mass	9,520	3,034	31.9	18,278	7,911	43.3
Memphis, Tenn	34,722	8,654	24.9	5,467	1,184	21.7
Milwaukee, Wis	44,370	14,513	32.7	90,106	28,578	31.7
Minneapolis, Minn	49,843	14,512	29.1	67,748	23,744	35.0
Nashville, Tenn	31,435	7,915	25.2	3,113	728	23.4
New Bedford, Mass	8,128	2,466	30.3	15,204	6,879	45.2
New Haven, Conn	18,182	5,468	30.1	23,233	8,188	35.2
New Orleans, La	75,100	18,725	24.9	33,595	6,908	20.6
New York, N. Y	446,962	146,240	32.7	795,806	264,175	33.2
Bronx borough	47,600	15,092	31.7	113,895	36,782	32.3
Brooklyn borough	172,639	54,098	31.3	301,542	94,203	31.2
Manhattan borough	161,189	59,564	37.0	285,436	106,774	37.4
Queens borough	52,255	14,187	27.1	79,496	22,448	28.2
Richmond borough	13,279	3,299	24.8	15,437	3,968	25.7
Newark, N. J	44,156	13,020	29.5	56,578	17,489	30.9
Norfolk, Va	23,052	4,995	21.7	2,705	605	22.4
Oakland, Calif	35,905	8,673	24.2	28,961	7,132	24.6
Omaha, Nebr	33,124	9,421	28.4	23,742	7,469	31.5
Paterson, N. J	12,671	4,303	34.0	20,908	8,362	40.0
Philadelphia, Pa	278,419	81,116	29.1	217,866	68,315	31.4
Pittsburgh, Pa	82,513	21,629	26.2	80,589	22,069	27.4
Portland, Oreg	56,113	15,430	27.5	29,247	8,679	29.7
Providence, R. I	26,473	8,613	32.5	36,383	14,676	40.3
Reading, Pa	34,495	10,852	31.5	5,793	1,845	31.8
Richmond, Va	44,416	12,095	27.2	4,367	1,026	23.5
Rochester, N. Y	44,928	14,994	33.4	43,122	14,598	33.9
St. Louis, Mo	142,568	45,782	32.1	111,066	31,757	28.6
St. Paul, Minn	26,652	8,055	30.2	44,962	15,391	34.2
Salt Lake City, Utah	19,705	4,286	21.8	17,323	3,932	22.7
San Antonio, Tex	30,453	6,955	22.8	12,856	2,761	21.5
San Francisco, Calif	63,677	21,121	33.2	77,342	24,283	31.4
Scranton, Pa	18,145	4,655	26.8	23,092	6,005	30.3
Seattle, Wash	55,290	14,988	27.1	36,133	10,642	29.5
Spokane, Wash	23,160	5,934	25.6	12,824	3,555	27.7
Springfield, Mass	20,270	6,291	31.0	17,461	6,504	37.2
Syracuse, N. Y	32,452	9,145	28.2	22,998	6,942	30.2
Toledo, Ohio	47,322	12,091	25.6	30,505	8,026	26.3
Trenton, N. J	18,003	4,778	26.5	13,001	4,006	30.8
Washington, D. C	112,079	48,594	43.4	27,501	11,535	41.9
Wilmington, Del	22,769	5,787	25.4	9,152	2,418	26.4
Worcester, Mass	20,011	5,920	29.6	26,475	9,817	37.1
Yonkers, N. Y	11,665	3,082	26.4	15,379	4,989	32.4
Youngstown, Ohio	16,948	3,668	21.6	14,495	3,034	20.9

THE POPULATION 10 YEARS OF AGE AND OVER ENGAGED IN GAINFUL OCCUPA-
INHABITANTS OR MORE: 1920.

CITY.	FOREIGN-BORN WHITE.			NEGRO.		
	Total number.	Engaged in gainful occupations.		Total number.	Engaged in gainful occupations.	
		Number.	Per ct.		Number.	Per ct.
Akron, Ohio	12,949	1,910	14.8	1,743	619	35.5
Albany, N. Y	8,578	1,632	19.0	518	193	37.3
Atlanta, Ga	2,009	348	17.3	28,917	16,743	57.9
Baltimore, Md	39,470	7,491	19.0	46,924	26,893	57.3
Birmingham, Ala	2,538	313	12.3	29,733	12,044	40.5
Boston, Mass	119,847	32,895	27.4	6,961	3,224	46.3
Bridgeport, Conn	20,828	4,450	21.4	847	370	43.7
Buffalo, N. Y	55,879	8,876	15.9	1,733	629	36.3
Cambridge, Mass	16,644	4,650	27.9	2,316	920	39.7
Camden, N. J	9,028	1,368	15.2	3,399	1,325	39.0
Chicago, Ill	369,798	74,586	20.2	47,150	20,755	44.0
Cincinnati, Ohio	20,895	4,005	19.2	12,853	5,926	46.1
Cleveland, Ohio	104,859	17,690	16.9	13,465	5,118	38.0
Columbus, Ohio	6,870	1,154	16.8	8,749	3,270	37.4
Dallas, Tex	3,468	639	18.4	10,549	6,002	56.9
Dayton, Ohio	5,648	920	16.3	3,533	1,491	42.2
Denver, Colo	16,515	3,267	19.8	2,678	1,200	44.8
Des Moines, Iowa	4,962	922	18.6	2,284	866	37.9
Detroit, Mich	116,707	19,295	16.5	14,820	4,969	33.5
Fall River, Mass	21,700	8,222	37.9	128	83	64.8
Fort Worth, Tex	2,388	371	15.5	6,803	3,145	46.2
Grand Rapids, Mich	13,223	2,256	17.1	444	150	33.8
Hartford, Conn	18,933	4,393	23.2	1,700	838	49.3
Houston, Tex	4,930	750	15.2	15,155	7,738	51.1
Indianapolis, Ind	7,548	1,152	15.3	14,692	5,931	40.4
Jersey City, N. J	35,373	5,185	14.7	3,229	1,133	35.1
Kansas City, Kans	4,597	621	13.5	6,066	1,838	30.3
Kansas City, Mo	11,691	2,001	17.1	13,651	6,405	46.9
Los Angeles, Calif	50,193	11,606	23.1	7,168	3,261	45.5
Louisville, Ky	5,710	937	16.4	18,498	11,246	60.8
Lowell, Mass	19,316	7,276	37.7	60	27	(1)
Memphis, Tenn	2,469	468	19.0	28,230	13,835	49.0
Milwaukee, Wis	48,795	7,956	16.3	853	289	33.9
Minneapolis, Minn	39,170	7,836	20.0	1,579	638	40.4
Nashville, Tenn	1,089	180	16.5	16,867	9,106	54.0
New Bedford, Mass	24,299	10,873	44.7	1,602	552	34.5
New Haven, Conn	21,858	4,395	20.1	1,893	903	47.7
New Orleans, La	10,325	1,812	17.5	45,608	22,305	48.9
New York, N. Y	959,953	240,663	25.1	69,873	40,484	57.9
Bronx borough	130,261	24,840	19.1	2,064	938	45.4
Brooklyn borough	314,048	59,379	18.9	14,293	7,438	52.0
Manhattan borough	447,754	145,455	32.5	50,474	30,592	60.6
Queens borough	54,112	8,929	16.5	2,436	1,224	50.2
Richmond borough	13,778	2,060	15.0	606	292	48.2
Newark, N. J	54,412	8,913	16.4	6,971	2,804	40.2
Norfolk, Va	2,113	359	17.0	18,214	8,665	47.6
Oakland, Calif	19,380	3,398	17.5	2,123	634	29.9
Omaha, Nebr	15,305	2,595	17.0	4,049	1,580	39.0
Paterson, N. J	21,654	5,838	27.0	706	378	53.5
Philadelphia, Pa	190,341	38,510	20.2	57,261	27,792	48.5
Pittsburgh, Pa	54,375	8,862	16.3	14,996	5,195	34.6
Portland, Oreg	19,371	4,029	20.8	633	252	39.8
Providence, R. I	34,567	9,052	26.2	2,285	1,084	47.4
Reading, Pa	4,045	804	19.9	350	123	35.1
Richmond, Va	2,074	429	20.7	24,551	13,084	53.3
Rochester, N. Y	33,712	7,696	22.8	732	336	45.9
St. Louis, Mo	46,605	8,713	18.7	30,095	13,526	44.9
St. Paul, Minn	23,318	4,190	18.0	1,352	476	35.2
Salt Lake City, Utah	9,578	1,726	18.0	287	110	38.3
San Antonio, Tex	15,836	3,612	22.8	6,448	3,475	53.9
San Francisco, Calif	56,429	14,445	25.6	937	491	52.4
Scranton, Pa	13,319	1,411	10.6	219	73	33.3
Seattle, Wash	29,156	6,538	22.4	1,087	466	42.9
Spokane, Wash	7,196	1,500	20.8	299	118	39.5
Springfield, Mass	15,176	3,933	25.9	1,130	571	50.5
Syracuse, N. Y	14,689	2,467	16.8	517	200	38.7
Toledo, Ohio	16,179	2,398	14.8	2,180	765	35.1
Trenton, N. J	13,379	2,344	17.5	1,674	706	42.2
Washington, D. C	13,270	3,889	29.3	50,803	28,588	56.3
Wilmington, Del	6,835	1,053	15.4	4,466	2,509	56.2
Worcester, Mass	25,247	5,029	19.9	530	237	44.7
Yonkers, N. Y	12,588	2,656	21.1	883	489	55.4
Youngstown, Ohio	12,883	1,403	10.9	2,328	547	23.5

[1] Per cent not shown, base being less than 100.

TABLE 23.—MALES AND FEMALES 10 YEARS OF AGE AND OVER ENGAGED IN GAIN-
FUL OCCUPATIONS, CLASSIFIED BY COLOR OR RACE, NATIVITY, AND PARENT-
AGE, AND BY MARITAL CONDITION, FOR CITIES HAVING FROM 25,000 TO 100,000
INHABITANTS: 1920.

CITY AND SEX.	Total.	Native white. Native parentage.	Native white. Foreign or mixed parentage.	Foreign-born white.	Negro.	Chinese.	Japanese.	Indian and all other.	Married.	Single, widowed, divorced, and unknown.
Alameda, Calif.:										
Male	9,273	3,505	2,777	2,658	56	73	199	5	6,217	3,056
Female	2,425	1,061	918	377	30	2	36	1	430	1,995
Allentown, Pa.:										
Male	23,466	16,370	2,776	4,241	78	1			15,913	7,553
Female	7,932	5,474	1,218	1,208	32				1,843	6,089
Altoona, Pa.:										
Male	19,193	13,337	2,763	2,756	327	9		1	12,492	6,701
Female	4,905	3,628	947	224	106				529	4,376
Amsterdam, N. Y.:										
Male	10,404	3,085	2,730	4,549	38	1	1		6,771	3,633
Female	5,314	1,719	1,737	1,836	22				1,824	3,490
Anderson, Ind.:										
Male	10,186	8,547	800	508	327	4			6,674	3,512
Female	2,954	2,514	268	57	115				756	2,198
Asheville, N. C.:										
Male	7,934	5,490	188	229	2,022	1	4		5,389	2,545
Female	3,474	1,600	87	73	1,714				971	2,503
Atlantic City, N. J.:										
Male	16,514	6,532	2,540	3,142	4,255	26	17	2	10,679	5,835
Female	7,386	2,357	1,130	827	3,069		3		2,071	5,315
Auburn, N. Y.:										
Male	12,119	4,857	3,271	3,773	215	1		2	7,598	4,521
Female	4,327	1,932	1,549	783	63				987	3,340
Augusta, Ga.:										
Male	17,378	8,426	611	492	7,789	57	2	1	10,942	6,436
Female	8,886	2,729	266	94	5,797				3,361	5,525
Aurora, Ill.:										
Male	12,116	4,766	3,940	3,172	233	5			7,880	4,236
Female	3,707	1,662	1,545	413	87				627	3,080
Austin, Tex.:										
Male	9,018	4,978	1,247	1,032	1,747	14			6,037	2,981
Female	4,059	1,962	538	196	1,362	1			928	3,131
Bangor, Me.:										
Male	7,521	4,435	1,482	1,515	67	22			4,954	2,567
Female	3,045	1,824	758	431	32				455	2,590
Battle Creek, Mich.:										
Male	12,625	8,545	1,932	1,717	407	20	3	1	8,548	4,077
Female	4,291	3,026	812	319	129	1	1	3	1,280	3,011
Bay City, Mich.:										
Male	14,705	4,106	6,494	4,037	61	1		6	9,347	5,358
Female	4,228	1,229	2,336	644	16			3	564	3,664
Bayonne, N. J.:										
Male	23,898	3,714	6,840	13,086	227	30	1		14,949	8,949
Female	5,341	1,115	2,865	1,273	87		1		525	4,816
Beaumont, Tex.:										
Male	14,029	7,351	890	1,063	4,711	13		1	8,714	5,315
Female	4,250	1,511	171	98	2,470				1,668	2,582
Bellingham, Wash.:										
Male	8,704	3,847	2,124	2,683	17	2	25	6	5,365	3,339
Female	1,974	952	709	299	6	1	4	3	457	1,517
Berkeley, Calif.:										
Male	16,846	7,109	4,061	4,013	161	176	339	17	11,066	5,182
Female	5,844	2,893	1,801	956	100	6	84	4	1,083	4,761
Bethlehem, Pa.:										
Male	16,326	7,926	2,294	5,946	149	8	3		10,922	5,404
Female	3,868	2,036	872	920	39		1		716	3,152
Binghamton, N. Y.:										
Male	21,060	12,332	3,838	4,654	214	13	3	6	13,875	7,185
Female	9,352	5,642	2,219	1,362	129				2,978	6,374
Bloomington, Ill.:										
Male	9,138	5,211	2,404	1,210	304	9			5,934	3,204
Female	2,985	1,798	853	203	130			1	471	2,514
Brockton, Mass.:										
Male	22,466	7,957	6,098	8,186	179	43		3	13,885	8,581
Female	10,127	3,753	3,783	2,489	99			3	2,955	7,172

TABLE 23.—MALES AND FEMALES 10 YEARS OF AGE AND OVER ENGAGED IN GAIN-FUL OCCUPATIONS, CLASSIFIED BY COLOR OR RACE, NATIVITY, AND PARENT-AGE, AND BY MARITAL CONDITION, FOR CITIES HAVING FROM 25,000 TO 100,000 INHABITANTS: 1920—Continued.

CITY AND SEX.	Total.	Native white. Native parentage.	Native white. Foreign or mixed parentage.	Foreign-born white.	Negro.	Chinese.	Japanese.	Indian and all other.	Married.	Single, widowed, divorced, and unknown.
Brookline town, Mass.:										
Male	9,833	4,371	2,775	2,611	54	10	12	.....	6,481	3,352
Female	7,545	1,725	1,813	3,753	252	.....	2	.....	551	6,994
Butte, Mont.:										
Male	15,851	4,366	4,680	6,518	96	174	11	6	8,435	7,416
Female	3,511	1,008	1,582	883	36	1	1	.....	609	2,902
Canton, Ohio:										
Male	33,172	18,470	4,702	9,331	636	32	.....	1	20,107	13,065
Female	6,587	4,584	1,298	581	124	.....	.....	.....	1,282	5,305
Cedar Rapids, Iowa:										
Male	14,954	8,191	3,861	2,654	247	1	.....	.....	9,854	5,100
Female	4,812	2,788	1,510	442	72	.....	.....	.....	940	3,872
Charleston, S. C.:										
Male	21,671	8,697	1,735	1,142	10,071	18	.....	8	13,352	8,319
Female	10,547	2,310	505	116	7,616	.....	.....	.....	3,264	7,283
Charleston, W. Va.:										
Male	13,032	9,861	795	734	1,632	9	.....	1	8,304	4,728
Female	3,858	2,613	213	99	933	.....	.....	.....	909	2,949
Charlotte, N. C.:										
Male	14,430	9,247	249	257	4,673	1	3	.....	9,228	5,202
Female	6,803	3,111	77	39	3,576	.....	.....	.....	2,204	4,599
Chattanooga, Tenn.										
Male	20,459	11,777	865	615	7,197	.....	.....	5	12,605	7,854
Female	8,137	3,820	295	78	3,944	.....	.....	.....	2,835	5,302
Chelsea, Mass.:										
Male	13,698	2,138	3,309	8,098	131	16	.....	6	8,242	5,456
Female	4,075	855	1,724	1,446	49	1	.....	.....	495	3,580
Chester, Pa.:										
Male	22,242	9,167	3,414	6,569	3,052	33	1	6	12,743	9,499
Female	4,705	2,183	1,152	499	870	.....	.....	1	971	3,734
Chicopee, Mass.:										
Male	11,200	1,616	3,645	5,925	6	8	.....	.....	6,900	4,300
Female	4,253	648	1,952	1,653	.....	.....	.....	.....	1,155	3,098
Cicero town, Ill.:										
Male	14,423	1,303	5,201	7,911	3	5	.....	.....	9,321	5,102
Female	4,254	526	2,479	1,248	1	.....	.....	.....	943	3,311
Clarksburg, W. Va.:										
Male	8,922	6,692	698	1,075	457	.....	.....	.....	5,844	3,078
Female	1,997	1,552	175	64	206	.....	.....	.....	359	1,638
Clifton, N. J.:										
Male	8,302	1,241	2,275	4,756	16	1	13	.....	5,523	2,779
Female	2,876	417	1,151	1,299	9	.....	.....	.....	833	2,043
Colorado Springs, Colo.:										
Male	8,369	5,510	1,520	1,045	286	3	1	4	5,802	2,567
Female	3,445	2,188	713	322	222	.....	.....	.....	688	2,757
Columbia, S. C.:										
Male	11,095	6,390	234	264	4,205	2	.....	.....	6,976	4,119
Female	5,081	2,040	72	27	2,942	.....	.....	.....	1,442	3,639
Columbus, Ga.:										
Male	9,756	6,474	241	192	2,847	2	.....	.....	6,100	3,656
Female	5,652	2,980	78	18	2,576	.....	.....	.....	2,171	3,481
Council Bluffs, Iowa:										
Male	11,644	6,980	2,503	1,911	248	.....	1	1	7,420	4,224
Female	3,399	2,034	1,066	232	66	.....	1	.....	620	2,779
Covington, Ky.:										
Male	18,770	11,218	5,250	1,175	1,122	5	.....	.....	11,496	7,274
Female	6,931	4,036	2,032	195	668	.....	.....	.....	969	5,962
Cranston, R. I.:										
Male	8,720	3,197	2,346	3,113	57	1	4	2	5,822	2,898
Female	2,957	1,029	1,144	754	28	.....	.....	2	602	2,355
Cumberland, Md.:										
Male	10,045	7,365	1,387	597	694	.....	1	1	5,846	4,199
Female	2,586	1,983	400	57	146	.....	.....	.....	275	2,311
Danville, Ill.:										
Male	11,124	7,567	1,821	887	838	7	.....	4	7,254	3,870
Female	3,287	2,144	611	137	391	.....	1	3	749	2,538
Davenport, Iowa:										
Male	18,842	8,463	6,826	3,233	305	8	3	4	11,571	7,271
Female	5,821	2,873	2,383	489	76	.....	.....	.....	1,081	4,740

TABLE 23.—MALES AND FEMALES 10 YEARS OF AGE AND OVER ENGAGED IN GAIN-
FUL OCCUPATIONS, CLASSIFIED BY COLOR OR RACE, NATIVITY, AND PARENT-
AGE, AND BY MARITAL CONDITION, FOR CITIES HAVING FROM 25,000 TO 100,000
INHABITANTS: 1920—Continued.

CITY AND SEX.	Total.	COLOR OR RACE, NATIVITY, AND PARENTAGE.							MARITAL CONDITION.	
		Native white.		Foreign-born white.	Negro.	Chinese.	Japanese.	Indian and all other.	Married.	Single, widowed, divorced, and unknown.
		Native parentage.	Foreign or mixed parentage.							
Decatur, Ill.:										
Male	14,515	10,611	2,279	1,199	422	4			9,538	4,977
Female	4,080	3,017	760	164	138			1	778	3,302
Dubuque, Iowa:										
Male	12,390	5,028	5,486	1,839	34	3			7,305	5,085
Female	4,508	2,192	2,035	271	10				346	4,162
Duluth, Minn.:										
Male	34,968	6,562	11,672	16,432	220	74	3	5	19,381	15,587
Female	10,034	2,056	5,712	2,208	56			2	1,150	8,884
East Chicago, Ind.:										
Male	13,689	2,151	1,752	9,039	715	22	5	5	8,230	5,459
Female	1,255	305	499	386	65				213	1,042
East Cleveland, Ohio:										
Male	8,766	4,472	2,581	1,677	36				6,448	2,318
Female	2,806	1,355	1,014	374	63				436	2,370
East Orange, N. J.:										
Male	15,459	7,790	4,188	2,755	704	22			11,191	4,268
Female	5,756	2,508	1,609	962	677				780	4,976
East St. Louis, Ill.:										
Male	23,860	13,102	4,292	3,694	2,761	11			14,512	9,348
Female	5,887	3,335	1,242	432	878				1,447	4,440
Easton, Pa.:										
Male	10,984	7,133	1,706	2,016	119	8	1	1	7,241	3,743
Female	3,571	2,512	644	360	55				655	2,916
El Paso, Tex.:										
Male	22,475	8,751	2,460	10,564	502	97	28	73	14,145	8,330
Female	7,048	2,538	810	3,474	205			21	1,357	5,691
Elgin, Ill.:										
Male	7,891	2,989	3,042	1,809	47	4			5,230	2,661
Female	4,058	1,719	1,845	473	21				882	3,176
Elizabeth, N. J.:										
Male	31,986	7,625	9,041	14,527	759	31	1	2	19,646	12,340
Female	8,200	2,370	3,660	1,837	331			2	1,106	7,094
Elmira, N. Y.:										
Male	15,143	9,481	3,384	2,074	197	6		1	9,634	5,509
Female	4,947	3,044	1,510	307	85			1	828	4,119
Erie, Pa.:										
Male	29,752	11,993	8,669	8,719	352	17		2	19,088	10,664
Female	7,644	3,597	3,102	861	84				875	6,769
Evanston, Ill.:										
Male	10,879	4,182	2,949	2,903	824	16	1	4	7,703	3,176
Female	5,133	1,548	1,754	1,180	650		1		860	4,273
Evansville, Ind.:										
Male	27,932	18,277	5,956	1,272	2,413		13	1	17,535	10,397
Female	9,879	6,678	1,708	154	1,339				1,719	8,160
Everett, Mass.:										
Male	12,523	3,442	3,774	4,942	355	10			8,062	4,461
Female	3,878	1,179	1,706	859	134				531	3,347
Everett, Wash.:										
Male	10,015	4,146	2,645	3,089	54	1	65	15	5,945	4,070
Female	2,138	992	783	339	23		1		500	1,638
Fitchburg, Mass.:										
Male	13,215	3,023	4,102	6,069	10	17	1		8,103	5,052
Female	5,671	1,194	2,501	1,965	11				1,270	4,206
Flint, Mich.:										
Male	38,047	19,263	9,079	8,695	974	26	1	9	21,459	16,588
Female	7,007	3,915	2,165	805	118			4	1,811	5,196
Fort Smith, Ark.:										
Male	8,960	6,485	858	421	1,193	1		2	5,945	3,015
Female	2,642	1,560	283	78	721				687	1,955
Fort Wayne, Ind.:										
Male	29,494	18,066	7,540	3,258	611	15	3	1	18,399	11,095
Female	10,319	7,174	2,606	349	190				1,422	8,897
Fresno, Calif.:										
Male	16,085	8,334	2,603	4,153	171	350	463	11	9,809	6,276
Female	4,046	2,514	915	481	79	8	47	2	1,128	2,918

TABLE 23.—MALES AND FEMALES 10 YEARS OF AGE AND OVER ENGAGED IN GAIN-FUL OCCUPATIONS, CLASSIFIED BY COLOR OR RACE, NATIVITY, AND PARENTAGE, AND BY MARITAL CONDITION, FOR CITIES HAVING FROM 25,000 TO 100,000 INHABITANTS: 1920—Continued.

| CITY AND SEX. | Total. | Native white. | | Foreign-born white. | Negro. | Chinese. | Japanese. | Indian and all other. | Married. | Single, widowed, divorced, and unknown. |
		Native parentage.	Foreign or mixed parentage.							
Galveston, Tex.:										
Male	16,967	5,753	3,222	3,849	4.099	35	7	2	8,925	8,042
Female	4,795	1,393	872	340	2,188			2	1,407	3,388
Gary, Ind.:										
Male	21,559	6,342	2,965	9,932	2,291	21	5	3	12,540	9,019
Female	2,415	947	679	481	308				581	1,834
Green Bay, Wis :										
Male	9,134	3,111	4,511	1,480	16	3		13	5,832	3,302
Female	3,155	1,388	1,524	220	5			18	287	2,868
Hagerstown, Md.:										
Male	8,914	7,714	379	253	562	5		1	5,893	3,021
Female	2,542	2,098	107	24	313				400	2,142
Hamilton, Ohio:										
Male	14,085	9,010	3,080	1,350	640	1		4	8,491	5,594
Female	3,312	2,257	803	111	141				433	2,879
Hammond, Ind.:										
Male	12,408	4,768	3,084	4,446	85	19	5	1	7,809	4,599
Female	2,221	987	922	307	5				354	1,867
Hamtramck village, Mich.:										
Male	16,183	485	1,701	13,220	777				10,318	5,865
Female	1,579	104	589	754	132				417	1,162
Harrisburg, Pa.:										
Male	25,484	19,284	2,150	2,087	1,949	11	3		17,163	8,321
Female	7,845	6,083	636	319	807				1,410	6,435
Haverhill, Mass.:										
Male	18,065	6,870	4,675	6,371	132	17			11,070	6,995
Female	8,854	3,545	3,122	2,106	81				2,833	6,021
Hazleton, Pa.:										
Male	9,243	2,778	3,487	2,961	13	3	1		5,652	3,591
Female	3,011	1,169	1,621	220	1				143	2,868
Highland Park, Mich.:										
Male	18,987	7,468	4,227	7,069	157	27	14	25	10,931	8,056
Female	3,434	1,481	1,157	741	54			1	696	2,738
Hoboken, N. J.:										
Male	24,264	4,313	7,842	11,970	99	36	2	2	13,106	11,158
Female	7,102	1,638	3,534	1,897	33				955	6,147
Holyoke, Mass.:										
Male	18,464	2,775	6,956	8,658	56	19			10,870	7,594
Female	10,168	1,363	5,033	3,743	29				2,158	8,010
Huntington, W. Va.:										
Male	15,733	13,647	579	413	1,086	8			10,547	5,186
Female	4,068	3,308	117	41	602				863	3,205
Irvington town, N. J.:										
Male	8,329	2,764	2,950	2,569	42	4			5,757	2,572
Female	2,054	802	954	279	19				242	1,812
Jackson, Mich.:										
Male	17,815	10,854	3,684	2,831	417	23	1	5	11,053	6,762
Female	4,622	2,965	1,164	403	89	1			1,203	3,419
Jacksonville, Fla.:										
Male	31,492	12,891	1,636	1,959	14,963	35		8	20,690	10,802
Female	13,310	3,389	565	295	9,059	2			5,981	7,329
Jamestown, N. Y.:										
Male	12,969	3,947	3,424	5,505	92			1	8,516	4,453
Female	4,759	1,607	1,869	1,251	30			2	1,170	3,589
Johnstown, Pa.:										
Male	21,614	9,973	3,837	6,817	968	19			13,377	8,237
Female	4,340	2,637	1,230	402	71				350	3,990
Joliet, Ill.:										
Male	12,537	3,630	4,328	4,273	293	12	1		7,481	5,056
Female	3,428	1,200	1,719	416	93				386	3,042
Joplin, Mo.:										
Male	9,146	7,717	776	357	285	8		3	6,317	2,829
Female	2,706	2,339	185	32	149			1	546	2,160
Kalamazoo, Mich.:										
Male	15,639	8,465	3,569	3,323	263	16	1	2	10,483	5,156
Female	5,726	3,383	1,576	665	102				1,599	4,127

Table 23.—MALES AND FEMALES 10 YEARS OF AGE AND OVER ENGAGED IN GAINFUL OCCUPATIONS, CLASSIFIED BY COLOR OR RACE, NATIVITY, AND PARENTAGE, AND BY MARITAL CONDITION, FOR CITIES HAVING FROM 25,000 TO 100,000 INHABITANTS: 1920—Continued.

CITY AND SEX.	Total.	Native white.		Foreign-born white.	Negro.	Chinese.	Japanese.	Indian and all other.	Married.	Single, widowed, divorced, and unknown.
		Native parentage.	Foreign or mixed parentage.							
Kearny town, N. J.:										
Male	8,605	2,172	2,688	3,720	17	6	2		5,384	3,221
Female	2,879	780	1,329	750	20				291	2,588
Kenosha, Wis.:										
Male	15,146	3,508	4,240	7,342	44	6	3	3	8,388	6,758
Female	3,172	1,047	1,451	663	11				472	2,700
Kingston, N. Y.:										
Male	8,494	4,812	2,242	1,246	192	2			5,234	3,260
Female	3,483	2,152	1,046	189	96				373	3,110
Knoxville, Tenn.:										
Male	23,728	19,017	591	396	3,723			1	16,097	7,631
Female	8,868	6,313	204	59	2,292				2,613	6,255
Kokomo, Ind.:										
Male	10,583	8,755	831	666	329	2			6,941	3,642
Female	2,211	1,869	196	56	90				616	1,595
La Crosse, Wis.:										
Male	9,099	2,977	4,338	1,768	14	2			5,738	3,361
Female	3,536	1,342	1,902	284	8				349	3,187
Lakewood, Ohio:										
Male	12,949	5,703	3,701	3,494	45	5	1		9,877	3,072
Female	3,601	1,637	1,338	595	31				574	3,027
Lancaster, Pa.:										
Male	16,824	12,865	2,400	1,247	307	5			10,900	5,924
Female	7,485	5,939	1,137	253	155			1	1,454	6,031
Lansing, Mich.:										
Male	21,046	13,389	4,261	3,103	272	21			13,607	7,439
Female	5,124	3,407	1,265	374	77	1			1,499	3,625
Lawrence, Mass.:										
Male	30,775	3,274	9,142	18,190	112	57			18,429	12,346
Female	16,221	1,730	6,582	7,875	34				5,460	10,761
Lewiston, Me.:										
Male	9,842	2,776	2,756	4,272	16	21	1		5,710	4,132
Female	5,480	1,487	1,792	2,187	14				1,409	4,071
Lexington, Ky.:										
Male	13,475	7,734	839	408	4,490	4			8,476	4,999
Female	6,500	2,579	381	56	3,483			1	2,276	4,224
Lima, Ohio:										
Male	13,430	10,090	1,923	943	456	15	3		9,140	4,290
Female	3,676	2,850	584	100	142				791	2,885
Lincoln, Nebr.:										
Male	16,281	9,568	3,386	2,929	380		16	2	11,240	5,041
Female	6,202	3,673	1,686	693	150				1,454	4,748
Little Rock, Ark.:										
Male	20,850	12,327	1,722	902	5,897	1		1	13,479	7,371
Female	8,399	4,041	525	156	3,677				2,666	5,733
Long Beach, Calif.:										
Male	14,409	9,495	2,601	2,055	55	28	174	1	10,094	4,315
Female	4,326	2,943	846	474	30		32	1	1,109	3,217
Lorain, Ohio:										
Male	19,797	3,408	2,287	6,851	240	1			8,118	4,669
Female	1,573	575	631	296	51				183	1,350
Lynchburg, Va.:										
Male	8,760	5,982	249	179	2,350				5,387	3,373
Female	5,294	2,946	93	32	2,223				1,400	3,894
Lynn, Mass.:										
Male	33,403	10,973	9,323	12,718	281	108			20,259	13,144
Female	14,629	4,978	5,415	4,094	140			2	3,874	10,755
McKeesport, Pa.:										
Male	15,191	4,625	3,716	6,476	354	19	1		9,629	5,562
Female	2,835	1,090	1,215	444	86				297	2,538
Macon, Ga.:										
Male	17,541	8,917	390	356	7,874	4			11,424	6,117
Female	8,816	2,563	125	62	6,066				3,701	5,115
Madison, Wis.:										
Male	11,559	4,754	4,461	2,220	89	20	15		7,665	3,894
Female	4,910	2,318	2,122	428	42				708	4,202

TABLE 23.—MALES AND FEMALES 10 YEARS OF AGE AND OVER ENGAGED IN GAINFUL OCCUPATIONS, CLASSIFIED BY COLOR OR RACE, NATIVITY, AND PARENTAGE, AND BY MARITAL CONDITION, FOR CITIES HAVING FROM 25,000 TO 100,000 INHABITANTS: 1920—Continued.

CITY AND SEX.	Total.	COLOR OR RACE, NATIVITY, AND PARENTAGE.							MARITAL CONDITION.	
		Native white.		Foreign-born white.	Negro.	Chinese.	Japanese.	Indian and all other.		
		Native parentage.	Foreign or mixed parentage.						Married.	Single, widowed, divorced, and unknown.
Malden, Mass.:										
Male	14,643	4,311	4,230	5,924	163	15			9,391	5,252
Female	5,978	1,788	2,503	1,602	85				698	5,280
Manchester, N. H.:										
Male	23,794	5,202	6,704	11,854	19	15			14,764	9,030
Female	13,756	2,695	5,091	5,962	8				3,943	9,813
Mansfield, Ohio:										
Male	9,817	6,489	1,538	1,661	126	3			6,328	3,489
Female	2,632	1,835	525	242	30				488	2,144
Marion, Ohio:										
Male	9,171	7,434	1,150	492	95				6,288	2,883
Female	2,138	1,786	269	44	39				423	1,715
Medford, Mass:										
Male	11,904	4,397	3,718	3,625	150	10	4		8,170	3,734
Female	4,205	1,514	1,814	813	63			1	549	3,656
Meriden, Conn.:										
Male	9,680	2,313	3,543	3,768	50	6			5,966	3,714
Female	3,401	907	1,823	655	16				394	3,007
Miami, Fla.:										
Male	10,229	4,709	1,041	1,179	3,280	13	4	3	6,542	3,687
Female	4,064	1,044	315	287	2,416		1	1	1,830	2,234
Mobile, Ala.:										
Male	19,816	8,916	1,815	1,021	8,054	8	1	1	12,287	7,529
Female	8,538	2,495	509	125	5,405			4	2,636	5,902
Moline, Ill.:										
Male	11,582	4,159	3,312	3,972	138		1		6,718	4,864
Female	2,650	1,007	1,173	434	36				505	2,145
Montclair town, N. J.:										
Male	7,996	3,201	1,661	2,132	974	17	11		5,704	2,292
Female	3,629	991	724	891	1,021	1	1		628	3,001
Montgomery, Ala.:										
Male	13,242	6,553	581	416	5,686	5		1	8,449	4,793
Female	7,620	2,013	134	61	5,412				2,673	4,947
Mount Vernon, N. Y.:										
Male	12,617	4,035	3,726	4,466	370	17	3		8,328	4,289
Female	4,961	1,648	1,708	1,129	476				780	4,181
Muncie, Ind.:										
Male	12,737	10,460	1,012	460	795	9		1	8,401	4,336
Female	3,413	2,844	247	42	280				951	2,462
Muskegon, Mich.:										
Male	13,080	4,627	4,909	3,443	83	6		12	7,823	5,257
Female	3,375	1,249	1,728	373	19			6	625	2,750
Muskogee, Okla.:										
Male	9,352	6,199	577	306	2,169	6		95	6,548	2,804
Female	2,829	1,691	141	31	941			25	765	2,064
Nashua, N. H.:										
Male	9,314	2,666	2,522	4,092	24	9	1		5,655	3,659
Female	3,947	966	1,497	1,484					1,136	2,811
New Britain, Conn.:										
Male	19,310	3,191	4,928	11,012	163	8	6	2	11,869	7,441
Female	5,945	1,256	2,818	1,838	33				1,226	4,719
New Brunswick, N. J.:										
Male	10,170	3,441	2,245	4,083	382	17	2		6,505	3,665
Female	3,707	1,293	993	1,245	176				878	2,829
New Castle, Pa.:										
Male	14,414	7,000	2,427	4,614	364	8		1	9,471	4,943
Female	2,849	1,696	706	369	78				357	2,492
New London, Conn.:										
Male	8,384	3,298	2,145	2,700	189	47	4	1	5,206	3,178
Female	2,356	907	903	428	118				300	2,056
New Rochelle, N. Y.:										
Male	11,226	3,515	3,109	3,819	755	12	15	1	6,983	4,243
Female	4,360	981	1,349	1,063	963		2	2	818	3,542
Newark, Ohio:										
Male	9,088	6,740	1,329	801	214	4			5,963	3,125
Female	2,364	1,827	382	73	82				392	1,972

75108°—22——34

TABLE 23.—MALES AND FEMALES 10 YEARS OF AGE AND OVER ENGAGED IN GAINFUL OCCUPATIONS, CLASSIFIED BY COLOR OR RACE, NATIVITY, AND PARENTAGE, AND BY MARITAL CONDITION, FOR CITIES HAVING FROM 25,000 TO 100,000 INHABITANTS: 1920—Continued.

CITY AND SEX.	Total.	COLOR OR RACE, NATIVITY, AND PARENTAGE.							MARITAL CONDITION.	
		Native white.		Foreign-born white.	Negro.	Chinese.	Japanese.	Indian and all other.	Married.	Single, widowed, divorced, and unknown.
		Native parentage.	Foreign or mixed parentage.							
Newburgh, N. Y.:										
Male	10,143	4,655	2,960	2,284	235	8	1	.....	6,213	3,930
Female	3,562	1,715	1,355	369	123	.....	.....	.....	572	2,990
Newport, Ky.:										
Male	9,693	5,401	3,151	839	307	.....	.....	.....	6,024	3,674
Female	3,567	2,037	1,195	158	177	.....	.....	.....	493	3,074
Newport, R. I.:										
Male	11,872	5,208	3,580	2,514	551	13	3	3	5,458	6,414
Female	2,872	795	1,097	662	317	.....	.....	1	358	2,514
Newport News, Va.:										
Male	15,190	7,276	810	1,194	5,867	42	.....	1	7,822	7,368
Female	3,257	941	156	86	2,074	.....	.....	.....	1,192	2,065
Newton, Mass.:										
Male	12,814	5,284	3,591	3,785	110	12	2	.....	8,511	4,303
Female	6,571	1,832	2,134	2,376	228	.....	1	.....	606	5,965
Niagara Falls, N. Y.:										
Male	17,931	4,689	3,659	9,335	241	5	.....	2	11,044	6,887
Female	3,888	1,249	1,375	1,213	47	.....	.....	4	599	3,289
Norristown borough, Pa.:										
Male	9,657	5,778	1,653	1,709	507	9	.....	1	6,010	3,647
Female	3,823	2,305	839	442	237	.....	.....	.....	752	3,071
Norwalk, Conn.:										
Male	8,857	3,525	2,354	2,710	252	9	4	3	5,622	3,235
Female	3,439	1,298	1,349	659	132	.....	.....	1	839	2,600
Oak Park village, Ill.:										
Male	11,951	5,068	4,398	2,402	64	19	.....	.....	8,621	3,330
Female	4,426	1,822	1,805	732	66	.....	1	.....	522	3,904
Ogden, Utah:										
Male	9,529	3,991	3,249	1,939	125	75	150	.....	6,675	2,854
Female	2,260	1,058	836	319	28	.....	19	.....	391	1,869
Oklahoma City, Okla.:										
Male	32,204	24,086	3,001	1,897	3,091	108	.....	21	20,258	11,946
Female	11,057	7,954	1,016	215	1,863	.....	.....	9	3,564	7,493
Orange, N. J.:										
Male	9,972	2,752	2,916	3,154	1,129	17	3	1	6,090	3,882
Female	4,049	1,026	1,533	657	833	.....	.....	.....	568	3,481
Oshkosh, Wis.:										
Male	10,005	2,729	4,741	2,515	13	2	.....	5	6,341	3,664
Female	3,643	1,165	2,108	366	3	.....	.....	1	331	3,312
Pasadena, Calif.:										
Male	11,720	6,760	2,141	2,212	324	89	180	14	8,087	3,633
Female	5,868	3,037	1,238	1,290	276	2	24	1	1,052	4,816
Passaic, N. J.:										
Male	19,330	2,457	4,135	12,490	226	19	1	2	12,934	6,396
Female	7,982	1,095	2,449	4,320	118	.....	.....	.....	2,393	5,589
Pawtucket, R. I.:										
Male	21,163	4,105	7,515	9,381	142	18	2	.....	12,537	8,626
Female	9,857	1,909	4,709	3,182	57	.....	.....	.....	2,024	7,833
Pensacola, Fla.:										
Male	10,821	5,300	913	1,000	3,603	5	.....	.....	6,445	4,376
Female	3,364	1,006	198	66	2,094	.....	.....	.....	1,197	2,167
Peoria, Ill.:										
Male	26,828	15,221	6,964	3,700	863	9	3	.....	16,124	10,704
Female	8,584	5,091	2,542	612	338	.....	.....	1	1,531	7,053
Perth Amboy, N. J.:										
Male	12,876	1,801	3,181	7,698	179	14	1	2	8,425	4,451
Female	3,130	521	1,574	982	53	.....	.....	.....	529	2,601
Petersburg, Va.:										
Male	9,453	4,880	170	277	4,122	4	.....	.....	5,948	3,505
Female	5,002	1,576	60	44	3,322	.....	.....	.....	1,661	3,341
Phoenix, Ariz.:										
Male	10,126	6,059	1,617	1,894	427	72	12	45	5,959	4,167
Female	2,618	1,601	465	283	227	3	2	37	749	1,869
Pittsfield, Mass.:										
Male	13,198	5,290	3,909	3,824	139	35	1	.....	8,372	4,826
Female	5,318	2,317	2,094	840	67	.....	.....	.....	852	4,466

Table 23.—MALES AND FEMALES 10 YEARS OF AGE AND OVER ENGAGED IN GAINFUL OCCUPATIONS, CLASSIFIED BY COLOR OR RACE, NATIVITY, AND PARENTAGE, AND BY MARITAL CONDITION, FOR CITIES HAVING FROM 25,000 TO 100,000 INHABITANTS: 1920—Continued.

CITY AND SEX.	Total.	Native white. Native parentage.	Native white. Foreign or mixed parentage.	Foreign-born white.	Negro.	Chinese.	Japanese.	Indian and all other.	Married.	Single, widowed, divorced, and unknown.
Plainfield, N. J.:										
Male	8,518	3,386	1,890	2,466	763	5	7	1	5,800	2,718
Female	3,247	1,083	843	627	693	1			695	2,552
Pontiac, Mich.:										
Male	13,156	7,257	2,943	2,653	295	8			7,726	5,430
Female	2,588	1,509	755	258	66				708	1,880
Port Huron, Mich.:										
Male	8,421	2,389	3,091	2,727	212	1		1	5,730	2,691
Female	1,913	603	855	429	26				244	1,669
Portland, Me.:										
Male	22,113	11,442	4,799	5,696	112	57	2	5	14,309	7,804
Female	8,179	4,269	2,301	1,550	59				1,426	6,753
Portsmouth, Ohio:										
Male	10,847	8,723	1,298	333	490	3			6,944	3,903
Female	3,055	2,499	372	31	153				509	2,546
Portsmouth, Va.:										
Male	19,341	9,298	893	808	8,319	3	4	16	11,353	7,988
Female	5,453	1,714	160	87	3,492				1,647	3,806
Poughkeepsie, N. Y.:										
Male	10,940	5,573	2,528	2,544	277	13	4	1	7,094	3,846
Female	4,331	2,398	1,225	514	194				784	3,547
Pueblo, Colo.:										
Male	14,048	7,409	2,443	3,600	533	8	53	2	8,812	5,236
Female	3,532	2,076	839	402	215				882	2,650
Quincy, Ill.:										
Male	11,965	6,609	3,958	917	473	5	1	2	7,248	4,717
Female	4,045	2,352	1,282	153	258				546	3,499
Quincy, Mass.:										
Male	15,573	4,528	4,468	6,536	14	23	3	1	9,906	5,667
Female	4,108	1,178	1,916	1,011	3				460	3,648
Racine, Wis.:										
Male	22,166	5,257	7,796	8,929	155	19		10	12,423	9,743
Female	5,395	1,581	2,877	894	43				779	4,616
Revere, Mass.:										
Male	8,611	1,957	2,558	4,074	15	7			5,658	2,953
Female	2,409	684	1,130	589	6				314	2,095
Richmond, Ind.:										
Male	9,271	6,678	1,384	576	624	9			5,909	3,362
Female	2,619	1,923	436	64	196				553	2,066
Roanoke, Va.:										
Male	15,783	11,940	483	458	2,892	10			10,399	5,384
Female	4,640	2,916	132	41	1,551				911	3,729
Rock Island, Ill.:										
Male	12,666	5,813	3,984	2,561	303	3	1	1	7,795	4,871
Female	3,394	1,621	1,320	342	111				691	2,703
Rockford, Ill.:										
Male	23,212	7,423	6,587	8,966	202	33		1	13,868	9,344
Female	7,179	2,735	3,032	1,350	62				1,549	5,630
Rome, N. Y.:										
Male	8,487	3,763	1,903	2,751	65	3		2	5,000	3,487
Female	2,410	1,399	729	266	16				463	1,947
Sacramento, Calif.:										
Male	24,419	10,715	6,189	5,776	288	535	778	138	14,151	10,268
Female	6,535	3,621	2,022	700	92	5	88	7	1,632	4,903
Saginaw, Mich.:										
Male	20,073	6,910	7,736	5,261	144	15		7	13,132	6,941
Female	5,608	2,155	2,684	729	40				796	4,812
St. Joseph, Mo.:										
Male	26,572	17,278	4,456	3,128	1,702	4	1	3	16,715	9,857
Female	9,070	5,759	1,988	554	767			2	2,334	6,736
Salem, Mass.:										
Male	13,329	3,618	4,578	5,052	34	47			7,712	5,617
Female	5,732	1,591	2,605	1,507	24	5			919	4,813
San Diego, Calif.:										
Male	23,398	11,994	4,978	5,391	363	187	437	48	14,232	9,166
Female	7,639	4,141	1,999	1,258	202	3	17	19	2,105	5,534

TABLE 23.—MALES AND FEMALES 10 YEARS OF AGE AND OVER ENGAGED IN GAIN-FUL OCCUPATIONS, CLASSIFIED BY COLOR OR RACE, NATIVITY, AND PARENT-AGE, AND BY MARITAL CONDITION, FOR CITIES HAVING FROM 25,000 TO 100,000 INHABITANTS: 1920—Continued.

CITY AND SEX.	Total.	Native white. Native parentage.	Native white. Foreign or mixed parentage.	Foreign-born white.	Negro.	Chinese.	Japanese.	Indian and all other.	Married.	Single, widowed, divorced, and unknown.
San Jose, Calif.:										
Male	12,135	4,940	3,300	3,494	58	212	129	2	7,539	4,596
Female	3,865	1,859	1,347	595	34	6	24		870	2,995
Savannah, Ga.:										
Male	28,986	11,070	1,890	1,619	14,375	27	2	3	17,900	11,086
Female	12,880	2,858	576	292	9,153	1			4,865	8,015
Schenectady, N. Y.:										
Male	29,164	11,472	7,219	10,243	148	75	6	1	19,284	9,880
Female	8,327	3,878	2,967	1,402	80				1,553	6,774
Sheboygan, Wis.:										
Male	10,207	1,834	4,263	4,108		2			6,429	3,778
Female	2,801	877	1,496	428					282	2,519
Shreveport, La.:										
Male	15,459	8,158	699	651	5,935	15	1		9,462	5,997
Female	6,343	1,966	150	105	4,121	1			2,267	4,076
Sioux City, Iowa:										
Male	25,859	13,245	6,135	5,885	548	26		20	14,494	11,365
Female	7,475	4,066	2,405	812	192				1,511	5,964
Sioux Falls, S. Dak.:										
Male	8,007	4,071	2,613	1,261	45	11	1	5	5,003	3,004
Female	2,668	1,326	1,071	250	18			3	545	2,123
Somerville, Mass.:										
Male	29,126	9,520	9,016	10,465	94	28	3		18,943	10,183
Female	10,912	3,729	4,873	2,261	49				1,383	9,529
South Bend, Ind.:										
Male	23,305	10,715	5,329	6,694	550	12	1	4	14,838	8,467
Female	6,674	3,345	2,371	839	119				1,235	5,439
Springfield, Ill.:										
Male	19,167	10,553	4,711	2,943	950	10			11,817	7,350
Female	6,893	3,992	2,070	512	319				994	5,899
Springfield, Mo.:										
Male	12,124	9,960	1,168	436	558	2			8,570	3,554
Female	3,793	3,059	322	53	358			1	799	2,994
Springfield, Ohio:										
Male	20,636	13,915	2,785	1,304	2,622	10			13,239	7,397
Female	5,781	3,956	926	142	757				1,219	4,562
Stamford, Conn.:										
Male	10,893	2,810	2,722	5,037	310	12	2		7,124	3,769
Female	3,507	1,005	1,331	957	214				761	2,746
Steubenville, Ohio:										
Male	9,766	4,513	1,613	3,190	443	4		3	5,967	3,799
Female	1,975	1,146	467	209	153				281	1,694
Stockton, Calif.:										
Male	13,998	6,666	3,388	3,225	110	282	301	26	8,063	5,935
Female	3,238	1,745	1,047	355	48	6	37		892	2,346
Superior, Wis.:										
Male	13,498	2,771	4,679	5,960	54	13	1	20	7,671	5,827
Female	3,019	754	1,665	572	26			2	374	2,645
Tacoma, Wash.:										
Male	35,229	14,515	8,622	10,886	377	42	738	49	20,838	14,391
Female	8,142	0,791	2,928	1,349	114	2	62	3	1,984	6,258
Tampa, Fla.:										
Male	16,659	5,488	1,728	5,203	4,156	99		2	10,090	6,909
Female	7,760	1,736	972	1,900	3,150	1		1	3,488	4,272
Taunton, Mass.:										
Male	11,301	3,492	3,466	4,187	152	4			6,789	4,512
Female	4,542	1,311	1,893	1,307	31				757	3,785
Terre Haute, Ind.:										
Male	22,441	15,874	3,387	1,885	1,283	10	2		14,551	7,890
Female	6,255	4,392	1,074	220	568		1		1,160	5,095
Topeka, Kans.:										
Male	15,517	9,965	2,435	1,721	1,375	2		19	10,626	4,891
Female	5,565	3,596	1,052	228	684			5	1,030	4,535
Troy, N. Y.:										
Male	22,270	9,029	8,294	4,702	215	28	2		13,072	9,198
Female	12,037	5,245	5,261	1,413	118				1,501	10,536

TABLE 23.—MALES AND FEMALES 10 YEARS OF AGE AND OVER ENGAGED IN GAINFUL OCCUPATIONS, CLASSIFIED BY COLOR OR RACE, NATIVITY, AND PARENTAGE, AND BY MARITAL CONDITION, FOR CITIES HAVING FROM 25,000 TO 100,000 INHABITANTS: 1920—Continued.

CITY AND SEX.	Total.	COLOR OR RACE, NATIVITY, AND PARENTAGE.							MARITAL CONDITION.	
		Native white.		Foreign-born white.	Negro.	Chinese.	Japanese.	Indian and all other.	Married.	Single, widowed, divorced, and unknown.
		Native parentage.	Foreign or mixed parentage.							
Tulsa, Okla.:										
Male	26,359	20,086	2,033	1,134	3,019	11	11	65	16,209	10,150
Female	7,864	5,405	469	180	1,796			14	2,203	5,661
Utica, N.Y.:										
Male	29,199	9,771	8,560	10,705	131	29	2	1	18,563	10,636
Female	12,273	4,844	4,583	2,766	80				2,892	9,381
Waco, Tex.:										
Male	11,651	7,577	865	861	2,336	12			7,987	3,664
Female	3,781	1,894	265	107	1,515				1,062	2,719
Waltham, Mass.:										
Male	9,549	3,053	3,037	3,421	11	27			5,690	3,859
Female	5,087	1,717	1,976	1,376	18				793	4,294
Warren, Ohio:										
Male	9,813	5,251	1,411	2,810	335	6			6,338	3,475
Female	2,018	1,418	368	149	83				381	1,637
Waterbury, Conn.:										
Male	31,078	6,939	8,228	15,493	383	33	1	1	18,260	12,818
Female	9,877	2,571	4,656	2,486	164				1,539	8,338
Waterloo, Iowa:										
Male	11,867	7,473	2,624	1,440	320	8		2	7,905	3,962
Female	3,411	2,268	916	155	71			1	787	2,624
Watertown, N.Y.:										
Male	10,146	5,080	2,413	2,595	46	3	4	5	6,769	3,377
Female	3,644	1,904	1,064	657	19				839	2,805
West Hoboken town, N.J.:										
Male	13,126	2,221	4,367	6,519	3	16			8,254	4,872
Female	4,160	856	1,980	1,322	2				770	3,390
West New York town, N.J.:										
Male	9,709	1,992	3,412	4,268	32	5			6,507	3,202
Female	2,852	742	1,371	724	15				469	2,383
Wheeling, W.Va.:										
Male	17,952	9,952	4,493	2,842	656	9			11,245	6,707
Female	5,267	3,135	1,492	391	249				559	4,708
Wichita, Kans.:										
Male	22,862	17,914	2,392	1,328	1,207	14	3	4	15,673	7,189
Female	7,008	5,562	798	206	433			9	1,745	5,263
Wichita Falls, Tex.:										
Male	17,344	14,093	952	1,230	1,058	8	1	2	8,872	8,472
Female	2,890	2,025	146	71	647	1			1,041	1,849
Wilkes-Barre, Pa.:										
Male	22,271	7,381	7,578	7,089	218	2	1	2	13,621	8,650
Female	6,791	2,671	3,255	797	68				428	6,363
Williamsport, Pa.:										
Male	11,983	8,686	1,886	1,108	302	1			7,711	4,272
Female	4,198	3,192	709	130	167				630	3,568
Wilmington, N.C.:										
Male	10,861	5,870	320	369	4,299	3			6,580	4,281
Female	4,450	1,413	77	28	2,932				1,364	3,086
Winston-Salem, N.C.:										
Male	16,761	8,932	119	173	7,529	7		1	9,405	7,356
Female	9,459	3,551	39	25	5,844				3,688	5,771
Woonsocket, R.I.:										
Male	13,770	1,657	5,012	7,049	35	17			7,893	5,877
Female	6,973	921	3,362	2,686	4				1,452	5,521
York, Pa.:										
Male	15,590	13,295	1,243	555	495	1	1		10,266	5,324
Female	5,932	5,147	401	86	297	1			1,413	4,519
Zanesville, Ohio:										
Male	9,554	7,083	1,296	653	519	2		1	6,360	3,194
Female	2,785	2,136	392	72	184			1	461	2,324

TABLE 24.—NUMBER AND PROPORTION OF PERSONS OCCUPIED, BY AGE PERIODS, FOR THE UNITED STATES: 1920 AND 1910.

CENSUS YEAR AND AGE PERIOD.	MALES 10 YEARS OF AGE AND OVER.			FEMALES 10 YEARS OF AGE AND OVER.		
	Total. number.	Engaged in gainful occupations.		Total. number.	Engaged in gainful occupations.	
		Number.	Per cent.		Number.	Per cent.
1920						
10 years and over.........	42,289,969	33,064,737	78.2	40,449,346	8,549,511	21.1
10 to 13 years..............	4,336,009	258,259	6.0	4,258,863	119,804	2.8
14 and 15 years...............	1,958,976	455,989	23.3	1,948,734	226,806	11.6
14 years...................	1,033,297	174,683	16.9	1,012,968	82,911	8.2
15 years...................	925,679	281,306	30.4	935,766	143,895	15.4
16 and 17 years..............	1,902,867	1,103,456	58.0	1,925,264	609,192	31.6
16 years...................	976,834	501,134	51.3	996,124	277,823	27.9
17 years...................	926,033	602,322	65.0	929,140	331,369	35.7
18 and 19 years..............	1,845,246	1,443,968	78.3	1,895,734	802,235	42.3
20 to 24 years...............	4,527,045	4,121,392	91.0	4,749,976	1,809,075	38.1
25 to 44 years...............	16,028,920	15,579,586	97.2	15,249,602	3,417,373	22.4
45 to 64 years...............	9,114,960	8,552,175	93.8	7,915,205	1,352,479	17.1
65 years and over............	2,483,071	1,492,837	60.1	2,450,144	196,900	8.0
Age unknown.................	92,875	57,075	61.5	55,824	15,647	28.0
1910						
10 years and over..........	37,027,558	30,091,564	81.3	34,552,712	8,075,772	23.4
10 to 13 years..............	3,665,779	609,030	16.6	3,593,239	286,946	8.0
14 and 15 years...............	1,798,449	744,109	41.4	1,770,898	350,140	19.8
14 years...................	935,974	324,500	34.7	912.148	148,998	16.3
15 years...................	862,475	419,609	48.7	858,750	201,142	23.4
16 to 20 years..............	4,564,179	3,615,623	79.2	4,632,821	1,847,600	39.9
21 to 44 years[1]...............	17,849,843	17,262,209	96.7	16,331,449	4,302,969	26.3
45 years and over............	9,149,308	7,860,593	85.9	8,224,305	1,288,117	15.7

[1] Includes persons of unknown age.

TABLE 25.—NUMBER AND PER CENT DISTRIBUTION, BY AGE PERIODS, OF MALES AND OF FEMALES ENGAGED IN EACH GENERAL DIVISION OF OCCUPATIONS, FOR THE UNITED STATES: 1920.

SEX AND AGE PERIODS.	All occupations.	Agriculture, forestry, and animal husbandry.	Extraction of minerals.	Manufacturing and mechanical industries.	Transportation.	Trade.	Public service (not elsewhere classified).	Professional service.	Domestic and personal service.	Clerical occupations.
					NUMBER.					
Male	33,064,737	9,869,030	1,087,359	10,888,183	2,850,528	3,575,187	748,666	1,127,391	1,217,968	1,700,425
10 to 13 years...	258,259	221,409	598	6,737	1,682	16,369	136	325	4,880	6,123
14 years	174,683	109,360	1,465	27,039	3,907	11,835	199	504	4,299	16,075
15 years	281,306	128,469	4,982	70,559	10,028	21,030	750	1,150	6,903	37,435
16 years	501,134	186,368	19,639	162,781	23,844	36,044	2,428	2,294	11,218	56,518
17 years	602,322	210,116	23,267	203,434	37,145	43,576	8,405	3,480	13,170	59,729
18 and 19 years.	1,443,968	457,588	54,024	475,401	120,285	104,222	50,993	17,792	32,940	130,723
20 to 24 years...	4,121,392	1,134,649	143,920	1,395,784	404,352	372,471	114,931	106,632	112,716	335,937
25 to 44 years...	15,579,586	3,966,116	577,472	5,461,425	1,503,895	1,799,041	306,491	605,682	603,619	755,845
45 to 64 years...	8,552,175	2,783,518	236,137	2,685,508	661,331	1,020,498	214,156	328,893	357,849	264,285
65 and over	1,492,837	662,046	22,356	378,673	76,619	144,500	47,415	58,614	66,685	35,929
Age unknown..	57,075	9,391	3,499	20,842	7,440	5,601	2,762	2,025	3,689	1,826
Female	8,549,511	1,084,128	2,864	1,930,341	213,054	667,792	21,794	1,016,498	2,186,924	1,426,116
10 to 13 years...	119,804	107,549	49	2,736	217	844	17	296	7,292	804
14 years	82,911	41,617	34	23,473	455	3,009	9	298	10,182	3,834
15 years	143,895	38,905	63	54,793	2,623	10,281	19	892	20,450	15,869
16 years	277,823	43,923	133	107,822	10,876	24,712	37	2,820	39,780	47,720
17 years	331,369	37,504	171	113,476	16,520	30,330	57	8,629	48,368	76,314
18 and 19 years.	802,235	71,497	299	214,340	39,966	67,744	547	69,450	118,729	219,663
20 to 24 years...	1,809,075	130,790	510	382,765	70,702	138,915	2,929	298,827	302,226	481,411
25 to 44 years...	3,417,373	337,087	1,125	730,250	63,266	291,658	12,096	490,894	972,489	518,508
45 to 64 years...	1,352,479	219,802	405	271,047	7,660	91,725	5,554	130,500	568,448	57,338
65 and over	196,900	54,356	66	26,986	547	7,408	471	10,976	93,135	2,955
Age unknown..	15,647	1,098	9	2,653	222	1,166	58	2,916	5,825	1,700
					PER CENT DISTRIBUTION.					
Male	100.0	100.0	100.0	100.0	100.0	100.0	100.0	100.0	100.0	100.0
10 to 13 years...	0.8	2.2	0.1	0.1	0.1	0.5	(1)	(1)	0.4	0.4
14 years	0.5	1.1	0.1	0.2	0.1	0.3	(1)	(1)	0.4	0.9
15 years	0.9	1.3	0.5	0.6	0.4	0.6	0.1	0.1	0.6	2.2
16 years	1.5	1.9	1.8	1.5	0.8	1.0	0.3	0.2	0.9	3.3
17 years	1.8	2.1	2.1	1.9	1.3	1.2	1.1	0.3	1.1	3.5
18 and 19 years.	4.4	4.6	5.0	4.4	4.2	2.9	6.8	1.6	2.7	7.7
20 to 24 years...	12.5	11.5	13.2	12.8	14.2	10.4	15.4	9.5	9.3	19.8
25 to 44 years...	47.1	40.2	53.1	50.2	52.8	50.3	40.9	53.7	49.6	44.5
45 to 64 years...	25.9	28.2	21.7	24.7	23.2	28.5	28.6	29.2	29.4	15.5
65 and over	4.5	6.7	2.1	3.5	2.7	4.0	6.3	5.2	5.5	2.1
Age unknown..	0.2	0.1	0.3	0.2	0.3	0.2	0.4	0.2	0.3	0.1
Female	100.0	100.0	100.0	100.0	100.0	100.0	100.0	100.0	100.0	100.0
10 to 13 years...	1.4	9.9	1.7	0.1	0.1	0.1	0.1	(1)	0.3	0.1
14 years	1.0	3.8	1.2	1.2	0.2	0.5	(1)	(1)	0.5	0.3
15 years	1.7	3.6	2.2	2.8	1.2	1.5	0.1	0.1	0.9	1.1
16 years	3.2	4.1	4.6	5.6	5.1	3.7	0.2	0.3	1.8	3.3
17 years	3.9	3.5	6.0	5.9	7.8	4.5	0.3	0.8	2.2	5.4
18 and 19 years.	9.4	6.6	10.4	11.1	18.8	10.1	2.5	6.8	5.4	15.4
20 to 24 years...	21.2	12.1	17.8	19.8	33.2	20.8	13.4	29.4	13.8	33.8
25 to 44 years...	40.0	31.1	39.3	37.8	29.7	43.7	55.5	48.3	44.5	36.4
45 to 64 years...	15.8	20.3	14.1	14.0	3.6	13.7	25.5	12.8	26.0	4.0
65 and over	2.3	5.0	2.3	1.4	0.3	1.1	2.2	1.1	4.3	0.2
Age unknown..	0.2	0.1	0.3	0.1	0.1	0.2	0.3	0.3	0.3	0.1

[1] Less than one-tenth of 1 per cent.

TABLE 26.—NUMBER AND PROPORTION OF MALES AND OF FEMALES IN EACH PRINCIPAL CLASS OF THE POPULATION ENGAGED IN GAINFUL OCCUPATIONS, BY AGE PERIODS, FOR THE UNITED STATES: 1920.

SEX AND AGE PERIODS.	NATIVE WHITE—NATIVE PARENTAGE.			NATIVE WHITE—FOREIGN OR MIXED PARENTAGE.		
	Total number.	Engaged in gainful occupations.		Total number.	Engaged in gainful occupations.	
		Number.	Per cent.		Number.	Per cent.
Males	22,361,495	16,788,668	75.1	8,289,550	6,237,012	75.2
10 to 13 years	2,637,668	144,605	5.5	1,061,824	13,150	1.2
14 years	631,720	95,919	15.2	236,786	27,117	11.5
15 years	561,320	149,720	26.7	217,665	67,143	30.8
16 years	588,313	272,619	46.3	229,349	129,044	56.3
17 years	554,815	335,386	60.5	216,114	150,894	69.8
18 and 19 years	1,093,029	823,481	75.3	421,956	341,770	81.0
20 to 24 years	2,546,818	2,289,446	89.9	1,014,770	925,130	91.2
25 to 44 years	7,968,863	7,726,512	97.0	3,003,679	2,910,176	96.9
45 to 64 years	4,354,663	4,088,668	93.9	1,628,009	1,508,153	92.6
65 years and over	1,365,527	831,456	60.9	253,564	160,123	63.1
Age unknown	58,759	30,856	52.5	5,834	4,312	73.9
Females	21,716,069	3,733,329	17.2	8,494,749	2,110,454	24.8
10 to 13 years	2,575,468	48,437	1.9	1,049,256	4,356	0.4
14 years	610,853	31,929	5.2	234,385	17,667	7.5
15 years	559,798	56,566	10.1	220,423	45,627	20.7
16 years	590,463	117,827	20.0	232,488	93,069	40.0
17 years	550,013	146,294	26.6	218,133	110,912	50.8
18 and 19 years	1,101,295	378,393	34.4	431,039	248,415	57.6
20 to 24 years	2,629,889	855,946	32.5	1,067,020	521,017	48.8
25 to 44 years	7,807,162	1,439,349	18.4	3,150,386	774,177	24.6
45 to 64 years	3,884,369	558,202	14.4	1,623,864	271,734	16.7
65 years and over	1,373,349	93,033	6.8	262,359	21,686	8.3
Age unknown	33,410	7,353	22.0	5,396	1,794	33.2

SEX AND AGE PERIODS.	FOREIGN-BORN WHITE.			NEGRO.		
	Total number.	Engaged in gainful occupations.		Total number.	Engaged in gainful occupations.	
		Number.	Per cent.		Number.	Per cent.
Males	7,419,691	6,627,997	89.3	4,009,462	3,252,862	81.1
10 to 13 years	127,961	3,269	2.6	494,192	96,470	19.5
14 years	39,191	5,488	14.0	122,059	45,751	37.5
15 years	40,280	14,169	35.2	103,063	49,656	48.2
16 years	49,626	32,072	64.6	106,028	66,351	62.6
17 years	51,561	40,389	78.3	100,059	74,217	74.2
18 and 19 years	117,803	102,814	87.3	204,266	171,209	83.8
20 to 24 years	456,988	435,548	95.3	487,169	455,308	93.5
25 to 44 years	3,550,778	3,484,701	98.1	1,415,444	1,376,666	97.3
45 to 64 years	2,292,387	2,143,433	93.5	789,791	767,459	97.2
65 years and over	679,384	355,075	52.3	173,881	139,476	80.2
Age unknown	13,732	11,039	80.4	13,510	10,299	76.2
Females	6,078,195	1,110,100	19.4	4,043,763	1,571,289	38.9
10 to 13 years	125,361	1,501	1.2	495,026	64,982	13.1
14 years	38,849	3,746	9.6	125,637	29,392	23.4
15 years	41,619	10,519	25.3	111,019	30,980	27.9
16 years	51,145	25,263	49.4	118,984	41,371	34.8
17 years	52,539	31,666	60.3	105,728	42,178	39.9
18 and 19 years	123,369	72,237	58.6	234,068	102,238	43.7
20 to 24 years	469,856	177,030	37.7	567,678	252,417	44.5
25 to 44 years	2,720,964	506,267	18.6	1,525,792	689,933	45.2
45 to 64 years	1,799,118	250,084	13.9	591,006	269,955	45.7
65 years and over	648,843	38,453	5.9	158,832	43,096	27.1
Age unknown	6,532	1,697	26.0	9,993	4,747	47.5

TABLE 27.—NUMBER AND PROPORTION OF CHILDREN 10 TO 15 YEARS OF AGE
ENGAGED IN GAINFUL OCCUPATIONS, BY SEX, AGE, AND POPULATION CLASSES,
FOR THE UNITED STATES: 1920 AND 1910.

[Per cent not shown where base is less than 100.]

SEX AND CLASS OF POPULATION.	CHILDREN 10 TO 15 YEARS OF AGE.					
	1920			1910		
	Total number.	Engaged in gainful occupations.		Total number.	Engaged in gainful occupations.	
		Number.	Per cent.		Number.	Per cent.
Both sexes	12,502,582	1,060,858	8.5	10,828,365	1,990,225	18.4
Native white—Native parentage	7,576,827	527,176	7.0	6,322,926	1,022,561	16.2
Native white—Foreign or mixed parentage	3,020,339	175,060	5.8	2,669,259	265,245	9.9
Foreign-born white	413,261	38,692	9.4	433,515	62,997	14.5
Negro	1,450,996	317,231	21.9	1,362,821	634,938	46.6
Indian, Chinese, Japanese, and all other[1]	41,159	2,699	6.6	39,844	4,484	11.3
Indian	35,503	2,359	6.6			
Chinese	2,411	158	6.6			
Japanese	3,067	169	5.5			
All other	178	13	7.3			
Male	6,294,985	714,248	11.3	5,464,228	1,353,139	24.8
Native white—Native parentage	3,830,708	390,244	10.2	3,205,203	771,904	24.1
Native white—Foreign or mixed parentage	1,516,275	107,410	7.1	1,339,593	176,042	13.1
Foreign-born white	207,432	22,926	11.1	218,372	36,159	16.6
Negro	719,314	191,877	26.7	679,995	365,709	53.8
Indian, Chinese, Japanese, and all other[1]	21,256	1,791	8.4	21,065	3,325	15.8
Indian	17,918	1,496	8.3			
Chinese	1,524	144	9.4			
Japanese	1,725	141	8.2			
All other	89	10				
Female	6,207,597	346,610	5.6	5,364,137	637,086	11.9
Native white—Native parentage	3,746,119	136,932	3.7	3,117,723	250,657	8.0
Native white—Foreign or mixed parentage	1,504,064	67,650	4.5	1,329,666	89,203	6.7
Foreign-born white	205,829	15,766	7.7	215,143	26,838	12.5
Negro	731,682	125,354	17.1	682,826	269,229	39.4
Indian, Chinese, Japanese, and all other[1]	19,903	908	4.6	18,779	1,159	6.2
Indian	17,585	863	4.9			
Chinese	887	14	1.6			
Japanese	1,342	28	2.1			
All other	89	3				

[1] Separate figures for Indian, Chinese, Japanese, and "all other" not available for 1910.

TABLE 28.—NUMBER OF MALES IN EACH AGE PERIOD ENGAGED

DIVISION AND STATE.	AGE PERIOD.					
	10 years and over.	10 to 13 years.	14 years.	15 years.	16 years.	17 years.
United States	33,064,737	258,259	174,683	281,306	501,134	602,322
GEOGRAPHIC DIVISIONS:						
New England	2,363,377	2,316	10,506	21,646	34,974	40,959
Middle Atlantic	7,122,699	6,425	17,976	52,630	113,285	131,532
East North Central	6,951,808	12,673	17,263	42,465	91,498	116,788
West North Central	3,815,681	10,972	11,824	23,049	47,481	61,355
South Atlantic	4,096,041	80,897	46,026	54,507	81,388	91,204
East South Central	2,608,411	77,390	35,462	38,923	54,519	60,669
West South Central	3,049,275	60,077	29,693	35,860	51,841	62,246
Mountain	1,077,774	4,039	3,046	5,430	10,525	14,321
Pacific	1,979,671	3,470	2,887	6,796	15,623	23,248
NEW ENGLAND:						
Maine	245,013	257	351	1,245	2,853	3,784
New Hampshire	143,525	144	234	624	1,938	2,408
Vermont	111,585	169	206	560	1,448	1,877
Massachusetts	1,225,163	1,144	6,193	12,377	18,174	20,465
Rhode Island	194,438	131	1,634	2,711	3,694	4,564
Connecticut	443,653	471	1,888	4,129	6,867	7,861
MIDDLE ATLANTIC:						
New York	3,367,909	2,088	5,097	22,197	47,411	58,484
New Jersey	1,014,663	829	3,860	9,507	16,567	18,557
Pennsylvania	2,740,127	3,508	9,019	20,926	49,307	54,491
EAST NORTH CENTRAL:						
Ohio	1,891,546	3,226	2,755	9,249	22,353	29,555
Indiana	931,647	2,632	3,221	6,575	13,201	16,339
Illinois	2,086,800	3,026	6,193	14,651	29,901	36,049
Michigan	1,228,631	2,291	2,086	5,514	14,968	19,830
Wisconsin	813,184	1,498	3,008	6,476	11,075	15,015
WEST NORTH CENTRAL:						
Minnesota	742,947	1,455	1,570	3,503	9,261	12,253
Iowa	717,377	1,758	1,891	3,832	8,361	10,953
Missouri	1,072,545	3,645	4,721	8,527	15,434	18,256
North Dakota	178,754	739	523	953	1,893	2,784
South Dakota	186,885	538	565	1,035	2,057	3,016
Nebraska	385,292	1,089	1,055	2,222	4,308	5,997
Kansas	531,881	1,748	1,499	2,977	6,167	8,096
SOUTH ATLANTIC:						
Delaware	73,122	191	248	513	1,023	1,262
Maryland	466,257	1,338	2,408	4,509	7,952	9,590
District of Columbia	143,401	196	340	736	1,464	1,879
Virginia	677,366	6,930	5,345	7,656	12,289	15,079
West Virginia	433,677	1,643	1,524	2,812	7,100	8,916
North Carolina	693,155	18,909	10,623	11,413	16,155	16,580
South Carolina	468,601	18,945	9,145	9,321	11,725	11,894
Georgia	840,412	29,458	14,306	14,997	19,082	20,201
Florida	300,050	3,287	2,087	2,550	4,598	5,803
EAST SOUTH CENTRAL:						
Kentucky	719,629	8,337	5,997	8,216	13,145	15,458
Tennessee	677,988	13,828	7,745	9,097	13,191	15,348
Alabama	684,348	30,078	11,810	11,956	16,442	17,271
Mississippi	526,446	25,147	9,910	9,654	11,741	12,592
WEST SOUTH CENTRAL:						
Arkansas	518,754	17,149	7,230	7,713	10,514	11,491
Louisiana	528,507	8,668	5,813	7,447	10,442	12,104
Oklahoma	586,834	7,889	4,073	5,117	8,205	10,595
Texas	1,415,180	26,371	12,577	15,583	22,680	28,056
MOUNTAIN:						
Montana	185,905	310	270	585	1,360	1,949
Idaho	135,950	462	335	624	1,284	1,854
Wyoming	72,134	118	132	263	602	780
Colorado	303,870	991	928	1,696	3,340	4,331
New Mexico	107,000	625	401	763	1,249	1,713
Arizona	112,193	788	418	601	1,123	1,448
Utah	127,418	716	529	881	1,397	2,015
Nevada	33,214	29	33	74	171	231
PACIFIC:						
Washington	485,767	986	817	2,033	4,190	5,795
Oregon	267,791	620	490	978	2,165	3,195
California	1,226,113	1,864	1,580	3,785	9,268	14,258

IN GAINFUL OCCUPATIONS, BY DIVISIONS AND STATES: 1920.

DIVISION AND STATE.	AGE PERIOD.					
	18 and 19 years.	20 to 24 years.	25 to 44 years.	45 to 64 years.	65 years and over.	Age unknown.
United States	1,443,968	4,121,392	15,579,586	8,552,175	1,492,837	57,075
GEOGRAPHIC DIVISIONS:						
New England	93,457	270,225	1,100,682	663,484	122,716	2,412
Middle Atlantic	296,070	856,781	3,505,015	1,848,905	285,726	8,354
East North Central	284,635	847,483	3,388,325	1,828,383	313,811	8,484
West North Central	155,234	476,722	1,819,383	1,027,203	176,557	5,901
South Atlantic	219,522	567,799	1,770,083	977,387	198,631	8,597
East South Central	133,378	341,642	1,082,216	643,823	136,188	4,201
West South Central	155,471	429,111	1,378,483	711,112	126,365	9,016
Mountain	40,518	128,249	544,826	280,700	43,242	2,878
Pacific	65,683	203,380	990,573	571,178	89,601	7,232
NEW ENGLAND:						
Maine	9,443	27,184	103,196	76,464	19,795	441
New Hampshire	5,580	15,695	61,231	44,692	10,689	290
Vermont	4,317	11,957	46,599	35,086	9,216	150
Massachusetts	47,266	140,965	582,335	340,058	55,244	942
Rhode Island	9,488	23,210	88,784	51,805	8,320	97
Connecticut	17,363	51,214	218,537	115,379	19,452	492
MIDDLE ATLANTIC:						
New York	133,501	402,733	1,678,342	879,709	134,208	4,139
New Jersey	42,217	122,311	504,965	258,587	36,308	955
Pennsylvania	120,352	331,737	1,321,708	710,609	115,210	3,260
EAST NORTH CENTRAL:						
Ohio	75,257	234,050	924,971	499,456	89,102	1,572
Indiana	38,824	109,719	420,836	265,350	53,498	1,452
Illinois	85,708	247,476	1,043,053	539,970	77,880	2,893
Michigan	49,310	153,083	615,872	306,382	57,700	1,595
Wisconsin	35,536	103,155	383,593	217,225	35,631	972
WEST NORTH CENTRAL:						
Minnesota	30,378	94,572	362,954	196,543	29,634	824
Iowa	28,089	90,614	341,625	196,289	33,014	951
Missouri	44,437	126,254	489,884	301,343	58,552	1,492
North Dakota	7,091	22,698	91,357	44,827	5,524	365
South Dakota	7,723	24,911	95,250	44,806	6,461	523
Nebraska	15,975	50,586	189,943	98,130	15,206	781
Kansas	21,541	67,087	248,370	145,265	28,166	965
SOUTH ATLANTIC:						
Delaware	2,843	9,332	33,739	19,978	3,823	170
Maryland	23,147	62,694	209,987	121,636	22,055	941
District of Columbia	5,761	20,069	71,191	35,590	5,478	697
Virginia	38,449	94,918	292,301	166,886	36,181	1,332
West Virginia	22,204	59,720	205,252	103,559	20,169	778
North Carolina	37,525	97,222	286,047	159,653	37,604	1,424
South Carolina	27,378	68,261	190,954	99,506	20,904	568
Georgia	47,984	118,131	345,549	191,371	37,966	1,367
Florida	14,231	37,452	135,063	79,208	14,451	1,320
EAST SOUTH CENTRAL:						
Kentucky	36,719	94,511	309,886	186,384	40,249	727
Tennessee	34,928	87,715	286,610	172,486	36,180	860
Alabama	35,784	90,958	273,645	163,384	31,660	1,360
Mississippi	25,947	68,458	212,075	121,569	28,099	1,254
WEST SOUTH CENTRAL:						
Arkansas	25,514	66,693	218,280	128,915	24,481	774
Louisiana	27,973	74,204	238,919	119,809	20,915	2,213
Oklahoma	28,006	80,393	273,266	145,094	22,969	1,227
Texas	73,978	207,821	648,018	317,294	58,000	4,802
MOUNTAIN:						
Montana	5,254	17,351	102,070	49,421	6,703	632
Idaho	5,089	15,920	67,938	36,879	5,418	147
Wyoming	2,420	8,723	40,120	16,392	2,086	498
Colorado	11,270	34,869	146,769	85,489	13,677	510
New Mexico	5,099	15,324	49,597	26,993	5,226	161
Arizona	4,727	15,887	57,719	25,172	3,728	579
Utah	5,862	17,172	63,258	30,552	4,837	199
Nevada	797	3,003	17,355	9,802	1,567	152
PACIFIC:						
Washington	15,575	50,186	244,677	138,567	21,128	1,813
Oregon	8,629	27,020	130,915	80,486	12,896	397
California	41,479	126,174	614,981	352,125	55,577	5,022

TABLE 29.—NUMBER OF FEMALES IN EACH AGE PERIOD ENGAGED

DIVISION AND STATE.	AGE PERIOD.					
	10 years and over.	10 to 13 years.	14 years.	15 years.	16 years.	17 years.
United States	8,549,511	119,804	82,911	143,895	277,823	331,369
GEOGRAPHIC DIVISIONS:						
New England	871,015	683	7,984	16,104	27,180	32,520
Middle Atlantic	2,117,517	2,471	12,933	39,106	86,951	101,629
East North Central	1,564,041	1,889	6,785	19,726	51,337	68,151
West North Central	772,315	1,887	2,751	7,423	18,632	26,273
South Atlantic	1,243,958	42,650	22,734	27,167	41,787	43,012
East South Central	702,433	37,742	15,645	16,180	22,393	22,489
West South Central	666,973	31,036	12,833	14,768	19,912	22,213
Mountain	177,220	967	698	1,432	3,134	4,742
Pacific	434,039	479	548	1,989	6,497	10,340
NEW ENGLAND:						
Maine	64,845	76	133	523	1,505	2,075
New Hampshire	49,302	50	114	360	1,343	1,792
Vermont	26,899	38	58	246	656	861
Massachusetts	503,155	287	4,610	9,112	14,478	17,605
Rhode Island	80,562	55	1,518	2,520	3,427	3,531
Connecticut	146,252	177	1,551	3,343	5,771	6,656
MIDDLE ATLANTIC:						
New York	1,135,295	734	3,057	16,673	41,440	51,274
New Jersey	295,990	399	3,433	7,996	14,367	15,373
Pennsylvania	686,232	1,338	6,443	14,437	31,144	34,982
EAST NORTH CENTRAL:						
Ohio	409,970	395	502	1,992	10,416	16,269
Indiana	185,385	315	1,188	2,980	6,457	7,882
Illinois	540,938	608	3,340	9,115	20,203	23,791
Michigan	245,383	367	501	2,395	8,524	11,338
Wisconsin	182,365	204	1,254	3,244	5,737	8,871
WEST NORTH CENTRAL:						
Minnesota	164,066	312	388	1,043	3,883	6,063
Iowa	141,321	209	351	1,080	2,931	4,230
Missouri	244,615	678	1,380	3,636	7,391	9,130
North Dakota	28,328	232	125	244	515	931
South Dakota	29,686	113	90	214	503	826
Nebraska	71,789	183	183	554	1,509	2,402
Kansas	92,510	160	234	652	1,900	2,691
SOUTH ATLANTIC:						
Delaware	18,102	48	107	299	613	702
Maryland	137,221	430	1,122	2,493	5,381	6,019
District of Columbia	92,626	63	138	398	1,166	1,657
Virginia	156,210	1,674	1,479	2,409	4,352	5,177
West Virginia	57,439	357	356	739	1,856	2,240
North Carolina	202,697	9,766	5,385	6,066	8,363	7,837
South Carolina	205,656	13,583	6,319	6,207	8,120	7,267
Georgia	288,745	15,539	7,113	7,521	10,012	9,788
Florida	85,262	1,190	715	1,035	1,924	2,325
EAST SOUTH CENTRAL:						
Kentucky	131,493	1,487	1,037	1,680	3,181	4,018
Tennessee	152,108	4,342	2,111	2,714	4,362	4,842
Alabama	223,868	17,518	6,599	6,436	8,435	7,543
Mississippi	194,964	14,395	5,898	5,350	6,415	6,086
WEST SOUTH CENTRAL:						
Arkansas	115,810	9,190	3,477	3,381	4,058	3,869
Louisiana	152,726	4,418	2,647	3,281	4,601	5,103
Oklahoma	94,594	3,240	1,206	1,456	2,294	2,947
Texas	303,843	14,188	5,503	6,650	8,959	10,294
MOUNTAIN:						
Montana	28,278	33	59	145	388	675
Idaho	17,509	35	39	113	275	487
Wyoming	9,402	24	22	49	152	219
Colorado	62,587	172	205	536	1,150	1,646
New Mexico	14,941	196	90	181	309	531
Arizona	18,386	480	199	222	356	105
Utah	21,783	22	53	160	462	847
Nevada	4,334	5	2	26	42	72
PACIFIC:						
Washington	92,900	119	169	526	1,512	2,479
Oregon	54,492	54	68	252	843	1,415
California	286,647	306	311	1,211	4,142	6,446

IN GAINFUL OCCUPATIONS, BY DIVISIONS AND STATES: 1920.

DIVISION AND STATE.	AGE PERIOD.					
	18 and 19 years.	20 to 24 years.	25 to 44 years.	45 to 64 years.	65 years and over.	Age un-known.
United States.................	802,235	1,809,075	3,417,373	1,352,479	196,900	15,647
GEOGRAPHIC DIVISIONS:						
New England..................	77,197	185,147	355,609	147,646	20,023	922
Middle Atlantic..............	220,958	473,555	823,751	313,107	40,750	2,306
East North Central............	168,758	357,045	615,258	238,656	34,130	2,306
West North Central............	77,263	189,619	310,982	118,688	17,092	1,705
South Atlantic...............	103,386	237,687	492,344	196,250	33,930	3,011
East South Central............	52,351	118,686	271,196	121,413	22,901	1,437
West South Central...........	56,025	127,585	265,645	100,006	14,747	2,203
Mountain...................	15,253	37,941	77,114	31,578	3,843	518
Pacific.....................	31,044	81,810	205,474	85,135	9,484	1,239
NEW ENGLAND:						
Maine......................	5,430	13,504	25,277	13,493	2,721	108
New Hampshire...............	4,123	10,015	19,653	9,902	1,853	97
Vermont...................	2,330	5,341	10,029	6,031	1,267	42
Massachusetts...............	43,119	106,596	212,130	84,869	9,937	412
Rhode Island...............	7,404	16,777	31,729	12,109	1,445	47
Connecticut.................	14,791	32,914	56,791	21,242	2,800	216
MIDDLE ATLANTIC:						
New York..................	112,512	257,234	458,725	171,254	21,203	1,189
New Jersey.................	32,496	66,294	110,389	40,053	4,890	300
Pennsylvania...............	75,950	150,027	254,637	101,800	14,657	817
EAST NORTH CENTRAL:						
Ohio......................	44,109	90,712	166,130	68,458	10,612	375
Indiana...................	19,209	39,031	69,255	33,006	5,680	382
Illinois....................	55,874	122,992	219,386	75,816	8,815	998
Michigan..................	27,390	56,894	95,486	36,729	5,416	343
Wisconsin.................	22,176	47,416	65,001	24,647	3,607	208
WEST NORTH CENTRAL:						
Minnesota.................	17,812	46,235	65,539	19,989	2,554	248
Iowa.....................	13,752	35,559	56,497	23,108	3,375	229
Missouri..................	22,391	49,944	100,685	42,170	6,666	544
North Dakota..............	3,383	8,746	10,262	3,377	413	100
South Dakota..............	3,129	8,502	11,659	3,993	503	154
Nebraska..................	7,751	18,557	29,118	10,171	1,185	176
Kansas...................	9,045	22,076	37,222	15,880	2,396	254
SOUTH ATLANTIC:						
Delaware..................	1,659	3,562	7,125	3,338	585	64
Maryland.................	12,926	26,271	54,448	24,130	3,880	121
District of Columbia..........	5,609	20,002	45,853	15,469	1,874	397
Virginia...................	13,415	31,756	61,226	28,388	5,803	531
West Virginia..............	6,180	13,026	21,306	9,214	2,022	143
North Carolina.............	18,391	39,766	71,501	29,285	5,808	529
South Carolina.............	16,731	36,669	77,240	28,366	4,867	287
Georgia...................	22,528	51,762	113,817	43,214	6,956	495
Florida...................	5,947	14,873	39,828	14,846	2,135	444
EAST SOUTH CENTRAL:						
Kentucky..................	9,750	22,999	52,293	28,723	6,078	247
Tennessee.................	11,869	27,675	61,660	26,879	5,297	357
Alabama..................	17,017	36,085	82,437	35,124	6,285	389
Mississippi................	13,715	31,927	74,806	30,687	5,241	444
WEST SOUTH CENTRAL:						
Arkansas..................	9,112	18,990	42,933	17,913	2,619	268
Louisiana.................	11,830	26,851	63,182	25,978	4,263	572
Oklahoma.................	9,168	20,904	37,898	13,670	1,570	241
Texas....................	25,915	60,840	121,632	42,445	6,295	1,122
MOUNTAIN:						
Montana..................	2,455	6,274	13,015	4,674	480	80
Idaho....................	1,684	4,321	7,256	2,954	320	25
Wyoming.................	752	2,077	4,426	1,439	184	58
Colorado.................	4,871	12,575	27,256	12,488	1,499	159
New Mexico...............	1,207	2,859	6,228	3,007	443	31
Arizona..................	1,321	3,363	8,719	2,878	332	111
Utah....................	2,719	5,737	8,111	3,195	436	41
Nevada..................	244	735	2,103	943	149	13
PACIFIC:						
Washington...............	7,723	19,839	42,543	16,031	1,629	330
Oregon...................	4,453	11,201	24,939	10,111	1,072	84
California.................	18,868	50,770	137,992	58,993	6,783	825

TABLE 30.—NUMBER AND PROPORTION OF CHILDREN OF EACH SEX 10 TO 15 YEARS OF

DIVISION AND STATE.	MALES 10 TO 15 YEARS OF AGE: 1920			MALES 10 TO 15 YEARS OF AGE 1910		
	Total number.	Engaged in gainful occupations.		Total number.	Engaged in gainful occupations.	
		Number.	Per cent.		Number.	Per cent.
United States	6,294,985	714,248	11.3	5,464,228	1,353,139	24.8
GEOGRAPHIC DIVISIONS:						
New England	384,222	34,468	9.0	334,762	38,096	11.4
Middle Atlantic	1,201,840	77,031	6.4	1,027,768	118,312	11.5
East North Central	1,166,568	72,401	6.2	1,025,615	133,003	13.0
West North Central	745,989	45,845	6.1	705,931	120,601	17.1
South Atlantic	961,537	181,430	18.9	835,646	364,529	43.6
East South Central	640,781	151,775	23.7	583,837	295,255	50.6
West South Central	731,028	125,630	17.2	609,507	248,765	40.8
Mountain	198,871	12,515	6.3	144,810	18,595	12.8
Pacific	264,149	13,153	5.0	196,352	15,983	8.1
NEW ENGLAND:						
Maine	41,486	1,853	4.5	38,826	3,710	9.6
New Hampshire	22,825	1,002	4.4	21,710	2,222	10.2
Vermont	19,638	935	4.8	19,107	1,967	10.3
Massachusetts	197,205	19,714	10.0	169,990	19,172	11.3
Rhode Island	31,346	4,476	14.3	28,095	4,350	15.5
Connecticut	71,722	6,488	9.0	57,034	6,675	11.7
MIDDLE ATLANTIC:						
New York	532,343	29,382	5.5	466,895	39,357	8.4
New Jersey	170,747	14,196	8.3	136,309	14,948	11.0
Pennsylvania	498,750	33,453	6.7	424,564	64,007	15.1
EAST NORTH CENTRAL:						
Ohio	300,942	15,230	5.1	255,713	31,906	12.5
Indiana	163,834	12,428	7.6	154,238	27,688	18.0
Illinois	351,552	23,870	6.8	311,761	41,912	13.4
Michigan	194,494	9,891	5.1	155,502	14,512	9.3
Wisconsin	155,746	10,982	7.1	148,401	16,985	11.4
WEST NORTH CENTRAL:						
Minnesota	140,111	6,528	4.7	129,031	14,707	11.4
Iowa	136,380	7,481	5.5	134,077	20,777	15.5
Missouri	199,657	16,893	8.5	195,183	44,373	22.7
North Dakota	44,613	2,215	5.0	35,848	5,929	16.5
South Dakota	39,830	2,138	5.4	36,521	6,953	19.0
Nebraska	78,981	4,366	5.5	73,615	10,865	14.8
Kansas	106,417	6,224	5.8	101,656	16,997	16.7
SOUTH ATLANTIC:						
Delaware	12,008	952	7.9	11,826	2,753	23.3
Maryland	82,847	8,255	10.0	77,358	16,336	21.1
District of Columbia	17,149	1,272	7.4	14,405	913	6.3
Virginia	157,364	19,931	12.7	142,317	47,204	33.2
West Virginia	96,362	5,979	6.2	79,343	20,548	25.9
North Carolina	188,538	40,945	21.7	159,276	91,649	57.5
South Carolina	130,337	37,411	28.7	114,019	66,382	58.2
Georgia	215,008	58,761	27.3	189,378	101,648	53.7
Florida	61,924	7,924	12.8	47,724	17,096	35.8
EAST SOUTH CENTRAL:						
Kentucky	161,285	22,550	14.0	152,511	53,838	35.3
Tennessee	164,155	30,670	18.7	147,323	64,035	43.5
Alabama	175,571	53,844	30.7	152,170	94,126	61.9
Mississippi	139,770	44,711	32.0	131,833	83,256	63.2
WEST SOUTH CENTRAL:						
Arkansas	130,853	32,092	24.5	107,875	60,109	55.7
Louisiana	128,369	21,928	17.1	114,766	38,830	33.8
Oklahoma	147,007	17,070	11.6	112,344	35,383	31.5
Texas	324,700	54,531	16.8	274,522	114,443	11.7
MOUNTAIN:						
Montana	30,450	1,165	3.8	17,894	1,448	8.1
Idaho	27,823	1,421	5.1	19,526	2,424	12.4
Wyoming	10,509	513	4.9	6,511	755	11.6
Colorado	52,681	3,615	6.9	41,983	4,683	11.2
New Mexico	24,082	1,729	7.2	20,811	4,942	23.7
Arizona	19,318	1,810	9.4	11,166	1,297	11.6
Utah	30,564	2,126	7.0	23,897	2,811	11.8
Nevada	3,444	136	3.9	3,022	235	7.8
PACIFIC:						
Washington	69,714	3,836	5.5	56,392	4,424	7.8
Oregon	41,134	2,088	5.1	33,959	2,970	8.7
California	153,301	7,229	4.7	106,001	8,589	8.1

AGE ENGAGED IN GAINFUL OCCUPATIONS, BY DIVISIONS AND STATES: 1920 AND 1910.

DIVISION AND STATE.	FEMALES 10 TO 15 YEARS OF AGE: 1920			FEMALES 10 TO 15 YEARS OF AGE: 1910		
	Total number.	Engaged in gainful occupations.		Total number.	Engaged in gainful occupations.	
		Number.	Per cent.		Number.	Per cent.
United States	6,207,597	346,610	5.6	5,364,137	637,086	11.9
GEOGRAPHIC DIVISIONS:						
New England	383,909	24,771	6.5	333,886	25,843	7.7
Middle Atlantic	1,195,896	54,510	4.6	1,025,227	69,469	6.8
East North Central	1,146,143	28,400	2.5	1,009,752	43,237	4.3
West North Central	731,374	12,061	1.6	689,453	21,445	3.1
South Atlantic	950,037	92,551	9.7	815,579	198,717	24.4
East South Central	626,494	69,567	11.1	564,753	146,635	26.0
West South Central	718,736	58,637	8.2	594,593	123,908	20.8
Mountain	194,692	3,097	1.6	139,410	3,593	2.6
Pacific	260,316	3,016	1.2	191,484	4,239	2.2
NEW ENGLAND:						
Maine	41,343	732	1.8	38,454	1,716	4.5
New Hampshire	22,866	524	2.3	21,725	1,537	7.1
Vermont	18,941	342	1.8	18,541	598	3.2
Massachusetts	196,821	14,009	7.1	170,042	13,573	8.0
Rhode Island	32,393	4,093	12.6	28,299	3,726	13.2
Connecticut	71,545	5,071	7.1	56,825	4,693	8.3
MIDDLE ATLANTIC:						
New York	527,292	20,464	3.9	467,191	25,737	5.5
New Jersey	170,438	11,828	6.9	135,993	10,844	8.0
Pennsylvania	498,166	22,218	4.5	422,043	32,888	7.8
EAST NORTH CENTRAL:						
Ohio	295,799	2,889	1.0	252,063	10,940	4.3
Indiana	160,145	4,483	2.8	150,889	6,005	4.0
Illinois	347,758	13,063	3.8	309,401	14,598	4.7
Michigan	189,719	3,263	1.7	152,193	4,781	3.1
Wisconsin	152,722	4,702	3.1	145,206	6,913	4.8
WEST NORTH CENTRAL:						
Minnesota	137,417	1,743	1.3	125,902	3,657	2.9
Iowa	133,837	1,640	1.2	131,631	3,608	2.7
Missouri	196,025	5,694	2.9	192,136	8,329	4.3
North Dakota	43,270	601	1.4	34,148	1,423	4.2
South Dakota	38,597	417	1.1	34,672	1,256	3.6
Nebraska	76,939	920	1.2	71,826	1,439	2.0
Kansas	105,289	1,046	1.0	99,138	1,733	1.7
SOUTH ATLANTIC:						
Delaware	11,801	454	3.8	11,259	903	8.0
Maryland	81,699	4,045	5.0	76,730	7,831	10.2
District of Columbia	18,081	599	3.3	15,060	432	2.9
Virginia	154,551	5,562	3.6	138,920	14,675	10.6
West Virginia	94,937	1,452	1.5	75,658	3,254	4.3
North Carolina	184,946	21,217	11.5	155,495	52,983	34.1
South Carolina	129,867	26,109	20.1	112,093	50,870	45.4
Georgia	212,227	30,173	14.2	183,323	59,941	32.7
Florida	61,928	2,940	4.7	47,041	7,828	16.6
EAST SOUTH CENTRAL:						
Kentucky	157,123	4,204	2.7	148,441	10,854	7.3
Tennessee	159,393	9,167	5.8	141,992	19,921	14.0
Alabama	173,966	30,553	17.6	146,795	60,586	41.3
Mississippi	136,012	25,643	18.9	127,525	55,274	43.3
WEST SOUTH CENTRAL:						
Arkansas	128,740	16,048	12.5	105,917	32,341	30.5
Louisiana	129,683	10,346	8.0	114,171	20,902	18.3
Oklahoma	142,466	5,902	4.1	107,760	10,728	10.0
Texas	317,847	26,341	8.3	266,745	59,937	22.5
MOUNTAIN:						
Montana	29,595	237	0.8	17,330	316	1.8
Idaho	26,818	187	0.7	18,249	274	1.5
Wyoming	9,878	95	1.0	6,243	111	1.8
Colorado	52,109	943	1.8	40,988	1,181	2.9
New Mexico	23,950	466	1.9	20,020	864	4.3
Arizona	18,960	901	4.8	10,369	376	3.6
Utah	30,111	235	0.8	23,406	420	1.8
Nevada	3,271	33	1.0	2,805	51	1.8
PACIFIC:						
Washington	68,931	814	1.2	54,930	1,042	1.9
Oregon	40,366	374	0.9	32,800	535	1.6
California	151,019	1,828	1.2	103,754	2,662	2.6

TABLE 31.—NUMBER OF MALES IN EACH AGE PERIOD ENGAGED IN GAIN-

CITY.	AGE PERIOD.					
	10 years and over.	10 to 13 years.	14 years.	15 years.	16 years.	17 years.
Akron, Ohio	92,082	79	53	266	771	1,251
Albany, N. Y	37,822	30	42	152	414	538
Atlanta, Ga	66,702	426	528	713	1,046	1,202
Baltimore, Md	245,122	222	1,142	2,370	3,999	4,650
Birmingham, Ala	59,070	196	192	362	751	1,031
Boston, Mass	245,905	250	799	1,817	3,157	3,742
Bridgeport, Conn	48,369	44	160	375	669	763
Buffalo, N. Y	165,362	79	215	1,038	2,289	2,795
Cambridge, Mass	34,025	28	153	326	520	616
Camden, N. J	39,336	23	124	339	719	825
Chicago, Ill	919,899	421	2,827	7,213	12,974	14,845
Cincinnati, Ohio	134,925	145	119	790	1,705	2,232
Cleveland, Ohio	273,715	282	190	1,425	3,432	4,248
Columbus, Ohio	80,726	158	109	354	778	1,031
Dallas, Tex	55,719	142	186	387	594	836
Dayton, Ohio	53,529	171	109	253	547	750
Denver, Colo	90,084	177	260	502	863	1,092
Des Moines, Iowa	41,301	86	90	190	491	589
Detroit, Mich	381,300	436	309	1,155	3,898	5,267
Fall River, Mass	36,094	21	563	792	933	897
Fort Worth, Tex	40,013	82	116	240	415	608
Grand Rapids, Mich	43,985	95	73	203	557	812
Hartford, Conn	46,347	47	106	314	584	667
Houston, Tex	48,749	203	208	461	707	818
Indianapolis, Ind	110,137	405	385	805	1,434	1,771
Jersey City, N. J	97,738	57	413	1,093	1,702	2,042
Kansas City, Kans	34,757	41	95	259	527	587
Kansas City, Mo	116,858	126	234	573	1,154	1,360
Los Angeles, Calif	197,700	277	198	566	1,400	2,014
Louisville, Ky	78,067	106	261	522	1,158	1,409
Lowell, Mass	35,771	20	151	402	584	640
Memphis, Tenn	56,428	169	201	410	661	929
Milwaukee, Wis	153,419	336	769	1,435	2,006	2,635
Minneapolis, Minn	127,549	187	147	380	1,126	1,486
Nashville, Tenn	37,325	200	240	380	608	752
New Bedford, Mass	39,796	44	392	696	824	794
New Haven, Conn	51,037	47	265	566	833	906
New Orleans, La	128,422	327	954	1,581	2,304	2,641
New York, N. Y	1,839,685	568	3,158	14,615	28,648	34,895
Bronx borough	230,546	55	329	1,719	3,522	4,572
Brooklyn borough	646,774	222	1,274	5,927	11,488	13,638
Manhattan borough	773,448	222	1,111	5,193	10,413	12,807
Queens borough	151,040	56	390	1,491	2,619	3,141
Richmond borough	37,877	13	54	285	606	737
Newark, N. J	136,095	90	503	1,346	2,258	2,415
Norfolk, Va	43,733	159	176	307	517	723
Oakland, Calif	78,354	106	94	247	635	832
Omaha, Nebr	67,869	123	117	303	693	939
Paterson, N. J	44,996	22	254	590	899	944
Philadelphia, Pa	603,237	330	1,702	3,964	9,387	11,027
Pittsburgh, Pa	191,989	105	365	1,006	2,750	3,315
Portland, Oreg	92,102	303	218	372	759	994
Providence, R. I	75,875	43	523	925	1,219	1,315
Reading, Pa	35,939	40	268	445	706	693
Richmond, Va	53,184	140	254	503	840	1,028
Rochester, N. Y	96,463	52	145	617	1,310	1,504
St. Louis, Mo	272,659	191	1,225	2,658	4,237	4,722
St. Paul, Minn	78,702	77	99	308	1,000	1,196
Salt Lake City, Utah	86,811	68	97	209	353	480
San Antonio, Tex	52,740	246	247	161	753	881
San Francisco, Calif	204,734	156	192	566	1,482	2,778
Scranton, Pa	41,453	19	160	387	902	1,034
Seattle, Wash	120,600	265	220	466	839	1,169
Spokane, Wash	34,737	83	59	173	286	415
Springfield, Mass	42,954	34	149	352	508	570
Syracuse, N. Y	58,546	69	85	272	620	808
Toledo, Ohio	86,846	130	116	448	1,094	1,436
Trenton, N. J	38,854	24	252	455	624	722
Washington, D. C	143,401	196	340	736	1,464	1,879
Wilmington, Del	38,552	41	131	300	554	676
Worcester, Mass	57,885	54	291	592	851	856
Yonkers, N. Y	30,187	9	29	151	426	548
Youngstown, Ohio	46,611	62	38	138	430	626

FUL OCCUPATIONS, FOR CITIES HAVING 100,000 INHABITANTS OR MORE: 1920.

CITY.	AGE PERIOD.					
	18 and 19 years.	20 to 24 years.	25 to 44 years.	45 to 64 years.	65 years and over.	Age unknown.
Akron, Ohio	4,969	20,236	50,469	12,725	1,103	160
Albany, N. Y	1,279	3,961	18,976	10,719	1,678	33
Atlanta, Ga	3,125	10,036	33,994	13,738	1,854	40
Baltimore, Md	10,858	33,210	118,730	60,963	8,921	57
Birmingham, Ala	2,692	8,647	31,031	12,681	1,295	192
Boston, Mass	9,278	29,023	121,890	66,778	8,761	410
Bridgeport, Conn	1,733	5,986	26,530	10,844	1,179	86
Buffalo, N. Y	6,354	20,262	85,571	41,637	4,995	127
Cambridge, Mass	1,340	3,967	16,485	9,206	1,377	7
Camden, N. J	1,699	4,978	19,667	9,589	1,324	49
Chicago, Ill	33,503	107,007	496,062	220,024	23,505	1,518
Cincinnati, Ohio	5,049	15,776	65,446	38,139	5,430	94
Cleveland, Ohio	9,941	34,586	155,614	57,704	6,113	180
Columbus, Ohio	3,111	9,725	40,843	21,368	3,085	164
Dallas, Tex	2,376	8,170	30,148	11,274	1,479	127
Dayton, Ohio	2,091	6,920	26,924	13,718	2,013	33
Denver, Colo	2,827	9,884	44,617	25,969	3,774	119
Des Moines, Iowa	1,367	4,925	21,153	10,658	1,689	63
Detroit, Mich	14,936	56,767	224,803	66,547	6,712	470
Fall River, Mass	1,748	4,583	16,011	9,340	1,198	8
Fort Worth, Tex	1,637	6,091	21,524	8,110	1,025	165
Grand Rapids, Mich	1,828	5,088	21,249	11,965	2,052	63
Hartford, Conn	1,679	5,736	24,365	11,401	1,420	28
Houston, Tex	2,055	6,777	25,494	10,628	1,323	75
Indianapolis, Ind	4,374	13,566	54,317	28,518	4,315	247
Jersey City, N. J	4,332	12,664	49,545	23,384	2,477	29
Kansas City, Kans	1,383	4,403	17,290	8,850	1,274	48
Kansas City, Mo	3,766	13,621	61,034	30,452	4,228	310
Los Angeles, Calif	5,877	20,231	103,394	55,053	7,930	760
Louisville, Ky	3,244	9,712	37,246	21,293	3,014	102
Lowell, Mass	1,516	4,362	16,961	9,719	1,392	24
Memphis, Tenn	2,318	7,284	29,318	13,238	1,626	274
Milwaukee, Wis	6,249	19,819	79,423	35,770	4,847	130
Minneapolis, Minn	3,955	14,756	68,160	32,547	4,684	121
Nashville, Tenn	1,733	4,900	16,902	10,054	1,513	43
New Bedford, Mass	1,817	5,202	19,580	9,251	1,188	8
New Haven, Conn	1,880	6,022	25,481	13,025	1,921	91
New Orleans, La	6,664	18,828	62,565	28,820	3,441	297
New York, N. Y	76,676	235,028	967,670	430,516	45,422	2,489
Bronx borough	9,653	29,432	126,202	50,210	4,738	114
Brooklyn borough	29,519	85,772	331,008	150,819	16,612	495
Manhattan borough	29,058	96,154	414,413	183,222	19,175	1,680
Queens borough	6,665	18,559	77,266	37,010	3,687	156
Richmond borough	1,781	5,111	18,781	9,255	1,210	44
Newark, N. J	5,732	17,217	70,622	32,281	3,567	64
Norfolk, Va	2,122	6,935	22,743	9,158	875	18
Oakland, Calif	2,296	7,878	41,268	21,898	2,939	161
Omaha, Nebr	2,640	8,653	35,196	16,737	2,232	236
Paterson, N. J	1,929	5,711	21,785	11,385	1,463	14
Philadelphia, Pa	24,966	75,960	299,787	154,308	21,235	571
Pittsburgh, Pa	7,668	23,727	99,838	47,683	5,287	245
Portland, Oreg	2,539	8,715	48,551	26,362	3,169	120
Providence, R. I	2,974	8,856	36,250	20,846	2,875	49
Reading, Pa	1,456	4,200	16,556	9,931	1,630	14
Richmond, Va	2,397	7,452	26,543	12,168	1,666	193
Rochester, N. Y	3,542	11,283	49,442	24,959	3,507	102
St. Louis, Mo	10,583	32,289	135,502	71,516	9,470	266
St. Paul, Minn	3,042	9,753	40,547	19,750	2,844	86
Salt Lake City, Utah	1,414	4,390	18,234	9,117	1,366	86
San Antonio, Tex	2,855	8,846	25,664	11,150	1,502	132
San Francisco, Calif	7,790	21,741	108,025	53,841	6,201	1,962
Scranton, Pa	2,060	5,071	20,018	10,565	1,215	22
Seattle, Wash	3,097	11,272	66,743	32,158	3,672	699
Spokane, Wash	996	3,303	17,031	10,922	1,427	42
Springfield, Mass	1,511	5,157	22,630	10,635	1,386	22
Syracuse, N. Y	1,894	6,857	29,740	15,935	2,223	43
Toledo, Ohio	3,477	11,458	44,718	20,988	2,914	67
Trenton, N. J	1,479	4,814	20,050	9,222	1,198	14
Washington, D. C	5,761	20,069	71,191	35,590	5,478	697
Wilmington, Del	1,492	5,378	19,204	9,348	1,318	110
Worcester, Mass	2,139	6,754	29,545	14,702	2,054	47
Yonkers, N. Y	1,271	3,732	15,347	7,871	784	19
Youngstown, Ohio	1,697	5,945	27,300	9,473	853	49

TABLE 32.—NUMBER OF FEMALES IN EACH AGE PERIOD ENGAGED IN GAIN-

CITY.	AGE PERIOD.					
	10 years and over.	10 to 13 years.	14 years.	15 years.	16 years.	17 years.
Akron, Ohio	16,021	12	12	38	329	695
Albany, N. Y	14,500	5	20	122	351	472
Atlanta, Ga	32,250	122	178	397	783	883
Baltimore, Md	92,632	127	773	1,785	3,886	4,181
Birmingham, Ala	20,082	70	91	184	481	527
Boston, Mass	104,302	49	470	1,222	2,537	3,354
Bridgeport, Conn	15,527	13	169	359	660	723
Buffalo, N. Y	49,981	21	164	921	2,178	2,653
Cambridge, Mass	15,984	7	89	235	413	549
Camden, N. J	10,758	2	89	318	597	655
Chicago, Ill	311,535	229	2,217	6,004	12,359	14,136
Cincinnati, Ohio	50,383	18	21	113	1,132	1,798
Cleveland, Ohio	73,531	50	56	282	2,207	3,564
Columbus, Ohio	25,479	8	13	62	391	660
Dallas, Tex	21,772	35	60	221	438	626
Dayton, Ohio	15,030	5	10	46	339	538
Denver, Colo	29,006	26	116	301	580	842
Des Moines, Iowa	15,350	11	17	85	286	458
Detroit, Mich	83,814	95	123	753	3,214	4,218
Fall River, Mass	20,404	9	513	771	884	899
Fort Worth, Tex	10,702	22	22	88	226	346
Grand Rapids, Mich	15,071	15	14	109	505	712
Hartford, Conn	17,599	15	101	255	502	719
Houston, Tex	17,181	44	72	174	360	530
Indianapolis, Ind	36,221	41	209	517	1,098	1,386
Jersey City, N. J	29,895	22	308	860	1,656	1,812
Kansas City, Kans	9,222	8	40	133	398	421
Kansas City, Mo	40,322	39	87	271	767	1,118
Los Angeles, Calif	68,400	46	55	238	866	1,351
Louisville, Ky	34,186	38	138	355	917	1,149
Lowell, Mass	18,248	17	103	329	598	659
Memphis, Tenn	24,143	50	107	202	447	640
Milwaukee, Wis	51,344	19	585	1,323	1,887	2,758
Minneapolis, Minn	46,740	26	73	197	885	1,610
Nashville, Tenn	17,929	55	75	178	405	533
New Bedford, Mass	20,773	9	380	612	782	822
New Haven, Conn	18,955	18	216	440	719	831
New Orleans, La	49,761	139	393	871	1,402	1,783
New York, N. Y	691,727	416	2,050	11,576	27,825	34,205
Bronx borough	77,658	42	207	1,329	3,547	4,515
Brooklyn borough	215,139	149	832	4,590	10,809	13,091
Manhattan borough	342,518	188	757	4,282	10,406	13,113
Queens borough	46,792	30	223	1,210	2,599	2,917
Richmond borough	9,620	7	31	165	464	569
Newark, N. J	42,235	47	403	1,164	2,196	2,359
Norfolk, Va	14,627	41	56	146	284	405
Oakland, Calif	20,119	9	11	98	366	544
Omaha, Nebr	21,066	22	40	196	547	762
Paterson, N. J	18,883	12	270	602	941	960
Philadelphia, Pa	215,763	144	1,387	3,420	8,267	9,683
Pittsburgh, Pa	57,759	50	249	676	2,185	2,837
Portland, Oreg	28,506	20	35	126	501	804
Providence, R. I	33,430	27	474	830	1,216	1,274
Reading, Pa	13,624	11	274	437	618	647
Richmond, Va	26,641	41	171	412	802	985
Rochester, N. Y	37,641	24	112	549	1,297	1,563
St. Louis, Mo	99,791	121	756	2,087	3,889	4,363
St. Paul, Minn	28,118	23	44	188	796	1,156
Salt Lake City, Utah	10,080	5	20	65	225	383
San Antonio, Tex	16,807	53	95	238	517	616
San Francisco, Calif	60,932	49	48	262	951	1,541
Scranton, Pa	13,334	13	132	325	781	866
Seattle, Wash	33,176	16	46	164	441	811
Spokane, Wash	11,121	7	21	35	183	280
Springfield, Mass	17,301	12	116	238	413	543
Syracuse, N. Y	18,759	29	56	248	561	689
Toledo, Ohio	23,283	15	42	143	676	1,019
Trenton, N. J	11,834	13	215	441	633	631
Washington, D. C	92,626	63	138	398	1,166	1,657
Wilmington, Del	11,767	23	86	226	463	479
Worcester, Mass	21,008	11	180	383	671	789
Yonkers, N. Y	11,218	5	29	146	417	561
Youngstown, Ohio	8,652	11	14	51	298	396

FUL OCCUPATIONS, FOR CITIES HAVING 100,000 INHABITANTS OR MORE: 1920.

CITY.	AGE PERIOD.					
	18 and 19 years.	20 to 24 years.	25 to 44 years.	45 to 64 years.	65 years and over.	Age unknown.
Akron, Ohio	2,022	4,480	6,901	1,418	105	9
Albany, N. Y	1,243	3,028	6,361	2,567	318	13
Atlanta, Ga	2,414	6,844	15,596	4,428	579	26
Baltimore, Md	8,659	17,839	38,208	15,212	1,929	33
Birmingham, Ala	1,686	4,263	9,797	2,648	251	84
Boston, Mass	8,725	21,994	44,951	18,803	2,065	132
Bridgeport, Conn	1,675	3,697	6,259	1,780	162	30
Buffalo, N. Y	5,558	11,765	19,446	6,579	655	41
Cambridge, Mass	1,363	3,349	6,929	2,755	291	4
Camden, N. J	1,249	2,244	3,893	1,513	190	8
Chicago, Ill	31,260	71,788	132,270	37,565	3,105	602
Cincinnati, Ohio	4,430	9,794	22,021	9,828	1,167	61
Cleveland, Ohio	8,716	17,480	32,259	8,144	719	54
Columbus, Ohio	2,131	5,184	11,799	4,718	485	28
Dallas, Tex	1,917	5,068	10,678	2,412	200	117
Dayton, Ohio	1,577	3,224	6,515	2,474	288	14
Denver, Colo	2,176	5,721	13,310	5,344	534	56
Des Moines, Iowa	1,329	3,793	7,019	2,133	194	25
Detroit, Mich	9,373	20,678	35,890	8,643	734	93
Fall River, Mass	1,933	4,259	8,003	2,884	242	7
Fort Worth, Tex	934	2,487	5,218	1,186	117	56
Grand Rapids, Mich	1,653	3,395	6,120	2,285	247	16
Hartford, Conn	1,750	4,277	7,294	2,436	226	24
Houston, Tex	1,495	3,604	8,456	2,182	230	34
Indianapolis, Ind	3,200	7,162	15,735	6,105	630	138
Jersey City, N. J	3,596	7,396	10,680	3,230	318	17
Kansas City, Kans	1,005	1,919	3,790	1,372	118	18
Kansas City, Mo	3,092	8,386	19,980	5,937	507	138
Los Angeles, Calif	4,021	11,056	34,825	14,317	1,433	192
Louisville, Ky	2,661	6,347	15,186	6,479	843	73
Lowell, Mass	1,474	3,756	7,928	3,107	267	10
Memphis, Tenn	1,652	4,623	12,070	3,772	474	106
Milwaukee, Wis	6,153	12,867	19,455	5,689	558	50
Minneapolis, Minn	4,555	12,686	21,023	5,207	423	55
Nashville, Tenn	1,418	3,378	8,265	3,131	456	35
New Bedford, Mass	1,821	4,481	9,046	2,602	210	8
New Haven, Conn	1,972	4,345	7,228	2,792	342	52
New Orleans, La	4,169	8,873	22,258	8,515	1,181	177
New York, N. Y	73,247	166,267	280,206	87,292	7,999	644
Bronx borough	10,087	22,877	27,940	6,505	568	41
Brooklyn borough	27,182	55,278	75,901	24,552	2,571	184
Manhattan borough	29,099	74,195	155,827	50,052	4,225	374
Queens borough	5,738	11,706	16,985	4,872	478	34
Richmond borough	1,141	2,211	3,553	1,311	157	11
Newark, N. J	5,004	9,881	15,471	5,186	481	43
Norfolk, Va	1,218	3,118	7,018	2,126	206	9
Oakland, Calif	1,586	3,913	9,556	3,599	393	44
Omaha, Nebr	2,040	5,033	9,522	2,649	188	67
Paterson, N. J	1,998	4,137	7,415	2,322	210	16
Philadelphia, Pa	21,005	45,455	87,554	34,714	3,833	301
Pittsburgh, Pa	6,224	13,013	23,823	7,957	682	83
Portland, Oreg	2,271	5,819	13,847	4,701	356	26
Providence, R. I	2,795	6,760	13,864	5,584	578	28
Reading, Pa	1,262	2,591	5,357	2,133	288	6
Richmond, Va	2,435	5,675	11,439	3,983	542	156
Rochester, N. Y	3,400	8,160	15,933	5,914	604	85
St. Louis, Mo	9,417	20,229	42,222	14,963	1,630	123
St. Paul, Minn	3,005	7,389	12,001	3,224	266	26
Salt Lake City, Utah	1,200	2,427	4,091	1,466	177	26
San Antonio, Tex	1,480	3,392	7,708	2,403	229	76
San Francisco, Calif	4,283	11,874	30,869	10,008	864	183
Scranton, Pa	1,848	3,434	4,640	1,183	106	6
Seattle, Wash	2,498	6,806	16,722	5,115	398	159
Spokane, Wash	1,004	2,421	5,216	1,780	155	19
Springfield, Mass	1,355	3,704	7,895	2,739	271	15
Syracuse, N. Y	1,640	3,971	7,814	3,364	382	5
Toledo, Ohio	2,664	5,159	9,798	3,389	357	21
Trenton, N. J	1,300	2,645	4,222	1,543	184	7
Washington, D. C	5,609	20,002	45,852	15,470	1,874	397
Wilmington, Del	1,145	2,430	4,726	1,882	273	34
Worcester, Mass	1,957	4,875	8,688	3,050	371	33
Yonkers, N. Y	1,223	2,626	4,548	1,548	108	7
Youngstown, Ohio	1,054	2,085	3,682	971	83	7

TABLE 33.—NUMBER AND PROPORTION OF CHILDREN OF EACH SEX 10 TO 15 YEARS OF AGE ENGAGED IN GAINFUL OCCUPATIONS, FOR CITIES HAVING, IN 1920, 100,000 INHABITANTS OR MORE: 1920 AND 1910.

CITY.	MALES 10 TO 15 YEARS OF AGE: 1920			MALES 10 TO 15 YEARS OF AGE: 1910			FEMALES 10 TO 15 YEARS OF AGE: 1920			FEMALES 10 TO 15 YEARS OF AGE: 1910		
	Total number.	Engaged in gainful occupations. Number.	Per cent.	Total number.	Engaged in gainful occupations. Number.	Per cent.	Total number.	Engaged in gainful occupations. Number.	Per cent.	Total number.	Engaged in gainful occupations. Number.	Per cent.
Akron, Ohio	7,170	398	5.6	2,977	381	12.8	7,237	62	0.9	3,056	216	7.1
Albany, N.Y	4,901	224	4.6	4,477	366	8.2	4,944	147	3.0	4,487	208	4.6
Atlanta, Ga	9,690	1,667	17.2	7,786	1,891	24.3	10,362	697	6.7	8,091	981	12.1
Baltimore, Md	35,788	3,734	10.4	28,254	4,728	16.7	36,937	2,685	7.3	29,952	4,122	13.8
Birmingham, Ala	9,406	750	8.0	6,621	1,267	19.1	10,011	345	3.4	6,953	531	7.6
Boston, Mass	36,206	2,866	7.9	32,684	3,208	9.8	36,148	1,741	4.8	32,998	2,028	6.1
Bridgeport, Conn	6,880	579	8.4	4,880	747	15.3	6,885	541	7.9	5,010	651	13.0
Buffalo, N.Y	24,832	1,332	5.4	23,053	2,086	9.0	25,372	1,106	4.4	23,448	1,320	5.6
Cambridge, Mass	5,480	507	9.3	5,237	510	9.7	5,558	331	6.0	5,398	406	7.5
Camden, N.J	5,957	486	8.2	4,700	654	13.9	6,107	*409	6.7	4,975	486	9.8
Chicago, Ill	130,042	10,461	8.0	110,610	11,772	10.6	130,954	8,450	6.5	111,782	8,718	7.8
Cincinnati, Ohio	17,669	1,054	6.0	17,664	2,380	13.5	17,831	152	0.9	17,801	1,706	9.6
Cleveland, Ohio	39,401	1,897	4.8	27,886	3,449	12.4	39,216	388	1.0	28,265	2,554	9.0
Columbus, Ohio	10,541	621	5.9	7,961	846	10.6	10,374	83	0.8	8,175	382	4.7
Dallas, Tex	7,119	715	10.0	4,263	644	15.1	7,578	316	4.2	4,571	276	6.0
Dayton, Ohio	6,684	533	8.0	5,123	598	11.7	6,717	61	0.9	5,214	234	4.5
Denver, Colo	10,726	939	8.8	9,798	880	9.0	11,259	443	3.9	9,885	389	3.9
Des Moines, Iowa	5,790	366	6.3	4,036	490	12.1	6,058	113	1.9	4,190	213	5.1
Detroit, Mich	40,153	1,900	4.7	21,954	2,937	13.4	39,973	971	2.4	22,395	2,120	9.5
Fall River, Mass	7,110	1,376	19.4	7,070	1,386	19.6	7,323	1,293	17.7	6,998	1,245	17.8
Fort Worth, Tex	4,686	438	9.3	3,500	415	11.9	4,996	132	2.6	3,567	151	4.2
Grand Rapids, Mich	6,694	371	5.5	5,513	343	6.2	7,065	138	2.0	5,566	179	3.2
Hartford, Conn	6,415	467	7.3	4,730	464	9.8	6,582	371	5.6	4,749	295	6.2
Houston, Tex	6,701	872	13.0	3,834	534	13.9	7,131	290	4.1	3,958	253	6.4
Indianapolis, Ind	10,600	1,595	11.7	10,379	1,635	15.8	13,852	767	5.5	10,678	787	7.4
Jersey City, N.J	15,920	1,563	9.8	15,064	1,264	8.4	16,131	1,190	7.4	15,177	992	6.5
Kansas City, Kans	5,178	395	7.6	4,214	429	10.2	5,341	181	3.4	4,406	204	4.6
Kansas City, Mo	13,055	933	7.1	10,033	1,130	11.3	13,210	397	3.0	10,475	510	4.9
Los Angeles, Calif	21,654	1,041	4.8	12,609	1,004	8.0	22,531	339	1.5	12,878	458	3.6
Louisville, Ky	11,025	889	8.1	11,262	1,543	13.7	11,537	531	4.6	11,781	955	8.1
Lowell, Mass	5,624	573	10.2	5,133	736	14.3	5,927	449	7.6	5,244	645	12.3
Memphis, Tenn	7,173	780	10.9	5,544	1,089	19.6	7,846	359	4.6	5,923	546	9.2
Milwaukee, Wis	22,133	2,540	11.5	21,166	2,448	11.6	22,914	1,927	8.4	21,185	2,158	10.2
Minneapolis, Minn	16,038	714	4.5	13,352	470	3.5	16,221	296	1.8	13,570	304	2.2
Nashville, Tenn	6,222	820	13.2	5,763	953	16.5	6,576	308	4.7	6,184	405	6.5
New Bedford, Mass	6,072	1,132	18.6	4,867	938	19.3	6,395	1,001	15.7	5,066	850	16.8
New Haven, Conn	8,422	878	10.4	7,117	887	12.5	8,590	674	7.8	6,968	674	9.7
New Orleans, La	20,384	2,862	14.0	18,796	2,670	14.2	21,605	1,403	6.5	19,680	1,457	7.4
New York, N.Y	291,164	18,341	6.3	248,927	21,408	8.6	289,513	14,042	4.9	251,961	17,161	6.8
Bronx borough	40,509	2,103	5.2	25,091	1,805	7.2	39,555	1,578	4.0	23,819	1,203	5.1
Brooklyn borough	111,681	7,423	6.6	90,033	7,725	8.6	111,630	5,571	5.0	91,756	5,508	6.0
Manhattan borough	106,297	6,526	6.1	111,315	10,199	9.2	106,423	5,227	4.9	114,273	9,223	8.1
Queens borough	25,940	1,937	7.5	17,218	1,436	8.3	25,594	1,463	5.7	17,216	1,093	6.3
Richmond borough	6,737	352	5.2	5,270	243	4.6	6,311	203	3.2	4,897	134	2.7
Newark, N.J	22,115	1,939	8.8	18,319	2,002	10.9	21,929	1,614	7.4	18,966	1,849	9.7
Norfolk, Va	5,171	642	12.4	3,115	513	16.5	5,349	243	4.5	3,313	282	8.5
Oakland, Calif	9,124	447	4.9	6,161	548	8.9	9,220	118	1.3	6,476	242	3.7
Omaha, Nebr	8,714	543	6.2	5,579	341	6.1	9,105	258	2.8	5,615	172	3.1
Paterson, N.J	7,397	866	11.7	6,991	964	13.8	7,529	884	11.7	6,997	964	13.8
Philadelphia, Pa	89,728	5,996	6.7	78,003	11,777	15.1	90,207	4,951	5.5	78,958	9,321	11.8
Pittsburgh, Pa	30,864	1,476	4.8	27,295	3,237	11.9	30,716	975	3.2	27,897	2,032	7.3
Portland, Oreg	10,767	893	8.3	7,479	456	6.1	11,233	181	1.6	7,532	152	2.0
Providence, R.I	11,824	1,491	12.6	10,876	1,622	14.9	12,283	1,331	10.8	11,041	1,315	11.9
Reading, Pa	5,005	732	14.1	4,877	888	18.4	5,752	722	12.6	4,926	797	16.5
Richmond, Va	8,042	907	11.2	6,500	1,237	19.0	8,870	624	7.0	6,682	791	11.8
Rochester, N.Y	13,306	814	6.1	10,270	934	9.1	13,494	685	5.1	10,250	805	7.8
St. Louis, Mo	36,062	4,074	11.3	33,667	4,933	14.7	36,647	2,964	8.1	34,236	3,327	9.7
St. Paul, Minn	10,613	484	4.6	10,515	547	5.2	10,664	255	2.4	10,595	345	3.3
Salt Lake City, Utah	6,664	374	5.6	4,879	321	6.6	6,724	90	1.3	4,861	137	2.8
San Antonio, Tex	8,679	957	11.0	5,386	654	12.1	9,051	386	4.3	5,565	348	6.3
San Francisco, Calif	18,429	914	5.0	15,167	1,574	10.4	18,755	359	1.9	15,104	657	4.3
Scranton, Pa	8,149	566	6.9	7,368	1,212	16.4	8,490	470	5.5	7,628	841	11.0
Seattle, Wash	11,996	951	7.9	8,748	628	7.2	12,359	226	1.8	8,852	239	2.7
Spokane, Wash	5,012	315	6.3	4,330	287	6.6	5,145	63	1.2	4,463	93	2.1
Springfield, Mass	5,816	535	9.2	4,153	460	11.1	5,949	366	6.2	4,241	318	7.5
Syracuse, N.Y	7,675	426	5.6	6,320	635	10.0	7,832	333	4.3	6,459	401	6.2
Toledo, Ohio	11,073	694	6.3	8,434	1,030	12.2	11,187	200	1.8	8,547	642	7.5
Trenton, N.J	6,052	731	12.1	4,957	801	16.2	6,248	669	10.7	5,027	514	10.2
Washington, D.C	17,149	1,272	7.4	14,405	913	6.3	18,081	599	3.3	15,060	432	2.9
Wilmington, Del	4,997	472	9.4	4,216	525	12.5	5,288	335	6.3	4,448	382	8.6
Worcester, Mass	8,799	937	10.6	7,119	829	11.6	8,827	574	6.5	7,301	604	8.3
Yonkers, N.Y	5,729	189	3.3	4,257	204	4.8	5,637	180	3.2	4,239	186	4.4
Youngstown, Ohio	6,286	238	3.8	3,572	297	8.3	6,340	76	1.2	3,566	147	4.1

TABLE **34.**—MALES AND FEMALES 10 YEARS OF AGE AND OVER ENGAGED IN GAINFUL OCCUPATIONS, CLASSIFIED BY AGE, FOR CITIES HAVING FROM 25,000 TO 100,000 INHABITANTS: 1920.

CITY AND SEX.	Total.	10 to 13	14	15	16	17	18 and 19	20 to 24	25 to 44	45 to 64	65 and over.	Unknown.
Alameda, Calif.:												
Male	9,273	39	17	40	92	114	267	878	4,779	2,639	400	8
Female	2,425	....	2	15	49	80	189	524	1,050	456	60	....
Allentown, Pa.:												
Male	23,466	19	163	270	424	391	954	2,710	11,811	5,751	949	24
Female	7,932	8	106	209	369	397	846	1,778	3,190	900	123	6
Altoona, Pa.:												
Male	19,193	50	60	130	281	321	898	2,463	9,512	4,941	519	18
Female	4,905	3	22	57	191	204	544	1,188	1,943	679	72	2
Amsterdam, N. Y.:												
Male	10,404	13	20	96	187	189	372	1,187	5,234	2,739	359	8
Female	5,314	4	25	102	200	209	382	1,051	2,436	829	75	1
Anderson, Ind.:												
Male	10,186	38	36	59	144	199	464	1,411	4,694	2,695	438	8
Female	2,954	4	6	21	133	136	340	602	1,153	511	45	3
Asheville, N. C.:												
Male	7,934	30	24	71	115	104	320	1,053	4,115	1,845	245	12
Female	3,474	9	11	22	62	75	256	757	1,683	523	62	14
Atlantic City, N. J.:												
Male	16,514	15	28	68	142	208	463	1,655	8,671	4,701	532	31
Female	7,386	5	15	62	129	156	438	1,157	3,716	1,548	140	20
Auburn, N. Y.:												
Male	12,119	17	18	68	157	149	411	1,428	6,160	3,202	498	11
Female	4,327	1	11	53	131	171	377	794	1,831	833	120	5
Augusta, Ga.:												
Male	17,378	74	80	142	255	281	818	2,537	8,665	3,989	499	38
Female	8,886	18	57	106	162	219	588	1,614	4,176	1,688	230	28
Aurora, Ill.:												
Male	12,116	16	41	89	173	188	428	1,339	5,986	3,332	516	8
Female	3,707	7	23	63	132	154	385	857	1,480	540	50	7
Austin, Tex.:												
Male	9,018	20	27	55	92	123	368	1,074	4,313	2,401	531	14
Female	4,059	8	17	21	47	81	266	777	1,963	750	111	18
Bangor, Me.:												
Male	7,521	1	5	21	37	74	216	738	3,421	2,528	474	6
Female	3,045	4	4	16	33	49	191	674	1,343	642	86	3
Battle Creek, Mich.:												
Male	12,625	47	30	51	138	177	441	1,485	6,166	3,465	614	11
Female	4,291	5	5	27	81	118	372	962	1,895	747	70	9
Bay City, Mich.:												
Male	14,705	16	26	121	265	328	708	1,829	6,553	3,889	959	11
Female	4,228	4	21	76	228	251	546	994	1,447	584	76	1
Bayonne, N. J.:												
Male	23,898	12	42	226	417	477	1,026	3,036	13,259	4,943	454	6
Female	5,341	2	66	169	362	390	819	1,511	1,579	397	44	2
Beaumont, Tex.:												
Male	14,029	49	52	100	165	241	572	2,178	7,533	2,806	318	15
Female	4,250	11	27	44	82	106	339	940	2,231	423	33	14
Bellingham, Wash.:												
Male	8,704	27	19	45	71	115	289	937	4,050	2,678	463	10
Female	1,974	1	3	5	28	55	183	494	827	343	29	6
Berkeley, Calif.:												
Male	16,248	36	26	58	115	181	458	1,581	8,203	4,938	629	23
Female	5,844	3	3	16	73	125	334	1,127	2,824	1,209	121	9
Bethlehem, Pa.:												
Male	16,326	15	40	94	266	267	614	1,964	8,984	3,637	435	10
Female	3,868	6	41	89	214	232	486	902	1,400	427	67	4
Binghamton, N. Y.:												
Male	21,060	22	25	104	248	313	745	2,604	10,387	5,718	890	4
Female	9,352	8	15	70	230	326	747	1,824	4,106	1,783	239	4
Bloomington, Ill.:												
Male	9,138	13	24	53	112	138	318	1,028	4,339	2,593	508	12
Female	2,985	1	8	30	72	117	269	649	1,236	527	62	14
Brockton, Mass.:												
Male	22,466	49	93	195	309	377	795	2,464	10,830	6,363	977	14
Female	10,127	5	62	164	256	299	739	1,955	4,598	1,861	184	4
Brookline town, Mass.:												
Male	9,833	19	12	25	72	67	204	850	4,657	3,356	564	7
Female	7,545	5	4	14	34	48	272	1,381	4,084	1,556	131	16
Butte, Mont.:												
Male	15,851	43	28	64	119	155	385	1,460	8,960	4,121	354	162
Female	3,511	2	10	26	70	105	308	813	1,588	526	63	....
Canton, Ohio:												
Male	33,172	38	39	176	365	452	1,310	4,646	18,185	7,030	923	8
Female	6,587	9	12	61	187	314	764	1,519	2,697	941	83	....

TABLE **34.**—MALES AND FEMALES 10 YEARS OF AGE AND OVER ENGAGED IN GAINFUL OCCUPATIONS, CLASSIFIED BY AGE, FOR CITIES HAVING FROM 25,000 TO 100,000 INHABITANTS: 1920—Continued.

CITY AND SEX.	Total.	AGE (YEARS OR PERIODS).										
		10 to 13	14	15	16	17	18 and 19	20 to 24	25 to 44	45 to 64	65 and over.	Unknown.
Cedar Rapids, Iowa:												
Male	14,954	60	40	88	165	242	538	1,802	7,509	3,905	590	15
Female	4,812	.....	9	40	144	172	452	1,117	2,099	707	59	13
Charleston, S. C.:												
Male	21,671	94	111	188	287	351	1,038	3,277	11,029	4,565	602	129
Female	10,547	39	68	121	232	301	816	1,962	4,937	1,778	221	72
Charleston, W. Va.:												
Male	13,032	30	28	63	139	190	515	1,800	6,963	2,914	354	36
Female	3,858	7	20	37	96	118	366	963	1,689	484	58	20
Charlotte, N. C.:												
Male	14,430	106	109	155	243	272	666	2,289	7,279	2,807	415	89
Female	6,803	46	71	119	194	217	598	1,625	2,933	822	123	55
Chattanooga, Tenn.:												
Male	20,459	52	75	136	252	354	936	3,154	10,499	4,419	555	27
Female	8,137	22	37	64	187	230	624	1,791	3,963	1,106	98	15
Chelsea, Mass.:												
Male	13,698	10	63	161	212	274	694	1,778	6,775	3,249	453	29
Female	4,075	2	34	74	173	206	529	1,140	1,341	512	58	6
Chester, Pa.:												
Male	22,242	14	39	102	304	391	962	3,316	11,887	4,639	559	29
Female	4,705	4	31	107	232	227	516	1,011	1,809	690	66	12
Chicopee, Mass.:												
Male	11,200	9	139	184	235	254	500	1,440	5,761	2,422	252	4
Female	4,253	7	105	181	222	233	473	989	1,578	431	33	1
Cicero town, Ill.:												
Male	14,423	8	101	194	336	335	645	1,799	8,137	2,659	198	11
Female	4,254	12	92	196	314	361	640	1,100	1,322	194	12	11
Clarksburg, W. Va.:												
Male	8,922	9	14	36	149	179	368	1,326	4,671	1,886	245	39
Female	1,997	4	4	14	44	74	201	525	839	244	39	9
Clifton, N. J.:												
Male	8,302	7	86	147	189	179	336	982	4,393	1,829	153	1
Female	2,876	7	69	115	175	169	358	740	1,011	210	22	....
Colorado Springs, Colo.:												
Male	8,369	20	32	50	93	112	241	791	3,654	2,878	471	27
Female	3,445	4	3	12	41	57	178	590	1,569	872	118	1
Columbia, S. C.:												
Male	11,095	39	59	80	151	145	466	1,816	5,937	2,123	259	20
Female	5,081	11	25	53	97	132	429	1,207	2,356	649	112	10
Columbus, Ga.:												
Male	9,756	56	71	109	188	231	603	*1,638	4,582	1,943	334	1
Female	5,652	24	44	89	216	219	493	1,201	2,417	823	121	2
Council Bluffs, Iowa:												
Male	11,644	17	28	60	142	190	449	1,484	5,712	3,041	492	29
Female	3,399	2	7	29	95	172	384	872	1,313	469	51	5
Covington, Ky.:												
Male	18,770	23	76	154	316	362	881	2,344	8,863	5,001	742	8
Female	6,931	6	30	88	239	302	689	1,345	2,831	1,242	152	7
Cranston, R. I.:												
Male	8,720	1	55	95	155	150	354	877	4,151	2,480	396	6
Female	2,957	1	49	79	133	125	262	626	1,084	529	67	2
Cumberland, Md.:												
Male	10,045	20	41	100	191	206	484	1,354	4,541	2,218	361	529
Female	2,586	7	18	39	126	131	285	595	991	349	44	1
Danville, Ill.:												
Male	11,124	33	49	88	155	195	429	1,257	5,349	3,104	460	5
Female	3,287	3	14	39	112	158	337	643	1,366	549	64	2
Davenport, Iowa:												
Male	18,842	32	43	109	235	270	651	2,007	8,415	5,017	741	41
Female	5,821	4	10	15	161	213	517	1,320	2,444	932	122	10
Decatur, Ill.:												
Male	14,515	29	71	118	241	271	668	1,880	6,821	3,807	597	12
Female	4,080	5	27	62	160	209	452	899	1,567	630	66	3
Dubuque, Iowa:												
Male	12,390	44	56	86	198	217	485	1,473	5,654	3,576	591	10
Female	4,508	6	17	81	191	210	443	1,050	1,761	658	90	1
Duluth, Minn.:												
Male	34,968	44	41	102	409	542	1,261	4,064	18,671	8,765	1,015	54
Female	10,034	5	10	62	339	475	1,318	3,043	3,802	893	65	22
East Chicago, Ind.:												
Male	13,689	8	14	54	146	178	405	1,561	8,412	2,451	317	143
Female	1,255	4	15	50	89	104	178	298	419	81	6	11
East Cleveland, Ohio:												
Male	8,766	23	15	30	70	76	235	929	5,009	2,127	249	3
Female	2,806	2	2	15	33	71	231	718	1,323	396	13	2

TABLE 34.—MALES AND FEMALES 10 YEARS OF AGE AND OVER ENGAGED IN GAINFUL OCCUPATIONS, CLASSIFIED BY AGE, FOR CITIES HAVING FROM 25,000 TO 100,000 INHABITANTS: 1920—Continued.

CITY AND SEX	Total.	AGE (YEARS OR PERIODS).										
		10 to 13	14	15	16	17	18 and 19	20 to 24	25 to 44	45 to 64	65 and over.	Unknown.
East Orange, N. J.:												
Male	15,459	5	19	46	141	155	480	1,466	8,239	4,310	594	4
Female	5,756	3	10	44	107	135	379	1,200	2,737	1,046	87	8
East St. Louis, Ill.:												
Male	23,860	24	76	180	400	442	1,016	3,104	12,328	5,694	584	12
Female	5,887	3	36	128	309	308	660	1,248	2,394	720	77	4
Easton, Pa.:												
Male	10,984	18	39	74	125	167	391	1,258	5,395	2,979	525	13
Female	3,571	8	27	62	125	167	341	722	1,404	627	82	6
El Paso, Tex.:												
Male	22,475	73	74	191	319	387	1,055	2,849	11,851	5,135	528	13
Female	7,048	14	28	92	198	253	686	1,463	3,380	866	62	6
Elgin, Ill.:												
Male	7,891	10	12	62	90	130	284	983	3,442	2,373	481	24
Female	4,058	3	9	48	108	165	415	901	1,658	661	71	19
Elizabeth, N. J.:												
Male	31,986	19	141	308	580	587	1,223	3,801	17,284	7,182	820	41
Female	8,200	12	111	257	471	506	1,008	1,892	2,885	949	98	11
Elmira, N. Y.:												
Male	15,143	19	19	57	163	222	589	1,869	7,060	4,395	738	12
Female	4,947	2	9	48	132	153	438	1,073	2,024	923	138	7
Erie, Pa.:												
Male	29,752	19	47	135	418	492	1,128	3,716	15,471	7,329	985	12
Female	7,644	8	18	80	300	430	914	1,837	2,962	987	105	3
Evanston, Ill.:												
Male	10,879	12	24	40	102	118	301	1,061	5,643	3,202	364	12
Female	5,133	2	7	29	91	120	338	1,066	2,452	925	84	19
Evansville, Ind.:												
Male	27,932	80	98	199	465	602	1,270	3,549	13,144	7,358	1,155	12
Female	9,879	8	40	114	389	527	1,150	2,207	3,830	1,403	207	4
Everett, Mass.:												
Male	12,523	9	42	106	195	229	508	1,563	5,902	3,473	494	2
Female	3,878	1	32	54	110	170	445	1,011	1,467	526	62	....
Everett, Wash.:												
Male	10,015	49	37	66	125	144	351	1,064	4,926	2,858	374	21
Female	2,138	3	3	17	42	75	204	454	944	354	37	5
Fitchburg, Mass.:												
Male	13,215	18	130	236	237	240	534	1,601	6,349	3,329	535	6
Female	5,671	.....	96	166	196	217	535	1,245	2,327	769	111	9
Flint, Mich.:												
Male	38,047	138	81	127	350	595	2,055	6,913	19,769	6,982	888	149
Female	7,007	6	18	71	217	385	969	1,927	2,628	704	68	14
Fort Smith, Ark.:												
Male	8,960	27	29	63	160	176	378	1,166	4,321	2,290	327	23
Female	2,642	5	9	16	51	81	242	583	1,177	427	39	12
Fort Wayne, Ind.:												
Male	29,494	91	153	292	511	538	1,381	4,017	14,149	7,297	1,048	17
Female	10,319	15	106	224	459	475	1,133	2,429	4,001	1,327	138	12
Fresno, Calif.:												
Male	16,085	32	18	66	137	215	479	1,742	8,758	4,079	541	18
Female	4,046	3	6	19	73	114	352	897	2,006	522	45	9
Galveston, Tex.:												
Male	16,967	64	67	158	223	283	720	2,345	8,569	3,952	534	52
Female	4,795	12	11	50	127	163	331	871	2,335	782	101	12
Gary, Ind.:												
Male	21,559	20	17	52	169	216	602	2,993	13,784	3,475	174	57
Female	2,415	5	10	49	125	135	254	546	1,038	229	17	7
Green Bay, Wis.:												
Male	9,134	15	31	60	112	152	442	1,252	4,395	2,338	326	11
Female	3,155	4	10	25	75	168	471	868	1,159	341	29	5
Hagerstown, Md.:												
Male	8,914	18	33	70	139	190	390	1,178	4,309	2,147	365	75
Female	2,542	1	23	43	114	127	270	499	982	389	60	34
Hamilton, Ohio:												
Male	14,085	31	21	96	206	294	767	1,941	6,490	3,668	570	1
Female	3,312	1	4	22	103	156	422	714	1,240	580	70	....
Hammond, Ind.:												
Male	12,408	6	31	92	195	195	507	1,549	6,955	2,600	257	21
Female	2,221	1	17	56	126	178	341	579	694	207	20	2
Hamtramck village, Mich.:												
Male	16,183	5	7	50	183	201	431	1,834	11,684	1,686	94	8
Female	1,579	4	17	49	161	171	278	334	488	74	3	....
Harrisburg, Pa.:												
Male	25,484	32	42	86	295	366	881	3,082	12,598	6,990	1,057	55
Female	7,845	8	26	52	203	248	714	1,625	3,416	1,388	149	16

TABLE **34.**—MALES AND FEMALES 10 YEARS OF AGE AND OVER ENGAGED IN GAINFUL OCCUPATIONS, CLASSIFIED BY AGE, FOR CITIES HAVING FROM 25,000 TO 100,000 INHABITANTS: 1920—Continued.

CITY AND SEX.	Total.	10 to 13	14	15	16	17	18 and 19	20 to 24	25 to 44	45 to 64	65 and over.	Unknown.
Haverhill, Mass.:												
Male	18,065	34	92	224	279	294	667	2,141	8,626	4,891	797	20
Female	8,854	6	66	151	209	265	668	1,655	3,863	1,744	212	15
Hazleton, Pa.:												
Male	9,243	4	44	122	209	251	488	1,237	4,219	2,374	290	5
Female	3,011	4	52	138	224	239	453	747	904	224	26	
Highland Park, Mich.:												
Male	18,987	25	22	39	129	183	674	2,935	11,502	3,204	262	12
Female	3,434	1	3	10	96	119	358	886	1,594	344	22	1
Hoboken, N. J.:												
Male	24,264	15	108	267	452	464	1,069	3,158	12,327	5,737	649	18
Female	7,102	13	103	240	432	415	843	1,534	2,553	882	86	1
Holyoke, Mass.:												
Male	18,464	15	163	258	305	362	815	2,415	8,912	4,640	571	8
Female	10,168	7	153	251	336	369	885	2,200	4,567	1,290	101	9
Huntington, W. Va.:												
Male	15,733	37	44	106	240	290	801	2,193	7,800	3,689	498	35
Female	4,068	9	21	47	155	202	470	914	1,706	484	41	19
Irvington town, N. J.:												
Male	8,329	8	21	79	132	121	326	982	4,330	2,093	235	2
Female	2,054	2	24	58	148	136	310	486	674	199	17	
Jackson, Mich.:												
Male	17,815	50	24	62	203	293	721	2,535	8,964	4,250	704	9
Female	4,622	5	5	39	131	187	428	913	1,973	837	102	2
Jacksonville, Fla.:												
Male	31,492	142	157	211	351	466	1,179	4,075	16,835	6,982	780	314
Female	13,310	35	41	103	248	306	904	2,493	7,097	1,767	185	131
Jamestown, N. Y.:												
Male	12,969	8	24	84	196	213	555	1,521	6,028	3,680	652	8
Female	4,759	3	6	48	187	210	465	993	1,949	775	117	6
Johnstown, Pa.:												
Male	21,614	29	49	151	411	405	943	2,748	11,491	4,831	553	3
Female	4,340	6	28	77	249	273	617	1,082	1,522	446	37	3
Joliet, Ill.:												
Male	12,537	15	14	52	184	228	562	1,639	6,284	3,160	390	9
Female	3,428	3	11	38	128	157	406	822	1,385	423	51	4
Joplin, Mo.:												
Male	9,146	12	23	47	117	139	337	990	4,503	2,568	407	3
Female	2,706	6	9	31	97	127	290	502	1,184	411	47	2
Kalamazoo, Mich.:												
Male	15,639	12	17	58	193	237	599	1,977	7,475	4,308	730	33
Female	5,726	2	4	48	156	222	516	1,134	2,350	1,130	149	15
Kearny town, N. J.:												
Male	8,605	6	49	85	188	199	362	1,132	4,274	2,066	241	3
Female	2,879	2	53	95	164	194	402	736	967	241	25	
Kenosha, Wis.:												
Male	15,146	8	47	87	144	216	652	2,315	8,565	2,772	299	41
Female	3,172	6	32	81	141	213	475	887	1,063	248	22	4
Kingston, N. Y.:												
Male	8,494	9	11	58	141	164	330	940	3,589	2,719	529	4
Female	3,483		10	52	123	172	348	732	1,352	623	67	4
Knoxville, Tenn.:												
Male	23,728	65	84	194	445	520	1,165	3,422	11,338	5,747	715	33
Female	8,868	25	47	151	323	372	929	1,916	3,812	1,162	115	16
Kokomo, Ind.:												
Male	10,583	20	28	92	153	191	504	1,519	5,004	2,653	417	2
Female	2,211	4	15	36	97	95	253	482	829	354	44	2
La Crosse, Wis.:												
Male	9,099	5	16	57	92	171	350	1,074	4,218	2,660	450	6
Female	3,536		18	48	80	165	381	939	1,535	515	48	7
Lakewood, Ohio:												
Male	12,949	1	9	29	79	127	292	1,224	7,704	3,192	291	1
Female	3,601	2	5	15	77	145	316	842	1,761	400	37	1
Lancaster, Pa.:												
Male	16,824	39	115	156	314	298	681	1,972	7,429	4,844	972	4
Female	7,485	10	90	159	297	297	745	1,396	2,926	1,348	214	3
Lansing, Mich.:												
Male	21,046	124	128	185	280	346	926	3,000	10,279	4,974	747	57
Female	5,124	3	8	28	126	197	516	1,124	2,235	809	66	12
Lawrence, Mass.:												
Male	30,775	19	346	494	630	589	1,198	3,628	15,319	7,602	938	12
Female	16,221	6	329	509	588	586	1,370	3,365	7,175	2,128	158	7
Lewiston, Me.:												
Male	9,842	2	5	34	232	234	469	1,331	4,529	2,544	443	19
Female	5,480	5	18	38	193	243	540	1,178	2,297	861	105	2

TABLE 34.—MALES AND FEMALES 10 YEARS OF AGE AND OVER ENGAGED IN GAINFUL OCCUPATIONS, CLASSIFIED BY AGE, FOR CITIES HAVING FROM 25,000 TO 100,000 INHABITANTS: 1920—Continued.

CITY AND SEX.	Total.	AGE (YEARS OR PERIODS).										Unknown.
		10 to 13	14	15	16	17	18 and 19	20 to 24	25 to 44	45 to 64	65 and over.	
Lexington, Ky.:												
Male	13,475	28	42	49	157	206	490	1,475	6,430	3,982	599	17
Female	6,500	4	6	29	70	132	352	999	3,115	1,577	207	9
Lima, Ohio:												
Male	13,430	27	25	79	147	227	540	1,684	6,484	3,699	517	1
Female	3,676	1	9	25	101	156	419	864	1,515	536	49	1
Lincoln, Nebr.:												
Male	16,281	42	30	82	165	210	557	1,995	8,042	4,391	724	43
Female	6,202	4	7	20	125	167	536	1,437	2,817	982	76	31
Little Rock, Ark.:												
Male	20,850	43	45	132	210	311	797	2,686	11,041	4,885	599	101
Female	8,399	12	19	53	146	213	670	1,804	4,070	1,215	131	66
Long Beach, Calif.:												
Male	14,409	32	27	49	83	154	448	1,535	6,885	4,496	679	21
Female	4,326	3	4	10	36	57	238	639	2,118	1,085	126	10
Lorain, Ohio:												
Male	12,787	6	8	61	124	188	404	1,423	7,355	2,940	272	6
Female	1,533	3	1	21	81	121	240	358	523	162	22	1
Lynchburg, Va.:												
Male	8,760	43	86	104	184	187	452	1,298	4,117	1,993	273	23
Female	5,294	15	22	74	149	189	546	1,156	2,214	795	102	32
Lynn, Mass.:												
Male	33,403	24	80	199	432	510	1,139	3,872	16,460	9,265	1,407	15
Female	14,629	4	43	154	300	420	1,096	2,795	6,604	2,864	342	7
McKeesport, Pa.:												
Male	15,191	11	36	104	280	290	651	1,972	7,923	3,570	320	34
Female	2,835	4	19	59	155	178	381	777	973	268	20	1
Macon, Ga.:												
Male	17,541	174	145	187	283	327	878	2,616	8,865	3,599	451	16
Female	8,816	49	44	115	182	233	624	1,703	4,155	1,480	224	7
Madison, Wis.:												
Male	11,559	23	25	55	82	145	347	1,346	5,961	3,140	419	16
Female	4,910	3	6	21	45	110	404	1,248	2,265	724	72	12
Malden, Mass.:												
Male	14,643	7	41	102	204	221	581	1,759	6,774	4,314	638	2
Female	5,978	2	28	59	138	228	593	1,463	2,403	961	100	3
Manchester, N. H.:												
Male	23,794	30	57	134	404	502	1,046	2,965	11,393	6,271	971	21
Female	13,756	20	28	99	427	528	1,181	3,008	5,910	2,277	253	25
Mansfield, Ohio:												
Male	9,817	33	30	69	133	154	400	1,262	4,682	2,565	460	29
Female	2,632	6	1	20	60	119	305	528	1,056	475	52	10
Marion, Ohio:												
Male	9,171	37	21	65	101	145	368	1,119	4,380	2,529	402	4
Female	2,138	1	.....	9	57	82	237	496	814	395	47	....
Medford, Mass.:												
Male	11,904	4	27	88	154	177	430	1,330	6,013	3,215	466	....
Female	4,205	2	12	43	86	150	410	1,093	1,711	631	64	3
Meriden, Conn.:												
Male	9,680	9	40	111	151	189	394	1,151	4,477	2,602	548	8
Female	3,401	1	39	79	142	196	333	803	1,270	465	65	8
Miami, Fla.:												
Male	10,229	32	26	40	107	132	367	1,341	5,485	2,347	285	67
Female	4,064	5	11	20	68	111	266	769	2,132	607	59	16
Mobile, Ala.:												
Male	19,816	73	80	159	312	387	948	2,736	9,679	4,780	598	64
Female	8,538	30	28	76	159	206	635	1,540	3,975	1,615	244	30
Moline, Ill.:												
Male	11,582	37	31	66	136	177	427	1,326	6,235	2,779	358	10
Female	2,650	4	10	26	83	136	298	642	1,070	349	30	2
Montclair town, N. J.:												
Male	7,996	1	2	16	51	72	200	801	4,109	2,465	276	3
Female	3,629	4	9	16	56	67	221	716	1,824	658	57	1
Montgomery, Ala.:												
Male	13,242	74	57	89	185	218	544	1,800	6,628	3,217	420	10
Female	7,620	26	36	61	142	158	535	1,484	3,694	1,284	194	6
Mount Vernon, N. Y.:												
Male	12,617	9	13	76	155	180	445	1,435	6,315	3,492	492	5
Female	4,961	4	8	54	115	180	476	1,142	2,176	749	56	1
Muncie, Ind.:												
Male	12,737	35	54	93	220	245	572	1,535	5,830	3,507	600	46
Female	3,413	3	17	52	164	171	360	679	1,320	567	71	9
Muskegon, Mich.:												
Male	13,080	27	20	65	211	252	667	1,907	6,166	3,117	586	62
Female	3,375	1	10	43	191	224	451	832	1,172	393	46	12

TABLE 34.—MALES AND FEMALES 10 YEARS OF AGE AND OVER ENGAGED IN GAINFUL OCCUPATIONS, CLASSIFIED BY AGE, FOR CITIES HAVING FROM 25,000 TO 100,000 INHABITANTS: 1920—Continued.

CITY AND SEX.	Total.	10 to 13	14	15	16	17	18 and 19	20 to 24	25 to 44	45 to 64	65 and over.	Unknown.
Muskogee, Okla.:												
Male	9,352	24	18	52	87	139	339	1,171	4,798	2,383	322	19
Female	2,829	2	6	14	57	71	260	638	1,372	372	26	11
Nashua, N. H.:												
Male	9,314	9	19	40	150	163	375	1,179	4,525	2,437	399	18
Female	3,947	5	6	29	121	170	367	893	1,691	583	75	7
New Britain, Conn.:												
Male	19,310	18	84	185	302	338	752	2,289	10,583	4,217	534	8
Female	5,945	6	81	213	288	318	645	1,478	2,311	551	54	....
New Brunswick, N. J.:												
Male	10,170	4	14	62	126	159	374	1,248	5,510	2,334	332	7
Female	3,707	4	21	82	130	149	351	853	1,571	496	45	5
New Castle, Pa.:												
Male	14,414	30	22	74	228	230	570	1,757	7,660	3,398	385	60
Female	2,849	1	13	47	129	123	310	678	1,115	393	40	....
New London, Conn.:												
Male	8,384	7	13	42	102	128	420	1,101	3,987	2,235	348	1
Female	2,356	2	11	19	96	78	247	555	897	401	50	....
New Rochelle, N. Y.:												
Male	11,226	7	10	58	102	139	473	1,409	5,484	2,964	298	282
Female	4,360	3	9	45	129	145	362	931	1,969	698	59	10
Newark, Ohio:												
Male	9,088	22	23	61	128	167	366	1,029	4,225	2,622	440	5
Female	2,364	3	2	13	52	89	219	476	950	499	61	....
Newburgh, N. Y.:												
Male	10,143	7	22	58	162	177	454	1,228	4,674	2,942	414	5
Female	3,562	1	8	54	119	168	347	727	1,366	692	76	4
Newport, Ky.:												
Male	9,698	15	27	106	179	183	427	1,231	4,587	2,563	377	3
Female	3,567	4	34	71	113	184	337	702	1,401	639	82	....
Newport, R. I.:												
Male	11,872	15	20	48	123	864	1,093	1,544	4,615	2,555	387	8
Female	2,872	4	7	18	61	70	207	576	1,188	645	96	....
Newport News, Va.:												
Male	15,190	31	39	82	176	213	843	3,139	7,608	2,570	229	200
Female	3,257	10	16	33	83	109	277	862	1,459	339	18	51
Newton, Mass.:												
Male	12,814	9	21	68	102	161	386	1,328	5,894	4,178	663	4
Female	6,571	3	15	54	90	124	438	1,351	3,154	1,210	126	6
Niagara Falls, N. Y.:												
Male	17,931	6	14	57	172	256	631	2,189	10,117	4,076	394	19
Female	3,888	3	9	52	162	220	453	943	1,497	494	45	10
Norristown borough, Pa.:												
Male	9,657	9	43	69	147	161	394	1,219	4,535	2,622	458	....
Female	3,823	1	37	70	160	150	291	653	1,498	869	92	2
Norwalk, Conn.:												
Male	8,857	24	71	122	136	159	330	980	4,017	2,515	490	13
Female	3,439	6	49	83	131	152	325	657	1,323	632	75	6
Oak Park village, Ill.:												
Male	11,951	6	12	48	93	126	349	1,076	6,013	3,774	444	10
Female	4,426	3	4	26	86	118	309	1,082	2,086	641	57	14
Ogden, Utah:												
Male	9,529	40	27	58	85	154	390	1,203	4,848	2,360	355	9
Female	2,260	1	4	22	57	101	302	576	885	285	25	2
Oklahoma City, Okla.:												
Male	32,204	87	75	127	315	482	1,293	4,624	16,916	7,362	870	53
Female	11,057	10	18	53	201	339	985	2,671	5,417	1,250	86	27
Orange, N. J.:												
Male	9,972	4	32	72	210	202	449	1,232	4,862	2,548	357	4
Female	4,049	4	23	77	151	164	366	868	1,663	660	70	3
Oshkosh, Wis.:												
Male	10,005	19	72	115	134	177	453	1,144	4,240	3,068	568	15
Female	3,643	5	42	88	124	182	443	878	1,370	448	58	5
Pasadena, Calif.:												
Male	11,720	31	32	42	78	119	287	1,038	5,477	3,885	708	23
Female	5,868	3	6	6	39	74	226	704	2,852	1,750	190	18
Passaic, N. J.:												
Male	19,330	6	122	214	367	319	725	2,430	10,676	4,074	393	4
Female	7,982	9	151	227	344	408	820	2,103	3,228	639	49	4
Pawtucket, R. I.:												
Male	21,163	15	233	340	478	471	944	2,661	9,904	5,394	713	10
Female	9,857	3	209	352	446	459	942	2,138	3,907	1,270	128	3
Pensacola, Fla.:												
Male	10,821	68	54	92	154	208	538	1,627	5,290	2,431	319	40
Female	3,364	10	13	34	79	102	278	620	1,572	568	80	8

TABLE 34.—MALES AND FEMALES 10 YEARS OF AGE AND OVER ENGAGED IN GAIN-FUL OCCUPATIONS, CLASSIFIED BY AGE, FOR CITIES HAVING FROM 25,000 TO 100,000 INHABITANTS: 1920—Continued.

CITY AND SEX.	Total.	AGE (YEARS OR PERIODS).										
		10 to 13	14	15	16	17	18 and 19	20 to 24	25 to 44	45 to 64	65 and over.	Un-known.
Peoria, Ill.:												
Male	26,828	32	60	154	336	391	995	3,046	13,243	7,481	1,061	29
Female	8,584	9	33	106	246	323	750	1,861	3,757	1,357	113	29
Perth Amboy, N.J.:												
Male	12,876	18	49	141	243	229	508	1,533	7,153	2,726	274	8
Female	3,130	11	90	179	245	229	427	754	961	211	20	3
Petersburg, Va.:												
Male	9,453	27	34	60	171	192	486	1,432	4,588	2,051	316	96
Female	5,002	16	36	65	159	183	442	1,055	2,092	736	144	71
Phoenix, Ariz.:												
Male	10,126	16	25	44	103	142	361	1,173	5,393	2,510	353	....
Female	2,618	1	4	12	34	49	183	520	1,387	398	23	7
Pittsfield, Mass.:												
Male	13,198	11	38	120	200	233	448	1,531	6,614	3,492	490	21
Female	5,318	3	34	110	165	209	527	1,140	2,258	790	76	6
Plainfield, N.J.:												
Male	8,518	12	17	36	104	139	293	935	4,420	2,211	328	23
Female	3,247	3	16	39	93	93	272	636	1,402	608	74	11
Pontiac, Mich.:												
Male	13,156	6	7	39	112	189	642	2,184	6,796	2,776	378	27
Female	2,588	2	5	22	76	99	299	703	967	378	34	3
Port Huron, Mich.:												
Male	8,421	8	11	32	99	159	385	1,009	3,834	2,447	432	5
Female	1,913	1	6	20	93	122	244	402	643	310	41	31
Portland, Me.:												
Male	22,113	30	30	90	181	285	712	2,437	10,540	6,589	1,190	29
Female	8,179	2	10	36	121	202	574	1,677	3,565	1,746	233	13
Portsmouth, Ohio:												
Male	10,847	13	21	64	182	223	552	1,594	5,332	2,501	359	6
Female	3,055	1	2	15	83	111	424	718	1,181	467	50	3
Portsmouth, Va.:												
Male	19,341	99	89	170	279	381	1,031	3,297	9,397	4,149	443	6
Female	5,453	16	33	62	147	169	539	1,163	2,455	775	93	1
Poughkeepsie, N.Y.:												
Male	10,940	10	16	50	154	174	431	1,268	5,200	3,132	495	10
Female	4,331	2	7	54	134	149	396	770	1,735	938	140	6
Pueblo, Colo.:												
Male	14,048	28	47	89	187	212	511	1,576	6,985	3,812	548	53
Female	3,532	3	13	35	96	120	295	676	1,492	707	73	22
Quincy, Ill.:												
Male	11,965	31	53	125	198	219	501	1,382	5,303	3,520	621	12
Female	4,045	3	21	45	169	132	387	773	1,622	798	89	6
Quincy, Mass.:												
Male	15,573	6	37	125	165	245	611	1,769	8,115	3,984	514	2
Female	4,108	2	24	52	115	186	439	1,043	1,608	521	56	2
Racine, Wis.:												
Male	22,166	36	60	171	271	374	996	3,409	11,538	4,675	605	31
Female	5,395	9	35	105	207	320	704	1,421	1,994	537	66	3
Revere, Mass.:												
Male	8,611	1	37	82	122	162	371	1,069	4,402	2,114	248	3
Female	2,409	1	32	50	109	161	274	641	862	249	27	3
Richmond, Ind.:												
Male	9,271	49	53	67	121	160	373	1,064	4,265	2,625	486	8
Female	2,619	3	20	53	89	95	227	479	1,009	560	82	2
Roanoke, Va.:												
Male	15,783	53	74	169	236	275	749	2,319	7,986	3,521	355	46
Female	4,640	12	24	54	126	198	499	1,272	1,816	542	66	31
Rock Island, Ill.:												
Male	12,666	44	32	81	158	190	471	1,494	6,366	3,316	460	54
Female	3,394	6	15	40	97	140	356	746	1,444	505	39	6
Rockford, Ill.:												
Male	23,212	68	53	66	296	378	897	3,025	12,006	5,551	822	50
Female	7,179	4	5	36	249	319	768	1,823	2,942	908	98	27
Rome, N.Y.:												
Male	8,487	24	18	60	109	144	342	1,038	4,154	2,239	357	2
Female	2,410	5	15	39	107	121	232	479	919	424	69	....
Sacramento, Calif.:												
Male	24,419	59	39	82	228	251	777	2,473	12,606	6,980	910	14
Female	6,535	2	6	42	115	185	595	1,381	3,013	1,077	113	6
Saginaw, Mich.:												
Male	20,073	53	25	93	315	380	882	2,476	9,586	5,249	985	29
Female	5,608	6	4	55	277	281	718	1,317	2,055	779	106	10
St. Joseph, Mo.:												
Male	26,572	57	85	156	372	442	1,178	3,351	12,416	7,258	1,146	111
Female	9,070	10	27	80	271	326	799	1,791	3,947	1,608	166	45

TABLE **34.**—MALES AND FEMALES 10 YEARS OF AGE AND OVER ENGAGED IN GAIN-
FUL OCCUPATIONS, CLASSIFIED BY AGE, FOR CITIES HAVING FROM 25,000 TO 100,000
INHABITANTS: 1920—Continued.

CITY AND SEX.	Total.	AGE (YEARS OR PERIODS).										
		10 to 13	14	15	16	17	18 and 19	20 to 24	25 to 44	45 to 64	65 and over.	Un-known.
Salem, Mass.:												
Male	13,329	3	79	171	222	253	577	1,582	6,240	3,625	571	6
Female	5,732	1	45	111	213	217	503	1,203	2,348	977	111	3
San Diego, Calif.:												
Male	23,398	66	54	77	174	250	682	2,250	10,872	7,467	1,421	85
Female	7,639	3	7	26	87	121	440	1,170	3,624	1,895	245	21
San Jose, Calif.:												
Male	12,135	13	16	43	86	156	324	1,222	5,699	3,819	648	109
Female	3,865	1	3	15	58	97	241	690	1,731	905	86	38
Savannah, Ga.:												
Male	28,986	149	148	265	375	495	1,366	4,420	15,128	5,934	658	48
Female	12,880	45	84	143	292	323	1,003	2,581	6,218	1,899	256	36
Schenectady, N. Y.:												
Male	29,164	12	23	128	336	391	972	3,338	15,387	7,730	806	41
Female	8,327	7	3	73	329	373	926	2,004	3,424	1,068	97	23
Sheboygan, Wis.:												
Male	10,207	22	85	136	182	229	459	1,218	4,685	2,709	478	4
Female	2,801	2	53	88	168	223	404	712	854	266	30	1
Shreveport, La.:												
Male	15,459	62	72	109	164	219	677	2,212	8,337	3,040	362	205
Female	6,343	26	23	41	99	166	469	1,398	3,124	859	102	36
Sioux City, Iowa:												
Male	25,859	43	31	95	256	352	943	3,601	13,815	5,886	808	29
Female	7,475	6	11	63	175	237	718	2,042	3,348	802	56	17
Sioux Falls, S. Dak.:												
Male	8,007	9	11	20	70	95	296	1,046	4,245	1,904	235	76
Female	2,668	2	1	20	51	79	234	710	1,202	301	23	45
Somerville, Mass.:												
Male	29,126	24	80	227	372	419	1,003	3,418	13,987	8,298	1,298	......
Female	10,912	7	39	133	280	400	1,010	2,561	4,563	1,743	175	1
South Bend, Ind.:												
Male	23,305	30	120	225	407	492	1,032	3,004	11,626	5,593	737	39
Female	6,674	8	100	206	347	453	865	1,532	2,344	726	83	10
Springfield, Ill.:												
Male	19,167	24	54	164	337	360	785	2,067	9,136	5,356	872	12
Female	6,893	7	27	97	262	318	751	1,412	2,887	1,011	117	4
Springfield, Mo.:												
Male	12,124	21	38	64	140	185	522	1,466	5,718	3,378	539	53
Female	3,793	5	11	28	89	121	359	880	1,587	615	70	28
Springfield, Ohio:												
Male	20,636	64	42	99	205	340	886	2,538	9,785	5,635	1,016	26
Female	5,781	2	2	8	105	213	667	1,233	2,380	1,026	134	11
Stamford, Conn.:												
Male	10,893	10	32	86	192	186	398	1,185	5,698	2,725	350	31
Female	3,507	1	30	74	139	166	369	765	1,430	468	52	13
Steubenville, Ohio:												
Male	9,766	23	19	53	139	124	357	1,175	5,490	2,110	275	1
Female	1,975	4	5	25	55	102	217	437	774	322	33	1
Stockton, Calif.:												
Male	13,998	39	20	38	129	162	474	1,445	7,165	3,929	580	17
Female	3,238	3	3	20	51	107	275	650	1,490	581	58	......
Superior, Wis.:												
Male	13,498	19	16	35	80	203	533	1,615	6,877	3,695	399	26
Female	3,019	2	5	10	33	141	396	935	1,161	307	27	2
Tacoma, Wash.:												
Male	35,229	88	72	203	391	444	1,129	3,682	17,531	9,826	1,347	516
Female	8,242	9	14	71	175	259	789	1,799	3,626	1,315	128	57
Tampa, Fla.:												
Male	10,659	41	37	130	301	333	779	2,120	8,790	3,764	357	57
Female	7,760	6	51	101	232	287	622	1,465	3,956	965	61	14
Taunton, Mass.:												
Male	11,301	14	92	155	191	217	469	1,311	5,149	3,139	560	4
Female	4,542	3	78	138	163	184	421	1,009	1,724	735	87	......
Terre Haute, Ind.:												
Male	22,441	53	55	146	325	385	957	2,597	10,700	6,211	985	27
Female	6,255	3	28	69	204	264	626	1,286	2,583	1,073	116	3
Topeka, Kans.:												
Male	15,517	23	29	79	193	252	608	1,793	7,158	4,416	935	31
Female	5,565	5	11	35	149	156	473	1,294	2,431	898	96	17
Troy, N. Y.:												
Male	22,270	12	29	96	298	322	832	2,558	10,256	6,743	1,109	15
Female	12,037	4	25	105	323	395	878	2,237	5,231	2,552	255	32
Tulsa, Okla.:												
Male	26,359	30	48	83	207	307	1,005	3,976	15,066	5,070	486	81
Female	7,864	9	14	47	116	209	718	2,013	3,959	708	52	19

TABLE **34.**—MALES AND FEMALES 10 YEARS OF AGE AND OVER ENGAGED IN GAINFUL OCCUPATIONS, CLASSIFIED BY AGE, FOR CITIES HAVING FROM 25,000 TO 100,000 INHABITANTS: 1920—Continued.

CITY AND SEX.	Total.	AGE (YEARS OR PERIODS).										
		10 to 13	14	15	16	17	18 and 19	20 to 24	25 to 44	45 to 64	65 and over.	Unknown.
Utica, N. Y.:												
Male	29,199	39	56	214	432	477	1,102	3,318	14,908	7,580	1,070	3
Female	12,273	8	28	188	410	493	1,088	2,521	5,308	2,030	197	2
Waco, Tex.:												
Male	11,651	30	40	69	146	198	435	1,485	5,934	2,850	400	64
Female	3,781	6	11	41	70	104	259	820	1,850	533	57	30
Waltham, Mass.:												
Male	9,549	15	29	100	144	170	391	1,147	4,379	2,708	463	3
Female	5,087	1	16	39	112	156	410	1,048	2,291	912	102	....
Warren, Ohio:												
Male	9,813	11	6	18	69	114	348	1,370	5,422	2,167	282	6
Female	2,018	1	2	11	40	85	256	548	788	254	28	5
Waterbury, Conn.:												
Male	31,078	34	114	274	487	564	1,292	3,996	16,810	6,755	719	33
Female	9,877	13	53	195	408	511	1,036	2,509	4,057	1,007	83	5
Waterloo, Iowa:												
Male	11,867	70	44	68	146	165	446	1,461	6,180	2,888	385	14
Female	3,411	7	7	23	77	111	324	828	1,509	472	42	11
Watertown, N. Y.:												
Male	10,146	21	17	52	97	151	327	1,177	4,700	3,080	521	3
Female	3,644	.....	1	28	94	134	310	736	1,504	731	104	2
West Hoboken town, N. J.:												
Male	13,126	13	45	152	220	257	582	1,653	6,609	3,255	330	10
Female	4,160	1	50	109	238	259	521	1,019	1,483	438	42	....
West New York town, N. J.:												
Male	9,709	2	56	133	183	218	388	1,254	5,325	1,992	153	5
Female	2,852	5	42	145	190	201	391	710	938	216	13	1
Wheeling, W. Va.:												
Male	17,952	17	33	110	279	294	728	2,037	8,903	4,817	678	56
Female	5,267	7	29	78	237	247	553	1,128	2,007	831	139	11
Wichita, Kans.:												
Male	22,862	31	28	91	222	317	781	2,822	11,734	5,900	897	39
Female	7,008	4	7	34	150	214	559	1,640	3,287	1,005	88	20
Wichita Falls, Tex.:												
Male	17,344	30	44	66	142	236	706	2,604	9,064	2,662	222	1,568
Female	2,890	9	14	22	49	85	263	710	1,312	191	23	212
Wilkes-Barre, Pa.:												
Male	22,271	26	110	209	446	497	1,032	2,713	10,642	5,789	793	14
Female	6,791	8	54	166	362	373	858	1,742	2,422	728	70	8
Williamsport, Pa.:												
Male	11,983	5	27	81	196	211	513	1,545	5,205	3,484	703	13
Female	4,198	3	23	36	125	173	371	838	1,734	796	94	5
Wilmington, N. C.:												
Male	10,861	84	103	107	167	220	532	1,801	5,256	2,194	359	38
Female	4,450	22	30	63	102	120	323	899	1,990	745	135	21
Winston-Salem, N. C.:												
Male	16,761	39	116	183	369	475	1,379	3,868	7,323	2,643	333	33
Female	9,459	22	83	161	286	403	1,110	2,617	3,786	887	88	16
Woonsocket, R. I.:												
Male	13,770	12	174	250	381	356	758	1,883	6,195	3,334	424	3
Female	6,973	5	203	282	371	400	729	1,583	2,630	706	60	4
York, Pa.:												
Male	15,590	44	110	154	275	322	724	1,990	6,803	4,336	827	5
Female	5,932	9	79	135	282	298	558	1,138	2,344	959	127	3
Zanesville, Ohio:												
Male	9,554	47	17	71	137	155	363	1,030	4,364	2,886	474	10
Female	2,785	4	3	13	78	107	270	491	1,160	572	84	3

TABLE 35.—NUMBER AND PROPORTION OF CHILDREN OF EACH SEX 10 TO 15 YEARS OF AGE ENGAGED IN GAINFUL OCCUPATIONS, FOR CITIES HAVING FROM 25,000 TO 100,000 INHABITANTS: 1920.

CITY.	MALES 10 TO 15 YEARS OF AGE: 1920			FEMALES 10 TO 15 YEARS OF AGE: 1920			CITY.	MALES 10 TO 15 YEARS OF AGE: 1920			FEMALES 10 TO 15 YEARS OF AGE: 1920		
	Total number.	Number.	Per cent.	Total number.	Number.	Per cent.		Total number.	Number.	Per cent.	Total number.	Number.	Per cent.
Alameda, Calif.....	1,377	96	7.0	1,367	17	1.2	Elizabeth, N.J.....	5,070	468	9.2	4,977	380	7.6
Allentown, Pa.....	3,752	452	12.0	3,865	323	8.4	Elmira, N.Y.....	1,825	95	5.2	1,851	59	3.2
Altoona, Pa.....	3,131	240	7.7	3,224	82	2.5	Erie, Pa.....	4,842	201	4.2	4,995	106	2.1
Amsterdam, N.Y..	1,635	129	7.9	1,747	131	7.5	Evanston, Ill.......	1,674	76	4.5	1,769	38	2.1
Anderson, Ind.....	1,501	133	8.9	1,399	31	2.2	Evansville, Ind....	4,175	377	9.0	4,264	162	3.8
Asheville, N.C....	1,545	125	8.1	1,571	42	2.7	Everett, Mass.....	2,180	157	7.2	2,239	87	3.9
Atlantic City, N.J.	2,364	111	4.7	2,330	82	3.5	Everett, Wash....	1,426	152	10.7	1,380	23	1.7
Auburn, N.Y.....	1,671	103	6.2	1,752	65	3.7	Fitchburg, Mass...	2,197	384	17.5	2,303	262	11.4
Augusta, Ga....	2,541	296	11.6	2,766	181	6.5	Flint, Mich.....	3,486	346	9.9	3,545	95	2.7
Aurora, Ill.........	1,685	146	8.7	1,686	93	5.5	Fort Smith, Ark...	1,594	119	7.5	1,772	30	1.7
Austin, Tex........	1,963	102	5.2	2,069	46	2.2	Fort Wayne, Ind...	3,891	536	13.8	4,102	345	8.4
Bangor, Me........	1,168	27	2.3	1,322	24	1.8	Fresno, Calif....	2,076	116	5.6	2,117	28	1.3
Battle Creek, Mich.	1,470	128	8.7	1,550	37	2.4	Galveston, Tex....	2,047	289	14.1	2,181	73	3.3
Bay City, Mich....	2,941	163	5.5	2,779	101	3.6	Gary, Ind.........	2,439	89	3.6	2,383	64	2.7
Bayonne, N.J....	4,481	280	6.2	4,617	237	5.1	Green Bay, Wis...	1,807	106	5.9	1,841	39	2.1
Beaumont, Tex....	2,195	201	9.2	2,238	82	3.7	Hagerstown, Md...	1,352	121	8.9	1,485	67	4.5
Bellingham, Wash.	1,303	91	7.0	1,311	9	0.7	Hamilton, Ohio....	1,905	148	7.8	1,971	27	1.4
Berkeley, Calif....	2,542	120	4.7	2,636	22	0.8	Hammond, Ind....	1,986	129	6.5	1,958	74	3.8
Bethlehem, Pa....	2,450	149	6.1	2,489	136	5.5	Hamtramck, Mich.	2,064	62	3.0	1,983	70	3.5
Binghamton, N.Y.	2,713	151	5.6	2,677	93	3.5	Harrisburg, Pa.....	3,545	160	4.5	3,575	86	2.4
Bloomington, Ill....	1,299	90	6.9	1,407	39	2.8	Haverhill, Mass....	2,653	350	13.2	2,626	223	8.5
Brockton, Mass....	3,204	337	10.5	3,253	231	7.1	Hazleton, Pa......	2,126	170	8.0	2,171	194	8.9
Brookline, Mass....	1,323	56	4.2	1,474	23	1.6	Highland Pk.,Mich.	1,629	86	5.3	1,669	14	0.8
Butte, Mont.......	1,934	135	7.0	1,943	38	2.0	Hoboken, N.J.....	3,424	390	11.4	3,700	356	9.6
Canton, Ohio......	3,666	253	6.9	3,803	82	2.2	Holyoke, Mass....	3,240	436	13.5	3,297	411	12.5
Cedar Rapids, Iowa.	2,034	188	9.2	2,230	49	2.2	Huntington, W.Va.	2,764	187	6.8	2,800	77	2.8
Charleston, S.C....	3,499	393	11.2	3,582	228	6.4	Irvington, N.J.....	1,335	108	8.1	1,354	84	6.2
Charleston, W.Va..	2,000	121	6.1	2,094	64	3.1	Jackson, Mich.....	1,970	136	6.9	2,089	49	2.3
Charlotte, N.C.....	2,410	370	15.4	2,683	236	8.8	Jacksonville, Fla...	4,121	510	12.4	4,605	179	3.9
Chattanooga, Tenn.	2,839	263	9.3	2,859	123	4.3	Jamestown, N.Y...	1,944	116	6.0	1,875	57	3.0
Chelsea, Mass......	2,501	234	9.4	2,460	110	4.5	Johnstown, Pa.....	3,839	229	6.0	3,856	111	2.9
Chester, Pa........	2,301	155	6.7	2,457	142	5.8	Joliet, Ill..........	2,019	81	4.0	2,046	52	2.5
Chicopee, Mass....	2,094	332	15.9	2,134	293	13.7	Joplin, Mo........	1,676	82	4.9	1,713	46	2.7
Cicero town, Ill....	2,739	303	11.1	2,692	300	11.1	Kalamazoo, Mich...	2,196	87	4.0	2,202	54	2.5
Clarksburg, W.Va.	1,501	59	3.9	1,517	22	1.5	Kearny, N.J.......	1,513	140	9.3	1,460	150	10.3
Clifton, N.J........	1,608	240	14.9	1,577	191	12.1	Kenosha, Wis.....	1,886	142	7.5	1,995	119	6.0
Colorado Spgs.,Colo.	1,419	102	7.2	1,502	19	1.3	Kingston, N.Y.....	1,297	78	6.0	1,351	62	4.6
Columbia, S.C.....	1,864	178	9.5	2,027	89	4.4	Knoxville, Tenn...	4,242	343	8.1	4,544	223	4.9
Columbus, Ga.....	1,660	236	14.2	1,896	157	8.3	Kokomo, Ind......	1,375	140	10.2	1,449	55	3.8
Council Bluffs,Iowa	1,793	105	5.9	1,751	38	2.2	La Crosse, Wis....	1,479	78	5.3	1,550	66	4.3
Covington, Ky.....	2,782	253	9.1	2,833	124	4.4	Lakewood, Ohio....	1,946	39	2.0	2,012	22	1.1
Cranston, R.I.....	1,597	151	9.8	1,450	120	8.0	Lancaster, Pa......	2,173	310	10.5	2,501	250	10.0
Cumberland, Md..	1,597	161	10.1	1,616	64	4.0	Lansing, Mich.....	2,766	427	15.8	2,402	30	1.6
Danville, Ill.......	1,745	170	9.7	1,712	56	3.3	Lawrence, Mass....	5,004	859	17.2	5,003	844	16.9
Davenport, Iowa...	2,609	206	7.9	2,662	62	2.3	Lewiston, Me......	1,625	41	2.5	1,725	61	3.5
Decatur, Ill........	2,186	218	10.0	2,247	94	4.2	Lexington, Ky.....	1,750	119	6.8	1,839	39	2.1
Dubuque, Iowa....	1,776	186	10.5	1,901	104	5.5	Lima, Ohio.......	2,059	131	6.4	2,086	35	1.7
Duluth, Minn.....	4,760	187	3.9	4,848	77	1.6	Lincoln, Nebr.....	2,624	154	5.9	2,722	31	1.1
E. Chicago, Ind...	1,789	76	4.2	1,684	69	4.1	Little Rock, Ark...	3,164	220	7.0	3,299	84	2.5
E. Cleveland, Ohio.	1,097	68	6.2	1,150	19	1.7	Long Beach, Calif.	2,183	108	4.9	2,241	17	0.8
E. Orange, N.J....	2,150	70	3.3	2,279	57	2.5	Lorain, Ohio......	2,062	75	3.6	2,108	25	1.2
E. St. Louis, Ill....	3,458	280	8.1	3,539	167	4.7	Lynchburg, Va....	1,606	233	14.5	1,752	111	6.3
Easton, Pa........	1,551	131	8.4	1,569	97	6.2	Lynn, Mass.......	4,546	303	6.7	4,776	201	4.2
El Paso, Tex.......	4,321	338	7.8	4,698	134	2.9	McKeesport, Pa...	2,722	151	5.5	2,748	82	3.0
Elgin, Ill...........	1,132	84	7.4	1,163	60	5.2	Macon, Ga........	2,823	506	17.9	2,964	208	7.0

TABLE 35.—NUMBER AND PROPORTION OF CHILDREN OF EACH SEX 10 TO 15 YEARS OF AGE ENGAGED IN GAINFUL OCCUPATIONS, FOR CITIES HAVING FROM 25,000 TO 100,000 INHABITANTS: 1920—Continued.

CITY.	MALES 10 TO 15 YEARS OF AGE: 1920			FEMALES 10 TO 15 YEARS OF AGE: 1920			CITY.	MALES 10 TO 15 YEARS OF AGE: 1920			FEMALES 10 TO 15 YEARS OF AGE: 1920		
	Total number.	Engaged in gainful occupations. Number.	Per cent.	Total number.	Engaged in gainful occupations. Number.	Per cent.		Total number.	Engaged in gainful occupations. Number.	Per cent.	Total number.	Engaged in gainful occupations. Number.	Per cent.
Madison, Wis........	1,658	103	6.2	1,794	30	1.7	Racine, Wis.........	2,702	267	9.9	2,682	143	5.3
Malden, Mass.......	2,678	150	5.6	2,702	89	3.3	Revere, Mass.......	1,730	120	6.9	1,767	83	4.7
Manchester, N.H..	4,152	221	5.3	4,301	147	3.4	Richmond, Ind....	1,211	169	14.0	1,239	76	6.1
Mansfield, Ohio....	1,218	132	10.8	1,232	27	2.2	Roanoke, Va.......	2,653	296	11.2	2,762	90	3.3
Marion, Ohio.......	1,378	123	8.9	1,434	10	0.7	Rock Island, Ill....	1,583	157	9.9	1,641	61	3.7
Medford, Mass.....	1,888	119	6.3	1,900	57	3.0	Rockford, Ill.......	2,869	187	6.5	2,959	45	1.5
Meriden, Conn.....	1,835	160	8.7	1,486	119	8.0	Rome, N.Y........	1,430	102	7.1	1,343	59	4.4
Miami, Fla.........	1,224	98	8.0	1,239	36	2.9	Sacramento, Calif..	2,687	180	6.7	2,861	50	1.7
Mobile, Ala........	3,113	312	10.0	3,337	134	4.0	Saginaw, Mich.....	3,166	171	5.4	3,289	65	2.0
Moline, Ill.........	1,373	134	9.8	1,390	40	2.9	St. Joseph, Mo.....	3,536	298	8.4	3,705	117	3.2
Montclair, N.J.....	1,449	19	1.3	1,470	29	2.0	Salem, Mass........	2,319	253	10.9	2,293	157	6.8
Montgomery, Ala...	2,167	220	10.2	2,567	123	4.8	San Diego, Calif....	2,792	197	7.1	2,918	36	1.2
Mount Vernon, N.Y.	2,385	98	4.1	2,255	66	2.9	San Jose, Calif.....	1,961	72	3.7	2,015	19	0.9
Muncie, Ind........	1,849	182	9.8	1,839	72	3.9	Savannah, Ga......	3,811	562	14.7	4,385	272	6.2
Muskegon, Mich...	1,699	112	6.6	1,710	54	3.2	Schenectady, N.Y.	4,490	163	3.6	4,604	83	1.8
Muskogee, Okla....	1,655	94	5.7	1,726	22	1.3	Sheboygan, Wis....	1,761	243	13.8	1,632	143	8.8
Nashua, N.H......	1,335	68	5.1	1,510	40	2.6	Shreveport, La.....	2,048	243	11.9	2,323	90	3.9
New Britain, Conn.	3,076	287	9.3	3,221	300	9.3	Sioux City, Iowa...	3,013	169	5.6	3,145	80	2.5
New Brunswick, N.J	1,695	80	4.7	1,685	107	6.4	Sioux Falls, S. Dak.	1,130	40	3.5	1,192	23	1.9
New Castle, Pa.....	2,356	126	5.3	2,407	61	2.5	Somerville, Mass...	4,363	331	7.6	4,558	179	3.9
New London, Conn.	1,241	62	5.0	1,270	32	2.5	South Bend, Ind...	3,808	375	9.8	3,954	314	7.9
New Rochelle, N.Y.	1,951	75	3.8	1,923	57	3.0	Springfield, Ill.....	2,981	242	8.1	3,126	131	4.2
Newark, Ohio......	1,312	106	8.1	1,252	18	1.4	Springfield, Mo.....	2,054	123	6.0	2,219	44	2.0
Newburgh, N.Y....	1,419	87	6.1	1,433	63	4.4	Springfield, Ohio..	2,836	205	7.2	2,988	12	0.4
Newport, Ky.......	1,379	148	10.7	1,476	109	7.4	Stamford, Conn....	1,827	128	7.0	1,950	105	5.4
Newport, R.I......	1,322	83	6.3	1,354	29	2.1	Steubenville, Ohio.	1,423	95	6.7	1,425	34	2.4
Newport News, Va.	1,453	152	10.5	1,600	59	3.7	Stockton, Calif.....	1,615	97	6.0	1,623	26	1.6
Newton, Mass.....	2,336	98	4.2	2,339	72	3.1	Superior, Wis......	2,146	70	3.3	2,300	17	0.7
Niagara Falls, N.Y.	2,463	77	3.1	2,330	64	2.7	Tacoma, Wash.....	4,310	363	8.4	4,569	94	2.1
Norristown, Pa....	1,477	121	8.2	1,489	108	7.3	Tampa, Fla........	3,063	228	7.4	3,063	138	4.5
Norwalk, Conn.....	1,445	217	15.0	1,426	138	9.7	Taunton, Mass.....	1,921	261	13.6	1,898	219	11.5
Oak Park, Ill......	1,984	66	3.3	1,897	33	1.7	Terre Haute, Ind..	3,336	254	7.6	3,441	100	2.9
Ogden, Utah.......	2,088	125	6.0	1,992	27	1.4	Topeka, Kans......	2,267	131	5.8	2,393	51	2.1
Oklahoma City, Okla.............	4,227	289	6.8	4,389	81	1.8	Troy, N.Y.........	3,205	137	4.3	3,330	134	4.0
Orange, N.J........	1,859	108	5.8	1,859	104	5.6	Tulsa, Okla........	3,244	161	5.0	3,250	70	2.2
Oshkosh, Wis......	1,799	206	11.5	1,856	135	7.3	Utica, N.Y.........	4,577	309	6.8	4,623	224	4.8
Pasadena, Calif....	1,820	105	5.8	1,760	15	0.9	Waco, Tex.........	2,299	139	6.0	2,313	58	2.5
Passaic, N.J.......	3,575	342	9.6	3,672	387	10.5	Waltham, Mass.....	1,679	144	8.6	1,360	56	4.1
Pawtucket, R.I....	3,188	588	18.4	3,451	564	16.3	Warren, Ohio......	1,175	35	3.0	1,086	14	1.3
Pensacola, Fla.....	1,549	214	13.8	1,739	57	3.3	Waterbury, Conn...	4,822	422	8.8	4,763	261	5.5
Peoria, Ill.........	3,275	246	7.5	3,551	148	4.2	Waterloo, Iowa....	1,694	182	10.7	1,789	37	2.1
Perth Amboy, N.J.	2,438	208	8.5	2,476	280	11.3	Watertown, N.Y...	1,416	90	6.4	1,494	29	1.9
Petersburg, Va....	1,520	121	8.0	1,760	117	6.6	W. Hoboken, N.J...	2,268	210	9.3	2,271	160	7.0
Phoenix, Ariz.....	1,281	85	6.6	1,317	17	1.3	W. New York, N.J.	1,648	191	11.6	1,717	192	11.2
Pittsfield, Mass....	2,026	169	8.3	2,116	147	6.9	Wheeling, W. Va...	2,863	160	5.6	2,996	114	3.8
Plainfield, N.J.....	1,331	65	4.9	1,324	58	4.4	Wichita, Kans.....	3,445	150	4.4	3,443	45	1.3
Pontiac, Mich......	1,320	52	3.9	1,322	29	2.2	Wichita Falls, Tex.	1,619	140	8.6	1,580	45	2.8
Port Huron, Mich..	1,316	51	3.9	1,322	27	2.0	Wilkes-Barre, Pa...	4,471	345	7.7	4,346	228	5.2
Portland, Me......	3,002	150	5.0	3,173	48	1.5	Williamsport, Pa...	1,684	113	6.7	1,718	62	3.6
Portsmouth, Ohio.	1,531	98	6.4	1,694	18	1.1	Wilmington, N.C...	1,694	294	17.4	1,941	115	5.9
Portsmouth, Va....	2,682	358	13.3	3,007	111	3.7	Winston-Salem N.C	2,360	338	14.3	2,507	266	10.6
Poughkeepsie, N.Y.	1,642	76	4.6	1,649	63	3.8	Woonsocket, R.I...	2,348	436	18.6	2,613	490	18.8
Pueblo, Colo.......	2,225	164	7.4	2,281	51	2.2	York, Pa...........	2,343	308	13.1	2,454	223	9.1
Quincy, Ill.........	1,698	209	12.3	1,670	69	4.1	Zanesville, Ohio...	1,441	135	9.4	1,412	20	1.4
Quincy, Mass......	2,542	168	6.6	2,452	78	3.2							

TABLE **36.**—NUMBER AND PROPORTION OF WOMEN 15 YEARS OF AGE AND OVER, IN EACH SPECIFIED MARITAL CLASS, ENGAGED IN GAINFUL OCCUPATIONS, FOR THE UNITED STATES: 1890–1920.

CENSUS YEAR AND MARITAL CONDITION.	WOMEN 15 YEARS OF AGE AND OVER.		
	Total number.	Engaged in gainful occupations.	
		Number.	Per cent.
1920			
Aggregate	35,177,515	8,346,796	23.7
Married	21,318,933	1,920,281	9.0
Single, widowed, divorced, and unknown	13,858,582	6,426,515	46.4
1910			
Aggregate	30,047,325	7,639,828	25.4
Married	17,684,687	1,890,661	10.7
Single, widowed, divorced, and unknown	12,362,638	5,749,167	46.5
1900			
Aggregate	24,249,191	4,997,415	20.6
Married	13,810,057	769,477	5.6
Single, widowed, divorced, and unknown	10,439,134	4,227,938	40.5
1890			
Aggregate	19,602,178	3,712,144	18.9
Married	11,124,785	515,260	4.6
Single, widowed, divorced, and unknown	8,477,393	3,196,884	37.7

TABLE **37.**—NUMBER AND PER CENT DISTRIBUTION, BY MARITAL CONDITION, OF THE GAINFULLY OCCUPIED WOMEN 15 YEARS OF AGE AND OVER, FOR THE UNITED STATES: 1890–1920.

CENSUS YEAR AND MARITAL CONDITION.	WOMEN 15 YEARS OF AGE AND OVER ENGAGED IN GAINFUL OCCUPATIONS.	
	Number.	Per cent distribution.
1920		
Aggregate	8,346,796	100.0
Married	1,920,281	23.0
Single, widowed, divorced, and unknown	6,426,515	77.0
1910		
Aggregate	7,639,828	100.0
Married	1,890,661	24.7
Single, widowed, divorced, and unknown	5,749,167	75.3
1900		
Aggregate	4,997,415	100.0
Married	769,477	15.4
Single, widowed, divorced, and unknown	4,227,938	84.6
1890		
Aggregate	3,712,144	100.0
Married	515,260	13.9
Single, widowed, divorced, and unknown	3,196,884	86.1

TABLE **38.**—NUMBER AND PER CENT DISTRIBUTION, BY MARITAL CONDITION, OF THE WOMEN 15 YEARS OF AGE AND OVER IN EACH GENERAL DIVISION OF OCCUPATIONS, FOR THE UNITED STATES: 1920 AND 1910.

CENSUS YEAR AND GENERAL DIVISION OF OCCUPATIONS.	Total number.	MARRIED.		SINGLE, WIDOWED, DIVORCED, AND UNKNOWN.	
		Number.	Per cent of total.	Number.	Per cent of total.
1920					
All occupations...................	8,346,796	1,920,281	23.0	6,426,515	77.0
Agriculture, forestry, and animal husbandry...	934,962	371,537	39.7	563,425	60.3
Extraction of minerals...................	2,781	1,278	46.0	1,503	54.0
Manufacturing and mechanical industries......	1,904,132	466,663	24.5	1,437,469	75.5
Transportation........................	212,382	26,480	12.5	185,902	87.5
Trade.................................	663,939	156,490	23.6	507,449	76.4
Public service (not elsewhere classified)........	21,768	7,542	34.6	14,226	65.4
Professional service....................	1,015,904	123,578	12.2	892,326	87.8
Domestic and personal service...............	2,169,450	637,675	29.4	1,531,775	70.6
Clerical occupations......................	1,421,478	129,038	9.1	1,292,440	90.9
1910					
All occupations...................	7,639,828	1,890,661	24.7	5,749,167	75.3
Agriculture, forestry, and animal husbandry..	1,473,261	692,745	47.0	780,516	53.0
Extraction of minerals...................	1,060	371	35.0	689	65.0
Manufacturing and mechanical industries......	1,775,917	330,914	18.6	1,445,003	81.4
Transportation........................	106,034	8,602	8.1	97,432	91.9
Trade.................................	464,173	83,089	17.9	381,084	82.1
Public service (not elsewhere classified)........	13,555	4,377	32.3	9,178	67.7
Professional service....................	733,342	76,287	10.4	657,055	89.6
Domestic and personal service...............	2,483,277	661,199	26.6	1,822,078	73.4
Clerical occupations......................	589,209	33,077	5.6	556,132	94.4

TABLE **39.**—NUMBER AND PER CENT DISTRIBUTION, BY GENERAL DIVISIONS OF OCCUPATIONS, OF THE GAINFULLY OCCUPIED WOMEN 15 YEARS OF AGE AND OVER IN EACH SPECIFIED MARITAL CLASS, FOR THE UNITED STATES: 1920 AND 1910.

CENSUS YEAR AND GENERAL DIVISION OF OCCUPATIONS.	TOTAL NUMBER.		MARRIED.		SINGLE, WIDOWED, DIVORCED, AND UNKNOWN.	
	Number.	Per cent distribution.	Number.	Per cent distribution.	Number.	Per cent distribution.
1920						
All occupations...................	8,346,796	100.0	1,920,281	100.0	6,426,515	100.0
Agriculture, forestry, and animal husbandry.	934,962	11.2	371,537	19.3	563,425	8.8
Extraction of minerals...................	2,781	(1)	1,278	0.1	1,503	(1)
Manufacturing and mechanical industries...	1,904,132	22.8	466,663	24.3	1,437,469	22.4
Transportation........................	212,382	2.5	26,480	1.4	185,902	2.9
Trade.................................	663,939	8.0	156,490	8.1	507,449	7.9
Public service (not elsewhere classified).....	21,768	0.3	7,542	0.4	14,226	0.2
Professional service.....................	1,015,904	12.2	123,578	6.4	892,326	13.9
Domestic and personal service..............	2,169,450	26.0	637,675	33.2	1,531,775	23.8
Clerical occupations.....................	1,421,478	17.0	129,038	6.7	1,292,440	20.1
1910						
All occupations...................	7,639,828	100.0	1,890,661	100.0	5,749,167	100.0
Agriculture, forestry, and animal husbandry.	1,473,261	19.3	692,745	36.6	780,516	13.6
Extraction of minerals...................	1,060	(1)	371	(1)	689	(1)
Manufacturing and mechanical industries...	1,775,917	23.2	330,914	17.5	1,445,003	25.1
Transportation........................	106,034	1.4	8,602	0.5	97,432	1.7
Trade.................................	464,173	6.1	83,089	4.4	381,084	6.6
Public service (not elsewhere classified).....	13,555	0.2	4,377	0.2	9,178	0.2
Professional service.....................	733,342	9.6	76,287	4.0	657,055	11.4
Domestic and personal service..............	2,483,277	32.5	661,199	35.0	1,822,078	31.7
Clerical occupations.....................	589,209	7.7	33,077	1.7	556,132	9.7

[1] Less than one-tenth of 1 per cent.

TABLE **40.**—NUMBER AND PROPORTION OF WOMEN 15 YEARS OF AGE AND OVER IN EACH SPECIFIED MARITAL CLASS ENGAGED IN GAINFUL OCCUPATIONS, BY CLASS OF POPULATION AND AGE PERIODS, FOR THE UNITED STATES: 1920.

CLASS OF POPULATION AND AGE PERIOD.	ALL CLASSES.			MARRIED.			SINGLE, WIDOWED, DIVORCED, AND UNKNOWN.		
	Total number.	Engaged in gainful occupations. Number.	Per cent.	Total. number.	Engaged in gainful occupations. Number.	Per cent.	Total number.	Engaged in gainful occupations. Number.	Per cent.
All classes..............	35,177,515	8,346,796	23.7	21,318,933	1,920,281	9.0	13,858,582	6,426,515	46.4
15 to 19 years..........	4,756,764	1,555,322	32.7	596,542	74,305	12.5	4,160,222	1,481,017	35.6
20 to 24 years..........	4,749,976	1,809,075	38.1	2,483,697	283,870	11.4	2,266,279	1,525,205	67.3
25 to 44 years..........	15,249,602	3,417,373	22.4	11,918,789	1,143,706	9.6	3,330,813	2,273,667	68.3
25 to 34 years........	8,488,668	(1)	......	6,492,355	627,580	9.7	1,996,313	(1)	......
35 to 44 years........	6,760,934	(1)	......	5,426,434	516,126	9.5	1,334,500	(1)	......
45 years and over [2].....	10,421,173	1,565,026	15.0	6,319,905	418,400	6.6	4,101,268	1,146,626	28.0
Native white—Native parentage..........	18,529,748	3,652,963	19.7	11,195,865	707,503	6.3	7,333,883	2,945,460	40.2
15 to 19 years..........	2,801,569	699,080	25.0	372,924	29,980	8.0	2,428,645	669,100	27.6
20 to 24 years..........	2,629,889	855,946	32.5	1,404,020	106,191	7.6	1,225,869	749,755	61.2
25 to 44 years..........	7,807,162	1,439,349	18.4	6,169,355	407,769	6.6	1,637,807	1,031,580	63.0
25 to 34 years........	4,438,860	(1)	......	3,421,662	225,760	6.6	1,017,198	(1)	......
35 to 44 years........	3,368,302	(1)	......	2,747,693	182,009	6.6	620,609	(1)	......
45 years and over [2].....	5,291,128	658,588	12.4	3,249,566	163,563	5.0	2,041,562	495,025	24.2
Native white—Foreign or mixed parentage.	7,211,108	2,088,431	29.0	3,890,870	245,311	6.3	3,320,238	1,843,120	55.5
15 to 19 years..........	1,102,083	498,023	45.2	68,151	7,677	11.3	1,033,932	490,346	47.4
20 to 24 years..........	1,067,020	521,017	48.8	422,358	37,284	8.8	644,662	483,733	75.0
25 to 44 years..........	3,150,386	774,177	24.6	2,251,596	146,385	6.5	898,790	627,792	69.8
25 to 34 years........	1,804,121	(1)	......	1,245,794	83,255	6.7	558,327	(1)	......
35 to 44 years........	1,346,265	(1)	......	1,005,802	63,130	6.3	340,463	(1)	......
45 years and over [2].....	1,891,619	295,214	15.6	1,148,765	53,965	4.7	742,854	241,249	32.5
Foreign-born white.....	5,913,985	1,113,216	18.8	4,123,503	296,126	7.2	1,790,482	817,090	45.6
15 to 19 years..........	268,672	139,685	52.0	38,477	4,382	11.4	230,195	135,303	58.8
20 to 24 years..........	469,856	177,030	37.7	289,349	27,876	9.6	180,507	149,154	82.6
25 to 44 years..........	2,720,964	506,267	18.6	2,299,018	189,138	8.2	421,946	317,129	75.2
25 to 34 years........	1,366,932	(1)	......	1,150,570	95,802	8.3	216,362	(1)	......
35 to 44 years........	1,354,032	(1)	......	1,148,448	93,336	8.1	205,584	(1)	......
45 years and over [2].....	2,454,493	290,234	11.8	1,496,659	74,730	5.0	957,834	215,504	22.5
Negro.....	3,423,100	1,476,915	43.1	2,039,181	662,684	32.5	1,383,919	814,231	58.8
15 to 19 years..........	569,799	216,767	38.0	114,169	31,911	28.0	455,630	184,856	40.6
20 to 24 years..........	567,678	252,417	44.5	356,740	111,095	31.1	210,938	141,322	67.0
25 to 44 years..........	1,525,792	689,933	45.2	1,158,765	394,916	34.1	367,027	295,017	80.4
25 to 34 years........	851,673	(1)	......	650,348	219,432	33.7	201,325	(1)	......
35 to 44 years........	674,119	(1)	......	508,417	175,484	34.5	165,702	(1)	......
45 years and over [2].....	759,831	317,798	41.8	409,507	124,762	30.5	350,324	193,036	55.1
Indian.....	70,431	9,168	13.0	43,923	3,929	8.9	26,508	5,239	19.8
15 to 19 years..........	12,707	1,372	10.8	2,279	258	11.3	10,428	1,114	10.7
20 to 24 years..........	9,596	1,449	15.1	6,005	548	9.1	3,591	901	25.1
25 to 44 years..........	26,531	3,764	14.2	22,209	2,169	9.8	4,322	1,595	36.9
25 to 34 years........	14,490	(1)	......	11,923	1,210	10.1	2,567	(1)	......
35 to 44 years........	12,041	(1)	......	10,286	959	9.3	1,755	(1)	......
45 years and over [2].....	21,597	2,583	12.0	13,430	954	7.1	8,167	1,629	19.9
Chinese, Japanese, and all other..........	29,143	6,103	20.9	25,591	4,728	18.5	3,552	1,375	38.7
15 to 19 years..........	1,934	395	20.4	542	97	17.9	1,392	298	21.4
20 to 24 years..........	5,937	1,016	20.5	5,225	876	16.8	712	340	47.8
25 to 44 years..........	18,767	3,883	20.7	17,840	3,329	18.7	921	554	60.2
25 to 34 years........	12,592	(1)	......	12,058	2,121	17.6	534	(1)	......
35 to 44 years........	6,175	(1)	......	5,788	1,208	20.9	387	(1)	......
45 years and over [2].....	2,505	609	24.3	1,978	426	21.5	527	183	34.7

[1] Figures not available.   [2] Includes age unknown.

TABLE 41.—NUMBER AND PROPORTION OF THE GAINFULLY OCCUPIED WOMEN 15 YEARS OF AGE AND OVER IN EACH SPECIFIED MARITAL CLASS, BY CLASS OF POPULATION AND AGE PERIODS, FOR THE UNITED STATES: 1920.

CLASS OF POPULATION AND AGE PERIOD.	Total number.	MARRIED.		SINGLE, WIDOWED, DIVORCED, AND UNKNOWN.	
		Number.	Per cent of total.	Number.	Per cent of total.
All classes	8,346,796	1,920,281	23.0	6,426,515	77.0
15 to 19 years	1,555,322	74,305	4.8	1,481,017	95.2
20 to 24 years	1,809,075	283,870	15.7	1,525,205	84.3
25 to 44 years	3,417,373	1,143,706	33.5	2,273,667	66.5
25 to 34 years	(1)	627,580		(1)	
35 to 44 years	(1)	516,126		(1)	
45 years and over [2]	1,565,026	418,400	26.7	1,146,626	73.3
Native white—Native parentage	3,652,963	707,503	19.4	2,945,460	80.6
15 to 19 years	699,080	29,980	4.3	669,100	95.7
20 to 24 years	855,946	106,191	12.4	749,755	87.6
25 to 44 years	1,439,349	407,769	28.3	1,031,580	71.7
25 to 34 years	(1)	225,760		(1)	
35 to 44 years	(1)	182,009		(1)	
45 years and over [2]	658,588	163,563	24.8	495,025	75.2
Native white—Foreign or mixed parentage	2,088,431	245,311	11.7	1,843,120	88.3
15 to 19 years	498,023	7,677	1.5	490,346	98.5
20 to 24 years	521,017	37,284	7.2	483,733	92.8
25 to 44 years	774,177	146,385	18.9	627,792	81.1
25 to 34 years	(1)	83,255		(1)	
35 to 44 years	(1)	63,130		(1)	
45 years and over [2]	295,214	53,965	18.3	241,249	81.7
Foreign-born white	1,113,216	296,126	26.6	817,090	73.4
15 to 19 years	139,685	4,382	3.1	135,303	96.9
20 to 24 years	177,030	27,876	15.7	149,154	84.3
25 to 44 years	506,267	189,138	37.4	317,129	62.6
25 to 34 years	(1)	95,802		(1)	
35 to 44 years	(1)	93,336		(1)	
45 years and over [2]	290,234	74,730	25.7	215,504	74.3
Negro	1,476,915	662,684	44.9	814,231	55.1
15 to 19 years	216,767	31,911	14.7	184,856	85.3
20 to 24 years	252,417	111,095	44.0	141,322	56.0
25 to 44 years	689,933	394,916	57.2	295,017	42.8
25 to 34 years	(1)	219,432		(1)	
35 to 44 years	(1)	175,484		(1)	
45 years and over [2]	317,798	124,762	39.3	193,036	60.7
Indian	9,168	3,929	42.9	5,239	57.1
15 to 19 years	1,372	258	18.8	1,114	81.2
20 to 24 years	1,449	548	37.8	901	62.2
25 to 44 years	3,764	2,169	57.6	1,595	42.4
25 to 34 years	(1)	1,210		(1)	
35 to 44 years	(1)	959		(1)	
45 years and over [2]	2,583	954	36.9	1,629	63.1
Chinese, Japanese, and all other	6,103	4,728	77.5	1,375	22.5
15 to 19 years	395	97	24.6	298	75.4
20 to 24 years	1,216	876	72.0	340	28.0
25 to 44 years	3,883	3,329	85.7	554	14.3
25 to 34 years	(1)	2,121		(1)	
35 to 44 years	(1)	1,208		(1)	
45 years and over [2]	609	426	70.0	183	30.0

[1] Figures not available.   [3] Includes age unknown.

TABLE **42.**—PER CENT DISTRIBUTION, BY AGE PERIODS, FOR EACH PRINCIPAL CLASS OF THE POPULATION, OF ALL WOMEN AND OF THE GAINFULLY OCCUPIED WOMEN 15 YEARS OF AGE AND OVER, IN EACH SPECIFIED MARITAL CLASS, FOR THE UNITED STATES: 1920.

| CLASS OF POPULATION AND AGE PERIOD. | WOMEN 15 YEARS OF AGE AND OVER: 1920. | | | | | |
| | Aggregate. | | | Engaged in gainful occupations. | | |
	Total number.	Married.	Single, widowed, divorced, and unknown.	Total number.	Married.	Single, widowed, divorced, and unknown.
All classes..................	100. 0	100. 0	100. 0	100. 0	100. 0	100. 0
15 to 19 years..............	13. 5	2. 8	30. 0	18. 6	3. 9	23. 0
20 to 24 years..............	13. 5	11. 7	16. 4	21. 7	14. 8	23. 7
25 to 44 years..............	43. 4	55. 9	24. 0	40. 9	59. 6	35. 4
25 to 34 years.........	24. 1	30. 5	14. 4	(1)	32. 7	(1)
35 to 44 years.........	19. 2	25. 5	9. 6	(1)	26. 9	(1)
45 years and over [2]........	29. 6	29. 6	29. 6	18. 8	21. 8	17. 8
Native white—Native parentage..................	100. 0	100. 0	100. 0	100. 0	100. 0	100. 0
15 to 19 years..............	15. 1	3. 3	33. 1	19. 1	4. 2	22. 7
20 to 24 years..............	14. 2	12. 5	16. 7	23. 4	15. 0	25. 5
25 to 44 years..............	42. 1	55. 1	22. 3	39. 4	57. 6	35. 0
25 to 34 years.........	24. 0	30. 6	13. 9	(1)	31. 9	(1)
35 to 44 years.........	18. 2	24. 5	8. 5	(1)	25. 7	(1)
45 years and over [2]........	28. 6	29. 0	27. 8	18. 0	23. 1	16. 8
Native white—Foreign or mixed parentage..........	100. 0	100. 0	100. 0	100. 0	100. 0	100. 0
15 to 19 years..............	15. 3	1. 8	31. 1	23. 8	3. 1	26. 6
20 to 24 years..............	14. 8	10. 9	19. 4	24. 9	15. 2	26. 2
25 to 44 years..............	43. 7	57. 9	27. 1	37. 1	59. 7	34. 1
25 to 34 years.........	25. 0	32. 0	16. 8	(1)	33. 9	(1)
35 to 44 years.........	18. 7	25. 9	10. 3	(1)	25. 7	(1)
45 years and over [2]........	26. 2	29. 5	22. 4	14. 1	22. 0	13. 1
Foreign-born white..........	100. 0	100. 0	100. 0	100. 0	100. 0	100. 0
15 to 19 years..............	4. 5	0. 9	12. 9	12. 5	1. 5	16. 6
20 to 24 years..............	7. 9	7. 0	10. 1	15. 9	9. 4	18. 3
25 to 44 years..............	46. 0	55. 8	23. 6	45. 5	63. 9	38. 8
25 to 34 years.........	23. 1	27. 9	12. 1	(1)	32. 4	(1)
35 to 44 years.........	22. 9	27. 9	11. 5	(1)	31. 5	(1)
45 years and over [2]........	41. 5	36. 3	53. 5	26. 1	25. 2	26. 4
Negro..................	100. 0	100. 0	100. 0	100. 0	100. 0	100. 0
15 to 19 years..............	16. 6	5. 6	32. 9	14. 7	4. 8	22. 7
20 to 24 years..............	16. 6	17. 5	15. 2	17. 1	16. 8	17. 4
25 to 44 years..............	44. 6	56. 8	26. 5	46. 7	59. 6	36. 2
25 to 34 years.........	24. 9	31. 9	14. 5	(1)	33. 1	(1)
35 to 44 years.........	19. 7	24. 9	12. 0	(1)	26. 5	(1)
45 years and over [2]........	22. 2	20. 1	25. 3	21. 5	18. 8	23. 7
Indian.................	100. 0	100. 0	100. 0	100. 0	100. 0	100. 0
15 to 19 years..............	18. 0	5. 2	39. 3	15. 0	6. 6	21. 3
20 to 24 years..............	13. 6	13. 7	13. 5	15. 8	13. 9	17. 2
25 to 44 years..............	37. 7	50. 6	16. 3	41. 1	55. 2	30. 4
25 to 34 years.........	20. 6	27. 1	9. 7	(1)	30. 8	(1)
35 to 44 years.........	17. 1	23. 4	6. 6	(1)	24. 4	(1)
45 years and over [2]........	30. 7	30. 6	30. 8	28. 2	24. 3	31. 1
Chinese, Japanese, and all other.................	100. 0	100. 0	100. 0	100. 0	100. 0	100. 0
15 to 19 years..............	6. 0	2. 1	39. 2	6. 5	2. 1	21. 7
20 to 24 years..............	20. 4	20. 4	20. 0	19. 9	18. 5	24. 7
25 to 44 years..............	64. 4	69. 7	25. 9	63. 6	70. 4	40. 3
25 to 34 years.........	43. 2	47. 1	15. 0	(1)	44. 5	(1)
35 to 44 years.........	21. 2	22. 6	10. 9	(1)	25. 5	(1)
45 years and over [2]........	8. 6	7. 7	14. 8	10. 0	9. 0	13. 3

[1] Figures not available.   [2] Includes age unknown.

TABLE 43.—PER CENT DISTRIBUTION, BY POPULATION CLASSES, OF ALL WOMEN AND OF THE GAINFULLY OCCUPIED WOMEN 15 YEARS OF AGE AND OVER, IN EACH SPECIFIED MARITAL CLASS, FOR THE UNITED STATES: 1920.

CLASS OF POPULATION.	WOMEN 15 YEARS OF AGE AND OVER: 1920.					
	Aggregate.			Engaged in gainful occupations.		
	Total number.	Married.	Single, widowed, divorced, and unknown.	Total number.	Married.	Single, widowed, divorced, and unknown.
All classes.............	100.0	100.0	100.0	100.0	100.0	100.0
Native white—Native parentage......................	52.7	52.5	52.9	43.8	36.8	45.8
Native white—Foreign or mixed parentage............	20.5	18.3	24.0	25.0	12.8	28.7
Foreign-born white............	16.8	19.3	12.9	13.3	15.4	12.7
Negro.........................	9.7	9.6	10.0	17.7	34.5	12.7
Indian........................	0.2	0.2	0.2	0.1	0.2	0.1
Chinese, Japanese, and all other.......................	0.1	0.1	(1)	0.1	0.2	(1)

[1] Less than one-tenth of 1 per cent.

TABLE **44.**—NUMBER AND PROPORTION OF WOMEN 15 YEARS OF AGE AND OVER, IN EACH SPECIFIED MARITAL CLASS, ENGAGED IN GAINFUL OCCUPATIONS, BY DIVISIONS AND STATES: 1920.

DIVISION AND STATE.	AGGREGATE.			MARRIED.			SINGLE, WIDOWED, DIVORCED, AND UNKNOWN.		
	Total number.	Engaged in gainful occupations. Number.	Per cent.	Total number.	Engaged in gainful occupations. Number.	Per cent.	Total number.	Engaged in gainful occupations. Number.	Per cent.
United States	35,177,515	8,346,796	23.7	21,318,933	1,920,281	9.0	13,858,582	6,426,515	46.4
GEOGRAPHIC DIVISIONS:									
New England........	2,681,138	862,348	32.2	1,485,377	175,568	11.8	1,195,761	686,780	57.4
Middle Atlantic......	7,757,457	2,102,113	27.1	4,518,248	348,128	7.7	3,239,209	1,753,985	54.1
East North Central..	7,321,833	1,555,367	21.2	4,545,175	282,285	6.2	2,776,658	1,273,082	45.8
West North Central..	4,159,479	767,677	18.5	2,555,896	137,368	5.4	1,603,583	630,309	39.3
South Atlantic.......	4,420,837	1,178,574	26.7	2,654,236	394,664	14.9	1,766,601	783,910	44.4
East South Central...	2,794,845	649,046	23.2	1,725,179	225,222	13.1	1,069,666	423,824	39.6
West South Central..	3,131,029	623,104	19.9	1,988,774	201,013	10.1	1,142,255	422,091	37.0
Mountain............	1,000,086	175,555	17.6	654,476	43,152	6.6	345,610	132,403	38.3
Pacific..............	1,910,811	433,012	22.7	1,191,572	112,881	9.5	719,239	320,131	44.5
NEW ENGLAND:									
Maine................	271,764	64,636	23.8	162,623	16,288	10.0	109,141	48,348	44.3
New Hampshire.....	161,208	49,138	30.5	92,353	13,308	14.4	68,855	35,830	52.0
Vermont............	123,982	26,803	21.6	74,505	6,011	8.1	49,477	20,792	42.0
Massachusetts......	1,425,443	498,258	35.0	758,897	96,496	12.7	666,546	401,762	60.3
Rhode Island.......	219,409	78,989	36.0	118,772	15,530	13.1	100,637	63,459	63.1
Connecticut.........	479,332	144,524	30.2	278,227	27,935	10.0	201,105	116,589	58.0
MIDDLE ATLANTIC:									
New York..........	3,767,540	1,131,504	30.0	2,134,604	194,305	9.1	1,632,936	937,199	57.4
New Jersey.........	1,092,623	292,158	26.7	653,587	50,451	7.7	439,036	241,707	55.1
Pennsylvania.......	2,897,294	678,451	23.4	1,730,057	103,372	6.0	1,167,237	575,079	49.3
EAST NORTH CENTRAL:									
Ohio................	1,990,701	409,073	20.5	1,241,451	76,655	6.2	749,250	332,418	44.4
Indiana.............	1,021,915	183,882	18.0	650,187	34,848	5.4	371,728	149,034	40.1
Illinois.............	2,242,120	536,990	24.0	1,353,118	96,448	7.1	889,002	440,542	49.6
Michigan...........	1,198,037	244,515	20.4	782,648	52,097	6.7	415,389	192,418	46.3
Wisconsin..........	869,060	180,907	20.8	517,771	22,237	4.3	351,289	158,670	45.2
WEST NORTH CENTRAL:									
Minnesota..........	774,433	163,366	21.1	450,785	20,170	4.5	323,648	143,196	44.2
Iowa................	819,947	140,761	17.2	505,294	24,200	4.8	314,653	116,561	37.0
Missouri............	1,186,407	242,557	20.4	724,886	50,414	7.0	461,521	192,143	41.6
North Dakota.......	181,450	27,971	15.4	113,843	3,910	3.4	67,607	24,061	35.6
South Dakota.......	190,812	29,483	15.5	121,408	5,231	4.3	69,404	24,252	34.9
Nebraska...........	419,146	71,423	17.0	263,890	13,967	5.3	155,256	57,456	37.0
Kansas.............	587,284	92,116	15.7	375,790	19,476	5.2	211,494	72,640	34.3
SOUTH ATLANTIC:									
Delaware...........	77,105	17,947	23.3	47,469	4,413	9.3	29,636	13,534	45.7
Maryland...........	506,569	135,669	26.8	294,043	32,262	11.0	212,526	103,407	48.7
District of Columbia .	188,466	92,425	49.0	88,602	22,871	25.8	99,864	69,554	69.6
Virginia....../......	730,985	153,057	20.9	432,557	41,555	9.6	298,428	111,502	37.4
West Virginia.......	431,564	56,726	13.1	280,811	10,499	3.7	150,753	46,227	30.7
North Carolina......	769,185	187,546	24.4	460,742	60,951	13.2	308,443	126,595	41.0
South Carolina......	504,048	185,754	36.9	298,648	79,526	26.6	205,400	106,228	51.7
Georgia.............	900,117	266,093	29.6	551,522	107,275	19.5	348,595	158,818	45.6
Florida.............	312,798	83,357	26.6	199,842	35,312	17.7	112,956	48,045	42.5
EAST SOUTH CENTRAL:									
Kentucky...........	770,695	128,969	16.7	481,060	31,280	6.5	289,635	97,689	33.7
Tennessee..........	749,045	145,655	19.4	461,883	44,262	9.6	287,162	101,393	35.3
Alabama............	720,780	199,751	27.7	440,207	72,733	16.5	280,573	127,018	45.3
Mississippi.........	554,325	174,671	31.5	342,029	76,947	22.5	212,296	97,724	46.0
WEST SOUTH CENTRAL:									
Arkansas...........	525,477	103,143	19.6	344,325	36,919	10.7	181,152	66,224	36.6
Louisiana...........	571,359	145,661	25.5	338,897	50,112	14.8	232,442	95,549	41.1
Oklahoma...........	594,673	90,149	15.2	402,863	20,550	7.7	191,816	63,195	32.9
Texas..............	1,439,534	284,152	19.7	902,689	87,020	9.6	536,845	197,123	36.7
MOUNTAIN:									
Montana............	160,625	28,186	17.5	108,119	6,508	6.0	52,506	21,678	41.3
Idaho..............	123,287	17,435	14.1	84,554	4,408	5.2	38,733	13,027	33.6
Wyoming...........	54,169	9,356	17.3	38,172	2,666	7.0	15,997	6,690	41.8
Colorado...........	307,458	62,180	20.2	195,193	14,462	7.4	112,265	47,718	42.5
New Mexico........	103,503	14,656	14.2	66,577	3,715	5.6	36,926	10,941	29.6
Arizona............	95,671	17,707	18.5	63,685	6,174	9.7	31,986	11,533	36.1
Utah...............	133,642	21,708	16.2	83,713	3,779	4.5	49,929	17,929	35.9
Nevada............	21,731	4,327	19.9	14,463	1,440	10.0	7,268	2,887	39.7
PACIFIC:									
Washington.........	438,357	92,612	21.1	287,871	24,172	8.4	150,486	68,440	45.5
Oregon.............	261,847	54,370	20.8	170,069	15,155	8.9	91,778	39,215	42.7
California..........	1,210,607	286,030	23.6	733,632	73,554	10.0	476,975	212,476	44.5

TABLE 45.—NUMBER AND PER CENT DISTRIBUTION, BY MARITAL CONDITION, OF THE GAINFULLY OCCUPIED WOMEN 15 YEARS OF AGE AND OVER, BY DIVISIONS AND STATES: 1920 AND 1910.

DIVISION AND STATE.	1920					1910				
	Total number.	Married.		Single, widowed, divorced, and unknown.		Total number.	Married.		Single, widowed, divorced, and unknown.	
		Number.	Per cent of total.	Number.	Per cent of total.		Number.	Per cent of total.	Number.	Per cent of total.
United States..	8,346,796	1,920,281	23.0	6,426,515	77.0	7,639,828	1,890,661	24.7	5,749,167	75.3
GEOGRAPHIC DIVISIONS:										
New England........	862,348	175,568	20.4	686,780	79.6	766,159	137,452	17.9	628,707	82.1
Middle Atlantic.....	2,102,113	348,128	16.6	1,753,985	83.4	1,802,514	280,550	15.6	1,521,964	84.4
East North Central..	1,555,367	282,285	18.1	1,273,082	81.9	1,265,997	192,518	15.2	1,073,479	84.8
West North Central.	767,677	137,368	17.9	630,309	82.1	679,714	112,711	16.6	567,003	83.4
South Atlantic......	1,178,574	394,664	33.5	783,910	66.5	1,235,970	470,833	38.1	765,137	61.9
East South Central.	649,046	225,222	34.7	423,824	65.3	823,661	348,419	42.3	475,242	57.7
West South Central.	623,104	201,013	32.3	422,091	67.7	647,914	251,264	38.8	396,650	61.2
Mountain............	175,555	43,152	24.6	132,403	75.4	137,965	35,954	26.1	102,011	73.9
Pacific.............	433,012	112,881	26.1	320,131	73.9	279,934	60,960	21.8	218,974	78.2
NEW ENGLAND:										
Maine...............	64,636	16,288	25.2	48,348	74.8	62,631	14,281	22.8	48,350	77.2
New Hampshire.....	49,138	13,308	27.1	35,830	72.9	47,797	12,044	25.2	35,753	74.8
Vermont............	26,803	6,011	22.4	20,792	77.6	28,123	6,724	23.9	21,399	76.1
Massachusetts......	498,258	96,496	19.4	401,762	80.6	439,607	74,815	17.0	364,792	83.0
Rhode Island........	78,989	15,530	19.7	63,459	80.3	69,520	11,393	16.4	58,127	83.6
Connecticut.........	144,524	27,935	19.3	116,589	80.7	118,481	18,195	15.4	100,286	84.6
MIDDLE ATLANTIC:										
New York...........	1,131,504	194,305	17.2	937,199	82.8	976,098	156,515	16.0	819,583	84.0
New Jersey..........	292,158	50,451	17.3	241,707	82.7	235,602	37,653	16.0	197,949	84.0
Pennsylvania........	678,451	103,372	15.2	575,079	84.8	590,814	86,382	14.6	504,432	85.4
E. NORTH CENTRAL:										
Ohio................	409,073	76,655	18.7	332,418	81.3	342,573	53,958	15.8	288,615	84.2
Indiana.............	183,882	34,848	19.0	149,034	81.0	153,137	26,433	17.3	126,704	82.7
Illinois.............	536,990	96,448	18.0	440,542	82.0	426,058	60,305	14.2	365,753	85.8
Michigan............	244,515	52,097	21.3	192,418	78.7	184,452	31,414	17.0	153,038	83.0
Wisconsin...........	180,907	22,237	12.3	158,670	87.7	159,777	20,408	12.8	139,369	87.2
W. NORTH CENTRAL:										
Minnesota...........	163,366	20,170	12.3	143,196	87.7	143,796	16,938	11.8	126,858	88.2
Iowa...............	140,761	24,200	17.2	116,561	82.8	129,883	20,049	15.4	109,834	84.6
Missouri...........	242,557	50,414	20.8	192,143	79.2	207,496	40,205	19.4	167,291	80.6
North Dakota.......	27,971	3,910	14.0	24,061	86.0	28,145	4,546	16.2	23,599	83.8
South Dakota.......	29,483	5,231	17.7	24,252	82.3	27,936	4,588	16.4	23,348	83.6
Nebraska............	71,423	13,967	19.6	57,456	80.4	62,632	10,341	16.5	52,291	83.5
Kansas.............	92,116	19,476	21.1	72,640	78.9	79,826	16,044	20.1	63,782	79.9
SOUTH ATLANTIC:										
Delaware...........	17,947	4,413	24.6	13,534	75.4	17,037	4,272	25.1	12,765	74.9
Maryland...........	135,669	32,262	23.8	103,407	76.2	125,801	30,662	24.4	95,139	75.6
District of Columbia.	92,425	22,871	24.7	69,554	75.3	52,762	14,006	26.5	38,756	73.5
Virginia............	153,057	41,555	27.2	111,502	72.8	158,321	45,814	28.9	112,507	71.1
West Virginia.......	56,726	10,499	18.5	46,227	81.5	52,038	11,551	22.2	40,487	77.8
North Carolina......	187,546	60,951	32.5	126,595	67.5	231,002	86,507	37.4	144,495	62.6
South Carolina.....	185,754	79,526	42.8	106,228	57.2	226,843	110,293	48.6	116,550	51.4
Georgia.............	266,093	107,275	40.3	158,818	59.7	305,073	137,240	45.0	167,833	55.0
Florida............	83,357	35,312	42.4	48,045	57.6	67,093	30,488	45.4	36,605	54.6
E. SOUTH CENTRAL:										
Kentucky...........	128,969	31,280	24.3	97,689	75.7	140,242	37,873	27.0	102,369	73.0
Tennessee..........	145,655	44,262	30.4	101,393	69.6	158,147	54,596	34.5	103,551	65.5
Alabama...........	199,751	72,733	36.4	127,018	63.6	264,954	120,342	45.4	144,612	54.6
Mississippi.........	174,671	76,947	44.1	97,724	55.9	260,318	135,608	52.1	124,710	47.9
W. SOUTH CENTRAL:										
Arkansas...........	103,143	36,919	35.8	66,224	64.2	135,869	59,179	43.6	76,690	56.4
Louisiana..........	145,661	50,112	34.4	95,549	65.6	162,005	63,708	39.3	98,297	60.7
Oklahoma..........	90,148	26,953	29.9	63,195	70.1	69,856	23,090	33.1	46,766	66.9
Texas..............	284,152	87,029	30.6	197,123	69.4	280,184	105,287	37.6	174,897	62.4
MOUNTAIN:										
Montana............	28,186	6,508	23.1	21,678	76.9	18,700	4,235	22.6	14,465	77.4
Idaho..............	17,435	4,408	25.3	13,027	74.7	12,879	3,621	28.1	9,258	71.9
Wyoming...........	9,356	2,666	28.5	6,690	71.5	5,955	1,674	28.1	4,281	71.9
Colorado...........	62,180	14,462	23.3	47,718	76.7	53,004	12,211	23.0	40,793	77.0
New Mexico........	14,656	3,715	25.3	10,941	74.7	14,487	4,899	33.8	9,588	66.2
Arizona............	17,707	6,174	34.9	11,533	65.1	10,357	4,159	40.2	6,198	59.8
Utah...............	21,708	3,779	17.4	17,929	82.6	18,235	3,506	19.2	14,729	80.8
Nevada............	4,327	1,440	33.3	2,887	66.7	4,348	1,649	37.9	2,699	62.1
PACIFIC:										
Washington.........	92,612	24,172	26.1	68,440	73.9	65,771	14,356	21.8	51,415	78.2
Oregon.............	54,370	15,155	27.9	39,215	72.1	40,225	9,184	22.8	31,041	77.2
California..........	286,030	73,554	25.7	212,476	74.3	173,938	37,420	21.5	136,518	78.5

TABLE 46.—NUMBER AND PROPORTION OF MARRIED WOMEN 15 YEARS OF AGE AND

DIVISION AND STATE.	1920			1910		
	Total number.	Engaged in gainful occupations.		Total number.	Engaged in gainful occupations.	
		Number.	Per cent.		Number.	Per cent.
United States..........	21,318,933	1,920,281	9.0	17,684,687	1,890,661	10.7
GEOGRAPHIC DIVISIONS:						
New England..............	1,485,377	175,568	11.8	1,286,344	137,452	10.7
Middle Atlantic...........	4,518,248	348,128	7.7	3,774,008	280,550	7.4
East North Central........	4,545,175	282,285	6.2	3,704,975	192,518	5.2
West North Central.......	2,555,896	137,368	5.4	2,241,834	112,711	5.0
South Atlantic............	2,654,236	394,664	14.9	2,216,806	470,833	21.2
East South Central........	1,725,179	225,222	13.1	1,559,716	348,419	22.3
West South Central.......	1,988,774	201,013	10.1	1,614,155	251,264	15.6
Mountain.................	654,476	43,152	6.6	484,847	35,954	7.4
Pacific...................	1,191,572	112,881	9.5	802,002	60,960	7.6
NEW ENGLAND:						
Maine....................	162,623	16,288	10.0	156,535	14,281	9.1
New Hampshire...........	92,353	13,308	14.4	89,357	12,044	13.5
Vermont..................	74,505	6,011	8.1	75,681	6,724	8.9
Massachusetts............	758,897	96,496	12.7	644,531	74,815	11.6
Rhode Island.............	118,772	15,530	13.1	102,938	11,393	11.1
Connecticut..............	278,227	27,935	10.0	217,302	18,195	8.4
MIDDLE ATLANTIC:						
New York................	2,134,604	194,305	9.1	1,793,558	156,515	8.7
New Jersey...............	653,587	50,451	7.7	506,985	37,653	7.4
Pennsylvania.............	1,730,057	103,372	6.0	1,473,465	86,382	5.9
EAST NORTH CENTRAL:						
Ohio.....................	1,241,451	76,655	6.2	991,870	53,958	5.4
Indiana..................	650,187	34,848	5.4	576,524	26,433	4.6
Illinois..................	1,353,118	96,448	7.1	1,113,992	60,305	5.4
Michigan.................	782,648	52,097	6.7	587,253	31,414	5.3
Wisconsin................	517,771	22,237	4.3	435,336	20,408	4.7
WEST NORTH CENTRAL:						
Minnesota................	450,785	20,170	4.5	360,136	16,938	4.7
Iowa.....................	505,294	24,200	4.8	442,599	20,049	4.5
Missouri.................	724,886	50,414	7.0	660,819	40,205	6.1
North Dakota.............	113,843	3,910	3.4	98,370	4,546	4.6
South Dakota.............	121,408	5,231	4.3	105,949	4,588	4.3
Nebraska.................	263,890	13,967	5.3	230,441	10,341	4.5
Kansas...................	375,790	19,476	5.2	343,520	16,044	4.7
SOUTH ATLANTIC:						
Delaware.................	47,469	4,413	9.3	40,915	4,272	10.4
Maryland.................	294,043	32,262	11.0	247,837	30,662	12.4
District of Columbia.......	88,602	22,871	25.8	65,688	14,006	21.3
Virginia..................	432,557	41,555	9.6	366,488	45,814	12.5
West Virginia.............	280,811	10,499	3.7	225,691	11,551	5.1
North Carolina...........	460,742	60,951	13.2	386,528	86,507	22.4
South Carolina...........	298,648	79,526	26.6	263,611	110,293	41.8
Georgia..................	551,522	107,275	19.5	475,941	137,240	28.8
Florida..................	199,842	35,312	17.7	144,107	30,488	21.2
EAST SOUTH CENTRAL:						
Kentucky.................	481,060	31,280	6.5	436,478	37,873	8.7
Tennessee................	461,883	44,262	9.6	411,118	54,596	13.3
Alabama.................	440,207	72,733	16.5	388,191	120,342	31.0
Mississippi..............	342,029	76,947	22.5	323,929	135,608	41.9
WEST SOUTH CENTRAL:						
Arkansas.................	344,325	36,919	10.7	292,600	59,179	20.2
Louisiana................	338,897	50,112	14.8	290,536	63,708	21.9
Oklahoma................	402,863	26,953	6.7	317,450	23,090	7.3
Texas...................	902,689	87,029	9.6	713,569	105,287	14.8
MOUNTAIN:						
Montana.................	100,110	6,508	6.0	64,185	4,235	6.6
Idaho...................	84,554	4,408	5.2	58,904	3,621	6.1
Wyoming.................	38,172	2,666	7.0	24,199	1,074	4.0
Colorado.................	195,193	14,462	7.4	160,546	12,211	7.6
New Mexico..............	66,577	3,715	5.6	61,048	4,899	8.0
Arizona..................	63,685	6,174	9.7	35,601	4,159	11.7
Utah....................	83,713	3,779	4.5	66,255	3,506	5.3
Nevada..................	14,463	1,440	10.0	14,109	1,649	11.7
PACIFIC:						
Washington..............	287,871	24,172	8.4	214,653	14,356	6.7
Oregon..................	170,069	15,155	8.9	128,182	9,184	7.2
California...............	733,632	73,554	10.0	459,167	37,420	8.1

OVER ENGAGED IN GAINFUL OCCUPATIONS, BY DIVISIONS AND STATES: 1890–1920.

DIVISION AND STATE.	1900			1890		
	Total number.	Engaged in gainful occupations.		Total number.	Engaged in gainful occupations.	
		Number.	Per cent.		Number.	Per cent.
United States	13,810,057	769,477	5.6	11,124,785	515,260	4.6
GEOGRAPHIC DIVISIONS:						
New England	1,078,704	71,818	6.7	914,995	51,033	5.6
Middle Atlantic	2,923,463	115,549	4.0	2,378,820	74,530	3.1
East North Central	3,073,297	77,385	2.5	2,516,482	45,844	1.8
West North Central	1,879,354	48,868	2.6	1,581,777	32,199	2.0
South Atlantic	1,757,898	207,537	11.8	1,448,075	143,495	9.9
East South Central	1,282,274	136,806	10.7	1,055,338	93,737	8.9
West South Central	1,100,267	78,172	7.1	738,660	56,911	7.7
Mountain	292,622	14,452	4.9	187,347	6,440	3.4
Pacific	422,178	18,890	4.5	303,291	11,071	3.7
NEW ENGLAND:						
Maine	143,550	7,991	5.6	137,175	5,770	4.2
New Hampshire	84,475	7,783	9.2	78,522	5,941	7.6
Vermont	72,479	3,298	4.6	69,949	2,276	3.3
Massachusetts	524,893	38,555	7.3	421,254	27,145	6.4
Rhode Island	79,798	5,505	6.9	64,836	4,211	6.5
Connecticut	173,509	8,686	5.0	143,259	5,690	4.0
MIDDLE ATLANTIC:						
New York	1,393,915	66,090	4.7	1,149,954	42,968	3.7
New Jersey	364,239	15,112	4.1	276,336	9,249	3.3
Pennsylvania	1,165,309	34,347	2.9	952,530	22,313	2.3
EAST NORTH CENTRAL:						
Ohio	813,106	20,429	2.5	689,331	12,567	1.8
Indiana	501,303	11,556	2.3	413,501	6,685	1.6
Illinois	900,138	24,186	2.7	694,507	13,212	1.9
Michigan	487,297	13,911	2.9	416,295	8,839	2.1
Wisconsin	371,453	7,303	2.0	302,848	4,541	1.5
WEST NORTH CENTRAL:						
Minnesota	297,071	7,057	2.4	223,461	4,345	1.9
Iowa	419,512	9,583	2.3	349,971	5,380	1.5
Missouri	568,817	17,567	3.1	467,825	11,300	2.4
North Dakota	51,444	1,346	2.6	31,171	733	2.4
South Dakota	69,816	1,557	2.2	58,289	1,213	2.1
Nebraska	193,639	4,904	2.5	187,572	3,819	2.0
Kansas	279,055	6,854	2.5	263,488	5,409	2.1
SOUTH ATLANTIC:						
Delaware	34,955	1,855	5.3	31,191	1,201	3.9
Maryland	210,858	15,267	7.2	179,885	13,897	7.7
District of Columbia	50,378	8,840	17.5	39,674	6,879	17.3
Virginia	302,631	22,423	7.4	258,083	16,447	6.4
West Virginia	166,049	3,386	2.0	127,560	1,915	1.5
North Carolina	309,388	36,497	11.8	257,853	18,010	7.0
South Carolina	218,688	52,310	23.9	184,898	38,246	20.7
Georgia	373,122	56,643	15.2	301,935	39,540	13.1
Florida	91,829	10,316	11.2	66,996	7,360	11.0
EAST SOUTH CENTRAL:						
Kentucky	377,977	17,434	4.6	313,781	11,660	3.7
Tennessee	345,842	21,167	6.1	291,554	13,367	4.6
Alabama	304,038	49,089	16.1	245,861	30,440	12.4
Mississippi	254,417	49,116	19.3	204,142	38,270	18.7
WEST SOUTH CENTRAL:						
Arkansas	223,313	13,493	6.0	187,397	10,080	5.4
Louisiana	225,406	35,384	15.7	179,414	30,299	16.9
Oklahoma	141,220	3,658	2.6	11,241	153	1.4
Texas	510,328	25,637	5.0	360,608	16,379	4.5
MOUNTAIN:						
Montana	38,755	1,734	4.5	18,765	780	4.2
Idaho	26,882	905	3.4	12,985	415	3.2
Wyoming	14,033	541	3.9	8,777	266	3.0
Colorado	102,388	4,890	4.8	69,090	2,765	4.0
New Mexico	36,439	1,386	3.8	28,903	669	2.3
Arizona	20,390	2,697	13.2	8,759	302	3.4
Utah	46,888	1,732	3.7	33,788	905	2.7
Nevada	6,847	567	8.3	6,280	338	5.4
PACIFIC:						
Washington	89,151	3,869	4.3	56,370	1,979	3.5
Oregon	72,750	2,825	3.9	52,308	1,531	2.9
California	260,277	12,196	4.7	194,613	7,561	3.9

TABLE 47.—NUMBER AND PROPORTION OF MARRIED WOMEN 15 YEARS OF AGE AND OCCUPATIONS, BY

	DIVISION AND STATE.	NATIVE WHITE—NATIVE PARENTAGE.			NATIVE WHITE—FOREIGN OR MIXED PARENTAGE.		
		Total number.	Engaged in gainful occupations.		Total number.	Engaged in gainful occupations.	
			Number.	Per cent.		Number.	Per cent.
1	United States...........	11,195,865	707,503	6.3	3,890,870	245,311	6.3
	GEOGRAPHIC DIVISIONS:						
2	New England..............	534,679	53,955	10.1	331,003	40,863	12.3
3	Middle Atlantic............	1,852,408	128,914	7.0	987,130	62,990	6.4
4	East North Central.........	2,292,058	131,837	5.8	1,156,234	60,811	5.3
5	West North Central.......	1,379,396	75,291	5.5	702,907	29,359	4.2
6	South Atlantic.............	1,669,800	111,538	6.7	98,424	6,754	6.9
7	East South Central.........	1,174,207	54,980	4.7	46,344	2,205	4.8
8	West South Central........	1,331,436	68,620	5.2	130,912	7,991	6.1
9	Mountain..................	364,567	23,592	6.5	150,620	8,760	5.8
10	Pacific....................	597,314	58,776	9.8	287,296	25,578	8.9
	NEW ENGLAND:						
11	Maine.....................	105,396	9,793	9.3	23,188	2,665	11.5
12	New Hampshire............	46,867	5,270	11.2	16,667	2,844	17.1
13	Vermont...................	46,303	3,870	8.4	14,758	1,292	8.8
14	Massachusetts.............	220,932	24,173	10.9	182,000	23,522	12.9
15	Rhode Island..............	30,374	3,136	10.3	30,269	4,208	13.9
16	Connecticut...............	84,807	7,713	9.1	64,121	6,332	9.9
	MIDDLE ATLANTIC:						
17	New York.................	692,314	62,953	9.1	528,974	40,166	7.6
18	New Jersey................	233,470	13,866	5.9	149,351	9,012	6.0
19	Pennsylvania..............	926,624	52,095	5.6	308,805	13,812	4.5
	EAST NORTH CENTRAL:						
20	Ohio......................	756,513	41,093	5.4	242,606	11,589	4.8
21	Indiana...................	503,009	24,839	4.9	86,285	3,494	4.0
22	Illinois...................	573,176	34,380	6.0	364,441	23,372	6.4
23	Michigan..................	319,367	24,690	7.7	226,386	13,009	5.7
24	Wisconsin.................	139,993	6,835	4.9	236,516	9,347	4.0
	WEST NORTH CENTRAL:						
25	Minnesota.................	109,161	6,292	5.8	193,538	8,339	4.3
26	Iowa......................	284,197	15,533	5.5	151,068	5,637	3.7
27	Missouri..................	511,735	27,915	5.5	123,177	6,521	5.3
28	North Dakota.............	27,726	1,494	5.4	43,326	1,476	3.4
29	South Dakota.............	47,389	2,745	5.8	45,430	1,710	3.8
30	Nebraska..................	135,106	8,003	5.9	79,330	3,208	4.0
31	Kansas....................	264,082	13,309	5.0	67,038	2,468	3.7
	SOUTH ATLANTIC:						
32	Delaware..................	30,292	1,709	5.6	5,219	295	5.7
33	Maryland.................	174,908	8,979	5.1	39,635	2,042	5.2
34	District of Columbia.......	46,059	8,558	18.6	11,201	1,651	14.7
35	Virginia..................	290,007	12,236	4.2	8,650	537	6.2
36	West Virginia.............	236,389	7,281	3.1	11,960	396	3.3
37	North Carolina............	324,426	24,327	7.5	2,040	135	6.6
38	South Carolina............	145,679	17,215	11.8	2,255	127	5.6
39	Georgia...................	313,576	24,432	7.8	5,636	386	6.8
40	Florida...................	108,464	6,801	6.3	11,828	1,185	10.0
	EAST SOUTH CENTRAL:						
41	Kentucky..................	397,984	13,636	3.4	27,570	1,174	4.3
42	Tennessee.:..............	359,211	15,157	4.2	8,213	433	5.3
43	Alabama..................	262,307	16,483	6.3	6,637	349	5.3
44	Mississippi...............	154,705	9,704	6.3	3,924	249	6.3
	WEST SOUTH CENTRAL:						
45	Arkansas..................	236,299	11,674	4.9	8,419	448	5.3
46	Louisiana.................	168,859	7,030	4.2	21,660	1,054	4.9
47	Oklahoma.................	330,520	18,359	5.6	23,104	1,306	5.7
48	Texas....................	595,758	31,557	5.3	77,729	5,183	6.7
	MOUNTAIN:						
49	Montana..................	50,029	3,391	6.8	30,508	1,845	6.0
50	Idaho.....................	52,351	2,888	5.5	20,948	984	4.7
51	Wyoming..................	23,042	1,692	7.3	8,388	538	6.4
52	Colorado..................	120,254	9,006	7.5	39,208	2,797	7.1
53	New Mexico...............	50,508	2,149	4.3	5,127	314	6.1
54	Arizona...................	28,758	2,153	7.5	9,465	665	7.0
55	Utah......................	33,200	1,671	5.0	32,970	1,259	3.8
56	Nevada...................	6,425	642	10.0	4,006	358	8.9
	PACIFIC:						
57	Washington...............	144,170	13,044	9.0	69,321	5,782	8.3
58	Oregon....................	104,569	9,796	9.4	36,061	3,206	8.9
59	California.................	348,575	35,936	10.3	181,914	16,590	9.1

¹ Per cent not shown where base is less than 100.

OVER, IN EACH PRINCIPAL CLASS OF THE POPULATION, ENGAGED IN GAINFUL DIVISIONS AND STATES: 1920.

FOREIGN-BORN WHITE.			NEGRO.			INDIAN, CHINESE, JAPANESE, AND ALL OTHER.			
Total number.	Engaged in gainful occupations.		Total number.	Engaged in gainful occupations.		Total number.	Engaged in gainful occupations.		
	Number.	Per cent.		Number.	Per cent.		Number.	Per cent.	
4,123,503	296,126	7.2	2,039,181	662,684	32.5	69,514	8,657	12.5	1
603,268	75,446	12.5	15,954	5,205	32.6	473	99	20.9	2
1,541,876	107,143	6.9	135,197	48,833	36.1	1,637	248	15.1	3
974,174	56,092	5.8	119,604	33,328	27.9	3,105	217	7.0	4
404,122	14,434	3.6	62,061	18,112	29.2	7,410	172	2.3	5
86,322	6,986	8.1	797,273	269,074	33.7	2,417	312	12.9	6
17,907	1,243	6.9	486,417	166,730	34.3	304	64	21.1	7
109,951	7,664	7.0	406,214	116,388	28.7	10,261	350	3.4	8
117,521	6,649	5.7	5,645	1,600	28.3	16,123	2,551	15.8	9
268,362	20,469	7.6	10,816	3,414	31.6	27,784	4,644	16.7	10
33,639	3,742	11.1	228	43	18.9	172	45	26.2	11
28,701	5,172	18.0	108	17	15.7	10	5	(1)	12
13,353	822	6.2	88	25	(1)	3	2	(1)	13
346,595	45,935	13.3	9,159	2,831	30.9	211	35	16.6	14
56,189	7,624	13.6	1,913	558	29.2	27	4	(1)	15
124,791	12,151	9.7	4,458	1,731	38.8	50	8	(1)	16
866,376	70,860	8.2	45,512	20,112	44.2	1,428	214	15.0	17
244,684	18,708	7.6	26,001	8,850	34.0	81	15	(1)	18
430,816	17,575	4.1	63,684	19,871	31.2	128	19	14.8	19
199,510	12,120	6.1	42,745	11,835	27.7	77	18	(1)	20
42,614	1,605	3.8	18,254	4,907	26.9	25	3	(1)	21
372,439	25,758	6.9	42,872	12,906	30.1	190	32	16.8	22
221,204	10,872	4.9	14,622	3,427	23.4	1,069	99	9.3	23
138,407	5,737	4.1	1,111	253	22.8	1,744	65	3.7	24
144,330	4,921	3.4	2,063	553	26.8	1,693	65	3.8	25
65,639	1,978	3.0	4,279	1,046	24.4	111	6	5.4	26
50,142	3,154	6.3	39,772	12,811	32.2	60	13	(1)	27
41,525	916	2.2	85	11	(1)	1,181	13	1.1	28
25,052	697	2.8	146	43	29.5	3,391	36	1.1	29
45,623	1,758	3.9	3,125	979	31.3	706	19	2.7	30
31,811	1,010	3.2	12,591	2,669	21.2	268	20	7.5	31
5,959	308	5.2	5,998	2,101	35.0	1			32
30,757	1,955	6.4	48,723	19,281	39.6	20	5	(1)	33
7,618	877	11.5	23,686	11,779	49.7	38	6	(1)	34
8,201	495	6.0	125,550	28,278	22.5	149	9	6.0	35
14,801	485	3.3	17,652	2,335	13.2	9	2	(1)	36
1,734	123	7.1	130,537	36,095	27.7	2,005	271	13.5	37
1,468	137	9.3	149,187	62,039	41.6	59	8	(1)	38
3,932	337	8.6	228,351	82,114	36.0	27	6	(1)	39
11,852	2,269	19.1	67,589	25,052	37.1	109	5	4.6	40
7,148	366	5.1	48,345	16,098	33.3	13	6	(1)	41
3,996	306	7.7	90,448	28,365	31.4	15	1	(1)	42
4,765	298	6.3	166,443	55,600	33.4	55	3	(1)	43
1,998	273	13.7	181,181	66,667	36.8	221	54	24.4	44
3,461	247	7.1	96,121	24,549	25.5	25	1	(1)	45
10,740	742	6.9	137,442	41,274	30.0	196	12	6.1	46
10,626	508	4.8	29,013	6,495	22.4	9,600	285	3.0	47
85,124	6,167	7.2	143,638	44,070	30.7	440	52	11.8	48
24,805	1,145	4.6	347	68	19.6	2,430	59	2.4	49
10,092	446	4.4	189	36	19.0	974	54	5.5	50
6,010	305	5.1	279	103	36.9	453	28	6.2	51
32,402	1,842	5.7	2,577	765	29.7	752	52	6.9	52
7,055	261	3.7	648	172	26.5	3,239	819	25.3	53
18,030	1,753	9.7	1,160	336	29.0	6,272	1,267	20.2	54
16,293	686	4.2	368	81	22.0	882	82	9.3	55
2,834	211	7.4	77	39	(1)	1,121	190	16.9	56
67,306	4,096	6.1	1,545	441	28.5	5,529	809	14.6	57
27,190	1,788	6.6	511	168	32.9	1,738	197	11.3	58
173,866	14,585	8.4	8,760	2,805	32.0	20,517	3,638	17.7	59

TABLE 48.—NUMBER AND PROPORTION OF WOMEN 15 YEARS OF AGE AND OVER, IN EACH SPECIFIED MARITAL CLASS, ENGAGED IN GAINFUL OCCUPATIONS, FOR CITIES HAVING 100,000 INHABITANTS OR MORE: 1920.

CITY.	AGGREGATE.			MARRIED.			SINGLE, WIDOWED, DIVORCED, AND UNKNOWN.		
	Total number.	Engaged in gainful occupations.		Total number.	Engaged in gainful occupations.		Total number.	Engaged in gainful occupations.	
		Number.	Per cent.		Number.	Per cent.		Number.	Per cent.
Akron, Ohio	62,699	15,997	25.5	42,734	4,282	10.0	19,965	11,715	58.7
Albany, N. Y	46,117	14,475	31.4	22,530	1,311	5.8	23,587	13,164	55.8
Atlanta, Ga	78,161	31,950	40.9	44,425	11,112	25.0	33,736	20,838	61.8
Baltimore, Md	274,258	91,732	33.4	152,688	20,957	13.7	121,570	70,775	58.2
Birmingham, Ala	64,178	19,921	31.0	39,049	6,523	16.7	25,129	13,398	53.3
Boston, Mass	280,922	103,783	36.9	137,853	13,583	9.9	143,069	90,200	63.0
Bridgeport, Conn	48,443	15,345	31.7	29,741	3,669	12.3	18,702	11,676	62.4
Buffalo, N. Y	182,246	49,796	27.3	104,353	5,166	5.0	77,893	44,630	57.3
Cambridge, Mass	42,479	15,888	37.4	20,658	2,220	10.7	21,821	13,668	62.6
Camden, N. J	39,535	10,667	27.0	25,128	2,217	8.8	14,407	8,450	58.7
Chicago, Ill	956,800	309,089	32.3	560,645	58,438	10.4	396,155	250,651	63.3
Cincinnati, Ohio	160,893	50,344	31.3	84,733	8,403	9.9	76,160	41,941	55.1
Cleveland, Ohio	266,322	73,425	27.6	168,144	16,153	9.6	98,178	57,272	58.3
Columbus, Ohio	90,919	25,458	28.0	52,357	5,445	10.4	38,562	20,013	51.9
Dallas, Tex	60,572	21,677	35.8	35,146	6,845	19.5	25,426	14,832	58.3
Dayton, Ohio	56,493	15,015	26.6	34,904	3,140	9.0	21,589	11,875	55.0
Denver, Colo	97,101	28,864	29.7	54,996	6,205	11.3	42,105	22,659	53.8
Des Moines, Iowa	48,449	15,322	31.6	28,263	3,554	12.6	20,186	11,768	58.3
Detroit, Mich	319,853	83,596	26.1	209,219	17,105	8.2	110,634	66,491	60.1
Fall River, Mass	43,002	19,882	46.2	22,376	5,489	24.5	20,626	14,393	69.8
Fort Worth, Tex	37,396	10,658	28.5	23,253	3,408	14.7	14,143	7,250	51.3
Grand Rapids, Mich	50,857	15,042	29.6	30,200	3,045	10.1	20,657	11,997	58.1
Hartford, Conn	50,298	17,483	34.8	27,885	3,183	11.4	22,413	14,300	63.8
Houston, Tex	51,806	17,065	32.9	31,211	5,787	18.5	20,595	11,278	54.8
Indianapolis, Ind	121,688	35,971	29.6	73,583	8,876	12.1	48,105	27,095	56.3
Jersey City, N. J	102,266	29,565	28.9	58,551	3,467	5.9	43,715	26,098	59.7
Kansas City, Kans	34,979	9,174	26.2	22,749	2,499	11.0	12,230	6,675	54.6
Kansas City, Mo	127,444	40,196	31.5	75,256	10,347	13.7	52,188	29,849	57.2
Los Angeles, Calif	233,883	68,299	29.2	132,890	18,174	13.7	100,993	50,125	49.6
Louisville, Ky	94,544	34,010	36.0	49,685	8,078	16.3	44,859	25,932	57.8
Lowell, Mass	42,212	18,128	42.9	21,353	4,458	20.9	20,859	13,670	65.5
Memphis, Tenn	64,269	23,986	37.3	36,279	7,717	21.3	27,990	16,269	58.1
Milwaukee, Wis	164,908	50,740	30.8	94,036	6,370	6.8	70,872	44,370	62.6
Minneapolis, Minn	144,582	46,641	32.3	80,173	6,441	8.0	64,409	40,200	62.4
Nashville, Tenn	47,014	17,799	37.9	25,151	5,347	21.3	21,863	12,452	57.0
New Bedford, Mass	43,845	20,384	46.5	24,592	7,200	29.3	19,253	13,184	68.5
New Haven, Conn	57,912	18,721	32.3	32,171	2,844	8.8	25,741	15,877	61.7
New Orleans, La	146,515	49,229	33.6	74,831	12,375	16.5	71,684	36,854	51.4
New York, N. Y	2,026,797	689,261	34.0	1,115,670	107,315	9.6	911,127	581,946	63.9
Bronx borough	260,085	77,409	29.8	152,172	9,485	6.2	107,913	67,924	62.9
Brooklyn borough	707,341	214,158	30.3	399,517	26,717	6.7	307,824	187,441	60.9
Manhattan borough	855,130	341,573	39.9	441,585	63,012	14.3	413,545	278,561	67.4
Queens borough	166,545	46,539	27.9	100,679	7,063	7.0	65,866	39,476	59.9
Richmond borough	37,696	9,582	25.4	21,717	1,038	4.8	15,979	8,544	53.5
Newark, N. J	143,424	41,785	29.1	84,071	5,728	6.8	59,353	36,057	60.8
Norfolk, Va	41,555	14,530	35.0	25,306	5,128	20.3	16,249	9,402	57.9
Oakland, Calif	79,813	20,099	25.2	47,873	4,820	10.1	31,940	15,279	47.8
Omaha, Nebr	68,516	21,004	30.7	40,719	4,759	11.7	27,797	16,245	58.4
Paterson, N. J	49,605	18,601	37.5	27,887	4,243	15.2	21,718	14,358	66.1
Philadelphia, Pa	667,074	214,232	32.1	373,687	37,402	10.0	293,387	176,830	60.3
Pittsburgh, Pa	206,266	57,460	27.9	115,400	6,968	6.0	90,866	50,492	55.6
Portland, Oreg	96,540	28,451	29.5	58,553	7,423	12.7	37,987	21,028	55.4
Providence, R. I	89,342	32,929	36.9	46,225	5,433	11.8	43,117	27,496	63.8
Reading, Pa	39,824	13,339	33.5	23,648	3,312	14.0	16,176	10,027	62.0
Richmond, Va	67,978	26,429	38.9	35,171	6,985	19.9	32,807	19,444	59.3
Rochester, N. Y	111,108	37,505	33.8	62,523	7,587	12.1	48,585	29,918	61.6
St. Louis, Mo	299,442	98,011	33.0	165,846	18,623	11.2	133,596	80,291	60.1
St. Paul, Minn	67,005	28,051	32.1	47,815	3,000	7.7	39,480	24,352	61.7
Salt Lake City, Utah	41,288	10,060	24.4	24,381	1,769	7.3	16,907	8,292	48.0
San Antonio, Tex	57,986	16,659	28.7	32,539	4,003	12.3	25,447	12,656	49.7
San Francisco, Calif	185,109	60,835	32.9	100,816	13,189	13.1	84,293	47,646	56.5
Scranton, Pa	47,492	13,189	27.8	25,807	671	2.6	21,685	12,518	57.7
Seattle, Wash	113,606	33,114	29.1	70,054	8,203	11.7	43,552	24,911	57.2
Spokane, Wash	39,214	11,093	28.3	23,444	2,676	11.4	15,770	8,417	53.4
Springfield, Mass	49,027	17,173	35.0	27,349	3,768	13.8	21,678	13,405	61.8
Syracuse, N. Y	64,035	18,674	29.2	37,461	3,369	9.0	26,574	15,305	57.6
Toledo, Ohio	86,698	23,226	26.8	53,870	4,834	9.0	32,828	18,392	56.0
Trenton, N. J	40,773	11,606	28.5	24,342	2,032	8.3	16,431	9,574	58.3
Washington, D. C	188,466	92,425	49.0	88,602	22,871	25.8	99,864	69,554	69.6
Wilmington, Del	38,731	11,658	30.1	23,019	2,636	11.5	15,712	9,022	57.4
Worcester, Mass	64,823	20,817	32.1	35,426	2,873	• 8.1	29,397	17,944	61.0
Yonkers, N. Y	35,697	11,184	31.3	19,935	1,626	8.2	15,762	9,558	60.6
Youngstown, Ohio	41,248	8,627	20.9	26,984	1,387	5.1	14,264	7,240	50.8

TABLE 49.—NUMBER AND PROPORTION OF MARRIED WOMEN 15 YEARS OF AGE AND OVER, IN EACH PRINCIPAL CLASS OF THE POPULATION, ENGAGED IN GAINFUL OCCUPATIONS, FOR CITIES HAVING 100,000 INHABITANTS OR MORE: 1920.

CITY.	NATIVE WHITE—NATIVE PARENTAGE.			NATIVE WHITE—FOREIGN OR MIXED PARENTAGE.			FOREIGN-BORN WHITE.			NEGRO.		
	Total number.	Engaged in gainful occupations.		Total number.	Engaged in gainful occupations.		Total number.	Engaged in gainful occupations.		Total number.	Engaged in gainful occupations.	
		Number.	Per cent.		Number.	Per cent.		Number.	Per cent.		Number.	Per cent.
Akron, Ohio	24,975	2,658	10.6	6,771	458	6.8	9,788	803	8.2	1,199	363	30.3
Albany, N.Y.	9,983	640	6.4	7,286	389	5.3	5,007	228	4.6	252	54	21.4
Atlanta, Ga.	27,149	3,278	12.1	1,615	117	7.2	1,328	84	6.3	14,333	7,633	53.3
Baltimore, Md.	73,045	4,970	6.8	29,725	1,681	5.7	25,690	1,736	6.8	24,213	12,566	51.9
Birmingham, Ala.	19,583	1,302	6.6	1,670	87	5.2	1,776	99	5.6	16,020	5,035	31.4
Boston, Mass.	26,840	3,401	12.7	34,927	3,302	9.5	72,526	5,743	7.9	3,496	1,131	32.4
Bridgeport, Conn.	6,958	918	13.2	6,936	769	11.1	15,332	1,792	11.7	514	190	37.0
Buffalo, N.Y.	28,323	1,726	6.1	37,223	1,546	4.2	37,678	1,625	4.3	1,105	263	23.8
Cambridge, Mass.	4,606	483	10.5	4,782	498	10.4	10,123	940	9.3	1,139	296	26.0
Camden, N.J.	11,623	928	8.0	4,865	306	6.3	6,737	419	6.2	1,902	564	29.7
Chicago, Ill.	106,190	12,905	12.2	173,778	15,522	8.9	253,443	20,521	8.1	27,084	9,463	34.9
Cincinnati, Ohio	37,532	3,072	8.2	28,511	1,499	5.3	11,294	882	7.8	7,388	2,947	39.9
Cleveland, Ohio	39,398	4,252	10.8	44,073	3,153	7.2	75,960	5,993	7.9	8,696	2,752	31.6
Columbus, Ohio	33,896	3,048	9.0	9,068	553	6.1	4,220	245	5.8	5,167	1,598	30.9
Dallas, Tex.	24,354	3,336	13.7	2,902	270	9.3	2,202	171	7.8	5,679	3,065	54.0
Dayton, Ohio	22,044	1,701	7.7	6,844	304	4.4	3,825	341	8.9	2,187	793	36.3
Denver, Colo.	28,920	3,566	12.3	14,201	1,394	9.8	10,366	751	7.2	1,428	485	34.0
Des Moines, Iowa	18,017	2,357	13.1	5,704	564	9.9	3,205	214	6.7	1,336	418	31.3
Detroit, Mich.	58,703	5,926	10.1	57,453	3,951	6.9	82,713	4,588	5.5	10,294	2,627	25.5
Fall River, Mass.	2,403	334	13.9	6,200	1,537	24.8	13,703	3,583	26.1	68	34	(1)
Fort Worth, Tex.	16,386	1,641	10.0	1,536	112	7.3	1,560	118	7.6	3,765	1,536	40.8
Grand Rapids, Mich.	10,767	1,442	13.4	10,015	852	8.5	9,157	689	7.5	257	62	24.1
Hartford, Conn.	7,397	948	12.8	6,703	726	10.8	12,838	1,097	8.5	941	412	43.8
Houston, Tex.	15,470	1,525	9.9	4,373	285	6.5	3,200	207	6.5	8,160	3,765	46.1
Indianapolis, Ind.	50,023	5,307	10.6	10,625	708	6.7	4,690	287	6.1	8,243	2,572	31.2
Jersey City, N.J.	13,173	815	6.2	18,396	949	5.2	25,120	1,270	5.1	1,859	433	23.3
Kansas City, Kans.	12,376	1,184	9.6	3,534	282	8.0	3,341	236	7.1	3,493	796	22.8
Kansas City, Mo.	47,398	6,099	12.9	12,958	1,135	8.8	7,467	470	6.3	7,420	2,639	35.6
Los Angeles, Calif.	66,613	9,263	13.9	29,959	3,659	12.2	29,806	3,188	10.7	3,800	1,430	37.6
Louisville, Ky.	26,861	2,385	8.9	10,903	547	5.0	2,935	174	5.9	8,983	4,969	55.3
Lowell, Mass.	3,840	546	14.2	5,602	1,066	19.0	11,876	2,840	23.9	32	6	(1)
Memphis, Tenn.	17,596	1,731	9.8	2,678	165	6.2	1,525	113	7.4	14,475	5,707	39.4
Milwaukee, Wis.	17,603	1,390	7.9	43,124	2,591	6.0	32,760	2,259	6.9	541	127	23.5
Minneapolis, Minn.	22,965	2,215	9.6	30,471	2,481	8.1	25,770	1,462	5.7	943	279	29.6
Nashville, Tenn.	15,284	1,483	9.7	1,413	76	5.4	612	50	8.2	7,842	3,738	47.7
New Bedford, Mass.	3,619	495	13.7	4,923	1,346	27.3	15,157	5,123	33.8	890	236	26.5
New Haven, Conn.	8,026	767	9.6	8,114	651	8.0	15,018	1,068	7.1	1,005	357	35.5
New Orleans, La.	32,189	1,996	6.2	15,384	802	5.2	5,308	397	7.5	21,931	9,178	41.8
New York, N.Y.	183,567	18,558	10.1	278,650	21,928	7.9	617,211	50,134	8.1	35,795	16,623	46.4
Bronx borough	19,948	1,616	8.1	41,431	2,554	6.2	89,827	4,999	5.6	954	312	32.7
Brooklyn borough	71,406	5,924	8.3	107,236	6,871	6.4	213,615	11,233	5.3	7,212	2,680	37.2
Manhattan borough	63,204	9,148	14.5	86,001	9,968	11.6	265,819	30,716	11.6	26,194	13,122	50.1
Queens borough	23,270	1,587	6.8	37,788	2,247	5.9	38,465	2,796	7.3	1,137	433	38.1
Richmond borough	5,739	283	4.9	6,194	288	4.6	9,485	390	4.1	298	76	25.5
Newark, N.J.	19,948	1,467	7.4	21,513	1,220	5.7	38,524	1,794	4.7	4,075	1,244	30.5
Norfolk, Va.	12,741	1,053	8.3	1,250	121	9.7	1,556	132	8.5	9,753	3,821	39.2
Oakland, Calif.	18,255	2,057	11.3	15,009	1,308	8.7	12,477	1,013	8.1	1,230	238	19.3
Omaha, Nebr.	16,896	2,146	12.7	10,962	1,076	9.8	10,319	695	6.7	2,527	841	33.3
Paterson, N.J.	5,466	717	13.1	7,357	1,086	14.8	14,711	2,288	15.6	351	152	43.3
Philadelphia, Pa.	128,726	11,054	8.6	87,178	6,298	7.2	125,730	7,502	6.0	31,992	12,538	39.2
Pittsburgh, Pa.	37,326	2,135	5.7	32,218	1,199	3.7	36,907	1,385	3.8	8,931	2,246	25.1
Portland, Oreg.	30,132	4,404	14.6	14,919	1,745	11.7	12,600	1,066	8.5	414	134	32.4
Providence, R.I.	10,946	1,300	11.9	11,960	1,486	12.4	22,213	2,283	10.3	1,094	362	33.1
Reading, Pa.	18,053	2,648	14.7	2,477	314	12.7	2,920	296	10.1	198	54	27.3
Richmond, Va.	20,587	1,511	7.3	1,960	108	5.5	1,285	89	6.9	11,335	5,276	46.5
Rochester, N.Y.	20,846	2,989	14.3	19,159	2,065	10.8	22,115	2,382	10.8	398	149	37.4
St. Louis, Mo.	65,681	6,952	10.6	55,370	3,586	6.5	28,131	2,072	7.4	16,644	6,008	36.1
St. Paul, Minn.	11,623	1,129	9.7	20,313	1,475	7.3	15,043	883	5.9	818	209	25.6
Salt Lake City, Utah	8,953	781	8.7	9,322	565	6.1	5,828	341	5.9	187	55	29.4
San Antonio, Tex.	15,032	1,333	8.9	6,202	431	6.9	8,010	657	8.2	3,282	1,581	48.2
San Francisco, Calif.	29,333	4,590	15.7	35,719	4,003	11.2	33,441	4,056	12.1	493	199	40.4
Scranton, Pa.	7,533	257	3.4	8,799	242	2.8	9,353	149	1.6	122	23	18.9
Seattle, Wash.	29,925	3,903	13.0	18,284	2,057	11.3	19,230	1,625	8.5	695	236	34.0
Spokane, Wash.	12,016	1,518	12.6	6,507	687	10.6	4,695	402	8.6	182	60	33.0
Springfield, Mass.	9,674	1,369	14.2	7,112	996	14.0	9,969	1,142	11.5	588	260	44.2
Syracuse, N.Y.	16,300	1,831	11.2	10,710	854	8.0	10,153	597	5.9	283	84	29.7
Toledo, Ohio	25,485	2,604	10.2	15,765	1,137	7.2	11,203	695	6.2	1,412	396	28.0
Trenton, N.J.	8,839	672	7.6	4,823	329	6.8	9,746	689	7.1	933	342	36.7
Washington, D.C.	46,059	8,558	18.6	11,201	1,651	14.7	7,618	877	11.5	23.686	11,779	49.7
Wilmington, Del.	11,943	964	8.1	3,890	249	6.4	4,916	279	5.7	2,269	1,144	50.4
Worcester, Mass.	8,781	867	9.9	9,079	849	9.4	17,287	1,063	6.1	265	92	34.7
Yonkers, N.Y.	5,175	334	6.5	5,574	375	6.7	8,771	738	8.4	411	177	43.1
Youngstown, Ohio	9,023	553	6.1	6,667	255	3.8	9,730	359	3.7	1,563	220	14.1

1 Per cent not shown where base is less than 100.

AGRICULTURE

(575)

CONTENTS.

Page.

DEFINITIONS AND EXPLANATION OF TERMS 581

GENERAL INFORMATION.

FARMS AND FARM PROPERTY.

Table.

1. Population, farms, and farm property in the United States: 1920 and 1910 583
2. Population, farms, and farm property in the United States: 1850 to 1920 584
3. Farm population and total population, by divisions and states: 1920 585
4. Farm population, by age and sex, by divisions and states: 1920 586
5. Farm population, by race, nativity, and parentage, by divisions and states: 1920 587
6. Population, number of farms, and farm acreage, by divisions and states: 1920 and 1910 588
7. Population, number of farms, and farm acreage, by divisions and states: 1850 to 1920 590
8. Value of all farm property and of the several classes, by divisions and states: 1920 and 1910 600
9. Value of all farm property and of the several classes, by divisions: 1850 to 1920 602
10. Per cent distribution of farms, farm land, and value of farm property, by divisions and states: 1920 and 1910 604
11. Average acreage per farm, per cent of farm land improved, and average value of farm property per acre, by divisions and states: 1920 and 1910 605

SIZE OF FARMS.

12. Number of farms in the United States, with per cent distribution, by size: 1880 to 1920 606
13. Farm acreage, with per cent distribution and percentage of farm land improved, by size of farm, for the United States: 1920 and 1910 606
14. Value of farm property in the United States, by size of farm: 1920 and 1910 607
15. Farms and farm acreage, and value of farm property, by classes, by size of farm, by divisions and states: 1920 and 1910 608

FARM TENURE.

16. Number and acreage of farms in the United States, by tenure: 1920 and 1910 626
17. Percentage of farm land improved, average acreage per farm, and per cent distribution, by tenure, for the United States: 1920 and 1910 626
18. Number of farms in the United States, with per cent distribution, by tenure: 1880 to 1920 627
19. Number and acreage of farms in the South, with averages and percentages, by tenure: 1920 627
20. Value of farm property in the United States, by tenure: 1920 and 1910 628
21. Value of farm property in the South, by tenure: 1920 629
22. Average value of farm property per farm and per acre, by tenure, for the United States: 1920 and 1910 629
23. Number of farms, with per cent distribution, by tenure, by divisions and states: 1920 and 1910 ... 630
24. Tenant farms classified according to form of tenancy, by divisions and states: 1920 and 1910 632
25. Acreage of farm land, with percentages and averages, by tenure, by divisions and states: 1920 and 1910 634
26. Value of all farm property and of the several classes, by tenure, by divisions and states: 1920 and 1910 640
27. Average value of land and buildings per farm, by tenure, by divisions and states: 1920 and 1910 . 650
28. Average value of land and buildings per acre, by tenure, by divisions and states: 1920 and 1910 . 651

COLOR AND TENURE OF FARMERS.

29. Number and acreage of farms in the United States, by color and tenure: 1920 and 1910 652
30. Percentage of farm land improved, average acreage per farm, and per cent distribution, by color and tenure, for the United States: 1920 and 1910 653
31. Number of farms in the United States, with per cent distribution, by color and tenure: 1900 to 1920 . 653
32. Number and acreage of farms in the South, with averages and percentages, by color and tenure: 1920 654
33. Number of farms in the South, with per cent distribution, by color and tenure: 1900 to 1920 654
34. Value of farm property in the United States, by color and tenure: 1920 and 1910 655
35. Value of farm property in the South, by color and tenure: 1920 656
36. Average value of farm property per farm and per acre, by color and tenure, for the United States: 1920 and 1910 657
37. Number of farms, by color and tenure, with per cent distribution by tenure, by divisions and states: 1920 and 1910 660
38. Farms operated by white and colored tenants classified according to form of tenancy, by divisions and states: 1920 and 1910 664
39. Acreage of farm land, with percentages and averages, by color and tenure, by divisions and states: 1920 and 1910 670
40. Value of all farm property and of the several classes, by color and tenure, by divisions and states: 1920 and 1910 682
41. Average value of land and buildings per farm, by color and tenure, by divisions and states: 1920 and 1910 704
42. Average value of land and buildings per acre, by color and tenure, by divisions and states: 1920 and 1910 706

(576)

CONTENTS.

CONTENTS.

578

CROPS AND MISCELLANEOUS PRODUCTS.

ACREAGE, PRODUCTION, AND VALUE OF ALL CROPS.

CONTENTS.

580

AGRICULTURE.

DEFINITIONS AND EXPLANATIONS OF TERMS.

Farm.—A "farm" for census purposes is all the land which is directly farmed by one person managing and conducting agricultural operations, either by his own labor alone or with the assistance of members of his household or hired employees. The term "agricultural operations" is used as a general term, referring to the work of growing crops, producing other agricultural products, and raising domestic animals, poultry, and bees. A "farm" as thus defined may consist of a single tract of land or of a number of separate and distinct tracts, and these several tracts may be held under different tenures, as where one tract is owned by the farmer and another tract is hired by him. When a landowner has one or more tenants, renters, croppers, or managers, the land operated by each is considered a "farm."

In applying the foregoing definition of a "farm" for census purposes, enumerators were instructed to report as a "farm" any tract of 3 or more acres used for agricultural purposes, and also any tract containing less than 3 acres which produced at least $250 worth of farm products in the year 1919, or required for its agricultural operations the continuous services of at least one person.

Farm population—definition.—The farm population, as the term is here used, includes all persons actually living on farms, without regard to occupation, and also those farm laborers (and their families) who, while not living on a farm, nevertheless live in strictly rural territory, outside the limits of any village or other incorporated place.

Farmer.—A "farmer" or "farm operator," according to the census definition, is a person who directs the operation of a farm. The number of farmers shown by the census of agriculture is, therefore, the same as the number of farms. Owners of farms who do not themselves direct the farm operations are not reported as farmers.

Tenure classification.—Farm operators are classified according to tenure as follows:

Farm owners include (1) farmers operating their own land only and (2) those operating both their own land and some land hired from others. The latter are sometimes referred to in the census reports as "part owners," the term "full owners" being used for those owning all the land which they operate.

Managers are farmers who are conducting farm operations for the owner for wages or a salary.

Farm tenants are farmers who, as tenants, renters, or croppers, operate hired land only. They were reported in 1920 in five classes: (1) Share tenants—those who pay a certain share of the products, as one-half, one-third, or one-quarter, for the use of the farm but furnish their own equipment and animals; (2) croppers—share tenants who do not furnish their work animals; (3) share-cash tenants—those who pay a share of the products for part of the land rented by them and cash for part; (4) cash tenants—those who pay a cash rental, as $7 per acre of crop land or $500 for the use of the whole farm; (5) standing renters—those who pay a stated amount of farm products for the use of the farm, as 3 bales of cotton or 500 bushels of corn. In some cases the character of the tenancy was not ascertained by the enumerator; such tenants are designated "unspecified."

Farm land.—Farm land is divided into (1) improved land, (2) woodland, and (3) other unimproved land.

Improved land includes all land regularly tilled or mowed, land in pasture which has been cleared or tilled, land lying fallow, land in gardens, orchards, vineyards, and nurseries, and land occupied by farm buildings.

Woodland includes all land covered with natural or planted forest trees which produce, or later may produce, firewood or other forest products.

All other unimproved land includes brush land, rough or stony land, swamp land, and any other land which is not improved or in forest.

Farm mortgages.—Three points should be kept in mind in using the census statistics for farm mortgages. First, the statistics are limited to farms operated by their owners, and no figures whatever are given for farms operated by tenants or hired managers. Second, the mortgage debt represented by the figures is that debt secured by real-estate mortgage, not including indebtedness secured by chattel mortgage, crop mortgage, or collateral or personal security. Third, while the figures representing the number of mortgaged farms include farms whose owners hire and operate some land in addition to that which they own, the statistics for the amount of the mortgage debt cover only those farms which consist wholly of land owned by the operator.

Live stock on farms.—The term "live stock," as it is used in the census reports, includes not only the common domestic animals (horses, mules, asses and burros, cattle, sheep, goats, and swine) but also poultry and bees. The figures for the value of live stock which are given in a number of the tables in connection with the value of other classes of farm property represent the value of the whole group as above defined. Certain totals are also given for domestic animals alone.

The comparability of the figures for live stock as reported for 1920 and 1910 is seriously affected by the change in the date of enumeration from April 15 in 1910 to January 1 in 1920. The 1910 census, by reason of its later date of enumeration, gained the large numbers of domestic animals born between January 1 and April 15, which would not have been reported, of course, if the census had been taken as of January 1. On the other hand, a group of considerable importance was omitted from the 1910 enumeration on account of the later date, namely, those animals which were sold or slaughtered (or which died) during the first 3½ months of the year—animals which were on the farms on January 1, 1910, but not on April 15. In most cases the gain from the animals born would considerably exceed the loss from animals marketed or otherwise disposed of. Hence the 1910 totals are, in general, somewhat too large for fair comparison with 1920, while the 1910 figures, omitting those animals born subsequent to January 1, 1910, are too small. This question is discussed in detail in the general reports of the census of agriculture.

Dairy cows.—Dairy cows, as reported for 1920, included all cows and heifers 2 years old and over kept mainly for milk production. The figures obtained under this classification are not closely comparable with the figures reported at the census of 1910, particularly because the age limits employed in 1910 included all cows and heifers 15½ months old and over on April 15, 1910 (1 year old and over on Jan. 1). An estimate of the number of dairy cows 2 years old and over on January 1, 1910, has been made, however, and is given in the tables.

Gross value of farm products.—The "gross value of farm products" which is shown in Table 210 is obtained by adding together the value of live-stock products, domestic animals sold or slaughtered, farm crops, forest products of farms, and nursery and greenhouse products. This figure corresponds approximately with the gross value of products for a manufacturing industry, and for many purposes forms a fairly satisfactory index of the progress of agriculture or of the relative importance of the agricultural industry in different areas. It contains, however, two serious elements of duplication. First, when the value of all crops produced is added to the value of all live-stock products, the value of the crops which are fed to live stock is duplicated. Second, in the total value of live stock sold there is duplication, because animals are frequently sold by one farmer to another and again sold by the second farmer. The duplication is more serious in the states where live-stock products form a large part of the total gross value than in those states where crops are the principal product.

GENERAL FARM INFORMATION.

TABLE 1.—POPULATION, FARMS, AND FARM PROPERTY IN THE UNITED STATES: 1920 AND 1910.

ITEM.	1920 (January 1)	1910 (April 15)	INCREASE.[1] Amount.	Per cent.
Population, total	105,710,620	91,972,266	13,738,354	14.9
Rural[2]	51,406,017	49,806,146	1,599,871	3.2
Urban	54,304,603	42,166,120	12,138,483	28.8
Per cent rural	48.6	54.2		
Farm population	31,614,269			
Per cent of total population	29.9			
Number of farms	6,448,343	6,361,502	86,841	1.4
Approximate land area of the country .acres	1,903,215,360	1,903,289,600	[3] −74,240	([4])
All land in farms acres	955,883,715	878,798,325	77,085,390	8.8
Improved land acres	503,073,007	478,451,750	24,621,257	5.1
Woodland acres	167,730,794	190,865,553	−23,134,759	−12.1
Other unimproved land acres	285,079,914	209,481,022	75,598,892	36.1
Per cent of total land area represented by—				
All land in farms	50.2	46.2		
Improved land in farms	26.4	25.1		
Woodland in farms	8.8	10.0		
Other unimproved land in farms	15.0	11.1		
Per cent of all land in farms:				
Improved land	52.6	54.4		
Woodland	17.5	21.7		
Other unimproved land	29.8	23.8		
Average acreage per farm:				
All land	148.2	138.1	10.1	7.3
Improved land	78.0	75.2	2.8	3.7
Woodland	26.0	30.0	−4.0	−13.3
Other unimproved land	44.2	32.9	11.3	34.3
Value of all farm property	$77,924,100,338	$40,991,449,090	$36,932,651,248	90.1
Land and buildings	66,316,002,602	34,801,125,697	31,514,876,905	90.6
Land alone[5]	54,829,563,059	28,475,674,169	26,353,888,890	92.5
Buildings	11,486,439,543	6,325,451,528	5,160,988,015	81.6
Implements and machinery	3,594,772,928	1,265,149,783	2,329,623,145	184.1
Live stock	8,013,324,808	4,925,173,610	3,088,151,198	62.7
Per cent of value of all farm property represented by—				
Land and buildings	85.1	84.9		
Land alone	70.4	69.5		
Buildings	14.7	15.4		
Implements and machinery	4.6	3.1		
Live stock	10.3	12.0		
Average value per farm:				
All farm property	$12,084	$6,444	$5,640	87.5
Land and buildings	10,284	5,471	4,813	88.0
Land alone	8,503	4,476	4,027	90.0
Buildings	1,781	994	787	79.2
Implements and machinery	557	199	358	179.9
Live stock	1,243	774	469	60.6
Average value per acre of all land in farms:				
All farm property	$81.52	$46.64	$34.88	74.8
Land and buildings	69.38	39.60	29.78	75.2
Land alone	57.36	32.40	24.96	77.0
Buildings	12.02	7.20	4.82	66.9
Implements and machinery	3.76	1.44	2.32	161.1
Live stock	8.38	5.60	2.78	49.6

[1] A minus sign (−) denotes decrease.
[2] Population residing outside of incorporated places having 2,500 inhabitants or over.
[3] Decrease in land area due to the building of the Pathfinder and Shoshone Reservoirs in Wyoming and several reservoirs in connection with irrigation projects in Montana.
[4] Less than one-tenth of 1 per cent decrease.
[5] These figures include the value of fences, tile drains, and other incidental improvements on the land, excluding only the value of buildings.

TABLE 2.—POPULATION, FARMS, AND FARM PROPERTY IN THE UNITED STATES:
1850 TO 1920.

[Figures for 1920 relate to Jan. 1; for 1910, to Apr. 15; and for earlier years to June 1.]

ITEM.	1920	1910	1900	1890
Population	105,710,620	91,972,266	75,994,575	62,947,714
Number of farms	6,448,343	6,361,502	5,737,372	4,564,641
Approx. land area of country....acres..	1,903,215,360	1,903,289,600	1,903,461,760	1,903,337,600
All land in farms....................acres.	955,883,715	878,798,325	838,591,774	623,218,619
Improved land...............acres..	503,073,007	478,451,750	414,498,487	357,616,755
Unimproved land...........acres..	452,810,708	400,346,575	424,093,287	265,601,864
Per cent of total land area represented by—				
All land in farms....................	50.2	46.2	44.1	32.7
Improved land in farms.........	26.4	25.1	21.8	18.8
Unimproved land in farms......	23.8	21.0	22.3	14.0
Per cent of all land in farms:				
Improved land....................	52.6	54.4	49.4	57.4
Unimproved land.................	47.4	45.6	50.6	42.6
Average acreage per farm:				
All land............................	148.2	138.1	146.2	136.5
Improved land..................	78.0	75.2	72.2	78.3
Unimproved land...............	70.2	62.9	73.9	58.2
Value of all farm property...............	$77,924,100,338	$40,991,449,090	$20,439,901,164	$16,082,267,689
Land and buildings.................	66,316,002,602	34,801,125,697	16,614,647,491	13,279,252,649
Implements and machinery.........	3,594,772,928	1,265,149,783	749,775,970	494,247,467
Live stock........................	8,013,324,808	4,925,173,610	3,075,477,703	2,308,767,573
Per cent of value of all farm property represented by—				
Land and buildings.................	85.1	84.9	81.3	82.6
Implements and machinery.........	4.6	3.1	3.7	3.1
Live stock..........................	10.3	12.0	15.0	14.4
Av. value of all farm property per farm..	$12,084	$6,444	$3,563	$3,523
Av. value of all farm property per acre..	81.52	46.64	24.37	25.81
Av. value of land and buildings per acre.	69.38	39.60	19.81	21.31

ITEM.	1880	1870	1860	1850
Population...............................	50,155,783	38,558,371	31,443,321	23,191,876
Number of farms......................	4,008,907	2,659,985	2,044,077	1,449,073
Approx. land area of country....acres..	1,903,337,600	1,903,337,600	1,903,337,600	1,884,375,680
All land in farms.................acres.	536,081,835	407,735,041	407,212,538	293,560,614
Improved land..............acres..	284,771,042	188,921,099	163,110,720	113,032,614
Unimproved land...........acres..	251,310,793	218,813,942	244,101,818	180,528,000
Per cent of total land area represented by—				
All land in farms....................	28.2	21.4	21.4	15.6
Improved land in farms.........	15.0	9.9	8.6	6.0
Unimproved land in farms......	13.2	11.5	12.8	9.6
Per cent of all land in farms:				
Improved land....................	53.1	46.3	40.1	38.5
Unimproved land.................	46.9	53.7	59.9	61.5
Average acreage per farm:				
All land............................	133.7	153.3	199.2	202.6
Improved land..................	71.0	71.0	79.8	78.0
Unimproved land...............	62.7	82.3	119.4	124.6
Value of all farm property...............	$12,180,501,538	$8,944,857,749	$7,980,493,063	$3,967,343,580
Land and buildings.................	10,197,096,776	7,444,054,462	6,645,045,007	3,271,575,426
Implements and machinery.........	406,520,055	270,913,678	246,118,141	151,587,638
Live stock........................	1,576,884,707	1,229,889,609	1,089,329,915	544,180,516
Per cent of value of all farm property represented by—				
Land and buildings.................	83.7	83.2	83.3	82.5
Implements and machinery.........	3.3	3.0	3.1	3.8
Live stock..........................	12.9	13.7	13.6	13.7
Av. value of all farm property per farm..	$3,038	$3,363	$3,904	$2,738
Av. value of all farm property per acre..	22.72	21.94	19.60	13.51
Av. value of land and buildings per acre.	19.02	18.26	16.32	11.14

TABLE 3.—FARM POPULATION AND TOTAL POPULATION, BY DIVISIONS AND STATES: 1920.

DIVISION AND STATE.	Total population.	FARM POPULATION.				
		Total.		In cities and other incorporated places of 2,500 and over.	In rural territory.	
		Number.	Per cent of total population.		Number.	Per cent of rural population.
United States........	105,710,620	31,614,269	29.9	255,629	31,358,640	61.0
GEOGRAPHIC DIVISIONS:						
New England............	7,400,909	625,877	8.5	90,455	535,422	34.9
Middle Atlantic.........	22,261,144	1,892,789	8.5	31,628	1,861,161	33.3
East North Central.....	21,475,543	4,913,633	22.9	26,429	4,887,204	58.0
West North Central.....	12,544,249	5,171,596	41.2	18,413	5,153,183	65.9
South Atlantic.........	13,990,272	6,416,698	45.9	18,941	6,397,757	66.3
East South Central......	8,893,307	5,182,937	58.3	8,131	5,174,806	75.0
West South Central.....	10,242,224	5,228,199	51.0	17,629	5,210,570	71.7
Mountain...............	3,336,101	1,168,367	35.0	15,374	1,152,993	54.4
Pacific.................	5,566,871	1,014,173	18.2	28,629	985,544	47.0
NEW ENGLAND:						
Maine..................	768,014	197,601	25.7	8,575	189,026	40.4
New Hampshire........	443,083	76,021	17.2	11,414	64,607	39.6
Vermont..............	352,428	125,263	35.5	818	124,445	51.3
Massachusetts..........	3,852,356	118,554	3.1	56,822	61,732	30.5
Rhode Island..........	604,397	15,136	2.5	9,821	5,315	34.9
Connecticut...........	1,380,631	93,302	6.8	3,005	90,297	20.3
MIDDLE ATLANTIC:						
New York..............	10,385,227	800,747	7.7	17,793	782,954	43.6
New Jersey............	3,155,900	143,708	4.6	6,861	136,847	20.1
Pennsylvania..........	8,720,017	948,334	10.9	6,974	941,360	30.2
EAST NORTH CENTRAL:						
Ohio..................	5,759,394	1,139,329	19.8	5,417	1,133,912	54.5
Indiana...............	2,930,390	907,295	31.0	4,475	902,820	62.4
Illinois...............	6,485,280	1,098,262	16.9	7,526	1,090,736	52.4
Michigan..............	3,668,412	848,710	23.1	4,211	844,499	59.2
Wisconsin.............	2,632,067	920,037	35.0	4,800	915,237	66.0
WEST NORTH CENTRAL:						
Minnesota.............	2,387,125	897,181	37.6	3,721	893,460	66.9
Iowa..................	2,404,021	984,799	41.0	7,105	977,694	64.0
Missouri..............	3,404,055	1,211,346	35.6	3,447	1,207,899	66.5
North Dakota..........	646,872	394,500	61.0	878	393,622	70.5
South Dakota..........	636,547	362,221	56.9	335	361,886	67.7
Nebraska..............	1,296,372	584,172	45.1	1,434	582,738	65.4
Kansas................	1,769,257	737,377	41.7	1,493	735,884	63.9
SOUTH ATLANTIC:						
Delaware..............	223,003	51,212	23.0	61	51,151	50.0
Maryland..............	1,449,661	279,225	19.3	1,569	277,656	47.9
District of Columbia....	437,571	894	0.2	894	....	....
Virginia..............	2,309,187	1,064,417	46.1	4,504	1,059,913	64.8
West Virginia..........	1,463,701	477,924	32.7	1,293	476,631	43.5
North Carolina........	2,559,123	1,501,227	58.7	1,281	1,499,946	72.5
South Carolina........	1,683,724	1,074,693	63.8	2,214	1,072,479	77.2
Georgia..............	2,895,832	1,685,213	58.2	4,602	1,680,611	77.5
Florida..............	968,470	281,893	29.1	2,523	279,370	45.6
EAST SOUTH CENTRAL:						
Kentucky..............	2,416,630	1,304,862	54.0	2,520	1,302,342	73.0
Tennessee.............	2,337,885	1,271,708	54.4	2,529	1,269,179	73.5
Alabama..............	2,348,174	1,335,885	56.9	1,372	1,334,513	72.6
Mississippi...........	1,790,618	1,270,482	71.0	1,710	1,268,772	81.8
WEST SOUTH CENTRAL:						
Arkansas..............	1,752,204	1,147,049	65.5	2,567	1,144,482	78.3
Louisiana.............	1,798,509	786,050	43.7	1,595	784,455	67.0
Oklahoma.............	2,028,283	1,017,327	50.2	1,428	1,015,899	68.2
Texas................	4,663,228	2,277,773	48.8	12,039	2,265,734	71.9
MOUNTAIN:						
Montana..............	548,889	225,667	41.1	278	225,389	59.8
Idaho................	431,866	200,902	46.5	4,339	196,563	62.8
Wyoming.............	194,402	67,306	34.6	230	67,076	48.9
Colorado.............	939,629	266,073	28.3	792	265,281	54.5
New Mexico..........	360,350	161,446	44.8	904	160,542	54.3
Arizona.............	334,162	90,560	27.1	393	90,167	41.6
Utah................	449,396	140,249	31.2	8,377	131,872	56.4
Nevada..............	77,407	16,164	20.9	61	16,103	25.9
PACIFIC:						
Washington............	1,356,621	283,382	20.9	3,360	280,022	46.1
Oregon................	783,389	214,021	27.3	2,012	212,009	54.0
California..............	3,426,861	516,770	15.1	23,257	493,513	45.1

TABLE 4.—FARM POPULATION, BY AGE AND SEX, BY DIVISIONS AND STATES: 1920.

DIVISION AND STATE.	Total.	BY SEX.			BY AGE.			Per cent of total.		
		Male.	Female.	Males per 100 females.	Under 10 years.	10 to 20 years.	21 years and over.	Under 10.	10 to 20.	21 and over.
United States..	31,614,269	16,496,338	15,117,931	109.1	8,138,070	7,824,106	15,652,093	25.7	24.7	49.5
GEOG. DIVISIONS:										
New England.....	625,877	330,206	295,671	111.7	117,627	124,102	384,148	18.8	19.8	61.4
Middle Atlantic...	1,892,789	993,979	898,810	110.6	380,852	405,174	1,106,763	20.1	21.4	58.5
E. North Central..	4,913,633	2,590,945	2,322,688	111.5	1,103,609	1,107,005	2,703,019	22.5	22.5	55.0
W. North Central.	5,171,596	2,760,145	2,411,451	114.5	1,288,322	1,221,719	2,661,555	24.9	23.6	51.5
South Atlantic....	6,416,698	3,264,380	3,152,318	103.6	1,835,747	1,716,854	2,864,097	28.6	26.8	44.6
E. South Central..	5,182,937	2,640,245	2,542,692	103.8	1,426,053	1,363,697	2,393,187	27.5	26.3	46.2
W. South Central.	5,228,199	2,713,605	2,514,594	107.9	1,457,125	1,413,762	2,357,312	27.9	27.0	45.1
Mountain.........	1,168,367	636,150	532,217	119.5	314,350	267,584	586,433	26.9	22.9	50.2
Pacific............	1,014,173	566,683	447,490	126.6	214,385	204,209	595,579	21.1	20.1	58.7
NEW ENGLAND:										
Maine............	197,601	104,107	93,494	111.4	37,622	40,228	119,751	19.0	20.4	60.6
New Hampshire..	76,021	39,976	36,045	110.9	12,679	13,775	49,567	16.7	18.1	65.2
Vermont..........	125,263	66,545	58,718	113.3	24,842	26,009	74,412	19.8	20.8	59.4
Massachusetts....	118,554	62,517	56,037	111.6	21,729	23,101	73,724	18.3	19.5	62.2
Rhode Island.....	15,136	8,037	7,099	113.2	2,643	2,904	9,589	17.5	19.2	63.4
Connecticut.......	93,302	49,024	44,278	110.7	18,112	18,085	57,105	19.4	19.4	61.2
MIDDLE ATLANTIC:										
New York........	800,747	423,511	377,236	112.3	147,576	154,011	499,160	18.4	19.2	62.3
New Jersey.......	143,708	76,745	66,963	114.6	27,574	30,008	86,126	19.2	20.9	59.9
Pennsylvania.....	948,334	493,723	454,611	108.6	205,702	221,155	521,477	21.7	23.3	55.0
E. NORTH CENTRAL:										
Ohio.............	1,139,329	595,470	543,859	109.5	241,543	249,203	648,583	21.2	21.9	56.9
Indiana..........	907,295	472,628	434,667	108.7	194,370	201,157	511,768	21.4	22.2	56.4
Illinois..........	1,098,262	577,824	520,438	111.0	249,818	252,905	595,539	22.7	23.0	54.2
Michigan.........	848,710	451,555	397,155	113.7	194,753	186,073	467,884	22.9	21.9	55.1
Wisconsin........	920,037	493,468	426,569	115.7	223,125	217,667	479,245	24.3	23.7	52.1
W. NORTH CENTRAL:										
Minnesota........	897,181	486,048	411,133	118.2	219,221	221,345	456,615	24.4	24.7	50.9
Iowa............	984,799	523,710	461,089	113.6	240,470	224,609	519,720	24.4	22.8	52.8
Missouri.........	1,211,346	635,263	576,083	110.3	285,441	286,949	638,986	23.6	23.7	52.7
North Dakota.....	394,500	213,837	180,663	118.4	116,061	95,377	183,062	29.4	4.2	46.4
South Dakota.....	362,221	197,043	165,178	119.3	97,885	83,353	180,983	27.0	23.0	50.0
Nebraska.........	584,172	313,706	270,466	116.0	151,335	137,837	295,000	25.9	23.6	50.5
Kansas..........	737,377	390,538	346,839	112.6	177,939	172,249	387,189	24.1	23.4	52.5
SOUTH ATLANTIC:										
Delaware.........	51,212	26,954	24,258	111.1	11,506	12,051	27,655	22.5	23.5	54.0
Maryland.........	279,225	146,087	133,138	109.7	65,438	68,185	145,602	23.4	24.4	52.1
Dist. of Columbia.	894	627	267	234.8	76	464	354	8.5	51.9	39.6
Virginia..........	1,064,417	543,692	520,725	104.4	286,167	276,190	502,060	26.9	25.9	47.2
West Virginia....	477,924	248,985	228,939	108.8	125,289	125,725	226,910	26.2	26.3	47.5
North Carolina....	1,501,227	761,130	740,097	102.8	451,199	394,339	655,689	30.1	26.3	43.7
South Carolina....	1,074,693	539,603	535,090	100.8	325,720	300,012	448,961	30.3	27.9	41.8
Georgia..........	1,685,213	851,915	833,298	102.2	495,973	464,560	724,680	29.4	27.6	43.0
Florida..........	281,893	145,387	136,506	106.5	74,379	75,328	132,186	26.4	26.7	46.9
E. SOUTH CENTRAL:										
Kentucky.........	1,304,862	676,428	628,434	107.6	350,746	327,472	626,644	26.9	25.1	48.0
Tennessee........	1,271,708	650,529	621,179	104.7	342,582	326,725	602,401	26.9	25.7	47.4
Alabama.........	1,335,885	670,829	665,056	100.9	389,350	363,058	583,477	29.1	27.2	43.7
Mississippi.......	1,270,482	642,459	628,023	102.3	343,375	346,442	580,665	27.0	27.3	45.7
W. SOUTH CENTRAL:										
Arkansas.........	1,147,049	591,198	555,851	106.4	319,138	306,047	521,864	27.8	26.7	45.5
Louisiana........	786,050	400,200	385,850	103.7	222,308	219,008	344,734	28.3	27.9	43.9
Oklahoma........	1,017,327	537,002	480,325	111.8	290,828	274,495	452,004	28.6	27.0	44.4
Texas...........	2,277,773	1,185,205	1,092,568	108.5	624,851	614,212	1,038,710	27.4	27.0	45.6
MOUNTAIN:										
Montana.....	225,667	126,198	99,469	126.9	59,218	43,726	122,723	26.2	19.4	54.4
Idaho...........	200,802	109,641	91,201	120.1	54,989	47,300	98,613	27.4	23.5	49.1
Wyoming.........	67,306	37,620	29,686	126.7	17,230	14,076	35,994	25.6	20.9	53.5
Colorado.........	266,073	143,987	122,086	117.9	68,977	60,061	137,035	25.9	22.6	51.5
New Mexico......	161,446	86,209	75,237	114.6	44,193	39,642	77,611	27.4	24.6	48.1
Arizona..........	90,560	49,140	41,420	118.6	24,874	21,928	43,758	27.5	24.2	48.0
Utah............	140,249	73,672	66,577	110.6	41,343	37,821	61,085	29.5	27.0	43.6
Nevada..........	16,164	9,683	6,481	149.4	3,520	3,030	9,614	21.8	18.7	59.5
PACIFIC:										
Washington.......	283,382	155,594	127,788	121.8	62,947	62,681	157,754	22.2	22.1	55.7
Oregon..........	214,021	117,973	96,048	122.8	45,548	45,572	122,901	21.3	21.3	57.4
California........	516,770	293,116	223,654	131.1	105,890	95,956	314,924	20.5	18.6	60.9

TABLE 5.—FARM POPULATION, BY RACE, NATIVITY, AND PARENTAGE, BY DIVISIONS AND STATES: 1920.

DIVISION AND STATE.	Total.	NATIVE WHITE. Total.	Native parentage.	Foreign and mixed parentage.	Foreign-born white.	Colored.	PER CENT OF TOTAL. Native white	Foreign-born white	Colored.
United States....	31,614,269	24,842,614	21,045,836	3,796,778	1,471,040	5,300,615	78.6	4.7	16.8
GEOGRAPHIC DIVISIONS:									
New England.......	625,877	546,178	417,747	128,431	77,844	1,855	87.3	12.4	0.3
Middle Atlantic.....	1,892,789	1,750,182	1,469,287	280,895	127,563	15,044	92.5	6.7	0.8
East North Central..	4,913,633	4,535,793	3,457,822	1,077,971	350,512	27,328	92.3	7.1	0.6
West North Central.	5,171,596	4,644,672	3,161,917	1,482,755	479,917	47,007	89.8	9.3	0.9
South Atlantic......	6,416,698	4,048,438	4,008,035	40,403	18,405	2,349,855	63.1	0.3	36.6
East South Central..	5,182,937	3,658,174	3,629,842	28,332	8,399	1,516,364	70.6	0.2	29.3
West South Central.	5,228,199	3,858,811	3,586,617	272,194	138,621	1,230,767	73.8	2.7	23.5
Mountain...........	1,168,367	1,003,702	767,688	236,014	109,688	54,977	85.9	9.4	4.7
Pacific.............	1,014,173	796,664	546,881	249,783	160,091	57,418	78.6	15.8	5.7
NEW ENGLAND:									
Maine..............	197,601	183,333	155,418	27,915	14,131	137	92.8	7.2	0.1
New Hampshire....	76,021	68,437	55,746	12,691	7,498	86	90.0	9.9	0.1
Vermont...........	125,263	112,669	90,996	21,673	12,491	163	89.9	9.9	0.1
Massachusetts.......	118,554	95,671	61,453	34,218	22,246	637	80.7	18.8	0.5
Rhode Island.......	15,136	12,751	9,191	3,560	2,173	212	84.2	14.4	1.4
Connecticut.........	93,302	73,317	44,943	28,374	19,365	620	78.6	20.8	0.7
MIDDLE ATLANTIC:									
New York..........	800,747	725,121	561,749	163,372	71,276	4,350	90.6	8.9	0.5
New Jersey.........	143,708	118,963	89,132	29,831	19,393	5,352	82.8	13.5	3.7
Pennsylvania.......	948,334	906,098	818,406	87,692	36,894	5,342	95.5	3.9	0.6
EAST NORTH CENTRAL:									
Ohio..............	1,139,329	1,091,988	957,414	134,574	37,765	9,576	95.8	3.3	0.8
Indiana............	907,295	887,471	810,444	77,027	16,271	3,553	97.8	1.8	0.4
Illinois............	1,098,262	1,037,744	827,593	210,151	54,390	6,128	94.5	5.0	0.6
Michigan...........	848,710	732,397	464,785	267,612	112,358	3,955	86.3	13.2	0.5
Wisconsin..........	920,037	786,193	397,586	388,607	129,728	4,116	85.5	14.1	0.4
WEST NORTH CENTRAL:									
Minnesota..........	897,181	738,921	308,505	430,416	155,846	2,414	82.4	17.4	0.3
Iowa..............	984,799	905,752	622,532	283,220	78,385	662	92.0	8.0	0.1
Missouri...........	1,211,346	1,171,082	1,076,260	94,822	20,131	20,133	96.7	1.7	1.7
North Dakota......	394,500	306,981	111,357	195,624	82,859	4,660	77.8	21.0	1.2
South Dakota......	362,221	304,431	162,247	142,184	47,221	10,569	84.0	13.0	2.9
Nebraska..........	584,172	525,815	334,066	191,749	56,084	2,273	90.0	9.6	0.4
Kansas............	737,377	691,690	546,950	144,740	39,391	6,296	93.8	5.3	0.9
SOUTH ATLANTIC:									
Delaware..........	51,212	41,100	38,950	2,150	1,150	8,962	80.3	2.2	17.5
Maryland..........	279,225	211,859	200,356	11,503	4,372	62,994	75.9	1.6	22.6
Dist. of Columbia...	894	622	516	106	54	218	69.6	6.0	24.4
Virginia............	1,064,417	750,745	742,497	8,248	4,445	309,227	70.5	0.4	29.1
West Virginia......	477,924	472,211	465,789	6,422	1,661	4,052	98.8	0.3	0.8
North Carolina.....	1,501,227	1,022,214	1,020,406	1,808	897	478,116	68.1	0.1	31.8
South Carolina.....	1,074,693	433,775	432,816	959	356	640,562	40.4	(1)	59.6
Georgia............	1,685,213	927,071	924,637	2,434	838	757,304	55.0	(1)	44.9
Florida............	281,893	188,841	182,068	6,773	4,632	88,420	67.0	1.6	31.4
EAST SOUTH CENTRAL:									
Kentucky..........	1,304,862	1,228,769	1,215,435	13,334	2,665	73,428	94.2	0.2	5.6
Tennessee.........	1,271,708	1,066,374	1,061,037	5,337	1,656	203,678	83.9	0.1	16.0
Alabama..........	1,335,885	817,643	812,282	5,361	2,379	515,863	61.2	0.2	38.6
Mississippi........	1,270,482	545,388	541,088	4,300	1,699	723,395	42.9	0.1	56.9
WEST SOUTH CENTRAL:									
Arkansas...........	1,147,049	807,892	792,613	15,279	4,939	334,218	70.4	0.4	29.1
Louisiana..........	786,050	418,327	405,345	12,982	5,813	361,910	53.2	0.7	46.0
Oklahoma..........	1,017,327	887,615	842,893	44,722	13,362	116,350	87.2	1.3	11.4
Texas.............	2,277,773	1,744,977	1,545,766	199,211	114,507	418,289	76.6	5.0	18.4
MOUNTAIN:									
Montana...........	225,667	184,692	119,891	64,801	33,642	7,333	81.8	14.9	3.2
Idaho.............	200,902	183,087	139,747	43,340	14,705	3,110	91.1	7.3	1.5
Wyoming..........	67,306	60,808	47,562	13,246	5,594	904	90.3	8.3	1.3
Colorado..........	266,073	239,456	187,995	51,461	24,357	2,260	90.0	9.2	0.8
New Mexico........	161,446	143,707	134,730	8,977	5,360	12,379	89.0	3.3	7.7
Arizona...........	90,560	52,151	42,206	9,945	13,711	24,698	57.6	15.1	27.3
Utah.............	140,249	128,373	88,160	40,213	9,540	2,336	91.5	6.8	1.7
Nevada............	16,164	11,428	7,397	4,031	2,779	1,957	70.7	17.2	12.1
PACIFIC:									
Washington........	283,382	231,444	155,559	75,885	44,064	7,874	81.7	15.5	2.8
Oregon...........	214,021	188,953	145,729	43,224	21,117	3,951	88.3	9.9	1.8
California..........	516,770	376,267	245,593	130,674	94,910	45,593	72.8	18.4	8.8

[1] Less than one-tenth of 1 per cent.

TABLE 6.—POPULATION, NUMBER OF FARMS, AND FARM ACREAGE,

[A minus sign (—) denotes decrease.]

	DIVISION AND STATE.	TOTAL POPULATION.			RURAL POPULATION.			NUMBER OF FARMS.		
		1920	1910	Per cent of increase	1920	1910	Per cent of increase	1920	1910	Per cent of increase
1	United States.	105,710,620	91,972,266	14.9	51,406,017	49,806,146	3.2	6,448,343	6,361,502	1.4
	GEOG. DIVISIONS:									
2	New England....	7,400,909	6,552,681	12.9	1,535,836	1,554,599	—1.2	156,564	188,802	—17.1
3	Middle Atlantic..	22,261,144	19,315,892	15.2	5,588,549	5,592,519	—0.1	425,147	468,379	—9.2
4	E. North Central.	21,475,543	18,250,621	17.7	8,426,271	8,633,350	—2.4	1,084,744	1,123,489	—3.4
5	W. North Central	12,544,249	11,637,921	7.8	7,816,877	7,764,205	0.7	1,096,951	1,109,948	—1.2
6	South Atlantic...	13,990,272	12,194,895	14.7	9,651,480	9,102,742	6.0	1,158,976	1,111,881	4.2
7	E. South Central.	8,893,307	8,409,901	5.7	6,899,100	6,835,672	0.9	1,051,600	1,042,480	0.9
8	W. South Central.	10,242,224	8,784,534	16.6	7,271,395	6,827,078	6.5	996,088	943,186	5.6
9	Mountain........	3,336,101	2,633,517	26.7	2,121,121	1,686,006	25.8	244,109	183,446	33.1
10	Pacific..........	5,566,871	4,192,304	32.8	2,095,388	1,809,975	15.8	234,164	189,891	23.3
	NEW ENGLAND:									
11	Maine.........	768,014	742,371	3.5	468,445	480,123	—2.4	48,227	60,016	—19.6
12	New Hampshire.	443,083	430,572	2.9	163,322	175,473	—6.9	20,523	27,053	—24.1
13	Vermont.........	352,428	355,956	—1.0	242,452	257,039	—5.7	29,075	32,709	—11.1
14	Massachusetts...	3,852,356	3,366,416	14.4	202,108	241,049	—16.2	32,001	36,917	—13.3
15	Rhode Island....	604,397	542,610	11.4	15,217	17,956	—15.3	4,083	5,292	—22.8
16	Connecticut......	1,380,631	1,114,756	23.9	444,292	382,959	16.0	22,655	26,815	—15.5
	MIDDLE ATLANTIC:									
17	New York......	10,385,227	9,113,614	14.0	1,795,383	1,928,120	—6.9	193,195	215,597	—10.4
18	New Jersey......	3,155,900	2,537,167	24.4	680,964	629,957	8.1	29,702	33,487	—11.3
19	Pennsylvania....	8,720,017	7,665,111	13.8	3,112,202	3,034,442	2.6	202,250	219,295	—7.8
	E. NORTH CENTRAL:									
20	Ohio............	5,759,394	4,767,121	20.8	2,082,258	2,101,978	—0.9	256,695	272,045	—5.6
21	Indiana..........	2,930,390	2,700,876	8.5	1,447,535	1,557,041	—7.0	205,126	215,485	—4.8
22	Illinois..........	6,485,280	5,638,591	15.0	2,082,127	2,161,662	—3.7	237,181	251,872	—5.8
23	Michigan........	3,668,412	2,810,173	30.5	1,426,852	1,483,129	—3.8	196,447	206,960	—5.1
24	Wisconsin.......	2,632,067	2,333,860	12.8	1,387,499	1,329,540	4.4	189,295	177,127	6.9
	W. NORTH CENTRAL:									
25	Minnesota.......	2,387,125	2,075,708	15.0	1,335,532	1,225,414	9.0	178,478	156,137	14.3
26	Iowa............	2,404,021	2,224,771	8.1	1,528,526	1,544,717	—1.0	213,439	217,044	—1.7
27	Missouri........	3,404,055	3,293,335	3.4	1,817,152	1,894,518	—4.1	263,004	277,244	—5.1
28	North Dakota....	646,872	577,056	12.1	558,633	513,820	8.7	77,690	74,360	4.5
29	South Dakota....	636,547	583,888	9.0	534,675	507,215	5.4	74,637	77,644	—3.9
30	Nebraska......	1,296,372	1,192,214	8.7	891,066	881,362	1.1	124,417	129,678	—4.1
31	Kansas.........	1,769,257	1,690,949	4.6	1,151,293	1,197,159	—3.8	165,286	177,841	—7.1
	SOUTH ATLANTIC:									
32	Delaware........	223,003	202,322	10.2	102,236	105,237	—2.9	10,140	10,836	—6.4
33	Maryland........	1,449,661	1,295,346	11.9	580,239	637,154	—8.9	47,908	48,923	—2.1
34	Dist. of Columbia.	437,571	331,069	32.2				204	217	—6.0
35	Virginia........	2,309,187	2,061,612	12.0	1,635,203	1,585,083	3.2	186,242	184,018	1.2
36	West Virginia....	1,463,701	1,221,119	19.9	1,094,694	992,877	10.3	87,289	96,685	—9.7
37	North Carolina..	2,559,123	2,206,287	16.0	2,068,753	1,887,813	9.6	269,763	253,725	6.3
38	South Carolina...	1,683,724	1,515,400	11.1	1,389,737	1,290,568	7.7	192,693	176,434	9.2
39	Georgia..........	2,895,832	2,609,121	11.0	2,167,973	2,070,471	4.7	310,732	291,027	6.8
40	Florida..........	968,470	752,619	28.7	612,645	533,539	14.8	54,005	50,016	8.0
	E. SOUTH CENTRAL:									
41	Kentucky......	2,416,630	2,289,905	5.5	1,783,087	1,734,463	2.8	270,626	259,185	4.4
42	Tennessee.......	2,337,885	2,184,789	7.0	1,726,659	1,743,744	—1.0	252,774	246,012	2.7
43	Alabama........	2,348,174	2,138,093	9.8	1,838,857	1,767,662	4.0	256,099	262,901	—2.6
44	Mississippi......	1,790,618	1,797,114	—0.4	1,550,497	1,589,803	—2.5	272,101	274,382	—0.8
	W. SOUTH CENTRAL:									
45	Arkansas........	1,752,204	1,574,449	11.3	1,461,707	1,371,768	6.6	232,604	214,678	8.4
46	Louisiana	1,798,509	1,656,388	8.6	1,170,346	1,159,872	0.9	135,463	120,546	12.4
47	Oklahoma	2,028,283	1,657,155	22.4	1,488,803	1,337,000	11.4	191,988	190,192	0.9
48	Texas..........	4,663,220	3,896,542	19.7	3,150,539	2,958,438	6.5	436,033	417,770	4.4
	MOUNTAIN:									
49	Montana........	548,889	376,053	46.0	376,878	242,633	55.3	57,677	26,214	120.0
50	Idaho..........	431,866	325,594	32.6	312,829	255,696	22.3	42,106	30,807	36.7
51	Wyoming.......	194,402	145,965	33.2	137,054	102,744	33.4	15,748	10,987	43.3
52	Colorado.......	939,629	799,024	17.6	486,370	394,184	23.4	59,934	46,170	29.8
53	New Mexico.....	360,350	327,301	10.1	295,390	280,730	5.2	29,844	35,676	—16.3
54	Arizona........	334,162	204,354	63.5	216,635	141,094	53.5	9,975	9,227	8.1
55	Utah...........	449,396	373,351	20.4	233,812	200,417	16.7	25,662	21,676	18.4
56	Nevada.........	77,407	81,875	—5.5	62,153	68,508	—9.3	3,163	2,689	17.6
	PACIFIC:									
57	Washington	1,356,621	1,141,990	18.8	607,886	536,460	13.3	66,288	56,192	18.0
58	Oregon.........	783,389	672,765	16.4	392,370	365,705	7.3	50,206	45,502	10.3
59	California.......	3,426,861	2,377,549	44.1	1,095,132	907,810	20.6	117,670	88,197	33.4

BY DIVISIONS AND STATES: 1920 AND 1910.

[A minus sign (−) denotes decrease.]

ALL LAND IN FARMS (ACRES).			IMPROVED LAND IN FARMS (ACRES).[1]		WOODLAND IN FARMS (ACRES).		OTHER UNIMPROVED LAND IN FARMS (ACRES).		
1920	1910	Per cent of increase.	1920	1910	1920	1910	1920	1910	
955,883,715	878,798,325	8.8	503,073,007	478,451,750	167,730,794	190,865,553	285,079,914	209,481,022	1
16,990,642	19,714,931	−13.8	6,114,601	7,254,904	7,020,311	7,852,913	3,855,730	4,607,114	2
40,572,901	43,191,056	−6.1	26,562,107	29,320,894	8,659,237	9,255,715	5,351,557	4,614,447	3
117,735,179	117,929,148	−0.2	87,894,835	88,947,228	18,061,460	18,109,180	11,778,884	10,872,740	4
256,973,229	232,648,121	10.5	171,394,439	164,284,862	18,761,832	17,969,615	66,816,958	50,393,644	5
97,775,243	103,782,255	−5.8	48,509,886	48,479,733	41,802,263	48,904,830	7,463,094	6,397,692	6
78,897,463	81,520,629	−3.2	44,380,132	43,946,846	28,414,524	32,287,681	6,102,807	5,286,102	7
173,449,127	169,149,976	2.5	64,189,006	58,264,273	29,749,152	44,055,394	79,510,369	66,830,309	8
117,337,226	59,533,420	97.1	30,105,868	15,915,002	6,887,071	4,169,081	80,344,287	39,509,337	9
56,152,705	51,328,789	9.4	23,921,533	22,038,008	8,374,944	8,321,144	23,856,228	20,969,637	10
5,425,968	6,296,859	−13.8	1,977,329	2,360,657	2,447,597	2,775,621	1,001,042	1,160,581	11
2,603,806	3,249,458	−19.9	702,962	929,185	1,299,838	1,502,389	601,066	817,884	12
4,235,811	4,663,577	−9.2	1,691,595	1,633,965	1,428,309	1,566,698	1,115,907	1,462,914	13
2,494,477	2,875,941	−13.3	908,834	1,164,501	1,030,386	1,064,553	555,257	646,887	14
331,600	443,308	−25.2	132,855	178,344	130,462	185,909	68,283	79,055	15
1,898,980	2,185,788	−13.1	701,086	988,252	683,719	757,743	514,175	439,793	16
20,632,803	22,030,367	−6.3	13,158,781	14,844,039	4,160,567	4,436,145	3,313,455	2,750,183	17
2,282,585	2,573,857	−11.3	1,555,607	1,803,336	454,768	538,131	272,210	232,390	18
17,657,513	18,586,832	−5.0	11,847,719	12,673,519	4,043,902	4,281,439	1,765,892	1,631,874	19
23,515,888	24,105,708	−2.4	18,542,353	19,227,969	3,198,929	3,285,376	1,774,606	1,592,363	20
21,063,332	21,299,823	−1.1	16,680,212	16,931,252	3,141,042	3,370,791	1,242,078	997,780	21
31,974,775	32,522,937	−1.7	27,294,533	28,048,323	3,102,579	3,147,879	1,577,663	1,326,735	22
19,032,961	18,940,614	0.5	12,925,521	12,832,078	3,217,000	2,927,554	2,890,440	3,180,982	23
22,148,223	21,060,066	5.2	12,452,216	11,907,606	5,401,910	5,377,580	4,294,097	3,774,880	24
30,221,758	27,675,823	9.2	21,481,710	19,643,533	4,482,656	3,922,391	4,257,392	4,109,899	25
33,474,896	33,930,688	−1.3	28,606,951	29,491,199	2,295,274	2,314,115	2,572,671	2,125,374	26
34,774,679	34,591,248	0.5	24,832,966	24,581,186	8,553,857	8,918,972	1,387,856	1,091,090	27
36,214,751	28,426,650	27.4	24,563,178	20,455,082	679,836	421,877	10,971,737	7,549,681	28
34,636,491	26,016,892	33.1	18,199,250	15,827,208	536,183	383,144	15,901,058	9,806,540	29
42,225,475	38,622,021	9.3	23,109,624	24,382,577	900,933	803,206	18,214,918	13,436,238	30
45,425,179	43,384,799	4.7	30,600,760	29,904,067	1,313,093	1,205,910	13,511,326	12,274,822	31
944,511	1,038,866	−9.1	653,052	713,538	222,658	252,032	68,801	73,296	32
4,757,999	5,057,140	−5.9	3,136,728	3,354,767	1,327,221	1,467,333	294,050	235,040	33
5,668	6,063	−6.5	4,258	5,133	828	689	582	241	34
18,561,112	19,495,636	−4.8	9,460,492	9,870,058	7,907,352	8,414,680	1,193,268	1,210,898	35
9,569,790	10,026,442	−4.6	5,520,308	5,521,757	3,469,444	3,968,836	580,038	535,849	36
20,021,736	22,439,129	−10.8	8,198,409	8,813,056	10,299,547	12,451,739	1,523,780	1,174,334	37
12,426,675	13,512,028	−8.0	6,184,159	6,097,999	5,302,575	6,339,142	939,941	1,074,887	38
25,441,061	26,953,413	−5.6	13,055,219	12,298,017	10,491,848	13,002,741	1,894,004	1,652,655	39
6,046,691	5,253,538	15.1	2,297,271	1,805,408	2,780,790	3,007,638	968,630	440,492	40
21,612,772	22,189,127	−2.6	13,975,746	14,354,471	6,018,280	6,951,626	1,618,746	883,030	41
19,510,856	20,041,657	−2.6	11,185,302	10,890,484	7,080,169	8,007,733	1,245,385	1,143,440	42
19,576,856	20,732,312	−5.6	9,893,407	9,693,581	8,301,177	9,444,764	1,382,272	1,593,967	43
18,196,979	18,557,533	−1.9	9,325,677	9,008,310	7,014,898	7,883,558	1,856,404	1,665,665	44
17,456,750	17,416,075	0.2	9,210,556	8,076,254	7,396,028	8,511,510	850,166	828,311	45
10,019,822	10,439,481	−4.0	5,626,226	5,276,016	3,614,040	4,316,561	779,556	846,904	46
31,951,934	28,859,353	10.7	18,125,321	17,551,337	4,206,171	3,568,910	9,620,442	7,739,106	47
114,020,621	112,435,067	1.4	31,227,503	27,360,666	14,532,913	27,658,413	68,260,205	57,415,988	48
35,070,656	13,545,603	158.9	11,007,278	3,640,309	1,646,462	595,870	22,416,916	9,309,424	49
8,375,873	5,283,604	58.5	4,511,680	2,778,740	820,876	584,556	3,043,317	1,920,308	50
11,809,351	8,543,010	38.2	2,102,005	1,256,160	421,806	252,152	9,285,540	7,034,698	51
24,462,014	13,532,113	80.8	7,744,757	4,302,101	1,415,420	891,698	15,301,837	8,338,314	52
24,409,633	11,270,021	116.6	1,717,224	1,467,191	1,817,460	1,491,025	20,874,949	8,311,805	53
5,802,126	1,246,613	365.4	712,803	350,173	523,648	100,061	4,565,675	796,379	54
5,050,410	3,397,699	48.6	1,715,380	1,368,211	212,762	145,510	3,122,268	1,883,978	55
2,357,163	2,714,757	−13.2	594,741	752,117	28,637	48,209	1,733,785	1,914,431	56
13,244,720	11,712,235	13.1	7,129,343	6,373,311	1,813,061	1,541,551	4,302,316	3,797,373	57
13,542,318	11,685,110	15.9	4,913,851	4,274,803	2,309,596	2,237,826	6,318,871	5,172,481	58
29,365,667	27,931,444	5.1	11,878,339	11,389,894	4,252,287	4,541,767	13,235,041	11,999,783	59

[1] For per cent of increase or decrease, 1910–1920, see Table 7.

TABLE 7.—POPULATION, NUMBER OF FARMS, AND FARM ACREAGE, BY DIVISIONS AND STATES: 1850 TO 1920.

[A minus sign (−) denotes decrease.]

DIVISION OR STATE AND CENSUS YEAR.	POPULATION.		NUMBER OF FARMS.		ALL LAND IN FARMS.		IMPROVED LAND IN FARMS.	
	Number.	Per cent of increase.	Number.	Per cent of increase.	Acres.	Per cent of increase.	Acres.	Per cent of increase.
UNITED STATES.								
1920	105,710,620	14.9	6,448,343	1.4	955,883,715	8.8	503,073,007	5.1
1910	91,972,266	21.0	6,361,502	10.9	878,798,325	4.8	478,451,750	15.4
1900	75,994,575	20.7	5,737,372	25.7	838,591,774	34.6	414,498,487	15.9
1890	62,947,714	25.5	4,564,641	13.9	623,218,619	16.3	357,616,755	25.6
1880	50,155,783	30.1	4,008,907	50.7	536,081,835	31.5	284,771,042	50.7
1870	38,558,371	22.6	2,659,985	30.1	407,735,041	0.1	188,921,099	15.8
1860	31,443,321	35.6	2,044,077	41.1	407,212,538	38.7	163,110,720	44.3
1850	23,191,876	....	1,449,073	....	293,560,614	....	113,032,614	....
GEOGRAPHIC DIVISIONS.								
NEW ENGLAND.								
1920	7,400,909	12.9	156,564	−17.1	16,990,642	−13.8	6,114,601	−15.7
1910	6,552,681	17.2	188,802	−1.6	19,714,931	−4.1	7,254,904	−10.8
1900	5,592,017	19.0	191,888	1.0	20,548,999	4.0	8,134,403	−24.3
1890	4,700,749	17.2	189,961	−8.3	19,755,584	−8.0	10,738,930	−18.3
1880	4,010,529	15.0	207,232	14.7	21,483,772	9.8	13,148,466	9.6
1870	3,487,924	11.2	180,649	−1.8	19,569,863	−2.7	11,997,540	−1.8
1860	3,135,283	14.9	183,942	9.7	20,110,922	9.5	12,215,771	9.6
1850	2,728,116	....	167,651	....	18,367,458	....	11,150,594	....
MIDDLE ATLANTIC.								
1920	22,261,144	15.2	425,147	−9.2	40,572,901	−6.1	26,562,107	−9.4
1910	19,315,892	25.0	468,379	−3.5	43,191,056	−3.7	29,320,894	−4.8
1900	15,454,678	21.6	485,618	3.6	44,860,090	4.4	30,786,211	−2.6
1890	12,706,220	21.0	468,608	−4.2	42,987,941	−7.6	31,599,094	−4.9
1880	10,496,878	19.1	488,907	16.1	46,501,868	7.7	33,237,166	14.1
1870	8,810,806	18.1	420,946	10.5	43,174,521	5.4	29,119,645	8.8
1860	7,458,985	26.4	380,993	18.3	40,970,623	11.3	26,766,140	17.4
1850	5,898,735	....	322,103	....	36,795,377	....	22,805,574	....
EAST NORTH CENTRAL.								
1920	21,475,543	17.7	1,084,744	−3.4	117,735,179	−0.2	87,894,835	−1.2
1910	18,250,621	14.2	1,123,489	−1.1	117,929,148	1.4	88,947,228	2.6
1900	15,985,581	18.6	1,135,823	12.6	116,340,761	10.0	86,670,271	10.0
1890	13,478,305	20.3	1,009,031	2.4	105,786,825	(¹)	78,774,647	4.2
1880	11,206,668	22.8	985,273	29.3	105,784,212	21.0	75,589,373	37.7
1870	9,124,517	31.7	761,735	29.8	87,449,392	20.3	54,899,646	33.3
1860	6,926,884	53.1	586,717	59.4	72,696,843	44.8	41,186,414	79.8
1850	4,523,260	....	368,177	....	50,188,875	....	22,912,190	....
WEST NORTH CENTRAL.								
1920	12,544,249	7.8	1,096,951	−1.2	256,973,229	10.5	171,394,439	4.3
1910	11,637,921	12.5	1,109,948	4.6	232,648,121	15.7	164,284,862	21.1
1900	10,347,423	15.8	1,060,744	16.0	201,008,713	33.3	135,643,828	28.6
1890	8,932,112	45.1	914,791	28.4	150,800,169	49.0	105,517,479	72.3
1880	6,157,443	59.7	712,695	96.1	101,197,945	95.5	61,252,946	160.5
1870	3,856,601	77.7	363,343	95.9	51,765,877	47.1	23,509,863	111.4
1860	2,169,832	146.5	185,448	167.1	18,200,747	181.7	11,122,285	195.2
1850	880,335	....	69,420	....	12,497,615	....	3,766,113	....
SOUTH ATLANTIC.								
1920	13,990,272	14.7	1,158,976	4.2	97,775,243	−5.8	48,509,886	0.1
1910	12,194,895	16.8	1,111,881	15.6	103,782,255	−0.5	48,479,733	5.2
1900	10,443,480	17.9	962,225	28.4	104,297,506	4.1	46,100,226	10.6
1890	8,857,922	16.6	749,600	16.3	100,157,573	−1.2	41,677,371	15.2
1880	7,597,197	29.8	644,429	72.3	101,419,563	12.4	36,170,331	19.8
1870	5,853,610	9.1	374,102	23.9	90,213,055	−15.3	30,202,991	−13.5
1860	5,364,703	14.7	301,940	21.7	106,520,771	14.0	34,900,942	16.3
1850	4,679,090	....	248,196	....	93,401,610	....	30,009,323	....

¹ Less than one-tenth of 1 per cent.

TABLE 7.—POPULATION, NUMBER OF FARMS, AND FARM ACREAGE, BY DIVISIONS AND STATES: 1850 TO 1920—Continued.

[A minus sign (−) denotes decrease. Per cent not shown when more than 1,000.]

DIVISION OR STATE AND CENSUS YEAR.	POPULATION.		NUMBER OF FARMS.		ALL LAND IN FARMS.		IMPROVED LAND IN FARMS.	
	Number.	Per cent of increase.	Number.	Per cent of increase.	Acres.	Per cent of increase.	Acres.	Per cent of increase.
GEOGRAPHIC DIVISIONS—Con.								
EAST SOUTH CENTRAL.								
1920	8,893,307	5.7	1,051,600	0.9	78,897,463	−3.2	44,380,132	1.0
1910	8,409,901	11.4	1,042,480	15.4	81,520,629	0.3	43,946,846	9.2
1900	7,547,757	17.4	903,313	37.7	81,247,643	2.8	40,237,337	12.6
1890	6,429,154	15.1	655,766	15.1	78,999,359	2.8	35,729,170	15.9
1880	5,585,151	26.8	569,739	53.2	76,872,951	15.9	30,820,882	27.3
1870	4,404,445	9.5	371,968	37.2	66,323,611	−11.3	24,218,478	−6.5
1860	4,020,991	19.6	271,150	21.4	74,776,655	27.7	25,891,024	36.1
1850	3,363,271	....	223,436	....	58,561,870	....	19,023,415	....
WEST SOUTH CENTRAL.								
1920	10,242,224	16.6	996,088	5.6	173,449,127	2.5	64,189,606	10.2
1910	8,784,534	34.5	943,186	24.9	169,149,976	−4.2	58,264,273	46.5
1900	6,532,290	37.8	754,853	75.1	176,491,202	127.9	39,770,530	30.1
1890	4,740,983	42.2	431,006	36.0	77,448,935	36.8	30,559,654	61.0
1880	3,334,220	64.2	316,909	127.9	56,627,272	71.5	18,985,889	176.3
1870	2,029,965	16.2	139,030	40.1	33,019,636	−25.3	6,870,297	−6.4
1860	1,747,667	85.9	99,223	128.7	44,216,310	131.7	7,341,202	143.4
1850	940,251	....	43,378	....	19,083,596	....	3,015,531	....
MOUNTAIN.								
1920	3,336,101	26.7	244,109	33.1	117,337,226	97.1	30,105,868	89.2
1910	2,633,517	57.3	183,446	81.0	59,533,420	28.3	15,915,002	89.4
1900	1,674,657	38.0	101,327	105.1	46,397,284	214.2	8,402,576	53.9
1890	1,213,935	85.9	49,398	97.3	14,765,862	271.3	5,460,739	146.7
1880	653,119	107.1	25,043	81.8	3,976,377	126.8	2,213,300	284.1
1870	315,385	80.3	13,774	56.3	1,753,590	12.3	576,200	139.5
1860	174,923	139.9	8,812	88.5	1,560,938	362.6	240,625	31.8
1850	72,927	....	4,676	....	337,420	....	182,534	....
PACIFIC.								
1920	5,566,871	32.8	234,164	23.3	56,152,705	9.4	23,921,533	8.5
1910	4,192,304	73.5	189,891	34.1	51,328,789	8.3	22,038,008	17.5
1900	2,416,692	28.0	141,581	46.7	47,399,576	45.8	18,753,105	6.8
1890	1,888,334	69.4	96,480	64.4	32,516,371	46.4	17,559,671	31.5
1880	1,114,578	65.1	58,680	70.4	22,217,875	53.6	13,352,689	77.4
1870	675,125	52.0	34,438	33.2	14,465,496	29.7	7,526,439	118.4
1860	444,053	319.4	25,852	....	11,156,729	157.9	3,446,317	....
1850	105,891	....	2,036	....	4,326,793	....	165,311	....
NEW ENGLAND.								
MAINE.								
1920	768,014	3.5	48,227	−19.6	5,425,968	−13.8	1,977,329	−16.2
1910	742,371	6.9	60,016	1.2	6,296,859	(1)	2,360,657	−1.1
1900	694,466	5.0	59,299	−4.4	6,299,946	1.9	2,386,889	−21.6
1890	661,086	1.9	62,013	−3.6	6,179,925	−5.7	3,044,666	−12.6
1880	648,936	3.5	64,309	7.5	6,552,578	12.2	3,484,908	19.4
1870	626,915	−0.2	59,804	7.4	5,838,058	1.9	2,917,793	7.9
1860	628,279	7.7	55,698	19.1	5,727,671	25.7	2,704,133	32.6
1850	583,169	....	46,760	....	4,555,393	....	2,039,596	....
NEW HAMPSHIRE.								
1920	443,083	2.9	20,523	−24.1	2,603,806	−19.9	702,902	−24.4
1910	430,572	4.6	27,053	−7.7	3,219,458	−10.0	929,185	−13.7
1900	411,588	9.3	29,324	0.6	3,609,864	4.4	1,076,879	−37.7
1890	376,530	8.5	29,151	−9.4	3,459,018	−7.0	1,727,387	−25.2
1880	346,991	9.0	32,181	8.6	3,721,173	3.2	2,308,112	−1.1
1870	318,300	−2.4	29,642	−2.8	3,605,994	−3.7	2,334,487	−1.4
1860	326,073	2.5	30,501	4.4	3,744,625	10.4	2,367,034	5.1
1850	317,976	....	29,229	....	3,392,414	....	2,251,488	....

[1] Less than one-tenth of 1 per cent decrease.

TABLE **7.**—POPULATION, NUMBER OF FARMS, AND FARM ACREAGE, BY DIVISIONS AND STATES: 1850 TO 1920—Continued.

[A minus sign (−) denotes decrease.]

DIVISION OR STATE AND CENSUS YEAR.	POPULATION.		NUMBER OF FARMS.		ALL LAND IN FARMS.		IMPROVED LAND IN FARMS.	
	Number.	Per cent of increase.	Number.	Per cent of increase.	Acres.	Per cent of increase.	Acres.	Per cent of increase.
NEW ENGLAND—Con.								
VERMONT.								
1920	352,428	−1.0	29,075	−11.1	4,235,811	−9.2	1,691,595	3.5
1910	355,956	3.6	32,709	−1.2	4,663,577	−1.3	1,633,965	−23.2
1900	343,641	3.4	33,104	1.6	4,724,440	7.5	2,126,624	−19.9
1890	332,422	(¹)	32,573	−8.3	4,395,646	−10.0	2,655,943	−19.2
1880	332,286	0.5	35,522	5.0	4,882,588	7.8	3,286,461	6.9
1870	330,551	4.9	33,827	7.2	4,528,804	6.0	3,073,257	8.9
1860	315,098	0.3	31,556	6.0	4,274,414	3.6	2,823,157	8.5
1850	314,120	....	29,763	....	4,125,822	....	2,601,409	....
MASSACHUSETTS.								
1920	3,852,356	14.4	32,001	−13.3	2,494,477	−13.3	908,834	−22.0
1910	3,366,416	20.0	36,917	−2.1	2,875,941	−8.6	1,164,501	−9.9
1900	2,805,346	25.3	37,715	9.7	3,147,064	5.0	1,292,132	−22.0
1890	2,238,947	25.6	34,374	−10.5	2,998,282	−10.7	1,657,024	−22.1
1880	1,783,085	22.4	38,406	44.9	3,359,079	23.0	2,128,311	22.6
1870	1,457,351	18.4	26,500	−25.6	2,730,283	−18.2	1,736,221	−19.5
1860	1,231,066	23.8	35,601	4.5	3,338,724	−0.5	2,155,512	1.0
1850	994,514	....	34,069	....	3,356,012	....	2,133,436	....
RHODE ISLAND.								
1920	604,397	11.4	4,083	−22.8	331,600	−25.2	132,855	−25.5
1910	542,610	26.6	5,292	−3.7	443,308	−2.7	178,344	−4.8
1900	428,556	24.0	5,498	(²)	455,602	−2.9	187,354	−31.7
1890	345,506	24.9	5,500	−11.5	469,281	−8.8	274,491	−8.0
1880	276,531	27.2	6,216	15.8	514,813	2.5	298,486	3.3
1870	217,353	24.5	5,368	−0.7	502,308	−3.6	289,030	−13.8
1860	174,620	18.4	5,406	0.4	521,224	−5.9	335,128	−6.0
1850	147,545	....	5,385	....	553,938	....	356,487	....
CONNECTICUT.								
1920	1,380,631	23.9	22,655	−15.5	1,898,980	−13.1	701,086	−29.1
1910	1,114,756	22.7	26,815	−0.5	2,185,788	−5.5	988,252	−7.2
1900	908,420	21.7	26,948	2.3	2,312,083	2.6	1,064,525	−22.8
1890	746,258	19.8	26,350	−13.9	2,253,432	−8.2	1,379,419	−16.0
1880	622,700	15.9	30,598	20.0	2,453,541	3.8	1,642,188	−0.3
1870	537,454	16.8	25,508	1.3	2,364,416	−5.6	1,646,752	−10.1
1860	460,147	24.1	25,180	12.2	2,504,264	5.0	1,830,807	3.5
1850	370,792	....	22,445	....	2,383,879	....	1,768,178	....
MIDDLE ATLANTIC.								
NEW YORK.								
1920	10,385,227	14.0	193,195	−10.4	20,632,803	−6.3	13,158,781	−11.4
1910	9,113,614	25.4	215,597	−4.9	22,030,367	−2.7	14,844,039	−4.8
1900	7,268,894	21.1	226,720	0.2	22,648,109	3.1	15,599,986	−4.8
1890	6,003,174	18.1	226,223	−6.2	21,961,562	−7.6	16,389,380	−7.5
1880	5,082,871	16.0	241,058	11.5	23,780,754	7.2	17,717,862	13.4
1870	4,382,759	12.9	216,253	9.8	22,190,810	5.8	15,627,206	8.8
1860	3,880,735	25.3	196,990	15.5	20,974,958	9.7	14,358,403	15.7
1850	3,097,394	....	170,621	....	19,119,084	....	12,408,964	....
NEW JERSEY.								
1920	3,155,900	24.4	29,702	−11.3	2,282,585	−11.3	1,555,907	−13.7
1910	2,537,167	34.7	33,487	−3.4	2,573,857	−9.4	1,803,336	−8.8
1900	1,883,669	30.4	34,650	12.4	2,840,966	6.7	1,977,042	−1.1
1890	1,444,933	27.7	30,828	−10.1	2,662,009	−9.1	1,999,117	−4.6
1880	1,131,116	24.8	34,307	11.9	2,929,773	−2.0	2,096,297	6.1
1870	906,096	34.8	30,652	10.9	2,989,511	0.2	1,976,474	1.6
1860	672,035	37.3	27,646	15.6	2,983,525	8.4	1,944,441	10.0
1850	489,555	....	23,905	....	2,752,946	....	1,767,991	....

¹ Less than one-tenth of 1 per cent.   ² Less than one-tenth of 1 per cent decrease.

TABLE 7.—POPULATION, NUMBER OF FARMS, AND FARM ACREAGE, BY DIVISIONS AND STATES: 1850 TO 1920—Continued.

[A minus sign (−) denotes decrease.]

DIVISION OR STATE AND CENSUS YEAR.	POPULATION.		NUMBER OF FARMS.		ALL LAND IN FARMS.		IMPROVED LAND IN FARMS.	
	Number.	Per cent of increase.	Number.	Per cent of increase.	Acres.	Per cent of increase.	Acres.	Per cent of increase.
MIDDLE ATLANTIC— Continued.								
PENNSYLVANIA.								
1920	8,720,017	13.8	202,250	−7.8	17,657,513	−5.0	11,847,719	−6.5
1910	7,665,111	21.6	219,295	−2.2	18,586,832	−4.0	12,673,519	−4.1
1900	6,302,115	19.9	224,248	6.0	19,371,015	5.5	13,209,183	(1)
1890	5,258,113	22.8	211,557	−0.9	18,364,370	−7.2	13,210,597	−1.6
1880	4,282,891	21.6	213,542	22.7	19,791,341	10.0	13,423,007	16.6
1870	3,521,951	21.2	174,041	11.3	17,994,200	5.8	11,515,965	10.1
1860	2,906,215	25.7	156,357	22.6	17,012,140	14.0	10,463,296	21.3
1850	2,311,786	......	127,577	......	14,923,347	......	8,628,619	......
EAST NORTH CENTRAL.								
OHIO.								
1920	5,759,394	20.8	256,695	−5.6	23,515,888	−2.4	18,542,353	−3.6
1910	4,767,121	14.7	272,045	−1.7	24,105,708	−1.6	19,227,969	−0.1
1900	4,157,545	13.2	276,719	10.1	24,501,985	4.9	19,244,472	4.9
1890	3,672,329	14.8	251,430	1.7	23,352,408	−4.8	18,338,824	1.4
1880	3,198,062	20.0	247,189	26.1	24,529,226	13.0	18,081,091	25.0
1870	2,665,260	13.9	195,953	8.9	21,712,420	6.1	14,469,133	14.6
1860	2,339,511	18.1	179,889	25.1	20,472,141	13.7	12,625,394	28.2
1850	1,980,329	......	143,807	......	17,997,493	......	9,851,493	......
INDIANA.								
1920	2,930,390	8.5	205,126	−4.8	21,063,332	−1.1	16,680,212	−1.5
1910	2,700,876	7.3	215,485	−2.9	21,299,823	−1.5	16,931,252	1.5
1900	2,516,462	14.8	221,897	12.0	21,619,623	6.2	16,680,358	10.4
1890	2,192,404	10.8	198,167	2.1	20,362,516	−0.3	15,107,482	8.4
1880	1,978,301	17.7	194,013	20.3	20,420,983	12.7	13,933,738	37.9
1870	1,680,637	24.5	161,289	22.3	18,119,648	10.6	10,104,279	22.6
1860	1,350,428	36.6	131,826	40.4	16,388,292	28.1	8,242,183	63.3
1850	988,416	......	93,896	......	12,793,422	......	5,046,543	......
ILLINOIS.								
1920	6,485,280	15.0	237,181	−5.8	31,974,775	−1.7	27,294,533	−2.7
1910	5,638,591	16.9	251,872	−4.6	32,522,937	−0.8	28,048,323	1.3
1900	4,821,550	26.0	264,151	9.8	32,794,728	7.5	27,699,219	7.9
1890	3,826,352	24.3	240,681	−5.9	30,498,277	−3.7	25,669,060	−1.7
1880	3,077,871	21.2	255,741	26.1	31,673,645	22.4	26,115,154	35.1
1870	2,539,891	48.4	202,803	41.5	25,882,861	23.8	19,329,952	47.6
1860	1,711,951	101.1	143,310	88.1	20,911,989	73.7	13,096,374	159.9
1850	851,470	......	76,208	......	12,037,412	......	5,039,545	......
MICHIGAN.								
1920	3,668,412	30.5	196,447	−5.1	19,032,961	0.5	12,925,521	0.7
1910	2,810,173	16.1	206,960	1.8	18,940,614	7.9	12,832,078	8.8
1900	2,420,982	15.6	203,261	17.9	17,561,698	18.8	11,799,250	19.6
1890	2,093,890	27.9	172,344	11.9	14,785,636	7.1	9,865,350	18.9
1880	1,636,937	38.2	154,008	55.9	13,807,240	37.8	8,296,862	62.8
1870	1,184,059	58.1	98,786	58.3	10,019,142	42.5	5,096,939	46.6
1860	749,113	88.4	62,422	83.1	7,030,834	60.4	3,476,296	80.2
1850	397,654	......	34,089	......	4,383,890	......	1,929,110	......
WISCONSIN.								
1920	2,632,067	12.8	189,295	6.9	22,148,223	5.2	12,452,216	4.6
1910	2,333,860	12.8	177,127	4.3	21,060,066	6.0	11,907,606	5.9
1900	2,069,042	22.2	169,795	16.0	19,862,727	18.3	11,246,972	14.8
1890	1,693,330	28.7	146,409	9.0	16,787,988	9.3	9,793,931	6.9
1880	1,315,497	24.7	134,322	30.5	15,353,118	31.1	9,162,528	55.3
1870	1,054,670	35.9	102,904	48.6	11,715,321	48.4	5,899,343	57.5
1860	775,881	154.1	69,270	243.3	7,893,587	165.2	3,746,167	258.3
1850	305,391	......	20,177	......	2,976,658	......	1,045,499	......

1 Less than one-tenth of 1 per cent decrease.

TABLE 7.—POPULATION, NUMBER OF FARMS, AND FARM ACREAGE, BY DIVISIONS AND STATES: 1850 TO 1920—Continued.

[A minus sign (−) denotes decrease. Per cent not shown when more than 1,000.]

DIVISION OR STATE AND CENSUS YEAR.	POPULATION.		NUMBER OF FARMS.		ALL LAND IN FARMS.		IMPROVED LAND IN FARMS.	
	Number.	Per cent of increase.	Number.	Per cent of increase.	Acres.	Per cent of increase.	Acres.	Per cent of increase.
WEST NORTH CENTRAL.								
MINNESOTA.								
1920	2,387,125	15.0	178,478	14.3	30,221,758	9.2	21,481,710	9.4
1910	2,075,708	18.5	156,137	1.0	27,675,823	5.4	19,643,533	6.5
1900	1,751,394	33.7	154,659	32.4	26,248,498	40.6	18,442,585	65.7
1890	1,310,283	67.8	116,851	26.5	18,663,645	39.2	11,127,953	53.6
1880	780,773	77.6	92,386	98.7	13,403,019	106.7	7,246,693	212.1
1870	439,706	155.6	46,500	155.8	6,483,828	139.1	2,322,102	317.4
1860	172,023	....	18,181	....	2,711,968	....	556,250	....
1850	6,077	....	157	....	28,881	....	5,035	....
IOWA.								
1920	2,404,021	8.1	213,439	−1.7	33,474,896	−1.3	28,606,951	−3.0
1910	2,224,771	−0.3	217,044	−5.1	33,930,688	−1.9	29,491,199	−1.4
1900	2,231,853	16.7	228,622	13.2	34,574,337	13.4	29,897,552	17.6
1890	1,912,297	17.7	201,903	8.9	30,491,541	23.2	25,428,899	28.0
1880	1,624,615	36.1	185,351	59.4	24,752,700	59.3	19,866,541	111.4
1870	1,194,020	76.9	116,292	90.1	15,541,793	54.3	9,396,467	147.7
1860	674,913	251.1	61,163	313.1	10,069,907	268.0	3,792,792	359.9
1850	192,214	....	14,805	....	2,736,064	....	824,682	....
MISSOURI.								
1920	3,404,055	3.4	263,004	−5.1	34,774,679	0.5	24,832,966	1.0
1910	3,293,335	6.0	277,244	−2.7	34,591,248	1.7	24,581,186	7.3
1900	3,106,665	16.0	284,886	19.7	33,997,873	10.5	22,900,043	15.7
1890	2,679,185	23.6	238,043	10.4	30,780,290	10.4	19,792,313	18.2
1880	2,168,380	26.0	215,575	45.3	27,879,276	28.4	16,745,031	83.4
1870	1,721,295	45.6	148,328	59.8	21,707,220	8.6	9,130,615	46.2
1860	1,182,012	73.3	92,792	70.4	19,984,810	105.3	6,246,871	112.6
1850	682,044	....	54,458	....	9,732,670	....	2,938,425	....
NORTH DAKOTA.								
1920	646,872	12.1	77,690	4.5	36,214,751	27.4	24,563,178	20.1
1910	577,056	80.8	74,360	64.0	28,426,650	82.9	20,455,092	112.1
1900	319,146	67.1	45,332	64.2	15,542,640	102.9	9,644,520	107.1
1890	190,983	417.4	27,611	628.5	7,660,333	645.3	4,658,015	....
1880 [1]	36,909	160.3	3,790	120.3	1,027,845	239.9	259,543	508.6
1870 [2]	14,181	193.2	1,720	....	302,376	....	42,645	....
1860 [2]	4,837	....	123	....	26,448	....	2,115	....
SOUTH DAKOTA.								
1920	636,547	9.0	74,637	−3.9	34,636,491	33.1	18,199,250	15.0
1910	583,888	45.4	77,644	47.6	26,016,892	36.4	15,827,208	40.2
1900	401,570	15.2	52,622	4.9	19,070,616	67.3	11,285,983	62.2
1890	348,600	254.7	50,158	267.6	11,396,460	311.0	6,959,293	681.2
1880 [1]	98,268	....	13,645	....	2,772,811	....	890,870	....
NEBRASKA.								
1920	1,296,372	8.7	124,417	−4.1	42,225,475	9.3	23,109,624	−5.2
1910	1,192,214	11.8	129,678	6.7	38,622,021	29.1	24,382,577	32.3
1900	1,066,300	0.3	121,525	7.0	29,911,779	38.5	18,432,595	20.9
1890	1,062,656	134.9	113,608	79.2	21,593,444	117.1	15,247,705	177.0
1880	452,402	267.8	63,387	415.3	9,944,826	379.6	5,504,702	750.8
1870	122,993	326.5	12,301	611.1	2,073,781	228.5	647,031	444.7
1860	28,841	....	2,789	....	631,214	....	118,789	....
KANSAS.								
1920	1,769,257	4.6	165,286	−7.1	45,425,179	4.7	30,600,760	2.3
1910	1,690,949	15.0	177,841	2.7	43,384,799	4.1	29,904,067	19.4
1900	1,470,495	3.0	173,098	3.9	41,662,970	37.9	25,040,550	12.3
1890	1,428,108	43.4	166,617	20.2	30,214,456	41.1	22,303,301	107.7
1880	996,096	173.4	138,561	262.7	21,417,468	278.6	10,739,566	444.9
1870	364,399	239.9	38,202	267.3	5,656,879	218.1	1,971,003	386.1
1860	107,206	....	10,400	....	1,778,400	....	405,468	....

[1] North Dakota and South Dakota admitted as states in 1889. Figures for 1880 obtained by consolidating data for the counties which then occupied the areas now known as North and South Dakota, respectively.
[2] The 1870 and 1860 figures are for Dakota Territory.

TABLE 7.—POPULATION, NUMBER OF FARMS, AND FARM ACREAGE, BY DIVISIONS AND STATES: 1850 TO 1920—Continued.

[A minus sign (−) denotes decrease.]

DIVISION OR STATE AND CENSUS YEAR.	POPULATION.		NUMBER OF FARMS.		ALL LAND IN FARMS.		IMPROVED LAND IN FARMS.	
	Number.	Per cent of increase.	Number.	Per cent of increase.	Acres.	Per cent of increase.	Acres.	Per cent of increase.
SOUTH ATLANTIC.								
DELAWARE.								
1920	223,003	10.2	10,140	−6.4	944,511	−9.1	653,052	−8.5
1910	202,322	9.5	10,836	11.9	1,038,866	−2.6	713,538	−5.4
1900	184,735	9.6	9,687	3.3	1,066,228	1.0	754,010	−1.1
1890	168,493	14.9	9,381	7.2	1,055,692	−3.2	762,655	2.1
1880	146,608	17.3	8,749	14.9	1,090,245	3.6	746,958	7.0
1870	125,015	11.4	7,615	14.4	1,052,322	4.8	698,115	9.6
1860	112,216	22.6	6,658	9.8	1,004,295	5.0	637,065	9.7
1850	91,532	......	6,063	......	956,144	......	580,862	......
MARYLAND.								
1920	1,449,661	11.9	47,908	−2.1	4,757,999	−5.9	3,136,728	−6.5
1910	1,295,346	9.0	48,923	6.3	5,057,140	−2.2	3,354,767	−4.6
1900	1,188,044	14.0	46,012	12.8	5,170,075	4.4	3,516,352	3.0
1890	1,042,390	11.5	40,798	0.7	4,952,390	−3.3	3,412,908	2.1
1880	934,943	19.7	40,517	50.1	5,119,831	13.5	3,342,700	14.7
1870	780,894	13.7	27,000	5.9	4,512,579	−6.7	2,914,007	−2.9
1860	687,049	17.8	25,494	16.6	4,835,571	4.3	3,002,267	7.3
1850	583,034	......	21,860	......	4,634,350	......	2,797,905	......
DISTRICT OF COLUMBIA.								
1920	437,571	32.2	204	−6.0	5,668	−6.5	4,258	−17.0
1910	331,069	18.8	217	−19.3	6,063	−28.6	5,133	−13.5
1900	278,718	21.0	269	−29.6	8,489	−27.7	5,934	−40.0
1890	230,392	29.7	382	−12.2	11,745	−35.3	9,898	−21.6
1880	177,624	34.9	435	108.1	18,146	55.4	12,632	52.8
1870	131,700	75.4	209	−12.2	11,677	−65.9	8,266	−52.7
1860	75,080	45.3	238	−10.9	34,263	24.8	17,474	7.4
1850	51,687	......	267	......	27,454	......	16,267	......
VIRGINIA.								
1920	2,309,187	12.0	186,242	1.2	18,561,112	−4.8	9,460,492	−4.1
1910	2,061,612	11.2	184,018	9.6	19,495,636	−2.1	9,870,058	−2.2
1900	1,854,184	12.0	167,886	31.6	19,907,883	4.2	10,094,805	10.6
1890	1,655,980	9.5	127,600	7.7	19,104,951	−3.7	9,125,545	7.2
1880	1,512,565	23.5	118,517	60.5	19,835,785	9.3	8,510,113	4.2
1870	1,225,163	−23.3	73,849	−20.3	18,145,911	−41.7	8,165,040	−28.6
1860 [1]	1,596,318	12.3	92,605	20.2	31,117,036	19.0	11,437,821	10.4
1850 [1]	1,421,661	......	77,013	......	26,152,311	......	10,360,135	......
WEST VIRGINIA.								
1920	1,463,701	19.9	87,289	−9.7	9,569,790	−4.6	5,520,308	(2)
1910	1,221,119	27.4	96,685	4.1	10,026,442	−5.9	5,521,757	0.4
1900	958,800	25.7	92,874	27.6	10,654,513	3.2	5,498,981	20.8
1890	762,794	23.3	72,773	16.1	10,321,326	1.3	4,554,000	20.1
1880	618,457	39.9	62,674	57.6	10,193,779	19.5	3,792,327	47.0
1870	442,014	......	39,778	......	8,528,394	......	2,580,254	......
NORTH CAROLINA.								
1920	2,559,123	16.0	269,763	6.3	20,021,736	−10.8	8,198,409	−7.0
1910	2,206,287	16.5	253,725	12.9	22,439,129	−1.4	8,813,056	5.8
1900	1,893,810	17.1	224,637	25.9	22,749,356	0.4	8,327,106	6.4
1890	1,617,949	15.6	178,359	13.2	22,651,896	1.3	7,828,569	20.8
1880	1,399,750	30.7	157,609	68.4	22,363,558	12.7	6,481,191	23.2
1870	1,071,361	7.9	93,565	24.4	19,835,410	−16.5	5,258,742	−19.3
1860	992,622	14.2	75,203	32.0	23,762,969	13.2	6,517,284	19.5
1850	869,039	......	56,963	......	20,996,983	......	5,453,975	......

[1] In 1860 and 1850 Virginia included the area now known as West Virginia.
[2] Less than one-tenth of 1 per cent decrease.

Table 7.—POPULATION, NUMBER OF FARMS, AND FARM ACREAGE, BY DIVISIONS AND STATES : 1850 TO 1920—Continued.

[A minus sign (−) denotes decrease.]

DIVISION OR STATE AND CENSUS YEAR.	POPULATION.		NUMBER OF FARMS.		ALL LAND IN FARMS.		IMPROVED LAND IN FARMS.	
	Number.	Per cent of increase.	Number.	Per cent of increase.	Acres.	Per cent of increase.	Acres.	Per cent of increase.
SOUTH ATLANTIC— Continued.								
SOUTH CAROLINA.								
1920	1,683,724	11.1	192,693	9.2	12,426,675	−8.0	6,184,159	1.4
1910	1,515,400	13.1	176,434	13.6	13,512,028	−3.4	6,097,999	5.6
1900	1,340,316	16.4	155,355	35.1	13,985,014	6.1	5,775,741	9.9
1890	1,151,149	15.6	115,008	22.5	13,184,652	−2.0	5,255,237	27.2
1880	995,577	41.1	93,864	80.9	13,457,613	11.2	4,132,050	37.3
1870	705,606	0.3	51,889	56.4	12,105,280	−25.3	3,010,539	−34.2
1860	703,708	5.3	33,171	10.7	16,195,919	−0.1	4,572,060	12.3
1850	668,507	......	29,967	......	16,217,700	......	4,072,651	......
GEORGIA.								
1920	2,895,832	11.0	310,732	6.8	25,441,061	−5.6	13,055,209	6.2
1910	2,609,121	17.7	291,027	29.5	26,953,413	2.1	12,298,017	15.8
1900	2,216,331	20.6	224,691	31.3	26,392,057	4.7	10,615,644	10.8
1890	1,837,353	19.1	171,071	23.4	25,200,435	−3.2	9,582,866	16.8
1880	1,542,180	30.2	138,626	98.2	26,043,282	10.1	8,204,720	20.1
1870	1,184,109	12.0	69,956	12.8	23,647,941	−11.3	6,831,856	−15.3
1860	1,057,286	16.7	62,003	19.8	26,650,490	16.8	8,062,758	26.4
1850	906,185	......	51,759	......	22,821,379	......	6,378,479	......
FLORIDA.								
1920	968,470	28.7	54,005	8.0	6,046,691	15.1	2,297,271	27.2
1910	752,619	42.4	50,016	22.5	5,253,538	20.4	1,805,408	19.4
1900	528,542	35.0	40,814	19.2	4,363,891	18.8	1,511,653	31.9
1890	391,422	45.2	34,228	46.0	3,674,486	11.4	1,145,693	20.9
1880	269,493	43.5	23,438	128.9	3,297,324	38.9	947,640	28.7
1870	187,748	33.7	10,241	55.9	2,373,541	−18.7	736,172	12.5
1860	140,424	60.6	6,568	52.6	2,920,228	83.1	654,213	87.4
1850	87,445	......	4,304	......	1,595,289	......	349,049	......
EAST SOUTH CENTRAL.								
KENTUCKY.								
1920	2,416,630	5.5	270,626	4.4	21,612,772	−2.6	13,975,746	−2.6
1910	2,289,905	6.6	259,185	10.4	22,189,127	1.0	14,354,471	4.5
1900	2,147,174	15.5	234,667	30.9	21,979,422	2.6	13,741,968	16.3
1890	1,858,635	12.7	179,264	7.7	21,412,229	−0.4	11,818,882	10.1
1880	1,648,690	24.8	166,453	40.6	21,495,240	15.2	10,731,683	32.4
1870	1,321,011	14.3	118,422	30.4	18,660,106	−2.6	8,103,850	6.0
1860	1,155,684	17.6	90,814	21.4	19,163,261	13.1	7,644,208	28.1
1850	982,405	......	74,777	......	16,949,748	......	5,968,270	......
TENNESSEE.								
1920	2,337,885	7.0	252,774	2.7	19,510,856	−2.6	11,185,302	2.7
1910	2,184,789	8.1	246,012	9.5	20,041,657	−1.5	10,890,484	6.3
1900	2,020,616	14.3	224,623	28.8	20,342,058	0.9	10,245,950	9.4
1890	1,767,518	14.6	174,412	5.3	20,161,583	−2.4	9,362,555	10.2
1880	1,542,359	22.6	165,650	40.2	20,666,915	5.5	8,496,556	24.2
1870	1,258,520	13.4	118,141	43.4	19,581,214	−5.3	6,843,278	0.7
1860	1,100,891	10.7	82,368	13.2	20,669,165	8.9	6,795,337	31.3
1850	1,002,717	......	72,735	...	18,984,022	......	5,175,173	......
ALABAMA.								
1920	2,348,174	9.8	256,099	−2.6	19,576,856	−5.6	9,893,407	2.1
1910	2,138,093	16.9	262,901	17.8	20,732,312	0.2	9,693,581	12.0
1900	1,828,697	20.8	223,220	41.5	20,685,427	4.2	8,654,991	12.4
1890	1,513,401	19.9	157,772	16.1	19,853,000	5.3	7,698,343	20.7
1880	1,262,505	26.6	135,864	101.6	18,855,334	26.0	6,375,706	25.9
1870	996,992	3.4	67,382	22.2	14,961,178	−21.7	5,062,204	−20.7
1860	964,201	25.0	55,128	31.4	19,104,545	57.4	6,385,724	44.0
1850	771,623	......	41,964	......	12,137,681	......	4,435,614	......

TABLE 7.—POPULATION, NUMBER OF FARMS, AND FARM ACREAGE, BY DIVISIONS AND STATES: 1850 TO 1920—Continued.

[A minus sign (−) denotes decrease. Per cent not shown when more than 1,000.]

DIVISION OR STATE AND CENSUS YEAR.	POPULATION.		NUMBER OF FARMS.		ALL LAND IN FARMS.		IMPROVED LAND IN FARMS.	
	Number.	Per cent of increase.	Number.	Per cent of increase.	Acres.	Per cent of increase.	Acres.	Per cent of increase.
EAST SOUTH CENTRAL—Con.								
MISSISSIPPI.								
1920	1,790,618	−0.4	272,101	−0.8	18,196,979	−1.9	9,325,677	3.5
1910	1,797,114	15.8	274,382	24.3	18,557,533	1.7	9,008,310	18.6
1900	1,551,270	20.3	220,803	53.0	18,240,736	3.8	7,594,428	10.9
1890	1,289,600	14.0	144,318	41.8	17,572,547	10.8	6,849,390	31.3
1880	1,131,597	36.7	101,772	49.6	15,855,462	20.8	5,216,937	23.9
1870	827,922	4.6	68,023	58.8	13,121,113	−17.2	4,209,146	−16.9
1860	791,305	30.5	42,840	26.1	15,839,684	51.0	5,065,755	47.1
1850	606,526	....	33,960	....	10,490,419	....	3,444,358	....
WEST SOUTH CENTRAL.								
ARKANSAS.								
1920	1,752,204	11.3	232,604	8.4	17,456,750	0.2	9,210,556	14.0
1910	1,574,449	20.0	214,678	20.1	17,416,075	4.7	8,076,254	16.1
1900	1,311,564	16.3	178,694	43.2	16,636,719	11.7	6,953,735	27.0
1890	1,128,211	40.6	124,760	32.1	14,891,356	23.5	5,475,043	52.3
1880	802,525	65.6	94,433	91.1	12,061,547	58.8	3,595,603	93.3
1870	484,471	11.3	49,424	26.7	7,597,296	−20.6	1,859,821	−6.2
1860	435,450	107.5	39,004	119.6	9,573,706	268.5	1,983,313	153.8
1850	209,897	....	17,758	....	2,598,214	....	781,530	....
LOUISIANA.								
1920	1,798,509	8.6	135,463	12.4	10,019,822	−4.0	5,626,226	6.6
1910	1,656,388	19.9	120,546	3.9	10,439,481	−5.6	5,276,016	13.1
1900	1,381,625	23.5	115,969	67.4	11,059,127	15.9	4,666,532	23.6
1890	1,118,588	19.0	69,294	43.5	9,544,219	15.4	3,774,668	37.8
1880	939,946	29.3	48,292	69.6	8,273,506	17.8	2,739,972	33.9
1870	726,915	2.7	28,481	64.4	7,025,817	−24.4	2,045,640	−24.4
1860	708,002	36.7	17,328	29.1	9,298,576	86.4	2,707,108	70.3
1850	517,762	....	13,422	....	4,989,043	....	1,590,025	....
OKLAHOMA.								
1920	2,028,283	22.4	191,988	0.9	31,951,934	10.7	18,125,321	3.3
1910	1,657,155	109.7	190,192	76.1	28,859,353	25.5	17,551,337	104.7
1900 [1]	790,391	205.6	108,000	....	22,988,339	....	8,574,187	....
1890 [2]	258,657	....	8,826	....	1,606,423	....	563,728	....
TEXAS.								
1920	4,663,228	19.7	436,033	4.4	114,020,621	1.4	31,227,503	14.1
1910	3,896,542	27.8	417,770	18.6	112,435,067	−10.6	27,360,666	39.8
1900	3,048,710	36.4	352,190	54.4	125,807,017	144.7	19,576,076	−5.6
1890	2,235,527	40.4	228,126	31.0	51,406,937	41.6	20,746,215	64.0
1880	1,591,749	94.5	174,184	185.0	36,292,219	97.3	12,650,314	326.7
1870	818,579	35.5	61,125	42.5	18,396,523	−27.4	2,964,836	11.8
1860	604,215	184.2	42,891	251.6	25,344,028	120.5	2,650,781	311.6
1850	212,592	....	12,198	....	11,496,339	....	643,976	....
MOUNTAIN.								
MONTANA.								
1920	548,889	46.0	57,677	120.0	35,070,656	158.9	11,007,278	202.4
1910	376,053	54.5	26,214	96.1	13,545,603	14.4	3,640,309	109.6
1900	243,329	70.3	13,370	138.6	11,844,454	503.0	1,736,701	89.7
1890	142,924	265.0	5,603	268.9	1,964,197	384.2	915,517	248.6
1880	39,159	90.1	1,519	78.5	405,683	190.7	202,611	210.1
1870	20,595	....	851	....	139,537	....	84,674	....

[1] Figures for 1900 include Indian Territory.
[2] The 1890 figures for population include Indian Territory; those for number of farms and farm acreage are for Oklahoma Territory alone, no data being available for Indian Territory.

TABLE 7.—POPULATION, NUMBER OF FARMS, AND FARM ACREAGE, BY DIVISIONS AND STATES: 1850 TO 1920—Continued.

[A minus sign (−) denotes decrease. Per cent not shown when base is less than 100 or when per cent is more than 1,000.]

DIVISION OR STATE AND CENSUS YEAR.	POPULATION.		NUMBER OF FARMS.		ALL LAND IN FARMS.		IMPROVED LAND IN FARMS.	
	Number.	Per cent of increase.	Number.	Per cent of increase.	Acres.	Per cent of increase.	Acres.	Per cent of increase.
MOUNTAIN—Con.								
IDAHO.								
1920	431,866	32.6	42,106	36.7	8,375,873	58.5	4,511,680	62.4
1910	325,594	101.3	30,807	76.3	5,283,604	64.9	2,778,740	96.6
1900	161,772	82.7	17,471	164.6	3,204,903	146.1	1,413,118	133.0
1890	88,548	171.5	6,603	250.3	1,302,256	297.3	606,362	207.2
1880	32,610	117.4	1,885	355.3	327,798	324.9	197,407	642.0
1870	14,999	......	414	......	77,139	......	26,603	......
WYOMING.								
1920	194,402	33.2	15,748	43.3	11,809,351	38.2	2,102,005	67.3
1910	145,965	57.7	10,987	80.3	8,543,010	5.2	1,256,160	58.5
1900	92,531	47.9	6,095	95.0	8,124,536	343.9	792,332	66.2
1890	62,555	200.9	3,125	583.8	1,830,432	......	476,831	473.6
1880	20,789	128.0	457	161.1	124,433	......	83,122	......
1870	9,118	......	175	......	4,341	......	338	......
COLORADO.								
1920	939,629	17.6	59,934	29.8	24,462,014	80.8	7,744,757	80.0
1910	799,024	48.0	46,170	86.9	13,532,113	42.8	4,302,101	89.2
1900	539,700	30.6	24,700	50.7	9,474,588	106.0	2,273,968	24.7
1890	413,249	112.7	16,389	263.7	4,598,941	294.6	1,823,520	195.9
1880	194,327	387.5	4,506	159.3	1,165,373	263.8	616,169	544.6
1870	39,864	16.3	1,738	......	320,346	......	95,594	......
1860	34,277	......						
NEW MEXICO.								
1920	360,350	10.1	29,844	−16.3	24,409,633	116.6	1,717,224	17.0
1910	327,301	67.6	35,676	189.8	11,270,021	119.7	1,467,191	348.9
1900	195,310	21.9	12,311	176.2	5,130,878	551.2	326,873	24.2
1890	160,282	34.1	4,458	−11.8	787,882	24.8	263,106	10.8
1880	119,565	30.1	5,053	12.8	631,131	−24.3	237,392	66.0
1870	91,874	−1.8	4,480	−11.9	833,549	−41.1	143,007	−4.2
1860	93,516	51.9	5,086	35.6	1,414,909	386.9	149,274	−10.2
1850	61,547	......	3,750	......	290,571	......	166,201	......
ARIZONA.								
1920	334,162	63.5	9,975	8.1	5,802,126	365.4	712,803	103.6
1910	204,354	66.2	9,227	58.8	1,246,613	−35.6	350,173	37.6
1900	122,931	39.3	5,809	307.4	1,935,327	49.2	254,521	144.4
1890	88,243	118.2	1,426	85.9	1,297,033	856.7	104,128	85.7
1880	40,440	318.7	767	345.9	135,573	521.7	56,071	284.4
1870	9,658	......	172	......	21,807	......	14,585	......
UTAH.								
1920	449,396	20.4	25,662	18.4	5,050,410	48.6	1,715,380	25.4
1910	373,351	34.9	21,676	11.8	3,397,699	−17.5	1,368,211	32.6
1900	276,749	31.3	19,387	84.3	4,116,951	211.0	1,032,117	88.3
1890	210,779	46.4	10,517	11.3	1,323,705	101.9	548,223	31.7
1880	143,963	65.9	9,452	92.6	655,524	341.8	416,105	250.4
1870	86,786	115.5	4,908	35.0	118,261	65.0	118,755	53.8
1860	40,273	253.9	3,635	292.5	89,911	91.9	77,219	372.8
1850	11,380	......	926	......	46,849	......	16,333	......
NEVADA.								
1920	77,407	−5.5	3,163	17.6	2,357,163	−13.2	594,741	−20.9
1910	81,875	93.4	2,689	23.1	2,714,757	5.8	752,117	31.3
1900	42,335	−10.6	2,184	71.0	2,565,647	54.4	572,946	−20.8
1890	47,355	−23.9	1,277	−9.0	1,661,416	213.0	723,052	109.9
1880	62,266	46.5	1,404	35.5	530,862	154.6	344,423	271.8
1870	42,491	519.7	1,036	......	208,510	271.6	92,644	555.6
1860	6,857	......	91	......	56,118	......	14,132	......

TABLE 7.—POPULATION, NUMBER OF FARMS AND FARM ACREAGE, BY DIVISIONS AND STATES: 1850 TO 1920—Continued.

[A minus sign (—) denotes decrease. Per cent not shown when more than 1,000.]

DIVISION OR STATE AND CENSUS YEAR.	POPULATION.		NUMBER OF FARMS.		ALL LAND IN FARMS.		IMPROVED LAND IN FARMS.	
	Number.	Per cent of increase.	Number.	Per cent of increase.	Acres.	Per cent of increase.	Acres.	Per cent of increase.
PACIFIC.								
WASHINGTON.								
1920	1,356,621	18.8	66,288	18.0	13,244,720	13.1	7,129,343	11.9
1910	1,141,990	120.4	56,192	69.2	11,712,235	37.8	6,373,311	83.9
1900	518,103	45.0	33,202	83.9	8,499,297	103.4	3,465,960	90.4
1890	357,232	375.6	18,056	176.6	4,179,190	196.5	1,820,832	275.9
1880	75,116	213.6	6,529	108.8	1,409,421	117.1	484,346	152.2
1870	23,955	106.6	3,127	135.1	649,139	77.3	192,016	134.5
1860	11,594	......	1,330	......	366,156	......	81,869	......
OREGON.								
1920	783,389	16.4	50,206	10.3	13,542,318	15.9	4,913,851	14.9
1910	672,765	62.7	45,502	27.0	11,685,110	16.0	4,274,803	28.4
1900	413,536	30.2	35,837	40.4	10,071,328	45.8	3,328,308	−5.3
1890	317,704	81.8	25,530	57.4	6,909,888	63.9	3,516,000	59.9
1880	174,768	92.2	16,217	113.7	4,214,712	76.4	2,198,645	97.0
1870	90,923	73.3	7,587	30.7	2,389,252	16.0	1,116,290	24.5
1860	52,465	294.7	5,806	398.8	2,060,539	376.1	896,414	574.7
1850	13,294	......	1,164	......	432,808	......	132,857	......
CALIFORNIA.								
1920	3,426,861	44.1	117,670	33.4	29,365,667	5.1	11,878,339	4.3
1910	2,377,549	60.1	88,197	21.6	27,931,444	−3.1	11,389,894	−4.8
1900	1,485,053	22.4	72,542	37.1	28,828,951	34.5	11,958,837	−2.2
1890	1,213,398	40.3	52,894	47.2	21,427,293	29.1	12,222,839	14.6
1880	864,694	54.3	35,934	51.5	16,593,742	45.2	10,669,698	71.6
1870	560,247	47.4	23,724	26.8	11,427,105	30.9	6,218,133	151.9
1860	379,994	310.4	18,716	......	8,730,034	124.2	2,468,034	......
1850	92,597	......	872	......	3,893,985	......	32,454	......

TABLE 8.—VALUE OF ALL FARM PROPERTY AND OF THE SEVERAL

[A minus sign (−) denotes decrease.]

	DIVISION AND STATE.	ALL FARM PROPERTY.			LAND.		
		1920	1910	Per cent of increase	1920	1910	Per cent of increase
1	United States....	$77,924,100,338	$40,991,449,090	90.1	$54,829,563,059	$28,475,674,169	92.5
	GEOGRAPHIC DIVISIONS:						
2	New England	1,173,019,594	867,240,457	35.3	488,125,250	382,134,424	27.7
3	Middle Atlantic	3,949,684,183	2,959,589,022	33.5	1,661,676,107	1,462,321,005	13.6
4	East North Central..	17,245,362,593	10,119,128,066	70.4	12,046,073,684	7,231,699,114	66.6
5	West North Central .	27,991,434,545	13,535,309,511	106.8	21,310,145,142	10,052,560,913	112.3
6	South Atlantic......	6,132,917,760	2,951,200,773	107.8	4,000,681,904	1,883,349,675	112.4
7	East South Central .	4,419,466,237	2,182,771,779	102.5	2,916,141,232	1,326,826,864	119.8
8	West South Central .	7,622,066,027	3,838,154,337	98.6	5,408,059,615	2,716,098,530	99.1
9	Mountain	4,083,137,939	1,757,573,368	132.3	2,801,712,079	1,174,370,096	138.6
10	Pacific	5,307,011,460	2,780,481,777	90.9	4,166,948,046	2,246,313,548	85.5
	NEW ENGLAND:						
11	Maine	270,526,733	199,271,998	35.8	114,411,871	86,481,395	32.3
12	New Hampshire	118,656,115	103,704,196	14.4	47,425,331	44,519,047	6.5
13	Vermont	222,736,620	145,399,728	53.2	82,938,253	58,385,327	42.1
14	Massachusetts	300,471,743	226,474,025	32.7	127,653,607	105,532,616	21.0
15	Rhode Island	33,636,766	32,990,739	2.0	14,509,073	15,009,981	−3.3
16	Connecticut	226,991,617	159,399,771	42.4	101,187,115	72,206,058	40.1
	MIDDLE ATLANTIC:						
17	New York	1,908,483,201	1,451,481,495	31.5	793,335,558	707,747,828	12.1
18	New Jersey	311,847,948	254,832,665	22.4	142,182,498	124,143,167	14.5
19	Pennsylvania	1,729,353,034	1,253,274,862	38.0	726,158,051	630,430,010	15.2
	EAST NORTH CENTRAL:						
20	Ohio	3,095,666,336	1,902,694,589	62.7	2,015,112,999	1,285,894,812	56.7
21	Indiana	3,042,311,247	1,809,135,238	68.2	2,202,566,336	1,328,196,545	65.8
22	Illinois	6,666,767,235	3,905,321,075	70.7	5,250,294,752	3,090,411,148	69.9
23	Michigan	1,763,334,778	1,088,858,379	61.9	959,186,538	615,258,348	55.9
24	Wisconsin	2,677,282,997	1,413,118,785	89.5	1,618,913,059	911,938,261	77.5
	WEST NORTH CENTRAL:						
25	Minnesota	3,787,420,118	1,476,411,737	156.5	2,750,328,432	1,019,102,027	169.9
26	Iowa	8,524,870,956	3,745,860,544	127.6	6,679,020,577	2,801,973,729	138.4
27	Missouri	3,591,068,085	2,052,917,488	74.9	2,594,193,271	1,445,982,389	79.4
28	North Dakota	1,759,742,995	974,814,205	80.5	1,279,313,627	730,380,131	75.2
29	South Dakota	2,823,870,212	1,166,096,980	142.2	2,231,431,723	902,606,751	147.2
30	Nebraska	4,201,655,992	2,079,818,647	102.0	3,330,222,340	1,614,539,313	106.3
31	Kansas	3,302,806,187	2,039,389,910	62.0	2,475,635,172	1,537,976,573	61.0
	SOUTH ATLANTIC:						
32	Delaware	80,137,614	63,179,201	26.8	42,115,802	34,938,161	20.5
33	Maryland	463,638,120	286,167,028	62.0	259,904,047	163,451,614	59.0
34	District of Columbia.	5,927,987	8,476,533	−30.1	4,156,148	7,193,950	−42.2
35	Virginia	1,196,555,772	625,065,383	91.4	756,354,277	394,658,912	91.6
36	West Virginia	496,439,617	314,738,540	57.7	307,309,704	207,075,759	48.4
37	North Carolina	1,250,166,995	537,716,210	132.5	857,815,016	343,164,945	150.0
38	South Carolina	953,064,742	392,128,314	143.0	647,157,209	268,774,854	140.8
39	Georgia	1,356,685,196	580,546,381	133.7	897,444,961	370,353,415	142.3
40	Florida	330,301,717	143,183,183	130.7	228,424,740	93,738,065	143.7
	EAST SOUTH CENTRAL:						
41	Kentucky	1,511,901,077	773,797,880	95.4	1,050,752,680	484,464,617	116.9
42	Tennessee	1,251,964,585	612,520,836	104.4	807,782,296	371,415,783	117.5
43	Alabama	690,848,720	370,138,429	86.6	415,763,862	216,944,175	91.6
44	Mississippi	964,751,855	426,314,634	126.3	641,842,394	254,002,289	152.7
	WEST SOUTH CENTRAL:						
45	Arkansas	924,395,483	400,089,303	131.0	607,773,440	246,021,450	147.0
46	Louisiana	589,826,679	301,220,988	95.8	383,618,162	187,803,277	104.3
47	Oklahoma	1,660,423,544	918,198,882	80.8	1,171,459,364	649,066,668	80.5
48	Texas	4,447,420,321	2,218,645,164	100.5	3,245,208,649	1,633,207,135	98.7
	MOUNTAIN:						
49	Montana	985,961,308	347,828,770	160.5	691,912,265	226,771,302	205.1
50	Idaho	716,137,910	305,017,185	117.6	511,865,869	219,953,316	132.7
51	Wyoming	334,410,590	167,189,081	100.0	210,947,494	88,808,273	107.0
52	Colorado	1,076,794,749	491,471,806	119.1	763,722,716	362,822,205	110.5
53	New Mexico	325,185,999	159,447,990	103.9	196,341,050	98,806,497	98.7
54	Arizona	233,592,989	75,123,970	210.9	156,562,606	42,349,737	269.7
55	Utah	311,274,728	150,795,201	106.4	210,997,840	99,482,164	112.1
56	Nevada	99,779,666	60,399,365	65.2	59,362,239	35,276,599	68.3
	PACIFIC:						
57	Washington	1,057,429,848	637,543,411	65.9	797,651,020	517,421,998	54.2
58	Oregon	818,559,751	528,243,782	55.0	586,242,049	411,696,102	42.4
59	California	3,431,021,861	1,614,694,584	112.5	2,783,054,977	1,317,195,448	111.3

CLASSES, BY DIVISIONS AND STATES: 1920 AND 1910.

[A minus sign (−) denotes decrease.]

BUILDINGS.			IMPLEMENTS AND MACHINERY.			LIVE STOCK.			
1920	1910	Per cent of increase	1920	1910	Per cent of increase	1920	1910	Per cent of increase	
$11,486,439,543	$6,325,451,528	81.6	$3,594,772,928	$1,265,149,783	184.1	$8,013,324,808	$4,925,173,610	62.7	1
429,343,334	336,410,384	27.6	92,387,525	50,798,826	81.9	163,163,485	97,896,823	66.7	2
1,340,461,647	980,628,098	36.7	359,152,336	167,480,384	114.4	588,394,093	349,159,535	68.5	3
2,891,567,987	1,642,292,480	76.1	786,076,805	268,806,550	192.4	1,521,644,117	976,329,922	55.9	4
3,129,350,027	1,562,104,957	100.3	1,162,938,264	368,935,544	215.2	2,359,001,112	1,551,708,097	52.0	5
1,201,091,568	603,086,799	99.2	283,980,857	98,230,147	189.1	647,163,431	366,534,152	76.6	6
747,552,131	411,570,975	81.6	176,064,886	75,339,333	133.7	579,707,988	369,034,607	57.1	7
883,128,457	412,498,352	114.1	311,098,790	119,720,377	159.9	1,019,779,165	589,837,078	72.9	8
361,475,704	145,026,777	149.2	190,715,673	49,429,975	285.8	729,234,483	388,746,520	87.6	9
502,468,688	231,832,706	116.7	232,357,792	66,408,647	249.9	405,236,934	235,926,876	71.8	10
89,697,100	73,138,231	22.6	26,637,660	14,490,533	83.8	39,780,102	25,161,839	58.1	11
42,570,539	41,397,014	2.8	9,499,322	5,877,657	61.6	19,160,923	11,910,478	60.9	12
76,178,906	54,202,948	40.5	21,234,130	10,168,687	108.8	42,385,331	22,642,766	87.2	13
119,934,224	88,636,149	35.3	19,359,755	11,563,894	67.4	33,524,157	20,741,366	61.6	14
11,878,853	12,922,879	−8.1	2,408,561	1,781,407	35.2	4,840,279	3,276,472	47.7	15
89,083,712	66,113,163	34.7	13,248,097	6,916,648	91.5	23,472,693	14,163,902	65.7	16
631,726,182	476,998,001	32.4	169,866,766	83,644,822	103.1	313,554,695	183,090,844	71.3	17
108,141,488	92,991,352	16.3	25,459,205	13,109,507	94.2	36,064,757	24,588,639	46.7	18
600,593,977	410,638,745	46.3	163,826,365	70,726,055	131.6	238,774,641	141,480,052	68.8	19
646,322,950	368,257,594	75.5	146,575,269	51,210,071	186.2	287,655,118	197,332,112	45.8	20
451,077,637	266,079,051	69.5	127,403,086	40,999,541	210.7	261,264,188	173,860,101	50.3	21
747,698,814	432,381,422	72.9	222,619,605	73,724,074	202.0	446,154,064	308,804,431	44.5	22
477,499,672	285,879,951	67.0	122,389,936	49,916,285	145.2	204,258,632	137,803,795	48.2	23
568,962,914	289,694,462	96.4	167,088,909	52,956,579	215.5	322,312,115	158,529,483	103.3	24
550,839,893	243,339,399	126.4	181,087,968	52,329,165	246.1	305,163,825	161,641,146	88.8	25
922,751,713	455,405,671	102.6	309,172,398	95,477,948	223.8	613,926,268	393,003,196	56.2	26
468,774,449	270,221,997	73.5	138,261,340	50,873,994	171.8	389,839,045	285,839,108	36.4	27
209,207,868	92,276,613	126.7	114,186,865	43,907,595	160.1	157,034,635	108,249,866	45.1	28
241,461,958	102,474,056	135.6	112,408,268	33,786,973	232.7	238,568,263	127,229,200	87.5	29
391,885,420	198,807,622	92.1	153,104,448	44,249,708	246.0	336,443,784	222,222,000	51.4	30
354,428,746	199,579,599	77.6	154,716,977	48,310,161	220.3	318,025,292	253,523,577	25.4	31
22,639,829	18,217,822	24.3	6,781,318	3,206,095	111.5	8,600,665	6,817,123	26.2	32
126,692,803	78,285,509	61.8	28,970,020	11,859,771	144.3	48,071,250	32,570,134	47.6	33
1,421,221	1,037,393	37.0	104,252	92,350	12.9	246,366	152,840	61.2	34
268,080,748	137,399,150	95.1	50,151,466	18,115,883	176.8	121,969,281	74,891,438	62.9	35
103,473,702	57,315,195	80.5	18,395,058	7,011,513	162.4	67,261,153	43,336,073	55.2	36
218,577,944	113,459,662	92.6	54,621,363	18,441,619	196.2	119,152,672	62,649,984	90.2	37
166,326,991	64,113,227	159.4	48,062,387	14,108,653	240.7	91,518,155	45,131,380	102.8	38
240,853,666	108,850,917	121.3	63,343,220	20,948,056	202.4	155,043,349	80,393,993	92.9	39
53,024,664	24,407,924	117.2	13,551,773	4,446,007	204.8	35,300,540	20,591,187	71.4	40
254,406,256	150,994,755	68.5	48,354,857	20,851,846	131.9	158,387,284	117,486,662	34.8	41
217,197,598	109,106,804	99.1	53,462,556	21,292,171	151.1	173,522,135	110,706,078	56.7	42
127,893,893	71,309,416	79.4	34,366,217	16,290,004	111.0	112,824,748	65,594,834	72.0	43
148,054,384	80,160,000	84.7	39,881,256	16,905,312	135.9	134,973,821	75,247,033	79.4	44
145,337,226	63,145,363	130.2	43,432,237	16,864,198	157.5	127,852,580	74,058,292	72.6	45
90,420,631	49,741,173	81.8	32,715,010	18,977,053	72.4	83,072,876	44,699,485	85.8	46
192,405,930	89,610,556	114.7	80,630,547	27,088,866	197.7	215,927,703	152,432,792	41.7	47
454,964,670	210,001,260	116.6	154,320,996	56,790,260	171.7	592,926,006	318,646,509	86.1	48
84,855,264	24,854,628	241.4	55,004,212	10,539,653	421.9	154,189,567	85,663,187	80.0	49
69,646,095	25,112,509	177.3	38,417,253	10,476,051	266.7	96,208,693	49,775,309	93.3	50
23,800,631	9,007,001	164.2	11,777,949	3,668,294	221.1	87,884,516	65,605,510	34.0	51
102,290,944	45,696,656	123.8	49,804,509	12,791,601	289.4	160,976,580	70,161,344	129.4	52
25,473,162	13,024,502	95.6	9,745,369	4,122,312	136.4	93,626,418	43,494,679	115.3	53
15,762,715	4,935,573	219.4	8,820,667	1,787,790	393.4	52,447,001	26,050,870	101.3	54
32,753,918	18,063,168	81.3	13,514,787	4,468,178	202.5	54,008,183	28,781,691	87.6	55
6,892,975	4,332,740	59.1	3,630,927	1,576,096	130.4	29,893,525	19,213,930	55.6	56
122,741,321	54,546,459	125.0	54,721,377	16,709,844	227.5	82,316,130	48,865,110	68.5	57
88,971,235	43,880,207	102.8	41,567,125	13,205,645	214.8	101,779,342	59,461,828	71.2	58
290,756,132	133,406,040	117.9	136,069,290	36,493,158	272.9	221,141,462	127,599,938	73.3	59

TABLE 9.—VALUE OF ALL FARM PROPERTY AND OF THE SEVERAL CLASSES, BY DIVISIONS: 1850 TO 1920.

[Figures for 1870 are computed gold values, being 80 per cent of the currency values reported. A minus sign (−) denotes decrease.]

DIVISION AND CENSUS YEAR.	ALL FARM PROPERTY.		LAND AND BUILDINGS.		IMPLEMENTS AND MACHINERY.		LIVE STOCK.	
	Value.	Per cent of increase	Value.	Per cent of increase	Value.	Per cent of increase	Value.	Per cent of increase
UNITED STATES.								
1920	$77,924,100,338	90.1	$66,316,002,602	90.6	$3,594,772,928	184.1	$8,013,324,808	62.7
1910	40,991,449,090	100.5	34,801,125,697	109.5	1,265,149,783	68.7	4,925,173,610	60.1
1900	20,439,901,164	27.1	16,614,647,491	25.1	749,775,970	51.7	3,075,477,703	33.2
1890	16,082,267,689	32.0	13,279,252,649	30.2	494,247,467	21.6	2,308,767,573	46.4
1880	12,180,501,538	36.2	10,197,096,776	37.0	406,520,055	50.1	1,576,884,707	28.2
1870	8,944,857,749	12.1	7,444,054,462	12.0	270,913,678	10.1	1,229,889,609	12.9
1860	7,980,493,063	101.2	6,645,045,007	103.1	246,118,141	62.4	1,089,329,915	100.2
1850	3,967,343,580	......	3,271,575,426	......	151,587,638	......	544,180,516	......
GEOGRAPHIC DIVISIONS.								
NEW ENGLAND.								
1920	1,173,019,594	35.3	917,468,584	27.7	92,387,525	81.9	163,163,485	66.7
1910	867,240,457	35.6	718,544,808	36.0	50,798,826	39.0	97,896,823	30.8
1900	639,645,900	9.3	528,267,748	7.9	36,551,820	53.7	74,826,332	4.0
1890	585,267,817	−12.9	489,570,178	−15.7	23,783,288	7.6	71,914,351	4.1
1880	671,846,058	18.6	580,681,418	24.0	22,096,563	22.5	69,068,077	−13.9
1870	566,353,951	0.9	468,133,979	−1.7	18,042,446	9.6	80,177,526	16.7
1860	561,467,417	29.0	476,303,837	27.9	16,468,564	27.3	68,695,016	37.8
1850	435,154,525	......	372,348,543	......	12,937,290	......	49,868,692	......
MIDDLE ATLANTIC.								
1920	3,949,684,183	33.5	3,002,137,754	22.9	359,152,336	114.4	588,394,093	68.5
1910	2,959,589,022	28.1	2,442,949,103	25.3	167,480,384	44.1	349,159,535	42.1
1900	2,310,886,728	−3.1	1,948,997,940	−4.9	116,253,270	24.9	245,635,518	15.1
1890	2,384,703,476	−5.5	2,049,630,359	−7.8	93,084,964	9.5	241,988,153	11.5
1880	2,524,721,419	6.0	2,222,761,984	7.9	84,986,863	18.6	216,972,572	−13.3
1870	2,381,103,898	25.8	2,059,090,179	25.1	71,635,120	24.9	250,378,599	32.0
1860	1,892,664,457	51.5	1,645,644,638	52.0	57,356,104	39.1	189,663,715	50.8
1850	1,249,643,065	......	1,082,660,252	......	41,232,970	......	125,749,843	......
EAST NORTH CENTRAL.								
1920	17,245,362,593	70.4	14,937,641,671	68.3	786,076,805	192.4	1,521,644,117	55.9
1910	10,119,128,066	78.0	8,873,991,594	80.6	268,806,550	61.3	976,329,922	61.5
1900	5,683,925,367	19.6	4,912,597,440	19.8	166,694,220	31.8	604,633,707	15.5
1890	4,751,184,987	14.3	4,101,406,702	13.0	126,454,149	5.6	523,324,136	27.8
1880	4,158,388,413	34.5	3,629,140,732	37.1	119,804,675	41.4	409,443,006	14.0
1870	3,090,625,976	52.3	2,646,744,323	52.5	84,717,847	49.1	359,163,806	52.0
1860	2,028,817,467	151.8	1,735,742,858	158.4	56,810,880	86.9	236,263,729	127.8
1850	805,787,277	......	671,678,075	......	30,393,529	......	103,715,673	......
WEST NORTH CENTRAL.								
1920	27,991,434,545	106.8	24,469,495,169	110.7	1,162,938,264	215.2	2,359,001,112	52.0
1910	13,535,309,511	132.5	11,614,665,870	149.7	368,935,544	86.9	1,551,708,097	59.6
1900	5,820,994,481	54.5	4,651,282,998	56.7	197,367,840	56.9	972,343,643	44.6
1890	3,766,511,744	93.2	2,968,300,452	97.8	125,771,166	45.5	672,380,126	85.2
1880	1,949,743,846	91.5	1,500,000,755	86.4	86,428,597	122.4	363,014,894	108.2
1870	1,018,032,607	105.8	804,857,937	104.1	38,858,215	142.0	174,316,455	109.7
1860	494,589,405	354.2	394,270,605	392.6	16,005,656	209.6	84,313,144	256.2
1850	108,885,147	......	80,045,058	......	5,170,375	......	23,669,714	......
SOUTH ATLANTIC.								
1920	6,132,917,760	107.8	5,201,773,472	109.2	283,980,857	189.1	647,163,431	76.6
1910	2,951,200,773	103.0	2,486,436,474	106.1	98,230,147	84.2	366,534,152	88.6
1900	1,454,031,316	9.0	1,206,349,618	6.3	53,318,890	46.3	194,362,808	20.3
1890	1,333,395,489	26.6	1,135,319,670	27.3	36,444,018	18.3	161,631,801	23.8
1880	1,053,156,575	42.2	891,774,157	46.1	30,812,107	53.9	130,570,311	18.3
1870	740,833,437	−38.6	610,428,194	−39.5	20,025,259	−41.2	110,379,984	−33.0
1860	1,207,375,444	71.0	1,008,613,065	74.9	34,045,771	38.1	164,716,608	56.9
1850	706,208,481	......	576,590,583	......	24,656,545	......	104,961,353	......

TABLE 9.—VALUE OF ALL FARM PROPERTY AND OF THE SEVERAL CLASSES, BY DIVISIONS: 1850 TO 1920—Continued.

[Figures for 1870 are computed gold values, being 80 per cent of the currency values reported. A minus sign (−) denotes decrease. Per cent not shown when more than 1,000.]

DIVISION AND CENSUS YEAR.	ALL FARM PROPERTY.		LAND AND BUILDINGS.		IMPLEMENTS AND MACHINERY.		LIVE STOCK.	
	Value.	Per cent of increase	Value.	Per cent of increase	Value.	Per cent of increase	Value.	Per cent of increase
EAST SOUTH CENTRAL.								
1920	$4,419,466,237	102.5	$3,663,693,363	110.8	$176,064,886	133.7	$579,707,988	57.1
1910	2,182,771,779	82.5	1,738,397,839	86.2	75,339,333	54.5	369,034,607	73.0
1900	1,195,868,790	13.4	933,780,823	12.8	48,767,235	55.7	213,320,732	8.9
1890	1,054,730,138	24.6	827,514,447	22.1	31,323,896	14.1	195,891,795	38.5
1880	846,707,577	20.0	677,848,031	24.7	27,464,111	40.0	141,395,435	−0.7
1870	705,564,773	−39.6	543,550,620	−41.5	19,612,753	−39.1	142,401,400	−31.3
1860	1,169,024,049	136.6	929,440,929	149.9	32,200,055	50.3	207,383,065	105.9
1850	494,085,395	......	371,934,332	......	21,417,837	......	100,733,226	......
WEST SOUTH CENTRAL.								
1920	7,622,066,027	98.6	6,291,188,072	101.1	311,098,790	159.9	1,019,779,165	72.9
1910	3,838,154,337	136.9	3,128,596,882	174.7	119,720,377	53.6	589,837,078	46.3
1900	1,619,954,613	93.8	1,138,891,068	85.9	77,925,050	188.4	403,138,495	105.4
1890	835,791,560	88.4	612,508,151	101.7	27,019,876	41.3	196,263,533	62.5
1880	443,589,488	120.2	303,707,658	125.4	19,124,513	86.9	120,757,317	113.9
1870	201,412,394	−60.0	134,716,055	−65.0	10,234,828	−64.8	56,461,511	−36.9
1860	503,093,122	232.8	384,540,755	257.3	29,083,003	89.7	89,469,364	217.1
1850	151,172,760	......	107,629,651	......	15,329,938	......	28,213,171	......
MOUNTAIN.								
1920	4,083,137,939	132.3	3,163,187,783	139.7	190,715,673	285.8	729,234,483	87.6
1910	1,757,573,368	192.3	1,319,396,873	289.6	49,429,975	162.8	388,746,520	59.4
1900	601,264,180	72.0	338,619,672	70.6	18,807,620	136.0	243,836,888	70.5
1890	349,550,941	185.1	198,545,200	241.8	7,969,430	131.7	143,026,311	134.2
1880	122,598,535	526.4	58,078,360	548.1	3,440,196	283.8	61,079,979	528.8
1870	19,571,627	78.2	8,961,817	106.3	896,252	100.6	9,713,558	56.8
1860	10,984,059	163.4	4,343,081	120.9	446,887	175.4	6,194,091	203.4
1850	4,169,566	......	1,965,721	......	162,248	......	2,041,597	......
PACIFIC.								
1920	5,307,011,460	90.9	4,669,416,734	88.4	232,357,792	249.9	405,236,934	71.8
1910	2,780,481,777	149.7	2,478,146,254	159.2	66,408,647	94.8	235,926,876	91.2
1900	1,113,329,789	9.0	955,860,184	6.6	34,090,025	52.2	123,379,580	20.6
1890	1,021,131,537	149.2	896,397,490	169.3	22,396,680	81.2	102,337,367	58.5
1880	409,749,627	85.1	332,804,081	98.6	12,362,430	79.4	64,583,116	37.7
1870	221,359,086	96.8	167,571,358	153.3	6,890,958	86.2	46,896,770	10.0
1860	112,477,643	819.2	66,145,239	883.8	3,701,221	......	42,631,183	715.5
1850	12,237,364	......	6,723,211	......	286,906	......	5,227,247	......

TABLE 10.—PER CENT DISTRIBUTION OF FARMS, FARM LAND, AND VALUE OF FARM PROPERTY, BY DIVISIONS AND STATES: 1920 AND 1910.

DIVISION AND STATE.	NUMBER OF FARMS.		ALL LAND IN FARMS.		IMPROVED LAND IN FARMS.		ALL FARM PROPERTY.		LAND AND BUILDINGS.		IMPLEMENTS AND MACHINERY.		LIVE STOCK.	
	1920	1910	1920	1910	1920	1910	1920	1910	1920	1910	1920	1910	1920	1910
United States	100.0	100.0	100.0	100.0	100.0	100.0	100.0	100.0	100.0	100.0	100.0	100.0	100.0	100.0
GEOGRAPHIC DIVISIONS:														
New England	2.43	2.97	1.78	2.24	1.22	1.52	1.51	2.12	1.38	2.06	2.57	4.02	2.04	1.99
Middle Atlantic	6.59	7.36	4.24	4.91	5.28	6.13	5.07	7.22	4.53	7.02	9.99	13.24	7.34	7.09
East North Central	16.82	17.66	12.32	13.42	17.47	18.59	22.13	24.69	22.52	25.50	21.87	21.25	18.99	19.82
West North Central	17.01	17.45	26.88	26.47	34.07	34.34	35.92	33.02	36.90	33.37	32.35	29.16	29.44	31.51
South Atlantic	17.97	17.48	10.23	11.81	9.64	10.13	7.87	7.20	7.84	7.14	7.90	7.76	8.08	7.44
East South Central	16.31	16.39	8.25	9.28	8.82	9.19	5.67	5.32	5.52	4.99	4.90	5.96	7.23	7.49
West South Central	15.45	14.83	18.15	19.25	12.76	12.18	9.78	9.36	9.49	8.99	8.65	9.46	12.73	11.98
Mountain	3.79	2.88	12.28	6.77	5.98	3.33	5.24	4.29	4.77	3.79	5.31	3.91	9.10	7.89
Pacific	3.63	2.98	5.87	5.84	4.76	4.61	6.81	6.78	7.04	7.12	6.46	5.25	5.06	4.79
NEW ENGLAND:														
Maine	0.75	0.94	0.57	0.72	0.39	0.49	0.35	0.49	0.31	0.46	0.74	1.15	0.50	0.51
New Hampshire	0.32	0.43	0.27	0.37	0.14	0.19	0.15	0.25	0.14	0.25	0.26	0.46	0.24	0.24
Vermont	0.45	0.51	0.44	0.53	0.34	0.34	0.29	0.35	0.24	0.32	0.59	0.80	0.53	0.46
Massachusetts	0.50	0.58	0.26	0.33	0.18	0.24	0.39	0.55	0.37	0.56	0.54	0.91	0.42	0.42
Rhode Island	0.06	0.08	0.03	0.05	0.03	0.04	0.04	0.08	0.04	0.08	0.07	0.14	0.06	0.07
Connecticut	0.35	0.42	0.20	0.25	0.14	0.21	0.29	0.39	0.29	0.40	0.37	0.55	0.29	0.29
MIDDLE ATLANTIC:														
New York	3.00	3.39	2.16	2.51	2.62	3.10	2.45	3.54	2.15	3.40	4.73	6.61	3.91	3.72
New Jersey	0.46	0.53	0.24	0.29	0.31	0.38	0.40	0.62	0.38	0.62	0.71	1.04	0.45	0.50
Pennsylvania	3.14	3.45	1.85	2.11	2.36	2.65	2.22	3.06	2.00	2.99	4.56	5.59	2.98	2.87
EAST NORTH CENTRAL:														
Ohio	3.98	4.28	2.46	2.74	3.69	4.02	3.97	4.64	4.01	4.75	4.08	4.05	3.59	4.01
Indiana	3.18	3.39	2.20	2.42	3.32	3.54	3.90	4.41	4.00	4.58	3.54	3.24	3.26	3.53
Illinois	3.68	3.96	3.35	3.70	5.43	5.86	8.56	9.53	9.04	10.12	6.19	5.83	5.57	6.27
Michigan	3.05	3.25	1.99	2.16	2.57	2.68	2.26	2.66	2.17	2.59	3.40	3.95	2.55	2.80
Wisconsin	2.94	2.78	2.32	2.40	2.48	2.49	3.44	3.45	3.30	3.45	4.65	4.19	4.02	3.22
WEST NORTH CENTRAL:														
Minnesota	2.77	2.45	3.16	3.15	4.27	4.11	4.86	3.60	4.98	3.63	5.04	4.14	3.81	3.28
Iowa	3.31	3.41	3.50	3.86	5.69	6.16	10.94	9.14	11.46	9.36	8.60	7.55	7.66	7.98
Missouri	4.08	4.36	3.64	3.94	4.94	5.14	4.61	5.01	4.62	4.93	3.54	4.02	4.86	5.80
North Dakota	1.20	1.17	3.79	3.23	4.88	4.28	2.26	2.38	2.24	2.36	3.18	3.47	1.96	2.20
South Dakota	1.16	1.22	3.62	2.96	3.62	3.31	3.62	2.84	3.73	2.89	3.13	2.67	2.98	2.58
Nebraska	1.93	2.04	4.42	4.39	4.59	5.10	5.39	5.07	5.60	5.21	4.26	3.50	4.20	4.51
Kansas	2.56	2.80	4.75	4.94	6.08	6.25	4.24	4.97	4.27	4.99	4.30	3.82	3.97	5.15
SOUTH ATLANTIC:														
Delaware	0.16	0.17	0.10	0.12	0.13	0.15	0.10	0.15	0.10	0.15	0.19	0.25	0.11	0.14
Maryland	0.74	0.77	0.50	0.58	0.62	0.70	0.59	0.70	0.58	0.69	0.81	0.94	0.60	0.66
District of Columbia	(1)	(1)	(1)	(1)	(1)	(1)	0.01	0.02	0.01	0.02	(1)	0.01	(1)	(1)
Virginia	2.89	2.89	1.94	2.22	1.88	2.06	1.54	1.52	1.54	1.53	1.40	1.43	1.52	1.52
West Virginia	1.35	1.52	1.00	1.14	1.10	1.15	0.64	0.77	0.62	0.76	0.51	0.55	0.84	0.88
North Carolina	4.18	3.99	2.09	2.55	1.63	1.84	1.60	1.31	1.62	1.31	1.52	1.46	1.49	1.27
South Carolina	2.99	2.77	1.30	1.54	1.23	1.27	1.22	0.96	1.23	0.96	1.34	1.12	1.14	0.92
Georgia	4.82	4.57	2.66	3.07	2.60	2.57	1.74	1.42	1.72	1.38	1.76	1.66	1.93	1.63
Florida	0.84	0.79	0.63	0.60	0.46	0.38	0.42	0.35	0.42	0.34	0.38	0.35	0.44	0.42
EAST SOUTH CENTRAL:														
Kentucky	4.20	4.07	2.26	2.52	2.78	3.00	1.94	1.89	1.97	1.83	1.35	1.65	1.98	2.39
Tennessee	3.92	3.87	2.04	2.28	2.22	2.28	1.61	1.49	1.55	1.38	1.49	1.68	2.17	2.25
Alabama	3.97	4.13	2.05	2.36	1.97	2.03	0.89	0.90	0.82	0.83	0.96	1.29	1.41	1.33
Mississippi	4.22	4.31	1.90	2.11	1.85	1.88	1.24	1.04	1.19	0.96	1.11	1.34	1.68	1.53
WEST SOUTH CENTRAL:														
Arkansas	3.61	3.37	1.83	1.98	1.83	1.69	1.19	0.98	1.14	0.89	1.21	1.33	1.60	1.50
Louisiana	2.10	1.89	1.05	1.19	1.12	1.10	0.76	0.73	0.71	0.68	0.91	1.50	1.04	0.91
Oklahoma	2.98	2.99	3.34	3.28	3.60	3.67	2.13	2.24	2.06	2.12	2.24	2.14	2.69	3.09
Texas	6.76	6.57	11.93	12.79	6.21	5.72	5.71	5.41	5.58	5.30	4.29	4.49	7.40	6.47
MOUNTAIN:														
Montana	0.89	0.41	3.67	1.54	2.13	0.70	1.97	0.85	1.17	0.72	1.53	0.83	1.92	1.74
Idaho	0.65	0.48	0.88	0.60	0.90	0.58	0.92	0.74	0.83	0.60	1.07	0.80	1.09	1.01
Wyoming	0.24	0.17	1.24	0.97	0.42	0.26	0.43	0.41	0.35	0.28	0.33	0.29	1.10	1.33
Colorado	0.93	0.73	2.56	1.54	1.54	0.90	1.38	1.20	1.31	1.17	1.39	1.01	2.01	1.42
New Mexico	0.46	0.56	2.55	1.28	0.34	0.31	0.42	0.39	0.33	0.32	0.27	0.33	1.17	0.88
Arizona	0.15	0.15	0.61	0.14	0.14	0.07	0.30	0.18	0.26	0.14	0.25	0.14	0.65	0.53
Utah	0.40	0.34	0.53	0.39	0.34	0.29	0.40	0.37	0.37	0.34	0.38	0.35	0.67	0.53
Nevada	0.05	0.04	0.25	0.31	0.12	0.16	0.13	0.15	0.10	0.11	0.10	0.12	0.37	0.39
PACIFIC:														
Washington	1.03	0.88	1.39	1.33	1.42	1.33	1.36	1.56	1.39	1.64	1.52	1.32	1.03	0.99
Oregon	0.78	0.72	1.42	1.33	0.98	0.89	1.05	1.29	1.02	1.31	1.16	1.04	1.27	1.21
California	1.82	1.39	3.07	3.18	2.36	2.38	4.40	3.94	4.64	4.17	3.79	2.88	2.76	2.59

¹ Less than one-hundredth of 1 per cent.

TABLE 11.—AVERAGE ACREAGE PER FARM, PER CENT OF FARM LAND IMPROVED, AND AVERAGE VALUE OF FARM PROPERTY PER ACRE, BY DIVISIONS AND STATES: 1920 AND 1910.

DIVISION AND STATE.	AVERAGE ACREAGE PER FARM.				PER CENT OF FARM LAND IMPROVED.		AVERAGE VALUE PER ACRE.					
	All land.		Improved land.				All farm property.		Land and buildings.		Land alone.	
	1920	1910	1920	1910	1920	1910	1920	1910	1920	1910	1920	1910
United States.	148.2	138.1	78.0	75.2	52.6	54.4	$81.52	$46.64	$69.38	$39.60	$57.36	$32.40
GEOG. DIVISIONS:												
New England..	108.5	104.4	39.1	38.4	36.0	36.8	69.04	43.99	54.00	36.45	28.73	19.38
Middle Atlantic	95.4	92.2	62.5	62.6	65.5	67.9	97.35	68.52	73.99	56.56	40.96	33.86
E. N. Central..	108.5	105.0	81.0	79.2	74.7	75.4	146.48	85.81	126.87	75.25	102.31	61.32
W. N. Central..	234.3	209.6	156.2	148.0	66.7	70.6	108.93	58.18	95.22	49.92	83.04	43.21
South Atlantic.	84.4	93.3	41.9	43.6	49.6	46.7	62.72	28.44	53.20	23.96	40.92	18.15
E. S. Central...	75.0	78.2	42.2	42.2	56.3	53.9	56.02	26.78	46.44	21.32	36.96	16.28
W. S. Central...	174.1	179.3	64.4	61.8	37.0	34.4	43.94	22.69	36.27	18.50	31.18	16.06
Mountain......	480.7	324.5	123.3	86.8	25.7	26.7	34.80	29.52	26.96	22.16	23.88	19.73
Pacific.........	239.8	270.3	102.2	116.1	42.6	42.9	94.51	54.17	83.16	48.28	74.21	43.76
NEW ENGLAND:												
Maine..........	112.5	104.9	41.0	39.3	36.4	37.5	49.86	31.65	37.62	25.35	21.09	13.73
NewHampshire	126.9	120.1	34.2	34.3	27.0	28.6	45.57	31.91	34.56	26.44	18.21	13.70
Vermont........	145.7	142.6	58.2	50.0	39.9	35.0	52.58	31.18	37.56	24.14	19.58	12.52
Massachusetts..	77.9	77.9	28.4	31.5	36.4	40.5	120.45	78.75	99.25	67.51	51.17	36.69
Rhode Island..	81.2	83.8	32.5	33.7	40.1	40.2	101.44	74.42	79.58	63.01	43.75	33.86
Connecticut....	83.8	81.5	30.9	36.9	36.9	45.2	119.53	72.93	100.20	63.28	53.28	33.03
MID. ATLANTIC:												
New York.....	106.8	102.2	68.1	68.8	63.8	67.4	92.50	65.89	69.07	53.78	38.45	32.13
New Jersey....	76.8	76.9	52.4	53.9	68.2	70.1	136.62	99.01	109.67	84.36	62.29	48.23
Pennsylvania...	87.3	84.8	58.6	57.8	67.1	68.2	97.94	67.43	75.14	56.01	41.12	33.92
E. N. CENTRAL:												
Ohio..........	91.6	88.6	72.2	70.7	78.9	79.8	131.64	78.93	113.18	68.62	85.69	53.34
Indiana........	102.7	98.8	81.3	78.6	79.2	79.5	144.44	84.94	125.98	74.85	104.57	62.36
Illinois........	134.8	129.1	115.1	111.4	85.4	86.2	208.50	120.08	187.59	108.32	164.20	95.02
Michigan.......	96.9	91.5	65.8	62.0	67.9	67.8	92.65	57.49	75.48	47.58	50.40	32.48
Wisconsin.....	117.0	118.9	65.8	67.2	56.2	56.5	120.88	67.10	98.78	57.06	73.09	43.30
W. N. CENTRAL:												
Minnesota.....	169.3	177.3	120.4	125.8	71.1	71.0	125.32	53.35	109.23	45.62	91.00	36.82
Iowa..........	156.8	156.3	134.0	135.9	85.5	86.9	254.66	110.40	227.09	96.00	199.52	82.58
Missouri.......	132.2	124.8	94.4	88.7	71.4	71.1	103.27	59.35	88.08	49.61	74.60	41.80
North Dakota..	466.1	382.3	316.2	275.1	67.8	72.0	48.59	34.29	41.10	28.94	35.33	25.69
South Dakota..	464.1	335.1	243.8	203.8	52.5	60.8	81.53	44.82	71.40	38.63	64.42	34.69
Nebraska......	339.4	297.8	185.7	188.0	54.7	63.1	99.51	53.85	87.91	46.95	78.87	41.80
Kansas........	274.8	244.0	185.1	168.2	67.4	68.9	72.71	47.01	62.30	40.05	54.50	35.45
SOUTH ATLANTIC:												
Delaware......	93.1	95.9	64.4	65.8	69.1	68.7	84.85	60.82	68.56	51.17	44.59	33.63
Maryland......	99.3	103.4	65.5	68.6	65.9	66.3	97.44	56.59	81.25	47.80	54.62	32.32
Dist. Columbia.	27.8	27.9	20.9	23.7	75.1	84.7	1,045.87	1,398.08	984.01	1,357.64	733.27	1,186.53
Virginia........	99.7	105.9	50.8	53.6	51.0	50.6	64.47	32.06	55.19	27.29	40.75	20.24
West Virginia..	109.6	103.7	63.2	57.1	57.7	55.1	51.88	31.39	42.93	26.37	32.11	20.65
North Carolina.	74.2	88.4	30.4	34.7	40.9	39.3	62.44	23.96	53.76	20.35	42.84	15.29
South Carolina.	64.5	76.6	32.1	34.6	49.8	45.1	76.70	29.02	65.46	24.64	52.08	19.89
Georgia.......	81.9	92.6	42.0	42.3	51.3	45.6	53.33	21.54	44.74	17.78	35.28	13.74
Florida........	112.0	105.0	42.5	36.1	38.0	34.4	54.63	27.25	46.55	22.49	37.78	17.84
E. S. CENTRAL:												
Kentucky......	79.9	85.6	51.6	55.4	64.7	64.7	69.95	34.87	60.39	28.64	48.62	21.83
Tennessee.....	77.2	81.5	44.3	44.3	57.3	54.3	64.17	30.56	52.53	23.98	41.40	18.53
Alabama.......	76.4	78.9	38.6	36.9	50.5	46.8	35.29	17.85	27.77	13.90	21.24	10.46
Mississippi.....	66.9	67.6	34.3	32.8	51.2	48.5	53.02	22.97	43.41	18.01	35.27	13.69
W. S. CENTRAL:												
Arkansas.......	75.0	81.1	39.6	37.6	52.8	46.4	52.95	22.97	43.14	17.75	34.82	14.13
Louisiana......	74.0	86.6	41.5	43.8	56.2	50.5	58.87	28.85	47.31	22.75	38.29	17.99
Oklahoma.....	166.4	151.7	94.4	92.3	56.7	60.8	51.97	31.82	42.68	25.60	36.66	22.49
Texas.........	261.5	269.1	71.6	65.5	27.4	24.3	39.01	19.73	32.45	16.39	28.46	14.53
MOUNTAIN:												
Montana.......	608.1	516.7	190.8	138.9	31.4	26.9	28.11	25.68	22.15	18.58	19.73	16.74
Idaho.........	198.9	171.5	107.2	90.2	53.9	52.6	85.50	57.79	69.43	46.38	61.11	41.63
Wyoming......	749.9	777.6	133.5	114.3	17.8	14.7	28.32	19.57	19.88	11.46	17.86	10.41
Colorado......	408.1	293.1	129.2	93.2	31.7	31.8	44.02	36.32	35.40	30.19	31.22	26.81
New Mexico...	817.9	315.9	57.5	41.1	7.0	13.0	13.32	14.15	9.09	9.92	8.04	8.77
Arizona........	581.7	135.1	71.5	38.0	12.3	28.1	40.26	60.26	29.70	37.93	26.98	33.97
Utah..........	196.8	156.7	66.8	63.1	34.0	40.3	61.63	44.38	48.26	34.60	41.78	29.28
Nevada........	745.2	1,009.6	188.0	279.7	25.2	27.7	42.33	22.25	28.11	14.59	25.18	12.99
PACIFIC:												
Washington....	199.8	208.4	107.6	113.4	53.8	54.4	79.84	54.43	69.49	48.84	60.22	44.18
Oregon.........	269.7	256.8	97.9	93.9	36.3	36.6	60.44	45.21	49.86	38.99	43.29	35.23
California......	249.6	316.7	100.9	129.1	40.4	40.8	116.84	57.81	104.67	51.93	94.77	47.16

TABLE 12.—NUMBER OF FARMS IN THE UNITED STATES, WITH PER CENT DISTRIBUTION, BY SIZE: 1880 TO 1920.

SIZE GROUP.	NUMBER OF FARMS.					PER CENT DISTRIBUTION.				
	1920	1910	1900	1890	1880	1920	1910	1900	1890	1880
Total........	6,448,343	6,361,502	5,737,372	4,564,641	4,008,907	100.0	100.0	100.0	100.0	100.0
Under 10 acres....	288,772	335,043	267,229	150,194	139,241	4.5	5.3	4.7	3.3	3.5
Under 3 acres...	20,350	18,033	41,385	....	4,352	0.3	0.3	0.7	......	0.1
3 to 9 acres......	268,422	317,010	225,844	....	134,889	4.2	5.0	3.9	......	3.4
10 to 19 acres......	507,763	504,123	406,641	265,550	254,749	7.9	7.9	7.1	5.8	6.4
20 to 49 acres......	1,503,732	1,414,376	1,257,496	902,777	781,574	23.3	22.2	21.9	19.8	19.5
50 to 99 acres......	1,474,745	1,438,069	1,366,038	1,121,485	1,032,810	22.9	22.6	23.8	24.6	25.8
100 to 499 acres....	2,456,107	2,494,461	2,290,282	2,008,694	1,695,983	38.1	39.2	39.9	44.0	42.3
100 to 174 acres .	1,449,630	1,516,286	1,422,262	....	....	22.5	23.8	24.8	......	......
175 to 259 acres..	530,800	534,191	490,069	....	....	8.2	8.4	8.5	......	......
260 to 499 acres..	475,677	443,984	377,951	....	....	7.4	7.0	6.6	......	......
500 to 999 acres....	149,819	125,295	102,526	84,395	75,972	2.3	2.0	1.8	1.8	1.9
1,000 acres and over.............	67,405	50,135	47,160	31,546	28,578	1.0	0.8	0.8	0.7	0.7

TABLE 13.—FARM ACREAGE, WITH PER CENT DISTRIBUTION AND PERCENTAGE OF FARM LAND IMPROVED, BY SIZE OF FARM, FOR THE UNITED STATES: 1920 AND 1910.

SIZE GROUP.	ALL LAND IN FARMS (ACRES).		IMPROVED LAND IN FARMS (ACRES).		PER CENT DISTRIBUTION.				PER CENT OF FARM LAND IMPROVED.	
					All land.		Improved land.			
	1920	1910	1920	1910	1920	1910	1920	1910	1920	1910
Total.....	955,883,715	878,798,325	503,073,007	478,451,750	100.0	100.0	100.0	100.0	52.6	54.4
Under 20 acres...	8,688,899	8,793,820	7,803,761	7,991,543	0.9	1.0	1.6	1.7	89.8	90.9
20 to 49 acres...	48,464,330	45,378,449	38,507,730	36,596,032	5.1	5.2	7.7	7.6	79.5	80.6
50 to 99 acres...	105,630,796	103,120,868	72,621,719	71,155,246	11.1	11.7	14.4	14.9	68.8	69.0
100 to 174 acres.	194,681,260	205,480,585	128,200,972	128,853,538	20.4	23.4	25.5	26.9	65.9	62.7
175 to 499 acres.	276,806,995	265,289,069	170,074,735	161,775,502	29.0	30.2	33.8	33.8	61.4	61.0
500 to 999 acres.	100,975,916	83,653,487	48,134,952	40,817,118	10.6	9.5	9.6	8.5	47.7	48.8
1,000 and over.	220,635,519	167,082,047	37,729,138	31,262,771	23.1	19.0	7.5	6.5	17.1	18.7

TABLE 14.—VALUE OF FARM PROPERTY IN THE UNITED STATES, BY SIZE OF FARM: 1920 AND 1910.

SIZE GROUP (ACRES).	ALL FARM PROPERTY.		LAND AND BUILDINGS.		LAND ALONE.	
	1920	1910	1920	1910	1920	1910
Total..	$77,924,100,338	$40,991,449,090	$66,316,002,602	$34,801,125,697	$54,829,563,059	$28,475,674,169
Under 20...	2,452,977,205	1,520,384,193	2,093,165,093	1,309,907,611	1,322,556,907	802,210,953
20 to 49.....	5,864,412,204	2,974,490,664	4,921,514,885	2,485,471,119	3,678,033,741	1,815,363,083
50 to 99.....	11,183,267,488	6,003,926,775	9,345,378,110	5,029,510,723	7,137,366,114	3,809,362,679
100 to 174...	20,901,789,301	11,089,188,836	17,820,667,684	9,405,391,855	14,566,824,506	7,613,104,371
175 to 499...	26,389,647,868	13,650,063,506	22,879,246,128	11,762,614,964	19,750,806,952	10,066,760,353
500 to 999...	5,533,774,473	2,907,900,770	4,725,558,030	2,483,160,122	4,192,956,165	2,210,728,394
1,000 and over......	5,598,231,799	2,845,494,346	4,530,472,672	2,325,069,303	4,181,018,674	2,158,144,336

SIZE GROUP (ACRES).	BUILDINGS.		IMPLEMENTS AND MACHINERY.		LIVE STOCK.	
	1920	1910	1920	1910	1920	1910
Total..	$11,486,439,543	$6,325,451,528	$3,594,772,928	$1,265,149,783	$8,013,324,808	$4,925,173,610
Under 20...	770,608,186	507,696,658	115,976,829	47,198,043	243,835,283	163,278,539
20 to 49.....	1,243,481,144	670,108,036	290,712,393	107,014,301	652,184,926	382,005,244
50 to 99.....	2,208,011,996	1,220,148,044	608,088,704	224,064,159	1,229,800,674	750,351,893
100 to 174...	3,253,843,178	1,792,287,484	1,031,828,610	365,417,498	2,049,293,007	1,318,379,483
175 to 499...	3,128,439,176	1,695,854,611	1,141,309,585	381,446,010	2,369,092,155	1,506,002,532
500 to 999...	532,601,865	272,431,728	242,492,917	80,052,723	565,723,526	344,687,925
1,000 and over......	349,453,998	166,924,967	164,363,890	59,957,049	903,395,237	460,467,994

TABLE 15.—FARMS AND FARM ACREAGE, AND VALUE OF FARM PROPERTY, BY

DIVISION OR STATE AND SIZE GROUP.	NUMBER OF FARMS.		ALL LAND IN FARMS (ACRES).		IMPROVED LAND IN FARMS (ACRES).	
	1920	1910	1920	1910	1920	1910
UNITED STATES.						
1 Total	6,448,343	6,361,502	955,883,715	878,798,325	503,073,007	478,451,750
2 Under 20 acres	796,535	839,166	8,688,899	8,793,820	7,803,761	7,991,543
3 20 to 49 acres	1,503,732	1,414,376	48,464,330	45,378,449	38,507,730	36,596,032
4 50 to 99 acres	1,474,745	1,438,069	105,630,796	103,120,868	72,621,719	71,155,246
5 100 to 174 acres	1,449,630	1,516,286	194,681,260	205,480,585	128,200,972	128,853,538
6 175 to 499 acres	1,006,477	978,175	276,806,995	265,289,069	170,074,735	161,775,502
7 500 to 999 acres	149,819	125,295	100,975,916	83,653,487	48,134,952	40,817,118
8 1,000 acres and over	67,405	50,135	220,635,519	167,082,047	37,729,138	31,262,771
GEOGRAPHIC DIVISIONS.						
NEW ENGLAND.						
9 Total	156,564	188,802	16,990,642	19,714,931	6,114,601	7,254,904
10 Under 20 acres	25,886	34,304	244,585	317,557	170,621	231,463
11 20 to 49 acres	27,117	33,822	889,873	1,101,352	449,163	575,903
12 50 to 99 acres	38,036	45,932	2,675,297	3,210,561	1,122,957	1,427,597
13 100 to 174 acres	37,993	44,019	4,837,480	5,575,475	1,843,654	2,198,055
14 175 to 499 acres	25,173	28,008	6,359,454	7,062,543	2,106,513	2,334,708
15 500 to 999 acres	1,916	2,139	1,179,292	1,324,559	294,094	312,640
16 1,000 acres and over	443	578	804,661	1,122,884	127,599	174,538
MIDDLE ATLANTIC.						
17 Total	425,147	468,379	40,572,901	43,191,056	26,562,107	29,320,894
18 Under 20 acres	65,725	80,919	625,807	751,343	527,333	645,000
19 20 to 49 acres	70,492	78,375	2,359,653	2,596,184	1,807,576	2,014,736
20 50 to 99 acres	120,323	130,702	8,636,151	9,335,076	6,365,742	7,028,777
21 100 to 174 acres	116,009	123,756	14,768,937	15,710,409	10,165,376	11,230,267
22 175 to 499 acres	50,437	52,310	12,148,275	12,531,376	7,069,779	7,720,162
23 500 to 999 acres	1,736	1,848	1,068,668	1,154,723	444,423	494,032
24 1,000 acres and over	425	469	965,410	1,111,945	181,878	187,920
EAST NORTH CENTRAL.						
25 Total	1,084,744	1,123,489	117,735,179	117,929,148	87,894,835	88,947,228
26 Under 20 acres	90,703	108,283	864,702	1,002,397	750,504	893,205
27 20 to 49 acres	172,052	197,164	6,118,911	6,907,601	4,733,625	5,437,794
28 50 to 99 acres	335,439	340,940	25,198,225	25,448,406	19,369,470	19,692,117
29 100 to 174 acres	325,390	315,607	43,040,457	41,708,394	32,715,984	31,821,219
30 175 to 499 acres	155,489	155,585	38,071,074	38,250,593	27,953,290	28,505,359
31 500 to 999 acres	4,912	5,147	3,027,709	3,205,712	1,836,723	2,027,345
32 1,000 acres and over	759	763	1,414,101	1,406,045	535,239	570,189
WEST NORTH CENTRAL.						
33 Total	1,096,951	1,109,948	256,973,229	232,648,121	171,394,439	164,284,862
34 Under 20 acres	46,093	52,536	422,589	475,532	365,719	423,462
35 20 to 49 acres	81,820	91,971	2,911,141	3,206,053	2,189,555	2,500,290
36 50 to 99 acres	170,896	181,843	13,083,750	13,808,123	10,112,177	10,848,559
37 100 to 174 acres	351,003	368,669	50,322,130	53,137,842	39,768,680	39,724,322
38 175 to 499 acres	366,438	346,875	106,104,113	99,858,046	80,515,564	76,716,957
39 500 to 999 acres	60,561	55,179	41,245,581	37,138,135	25,376,134	23,210,837
40 1,000 acres and over	20,140	12,875	42,883,925	25,024,390	13,066,610	10,860,435
SOUTH ATLANTIC.						
41 Total	1,158,976	1,111,881	97,775,243	100,700,955	48,509,886	44,470,727
42 Under 20 acres	187,326	186,956	2,152,615	1,991,481	1,890,710	1,760,123
43 20 to 49 acres	401,259	354,207	12,553,867	11,035,210	9,680,582	8,821,385
44 50 to 99 acres	280,114	251,901	18,939,611	17,173,796	11,034,277	10,013,755
45 100 to 174 acres	175,311	181,336	22,025,845	22,907,206	10,611,747	10,855,205
46 175 to 499 acres	99,833	117,899	25,903,020	31,000,073	10,911,152	12,264,756
47 500 to 999 acres	11,269	14,555	7,214,715	9,454,383	2,501,953	2,879,471
48 1,000 acres and over	3,864	5,027	8,985,570	10,220,106	1,874,459	1,885,038

CLASSES, BY SIZE OF FARM, BY DIVISIONS AND STATES: 1920 AND 1910.

	VALUE OF FARM PROPERTY.					
	All farm property.		Land and buildings.		Implements and machinery, 1920	Live stock, 1920
	1920	1910	1920	1910		
$77,924,100,338	$40,991,449,090	$66,316,002,602	$34,801,125,697	$3,594,772,928	$8,013,324,808	1
2,452,977,205	1,520,384,193	2,093,165,093	1,309,907,611	115,976,829	243,835,283	2
5,864,412,204	2,974,490,664	4,921,514,885	2,485,471,119	290,712,393	652,184,926	3
11,183,267,488	6,003,926,775	9,345,378,110	5,029,510,723	608,088,704	1,229,800,674	4
20,901,789,301	11,089,188,836	17,820,667,684	9,405,391,855	1,031,828,610	2,049,293,007	5
26,389,647,868	13,650,063,506	22,879,246,128	11,762,614,964	1,141,309,585	2,369,092,155	6
5,533,774,473	2,907,900,770	4,725,558,030	2,483,160,122	242,492,917	565,723,526	7
5,598,231,799	2,845,494,346	4,530,472,672	2,325,069,303	164,363,890	903,395,237	8
1,173,019,594	867,240,457	917,468,584	718,544,808	92,387,525	163,163,485	9
117,282,558	103,684,445	102,930,777	93,749,802	5,869,324	8,482,457	10
145,895,846	115,060,073	120,904,586	99,415,227	9,612,265	15,378,995	11
228,990,073	173,183,103	179,361,406	143,027,415	18,107,210	31,521,457	12
293,219,534	209,626,771	219,528,111	167,577,293	26,519,229	47,172,194	13
310,862,500	211,215,873	232,136,573	168,134,552	27,465,150	51,260,777	14
49,351,224	33,546,848	39,248,124	27,992,625	3,403,009	6,700,091	15
27,417,859	20,923,344	23,359,007	18,647,894	1,411,338	2,647,514	16
3,949,684,183	2,959,589,022	3,002,137,754	2,442,949,103	359,152,336	588,394,093	17
285,988,337	262,182,753	246,241,639	235,705,545	18,536,155	21,210,543	18
419,065,701	334,871,082	338,345,820	287,713,829	35,192,550	45,527,331	19
998,579,879	729,373,201	759,290,542	597,452,188	97,178,478	142,110,859	20
1,297,836,276	942,702,370	952,456,523	757,538,229	127,564,673	217,815,080	21
829,206,769	602,201,806	607,765,251	487,133,975	73,916,650	147,524,868	22
72,400,233	54,091,937	57,504,141	46,416,557	4,938,517	9,957,575	23
46,606,988	34,165,873	40,533,838	30,988,780	1,825,313	4,247,837	24
17,245,362,593	10,119,128,066	14,937,641,671	8,873,991,594	786,076,805	1,521,644,117	25
358,320,128	269,634,199	314,245,145	240,935,704	17,261,304	26,813,679	26
948,747,487	641,208,222	801,012,583	547,475,778	50,922,988	96,811,916	27
3,484,433,247	2,068,992,156	2,942,580,223	1,776,191,397	191,185,891	350,667,133	28
6,175,667,327	3,475,729,461	5,328,277,223	3,040,388,836	293,938,517	553,451,587	29
5,790,164,018	3,348,816,072	5,120,305,700	2,985,416,667	217,515,216	452,343,102	30
376,702,640	246,283,605	332,595,981	221,406,654	11,909,338	32,197,321	31
111,327,746	68,464,351	98,624,816	62,176,558	3,343,551	9,359,379	32
27,991,434,545	13,535,309,511	24,469,495,169	11,614,665,870	1,162,938,264	2,359,001,112	33
222,043,877	151,054,813	192,926,527	132,495,516	10,282,084	18,835,266	34
493,698,114	299,200,188	417,456,245	250,463,450	23,543,863	52,698,006	35
2,007,063,103	1,065,153,850	1,724,388,662	897,439,966	93,975,887	188,698,554	36
7,901,682,732	3,648,055,794	6,928,263,659	3,121,921,068	339,213,792	634,205,281	37
13,293,211,632	6,285,529,579	11,718,597,795	5,437,429,168	533,594,275	1,041,019,562	38
2,671,677,239	1,432,013,395	2,314,566,806	1,230,317,448	116,628,410	240,482,014	39
1,402,057,848	654,301,892	1,173,295,475	544,599,254	45,699,944	183,062,429	40
6,132,917,760	2,951,200,773	5,201,773,472	2,486,436,474	283,980,857	647,163,431	41
366,474,995	174,556,023	309,946,850	148,599,191	17,080,609	39,447,536	42
1,160,620,766	443,840,688	974,052,677	365,777,254	52,380,494	134,187,595	43
1,355,953,843	564,548,469	1,137,834,706	467,510,682	66,154,160	151,964,977	44
1,300,556,922	640,491,377	1,098,039,216	534,692,343	64,289,237	138,228,469	45
1,361,490,529	772,173,629	1,165,596,871	657,034,694	63,087,394	132,806,264	46
327,229,159	198,542,197	284,954,968	172,377,094	12,745,101	29,529,090	47
260,591,546	157,048,390	231,348,184	140,445,216	8,243,862	20,999,500	48

TABLE 15.—FARMS AND FARM ACREAGE, AND VALUE OF FARM PROPERTY, BY

	DIVISION OR STATE AND SIZE GROUP.	NUMBER OF FARMS.		ALL LAND IN FARMS (ACRES).		IMPROVED LAND IN FARMS (ACRES).	
		1920	1910	1920	1910	1920	1910
	GEOGRAPHIC DIVISIONS—Con.						
	EAST SOUTH CENTRAL.						
1	Total..........	1,051,600	1,042,480	78,897,463	81,520,629	44,380,132	43,946,846
2	Under 20 acres....	203,187	211,614	2,450,056	2,485,330	2,306,412	2,380,281
3	20 to 49 acres......	373,138	350,256	11,490,514	10,670,111	9,381,822	8,931,163
4	50 to 99 acres......	235,444	225,976	16,327,012	15,708,129	10,102,504	9,740,827
5	100 to 174 acres....	152,992	157,414	19,467,801	20,216,555	10,165,674	10,281,319
6	175 to 499 acres....	77,078	86,297	19,735,293	22,187,511	9,095,798	9,710,562
7	500 to 999 acres....	7,245	8,396	4,649,488	5,421,938	1,839,049	1,860,628
8	1,000 acres and over	2,516	2,527	4,777,299	4,831,055	1,488,873	1,042,066
	WEST SOUTH CENTRAL.						
9	Total..........	996,088	943,186	173,449,127	169,149,976	64,189,606	58,264,273
10	Under 20 acres....	97,878	102,044	1,224,899	1,242,449	1,174,752	1,197,062
11	20 to 49 acres......	296,729	251,444	9,517,329	8,037,214	8,264,205	6,966,847
12	50 to 99 acres......	235,213	216,860	16,474,756	15,230,102	11,557,320	10,409,053
13	100 to 174 acres....	212,167	222,794	28,772,928	30,702,647	17,127,130	16,991,457
14	175 to 499 acres....	120,429	118,416	33,091,746	31,958,649	16,896,030	14,780,491
15	500 to 999 acres....	19,717	18,232	13,109,211	12,188,175	4,548,480	3,620,037
16	1,000 acres and over	13,955	13,396	71,258,258	69,790,740	4,621,689	4,299,326
	MOUNTAIN.						
17	Total..........	244,109	183,446	117,337,226	59,533,420	30,105,868	15,915,002
18	Under 20 acres....	22,071	23,426	191,811	180,499	170,349	162,718
19	20 to 49 acres......	25,392	19,383	863,634	642,802	686,378	497,568
20	50 to 99 acres......	26,896	19,330	1,995,062	1,434,802	1,457,778	937,086
21	100 to 174 acres....	45,855	64,783	6,808,603	9,976,088	3,478,226	3,495,991
22	175 to 499 acres....	77,982	41,676	25,196,184	12,933,226	10,217,940	4,682,626
23	500 to 999 acres....	30,005	8,483	20,869,699	5,910,654	6,720,399	2,036,857
24	1,000 acres and over	15,908	6,365	61,412,233	28,455,350	7,374,798	4,102,156
	PACIFIC.						
25	Total..........	234,164	189,891	56,152,705	51,328,789	23,921,533	22,038,008
26	Under 20 acres....	57,666	39,084	511,835	347,232	442,355	298,229
27	20 to 49 acres......	55,733	37,754	1,759,408	1,181,922	1,314,824	850,346
28	50 to 99 acres......	32,384	24,585	2,300,932	1,771,873	1,499,494	1,057,475
29	100 to 174 acres....	32,910	37,908	4,637,079	5,545,969	2,324,501	2,255,703
30	175 to 499 acres....	33,618	31,109	10,197,836	9,507,053	5,308,669	5,059,881
31	500 to 999 acres....	12,458	11,316	8,611,553	7,855,208	4,573,697	4,375,271
32	1,000 acres and over	9,395	8,135	28,134,062	25,119,532	8,457,993	8,141,103
	NEW ENGLAND.						
33	Maine, total....	48,227	60,016	5,425,968	6,296,859	1,977,329	2,360,657
34	Under 20 acres....	4,525	7,113	44,723	67,517	31,198	49,008
35	20 to 49 acres......	6,768	9,492	226,831	314,397	109,899	154,846
36	50 to 99 acres......	14,277	17,895	1,002,134	1,246,571	427,438	553,516
37	100 to 174 acres....	14,425	16,633	1,815,473	2,078,196	706,008	838,328
38	175 to 499 acres....	7,683	8,293	1,893,306	2,041,995	613,714	678,640
39	500 to 999 acres....	459	461	282,488	284,828	67,648	61,914
40	1,000 acres and over	90	129	161,013	263,355	21,424	24,405
41	New Hampshire, total....	20,523	27,053	2,603,806	3,249,458	702,902	929,185
42	Under 20 acres....	2,897	4,595	27,608	42,565	18,749	30,314
43	20 to 49 acres......	3,375	4,509	111,567	140,013	49,936	68,056
44	50 to 99 acres......	4,888	6,248	344,807	434,835	101,908	164,514
45	100 to 174 acres....	4,986	6,247	631,682	787,462	191,338	266,961
46	175 to 499 acres....	3,809	4,774	990,126	1,221,669	243,410	314,777
47	500 to 999 acres....	433	513	267,007	322,557	47,013	58,667
48	1,000 acres and over	135	167	230,789	294,357	31,148	37,296

CLASSES, BY SIZE OF FARM, BY DIVISIONS AND STATES: 1920 AND 1910—Continued.

VALUE OF FARM PROPERTY.						
All farm property.		Land and buildings.		Implements and machinery, 1920	Live stock, 1920	
1920	1910	1920	1910			
$4,419,466,237	$2,182,771,779	$3,663,693,363	$1,738,397,839	$176,064,886	$579,707,938	1
331,009,396	152,983,691	278,892,652	122,796,696	11,544,644	40,572,100	2
890,301,106	390,932,384	723,647,323	300,677,928	34,989,677	131,664,106	3
917,411,024	441,908,422	741,251,211	341,585,076	40,988,511	135,171,302	4
937,942,592	477,645,909	773,356,259	377,318,696	39,528,653	125,057,680	5
953,183,487	518,269,413	807,567,327	424,085,873	36,153,704	109,462,456	6
216,791,594	118,851,954	187,102,779	100,346,667	7,615,417	22,073,398	7
172,827,038	82,180,006	151,875,812	71,586,903	5,244,280	15,706,946	8
7,622,066,027	3,838,154,337	6,291,188,072	3,128,596,882	311,098,790	1,019,779,165	9
177,233,986	92,025,420	144,253,094	72,535,495	7,980,229	25,000,663	10
814,478,166	328,918,382	666,927,717	254,640,834	34,616,784	112,933,665	11
1,233,773,314	547,785,092	1,029,654,155	439,513,149	53,414,726	150,704,433	12
1,784,007,995	955,057,901	1,502,914,643	785,668,672	80,019,568	201,073,784	13
1,750,207,689	884,761,185	1,475,985,451	735,359,191	83,233,134	190,989,104	14
543,539,870	276,894,479	450,937,758	229,842,248	24,172,736	68,429,376	15
1,318,825,007	752,711,878	1,020,515,254	611,037,293	27,661,613	270,648,140	16
4,083,137,939	1,757,573,368	3,163,187,783	1,319,396,873	190,715,673	729,234,483	17
109,380,022	91,026,992	69,286,413	54,910,190	4,988,872	35,104,737	18
201,979,045	103,745,173	166,535,182	87,355,935	11,062,682	24,381,181	19
338,225,234	137,817,598	280,555,602	115,954,389	17,813,587	39,105,944	20
564,330,039	361,153,266	450,095,418	282,364,876	30,067,748	84,166,873	21
1,084,422,479	434,117,572	857,908,592	339,662,884	59,867,792	166,646,095	22
657,928,535	191,913,186	514,878,994	140,170,868	33,606,375	109,443,166	23
1,126,872,585	437,799,581	823,927,582	298,977,731	33,308,617	269,636,386	24
5,307,011,460	2,780,481,777	4,669,416,734	2,478,146,254	232,357,792	405,236,934	25
485,243,906	223,235,857	434,441,996	208,179,472	22,433,608	28,368,302	26
789,625,973	316,714,472	712,632,752	291,950,884	38,391,090	38,602,131	27
618,837,771	275,164,884	550,461,603	250,836,461	29,270,254	39,105,914	28
646,545,884	378,725,987	567,736,632	337,921,842	30,687,193	48,122,059	29
1,016,898,765	592,978,377	893,382,568	528,357,960	46,476,270	77,039,927	30
618,153,979	355,763,169	543,768,479	314,289,961	27,474,005	46,911,495	31
1,131,705,182	637,899,031	966,992,704	546,609,674	37,625,372	127,087,106	32
270,526,733	199,271,998	204,108,971	159,619,626	26,637,660	39,780,102	33
11,858,781	13,043,656	9,941,270	11,570,427	746,037	1,171,474	34
21,543,957	18,349,654	17,043,842	15,302,117	1,737,785	2,762,330	35
58,505,870	46,032,860	43,334,653	36,562,364	5,930,277	9,240,940	36
90,932,944	64,458,680	67,458,814	50,555,750	9,601,430	13,872,700	37
76,143,275	49,708,232	57,020,492	39,190,736	7,752,326	11,370,457	38
8,312,451	5,012,347	6,585,475	4,161,055	681,960	1,045,016	39
3,229,455	2,666,569	2,724,425	2,277,177	187,845	317,185	40
118,656,115	103,704,196	89,995,870	85,916,061	9,499,322	19,160,923	41
7,759,575	9,143,664	6,406,699	8,104,281	484,804	868,072	42
10,890,484	10,749,482	8,577,375	9,187,967	825,064	1,488,045	43
20,166,290	17,562,206	15,150,079	14,413,621	1,658,248	3,357,563	44
27,502,457	23,653,963	19,980,665	19,065,747	2,446,666	5,075,126	45
36,784,805	30,235,377	27,150,090	24,369,313	3,159,720	6,474,995	46
8,429,495	7,258,393	6,669,157	6,197,466	572,700	1,187,638	47
7,123,009	5,101,111	6,061,405	4,577,666	352,120	709,484	48

TABLE 15.—FARMS AND FARM ACREAGE, AND VALUE OF FARM PROPERTY, BY

	DIVISION OR STATE AND SIZE GROUP.	NUMBER OF FARMS.		ALL LAND IN FARMS (ACRES).		IMPROVED LAND IN FARMS (ACRES).	
		1920	1910	1920	1910	1920	1910
	NEW ENGLAND— Continued.						
1	Vermont, total.	29,075	32,709	4,235,811	4,663,577	1,691,595	1,633,965
2	Under 20 acres....	3,350	4,578	31,742	40,250	23,447	29,952
3	20 to 49 acres......	2,924	3,481	96,673	112,129	51,948	58,062
4	50 to 99 acres......	5,199	5,910	377,986	424,012	172,409	182,638
5	100 to 174 acres....	8,777	9,492	1,150,485	1,238,117	490,186	480,120
6	175 to 499 acres....	8,196	8,516	2,097,010	2,187,113	814,429	757,888
7	500 to 999 acres....	544	607	327,288	371,849	107,338	95,940
8	1,000 acres and over	85	125	154,627	290,107	31,838	29,365
9	Massachusetts, total..........	32,001	36,917	2,494,477	2,875,941	908,834	1,164,501
10	Under 20 acres....	9,505	10,606	84,533	96,041	59,044	69,869
11	20 to 49 acres......	7,532	8,890	242,466	287,509	124,838	156,902
12	50 to 99 acres......	6,834	7,981	474,580	554,699	202,486	252,447
13	100 to 174 acres....	4,888	5,703	618,820	721,710	227,593	290,707
14	175 to 499 acres....	2,895	3,325	733,572	840,139	226,702	278,531
15	500 to 999 acres....	265	319	168,420	197,218	38,719	47,817
16	1,000 acres and over	82	93	172,086	178,625	29,452	68,228
17	Rhode Island, total..........	4,083	5,292	331,600	443,308	132,855	178,344
18	Under 20 acres....	936	1,377	9,087	12,387	6,890	9,873
19	20 to 49 acres......	983	1,144	31,740	36,603	18,436	22,097
20	50 to 99 acres......	1,031	1,264	70,151	87,794	32,193	41,493
21	100 to 174 acres....	718	945	88,382	117,094	35,640	47,500
22	175 to 499 acres....	357	487	89,728	121,822	29,326	42,914
23	500 to 999 acres....	46	51	27,012	30,875	7,190	10,577
24	1,000 acres and over	12	24	15,500	36,733	3,180	3,890
25	Connecticut, total..........	22,655	26,815	1,898,980	2,185,788	701,086	988,252
26	Under 20 acres....	4,673	6,035	46,672	58,797	31,293	42,447
27	20 to 49 acres......	5,535	6,306	180,596	204,701	94,106	115,940
28	50 to 99 acres......	5,807	6,634	405,639	462,650	167,123	232,989
29	100 to 174 acres....	4,199	4,999	532,638	632,896	192,889	285,839
30	175 to 499 acres....	2,233	2,613	555,712	649,805	178,932	261,958
31	500 to 999 acres....	169	188	107,077	117,232	26,186	37,725
32	1,000 acres and over	39	40	70,646	59,707	10,557	11,354
	MIDDLE ATLANTIC.						
33	New York, total..........	193,195	215,597	20,632,803	22,030,367	13,158,781	14,844,039
34	Under 20 acres......	26,540	34,188	248,049	307,362	209,843	267,909
35	20 to 49 acres......	27,267	31,047	914,599	1,028,991	694,860	801,480
36	50 to 99 acres......	50,784	56,821	3,661,658	4,068,580	2,651,613	3,053,725
37	100 to 174 acres....	56,929	61,031	7,317,041	7,804,307	4,911,933	5,540,335
38	175 to 499 acres....	30,461	31,163	7,416,504	7,550,324	4,325,013	4,746,402
39	500 to 999 acres....	999	1,104	616,743	685,906	269,368	316,532
40	1,000 acres and over	215	243	458,209	584,897	96,151	117,656
41	New Jersey, total..........	29,702	33,487	2,282,585	2,573,857	1,555,607	1,803,336
42	Under 20 acres....	7,222	8,073	69,675	77,541	57,110	64,420
43	20 to 49 acres......	6,763	7,607	215,735	243,806	162,830	187,500
44	50 to 99 acres......	7,367	8,194	526,424	585,063	405,887	458,015
45	100 to 174 acres....	6,251	7,207	789,749	911,564	591,477	698,575
46	175 to 499 acres....	1,950	2,235	461,278	524,918	284,779	337,874
47	500 to 999 acres....	93	112	58,700	70,426	23,872	30,988
48	1,000 acres and over	56	59	161,016	100,600	29,652	25,964
49	Pennsylvania, total..........	202,250	219,295	17,657,513	18,586,832	11,847,719	12,673,519
50	Under 20 acres....	31,963	38,658	308,083	366,440	260,380	312,671
51	20 to 49 acres......	36,462	39,721	1,229,319	1,323,387	949,886	1,025,756
52	50 to 99 acres......	62,172	65,687	4,448,069	4,681,433	3,308,242	3,517,037
53	100 to 174 acres....	52,829	55,518	6,662,147	6,994,538	4,661,966	4,991,357
54	175 to 499 acres....	18,026	18,912	4,270,493	4,456,134	2,459,987	2,635,886
55	500 to 999 acres....	644	632	393,217	398,391	151,183	146,512
56	1,000 acres and over	154	167	346,185	366,509	56,075	44,300

CLASSES, BY SIZE OF FARM, BY DIVISIONS AND STATES: 1920 AND 1910—Continued.

VALUE OF FARM PROPERTY.						
All farm property.		Land and buildings.		Implements and machinery, 1920	Live stock, 1920	
1920	1910	1920	1910			
$222,736,620	$145,399,728	$159,117,159	$112,588,275	$21,234,130	$42,385,331	1
9,315,297	8,736,510	7,768,711	7,692,142	624,275	922,311	2
10,529,179	8,405,909	8,249,831	7,038,230	859,533	1,419,815	3
24,512,344	16,792,321	17,641,417	13,057,680	2,336,710	4,534,217	4
62,628,755	39,031,989	43,420,913	29,253,559	6,367,258	12,840,584	5
98,728,429	58,539,892	68,960,062	43,794,392	9,777,108	19,991,259	6
11,875,948	7,718,279	8,724,370	6,114,956	974,304	2,177,274	7
5,146,668	6,174,828	4,351,855	5,637,316	294,942	499,871	8
300,471,743	226,474,025	247,587,831	194,168,765	19,359,755	33,524,157	9
53,297,510	43,185,824	47,229,906	39,272,556	2,473,335	3,594,269	10
54,382,709	42,253,072	45,327,151	36,665,199	3,564,472	5,491,086	11
62,366,790	48,436,136	50,631,464	40,939,114	4,346,255	7,389,071	12
56,739,563	42,117,630	44,674,543	34,863,149	4,248,668	7,816,352	13
53,151,633	38,423,138	42,451,799	32,098,128	3,636,022	7,063,812	14
11,605,010	7,619,198	9,549,210	6,375,095	685,547	1,370,253	15
8,928,528	4,439,027	7,723,758	3,955,524	405,456	799,314	16
33,636,766	32,990,739	26,387,926	27,932,860	2,408,561	4,840,279	17
4,659,386	5,758,365	3,900,539	5,169,439	302,427	456,420	18
5,963,959	6,144,523	4,697,856	5,309,083	414,213	851,890	19
8,000,218	7,355,731	6,154,134	6,140,626	555,765	1,290,319	20
7,102,940	5,853,406	5,322,994	4,789,185	608,460	1,171,486	21
5,273,776	6,170,795	4,104,038	5,056,297	363,304	806,434	22
1,887,936	1,267,468	1,547,305	1,101,300	129,792	210,839	23
748,551	440,451	661,060	366,930	34,600	52,891	24
226,991,617	159,399,771	190,270,827	138,319,221	13,248,097	23,472,693	25
30,392,009	23,816,426	27,683,652	21,940,957	1,238,446	1,469,911	26
42,585,558	29,157,433	37,008,531	25,912,631	2,211,198	3,365,829	27
55,438,561	37,003,849	46,449,259	31,914,010	3,279,955	5,709,347	28
48,312,875	34,511,103	38,670,182	29,049,903	3,246,747	6,395,946	29
40,780,582	28,138,439	32,450,092	23,625,686	2,776,670	5,553,820	30
7,240,384	4,671,163	6,172,607	4,042,753	358,706	709,071	31
2,241,648	2,101,358	1,836,504	1,833,281	136,375	268,769	32
1,908,483,201	1,451,481,495	1,425,061,740	1,184,745,829	169,866,766	313,554,695	33
125,423,228	120,842,027	107,997,044	108,633,214	8,137,192	9,288,992	34
182,169,457	149,968,097	148,987,988	129,618,019	14,570,261	18,611,208	35
420,780,087	323,753,415	317,697,839	264,212,934	39,829,833	63,252,415	36
621,277,225	454,827,056	445,882,444	360,162,667	59,728,661	115,666,120	37
496,035,302	350,307,374	353,816,726	277,308,685	43,939,127	98,279,449	38
39,855,838	32,192,444	31,179,064	27,143,232	2,749,303	5,927,471	39
22,942,064	19,591,082	19,500,635	17,667,078	912,389	2,529,040	40
311,847,948	254,832,665	250,323,986	217,134,519	25,459,205	36,064,757	41
38,111,983	34,404,869	33,128,566	31,003,585	2,240,338	2,743,079	42
48,534,920	38,672,575	40,646,179	33,700,754	3,685,905	4,202,836	43
76,219,588	60,989,404	60,591,591	51,375,789	6,841,825	8,786,172	44
89,116,688	71,859,141	68,140,084	59,041,617	8,365,934	12,610,670	45
44,435,139	37,125,207	34,535,386	31,466,639	3,551,061	6,348,692	46
5,844,231	5,809,002	4,602,550	5,129,585	418,368	823,313	47
9,585,399	5,972,467	8,679,630	5,416,550	355,774	549,995	48
1,729,353,034	1,253,274,862	1,326,752,028	1,041,068,755	163,826,365	238,774,641	49
122,453,126	106,935,857	105,116,029	96,068,746	8,158,625	9,178,472	50
188,361,324	146,230,410	148,711,653	124,395,056	16,936,384	22,713,287	51
501,580,204	344,630,382	381,001,112	281,863,465	50,506,820	70,072,272	52
587,442,363	416,016,173	438,433,995	338,333,945	59,470,078	89,538,290	53
288,736,328	214,769,225	219,413,139	178,358,651	26,426,462	42,896,727	54
26,700,164	16,090,491	21,722,527	14,143,740	1,770,846	3,206,791	55
14,079,525	8,602,324	12,353,573	7,905,152	557,150	1,168,802	56

TABLE 15.—FARMS AND FARM ACREAGE, AND VALUE OF FARM PROPERTY, BY

DIVISION OR STATE AND SIZE GROUP.	NUMBER OF FARMS.		ALL LAND IN FARMS (ACRES).		IMPROVED LAND IN FARMS (ACRES).	
	1920	1910	1920	1910	1920	1910
EAST NORTH CENTRAL.						
1 Ohio, total......	256,695	272,045	23,515,888	24,105,708	18,542,353	19,227,969
2 Under 20 acres....	31,479	38,913	309,944	363,977	269,835	327,189
3 20 to 49 acres....	44,535	50,331	1,558,326	1,719,606	1,278,657	1,441,294
4 50 to 99 acres......	86,337	88,047	6,372,019	6,444,930	5,191,712	5,288,437
5 100 to 174 acres....	69,738	68,746	8,969,102	8,850,408	7,098,910	7,053,181
6 175 to 499 acres....	23,773	25,113	5,677,796	6,020,366	4,297,908	4,641,288
7 500 to 999 acres....	728	783	446,953	488,963	311,411	355,502
8 1,000 acres and over	105	112	181,748	217,458	93,920	121,078
9 **Indiana, total...**	205,126	215,485	21,063,332	21,299,823	16,680,212	16,931,252
10 Under 20 acres....	19,916	23,644	189,627	221,480	164,487	196,615
11 20 to 49 acres....	34,949	40,161	1,227,117	1,384,816	1,006,186	1,155,565
12 50 to 99 acres......	65,066	67,221	4,859,427	4,977,801	3,992,245	4,097,432
13 100 to 174 acres....	57,895	57,261	7,591,255	7,485,481	6,072,468	5,996,101
14 175 to 499 acres....	26,265	26,107	6,433,804	6,400,036	4,945,009	4,923,766
15 500 to 999 acres....	905	949	553,839	591,015	378,543	418,564
16 1,000 acres and over	130	142	208,263	239,194	121,274	143,209
17 **Illinois, total....**	237,181	251,872	31,974,775	32,522,937	27,294,533	28,048,323
18 Under 20 acres....	16,710	20,294	156,187	186,520	139,166	169,516
19 20 to 49 acres......	26,989	33,322	925,154	1,129,398	783,957	973,339
20 50 to 99 acres......	51,920	57,917	3,925,671	4,337,599	3,402,203	3,795,685
21 100 to 174 acres....	81,459	80,539	11,133,433	10,964,517	9,759,866	9,672,197
22 175 to 499 acres....	58,186	57,755	14,501,272	14,446,916	12,261,939	12,384,215
23 500 to 999 acres....	1,733	1,842	1,057,205	1,135,951	768,254	849,906
24 1,000 acres and over	184	203	275,853	322,036	179,148	203,465
25 **Michigan, total.**	196,447	206,960	19,032,961	18,940,614	12,925,521	12,832,078
26 Under 20 acres....	12,744	14,785	120,664	137,131	104,690	121,750
27 20 to 49 acres....	40,765	49,890	1,489,135	1,814,802	1,126,919	1,351,445
28 50 to 99 acres......	71,391	73,748	5,369,830	5,537,099	3,974,153	3,998,814
29 100 to 174 acres....	52,645	50,622	6,856,373	6,591,003	4,796,617	4,539,148
30 175 to 499 acres....	18,075	17,143	4,335,771	4,125,482	2,675,770	2,602,019
31 500 to 999 acres....	634	607	404,907	391,180	165,962	159,477
32 1,000 acres and over	193	165	456,281	343,917	81,410	59,425
33 **Wisconsin, total**	189,295	177,127	22,148,223	21,060,066	12,452,216	11,907,606
34 Under 20 acres....	9,854	10,647	88,280	93,289	72,326	78,135
35 20 to 49 acres......	24,814	23,460	919,179	858,979	537,906	516,151
36 50 to 99 acres......	60,725	54,007	4,671,278	4,150,977	2,809,157	2,511,749
37 100 to 174 acres....	63,653	58,439	8,490,294	7,816,985	4,988,123	4,560,592
38 175 to 499 acres....	29,190	29,467	7,122,431	7,257,793	3,772,664	3,954,071
39 500 to 999 acres....	912	966	564,805	598,603	212,553	243,896
40 1,000 acres and over	147	141	291,956	283,440	59,487	43,012
WEST NORTH CENTRAL.						
41 **Minnesota, total..........**	178,478	156,137	30,221,758	27,675,823	21,481,710	19,643,533
42 Under 20 acres....	6,160	5,619	54,918	49,878	42,061	39,373
43 20 to 49 acres......	14,111	12,028	520,468	435,963	289,773	244,221
44 50 to 99 acres......	32,743	26,571	2,539,514	2,055,944	1,559,948	1,258,358
45 100 to 174 acres....	65,793	55,424	9,502,408	8,031,778	6,489,189	5,245,521
46 175 to 499 acres....	56,353	52,836	15,279,791	14,515,821	11,393,210	10,910,810
47 500 to 999 acres....	3,046	3,359	1,916,545	2,118,081	1,433,302	1,617,491
48 1,000 acres and over	272	300	408,114	468,358	274,227	327,759
49 **Iowa, total.....**	213,439	217,044	33,474,896	33,930,688	28,606,951	29,491,199
50 Under 20 acres....	11,521	13,724	102,480	117,505	87,747	102,881
51 20 to 49 acres......	13,117	15,678	458,651	537,644	370,292	430,517
52 50 to 99 acres......	35,959	38,712	2,782,734	2,980,189	2,420,641	2,619,874
53 100 to 174 acres....	85,549	80,121	12,052,654	11,243,738	10,600,330	10,009,429
54 175 to 499 acres....	65,279	66,165	16,712,805	17,206,099	14,124,470	14,875,500
55 500 to 999 acres....	1,877	2,430	1,151,201	1,513,469	864,587	1,203,407
56 1,000 acres and over	137	214	214,371	331,584	138,884	229,591

CLASSES, BY SIZE OF FARM, BY DIVISIONS AND STATES: 1920 AND 1910—Continued.

	VALUE OF FARM PROPERTY.					
All farm property.		Land and buildings.		Implements and machinery, 1920	Live stock, 1920	
1920	1910	1920	1910			
$3,095,666,336	$1,902,694,589	$2,661,435,949	$1,654,152,406	$146,575,269	$287,655,118	1
117,933,347	90,261,569	104,365,453	81,009,747	5,491,570	8,076,324	2
257,255,622	172,563,402	221,038,609	149,415,179	12,643,317	23,573,696	3
881,586,095	527,673,508	752,479,545	454,592,415	45,395,269	83,711,281	4
1,107,714,421	656,815,339	949,553,636	569,462,824	53,387,596	104,773,189	5
660,948,964	411,552,516	572,502,799	360,285,828	27,296,384	61,149,781	6
53,348,160	32,959,856	46,568,014	29,425,733	1,725,975	5,054,171	7
16,879,727	10,868,399	14,927,893	9,960,680	635,158	1,316,676	8
3,042,311,247	1,809,135,238	2,653,643,973	1,594,275,596	127,403,086	261,264,188	9
68,324,284	49,368,084	58,725,125	43,197,215	3,295,466	6,303,693	10
195,360,879	130,613,036	165,813,204	111,641,607	9,359,677	20,187,998	11
718,116,861	427,573,278	617,899,988	371,629,800	33,732,754	66,484,119	12
1,073,709,741	622,912,383	936,277,150	549,502,724	46,177,211	91,255,380	13
897,712,086	520,695,792	796,084,561	465,787,540	32,268,007	69,359,518	14
67,112,281	44,353,853	59,369,828	40,161,060	1,989,379	5,753,074	15
21,975,115	13,618,818	19,474,117	12,355,650	580,592	1,920,406	16
6,666,767,235	3,905,321,075	5,997,993,566	3,522,792,570	222,619,605	446,154,064	17
84,190,785	65,823,456	73,940,004	59,074,577	4,002,443	6,248,338	18
173,432,727	129,353,311	148,577,095	111,860,899	7,919,128	16,936,504	19
707,237,996	459,661,046	620,974,020	405,785,654	28,407,528	57,856,448	20
2,321,586,190	1,303,933,769	2,084,224,974	1,174,168,111	81,845,245	155,515,971	21
3,144,857,401	1,787,900,988	2,857,902,028	1,627,581,457	94,448,496	192,506,877	22
190,945,915	127,938,305	172,057,852	116,284,511	5,070,294	13,817,769	23
44,516,221	30,710,200	40,317,593	28,037,361	926,471	3,272,157	24
1,763,334,778	1,088,858,379	1,436,686,210	901,138,299	122,389,936	204,258,632	25
44,595,826	31,976,581	38,961,427	28,255,364	2,566,820	3,067,579	26
182,264,339	129,751,200	150,269,336	106,804,968	12,459,577	19,535,426	27
533,291,946	331,890,216	431,375,137	271,485,989	38,801,733	63,115,076	28
619,723,580	365,150,937	502,195,333	301,276,358	44,049,669	73,478,578	29
346,007,009	208,536,983	282,847,645	174,584,535	22,561,769	40,597,595	30
23,167,933	15,061,629	19,117,412	13,040,547	1,275,353	2,775,168	31
14,284,145	6,490,833	11,919,920	5,690,538	675,015	1,689,210	32
2,677,282,997	1,413,118,785	2,187,881,973	1,201,632,723	167,088,909	322,312,115	33
43,275,886	32,204,509	38,253,136	29,398,801	1,905,005	3,117,745	34
140,433,920	78,927,279	115,314,339	67,753,125	8,541,289	16,578,292	35
644,200,349	322,194,108	519,851,533	272,697,539	44,848,607	79,500,209	36
1,052,933,395	526,917,033	856,026,130	445,978,819	68,478,796	128,428,469	37
740,638,555	420,129,793	610,968,667	357,177,307	40,940,560	88,729,331	38
42,128,351	25,969,962	35,482,875	22,494,803	1,848,337	4,797,139	39
13,672,538	6,776,101	11,985,293	6,132,329	526,315	1,160,930	40
3,787,420,118	1,476,411,737	3,301,168,325	1,262,441,426	181,087,968	305,163,825	41
29,456,529	16,009,503	25,993,609	14,224,838	1,305,742	2,157,178	42
77,269,558	34,382,024	64,661,334	28,966,718	4,306,020	8,302,204	43
339,613,389	127,892,388	286,331,943	106,823,204	19,401,020	33,880,426	44
1,230,611,629	421,275,955	1,063,975,693	355,727,207	61,962,011	104,673,925	45
1,894,666,526	759,178,062	1,668,275,582	653,616,766	84,539,790	141,851,154	46
183,808,962	97,954,894	163,622,738	85,072,938	8,068,532	12,117,692	47
31,993,525	19,718,911	28,307,426	17,409,755	1,504,853	2,181,246	48
8,524,870,956	3,745,860,544	7,601,772,290	3,257,379,400	309,172,398	613,926,268	49
72,142,689	44,556,723	63,673,895	39,306,861	3,296,192	5,172,602	50
135,640,415	74,962,916	117,881,873	63,692,308	6,075,892	11,682,650	51
720,398,778	345,226,449	632,355,272	295,461,882	31,869,033	56,174,473	52
3,136,711,110	1,263,422,121	2,792,174,568	1,096,625,573	122,311,246	222,225,296	53
4,175,324,923	1,847,414,631	3,741,311,488	1,614,102,750	138,534,425	295,479,010	54
247,667,449	141,479,947	221,595,887	122,994,559	6,341,359	19,730,203	55
36,985,592	28,797,757	32,779,307	25,195,467	744,251	3,462,034	56

TABLE 15.—FARMS AND FARM ACREAGE, AND VALUE OF FARM PROPERTY, BY

	DIVISION OR STATE AND SIZE GROUP.	NUMBER OF FARMS.		ALL LAND IN FARMS (ACRES).		IMPROVED LAND IN FARMS (ACRES).	
		1920	1910	1920	1910	1920	1910
	WEST NORTH CENTRAL—Con.						
1	Missouri, total..	263,004	277,244	34,774,679	34,591,248	24,832,966	24,581,186
2	Under 20 acres....	16,641	19,756	163,519	192,760	145,462	176,479
3	20 to 49 acres......	41,116	47,398	1,470,343	1,657,429	1,151,634	1,312,077
4	50 to 99 acres......	67,446	74,178	5,080,089	5,524,548	3,879,808	4,184,784
5	100 to 174 acres....	79,507	80,020	10,669,125	10,701,983	7,888,573	7,666,746
6	175 to 499 acres....	53,961	51,921	13,950,052	13,374,223	9,834,949	9,356,608
7	500 to 999 acres....	3,684	3,427	2,334,718	2,180,501	1,444,349	1,412,313
8	1,000 acres and over	649	544	1,106,833	959,804	488,191	472,179
9	North Dakota, total..........	77,690	74,360	36,214,751	28,426,650	24,563,178	20,455,092
10	Under 20 acres....	314	229	2,739	1,601	2,242	1,224
11	20 to 49 acres......	505	450	19,214	16,687	12,139	10,718
12	50 to 99 acres......	917	1,207	72,244	94,199	44,308	53,653
13	100 to 174 acres....	11,490	23,003	1,811,850	3,640,003	1,309,334	2,124,647
14	175 to 499 acres....	42,078	34,393	14,982,215	12,000,916	11,179,876	9,063,590
15	500 to 999 acres....	18,442	12,662	12,773,126	8,783,550	8,871,108	6,675,379
16	1,000 acres and over	3,944	2,416	6,553,363	3,889,694	3,144,171	2,525,881
17	South Dakota, total..........	74,637	77,644	34,636,491	26,016,892	18,199,250	15,827,208
18	Under 20 acres....	766	808	6,243	6,612	5,351	5,685
19	20 to 49 acres......	993	1,121	34,944	39,475	28,057	30,001
20	50 to 99 acres......	2,381	2,406	183,120	183,202	149,375	134,340
21	100 to 174 acres....	16,463	28,396	2,546,272	4,458,036	2,005,301	2,113,308
22	175 to 499 acres....	37,343	33,041	12,222,971	10,819,704	9,020,473	8,064,822
23	500 to 999 acres....	11,641	9,698	8,124,859	6,583,127	4,439,101	3,886,801
24	1,000 acres and over	5,050	2,174	11,518,082	3,926,736	2,551,592	1,592,251
25	Nebraska, total..........	124,417	129,678	42,225,475	38,622,021	23,109,624	24,382,577
26	Under 20 acres....	3,361	4,358	29,549	37,150	26,381	34,074
27	20 to 49 acres......	3,701	4,558	125,451	152,474	106,012	134,271
28	50 to 99 acres......	11,163	12,618	868,651	971,897	768,189	879,406
29	100 to 174 acres....	43,157	43,916	6,475,703	6,543,429	5,586,170	5,675,821
30	175 to 499 acres....	47,377	47,233	13,809,256	13,923,207	10,473,340	10,633,939
31	500 to 999 acres....	9,744	13,128	6,679,959	8,837,526	3,042,210	3,888,358
32	1,000 acres and over	5,914	3,867	14,236,906	8,156,338	3,107,322	3,136,708
33	Kansas, total...	165,286	177,841	45,425,179	43,384,799	30,600,760	29,904,067
34	Under 20 acres....	7,330	8,042	63,141	69,566	56,475	63,746
35	20 to 49 acres......	8,277	10,738	282,070	366,381	231,648	318,485
36	50 to 99 acres......	20,287	26,151	1,557,398	1,998,144	1,289,908	1,718,144
37	100 to 174 acres....	49,044	57,789	7,264,118	8,518,875	5,889,783	6,888,850
38	175 to 499 acres....	64,047	61,286	19,147,023	18,018,076	14,489,246	13,811,688
39	500 to 999 acres....	12,127	10,475	8,265,173	7,121,881	5,281,477	4,527,088
40	1,000 acres and over	4,174	3,360	8,846,256	7,291,876	3,362,223	2,576,066
	SOUTH ATLANTIC.						
41	Delaware, total..........	10,140	10,836	944,511	1,038,866	653,052	713,538
42	Under 20 acres....	1,226	1,535	13,906	15,185	12,085	13,404
43	20 to 49 acres......	2,182	1,988	74,064	66,119	59,418	52,746
44	50 to 99 acres......	2,952	2,977	208,105	211,100	150,878	154,027
45	100 to 174 acres....	2,510	2,849	320,645	359,476	222,948	249,355
46	175 to 499 acres....	1,218	1,429	292,886	345,465	193,106	226,100
47	500 to 999 acres....	47	52	28,007	32,310	12,487	14,083
48	1,000 acres and over	5	6	6,899	9,311	2,130	3,823
49	Maryland, total..........	47,908	48,923	4,757,999	5,057,140	3,136,728	3,354,767
50	Under 20 acres....	9,473	10,232	92,393	97,263	75,315	80,696
51	20 to 49 acres......	9,003	8,629	292,558	278,402	205,921	209,115
52	50 to 99 acres......	10,452	9,946	741,162	700,098	518,872	497,340
53	100 to 174 acres....	11,178	11,457	1,451,857	1,486,215	1,010,626	1,049,206
54	175 to 499 acres....	7,344	8,070	1,843,500	2,055,882	1,179,057	1,329,921
55	500 to 999 acres....	392	506	238,075	312,911	115,134	151,285
56	1,000 acres and over	66	83	98,454	126,369	31,803	37,204

CLASSES, BY SIZE OF FARM, BY DIVISIONS AND STATES: 1920 AND 1910—Continued.

VALUE OF FARM PROPERTY.						
All farm property.		Land and buildings.		Implements and machinery, 1920	Live stock, 1920	
1920	1910	1920	1910			
$3,591,068,085	$2,052,917,488	$3,062,967,700	$1,716,204,386	$138,261,340	$389,839,045	1
62,845,038	48,908,308	54,444,693	42,818,101	2,733,950	5,666,395	2
185,355,984	123,626,921	154,227,316	101,486,534	8,341,090	22,787,578	3
536,795,812	336,061,373	451,188,861	276,273,994	23,162,784	62,444,167	4
1,087,951,050	604,876,830	925,727,218	503,288,840	44,985,493	117,238,339	5
1,419,855,599	772,162,767	1,220,018,422	649,467,153	51,296,138	148,541,039	6
221,754,920	124,425,746	191,732,903	105,685,100	6,030,421	23,991,596	7
76,509,682	42,855,543	65,628,287	37,184,664	1,711,464	9,169,931	8
1,759,742,995	974,814,205	1,488,521,495	822,656,744	114,186,865	157,034,635	9
1,147,212	817,723	744,652	364,599	82,132	320,428	10
2,354,761	1,011,619	1,732,546	739,953	164,067	458,148	11
5,064,354	3,396,393	3,902,911	2,539,341	374,653	786,790	12
103,435,734	107,339,232	83,895,630	83,425,352	8,103,788	11,436,316	13
808,926,563	420,353,851	684,846,823	354,271,009	53,710,772	70,368,968	14
610,565,650	314,962,955	521,485,186	271,500,607	38,762,441	50,318,023	15
228,248,721	126,932,432	191,913,747	109,815,883	12,989,012	23,345,962	16
2,823,870,212	1,166,096,980	2,472,893,681	1,005,080,807	112,408,268	238,568,263	17
4,626,359	2,361,267	3,412,065	1,868,680	210,077	1,004,217	18
8,325,521	3,802,990	6,852,425	3,061,278	426,003	1,047,093	19
37,012,400	12,500,857	31,933,955	10,407,857	1,732,484	3,345,961	20
404,170,107	177,913,734	354,959,385	149,337,025	17,820,191	31,390,531	21
1,487,381,129	580,338,548	1,321,616,325	504,518,418	60,101,205	105,663,599	22
550,983,487	274,700,266	480,113,395	239,012,732	22,356,818	48,513,274	23
331,371,209	114,479,318	274,006,131	96,874,817	9,761,490	47,603,588	24
4,201,655,992	2,079,818,647	3,712,107,760	1,813,346,935	153,104,448	336,443,784	25
20,880,695	16,106,506	18,235,760	14,379,350	931,944	1,712,991	26
36,121,080	22,534,942	31,288,993	19,378,544	1,620,189	3,211,898	27
185,091,514	100,753,600	163,336,396	88,286,663	7,965,580	13,789,538	28
1,201,023,240	574,221,177	1,073,256,586	507,591,497	46,922,326	80,844,328	29
1,958,973,645	993,706,922	1,747,788,207	878,937,406	71,117,928	140,067,510	30
400,453,546	219,660,983	347,430,278	185,509,755	14,557,778	38,465,490	31
399,112,272	152,834,517	330,771,540	119,263,720	9,988,703	58,352,029	32
3,302,806,187	2,039,389,910	2,830,063,918	1,737,556,172	154,716,977	318,025,292	33
30,945,355	22,294,783	26,421,853	19,533,087	1,722,047	2,801,455	34
48,630,795	38,878,776	40,811,758	33,138,115	2,610,602	5,208,435	35
183,086,856	139,322,790	155,339,324	117,647,025	9,470,333	18,277,199	36
737,779,862	499,006,745	634,274,579	425,925,574	37,108,737	66,396,546	37
1,548,083,247	912,374,798	1,334,740,948	782,515,666	74,294,017	139,048,282	38
456,443,225	258,828,604	388,586,419	219,941,757	20,511,070	47,345,736	39
297,836,847	168,683,414	249,889,037	138,854,948	9,000,171	38,947,639	40
80,137,614	63,179,201	64,755,631	53,155,983	6,781,318	8,600,665	41
3,990,343	4,465,760	3,408,687	3,913,303	289,462	292,194	42
9,327,739	6,535,139	7,646,250	5,559,301	797,408	884,081	43
17,878,554	13,195,308	14,306,827	10,989,516	1,645,356	1,926,371	44
24,708,528	18,964,997	19,683,597	15,699,201	2,198,791	2,826,140	45
22,552,029	18,755,902	18,264,070	15,893,322	1,757,576	2,530,383	46
1,399,944	1,205,357	1,200,200	1,053,950	77,525	122,219	47
280,477	56,738	246,000	47,300	15,200	19,277	48
463,638,120	286,167,028	386,596,850	241,737,123	28,970,020	48,071,250	49
29,728,087	20,288,902	25,778,323	17,813,279	1,736,533	2,213,231	50
45,212,650	26,612,137	38,357,131	22,791,832	2,848,247	4,007,272	51
77,456,136	43,585,736	63,813,017	36,304,852	5,361,923	8,281,196	52
134,479,536	77,263,306	110,318,638	63,818,929	8,831,610	15,329,288	53
154,447,023	102,890,168	128,926,821	87,550,094	9,089,454	16,430,748	54
17,488,405	12,388,300	15,108,440	10,724,022	887,783	1,492,182	55
4,826,283	3,138,479	4,294,480	2,734,115	214,470	317,333	56

TABLE 15.—FARMS AND FARM ACREAGE, AND VALUE OF FARM PROPERTY, BY

	DIVISION OR STATE AND SIZE GROUP.	NUMBER OF FARMS.		ALL LAND IN FARMS (ACRES).		IMPROVED LAND IN FARMS (ACRES).	
		1920	1910	1920	1910	1920	1910
	SOUTH ATLANTIC— Continued.						
1	Dist. Columbia, total...	204	217	5,668	6,063	4,258	5,133
2	Under 20 acres....	127	122	1,071	1,039	939	1,001
3	20 to 49 acres......	50	65	1,492	1,878	1,139	1,650
4	50 to 99 acres......	18	17	1,099	1,114	856	812
5	100 to 174 acres....	5	10	597	1,115	210	813
6	175 to 499 acres....	4	3	1,409	917	1,114	857
7	500 to 999 acres....						
8	1,000 acres and over						
9	Virginia, total.	186,242	184,018	18,561,112	19,495,636	9,460,492	9,870,058
10	Under 20 acres....	36,402	39,746	383,256	397,425	306,179	321,370
11	20 to 49 acres......	45,884	42,390	1,461,041	1,332,113	963,634	894,682
12	50 to 99 acres......	42,714	38,342	2,949,407	2,648,520	1,635,182	1,495,798
13	100 to 174 acres....	34,011	32,997	4,323,469	4,191,039	2,225,483	2,194,055
14	175 to 499 acres....	23,601	26,101	6,196,299	6,937,154	3,018,981	3,382,003
15	500 to 999 acres....	2,833	3,450	1,821,085	2,216,101	798,969	973,035
16	1,000 acres and over	779	992	1,426,555	1,773,284	512,064	609,115
17	West Virginia, total............	87,289	96,685	9,569,790	10,026,442	5,520,308	5,521,757
18	Under 20 acres....	10,410	15,399	106,922	149,047	90,462	128,207
19	20 to 49 acres......	18,155	20,323	612,971	676,989	425,127	456,945
20	50 to 99 acres......	25,587	26,806	1,794,165	1,875,754	1,142,979	1,155,188
21	100 to 174 acres....	19,539	20,156	2,480,455	2,557,005	1,506,732	1,509,134
22	175 to 499 acres....	11,990	12,248	3,091,882	3,179,329	1,734,242	1,695,072
23	500 to 999 acres....	1,227	1,316	786,048	849,970	375,517	366,356
24	1,000 acres and over	381	437	697,347	738,348	245,249	210,855
25	North Carolina, total..	269,763	253,725	20,021,736	22,439,129	8,198,409	8,813,056
26	Under 20 acres....	51,336	43,224	618,757	485,387	545,041	427,423
27	20 to 49 acres......	87,239	75,629	2,747,018	2,326,984	1,852,952	1,705,751
28	50 to 99 acres......	68,903	62,157	4,697,176	4,253,522	2,172,800	2,086,897
29	100 to 174 acres....	41,082	43,987	5,119,334	5,532,657	1,853,395	2,098,630
30	175 to 499 acres....	19,094	25,254	4,823,859	6,504,207	1,395,504	1,906,623
31	500 to 999 acres....	1,629	2,669	1,027,735	1,724,796	226,997	365,077
32	1,000 acres and over	480	805	987,857	1,611,576	151,720	222,655
33	South Carolina, total..	192,693	176,434	12,426,675	13,512,028	6,184,159	6,097,999
34	Under 20 acres....	40,825	37,985	497,619	412,235	467,654	391,563
35	20 to 49 acres......	84,893	70,582	2,533,757	2,072,476	2,097,908	1,791,196
36	50 to 99 acres......	37,530	33,147	2,464,832	2,205,541	1,444,956	1,293,355
37	100 to 174 acres....	18,166	19,427	2,250,658	2,433,404	928,937	1,005,949
38	175 to 499 acres....	9,352	12,539	2,448,485	3,349,902	786,668	1,046,858
39	500 to 999 acres....	1,343	1,942	859,101	1,277,578	227,304	306,337
40	1,000 acres and over	584	812	1,372,023	1,760,892	230,732	262,741
41	Georgia, total.	310,732	291,027	25,441,061	26,953,413	13,055,209	12,298,017
42	Under 20 acres....	26,969	29,629	335,365	348,103	312,835	327,212
43	20 to 49 acres......	134,471	117,432	4,189,977	3,709,289	3,613,514	3,318,067
44	50 to 99 acres......	81,112	68,510	5,304,281	4,553,582	3,516,013	2,968,547
45	100 to 174 acres....	41,183	42,275	5,047,941	5,223,132	2,403,565	2,367,863
46	175 to 499 acres....	22,753	27,710	6,012,780	7,412,596	2,113,672	2,288,329
47	500 to 999 acres....	3,091	3,950	1,995,069	2,604,839	597,163	595,659
48	1,000 acres and over	1,153	1,521	2,555,648	3,101,872	498,447	432,340
49	Florida, total.	54,005	50,016	6,046,691	5,253,528	2,297,271	1,805,408
50	Under 20 acres....	10,558	9,084	103,326	87,797	85,206	69,247
51	20 to 49 acres......	19,382	17,169	640,989	570,960	460,369	391,233
52	50 to 99 acres......	10,846	9,999	779,384	724,565	451,741	361,791
53	100 to 174 acres....	7,637	8,178	1,030,889	1,123,163	459,851	380,200
54	175 to 499 acres....	4,477	4,545	1,191,720	1,214,621	488,808	388,993
55	500 to 999 acres....	707	670	458,265	435,978	148,382	107,639
56	1,000 acres and over	398	371	1,842,118	1,098,454	202,314	106,305

CLASSES, BY SIZE OF FARM, BY DIVISIONS AND STATES: 1920 AND 1910—Continued.

VALUE OF FARM PROPERTY.						
All farm property.		Land and buildings.		Implements and machinery, 1920	Live stock, 1920	
1920	1910	1920	1910			
$5,927,987	$8,476,533	$5,577,369	$8,231,343	$104,252	$246,366	1
1,852,500	3,795,076	1,777,389	3,723,300	38,778	36,333	2
1,824,045	2,075,651	1,765,500	2,034,300	21,474	37,071	3
836,582	1,010,015	792,530	987,000	17,450	26,602	4
252,080	984,612	242,000	936,743	5,850	4,230	5
1,162,780	611,179	999,950	550,000	20,700	142,130	6
						7
						8
1,196,555,772	625,065,383	1,024,435,025	532,058,062	50,151,466	121,969,281	9
66,694,605	37,096,342	56,561,206	31,523,270	2,986,749	7,146,650	10
126,554,075	59,873,583	106,201,054	49,994,079	5,611,142	14,741,879	11
203,258,122	92,222,535	172,186,184	77,362,360	9,177,053	21,894,885	12
269,413,392	128,431,431	230,578,541	108,368,330	12,137,966	26,696,885	13
365,580,834	199,825,958	314,882,596	170,377,481	15,343,596	35,354,642	14
99,626,854	61,116,944	86,797,439	53,041,674	3,095,574	9,733,841	15
65,427,890	46,498,590	57,228,005	41,390,868	1,799,386	6,400,499	16
496,439,617	314,738,540	410,783,406	264,390,954	18,395,058	67,261,153	17
20,016,982	14,293,985	16,830,461	12,055,803	660,523	2,525,998	18
44,399,217	27,877,303	36,149,403	22,929,321	1,659,683	6,590,131	19
96,692,104	59,989,120	78,335,137	49,093,413	3,723,874	14,633,093	20
125,581,996	78,331,847	103,026,909	64,873,363	5,116,171	17,438,916	21
154,260,112	94,982,622	128,909,805	80,792,565	5,819,851	19,530,456	22
34,432,375	22,514,231	29,127,725	19,609,782	994,902	4,309,748	23
21,056,831	16,749,432	18,403,966	15,036,707	420,054	2,232,811	24
1,250,166,995	537,716,210	1,076,392,960	456,624,607	54,621,363	119,152,672	25
89,233,345	29,311,954	75,189,066	24,749,610	4,065,298	9,978,981	26
268,649,473	87,389,402	227,661,828	72,871,655	11,513,245	29,519,400	27
320,481,739	121,671,335	272,469,348	101,807,106	14,913,378	33,099,013	28
276,008,071	127,111,341	237,905,284	107,303,214	12,489,146	25,613,641	29
227,298,865	124,665,376	200,925,811	107,251,793	9,314,829	17,058,225	30
42,550,767	27,977,039	38,318,225	24,677,277	1,603,519	2,629,023	31
25,899,735	19,589,763	23,923,398	17,963,952	721,948	1,254,389	32
953,064,742	392,128,314	813,484,200	332,888,081	48,062,387	91,518,155	33
68,816,551	23,859,056	56,909,873	19,781,861	3,292,279	8,614,399	34
275,313,848	86,191,719	232,212,508	71,354,028	13,120,046	29,981,294	35
228,067,649	81,409,887	193,531,786	68,415,043	12,070,489	22,465,374	36
160,439,030	71,213,096	137,461,439	60,528,192	8,547,053	14,430,538	37
138,927,882	81,063,916	120,697,969	69,933,577	7,584,239	10,645,674	38
40,803,194	25,848,077	35,978,068	22,659,523	2,006,353	2,818,773	39
40,696,588	22,542,563	36,692,557	20,215,857	1,441,928	2,562,103	40
1,356,685,196	580,546,381	1,138,298,627	479,204,332	63,343,220	155,043,349	41
46,634,215	23,869,880	38,409,506	19,929,323	2,482,094	5,742,615	42
322,779,296	119,736,720	267,507,035	96,117,977	13,962,506	41,309,755	43
355,382,277	127,174,911	295,594,023	102,927,993	16,845,385	42,942,869	44
256,991,400	112,789,791	215,069,955	92,772,819	12,656,918	29,264,527	45
238,053,338	122,928,217	202,073,127	102,831,020	11,556,316	24,423,895	46
70,556,410	37,957,082	60,822,694	32,471,115	3,311,379	6,422,337	47
66,288,260	36,089,780	58,822,287	32,154,085	2,528,622	4,937,351	48
330,301,717	143,183,183	281,449,404	118,145,989	13,551,773	35,300,540	49
39,508,367	17,575,068	35,082,339	15,109,442	1,528,893	2,897,135	50
66,515,423	27,549,034	56,551,968	22,124,761	2,846,743	7,116,712	51
55,900,680	24,289,622	46,805,854	19,623,399	2,399,252	6,695,574	52
52,682,889	25,400,956	43,752,853	20,391,462	2,305,732	6,624,304	53
59,207,666	26,450,291	49,916,722	21,854,842	2,600,833	6,690,111	54
20,371,210	9,535,167	17,602,177	8,139,751	768,066	2,000,967	55
36,115,482	12,383,045	31,737,491	10,902,332	1,102,254	3,275,737	56

TABLE 15.—FARMS AND FARM ACREAGE, AND VALUE OF FARM PROPERTY, BY

	DIVISION OR STATE AND SIZE GROUP.	NUMBER OF FARMS.		ALL LAND IN FARMS (ACRES).		IMPROVED LAND IN FARMS (ACRES).	
		1920	1910	1920	1910	1920	1910
	EAST SOUTH CENTRAL.						
1	**Kentucky,** total..........	270,626	259,185	21,612,772	22,189,127	13,975,746	14,354,471
2	Under 20 acres....	58,965	55,472	612,018	585,546	567,163	554,143
3	20 to 49 acres......	63,571	58,537	2,035,960	1,854,214	1,611,014	1,495,951
4	50 to 99 acres......	71,200	65,778	4,920,991	4,556,297	3,362,126	3,174,258
5	100 to 174 acres....	50,991	50,134	6,366,452	6,282,939	4,077,452	4,117,357
6	175 to 499 acres....	23,843	26,639	5,966,493	6,711,828	3,609,207	4,077,796
7	500 to 999 acres....	1,690	2,181	1,057,923	1,370,115	529,914	688,727
8	1,000 acres and over	366	444	652,935	828,188	218,870	246,239
9	**Tennessee,** total..........	252,774	246,012	19,510,856	20,041,657	11,185,302	10,890,484
10	Under 20 acres....	44,528	47,341	537,182	547,322	480,320	501,007
11	20 to 49 acres......	79,924	72,212	2,501,680	2,240,374	1,995,349	1,800,374
12	50 to 99 acres......	64,940	60,105	4,458,127	4,147,088	2,832,874	2,581,648
13	100 to 174 acres....	41,283	41,545	5,185,816	5,256,026	2,860,068	2,802,232
14	175 to 499 acres....	20,172	22,450	5,092,780	5,724,087	2,484,810	2,619,991
15	500 to 999 acres....	1,524	1,878	960,046	1,189,042	373,701	422,571
16	1,000 acres and over	403	481	775,225	937,718	158,180	162,661
17	**Alabama,** total..........	256,099	262,901	19,576,856	20,732,312	9,893,407	9,693,581
18	Under 20 acres....	33,741	41,858	406,961	477,518	383,433	461,806
19	20 to 49 acres......	112,848	106,841	3,564,798	3,294,559	2,910,326	2,803,670
20	50 to 99 acres......	57,404	55,448	4,002,957	3,862,717	2,345,600	2,289,469
21	100 to 174 acres....	32,500	35,563	4,210,290	4,674,360	1,774,266	1,857,959
22	175 to 499 acres....	16,733	20,093	4,372,952	5,257,792	1,483,031	1,602,363
23	500 to 999 acres....	1,991	2,276	1,298,224	1,497,299	447,263	374,410
24	1,000 acres and over	882	822	1,720,674	1,668,067	549,488	303,904
25	**Mississippi,** total..........	272,101	274,382	18,196,979	18,557,533	9,325,677	9,008,310
26	Under 20 acres....	65,953	66,943	893,895	874,944	875,496	863,325
27	20 to 49 acres......	116,795	112,666	3,388,076	3,280,964	2,865,133	2,831,168
28	50 to 99 acres......	41,900	44,645	2,944,937	3,142,027	1,561,904	1,695,452
29	100 to 174 acres....	28,218	30,172	3,705,243	4,003,230	1,453,888	1,503,771
30	175 to 499 acres....	16,330	17,115	4,303,068	4,493,804	1,518,750	1,410,412
31	500 to 999 acres....	2,040	2,061	1,333,295	1,365,482	488,171	374,920
32	1,000 acres and over	865	780	1,628,465	1,397,082	562,335	329,262
	WEST SOUTH CENTRAL.						
33	**Arkansas,** total.	232,604	214,678	17,456,750	17,416,075	9,210,556	8,076,254
34	Under 20 acres....	35,943	36,259	475,109	476,539	463,317	467,555
35	20 to 49 acres......	92,438	74,983	2,914,479	2,343,264	2,438,209	1,944,165
36	50 to 99 acres......	50,619	45,373	3,658,894	3,299,148	2,135,253	1,799,792
37	100 to 174 acres....	36,275	39,353	4,870,400	5,395,529	2,089,270	1,993,878
38	175 to 499 acres....	15,732	17,149	4,011,210	4,316,389	1,567,467	1,455,435
39	500 to 999 acres....	1,195	1,163	754,347	763,283	276,207	228,306
40	1,000 acres and over	402	398	772,311	821,923	240,833	187,123
41	**Louisiana,** total.	135,463	120,546	10,019,822	10,439,481	5,626,226	5,276,016
42	Under 20 acres....	30,033	29,256	397,061	355,220	385,573	345,303
43	20 to 49 acres......	61,346	46,389	1,830,508	1,397,534	1,566,156	1,164,909
44	50 to 99 acres......	21,715	20,248	1,497,637	1,418,628	905,883	821,543
45	100 to 174 acres....	12,855	13,681	1,672,723	1,817,211	797,920	789,583
46	175 to 499 acres....	7,472	8,406	1,998,647	2,274,598	919,981	958,320
47	500 to 999 acres....	1,247	1,340	821,976	1,030,218	395,158	453,758
48	1,000 acres and over	795	1,018	1,801,270	2,110,079	655,555	719,600
49	**Oklahoma,** total.	191,988	190,192	31,951,934	28,859,353	18,125,321	17,551,337
50	Under 20 acres....	6,024	7,158	62,795	80,936	57,558	76,769
51	20 to 49 acres......	32,558	31,489	1,132,092	1,065,835	957,758	930,731
52	50 to 99 acres......	43,452	39,002	3,150,650	2,798,885	2,233,932	2,042,852
53	100 to 174 acres....	66,245	75,186	9,730,995	11,217,523	6,183,134	7,118,362
54	175 to 499 acres....	37,652	33,812	10,936,409	9,429,784	6,655,034	5,914,539
55	500 to 999 acres....	4,566	2,688	3,002,101	1,767,120	1,359,281	876,997
56	1,000 acres and over	1,491	857	3,936,892	2,499,270	678,624	591,087

CLASSES, BY SIZE OF FARM, BY DIVISIONS AND STATES: 1920 AND 1910—Continued.

	VALUE OF FARM PROPERTY.					
All farm property.		Land and buildings.		Implements and machinery, 1920	Live stock, 1920	
1920	1910	1920	1910			
$1,511,901,077	$773,797,880	$1,305,158,936	$635,459,372	$48,354,857	$158,387,284	1
89,747,761	45,077,941	75,325,782	36,723,010	3,256,132	11,165,847	2
176,914,790	85,529,515	148,451,363	68,341,744	6,199,006	22,264,421	3
320,805,307	150,425,812	271,368,077	119,994,284	11,571,683	37,865,547	4
388,614,523	192,450,444	334,325,404	156,477,645	13,039,814	41,249,305	5
418,011,087	229,882,678	368,912,909	193,447,982	11,956,448	37,141,730	6
78,255,718	47,327,357	70,462,079	40,615,629	1,810,433	5,983,206	7
39,551,891	23,104,133	36,313,322	19,859,078	521,341	2,717,228	8
1,251,964,585	612,520,836	1,024,979,894	480,522,587	53,462,556	173,522,135	9
72,103,183	39,884,943	57,981,533	31,506,673	3,219,679	10,901,971	10
213,911,990	97,599,771	170,536,660	74,475,941	9,622,651	33,752,679	11
301,539,713	136,382,564	242,315,858	104,019,256	14,091,730	45,132,125	12
303,599,927	145,696,692	249,029,156	113,199,169	13,161,369	41,409,402	13
288,127,635	149,585,913	242,076,907	120,220,288	11,195,581	34,855,147	14
50,180,671	28,241,155	43,172,755	23,618,950	1,608,929	5,398,987	15
22,501,466	15,129,798	19,867,025	13,482,310	562,617	2,071,824	16
690,848,720	370,138,429	543,657,755	288,253,591	34,366,217	112,824,748	17
33,466,135	22,615,720	25,829,557	17,732,596	1,703,483	5,933,095	18
181,492,083	87,334,591	138,767,831	65,174,986	8,604,557	34,119,695	19
163,674,932	81,225,417	127,250,597	61,745,865	8,550,934	27,873,401	20
129,525,934	72,073,360	102,511,870	56,058,111	6,762,136	20,251,928	21
110,359,121	69,236,239	88,753,849	55,450,822	5,713,585	15,891,687	22
33,611,108	19,293,208	27,542,246	16,116,822	1,636,170	4,432,692	23
38,719,407	18,359,894	33,001,805	15,974,389	1,395,352	4,322,250	24
964,751,855	426,314,634	789,896,778	344,162,289	39,881,256	134,973,821	25
135,692,317	45,405,087	119,755,780	36,834,417	3,365,350	12,571,187	26
317,982,243	120,468,507	265,891,469	92,685,257	10,563,463	41,527,311	27
131,391,072	73,874,629	100,316,679	55,825,671	6,774,164	24,300,229	28
116,202,208	67,425,413	87,489,829	51,583,771	6,565,334	22,147,045	29
136,685,644	69,564,583	107,823,662	54,966,781	7,288,090	21,573,892	30
54,744,097	23,990,234	45,925,699	19,995,266	2,559,885	6,258,513	31
72,054,274	25,586,181	62,693,660	22,271,126	2,764,970	6,595,644	32
924,395,483	400,089,303	753,110,666	309,166,813	43,432,237	127,852,580	33
61,483,776	26,568,133	52,658,666	21,086,055	1,961,106	6,864,004	34
248,465,696	93,119,636	203,019,999	70,534,909	10,066,450	35,379,247	35
197,353,451	84,071,568	156,022,219	63,280,020	9,761,822	31,569,410	36
179,991,295	88,150,786	142,550,313	66,823,373	9,351,673	28,089,309	37
153,700,844	73,246,365	125,499,006	57,492,644	8,537,248	19,664,590	38
40,667,541	16,834,101	35,132,895	14,164,369	2,092,933	3,441,713	39
42,732,880	18,098,714	38,227,568	15,785,443	1,661,005	2,844,307	40
589,826,679	301,220,988	474,038,793	237,544,450	32,715,010	83,072,876	41
44,534,273	22,332,106	35,426,473	17,800,570	1,913,397	7,194,403	42
142,640,946	53,743,789	112,397,403	41,491,842	6,140,282	24,103,261	43
90,395,038	41,870,365	71,412,237	32,597,748	4,163,101	14,819,700	44
77,601,632	38,458,364	61,147,481	30,213,391	4,225,972	12,228,179	45
98,006,965	49,439,964	79,769,690	39,499,613	5,931,190	12,306,085	46
47,080,250	29,084,945	39,223,106	23,317,045	3,141,692	4,715,452	47
89,567,575	66,291,455	74,662,403	52,624,241	7,199,376	7,705,796	48
1,660,423,544	918,198,882	1,363,865,294	738,677,224	80,630,547	215,927,703	49
12,874,329	8,967,361	9,840,509	6,672,521	825,153	2,208,667	50
85,731,005	40,768,830	67,006,181	30,170,704	4,393,603	14,331,221	51
206,158,815	97,721,230	166,956,748	75,944,069	9,252,080	29,949,987	52
569,076,795	383,857,769	473,128,266	314,897,360	27,233,983	68,714,546	53
573,526,209	302,168,059	477,399,860	248,431,705	30,325,157	65,801,192	54
117,711,253	44,430,982	95,576,957	35,255,653	6,032,232	16,102,064	55
95,345,138	40,284,651	73,956,773	26,805,212	2,568,339	18,820,026	56

TABLE 15.—FARMS AND FARM ACREAGE, AND VALUE OF FARM PROPERTY, BY

	DIVISION OR STATE AND SIZE GROUP.	NUMBER OF FARMS.		ALL LAND IN FARMS (ACRES).		IMPROVED LAND IN FARMS (ACRES).	
		1920	1910	1920	1910	1920	1910
	WEST SOUTH CENTRAL—Contd.						
1	Texas, total.....	436,033	417,770	114,020,621	112,435,067	31,227,503	27,360,666
2	Under 20 acres....	25,878	29,371	289,934	329,754	268,304	307,435
3	20 to 49 acres......	110,387	98,583	3,640,250	3,230,581	3,302,082	2,927,042
4	50 to 99 acres......	119,427	112,237	8,167,575	7,713,441	6,282,252	5,744,866
5	100 to 174 acres....	96,792	94,574	12,498,810	12,272,384	8,056,806	7,089,634
6	175 to 499 acres....	59,573	59,049	16,145,480	15,937,878	7,753,548	6,452,197
7	500 to 999 acres....	12,709	12,833	8,530,787	8,621,554	2,517,834	2,060,976
8	1,000 acres and over	11,267	11,123	64,747,785	64,329,475	3,046,677	2,778,516
	MOUNTAIN.						
9	Montana, total.	57,677	26,214	35,070,656	13,545,603	11,007,278	3,640,309
10	Under 20 acres....	930	755	7,479	4,382	6,400	3,842
11	20 to 49 acres......	1,279	956	45,081	33,662	30,203	21,399
12	50 to 99 acres......	2,141	1,260	164,200	96,034	103,363	55,645
13	100 to 174 acres....	8,735	10,552	1,334,502	1,648,834	661,443	614,349
14	175 to 499 acres....	26,988	8,339	8,958,493	2,668,526	3,776,985	923,664
15	500 to 999 acres....	11,982	2,353	8,436,043	1,654,257	3,108,747	599,093
16	1,000 acres and over	5,622	1,999	16,124,858	7,439,908	3,320,137	1,422,317
17	Idaho, total....	42,106	30,807	8,375,873	5,283,604	4,511,680	2,778,740
18	Under 20 acres....	2,917	2,005	26,151	16,286	22,795	14,963
19	20 to 49 acres......	6,819	4,048	246,810	144,087	200,840	111,568
20	50 to 99 acres......	8,502	5,820	640,094	443,682	500,157	280,371
21	100 to 174 acres....	10,565	11,891	1,544,269	1,793,755	900,060	792,797
22	175 to 499 acres....	10,488	5,866	3,174,632	1,708,591	1,704,430	977,778
23	500 to 999 acres....	2,209	921	1,475,446	610,397	761,468	344,077
24	1,000 acres and over	606	256	1,268,471	566,806	421,930	257,186
25	Wyoming, total.	15,748	10,987	11,809,351	8,543,010	2,102,005	1,256,160
26	Under 20 acres....	196	420	1,193	1,116	988	951
27	20 to 49 acres......	399	338	14,648	12,610	11,209	8,941
28	50 to 99 acres......	994	645	76,717	49,985	55,608	33,007
29	100 to 174 acres....	2,551	3,816	382,853	595,182	181,491	174,978
30	175 to 499 acres....	6,011	3,629	1,964,549	1,166,263	598,326	330,228
31	500 to 999 acres....	3,521	984	2,413,074	703,831	466,127	189,064
32	1,000 acres and over	2,076	1,155	6,956,317	6,014,023	788,256	518,991
33	Colorado, total.	59,934	46,170	24,462,014	13,532,113	7,744,757	4,302,101
34	Under 20 acres....	4,932	5,070	40,820	40,432	37,671	37,538
35	20 to 49 acres......	4,449	3,882	147,114	126,209	120,393	99,671
36	50 to 99 acres......	5,913	4,384	442,875	328,961	342,449	235,870
37	100 to 174 acres....	12,139	16,355	1,818,972	2,526,569	1,022,382	978,512
38	175 to 499 acres....	21,611	12,476	7,064,941	3,929,716	2,908,587	1,456,957
39	500 to 999 acres....	7,482	2,426	5,189,387	1,699,403	1,733,574	557,631
40	1,000 acres and over	3,408	1,577	9,757,905	4,880,823	1,579,701	935,922
41	New Mexico, total..........	29,844	35,676	24,409,633	11,270,021	1,717,224	1,467,191
42	Under 20 acres....	6,789	6,885	56,479	55,286	48,020	46,776
43	20 to 49 acres......	3,095	2,812	96,741	87,971	63,733	57,882
44	50 to 99 acres......	2,008	1,820	144,016	132,025	68,557	62,466
45	100 to 174 acres....	4,929	15,363	745,904	2,418,328	209,581	545,207
46	175 to 499 acres....	7,015	7,388	2,319,283	2,322,242	524,086	504,519
47	500 to 999 acres....	3,196	836	2,235,058	584,375	319,610	96,895
48	1,000 acres and over	2,812	572	18,812,152	5,669,794	483,637	153,446
49	Arizona, total..	9,975	9,227	5,802,126	1,246,613	712,803	350,173
50	Under 20 acres....	1,436	3,946	12,250	15,496	11,477	14,367
51	20 to 49 acres......	2,367	1,477	77,030	46,757	65,923	37,271
52	50 to 99 acres......	1,703	820	122,060	59,047	93,429	38,273
53	100 to 174 acres....	2,239	2,591	329,017	309,210	152,782	95,142
54	175 to 499 acres....	1,351	757	413,992	225,491	150,413	70,633
55	500 to 999 acres....	478	164	342,213	112,612	68,318	37,001
56	1,000 acres and over	401	72	4,504,765	388,000	170,461	48,186

CLASSES, BY SIZE OF FARM, BY DIVISIONS AND STATES: 1920 AND 1910—Continued.

VALUE OF FARM PROPERTY.

All farm property.		Land and buildings.		Implements and machinery, 1920	Live stock, 1920	
1920	1910	1920	1910			
$4,447,420,321	$2,218,645,164	$3,700,173,319	$1,843,208,395	$154,320,996	$592,926,006	1
58,341,608	34,157,820	46,327,446	26,976,349	3,280,573	8,733,589	2
337,640,519	141,286,127	284,504,134	112,443,379	14,016,449	39,119,936	3
739,866,010	324,121,929	635,262,951	267,691,312	30,237,723	74,365,336	4
957,338,273	444,590,982	826,088,583	373,734,548	39,207,940	92,041,750	5
924,973,671	459,906,797	793,316,895	389,435,229	38,439,539	93,217,237	6
338,080,826	186,544,451	281,004,800	157,105,181	12,905,879	44,170,147	7
1,091,179,414	628,037,058	833,668,510	515,822,397	16,232,893	241,278,011	8
985,961,308	347,828,770	776,767,529	251,625,930	55,004,212	154,189,567	9
5,169,480	5,300,893	3,003,825	1,917,013	229,313	1,936,342	10
6,531,162	4,254,513	5,028,645	3,462,310	426,906	1,075,611	11
15,784,223	8,200,648	12,535,913	6,799,281	985,736	2,262,574	12
69,252,074	57,987,805	55,033,292	43,134,560	4,470,088	9,748,694	13
289,726,272	85,130,955	229,704,576	64,052,439	19,790,091	40,231,605	14
237,642,295	52,686,766	191,353,086	38,615,276	14,974,745	31,314,464	15
361,855,802	134,267,190	280,108,192	93,645,051	14,127,333	67,620,277	16
716,137,910	305,317,185	581,511,964	245,065,825	38,417,253	96,208,693	17
21,211,064	10,906,254	11,350,512	6,167,205	844,964	9,015,588	18
60,509,629	22,596,683	50,608,301	19,458,414	3,676,276	6,225,052	19
125,189,893	40,125,673	106,018,994	34,251,759	6,899,636	12,271,263	20
156,785,486	85,480,760	130,568,796	69,712,591	8,585,162	17,631,528	21
216,914,202	91,163,181	176,119,945	73,842,412	11,828,525	28,965,732	22
83,579,406	31,689,594	67,519,442	24,255,139	4,346,958	11,713,006	23
51,948,230	23,355,040	39,325,974	17,378,305	2,235,732	10,386,524	24
334,410,590	167,189,081	234,748,125	97,915,277	11,777,949	87,884,516	25
2,153,139	7,474,636	422,628	389,589	37,301	1,693,210	26
2,742,747	1,080,515	1,949,767	794,290	166,113	626,867	27
10,398,027	3,090,267	8,223,153	2,310,865	547,921	1,626,953	28
27,735,478	18,223,812	20,609,851	12,457,188	1,387,286	5,738,341	29
72,981,849	33,964,567	53,864,259	22,562,822	3,395,238	15,722,352	30
62,030,272	20,540,472	45,021,844	13,119,697	2,351,881	14,656,547	31
156,369,078	82,814,812	104,656,623	46,280,826	3,892,209	47,820,246	32
1,076,794,749	491,471,806	866,013,660	408,518,861	49,804,509	160,976,580	33
27,601,279	29,052,220	22,589,999	25,630,351	1,606,380	3,404,900	34
37,473,566	31,496,000	31,109,820	28,470,967	2,176,797	4,186,949	35
79,096,238	42,738,865	65,005,488	37,509,580	4,400,217	9,690,533	36
176,029,478	111,747,447	141,440,011	93,753,309	9,365,509	25,223,958	37
334,082,042	138,567,002	269,798,871	115,238,983	17,157,150	47,126,021	38
180,953,736	51,291,200	146,769,447	40,327,319	8,504,317	25,679,972	39
241,558,410	86,579,072	189,300,024	67,588,352	6,594,139	45,664,247	40
325,185,999	159,447,990	221,814,212	111,830,999	9,745,369	93,626,418	41
16,849,642	11,616,687	8,182,444	5,584,194	807,375	7,859,823	42
12,768,986	8,314,760	9,219,075	6,132,982	641,760	2,908,151	43
10,934,580	7,861,327	7,938,860	6,281,688	580,379	2,415,341	44
28,263,266	39,420,116	19,679,295	27,994,954	1,362,946	7,221,025	45
52,619,835	35,064,728	37,640,608	26,054,455	2,427,534	12,551,693	46
40,034,119	11,242,495	26,747,377	7,548,783	1,367,438	11,919,304	47
163,715,571	45,927,877	112,406,553	32,233,943	2,557,937	48,751,081	48
233,592,989	75,123,970	172,325,321	47,285,310	8,820,667	52,447,001	49
10,677,428	9,858,717	5,590,347	2,623,273	443,624	4,643,457	50
26,493,546	7,785,116	22,194,449	5,824,965	1,197,120	3,101,977	51
34,347,621	7,418,416	29,187,832	5,862,640	1,382,357	3,727,432	52
47,249,052	18,366,850	37,077,885	12,157,575	2,089,842	8,081,325	53
40,262,924	13,584,361	31,182,299	10,120,344	1,765,525	7,315,100	54
17,228,289	7,228,563	10,976,598	3,873,652	569,895	5,681,796	55
57,384,129	10,881,947	36,115,911	6,822,861	1,372,304	19,895,914	56

TABLE 15.—FARMS AND FARM ACREAGE, AND VALUE OF FARM PROPERTY, BY

	DIVISION OR STATE AND SIZE GROUP.	NUMBER OF FARMS.		ALL LAND IN FARMS (ACRES).		IMPROVED LAND IN FARMS (ACRES).	
		1920	1910	1920	1910	1920	1910
	MOUNTAIN—Con.						
1	Utah, total.....	25,662	21,676	5,050,410	3,397,639	1,715,380	1,368,211
2	Under 20 acres....	4,610	4,674	45,394	45,627	41,282	42,696
3	20 to 49 acres......	6,549	5,550	221,278	181,178	183,929	153,899
4	50 to 99 acres......	5,080	4,170	362,377	293,613	268,747	214,976
5	100 to 174 acres....	4,086	3,660	563,226	512,595	313,193	256,127
6	175 to 499 acres....	3,867	2,681	1,101,829	745,164	481,314	328,168
7	500 to 999 acres....	852	551	581,606	370,088	199,460	133,974
8	1,000 acres and over	618	390	2,174,700	1,249,434	227,455	238,371
9	Nevada, total...	3,163	2,689	2,357,163	2,714,757	594,741	752,117
10	Under 20 acres....	261	271	2,045	1,874	1,716	1,585
11	20 to 49 acres......	435	320	14,926	10,328	10,148	6,937
12	50 to 99 acres......	555	411	41,930	31,455	25,468	16,478
13	100 to 174 acres....	611	555	89,860	81,615	37,294	38,579
14	175 to 499 acres....	651	540	198,465	167,232	73,799	81,679
15	500 to 999 acres....	285	248	196,872	175,691	63,095	79,122
16	1,000 acres and over	365	344	1,813,065	2,246,562	383,221	527,737
	PACIFIC.						
17	Washington, total..........	66,288	56,192	13,244,720	11,712,235	7,129,343	6,373,311
18	Under 20 acres....	16,073	10,529	144,283	91,282	106,254	66,475
19	20 to 49 acres......	15,255	10,252	488,310	328,883	271,142	164,236
20	50 to 99 acres......	9,048	7,105	654,446	523,088	316,424	218,786
21	100 to 174 acres....	9,958	13,884	1,431,398	2,082,832	580,420	700,073
22	175 to 499 acres....	9,637	9,215	3,014,393	2,898,427	1,666,553	1,692,749
23	500 to 999 acres....	4,042	3,481	2,824,573	2,442,948	1,867,333	1,709,798
24	1,000 acres and over	2,275	1,726	4,687,317	3,344,775	2,321,217	1,821,194
25	Oregon, total...	50,206	45,502	13,542,318	11,685,110	4,913,851	4,274,803
26	Under 20 acres....	7,526	6,030	71,149	55,128	55,593	42,075
27	20 to 49 acres......	8,755	6,888	289,943	227,085	182,195	127,814
28	50 to 99 acres......	8,302	6,800	600,514	495,834	327,878	238,549
29	100 to 174 acres....	9,735	12,009	1,363,834	1,753,678	591,348	583,111
30	175 to 499 acres....	10,310	9,343	3,087,764	2,791,920	1,255,381	1,140,175
31	500 to 999 acres....	3,364	2,716	2,320,568	1,876,662	953,027	818,971
32	1,000 acres and over	2,214	1,716	5,808,546	4,484,803	1,548,429	1,324,108
33	California, total.	117,670	88,197	29,365,667	27,931,444	11,878,339	11,389,894
34	Under 20 acres....	34,067	22,525	296,403	200,822	280,508	189,679
35	20 to 49 acres......	31,723	20,614	981,155	625,954	861,487	558,296
36	50 to 99 acres......	15,034	10,680	1,045,972	752,951	855,192	600,140
37	100 to 174 acres....	13,217	12,015	1,841,847	1,709,459	1,152,733	972,519
38	175 to 499 acres....	13,671	12,551	4,095,679	3,816,706	2,386,735	2,226,957
39	500 to 999 acres....	5,052	5,119	3,466,412	3,535,598	1,753,337	1,846,502
40	1,000 acres and over	4,906	4,693	17,638,199	17,289,954	4,588,347	4,995,801

CLASSES, BY SIZE OF FARM, BY DIVISIONS AND STATES: 1920 AND 1910—Continued.

VALUE OF FARM PROPERTY.						
All farm property.		Land and buildings.		Implements and machinery, 1920	Live stock, 1920	
1920	1910	1920	1910			
$311,274,728	$150,795,201	$243,751,758	$117,545,332	$13,514,787	$54,008,183	1
23,422,329	15,420,726	17,494,963	11,996,852	964,193	4,963,173	2
52,881,621	26,878,028	44,596,545	22,188,727	2,629,695	5,655,381	3
56,853,351	25,920,695	47,158,810	20,965,001	2,684,815	7,009,726	4
49,970,887	24,847,468	39,430,291	19,690,152	2,313,483	8,227,113	5
62,680,365	28,096,118	48,640,507	21,359,510	2,805,515	11,234,343	6
24,653,243	10,339,220	18,648,865	7,626,182	994,830	5,009,548	7
40,812,932	19,292,946	27,781,777	13,718,908	1,122,256	11,908,899	8
99,779,666	60,399,365	66,255,214	39,609,339	3,630,927	29,893,525	9
2,295,661	1,396,859	651,695	601,713	55,722	1,588,244	10
2,577,788	1,339,558	1,828,580	1,023,280	148,015	601,193	11
5,671,301	2,461,707	4,486,552	1,973,575	332,526	852,223	12
9,044,318	5,079,008	6,255,997	3,464,547	493,432	2,294,889	13
15,154,990	8,546,660	10,957,527	6,431,919	698,214	3,499,249	14
11,807,175	6,894,876	7,842,335	4,804,820	496,311	3,468,529	15
53,228,433	34,680,697	34,232,528	21,309,485	1,406,707	17,589,198	16
1,057,429,848	637,543,411	920,392,341	571,968,457	54,721,377	82,316,130	17
91,771,197	54,058,886	80,336,316	50,780,592	5,221,444	6,213,437	18
126,753,983	67,258,059	109,039,485	61,496,331	7,453,245	10,261,253	19
104,915,499	58,643,672	88,949,239	52,667,859	5,938,084	10,028,176	20
132,908,568	105,865,993	113,466,727	94,207,452	6,978,324	12,463,517	21
232,242,015	148,889,394	203,720,345	132,453,455	11,675,574	16,846,096	22
178,487,667	101,348,695	158,664,229	90,553,407	8,680,998	11,142,440	23
190,350,919	101,478,712	166,216,000	89,809,361	8,773,708	15,361,211	24
818,559,751	528,243,782	675,213,284	455,576,309	41,567,125	101,779,342	25
39,142,123	26,140,898	32,360,252	23,517,363	2,007,824	4,774,047	26
68,666,806	41,300,528	59,777,458	37,654,879	3,718,783	5,170,565	27
93,510,154	54,328,126	79,128,890	48,774,337	5,091,417	9,289,847	28
126,838,048	94,747,031	106,660,856	82,682,016	6,917,185	13,260,007	29
203,392,474	142,264,007	168,671,562	124,131,252	10,700,159	24,020,753	30
113,723,479	69,707,196	94,860,231	59,579,881	5,691,683	13,171,565	31
173,286,667	99,755,996	133,754,035	79,236,581	7,440,074	32,092,558	32
3,431,021,861	1,614,694,584	3,073,811,109	1,450,601,488	136,069,290	221,141,462	33
354,330,586	143,036,073	321,745,428	133,881,517	15,204,340	17,380,818	34
594,205,184	208,155,885	543,815,809	192,799,674	27,219,062	23,170,313	35
420,412,118	162,193,086	382,383,474	149,394,265	18,240,753	19,787,891	36
386,799,268	178,112,963	347,609,049	161,032,374	16,791,684	22,398,535	37
581,264,276	301,824,976	520,990,661	271,773,253	24,100,537	36,173,078	38
325,942,833	184,707,278	290,244,019	164,156,673	13,101,324	22,597,490	39
768,067,596	436,664,323	667,022,669	377,563,732	21,411,590	79,633,337	40

TABLE 16.—NUMBER AND ACREAGE OF FARMS IN THE UNITED STATES, BY TENURE: 1920 AND 1910.

TENURE.	NUMBER OF FARMS.			ALL LAND IN FARMS (ACRES).			IMPROVED LAND IN FARMS (ACRES).		
	1920	1910	Per cent of increase.[1]	1920	1910	Per cent of increase.[1]	1920	1910	Per cent of increase.[1]
Total....	6,448,343	6,361,502	1.4	955,883,715	878,798,325	8.8	503,073,007	478,451,750	5.1
Owners........	3,925,090	3,948,722	-0.6	636,775,015	598,554,617	6.4	314,107,483	309,850,421	1.4
Owning entire farm..	3,366,510	3,354,897	0.3	461,250,133	464,923,315	-0.8	235,177,464	233,808,597	0.6
Hiring additional land......	558,580	593,825	-5.9	175,524,882	133,631,302	31.4	78,930,019	76,041,824	3.8
Managers.....	68,449	58,104	17.8	54,129,157	53,730,865	0.7	13,210,999	12,314,015	7.3
Tenants......	2,454,804	2,354,676	4.3	264,979,543	226,512,843	17.0	175,754,525	156,287,314	12.5
Share[2].....	1,678,812	1,399,923	19.9	160,722,551	123,053,718	30.6	112,879,950	89,737,744	25.8
Share-cash..	127,822	128,466	-0.5	24,334,428	19,389,868	25.5	19,933,107	15,923,917	25.2
Cash[2]......	585,005	712,294	-17.9	71,481,655	67,846,851	5.4	38,386,494	41,566,162	-7.6
Unspecified.	63,165	113,993	-44.6	8,440,909	16,222,406	-48.0	4,554,974	9,059,491	-49.7

[1] A minus sign (−) denotes decrease.
[2] Share tenants include croppers reported in the Southern states in 1920, and cash tenants likewise include standing renters.

TABLE 17.—PERCENTAGE OF FARM LAND IMPROVED, AVERAGE ACREAGE PER FARM, AND PER CENT DISTRIBUTION, BY TENURE, FOR THE UNITED STATES: 1920 AND 1910.

TENURE.	PER CENT OF FARM LAND IMPROVED.		AVERAGE ACREAGE PER FARM.				PER CENT DISTRIBUTION.			
			All land.		Improved land.		All land in farms.		Improved land in farms.	
	1920	1910	1920	1910	1920	1910	1920	1910	1920	1910
Total.................	52.6	54.4	148.2	138.1	78.0	75.2	100.0	100.0	100.0	100.0
Owners...................	49.3	51.8	162.2	151.6	80.0	78.5	66.6	68.1	62.4	64.8
Owning entire farm.......	51.0	50.3	137.0	138.6	69.9	69.7	48.3	52.9	46.7	48.9
Hiring additional land....	45.0	56.9	314.2	225.0	141.3	128.1	18.4	15.2	15.7	15.9
Managers.....................	24.4	22.9	790.8	924.7	193.0	211.9	5.7	6.1	2.6	2.6
Tenants.....................	66.3	69.0	107.9	96.2	71.6	66.4	27.7	25.8	34.9	32.7
Share[1]....................	70.2	72.9	95.7	87.9	67.2	64.1	16.8	14.0	22.4	18.8
Share-cash................	81.9	82.1	190.4	150.9	155.9	124.0	2.5	2.2	4.0	3.3
Cash[1]....................	53.7	61.3	122.2	95.3	65.6	58.4	7.5	7.7	7.6	8.7
Unspecified...............	54.0	55.8	133.6	142.3	72.1	79.5	0.9	1.8	0.9	1.9

[1] Share tenants include croppers reported in the Southern states in 1920, and cash tenants likewise include standing renters.

TABLE 18.—NUMBER OF FARMS IN THE UNITED STATES, WITH PER CENT DISTRIBUTION, BY TENURE: 1880 TO 1920.

TENURE.	NUMBER OF FARMS.					PER CENT DISTRIBUTION.				
	1920	1910	1900	1890	1880	1920	1910	1900	1890	1880
Total...............	6,448,343	6,361,502	5,737,372	4,564,641	4,008,907	100.0	100.0	100.0	100.0	100.0
Owners and managers...	3,993,539	4,006,826	3,712,408	3,269,728	2,984,306	61.9	63.0	64.7	71.6	74.4
Owners.................	3,925,090	3,948,722	3,653,323	....	....	60.9	62.1	63.7	.....	.....
Owning entire farm..	3,366,510	3,354,897	3,201,947	....	....	52.2	52.7	55.8	.....	.....
Hiring additional land	558,580	593,825	451,376	....	....	8.7	9.3	7.9	.....	.....
Managers..............	68,449	58,104	59,085	....	....	1.1	0.9	1.0	.....	.....
Tenants...............	2,454,804	2,354,676	2,024,964	4,294,913	1,024,601	38.1	37.0	35.3	28.4	25.6
Share and share-cash..	1,806,634	1,528,389	1,273,299	840,254	702,244	28.0	24.0	22.2	18.4	17.5
Share [1]	1,678,812	1,399,923	....	....	....	26.0	22.0	.....	.....	.....
Share-cash..........	127,822	128,466	....	....	....	2.0	2.0	.....	.....	.....
Cash and unspecified..	648,170	826,287	751,665	454,659	322,357	10.1	13.0	13.1	10.0	8.0
Cash [1]	585,005	712,294	....	....	....	9.1	11.2	.....	.....	.....
Unspecified..........	63,165	113,993	....	....	....	1.0	1.8	.....	.....	.....

[1] Share tenants include croppers reported in the Southern states in 1920, and cash tenants likewise include standing renters.

TABLE 19.—NUMBER AND ACREAGE OF FARMS IN THE SOUTH, WITH AVERAGES AND PERCENTAGES, BY TENURE: 1920.

TENURE.	Number of farms.	All land in farms (acres).	Improved land in farms (acres).	Per cent of farm land improved.	AVERAGE ACREAGE PER FARM.		PER CENT DISTRIBUTION.		
					All land.	Improved land.	Number of farms.	All land.	Improved land.
The South, total.............	3,206,664	350,121,833	157,079,624	44.9	109.2	49.0	100.0	100.0	100.0
Owners...................	1,597,225	220,601,656	89,545,302	40.6	138.1	56.1	49.8	63.0	57.0
Owning entire farm........	1,405,762	181,653,185	76,490,551	42.1	129.2	54.4	43.8	51.9	48.7
Hiring additional land.........	191,463	38,948,471	13,054,751	33.5	203.4	68.2	6.0	11.1	8.3
Managers....................	18,318	22,441,164	3,494,283	15.6	1,225.1	190.8	0.6	6.4	2.2
Tenants.....................	1,591,121	107,079,013	64,040,039	59.8	67.3	40.2	49.6	30.6	40.8
Share tenants, including croppers..	1,212,315	73,428,165	48,565,911	66.1	60.6	40.1	37.8	21.0	30.9
Share tenants proper...........	651,224	50,897,112	31,907,797	62.7	78.2	49.0	20.3	14.5	20.3
Croppers....................	561,091	22,531,053	16,658,114	73.9	40.2	29.7	17.5	6.4	10.6
Share-cash tenants.............	22,672	2,116,471	1,416,438	66.9	93.4	62.5	0.7	0.6	0.9
Cash tenants, including standing renters...................	324,184	28,606,529	12,754,123	44.6	88.2	39.3	10.1	8.2	8.1
Cash tenants proper...........	219,188	22,219,722	8,765,026	39.4	101.4	40.0	6.8	6.3	5.6
Standing renters.............	104,996	6,386,807	3,989,097	62.5	60.8	38.0	3.3	1.8	2.5
Unspecified tenants...........	31,950	2,927,848	1,303,567	44.5	91.6	40.8	1.0	0.8	0.8

TABLE 20.—VALUE OF FARM PROPERTY IN THE UNITED STATES, BY TENURE: 1920 AND 1910.

TENURE.	ALL FARM PROPERTY.			LAND AND BUILDINGS.		
	1920	1910	Per cent of increase.	1920	1910	Per cent of increase.
Total	$77,924,100,338	$40,991,449,090	90.1	$66,316,002,602	$34,801,125,697	90.6
Owners	47,611,545,944	26,669,634,373	78.5	39,864,222,907	22,366,934,278	78.2
Owning entire farm	36,837,394,179	20,730,867,111	77.7	30,710,720,764	17,310,639,016	77.4
Hiring additional land	10,774,151,765	5,938,767,262	81.4	9,153,502,143	5,056,295,262	81.0
Managers	3,132,273,005	1,700,624,936	84.2	2,665,216,465	1,456,958,992	82.9
Tenants	27,180,281,389	12,621,189,781	115.4	23,786,563,230	10,977,232,427	116.7
Share[1]	15,157,085,982	} 7,981,203,217	140.4	13,221,673,341	} 6,969,948,650	142.3
Share-cash	4,030,760,602			3,668,741,782		
Cash[1]	7,320,236,819	} 4,639,986,564	72.3	6,318,247,496	} 4,007,283,777	72.1
Unspecified	672,197,986			577,900,611		

TENURE.	LAND ALONE.			BUILDINGS.		
	1920	1910	Per cent of increase.	1920	1910	Per cent of increase.
Total	$54,829,563,059	$28,475,674,169	92.5	$11,486,439,543	$6,325,451,528	81.6
Owners	31,984,781,634	17,806,121,628	79.6	7,879,441,273	4,560,812,650	72.8
Owning entire farm	24,058,745,303	13,441,834,689	79.0	6,651,975,461	3,868,804,327	71.9
Hiring additional land	7,926,036,331	4,364,286,939	81.6	1,227,465,812	692,008,323	77.4
Managers	2,207,651,020	1,218,859,265	81.1	457,565,445	238,099,727	92.2
Tenants	20,637,130,405	9,450,693,276	118.4	3,149,432,825	1,526,539,151	106.3
Share[1]	11,360,487,099	} 6,030,006,141	143.9	1,861,186,242	} 939,942,509	132.3
Share-cash	3,346,643,058			322,098,724		
Cash[1]	5,442,946,372	} 3,420,687,135	73.4	875,301,124	} 586,596,642	64.7
Unspecified	487,053,876			90,846,735		

TENURE.	IMPLEMENTS AND MACHINERY.			LIVE STOCK.		
	1920	1910	Per cent of increase.	1920	1910	Per cent of increase.
Total	$3,594,772,928	$1,265,149,783	184.1	$8,013,324,808	$4,925,173,610	62.7
Owners	2,447,792,781	900,672,541	171.8	5,299,530,256	3,402,027,554	55.8
Owning entire farm	1,958,178,820	731,851,754	167.6	4,168,494,595	2,688,376,341	55.1
Hiring additional land	489,613,961	168,820,787	190.0	1,131,035,661	713,651,213	58.5
Managers	103,773,702	42,908,500	141.8	363,282,838	200,757,444	81.0
Tenants	1,043,206,445	321,568,742	224.4	2,350,511,714	1,322,388,612	77.7
Share[1]	594,777,370	} 200,889,301	262.1	1,340,635,271	} 810,365,266	93.7
Share-cash	132,613,385			229,405,435		
Cash[1]	289,853,058	} 120,679,441	161.7	712,136,265	} 512,023,346	52.4
Unspecified	25,962,632			68,334,743		

[1] Share tenants include croppers reported in the Southern states in 1920, and cash tenants likewise include standing renters.

TABLE **21.**—VALUE OF FARM PROPERTY IN THE SOUTH, BY TENURE: 1920.

TENURE.	All farm property.	Land.	Buildings.	Implements and machinery.	Live stock.
The South, total	$18,174,450,024	$12,324,882,751	$2,831,772,156	$771,144,533	$2,246,650,584
Owners	10,605,235,862	6,852,424,081	1,847,456,083	508,825,552	1,396,530,146
Owning entire farm	9,099,251,139	5,815,704,511	1,659,672,272	444,294,872	1,179,579,484
Hiring additional land	1,505,984,723	1,036,719,570	187,783,811	64,530,680	216,950,662
Managers	796,894,078	574,160,283	95,236,202	25,531,088	101,966,505
Tenants	6,772,320,084	4,898,298,387	889,079,871	236,787,893	748,153,933
Share tenants, including croppers	5,054,014,420	3,709,004,584	662,693,651	170,813,044	511,503,141
Share tenants proper	3,392,565,740	2,457,932,861	436,172,517	127,395,972	371,064,390
Croppers	1,661,448,680	1,251,071,723	226,521,134	43,417,072	140,438,751
Share-cash tenants	181,370,964	136,869,249	19,220,682	6,754,459	18,526,574
Cash tenants, including standing renter	1,396,245,905	956,784,441	185,902,327	54,187,659	199,371,478
Cash tenants proper	1,027,195,230	705,656,622	131,601,478	38,020,019	151,917,111
Standing renters	369,050,675	251,127,819	54,300,849	16,167,640	47,454,367
Unspecified tenants	140,688,795	95,640,113	21,263,211	5,032,731	18,752,740

TABLE **22.**—AVERAGE VALUE OF FARM PROPERTY PER FARM AND PER ACRE, BY TENURE, FOR THE UNITED STATES: 1920 AND 1910.

ITEM.	TOTAL.		Owners.		Managers.		Tenants.	
	1920	1910	1920	1910	1920	1910	1920	1910
Average value per farm:								
All farm property	$12,084	$6,444	$12,130	$6,754	$45,761	$29,269	$11,072	$5,360
Land and buildings	10,284	5,471	10,156	5,664	38,937	25,075	9,690	4,662
Land alone	8,503	4,476	8,149	4,509	32,252	20,977	8,407	4,014
Buildings	1,781	994	2,007	1,155	6,685	4,098	1,283	648
Implements and machinery	557	199	624	228	1,516	738	425	137
Live stock	1,243	774	1,350	862	5,307	3,455	958	562
Average value per acre:								
All farm property	81.52	46.64	74.77	44.56	57.87	31.65	102.58	55.72
Land and buildings	69.38	39.60	62.60	37.37	49.24	27.12	89.77	48.46
Land alone	57.36	32.40	50.23	29.75	40.78	22.68	77.88	41.72
Buildings	12.02	7.20	12.37	7.62	8.45	4.43	11.89	6.74
Implements and machinery	3.76	1.44	3.84	1.50	1.92	0.80	3.94	1.42
Live stock	8.38	5.60	8.32	5.68	6.71	3.74	8.87	5.84

TABLE 23.—NUMBER OF FARMS, WITH PER CENT DISTRIBU-

	DIVISION AND STATE.	TOTAL NUMBER OF FARMS.		NUMBER OF FARMS OPERATED BY—			
				All owners.		Full owners (owning entire farm).	
		1920	1910	1920	1910	1920	1910
1	United States...	6,448,343	6,361,502	3,925,090	3,948,722	3,366,510	3,354,897
	GEOGRAPHIC DIVISIONS:						
2	New England.......	156,564	188,802	140,160	168,408	133,841	162,539
3	Middle Atlantic.....	425,147	468,379	327,104	355,036	304,603	329,423
4	East North Central..	1,084,744	1,123,489	766,786	809,044	659,947	677,239
5	West North Central.	1,096,951	1,109,948	711,156	758,946	543,249	580,066
6	South Atlantic......	1,158,976	1,111,881	607,089	593,154	546,563	521,558
7	East South Central..	1,051,600	1,042,480	525,808	510,452	468,054	438,977
8	West South Central.	996,088	943,186	464,328	440,905	391,145	368,855
9	Mountain............	244,109	183,446	202,515	160,844	165,094	145,029
10	Pacific.............	234,164	189,891	180,144	151,933	154,014	131,211
	NEW ENGLAND:						
11	Maine...............	48,227	60,016	45,437	56,454	44,224	55,349
12	New Hampshire.....	20,523	27,053	18,604	24,493	17,836	23,714
13	Vermont............	29,075	32,709	25,121	28,065	23,926	26,793
14	Massachusetts.......	32,001	36,917	28,087	32,075	26,515	30,705
15	Rhode Island........	4,083	5,292	3,245	4,087	2,971	3,831
16	Connecticut.........	22,655	26,815	19,666	23,234	18,369	22,147
	MIDDLE ATLANTIC:						
17	New York...........	193,195	215,597	151,717	166,674	139,153	152,343
18	New Jersey.........	29,702	33,487	21,889	24,133	20,752	22,992
19	Pennsylvania.......	202,250	219,295	153,498	164,229	144,698	154,088
	EAST NORTH CENTRAL:						
20	Ohio................	256,695	272,045	177,986	192,104	157,116	162,982
21	Indiana.............	205,126	215,485	137,210	148,501	112,664	115,424
22	Illinois.............	237,181	251,872	132,574	145,107	100,903	107,300
23	Michigan............	196,447	206,960	159,406	172,310	139,874	151,005
24	Wisconsin...........	189,295	177,127	159,610	151,022	149,390	140,528
	WEST NORTH CENTRAL:						
25	Minnesota...........	178,478	156,137	132,744	122,104	112,880	99,493
26	Iowa...............	213,439	217,044	121,888	133,003	99,008	106,464
27	Missouri...........	263,004	277,244	185,030	192,285	153,852	152,807
28	North Dakota.......	77,690	74,360	56,917	63,212	34,051	44,667
29	South Dakota.......	74,637	77,644	47,815	57,984	27,253	40,405
30	Nebraska............	124,417	129,678	69,672	79,250	50,565	58,222
31	Kansas.............	165,286	177,841	97,090	111,108	65,640	78,008
	SOUTH ATLANTIC:						
32	Delaware...........	10,140	10,836	6,010	6,178	5,688	5,865
33	Maryland...........	47,908	48,923	32,805	33,519	30,842	31,120
34	District of Columbia.	204	217	100	118	91	111
35	Virginia............	186,242	184,018	136,363	133,664	121,454	117,964
36	West Virginia......	87,289	96,685	72,101	75,978	66,220	68,318
37	North Carolina......	269,763	253,725	151,376	145,320	131,847	121,382
38	South Carolina......	192,693	176,434	67,724	64,350	60,089	55,523
39	Georgia.............	310,732	291,027	102,123	98,628	94,575	88,768
40	Florida.............	54,005	50,016	38,487	35,399	35,757	32,507
	EAST SOUTH CENTRAL:						
41	Kentucky...........	270,626	259,185	179,327	170,332	159,206	148,832
42	Tennessee..........	252,774	246,012	148,082	144,125	129,532	120,081
43	Alabama............	256,099	262,901	107,089	103,929	95,548	87,589
44	Mississippi.........	272,101	274,382	91,310	92,066	83,768	82,475
	WEST SOUTH CENTRAL:						
45	Arkansas............	232,604	214,678	112,647	106,649	98,037	87,866
46	Louisiana...........	135,463	120,546	57,254	52,989	51,895	48,590
47	Oklahoma...........	191,988	190,192	93,217	85,404	69,786	64,884
48	Texas..............	436,033	417,770	201,210	195,863	171,427	167,515
	MOUNTAIN:						
49	Montana............	57,677	26,214	50,271	23,365	38,431	21,525
50	Idaho..............	42,106	30,807	34,647	27,100	30,200	24,940
51	Wyoming...........	15,748	10,987	13,408	9,770	10,681	8,677
52	Colorado...........	59,934	46,170	45,291	36,993	35,553	32,474
53	New Mexico........	29,844	35,676	25,756	33,398	21,533	30,417
54	Arizona............	9,975	9,227	7,869	8,203	6,970	7,759
55	Utah...............	25,662	21,676	22,579	19,762	19,134	17,176
56	Nevada.............	3,163	2,689	2,699	2,175	2,493	2,061
	PACIFIC:						
57	Washington........	66,288	56,192	52,701	47,505	44,832	41,729
58	Oregon.............	50,206	45,502	39,863	37,796	33,300	32,982
59	California...........	117,670	88,197	87,580	66,632	75,882	56,500

TION, BY TENURE, BY DIVISIONS AND STATES: 1920 AND 1910.

| NUMBER OF FARMS OPERATED BY— | | | | | | PER CENT OF ALL FARMS OPERATED BY— | | | | | | |
| Part owners (hiring additional land). | | Managers. | | Tenants. | | Owners. | | Managers. | | Tenants. | | |
1920	1910	1920	1910	1920	1910	1920	1910	1920	1910	1920	1910	
558,580	593,825	68,449	58,104	2,454,804	2,354,676	60.9	62.1	1.1	0.9	38.1	37.0	1
6,319	5,869	4,802	5,379	11,602	15,015	89.5	89.2	3.1	2.8	7.4	8.0	2
22,501	25,613	9,853	9,072	88,190	104,271	76.9	75.8	2.3	1.9	20.7	22.3	3
106,839	131,805	13,551	10,848	304,407	303,597	70.7	72.0	1.2	1.0	28.1	27.0	4
167,907	178,880	10,776	8,384	375,019	342,618	64.8	68.4	1.0	0.8	34.2	30.9	5
60,526	71,596	9,799	8,298	542,088	510,429	52.4	53.3	0.8	0.7	46.8	45.9	6
57,754	71,475	3,506	3,290	522,286	528,738	50.0	49.0	0.3	0.3	49.7	50.7	7
73,183	72,050	5,013	4,696	526,747	497,585	46.6	46.7	0.5	0.5	52.9	52.8	8
37,421	15,815	4,116	2,912	37,478	19,690	83.0	87.7	1.7	1.6	15.4	10.7	9
26,130	20,722	7,033	5,225	46,987	32,733	76.9	80.0	3.0	2.8	20.1	17.2	10
1,213	1,105	786	999	2,004	2,563	94.2	94.1	1.6	1.7	4.2	4.3	11
768	779	546	681	1,373	1,879	90.6	90.5	2.7	2.5	6.7	6.9	12
1,195	1,272	568	636	3,386	4,008	86.4	85.8	2.0	1.9	11.6	12.3	13
1,572	1,370	1,627	1,863	2,287	2,979	87.8	86.9	5.1	5.0	7.1	8.1	14
274	256	205	251	633	954	79.5	77.2	5.0	4.7	15.5	18.0	15
1,297	1,087	1,070	949	1,919	2,632	86.8	86.6	4.7	3.5	8.5	9.8	16
12,564	14,331	4,376	4,051	37,102	44,872	78.5	77.3	2.3	1.9	19.2	20.8	17
1,137	1,141	987	1,060	6,826	8,294	73.7	72.1	3.3	3.2	23.0	24.8	18
8,800	10,141	4,490	3,961	44,262	51,105	75.9	74.9	2.2	1.8	21.9	23.3	19
20,870	29,122	3,065	2,753	75,644	77,188	69.3	70.6	1.2	1.0	29.5	28.4	20
24,546	33,077	2,329	2,297	65,587	64,687	66.9	68.9	1.1	1.1	32.0	30.0	21
31,671	37,807	3,411	2,386	101,196	104,379	55.9	57.6	1.4	0.9	42.7	41.4	22
19,532	21,305	2,319	1,961	34,722	32,689	81.1	83.3	1.2	0.9	17.7	15.8	23
10,220	10,494	2,427	1,451	27,258	24,654	84.3	85.3	1.3	0.8	14.4	13.9	24
19,864	22,611	1,596	1,222	44,138	32,811	74.4	78.2	0.9	0.8	24.7	21.0	25
22,880	26,539	2,487	1,926	89,064	82,115	57.1	61.3	1.2	0.9	41.7	37.8	26
31,178	39,478	2,247	2,001	75,727	82,958	70.4	69.4	0.9	0.7	28.8	29.9	27
22,866	18,545	855	484	19,918	10,664	73.3	85.0	1.1	0.7	25.6	14.3	28
20,562	17,579	781	429	26,041	19,231	64.1	74.7	1.0	0.6	34.9	24.8	29
19,107	21,028	1,315	987	53,430	49,441	56.0	61.1	1.1	0.8	42.9	38.1	30
31,450	33,100	1,495	1,335	66,701	65,398	58.7	62.5	0.9	0.8	40.4	36.8	31
322	313	144	123	3,986	4,535	59.3	57.0	1.4	1.1	39.3	41.9	32
1,963	2,399	1,262	988	13,841	14,416	68.5	68.5	2.6	2.0	28.9	29.5	33
9	7	19	15	85	84	49.0	54.4	9.3	6.9	41.7	38.7	34
14,909	15,700	2,134	1,625	47,745	48,729	73.2	72.6	1.1	0.9	25.6	26.5	35
5,881	7,660	1,090	872	14,098	19,835	82.6	78.6	1.2	0.9	16.2	20.5	36
19,529	23,938	928	1,118	117,459	107,287	56.1	57.3	0.3	0.4	43.5	42.3	37
7,635	8,827	738	863	124,231	111,221	35.1	36.5	0.4	0.5	64.5	63.0	38
7,548	9,860	1,655	1,419	206,954	190,980	32.9	33.9	0.5	0.5	66.6	65.6	39
2,730	2,892	1,829	1,275	13,689	13,342	71.3	70.8	3.4	2.5	25.3	26.7	40
20,121	21,500	969	993	90,330	87,860	66.3	65.7	0.4	0.4	33.4	33.9	41
18,550	24,044	807	826	103,885	101,061	58.6	58.6	0.3	0.3	41.1	41.1	42
11,541	16,340	741	646	148,269	158,326	41.8	39.5	0.3	0.2	57.9	60.2	43
7,542	9,591	989	825	179,802	181,491	33.6	33.6	0.4	0.3	66.1	66.1	44
14,610	18,783	736	763	119,221	107,266	48.4	49.7	0.3	0.4	51.3	50.0	45
5,359	4,399	828	950	77,381	66,607	42.3	44.0	0.6	0.8	57.1	55.3	46
23,431	20,520	935	651	97,836	104,137	48.6	44.9	0.5	0.3	51.0	54.8	47
29,783	28,348	2,514	2,332	232,309	219,575	46.1	46.9	0.6	0.6	53.3	52.6	48
11,840	1,840	899	505	6,507	2,344	87.2	89.1	1.6	1.9	11.3	8.9	49
4,348	2,229	758	450	6,701	3,188	82.3	88.2	1.8	1.5	15.9	10.3	50
2,722	1,102	377	311	1,968	897	85.1	89.0	2.4	2.8	12.5	8.2	51
9,738	4,519	880	787	13,763	8,390	75.6	80.1	1.5	1.7	23.0	18.2	52
4,223	2,981	433	321	3,655	1,957	86.3	93.6	1.5	0.9	12.2	5.5	53
899	444	305	163	1,801	861	78.9	88.9	3.1	1.8	18.1	9.3	54
3,445	2,586	296	194	2,787	1,720	88.0	91.2	1.2	0.9	10.9	7.9	55
206	114	168	181	296	333	85.3	80.9	5.3	6.7	9.4	12.4	56
7,869	5,776	1,168	961	12,419	7,726	79.5	84.5	1.8	1.7	18.7	13.7	57
6,563	4,814	916	847	9,427	6,859	79.4	83.1	1.8	1.9	18.8	15.1	58
11,698	10,132	4,949	3,417	25,141	18,148	74.4	75.5	4.2	3.9	21.4	20.6	59

TABLE 24.—TENANT FARMS CLASSIFIED ACCORDING TO FORM

	DIVISION AND STATE.	TOTAL NUMBER OF FARMS OPERATED BY TENANTS.		SHARE TENANTS. 1920			1910
		1920	1910	Total, including croppers.	Share tenants proper.	Croppers.[1]	
1	United States.........	2,454,804	2,354,676	1,678,812	1,117,721	561,091	1,399,923
	GEOGRAPHIC DIVISIONS:						
2	New England............	11,602	15,015	2,698	2,698	....	2,611
3	Middle Atlantic..........	88,190	104,271	51,174	51,174	....	54,958
4	East North Central.....	304,407	303,597	182,283	182,283	....	170,712
5	West North Central.....	375,019	342,618	186,704	186,704	....	167,096
6	South Atlantic..........	542,088	510,429	389,512	186,986	202,526	299,381
7	East South Central......	522,286	528,738	377,725	175,441	202,284	307,923
8	West South Central.....	526,747	497,585	445,078	288,797	156,281	374,372
9	Mountain...............	37,478	19,690	23,968	23,968	....	10,349
10	Pacific.................	46,987	32,733	19,670	19,670	....	12,521
	NEW ENGLAND:						
11	Maine................	2,004	2,563	292	292	....	289
12	New Hampshire........	1,373	1,879	120	120	....	151
13	Vermont.............	3,386	4,008	1,621	1,621	....	1,642
14	Massachusetts...........	2,287	2,979	330	330	....	214
15	Rhode Island..........	633	954	22	22	....	27
16	Connecticut..........	1,919	2,632	313	313	....	288
	MIDDLE ATLANTIC:						
17	New York............	37,102	44,872	20,864	20,864	....	23,086
18	New Jersey...........	6,826	8,294	3,600	3,600	....	3,921
19	Pennsylvania.........	44,262	51,105	26,710	26,710	....	27,951
	EAST NORTH CENTRAL:						
20	Ohio................	75,644	77,188	50,665	50,665	....	49,972
21	Indiana.............	65,587	64,687	48,473	48,473	....	45,573
22	Illinois..............	101,196	104,379	45,281	45,281	....	43,551
23	Michigan............	34,722	32,689	23,280	23,280	....	20,378
24	Wisconsin............	27,258	24,654	14,584	14,584	....	11,238
	WEST NORTH CENTRAL:						
25	Minnesota............	44,138	32,811	18,976	18,976	....	18,471
26	Iowa.................	89,064	82,115	25,606	25,606	....	20,935
27	Missouri.............	75,727	82,958	46,245	46,245	....	46,744
28	North Dakota.........	19,918	10,664	16,943	16,943	....	8,086
29	South Dakota.........	26,041	19,231	12,269	12,269	....	11,156
30	Nebraska.............	53,430	49,441	25,536	25,536	....	24,771
31	Kansas...............	66,701	65,398	41,129	41,129	....	36,933
	SOUTH ATLANTIC:						
32	Delaware.............	3,986	4,535	3,314	3,106	208	3,622
33	Maryland.............	13,841	14,416	11,011	9,552	1,459	10,118
34	District of Columbia....	85	84	6	6	....	2
35	Virginia.............	47,745	48,729	37,761	24,046	13,715	33,472
36	West Virginia..........	14,098	19,835	6,959	5,331	1,628	9,576
37	North Carolina........	117,459	107,287	98,758	58,819	39,939	80,215
38	South Carolina........	124,231	111,221	82,212	38,423	43,789	52,640
39	Georgia..............	206,954	190,980	142,532	45,035	97,497	105,504
40	Florida..............	13,689	13,342	6,959	2,668	4,291	4,232
	EAST SOUTH CENTRAL:						
41	Kentucky.............	90,330	87,860	73,655	44,205	29,450	69,176
42	Tennessee............	103,885	101,061	81,235	43,157	38,078	68,247
43	Alabama.............	148,269	158,326	87,676	39,779	47,897	67,352
44	Mississippi...........	179,802	181,491	135,159	48,300	86,859	103,148
	WEST SOUTH CENTRAL:						
45	Arkansas.............	119,221	107,266	94,884	47,219	47,665	68,553
46	Louisiana............	77,381	66,607	61,808	30,499	31,309	48,710
47	Oklahoma............	97,836	104,137	77,364	68,438	8,926	72,356
48	Texas...............	232,309	219,575	211,022	142,641	68,381	184,753
	MOUNTAIN:						
49	Montana.............	6,507	2,344	4,398	4,398	....	952
50	Idaho...............	6,701	3,100	4,023	4,023	....	1,639
51	Wyoming............	1,908	907	1,125	1,125	....	407
52	Colorado............	13,763	8,390	9,575	9,575	....	4,913
53	New Mexico..........	3,655	1,957	2,469	2,469	....	1,255
54	Arizona.............	1,801	861	887	887	....	272
55	Utah................	2,787	1,720	1,369	1,369	....	837
56	Nevada..............	296	333	122	122	....	96
	PACIFIC:						
57	Washington..........	12,419	7,726	5,851	5,851	....	3,459
58	Oregon..............	9,427	6,859	4,176	4,176	....	2,927
59	California...........	25,141	18,148	9,643	9,643	....	6,135

[1] Reported in the Southern states only.

OF TENANCY, BY DIVISIONS AND STATES: 1920 AND 1910.

SHARE-CASH TENANTS.		CASH TENANTS.				UNSPECIFIED TENANTS.		
		1920			1910			
1920	1910	Total, including standing renters.	Cash tenants proper.	Standing renters.¹		1920	1910	
127,822	128,466	585,005	480,009	104,996	712,294	63,165	113,993	1
95	216	8,071	8,071	....	9,787	738	2,401	2
1,127	2,232	32,879	32,879	....	40,958	3,010	6,123	3
33,537	33,551	76,945	76,945	....	84,082	11,642	15,252	4
68,316	50,983	107,568	107,568	....	102,883	12,431	21,656	5
1,977	10,117	139,907	64,594	75,313	176,617	10,692	24,314	6
6,795	12,555	124,478	99,227	25,251	192,252	13,288	16,008	7
13,900	16,993	59,799	55,367	4,432	84,191	7,970	22,029	8
786	615	10,916	10,916	....	5,661	1,808	3,065	9
1,289	1,204	24,442	24,442	....	15,863	1,586	3,145	10
11	44	1,569	1,569	....	1,733	132	497	11
5	29	1,073	1,073	....	1,224	175	475	12
26	50	1,489	1,489	....	2,182	250	134	13
23	43	1,766	1,766	....	2,115	168	607	14
....	8	609	609	....	738	2	181	15
30	42	1,565	1,565	....	1,795	11	507	16
356	1,013	14,676	14,676	....	18,519	1,206	2,254	17
40	177	2,983	2,983	....	3,499	203	697	18
731	1,042	15,220	15,220	....	18,940	1,601	3,172	19
1,578	3,462	19,298	19,298	....	21,068	4,103	2,686	20
3,800	4,896	10,615	10,615	....	10,636	2,699	3,582	21
27,379	23,665	26,300	26,300	....	32,120	2,236	5,043	22
422	870	9,312	9,312	....	9,629	1,708	1,812	23
358	658	11,420	11,420	....	10,629	896	2,129	24
8,375	3,774	15,251	15,251	....	7,918	1,536	2,648	25
16,401	14,129	44,586	44,586	....	43,394	2,471	3,657	26
6,995	8,553	17,292	17,292	....	24,461	5,195	3,200	27
891	178	1,175	1,175	....	324	909	2,076	28
7,891	3,668	5,328	5,328	....	2,301	553	2,106	29
14,773	11,069	12,307	12,307	....	10,701	814	2,900	30
12,990	9,612	11,629	11,629	....	13,784	953	5,069	31
11	47	484	482	2	619	177	247	32
38	204	2,306	2,288	18	2,938	486	1,156	33
2	....	71	71	....	82	6	....	34
337	1,208	7,616	7,577	39	11,413	2,031	2,636	35
212	923	5,627	5,616	11	8,560	1,300	776	36
468	2,033	15,916	9,425	6,491	20,708	2,317	4,331	37
521	2,326	40,072	15,769	24,303	50,268	1,426	5,987	38
355	3,089	61,820	18,178	43,642	75,223	2,247	7,164	39
33	287	5,995	5,188	807	6,806	702	2,017	40
2,221	3,424	9,929	9,618	311	12,701	4,525	2,559	41
836	2,884	17,883	14,811	3,072	27,436	3,931	2,494	42
430	2,428	57,694	46,494	11,200	83,360	2,469	5,186	43
3,308	3,819	38,972	28,304	10,668	68,755	2,363	5,769	44
3,837	3,030	18,171	17,419	752	30,405	2,329	5,278	45
1,193	1,362	13,505	10,905	2,600	14,486	875	2,049	46
3,902	3,962	15,710	15,680	30	21,751	860	6,068	47
4,968	8,639	12,413	11,363	1,050	17,549	3,906	8,634	48
160	51	1,757	1,757	....	790	192	551	49
154	131	2,089	2,089	....	807	435	611	50
43	27	604	604	....	266	196	197	51
304	233	3,375	3,375	....	2,211	509	1,033	52
39	51	894	894	....	440	253	233	53
27	18	853	853	....	466	34	105	54
56	97	1,176	1,176	....	490	186	296	55
3	7	168	168	....	191	3	39	56
269	255	5,830	5,830	....	3,089	469	923	57
278	245	4,382	4,382	....	3,037	591	650	58
742	704	14,230	14,230	....	9,737	526	1,572	59

TABLE 25.—ACREAGE OF FARM LAND, WITH PERCENTAGES AND AVERAGES, BY TENURE, BY DIVISIONS AND STATES: 1920 AND 1910.

DIVISION OR STATE AND TENURE.	ALL LAND IN FARMS (ACRES).		IMPROVED LAND IN FARMS (ACRES).		PER CENT OF FARM LAND IMPROVED.		AVERAGE ACREAGE PER FARM.			
							All land.		Improved land.	
	1920	1910	1920	1910	1920	1910	1920	1910	1920	1910
UNITED STATES.										
Total	955,883,715	878,798,325	503,073,007	478,451,750	52.6	54.4	148.2	138.1	78.0	75.2
Owners	636,775,015	598,554,617	314,107,483	309,850,421	49.3	51.8	162.2	151.6	80.0	78.5
Managers	54,129,157	53,730,865	13,210,999	12,314,015	24.4	22.9	790.8	924.7	193.0	211.9
Tenants	264,979,543	226,512,843	175,754,525	156,287,314	66.3	69.0	107.9	96.2	71.6	66.4
GEOGRAPHIC DIVISIONS.										
NEW ENGLAND.										
Total	16,990,642	19,714,931	6,114,601	7,254,904	36.0	36.8	108.5	104.4	39.1	38.4
Owners	14,704,536	17,089,125	5,279,659	6,259,844	35.9	36.6	104.9	101.5	37.7	37.2
Managers	980,426	1,087,463	323,146	376,404	33.0	34.6	204.2	202.2	67.3	70.0
Tenants	1,305,680	1,538,343	511,796	618,656	39.2	40.2	112.5	102.5	44.1	41.2
MIDDLE ATLANTIC.										
Total	40,572,901	43,191,056	26,562,107	29,320,894	65.5	67.9	95.4	92.2	62.5	62.6
Owners	29,018,681	30,283,268	18,776,624	20,288,060	64.7	67.0	88.7	85.3	57.4	57.1
Managers	1,923,037	1,714,084	1,027,679	910,418	53.4	53.1	195.2	188.9	104.3	100.4
Tenants	9,631,183	11,193,704	6,757,804	8,122,416	70.2	72.6	109.2	107.4	76.6	77.9
EAST NORTH CENTRAL.										
Total	117,735,179	117,929,148	87,894,835	88,947,228	74.7	75.4	108.5	105.0	81.0	79.2
Owners	76,518,051	80,234,320	55,129,801	58,470,026	72.0	72.9	99.8	99.2	71.9	72.3
Managers	2,867,235	2,354,205	1,828,791	1,493,321	63.8	63.4	211.6	217.0	135.0	137.7
Tenants	38,349,893	35,340,623	30,936,243	28,983,881	80.7	82.0	126.0	116.4	101.6	95.5
WEST NORTH CENTRAL.										
Total	256,973,229	232,648,121	171,394,439	164,284,862	66.7	70.6	234.3	209.6	156.2	148.0
Owners	168,570,080	164,789,865	107,103,336	111,279,585	63.5	67.5	237.0	217.1	150.6	146.6
Managers	6,079,202	5,005,299	2,856,089	2,726,669	47.0	54.5	564.1	597.0	265.0	325.2
Tenants	82,323,947	62,852,957	61,435,014	50,278,608	74.6	80.0	219.5	183.4	163.8	146.7
SOUTH ATLANTIC.										
Total	97,775,243	103,782,255	48,509,886	48,479,733	49.6	46.7	84.4	93.3	41.9	43.6
Owners	61,798,370	69,129,783	28,028,682	28,844,267	45.4	41.7	101.8	116.5	46.2	48.6
Managers	4,402,027	3,364,390	1,470,268	1,229,084	33.4	36.5	449.2	405.4	150.0	148.1
Tenants	31,574,846	31,288,082	19,010,936	18,406,382	60.2	58.8	58.2	61.3	35.1	36.1
EAST SOUTH CENTRAL.										
Total	78,897,463	81,520,629	44,380,132	43,946,846	56.3	53.9	75.0	78.2	42.2	42.2
Owners	54,021,795	57,131,972	27,730,393	27,383,922	51.3	47.9	102.7	111.9	52.7	53.6
Managers	1,528,565	1,603,467	685,091	578,791	44.8	36.1	436.0	487.4	195.4	175.9
Tenants	23,347,103	22,785,190	15,964,648	15,984,133	68.4	70.2	44.7	43.1	30.6	30.2
WEST SOUTH CENTRAL.										
Total	173,449,127	169,149,976	64,183,600	50,061,073	27.0	34.4	174.1	179.3	64.4	61.8
Owners	104,781,491	104,355,474	33,700,007	20,885,471	32.2	29.6	295.7	236.7	67.8	70.1
Managers	16,510,572	19,698,171	1,338,924	1,426,467	8.1	7.2	3253.6	4194.7	267.1	303.8
Tenants	52,157,064	45,098,331	29,064,455	25,952,335	55.7	57.5	99.0	90.6	55.2	52.2
MOUNTAIN.										
Total	117,337,226	59,533,420	30,105,868	15,915,002	25.7	26.7	480.7	324.5	123.3	86.8
Owners	90,888,734	42,265,930	23,592,819	12,152,588	26.0	28.8	448.8	262.8	116.5	75.6
Managers	12,973,586	11,003,725	1,536,415	1,471,963	11.8	13.4	3152.0	3778.8	373.3	505.5
Tenants	13,474,906	6,263,765	4,976,634	2,290,451	36.9	36.6	359.5	318.1	132.8	116.3
PACIFIC.										
Total	56,152,705	51,328,789	23,921,533	22,038,008	42.6	42.9	239.8	270.3	102.2	116.1
Owners	36,473,277	33,276,880	14,679,942	14,286,658	40.2	42.9	202.5	219.0	81.5	94.0
Managers	6,864,507	7,900,061	2,144,596	2,100,898	31.2	26.6	976.0	152.0	304.9	402.1
Tenants	12,814,921	10,151,848	7,096,995	5,650,452	55.4	55.7	272.7	310.1	151.0	172.6

TABLE 25.—ACREAGE OF FARM LAND, WITH PERCENTAGES AND AVERAGES, BY TENURE, BY DIVISIONS AND STATES: 1920 AND 1910—Continued.

DIVISION OR STATE AND TENURE.	ALL LAND IN FARMS (ACRES).		IMPROVED LAND IN FARMS (ACRES).		PER CENT OF FARM LAND IMPROVED.		AVERAGE ACREAGE PER FARM.			
							All land.		Improved land.	
	1920	1910	1920	1910	1920	1910	1920	1910	1920	1910
NEW ENGLAND.										
Maine, total	5,425,968	6,296,859	1,977,329	2,360,657	36.4	37.5	112.5	104.9	41.0	39.3
Owners	5,073,856	5,915,822	1,853,224	2,222,452	36.5	37.6	111.7	104.8	40.8	39.4
Managers	145,793	156,901	49,431	53,352	33.9	34.0	185.5	157.1	62.9	53.4
Tenants	206,319	224,136	74,674	84,853	36.2	37.9	103.0	87.4	37.3	33.1
New Hampshire, total	2,603,806	3,249,458	702,902	929,185	27.0	28.6	126.9	120.1	34.2	34.3
Owners	2,296,383	2,863,633	623,673	829,301	27.2	29.0	123.4	116.9	33.5	33.9
Managers	154,358	209,625	33,821	42,790	21.9	20.4	282.7	307.8	61.9	62.8
Tenants	153,065	176,200	45,408	57,094	29.7	32.4	111.5	93.8	33.1	30.4
Vermont, total	4,235,811	4,663,577	1,691,595	1,633,965	39.9	35.0	145.7	142.6	58.2	50.0
Owners	3,520,899	3,816,498	1,387,502	1,321,497	39.4	34.6	140.2	136.0	55.2	47.1
Managers	150,197	208,938	55,962	52,584	37.3	25.2	264.4	328.5	98.5	82.7
Tenants	564,715	638,141	248,131	259,884	43.9	40.7	166.8	159.2	73.3	64.8
Massachusetts, total	2,494,477	2,875,941	908,834	1,164,501	36.4	40.5	77.9	77.9	28.4	31.5
Owners	2,021,920	2,343,103	744,523	931,621	36.8	39.8	72.0	73.1	26.5	29.0
Managers	313,095	330,914	104,650	150,206	33.4	45.4	192.4	177.6	64.3	80.6
Tenants	159,462	201,924	59,661	82,674	37.4	40.9	69.7	67.8	26.1	27.8
Rhode Island, total	331,600	443,308	132,855	178,344	40.1	40.2	81.2	83.8	32.5	33.7
Owners	248,934	318,262	97,719	127,964	39.3	40.2	76.7	77.9	30.1	31.3
Managers	29,792	44,436	13,943	15,914	46.8	35.8	145.3	177.0	68.0	63.4
Tenants	52,874	80,610	21,193	34,466	40.1	42.8	83.5	84.5	33.5	36.1
Connecticut, total	1,898,980	2,185,788	701,086	988,252	36.9	45.2	83.8	81.5	30.9	36.9
Owners	1,542,544	1,831,807	573,018	827,009	37.1	45.1	78.4	78.8	29.1	35.6
Managers	187,191	136,649	65,339	61,558	34.9	45.1	174.9	144.0	61.1	64.9
Tenants	169,245	217,332	62,729	99,685	37.1	45.9	88.2	82.6	32.7	37.9
MIDDLE ATLANTIC.										
New York, total	20,632,803	22,030,367	13,158,781	14,844,039	63.8	67.4	106.8	102.2	68.1	68.8
Owners	15,084,383	15,824,840	9,600,996	10,606,157	63.6	67.0	99.4	94.9	63.3	63.6
Managers	932,355	838,476	462,387	431,936	49.6	51.5	213.1	207.0	105.7	106.6
Tenants	4,616,065	5,367,051	3,095,398	3,805,946	67.1	70.9	124.4	119.6	83.4	84.8
New Jersey, total	2,282,585	2,573,857	1,555,607	1,803,336	68.2	70.1	76.8	76.9	52.4	53.9
Owners	1,424,791	1,562,906	971,819	1,105,612	68.2	70.7	65.1	64.8	44.4	45.8
Managers	208,391	227,340	101,871	106,528	48.9	46.9	211.1	214.5	103.2	100.5
Tenants	649,403	783,611	481,917	591,196	74.2	75.4	95.1	94.5	70.6	71.3
Pennsylvania, total	17,657,513	18,586,832	11,847,719	12,673,519	67.1	68.2	87.3	84.8	58.6	57.8
Owners	12,509,507	12,895,522	8,203,809	8,576,291	65.6	66.5	81.5	78.5	53.4	52.2
Managers	782,291	648,268	463,421	371,954	59.2	57.4	174.2	163.7	103.2	93.9
Tenants	4,365,715	5,043,042	3,180,489	3,725,274	72.9	73.9	98.6	98.7	71.9	72.9
EAST NORTH CENTRAL.										
Ohio, total	23,515,888	24,105,708	18,542,353	19,227,969	78.9	79.8	91.6	88.6	72.2	70.7
Owners	15,000,053	16,031,682	11,746,480	12,724,672	78.3	79.4	84.3	83.5	66.0	66.2
Managers	561,724	504,636	390,147	349,442	69.5	69.2	183.3	183.3	127.3	126.9
Tenants	7,954,111	7,569,390	6,405,726	6,153,855	80.5	81.3	105.2	98.1	84.7	79.7
Indiana, total	21,063,332	21,299,823	16,680,212	16,931,252	79.2	79.5	102.7	98.8	81.3	78.6
Owners	12,870,464	13,938,925	10,025,972	10,943,297	77.9	78.5	93.8	93.9	73.1	73.7
Managers	472,916	483,469	346,707	343,151	73.3	71.0	203.1	210.5	148.9	149.4
Tenants	7,719,952	6,877,429	6,307,533	5,644,804	81.7	82.1	117.7	106.3	96.2	87.3

TABLE 25.—ACREAGE OF FARM LAND, WITH PERCENTAGES AND AVERAGES, BY TENURE, BY DIVISIONS AND STATES: 1920 AND 1910—Continued.

DIVISION OR STATE AND TENURE.	ALL LAND IN FARMS (ACRES).		IMPROVED LAND IN FARMS (ACRES).		PER CENT OF FARM LAND IMPROVED.		AVERAGE ACREAGE PER FARM.			
							All land.		Improved land.	
	1920	1910	1920	1910	1920	1910	1920	1910	1920	1910
EAST NORTH CENTRAL—Con.										
Illinois, total	31,974,775	32,522,937	27,294,533	28,048,323	85.4	86.2	134.8	129.1	115.1	111.4
Owners	16,265,076	17,787,063	13,621,331	15,033,192	83.7	84.5	122.7	122.6	102.7	103.6
Managers	712,850	558,463	577,654	428,467	81.0	76.7	209.0	234.1	169.4	179.6
Tenants	14,996,849	14,177,411	13,095,548	12,586,664	87.3	88.8	148.2	135.8	129.4	120.6
Michigan, total	19,032,961	18,940,614	12,925,521	12,832,078	67.9	67.8	96.9	91.5	65.8	62.0
Owners	14,541,461	15,107,494	9,846,841	10,142,159	67.7	67.1	91.2	87.7	61.8	58.9
Managers	587,891	452,504	272,352	217,109	46.3	48.0	253.5	230.8	117.4	110.7
Tenants	3,903,609	3,380,616	2,806,328	2,472,810	71.9	73.1	112.4	103.4	80.8	75.6
Wisconsin, total	22,148,223	21,060,066	12,452,216	11,907,606	56.2	56.5	117.0	118.9	65.8	67.2
Owners	17,840,997	17,369,156	9,889,177	9,626,706	55.4	55.4	111.8	115.0	62.0	63.7
Managers	531,854	355,133	241,931	155,152	45.5	43.7	219.1	244.8	99.7	106.9
Tenants	3,775,372	3,335,777	2,321,108	2,125,748	61.5	63.7	138.5	135.3	85.2	86.2
WEST NORTH CENTRAL.										
Minnesota, total	30,221,758	27,675,823	21,481,710	19,643,533	71.1	71.0	169.3	177.3	120.4	125.8
Owners	21,014,164	20,668,885	14,254,641	14,153,505	67.8	68.5	158.3	169.3	107.4	115.9
Managers	443,089	413,734	283,869	285,241	64.1	68.9	277.6	338.6	177.9	233.4
Tenants	8,764,505	6,593,204	6,943,200	5,204,787	79.2	78.9	198.6	200.9	157.3	158.6
Iowa, total	33,474,896	33,930,688	28,606,951	29,491,199	85.5	86.9	156.8	156.3	134.0	135.9
Owners	18,051,121	20,214,337	15,319,624	17,432,235	84.9	86.2	148.1	152.0	125.7	131.1
Managers	569,086	490,805	445,897	383,977	78.4	78.2	228.8	254.8	179.3	199.4
Tenants	14,854,689	13,225,546	12,841,430	11,674,987	86.4	88.3	166.8	161.1	144.2	142.2
Missouri, total	34,774,679	34,591,248	24,832,966	24,581,186	71.4	71.1	132.2	124.8	94.4	88.7
Owners	24,686,797	25,189,241	17,466,971	17,694,543	70.8	70.2	133.4	131.0	94.4	92.0
Managers	664,447	629,845	428,977	396,712	64.6	63.0	295.7	314.8	190.9	198.3
Tenants	9,423,435	8,772,162	6,937,018	6,489,931	73.6	74.0	124.4	105.7	91.6	78.2
North Dakota, total	36,214,751	28,426,650	24,563,178	20,455,092	67.8	72.0	466.1	382.3	316.2	275.1
Owners	26,850,085	23,586,728	17,457,329	16,407,698	65.0	69.6	471.7	373.1	306.7	259.6
Managers	811,467	477,213	482,855	374,882	59.5	78.6	949.1	986.0	564.7	774.5
Tenants	8,553,199	4,362,709	6,622,994	3,672,512	77.4	84.2	429.4	409.1	332.5	344.4
South Dakota, total	34,636,491	26,016,892	18,199,250	15,827,208	52.5	60.8	464.1	335.1	243.8	203.8
Owners	24,169,377	19,314,938	11,483,257	10,779,500	47.5	55.8	505.5	333.1	240.2	185.9
Managers	889,717	635,199	278,756	288,166	31.3	45.4	1139.2	1480.7	356.9	671.7
Tenants	9,577,397	6,066,755	6,437,237	4,759,542	67.2	78.5	367.8	315.5	247.2	247.5
Nebraska, total	42,225,475	38,622,021	23,109,624	24,382,577	54.7	63.1	339.4	297.8	185.7	188.0
Owners	26,421,765	26,975,554	13,178,570	15,463,311	49.9	57.3	379.2	340.4	189.2	195.1
Managers	1,480,485	1,094,812	432,464	562,829	29.2	51.4	1125.8	1109.2	328.9	570.2
Tenants	14,323,225	10,551,655	9,498,590	8,356,437	66.3	79.2	268.1	213.4	177.8	169.0
Kansas, total	45,425,179	43,384,799	30,600,760	29,904,067	67.4	68.9	274.8	244.0	185.1	168.2
Owners	27,376,771	28,840,182	17,942,944	19,348,793	65.5	67.1	282.0	259.6	184.8	174.1
Managers	1,220,911	1,263,691	503,271	434,862	41.2	34.4	816.7	946.6	336.6	325.7
Tenants	16,827,497	13,280,926	12,154,545	10,120,412	72.2	76.2	252.3	203.1	182.2	154.7
SOUTH ATLANTIC.										
Delaware, total	944,511	1,038,866	653,052	713,538	69.1	68.7	93.1	95.9	64.4	65.8
Owners	451,476	476,827	302,219	322,077	66.9	67.5	75.1	77.2	50.3	52.1
Managers	21,485	21,164	16,544	17,587	77.0	83.1	149.2	172.1	114.9	143.0
Tenants	471,550	540,875	334,289	373,874	70.9	69.1	118.3	119.3	83.9	82.4
Maryland, total	4,757,999	5,057,140	3,136,728	3,354,767	65.9	66.3	99.3	103.4	65.5	68.6
Owners	2,750,870	2,905,318	1,759,988	1,883,482	64.0	64.8	83.9	86.7	53.6	56.2
Managers	259,426	207,291	168,518	129,269	65.0	62.4	205.6	209.8	133.5	130.8
Tenants	1,747,703	1,944,531	1,208,222	1,342,016	69.1	69.0	126.3	134.9	87.3	93.1

TABLE 25.—ACREAGE OF FARM LAND, WITH PERCENTAGES AND AVERAGES, BY TENURE, BY DIVISIONS AND STATES: 1920 AND 1910—Continued.

DIVISION OR STATE AND TENURE.	ALL LAND IN FARMS (ACRES).		IMPROVED LAND IN FARMS (ACRES).		PER CENT OF FARM LAND IMPROVED.		AVERAGE ACREAGE PER FARM.			
							All land.		Improved land.	
	1920	1910	1920	1910	1920	1910	1920	1910	1920	1910
SOUTH ATLANTIC—Continued.										
Dist. Columbia, total	5,668	6,063	4,258	5,133	75.1	84.7	27.8	27.9	20.9	23.7
Owners	1,729	2,429	1,311	2,127	75.8	87.6	17.3	20.6	13.1	18.0
Managers	1,951	1,456	1,519	1,263	77.9	86.7	102.7	97.1	79.9	84.2
Tenants	1,988	2,178	1,428	1,743	71.8	80.0	23.4	25.9	16.8	20.8
Virginia, total	18,561,112	19,495,636	9,460,492	9,870,058	51.0	50.6	99.7	105.9	50.8	53.6
Owners	13,760,903	14,715,345	7,042,904	7,471,786	51.2	50.8	100.9	110.1	51.6	55.9
Managers	823,750	660,325	415,481	320,528	50.4	48.5	386.0	406.4	194.7	197.2
Tenants	3,976,459	4,119,966	2,002,107	2,077,744	50.3	50.4	83.3	84.5	41.9	42.6
West Virginia, total	9,569,790	10,026,442	5,520,308	5,521,757	57.7	55.1	109.6	103.7	63.2	57.1
Owners	7,813,342	8,184,195	4,587,648	4,606,103	58.7	56.3	108.4	107.7	63.6	60.6
Managers	356,083	284,502	184,148	133,834	51.7	47.0	326.7	326.3	168.9	153.5
Tenants	1,400,365	1,557,745	748,512	781,820	53.5	50.2	99.3	78.5	53.1	39.4
North Carolina, total	20,021,736	22,439,129	8,198,409	8,813,056	40.9	39.3	74.2	88.4	30.4	34.7
Owners	13,441,509	15,656,323	4,966,358	5,539,783	36.9	35.4	88.8	107.7	32.8	38.1
Managers	386,449	582,377	112,279	159,982	29.1	27.5	416.4	520.9	121.0	143.1
Tenants	6,193,778	6,200,429	3,119,772	3,113,291	50.4	50.2	52.7	57.8	26.6	29.0
South Carolina, total	12,426,675	13,512,028	6,184,159	6,097,999	49.8	45.1	64.5	76.6	32.1	34.6
Owners	6,717,237	8,051,503	2,622,929	2,800,778	39.0	34.8	99.2	125.1	38.7	43.5
Managers	424,522	547,412	116,442	141,806	27.4	25.9	575.2	634.3	157.8	164.3
Tenants	5,284,916	4,913,113	3,444,788	3,155,415	65.2	64.2	42.5	44.2	27.7	28.4
Georgia, total	25,441,061	26,953,413	13,055,209	12,298,017	51.3	45.6	81.9	92.6	42.0	42.3
Owners	12,800,859	14,851,292	5,108,353	4,931,295	39.9	33.2	125.3	150.6	50.0	50.0
Managers	925,989	779,122	319,099	248,350	34.5	31.9	559.5	549.1	192.8	175.0
Tenants	11,714,213	11,322,999	7,627,757	7,118,372	65.1	62.9	56.6	59.3	36.9	37.3
Florida, total	6,046,691	5,253,538	2,297,271	1,805,408	38.0	34.4	112.0	105.0	42.5	36.1
Owners	4,060,445	4,286,551	1,636,972	1,286,836	40.3	30.0	105.5	121.1	42.5	36.4
Managers	1,202,372	280,741	136,238	76,465	11.3	27.2	657.4	220.2	74.5	60.0
Tenants	783,874	686,246	524,061	442,107	66.9	64.4	57.3	51.4	38.3	33.1
EAST SOUTH CENTRAL.										
Kentucky, total	21,612,772	22,189,127	13,975,746	14,354,471	64.7	64.7	79.9	85.6	51.6	55.4
Owners	16,791,715	17,462,755	10,694,025	11,086,744	63.7	63.5	93.6	102.5	59.6	65.1
Managers	269,839	315,260	162,575	174,708	60.2	55.4	278.5	317.5	167.8	175.9
Tenants	4,551,218	4,411,112	3,119,146	3,093,019	68.5	70.1	50.4	50.2	34.5	35.2
Tennessee, total	19,510,856	20,041,657	11,185,302	10,890,484	57.3	54.3	77.2	81.5	44.3	44.3
Owners	13,778,809	14,672,637	7,506,987	7,461,499	54.5	50.9	93.0	101.8	50.7	51.8
Managers	220,879	334,929	107,729	115,918	48.8	34.6	273.7	405.5	133.5	140.3
Tenants	5,511,168	5,034,091	3,570,586	3,313,067	64.8	65.8	53.1	49.8	34.4	32.8
Alabama, total	19,576,856	20,732,312	9,893,407	9,663,581	50.5	46.8	76.4	78.9	38.6	36.9
Owners	12,117,491	13,280,106	4,986,369	4,620,232	41.2	34.8	113.2	127.8	46.6	44.5
Managers	455,098	366,767	184,306	120,099	40.5	32.7	614.2	567.8	248.7	185.9
Tenants	7,004,267	7,085,439	4,722,732	4,953,250	67.4	69.9	47.2	44.8	31.9	31.3
Mississippi, total	18,196,979	18,557,533	9,325,677	9,008,310	51.2	48.5	66.9	67.6	34.3	32.8
Owners	11,333,780	11,716,474	4,543,012	4,215,447	40.1	36.0	124.1	127.3	49.8	45.8
Managers	582,749	586,511	230,481	168,066	39.6	28.7	589.2	710.9	233.0	203.7
Tenants	6,280,450	6,254,548	4,552,184	4,624,797	72.5	73.9	34.9	34.5	25.3	25.5

TABLE 25.—ACREAGE OF FARM LAND, WITH PERCENTAGES AND AVERAGES, BY TENURE, BY DIVISIONS AND STATES: 1920 AND 1910—Continued.

DIVISION OR STATE AND TENURE.	ALL LAND IN FARMS (ACRES).		IMPROVED LAND IN FARMS (ACRES).		PER CENT OF FARM LAND IMPROVED.		AVERAGE ACREAGE PER FARM.			
							All land.		Improved land.	
	1920	1910	1920	1910	1920	1910	1920	1910	1920	1910
WEST SOUTH CENTRAL.										
Arkansas, total...	17,456,750	17,416,075	9,210,556	8,076,254	52.8	46.4	75.0	81.1	39.6	37.6
Owners............	11,810,397	12,389,542	5,340,197	4,815,122	45.2	38.9	104.8	116.2	47.4	45.2
Managers..........	351,565	328,186	143,616	112,699	40.9	34.3	477.7	430.1	195.1	147.7
Tenants...........	5,294,788	4,698,347	3,726,743	3,148,433	70.4	67.0	44.4	43.8	31.3	29.4
Louisiana, total...	10,019,822	10,439,481	5,626,226	5,276,016	56.2	50.5	74.0	86.6	41.5	43.8
Owners............	6,255,255	6,766,123	2,979,005	2,865,762	47.6	42.3	109.3	127.7	52.0	54.1
Managers..........	900,121	986,357	362,025	414,442	40.2	42.0	1087.1	1038.3	437.2	436.3
Tenants...........	2,864,446	2,687,001	2,285,196	1,995,812	79.8	74.3	37.0	40.3	29.5	30.0
Oklahoma, total...	31,951,934	28,859,353	18,125,321	17,551,337	56.7	60.8	166.4	151.7	94.4	92.3
Owners............	18,471,693	15,996,795	9,885,001	9,322,165	53.5	58.3	198.2	187.3	106.0	109.2
Managers..........	926,026	428,679	196,293	176,927	21.2	41.3	990.4	658.5	209.9	271.8
Tenants...........	12,554,215	12,433,879	8,044,027	8,052,245	64.1	64.8	128.3	119.4	82.2	77.3
Texas, total.......	114,020,621	112,435,067	31,227,503	27,360,666	27.4	24.3	261.5	269.1	71.6	65.5
Owners............	68,244,146	69,201,014	15,582,024	13,882,422	22.8	20.1	339.2	353.3	77.4	70.9
Managers..........	14,332,860	17,954,949	636,990	722,399	4.4	4.0	5701.2	7699.4	253.4	309.8
Tenants...........	31,443,615	25,279,104	15,008,489	12,755,845	47.7	50.5	135.4	115.1	64.6	58.1
MOUNTAIN.										
Montana, total....	35,070,656	13,545,603	11,007,278	3,640,309	31.4	26.9	608.1	516.7	190.8	138.9
Owners............	28,952,950	10,640,902	9,114,756	2,894,823	31.5	27.2	575.9	455.4	181.3	123.9
Managers..........	2,859,873	1,429,990	489,333	357,840	17.1	25.0	3181.2	2831.7	544.3	708.6
Tenants...........	3,257,833	1,474,711	1,403,189	387,646	43.1	26.3	500.7	629.1	215.6	165.4
Idaho, total.......	8,375,873	5,283,604	4,511,680	2,778,740	53.9	52.6	198.9	171.5	107.2	90.2
Owners............	6,798,893	4,446,313	3,544,027	2,268,114	52.1	51.0	196.2	163.7	102.3	83.5
Managers..........	385,718	270,234	181,096	126,814	47.0	46.9	508.9	600.5	238.9	281.8
Tenants...........	1,191,262	567,057	786,557	383,812	66.0	67.7	177.8	177.9	117.4	120.4
Wyoming, total....	11,809,351	8,543,010	2,102,005	1,256,160	17.8	14.7	749.9	777.6	133.5	114.3
Owners............	9,359,517	5,152,581	1,663,148	940,372	17.8	18.3	698.3	526.9	124.1	96.2
Managers..........	1,465,993	2,862,992	148,024	189,900	10.1	6.6	3888.6	9205.8	392.6	610.6
Tenants...........	983,841	527,437	290,833	125,888	29.6	23.9	499.9	588.0	147.8	140.3
Colorado, total...	24,462,014	13,532,113	7,744,757	4,302,101	31.7	31.8	408.1	293.1	129.2	93.2
Owners............	18,621,678	10,134,797	5,582,447	2,907,897	30.0	28.7	411.2	274.0	123.3	78.6
Managers..........	1,595,853	1,140,446	297,802	310,402	18.7	27.2	1813.5	1449.1	338.4	394.4
Tenants...........	4,244,483	2,256,870	1,864,508	1,083,802	43.9	48.0	308.4	269.0	135.5	129.2
New Mexico, total.	24,409,633	11,270,021	1,717,224	1,467,191	7.0	13.0	817.9	315.9	57.5	41.1
Owners............	17,854,006	7,095,901	1,393,083	1,298,739	7.8	18.3	693.2	212.5	54.1	38.9
Managers..........	3,862,989	3,195,759	76,366	74,147	2.0	2.3	8921.5	9955.6	176.4	231.0
Tenants...........	2,692,638	978,361	247,775	94,305	9.2	9.6	736.7	499.9	67.8	48.2
Arizona, total....	5,802,126	1,246,613	712,803	350,173	12.3	28.1	581.7	135.1	71.5	38.0
Owners............	3,819,651	874,914	442,010	254,439	11.6	29.1	485.4	106.7	56.2	31.0
Managers..........	1,390,949	264,798	119,215	35,871	8.6	13.5	4560.5	1624.5	390.9	220.1
Tenants...........	591,526	106,901	151,578	59,863	25.6	56.0	328.4	124.2	84.2	69.5
Utah, total........	5,050,410	3,397,699	1,715,380	1,368,211	34.0	40.3	196.8	156.7	66.8	63.1
Owners............	4,062,508	2,888,090	1,457,096	1,202,072	35.9	41.6	179.9	146.1	64.5	60.8
Managers..........	615,734	315,376	79,344	66,462	12.9	21.1	2050.2	1625.6	268.1	342.6
Tenants...........	372,168	194,233	178,940	99,677	48.1	51.3	133.5	112.9	64.2	58.0
Nevada, total.....	2,357,163	2,714,757	594,741	752,117	25.2	27.7	745.2	1009.6	188.0	279.7
Owners............	1,419,531	1,032,432	396,252	386,132	27.9	37.4	525.9	474.7	146.8	177.5
Managers..........	796,477	1,524,130	145,235	310,527	18.2	20.4	4740.9	8420.4	864.5	1715.6
Tenants...........	141,155	158,195	53,254	55,458	37.7	35.1	476.9	475.0	179.9	166.5

TABLE 25.—ACREAGE OF FARM LAND, WITH PERCENTAGES AND AVERAGES, BY TENURE, BY DIVISIONS AND STATES: 1920 AND 1910—Continued.

DIVISION OR STATE AND TENURE.	ALL LAND IN FARMS (ACRES).		IMPROVED LAND IN FARMS (ACRES).		PER CENT OF FARM LAND IMPROVED.		AVERAGE ACREAGE PER FARM.			
							All land.		Improved land.	
	1920	1910	1920	1910	1920	1910	1920	1910	1920	1910
PACIFIC.										
Washington, total.	13,244,720	11,712,235	7,129,343	6,373,311	53.8	54.4	199.8	208.4	107.6	113.4
Owners.............	9,259,800	9,115,171	4,529,580	4,760,836	48.9	52.2	175.7	191.9	85.9	100.2
Managers...........	541,136	529,082	256,391	159,461	47.4	30.1	463.3	550.6	219.5	165.9
Tenants............	3,443,784	2,067,982	2,343,372	1,453,014	68.0	70.3	277.3	267.7	188.7	188.1
Oregon, total......	13,542,318	11,685,110	4,913,851	4,274,803	36.3	36.6	269.7	256.8	97.9	93.9
Owners.............	10,017,262	9,036,370	3,331,150	3,061,350	33.3	33.9	251.3	239.1	83.6	81.0
Managers...........	837,924	766,007	300,687	212,812	35.9	27.8	914.8	904.4	328.3	251.3
Tenants............	2,687,132	1,882,733	1,282,014	1,000,641	47.7	53.1	285.0	274.5	136.0	145.9
California, total...	29,365,667	27,931,444	11,878,339	11,389,894	40.4	40.8	249.6	316.7	100.9	129.1
Owners.............	17,196,215	15,125,339	6,819,212	6,464,472	39.7	42.7	196.3	227.0	77.9	97.0
Managers...........	5,485,447	6,604,972	1,587,518	1,728,625	28.9	26.2	1108.4	1933.0	320.8	505.9
Tenants............	6,684,005	6,201,133	3,471,609	3,196,797	51.9	51.6	265.9	341.7	138.1	176.1

TABLE 26.—VALUE OF ALL FARM PROPERTY AND OF THE SEVERAL

DIVISION OR STATE AND TENURE.	ALL FARM PROPERTY.		LAND AND BUILDINGS.		
			Total.		Land alone.
	1920	1910	1920	1910	1920
UNITED STATES.					
1 Total	$77,924,100,338	$40,991,449,090	$66,316,002,602	$34,801,125,697	$54,829,563,059
2 Owners	47,611,545,944	26,669,634,373	39,864,222,907	22,366,934,278	31,984,781,634
3 Managers	3,132,273,005	1,700,624,936	2,665,216,465	1,456,958,992	2,207,651,020
4 Tenants	27,180,281,389	12,621,189,781	23,786,563,230	10,977,232,427	20,637,130,405
GEOGRAPHIC DIVISIONS.					
NEW ENGLAND.					
5 Total	1,173,019,594	867,240,457	917,468,584	718,544,808	488,125,250
6 Owners	949,587,985	707,087,858	732,985,945	579,951,343	384,238,323
7 Managers	133,522,014	91,617,841	115,122,376	81,663,226	64,051,157
8 Tenants	89,909,595	68,534,758	69,360,263	56,930,239	39,835,770
MIDDLE ATLANTIC.					
9 Total	3,949,684,183	2,959,589,022	3,002,137,754	2,442,949,103	1,661,676,107
10 Owners	2,663,591,574	1,956,906,352	1,987,775,786	1,594,225,109	1,041,704,049
11 Managers	302,070,412	199,378,007	256,451,780	178,283,750	149,748,070
12 Tenants	984,022,197	803,304,663	757,910,188	670,440,244	470,223,988
EAST NORTH CENTRAL.					
13 Total	17,245,362,593	10,119,128,066	14,937,641,671	8,873,991,594	12,046,073,684
14 Owners	10,058,142,054	6,314,009,403	8,547,956,861	5,458,959,257	6,576,977,706
15 Managers	477,058,724	222,456,873	421,031,710	198,347,752	335,754,996
16 Tenants	6,710,161,815	3,582,661,790	5,968,653,100	3,216,684,585	5,133,340,982
WEST NORTH CENTRAL.					
17 Total	27,991,434,545	13,535,309,511	24,469,495,169	11,614,665,870	21,340,145,142
18 Owners	16,841,094,799	8,981,852,218	14,546,115,223	7,615,880,376	12,444,869,417
19 Managers	517,018,682	234,979,209	445,906,192	199,611,857	387,067,373
20 Tenants	10,633,321,064	4,318,478,084	9,477,473,754	3,799,173,637	8,508,208,352
SOUTH ATLANTIC.					
21 Total	6,132,917,760	2,951,200,773	5,201,773,472	2,486,436,474	4,000,681,904
22 Owners	3,668,836,823	1,905,397,469	3,071,638,805	1,593,294,281	2,277,406,304
23 Managers	305,470,576	139,453,227	272,176,404	125,539,290	215,456,350
24 Tenants	2,158,610,361	906,350,077	1,857,958,263	767,602,903	1,507,819,250
EAST SOUTH CENTRAL.					
25 Total	4,419,466,237	2,182,771,779	3,663,693,363	1,738,397,839	2,916,141,232
26 Owners	2,758,397,331	1,432,645,781	2,259,091,657	1,135,752,526	1,750,557,989
27 Managers	110,765,776	56,250,544	94,822,369	47,597,661	78,827,578
28 Tenants	1,550,303,130	693,875,454	1,309,779,337	555,047,652	1,086,755,665
WEST SOUTH CENTRAL.					
29 Total	7,622,066,027	3,838,154,337	6,291,188,072	3,128,596,882	5,408,059,615
30 Owners	4,178,001,708	2,195,591,300	3,369,149,702	1,767,880,518	2,824,459,788
31 Managers	380,657,726	248,191,089	302,397,712	205,183,145	279,876,355
32 Tenants	3,063,406,593	1,394,371,948	2,619,640,658	1,155,533,219	2,303,723,472
MOUNTAIN.					
33 Total	4,083,137,939	1,757,573,368	3,163,187,783	1,319,396,873	2,801,712,079
34 Owners	3,062,853,906	1,318,669,728	2,351,059,166	972,132,526	2,064,154,166
35 Managers	323,137,311	186,576,669	233,107,982	133,047,729	212,352,569
36 Tenants	697,146,722	252,326,971	579,020,635	214,216,618	525,205,344
PACIFIC.					
37 Total	5,307,011,460	2,780,481,777	4,669,416,734	2,478,146,254	4,166,948,046
38 Owners	3,431,039,764	1,857,474,264	2,998,449,762	1,648,858,342	2,620,413,892
39 Managers	582,571,784	321,721,477	524,199,940	287,684,582	484,516,572
40 Tenants	1,293,399,912	601,286,036	1,146,767,032	541,603,330	1,062,017,582

CLASSES, BY TENURE, BY DIVISIONS AND STATES: 1920 and 1910.

LAND AND BUILDINGS—continued.			IMPLEMENTS AND MACHINERY.		LIVE STOCK.		
Land alone— Continued.	Buildings.						
1910	1920	1910	1920	1910	1920	1910	
$28,475,674,169	$11,486,439,543	$6,325,451,528	$3,594,772,928	$1,265,149,783	$8,013,324,808	$4,925,173,610	1
17,806,121,628	7,879,441,273	4,560,812,650	2,447,792,781	900,672,541	5,299,530,256	3,402,027,554	2
1,218,859,265	457,565,445	238,099,727	103,773,702	42,908,500	363,282,838	200,757,444	3
9,450,693,276	3,149,432,825	1,526,539,151	1,043,206,445	321,568,742	2,350,511,714	1,322,388,612	4
382,134,424	429,343,334	336,410,384	92,387,525	50,798,826	163,163,485	97,896,823	5
302,178,221	348,747,622	277,773,122	79,706,212	43,954,140	136,895,828	83,182,375	6
46,985,629	51,071,219	34,677,597	6,757,841	3,572,404	11,641,797	6,382,211	7
32,970,574	29,524,493	23,959,665	5,923,472	3,272,282	14,625,860	8,332,237	8
1,462,321,005	1,340,461,647	980,628,098	359,152,336	167,480,384	588,394,093	349,159,535	9
906,817,086	946,071,737	687,408,023	262,569,221	120,120,580	413,246,567	242,560,663	10
111,484,860	106,703,710	66,798,890	16,500,578	7,387,337	29,118,054	13,706,920	11
444,019,059	287,686,200	226,421,185	80,082,537	39,972,467	146,029,472	92,891,952	12
7,231,699,114	2,891,567,987	1,642,292,480	786,076,805	268,806,550	1,521,644,117	976,329,922	13
4,281,681,370	1,970,979,155	1,177,277,887	521,674,491	189,017,199	988,510,702	666,032,947	14
161,093,641	85,276,714	37,254,111	16,310,480	5,044,543	39,716,534	19,064,578	15
2,788,924,103	835,312,118	427,760,482	248,091,834	74,744,808	493,416,881	291,232,397	16
10,052,560,913	3,129,350,027	1,562,104,957	1,162,938,264	368,935,544	2,359,001,112	1,551,708,097	17
6,488,097,834	2,101,245,806	1,127,782,542	757,245,213	263,272,264	1,537,734,363	1,102,699,578	18
175,873,175	58,838,819	23,738,682	14,269,699	4,675,495	56,842,791	30,691,857	19
3,388,589,904	969,265,402	410,583,733	391,423,352	100,987,785	764,423,958	418,316,662	20
1,883,349,675	1,201,091,568	603,086,799	283,980,857	98,230,147	647,163,431	366,534,152	21
1,166,109,665	794,232,501	427,184,616	192,278,230	69,109,744	404,919,788	242,993,444	22
99,401,097	56,720,054	26,138,193	10,888,762	3,940,904	22,405,410	9,973,033	23
617,838,913	350,139,013	149,763,990	80,813,865	25,179,499	219,838,233	113,567,675	24
1,326,826,864	747,552,131	411,570,975	176,064,886	75,339,333	579,707,988	369,034,607	25
838,195,980	508,533,668	297,556,546	122,132,015	53,489,572	377,173,659	243,403,683	26
38,109,604	15,994,791	9,488,057	3,920,323	1,939,456	12,023,084	6,713,427	27
450,521,280	223,023,672	104,526,372	50,012,548	19,910,305	190,511,245	118,917,497	28
2,716,098,530	883,128,457	412,498,352	311,098,790	119,720,377	1,019,779,165	589,837,078	29
1,498,682,703	544,689,914	269,197,815	194,415,307	72,917,442	614,436,699	354,793,340	30
192,217,250	22,521,357	12,965,895	10,722,003	7,692,277	67,538,011	35,315,667	31
1,025,198,577	315,917,186	130,334,642	105,961,480	39,110,658	337,804,455	199,728,071	32
1,174,370,096	361,475,704	145,026,777	190,715,673	49,429,975	729,234,483	388,746,520	33
855,897,132	286,905,000	116,235,394	152,844,998	40,451,977	558,949,742	306,085,225	34
122,924,070	20,755,413	10,123,659	8,381,048	3,105,741	81,648,281	50,423,199	35
195,548,894	53,815,291	18,667,724	29,489,627	5,872,257	88,636,460	32,238,096	36
2,246,313,548	502,468,688	231,832,706	232,357,792	66,408,647	405,236,934	235,926,876	37
1,468,461,637	378,035,870	180,396,705	164,927,094	48,339,623	267,662,908	160,276,299	38
270,769,939	39,683,368	16,914,643	16,022,968	5,550,343	42,348,876	28,480,552	39
507,081,972	84,749,450	34,521,358	51,407,730	12,518,681	95,225,150	47,164,025	40

TABLE 26.—VALUE OF ALL FARM PROPERTY AND OF THE SEVERAL

	DIVISION OR STATE AND TENURE.	ALL FARM PROPERTY.		LAND AND BUILDINGS.		
				Total.		Land alone.
		1920	1910	1920	1910	1920
	NEW ENGLAND.					
1	**Maine,** total........	$270,526,733	$199,271,998	$204,108,971	$159,619,626	$114,411,871
2	Owners..............	249,818,888	185,087,053	187,505,075	147,713,769	104,931,613
3	Managers............	10,634,334	6,437,841	8,764,123	5,375,570	4,655,990
4	Tenants.............	10,073,511	7,747,104	7,839,773	6,530,287	4,824,268
5	**N. Hampshire,** total	118,656,115	103,704,196	89,995,870	85,916,061	47,425,331
6	Owners..............	100,505,865	90,302,512	75,518,677	74,451,558	39,941,908
7	Managers............	11,217,649	7,766,347	9,351,273	6,767,633	4,738,683
8	Tenants.............	6,932,601	5,635,337	5,125,920	4,696,870	2,744,740
9	**Vermont,** total.....	222,736,620	145,399,728	159,117,159	112,588,275	82,938,253
10	Owners..............	179,276,757	115,641,507	126,686,877	88,566,017	65,644,314
11	Managers............	11,931,712	9,164,766	9,611,978	7,926,085	4,811,403
12	Tenants.............	31,528,151	20,593,455	22,818,304	16,096,173	12,482,536
13	**Massachusetts,** total	300,471,743	226,474,025	247,587,831	194,168,765	127,653,607
14	Owners..............	224,111,334	170,007,332	182,098,530	144,241,398	90,526,284
15	Managers............	58,525,749	41,005,384	50,988,024	36,745,990	28,705,631
16	Tenants.............	17,834,660	15,461,309	14,501,277	13,181,377	8,421,692
17	**Rhode Island,** total	33,636,766	32,990,739	26,387,926	27,932,860	14,509,073
18	Owners..............	23,069,059	21,638,781	17,941,656	18,137,295	9,481,893
19	Managers............	5,548,971	5,915,923	4,616,373	5,175,000	2,584,498
20	Tenants.............	5,018,736	5,436,035	3,829,897	4,620,565	2,442,682
21	**Connecticut,** total..	226,991,617	159,399,771	190,270,827	138,319,221	101,187,115
22	Owners..............	172,806,082	124,410,673	143,235,130	106,841,306	73,712,311
23	Managers............	35,663,599	21,327,580	31,790,605	19,672,948	18,554,952
24	Tenants.............	18,521,936	13,661,518	15,245,092	11,804,967	8,919,852
	MIDDLE ATLANTIC.					
25	**New York,** total....	1,908,483,201	1,451,481,495	1,425,061,740	1,184,745,829	793,335,558
26	Owners..............	1,321,699,217	990,431,448	966,593,359	797,712,574	509,583,419
27	Managers............	147,440,824	99,630,064	125,574,461	89,015,220	73,549,665
28	Tenants.............	439,343,160	361,419,983	332,893,920	298,018,035	210,202,474
29	**New Jersey,** total..	311,847,948	254,832,665	250,323,986	217,134,519	142,182,498
30	Owners..............	198,739,650	157,016,172	159,298,815	133,121,579	86,570,766
31	Managers............	33,867,702	30,182,254	29,039,041	27,319,227	17,368,367
32	Tenants.............	79,240,596	67,634,239	61,986,130	56,693,713	38,243,365
33	**Pennsylvania,** total	1,729,353,034	1,253,274,862	1,326,752,028	1,041,068,755	726,158,051
34	Owners..............	1,143,152,707	809,458,732	861,883,612	663,390,956	445,549,864
35	Managers............	120,761,886	69,565,689	101,838,278	61,949,303	58,830,038
36	Tenants.............	465,438,441	374,250,441	363,030,138	315,728,496	221,778,149
	EAST NORTH CENTRAL.					
37	**Ohio,** total.........	3,095,666,336	1,902,694,589	2,661,435,949	1,654,152,406	2,015,112,999
38	Owners..............	1,846,805,911	1,216,102,316	1,572,254,047	1,047,849,280	1,145,259,222
39	Managers............	98,711,531	53,025,580	87,411,346	47,935,700	65,381,979
40	Tenants.............	1,150,148,894	633,566,693	1,001,770,556	558,367,426	804,471,798
41	**Indiana,** total......	3,043,011,247	1,860,185,990	2,653,040,070	1,601,075,500	2,002,500,000
42	Owners..............	1,749,075,832	1,189,105,749	1,507,782,478	999,740,881	1,014,770,972
43	Managers............	74,514,423	42,731,998	65,509,416	37,817,116	54,562,953
44	Tenants.............	1,218,720,992	628,220,491	1,080,349,079	563,317,559	933,223,405
45	**Illinois,** total.......	6,666,767,235	3,905,321,075	5,997,993,566	3,522,792,570	5,250,294,752
46	Owners..............	3,040,416,791	1,983,423,213	2,691,762,986	1,765,992,310	2,275,943,663
47	Managers............	179,145,349	72,216,587	162,318,962	65,008,033	139,671,781
48	Tenants.............	3,447,205,095	1,849,681,275	3,143,911,618	1,691,792,227	2,834,679,308
49	**Michigan,** total.....	1,763,334,778	1,088,858,379	1,436,686,210	901,138,299	959,186,538
50	Owners..............	1,307,774,069	850,444,870	1,056,478,928	699,059,567	687,319,570
51	Managers............	58,510,839	26,387,458	50,198,044	22,981,178	35,680,447
52	Tenants.............	397,049,870	212,026,051	330,009,238	179,097,554	236,186,521
53	**Wisconsin,** total....	2,677,282,997	1,413,118,785	2,187,881,973	1,201,632,723	1,618,913,059
54	Owners..............	2,114,069,451	1,125,856,255	1,719,625,423	952,917,179	1,253,675,273
55	Managers............	66,176,582	28,095,250	55,593,942	24,605,725	40,457,836
56	Tenants.............	497,036,964	259,167,280	412,612,609	224,109,819	324,779,950

CLASSES, BY TENURE, BY DIVISIONS AND STATES: 1920 and 1910—Continued.

LAND AND BUILDINGS—continued.			IMPLEMENTS AND MACHINERY.		LIVE STOCK.		
Land alone—Continued.	Buildings.						
1910	1920	1910	1920	1910	1920	1910	
$86,481,395	$89,697,100	$73,138,231	$26,637,660	$14,490,533	$39,780,102	$25,161,839	1
79,807,441	82,573,462	67,906,328	25,106,305	13,713,140	37,207,508	23,660,144	2
2,724,800	4,108,133	2,650,770	724,167	354,284	1,146,044	707,987	3
3,949,154	3,015,505	2,581,133	807,188	423,109	1,426,550	793,708	4
44,519,047	42,570,539	41,397,014	9,499,322	5,877,657	19,160,923	11,910,478	5
38,498,150	35,576,769	35,953,408	8,378,510	5,282,127	16,608,678	10,568,827	6
3,583,654	4,612,590	3,183,979	634,459	329,630	1,231,917	669,084	7
2,437,243	2,381,180	2,259,627	486,353	265,900	1,320,328	672,567	8
58,385,327	76,178,906	54,202,948	21,234,130	10,168,687	42,385,331	22,642,766	9
45,045,899	61,042,563	43,520,118	18,084,328	8,602,264	34,505,552	18,473,226	10
4,273,240	4,800,575	3,652,845	740,797	385,225	1,578,937	853,456	11
9,066,188	10,335,768	7,029,985	2,409,005	1,181,198	6,300,842	3,316,084	12
105,532,616	119,934,224	88,636,149	19,359,755	11,563,894	33,524,157	20,741,366	13
74,660,058	91,572,246	69,581,340	15,807,272	9,344,827	26,205,532	16,421,107	14
22,894,906	22,282,393	13,851,084	2,623,637	1,541,741	4,914,088	2,717,653	15
7,977,652	6,079,585	5,203,725	928,846	677,326	2,404,537	1,602,606	16
15,009,981	11,878,853	12,922,879	2,408,561	1,781,407	4,840,279	3,276,472	17
9,023,408	8,459,763	9,113,887	1,766,481	1,244,094	3,360,922	2,257,392	18
3,210,643	2,031,875	1,964,357	315,878	291,870	616,720	449,053	19
2,775,930	1,387,215	1,844,635	326,202	245,443	862,637	570,027	20
72,206,058	89,083,712	66,113,163	13,248,097	6,916,648	23,472,693	14,163,902	21
55,143,265	69,522,819	51,698,041	10,563,316	5,767,688	19,007,636	11,801,679	22
10,298,386	13,235,653	9,374,562	1,718,903	669,654	2,154,091	984,978	23
6,764,407	6,325,240	•5,040,560	965,878	479,306	2,310,966	1,377,245	24
707,747,828	631,726,182	476,998,001	169,866,766	83,644,822	313,554,695	183,090,844	25
451,980,742	457,009,940	345,731,832	127,966,863	61,961,975	227,138,995	130,756,899	26
56,075,270	52,024,796	32,939,950	7,407,048	3,536,433	14,459,315	7,078,411	27
199,691,816	122,691,446	98,326,219	34,492,855	18,146,414	71,956,385	45,255,534	28
124,143,167	108,141,488	92,991,352	25,459,205	13,109,507	36,064,757	24,588,639	29
72,210,895	72,728,049	60,910,684	17,202,243	8,701,311	22,238,592	15,193,282	30
16,106,372	11,670,674	11,212,855	1,945,358	1,054,336	2,883,303	1,808,691	31
35,825,900	23,742,765	20,867,813	6,311,604	3,353,860	10,942,862	7,586,666	32
630,430,010	600,593,977	410,638,745	163,826,365	70,726,055	238,774,641	141,480,052	33
382,625,449	416,333,748	280,765,507	117,400,115	49,457,294	163,868,980	96,610,482	34
39,303,218	43,008,240	22,646,085	7,148,172	2,796,568	11,775,436	4,819,818	35
208,501,343	141,251,989	107,227,153	39,278,078	18,472,193	63,130,225	40,049,752	36
1,285,894,812	646,322,950	368,257,594	146,575,269	51,210,071	287,655,118	197,332,112	37
791,016,912	426,994,825	256,832,368	93,679,423	34,698,593	180,872,441	133,554,443	38
36,878,219	22,029,367	11,057,481	3,556,341	1,202,403	7,743,844	3,887,477	39
457,999,681	197,298,758	100,367,745	49,339,505	15,309,075	99,038,833	59,890,192	40
1,328,196,545	451,077,637	266,079,051	127,403,086	40,999,541	261,264,188	173,860,101	41
804,578,413	293,005,500	188,562,508	79,775,186	27,818,398	161,515,168	117,223,430	42
32,619,174	10,946,463	5,197,942	2,335,351	762,861	6,669,656	4,152,021	43
490,998,958	147,125,674	72,318,601	45,292,549	12,418,282	93,079,364	52,484,650	44
3,090,411,148	747,698,814	432,381,422	222,619,605	73,724,074	446,154,064	308,804,431	45
1,503,905,887	415,819,323	262,086,423	113,435,410	41,321,035	235,218,395	176,109,868	46
56,507,607	22,647,181	8,500,426	4,381,612	1,270,842	12,444,775	5,937,712	47
1,529,997,654	309,232,310	161,794,573	104,802,583	31,132,197	198,490,894	126,756,851	48
615,258,348	477,499,672	285,879,951	122,389,936	49,916,285	204,258,632	137,803,795	49
469,027,547	369,159,358	230,032,020	96,083,962	40,879,537	155,211,179	110,505,766	50
16,805,089	14,517,597	6,176,089	2,867,728	909,861	5,445,067	2,496,419	51
129,425,712	93,822,717	49,671,842	23,438,246	8,126,887	43,602,386	24,801,610	52
911,938,261	568,968,914	289,694,462	167,088,909	52,956,579	322,312,115	158,529,483	53
713,152,611	466,000,149	239,764,568	138,700,510	44,299,636	255,693,519	128,639,440	54
18,283,552	15,136,106	6,322,173	3,169,448	898,576	7,413,192	2,590,949	55
180,502,098	87,832,659	43,607,721	25,218,951	7,758,367	59,205,404	27,299,094	56

TABLE 26.—VALUE OF ALL FARM PROPERTY AND OF THE SEVERAL

	DIVISION OR STATE AND TENURE.	ALL FARM PROPERTY.		LAND AND BUILDINGS.		
				Total.		Land alone.
		1920	1910	1920	1910	1920
	WEST NORTH CENTRAL.					
1	**Minnesota, total**...	$3,787,420,118	$1,476,411,737	$3,301,168,325	$1,262,441,426	$2,750,328,432
2	Owners..............	2,537,589,486	1,083,350,056	2,191,751,054	920,359,347	1,789,039,414
3	Managers............	58,162,979	24,167,277	50,234,658	20,909,251	40,230,519
4	Tenants.............	1,191,667,653	368,894,404	1,059,182,613	321,172,828	921,058,499
5	**Iowa, total**........	8,524,870,956	3,745,860,544	7,601,772,290	3,257,379,400	6,679,020,577
6	Owners..............	4,544,498,718	2,257,685,527	4,011,441,160	1,942,594,349	3,448,299,333
7	Managers............	140,772,728	51,930,206	125,900,751	44,993,925	110,594,202
8	Tenants.............	3,839,599,510	1,436,244,811	3,464,430,379	1,269,791,126	3,120,127,042
9	**Missouri, total**.....	3,591,068,085	2,052,917,488	3,062,967,700	1,716,204,386	2,594,193,271
10	Owners..............	2,476,531,087	1,460,538,331	2,089,419,403	1,206,020,845	1,741,864,360
11	Managers............	85,927,126	46,017,055	74,678,836	40,361,980	61,664,535
12	Tenants.............	1,028,609,872	546,362,102	898,869,461	469,821,561	790,664,376
	North Dakota,					
13	total..............	1,759,742,995	974,814,205	1,488,521,495	822,656,744	1,279,313,627
14	Owners..............	1,243,907,545	787,521,495	1,040,855,450	658,809,090	886,960,902
15	Managers............	41,100,933	19,296,374	35,108,503	16,898,168	29,758,105
16	Tenants.............	474,734,517	167,996,336	412,557,542	146,949,486	362,594,620
17	**South Dakota,**					
	total..............	2,823,870,212	1,166,096,980	2,472,893,681	1,005,080,807	2,231,431,723
18	Owners..............	1,733,696,642	814,235,325	1,499,919,420	694,509,873	1,340,434,697
19	Managers............	46,833,841	16,828,257	38,900,410	13,918,757	35,176,117
20	Tenants.............	1,043,339,729	335,033,398	934,073,851	296,652,177	855,820,909
21	**Nebraska, total**....	4,201,655,992	2,079,818,647	3,712,107,760	1,813,346,935	3,330,222,340
22	Owners..............	2,358,820,323	1,261,875,866	2,060,996,545	1,084,248,917	1,819,193,473
23	Managers............	78,403,678	37,563,134	65,693,263	30,056,713	59,999,794
24	Tenants.............	1,764,431,991	780,379,647	1,585,417,952	699,041,305	1,451,029,073
25	**Kansas, total**......	3,302,806,187	2,039,389,910	2,830,063,918	1,737,556,172	2,475,635,172
26	Owners..............	1,946,050,998	1,316,645,618	1,651,732,191	1,109,337,955	1,419,077,238
27	Managers............	65,817,397	39,176,906	55,389,771	32,473,063	49,644,101
28	Tenants.............	1,290,937,792	683,567,386	1,122,941,956	595,745,154	1,006,913,833
	SOUTH ATLANTIC.					
29	**Delaware, total**....	80,137,614	63,179,201	64,755,631	53,155,983	42,115,802
30	Owners..............	38,521,671	32,461,054	30,649,497	27,175,067	18,016,328
31	Managers............	3,757,021	2,061,694	3,230,767	1,776,280	2,292,725
32	Tenants.............	37,858,922	28,656,453	30,875,367	24,204,636	21,806,749
33	**Maryland, total**....	463,638,120	286,167,028	386,596,850	241,737,123	259,904,047
34	Owners..............	267,872,899	160,068,263	220,743,136	132,810,705	141,685,771
35	Managers............	39,599,739	26,573,399	34,526,139	24,468,741	21,994,101
36	Tenants.............	156,165,482	99,525,366	131,327,575	84,457,677	96,224,175
37	**District of Columbia, total**.........	5,927,987	8,476,533	5,577,369	8,231,343	4,156,148
38	Owners..............	1,800,669	2,335,216	1,712,819	2,279,800	1,181,469
39	Managers............	2,542,914	3,381,067	2,347,850	3,240,843	1,674,219
40	Tenants.............	1,584,404	2,760,250	1,516,700	2,710,700	1,300,460
41	**Virginia, total**......	1,196,555,779	695,065,777	1,094,435,025	532,058,069	756,254,977
42	Owners.............	878,456,395	476,503,394	746,599,004	402,841,295	539,695,755
43	Managers............	71,007,739	30,868,847	62,720,066	27,354,426	47,269,720
44	Tenants.............	247,091,638	117,693,142	215,115,955	101,862,341	169,388,802
45	**West Virginia,** total............	496,439,617	314,738,540	410,783,406	264,390,954	307,309,704
46	Owners..............	393,058,740	250,599,816	321,094,958	207,994,468	234,589,999
47	Managers............	25,733,496	10,285,735	23,051,738	9,135,665	19,322,852
48	Tenants.............	77,647,381	53,852,989	66,636,710	47,260,821	53,396,853
49	**North Carolina,** total............	1,250,166,995	537,716,210	1,076,392,960	456,624,607	857,815,016
50	Owners..............	754,437,708	362,563,593	639,114,219	305,334,091	494,942,893
51	Managers............	26,359,678	15,848,361	23,525,086	14,209,244	18,372,540
52	Tenants.............	469,369,609	159,304,256	413,753,655	137,081,272	344,499,583

CLASSES, BY TENURE, BY DIVISIONS AND STATES: 1920 AND 1910—Continued.

| LAND AND BUILDINGS—continued. | | | IMPLEMENTS AND MACHINERY. | | LIVE STOCK. | | |
| Land alone—Continued. | Buildings. | | | | | | |
1910	1920	1910	1920	1910	1920	1910	
$1,019,102,027	$550,839,893	$243,339,399	$181,087,968	$52,329,165	$305,163,825	$161,641,146	1
731,554,845	402,711,640	188,804,502	130,388,874	40,312,954	215,449,558	122,677,755	2
16,875,616	10,004,139	4,033,635	2,145,474	769,853	5,782,847	2,488,173	3
270,671,566	138,124,114	50,501,262	48,553,620	11,246,358	83,931,420	36,475,218	4
2,801,973,729	922,751,713	455,405,671	309,172,398	95,477,948	613,926,268	393,003,196	5
1,637,406,979	563,141,827	305,187,370	179,054,709	61,391,989	354,002,849	253,699,189	6
39,199,222	15,306,549	5,794,703	3,090,470	1,033,232	11,781,507	5,903,049	7
1,125,367,528	344,303,337	144,423,598	127,027,219	33,052,727	248,141,912	133,400,958	8
1,445,982,389	468,774,429	270,221,997	138,261,340	50,873,994	389,839,045	285,839,108	9
998,034,801	347,555,043	207,986,044	101,198,408	37,963,319	285,913,276	216,554,167	10
35,187,133	13,014,301	5,174,847	2,162,422	720,402	9,085,868	4,934,673	11
412,760,455	108,205,085	57,061,106	34,900,510	12,190,273	94,839,901	64,350,268	12
730,380,131	209,207,868	92,276,613	114,186,865	43,907,595	157,034,635	108,249,866	13
582,861,877	153,894,548	75,947,213	86,070,844	37,199,449	116,981,251	91,512,956	14
15,092,453	5,350,398	1,805,715	2,076,252	742,463	3,916,178	1,655,743	15
132,425,801	49,962,922	14,523,685	26,039,769	5,965,683	36,137,206	15,081,167	16
902,606,751	241,461,958	102,474,056	112,408,268	33,786,973	238,568,263	127,229,200	17
619,845,137	159,484,723	74,664,736	73,011,060	24,572,061	160,766,162	95,153,391	18
12,713,942	3,724,293	1,204,815	1,297,558	333,471	6,635,873	2,576,029	19
270,047,672	78,252,942	26,604,505	38,099,650	8,881,441	71,166,228	29,499,780	20
1,614,539,313	381,885,420	198,807,622	153,104,448	44,249,708	336,443,784	222,222,004	21
950,289,391	241,803,072	133,959,526	91,565,876	28,608,676	206,257,902	149,018,273	22
27,025,908	5,693,469	3,030,805	1,677,720	542,819	11,032,695	6,963,602	23
637,224,014	134,388,879	61,817,291	59,860,852	15,098,213	119,153,187	66,240,129	24
1,537,976,573	354,428,746	199,579,599	154,716,977	48,310,161	318,025,292	253,523,577	25
968,104,804	232,654,953	141,233,151	95,955,442	33,223,816	198,363,365	174,083,847	26
29,778,901	5,745,670	2,694,162	1,819,803	533,255	8,607,823	6,170,588	27
540,092,868	116,028,123	55,652,286	56,941,732	14,553,090	111,054,104	73,269,142	28
34,938,161	22,639,829	18,217,822	6,781,318	3,206,095	8,600,665	6,817,123	29
16,180,799	12,633,169	10,994,268	3,740,377	1,850,410	4,131,797	3,435,577	30
1,111,205	938,042	665,075	242,768	94,379	283,486	191,035	31
17,646,157	9,068,618	6,558,479	2,798,173	1,261,306	4,185,382	3,190,511	32
163,451,614	126,692,803	78,285,509	28,970,020	11,859,771	48,071,250	32,570,134	33
83,429,643	79,057,365	49,381,062	18,840,230	7,684,897	28,289,533	19,572,661	34
17,973,915	12,532,038	6,494,826	1,817,972	661,144	3,255,628	1,443,514	35
62,048,056	35,103,400	22,409,621	8,311,818	3,513,730	16,526,089	11,553,959	36
7,193,950	1,421,221	1,037,393	104,252	92,350	246,366	152,840	37
1,876,100	531,350	403,700	41,687	19,685	46,163	35,731	38
2,929,600	673,631	311,243	36,415	61,100	158,649	79,124	39
2,388,250	216,240	322,450	26,150	11,565	41,554	37,985	40
394,658,912	268,080,748	137,399,150	50,151,466	18,115,883	121,969,281	74,891,438	41
292,888,081	206,903,249	110,003,214	39,088,590	14,395,201	92,768,801	59,266,898	42
21,106,420	15,450,346	6,248,006	2,357,762	803,741	5,929,911	2,710,680	43
80,714,411	45,727,153	21,147,930	8,705,114	2,916,941	23,270,569	12,913,860	44
207,075,759	103,473,702	57,315,195	18,395,058	7,011,513	67,261,153	43,336,073	45
159,475,370	86,504,959	48,519,098	15,445,375	6,002,017	56,518,407	36,603,331	46
7,612,055	3,728,886	1,523,610	740,899	162,204	1,940,859	987,866	47
39,988,334	13,239,857	7,272,487	2,208,784	847,292	8,801,887	5,744,876	48
343,164,945	218,577,944	113,459,662	54,621,363	18,441,619	119,152,672	62,649,984	49
221,658,135	144,171,326	83,675,956	38,288,083	13,897,746	77,035,406	43,331,756	50
11,734,529	5,152,546	2,474,715	946,534	492,607	1,888,058	1,146,510	51
109,772,281	69,254,072	27,308,991	15,386,746	4,051,266	40,229,208	18,171,718	52

TABLE 26.—VALUE OF ALL FARM PROPERTY AND OF THE SEVERAL

DIVISION OR STATE AND TENURE.	ALL FARM PROPERTY.		LAND AND BUILDINGS.		
			Total.		Land alone.
	1920	1910	1920	1910	1920
SOUTH ATLANTIC—Con.					
1 South Carolina, total............	$953,064,742	$392,128,314	$813,484,200	$332,888,081	$647,157,209
2 Owners...............	481,877,210	219,268,275	406,630,568	185,703,312	309,991,708
3 Managers..............	22,653,642	12,803,179	19,742,432	11,286,139	15,935,497
4 Tenants...............	448,533,890	160,056,860	387,111,200	135,898,630	321,230,004
5 Georgia, total......	1,356,685,196	580,546,381	1,138,298,627	479,204,332	897,444,961
6 Owners...............	615,657,538	291,426,602	506,548,019	239,621,776	380,860,366
7 Managers..............	54,787,814	20,195,588	47,833,256	17,653,921	38,954,800
8 Tenants...............	686,239,844	268,924,191	583,917,352	221,928,635	477,629,795
9 Florida, total......	330,301,717	143,183,183	281,449,404	118,145,989	228,424,740
10 Owners...............	237,153,993	110,171,256	198,546,585	89,533,767	156,442,015
11 Managers..............	59,028,533	17,435,357	55,199,070	16,414,031	49,639,896
12 Tenants...............	34,119,191	15,576,570	27,703,749	12,198,191	22,342,829
EAST SOUTH CENTRAL.					
13 Kentucky, total...	1,511,901,077	773,797,880	1,305,158,936	635,459,372	1,050,752,680
14 Owners...............	1,098,190,026	571,571,451	940,991,765	464,838,303	748,405,731
15 Managers..............	31,669,080	20,321,409	27,807,376	16,836,522	22,709,362
16 Tenants...............	382,041,971	181,905,020	336,359,795	153,784,547	279,637,587
17 Tennessee, total....	1,251,964,585	612,520,836	1,024,979,894	480,522,587	807,782,296
18 Owners...............	845,929,877	426,686,809	686,058,886	332,367,652	528,777,934
19 Managers..............	20,391,040	12,582,286	17,490,795	10,992,818	13,577,489
20 Tenants...............	385,643,668	173,251,741	321,430,213	137,162,117	265,426,873
21 Alabama, total.....	690,848,720	370,138,429	543,657,755	288,253,591	415,763,862
22 Owners...............	394,154,888	212,952,932	308,519,136	166,872,298	229,228,335
23 Managers..............	17,803,332	8,229,582	15,091,316	6,965,693	12,748,938
24 Tenants...............	278,890,500	148,955,915	220,047,303	114,415,600	173,786,589
25 Mississippi, total...	964,751,855	426,314,634	789,896,778	334,162,289	641,842,394
26 Owners...............	420,122,540	221,434,589	323,521,870	171,674,273	244,145,989
27 Managers..............	40,902,324	15,117,267	34,432,882	12,802,628	29,791,789
28 Tenants...............	503,726,991	189,762,778	431,942,026	149,685,388	367,904,616
WEST SOUTH CENTRAL.					
29 Arkansas, total....	924,395,483	400,089,303	753,110,666	309,166,813	607,773,440
30 Owners...............	516,331,819	240,112,532	407,346,897	181,882,010	315,494,861
31 Managers..............	29,120,363	12,098,030	25,327,476	10,440,663	22,485,051
32 Tenants...............	378,943,301	147,878,741	320,436,293	116,844,140	269,793,528
33 Louisiana, total....	589,826,679	301,220,988	474,038,793	237,544,450	383,618,162
34 Owners...............	331,764,023	171,395,396	261,827,217	134,121,536	206,821,658
35 Managers..............	53,328,365	38,680,084	43,911,266	29,902,294	37,398,511
36 Tenants...............	204,734,291	91,145,508	168,300,310	73,520,620	139,397,993
37 Oklahoma, total....	1,660,423,544	918,198,882	1,363,865,294	738,677,224	1,171,459,364
38 Owners...............	925,797,877	518,708,930	748,035,636	417,862,302	630,495,315
39 Managers..............	33,015,885	12,162,250	26,634,240	8,748,571	23,603,317
40 Tenants...............	701,609,782	387,327,702	589,195,418	312,066,351	517,360,732
41 Texas, total........	4,447,420,321	2,218,645,164	3,700,173,319	1,843,208,395	3,245,208,649
42 Owners...............	2,404,107,989	1,265,274,442	1,051,030,050	1,004,014,070	1,671,047,954
43 Managers..............	265,193,113	185,350,725	306,524,720	156,091,617	100,080,470
44 Tenants..............	1,778,119,219	768,019,997	1,541,708,637	653,102,108	1,377,171,219

CLASSES, BY TENURE, BY DIVISIONS AND STATES: 1920 and 1910—Continued.

LAND AND BUILDINGS—continued.			IMPLEMENTS AND MACHINERY.		LIVE STOCK.		
Land alone—Continued.	Buildings.						
1910	1920	1910	1920	1910	1920	1910	
$268,774,854	$166,326,991	$64,113,227	$48,062,387	$14,108,853	$91,518,155	$45,131,380	1
143,847,030	96,638,860	41,856,282	29,471,629	9,268,550	45,775,013	24,296,413	2
9,492,287	3,806,935	1,793,852	986,785	489,002	1,924,425	1,028,038	3
115,435,537	65,881,196	20,463,093	17,603,973	4,351,301	43,818,717	19,806,929	4
370,353,415	240,853,666	108,850,917	63,343,220	20,948,056	155,043,349	80,393,993	5
176,485,458	125,687,653	63,136,318	36,626,486	12,446,311	72,483,033	39,358,515	6
13,832,045	8,878,456	3,821,876	2,246,452	804,572	4,708,106	1,737,095	7
180,035,912	106,287,557	41,892,723	24,470,282	7,697,173	77,852,210	39,298,383	8
93,738,065	53,024,664	24,407,924	13,551,773	4,446,007	35,300,540	20,591,187	9
70,319,049	42,104,570	19,214,718	10,735,773	3,544,927	27,871,635	17,092,562	10
13,609,041	5,559,174	2,804,990	1,513,175	372,155	2,316,288	649,171	11
9,809,975	5,360,920	2,388,216	1,302,825	528,925	5,112,617	2,849,454	12
484,464,617	254,406,256	150,994,755	48,354,857	20,851,846	158,387,284	117,486,662	13
346,898,655	192,586,034	117,939,648	37,167,334	16,284,290	120,030,927	90,448,858	14
12,763,682	5,098,014	4,072,840	742,294	580,625	3,119,410	2,904,262	15
124,802,280	56,722,208	28,982,267	10,445,229	3,986,931	35,236,947	24,133,542	16
371,415,783	217,197,598	109,106,804	53,462,556	21,292,171	173,522,135	110,706,078	17
249,129,676	157,280,952	83,237,976	39,065,380	15,704,129	120,805,611	78,615,028	18
9,008,950	3,913,306	1,983,868	625,451	285,699	2,274,794	1,303,769	19
113,277,157	56,003,340	23,884,960	13,771,725	5,302,343	50,441,730	30,787,281	20
216,944,175	127,893,893	71,309,416	34,366,217	16,290,004	112,824,748	65,594,834	21
120,248,304	79,290,801	46,623,994	22,300,787	10,756,058	63,334,965	35,324,576	22
5,569,349	2,342,378	1,396,344	664,577	341,044	2,047,439	922,845	23
91,126,522	46,260,714	23,289,078	11,400,853	5,192,902	47,442,344	29,347,413	24
254,002,289	148,054,384	80,160,000	39,881,256	16,905,312	134,973,821	75,247,033	25
121,919,345	79,375,881	49,754,928	23,598,514	10,745,095	73,002,156	39,015,221	26
10,767,623	4,641,093	2,035,005	1,888,001	732,088	4,581,441	1,582,551	27
121,315,321	64,037,410	28,370,067	14,394,741	5,428,129	57,390,224	34,649,261	28
246,021,450	145,337,226	63,145,363	43,432,237	16,864,198	127,852,580	74,058,292	29
138,809,633	91,852,036	43,072,377	28,285,260	11,462,887	80,699,662	46,767,635	30
9,283,914	2,842,425	1,156,749	1,369,717	568,470	2,423,170	1,088,897	31
97,927,903	50,642,765	18,916,237	13,777,260	4,832,841	44,729,748	26,201,760	32
187,803,277	90,420,631	49,741,173	32,715,010	18,977,053	83,072,876	44,699,485	33
102,960,658	55,005,559	31,160,878	20,065,262	10,393,150	49,871,544	26,880,710	34
24,205,148	6,512,755	5,697,146	4,703,512	5,271,288	4,713,587	3,506,502	35
60,637,471	28,902,317	12,883,149	7,946,236	3,312,615	28,487,745	14,312,273	36
649,066,668	192,405,930	89,610,556	80,630,547	27,088,866	215,927,703	152,432,792	37
360,921,413	117,540,321	56,940,889	50,790,993	16,235,088	126,971,248	84,611,540	38
7,596,232	3,030,923	1,152,339	894,028	247,801	5,487,617	3,165,878	39
280,549,023	71,834,686	31,517,328	28,945,526	10,605,977	83,468,838	64,655,374	40
1,633,207,135	454,964,670	210,001,260	154,320,996	56,790,260	592,926,006	318,646,509	41
895,990,999	280,291,998	138,023,671	95,273,792	34,826,317	356,894,245	196,533,455	42
151,131,956	10,135,254	4,959,661	3,754,746	1,604,718	54,913,637	27,554,390	43
586,084,180	164,537,418	67,017,928	55,292,458	20,359,225	181,118,124	94,558,664	44

TABLE **26.**—VALUE OF ALL FARM PROPERTY AND OF THE SEVERAL

	DIVISION OR STATE AND TENURE.	ALL FARM PROPERTY.		LAND AND BUILDINGS.		
				Total.		Land alone.
		1920	1910	1920	1910	1920
	MOUNTAIN.					
1	**Montana, total**	$985,961,308	$347,828,770	$776,767,529	$251,625,930	$691,912,265
2	Owners	799,284,616	276,043,948	627,015,111	196,511,859	556,658,369
3	Managers	65,411,397	35,639,141	50,462,230	26,293,008	45,801,316
4	Tenants	121,265,295	36,145,681	99,290,188	28,821,063	89,452,580
5	**Idaho, total**	716,137,910	305,317,185	581,511,964	245,065,825	511,865,869
6	Owners	546,742,786	248,671,571	437,588,136	196,806,545	380,701,447
7	Managers	36,990,860	17,222,431	29,121,176	13,627,913	26,216,759
8	Tenants	132,404,264	39,423,183	114,802,652	34,631,367	104,947,663
9	**Wyoming, total**	334,410,590	167,189,081	234,748,125	97,915,277	210,947,494
10	Owners	252,838,359	123,022,941	174,279,727	71,276,554	155,544,573
11	Managers	42,280,712	31,092,474	30,491,658	17,184,459	28,266,977
12	Tenants	39,291,519	13,073,666	29,976,740	9,454,264	27,135,944
13	**Colorado, total**	1,076,794,749	491,471,806	866,013,660	408,518,861	763,722,716
14	Owners	738,655,401	332,301,156	587,657,108	270,209,463	513,418,657
15	Managers	57,539,844	36,507,244	42,106,600	29,343,653	37,269,141
16	Tenants	280,599,504	122,663,406	236,249,952	108,965,745	213,034,918
17	**New Mexico, total**	325,185,999	159,447,990	221,814,212	111,830,999	196,341,050
18	Owners	248,993,411	118,905,010	168,369,177	80,982,225	147,198,029
19	Managers	35,634,185	27,489,143	23,556,840	20,343,772	21,889,439
20	Tenants	40,558,403	13,053,837	29,888,195	10,505,002	27,253,582
21	**Arizona, total**	233,592,989	75,123,970	172,325,321	47,285,310	156,562,606
22	Owners	144,937,086	54,554,546	105,646,848	33,196,611	94,493,035
23	Managers	45,697,834	8,953,582	30,826,729	5,800,694	28,218,077
24	Tenants	42,958,069	11,615,842	35,851,744	8,288,005	33,851,494
25	**Utah, total**	311,274,728	150,795,201	243,751,758	117,545,332	210,997,840
26	Owners	265,098,820	131,563,980	206,623,839	101,417,754	177,372,208
27	Managers	13,866,226	7,943,361	9,737,800	6,545,737	8,987,614
28	Tenants	32,309,682	11,287,860	27,390,119	9,581,841	24,638,018
29	**Nevada, total**	99,779,666	60,399,365	66,255,214	39,609,339	59,362,239
30	Owners	66,303,427	33,606,576	43,879,220	21,731,515	38,767,848
31	Managers	25,716,253	21,729,293	16,804,949	13,908,493	15,703,246
32	Tenants	7,759,986	5,063,496	5,571,045	3,969,331	4,891,145
	PACIFIC.					
33	**Washington, total**	1,057,429,848	637,543,411	920,392,341	571,968,457	797,651,020
34	Owners	716,451,665	481,938,334	618,999,617	430,624,440	524,227,132
35	Managers	51,703,647	31,602,794	45,722,744	29,414,474	40,231,579
36	Tenants	289,274,536	124,002,283	255,669,980	111,929,543	233,192,309
37	**Oregon, total**	818,559,751	528,243,782	675,213,284	455,576,309	586,242,049
38	Owners	587,481,551	393,458,262	478,525,734	335,786,072	409,134,569
39	Managers	44,136,532	33,164,864	36,444,760	28,725,693	32,225,853
40	Tenants	186,941,668	101,620,656	160,242,790	91,064,544	144,881,627
41	**California, total**	3,431,021,861	1,614,694,584	3,073,811,109	1,450,601,488	2,783,054,977
42	Owners	2,127,106,548	982,077,668	1,900,924,411	882,447,830	1,687,052,191
43	Managers	486,731,605	256,953,819	442,032,436	229,544,415	412,059,140
44	Tenants	817,183,708	375,663,097	730,854,262	338,609,243	683,943,646

CLASSES, BY TENURE, BY DIVISIONS AND STATES: 1920 AND 1910—Continued.

LAND AND BUILDINGS—continued.			IMPLEMENTS AND MACHINERY.		LIVE STOCK.		
Land alone—Continued.	Buildings.						
1910	1920	1910	1920	1910	1920	1910	
$226,771,302	$84,855,264	$24,854,628	$55,004,212	$10,539,653	$154,189,567	$85,663,187	1
176,221,974	70,356,742	20,289,885	46,652,539	8,939,452	125,616,966	70,592,637	2
24,435,030	4,660,914	1,857,978	2,086,510	624,947	12,862,657	8,721,186	3
26,114,298	9,837,608	2,706,765	6,265,163	975,254	15,709,944	6,349,364	4
219,953,316	69,646,095	25,112,509	38,417,253	10,476,051	96,208,693	49,775,309	5
175,245,292	56,886,689	21,561,253	31,630,440	9,019,045	77,524,210	42,845,981	6
12,584,143	2,904,417	1,043,770	1,219,026	380,068	6,650,658	3,214,450	7
32,123,881	9,854,989	2,507,486	5,567,787	1,076,938	12,033,825	3,714,878	8
88,908,276	23,800,631	9,007,001	11,777,949	3,668,294	87,884,516	65,605,510	9
64,244,288	18,735,154	7,032,266	9,549,532	2,941,958	69,009,100	48,804,429	10
15,985,174	2,224,681	1,199,285	802,816	446,532	10,986,238	13,461,483	11
8,678,814	2,840,796	775,450	1,425,601	279,804	7,889,178	3,339,598	12
362,822,205	102,290,944	45,696,656	49,804,509	12,791,601	160,976,580	70,161,344	13
237,268,627	74,238,451	32,940,836	35,901,170	9,401,352	115,097,123	52,690,341	14
26,384,022	4,837,459	2,959,631	1,711,392	741,543	13,721,852	6,422,048	15
99,169,556	23,215,034	9,796,189	12,191,947	2,648,706	32,157,605	11,048,955	16
98,806,497	25,473,162	13,024,502	9,745,369	4,122,312	93,626,418	43,494,679	17
69,915,686	21,171,148	11,066,539	8,031,292	3,608,024	72,592,942	34,314,761	18
19,185,727	1,667,401	1,158,045	506,232	271,228	11,571,113	6,874,143	19
9,705,084	2,634,613	799,918	1,207,845	243,060	9,462,363	2,305,775	20
42,349,737	15,762,715	4,935,573	8,820,667	1,787,790	52,447,001	26,050,870	21
29,112,511	11,153,813	4,084,100	6,246,070	1,428,645	33,044,168	19,929,290	22
5,473,757	2,608,652	326,937	1,210,506	150,484	13,660,599	3,002,404	23
7,763,469	2,000,250	524,536	1,364,091	208,661	5,742,234	3,119,176	24
99,482,164	32,753,918	18,063,168	13,514,787	4,468,178	54,008,183	28,781,691	25
84,966,384	29,251,631	16,451,370	12,035,333	3,996,950	46,439,648	26,149,276	26
6,087,097	750,186	458,640	350,125	176,622	3,778,301	1,221,002	27
8,428,683	2,752,101	1,153,158	1,129,329	294,606	3,790,234	1,411,413	28
35,276,599	6,892,975	4,332,740	3,630,927	1,576,096	29,893,525	19,213,930	29
18,922,370	5,111,372	2,809,145	2,798,622	1,116,551	19,625,585	10,758,510	30
12,789,120	1,101,703	1,119,373	494,441	314,317	8,416,863	7,506,483	31
3,565,109	679,900	404,222	337,864	145,228	1,851,077	948,937	32
517,421,998	122,741,321	54,546,459	54,721,377	16,709,844	82,316,130	48,865,110	33
385,189,422	94,772,485	45,435,018	39,648,563	13,165,701	57,803,485	38,148,193	34
27,547,411	5,491,165	1,867,063	2,011,034	545,006	3,969,869	1,643,314	35
104,685,165	22,477,671	7,244,378	13,061,780	2,999,137	20,542,776	9,073,603	36
411,696,102	88,971,235	43,880,207	41,567,125	13,205,645	101,779,342	59,461,828	37
299,901,667	69,391,165	35,884,405	31,291,853	10,503,437	77,663,964	47,168,753	38
27,019,256	4,218,907	1,706,437	1,503,269	507,398	6,188,503	3,931,773	39
84,775,179	15,361,163	6,289,365	8,772,003	2,194,810	17,926,875	8,361,302	40
1,317,195,448	290,756,132	133,406,040	136,069,290	36,493,158	221,141,462	127,599,938	41
783,370,548	213,872,220	99,077,282	93,986,678	24,670,485	132,195,459	74,959,353	42
216,203,272	29,973,296	13,341,143	12,508,665	4,497,939	32,190,504	22,911,465	43
317,621,628	46,910,616	20,987,615	29,573,947	7,324,734	•56,755,499	29,729,120	44

TABLE 27.—AVERAGE VALUE OF LAND AND BUILDINGS PER FARM, BY TENURE, BY DIVISIONS AND STATES: 1920 AND 1910.

DIVISION AND STATE.	TOTAL.		OWNERS.		MANAGERS.		TENANTS.	
	1920	1910	1920	1910	1920	1910	1920	1910
United States....	$10,284	$5,471	$10,156	$5,664	$38,937	$25,075	$9,690	$4,662
GEOGRAPHIC DIVISIONS:								
New England.........	5,860	3,806	5,230	3,444	23,974	15,182	5,978	3,792
Middle Atlantic......	7,061	5,216	6,077	4,490	26,028	19,652	8,594	6,430
East North Central..	13,771	7,899	11,148	6,747	31,070	18,284	19,607	10,595
West North Central..	22,307	10,464	20,454	10,035	41,380	23,809	25,272	11,089
South Atlantic.......	4,488	2,236	5,060	2,686	27,776	15,129	3,427	1,504
East South Central..	3,484	1,668	4,296	2,225	27,046	14,467	2,508	1,050
West South Central..	6,316	3,317	7,256	4,010	60,323	43,693	4,973	2,322
Mountain............	12,958	7,192	11,609	6,044	56,635	45,689	15,450	10,879
Pacific..............	19,941	13,050	16,645	10,853	74,534	55,059	24,406	16,546
NEW ENGLAND:								
Maine...............	4,232	2,660	4,127	2,617	11,150	5,381	3,912	2,548
New Hampshire.....	4,385	3,176	4,059	3,040	17,127	9,938	3,733	2,500
Vermont............	5,473	3,442	5,043	3,156	16,922	12,462	6,739	4,016
Massachusetts......	7,737	5,260	6,483	4,497	31,339	19,724	6,341	4,425
Rhode Island........	6,463	5,278	5,529	4,438	22,519	20,618	6,050	4,843
Connecticut.........	8,399	5,158	7,283	4,598	29,711	20,730	7,944	4,485
MIDDLE ATLANTIC:								
New York...........	7,376	5,495	6,371	4,786	28,696	21,974	8,972	6,642
New Jersey.........	8,428	6,484	7,278	5,516	29,422	25,773	9,081	6,836
Pennsylvania........	6,560	4,747	5,615	4,039	22,681	15,640	8,202	6,178
EAST NORTH CENTRAL:								
Ohio................	10,368	6,080	8,834	5,455	28,519	17,412	13,243	7,234
Indiana.............	12,937	7,399	10,989	6,688	28,128	16,464	16,472	8,708
Illinois.............	25,289	13,986	20,304	12,170	47,587	27,246	31,068	16,208
Michigan...........	7,313	4,354	6,628	4,057	21,646	11,719	9,504	5,479
Wisconsin..........	11,558	6,784	10,774	6,310	22,906	16,958	15,137	9,090
WEST NORTH CENTRAL:								
Minnesota..........	18,496	8,085	16,511	7,538	31,475	17,111	23,997	9,789
Iowa...............	35,616	15,008	32,911	14,606	50,624	23,361	38,898	15,464
Missouri...........	11,646	6,190	11,292	6,272	33,235	20,171	11,970	5,663
North Dakota.......	19,160	11,063	18,287	10,422	41,063	34,914	20,713	13,780
South Dakota.......	33,132	12,945	31,369	11,978	49,808	32,445	35,869	15,426
Nebraska...........	29,836	13,983	29,581	13,681	49,957	30,453	29,673	14,139
Kansas.............	17,122	9,770	17,012	9,984	37,050	24,324	16,835	9,110
SOUTH ATLANTIC:								
Delaware...........	6,386	4,905	5,100	4,399	22,436	14,441	7,746	5,337
Maryland...........	8,070	4,941	6,729	3,962	27,358	24,766	9,488	5,859
District of Columbia.	27,340	37,932	17,128	19,320	123,571	216,056	17,844	32,270
Virginia............	5,501	2,891	5,475	3,014	29,391	16,833	4,506	2,090
West Virginia.......	4,706	2,735	4,453	2,738	21,148	10,477	4,727	2,383
North Carolina......	3,990	1,800	4,222	2,101	25,350	12,710	3,523	1,278
South Carolina.......	4,222	1,887	6,004	2,886	26,751	13,078	3,116	1,222
Georgia.............	3,663	1,647	4,960	2,430	28,902	12,441	2,821	1,162
Florida.............	5,212	2,362	5,159	2,529	30,180	12,874	2,024	914
EAST SOUTH CENTRAL:								
Kentucky...........	4,823	2,452	5,247	2,729	28,697	16,955	3,724	1,750
Tennessee..........	4,055	1,953	4,633	2,306	21,674	13,308	3,094	1,357
Alabama............	2,123	1,096	2,881	1,606	20,366	10,783	1,484	723
Mississippi.........	2,903	1,218	3,543	1,865	34,816	15,518	2,402	825
WEST SOUTH CENTRAL:								
Arkansas...........	3,238	1,440	3,616	1,705	34,412	13,684	2,688	1,089
Louisiana...........	3,499	1,971	4,573	2,531	53,033	31,476	2,175	1,104
Oklahoma...........	7,104	3,884	8,025	4,893	28,486	13,439	6,022	2,997
Texas..............	8,486	4,412	9,701	5,279	82,150	66,935	6,636	2,974
MOUNTAIN:								
Montana............	13,468	9,599	12,473	8,411	56,132	52,065	15,259	12,206
Idaho..............	13,811	7,955	12,620	7,011	38,418	30,284	17,132	10,863
Wyoming...........	14,907	8,912	13,003	7,390	60,000	53,235	15,232	10,540
Colorado...........	14,449	8,848	12,975	7,304	47,848	37,285	17,166	12,988
New Mexico.........	7,432	3,135	6,537	2,425	54,404	63,376	8,177	5,368
Arizona............	17,276	5,125	13,426	4,047	101,071	35,587	19,907	9,626
Utah...............	9,499	5,423	9,151	5,132	32,898	33,741	9,828	5,571
Nevada.............	20,947	14,730	16,258	9,992	100,029	76,843	18,821	11,920
PACIFIC:								
Washington.........	13,885	10,179	11,746	9,065	39,146	30,608	20,587	14,487
Oregon.............	13,449	10,012	12,004	8,884	39,787	33,915	16,998	13,277
California..........	26,122	16,447	21,705	13,244	89,318	67,177	29,070	18,658

TABLE 28.—AVERAGE VALUE OF LAND AND BUILDINGS PER ACRE, BY TENURE, BY DIVISIONS AND STATES: 1920 AND 1910.

DIVISION AND STATE.	TOTAL.		OWNERS.		MANAGERS.		TENANTS.	
	1920	1910	1920	1910	1920	1910	1920	1910
United States........	$69.38	$39.60	$62.60	$37.37	$49.24	$27.12	$89.77	$48.46
GEOGRAPHIC DIVISIONS:								
New England............	54.00	36.45	49.85	33.94	117.42	75.10	53.12	37.01
Middle Atlantic..........	73.99	56.56	68.50	52.64	133.36	104.01	78.69	59.89
East North Central......	126.87	75.25	111.71	68.04	146.84	84.25	155.64	91.02
West North Central.....	95.22	49.92	86.29	46.22	73.35	39.88	115.12	60.45
South Atlantic..........	53.20	23.96	49.70	23.05	61.83	37.31	58.84	24.53
East South Central......	46.44	21.32	41.82	19.88	62.03	29.68	56.10	24.36
West South Central.....	36.27	18.50	32.15	16.94	18.32	10.42	50.23	25.62
Mountain...............	26.96	22.16	25.87	23.00	17.97	12.09	42.97	34.20
Pacific.................	83.16	48.28	82.21	49.55	76.36	36.42	89.49	53.35
NEW ENGLAND:								
Maine..................	37.62	25.35	36.96	24.97	60.11	34.26	38.00	29.14
New Hampshire.........	34.56	26.44	32.89	26.00	60.58	32.28	33.49	26.66
Vermont...............	37.56	24.14	35.98	23.21	64.00	37.94	40.41	25.22
Massachusetts..........	99.25	67.51	90.06	61.56	162.85	111.04	90.94	65.28
Rhode Island...........	79.58	63.01	72.07	56.99	154.95	116.46	72.43	57.32
Connecticut............	100.20	63.28	92.86	58.33	169.83	143.97	90.08	54.32
MIDDLE ATLANTIC:								
New York..............	69.07	53.78	64.08	50.41	134.69	106.16	72.12	55.53
New Jersey.............	109.67	84.36	111.81	85.18	139.35	120.17	95.45	72.35
Pennsylvania...........	75.14	56.01	68.90	51.44	130.18	95.56	83.15	62.61
EAST NORTH CENTRAL:								
Ohio...................	113.18	68.62	104.82	65.36	155.61	94.99	125.94	73.77
Indiana................	125.98	74.85	117.15	71.25	138.52	78.22	139.94	81.91
Illinois................	187.59	108.32	165.49	99.29	227.70	116.41	209.64	119.33
Michigan...............	75.48	47.58	72.65	46.27	85.39	50.79	84.54	52.98
Wisconsin..............	98.78	57.06	96.39	54.86	104.53	69.29	109.29	67.18
WEST NORTH CENTRAL:								
Minnesota..............	109.23	45.62	104.30	44.53	113.37	50.54	120.85	48.71
Iowa...................	227.09	96.00	222.23	96.10	221.23	91.67	233.22	96.01
Missouri...............	88.08	49.61	84.64	47.88	112.39	64.08	95.39	53.56
North Dakota...........	41.10	28.94	38.77	27.93	43.27	35.41	48.23	33.68
South Dakota...........	71.40	38.63	62.06	35.96	43.72	21.91	97.53	48.90
Nebraska...............	87.91	46.95	78.00	40.19	44.37	27.45	110.69	66.25
Kansas.................	62.30	40.05	60.33	38.47	45.37	25.70	66.73	44.86
SOUTH ATLANTIC:								
Delaware...............	68.56	51.17	67.89	56.99	150.37	83.93	65.48	44.75
Maryland...............	81.25	47.80	80.24	45.71	133.09	118.04	75.14	43.43
District of Columbia.....	984.01	1,357.64	990.64	938.58	1,203.41	2,225.85	762.93	1,244.58
Virginia...............	55.19	27.29	54.26	27.38	76.14	41.43	54.10	24.72
West Virginia..........	42.93	26.37	41.10	25.41	64.74	32.11	47.59	30.34
North Carolina.........	53.76	20.35	47.55	19.50	60.88	24.40	66.80	22.11
South Carolina.........	65.46	24.64	60.54	23.06	46.51	20.62	73.25	27.66
Georgia................	44.74	17.78	39.57	16.13	51.66	22.66	49.85	19.60
Florida................	46.55	22.49	48.90	20.89	45.91	58.47	35.34	17.78
EAST SOUTH CENTRAL:								
Kentucky...............	60.39	28.64	56.04	26.62	103.05	53.41	73.91	34.86
Tennessee..............	52.53	23.98	49.79	22.65	79.19	32.82	58.32	27.25
Alabama...............	27.77	13.90	25.46	12.57	33.16	18.99	31.42	16.15
Mississippi............	43.41	18.01	28.54	14.65	59.09	21.83	68.78	23.93
WEST SOUTH CENTRAL:								
Arkansas...............	43.14	17.75	34.49	14.68	72.04	31.81	60.52	24.87
Louisiana..............	47.31	22.75	41.86	19.82	48.78	30.32	58.75	27.36
Oklahoma..............	42.68	25.60	40.50	26.12	28.76	20.41	46.93	25.10
Texas..................	32.45	16.39	28.60	14.94	14.41	8.69	49.03	25.84
MOUNTAIN:								
Montana................	22.15	18.58	21.66	18.47	17.64	18.39	30.48	19.54
Idaho..................	69.43	46.38	64.36	44.26	75.50	50.43	96.37	61.07
Wyoming...............	19.88	11.46	18.62	13.83	20.80	6.00	30.47	17.92
Colorado...............	35.40	30.19	31.56	26.66	26.39	25.73	55.66	48.28
New Mexico............	9.09	9.92	9.43	11.41	6.10	6.37	11.10	10.74
Arizona................	29.70	37.93	27.66	37.94	22.16	21.91	60.61	77.53
Utah..................	48.26	34.60	50.86	35.12	15.81	20.76	73.60	49.33
Nevada................	28.11	14.59	30.91	21.05	21.10	9.13	39.47	25.09
PACIFIC:								
Washington............	69.49	48.84	66.85	47.24	84.49	55.60	74.24	54.13
Oregon................	49.86	38.99	47.77	37.16	43.49	37.50	59.63	48.37
California..............	104.67	51.93	110.54	58.34	80.58	34.75	109.34	54.60

TABLE 29.—NUMBER AND ACREAGE OF FARMS IN THE UNITED STATES, BY COLOR AND TENURE: 1920 AND 1910.

[Corresponding figures for all farmers, by tenure, in Table 16.]

COLOR AND TENURE.	NUMBER OF FARMS.			ALL LAND IN FARMS (ACRES).			IMPROVED LAND IN FARMS (ACRES).		
	1920	1910	Per cent of inc.[1]	1920	1910	Per cent of inc.[1]	1920	1910	Per cent of inc.[1]
WHITE FARMERS.									
Total....	5,498,454	5,440,619	1.1	910,939,194	832,166,020	9.5	473,774,566	449,418,265	5.4
Owners.......	3,691,868	3,707,501	−0.4	620,070,823	579,478,154	7.0	306,029,220	301,504,138	1.5
Owning entire farm..	3,174,109	3,159,088	0.5	447,244,925	448,961,809	−0.4	228,667,878	227,265,911	0.6
Hiring addit. land..	517,759	548,413	−5.6	172,825,898	130,516,345	32.4	77,361,342	74,238,227	4.2
Managers.....	66,223	56,560	17.1	53,653,478	53,304,976	0.7	13,009,436	12,166,563	6.9
Tenants......	1,740,363	1,676,558	3.8	237,214,893	199,382,890	19.0	154,735,910	135,747,564	14.0
Share[2].....	1,163,942	1,026,372	13.4	142,337,408	109,695,138	29.8	98,410,006	79,093,004	24.4
Share-cash..	119,395	113,843	4.9	24,025,817	18,734,775	28.2	19,668,931	15,425,303	27.5
Cash[2].......	400,907	447,851	−10.5	62,762,080	55,948,318	12.2	32,318,657	33,014,406	−2.1
Unspecified.	56,119	88,492	−36.6	8,089,588	15,004,659	−46.1	4,338,316	8,214,851	−47.2
COLORED FARMERS.									
Total....	949,889	920,883	3.2	44,944,521	46,632,305	−3.6	29,298,441	29,033,485	0.9
Owners.......	233,222	241,221	−3.3	16,704,192	19,076,463	−12.4	8,078,263	8,346,283	−3.2
Owning entire farm..	192,401	195,809	−1.7	14,005,208	15,961,506	−12.3	6,509,586	6,542,686	−0.5
Hiring addit. land..	40,821	45,412	−10.1	2,698,984	3,114,957	−13.4	1,568,677	1,803,597	−13.0
Managers.....	2,226	1,544	44.2	475,679	425,889	11.7	201,563	147,452	36.7
Tenants......	714,441	678,118	5.4	27,764,650	27,129,953	2.3	21,018,615	20,539,750	2.3
Share[2]......	514,870	373,551	37.8	18,385,143	13,358,580	37.6	14,469,944	10,644,740	35.9
Share-cash..	8,427	14,623	−42.4	308,611	655,093	−52.9	264,176	498,614	−47.0
Cash[2].......	184,098	264,443	−30.4	8,719,575	11,898,533	−26.7	6,067,837	8,551,756	−29.0
Unspecified.	7,046	25,501	−72.4	351,321	1,217,747	−71.1	216,658	844,640	−74.3

[1] A minus sign (−) denotes decrease.
[2] Share tenants include croppers reported in the Southern states in 1920, and cash tenants likewise include standing renters.

TABLE 30.—PERCENTAGE OF FARM LAND IMPROVED, AVERAGE ACREAGE PER FARM, AND PER CENT DISTRIBUTION, BY COLOR AND TENURE, FOR THE UNITED STATES: 1920 AND 1910.

[Corresponding figures for all farmers, by tenure, in Table 17.]

COLOR AND TENURE.	PER CENT OF FARM LAND IMPROVED.		AVERAGE ACREAGE PER FARM.				PER CENT DISTRIBUTION.			
			All land.		Improved land.		All land in farms.		Improved land in farms.	
	1920	1910	1920	1910	1920	1910	1920	1910	1920	1910
WHITE FARMERS.										
Total	52.0	54.0	165.7	153.0	86.2	82.6	100.0	100.0	100.0	100.0
Owners	49.4	52.0	168.0	156.3	82.9	81.3	68.1	69.6	64.6	67.1
Owning entire farm	51.1	50.6	140.9	142.1	72.0	71.9	49.1	54.0	48.3	50.6
Hiring additional land	44.8	56.9	333.8	238.0	149.4	135.4	19.0	15.7	16.3	16.5
Managers	24.2	22.8	810.2	942.5	196.4	215.1	5.9	6.4	2.7	2.7
Tenants	65.2	68.1	136.3	118.9	88.9	81.0	26.0	24.0	32.7	30.2
Share [1]	69.1	72.1	122.3	106.9	84.5	77.1	15.6	13.2	20.8	17.6
Share-cash	81.9	82.3	201.2	164.6	164.7	135.5	2.6	2.3	4.2	3.4
Cash [1]	51.5	59.0	156.6	124.9	80.6	73.7	6.9	6.7	6.8	7.3
Unspecified	53.6	54.7	144.2	169.6	77.3	92.8	0.9	1.8	0.9	1.8
COLORED FARMERS.										
Total	65.2	62.3	47.3	50.6	30.8	31.5	100.0	100.0	100.0	100.0
Owners	48.4	43.8	71.6	79.1	34.6	34.6	37.2	40.9	27.6	28.7
Owning entire farm	46.5	41.0	72.8	81.5	33.8	33.4	31.2	34.2	22.2	22.5
Hiring additional land	58.1	57.9	66.1	68.6	38.4	39.7	6.0	6.7	5.4	6.2
Managers	42.4	34.6	213.7	275.8	90.5	95.5	1.1	0.9	0.7	0.5
Tenants	75.7	75.7	38.9	40.0	29.4	30.3	61.8	58.2	71.7	70.7
Share [1]	78.7	79.7	35.7	35.8	28.1	28.5	40.9	28.6	49.4	36.7
Share-cash	85.6	76.1	36.6	44.8	31.3	34.1	0.7	1.4	0.9	1.7
Cash [1]	69.6	71.9	47.4	45.0	33.0	32.3	19.4	25.5	20.7	29.5
Unspecified	61.7	69.4	49.9	47.8	30.7	33.1	0.8	2.6	0.7	2.9

[1] Share tenants include croppers reported in the Southern states in 1920, and cash tenants likewise include standing renters.

TABLE 31.—NUMBER OF FARMS IN THE UNITED STATES, WITH PER CENT DISTRIBUTION, BY COLOR AND TENURE: 1900 TO 1920.

[Corresponding figures for all farmers, by tenure, in Table 18.]

COLOR AND TENURE.	NUMBER OF FARMS.			PER CENT DISTRIBUTION.		
	1920	1910	1900	1920	1910	1900
WHITE FARMERS.						
Total	5,498,454	5,440,619	4,969,608	100.0	100.0	100.0
Owners	3,691,868	3,707,501	3,446,806	67.1	68.1	69.4
Managers	66,223	56,560	57,261	1.2	1.0	1.2
Tenants	1,740,363	1,676,558	1,465,541	31.7	30.8	29.5
COLORED FARMERS.						
Total	949,889	920,883	767,764	100.0	100.0	100.0
Owners	233,222	241,221	206,517	24.6	26.2	26.9
Managers	2,226	1,544	1,824	0.2	0.2	0.2
Tenants	714,441	678,118	559,423	75.2	73.6	72.9

TABLE 32.—NUMBER AND ACREAGE OF FARMS IN THE SOUTH, WITH AVERAGES AND PERCENTAGES, BY COLOR AND TENURE. 1920.

[Corresponding figures for all farmers, by tenure, in Table 19.]

COLOR AND TENURE.	Number of farms.	All land in farms (acres).	Improved land in farms (acres).	Per cent of farm land improved.	AVERAGE ACREAGE PER FARM.		PER CENT. DISTRIBUTION.		
					All land.	Improved land.	Number of farms.	All land.	Improved land.
THE SOUTH.									
WHITE FARMERS.									
Total	2,283,750	308,803,337	129,335,864	41.9	135.2	56.6	100.0	100.0	100.0
Owners	1,379,636	206,525,033	82,297,960	39.8	149.7	59.7	60.4	66.9	63.6
Owning entire farm	1,227,204	169,703,027	70,567,733	41.6	138.3	57.5	53.7	55.0	54.6
Hiring additional land	152,432	36,822,006	11,730,227	31.9	241.6	77.0	6.7	11.9	9.1
Managers	16,548	22,073,344	3,345,166	15.2	1,333.9	202.1	0.7	7.1	2.6
Tenants	887,566	80,204,960	43,692,738	54.5	90.4	49.2	38.9	26.0	33.8
Share tenants, including croppers	701,891	55,472,862	34,436,595	62.1	79.0	49.1	30.7	18.0	26.6
Share tenants proper	474,513	43,082,592	26,275,314	61.0	90.8	55.4	20.8	14.0	20.3
Croppers	227,378	12,390,270	8,161,281	65.9	54.5	35.9	10.0	4.0	6.3
Share-cash tenants	14,465	1,844,801	1,179,861	64.0	127.5	81.6	0.6	0.6	0.9
Cash tenants, including standing renters	145,985	20,264,957	6,969,701	34.4	138.8	47.7	6.4	6.6	5.4
Cash tenants proper	118,913	18,209,123	5,852,029	32.1	153.1	49.2	5.2	5.9	4.5
Standing renters	27,072	2,055,834	1,117,672	54.4	75.9	41.3	1.2	0.7	0.9
Unspecified tenants	25,225	2,622,340	1,106,581	42.2	104.0	43.9	1.1	0.8	0.9
COLORED FARMERS.									
Total	922,914	41,318,496	27,743,760	67.1	44.8	30.1	100.0	100.0	100.0
Owners	217,589	14,076,623	7,247,342	51.5	64.7	33.3	23.6	34.1	26.1
Owning entire farm	178,558	11,950,158	5,922,818	49.6	66.9	33.2	19.3	28.9	21.3
Hiring additional land	39,031	2,126,465	1,324,524	62.3	54.5	33.9	4.2	5.1	4.8
Managers	1,770	367,820	149,117	40.5	207.8	84.2	0.2	0.9	0.5
Tenants	703,555	26,874,053	20,347,301	75.7	38.2	28.9	76.2	65.0	73.3
Share tenants, including croppers	510,424	17,955,303	14,129,316	78.7	35.2	27.7	55.3	43.5	50.9
Share tenants proper	176,711	7,814,520	5,632,483	72.1	44.2	31.9	19.1	18.9	20.3
Croppers	333,713	10,140,783	8,496,833	83.8	30.4	25.5	36.2	24.5	30.6
Share-cash tenants	8,207	271,670	236,577	87.1	33.1	28.8	0.9	0.7	0.9
Cash tenants, including standing renters	178,199	8,341,572	5,784,422	69.3	46.8	32.5	19.3	20.2	20.8
Cash tenants proper	100,275	4,010,599	2,912,997	72.6	40.0	29.1	10.9	9.7	10.5
Standing renters	77,924	4,330,973	2,871,425	66.3	55.6	36.8	8.4	10.5	10.3
Unspecified tenants	6,725	305,508	196,986	64.5	45.4	29.3	0.7	0.7	0.7

TABLE 33.—NUMBER OF FARMS IN THE SOUTH, WITH PER CENT DISTRIBUTION, BY COLOR AND TENURE: 1900 TO 1920.

COLOR AND TENURE.	NUMBER OF FARMS.			PER CENT DISTRIBUTION.		
	1920	1910	1900	1920	1910	1900
THE SOUTH.						
WHITE FARMERS.						
Total	2,283,750	2,207,406	1,879,721	100.0	100.0	100.0
Owners	1,379,636	1,326,044	1,183,806	60.4	60.1	63.0
Managers	16,548	15,084	17,172	0.7	0.7	0.9
Tenants	887,566	866,278	678,743	38.9	39.2	36.1
COLORED FARMERS.						
Total	922,914	890,141	740,670	100.0	100.0	100.0
Owners	217,589	218,467	186,676	23.6	24.5	25.2
Managers	1,770	1,200	1,593	0.2	0.1	0.2
Tenants	703,555	670,474	552,401	76.2	75.3	74.6

TABLE 34.—VALUE OF FARM PROPERTY IN THE UNITED STATES, BY COLOR AND TENURE: 1920 AND 1910.

[Corresponding figures for all farmers, by tenure, in Table 20.]

COLOR AND TENURE.	ALL FARM PROPERTY.			LAND AND BUILDINGS.		
	1920	1910	Per cent of increase.	1920	1910	Per cent of increase.
WHITE FARMERS.						
Total	$74,955,403,721	$39,712,214,845	88.7	$63,786,058,855	$33,764,392,187	88.9
Owners	46,810,947,920	26,228,711,934	78.5	39,215,462,823	22,020,188,824	78.1
Owning entire farm	36,176,166,655	20,374,872,924	77.6	30,176,281,465	17,032,045,135	77.2
Hiring additional land	10,634,781,265	5,853,839,010	81.7	9,039,181,358	4,988,143,689	81.2
Managers	3,091,165,814	1,681,895,418	83.8	2,629,284,676	1,440,643,081	82.5
Tenants	25,053,289,987	11,801,607,493	112.3	21,941,311,356	10,303,560,282	112.9
Share [1]	13,682,864,376	} 7,538,264,668	134.4	11,921,171,797	} 6,596,004,373	135.8
Share-cash	3,989,058,066			3,632,413,956		
Cash [1]	6,728,610,115	} 4,263,342,825	73.1	5,826,072,815	} 3,707,555,909	72.3
Unspecified	652,757,430			561,652,788		
COLORED FARMERS.						
Total	2,968,696,617	1,279,234,245	132.1	2,529,943,747	1,036,733,510	144.0
Owners	800,598,024	440,922,439	81.6	648,760,084	346,745,454	87.1
Owning entire farm	661,227,524	355,994,187	85.7	534,439,299	278,593,881	91.8
Hiring additional land	139,370,500	84,928,252	64.1	114,320,785	68,151,573	67.7
Managers	41,107,191	18,729,518	119.5	35,931,789	16,315,911	120.2
Tenants	2,126,991,402	819,582,288	159.5	1,845,251,874	673,672,145	173.9
Share [1]	1,474,221,606	} 442,938,549	242.2	1,300,501,544	} 373,944,277	257.5
Share-cash	41,702,536			36,327,826		
Cash [1]	591,626,704	} 376,643,739	62.2	492,174,681	} 299,727,868	69.6
Unspecified	19,440,556			16,247,823		

COLOR AND TENURE.	LAND ALONE.			BUILDINGS.		
	1920	1910	Per cent of increase.	1920	1910	Per cent of increase.
WHITE FARMERS.						
Total	$52,707,641,140	$27,615,515,334	90.9	$11,078,417,715	$6,148,876,853	80.2
Owners	31,471,590,402	17,528,730,187	79.5	7,743,872,421	4,491,458,637	72.4
Owning entire farm	23,638,999,408	13,220,114,695	78.8	6,537,282,057	3,811,930,440	71.5
Hiring additional land	7,832,590,994	4,308,615,492	81.8	1,206,590,364	679,528,197	77.6
Managers	2,178,344,776	1,205,653,349	80.7	450,939,900	234,989,732	91.9
Tenants	19,057,705,962	8,881,131,798	114.6	2,883,605,394	1,422,428,484	102.7
Share [1]	10,249,405,206	} 5,713,371,914	137.4	1,671,766,591	} 882,632,459	125.4
Share-cash	3,314,287,619			318,126,337		
Cash [1]	5,020,508,499	} 3,167,759,884	73.4	805,564,316	} 539,796,025	65.6
Unspecified	473,504,638			88,148,150		
COLORED FARMERS.						
Total	2,121,921,919	860,158,835	146.7	408,021,828	176,574,675	131.1
Owners	513,191,232	277,391,441	85.0	135,568,852	69,354,013	95.5
Owning entire farm	419,745,895	221,719,994	89.3	114,693,404	56,873,887	101.7
Hiring additional land	93,445,337	55,671,447	67.9	20,875,448	12,480,126	67.3
Managers	29,306,244	13,205,916	121.9	6,625,545	3,109,995	113.0
Tenants	1,579,424,443	569,561,478	177.3	265,827,431	104,110,667	155.3
Share [1]	1,111,081,893	} 316,634,227	261.1	189,419,651	} 57,310,050	237.4
Share-cash	32,355,439			3,972,387		
Cash [1]	422,437,873	} 252,927,251	72.4	69,736,808	} 46,800,617	54.8
Unspecified	13,549,238			2,698,585		

[1] Share tenants include croppers reported in the Southern States in 1920, and cash tenants likewise include standing renters.

TABLE 34.—VALUE OF FARM PROPERTY IN THE UNITED STATES, BY COLOR AND TENURE: 1920 AND 1910—Continued.

[Corresponding figures for all farmers, by tenure, in Table 20.]

COLOR AND TENURE.	IMPLEMENTS AND MACHINERY.			LIVE STOCK.		
	1920	1910	Per cent of increase.	1920	1910	Per cent of increase.
WHITE FARMERS.						
Total	$3,491,321,159	$1,227,407,744	184.4	$7,678,023,707	$4,720,414,914	62.7
Owners	2,411,134,220	884,819,727	172.5	5,184,350,877	3,323,703,383	56.0
Owning entire farm	1,927,214,682	718,866,096	168.1	4,072,670,508	2,623,961,693	55.2
Hiring additional land	483,919,538	165,953,631	191.6	1,111,680,369	699,741,690	58.9
Managers	102,231,072	42,473,043	140.7	359,650,066	198,779,294	80.9
Tenants	977,955,867	300,114,974	225.9	2,134,022,764	1,197,932,237	78.1
Share [1]	554,897,105	} 191,476,447	258.5	1,206,795,474	} 750,783,848	90.7
Share-cash	131,463,184			225,180,926		
Cash [1]	266,270,857	} 108,638,527	168.4	636,266,443	} 447,148,389	57.0
Unspecified	25,324,721			65,779,921		
COLORED FARMERS.						
Total	103,451,769	37,742,039	174.1	335,301,101	204,758,696	63.8
Owners	36,658,561	15,852,814	131.2	115,179,379	78,324,171	47.1
Owning entire farm	30,964,138	12,985,658	138.4	95,824,087	64,414,648	48.8
Hiring additional land	5,694,423	2,867,156	98.6	19,355,292	13,909,523	39.2
Managers	1,542,630	435,457	254.3	3,632,772	1,978,150	83.6
Tenants	65,250,578	21,453,768	204.1	216,488,950	124,456,375	73.9
Share [1]	39,880,265	} 9,412,854	335.9	133,839,797	} 59,581,418	131.7
Share-cash	1,150,201			4,224,509		
Cash [1]	23,582,201	} 12,040,914	101.1	75,869,822	} 64,874,957	20.9
Unspecified	637,911			2,554,822		

[1] Share tenants include croppers reported in the Southern states in 1920, and cash tenants likewise include standing renters.

TABLE 35.—VALUE OF FARM PROPERTY IN THE SOUTH, BY COLOR AND TENURE: 1920.

[Corresponding figures for all farmers, by tenure, in Table 21.]

COLOR AND TENURE.	All farm property.	Land.	Buildings.	Implements and machinery.	Live stock.
THE SOUTH.					
WHITE FARMERS.					
Total	$15,547,590,202	$10,477,276,809	$2,451,526,481	$680,756,446	$1,938,030,466
Owners	9,924,590,749	6,422,405,001	1,723,054,101	477,494,986	1,298,946,661
Owning entire farm	8,534,027,597	5,461,497,477	1,550,054,189	417,802,433	1,098,073,388
Hiring additional land	1,390,563,152	960,997,524	168,999,802	59,692,553	200,873,273
Managers	771,799,018	557,140,666	90,721,921	24,628,189	99,308,242
Tenants	4,851,200,435	3,497,641,142	635,150,459	178,633,271	539,775,563
Share tenants, including croppers	3,667,065,462	2,673,058,147	479,132,402	133,734,356	381,140,557
Share tenants proper	2,817,302,611	2,043,114,693	362,356,546	108,420,770	303,410,602
Croppers	849,762,851	629,943,454	116,775,856	25,313,586	77,729,955
Share-cash tenants	146,290,829	110,385,880	15,601,565	5,788,498	14,514,886
Cash tenants, including standing renters	913,101,289	629,344,024	121,554,036	34,589,791	127,613,438
Cash tenants proper	775,786,631	535,941,040	99,203,226	28,068,871	112,573,494
Standing renters	137,314,658	93,402,984	22,350,810	6,520,920	15,039,944
Unspecified tenants	124,742,855	84,853,091	18,862,456	4,520,626	16,506,682

TABLE 35.—VALUE OF FARM PROPERTY IN THE SOUTH, BY COLOR AND TENURE: 1920—Continued.

[Corresponding figures for all farmers, by tenure, in Table 21.]

COLOR AND TENURE.	All farm property.	Land.	Buildings.	Implements and machinery.	Live stock.
THE SOUTH—Con.					
COLORED FARMERS.					
Total.................	$2,626,859,822	$1,847,605,942	$380,245,675	$90,388,087	$308,620,118
Owners.................	680,645,113	429,929,080	121,801,982	31,330,566	97,583,485
Owning entire farm......	565,223,542	354,207,034	103,017,973	26,492,439	81,506,096
Hiring additional land...	115,421,571	75,722,046	18,784,009	4,838,127	16,077,389
Managers................	25,095,060	17,019,617	4,514,281	902,899	2,658,263
Tenants.................	1,921,119,649	1,400,657,245	253,929,412	58,154,622	208,378,370
Share tenants, including croppers.............	1,386,948,958	1,035,946,437	183,561,249	37,078,688	130,362,584
Share tenants proper...	575,263,129	414,818,168	73,815,971	18,975,202	67,653,788
Croppers...............	811,685,829	621,128,269	109,745,278	18,103,486	62,708,796
Share-cash tenants.......	35,080,135	26,483,369	3,619,117	965,961	4,011,688
Cash tenants, including standing renters......	483,144,616	327,440,417	64,348,291	19,597,868	71,758,040
Cash tenants proper....	251,408,599	169,715,582	32,398,252	9,951,148	39,343,617
Standing renters........	231,736,017	157,724,835	31,950,039	9,646,720	32,414,423
Unspecified tenants......	15,945,940	10,787,022	2,400,755	512,105	2,246,058

TABLE 36.—AVERAGE VALUE OF FARM PROPERTY PER FARM AND PER ACRE, BY COLOR AND TENURE, FOR THE UNITED STATES: 1920 AND 1910.

[Corresponding figures for all farmers, by tenure, in Table 22.]

| COLOR AND ITEM. | TOTAL. | | FARMS OPERATED BY— | | | | | |
| | | | Owners. | | Managers. | | Tenants. | |
	1920	1910	1920	1910	1920	1910	1920	1910
WHITE FARMERS.								
Average value per farm:								
All farm property.......	$13,632	$7,299	$12,679	$7,075	$46,678	$29,736	$14,395	$7,039
Land and buildings...........	11,601	6,206	10,622	5,939	39,703	25,471	12,607	6,146
Land alone.................	9,586	5,076	8,525	4,728	32,894	21,316	10,950	5,297
Buildings..................	2,015	1,130	2,098	1,211	6,809	4,155	1,657	848
Implements and machinery....	635	226	653	239	1,544	751	562	179
Live stock.....................	1,396	868	1,404	896	5,431	3,514	1,226	715
Average value per acre:								
All farm property.......	82.28	47.72	75.49	45.26	57.61	31.55	105.61	59.19
Land and buildings...........	70.02	40.57	63.24	38.00	49.00	27.03	92.50	51.68
Land alone.................	57.86	33.19	50.75	30.25	40.60	22.62	80.34	44.54
Buildings..................	12.16	7.39	12.49	7.75	8.40	4.41	12.16	7.13
Implements and machinery....	3.83	1.47	3.89	1.53	1.91	0.80	4.12	1.51
Live stock..................	8.43	5.67	8.36	5.74	6.70	3.73	9.00	6.01
COLORED FARMERS.								
Average value per farm:								
All farm property.......	3,125	1,389	3,433	1,828	18,467	12,131	2,977	1,209
Land and buildings...........	2,663	1,126	2,782	1,437	16,142	10,567	2,583	993
Land alone.................	2,234	934	2,200	1,150	13,165	8,553	2,211	840
Buildings..................	430	192	581	288	2,976	2,014	372	154
Implements and machinery....	109	41	157	66	693	282	91	32
Live stock..................	353	222	494	325	1,632	1,281	303	184
Average value per acre:								
All farm property.......	66.05	27.43	47.93	23.11	86.42	43.98	76.61	30.21
Land and buildings...........	56.29	22.23	38.84	18.18	75.54	38.31	66.46	24.83
Land alone.................	47.21	18.45	30.72	14.54	61.61	31.01	56.89	20.99
Buildings..................	9.08	3.79	8.12	3.64	13.93	7.30	9.57	3.84
Implements and machinery....	2.30	0.81	2.19	0.83	3.24	1.02	2.35	0.79
Live stock..................	7.46	4.39	6.90	4.11	7.64	4.64	7.80	4.59

TABLE 37.—NUMBER OF FARMS, BY COLOR AND TENURE, WITH PER CENT

[Corresponding figures for all

DIVISION OR STATE AND COLOR.	TOTAL NUMBER OF FARMS.		NUMBER OF FARMS OPERATED BY—			
			All owners.		Full owners (owning entire farm).	
	1920	1910	1920	1910	1920	1910
UNITED STATES.						
1 White	5,498,454	5,440,619	3,691,868	3,707,501	3,174,109	3,159,088
2 Colored	949,889	920,883	233,222	241,221	192,401	195,809
GEOGRAPHIC DIVISIONS.						
NEW ENGLAND:						
3 White	156,293	188,460	139,942	168,137	133,633	162,282
4 Colored	271	342	218	271	208	257
MIDDLE ATLANTIC:						
5 White	423,611	466,418	326,129	353,622	303,715	328,138
6 Colored	1,536	1,961	975	1,414	888	1,285
EAST NORTH CENTRAL:						
7 White	1,080,267	1,117,772	763,702	805,136	657,369	674,220
8 Colored	4,477	5,717	3,084	3,908	2,578	3,019
WEST NORTH CENTRAL:						
9 White	1,090,032	1,100,084	706,280	751,577	539,189	573,778
10 Colored	6,919	9,864	4,876	7,369	4,060	6,288
SOUTH ATLANTIC:						
11 White	775,144	756,019	504,426	491,193	463,541	440,644
12 Colored	383,832	355,862	102,663	101,961	83,022	80,914
EAST SOUTH CENTRAL:						
13 White	744,368	717,262	470,268	451,715	422,252	392,657
14 Colored	307,232	325,218	55,540	58,737	45,802	46,320
WEST SOUTH CENTRAL:						
15 White	764,238	734,125	404,942	383,136	341,411	320,799
16 Colored	231,850	209,061	59,386	57,769	49,734	48,056
MOUNTAIN:						
17 White	238,662	175,418	198,153	153,169	160,854	137,388
18 Colored	5,447	8,028	4,362	7,675	4,240	7,641
PACIFIC:						
19 White	225,839	185,061	178,026	149,816	152,145	129,182
20 Colored	8,325	4,830	2,118	2,117	1,869	2,029
NEW ENGLAND.						
MAINE:						
21 White	48,214	59,987	45,424	56,429	44,211	55,324
22 Colored	13	29	13	25	13	25
NEW HAMPSHIRE:						
23 White	20,509	27,038	18,592	24,481	17,824	23,702
24 Colored	14	15	12	12	12	12
VERMONT:						
25 White	29,047	32,689	25,100	28,048	23,906	26,777
26 Colored	28	20	21	17	20	16
MASSACHUSETTS:						
27 White	31,880	36,793	27,980	31,966	26,411	30,599
28 Colored	121	124	107	109	104	106
RHODE ISLAND:						
29 White	4,063	5,251	3,231	4,058	2,957	3,806
30 Colored	20	41	14	29	14	25
CONNECTICUT:						
31 White	22,580	26,702	19,615	23,155	18,324	22,074
32 Colored	75	113	51	79	15	73
MIDDLE ATLANTIC.						
NEW YORK:						
33 White	192,645	214,658	151,288	165,866	138,762	151,616
34 Colored	550	939	429	808	391	727
NEW JERSEY:						
35 White	29,167	33,011	21,604	23,868	20,493	22,750
36 Colored	535	476	285	265	259	242
PENNSYLVANIA:						
37 White	201,799	218,749	153,237	163,888	144,460	153,772
38 Colored	451	546	261	341	238	316

DISTRIBUTION BY TENURE, BY DIVISIONS AND STATES: 1920 AND 1910.

farmers, by tenure, in Table 23.]

| NUMBER OF FARMS OPERATED BY— | | | | | | PER CENT OF ALL FARMS OPERATED BY— | | | | | | |
| Part owners (hiring additional land). | | Managers. | | Tenants. | | Owners. | | Managers. | | Tenants. | | |
1920	1910	1920	1910	1920	1910	1920	1910	1920	1910	1920	1910	
517,759	548,413	66,223	56,560	1,740,363	1,676,558	67.1	68.1	1.2	1.0	31.7	30.8	1
40,821	45,412	2,226	1,544	714,441	678,118	24.6	26.2	0.2	0.2	75.2	73.6	2
6,309	5,855	4,784	5,360	11,567	14,963	89.5	89.2	3.1	2.8	7.4	7.9	3
10	14	18	19	35	52	80.4	79.2	6.6	5.6	12.9	15.2	4
22,414	25,484	9,763	9,000	87,719	103,796	77.0	75.8	2.3	1.9	20.7	22.3	5
87	129	90	72	471	475	63.5	72.1	5.9	3.7	30.7	24.2	6
106,333	130,916	13,480	10,774	303,085	301,862	70.7	72.0	1.2	1.0	28.1	27.0	7
506	889	71	74	1,322	1,735	68.9	68.4	1.6	1.3	29.5	30.3	8
167,091	177,799	10,692	8,318	373,060	340,199	64.8	68.3	1.0	0.8	34.2	30.9	9
816	1,081	84	76	1,959	2,419	70.5	74.7	1.2	0.8	28.3	24.5	10
40,885	50,549	8,842	7,578	261,876	257,248	65.1	65.0	1.1	1.0	33.8	34.0	11
19,641	21,047	957	720	280,212	253,181	26.7	28.7	0.2	0.2	73.0	71.1	12
48,016	59,058	3,099	3,041	271,001	262,506	63.2	63.0	0.4	0.4	36.4	36.6	13
9,738	12,417	407	249	251,285	266,232	18.1	18.1	0.1	0.1	81.8	81.9	14
63,531	62,337	4,607	4,465	354,689	346,524	53.0	52.2	0.6	0.6	46.4	47.2	15
9,652	9,713	406	231	172,058	151,061	25.6	27.6	0.2	0.1	74.2	72.3	16
37,299	15,781	4,089	2,890	36,420	19,359	83.0	87.3	1.7	1.6	15.3	11.0	17
122	34	27	22	1,058	331	80.1	95.6	0.5	0.3	19.4	4.1	18
25,881	20,634	6,867	5,144	40,946	30,101	78.8	81.0	3.0	2.8	18.1	16.3	19
249	88	166	81	6,041	2,632	25.4	43.8	2.0	1.7	72.6	54.5	20
1,213	1,105	786	998	2,004	2,560	94.2	94.1	1.6	1.7	4.2	4.3	21
....	....	....	1	....	3	100.0	86.2	......	3.4	....	10.3	22
768	779	545	680	1,372	1,877	90.7	90.5	2.7	2.5	6.7	6.9	23
....	....	1	1	1	2	85.7	80.0	7.1	6.7	7.1	13.3	24
1,194	1,271	565	635	3,382	4,006	86.4	85.8	1.9	1.9	11.6	12.3	25
1	1	3	1	4	2	75.0	85.0	10.7	5.0	14.3	10.0	26
1,569	1,367	1,620	1,859	2,280	2,968	87.8	86.9	5.1	5.1	7.2	8.1	27
3	3	7	4	7	11	88.4	87.9	5.8	3.2	5.8	8.9	28
274	252	204	251	628	942	79.5	77.3	5.0	4.8	15.5	17.9	29
....	4	1	....	....	5	70.0	70.7	5.0	......	25.0	29.3	30
1,291	1,081	1,064	937	1,901	2,610	86.9	86.7	4.7	3.5	8.4	9.8	31
6	6	6	12	18	22	68.0	69.9	8.0	10.6	24.0	19.5	32
12,526	14,250	4,351	4,037	37,006	44,755	78.5	77.3	2.3	1.9	19.2	20.8	33
38	81	25	14	96	117	78.0	86.0	4.5	1.5	17.5	12.5	34
1,111	1,118	967	1,033	6,596	8,110	74.1	72.3	3.3	3.1	22.6	24.6	35
26	23	20	27	230	184	53.3	55.7	3.7	5.7	43.0	38.7	36
8,777	10,116	4,445	3,930	44,117	50,931	75.9	74.9	2.2	1.8	21.9	23.3	37
23	25	45	31	145	174	57.9	62.5	10.0	5.7	32.2	31.9	38

TABLE 37.—NUMBER OF FARMS, BY COLOR AND TENURE, WITH PER CENT DIS-

Corresponding figures for all

| | DIVISION OR STATE AND COLOR. | TOTAL NUMBER OF FARMS. | | NUMBER OF FARMS OPERATED BY— | | | |
| | | | | All owners. | | Full owners (owning entire farm). | |
		1920	1910	1920	1910	1920	1910
	EAST NORTH CENTRAL.						
	OHIO:						
1	White	255,079	270,095	176,933	190,791	156,214	161,999
2	Colored	1,616	1,950	1,053	1,313	902	983
	INDIANA:						
3	White	204,554	214,680	136,904	148,029	112,452	115,110
4	Colored	572	805	306	472	212	314
	ILLINOIS:						
5	White	236,288	250,447	132,040	144,318	100,521	106,730
6	Colored	893	1,425	534	789	382	570
	MICHIGAN:						
7	White	195,714	206,014	158,843	171,525	139,388	150,337
8	Colored	733	946	563	785	486	668
	WISCONSIN:						
9	White	188,632	176,536	158,982	150,473	148,794	140,044
10	Colored	663	591	628	549	596	484
	WEST NORTH CENTRAL.						
	MINNESOTA:						
11	White	178,271	155,844	132,567	121,910	112,721	99,320
12	Colored	207	293	177	194	159	173
	IOWA:						
13	White	213,330	216,843	121,814	132,867	98,948	106,369
14	Colored	109	201	74	136	60	95
	MISSOURI:						
15	White	260,178	273,578	183,386	190,176	152,547	151,318
16	Colored	2,826	3,666	1,644	2,109	1,305	1,489
	NORTH DAKOTA:						
17	White	77,147	73,617	56,448	62,485	33,627	43,950
18	Colored	543	743	469	727	424	717
	SOUTH DAKOTA:						
19	White	73,025	74,836	46,350	55,248	25,913	37,733
20	Colored	1,612	2,808	1,465	2,736	1,340	2,672
	NEBRASKA:						
21	White	124,033	129,216	69,418	78,881	50,352	57,869
22	Colored	384	462	254	369	213	353
	KANSAS:						
23	White	164,048	176,150	96,297	110,010	65,081	77,219
24	Colored	1,238	1,691	793	1,098	559	789
	SOUTH ATLANTIC.						
	DELAWARE:						
25	White	9,268	9,914	5,655	5,772	5,383	5,518
26	Colored	872	922	355	406	305	347
	MARYLAND:						
27	White	41,699	42,551	29,256	29,569	27,751	27,819
28	Colored	6,209	6,372	3,549	3,950	3,091	3,301
	DISTRICT OF COLUMBIA:						
29	White	184	205	91	110	83	105
30	Colored	20	12	9	8	8	0
	VIRGINIA:						
31	White	138,456	135,904	105,414	101,430	95,934	91,144
32	Colored	47,180	48,114	30,949	32,228	25,520	26,820
	WEST VIRGINIA:						
33	White	86,785	95,977	71,698	75,420	65,854	67,831
34	Colored	504	708	403	558	366	487
	NORTH CAROLINA:						
35	White	193,473	188,069	129,099	123,877	115,482	106,560
36	Colored	76,290	65,656	22,277	21,443	16,365	14,822
	SOUTH CAROLINA:						
37	White	83,683	79,636	44,965	43,978	41,811	39,446
38	Colored	109,010	96,798	22,759	20,372	18,278	16,077
	GEORGIA:						
39	White	180,545	168,468	86,081	82,930	80,891	75,909
40	Colored	130,187	122,559	16,042	15,698	13,684	12,859
	FLORIDA:						
41	White	41,051	35,295	32,167	28,101	30,352	26,312
42	Colored	12,954	14,721	6,320	7,298	5,405	6,195

TRIBUTION BY TENURE, BY DIVISIONS AND STATES: 1920 AND 1910—Continued.

farmers, by tenure, in Table 23.]

NUMBER OF FARMS OPERATED BY—						PER CENT OF ALL FARMS OPERATED BY—						
Part owners (hiring additional land).		Managers.		Tenants.		Owners.		Managers.		Tenants.		
1920	1910	1920	1910	1920	1910	1920	1910	1920	1910	1920	1910	
20,719	28,792	3,029	2,725	75,117	76,579	69.4	70.6	1.2	1.0	29.4	28.4	1
151	330	36	28	527	609	65.2	67.3	2.2	1.4	32.6	31.2	2
24,452	32,919	2,315	2,282	65,335	64,369	66.9	68.9	1.1	1.1	31.9	30.0	3
94	158	14	15	252	318	53.5	58.6	2.4	1.9	44.1	39.5	4
31,519	37,588	3,402	2,368	100,846	103,761	55.9	57.6	1.4	0.9	42.7	41.4	5
152	219	9	18	350	618	59.8	55.4	1.0	1.3	39.2	43.4	6
19,455	21,188	2,310	1,952	34,561	32,537	81.2	83.3	1.2	0.9	17.7	15.8	7
77	117	9	9	161	152	76.8	83.0	1.2	1.0	22.0	16.1	8
10,188	10,429	2,424	1,447	27,226	24,616	84.3	85.2	1.3	0.8	14.4	13.9	9
32	65	3	4	32	38	94.7	92.9	0.5	0.7	4.8	6.4	10
19,846	22,590	1,595	1,220	44,109	32,714	74.4	78.2	0.9	0.8	24.7	21.0	11
18	21	1	2	29	97	85.5	66.2	0.5	0.7	14.0	33.1	12
22,866	26,498	2,486	1,924	89,030	82,052	57.1	61.3	1.2	0.9	41.7	37.8	13
14	41	1	2	34	63	67.9	67.7	0.9	1.0	31.2	31.3	14
30,839	38,858	2,199	1,960	74,593	81,442	70.5	69.5	0.8	0.7	28.7	29.8	15
339	620	48	41	1,134	1,516	58.2	57.5	1.7	1.1	40.1	41.4	16
22,821	18,535	853	482	19,846	10,650	73.2	84.9	1.1	0.7	25.7	14.5	17
45	10	2	2	72	14	86.4	97.8	0.4	0.3	13.3	1.9	18
20,437	17,515	771	422	25,904	19,166	63.5	73.8	1.1	0.6	35.5	25.6	19
125	64	10	7	137	65	90.9	97.4	0.6	0.2	8.5	2.3	20
19,066	21,012	1,311	986	53,304	49,349	56.0	61.0	1.1	0.8	43.0	38.2	21
41	16	4	1	126	92	66.1	79.9	1.0	0.2	32.8	19.9	22
31,216	32,791	1,477	1,314	66,274	64,826	58.7	62.5	0.9	0.7	40.4	36.8	23
234	309	18	21	427	572	64.1	64.9	1.5	1.2	34.5	33.8	24
272	254	131	107	3,482	4,035	61.0	58.2	1.4	1.1	37.6	40.7	25
50	59	13	16	504	500	40.7	44.0	1.5	1.7	57.8	54.2	26
1,505	1,750	1,111	901	11,332	12,081	70.2	69.5	2.7	2.1	27.2	28.4	27
458	649	151	87	2,509	2,335	57.2	62.0	2.4	1.4	40.4	36.6	28
8	5	18	14	75	81	49.5	53.7	9.8	6.8	40.8	39.5	29
1	2	1	1	10	3	45.0	66.7	5.0	8.3	50.0	25.0	30
9,480	10,292	1,937	1,445	31,105	33,023	76.1	74.6	1.4	1.1	22.5	24.3	31
5,429	5,408	197	180	16,640	15,706	64.8	67.0	0.4	0.4	34.8	32.6	32
5,844	7,589	1,082	865	14,005	19,692	82.6	78.6	1.2	0.9	16.1	20.5	33
37	71	8	7	93	143	80.0	78.8	1.6	1.0	18.5	20.2	34
13,617	17,317	832	1,044	63,542	63,148	66.7	65.9	0.4	0.6	32.8	33.6	35
5,912	6,621	96	74	53,917	44,139	29.2	32.7	0.1	0.1	70.7	67.2	36
3,154	4,532	555	732	38,163	34,926	53.7	55.2	0.7	0.9	45.6	43.9	37
4,481	4,295	183	131	86,068	76,295	20.9	21.0	0.2	0.1	79.0	78.8	38
5,190	7,021	1,448	1,296	93,016	84,242	47.7	49.2	0.8	0.8	51.5	50.0	39
2,358	2,839	207	123	113,938	106,738	12.3	12.8	0.2	0.1	87.5	87.1	40
1,815	1,789	1,728	1,174	7,156	6,020	78.4	79.6	4.2	3.3	17.4	17.1	41
915	1,103	101	101	6,533	7,322	48.8	49.6	0.8	0.7	50.4	49.7	42

TABLE **37.**—NUMBER OF FARMS, BY COLOR AND TENURE, WITH PER CENT DIS-

[Corresponding figures for all

	DIVISION OR STATE AND COLOR.	TOTAL NUMBER OF FARMS.		NUMBER OF FARMS OPERATED BY—			
				All owners.		Full owners (owning entire farm).	
		1920	1910	1920	1910	1920	1910
	EAST SOUTH CENTRAL.						
	KENTUCKY:						
1	White	257,998	247,455	174,008	164,403	155,026	144,366
2	Colored	12,628	11,730	5,319	5,929	4,180	4,466
	TENNESSEE:						
3	White	214,592	207,704	138,242	133,425	121,661	112,341
4	Colored	38,182	38,308	9,840	10,700	7,871	7,740
	ALABAMA:						
5	White	160,896	152,458	89,887	86,847	81,885	74,580
6	Colored	95,203	110,443	17,202	17,082	13,663	13,009
	MISSISSIPPI:						
7	White	110,882	109,645	68,131	67,040	63,680	61,370
8	Colored	161,219	164,737	23,179	25,026	20,088	21,105
	WEST SOUTH CENTRAL.						
	ARKANSAS:						
9	White	160,322	151,085	97,274	91,987	85,171	76,006
10	Colored	72,282	63,593	15,373	14,662	12,866	11,860
	LOUISIANA:						
11	White	73,404	65,667	46,268	42,264	42,422	38,991
12	Colored	62,059	54,879	10,986	10,725	9,473	9,599
	OKLAHOMA:						
13	White	173,263	169,521	83,729	74,254	61,784	54,965
14	Colored	18,725	20,671	9,488	11,150	8,002	9,919
	TEXAS:						
15	White	357,249	347,852	177,671	174,631	152,034	150,837
16	Colored	78,784	69,918	23,539	21,232	19,393	16,678
	MOUNTAIN.						
	MONTANA:						
17	White	56,614	25,018	49,286	22,198	37,491	20,359
18	Colored	1,063	1,196	985	1,167	940	1,166
	IDAHO:						
19	White	41,598	30,402	34,284	26,826	29,948	24,604
20	Colored	508	405	363	343	351	336
	WYOMING:						
21	White	15,579	10,922	13,280	9,718	10,563	8,617
22	Colored	169	65	123	61	118	60
	COLORADO:						
23	White	59,381	45,596	45,043	36,527	35,339	32,016
24	Colored	553	574	248	466	214	458
	NEW MEXICO:						
25	White	27,969	33,528	24,113	31,277	19,894	28,306
26	Colored	1,875	2,148	1,643	2,121	1,639	2,111
	ARIZONA:						
27	White	9,329	6,024	7,316	5,054	6,423	4,610
28	Colored	646	3,203	553	3,149	547	3,149
	UTAH:						
29	White	25,248	21,400	22,340	19,546	18,908	16,967
30	Colored	414	276	239	216	226	200
	NEVADA:						
31	White	2,944	2,528	2,491	2,020	2,288	1,909
32	Colored	215	161	208	152	205	152
	PACIFIC.						
	WASHINGTON:						
33	White	65,022	55,067	52,184	46,804	44,355	41,046
34	Colored	1,266	1,125	517	701	477	683
	OREGON:						
35	White	49,633	44,875	39,505	37,318	32,989	32,515
36	Colored	573	627	358	478	311	467
	CALIFORNIA:						
37	White	111,184	85,119	86,337	65,694	74,801	55,621
38	Colored	6,486	3,078	1,243	938	1,081	879

[1]Less than one-tenth of 1 per cent.

TRIBUTION BY TENURE, BY DIVISIONS AND STATES: 1920 AND 1910—Continued.

farmers, by tenure, in Table 23.]

| NUMBER OF FARMS OPERATED BY— | | | | | | PER CENT OF ALL FARMS OPERATED BY— | | | | | | |
| Part owners (hiring additional land). | | Managers. | | Tenants. | | Owners. | | Managers. | | Tenants. | | |
1920	1910	1920	1910	1920	1910	1920	1910	1920	1910	1920	1910	
18,982	20,037	934	953	83,056	82,099	67.4	66.4	0.4	0.4	32.2	33.2	1
1,139	1,463	35	40	7,274	5,761	42.1	50.5	0.3	0.3	57.6	49.1	2
16,581	21,084	754	775	75,596	73,504	64.4	64.2	0.4	0.4	35.2	35.4	3
1,969	2,960	53	51	28,289	27,557	25.8	27.9	0.1	0.1	74.1	71.9	4
8,002	12,267	614	594	70,395	65,017	55.9	57.0	0.4	0.4	43.8	42.6	5
3,539	4,073	127	52	77,874	93,309	18.1	15.5	0.1	(1)	81.8	84.5	6
4,451	5,670	797	719	41,954	41,886	61.4	61.1	0.7	0.7	37.8	38.2	7
3,091	3,921	192	106	137,848	139,605	14.4	15.2	0.1	0.1	85.5	84.7	8
12,103	15,981	641	717	62,407	58,381	60.7	60.9	0.4	0.5	38.9	38.6	9
2,507	2,802	95	46	56,814	48,885	21.3	23.1	0.1	0.1	78.6	76.9	10
3,846	3,273	736	873	26,400	22,530	63.0	64.4	1.0	1.3	36.0	34.3	11
1,513	1,126	92	77	50,981	44,077	17.7	19.5	0.1	0.1	82.1	80.3	12
21,945	19,289	850	624	88,684	94,643	48.3	43.8	0.5	0.4	51.2	55.8	13
1,486	1,231	85	27	9,152	9,494	50.7	53.9	0.5	0.1	48.9	45.9	14
25,637	23,794	2,380	2,251	177,198	170,970	49.7	50.2	0.7	0.6	49.6	49.2	15
4,146	4,554	134	81	55,111	48,605	29.9	30.4	0.2	0.1	70.0	69.5	16
11,795	1,839	889	502	6,439	2,318	87.1	88.7	1.6	2.0	11.4	9.3	17
45	1	10	3	68	26	92.7	97.6	0.9	0.3	6.4	2.2	18
4,336	2,222	758	450	6,556	3,126	82.4	88.2	1.8	1.5	15.8	10.3	19
12	7	....	....	145	62	71.5	84.7	....	....	28.5	15.3	20
2,717	1,101	377	310	1,922	894	85.2	89.0	2.4	2.8	12.3	8.2	21
5	1	....	1	46	3	72.8	93.8	....	1.5	27.2	4.6	22
9,704	4,511	874	786	13,464	8,283	75.9	80.1	1.5	1.7	22.7	18.2	23
34	8	6	1	299	107	44.8	81.2	1.1	0.2	54.1	18.6	24
4,219	2,971	431	317	3,425	1,934	86.2	93.3	1.5	0.9	12.2	5.8	25
4	10	2	4	230	23	87.6	98.7	0.1	0.2	12.3	1.1	26
893	444	300	152	1,713	818	78.4	83.9	3.2	2.5	18.4	13.6	27
6	....	5	11	88	43	85.6	98.3	0.8	0.3	13.6	1.3	28
3,432	2,579	293	193	2,615	1,661	88.5	91.3	1.2	0.9	10.4	7.8	29
13	7	3	1	172	59	57.7	78.3	0.7	0.4	41.5	21.4	30
203	114	167	180	286	325	84.6	80.0	5.7	7.1	9.7	12.9	31
3	....	1	1	10	8	95.0	94.4	0.5	0.6	4.6	5.0	32
7,829	5,758	1,159	950	11,679	7,313	80.3	85.0	1.8	1.7	18.0	13.3	33
40	18	9	11	740	413	40.8	62.3	0.7	1.0	58.5	36.7	34
6,516	4,803	908	839	9,220	6,718	79.6	83.2	1.8	1.9	18.6	15.0	35
47	11	8	8	207	141	62.5	76.2	1.4	1.3	36.1	22.5	36
11,536	10,073	4,800	3,355	20,047	16,070	77.7	77.2	4.3	3.9	18.0	18.9	37
162	59	149	62	5,094	2,078	19.2	30.5	2.3	2.0	78.5	67.5	38

TABLE 38.—FARMS OPERATED BY WHITE AND COLORED TENANTS CLASSIFIED

[Corresponding figures for all

	DIVISION OR STATE AND COLOR.	TOTAL NUMBER OF FARMS OPERATED BY TENANTS.		SHARE TENANTS.			
				1920			1910
		1920	1910	Total, including croppers.	Share tenants proper.	Croppers.[1]	
	UNITED STATES.						
1	White..............	1,740,363	1,676,558	1,163,942	936,564	227,378	1,026,372
2	Colored............	714,441	678,118	514,870	181,157	333,713	373,551
	GEOGRAPHIC DIVISIONS.						
	NEW ENGLAND:						
3	White..........	11,567	14,963	2,691	2,691	....	2,607
4	Colored........	35	52	7	7	....	4
	MIDDLE ATLANTIC:						
5	White..........	87,719	103,796	50,933	50,933	....	54,748
6	Colored........	471	475	241	241	....	210
	EAST NORTH CENTRAL:						
7	White..........	303,085	301,862	181,354	181,354	....	169,637
8	Colored........	1,322	1,735	929	929	....	1,075
	WEST NORTH CENTRAL:						
9	White..........	373,060	340,199	185,362	185,362	....	165,699
10	Colored........	1,959	2,419	1,342	1,342	....	1,397
	SOUTH ATLANTIC:						
11	White..........	261,876	257,248	192,205	115,907	76,298	164,178
12	Colored........	280,212	253,181	197,307	71,079	126,228	135,203
	EAST SOUTH CENTRAL:						
13	White..........	271,001	262,506	210,698	129,217	81,481	181,694
14	Colored........	251,285	266,232	167,027	46,224	120,803	126,229
	WEST SOUTH CENTRAL:						
15	White..........	354,689	346,524	298,988	229,389	69,599	265,498
16	Colored........	172,058	151,061	146,090	59,408	86,682	108,874
	MOUNTAIN:						
17	White..........	36,420	19,359	23,524	23,524	....	10,256
18	Colored........	1,058	331	444	444	....	93
	PACIFIC:						
19	White..........	40,946	30,101	18,187	18,187	....	12,055
20	Colored........	6,041	2,632	1,483	1,483	....	466
	NEW ENGLAND.						
	MAINE:						
21	White..........	2,004	2,560	292	292	....	289
22	Colored........	....	3	....	....		
	NEW HAMPSHIRE:						
23	White..........	1,372	1,877	120	120	....	151
24	Colored........	1	2				
	VERMONT:						
25	White..........	3,382	4,006	1,620	1,620	....	1,641
26	Colored........	4	2	1	1	....	1
	MASSACHUSETTS:						
27	White..........	2,280	2,968	330	330	....	214
28	Colored........	7	11				
	RHODE ISLAND:						
29	White..........	628	942	22	22	....	27
30	Colored........	5	12	......	....	....	
	CONNECTICUT:						
31	White..........	1,001	1,810	307	307	....	285
32	Colored........	18	22	6	6	....	3
	MIDDLE ATLANTIC.						
	NEW YORK:						
33	White..........	37,006	44,755	20,818	20,818	....	23,033
34	Colored........	96	117	46	46	....	53
	NEW JERSEY:						
35	White..........	6,596	8,110	3,466	3,466	....	3,816
36	Colored........	230	184	134	134	....	105
	PENNSYLVANIA:						
37	White..........	44,117	50,931	26,649	26,649	....	27,899
38	Colored........	145	174	61	61	....	52

[1] Reported in the Southern states only.

ACCORDING TO FORM OF TENANCY, BY DIVISIONS AND STATES: 1920 AND 1910.

farmers, by tenure, in Table 24.]

SHARE-CASH TENANTS.		CASH TENANTS.				UNSPECIFIED TENANTS.		
		1920			1910			
1920	1910	Total, including standing renters.	Cash tenants proper.	Standing renters.[1]	1910	1920	1910	
119,395	113,843	400,907	373,835	27,072	447,851	56,119	88,492	1
8,427	14,623	184,098	106,174	77,924	264,443	7,046	25,501	2
95	215	8,045	8,045	....	9,750	736	2,391	3
....	1	26	26	....	37	2	10	4
1,122	2,224	32,671	32,671	....	40,742	2,993	6,082	5
5	8	208	208	....	216	17	41	6
33,487	33,427	76,650	76,650	....	83,641	11,594	15,157	7
50	124	295	295	....	441	48	95	8
68,235	50,812	107,148	107,148	....	102,170	12,315	21,518	9
81	171	420	420	....	713	116	138	10
1,241	5,336	60,515	37,685	22,830	74,953	7,915	12,781	11
736	4,781	79,392	26,909	52,483	101,664	2,777	11,533	12
3,279	7,565	46,162	42,671	3,491	65,284	10,862	7,963	13
3,516	4,990	78,316	56,556	21,760	126,968	2,426	8,045	14
9,945	12,546	39,308	38,557	751	51,857	6,448	16,623	15
3,955	4,447	20,491	16,810	3,681	32,334	1,522	5,406	16
777	606	10,363	10,363	....	5,504	1,756	2,993	17
9	9	553	553	....	157	52	72	18
1,214	1,112	20,045	20,045	....	13,950	1,500	2,984	19
75	92	4,397	4,397	....	1,913	86	161	20
11	44	1,569	1,569	....	1,731	132	496	21
....	....	....	....	....	2	....	1	22
5	29	1,073	1,073	....	1,223	174	474	23
....	....	....	....	....	1	1	1	24
26	50	1,487	1,487	....	2,181	249	134	25
....	....	2	2	....	1	1	....	26
23	42	1,759	1,759	....	2,107	168	605	27
....	1	7	7	....	8	....	2	28
....	8	604	604	....	728	2	179	29
....	....	5	5	....	10	....	2	30
30	42	1,553	1,553	....	1,780	11	503	31
....	....	12	12	....	15	....	4	32
355	1,013	14,634	14,634	....	18,461	1,199	2,248	33
1	....	42	42	....	58	7	6	34
39	171	2,896	2,896	....	3,445	195	678	35
1	6	87	87	....	54	8	19	36
728	1,040	15,141	15,141	....	18,836	1,599	3,156	37
3	2	79	79	....	104	2	16	38

Table 38.—FARMS OPERATED BY WHITE AND COLORED TENANTS CLASSIFIED

[Corresponding figures for all

	DIVISION OR STATE AND COLOR.	TOTAL NUMBER OF FARMS OPERATED BY TENANTS.		SHARE TENANTS.			
					1920		1910
		1920	1910	Total, including croppers.	Share tenants proper.	Croppers.[1]	
	EAST NORTH CENTRAL.						
	OHIO:						
1	White	75,117	76,579	50,291	50,291	....	49,577
2	Colored	527	609	374	374	....	395
	INDIANA:						
3	White	65,335	64,369	48,287	48,287	....	45,343
4	Colored	252	318	186	186	....	230
	ILLINOIS:						
5	White	100,846	102,761	45,037	45,037	....	43,220
6	Colored	350	618	244	244	....	331
	MICHIGAN:						
7	White	34,561	32,537	23,164	23,164	....	20,270
8	Colored	161	152	116	116	....	108
	WISCONSIN:						
9	White	27,226	24,616	14,575	14,575	....	11,227
10	Colored	32	38	9	9	....	11
	WEST NORTH CENTRAL.						
	MINNESOTA:						
11	White	44,109	32,714	18,967	18,967	....	18,453
12	Colored	29	97	9	9	....	18
	IOWA:						
13	White	89,030	82,052	25,590	25,590	....	20,908
14	Colored	34	63	16	16	....	27
	MISSOURI:						
15	White	74,593	81,442	45,367	45,367	....	45,785
16	Colored	1,134	1,516	878	878	....	959
	NORTH DAKOTA:						
17	White	19,846	10,650	16,909	16,909	....	8,079
18	Colored	72	14	34	34	....	7
	SOUTH DAKOTA:						
19	White	25,904	19,166	12,209	12,209	....	11,137
20	Colored	137	65	60	60	....	19
	NEBRASKA:						
21	White	53,304	49,349	25,477	25,477	....	24,743
22	Colored	126	92	59	59	....	28
	KANSAS:						
23	White	66,274	64,826	40,843	40,843	....	36,594
24	Colored	427	572	286	286	....	339
	SOUTH ATLANTIC.						
	DELAWARE:						
25	White	3,482	4,035	2,882	2,748	134	3,201
26	Colored	504	500	432	358	74	421
	MARYLAND:						
27	White	11,332	12,081	8,906	8,048	858	8,433
28	Colored	2,509	2,335	2,105	1,504	601	1,685
	DISTRICT OF COLUMBIA:						
29	White	75	81	5	5	....	2
30	Colored	10	3	1	1	....	....
	VIRGINIA:						
31	White	31,105	33,023	23,840	16,140	7,700	22,566
32	Colored	16,640	15,706	13,921	7,906	6,015	10,906
	WEST VIRGINIA:						
33	White	14,005	19,692	6,913	5,297	1,616	9,498
34	Colored	93	143	46	34	12	78
	NORTH CAROLINA:						
35	White	63,542	63,148	52,565	35,990	16,575	48,606
36	Colored	53,917	44,139	46,193	22,829	23,364	31,609
	SOUTH CAROLINA:						
37	White	38,163	34,926	25,854	14,900	10,954	18,471
38	Colored	86,068	76,295	56,358	23,523	32,835	34,169
	GEORGIA:						
39	White	93,016	84,242	67,160	30,938	36,222	51,040
40	Colored	113,938	106,738	75,372	14,097	61,275	54,464
	FLORIDA:						
41	White	7,156	6,020	4,080	1,841	2,239	2,361
42	Colored	6,533	7,322	2,879	827	2,052	1,871

[1] Reported in the Southern states only.

ACCORDING TO FORM OF TENANCY, BY DIVISIONS AND STATES: 1920 AND 1910—Con.

farmers, by tenure, in Table 24.]

SHARE-CASH TENANTS.		CASH TENANTS.				UNSPECIFIED TENANTS.		
		1920			1910			
1920	1910	Total, including standing renters.	Cash tenants proper.	Standing renters.[1]		1920	1910	
1,562	3,428	19,181	19,181	....	20,914	4,083	2,660	1
16	34	117	117	....	154	20	26	2
3,795	4,874	10,564	10,564	....	10,575	2,689	3,577	3
5	22	51	51	....	61	10	5	4
27,352	23,605	26,230	26,230	....	31,947	2,227	4,989	5
27	60	70	70	....	173	9	54	6
421	864	9,277	9,277	....	9,592	1,699	1,811	7
1	6	35	35	....	37	9	1	8
357	656	11,398	11,398	....	10,613	896	2,120	9
1	2	22	22	....	16	....	9	10
8,374	3,772	15,237	15,237	....	7,846	1,531	2,643	11
1	2	14	14	....	72	5	5	12
16,399	14,120	44,572	44,572	....	43,367	2,469	3,657	13
2	9	14	14	....	27	2	....	14
6,948	8,439	17,133	17,133	....	24,051	5,145	3,167	15
47	114	159	159	....	410	50	33	16
890	178	1,151	1,151	....	322	896	2,071	17
1	....	24	24	....	2	13	5	18
7,888	3,665	5,278	5,278	....	2,281	529	2,083	19
3	3	50	50	....	20	24	23	20
14,763	11,060	12,253	12,253	....	10,667	811	2,879	21
10	9	54	54	....	34	3	21	22
12,973	9,578	11,524	11,524	....	13,636	934	5,018	23
17	34	105	105	....	148	19	51	24
9	43	445	444	1	564	146	227	25
2	4	39	38	1	55	31	20	26
32	169	2,002	1,991	11	2,533	392	946	27
6	35	304	297	7	405	94	210	28
1	....	65	65	....	79	4	....	29
1	....	6	6	....	3	2	....	30
265	826	5,369	5,338	31	7,752	1,631	1,879	31
72	382	2,247	2,239	8	3,661	400	757	32
211	921	5,592	5,581	11	8,498	1,289	775	33
1	2	35	35	....	62	11	1	34
304	1,112	8,798	6,212	2,586	10,598	1,875	2,832	35
164	921	7,118	3,213	3,905	10,110	442	1,499	36
167	830	11,457	4,742	6,715	13,610	685	2,015	37
354	1,496	28,615	11,027	17,588	36,658	741	3,972	38
226	1,294	24,156	10,718	13,438	28,772	1,474	3,136	39
129	1,795	37,664	7,460	30,204	46,451	773	4,028	40
26	141	2,631	2,594	37	2,547	419	971	41
7	146	3,364	2,594	770	4,259	283	1,046	42

TABLE **38.**—FARMS OPERATED BY WHITE AND COLORED TENANTS CLASSIFIED

[Corresponding figures for all

	DIVISION OR STATE AND COLOR.	TOTAL NUMBER OF FARMS OPERATED BY TENANTS.		SHARE TENANTS.			
				1920			1910
		1920	1910	Total, including croppers.	Share tenants proper.	Croppers.[1]	
	EAST SOUTH CENTRAL.						
	KENTUCKY:						
1	White...............	83,056	82,099	66,959	42,346	24,613	64,163
2	Colored..............	7,274	5,761	6,696	1,859	4,837	5,013
	TENNESSEE:						
3	White...............	75,596	73,504	60,864	37,405	23,459	52,990
4	Colored..............	28,289	27,557	20,371	5,752	14,619	15,257
	ALABAMA:						
5	White...............	70,395	65,017	51,209	30,496	20,713	39,665
6	Colored..............	77,874	93,309	36,467	9,283	27,184	27,687
	MISSISSIPPI:						
7	White...............	41,954	41,886	31,666	18,970	12,696	24,876
8	Colored..............	137,848	139,605	103,493	29,330	74,163	78,272
	WEST SOUTH CENTRAL.						
	ARKANSAS:						
9	White...............	62,407	58,381	49,970	34,993	14,977	40,971
10	Colored..............	56,814	48,885	44,914	12,226	32,688	27,582
	LOUISIANA:						
11	White...............	26,400	22,530	20,226	12,973	7,253	15,114
12	Colored..............	50,981	44,077	41,582	17,526	24,056	33,596
	OKLAHOMA:						
13	White...............	88,684	94,643	69,429	62,442	6,987	65,107
14	Colored..............	9,152	9,494	7,935	5,996	1,939	7,249
	TEXAS:						
15	White...............	177,198	170,970	159,363	118,981	40,382	144,306
16	Colored..............	55,111	48,605	51,659	23,660	27,999	40,447
	MOUNTAIN.						
	MONTANA:						
17	White...............	6,439	2,318	4,368	4,368	....	947
18	Colored..............	68	26	30	30	....	5
	IDAHO:						
19	White...............	6,556	3,126	4,007	4,007	....	1,632
20	Colored..............	145	62	16	16	....	7
	WYOMING:						
21	White...............	1,922	894	1,114	1,114	....	405
22	Colored..............	46	3	11	11	....	2
	COLORADO:						
23	White...............	13,464	8,283	9,451	9,451	....	4,853
24	Colored..............	299	107	124	124	....	60
	NEW MEXICO:						
25	White...............	3,425	1,934	2,250	2,250	....	1,222
26	Colored..............	230	23	219	219	....	11
	ARIZONA:						
27	White...............	1,713	818	871	871	....	270
28	Colored..............	88	43	16	16	....	2
	UTAH:						
29	White...............	2,615	1,661	1,346	1,346	....	833
30	Colored..............	172	59	23	23	....	4
	NEVADA:						
31	White...........	996	813	117	117	....	94
32	Colored..............	10	8	5	5	....	2
	PACIFIC.						
	WASHINGTON:						
33	White...............	11,679	7,313	5,816	5,816	....	3,429
34	Colored..............	740	413	35	35	....	30
	OREGON:						
35	White...............	9,220	6,718	4,054	4,054	....	2,890
36	Colored..............	207	141	122	122	....	37
	CALIFORNIA:						
37	White...............	20,047	16,070	8,317	8,317	....	5,736
38	Colored..............	5,094	2,078	1,326	1,326	....	399

[1] Reported in the Southern states only.

ACCORDING TO FORM OF TENANCY, BY DIVISIONS AND STATES: 1920 AND 1910—Con.

farmers, by tenure, in Table 24.]

SHARE-CASH TENANTS.		CASH TENANTS.				UNSPECIFIED TENANTS.		
		1920			1910			
1920	1910	Total, including standing renters.	Cash tenants proper.	Standing renters.¹		1920	1910	
2,124	3,278	9,689	9,382	307	12,228	4,284	2,430	1
97	146	240	236	4	473	241	129	2
733	2,385	10,518	9,961	557	16,398	3,481	1,731	3
103	499	7,365	4,850	2,515	11,038	450	763	4
219	1,139	17,287	15,675	1,612	22,125	1,680	2,088	5
211	1,289	40,407	30,819	9,588	61,235	789	3,098	6
203	763	8,668	7,653	1,015	14,533	1,417	1,714	7
3,105	3,056	30,304	20,651	9,653	54,222	946	4,055	8
1,552	1,530	8,913	8,523	390	13,301	1,972	2,579	9
2,285	1,500	9,258	8,896	362	17,104	357	2,699	10
200	454	5,548	5,358	190	5,763	426	1,199	11
993	908	7,957	5,547	2,410	8,723	449	850	12
3,800	3,714	14,675	14,654	21	20,353	780	5,469	13
102	248	1,035	1,026	9	1,398	80	599	14
4,393	6,848	10,172	10,022	150	12,440	3,270	7,376	15
575	1,791	2,241	1,341	900	5,109	636	1,258	16
160	51	1,722	1,722	....	780	189	540	17
....	....	35	35	....	10	3	11	18
153	130	1,972	1,972	....	764	424	600	19
1	1	117	117	....	43	11	11	20
43	27	594	594	....	265	171	197	21
....	....	10	10	....	1	25	....	22
300	227	3,212	3,212	....	2,191	501	1,012	23
4	6	163	163	....	20	8	21	24
39	50	884	884	....	436	252	226	25
....	1	10	10	....	4	1	7	26
27	18	783	783	....	434	32	96	27
....	....	70	70	....	32	2	9	28
53	96	1,032	1,032	....	448	184	284	29
3	1	144	144	....	42	2	12	30
2	7	164	164	....	186	3	38	31
1	....	4	4	....	5	....	1	32
268	197	5,144	5,144	....	2,799	451	888	33
1	58	686	686	....	290	18	35	34
276	244	4,307	4,307	....	2,941	583	643	35
2	1	75	75	....	96	8	7	36
670	671	10,594	10,594	....	8,210	466	1,453	37
72	33	3,636	3,636	....	1,527	60	119	38

TABLE 39.—ACREAGE OF FARM LAND, WITH PERCENTAGES AND AVERAGES, BY COLOR AND TENURE, BY DIVISIONS AND STATES: 1920 AND 1910.

[Corresponding figures for all farmers, by tenure, in Table 25.]

DIVISION OR STATE AND COLOR AND TENURE.	ALL LAND IN FARMS (ACRES).		IMPROVED LAND IN FARMS (ACRES).		PER CENT OF FARM LAND IMPROVED.		AVERAGE ACREAGE PER FARM.			
							All land.		Improved land.	
	1920	1910	1920	1910	1920	1910	1920	1910	1920	1910
UNITED STATES.										
White farmers:										
Total	910,939,194	832,166,020	473,774,566	449,418,265	52.0	54.0	165.7	153.0	86.2	82.6
Owners	620,070,823	579,478,154	306,029,220	301,504,138	49.4	52.0	168.0	156.3	82.9	81.3
Managers	53,653,478	53,304,976	13,009,436	12,166,563	24.2	22.8	810.2	942.5	196.4	215.1
Tenants	237,214,893	199,382,890	154,735,910	135,747,564	65.2	68.1	136.3	118.9	88.9	81.0
Colored farmers:										
Total	44,944,521	46,632,305	29,298,441	29,033,485	65.2	62.3	47.3	50.6	30.8	31.5
Owners	16,704,192	19,076,463	8,078,263	8,346,283	48.4	43.8	71.6	79.1	34.6	34.6
Managers	475,679	425,889	201,563	147,452	42.4	34.6	213.7	275.8	90.5	95.5
Tenants	27,764,650	27,129,953	21,018,615	20,539,750	75.7	75.7	38.9	40.0	29.4	30.3
GEOGRAPHIC DIVISIONS.										
NEW ENGLAND.										
White farmers:										
Total	16,969,976	19,698,623	6,107,456	7,248,822	36.0	36.8	108.6	104.5	39.1	38.5
Owners	14,693,218	17,077,699	5,275,353	6,255,311	35.9	36.6	105.0	101.6	37.7	37.2
Managers	976,421	1,085,389	321,871	376,001	33.0	34.6	204.1	202.5	67.3	70.1
Tenants	1,300,337	1,535,535	510,232	617,510	39.2	40.2	112.4	102.6	44.1	41.3
Colored farmers:										
Total	20,666	16,308	7,145	6,082	34.6	37.3	76.3	47.7	26.4	17.8
Owners	11,318	11,426	4,306	4,533	38.0	39.7	51.9	42.2	19.8	16.7
Managers	4,005	2,074	1,275	403	31.8	19.4	222.5	109.2	70.8	21.2
Tenants	5,343	2,808	1,564	1,146	29.3	40.8	152.7	54.0	44.7	22.0
MIDDLE ATLANTIC.										
White farmers:										
Total	40,476,772	43,078,966	26,499,833	29,250,638	65.5	67.9	95.6	92.4	62.6	62.7
Owners	28,969,267	30,212,503	18,745,081	20,246,673	64.7	67.0	88.8	85.4	57.5	57.3
Managers	1,913,201	1,707,010	1,020,914	905,549	53.4	53.0	196.0	189.7	104.6	100.6
Tenants	9,594,304	11,159,453	6,733,838	*8,098,416	70.2	72.6	109.4	107.5	76.8	78 0
Colored farmers:										
Total	96,129	112,090	62,274	70,256	64.8	62.7	62.6	57.2	40.5	35.8
Owners	49,414	70,765	31,543	41,387	63.8	58.5	50.7	50.0	32.4	29.3
Managers	9,836	7,074	6,765	4,869	68.8	68.8	109.3	98.3	75.2	67.6
Tenants	36,879	34,251	23,966	24,000	65.0	70.1	78.3	72.1	50.9	50.5
EAST NORTH CENTRAL.										
White farmers:										
Total	117,457,542	117,589,897	87,694,022	88,702,567	74.7	75.4	108.7	105.2	81.2	79.4
Owners	76,345,020	80,020,865	55,012,376	58,324,786	72.1	72.9	100.0	99.4	72.0	72.4
Managers	2,857,754	2,342,717	1,821,109	1,484,701	63.7	63.4	212.0	217.4	135.1	137.8
Tenants	38,254,768	35,226,315	30,860,537	28,893,080	80.7	82.0	126.2	116.7	101.8	95.7
Colored farmers:										
Total	277,637	339,751	200,813	244,661	72.3	72.1	69.0	59.3	44.9	42.8
Owners	173,031	213,455	117,125	145,240	67.9	68.0	56.1	54.6	38.1	37.2
Managers	9,481	11,488	7,682	8,620	81.0	75.0	133.5	155.2	108.2	116.5
Tenants	95,125	114,308	75,706	90,801	79.6	79.4	72.0	65.9	57.3	52.3
WEST NORTH CENTRAL.										
White farmers:										
Total	255,461,338	230,456,459	170,879,480	163,735,756	66.9	71.0	234.4	209.5	156.8	148.8
Owners	167,310,284	162,815,991	106,743,983	110,887,369	63.8	68.1	236.9	216.6	151.1	147.5
Managers	6,056,041	4,975,801	2,843,182	2,712,086	46.9	54.5	566.4	598.9	265.9	326.4
Tenants	82,095,013	62,664,667	61,292,315	50,136,301	74.7	80.0	220.1	184.2	164.3	147.4
Colored farmers:										
Total	1,511,891	2,191,662	514,959	549,106	34.1	25.1	218.5	222.2	74.4	55.7
Owners	1,259,796	1,973,874	359,353	392,216	28.5	19.9	258.4	267.9	73.7	53.2
Managers	23,161	29,498	12,907	14,583	55.7	49.4	275.7	388.1	153.7	191.9
Tenants	228,934	188,290	142,699	142,307	62.3	75.6	116.9	77.8	72.8	58.8

TABLE 39.—ACREAGE OF FARM LAND, WITH PERCENTAGES AND AVERAGES, BY COLOR AND TENURE, BY DIVISIONS AND STATES: 1920 AND 1910—Continued.

[Corresponding figures for all farmers, by tenure, in Table 25.]

DIVISION OR STATE AND COLOR AND TENURE.	ALL LAND IN FARMS (ACRES).		IMPROVED LAND IN FARMS (ACRES).		PER CENT OF FARM LAND IMPROVED.		AVERAGE ACREAGE PER FARM.			
							All land.		Improved land.	
	1920	1910	1920	1910	1920	1910	1920	1910	1920	1910
GEOGRAPHIC DIVISIONS—Con.										
SOUTH ATLANTIC.										
White farmers:										
Total	79,550,302	86,106,873	37,055,998	37,489,664	46.6	43.5	102.6	113.9	47.8	49.6
Owners	56,279,975	63,483,405	25,284,578	26,148,320	44.9	41.2	111.6	129.2	50.1	53.2
Managers	4,256,060	3,219,019	1,398,607	1,167,797	32.9	36.3	481.3	424.8	158.2	154.1
Tenants	19,014,267	19,404,449	10,372,813	10,173,547	54.6	52.4	72.6	75.4	39.6	39.5
Colored farmers:										
Total	18,224,941	17,675,382	11,453,888	10,990,069	62.8	62.2	47.5	49.7	29.8	30.9
Owners	5,518,395	5,646,378	2,744,104	2,695,947	49.7	47.7	53.8	55.4	26.7	26.4
Managers	145,967	145,371	71,661	61,287	49.1	42.2	152.5	201.9	74.9	85.1
Tenants	12,560,579	11,883,633	8,638,123	8,232,835	68.8	69.3	44.8	46.9	30.8	32.5
EAST SOUTH CENTRAL.										
White farmers:										
Total	66,783,791	67,924,912	35,838,577	34,390,317	53.7	50.6	89.7	94.7	48.1	47.9
Owners	50,088,549	52,592,020	25,739,456	25,170,277	51.4	47.9	106.5	116.4	54.7	55.7
Managers	1,442,654	1,527,107	647,717	552,554	44.9	36.2	465.5	502.2	209.0	181.7
Tenants	15,252,588	13,805,785	9,451,404	8,667,486	62.0	62.8	56.3	52.6	34.9	33.0
Colored farmers:										
Total	12,113,672	13,595,717	8,541,555	9,556,529	70.5	70.3	39.4	41.8	27.8	29.4
Owners	3,933,246	4,539,952	1,990,937	2,213,645	50.6	48.8	70.8	77.3	35.8	37.7
Managers	85,911	76,360	37,374	26,237	43.5	34.4	211.1	306.7	91.8	105.4
Tenants	8,094,515	8,979,405	6,513,244	7,316,647	80.5	81.5	32.2	33.7	25.9	27.5
WEST SOUTH CENTRAL.										
White farmers:										
Total	162,469,244	157,811,958	56,441,289	51,075,128	34.7	32.4	212.6	215.0	73.9	69.6
Owners	100,156,509	98,848,268	31,273,926	28,263,944	31.2	28.6	247.3	258.0	77.2	73.8
Managers	16,374,630	19,570,123	1,298,842	1,405,742	7.9	7.2	3,554.3	4,383.0	281.9	314.8
Tenants	45,938,105	39,393,567	23,868,521	21,405,442	52.0	54.3	129.5	113.7	67.3	61.8
Colored farmers:										
Total	10,979,883	11,338,018	7,748,317	7,189,145	70.6	63.4	47.4	54.2	33.4	34.4
Owners	4,624,982	5,505,206	2,512,301	2,621,527	54.3	47.6	77.9	95.3	42.3	45.4
Managers	135,942	128,048	40,082	20,725	29.5	16.2	334.8	554.5	98.7	89.7
Tenants	6,218,959	5,704,764	5,195,934	4,546,893	83.5	79.7	36.1	37.8	30.2	30.1
MOUNTAIN.										
White farmers:										
Total	116,339,757	58,748,762	29,810,696	15,773,427	25.6	26.8	487.5	334.9	124.9	89.9
Owners	90,040,400	41,531,923	23,367,187	12,037,033	26.0	29.0	454.4	271.2	117.9	78.0
Managers	12,939,972	10,987,740	1,533,869	1,467,173	11.9	13.4	3,166.4	3,802.0	375.1	507.7
Tenants	13,359,385	6,229,099	4,909,640	2,269,221	36.8	36.4	366.8	321.8	134.8	117.2
Colored farmers:										
Total	997,469	784,658	295,172	141,575	29.6	18.0	183.1	97.7	54.2	17.6
Owners	848,334	734,007	225,632	115,555	26.6	15.7	194.5	95.6	51.7	15.1
Managers	33,614	15,985	2,546	4,790	7.6	30.0	1,245.0	726.6	94.3	217.7
Tenants	115,521	34,666	66,994	21,230	58.0	61.2	109.2	104.7	63.3	64.1
PACIFIC.										
White farmers:										
Total	55,430,472	50,749,570	23,447,215	21,751,946	42.3	42.9	245.4	274.2	103.8	117.5
Owners	36,187,601	32,895,480	14,587,280	14,170,425	40.3	43.1	203.3	219.6	81.9	94.6
Managers	6,836,745	7,890,070	2,123,325	2,094,960	31.1	26.6	995.6	1,533.8	309.2	407.3
Tenants	12,406,126	9,964,020	6,736,610	5,486,561	54.3	55.1	303.0	331.0	164.5	182.3
Colored farmers:										
Total	722,233	579,219	474,318	286,062	65.7	49.4	86.8	119.9	57.0	59.2
Owners	285,676	381,400	92,662	116,233	32.4	30.5	134.9	180.2	43.7	54.9
Managers	27,762	9,991	21,271	5,938	76.6	59.4	167.2	123.3	128.1	73.3
Tenants	408,795	187,828	360,385	163,891	88.2	87.3	67.7	71.4	59.7	62.3

TABLE 39.—ACREAGE OF FARM LAND, WITH PERCENTAGES AND AVERAGES, BY COLOR AND TENURE, BY DIVISIONS AND STATES: 1920 AND 1910—Continued.

[Corresponding figures for all farmers, by tenure, in Table 25.]

DIVISION OR STATE AND COLOR AND TENURE.	ALL LAND IN FARMS (ACRES).		IMPROVED LAND IN FARMS (ACRES).		PER CENT OF FARM LAND IM- PROVED.		AVERAGE ACREAGE PER FARM.			
							All land.		Improved land.	
	1920	1910	1920	1910	1920	1910	1920	1910	1920	1910
NEW ENGLAND.										
MAINE.										
White farmers:										
Total	5,425,015	6,295,369	1,976,884	2,359,993	36.4	37.5	112.5	104.9	41.0	39.3
Owners	5,072,903	5,914,533	1,852,779	2,221,880	36.5	37.6	111.7	104.8	40.8	39.4
Managers	145,793	156,864	49,431	53,351	33.9	34.0	185.5	157.2	62.9	53.5
Tenants	206,319	223,972	74,674	84,762	36.2	37.8	103.0	87.5	37.3	33.1
Colored farmers:										
Total	953	1,490	445	664	46.7	44.6	73.3	51.4	34.2	22.9
Owners	953	1,289	445	572	46.7	44.4	73.3	51.6	34.2	22.9
Managers		37		1		2.7		37.0		1.0
Tenants		164		91		55.5		54.7		30.3
NEW HAMPSHIRE.										
White farmers:										
Total	2,602,330	3,248,530	702,387	928,887	27.0	28.6	126.9	120.1	34.2	34.4
Owners	2,295,262	2,863,072	623,263	829,074	27.2	29.0	123.5	117.0	33.5	33.9
Managers	154,033	209,623	33,721	42,788	21.9	20.4	282.6	308.3	61.9	62.9
Tenants	153,035	175,835	45,403	57,025	29.7	32.4	111.5	93.7	33.1	30.4
Colored farmers:										
Total	1,476	928	515	298	34.9	32.1	105.4	61.9	36.8	19.9
Owners	1,121	561	410	227	36.6	40.5	93.4	46.8	34.2	18.9
Managers	325	2	100	2	30.8	100.0	325.0	2.0	100.0	2.0
Tenants	30	365	5	69	16.7	18.9	30.0	182.5	5.0	34.5
VERMONT.										
White farmers:										
Total	4,231,361	4,661,660	1,690,173	1.633,331	39.9	35.0	145.7	142.6	58.2	50.0
Owners	3,517,824	3,814,804	1,386,421	1,320,934	39.4	34.6	140.2	136.0	55.2	47.1
Managers	149,783	208,840	55,850	52.575	37.3	25.2	265.1	328.9	98.8	82.8
Tenants	563,754	638,016	247,902	259,822	44.0	40.7	166.7	159.3	73.3	64.9
Colored farmers:										
Total	4,450	1,917	1.422	634	32.0	33.1	158.9	95.9	50.8	31.7
Owners	3,075	1,694	1,081	563	35.2	33.2	146.4	99.6	51.5	33.1
Managers	414	98	112	9	27.1	9.2	138.0	98.0	37.3	9.0
Tenants	961	125	229	62	23.8	49.6	240.3	62.5	57.3	31.0
MASSACHUSETTS.										
White farmers:										
Total	2,488,887	2,871,377	906,399	1,162,960	36.4	40.5	78.1	78.0	28.4	31.6
Owners	2,018,142	2,339,252	743,053	930,323	36.8	39.8	72.1	73.2	26.6	29.1
Managers	311,884	330,644	103,844	150,105	33.3	45.4	192.5	177.9	64.1	80.7
Tenants	158,861	201,481	59,502	82,532	37.5	41.0	69.7	67.9	26.1	27.8
Colored farmers:										
Total	5,590	4,564	2,435	1,541	43.6	33.8	46.2	36.8	20.1	12.4
Owners	3,778	3,851	1,470	1,298	38.9	33.7	35.3	35.3	13.7	11.9
Managers	1,211	270	806	101	66.6	37.4	173.0	67.5	115.1	25.3
Tenants	601	443	159	142	26.5	32.1	85.9	40.3	22.7	12.9
RHODE ISLAND.										
White farmers:										
Total	330,648	441,634	132,543	177,752	40.1	40.2	81.4	84.1	32.6	33.9
Owners	248,296	317,157	97,523	127,577	39.3	40.2	76.8	78.2	30.2	31.4
Managers	29,702	44,436	13,913	15,914	46.8	35.8	145.6	177.0	68.2	63.4
Tenants	52,650	80,041	21,107	34,261	40.1	42.8	83.8	85.0	33.6	36.4
Colored farmers:										
Total	952	1,674	312	592	32.8	35.4	47.6	40.8	15.6	14.4
Owners	638	1,105	196	387	30.7	35.0	45.6	38.1	14.0	13.3
Managers	90		30		33.3		90.0		30.0	
Tenants	224	569	86	205	38.4	36.0	44.8	47.4	17.2	17.1

TABLE 39.—ACREAGE OF FARM LAND, WITH PERCENTAGES AND AVERAGES, BY COLOR AND TENURE, BY DIVISIONS AND STATES: 1920 AND 1910—Continued.

[Corresponding figures for all farmers, by tenure, in Table 25.]

DIVISION OR STATE AND COLOR AND TENURE.	ALL LAND IN FARMS (ACRES).		IMPROVED LAND IN FARMS (ACRES).		PER CENT OF FARM LAND IMPROVED.		AVERAGE ACREAGE PER FARM.			
							All land.		Improved land.	
	1920	1910	1920	1910	1920	1910	1920	1910	1920	1910
NEW ENGLAND—Continued.										
CONNECTICUT.										
White farmers:										
Total	1,891,735	2,180,053	699,070	985,899	37.0	45.2	83.8	81.6	31.0	36.9
Owners	1,540,791	1,828,881	572,314	825,523	37.1	45.1	78.6	79.0	29.2	35.7
Managers	185,226	134,982	65,112	61,268	35.2	45.4	174.1	144.1	61.2	65.4
Tenants	165,718	216,190	61,644	99,108	37.2	45.8	87.2	82.8	32.4	38.0
Colored farmers:										
Total	7,245	5,735	2,016	2,353	27.8	41.0	96.6	50.8	26.9	20.8
Owners	1,753	2,926	704	1,486	40.2	50.8	34.4	37.0	13.8	18.8
Managers	1,965	1,667	227	290	11.6	17.4	327.5	138.9	37.8	24.2
Tenants	3,527	1,142	1,085	577	30.8	50.5	195.9	51.9	60.3	26.2
MIDDLE ATLANTIC.										
NEW YORK.										
White farmers:										
Total	20,589,928	21,971,024	13,131,646	14,808,120	63.8	67.4	106.9	102.4	68.2	69.0
Owners	15,054,158	15,776,790	9,582,336	10,578,703	63.7	67.1	99.5	95.1	63.3	63.8
Managers	928,660	837,077	460,201	430,898	49.6	51.5	213.4	207.4	105.8	106.7
Tenants	4,607,110	5,357,157	3,089,109	3,798,519	67.1	70.9	124.5	119.7	83.5	84.9
Colored farmers:										
Total	42,875	59,343	27,135	35,919	63.3	60.5	78.0	63.2	49.3	38.3
Owners	30,225	48,050	18,660	27,454	61.7	57.1	70.5	59.5	43.5	34.0
Managers	3,695	1,399	2,186	1,038	59.2	74.2	147.8	99.9	87.4	74.1
Tenants	8,955	9,894	6,289	7,427	70.2	75.1	93.3	84.6	65.5	63.5
NEW JERSEY.										
White farmers:										
Total	2,256,265	2,551,497	1,539,147	1,788,211	68.2	70.1	77.4	77.3	52.8	54.2
Owners	1,415,789	1,556,103	966,582	1,100,750	68.3	70.7	65.5	65.2	44.7	46.1
Managers	206,413	225,099	100,342	104,867	48.6	46.6	213.5	217.9	103.8	101.5
Tenants	634,063	770,295	472,223	582,594	74.5	75.6	96.1	95.0	71.6	71.8
Colored farmers:										
Total	26,320	22,360	16,460	15,125	62.5	67.6	49.2	47.0	30.8	31.8
Owners	9,002	6,803	5,237	4,862	58.2	71.5	31.6	25.7	18.4	18.3
Managers	1,978	2,241	1,529	1,661	77.3	74.1	98.9	83.0	76.5	61.5
Tenants	15,340	13,316	9,694	8,602	63.2	64.6	66.7	72.4	42.1	46.8
PENNSYLVANIA.										
White farmers:										
Total	17,630,579	18,556,445	11,829,040	12,654,307	67.1	68.2	87.4	84.8	58.6	57.8
Owners	12,499,320	12,879,610	8,196,163	8,567,220	65.6	66.5	81.6	78.6	53.5	52.3
Managers	778,128	644,834	460,371	369,784	59.2	57.3	175.1	164.1	103.6	94.1
Tenants	4,353,131	5,032,001	3,172,506	3,717,303	72.9	73.9	98.7	98.8	71.9	73.0
Colored farmers:										
Total	26,934	30,387	18,679	19,212	69.4	63.2	59.7	55.7	41.4	35.2
Owners	10,187	15,912	7,646	9,071	75.1	57.0	39.0	46.7	29.3	26.6
Managers	4,163	3,434	3,050	2,170	73.3	63.2	92.5	110.8	67.8	70.0
Tenants	12,584	11,041	7,983	7,971	63.4	72.2	86.8	63.5	55.1	45.8
EAST NORTH CENTRAL.										
OHIO.										
White farmers:										
Total	23,415,476	23,998,961	18,465,916	19,144,653	78.9	79.8	91.8	88.9	72.4	70.9
Owners	14,944,527	15,970,297	11,705,310	12,678,068	78.3	79.4	84.5	83.7	66.2	66.5
Managers	557,191	501,536	386,592	347,033	69.4	69.2	184.0	184.0	127.6	127.4
Tenants	7,913,758	7,527,128	6,374,014	6,119,552	80.5	81.3	105.4	98.3	84.9	79.9
Colored farmers:										
Total	100,412	106,747	76,437	83,316	76.1	78.1	62.1	54.7	47.3	42.7
Owners	55,526	61,385	41,170	46,604	74.1	75.9	52.7	46.8	39.1	35.5
Managers	4,533	3,100	3,555	2,409	78.4	77.7	125.9	110.7	98.8	86.0
Tenants	40,353	42,262	31,712	34,303	78.6	81.2	76.6	69.4	60.2	56.3

TABLE **39.**—ACREAGE OF FARM LAND, WITH PERCENTAGES AND AVERAGES, BY COLOR AND TENURE, BY DIVISIONS AND STATES: 1920 AND 1910—Continued.

[Corresponding figures for all farmers, by tenure, in Table 25.]

DIVISION OR STATE AND COLOR AND TENURE.	ALL LAND IN FARMS (ACRES).		IMPROVED LAND IN FARMS (ACRES).		PER CENT OF FARM LAND IMPROVED.		AVERAGE ACREAGE PER FARM.			
							All land.		Improved land.	
	1920	1910	1920	1910	1920	1910	1920	1910	1920	1910
EAST NORTH CENTRAL—Con.										
INDIANA.										
White farmers:										
Total	21,026,616	21,254,834	16,649,507	16,893,488	79.2	79.5	102.8	99.0	81.4	78.7
Owners	12,853,162	13,913,726	10,011,639	10,922,085	77.9	78.5	93.9	94.0	73.1	73.8
Managers	470,497	481,387	344,647	341,668	73.3	71.0	203.2	210.9	148.9	149.7
Tenants	7,702,957	6,859,721	6,293,221	5,629,735	81.7	82.1	117.9	106.6	96.3	87.5
Colored farmers:										
Total	36,716	44,989	30,705	37,764	83.6	83.9	64.2	55.9	53.7	46.9
Owners	17,302	25,199	14,333	21,212	82.8	84.2	56.5	53.4	46.8	44.9
Managers	2,419	2,082	2,060	1,483	85.2	71.2	172.8	138.8	147.1	98.9
Tenants	16,995	17,708	14,312	15,069	84.2	85.1	67.4	55.7	56.8	47.4
ILLINOIS.										
White farmers:										
Total	31,917,073	32,435,051	27,247,436	27,979,926	85.4	86.3	135.1	129.5	115.3	111.7
Owners	16,231,619	17,743,314	13,595,050	14,999,471	83.8	84.5	122.9	122.9	103.0	103.9
Managers	711,773	553,275	576,713	424,551	81.0	76.7	209.2	233.6	169.5	179.3
Tenants	14,973,681	14,138,462	13,075,673	12,555,904	87.3	88.8	148.5	136.3	129.7	121.0
Colored farmers:										
Total	57,702	87,886	47,097	68,397	81.6	77.8	64.6	61.7	52.7	48.0
Owners	33,457	43,749	26,281	33,721	78.6	77.1	62.7	55.4	49.2	42.7
Managers	1,077	5,188	941	3,916	87.4	75.5	119.7	288.2	104.6	217.6
Tenants	23,168	38,949	19,875	30,760	85.8	79.0	66.2	63.0	56.8	49.8
MICHIGAN.										
White farmers:										
Total	18,984,248	18,880,909	12,893,814	12,792,283	67.9	67.8	97.0	91.6	65.9	62.1
Owners	14,506,732	15,061,387	9,824,920	10,112,470	67.7	67.1	91.3	87.8	61.9	59.0
Managers	587,044	451,689	271,683	216,459	46.3	47.9	254.1	231.4	117.6	110.9
Tenants	3,890,472	3,367,833	2,797,211	2,463,354	71.9	73.1	112.6	103.5	80.9	75.7
Colored farmers:										
Total	48,713	59,705	31,707	39,795	65.1	66.7	66.5	63.1	43.3	42.1
Owners	34,729	46,107	21,921	29,689	63.1	64.4	61.7	58.7	38.9	37.8
Managers	847	815	669	650	79.0	79.8	94.1	90.6	74.3	72.2
Tenants	13,137	12,783	9,117	9,456	69.4	74.0	81.6	84.1	56.6	62.2
WISCONSIN.										
White farmers:										
Total	22,114,129	21,020,142	12,437,349	11,892,217	56.2	56.6	117.2	119.1	65.9	67.4
Owners	17,808,980	17,332,141	9,875,457	9,612,692	55.5	55.5	112.0	115.2	62.1	63.9
Managers	531,249	354,830	241,474	154,990	45.5	43.7	219.2	245.2	99.6	107.1
Tenants	3,773,900	3,333,171	2,320,418	2,124,535	61.5	63.7	138.6	135.4	85.2	86.3
Colored farmers:										
Total	34,094	39,924	14,867	15,389	43.6	38.5	51.4	67.6	22.4	26.0
Owners	32,017	37,015	13,720	14,014	42.9	37.9	51.0	67.4	21.8	25.5
Managers	605	303	457	162	75.5	53.5	201.7	75.8	152.3	40.5
Tenants	1,472	2,606	690	1,213	46.9	46.5	46.0	68.6	21.6	31.9
WEST NORTH CENTRAL.										
MINNESOTA.										
White farmers:										
Total	30,201,479	27,652,207	21,474,366	19,628,989	71.1	71.0	169.4	177.4	120.5	126.0
Owners	20,996,110	20,649,735	14,248,621	14,141,833	67.9	68.5	158.4	169.4	107.5	116.0
Managers	443,065	413,283	283,845	285,037	64.1	69.0	277.8	338.8	178.0	233.6
Tenants	8,762,304	6,589,189	6,941,900	5,202,119	79.2	79.0	198.7	201.4	157.4	159.0
Colored farmers:										
Total	20,279	23,616	7,344	14,544	36.2	61.6	98.0	80.6	35.5	49.6
Owners	18,054	19,150	6,020	11,672	33.3	61.0	102.0	98.7	34.0	60.2
Managers	24	451	24	204	100.0	45.2	24.0	225.5	24.0	102.0
Tenants	2,201	4,015	1,300	2,668	59.1	66.5	75.9	41.4	44.8	27.5

TABLE 39.—ACREAGE OF FARM LAND, WITH PERCENTAGES AND AVERAGES, BY COLOR AND TENURE, BY DIVISIONS AND STATES: 1920 AND 1910—Continued.

[Corresponding figures for all farmers, by tenure, in Table 25.]

DIVISION OR STATE AND COLOR AND TENURE.	ALL LAND IN FARMS (ACRES).		IMPROVED LAND IN FARMS (ACRES).		PER CENT OF FARM LAND IMPROVED.		AVERAGE ACREAGE PER FARM.			
							All land.		Improved land.	
	1920	1910	1920	1910	1920	1910	1920	1910	1920	1910
WEST NORTH CENTRAL—Con.										
IOWA.										
White farmers:										
Total	33,466,049	33,916,710	28,600,734	29,480,206	85.5	86.9	156.9	156.4	134.1	136.0
Owners	18,045,981	20,207,822	15,316,174	17,427,080	84.9	86.2	148.1	152.1	125.7	131.2
Managers	568,836	489,789	445,737	383,331	78.4	78.3	228.8	254.6	179.3	199.2
Tenants	14,851,232	13,219,099	12,838,823	11,669,795	86.4	88.3	166.8	161.1	144.2	142.2
Colored farmers:										
Total	8,847	13,978	6,217	10,993	70.3	78.6	81.2	69.5	57.0	54.7
Owners	5,140	6,515	3,450	5,155	67.1	79.1	69.5	47.9	46.6	37.9
Managers	250	1,016	160	646	64.0	63.6	250.0	508.0	160.0	323.0
Tenants	3,457	6,447	2,607	5,192	75.4	80.5	101.7	102.3	76.7	82.4
MISSOURI.										
White farmers:										
Total	34,584,245	34,361,183	24,690,967	24,408,746	71.4	71.0	132.9	125.6	94.9	89.2
Owners	24,574,801	25,057,644	17,389,055	17,602,014	70.8	70.2	134.0	131.8	94.8	92.6
Managers	653,390	622,313	419,598	390,006	64.2	62.7	297.1	317.5	190.8	199.0
Tenants	9,356,054	8,681,226	6,882,314	6,416,726	73.6	73.9	125.4	106.6	92.3	78.8
Colored farmers:										
Total	190,434	230,065	141,999	172,440	74.6	75.0	67.4	62.8	50.2	47.0
Owners	111,996	131,597	77,916	92,529	69.6	70.3	68.1	62.4	47.4	43.9
Managers	11,057	7,532	9,379	6,706	84.8	89.0	230.4	183.7	195.4	163.6
Tenants	67,381	90,936	54,704	73,205	81.2	80.5	59.4	60.0	48.2	48.3
NORTH DAKOTA.										
White farmers:										
Total	36,028,299	28,231,630	24,517,007	20,406,121	68.0	72.3	467.0	383.5	317.8	277.2
Owners	26,684,516	23,395,028	17,419,933	16,360,242	65.3	69.9	472.7	374.4	308.6	261.8
Managers	810,667	476,733	482,405	374,572	59.5	78.6	950.4	989.1	565.5	777.1
Tenants	8,533,116	4,359,869	6,614,669	3,671,307	77.5	84.2	430.0	409.4	333.3	344.7
Colored farmers:										
Total	186,452	195,020	46,171	48,971	24.8	25.1	343.4	262.5	85.0	65.9
Owners	165,569	191,700	37,396	47,456	22.6	24.8	353.0	263.7	79.7	65.3
Managers	800	480	450	310	56.3	64.6	400.0	240.0	225.0	155.0
Tenants	20,083	2,840	8,325	1,205	41.5	42.4	278.9	202.9	115.6	86.1
SOUTH DAKOTA.										
White farmers:										
Total	33,786,349	24,571,572	18,048,481	15,706,380	53.4	63.9	462.7	328.3	247.2	209.9
Owners	23,364,878	17,892,408	11,344,964	10,665,903	48.6	59.6	504.1	323.9	244.8	193.1
Managers	883,213	626,827	278,302	287,066	31.5	45.8	1,145.5	1,485.4	361.0	680.3
Tenants	9,538,258	6,052,337	6,425,215	4,753,411	67.4	78.5	368.2	315.8	248.0	248.0
Colored farmers:										
Total	850,142	1,445,320	150,769	120,828	17.7	8.4	527.4	514.7	93.5	43.0
Owners	804,499	1,422,530	138,293	113,597	17.2	8.0	549.1	519.9	94.4	41.5
Managers	6,504	8,372	454	1,100	7.0	13.1	650.4	1,196.0	45.4	157.1
Tenants	39,139	14,418	12,022	6,131	30.7	42.5	285.7	221.8	87.8	94.3
NEBRASKA.										
White farmers:										
Total	42,158,793	38,541,471	23,077,258	24,341,688	54.7	63.2	339.9	298.3	186.1	188.4
Owners	26,384,910	26,908,314	13,161,040	15,431,091	49.9	57.3	380.1	341.1	189.6	195.6
Managers	1,478,572	1,093,212	432,101	561,929	29.2	51.4	1,127.8	1,108.7	329.6	569.9
Tenants	14,295,311	10,539,945	9,484,117	8,348,668	66.3	79.2	268.2	213.6	177.9	169.2
Colored farmers:										
Total	66,682	80,550	32,366	40,889	48.5	50.8	173.7	174.4	84.3	88.5
Owners	36,855	67,240	17,530	32,220	47.6	47.9	145.1	182.2	69.0	87.3
Managers	1,913	1,600	363	900	19.0	56.3	478.3	1,600.0	90.8	900.0
Tenants	27,914	11,710	14,473	7,769	51.8	66.3	221.5	127.3	114.9	84.4

TABLE 39.—ACREAGE OF FARM LAND, WITH PERCENTAGES AND AVERAGES, BY COLOR AND TENURE, BY DIVISIONS AND STATES: 1920 AND 1910—Continued.

[Corresponding figures for all farmers, by tenure, in Table 25.]

DIVISION OR STATE AND COLOR AND TENURE.	ALL LAND IN FARMS (ACRES).		IMPROVED LAND IN FARMS (ACRES).		PER CENT OF FARM LAND IMPROVED.		AVERAGE ACREAGE PER FARM.			
							All land.		Improved land.	
	1920	1910	1920	1910	1920	1910	1920	1910	1920	1910
WEST NORTH CENTRAL—Con.										
KANSAS.										
White farmers:										
Total	45,236,124	43,181,686	30,470,667	29,763,626	67.4	68.9	275.7	245.1	185.7	169.0
Owners	27,259,088	28,705,040	17,864,196	19,259,206	65.5	67.1	283.1	260.9	185.5	175.1
Managers	1,218,298	1,253,644	501,194	430,145	41.1	34.3	824.8	954.1	339.3	327.4
Tenants	16,758,738	13,223,002	12,105,277	10,074,275	72.2	76.2	252.9	204.0	182.7	155.4
Colored farmers:										
Total	189,055	203,113	130,093	140,441	68.8	69.1	152.7	120.1	105.1	83.1
Owners	117,683	135,142	78,748	89,587	66.9	66.3	148.4	123.1	99.3	81.6
Managers	2,613	10,047	2,077	4,717	79.5	46.9	145.2	478.4	115.4	224.6
Tenants	68,759	57,924	49,268	46,137	71.7	79.7	161.0	101.3	115.4	80.7
SOUTH ATLANTIC.										
DELAWARE.										
White farmers:										
Total	889,623	981,893	615,117	676,462	69.1	68.9	96.0	99.0	66.4	68.2
Owners	438,964	463,212	293,795	312,803	66.9	67.5	77.6	80.3	52.0	54.2
Managers	20,191	18,769	15,611	15,553	77.3	82.9	154.1	175.4	119.2	145.4
Tenants	430,468	499,912	305,711	348,106	71.0	69.6	123.6	123.9	87.8	86.3
Colored farmers:										
Total	54,888	56,973	37,935	37,076	69.1	65.1	62.9	61.8	43.5	40.2
Owners	12,512	13,615	8,424	9,274	67.3	68.1	35.2	33.5	23.7	22.8
Managers	1,294	2,395	933	2,034	72.1	84.9	99.5	149.7	71.8	127.1
Tenants	41,082	40,963	28,578	25,768	69.6	62.9	81.5	81.9	56.7	51.5
MARYLAND.										
White farmers:										
Total	4,406,422	4,698,623	2,919,042	3,136,185	66.2	66.7	105.7	110.4	70.0	73.7
Owners	2,631,595	2,783,279	1,686,704	1,806,918	64.1	64.9	90.0	94.1	57.7	61.1
Managers	237,344	193,930	152,839	120,254	64.4	62.0	213.6	215.2	137.6	133.5
Tenants	1,537,483	1,721,414	1,079,499	1,209,013	70.2	70.2	135.7	142.5	95.3	100.1
Colored farmers:										
Total	351,577	358,517	217,686	218,582	61.9	61.0	56.6	56.3	35.1	34.3
Owners	119,275	122,039	73,284	76,564	61.4	62.7	33.6	30.9	20.6	19.4
Managers	22,082	13,361	15,679	9,015	71.0	67.5	146.2	153.6	103.8	103.6
Tenants	210,220	223,117	128,723	133,003	61.2	59.6	83.8	95.6	51.3	57.0
DIST. OF COLUMBIA.										
White farmers:										
Total	5,380	5,968	3,985	5,038	74.1	84.4	29.2	29.1	21.7	24.6
Owners	1,704	2,371	1,287	2,069	75.5	87.3	18.7	21.6	14.1	18.8
Managers	1,856	1,452	1,429	1,259	77.0	86.7	103.1	103.7	79.4	89.9
Tenants	1,820	2,145	1,269	1,710	69.7	79.7	24.3	26.5	16.9	21.1
Colored farmers:										
Total	288	95	273	95	94.8	100.0	14.4	7.9	13.7	7.9
Owners	25	58	24	58	96.0	100.0	2.8	7.3	2.7	7.3
Managers	95	4	90	4	94.7	100.0	95.0	4.0	90.0	4.0
Tenants	168	33	159	33	94.6	100.0	16.8	11.0	15.9	11.0
VIRGINIA.										
White farmers:										
Total	16,297,693	17,257,416	8,356,031	8,758,850	51.3	50.8	117.7	127.0	60.4	64.4
Owners	12,387,142	13,334,122	6,388,686	6,802,428	51.6	51.0	117.5	131.5	60.6	67.1
Managers	792,456	630,340	398,326	306,482	50.3	48.6	409.1	436.2	205.6	212.1
Tenants	3,118,095	3,292,954	1,569,019	1,649,940	50.3	50.1	100.2	99.7	50.4	50.0
Colored farmers:										
Total	2,263,419	2,238,220	1,104,461	1,111,208	48.8	49.6	47.4	46.5	23.1	23.1
Owners	1,373,761	1,381,248	654,218	669,358	47.6	48.5	44.4	42.9	21.1	20.8
Managers	31,294	29,985	17,155	14,046	54.8	46.8	158.9	166.6	87.1	78.0
Tenants	858,364	827,012	433,088	427,804	50.5	51.7	51.6	52.7	26.0	27.2

TABLE 39.—ACREAGE OF FARM LAND, WITH PERCENTAGES AND AVERAGES, BY COLOR AND TENURE, BY DIVISIONS AND STATES: 1920 AND 1910—Continued.

[Corresponding figures for all farmers, by tenure, in Table 25.]

DIVISION OR STATE AND COLOR AND TENURE.	ALL LAND IN FARMS (ACRES).		IMPROVED LAND IN FARMS (ACRES).		PER CENT OF FARM LAND IMPROVED.		AVERAGE ACREAGE PER FARM.			
							All land.		Improved land.	
	1920	1910	1920	1910	1920	1910	1920	1910	1920	1910
SOUTH ATLANTIC—Continued.										
WEST VIRGINIA.										
White farmers:										
Total	9,542,246	9,991,901	5,503,202	5,501,500	57.7	55.1	110.0	104.1	63.4	57.3
Owners	7,794,290	8,158,238	4,576,437	4,591,581	58.7	56.3	108.7	108.2	63.8	60.9
Managers	354,563	283,847	182,909	133,232	51.6	46.9	327.7	328.1	169.0	154.0
Tenants	1,393,393	1,549,816	743,856	776,687	53.4	50.1	99.5	78.7	53.1	39.4
Colored farmers:										
Total	27,544	34,541	17,106	20,257	62.1	58.6	54.7	48.8	33.9	28.6
Owners	19,052	25,957	11,211	14,522	58.8	55.9	47.3	46.5	27.8	26.0
Managers	1,520	655	1,239	602	81.5	91.9	190.0	93.6	154.9	86.0
Tenants	6,972	7,929	4,656	5,133	66.8	64.7	75.0	55.4	50.1	35.9
NORTH CAROLINA.										
White farmers:										
Total	16,584,294	19,253,325	6,341,309	7,082,344	38.2	36.8	85.7	102.4	32.8	37.7
Owners	12,282,645	14,458,827	4,458,019	5,027,216	36.3	34.8	95.1	116.7	34.5	40.6
Managers	373,582	563,385	105,916	154,738	28.4	27.5	449.0	539.6	127.3	148.2
Tenants	3,928,067	4,231,113	1,777,374	1,900,390	45.2	44.9	61.8	67.0	28.0	30.1
Colored farmers:										
Total	3,437,442	3,185,804	1,857,100	1,730,712	54.0	54.3	45.1	48.5	24.3	26.4
Owners	1,158,864	1,197,496	508,339	512,567	43.9	42.8	52.0	55.8	22.8	23.9
Managers	12,867	18,992	6,363	5,244	49.5	27.6	134.0	256.6	66.3	70.9
Tenants	2,265,711	1,969,316	1,342,398	1,212,901	59.2	61.6	42.0	44.6	24.9	27.5
SOUTH CAROLINA.										
White farmers:										
Total	8,046,672	9,571,552	3,280,566	3,499,775	40.8	36.6	96.2	120.2	39.2	43.9
Owners	5,570,841	6,953,459	2,032,048	2,261,431	36.5	32.5	123.9	158.1	45.2	51.4
Managers	387,427	504,958	104,990	126,932	27.1	25.1	698.1	689.8	189.2	173.4
Tenants	2,088,404	2,113,135	1,143,528	1,111,412	54.8	52.6	54.7	60.5	30.0	31.8
Colored farmers:										
Total	4,380,003	3,940,476	2,903,593	2,598,224	66.3	65.9	40.2	40.7	26.6	26.8
Owners	1,146,396	1,098,044	590,881	539,347	51.5	49.1	50.4	53.9	26.0	26.5
Managers	37,095	42,454	11,452	14,874	30.9	35.0	202.7	324.1	62.6	113.5
Tenants	3,196,512	2,799,978	2,301,260	2,044,003	72.0	73.0	37.1	36.7	26.7	26.8
GEORGIA.										
White farmers:										
Total	18,369,149	19,861,362	8,177,099	7,506,455	44.5	37.8	101.7	117.9	45.3	44.6
Owners	11,469,031	13,501,789	4,414,710	4,286,899	38.5	31.8	133.2	162.8	51.3	51.7
Managers	896,951	751,571	305,801	237,134	34.1	31.6	619.4	579.9	211.2	183.0
Tenants	6,003.167	5,608,002	3,456,588	2,982,422	57.6	53.2	64.5	66.6	37.2	35.4
Colored farmers:										
Total	7,071,912	7,092,051	4,878,110	4,791,562	69.0	67.6	54.3	57.9	37.5	39.1
Owners	1,331,828	1,349,503	693,643	644,396	52.1	47.8	83.0	86.0	43.2	41.0
Managers	29,038	27,551	13,298	11,216	45.8	40.7	140.3	224.0	64.2	91.2
Tenants	5,711,046	5,714,997	4,171,169	4,135,950	73.0	72.4	50.1	53.5	36.6	38.7
FLORIDA.										
White farmers:										
Total	5,408,823	4,484,833	1,859,647	1,323,055	34.4	29.5	131.8	127.1	45.3	37.5
Owners	3,703,763	3,828,108	1,432,892	1,056,975	38.7	27.6	115.1	136.2	44.5	37.6
Managers	1,191,690	270,767	130,786	72,213	11.0	26.7	689.6	230.6	75.7	61.5
Tenants	513,370	385,958	295,969	193,867	57.7	50.2	71.7	64.1	41.4	32.2
Colored farmers:										
Total	637,868	768,705	437,624	482,353	68.6	62.7	49.2	52.2	33.8	32.8
Owners	356,682	458,443	204,080	229,861	57.2	50.1	56.4	62.8	32.3	31.5
Managers	10,682	9,974	5,452	4,252	51.0	42.6	105.8	98.8	54.0	42.1
Tenants	270,504	300,288	228,092	248,240	84.3	82.7	41.4	41.0	34.9	33.9

TABLE 39.—ACREAGE OF FARM LAND, WITH PERCENTAGES AND AVERAGES, BY COLOR AND TENURE, BY DIVISIONS AND STATES: 1920 AND 1910—Continued.

[Corresponding figures for all farmers, by tenure, in Table 25.]

DIVISION OR STATE AND COLOR AND TENURE.	ALL LAND IN FARMS (ACRES).		IMPROVED LAND IN FARMS (ACRES).		PER CENT OF FARM LAND IMPROVED.		AVERAGE ACREAGE PER FARM.			
							All land.		Improved land.	
	1920	1910	1920	1910	1920	1910	1920	1910	1920	1910
EAST SOUTH CENTRAL.										
KENTUCKY.										
White farmers:										
Total	21,185,813	21,748,350	13,641,230	14,010,777	64.4	64.4	82.1	87.9	52.9	56.6
Owners	16,551,588	17,207,392	10,522,346	10,900,955	63.6	63.3	95.1	104.7	60.5	66.3
Managers	265,130	310,942	158,977	171,131	60.0	55.0	283.9	326.3	170.2	179.6
Tenants	4,369,095	4,230,016	2,959,907	2,938,691	67.7	69.5	52.6	51.5	35.6	35.8
Colored farmers:										
Total	426,959	440,777	334,516	343,694	78.3	78.0	33.8	37.6	26.5	29.3
Owners	240,127	255,363	171,679	185,789	71.5	72.8	45.1	43.1	32.3	31.3
Managers	4,709	4,318	3,598	3,577	76.4	82.8	134.5	108.0	102.8	89.4
Tenants	182,123	181,096	159,239	154,328	87.4	85.2	25.0	31.4	21.9	26.8
TENNESSEE.										
White farmers:										
Total	17,987,053	18,435,579	10,066,270	9,728,208	56.0	52.8	83.8	88.8	46.9	46.8
Owners	13,243,529	14,081,961	7,185,542	7,111,807	54.3	50.5	95.8	105.5	52.0	53.3
Managers	211,608	317,247	103,376	109,140	48.9	34.4	280.6	409.4	137.1	140.8
Tenants	4,531,916	4,036,371	2,777,352	2,507,261	61.3	62.1	59.9	54.9	36.7	34.1
Colored farmers:										
Total	1,523,803	1,606,078	1,119,032	1,162,276	73.4	72.4	39.9	41.9	29.3	30.3
Owners	535,280	590,676	321,445	349,692	60.1	59.2	54.4	55.2	32.7	32.7
Managers	9,271	17,682	4,353	6,778	47.0	38.3	174.9	346.7	82.1	132.9
Tenants	979,252	997,720	793,234	805,806	81.0	80.8	34.6	36.2	28.0	29.2
ALABAMA.										
White farmers:										
Total	15,228,611	15,640,877	6,929,437	6,130,405	45.5	39.2	94.6	102.6	43.1	40.2
Owners	10,784,790	11,813,387	4,338,484	3,944,413	40.2	33.4	120.0	136.0	48.3	45.4
Managers	422,952	349,285	167,681	115,087	39.6	32.9	688.8	588.0	273.1	193.7
Tenants	4,020,869	3,478,205	2,423,272	2,070,905	60.3	59.5	57.1	53.5	34.4	31.9
Colored farmers:										
Total	4,348,245	5,091,435	2,963,970	3,563,176	68.2	70.0	45.7	46.1	31.1	32.3
Owners	1,332,701	1,466,719	647,885	675,819	48.6	46.1	77.5	85.9	37.7	39.6
Managers	32,146	17,482	16,625	5,012	51.7	28.7	253.1	336.2	130.9	96.4
Tenants	2,983,398	3,607,234	2,299,460	2,882,345	77.1	79.9	38.3	38.7	29.5	30.9
MISSISSIPPI.										
White farmers:										
Total	12,382,314	12,100,106	5,201,640	4,520,927	42.0	37.4	111.7	110.4	46.9	41.2
Owners	9,508,642	9,489,280	3,693,084	3,213,102	38.8	33.9	139.6	141.5	54.2	47.9
Managers	542,964	549,633	217,683	157,196	40.1	28.6	681.3	764.4	273.1	218.6
Tenants	2,330,708	2,061,193	1,290,873	1,150,629	55.4	55.8	55.6	49.2	30.8	27.5
Colored farmers:										
Total	5,814,665	6,457,427	4,124,037	4,487,383	70.9	69.5	36.1	39.2	25.6	27.2
Owners	1,825,138	2,227,194	849,928	1,002,345	46.6	45.0	78.7	89.0	36.7	40.1
Managers	39,785	36,878	12,798	10,870	32.2	29.5	207.2	347.9	66.7	102.5
Tenants	3,949,742	4,193,355	3,261,311	3,474,168	82.6	82.8	28.7	30.0	23.7	24.9
WEST SOUTH CENTRAL.										
ARKANSAS.										
White farmers:										
Total	14,831,988	14,762,752	7,266,816	6,303,048	49.0	42.7	92.5	97.7	45.3	41.7
Owners	10,767,826	11,185,428	4,799,531	4,273,857	44.6	38.2	110.7	121.6	49.3	46.5
Managers	338,354	322,093	137,913	109,631	40.8	34.0	527.9	449.2	215.2	152.9
Tenants	3,725,808	3,255,231	2,329,372	1,919,560	62.5	59.0	59.7	55.8	37.3	32.9
Colored farmers:										
Total	2,624,762	2,653,323	1,943,740	1,773,206	74.1	66.8	36.3	41.7	26.9	27.9
Owners	1,042,571	1,204,114	540,666	541,265	51.9	45.0	67.8	82.1	35.2	36.9
Managers	13,211	6,093	5,703	3,068	43.2	50.4	139.1	132.5	60.0	66.7
Tenants	1,568,980	1,443,116	1,397,371	1,228,873	89.1	85.2	27.6	29.5	24.6	25.1

TABLE 39.—ACREAGE OF FARM LAND, WITH PERCENTAGES AND AVERAGES, BY COLOR AND TENURE, BY DIVISIONS AND STATES: 1920 AND 1910—Continued.

[Corresponding figures for all farmers, by tenure, in Table 25.]

DIVISION OR STATE AND COLOR AND TENURE.	ALL LAND IN FARMS (ACRES).		IMPROVED LAND IN FARMS (ACRES).		PER CENT OF FARM LAND IMPROVED.		AVERAGE ACREAGE PER FARM.			
							All land.		Improved land.	
	1920	1910	1920	1910	1920	1910	1920	1910	1920	1910
WEST SOUTH CENTRAL—Con.										
LOUISIANA.										
White farmers:										
Total	7,837,244	8,315,160	3,986,133	3,809,409	50.9	45.8	106.8	126.6	54.3	58.0
Owners	5,507,512	5,931,428	2,595,779	2,466,112	47.1	41.6	119.0	140.3	56.1	58.4
Managers	885,656	965,381	354,550	406,395	40.0	42.1	1,203.3	1,105.8	481.7	465.5
Tenants	1,444,076	1,418,351	1,035,804	936,902	71.7	66.1	54.7	63.0	39.2	41.6
Colored farmers:										
Total	2,182,578	2,124,321	1,640,093	1,466,607	75.1	69.0	35.2	38.7	26.4	26.7
Owners	747,743	834,695	383,226	399,650	51.3	47.9	68.1	77.8	34.9	37.3
Managers	14,465	20,976	7,475	8,047	51.7	38.4	157.2	272.4	81.3	104.5
Tenants	1,420,370	1,268,650	1,249,392	1,058,910	88.0	83.5	27.9	28.8	24.5	24.0
OKLAHOMA.										
White farmers:										
Total	30,238,531	26,582,642	17,121,391	16,378,518	56.6	61.6	174.5	156.8	98.8	96.6
Owners	17,442,221	14,397,140	9,332,156	8,587,571	53.5	59.6	208.3	193.9	111.5	115.7
Managers	901,363	422,384	186,922	175,443	20.7	41.5	1,060.4	676.9	219.9	281.2
Tenants	11,894,947	11,763,118	7,602,313	7,615,504	63.9	64.7	134.1	124.3	85.7	80.5
Colored farmers:										
Total	1,713,403	2,276,711	1,003,930	1,172,819	58.6	51.5	91.5	110.1	53.6	56.7
Owners	1,029,472	1,599,655	552,845	734,594	53.7	45.9	108.5	143.5	58.3	65.9
Managers	24,663	6,295	9,371	1,484	38.0	23.6	290.2	233.1	110.2	55.0
Tenants	659,268	670,761	441,714	436,741	67.0	65.1	72.0	70.7	48.3	46.0
TEXAS.										
White farmers:										
Total	109,561,481	108,151,404	28,066,949	24,584,153	25.6	22.7	306.7	310.9	78.6	70.7
Owners	66,438,950	67,334,272	14,546,460	12,936,404	21.9	19.2	373.9	385.6	81.9	74.1
Managers	14,249,257	17,860,265	619,457	714,273	4.3	4.0	5,987.1	7,934.4	260.3	317.3
Tenants	28,873,274	22,956,867	12,901,032	10,933,476	44.7	47.6	162.9	134.3	72.8	63.9
Colored farmers:										
Total	4,459,140	4,283,663	3,160,554	2,776,513	70.9	64.8	56.6	61.3	40.1	39.7
Owners	1,805,196	1,866,742	1,035,564	946,018	57.4	50.7	76.7	87.9	44.0	44.6
Managers	83,603	94,684	17,533	8,126	21.0	8.6	623.9	1,168.9	130.8	100.3
Tenants	2,570,341	2,322,237	2,107,457	1,822,369	82.0	78.5	46.6	47.8	38.2	37.5
MOUNTAIN.										
MONTANA.										
White farmers:										
Total	34,419,041	13,253,237	10,859,296	3,609,567	31.6	27.2	608.0	529.7	191.8	144.3
Owners	28,346,665	10,354,149	8,978,081	2,865,771	31.7	27.7	575.1	466.4	182.2	129.1
Managers	2,855,278	1,426,650	488,648	357,140	17.1	25.0	3,211.8	2,841.9	549.7	711.4
Tenants	3,217,098	1,472,438	1,392,567	386,656	43.3	26.3	499.6	635.2	216.3	166.8
Colored farmers:										
Total	651,615	292,366	147,982	30,742	22.7	10.5	613.0	244.5	139.2	25.7
Owners	606,285	286,753	136,675	29,052	22.5	10.1	615.5	245.7	138.8	24.9
Managers	4,595	3,340	685	700	14.9	21.0	459.5	1,113.3	68.5	233.3
Tenants	40,735	2,273	10,622	990	26.1	43.6	599.0	87.4	156.2	38.1
IDAHO.										
White farmers:										
Total	8,327,986	5,224,913	4,482,946	2,751,145	53.8	52.7	200.2	171.9	107.8	90.5
Owners	6,762,649	4,391,818	3,524,814	2,244,062	52.1	51.1	197.3	163.7	102.8	83.7
Managers	385,718	270,234	181,096	126,814	47.0	46.9	508.9	600.5	238.9	281.8
Tenants	1,179,619	562,861	777,036	380,269	65.9	67.6	179.9	180.1	118.5	121.6
Colored farmers:										
Total	47,887	58,691	28,734	27,595	60.0	47.0	94.3	144.9	56.6	68.1
Owners	36,244	54,495	19,213	24,052	53.0	44.1	99.8	158.9	52.9	70.1
Managers										
Tenants	11,643	4,196	9,521	3,543	81.8	84.4	80.3	67.7	65.7	57.1

TABLE 39.—ACREAGE OF FARM LAND, WITH PERCENTAGES AND AVERAGES, BY COLOR AND TENURE, BY DIVISIONS AND STATES: 1920 AND 1910—Continued.

[Corresponding figures for all farmers, by tenure, in Table 25.]

DIVISION OR STATE AND COLOR AND TENURE.	ALL LAND IN FARMS (ACRES).		IMPROVED LAND IN FARMS (ACRES).		PER CENT OF FARM LAND IMPROVED.		AVERAGE ACREAGE PER FARM.			
							All land.		Improved land.	
	1920	1910	1920	1910	1920	1910	1920	1910	1920	1910
MOUNTAIN—Con.										
WYOMING.										
White farmers:										
Total	11,786,483	8,532,201	2,093,662	1,251,126	17.8	14.7	756.6	781.2	134.4	114.6
Owners	9,341,381	5,142,112	1,657,632	935,618	17.7	18.2	703.4	529.1	124.8	96.3
Managers	1,465,993	2,862,912	148,024	189,820	10.1	6.6	3,888.6	9,235.2	392.6	612.3
Tenants	979,109	527,177	288,006	125,688	29.4	23.8	509.4	589.7	149.8	140.6
Colored farmers:										
Total	22,868	10,809	8,343	5,034	36.5	46.6	135.3	166.3	49.4	77.4
Owners	18,136	10,469	5,516	4,754	30.4	45.4	147.4	171.6	44.8	77.9
Managers		80		80		100.0		80.0		80.0
Tenants	4,732	260	2,827	200	59.7	76.9	102.9	86.7	61.5	66.7
COLORADO.										
White farmers:										
Total	24,374,636	13,424,263	7,700,761	4,287,410	31.6	31.9	410.5	294.4	129.7	94.0
Owners	18,574,947	10,048,059	5,566,744	2,903,840	30.0	28.9	412.4	275.1	123.6	79.5
Managers	1,593,463	1,137,746	296,707	310,302	18.6	27.3	1,823.2	1,447.5	339.5	394.8
Tenants	4,206,226	2,238,458	1,837,310	1,073,268	43.7	47.9	312.4	270.2	136.5	129.6
Colored farmers:										
Total	87,378	107,850	43,996	14,691	50.4	13.6	158.0	187.9	79.6	25.6
Owners	46,731	86,738	15,703	4,057	33.6	4.7	188.4	186.1	63.3	8.7
Managers	2,390	2,700	1,095	100	45.8	3.7	398.3	2,700.0	182.5	100.0
Tenants	38,257	18,412	27,198	10,534	71.1	57.2	127.9	172.1	91.0	98.4
NEW MEXICO.										
White farmers:										
Total	24,345,274	11,086,792	1,696,964	1,446,220	7.0	13.0	870.4	330.7	60.7	43.1
Owners	17,794,166	6,921,976	1,376,527	1,279,154	7.7	18.5	737.9	221.3	57.1	40.9
Managers	3,862,963	3,190,229	76,340	73,887	2.0	2.3	8,962.8	10,063.8	177.1	233.1
Tenants	2,688,145	974,587	244,097	93,179	9.1	9.6	784.9	503.9	71.3	48.2
Colored farmers:										
Total	64,359	183,229	20,260	20,971	31.5	11.4	34.3	85.3	10.8	9.8
Owners	59,840	173,925	16,556	19,585	27.7	11.3	36.4	82.0	10.1	9.2
Managers	26	5,530	26	260	100.0	4.7	13.0	1,382.5	13.0	65.0
Tenants	4,493	3,774	3,678	1,126	81.9	29.8	19.5	164.1	16.0	49.0
ARIZONA.										
White farmers:										
Total	5,741,704	1,145,737	693,184	323,767	12.1	28.3	615.5	190.2	74.3	53.7
Owners	3,765,468	777,207	427,255	230,530	11.3	29.7	514.7	153.8	58.4	45.6
Managers	1,389,819	263,123	118,845	34,761	8.6	13.2	4,632.7	1,731.1	396.2	228.7
Tenants	586,417	105,407	147,084	58,476	25.1	55.5	342.3	128.9	85.9	71.5
Colored farmers:										
Total	60,422	100,876	19,619	26,406	32.5	26.2	93.5	31.5	30.4	8.2
Owners	54,183	97,707	14,755	23,909	27.2	24.5	98.0	31.0	26.7	7.6
Managers	1,130	1,675	370	1,110	32.7	66.3	226.0	152.3	74.0	100.9
Tenants	5,109	1,494	4,494	1,387	88.0	92.8	58.1	34.7	51.1	32.3
UTAH.										
White farmers:										
Total	4,999,240	3,374,792	1,696,794	1,356,600	33.9	40.5	198.9	197.7	67.4	81.1
Owners	4,046,688	2,871,213	1,447,206	1,196,234	35.8	41.7	181.1	146.9	64.8	61.9
Managers	590,341	312,876	78,994	63,962	13.4	20.4	2,014.8	1,621.1	269.6	331.4
Tenants	362,211	190,703	170,594	96,464	47.1	50.6	138.5	114.8	65.2	58.1
Colored farmers:										
Total	51,170	22,907	18,586	11,551	36.3	50.4	123.6	83.0	44.9	41.9
Owners	15,820	16,877	9,890	5,838	62.5	34.6	66.2	78.1	41.4	27.0
Managers	25,393	2,500	350	2,500	1.4	100.0	8,464.3	2,500.0	116.7	2,500.0
Tenants	9,957	3,530	8,346	3,213	83.8	91.0	57.9	59.8	48.5	54.5

TABLE 39.—ACREAGE OF FARM LAND, WITH PERCENTAGES AND AVERAGES, BY COLOR AND TENURE, BY DIVISIONS AND STATES: 1920 AND 1910—Continued.

[Corresponding figures for all farmers, by tenure, in Table 25.]

DIVISION OR STATE AND COLOR AND TENURE.	ALL LAND IN FARMS (ACRES).		IMPROVED LAND IN FARMS (ACRES).		PER CENT OF FARM LAND IMPROVED.		AVERAGE ACREAGE PER FARM.			
							All land.		Improved land.	
	1920	1910	1920	1910	1920	1910	1920	1910	1920	1910
MOUNTAIN—Con.										
NEVADA.										
White farmers:										
Total	2,345,393	2,706,827	587,089	747,532	25.0	27.6	796.7	1,070.7	199.4	295.7
Owners	1,408,436	1,025,389	388,928	381,824	27.6	37.2	565.4	506.9	156.1	188.7
Managers	796,397	1,523,970	145,215	310,487	18.2	20.4	4,768.8	8,466.5	869.6	1,724.9
Tenants	140,560	157,468	52,946	55,221	37.7	35.1	491.5	484.5	185.1	169.9
Colored farmers:										
Total	11,770	7,930	7,652	4,585	65.0	57.8	53.7	49.3	34.9	28.5
Owners	11,095	7,043	7,324	4,308	66.0	61.2	53.3	46.3	35.2	28.3
Managers	80	160	20	40	25.0	25.0	80.0	160.0	20.0	40.0
Tenants	595	727	308	237	51.8	32.6	59.5	90.9	30.8	29.6
PACIFIC.										
WASHINGTON.										
White farmers:										
Total	13,143,321	11,611,390	7,085,158	6,340,269	53.9	54.6	202.1	210.9	109.0	115.1
Owners	9,190,187	9,032,286	4,508,944	4,737,809	49.1	52.5	176.1	193.0	86.4	101.2
Managers	539,938	528,561	255,685	159,096	47.4	30.1	465.9	556.4	220.6	167.5
Tenants	3,413,196	2,050,543	2,320,529	1,443,364	68.0	70.4	292.3	280.4	198.7	197.4
Colored farmers:										
Total	101,399	100,845	44,185	33,042	43.6	32.8	80.1	89.6	34.9	29.4
Owners	69,613	82,885	20,636	23,027	29.6	27.8	134.6	118.2	39.9	32.8
Managers	1,198	521	706	365	58.9	70.1	133.1	47.4	78.4	33.2
Tenants	30,588	17,439	22,843	9,650	74.7	55.3	41.3	42.2	30.9	23.4
OREGON.										
White farmers:										
Total	13,442,465	11,469,729	4,884,562	4,203,339	36.3	36.6	270.8	255.6	98.4	93.7
Owners	9,927,903	8,830,931	3,308,747	2,996,338	33.3	33.9	251.3	236.6	83.8	80.3
Managers	836,557	763,539	299,973	211,852	35.9	27.7	921.3	910.1	330.4	252.5
Tenants	2,678,005	1,875,259	1,275,842	995,149	47.6	53.1	290.5	279.1	138.4	148.1
Colored farmers:										
Total	99,853	215,381	29,289	71,464	29.3	33.2	174.3	343.5	51.1	114.0
Owners	89,359	205,439	22,403	65,012	25.1	31.6	249.6	429.8	62.6	136.0
Managers	1,367	2,468	714	960	52.2	38.9	170.9	308.5	89.3	120.0
Tenants	9,127	7,474	6,172	5,492	67.6	73.5	44.1	53.0	29.8	39.0
CALIFORNIA.										
White farmers:										
Total	28,844,686	27,668,451	11,477,495	11,208,338	39.8	40.5	259.4	325.1	103.2	131.7
Owners	17,069,511	15,032,263	6,769,589	6,436,278	39.7	42.8	197.7	228.8	78.4	98.0
Managers	5,460,250	6,597,970	1,567,667	1,724,012	28.7	26.1	1,137.6	1,966.6	326.6	513.9
Tenants	6,314,925	6,038,218	3,140,239	3,048,048	49.7	50.5	315.0	375.7	156.6	189.7
Colored farmers:										
Total	520,981	262,993	400,844	181,556	76.9	69.0	80.3	85.4	61.8	59.0
Owners	126,704	93,076	49,623	28,194	39.2	30.3	101.9	99.2	39.9	30.1
Managers	25,197	7,002	19,851	4,613	78.8	65.9	169.1	112.9	133.2	74.4
Tenants	369,080	162,915	331,370	148,749	89.8	91.3	72.5	78.4	65.1	71.6

TABLE **40.**—VALUE OF ALL FARM PROPERTY AND OF THE SEVERAL CLASSES,

[Corresponding figures for all farmers,

DIVISION OR STATE AND COLOR AND TENURE.	ALL FARM PROPERTY.		LAND AND BUILDINGS.		
			Total.		Land alone.
	1920	1910	1920	1910	1920
UNITED STATES.					
White farmers:					
1 Total..........	$74,955,403,721	$39,712,214,845	$63,786,058,855	$33,764,392,187	$52,707,641,140
2 Owners..........	46,810,947,920	26,228,711,934	39,215,462,823	22,020,188,824	31,471,590,402
3 Managers.........	3,091,165,814	1,681,895,418	2,629,284,676	1,440,643,081	2,178,344,776
4 Tenants..........	25,053,289,987	11,801,607,493	21,941,311,356	10,303,560,282	19,057,705,962
Colored farmers:					
5 Total..........	2,968,696,617	1,279,234,245	2,529,943,747	1,036,733,510	2,121,921,919
6 Owners..........	800,598,024	440,922,439	648,760,084	346,745,454	513,191,232
7 Managers..........	41,107,191	18,729,518	35,931,789	16,315,911	29,306,244
8 Tenants..........	2,126,991,402	819,582,288	1,845,251,874	673,672,145	1,579,424,443
GEOGRAPHIC DIVISIONS.					
NEW ENGLAND.					
White farmers:					
9 Total..........	1,171,606,271	866,221,490	916,313,274	717,679,060	487,501,110
10 Owners..........	948,743,034	706,438,885	732,311,285	579,415,085	383,896,933
11 Managers..........	133,236,621	91,434,284	114,885,476	81,494,826	63,931,157
12 Tenants..........	89,626,616	68,348,321	69,116,513	56,769,149	39,673,020
Colored farmers:					
13 Total..........	1,413,323	1,018,967	1,155,310	865,748	624,140
14 Owners..........	844,951	648,973	674,660	536,258	341,390
15 Managers..........	285,393	183,557	236,900	168,400	120,000
16 Tenants..........	282,979	186,437	243,750	161,090	162,750
MIDDLE ATLANTIC.					
White farmers:					
17 Total..........	3,939,421,666	2,951,859,412	2,994,027,569	2,436,301,466	1,656,863,858
18 Owners..........	2,659,326,425	1,953,245,680	1,984,594,546	1,591,201,784	1,039,983,670
19 Managers..........	299,949,236	198,277,519	254,648,815	177,279,093	148,783,955
20 Tenants..........	980,146,005	800,336,213	754,784,208	667,820,589	468,096,233
Colored farmers:					
21 Total..........	10,262,517	7,729,610	8,110,185	6,647,637	4,812,249
22 Owners..........	4,265,149	3,660,672	3,181,240	3,023,325	1,720,379
23 Managers..........	2,121,176	1,100,488	1,802,965	1,004,657	964,115
24 Tenants..........	3,876,192	2,968,450	3,125,980	2,619,655	2,127,755
EAST NORTH CENTRAL.					
White farmers:					
25 Total..........	17,216,409,359	10,096,755,805	14,913,047,970	8,854,513,191	12,026,451,412
26 Owners..........	10,043,050,901	6,301,649,359	8,535,502,609	5,448,421,817	6,567,616,302
27 Managers..........	475,338,563	221,216,313	419,553,629	197,256,127	334,600,649
28 Tenants..........	6,698,019,895	3,573,890,133	5,957,991,732	3,208,835,247	5,124,234,461
Colored farmers:					
29 Total..........	28,953,234	22,372,261	24,593,701	19,478,403	19,622,272
30 Owners..........	15,091,153	12,360,044	12,454,252	10,537,440	9,361,404
31 Managers..........	1,720,161	1,240,560	1,478,081	1,091,625	1,154,347
32 Tenants..........	12,141,920	8,771,657	10,661,368	7,849,338	9,106,521
WEST NORTH CENTRAL.					
White farmers:					
33 Total..........	27,924,140,000	13,470,577,969	24,412,768,920	11,568,497,127	21,290,066,058
34 Owners..........	16,795,115,502	8,939,619,373	14,508,000,491	7,581,431,104	12,411,500,280
35 Managers..........	514,843,581	233,149,336	444,064,157	198,076,577	385,431,288
36 Tenants..........	10,614,189,905	4,306,809,160	9,460,704,272	3,788,989,446	8,493,134,490
Colored farmers:					
37 Total..........	67,285,556	55,731,642	56,726,249	46,168,743	50,079,084
38 Owners..........	45,979,296	42,232,845	38,114,732	34,449,272	33,369,137
39 Managers..........	2,175,101	1,829,873	1,842,035	1,535,280	1,636,085
40 Tenants..........	19,131,159	11,668,924	16,769,482	10,184,191	15,073,862
SOUTH ATLANTIC.					
White farmers:					
41 Total..........	4,975,830,728	2,507,381,097	4,214,016,606	2,118,729,406	3,196,691,946
42 Owners..........	3,377,197,368	1,774,857,545	2,831,898,133	1,487,725,662	2,097,506,487
43 Managers..........	292,741,327	133,083,247	261,025,722	119,811,609	207,364,286
44 Tenants..........	1,305,892,033	599,440,305	1,121,092,751	511,192,135	891,821,173

BY COLOR AND TENURE, BY DIVISIONS AND STATES: 1920 AND 1910.

by tenure, in Table 26.]

LAND AND BUILDINGS—continued.			IMPLEMENTS AND MACHINERY.		LIVE STOCK.		
Land alone—Continued.	Buildings.						
1910	1920	1910	1920	1910	1920	1910	
$27,615,515,334	$11,078,417,715	$6,148,876,853	$3,491,321,159	$1,227,407,744	$7,678,023,707	$4,720,414,914	1
17,528,730,187	7,743,872,421	4,491,458,637	2,411,134,220	884,819,727	5,184,350,877	3,323,703,383	2
1,205,653,349	450,939,900	234,989,732	102,231,072	42,473,043	359,650,066	198,779,294	3
8,881,131,798	2,883,605,394	1,422,428,484	977,955,867	300,114,974	2,134,022,764	1,197,932,237	4
860,158,835	408,021,828	176,574,675	103,451,769	37,742,039	335,301,101	204,758,696	5
277,391,441	135,568,852	69,354,013	36,658,561	15,852,814	115,179,379	78,324,171	6
13,205,916	6,625,545	3,109,995	1,542,630	435,457	3,632,772	1,978,150	7
569,561,478	265,827,431	104,110,667	65,250,578	21,453,768	216,488,950	124,456,375	8
381,669,966	428,812,164	336,009,094	92,318,985	50,751,863	162,974,012	97,790,567	9
301,890,603	348,414,352	277,524,482	79,655,997	43,919,419	136,775,752	83,104,381	10
46,906,729	50,954,319	34,588,097	6,749,341	3,568,179	11,601,804	6,371,279	11
32,872,634	29,443,493	23,896,515	5,913,647	3,264,265	14,596,456	8,314,907	12
464,458	531,170	401,290	68,540	46,963	189,473	106,256	13
287,618	333,270	248,640	50,215	34,721	120,076	77,994	14
78,900	116,900	89,500	8,500	4,225	39,993	10,932	15
97,940	81,000	63,150	9,825	8,017	29,404	17,330	16
1,457,962,424	1,337,163,711	978,339,042	358,461,081	167,150,284	586,933,016	348,407,662	17
904,928,832	944,610,876	686,272,952	262,220,457	119,928,613	412,511,422	242,115,283	18
110,852,178	105,864,860	66,426,915	16,375,418	7,351,062	28,925,003	13,647,364	19
442,181,414	286,687,975	225,639,175	79,865,206	39,870,609	145,496,591	92,645,015	20
4,358,581	3,297,936	2,289,056	691,255	330,100	1,461,077	751,873	21
1,888,254	1,460,861	1,135,071	348,764	191,967	735,145	445,380	22
632,682	838,850	371,975	125,160	36,275	193,051	59,556	23
1,837,645	998,225	782,010	217,331	101,858	532,881	246,937	24
7,215,452,063	2,886,596,558	1,639,061,128	784,896,834	268,280,588	1,518,464,555	973,962,026	25
4,273,324,867	1,967,886,307	1,175,096,950	520,972,145	188,663,765	986,576,147	664,563,777	26
160,145,326	84,952,980	84,110,801	16,229,805	5,028,731	39,555,129	18,931,455	27
2,781,981,870	833,757,271	426,853,377	247,694,884	74,588,092	492,333,279	290,466,794	28
16,247,051	4,971,429	3,231,352	1,179,971	525,962	3,179,562	2,367,896	29
8,356,503	3,092,848	2,180,937	702,346	353,434	1,934,555	1,469,170	30
948,315	323,734	143,310	80,675	15,812	161,405	133,123	31
6,942,233	1,554,847	907,105	396,950	156,716	1,083,602	765,603	32
10,010,918,131	3,122,702,862	1,557,578,996	1,160,502,401	367,587,275	2,350,877,668	1,543,493,467	33
6,457,081,390	2,096,500,211	1,124,349,714	755,425,094	262,198,019	1,531,689,918	1,095,990,250	34
174,500,165	58,632,869	23,576,412	14,220,499	4,655,030	56,558,925	30,417,729	35
3,379,336,576	967,569,782	409,652,870	390,856,808	100,734,226	762,628,825	417,085,488	36
41,642,782	6,647,165	4,525,961	2,435,863	1,348,269	8,123,444	8,214,630	37
31,016,444	4,745,595	3,432,828	1,820,119	1,074,245	6,044,445	6,709,328	38
1,373,010	205,950	162,270	49,200	20,465	283,866	274,128	39
9,253,328	1,695,620	930,863	566,544	253,559	1,795,133	1,231,174	40
1,586,788,567	1,017,324,660	531,940,839	241,801,676	85,015,410	520,012,446	303,636,281	41
1,088,123,244	734,391,646	399,602,418	178,386,882	64,033,588	366,912,353	223,098,295	42
94,980,026	53,661,436	24,831,583	10,392,845	3,777,396	21,322,760	9,494,242	43
403,685,297	229,271,578	107,506,838	53,021,949	17,204,426	131,777,333	71,043,744	44

Table 40.—VALUE OF ALL FARM PROPERTY AND OF THE SEVERAL CLASSES,

[Corresponding figures for all farmers,

| | DIVISION OR STATE AND COLOR AND TENURE. | ALL FARM PROPERTY. | | LAND AND BUILDINGS. | | |
| | | | | Total. | | Land alone. |
		1920	1910	1920	1910	1920
	GEOG. DIVISIONS—Con.					
	SOUTH ATLANTIC—Con.					
	Colored farmers:					
1	Total	$1,157,087,032	$443,819,676	$987,756,856	$367,707,068	$803,989,958
2	Owners	291,639,455	130,539,924	239,740,672	105,568,619	179,899,817
3	Managers	12,729,249	6,369,980	11,150,682	5,727,681	8,092,064
4	Tenants	852,718,328	306,909,772	736,865,512	256,410,768	615,998,077
	EAST SOUTH CENTRAL.					
	White farmers:					
5	Total	3,651,406,813	1,825,482,285	3,017,686,597	1,458,730,081	2,375,799,593
6	Owners	2,597,652,955	1,340,401,654	2,131,646,950	1,064,815,312	1,650,818,824
7	Managers	105,180,741	52,977,285	90,169,108	45,025,391	75,054,392
8	Tenants	948,573,117	432,103,346	795,870,539	348,889,378	649,926,377
	Colored farmers:					
9	Total	768,059,424	357,289,494	646,006,766	279,667,758	540,341,639
10	Owners	160,744,376	92,244,127	127,444,707	70,937,214	99,739,165
11	Managers	5,585,035	3,273,259	4,653,261	2,572,270	3,773,186
12	Tenants	601,730,013	261,772,108	513,908,798	206,158,274	436,829,288
	WEST SOUTH CENTRAL.					
	White farmers:					
13	Total	6,920,352,661	3,522,621,931	5,697,100,087	2,875,839,374	4,904,785,270
14	Owners	3,949,740,426	2,071,494,081	3,184,604,019	1,671,394,113	2,674,169,690
15	Managers	373,876,950	245,774,925	296,667,757	203,111,147	274,721,988
16	Tenants	2,596,735,285	1,205,352,925	2,215,828,311	1,001,334,114	1,955,893,592
	Colored farmers:					
17	Total	701,713,366	315,532,406	594,087,985	252,757,508	503,274,345
18	Owners	228,261,282	124,097,219	184,545,683	96,486,405	150,290,098
19	Managers	6,780,776	2,416,164	5,729,955	2,071,998	5,154,367
20	Tenants	466,671,308	189,019,023	403,812,347	154,199,105	347,829,880
	MOUNTAIN.					
	White farmers:					
21	Total	4,040,266,794	1,732,578,273	3,130,443,403	1,302,812,786	2,771,945,669
22	Owners	3,035,944,294	1,296,929,471	2,332,192,366	958,442,520	2,047,203,237
23	Managers	322,255,011	186,025,701	232,410,007	132,587,229	211,830,464
24	Tenants	682,067,489	249,623,101	565,841,030	211,783,037	512,911,968
	Colored farmers:					
25	Total	42,871,145	24,995,095	32,744,380	16,584,087	29,766,410
26	Owners	26,909,612	21,740,257	18,866,800	13,690,006	16,950,929
27	Managers	882,300	550,968	697,975	460,500	522,105
28	Tenants	15,079,233	2,703,870	13,179,605	2,433,581	12,293,376
	PACIFIC.					
	White farmers:					
29	Total	5,115,960,440	2,729,736,683	4,490,654,429	2,431,289,696	3,997,536,224
30	Owners	3,404,177,014	1,844,075,886	2,974,712,424	1,637,341,427	2,598,894,979
31	Managers	573,743,784	319,956,808	515,860,005	286,001,082	476,626,597
32	Tenants	1,138,039,642	565,703,989	1,000,082,000	507,947,187	922,014,648
	Colored farmers:					
33	Total	191,051,020	50,745,094	178,762,305	46,856,558	169,411,822
34	Owners	26,862,750	13,383,378	20,737,738	11,516,915	21,518,913
35	Managers	8,828,000	1,704,669	8,329,935	1,683,500	7,889,975
36	Tenants	155,360,270	35,582,047	146,685,032	33,656,143	140,002,934
	NEW ENGLAND.					
	MAINE.					
	White farmers:					
37	Total	270,461,895	199,218,941	204,054,571	159,576,776	114,379,071
38	Owners	249,754,050	185,040,067	187,450,675	147,676,269	104,898,813
39	Managers	10,634,334	6,436,921	8,764,123	5,374,670	4,655,990
40	Tenants	10,073,511	7,741,953	7,839,773	6,525,837	4,824,268

BY COLOR AND TENURE, BY DIVISIONS AND STATES: 1920 AND 1910—Continued.

by tenure, in Table 26.]

LAND AND BUILDINGS—continued.			IMPLEMENTS AND MACHINERY.		LIVE STOCK.		
Land alone—Continued.	Buildings.						
1910	1920	1910	1920	1910	1920	1910	
$296,561,108	$183,766,908	$71,145,960	$42,179,181	$13,214,737	$127,150,985	$62,897,871	1
77,986,421	59,840,855	27,582,198	13,891,348	5,076,156	38,007,435	19,895,149	2
4,421,071	3,058,618	1,306,610	495,917	163,508	1,082,650	478,791	3
214,153,616	120,867,435	42,257,152	27,791,916	7,975,073	88,060,900	42,523,931	4
1,099,625,442	641,887,004	359,104,639	151,269,115	64,162,382	482,451,101	302,589,822	5
783,373,358	480,828,126	281,411,954	114,841,715	49,720,287	351,164,290	225,866,055	6
36,127,839	15,114,716	8,897,552	3,696,750	1,861,178	11,314,883	6,090,716	7
280,124,245	145,944,162	68,765,133	32,730,650	12,580,917	119,971,928	70,633,051	8
227,201,422	105,665,127	52,466,336	24,795,771	11,176,951	97,256,887	66,444,785	9
54,822,622	27,705,542	16,114,592	7,290,300	3,769,285	26,009,369	17,537,628	10
1,981,765	880,075	590,505	223,573	78,278	708,201	622,711	11
170,397,035	77,079,510	35,761,239	17,281,898	7,329,388	70,539,317	48,284,446	12
2,502,228,938	792,314,817	373,610,436	287,685,655	110,334,947	935,566,919	536,447,610	13
1,419,216,175	510,434,329	252,177,938	184,266,389	68,473,621	580,870,018	331,626,347	14
190,363,232	21,945,769	12,747,915	10,538,594	7,625,159	66,670,599	35,038,619	15
892,649,531	259,934,719	108,684,583	92,880,672	34,236,167	288,026,302	169,782,644	16
213,869,592	90,813,640	38,887,916	23,413,135	9,385,430	84,212,246	53,389,468	17
79,466,528	34,255,585	17,019,877	10,148,918	4,443,821	33,566,681	23,166,993	18
1,854,018	575,588	217,980	183,409	67,118	867,412	277,048	19
132,549,046	55,982,467	21,650,059	13,080,808	4,874,491	49,778,153	29,945,427	20
1,158,747,365	358,497,734	144,065,421	188,660,056	48,828,852	721,163,335	380,936,635	21
843,019,886	284,989,129	115,422,634	151,525,199	39,936,062	552,226,729	298,550,889	22
122,490,795	20,579,543	10,096,434	8,349,147	3,090,980	81,495,857	50,347,492	23
193,236,684	52,929,062	18,546,353	28,785,710	5,801,810	87,440,749	32,038,254	24
15,622,731	2,977,970	961,356	2,055,617	601,123	8,071,148	7,809,885	25
12,877,246	1,915,871	812,760	1,319,799	515,915	6,723,013	7,534,336	26
433,275	175,870	27,225	31,901	14,761	152,424	75,707	27
2,312,210	886,229	121,371	703,917	70,447	1,195,711	199,842	28
2,202,122,438	493,118,205	229,167,258	225,725,356	65,296,143	399,580,655	233,150,844	29
1,457,771,832	375,817,445	179,569,595	163,840,342	47,946,353	265,624,248	158,788,106	30
269,287,059	39,233,408	16,714,023	15,678,673	5,515,328	42,205,106	28,440,398	31
475,063,547	78,067,352	32,883,640	46,206,341	11,834,462	91,751,301	45,922,340	32
44,191,110	9,350,483	2,665,448	6,632,436	1,112,504	5,656,279	2,776,032	33
10,169,805	2,218,425	827,110	1,086,752	393,270	2,038,660	1,488,193	34
1,482,880	449,960	200,620	344,295	35,015	143,770	46,154	35
32,018,425	6,682,098	1,637,718	5,201,389	684,219	3,473,849	1,241,685	36
86,461,820	89,675,500	73,114,956	26,635,535	14,486,603	39,771,789	25,155,562	37
79,790,266	82,551,862	67,886,003	25,104,180	13,709,630	37,199,195	23,654,168	38
2,724,500	4,108,133	2,650,170	724,167	354,264	1,146,044	707,987	39
3,947,054	3,015,505	2,578,783	807,188	422,709	1,426,550	793,407	40

TABLE 40.—VALUE OF ALL FARM PROPERTY AND OF THE SEVERAL CLASSES,

[Corresponding figures for all farmers,

DIVISION OR STATE AND COLOR AND TENURE.	ALL FARM PROPERTY.		LAND AND BUILDINGS.		
			Total.		Land alone.
	1920	1910	1920	1910	1920
NEW ENGLAND—Con.					
MAINE—con.					
Colored farmers:					
1 Total............	$64,838	$53,057	$54,400	$42,850	$32,800
2 Owners...........	64,838	46,986	54,400	37,500	32,800
3 Managers.........		920		900	
4 Tenants..........		5,151		4,450	
NEW HAMPSHIRE.					
White farmers:					
5 Total............	118,596,899	103,630,603	89,966,470	85,853,261	47,414,381
6 Owners...........	100,478,315	90,287,937	75,500,477	74,439,558	39,934,558
7 Managers.........	11,190,713	7,754,322	9,341,273	6,757,633	4,735,683
8 Tenants..........	6,927,871	5,588,344	5,124,720	4,656,070	2,744,140
Colored farmers:					
9 Total............	59,216	73,593	29,400	62,800	10,950
10 Owners...........	27,550	14,575	18,200	12,000	7,350
11 Managers.........	26,936	12,025	10,000	10,000	3,000
12 Tenants..........	4,730	46,993	1,200	40,800	600
VERMONT.					
White farmers:					
13 Total............	222,574,834	145,346,562	159,000,434	112,545,925	82,863,428
14 Owners...........	179,155,978	115,596,874	126,599,752	88,530,867	65,588,889
15 Managers.........	11,919,611	9,163,066	9,603,078	7,924,385	4,806,203
16 Tenants..........	31,499,245	20,586,622	22,797,604	16,090,673	12,468,336
Colored farmers:					
17 Total............	161,786	53,166	116,725	42,350	74,825
18 Owners...........	120,779	44,633	87,125	35,150	55,425
19 Managers.........	12,101	1,700	8,900	1,700	5,200
20 Tenants..........	28,906	6,833	20,700	5,500	14,200
MASSACHUSETTS.					
White farmers:					
21 Total............	300,008,689	226,126,582	247,214,036	193,867,012	127,473,632
22 Owners...........	223,762,381	169,724,030	181,827,185	143,998,535	90,403,709
23 Managers.........	58,435,338	40,967,349	50,906,024	36,709,690	28,659,331
24 Tenants..........	17,810,970	15,435,203	14,480,827	13,158,787	8,410,592
Colored farmers:					
25 Total............	463,054	347,443	373,795	301,753	179,975
26 Owners...........	348,953	283,302	271,345	242,863	122,575
27 Managers.........	90,411	38,035	82,000	36,300	46,300
28 Tenants..........	23,690	26,106	20,450	22,590	11,100
RHODE ISLAND.					
White farmers:					
29 Total............	33,585,186	32,907,783	26,348,426	27,868,260	14,483,223
30 Owners...........	23,037,876	21,577,746	17,916,756	18,090,945	9,465,493
31 Managers.........	5,541,030	5,915,923	4,609,373	5,175,000	2,579,998
32 Tenants..........	5,006,280	5,414,114	3,822,297	4,602,315	2,437,732
Colored farmers:					
33 Total............	51,580	82,956	39,500	64,600	25,850
34 Owners...........	31,183	61,035	24,900	46,350	16,400
35 Managers.........	7,941		7,000		4,500
36 Tenants..........	12,456	21,921	7,600	18,250	4,950
CONNECTICUT.					
White farmers:					
37 Total............	226,378,768	158,991,019	189,729,337	137,967,826	100,887,375
38 Owners...........	172,554,434	124,212,231	143,016,440	106,678,911	73,605,471
39 Managers.........	35,515,595	21,196,703	31,661,605	19,553,448	18,493,952
40 Tenants..........	18,308,739	13,582,085	15,051,292	11,735,467	8,787,952
Colored farmers:					
41 Total............	612,849	408,752	541,490	351,395	299,740
42 Owners...........	251,648	198,442	218,690	162,395	106,840
43 Managers.........	148,004	130,877	129,000	119,500	61,000
44 Tenants..........	213,197	79,433	193,800	69,600	131,900

BY COLOR AND TENURE, BY DIVISIONS AND STATES: 1920 AND 1910—Continued.

by tenure, in Table 26.]

| LAND AND BUILDINGS—continued. | | | IMPLEMENTS AND MACHINERY. | | LIVE STOCK. | | |
| Land alone— Continued. | Buildings. | | | | | | |
1910	1920	1910	1920	1910	1920	1910	
$19,575	$21,600	$23,275	$2,125	$3,930	$8,313	$6,277	1
17,175	21,600	20,325	2,125	3,510	8,313	5,976	2
300	....	600	....	20	....	....	3
2,100	....	2,350	....	400	....	301	4
44,487,297	42,552,089	41,365,964	9,496,647	5,874,452	19,133,782	11,902,890	5
38,491,600	35,565,919	35,947,958	8,376,335	5,281,147	16,601,503	10,567,232	6
3,578,654	4,605,590	3,178,979	633,959	329,605	1,215,481	667,084	7
2,417,043	2,380,580	2,239,027	486,353	263,700	1,316,798	668,574	8
31,750	18,450	31,050	2,675	3,205	27,141	7,588	9
6,550	10,850	5,450	2,175	980	7,175	1,595	10
5,000	7,000	5,000	500	25	16,436	2,000	11
20,200	600	20,600	....	2,200	3,530	3,993	12
58,365,227	76,137,006	54,180,698	21,216,990	10,165,727	42,357,410	22,634,910	13
45,029,999	61,010,863	43,500,868	18,070,388	8,599,604	34,485,838	18,466,403	14
4,272,040	4,796,875	3,652,345	740,397	385,225	1,576,136	853,456	15
9,063,188	10,329,268	7,027,485	2,406,205	1,180,898	6,295,436	3,315,051	16
20,100	41,900	22,250	17,140	2,960	27,921	7,856	17
15,900	31,700	19,250	13,940	2,660	19,714	6,823	18
1,200	3,700	500	400	....	2,801	....	19
3,000	6,500	2,500	2,800	300	5,406	1,033	20
105,375,928	119,740,404	88,491,084	19,337,590	11,549,835	33,457,063	20,709,735	21
74,535,960	91,423,476	69,462,575	15,790,507	9,332,521	26,144,689	16,392,974	22
22,875,406	22,246,693	13,834,284	2,619,537	1,541,091	4,909,777	2,716,568	23
7,964,562	6,070,235	5,194,225	927,546	676,223	2,402,597	1,600,193	24
156,688	193,820	145,065	22,165	14,059	67,094	31,631	25
124,098	148,770	118,765	16,765	12,306	60,843	28,133	26
19,500	35,700	16,800	4,100	650	4,311	1,085	27
13,090	9,350	9,500	1,300	1,103	1,940	2,413	28
14,971,131	11,865,203	12,897,129	2,405,186	1,775,087	4,831,574	3,264,436	29
8,994,908	8,451,263	9,096,037	1,764,256	1,239,129	3,356,864	2,247,672	30
3,210,643	2,029,375	1,964,357	315,378	291,870	616,279	449,053	31
2,765,580	1,384,565	1,836,735	325,552	244,088	858,431	567,711	32
38,850	13,650	25,750	3,375	6,320	8,705	12,036	33
28,500	8,500	17,850	2,225	4,965	4,058	9,720	34
....	2,500	....	500	....	441	....	35
10,350	2,650	7,900	650	1,355	4,206	2,316	36
72,008,563	88,841,962	65,959,263	13,227,037	6,900,159	23,422,394	14,123,034	37
55,047,870	69,410,969	51,631,041	10,550,331	5,757,388	18,987,663	11,775,932	38
10,245,486	13,167,653	9,307,962	1,715,903	666,124	2,138,087	977,131	39
6,715,207	6,263,340	5,020,260	960,803	476,647	2,296,644	1,369,971	40
197,495	241,750	153,900	21,060	16,489	50,299	40,868	41
95,395	111,850	67,000	12,985	10,300	19,973	25,747	42
52,900	68,000	66,600	3,000	3,530	16,004	7,847	43
49,200	61,900	20,300	5,075	2,659	14,322	7,274	44

TABLE **40.**—VALUE OF ALL FARM PROPERTY AND OF THE SEVERAL CLASSES,

[Corresponding figures for all farmers,

	DIVISION OR STATE AND COLOR AND TENURE.	ALL FARM PROPERTY.		LAND AND BUILDINGS.		
				Total.		Land alone.
		1920	1910	1920	1910	1920
	MIDDLE ATLANTIC.					
	NEW YORK.					
	White farmers:					
1	Total............	$1,904,843,484	$1,448,409,435	$1,422,362,205	$1,182,175,509	$791,805,268
2	Owners............	1,319,587,966	988,371,760	965,090,744	796,032,844	508,749,149
3	Managers...........	146,829,370	99,452,150	125,107,521	88,857,170	73,333,875
4	Tenants............	438,426,148	360,585,525	332,163,940	297,285,495	209,722,244
	Colored farmers:					
5	Total............	3,639,717	3,072,060	2,699,535	2,570,320	1,530,290
6	Owners............	2,111,251	2,059,688	1,502,615	1,679,730	834,270
7	Managers...........	611,454	177,914	466,940	158,050	215,790
8	Tenants............	917,012	834,458	729,980	732,540	480,230
	NEW JERSEY.					
	White farmers:					
9	Total............	309,193,917	252,858,966	248,174,396	215,434,782	140,827,209
10	Owners............	197,808,238	156,440,367	158,539,100	132,644,399	86,134,502
11	Managers...........	33,555,909	29,727,935	28,781,541	26,903,070	17,222,667
12	Tenants............	77,829,770	66,690,664	60,853,755	55,887,313	37,470,040
	Colored farmers:					
13	Total...........	2,654,031	1,973,699	2,149,590	1,699,737	1,355,289
14	Owners............	931,412	575,805	759,715	477,180	436,264
15	Managers...........	311,793	454,319	257,500	416,157	145,700
16	Tenants............	1,410,826	943,575	1,132,375	806,400	773,325
	PENNSYLVANIA.					
	White farmers:					
17	Total............	1,725,384,265	1,250,591,011	1,323,490,968	1,038,691,175	724,231,381
18	Owners............	1,141,930,221	808,433,553	860,964,702	662,524,541	415,100,019
19	Managers...........	119,563,957	69,097,434	100,759,753	61,518,853	58,227,413
20	Tenants............	463,890,087	373,060,024	361,766,513	314,647,781	220,903,949
	Colored farmers:					
21	Total...........	3,968,769	2,683,851	3,261,060	2,377,580	1,926,670
22	Owners............	1,222,486	1,025,179	918,910	866,415	449,845
23	Managers...........	1,197,929	468,255	1,078,525	430,450	602,625
24	Tenants............	1,548,354	1,190,417	1,263,625	1,080,715	874,200
	EAST NORTH CENTRAL.					
	OHIO.					
	White farmers:					
25	Total............	3,084,992,339	1,895,787,443	2,652,309,467	1,648,158,531	2,008,056,504
26	Owners............	1,841,805,135	1,212,597,916	1,568,080,923	1,044,884,584	1,142,219,120
27	Managers...........	97,860,349	52,659,573	86,673,986	47,630,020	64,824,169
28	Tenants............	1,145,326,855	630,529,954	997,554,558	555,643,927	801,013,215
	Colored farmers:					
29	Total............	10,673,997	6,907,146	9,126,482	5,993,875	7,056,495
30	Owners............	5,000,776	3,504,400	4,173,124	2,964,696	3,040,102
31	Managers...........	851,182	366,007	737,360	305,680	557,810
32	Tenants............	4,822,039	3,036,739	4,215,998	2,723,499	3,458,583
	INDIANA					
	White farmers:					
33	Total............	3,037,485,093	1,805,312,131	2,649,387,943	1,590,871,449	2,198,942,016
34	Owners............	1,746,939,544	1,136,135,608	1,505,952,568	991,333,749	1,213,305,413
35	Managers...........	74,221,537	42,493,445	65,245,276	37,595,791	54,335,613
36	Tenants............	1,216,324,012	626,683,078	1,078,190,099	561,941,909	931,300,990
	Colored farmers:					
37	Total............	4,826,154	3,823,107	4,256,030	3,404,147	3,624,320
38	Owners............	2,136,288	2,047,141	1,832,910	1,807,172	1,474,565
39	Managers...........	292,886	238,553	264,140	221,325	227,340
40	Tenants............	2,396,980	1,537,413	2,158,980	1,375,650	1,922,415

BY COLOR AND TENURE, BY DIVISIONS AND STATES: 1920 AND 1910—Continued.

by tenure, in Table 26.]

LAND AND BUILDINGS—continued.			IMPLEMENTS AND MACHINERY.		LIVE STOCK.		
Land alone— Continued.	Buildings.						
1910	1920	1910	1920	1910	1920	1910	
$706,075,459	$630,556,937	$476,100,050	$169,590,151	$83,493,538	$312,891,128	$182,740,388	1
450,892,148	456,341,595	345,140,696	127,779,338	61,850,120	226,717,884	130,488,796	2
55,972,220	51,773,646	32,884,950	7,367,788	3,527,133	14,354,061	7,067,847	3
199,211,091	122,441,696	98,074,404	34,443,025	18,116,285	71,819,183	45,183,745	4
1,672,369	1,169,245	897,951	276,615	151,284	663,567	350,456	5
1,088,594	668,345	591,136	187,525	111,855	421,111	268,103	6
103,050	251,150	55,000	39,260	9,300	105,254	10,564	7
480,725	249,750	251,815	49,830	30,129	137,202	71,789	8
123,112,050	107,347,187	92,322,732	25,273,751	13,024,911	35,745,770	24,399,273	9
71,939,175	72,404,598	60,705,224	17,135,263	8,667,416	22,133,875	15,128,552	10
15,853,415	11,558,874	11,049,655	1,927,433	1,040,076	2,846,935	1,784,789	11
35,319,460	23,383,715	20,567,853	6,211,055	3,317,419	10,764,960	7,485,932	12
1,031,117	794,301	668,620	185,454	84,596	318,987	189,366	13
271,720	323,451	205,460	66,980	33,895	104,717	64,730	14
252,957	111,800	163,200	17,925	14,260	36,368	23,902	15
506,440	359,050	299,960	100,549	36,441	177,902	100,734	16
628,774,915	599,259,587	409,916,260	163,597,179	70,631,835	238,296,118	141,268,001	17
382,097,509	415,864,683	280,427,032	117,305,856	49,411,077	163,659,663	96,497,935	18
39,026,543	42,532,340	22,492,310	7,080,197	2,783,853	11,724,007	4,794,728	19
207,650,863	140,862,564	106,996,918	39,211,126	18,436,905	62,912,448	39,975,338	20
1,655,095	1,334,390	722,485	229,186	94,220	478,523	212,051	21
527,940	469,065	338,475	94,259	46,217	209,317	112,547	22
276,675	475,900	153,775	67,975	12,715	51,429	25,090	23
850,480	389,425	230,235	66,952	35,288	217,777	74,414	24
1,281,029,174	644,252,963	367,129,357	146,148,088	51,061,393	286,534,784	196,567,519	25
788,752,728	425,861,803	256,131,856	93,461,670	34,605,053	180,262,542	133,108,279	26
36,633,079	21,849,817	10,996,941	3,516,576	1,198,683	7,669,787	3,830,870	27
455,643,367	196,541,343	100,000,560	49,169,842	15,257,657	98,602,455	59,628,370	28
4,865,638	2,069,987	1,128,237	427,181	148,678	1,120,334	764,593	29
2,264,184	1,133,022	700,512	217,753	93,540	609,899	446,164	30
245,140	179,550	60,540	39,765	3,720	74,057	56,607	31
2,356,314	757,415	367,185	169,663	51,418	436,378	261,822	32
1,325,245,358	450,445,927	265,626,091	127,272,631	40,934,436	260,824,519	173,506,246	33
803,041,066	292,647,155	188,292,683	79,712,881	27,779,376	161,274,095	117,022,483	34
32,437,669	10,909,663	5,158,122	2,324,051	760,996	6,652,210	4,136,658	35
489,766,623	146,889,109	72,175,286	45,235,699	12,394,064	92,898,214	52,347,105	36
2,951,187	631,710	452,960	130,455	65,105	439,669	353,855	37
1,537,347	358,345	269,825	62,305	39,022	241,073	200,947	38
181,505	36,800	39,820	11,300	1,865	17,446	15,363	39
1,232,335	236,565	143,315	56,850	24,218	181,150	137,545	40

75108°—23——44

TABLE 40.—VALUE OF ALL FARM PROPERTY AND OF THE SEVERAL CLASSES,

[Corresponding figures for all farmers,

	DIVISION OR STATE AND COLOR AND TENURE.	ALL FARM PROPERTY.		LAND AND BUILDINGS.		
				Total.		Land alone.
		1920	1910	1920	1910	1920
	EAST NORTH CENTRAL—Con.					
	ILLINOIS.					
	White farmers:					
1	Total	$6,659,697,065	$3,898,523,405	$5,991,909,691	$3,516,801,778	$5,244,998,200
2	Owners	3,037,357,822	1,980,515,101	2,689,220,786	1,763,516,457	2,273,876,661
3	Managers	178,864,629	71,645,528	162,074,362	64,498,713	139,447,281
4	Tenants	3,443,474,614	1,846,362,776	3,140,614,543	1,688,786,608	2,831,674,258
	Colored farmers:					
5	Total	7,070,170	6,797,670	6,083,875	5,990,792	5,296,552
6	Owners	3,058,969	2,908,112	2,542,200	2,475,853	2,067,002
7	Managers	280,720	571,059	244,600	509,320	224,500
8	Tenants	3,730,481	3,318,499	3,297,075	3,005,619	3,005,050
	MICHIGAN.					
	White farmers:					
9	Total	1,759,620,834	1,085,883,399	1,433,681,404	898,674,084	957,087,025
10	Owners	1,305,312,622	848,265,597	1,054,527,393	697,276,022	685,965,937
11	Managers	58,322,245	26,334,596	50,032,563	22,934,178	35,581,250
12	Tenants	395,985,967	211,283,206	329,121,448	178,463,884	235,539,838
	Colored farmers:					
13	Total	3,713,944	2,974,980	3,004,806	2,464,215	2,099,513
14	Owners	2,461,447	2,179,273	1,951,535	1,783,545	1,353,633
15	Managers	188,594	52,862	165,481	47,000	99,197
16	Tenants	1,063,903	742,845	887,790	633,670	646,683
	WISCONSIN.					
	White farmers:					
17	Total	2,674,614,028	1,411,249,427	2,185,759,465	1,200,007,349	1,617,367,667
18	Owners	2,111,635,778	1,124,135,137	1,717,720,939	951,411,005	1,252,249,171
19	Managers	66,069,803	28,083,171	55,527,442	24,597,425	40,412,336
20	Tenants	496,908,447	259,031,119	412,511,084	223,998,919	324,706,160
	Colored farmers:					
21	Total	2,668,969	1,869,358	2,122,508	1,625,374	1,545,392
22	Owners	2,433,673	1,721,118	1,954,483	1,506,174	1,426,102
23	Managers	106,779	12,079	66,500	8,300	45,500
24	Tenants	128,517	136,161	101,525	110,900	73,790
	WEST NORTH CENTRAL.					
	MINNESOTA.					
	White farmers:					
25	Total	3,786,230,388	1,475,524,942	3,300,302,223	1,261,737,765	2,749,640,002
26	Owners	2,536,609,747	1,082,713,358	2,191,052,872	919,852,474	1,788,482,079
27	Managers	58,155,402	24,153,161	50,230,658	20,896,011	40,228,519
28	Tenants	1,191,465,239	368,658,423	1,059,018,693	320,989,280	920,929,404
	Colored farmers:					
29	Total	1,189,730	886,795	866,102	703,661	688,430
30	Owners	979,739	636,698	698,182	506,873	557,335
31	Managers	7,577	14,116	4,000	13,240	2,000
32	Tenants	202,414	235,981	163,920	183,548	129,095
	IOWA.					
	White farmers:					
33	Total	8,523,312,759	3,744,583,913	7,600,441,690	3,256,290,815	6,677,866,277
34	Owners	4,543,714,016	2,257,063,692	4,010,757,910	1,942,080,289	3,447,714,783
35	Managers	140,718,205	51,831,112	125,849,751	44,907,725	110,545,702
36	Tenants	3,838,880,538	1,435,689,109	3,463,834,029	1,269,302,801	3,119,605,792
	Colored farmers:					
37	Total	1,558,197	1,276,631	1,330,600	1,088,585	1,154,300
38	Owners	784,702	621,835	683,250	514,060	584,550
39	Managers	54,523	99,094	51,000	86,200	48,500
40	Tenants	718,972	555,702	596,350	488,325	521,250

BY COLOR AND TENURE, BY DIVISIONS AND STATES: 1920 AND 1910—Continued.

by tenure, in Table 26.]

LAND AND BUILDINGS—continued.			IMPLEMENTS AND MACHINERY.		LIVE STOCK.		
Land alone—Continued.	Buildings.						
1910	1920	1910	1920	1910	1920	1910	
$3,085,093,580	$746,911,491	$431,708,198	$222,402,367	$73,590,331	$445,385,007	$308,131,296	1
1,501,844,713	415,344,125	261,671,744	113,325,122	41,249,404	234,811,914	175,749,240	2
56,025,287	22,627,081	8,473,426	4,374,392	1,263,302	12,415,875	5,883,513	3
1,527,223,580	308,940,285	161,563,028	104,702,853	31,077,625	198,157,218	126,498,543	4
5,317,568	787,323	673,224	217,238	133,743	769,057	673,135	5
2,061,174	475,198	414,679	110,288	71,631	406,481	360,628	6
482,320	20,100	27,000	7,220	7,540	28,900	54,199	7
2,774,074	292,025	231,545	99,730	54,572	333,676	258,308	8
613,443,483	476,594,379	285,230,601	122,155,226	49,801,094	203,784,204	137,408,221	9
467,740,482	368,561,456	229,535,540	95,930,199	40,786,047	154,855,030	110,203,528	10
16,771,239	14,451,313	6,162,939	2,850,328	908,266	5,439,354	2,492,152	11
128,931,762	93,581,610	49,532,122	23,374,699	8,106,781	43,489,820	24,712,541	12
1,814,865	905,293	649,350	234,710	115,191	474,428	395,574	13
1,287,065	597,902	496,480	153,763	93,490	356,149	302,238	14
33,850	66,284	13,150	17,400	1,595	5,713	4,267	15
493,950	241,107	139,720	63,547	20,106	112,566	89,069	16
910,640,468	568,391,798	289,366,881	166,918,522	52,893,334	321,936,041	158,348,744	17
711,945,878	465,471,768	239,465,127	138,542,273	44,243,885	255,372,566	128,480,247	18
18,278,052	15,115,106	6,319,373	3,164,458	897,484	7,377,903	2,588,262	19
180,416,538	87,804,924	43,582,381	25,211,791	7,751,965	59,185,572	27,280,235	20
1,297,793	577,116	327,581	170,387	63,245	376,074	180,739	21
1,206,733	528,381	299,441	158,237	55,751	320,953	159,193	22
5,500	21,000	2,800	4,990	1,092	35,289	2,687	23
85,560	27,735	25,340	7,160	6,402	19,832	18,859	24
1,018,550,643	550,662,221	243,187,122	181,021,121	52,282,127	304,907.044	161,505,050	25
731,157,154	402,570,793	188,695,320	130,330,718	40,279,614	215,226,157	122,581,270	26
16,863,176	10,002,139	4,032,835	2,144,474	769,578	5,780,270	2,487,572	27
270,530,313	138,089,289	50,458,967	48,545,929	11,232,935	83,900,617	36,436,208	28
551,384	177,672	152,277	66,847	47,038	256,781	136,096	29
397,691	140,487	109,182	58,156	33,340	223,401	96,485	30
12,440	2,000	800	1,000	275	2,577	601	31
141,253	34,825	42,295	7,691	13,423	30,803	39,010	32
2,801,073,364	922,575,413	455,217,451	309,122,421	95,437,450	613,748,648	392,855,648	33
1,637,013,594	563,043,127	305,066,695	179,025,967	61,368,226	353,930,139	253,615,177	34
39,127,022	15,304,049	5,780,703	3,089,670	1,030,532	11,778,784	5,892,855	35
1,124,932,748	344,228,237	144,370,053	127,006,784	33,038,692	248,039,725	133,347,616	36
900,365	176,300	188,220	49,977	40,498	177,620	147,548	37
393,385	98,700	120,675	28,742	23,763	72,710	84,012	38
72,200	2,500	14,000	800	2,700	2,723	10,194	39
434,780	75,100	53,545	20,435	14,035	102,187	53,342	40

TABLE 40.—VALUE OF ALL FARM PROPERTY AND OF THE SEVERAL CLASSES,

[Corresponding figures for all farmers,

	DIVISION OR STATE AND COLOR AND TENURE.	ALL FARM PROPERTY.		LAND AND BUILDINGS.		
				Total.		Land alone.
		1920	1910	1920	1910	1920
	WEST NORTH CENTRAL—Con.					
	MISSOURI.					
	White farmers:					
1	Total............	$3,571,957,295	$2,038,795,640	$3,046,425,093	$1,704,175,048	$2,579,804,597
2	Owners.............	2,466,597,321	1,453,650,819	2,080,967,866	1,200,375,407	1,734,640,306
3	Managers............	84,465,973	45,095,461	73,402,741	39,528,525	60,529,190
4	Tenants.............	1,020,894,001	540,049,360	892,054,486	464,271,116	784,635,101
	Colored farmers:					
5	Total............	19,110,790	14,121,848	16,542,607	12,029,338	14,388,674
6	Owners.............	9,933,766	6,887,512	8,451,537	5,645,438	7,224,054
7	Managers...........	1,461,153	921,594	1,276,095	833,455	1,135,345
8	Tenants.............	7,715,871	6,312,742	6,814,975	5,550,445	6,029,275
	NORTH DAKOTA.					
	White farmers:					
9	Total............	1,755,241,354	970,794,963	1,484,992,639	819,548,724	1,276,184,609
10	Owners.............	1,240,050,699	783,580,686	1,037,814,394	655,758,685	884,265,819
11	Managers...........	41,061,337	19,284,824	35,085,503	16,889,168	29,736,605
12	Tenants.............	474,129,318	167,929,453	412,092,742	146,900,871	362,182,185
	Colored farmers:					
13	Total............	4,501,641	4,019,242	3,528,856	3,108,020	3,129,018
14	Owners.............	3,856,846	3,940,809	3,041,056	3,050,405	2,695,083
15	Managers............	39,596	11,550	23,000	9,000	21,500
16	Tenants.............	605,199	66,883	464,800	48,615	412,435
	SOUTH DAKOTA.					
	White farmers:					
17	Total............	2,802,380,979	1,143,313,772	2,455,467,682	986,809,093	2,215,845,271
18	Owners.............	1,714,124,726	792,162,123	1,484,093,143	676,693,233	1,326,284,927
19	Managers...........	46,668,342	16,582,166	38,802,470	13,791,687	35,093,277
20	Tenants.............	1,041,587,911	334,569,483	932,572,069	296,324,173	854,467,067
	Colored farmers:					
21	Total...........	21,489,233	22,783,208	17,425,999	18,271,714	15,586,452
22	Owners.............	19,571,916	22,073,202	15,826,277	17,816,640	14,149,770
23	Managers...........	165,499	246,091	97,940	127,070	82,840
24	Tenants.............	1,751,818	463,915	1,501,782	328,004	1,353,842
	NEBRASKA.					
	White farmers:					
25	Total...........	4,194,397,347	2,076,690,898	3,705,654,150	1,810,628,865	3,324,390,695
26	Owners.............	2,354,826,114	1,259,674,939	2,057,471,600	1,082,358,527	1,816,110,208
27	Managers...........	78,279,737	37,412,466	65,593,263	29,928,713	59,912,694
28	Tenants.............	1,761,291,496	779,603,493	1,582,589,287	698,341,625	1,448,367,793
	Colored farmers:					
29	Total...........	7,258,645	3,127,749	6,453,610	2,718,070	5,831,645
30	Owners.............	3,994,209	2,200,927	3,524,945	1,890,390	3,083,265
31	Managers...........	123,941	150,668	100,000	128,000	87,100
32	Tenants.............	3,140,495	776,154	2,828,665	699,680	2,661,280
	KANSAS.					
	White farmers:					
33	Total...........	3,290,628,867	2,029,873,741	2,819,485,443	1,729,306,817	2,466,334,607
34	Owners.............	1,939,192,880	1,310,773,756	1,645,842,706	1,104,312,489	1,414,002,158
35	Managers...........	65,494,585	38,790,140	55,000,771	32,134,748	49,385,301
36	Tenants.............	1,285,941,402	680,000,000	1,118,542,966	592,859,580	1,002,947,148
	Colored farmers:					
37	Total...........	12,177,320	9,516,169	10,578,475	8,249,355	9,300,565
38	Owners.............	6,858,118	5,871,862	5,889,485	5,025,466	5,075,080
39	Managers...........	322,812	386,760	290,000	338,315	258,800
40	Tenants.............	4,996,390	3,257,547	4,398,990	2,885,574	3,966,685
	SOUTH ATLANTIC.					
	DELAWARE.					
	White farmers:					
41	Total...........	76,642,235	60,828,356	61,870,186	51,174,267	40,131,412
42	Owners.............	37,661,807	31,774,732	29,968,197	26,627,516	17,583,258
43	Managers...........	3,580,311	1,895,323	3,087,117	1,630,480	2,205,675
44	Tenants.............	35,400,117	27,158,301	28,814,872	22,916,271	20,342,479

BY COLOR AND TENURE, BY DIVISIONS AND STATES: 1920 AND 1910—Continued.

by tenure, in Table 26.]

| LAND AND BUILDINGS—continued. | | | IMPLEMENTS AND MACHINERY. | | LIVE STOCK. | | |
| Land alone—Continued. | Buildings. | | | | | | |
1910	1920	1910	1920	1910	1920	1910	
$1,435,404,619	$466,620,496	$268,770,429	$137,706,398	$50,557,774	$387,825,804	$284,062,818	1
993,235,101	346,327,560	207,140,306	100,862,127	37,780,059	284,767,328	215,495,353	2
34,447,828	12,873,551	5,080,697	2,135,177	712,467	8,928,055	4,854,469	3
407,721,690	107,419,385	56,549,426	34,709,094	12,065,248	94,130,421	63,712,996	4
10,577,770	2,153,933	1,451,568	554,942	316,220	2,013,241	1,776,290	5
4,799,700	1,227,483	845,738	336,281	183,260	1,145,948	1,058,814	6
739,305	140,750	94,150	27,245	7,935	157,813	80,204	7
5,038,765	785,700	511,680	191,416	125,025	709,480	637,272	8
727,512,290	208,808,030	92,036,434	113,967,135	43,733,892	156,281,580	107,512,347	9
580,042,676	153,548,575	75,716,009	85,885,192	37,031,550	116,351,113	90,790,451	10
15,085,153	5,348,898	1,804,015	2,075,202	741,663	3,900,632	1,653,993	11
132,384,461	49,910,557	14,516,410	26,006,741	5,960,679	36,029,835	15,067,903	12
2,867,841	399,838	240,179	219,730	173,703	753,055	737,519	13
2,819,201	345,973	231,204	185,652	167,899	630,138	722,505	14
7,300	1,500	1,700	1,050	800	15,546	1,750	15
41,340	52,365	7,275	33,028	5,004	107,371	13,264	16
885,534,462	239,622,411	101,274,631	111,581,077	33,308,293	235,332,220	123,196,386	17
603,193,174	157,808,216	73,500,059	72,257,726	24,111,686	157,773,857	91,357,204	18
12,590,492	3,709,193	1,201,195	1,287,113	331,541	6,578,759	2,458,938	19
269,750,796	78,105,002	26,573,377	38,036,238	8,865,066	70,979,604	29,380,244	20
17,072,289	1,839,547	1,199,425	827,191	478,680	3,236,043	4,032,814	21
16,651,963	1,676,507	1,164,677	753,334	460,375	2,992,305	3,796,187	22
123,450	15,100	3,620	10,445	1,930	57,114	117,091	23
296,876	147,940	31,128	63,412	16,375	186,624	119,536	24
1,612,150,758	381,263,455	198,478,107	152,850,017	44,172,323	335,893,180	221,889,710	25
948,659,816	241,361,392	133,698,711	91,403,339	28,548,651	205,951,175	148,767,761	26
26,912,908	5,680,569	3,015,805	1,676,770	540,319	11,009,704	6,943,434	27
636,578,034	134,221,494	61,763,591	59,769,908	15,083,353	118,932,301	66,178,515	28
2,388,555	621,965	329,515	254,431	77,385	550,604	332,294	29
1,629,575	441,680	260,815	162,537	60,025	306,727	250,512	30
113,000	12,900	15,000	950	2,500	22,991	20,168	31
645,980	167,385	53,700	90,944	14,860	220,886	61,614	32
1,530,691,995	353,150,836	198,614,822	154,254,232	48,095,416	316,889,192	252,471,508	33
963,779,875	231,840,548	140,532,614	95,660,025	33,078,233	197,690,149	173,383,034	34
29,473,586	5,714,470	2,661,162	1,812,093	528,930	8,582,721	6,126,468	35
537,438,534	115,595,818	55,421,046	56,782,114	14,488,253	110,616,322	72,962,006	36
7,284,578	1,277,910	964,777	462,745	214,745	1,136,100	1,052,069	37
4,324,929	814,405	700,537	295,417	145,583	673,216	700,813	38
305,315	31,200	33,000	7,710	4,325	25,102	44,120	39
2,654,334	432,305	231,240	159,618	64,837	437,782	307,136	40
33,486,704	21,738,774	17,687,563	6,549,214	3,106,005	8,222,835	6,548,084	41
15,818,208	12,384,939	10,809,308	3,669,939	1,809,305	4,023,671	3,337,911	42
1,011,305	881,442	619,175	226,524	88,889	266,670	175,954	43
16,657,191	8,472,393	6,259,080	2,652,751	1,207,811	3,932,494	3,034,219	44

TABLE **40.**—VALUE OF ALL FARM PROPERTY AND OF THE SEVERAL CLASSES,

[Corresponding figures for all farmers,

	DIVISION OR STATE AND COLOR AND TENURE.	ALL FARM PROPERTY.		LAND AND BUILDINGS.		
				Total.		Land alone.
		1920	1910	1920	1910	1920
	SOUTH ATLANTIC—Con.					
	DELAWARE—con.					
	Colored farmers:					
1	Total	$3,495,379	$2,350,845	$2,885,445	$1,981,716	$1,984,390
2	Owners	859,864	686,322	681,300	547,551	433,070
3	Managers	176,710	166,371	143,650	145,800	87,050
4	Tenants	2,458,805	1,498,152	2,060,495	1,288,365	1,464,270
	MARYLAND.					
	White farmers:					
5	Total	438,439,834	273,915,229	364,941,929	231,467,339	244,730,392
6	Owners	258,284,003	155,188,547	212,779,739	128,885,932	136,480,551
7	Managers	36,958,215	25,274,878	32,189,489	23,296,191	20,467,676
8	Tenants	143,197,616	93,451,804	119,972,701	79,285,216	87,782,165
	Colored farmers:					
9	Total	25,198,286	12,251,799	21,654,921	10,269,784	15,173,655
10	Owners	9,588,896	4,879,716	7,963,397	3,924,773	5,205,220
11	Managers	2,641,524	1,298,521	2,336,650	1,172,550	1,526,425
12	Tenants	12,967,866	6,073,562	11,354,874	5,172,461	8,442,010
	DIST. OF COLUMBIA.					
	White farmers:					
13	Total	5,682,274	8,382,862	5,344,069	8,141,943	4,022,598
14	Owners	1,757,369	2,283,304	1,672,519	2,231,400	1,151,169
15	Managers	2,431,709	3,372,882	2,242,150	3,232,843	1,643,019
16	Tenants	1,493,196	2,726,676	1,429,400	2,677,700	1,228,410
	Colored farmers:					
17	Total	245,713	93,671	233,300	89,400	133,550
18	Owners	43,300	51,912	40,300	48,400	30,300
19	Managers	111,205	8,185	105,700	8,000	31,200
20	Tenants	91,208	33,574	87,300	33,000	72,050
	VIRGINIA.					
	White farmers:					
21	Total	1,077,230,705	570,316,476	923,443,114	486,833,558	682,763,115
22	Owners	809,252,942	441,729,244	689,513,531	374,781,761	500,984,650
23	Managers	68,337,222	29,386,923	60,387,017	26,023,611	45,604,085
24	Tenants	199,640,541	99,200,309	173,542,566	86,028,186	136,174,380
	Colored farmers:					
25	Total	119,325,067	54,748,907	100,991,911	45,224,504	73,591,162
26	Owners	69,203,453	34,774,150	57,085,473	28,059,534	38,711,105
27	Managers	2,670,517	1,481,924	2,333,049	1,330,815	1,665,635
28	Tenants	47,451,097	18,492,833	41,573,389	15,834,155	33,214,422
	WEST VIRGINIA.					
	White farmers:					
29	Total	494,390,682	313,432,473	409,055,516	263,314,560	306,000,505
30	Owners	391,880,827	249,700,859	320,138,396	207,256,207	233,898,778
31	Managers	25,495,705	10,242,372	22,828,038	9,099,970	19,140,352
32	Tenants	77,014,150	53,489,242	66,089,082	46,958,383	52,961,375
	Colored farmers:					
33	Total	2,048,935	1,306,067	1,727,890	1,076,394	1,309,199
34	Owners	1,177,913	898,957	956,562	738,261	691,221
35	Managers	237,791	43,363	223,700	35,695	182,500
36	Tenants	633,231	363,747	547,628	302,438	435,478
	NORTH CAROLINA.					
	White farmers:					
37	Total	988,278,052	456,291,410	846,858,683	387,358,391	665,675,111
38	Owners	684,982,141	335,115,183	580,454,351	282,524,002	448,483,602
39	Managers	25,194,723	15,228,392	22,495,491	13,652,244	17,570,620
40	Tenants	278,101,188	105,947,835	243,908,841	91,182,145	199,620,889
	Colored farmers:					
41	Total	261,888,943	81,424,800	229,534,277	69,266,216	192,139,905
42	Owners	69,455,567	27,448,410	58,659,868	22,810,089	46,459,291
43	Managers	1,164,955	619,969	1,029,595	557,000	801,920
44	Tenants	191,268,421	53,356,421	169,844,814	45,899,127	144,878,694

BY COLOR AND TENURE, BY DIVISIONS AND STATES: 1920 AND 1910—Continued.

by tenure, in Table 26.]

LAND AND BUILDINGS—continued.			IMPLEMENTS AND MACHINERY.		LIVE STOCK.		
Land alone—Continued.	Buildings.						
1910	1920	1910	1920	1910	1920	1910	
$1,451,457	$901,055	$530,259	$232,104	$100,090	$377,830	$269,039	1
362,591	248,230	184,960	70,438	41,105	108,126	97,666	2
99,900	56,600	45,900	16,244	5,490	16,816	15,081	3
988,966	596,225	299,399	145,422	53,495	252,888	156,292	4
156,352,922	120,211,537	75,114,417	27,801,147	11,422,701	45,696,758	31,025,189	5
80,918,963	76,299,188	47,966,969	18,264,996	7,467,382	27,239,268	18,835,233	6
17,207,085	11,721,813	6,089,105	1,718,361	619,938	3,050,365	1,358,749	7
58,226,874	32,190,536	21,058,342	7,817,790	3,335,381	15,407,125	10,831,207	8
7,098,692	6,481,266	3,171,092	1,168,873	437,070	2,374,492	1,544,945	9
2,510,680	2,758,177	1,414,093	575,234	217,515	1,050,265	737,428	10
766,830	810,225	405,720	99,611	41,206	205,263	84,765	11
3,821,182	2,912,864	1,351,279	494,028	178,349	1,118,964	722,752	12
7,127,350	1,321,471	1,014,593	100,067	91,395	238,138	149,524	13
1,844,300	521,350	387,100	41,097	18,935	43,753	32,969	14
2,922,800	599,131	310,043	33,915	61,050	155,644	78,989	15
2,360,250	200,990	317,450	25,055	11,410	38,741	37,566	16
66,600	99,750	22,800	4,185	955	8,228	3,316	17
31,800	10,000	16,600	590	750	2,410	2,762	18
6,800	74,500	1,200	2,500	50	3,005	135	19
28,000	15,250	5,000	1,095	155	2,813	419	20
362,105,272	240,679,999	124,728,286	45,381,173	16,263,380	108,406,418	67,219,538	21
273,977,750	188,528,881	100,804,011	35,903,185	13,067,126	83,836,226	53,880,357	22
20,075,295	14,782,932	5,948,316	2,249,999	774,883	5,700,206	2,588,429	23
68,052,227	37,368,186	17,975,959	7,227,989	2,421,371	18,869,986	10,750,752	24
32,553,640	27,400,749	12,670,864	4,770,293	1,852,503	13,562,863	7,671,900	25
18,860,331	18,374,368	9,199,203	3,185,405	1,328,075	8,932,575	5,386,541	26
1,031,125	667,414	299,690	107,763	28,858	229,705	122,251	27
12,662,184	8,358,967	3,171,971	1,477,125	495,570	4,400,583	2,163,108	28
206,247,170	103,055,011	57,067,390	18,328,028	6,979,820	67,007,138	43,138,093	29
158,914,608	86,239,618	48,341,599	15,402,697	5,980,122	56,339,734	36,464,530	30
7,586,355	3,687,686	1,513,615	735,474	161,456	1,932,193	980,946	31
39,746,207	13,127,707	7,212,176	2,189,857	838,242	8,735,211	5,692,617	32
828,589	418,691	247,805	67,030	31,693	254,015	197,980	33
560,762	265,341	177,499	42,678	21,895	178,673	138,801	34
25,700	41,200	9,995	5,425	748	8,666	6,920	35
242,127	112,150	60,311	18,927	9,050	66,676	52,259	36
287,802,767	181,183,572	99,555,624	46,265,515	16,180,149	95,153,854	52,752,870	37
204,594,547	131,970,749	77,929,455	35,428,768	12,908,504	69,099,022	39,682,677	38
11,367,279	4,924,871	2,284,965	900,367	475,712	1,798,865	1,100,436	39
71,840,941	44,287,952	19,341,204	9,936,380	2,795,933	24,255,967	11,969,757	40
55,362,178	37,394,372	13,904,038	8,355,848	2,261,470	23,998,818	9,897,114	41
17,063,588	12,200,577	5,746,501	2,859,315	989,242	7,936,384	3,649,079	42
367,250	227,675	189,750	46,167	16,895	89,193	46,074	43
37,931,340	24,966,120	7,967,787	5,450,366	1,255,333	15,973,241	6,201,961	44

TABLE **40.**—VALUE OF ALL FARM PROPERTY AND OF THE SEVERAL CLASSES,

[Corresponding figures for all farmers,

DIVISION OR STATE AND COLOR AND TENURE.	ALL FARM PROPERTY.		LAND AND BUILDINGS.		
			Total.		Land alone.
	1920	1910	1920	1910	1920
SOUTH ATLANTIC—Con.					
SOUTH CAROLINA.					
White farmers:					
1 Total............	$611,327,079	$273,774,540	$523,070,165	$233,888,327	$407,092,648
2 Owners.............	408,059,177	191,927,325	346,790,985	163,591,021	263,504,088
3 Managers...........	20,129,913	11,730,892	17,531,604	10,305,245	14,209,478
4 Tenants...........	183,137,989	70,116,323	158,747,576	59,992,061	129,379,082
Colored farmers:					
5 Total............	341,737,663	118,353,774	290,414,035	98,999,754	240,064,561
6 Owners.............	73,818,033	27,340,950	59,839,583	22,112,291	46,487,620
7 Managers...........	2,523,729	1,072,287	2,210,828	980,894	1,726,019
8 Tenants...........	265,395,901	89,940,537	228,363,624	75,906,569	191,850,922
GEORGIA.					
White farmers:					
9 Total............	975,982,644	422,667,196	815,544,918	350,320,600	631,406,410
10 Owners.............	559,801,554	265,746,680	461,061,783	219,080,866	345,688,891
11 Managers...........	52,714,961	19,304,672	46,076,256	16,895,884	37,674,405
12 Tenants...........	363,466,129	137,615,844	308,406,879	114,343,850	248,043,114
Colored farmers:					
13 Total............	380,702,552	157,879,185	322,753,709	128,883,732	266,038,551
14 Owners.............	55,855,984	25,679,922	45,486,236	20,540,910	35,171,475
15 Managers...........	2,072,853	890,916	1,757,000	758,037	1,280,395
16 Tenants...........	322,773,715	131,308,347	275,510,473	107,584,785	229,586,681
FLORIDA.					
White farmers:					
17 Total............	307,857,223	127,772,555	263,888,026	106,230,421	214,869,755
18 Owners.............	225,517,548	101,391,671	189,518,632	82,746,957	149,731,500
19 Managers...........	57,898,568	16,646,913	54,188,560	15,675,141	48,848,976
20 Tenants...........	24,441,107	9,733,971	20,180,834	7,808,323	16,289,279
Colored farmers:					
21 Total............	22,444,494	15,410,628	17,561,378	11,915,568	13,554,985
22 Owners.............	11,636,445	8,779,585	9,027,953	6,786,810	6,710,515
23 Managers...........	1,129,965	788,444	1,010,510	738,890	790,920
24 Tenants...........	9,678,084	5,842,599	7,522,915	4,389,868	6,053,550
EAST SOUTH CENTRAL.					
KENTUCKY.					
White farmers:					
25 Total............	1,471,386,618	755,526,390	1,269,086,758	620,427,464	1,021,155,466
26 Owners.............	1,079,335,762	562,662,524	924,600,468	457,684,135	735,437,534
27 Managers...........	30,896,325	19,569,231	27,122,830	16,459,067	22,182,803
28 Tenants...........	361,154,531	173,294,635	317,363,460	146,284,262	263,535,129
Colored farmers:					
29 Total............	40,514,459	18,271,490	36,072,178	15,031,908	29,597,214
30 Owners.............	18,854,264	8,908,927	16,391,297	7,154,168	12,968,197
31 Managers...........	772,755	752,178	684,546	377,455	526,559
32 Tenants...........	20,887,440	8,610,385	18,996,335	7,500,285	16,102,458
TENNESSEE.					
White farmers:					
33 Total............	1,112,501,105	550,191,600	931,551,640	478,320,091	783,071,907
34 Owners.............	813,730,477	410,275,459	660,781,541	320,187,872	509,008,086
35 Managers..........	19,422,158	11,677,418	16,689,095	10,188,313	12,887,819
36 Tenants	309,381,770	136,481,729	257,081,013	107,953,836	211,076,002
Colored farmers:					
37 Total............	109,430,180	54,086,230	90,428,245	42,192,566	74,810,389
38 Owners.............	32,199,400	16,411,350	25,277,345	12,179,780	19,769,848
39 Managers...........	968,882	904,868	801,700	804,505	689,670
40 Tenants...........	76,261,898	36,770,012	64,349,200	29,208,281	54,350,871
ALABAMA.					
White farmers:					
41 Total..........	539,956,015	272,767,681	426,752,943	214,334,864	323,564,185
42 Owners.............	356,502,632	190,446,505	279,494,456	149,586,796	207,184,872
43 Managers..........	16,542,952	7,715,519	14,037,411	6,550,964	11,903,651
44 Tenants.............	166,910,431	74,605,657	133,221,076	58,197,104	104,475,662

BY COLOR AND TENURE, BY DIVISIONS AND STATES: 1920 AND 1910—Continued.

by tenure, in Table 26.]

LAND AND BUILDINGS—continued.			IMPLEMENTS AND MACHINERY.		LIVE STOCK.		
Land alone—Continued.	Buildings.						
1910	1920	1910	1920	1910	1920	1910	
$184,728,209	$115,977,517	$49,160,118	$34,247,634	$10,740,390	$54,009,280	$29,145,823	1
126,304,187	83,286,897	37,286,834	25,545,485	8,168,402	35,722,707	20,167,902	2
8,604,978	3,322,126	1,700,267	895,090	460,348	1,703,219	965,299	3
49,819,044	29,368,494	10,173,017	7,807,059	2,111,640	16,583,354	8,012,622	4
84,046,645	50,349,474	14,953,109	13,814,753	3,368,463	37,508,875	15,985,557	5
17,542,843	13,351,963	4,569,448	3,926,144	1,100,148	10,052,306	4,128,511	6
887,309	484,809	93,585	91,695	28,654	221,206	62,739	7
65,616,493	36,512,702	10,290,076	9,796,914	2,239,661	27,235,363	11,794,307	8
264,497,825	184,138,508	85,822,775	50,461,755	16,388,094	109,975,971	55,958,502	9
160,527,381	115,372,892	58,553,485	33,880,275	11,426,928	64,859,496	35,238,886	10
13,235,053	8,401,851	3,660,831	2,170,655	778,371	4,468,050	1,630,417	11
90,735,391	60,363,765	23,608,459	14,410,825	4,182,795	40,648,425	19,089,199	12
105,855,590	56,715,158	23,028,142	12,881,465	4,559,962	45,067,378	24,435,491	13
15,958,077	10,314,761	4,582,833	2,746,211	1,019,383	7,623,537	4,119,629	14
596,992	476,605	161,045	75,797	26,201	240,056	106,678	15
89,300,521	45,923,792	18,284,264	10,059,457	3,514,378	37,203,785	20,209,184	16
84,440,348	49,018,271	21,790,073	12,667,143	3,843,476	31,302,054	17,698,658	17
65,223,300	39,787,132	17,523,657	10,250,440	3,186,884	25,748,476	15,457,830	18
12,969,876	5,339,584	2,705,265	1,462,460	356,749	2,247,548	615,023	19
6,247,172	3,891,555	1,561,151	954,243	299,843	3,306,030	1,625,805	20
9,297,717	4,006,393	2,617,851	884,630	602,531	3,998,486	2,892,529	21
5,095,749	2,317,438	1,691,061	485,333	358,043	2,123,159	1,634,732	22
639,165	219,590	99,725	50,715	15,406	68,740	34,148	23
3,562,803	1,469,365	827,065	348,582	229,082	1,806,587	1,223,649	24
472,225,751	247,931,292	148,201,713	47,378,364	20,430,937	154,921,496	114,667,989	25
341,365,771	189,162,934	116,318,364	36,637,696	16,020,230	118,097,598	88,958,159	26
12,476,022	4,940,027	3,983,045	717,797	572,888	3,055,698	2,537,276	27
118,383,958	53,828,331	27,900,304	10,022,871	3,837,819	33,768,200	23,172,554	28
12,238,866	6,474,964	2,793,042	976,493	420,909	3,465,788	2,818,673	29
5,532,884	3,423,100	1,621,284	529,638	264,060	1,933,329	1,490,699	30
287,660	157,987	89,795	24,497	7,737	63,712	366,986	31
6,418,322	2,893,877	1,081,963	422,358	149,112	1,468,747	960,988	32
336,171,390	201,579,742	102,158,631	49,227,039	19,470,933	158,755,717	100,633,652	33
239,598,635	151,773,455	80,589,237	37,518,752	15,004,222	115,430,184	75,083,365	34
8,322,015	3,801,276	1,866,298	596,901	273,330	2,136,162	1,215,775	35
88,250,740	46,005,011	19,703,096	11,111,386	4,193,381	41,189,371	24,334,512	36
35,244,393	15,617,856	6,948,173	4,235,517	1,821,238	14,766,418	10,072,426	37
9,531,041	5,507,497	2,648,739	1,546,628	699,907	5,375,427	3,531,663	38
686,935	112,030	117,570	28,550	12,369	138,632	87,994	39
25,026,417	9,998,329	4,181,864	2,660,339	1,108,962	9,252,359	6,452,769	40
157,619,496	103,188,758	56,715,368	28,156,938	12,957,495	85,046,134	45,475,322	41
106,940,798	72,309,584	42,645,998	20,546,337	9,819,496	56,461,839	31,040,213	42
5,314,785	2,133,760	1,236,179	624,397	325,287	1,881,144	839,268	43
45,363,913	28,745,414	12,833,191	6,986,204	2,812,712	26,703,151	13,595,841	44

TABLE **40.**—VALUE OF ALL FARM PROPERTY AND OF THE SEVERAL CLASSES,

[Corresponding figures for all farmers,

	DIVISION OR STATE AND COLOR AND TENURE.	ALL FARM PROPERTY.		LAND AND BUILDINGS.		
				Total.		Land alone.
		1920	1910	1920	1910	1920
	EAST SOUTH CENTRAL—Con.					
	ALABAMA—con.					
	Colored farmers:					
1	Total	$150,892,705	$97,370,748	$116,904,812	$73,918,727	$92,199,677
2	Owners	37,652,256	22,506,427	29,024,680	17,285,502	22,043,463
3	Managers	1,260,380	514,063	1,053,905	414,729	845,287
4	Tenants	111,980,069	74,350,258	86,826,227	56,218,496	69,310,927
	MISSISSIPPI.					
	White farmers:					
5	Total	497,529,775	238,753,608	387,295,247	185,637,732	298,108,035
6	Owners	348,084,084	177,017,166	266,770,485	137,356,509	199,188,332
7	Managers	38,319,306	14,015,117	32,319,772	11,827,047	28,080,119
8	Tenants	111,126,385	47,721,325	88,204,990	36,454,176	70,839,584
	Colored farmers:					
9	Total	467,222,080	187,561,026	402,601,531	148,524,557	343,734,359
10	Owners	72,038,456	44,417,423	56,751,385	34,317,764	44,957,657
11	Managers	2,583,018	1,102,150	2,113,110	975,581	1,711,670
12	Tenants	392,600,606	142,041,453	343,737,036	113,231,212	297,065,032
	WEST SOUTH CENTRAL.					
	ARKANSAS.					
	White farmers:					
13	Total	712,090,762	312,931,573	570,653,057	240,153,704	453,235,261
14	Owners	459,978,971	212,972,643	361,754,359	161,187,795	278,304,146
15	Managers	27,767,282	11,811,473	24,139,921	10,201,748	21,403,331
16	Tenants	224,344,509	88,147,457	184,758,777	68,764,161	153,527,784
	Colored farmers:					
17	Total	212,304,721	87,157,730	182,457,609	69,013,109	154,538,179
18	Owners	56,352,848	27,139,889	45,592,538	20,694,215	37,190,715
19	Managers	1,353,081	286,557	1,187,555	238,915	1,081,720
20	Tenants	154,598,792	59,731,284	135,677,516	48,079,979	116,265,744
	LOUISIANA.					
	White farmers:					
21	Total	457,911,706	244,697,247	366,365,525	192,610,792	295,776,756
22	Owners	299,440,327	154,901,321	236,354,594	121,341,966	186,494,967
23	Managers	52,336,807	37,990,657	43,057,956	29,298,223	36,647,987
24	Tenants	106,134,572	51,805,269	86,952,975	41,970,603	72,633,802
	Colored farmers:					
25	Total	131,914,973	56,523,741	107,673,268	44,933,658	87,841,406
26	Owners	32,323,696	16,494,075	25,472,623	12,779,570	20,326,691
27	Managers	991,558	689,427	853,310	604,071	750,524
28	Tenants	98,599,719	39,340,239	81,347,335	31,550,017	66,764,191
	OKLAHOMA.					
	White farmers:					
29	Total	1,566,708,361	859,340,810	1,286,081,414	691,455,431	1,105,078,897
30	Owners	870,363,408	478,118,900	702,725,632	385,536,954	592,955,865
31	Managers	31,957,102	11,978,671	25,772,475	8,612,109	22,853,464
32	Tenants	664,387,851	369,243,239	557,583,307	297,306,368	489,269,568
	Colored farmers:					
00	Total	85,713,185	58,808,072	77,183,880	47,221,793	66,380,467
34	Owners	55,434,469	40,590,030	45,310,004	32,325,348	37,539,450
35	Managers	1,058,783	183,579	861,765	136,462	749,853
36	Tenants	37,221,931	18,084,463	31,612,111	14,759,983	28,091,164
	TEXAS.					
	White farmers:					
37	Total	4,183,641,832	2,105,652,301	3,474,000,091	1,751,619,447	3,050,694,356
38	Owners	2,319,957,720	1,225,501,217	1,883,769,434	1,003,327,398	1,616,414,712
39	Managers	261,815,759	183,994,124	203,697,405	154,999,067	193,817,206
40	Tenants	1,601,868,353	696,156,960	1,386,533,252	593,292,982	1,240,462,438
	Colored farmers:					
41	Total	263,778,489	112,992,863	226,173,228	91,588,948	194,514,293
42	Owners	84,150,269	39,873,225	68,170,518	30,687,272	55,233,242
43	Managers	3,377,354	1,256,601	2,827,325	1,092,550	2,572,270
44	Tenants	176,250,866	71,863,037	155,175,385	59,809,126	136,708,781

BY COLOR AND TENURE, BY DIVISIONS AND STATES: 1920 AND 1910—Continued.

by tenure, in Table 26.]

| LAND AND BUILDINGS—continued. | | | IMPLEMENTS AND MACHINERY. | | LIVE STOCK. | | |
| Land alone—Continued. | Buildings. | | | | | | |
1910	1920	1910	1920	1910	1920	1910	
$59,324,679	$24,705,135	$14,594,048	$6,209,279	$3,332,509	$27,778,614	$20,119,512	1
13,307,506	6,981,217	3,977,996	1,754,450	936,562	6,873,126	4,284,363	2
254,564	208,618	160,165	40,180	15,757	166,295	83,577	3
45,762,609	17,515,300	10,455,887	4,414,649	2,380,190	20,739,193	15,751,572	4
133,608,805	89,187,212	52,028,927	26,506,774	11,303,017	83,727,754	41,812,859	5
95,468,154	67,582,153	41,888,355	20,138,930	8,876,339	61,174,669	30,784,318	6
10,015,017	4,239,653	1,812,030	1,757,655	689,673	4,241,879	1,498,397	7
28,125,634	17,365,406	8,328,542	4,610,189	1,737,005	18,311,206	9,530,144	8
120,393,484	58,867,172	28,131,073	13,374,482	5,602,295	51,246,067	33,434,174	9
26,451,191	11,793,728	7,866,573	3,459,584	1,868,756	11,827,487	8,230,903	10
752,606	401,440	222,975	130,346	42,415	339,562	84,154	11
93,189,687	46,672,004	20,041,525	9,784,552	3,691,124	39,079,018	25,119,117	12
188,068,595	117,417,796	52,085,109	37,126,771	14,075,041	104,310,934	58,702,828	13
122,092,206	83,450,213	39,095,589	25,904,055	10,326,004	72,320,557	41,458,844	14
9,075,999	2,736,590	1,125,749	1,318,398	553,011	2,308,963	1,056,714	15
56,900,390	31,230,993	11,863,771	9,904,318	3,196,026	29,681,414	16,187,270	16
57,952,855	27,919,430	11,060,254	6,305,466	2,789,157	23,541,646	15,355,464	17
16,717,427	8,401,823	3,976,788	2,381,205	1,136,883	8,379,105	5,308,791	18
207,915	105,835	31,000	51,319	15,459	114,207	32,183	19
41,027,513	19,411,772	7,052,466	3,872,942	1,636,815	15,048,334	10,014,490	20
151,600,372	70,588,769	41,010,420	28,003,936	17,292,480	63,542,245	34,793,975	21
92,958,898	49,859,627	28,383,068	18,685,419	9,751,096	44,400,314	23,808,259	22
23,689,102	6,409,969	5,609,121	4,670,006	5,250,609	4,608,845	3,441,825	23
34,952,372	14,319,173	7,018,231	4,648,511	2,290,775	14,533,086	7,543,891	24
36,202,905	19,831,862	8,730,753	4,711,074	1,684,573	19,530,631	9,905,510	25
10,001,760	5,145,932	2,777,810	1,379,843	642,054	5,471,230	3,072,451	26
516,046	102,786	88,025	33,506	20,679	104,742	64,677	27
25,685,099	14,583,144	5,864,918	3,297,725	1,021,840	13,954,659	6,768,382	28
608,094,918	181,002,517	83,360,513	76,712,166	25,451,097	203,914,781	142,434,282	29
333,397,812	109,769,767	52,139,142	48,137,128	15,074,889	119,500,648	77,507,057	30
7,478,510	2,919,011	1,133,599	850,671	244,629	5,333,956	3,121,933	31
267,218,596	68,313,739	30,087,772	27,724,367	10,131,579	79,080,177	61,805,292	32
40,971,750	11,403,413	6,250,043	3,918,381	1,637,769	12,012,922	9,998,510	33
27,523,601	7,770,554	4,801,747	2,653,865	1,160,199	7,470,600	7,104,483	34
117,722	111,912	18,740	43,357	3,172	153,661	43,945	35
13,330,427	3,520,947	1,429,556	1,221,159	474,398	4,388,661	2,850,082	36
1,554,465,053	423,305,735	197,154,394	145,842,782	53,516,329	563,798,959	300,516,525	37
870,767,259	267,354,722	132,560,139	91,539,787	33,321,632	344,648,499	188,852,187	38
150,119,621	9,880,199	4,879,446	3,699,519	1,576,910	54,418,835	27,418,147	39
533,578,173	146,070,814	59,714,809	50,603,476	18,617,787	164,731,625	84,246,191	40
78,742,082	31,658,935	12,846,866	8,478,214	3,273,931	29,127,047	18,129,984	41
25,223,740	12,937,276	5,463,532	3,734,005	1,504,685	12,245,746	7,681,268	42
1,012,335	255,055	80,215	55,227	27,808	494,802	136,243	43
52,506,007	18,466,604	7,303,119	4,688,982	1,741,438	16,386,499	10,312,473	44

TABLE 40.—VALUE OF ALL FARM PROPERTY AND OF THE SEVERAL CLASSES,

[Corresponding figures for all farmers,

| DIVISION OR STATE AND COLOR AND TENURE. | ALL FARM PROPERTY. | | LAND AND BUILDINGS. | | |
| | | | Total. | | Land alone. |
	1920	1910	1920	1910	1920
MOUNTAIN.					
MONTANA.					
White farmers:					
1 Total	$973,337,451	$341,516,469	$767,439,420	$247,484,190	$683,538,978
2 Owners	787,829,756	269,979,721	618,493,954	192,553,254	548,887,119
3 Managers	65,167,367	35,536,731	50,240,105	26,236,608	45,694,591
4 Tenants	120,340,328	36,000,017	98,705,361	28,694,328	88,957,268
Colored farmers:					
5 Total	12,623,857	6,312,301	9,328,109	4,141,740	8,373,287
6 Owners	11,454,860	6,064,227	8,521,157	3,958,605	7,771,250
7 Managers	244,030	102,410	222,125	56,400	106,725
8 Tenants	924,967	145,664	584,827	126,735	495,312
IDAHO.					
White farmers:					
9 Total	710,441,620	302,553,671	576,470,350	242,839,338	507,180,172
10 Owners	543,436,183	246,346,662	434,749,536	194,970,158	378,080,444
11 Managers	36,990,860	17,222,431	29,121,176	13,627,913	26,216,759
12 Tenants	130,014,577	38,984,578	112,599,638	34,241,267	102,882,969
Colored farmers:					
13 Total	5,696,290	2,763,514	5,041,614	2,226,487	4,685,697
14 Owners	3,306,603	2,324,909	2,838,600	1,836,387	2,621,003
15 Managers					
16 Tenants	2,389,687	438,605	2,203,014	390,100	2,064,694
WYOMING.					
White farmers:					
17 Total	332,982,612	166,889,911	233,689,165	97,707,277	209,981,172
18 Owners	251,833,183	122,740,497	173,572,717	71,082,554	154,902,101
19 Managers	42,280,712	31,083,615	30,491,658	17,176,459	28,266,977
20 Tenants	38,868,717	13,065,799	29,624,790	9,448,264	26,812,094
Colored farmers:					
21 Total	1,427,978	299,170	1,058,960	208,000	966,322
22 Owners	1,005,176	282,444	707,010	194,000	642,472
23 Managers		8,859		8,000	
24 Tenants	422,802	7,867	351,950	6,000	323,850
COLORADO.					
White farmers:					
25 Total	1,068,154,527	487,204,788	858,500,595	404,493,616	756,829,126
26 Owners	736,704,709	329,320,316	586,046,043	267,347,078	511,990,517
27 Managers	57,288,605	36,489,813	41,916,400	29,330,153	37,099,941
28 Tenants	274,161,213	121,394,659	230,538,152	107,816,385	207,738,668
Colored farmers:					
29 Total	8,640,222	4,267,018	7,513,065	4,025,245	6,893,590
30 Owners	1,950,692	2,980,840	1,611,065	2,862,385	1,428,140
31 Managers	251,239	17,431	190,200	13,500	169,200
32 Tenants	6,438,291	1,268,747	5,711,800	1,149,360	5,296,250
NEW MEXICO.					
White farmers:					
33 Total	320,212,374	155,380,360	219,443,079	100,507,000	194,411,823
34 Owners	244,803,636	115,084,108	166,457,042	78,938,055	145,702,346
35 Managers	35,618,873	27,376,669	23,544,090	20,250,622	21,879,689
36 Tenants	39,789,965	12,919,583	29,442,806	10,398,661	26,829,888
Colored farmers:					
37 Total	4,973,625	4,067,630	2,370,274	2,243,661	1,929,127
38 Owners	4,189,875	3,820,902	1,912,135	2,044,170	1,495,683
39 Managers	15,312	112,474	12,750	93,150	9,750
40 Tenants	768,438	134,254	445,389	106,341	423,694
ARIZONA.					
White farmers:					
41 Total	229,055,446	69,716,204	168,903,633	44,966,301	153,348,539
42 Owners	142,112,010	49,453,207	103,841,290	31,139,862	92,810,983
43 Managers	45,586,810	8,898,273	30,729,829	5,764,744	28,142,047
44 Tenants	41,356,626	11,364,724	34,332,514	8,061,695	32,395,509

BY COLOR AND TENURE, BY DIVISIONS AND STATES: 1920 AND 1910—Continued.

by tenure, in Table 26.]

LAND AND BUILDINGS—continued.			IMPLEMENTS AND MACHINERY.		LIVE STOCK.		
Land alone—Continued.	Buildings.						
1910	1920	1910	1920	1910	1920	1910	
$222,856,773	$83,900,442	$24,627,417	$54,440,646	$10,389,789	$151,457,385	$83,642,490	1
172,470,405	69,606,835	20,082,849	46,137,279	8,806,308	123,198,523	68,620,159	2
24,389,680	4,545,514	1,846,928	2,081,654	612,914	12,845,608	8,687,176	3
25,996,688	9,748,093	2,697,640	6,221,713	970,534	15,413,254	6,335,155	4
3,914,529	954,822	227,211	563,566	149,864	2,732,182	2,020,697	5
3,751,569	749,907	207,036	515,260	133,144	2,418,443	1,972,478	6
45,350	115,400	11,050	4,856	12,000	17,049	34,010	7
117,610	89,515	9,125	43,450	4,720	296,690	14,209	8
217,896,691	69,290,178	24,942,647	38,166,519	10,356,318	95,804,751	49,358,015	9
173,554,492	56,669,092	21,415,666	31,464,230	8,921,120	77,222,417	42,455,384	10
12,584,143	2,904,417	1,043,770	1,219,026	380,068	6,650,658	3,214,450	11
31,758,056	9,716,669	2,483,211	5,483,263	1,055,130	11,931,676	3,688,181	12
2,056,625	355,917	169,862	250,734	119,733	403,942	417,294	13
1,690,800	217,597	145,587	166,210	97,925	301,793	390,597	14
							15
365,825	138,320	24,275	84,524	21,808	102,149	26,697	16
88,714,541	23,707,993	8,992,736	11,702,201	3,659,359	87,591,246	65,523,275	17
64,063,003	18,670,616	7,019,551	9,501,004	2,933,973	68,759,462	48,723,970	18
15,978,174	2,224,681	1,198,285	802,816	446,232	10,986,238	13,460,924	19
8,673,364	2,812,696	774,900	1,398,381	279,154	7,845,546	3,338,381	20
193,735	92,638	14,265	75,748	8,935	293,270	82,235	21
181,285	64,538	12,715	48,528	7,985	249,638	80,459	22
7,000	....	1,000	....	300	....	559	23
5,450	28,100	550	27,220	650	43,632	1,217	24
358,897,925	101,671,469	45,595,691	49,320,664	12,754,837	160,333,268	69,956,335	25
234,455,232	74,055,526	32,891,846	35,797,105	9,385,017	114,861,561	52,588,221	26
26,370,622	4,816,459	2,959,531	1,700,907	741,493	13,671,298	6,418,167	27
98,072,071	22,799,484	9,744,314	11,822,652	2,628,327	31,800,409	10,949,947	28
3,924,280	619,475	100,965	483,845	36,764	643,312	205,009	29
2,813,395	182,925	48,990	104,065	16,335	235,562	102,120	30
13,400	21,000	100	10,485	50	50,554	3,881	31
1,097,485	415,550	51,875	369,295	20,379	357,196	99,008	32
96,767,969	25,032,015	12,819,369	9,441,798	4,004,994	91,326,638	41,788,028	33
68,064,349	20,754,696	10,873,706	7,783,430	3,499,079	70,563,064	32,646,974	34
19,096,977	1,664,401	1,153,645	504,672	269,442	11,570,111	6,856,605	35
9,606,643	2,612,918	792,018	1,153,696	236,473	9,193,463	2,284,449	36
2,038,528	441,147	205,133	303,571	117,318	2,299,780	1,706,651	37
1,851,337	416,452	192,833	247,862	108,945	2,029,878	1,667,787	38
88,750	3,000	4,400	1,560	1,786	1,002	17,538	39
98,441	21,695	7,900	54,149	6,587	268,900	21,326	40
40,164,186	15,555,094	4,802,115	8,643,569	1,681,472	51,508,244	23,068,431	41
27,174,954	11,030,307	3,964,908	6,123,371	1,331,195	32,147,349	16,982,150	42
5,446,382	2,587,782	318,362	1,201,106	149,934	13,655,875	2,983,595	43
7,542,850	1,937,005	518,845	1,319,092	200,343	5,705,020	3,102,686	44

TABLE **40.**—VALUE OF ALL FARM PROPERTY AND OF THE SEVERAL CLASSES,

[Corresponding figures for all farmers,

DIVISION OR STATE AND COLOR AND TENURE.	ALL FARM PROPERTY.		LAND AND BUILDINGS.		
			Total.		Land alone.
	1920	1910	1920	1910	1920
MOUNTAIN—Continued.					
ARIZONA—continued.					
Colored farmers:					
1 Total............	$4,537,543	$5,407,766	$3,421,688	$2,319,009	$3,214,067
2 Owners.............	2,825,076	5,101,339	1,805,558	2,056,749	1,682,052
3 Managers............	• 111,024	55,309	96,900	35,950	76,030
4 Tenants............	1,601,443	251,118	1,519,230	226,310	1,455,985
UTAH.					
White farmers:					
5 Total............	307,147,614	149,315,534	240,375,568	116,398,862	207,861,024
6 Owners.............	263,638,411	130,768,381	205,669,094	100,928,169	176,513,933
7 Managers............	13,611,379	7,692,661	9,566,800	6,295,737	8,832,114
8 Tenants............	29,897,824	10,854,492	25,139,674	9,174,956	22,514,977
Colored farmers:					
9 Total............	4,127,114	1,479,667	3,376,190	1,146,470	3,136,816
10 Owners.............	1,460,409	795,599	954,745	489,585	858,275
11 Managers............	254,847	250,700	171,000	250,000	155,500
12 Tenants............	2,411,858	433,368	2,250,445	406,885	2,123,041
NEVADA.					
White farmers:					
13 Total............	98,935,150	60,001,336	65,620,734	39,335,864	58,794,735
14 Owners.............	65,586,506	33,236,579	43,362,690	21,483,390	38,315,794
15 Managers............	25,710,405	21,725,508	16,799,949	13,904,993	15,698,346
16 Tenants............	7,638,239	5,039,249	5,458,095	3,947,481	4,780,595
Colored farmers:					
17 Total............	844,516	398,029	634,480	273,475	567,504
18 Owners.............	716,921	369,997	516,530	248,125	452,054
19 Managers............	5,848	3,785	5,000	3,500	4,900
20 Tenants............	121,747	24,247	112,950	21,850	110,550
PACIFIC.					
WASHINGTON.					
White farmers:					
21 Total............	1,042,765,610	627,864,255	907,801,691	563,157,981	786,144,835
22 Owners.............	711,982,611	477,570,898	615,279,267	426,856,472	520,962,627
23 Managers............	51,505,430	31,477,031	45,559,894	29,293,274	40,077,229
24 Tenants............	279,277,569	118,816,326	246,962,530	107,008,235	225,104,979
Colored farmers:					
25 Total............	14,664,238	9,679,156	12,590,650	8,810,476	11,506,185
26 Owners.............	4,469,054	4,367,436	3,720,350	3,767,968	3,264,505
27 Managers............	198,217	125,763	162,850	121,200	154,350
28 Tenants............	9,996,967	5,185,957	8,707,450	4,921,308	8,087,330
OREGON.					
White farmers:					
29 Total............	812,345,801	522,338,795	669,826,485	450,408,204	581,387,657
30 Owners.............	584,201,729	389,312,934	475,825,872	332,281,402	406,750,289
31 Managers............	43,939,850	33,019,124	36,261,485	28,593,193	32,062,328
32 Tenants............	184,204,222	100,006,737	157,739,128	89,533,609	142,575,040
Colored farmers:					
33 Total............	6,213,950	5,904,987	5,386,799	5,168,105	4,854,392
34 Owners.............	3,279,822	4,145,328	2,699,862	3,504,670	2,384,280
35 Managers............	196,682	145,740	183,275	132,500	163,525
36 Tenants............	2,737,446	1,613,919	2,503,662	1,530,935	2,306,587
CALIFORNIA.					
White farmers:					
37 Total............	3,260,849,029	1,579,533,633	2,913,026,253	1,417,723,511	2,630,003,732
38 Owners.............	2,107,992,674	977,192,054	1,883,607,285	878,203,553	1,671,182,063
39 Managers............	478,298,504	255,460,653	434,038,626	228,114,615	404,487,040
40 Tenants....	674,557,851	346,880,926	595,380,342	311,405,343	554,334,629
Colored farmers:					
41 Total............	170,172,832	35,160,951	160,784,856	32,877,977	153,051,245
42 Owners.............	19,113,874	4,885,614	17,317,126	4,244,277	15,870,128
43 Managers............	8,433,101	1,493,166	7,993,810	1,429,800	7,572,100
44 Tenants............	142,625,857	28,782,171	135,473,920	27,203,900	129,609,017

BY COLOR AND TENURE, BY DIVISIONS AND STATES: 1920 AND 1910—Continued.

by tenure, in Table 26.]

LAND AND BUILDINGS—continued.			IMPLEMENTS AND MACHINERY.		LIVE STOCK.		
Land alone—Continued.	Buildings.						
1910	1920	1910	1920	1910	1920	1910	
$2,185,551	$207,621	$133,458	$177,098	$106,318	$938,757	$2,982,439	1
1,937,557	123,506	119,192	122,699	97,450	896,819	2,947,140	2
27,375	20,870	8,575	9,400	550	4,724	18,809	3
220,619	63,245	5,691	44,999	8,318	37,214	16,490	4
98,407,974	32,514,544	17,990,888	13,363,167	4,430,517	53,408,879	28,486,155	5
84,526,774	29,155,161	16,401,395	11,967,463	3,966,714	46,001,854	25,873,498	6
5,839,097	734,686	456,640	344,825	176,622	3,699,754	1,220,302	7
8,042,103	2,624,697	1,132,853	1,050,879	287,181	3,707,271	1,392,355	8
1,074,190	239,374	72,280	151,620	37,661	599,304	295,536	9
439,610	96,470	49,975	67,870	30,236	437,794	275,778	10
248,000	15,500	2,000	5,300	....	78,547	700	11
386,580	127,404	20,305	78,450	7,425	82,963	19,058	12
35,041,306	6,825,999	4,294,558	3,581,492	1,551,566	29,732,924	19,113,906	13
18,710,677	5,046,896	2,772,713	2,751,317	1,092,656	19,472,499	10,660,533	14
12,785,720	1,101,603	1,119,273	494,141	314,242	8,416,315	7,506,273	15
3,544,909	677,500	402,572	336,034	144,668	1,844,110	947,100	16
235,293	66,976	38,182	49,435	24,530	160,601	100,024	17
211,693	64,476	36,432	47,305	23,895	153,086	97,977	18
3,400	100	100	300	75	548	210	19
20,200	2,400	1,650	1,830	560	6,967	1,837	20
509,083,987	121,656,856	54,073,994	54,020,215	16,549,230	80,943,704	48,157,044	21
381,682,024	94,316,640	45,174,448	39,425,243	13,058,275	57,278,101	37,656,151	22
27,440,781	5,482,665	1,852,493	2,005,884	543,966	3,939,652	1,639,791	23
99,961,182	21,857,551	7,047,053	12,589,088	2,946,989	19,725,951	8,861,102	24
8,338,011	1,084,465	472,465	701,162	160,614	1,372,426	708,066	25
3,507,398	455,845	260,570	223,320	107,426	525,384	492,042	26
106,630	8,500	14,570	5,150	1,040	30,217	3,523	27
4,723,983	620,120	197,325	472,692	52,148	816,825	212,501	28
406,795,227	88,438,828	43,612,977	41,289,743	13,075,654	101,229,573	58,854,937	29
296,540,617	69,075,583	35,740,785	31,170,364	10,403,833	77,205,493	46,627,699	30
26,901,856	4,199,157	1,691,337	1,496,719	505,023	6,181,646	3,920,908	31
83,352,754	15,164,088	6,180,855	8,622,660	2,166,798	17,842,434	8,306,330	32
4,900,875	532,407	267,230	277,382	129,991	549,769	606,891	33
3,361,050	315,582	143,620	121,489	99,604	458,471	541,054	34
117,400	19,750	15,100	6,550	2,375	6,857	10,865	35
1,422,425	197,075	108,510	149,343	28,012	84,441	54,972	36
1,286,243,224	283,022,521	131,480,287	130,415,398	35,671,259	217,407,378	126,138,863	37
779,549,191	212,425,222	98,654,362	93,244,735	24,484,245	131,140,654	74,504,256	38
214,944,422	29,551,586	13,170,193	12,176,070	4,466,339	32,083,808	22,879,699	39
291,749,611	41,045,713	19,655,732	24,994,593	6,720,675	54,182,916	28,754,908	40
30,952,224	7,733,611	1,925,753	5,653,892	821,899	3,734,084	1,461,075	41
3,821,357	1,446,998	422,920	741,943	186,240	1,054,805	455,097	42
1,258,850	421,710	170,950	332,595	31,600	106,696	31,766	43
25,872,017	5,864,903	1,331,883	4,579,354	604,059	2,572,583	974,212	44

TABLE **41.**—AVERAGE VALUE OF LAND AND BUILDINGS PER FARM,

[Corresponding figures for all farmers,

DIVISION AND STATE.	FARMS OPERATED BY WHITE FARMERS.							
	Total.		Owners.		Managers.		Tenants.	
	1920	1910	1920	1910	1920	1910	1920	1910
United States......	$11,601	$6,206	$10,622	$5,939	$39,703	$25,471	$12,607	$6,146
GEOGRAPHIC DIVISIONS:								
New England............	5,863	3,808	5,233	3,446	24,015	15,204	5,975	3,794
Middle Atlantic.........	7,068	5,223	6,085	4,500	26,083	19,698	8,605	6,434
East North Central.....	13,805	7,922	11,176	6,767	31,124	18,309	19,658	10,630
West North Central....	22,396	10,516	20,541	10,087	41,532	23,842	25,360	11,138
South Atlantic.........	5,436	2,802	5,614	3,029	29,521	15,810	4,281	1,987
East South Central.....	4,054	2,034	4,533	2,357	29,096	14,806	2,937	1,329
West South Central....	7,455	3,917	7,864	4,362	64,395	45,490	6,247	2,890
Mountain...............	13,117	7,427	11,770	6,257	56,838	45,878	15,537	10,940
Pacific.................	19,884	13,138	16,709	10,929	75,122	55,599	24,424	16,875
NEW ENGLAND:								
Maine.................	4,232	2,660	4,127	2,617	11,150	5,385	3,912	2,549
New Hampshire........	4,387	3,175	4,061	3,041	17,140	9,938	3,735	2,481
Vermont..............	5,474	3,443	5,044	3,156	16,997	12,479	6,741	4,017
Massachusetts.........	7,755	5,269	6,498	4,505	31,423	19,747	6,351	4,434
Rhode Island.........	6,485	5,307	5,545	4,458	22,595	20,618	6,086	4,886
Connecticut..........	8,403	5,167	7,291	4,607	29,757	20,868	7,918	4,496
MIDDLE ATLANTIC:								
New York............	7,383	5,507	6,379	4,799	28,754	22,011	8,976	6,643
New Jersey...........	8,509	6,526	7,338	5,557	29,764	26,044	9,226	6,891
Pennsylvania.........	6,558	4,748	5,619	4,043	22,668	15,654	8,200	6,178
EAST NORTH CENTRAL:								
Ohio.................	10,398	6,102	8,863	5,477	28,615	17,479	13,280	7,256
Indiana..............	12,952	7,410	11,000	6,697	28,184	16,475	16,502	8,730
Illinois.............	25,359	14,042	20,367	12,220	47,641	27,238	31,143	16,276
Michigan.............	7,325	4,362	6,639	4,065	21,659	11,749	9,523	5,485
Wisconsin............	11,587	6,798	10,804	6,323	22,907	16,999	15,151	9,100
WEST NORTH CENTRAL:								
Minnesota............	18,513	8,096	16,528	7,545	31,493	17,128	24,009	9,812
Iowa.................	35,628	15,017	32,925	14,617	50,623	23,341	38,906	15,469
Missouri.............	11,709	6,229	11,347	6,312	33,380	20,168	11,959	5,701
North Dakota.........	19,249	11,133	18,385	10,495	41,132	35,040	20,765	13,794
South Dakota.........	33,625	13,186	32,019	12,248	50,327	32,682	36,001	15,461
Nebraska.............	29,876	14,012	29,639	13,721	50,033	30,354	29,690	14,151
Kansas...............	17,187	9,817	17,091	10,038	37,305	24,456	16,878	9,145
SOUTH ATLANTIC:								
Delaware.............	6,676	5,162	5,299	4,613	23,566	15,238	8,275	5,679
Maryland.............	8,752	5,440	7,273	4,359	28,973	25,856	10,587	6,563
District of Columbia....	29,044	39,717	18,379	20,285	124,564	230,917	19,059	33,058
Virginia.............	6,670	3,582	6,541	3,695	31,176	18,009	5,579	2,605
West Virginia........	4,713	2,744	4,465	2,748	21,098	10,520	4,719	2,385
North Carolina.......	4,377	2,060	4,496	2,281	27,038	13,077	3,839	1,444
South Carolina.......	6,251	2,937	7,712	3,720	31,588	14,078	4,160	1,718
Georgia..............	4,517	2,079	5,356	2,642	31,321	13,037	3,316	1,357
Florida..............	6,428	3,010	5,892	2,945	31,359	13,352	2,820	1,297
EAST SOUTH CENTRAL:								
Kentucky.............	4,919	2,507	5,314	2,784	29,039	17,271	3,821	1,782
Tennessee............	4,355	2,110	4,780	2,400	22,134	13,146	3,401	1,469
Alabama.............	2,652	1,406	3,109	1,722	22,862	11,029	1,892	895
Mississippi..........	3,493	1,693	3,916	2,049	40,552	16,449	2,102	870
WEST SOUTH CENTRAL:								
Arkansas.............	3,559	1,590	3,719	1,752	37,660	14,228	2,961	1,178
Louisiana............	4,991	2,933	5,108	2,871	58,503	33,560	3,204	1,000
Oklahoma............	7,423	4,079	8,393	5,192	30,321	13,801	6,287	2,141
Texas...............	6,791	5,050	10,003	5,745	85,537	68,858	7,825	3,470
MOUNTAIN:								
Montana.............	13,556	9,892	12,549	8,674	56,513	52,264	15,329	12,379
Idaho...............	13,858	7,988	12,681	7,268	38,418	30,284	17,175	10,954
Wyoming.............	15,000	8,946	13,070	7,315	80,880	55,408	15,414	10,569
Colorado............	14,457	8,871	13,011	7,319	47,959	37,316	17,123	13,017
New Mexico..........	7,846	3,269	6,903	2,524	54,627	63,882	8,596	5,377
Arizona.............	18,105	7,465	14,194	6,161	102,433	37,926	20,042	9,855
Utah................	9,521	5,439	9,206	5,164	32,651	32,620	9,614	5,524
Nevada..............	22,290	15,560	17,408	10,620	100,598	77,250	19,084	12,146
PACIFIC:								
Washington..........	13,961	10,227	11,791	9,120	39,310	30,835	21,146	14,633
Oregon..............	13,496	10,037	12,045	8,904	39,936	34,080	17,108	13,327
California...........	26,200	16,656	21,817	13,368	90,425	67,992	29,699	19,378

BY COLOR AND TENURE, BY DIVISIONS AND STATES: 1920 AND 1910.

by tenure, in Table 27.]

DIVISION AND STATE.	FARMS OPERATED BY COLORED FARMERS.							
	Total.		Owners.		Managers.		Tenants.	
	1920	1910	1920	1910	1920	1910	1920	1910
United States.......	$2,663	$1,126	$2,782	$1,437	$16,142	$10,567	$2,583	$993
GEOGRAPHIC DIVISIONS:								
New England..........	4,263	2,531	3,095	1,979	13,161	8,863	6,964	3,098
Middle Atlantic.........	5,280	3,390	3,263	2,138	20,033	13,954	6,637	5,515
East North Central......	5,493	3,407	4,038	2,696	20,818	14,752	8,065	4,524
West North Central.....	8,199	4,681	7,817	4,675	21,929	20,201	8,560	4,210
South Atlantic..........	2,573	1,033	2,335	1,035	11,652	7,955	2,630	1,013
East South Central......	2,103	860	2,295	1,208	11,433	10,330	2,045	774
West South Central.....	2,562	1,209	3,108	1,670	14,113	8,970	2,347	1,021
Mountain..............	6,011	2,066	4,325	1,784	25,851	20,932	12,457	7,352
Pacific.................	21,473	9,701	11,207	5,440	50,241	20,784	24,282	12,787
NEW ENGLAND:								
Maine...................	4,185	1,478	4,185	1,500	....	900	....	1,483
New Hampshire........	2,100	4,187	1,517	1,000	10,000	10,000	1,200	20,400
Vermont...............	4,169	2,118	4,149	2,068	2,967	1,700	5,175	2,750
Massachusetts..........	3,089	2,433	2,536	2,228	11,714	9,075	2,921	2,054
Rhode Island..........	1,975	1,576	1,779	1,598	7,000	....	1,520	1,521
Connecticut...........	7,220	3,110	4,288	2,056	21,500	9,958	10,767	3,159
MIDDLE ATLANTIC:								
New York.............	4,908	2,737	3,503	2,079	18,678	11,289	7,604	6,261
New Jersey............	4,018	3,571	2,666	1,801	12,875	15,413	4,923	4,383
Pennsylvania..........	7,231	4,355	3,521	2,541	23,967	13,885	8,715	6,211
EAST NORTH CENTRAL:								
Ohio...................	5,648	3,074	3,963	2,258	20,482	10,917	8,000	4,472
Indiana...............	7,441	4,229	5,990	3,829	18,867	14,755	8,567	4,326
Illinois................	6,813	4,204	4,761	3,138	27,178	28,296	9,420	4,863
Michigan..............	4,099	2,605	3,466	2,272	18,387	5,222	5,514	4,169
Wisconsin.............	3,201	2,750	3,112	2,743	22,167	2,075	3,173	2,918
WEST NORTH CENTRAL:								
Minnesota.............	4,184	2,402	3,945	2,613	4,000	6,620	5,652	1,892
Iowa..................	12,207	5,416	9,233	3,780	51,000	43,100	17,540	7,751
Missouri..............	5,854	3,281	5,141	2,677	26,585	20,328	6,010	3,661
North Dakota..........	6,499	4,183	6,484	4,196	11,500	4,500	6,456	3,473
South Dakota..........	10,810	6,507	10,803	6,512	9,794	18,153	10,962	5,046
Nebraska.............	16,806	5,883	13,878	5,123	25,000	128,000	22,450	7,605
Kansas................	8,545	4,878	7,427	4,577	16,111	16,110	10,302	5,045
SOUTH ATLANTIC:								
Delaware..............	3,309	2,149	1,919	1,349	11,050	9,113	4,088	2,577
Maryland.............	3,488	1,612	2,244	994	15,475	13,478	4,526	2,215
District of Columbia....	11,665	7,450	4,478	6,050	105,700	8,000	8,730	11,000
Virginia...............	2,113	940	1,845	871	11,843	7,393	2,498	1,008
West Virginia..........	3,428	1,520	2,374	1,323	27,963	5,099	5,888	2,115
North Carolina.........	3,009	1,055	2,633	1,064	10,725	7,527	3,150	1,040
South Carolina.........	2,664	1,023	2,629	1,085	12,081	7,488	2,653	995
Georgia...............	2,479	1,052	2,835	1,309	8,488	6,163	2,418	1,008
Florida...............	1,356	809	1,428	930	10,005	7,316	1,152	600
EAST SOUTH CENTRAL:								
Kentucky..............	2,857	1,281	3,082	1,207	19,558	9,436	2,612	1,302
Tennessee.............	2,368	1,101	2,569	1,138	15,126	15,775	2,275	1,060
Alabama..............	1,228	669	1,687	1,012	8,298	7,976	1,115	602
Mississippi............	2,497	902	2,448	1,371	11,006	9,204	2,494	811
WEST SOUTH CENTRAL:								
Arkansas..............	2,524	1,085	2,966	1,411	12,501	5,194	2,388	984
Louisiana.............	1,735	819	2,319	1,192	9,275	7,845	1,596	716
Oklahoma.............	4,154	2,284	4,776	2,899	10,138	5,054	3,454	1,555
Texas.................	2,871	1,310	2,896	1,445	21,099	13,488	2,816	1,231
MOUNTAIN:								
Montana...............	8,775	3,463	8,651	3,392	22,213	18,800	8,600	4,874
Idaho.................	9,924	5,497	7,820	5,354	....	....	15,193	6,292
Wyoming..............	6,266	3,200	5,748	3,180	....	8,000	7,651	2,000
Colorado..............	13,586	7,013	6,496	6,142	31,700	13,500	19,103	10,742
New Mexico...........	1,264	1,045	1,164	964	6,375	23,288	1,936	4,624
Arizona...............	5,297	724	3,265	653	19,380	3,268	17,264	5,263
Utah..................	8,155	4,154	3,995	2,267	57,000	250,000	13,084	6,896
Nevada...............	2,897	1,699	2,483	1,632	5,000	3,500	11,295	2,731
PACIFIC:								
Washington...........	9,945	7,832	7,196	5,375	18,094	11,018	11,767	11,916
Oregon...............	9,401	8,243	7,542	7,332	22,909	16,563	12,095	10,858
California.............	21,790	10,682	13,932	4,525	53,650	23,061	26,595	13,091

TABLE 42.—AVERAGE VALUE OF LAND AND BUILDINGS PER ACRE,

[Corresponding figures for all farmers,

DIVISION AND STATE.	FARMS OPERATED BY WHITE FARMERS.							
	Total.		Owners.		*Managers.		Tenants.	
	1920	1910	1920	1910	1920	1910	1920	1910
United States........	$70.02	$40.57	$63.24	$38.00	$49.00	$27.03	$92.50	$51.68
GEOGRAPHIC DIVISIONS:								
New England.............	54.00	36.43	49.84	33.93	117.66	75.08	53.15	36.97
Middle Atlantic..........	73.97	56.55	68.51	52.67	133.10	103.85	78.67	59.84
East North Central.......	126.97	75.30	111.80	68.09	146.81	84.20	155.75	91.09
West North Central.......	95.56	50.20	86.71	46.56	73.33	39.81	115.24	60.46
South Atlantic...........	52.97	24.61	50.32	23.43	61.33	37.22	58.96	26.34
East South Central.......	45.19	21.48	42.56	20.25	62.50	29.48	52.18	25.27
West South Central.......	35.07	18.22	31.80	16.91	18.12	10.38	48.24	25.42
Mountain.................	26.91	22.18	25.90	23.08	17.96	12.07	42.36	34.00
Pacific..................	81.01	47.91	82.20	49.77	75.45	36.25	80.61	50.98
NEW ENGLAND:								
Maine....................	37.61	25.35	36.95	24.97	60.11	34.26	38.00	29.14
New Hampshire...........	34.57	26.43	32.89	26.00	60.64	32.24	33.49	26.48
Vermont.................	37.58	24.14	35.99	23.21	64.11	37.94	40.44	25.22
Massachusetts............	99.33	67.52	90.10	61.56	163.22	111.02	91.15	65.31
Rhode Island.............	79.69	63.10	72.16	57.04	155.19	116.46	72.60	57.50
Connecticut..............	100.29	63.29	92.82	58.33	170.93	144.86	90.82	54.28
MIDDLE ATLANTIC:								
New York................	69.08	53.81	64.11	50.46	134.72	106.15	72.10	55.49
New Jersey...............	109.99	84.43	111.98	85.24	139.44	119.52	95.97	72.55
Pennsylvania.............	75.07	55.97	68.88	51.44	129.49	95.40	83.10	62.53
EAST NORTH CENTRAL:								
Ohio.....................	113.27	68.68	104.93	65.43	155.56	94.97	126.05	73.82
Indiana..................	126.00	74.85	117.17	71.25	138.67	78.10	139.97	81.92
Illinois.................	187.73	108.43	165.68	99.39	227.71	116.58	209.74	119.45
Michigan.................	75.52	47.60	72.69	46.30	85.23	50.77	84.60	52.99
Wisconsin................	98.84	57.09	96.45	54.89	104.52	69.32	109.31	67.20
WEST NORTH CENTRAL:								
Minnesota................	109.28	45.63	104.36	44.55	113.37	50.56	120.86	48.71
Iowa.....................	227.11	96.01	222.25	96.11	221.24	91.69	233.24	95.02
Missouri.................	88.09	49.60	84.68	47.90	112.34	63.52	95.35	53.48
North Dakota.............	41.22	29.03	38.89	28.03	43.28	35.43	48.29	33.69
South Dakota.............	72.68	40.16	63.52	37.82	43.93	22.00	97.77	48.96
Nebraska.................	87.90	46.98	77.98	40.22	44.36	27.38	110.71	66.26
Kansas...................	62.33	40.05	60.38	38.47	45.23	25.63	66.74	44.84
SOUTH ATLANTIC:								
Delaware.................	69.55	52.12	68.27	57.48	152.90	86.87	66.94	45.84
Maryland.................	82.82	49.26	80.86	46.31	135.62	120.13	78.03	46.06
District of Columbia......	993.32	1,364.27	981.53	941.12	1,208.05	2,226.48	785.38	1,248.34
Virginia.................	56.66	28.21	55.66	28.11	76.20	41.29	55.66	26.12
West Virginia............	42.87	26.35	41.07	25.40	64.38	32.06	47.43	30.30
North Carolina...........	51.06	20.12	47.26	19.54	60.22	24.23	62.09	21.55
South Carolina...........	65.00	24.44	62.25	23.53	45.25	20.41	76.01	28.39
Georgia..................	44.40	17.64	40.20	16.23	51.37	22.48	51.37	20.39
Florida..................	48.79	23.69	51.17	21.62	45.47	57.89	39.31	20.23
EAST SOUTH CENTRAL:								
Kentucky.................	59.90	28.53	55.86	26.60	102.30	52.93	72.64	34.58
Tennessee................	51.96	23.78	49.89	22.74	78.87	32.11	56.73	26.75
Alabama..................	28.02	13.70	25.92	12.66	33.19	18.76	33.13	16.73
Mississippi..............	31.28	15.34	28.06	14.47	59.52	21.52	37.84	17.69
WEST SOUTH CENTRAL:								
Arkansas.................	38.47	16.27	33.60	14.41	71.35	31.67	49.59	21.12
Louisiana................	46.75	23.16	42.91	20.46	48.69	30.33	60.21	29.59
Oklahoma.................	42.33	26.01	40.29	26.78	78.50	20.00	40.88	25.27
Texas....................	31.71	16.20	28.35	14.90	14.30	8.68	48.02	25.84
MOUNTAIN:								
Montana..................	22.30	18.67	21.82	18.60	17.60	18.39	30.68	19.49
Idaho....................	69.22	46.48	64.29	44.39	75.50	50.43	95.45	60.83
Wyoming.................	19.83	11.45	18.58	13.82	20.80	6.00	30.26	17.92
Colorado.................	35.22	30.13	31.55	26.61	26.31	25.78	54.81	48.17
New Mexico...............	9.01	9.88	9.35	11.40	6.09	6.35	10.95	10.67
Arizona..................	29.42	39.25	27.58	40.07	22.11	21.91	58.55	76.48
Utah.....................	48.08	34.49	50.82	35.15	16.21	20.12	69.41	48.11
Nevada...................	27.98	14.53	30.79	20.95	21.09	9.12	38.83	25.07
PACIFIC:								
Washington...............	69.07	48.50	66.95	47.26	84.38	55.42	72.36	52.19
Oregon...................	49.83	39.27	47.93	37.63	43.35	37.45	58.90	47.74
California...............	100.99	51.24	110.35	58.42	79.49	34.57	94.28	51.57

BY COLOR AND TENURE, BY DIVISIONS AND STATES: 1920 AND 1910.

by tenure, in Table 28.]

DIVISION AND STATE.	FARMS OPERATED BY COLORED FARMERS.							
	Total.		Owners.		Managers.		Tenants.	
	1920	1910	1920	1910	1920	1910	1920	1910
United States..........	$56.29	$22.23	$38.84	$18.18	$75.54	$38.31	$66.46	$24.83
GEOGRAPHIC DIVISIONS:								
New England.............	55.90	53.09	59.61	46.93	59.15	81.20	45.62	57.37
Middle Atlantic.........	84.37	59.31	64.38	42.72	183.30	142.02	84.76	76.48
East North Central.......	88.58	57.42	71.98	49.37	155.90	95.02	112.08	68.67
West North Central......	37.52	21.07	30.25	17.45	79.53	52.05	73.25	54.09
South Atlantic............	54.20	20.80	43.44	18.70	76.39	39.40	58.66	21.58
East South Central........	53.33	20.57	32.40	15.63	54.16	33.69	63.49	22.96
West South Central.......	54.11	22.29	39.90	17.53	42.15	16.18	64.93	27.03
Mountain.................	32.83	21.14	22.24	18.65	20.76	28.81	114.09	70.20
Pacific...................	247.51	80.90	83.09	30.20	300.41	168.50	358.82	179.19
NEW ENGLAND:								
Maine.....................	57.08	28.76	57.08	29.09	....	24.32	....	27.13
New Hampshire..........	19.92	67.67	16.24	21.39	30.77	5,000.00	40.00	111.78
Vermont................	26.23	22.09	28.33	20.75	21.50	17.35	21.54	44.00
Massachusetts...........	66.87	66.12	71.82	63.06	67.71	134.44	34.03	50.99
Rhode Island.............	41.49	38.59	39.03	41.95	77.78	....	33.93	32.07
Connecticut..............	74.74	61.27	124.75	55.50	65.65	71.69	54.95	60.86
MIDDLE ATLANTIC:								
New York...............	62.96	43.31	49.71	34.96	126.37	112.97	81.52	74.04
New Jersey..............	81.67	76.02	84.39	70.14	130.18	185.70	73.82	60.56
Pennsylvania............	121.08	78.24	90.20	54.45	259.07	125.35	100.42	97.88
EAST NORTH CENTRAL:								
Ohio....................	90.89	56.15	75.16	48.30	162.66	98.61	104.48	64.44
Indiana.................	115.92	75.67	105.94	71.72	109.19	106.30	127.04	77.69
Illinois.................	105.44	68.17	75.98	56.59	227.11	98.17	142.31	77.17
Michigan................	61.68	41.27	56.19	38.68	195.37	57.67	67.58	49.57
Wisconsin...............	62.25	40.71	61.05	40.69	109.92	27.39	68.97	42.56
WEST NORTH CENTRAL:								
Minnesota...............	42.71	29.80	38.67	26.47	166.67	29.36	74.48	45.72
Iowa....................	150.40	77.88	132.93	78.90	204.00	84.84	172.51	75.74
Missouri................	86.87	52.29	75.46	42.90	115.41	110.66	101.14	61.04
North Dakota............	18.93	15.94	18.37	15.91	28.75	18.75	23.14	17.12
South Dakota............	20.50	12.64	19.67	12.52	15.06	15.18	38.37	22.75
Nebraska................	96.78	33.74	95.64	28.11	52.27	80.00	101.33	59.75
Kansas..................	55.95	40.61	50.05	37.19	110.98	33.67	63.98	49.82
SOUTH ATLANTIC:								
Delaware.............:	52.57	34.78	54.45	40.22	111.01	60.88	50.16	31.45
Maryland................	61.59	28.65	66.77	32.16	105.82	87.76	54.01	23.18
District of Columbia......	810.07	941.05	1,612.00	834.48	1,112.63	2,000.00	519.64	1,000.00
Virginia.................	44.62	20.21	41.55	20.31	74.55	44.38	48.43	19.15
West Virginia...........	62.73	31.16	50.21	28.44	147.17	54.50	78.55	38.14
North Carolina..........	66.77	21.74	50.62	19.05	80.02	29.33	74.96	23.31
South Carolina..........	66.30	25.12	52.20	20.14	59.60	23.10	71.44	27.11
Georgia.............. ..	45.64	18.17	34.15	15.22	60.51	27.51	48.24	18.82
Florida.................	27.53	15.50	25.31	14.80	94.60	74.08	27.81	14.62
EAST SOUTH CENTRAL:								
Kentucky................	84.49	34.10	68.26	28.02	145.37	87.41	104.30	41.42
Tennessee...............	59.34	26.27	47.22	20.62	86.47	45.50	65.71	29.28
Alabama.................	26.89	14.52	21.78	11.79	32.78	23.72	29.10	15.58
Mississippi..............	69.24	23.00	31.09	15.41	53.11	26.45	87.03	27.00
WEST SOUTH CENTRAL:								
Arkansas................	69.51	26.01	43.73	17.19	89.89	39.21	86.47	33.32
Louisiana...............	49.33	21.15	34.07	15.31	59.89	28.80	57.27	24.87
Oklahoma...............	45.40	20.74	44.01	20.21	34.94	21.68	47.95	22.00
Texas...................	50.72	21.38	37.76	16.44	33.82	11.54	60.37	25.75
MOUNTAIN:								
Montana.................	14.32	14.17	14.05	13.80	48.34	16.89	14.36	55.76
Idaho...................	105.28	37.94	78.32	33.70	....	....	189.21	92.97
Wyoming................	46.31	19.24	38.98	18.53	....	100.00	74.38	23.08
Colorado................	85.98	37.32	34.48	33.00	79.58	5.00	149.30	62.42
New Mexico.............	36.83	12.25	31.95	11.75	490.38	16.84	99.13	28.18
Arizona.................	56.63	22.99	33.32	21.05	85.75	21.46	297.36	151.48
Utah....................	65.98	50.05	60.35	29.01	6.73	100.00	226.02	115.26
Nevada..................	53.91	34.49	46.56	35.23	62.50	21.88	189.83	30.06
PACIFIC:								
Washington.............	124.17	87.37	53.44	45.46	135.93	232.63	284.67	282.20
Oregon.-...............	53.95	24.00	30.21	17.06	134.07	53.69	274.31	204.83
California...............	308.62	125.01	136.67	45.60	317.25	204.20	367.06	166.98

TABLE 43.—NUMBER OF FARM OPERATORS IN THE UNITED STATES, WITH PER CENT DISTRIBUTION, BY COLOR, NATIVITY, AND TENURE: 1920 AND 1910.

COLOR AND NATIVITY.	TOTAL.		OWNERS.		MANAGERS.		TENANTS.	
	1920	1910	1920	1910	1920	1910	1920	1910
All farm operators.	6,448,343	6,361,502	3,925,090	3,948,722	68,449	58,104	2,454,804	2,354,676
White farm operators....	5,498,454	5,440,619	3,691,868	3,707,501	66,223	56,560	1,740,363	1,676,558
Native [1]	4,917,386	4,771,063	3,227,521	3,162,584	59,035	50,087	1,630,830	1,558,392
Foreign born..........	581,068	669,556	464,347	544,917	7,188	6,473	109,533	118,166
Colored farm operators...	919,889	920,883	233,222	241,221	2,226	1,544	714,441	678,118
	PER CENT DISTRIBUTION BY COLOR AND NATIVITY.							
All farm operators.	100.0	100.0	100.0	100.0	100.0	100.0	100.0	100.0
White farm operators....	85.3	85.5	94.1	93.9	96.7	97.3	70.9	71.2
Native [1]	76.3	75.0	82.2	80.1	86.2	86.2	66.4	66.2
Foreign born..........	9.0	10.5	11.8	13.8	10.5	11.1	4.5	5.0
Colored farm operators...	14.7	14.5	5.9	6.1	3.3	2.7	29.1	28.8
	PER CENT DISTRIBUTION BY TENURE.							
All farm operators.	100.0	100.0	60.9	62.1	1.1	0.9	38.1	37.0
White farm operators....	100.0	100.0	67.1	68.1	1.2	1.0	31.7	30.8
Native [1]	100.0	100.0	65.6	66.3	1.2	1.0	33.2	32.7
Foreign born..........	100.0	100.0	79.9	81.4	1.2	1.0	18.9	17.6
Colored farm operators ..	100.0	100.0	24.6	26.2	0.2	0.2	75.2	73.6

[1] Includes farmers with country of birth not reported, as follows: For 1920, 99,540; for 1910, 7,807.

TABLE 44.—ACREAGE AND VALUE OF FARMS IN THE UNITED STATES, BY COLOR, NATIVITY, AND TENURE OF FARMER: 1920.

COLOR, NATIVITY, AND TENURE.	All land in farms (acres).	Improved land in farms (acres).	Value of farms (land and buildings).
All farm operators	**955,883,715**	**503,073,007**	**$66,316,002,602**
Owners	636,775,015	314,107,483	39,864,222,907
Managers	54,129,157	13,210,999	2,665,216,465
Tenants	264,979,543	175,754,525	23,786,563,230
White farm operators, total	910,939,194	473,774,566	63,786,058,855
Owners	620,070,823	306,029,220	39,215,462,823
Managers	53,653,478	13,009,436	2,629,284,676
Tenants	237,214,893	154,735,910	21,941,311,356
Native white farm operators	799,767,149	411,266,350	54,800,517,317
Owners	534,507,308	259,480,553	32,954,157,743
Managers	48,956,294	11,674,897	2,283,109,796
Tenants	216,303,547	140,110,900	19,563,249,778
Foreign-born white farm operators	111,172,045	62,508,216	8,985,541,538
Owners	85,563,515	46,548,667	6,261,305,080
Managers	4,697,184	1,334,539	346,174,880
Tenants	20,911,346	14,625,010	2,378,061,578
Colored farm operators	44,944,521	29,298,441	2,529,943,747
Owners	16,704,192	8,078,263	648,760,084
Managers	475,679	201,563	35,931,789
Tenants	27,764,650	21,018,615	1,845,251,874

PER CENT DISTRIBUTION.

All farm operators	**100.0**	**100.0**	**100.0**
White farm operators	95.3	94.2	96.2
Native	83.7	81.8	82.6
Foreign born	11.6	12.4	13.5
Colored farm operators	4.7	5.8	3.8

AVERAGE PER FARM.

All farm operators	**148.2**	**78.0**	**$10,284**
White farm operators	165.7	86.2	11,601
Native	162.6	83.6	11,144
Foreign born	191.3	107.6	15,464
Colored farm operators	47.3	30.8	2,663

TABLE 45.—NUMBER OF FARM OPERATORS IN THE UNITED STATES, BY RACE AND TENURE: 1920 AND 1910.

RACE.	TOTAL.		OWNERS.		MANAGERS.		TENANTS.	
	1920	1910	1920	1910	1920	1910	1920	1910
All farm operators.	6,448,343	6,361,502	3,925,090	3,948,722	68,449	58,104	2,454,804	2,354,676
White farm operators....	5,498,454	5,440,619	3,691,868	3,707,501	66,223	56,560	1,740,363	1,676,558
Colored farm operators...	949,889	920,883	233,222	*241,221	2,226	1,544	714,441	678,118
Negroes...............	925,708	893,370	218,612	218,972	2,026	1,434	705,070	672,964
Indians...............	16,680	24,251	13,821	21,892	54	47	2,805	2,312
Japanese.............	6,892	2,502	717	294	123	45	6,052	2,163
Chinese	609	760	72	63	23	18	514	679

TABLE 46.—ACREAGE AND VALUE OF FARMS IN THE UNITED STATES, BY RACE OF FARMER: 1920.

RACE.	All land in farms (acres).	Improved land in farms (acres).	Value of farms (land and buildings).
All farm operators.....................	955,883,715	503,073,007	$66,316,002,602
White farm operators......................	910,939,194	473,774,566	63,786,058,855
Colored farm operators......................	44,944,521	29,298,441	2,529,943,747
Negroes......................................	41,432,182	27,928,900	2,257,645,325
Indians.......................................	2,962,313	895,898	89,399,963
Japanese.....................................	491,625	422,768	164,109,442
Chinese	58,401	50,875	18,789,017

TABLE 47.—NUMBER OF FARM OPERATORS, BY COLOR AND NATIVITY, BY DIVISIONS AND STATES: 1920 AND 1910.

DIVISION AND STATE.	ALL FARM OPERATORS.		NATIVE WHITE FARM OPERATORS.[1]		FOREIGN-BORN WHITE FARM OPERATORS.		COLORED FARM OPERATORS.	
	1920	1910	1920	1910	1920	1910	1920	1910
United States ...	6,448,343	6,361,502	4,917,386	4,771,063	581,068	669,556	949,889	920,883
GEOGRAPHIC DIVISIONS:								
New England......	156,564	188,802	128,028	161,009	28,265	27,451	271	342
Middle Atlantic....	425,147	468,379	376,701	419,342	46,910	47,076	1,536	1,961
East North Central.	1,084,744	1,123,489	935,492	929,619	144,775	188,153	4,477	5,717
West North Central.	1,096,951	1,109,948	883,809	830,642	206,223	269,442	6,919	9,864
South Atlantic.....	1,158,976	1,111,881	767,771	748,878	7,373	7,141	383,832	355,862
East South Central.	1,051,600	1,042,480	740,862	712,443	3,506	4,819	307,232	325,218
West South Central.	996,088	943,186	724,301	692,624	39,937	41,501	231,850	209,061
Mountain..........	244,109	183,446	197,678	143,991	40,984	31,427	5,447	8,028
Pacific............	234,164	189,891	162,744	132,515	63,095	52,546	8,325	4,830
NEW ENGLAND:								
Maine..............	48,227	60,016	43,830	55,014	4,384	4,973	13	29
New Hampshire....	20,523	27,053	17,890	24,347	2,619	2,691	14	15
Vermont...........	29,075	32,709	25,280	28,968	3,767	3,721	28	20
Massachusetts......	32,001	36,917	22,950	28,431	8,930	8,362	121	124
Rhode Island......	4,083	5,292	3,123	4,408	940	843	20	41
Connecticut........	22,655	26,815	14,955	19,841	7,625	6,861	75	113
MIDDLE ATLANTIC:								
New York..........	193,195	215,597	166,869	187,629	25,776	27,029	550	939
New Jersey.........	29,702	33,487	22,555	26,796	6,612	6,215	535	476
Pennsylvania.......	202,250	219,295	187,277	204,917	14,522	13,832	451	546
EAST NORTH CENTRAL:								
Ohio..............	256,695	272,045	241,075	252,645	14,004	17,450	1,616	1,950
Indiana...........	205,126	215,485	198,156	204,951	6,398	9,729	572	805
Illinois...........	237,181	251,872	214,177	217,053	22,111	33,394	893	1,425
Michigan..........	196,447	206,960	147,450	147,790	48,264	58,224	733	946
Wisconsin.........	189,295	177,127	134,634	107,180	53,998	69,356	663	591
WEST NORTH CENTRAL:								
Minnesota.........	178,478	156,137	110,966	74,710	67,305	81,134	207	293
Iowa..............	213,439	217,044	181,109	167,856	32,221	48,987	109	201
Missouri..........	263,004	277,244	251,835	259,111	8,343	14,467	2,826	3,666
North Dakota......	77,690	74,360	40,899	35,750	36,248	37,867	543	743
South Dakota......	74,637	77,644	52,700	49,360	20,325	25,476	1,612	2,808
Nebraska..........	124,417	129,678	99,441	93,509	24,592	35,707	384	462
Kansas............	165,286	177,841	146,859	150,346	17,189	25,804	1,238	1,691
SOUTH ATLANTIC:								
Delaware..........	10,140	10,836	8,905	9,504	363	410	872	922
Maryland..........	47,908	48,923	40,130	40,669	1,569	1,882	6,209	6,372
Dist. of Columbia...	204	217	153	168	31	37	20	12
Virginia...........	186,242	184,018	136,874	134,155	1,582	1,749	47,786	48,114
West Virginia......	87,289	96,685	86,033	95,138	752	839	504	708
North Carolina.....	269,763	253,725	193,081	187,657	392	412	76,290	65,656
South Carolina.....	192,693	176,434	83,542	79,424	141	212	109,010	96,798
Georgia...........	310,732	291,027	180,217	168,083	328	385	130,187	122,559
Florida............	54,005	50,016	38,836	34,080	2,215	1,215	12,954	14,721
EAST SOUTH CENTRAL:								
Kentucky..........	270,626	259,185	256,886	245,499	1,112	1,956	12,628	11,730
Tennessee.........	252,774	246,012	213,832	206,821	760	883	38,182	38,308
Alabama...........	256,099	262,901	159,865	151,214	1,031	1,244	95,203	110,443
Mississippi........	272,101	274,382	110,279	108,909	603	736	161,219	164,737
WEST SOUTH CENTRAL:								
Arkansas..........	232,604	214,678	158,273	148,627	2,049	2,458	72,282	63,593
Louisiana..........	135,463	120,546	71,081	63,236	2,323	2,431	62,059	54,879
Oklahoma.........	191,988	190,192	167,472	161,773	5,791	7,748	18,725	20,671
Texas.............	436,033	417,770	327,475	318,988	29,774	28,864	78,784	69,918
MOUNTAIN:								
Montana...........	57,677	26,214	41,051	18,165	15,563	6,852	1,063	1,196
Idaho.............	42,106	30,807	35,284	24,694	6,314	5,708	508	405
Wyoming..........	15,748	10,987	13,306	9,019	2,273	1,903	169	65
Colorado..........	59,934	46,170	49,846	37,198	9,535	8,398	553	574
New Mexico........	29,844	35,676	26,593	32,088	1,376	1,440	1,875	2,148
Arizona...........	9,975	9,227	8,262	5,218	1,067	806	646	3,203
Utah..............	25,662	21,676	21,276	15,948	3,972	5,452	414	276
Nevada............	3,163	2,689	2,060	1,661	884	867	219	161
PACIFIC:								
Washington........	66,288	56,192	45,265	37,770	19,757	17,297	1,266	1,125
Oregon............	50,206	45,502	40,484	35,819	9,149	9,056	573	627
California.........	117,670	88,197	76,995	58,926	34,189	26,193	6,486	3,078

[1] Includes farmers with country of birth not reported.

TABLE 48.—NUMBER OF FARM OPERATORS, BY COLOR,

DIVISION AND STATE.	ALL FARM OPERATORS.				NATIVE WHITE FARM OPERATORS.[1]			
	Total.	Owners.	Managers.	Tenants.	Total.	Owners.	Managers.	Tenants.
United States....	6,448,343	3,925,090	68,449	2,454,804	4,917,386	3,227,521	59,035	1,630,830
GEOGRAPHIC DIVISIONS:								
New England........	156,564	140,160	4,802	11,602	128,028	114,804	3,754	9,470
Middle Atlantic.....	425,147	327,104	9,853	88,190	376,701	287,821	8,478	80,402
East North Central..	1,084,744	766,786	13,551	304,407	935,492	641,233	12,086	282,173
West North Central..	1,096,951	711,156	10,776	375,019	883,809	545,283	9,509	329,017
South Atlantic......	1,158,976	607,089	9,799	542,088	767,771	498,214	8,508	261,049
East South Central..	1,051,600	525,808	3,506	522,286	740,862	467,447	3,045	270,370
West South Central..	996,088	464,328	5,013	526,747	724,301	382,668	4,407	337,226
Mountain............	244,109	202,515	4,116	37,478	197,678	163,248	3,592	30,838
Pacific.............	234,164	180,144	7,033	46,987	162,744	126,803	5,656	30,285
NEW ENGLAND:								
Maine...............	48,227	45,437	786	2,004	43,830	41,338	689	1,803
New Hampshire.....	20,523	18,604	546	1,373	17,890	16,225	472	1,193
Vermont...........	29,075	25,121	568	3,386	25,280	21,719	506	3,055
Massachusetts.......	32,001	28,087	1,627	2,287	22,950	20,157	1,191	1,602
Rhode Island.......	4,083	3,245	205	633	3,123	2,521	153	449
Connecticut.........	22,655	19,666	1,070	1,919	14,955	12,844	743	1,368
MIDDLE ATLANTIC:								
New York...........	193,195	151,717	4,376	37,102	166,869	130,404	3,586	32,879
New Jersey.........	29,702	21,889	987	6,826	22,555	16,046	779	5,730
Pennsylvania........	202,250	153,498	4,490	44,262	187,277	141,371	4,113	41,793
EAST NORTH CENTRAL:								
Ohio...............	256,695	177,986	3,065	75,644	241,075	165,688	2,842	72,545
Indiana.............	205,126	137,210	2,329	65,587	198,156	131,737	2,251	64,168
Illinois............	237,181	132,574	3,411	101,196	214,177	118,774	3,124	92,279
Michigan...........	196,447	159,406	2,319	34,722	147,450	115,624	1,925	29,901
Wisconsin..........	189,295	159,610	2,427	27,258	134,634	109,410	1,944	23,280
WEST NORTH CENTRAL:								
Minnesota..........	178,478	132,744	1,596	44,138	110,966	74,871	1,227	34,868
Iowa...............	213,439	121,888	2,487	89,064	181,109	100,741	2,278	78,090
Missouri...........	263,004	185,030	2,247	75,727	251,835	176,040	2,124	73,671
North Dakota.......	77,690	56,917	855	19,918	40,899	27,489	627	12,783
South Dakota.......	74,637	47,815	781	26,041	52,700	31,450	654	20,596
Nebraska...........	124,417	69,672	1,315	53,430	99,441	51,829	1,183	46,429
Kansas.............	165,286	97,090	1,495	66,701	146,859	82,863	1,416	62,580
SOUTH ATLANTIC:								
Delaware...........	10,140	6,010	144	3,986	8,905	5,334	125	3,446
Maryland...........	47,908	32,805	1,262	13,841	40,130	27,914	1,056	11,160
District of Columbia.	204	100	19	85	153	72	14	67
Virginia...........	186,242	136,363	2,134	47,745	136,874	103,988	1,904	30,982
West Virginia......	87,289	72,101	1,090	14,098	86,033	71,181	1,071	13,781
North Carolina.....	269,763	151,376	928	117,459	193,081	128,774	820	63,487
South Carolina.....	192,693	67,724	738	124,231	83,542	44,859	551	38,132
Georgia............	310,732	102,123	1,655	206,954	180,217	85,836	1,432	92,949
Florida............	54,005	38,487	1,829	13,689	38,836	30,256	1,535	7,045
EAST SOUTH CENTRAL:								
Kentucky...........	270,626	179,327	969	90,330	256,886	173,070	918	82,898
Tennessee..........	252,774	148,082	807	103,885	213,832	137,644	748	75,440
Alabama............	256,099	107,089	741	148,269	159,865	88,974	600	70,291
Mississippi........	272,101	91,310	989	179,802	110,279	67,759	779	41,741
WEST SOUTH CENTRAL:								
Arkansas...........	232,604	112,647	736	119,221	158,273	95,539	637	62,097
Louisiana..........	135,463	57,254	828	77,381	71,081	44,727	721	25,633
Oklahoma..........	191,988	93,217	935	97,836	167,472	79,136	833	87,503
Texas..............	436,033	201,210	2,514	232,309	327,475	163,266	2,216	161,993
MOUNTAIN:								
Montana............	57,677	50,271	899	6,507	41,031	35,301	722	5,008
Idaho	42,106	34,647	758	6,701	95,001	28,748	660	5,876
Wyoming...........	15,718	13,403	377	1,968	13,306	11,340	340	1,626
Colorado...........	59,934	45,291	880	13,763	49,846	37,750	807	11,289
New Mexico........	29,844	25,756	433	3,655	26,593	23,202	401	2,990
Arizona............	9,975	7,869	305	1,801	8,262	6,482	270	1,510
Utah...............	25,662	22,579	296	2,787	21,276	18,688	268	2,320
Nevada.............	3,163	2,699	168	296	2,060	1,737	124	199
PACIFIC:								
Washington.........	66,288	52,701	1,168	12,419	45,265	34,970	941	9,354
Oregon.............	50,206	39,863	916	9,427	40,484	31,569	802	8,113
California..........	117,670	87,580	4,949	25,141	76,995	60,264	3,913	12,818

[1] Includes farmers with country of birth not reported.

NATIVITY, AND TENURE, BY DIVISIONS AND STATES: 1920.

DIVISION AND STATE.	FOREIGN-BORN WHITE FARM OPERATORS.				COLORED FARM OPERATORS.			
	Total.	Owners.	Managers.	Tenants.	Total.	Owners.	Managers.	Tenants.
United States	581,068	464,347	7,188	109,533	949,889	233,222	2,226	714,441
GEOGRAPHIC DIVISIONS:								
New England	28,265	25,138	1,030	2,097	271	218	18	35
Middle Atlantic	46,910	38,308	1,285	7,317	1,536	975	90	471
East North Central	144,775	122,469	1,394	20,912	4,477	3,084	71	1,322
West North Central	206,223	150,997	1,183	44,043	6,919	4,876	84	1,959
South Atlantic	7,373	6,212	334	827	383,832	102,663	957	280,212
East South Central	3,506	2,821	54	631	307,232	55,540	407	251,285
West South Central	39,937	22,274	200	17,463	231,850	59,386	406	172,058
Mountain	40,984	34,905	497	5,582	5,447	4,362	27	1,058
Pacific	63,095	51,223	1,211	10,661	8,325	2,118	166	6,041
NEW ENGLAND:								
Maine	4,384	4,086	97	201	13	13		1
New Hampshire	2,619	2,367	73	179	14	12	1	1
Vermont	3,767	3,381	59	327	28	21	3	4
Massachusetts	8,930	7,823	429	678	121	107	7	7
Rhode Island	940	710	51	179	20	14	1	5
Connecticut	7,625	6,771	321	533	75	51	6	18
MIDDLE ATLANTIC:								
New York	25,776	20,884	765	4,127	550	429	25	96
New Jersey	6,612	5,558	188	866	535	285	20	230
Pennsylvania	14,522	11,866	332	2,324	451	261	45	145
EAST NORTH CENTRAL:								
Ohio	14,004	11,245	187	2,572	1,616	1,053	36	527
Indiana	6,398	5,167	64	1,167	572	306	14	252
Illinois	22,111	13,266	278	8,567	893	534	9	350
Michigan	48,264	43,219	385	4,660	733	563	9	161
Wisconsin	53,998	49,572	480	3,946	663	628	3	32
WEST NORTH CENTRAL:								
Minnesota	67,305	57,696	368	9,241	207	177	1	29
Iowa	32,221	21,073	208	10,940	109	74	1	34
Missouri	8,343	7,346	75	922	2,826	1,644	48	1,134
North Dakota	36,248	28,959	226	7,063	543	469	2	72
South Dakota	20,325	14,900	117	5,308	1,612	1,465	10	137
Nebraska	24,592	17,589	128	6,875	384	254	4	126
Kansas	17,189	13,434	61	3,694	1,238	793	18	427
SOUTH ATLANTIC:								
Delaware	363	321	6	36	872	355	13	504
Maryland	1,569	1,342	55	172	6,209	3,549	151	2,509
District of Columbia	31	19	4	8	20	9	1	10
Virginia	1,582	1,426	33	123	47,786	30,949	197	16,640
West Virginia	752	517	11	224	504	403	8	93
North Carolina	392	325	12	55	76,290	22,277	96	53,917
South Carolina	141	106	4	31	109,010	22,759	183	86,068
Georgia	328	245	16	67	130,187	16,042	207	113,938
Florida	2,215	1,911	193	111	12,954	6,320	101	6,533
EAST SOUTH CENTRAL:								
Kentucky	1,112	938	16	158	12,628	5,319	35	7,274
Tennessee	760	598	6	156	38,182	9,840	53	28,289
Alabama	1,031	913	14	104	95,203	17,202	127	77,874
Mississippi	603	372	18	213	161,219	23,179	192	137,848
WEST SOUTH CENTRAL:								
Arkansas	2,049	1,735	4	310	72,282	15,373	95	56,814
Louisiana	2,323	1,541	15	767	62,059	10,986	92	50,981
Oklahoma	5,791	4,593	17	1,181	18,725	9,488	85	9,152
Texas	29,774	14,405	164	15,205	78,784	23,539	134	55,111
MOUNTAIN:								
Montana	15,563	13,985	167	1,411	1,063	985	10	68
Idaho	6,314	5,536	98	680	508	363		145
Wyoming	2,273	1,940	37	296	169	123		46
Colorado	9,535	7,293	67	2,175	553	248	6	299
New Mexico	1,376	911	30	435	1,875	1,643	2	230
Arizona	1,067	834	30	203	646	553	5	88
Utah	3,972	3,652	25	295	414	239	3	172
Nevada	884	754	43	87	219	208	1	10
PACIFIC:								
Washington	19,757	17,214	218	2,325	1,266	517	9	740
Oregon	9,149	7,936	106	1,107	573	358	8	207
California	34,189	26,073	887	7,229	6,486	1,243	149	5,094

TABLE 49.—ACREAGE OF FARM LAND, BY COLOR AND NATIVITY OF FARMER, BY DIVISIONS AND STATES: 1920.

[Acreage of land operated by all farmers in Table 58.]

DIVISION AND STATE.	ACREAGE OF ALL LAND IN FARMS OPERATED BY—			ACREAGE OF IMPROVED LAND IN FARMS OPERATED BY—		
	Native white farmers.	Foreign-born white farmers.	Colored farmers.	Native white farmers.	Foreign-born white farmers.	Colored farmers.
United States	799,767,149	111,172,045	44,944,521	411,266,350	62,508,216	29,298,441
GEOGRAPHIC DIVISIONS:						
New England	14,577,167	2,392,809	20,666	5,161,809	945,647	7,145
Middle Atlantic	36,926,113	3,550,659	96,129	24,276,451	2,223,382	62,274
East North Central	103,322,178	14,235,364	277,637	78,846,396	8,847,626	200,813
West North Central	201,588,879	53,872,459	1,511,891	134,286,249	36,593,231	514,959
South Atlantic	78,825,092	725,210	18,224,941	36,743,177	312,821	11,453,888
East South Central	66,455,226	328,565	12,113,672	35,661,235	177,342	8,541,555
West South Central	155,099,848	7,369,396	10,979,883	53,277,523	3,163,766	7,748,317
Mountain	99,283,989	17,055,768	997,469	24,614,210	5,196,486	295,172
Pacific	43,788,657	11,641,815	722,233	18,399,300	5,047,915	474,318
NEW ENGLAND:						
Maine	4,960,209	464,806	953	1,768,011	208,873	445
New Hampshire	2,336,254	266,076	1,476	621,913	80,474	515
Vermont	3,674,319	557,042	4,450	1,449,131	241,042	1,422
Massachusetts	1,968,970	519,917	5,590	701,343	205,056	2,435
Rhode Island	276,543	54,105	952	108,607	23,936	312
Connecticut	1,360,872	530,863	7,245	512,804	186,266	2,016
MIDDLE ATLANTIC:						
New York	18,344,237	2,245,691	42,875	11,702,092	1,429,554	27,135
New Jersey	1,928,591	327,674	26,320	1,321,886	217,261	16,460
Pennsylvania	16,653,285	977,294	26,934	11,252,473	576,567	18,679
EAST NORTH CENTRAL:						
Ohio	22,462,603	952,873	100,412	17,761,878	704,038	76,437
Indiana	20,405,497	621,119	36,716	16,166,647	482,860	30,705
Illinois	29,140,069	2,777,004	57,702	25,055,326	2,192,110	47,097
Michigan	14,709,946	4,274,302	48,713	10,251,673	2,642,141	31,707
Wisconsin	16,504,063	5,610,066	34,094	9,610,872	2,826,477	14,867
WEST NORTH CENTRAL:						
Minnesota	19,362,288	10,839,191	20,279	14,212,197	7,262,169	7,344
Iowa	28,405,463	5,060,586	8,847	24,198,486	4,402,248	6,217
Missouri	33,471,859	1,112,386	190,434	23,920,895	770,072	141,999
North Dakota	19,393,945	16,634,354	186,452	13,158,149	11,358,858	46,171
South Dakota	25,372,917	8,413,432	850,142	13,012,519	5,035,962	150,769
Nebraska	35,198,035	6,960,758	66,682	18,674,678	4,402,580	32,366
Kansas	40,384,372	4,851,752	189,055	27,109,325	3,361,342	130,093
SOUTH ATLANTIC:						
Delaware	861,124	28,499	54,888	596,080	19,037	37,935
Maryland	4,277,868	128,554	351,577	2,845,259	73,783	217,686
District of Columbia	4,912	468	288	3,626	39	273
Virginia	16,085,118	212,575	2,263,419	8,265,401	90,630	1,104,461
West Virginia	9,479,825	62,421	27,544	5,468,291	34,911	17,105
North Carolina	16,538,442	45,852	3,437,442	6,325,745	15,564	1,857,100
South Carolina	8,009,681	36,991	4,380,003	3,267,931	12,635	2,903,593
Georgia	18,296,541	72,608	7,071,912	8,159,601	17,498	4,878,110
Florida	5,271,581	137,242	637,868	1,811,243	48,404	437,624
EAST SOUTH CENTRAL:						
Kentucky	21,088,067	97,746	426,959	13,572,256	68,974	334,516
Tennessee	17,920,245	66,808	1,523,803	10,029,097	37,173	1,119,032
Alabama	15,143,115	85,496	4,348,245	6,897,150	32,287	2,963,970
Mississippi	12,303,799	78,515	5,814,665	5,162,732	38,908	4,124,037
WEST SOUTH CENTRAL:						
Arkansas	14,606,175	225,813	2,624,762	7,153,704	110,022	1,843,740
Louisiana	7,663,058	170,286	2,182,578	3,886,006	100,127	1,640,093
Oklahoma	28,870,010	1,368,521	1,713,403	16,284,570	836,821	1,003,930
Texas	103,959,705	5,601,776	4,459,140	25,953,153	2,113,796	3,160,554
MOUNTAIN:						
Montana	25,960,310	8,458,731	651,615	8,174,686	2,684,610	147,982
Idaho	7,167,170	1,160,816	47,887	3,858,416	624,530	28,734
Wyoming	10,094,051	1,692,432	22,868	1,794,414	299,248	8,343
Colorado	21,493,748	2,880,888	87,378	6,642,114	1,058,647	43,996
New Mexico	22,882,250	1,463,024	64,359	1,612,854	84,110	20,260
Arizona	5,310,845	430,859	60,422	614,006	79,178	19,619
Utah	4,531,616	467,624	51,170	1,475,865	220,929	18,586
Nevada	1,843,999	501,394	11,770	441,855	145,234	7,652
PACIFIC:						
Washington	10,237,175	2,906,146	101,399	5,523,148	1,562,010	44,185
Oregon	11,432,137	2,010,328	99,853	4,273,552	611,010	29,289
California	22,119,345	6,725,341	520,981	8,602,600	2,874,895	400,844

TABLE 50.—NUMBER OF COLORED FARM OPERATORS, BY RACE, BY DIVISIONS AND STATES: 1920 AND 1910.

DIVISION AND STATE.	ALL COLORED FARM OPERATORS.		NEGROES.		INDIANS.		JAPANESE.		CHINESE.	
	1920	1910	1920	1910	1920	1910	1920	1910	1920	1910
United States	949,889	920,883	925,708	893,370	16,680	24,251	6,892	2,502	609	760
GEOGRAPHIC DIVISIONS:										
New England	271	342	242	310	29	32				
Middle Atlantic	1,536	1,961	1,227	1,310	300	638	7	8	2	5
East North Central	4,477	5,717	3,674	4,843	800	870	2	2	1	2
West North Central	6,919	9,864	4,237	5,589	2,618	4,252	62	21	2	2
South Atlantic	383,832	355,862	382,278	354,530	1,549	1,303	3	16	2	13
East South Central	307,232	325,218	307,006	324,884	222	333			4	1
West South Central	231,850	209,061	226,311	201,422	5,497	7,584	33	45	9	10
Mountain	5,447	8,028	349	219	4,327	7,523	710	195	61	91
Pacific	8,325	4,830	384	263	1,338	1,716	6,075	2,215	528	636
NEW ENGLAND:										
Maine	13	29	13	28		1				
New Hampshire	14	15	14	14		1				
Vermont	28	20	28	20						
Massachusetts	121	124	103	103	18	21				
Rhode Island	20	41	19	40	1	1				
Connecticut	75	113	65	105	10	8				
MIDDLE ATLANTIC:										
New York	550	939	245	295	299	635	5	5	1	4
New Jersey	535	476	531	472	1		2	3	1	1
Pennsylvania	451	546	451	543		3				
EAST NORTH CENTRAL:										
Ohio	1,616	1,950	1,616	1,948		1		1		
Indiana	572	805	570	785	2	20				
Illinois	893	1,425	892	1,422	1	2				1
Michigan	733	916	549	640	182	306	1		1	
Wisconsin	663	591	47	48	615	541	1	1		1
WEST NORTH CENTRAL:										
Minnesota	207	293	33	29	174	264				
Iowa	109	201	109	187		14			1	1
Missouri	2,826	3,666	2,824	3,656	1	9			1	1
North Dakota	543	743	26	22	517	721				
South Dakota	1,612	2,808	47	67	1,563	2,740	1		1	1
Nebraska	384	462	63	96	260	347	61	19		
Kansas	1,238	1,691	1,135	1,532	103	157		2		
SOUTH ATLANTIC:										
Delaware	872	922	872	922						
Maryland	6,209	6,372	6,208	6,370	1	1				1
District of Columbia	20	12	20	12						
Virginia	47,786	48,114	47,690	48,039	96	74				1
West Virginia	504	708	504	707		1				
North Carolina	76,290	65,656	74,849	64,456	1,440	1,197			1	3
South Carolina	109,010	96,798	109,005	96,772	1	25	3		1	1
Georgia	130,187	122,559	130,176	122,554	11	3				2
Florida	12,954	14,721	12,954	14,698		2		16		5
EAST SOUTH CENTRAL:										
Kentucky	12,628	11,730	12,624	11,709	3	21			1	
Tennessee	38,182	38,308	38,181	38,300	1	8				
Alabama	95,203	110,443	95,200	110,387		56			3	
Mississippi	161,219	164,737	161,001	164,488	218	248				1
WEST SOUTH CENTRAL:										
Arkansas	72,282	63,593	72,275	63,578	7	15				
Louisiana	62,059	54,879	62,036	54,819	22	58	1			2
Oklahoma	18,725	20,671	13,403	13,209	5,315	7,459	3	1	4	2
Texas	78,784	69,918	78,597	69,816	153	52	29	44	5	6
MOUNTAIN:										
Montana	1,063	1,196	31	29	987	1,146	29	4	16	17
Idaho	508	405	23	13	336	334	129	36	20	22
Wyoming	169	65	17	19	134	44	15	1	3	1
Colorado	553	574	148	81	83	405	321	87	1	1
New Mexico	1,875	2,148	32	48	1,833	2,087	9	10	1	3
Arizona	646	3,203	32	12	537	3,159	69	5	8	27
Utah	414	276	61	11	209	200	133	52	11	13
Nevada	219	161	5	6	208	148	5		1	7
PACIFIC:										
Washington	1,266	1,125	79	77	460	673	699	316	28	59
Oregon	573	627	15	27	300	452	224	83	34	65
California	6,486	3,078	290	159	578	591	5,152	1,816	466	512

TABLE 51.—NUMBER OF COLORED FARM OPERATORS, BY RACE AND TENURE, BY DIVISIONS AND STATES: 1920.

[Total number of colored farm operators, by race, in Table 50.]

DIVISION AND STATE.	NEGRO FARM OPERATORS.			INDIAN FARM OPERATORS.			JAPANESE FARM OPERATORS.			CHINESE FARM OPERATORS.		
	Owners.	Managers.	Tenants.	Owners.	Managers.	Tenants.	Owners.	Managers.	Tenants.	Owners.	Managers.	Tenants.
United States ...	218,612	2,026	705,070	13,821	54	2,805	717	123	6,052	72	23	514
GEOGRAPHIC DIVISIONS:												
New England	192	17	33	26	1	2						
Middle Atlantic	697	86	444	276	3	21	2		5		1	1
East North Central	2,335	66	1,273	748	5	47			2		1	
West North Central	2,525	73	1,639	2,345	11	262	5		57	1		1
South Atlantic	102,056	956	279,266	607	1	941			3			2
East South Central	55,488	406	251,112	51		171				1	1	2
West South Central	54,821	397	171,093	4,546	8	943	14	1	18	5		4
Mountain	239	10	100	4,017	14	296	102	2	606	4	1	56
Pacific	259	15	110	1,205	11	122	594	120	5,361	60	20	448
NEW ENGLAND:												
Maine	13											
New Hampshire	12	1	1									
Vermont	21	3	4									
Massachusetts	89	7	7	18								
Rhode Island	13	1	5	1								
Connecticut	44	5	16	7	1	2						
MIDDLE ATLANTIC:												
New York	152	22	71	275	3	21	2		3			1
New Jersey	284	19	228	1					2		1	
Pennsylvania	261	45	145									
EAST NORTH CENTRAL:												
Ohio	1,053	36	527									
Indiana	305	14	251	1		1						
Illinois	533	9	350	1								
Michigan	403	7	139	159	2	21			1	1		
Wisconsin	41		6	587	3	25			1			
WEST NORTH CENTRAL:												
Minnesota	24		9	153	1	20						
Iowa	74	1	34									
Missouri	1,643	48	1,133	1								1
North Dakota	11	2	13	458		59						
South Dakota	33	1	13	1,430	9	124	1					
Nebraska	31	4	28	219		41	4		57	1		
Kansas	709	17	409	84	1	18						
SOUTH ATLANTIC:												
Delaware	355	13	504									
Maryland	3,548	151	2,509	1								
Dist. of Columbia	9	1	10									
Virginia	30,908	197	16,585	41		55						
West Virginia	403	8	93									
North Carolina	21,714	95	53,040	563	1	876						1
South Carolina	22,759	183	86,063			1			3			1
Georgia	16,040	207	113,929	2		9						
Florida	6,320	101	6,533									
EAST SOUTH CENTRAL:												
Kentucky	5,318	35	7,271	1		2						
Tennessee	9,839	53	28,289	1								1
Alabama	17,201	126	77,873									
Mississippi	23,130	192	137,679	49		169				1	1	1
WEST SOUTH CENTRAL:												
Arkansas	15,009	95	56,811	4		0						
Louisiana	10,075	51	50,969	11		11						
Oklahoma	4,958	77	8,368	4,526	8	781	1		2	3		1
Texas	23,519	133	54,945	5		148	13	1	15	2		3
MOUNTAIN:												
Montana	26	1	4	951	9	27	8		21			16
Idaho	16		7	329		7	18		111			20
Wyoming	17			103		31	2		13	1		2
Colorado	115	5	28	81		2	51	1	269	1		
New Mexico	24		8	1,619	1	213			9		1	
Arizona	19	3	10	530	2	5	2		67	2		6
Utah	19	1	41	200	1	8	20	1	112			11
Nevada	3		2	204	1	3	1		4			1
PACIFIC:												
Washington	65		14	423	4	33	27	5	667	2		26
Oregon	11	2	2	281	2	17	61	2	161	5	2	27
California	183	13	94	501	5	72	506	113	4,533	53	18	395

TABLE 52.—NUMBER OF WHITE FARM OPERATORS IN THE UNITED STATES, BY COUNTRY OF BIRTH, 1920 AND 1910, WITH FARM ACREAGE AND VALUE FOR 1920.

NATIVITY OF FARMER.	NUMBER OF FARM OPERATORS.				LAND IN FARMS, 1920.		Value of farms (land and buildings), 1920
	1920	1910	Per cent distribution of foreign-born white.		All land (acres).	Improved land (acres).	
			1920	1910			
All white farmers	5,498,454	5,440,619			910,939,194	473,774,566	$63,786,058,855
Born in the United States	4,817,846	4,763,256			780,710,497	402,727,922	53,591,410,431
Born in foreign countries, total.	581,068	669,556	100.0	100.0	111,172,045	62,508,216	8,985,541,538
England	26,614	39,728	4.6	5.9	5,036,138	2,207,529	384,492,414
Scotland	7,605	10,220	1.3	1.5	2,738,653	928,047	162,473,851
Wales	2,472	4,110	0.4	0.6	482,178	261,242	37,675,623
Ireland	16,562	33,480	2.9	5.0	4,065,473	1,782,471	308,442,116
Norway	51,599	59,742	8.9	8.9	12,726,884	7,810,200	878,081,731
Sweden	60,461	67,453	10.4	10.1	10,978,905	6,409,960	978,605,102
Denmark	25,565	28,375	4.4	4.2	5,148,940	3,123,667	517,475,883
Netherlands (Holland)	15,589	13,790	2.7	2.1	2,403,030	1,667,185	321,996,268
Switzerland	13,051	14,333	2.2	2.1	2,569,288	1,325,241	225,299,776
France	6,119	5,832	1.1	0.9	1,620,047	553,245	100,803,220
Germany	140,667	221,800	24.2	33.1	25,386,893	15,694,131	2,520,600,623
Poland	17,352	7,228	3.0	1.1	2,006,227	1,129,483	153,643,629
Austria	30,172	33,336	5.2	5.0	4,455,775	2,477,405	329,585,942
Hungary	7,122	3,827	1.2	0.6	977,986	548,012	60,127,807
Russia	32,388	25,788	5.6	3.9	9,946,798	6,260,226	516,677,023
Finland	14,988	(1)	2.6		1,694,743	689,720	82,981,388
Rumania	693	(1)	0.1		184,158	118,699	7,667,840
Greece	846	(1)	0.1		121,223	54,378	9,306,242
Italy	18,267	10,614	3.1	1.6	1,903,900	852,894	181,425,476
Portugal	4,254	(1)	0.7		613,130	300,200	75,931,189
Other European countries	20,107	17,689	3.5	2.6	3,771,490	2,042,110	340,541,459
Mexico	12,142	(2)	2.1		1,576,722	700,116	71,207,258
Canada	48,668	61,878	8.4	9.2	9,227,880	4,834,030	576,841,162
Other countries	7,765	10,333	1.3	1.5	1,535,584	738,025	143,658,516
Country of birth not reported	99,540	7,807			19,056,652	8,538,428	1,209,106,886

[1] Included with "Other European countries."   [2] Included with "Other countries."

718   ABSTRACT OF THE CENSUS—AGRICULTURE.

TABLE **53.**—NUMBER AND VALUE OF FARMS IN THE UNITED STATES OPERATED
BY WHITE FARMERS, BY COUNTRY OF BIRTH AND TENURE OF FARMER: 1920.

[Totals for white farmers, by country of birth, in Table 52.]

NATIVITY OF FARMER.	NUMBER OF FARMS.			VALUE OF FARMS (LAND AND BUILDINGS).		
	Owners.	Managers.	Tenants.	Owners.	Managers.	Tenants.
All white farmers....	3,691,868	66,223	1,740,363	$39,215,462,823	$2,629,284,676	$21,941,311,356
Born in the United States..	3,162,223	57,440	1,598,183	32,224,972,299	2,195,639,342	19,170,798,790
Born in foreign countries, total......................	464,347	7,188	109,533	6,261,305,080	346,174,880	2,378,061,578
England................	21,840	858	3,916	259,698,564	49,474,775	75,319,075
Scotland...............	6,004	414	1,187	97,311,209	40,553,962	24,608,680
Wales..................	2,071	53	348	28,747,948	2,502,945	6,424,730
Ireland................	13,925	581	2,056	218,449,446	37,416,312	52,576,358
Norway................	43,815	361	7,423	670,681,449	11,291,280	196,109,002
Sweden................	50,114	622	9,725	662,305,841	23,284,419	293,014,842
Denmark...............	19,523	336	5,706	328,542,491	14,921,703	174,011,689
Netherlands (Holland).	10,364	197	5,028	154,825,973	7,535,855	159,634,440
Switzerland............	10,324	166	2,561	151,657,764	8,536,259	65,105,753
France.................	4,942	100	1,077	65,375,414	3,395,230	32,032,576
Germany...............	116,962	1,203	22,502	1,874,800,267	50,095,598	595,704,758
Poland................	14,874	114	2,364	110,329,504	3,281,638	40,032,487
Austria................	24,534	235	5,403	242,933,374	5,759,649	80,892,919
Hungary...............	5,439	80	1,603	38,935,017	1,654,320	19,538,470
Russia.................	24,244	179	7,965	370,115,899	4,909,330	141,651,794
Finland................	13,730	46	1,212	70,040,299	543,175	12,397,914
Rumania...............	533	7	153	5,655,380	151,850	1,860,610
Greece.................	540	13	293	4,620,270	141,200	4,544,772
Italy..................	13,403	234	4,630	100,945,723	8,725,826	71,753,927
Portugal..............	2,896	49	1,309	39,051,251	2,421,450	34,458,488
Other European countries.	15,238	180	4,689	220,391,049	19,189,386	100,961,024
Mexico................	1,625	117	10,400	12,036,003	5,598,026	53,573,229
Canada................	41,864	910	5,894	443,791,751	40,640,375	92,409,036
Other countries.........	5,543	133	2,089	90,063,194	4,150,317	49,445,005
Country of birth not reported..................	65,298	1,595	32,647	729,185,444	87,470,454	392,450,988

TABLE 54.—FARM ACREAGE OPERATED BY WHITE FARMERS IN THE UNITED STATES, BY COUNTRY OF BIRTH AND TENURE OF FARMER: 1920.

[Totals for white farmers, by country of birth, in Table 52.]

NATIVITY OF FARMER.	ALL LAND IN FARMS (ACRES).			IMPROVED LAND IN FARMS (ACRES).		
	Owners.	Managers.	Tenants.	Owners.	Managers.	Tenants.
All white farmers..........	620,070,823	53,653,478	237,214,893	306,029,220	13,009,436	154,735,910
Born in the United States.......	521,930,228	46,936,368	211,843,901	254,119,496	11,287,649	137,320,777
Born in foreign countries, total..	85,563,515	4,697,184	20,911,346	46,548,667	1,334,539	14,625,010
England.....................	3,795,860	518,843	721,435	1,643,463	121,703	442,363
Scotland...................	1,909,150	537,878	291,625	628,587	143,134	156,326
Wales.....................	394,144	24,831	63,203	207,212	12,662	41,368
Ireland....................	3,285,888	250,590	528,995	1,431,820	76,607	274,044
Norway....................	10,602,974	204,383	1,919,527	6,232,391	102,667	1,475,142
Sweden....................	8,394,038	491,130	2,093,737	4,735,034	103,292	1,571,634
Denmark....................	3,763,214	175,284	1,210,442	2,144,099	71,660	907,908
Netherlands (Holland)......	1,409,767	65,947	927,316	921,069	36,170	709,946
Switzerland................	1,885,980	91,928	591,380	951,911	29,575	343,755
France....................	1,113,958	59,585	446,504	394,451	10,305	148,489
Germany....................	20,457,358	702,638	4,226,897	12,201,923	260,829	3,231,379
Poland....................	1,674,543	15,191	316,493	902,841	8,001	218,641
Austria....................	3,651,844	64,074	739,857	1,923,164	26,352	527,889
Hungary....................	764,525	14,480	198,981	410,583	6,925	130,504
Russia....................	7,652,387	86,987	2,207,424	4,653,372	24,056	1,582,798
Finland....................	1,508,954	8,060	177,729	573,922	2,440	113,358
Rumania....................	144,386	1,518	38,254	89,641	1,249	27,809
Greece....................	77,648	2,225	41,350	30,806	446	23,126
Italy.....................	1,233,023	128,047	542,830	508,393	29,414	315,087
Portugal..................	353,396	27,728	232,006	151,092	8,950	140,158
Other European countries...	2,604,704	252,709	914,077	1,425,500	58,383	558,227
Mexico....................	444,435	351,310	780,977	83,645	15,301	601,170
Canada....................	7,411,207	559,703	1,256,970	3,871,562	170,455	792,013
Other countries.............	1,030,132	62,115	443,337	432,186	13,963	291,876
Country of birth not reported....	12,577,080	2,019,926	4,459,646	5,361,057	387,248	2,790,123

TABLE 55.—WHITE FARM OPERATORS, BY COUNTRY OF BIRTH,

[Total number of white farm

DIVISION OR STATE AND CENSUS YEAR.	White farmers born in the United States.	WHITE FARMERS BORN IN FOREIGN COUNTRIES.									
		Total.	England.	Scotland.	Wales.	Ireland.	Norway.	Sweden.	Denmark.	Netherlands (Holland).	Switzerland.
1 United States..1920..	4,817,846	581,068	26,614	7,605	2,472	16,562	51,599	60,461	25,565	15,589	13,051
2 1910..	4,763,256	669,556	39,728	10,220	4,110	33,480	59,742	67,453	28,375	13,790	14,333
GEOGRAPHIC DIVISIONS.											
3 New England......1920..	125,525	28,265	1,786	594	49	1,924	178	1,784	383	98	206
4 1910..	160,196	27,451	2,429	714	198	3,751	141	1,747	390	75	207
5 Middle Atlantic....1920..	369,122	46,910	4,061	797	384	3,522	354	2,095	689	1,320	811
6 1910..	417,730	47,076	5,716	999	652	7,103	109	2,246	553	1,143	895
7 East North Central.1920..	918,467	144,775	5,856	1,257	487	2,973	10,048	11,928	4,538	5,874	3,381
8 1910..	927,524	188,153	10,332	2,080	922	7,466	13,330	13,491	5,739	6,710	4,062
9 West North Central.1920..	864,735	206,223	5,100	1,580	650	3,890	33,543	32,180	12,532	6,027	2,810
10 1910..	829,467	269,442	8,805	2,786	1,265	9,094	41,015	39,614	14,846	4,827	3,863
11 South Atlantic......1920..	750,533	7,373	952	234	44	331	104	301	169	156	195
12 1910..	748,411	7,141	1,134	313	61	633	93	190	124	52	247
13 East South Central.1920..	723,593	3,506	267	64	10	188	47	229	72	46	297
14 1910..	712,116	4,819	467	120	18	467	64	245	73	26	391
15 West South Central.1920..	708,363	39,937	980	463	56	399	312	1,123	578	171	713
16 1910..	691,971	41,501	1,558	417	97	781	404	1,381	491	139	712
17 Mountain..........1920..	193,352	40,984	3,718	1,299	464	1,306	3,529	4,388	3,162	908	1,175
18 1910..	143,699	31,427	4,932	1,362	562	1,484	1,683	3,627	3,097	393	1,023
19 Pacific............1920..	159,156	63,095	3,894	1,317	328	2,029	3,484	6,433	3,442	989	3,460
20 1910..	132,142	52,546	4,355	1,429	335	2,701	2,903	4,912	3,062	425	2,933
NEW ENGLAND.											
21 Maine............1920..	43,238	4,384	188	68	9	96	28	284	104	3	4
22 1910..	54,885	4,973	277	106	12	174	27	351	116	4	7
23 New Hampshire....1920..	17,275	2,619	210	84	1	124	23	111	17	1	7
24 1910..	24,283	2,691	236	92	3	263	18	88	11	2	11
25 Vermont..........1920..	24,952	3,767	182	96	26	199	15	78	30	8	16
26 1910..	28,922	3,721	210	118	158	463	5	61	23	2	4
27 Massachusetts......1920..	22,387	8,930	740	221	6	796	67	577	92	69	40
28 1910..	28,110	8,362	994	231	12	1,572	56	520	99	53	35
29 Rhode Island.......1920..	3,007	940	105	27	.....	59	5	62	7	3	9
30 1910..	4,336	843	161	46	.....	115	2	52	6	4	7
31 Connecticut.......1920..	14,666	7,625	361	98	7	650	40	672	133	14	130
32 1910..	19,660	6,861	551	121	13	1,164	33	675	135	10	143
MIDDLE ATLANTIC.											
33 New York..........1920..	163,977	25,776	2,728	413	255	2,354	269	919	468	1,068	444
34 1910..	186,948	27,029	3,710	491	404	4,770	41	785	308	978	424
35 New Jersey.........1920..	22,012	6,612	409	98	10	309	42	113	101	180	98
36 1910..	26,526	6,215	606	128	18	579	30	92	105	133	136
37 Pennsylvania.......1920..	183,133	14,522	924	286	119	859	43	1,063	120	72	269
38 1910..	204,256	13,832	1,400	380	230	1,754	38	1,369	140	32	335
EAST NORTH CENTRAL.											
39 Ohio.............1920..	236,613	14,004	1,124	194	193	464	14	195	98	115	942
40 1910..	252,213	17,450	1,869	297	397	1,019	16	199	125	80	1,256
41 Indiana...........1920..	194,897	6,398	310	93	25	219	19	522	93	354	343
42 1910..	204,651	9,729	550	131	34	547	30	642	95	369	457
43 Illinois...........1920..	210,192	22,111	1,368	320	65	916	709	3,285	743	964	421
44 1910..	216,471	33,394	2,422	450	123	2,185	982	4,267	878	000	620
45 Michigan..........1920..	144,930	48,964	2,003	400	32	819	654	3,088	1,142	3,370	971
46 1910..	147,378	58,224	3,912	959	57	2,011	817	3,330	1,381	3,931	449
47 Wisconsin.......1920..	131,835	53,998	851	214	172	555	8,652	4,838	2,462	1,162	1,307
48 1910..	106,811	69,356	1,578	343	311	1,704	11,485	5,053	3,260	1,332	1,274
WEST NORTH CENTRAL.											
49 Minnesota.........1920..	108,042	67,305	655	254	74	634	14,925	16,934	3,126	1,610	433
50 1910..	74,528	81,134	944	381	138	1,556	19,206	19,760	3,432	783	499
51 Iowa.............1920..	177,401	32,221	1,267	343	118	1,080	3,094	3,318	3,273	2,674	533
52 1910..	167,432	48,987	2,374	676	308	2,592	4,614	4,570	4,061	2,479	777
53 Missouri..........1920..	246,907	8,343	555	141	94	365	29	411	164	99	492
54 1910..	258,912	14,467	1,048	291	163	883	42	551	190	103	850
55 North Dakota......1920..	39,447	36,248	431	238	27	335	10,900	3,377	1,237	296	142
56 1910..	35,689	37,867	627	359	41	839	10,886	3,635	1,318	216	151
57 South Dakota......1920..	51,450	20,325	465	147	82	314	4,025	2,265	1,703	996	192
58 1910..	49,287	25,476	676	213	118	619	5,381	2,708	1,811	780	199

[1] In 1910 farmers born in Finland, Rumania, Greece, and Portugal were included with "Other European countries."

BY DIVISIONS AND STATES: 1920 AND 1910.

operators in Table 37.]

France.	Germany.	Poland.	Austria.	Hungary.	Russia.	Finland.[1]	Rumania.[1]	Greece.[1]	Italy.	Portugal.[1]	Other European countries.[1]	Mexico.[2]	Canada.	Other countries.[2]	Country of birth not reported.	
6,119	140,667	17,352	30,172	7,122	32,388	14,988	693	846	18,267	4,254	20,107	12,142	48,668	7,765	99,540	1
5,832	221,800	7,228	33,336	3,827	25,788	...	...	...	10,614	...	17,689	...	61,878	10,333	7,807	2
313	1,840	1,502	1,157	312	1,812	957	14	64	1,670	458	575	2	9,884	703	2,503	3
306	2,481	372	843	248	1,169	...	...	...	652	...	948	...	10,611	169	813	4
806	10,456	2,955	4,392	1,507	2,638	272	144	65	4,479	8	1,311	5	3,527	312	7,579	5
668	15,601	411	1,868	538	1,919	...	...	...	2,370	...	379	...	3,807	99	1,612	6
1,332	45,840	7,664	7,854	2,694	3,434	5,618	116	158	1,400	152	5,503	37	15,947	681	17,025	7
1,353	79,813	3,466	6,874	840	1,941	...	...	...	654	...	4,527	...	24,262	291	2,095	8
1,050	54,653	2,981	8,013	1,407	16,377	5,549	324	72	596	56	6,826	46	8,713	1,248	19,074	9
1,173	87,935	2,179	14,761	1,394	16,245	...	...	...	404	...	5,331	...	13,356	549	1,175	10
131	1,889	227	686	258	229	40	10	45	310	3	221	2	629	207	17,238	11
112	2,635	69	344	165	143	...	...	...	214	...	75	...	443	94	467	12
97	1,083	39	149	85	59	28	4	12	416	1	109	3	159	42	12,269	13
108	1,920	27	121	62	44	...	...	...	392	...	84	...	148	42	327	14
609	10,348	909	4,146	274	1,661	34	3	27	2,497	15	2,558	10,977	565	519	15,938	15
650	15,420	562	6,173	264	1,686	...	...	...	2,089	...	842	...	847	6,988	653	16
495	5,413	333	2,005	296	3,647	621	44	187	1,896	64	1,158	781	3,532	563	4,326	17
355	5,147	47	1,021	147	1,058	...	...	...	1,067	...	593	...	3,038	791	292	18
1,286	9,145	742	1,770	289	2,531	1,869	34	216	5,003	3,497	1,846	289	5,712	3,490	3,588	19
1,107	10,848	95	1,331	169	1,583	...	...	...	2,772	...	4,910	...	5,366	1,310	373	20
14	74	20	19	2	57	220	...	3	40	2	20	...	3,088	41	592	21
25	100	2	9	10	25	...	...	...	12	...	80	...	3,628	8	129	22
13	74	72	51	3	80	123	2	10	21	4	16	1	1,514	57	615	23
15	90	15	14	6	21	...	...	...	21	...	67	...	1,697	21	64	24
24	98	46	35	14	28	81	...	1	62	21	26	...	2,663	18	328	25
18	102	9	15	3	24	...	...	...	22	...	19	...	2,463	2	46	26
136	380	557	352	84	628	434	1	40	687	368	185	...	2,076	394	563	27
114	598	203	255	36	421	...	...	...	195	...	585	...	2,277	106	321	28
9	103	12	13	1	22	11	1	...	131	52	9	...	162	137	116	29
9	53	...	6	2	2	...	...	...	83	...	142	...	150	3	72	30
117	1,111	795	687	208	997	88	10	10	729	11	319	1	381	56	289	31
125	1,538	143	544	191	676	...	...	...	319	...	55	...	396	29	181	32
442	5,838	1,655	1,182	407	1,346	179	97	32	1,782	5	532	2	3,188	171	2,892	33
291	8,551	171	585	135	917	...	...	...	825	...	173	...	3,414	56	681	34
122	1,453	314	399	315	596	13	22	11	1,745	...	128	...	75	59	543	35
129	2,002	72	215	84	600	...	...	...	1,134	...	65	...	75	12	270	36
242	3,165	986	2,811	785	696	80	25	22	952	3	651	3	264	82	4,144	37
248	5,048	168	1,068	319	402	...	...	...	411	...	141	...	318	31	661	38
270	5,289	593	1,685	942	327	211	58	53	311	2	460	6	345	113	4,462	39
340	9,872	66	686	327	163	...	...	...	128	...	149	...	431	30	432	40
178	3,048	236	229	126	65	4	9	10	80	...	247	1	131	56	3,259	41
166	5,863	145	216	35	64	...	...	...	38	...	124	...	201	22	300	42
401	9,725	472	477	144	209	23	5	39	435	3	921	1	350	115	3,985	43
370	17,811	228	427	58	122	...	...	...	208	...	487	...	679	73	582	44
264	9,746	2,479	2,034	933	1,538	3,947	33	37	298	2	1,341	3	13,393	192	2,520	45
295	15,788	737	1,118	181	746	...	...	...	110	...	2,301	...	20,129	71	412	46
219	18,032	3,884	3,429	549	1,295	1,433	11	19	276	145	2,534	26	1,728	205	2,799	47
182	30,479	2,290	4,427	239	846	...	...	...	170	...	1,466	...	2,822	95	369	48
148	14,731	1,386	2,246	281	671	4,703	11	12	71	4	1,586	1	2,527	282	2,924	49
125	22,011	1,161	3,385	243	700	...	...	...	28	...	3,091	...	3,583	108	182	50
274	12,730	59	926	53	119	49	2	6	116	6	1,182	4	752	243	3,708	51
248	21,940	24	2,279	91	73	...	...	...	46	...	300	...	1,433	102	424	52
175	4,328	84	425	82	87	10	5	13	190	...	201	4	296	93	4,928	53
248	8,453	86	504	109	74	...	...	...	167	...	103	...	546	56	199	54
79	3,694	516	849	697	8,590	432	284	3	12	43	656	3	3,125	282	1,452	55
65	4,825	286	1,304	513	7,734	...	...	...	14	...	689	...	4,251	114	61	56
57	4,400	191	587	167	2,977	321	18	9	28	...	638	3	666	74	1,250	57
65	6,523	121	1,204	161	3,240	...	...	...	30	...	425	...	1,152	50	73	58

[2] In 1910 farmers born in Mexico were included with "Other countries."

TABLE 55.—WHITE FARM OPERATORS, BY COUNTRY OF BIRTH,

[Total number of white farm

	DIVISION OR STATE AND CENSUS YEAR.	White farmers born in the United States.	WHITE FARMERS BORN IN FOREIGN COUNTRIES.									
			Total.	England.	Scotland.	Wales.	Ireland.	Norway.	Sweden.	Denmark.	Netherlands (Holland).	Switzerland.
	WEST NORTH CENTRAL–Con.											
1	Nebraska....1920..	97,335	24,592	710	163	80	584	360	3,578	2,487	183	427
2	1910..	93,436	35,707	1,315	329	201	1,274	559	5,139	3,214	222	543
3	Kansas....1920..	144,153	17,189	1,017	294	175	578	210	2,297	542	169	591
4	1910..	150,183	25,804	1,821	537	296	1,331	327	3,251	820	244	844
	SOUTH ATLANTIC.											
5	Delaware....1920..	8,411	363	35	7	1	27	.....	9	4	4	5
6	1910..	9,475	410	55	5	2	72	3	12	3	2	5
7	Maryland....1920..	39,380	1,569	119	34	6	73	4	18	17	25	25
8	1910..	40,560	1,882	153	54	11	151	6	16	13	16	37
9	District of Columbia.1920..	150	31	5	1	.....	3				1	1
10	1910..	167	37	6	4	.....	4				1	2
11	Virginia....1920..	134,068	1,582	264	60	8	75	36	31	47	31	30
12	1910..	134,113	1,749	348	93	14	112	63	29	35	11	41
13	West Virginia......1920..	84,407	752	105	15	9	46	2	7	3	14	65
14	1910..	95,089	839	95	31	20	131	2	6	3	3	111
15	North Carolina.....1920..	188,458	392	50	30	4	11	3	8	9	29	7
16	1910..	187,611	412	73	34	4	21	.....	3	5	6	13
17	South Carolina....1920..	81,941	141	13	3	.....	12	3	2	3	6	2
18	1910..	79,371	212	21	4	.....	29	.....	7	6	2	3
19	Georgia....1920..	176,275	328	51	13	2	14	4	16	3	14	14
20	1910..	167,993	385	80	20	2	41	4	9	2	.....	14
21	Florida....1920..	37,443	2,215	310	71	14	70	52	210	83	33	45
22	1910..	34,032	1,215	303	68	8	72	15	108	57	11	22
	EAST SOUTH CENTRAL.											
23	Kentucky....1920..	252,746	1,112	66	14	3	83	1	10	13	15	168
24	1910..	245,332	1,956	130	32	9	280	2	11	3	4	211
25	Tennessee....1920..	210,926	760	75	12	3	41	13	36	14	11	91
26	1910..	208,770	883	110	23	6	80	23	31	16	6	131
27	Alabama....1920..	157,533	1,031	68	26	1	23	27	152	27	13	27
28	1910..	151,180	1,244	144	45	2	21	33	167	44	12	41
29	Mississippi....1920..	107,388	603	58	12	3	41	6	31	18	7	11
30	1910..	108,834	736	83	20	1	86	6	36	10	4	8
	WEST SOUTH CENTRAL.											
31	Arkansas....1920..	155,140	2,049	132	24	10	38	10	52	42	26	124
32	1910..	148,559	2,458	201	46	15	117	13	69	45	20	142
33	Louisiana....1920..	69,098	2,323	46	20	5	34	9	37	14	8	15
34	1910..	63,125	2,431	78	23	6	62	13	28	17	7	21
35	Oklahoma....1920..	162,697	5,791	259	76	18	143	48	165	130	44	168
36	1910..	161,677	7,748	454	128	37	285	74	258	172	47	228
37	Texas....1920..	321,428	29,774	543	343	23	184	245	869	392	93	406
38	1910..	318,610	28,864	825	220	39	317	304	1,026	257	65	321
	MOUNTAIN.											
39	Montana....1920..	40,277	15,563	807	515	81	552	2,796	1,364	943	514	240
40	1910..	18,111	6,853	616	339	64	456	854	535	375	186	135
41	Idaho....1920..	34,423	6,314	655	211	107	166	337	934	536	93	385
42	1910..	24,679	5,708	854	204	128	211	400	859	574	54	289
43	Wyoming....1920..	12,950	2,273	274	150	20	85	69	295	153	32	68
44	1910..	8,925	1,903	324	178	34	122	55	252	147	6	52
45	Colorado....1920..	49,173	9,535	623	222	109	335	162	1,145	442	173	208
46	1910..	37,129	8,398	882	294	111	451	176	1,128	434	87	242
47	New Mexico......1920..	65,050	1,070	86	61	7	43	17	30	71	10	32
48	1910..	32,067	1,440	169	47	8	61	11	55	25	14	32
49	Arizona....1920..	8,076	1,067	75	17	8	44	10	35	61	11	41
50	1910..	5,207	806	95	22	12	45	8	28	51	......	40
51	Utah....1920..	20,815	3,972	1,126	138	127	34	125	528	904	74	143
52	1910..	15,927	5,452	1,922	257	202	65	168	742	1,420	43	173
53	Nevada....1920..	1,982	884	65	15	5	45	13	37	52	1	58
54	1910..	1,654	867	70	21	3	73	11	28	71	3	60
	PACIFIC.											
55	Washington........1920..	44,353	19,757	1,126	413	107	524	2,492	3,231	995	540	679
56	1910..	37,668	17,297	1,206	452	130	736	2,030	2,399	945	230	538
57	Oregon....1920..	39,529	9,149	620	317	77	348	518	957	530	121	793
58	1910..	35,728	9,056	784	350	68	410	533	866	498	80	680
59	California....1920..	75,274	34,189	2,148	587	144	1,157	474	2,245	1,917	328	1,988
60	1910..	58,746	26,193	2,365	627	131	1,555	340	1,647	1,619	115	1,715

1 In 1910 farmers born in Finland, Rumania, Greece, and Portugal were included with "Other European countries."

BY DIVISIONS AND STATES: 1920 AND 1910—Continued.

operators in Table 37.]

WHITE FARMERS BORN IN FOREIGN COUNTRIES—continued.

France.	Germany.	Poland.	Austria.	Hungary.	Russia.	Finland.[1]	Rumania.[1]	Greece.[1]	Italy.	Portugal.[1]	Other European countries.[1]	Mexico.[2]	Canada.	Other countries.[2]	Country of birth not reported.	
98	9,505	583	1,871	48	1,294	13	3	22	62		1,746	7	632	136	2,106	1
115	15,478	449	4,216	70	880				20		485		1,139	59	73	2
219	5,265	162	1,109	79	2,639	21	1	7	117	3	817	24	715	138	2,706	3
307	8,705	52	1,869	207	3,544				99		238		1,252	60	163	4
6	88	18	24	16	14		1	2	44		20		36	2	494	5
14	131	4	18	6	6				12		7		52	1	29	6
30	722	73	146	55	73	3	3	1	34		39		53	16	750	7
18	1,126	38	88	29	51				13		9		47	6	109	8
	15		1	1					3						3	9
	21														1	10
20	259	51	253	85	56	2	3	5	28		87		105	46	2,806	11
17	436	5	187	93	47				28		18		145	27	42	12
12	165	23	144	19	14	1		2	70		7	1	24	4	1,626	13
16	336	1	21	5	6				27		4		20	1	49	14
10	61	16	25	13	6	1	1	14	50		8		31	5	4,623	15
12	74	12	6	11	11				87		8		29	3	46	16
3	59	4	4		6				3		3		12	3	1,601	17
4	101	2	7	1	5				4		4		6	6	53	18
8	81	3	13	11	11	2		3	4	1	11		29	20	3,942	19
10	117	3	4	16	9				5		6		31	12	90	20
42	439	39	76	58	49	31	2	18	74	2	46	1	339	111	1,393	21
21	293	4	13	4	8				38		19		113	38	48	22
44	508	5	39	5	10	6	1		19	1	38	1	46	16	4,140	23
60	1,063	2	47	1	10				17		22		43	9	167	24
15	140	14	34	6	23	5		7	146		15		48	11	2,906	25
7	248	17	14	4	11				99		5		42	10	51	26
22	333	14	67	68	14	11	1	3	49		35		41	9	2,332	27
21	462	6	48	53	15				42		30		43	15	34	28
16	102	6	9	6	12	6	2		202		21	2	24	6	2,891	29
20	147	2	12	4	8				234		27		20	8	75	30
51	856	22	152	20	37	5		5	187	1	135	11	85	24	3,133	31
69	1,247	7	105	57	32				91		51		113	18	68	32
149	244	4	57	96	19	5			1,336	2	126	30	50	17	1,983	33
270	343	9	29	63	6				1,256		96		59	111		34
162	1,864	143	402	37	1,216	6	1	6	68	4	440	59	230	102	4,775	35
140	3,015	92	808	34	1,391				32		40		441	77	96	36
247	7,384	740	3,535	121	389	18	2	16	906	8	1,857	10,877	200	376	6,047	37
171	10,815	454	5,236	110	237				710		655		234	6,848	378	38
146	1,942	174	870	145	1,230	333	25	27	260	10	523	1	1,947	118	774	39
59	1,146	13	289	48	122				86		200		1,320	10	54	40
67	975	19	215	31	355	162	12	22	129	11	109	16	624	143	861	41
42	1,046	2	108	18	147				65		87		560	60	15	42
33	322	42	99	25	222	25	3	13	58	4	64	2	161	54	356	43
26	321	16	79	15	32				29		45		160	10	94	44
103	1,560	70	674	71	1,670	45	2	25	967	7	248	53	527	10	673	45
101	1,926	12	462	41	734				539		107		643	28	69	46
52	178	12	46	15	38	3		7	97	7	51	404	74	36	937	47
56	274	1	41	17	14				61		32		123	399	21	48
20	102	2	47	4	101	10	2		39	5	26	280	98	29	186	49
17	116	2	25	4	3				24		22		86	206	11	50
25	210	8	38	4	28	33		89	148	3	46	22	50	69	461	51
21	175		11	3	4				67		43		74	62	21	52
49	124	6	16	1	3	10		4	198	17	91	3	51	20	78	53
33	143	1	6	1	2				196		57		72	16	7	54
167	3,001	284	681	70	1,010	1,206	4	27	386	33	242	2	2,279	258	912	55
155	3,687	44	515	33	871				231		643		2,218	228	102	56
125	1,945	73	261	75	355	396	14	25	164	24	311	14	972	114	955	57
93	2,492	29	286	53	218				84		473		1,024	35	91	58
994	4,199	385	828	144	1,166	267	16	164	4,453	3,440	1,293	273	2,461	3,118	1,721	59
859	4,669	22	530	83	494				2,457		3,794		2,124	1,047	180	60

[2] In 1910 farmers born in Mexico were included with "Other countries."

TABLE 56.—NUMBER, ACREAGE, AND VALUE OF FARMS IN THE UNITED STATES, WITH PERCENTAGES AND AVERAGES, BY SEX AND TENURE OF FARMER: 1920.

SEX AND TENURE OF FARMER.	Number of farms.	ALL LAND IN FARMS (ACRES).		IMPROVED LAND IN FARMS (ACRES).	
		Total.	Average per farm.	Total.	Average per farm.
Total	6,448,343	955,883,715	148.2	503,073,007	78.0
Male	6,186,624	929,779,029	150.3	489,966,522	79.2
Female	261,719	26,104,686	99.7	13,106,485	50.1
Owners	3,925,090	636,775,015	162.2	314,107,483	80.0
Male	3,737,222	614,185,155	164.3	303,405,613	81.2
Female	187,868	22,589,860	120.2	10,701,870	57.0
Managers	68,449	54,129,157	790.8	13,210,999	193.0
Male	67,679	53,943,874	797.1	13,140,138	194.2
Female	770	185,283	240.6	70,861	92.0
Tenants	2,454,804	264,979,543	107.9	175,754,525	71.6
Male	2,381,723	261,650,000	109.9	173,420,771	72.8
Female	73,081	3,329,543	45.6	2,333,754	31.9

SEX AND TENURE OF FARMER.	VALUE OF FARMS (LAND AND BUILDINGS).		PER CENT DISTRIBUTION BY SEX OF FARMER.			
	Total.	Average per farm.	Number of farms.	All land.	Improved land.	Value of land and buildings.
Total	$66,316,002,602	$10,284	100.0	100.0	100.0	100.0
Male	64,636,346,544	10,448	95.9	97.3	97.4	97.5
Female	1,679,656,058	6,418	4.1	2.7	2.6	2.5
Owners	39,864,222,907	10,156	100.0	100.0	100.0	100.0
Male	38,442,098,373	10,286	95.2	96.5	96.6	96.4
Female	1,422,124,534	7,570	4.8	3.5	3.4	3.6
Managers	2,665,216,465	38,937	100.0	100.0	100.0	100.0
Male	2,651,176,139	39,173	98.9	99.7	99.5	99.5
Female	14,040,326	18,234	1.1	0.3	0.5	0.5
Tenants	23,786,563,230	9,690	100.0	100.0	100.0	100.0
Male	23,543,072,032	9,885	97.0	98.7	98.7	99.0
Female	243,491,198	3,332	3.0	1.3	1.3	1.0

TABLE 57.—NUMBER OF FARM OPERATORS, BY SEX AND TENURE, BY DIVISIONS AND STATES: 1920.

[Totals for owners, managers, and tenants in Table 48.]

DIVISION AND STATE.	ALL FARMERS.			OWNERS.		MANAGERS.		TENANTS.	
	Total.	Male.	Female.	Male.	Female.	Male.	Female.	Male.	Female.
United States....	6,448,343	6,186,624	261,719	3,737,222	187,868	67,679	770	2,381,723	73,081
GEOGRAPHIC DIVISIONS:									
New England......	156,564	147,585	8,979	131,510	8,650	4,750	52	11,325	277
Middle Atlantic.....	425,147	408,312	16,835	311,286	15,818	9,764	89	87,262	928
East North Central..	1,084,744	1,051,198	33,546	735,474	31,312	13,426	125	302,298	2,109
West North Central..	1,096,951	1,068,653	28,298	685,672	25,484	10,688	88	372,293	2,726
South Atlantic......	1,158,976	1,101,399	57,577	571,142	35,947	9,675	124	520,582	21,506
East South Central..	1,051,600	993,631	57,969	495,236	30,572	3,439	67	494,956	27,330
West South Central..	996,088	955,637	40,451	441,204	23,124	4,937	76	509,496	17,251
Mountain............	244,109	235,901	8,208	194,739	7,776	4,050	66	37,112	366
Pacific..............	234,164	224,308	9,856	170,959	9,185	6,950	83	46,399	588
NEW ENGLAND:									
Maine................	48,227	45,702	2,525	42,964	2,473	780	6	1,958	46
New Hampshire.....	20,523	19,091	1,432	17,214	1,390	533	13	1,344	29
Vermont.............	29,075	27,884	1,191	23,972	1,149	562	6	3,350	36
Massachusetts.......	32,001	30,026	1,975	26,205	1,882	1,618	9	2,203	84
Rhode Island........	4,083	3,788	295	2,976	269	201	4	611	22
Connecticut.........	22,655	21,094	1,561	18,179	1,487	1,056	14	1,859	60
MIDDLE ATLANTIC:									
New York...........	193,195	185,718	7,477	144,653	7,064	4,332	44	36,733	369
New Jersey..........	29,702	28,599	1,103	20,872	1,017	982	5	6,745	81
Pennsylvania........	202,250	193,995	8,255	145,761	7,737	4,450	40	43,784	478
EAST NORTH CENTRAL:									
Ohio.................	256,695	247,676	9,019	169,572	8,414	3,031	34	75,073	571
Indiana.............	205,126	198,867	6,259	131,308	5,902	2,311	18	65,248	339
Illinois.............	237,181	230,495	6,686	126,691	5,883	3,387	24	100,417	779
Michigan............	196,447	190,671	5,776	153,872	5,534	2,300	19	34,499	223
Wisconsin...........	189,295	183,489	5,806	154,031	5,579	2,397	30	27,061	197
WEST NORTH CENTRAL:									
Minnesota...........	178,478	172,897	5,581	127,554	5,190	1,585	11	43,758	380
Iowa................	213,439	209,232	4,207	118,177	3,711	2,467	20	88,588	476
Missouri............	263,004	254,206	8,798	177,020	8,010	2,214	33	74,972	755
North Dakota.......	77,690	76,016	1,674	55,389	1,528	851	4	19,776	142
South Dakota.......	74,637	73,059	1,578	46,403	1,412	776	5	25,880	161
Nebraska............	124,417	122,103	2,314	67,699	1,973	1,310	5	53,094	336
Kansas..............	165,286	161,140	4,146	93,430	3,660	1,485	10	66,225	476
SOUTH ATLANTIC:									
Delaware............	10,140	9,933	207	5,844	166	144		3,945	41
Maryland............	47,908	46,080	1,828	31,127	1,678	1,254	8	13,699	142
Dist. of Columbia....	204	193	11	96	4	17	2	80	5
Virginia.............	186,242	176,214	10,028	127,476	8,887	2,111	23	46,627	1,118
West Virginia.......	87,289	82,775	4,514	67,931	4,170	1,065	25	13,779	319
North Carolina.....	269,763	257,612	12,151	142,999	8,377	911	17	113,702	3,757
South Carolina......	192,693	181,107	11,586	62,917	4,807	730	8	117,460	6,771
Georgia.............	310,732	296,688	14,044	96,758	5,365	1,641	14	198,289	8,665
Florida.............	54,005	50,797	3,208	35,994	2,493	1,802	27	13,001	688
EAST SOUTH CENTRAL:									
Kentucky...........	270,626	259,227	11,399	169,246	10,081	948	21	89,033	1,297
Tennessee...........	252,774	241,400	11,374	139,455	8,627	799	8	101,146	2,739
Alabama............	256,099	239,835	16,264	100,832	6,257	719	22	138,284	9,985
Mississippi..........	272,101	253,169	18,932	85,703	5,607	973	16	166,493	13,309
WEST SOUTH CENTRAL:									
Arkansas............	232,604	221,577	11,027	106,848	5,799	722	14	114,007	5,214
Louisiana...........	135,463	127,777	7,686	54,175	3,079	819	9	72,783	4,598
Oklahoma...........	191,988	186,475	5,513	89,528	3,689	916	19	96,031	1,805
Texas...............	436,033	419,808	16,225	190,653	10,557	2,480	34	226,675	5,634
MOUNTAIN:									
Montana............	57,677	55,625	2,052	48,302	1,969	886	13	6,437	70
Idaho..............	42,106	40,940	1,166	33,569	1,078	723	35	6,648	53
Wyoming	15,748	15,082	666	12,777	626	375	2	1,930	38
Colorado............	59,934	58,138	1,796	43,617	1,674	876	4	13,645	118
New Mexico........	29,844	28,447	1,397	24,418	1,338	426	7	3,603	52
Arizona.............	9,975	9,608	367	7,519	350	305		1,784	17
Utah...............	25,662	25,035	627	21,970	609	295	1	2,770	17
Nevada.............	3,163	3,026	137	2,567	132	164	4	295	1
PACIFIC:									
Washington.........	66,288	63,855	2,433	50,440	2,261	1,149	19	12,266	153
Oregon.............	50,206	48,557	1,649	38,345	1,518	904	12	9,308	119
California...........	117,670	111,896	5,774	82,174	5,406	4,897	52	24,825	316

TABLE 58.—ACREAGE OF FARM LAND, BY SEX OF FARMER, BY DIVISIONS AND STATES: 1920.

DIVISION AND STATE.	ACREAGE OF ALL LAND IN FARMS OPERATED BY—			ACREAGE OF IMPROVED LAND IN FARMS OPERATED BY—		
	All farmers.	Males.	Females.	All farmers.	Males.	Females.
United States.....	955,883,715	929,779,029	26,104,686	503,073,007	489,966,522	13,106,485
GEOGRAPHIC DIVISIONS:						
New England........	16,990,642	16,259,409	731,233	6,114,601	5,849,671	264,930
Middle Atlantic......	40,572,901	39,301,311	1,271,590	26,562,107	25,769,579	792,528
East North Central...	117,735,179	115,044,014	2,691,165	87,894,835	86,007,214	1,887,621
West North Central..	256,973,229	251,917,553	5,055,676	171,394,439	168,149,086	3,245,353
South Atlantic.......	97,775,243	93,823,273	3,951,970	48,509,886	46,583,960	1,925,926
East South Central...	78,897,463	75,393,906	3,503,557	44,380,132	42,482,314	1,897,818
West South Central...	173,449,127	168,571,234	4,877,893	64,189,606	62,367,991	1,821,615
Mountain.............	117,337,226	114,685,201	2,652,025	30,105,868	29,415,674	690,194
Pacific..............	56,152,705	54,783,128	1,369,577	23,921,533	23,341,033	580,500
NEW ENGLAND:						
Maine...............	5,425,968	5,202,699	223,269	1,977,329	1,897,519	79,810
New Hampshire......	2,603,806	2,463,555	140,251	702,902	656,499	46,403
Vermont.............	4,235,811	4,116,589	119,222	1,691,595	1,643,165	48,430
Massachusetts........	2,494,477	2,376,233	118,244	908,834	864,452	44,382
Rhode Island.........	331,600	308,368	23,232	132,855	124,262	8,593
Connecticut..........	1,898,980	1,791,965	107,015	701,086	663,774	37,312
MIDDLE ATLANTIC:						
New York............	20,632,803	20,014,764	618,039	13,158,781	12,784,721	374,060
New Jersey..........	2,282,585	2,214,877	67,708	1,555,607	1,509,687	45,920
Pennsylvania........	17,657,513	17,071,670	585,843	11,847,719	11,475,171	372,548
EAST NORTH CENTRAL:						
Ohio................	23,515,888	22,907,463	608,425	18,542,353	18,085,151	457,202
Indiana.............	21,063,332	20,616,279	447,053	16,680,212	16,355,570	324,642
Illinois............	31,974,775	31,352,694	622,081	27,294,533	26,783,224	511,309
Michigan............	19,032,961	18,592,535	440,426	12,925,521	12,639,675	285,846
Wisconsin...........	22,148,223	21,575,043	573,180	12,452,216	12,143,594	308,622
WEST NORTH CENTRAL:						
Minnesota...........	30,221,758	29,374,213	847,545	21,481,710	20,897,095	584,615
Iowa................	33,474,896	32,973,103	501,793	28,606,951	28,192,563	414,388
Missouri............	34,774,679	33,894,069	880,610	24,832,966	24,246,000	586,966
North Dakota........	36,214,751	35,497,465	717,286	24,563,178	24,130,154	433,024
South Dakota........	34,636,491	33,996,948	639,543	18,199,250	17,870,739	328,511
Nebraska............	42,225,475	41,551,704	673,771	23,109,624	22,748,728	360,896
Kansas..............	45,425,179	44,630,051	795,128	30,600,760	30,063,807	536,953
SOUTH ATLANTIC:						
Delaware............	944,511	929,032	15,479	653,052	641,987	11,065
Maryland............	4,757,999	4,613,728	144,271	3,136,728	3,047,098	89,630
District of Columbia..	5,668	5,313	355	4,258	4,054	204
Virginia............	18,561,112	17,729,231	831,881	9,460,492	9,044,040	416,452
West Virginia.......	9,569,790	9,166,727	403,063	5,520,308	5,287,265	233,043
North Carolina......	20,021,736	19,204,073	817,663	8,195,409	7,886,848	311,561
South Carolina......	12,426,675	11,890,205	536,470	6,184,159	5,906,465	277,694
Georgia.............	25,441,061	24,492,996	948,065	13,055,209	12,572,987	482,222
Florida.............	6,046,691	5,791,968	254,723	2,297,271	2,193,216	104,055
EAST SOUTH CENTRAL:						
Kentucky............	21,612,772	20,741,365	871,407	13,975,746	13,450,433	525,313
Tennessee...........	19,510,856	18,729,118	781,738	11,185,302	10,756,933	428,369
Alabama.............	19,576,856	18,657,474	919,382	9,893,407	9,433,670	459,737
Mississippi.........	18,196,979	17,265,949	931,030	9,325,677	8,841,278	484,399
WEST SOUTH CENTRAL:						
Arkansas............	17,456,750	16,804,965	651,785	9,210,556	8,878,193	332,363
Louisiana...........	10,019,822	9,603,417	416,405	5,626,226	5,403,745	222,481
Oklahoma............	31,951,934	31,256,894	695,040	18,125,321	17,732,653	392,668
Texas..............	114,020,621	110,905,958	3,114,663	31,227,503	30,353,400	874,103
MOUNTAIN:						
Montana.............	35,070,656	34,161,895	908,761	11,007,278	10,762,873	244,405
Idaho...............	8,375,873	8,156,306	219,567	4,511,680	4,404,653	107,027
Wyoming.............	11,809,351	11,389,053	420,298	2,102,005	2,039,332	62,673
Colorado............	24,462,014	23,927,744	534,270	7,744,757	7,579,118	165,639
New Mexico..........	24,100,633	24,019,994	660,000	1,717,224	1,664,253	52,971
Arizona.............	5,802,126	5,727,306	74,820	712,803	697,010	15,793
Utah................	5,050,410	4,991,528	58,882	1,715,380	1,689,554	25,826
Nevada.............	2,357,163	2,311,375	45,788	594,741	578,881	15,860
PACIFIC:						
Washington..........	13,244,720	12,982,616	262,104	7,129,343	7,005,131	124,212
Oregon.............	13,542,318	13,269,636	272,682	4,913,851	4,819,576	94,275
California..........	29,365,667	28,530,876	834,791	11,878,339	11,516,326	362,013

TABLE 59.—VALUE AND PER CENT DISTRIBUTION OF FARMS, AND AVERAGE ACRE AGE PER FARM, BY SEX OF FARMER, BY DIVISIONS AND STATES: 1920.

DIVISION AND STATE.	VALUE OF FARMS (LAND AND BUILDINGS) OPERATED BY—		PER CENT OF ALL FARMS OPERATED BY—		AVERAGE ACREAGE OF ALL LAND PER FARM OPERATED BY—		AVERAGE ACREAGE OF IMPROVED LAND PER FARM OPERATED BY—	
	Males.	Females.	Males.	Females.	Males.	Females.	Males.	Females.
United States	$64,636,346,544	$1,679,656,058	95.9	4.1	150.3	99.7	79.2	50.1
GEOGRAPHIC DIVISIONS:								
New England	875,593,287	41,875,297	94.3	5.7	110.2	81.4	39.6	29.5
Middle Atlantic	2,900,080,835	102,056,919	96.0	4.0	96.3	75.5	63.1	47.1
East North Central	14,624,133,431	313,508,240	96.9	3.1	109.4	80.2	81.8	56.3
West North Central	24,004,579,920	464,915,249	97.4	2.6	235.7	178.7	157.3	114.7
South Atlantic	4,992,527,200	209,246,272	95.0	5.0	85.2	68.6	42.3	33.4
East South Central	3,511,983,369	151,709,994	94.5	5.5	75.9	60.4	42.8	32.7
West South Central	6,113,934,821	177,253,251	95.9	4.1	176.4	120.6	65.3	45.0
Mountain	3,092,798,907	70,388,876	96.6	3.4	486.2	323.1	124.7	84.1
Pacific	4,520,714,774	148,701,960	95.8	4.2	244.2	139.0	104.1	58.9
NEW ENGLAND:								
Maine	196,065,751	8,043,220	94.8	5.2	113.8	88.4	41.5	31.6
New Hampshire	84,811,888	5,183,982	93.0	7.0	129.0	97.9	34.4	32.4
Vermont	154,268,890	4,848,269	95.9	4.1	147.6	100.1	58.9	40.7
Massachusetts	235,500,822	12,087,009	93.8	6.2	79.1	59.9	28.8	22.5
Rhode Island	24,990,858	1,397,068	92.8	7.2	81.4	78.8	32.8	29.1
Connecticut	179,955,078	10,315,749	93.1	6.9	85.0	68.6	31.5	23.9
MIDDLE ATLANTIC:								
New York	1,378,170,515	46,891,225	96.1	3.9	107.8	82.7	68.8	50.0
New Jersey	241,962,168	8,361,818	96.3	3.7	77.4	61.4	52.8	41.6
Pennsylvania	1,279,948,152	46,803,876	95.9	4.1	88.0	71.0	59.2	45.1
EAST NORTH CENTRAL:								
Ohio	2,599,841,126	61,594,823	96.5	3.5	92.5	67.5	73.0	50.7
Indiana	2,593,789,695	59,854,278	96.9	3.1	103.7	71.4	82.2	51.9
Illinois	5,894,957,688	103,035,878	97.2	2.8	136.0	93.0	116.2	76.5
Michigan	1,404,325,237	32,360,973	97.1	2.9	97.5	76.3	66.3	49.5
Wisconsin	2,131,219,685	56,662,288	96.9	3.1	117.6	98.7	66.2	53.2
WEST NORTH CENTRAL:								
Minnesota	3,211,148,661	90,019,664	96.9	3.1	169.9	151.9	120.9	104.8
Iowa	7,488,320,850	113,451,440	98.0	2.0	157.6	119.3	134.7	98.5
Missouri	2,987,341,373	75,626,327	96.7	3.3	133.3	100.1	95.4	66.7
North Dakota	1,460,629,954	27,891,541	97.8	2.2	467.0	428.5	317.4	258.7
South Dakota	2,429,093,600	43,800,081	97.9	2.1	465.3	405.3	244.6	208.2
Nebraska	3,652,334,918	59,772,842	98.1	1.9	340.3	291.2	186.3	156.0
Kansas	2,775,710,564	54,353,354	97.5	2.5	277.0	191.8	186.6	129.5
SOUTH ATLANTIC:								
Delaware	63,446,776	1,308,855	98.0	2.0	93.5	74.8	64.6	53.5
Maryland	373,951,719	12,645,131	96.2	3.8	100.1	78.9	66.1	49.0
District of Columbia	5,015,369	562,000	94.6	5.4	27.5	32.3	21.0	18.5
Virginia	979,071,830	45,363,195	94.6	5.4	100.6	83.0	51.3	41.5
West Virginia	388,077,353	22,706,053	94.8	5.2	110.7	89.3	63.9	51.6
North Carolina	1,037,185,550	39,207,410	95.5	4.5	74.5	67.3	30.6	25.6
South Carolina	778,542,864	34,941,336	94.0	6.0	65.7	46.3	32.6	24.0
Georgia	1,099,285,515	39,013,112	95.5	4.5	82.6	67.5	42.4	34.3
Florida	267,950,224	13,499,180	94.1	5.9	114.0	79.4	43.2	32.4
EAST SOUTH CENTRAL:								
Kentucky	1,258,250,063	46,908,873	95.8	4.2	80.0	76.4	51.9	46.1
Tennessee	985,566,732	39,413,162	95.5	4.5	77.6	68.7	44.6	37.7
Alabama	518,875,552	24,782,203	93.6	6.4	77.8	56.5	39.3	28.3
Mississippi	749,291,022	40,605,756	93.0	7.0	68.2	49.2	34.9	25.6
WEST SOUTH CENTRAL:								
Arkansas	726,557,531	26,553,135	95.3	4.7	75.8	59.1	40.1	30.1
Louisiana	455,641,788	18,397,005	94.3	5.7	75.2	54.2	42.3	28.9
Oklahoma	1,333,040,048	30,825,246	97.1	2.9	167.6	126.1	95.1	71.2
Texas	3,598,695,454	101,477,865	96.3	3.7	264.2	192.0	72.3	53.9
MOUNTAIN:								
Montana	757,476,975	19,290,554	96.4	3.6	614.1	442.9	193.5	119.1
Idaho	569,058,947	12,453,017	97.2	2.8	199.2	188.3	107.6	91.8
Wyoming	227,554,676	7,193,449	95.8	4.2	755.1	631.1	135.2	94.1
Colorado	848,728,013	17,285,647	97.0	3.0	411.6	297.5	130.4	92.2
New Mexico	217,083,309	4,730,903	95.3	4.7	844.4	278.9	58.5	37.9
Arizona	169,468,458	2,856,863	96.3	3.7	596.1	203.9	72.5	43.0
Utah	239,287,190	4,464,568	97.6	2.4	199.4	93.9	67.5	41.2
Nevada	64,141,339	2,113,875	95.7	4.3	763.8	334.2	191.3	115.8
PACIFIC:								
Washington	898,424,475	21,967,866	96.3	3.7	203.3	107.7	109.7	51.1
Oregon	659,338,518	15,874,766	96.7	3.3	273.3	165.4	99.3	57.2
California	2,962,951,781	110,859,328	95.1	4.9	255.0	144.6	102.9	62.7

TABLE 60.—FARM OPERATORS IN THE UNITED STATES, WITH PER CENT DISTRIBUTION, BY AGE AND TENURE: 1920 AND 1910.

AGE AND CENSUS YEAR.	Total.	OWNERS.				Managers.	TENANTS		
		All owners.	Full owners, free.[1]	Full owners, mortgaged.	Part owners.		All tenants.	Share and share-cash.	Cash and unspecified.
NUMBER.									
All farmers:									
1920	6,448,343	3,925,090	2,149,276	1,217,234	558,580	68,449	2,454,804	1,806,634	648,170
1910	6,361,502	3,948,722	2,295,277	1,059,620	593,825	58,104	2,354,676	1,528,389	826,287
Reporting age:									
1920	6,364,163	3,873,034	2,117,459	1,203,190	552,385	66,636	2,424,493	1,785,352	639,141
1910	6,339,476	3,934,968	2,284,343	1,058,018	592,607	56,846	2,347,662	1,524,494	823,168
Under 25 years—									
1920	383,680	87,400	39,111	28,970	19,319	5,484	290,796	243,316	47,480
1910	419,330	97,690	54,415	23,715	19,560	4,820	316,820	236,374	80,446
25 to 34 years—									
1920	1,333,020	561,442	215,759	227,513	118,170	17,983	753,595	569,834	183,761
1910	1,413,876	620,961	297,261	192,747	130,953	15,700	777,215	524,916	252,299
35 to 44 years—									
1920	1,587,519	938,174	422,864	348,618	166,692	18,757	630,588	455,064	175,524
1910	1,571,469	969,859	487,141	301,674	181,044	16,212	585,398	368,960	216,438
45 to 54 years—									
1920	1,482,494	1,021,445	556,833	319,980	144,632	14,063	446,986	313,198	133,788
1910	1,432,707	1,036,493	592,148	287,992	156,353	11,724	384,490	231,721	152,769
55 to 64 years—									
1920	993,771	780,579	508,786	195,740	76,053	7,226	205,966	140,913	65,053
1910	947,524	741,614	490,910	172,197	78,507	5,840	200,070	117,709	82,361
65 years and over—									
1920	583,679	483,994	374,106	82,369	27,519	3,123	96,562	63,027	33,535
1910	554,570	468,351	362,468	79,693	26,190	2,550	83,669	44,814	38,855
Not reporting age:									
1920	84,180	52,056	31,817	14,044	6,195	1,813	30,311	21,282	9,029
1910	22,026	13,754	10,934	1,602	1,218	1,258	7,014	3,895	3,119
PER CENT DISTRIBUTION OF TENURE CLASSES BY AGE.[2]									
All farmers:									
1920	100.0	100.0	100.0	100.0	100.0	100.0	100.0	100.0	100.0
1910	100.0	100.0	100.0	100.0	100.0	100.0	100.0	100.0	100.0
Under 25 years:									
1920	6.0	2.3	1.8	2.4	3.5	8.2	12.0	13.6	7.4
1910	6.6	2.5	2.4	2.2	3.3	8.5	13.5	15.5	9.8
25 to 34 years:									
1920	20.9	14.5	10.2	18.9	21.4	27.0	31.1	31.9	28.8
1910	22.3	15.8	13.0	18.2	22.1	27.6	33.1	34.4	30.6
35 to 44 years:									
1920	24.9	24.2	20.0	29.0	30.2	28.1	26.0	25.5	27.5
1910	24.8	24.6	21.3	28.5	30.6	28.5	24.9	24.2	26.3
45 to 54 years:									
1920	23.3	26.4	26.3	26.6	26.2	21.1	18.4	17.5	20.9
1910	22.6	26.3	25.9	27.2	26.4	20.6	16.4	15.2	18.6
55 to 64 years:									
1920	15.6	20.2	24.0	16.3	13.8	10.8	8.5	7.9	10.2
1910	14.9	18.8	21.5	16.3	13.2	10.3	8.5	7.7	10.0
65 years and over:									
1920	9.2	12.5	17.7	6.8	5.0	4.7	4.0	3.5	5.2
1910	0.7	11.9	15.9	7.5	4.4	4.5	3.6	2.9	4.7

[1] Includes full owners whose mortgage status was not reported.
[2] Percentages based on number of farm operators reporting age.

TABLE 60.—FARM OPERATORS IN THE UNITED STATES, WITH PER CENT DISTRIBUTION, BY AGE AND TENURE; 1920 AND 1910—Continued.

AGE AND CENSUS YEAR.	Total.	OWNERS.				Managers.	TENANTS.		
		All owners.	Full owners, free.[1]	Full owners, mortgaged.	Part owners.		All tenants.	Share and share-cash.	Cash and unspecified.
		PER CENT DISTRIBUTION OF AGE GROUPS BY TENURE.[2]							
All farmers:									
1920	100.0	60.9	33.3	18.9	8.7	1.0	38.1	28.1	10.0
1910	100.0	62.1	36.0	16.7	9.3	0.9	37.0	24.0	13.0
Under 25 years:									
1920	100.0	22.8	10.2	7.6	5.0	1.4	75.8	63.4	12.4
1910	100.0	23.3	13.0	5.7	4.7	1.1	75.6	56.4	19.2
25 to 34 years:									
1920	100.0	42.1	16.2	17.1	8.9	1.3	56.5	42.7	13.8
1910	100.0	43.9	21.0	13.6	9.3	1.1	55.0	37.1	17.8
35 to 44 years:									
1920	100.0	59.1	26.6	22.0	10.5	1.2	39.7	28.7	11.1
1910	100.0	61.7	31.0	19.2	11.5	1.0	37.3	23.5	13.8
45 to 54 years:									
1920	100.0	68.9	37.6	21.6	9.8	0.9	30.2	21.1	9.0
1910	100.0	72.3	41.3	20.1	10.9	0.8	26.8	16.2	10.7
55 to 64 years:									
1920	100.0	78.5	51.2	19.7	7.7	0.7	20.7	14.2	6.5
1910	100.0	78.3	51.8	18.2	8.3	0.6	21.1	12.4	8.7
65 years and over:									
1920	100.0	82.9	64.1	14.1	4.7	0.5	16.5	10.8	5.7
1910	100.0	84.5	65.4	14.4	4.7	0.5	15.1	8.1	7.0

[1] Includes full owners whose mortgage status was not reported.
[2] Percentages based on number of farm operators reporting age.

TABLE 61.—WHITE AND COLORED FARM OPERATORS IN THE SOUTH, WITH PER CENT DISTRIBUTION, BY AGE AND TENURE: 1920 AND 1910.

COLOR, TENURE, AND CENSUS YEAR.	All farm operators.	FARM OPERATORS REPORTING AGE.							Not reporting age.
		Total.	Under 25 years.	25 to 34 years.	35 to 44 years.	45 to 54 years.	55 to 64 years.	65 years and over.	
THE SOUTH.				NUMBER.					
White farmers, total:									
1920	2,283,750	2,258,017	175,320	496,689	567,049	489,947	325,140	203,872	25,733
1910	2,207,406	2,202,933	190,505	541,198	536,366	459,655	312,423	162,786	4,473
Owners:									
1920	1,379,636	1,364,199	42,543	217,055	339,871	340,895	253,362	170,473	15,437
1910	1,326,044	1,323,794	43,418	243,931	332,768	326,569	240,388	136,720	2,250
Full owners, free [1]—									
1920	916,204	905,404	22,940	115,999	203,883	226,809	191,382	144,391	10,805
1910	908,211	906,514	26,511	144,086	209,315	225,454	184,080	117,068	1,697
Full owners, mortgaged—									
1920	310,995	307,943	11,083	66,105	91,150	77,367	43,661	18,577	3,052
1910	245,889	245,607	8,515	56,668	71,219	60,432	35,426	13,347	282
Part owners—									
1920	152,432	150,852	8,520	34,951	44,838	36,719	18,319	7,505	1,580
1910	171,944	171,673	8,392	43,177	52,234	40,683	20,882	6,305	271
Managers:									
1920	16,548	16,092	1,266	4,177	4,484	3,556	1,726	883	456
1910	15,084	14,736	1,274	4,203	4,091	2,941	1,535	692	348
Tenants:									
1920	887,566	877,726	131,511	275,457	222,694	145,496	70,052	32,516	9,840
1910	866,278	864,403	145,813	293,064	199,507	130,145	70,500	25,374	1,875
Share and share-cash—									
1920	716,356	708,729	113,875	226,174	176,944	114,305	53,757	23,674	7,627
1910	636,817	635,651	115,386	219,548	144,336	91,531	48,289	16,561	1,166
Cash and unspecified—									
1920	171,210	168,997	17,636	49,283	45,750	31,191	16,295	8,842	2,213
1910	229,461	228,752	30,427	73,516	55,171	38,614	22,211	8,813	709

[1] Includes full owners whose mortgage status was not reported.

TABLE 61.—WHITE AND COLORED FARM OPERATORS IN THE SOUTH, WITH PER CENT DISTRIBUTION, BY AGE AND TENURE: 1920 AND 1910—Continued.

COLOR, TENURE, AND CENSUS YEAR.	All farm operators.	FARM OPERATORS REPORTING AGE.							Not reporting age.
		Total.	Under 25 years.	25 to 34 years.	35 to 44 years.	45 to 54 years.	55 to 64 years.	65 years and over.	
				NUMBER—continued.					
THE SOUTH—Continued.									
Colored farmers, total:									
1920	922,914	912,122	89,112	186,489	216,383	229,460	116,963	73,715	10,792
1910	890,141	886,976	87,728	220,911	220,133	182,307	110,460	65,437	3,165
Owners:									
1920	217,589	215,202	6,011	24,524	46,102	63,774	42,788	32,003	2,387
1910	218,467	217,908	6,100	32,174	50,051	58,453	41,944	29,186	559
Full owners, free [1]—									
1920	135,944	134,441	3,447	13,440	26,529	38,106	28,693	24,226	1,503
1910	128,557	128,221	3,701	17,942	27,265	32,810	25,685	20,818	336
Full owners, mortgaged—									
1920	42,614	42,159	928	5,166	9,757	13,786	7,992	4,530	455
1910	46,733	46,632	1,155	7,203	11,225	13,250	8,781	5,018	101
Part owners—									
1920	39,031	38,602	1,636	5,918	9,816	11,882	6,103	3,247	429
1910	43,177	43,055	1,244	7,029	11,561	12,393	7,478	3,350	122
Managers:									
1920	1,770	1,728	159	372	443	444	212	98	42
1910	1,200	1,185	94	294	327	263	141	66	15
Tenants:									
1920	703,555	695,192	82,942	161,593	169,838	165,242	73,963	41,614	8,363
1910	870,474	667,883	81,534	188,443	169,755	123,591	68,375	36,185	2,591
Share and share-cash—									
1920	518,631	512,170	71,460	126,791	125,412	112,635	48,888	26,984	6,461
1910	384,524	382,900	56,781	116,047	94,781	63,344	34,423	17,524	1,624
Cash and unspecified—									
1920	184,924	183,022	11,482	34,802	44,426	52,607	25,075	14,630	1,902
1910	285,950	284,983	24,753	72,396	74,974	60,247	33,952	18,661	967
		PER CENT DISTRIBUTION BY AGE: 1920.							
White farmers, total		100.0	7.8	22.0	25.1	21.7	14.4	9.0	
Owners		100.0	3.1	15.9	24.9	25.0	18.6	12.5	
Full owners, free [1]		100.0	2.5	12.8	22.5	25.1	21.1	15.9	
Full owners, mortgaged		100.0	3.6	21.5	29.6	25.1	14.2	6.0	
Part owners		100.0	5.6	23.2	29.7	24.3	12.1	5.0	
Managers		100.0	7.9	26.0	27.9	22.1	10.7	5.5	
Tenants		100.0	15.0	31.4	25.4	16.6	8.0	3.7	
Share and share-cash		100.0	16.1	31.9	25.0	16.1	7.6	3.3	
Cash and unspecified		100.0	10.4	29.2	27.1	18.5	9.6	5.2	
Colored farmers, total		100.0	9.8	20.4	23.7	25.2	12.8	8.1	
Owners		100.0	2.8	11.4	21.4	29.6	19.9	14.9	
Full owners, free [1]		100.0	2.6	10.0	19.7	28.3	21.3	18.0	
Full owners, mortgaged		100.0	2.2	12.3	23.1	32.7	19.0	10.7	
Part owners		100.0	4.2	15.3	25.4	30.8	15.8	8.4	
Managers		100.0	9.2	21.5	25.6	25.7	12.3	5.7	
Tenants		100.0	11.9	23.8	24.1	23.8	10.6	6.0	
Share and share-cash		100.0	14.0	24.8	24.5	22.0	9.5	5.3	
Cash and unspecified		100.0	6.3	19.0	24.3	28.7	13.7	8.0	

[1] Includes full owners whose mortgage status was not reported.

TABLE 62.—FARM OPERATORS CLASSIFIED ACCORDING TO AGE AND TENURE, BY DIVISIONS AND STATES: 1920.

DIVISION OR STATE AND TENURE.	All farm operators.	FARM OPERATORS REPORTING AGE.							Not reporting age.
		Total.	Under 25 years.	25 to 34 years.	35 to 44 years.	45 to 54 years.	55 to 64 years.	65 years and over.	
UNITED STATES.									
Total	6,448,343	6,364,163	383,680	1,333,020	1,587,519	1,482,494	993,771	583,679	84,180
Owners	3,925,090	3,873,034	87,400	561,442	938,174	1,021,445	780,579	483,994	52,056
Managers	68,449	66,636	5,484	17,983	18,757	14,063	7,226	3,123	1,813
Tenants	2,454,804	2,424,493	290,796	753,595	630,588	446,986	205,966	96,562	30,311
GEOGRAPHIC DIVISIONS.									
NEW ENGLAND.									
Total	156,564	153,455	2,593	17,437	31,801	39,603	34,057	27,964	3,109
Owners	140,160	137,409	1,783	13,554	27,270	35,935	32,055	26,812	2,751
Managers	4,802	4,669	232	923	1,264	1,170	725	355	133
Tenants	11,602	11,377	578	2,960	3,267	2,498	1,277	797	225
MIDDLE ATLANTIC.									
Total	425,147	417,237	10,509	62,145	96,169	106,848	85,206	56,360	7,910
Owners	327,104	321,102	4,166	33,731	68,401	87,411	75,224	52,169	6,002
Managers	9,853	9,567	530	2,324	2,712	2,223	1,283	495	286
Tenants	88,190	86,568	5,813	26,090	25,056	17,214	8,699	3,696	1,622
EAST NORTH CENTRAL.									
Total	1,084,744	1,069,490	37,753	209,815	264,839	258,619	191,537	106,927	15,254
Owners	766,786	756,098	11,344	96,244	175,264	206,616	168,037	98,593	10,688
Managers	13,551	13,207	1,198	3,846	3,775	2,561	1,328	499	344
Tenants	304,407	300,185	25,211	109,725	85,800	49,442	22,172	7,835	4,222
WEST NORTH CENTRAL.									
Total	1,096,951	1,083,672	52,794	263,565	284,126	244,728	161,085	77,374	13,279
Owners	711,156	702,546	12,898	108,777	182,862	190,966	137,539	69,504	8,610
Managers	10,776	10,570	1,340	3,430	2,802	1,889	802	307	206
Tenants	375,019	370,556	38,556	151,358	98,462	51,873	22,744	7,563	4,463
SOUTH ATLANTIC.									
Total	1,158,976	1,143,758	82,996	227,643	282,403	266,073	172,574	112,069	15,218
Owners	607,089	599,815	15,559	83,848	144,775	154,579	118,052	83,002	7,274
Managers	9,799	9,523	629	2,214	2,703	2,289	1,112	576	276
Tenants	542,088	534,420	66,808	141,581	134,925	109,205	53,410	28,491	7,668
EAST SOUTH CENTRAL.									
Total	1,051,600	1,040,712	92,899	224,193	250,689	234,293	143,308	95,330	10,888
Owners	525,808	520,373	17,386	82,247	125,058	131,068	95,633	68,981	5,435
Managers	3,506	3,419	333	883	911	755	349	188	87
Tenants	522,286	516,920	75,180	141,063	124,720	102,470	47,326	26,161	5,366
WEST SOUTH CENTRAL.									
Total	996,088	985,669	88,537	231,342	250,340	219,041	126,221	70,188	10,419
Owners	464,328	459,213	15,609	75,484	116,140	119,022	82,465	50,493	5,115
Managers	5,013	4,878	463	1,452	1,313	956	477	217	135
Tenants	526,747	521,578	72,465	154,406	132,887	99,063	43,279	19,478	5,169
MOUNTAIN.									
Total	244,109	240,015	9,446	57,741	66,936	54,556	35,930	15,406	4,094
Owners	202,515	199,188	5,775	44,310	55,223	47,222	32,455	14,203	3,327
Managers	4,116	3,968	381	1,268	1,115	707	359	138	148
Tenants	37,478	36,859	3,290	12,163	10,598	6,627	3,116	1,065	619
PACIFIC.									
Total	234,164	230,155	6,153	39,139	60,216	58,733	43,853	22,061	4,009
Owners	180,144	177,290	2,880	23,247	43,181	48,626	39,119	20,237	2,854
Managers	7,033	6,835	378	1,643	2,162	1,513	791	348	198
Tenants	46,987	46,030	2,895	14,249	14,873	8,594	3,943	1,476	957

TABLE 62.—FARM OPERATORS CLASSIFIED ACCORDING TO AGE AND TENURE, BY DIVISIONS AND STATES: 1920—Continued.

DIVISION OR STATE AND TENURE.	All farm operators.	FARM OPERATORS REPORTING AGE.							Not reporting age.
		Total.	Under 25 years.	25 to 34 years.	35 to 44 years.	45 to 54 years.	55 to 64 years.	65 years and over.	
NEW ENGLAND.									
Maine, total	48,227	47,484	867	5,529	9,617	11,858	10,706	8,907	743
Owners	45,437	44,739	699	4,829	8,915	11,277	10,353	8,666	698
Managers	786	769	47	128	187	193	143	71	17
Tenants	2,004	1,976	121	572	515	388	210	170	28
New Hampshire, total	20,523	20,006	291	1,954	3,811	4,961	4,733	4,256	517
Owners	18,604	18,147	191	1,526	3,311	4,510	4,498	4,111	457
Managers	546	528	36	110	127	132	79	44	18
Tenants	1,373	1,331	64	318	373	319	156	101	42
Vermont, total	29,075	28,561	696	3,986	6,375	7,299	5,707	4,498	514
Owners	25,121	24,674	427	2,880	5,229	6,503	5,321	4,314	447
Managers	568	556	44	142	150	118	70	32	12
Tenants	3,386	3,331	225	964	996	678	316	152	55
Massachusetts, total	32,001	31,192	393	3,072	6,388	8,580	7,146	5,613	809
Owners	28,087	27,393	250	2,315	5,312	7,594	6,606	5,316	694
Managers	1,627	1,569	56	289	440	419	250	115	58
Tenants	2,287	2,230	87	468	636	567	290	182	57
Rhode Island, total	4,083	3,991	49	363	774	1,064	916	825	92
Owners	3,245	3,166	21	198	542	848	802	755	79
Managers	205	201	12	32	53	47	32	25	4
Tenants	633	624	16	133	179	169	82	45	9
Connecticut, total	22,655	22,221	297	2,533	4,836	5,841	4,849	3,865	434
Owners	19,666	19,290	195	1,806	3,961	5,203	4,475	3,650	376
Managers	1,070	1,046	37	222	307	261	151	68	24
Tenants	1,919	1,885	65	505	568	377	223	147	34
MIDDLE ATLANTIC.									
New York, total	193,195	189,765	4,733	28,144	43,170	48,220	39,248	26,250	3,430
Owners	151,717	149,074	2,057	16,185	31,466	40,155	34,788	24,423	2,643
Managers	4,376	4,240	197	996	1,189	1,002	622	234	136
Tenants	37,102	36,451	2,479	10,963	10,515	7,063	3,838	1,593	651
New Jersey, total	29,702	29,071	645	4,186	6,833	7,845	5,987	3,575	631
Owners	21,889	21,432	270	2,118	4,655	6,092	5,108	3,189	457
Managers	987	961	54	217	241	266	134	49	26
Tenants	6,826	6,678	321	1,851	1,937	1,487	745	337	148
Pennsylvania, total	202,250	198,401	5,131	29,815	46,166	50,783	39,971	26,535	3,849
Owners	153,498	150,596	1,839	15,428	32,280	41,164	35,328	24,557	2,902
Managers	4,490	4,366	279	1,111	1,282	955	527	212	124
Tenants	44,262	43,439	3,013	13,276	12,604	8,664	4,116	1,766	823
EAST NORTH CENTRAL.									
Ohio, total	256,695	252,860	8,112	43,721	60,308	62,186	48,175	30,358	3,835
Owners	177,986	175,352	1,856	17,080	37,937	48,506	41,915	28,058	2,634
Managers	3,065	2,972	240	744	855	643	372	118	93
Tenants	75,644	74,536	6,016	25,897	21,516	13,037	5,888	2,182	1,108
Indiana, total	205,126	202,139	8,335	39,052	47,704	47,925	36,926	22,167	2,987
Owners	137,210	135,137	1,942	15,081	29,196	36,867	31,769	20,282	2,073
Managers	2,329	2,271	187	604	644	489	257	90	58
Tenants	65,587	64,701	6,206	23,397	17,864	10,569	4,900	1,795	856
Illinois, total	237,181	233,755	9,202	51,300	60,178	59,177	37,920	18,928	3,426
Owners	132,574	130,629	1,959	14,284	29,399	38,355	30,162	16,170	1,940
Managers	3,411	3,324	274	1,084	1,022	598	255	91	87
Tenants	101,196	99,802	6,969	35,988	29,755	17,220	7,503	2,367	1,394
Michigan, total	196,447	194,077	5,775	34,327	47,591	47,260	37,474	21,650	2,370
Owners	159,406	157,539	2,307	21,193	37,388	41,498	34,674	20,479	1,867
Managers	2,319	2,268	204	629	629	442	252	117	51
Tenants	34,722	34,270	3,264	12,510	9,574	5,320	2,548	1,054	452
Wisconsin, total	189,295	186,659	6,329	41,329	49,060	45,075	31,042	13,824	2,636
Owners	159,610	157,441	3,280	28,606	41,344	41,390	29,517	13,304	2,169
Managers	2,427	2,372	293	790	625	389	192	83	55
Tenants	27,258	26,846	2,756	11,933	7,091	3,296	1,333	437	412

TABLE 62.—FARM OPERATORS CLASSIFIED ACCORDING TO AGE AND TENURE, BY DIVISIONS AND STATES: 1920—Continued.

DIVISION OR STATE AND TENURE.	All farm operators.	FARM OPERATORS REPORTING AGE.							Not reporting age.
		Total.	Under 25 years.	25 to 34 years.	35 to 44 years.	45 to 54 years.	55 to 64 years.	65 years and over.	
WEST NORTH CENTRAL.									
Minnesota, total	178,478	176,139	6,645	40,281	45,349	42,790	29,376	11,698	2,339
Owners	132,744	131,091	2,154	20,828	33,496	36,787	26,842	10,984	1,653
Managers	1,596	1,563	188	562	411	256	107	39	33
Tenants	44,138	43,485	4,303	18,891	11,442	5,747	2,427	675	653
Iowa, total	213,439	210,705	9,865	55,121	56,282	48,592	28,609	12,236	2,734
Owners	121,888	120,322	1,505	16,216	31,824	36,135	23,798	10,844	1,566
Managers	2,487	2,429	348	842	620	423	154	42	58
Tenants	89,064	87,954	8,012	38,063	23,838	12,034	4,657	1,350	1,110
Missouri, total	263,004	259,991	12,934	52,622	62,399	59,523	44,405	28,108	3,013
Owners	185,030	182,856	4,355	26,412	42,113	46,793	37,874	25,309	2,174
Managers	2,247	2,204	195	589	602	475	226	117	43
Tenants	75,727	74,931	8,384	25,621	19,684	12,255	6,305	2,682	796
North Dakota, total	77,690	76,923	3,668	20,176	23,122	17,291	9,468	3,198	767
Owners	56,917	56,354	1,244	11,166	17,941	14,639	8,429	2,935	563
Managers	855	845	130	323	197	138	47	10	10
Tenants	19,918	19,724	2,294	8,687	4,984	2,514	992	253	194
South Dakota, total	74,637	73,703	3,946	21,374	21,177	15,106	8,791	3,309	934
Owners	47,815	47,226	1,091	9,671	14,111	11,833	7,556	2,964	589
Managers	781	772	116	280	197	124	41	14	9
Tenants	26,041	25,705	2,739	11,423	6,869	3,149	1,194	331	336
Nebraska, total	124,417	122,902	7,218	34,956	33,503	25,439	15,786	6,000	1,515
Owners	69,672	68,816	1,158	11,730	19,250	18,555	12,905	5,218	856
Managers	1,315	1,286	198	403	344	218	90	33	29
Tenants	53,430	52,800	5,862	22,823	13,909	6,666	2,791	749	630
Kansas, total	165,286	163,309	8,518	39,035	42,294	35,987	24,650	12,825	1,977
Owners	97,090	95,881	1,391	12,754	24,127	26,224	20,135	11,250	1,209
Managers	1,495	1,471	165	431	431	255	137	52	24
Tenants	66,701	65,957	6,962	25,850	17,736	9,508	4,378	1,523	744
SOUTH ATLANTIC.									
Delaware, total	10,140	9,973	444	1,914	2,365	2,397	1,825	1,028	167
Owners	6,010	5,899	117	775	1,298	1,572	1,321	816	111
Managers	144	140	8	24	37	42	23	6	4
Tenants	3,986	3,934	319	1,115	1,030	783	481	206	52
Maryland, total	47,908	47,328	1,502	7,841	11,171	12,476	8,958	5,380	580
Owners	32,805	32,430	487	3,594	7,126	9,239	7,301	4,683	375
Managers	1,262	1,231	73	318	356	293	140	51	31
Tenants	13,841	13,667	942	3,929	3,689	2,944	1,517	646	174
District of Columbia, total	204	196	4	20	43	56	47	26	8
Owners	100	98	1	7	18	26	24	22	2
Managers	19	14		2	4	4	2	2	5
Tenants	85	84	3	11	21	26	21	2	1
Virginia, total	186,242	184,022	7,771	30,120	45,055	46,183	31,785	23,108	2,220
Owners	136,363	134,870	2,899	16,806	31,752	36,097	27,014	20,302	1,493
Managers	2,134	2,089	162	474	614	492	218	129	45
Tenants	47,745	47,063	4,710	12,840	12,689	9,594	4,553	2,677	682
West Virginia, total	87,289	86,329	2,233	12,457	21,211	22,076	16,212	12,140	960
Owners	72,101	71,335	1,271	8,564	16,868	18,843	14,576	11,213	766
Managers	1,090	1,058	52	250	322	256	119	59	32
Tenants	14,098	13,936	910	3,643	4,021	2,977	1,517	868	162
North Carolina, total	269,763	266,181	17,944	55,729	66,867	58,748	40,147	26,746	3,582
Owners	151,376	149,656	4,198	23,079	36,581	36,358	28,813	20,627	1,720
Managers	928	889	71	246	246	196	89	43	39
Tenants	117,459	115,636	13,675	32,404	30,042	22,194	11,245	6,076	1,823
South Carolina, total	192,693	190,645	18,301	42,529	49,642	42,120	23,394	14,659	2,048
Owners	67,724	67,087	2,189	10,250	17,549	17,025	11,969	8,105	637
Managers	738	723	61	188	220	149	75	30	15
Tenants	124,231	122,835	16,051	32,091	31,873	24,946	11,350	6,524	1,396

Table 62.—FARM OPERATORS CLASSIFIED ACCORDING TO AGE AND TENURE, BY DIVISIONS AND STATES: 1920—Continued.

DIVISION OR STATE AND TENURE.	All farm opera-tors.	FARM OPERATORS REPORTING AGE.							Not re-port-ing age.
		Total.	Under 25 years.	25 to 34 years.	35 to 44 years.	45 to 54 years.	55 to 64 years.	65 years and over.	
SOUTH ATLANTIC—Con.									
Georgia, total	310,732	306,258	32,520	68,734	73,472	68,249	40,598	22,685	4,474
Owners	102,123	100,850	3,414	15,781	24,941	25,470	19,232	12,012	1,273
Managers	1,655	1,618	134	432	464	345	164	79	37
Tenants	206,954	203,790	28,972	52,521	48,067	42,434	21,202	10,594	3,164
Florida, total	54,005	52,826	2,277	8,299	12,577	13,768	9,608	6,297	1,179
Owners	38,487	37,590	983	4,992	8,642	9,949	7,802	5,222	897
Managers	1,829	1,761	68	280	442	512	282	177	68
Tenants	13,689	13,475	1,226	3,027	3,493	3,307	1,524	898	214
EAST SOUTH CENTRAL.									
Kentucky, total	270,626	267,496	21,870	57,098	63,876	58,737	38,934	26,981	3,130
Owners	179,327	177,295	6,170	29,126	42,393	43,992	31,955	23,659	2,032
Managers	969	937	108	266	222	181	91	69	32
Tenants	90,330	89,264	15,592	27,706	21,261	14,564	6,888	3,253	1,066
Tennessee, total	252,774	249,967	19,935	52,231	59,098	56,606	37,209	24,838	2,807
Owners	148,082	146,526	4,187	21,142	34,554	37,894	28,199	20,550	1,556
Managers	807	788	98	185	209	182	76	38	19
Tenants	103,885	102,653	15,650	30,954	24,335	18,530	8,934	4,250	1,232
Alabama, total	256,099	253,671	22,640	54,643	58,481	61,685	34,407	21,815	2,428
Owners	107,089	106,151	3,626	17,228	25,428	27,304	19,432	13,133	938
Managers	741	730	54	181	195	184	72	44	11
Tenants	148,269	146,790	18,960	37,234	32,858	34,197	14,903	8,638	1,479
Mississippi, total	272,101	269,578	28,454	60,171	69,234	57,265	32,758	21,696	2,523
Owners	91,310	90,401	3,403	14,751	22,683	21,878	16,047	11,639	9C?
Managers	989	964	73	251	285	208	110	37	25
Tenants	179,802	178,213	24,978	45,169	46,266	35,179	16,601	10,020	1,589
WEST SOUTH CENTRAL.									
Arkansas, total	232,604	230,426	21,327	53,034	56,638	53,614	28,857	16,956	2,178
Owners	112,647	111,577	4,326	19,774	27,660	28,328	18,904	12,585	1,070
Managers	736	717	55	192	213	149	61	47	19
Tenants	119,221	118,132	16,946	33,068	28,765	25,137	9,892	4,324	1,089
Louisiana, total	135,463	134,036	12,183	23,473	35,442	29,873	16,626	10,439	1,427
Owners	57,254	56,588	2,090	9,845	15,032	14,070	9,304	6,247	666
Managers	828	805	46	200	216	197	108	38	23
Tenants	77,381	76,643	10,047	19,428	20,194	15,606	7,214	4,154	738
Oklahoma, total	191,988	189,577	14,165	44,056	49,333	44,076	26,120	11,827	2,411
Owners	93,217	91,883	3,203	14,530	23,234	25,719	16,909	8,288	1,334
Managers	935	910	91	291	222	170	105	31	25
Tenants	97,836	96,784	10,871	29,235	25,877	18,187	9,106	3,508	1,052
Texas, total	436,033	431,630	40,862	104,779	108,927	91,478	54,618	30,966	4,403
Owners	201,210	199,165	5,990	31,335	50,214	50,905	37,348	23,373	2,045
Managers	2,514	2,446	271	769	662	440	203	101	68
Tenants	232,309	230,019	34,601	72,675	58,051	40,133	17,067	7,492	2,290
MOUNTAIN.									
Montana, total	57,677	56,980	1,654	10,950	17,125	11,701	7,700	3,770	007
Owners	50,271	49,668	1,101	10,119	14,070	10,450	7,130	3,502	602
Managers	899	874	73	284	240	156	93	28	25
Tenants	6,507	6,438	477	2,259	1,915	1,125	504	158	69
Idaho, total	42,106	41,150	1,689	9,599	11,753	9,680	6,075	2,354	956
Owners	34,647	33,830	988	7,010	9,673	8,476	5,510	2,173	817
Managers	758	733	68	248	217	111	58	31	25
Tenants	6,701	6,587	633	2,341	1,863	1,093	507	150	114
Wyoming, total	15,748	15,456	616	4,090	4,557	3,300	2,049	844	292
Owners	13,403	13,163	465	3,375	3,798	2,868	1,876	781	240
Managers	377	367	32	128	115	65	18	9	10
Tenants	1,968	1,926	119	587	644	367	155	54	42

TABLE 62.—FARM OPERATORS CLASSIFIED ACCORDING TO AGE AND TENURE, BY DIVISIONS AND STATES: 1920—Continued.

DIVISION OR STATE AND TENURE.	All farm operators.	FARM OPERATORS REPORTING AGE.							Not reporting age.
		Total.	Under 25 years.	25 to 34 years.	35 to 44 years.	45 to 54 years.	55 to 64 years.	65 years and over.	
MOUNTAIN—Con.									
Colorado, total	59,934	59,000	2,414	13,965	15,885	13,702	9,082	3,952	934
Owners	45,291	44,599	1,175	9,265	11,766	11,048	7,830	3,515	692
Managers	880	855	72	278	216	166	88	35	25
Tenants	13,763	13,546	1,167	4,422	3,903	2,488	1,164	402	217
New Mexico, total	29,844	29,437	1,354	5,965	7,207	7,048	5,098	2,765	407
Owners	25,756	25,419	968	4,886	6,189	6,232	4,596	2,548	337
Managers	433	422	51	128	107	75	44	17	11
Tenants	3,655	3,596	335	951	911	741	458	200	59
Arizona, total	9,975	9,700	373	2,013	2,815	2,359	1,458	682	275
Owners	7,869	7,671	229	1,439	2,181	1,910	1,288	624	198
Managers	305	275	20	82	88	53	23	9	30
Tenants	1,801	1,754	124	492	546	396	147	49	47
Utah, total	25,662	25,219	1,265	5,556	6,667	5,973	3,984	1,774	443
Owners	22,579	22,212	792	4,463	5,862	5,561	3,811	1,723	367
Managers	296	283	58	86	72	45	17	5	13
Tenants	2,787	2,724	415	1,007	733	367	156	46	63
Nevada, total	3,163	3,073	81	597	927	763	448	257	90
Owners	2,699	2,626	54	459	784	677	405	247	73
Managers	168	159	7	34	60	36	18	4	9
Tenants	296	288	20	104	83	50	25	6	8
PACIFIC.									
Washington, total	66,288	65,422	1,878	10,906	16,736	16,650	13,079	6,173	866
Owners	52,701	52,052	830	6,591	12,715	14,254	11,958	5,704	649
Managers	1,168	1,135	96	301	331	242	109	56	33
Tenants	12,419	12,235	952	4,014	3,690	2,154	1,012	413	184
Oregon, total	50,206	49,476	1,424	8,911	12,608	12,213	9,504	4,816	730
Owners	39,863	39,293	674	5,655	9,682	10,400	8,472	4,410	570
Managers	916	893	53	245	250	198	109	38	23
Tenants	9,427	9,290	697	3,011	2,676	1,615	923	368	137
California, total	117,670	115,257	2,851	19,322	30,872	29,870	21,270	11,072	2,413
Owners	87,580	85,945	1,376	11,001	20,784	23,972	18,689	10,123	1,635
Managers	4,949	4,807	229	1,097	1,581	1,073	573	254	142
Tenants	25,141	24,505	1,246	7,224	8,507	4,825	2,008	695	636

TABLE 63.—PER CENT DISTRIBUTION OF FARM OWNERS AND TENANTS, BY AGE, BY DIVISIONS AND STATES: 1920.

[Percentages based on number of owners or tenants reporting age.]

DIVISION AND STATE.	OWNERS.						TENANTS.					
	Under 25 years.	25 to 34 years.	35 to 44 years.	45 to 54 years.	55 to 64 years.	65 years and over.	Under 25 years.	25 to 34 years.	35 to 44 years.	45 to 54 years.	55 to 64 years.	65 years and over.
United States	2.3	14.5	24.2	26.4	20.2	12.5	12.0	31.1	26.0	18.4	8.5	4.0
GEOGRAPHIC DIVISIONS:												
New England	1.3	9.9	19.8	26.2	23.3	19.5	5.1	26.0	28.7	22.0	11.2	7.0
Middle Atlantic	1.3	10.5	21.3	27.2	23.4	16.2	6.7	30.1	28.9	19.9	10.0	4.3
East North Central	1.5	12.7	23.2	27.3	22.2	13.0	8.4	36.6	28.6	16.5	7.4	2.6
West North Central	1.8	15.5	26.0	27.2	19.6	9.9	10.4	40.8	26.6	14.0	6.1	2.0
South Atlantic	2.6	14.0	24.1	25.8	19.7	13.8	12.5	26.5	25.2	20.4	10.0	5.3
East South Central	3.3	15.8	24.0	25.2	18.4	13.3	14.5	27.3	24.1	19.8	9.2	5.1
West South Central	3.4	16.4	25.3	25.9	18.0	11.0	13.9	29.6	25.5	19.0	8.3	3.7
Mountain	2.9	22.2	27.7	23.7	16.3	7.1	8.9	33.0	28.8	18.0	8.5	2.9
Pacific	1.6	13.1	24.4	27.4	22.1	11.4	6.3	31.0	32.3	18.7	8.6	3.2
NEW ENGLAND:												
Maine	1.6	10.8	19.9	25.2	23.1	19.4	6.1	28.9	26.1	19.6	10.6	8.6
New Hampshire	1.1	8.4	18.2	24.9	24.8	22.7	4.8	23.9	28.0	24.0	11.7	7.6
Vermont	1.7	11.7	21.2	26.4	21.6	17.5	6.8	28.9	29.9	20.4	9.5	4.6
Massachusetts	0.9	8.5	19.4	27.7	24.1	19.4	3.9	21.0	28.5	25.4	13.0	8.2
Rhode Island	0.7	6.3	17.1	26.8	25.3	23.8	2.6	21.3	28.7	27.1	13.1	7.2
Connecticut	1.0	9.4	20.5	27.0	23.2	18.9	3.4	26.8	30.1	20.0	11.8	7.8
MIDDLE ATLANTIC:												
New York	1.4	10.9	21.1	26.9	23.3	16.4	6.8	30.1	28.8	19.4	10.5	4.4
New Jersey	1.3	9.9	21.7	28.4	23.8	14.9	4.8	27.7	29.0	22.3	11.2	5.0
Pennsylvania	1.2	10.2	21.4	27.3	23.5	16.3	6.9	30.6	29.0	19.9	9.5	4.1
EAST NORTH CENTRAL:												
Ohio	1.1	9.7	21.6	27.7	23.9	16.0	8.1	34.7	28.9	17.5	7.9	2.9
Indiana	1.4	11.2	21.6	27.3	23.5	15.0	9.6	36.1	27.6	16.3	7.6	2.8
Illinois	1.5	10.9	22.5	29.4	23.1	12.6	7.0	36.1	29.8	17.3	7.5	2.4
Michigan	1.5	13.5	23.7	26.3	22.0	13.0	9.5	36.5	27.9	15.5	7.4	3.1
Wisconsin	2.1	18.2	26.3	26.3	18.7	8.5	10.3	44.4	26.4	12.3	5.0	1.6
WEST NORTH CENTRAL:												
Minnesota	1.6	15.9	25.6	28.1	20.5	8.4	9.9	43.4	26.3	13.2	5.6	1.6
Iowa	1.3	13.5	26.4	30.0	19.8	9.0	9.1	43.3	27.1	13.7	5.3	1.5
Missouri	2.4	14.4	23.0	25.6	20.7	13.8	11.2	34.2	26.3	16.4	8.4	3.6
North Dakota	2.2	19.8	31.8	26.0	15.0	5.2	11.6	44.0	25.3	12.7	5.0	1.3
South Dakota	2.3	20.5	29.9	25.1	16.0	6.3	10.7	44.4	26.7	12.3	4.6	1.3
Nebraska	1.7	17.0	28.0	27.0	18.8	7.6	11.1	43.2	26.3	12.6	5.3	1.4
Kansas	1.5	13.3	25.2	27.4	21.0	11.7	10.6	39.2	26.9	14.4	6.6	2.3
SOUTH ATLANTIC:												
Delaware	2.0	13.1	22.0	26.6	22.4	13.8	8.1	28.3	26.2	19.9	12.2	5.2
Maryland	1.5	11.1	22.0	28.5	22.5	14.4	6.9	28.7	27.0	21.5	11.1	4.7
District of Columbia	1.0	7.1	18.4	26.5	24.5	22.4	3.6	13.1	25.0	31.0	25.0	2.4
Virginia	2.1	12.5	23.5	26.8	20.0	15.1	10.0	27.3	27.0	20.4	9.7	5.7
West Virginia	1.8	12.0	23.6	26.4	20.4	15.7	6.5	26.1	28.9	21.4	10.9	6.2
North Carolina	2.8	15.4	24.4	24.3	19.3	13.8	11.8	28.0	26.0	19.2	9.7	5.3
South Carolina	3.3	15.3	26.2	25.4	17.8	12.1	13.1	26.1	25.9	20.3	9.2	5.3
Georgia	3.4	15.4	24.7	25.3	19.1	11.9	14.2	25.8	23.6	20.8	10.4	5.2
Florida	2.6	13.3	23.0	26.5	20.8	13.9	9.1	22.5	25.9	24.5	11.3	6.7
EAST SOUTH CENTRAL:												
Kentucky	3.5	16.4	23.9	24.8	18.0	13.3	17.5	31.0	23.8	16.3	7.7	3.6
Tennessee	2.9	14.4	23.6	25.9	19.2	14.0	15.2	30.2	23.7	18.1	8.7	4.1
Alabama	3.4	16.2	24.0	25.7	18.3	12.4	12.9	25.4	22.4	23.3	10.2	5.9
Mississippi	3.8	16.3	25.1	24.2	17.8	12.9	14.0	25.3	26.0	19.7	9.3	5.6
WEST SOUTH CENTRAL:												
Arkansas	3.9	17.7	24.8	25.4	16.9	11.3	14.3	28.0	24.3	21.3	8.4	3.7
Louisiana	3.7	17.1	26.6	24.9	16.4	11.0	13.3	20.0	20.4	20.4	9.4	5.4
Oklahoma	3.5	15.8	25.3	25.8	18.4	8.0	11.0	29.0	26.7	18.8	9.4	3.6
Texas	3.0	15.7	25.2	25.6	18.8	11.7	15.0	31.6	25.2	17.4	7.4	3.3
MOUNTAIN:												
Montana	2.2	27.0	30.1	21.0	14.4	5.2	7.4	35.1	29.7	17.5	7.8	2.5
Idaho	2.9	20.7	28.6	25.1	16.3	6.4	9.6	35.5	28.3	16.6	7.7	2.3
Wyoming	3.5	25.6	28.9	21.8	14.3	5.9	6.2	30.5	33.4	19.1	8.0	2.8
Colorado	2.6	20.8	26.4	24.8	17.6	7.9	8.6	32.6	28.8	18.4	8.6	3.0
New Mexico	3.8	19.2	24.3	24.5	18.1	10.0	9.3	26.4	25.3	20.6	12.7	5.6
Arizona	3.0	18.8	28.4	24.9	16.8	8.1	7.1	28.1	31.1	22.6	8.4	2.8
Utah	3.6	20.1	26.4	25.0	17.2	7.8	15.2	37.0	26.9	13.5	5.7	1.7
Nevada	2.1	17.5	29.9	25.8	15.4	9.4	6.9	36.1	28.8	17.4	8.7	2.1
PACIFIC:												
Washington	1.6	12.7	24.4	27.4	23.0	11.0	7.8	32.8	30.2	17.6	8.3	3.4
Oregon	1.7	14.4	24.6	26.5	21.6	11.2	7.5	32.4	28.8	17.4	9.9	4.0
California	1.6	12.8	24.2	27.9	21.7	11.8	5.1	29.5	34.7	19.7	8.2	2.8

TABLE 64.—NUMBER OF OWNED FARMS IN THE UNITED STATES CLASSIFIED ACCORD-
ING TO MORTGAGE STATUS: 1890 TO 1920.

ITEM.	FARMS OPERATED BY THEIR OWNERS.		OWNED FARM HOMES.	
	1920	1910	1900	1890
Total..............................	3,925,090	3,948,722	3,638,403	3,142,746
Increase over preceding census [1].	−23,632	310,319	495,657	....
Per cent of increase [1].......	−0.6	8.5	15.8	....
Reported as free from mortgage.........	2,074,325	2,588,596	2,419,180	2,228,806
Increase over preceding census [1]....	−514,271	169,416	190,374	....
Per cent of increase [1]...........	−19.9	7.0	8.5	....
Reported as mortgaged..................	1,461,306	1,312,034	1,093,164	874,215
Increase over preceding census......	149,272	218,870	218,949	....
Per cent of increase..............	11.4	20.0	25.0	....
Unknown (no report)...................	389,459	48,092	126,059	39,725
Increase over preceding census [1]....	341,367	−77,967	86,334	....
Per cent of increase [1]...........	709.8	−61.8	217.3	....
Per cent of total—				
Free from mortgage................	52.8	65.6	66.5	70.9
Mortgaged........................	37.2	33.2	30.0	27.8
Unknown (no report)..............	9.9	1.2	3.5	1.3

[1] A minus sign (−) denotes decrease. The comparative figures shown for farms free from mortgage and mortgaged are affected somewhat by the fact that more farms were tabulated as "unknown" in 1920 than at earlier censuses.

TABLE 65.—FARM MORTGAGE DEBT IN THE UNITED STATES, VALUE OF FARMS REPORTING AMOUNT OF DEBT, RATIO OF DEBT TO VALUE, AVERAGES PER FARM, AND INTEREST RATE: 1890, 1910, AND 1920.

ITEM.	OWNED FARMS MORTGAGED.[1]		Owned farm homes mortgaged, 1890.[2]
	1920	1910	
Number of farms reporting amount of debt.....	1,193,047	1,006,511	886,957
Increase over preceding census..................	186,536	119,554	....
Per cent of increase......................	18.5	13.5	....
Value of mortgaged farms (land and buildings).	$13,775,500,013	$6,330,236,951	$3,054,923,165
Increase over preceding census..................	$7,445,263,062	$3,275,313,786	....
Per cent of increase......................	117.6	107.2	....
Amount of mortgage debt......................	$4,003,767,192	$1,726,172,851	$1,085,995,960
Increase over preceding census..................	$2,277,594,341	$640,176,891	....
Per cent of increase......................	131.9	58.9	....
Ratio of debt to value, per cent.............	29.1	27.3	35.5
Average per farm:			
Value of land and buildings....................	$11,546	$6,289	$3,444
Amount of debt...............................	$3,356	$1,715	$1,224
Owner's equity...............................	$8,191	$4,574	$2,220
Average rate of interest paid, per cent..............	6.1	....	7.1

[1] Figures include only farms consisting wholly of land owned by the operator and reporting amount of mortgage debt.
[2] The figures for 1890 cover the estimated total number of owned farm homes mortgaged, including a part of those shown in Table 64 as "unknown."

75108°—23——47

TABLE 66.—FARM MORTGAGE DEBT IN THE UNITED STATES CLASSIFIED ACCORDING TO INTEREST RATE, WITH ANNUAL INTEREST CHARGE: 1920.

INTEREST RATE.	FARM MORTGAGE DEBT.[1]		Annual interest charge.
	Amount.	Per cent distribution.	
Total farm mortgage debt...................	$4,003,767,192	....	....
With interest rate reported........................	3,941,225,978	100.00	$238,501,748
Less than 4 per cent.....................	13,246,285	0.34	410,545
4 per cent...........................	73,459,416	1.86	2,938,363
Between 4 and 5 per cent........................	45,589,167	1.16	2,067,925
5 per cent...........................	751,700,696	19.07	37,585,268
Between 5 and 5½ per cent....................	35,360,355	0.90	1,856,524
5½ per cent.............................	484,539,054	12.29	26,649,872
Between 5½ and 6 per cent....................	36,900,708	0.94	2,121,921
6 per cent.............................	1,542,244,146	39.13	92,534,699
Between 6 and 6½ per cent....................	15,253,551	0.39	953,443
6½ per cent.............................	108,555,481	2.75	7,056,392
Between 6½ and 7 per cent....................	9,713,563	0.25	655,757
7 per cent.............................	364,088,503	9.24	25,486,330
Between 7 and 8 per cent....................	35,023,795	0.89	2,624,210
8 per cent.............................	335,466,201	8.51	26,837,272
Between 8 and 10 per cent....................	28,923,338	0.73	2,572,725
10 per cent.............................	59,092,008	1.50	5,909,317
More than 10 per cent.....................	2,069,711	0.05	241,185
Interest rate not reported.....................	62,541,214	....	....

[1] Reported debt on fully owned farms only. The total debt on all farms in 1920, including those operated by tenants, part owners, and managers, has been estimated at $7,857,700,000.

TABLE 67.—FARM MORTGAGE DEBT IN THE UNITED STATES CLASSIFIED ACCORDING TO VALUE OF FARM, WITH RATIO OF DEBT TO VALUE AND AVERAGE INTEREST RATE: 1920.

VALUE GROUP.	FARMS REPORTING AMOUNT OF DEBT.		FARM MORTGAGE DEBT.[1]		Ratio of debt to value (per cent).	Average interest rate (per cent).
	Number.	Per cent distribution.	Amount.	Per cent distribution.		
Total..	1,193,047	100.0	$4,003,767,192	100.0	29.1	6.1
Under $5,000	474,649	39.8	467,449,381	11.7	38.7	6.6
Under $2,500	213,844	17.9	129,263,438	3.2	42.2	6.8
$2,500 to $4,999	260,805	21.9	338,185,943	8.4	37.4	6.5
$5,000 to $9,999	295,814	24.8	703,854,308	17.6	35.2	6.2
$5,000 to $7,499	191,406	16.0	402,781,862	10.1	35.7	6.2
$7,500 to $9,999	104,408	8.8	301,072,446	7.5	34.6	6.2
$10,000 to $14,999	147,029	12.3	573,984,642	14.3	34.0	6.0
$15,000 to $19,999	84,909	7.1	428,312,701	10.7	30.7	6.0
$20,000 to $24,999	57,990	4.9	366,129,944	9.1	29.2	5.9
$25,000 to $29,999	28,620	2.4	215,366,895	5.4	28.5	5.9
$30,000 to $34,999	27,921	2.3	238,533,885	6.0	27.3	5.9
$35,000 to $39,999	14,862	1.2	142,131,377	3.5	26.3	5.9
$40,000 to $44,999	14,967	1.3	156,113,481	3.9	25.4	5.8
$45,000 to $49,999	10,354	0.9	117,925,985	2.9	24.2	5.7
$50,000 and over	35,932	3.0	593,964,593	14.8	20.1	5.9

[1] Reported debt on fully owned farms only.

TABLE 68.—OWNED FARMS REPORTED AS FREE FROM MORTGAGE AND MORT-
GAGED, BY DIVISIONS AND STATES: 1920 AND 1910.

[Farms owned wholly or in part by the operator.]

DIVISION AND STATE.	1920				1910			
	Total.	Free from mortgage.	Mort- gaged.	Un- known (no report).	Total.	Free from mortgage.	Mort- gaged.	Un- known (no report).
United States....	3,925,090	2,074,325	1,461,306	389,459	3,948,722	2,588,596	1,312,034	48,092
GEOGRAPHIC DIVISIONS:								
New England.......	140,160	80,412	53,138	6,610	168,408	108,938	58,474	996
Middle Atlantic.....	327,104	179,326	125,216	22,562	355,036	217,257	134,803	2,976
East North Central..	766,786	382,771	326,313	57,702	809,044	473,822	327,463	7,759
West North Central..	711,156	278,906	368,158	64,092	758,946	404,555	346,182	8,209
South Atlantic......	607,089	408,804	118,026	80,259	593,154	474,742	110,198	8,214
East South Central..	525,808	339,312	124,723	61,773	510,452	388,837	114,195	7,420
West South Central..	464,328	236,932	162,738	64,658	440,905	299,303	132,252	9,350
Mountain..........	202,515	88,731	97,038	16,746	160,844	125,940	33,060	1,844
Pacific..............	180,144	79,131	85,956	15,057	151,933	95,202	55,407	1,324
NEW ENGLAND:								
Maine.............	45,437	30,665	13,023	1,749	56,454	41,309	14,948	197
New Hampshire.....	18,604	11,992	5,389	1,223	24,493	18,119	6,234	140
Vermont...........	25,121	12,132	12,225	764	28,065	14,851	13,140	74
Massachusetts......	28,087	14,055	12,632	1,400	32,075	18,768	13,014	293
Rhode Island.......	3,245	1,971	949	325	4,087	2,811	1,180	96
Connecticut........	19,666	9,597	8,920	1,149	23,234	13,080	9,958	196
MIDDLE ATLANTIC:								
New York..........	151,717	75,522	66,633	9,562	166,674	93,118	72,311	1,245
New Jersey.........	21,889	10,000	10,085	1,804	24,133	11,983	11,793	357
Pennsylvania.......	153,498	93,804	48,498	11,196	164,229	112,156	50,699	1,374
EAST NORTH CENTRAL:								
Ohio...............	177,986	110,004	50,784	17,198	192,104	135,616	54,997	1,491
Indiana............	137,210	73,233	51,474	12,503	148,501	89,847	56,914	1,740
Illinois............	132,574	68,892	51,039	12,643	145,107	86,713	55,792	2,602
Michigan..........	159,406	72,869	78,758	7,779	172,310	88,705	82,631	974
Wisconsin..........	159,610	57,773	94,258	7,579	151,022	72,941	77,129	952
WEST NORTH CENTRAL:								
Minnesota..........	132,744	54,086	69,545	9,113	122,104	65,038	56,145	921
Iowa..............	121,888	45,807	66,096	9,985	133,003	63,234	68,045	1,724
Missouri...........	185,030	82,099	85,538	17,393	192,285	102,514	88,486	1,285
North Dakota......	56,917	12,833	40,462	3,622	63,212	30,651	31,727	834
South Dakota......	47,815	16,037	27,262	4,516	57,984	35,101	21,691	1,192
Nebraska..........	69,672	27,065	35,191	7,416	79,250	47,435	30,839	976
Kansas............	97,090	40,979	44,064	12,047	111,108	60,582	49,249	1,277
SOUTH ATLANTIC:								
Delaware...........	6,010	3,504	2,018	488	6,178	3,817	2,264	97
Maryland..........	32,805	19,292	11,339	2,174	33,519	21,084	12,127	308
District of Columbia.	100	53	29	18	118	93	21	4
Virginia...........	136,363	98,470	24,331	13,562	133,664	111,474	21,182	1,008
West Virginia......	72,101	52,617	10,274	9,210	75,978	66,093	9,525	360
North Carolina.....	151,376	102,950	24,499	23,927	145,320	117,028	26,642	1,650
South Carolina.....	67,724	42,847	14,299	10,578	64,350	47,535	15,020	1,795
Georgia............	102,123	64,061	23,135	14,927	98,628	78,004	18,257	2,367
Florida............	38,487	25,010	8,102	5,375	35,399	29,614	5,160	625
EAST SOUTH CENTRAL:								
Kentucky..........	179,327	116,613	40,615	22,099	170,332	135,505	33,039	1,788
Tennessee..........	148,082	105,128	32,264	10,690	144,125	118,285	24,006	1,834
Alabama...........	107,089	64,498	27,854	14,737	103,929	74,504	27,457	1,968
Mississippi.........	91,310	53,073	23,990	14,247	92,066	60,543	29,693	1,830
WEST SOUTH CENTRAL:								
Arkansas..........	112,647	64,881	33,990	13,776	106,649	82,321	22,374	1,954
Louisiana	57,254	36,010	11,783	9,461	52,989	42,011	9,834	1,144
Oklahoma...........	93,217	30,551	47,025	15,641	85,404	46,889	36,036	2,479
Texas.............	201,010	105,490	69,940	25,780	195,800	128,082	64,008	3,773
MOUNTAIN:								
Montana...........	50,271	16,365	29,897	4,009	23,365	18,014	4,820	901
Idaho.............	34,647	11,872	20,060	2,715	27,169	17,933	9,010	226
Wyoming..........	13,403	6,816	5,513	1,074	9,779	7,815	1,923	41
Colorado..........	45,291	20,965	21,131	3,195	36,993	26,822	9,636	535
New Mexico........	25,756	16,650	6,257	2,849	33,398	31,382	1,775	241
Arizona...........	7,869	3,708	3,380	781	8,203	7,038	1,043	122
Utah..............	22,579	10,756	9,916	1,907	19,762	15,131	4,492	139
Nevada............	2,699	1,599	884	216	2,175	1,805	361	9
PACIFIC:								
Washington........	52,701	25,012	24,004	3,685	47,505	30,979	16,026	500
Oregon............	39,863	18,077	17,843	3,943	37,796	24,855	12,632	309
California..........	87,580	36,042	44,109	7,429	66,632	39,368	26,749	515

TABLE 69.—MORTGAGED FARMS CLASSIFIED ACCORDING TO CHARACTER OF OWNERSHIP, BY DIVISIONS AND STATES: 1920 AND 1910.

DIVISION AND STATE.	OWNED FARMS REPORTED AS MORTGAGED, 1920.					OWNED FARMS REPORTED AS MORTGAGED, 1910.	
	Total.	Operated by full owners.			Operated by part owners.	Total.	Operated by full owners reporting amount of debt.
		Total.	Reporting amount of debt.	Not reporting amount of debt.			
United States..........	1,461,306	1,217,234	1,193,047	24,187	244,072	1,312,034	1,006,511
GEOGRAPHIC DIVISIONS:							
New England..............	53,138	50,571	49,456	1,115	2,567	58,474	53,791
Middle Atlantic............	125,216	116,402	113,441	2,961	8,814	134,803	118,220
East North Central........	326,313	278,777	274,347	4,430	47,536	327,463	257,884
West North Central.......	368,158	269,846	266,281	3,565	98,312	346,182	236,975
South Atlantic.............	118,026	106,929	103,039	3,890	11,097	110,198	86,522
East South Central........	124,723	111,814	109,619	2,195	12,909	114,195	85,282
West South Central.......	162,738	134,866	131,550	3,316	27,872	132,252	96,687
Mountain..................	97,038	75,590	74,118	1,472	21,448	33,060	26,731
Pacific....................	85,956	72,439	71,196	1,243	13,517	55,407	44,419
NEW ENGLAND:							
Maine....................	13,023	12,693	12,345	348	330	14,948	13,894
New Hampshire...........	5,389	5,126	4,951	175	263	6,234	5,666
Vermont..................	12,225	11,654	11,504	150	571	13,140	12,138
Massachusetts............	12,632	11,921	11,663	258	711	13,014	12,030
Rhode Island.............	949	879	856	23	70	1,180	1,001
Connecticut..............	8,920	8,298	8,137	161	622	9,958	9,062
MIDDLE ATLANTIC:							
New York................	66,633	61,095	59,735	1,360	5,538	72,311	62,555
New Jersey...............	10,085	9,580	9,296	284	505	11,793	10,666
Pennsylvania.............	48,498	45,727	44,410	1,317	2,771	50,699	44,999
EAST NORTH CENTRAL:							
Ohio.....................	50,784	43,940	43,068	872	6,844	54,997	42,785
Indiana..................	51,474	40,954	40,416	538	10,520	56,914	40,108
Illinois..................	51,039	37,249	36,663	586	13,790	55,792	36,938
Michigan.................	78,758	68,448	67,119	1,329	10,310	82,631	68,655
Wisconsin................	94,258	88,186	87,081	1,105	6,072	77,129	69,398
WEST NORTH CENTRAL:							
Minnesota................	69,545	58,350	57,585	765	11,195	56,145	41,775
Iowa.....................	66,096	52,985	52,341	644	13,111	68,045	50,452
Missouri.................	85,538	69,644	68,784	860	15,894	88,486	64,028
North Dakota............	40,462	22,918	22,623	295	17,544	31,727	19,187
South Dakota............	27,262	14,256	14,039	217	13,006	21,691	11,313
Nebraska................	35,191	24,357	23,986	371	10,834	30,839	19,778
Kansas...................	44,064	27,336	26,923	413	16,728	49,249	30,442
SOUTH ATLANTIC:							
Delaware.................	2,018	1,943	1,903	40	75	2,264	2,021
Maryland................	11,339	10,749	10,407	342	590	12,127	10,754
District of Columbia......	29	25	24	1	4	21	20
Virginia..................	24,331	21,865	21,155	710	2,466	21,182	17,410
West Virginia............	10,274	9,376	9,031	345	898	9,525	7,878
North Carolina...........	24,499	20,908	20,149	759	3,591	26,642	19,252
South Carolina...........	14,299	12,884	12,265	619	1,415	15,020	11,189
Georgia..................	23,135	21,693	20,797	896	1,442	18,257	13,839
Florida..................	8,102	7,486	7,308	178	616	5,160	4,159
EAST SOUTH CENTRAL:							
Kentucky.................	40,615	36,304	35,531	773	4,311	33,039	25,846
Tennessee................	32,264	28,001	27,496	505	4,263	24,006	17,362
Alabama.................	27,854	25,136	24,748	388	2,718	27,457	19,230
Mississippi..............	23,990	22,373	21,844	529	1,617	29,693	22,844
WEST SOUTH CENTRAL:							
Arkansas.................	33,990	30,012	29,504	508	3,978	22,374	16,555
Louisiana................	11,783	10,751	10,301	450	1,032	9,834	7,520
Oklahoma................	47,025	34,740	34,045	695	12,285	36,036	24,588
Texas....................	69,940	59,363	57,700	1,663	10,577	64,008	48,024
MOUNTAIN:							
Montana.................	29,897	21,786	21,244	542	8,111	4,820	3,990
Idaho....................	20,060	17,383	17,142	241	2,677	9,010	7,594
Wyoming.................	5,513	4,057	3,937	120	1,456	1,923	1,531
Colorado.................	21,131	15,955	15,735	220	5,176	9,636	7,571
New Mexico..............	6,257	4,458	4,331	127	1,799	1,775	1,397
Arizona..................	3,380	2,962	2,876	86	418	1,043	813
Utah.....................	9,916	8,200	8,086	114	1,716	4,492	3,526
Nevada..................	884	789	767	22	95	361	309
PACIFIC:							
Washington..............	24,004	19,780	19,503	277	4,224	16,026	12,715
Oregon..................	17,843	14,565	14,355	210	3,278	12,632	10,274
California...............	44,109	38,094	37,338	756	6,015	26,749	21,430

TABLE 70.—FARM MORTGAGE DEBT, VALUE OF FARMS REPORTING AMOUNT OF DEBT, AND RATIO OF DEBT TO VALUE, BY DIVISIONS AND STATES: 1920 AND 1910.

[Figures include only farms consisting wholly of land owned by the operator and reporting amount of mortgage debt.]

DIVISION AND STATE.	VALUE OF FARMS (LAND AND BUILDINGS).		AMOUNT OF DEBT.		RATIO OF DEBT TO VALUE (PER CENT).	
	1920	1910	1920	1910	1920	1910
United States.....	$13,775,500,013	$6,330,236,951	$4,003,767,192	$1,726,172,851	29.1	27.3
GEOGRAPHIC DIVISIONS:						
New England........	271,162,739	183,826,183	91,756,058	58,535,508	33.8	31.8
Middle Atlantic......	711,867,559	516,334,528	258,397,005	178,326,219	36.3	34.5
East North Central...	2,959,228,357	1,605,964,728	922,266,312	459,886,968	31.2	28.6
West North Central..	5,414,232,364	2,361,540,675	1,437,337,392	608,480,562	26.5	25.8
South Atlantic.......	652,812,215	270,317,105	192,668,718	73,597,258	29.5	27.2
East South Central...	570,595,365	203,125,373	176,102,120	59,769,643	30.9	29.4
West South Central..	1,134,847,511	484,014,790	304,631,634	121,365,670	26.8	25.1
Mountain...........	927,906,171	247,994,132	283,423,921	59,364,185	30.5	23.9
Pacific.............	1,132,847,732	457,119,437	337,184,032	106,846,838	29.8	23.4
NEW ENGLAND:						
Maine..............	58,427,088	39,774,005	18,592,225	11,738,529	31.8	29.5
New Hampshire.....	20,274,025	15,457,040	6,820,501	4,773,610	33.6	30.9
Vermont...........	61,070,552	36,858,501	23,575,778	12,436,091	38.6	33.7
Massachusetts.......	70,745,237	49,742,396	23,412,188	16,371,484	33.1	32.9
Rhode Island........	4,864,643	4,087,933	1,494,367	1,356,326	30.7	33.2
Connecticut.........	55,781,194	37,906,308	17,860,949	11,859,468	32.0	31.3
MIDDLE ATLANTIC:						
New York...........	388,114,245	284,659,163	145,533,268	97,309,848	37.5	34.2
New Jersey.........	67,175,967	55,507,006	25,122,582	19,476,938	37.4	35.1
Pennsylvania........	256,577,347	176,168,359	87,741,155	61,539,433	34.2	34.9
EAST NORTH CENTRAL:						
Ohio................	387,187,747	220,749,834	121,120,774	63,788,397	31.3	28.9
Indiana.............	439,152,507	251,961,241	105,256,239	57,486,582	24.0	22.8
Illinois.............	775,394,589	454,857,222	197,211,841	115,799,646	25.4	25.5
Michigan...........	420,108,156	250,874,010	144,103,067	75,997,030	34.3	30.3
Wisconsin..........	937,385,358	427,522,421	354,574,391	146,815,313	37.8	34.3
WEST NORTH CENTRAL:						
Minnesota..........	925,963,060	295,015,775	254,475,222	77,866,283	27.5	26.4
Iowa...............	1,814,260,136	735,265,320	489,816,739	204,242,722	27.0	27.8
Missouri............	752,008,050	389,476,000	216,463,380	112,565,403	28.8	28.9
North Dakota........	380,132,941	213,642,953	108,284,682	47,841,587	28.5	22.4
South Dakota.......	411,837,314	154,749,490	89,875,046	32,771,359	21.8	21.2
Nebraska...........	705,561,409	286,308,920	168,507,859	62,373,472	23.9	21.8
Kansas.............	424,469,454	287,082,217	109,914,464	70,819,736	25.9	24.7
SOUTH ATLANTIC:						
Delaware...........	11,422,387	8,801,976	4,460,416	3,068,721	39.0	34.9
Maryland...........	75,082,413	44,398,721	27,481,197	15,673,773	36.6	35.3
Dist. of Columbia....	237,900	233,400	92,900	56,100	39.1	24.0
Virginia............	151,585,109	62,377,247	41,725,542	15,440,291	27.5	24.8
West Virginia.......	43,989,441	21,549,125	11,205,953	5,592,533	25.5	26.0
North Carolina......	103,282,055	42,952,440	31,968,285	9,958,389	31.0	23.2
South Carolina......	92,052,935	39,593,747	25,153,227	10,109,072	27.3	25.5
Georgia............	124,579,125	37,526,424	37,671,385	10,988,409	30.2	29.3
Florida.............	50,580,850	12,884,025	12,909,813	2,709,970	25.5	21.0
EAST SOUTH CENTRAL:						
Kentucky...........	230,557,435	81,315,441	67,116,481	23,411,430	29.1	28.8
Tennessee.........:.	159,000,504	47,232,059	49,836,266	12,626,330	31.3	26.7
Alabama...........	81,888,501	32,311,461	29,103,101	10,350,577	35.5	32.0
Mississippi..........	99,148,925	42,266,412	30,046,272	13,381,306	30.3	31.7
WEST SOUTH CENTRAL:						
Arkansas...........	129,347,657	35,035,023	38,539,428	8,941,332	29.8	25.5
Louisiana...........	68,361,653	28,771,635	20,490,966	8,950,301	30.0	31.1
Oklahoma..........	272,613,022	190,397,200	73,434,422	27,384,765	26.9	22.4
Texas..............	664,100,170	207,880,832	172,166,818	76,089,272	25.9	25.5
MOUNTAIN:						
Montana...........	240,549,778	44,615,154	77,949,679	10,741,280	32.4	24.1
Idaho..............	223,648,851	64,376,068	69,868,243	14,557,103	31.2	22.6
Wyoming...........	55,609,834	16,675,387	15,303,106	4,207,983	27.5	25.2
Colorado...........	211,700,699	77,332,068	62,623,338	18,986,026	29.6	24.6
New Mexico........	43,085,327	10,683,233	11,178,034	2,590,282	25.9	24.2
Arizona............	50,452,989	8,695,498	15,648,280	2,253,252	31.0	25.9
Utah...............	84,578,191	21,319,580	24,334,636	4,564,175	28.8	21.4
Nevada............	18,280,502	4,297,144	6,518,605	1,464,084	35.7	34.1
PACIFIC:						
Washington.........	202,018,288	113,394,798	61,120,951	25,644,551	30.3	22.6
Oregon............	166,663,433	93,525,449	51,999,178	21,165,627	31.2	22.6
California..........	764,166,011	250,199,190	224,063,903	60,036,660	29.3	24.0

TABLE 71.—AVERAGE VALUE OF MORTGAGED FARMS, AVERAGE DEBT, AND AVER-
AGE EQUITY PER FARM, BY DIVISIONS AND STATES: 1920 AND 1910.

[A minus sign (−) denotes decrease.]

DIVISION AND STATE.	AVERAGE VALUE OF LAND AND BUILDINGS PER FARM.			AVERAGE MORTGAGE DEBT PER FARM.			AVERAGE EQUITY PER FARM.		
	1920	1910	Per cent of increase.	1920	1910	Per cent of increase.	1920	1910	Per cent of increase.
United States	$11,546	$6,289	83.6	$3,356	$1,715	95.7	$8,191	$4,574	79.1
GEOGRAPHIC DIVISIONS:									
New England	5,483	3,417	60.5	1,855	1,088	70.5	3,628	2,329	55.8
Middle Atlantic	6,275	4,368	43.7	2,278	1,508	51.1	3,997	2,860	39.8
East North Central	10,786	6,227	73.2	3,362	1,783	88.6	7,425	4,444	67.1
West North Central	20,333	9,965	104.0	5,398	2,568	110.2	14,935	7,397	101.9
South Atlantic	6,336	3,124	102.8	1,870	851	119.7	4,466	2,273	96.5
East South Central	5,205	2,382	118.5	1,606	701	129.1	3,599	1,681	114.1
West South Central	8,627	5,006	72.3	2,316	1,255	84.5	6,311	3,751	68.2
Mountain	12,519	9,277	34.9	3,824	2,221	72.2	8,695	7,056	23.2
Pacific	15,912	10,291	54.6	4,736	2,405	96.9	11,176	7,886	41.7
NEW ENGLAND:									
Maine	4,733	2,863	65.3	1,506	845	78.2	3,227	2,018	59.9
New Hampshire	4,095	2,728	50.1	1,378	842	63.7	2,717	1,886	44.1
Vermont	5,309	3,037	74.8	2,049	1,025	99.9	3,259	2,012	62.0
Massachusetts	6,066	4,135	46.7	2,007	1,361	47.5	4,058	2,774	46.3
Rhode Island	5,683	4,084	39.2	1,746	1,355	28.9	3,937	2,729	44.3
Connecticut	6,855	4,183	63.9	2,195	1,309	67.7	4,660	2,874	62.1
MIDDLE ATLANTIC:									
New York	6,497	4,551	42.8	2,436	1,556	56.6	4,061	2,995	35.6
New Jersey	7,226	5,204	38.9	2,703	1,826	48.0	4,524	3,378	33.9
Pennsylvania	5,777	3,915	47.6	1,976	1,368	44.4	3,802	2,547	49.3
EAST NORTH CENTRAL:									
Ohio	8,990	5,160	74.2	2,812	1,491	88.6	6,178	3,669	68.4
Indiana	10,866	6,282	73.0	2,604	1,433	81.7	8,261	4,849	70.4
Illinois	21,149	12,314	71.7	5,379	3,135	71.6	15,770	9,179	71.8
Michigan	6,259	3,654	71.3	2,147	1,107	93.9	4,112	2,547	61.4
Wisconsin	10,765	6,160	74.8	4,072	2,116	92.4	6,693	4,044	65.5
WEST NORTH CENTRAL:									
Minnesota	16,080	7,062	127.7	4,419	1,864	137.1	11,661	5,198	124.3
Iowa	34,662	14,574	137.8	9,358	4,048	131.2	25,304	10,526	140.4
Missouri	10,933	6,083	79.7	3,147	1,758	79.0	7,786	4,325	80.0
North Dakota	16,803	11,135	50.9	4,786	2,493	92.0	12,016	8,642	39.0
South Dakota	29,335	13,679	114.5	6,402	2,897	121.0	22,933	10,782	112.7
Nebraska	29,416	14,476	103.2	7,025	3,154	122.7	22,390	11,322	97.8
Kansas	15,766	9,430	67.2	4,083	2,326	75.5	11,684	7,104	64.5
SOUTH ATLANTIC:									
Delaware	6,002	4,355	37.8	2,344	1,518	54.4	3,658	2,837	28.9
Maryland	7,215	4,129	74.7	2,641	1,457	81.3	4,574	2,672	71.2
District of Columbia	9,913	11,670	−15.1	3,871	2,805	38.0	6,042	8,865	−31.8
Virginia	7,165	3,583	100.0	1,972	887	122.3	5,193	2,696	92.6
West Virginia	4,871	2,735	78.1	1,241	710	74.8	3,630	2,025	79.3
North Carolina	5,126	2,231	129.8	1,587	517	207.0	3,539	1,714	106.5
South Carolina	7,505	3,539	112.1	2,051	903	127.1	5,455	2,636	106.9
Georgia	5,990	2,712	120.9	1,811	794	128.1	4,179	1,918	117.9
Florida	6,921	3,098	123.4	1,767	652	171.0	5,155	2,446	110.8
EAST SOUTH CENTRAL:									
Kentucky	6,489	3,146	106.3	1,889	906	108.5	4,600	2,240	105.4
Tennessee	5,783	2,720	112.6	1,812	727	149.2	3,970	1,993	99.2
Alabama	3,309	1,680	97.0	1,176	538	118.6	2,133	1,142	86.8
Mississippi	4,539	1,850	145.4	1,375	586	134.6	3,163	1,264	150.2
WEST SOUTH CENTRAL:									
Arkansas	4,384	2,116	107.2	1,306	540	141.9	3,078	1,576	95.3
Louisiana	6,636	3,826	73.4	1,989	1,190	67.1	4,647	2,636	76.3
Oklahoma	8,008	4,975	61.0	2,157	1,114	93.6	5,851	3,861	51.5
Texas	11,517	6,203	85.7	2,984	1,584	88.4	8,533	4,619	84.7
MOUNTAIN:									
Montana	11,323	11,182	1.3	3,669	2,692	36.3	7,654	8,490	−9.8
Idaho	13,047	8,477	53.9	4,076	1,917	112.6	8,971	6,560	36.8
Wyoming	14,125	10,892	29.7	3,887	2,749	41.4	10,238	8,143	25.7
Colorado	13,454	10,214	31.7	3,980	2,508	58.7	9,474	7,706	22.9
New Mexico	9,948	7,647	30.1	2,581	1,854	39.2	7,367	5,793	27.2
Arizona	17,543	10,696	64.0	5,441	2,772	96.3	12,102	7,924	52.7
Utah	10,460	6,046	73.0	3,009	1,294	132.5	7,450	4,752	56.8
Nevada	23,834	13,907	71.4	8,499	4,738	79.4	15,335	9,169	67.2
PACIFIC:									
Washington	10,358	8,918	16.1	3,134	2,017	55.4	7,224	6,901	4.7
Oregon	11,610	9,103	27.5	3,622	2,060	75.8	7,988	7,043	13.4
California	20,466	11,675	75.3	6,001	2,802	114.2	14,465	8,873	63.0

TABLE 72.—FARM MORTGAGE DEBT CLASSIFIED ACCORDING TO RATE OF INTEREST,

[Mortgage debt on farms consisting wholly of land

	DIVISION AND STATE.	AMOUNT OF FARM MORTGAGE DEBT.				
		Total.	Interest rate reported.			
			Total.	Less than 5 per cent.	5 per cent.	Between 5 and 6 per cent.
1	United States.......	$4,003,767,192	$3,941,225,978	$132,294,868	$751,700,696	$556,800,117
	GEOGRAPHIC DIVISIONS:					
2	New England...........	91,756,058	90,285,144	1,443,013	28,626,572	9,866,905
3	Middle Atlantic........	258,397,005	253,262,316	17,496,170	107,527,546	26,470,580
4	East North Central....	922,266,312	910,815,941	67,438,814	262,639,830	124,833,818
5	West North Central....	1,437,337,392	1,418,591,954	31,306,158	301,638,687	333,151,745
6	South Atlantic.........	192,668,718	188,249,396	1,894,261	9,918,273	12,861,646
7	East South Central.....	176,102,120	172,416,731	1,152,995	6,221,868	10,346,567
8	West South Central.....	304,631,634	296,400,545	6,708,736	16,168,793	16,756,006
9	Mountain..............	283,423,921	279,360,646	2,390,818	5,829,673	10,810,449
10	Pacific................	337,184,032	331,843,305	2,463,903	13,129,454	11,702,401
	NEW ENGLAND:					
11	Maine.................	18,592,225	18,203,988	275,859	979,408	834,476
12	New Hampshire........	6,820,551	6,676,055	165,457	5,335,056	308,982
13	Vermont..............	23,575,778	23,167,085	295,480	12,312,094	2,060,047
14	Massachusetts.........	23,412,188	23,177,684	416,525	5,392,910	4,918,951
15	Rhode Island..........	1,494,367	1,471,208	25,552	198,362	107,417
16	Connecticut...........	17,860,949	17,589,124	264,140	4,408,742	1,637,032
	MIDDLE ATLANTIC:					
17	New York.............	145,533,268	143,338,267	4,127,610	65,955,014	14,489,939
18	New Jersey............	25,122,582	24,738,573	773,621	11,581,382	1,719,945
19	Pennsylvania..........	87,741,155	85,185,476	12,594,939	29,991,150	10,260,696
	EAST NORTH CENTRAL:					
20	Ohio.................	121,120,774	119,763,387	2,286,130	14,872,198	8,664,426
21	Indiana..............	105,256,239	104,310,977	1,030,337	12,563,408	18,139,405
22	Illinois..............	197,211,841	192,599,846	4,273,321	66,331,828	55,513,697
23	Michigan.............	144,103,067	142,741,028	2,894,972	21,135,056	8,487,908
24	Wisconsin............	354,574,391	351,400,703	56,954,054	147,737,340	34,028,382
	WEST NORTH CENTRAL:					
25	Minnesota.............	254,475,222	251,952,399	10,704,634	54,864,025	46,584,208
26	Iowa.................	489,816,739	485,836,865	13,361,853	158,876,164	179,443,592
27	Missouri.............	216,463,380	214,330,907	1,908,998	20,950,520	24,746,784
28	North Dakota........	108,284,682	107,330,982	306,285	3,949,636	5,012,384
29	South Dakota........	89,875,046	88,403,941	863,708	13,799,907	21,583,851
30	Nebraska.............	168,507,859	161,898,670	3,265,938	38,999,403	41,964,873
31	Kansas...............	109,914,464	108,838,190	894,742	10,199,032	13,816,053
	SOUTH ATLANTIC:					
32	Delaware.............	4,460,416	4,436,916	63,735	1,011,750	408,500
33	Maryland.............	27,481,197	27,010,373	742,291	4,587,053	3,140,438
34	District of Columbia....	92,900	92,100	....	17,200	6,000
35	Virginia..............	41,725,542	40,743,839	399,839	1,699,435	2,810,487
36	West Virginia.........	11,205,953	10,872,437	341,522	774,417	922,637
37	North Carolina........	31,968,285	31,142,238	112,014	456,262	1,729,618
38	South Carolina........	25,153,227	24,705,550	90,829	391,515	1,344,565
39	Georgia..............	37,671,385	36,708,833	94,839	579,221	1,699,716
40	Florida..............	12,909,813	12,537,110	49,192	401,420	799,685
	EAST SOUTH CENTRAL:					
41	Kentucky.............	67,116,481	65,948,273	482,326	2,760,634	3,227,615
42	Tennessee............	49,836,266	48,917,964	220,956	1,347,323	3,523,881
43	Alabama.............	29,103,101	28,152,235	202,403	754,639	1,429,744
44	Mississippi...........	30,046,272	29,398,259	247,310	1,359,272	2,165,327
	WEST SOUTH CENTRAL:					
45	Arkansas.............	38,539,428	37,936,348	180,630	845,743	2,503,225
46	Louisiana.............	20,490,066	10,001,820	96,475	525,386	988,909
47	Oklahoma.............	70,404,422	73,501,084	373,926	12,073,305	5,503,612
48	Texas...............	172,166,818	165,880,384	6,057,745	6,773,209	7,760,610
	MOUNTAIN:					
49	Montana.............	77,949,679	77,348,718	238,084	1,743,837	2,818,187
50	Idaho...............	69,868,243	69,282,713	156,160	882,750	2,809,167
51	Wyoming.............	15,303,106	14,493,100	226,330	238,168	331,847
52	Colorado.............	62,623,338	62,005,776	284,612	1,281,184	2,081,791
53	New Mexico..........	11,178,034	10,970,988	1,092,675	383,343	891,896
54	Arizona..............	15,648,280	15,164,436	58,608	237,603	197,769
55	Utah................	24,334,636	23,958,070	292,525	746,113	1,588,542
56	Nevada..............	6,518,605	6,136,845	41,824	316,675	91,250
	PACIFIC:					
57	Washington...........	61,120,951	60,322,532	620,947	3,288,990	3,752,328
58	Oregon..............	51,999,178	51,259,391	716,806	3,161,406	3,483,469
59	California...........	224,063,903	220,261,382	1,126,150	6,679,058	4,466,604

1920, AND AVERAGE RATE OF INTEREST, 1920 AND 1890, BY DIVISIONS AND STATES.

owned by the operator and reporting amount of debt.]

| | AMOUNT OF FARM MORTGAGE DEBT—continued. | | | | | Interest rate not reported. | AVERAGE RATE OF INTEREST (PER CENT). | | |
| | Interest rate reported—continued. | | | | | | | | |
6 per cent.	Between 6 and 7 per cent.	7 per cent.	Between 7 and 8 per cent.	8 per cent.	More than 8 per cent.		1920	1890	
$1,542,244,146	$133,522,595	$364,088,503	$35,023,795	$335,466,201	$90,085,057	$62,541,214	6.1	7.1	1
46,928,144	766,745	1,270,986	87,362	1,092,952	202,465	1,470,914	5.7	5.8	2
100,759,658	399,365	169,337	38,507	102,663	298,490	5,134,689	5.4	5.6	3
392,818,144	14,470,433	43,812,959	446,544	2,572,614	1,782,785	11,450,371	5.6	6.9	4
532,563,417	69,725,942	83,676,381	9,537,520	44,178,892	12,813,212	18,745,438	5.8	8.0	5
105,159,650	1,973,465	14,121,036	993,552	39,032,357	2,295,156	4,419,322	6.4	6.6	6
113,217,912	1,535,210	4,929,735	337,450	30,968,792	3,706,202	3,685,389	6.4	7.7	7
64,206,492	9,895,981	38,928,378	8,147,604	104,739,664	30,848,891	8,231,089	7.2	8.5	8
65,176,785	12,173,697	50,876,602	10,343,532	86,269,689	35,489,401	4,063,275	7.3	9.9	9
121,413,944	22,581,757	126,303,089	5,091,724	26,508,578	2,648,455	5,340,727	6.6	8.9	10
13,660,534	283,384	1,044,015	59,400	1,009,191	57,721	388,237	6.1	6.3	11
836,060	8,550	10,600	....	11,350	....	144,496	5.1	5.9	12
8,323,661	42,056	1,740	300	22,350	109,357	408,693	5.4	5.9	13
11,871,975	322,225	176,331	23,462	31,286	24,019	234,504	5.7	5.6	14
1,096,277	11,900	27,900	....	3,800	....	23,159	5.8	5.8	15
11,139,637	98,630	10,400	4,200	14,975	11,368	271,825	5.7	5.6	16
58,286,271	231,020	40,187	7,035	43,568	157,623	2,195,001	5.4	5.7	17
10,551,170	44,100	19,000	6,325	22,325	20,705	384,009	5.4	5.7	18
31,922,217	124,245	110,150	25,147	36,770	120,162	2,555,679	5.3	5.4	19
88,006,982	1,704,654	3,608,821	32,320	501,930	85,926	1,357,387	5.9	6.7	20
66,324,382	1,374,728	3,483,451	89,899	956,119	349,248	945,262	5.8	6.9	21
57,037,518	1,551,040	7,312,967	18,100	105,758	455,617	4,611,995	5.5	6.9	22
83,902,400	4,608,668	21,381,009	51,433	131,886	147,696	1,362,039	6.0	7.1	23
97,546,862	5,231,343	8,026,711	254,792	876,921	744,298	3,173,688	5.3	6.6	24
104,926,611	12,818,582	14,914,589	1,399,232	4,499,641	1,240,877	2,522,823	5.8	8.2	25
115,309,177	10,719,731	5,672,132	441,823	1,296,877	715,516	3,979,874	5.5	7.4	26
112,163,690	15,866,474	22,731,016	1,724,228	13,744,344	494,853	2,132,473	6.1	7.9	27
42,146,337	10,275,331	19,531,561	4,075,346	14,506,928	7,527,174	953,700	6.7	9.5	28
40,640,034	3,322,771	3,905,884	464,354	2,672,769	1,150,663	1,471,105	5.9	9.5	29
59,006,768	4,739,017	7,283,689	783,082	4,613,042	1,242,858	6,609,189	5.7	8.2	30
58,370,800	11,984,036	9,637,510	649,455	2,845,291	441,271	1,076,274	6.0	8.2	31
2,945,890	....	600	....	2,000	4,441	23,500	5.7	5.7	32
18,437,963	59,006	8,805	1,000	14,202	19,615	470,824	5.6	5.8	33
68,900						800	5.8	6.0	34
35,129,537	161,194	179,178	700	222,799	140,670	981,703	5.9	6.1	35
8,392,024	274,399	47,689	2,296	67,249	50,204	333,516	5.9	6.2	36
28,309,949	61,260	52,266	35,000	281,195	104,674	826,047	6.0	8.0	37
2,541,599	412,976	6,452,481	218,071	12,988,806	264,708	447,677	7.3	8.6	38
6,311,363	851,964	6,295,412	575,195	19,801,046	500,077	962,552	7.3	8.3	39
3,022,425	152,666	1,084,605	161,290	5,655,060	1,210,767	372,703	7.3	10.7	40
55,169,627	181,218	906,441	16,695	2,721,974	481,743	1,168,208	6.0	6.7	41
37,598,270	234,314	755,156	51,175	4,095,554	1,091,335	918,302	6.2	6.2	42
3,985,298	692,358	2,282,467	175,955	17,163,742	1,465,629	950,866	7.5	8.9	43
16,464,717	427,320	985,671	93,625	6,987,522	667,495	648,013	6.5	9.8	44
5,730,133	685,583	4,134,526	587,387	12,584,611	10,684,510	603,080	7.8	9.4	45
4,868,257	290,196	1,421,063	378,438	10,951,452	471,693	499,137	7.2	8.1	46
27,405,105	2,718,248	6,955,442	954,255	14,997,735	3,664,218	842,438	6.6	....	47
26,202,997	6,201,954	26,417,347	6,227,524	66,205,866	16,028,470	6,286,434	7.3	8.4	48
16,764,448	2,874,400	9,620,515	3,127,035	21,013,459	19,148,753	600,961	7.6	11.0	49
11,528,015	3,934,089	16,120,799	3,914,224	24,723,199	5,214,310	585,530	7.3	10.6	50
2,191,302	228,410	1,817,697	258,170	6,498,960	2,702,216	810,006	7.7	10.9	51
23,825,643	2,948,005	14,128,584	1,483,803	13,371,580	2,600,574	617,562	6.8	9.2	52
1,495,411	634,234	1,052,529	136,877	2,410,821	2,873,202	207,046	7.3	10.1	53
2,414,518	190,230	2,224,144	643,563	8,099,635	1,098,366	483,844	7.5	12.6	54
4,870,570	913,829	4,335,388	723,760	8,738,878	1,748,465	376,566	7.1	10.1	55
2,086,878	450,500	1,576,946	56,100	1,413,157	103,515	381,760	6.7	9.6	56
19,031,671	4,940,302	15,910,351	1,552,195	10,341,850	883,898	798,419	6.6	9.9	57
22,099,957	2,806,029	9,226,651	1,034,263	7,892,973	837,837	739,787	6.5	9.1	58
80,282,316	14,835,426	101,166,087	2,505,266	8,273,755	926,720	3,802,521	6.6	8.8	59

TABLE 73.—FARM EXPENDITURES FOR LABOR, FERTILIZER, AND FEED, BY DIVISIONS AND STATES: 1919 AND 1909.

DIVISION AND STATE.	LABOR.[1]		FERTILIZER.		FEED.	
	1919	1909	1919	1909	1919	1909
United States....	$1,356,403,452	$651,611,287	$326,399,800	$114,882,541	$1,097,452,187	$299,839,857
GEOGRAPHIC DIVISIONS:						
New England.......	53,756,424	34,500,407	18,322,697	9,407,759	69,538,522	34,613,964
Middle Atlantic......	124,005,769	78,021,579	41,438,394	18,221,474	149,363,497	54,696,044
East North Central..	238,760,412	117,880,195	30,589,412	8,058,881	197,070,423	40,611,121
West North Central..	342,082,814	135,924,234	6,168,742	983,216	307,390,867	76,207,557
South Atlantic.......	103,007,774	66,607,245	185,700,177	59,625,130	60,504,537	19,255,280
East South Central...	44,136,117	35,308,883	25,476,855	12,901,239	43,363,604	15,607,673
West South Central..	162,986,652	59,980,738	8,696,846	3,225,927	121,091,954	24,723,146
Mountain..........	106,419,196	46,939,012	808,518	159,342	68,635,906	13,204,509
Pacific..............	181,248,294	76,448,994	9,198,159	2,299,573	80,492,877	20,920,563
NEW ENGLAND:						
Maine...............	9,641,064	5,633,106	7,759,067	4,069,479	14,858,557	7,267,854
New Hampshire.....	4,520,816	3,374,126	526,180	512,580	8,725,716	4,614,938
Vermont...........	7,712,305	4,748,003	857,273	570,752	11,070,656	4,758,703
Massachusetts........	16,577,123	12,101,959	3,906,733	1,965,682	20,272,851	10,878,178
Rhode Island........	2,102,397	1,761,594	379,786	335,103	2,889,450	1,678,183
Connecticut.........	13,202,719	6,881,619	4,893,658	1,954,163	11,721,292	5,416,108
MIDDLE ATLANTIC:						
New York..........	64,324,931	41,312,014	15,067,371	7,142,265	82,966,321	29,545,703
New Jersey.........	18,074,198	11,097,727	10,742,682	4,277,604	14,719,159	5,947,181
Pennsylvania........	41,606,640	25,611,838	15,628,341	6,801,605	51,678,017	19,203,160
EAST NORTH CENTRAL:						
Ohio...............	46,427,807	25,631,185	13,206,018	4,180,485	40,378,027	8,445,761
Indiana.............	32,867,304	17,682,079	8,734,698	2,189,695	42,306,030	6,893,901
Illinois.............	79,383,697	36,308,376	2,996,403	615,594	64,528,040	13,915,628
Michigan............	31,944,861	19,063,082	4,872,543	945,354	21,938,870	5,682,915
Wisconsin............	48,136,743	19,195,473	779,750	127,753	27,919,456	5,672,916
WEST NORTH CENTRAL:						
Minnesota...........	49,811,218	22,330,149	432,680	74,653	22,940,650	5,041,925
Iowa...............	70,698,060	24,781,592	596,537	109,570	79,068,535	18,582,251
Missouri............	40,015,464	18,644,695	3,941,488	671,073	60,171,516	17,148,008
North Dakota.......	37,063,815	21,740,149	119,782	10,003	12,382,661	2,003,028
South Dakota.......	31,751,355	12,831,944	34,466	11,294	16,689,237	3,049,255
Nebraska...........	44,769,418	15,028,468	64,752	31,021	58,623,746	12,567,838
Kansas.............	67,873,484	20,567,237	979,037	75,602	57,514,522	17,815,252
SOUTH ATLANTIC:						
Delaware...........	2,807,879	1,612,471	1,222,329	864,577	1,490,252	337,841
Maryland...........	16,721,294	8,802,172	7,610,478	3,387,634	8,044,715	2,445,065
Dist. of Columbia....	173,066	238,833	23,267	16,975	170,758	130,077
Virginia............	20,422,610	13,354,194	17,277,705	6,932,455	12,400,193	3,504,660
West Virginia.......	5,815,727	4,035,764	1,709,546	528,937	5,639,713	1,938,233
North Carolina......	12,035,960	9,220,564	48,786,694	12,262,533	12,291,850	3,151,190
South Carolina......	15,184,138	10,770,758	52,546,795	15,162,017	5,903,625	1,830,815
Georgia.............	19,016,703	13,218,113	46,196,434	16,860,149	9,538,763	4,097,043
Florida.............	10,830,397	5,354,376	10,316,929	3,609,853	5,024,668	1,820,356
EAST SOUTH CENTRAL:						
Kentucky...........	18,152,309	12,243,851	3,597,449	1,350,720	16,016,669	4,014,998
Tennessee..........	11,226,472	8,448,059	3,525,133	1,216,296	11,165,456	3,570,551
Alabama............	7,724,138	7,454,748	14,066,108	7,630,952	5,920,837	4,041,486
Mississippi.........	7,033,198	7,162,225	4,288,165	2,703,271	10,260,642	3,980,638
WEST SOUTH CENTRAL:						
Arkansas...........	13,207,550	7,654,571	2,572,678	596,553	17,725,489	4,275,587
Louisiana...........	21,418,393	16,704,125	3,840,469	2,004,919	12,232,235	3,784,140
Oklahoma..........	40,615,418	9,837,541	452,492	29,092	30,372,146	5,863,373
Texas..............	87,745,291	25,784,501	1,831,207	595,363	60,762,084	10,800,046
MOUNTAIN:						
Montana............	21,344,016	10,930,477	126,232	12,323	19,791,034	1,741,071
Idaho..............	18,303,152	6,701,604	106,121	20,737	10,709,475	2,122,709
Wyoming..........	9,300,390	6,174,164	8,489	5,302	6,909,684	1,508,828
Colorado...........	28,292,008	10,818,403	284,448	67,118	10,400,076	1,032,155
New Mexico........	6,488,120	3,645,423	113,483	25,371	5,370,823	1,527,037
Arizona............	8,442,276	2,504,984	40,892	6,080	2,059,855	541,371
Utah...............	8,490,146	3,169,917	108,956	20,037	3,941,388	727,409
Nevada............	5,808,487	2,993,978	9,897	8,379	1,422,672	443,285
PACIFIC:						
Washington.........	34,121,457	15,370,931	525,637	87,023	20,721,880	5,045,297
Oregon............	21,030,685	11,101,864	489,524	68,557	13,390,428	3,198,363
California..........	126,096,152	49,976,199	8,182,998	2,143,993	46,380,569	12,676,903

[1] Represents expenditure in cash and value of rent and board furnished. For the United States, the amount expended in cash in 1919 was $1,098,604,590, and in 1909, $521,729,941; the value of rent and board furnished in 1919 was $257,798,862, and in 1909, $129,881,346.

TABLE 74.—COOPERATIVE MARKETING AND PURCHASING THROUGH FARMERS' ORGANIZATIONS, BY DIVISIONS AND STATES: 1919.

DIVISION AND STATE.	SALES THROUGH FARMERS' MARKETING ORGANIZATIONS.				PURCHASES THROUGH FARMERS' MARKETING ORGANIZATIONS.			
	Farms reporting.		Amount.		Farms reporting.		Amount.	
	Number.	Per cent of all farms.	Total.	Average per farm.	Number.	Per cent of all farms.	Total.	Average per farm.
United States.........	511,383	7.9	$721,983,639	$1,412	329,449	5.1	$84,615,669	$257
GEOGRAPHIC DIVISIONS:								
New England............	4,060	2.6	5,916,681	1,457	7,579	4.8	3,035,806	401
Middle Atlantic.........	33,854	8.0	61,224,128	1,808	17,884	4.2	6,193,647	346
East North Central......	144,339	13.3	132,639,450	919	83,518	7.7	14,305,931	171
West North Central.....	243,288	22.2	300,820,976	1,236	166,084	15.1	43,115,568	260
South Atlantic..........	9,517	0.8	20,639,686	2,169	12,230	1.1	2,607,639	213
East South Central......	12,705	1.2	5,271,001	415	5,285	0.5	763,054	144
West South Central.....	15,635	1.6	26,934,455	1,723	9,332	0.9	2,803,314	300
Mountain...............	12,785	5.2	17,443,431	1,364	13,875	5.7	3,769,213	272
Pacific................	35,200	15.0	151,093,831	4,292	13,662	5.8	8,021,497	587
NEW ENGLAND:								
Maine.................	1,264	2.6	1,421,022	1,124	3,407	7.1	1,498,395	440
New Hampshire.........	122	0.6	120,427	987	946	4.6	246,059	260
Vermont..............	1,239	4.3	1,449,389	1,170	1,672	5.8	510,305	305
Massachusetts.........	747	2.3	1,671,099	2,237	1,009	3.2	521,547	517
Rhode Island..........	95	2.3	222,078	2,338	86	2.1	30,534	355
Connecticut...........	593	2.6	1,032,666	1,741	459	2.0	228,966	499
MIDDLE ATLANTIC:								
New York.............	23,494	12.2	44,906,247	1,911	7,106	3.7	2,270,976	320
New Jersey...........	2,758	9.3	6,603,253	2,394	2,798	9.4	2,093,705	748
Pennsylvania..........	7,602	3.8	9,714,628	1,278	7,980	3.9	1,828,966	229
EAST NORTH CENTRAL:								
Ohio.................	19,952	7.8	18,762,020	940	21,250	8.3	3,197,047	150
Indiana..............	14,638	7.1	12,778,040	873	10,019	4.9	1,766,268	176
Illinois..............	24,797	10.5	47,920,487	1,933	12,303	5.2	3,333,667	271
Michigan.............	42,104	21.4	24,294,688	577	18,154	9.2	2,445,953	135
Wisconsin............	42,848	22.6	28,884,215	674	21,792	11.5	3,562,996	164
WEST NORTH CENTRAL:								
Minnesota............	78,314	43.9	82,760,459	1,057	29,611	16.6	6,642,162	224
Iowa................	43,350	20.3	59,403,626	1,370	32,530	15.2	6,760,952	208
Missouri.............	17,748	6.7	13,474,992	759	17,954	6.8	2,964,714	165
North Dakota.........	17,438	22.4	24,484,558	1,404	12,579	16.2	3,840,811	305
South Dakota.........	20,241	27.1	31,651,244	1,564	13,754	18.4	3,583,771	261
Nebraska............	32,543	26.2	44,755,140	1,375	27,335	22.0	9,660,107	353
Kansas..............	33,654	20.4	44,290,957	1,316	32,321	19.6	9,663,051	299
SOUTH ATLANTIC:								
Delaware.............	548	5.4	218,034	398	275	2.7	29,554	107
Maryland............	1,865	3.9	3,089,200	1,656	637	1.3	272,420	428
District of Columbia....								
Virginia.............	3,849	2.1	10,186,092	2,646	5,161	2.8	1,205,659	234
West Virginia.........	625	0.7	284,150	455	2,203	2.5	218,219	99
North Carolina........	850	0.3	663,227	780	2,976	1.1	421,142	142
South Carolina........	203	0.1	961,999	4,739	186	0.1	126,190	678
Georgia.............	210	0.1	890,605	4,241	411	0.1	65,446	159
Florida..............	1,367	2.5	4,346,379	3,180	381	0.7	269,009	706
EAST SOUTH CENTRAL:								
Kentucky.............	3,498	1.3	2,430,792	695	2,344	0.9	381,406	163
Tennessee............	1,255	0.5	607,671	484	1,174	0.5	133,270	114
Alabama.............	2,678	1.0	837,498	313	422	0.2	72,287	171
Mississippi...........	5,274	1.9	1,395,040	265	1,345	0.5	176,091	131
WEST SOUTH CENTRAL:								
Arkansas.............	2,885	1.2	4,726,491	1,638	1,072	0.5	173,722	162
Louisiana............	4,284	3.2	9,715,844	2,268	1,591	1.2	869,389	546
Oklahoma............	5,980	3.1	8,055,084	1,347	4,900	2.6	1,106,270	226
Texas...............	2,486	0.6	4,437,036	1,785	1,769	0.4	653,933	370
MOUNTAIN:								
Montana.............	1,948	3.4	1,538,303	790	2,926	5.1	871,192	298
Idaho...............	2,336	5.5	3,399,598	1,455	2,653	6.3	657,952	248
Wyoming............	370	2.3	646,748	1,748	611	3.9	137,403	225
Colorado............	5,847	9.8	9,303,346	1,591	5,613	9.4	1,658,358	295
New Mexico..........	975	3.3	1,047,105	1,074	574	1.9	220,026	383
Arizona.............	180	1.8	394,508	2,192	121	1.2	41,170	340
Utah................	1,127	4.4	1,105,523	981	1,377	5.4	183,112	133
Nevada.............	2	0.1	8,300	4,150				
PACIFIC:								
Washington..........	5,583	8.4	15,356,226	2,751	5,355	8.1	2,710,202	506
Oregon.............	3,845	7.7	7,746,624	2,015	2,515	5.0	990,166	394
California...........	25,772	21.9	127,990,981	4,966	5,792	4.9	4,321,129	746

TABLE 75.—MOTOR VEHICLES (AUTOMOBILES, MOTOR TRUCKS, AND TRACTORS) ON FARMS, BY DIVISIONS AND STATES: 1920.

DIVISION AND STATE.	AUTOMOBILES.			MOTOR TRUCKS.			TRACTORS.		
	Farms reporting.		Number of auto-mobiles.	Farms reporting.		Number of motor trucks.	Farms reporting.		Number of trac-tors.
	Number.	Per cent of all farms.		Number	Per cent of all farms.		Number.	Per cent of all farms.	
United States	1,979,564	30.7	2,146,362	131,551	2.0	139,169	229,332	3.6	246,083
GEOGRAPHIC DIVISIONS:									
New England	40,269	25.7	44,754	7,284	4.7	8,119	2,245	1.4	2,397
Middle Atlantic	149,599	35.2	164,939	20,472	4.8	22,011	13,240	3.1	14,140
East North Central	513,052	47.3	550,858	24,942	2.3	26,074	55,413	5.1	58,092
West North Central	631,631	57.6	693,032	32,331	2.9	33,375	92,123	8.4	97,884
South Atlantic	187,236	16.2	200,103	14,716	1.3	15,787	10,460	0.9	11,229
East South Central	81,830	7.8	86,141	4,869	0.5	5,153	5,044	0.5	5,379
West South Central	173,609	17.4	184,275	8,960	0.9	9,455	17,435	1.8	19,892
Mountain	91,698	37.6	98,727	7,168	2.9	7,589	15,865	6.5	17,513
Pacific	110,640	47.2	123,533	10,809	4.6	11,606	17,507	7.5	19,557
NEW ENGLAND:									
Maine	11,686	24.2	12,569	1,061	2.2	1,120	605	1.3	635
New Hampshire	4,797	23.4	5,263	663	3.2	717	196	1.0	207
Vermont	7,611	26.2	8,172	576	2.0	616	424	1.5	444
Massachusetts	8,181	25.6	9,309	3,136	9.8	3,535	540	1.7	592
Rhode Island	1,198	29.3	1,395	471	11.5	536	69	1.7	79
Connecticut	6,796	30.0	8,046	1,377	6.1	1,595	411	1.8	440
MIDDLE ATLANTIC:									
New York	68,003	35.2	74,753	8,636	4.5	9,259	7,021	3.6	7,497
New Jersey	11,731	39.5	13,695	3,075	10.4	3,380	845	2.8	946
Pennsylvania	69,865	34.5	76,491	8,761	4.3	9,372	5,374	2.7	5,697
EAST NORTH CENTRAL:									
Ohio	119,511	46.6	128,384	6,960	2.7	7,319	9,934	3.9	10,469
Indiana	95,238	46.4	102,122	3,501	1.7	3,671	8,871	4.3	9,230
Illinois	125,586	52.9	139,090	5,907	2.5	6,154	21,932	9.2	23,102
Michigan	78,919	40.2	82,437	4,681	2.4	4,886	5,584	2.8	5,884
Wisconsin	93,798	49.6	98,825	3,893	2.1	4,044	9,092	4.8	9,407
WEST NORTH CENTRAL:									
Minnesota	101,847	57.1	107,824	3,677	2.1	3,803	14,794	8.3	15,503
Iowa	156,081	73.1	177,558	8,669	4.1	8,910	19,427	9.1	20,270
Missouri	81,392	30.9	86,229	4,878	1.9	5,059	7,438	2.8	7,889
North Dakota	44,010	56.6	47,711	743	1.0	774	11,834	15.2	13,006
South Dakota	51,780	69.4	58,202	4,249	5.7	4,353	12,160	16.3	12,939
Nebraska	94,004	75.6	104,453	6,333	5.1	6,548	10,342	8.3	11,100
Kansas	102,517	62.0	111,055	3,782	2.3	3,928	16,128	9.8	17,177
SOUTH ATLANTIC:									
Delaware	3,693	36.4	4,014	283	2.8	304	220	2.2	239
Maryland	16,049	33.5	17,702	2,556	5.3	2,805	1,410	2.9	1,525
District of Columbia	50	24.5	58	29	14.2	29	1	0.5	1
Virginia	28,557	15.3	30,959	2,389	1.3	2,544	2,206	1.2	2,379
West Virginia	10,405	11.9	11,127	886	1.0	936	541	0.6	572
North Carolina	41,839	15.5	44,207	2,551	0.9	2,671	2,184	0.8	2,277
South Carolina	30,709	15.9	32,812	1,609	0.8	1,736	1,213	0.6	1,304
Georgia	47,173	15.2	49,841	2,913	0.9	3,145	2,083	0.7	2,252
Florida	8,761	16.2	9,383	1,500	2.8	1,617	602	1.1	680
EAST SOUTH CENTRAL:									
Kentucky	28,532	10.5	30,146	1,455	0.5	1,538	1,913	0.7	2,029
Tennessee	22,446	8.9	23,550	1,362	0.5	1,430	1,796	0.7	1,872
Alabama	15,906	6.2	16,592	1,114	0.4	1,180	737	0.3	811
Mississippi	14,946	5.5	15,853	938	0.3	1,005	598	0.2	667
WEST SOUTH CENTRAL:									
Arkansas	15,401	6.6	16,408	973	0.4	1,027	1,423	0.6	1,822
Louisiana	9,491	7.0	10,612	700	0.5	871	1,118	0.8	2,012
Oklahoma	49,017	25.5	52,063	2,070	1.1	2,155	5,786	3.0	6,210
Texas	99,697	22.9	105,292	5,124	1.2	5,399	8,084	1.9	9,048
MOUNTAIN:									
Montana	20,749	36.0	22,072	1,167	2.0	1,225	6,890	11.9	7,647
Idaho	16,651	39.5	17,646	779	1.9	837	1,468	3.5	1,587
Wyoming	6,180	39.2	6,705	554	3.5	591	969	6.2	1,075
Colorado	28,356	47.3	30,830	2,884	4.8	3,016	4,526	7.6	4,990
New Mexico	5,546	18.6	6,018	552	1.8	593	457	1.5	491
Arizona	4,534	45.5	5,082	527	5.3	581	820	8.2	930
Utah	8,246	32.1	8,657	544	2.1	572	553	2.2	583
Nevada	1,436	45.4	1,717	161	5.1	174	182	5.8	210
PACIFIC:									
Washington	27,626	41.7	29,792	3,172	4.8	3,371	2,474	3.7	2,635
Oregon	20,561	41.0	22,223	1,728	3.4	1,819	2,902	5.8	3,070
California	62,453	53.1	71,518	5,909	5.0	6,416	12,131	10.3	13,852

TABLE 76.—TELEPHONES, WATER, AND LIGHT ON FARMS, BY DIVISIONS AND STATES: 1920.

DIVISION AND STATE.	FARMS REPORTING TELEPHONES.		FARMS REPORTING WATER PIPED INTO HOUSE.		FARMS REPORTING GAS OR ELECTRIC LIGHT.	
	Number.	Per cent of all farms.	Number.	Per cent of all farms.	Number.	Per cent of all farms.
United States	2,498,493	38.7	643,899	10.0	452,620	7.0
GEOGRAPHIC DIVISIONS:						
New England	80,510	51.4	74,954	47.9	24,000	15.3
Middle Atlantic	189,344	44.5	98,936	23.3	60,102	14.1
East North Central	678,862	62.6	134,877	12.4	113,871	10.5
West North Central	762,442	69.5	107,015	9.8	97,847	8.9
South Atlantic	164,213	14.2	38,775	3.3	45,407	3.9
East South Central	196,692	18.7	15,999	1.5	21,720	2.1
West South Central	273,315	27.4	49,191	4.9	19,352	1.9
Mountain	62,503	25.6	26,343	10.8	25,161	10.3
Pacific	90,612	38.7	97,809	41.8	45,160	19.3
NEW ENGLAND:						
Maine	23,632	49.0	18,020	37.4	4,625	9.6
New Hampshire	10,166	49.5	10,765	52.5	2,322	11.3
Vermont	16,752	57.6	18,301	62.9	3,328	11.4
Massachusetts	16,537	51.7	16,893	52.8	9,062	28.3
Rhode Island	1,685	41.3	1,451	35.5	700	17.1
Connecticut	11,738	51.8	9,524	42.0	3,963	17.5
MIDDLE ATLANTIC:						
New York	91,973	47.6	45,487	23.5	24,882	12.9
New Jersey	9,484	31.9	7,047	27.7	4,551	15.3
Pennsylvania	87,887	43.5	46,402	22.9	30,669	15.2
EAST NORTH CENTRAL:						
Ohio	159,478	62.1	41,531	16.2	37,745	14.7
Indiana	136,140	66.4	23,476	11.4	20,584	10.0
Illinois	173,572	73.2	26,676	11.2	23,273	9.8
Michigan	97,874	49.8	29,729	15.1	15,695	8.0
Wisconsin	111,798	59.1	13,465	7.1	16,574	8.8
WEST NORTH CENTRAL:						
Minnesota	110,568	62.0	11,392	6.4	13,539	7.6
Iowa	183,852	86.1	33,851	15.9	32,552	15.3
Missouri	163,543	62.2	11,901	4.5	14,341	5.5
North Dakota	36,349	46.8	4,684	6.0	4,518	5.8
South Dakota	44,327	59.4	9,157	12.3	6,445	8.6
Nebraska	95,050	76.4	20,691	16.6	12,062	9.7
Kansas	128,753	77.9	15,339	9.3	14,390	8.7
SOUTH ATLANTIC:						
Delaware	2,763	27.2	752	7.4	397	3.9
Maryland	11,755	24.5	6,702	14.0	3,330	7.0
District of Columbia	67	32.8	51	25.0	52	25.5
Virginia	33,482	18.0	9,474	5.1	7,874	4.2
West Virginia	37,789	43.3	4,974	5.7	12,900	14.8
North Carolina	33,029	12.2	4,423	1.6	7,816	2.9
South Carolina	10,943	5.7	3,443	1.8	5,170	2.7
Georgia	29,861	9.6	5,615	1.8	5,826	1.9
Florida	4,524	8.4	3,341	6.2	2,042	3.8
EAST SOUTH CENTRAL:						
Kentucky	73,145	27.0	5,139	1.9	5,925	2.2
Tennessee	56,880	22.5	4,890	1.9	4,554	1.8
Alabama	38,407	15.0	2,987	1.2	8,345	3.3
Mississippi	28,260	10.4	2,983	1.1	2,896	1.1
WEST SOUTH CENTRAL:						
Arkansas	52,869	22.7	1,780	0.8	2,643	1.1
Louisiana	8,599	6.3	2,185	1.6	1,471	1.1
Oklahoma	71,613	37.3	6,646	3.5	7,010	3.7
Texas	140,234	32.2	38,580	8.8	8,228	1.9
MOUNTAIN:						
Montana	9,781	17.0	3,055	5.3	2,013	3.5
Idaho	13,837	32.9	5,240	12.4	5,982	14.2
Wyoming	4,449	28.3	1,035	6.6	717	4.6
Colorado	22,022	36.7	6,806	11.4	3,925	6.5
New Mexico	3,359	11.3	1,460	4.9	422	1.4
Arizona	1,638	16.4	1,988	19.9	592	5.9
Utah	6,295	24.5	6,179	24.1	11,125	43.4
Nevada	1,122	35.5	580	18.3	385	12.2
PACIFIC:						
Washington	27,952	42.2	18,967	28.6	9,178	13.8
Oregon	25,351	50.5	12,914	25.7	5,463	10.9
California	37,309	31.7	65,928	56.0	30,519	25.9

LIVE STOCK ON FARMS AND NOT ON FARMS.

TABLE 77.—VALUE OF LIVE STOCK ON FARMS IN THE UNITED STATES, BY CLASSES: 1920 AND 1910.

CLASS.	1920	1910	INCREASE.[1] Amount.	INCREASE.[1] Per cent.	PER CENT OF TOTAL. 1920	PER CENT OF TOTAL. 1910
Total..............	$8,013,324,808	[2] $4,925,173,610	$3,088,151,198	62.7	100.0	100.0
Domestic animals, total.....	7,623,089,398	4,760,060,093	2,863,029,305	60.1	95.1	96.6
Horses................	1,782,077,487	2,083,588,195	−301,510,708	−14.5	22.2	42.3
Mules.................	779,294,411	525,391,863	253,902,548	48.3	9.7	10.7
Asses and burros.........	8,198,242	13,200,112	−5,001,870	−37.9	0.1	0.3
Cattle..................	3,651,970,229	1,499,523,607	2,152,446,622	143.5	45.6	30.4
Sheep..................	395,401,286	232,841,585	162,559,701	69.8	4.9	4.7
Goats..................	17,565,363	6,176,423	11,388,940	184.4	0.2	0.1
Swine.................	988,582,380	399,338,308	589,244,072	147.6	12.3	8.1
Poultry, total..............	373,394,057	[3] 154,663,220	218,730,837	141.4	4.7	3.1
Chickens..............	349,508,867	140,193,129	209,315,738	149.3	4.4	2.8
Turkeys...............	12,904,989	6,605,818	6,299,171	95.4	0.2	0.1
Ducks.................	3,373,966	1,567,164	1,806,802	115.3	(4)	(4)
Geese.................	5,428,806	3,194,507	2,234,299	69.9	0.1	0.1
Guinea fowls..........	1,582,313	613,282	969,031	158.0	(4)	(4)
Pigeons...............	537,576	762,374	−224,798	−29.5	(4)	(4)
Ostriches.............	57,540	1,696,140	−1,638,600	−96.6	(4)	(4)
Hives of bees..............	16,841,353	10,373,615	6,467,738	62.3	0.2	0.2

[1] A minus sign (−) denotes decrease.
[2] Includes the value of special classes of animals (buffaloes, deer, etc.), not included under "Domestic animals," to the amount of $76,682.
[3] Includes the value of special classes of poultry (peafowls, pheasants), etc., to the amount of $30,806.
[4] Less than one-tenth of 1 per cent.

TABLE 78.—NUMBER AND VALUE OF LIVE STOCK ON FARMS IN THE UNITED STATES, BY CLASSES, AND NUMBER OF FARMS REPORTING: 1920 AND 1910.

[Figures for 1920 relate to Jan. 1; for 1910, to Apr. 15.]

CLASS.	FARMS REPORTING. 1920	FARMS REPORTING. 1910	NUMBER. 1920	NUMBER. 1910	VALUE. 1920	VALUE. 1910
Horses................	4,704,235	4,692,814	19,767,161	19,833,113	$1,782,077,487	$2,083,588,195
Mules.................	2,259,746	1,869,005	5,432,391	4,209,769	779,294,411	525,391,863
Asses and burros........	33,308	43,927	72,491	105,698	8,198,242	13,200,112
Cattle, total............	5,358,243	5,284,916	66,652,559	61,803,866	3,651,970,229	1,499,523,607
Beef cattle..........	1,841,053	....	35,288,100	....	1,766,550,258	....
Dairy cattle.........	4,565,753	....	31,364,459	....	1,885,419,971	....
Sheep.................	538,593	610,894	35,033,516	52,447,861	395,401,286	232,841,585
Goats.................	107,267	82,755	3,458,925	2,915,195	17,565,363	6,176,423
Swine.................	4,850,807	4,351,751	59,346,409	58,185,676	988,582,380	399,338,308
Poultry, total [1].........	5,852,040	5,585,032	372,825,264	295,880,190	373,394,057	154,663,220
Chickens.............	5,837,367	5,578,425	359,537,127	280,340,959	349,508,867	140,193,129
Turkeys..............	670,834	871,123	3,627,028	3,688,708	12,904,989	6,605,818
Ducks................	461,363	503,704	2,817,624	2,906,525	3,373,966	1,567,164
Geese................	527,836	662,324	2,939,203	4,431,980	5,428,806	3,194,507
Guinea fowls........	383,632	339,538	2,410,421	1,765,031	1,582,313	613,282
Pigeons..............	77,769	109,407	1,493,630	2,730,994	537,576	762,374
Ostriches............	4	29	231	5,361	57,540	1,696,140
Hives of bees..........	540,917	585,955	3,467,396	3,445,006	16,841,353	10,373,615

[1] Figures for 1910 include special classes of poultry (peafowls, pheasants, etc.).

TABLE 79.—NUMBER OF EACH CLASS OF LIVE STOCK ON FARMS IN THE UNITED STATES: 1850 TO 1920.

[Figures for 1920 relate to Jan. 1; for 1910, to Apr. 15; and for earlier years, to June 1.]

CLASS.	1920	1910	1900	1890	1880	1870	1860	1850
All horses, mules, and asses and burros....	25,272,043	24,148,580	21,625,800	17,581,318	12,170,296	8,270,785	7,400,322	4,896,050
Horses...........	19,767,161	19,833,113	18,267,020	15,266,244	10,357,488	7,145,370	6,249,174	4,336,719
Mules [1]...........	5,432,391	4,209,769	3,264,615	2,251,876	1,812,808	1,125,415	1,151,148	559,331
Asses and burros [1]	72,491	105,698	94,165	63,198	....	....	....	....
All cattle..............	66,652,559	61,803,866	67,719,410	57,648,792	39,675,533	23,820,608	25,620,019	17,778,907
Dairy cows [2].....	19,675,297	20,625,432	17,135,633	16,511,950	12,443,120	8,935,332	8,585,735	6,385,094
Sheep..............	35,033,516	52,447,861	61,503,713	40,876,312	42,192,074	28,477,951	22,471,275	21,723,220
Goats [3]...............	3,458,925	2,915,125	1,870,599	....	....	....	....	....
Swine..............	59,346,409	58,185,676	62,868,041	57,426,859	49,772,670	25,134,569	33,512,867	30,354,213
Poultry [4]...........	372,825,264	295,880,190	250,624,038	285,609,440	125,507,322	....	....	....
Hives of bees [5]......	3,467,396	3,445,006	4,108,239	....	....	....	....	....

[1] Prior to 1890 asses and burros were included with mules.
[2] Figures for all years except 1910 represent dairy cows and heifers 2 years old and over on the census date; for 1910, cows and heifers 15½ months old and over. For comparison with 1920, the number of dairy cows and heifers 2 years old and over on Jan. 1, 1910, has been estimated at 17,125,471.
[3] Goats not reported prior to 1900. [4] Poultry not reported prior to 1880. [5] Bees not reported prior to 1900.

TABLE 80.—NUMBER AND VALUE OF LIVE STOCK ON FARMS IN THE UNITED STATES (DETAILED CLASSIFICATION): 1920.

CLASS.	Number.	Value.
Total..........	....	$8,013,324,808
Domestic animals, total..........	....	7,623,089,398
Horses, total..........	19,767,161	1,782,077,487
Colts under 1 year of age..........	1,198,236	42,635,364
Colts 1 year old and under 2 years..........	1,333,480	68,629,105
Mares 2 years old and over..........	9,035,949	870,611,458
Geldings 2 years old and over..........	8,055,590	769,427,198
Stallions 2 years old and over..........	129,361	30,322,300
Unclassified..........	14,545	452,062
Mules, total..........	5,432,391	779,294,411
Mule colts under 1 year of age..........	389,279	24,285,116
Mule colts 1 year old and under 2 years..........	391,418	38,692,981
Mules 2 years old and over..........	4,651,694	716,316,314
Asses and burros..........	72,491	8,198,242
Cattle, total..........	66,652,559	3,651,970,229
Beef cattle, total..........	35,288,100	1,766,550,258
Calves under 1 year of age..........	8,607,938	213,163,872
Heifers 1 year old and under 2 years..........	3,981,205	158,519,176
Cows and heifers 2 years old and over..........	12,624,996	739,153,095
Steers 1 year old and under 2 years..........	4,650,347	225,197,635
Steers 2 years old and over..........	4,629,778	350,217,938
Bulls 1 year old and over..........	725,165	77,809,896
Unclassified..........	68,671	2,488,646
Dairy cattle, total..........	31,364,459	1,885,419,971
Calves under 1 year of age..........	6,867,991	142,374,321
Heifers 1 year old and under 2 years..........	4,048,851	169,159,243
Cows and heifers 2 years old and over..........	19,675,297	1,507,513,140
Bulls 1 year old and over..........	772,320	66,373,267
Sheep, total..........	35,033,516	395,401,286
Lambs under 1 year of age..........	8,925,815	78,203,972
Ewes 1 year old and over..........	23,518,631	283,564,609
Rams 1 year old and over..........	808,808	17,022,643
Wethers 1 year old and over..........	1,496,576	14,318,301
Unclassified..........	283,686	2,291,761
Goats, total..........	3,458,925	17,565,363
Kids under 1 year of age, raised for fleeces..........	511,573	2,240,572
Goats 1 year old and over, raised for fleeces..........	1,590,018	9,970,206
All other goats..........	1,357,334	5,354,585
Swine, total..........	59,346,409	988,582,380
Pigs under 6 months old..........	26,172,239	190,251,923
Sows and gilts for breeding, 6 months old and over..........	11,416,471	336,249,473
Boars for breeding, 6 months old and over..........	925,340	37,542,944
All other hogs, 6 months old and over..........	20,827,938	424,485,466
Unclassified..........	4,421	52,574
Poultry, total..........	372,825,264	373,394,057
Chickens..........	359,537,127	349,508,867
Turkeys..........	3,627,028	12,904,989
Ducks..........	2,817,624	3,373,966
Geese..........	2,939,203	5,428,806
Guinea fowls..........	2,410,421	1,582,313
Pigeons..........	1,493,630	537,576
Ostriches..........	231	57,540
Hives of bees..........	3,467,396	16,841,353

TABLE 81.—VALUE OF LIVE STOCK ON FARMS, BY CLASSES, WITH AVERAGE PER

	DIVISION AND STATE.	ALL LIVE STOCK.		DOMESTIC ANIMALS.	
		1920	1910 [1]	1920	1910
1	United States	$8,013,324,808	$4,925,173,610	$7,623,089,398	$4,760,060,093
	GEOGRAPHIC DIVISIONS:				
2	New England	163,163,485	97,896,823	152,694,393	92,462,323
3	Middle Atlantic	588,394,093	349,159,535	548,307,178	330,213,413
4	East North Central	1,521,644,117	976,329,922	1,434,093,602	935,456,253
5	West North Central	2,359,001,112	1,551,708,097	2,256,619,648	1,505,717,901
6	South Atlantic	647,163,431	366,534,152	606,008,093	351,328,058
7	East South Central	579,707,988	369,034,607	546,400,792	356,043,964
8	West South Central	1,019,779,165	589,837,078	980,513,030	576,926,692
9	Mountain	729,234,483	388,746,520	718,044,372	383,272,141
10	Pacific	405,236,934	235,926,876	380,408,290	228,639,348
	NEW ENGLAND:				
11	Maine	39,780,102	25,161,839	37,458,596	23,989,561
12	New Hampshire	19,160,923	11,910,478	17,799,036	11,237,764
13	Vermont	42,385,331	22,642,766	41,151,827	21,990,630
14	Massachusetts	33,524,157	20,741,366	30,512,291	19,208,712
15	Rhode Island	4,840,279	3,276,472	4,335,833	2,902,316
16	Connecticut	23,472,693	14,163,902	21,436,810	13,133,340
	MIDDLE ATLANTIC:				
17	New York	313,554,695	183,090,844	297,224,282	174,560,658
18	New Jersey	33,064,757	24,588,639	31,662,357	22,325,469
19	Pennsylvania	238,774,641	141,480,052	219,420,539	133,327,286
	EAST NORTH CENTRAL:				
20	Ohio	287,655,118	197,332,112	266,551,496	187,523,324
21	Indiana	261,264,188	173,860,101	244,164,616	165,867,178
22	Illinois	446,154,064	308,804,431	420,213,170	296,619,153
23	Michigan	204,258,632	137,803,795	192,145,492	131,746,348
24	Wisconsin	322,312,115	158,529,483	311,018,828	153,700,250
	WEST NORTH CENTRAL:				
25	Minnesota	305,163,825	161,641,146	293,373,818	156,771,855
26	Iowa	613,926,268	393,003,196	585,489,568	380,201,586
27	Missouri	389,839,045	285,839,108	363,734,334	273,366,662
28	North Dakota	157,034,635	108,249,866	153,361,490	106,761,317
29	South Dakota	238,568,263	127,229,200	232,364,625	124,841,010
30	Nebraska	336,443,784	222,222,004	326,014,912	217,849,050
31	Kansas	318,025,292	253,523,577	302,280,901	245,926,421
	SOUTH ATLANTIC:				
32	Delaware	8,600,665	6,817,123	7,373,260	6,243,368
33	Maryland	48,071,250	32,570,134	43,784,464	30,649,961
34	District of Columbia	246,366	152,840	230,183	145,573
35	Virginia	121,969,281	74,891,438	112,561,591	71,192,843
36	West Virginia	67,261,153	43,336,073	62,571,449	41,318,436
37	North Carolina	119,152,672	62,649,984	111,295,312	60,050,731
38	South Carolina	91,518,155	45,131,380	87,073,365	43,790,143
39	Georgia	155,043,349	80,393,993	147,813,842	78,118,098
40	Florida	35,300,540	20,561,187	33,304,627	19,818,905
	EAST SOUTH CENTRAL:				
41	Kentucky	158,387,284	117,486,662	148,563,339	112,605,412
42	Tennessee	173,522,135	110,706,078	162,232,187	106,608,122
43	Alabama	112,824,748	65,594,834	107,342,204	63,574,674
44	Mississippi	134,973,821	75,247,033	128,263,062	73,255,756
	WEST SOUTH CENTRAL:				
45	Arkansas	127,852,580	74,058,292	121,372,537	71,794,486
46	Louisiana	83,072,876	44,699,485	79,208,305	43,314,683
47	Oklahoma	215,927,703	152,432,792	204,869,158	148,652,983
48	Texas	592,926,006	318,646,509	575,063,030	313,164,540
	MOUNTAIN;				
49	Montana	154,189,567	85,662,107	149,653,210	84,999,659
50	Idaho	96,208,693	49,775,309	94,438,910	49,076,971
51	Wyoming	87,884,516	65,605,510	87,093,572	65,384,559
52	Colorado	160,976,580	70,161,344	157,619,235	68,840,485
53	New Mexico	93,626,418	43,494,679	92,756,492	43,191,913
54	Arizona	52,447,001	26,050,870	51,555,815	24,376,530
55	Utah	54,008,183	28,781,691	52,973,251	28,330,215
56	Nevada	29,893,525	19,213,930	29,540,877	19,071,809
	PACIFIC:				
57	Washington	82,316,130	48,865,110	77,572,066	47,370,775
58	Oregon	101,779,342	59,461,828	98,457,779	58,243,921
59	California	221,141,462	127,599,938	204,378,445	123,024,652

[1] Includes the value of special classes of animals (buffaloes, deer, etc.), not included under "Domestic animals," to the amount of $76,682.

FARM AND PER CENT DISTRIBUTION, BY DIVISIONS AND STATES: 1920 AND 1910.

POULTRY.		BEES.		AVERAGE VALUE OF ALL LIVE STOCK PER FARM.		PER CENT DISTRIBUTION OF VALUE OF ALL LIVE STOCK.		
1920	1910 ²	1920	1910	1920	1910	1920	1910	
$373,394,057	$154,663,220	$16,841,353	$10,373,615	$1,243	$774	100.0	100.0	1
10,150,242	5,238,461	318,850	195,959	1,042	519	2.04	1.99	2
38,312,719	17,775,385	1,774,196	1,166,587	1,384	745	7.34	7.09	3
84,999,901	39,070,998	2,550,614	1,800,931	1,403	869	18.99	19.82	4
100,125,035	44,226,368	2,256,429	1,729,683	2,151	1,398	29.44	31.51	5
38,825,235	13,631,507	2,330,103	1,574,577	558	330	8.08	7.44	6
31,412,143	11,873,198	1,895,053	1,117,145	551	354	7.23	7.49	7
37,393,990	11,910,631	1,872,145	997,825	1,024	625	12.73	11.98	8
9,432,948	4,656,963	1,757,163	784,056	2,987	2,119	9.10	7.89	9
22,741,844	6,279,709	2,086,800	1,006,852	1,731	1,242	5.06	4.79	10
2,219,332	1,131,921	102,174	40,357	825	419	0.50	0.51	11
1,334,836	649,121	27,051	23,593	934	440	0.24	0.24	12
1,167,717	607,787	65,787	44,349	1,458	692	0.53	0.46	13
2,951,001	1,492,961	60,865	39,683	1,048	562	0.42	0.42	14
498,257	368,018	6,189	6,138	1,185	619	0.06	0.07	15
1,979,099	988,653	56,784	41,839	1,036	528	0.29	0.29	16
15,348,600	7,879,388	981,813	646,848	1,623	849	3.91	3.72	17
4,324,584	2,221,610	77,816	41,560	1,214	734	0.45	0.50	18
18,639,535	7,674,387	714,567	478,179	1,181	645	2.98	2.87	19
20,693,940	9,532,672	409,682	275,726	1,121	725	3.59	4.01	20
16,757,365	7,762,015	342,207	230,478	1,274	807	3.26	3.53	21
25,234,061	11,696,650	706,833	487,733	1,881	1,226	5.57	6.27	22
11,587,814	5,610,958	525,326	446,464	1,040	666	2.55	2.80	23
10,726,721	4,468,703	566,566	360,530	1,703	895	4.02	3.22	24
11,405,427	4,646,960	384,580	221,781	1,710	1,035	3.81	3.28	25
27,779,633	12,269,881	657,067	517,329	2,876	1,811	7.66	7.98	26
25,470,023	11,870,972	634,688	584,549	1,482	1,031	4.86	5.80	27
3,667,531	1,485,463	5,614	3,086	2,021	1,456	1.96	2.20	28
6,126,335	2,356,465	77,303	31,650	3,196	1,639	2.98	2.58	29
10,222,546	4,219,158	206,326	152,676	2,704	1,714	4.20	4.51	30
15,453,540	7,377,469	290,851	218,612	1,924	1,426	3.97	5.15	31
1,215,586	560,146	11,819	13,609	848	629	0.11	0.14	32
4,216,105	1,858,570	70,681	61,603	1,003	666	0.60	0.66	33
16,013	6,477	170	790	1,208	704	(³)	(³)	34
8,909,808	3,395,962	497,882	302,623	655	407	1.52	1.52	35
4,230,975	1,628,700	458,729	388,937	771	448	0.84	0.88	36
7,324,880	2,212,570	532,480	386,683	442	247	1.49	1.27	37
4,263,068	1,206,615	181,722	134,622	475	256	1.14	0.92	38
6,879,535	2,088,653	349,972	187,242	499	276	1.93	1.63	39
1,769,265	673,814	226,648	98,468	654	412	0.44	0.42	40
9,256,715	4,461,871	567,230	419,379	585	453	1.98	2.39	41
10,591,690	3,757,337	698,258	340,619	686	450	2.17	2.25	42
5,098,288	1,807,239	384,256	212,921	441	250	1.41	1.33	43
6,465,450	1,846,751	245,309	144,226	496	274	1.68	1.53	44
6,143,635	2,063,432	336,408	200,049	550	345	1.60	1.50	45
3,738,883	1,326,614	125,688	58,188	613	371	1.04	0.91	46
10,836,525	3,713,943	222,020	64,261	1,125	801	2.69	3.09	47
16,674,947	4,806,642	1,188,029	675,327	1,360	763	7.40	6.47	48
1,994,289	628,436	129,058	32,112	2,673	3,268	1.92	1.74	49
1,489,053	598,190	280,730	100,148	2,285	1,616	1.20	1.01	50
634,793	194,078	156,151	20,493	5,581	5,971	1.10	1.33	51
2,924,006	1,012,251	433,339	308,608	2,686	1,520	2.01	1.42	52
752,235	256,466	117,691	46,300	3,137	1,219	1.17	0.88	53
640,595	1,545,966	250,591	104,374	5,258	2,823	0.65	0.53	54
814,566	327,908	220,366	123,568	2,105	1,328	0.67	0.58	55
183,411	93,668	169,237	48,453	9,451	7,145	0.37	0.39	56
4,389,759	1,367,440	354,305	126,895	1,242	870	1.03	0.99	57
3,058,515	1,067,743	263,048	150,164	2,027	1,307	1.27	1.21	58
15,293,570	3,844,526	1,469,447	729,793	1,879	1,447	2.76	2.59	59

² Includes the value of peafowls, pheasants, and India jungle fowls to the amount of $30,806.
³ Less than one-hundredth of 1 per cent.

TABLE 82.—AVERAGE VALUE OF SPECIFIED CLASSES OF DOMESTIC ANIMALS ON FARMS, BY DIVISIONS AND STATES: 1920 AND 1910.

DIVISION AND STATE.	HORSES.		MULES.		ALL CATTLE.		SHEEP.		SWINE.	
	1920	1910	1920	1910	1920	1910	1920	1910	1920	1910
United States.....	$90.15	$105.06	$143.45	$124.80	$54.79	$24.26	$11.29	$4.44	$16.66	$6.86
GEOGRAPHIC DIVISIONS:										
New England.........	149.71	124.19	150.51	163.64	72.39	31.60	10.95	4.29	21.74	10.09
Middle Atlantic.......	132.98	130.21	150.80	146.83	87.93	32.77	11.88	4.85	18.86	8.18
East North Central....	93.63	111.17	120.50	121.05	64.76	27.70	10.56	4.09	17.72	7.10
West North Central...	82.21	110.91	124.58	126.47	53.26	25.48	11.86	4.60	20.42	8.62
South Atlantic........	113.57	109.22	180.34	143.87	44.21	18.50	9.82	3.61	11.13	3.83
East South Central...	105.26	103.16	144.30	124.63	38.62	19.13	10.08	3.73	10.47	4.70
West South Central...	83.72	77.74	136.31	112.99	44.96	18.96	11.78	3.29	11.86	4.65
Mountain.............	69.20	78.91	104.25	106.78	51.69	24.13	11.35	4.90	16.33	7.98
Pacific..............	82.15	99.85	116.39	130.38	59.75	25.76	11.56	4.02	16.36	7.02
NEW ENGLAND:										
Maine................	169.38	133.53	158.41	202.36	60.75	30.35	9.98	3.94	21.25	10.88
New Hampshire......	136.64	113.92	139.90	152.21	69.15	31.22	11.15	4.39	21.39	11.15
Vermont.............	134.93	106.35	152.94	124.80	65.45	27.49	11.53	4.55	19.34	10.28
Massachusetts........	153.56	134.90	133.29	161.88	92.98	37.03	12.55	4.78	22.45	9.50
Rhode Island.........	148.64	149.18	120.49	177.06	97.78	38.34	13.64	4.81	25.73	8.81
Connecticut.........	139.11	123.85	156.99	174.81	82.87	34.46	14.31	5.01	23.48	9.03
MIDDLE ATLANTIC:										
New York...........	145.03	135.44	163.28	160.54	92.73	34.28	13.30	5.20	19.47	8.86
New Jersey..........	132.93	135.09	158.35	153.87	102.24	37.64	13.92	5.25	18.70	7.67
Pennsylvania........	120.22	123.79	148.36	144.94	79.63	29.77	10.21	4.46	18.57	7.80
EAST NORTH CENTRAL:										
Ohio................	94.65	108.67	115.35	121.48	61.54	27.97	9.05	3.82	15.72	6.25
Indiana.............	93.00	107.07	119.46	117.78	61.14	28.69	11.85	4.42	16.79	6.57
Illinois.............	91.54	112.44	122.59	122.71	65.37	30.10	12.46	4.57	19.44	7.73
Michigan............	93.20	116.90	112.36	133.47	64.13	27.04	11.32	4.18	17.74	7.83
Wisconsin...........	97.44	111.58	112.33	110.05	68.40	25.18	11.02	3.95	18.76	7.53
WEST NORTH CENTRAL:										
Minnesota...........	89.01	118.26	103.83	126.88	50.06	21.43	11.29	4.22	21.94	9.16
Iowa................	91.81	119.28	123.18	136.01	56.76	26.72	11.80	5.02	22.41	9.24
Missouri............	82.19	106.18	131.02	126.75	57.15	28.45	12.39	4.36	15.83	7.20
North Dakota........	84.34	128.28	99.14	149.32	50.89	23.81	11.96	4.29	19.39	9.51
South Dakota........	69.83	109.72	108.42	134.31	51.10	23.62	12.61	4.91	22.01	10.29
Nebraska............	75.21	101.95	117.08	124.38	51.89	24.92	10.34	5.07	20.98	8.63
Kansas..............	77.93	98.30	120.55	122.98	51.76	26.16	11.54	4.44	16.96	8.24
SOUTH ATLANTIC:										
Delaware............	78.29	104.39	123.09	128.75	72.98	29.98	11.92	4.73	15.62	6.86
Maryland............	97.89	108.00	126.87	134.27	71.86	27.35	12.26	4.82	13.61	5.86
District of Columbia..	118.05	97.56	143.31	110.57	167.98	76.69	13.00	......	20.00	14.11
Virginia.............	104.95	105.49	139.66	126.55	56.38	24.59	11.66	4.10	11.54	5.22
West Virginia........	105.41	103.25	122.77	114.34	57.41	25.57	9.90	3.74	13.26	6.36
North Carolina.......	127.79	110.91	170.21	135.65	44.66	17.91	8.65	2.61	12.59	3.78
South Carolina.......	147.61	127.08	202.12	153.28	46.51	18.18	4.63	2.17	12.68	3.81
Georgia.............	133.67	118.22	191.92	148.89	30.46	13.02	4.48	1.64	9.93	3.04
Florida.............	118.03	106.37	184.89	151.97	23.09	10.96	4.92	2.25	7.60	2.28
EAST SOUTH CENTRAL:										
Kentucky............	96.94	101.11	120.82	117.32	47.82	25.95	11.17	4.09	10.28	6.00
Tennessee...........	111.92	112.44	144.80	127.24	44.21	20.76	11.04	3.78	10.63	5.28
Alabama.............	111.06	100.65	150.64	127.77	30.73	14.45	5.92	2.10	10.24	3.44
Mississippi..........	106.69	93.90	159.95	125.23	31.95	15.08	5.34	2.13	10.71	3.80
WEST SOUTH CENTRAL:										
Arkansas............	95.87	90.89	147.99	122.09	32.64	15.04	8.26	2.27	9.30	3.40
Louisiana...........	87.88	65.03	157.39	118.77	33.10	14.42	5.18	1.92	8.87	2.88
Oklahoma...........	79.54	85.67	118.50	111.33	42.05	22.11	10.66	4.06	13.04	6.52
Texas...............	82.99	71.81	134.45	109.51	49.64	19.18	12.30	3.48	13.90	4.98
MOUNTAIN:										
Montana............	72.19	85.82	118.33	106.68	58.29	29.13	12.37	5.39	17.29	8.65
Idaho..............	83.13	100.28	104.82	119.25	50.89	24.97	12.41	5.28	14.86	7.84
Wyoming...........	56.89	79.63	100.22	121.55	57.10	29.38	13.04	5.50	16.26	8.89
Colorado...........	75.63	93.13	108.75	122.02	54.04	27.50	10.07	4.81	17.34	8.75
New Mexico........	33.08	43.83	92.04	97.95	48.53	18.87	9.40	3.61	16.64	6.07
Arizona............	42.19	42.28	118.03	100.79	43.19	17.73	8.08	3.59	17.85	6.61
Utah...............	76.85	86.45	68.10	69.17	44.76	21.70	11.16	4.73	13.61	6.93
Nevada.............	55.63	55.08	71.74	83.92	45.75	21.72	11.21	4.42	12.92	6.56
PACIFIC:										
Washington.........	84.58	105.79	126.92	145.78	63.84	30.32	12.42	4.06	19.07	8.13
Oregon.............	70.80	92.68	110.58	119.45	56.18	24.23	12.20	4.53	17.48	7.22
California...........	88.01	100.45	113.88	129.25	60.10	25.41	10.79	3.45	15.23	6.66

TABLE 83.—HORSES ON FARMS—FARMS REPORTING, NUMBER, AND VALUE, BY DIVISIONS AND STATES: 1920 AND 1910.

DIVISION AND STATE.	FARMS REPORTING.		NUMBER.		VALUE.	
	1920	1910	1920	1910	1920	1910
United States	4,704,235	4,692,814	19,767,161	19,833,113	$1,782,077,487	$2,083,588,195
GEOGRAPHIC DIVISIONS:						
New England	127,369	149,651	305,045	354,755	45,667,281	44,058,076
Middle Atlantic	370,349	399,530	1,114,758	1,229,686	148,244,453	160,111,303
East North Central	989,270	1,018,820	4,113,650	4,401,442	385,162,836	489,290,485
West North Central	1,026,318	1,032,768	6,942,499	6,794,192	570,718,067	753,512,291
South Atlantic	534,527	535,349	1,039,043	1,111,187	118,002,739	121,359,125
East South Central	563,532	549,941	1,045,677	1,144,599	110,068,837	118,071,299
West South Central	688,126	686,369	2,160,487	2,349,029	180,865,938	182,618,200
Mountain	221,720	159,890	2,075,655	1,427,057	143,635,651	112,606,228
Pacific	183,024	160,556	970,347	1,021,166	79,711,685	101,961,188
NEW ENGLAND:						
Maine	40,238	47,292	94,350	107,574	15,980,681	14,364,756
New Hampshire	16,673	20,960	38,194	46,229	5,218,893	5,266,389
Vermont	25,789	28,147	77,231	80,781	10,421,141	8,591,357
Massachusetts	23,671	28,173	50,605	64,283	7,771,029	8,671,997
Rhode Island	3,176	4,113	6,540	9,547	972,111	1,424,177
Connecticut	17,822	20,966	38,125	46,341	5,303,426	5,739,400
MIDDLE ATLANTIC:						
New York	171,524	186,435	536,171	591,008	77,762,412	80,043,302
New Jersey	24,935	28,732	72,621	88,922	9,653,169	12,012,512
Pennsylvania	173,890	184,363	505,966	549,756	60,828,872	68,055,489
EAST NORTH CENTRAL:						
Ohio	231,451	243,301	810,692	910,224	76,729,266	98,910,638
Indiana	185,784	195,268	717,233	813,644	66,703,216	87,118,468
Illinois	217,807	235,407	1,296,852	1,452,887	118,708,874	163,363,400
Michigan	176,259	184,267	605,509	610,033	56,433,765	71,312,474
Wisconsin	177,969	160,577	683,364	614,654	66,587,715	68,585,505
WEST NORTH CENTRAL:						
Minnesota	167,344	142,846	932,794	753,184	83,027,777	89,068,872
Iowa	203,642	209,812	1,386,522	1,492,226	127,297,231	177,999,124
Missouri	232,866	246,865	906,220	1,073,387	74,482,800	113,976,563
North Dakota	75,601	69,945	855,682	650,599	72,168,452	83,461,739
South Dakota	72,156	70,782	817,058	669,362	57,051,132	73,442,978
Nebraska	118,764	123,977	961,396	1,008,378	72,306,803	102,804,907
Kansas	155,945	168,481	1,082,827	1,147,056	84,383,872	112,758,108
SOUTH ATLANTIC:						
Delaware	9,220	9,857	27,752	33,065	2,172,609	3,451,791
Maryland	41,973	42,374	141,341	155,438	13,835,411	16,787,467
District of Columbia	140	195	311	564	36,712	55,026
Virginia	133,570	127,758	312,465	330,424	32,791,799	34,857,610
West Virginia	69,021	70,777	169,148	179,991	17,829,634	18,583,381
North Carolina	116,508	109,208	171,436	166,151	21,907,650	18,428,134
South Carolina	61,932	58,633	77,517	79,847	11,442,492	10,147,178
Georgia	76,783	87,257	100,503	120,067	13,434,117	14,193,839
Florida	25,380	29,290	38,570	45,640	4,552,315	4,854,699
EAST SOUTH CENTRAL:						
Kentucky	181,378	175,945	382,442	443,034	37,075,671	44,796,120
Tennessee	161,743	153,838	317,921	349,709	35,582,960	39,320,044
Alabama	89,542	91,508	130,462	135,636	14,488,541	13,651,284
Mississippi	130,869	128,650	214,852	216,220	22,921,665	20,303,851
WEST SOUTH CENTRAL:						
Arkansas	125,706	124,393	251,926	254,716	24,151,061	23,152,209
Louisiana	88,672	79,565	178,756	181,286	15,709,070	11,789,695
Oklahoma	160,852	163,204	738,443	742,959	58,734,170	63,651,661
Texas	312,896	319,207	991,362	1,170,068	82,271,637	84,024,635
MOUNTAIN:						
Montana	53,019	22,883	668,723	315,956	48,277,891	27,115,764
Idaho	38,067	27,367	293,123	197,772	24,368,376	19,832,423
Wyoming	14,325	9,763	198,295	156,062	11,281,294	12,426,838
Colorado	54,728	41,607	420,704	294,035	31,816,018	27,382,926
New Mexico	27,053	27,812	182,686	179,525	9,696,377	7,868,314
Arizona	8,500	8,309	136,167	99,578	5,744,671	4,209,726
Utah	23,111	19,684	125,471	115,676	9,642,418	9,999,835
Nevada	2,917	2,465	50,486	68,453	2,808,606	3,770,402
PACIFIC:						
Washington	52,569	45,634	296,381	280,572	25,069,336	29,680,849
Oregon	42,641	38,803	271,559	271,708	19,225,842	25,181,143
California	87,814	76,119	402,407	468,886	35,416,507	47,099,196

TABLE 84.—HORSES ON FARMS—NUMBER, BY AGE AND SEX, BY DIVISIONS AND STATES: 1920.

DIVISION AND STATE.	Total.[1]	Colts under 1 year of age.	Colts 1 year old and under 2 years.	Mares 2 years old and over.	Geldings 2 years old and over.	Stallions 2 years old and over.
United States	19,767,161	1,198,236	1,333,480	9,035,949	8,055,590	129,361
GEOGRAPHIC DIVISIONS:						
New England	305,045	6,670	5,739	106,406	183,601	2,629
Middle Atlantic	1,114,758	27,779	29,734	446,171	604,749	6,325
East North Central	4,113,650	173,546	223,892	2,028,965	1,669,486	17,761
West North Central	6,942,499	476,314	565,879	3,280,722	2,582,714	36,870
South Atlantic	1,039,043	34,319	41,892	460,475	491,103	11,254
East South Central	1,045,677	53,775	46,624	495,629	439,852	9,797
West South Central	2,160,487	133,044	136,312	948,752	924,957	17,422
Mountain	2,075,655	231,542	217,144	846,751	744,260	21,413
Pacific	970,347	61,247	66,264	422,078	414,868	5,890
NEW ENGLAND:						
Maine	94,350	1,732	1,894	33,703	56,301	720
New Hampshire	38,194	851	649	13,492	22,894	308
Vermont	77,231	2,250	2,272	31,740	40,335	634
Massachusetts	50,605	1,111	529	14,980	33,461	524
Rhode Island	6,540	129	63	2,042	4,189	117
Connecticut	38,125	597	332	10,449	26,421	326
MIDDLE ATLANTIC:						
New York	536,171	12,952	12,890	223,077	284,333	2,919
New Jersey	72,621	954	791	19,731	50,861	284
Pennsylvania	505,966	13,873	16,053	203,363	269,555	3,122
EAST NORTH CENTRAL:						
Ohio	810,692	29,265	39,415	403,290	335,261	3,461
Indiana	717,233	31,915	39,090	368,725	274,232	3,271
Illinois	1,296,852	71,008	89,926	650,248	479,397	6,273
Michigan	605,509	17,526	24,170	284,014	277,806	1,993
Wisconsin	683,364	23,832	31,291	322,688	302,790	2,763
WEST NORTH CENTRAL:						
Minnesota	932,794	46,587	60,272	432,615	389,347	3,973
Iowa	1,386,522	79,547	108,176	693,831	498,975	5,993
Missouri	906,120	55,805	62,824	461,632	321,028	4,931
North Dakota	855,682	69,250	73,422	361,070	347,151	4,789
South Dakota	817,058	73,100	82,158	364,249	291,846	5,705
Nebraska	961,396	70,075	82,149	441,599	362,240	5,333
Kansas	1,082,827	81,950	96,878	525,726	372,127	6,146
SOUTH ATLANTIC:						
Delaware	27,752	660	931	11,654	14,334	173
Maryland	141,341	5,094	6,898	62,694	65,706	949
District of Columbia	311	1		96	214	
Virginia	312,465	12,962	16,417	138,835	142,782	1,469
West Virginia	169,148	6,331	8,579	78,660	74,842	736
North Carolina	171,436	3,487	3,139	71,061	91,242	2,507
South Carolina	77,517	1,876	1,941	36,828	34,930	1,942
Georgia	100,503	2,311	2,514	45,364	47,670	2,644
Florida	38,570	1,597	1,473	15,283	19,383	834
EAST SOUTH CENTRAL:						
Kentucky	382,442	18,526	17,018	178,225	165,940	2,733
Tennessee	317,921	16,365	14,328	157,050	128,059	2,119
Alabama	130,462	6,370	5,161	60,133	56,170	2,628
Mississippi	214,852	12,514	10,117	100,221	89,683	2,317
WEST SOUTH CENTRAL:						
Arkansas	251,926	12,808	12,246	119,672	104,861	2,339
Louisiana	178,756	10,308	9,017	75,686	81,726	2,019
Oklahoma	738,443	57,482	64,167	345,888	265,903	5,003
Texas	991,362	52,446	50,882	407,506	472,467	8,061
MOUNTAIN:						
Montana	668,723	85,513	75,731	262,090	235,948	6,103
Idaho	293,123	28,015	27,774	124,488	110,694	2,152
Wyoming	198,295	27,547	26,341	76,506	65,642	2,058
Colorado	420,704	41,429	44,140	180,681	150,660	3,788
New Mexico	182,686	15,083	16,157	71,375	77,927	2,144
Arizona	136,167	15,319	8,318	59,689	38,236	3,398
Utah	125,471	12,989	12,573	51,841	47,043	1,025
Nevada	50,486	5,647	6,104	20,081	18,109	545
PACIFIC:						
Washington	296,381	19,524	21,529	126,403	127,392	1,533
Oregon	271,559	23,464	24,393	119,500	102,113	2,089
California	402,407	18,259	20,342	176,175	185,363	2,268

[1] Includes 14,545 horses, not classified by age or sex, distributed as follows: Montana, 3,338, and Arizona, 11,207.

TABLE 85.—MULES ON FARMS—FARMS REPORTING, NUMBER, AND VALUE, BY DIVISIONS AND STATES: 1920 AND 1910.

DIVISION AND STATE.	FARMS REPORTING.		NUMBER.		VALUE.	
	1920	1910	1920	1910	1920	1910
United States.........	2,259,746	1,869,005	5,432,391	4,209,769	$779,294,411	$525,391,863
GEOGRAPHIC DIVISIONS:						
New England............	1,281	897	2,569	1,729	386,657	282,928
Middle Atlantic........	28,960	21,664	68,109	52,416	10,271,127	7,696,310
East North Central......	117,912	101,835	310,426	259,423	37,407,187	31,404,071
West North Central......	272,911	234,628	846,948	715,932	105,515,383	90,544,355
South Atlantic..........	604,061	458,426	1,079,033	749,257	194,597,415	107,799,330
East South Central......	579,463	525,208	1,249,721	1,003,804	180,334,666	125,108,538
West South Central......	602,831	494,748	1,685,359	1,286,378	229,725,990	145,350,358
Mountain...............	30,795	16,257	89,341	48,957	9,313,691	5,227,444
Pacific.................	21,532	15,342	100,885	91,873	11,742,295	11,978,529
NEW ENGLAND:						
Maine..................	264	212	444	358	70,336	72,446
New Hampshire.........	127	104	248	195	34,694	29,681
Vermont...............	305	206	601	429	91,916	53,540
Massachusetts..........	177	155	332	268	44,251	43,385
Rhode Island..........	35	34	75	63	9,037	11,155
Connecticut............	373	186	869	416	136,423	72,721
MIDDLE ATLANTIC:						
New York..............	3,671	1,890	7,323	4,052	1,195,696	650,497
New Jersey............	2,451	1,878	5,705	4,041	903,374	621,774
Pennsylvania..........	22,838	17,896	55,081	44,323	8,172,057	6,424,039
EAST NORTH CENTRAL:						
Ohio..................	14,748	10,628	31,626	22,850	3,647,955	2,775,831
Indiana...............	38,581	33,225	100,358	82,168	11,988,392	9,678,014
Illinois...............	59,636	54,572	168,274	147,833	20,628,517	18,140,335
Michigan..............	2,852	1,865	5,884	3,700	661,115	493,825
Wisconsin.............	2,095	1,545	4,284	2,872	481,208	316,066
WEST NORTH CENTRAL:						
Minnesota.............	5,014	2,813	10,238	5,775	1,062,973	732,723
Iowa.................	30,585	21,872	81,520	55,524	10,041,522	7,551,818
Missouri..............	123,418	112,285	389,045	342,700	50,971,253	43,438,702
North Dakota..........	3,173	2,800	7,873	7,695	780,508	1,149,001
South Dakota..........	5,814	5,025	15,093	12,424	1,636,376	1,668,617
Nebraska.............	37,142	28,438	99,847	83,405	11,690,082	10,374,076
Kansas...............	67,765	61,395	243,332	208,409	29,332,669	25,629,418
SOUTH ATLANTIC:						
Delaware.............	4,052	2,722	9,439	5,935	1,161,877	764,133
Maryland.............	12,589	8,869	32,621	22,667	4,138,764	3,043,581
District of Columbia......	16	17	32	53	4,586	5,860
Virginia..............	49,322	30,688	96,830	60,022	13,523,682	7,595,516
West Virginia..........	8,355	6,629	14,981	11,717	1,839,287	1,339,760
North Carolina.........	148,537	110,747	256,569	174,711	43,670,026	23,699,687
South Carolina.........	128,183	97,799	220,164	155,471	44,499,036	23,830,361
Georgia...............	229,207	186,512	406,351	295,348	77,986,306	43,974,611
Florida...............	23,800	14,443	42,046	23,333	7,773,851	3,545,821
EAST SOUTH CENTRAL:						
Kentucky.............	123,823	97,796	292,857	225,043	35,381,809	26,402,090
Tennessee............	141,626	123,887	352,510	275,855	51,042,649	35,100,810
Alabama..............	165,722	155,673	296,138	247,146	44,611,624	31,577,217
Mississippi...........	148,292	147,852	308,216	255,760	49,298,584	32,028,421
WEST SOUTH CENTRAL:						
Arkansas.............	134,819	110,014	322,677	222,200	47,751,655	27,128,027
Louisiana.............	72,278	51,668	180,115	131,554	28,348,039	15,624,962
Oklahoma.............	113,973	90,488	336,635	257,066	39,892,069	28,618,224
Texas................	281,761	242,578	845,932	675,558	113,734,227	73,979,145
MOUNTAIN:						
Montana..............	3,453	1,058	9,462	4,174	1,119,630	445,278
Idaho................	2,605	1,401	7,735	4,036	810,787	481,301
Wyoming.............	1,245	622	3,415	2,045	342,241	248,572
Colorado.............	11,108	4,802	31,125	14,739	3,384,824	1,798,535
New Mexico...........	7,808	5,950	20,369	14,937	1,874,836	1,463,012
Arizona..............	2,864	1,194	11,992	3,963	1,415,397	399,449
Utah.................	1,153	814	2,793	2,277	190,211	157,497
Nevada...............	559	416	2,450	2,786	175,765	233,800
PACIFIC:						
Washington...........	3,677	2,447	23,091	12,185	2,930,813	1,776,297
Oregon...............	3,252	1,880	14,375	9,927	1,589,552	1,185,788
California.............	14,603	11,015	63,419	69,761	7,221,930	9,016,444

Table 86.—MULES ON FARMS—NUMBER, BY AGE, BY DIVISIONS AND STATES: 1920.

DIVISION AND STATE.	Total.	Mule colts under 1 year of age.	Mule colts 1 year old and under 2 years.	Mules 2 years old and over.
United States	5,432,391	389,279	391,418	4,651,694
GEOGRAPHIC DIVISIONS:				
New England	2,569	70	132	2,367
Middle Atlantic	68,109	2,170	4,546	61,393
East North Central	310,426	47,074	43,566	219,786
West North Central	846,948	149,893	137,742	559,313
South Atlantic	1,079,033	12,013	23,984	1,043,036
East South Central	1,249,721	71,252	70,004	1,108,465
West South Central	1,685,359	88,550	92,154	1,504,655
Mountain	89,341	9,862	9,981	69,498
Pacific	100,885	8,395	9,309	83,181
NEW ENGLAND:				
Maine	444	26	31	387
New Hampshire	248	3	18	227
Vermont	601	23	34	544
Massachusetts	332	6	16	310
Rhode Island	75		5	70
Connecticut	869	12	28	829
MIDDLE ATLANTIC:				
New York	7,323	233	475	6,615
New Jersey	5,705	50	263	5,392
Pennsylvania	55,081	1,887	3,808	49,386
EAST NORTH CENTRAL:				
Ohio	31,626	2,791	3,340	25,495
Indiana	100,358	14,509	13,687	72,162
Illinois	168,274	29,224	25,779	113,271
Michigan	5,884	290	429	5,165
Wisconsin	4,284	260	331	3,693
WEST NORTH CENTRAL:				
Minnesota	10,238	1,055	1,030	8,153
Iowa	81,520	16,819	13,496	51,205
Missouri	389,045	68,457	65,133	255,455
North Dakota	7,873	808	691	6,374
South Dakota	15,093	1,936	2,076	11,081
Nebraska	99,847	15,782	14,422	69,643
Kansas	243,332	45,036	40,894	157,402
SOUTH ATLANTIC:				
Delaware	9,439	158	358	8,923
Maryland	32,621	912	1,676	30,033
District of Columbia	32	1	1	30
Virginia	96,830	3,437	5,351	88,042
West Virginia	14,981	604	1,091	13,286
North Carolina	256,569	3,435	6,922	246,212
South Carolina	220,164	1,040	3,412	215,712
Georgia	406,351	2,141	4,409	399,801
Florida	42,046	285	764	40,997
EAST SOUTH CENTRAL:				
Kentucky	292,857	23,450	23,690	245,717
Tennessee	352,510	33,217	31,354	287,939
Alabama	296,138	4,533	5,767	285,838
Mississippi	308,216	10,052	9,193	288,971
WEST SOUTH CENTRAL:				
Arkansas	322,677	14,625	15,394	292,658
Louisiana	180,115	3,272	4,496	172,347
Oklahoma	336,635	35,354	36,148	265,133
Texas	845,932	35,299	36,116	774,517
MOUNTAIN:				
Montana	9,462	753	663	8,046
Idaho	7,735	1,029	779	5,927
Wyoming	3,415	430	457	2,528
Colorado	31,125	4,201	3,801	23,123
New Mexico	20,369	2,002	2,000	16,104
Arizona	11,992	515	1,049	10,428
Utah	2,793	570	483	1,740
Nevada	2,450	362	486	1,602
PACIFIC:				
Washington	23,091	1,878	1,664	19,549
Oregon	14,375	1,649	1,555	11,171
California	63,419	4,868	6,090	52,461

TABLE 87.—ASSES AND BURROS ON FARMS—FARMS REPORTING, NUMBER, AND VALUE, BY DIVISIONS AND STATES: 1920 AND 1910.

DIVISION AND STATE.	FARMS REPORTING.		NUMBER.		VALUE.	
	1920	1910	1920	1910	1920	1910
United States.........	33,308	43,927	72,491	105,698	$8,198,242	$13,200,112
GEOGRAPHIC DIVISIONS:						
New England...............	149	115	187	147	12,596	12,823
Middle Atlantic...........	334	431	464	685	49,004	86,974
East North Central..........	2,434	2,737	4,581	5,426	684,980	958,698
West North Central.........	7,870	9,320	17,869	22,254	3,092,332	4,938,155
South Atlantic.............	1,491	2,077	1,988	3,373	252,230	474,208
East South Central.........	5,450	7,858	9,453	15,731	1,111,409	2,347,454
West South Central........	9,688	13,175	18,036	29,760	2,009,209	3,141,343
Mountain..................	4,433	6,724	16,512	25,009	529,709	659,960
Pacific...................	1,459	1,490	3,401	3,313	456,773	580,497
NEW ENGLAND:						
Maine.....................	39	18	46	22	3,055	3,728
New Hampshire............	22	17	26	30	1,026	1,593
Vermont..................	19	18	27	22	2,460	2,038
Massachusetts.............	40	19	52	21	4,270	1,777
Rhode Island.............	7	7	11	11	495	630
Connecticut..............	22	36	25	41	1,290	3,057
MIDDLE ATLANTIC:						
New York.................	164	190	211	284	18,145	38,262
New Jersey...............	14	31	17	53	2,415	5,274
Pennsylvania.............	156	210	236	348	28,444	43,438
EAST NORTH CENTRAL:						
Ohio.....................	326	259	577	488	63,344	61,560
Indiana..................	694	834	1,211	1,646	181,642	291,217
Illinois.................	1,231	1,381	2,554	2,863	419,698	568,194
Michigan.................	105	144	145	233	11,511	23,932
Wisconsin................	78	119	94	196	8,785	13,795
WEST NORTH CENTRAL:						
Minnesota................	156	144	201	219	26,794	22,857
Iowa.....................	719	832	1,141	1,614	265,635	280,212
Missouri.................	3,584	4,562	9,427	12,877	1,434,285	3,053,873
North Dakota.............	102	94	142	133	34,146	22,915
South Dakota.............	171	186	220	333	55,528	71,628
Nebraska.................	912	1,036	1,622	2,118	323,084	447,635
Kansas...................	2,226	2,466	5,116	4,960	952,860	1,039,035
SOUTH ATLANTIC:						
Delaware.................	12	17	12	18	2,320	3,975
Maryland.................	53	65	64	101	7,798	35,450
District of Columbia......	......	......	......	......	......	......
Virginia.................	277	450	366	783	59,385	121,654
West Virginia............	140	124	177	160	18,450	25,556
North Carolina...........	448	775	542	1,017	57,064	132,554
South Carolina...........	157	228	247	401	30,767	62,911
Georgia..................	300	328	427	765	63,385	81,403
Florida..................	104	90	153	128	13,061	10,705
EAST SOUTH CENTRAL:						
Kentucky.................	1,683	2,124	2,890	4,677	312,786	848,276
Tennessee................	2,439	3,785	4,480	7,989	490,357	1,075,066
Alabama..................	530	893	782	1,272	88,173	143,747
Mississippi..............	798	1,056	1,301	1,793	220,093	280,365
WEST SOUTH CENTRAL:						
Arkansas.................	1,843	1,815	3,218	3,098	348,757	469,738
Louisiana................	271	329	433	531	87,059	70,226
Oklahoma.................	2,699	2,880	5,159	5,723	689,921	881,305
Texas....................	4,875	8,151	9,226	20,408	883,472	1,720,074
MOUNTAIN:						
Montana..................	119	106	240	160	53,735	55,181
Idaho....................	198	147	451	347	46,209	99,992
Wyoming..................	90	92	165	241	23,438	27,690
Colorado.................	1,239	965	3,099	3,233	166,019	136,732
New Mexico...............	1,987	3,645	5,937	11,852	116,763	163,032
Arizona..................	500	1,338	5,240	7,104	68,886	73,092
Utah.....................	155	210	609	1,160	26,243	68,246
Nevada...................	145	221	771	912	28,416	35,995
PACIFIC:						
Washington...............	175	121	399	173	135,006	82,405
Oregon...................	334	270	737	548	150,592	150,777
California...............	950	1,099	2,265	2,592	171,175	347,315

TABLE 88.—CATTLE ON FARMS—FARMS REPORTING, NUMBER, AND VALUE, BY DIVISIONS AND STATES: 1920 AND 1910.

DIVISION AND STATE.	FARMS REPORTING.		NUMBER.		VALUE.	
	1920	1910	1920	1910	1920	1910
United States	5,358,243	5,284,916	66,652,559	61,803,866	$3,651,970,229	$1,499,523,607
GEOGRAPHIC DIVISIONS:						
New England	129,823	149,279	1,320,262	1,336,550	95,568,447	42,240,849
Middle Atlantic	364,917	404,325	3,869,251	4,232,521	340,239,350	138,685,253
East North Central	989,542	1,019,781	10,898,027	9,819,097	705,761,688	271,944,120
West North Central	1,018,207	1,009,077	20,173,185	17,647,714	1,074,478,824	449,654,307
South Atlantic	871,465	841,737	4,702,703	4,839,321	207,920,207	89,539,532
East South Central	849,466	838,167	4,549,786	3,942,526	175,690,454	75,401,279
West South Central	764,506	746,398	10,107,867	10,721,012	454,455,343	203,239,500
Mountain	198,117	132,466	7,599,689	6,060,725	392,797,035	146,269,549
Pacific	172,200	143,686	3,431,789	3,204,400	205,058,881	82,549,218
NEW ENGLAND:						
Maine	41,239	47,664	300,747	256,523	18,270,810	7,784,384
New Hampshire	16,776	20,496	163,653	167,831	11,317,213	5,240,122
Vermont	26,050	28,271	435,480	430,314	28,502,803	11,828,892
Massachusetts	23,900	27,532	216,099	252,416	20,093,098	9,348,076
Rhode Island	3,318	4,001	30,519	34,148	2,984,096	1,309,088
Connecticut	18,540	21,315	173,764	195,318	14,400,427	6,730,287
MIDDLE ATLANTIC:						
New York	167,801	185,664	2,144,244	2,423,003	198,826,728	83,062,242
New Jersey	21,535	25,713	179,459	222,999	18,347,004	8,393,117
Pennsylvania	175,581	192,948	1,545,548	1,586,519	123,065,618	47,229,894
EAST NORTH CENTRAL:						
Ohio	232,472	244,224	1,926,823	1,837,607	118,581,927	51,403,341
Indiana	187,780	193,876	1,546,095	1,363,016	94,529,884	39,110,492
Illinois	217,195	231,000	2,788,238	2,440,577	182,258,690	73,454,745
Michigan	173,417	185,081	1,586,042	1,497,823	101,717,971	40,500,318
Wisconsin	178,678	165,600	3,050,829	2,680,074	208,673,216	67,475,224
WEST NORTH CENTRAL:						
Minnesota	168,286	146,703	3,021,469	2,347,435	151,243,703	50,306,372
Iowa	201,521	205,554	4,557,708	4,448,006	258,677,963	118,864,139
Missouri	241,497	249,971	2,781,644	2,561,482	158,976,138	72,883,664
North Dakota	72,021	64,224	1,334,552	743,762	67,911,737	17,711,398
South Dakota	67,964	65,047	2,348,157	1,535,276	119,980,683	36,257,234
Nebraska	113,851	117,440	3,154,265	2,932,350	163,683,769	73,074,057
Kansas	153,067	160,138	2,975,390	3,079,403	154,004,831	80,557,443
SOUTH ATLANTIC:						
Delaware	7,944	8,498	46,509	54,986	3,394,160	1,648,333
Maryland	38,619	39,653	283,377	287,751	20,363,801	7,869,526
District of Columbia	101	109	965	982	162,097	75,305
Virginia	151,283	153,772	909,795	859,067	51,296,032	21,124,071
West Virginia	81,368	88,759	587,462	620,288	33,727,219	15,860,764
North Carolina	192,648	186,158	644,779	700,861	28,797,982	12,550,054
South Carolina	136,750	120,034	434,097	389,882	20,187,834	7,088,259
Georgia	230,864	213,203	1,156,738	1,080,316	35,235,147	14,060,958
Florida	31,888	31,551	638,981	845,188	14,755,935	9,262,262
EAST SOUTH CENTRAL:						
Kentucky	231,264	220,608	1,093,453	1,000,937	52,291,343	25,971,571
Tennessee	219,841	209,990	1,161,846	996,529	51,370,208	20,690,718
Alabama	208,603	212,231	1,044,008	932,428	32,078,763	13,469,626
Mississippi	189,758	195,338	1,250,479	1,012,632	39,950,140	15,269,364
WEST SOUTH CENTRAL:						
Arkansas	175,614	167,494	1,072,966	1,028,071	35,023,854	15,460,666
Louisiana	89,744	85,355	804,241	804,795	26,620,595	11,605,354
Oklahoma	164,578	156,842	2,073,945	1,953,560	87,199,975	43,187,601
Texas	334,570	336,707	6,156,715	6,934,586	305,610,919	132,985,879
MOUNTAIN:						
Montana	45,475	18,854	1,268,516	943,147	73,938,253	27,474,122
Idaho	35,494	22,844	711,000	433,807	36,382,229	11,330,639
Wyoming	12,742	8,045	875,122	707,121	50,012,404	22,697,387
Colorado	50,538	34,202	1,756,616	1,127,737	94,929,748	31,017,303
New Mexico	21,446	20,105	1,300,335	1,081,663	63,101,300	20,409,965
Arizona	7,768	6,225	821,918	824,929	35,500,759	14,624,708
Utah	22,138	19,053	505,578	412,334	22,627,870	8,948,702
Nevada	2,516	2,138	356,390	449,681	16,304,472	9,766,723
PACIFIC:						
Washington	54,513	42,885	572,644	402,120	36,558,949	12,193,465
Oregon	43,037	37,748	851,108	725,255	47,818,486	17,570,685
California	74,650	63,053	2,008,037	2,077,025	120,681,446	52,785,068

TABLE 89.—DAIRY COWS ON FARMS—FARMS REPORTING, NUMBER, AND VALUE, BY DIVISIONS AND STATES: 1920 AND 1910.

DIVISION AND STATE.	DAIRY COWS 2 YEARS OLD AND OVER ON JAN. 1 OF CENSUS YEAR.					DAIRY COWS AND HEIFERS 15½ MOS. OLD AND OVER ON APR. 15, 1910, AS REPORTED.	
	Farms reporting, 1920	Number.		Value.		Farms reporting.	Number.
		1920	1910 (estimated).[1]	1920	1910 (estimated).[1]		
United States	4,461,296	19,675,297	17,125,471	$1,507,513,140	$634,704,097	5,140,869	20,625,432
GEOGRAPHIC DIVISIONS:							
New England	124,024	842,928	699,421	73,349,974	30,082,940	147,028	841,698
Middle Atlantic	349,196	2,498,270	2,216,954	263,029,753	102,363,057	400,473	2,597,652
East North Central	889,353	5,050,798	4,013,904	419,676,828	160,930,258	1,009,479	4,839,527
West North Central	735,023	4,509,121	4,395,772	314,042,374	157,878,909	989,135	5,327,606
South Atlantic	741,269	1,673,035	1,506,947	107,220,209	43,194,333	794,716	1,810,754
East South Central	744,076	1,677,992	1,344,914	93,602,127	39,683,160	815,423	1,628,061
West South Central	592,605	1,882,361	1,845,402	103,174,475	52,822,323	724,466	2,249,553
Mountain	135,769	619,645	422,678	49,167,593	18,215,234	120,328	514,466
Pacific	149,981	921,147	679,479	84,249,807	29,533,883	139,821	826,115
NEW ENGLAND:							
Maine	39,346	175,425	126,762	12,847,993	5,218,312	46,944	156,819
New Hampshire	15,925	95,997	81,561	8,043,914	3,468,596	20,168	101,278
Vermont	25,336	290,122	222,838	23,027,209	8,692,942	27,947	265,483
Massachusetts	22,551	147,331	145,714	15,993,976	7,104,863	27,193	171,936
Rhode Island	3,126	21,431	20,068	2,393,801	995,610	3,932	23,329
Connecticut	17,740	112,622	102,478	11,043,081	4,602,617	20,844	122,853
MIDDLE ATLANTIC:							
New York	162,367	1,481,918	1,293,058	162,165,593	63,139,451	184,024	1,509,594
New Jersey	20,291	130,497	136,035	15,120,294	6,576,245	25,275	154,418
Pennsylvania	166,538	885,855	787,861	85,743,866	32,647,361	191,174	933,640
EAST NORTH CENTRAL:							
Ohio	206,669	888,057	758,676	69,081,634	30,481,197	241,736	905,125
Indiana	160,561	608,211	530,157	46,749,690	21,399,608	191,828	633,591
Illinois	183,501	957,313	875,644	80,021,373	36,953,194	228,267	1,050,223
Michigan	167,274	802,095	635,966	68,324,990	26,343,800	183,098	767,083
Wisconsin	171,348	1,795,122	1,213,461	155,499,141	45,752,459	164,550	1,473,505
WEST NORTH CENTRAL:							
Minnesota	144,948	1,229,179	870,590	83,888,246	29,594,924	145,584	1,085,388
Iowa	135,204	897,668	1,153,935	65,751,288	43,185,918	202,539	1,406,792
Missouri	169,002	661,959	714,657	47,383,419	27,275,158	245,403	856,430
North Dakota	53,745	370,707	208,367	25,508,598	7,658,306	62,977	259,173
South Dakota	43,406	336,892	306,767	22,136,640	10,264,773	61,046	369,764
Nebraska	80,470	438,459	520,969	29,953,940	18,094,139	114,467	613,952
Kansas	108,248	574,257	620,487	39,420,243	21,805,691	157,119	736,107
SOUTH ATLANTIC:							
Delaware	7,521	33,026	31,134	2,729,742	1,207,888	8,259	35,708
Maryland	35,113	161,972	143,349	13,499,901	5,081,004	38,826	166,859
District of Columbia	94	704	755	114,052	59,691	108	857
Virginia	140,368	357,969	305,321	23,648,157	9,328,261	148,565	356,284
West Virginia	65,621	181,206	206,878	12,800,247	6,871,273	87,004	239,539
North Carolina	163,866	290,223	252,862	18,109,871	7,051,308	173,635	308,914
South Carolina	115,159	187,846	148,621	12,923,805	4,286,092	109,179	180,842
Georgia	195,259	388,448	325,534	19,936,090	7,528,573	202,650	405,710
Florida	18,268	71,641	92,493	3,458,344	1,780,243	26,490	116,041
EAST SOUTH CENTRAL:							
Kentucky	206,048	441,346	351,277	28,063,355	12,556,149	216,181	409,834
Tennessee	193,509	415,128	333,214	26,631,983	10,849,098	205,360	397,104
Alabama	185,481	394,112	314,172	18,381,500	7,681,391	203,939	391,536
Mississippi	159,038	427,406	346,251	20,525,289	8,596,522	189,943	429,587
WEST SOUTH CENTRAL:							
Arkansas	150,174	415,507	342,410	19,326,991	8,473,003	163,643	425,793
Louisiana	56,544	176,936	226,847	8,755,744	5,293,179	82,147	279,097
Oklahoma	119,044	456,332	432,445	26,136,555	14,194,789	153,693	530,796
Texas	266,843	833,586	843,700	48,955,185	24,861,352	324,983	1,013,867
MOUNTAIN:							
Montana	29,393	127,581	64,468	10,847,070	3,051,356	16,774	77,527
Idaho	29,461	115,336	69,628	9,134,453	3,055,349	23,116	86,299
Wyoming	6,818	34,997	27,499	2,885,770	1,252,139	7,407	32,699
Colorado	36,102	192,234	119,029	15,002,071	5,307,598	32,660	144,734
New Mexico	8,799	37,805	42,445	2,671,549	1,503,880	15,869	51,451
Arizona	5,433	31,619	23,170	2,655,519	1,145,437	4,000	28,862
Utah	17,880	66,724	62,602	4,609,423	2,310,793	18,524	75,810
Nevada	1,883	13,349	13,837	1,161,738	588,682	1,978	17,084
PACIFIC:							
Washington	49,439	238,270	153,206	21,214,569	7,165,994	42,036	186,233
Oregon	36,925	180,462	143,846	14,629,375	5,662,467	36,684	172,550
California	63,617	502,415	382,427	48,405,863	16,705,422	61,101	467,332

[1] Estimated on the basis of the ratio between dairy heifers 1 year old and under 2 years and dairy cows 2 years old and over, as reported for 1920.

TABLE 90.—BEEF AND DAIRY CATTLE ON FARMS—NUMBER, BY

DIVISION AND STATE.	Total.[1]	NUMBER OF BEEF CATTLE ON FARMS.					
		Calves under 1 year of age.	Heifers 1 year old and under 2 years.	Cows and heifers 2 years old and over.	Steers 1 year old and under 2 years.	Steers 2 years old and over.	Bulls 1 year old and over.
United States	35,288,100	8,607,938	3,981,205	12,624,996	4,650,347	4,629,778	725,165
GEOGRAPHIC DIVISIONS:							
New England	88,771	15,530	7,790	22,437	14,522	25,241	3,251
Middle Atlantic	299,681	64,200	27,570	59,763	59,165	83,860	5,123
East North Central	3,077,569	819,165	356,058	794,694	595,016	443,922	68,714
West North Central	12,680,556	3,443,039	1,473,668	3,920,321	1,922,745	1,656,893	263,890
South Atlantic	2,088,898	468,333	249,102	730,111	262,403	296,009	43,440
East South Central	1,709,820	466,922	507,660	264,370	216,498	35,483
West South Central	6,792,009	1,399,243	665,006	3,044,553	627,560	918,100	137,547
Mountain	6,557,194	1,503,381	752,666	2,813,766	653,015	672,207	132,988
Pacific	1,993,602	428,125	230,458	731,691	251,551	317,048	34,729
NEW ENGLAND:							
Maine	33,474	6,046	2,864	7,092	6,509	9,701	1,262
New Hampshire	18,277	3,019	1,424	3,631	3,337	6,270	596
Vermont	14,200	2,501	1,023	3,219	2,568	4,347	542
Massachusetts	10,089	1,823	1,317	4,533	760	1,242	414
Rhode Island	1,706	244	164	837	97	288	76
Connecticut	11,025	1,897	998	3,125	1,251	3,393	361
MIDDLE ATLANTIC:							
New York	63,170	14,737	6,257	20,407	11,164	9,328	1,277
New Jersey	6,766	1,793	573	2,656	573	813	358
Pennsylvania	229,745	47,670	20,740	36,700	47,428	73,719	3,488
EAST NORTH CENTRAL:							
Ohio	577,450	148,118	71,321	137,415	119,977	86,909	13,710
Indiana	599,694	158,923	75,683	171,171	109,333	70,047	14,537
Illinois	1,283,178	340,425	139,125	361,909	208,533	203,591	29,595
Michigan	329,901	100,592	38,660	50,617	91,265	43,928	4,839
Wisconsin	287,346	71,107	31,269	73,582	65,908	39,447	6,033
WEST NORTH CENTRAL:							
Minnesota	940,842	248,319	112,417	252,183	182,242	120,620	25,061
Iowa	3,038,198	844,656	338,641	848,914	519,596	421,028	65,363
Missouri	1,714,894	445,199	181,048	533,675	267,127	255,250	32,595
North Dakota	674,529	212,398	85,051	211,084	99,204	50,669	16,123
South Dakota	1,801,899	467,986	222,931	573,589	246,428	258,778	32,187
Nebraska	2,464,557	682,265	292,711	828,853	324,786	287,749	48,193
Kansas	2,045,637	542,216	240,869	672,023	283,362	262,799	44,368
SOUTH ATLANTIC:							
Delaware	1,752	416	162	749	142	214	69
Maryland	53,666	6,177	3,308	10,396	8,414	23,272	2,099
District of Columbia	19	3	3	10	3		
Virginia	400,490	100,731	41,369	61,041	76,198	115,522	5,629
West Virginia	332,441	91,696	45,553	71,664	63,191	55,352	4,985
North Carolina	182,702	56,306	24,492	58,136	20,289	19,003	4,476
South Carolina	117,603	30,080	15,283	49,666	7,770	10,613	4,191
Georgia	481,875	104,224	65,549	216,518	45,216	36,739	13,629
Florida	518,350	78,700	53,383	261,931	41,180	35,294	8,362
EAST SOUTH CENTRAL:							
Kentucky	433,659	129,036	55,362	79,318	92,743	70,073	7,127
Tennessee	492,486	155,996	64,345	95,373	96,028	71,609	9,135
Alabama	322,434	71,693	42,117	128,350	35,971	35,191	9,112
Mississippi	461,241	110,197	57,063	204,619	39,628	39,625	10,109
WEST SOUTH CENTRAL:							
Arkansas	345,806	86,791	43,466	119,843	50,011	39,531	6,164
Louisiana	487,709	100,343	63,856	252,662	31,259	30,276	9,313
Oklahoma	1,265,486	309,025	157,342	490,033	146,500	136,645	25,285
Texas	4,693,008	903,084	400,342	2,161,050	399,790	711,648	96,785
MOUNTAIN:							
Montana	1,057,418	275,564	130,705	384,148	118,516	108,544	16,423
Idaho	512,512	129,276	63,508	187,006	71,976	49,740	8,678
Wyoming	817,241	206,741	93,241	299,126	85,142	119,104	13,887
Colorado	1,434,423	325,033	162,545	529,186	191,701	200,026	25,932
New Mexico	1,237,541	249,545	127,748	664,329	67,242	97,446	31,231
Arizona	768,191	153,137	76,497	429,480	41,165	41,819	22,774
Utah	397,563	94,528	53,825	175,128	41,917	24,557	7,608
Nevada	332,299	69,557	44,597	145,363	35,356	30,971	6,455
PACIFIC:							
Washington	193,819	51,062	24,045	64,924	26,861	23,668	3,259
Oregon	570,697	134,748	72,193	225,708	66,380	61,113	10,555
California	1,229,086	242,315	134,220	441,059	158,310	232,267	20,915

[1] Includes 68,671 cattle, not classified by age or sex, distributed by states as follows: Florida, 39,500; Montana, 23,518; Idaho, 2,328; and Arizona, 3,325.

AGE AND SEX, AND VALUE, BY DIVISIONS AND STATES: 1920.

DIVISION AND STATE.	NUMBER OF DAIRY CATTLE ON FARMS.					VALUE.	
	Total.	Calves under 1 year of age.	Heifers 1 year old and under 2 years.	Cows and heifers 2 years old and over.	Bulls 1 year old and over.	All beef cattle.	All dairy cattle.
United States........	31,364,459	6,867,991	4,048,851	19,675,297	772,320	$1,766,550,258	$1,885,419,971
GEOGRAPHIC DIVISIONS:							
New England............	1,231,491	183,934	172,711	842,928	31,918	6,259,488	89,308,959
Middle Atlantic.........	3,569,570	514,620	429,707	2,498,270	126,973	21,357,400	318,881,950
East North Central......	7,820,458	1,542,609	1,031,007	5,050,798	196,044	182,395,533	523,366,155
West North Central.....	7,492,629	1,807,382	976,139	4,509,121	199,987	667,816,123	406,662,701
South Atlantic..........	2,613,805	545,228	338,840	1,673,035	56,702	76,997,821	130,922,386
East South Central......	2,839,966	758,524	353,085	1,677,992	50,365	60,072,635	115,617,819
West South Central......	3,315,858	957,025	413,852	1,882,361	62,620	321,167,937	133,287,406
Mountain	1,042,495	269,720	134,591	619,645	18,539	329,709,379	63,087,656
Pacific.................	1,438,187	288,949	198,919	921,147	29,172	100,773,942	104,284,939
NEW ENGLAND:							
Maine.................	267,273	43,898	41,596	175,425	6,354	2,230,336	16,040,474
New Hampshire........	145,376	22,482	23,206	95,997	3,691	1,269,067	10,048,146
Vermont..............	421,280	64,147	55,521	290,122	11,490	906,462	27,596,341
Massachusetts.........	206,010	26,618	26,513	147,331	5,548	760,228	19,332,870
Rhode Island..........	28,813	3,183	3,483	21,431	716	165,194	2,818,902
Connecticut...........	162,739	23,606	22,392	112,622	4,119	928,201	13,472,226
MIDDLE ATLANTIC:							
New York.............	2,081,074	291,721	248,164	1,481,918	59,271	4,469,611	194,357,117
New Jersey...........	172,693	18,764	17,635	130,497	5,797	498,720	17,848,284
Pennsylvania..........	1,315,803	204,135	163,908	885,855	61,905	16,389,069	106,676,549
EAST NORTH CENTRAL:							
Ohio..................	1,349,373	261,003	171,426	888,057	28,887	32,296,064	86,285,863
Indiana...............	946,401	200,243	118,662	608,211	19,285	35,859,678	58,670,206
Illinois...............	1,505,060	314,196	190,860	957,313	42,691	81,306,470	100,952,220
Michigan.............	1,256,141	263,911	165,364	802,095	24,771	17,299,094	84,418,877
Wisconsin............	2,763,483	503,256	384,695	1,795,122	80,410	15,634,227	193,038,989
WEST NORTH CENTRAL:							
Minnesota.............	2,080,627	479,210	303,279	1,229,179	68,959	42,804,768	108,438,935
Iowa.................	1,519,510	385,628	196,707	897,668	39,507	172,373,106	86,304,857
Missouri.............	1,066,750	254,069	131,317	661,959	19,405	98,328,234	60,647,904
North Dakota.........	660,023	181,739	90,386	370,707	17,191	33,667,119	34,244,618
South Dakota.........	546,258	126,074	69,183	336,892	14,109	91,288,295	28,692,388
Nebraska.............	689,708	153,231	78,257	438,459	19,761	125,691,097	37,992,672
Kansas...............	929,753	227,431	107,010	574,257	21,055	103,663,504	50,341,327
SOUTH ATLANTIC:							
Delaware.............	44,757	5,141	4,852	33,026	1,738	103,687	3,290,473
Maryland.............	229,711	31,345	26,565	161,972	9,829	3,808,079	16,555,722
District of Columbia.....	946	118	95	704	29	1,483	160,614
Virginia..............	509,305	83,379	59,750	357,969	8,207	22,699,853	28,596,179
West Virginia.........	255,021	41,558	28,608	181,206	3,649	18,419,657	15,307,562
North Carolina........	462,077	99,222	64,334	290,223	8,298	6,666,483	22,131,499
South Carolina........	316,494	81,723	40,723	187,846	6,202	4,439,383	15,748,451
Georgia..............	674,863	174,747	95,674	388,448	15,994	10,545,737	24,689,410
Florida..............	120,631	27,995	18,239	71,641	2,756	10,313,459	4,442,476
EAST SOUTH CENTRAL:							
Kentucky.............	659,794	137,312	73,571	441,346	7,565	18,678,186	33,613,157
Tennessee............	669,360	165,877	79,595	415,128	8,760	18,739,997	32,630,211
Alabama.............	721,574	214,219	97,051	394,112	16,192	8,895,187	23,183,576
Mississippi...........	789,238	241,116	102,868	427,406	17,848	13,759,265	26,190,875
WEST SOUTH CENTRAL:							
Arkansas.............	727,160	198,445	101,182	415,507	12,026	10,476,051	24,547,803
Louisiana.............	316,532	92,886	40,754	176,936	5,956	15,438,764	11,181,831
Oklahoma............	808,459	232,543	103,787	456,332	15,797	52,703,130	34,496,845
Texas................	1,463,707	433,151	168,129	833,586	28,841	242,549,992	63,060,927
MOUNTAIN:							
Montana.............	211,098	54,422	25,844	127,581	3,251	60,118,952	13,819,301
Idaho...............	202,391	56,207	27,616	115,336	3,232	24,660,268	11,721,961
Wyoming............	58,192	15,655	6,618	34,997	922	46,351,697	3,660,707
Colorado............	322,193	81,447	41,513	192,234	6,999	75,480,127	19,449,621
New Mexico..........	62,794	15,779	8,022	37,805	1,188	59,580,397	3,520,903
Arizona.............	53,721	13,293	7,768	31,619	1,041	31,930,866	3,569,893
Utah................	108,015	25,794	14,077	66,724	1,420	16,806,429	5,821,441
Nevada.............	24,091	7,123	3,133	13,349	486	14,780,643	1,523,829
PACIFIC:							
Washington...........	378,825	80,990	51,365	238,270	8,200	10,066,144	26,492,805
Oregon..............	280,411	57,840	36,011	180,462	6,098	29,427,505	18,390,981
California............	778,951	150,119	111,543	502,415	14,874	61,280,293	59,401,153

TABLE 91.—SHEEP ON FARMS—FARMS REPORTING, NUMBER, AND VALUE, BY DIVISIONS AND STATES: 1920 AND 1910.

DIVISION AND STATE.	FARMS REPORTING.		NUMBER.		VALUE.	
	1920	1910	1920	1910	1920	1910
United States	538,593	610,894	35,033,516	52,447,861	$395,401,286	$232,841,585
GEOGRAPHIC DIVISIONS:						
New England	15,255	20,340	242,706	430,672	2,657,396	1,846,797
Middle Atlantic	38,389	51,168	1,097,908	1,844,057	13,038,280	8,934,933
East North Central	170,177	220,914	5,073,306	9,542,234	53,575,346	39,009,830
West North Central	123,655	105,482	4,949,702	5,065,009	58,689,277	23,287,792
South Atlantic	55,726	76,446	1,209,424	2,513,553	11,876,637	9,085,747
East South Central	62,775	88,039	1,318,349	2,496,221	13,288,976	9,299,829
West South Central	22,057	19,809	2,908,830	2,193,657	34,274,267	7,226,258
Mountain	30,093	16,328	13,206,983	22,770,291	149,920,711	111,656,290
Pacific	20,466	12,368	5,026,308	5,592,167	58,080,396	22,494,109
NEW ENGLAND:						
Maine	8,829	11,060	119,471	206,434	1,191,780	813,976
New Hampshire	1,644	2,236	28,021	43,772	312,490	192,346
Vermont	3,051	5,033	62,756	118,551	723,683	538,991
Massachusetts	939	1,028	18,880	32,708	237,023	156,498
Rhode Island	146	242	2,736	6,789	37,319	32,637
Connecticut	646	741	10,842	22,418	155,101	112,349
MIDDLE ATLANTIC:						
New York	18,828	24,854	578,726	930,300	7,699,791	4,839,651
New Jersey	554	878	10,471	30,683	145,785	161,138
Pennsylvania	19,007	25,436	508,711	883,074	5,192,704	3,934,144
EAST NORTH CENTRAL:						
Ohio	55,246	71,556	2,102,550	3,909,162	19,020,588	14,941,381
Indiana	30,074	38,191	643,889	1,336,967	7,628,968	5,908,496
Illinois	26,637	26,262	637,685	1,059,846	7,946,064	4,843,736
Michigan	35,454	54,865	1,209,191	2,306,476	13,688,379	9,646,565
Wisconsin	22,766	30,040	479,991	929,783	5,291,347	3,669,652
WEST NORTH CENTRAL:						
Minnesota	24,238	24,565	509,064	637,582	5,748,518	2,693,424
Iowa	30,455	21,810	1,092,095	1,145,549	12,883,597	5,748,836
Missouri	40,304	44,081	1,271,616	1,811,268	15,755,632	7,888,878
North Dakota	6,867	3,671	298,912	293,371	3,573,689	1,257,737
South Dakota	8,094	5,159	843,696	611,264	10,635,258	3,002,038
Nebraska	5,902	3,043	573,217	593,500	5,926,861	1,486,948
Kansas	7,795	3,153	361,102	272,475	4,165,722	1,209,931
SOUTH ATLANTIC:						
Delaware	135	266	3,220	7,806	38,397	36,898
Maryland	4,739	6,228	103,027	237,137	1,262,798	1,142,965
District of Columbia	3	....	10	....	130	....
Virginia	16,242	21,514	342,367	804,873	3,990,929	3,300,026
West Virginia	22,234	26,179	509,831	910,360	5,049,727	3,400,901
North Carolina	7,741	14,710	90,556	214,473	783,668	559,217
South Carolina	1,275	1,731	23,581	37,559	109,131	81,362
Georgia	2,874	5,167	72,173	187,644	323,615	308,212
Florida	483	651	64,659	113,701	318,242	256,166
EAST SOUTH CENTRAL:						
Kentucky	35,797	45,697	707,845	1,363,013	7,905,169	5,573,998
Tennessee	19,616	29,987	364,196	795,033	4,021,678	3,009,196
Alabama	3,021	6,628	81,868	142,930	484,424	299,919
Mississippi	4,341	5,727	164,440	195,245	877,705	416,716
WEST SOUTH CENTRAL:						
Arkansas	6,271	8,397	100,159	144,189	827,294	327,984
Louisiana	3,181	3,656	129,816	178,287	672,159	343,046
Oklahoma	2,722	880	105,370	62,472	1,123,033	253,864
Texas	9,883	6,876	2,573,485	1,808,709	31,651,781	6,301,364
MOUNTAIN:						
Montana	5,037	2,252	2,082,919	5,380,746	25,775,607	29,028,069
Idaho	6,007	2,952	2,356,270	3,010,478	29,249,088	16,007,132
Wyoming	3,694	1,040	1,809,775	5,397,161	24,250,274	29,666,228
Colorado	4,088	1,794	1,813,255	1,426,214	19,355,618	6,856,187
New Mexico	3,381	3,378	1,640,475	3,346,984	15,413,670	12,072,037
Arizona	760	1,627	881,914	1,226,733	7,123,719	4,400,514
Utah	5,436	2,388	1,691,795	1,827,180	18,881,529	8,634,735
Nevada	730	314	880,580	1,154,795	9,871,206	5,101,328
PACIFIC:						
Washington	4,244	2,155	623,779	475,555	7,750,407	1,931,170
Oregon	9,047	6,356	2,002,378	2,699,135	24,423,544	12,213,942
California	7,175	3,857	2,400,151	2,417,477	25,906,445	8,348,997

TABLE 92.—SHEEP ON FARMS—NUMBER, BY AGE AND SEX, BY DIVISIONS AND STATES: 1920.

DIVISION AND STATE.	Total.[1]	Lambs under 1 year of age.	Ewes 1 year old and over.	Rams 1 year old and over.	Wethers 1 year old and over.
United States	35,033,516	8,925,815	23,518,631	808,808	1,496,576
GEOGRAPHIC DIVISIONS:					
New England	242,706	51,015	178,657	7,908	5,126
Middle Atlantic	1,097,908	262,905	729,593	26,946	78,464
East North Central	5,073,306	1,341,397	3,379,021	120,749	232,139
West North Central	4,949,702	1,579,291	3,195,220	108,798	66,393
South Atlantic	1,209,424	182,454	929,182	49,157	44,796
East South Central	1,318,349	195,095	1,017,315	63,786	42,153
West South Central	2,908,830	704,839	1,684,100	54,367	465,524
Mountain	13,206,983	3,288,986	9,048,121	270,663	319,362
Pacific	5,026,308	1,319,833	3,357,422	106,434	242,619
NEW ENGLAND:					
Maine	119,471	23,660	90,049	3,967	1,795
New Hampshire	28,021	6,291	20,257	861	612
Vermont	62,756	12,940	47,088	1,895	833
Massachusetts	18,880	4,748	11,896	692	1,544
Rhode Island	2,736	684	1,814	104	134
Connecticut	10,842	2,692	7,553	389	208
MIDDLE ATLANTIC:					
New York	578,726	152,124	400,402	14,000	12,200
New Jersey	10,471	2,129	7,773	383	186
Pennsylvania	508,711	108,652	321,418	12,563	66,078
EAST NORTH CENTRAL:					
Ohio	2,102,550	536,023	1,336,429	42,623	187,475
Indiana	643,889	152,832	463,725	19,298	8,034
Illinois	637,685	181,671	423,199	18,805	14,010
Michigan	1,209,191	359,175	809,125	26,651	14,240
Wisconsin	479,991	111,696	346,543	13,372	8,380
WEST NORTH CENTRAL:					
Minnesota	509,064	136,685	351,691	14,073	6,615
Iowa	1,092,095	359,754	691,288	26,121	14,932
Missouri	1,271,616	314,127	910,257	32,786	14,446
North Dakota	298,912	75,812	209,323	6,955	6,822
South Dakota	843,696	227,289	587,597	15,821	12,989
Nebraska	573,217	348,638	213,541	5,603	5,435
Kansas	361,102	116,986	231,523	7,439	5,154
SOUTH ATLANTIC:					
Delaware	3,220	703	2,331	129	57
Maryland	103,027	13,031	85,480	3,895	621
District of Columbia	10		8	2	
Virginia	342,367	40,845	285,040	14,310	2,172
West Virginia	509,831	82,858	392,790	15,722	18,461
North Carolina	90,556	17,459	65,562	5,214	2,321
South Carolina	23,581	4,380	16,155	1,468	1,578
Georgia	72,173	13,889	45,897	4,388	7,999
Florida	64,659	9,289	35,919	4,029	11,587
EAST SOUTH CENTRAL:					
Kentucky	707,845	88,452	583,997	28,864	6,532
Tennessee	364,196	59,922	281,774	17,770	4,730
Alabama	81,868	15,187	51,728	4,989	9,964
Mississippi	164,440	31,534	99,816	12,163	20,927
WEST SOUTH CENTRAL:					
Arkansas	100,159	22,352	68,882	5,104	3,821
Louisiana	129,816	22,522	81,658	7,271	18,365
Oklahoma	105,370	29,753	69,415	2,857	3,345
Texas	2,573,485	630,212	1,464,145	39,135	439,993
MOUNTAIN:					
Montana	2,082,919	509,400	1,468,732	32,736	72,051
Idaho	2,356,270	446,449	1,789,631	53,634	36,756
Wyoming	1,859,775	376,594	1,362,336	48,758	10,087
Colorado	1,813,255	844,568	876,416	25,084	13,165
New Mexico	1,640,475	375,958	1,172,525	28,345	63,647
Arizona	881,914	118,776	531,818	37,880	59,411
Utah	1,691,795	407,622	1,231,341	25,162	27,670
Nevada	880,580	209,619	615,322	19,064	36,575
PACIFIC:					
Washington	623,779	151,969	438,571	10,573	22,666
Oregon	2,002,378	551,313	1,302,142	32,941	115,982
California	2,400,151	616,551	1,616,709	62,920	103,971

[1] Includes 283,686 sheep not classified by age or sex, distributed by states as follows: Florida, 3,835; Idaho, 29,800; Wyoming, 62,000; Colorado, 54,022; and Arizona, 134,029.

TABLE 93.—GOATS ON FARMS—FARMS REPORTING, NUMBER, AND VALUE, BY
DIVISIONS AND STATES: 1920 AND 1910.

DIVISION AND STATE.	FARMS REPORTING.		NUMBER.		VALUE.	
	1920	1910	1920	1910	1920	1910
United States	107,267	82,755	3,458,925	2,915,125	$17,565,363	$6,176,423
GEOGRAPHIC DIVISIONS:						
New England	689	660	6,033	3,195	60,977	18,426
Middle Atlantic	1,957	1,821	5,800	7,588	59,077	41,834
East North Central	4,367	6,230	25,967	35,059	140,306	110,771
West North Central	10,025	9,894	146,042	113,215	705,551	324,714
South Atlantic	21,964	17,026	227,508	211,101	629,894	235,758
East South Central	26,245	17,278	325,698	198,647	918,300	264,565
West South Central	27,429	17,717	2,013,986	1,276,231	10,886,947	2,719,056
Mountain	5,238	5,854	451,617	737,644	2,370,514	1,738,171
Pacific	9,353	6,275	256,274	332,445	1,793,797	723,128
NEW ENGLAND:						
Maine	110	147	476	582	3,809	2,177
New Hampshire	85	96	3,574	495	23,699	3,459
Vermont	46	69	124	261	2,414	1,033
Massachusetts	271	201	1,296	1,251	23,506	7,900
Rhode Island	35	49	116	106	1,637	982
Connecticut	142	98	447	500	5,912	2,785
MIDDLE ATLANTIC:						
New York	924	719	2,580	3,475	29,797	21,432
New Jersey	298	157	642	574	7,713	4,614
Pennsylvania	735	945	2,578	3,539	21,567	15,788
EAST NORTH CENTRAL:						
Ohio	626	918	4,027	5,379	23,165	17,843
Indiana	1,161	1,723	7,872	7,290	37,294	20,905
Illinois	1,474	2,040	9,977	12,435	48,291	38,564
Michigan	415	686	1,607	5,080	11,037	14,192
Wisconsin	691	863	2,484	4,875	20,519	19,267
WEST NORTH CENTRAL:						
Minnesota	690	784	2,745	4,588	18,180	18,480
Iowa	1,195	2,400	10,526	20,664	59,594	64,239
Missouri	5,225	3,947	121,012	72,415	558,520	187,409
North Dakota	410	294	1,250	1,074	7,972	5,618
South Dakota	469	660	1,286	2,337	7,949	11,422
Nebraska	933	892	2,286	3,290	12,807	11,945
Kansas	1,103	917	6,937	8,847	40,529	25,601
SOUTH ATLANTIC:						
Delaware	29	35	91	88	574	328
Maryland	171	198	873	1,182	5,918	5,115
District of Columbia	2		7		35	
Virginia	1,032	738	7,469	7,327	39,227	28,286
West Virginia	336	385	7,003	5,748	64,000	20,682
North Carolina	4,073	4,247	23,912	35,019	72,027	43,039
South Carolina	4,696	3,175	31,774	24,750	93,463	27,728
Georgia	9,326	6,301	110,489	89,616	211,319	70,059
Florida	2,299	1,947	45,890	47,371	146,331	40,521
EAST SOUTH CENTRAL:						
Kentucky	3,334	2,713	35,045	29,869	125,047	61,665
Tennessee	6,836	4,859	73,228	43,560	246,560	82,666
Alabama	8,195	5,667	104,148	79,347	255,468	76,361
Mississippi	7,880	4,039	113,277	45,871	291,225	43,873
WEST SOUTH CENTRAL:						
Arkansas	7,683	4,790	123,800	58,294	460,003	84,938
Louisiana	5,611	3,554	91,249	57,102	229,940	57,354
Oklahoma	2,798	1,436	45,825	25,591	229,635	62,687
Texas	11,337	7,937	1,753,112	1,135,244	9,967,369	2,514,077
MOUNTAIN:						
Montana	212	176	1,232	5,045	12,410	90,110
Idaho	274	98	1,515	3,719	14,808	36,697
Wyoming	94	72	1,511	2,739	9,341	16,128
Colorado	1,281	959	28,688	31,611	164,924	80,644
New Mexico	2,741	3,440	226,862	412,050	1,091,076	939,702
Arizona	242	911	161,124	246,617	816,793	555,327
Utah	305	134	29,512	29,014	253,100	75,547
Nevada	89	64	1,123	4,849	8,062	11,710
PACIFIC:						
Washington	559	417	6,830	8,621	78,306	31,662
Oregon	3,597	4,144	133,685	185,411	585,456	370,637
California	5,197	1,714	115,759	138,413	1,130,035	320,829

TABLE 94.—GOATS ON FARMS—NUMBER, BY CLASSES, BY DIVISIONS AND STATES: 1920.

DIVISION AND STATE.	Total.	Kids under 1 year of age, raised for fleeces.	Goats 1 year old and over, raised for fleeces.	All other goats.
United States	**3,458,925**	**511,573**	**1,590,018**	**1,357,334**
GEOGRAPHIC DIVISIONS:				
New England	6,033	3,215	629	2,189
Middle Atlantic	5,800	282	650	4,868
East North Central	25,967	1,301	4,469	20,197
West North Central	146,042	14,319	56,639	75,084
South Atlantic	227,508	2,609	12,528	212,371
East South Central	325,698	8,918	19,984	296,796
West South Central	2,013,986	366,612	1,141,565	505,809
Mountain	451,617	67,216	193,096	191,305
Pacific	256,274	47,101	160,458	48,715
NEW ENGLAND:				
Maine	476	49	62	365
New Hampshire	3,574	3,082	283	209
Vermont	124	26	61	37
Massachusetts	1,296	38	149	1,109
Rhode Island	116	6	22	88
Connecticut	447	14	52	381
MIDDLE ATLANTIC:				
New York	2,580	127	308	2,145
New Jersey	642	12	15	615
Pennsylvania	2,578	143	327	2,108
EAST NORTH CENTRAL:				
Ohio	4,027	88	398	3,541
Indiana	7,872	394	1,078	6,400
Illinois	9,977	523	1,803	7,651
Michigan	1,607	104	331	1,172
Wisconsin	2,484	192	859	1,433
WEST NORTH CENTRAL:				
Minnesota	2,745	292	758	1,695
Iowa	10,526	443	1,808	8,275
Missouri	121,012	12,385	51,745	56,882
North Dakota	1,250	80	149	1,021
South Dakota	1,286	93	209	984
Nebraska	2,286	119	209	984
Kansas	6,937	907	1,626	4,404
SOUTH ATLANTIC:				
Delaware	91	11	51	29
Maryland	873	43	190	640
District of Columbia	7			7
Virginia	7,469	600	1,866	5,003
West Virginia	7,003	1,202	3,341	2,460
North Carolina	23,912	129	290	23,493
South Carolina	31,774	56	186	31,532
Georgia	110,489	55	281	110,153
Florida	45,890	513	6,323	39,054
EAST SOUTH CENTRAL:				
Kentucky	35,045	1,298	4,409	29,338
Tennessee	73,228	7,139	13,782	52,307
Alabama	104,148	190	956	103,002
Mississippi	113,277	291	837	112,149
WEST SOUTH CENTRAL:				
Arkansas	123,800	4,713	15,121	103,966
Louisiana	91,249	165	904	90,180
Oklahoma	45,825	4,162	13,229	28,434
Texas	1,753,112	357,572	1,112,311	283,229
MOUNTAIN:				
Montana	1,282	184	601	497
Idaho	1,515	200	615	700
Wyoming	1,511	236	256	1,019
Colorado	28,688	1,398	4,995	22,295
New Mexico	226,862	34,655	97,478	94,729
Arizona	161,124	22,803	71,138	67,183
Utah	29,512	7,510	17,596	4,406
Nevada	1,123	230	417	476
PACIFIC:				
Washington	6,830	656	2,119	4,055
Oregon	133,685	25,867	99,699	8,119
California	115,759	20,578	58,640	36,541

TABLE 95.—SWINE ON FARMS—FARMS REPORTING, NUMBER, AND VALUE, BY DIVISIONS AND STATES: 1920 AND 1910.

DIVISION AND STATE.	FARMS REPORTING.		NUMBER.		VALUE.	
	1920	1910	1920	1910	1920	1910
United States	4,850,807	4,351,751	59,346,409	58,185,676	$988,582,380	$399,338,308
GEOGRAPHIC DIVISIONS:						
New England	85,729	74,938	383,752	396,642	8,341,039	4,002,424
Middle Atlantic	278,842	266,078	1,930,733	1,790,821	36,405,887	14,656,806
East North Central	860,574	797,844	14,182,648	14,461,059	251,361,259	102,738,278
West North Central	902,079	832,199	21,714,826	21,281,509	443,420,214	183,456,287
South Atlantic	933,143	819,267	6,535,706	5,963,920	72,728,971	22,834,358
East South Central	817,300	738,470	6,206,942	5,438,606	64,988,150	25,551,000
West South Central	717,794	673,104	5,758,305	7,021,945	68,295,336	32,631,977
Mountain	139,572	72,728	1,192,700	640,911	19,477,061	5,114,499
Pacific	115,774	77,123	1,440,797	1,190,263	23,564,463	8,352,679
NEW ENGLAND:						
Maine	27,996	24,852	91,204	87,156	1,938,125	948,094
New Hampshire	11,203	10,567	41,655	45,237	891,021	504,174
Vermont	17,556	17,995	72,761	94,821	1,407,410	974,779
Massachusetts	15,489	11,005	104,192	103,018	2,339,114	978,989
Rhode Island	2,097	1,665	12,869	14,038	331,138	123,647
Connecticut	11,388	8,854	61,071	52,372	1,434,231	472,741
MIDDLE ATLANTIC:						
New York	113,694	107,372	600,560	666,179	11,691,713	5,905,272
New Jersey	17,028	16,051	139,222	147,005	2,602,897	1,127,040
Pennsylvania	148,120	142,655	1,190,951	977,637	22,111,277	7,624,494
EAST NORTH CENTRAL:						
Ohio	199,402	190,850	3,083,846	3,105,627	48,485,251	19,412,730
Indiana	172,206	159,137	3,757,135	3,613,906	63,095,220	23,739,586
Illinois	198,718	191,028	4,639,182	4,686,362	90,203,036	36,210,179
Michigan	138,170	131,658	1,106,066	1,245,833	19,621,714	9,755,042
Wisconsin	152,078	125,171	1,596,419	1,809,331	29,956,038	13,620,741
WEST NORTH CENTRAL:						
Minnesota	144,411	108,609	2,380,862	1,520,257	52,245,873	13,929,127
Iowa	189,781	184,002	7,864,304	7,545,853	176,264,026	69,693,218
Missouri	217,396	214,424	3,888,677	4,438,194	61,555,706	31,937,573
North Dakota	59,183	42,972	458,265	331,603	8,884,986	3,152,909
South Dakota	62,174	48,029	1,953,826	1,009,721	42,997,699	10,387,093
Nebraska	106,282	102,832	3,435,690	3,435,724	72,071,506	29,649,482
Kansas	122,852	131,331	1,733,202	3,000,157	29,400,418	24,706,885
SOUTH ATLANTIC:						
Delaware	7,236	7,926	38,621	49,260	603,323	337,910
Maryland	35,926	35,194	306,452	301,583	4,169,974	1,765,857
District of Columbia	97	50	1,331	665	26,623	9,382
Virginia	151,223	140,176	941,308	797,635	10,860,537	4,165,680
West Virginia	67,897	66,884	305,211	328,188	4,046,132	2,087,392
North Carolina	222,030	198,127	1,271,270	1,227,625	16,006,895	4,638,046
South Carolina	155,775	121,870	844,981	665,211	10,710,642	2,552,344
Georgia	252,896	213,447	2,071,051	1,783,684	20,559,953	5,429,016
Florida	40,063	35,593	755,481	810,069	5,744,892	1,848,731
EAST SOUTH CENTRAL:						
Kentucky	188,103	172,846	1,504,431	1,491,816	15,471,514	8,951,692
Tennessee	204,565	181,844	1,832,307	1,387,938	19,477,775	7,329,622
Alabama	213,840	190,251	1,496,893	1,266,733	15,335,211	4,356,520
Mississippi	210,792	193,529	1,373,311	1,292,119	14,703,650	4,913,166
WEST SOUTH CENTRAL:						
Arkansas	172,959	157,209	1,378,091	1,518,947	12,809,913	5,170,924
Louisiana	101,415	86,568	850,562	1,327,605	7,541,443	3,824,046
Oklahoma	137,321	135,741	1,304,094	1,839,030	17,000,355	11,997,641
Texas	306,099	293,586	2,225,558	2,336,363	30,943,625	11,639,366
MOUNTAIN:						
Montana	26,065	9,160	167,060	99,261	2,809,004	858,829
Idaho	26,708	15,000	240,030	178,346	3,567,412	1,638,121
Wyoming	8,619	3,042	72,233	33,947	1,174,580	301,710
Colorado	38,789	18,979	449,866	179,294	7,802,084	1,568,158
New Mexico	15,743	10,389	87,906	45,409	1,462,470	275,851
Arizona	4,022	1,681	49,599	17,208	885,590	112,714
Utah	17,897	12,200	99,361	64,286	1,351,880	445,653
Nevada	1,729	1,317	26,645	23,160	344,350	151,851
PACIFIC:						
Washington	35,715	23,049	264,747	206,135	5,049,249	1,674,927
Oregon	30,201	22,465	266,778	217,577	4,664,307	1,570,949
California	49,858	31,609	909,272	766,551	13,850,907	5,106,803

TABLE 96.—SWINE ON FARMS—NUMBER, BY AGE AND SEX, BY DIVISIONS AND STATES: 1920.

DIVISION AND STATE.	Total.[1]	Pigs under 6 months old.	Sows and gilts for breeding, 6 months old and over.	Boars for breeding, 6 months old and over.	All other hogs, 6 months old and over.
United States.............	59,346,409	26,172,239	11,416,471	925,340	20,827,938
GEOGRAPHIC DIVISIONS:					
New England.................	383,752	219,624	57,224	6,834	100,070
Middle Atlantic..............	1,930,733	1,158,041	254,781	31,217	486,694
East North Central...........	14,182,648	7,371,399	2,645,896	229,728	3,935,625
West North Central..........	21,714,826	6,814,843	4,968,348	361,063	9,570,572
South Atlantic...............	6,535,706	3,407,765	1,050,373	102,410	1,970,737
East South Central...........	6,206,942	3,045,326	918,442	71,322	2,171,852
West South Central..........	5,758,305	2,885,260	1,086,949	82,687	1,703,409
Mountain....................	1,192,700	538,341	214,208	18,497	421,654
Pacific......................	1,440,797	731,640	220,250	21,582	467,325
NEW ENGLAND:					
Maine.......................	91,204	53,036	12,414	1,553	24,201
New Hampshire..............	41,655	25,053	5,765	754	10,083
Vermont....................	72,761	46,386	10,779	1,087	14,509
Massachusetts...............	104,192	53,757	17,742	2,042	30,651
Rhode Island...............	12,869	6,833	1,701	261	4,074
Connecticut.................	61,071	34,559	8,823	1,137	16,552
MIDDLE ATLANTIC:					
New York...................	600,560	379,413	90,368	8,898	121,881
New Jersey.................	139,222	74,817	21,174	2,659	40,572
Pennsylvania...............	1,190,951	703,811	143,239	19,660	324,241
EAST NORTH CENTRAL:					
Ohio.......................	3,083,846	1,888,040	493,603	44,823	657,380
Indiana....................	3,757,135	2,171,143	636,025	59,888	890,079
Illinois....................	4,639,182	1,887,329	929,826	76,148	1,745,879
Michigan...................	1,106,066	687,089	184,556	14,199	220,222
Wisconsin..................	1,596,419	737,798	401,886	34,670	422,065
WEST NORTH CENTRAL:					
Minnesota..................	2,380,862	627,745	617,538	52,436	1,083,143
Iowa......................	7,864,304	2,116,191	1,937,351	124,981	3,685,781
Missouri...................	3,888,677	1,937,526	677,481	57,665	1,216,005
North Dakota..............	458,265	133,870	126,760	11,614	186,021
South Dakota..............	1,953,826	373,270	545,725	37,154	997,677
Nebraska..................	3,435,690	802,342	781,036	51,966	1,800,346
Kansas....................	1,733,202	823,899	282,457	25,247	601,599
SOUTH ATLANTIC:					
Delaware..................	38,621	21,814	4,602	603	11,602
Maryland..................	306,452	181,938	41,320	6,042	77,152
District of Columbia........	1,331	540	295	42	454
Virginia...................	941,308	562,693	119,494	14,384	244,737
West Virginia..............	305,211	192,838	44,661	5,109	62,603
North Carolina.............	1,271,270	642,121	180,954	20,653	427,542
South Carolina.............	844,981	388,595	129,154	12,792	314,440
Georgia...................	2,071,051	1,034,173	363,729	30,170	642,979
Florida....................	755,481	383,053	166,164	12,615	189,228
EAST SOUTH CENTRAL:					
Kentucky..................	1,504,431	819,043	218,714	16,408	450,266
Tennessee.................	1,832,307	950,487	253,629	19,662	608,529
Alabama..................	1,496,893	679,910	228,281	19,373	569,329
Mississippi................	1,373,311	595,886	217,818	15,879	543,728
WEST SOUTH CENTRAL:					
Arkansas..................	1,378,091	699,946	266,185	15,574	396,386
Louisiana.................	850,562	384,450	196,955	14,527	254,630
Oklahoma.................	1,304,094	687,831	234,145	20,196	361,922
Texas....................	2,225,558	1,113,033	389,664	32,390	690,471
MOUNTAIN:					
Montana..................	167,060	69,509	33,975	3,000	60,576
Idaho....................	240,030	106,500	43,084	3,040	87,406
Wyoming.................	72,233	29,888	14,166	1,241	26,938
Colorado.................	449,866	200,027	79,658	7,166	163,015
New Mexico..............	87,906	44,360	16,249	1,502	25,795
Arizona..................	49,599	24,935	9,811	843	14,010
Utah....................	99,361	51,224	13,170	1,184	33,783
Nevada..................	26,645	11,898	4,095	521	10,131
PACIFIC:					
Washington...............	264,747	138,128	42,910	4,782	78,927
Oregon...................	266,778	140,656	38,472	4,219	83,431
California.................	909,272	452,856	138,868	12,581	304,967

[1] Includes 4,421 swine, not classified by age or sex, reported in Florida.

75108°—23——49

770 ABSTRACT OF THE CENSUS—AGRICULTURE.

TABLE 97.—POULTRY ON FARMS—FARMS REPORTING, NUMBER, AND VALUE, BY DIVISIONS AND STATES: 1920 AND 1910.

DIVISION AND STATE.	FARMS REPORTING.		NUMBER.		VALUE.	
	1920	1910[1]	1920	1910[1]	1920	1910[1]
United States	5,852,040	5,585,032	372,825,264	295,880,190	$373,394,057	$154,663,220
GEOGRAPHIC DIVISIONS:						
New England	129,219	150,643	5,953,355	7,078,636	10,150,242	5,238,461
Middle Atlantic	391,258	428,443	28,651,891	26,004,625	38,312,719	17,775,385
East North Central	1,022,190	1,045,736	86,561,574	71,941,382	84,999,901	39,070,998
West North Central	1,026,154	1,007,771	108,433,294	88,684,488	100,125,035	44,226,368
South Atlantic	1,053,743	971,758	38,477,792	27,858,263	38,825,235	13,631,507
East South Central	948,069	897,145	35,821,136	26,918,569	31,412,143	11,873,198
West South Central	890,206	808,267	42,045,411	31,501,899	37,393,990	11,910,631
Mountain	197,886	126,986	9,881,617	5,708,606	9,432,948	4,656,963
Pacific	193,315	148,283	16,999,194	10,183,722	22,741,844	6,279,709
NEW ENGLAND:						
Maine	38,923	46,440	1,418,342	1,735,962	2,219,332	1,131,921
New Hampshire	16,566	20,966	782,775	924,859	1,334,836	649,121
Vermont	24,704	27,528	815,085	938,524	1,167,717	607,787
Massachusetts	25,650	28,154	1,517,477	1,798,380	2,951,001	1,492,961
Rhode Island	3,560	4,341	266,009	415,209	498,257	368,018
Connecticut	19,816	23,214	1,153,667	1,265,702	1,979,099	988,653
MIDDLE ATLANTIC:						
New York	175,022	193,141	10,759,268	10,678,836	15,348,600	7,879,388
New Jersey	27,087	30,144	2,665,662	2,597,448	4,324,584	2,221,610
Pennsylvania	189,149	205,158	15,226,961	12,728,341	18,639,535	7,674,387
EAST NORTH CENTRAL:						
Ohio	241,940	253,685	20,604,103	17,342,289	20,693,940	9,532,672
Indiana	194,510	202,362	17,147,576	13,789,109	16,757,365	7,762,015
Illinois	227,105	237,165	25,864,558	21,409,835	25,234,061	11,696,650
Michigan	180,693	189,417	11,183,064	9,967,039	11,587,814	5,610,958
Wisconsin	177,942	163,107	11,762,273	9,433,110	10,726,721	4,468,703
WEST NORTH CENTRAL:						
Minnesota	184,507	142,659	13,663,443	10,697,075	11,405,427	4,646,960
Iowa	233,264	204,635	28,352,515	23,482,880	27,779,633	12,269,881
Missouri	243,908	259,628	25,610,515	20,897,208	25,470,023	11,870,972
North Dakota	70,193	61,532	4,608,449	3,268,109	3,667,531	1,485,463
South Dakota	67,829	61,561	6,968,088	5,251,348	6,126,335	2,356,465
Nebraska	113,409	115,591	11,932,243	9,351,830	10,222,546	4,219,158
Kansas	155,044	162,165	17,298,041	15,736,038	15,453,540	7,377,469
SOUTH ATLANTIC:						
Delaware	9,750	10,095	1,000,287	876,081	1,215,586	560,146
Maryland	45,621	46,054	3,688,566	2,908,958	4,216,105	1,858,570
District of Columbia	170	159	11,066	8,349	16,013	6,477
Virginia	175,184	170,207	8,286,676	6,099,581	8,909,808	3,395,962
West Virginia	82,451	89,203	4,179,658	3,310,155	4,230,975	1,628,700
North Carolina	247,322	223,808	7,827,935	5,053,870	7,324,880	2,212,570
South Carolina	189,627	146,855	4,240,009	2,946,414	4,263,068	1,206,615
Georgia	278,441	244,719	7,621,158	5,328,584	6,879,535	2,088,653
Florida	45,177	40,658	1,622,437	1,326,271	1,769,265	673,814
EAST SOUTH CENTRAL:						
Kentucky	241,489	231,462	11,020,231	8,764,204	9,256,715	4,461,871
Tennessee	234,207	222,711	11,835,303	8,056,145	10,591,690	3,757,337
Alabama	234,717	221,482	6,266,756	5,028,104	5,098,288	1,807,239
Mississippi	237,656	221,490	6,698,846	5,070,116	6,465,450	1,846,751
WEST SOUTH CENTRAL:						
Arkansas	208,119	183,816	7,395,654	5,788,570	6,143,635	2,063,432
Louisiana	120,257	98,439	4,010,782	3,542,447	3,738,883	1,326,614
Oklahoma	176,952	168,649	11,614,851	8,501,237	10,836,525	3,713,943
Texas	384,878	357,363	19,024,124	13,669,645	16,674,947	4,806,642
MOUNTAIN:						
Montana	44,629	17,629	2,127,854	966,690	1,994,289	628,436
Idaho	35,257	23,446	1,711,884	1,053,876	1,489,050	508,190
Wyoming	19,070	7,415	646,357	341,050	634,702	101,070
Colorado	51,894	24,401	2,554,041	1,721,445	2,924,006	1,012,251
New Mexico	22,183	19,540	739,782	531,625	752,235	256,466
Arizona	7,884	5,040	517,312	268,762	640,595	1,545,966
Utah	21,177	17,443	980,097	691,941	814,566	327,908
Nevada	2,594	1,982	163,984	133,217	183,411	93,668
PACIFIC:						
Washington	57,082	44,906	3,614,475	2,272,775	4,389,759	1,367,440
Oregon	43,824	37,126	2,573,536	1,823,680	3,058,515	1,067,743
California	92,409	66,251	10,811,183	6,087,267	15,293,570	3,844,526

[1] Figures for 1910 include special classes of poultry (peafowls, pheasants, etc.).

TABLE 98.—CHICKENS ON FARMS—FARMS REPORTING, NUMBER, AND VALUE, BY DIVISIONS AND STATES: 1920 AND 1910.

DIVISION AND STATE.	FARMS REPORTING.		NUMBER.		VALUE.	
	1920	1910	1920	1910	1920	1910
United States........	5,837,367	5,578,425	359,537,127	280,340,959	$349,508,867	$140,193,129
GEOGRAPHIC DIVISIONS:						
New England............	127,888	150,010	5,803,507	6,840,404	9,798,440	4,971,233
Middle Atlantic.........	389,651	427,938	27,452,439	24,448,840	36,189,656	16,344,122
East North Central......	1,020,865	1,045,350	84,516,275	69,471,093	81,154,370	36,607,898
West North Central.....	1,023,685	1,007,146	105,347,758	85,192,266	94,292,692	41,206,091
South Atlantic...........	1,052,718	970,381	36,407,610	25,626,503	35,291,681	11,894,200
East South Central......	946,904	895,734	34,091,878	24,495,050	28,946,802	10,272,626
West South Central.....	886,673	807,121	39,919,045	29,176,267	33,830,478	10,393,282
Mountain................	196,768	126,757	9,524,240	5,467,234	8,658,679	3,004,694
Pacific.................	192,215	147,988	16,474,375	9,623,302	21,346,069	5,498,983
NEW ENGLAND:						
Maine...................	38,464	46,185	1,403,284	1,704,900	2,178,964	1,098,954
New Hampshire.........	16,359	20,868	771,233	903,413	1,305,602	627,507
Vermont................	24,451	27,463	799,797	911,730	1,120,247	560,642
Massachusetts...........	25,425	28,018	1,455,193	1,709,934	2,823,802	1,402,977
Rhode Island...........	3,534	4,315	253,607	392,704	471,456	344,452
Connecticut............	19,655	23,161	1,120,393	1,217,723	1,898,369	936,701
MIDDLE ATLANTIC:						
New York..............	174,047	192,836	10,414,600	10,232,498	14,571,301	7,311,027
New Jersey	26,972	30,076	2,534,371	2,320,439	4,131,227	2,012,792
Pennsylvania..........	188,632	205,026	14,503,468	11,895,903	17,487,128	7,020,303
EAST NORTH CENTRAL:						
Ohio....................	241,578	253,608	20,232,637	16,850,099	19,939,378	9,010,277
Indiana................	194,239	202,317	16,754,293	13,216,024	16,007,088	7,168,901
Illinois................	226,740	237,067	25,120,643	20,563,850	24,012,534	10,941,491
Michigan...............	180,664	189,315	10,913,645	9,698,401	11,002,012	5,306,517
Wisconsin..............	177,644	163,043	11,495,057	9,142,719	10,193,358	4,180,712
WEST NORTH CENTRAL:						
Minnesota..............	163,818	142,581	13,212,619	10,293,843	10,456,950	4,231,719
Iowa...................	203,077	204,569	27,746,510	22,691,641	26,701,167	11,632,064
Missouri...............	248,575	259,450	24,883,985	19,910,221	23,844,730	10,822,952
North Dakota..........	69,722	61,452	4,328,567	3,095,026	3,115,012	1,327,727
South Dakota..........	67,687	61,492	6,641,572	4,924,349	5,559,307	2,147,380
Nebraska...............	116,083	115,512	11,615,257	9,010,945	9,810,988	4,013,893
Kansas.................	154,723	162,090	16,919,248	15,266,241	14,804,538	7,030,356
SOUTH ATLANTIC:						
Delaware...............	9,749	10,090	948,656	785,591	1,105,563	498,250
Maryland...............	45,564	46,008	3,436,376	2,650,750	3,724,798	1,616,010
District of Columbia....	170	159	10,370	7,405	15,194	5,820
Virginia...............	175,167	169,991	7,860,488	5,684,703	8,000,355	2,973,874
West Virginia..........	82,389	89,099	4,027,510	3,106,907	3,881,016	1,435,969
North Carolina.........	247,062	223,457	7,393,161	4,566,428	6,685,643	1,924,606
South Carolina.........	169,590	146,487	3,954,365	2,694,970	3,819,847	1,035,891
Georgia................	278,004	244,453	7,221,788	4,890,069	6,397,024	1,832,880
Florida................	45,023	40,637	1,554,896	1,239,680	1,662,241	570,900
EAST SOUTH CENTRAL:						
Kentucky...............	241,313	231,031	10,477,598	8,000,457	8,407,680	3,857,456
Tennessee.............	233,772	222,447	11,353,647	7,341,469	9,948,656	3,299,008
Alabama...............	234,173	221,101	5,918,429	4,589,660	4,663,423	1,566,188
Mississippi............	237,646	221,153	6,342,204	4,563,464	5,927,043	1,549,974
WEST SOUTH CENTRAL:						
Arkansas...............	208,031	183,480	6,955,132	5,182,670	5,560,070	1,682,112
Louisiana..............	119,607	98,304	3,763,910	3,259,087	3,392,412	1,157,505
Oklahoma..............	176,210	168,462	11,137,259	8,014,938	10,028,566	3,414,215
Texas..................	382,825	356,875	18,062,744	12,719,572	14,849,430	4,139,450
MOUNTAIN:						
Montana	44,266	17,595	2,055,120	922,540	1,847,287	565,337
Idaho..................	35,167	23,412	1,654,771	1,012,431	1,360,514	547,647
Wyoming...............	12,262	7,407	620,734	324,984	581,235	175,030
Colorado...............	51,693	34,427	2,874,721	1,644,471	2,680,983	927,977
New Mexico............	21,982	19,495	713,937	509,890	698,294	238,179
Arizona................	7,844	5,020	495,065	252,657	575,510	164,327
Utah...................	21,016	17,424	954,695	673,662	755,379	303,380
Nevada................	2,538	1,977	155,197	126,599	159,477	82,817
PACIFIC:						
Washington............	56,724	44,862	3,547,604	2,204,114	4,235,977	1,289,328
Oregon................	43,576	37,071	2,500,123	1,753,224	2,846,324	972,606
California.............	91,915	66,055	10,426,648	5,665,964	14,263,768	3,237,049

TABLE 99.—POULTRY ON FARMS—NUMBER OF SPECIFIED KINDS OF

[Figures for chickens

	DIVISION AND STATE.	TURKEYS. Number. 1920	TURKEYS. Number. 1910	TURKEYS. Value, 1920	DUCKS. Number. 1920	DUCKS. Number. 1910	DUCKS. Value, 1920
1	United States.........	3,627,028	3,688,708	$12,904,989	2,817,624	2,906,525	$3,373,966
	GEOGRAPHIC DIVISIONS:						
2	New England............	21,282	24,255	114,402	66,851	51,929	123,273
3	Middle Atlantic..........	152,973	252,546	760,965	391,119	369,706	665,434
4	East North Central.......	427,117	701,342	1,540,355	594,790	545,672	755,272
5	West North Central......	859,697	833,472	2,990,925	815,631	809,620	910,663
6	South Atlantic...........	550,004	526,518	2,129,653	287,167	330,054	300,506
7	East South Central.......	428,743	483,741	1,355,329	286,868	344,453	232,821
8	West South Central.......	780,676	620,791	2,449,929	225,306	348,852	184,549
9	Mountain................	172,834	86,703	560,987	55,291	42,242	64,713
10	Pacific..................	233,702	159,340	1,002,444	94,601	63,997	136,735
	NEW ENGLAND:						
11	Maine..................	3,531	2,948	15,391	5,455	6,311	9,895
12	New Hampshire.........	2,363	1,949	13,260	3,214	3,572	5,935
13	Vermont...............	5,514	11,693	30,757	4,511	4,561	7,142
14	Massachusetts..........	4,808	2,645	24,858	36,478	23,153	66,726
15	Rhode Island...........	1,310	1,109	7,996	4,646	4,519	8,534
16	Connecticut............	3,756	3,911	22,140	12,547	9,813	25,041
	MIDDLE ATLANTIC:						
17	New York..............	57,644	104,957	291,535	165,405	166,488	295,321
18	New Jersey.............	7,925	10,647	42,161	34,839	39,441	57,259
19	Pennsylvania...........	87,404	136,942	427,269	190,875	163,777	312,854
	EAST NORTH CENTRAL:						
20	Ohio..................	93,928	162,664	348,856	116,311	106,958	154,605
21	Indiana................	105,713	202,977	382,518	104,961	121,306	135,356
22	Illinois................	107,876	189,418	403,275	226,791	201,505	258,255
23	Michigan..............	74,780	81,263	258,857	69,960	54,723	99,932
24	Wisconsin.............	44,820	65,020	146,849	76,767	61,180	107,124
	WEST NORTH CENTRAL:						
25	Minnesota.............	142,896	147,335	441,322	122,579	94,269	148,426
26	Iowa..................	78,126	124,164	296,543	235,249	225,284	292,852
27	Missouri...............	218,057	311,575	1,057,220	125,082	155,129	128,694
28	North Dakota..........	139,179	61,621	379,204	42,475	39,938	46,976
29	South Dakota..........	83,866	51,992	260,367	111,687	87,544	122,757
30	Nebraska..............	48,345	32,364	140,688	100,765	92,524	101,145
31	Kansas................	119,228	104,421	415,581	77,794	114,932	69,813
	SOUTH ATLANTIC:						
32	Delaware..............	7,977	8,181	42,195	15,636	9,790	27,203
33	Maryland..............	55,323	60,260	262,901	53,556	50,232	72,885
34	District of Columbia.....	57	29	310	106	127	158
35	Virginia...............	159,687	148,386	667,410	94,503	94,451	92,069
36	West Virginia..........	61,800	72,752	250,080	28,610	35,576	29,537
37	North Carolina.........	96,770	70,009	331,070	56,003	75,786	42,298
38	South Carolina.........	73,340	64,396	271,029	10,756	15,653	10,927
39	Georgia...............	76,892	79,634	243,026	23,908	42,221	19,050
40	Florida...............	18,158	22,871	61,632	4,089	6,218	6,379
	EAST SOUTH CENTRAL:						
41	Kentucky..............	168,326	188,292	533,065	99,577	98,706	76,508
42	Tennessee.............	87,448	118,514	289,498	121,491	142,292	100,568
43	Alabama..............	92,733	84,487	258,221	34,993	59,227	26,900
44	Mississippi............	80,236	92,448	274,545	30,807	44,228	28,845
	WEST SOUTH CENTRAL:						
45	Arkansas..............	73,368	83,550	222,161	81,435	109,483	63,356
46	Louisiana.............	36,386	53,251	120,792	56,240	51,473	52,724
47	Oklahoma.............	192,721	120,324	604,085	46,562	112,986	36,118
48	Texas................	478,201	363,666	1,502,891	41,009	74,010	30,351
	MOUNTAIN:						
49	Montana..............	29,432	16,475	87,873	11,400	8,243	14,522
50	Idaho.................	25,982	14,274	85,450	9,994	8,900	12,464
51	Wyoming..............	12,560	5,883	37,534	3,570	3,411	4,187
52	Colorado..............	57,687	26,430	183,113	20,687	12,250	22,391
53	New Mexico............	13,771	7,308	44,508	2,840	2,693	3,038
54	Arizona...............	13,937	5,498	57,029	2,116	1,824	2,741
55	Utah.................	14,896	7,996	46,449	3,233	3,782	3,658
56	Nevada...............	4,569	2,839	19,031	1,451	1,139	1,712
	PACIFIC:						
57	Washington............	20,621	16,049	84,859	15,643	13,179	21,640
58	Oregon...............	38,373	26,689	159,016	14,166	10,757	18,546
59	California.............	174,708	116,602	758,569	64,792	40,061	96,549

FOWLS, 1920 AND 1910, AND VALUE, 1920, BY DIVISIONS AND STATES.
in Table 98.]

GEESE.			GUINEA FOWLS.			PIGEONS.			
Number.		Value, 1920	Number.		Value, 1920	Number.		Value, 1920	
1920	1910		1920	1910		1920	1910		
2,939,203	4,431,980	$5,428,806	2,410,421	1,765,031	$1,582,313	1,493,630	2,730,994	$537,576	1
18,939	27,202	76,321	14,765	37,852	17,809	28,011	95,451	19,997	2
101,081	84,797	352,522	252,910	166,729	216,035	301,369	680,996	128,107	3
542,080	638,907	1,323,986	287,633	232,312	171,090	193,679	351,162	54,828	4
798,523	961,045	1,682,296	307,148	223,998	179,569	304,537	662,492	68,890	5
392,645	679,872	554,940	651,541	413,032	469,654	188,825	280,517	78,801	6
505,441	1,145,929	585,981	420,371	342,026	260,952	87,835	105,950	30,258	7
492,785	824,120	628,445	442,753	333,408	236,572	184,786	197,155	46,017	8
47,133	26,946	114,256	17,663	8,383	14,974	64,433	72,741	19,109	9
40,576	43,162	110,059	15,637	7,291	15,658	140,155	284,530	91,569	10
3,480	4,021	12,785	1,426	13,340	1,689	1,166	4,436	608	11
1,349	1,438	4,875	1,512	4,394	1,779	3,104	10,092	3,385	12
1,813	2,505	6,710	2,062	3,742	2,182	1,388	4,232	679	13
4,896	12,313	21,292	3,717	4,446	4,727	12,385	44,830	9,596	14
1,419	2,725	6,042	1,383	4,277	1,652	3,644	9,873	2,577	15
5,982	4,200	24,617	4,665	7,653	5,780	6,324	21,988	3,152	16
32,045	29,310	121,953	32,265	33,020	33,162	57,309	111,954	35,328	17
12,655	9,166	44,403	32,018	21,994	28,890	43,854	195,738	20,644	18
56,381	46,321	186,166	188,627	111,715	153,983	200,206	373,304	72,135	19
84,785	112,706	205,858	50,848	53,953	36,278	25,594	55,678	8,965	20
89,216	139,081	183,818	70,755	57,433	40,440	22,638	51,929	8,145	21
195,769	226,546	469,127	131,315	84,057	70,777	82,164	144,268	20,093	22
73,205	66,792	200,413	26,365	26,274	17,522	25,109	39,510	9,078	23
99,105	93,782	264,770	8,350	10,595	6,073	38,174	59,777	8,547	24
146,906	105,161	344,523	10,503	10,927	7,147	27,940	45,266	7,059	25
187,270	215,221	441,163	57,595	38,448	35,859	47,765	187,994	12,049	26
191,479	365,866	355,209	120,409	81,848	72,843	41,503	71,821	11,327	27
54,951	30,456	114,943	3,930	2,666	2,976	39,347	38,360	8,420	28
73,093	59,991	165,493	16,902	12,465	10,544	40,968	114,935	7,867	29
75,253	89,128	141,512	31,628	22,408	17,281	60,995	104,401	10,932	30
69,571	95,222	119,453	66,181	55,236	32,919	46,019	99,715	11,236	31
4,006	5,111	15,233	15,613	12,754	16,759	8,399	54,654	8,633	32
20,014	23,606	73,132	85,130	51,653	65,276	38,167	72,435	17,113	33
26	40	49	259	28	217	248	720	85	34
46,985	79,093	73,754	99,970	53,308	67,466	25,043	39,521	8,754	35
33,379	72,972	50,384	23,159	14,148	17,806	5,200	7,698	2,152	36
143,006	238,205	181,658	118,683	76,519	77,452	20,312	26,043	6,759	37
30,437	59,664	41,226	136,046	83,152	107,010	35,065	28,378	13,029	38
104,612	171,625	107,665	146,511	101,543	96,938	47,447	43,193	15,832	39
10,180	29,556	11,839	26,170	19,927	20,730	8,944	7,875	6,444	40
177,420	399,932	191,311	74,698	46,721	41,185	22,612	29,613	6,966	41
158,156	366,687	183,475	90,821	68,841	60,330	23,740	17,688	9,163	42
51,671	142,519	54,159	143,417	118,814	87,158	25,513	33,232	8,427	43
118,194	236,791	157,036	111,435	107,650	72,279	15,970	25,417	5,702	44
191,171	343,995	230,777	78,908	52,287	44,825	15,580	16,339	4,446	45
95,955	121,534	136,497	43,798	32,041	31,209	14,493	25,032	5,249	46
77,266	113,594	100,616	128,508	78,973	58,469	32,535	60,159	8,671	47
128,393	244,997	160,555	191,539	170,107	102,069	122,178	95,625	27,651	48
15,435	7,013	37,983	1,631	633	1,830	14,836	11,736	4,794	49
12,190	8,842	26,470	2,304	970	2,273	6,643	8,440	1,882	50
3,633	1,708	9,452	719	381	649	5,141	4,677	1,736	51
10,296	4,455	25,879	7,317	3,668	5,326	23,639	29,998	6,314	52
921	779	2,306	3,005	1,953	2,300	5,308	8,954	1,789	53
716	701	1,866	1,987	461	2,038	3,468	3,568	1,181	54
3,040	2,938	7,743	561	249	443	3,672	3,306	894	55
902	510	2,557	139	68	115	1,726	2,062	519	56
13,935	14,858	39,369	3,922	1,763	3,777	12,750	22,701	4,137	57
11,727	14,109	29,818	2,728	2,608	2,419	6,419	15,764	2,392	58
14,914	14,195	40,872	8,987	2,920	9,462	120,986	246,065	85,040	59

TABLE 100.—BEES ON FARMS—FARMS REPORTING, NUMBER OF HIVES, AND VALUE, BY DIVISIONS AND STATES: 1920 AND 1910.

DIVISION AND STATE.	FARMS REPORTING.		NUMBER OF HIVES.		VALUE.	
	1920	1910	1920	1910	1920	1910
United States..........	540,917	585,955	3,467,396	3,445,006	$16,841,353	$10,373,615
GEOGRAPHIC DIVISIONS:						
New England.............	6,449	7,177	41,073	40,627	318,850	195,959
Middle Atlantic..........	32,971	39,183	262,728	291,659	1,774,196	1,166,587
East North Central.......	83,373	99,714	556,344	545,938	2,550,614	1,800,931
West North Central.......	85,228	109,408	497,471	546,693	2,256,429	1,729,683
South Atlantic...........	112,036	128,078	613,171	678,439	2,330,103	1,574,577
East South Central.......	108,113	103,248	585,323	506,962	1,895,053	1,117,145
West South Central.......	75,530	67,317	422,492	379,842	1,872,145	997,825
Mountain................	12,621	10,213	206,005	172,654	1,757,163	784,056
Pacific..................	24,596	21,617	282,789	282,192	2,086,800	1,006,852
NEW ENGLAND:						
Maine...................	2,009	1,371	12,639	7,592	102,174	40,357
New Hampshire..........	806	1,002	4,191	4,644	27,051	23,593
Vermont................	1,038	1,124	10,024	10,215	65,787	44,349
Massachusetts..........	1,341	1,597	6,573	7,464	60,865	39,683
Rhode Island...........	168	285	686	1,267	6,189	6,138
Connecticut............	1,087	1,798	6,960	9,445	56,784	41,839
MIDDLE ATLANTIC:						
New York...............	11,667	15,259	127,858	156,360	981,813	646,848
New Jersey.............	1,564	1,627	12,451	10,484	77,816	41,560
Pennsylvania...........	19,740	22,297	122,419	124,815	714,567	478,179
EAST NORTH CENTRAL:						
Ohio...................	17,250	23,203	105,675	98,242	409,682	275,726
Indiana................	15,942	19,487	87,045	80,938	342,207	230,478
Illinois...............	27,830	29,741	162,630	155,846	706,833	487,733
Michigan...............	11,724	16,892	93,348	115,274	525,326	446,464
Wisconsin..............	10,627	10,391	107,646	95,638	566,566	360,530
WEST NORTH CENTRAL:						
Minnesota..............	9,665	9,522	67,344	56,677	384,580	221,781
Iowa...................	18,280	28,935	138,319	160,025	657,067	517,329
Missouri...............	32,483	40,110	157,678	203,569	634,688	584,549
North Dakota...........	75	79	708	495	5,614	3,086
South Dakota...........	1,851	1,355	11,114	6,565	77,303	31,650
Nebraska...............	9,113	12,538	40,971	45,625	206,326	152,676
Kansas.................	13,761	16,869	81,337	73,737	290,851	218,612
SOUTH ATLANTIC:						
Delaware...............	446	1,119	2,976	6,410	11,819	13,609
Maryland...............	2,720	4,186	16,117	23,156	70,681	61,603
District of Columbia......	4	13	19	151	170	790
Virginia...............	20,221	22,437	104,267	104,005	497,882	302,623
West Virginia..........	18,620	24,035	89,873	110,673	458,729	388,937
North Carolina.........	32,044	36,248	163,956	189,178	532,480	386,683
South Carolina.........	10,376	12,528	58,028	75,422	181,722	134,622
Georgia................	23,171	23,167	136,698	130,549	349,972	187,242
Florida................	4,434	4,345	41,237	38,895	226,648	98,468
EAST SOUTH CENTRAL:						
Kentucky...............	34,665	35,603	156,889	152,991	567,230	419,379
Tennessee..............	30,961	27,706	191,898	144,481	698,258	340,619
Alabama................	25,266	23,911	153,766	135,140	384,256	212,921
Mississippi............	17,221	16,028	82,770	74,350	245,309	144,226
WEST SOUTH CENTRAL:						
Arkansas...............	22,993	19,692	112,475	92,731	336,408	200,049
Louisiana..............	5,522	4,928	31,079	29,591	125,688	58,188
Oklahoma...............	10,732	4,816	46,743	19,413	222,020	64,261
Texas..................	36,283	37,881	232,195	238,107	1,188,029	675,327
MOUNTAIN:						
Montana................	1,199	795	11,918	6,313	129,058	32,112
Idaho..................	3,416	2,368	35,900	21,903	280,730	100,148
Wyoming...............	842	579	13,968	4,596	156,151	20,493
Colorado...............	3,990	3,563	63,253	71,434	433,539	308,608
New Mexico.............	750	418	15,733	10,052	117,691	46,300
Arizona................	809	441	28,174	23,770	250,591	104,374
Utah...................	1,453	1,873	25,061	26,185	220,366	123,568
Nevada.................	162	176	11,998	8,401	169,237	48,453
PACIFIC:						
Washington.............	8,068	5,886	56,806	33,884	354,305	126,895
Oregon.................	7,702	8,861	45,264	47,285	263,048	150,164
California.............	8,826	6,870	180,719	201,023	1,469,447	729,793

TABLE 101.—DOMESTIC ANIMALS NOT ON FARMS IN THE UNITED STATES: 1920 AND 1910.

CLASS.	INCLOSURES REPORTING.		NUMBER OF ANIMALS REPORTED.	
	1920	1910	1920	1910
Horses, mules, and asses and burros......			2,098,846	3,469,662
Horses...............................	787,206	1,392,771	1,705,611	3,182,789
Mules................................	104,416	74,666	378,250	270,371
Asses and burros.....................	7,681	8,216	14,985	16,502
All cattle.............................	943,410	899,346	2,111,527	1,878,782
Dairy cows............................	866,609	867,226	1,220,564	1,170,338
Sheep and goats.......................			554,776	505,557
Sheep................................	11,357	6,140	450,042	390,887
Goats................................	30,370	23,745	104,734	114,670
Swine.................................	717,467	347,936	2,638,389	1,287,960

TABLE 102.—DOMESTIC ANIMALS ON FARMS AND NOT ON FARMS IN THE UNITED STATES: 1920 AND 1910.

CLASS.	TOTAL.		ON FARMS.		NOT ON FARMS.	
	1920	1910	1920	1910	1920	1910
Horses, mules, and asses and burros...................	27,370,889	27,618,242	25,272,043	24,148,580	2,098,846	3,469,662
Horses......................	21,472,772	23,015,902	19,767,161	19,833,113	1,705,611	3,182,789
Mules.......................	5,810,641	4,480,140	5,432,391	4,209,769	378,250	270,371
Asses and burros............	87,476	122,200	72,491	105,698	14,985	16,502
All cattle....................	68,764,086	63,682,648	66,652,559	61,803,866	2,111,527	1,878,782
Dairy cows..................	20,895,861	21,795,770	19,675,297	20,625,432	1,220,564	1,170,338
Sheep and goats.............	39,047,217	55,868,543	38,492,441	55,362,986	554,776	505,557
Sheep......................	35,483,558	52,838,748	35,033,516	52,447,861	450,042	390,887
Goats......................	3,563,659	3,029,795	3,458,925	2,915,125	104,734	114,670
Swine......................	61,984,798	59,473,636	59,346,409	58,185,676	2,638,389	1,287,960

TABLE **103.**—DOMESTIC ANIMALS NOT ON FARMS—NUMBER OF THE

	DIVISION AND STATE.	HORSES.		MULES.		ASSES AND BURROS.	
		1920	1910	1920	1910	1920	1910
1	United States..............	1,705,611	3,182,789	378,250	270,371	14,985	16,502
	GEOGRAPHIC DIVISIONS:						
2	New England..................	125,544	238,037	1,220	834	131	96
3	Middle Atlantic..............	291,496	626,990	17,988	25,127	529	387
4	East North Central...........	378,362	732,992	31,467	24,933	941	934
5	West North Central..........	292,091	571,221	36,069	31,054	1,606	2,198
6	South Atlantic...............	143,248	203,928	88,908	55,285	1,283	524
7	East South Central..........	103,323	143,383	76,595	45,229	1,142	974
8	West South Central..........	198,403	297,686	108,534	64,625	5,324	3,750
9	Mountain....................	98,602	161,211	7,970	9,491	3,104	6,395
10	Pacific.....................	74,542	207,341	9,499	13,793	925	1,244
	NEW ENGLAND:						
11	Maine......................	24,972	29,622	84	67	16	19
12	New Hampshire..............	14,722	18,101	74	45	15	5
13	Vermont....................	12,733	18,806	268	192	....	2
14	Massachusetts..............	50,775	115,186	534	271	79	36
15	Rhode Island...............	6,940	17,802	68	76	6	8
16	Connecticut................	15,402	38,520	192	183	15	26
	MIDDLE ATLANTIC:						
17	New York...................	141,648	303,256	2,972	3,490	135	144
18	New Jersey.................	38,178	96,384	1,054	1,519	78	55
19	Pennsylvania...............	111,670	227,350	13,962	20,118	316	188
	EAST NORTH CENTRAL:						
20	Ohio.......................	89,616	188,041	5,590	6,840	198	139
21	Indiana....................	59,619	120,632	5,557	5,710	229	243
22	Illinois...................	119,166	234,629	18,630	10,838	402	412
23	Michigan...................	58,474	100,238	894	700	66	74
24	Wisconsin..................	51,487	89,452	796	845	46	66
	WEST NORTH CENTRAL:						
25	Minnesota..................	56,746	83,654	1,306	1,017	51	100
26	Iowa.......................	54,411	123,370	2,987	3,477	123	199
27	Missouri...................	68,327	132,068	18,869	15,245	652	710
28	North Dakota...............	19,040	22,214	433	716	22	23
29	South Dakota...............	19,357	34,622	634	794	39	65
30	Nebraska...................	27,938	69,762	4,678	2,859	191	326
31	Kansas.....................	46,272	105,531	7,162	6,946	528	775
	SOUTH ATLANTIC:						
32	Delaware...................	3,022	7,219	343	353	3	4
33	Maryland...................	23,686	40,121	3,572	3,569	92	55
34	District of Columbia...........	4,015	11,604	323	1,154	1	6
35	Virginia...................	32,570	35,908	9,177	6,629	169	71
36	West Virginia..............	23,326	22,256	8,632	6,508	322	56
37	North Carolina.............	22,019	26,702	18,112	8,436	273	74
38	South Carolina.............	11,361	14,517	13,576	5,474	75	54
39	Georgia....................	15,653	31,528	27,203	15,556	246	162
40	Florida....................	7,596	14,073	7,970	7,606	102	42
	EAST SOUTH CENTRAL:						
41	Kentucky...................	34,422	49,462	16,582	11,061	284	245
42	Tennessee..................	34,095	43,753	19,936	14,302	476	453
43	Alabama....................	19,149	26,965	25,715	12,907	201	141
44	Mississippi................	15,657	23,203	14,362	6,959	181	135
	WEST SOUTH CENTRAL:						
45	Arkansas...................	26,829	33,040	24,973	9,728	655	269
46	Louisiana..................	27,885	33,281	17,479	12,226	326	112
47	Oklahoma...................	52,227	77,852	15,626	11,696	780	671
48	Texas......................	91,462	153,513	50,456	30,975	3,563	2,698
	MOUNTAIN:						
49	Montana....................	15,121	24,366	415	491	9	22
50	Idaho......................	19,414	20,620	702	679	59	41
51	Wyoming....................	6,053	10,484	469	728	15	28
52	Colorado...................	20,005	40,130	2,401	3,074	773	1,302
53	New Mexico.................	12,620	17,350	1,791	1,520	1,257	1,662
54	Arizona....................	6,107	15,031	1,503	1,321	876	2,878
55	Utah.......................	13,097	18,287	305	488	31	53
56	Nevada.....................	1,785	6,944	304	931	84	349
	PACIFIC:						
57	Washington.................	18,359	44,617	1,257	1,804	104	114
58	Oregon.....................	10,575	30,203	524	1,377	53	73
59	California.................	45,608	132,521	7,718	10,612	768	1,057

DIFFERENT KINDS OF ANIMALS, BY DIVISIONS AND STATES: 1920 AND 1910.

ALL CATTLE.		DAIRY COWS.		SHEEP.		GOATS.		SWINE.		
1920	1910	1920	1910	1920	1910	1920	1910	1920	1910	
2,111,527	1,878,782	1,220,564	1,170,338	450,042	390,887	104,734	114,670	2,638,389	1,287,960	1
71,234	50,495	51,207	40,654	6,067	7,495	2,214	1,399	103,151	32,063	2
148,754	153,719	110,873	115,973	15,348	28,392	12,372	8,932	258,458	142,821	3
283,231	283,200	181,372	199,433	63,494	55,472	4,709	6,747	480,674	179,397	4
337,768	317,753	188,405	226,109	120,821	53,650	5,618	3,115	433,193	223,522	5
302,097	233,996	196,173	151,775	13,984	10,195	11,743	9,663	492,182	230,418	6
287,741	258,464	164,820	136,193	8,313	12,360	15,454	9,661	415,049	192,852	7
436,518	399,326	227,629	199,972	23,788	8,058	19,844	22,245	343,865	238,836	8
143,378	96,917	48,004	42,987	124,050	145,922	12,097	43,322	55,584	28,549	9
100,806	84,912	52,081	57,242	74,177	69,343	20,683	9,586	56,233	19,502	10
19,775	9,700	14,271	7,879	3,936	2,023	150	39	15,473	5,668	11
9,210	4,473	6,369	3,653	477	345	116	59	9,636	4,012	12
7,940	5,876	5,879	4,848	395	201	52	20	6,374	3,522	13
21,500	19,896	15,421	16,082	972	4,329	1,016	643	51,498	12,010	14
3,003	2,654	2,257	2,040	113	108	253	243	5,297	2,969	15
9,806	7,896	7,010	6,152	174	489	627	395	14,873	3,882	16
44,898	47,508	31,202	32,225	5,827	23,608	3,872	2,523	56,050	32,316	17
13,907	14,512	9,945	11,869	4,415	207	2,917	2,111	24,076	9,264	18
89,949	91,699	69,726	71,879	5,106	4,577	5,583	4,298	178,332	101,241	19
64,566	62,388	46,579	47,054	10,248	8,868	815	1,134	113,606	47,125	20
45,276	54,157	32,323	34,421	4,339	5,633	671	922	99,064	36,549	21
96,014	77,255	49,334	51,192	37,194	31,069	2,385	1,900	215,478	70,973	22
42,061	47,385	29,114	35,345	7,465	6,453	420	2,116	23,970	13,894	23
35,314	42,015	24,022	31,421	4,248	3,449	418	675	28,556	10,856	24
55,986	53,946	36,185	40,979	6,973	2,162	306	373	33,339	10,365	25
42,545	61,705	28,354	45,754	2,706	1,206	529	417	81,316	45,427	26
96,880	75,941	55,536	54,218	16,154	17,850	2,682	1,422	147,622	78,557	27
16,471	12,429	10,088	8,640	2,164	1,188	36	133	5,835	2,461	28
20,241	17,033	10,699	12,275	7,447	884	112	105	19,312	7,426	29
48,192	40,488	16,331	26,074	59,024	20,029	836	304	62,688	42,379	30
57,453	56,211	31,212	38,169	26,353	10,331	1,117	361	83,081	36,907	31
781	1,172	635	947	6	15	3	39	2,378	3,729	32
11,754	14,710	8,649	11,009	861	671	376	384	33,594	24,424	33
398	629	199	513	37	1	53	78	1,637	170	34
48,320	36,661	36,637	27,210	2,483	2,882	528	513	84,944	38,771	35
55,462	31,524	42,555	24,052	4,253	1,358	574	255	77,873	25,406	36
52,246	36,528	36,079	25,667	1,623	1,579	1,323	1,744	90,293	50,241	37
35,310	22,396	21,002	16,231	1,190	369	2,281	1,044	47,033	13,017	38
70,853	63,172	40,018	36,295	2,580	2,914	4,214	3,257	107,863	52,562	39
26,973	27,204	10,399	9,851	951	406	2,391	2,349	46,567	22,098	40
53,693	55,719	38,504	29,179	2,323	1,954	813	907	80,130	40,117	41
75,916	55,292	48,532	36,854	2,777	3,487	2,996	2,066	145,800	55,729	42
88,029	75,297	45,216	38,105	1,498	1,783	8,273	4,918	118,293	53,283	43
70,103	72,156	32,568	32,055	1,715	5,136	3,372	1,770	70,826	43,723	44
74,185	63,632	38,697	34,670	1,244	1,187	3,230	2,084	78,533	56,173	45
74,751	57,900	33,119	26,442	4,294	2,602	3,778	3,775	61,077	40,564	46
81,498	72,980	45,241	36,511	654	261	946	1,485	62,628	48,404	47
206,084	204,814	110,572	102,349	17,596	4,008	11,890	14,901	141,627	93,695	48
20,266	11,200	5,646	5,465	28,913	33,579	88	60	6,702	2,538	49
23,475	10,040	9,120	6,138	39,552	7,874	205	94	9,566	2,851	50
7,105	4,536	2,254	2,392	7,986	11,080	725	541	2,122	743	51
44,259	30,498	11,551	11,772	28,799	8,473	2,550	4,008	15,155	13,957	52
11,023	13,649	4,379	4,377	6,392	23,938	6,677	24,410	5,296	2,312	53
8,378	8,529	2,472	2,150	777	1,131	988	12,779	2,017	1,304	54
26,448	16,459	12,137	9,851	11,110	39,789	814	1,368	14,203	4,252	55
2,424	2,006	445	842	521	20,058	50	62	523	592	56
32,909	21,730	18,448	15,266	24,506	2,957	810	789	16,910	4,274	57
21,350	17,006	14,193	12,014	11,191	1,755	1,480	1,684	5,942	3,060	58
46,547	46,176	19,440	29,962	38,480	64,631	18,393	7,113	33,381	12,168	59

TABLE 104.—DOMESTIC ANIMALS ON FARMS AND NOT ON FARMS—NUMBER OF

	DIVISION AND STATE.	HORSES.		MULES.		ASSES AND BURROS.	
		1920	1910	1920	1910	1920	1910
1	United States	21,472,772	23,015,902	5,810,641	4,480,140	87,476	122,200
	GEOGRAPHIC DIVISIONS:						
2	New England	430,589	592,792	3,789	2,563	318	243
3	Middle Atlantic	1,406,254	1,856,676	86,097	77,543	993	1,072
4	East North Central	4,492,012	5,134,434	341,893	284,356	5,522	6,360
5	West North Central	7,234,590	7,365,413	883,017	746,986	19,475	24,452
6	South Atlantic	1,182,291	1,315,115	1,167,941	804,542	3,271	3,897
7	East South Central	1,149,000	1,287,982	1,326,316	1,049,033	10,595	16,705
8	West South Central	2,358,890	2,646,715	1,793,893	1,351,003	23,360	33,510
9	Mountain	2,174,257	1,588,268	97,311	58,448	19,616	31,404
10	Pacific	1,044,889	1,228,507	110,384	105,666	4,326	4,557
	NEW ENGLAND:						
11	Maine	119,322	137,196	528	425	62	41
12	New Hampshire	52,916	64,330	322	240	41	35
13	Vermont	89,964	99,587	869	621	27	24
14	Massachusetts	101,380	179,469	866	539	131	57
15	Rhode Island	13,480	27,349	143	139	17	19
16	Connecticut	53,527	84,861	1,061	599	40	67
	MIDDLE ATLANTIC:						
17	New York	677,819	894,264	10,295	7,542	346	428
18	New Jersey	110,799	185,306	6,759	5,560	95	108
19	Pennsylvania	617,636	777,106	69,043	64,441	552	536
	EAST NORTH CENTRAL:						
20	Ohio	900,308	1,098,265	37,216	29,690	775	627
21	Indiana	776,852	934,276	105,915	87,878	1,440	1,889
22	Illinois	1,416,018	1,687,516	186,904	158,671	2,956	3,275
23	Michigan	663,983	710,271	6,778	4,400	211	307
24	Wisconsin	734,851	704,106	5,080	3,717	140	262
	WEST NORTH CENTRAL:						
25	Minnesota	989,540	836,838	11,544	6,792	252	319
26	Iowa	1,440,933	1,615,596	84,507	59,001	1,264	1,813
27	Missouri	974,547	1,205,455	407,914	357,945	10,079	13,587
28	North Dakota	874,722	672,813	8,306	8,411	164	156
29	South Dakota	836,415	703,984	15,727	13,218	259	398
30	Nebraska	989,334	1,078,140	101,525	86,264	1,813	2,444
31	Kansas	1,129,099	1,252,587	250,494	215,355	5,644	5,735
	SOUTH ATLANTIC:						
32	Delaware	30,774	40,284	9,782	6,288	15	22
33	Maryland	165,027	195,559	36,193	26,236	156	156
34	District of Columbia	4,326	12,168	355	1,207	1	6
35	Virginia	345,035	366,332	106,007	66,651	535	854
36	West Virginia	192,474	202,247	23,613	18,225	499	216
37	North Carolina	193,455	192,853	274,681	183,147	815	1,091
38	South Carolina	88,878	94,364	233,740	160,945	322	455
39	Georgia	116,156	151,595	433,554	310,904	673	927
40	Florida	46,166	59,713	50,016	30,939	255	170
	EAST SOUTH CENTRAL:						
41	Kentucky	416,864	492,496	309,439	236,104	3,174	4,922
42	Tennessee	352,016	393,462	372,446	290,157	4,956	8,442
43	Alabama	149,611	162,601	321,853	260,053	983	1,413
44	Mississippi	230,509	239,423	322,578	262,719	1,482	1,928
	WEST SOUTH CENTRAL:						
45	Arkansas	278,755	287,756	347,650	231,928	3,873	3,367
46	Louisiana	206,641	214,567	197,594	143,780	759	643
47	Oklahoma	790,670	820,811	352,261	268,762	5,939	6,394
48	Texas	1,082,824	1,323,581	896,388	706,533	12,789	23,106
	MOUNTAIN:						
49	Montana	683,844	340,322	9,877	4,665	240	102
50	Idaho	312,507	218,392	8,437	4,715	510	200
51	Wyoming	201,948	100,516	3,884	2,773	180	269
52	Colorado	444,509	342,164	33,000	18,063	3,872	4,595
53	New Mexico	195,306	196,875	22,160	16,466	7,194	13,514
54	Arizona	142,274	114,609	13,495	5,284	6,116	9,982
55	Utah	138,568	133,963	3,098	2,765	640	1,213
56	Nevada	52,271	75,397	2,754	3,717	855	1,261
	PACIFIC:						
57	Washington	314,740	325,189	24,348	13,989	503	287
58	Oregon	282,134	301,911	14,899	11,304	790	621
59	California	448,015	601,407	71,137	80,373	3,033	3,649

THE DIFFERENT KINDS OF ANIMALS, BY DIVISIONS AND STATES: 1920 AND 1910.

CATTLE.		SHEEP.		GOATS.		SWINE.		
1920	1910	1920	1910	1920	1910	1920	1910	
68,764,086	63,682,648	35,483,558	52,838,748	3,563,659	3,029,795	61,984,798	59,473,636	1
1,391,496	1,387,045	248,773	438,167	8,247	4,594	486,903	428,705	2
4,018,005	4,386,240	1,113,256	1,872,449	18,172	16,520	2,189,191	1,933,642	3
11,181,258	10,102,297	5,136,800	9,597,706	30,676	41,806	14,663,322	14,640,456	4
20,510,953	17,965,467	5,070,523	5,118,659	151,660	116,330	22,148,019	21,505,031	5
5,004,800	5,073,317	1,223,408	2,523,748	239,251	220,764	7,027,888	6,194,338	6
4,837,527	4,200,990	1,326,662	2,508,581	341,152	208,308	6,621,991	5,631,458	7
10,544,385	11,120,338	2,932,618	2,201,715	2,033,830	1,298,476	6,102,170	7,260,781	8
7,743,067	6,157,642	13,331,033	22,916,213	463,714	780,966	1,248,284	669,460	9
3,532,595	3,289,312	5,100,485	5,661,510	276,957	342,031	1,497,030	1,209,765	10
320,522	266,223	123,407	208,457	626	621	106,677	92,824	11
172,863	172,304	28,498	44,117	3,690	554	51,291	49,249	12
443,420	436,190	63,151	118,752	176	281	79,135	98,343	13
237,599	272,312	19,852	37,037	2,312	1,894	155,690	115,028	14
33,522	36,802	2,849	6,897	369	349	18,166	17,007	15
183,570	203,214	11,016	22,907	1,074	895	75,944	56,254	16
2,189,142	2,470,511	584,553	953,908	6,452	5,998	656,610	698,495	17
193,366	237,511	14,886	30,890	3,559	2,685	163,298	156,269	18
1,635,497	1,678,218	513,817	887,651	8,161	7,837	1,369,283	1,078,878	19
1,991,389	1,899,995	2,112,798	3,918,030	4,842	6,513	3,197,452	3,152,752	20
1,591,371	1,417,173	648,228	1,342,600	8,543	8,212	3,856,199	3,650,455	21
2,884,252	2,517,832	674,879	1,090,915	12,362	14,335	4,854,660	4,757,335	22
1,628,103	1,545,208	1,216,656	2,312,929	2,027	7,196	1,130,036	1,259,727	23
3,086,143	2,722,089	484,239	933,232	2,902	5,550	1,624,975	1,820,187	24
3,077,455	2,401,381	516,037	639,744	3,051	4,961	2,414,201	1,530,622	25
4,600,253	4,509,711	1,094,801	1,146,755	11,055	21,081	7,945,620	7,591,280	26
2,878,524	2,637,423	1,287,770	1,829,118	123,694	73,837	4,036,299	4,516,751	27
1,351,023	756,191	301,076	294,559	1,286	1,207	464,100	334,064	28
2,368,398	1,552,309	851,143	612,148	1,398	2,442	1,973,138	1,017,147	29
3,202,457	2,972,838	632,241	313,529	3,122	3,594	3,498,378	3,478,103	30
3,032,843	3,135,614	387,455	282,806	8,054	9,208	1,816,283	3,037,064	31
47,290	56,158	3,226	7,821	94	127	40,999	52,989	32
295,131	302,461	103,888	237,808	1,249	1,566	340,046	326,007	33
1,363	1,611	47	1	60	78	2,968	835	34
958,115	895,728	344,850	807,755	7,997	7,840	1,026,252	836,406	35
642,924	651,812	514,084	911,718	7,577	6,003	383,084	353,594	36
697,025	737,389	92,179	216,052	25,235	36,763	1,361,563	1,277,866	37
469,407	412,278	24,771	37,928	34,055	25,794	892,014	678,228	38
1,227,591	1,143,488	74,753	190,558	114,703	92,873	2,178,914	1,836,246	39
665,954	872,392	65,610	114,107	48,281	49,720	802,048	832,167	40
1,147,146	1,056,656	710,168	1,364,967	35,858	30,776	1,584,561	1,531,933	41
1,237,762	1,051,821	366,973	798,520	76,224	45,626	1,978,107	1,443,667	42
1,132,037	1,007,725	83,366	144,713	112,421	84,265	1,615,186	1,320,016	43
1,320,582	1,084,788	166,155	200,381	116,649	47,641	1,444,137	1,335,842	44
1,147,151	1,091,703	101,403	145,376	127,030	60,378	1,456,624	1,575,120	45
878,992	862,695	134,110	180,889	95,027	60,877	911,639	1,368,169	46
2,155,443	2,026,540	106,024	62,733	46,771	27,076	1,366,722	1,887,434	47
6,362,799	7,139,400	2,591,081	1,812,717	1,765,002	1,150,145	2,367,185	2,430,058	48
1,288,782	954,347	2,111,832	5,414,325	1,370	5,105	173,762	101,799	49
738,378	463,847	2,395,822	3,018,352	1,720	5,813	249,596	181,197	50
882,538	771,963	1,867,761	5,408,241	2,236	3,280	74,355	34,690	51
1,800,875	1,158,235	1,842,054	1,434,687	31,238	35,619	465,021	193,251	52
1,311,358	1,095,312	1,646,867	3,370,922	233,539	436,460	93,202	47,721	53
830,296	833,458	882,691	1,227,864	162,112	259,396	51,616	18,512	54
532,026	428,793	1,702,905	1,866,969	30,326	30,382	113,564	68,538	55
358,814	451,687	881,101	1,174,853	1,173	4,911	27,168	23,752	56
605,553	423,850	648,285	478,512	7,640	9,410	281,657	210,409	57
872,458	742,261	2,013,569	2,700,890	135,165	187,095	272,720	220,637	58
2,054,584	2,123,201	2,438,631	2,482,108	134,152	145,526	942,653	778,719	59

TABLE 105.—NUMBER OF HORSES AND MULES IN CITIES OF 25,000 INHABITANTS OR MORE: 1920 AND 1910.

STATE AND CITY.	HORSES.		MULES.	
	1920	1910	1920	1910
ALABAMA:				
Birmingham	1,942	3,870	1,136	1,765
Mobile	518	1,647	82	592
Montgomery	1,040	1,888	1,074	637
ARIZONA:				
Phoenix	652		343	
ARKANSAS:				
Fort Smith	484		207	
Little Rock	822	2,321	577	613
CALIFORNIA:				
Alameda	84			
Berkeley	260	1,340		2
Fresno	366		103	
Long Beach	217		19	
Los Angeles	4,301	16,600	889	2,054
Oakland	1,567	7,419	72	164
Pasadena	265	1,859	7	71
Sacramento	738	2,729	129	8
San Diego	539	2,657	56	163
San Francisco	5,491	21,511	234	317
San Jose	575	2,458		15
Stockton	379		120	
COLORADO:				
Colorado Springs	611	1,783	26	44
Denver	3,716	11,232	102	373
Pueblo	453	2,450	16	51
CONNECTICUT:				
Bridgeport	1,353	3,739	15	2
Hartford	1,266	3,629	15	9
Meriden	263	907		
New Britain	495	1,052	5	
New Haven	1,558	4,316	17	22
New London	232			
Norwalk	132		5	
Stamford	397	1,245	5	
Waterbury	687	2,563	4	33
DELAWARE:				
Wilmington	393	2,627	1	101
DISTRICT OF COLUMBIA:				
Washington	4,015	12,161	323	1,207
FLORIDA:				
Jacksonville	932	1,970	519	724
Miami	2		37	
Pensacola	343		74	
Tampa	238	1,049	375	345
GEORGIA:				
Atlanta	1,121	967	3,196	1,123
Augusta	789	1,201	460	578
Columbus	179		405	
Macon	447	926	643	442
Savannah	534	1,617	245	492
ILLINOIS:				
Aurora	261	1,104	8	24
Bloomington	308	1,976	15	122
Chicago	30,388	68,122	785	1,176
Cicero (town)	196		6	
Danville	819	1,688	39	42
Decatur	546	2,059	24	107
East St. Louis	1,286	2,531	2,126	932
Elgin	402	1,142		27
Evanston	193		6	
Joliet	409	1,697	12	1
Moline	365		3	
Oak Park (village)	355		9	
Peoria	1,534	2,374	100	40
Quincy	850	2,098	41	77
Rock Island	562		28	
Rockford	583	2,147	6	61
Springfield	992	3,120	126	71

STATE AND CITY.	HORSES.		MULES.	
	1920	1910	1920	1910
INDIANA:				
Anderson	607		12	
East Chicago	217		7	
Evansville	1,605	4,096	283	614
Fort Wayne	1,206	2,559	19	22
Gary	510		2	
Hammond	435		9	
Indianapolis	4,535	10,099	536	763
Kokomo	436		7	
Muncie	653		13	
Richmond	320		25	
South Bend	1,298	2,086	38	84
Terre Haute	1,049	2,685	121	103
IOWA:				
Cedar Rapids	739	1,815	110	57
Council Bluffs	688	1,921	60	27
Davenport	627	1,733	58	39
Des Moines	2,463	6,659	119	242
Dubuque	480	2,162	9	22
Sioux City	985	2,644	26	52
Waterloo	699	2,009	10	40
KANSAS:				
Kansas City	1,419	3,293	94	228
Topeka	926	2,936	48	96
Wichita	1,232	5,301	125	143
KENTUCKY:				
Covington	450	1,344	26	41
Lexington	1,211	2,413	927	530
Louisville	2,590	7,756	1,292	2,518
Newport	236	728	4	24
LOUISIANA:				
New Orleans	4,829	7,209	2,838	6,084
Shreveport	589	1,500	374	263
MAINE:				
Bangor	767		2	
Lewiston	661	1,302		
Portland	1,159	2,890	15	13
MARYLAND:				
Baltimore	7,378	15,346	821	1,800
Cumberland	132		45	
Hagerstown	524		20	
MASSACHUSETTS:				
Boston	10,093	23,007	44	26
Brockton	725	2,034	1	1
Brookline (town)	404	1,127		
Cambridge	2,032	4,294	202	9
Chelsea	744	1,068	2	9
Chicopee	338	725		2
Everett	130	770		
Fall River	1,236	3,687	5	2
Fitchburg	574	1,381		4
Haverhill	550	1,707	4	5
Holyoke	535	1,301	34	
Lawrence	852	2,190		10
Lowell	1,149	3,049	26	6
Lynn	905	2,575		8
Malden	566	1,129		
Medford	252		2	
New Bedford	1,805	2,644	35	3
Newton	472	1,797	1	
Pittsfield	569	1,875	1	2
Quincy	433	1,057		10
Revere	170		1	
Salem	431	1,367	23	11
Somerville	1,325	2,799	1	2
Springfield	1,126	3,198	6	15
Taunton	301	1,313	1	2
Waltham	338	1,083		
Worcester	1,832	4,469	12	12

TABLE 105.—NUMBER OF HORSES AND MULES IN CITIES OF 25,000 INHABITANTS OR MORE: 1920 AND 1910—Continued.

STATE AND CITY.	HORSES 1920	HORSES 1910	MULES 1920	MULES 1910
MICHIGAN:				
Battle Creek	537	1,183	9	16
Bay City	699	1,718	10	12
Detroit	7,124	13,849	51	70
Flint	746	1,604	2	13
Grand Rapids	1,591	4,540	45	27
Hamtramck (village)	132			
Highland Park	312			
Jackson	637	1,431	14	6
Kalamazoo	556	1,776		26
Lansing	772	2,122	12	2
Muskegon	296		5	
Pontiac	239		16	
Port Huron	407			
Saginaw	849	1,939	6	27
MINNESOTA:				
Duluth	1,193	2,991	22	24
Minneapolis	4,660	12,835	19	68
St. Paul	3,438	8,900	111	161
MISSOURI:				
Joplin	707	2,972	182	74
Kansas City	3,499	12,989	310	1,345
St. Joseph	1,247	4,623	132	427
St. Louis	11,071	27,204	2,205	4,135
Springfield	728	2,613	416	200
MONTANA:				
Butte	516	1,809		2
NEBRASKA:				
Lincoln	761	2,587	13	104
Omaha	1,496	5,752	83	160
NEW HAMPSHIRE:				
Manchester	1,163	1,730		1
Nashua	401	1,097	4	1
NEW JERSEY:				
Atlantic City	512	1,840	13	41
Bayonne	358	1,002		4
Camden	1,309	2,150	15	56
Clifton	165			
East Orange	127	1,375		5
Elizabeth	934	1,747	18	143
Hoboken	1,339	2,376	2	3
Irvington (town)	136			
Jersey City	3,827	10,233	17	103
Kearny (town)	241		1	
Montclair (town)	228		4	
New Brunswick	299		7	
Newark	4,457	12,863	72	239
Orange	233	1,225	2	9
Passaic	959	1,405	17	1
Paterson	1,036	3,534	32	83
Perth Amboy	294	812	2	4
Plainfield	253		10	
Trenton	1,094	2,705	34	54
West Hoboken (town)	230	619		
West New York (town)	189			
NEW YORK:				
Albany	1,638	3,850	5	4
Amsterdam	390	1,125	4	9
Auburn	555	1,410	10	2
Binghamton	871	1,626	20	27
Buffalo	5,267	14,131	171	245
Elmira	348	1,454	15	16
Jamestown	484	1,103	4	6
Kingston	510	1,313	5	6
Mount Vernon	431	1,370		14
New Rochelle	304	1,459	30	22

STATE AND CITY.	HORSES 1920	HORSES 1910	MULES 1920	MULES 1910
NEW YORK—Continued.				
New York	56,539	128,224	1,173	1,107
Newburgh	207	1,005	9	8
Niagara Falls	436	998		
Poughkeepsie	223	1,155	4	11
Rochester	3,139	6,802	23	53
Rome	465		2	
Schenectady	687	1,662	19	2
Syracuse	2,135	5,063	16	8
Troy	959	2,843	2	2
Utica	1,222	2,471	4	23
Watertown	620	1,490	12	1
Yonkers	665	2,844	7	22
NORTH CAROLINA:				
Asheville	338		102	
Charlotte	482	1,169	397	365
Wilmington	329	718	183	50
Winston-Salem	600		120	
OHIO:				
Akron	1,413	2,319	37	31
Canton	922	1,963	48	26
Cincinnati	5,031	13,901	550	1,201
Cleveland	4,924	16,839	208	164
Columbus	2,395	7,065	141	189
Dayton	1,409	5,227	79	187
East Cleveland	110		1	
Hamilton	439	1,337	23	20
Lakewood	165		42	
Lima	589	1,364	11	21
Lorain	171	659	2	7
Mansfield	356		18	
Marion	502		34	
Newark	512	1,969	27	19
Portsmouth	259		19	
Springfield	1,031	2,025	63	85
Steubenville	227		12	
Toledo	1,657	4,916	25	43
Warren	283		4	
Youngstown	951	2,403	19	49
Zanesville	489	1,242	123	147
OKLAHOMA:				
Muskogee	627	1,655	200	224
Oklahoma City	962	4,897	200	879
Tulsa	1,099		184	
OREGON:				
Portland	1,502	7,893	30	173
PENNSYLVANIA:				
Allentown	840	1,890	5	20
Altoona	435	1,234	11	36
Bethlehem	433		3	
Chester	645	1,476	16	61
Easton	335	1,100	15	33
Erie	807	1,918	8	29
Harrisburg	622	1,889		86
Hazleton	499	886	215	24
Johnstown	652	1,212	104	80
Lancaster	718	1,614	43	73
McKeesport	235	796	10	43
New Castle	271	1,103	16	68
Norristown (borough)	299	931	2	10
Philadelphia	19,472	50,461	756	1,304
Pittsburgh	6,032	12,845	476	603
Reading	905	2,735	16	49
Scranton	1,166	3,985	273	1,119
Wilkes-Barre	1,024	2,540	277	343
Williamsport	372	863	3	10
York	819	1,535	239	50

TABLE 105.—NUMBER OF HORSES AND MULES IN CITIES OF 25,000 INHABITANTS OR MORE: 1920 AND 1910—Continued.

STATE AND CITY.	HORSES. 1920	HORSES. 1910	MULES. 1920	MULES. 1910	STATE AND CITY.	HORSES. 1920	HORSES. 1910	MULES. 1920	MULES. 1910
RHODE ISLAND:					VIRGINIA:				
Cranston	242				Lynchburg	337	1,032	44	127
Newport	289	1,379	1	16	Newport News	73		57	
Pawtucket	663	2,082	1	6	Norfolk	1,308	1,909	197	233
Providence	2,646	7,392	10	27	Petersburg	40		11	
Woonsocket	576	1,110		2	Portsmouth	760	797	237	106
					Richmond	1,359	3,413	554	1,123
SOUTH CAROLINA:					Roanoke	532	1,262	68	100
Charleston	646	901	419	348					
Columbia	319	587	342	213	WASHINGTON:				
					Bellingham	179			
SOUTH DAKOTA:					Everett	134		2	
Sioux Falls	510		29		Seattle	1,254	8,419	18	499
					Spokane	903	4,973	55	64
TENNESSEE:					Tacoma	369	2,954		20
Chattanooga	369	1,597	344	644					
Knoxville	935	1,406	381	187	WEST VIRGINIA:				
Memphis	2,233	4,931	2,703	3,327	Charleston	348		59	
Nashville	2,711	5,622	1,429	777	Clarksburg	283		15	
					Huntington	585	988	53	82
TEXAS:					Wheeling	197	1,179	38	70
Austin	706	2,727	341	547					
Beaumont	397		74		WISCONSIN:				
Dallas	1,564	5,037	693	1,065	Green Bay	505	1,162	18	
El Paso	676	1,732	123	239	Kenosha	402		2	
Fort Worth	1,081	4,903	266	502	La Crosse	524	1,264	13	20
Galveston	847	1,802	642	519	Madison	412	1,523	16	6
Houston	3,295	5,337	1,352	1,204	Milwaukee	4,236	12,733	23	32
San Antonio	4,125	8,699	1,680	1,613	Oshkosh	501	982	2	3
Waco	678	2,384	544	423	Racine	606	1,312		
Wichita Falls	715		208		Sheboygan	447	1,051	20	34
					Superior	349	1,005		
UTAH:									
Ogden	417	1,773	10	3					
Salt Lake City	1,515	4,319	47	157					

TABLE 106.—PURE-BRED LIVE STOCK ON FARMS IN THE UNITED STATES, CLASSIFIED ACCORDING TO BREED: 1920.

BREED.	Number.	BREED.	Number.
Horses, total	120,540	Sheep, total	463,504
American Saddler	1,459	Cheviot	3,000
Belgian	10,838	Dorset Horn	8,458
Clydesdale	4,248	Hampshire Down	51,813
French Draft	2,964	Leicester	767
German Coach	697	Lincoln	13,903
Hackney	564	Merino	59,920
Percheron	70,613	Oxford	16,601
Shire	5,617	Rambouillet	106,849
Standard Bred	4,021	Shropshire	124,454
Thoroughbred	3,801	Southdown	8,451
All other breeds [1]	15,718	Suffolk	805
		All other breeds [1]	68,483
Cattle, total	1,981,514		
		Swine, total	2,040,000
Beef breeds, total	1,064,912	Berkshire	86,676
Aberdeen Angus	108,524	Chester White	191,207
Galloway	7,225	Duroc-Jersey	819,117
Hereford	405,582	Essex	1,771
Polled Durham	61,764	Hampshire	108,782
Shorthorn	416,995	Poland China	726,504
All other beef breeds [1]	64,822	Spotted Poland China	47,703
		Tamworth	5,639
Dairy breeds, total	916,602	Yorkshire	6,353
Ayrshire	30,509	All other breeds [1]	56,148
Brown Swiss	8,283		
Guernsey	79,446		
Holstein-Friesian	528,621		
Jersey	231,834		
All other dairy breeds [1]	37,909		

[1] Includes animals reported as pure bred, with breed not specified.

TABLE 107.—PURE-BRED LIVE STOCK ON FARMS, BY DIVISIONS AND STATES: 1920.

DIVISION AND STATE.	NUMBER OF FARMS REPORTING—		PURE-BRED HORSES.		PURE-BRED CATTLE.		PURE-BRED SHEEP.		PURE-BRED SWINE.	
	Domestic animals.	Pure-bred live stock.	Number.	Per cent of all horses.	Number.	Per cent of all cattle.	Number.	Per cent of all sheep.	Number.	Per cent of all swine.
United States	6,118,956	693,724	120,540	0.6	1,981,514	3.0	463,504	1.3	2,049,900	3.5
GEOGRAPHIC DIVISIONS:										
New England	141,499	19,496	2,017	0.7	93,289	7.1	8,314	3.4	17,535	4.6
Middle Atlantic	396,445	53,368	6,788	0.6	248,106	6.4	35,241	3.2	58,627	3.0
East North Central	1,045,438	177,576	34,090	0.8	457,331	4.2	94,028	1.9	558,333	3.9
West North Central	1,069,726	215,739	49,410	0.7	639,219	3.2	63,123	1.3	829,597	3.8
South Atlantic	1,103,360	52,298	3,775	0.4	76,851	1.6	12,231	1.0	149,313	2.3
East South Central	990,158	49,682	4,994	0.5	70,993	1.6	9,047	0.7	156,510	2.5
West South Central	934,341	67,415	5,287	0.2	181,343	1.8	21,054	0.7	182,422	3.2
Mountain	230,504	33,276	9,782	0.5	138,722	1.8	143,947	1.1	40,199	3.4
Pacific	207,485	24,874	4,397	0.5	75,660	2.2	76,519	1.5	57,364	4.0
NEW ENGLAND:										
Maine	44,103	4,912	299	0.3	18,202	6.1	2,361	2.0	2,913	3.2
New Hampshire	18,404	2,775	265	0.7	12,656	7.7	739	2.6	2,099	5.0
Vermont	27,269	5,747	661	0.9	29,758	6.8	3,035	4.8	2,111	2.9
Massachusetts	27,508	3,546	510	1.0	19,993	9.3	1,245	6.6	6,533	6.3
Rhode Island	3,704	367	75	1.1	1,719	5.6	93	3.4	513	4.0
Connecticut	20,511	2,149	207	0.5	10,961	6.3	841	7.8	3,366	5.5
MIDDLE ATLANTIC:										
New York	180,841	28,566	2,693	0.5	155,185	7.2	18,338	3.2	19,230	3.2
New Jersey	26,783	2,346	463	0.6	11,631	6.5	1,122	10.7	4,622	3.3
Pennsylvania	188,821	22,456	3,632	0.7	81,290	5.3	15,781	3.1	34,775	2.9
EAST NORTH CENTRAL:										
Ohio	245,572	33,365	7,257	0.9	96,384	5.0	39,444	1.9	96,908	3.1
Indiana	197,929	31,127	5,265	0.7	50,624	3.3	9,282	1.4	159,696	4.3
Illinois	231,744	52,545	15,559	1.2	109,996	3.9	13,300	2.1	215,965	4.7
Michigan	186,354	21,873	2,779	0.5	62,800	4.0	21,342	1.8	33,527	3.0
Wisconsin	183,839	38,666	3,230	0.5	137,527	4.5	10,660	2.2	52,237	3.3
WEST NORTH CENTRAL:										
Minnesota	173,034	32,227	4,500	0.5	88,696	2.9	8,729	1.7	99,443	4.2
Iowa	208,534	56,074	15,450	1.1	171,645	3.8	19,522	1.8	289,042	3.7
Missouri	256,236	38,374	4,480	0.5	102,939	3.7	15,383	1.2	148,811	3.8
North Dakota	76,110	13,535	5,636	0.7	33,821	2.5	4,989	1.7	22,076	4.8
South Dakota	73,203	23,286	5,321	0.7	62,348	2.7	6,487	0.8	91,853	4.7
Nebraska	121,870	25,472	5,654	0.6	82,047	2.6	3,448	0.6	112,502	3.3
Kansas	160,739	26,771	8,369	0.8	97,723	3.3	4,565	1.3	65,870	3.8
SOUTH ATLANTIC:										
Delaware	9,816	637	46	0.2	1,707	3.7	12	0.4	653	1.7
Maryland	45,674	3,179	821	0.6	9,588	3.4	1,092	1.1	5,860	1.9
District of Columbia	167	19			186	19.3			59	4.4
Virginia	179,200	8,875	1,809	0.6	17,777	2.0	3,785	1.1	20,867	2.2
West Virginia	84,310	7,136	546	0.3	12,485	2.1	5,424	1.1	7,820	2.6
North Carolina	257,573	10,057	193	0.1	10,782	1.7	1,207	1.3	27,374	2.2
South Carolina	181,452	6,188	110	0.1	6,864	1.6	192	0.8	21,282	2.5
Georgia	297,678	12,321	192	0.2	13,124	1.1	420	0.6	46,760	2.3
Florida	47,490	3,886	58	0.2	4,338	0.7	99	0.2	18,638	2.5
EAST SOUTH CENTRAL:										
Kentucky	253,144	11,379	3,491	0.9	19,693	1.8	5,549	0.8	33,619	2.2
Tennessee	242,630	15,800	832	0.3	24,666	2.1	2,694	0.7	47,571	2.6
Alabama	245,574	9,744	366	0.3	10,633	1.0	323	0.4	32,397	2.2
Mississippi	248,810	12,759	305	0.1	16,001	1.3	481	0.3	42,923	3.1
WEST SOUTH CENTRAL:										
Arkansas	214,163	15,475	446	0.2	13,486	1.3	799	0.8	46,006	3.3
Louisiana	125,648	3,807	262	0.1	6,498	0.8	194	0.1	11,675	1.4
Oklahoma	185,329	21,228	2,786	0.4	48,252	2.3	2,942	2.8	53,888	4.1
Texas	409,201	26,905	1,793	0.2	113,107	1.8	17,119	0.7	70,853	3.2
MOUNTAIN:										
Montana	54,017	7,142	3,585	0.5	22,994	1.8	24,208	1.2	5,351	3.2
Idaho	39,553	6,431	1,699	0.6	19,376	2.7	47,107	2.0	7,299	3.0
Wyoming	14,622	2,655	1,060	0.5	17,530	2.0	15,612	0.8	1,498	2.1
Colorado	56,938	8,781	2,043	0.5	33,610	1.9	7,982	0.4	17,951	4.0
New Mexico	28,532	2,331	261	0.1	18,727	1.4	10,478	0.6	3,245	3.7
Arizona	9,355	1,059	178	0.1	8,455	1.0	2,205	0.3	1,914	3.9
Utah	24,463	4,379	635	0.5	13,856	2.7	30,013	1.8	2,492	2.5
Nevada	3,024	498	321	0.6	4,174	1.2	6,342	0.7	449	1.7
PACIFIC:										
Washington	60,821	7,075	1,244	0.4	18,560	3.2	8,950	1.4	10,006	3.8
Oregon	47,003	8,293	1,538	0.6	24,712	2.9	38,738	1.9	11,617	4.4
California	99,661	9,506	1,615	0.4	32,388	1.6	28,831	1.2	35,741	3.9

TABLE 108.—PURE-BRED HORSES ON FARMS, CLASSIFIED ACCORDING TO BREED, BY DIVISIONS AND STATES: 1920.

DIVISION AND STATE.	Total.	American Saddler.	Belgian.	Clydesdale.	French Draft.	Percheron.	Shire.	Standard Bred.	Thoroughbred.	All other breeds. (1)
United States....	120,540	1,459	10,838	4,248	2,964	70,613	5,617	4,021	3,801	16,979
GEOGRAPHIC DIVISIONS:										
New England.......	2,017	27	91	157	10	418	4	178	23	1,109
Middle Atlantic.....	6,788	58	583	193	27	3,424	96	234	284	1,889
East North Central..	34,090	185	4,280	1,220	666	21,328	1,761	1,428	132	3,090
West North Central..	49,410	363	4,321	1,962	1,835	32,861	2,458	737	350	4,532
South Atlantic......	3,775	80	115	42	36	1,421	18	255	841	967
East South Central..	4,994	474	38	17	19	480	7	461	1,313	2,185
West South Central..	5,287	177	101	28	75	2,664	16	407	319	1,500
Mountain...........	9,782	63	902	323	257	5,966	654	243	369	1,005
Pacific.............	4,397	32	407	306	39	2,051	603	78	170	711
NEW ENGLAND:										
Maine..............	299	1	21	28	4	116	1	2	9	117
New Hampshire.....	265		22	26		27	1	72		117
Vermont...........	661	15	4	13	3	99	2	5	10	510
Massachusetts.....	510	11	39	72		92		98	3	195
Rhode Island.......	75			17		8				50
Connecticut........	207		5	1	3	76		1	1	120
MIDDLE ATLANTIC:										
New York..........	2,693	39	251	72	22	1,207	23	96	111	872
New Jersey........	463	15	3	33		111		15	21	265
Pennsylvania......	3,632	4	329	88	5	2,106	73	123	152	752
EAST NORTH CENTRAL:										
Ohio..............	7,257	12	1,411		109	4,846	105	227	13	534
Indiana...........	5,265	20	1,162	221	155	2,796	157	322	45	387
Illinois...........	15,559	138	1,023	612	322	9,772	1,399	610	61	1,622
Michigan..........	2,779	5	478	123	45	1,636	59	205	5	223
Wisconsin.........	3,230	10	206	264	35	2,278	41	64	8	324
WEST NORTH CENTRAL:										
Minnesota.........	4,500	9	553	249	78	3,148	65	20	12	366
Iowa.............	15,450	38	1,528	807	467	9,443	1,431	171	50	1,515
Missouri..........	4,480	247	160	43	98	2,564	56	128	111	1,073
North Dakota......	5,636	8	468	307	98	4,254	172	9	1	319
South Dakota......	5,321	20	742	288	224	3,529	176	49	12	281
Nebraska..........	5,654	9	552	220	121	3,786	419	139	70	338
Kansas............	8,369	32	318	48	749	6,137	139	221	94	631
SOUTH ATLANTIC:										
Delaware..........	46				1	14		14		17
Maryland..........	821	5	59	34		219	5	25	272	202
District of Columbia.										
Virginia...........	1,809	38	17		4	735	2	81	532	400
West Virginia......	546	17	36	6	24	271	11	70	8	103
North Carolina.....	193	5		1	5	94		17	1	70
South Carolina.....	110	7				13		29	10	51
Georgia...........	192	8	2	1	2	66		18	6	89
Florida...........	58		1			9		1	12	35
EAST SOUTH CENTRAL:										
Kentucky..........	3,491	373	26	4	4	174	2	329	1,247	1,332
Tennessee........	832	60	7	7	10	196	3	31	22	496
Alabama..........	366	18	3		1	40		67	42	195
Mississippi........	305	23	2	6	4	70	2	34	2	162
WEST SOUTH CENTRAL:										
Arkansas..........	446	54	10	5	3	124	2	26	7	215
Louisiana.........	262	31	1		3	45		50	3	129
Oklahoma.........	2,786	67	80	12	58	1,893	11	215	126	324
Texas............	1,793	25	10	11	11	602	3	116	183	832
MOUNTAIN:										
Montana..........	3,585	6	412	101	97	2,427	270	93	11	168
Idaho.............	1,699	5	145	75	25	1,095	150	38	20	146
Wyoming..........	1,060	9	92	42	40	571	87	31	16	142
Colorado..........	2,043	37	100	62	66	1,226	75	35	52	207
New Mexico........	261	?	9	1	4	128	1	15	44	58
Arizona...........	178	2	2	3	2	59	2	6	27	75
Utah.............	635		45	31	22	326	46	24	56	85
Nevada...........	321	2	5	8	1	134	23	1	113	34
PACIFIC:										
Washington........	1,244	4	123	64	8	535	312	14	33	151
Oregon...........	1,538	1	132	205	20	747	181	29	24	199
California.........	1,615	27	152	37	11	769	110	35	113	361

1 Includes animals reported as pure bred, with breed not specified.

TABLE 109.—PURE-BRED BEEF CATTLE ON FARMS, CLASSIFIED ACCORDING TO BREED, BY DIVISIONS AND STATES: 1920.

DIVISION AND STATE.	BEEF BREEDS.						
	Total.	Aberdeen Angus.	Gallo-way.	Hereford.	Polled Durham.	Shorthorn.	All other breeds.[1]
United States........	1,064,912	108,524	7,225	405,582	61,764	416,995	64,822
GEOGRAPHIC DIVISIONS:							
New England..........	7,565	285	....	3,335	841	2,538	566
Middle Atlantic........	8,342	688	47	748	1,394	4,865	600
East North Central.....	167,472	20,613	209	30,242	10,928	97,401	8,079
West North Central.....	532,252	63,023	5,323	179,155	20,488	230,693	33,570
South Atlantic..........	27,732	5,407	142	10,640	1,130	8,651	1,762
East South Central......	36,342	8,460	42	12,623	2,381	9,910	2,926
West South Central.....	138,075	5,687	910	85,220	8,775	29,358	8,125
Mountain..............	116,188	2,140	475	73,264	9,412	23,495	7,402
Pacific.................	30,944	2,221	77	10,355	6,415	10,084	1,792
NEW ENGLAND:							
Maine.................	2,519	63	....	1,530	466	442	18
New Hampshire........	1,906	11	....	888	54	676	277
Vermont..............	1,209	28	....	371	272	491	47
Massachusetts..........	1,186	112	....	344	....	717	13
Rhode Island...........	68	....	....	64	....	4	....
Connecticut...........	677	71	....	138	49	208	211
MIDDLE ATLANTIC:							
New York.............	2,148	248	23	60	457	1,118	242
New Jersey............	93	12	....	2	....	71	8
Pennsylvania..........	6,101	428	24	686	937	3,676	350
EAST NORTH CENTRAL:							
Ohio..................	25,502	2,642	31	3,229	1,542	17,324	734
Indiana...............	29,509	4,807	21	6,615	1,183	16,147	736
Illinois...............	73,584	10,106	94	16,370	3,147	39,093	4,774
Michigan..............	16,267	1,519	25	1,825	1,067	11,712	119
Wisconsin.............	22,610	1,539	38	2,203	3,989	13,125	1,716
WEST NORTH CENTRAL:							
Minnesota............	56,028	5,398	175	10,787	2,415	32,419	4,834
Iowa.................	151,359	27,457	286	40,894	5,475	69,560	7,687
Missouri.............	83,902	12,916	1,114	32,609	2,309	30,517	4,437
North Dakota.........	29,024	3,124	183	7,089	1,359	14,723	2,546
South Dakota.........	57,100	4,788	697	21,663	3,162	23,293	3,497
Nebraska.............	74,174	4,640	411	27,418	3,420	32,777	5,508
Kansas..............	80,665	4,700	2,457	38,695	2,348	27,404	5,061
SOUTH ATLANTIC:							
Delaware.............	16	1	....	....	....	15	....
Maryland.............	920	135	1	106	243	414	21
District of Columbia....	....	....	....	....	....	....	....
Virginia..............	8,191	1,121	62	2,135	380	4,289	204
West Virginia..........	8,035	1,962	37	4,118	80	1,709	129
North Carolina........	3,085	786	5	933	156	732	473
South Carolina........	1,680	328	2	862	36	103	349
Georgia..............	4,397	497	35	1,799	226	1,293	547
Florida...............	1,408	577	....	687	9	96	39
EAST SOUTH CENTRAL:							
Kentucky.............	10,864	1,706	....	4,375	353	3,536	894
Tennessee............	13,319	3,799	37	4,084	1,334	3,286	779
Alabama.............	4,525	883	1	1,524	379	1,508	230
Mississippi...........	7,634	2,072	4	2,640	315	1,580	1,023
WEST SOUTH CENTRAL:							
Arkansas.............	6,536	893	61	1,726	1,388	2,128	340
Louisiana............	3,083	313	....	1,340	226	840	364
Oklahoma............	38,713	1,876	319	12,133	1,217	22,019	1,149
Texas...............	89,743	2,605	530	70,021	5,944	4,371	6,272
MOUNTAIN:							
Montana.............	19,543	927	198	10,699	1,291	5,621	807
Idaho...............	15,238	295	27	5,464	2,540	6,298	614
Wyoming............	16,459	115	5	11,845	392	1,305	2,797
Colorado............	27,162	615	211	17,270	1,166	6,989	911
New Mexico..........	17,400	111	7	14,563	517	434	1,768
Arizona.............	5,683	....	....	5,023	117	224	319
Utah................	10,934	62	19	5,978	2,707	2,007	161
Nevada.............	3,769	15	8	2,422	682	617	25
PACIFIC:							
Washington..........	5,840	263	17	935	1,008	3,281	336
Oregon..............	11,860	776	13	4,182	2,307	3,758	824
California...........	13,244	1,182	47	5,238	3,100	3,045	632

[1] Includes animals reported as pure bred, with breed not specified.

75108°—22——50

TABLE 110.—PURE-BRED DAIRY CATTLE ON FARMS, CLASSIFIED ACCORDING TO BREED, BY DIVISIONS AND STATES: 1920.

DIVISION AND STATE.	DAIRY BREEDS.						
	Total.	Ayrshire.	Brown Swiss.	Guernsey.	Holstein-Friesian.	Jersey.	All other breeds.[1]
United States	916,602	30,509	8,283	79,446	528,621	231,834	37,909
GEOGRAPHIC DIVISIONS:							
New England	85,724	9,780	349	10,311	42,721	20,305	2,258
Middle Atlantic	239,764	12,883	1,904	21,114	171,124	25,815	6,924
East North Central	289,859	3,735	4,199	29,640	185,475	57,167	9,643
West North Central	106,967	1,859	1,386	8,250	62,055	23,697	9,720
South Atlantic	49,119	519	43	5,949	15,445	25,245	1,918
East South Central	34,651	27	3	298	5,902	27,024	1,397
West South Central	43,268	60	13	263	9,724	30,650	2,558
Mountain	22,534	324	146	838	12,689	6,926	1,611
Pacific	44,716	1,322	240	2,783	23,486	15,005	1,880
NEW ENGLAND:							
Maine	15,683	1,134	62	1,836	7,206	4,999	446
New Hampshire	10,750	1,214	75	1,151	6,695	1,348	267
Vermont	28,549	3,808	59	2,193	13,413	8,446	630
Massachusetts	18,807	1,880	80	3,348	10,006	2,904	589
Rhode Island	1,651	494	....	217	542	351	47
Connecticut	10,284	1,250	73	1,566	4,859	2,257	279
MIDDLE ATLANTIC:							
New York	153,037	9,521	1,347	9,749	114,662	13,411	4,347
New Jersey	11,538	265	23	1,747	7,810	1,368	325
Pennsylvania	75,189	3,097	534	9,618	48,652	11,036	2,252
EAST NORTH CENTRAL:							
Ohio	70,882	1,021	324	4,960	38,327	23,842	2,408
Indiana	21,115	509	131	1,215	8,477	9,921	862
Illinois	36,412	202	1,385	1,369	25,124	7,317	1,015
Michigan	46,533	291	429	3,369	32,702	8,296	1,446
Wisconsin	114,917	1,712	1,930	18,727	80,845	7,791	3,912
WEST NORTH CENTRAL:							
Minnesota	32,668	399	483	4,468	22,830	2,508	1,980
Iowa	20,286	271	447	1,716	10,916	3,629	3,307
Missouri	19,037	110	135	760	5,569	10,708	1,755
North Dakota	4,797	226	23	346	2,937	481	784
South Dakota	5,248	85	119	135	4,027	312	570
Nebraska	7,873	74	38	348	5,368	1,275	770
Kansas	17,058	694	141	477	10,408	4,784	554
SOUTH ATLANTIC:							
Delaware	1,691	1	....	246	1,245	172	27
Maryland	8,668	113	9	1,867	4,073	2,323	283
District of Columbia	186	....	....	1	175	10	....
Virginia	9,586	25	....	1,696	4,160	3,223	482
West Virginia	4,450	272	32	333	1,134	2,546	133
North Carolina	7,697	44	1	789	1,613	4,978	272
South Carolina	5,184	4	....	644	1,008	3,389	139
Georgia	8,727	14	1	305	1,700	6,224	483
Florida	2,930	46	....	68	337	2,380	99
EAST SOUTH CENTRAL:							
Kentucky	8,829	20	....	40	2,046	6,421	302
Tennessee	11,347	2	1	111	1,383	9,424	426
Alabama	6,108	4	2	46	1,142	4,608	306
Mississippi	8,367	1	....	101	1,331	6,571	363
WEST SOUTH CENTRAL:							
Arkansas	6,950	3	1	19	2,001	4,627	299
Louisiana	3,415	1	2	94	1,009	2,201	108
Oklahoma	9,539	37	3	91	3,741	5,104	563
Texas	23,364	19	7	59	2,973	18,718	1,588
MOUNTAIN:							
Montana	3,401	13	54	176	2,150	900	105
Idaho	1,100	46	48	197	2,049	1,579	219
Wyoming	1,071	21	14	31	747	167	91
Colorado	6,448	114	30	241	4,057	1,605	401
New Mexico	1,327	....	....	42	438	507	310
Arizona	2,772	109	....	48	1,778	669	168
Utah	2,922	....	....	93	970	1,706	153
Nevada	405	21	....	10	197	133	44
PACIFIC:							
Washington	12,720	404	69	941	7,673	3,402	231
Oregon	12,852	323	135	697	3,624	7,771	302
California	19,144	595	36	1,145	12,189	3,832	1,347

[1] Includes animals reported as pure bred, with breed not specified.

TABLE 111.—PURE-BRED SHEEP ON FARMS, CLASSIFIED ACCORDING TO BREED, BY DIVISIONS AND STATES: 1920.

DIVISION AND STATE.	Total.	Cheviot.	Dorset Horn.	Hampshire Down.	Lincoln.	Merino.	Oxford.	Rambouillet.	Shropshire.	Southdown.	All other breeds.[1]
United States.......	463,504	3,000	8,458	51,813	13,903	59,920	16,601	106,849	124,454	8,451	70,055
GEOGRAPHIC DIVISIONS:											
New England..........	8,314	536	890	585	19	618	891	88	3,220	532	935
Middle Atlantic........	35,241	935	4,755	6,620	299	3,688	1,440	903	9,519	1,569	5,513
East North Central.....	94,028	753	1,228	4,765	635	30,422	6,991	5,778	36,724	824	5,908
West North Central....	63,123	126	283	3,692	398	1,767	2,965	3,698	44,625	271	5,298
South Atlantic.........	12,231	162	852	2,582	51	1,775	169	33	4,221	1,676	710
East South Central.....	9,047	90	150	2,871	18	68	196	38	2,434	2,759	423
West South Central....	21,054	10	140	679	24	3,081	120	7,390	3,723	329	5,558
Mountain..............	143,947	388	28	22,626	6,414	7,227	2,416	66,379	7,865	341	30,263
Pacific...............	76,519	.....	132	7,393	6,045	11,274	1,413	22,542	12,123	150	15,447
NEW ENGLAND:											
Maine.................	2,361	235	84	259	1	81	710	4	551	132	304
New Hampshire.......	739	27	5	92	.....	2	60	9	372	19	153
Vermont..............	3,035	88	267	152	15	533	98	75	1,359	85	363
Massachusetts........	1,245	170	284	59	.....	2	23	....	550	54	103
Rhode Island.........	93	.....	.....	.....	.....	.....	.....	.....	47	36	10
Connecticut..........	841	16	250	23	3	.....	.....	.....	341	206	2
MIDDLE ATLANTIC:											
New York............	18,338	853	760	2,399	226	947	912	802	7,330	752	3,357
New Jersey...........	1,122	14	492	310	4	.....	.....	1	94	59	148
Pennsylvania.........	15,781	68	3,503	3,911	69	2,741	528	100	2,095	758	2,008
EAST NORTH CENTRAL:											
Ohio.................	39,444	138	355	458	258	24,170	892	2,765	8,164	431	1,813
Indiana..............	9,282	88	250	720	29	185	628	333	5,743	110	1,196
Illinois.............	13,300	308	449	811	.....	910	1,265	113	8,503	56	855
Michigan.............	21,342	24	72	1,910	268	4,998	2,800	2,267	7,942	.....	1,061
Wisconsin............	10,660	195	102	866	80	129	1,406	300	6,372	227	983
WEST NORTH CENTRAL:											
Minnesota............	8,729	.....	31	323	52	44	508	253	6,945	78	495
Iowa.................	19,522	112	81	509	65	1,523	821	16	14,404	22	1,969
Missouri.............	15,383	.....	58	1,235	86	117	798	308	11,423	128	1,230
North Dakota.........	4,989	.....	.....	427	108	3	428	159	3,583	2	279
South Dakota.........	6,487	2	.....	481	24	54	86	2,736	2,670	14	420
Nebraska.............	3,448	12	12	466	2	.....	271	202	2,040	26	417
Kansas...............	4,565	.....	101	251	61	26	53	24	3,560	1	488
SOUTH ATLANTIC:											
Delaware.............	12	.....	4	.....	.....	.....	.....	.....	1	7	.....
Maryland.............	1,092	9	109	19	.....	.....	15	7	635	259	39
District of Columbia...	.....	.....	.....	.....	.....	.....	.....	.....	.....	.....	.....
Virginia.............	3,785	80	241	1,678	48	7	56	.....	1,088	338	249
West Virginia........	5,424	69	479	613	3	1,725	75	11	1,479	712	258
North Carolina.......	1,207	2	19	209	.....	.....	.....	1	820	113	43
South Carolina.......	192	.....	.....	8	.....	.....	18	1	78	5	82
Georgia..............	420	2	.....	53	.....	42	.....	7	119	181	16
Florida..............	99	.....	.....	2	.....	1	5	6	1	61	23
EAST SOUTH CENTRAL:											
Kentucky.............	5,549	63	42	2,466	15	10	62	.....	1,331	1,349	211
Tennessee............	2,694	22	89	323	.....	9	127	17	840	1,216	51
Alabama..............	323	4	17	43	3	34	4	7	61	119	31
Mississippi..........	481	1	2	39	.....	15	3	14	202	75	130
WEST SOUTH CENTRAL:											
Arkansas.............	799	.....	6	82	1	45	35	59	293	24	254
Louisiana............	194	10	.....	.....	.....	5	.....	5	101	42	31
Oklahoma.............	2,942	.....	109	166	16	36	4	109	1,586	11	905
Texas................	17,119	.....	25	431	7	2,995	81	7,217	1,743	252	4,368
MOUNTAIN:											
Montana..............	24,208	20	.....	2,356	195	286	1,039	17,041	1,690	48	1,533
Idaho................	47,107	368	2	14,664	5,408	925	771	9,489	3,671	13	11,796
Wyoming.............	15,612	.....	.....	282	73	880	1	5,723	166	2	8,485
Colorado.............	7,982	.....	11	2,006	319	20	372	1,533	1,635	32	2,054
New Mexico...........	10,478	.....	1	92	182	2,991	166	6,492	80	33	441
Arizona..............	2,205	.....	6	10	1	753	.....	284	224	.....	927
Utah.................	30,013	.....	.....	2,145	236	48	67	25,094	86	193	2,144
Nevada...............	6,342	.....	8	1,071	.....	1,324	.....	723	313	20	2,883
PACIFIC:											
Washington...........	8,950	.....	5	1,257	919	111	592	4,421	841	20	784
Oregon...............	38,738	.....	79	4,764	4,978	6,153	821	2,946	5,040	62	13,895
California...........	28,831	.....	48	1,372	148	5,010	.....	15,175	6,242	68	768

[1] Includes animals reported as pure bred, with breed not specified.

TABLE **112.**—PURE-BRED SWINE ON FARMS, CLASSIFIED ACCORDING TO BREED, BY DIVISIONS AND STATES: 1920.

DIVISION AND STATE.	Total.	Berkshire.	Chester White.	Duroc-Jersey.	Essex.	Hampshire.	Poland China.	Spotted Poland China.	Tamworth.	Yorkshire.	All other breeds.[1]
United States...	2,049,900	86,676	191,207	819,117	1,771	108,782	726,504	47,703	5,639	6,353	56,148
GEOGRAPHIC DIVISIONS:											
New England......	17,535	9,300	4,139	1,357	13	524	606	17	78	618	883
Middle Atlantic....	58,627	22,864	13,681	10,705	62	2,373	5,387	118	418	903	2,116
East North Central.	558,333	12,657	68,852	186,470	5	28,014	215,465	29,713	1,395	1,897	13,865
West North Central.	829,597	5,520	83,841	329,633	34	44,501	326,210	15,751	1,258	1,787	21,062
South Atlantic.....	149,313	19,286	5,434	69,432	864	17,329	29,208	805	1,118	248	5,589
East South Central.	156,510	4,516	3,868	90,854	305	7,271	44,008	663	250	122	4,653
West South Central.	182,422	2,397	4,401	88,208	363	4,064	76,053	579	774	237	5,346
Mountain..........	40,199	2,314	2,072	20,469	83	1,266	12,499	46	59	110	1,281
Pacific............	57,364	7,822	4,919	21,989	42	3,440	17,068	11	289	431	1,353
NEW ENGLAND:											
Maine..............	2,913	1,205	1,254	113	.....	16	67	......	......	107	151
New Hampshire...	2,099	1,241	575	142	.....	51	38	......	2	17	33
Vermont...........	2,111	950	786	150	.....	7	87	......	21	6	104
Massachusetts.....	6,533	3,843	907	518	.....	88	206	17	52	413	489
Rhode Island......	513	377	52	33	.....	7	1	......	......	26	17
Connecticut.......	3,366	1,684	565	401	13	355	207	......	3	49	89
MIDDLE ATLANTIC:											
New York.........	19,230	6,624	5,596	4,309	34	710	570	......	140	598	649
New Jersey........	4,622	2,185	596	1,104	.....	163	148	......	258	58	110
Pennsylvania......	34,775	14,055	7,489	5,292	28	1,500	4,669	118	20	247	1,357
EAST NORTH CENTRAL:											
Ohio..............	96,908	3,605	12,851	34,478	2	3,299	34,597	4,332	84	334	3,326
Indiana...........	159,696	2,104	12,493	46,364	.....	6,858	66,786	21,123	77	27	3,864
Illinois...........	215,965	3,434	27,286	74,406	3	15,819	84,449	4,009	887	673	4,999
Michigan..........	33,527	1,618	7,869	12,842	.....	1,023	8,739	249	135	376	676
Wisconsin.........	52,237	1,896	8,353	18,380	.....	1,015	20,894	......	212	487	1,000
WEST NORTH CENTRAL:											
Minnesota.........	99,443	1,472	13,875	46,638	.....	1,906	32,208	27	17	1,052	2,248
Iowa..............	289,042	950	35,761	107,123	26	18,740	113,869	4,370	1,074	173	6,956
Missouri..........	148,811	1,182	8,306	47,986	6	5,133	74,139	8,696	52	9	3,302
North Dakota.....	22,076	710	3,840	10,152	.....	388	6,154	13	6	468	345
South Dakota.....	91,853	395	10,400	44,569	.....	8,479	26,045	65	43	59	1,798
Nebraska.........	112,502	319	6,732	50,193	2	8,051	42,212	283	61	18	4,631
Kansas............	65,870	492	4,927	22,972	.....	1,804	31,583	2,297	5	8	1,782
SOUTH ATLANTIC:											
Delaware..........	653	318	51	135	1	17	128	......	......	......	3
Maryland.........	5,860	2,326	775	1,669	1	195	727	30	......	8	129
Dist. of Columbia..	59	26	8	.....	.....	.....	25	......	......	......	......
Virginia..........	20,867	3,969	1,006	9,815	42	795	4,366	6	193	117	558
West Virginia......	7,820	1,338	1,445	1,315	1	150	3,292	31	64	31	153
North Carolina....	27,374	3,511	1,099	13,843	227	1,352	5,484	16	258	27	1,557
South Carolina....	21,282	2,202	567	12,078	190	906	4,253	2	221	.....	863
Georgia...........	46,760	4,254	414	19,184	275	12,150	8,025	715	244	21	1,478
Florida...........	18,638	1,342	69	11,393	127	1,764	2,908	5	138	44	848
EAST SOUTH CENTRAL:											
Kentucky..........	33,619	1,117	1,657	19,279	12	1,126	9,322	227	91	1	787
Tennessee.........	47,571	1,033	1,104	28,357	52	1,264	13,867	296	62	93	1,443
Alabama..........	32,397	1,047	445	17,887	97	3,406	7,915	119	55	10	1,416
Mississippi........	42,923	1,319	662	25,331	144	1,475	12,904	21	42	18	1,007
WEST SOUTH CENTRAL:											
Arkansas..........	46,006	399	1,085	23,886	100	1,036	18,155	258	121	4	962
Louisiana.........	11,073	236	102	7,167	30	656	2,843	11	50	210	894
Oklahoma........	53,000	255	1,357	26,268	34	1,292	21,728	294	143	3	1,014
Texas.............	70,853	1,507	1,257	30,887	199	1,080	33,327	16	452	12	2,116
MOUNTAIN:											
Montana..........	5,351	296	483	2,111	.....	390	1,941	......	22	6	102
Idaho.............	7,299	530	433	3,006	3	403	2,628	9	3	.....	284
Wyoming..........	1,498	19	88	542	.....	82	697	......	2	2	66
Colorado..........	17,951	422	686	10,678	78	270	5,291	37	4	2	483
New Mexico.......	3,245	148	160	1,617	2	90	858	......	19	100	251
Arizona...........	1,914	47	24	1,107	.....	10	688	......	1	.....	37
Utah..............	2,492	676	188	1,246	.....	11	307	......	8	.....	56
Nevada...........	449	176	10	162	.....	10	89	......	......	......	2
PACIFIC:											
Washington........	10,006	1,369	1,889	3,625	.....	408	2,297	......	190	28	200
Oregon...........	11,617	1,105	2,033	4,211	15	333	3,625	7	3	70	215
California.........	35,741	5,348	997	14,153	27	2,699	11,146	4	96	333	938

[1] Includes animals reported as pure bred, with breed not specified.

LIVE-STOCK PRODUCTS.

TABLE 113.—QUANTITY AND VALUE OF LIVE-STOCK PRODUCTS OF FARMS IN THE UNITED STATES: 1919 AND 1909.

ITEM.	Farms reporting, 1919	Unit.	NUMBER OR QUANTITY.		VALUE.	
			1919	1909	1919	1909
Total...................					$2,667,072,273	$1,177,974,703
Dairy products, total [1]........					1,481,462,091	596,413,463
Milk produced, as reported...	4,361,380	Gals.	6,893,727,418	5,813,699,474		
Total production of milk, including estimates [2]........		Gals.	7,805,143,792			
Butter made on farms........	3,565,305	Lbs.	707,666,492	994,650,610	346,355,759	222,861,440
Cheese made on farms........	17,956	Lbs.	6,371,396	9,405,864	2,268,025	1,148,708
Milk sold....................	710,694	Gals.	2,529,331,413	1,937,255,864	717,380,222	252,436,757
Cream sold..................	445,611	Gals.	82,247,580	54,933,583	111,905,929	37,655,047
Butter fat sold..............	875,200	Lbs.	532,244,072	305,662,587	303,552,156	82,311,511
Butter sold..................	1,269,814	Lbs.	207,859,564	415,080,489	106,973,742	100,378,123
Dairy products sold, total [3]..					1,239,812,049	473,769,412
Wool and mohair, total........					124,006,859	66,373,925
Wool, including estimates [2]...	[4]538,593	Lbs.	228,795,354	289,419,977	120,417,549	65,472,328
Mohair, as reported..........	12,403	Lbs.	6,808,890	3,778,706	3,589,310	901,597
Eggs and chickens, total.......					1,047,323,170	509,195,232
Chicken eggs produced, including estimates [2].........	[4]5,837,367	Doz.	1,654,044,932	1,574,979,416	661,082,803	[5]306,688,960
Chickens raised, including estimates [2].................	[4]5,837,367	No..	473,301,959	460,611,201	386,240,367	[6]202,506,272
Chicken eggs sold, as reported.	4,088,169	Doz.	1,010,813,258		404,562,912	
Chickens sold, as reported....	2,698,211	No..	140,811,045		119,722,603	
Eggs and chickens sold, total					524,285,515	
Honey and wax, total..........					14,280,153	5,992,083
Honey........................	312,997	Lbs.	55,224,061	54,814,890	13,988,670	5,762,869
Wax..........................		Lbs.	820,529	904,867	291,483	229,214
Calves, pigs, and lambs raised on farms:						
Calves......................	4,073,156	No..	21,133,385			
Pigs.........................	3,162,993	No..	62,072,829			
Lambs.......................	373,799	No..	13,653,130			
Domestic animals slaughtered on farms:						
Cattle and calves...........	887,611	No..	1,904,581	2,540,240		
Hogs and pigs...............	4,565,130	No..	16,800,230	15,378,517		
Sheep and lambs............	93,853	No..	434,608	529,526		
Meat and meat products sold:						
Beef and veal...............		Lbs.	224,780,189			
Pork........................		Lbs.	443,538,071			
Lamb and mutton...........		Lbs.	6,734,772			

[1] Value of milk, cream, and butter fat sold, and of butter and cheese made on farms.
[2] Estimates have been made for incomplete reports, as where a farmer reported dairy cows but no milk production, or chickens but no egg production. Chicken eggs and chickens for 1909 also involve estimated deductions from the published figures of the Thirteenth Census, which included all eggs and all kinds of fowls raised.
[3] Figures for 1919 do not include "cheese sold," as that item was not reported for 1919. The value of cheese sold in 1909 was $987,974.
[4] Includes farms for which estimates were made.
[5] Value of all eggs produced. The estimated value of chicken eggs produced in 1909 was $303,296,012.
[6] Value of all fowls raised. The estimated value of chickens raised in 1909 was $184,902,527.

TABLE 114.—VALUE OF LIVE-STOCK PRODUCTS OF

	DIVISION AND STATE.	TOTAL.		DAIRY PRODUCTS.[1]	
		1919	1909	1919	1909
1	United States	$2,667,072,273	$1,177,974,703	$1,481,462,091	$596,413,463
	GEOGRAPHIC DIVISIONS:				
2	New England	132,411,030	73,922,170	98,725,445	50,720,766
3	Middle Atlantic	412,960,765	192,977,646	298,511,901	130,772,563
4	East North Central	721,387,462	298,143,600	448,600,891	159,673,557
5	West North Central	550,742,614	245,673,372	263,048,219	108,824,533
6	South Atlantic	204,301,963	89,426,168	88,626,610	35,578,455
7	East South Central	159,643,789	73,815,566	70,130,277	30,200,917
8	West South Central	181,346,648	79,880,253	71,833,975	32,894,027
9	Mountain	121,132,969	55,917,961	41,070,484	12,991,603
10	Pacific	183,145,033	68,217,967	100,914,289	35,257,042
	NEW ENGLAND:				
11	Maine	26,075,219	13,613,815	17,772,370	8,079,692
12	New Hampshire	14,681,368	8,583,337	10,224,888	5,589,711
13	Vermont	31,573,340	14,821,352	27,207,813	12,128,465
14	Massachusetts	33,850,892	21,932,652	24,765,522	15,187,774
15	Rhode Island	5,367,881	3,406,278	3,830,881	2,065,941
16	Connecticut	20,862,330	11,564,736	14,923,971	7,669,183
	MIDDLE ATLANTIC:				
17	New York	225,465,739	104,867,285	179,695,810	77,807,161
18	New Jersey	31,482,945	17,951,089	19,198,718	10,156,600
19	Pennsylvania	156,012,081	70,159,272	99,617,373	42,808,802
	EAST NORTH CENTRAL:				
20	Ohio	155,587,919	68,500,279	81,148,586	30,869,408
21	Indiana	99,350,023	44,319,539	44,072,646	16,666,374
22	Illinois	142,351,262	67,390,680	71,998,333	31,542,209
23	Michigan	111,076,235	48,380,551	71,074,727	26,727,538
24	Wisconsin	213,022,023	69,552,551	180,306,599	53,868,028
	WEST NORTH CENTRAL:				
25	Minnesota	113,236,965	44,645,205	77,870,358	29,219,406
26	Iowa	130,250,447	66,053,869	55,408,744	31,196,883
27	Missouri	105,601,436	49,839,077	34,752,845	13,685,318
28	North Dakota	30,979,932	9,832,117	19,576,343	4,872,304
29	South Dakota	35,739,209	13,660,311	16,812,347	6,192,608
30	Nebraska	54,612,075	24,961,343	23,706,963	10,566,275
31	Kansas	80,322,550	36,681,450	34,920,619	13,091,739
	SOUTH ATLANTIC:				
32	Delaware	5,778,747	2,910,412	2,553,175	1,089,497
33	Maryland	25,522,172	11,967,668	13,407,526	5,480,900
34	District of Columbia	119,263	142,191	81,484	117,335
35	Virginia	46,311,494	21,473,064	19,167,935	7,704,326
36	West Virginia	26,332,970	11,984,911	11,390,209	5,000,138
37	North Carolina	35,860,056	14,904,898	14,912,137	5,789,583
38	South Carolina	20,354,060	7,611,077	7,995,753	2,800,605
39	Georgia	36,401,316	14,933,151	16,757,195	6,621,585
40	Florida	7,621,885	3,498,796	2,361,196	974,486
	EAST SOUTH CENTRAL:				
41	Kentucky	50,928,217	24,776,564	22,487,710	9,055,813
42	Tennessee	50,960,694	22,398,336	20,640,849	8,715,441
43	Alabama	30,426,993	13,513,006	15,229,517	6,396,198
44	Mississippi	27,327,885	13,127,660	11,772,201	6,033,465
	WEST SOUTH CENTRAL:				
45	Arkansas	30,083,950	14,115,791	13,445,124	6,587,428
46	Louisiana	13,613,465	7,286,958	4,509,985	2,761,380
47	Oklahoma	49,887,518	20,379,510	20,878,920	7,365,295
48	Texas	87,761,715	38,097,994	32,999,946	15,679,924
	MOUNTAIN:				
49	Montana	24,809,029	12,749,555	7,534,413	2,093,594
50	Idaho	22,225,355	9,740,404	8,065,646	1,962,500
51	Wyoming	14,004,109	10,734,548	2,143,020	539,423
52	Colorado	26,921,292	9,705,676	12,674,030	4,174,270
53	New Mexico	8,447,826	5,045,808	2,134,987	726,692
54	Arizona	6,294,886	2,769,881	2,745,329	909,411
55	Utah	13,735,823	5,664,682	4,809,087	2,067,534
56	Nevada	4,694,649	1,998,377	963,966	518,179
	PACIFIC:				
57	Washington	44,066,349	15,538,705	27,620,231	8,746,041
58	Oregon	35,146,671	14,401,942	17,651,409	6,067,024
59	California	103,932,013	38,277,320	55,642,649	20,443,977

[1] Value of milk, cream, and butter fat sold, and of butter and cheese made on farms.
[2] The figures represent the value of the total production of wool, including estimates, plus the value of mohair, as reported.

FARMS, BY DIVISIONS AND STATES: 1919 AND 1909.

WOOL AND MOHAIR.[2]		EGGS AND CHICKENS.[3]		HONEY AND WAX.		
1919	1909	1919	1909	1919	1909	
$124,006,859	$66,373,925	$1,047,323,170	$509,195,232	$14,280,153	$5,992,083	1
855,060	575,852	32,603,758	22,517,029	226,767	108,523	2
4,248,690	2,495,091	108,751,458	59,034,629	1,448,716	675,363	3
20,933,860	14,286,422	249,814,285	123,210,787	2,038,426	972,834	4
15,468,458	6,153,965	270,158,753	129,830,507	2,067,184	864,367	5
3,252,334	1,962,242	110,631,263	50,959,642	1,791,756	925,829	6
2,899,359	1,652,264	85,188,095	41,412,242	1,426,058	550,143	7
11,087,843	2,915,313	97,019,133	44,077,140	1,405,697	493,773	8
47,965,993	29,395,684	30,016,279	12,955,691	2,080,213	574,983	9
17,295,262	6,937,092	63,140,146	25,197,565	1,795,336	826,268	10
412,728	266,287	7,815,871	5,247,150	74,250	20,686	11
95,691	57,651	4,341,810	2,922,352	18,979	13,623	12
250,977	192,138	4,038,495	2,474,583	76,055	26,166	13
56,003	34,179	9,004,007	6,691,523	25,360	19,176	14
8,405	6,836	1,526,891	1,330,542	1,704	2,959	15
31,256	18,761	5,876,684	3,850,879	30,419	25,913	16
1,977,598	1,165,588	42,841,499	25,504,894	950,832	389,642	17
32,071	22,538	12,200,716	7,749,034	51,440	22,917	18
2,239,021	1,306,965	53,709,243	25,780,701	446,444	262,804	19
10,075,214	6,750,689	64,109,133	30,746,291	254,986	133,891	20
2,322,127	1,534,108	52,765,970	26,013,342	189,280	105,715	21
2,219,526	1,303,226	67,690,085	34,344,482	443,318	200,763	22
4,623,778	3,430,032	34,960,771	17,926,239	416,959	296,742	23
1,693,215	1,268,367	30,288,326	14,180,433	733,883	235,723	24
1,559,256	818,853	33,438,496	14,482,329	368,855	124,617	25
3,765,909	1,420,972	70,212,544	33,150,585	863,250	285,429	26
4,217,400	1,961,398	66,271,029	33,918,187	360,162	274,174	27
913,551	381,855	10,486,386	4,576,089	3,652	1,869	28
2,761,265	847,402	16,050,023	6,599,858	115,574	20,443	29
1,230,427	464,785	29,500,431	13,856,885	174,254	73,398	30
1,020,650	258,700	44,199,844	23,246,574	181,437	84,437	31
8,949	5,177	3,210,157	1,807,503	6,466	8,235	32
320,180	200,383	11,737,629	6,247,141	56,837	39,244	33
....	....	37,684	24,379	95	477	34
914,713	567,299	25,879,870	13,027,512	348,976	173,927	35
1,593,776	842,254	13,042,688	5,910,889	306,297	231,630	36
185,223	131,193	20,406,603	8,753,536	356,093	230,586	37
36,117	20,560	12,204,752	4,710,976	117,438	78,936	38
93,639	118,048	19,218,622	8,091,630	331,860	101,888	39
99,737	77,328	4,893,258	2,386,076	267,694	60,906	40
1,775,201	976,385	26,210,759	14,542,124	454,547	202,242	41
733,980	467,512	29,065,336	13,032,321	520,529	183,062	42
134,827	85,915	14,779,501	6,930,916	283,148	99,977	43
255,351	122,452	15,132,499	6,906,881	167,834	64,862	44
191,607	87,561	16,245,102	7,327,834	202,117	112,968	45
205,988	99,650	8,835,402	4,392,017	62,090	33,911	46
268,724	57,541	28,635,007	12,932,578	104,867	24,096	47
10,421,524	2,670,561	43,303,622	19,424,711	1,036,623	322,798	48
10,231,133	8,225,810	6,883,213	2,408,216	160,270	21,935	49
8,753,178	3,349,421	5,062,276	2,349,131	344,255	88,382	50
9,574,466	8,916,476	2,021,979	761,924	264,644	16,725	51
4,888,684	1,460,027	8,773,648	3,837,045	584,924	234,334	52
4,088,528	3,228,129	2,102,831	1,051,348	121,480	39,639	53
1,632,517	1,046,881	1,699,064	756,386	217,976	57,203	54
5,787,419	2,105,067	2,887,570	1,412,318	251,747	79,763	55
3,010,068	1,063,873	585,698	379,323	134,917	37,002	56
2,258,739	541,374	13,779,958	6,184,899	407,421	66,391	57
8,230,902	3,910,951	9,018,444	4,329,457	245,916	94,510	58
6,805,621	2,484,767	40,341,744	14,683,209	1,141,999	665,367	59

[3] The figures shown for 1919 represent the value of chicken eggs and chickens raised, while the 1909 figures include the value of the products of all kinds of poultry. The figures for both years represent the value of the total production, including estimates. The estimated value of chicken eggs produced in 1909 is shown in Table 123 and of chickens raised, in Table 124.

TABLE 115.—MILK PRODUCED ON FARMS, BY DIVISIONS AND STATES: 1919 AND 1909.

[A minus sign (−) denotes decrease.]

DIVISION AND STATE.	Total production of milk, including estimates, 1919 (gallons).[1]	Farms reporting, 1919	MILK PRODUCED, AS REPORTED.		Per cent of increase.
			Quantity (gallons).		
			1919	1909	
United States	7,805,143,792	4,361,380	6,893,727,418	5,813,699,474	18.6
GEOGRAPHIC DIVISIONS:					
New England	385,638,607	111,096	340,815,700	347,872,803	−2.0
Middle Atlantic	1,248,168,026	312,816	1,119,942,674	1,001,269,989	11.9
East North Central	2,246,679,781	849,101	2,008,013,552	1,564,282,966	28.4
West North Central	1,718,410,014	843,701	1,510,769,902	1,266,991,620	19.2
South Atlantic	517,728,377	680,259	449,716,323	418,843,384	7.4
East South Central	458,942,467	695,038	400,898,515	400,476,525	0.1
West South Central	459,370,676	587,085	396,679,416	416,401,603	−4.7
Mountain	260,412,164	147,231	231,237,131	116,468,996	98.5
Pacific	509,793,680	135,053	435,654,205	281,091,588	55.0
NEW ENGLAND:					
Maine	77,676,881	35,222	67,304,799	56,026,334	20.1
New Hampshire	42,556,285	13,843	36,456,334	35,033,153	4.1
Vermont	122,095,734	22,553	108,119,922	114,317,169	−5.4
Massachusetts	76,316,309	20,787	68,624,097	86,304,347	−20.5
Rhode Island	12,099,111	2,757	10,852,261	10,441,951	3.9
Connecticut	54,894,287	15,934	49,458,287	45,749,849	8.1
MIDDLE ATLANTIC:					
New York	756,045,942	142,540	675,923,730	597,363,198	13.2
New Jersey	70,490,729	17,982	64,135,989	67,698,219	−5.3
Pennsylvania	421,631,355	152,294	379,882,955	336,208,572	13.0
EAST NORTH CENTRAL:					
Ohio	396,317,787	193,896	347,869,655	307,590,755	13.1
Indiana	238,793,861	160,248	212,003,849	194,736,962	8.9
Illinois	370,486,981	187,206	333,234,145	320,240,399	4.1
Michigan	382,822,631	150,753	337,954,884	283,387,201	19.3
Wisconsin	858,258,521	156,998	776,951,019	458,327,649	69.5
WEST NORTH CENTRAL:					
Minnesota	475,506,689	131,906	388,217,369	273,319,603	42.0
Iowa	361,426,362	171,999	326,983,002	318,954,506	2.5
Missouri	228,907,721	205,549	208,471,273	188,297,972	10.7
North Dakota	138,606,540	58,757	124,365,039	70,637,899	76.1
South Dakota	124,424,918	55,688	113,486,710	82,428,514	37.7
Nebraska	168,083,367	95,468	151,352,415	160,610,359	−5.8
Kansas	221,454,417	124,334	197,894,094	172,742,767	14.6
SOUTH ATLANTIC:					
Delaware	11,356,313	5,851	9,412,193	7,859,857	19.8
Maryland	58,754,193	31,627	52,071,197	41,094,421	26.7
District of Columbia	512,074	91	505,567	555,342	−9.0
Virginia	110,942,113	133,285	100,816,137	95,555,051	5.5
West Virginia	73,690,103	71,032	67,161,992	71,230,033	−5.7
North Carolina	95,747,638	150,264	83,217,128	82,601,779	0.7
South Carolina	52,954,637	95,745	43,147,385	37,361,666	15.5
Georgia	101,615,773	175,427	84,348,991	74,908,776	12.6
Florida	12,155,533	16,937	9,035,733	7,676,459	17.7
EAST SOUTH CENTRAL:					
Kentucky	146,561,464	199,959	131,495,154	125,566,917	4.7
Tennessee	130,285,644	187,160	115,119,224	117,101,970	−1.7
Alabama	93,903,677	165,778	79,536,405	78,728,345	1.0
Mississippi	88,191,682	142,141	74,747,732	79,079,293	−5.5
WEST SOUTH CENTRAL:					
Arkansas	87,623,651	140,197	76,176,721	83,091,875	0.0
Louisiana	69,072,720	57,698	27,588,726	32,702,130	−15.6
Oklahoma	135,990,700	113,133	118,127,327	103,577,644	14.0
Texas	202,953,536	260,457	174,786,642	197,039,954	−11.3
MOUNTAIN:					
Montana	51,251,095	33,121	45,262,090	16,982,145	166.5
Idaho	52,365,498	28,786	45,748,122	20,861,072	119.3
Wyoming	14,542,841	8,917	13,175,031	6,453,634	104.1
Colorado	79,492,631	40,762	72,013,067	33,631,723	114.1
New Mexico	12,737,649	11,089	11,117,007	6,815,942	63.1
Arizona	14,370,833	4,776	12,908,592	6,881,608	87.6
Utah	29,339,512	17,924	25,602,493	20,486,317	25.0
Nevada	6,312,105	1,856	5,410,729	4,356,555	24.2
PACIFIC:					
Washington	140,524,518	45,971	124,019,763	70,083,033	77.0
Oregon	92,844,946	34,502	79,641,946	56,106,599	41.9
California	276,424,216	54,580	231,992,496	154,901,956	49.8

[1] Figures include estimates for farms which reported dairy cows on hand on January 1, 1920, but no milk production for the preceding calendar year.

TABLE 116.—BUTTER MADE ON FARMS, BY DIVISIONS AND STATES: 1919 AND 1909.

DIVISION AND STATE.	FARMS REPORTING.		QUANTITY (POUNDS).		VALUE.	
	1919	1909	1919	1909	1919	1909
United States........	3,565,305	3,787,749	707,666,492	994,650,610	$346,355,759	$222,861,440
GEOGRAPHIC DIVISIONS:						
New England............	62,951	83,010	22,093,227	40,732,783	13,146,301	11,704,089
Middle Atlantic.........	194,466	234,948	64,797,058	88,242,228	36,441,006	22,996,544
East North Central......	563,372	717,911	108,093,861	230,966,876	56,559,268	53,108,927
West North Central.....	726,739	711,499	130,995,829	201,172,278	66,387,407	44,748,964
South Atlantic..........	628,890	636,763	121,072,533	123,270,552	55,970,638	26,054,617
East South Central......	660,329	697,028	120,495,395	135,239,873	51,176,037	25,739,427
West South Central.....	531,609	560,724	101,443,114	128,188,799	46,134,284	25,838,528
Mountain..............	110,071	66,794	22,840,410	18,115,811	11,762,025	4,992,172
Pacific................	86,878	79,072	15,835,065	27,721,410	8,778,793	7,678,172
NEW ENGLAND:						
Maine..............	29,029	36,371	10,855,560	13,299,229	6,272,232	3,786,054
New Hampshire........	8,985	11,673	3,240,368	5,065,188	1,975,330	1,509,706
Vermont.............	8,780	15,102	3,877,039	15,165,692	2,301,863	4,185,028
Massachusetts..........	7,361	9,035	2,019,231	3,364,516	1,261,218	1,041,482
Rhode Island..........	1,033	1,633	174,902	339,607	105,834	104,161
Connecticut..........	7,763	9,196	1,926,127	3,498,551	1,229,824	1,077,658
MIDDLE ATLANTIC:						
New York.............	78,174	85,516	24,727,662	23,461,702	14,347,664	6,268,386
New Jersey............	7,783	12,328	1,600,789	3,622,411	955,624	1,059,935
Pennsylvania..........	108,509	137,104	38,468,607	61,158,115	21,137,718	15,668,223
EAST NORTH CENTRAL:						
Ohio................	143,448	188,481	30,264,265	63,569,132	15,967,415	14,305,607
Indiana..............	119,633	158,508	18,344,239	43,181,817	9,298,910	9,402,994
Illinois...............	146,524	168,485	25,063,897	46,609,992	12,853,175	10,493,217
Michigan.............	109,163	131,519	25,755,423	50,405,426	13,706,212	11,805,872
Wisconsin.............	44,604	70,918	8,666,037	27,200,509	4,733,556	7,101,237
WEST NORTH CENTRAL:						
Minnesota.............	92,867	85,001	20,205,076	34,708,669	10,345,233	8,593,233
Iowa................	134,357	124,881	25,422,675	38,679,568	13,411,842	9,061,041
Missouri.............	191,197	207,828	29,470,763	42,105,143	14,620,740	8,744,025
North Dakota..........	58,147	46,838	14,413,180	16,414,439	6,996,643	3,508,579
South Dakota..........	51,159	39,705	10,267,171	13,629,647	5,356,074	3,024,509
Nebraska.............	85,532	87,400	13,761,085	25,986,931	6,877,379	5,385,494
Kansas..............	113,480	119,846	17,455,879	29,647,881	8,779,496	6,432,083
SOUTH ATLANTIC:						
Delaware............	4,644	5,488	894,883	1,563,161	477,246	400,428
Maryland............	24,276	28,871	6,162,501	8,739,620	3,200,266	2,010,106
District of Columbia....	41	28	6,026	6,155	3,615	1,754
Virginia.............	130,652	134,222	25,476,621	26,651,244	11,720,110	5,683,060
West Virginia..........	70,650	81,070	17,715,107	18,969,699	8,227,663	4,054,498
North Carolina........	141,662	145,899	25,551,506	26,059,585	11,630,317	5,213,783
South Carolina........	81,659	73,029	13,846,353	12,329,567	6,632,222	2,562,561
Georgia.............	164,063	153,313	30,257,153	27,246,247	13,445,982	5,636,255
Florida.............	11,243	14,843	1,162,383	1,705,274	633,217	492,172
EAST SOUTH CENTRAL:						
Kentucky.............	191,825	194,299	34,080,415	38,130,687	14,355,559	7,117,905
Tennessee.............	182,940	188,629	37,166,063	39,827,906	15,769,833	7,392,901
Alabama..............	158,553	164,405	28,490,181	29,550,595	12,293,107	5,657,610
Mississippi............	127,011	149,695	20,758,736	28,730,685	8,757,538	5,571,011
WEST SOUTH CENTRAL:						
Arkansas.............	135,363	139,635	25,571,098	29,907,337	11,182,984	5,883,584
Louisiana.............	30,933	37,573	4,252,318	6,232,006	2,026,182	1,430,059
Oklahoma.............	120,422	116,792	22,214,546	27,056,242	10,754,197	5,613,253
Texas...............	244,891	266,724	49,405,152	64,993,214	22,170,921	12,911,632
MOUNTAIN:						
Montana..............	29,143	8,438	5,961,336	2,820,574	2,906,861	811,792
Idaho...............	24,032	13,622	4,540,364	3,542,135	2,443,454	982,397
Wyoming.............	7,686	4,065	1,422,822	1,192,122	744,630	331,021
Colorado.............	33,026	19,381	5,775,602	5,856,132	2,932,176	1,565,224
New Mexico..........	8,000	8,127	1,404,138	1,477,617	745,383	402,263
Arizona.............	2,846	1,566	593,446	325,980	336,146	105,347
Utah...............	4,185	10,606	2,876,675	2,497,366	1,503,563	672,479
Nevada.............	1,153	989	266,027	403,885	149,812	121,649
PACIFIC:						
Washington............	31,783	24,674	5,899,678	6,751,575	3,296,726	1,992,249
Oregon..............	25,124	23,053	4,177,628	5,667,964	2,369,219	1,599,931
California............	29,971	31,345	5,757,759	15,301,871	3,112,848	4,085,992

TABLE 117.—CHEESE MADE ON FARMS, BY DIVISIONS AND STATES: 1919 AND 1909.

DIVISION AND STATE.	FARMS REPORTING.		QUANTITY (POUNDS).		VALUE.	
	1919	1909	1919	1909	1919	1909
United States	17,956	12,054	6,371,396	9,405,864	$2,268,025	$1,148,708
GEOGRAPHIC DIVISIONS:						
New England	1,213	817	324,838	673,865	121,780	89,189
Middle Atlantic	2,836	2,283	1,146,667	1,910,549	393,433	194,472
East North Central	3,130	2,058	1,045,883	1,891,208	383,471	215,395
West North Central	3,738	2,011	318,958	473,196	124,679	59,999
South Atlantic	977	1,343	278,547	480,805	109,878	51,024
East South Central	482	340	136,022	93,971	56,815	9,703
West South Central	1,786	1,367	133,374	424,482	53,924	44,597
Mountain	2,177	1,114	512,669	457,740	207,040	70,897
Pacific	1,617	721	2,474,438	3,000,048	817,005	413,432
NEW ENGLAND:						
Maine	279	278	55,161	118,216	20,412	18,872
New Hampshire	124	206	32,469	180,996	12,339	24,456
Vermont	69	88	75,502	245,884	27,182	32,583
Massachusetts	314	80	60,796	45,753	23,709	5,311
Rhode Island	69	22	10,410	3,860	3,748	615
Connecticut	358	143	90,500	79,156	34,390	7,352
MIDDLE ATLANTIC:						
New York	1,030	522	521,445	390,049	172,076	33,195
New Jersey	447	228	92,984	77,824	29,755	9,277
Pennsylvania	1,359	1,533	532,238	1,442,676	191,602	152,000
EAST NORTH CENTRAL:						
Ohio	936	729	434,042	613,233	172,752	57,182
Indiana	575	291	109,234	63,619	39,325	7,800
Illinois	855	379	117,830	81,918	45,959	8,396
Michigan	377	246	76,660	291,176	26,836	36,228
Wisconsin	387	413	308,117	841,262	98,599	105,789
WEST NORTH CENTRAL:						
Minnesota	571	354	71,820	106,075	27,296	14,375
Iowa	512	341	53,273	78,538	20,248	16,689
Missouri	1,004	678	90,435	159,785	33,465	17,495
North Dakota	692	277	50,065	22,754	22,031	2,976
South Dakota	209	64	10,591	14,344	4,450	2,011
Nebraska	317	123	23,117	63,773	9,711	8,477
Kansas	433	174	19,657	27,927	7,478	3,976
SOUTH ATLANTIC:						
Delaware	9	4	3,170	700	1,173	114
Maryland	194	202	126,190	259,386	50,475	26,277
District of Columbia						
Virginia	333	609	39,765	97,263	13,926	9,191
West Virginia	237	222	88,562	70,473	36,638	9,063
North Carolina	162	278	16,168	39,353	5,662	3,729
South Carolina	1	16	171	12,909	72	2,542
Georgia	15	9	1,365	399	575	72
Florida	26	3	3,156	322	1,357	36
EAST SOUTH CENTRAL:						
Kentucky	150	122	13,643	56,148	5,596	4,843
Tennessee	233	140	114,386	18,592	48,036	2,168
Alabama	52	35	5,210	5,528	2,125	759
Mississippi	47	43	2,783	13,703	1,058	1,933
WEST SOUTH CENTRAL:						
Arkansas	104	120	8,603	20,435	3,441	3,027
Louisiana	40	68	5,972	190,089	2,628	18,065
Oklahoma	186	84	11,116	18,968	4,785	3,154
Texas	1,456	1,095	107,683	194,990	43,070	20,351
MOUNTAIN:						
Montana	327	52	43,223	49,988	16,601	8,195
Idaho	256	175	31,684	90,675	10,771	13,525
Wyoming	86	90	6,601	10,276	2,599	1,591
Colorado	440	122	157,186	69,895	70,739	10,045
New Mexico	466	503	87,087	81,869	31,351	13,515
Arizona	139	97	90,119	60,690	37,851	9,115
Utah	374	104	73,606	84,102	27,237	13,125
Nevada	89	32	22,927	10,245	9,628	1,786
PACIFIC:						
Washington	264	88	84,868	52,970	28,006	6,787
Oregon	238	153	43,898	169,205	14,926	23,151
California	1,115	480	2,345,672	2,777,873	774,073	383,494

TABLE 118.—MILK AND CREAM SOLD, BY DIVISIONS AND STATES: 1919 AND 1909.

[Figures for butter fat and butter sold in Table 120.]

DIVISION AND STATE.	MILK SOLD.			CREAM SOLD.		
	Farms reporting, 1919	Quantity (gallons).		Farms reporting, 1919	Quantity (gallons).	
		1919	1909		1919	1909
United States	710,694	2,529,331,413	1,937,255,864	445,611	82,247,580	54,933,583
GEOGRAPHIC DIVISIONS:						
New England	55,726	208,464,058	175,209,759	6,970	2,487,936	4,469,060
Middle Atlantic	176,950	879,984,088	750,556,634	9,424	3,116,194	2,446,696
East North Central	235,565	948,491,089	661,302,433	154,973	27,654,771	15,272,040
West North Central	58,605	129,303,194	144,537,918	192,794	31,949,388	22,599,643
South Atlantic	56,018	81,264,102	45,378,866	4,735	1,417,055	1,027,441
East South Central	44,846	32,803,250	22,593,214	17,433	2,616,454	368,959
West South Central	38,548	36,808,346	21,070,626	25,332	3,243,867	1,064,000
Mountain	15,289	47,821,325	31,108,665	19,817	3,952,032	1,549,881
Pacific	29,147	164,391,961	85,497,749	14,133	5,809,883	6,135,863
NEW ENGLAND:						
Maine	12,020	28,190,733	12,784,866	2,480	742,813	737,706
New Hampshire	7,728	23,043,256	21,132,268	993	264,635	380,944
Vermont	10,570	55,319,390	33,998,934	1,737	928,843	2,353,686
Massachusetts	14,681	55,676,858	64,496,692	991	310,918	501,876
Rhode Island	1,993	9,313,548	8,796,847	119	30,022	42,421
Connecticut	8,734	36,920,273	34,000,152	650	210,705	452,427
MIDDLE ATLANTIC:						
New York	94,263	573,161,952	524,279,723	5,257	1,815,983	1,207,174
New Jersey	10,807	56,377,196	56,856,550	189	51,114	79,485
Pennsylvania	71,880	250,444,940	169,420,361	3,978	1,249,097	1,160,037
EAST NORTH CENTRAL:						
Ohio	43,919	139,063,960	99,430,948	40,092	7,658,715	2,191,997
Indiana	22,397	45,167,166	32,562,414	39,365	5,907,414	1,347,660
Illinois	37,601	159,578,765	158,031,333	44,350	5,626,433	2,104,352
Michigan	44,380	130,864,366	74,025,769	21,978	4,459,626	2,485,081
Wisconsin	87,268	473,816,832	297,251,969	9,188	4,002,583	7,142,970
WEST NORTH CENTRAL:						
Minnesota	12,955	43,151,896	53,181,785	19,488	5,888,538	5,756,165
Iowa	14,158	31,355,659	55,241,511	38,597	6,784,753	8,062,449
Missouri	12,251	17,900,545	15,733,185	44,218	4,836,763	1,399,989
North Dakota	1,879	3,047,096	1,644,150	17,812	3,098,421	834,103
South Dakota	1,602	2,697,554	2,385,781	15,680	2,841,406	2,232,961
Nebraska	5,349	10,181,597	6,500,380	26,759	3,631,494	1,952,908
Kansas	10,411	20,968,847	9,851,126	30,240	4,868,013	2,361,068
SOUTH ATLANTIC:						
Delaware	1,936	6,876,251	4,425,909	139	34,252	25,809
Maryland	9,125	29,842,910	19,424,325	693	311,436	455,496
District of Columbia	31	129,170	339,345	1	25	
Virginia	8,939	17,009,435	8,577,893	1,895	556,583	302,217
West Virginia	5,735	6,778,970	4,050,741	963	292,106	104,696
North Carolina	11,578	7,060,063	2,380,029	651	100,933	21,329
South Carolina	5,581	2,870,607	919,745	137	18,155	11,282
Georgia	10,636	7,389,966	3,872,098	193	86,908	97,564
Florida	2,457	3,306,730	1,388,781	63	16,657	9,048
EAST SOUTH CENTRAL:						
Kentucky	15,952	12,469,133	10,415,482	13,238	1,581,285	159,016
Tennessee	12,406	9,831,349	6,814,209	2,057	490,112	145,976
Alabama	10,020	6,408,962	3,397,426	472	150,474	28,385
Mississippi	6,468	4,093,806	1,966,097	1,666	394,583	35,582
WEST SOUTH CENTRAL:						
Arkansas	10,162	4,332,116	3,952,322	1,875	234,791	53,302
Louisiana	3,591	5,334,031	4,501,119	75	19,459	32,433
Oklahoma	7,512	7,781,754	3,626,217	17,838	2,338,859	526,193
Texas	17,283	19,360,445	8,990,968	5,544	650,758	452,072
MOUNTAIN:						
Montana	1,752	5,101,542	3,584,689	4,991	926,842	274,979
Idaho	3,036	6,302,891	2,060,111	4,102	780,310	319,542
Wyoming	790	2,144,590	1,377,607	1,280	204,273	46,680
Colorado	4,996	16,086,983	10,037,067	7,046	1,381,758	440,257
New Mexico	1,055	1,626,479	1,036,922	1,324	198,098	9,679
Arizona	1,216	6,707,170	3,347,723	174	92,089	37,744
Utah	2,263	9,051,137	8,471,713	728	291,659	270,225
Nevada	181	800,533	1,192,833	172	77,003	150,775
PACIFIC:						
Washington	13,041	63,575,339	25,524,209	5,566	1,586,806	1,911,261
Oregon	6,590	22,878,290	14,640,108	4,173	1,106,341	827,541
California	9,516	77,938,332	45,333,432	4,394	3,116,736	3,397,061

TABLE **119.**—RECEIPTS FROM SALE OF DAIRY PRODUCTS,

	DIVISION AND STATE.	TOTAL.		MILK SOLD.	
		1919	1909	1919	1909
1	United States.............	$1,239,812,049	$473,769,412	$717,380,222	$252,436,757
	GEOGRAPHIC DIVISIONS:				
2	New England...............	94,240,873	47,538,217	71,144,292	31,344,948
3	Middle Atlantic............	285,223,148	122,989,049	249,921,321	93,644,462
4	East North Central.........	414,022,756	138,401,771	244,928,398	73,063,198
5	West North Central........	211,170,872	84,390,336	37,259,897	18,214,700
6	South Atlantic.............	47,807,452	17,137,738	28,832,599	8,603,975
7	East South Central........	27,430,954	9,301,281	10,683,233	4,126,971
8	West South Central........	33,256,045	11,922,158	14,892,395	4,700,646
9	Mountain..................	32,820,793	10,141,383	13,862,276	5,346,099
10	Pacific....................	93,839,156	31,947,479	45,855,811	13,391,758
	NEW ENGLAND:				
11	Maine.....................	15,543,524	6,722,779	8,881,006	2,518,384
12	New Hampshire............	9,627,286	5,130,057	7,389,956	3,613,676
13	Vermont..................	26,634,760	11,501,577	15,581,083	4,108,228
14	Massachusetts............	24,279,643	14,840,927	22,698,929	13,297,634
15	Rhode Island.............	3,770,528	2,017,444	3,667,306	1,903,546
16	Connecticut..............	14,385,132	7,325,433	12,926,012	5,903,480
	MIDDLE ATLANTIC:				
17	New York.................	174,155,050	74,939,815	159,005,454	60,593,426
18	New Jersey...............	18,617,574	9,685,352	18,056,363	8,937,246
19	Pennsylvania.............	92,450,524	38,363,882	72,859,504	24,113,790
	EAST NORTH CENTRAL:				
20	Ohio.....................	72,539,099	25,574,635	38,978,117	13,025,828
21	Indiana..................	38,003,286	12,768,710	12,612,103	4,717,136
22	Illinois..................	63,614,988	26,720,849	42,349,483	18,314,172
23	Michigan.................	62,783,113	22,099,178	34,335,072	8,365,401
24	Wisconsin................	177,082,270	51,238,399	116,653,623	28,640,661
	WEST NORTH CENTRAL:				
25	Minnesota................	69,768,098	25,214,222	11,583,626	6,146,512
26	Iowa....................	45,362,250	26,429,743	8,519,484	6,032,685
27	Missouri.................	23,600,175	8,187,856	5,691,864	2,756,163
28	North Dakota.............	13,956,477	2,876,298	998,961	293,956
29	South Dakota.............	12,222,562	4,501,430	842,421	350,303
30	Nebraska.................	17,982,199	7,631,658	3,136,984	1,001,081
31	Kansas..................	28,279,111	9,549,129	6,486,557	1,634,000
	SOUTH ATLANTIC:				
32	Delaware.................	2,442,253	966,173	1,993,745	665,963
33	Maryland.................	12,166,328	4,784,232	9,528,506	3,064,878
34	District of Columbia.......	77,918	116,116	77,774	115,581
35	Virginia.................	11,115,633	3,772,617	6,068,111	1,766,468
36	West Virginia............	6,470,872	2,532,324	2,466,158	864,958
37	North Carolina...........	5,938,555	1,787,245	2,679,728	548,526
38	South Carolina...........	2,306,536	626,305	1,285,534	218,857
39	Georgia..................	5,435,372	1,974,011	3,053,647	887,040
40	Florida..................	1,853,985	578,715	1,679,396	471,704
	EAST SOUTH CENTRAL:				
41	Kentucky.................	10,716,872	3,729,237	3,618,807	1,783,275
42	Tennessee................	8,537,425	3,211,978	3,172,241	1,210,092
43	Alabama.................	4,349,004	1,358,504	2,457,728	703,788
44	Mississippi..............	3,827,653	1,001,562	1,434,457	429,816
	WEST SOUTH CENTRAL:				
45	Arkansas.................	3,674,771	1,505,882	1,469,776	638,755
46	Louisiana................	2,714,391	1,588,338	2,409,576	1,277,122
47	Oklahoma................	11,998,313	3,366,515	2,738,708	715,455
48	Texas...................	14,868,570	5,461,423	8,274,335	2,069,314
	MOUNTAIN:				
49	Montana.................	5,620,378	1,646,693	1,821,781	872,201
50	Idaho...................	6,369,260	1,379,390	1,831,036	365,375
51	Wyoming................	1,605,083	1,000,035	577,347	155,882
52	Colorado................	10,555,075	3,407,723	4,624,288	1,988,153
53	New Mexico..............	1,538,162	434,199	725,419	295,634
54	Arizona.................	2,481,144	842,210	1,781,360	573,095
55	Utah...................	3,819,691	1,648,655	2,276,197	916,015
56	Nevada.................	832,991	443,588	224,848	219,554
	PACIFIC:				
57	Washington...............	25,412,685	7,693,479	16,363,465	3,889,006
58	Oregon..................	15,916,507	5,170,703	6,774,576	2,156,576
59	California...............	52,509,964	19,083,297	22,717,770	7,346,176

[1] No data were collected for cheese sold in 1919.

BY DIVISIONS AND STATES: 1919 AND 1909.

CREAM SOLD.		BUTTER FAT SOLD.		BUTTER SOLD.		Cheese sold, 1909 [i]	
1919	1909	1919	1909	1919	1909		
$111,905,929	$37,655,047	$303,552,156	$82,311,511	$106,973,742	$100,378,123	$987,974	1
3,565,193	3,168,909	10,747,879	4,413,631	8,783,509	8,533,864	76,865	2
4,389,553	1,713,979	7,366,588	12,223,106	23,545,686	15,229,862	177,640	3
38,026,639	10,157,366	108,703,115	23,128,671	22,364,604	31,855,809	196,727	4
41,499,188	14,530,377	117,777,048	31,270,493	14,634,739	20,333,127	41,639	5
1,863,063	743,112	1,850,432	125,727	15,261,358	7,622,916	42,008	6
3,621,192	265,754	4,593,000	59,062	8,533,529	4,842,959	6,535	7
4,508,407	795,188	6,244,965	1,015,068	7,610,278	5,381,690	29,566	8
5,547,491	1,230,340	9,691,652	1,352,095	3,719,374	2,166,918	45,931	9
8,885,203	5,050,022	36,577,477	8,723,658	2,520,665	4,410,978	371,063	10
959,335	499,365	1,639,385	1,257,017	4,063,798	2,433,332	14,681	11
408,456	273,714	438,807	168,159	1,390,067	1,052,226	22,282	12
1,264,889	1,537,698	8,032,796	2,264,928	1,755,992	3,559,314	31,409	13
472,840	475,824	308,826	367,523	799,048	696,336	3,610	14
43,522	55,997	10,471	1,622	49,229	55,955	324	15
416,151	326,311	317,594	354,382	725,375	736,701	4,559	16
2,614,759	904,502	3,555,857	10,007,652	8,978,980	3,407,122	27,113	17
125,711	76,399	31,265	73,743	404,235	593,826	4,138	18
1,649,083	733,078	3,779,466	2,141,711	14,162,471	11,228,914	146,389	19
10,131,885	1,498,138	15,898,417	1,982,653	7,530,680	9,021,150	46,866	20
8,255,252	920,369	13,867,056	1,618,075	3,268,875	5,508,198	4,932	21
7,893,871	1,515,676	8,855,845	1,210,748	4,515,789	5,674,830	5,423	22
5,964,703	1,675,024	17,041,904	4,845,013	5,441,434	7,178,433	35,307	23
5,780,928	4,548,159	53,039,893	13,472,182	1,607,826	4,473,198	104,199	24
7,380,909	3,542,993	48,533,294	10,922,293	2,270,269	4,591,554	10,870	25
8,379,826	5,071,600	25,077,344	11,020,868	3,385,596	4,296,424	8,166	26
6,627,837	938,157	7,778,939	1,229,478	3,501,535	3,253,565	10,493	27
4,062,780	528,977	7,495,928	537,816	1,398,808	1,514,215	1,334	28
3,681,313	1,436,094	6,928,089	1,379,691	770,739	1,334,308	1,034	29
4,993,050	1,399,408	8,689,839	2,771,815	1,162,326	2,451,987	7,367	30
6,373,473	1,613,148	13,273,615	3,408,532	2,145,466	2,891,074	2,375	31
41,685	18,666	39,326	4,326	367,497	277,202	16	32
378,956	295,963	249,323	83,676	2,009,543	1,313,822	25,893	33
63	....	32	....	49	535	....	34
726,105	220,274	639,683	25,333	3,681,734	1,756,000	4,542	35
355,093	69,116	304,657	2,503	3,344,964	1,588,613	7,134	36
160,758	21,399	435,672	2,146	2,662,397	1,212,464	2,710	37
29,556	13,721	48,369	2,924	943,077	389,134	1,669	38
141,000	94,031	115,991	4,187	2,124,734	988,723	30	39
29,847	9,942	17,379	632	127,363	96,423	14	40
2,232,182	108,334	2,275,566	41,456	2,590,317	1,793,142	3,030	41
587,514	101,266	1,063,225	9,014	3,714,445	1,890,272	1,334	42
207,137	28,115	269,420	5,926	1,414,719	620,177	498	43
594,359	28,039	984,789	2,666	814,048	539,368	1,673	44
332,771	43,642	456,152	18,420	1,416,072	803,841	1,224	45
35,797	34,306	35,802	1,828	233,216	257,750	17,332	46
3,248,949	362,612	4,132,281	670,821	1,878,375	1,615,694	1,933	47
890,890	354,628	1,620,730	323,999	4,082,615	2,704,405	9,077	48
1,247,557	248,397	1,541,353	192,819	1,009,687	365,916	7,170	49
1,113,079	265,025	2,667,303	336,178	756,851	403,744	9,068	50
290,704	33,181	527,740	17,748	209,292	131,116	998	51
1,920,574	299,626	3,126,259	311,222	883,954	800,740	7,982	52
284,154	11,998	348,680	3,282	179,909	119,468	3,817	53
131,988	37,280	457,984	184,574	109,812	39,924	7,337	54
436,118	223,840	565,972	242,075	541,404	257,379	9,346	55
123,317	110,993	456,361	64,197	28,465	48,631	213	56
2,233,112	1,486,924	5,698,922	1,371,075	1,117,186	941,285	5,189	57
1,635,358	701,177	6,857,330	1,586,189	649,243	706,301	20,460	58
5,016,733	2,861,921	24,021,225	5,766,394	754,236	2,763,392	345,414	59

TABLE 120.—BUTTER FAT AND BUTTER SOLD, BY DIVISIONS AND STATES: 1919 AND 1909.

DIVISION AND STATE.	BUTTER FAT SOLD.			BUTTER SOLD.		
	Farms reporting, 1919	Quantity (pounds).		Farms reporting, 1919	Quantity (pounds).	
		1919	1909		1919	1909
United States	875,200	532,244,072	305,662,587	1,269,814	207,859,564	415,080,489
GEOGRAPHIC DIVISIONS:						
New England	14,357	17,571,096	14,599,430	37,437	14,670,830	29,528,001
Middle Atlantic	14,851	12,490,752	44,023,628	139,125	41,855,538	57,828,247
East North Central	305,551	187,178,213	85,099,734	213,475	42,377,384	135,159,149
West North Central	398,706	214,581,923	123,176,904	202,020	28,883,728	88,186,732
South Atlantic	10,653	3,365,410	505,904	260,985	32,495,022	33,888,871
East South Central	23,583	8,548,193	217,860	198,398	19,418,492	22,688,468
West South Central	38,428	12,431,547	4,465,810	153,541	16,421,394	24,321,179
Mountain	31,518	17,884,633	4,799,182	37,463	7,196,857	7,635,775
Pacific	37,553	58,192,305	28,774,135	27,370	4,540,319	15,844,067
NEW ENGLAND:						
Maine	3,353	2,705,560	4,060,344	19,895	6,945,411	8,389,817
New Hampshire	705	758,782	566,229	5,685	2,272,752	3,510,593
Vermont	9,145	13,072,731	7,756,395	4,629	2,954,634	12,892,124
Massachusetts	629	506,851	1,148,019	3,358	1,282,887	2,220,311
Rhode Island	15	15,524	5,347	370	81,150	177,322
Connecticut	510	511,648	1,063,096	3,500	1,133,996	2,337,834
MIDDLE ATLANTIC:						
New York	7,228	6,298,760	36,249,617	52,429	15,455,725	12,630,113
New Jersey	98	61,579	249,557	3,624	674,267	2,003,029
Pennsylvania	7,525	6,130,413	7,524,454	83,072	25,725,546	43,195,105
EAST NORTH CENTRAL:						
Ohio	65,997	29,828,000	7,563,527	60,317	14,116,447	39,252,326
Indiana	65,541	25,922,440	6,361,831	37,809	6,438,298	24,715,894
Illinois	49,930	17,052,544	4,637,745	58,060	8,734,470	24,442,251
Michigan	58,378	31,647,906	18,287,691	44,874	10,154,869	30,010,783
Wisconsin	65,705	82,727,323	48,248,940	12,415	2,933,300	16,737,895
WEST NORTH CENTRAL:						
Minnesota	103,050	82,412,061	40,414,151	24,168	4,392,185	18,016,409
Iowa	81,340	45,411,147	42,917,696	40,015	6,463,846	17,917,387
Missouri	48,141	14,853,783	4,927,383	61,864	7,022,562	14,646,771
North Dakota	29,820	14,607,548	2,185,377	18,800	2,898,998	7,019,169
South Dakota	29,593	13,615,085	5,776,689	11,020	1,493,800	5,941,092
Nebraska	46,233	17,621,330	12,371,699	17,445	2,338,491	11,652,068
Kansas	60,529	26,060,969	14,583,909	28,708	4,273,846	12,993,836
SOUTH ATLANTIC:						
Delaware	164	76,232	18,149	3,234	675,359	1,024,945
Maryland	580	448,266	343,148	16,622	3,925,042	5,682,228
District of Columbia	1	50		4	81	1,800
Virginia	2,862	1,163,064	97,558	68,407	8,007,298	7,983,430
West Virginia	1,773	581,519	8,421	42,522	7,155,413	7,077,664
North Carolina	2,810	729,419	9,224	56,998	5,819,193	5,670,590
South Carolina	777	98,606	10,023	21,553	1,956,001	1,752,209
Georgia	1,510	240,456	17,286	48,841	4,728,372	4,385,354
Florida	176	27,798	2,095	2,804	228,263	310,651
EAST SOUTH CENTRAL:						
Kentucky	13,905	4,238,223	154,427	63,065	5,917,916	8,421,827
Tennessee	4,100	1,862,519	32,345	76,948	8,468,929	9,009,307
Alabama	1,605	582,858	21,744	36,083	3,160,572	2,805,021
Mississippi	3,973	1,864,593	9,344	22,302	1,871,075	2,452,313
WEST SOUTH CENTRAL:						
Arkansas	3,147	897,812	74,607	34,600	3,182,328	3,694,311
Louisiana	478	72,455	7,079	5,502	471,596	1,019,420
Oklahoma	23,942	8,357,831	3,137,112	32,300	6,820,173	7,465,824
Texas	10,861	9,100,449	1,247,018	81,136	8,947,297	12,141,624
MOUNTAIN:						
Montana	6,211	2,909,284	652,097	11,891	2,062,541	1,234,263
Idaho	8,937	4,951,818	1,191,867	8,188	1,381,995	1,417,663
Wyoming	2,249	1,005,907	67,303	2,183	395,135	461,952
Colorado	10,700	5,804,055	1,087,681	10,328	1,739,147	2,914,143
New Mexico	1,798	682,973	11,248	2,380	332,002	410,634
Arizona	462	762,599	665,850	897	193,597	120,951
Utah	758	1,049,559	914,133	1,393	1,040,581	919,581
Nevada	403	718,438	209,003	203	51,859	156,588
PACIFIC:						
Washington	11,707	9,738,094	4,386,283	12,244	2,012,530	3,112,326
Oregon	12,399	10,835,785	5,211,133	7,362	1,145,803	2,446,158
California	13,447	37,618,426	19,176,719	7,764	1,381,986	10,285,583

TABLE 121.—PRODUCTION AND VALUE OF WOOL, BY DIVISIONS AND STATES: 1919 AND 1909.

[A minus sign (−) denotes decrease.]

DIVISION AND STATE.	TOTAL PRODUCTION, INCLUDING ESTIMATES (POUNDS)[1].				VALUE.	
	1919	1909	Increase.		1919	1909
			Amount.	Per cent.		
United States	228,795,354	289,419,977	−60,624,623	−20.9	$120,417,549	$65,472,328
GEOGRAPHIC DIVISIONS:						
New England	1,399,736	2,006,040	−606,304	−30.2	853,928	574,577
Middle Atlantic	6,853,016	8,520,646	−1,667,630	−19.6	4,247,588	2,492,257
East North Central	34,544,603	48,670,564	−14,125,961	−29.0	20,925,934	14,276,742
West North Central	29,305,710	24,709,945	4,595,765	18.6	15,402,844	6,127,159
South Atlantic	5,268,497	6,677,028	−1,408,531	−21.1	3,233,092	1,955,262
East South Central	5,057,984	6,123,485	−1,065,501	−17.4	2,889,865	1,648,579
West South Central	16,282,327	11,359,271	4,923,056	43.3	8,383,574	2,442,998
Mountain	93,818,531	145,311,085	−51,492,554	−35.4	47,511,714	29,211,379
Pacific	36,264,950	36,041,913	223,037	0.6	16,969,010	6,743,375
NEW ENGLAND:						
Maine	665,453	947,622	−282,169	−29.8	412,581	266,080
New Hampshire	161,681	209,518	−47,837	−22.8	95,392	57,460
Vermont	417,955	625,722	−207,767	−33.2	250,773	192,002
Massachusetts	88,358	127,897	−39,539	−30.9	55,666	33,670
Rhode Island	13,488	24,009	−10,521	−43.8	8,363	6,835
Connecticut	52,801	71,272	−18,471	−25.9	31,153	18,530
MIDDLE ATLANTIC:						
New York	3,350,824	4,235,707	−884,883	−20.9	1,976,986	1,163,846
New Jersey	58,219	94,726	−36,507	−38.5	32,020	22,482
Pennsylvania	3,443,973	4,190,213	−746,240	−17.8	2,238,582	1,305,929
EAST NORTH CENTRAL:						
Ohio	15,264,513	21,685,258	−6,420,745	−29.6	10,074,579	6,749,005
Indiana	4,069,378	5,360,044	−1,290,666	−24.1	2,319,545	1,532,914
Illinois	4,183,214	4,971,380	−788,166	−15.9	2,217,103	1,299,218
Michigan	7,835,558	11,965,405	−4,129,847	−34.5	4,622,979	3,428,320
Wisconsin	3,191,940	4,688,477	−1,496,537	−31.9	1,691,728	1,267,285
WEST NORTH CENTRAL:						
Minnesota	3,054,384	3,259,282	−204,898	−6.3	1,557,736	816,866
Iowa	6,967,566	5,484,702	1,482,864	27.0	3,762,486	1,413,711
Missouri	7,705,993	7,343,222	362,771	4.9	4,161,236	1,947,060
North Dakota	1,826,352	1,676,830	149,522	8.9	913,176	381,722
South Dakota	5,112,798	3,598,246	1,514,552	42.1	2,760,911	847,012
Nebraska	2,562,280	2,177,355	384,925	17.7	1,229,894	464,183
Kansas	2,076,337	1,170,308	906,029	77.4	1,017,405	256,605
SOUTH ATLANTIC:						
Delaware	15,875	19,059	−3,184	−16.7	8,890	5,125
Maryland	551,194	705,320	−154,126	−21.9	319,693	199,909
District of Columbia						
Virginia	1,520,109	1,937,252	−417,143	−21.5	912,065	564,386
West Virginia	2,442,090	2,719,684	−277,594	−10.2	1,587,359	839,555
North Carolina	342,302	493,882	−151,580	−30.7	184,843	130,724
South Carolina	67,913	86,819	−18,906	−21.8	35,994	20,432
Georgia	166,720	427,943	−261,223	−61.0	93,363	117,871
Florida	162,294	287,069	−124,775	−43.5	90,885	77,260
EAST SOUTH CENTRAL:						
Kentucky	3,001,263	3,448,848	−447,585	−13.0	1,770,745	974,347
Tennessee	1,329,315	1,854,172	−524,857	−28.3	731,123	466,459
Alabama	247,241	339,884	−92,643	−27.3	133,510	85,677
Mississippi	480,165	480,581	−416	−0.1	254,487	122,096
WEST SOUTH CENTRAL:						
Arkansas	374,595	376,877	−2,282	−0.6	176,060	86,045
Louisiana	402,430	442,865	−40,435	−9.1	205,239	99,424
Oklahoma	604,824	281,750	323,074	114.7	254,026	55,187
Texas	14,900,478	10,257,779	4,642,699	45.3	7,748,249	2,202,342
MOUNTAIN:						
Montana	18,267,200	37,669,031	−19,401,831	−51.5	10,229,632	8,223,754
Idaho	17,860,527	16,377,265	1,483,262	9.1	8,751,658	3,345,037
Wyoming	18,411,773	42,827,866	−24,416,093	−57.0	9,574,122	8,912,608
Colorado	9,755,312	7,563,219	2,192,093	29.0	4,877,656	1,458,003
New Mexico	8,300,804	16,994,017	−8,693,213	−51.2	3,901,378	3,131,971
Arizona	3,130,795	5,503,800	−2,373,005	−43.1	1,440,166	983,761
Utah	11,690,303	12,102,220	−411,917	−3.4	5,728,248	2,093,827
Nevada	6,401,817	6,273,667	128,150	2.0	3,008,854	1,062,418
PACIFIC:						
Washington	5,008,945	3,135,348	1,873,597	59.8	2,254,025	536,708
Oregon	16,039,048	18,841,862	−2,802,814	−14.9	8,019,524	3,782,721
California	15,216,957	14,064,703	1,152,254	8.2	6,695,461	2,423,946

[1] Figures include estimates for farms which reported sheep on hand on the census date, but no wool production for the preceding calendar year.

Table 122.—PRODUCTION AND VALUE OF MOHAIR, BY DIVISIONS AND STATES: 1919 AND 1909.

[A minus sign (−) denotes decrease. Per cent not shown when base is less than 100 or when per cent is more than 1,000.]

DIVISION AND STATE.	PRODUCTION, AS REPORTED (POUNDS).		Increase.		VALUE.	
	1919	1909	Amount.	Per cent.	1919	1909
United States	6,808,890	3,778,706	3,030,184	80.2	$3,589,310	$901,597
GEOGRAPHIC DIVISIONS:						
New England	1,862	4,445	−2,583	−58.1	1,132	1,275
Middle Atlantic	2,042	8,797	−6,755	−76.8	1,102	2,834
East North Central	16,044	35,044	−19,000	−54.2	7,926	9,680
West North Central	137,720	116,057	21,663	18.7	65,614	26,806
South Atlantic	33,073	21,009	12,064	57.4	19,242	6,980
East South Central	19,158	13,241	5,917	44.7	9,494	3,685
West South Central	5,149,541	2,016,736	3,132,805	155.3	2,704,269	472,315
Mountain	838,762	738,226	100,536	13.6	454,279	184,305
Pacific	610,688	825,151	−214,463	−26.0	326,252	193,717
NEW ENGLAND:						
Maine	322	639	−317	−49.6	147	207
New Hampshire	452	629	−177	−28.1	299	191
Vermont	353	471	−118	−25.1	204	136
Massachusetts	468	1,695	−1,227	−72.4	337	509
Rhode Island	72	2	70		42	1
Connecticut	195	1,009	−814	−80.7	103	231
MIDDLE ATLANTIC:						
New York	1,093	5,412	−4,319	−79.8	612	1,742
New Jersey	85	187	−102	−54.5	51	56
Pennsylvania	864	3,198	−2,334	−73.0	439	1,036
EAST NORTH CENTRAL:						
Ohio	1,142	5,840	−4,698	−80.4	635	1,684
Indiana	5,215	4,472	743	16.6	2,582	1,194
Illinois	5,275	14,922	−9,647	−64.6	2,423	4,008
Michigan	1,617	5,677	−4,060	−71.5	799	1,712
Wisconsin	2,795	4,133	−1,338	−32.4	1,487	1,082
WEST NORTH CENTRAL:						
Minnesota	2,956	6,929	−3,973	−57.3	1,520	1,987
Iowa	6,938	29,206	−22,268	−76.2	3,423	7,261
Missouri	118,083	66,684	51,399	77.1	56,164	14,338
North Dakota	719	470	249	53.0	375	133
South Dakota	722	1,538	−816	−53.1	354	390
Nebraska	1,071	2,425	−1,354	−55.8	533	602
Kansas	7,231	8,805	−1,574	−17.9	3,245	2,095
SOUTH ATLANTIC:						
Delaware	99	210	−111	−52.9	59	52
Maryland	819	1,570	−751	−47.8	487	474
District of Columbia						
Virginia	5,015	8,047	−3,032	−37.7	2,648	2,913
West Virginia	10,757	8,991	1,766	19.6	6,417	2,699
North Carolina	630	1,020	−390	−38.2	380	469
South Carolina	257	486	−229	−47.1	123	128
Georgia	533	520	13	2.5	276	177
Florida	14,963	165	14,798		8,852	68
EAST SOUTH CENTRAL:						
Kentucky	9,305	7,702	1,603	20.8	4,456	2,038
Tennessee	5,878	3,428	2,450	71.5	2,857	1,053
Alabama	2,003	808	1,195	147.9	1,317	209
Mississippi	1,972	1,303	669	51.3	864	750
WEST SOUTH CENTRAL:						
Arkansas	33,770	7,265	26,505	364.8	15,547	1,516
Louisiana	1,353	1,044	309	29.6	749	226
Oklahoma	29,498	10,503	18,995	180.9	14,698	2,354
Texas	5,084,920	1,997,924	3,086,996	154.5	2,673,275	468,219
MOUNTAIN:						
Montana	2,628	8,328	−5,700	−68.4	1,501	2,056
Idaho	2,486	16,412	−13,926	−84.9	1,520	4,384
Wyoming	756	14,238	−13,482	−94.7	344	3,868
Colorado	21,895	7,894	14,001	177.4	11,028	2,024
New Mexico	369,711	394,895	−25,184	−6.4	187,150	96,158
Arizona	357,626	246,032	111,594	45.4	192,351	63,120
Utah	81,405	44,708	36,697	82.1	59,171	11,240
Nevada	2,255	5,719	−3,464	−60.6	1,214	1,455
PACIFIC:						
Washington	9,834	19,120	−9,286	−48.6	4,714	4,666
Oregon	380,675	523,435	−142,760	−27.3	211,378	128,230
California	220,179	282,596	−62,417	−22.1	110,160	60,821

TABLE **123.**—EGGS PRODUCED ON FARMS, BY DIVISIONS AND STATES: 1919 AND 1909.

[A minus sign (−) denotes decrease.]

DIVISION AND STATE.	TOTAL PRODUCTION OF CHICKEN EGGS, INCL. ESTIMATES (DOZENS).[1]			VALUE OF CHICKEN EGGS.[1]		Value of all eggs produced, 1909
	1919	1909	Per cent of increase.	1919	1909	
United States	1,654,044,932	1,574,979,416	5.0	$661,082,803	$303,296,012	$308,688,960
GEOGRAPHIC DIVISIONS:						
New England	37,631,896	54,668,994	−31.2	21,841,202	15,006,734	15,155,991
Middle Atlantic	151,453,438	159,465,468	−5.0	74,870,761	36,848,320	37,507,552
East North Central	400,445,456	389,256,925	2.9	159,334,852	74,595,257	75,237,900
West North Central	474,591,975	442,167,894	7.3	166,575,154	76,722,932	77,493,327
South Atlantic	144,662,300	134,289,761	7.7	62,037,007	26,211,141	26,545,679
East South Central	138,152,110	127,308,625	8.5	50,931,866	22,002,037	22,283,364
West South Central	157,008,422	163,644,118	−4.1	57,488,393	26,086,357	26,395,765
Mountain	49,993,154	35,233,191	41.9	20,109,956	8,489,470	8,582,548
Pacific	100,106,181	68,944,440	45.2	47,893,612	17,333,764	17,486,834
NEW ENGLAND:						
Maine	9,977,349	14,876,215	−32.9	5,487,542	3,769,581	3,792,335
New Hampshire	5,005,302	7,469,472	−33.0	2,853,022	2,033,121	2,043,338
Vermont	5,166,689	7,001,897	−26.2	2,738,345	1,703,214	1,715,221
Massachusetts	9,604,274	13,961,352	−31.2	6,050,693	4,211,958	4,280,445
Rhode Island	1,536,858	2,862,246	−46.3	906,746	837,496	848,527
Connecticut	6,341,424	8,497,812	−25.4	3,804,854	2,451,364	2,476,125
MIDDLE ATLANTIC:						
New York	62,175,162	71,191,449	−12.7	31,087,581	16,776,799	17,101,732
New Jersey	13,280,104	14,590,530	−9.0	7,304,057	3,832,751	3,903,005
Pennsylvania	75,998,172	73,683,489	3.1	36,479,123	16,238,770	16,502,815
EAST NORTH CENTRAL:						
Ohio	102,377,143	100,284,261	2.1	42,998,400	19,610,417	19,748,658
Indiana	83,101,293	80,028,638	3.8	32,409,504	15,149,620	15,287,205
Illinois	105,757,907	99,118,224	6.7	40,188,005	18,751,049	18,940,454
Michigan	55,986,999	59,556,356	−6.0	23,514,540	11,652,655	11,734,799
Wisconsin	53,222,114	50,269,446	5.9	20,224,403	9,431,516	9,526,784
WEST NORTH CENTRAL:						
Minnesota	60,249,543	53,323,702	13.0	21,689,835	9,640,434	9,767,410
Iowa	120,697,319	108,662,882	11.1	42,244,062	19,043,244	19,2.5,600
Missouri	117,203,569	110,922,159	5.7	42,193,285	19,229,528	19,345,602
North Dakota	20,820,407	17,069,496	22.0	7,078,938	2,984,773	3,045,687
South Dakota	30,351,984	24,641,342	23.2	10,016,155	4,155,161	4,244,291
Nebraska	49,132,537	46,460,624	5.8	16,705,063	7,902,483	7,990,377
Kansas	76,136,616	81,087,689	−6.1	26,647,816	13,767,309	13,864,360
SOUTH ATLANTIC:						
Delaware	3,908,463	4,395,100	−11.1	1,993,316	956,373	968,970
Maryland	15,085,691	15,238,591	−1.0	6,637,704	3,177,515	3,235,759
District of Columbia	42,932	51,062	−15.9	21,466	15,048	15,277
Virginia	36,551,269	34,539,082	5.8	15,351,533	6,779,042	6,882,276
West Virginia	21,708,279	18,948,259	14.6	8,900,394	3,628,127	3,672,193
North Carolina	24,841,021	23,179,226	7.2	10,433,229	4,197,174	4,256,769
South Carolina	12,812,143	10,983,171	16.7	5,893,586	2,147,657	2,162,797
Georgia	23,181,939	20,606,219	12.5	9,736,414	3,939,986	3,971,760
Florida	6,530,563	6,349,051	2.9	3,069,365	1,370,219	1,379,878
EAST SOUTH CENTRAL:						
Kentucky	42,224,720	43,781,616	−3.6	15,200,899	7,529,065	7,605,116
Tennessee	48,707,146	41,244,285	18.1	18,021,644	7,142,016	7,258,146
Alabama	23,436,979	21,945,662	6.8	8,671,682	3,713,533	3,762,445
Mississippi	23,783,265	20,337,062	16.9	9,037,641	3,617,423	3,657,657
WEST SOUTH CENTRAL:						
Arkansas	28,168,285	26,486,526	6.3	10,140,583	4,365,627	4,459,272
Louisiana	13,136,046	14,423,023	−8.9	4,991,697	2,406,877	2,448,502
Oklahoma	45,440,017	45,356,592	0.2	16,358,406	7,453,912	7,544,445
Texas	70,264,074	77,377,977	−9.2	25,997,707	11,859,941	11,943,546
MOUNTAIN:						
Montana	11,858,042	5,950,015	99.3	4,624,636	1,589,826	1,610,766
Idaho	8,604,809	6,433,840	33.7	3,441,924	1,531,398	1,548,431
Wyoming	3,165,743	2,070,799	52.9	1,297,955	493,865	501,386
Colorado	14,172,375	10,577,829	34.0	5,668,950	2,419,566	2,444,006
New Mexico	3,062,790	2,961,352	3.4	1,347,628	677,973	683,441
Arizona	2,524,832	1,731,872	45.8	1,186,671	526,500	530,746
Utah	5,709,076	4,644,829	22.9	2,112,358	989,959	999,959
Nevada	895,487	862,655	3.8	429,834	260,383	263,813
PACIFIC:						
Washington	21,356,576	16,373,740	30.4	10,037,591	4,276,801	4,311,291
Oregon	14,625,720	11,835,462	23.6	6,435,317	2,886,633	2,912,849
California	64,123,885	40,735,238	57.4	31,420,704	10,170,330	10,262,694

[1] Figures for both 1919 and 1909 include estimates for farms reporting chickens on hand on the census date but no eggs produced during the preceding calendar year. The returns for 1909 included all eggs produced. To obtain figures for chicken eggs alone in 1909, the quantity and value of eggs of other kinds have been estimated and deducted.

TABLE 124.—CHICKENS RAISED ON FARMS, BY DIVISIONS AND STATES: 1919 AND 1909.

[A minus sign (−) denotes decrease.]

DIVISION AND STATE.	TOTAL NUMBER OF CHICKENS RAISED, INCLUDING ESTIMATES.[1]			VALUE OF CHICKENS RAISED.[1]		Value of all fowls raised, 1909
	1919	1909	Per cent of increase.	1919	1909	
United States	473,301,959	460,611,201	2.8	$386,240,367	$184,902,527	$202,506,272
GEOGRAPHIC DIVISIONS:						
New England	8,477,360	10,756,947	−21.2	10,762,556	6,989,191	7,361,038
Middle Atlantic	31,059,155	34,070,656	−8.8	33,880,697	19,771,902	21,527,077
East North Central	99,251,552	98,895,698	0.4	90,479,433	44,919,397	47,972,887
West North Central	126,762,874	118,998,060	6.5	103,583,599	48,811,295	52,337,180
South Atlantic	65,374,047	65,058,950	0.5	48,594,256	21,353,022	24,413,963
East South Central	51,071,455	55,683,712	−8.3	34,256,229	16,543,401	19,128,878
West South Central	57,328,795	54,701,253	4.8	39,530,740	15,501,002	17,681,375
Mountain	13,037,295	8,431,522	54.6	9,906,323	3,993,778	4,373,143
Pacific	20,939,416	14,014,403	49.4	15,246,534	7,019,539	7,710,731
NEW ENGLAND:						
Maine	1,908,466	2,554,902	−25.3	2,328,329	1,412,625	1,454,815
New Hampshire	1,172,274	1,362,577	−14.0	1,488,788	850,007	879,014
Vermont	1,015,742	1,246,613	−18.5	1,300,150	700,891	759,302
Massachusetts	2,401,068	3,054,931	−21.4	2,953,314	2,271,235	2,411,078
Rhode Island	433,668	569,809	−23.9	620,145	451,166	482,015
Connecticut	1,546,142	1,968,112	−21.4	2,071,830	1,303,267	1,374,754
MIDDLE ATLANTIC:						
New York	11,872,644	13,393,599	−11.4	11,753,918	7,798,134	8,403,162
New Jersey	3,522,776	4,328,628	−18.6	4,896,659	3,484,502	3,846,029
Pennsylvania	15,663,745	16,348,429	−4.2	17,230,120	8,489,266	9,277,886
EAST NORTH CENTRAL:						
Ohio	22,458,227	22,776,881	−1.4	21,110,733	10,392,763	10,997,633
•Indiana	22,618,296	22,098,966	2.4	20,356,466	9,910,951	10,726,137
Illinois	29,893,565	31,058,772	−3.8	27,502,080	14,402,766	15,404,028
Michigan	12,441,555	12,529,844	−0.7	11,446,231	5,857,102	6,191,440
Wisconsin	11,839,909	10,431,235	13.5	10,063,923	4,355,815	4,653,649
WEST NORTH CENTRAL:						
Minnesota	15,062,386	11,412,001	32.0	11,748,661	4,295,291	4,714,919
Iowa	31,076,091	28,970,482	7.3	27,968,482	13,191,406	13,914,985
Missouri	29,363,102	30,413,289	−3.5	24,077,744	13,290,198	14,572,585
North Dakota	5,324,137	3,829,177	39.0	3,407,448	1,368,179	1,530,402
South Dakota	7,637,808	5,802,869	31.6	6,033,868	2,145,922	2,355,567
Nebraska	15,796,750	14,724,281	7.3	12,795,368	5,579,049	5,866,508
Kansas	22,502,600	23,845,961	−5.6	17,552,028	8,941,250	9,382,214
SOUTH ATLANTIC:						
Delaware	1,204,793	1,401,446	−14.0	1,216,841	746,294	838,533
Maryland	5,257,655	5,419,957	−3.0	5,099,925	2,616,891	3,011,382
District of Columbia	14,103	13,850	1.8	16,218	8,183	9,102
Virginia	14,227,483	15,182,753	−6.3	10,528,337	5,383,227	6,145,236
West Virginia	4,873,287	5,204,967	−6.4	4,142,294	1,974,530	2,238,696
North Carolina	14,047,006	13,765,827	2.0	9,973,374	3,912,187	4,496,767
South Carolina	9,015,952	8,062,383	11.8	6,311,166	2,188,886	2,548,179
Georgia	14,588,012	13,706,397	6.4	9,482,208	3,617,246	4,119,870
Florida	2,145,756	2,301,370	−6.8	1,823,893	905,578	1,006,198
EAST SOUTH CENTRAL:						
Kentucky	15,506,845	17,572,773	−11.8	11,009,860	6,000,512	6,937,008
Tennessee	15,554,496	15,865,254	−2.0	11,043,692	5,069,726	5,774,175
Alabama	10,179,698	11,382,815	−10.6	6,107,819	2,747,064	3,168,471
Mississippi	9,830,416	10,862,870	−9.5	6,094,858	2,726,099	3,249,224
WEST SOUTH CENTRAL:						
Arkansas	9,111,223	9,673,838	−5.8	6,104,519	2,403,855	2,868,562
Louisiana	5,570,587	5,830,049	−4.5	3,843,705	1,696,689	1,943,515
Oklahoma	16,817,261	15,336,955	9.7	12,276,601	4,951,694	5,388,133
Texas	25,829,724	23,860,411	8.3	17,305,915	6,140,704	7,481,165
MOUNTAIN:						
Montana	3,226,538	1,000,003	136.1	2,258,577	717,705	797,450
Idaho	2,250,489	1,588,794	41.6	1,620,352	733,441	800,700
Wyoming	893,857	494,768	80.7	724,024	235,005	260,538
Colorado	3,880,873	2,585,132	50.1	3,104,698	1,277,417	1,393,039
New Mexico	920,979	893,831	3.0	755,203	341,786	367,907
Arizona	569,325	374,241	52.1	512,393	204,881	225,640
Utah	1,107,446	946,647	17.0	775,212	381,432	412,359
Nevada	187,788	181,274	3.6	155,864	102,111	115,510
PACIFIC:						
Washington	4,860,217	3,610,589	34.6	3,742,367	1,766,812	1,873,608
Oregon	3,150,155	2,554,583	23.3	2,583,127	1,291,946	1,416,608
California	12,929,044	7,849,231	64.7	8,921,040	3,960,781	4,420,515

[1] Figures for both 1919 and 1909 include estimates for farms reporting chickens on hand on the census date but no chickens raised during the preceding calendar year. The returns for 1909 included all kinds of fowls raised. To obtain figures for chickens alone in 1909, the number and value of other fowls raised have been estimated and deducted.

TABLE 125.—EGGS AND CHICKENS SOLD, BY DIVISIONS AND STATES: 1919.

DIVISION AND STATE.	EGGS SOLD (AS REPORTED).			CHICKENS SOLD (AS REPORTED).		
	Farms reporting.	Quantity (dozens).	Value.	Farms reporting.	Number.	Value.
United States.......	4,088,169	1,010,813,258	$404,562,912	2,698,211	140,811,045	$119,722,603
GEOGRAPHIC DIVISIONS:						
New England............	86,473	24,212,749	14,086,764	53,882	3,177,497	4,006,975
Middle Atlantic........	313,023	104,302,743	51,059,828	217,091	12,240,154	13,455,574
East North Central....	882,318	274,303,755	108,342,696	674,774	38,988,942	35,616,945
West North Central....	869,234	306,832,765	107,921,254	621,624	40,711,378	33,761,568
South Atlantic.........	626,740	75,955,820	32,293,802	409,265	15,366,383	11,660,486
East South Central.....	641,435	75,555,136	27,564,260	366,088	11,491,779	7,881,340
West South Central.....	467,570	62,044,369	22,460,103	246,317	9,459,382	6,548,319
Mountain...............	98,318	21,310,233	8,515,629	48,764	2,626,550	2,007,829
Pacific................	103,058	66,295,688	32,318,576	60,406	6,748,980	4,783,567
NEW ENGLAND:						
Maine..................	27,855	6,770,370	3,735,171	17,676	736,742	907,087
New Hampshire........	11,069	3,299,639	1,865,739	6,548	432,771	538,007
Vermont...............	17,372	3,094,170	1,661,695	10,318	336,730	429,924
Massachusetts.........	15,244	6,022,298	3,827,993	9,893	996,275	1,218,653
Rhode Island..........	2,413	1,017,488	604,363	1,607	142,632	199,605
Connecticut...........	12,520	4,008,784	2,391,803	7,840	532,347	713,699
MIDDLE ATLANTIC:						
New York..............	133,808	40,455,153	20,185,619	76,508	4,105,159	4,067,469
New Jersey............	18,294	8,691,656	4,766,876	14,018	1,377,285	1,940,871
Pennsylvania..........	160,921	55,155,934	26,107,333	126,565	6,757,710	7,447,234
EAST NORTH CENTRAL:						
Ohio..................	214,069	74,898,009	31,092,151	164,607	9,196,928	8,668,429
Indiana...............	176,084	59,953,361	23,254,964	142,386	8,519,282	7,665,513
Illinois..............	202,259	70,011,698	26,387,664	173,671	12,482,811	11,477,038
Michigan..............	146,282	36,362,264	15,151,355	102,895	4,783,178	4,384,995
Wisconsin.............	143,624	33,078,423	12,456,562	91,215	4,006,743	3,420,970
WEST NORTH CENTRAL:						
Minnesota.............	134,608	37,639,899	13,531,653	92,269	5,022,749	3,975,196
Iowa..................	187,096	81,215,875	28,713,386	157,558	12,399,082	11,160,695
Missouri..............	219,991	84,327,264	30,429,597	169,323	10,400,818	8,499,119
North Dakota..........	46,459	8,498,671	2,886,246	17,331	846,410	552,426
South Dakota..........	52,180	17,427,479	5,809,376	29,598	1,846,268	1,477,500
Nebraska..............	94,644	27,114,878	9,221,227	65,130	4,090,398	3,333,801
Kansas................	134,256	50,608,699	17,329,769	90,415	6,105,653	4,762,831
SOUTH ATLANTIC:						
Delaware..............	8,568	2,811,908	1,439,544	6,596	434,970	440,763
Maryland..............	37,478	10,656,009	4,702,632	27,099	1,618,774	1,541,531
District of Columbia...	67	15,170	7,944	38	3,228	3,831
Virginia..............	141,112	23,213,608	9,786,435	100,638	4,700,493	3,467,581
West Virginia.........	68,434	14,358,172	5,846,359	50,779	1,772,170	1,512,954
North Carolina........	147,558	11,058,388	4,514,405	98,753	3,150,011	2,146,195
South Carolina........	67,298	3,342,717	1,509,588	37,240	1,113,236	765,521
Georgia...............	127,145	7,188,539	2,938,765	70,916	1,957,384	1,252,220
Florida...............	29,080	3,311,309	1,548,130	17,206	616,117	529,890
EAST SOUTH CENTRAL:						
Kentucky..............	196,370	25,631,564	9,238,447	115,617	3,713,172	2,625,124
Tennessee.............	187,594	31,241,103	11,459,007	124,569	4,429,422	3,167,433
Alabama...............	139,927	9,399,141	3,448,961	69,472	1,847,273	1,153,163
Mississippi...........	117,544	9,283,328	3,417,845	56,430	1,501,912	935,620
WEST SOUTH CENTRAL:						
Arkansas..............	111,486	12,048,940	4,158,751	61,434	1,815,467	1,225,772
Louisiana.............	48,828	4,915,384	1,846,947	16,540	474,844	322,241
Oklahoma..............	106,410	20,124,662	7,133,379	65,955	3,339,680	2,433,170
Texas.................	200,846	24,955,383	9,321,026	102,388	3,829,391	2,567,136
MOUNTAIN:						
Montana...............	23,692	4,387,077	1,735,867	11,693	604,435	424,342
Idaho.................	19,820	3,555,021	1,427,106	9,943	448,811	326,273
Wyoming...............	6,059	1,153,000	467,711	3,191	154,179	125,705
Colorado..............	30,164	6,352,073	2,485,694	15,509	784,711	635,954
New Mexico............	7,816	1,112,958	480,882	3,994	154,123	129,420
Arizona...............	3,618	1,320,387	605,040	2,323	147,519	131,781
Utah..................	6,193	3,059,845	1,137,528	1,288	275,650	188,236
Nevada................	956	369,872	175,801	823	57,122	46,118
PACIFIC:						
Washington............	33,003	13,107,150	6,299,710	18,491	1,482,355	1,141,058
Oregon................	27,522	8,426,715	3,740,429	16,192	909,249	733,950
California............	42,533	44,761,823	22,278,437	25,723	4,357,376	2,908,559

TABLE 126.—HONEY AND WAX PRODUCED ON FARMS, BY DIVISIONS AND STATES: 1919 AND 1909.

DIVISION AND STATE.	HONEY PRODUCED.				WAX PRODUCED.			
	Quantity (pounds).		Value (dollars).		Quantity (pounds).		Value (dollars).	
	1919	1909	1919	1909	1919	1909	1919	1909
United States....	55,224,061	54,814,890	13,988,670	5,762,869	820,529	904,867	291,483	229,214
GEOGRAPHIC DIVISIONS:								
New England.......	653,258	594,117	223,343	105,998	7,546	8,251	3,424	2,525
Middle Atlantic....	4,946,894	5,184,165	1,423,678	655,520	65,349	66,393	25,038	19,843
East North Central..	7,313,400	7,778,545	2,005,799	941,567	93,983	132,735	32,627	31,267
West North Central.	6,865,236	6,744,608	2,038,325	841,687	80,941	93,633	28,859	22,680
South Atlantic......	6,579,735	7,362,640	1,754,464	882,937	111,613	172,996	37,292	42,892
East South Central..	5,653,218	4,477,759	1,391,812	522,571	105,281	111,369	34,246	27,572
West South Central.	6,438,024	4,486,980	1,369,287	471,032	111,606	92,177	36,410	22,741
Mountain............	8,746,786	6,577,800	2,040,868	552,356	108,558	88,447	39,345	22,627
Pacific................	8,027,510	11,608,276	1,741,094	789,201	135,652	138,866	54,242	37,067
NEW ENGLAND:								
Maine	209,072	112,051	73,173	20,016	2,387	2,260	1,077	670
New Hampshire.....	49,512	65,038	18,815	13,363	386	792	164	260
Vermont.............	234,326	160,283	74,985	25,351	2,137	2,899	1,070	815
Massachusetts.......	70,769	96,802	24,770	18,806	1,312	1,019	590	370
Rhode Island........	6,488	14,221	1,687	2,904	57	185	17	55
Connecticut.........	83,091	145,722	29,913	25,558	1,267	1,096	506	355
MIDDLE ATLANTIC:								
New York...........	3,223,323	3,191,733	934,768	376,608	41,178	43,198	16,064	13,034
New Jersey..........	157,717	152,072	50,471	22,484	2,544	1,372	969	433
Pennsylvania	1,565,854	1,840,360	438,439	256,428	21,627	21,823	8,005	6,376
EAST NORTH CENTRAL:								
Ohio.................	835,894	1,001,179	250,774	131,710	10,790	7,454	4,212	2,181
Indiana..............	582,380	687,097	186,359	102,489	8,115	15,115	2,921	3,226
Illinois..............	1,896,996	1,428,640	436,310	194,625	21,908	26,240	7,008	6,138
Michigan............	1,321,447	2,507,810	409,649	289,137	20,304	28,524	7,310	7,605
Wisconsin...........	2,676,683	2,153,819	722,707	223,606	32,866	55,402	11,176	12,117
WEST NORTH CENTRAL:								
Minnesota...........	1,251,102	976,262	362,821	120,560	15,470	16,880	6,034	4,057
Iowa.................	2,840,025	2,374,080	852,015	275,418	33,041	44,266	11,235	10,011
Missouri.............	1,220,611	2,105,815	353,982	267,998	18,172	23,784	6,180	6,176
North Dakota.......	12,814	11,084	3,588	1,840	183	92	64	29
South Dakota.......	369,356	139,714	114,504	20,165	2,891	943	1,070	278
Nebraska............	573,453	527,868	172,042	72,463	6,144	3,336	2,212	935
Kansas..............	597,875	609,785	179,373	83,243	5,040	4,332	2,064	1,194
SOUTH ATLANTIC:								
Delaware............	27,703	62,777	6,371	7,770	317	2,756	95	465
Maryland............	215,685	306,367	56,076	38,164	1,947	4,358	761	1,080
District of Columbia.	315	3,657	95	477				
Virginia.............	1,267,300	1,344,360	342,168	167,971	19,441	23,883	6,808	5,956
West Virginia.......	919,689	1,556,739	303,495	228,843	7,786	11,090	2,802	2,787
North Carolina......	1,341,002	1,809,127	348,661	211,607	23,209	76,400	7,432	18,979
South Carolina......	441,684	653,119	114,837	75,941	7,866	12,440	2,601	2,995
Georgia.............	1,403,869	884,662	322,888	96,114	28,053	23,434	8,972	5,774
Florida..............	962,488	747,832	259,873	56,050	22,994	18,635	7,821	4,856
EAST SOUTH CENTRAL:								
Kentucky............	1,604,519	1,558,670	449,265	197,720	15,521	17,307	5,282	4,522
Tennessee...........	1,969,425	1,468,123	512,057	175,791	27,669	28,864	8,472	7,271
Alabama............	1,347,644	891,954	269,527	88,088	41,272	50,043	13,621	11,889
Mississippi.........	731,630	559,012	160,963	60,972	20,819	15,155	6,871	3,890
WEST SOUTH CENTRAL:								
Arkansas............	791,598	913,515	107,910	107,846	12,359	20,403	4,207	5,100
Louisiana...........	247,513	340,134	50,402	60,015	7,660	12,284	2,687	2,996
Oklahoma...........	357,677	140,234	103,728	23,783	2,916	1,088	1,139	313
Texas...............	5,041,236	3,093,097	1,008,246	308,488	88,671	58,402	28,377	14,310
MOUNTAIN:								
Montana............	630,608	163,510	157,656	21,802	7,682	394	2,614	133
Idaho...............	1,208,229	1,011,068	338,305	86,251	15,653	8,018	5,950	2,131
Wyoming............	1,084,273	138,924	260,225	16,248	14,257	1,563	4,419	477
Colorado............	2,493,950	2,306,492	573,610	225,832	28,282	33,682	11,314	8,502
New Mexico.........	593,290	439,528	118,658	38,113	7,051	5,345	2,822	1,526
Arizona.............	926,621	1,025,282	213,123	53,298	10,783	15,012	4,853	3,905
Utah................	1,232,239	1,138,091	246,447	75,892	18,933	16,667	5,300	3,871
Nevada.............	577,576	354,905	132,844	34,920	5,917	7,766	2,073	2,082
PACIFIC:								
Washington.........	1,596,206	503,580	399,059	65,196	17,420	4,038	8,362	1,195
Oregon.............	929,566	839,981	241,684	92,476	11,436	8,383	4,232	2,034
California...........	5,501,738	10,264,715	1,100,351	631,529	106,796	126,445	41,648	33,838

TABLE 127.—CALVES, PIGS, AND LAMBS RAISED ON FARMS, BY DIVISIONS AND STATES: 1919.

DIVISION AND STATE.	CALVES RAISED.		PIGS RAISED.		LAMBS RAISED.	
	Farms reporting.	Number.	Farms reporting.	Number.	Farms reporting.	Number.
United States	4,073,156	21,133,385	3,162,993	62,072,829	373,799	13,653,130
GEOGRAPHIC DIVISIONS:						
New England	87,870	477,699	32,355	464,688	10,238	116,640
Middle Atlantic	278,422	1,537,809	156,940	2,289,242	29,041	522,323
East North Central	860,004	4,380,052	678,244	17,809,790	123,926	2,397,946
West North Central	908,206	6,333,779	751,740	23,985,421	80,351	1,954,199
South Atlantic	528,868	1,303,804	468,439	5,480,150	42,913	743,540
East South Central	599,417	1,412,971	508,248	5,506,355	41,486	739,178
West South Central	535,621	2,807,336	420,226	4,069,218	12,929	651,331
Mountain	157,552	1,872,595	86,120	1,224,232	20,123	4,608,929
Pacific	117,196	1,007,340	60,681	1,243,733	12,792	1,919,044
NEW ENGLAND:						
Maine	30,973	124,924	10,266	122,691	6,179	59,683
New Hampshire	11,167	57,029	3,914	53,892	1,026	12,980
Vermont	20,622	166,388	7,142	98,022	1,954	30,800
Massachusetts	11,592	59,363	6,058	118,589	603	7,099
Rhode Island	1,995	10,524	763	12,446	90	1,102
Connecticut	11,521	59,471	4,212	59,048	386	4,976
MIDDLE ATLANTIC:						
New York	130,873	868,495	59,440	778,027	14,234	287,590
New Jersey	12,032	69,937	8,965	150,241	335	5,658
Pennsylvania	135,517	599,377	88,535	1,360,974	14,472	229,075
EAST NORTH CENTRAL:						
Ohio	191,147	751,061	152,440	3,989,970	42,094	884,414
Indiana	162,535	620,830	146,075	4,646,894	21,434	350,658
Illinois	193,702	1,004,521	169,831	5,364,756	17,404	291,920
Michigan	151,710	651,658	96,423	1,494,815	28,688	640,574
Wisconsin	160,910	1,351,982	113,475	2,313,355	14,306	230,380
WEST NORTH CENTRAL:						
Minnesota	150,710	1,047,150	114,659	2,863,418	14,133	214,164
Iowa	184,002	1,447,603	175,507	8,804,746	20,950	477,070
Missouri	209,052	913,843	180,329	4,484,884	28,697	642,525
North Dakota	64,686	422,883	43,425	620,998	4,089	99,466
South Dakota	62,962	615,796	55,228	2,022,991	4,572	275,379
Nebraska	104,413	920,826	92,712	3,335,006	2,953	69,128
Kansas	132,381	965,678	89,880	1,853,378	4,957	176,467
SOUTH ATLANTIC:						
Delaware	5,411	21,444	3,451	40,491	82	1,370
Maryland	27,204	113,120	21,301	347,491	3,842	72,307
District of Columbia	36	336	37	699		
Virginia	107,488	286,889	77,308	1,044,080	12,853	255,601
West Virginia	64,123	176,970	35,714	379,231	18,415	338,295
North Carolina	100,379	185,516	99,961	1,056,170	4,745	41,869
South Carolina	71,202	125,599	71,851	595,382	1,050	7,280
Georgia	135,551	296,641	131,847	1,549,428	1,579	15,620
Florida	17,474	97,289	26,969	467,178	347	11,198
EAST SOUTH CENTRAL:						
Kentucky	161,449	366,078	120,498	1,065,133	25,157	491,700
Tennessee	163,229	369,268	138,071	1,861,285	12,753	196,259
Alabama	137,897	299,761	117,462	1,026,350	1,576	19,907
Mississippi	136,842	377,864	132,217	1,013,587	2,000	31,312
WEST SOUTH CENTRAL:						
Arkansas	120,573	301,431	107,705	966,896	3,662	37,532
Louisiana	57,501	187,623	61,366	490,018	1,633	25,372
Oklahoma	124,214	635,752	83,821	1,031,300	2,188	44,898
Texas	233,333	1,682,530	167,334	1,581,004	5,446	543,529
MOUNTAIN:						
Montana	37,962	368,237	17,948	226,839	3,285	977,827
Idaho	28,967	194,856	17,765	263,610	5,769	786,780
Wyoming	10,721	245,289	5,683	81,682	1,767	773,286
Colorado	40,745	429,451	24,088	418,195	2,470	411,150
New Mexico	14,710	275,010	7,000	64,835	2,057	479,083
Arizona	4,679	136,981	1,797	31,432	304	124,494
Utah	17,753	140,426	10,705	115,645	3,968	694,298
Nevada	2,015	82,345	1,134	21,994	503	362,011
PACIFIC:						
Washington	41,385	206,554	19,396	301,767	2,688	258,018
Oregon	31,679	241,954	17,165	258,944	6,089	763,890
California	44,132	558,832	24,120	683,022	4,015	897,136

TABLE 128.—DOMESTIC ANIMALS SLAUGHTERED ON FARMS, BY DIVISIONS AND STATES: 1919 AND 1909.

DIVISION AND STATE.	CATTLE AND CALVES.			HOGS AND PIGS.			SHEEP AND LAMBS.		
	Farms reporting, 1919	Number. 1919	1909	Farms reporting, 1919	Number. 1919	1909	Farms reporting, 1919	Number. 1919	1909
United States...	887,611	1,904,581	2,540,240	4,565,130	16,800,230	15,378,517	93,853	434,608	529,526
GEOGRAPHIC DIVISIONS:									
New England......	25,732	81,512	177,377	80,297	194,306	177,154	3,584	20,514	41,719
Middle Atlantic....	98,191	272,534	456,396	291,531	1,162,255	1,135,912	8,398	52,151	80,724
East North Central.	194,105	411,392	503,340	824,093	2,824,044	2,944,811	14,138	37,269	57,686
West North Central.	260,168	387,429	463,481	853,378	2,708,636	2,664,171	20,539	50,455	45,612
South Atlantic.....	74,558	167,743	216,555	878,874	3,932,523	3,201,206	10,099	27,222	36,701
East South Central.	49,669	98,936	157,569	784,023	2,868,795	2,556,039	9,858	23,684	34,236
West South Central.	78,102	154,858	190,607	637,063	2,320,023	2,213,493	4,177	18,472	20,195
Mountain..........	62,158	153,760	153,685	127,415	443,567	208,106	16,901	159,674	153,572
Pacific............	44,928	176,417	221,230	88,456	346,081	277,625	6,159	45,167	59,081
NEW ENGLAND:									
Maine..............	10,357	35,660	46,151	27,898	54,529	47,319	2,007	12,326	23,277
New Hampshire....	3,135	8,965	19,766	10,783	23,545	22,563	467	2,655	5,987
Vermont..........	7,291	18,351	60,207	17,490	43,418	50,786	565	2,121	6,609
Massachusetts.....	2,553	8,263	27,708	11,749	36,413	27,754	266	1,601	2,412
Rhode Island......	231	827	7,874	1,507	4,167	3,674	36	167	749
Connecticut.......	2,165	9,446	15,671	10,870	32,234	25,058	243	1,644	2,685
MIDDLE ATLANTIC:									
New York..........	38,018	117,746	281,755	122,531	404,104	386,264	4,342	30,845	51,277
New Jersey........	1,747	5,924	17,200	15,003	64,745	73,709	185	975	1,229
Pennsylvania......	58,426	148,864	157,441	153,997	693,406	675,939	3,871	20,331	28,218
EAST NORTH CENTRAL:									
Ohio..............	42,667	78,074	85,220	199,228	732,636	768,195	3,297	10,778	16,754
Indiana...........	26,830	42,394	48,853	163,011	579,941	646,581	1,045	1,855	3,714
Illinois...........	34,791	71,732	119,545	192,950	723,838	762,545	2,062	4,376	4,284
Michigan..........	41,377	117,219	105,515	124,099	348,798	381,247	3,236	10,232	17,818
Wisconsin.........	48,440	101,973	144,207	144,805	438,831	386,243	4,498	10,028	15,116
WEST NORTH CENTRAL:									
Minnesota.........	64,087	111,276	159,719	134,856	379,611	314,590	5,142	12,332	16,231
Iowa..............	50,516	67,705	91,689	173,394	537,961	507,167	4,061	7,404	6,180
Missouri..........	28,350	43,909	40,838	210,494	796,082	949,318	3,630	8,207	7,461
North Dakota......	29,660	44,426	45,989	58,206	216,637	136,227	2,301	7,423	4,342
South Dakota......	22,291	30,516	35,509	54,749	161,885	117,781	2,218	7,237	7,246
Nebraska..........	31,563	41,350	47,541	96,961	268,025	261,515	1,382	3,160	1,753
Kansas............	33,701	48,247	42,196	124,718	348,435	377,566	1,805	4,692	2,399
SOUTH ATLANTIC:									
Delaware..........	298	1,035	965	7,674	27,553	27,588	25	158	87
Maryland..........	3,203	5,948	7,980	37,150	189,898	180,406	595	1,975	2,952
Dist. of Columbia...	4	59	36	64	501	383			
Virginia...........	11,508	21,328	25,144	157,369	655,627	537,797	2,878	7,786	9,185
West Virginia......	8,498	16,608	23,861	73,698	245,855	206,701	3,803	8,475	8,269
North Carolina....	17,372	35,492	50,734	208,602	934,320	783,247	1,775	5,292	9,763
South Carolina.....	8,360	18,029	24,326	132,709	431,217	309,922	364	1,175	1,409
Georgia...........	22,104	54,926	59,928	228,908	1,127,913	860,409	601	2,171	3,552
Florida...........	3,211	14,318	23,581	32,700	319,639	294,753	58	190	1,484
EAST SOUTH CENTRAL:									
Kentucky..........	12,293	19,984	23,557	206,113	721,263	733,642	5,023	9,503	10,650
Tennessee.........	13,509	27,657	43,031	201,960	783,197	742,123	3,312	8,322	13,490
Alabama..........	13,526	29,300	50,818	193,456	703,829	581,615	694	2,509	5,251
Mississippi........	10,341	21,995	40,163	182,494	660,506	498,659	829	3,350	4,845
WEST SOUTH CENTRAL:									
Arkansas..........	17,363	38,468	46,467	152,972	632,512	616,350	871	2,823	5,705
Louisiana.........	9,239	17,331	28,876	73,456	331,080	287,447	682	3,126	3,965
Oklahoma.........	21,933	37,516	28,788	130,444	438,185	101,400	1,133	3,364	1,129
Texas.............	29,567	61,540	80,476	280,191	918,246	895,000	1,491	9,159	9,396
MOUNTAIN:									
Montana..........	15,394	38,709	28,503	28,480	122,067	33,143	1,913	13,160	13,785
Idaho.............	11,654	24,119	17,005	24,389	81,520	47,437	4,361	21,583	8,494
Wyoming..........	4,319	10,802	11,758	8,171	31,476	13,064	1,380	13,175	20,832
Colorado..........	13,729	29,972	38,375	34,107	104,330	52,081	2,087	17,678	19,945
New Mexico........	6,988	17,957	19,974	10,309	27,935	21,929	2,753	48,924	58,839
Arizona...........	1,859	9,628	11,917	2,388	9,468	3,299	202	7,648	8,125
Utah..............	7,160	15,778	13,520	18,117	58,225	31,210	3,803	28,736	16,579
Nevada............	1,055	6,795	12,633	1,454	8,546	5,943	402	8,770	6,973
PACIFIC:									
Washington........	20,471	71,700	69,325	32,529	128,467	92,600	1,721	8,656	7,380
Oregon............	17,087	57,980	65,048	25,816	108,032	102,755	2,450	16,228	15,786
California.........	7,370	46,737	86,857	30,111	109,582	82,270	1,988	20,283	35,915

TABLE 129.—MEAT AND MEAT PRODUCTS SOLD, 1919, AND VALUE OF ALL DOMESTIC ANIMALS SOLD OR SLAUGHTERED ON FARMS, 1919 AND 1909, BY DIVISIONS AND STATES.

DIVISION AND STATE.	MEAT AND MEAT PRODUCTS SOLD BY FARMERS, 1919 (POUNDS).			VALUE OF ALL DOMESTIC ANIMALS SOLD OR SLAUGHTERED ON FARMS.	
	Beef and veal.	Pork.	Lamb and mutton.	1919 (estimated).[1]	1909 (as reported).
United States...........	224,780,189	443,538,071	6,734,772	$3,511,050,000	$1,833,175,487
GEOGRAPHIC DIVISIONS:					
New England...............	13,048,923	18,683,184	630,897	55,500,000	30,416,780
Middle Atlantic............	38,587,161	80,147,963	2,073,857	170,200,000	89,563,068
East North Central........	48,439,682	77,652,164	699,245	784,200,000	422,925,855
West North Central........	28,449,443	34,884,799	363,826	1,312,600,000	715,336,435
South Atlantic.............	23,232,863	89,963,090	563,070	221,550,000	102,508,692
East South Central........	12,767,425	57,559,258	382,033	256,500,000	129,996,105
West South Central........	17,764,913	48,907,473	190,833	352,200,000	181,003,205
Mountain..................	18,772,369	14,721,366	984,073	230,700,000	100,115,107
Pacific....................	23,717,410	21,018,774	846,938	127,600,000	61,310,240
NEW ENGLAND:					
Maine......................	5,432,085	5,233,720	378,934	15,700,000	8,419,921
New Hampshire............	1,502,542	2,405,790	80,324	7,700,000	4,329,750
Vermont...................	3,538,740	4,345,803	65,197	13,300,000	7,458,895
Massachusetts.............	985,897	3,475,055	47,550	10,900,000	6,020,530
Rhode Island..............	92,228	387,822	6,388	1,300,000	746,583
Connecticut...............	1,497,431	2,834,994	52,504	6,600,000	3,441,101
MIDDLE ATLANTIC:					
New York..................	16,660,983	31,826,854	1,265,237	71,000,000	39,261,111
New Jersey................	788,218	4,613,832	29,188	8,700,000	4,996,850
Pennsylvania..............	21,137,960	43,707,277	779,432	90,500,000	45,305,107
EAST NORTH CENTRAL:					
Ohio......................	10,479,748	18,265,203	175,768	159,400,000	89,596,986
Indiana...................	4,749,380	7,861,970	24,737	171,100,000	92,896,132
Illinois..................	7,582,210	13,475,480	35,626	274,800,000	147,060,674
Michigan..................	15,609,775	22,369,438	325,574	75,600,000	43,567,427
Wisconsin.................	10,018,569	15,680,073	137,540	103,300,000	49,804,636
WEST NORTH CENTRAL:					
Minnesota.................	8,181,397	9,162,008	132,365	104,000,000	41,064,015
Iowa......................	3,543,458	2,275,482	22,482	420,300,000	218,216,303
Missouri..................	5,424,009	12,593,599	85,354	270,800,000	159,239,222
North Dakota..............	3,141,414	3,326,483	54,287	34,900,000	14,456,748
South Dakota..............	1,519,967	1,528,839	17,208	63,700,000	38,359,140
Nebraska..................	2,331,358	1,411,883	9,781	208,700,000	106,077,755
Kansas....................	4,307,840	4,586,505	42,349	210,200,000	137,923,252
SOUTH ATLANTIC:					
Delaware..................	166,893	1,505,765	10,208	2,400,000	1,338,609
Maryland..................	1,110,480	5,885,569	52,438	16,800,000	8,469,767
District of Columbia......	....	30,086	....	50,000	24,456
Virginia..................	3,292,648	17,645,865	154,478	61,100,000	28,982,606
West Virginia.............	3,022,849	7,281,011	194,451	34,600,000	18,456,118
North Carolina............	4,085,821	23,406,140	93,474	41,600,000	18,526,988
South Carolina............	2,090,107	3,836,812	20,771	18,000,000	6,790,617
Georgia...................	7,034,301	17,185,081	34,325	39,000,000	15,869,720
Florida...................	2,429,764	13,186,761	2,925	8,000,000	4,049,811
EAST SOUTH CENTRAL:					
Kentucky..................	2,812,584	5,627,480	149,519	96,800,000	54,733,377
Tennessee.................	4,113,682	18,537,751	134,127	101,000,000	49,847,367
Alabama...................	3,125,916	17,187,482	49,862	29,100,000	13,150,064
Mississippi...............	2,715,243	16,206,545	48,525	29,600,000	12,265,297
WEST SOUTH CENTRAL:					
Arkansas..................	5,489,606	16,189,192	62,609	39,400,000	20,323,592
Louisiana.................	1,434,743	7,143,658	47,808	12,100,000	5,780,166
Oklahoma..................	4,390,967	4,795,513	27,538	103,800,000	61,099,694
Texas.....................	6,449,597	20,779,110	52,878	196,900,000	93,799,753
MOUNTAIN:					
Montana...................	5,583,828	4,788,791	184,350	46,000,000	21,609,099
Idaho.....................	3,302,145	2,045,781	177,449	30,500,000	12,865,703
Wyoming...................	1,027,164	1,005,783	90,851	23,700,000	14,224,680
Colorado..................	3,976,799	3,287,451	93,435	70,600,000	24,208,175
New Mexico................	1,509,566	858,269	151,110	25,700,000	10,941,885
Arizona...................	796,546	509,051	18,814	10,900,000	4,847,097
Utah......................	2,003,109	2,015,968	224,723	15,600,000	6,656,236
Nevada....................	573,212	210,272	43,341	7,700,000	4,762,232
PACIFIC:					
Washington................	10,064,599	9,424,841	262,890	23,900,000	10,249,346
Oregon....................	7,262,850	6,948,404	308,502	36,200,000	17,433,774
California................	6,389,961	4,645,529	275,546	67,500,000	33,627,120

[1] The value of domestic animals sold or slaughtered was not called for by the 1920 farm schedule. The estimate of the 1919 value was based on the ratio between the animals sold or slaughtered in 1909 and those on hand in 1910, and the changes in the number and average value of comparable classes of animals from 1910 to 1920.

CROPS AND MISCELLANEOUS PRODUCTS.

TABLE 130.—VALUE OF CROPS IN THE UNITED STATES, WITH PERCENTAGE OF TOTAL VALUE AND OF TOTAL CROP ACREAGE REPRESENTED BY EACH CROP: 1919 AND 1909.

CROP.	VALUE.		PER CENT OF TOTAL VALUE.		PER CENT OF TOTAL CROP ACREAGE.	
	1919	1909	1919	1909	1919	1909
All crops	$14,755,364,894	$5,231,850,683	100.0	100.0		
With acreage reports	13,638,197,008	5,018,074,443	92.4	95.9	100.0	100.0
With no acreage reports	1,117,167,886	213,776,240	7.6	4.1		
Cereals, total	6,941,257,254	2,665,539,714	47.0	50.9	62.8	61.5
Corn	3,507,797,102	1,438,553,919	23.8	27.5	25.2	31.6
Wheat	2,074,078,801	657,656,801	14.1	12.6	21.0	14.2
Oats	855,255,468	414,697,422	5.8	7.9	10.9	11.3
Barley	160,427,255	92,458,571	1.1	1.8	1.9	2.5
Rye	116,537,965	20,421,812	0.8	0.4	2.2	0.7
Buckwheat	19,715,305	9,330,592	0.1	0.2	0.2	0.3
Emmer and spelt	3,699,943	5,584,050	(1)	0.1	(1)	0.2
Kafir and milo	90,221,046	10,816,940	0.6	0.2	1.0	0.5
Rice (rough)	97,194,481	16,019,607	0.7	0.3	0.3	0.2
Mixed crops [2]	16,329,888		0.1		0.2	
Other grains and seeds with acreage reports, total	184,055,553	80,959,195	1.2	1.5	1.3	1.7
Dry edible beans	61,795,225	21,771,482	0.4	0.4	0.3	0.3
Soy beans	4,450,099	20,577	(1)	(1)	(1)	(1)
Other beans [3]	126,022	220,483	(1)	(1)	(1)	(1)
Dry peas	20,790,541	10,963,739	0.1	0.2	0.2	0.4
Peanuts	62,751,701	18,271,929	0.4	0.3	0.3	0.3
Flaxseed	29,360,998	28,970,554	0.2	0.6	0.4	0.7
Miscellaneous seeds [4]	4,780,967	740,431	(1)	(1)	(1)	(1)
Other seeds with no acreage reports, total	88,853,960	16,548,696	0.6	0.3		
Grass and clover seed	80,843,832	15,137,683	0.5	0.3		
Flower and vegetable seeds	8,010,128	1,411,013	0.1	(1)		
Hay and forage, total, including corn cut for forage	2,523,050,224		17.1		27.6	
Hay and forage, excluding corn cut for forage	2,316,115,574	826,401,175	15.7	15.8	23.4	23.3
Vegetables, total	1,302,199,688	418,110,154	8.8	8.0		
Potatoes (Irish or white)	639,440,521	166,423,910	4.3	3.2	0.9	1.2
Sweet potatoes and yams	124,844,475	35,429,176	0.8	0.7	0.2	0.2
Other vegetables [5]	193,248,964	216,257,068	1.3	4.1	0.4	0.9
Farm garden [6]	344,665,728		2.3			
Sugar crops, total	162,439,060	59,252,644	1.1	1.1		
Sugar cane	59,499,467	26,415,952	0.4	0.5	0.1	0.2
Sorghum grown for sirup	24,506,228	7,963,499	0.2	0.2	0.1	0.1
Sugar beets grown for sugar	66,051,989	19,695,384	0.4	0.4	0.2	0.1
Maple sugar and sirup	12,381,376	5,177,809	0.1	0.1		
Miscellaneous crops, total	2,820,510,172	943,014,889	19.1	18.0	10.3	10.8
Tobacco	444,047,481	104,302,856	3.0	2.0	0.5	0.4
Cotton and cottonseed	2,355,169,365	824,696,287	16.0	15.8	9.7	10.3
Lint cotton	2,007,430,242	703,619,303	13.6	13.4		
Cottonseed (estimated)	347,739,123	121,076,984	2.4	2.3		
Broom corn	7,945,163	5,134,434	0.1	0.1	0.1	0.1
Hops	10,364,464	7,844,745	0.1	0.1	(1)	(1)
Sundry minor crops [7]	2,983,699	1,036,567	(1)	(1)	(1)	(1)
Small fruits, total	61,732,161	29,974,481	0.4	0.6	0.1	0.1
Orchard fruits, total [8]	431,097,974	140,867,347	2.9	2.7		
Grapes	95,586,021	22,027,961	0.6	0.4		
Subtropical fruits, total	114,868,431	24,706,753	0.8	0.5		
Nuts, total [9]	29,714,396	4,447,674	0.2	0.1		

[1] Less than one-tenth of 1 per cent.
[2] Principally oats and barley, oats and wheat, and wheat and barley grown and harvested together.
[3] Includes castor beans, horse beans, and "other" beans.
[4] Includes broom-corn seed, hemp seed, mustard seed, sorghum seed, sunflower seed, and tobacco seed (1919 and 1909), sugar-beet seed (1919), and anise seed and golden-seal seed (1909).
[5] The 1919 figures represent vegetables raised for sale only.
[6] In 1909 the value of the farm garden was largely included in the value of "Other vegetables."
[7] Includes chufas, hemp, chicory, ginseng, mint, teasels, and willows (1919 and 1909), and cassava (1919).
[8] Includes apples, peaches, pears, plums and prunes, cherries, apricots, and small quantities of quinces.
[9] The 1909 figures include the value of wild nuts (black walnuts, butternuts, hickory nuts, etc.), which were not reported for 1919.

TABLE 131.— ACREAGE AND PRODUCTION OF SPECIFIED CROPS IN

[A minus sign (−) denotes decrease. Per

CROP.	FARMS REPORTING.				ACREAGE.		
	Number.		Per cent of all farms.		1919	1909	Per cent of increase.
	1919	1909	1919	1909			
All crops with acreage reports.................					[1] 348,551,669	311,194,516	12.0
Cereals, total.................					219,030,756	191,395,963	14.4
Corn............................	4,936,692	4,813,175	76.6	75.7	87,771,600	98,382,665	−10.8
Wheat........................	2,225,134	1,458,667	34.5	22.9	73,099,421	44,262,592	65.1
Oats..........................	2,238,102	2,174,006	34.7	34.2	37,991,002	35,159,441	8.1
Barley.......................	448,985	383,197	7.0	6.0	6,472,888	7,698,706	−15.9
Rye..........................	469,113	275,796	7.3	4.3	7,679,005	2,195,561	249.8
Buckwheat..................	171,166	197,789	2.7	3.1	742,627	878,048	−15.4
Emmer and spelt...........	11,922	37,609	0.2	0.6	166,829	573,022	−70.9
Kafir and milo..............	129,947	97,574	2.0	1.5	3,619,034	1,635,153	121.3
Rice (rough)................	20,310	13,708	0.3	0.2	911,272	610,175	49.3
Mixed crops [2].............	46,100	....	0.7	....	577,078	....	.....
Other grains and seeds with acreage reports, total.......					4,651,795	5,156,893	−9.8
Dry edible beans...........	168,185	185,934	2.6	2.9	1,161,682	802,991	44.7
Soy beans..................	31,124	339	0.5	([3])	112,826	1,629	.....
Other beans [4]............					1,631	13,318	−87.8
Dry peas...................	210,245	261,231	3.3	4.1	865,670	1,305,099	−33.7
Peanuts....................	230,380	219,003	3.6	3.4	1,125,100	869,887	29.3
Flaxseed...................	53,058	77,184	0.8	1.2	1,260,687	2,083,142	−39.5
Miscellaneous seeds [5]..					124,199	80,827	53.6
Other seeds with no acreage reports, total................							
Grass and clover seed...							
Hay and forage, total, including corn cut for forage.......	4,329,161	....	67.1	....	96,121,228	....	.....
Hay and forage, excluding corn cut for forage........	....	3,403,206	....	53.5	81,618,296	72,402,173	12.7
Vegetables, total............					5,530,704	7,073,379	−21.8
Potatoes (Irish or white)...	2,887,992	3,179,907	44.8	50.0	3,251,703	3,668,855	−11.4
Sweet potatoes and yams...	1,406,780	1,121,900	21.8	17.6	803,727	641,255	25.3
Other vegetables [6]......	488,254	4,261,776	7.6	67.0	1,475,274	2,763,269	.....
Farm garden...............	5,090,293	....	78.9	....			
Sugar crops, total..........					1,491,415	1,163,634	28.2
Sugar cane.................	271,278	278,233	4.2	4.4	372,938	476,849	−21.8
Sorghum grown for sirup...	560,057	399,297	8.7	6.3	482,043	326,352	47.7
Sugar beets grown for sugar..	47,211	33,307	0.7	0.5	636,434	360,432	76.6
Maple sugar and sirup	80,317	87,537	1.2	1.4			
Miscellaneous crops, total......					35,979,619	33,730,014	6.7
Tobacco....................	448,572	326,919	7.0	5.1	1,864,080	1,294,911	44.0
Cotton.....................	1,905,863	1,714,149	29.6	26.9	33,740,106	32,043,838	5.3
Cottonseed (estimated)							
Broom corn................	44,265	23,238	0.7	0.4	337,000	326,102	3.6
Hops......................	682	6,937	([3])	0.1	15,054	44,693	−64.3
Sundry minor crops [7].....					21,673	20,470	5.9
Small fruits, total	545,823	....	8.5	....	249,084	272,460	−8.6
Orchard fruits, total [8].........	3,124,225	....	48.5	....			.....
Grapes.......................	1,074,592	924,139	16.7	14.5			.....
Nuts, total [9].................							.....

[1] Excluding 14,502,932 acres reported for corn cut for forage, which is practically all duplicated in the acreage shown for corn harvested as grain.
[2] Principally oats and barley, oats and wheat, and wheat and barley grown and harvested together.
[3] Less than one-tenth of 1 per cent.
[4] Includes castor beans, horse beans, and " other " beans.

THE UNITED STATES, WITH NUMBER OF FARMS REPORTING: 1919 AND 1909.

cent not shown when more than 1,000.]

CROP.		PRODUCTION.			AVERAGE YIELD PER ACRE.	
	Unit.	1919	1909	Per cent of increase.	1919	1909
All crops with acreage reports						
Cereals, total..................	Bu....	4,680,986,419	4,512,564,465	3.7	21.4	23.6
Corn.......................	Bu....	2,345,832,507	2,552,189,630	—8.1	26.7	25.9
Wheat.....................	Bu....	945,403,215	683,379,259	38.3	12.9	15.4
Oats.......................	Bu....	1,055,182,798	1,007,142,980	4.8	27.8	28.6
Barley.....................	Bu....	122,024,773	173,344,212	—29.6	18.9	22.5
Rye........................	Bu....	75,992,223	29,520,457	157.4	9.9	13.4
Buckwheat.................	Bu....	12,690,384	14,849,332	—14.5	17.1	16.9
Emmer and spelt............	Bu....	2,607,868	12,702,710	—79.5	15.6	22.1
Kafir and milo.............	Bu....	72,085,954	17,597,305	309.6	19.9	10.8
Rice (rough)...............	Bu....	35,330,912	21,838,580	61.8	38.8	35.8
Mixed crops [2].............	Bu....	13,835,785	....	....	24.0	....
Other grains and seeds with acreage reports, total						
Dry edible beans...........	Bu....	14,079,093	11,251,160	25.1	12.1	14.0
Soy beans..................	Bu....	1,084,813	16,835	....	9.6	10.3
Other beans [4].............	Bu....	50,328	162,898	—69.1	30.9	12.2
Dry peas...................	Bu....	5,742,626	7,129,294	—19.5	6.6	5.5
Peanuts....................	Bu....	27,449,930	19,415,816	41.4	24.4	22.3
Flaxseed...................	Bu....	6,653,200	19,512,765	—65.9	5.3	9.4
Miscellaneous seeds [5].....						
Other seeds with no acreage reports, total	Bu....	7,851,698	6,671,348	17.7		
Grass and clover seed.......	Bu....	7,851,698	6,671,348	17.7		
Hay and forage, total, including corn cut for forage...	Tons..	146,343,241	....	....	1.52	....
Hay and forage, excluding corn cut for forage	Tons..	128,549,499	97,755,296	31.5	1.58	1.35
Vegetables, total..............						
Potatoes (Irish or white)....	Bu ...	290,427,580	389,194,965	—25.4	89.3	106.1
Sweet potatoes and yams....	Bu....	78,091,913	59,232,070	31.8	97.2	92.4
Other vegetables [6].........						
Farm garden...............						
Sugar crops, total..............	Tons..	11,182,188	11,518,818	—2.9	7.50	9.90
Sugar cane.................	Tons..	3,544,679	6,240,260	—43.2	9.50	13.09
Sorghum grown for sirup....	Tons..	1,644,100	1,376,487	19.4	3.41	4.22
Sugar beets grown for sugar..	Tons..	5,993,409	3,902,071	53.6	9.42	10.83
Maple sugar and sirup.......						
Miscellaneous crops, total.....						
Tobacco....................	Lbs..	1,372,993,261	1,055,764,806	30.0	737	815
Cotton.....................	Bales.	11,376,130	10,649,268	6.8	0.34	0.33
Cottonseed (estimated)......	Tons..	5,327,721	5,324,622	0.1		
Broom corn................	Lbs...	113,031,132	78,959,958	43.1	335	242
Hops.......................	Lbs...	19,760,793	40,718,748	—51.5	1,239	911
Sundry minor crops [7]......						
Small fruits, total..............	Qts...	324,988,968	426,565,863	—23.8	1,304.74	1,565.61
Orchard fruits, total [8]..........	Bu....	230,681,707	213,973,695	7.8		
Grapes..........................	Lbs...	2,516,840,387	2,265,065,205	11.1		
Nuts, total [9]..................	Lbs...	107,501,920	62,328,010	72.5		

[5] Includes broom-corn seed, hemp seed, mustard seed, sorghum seed, sunflower seed, and tobacco seed (1919 and 1909), sugar-beet seed (1919), and anise seed and golden-seal seed (1909).
[6] The 1919 figures represent vegetables raised for sale only.
[7] Includes chufas, hemp, chicory, ginseng, mint, teasels, and willows (1919 and 1909), and cassava (1919).
[8] Includes apples, peaches, pears, plums and prunes, cherries, apricots, and small quantities of quinces.
[9] Exclusive of coconuts which were reported by number. The 1909 figures include wild nuts (black walnuts, butternuts, and hickory nuts, etc.), which were not reported for 1919.

TABLE 132.—COMPARATIVE STATEMENT SHOWING INCREASE IN VALUE OF CROPS
HIGHER

	CROP.	Unit.	AVERAGE VALUE PER UNIT.			VALUE OF CROPS.
			1919	1909	Per cent of increase.	As reported, 1919
1	**All crops**					$14,755,364,894
2	**Crops compared**					13,995,911,487
3	**Crops not compared**					759,453,407
4	**Cereals, total** [5]					6,937,557,311
5	Corn	Bu....	$1.49533	$0.56365	165.3	3,507,797,102
6	Wheat	Bu....	2.19386	0.96236	128.0	2,074,078,801
7	Oats	Bu....	0.81053	0.41176	96.8	855,255,468
8	Barley	Bu....	1.31471	0.53338	146.5	160,427,255
9	Rye	Bu....	1.53355	0.69179	121.7	116,537,965
10	Buckwheat	Bu....	1.55356	0.62835	147.2	19,715,305
11	Kafir and milo	Bu....	1.25158	0.61469	103.6	90,221,046
12	Rice (rough)	Bu....	2.75098	0.73355	275.0	97,194,481
13	Mixed crops [6]	Bu....	1.18026	0.53893	119.0	16,329,888
14	**Other grains and seeds, total**					182,042,587
15	Dry edible beans	Bu....	4.38915	1.93504	126.8	61,795,225
16	Soy beans	Bu....	4.10218	1.22228	235.6	4,450,099
17	Other beans [7]	Bu....				125,198
18	Dry peas	Bu....	3.62039	1.53784	135.4	20,790,541
19	Peanuts	Bu....	2.28604	0.94108	142.9	62,751,701
20	Flaxseed	Bu....	4.41306	1.48470	197.2	29,360,998
21	Minor seeds [8]					2,768,825
22	**Clover and grass seeds, total**					80,843,832
23	Clover and alfalfa seed	Bu....	27.10828	6.96351	289.3	55,416,726
24	Timothy seed	Bu....	5.28508	1.39606	278.6	13,673,913
25	Millet seed	Bu....	2.80940	0.83561	236.2	3,682,987
26	Other grass seed	Bu....	4.22700	0.86166	390.6	8,070,206
27	**Hay and forage, excluding corn cut for forage**	Tons..				2,316,115,574
28	**Sugar crops, total**					162,439,060
29	Sugar cane	Tons..	16.78557	4.23315	296.5	59,499,467
30	Sorghum grown for sirup	Tons..	14.90556	5.78538	157.6	24,506,228
31	Sugar beets grown for sugar	Tons..	11.02077	5.04742	118.3	66,051,989
32	Maple sugar	Lbs...	0.32461	0.09844	229.8	3,146,107
33	Maple sirup	Gal...	2.63282	0.92473	184.7	9,235,269
34	**Miscellaneous crops, total**					3,584,661,323
35	Potatoes (Irish or white)	Bu....	2.20172	0.42761	414.9	639,440,521
36	Sweet potatoes and yams	Bu....	1.59869	0.59814	167.3	124,844,475
37	Tobacco	Lbs...	0.32342	0.09879	227.4	444,047,481
38	Cotton	Bales.	176.45985	66.07208	167.1	2,007,430,242
39	Cottonseed (estimated)	Tons..	65.26977	22.73908	187.0	347,739,123
40	Sundry minor crops [9]					21,159,481
41	**Fruits and nuts, total**					732,251,800
42	Small fruits [10]	Qts...				61,128,229
43	Orchard fruits [11]	Bu....				430,956,831
44	Grapes	Lbs...	0.03798	0.00973	290.3	95,586,021
45	Subtropical fruits [12]					114,866,920
46	Nuts	Lbs...				29,714,206

[1] A minus sign ( ) denotes decrease.   Per cent not shown when more than 1,000.
[2] Due partly to increased production and partly to higher prices.
[3] Increase in value on basis of 1909 prices for 1919 crops.   The percentages in this section represent the *net increase in production.*
[4] Excess of actual 1919 values over values computed for 1919 on basis of 1909 prices.
[5] Exclusive of emmer and spelt.
[6] Principally oats and barley, oats and wheat, and wheat and barley grown and harvested together.

BETWEEN 1909 AND 1919 RESULTING (1) FROM GREATER PRODUCTION AND (2) FROM PRICES.

VALUE OF CROPS—continued.		INCREASE IN CROP VALUES, 1909 TO 1919.[1]						
Computed for 1919 on basis of 1909 prices.	As reported, 1909	Gross increase.[2]		Increase due to greater production.[3]		Increase due to higher prices.[4]		
		Amount.	Per cent.	Amount.	Per cent.	Amount.	Per cent.	
	$5,231,850,683	$9,523,514,211	.....	.....	.....	.....	.....	1
$5,457,511,832	5,007,238,561	8,988,672,926	179.5	$450,273,271	9.0	$8,538,399,655	156.5	2
	224,612,122	534,841,285	.....					3
2,869,843,061	2,659,955,664	4,277,601,647	160.8	209,887,397	7.9	4,067,714,250	141.7	4
1,322,228,493	1,438,553,919	2,069,243,183	143.8	−116,325,426	−8.1	2,185,568,609	165.3	5
909,818,238	657,656,801	1,416,422,000	215.4	252,161,437	38.3	1,164,260,563	128.0	6
434,482,069	414,697,422	440,558,046	106.2	19,784,647	4.8	420,773,399	96.8	7
65,085,573	92,458,571	67,968,684	73.5	−27,372,998	−29.6	95,341,682	146.5	8
52,570,660	20,421,812	96,116,153	470.7	32,148,848	157.4	63,967,305	121.7	9
7,974,003	9,330,592	10,384,713	111.3	−1,356,589	−14.5	11,741,302	147.2	10
44,310,515	10,816,940	79,404,106	734.1	33,493,575	309.6	45,910,531	103.6	11
25,916,990	16,019,607	81,174,874	506.7	9,897,383	61.8	71,277,491	275.0	12
7,456,520	.....	16,329,888	.....	7,456,520	.....	8,873,368	119.0	13
74,370,192	80,747,291	101,295,296	125.4	−6,377,099	−7.9	107,672,395	144.8	14
27,243,608	21,771,482	40,023,743	183.8	5,472,126	25.1	34,551,617	126.8	15
1,325,945	20,577	4,429,522	.....	1,305,368	.....	3,124,154	235.6	16
51,524	9,091	116,107	.....	42,433	−446.8	73,674	143.0	17
8,831,240	10,963,739	9,826,802	89.6	−2,132,499	−19.5	11,959,301	135.4	18
25,832,580	18,271,929	44,479,772	243.4	7,560,651	41.4	36,919,121	142.9	19
9,878,006	28,970,554	390,444	1.3	−19,092,548	−65.9	19,482,992	197.2	20
1,207,289	739,919	2,028,906	274.2	467,370	63.2	1,561,536	129.3	21
20,587,826	15,137,683	65,706,149	434.1	5,450,143	36.0	60,256,006	292.7	22
14,235,315	8,976,962	46,439,764	517.3	5,258,353	58.6	41,181,411	289.3	23
3,611,981	4,018,951	9,654,962	240.2	−406,970	−10.1	10,061,932	278.6	24
1,095,445	481,566	3,191,421	649.2	603,879	122.8	2,587,542	236.2	25
1,645,085	1,650,204	6,420,002	389.0	−5,119	−0.3	6,425,121	390.6	26
988,399,235	826,401,175	1,489,714,399	180.3	161,998,060	19.6	1,327,716,339	134.3	27
58,965,936	59,252,644	103,186,416	174.1	−286,708	−0.5	103,473,124	175.5	28
15,005,158	26,415,952	33,083,515	125.2	−11,410,794	−43.2	44,494,309	296.5	29
9,511,743	7,963,499	16,542,729	207.7	1,548,244	19.4	14,994,485	157.6	30
30,251,252	19,695,384	46,356,605	235.4	10,555,868	53.6	35,800,737	118.3	31
954,066	1,380,492	1,765,615	127.9	−426,426	−30.9	2,192,041	229.8	32
3,243,717	3,797,317	5,437,952	143.2	−553,600	−14.6	5,991,552	184.7	33
1,191,481,631	1,144,716,087	2,439,945,236	213.1	46,765,544	4.1	2,393,179,692	200.9	34
124,189,737	166,423,910	473,016,611	284.2	−42,234,173	−25.4	515,250,784	414.9	35
46,709,897	35,429,176	89,415,299	252.4	11,280,721	31.8	78,134,578	167.3	36
135,638,004	104,302,856	339,744,625	325.7	31,335,148	30.0	308,409,477	227.4	37
751,644,571	703,619,303	1,303,810,939	185.3	48,025,268	6.8	1,255,785,671	167.1	38
121,147,474	121,076,984	226,662,139	187.2	70,490	0.1	226,591,649	187.0	39
12,151,948	13,863,858	7,295,623	52.6	−1,711,910	−12.3	9,007,533	74.1	40
253,863,951	221,028,017	511,223,783	231.3	32,835,934	14.9	478,387,849	188.4	41
22,580,153	29,502,078	31,626,151	107.2	−6,921,925	−23.5	38,548,076	170.7	42
155,873,932	140,350,104	290,606,727	207.1	15,523,828	11.1	275,082,899	176.5	43
24,488,857	22,027,961	73,558,060	333.9	2,460,896	11.2	71,097,164	290.3	44
39,875,667	24,700,200	90,166,123	365.0	15,175,467	61.4	74,990,656	188.1	45
11,045,342	4,447,674	25,266,722	568.1	6,597,668	148.3	18,669,054	169.0	46

7 Includes castor beans and horse beans.
8 Includes broom-corn seed, hemp seed, mustard seed, sorghum seed, sunflower seed, and tobacco seed.
9 Includes chufas, broom corn, hops, hemp, chicory, mint, teasels, and willows.
10 Exclusive of the group designated "Other berries."
11 Exclusive of quinces.
12 Exclusive of sugar apples and sapodillas (1919) and mandarins (1909).

TABLE 133.—ACREAGE AND PRODUCTION OF PRINCIPAL CROPS IN THE UNITED STATES: 1879 TO 1919.

CROP.	1919	1909	1899	1889	1879
			ACREAGE.		
Cereals:					
Corn	87,771,600	98,382,665	94,913,673	72,087,752	62,368,504
Wheat	73,099,421	44,262,592	52,588,574	33,579,514	35,430,333
Oats	37,991,002	35,159,441	29,539,698	28,320,677	16,144,593
Barley	6,472,888	7,698,706	4,470,196	3,220,834	1,997,727
Rye	7,679,005	2,195,561	2,054,292	2,171,604	1,842,233
Buckwheat	742,627	878,048	807,060	837,164	848,389
Kafir and milo	3,619,034	1,635,153	266,513		
Rice (rough)	911,272	610,175	342,214	161,312	174,173
Other grains and seeds:					
Dry edible beans	1,161,682	802,991	453,841		
Dry peas	865,670	1,305,099	968,370		
Peanuts	1,125,100	869,887	516,654	203,946	
Flaxseed	1,260,687	2,083,142	2,110,517	1,318,698	
Hay	72,779,888	68,227,310	58,583,847	52,948,797	30,631,054
Sugar crops:					
Sugar cane	372,938	476,849	386,986	274,975	227,776
Sorghum grown for sirup	482,043	326,352	293,152	415,691	
Sugar beets grown for sugar	636,434	360,433	110,170		
Miscellaneous crops:					
Tobacco	1,864,080	1,294,911	1,101,460	695,301	638,841
Cotton	33,740,106	32,043,838	24,275,101	20,175,270	14,480,019
Potatoes	3,251,703	3,668,855	2,938,778	2,600,750	(1)
Sweet potatoes and yams	803,727	641,255	537,312	524,588	(1)
			PRODUCTION.		
Cereals:	*Bushels.*	*Bushels.*	*Bushels.*	*Bushels.*	*Bushels.*
Corn	2,345,832,507	2,552,189,630	2,666,324,370	2,122,327,547	1,754,591,676
Wheat	945,403,215	683,379,259	658,534,252	468,373,968	459,483,137
Oats	1,055,182,798	1,007,142,980	943,389,375	809,250,666	407,858,999
Barley	122,024,773	173,344,212	119,634,877	78,332,976	43,997,495
Rye	75,992,223	29,520,457	25,568,625	28,421,398	19,831,595
Buckwheat	12,690,384	14,849,332	11,233,515	12,110,349	11,817,327
Kafir and milo	72,085,954	17,597,305	5,169,113		
Rice (rough)	35,330,912	21,838,580	9,002,886	4,625,573	3,961,560
Other grains and seeds:					
Dry edible beans	14,079,093	11,251,160	5,064,490	3,163,554	3,075,050
Dry peas	5,742,626	7,129,294	9,440,210	6,215,349	6,514,977
Peanuts	27,449,930	19,415,816	11,964,109	3,588,143	
Flaxseed	6,653,200	19,512,765	19,979,492	10,250,410	7,170,951
	Tons.	*Tons.*	*Tons.*	*Tons.*	*Tons.*
Hay	90,355,540	87,216,351	71,112,709	66,831,480	35,150,711
Sugar crops:					
Sugar cane	3,544,679	6,240,260	4,202,202		
Sorghum grown for sirup	1,644,100	1,376,487	1,910,046		
Sugar beets grown for sugar	5,993,409	3,902,071	793,353		
Miscellaneous crops:	*Pounds.*	*Pounds.*	*Pounds.*	*Pounds.*	*Pounds.*
Tobacco	1,372,993,261	1,055,764,806	868,112,865	488,256,646	472,661,157
	Bales.	*Bales.*	*Bales.*	*Bales.*	*Bales.*
Cotton	11,376,130	10,649,268	9,534,707	7,472,511	5,755,359
	Bushels.	*Bushels.*	*Bushels.*	*Bushels.*	*Bushels.*
Potatoes	290,427,580	389,194,965	273,318,167	217,546,362	169,458,539
Sweet potatoes and yams	78,091,913	59,232,070	42,517,412	43,950,261	33,378,693

[1] Acreage not completely reported.

TABLE 134.—VALUE OF ALL CROPS, WITH AVERAGE VALUE PER FARM AND PER ACRE, BY DIVISIONS AND STATES: 1919 AND 1909.

DIVISION AND STATE.	VALUE OF ALL CROPS.			AVERAGE VALUE PER FARM OF ALL FARM CROPS.		AVERAGE VALUE PER ACRE OF CROPS WITH ACREAGE REPORTS.	
	1919	1909	Per cent of increase.	1919	1909	1919	1909
United States......	$14,755,364,894	$5,231,850,683	182.0	$2,288	$822	$39.13	$16.13
GEOGRAPHIC DIVISIONS:							
New England..........	275,175,536	117,654,874	133.9	1,758	623	55.48	23.36
Middle Atlantic........	914,499,927	379,123,636	141.2	2,151	809	47.22	19.83
East North Central.....	2,818,367,792	1,072,080,129	162.9	2,598	954	42.52	17.33
West North Central....	3,676,902,149	1,419,131,769	159.1	3,352	1,279	28.04	12.18
South Atlantic.........	2,083,808,428	693,806,241	200.3	1,798	624	60.84	22.12
East South Central.....	1,306,179,289	519,800,422	151.3	1,242	499	46.17	19.69
West South Central....	2,168,622,649	604,643,008	258.7	2,177	641	41.13	15.22
Mountain..............	562,954,399	159,918,622	252.0	2,306	872	33.12	17.05
Pacific................	948,854,024	265,691,982	257.1	4,052	1,399	47.33	19.55
NEW ENGLAND:							
Maine................	100,152,324	33,386,440	200.0	2,077	556	59.12	19.60
New Hampshire........	23,509,665	12,112,260	94.1	1,146	448	36.99	18.88
Vermont..............	47,999,600	23,697,700	102.5	1,651	725	35.45	18.10
Massachusetts.........	53,700,925	26,191,705	105.0	1,678	709	77.55	36.81
Rhode Island..........	5,340,378	2,986,816	78.8	1,308	564	66.84	33.17
Connecticut...........	44,472,644	19,279,953	130.7	1,963	719	85.26	33.47
MIDDLE ATLANTIC:							
New York.............	417,046,864	190,002,693	119.5	2,159	881	43.60	19.89
New Jersey...........	87,484,186	35,648,849	145.4	2,945	1,065	76.74	30.11
Pennsylvania..........	409,968,877	153,472,094	167.1	2,027	700	47.24	18.31
EAST NORTH CENTRAL:							
Ohio.................	607,037,562	221,086,342	174.6	2,365	813	48.44	18.55
Indiana..............	497,229,719	196,869,691	152.6	2,424	914	40.49	16.93
Illinois..............	864,737,833	364,190,261	137.4	3,646	1,446	40.73	17.66
Michigan.............	404,014,810	152,102,869	165.6	2,057	735	40.16	17.11
Wisconsin............	445,347,868	137,830,966	223.1	2,353	778	43.81	15.67
WEST NORTH CENTRAL:							
Minnesota............	506,020,233	186,705,665	171.0	2,835	1,196	29.89	12.52
Iowa.................	890,391,299	309,376,240	187.8	4,172	1,425	42.26	14.87
Missouri.............	559,047,854	211,001,359	164.9	2,126	761	34.07	14.17
North Dakota.........	301,782,935	180,311,555	67.4	3,884	2,425	15.24	11.34
South Dakota.........	311,006,069	125,116,080	148.6	4,167	1,611	20.84	10.16
Nebraska.............	519,729,771	194,401,937	167.3	4,177	1,499	26.97	11.13
Kansas..............	588,923,248	212,218,933	177.5	3,563	1,193	26.25	10.57
SOUTH ATLANTIC:							
Delaware.............	23,058,906	8,650,192	166.6	2,274	798	45.44	19.12
Maryland............	109,858,608	40,330,688	172.4	2,293	824	50.99	20.05
District of Columbia....	307,614	242,582	26.8	1,508	1,118	118.55	86.92
Virginia..............	292,824,260	89,775,045	226.2	1,572	488	57.27	20.19
West Virginia.........	96,537,459	36,167,014	166.9	1,106	374	41.31	17.59
North Carolina........	503,229,313	131,071,959	283.9	1,865	517	82.31	22.21
South Carolina........	437,121,837	137,379,131	218.2	2,268	779	78.79	26.44
Georgia..............	540,613,626	216,971,974	149.2	1,740	746	49.20	22.13
Florida..............	80,256,806	33,217,656	141.6	1,486	664	43.83	21.14
EAST SOUTH CENTRAL:							
Kentucky.............	347,338,888	130,594,808	166.0	1,283	504	52.09	20.74
Tennessee............	318,285,307	111,133,210	186.4	1,259	452	43.83	16.90
Alabama.............	304,348,638	137,540,733	121.3	1,188	523	39.52	18.82
Mississippi..........	336,207,156	140,531,671	139.2	1,236	512	50.40	22.56
WEST SOUTH CENTRAL:							
Arkansas.............	340,813,256	112,129,230	203.9	1,465	522	48.27	20.27
Louisiana............	206,182,548	73,536,538	180.4	1,522	610	50.20	20.30
Oklahoma............	550,084,742	131,522,220	318.2	2,865	692	35.14	10.93
Texas...............	1,071,542,103	287,455,020	272.8	2,457	688	41.48	15.53
MOUNTAIN:							
Montana.............	69,975,185	28,886,689	142.2	1,213	1,102	17.40	15.25
Idaho...............	126,495,111	32,880,915	284.7	3,004	1,067	41.96	19.43
Wyoming............	30,270,630	9,903,071	205.7	1,922	901	25.34	12.43
Colorado.............	181,065,239	50,110,677	261.3	3,021	1,085	33.29	17.31
New Mexico..........	40,619,634	8,619,802	371.2	1,361	242	32.94	12.70
Arizona.............	42,481,230	5,434,664	681.7	4,259	589	90.83	25.89
Utah................	58,067,067	18,204,379	219.0	2,263	840	50.74	22.81
Nevada..............	13,980,303	5,878,425	137.8	4,420	2,186	34.97	14.73
PACIFIC:							
Washington..........	227,212,008	74,101,381	206.6	3,428	1,319	43.32	20.33
Oregon..............	131,884,639	45,064,450	192.7	2,627	990	39.30	18.10
California...........	589,757,377	146,526,151	302.5	5,012	1,661	54.02	19.68

Table 135.—ACREAGE AND VALUE OF ALL CROPS WITH ACREAGE REPORTS, BY DIVISIONS AND STATES: 1919 AND 1909.

[A minus sign (−) denotes decrease.]

DIVISION AND STATE.	ACREAGE OF ALL CROPS WITH ACREAGE REPORTS.			VALUE OF ALL CROPS WITH ACREAGE REPORTS.		
	1919	1909	Per cent of increase.	1919	1909	Per cent of increase.
United States	348,551,669	311,194,516	12.0	$13,638,197,008	$5,018,074,443	171.8
GEOGRAPHIC DIVISIONS:						
New England	4,262,104	4,653,922	−8.4	236,448,604	108,732,841	117.5
Middle Atlantic	17,007,595	17,309,074	−1.7	803,111,155	343,269,476	134.0
East North Central	62,757,917	59,772,909	5.0	2,668,365,141	1,035,922,245	157.6
West North Central	127,122,665	114,671,661	10.9	3,564,387,251	1,397,033,548	155.1
South Atlantic	31,859,714	30,267,979	5.3	1,938,236,668	669,441,705	189.5
East South Central	26,713,789	25,767,143	3.7	1,233,470,382	507,314,125	143.1
West South Central	50,548,349	39,267,232	28.7	2,079,022,461	597,575,820	247.9
Mountain	15,717,906	8,857,098	77.5	520,634,460	151,010,287	244.8
Pacific	12,561,630	10,627,498	18.2	594,520,886	207,774,396	186.1
NEW ENGLAND:						
Maine	1,529,941	1,587,896	−3.6	90,447,260	31,116,693	190.7
New Hampshire	508,168	592,976	−14.3	18,797,763	11,193,657	67.9
Vermont	1,143,304	1,203,735	−5.0	40,524,640	21,787,708	86.0
Massachusetts	560,647	652,094	−14.0	43,478,240	24,000,893	81.2
Rhode Island	61,733	83,705	−26.2	4,126,249	2,776,355	48.6
Connecticut	458,311	533,516	−14.1	39,074,452	17,857,535	118.8
MIDDLE ATLANTIC:						
New York	8,142,108	8,376,072	−2.8	354,988,170	166,575,783	113.1
New Jersey	994,004	1,111,300	−10.6	76,284,458	33,464,392	128.0
Pennsylvania	7,871,483	7,821,702	0.6	371,838,527	143,229,301	159.6
EAST NORTH CENTRAL:						
Ohio	11,780,554	11,425,822	3.1	570,665,227	212,005,794	169.2
Indiana	11,849,165	11,329,049	4.6	479,774,238	191,771,114	150.2
Illinois	20,370,027	20,269,123	0.5	829,618,809	357,947,866	131.8
Michigan	9,168,200	8,194,842	11.9	368,163,868	140,189,462	162.6
Wisconsin	9,589,971	8,554,073	12.1	420,142,999	134,008,009	213.5
WEST NORTH CENTRAL:						
Minnesota	16,362,970	14,727,447	11.1	489,070,789	184,365,249	165.3
Iowa	20,420,374	20,371,134	0.2	863,013,259	302,987,728	184.8
Missouri	15,418,596	14,332,746	7.6	525,244,769	203,102,959	158.6
North Dakota	19,422,463	15,888,280	22.2	295,936,991	180,201,654	64.2
South Dakota	14,654,636	12,226,354	19.9	305,379,973	124,279,954	145.7
Nebraska	18,935,849	17,229,114	9.9	510,659,673	191,832,489	166.2
Kansas	21,907,777	19,896,586	10.1	575,081,797	210,263,515	173.5
SOUTH ATLANTIC:						
Delaware	448,227	438,296	2.3	20,366,640	8,379,053	143.1
Maryland	1,987,965	1,927,254	3.2	101,367,369	38,636,747	162.4
District of Columbia	2,208	2,742	−19.5	261,749	238,337	9.8
Virginia	4,579,367	4,255,282	7.6	262,252,283	85,911,759	205.3
West Virginia	1,891,316	1,873,893	0.9	78,129,983	32,962,408	137.0
North Carolina	5,849,998	5,736,176	2.0	481,485,874	127,428,105	277.8
South Carolina	5,396,660	5,152,801	4.7	425,186,414	136,256,919	212.0
Georgia	10,468,834	9,660,737	8.4	515,056,531	213,825,377	140.9
Florida	1,235,139	1,220,798	1.2	54,129,825	25,803,000	109.8
EAST SOUTH CENTRAL:						
Kentucky	6,303,182	6,046,028	4.3	328,355,896	125,372,616	161.9
Tennessee	6,786,187	6,360,928	6.7	297,451,948	107,475,255	176.8
Alabama	7,265,035	7,202,040	0.9	287,135,779	135,515,382	111.9
Mississippi	6,359,385	6,158,147	3.3	320,526,759	138,950,872	130.7
WEST SOUTH CENTRAL:						
Arkansas	6,464,540	5,375,000	20.2	312,063,321	108,980,380	186.3
Louisiana	3,923,925	3,595,610	9.1	196,981,545	72,788,843	170.6
Oklahoma	15,132,111	11,920,773	26.9	531,759,411	130,238,187	308.3
Texas	25,027,773	18,384,910	36.1	1,038,212,184	285,568,410	263.6
MOUNTAIN:						
Montana	3,811,919	1,847,752	106.3	66,311,460	28,180,719	135.3
Idaho	2,706,212	1,637,931	65.2	113,561,245	31,820,979	256.9
Wyoming	1,153,624	786,644	46.7	29,233,036	9,777,870	199.0
Colorado	5,052,955	2,613,917	93.3	168,226,645	45,254,318	271.7
New Mexico	1,131,806	632,737	78.9	37,287,004	8,036,551	364.0
Arizona	441,712	190,958	131.3	40,118,635	4,943,226	711.6
Utah	1,030,398	754,773	36.5	52,281,459	17,218,700	203.6
Nevada	389,280	392,386	−0.8	13,614,976	5,777,924	135.6
PACIFIC:						
Washington	4,001,620	3,429,591	16.7	173,336,176	69,725,354	148.6
Oregon	2,803,016	2,278,990	23.0	110,169,711	41,241,304	167.1
California	5,756,994	4,918,917	17.0	311,014,999	96,807,738	221.3

TABLE 136.—FEED CROPS (CORN, OATS, BARLEY, AND HAY) SOLD BY FARMERS, BY DIVISIONS AND STATES: 1919.

[Figures for production in Tables 139, 143, 145, and 171.]

DIVISION AND STATE.	CORN SOLD.		OATS SOLD.		BARLEY SOLD.		HAY SOLD.	
	Quantity (bushels).	Per cent of production.	Quantity (bushels).	Per cent of production.	Quantity (bushels).	Per cent of production.	Quantity (tons).	Per cent of production.
United States...	460,997,139	19.7	277,214,402	26.3	44,945,358	36.8	13,137,181	14.5
GEOGRAPHIC DIVISIONS:								
New England......	139,961	2.5	196,828	2.8	14,167	4.1	356,438	9.2
Middle Atlantic....	12,355,150	14.7	3,495,912	6.7	219,462	8.6	1,412,215	13.9
East North Central.	171,878,225	25.1	103,797,672	31.1	3,700,221	14.8	2,331,470	13.1
West North Central.	220,622,399	24.6	122,345,352	24.8	20,910,741	36.1	3,347,182	10.9
South Atlantic.....	15,675,386	7.4	692,619	4.8	24,961	6.7	243,653	7.3
East South Central.	11,823,741	5.3	782,133	11.0	37,490	17.0	364,344	10.6
West South Central.	20,773,474	9.5	31,941,052	28.4	1,352,475	34.0	614,111	17.0
Mountain..........	5,221,315	31.2	4,188,328	29.0	2,083,644	34.9	2,554,009	27.0
Pacific.............	2,507,488	48.2	9,774,506	50.4	16,602,197	64.9	1,913,759	24.6
NEW ENGLAND:								
Maine..............	6,789	2.4	157,308	4.4	11,008	10.5	154,440	12.8
New Hampshire....	7,351	1.5	8,179	1.7	823	3.7	38,508	8.0
Vermont...........	7,841	0.8	23,360	1.0	1,897	1.0	80,662	6.7
Massachusetts.....	45,194	3.0	3,504	1.2	324	2.7	47,963	8.8
Rhode Island......	19,149	6.2	880	2.6	....	....	4,680	8.6
Connecticut.......	53,637	2.6	3,597	1.2	115	2.4	30,185	8.3
MIDDLE ATLANTIC:								
New York.........	592,067	4.2	622,031	2.9	195,576	8.6	928,874	14.8
New Jersey........	1,503,449	17.1	154,039	10.4	2,983	20.4	63,560	16.1
Pennsylvania......	10,259,634	16.7	2,719,842	9.3	20,903	8.0	419,781	12.0
EAST NORTH CENTRAL:								
Ohio..............	24,173,497	16.1	14,697,277	31.4	234,598	9.7	639,872	17.2
Indiana...........	26,862,498	16.9	20,978,977	39.9	135,418	9.5	313,670	13.8
Illinois...........	117,260,785	41.1	58,569,444	45.4	858,010	20.3	495,266	13.6
Michigan..........	2,398,624	5.3	4,673,381	12.6	557,446	11.6	570,066	18.0
Wisconsin.........	1,182,821	2.7	4,878,593	7.1	1,914,749	15.7	312,596	6.2
WEST NORTH CENTRAL:								
Minnesota.........	13,325,467	15.7	17,354,374	19.5	5,555,490	37.4	343,960	6.1
Iowa..............	106,547,801	28.7	67,776,982	36.2	2,010,569	37.6	646,650	12.1
Missouri..........	18,016,300	12.3	5,760,938	14.2	23,617	16.2	418,213	12.5
North Dakota.....	212,797	5.5	2,289,202	7.6	2,969,279	24.6	158,008	5.4
South Dakota......	20,018,300	29.0	13,615,620	26.6	6,197,002	48.4	298,245	7.6
Nebraska..........	48,297,859	30.1	11,629,834	19.4	1,535,730	34.9	659,286	12.4
Kansas............	14,203,875	23.8	3,918,402	10.8	2,619,054	31.5	822,820	19.0
SOUTH ATLANTIC:								
Delaware..........	852,188	23.1	8,595	12.1	310	49.6	8,766	9.9
Maryland..........	5,067,706	24.0	101,639	9.4	10,140	9.1	63,904	14.4
Dist. of Columbia...	2,285	14.6	....	....	....	....	18	2.1
Virginia...........	3,973,231	9.4	141,703	7.2	12,792	5.6	90,805	9.6
West Virginia......	994,003	5.8	116,111	3.8	1,659	6.7	31,786	4.6
North Carolina.....	1,617,099	3.9	78,292	4.7	60	1.7	17,179	3.8
South Carolina.....	467,419	1.7	59,024	1.6	....	....	4,652	1.7
Georgia...........	1,854,541	3.6	164,308	6.0	....	....	20,669	5.5
Florida............	846,914	9.6	22,947	10.3	....	....	5,874	8.3
EAST SOUTH CENTRAL:								
Kentucky..........	4,084,561	5.7	188,061	6.7	16,997	14.2	137,655	12.7
Tennessee.........	5,389,605	7.6	516,594	21.4	20,400	21.2	111,748	8.0
Alabama..........	1,708,903	3.9	36,544	3.3	93	1.8	52,627	11.9
Mississippi........	640,672	1.7	40,934	5.4	....	....	62,314	11.9
WEST SOUTH CENTRAL:								
Arkansas..........	1,147,945	3.4	219,762	8.1	157	5.4	91,961	11.9
Louisiana.........	647,194	3.0	16,551	3.4	....	....	23,189	9.4
Oklahoma.........	8,609,269	16.0	10,647,815	23.4	495,909	27.8	317,512	20.1
Texas.............	10,369,066	9.6	21,056,924	32.9	856,409	39.1	181,449	18.2
MOUNTAIN:								
Montana..........	22,280	14.0	518,954	20.1	66,711	19.2	227,081	17.0
Idaho.............	184,754	28.8	964,811	31.4	516,879	38.3	793,438	35.3
Wyoming..........	57,212	14.7	211,635	21.0	17,136	14.8	163,099	18.7
Colorado..........	3,237,481	32.0	1,373,687	30.3	810,635	28.9	770,793	28.5
New Mexico.......	1,542,104	32.0	464,840	42.8	71,687	36.9	156,289	39.7
Arizona...........	141,307	31.7	211,127	55.9	460,021	70.0	159,517	40.6
Utah..............	33,150	12.5	411,994	23.9	56,267	15.4	149,856	15.3
Nevada...........	3,027	20.6	31,280	41.7	84,308	56.9	133,936	24.5
PACIFIC:								
Washington........	220,325	24.4	4,672,749	57.9	994,877	44.2	477,171	27.3
Oregon............	116,752	13.8	3,113,113	37.2	591,366	41.4	458,794	24.0
California.........	2,170,411	62.9	1,988,644	67.0	15,015,954	68.6	977,794	23.8

TABLE 137.—POTATOES AND APPLES SOLD BY FARMERS, BY DIVISIONS AND STATES: 1919.

[Figures for production in Tables 172 and 191.]

DIVISION AND STATE.	POTATOES SOLD.		APPLES SOLD.		DIVISION AND STATE.	POTATOES SOLD.		APPLES SOLD.	
	Quantity (bushels).	Per cent of production.	Quantity (bushels).	Per cent of production.		Quantity (bushels.)	Per cent of production.	Quantity (bushels).	Per cent of production.
U. S.	169,523,734	58.4	98,582,854	72.2	SOUTH ATL.:				
GEOG. DIVS.:					Delaware	250,254	51.3	530,486	87.5
N. England	23,146,231	70.8	8,637,384	71.6	Maryland	3,280,675	66.7	998,572	65.7
Middle Atl.	41,163,813	63.5	16,113,156	74.8	Dist. of Col.	9,233	46.6	212	11.6
E. N. Cent.	33,788,686	52.0	9,905,570	63.0	Virginia	9,830,067	80.2	5,650,726	63.2
W. N. Cent.	24,273,805	48.3	5,664,919	52.4	W. Virginia	585,818	20.9	2,162,531	51.6
South Atl.	17,153,052	63.8	10,025,960	56.2	N. Carolina	1,443,577	50.6	506,398	26.1
E. S. Cent.	1,793,497	26.9	812,047	24.4	S. Carolina	533,535	49.5	17,458	8.1
W. S. Cent.	1,719,724	27.0	6,854,635	73.8	Georgia	162,603	23.4	159,576	38.3
Mountain	13,989,424	69.6	7,840,286	81.3	Florida	1,057,290	59.8	1	0.7
Pacific	12,495,502	70.9	32,728,897	90.1	E. S. CENT.:				
N. ENGLAND:					Kentucky	1,177,166	37.6	371,569	29.0
Maine	20,427,958	80.0	3,540,334	73.3	Tennessee	383,224	19.2	355,629	28.2
New Hamp.	441,769	32.9	961,286	70.5	Alabama	125,713	14.2	70,305	12.2
Vermont	621,288	27.3	474,955	49.5	Mississippi	107,394	16.5	14,544	6.7
Mass.	872,800	16.3	2,618,016	82.1	W. S. CENT.:				
Rhode Is.	179,752	61.3	230,861	69.1	Arkansas	260,796	14.8	5,704,867	79.6
Connecticut	602,655	43.9	811,932	58.2	Louisiana	349,515	36.0	2,576	5.9
MIDDLE ATL.:					Oklahoma	535,555	27.8	744,548	46.6
New York	20,199,931	62.2	11,769,151	82.0	Texas	573,858	33.6	402,644	82.7
New Jersey	9,155,883	88.7	1,356,258	81.4	MOUNTAIN:				
Penn	11,807,999	53.5	2,987,747	54.2	Montana	703,925	42.4	518,837	77.0
E. N. CENT.:					Idaho	4,664,483	74.0	3,021,446	82.9
Ohio	2,644,540	35.2	1,490,470	50.1	Wyoming	463,098	54.4	12,969	43.2
Indiana	497,072	20.1	388,013	41.9	Colorado	6,771,699	76.3	2,968,781	86.9
Illinois	1,146,895	24.4	3,265,017	69.9	New Mexico	22,169	20.0	674,624	71.8
Michigan	13,815,844	57.7	4,428,372	75.8	Arizona	110,465	63.4	71,911	59.5
Wisconsin	15,684,335	59.5	333,698	25.6	Utah	948,838	57.6	554,740	73.0
W. N. CENT.:					Nevada	304,747	62.1	16,978	32.3
Minnesota	16,987,336	63.6	226,672	22.0	PACIFIC:				
Iowa	651,890	14.7	461,662	25.5	Washington	3,585,633	61.1	20,845,774	96.6
Missouri	882,262	21.7	3,198,529	62.3	Oregon	1,742,478	49.2	5,054,500	73.0
N. Dakota	1,993,741	42.3	2,654	18.5	California	7,167,391	87.2	6,828,623	87.1
S. Dakota	1,034,095	36.1	63,959	38.0					
Nebraska	1,724,226	38.7	466,837	51.5					
Kansas	1,000,255	33.2	1,244,606	71.1					

TABLE 138.—EXPORTS OF PRINCIPAL CROPS FROM THE UNITED STATES DURING THE FISCAL YEARS ENDING JUNE 30, 1920 AND 1910.

CROP.	Unit.	QUANTITY.		VALUE.	
		1920	1910	1920	1910
Corn	Bu	14,467,926	36,802,374	$23,827,541	$25,427,993
Wheat	Bu	122,430,724	46,679,876	306,163,023	47,806,598
Oats	Bu	33,944,740	1,685,474	29,931,172	794,367
Barley	Bu	26,571,284	4,311,566	41,338,517	3,052,527
Rye	Bu	37,463,285	219,756	74,600,444	168,666
Buckwheat	Bu	244,785	158,160	440,312	103,138
Rice	Lbs	400,005,250	7,010,507	51,228,843	222,244
Hay	Tons	50,049	55,007	1,778,496	1,079,807
Tobacco (leaf)	Lbs	632,795,586	353,372,672	271,946,489	38,017,260
Cotton	Bales	6,915,408	6,263,293	1,381,707,502	450,447,243

TABLE 139.—CORN—ACREAGE AND PRODUCTION, BY DIVISIONS AND STATES: 1919 AND 1909.

[A minus sign (−) denotes decrease.]

DIVISION AND STATE.	ACREAGE.			PRODUCTION (BUSHELS).			AVERAGE YIELD PER ACRE (BUSHELS).	
	1919	1909	Per cent of increase.	1919	1909	Per cent of increase.	1919	1909
United States	87,771,600	98,382,665	−10. 8	2,345,832,507	2,552,189,630	−8. 1	26. 7	25. 9
GEOGRAPHIC DIVISIONS:								
New England	117,347	182,065	−35. 5	5,597,723	8,238,394	−32. 1	47. 7	45. 2
Middle Atlantic	1,900,324	2,158,554	−12. 0	84,335,321	69,610,602	21. 2	44. 4	32. 2
East North Central	18,349,075	21,910,191	−16. 3	683,430,905	845,298,285	−19. 1	37. 2	38. 6
West North Central	30,277,836	35,945,297	−15. 8	895,539,335	996,358,997	−10. 1	29. 6	27. 7
South Atlantic	12,288,485	11,386,984	7. 9	212,891,658	179,511,702	18. 6	17. 3	15 8
East South Central	12,539,455	11,328,268	10. 7	223,952,064	210,154,917	6. 6	17. 9	18. 6
West South Central	11,018,649	14,912,067	−26. 1	218,130,912	233,402,007	−6. 5	19. 8	15. 7
Mountain	1,096,918	463,991	136. 4	16,757,583	7,326,043	128. 7	15. 3	15. 8
Pacific	183,511	95,248	92. 7	5,197,006	2,288,683	127. 1	28. 3	24. 0
NEW ENGLAND:								
Maine	6,965	15,213	−54. 2	288,281	648,882	−55. 6	41. 4	42. 7
New Hampshire	10,433	19,814	−47. 3	482,738	916,263	−47. 3	46. 3	46. 2
Vermont	21,186	42,887	−50. 6	937,375	1,715,133	−45. 3	44. 2	40. 0
Massachusetts	28,953	41,755	−30. 7	1,515,933	2,029,381	−25. 3	52. 4	48. 6
Rhode Island	7,324	9,679	−24. 3	310,901	398,193	−21. 9	42. 4	41. 1
Connecticut	42,486	52,717	−19. 4	2,062,495	2,530,542	−18. 5	48. 5	48. 0
MIDDLE ATLANTIC:								
New York	320,325	512,442	−37. 5	14,109,202	18,115,634	−22. 1	44. 0	35. 4
New Jersey	233,595	265,441	−12. 0	8,776,107	10,000,731	−12. 2	37. 6	37. 7
Pennsylvania	1,346,404	1,380,671	−2. 5	61,450,012	41,494,237	48. 1	45. 6	30. 1
EAST NORTH CENTRAL:								
Ohio	3,563,352	3,916,050	−9. 0	149,844,626	157,513,300	−4. 9	42. 1	40. 2
Indiana	4,457,400	4,901,054	−9. 1	158,603,938	195,496,433	−18. 9	35. 6	39. 9
Illinois	7,908,385	10,045,839	−21. 3	285,346,031	390,218,676	−26. 9	36. 1	38. 8
Michigan	1,269,155	1,589,596	−20. 2	45,088,912	52,906,842	−14. 8	35. 5	33. 3
Wisconsin	1,150,783	1,457,652	−21. 1	44,547,398	49,163,034	−9. 4	38. 7	33. 7
WEST NORTH CENTRAL:								
Minnesota	2,380,838	2,004,068	18. 8	84,786,096	67,897,051	24. 9	35. 6	33. 9
Iowa	9,006,733	9,229,378	−2. 4	371,362,393	341,750,460	8. 7	41. 2	37. 1
Missouri	5,567,079	7,113,953	−21. 7	146,342,036	191,427,087	−23. 6	26. 3	26. 9
North Dakota	191,428	185,122	3. 4	3,876,883	4,941,152	−21. 5	20. 3	26. 7
South Dakota	2,756,234	2,037,658	35. 3	69,060,782	55,558,737	24. 3	25. 1	27. 3
Nebraska	6,699,450	7,266,057	−7. 8	160,391,314	180,132,807	−11. 0	23. 9	24. 8
Kansas	3,676,074	8,109,061	−54. 7	59,719,831	154,651,703	−61. 4	16. 2	19. 1
SOUTH ATLANTIC:								
Delaware	170,612	188,755	−9. 6	3,686,109	4,839,548	−23. 8	21. 6	25. 6
Maryland	619,265	647,012	−4. 3	21,083,076	17,911,436	17. 7	34. 0	27. 7
District of Columbia	370	426	−13. 1	15,663	12,667	23. 7	42. 3	29. 7
Virginia	1,804,802	1,860,359	−3. 0	42,302,978	38,295,141	10. 5	23. 4	20. 6
West Virginia	568,219	676,311	−16. 0	17,010,357	17,119,097	−0. 6	29. 9	25. 3
North Carolina	2,311,462	2,459,457	−6. 0	40,998,317	34,063,531	20. 4	17. 7	13. 8
South Carolina	1,753,813	1,565,832	12. 0	27,472,013	20,871,946	31. 6	15. 7	13. 3
Georgia	4,269,455	3,383,061	26. 2	51,492,033	39,374,569	30. 8	12. 1	11. 6
Florida	790,487	605,771	30. 5	8,831,112	7,023,767	25. 7	11. 2	11. 6
EAST SOUTH CENTRAL:								
Kentucky	3,247,167	3,436,340	−5. 5	71,518,484	83,348,024	−14. 2	22. 0	24. 3
Tennessee	3,301,075	3,146,348	4. 9	70,639,252	67,682,489	4. 4	21. 4	21. 5
Alabama	3,334,204	2,572,968	29. 6	43,699,100	30,695,737	42. 4	13. 1	11. 9
Mississippi	2,657,009	2,172,612	22. 3	38,095,228	28,428,667	34. 0	14. 3	13. 1
WEST SOUTH CENTRAL:								
Arkansas	2,292,119	2,277,116	0. 7	34,226,935	37,609,544	−9. 0	14. 9	16. 5
Louisiana	1,504,970	1,590,830	−5. 4	21,675,602	26,010,361	−16. 7	14. 4	16. 4
Oklahoma	2,472,905	5,914,069	−58. 2	53,851,093	94,283,407	−42. 9	21. 8	15. 9
Texas	4,748,655	5,130,052	−7. 4	108,377,282	75,498,695	43. 5	22. 8	14. 7
MOUNTAIN:								
Montana	18,717	9,514	96. 7	159,410	274,103	−41. 8	8. 5	28. 8
Idaho	23,277	9,194	153. 2	640,569	318,181	101. 3	27. 5	34. 6
Wyoming	38,575	9,268	316. 2	388,512	176,354	120. 3	10. 1	19. 0
Colorado	752,637	326,559	130. 5	10,105,627	4,903,304	106. 1	13. 4	15. 0
New Mexico	227,167	85,999	164. 2	4,737,182	1,164,970	306. 6	20. 9	13. 5
Arizona	22,150	15,605	41. 9	446,208	298,664	49. 4	20. 1	19. 1
Utah	13,848	7,267	90. 6	265,361	169,688	56. 4	19. 2	23. 4
Nevada	547	585	−6. 5	14,714	20,779	−29. 2	26. 9	35. 5
PACIFIC:								
Washington	34,799	26,033	33. 7	901,905	563,025	60. 2	25. 9	21. 6
Oregon	31,972	17,280	85. 0	846,642	451,757	87. 4	26. 5	26. 1
California	116,740	51,935	124. 8	3,448,459	1,273,901	170. 7	29. 5	24. 5

TABLE 140.—CORN—FARMS REPORTING AND VALUE, BY DIVISIONS AND STATES: 1919 AND 1909.

DIVISION AND STATE.	FARMS REPORTING.				VALUE.		AVERAGE VALUE PER BUSHEL.	
	Number.		Per cent of all farms.					
	1919	1909	1919	1909	1919	1909	1919	1909
United States	4,936,692	4,813,175	76.6	75.7	$3,507,797,102	$1,438,553,919	$1.50	$0.56
GEOGRAPHIC DIVISIONS:								
New England	45,610	67,712	29.1	35.9	10,338,708	5,560,074	1.85	0.67
Middle Atlantic	266,286	309,819	62.6	66.1	134,419,211	45,434,191	1.59	0.65
East North Central	886,094	940,681	81.7	83.7	993,229,282	434,424,336	1.45	0.51
West North Central	836,435	878,717	76.3	79.2	1,229,402,933	503,264,949	1.37	0.51
South Atlantic	1,070,408	974,833	92.4	87.7	385,762,628	149,479,304	1.81	0.83
East South Central	958,333	882,737	91.1	84.7	403,627,520	150,975,613	1.80	0.72
West South Central	798,947	713,996	80.2	75.7	317,465,328	143,035,538	1.46	0.61
Mountain	53,765	32,109	22.0	17.5	24,668,717	4,587,706	1.47	0.63
Pacific	20,814	12,571	8.9	6.6	8,882,775	1,792,208	1.71	0.78
NEW ENGLAND:								
Maine	4,214	9,801	8.7	16.3	504,495	434,834	1.75	0.67
New Hampshire	5,559	10,157	27.1	37.5	844,793	621,306	1.75	0.68
Vermont	8,888	13,761	30.6	42.1	1,687,275	1,102,222	1.80	0.64
Massachusetts	10,937	14,755	34.2	40.0	2,880,274	1,372,144	1.90	0.68
Rhode Island	2,211	2,898	54.2	54.8	606,256	335,629	1.95	0.84
Connecticut	13,801	16,340	60.9	60.9	3,815,615	1,693,939	1.85	0.67
MIDDLE ATLANTIC:								
New York	81,930	113,797	42.4	52.8	24,691,113	11,439,169	1.75	0.63
New Jersey	22,885	25,392	77.0	75.8	14,480,577	6,664,162	1.65	0.67
Pennsylvania	161,471	170,630	79.8	77.8	95,247,521	27,330,860	1.55	0.66
EAST NORTH CENTRAL:								
Ohio	225,568	233,102	87.9	85.7	217,274,709	82,327,269	1.45	0.52
Indiana	184,499	189,389	89.9	87.9	229,975,713	98,437,988	1.45	0.50
Illinois	208,777	226,954	88.0	90.1	413,751,746	198,350,496	1.45	0.51
Michigan	145,624	161,901	74.1	78.2	67,633,385	29,580,929	1.50	0.56
Wisconsin	121,626	129,335	64.3	73.0	64,593,729	25,727,654	1.45	0.52
WEST NORTH CENTRAL:								
Minnesota	121,511	113,061	68.1	72.4	110,221,931	30,510,145	1.30	0.45
Iowa	198,445	196,561	93.0	90.6	501,339,232	167,622,834	1.35	0.49
Missouri	227,045	241,192	86.3	87.0	219,513,084	107,347,033	1.50	0.56
North Dakota	10,408	15,025	13.4	20.2	5,427,636	2,403,303	1.40	0.49
South Dakota	54,602	49,277	73.2	63.5	89,779,016	26,395,985	1.30	0.48
Nebraska	111,970	113,214	90.0	87.3	216,528,274	88,234,846	1.35	0.49
Kansas	112,454	150,387	68.0	84.6	86,593,760	80,750,803	1.45	0.52
SOUTH ATLANTIC:								
Delaware	9,550	9,923	94.2	91.6	5,897,774	2,903,442	1.60	0.60
Maryland	42,389	42,084	88.5	86.0	32,678,769	11,015,298	1.55	0.61
Dist. of Columbia	73	68	35.8	31.3	25,844	9,635	1.65	0.76
Virginia	170,421	163,680	91.5	88.9	78,260,514	28,885,944	1.85	0.75
West Virginia	77,476	83,028	88.8	85.9	29,768,131	11,907,261	1.75	0.70
North Carolina	253,026	228,322	93.8	90.0	79,946,722	31,286,102	1.95	0.92
South Carolina	181,512	156,589	94.2	88.8	54,944,026	20,682,632	2.00	0.99
Georgia	294,987	253,410	94.9	87.1	90,111,074	37,079,981	1.75	0.94
Florida	40,974	37,729	75.9	75.4	14,129,774	5,709,009	1.60	0.81
EAST SOUTH CENTRAL:								
Kentucky	236,372	216,224	87.3	83.4	125,157,359	50,449,112	1.75	0.61
Tennessee	230,015	211,119	91.0	85.8	127,150,649	45,819,093	1.80	0.68
Alabama	245,928	229,113	96.0	87.1	80,843,335	28,677,032	1.85	0.93
Mississippi	246,018	226,281	90.4	82.5	70,476,177	26,030,376	1.85	0.92
WEST SOUTH CENTRAL:								
Arkansas	199,101	176,106	85.6	82.0	61,608,482	27,910,044	1.80	0.74
Louisiana	121,162	100,943	89.4	83.7	36,848,526	16,480,322	1.70	0.63
Oklahoma	137,371	148,590	71.6	78.1	72,698,979	48,080,554	1.35	0.51
Texas	341,313	288,357	78.3	69.0	146,309,341	50,564,618	1.35	0.67
MOUNTAIN:								
Montana	1,456	1,607	2.5	6.2	270,998	185,367	1.70	0.68
Idaho	3,320	1,751	8.4	4.4	1,000,079	191,395	1.70	0.60
Wyoming	1,835	1,065	11.7	9.7	641,046	101,465	1.65	0.58
Colorado	22,873	12,711	38.2	27.5	14,147,875	2,613,504	1.40	0.55
New Mexico	18,524	10,381	62.1	29.1	7,105,781	984,052	1.50	0.84
Arizona	2,074	2,266	20.8	24.6	870,105	293,847	1.95	0.98
Utah	3,331	2,533	13.0	10.7	517,456	134,396	1.95	0.79
Nevada	147	165	4.6	6.1	26,484	23,600	1.80	1.14
PACIFIC:								
Washington	5,271	3,128	8.0	5.6	1,623,433	404,367	1.80	0.72
Oregon	7,272	3,715	14.5	8.2	1,396,959	310,430	1.65	0.69
California	8,271	5,728	7.0	6.5	5,862,383	1,077,411	1.70	0.85

TABLE 141.—WHEAT—ACREAGE AND PRODUCTION, BY DIVISIONS AND STATES: 1919 AND 1909.

[A minus sign (−) denotes decrease. Per cent not shown when base is less than 100 or when per cent is more than 1,000.]

DIVISION AND STATE.	ACREAGE.			PRODUCTION (BUSHELS).			AVERAGE YIELD PER ACRE (BUSHELS).	
	1919	1909	Per cent of increase.	1919	1909	Per cent of increase.	1919	1909
United States	73,099,421	44,262,592	65.1	945,403,215	683,379,259	38.3	12.9	15.4
GEOGRAPHIC DIVISIONS:								
New England	31,864	4,893	551.2	544,786	114,998	373.7	17.1	23.5
Middle Atlantic	1,973,309	1,598,325	23.5	33,968,515	29,717,833	14.3	17.2	18.6
East North Central	11,410,716	7,038,364	62.1	201,963,399	121,097,675	66.8	17.7	17.2
West North Central	38,346,465	25,863,556	48.3	423,365,500	384,092,121	10.2	11.0	14.8
South Atlantic	2,924,762	2,241,345	30.5	32,847,792	26,650,768	23.3	11.2	11.9
East South Central	1,564,887	1,315,243	19.0	17,015,009	15,374,422	10.7	10.9	11.7
West South Central	7,374,160	1,556,087	373.9	104,246,291	17,096,127	509.8	14.1	11.0
Mountain	4,812,619	1,285,360	274.4	53,220,367	29,654,968	79.5	11.1	23.1
Pacific	4,660,639	3,359,419	38.7	78,231,556	59,580,347	31.3	16.8	17.7
NEW ENGLAND:								
Maine	14,464	3,407	324.5	261,185	85,119	206.8	18.1	25.0
New Hampshire	1,366	70		21,968	1,311		16.1	18.7
Vermont	11,276	678		176,003	14,087		15.6	20.8
Massachusetts	1,876	109		33,253	2,404		17.7	22.1
Rhode Island	106	13		2,275	208	993.8	21.5	16.0
Connecticut	2,776	616	350.6	50,102	11,869	322.1	18.0	19.3
MIDDLE ATLANTIC:								
New York	463,461	289,130	60.3	9,136,268	6,664,121	37.1	19.7	23.0
New Jersey	84,897	83,637	1.5	1,378,269	1,489,233	−7.5	16.2	17.8
Pennsylvania	1,424,951	1,225,558	16.3	23,453,978	21,564,479	8.8	16.5	17.6
EAST NORTH CENTRAL:								
Ohio	2,922,592	1,827,932	59.9	58,124,351	30,663,704	89.6	19.9	16.8
Indiana	2,798,657	2,082,835	34.4	45,207,862	33,935,972	33.2	16.2	16.3
Illinois	4,103,035	2,185,091	87.8	70,890,917	37,830,732	87.4	17.3	17.3
Michigan	1,056,687	802,137	31.7	20,411,825	16,025,791	27.4	19.3	20.0
Wisconsin	529,745	140,369	277.4	7,328,444	2,641,476	177.4	13.8	18.8
WEST NORTH CENTRAL:								
Minnesota	3,793,402	3,276,911	15.8	37,616,384	57,094,412	−34.1	9.9	17.4
Iowa	1,437,743	526,777	172.9	21,591,928	8,055,944	168.0	15.0	15.3
Missouri	4,564,990	2,017,128	126.3	65,210,462	29,837,429	118.6	14.3	14.8
North Dakota	9,098,042	8,188,782	11.1	61,540,404	116,781,886	−47.3	6.8	14.3
South Dakota	3,891,468	3,217,255	21.0	31,086,995	47,059,590	−33.9	8.0	14.6
Nebraska	4,294,156	2,662,918	61.3	57,843,598	47,685,745	21.3	13.5	17.9
Kansas	11,266,664	5,973,785	88.6	148,475,729	77,577,115	91.4	13.2	13.0
SOUTH ATLANTIC:								
Delaware	125,740	111,215	13.1	1,571,567	1,643,572	−4.4	12.5	14.8
Maryland	664,295	589,893	12.6	9,620,526	9,463,457	1.7	14.5	16.0
District of Columbia	18			200			11.1	
Virginia	990,506	692,907	42.9	11,446,027	8,076,989	41.7	11.6	11.7
West Virginia	298,036	209,315	42.4	3,747,812	2,575,996	45.5	12.6	12.3
North Carolina	620,659	501,912	23.7	4,744,528	3,827,145	24.0	7.6	7.6
South Carolina	84,621	43,028	96.7	630,911	310,614	103.1	7.5	7.2
Georgia	140,861	93,065	51.4	1,085,972	752,858	44.2	7.7	8.1
Florida	26	10		249	137	81.8	9.6	13.7
EAST SOUTH CENTRAL:								
Kentucky	839,987	681,323	23.3	10,375,129	8,739,260	18.7	12.4	12.8
Tennessee	684,497	619,861	10.4	6,362,357	6,516,539	−2.4	9.3	10.5
Alabama	34,017	13,665	148.9	222,838	113,953	95.6	6.6	8.3
Mississippi	6,386	394		54,685	4,670		8.6	11.9
WEST SOUTH CENTRAL:								
Arkansas	256,211	60,426	324.0	2,051,405	526,414	289.7	8.0	8.7
Louisiana	766	65		5,788	488		7.6	7.5
Oklahoma	4,702,280	1,169,420	302.1	65,761,843	14,008,334	369.4	14.0	12.0
Texas	2,414,903	326,176	640.4	36,427,255	2,560,891		15.1	7.9
MOUNTAIN:								
Montana	1,698,531	258,377	557.4	7,799,647	6,251,945	24.8	4.6	24.2
Idaho	1,141,295	399,234	185.9	17,877,113	10,237,609	74.6	15.7	25.6
Wyoming	181,420	41,968	332.3	1,445,227	738,698	95.6	8.0	17.6
Colorado	1,328,616	340,729	289.9	18,260,663	7,224,057	152.8	13.7	21.2
New Mexico	135,185	32,341	318.0	2,437,213	499,799	387.6	18.0	15.5
Arizona	37,131	20,028	85.4	835,374	362,875	130.2	22.5	18.1
Utah	268,457	178,423	50.5	4,100,979	3,943,910	4.0	15.3	22.1
Nevada	21,984	14,260	54.2	464,151	396,075	17.2	21.1	27.8
PACIFIC:								
Washington	2,494,160	2,118,015	17.8	41,837,909	40,920,390	2.2	16.8	19.3
Oregon	1,080,051	763,187	41.5	19,526,765	12,456,751	56.8	18.1	16.3
California	1,086,428	478,217	127.2	16,866,882	6,203,206	171.9	15.5	13.0

TABLE 142.—WHEAT—FARMS REPORTING AND VALUE, BY DIVISIONS AND STATES: 1919 AND 1909.

DIVISION AND STATE.	FARMS REPORTING.				VALUE.		AVERAGE VALUE PER BUSHEL.	
	Number.		Per cent of all farms.					
	1919	1909	1919	1909	1919	1909	1919	1909
United States...	2,225,134	1,458,667	34.5	22.9	$2,074,078,801	$657,656,801	$2.19	$0.96
GEOGRAPHIC DIVISIONS:								
New England.......	13,481	2,236	8.6	1.2	1,268,576	122,532	2.33	1.07
Middle Atlantic.....	189,989	158,480	44.7	33.8	76,415,411	31,665,041	2.25	1.07
East North Central..	632,344	432,165	58.3	38.5	444,146,148	121,885,650	2.20	1.01
West North Central.	653,240	446,974	59.6	40.3	935,172,662	363,923,162	2.21	0.95
South Atlantic......	305,821	212,246	26.4	19.1	76,313,751	28,725,004	2.32	1.08
East South Central..	126,023	83,775	12.0	8.0	38,086,974	15,851,025	2.24	1.03
West South Central.	153,987	35,048	15.5	3.7	220,415,296	17,278,603	2.11	1.01
Mountain..........	100,428	55,998	41.1	30.5	112,913,384	25,930,395	2.12	0.87
Pacific.............	49,821	31,745	21.3	16.7	169,346,599	52,275,389	2.16	0.88
NEW ENGLAND:								
Maine.............	4,961	1,433	10.3	2.4	613,785	91,554	2.35	1.08
New Hampshire....	912	62	4.4	0.2	50,526	1,406	2.30	1.07
Vermont..........	5,702	360	19.6	1.1	404,808	14,279	2.30	1.01
Massachusetts......	703	81	2.2	0.2	76,484	2,515	2.30	1.05
Rhode Island.......	40	7	1.0	0.1	5,232	211	2.30	1.01
Connecticut.........	1,163	293	5.1	1.1	117,741	12,567	2.35	1.06
MIDDLE ATLANTIC:								
New York.........	55,580	34,328	28.8	15.9	20,556,621	7,175,523	2.25	1.08
New Jersey........	8,124	8,401	27.4	25.1	3,087,324	1,568,880	2.24	1.05
Pennsylvania......	126,285	115,751	62.4	52.8	52,771,466	22,920,638	2.25	1.06
EAST NORTH CENTRAL:								
Ohio...............	176,421	137,523	68.7	50.6	127,873,574	31,112,975	2.20	1.01
Indiana...........	123,043	104,273	60.0	48.4	98,101,056	33,593,141	2.17	0.99
Illinois...........	136,079	76,434	57.4	30.3	155,960,014	38,000,712	2.20	1.00
Michigan..........	103,093	82,214	52.5	39.7	45,722,488	16,586,868	2.24	1.04
Wisconsin..........	93,708	31,721	49.5	17.9	16,489,016	2,591,954	2.25	0.98
WEST NORTH CENTRAL:								
Minnesota........	113,491	93,049	63.6	59.6	88,398,508	56,007,435	2.35	0.98
Iowa.............	76,219	36,284	35.7	16.7	44,479,372	7,703,205	2.06	0.96
Missouri..........	142,800	79,757	54.3	28.8	140,202,501	29,926,209	2.15	1.00
North Dakota......	67,724	59,365	87.2	79.8	147,696,970	109,129,869	2.40	0.93
South Dakota......	49,372	39,496	66.1	50.9	69,323,996	42,878,223	2.23	0.91
Nebraska..........	77,792	64,322	62.5	49.6	124,363,735	44,225,930	2.15	0.93
Kansas...........	125,842	74,701	76.1	42.0	320,707,580	74,052,291	2.16	0.95
SOUTH ATLANTIC:								
Delaware...........	5,312	4,827	52.4	44.5	3,457,447	1,697,539	2.20	1.03
Maryland.........	26,277	23,358	54.8	47.7	21,357,568	9,876,480	2.22	1.04
Dist. of Columbia...	3	....	1.5	......	446	......	2.23	......
Virginia...........	89,472	63,405	48.0	34.5	26,783,702	8,776,061	2.34	1.09
West Virginia......	35,203	22,344	40.3	23.1	8,395,097	2,697,141	2.24	1.05
North Carolina.....	89,388	65,124	33.1	25.7	11,861,354	4,420,322	2.50	1.15
South Carolina.....	24,433	11,356	12.7	6.4	1,634,062	385,835	2.59	1.24
Georgia...........	35,724	21,827	11.5	7.5	2,823,527	871,494	2.60	1.16
Florida............	9	5	(1)	(1)	548	132	2.20	0.96
EAST SOUTH CENTRAL:								
Kentucky..........	59,628	37,164	22.0	14.3	22,929,042	8,812,469	2.21	1.01
Tennessee.........	56,896	44,013	22.5	17.9	14,506,174	6,913,335	2.28	1.06
Alabama..........	8,473	2,463	3.3	0.9	530,356	120,873	2.38	1.06
Mississippi.........	1,026	135	0.4	(1)	121,402	4,348	2.22	0.93
WEST SOUTH CENTRAL:								
Arkansas..........	24,582	5,197	10.6	2.4	4,266,922	532,712	2.08	1.01
Louisiana.........	118	23	0.1	(1)	13,603	508	2.35	1.04
Oklahoma.........	66,953	23,003	34.9	12.1	140,730,350	13,854,322	2.14	0.99
Texas............	62,334	6,825	14.3	1.6	75,404,421	2,891,061	2.07	1.13
MOUNTAIN:								
Montana..........	93,136	8,164	40.1	31.1	18,641,156	5,329,389	2.39	0.85
Idaho............	27,629	12,676	53.7	41.1	36,648,087	8,412,587	2.05	0.82
Wyoming.........	4,468	2,138	20.4	24.9	3,121,693	644,251	2.16	0.87
Colorado..........	23,961	11,719	40.0	25.4	37,010,500	6,463,926	2.06	0.89
New Mexico.......	9,032	6,160	30.3	17.3	4,874,426	508,726	2.00	1.02
Arizona...........	1,764	1,409	17.7	15.3	1,921,358	410,214	2.30	1.13
Utah.............	14,488	12,387	56.5	57.1	9,022,154	3,765,017	2.20	0.95
Nevada...........	959	748	30.3	27.8	1,067,550	396,285	2.30	1.00
PACIFIC:								
Washington........	19,194	13,865	29.0	24.7	91,206,642	35,102,370	2.18	0.86
Oregon...........	20,666	13,202	41.2	29.0	41,201,480	10,849,036	2.11	0.87
California.........	9,961	4,678	8.5	5.3	36,938,477	6,323,983	2.19	1.02

¹Less than one-tenth of 1 per cent.

TABLE 143.—OATS—ACREAGE AND PRODUCTION, BY DIVISIONS AND STATES:
1919 AND 1909.

[A minus sign (−) denotes decrease. Per cent not shown when base is less than 100.]

DIVISION AND STATE.	ACREAGE.			PRODUCTION (BUSHELS).			AVERAGE YIELD PER ACRE (BUSHELS).	
	1919	1909	Per cent of increase.	1919	1909	Per cent of increase.	1919	1909
United States..	37,991,002	35,159,441	8.1	1,055,182,798	1,007,142,980	4.8	27.8	28.6
GEOGRAPHIC DIVISIONS:								
New England.....	236,113	223,221	5.8	7,099,771	7,350,601	−3.4	30.1	32.9
Middle Atlantic...	2,184,127	2,518,886	−13.3	52,255,952	64,344,715	−18.8	23.9	25.5
East North Central	11,228,593	11,225,445	(1)	333,705,369	373,803,573	−10.7	29.7	33.3
West North Central	17,978,166	15,710,495	14.4	494,110,435	432,660,477	14.2	27.5	27.5
South Atlantic....	886,071	1,368,832	−35.3	14,417,597	21,206,000	−32.0	16.3	15.5
East South Central	530,367	870,762	−39.1	7,085,657	11,646,687	−39.2	13.4	13.4
West South Central	3,642,748	1,276,534	185.4	112,652,747	27,273,695	313.0	30.9	21.4
Mountain..........	682,103	1,164,204	−41.4	14,457,607	40,604,255	−64.4	21.2	34.9
Pacific..........	622,714	801,062	−22.3	19,397,663	28,252,977	−31.3	31.2	35.3
NEW ENGLAND:								
Maine..............	116,691	120,991	−3.6	3,600,617	4,232,309	−14.9	30.9	35.0
New Hampshire..	14,688	10,860	35.2	485,367	386,419	25.6	33.0	35.6
Vermont..........	83,097	71,510	16.2	2,396,349	2,141,357	11.9	28.8	29.9
Massachusetts.....	9,533	7,927	20.3	287,881	268,500	7.2	30.2	33.9
Rhode Island.....	1,215	1,726	−29.6	34,507	48,212	−28.4	28.4	27.9
Connecticut.......	10,889	10,207	6.7	295,050	273,804	7.8	27.1	26.8
MIDDLE ATLANTIC:								
New York........	937,553	1,302,508	−28.0	21,595,461	34,795,277	−37.9	23.0	26.7
New Jersey.......	71,065	72,130	−1.5	1,477,319	1,376,752	7.3	20.8	19.1
Pennsylvania.....	1,175,509	1,144,248	2.7	29,183,172	28,172,686	3.6	24.8	24.6
EAST NORTH CENTRAL:								
Ohio.............	1,452,052	1,787,496	−18.8	46,818,330	57,591,046	−18.7	32.2	32.2
Indiana..........	1,718,748	1,667,818	3.1	52,529,723	50,607,913	3.8	30.6	30.3
Illinois..........	4,291,066	4,176,485	2.7	129,104,668	150,386,074	−14.2	30.1	36.0
Michigan..........	1,514,808	1,429,076	6.0	36,956,425	43,869,502	−15.8	24.4	30.7
Wisconsin..........	2,251,919	2,164,570	4.0	68,296,223	71,349,038	−4.3	30.3	33.0
WEST NORTH CENTRAL:								
Minnesota.........	3,429,079	2,977,258	15.2	89,108,151	93,897,717	−5.1	26.0	31.5
Iowa.............	5,484,113	4,655,154	17.8	187,045,705	128,198,055	45.9	34.1	27.5
Missouri..........	1,707,055	1,073,325	59.0	40,493,700	24,828,501	63.1	23.7	23.1
North Dakota.....	2,073,162	2,147,032	−3.4	30,294,074	65,886,702	−54.0	14.6	30.7
South Dakota.....	1,839,089	1,558,643	18.0	51,091,904	43,565,676	17.3	27.8	28.0
Nebraska..........	2,029,740	2,365,774	−14.2	59,819,545	53,360,185	12.1	29.5	22.6
Kansas............	1,415,928	933,309	51.7	36,257,356	22,923,641	58.2	25.6	24.6
SOUTH ATLANTIC:								
Delaware..........	4,736	4,226	12.1	70,791	98,239	−27.9	14.9	23.2
Maryland..........	48,891	49,210	−0.6	1,082,994	1,160,663	−6.7	22.2	23.6
Dist. of Columbia.	14	13	....	315	375	−16.0	22.5	28.8
Virginia..........	135,842	204,455	−33.6	1,958,609	2,884,495	−32.1	14.4	14.1
West Virginia.....	169,915	103,758	63.8	3,054,668	1,728,806	76.7	18.0	16.7
North Carolina....	125,885	228,120	−44.8	1,671,308	2,782,508	−39.9	13.3	12.2
South Carolina....	196,056	324,180	−39.5	3,597,835	5,745,291	−37.4	18.4	17.7
Georgia..........	187,525	411,664	−54.4	2,758,851	6,199,243	−55.5	14.7	15.1
Florida..........	17,207	43,206	−60.2	222,226	606,380	−63.4	12.9	14.0
EAST SOUTH CENTRAL:								
Kentucky..........	229,464	174,315	31.6	2,791,447	2,406,064	16.0	12.2	13.8
Tennessee.........	162,417	342,086	−52.5	2,413,409	4,720,692	−48.9	14.9	13.8
Alabama..........	85,398	257,276	−66.8	1,120,384	3,251,146	−65.5	13.1	12.6
Mississippi.......	53,088	97,085	−45.3	760,417	1,268,785	−40.1	14.3	13.1
WEST SOUTH CENTRAL:								
Arkansas.........	173,317	197,449	−12.2	2,703,753	3,212,891	−15.8	15.6	16.3
Louisiana.........	33,443	29,711	12.6	489,380	420,033	16.5	14.6	14.1
Oklahoma.........	1,573,055	609,373	158.1	45,470,191	16,606,154	173.8	28.9	27.3
Texas............	1,862,933	440,001	323.4	63,989,423	7,034,617	809.6	34.3	16.0
MOUNTAIN:								
Montana..........	191,096	333,195	−42.6	2,583,908	13,805,735	−81.3	13.5	41.4
Idaho.............	141,507	302,783	−53.3	3,069,132	11,328,106	−72.9	21.7	37.4
Wyoming..........	58,622	124,035	−52.7	1,006,552	3,361,425	−70.1	17.2	27.1
Colorado..........	174,189	275,948	−36.9	4,535,527	7,642,855	−40.7	26.0	27.7
New Mexico.......	40,029	33,707	18.8	1,085,311	720,560	50.6	27.1	21.4
Arizona...........	11,862	5,867	102.2	377,785	189,312	99.6	31.8	32.3
Utah.............	61,825	80,816	−23.5	1,724,392	3,221,289	−46.5	27.9	39.9
Nevada..........	2,973	7,853	−62.1	75,000	334,973	−77.6	25.2	42.7
PACIFIC:								
Washington.......	191,673	269,742	−28.9	8,073,481	13,228,003	−39.0	42.1	49.0
Oregon...........	284,152	339,162	−16.2	8,357,406	10,881,286	−23.2	29.4	32.1
California........	146,889	192,158	−23.6	2,966,776	4,143,688	−28.4	20.2	21.6

1 Less than one-tenth of 1 per cent.

TABLE 144.—OATS—FARMS REPORTING AND VALUE, BY DIVISIONS AND STATES: 1919 AND 1909.

DIVISION AND STATE.	FARMS REPORTING.				VALUE.		AVERAGE VALUE PER BUSHEL.	
	Number.		Per cent of all farms.					
	1919	1909	1919	1909	1919	1909	1919	1909
United States.....	2,238,102	2,174,006	34.7	34.2	$855,255,468	$414,697,422	$0.81	$0.41
GEOGRAPHIC DIVISIONS:								
New England........	41,896	43,579	26.8	23.1	7,312,401	4,027,338	1.03	0.55
Middle Atlantic......	267,496	298,684	62.9	63.8	49,263,771	33,111,736	0.94	0.51
East North Central..	693,318	668,954	63.9	59.5	274,567,854	149,004,329	0.82	0.40
West North Central..	683,192	588,275	62.3	53.0	375,935,127	162,647,073	0.76	0.38
South Atlantic.......	183,047	251,129	15.8	22.6	15,900,755	13,388,578	1.10	0.63
East South Central...	91,291	144,577	8.7	13.9	7,533,992	6,535,286	1.06	0.56
West South Central..	202,726	99,675	20.4	10.6	90,809,757	12,764,241	0.81	0.47
Mountain............	44,693	52,881	18.3	28.8	14,952,017	19,673,773	1.03	0.48
Pacific..............	30,443	26,252	13.0	13.8	18,979,794	13,545,068	0.98	0.48
NEW ENGLAND:								
Maine..............	18,337	22,029	38.0	36.7	3,780,648	2,293,947	1.05	0.54
New Hampshire.....	3,758	3,141	18.3	11.6	485,367	216,938	1.00	0.56
Vermont............	14,389	12,581	49.5	38.5	2,396,349	1,169,223	1.00	0.55
Massachusetts.......	2,214	2,181	6.9	5.9	302,276	157,381	1.05	0.59
Rhode Island........	321	455	7.9	8.6	37,958	28,661	1.10	0.59
Connecticut.........	2,877	3,192	12.7	11.9	309,803	161,188	1.05	0.59
MIDDLE ATLANTIC:								
New York..........	114,390	142,313	59.2	66.0	21,595,461	17,977,155	1.00	0.52
New Jersey.........	7,582	8,213	25.5	24.5	1,403,453	712,609	0.95	0.52
Pennsylvania.......	145,524	148,158	72.0	67.6	26,264,857	14,421,972	0.90	0.51
EAST NORTH CENTRAL:								
Ohio...............	137,099	150,180	53.4	55.2	39,795,590	23,212,352	0.85	0.40
Indiana............	101,522	101,199	49.5	47.0	42,023,780	18,928,706	0.80	0.37
Illinois............	157,879	139,156	66.6	55.2	103,283,734	59,693,819	0.80	0.40
Michigan...........	141,312	141,731	71.9	68.5	31,412,962	18,506,195	0.85	0.42
Wisconsin..........	155,506	136,688	82.2	77.2	58,051,788	28,663,257	0.85	0.40
WEST NORTH CENTRAL:								
Minnesota..........	140,876	118,692	78.9	76.0	66,831,124	34,023,389	0.75	0.36
Iowa..............	162,880	151,769	76.3	69.9	140,284,289	49,046,888	0.75	0.38
Missouri...........	117,497	80,308	44.7	29.0	32,394,961	10,253,990	0.80	0.41
North Dakota.......	51,160	56,903	65.9	76.5	24,235,260	24,114,345	0.80	0.37
South Dakota.......	49,921	45,127	66.9	58.1	38,318,937	16,044,785	0.75	0.37
Nebraska...........	77,510	81,466	62.3	62.8	44,864,671	19,443,570	0.75	0.36
Kansas............	83,348	54,010	50.4	30.4	29,005,885	9,720,106	0.80	0.42
SOUTH ATLANTIC:								
Delaware...........	769	698	7.6	6.4	67,251	51,022	0.95	0.52
Maryland..........	8,486	8,831	17.7	18.1	1,028,845	584,395	0.95	0.50
District of Columbia.	6	2	2.9	0.9	315	165	1.00	0.44
Virginia...........	28,275	36,306	15.2	19.7	2,154,475	1,609,973	1.10	0.56
West Virginia.......	34,600	22,412	39.6	23.2	3,054,668	912,388	1.00	0.53
North Carolina......	34,647	48,958	12.8	19.3	1,838,447	1,741,561	1.10	0.63
South Carolina......	43,462	57,398	22.6	32.5	4,317,400	3,809,345	1.20	0.66
Georgia............	30,505	70,379	9.8	24.2	3,172,680	4,236,625	1.15	0.68
Florida............	2,297	6,145	4.3	12.3	266,674	443,104	1.20	0.73
EAST SOUTH CENTRAL:								
Kentucky...........	37,887	25,548	14.0	9.9	2,931,018	1,216,187	1.05	0.51
Tennessee..........	23,860	44,432	9.4	18.1	2,534,082	2,378,464	1.05	0.50
Alabama...........	18,991	51,857	7.4	19.7	1,232,426	2,117,703	1.10	0.65
Mississippi.........	10,553	22,740	3.9	8.3	836,466	822,932	1.10	0.65
WEST SOUTH CENTRAL:								
Arkansas...........	25,549	31,836	11.0	14.8	2,703,753	1,641,752	1.00	0.51
Louisiana..........	5,456	4,579	4.0	3.8	538,319	250,588	1.10	0.60
Oklahoma..........	75,938	33,002	39.6	17.4	36,376,150	7,172,267	0.80	0.43
Texas..............	95,783	30,258	22.0	7.2	51,191,535	3,699,634	0.80	0.53
MOUNTAIN:								
Montana	8,451	10,450	14.7	39.9	2,583,908	6,148,021	1.00	0.45
Idaho.............	9,218	11,709	21.9	38.0	3,222,592	5,067,051	1.05	0.45
Wyoming...........	2,992	4,381	19.0	39.9	1,107,900	1,878,711	1.10	0.54
Colorado...........	11,711	12,844	19.5	27.8	4,308,752	4,177,267	0.95	0.55
New Mexico........	3,335	3,084	11.2	8.6	1,139,580	459,306	1.05	0.64
Arizona............	573	315	5.7	3.4	434,456	130,384	1.15	0.69
Utah..............	8,211	9,781	32.0	45.1	2,069,269	1,671,065	1.20	0.52
Nevada............	202	309	6.4	11.5	86,252	191,968	1.15	0.57
PACIFIC:								
Washington........	11,365	10,139	17.1	18.0	8,073,481	5,870,857	1.00	0.44
Oregon............	15,482	13,636	30.8	30.0	7,939,537	5,037,164	0.95	0.46
California..........	3,596	2,477	3.1	2.8	2,966,776	2,637,047	1.00	0.64

TABLE 145.—BARLEY—ACREAGE AND PRODUCTION, BY DIVISIONS AND STATES: 1919 AND 1909.

[A minus sign (−) denotes decrease. Per cent not shown when base is less than 100 or when per cent is more than 1,000.]

DIVISION AND STATE.	ACREAGE.			PRODUCTION (BUSHELS).			AVERAGE YIELD PER ACRE (BUSHELS).	
	1919	1909	Per cent of increase.	1919	1909	Per cent of increase.	1919	1909
United States.....	6,472,888	7,698,706	−15.9	122,024,773	173,344,212	−29.6	18.9	22.5
GEOGRAPHIC DIVISIONS:								
New England.......	14,767	16,242	−9.1	343,641	428,617	−19.8	23.3	26.4
Middle Atlantic......	130,788	87,733	49.1	2,549,471	2,062,189	23.6	19.5	23.5
East North Central...	1,160,055	1,007,102	15.2	25,061,508	26,705,278	−6.2	21.6	26.5
West North Central..	3,536,158	4,762,928	−25.8	57,946,122	98,997,430	−41.5	16.4	20.8
South Atlantic.......	14,593	15,561	−6.2	370,458	409,615	−9.6	25.4	26.3
East South Central...	12,083	5,388	124.3	221,027	119,922	84.3	18.3	22.3
West South Central..	155,766	14,253	992.9	3,979,068	181,346	....	25.5	12.7
Mountain............	310,447	313,606	−1.0	5,977,266	9,785,511	−38.9	19.3	31.2
Pacific..............	1,138,231	1,475,893	−22.9	25,576,212	34,654,304	−26.2	22.5	23.5
NEW ENGLAND:								
Maine...............	4,358	4,136	5.4	104,912	106,674	−1.7	24.1	25.8
New Hampshire.....	887	848	4.6	22,036	20,764	6.1	24.8	24.5
Vermont............	8,594	10,586	−18.8	196,815	285,008	−30.9	22.9	26.9
Massachusetts.......	509	349	45.8	11,832	9,021	31.2	23.2	25.8
Rhode Island........	145	182	−20.3	3,154	4,676	−32.5	21.8	25.7
Connecticut........	274	141	94.3	4,892	2,474	97.7	17.9	17.5
MIDDLE ATLANTIC:								
New York...........	116,109	79,956	45.2	2,273,011	1,922,868	18.2	19.6	24.0
New Jersey.........	894	152	488.2	14,613	3,082	374.1	16.3	20.3
Pennsylvania.......	13,785	7,625	80.8	261,847	136,239	92.2	19.0	17.9
EAST NORTH CENTRAL:								
Ohio...............	114,217	24,075	374.4	2,412,196	569,279	323.7	21.1	23.6
Indiana............	74,239	10,188	628.7	1,427,772	234,298	509.4	19.2	23.0
Illinois.............	176,792	63,325	179.2	4,226,911	1,613,559	162.0	23.9	25.5
Michigan...........	296,515	93,065	218.6	4,802,768	2,132,101	125.3	16.2	22.9
Wisconsin..........	498,292	816,449	−39.0	12,191,861	22,156,041	−45.0	24.5	27.1
WEST NORTH CENTRAL:								
Minnesota..........	814,381	1,573,761	−48.3	14,849,069	34,927,773	−57.5	18.2	22.2
Iowa...............	236,314	571,224	−58.6	5,352,802	10,964,184	−51.2	22.7	19.2
Missouri...........	8,930	7,915	12.8	145,496	134,253	8.4	16.3	17.0
North Dakota.......	1,085,329	1,215,811	−10.7	12,052,881	26,365,758	−54.3	11.1	21.7
South Dakota.......	754,929	1,114,531	−32.3	12,815,768	22,396,130	−42.8	17.0	20.1
Nebraska...........	211,242	113,571	86.0	4,405,323	1,987,516	121.6	20.9	17.5
Kansas.............	425,033	166,115	155.9	8,324,783	2,221,816	274.7	19.6	13.4
SOUTH ATLANTIC:								
Delaware...........	85	31	....	625	422	48.1	7.4	13.6
Maryland...........	3,888	4,494	−13.5	111,221	135,454	−17.9	28.6	30.1
Dist. of Columbia....	....	....	....	....	....	....	....	....
Virginia............	8,674	9,890	−12.3	229,301	253,649	−9.6	26.4	25.6
West Virginia.......	1,359	408	233.1	24,816	8,407	195.2	18.3	20.6
North Carolina......	429	504	−14.9	3,510	7,535	−53.4	8.2	15.0
South Carolina......	....	189	....	....	3,483	....	....	18.4
Georgia............	21	44	....	65	655	−90.1	3.1	14.9
Florida.............	137	1	....	920	10	....	6.7	10.0
EAST SOUTH CENTRAL:								
Kentucky...........	5,612	2,738	105.0	119,542	65,596	82.2	21.3	24.0
Tennessee..........	5,894	2,567	129.6	96,173	53,201	80.8	16.3	20.7
Alabama...........	577	41	....	5,312	372	....	9.2	9.1
Mississippi.........	....	42	....	....	753	....	....	17.9
WEST SOUTH CENTRAL:								
Arkansas...........	273	82	....	2,900	1,267	128.9	10.6	15.5
Louisiana..........	389	....	....	6,079	....	....	15.6	....
Oklahoma.........	77,324	10,283	652.0	1,781,839	127,641	....	23.0	12.4
Texas..............	77,780	3,888	....	2,188,250	52,438	....	28.1	13.5
MOUNTAIN:								
Montana...........	29,330	27,242	7.7	346,972	753,268	−53.9	11.8	27.6
Idaho..............	67,871	132,412	−48.7	1,348,876	4,598,292	−70.7	19.9	34.7
Wyoming..........	7,970	8,561	−6.9	115,624	189,057	−38.8	14.5	22.1
Colorado..........	153,015	71,411	114.3	2,801,498	1,889,342	48.3	18.3	26.5
New Mexico........	8,976	2,131	321.2	194,059	43,490	346.2	21.6	20.4
Arizona............	21,748	32,897	−33.9	656,835	1,008,442	−34.9	30.2	30.7
Utah..............	15,938	26,752	−40.4	365,186	891,471	−59.0	22.9	33.3
Nevada............	5,599	12,200	−54.1	148,216	412,149	−64.0	26.5	33.8
PACIFIC:								
Washington.........	84,568	171,888	−50.8	2,249,856	5,834,615	−61.4	26.6	33.9
Oregon............	66,595	108,847	−38.8	1,429,073	2,377,735	−39.9	21.5	21.8
California..........	987,068	1,195,158	−17.4	21,897,283	26,441,954	−17.2	22.2	22.1

TABLE 146.—BARLEY—FARMS REPORTING AND VALUE, BY DIVISIONS AND STATES: 1919 AND 1909.

DIVISION AND STATE.	FARMS REPORTING.				VALUE.		AVERAGE VALUE PER BUSHEL.	
	Number.		Per cent of all farms.					
	1919	1909	1919	1909	1919	1909	1919	1909
United States......	448,985	383,197	7.0	6.0	$160,427,255	$92,458,571	$1.31	$0.53
GEOGRAPHIC DIVISIONS:								
New England.........	5,722	6,593	3.7	3.5	591,771	342,659	1.72	0.80
Middle Atlantic.......	28,584	20,515	6.7	4.4	3,697,471	1,414,366	1.45	0.69
East North Central.....	182,536	122,864	16.8	10.9	33,693,097	15,240,518	1.34	0.57
West North Central....	176,703	196,723	16.1	17.7	68,015,039	47,400,962	1.17	0.48
South Atlantic.........	3,654	3,775	0.3	0.3	523,587	276,981	1.41	0.68
East South Central.....	1,551	442	0.1	(1)	360,046	79,171	1.63	0.66
West South Central....	11,403	1,074	1.1	0.1	4,470,878	107,835	1.12	0.59
Mountain............	20,861	16,998	8.5	9.3	8,449,855	5,566,331	1.41	0.57
Pacific...............	17,971	14,213	7.7	7.5	40,625,511	22,029,748	1.59	0.64
NEW ENGLAND:								
Maine................	1,629	2,258	3.4	3.8	183,597	86,230	1.75	0.81
New Hampshire.......	481	416	2.3	1.5	33,057	17,292	1.50	0.83
Vermont.............	3,160	3,569	10.9	10.9	344,431	225,803	1.75	0.79
Massachusetts........	260	197	0.8	0.5	18,930	7,177	1.60	0.80
Rhode Island.........	43	63	1.1	1.2	4,416	4,126	1.40	0.88
Connecticut..........	149	90	0.7	0.3	7,340	2,031	1.50	0.82
MIDDLE ATLANTIC:								
New York............	24,840	18,217	12.9	8.4	3,295,871	1,316,117	1.45	0.68
New Jersey...........	163	27	0.5	0.1	21,923	1,967	1.50	0.64
Pennsylvania.........	3,581	2,271	1.8	1.0	379,677	96,282	1.45	0.71
EAST NORTH CENTRAL:								
Ohio.................	19,601	4,753	7.6	1.7	3,256,468	311,741	1.35	0.55
Indiana..............	10,496	1,896	5.1	0.9	1,998,883	133,591	1.40	0.57
Illinois..............	17,653	7,074	7.4	2.8	5,494,990	880,706	1.30	0.55
Michigan.............	54,897	21,601	27.9	10.4	6,483,742	1,232,344	1.35	0.58
Wisconsin............	79,889	87,540	42.2	49.4	16,459,014	12,682,136	1.35	0.57
WEST NORTH CENTRAL:								
Minnesota...........	64,877	85,681	36.4	54.9	18,561,350	17,213,817	1.25	0.49
Iowa.................	19,016	36,435	8.9	16.8	6,423,366	5,320,708	1.20	0.49
Missouri.............	1,152	852	0.4	0.3	203,695	80,245	1.40	0.60
North Dakota.........	32,837	33,167	42.3	44.6	13,860,815	11,962,036	1.15	0.45
South Dakota.........	25,435	28,704	34.1	37.0	15,378,922	10,873,522	1.20	0.49
Nebraska.............	15,328	5,904	12.3	4.6	4,845,864	870,846	1.10	0.44
Kansas...............	18,058	5,980	10.9	3.4	8,741,027	1,079,788	1.05	0.49
SOUTH ATLANTIC:								
Delaware.............	10	8	0.1	0.1	812	288	1.30	0.68
Maryland............	1,099	1,215	2.3	2.5	144,589	79,231	1.30	0.58
District of Columbia...	....	....	....	....	....	....	....	....
Virginia.............	2,044	2,057	1.1	1.1	332,490	179,712	1.45	0.71
West Virginia.........	305	119	0.3	0.1	37,232	5,640	1.50	0.67
North Carolina........	179	149	0.1	0.1	6,494	6,863	1.85	0.91
South Carolina........	....	190	....	0.1	....	4,297	....	1.23
Georgia..............	5	36	(1)	(1)	130	942	2.00	1.44
Florida..............	12	1	(1)	(1)	1,840	8	2.00	0.80
EAST SOUTH CENTRAL:								
Kentucky............	508	175	0.2	0.1	191,266	42,929	1.60	0.65
Tennessee............	932	248	0.4	0.1	158,687	35,363	1.65	0.66
Alabama.............	111	14	(1)	(1)	10,093	336	1.90	0.90
Mississippi...........	....	5	....	(1)	....	543	....	0.72
WEST SOUTH CENTRAL:								
Arkansas.............	70	41	(1)	(1)	4,641	1,136	1.60	0.90
Louisiana............	35	....	(1)	......	10,032	....	1.65	....
Oklahoma............	5,450	834	2.8	0.4	2,049,119	75,059	1.15	0.59
Texas...............	5,848	199	1.3	(1)	2,407,086	31,640	1.10	0.60
MOUNTAIN:								
Montana	1,950	2,267	3.4	8.6	520,472	478,811	1.50	0.64
Idaho...............	1,577	3,955	10.9	12.8	2,030,320	2,322,705	1.50	0.51
Wyoming............	598	882	3.8	8.0	170,718	130,392	1.55	0.09
Colorado............	8,702	4,559	14.5	9.9	3,641,948	1,100,753	1.30	0.60
New Mexico..........	987	338	3.3	0.9	252,280	35,626	1.30	0.82
Arizona.............	934	983	9.4	10.7	952,415	714,834	1.45	0.71
Utah................	2,801	3,554	10.9	16.4	620,814	472,816	1.70	0.53
Nevada.............	312	460	9.9	17.1	259,379	310,394	1.75	0.75
PACIFIC:								
Washington..........	3,778	3,333	5.7	5.9	3,374,792	3,331,930	1.50	0.57
Oregon..............	3,450	3,283	6.9	7.2	2,215,065	1,513,310	1.55	0.64
California...........	10,743	7,597	9.1	8.6	35,035,654	17,184,508	1.60	0.65

1 Less than one-tenth of 1 per cent.

TABLE 147.—RYE—ACREAGE AND PRODUCTION, BY DIVISIONS AND STATES: 1919 AND 1909.

[A minus sign (−) denotes decrease. Per cent not shown when base is less than 100 or when per cent is more than 1,000.]

DIVISION AND STATE.	ACREAGE.			PRODUCTION (BUSHELS).			AVERAGE YIELD PER ACRE (BUSHELS).	
	1919	1909	Per cent of increase.	1919	1909	Per cent of increase.	1919	1909
United States....	7,679,005	2,195,561	249.8	75,992,223	29,520,457	157.4	9.9	13.4
GEOGRAPHIC DIVISIONS:								
New England........	10,282	13,221	−22.2	154,265	230,458	−33.1	15.0	17.4
Middle Atlantic......	432,824	472,132	−8.3	5,772,471	6,458,475	−10.6	13.3	13.7
East North Central...	2,229,022	968,558	130.1	28,811,726	13,443,196	114.3	12.9	13.9
West North Central..	4,282,616	470,582	810.1	35,963,450	6,907,788	420.6	8.4	14.7
South Atlantic.......	198,139	157,546	25.8	1,479,413	1,322,474	11.9	7.5	8.4
East South Central..	57,491	50,091	14.8	422,283	400,709	5.4	7.3	8.0
West South Central..	88,277	5,926	....	935,895	49,137	....	10.6	8.3
Mountain............	277,805	32,115	765.0	1,724,784	439,767	292.2	6.2	13.7
Pacific...............	102,549	25,390	303.9	727,936	268,453	171.2	7.1	10.6
. NEW ENGLAND:								
Maine................	272	292	−6.8	4,673	4,815	−2.9	17.2	16.5
New Hampshire.....	627	260	141.2	6,760	4,534	49.1	10.8	17.4
Vermont.............	527	1,115	−52.7	6,942	16,689	−58.4	13.2	15.0
Massachusetts.......	3,062	3,476	−11.9	46,261	59,183	−21.8	15.1	17.0
Rhode Island........	349	477	−26.8	5,650	7,545	−25.1	16.2	15.8
Connecticut.........	5,445	7,601	−28.4	83,979	137,692	−39.0	15.4	18.1
MIDDLE ATLANTIC:								
New York...........	115,661	130,540	−11.4	1,520,552	2,010,601	−24.4	13.1	15.4
New Jersey..........	74,174	69,032	7.4	1,043,916	951,271	9.7	14.1	13.8
Pennsylvania........	242,989	272,560	−10.8	3,208,003	3,496,603	−8.3	13.2	12.8
EAST NORTH CENTRAL:								
Ohio.................	116,464	67,912	71.5	1,666,449	921,919	80.8	14.3	13.6
Indiana..............	350,908	83,440	320.6	4,432,091	1,121,589	295.2	12.6	13.4
Illinois..............	319,636	58,973	442.0	3,872,621	787,519	391.7	12.1	13.4
Michigan............	912,951	419,020	117.9	12,168,182	5,814,394	109.3	13.3	13.9
Wisconsin...........	529,063	339,213	56.0	6,672,383	4,797,775	39.1	12.6	14.1
WEST NORTH CENTRAL:								
Minnesota...........	649,609	266,567	143.7	8,362,940	4,426,028	88.9	12.9	16.6
Iowa.................	89,458	42,042	112.8	1,110,739	570,996	94.5	12.4	13.6
Missouri.............	107,422	20,001	437.1	917,693	205,813	345.9	8.5	10.3
North Dakota........	2,422,563	48,188	....	16,294,377	689,233	....	6.7	14.3
South Dakota........	463,132	13,778	....	4,111,543	194,672	....	8.9	14.1
Nebraska............	359,926	62,827	472.9	3,259,390	660,631	393.4	9.1	10.5
Kansas..............	190,506	17,179	....	1,906,768	160,415	....	10.0	9.3
SOUTH ATLANTIC:								
Delaware............	6,198	1,017	509.4	58,235	11,423	409.8	9.4	11.2
Maryland............	21,196	28,093	−24.6	230,596	357,562	−35.5	10.9	12.7
Dist. of Columbia....	10	13	....	202	190	6.3	20.2	14.6
Virginia.............	57,018	47,890	19.1	456,689	438,345	4.2	8.0	9.2
West Virginia........	19,760	15,679	26.0	186,709	148,676	25.6	9.4	9.5
North Carolina......	67,871	48,685	39.4	390,123	280,431	39.1	5.7	5.8
South Carolina......	6,877	2,958	132.5	50,342	20,631	144.0	7.3	7.0
Georgia.............	18,041	12,352	46.1	100,209	59,937	67.2	5.6	4.9
Florida.............	1,168	859	36.0	6,308	5,279	19.5	5.4	6.1
EAST SOUTH CENTRAL:								
Kentucky............	27,678	26,813	3.2	240,555	255,532	−5.9	8.7	9.5
Tennessee...........	28,326	22,798	24.2	171,124	140,925	21.4	6.0	6.2
Alabama............	1,171	437	168.0	8,079	3,736	116.2	6.9	8.5
Mississippi..........	316	43	....	2,525	516	389.3	8.0	12.0
WEST SOUTH CENTRAL:								
Arkansas............	2,082	1,080	92.8	13,900	7,354	89.0	6.7	6.8
Louisiana...........	118	19	....	1,486	193	669.9	12.6	10.2
Oklahoma...........	71,680	4,291	....	705,124	37,240	....	9.8	8.7
Texas...............	14,397	536	....	215,385	4,350	....	15.0	8.1
MOUNTAIN:								
Montana............	75,979	6,034	....	227,948	111,214	105.0	3.0	18.4
Idaho...............	11,937	3,295	262.3	81,854	40,241	103.4	6.9	12.2
Wyoming............	41,879	1,516	....	192,532	20,479	840.1	4.6	13.5
Colorado............	133,131	15,715	747.2	1,088,564	198,025	449.7	8.2	12.6
New Mexico.........	3,751	257	....	53,797	2,913	....	14.3	11.3
Arizona.............	177	21	....	3,471	261	....	19.6	12.4
Utah................	10,378	5,234	98.3	72,507	65,754	10.3	7.0	12.6
Nevada.............	573	43	....	4,111	880	367.2	7.2	20.5
PACIFIC:								
Washington.........	41,677	5,450	664.7	229,653	50,746	352.6	5.5	9.3
Oregon.............	42,476	12,913	228.9	312,463	147,024	112.5	7.4	11.4
California...........	18,396	7,027	161.8	185,820	70,683	162.9	10.1	10.1

TABLE 148.—RYE—FARMS REPORTING AND VALUE, BY DIVISIONS AND STATES: 1919 AND 1909.

DIVISION AND STATE.	FARMS REPORTING.				VALUE.		AVERAGE VALUE PER BUSHEL.	
	Number.		Per cent of all farms.					
	1919	1909	1919	1909	1919	1909	1919	1909
United States	469,113	275,796	7.3	4.3	$116,537,965	$20,421,812	$1.53	$0.69
GEOGRAPHIC DIVISIONS:								
New England	4,348	5,674	2.8	3.0	294,137	206,852	1.91	0.90
Middle Atlantic	69,492	79,627	16.3	17.0	9,676,644	4,959,172	1.68	0.77
East North Central	193,235	113,438	17.8	10.1	44,161,824	9,011,568	1.53	0.67
West North Central	127,600	32,948	11.6	3.0	53,204,213	4,216,576	1.48	0.61
South Atlantic	46,325	32,982	4.0	3.0	2,836,161	1,106,617	1.92	0.84
East South Central	9,871	6,940	0.9	0.7	804,078	337,152	1.90	0.84
West South Central	6,174	847	0.6	0.1	1,409,048	41,165	1.51	0.84
Mountain	8,234	2,204	3.4	1.2	2,692,610	300,134	1.56	0.68
Pacific	3,834	1,136	1.6	0.6	1,459,250	242,576	2.00	0.90
NEW ENGLAND:								
Maine	133	109	0.3	0.2	9,346	4,388	2.00	0.91
New Hampshire	210	176	1.0	0.7	12,844	4,680	1.90	1.03
Vermont	206	278	0.7	0.8	13,190	14,533	1.90	0.87
Massachusetts	1,192	1,304	3.7	3.5	87,896	52,396	1.90	0.89
Rhode Island	120	176	2.9	3.3	11,300	7,007	2.00	0.93
Connecticut	2,487	3,631	11.0	13.5	159,561	123,848	1.90	0.90
MIDDLE ATLANTIC:								
New York	17,491	19,517	9.1	9.1	2,660,972	1,578,408	1.75	0.79
New Jersey	6,742	7,462	22.7	22.3	1,722,461	707,250	1.65	0.74
Pennsylvania	45,259	52,648	22.4	24.0	5,293,211	2,673,514	1.65	0.76
EAST NORTH CENTRAL:								
Ohio	15,860	10,224	6.2	3.8	2,582,991	636,276	1.55	0.69
Indiana	27,430	9,512	13.4	4.4	6,648,162	743,782	1.50	0.66
Illinois	19,569	4,643	8.3	1.8	6,002,566	523,374	1.55	0.66
Michigan	77,821	48,889	39.6	23.6	18,252,291	3,944,616	1.50	0.68
Wisconsin	52,555	40,170	27.8	22.7	10,675,814	3,163,520	1.60	0.66
WEST NORTH CENTRAL:								
Minnesota	40,500	18,777	22.7	12.0	12,962,560	2,679,987	1.55	0.61
Iowa	7,720	4,301	3.6	2.0	1,666,128	357,220	1.50	0.63
Missouri	9,582	2,601	3.6	0.9	1,468,304	156,852	1.60	0.76
North Dakota	35,041	1,463	45.1	2.0	23,626,848	411,728	1.45	0.60
South Dakota	10,677	679	14.3	0.9	5,961,741	115,126	1.45	0.59
Nebraska	12,951	3,887	10.4	3.0	4,563,143	383,736	1.40	0.58
Kansas	11,129	1,240	6.7	0.7	2,955,489	111,927	1.55	0.70
SOUTH ATLANTIC:								
Delaware	951	210	9.4	1.9	101,912	8,169	1.75	0.72
Maryland	4,178	5,181	8.7	10.6	380,486	252,691	1.65	0.71
District of Columbia	3	2	1.5	0.9	343	135	1.70	0.71
Virginia	11,655	8,509	6.3	4.6	822,039	344,241	1.80	0.79
West Virginia	3,900	2,774	4.5	2.9	326,749	122,258	1.75	0.82
North Carolina	19,637	12,830	7.3	5.1	819,263	269,566	2.10	0.96
South Carolina	2,134	1,043	1.1	0.6	143,477	32,197	2.85	1.56
Georgia	3,772	2,340	1.2	0.8	225,491	69,365	2.25	1.16
Florida	95	93	0.2	0.2	16,401	7,995	2.60	1.51
EAST SOUTH CENTRAL:								
Kentucky	4,090	3,488	1.5	1.3	445,032	202,534	1.85	0.79
Tennessee	5,240	3,166	2.1	1.3	333,693	129,845	1.95	0.92
Alabama	454	267	0.2	0.1	19,797	4,314	2.45	1.15
Mississippi	87	19	(1)	(1)	5,556	459	2.20	0.89
WEST SOUTH CENTRAL:								
Arkansas	614	303	0.3	0.1	27,800	6,834	2.00	0.93
Louisiana	25	9	(1)	(1)	3,419	236	2.30	1.22
Oklahoma	4,060	396	2.1	0.2	1,022,434	30,364	1.45	0.82
Texas	1,475	139	0.3	(1)	355,395	3,731	1.65	0.86
MOUNTAIN:								
Montana	1,863	395	3.2	1.5	376,115	82,669	1.65	0.74
Idaho	544	218	1.3	0.7	131,430	28,076	1.85	0.72
Wyoming	1,069	158	6.8	1.4	600,000	14,791	1.75	0.72
Colorado	3,945	992	6.6	2.1	1,578,424	123,530	1.45	0.62
New Mexico	240	28	0.8	0.1	86,074	2,650	1.60	0.91
Arizona	31	6	0.3	0.1	6,770	239	1.95	0.92
Utah	504	396	2.0	1.8	148,642	46,338	2.05	0.70
Nevada	38	11	1.2	0.4	8,222	941	2.00	1.07
PACIFIC:								
Washington	1,083	215	1.6	0.4	459,306	43,974	2.00	0.87
Oregon	2,288	728	4.6	1.6	656,174	132,756	2.10	0.90
California	463	193	0.4	0.2	343,770	65,846	1.85	0.93

1 Less than one-tenth of 1 per cent.

TABLE 149.—BUCKWHEAT—ACREAGE AND PRODUCTION, BY DIVISIONS AND STATES: 1919 AND 1909.

[A minus sign (−) denotes decrease. States not shown when acreage was less than 1,000 in 1919.]

DIVISION AND STATE.	ACREAGE.			PRODUCTION (BUSHELS).			AVERAGE YIELD PER ACRE (BUSHELS).	
	1919	1909	Per cent of increase.	1919	1909	Per cent of increase.	1919	1909
United States	742,627	878,048	−15.4	12,690,384	14,849,332	−14.5	17.1	16.9
GEOGRAPHIC DIVISIONS:								
New England	22,426	28,725	−21.9	456,762	602,715	−24.2	20.4	21.0
Middle Atlantic	475,822	592,159	−19.6	8,767,529	10,701,643	−18.1	18.4	18.1
East North Central	116,107	139,971	−17.0	1,763,820	1,897,474	−7.0	15.2	13.6
West North Central	40,570	25,955	56.3	487,761	349,316	39.6	12.0	13.5
South Atlantic	74,489	84,864	−12.2	1,079,834	1,216,608	−11.2	14.5	14.3
East South Central	11,212	4,772	135.0	119,859	51,525	132.6	10.7	10.8
West South Central	276	121	128.1	2,609	987	164.3	9.5	8.2
Mountain	1,086	316	243.7	7,308	7,931	−7.9	6.7	25.1
Pacific	639	1,165	−45.2	4,902	21,133	−76.8	7.7	18.1
NEW ENGLAND:								
Maine	14,364	15,552	−7.6	315,327	316,782	−0.5	22.0	20.4
Vermont	4,330	7,659	−43.5	81,346	174,394	−53.4	18.8	22.8
Massachusetts	1,304	1,630	−20.0	23,238	32,926	−29.4	17.8	20.2
Connecticut	1,768	2,797	−36.8	25,509	51,751	−50.7	14.4	18.5
MIDDLE ATLANTIC:								
New York	217,946	286,276	−23.9	3,901,481	5,691,745	−31.5	17.9	19.9
New Jersey	8,222	13,155	−37.5	110,309	212,548	−48.1	13.4	16.2
Pennsylvania	249,654	292,728	−14.7	4,755,739	4,797,350	−0.9	19.0	16.4
EAST NORTH CENTRAL:								
Ohio	30,413	26,073	16.6	640,662	483,410	32.5	21.1	18.5
Indiana	6,048	6,995	−13.5	73,260	84,991	−13.8	12.1	12.2
Illinois	4,138	4,696	−11.9	52,771	68,125	−22.5	12.8	14.5
Michigan	41,426	75,909	−45.4	524,004	958,119	−45.3	12.6	12.6
Wisconsin	34,082	26,298	29.6	473,123	302,829	56.2	13.9	11.5
WEST NORTH CENTRAL:								
Minnesota	26,022	10,309	152.4	321,688	144,861	122.1	12.4	14.1
Iowa	6,956	9,066	−23.3	99,587	120,559	−17.4	14.3	13.3
Missouri	1,119	1,676	−33.2	11,165	20,289	−45.0	10.0	12.1
North Dakota	1,286	1,039	23.8	7,368	17,066	−56.8	5.7	16.4
South Dakota	3,356	1,904	76.3	28,825	28,551	1.0	8.6	15.0
Nebraska	1,598	1,205	32.6	17,433	9,876	76.5	10.9	8.2
SOUTH ATLANTIC:								
Delaware	9,443	4,002	136.0	75,059	53,903	39.2	7.9	13.5
Maryland	8,736	10,388	−15.9	168,639	152,216	10.8	19.3	14.7
Virginia	19,354	25,481	−24.0	232,507	332,222	−30.0	12.0	13.0
West Virginia	31,095	33,323	−6.7	537,883	533,670	0.8	17.3	16.0
North Carolina	5,539	11,606	−52.3	63,478	144,186	−56.0	11.5	12.4
EAST SOUTH CENTRAL:								
Kentucky	7,605	1,887	303.0	73,364	18,074	305.9	9.6	9.6
Tennessee	3,532	2,867	23.2	46,032	33,249	38.4	13.0	11.6

TABLE 150.—BUCKWHEAT—FARMS REPORTING AND VALUE, BY DIVISIONS AND STATES: 1919 AND 1909.

[States not shown when acreage was less than 1,000 in 1919.]

DIVISION AND STATE.	FARMS REPORTING.				VALUE.		AVERAGE VALUE PER BUSHEL.	
	Number.		Per cent of all farms.					
	1919	1909	1919	1909	1919	1909	1919	1909
United States	171,166	197,789	2.7	3.1	$19,715,305	$9,330,592	$1.55	$0.63
GEOGRAPHIC DIVISIONS:								
New England............	9,074	12,838	5.8	6.8	776,174	400,081	1.70	0.66
Middle Atlantic..........	110,564	126,102	26.0	26.9	13,558,005	6,625,513	1.55	0.62
East North Central.......	25,349	32,005	2.3	2.8	2,731,308	1,222,109	1.55	0.64
West North Central......	4,899	3,906	0.4	0.4	746,802	230,356	1.53	0.66
South Atlantic...........	18,603	21,466	1.6	1.9	1,688,902	791,546	1.56	0.65
East South Central.......	2,432	1,296	0.2	0.1	185,610	37,268	1.55	0.72
West South Central......	64	31	(1)	(1)	4,482	854	1.72	0.87
Mountain.................	75	60	(1)	(1)	14,218	6,920	1.95	0.87
Pacific...................	106	85	(1)	(1)	9,804	15,945	2.00	0.75
NEW ENGLAND:								
Maine...................	4,788	5,981	9.9	10.0	520,291	189,516	1.65	0.60
Vermont.................	2,047	3,573	7.0	10.9	150,481	122,050	1.85	0.70
Massachusetts...........	679	867	2.1	2.3	40,668	24,678	1.75	0.75
Connecticut.............	1,107	1,649	4.9	6.1	43,365	45,532	1.70	0.88
MIDDLE ATLANTIC:								
New York................	53,061	62,601	27.5	29.0	6,242,370	3,587,558	1.60	0.63
New Jersey..............	1,793	2,850	6.0	8.5	182,009	141,997	1.65	0.67
Pennsylvania...........	55,710	60,651	27.5	27.7	7,133,626	2,895,958	1.50	0.60
EAST NORTH CENTRAL:								
Ohio....................	6,523	6,430	2.5	2.4	993,034	303,220	1.55	0.63
Indiana.................	899	1,289	0.4	0.6	113,558	56,617	1.55	0.67
Illinois.................	468	566	0.2	0.2	79,171	48,040	1.50	0.71
Michigan................	10,209	17,933	5.2	8.7	812,203	594,748	1.55	0.62
Wisconsin...............	7,250	5,787	3.8	3.3	733,342	219,484	1.55	0.72
WEST NORTH CENTRAL:								
Minnesota...............	3,172	1,516	1.8	1.0	466,449	89,058	1.45	0.61
Iowa....................	1,173	1,731	0.5	0.8	169,302	86,941	1.70	0.72
Missouri................	176	195	0.1	0.1	18,983	16,296	1.70	0.80
North Dakota...........	41	74	0.1	0.1	14,736	9,135	2.00	0.54
South Dakota...........	190	157	0.3	0.2	43,241	16,816	1.50	0.59
Nebraska...............	112	164	0.1	0.1	31,380	7,221	1.80	0.73
SOUTH ATLANTIC:								
Delaware................	1,042	743	10.3	6.9	108,836	30,839	1.45	0.57
Maryland...............	2,168	2,411	4.5	4.9	252,963	99,216	1.50	0.65
Virginia................	4,607	5,954	2.5	3.2	360,390	196,196	1.55	0.59
West Virginia...........	8,869	9,028	10.2	9.3	860,616	351,171	1.60	0.66
North Carolina..........	1,838	3,304	0.7	1.3	101,565	113,577	1.60	0.79
EAST SOUTH CENTRAL:								
Kentucky................	1,348	452	0.5	0.2	106,380	12,028	1.45	0.67
Tennessee...............	1,057	831	0.4	0.3	78,256	25,078	1.70	0.75

1 Less than one-tenth of 1 per cent.

TABLE 151.—EMMER AND SPELT—FARMS REPORTING, ACREAGE, PRODUCTION, AND VALUE, BY DIVISIONS AND STATES: 1919.

[States not shown when acreage was less than 1,000.]

DIVISION AND STATE.	Farms reporting.	Acreage.	Production (bushels).	Value.
United States	11,922	166,829	2,607,868	$3,699,943
GEOGRAPHIC DIVISIONS:				
New England	65	321	7,229	14,458
Middle Atlantic	111	405	6,875	12,251
East North Central	1,432	5,936	125,050	211,649
West North Central	9,566	150,704	2,327,102	3,234,157
South Atlantic	14	42	861	1,619
East South Central	2	2	26	48
West South Central	140	1,689	47,036	70,680
Mountain	530	7,359	86,478	142,311
Pacific	62	371	7,211	12,770
EAST NORTH CENTRAL:				
Michigan	649	2,674	51,353	87,307
Wisconsin	647	2,290	50,495	85,845
WEST NORTH CENTRAL:				
Minnesota	1,227	8,895	178,008	249,210
North Dakota	2,703	49,662	513,865	822,183
South Dakota	4,809	79,688	1,451,018	1,886,327
Nebraska	673	11,251	160,485	240,738
WEST SOUTH CENTRAL:				
Texas	101	1,453	43,040	64,565
MOUNTAIN:				
Montana	171	2,125	13,838	24,220
Colorado	225	3,701	52,832	84,529

TABLE 152.—KAFIR AND MILO—ACREAGE AND PRODUCTION, BY DIVISIONS AND STATES: 1919 AND 1909.

[A minus sign (—) denotes decrease. Per cent not shown when base is less than 100 or when per cent is more than 1,000. States not shown when acreage was less than 1,000 in 1919.]

DIVISION AND STATE.	ACREAGE.			PRODUCTION (BUSHELS).			AVERAGE YIELD PER ACRE (BUSHELS).	
	1919	1909	Per cent of increase.	1919	1909	Per cent of increase.	1919	1909
United States	3,619,034	1,635,153	121.3	72,085,954	17,597,305	309.6	19.9	10.8
GEOGRAPHIC DIVISIONS:								
New England	6	48	....	138	1,772	—92.2	23.0	36.9
Middle Atlantic	1,945	586	231.9	30,804	11,647	164.5	15.8	19.9
East North Central	600	1,185	—49.4	7,232	22,779	—68.3	12.1	19.2
West North Central	534,236	404,433	32.1	7,431,902	5,372,284	38.3	13.9	13.3
South Atlantic	265	230	15.2	3,896	3,561	9.4	14.7	15.5
East South Central	536	493	8.7	6,885	6,453	6.7	12.8	13.1
West South Central	2,636,051	1,107,406	138.0	54,371,423	10,536,612	416.0	20.6	9.5
Mountain	277,460	76,436	263.0	6,178,991	703,484	778.3	22.3	9.2
Pacific	167,935	44,336	278.8	4,054,683	938,713	331.9	24.1	21.2
MIDDLE ATLANTIC:								
Pennsylvania	1,769	283	525.1	27,901	5,129	440.0	15.8	18.1
WEST NORTH CENTRAL:								
Missouri	10,341	13,543	—23.6	151,367	228,386	—33.7	14.6	16.9
Nebraska	1,596	2,016	—20.8	22,106	20,212	9.4	13.9	10.0
Kansas	521,432	388,495	34.2	7,252,377	5,115,415	41.8	13.9	13.2
WEST SOUTH CENTRAL:								
Oklahoma	1,152,430	532,515	116.4	17,901,096	4,658,752	284.2	15.5	8.7
Texas	1,482,663	573,384	158.6	36,456,343	5,860,444	522.1	24.6	10.2
MOUNTAIN:								
Colorado	92,126	11,971	669.6	1,544,879	139,234	....	16.8	11.6
New Mexico	151,685	63,570	138.6	3,783,617	543,350	596.3	24.9	8.5
Arizona	33,608	801	....	849,994	18,739	....	25.3	23.4
PACIFIC:								
California	167,814	44,308	278.7	4,051,086	938,049	331.9	24.1	21.2

TABLE 153.—KAFIR AND MILO—FARMS REPORTING AND VALUE, BY DIVISIONS AND STATES: 1919 AND 1909.

[States not shown when acreage was less than 1,000 in 1919.]

DIVISION AND STATE.	FARMS REPORTING.				VALUE.		AVERAGE VALUE PER BUSHEL.	
	Number.		Per cent of all farms.					
	1919	1909	1919	1909	1919	1909	1919	1909
United States.........	129,947	97,574	2.0	1.5	$90,221,046	$10,816,940	$1.25	$0.61
GEOGRAPHIC DIVISIONS:								
New England............	4	16	(1)	(1)	207	1,084	1.50	0.61
Middle Atlantic..........	386	152	0.1	(1)	48,283	8,203	1.57	0.70
East North Central......	97	354	(1)	(1)	10,728	14,242	1.48	0.63
West North Central......	29,242	36,680	2.7	3.3	10,087,216	3,219,619	1.36	0.60
South Atlantic..........	124	125	(1)	(1)	6,810	2,918	1.75	0.82
East South Central......	147	215	(1)	(1)	14,039	4,998	2.04	0.77
West South Central......	84,797	53,853	8.5	5.7	65,223,938	6,330,665	1.20	0.60
Mountain................	7,953	3,651	3.3	2.0	7,936,502	509,163	1.28	0.72
Pacific..................	7,197	2,528	3.1	1.3	6,893,323	726,048	1.70	0.77
MIDDLE ATLANTIC:								
Pennsylvania...........	336	76	0.2	(1)	43,251	3,436	1.55	0.67
WEST NORTH CENTRAL:								
Missouri................	2,480	4,029	0.9	1.5	257,332	152,246	1.70	0.67
Nebraska...............	292	384	0.2	0.3	30,949	15,712	1.40	0.78
Kansas.................	26,380	32,160	16.0	18.1	9,790,707	3,046,799	1.35	0.60
WEST SOUTH CENTRAL:								
Oklahoma...............	41,824	29,660	21.8	15.6	23,271,427	2,531,036	1.30	0.54
Texas..................	42,544	23,631	9.8	5.7	41,924,803	3,785,463	1.15	0.65
MOUNTAIN:								
Colorado...............	2,785	783	4.6	1.7	1,931,104	94,486	1.25	0.68
New Mexico.............	3,610	2,741	12.1	7.7	4,729,524	392,393	1.25	0.72
Arizona................	1,545	109	15.5	1.2	1,274,994	20,355	1.50	1.09
PACIFIC:								
California...............	7,183	2,521	6.1	2.9	6,886,848	725,704	1.70	0.77

1 Less than one-tenth of 1 per cent.

TABLE 154.—RICE—ACREAGE AND PRODUCTION, BY DIVISIONS AND STATES: 1919 AND 1909.

[A minus sign (−) denotes decrease. Per cent not shown when base is less than 100. States not shown when acreage was less than 1,000 in 1919.]

DIVISION AND STATE.	ACREAGE.			PRODUCTION (BUSHELS).			AVERAGE YIELD PER ACRE (BUSHELS).	
	1919	1909	Per cent of increase.	1919	1909	Per cent of increase.	1919	1909
United States......	911,272	610,175	49.3	35,330,912	21,838,580	61.8	38.8	35.8
GEOGRAPHIC DIVISIONS:								
West North Central....	705	10	....	29,825	15	....	42.3	1.5
South Atlantic.........	13,213	27,080	−51.2	225,099	713,966	−68.5	17.0	26.4
East South Central.....	2,254	560	302.5	32,463	10,006	224.4	14.4	17.9
West South Central....	764,651	582,523	31.3	28,115,162	21,114,548	33.2	36.8	36.2
Mountain..............	82	2	....	2,050	45	....	25.0	22.5
Pacific................	130,367	....	....	6,926,313	....	....	53.1	......
SOUTH ATLANTIC:								
South Carolina.........	6,547	19,491	−66.4	122,465	541,570	77.4	18.7	27.8
Georgia...............	4,103	6,445	−36.3	59,711	148,698	−59.8	14.6	23.1
Florida................	2,391	623	283.8	39,157	12,341	217.3	16.4	19.8
EAST SOUTH CENTRAL:								
Alabama...............	1,038	279	272.0	14,279	5,170	176.2	13.8	18.5
Mississippi............	1,171	281	316.7	18,141	4,836	275.1	15.5	17.2
WEST SOUTH CENTRAL:								
Arkansas...............	143,211	27,419	422.3	6,797,126	1,282,830	429.9	47.5	46.8
Louisiana..............	456,959	317,518	43.9	16,011,667	10,839,973	47.7	35.0	34.1
Texas..................	164,481	237,586	−30.8	5,306,369	8,991,745	−41.0	32.3	37.8
PACIFIC:								
California.............	130,367	....	....	6,926,313	....	....	53.1	......

TABLE 155.—RICE—FARMS REPORTING AND VALUE, BY DIVISIONS AND STATES: 1919 AND 1909.

[States not shown when acreage was less than 1,000 in 1919.]

DIVISION AND STATE.	FARMS REPORTING.				VALUE.		AVERAGE VALUE PER BUSHEL.	
	Number.		Per cent of all farms.		1919	1909	1919	1909
	1919	1909	1919	1909				
United States	20,310	13,708	0.3	0.2	$97,194,481	$16,019,607	$2.75	$0.73
GEOGRAPHIC DIVISIONS:								
West North Central	3	1	(¹)	(¹)	79,036	10	2.65	0.67
South Atlantic	8,758	5,527	0.8	0.5	640,571	691,372	2.85	0.97
East South Central	2,000	596	0.2	0.1	75,592	10,547	2.33	1.05
West South Central	9,058	7,583	0.9	0.8	75,961,222	15,317,648	2.70	0.73
Mountain	1	1	(¹)	(¹)	5,433	30	2.65	0.67
Pacific	490		0.2		20,432,627		2.95	
SOUTH ATLANTIC:								
South Carolina	3,685	3,017	1.9	1.7	355,150	520,000	2.90	0.96
Georgia	3,064	1,740	1.0	0.6	167,189	145,813	2.80	0.38
Florida	1,893	609	3.5	1.2	107,687	15,290	2.75	1.24
EAST SOUTH CENTRAL:								
Alabama	778	238	0.3	0.1	32,846	5,179	2.30	1.30
Mississippi	1,217	358	0.4	0.1	42,631	5,368	2.35	1.11
WEST SOUTH CENTRAL:								
Arkansas	1,201	290	0.5	0.1	18,352,240	1,158,103	2.70	0.90
Louisiana	6,989	6,138	5.2	5.1	42,751,150	8,053,222	2.67	0.74
Texas	868	1,155	0.2	0.3	14,857,832	6,106,323	2.80	0.08
PACIFIC:								
California	490		0.4		20,432,627		2.95	

¹ Less than one-tenth of 1 per cent.

75108°—22——53

TABLE **156.**—MIXED CROPS—FARMS REPORTING, ACREAGE, PRODUCTION, AND VALUE, BY DIVISIONS AND STATES: 1919.

[Mixed crops consisted mainly of oats and barley, oats and wheat, and wheat and barley grown and harvested together.　States not shown when acreage was less than 1,000.]

DIVISION AND STATE.	Farms reporting.	Acreage.	Production (bushels).	Value.
United States	46,100	577,078	13,835,785	$16,329,888
GEOGRAPHIC DIVISIONS:				
New England	714	4,834	130,336	183,358
Middle Atlantic	13,517	130,096	2,928,944	3,515,343
East North Central	13,384	123,981	3,207,192	3,912,503
West North Central	14,806	278,567	6,760,352	7,544,953
South Atlantic	582	3,657	43,262	69,721
East South Central	164	1,446	28,684	42,312
West South Central	363	5,867	111,835	133,234
Mountain	325	6,592	90,619	134,035
Pacific	2,245	22,038	534,561	794,429
NEW ENGLAND:				
Vermont	576	4,298	115,055	161,076
MIDDLE ATLANTIC:				
New York	13,215	128,477	2,891,561	3,469,871
Pennsylvania	276	1,434	34,320	41,184
EAST NORTH CENTRAL:				
Ohio	198	1,475	36,049	48,669
Indiana	278	2,761	68,322	102,492
Illinois	439	4,564	134,692	161,631
Michigan	2,816	19,879	379,616	493,507
Wisconsin	9,653	95,302	2,588,513	3,106,204
WEST NORTH CENTRAL:				
Minnesota	9,741	193,864	4,579,897	5,037,894
Iowa	3,366	45,573	1,356,200	1,627,442
Missouri	146	2,311	46,405	55,687
North Dakota	235	7,900	65,480	78,574
South Dakota	320	7,996	164,919	197,905
Nebraska	774	16,230	448,835	448,835
Kansas	224	4,693	98,616	98,616
SOUTH ATLANTIC:				
North Carolina	366	1,854	19,856	31,770
WEST SOUTH CENTRAL:				
Oklahoma	220	4,043	75,508	75,508
Texas	113	1,537	34,342	54,947
MOUNTAIN:				
Montana	42	1,049	9,519	12,375
Colorado	142	3,205	46,454	69,686
PACIFIC:				
Washington	595	3,687	92,364	138,552
Oregon	1,602	15,591	367,958	551,943
California	48	2,760	74,239	103,934

TABLE 157.—DRY EDIBLE BEANS—ACREAGE AND PRODUCTION, BY DIVISIONS AND STATES: 1919 AND 1909.

[A minus sign (—) denotes decrease. Per cent not shown when more than 1,000. States not shown when acreage was less than 1,000 in 1919.]

DIVISION AND STATE.	ACREAGE.[1]			PRODUCTION (BUSHELS).			AVERAGE YIELD PER ACRE (BUSHELS).	
	1919	1909	Per cent of increase.	1919	1909	Per cent of increase.	1919	1909
United States	1,161,682	802,991	44.7	14,079,093	11,251,160	25.1	12.1	14.0
GEOGRAPHIC DIVISIONS:								
New England	12,989	16,619	—21.8	137,247	145,111	—5.4	10.6	8.7
Middle Atlantic	50,253	117,370	—57.2	736,871	1,696,468	—56.6	14.7	14.5
East North Central	335,630	422,256	—20.5	4,494,237	5,472,850	—17.9	13.4	13.0
West North Central	11,763	9,189	28.0	89,310	94,841	—5.8	7.6	10.3
South Atlantic	16,836	25,776	—34.7	98,308	162,853	—39.6	5.8	6.3
East South Central	19,266	18,488	4.2	106,448	114,022	—6.6	5.5	6.2
West South Central	12,103	3,551	240.8	90,271	25,052	260.3	7.5	7.1
Mountain	225,816	30,847	632.1	1,739,529	200,402	768.0	7.7	6.5
Pacific	477,026	158,902	200.2	6,586,872	3,339,561	97.2	13.8	21.0
NEW ENGLAND:								
Maine	5,689	10,341	—45.0	58,797	87,565	—32.9	10.3	8.5
New Hampshire	2,198	3,180	—30.9	18,488	22,546	—18.0	8.4	7.1
Vermont	3,696	2,390	54.6	45,696	26,359	73.4	12.4	11.0
Massachusetts	1,094	446	145.3	10,687	4,979	114.6	9.8	11.2
MIDDLE ATLANTIC:								
New York	45,897	115,698	—60.3	702,634	1,681,506	—58.2	15.3	14.5
Pennsylvania	3,516	1,269	177.1	27,520	12,021	128.9	7.8	9.5
EAST NORTH CENTRAL:								
Ohio	2,122	1,139	86.3	16,792	13,665	22.9	7.9	12.0
Indiana	3,016	1,721	75.2	14,011	15,238	—8.1	4.6	8.9
Illinois	1,516	1,153	31.5	8,293	6,866	20.8	5.5	6.0
Michigan	314,873	403,669	—22.0	4,332,317	5,282,511	—18.0	13.8	13.1
Wisconsin	14,103	14,574	—3.2	122,824	154,570	—20.5	8.7	10.6
WEST NORTH CENTRAL:								
Minnesota	4,735	4,697	0.8	50,471	62,822	—19.7	10.7	13.4
Missouri	3,422	1,281	167.1	16,070	9,385	71.2	4.7	7.3
SOUTH ATLANTIC:								
Maryland	1,632	196	732.7	11,769	1,833	542.1	7.2	9.4
Virginia	5,029	4,777	5.3	32,660	29,435	11.0	6.5	6.2
West Virginia	4,878	8,111	—39.9	26,709	39,794	—32.9	5.5	4.9
North Carolina	2,277	5,521	—58.8	12,334	35,937	—65.7	5.4	6.5
Georgia	2,463	2,947	—16.4	10,243	16,546	—38.1	4.2	5.6
EAST SOUTH CENTRAL:								
Kentucky	7,602	12,434	—38.9	43,154	70,557	—38.8	5.7	5.7
Tennessee	7,877	3,398	131.8	36,475	19,526	86.8	4.6	5.7
Alabama	3,671	1,557	135.8	25,398	15,212	67.0	6.9	9.8
WEST SOUTH CENTRAL:								
Louisiana	1,019	311	227.7	8,232	5,557	48.1	8.1	17.9
Oklahoma	1,544	575	168.5	12,046	2,520	378.0	7.8	4.4
Texas	9,479	1,846	397.2	67,638	12,895	424.5	7.4	7.0
MOUNTAIN:								
Montana	2,297	342	571.6	26,141	2,958	783.7	11.4	8.6
Idaho	33,941	1,915		344,432	33,816	918.5	10.1	17.7
Wyoming	1,046	273	283.2	4,712	1,876	151.2	4.5	6.9
Colorado	66,236	5,040		427,968	53,926	693.6	6.5	10.7
New Mexico	112,419	20,766	441.4	850,334	85,795	891.1	7.6	4.1
Arizona	9,438	2,301	310.2	82,090	18,457	344.8	8.7	8.0
PACIFIC:								
Washington	1,783	353	405.1	17,683	3,311	434.1	9.9	9.4
Oregon	3,569	562	535.1	16,238	8,032	102.2	4.5	14.3
California	471,674	157,987	198.6	6,552,951	3,328,218	96.9	13.9	21.1

[1] A considerable part of the acreage in the Southern states is probably a duplication of other crop acreage.

TABLE 158.—DRY EDIBLE BEANS—FARMS REPORTING AND VALUE, BY DIVISIONS AND STATES: 1919 AND 1909.

[States not shown when acreage was less than 1,000 in 1919.]

DIVISION AND STATE.	FARMS REPORTING.				VALUE.		AVERAGE VALUE PER BUSHEL.	
	Number.		Per cent of all farms.					
	1919	1909	1919	1909	1919	1909	1919	1909
United States.........	168,185	185,934	2.6	2.9	$61,795,225	$21,771,482	$4.39	$1.94
GEOGRAPHIC DIVISIONS:								
New England............	17,290	26,284	11.0	13.9	815,696	432,501	5.94	2.98
Middle Atlantic..........	20,910	24,798	4.9	5.3	3,723,334	3,723,350	5.05	2.19
East North Central.......	58,879	65,839	5.4	5.9	18,085,617	10,054,082	4.02	1.84
West North Central......	8,376	9,846	0.8	0.9	440,125	199,498	4.93	2.10
South Atlantic	12,974	25,544	1.1	2.3	548,653	291,885	5.58	1.79
East South Central.......	15,034	20,558	1.4	2.0	647,527	189,809	6.08	1.66
West South Central......	5,929	1,447	0.6	0 2	417,136	45,717	4.62	1.82
Mountain................	18,525	7,623	7.6	4.2	6,174,981	506,185	3.55	2.53
Pacific..................	10,268	3,995	4.4	2.1	30,942,156	6,328,455	4.70	1.89
NEW ENGLAND:								
Maine...................	8,956	15,788	18.6	26.3	358,661	275,334	6.10	3.14
New Hampshire..........	3,703	5,523	18.0	20.4	114,626	62,783	6.20	2.78
Vermont................	2,860	2,752	9.8	8.4	260,468	72,873	5.70	2.76
Massachusetts...........	1,166	1,252	3.6	3.4	58,244	12,382	5.45	2.49
MIDDLE ATLANTIC:								
New York...............	15,682	21,181	8.1	9.8	3,513,170	3,689,064	5.00	2.19
Pennsylvania...........	4,838	3,326	2.4	1.5	166,498	28,136	6.05	2.34
EAST NORTH CENTRAL:								
Ohio....................	2,058	2,108	0.8	0.8	105,799	30,082	6.30	2.20
Indiana............•......	2,124	1,982	1.0	0.9	81,264	30,929	5.80	2.03
Illinois..................	931	627	0.4	0.2	47,273	12,842	5.70	1.87
Michigan................	46,561	55,466	23.7	26.8	17,329,268	9,716,315	4.00	1.84
Wisconsin...............	7,205	5,656	3.8	3.2	522,013	263,914	4.25	1.71
WEST NORTH CENTRAL:								
Minnesota...............	3,217	4,587	1.8	2.9	219,550	124,996	4.35	1.99
Missouri................	2,622	2,391	1.0	0.9	97,227	20,354	6.05	2.17
SOUTH ATLANTIC:								
Maryland...............	670	312	1.4	0.6	75,912	3,342	6.45	1.82
Virginia.................	3,897	7,660	2.1	4.2	166,568	61,864	5.10	2.10
West Virginia...........	4,957	8,626	5.7	8.9	160,254	81,049	6.00	2.04
North Carolina..........	1,825	6,574	0.7	2.6	64,137	57,528	5.20	1.60
Georgia.................	1,391	1,329	0.4	0.5	51,215	30,018	5.00	1.81
EAST SOUTH CENTRAL:								
Kentucky...............	8,105	14,248	3.0	5.5	278,345	105,309	6.45	1.49
Tennessee...............	5,602	5,312	2.2	2.2	240,735	40,966	6.60	2.10
Alabama................	1,243	647	0.5	0.2	121,912	19,887	4.80	1.31
WEST SOUTH CENTRAL:								
Louisiana...............	445	78	0.3	0.1	41,160	6,982	5.00	1.26
Oklahoma...............	496	224	0.3	0.1	65,655	5,942	5.45	2.36
Texas...................	4,444	607	1.0	0.1	297,604	26,205	4.40	2.03
MOUNTAIN:								
Montana................	354	140	0.6	0.5	169,789	8,511	4.20	2.88
Idaho...................	1,557	293	3.7	1.0	1,205,519	76,314	3.50	2.26
Wyoming................	357	211	2.3	1.9	19,320	5,018	4.10	2.67
Colorado...............	5,661	1,387	9.4	3.0	1,455,091	128,701	3.40	2.39
New Mexico.............	9,395	4,593	31.5	12.9	2,976,176	232,023	3.50	2.70
Arizona.................	976	776	9.8	8.4	385,825	44,997	4.70	2.44
PACIFIC:								
Washington.............	732	266	1.1	0.5	74,269	9,656	4.20	2.92
Oregon.................	793	675	1.6	1.5	69,018	23,342	4.25	2.91
California...............	8,743	3,054	7.4	3.5	30,798,869	6,295,457	4.70	1.89

TABLE 159.—MISCELLANEOUS BEANS—ACREAGE, PRODUCTION, AND VALUE, BY STATES: 1919 AND 1909.

CROP AND STATE.	ACREAGE.[1]		PRODUCTION (BUSHELS).		VALUE.	
	1919	1909	1919	1909	1919	1909
United States	1,257,019	14,947	1,135,141	179,733	$4,576,121	$241,060
Soy beans, total	112,826	1,629	1,084,813	16,835	4,450,099	20,577
New York	1,387	1	16,556	5	86,926	10
Ohio	1,753	33	17,441	424	100,297	843
Indiana	2,807		23,010		132,316	
Illinois	3,288		23,812		123,820	
Michigan	6,257		78,515		384,726	
Wisconsin	1,942		16,838		92,626	
Missouri	2,682		18,315		94,329	
Virginia	10,283	29	111,353	415	517,794	695
North Carolina	47,041	1,249	498,048	13,313	1,743,194	14,141
Tennessee	7,649	256	49,731	2,037	236,235	3,387
Alabama	3,928	29	38,690	219	135,430	494
Mississippi	3,420	15	24,839	152	95,637	378
New Mexico	5,838		52,190		182,669	
All other states	14,551	17	115,475	270	524,100	629
Castor beans, total	133	565	428	2,077	963	3,432
Florida	129		389		875	
All other states	4	565	39	2,077	88	3,432
Velvet beans, total	1,142,562	12,560		154,767		210,837
North Carolina	3,153					
South Carolina	26,893					
Georgia	523,690	435		4,224		8,572
Florida	134,247	8,363		114,404		152,479
Alabama	336,292	3,638		34,398		44,899
Mississippi	81,691	124		1,741		4,887
Arkansas	4,236					
Louisiana	26,920					
Texas	4,101					
All other states	1,339					
Horse beans, total	1,459	150	49,694	5,534	124,235	5,659
Other beans, total	39	43	206	520	824	555

[1] A considerable part of the acreage in the Southern states is probably a duplication of other crop acreage.

TABLE 160.—DRY PEAS—ACREAGE AND PRODUCTION, BY DIVISIONS AND STATES: 1919 AND 1909.

[A minus sign (−) denotes decrease. Per cent not shown when more than 1,000. States not shown when acreage was less than 1,000 in 1919.]

DIVISION AND STATE.	ACREAGE.[1]			PRODUCTION (BUSHELS).			AVERAGE YIELD PER ACRE (BUSHELS).	
	1919	1909	Per cent of increase.	1919	1909	Per cent of increase.	1919	1909
United States.......	865,670	1,305,099	−33.7	5,742,626	7,129,294	−19.5	6.6	5.5
GEOGRAPHIC DIVISIONS:								
New England............	467	824	−43.3	5,705	7,784	−26.7	12.2	9.4
Middle Atlantic........	3,031	4,185	−27.6	39,795	73,358	−45.8	13.1	17.5
East North Central.....	119,788	227,430	−47.3	1,348,251	2,603,773	−48.2	11.3	11.4
West North Central....	9,956	27,635	−64.0	55,512	154,873	−64.2	5.6	5.6
South Atlantic.........	351,857	667,705	−47.3	1,561,085	2,242,244	−30.4	4.4	3.4
East South Central.....	176,833	203,229	−13.0	835,506	882,471	−5.3	4.7	4.3
West South Central....	84,925	138,902	−38.9	470,751	678,746	−30.6	5.5	4.9
Mountain..............	66,949	28,598	134.1	798,844	328,201	143.4	11.9	11.5
Pacific...............	51,864	6,591	686.9	627,177	157,844	297.3	12.1	23.9
MIDDLE ATLANTIC:								
New York............	2,876	4,007	−28.2	38,336	71,486	−46.4	13.3	17.8
EAST NORTH CENTRAL:								
Indiana...............	5,775	13,082	−55.9	29,405	88,254	−66.7	5.1	6.7
Illinois...............	15,958	41,076	−61.2	71,285	185,020	−61.5	4.5	4.5
Michigan..............	38,874	94,932	−59.1	454,639	1,162,403	−60.9	11.7	12.2
Wisconsin.............	58,554	78,017	−24.9	781,668	1,165,055	−32.9	13.3	14.9
WEST NORTH CENTRAL:								
Missouri..............	8,409	23,036	−63.5	38,426	109,357	−64.9	4.6	4.7
SOUTH ATLANTIC:								
Delaware.............	1,256	1,615	−22.2	10,667	12,521	−14.8	8.5	7.8
Maryland.............	1,418	742	91.1	12,061	5,603	115.3	8.5	7.6
Virginia..............	18,446	12,091	52.6	115,067	66,488	73.1	6.2	5.5
North Carolina........	49,513	169,934	−70.9	258,829	651,567	−60.3	5.2	3.8
South Carolina........	136,303	265,632	−48.7	599,245	711,853	−15.8	4.4	2.7
Georgia..............	138,481	210,315	−34.2	513,990	736,009	−30.2	3.7	3.5
Florida..............	6,087	7,144	−14.8	48,734	56,713	−14.1	8.0	7.9
EAST SOUTH CENTRAL:								
Kentucky.............	3,885	8,465	−54.1	22,763	44,772	−49.2	5.9	5.3
Tennessee.............	17,133	36,640	−53.2	82,677	133,924	−38.3	4.8	3.7
Alabama.............	96,582	85,034	13.6	486,126	418,007	16.3	5.0	4.9
Mississippi............	59,233	73,090	−19.0	243,940	285,768	−14.6	4.1	3.9
WEST SOUTH CENTRAL:								
Arkansas..............	26,107	52,730	−50.5	119,369	229,444	−48.0	4.6	4.4
Louisiana.............	22,230	33,150	−32.9	104,469	161,659	−35.4	4.7	4.9
Oklahoma.............	4,064	6,245	−34.9	26,925	33,282	−19.1	6.6	5.3
Texas................	32,524	46,777	−30.5	219,988	254,361	−13.5	6.8	5.4
MOUNTAIN:								
Montana..............	14,864	1,184	....	166,551	21,670	668.6	11.2	18.3
Idaho................	17,635	234	....	251,450	4,875	....	14.3	20.8
Colorado.............	27,798	24,230	14.7	295,751	258,281	14.5	10.6	10.7
New Mexico...........	5,750	2,485	131.4	70,013	30,829	127.1	12.2	12.4
PACIFIC:								
Washington...........	30,832	3,196	864.7	442,620	91,032	386.2	14.4	28.5
California............	20,893	2,959	606.1	182,779	57,468	218.1	8.7	19.4

[1] A considerable part of the acreage in the Southern states is probably a duplication of other crop acreage.

TABLE 161.—DRY PEAS—FARMS REPORTING AND VALUE, BY DIVISIONS AND STATES: 1919 AND 1909.

[States not shown when acreage was less than 1,000 in 1919.]

DIVISION AND STATE.	FARMS REPORTING.				VALUE.		AVERAGE VALUE PER BUSHEL.	
	Number.		Per cent of all farms.					
	1919	1909	1919	1909	1919	1909	1919	1909
United States......	210,245	261,231	3.3	4.1	$20,790,541	$10,963,739	$3.62	$1.54
GEOGRAPHIC DIVISIONS:								
New England..........	542	1,488	0.3	0.8	27,654	15,348	4.85	1.97
Middle Atlantic........	932	1,832	0.2	0.4	168,222	121,369	4.23	1.65
East North Central....	24,661	40,396	2.3	3.6	4,229,755	3,396,025	3.14	1.30
West North Central....	2,179	4,507	0.2	0.4	259,686	241,082	4.68	1.56
South Atlantic.........	92,118	118,172	7.9	10.6	6,371,230	3,805,792	4.08	1.70
East South Central.....	57,105	58,833	5.4	5.6	3,206,495	1,560,726	3.84	1.77
West South Central....	25,396	32,059	2.5	3.4	1,835,708	1,095,149	3.90	1.61
Mountain...............	5,045	2,612	2.1	1.4	2,686,534	495,132	3.36	1.51
Pacific.................	2,267	1,332	1.0	0.7	2,005,257	233,116	3.20	1.48
MIDDLE ATLANTIC:								
New York.............	879	1,661	0.5	0.8	161,011	117,558	4.20	1.64
EAST NORTH CENTRAL:								
Indiana.................	960	1,652	0.5	0.8	132,333	133,996	4.50	1.52
Illinois.................	1,972	4,534	0.8	1.8	335,039	273,373	4.70	1.48
Michigan...............	9,225	18,128	4.7	8.8	1,363,917	1,337,430	3.00	1.15
Wisconsin..............	12,366	15,950	6.5	9.0	2,345,004	1,645,928	3.00	1.41
WEST NORTH CENTRAL:								
Missouri................	1,480	3,462	0.6	1.2	182,535	180,391	4.75	1.65
SOUTH ATLANTIC:								
Delaware..............	291	523	2.9	4.8	53,335	25,278	5.00	2.02
Maryland..............	387	350	0.8	0.7	50,652	11,143	4.20	1.99
Virginia...............	6,009	4,462	3.2	2.4	489,045	127,211	4.25	1.91
North Carolina........	20,619	39,726	7.6	15.7	1,035,316	1,024,228	4.00	1.57
South Carolina........	33,919	35,660	17.6	20.2	2,426,944	1,311,454	4.05	1.84
Georgia...............	28,921	34,716	9.3	11.9	2,107,366	1,204,783	4.10	1.64
Florida............../...	1,807	2,642	3.3	5.3	194,936	98,383	4.00	1.73
EAST SOUTH CENTRAL:								
Kentucky..............	1,139	1,732	0.4	0.7	104,709	84,514	4.60	1.89
Tennessee.............	6,579	10,175	2.6	4.1	363,776	245,434	4.40	1.83
Alabama...............	32,435	26,905	12.7	10.2	1,750,050	660,270	3.60	1.58
Mississippi............	16,952	20,021	6.2	7.3	987,960	570,508	4.05	2.00
WEST SOUTH CENTRAL:								
Arkansas..............	9,442	13,821	4.1	6.4	519,258	376,076	4.35	1.64
Louisiana..............	5,993	6,330	4.4	5.3	438,769	252,362	4.20	1.56
Oklahoma.............	1,427	1,612	0.7	0.8	107,700	63,857	4.00	1.92
Texas.................	8,534	10,296	2.0	2.5	769,981	402,854	3.50	1.58
MOUNTAIN:								
Montana...............	620	180	1.1	0.7	516,310	37,757	3.10	1.74
Idaho..................	989	59	2.3	0.2	1,181,818	9,160	4.70	1.88
Colorado..............	1,306	832	2.2	1.8	739,389	397,540	2.50	1.54
New Mexico............	1,917	1,453	6.4	4.1	175,037	35,077	2.50	1.14
PACIFIC:								
Washington............	1,812	915	2.7	1.6	1,349,991	116,065	3.05	1.27
California.............	408	262	0.3	0.3	648,864	101,016	3.55	1.76

TABLE 162.—PEANUTS—ACREAGE AND PRODUCTION, BY STATES: 1919 AND 1909.

[A minus sign (−) denotes decrease.]

STATE.	ACREAGE.			PRODUCTION (BUSHELS).			AVERAGE YIELD PER ACRE (BUSHELS).	
	1919	1909	Per cent of increase.	1919	1909	Per cent of increase.	1919	1909
United States........	1,125,100	869,887	29.3	27,449,930	19,415,816	41.4	24.4	22.3
Virginia.................	133,162	145,213	−8.3	5,865,127	4,284,340	36.9	44.0	29.5
North Carolina...........	125,766	195,134	−35.5	5,854,689	5,980,919	−2.1	46.6	30.7
South Carolina...........	7,460	7,596	−1.8	112,578	154,822	−27.3	15.1	20.4
Georgia.................	201,786	160,317	25.9	3,826,505	2,569,787	48.9	19.0	16.0
Florida.................	77,416	126,150	−38.6	1,365,063	2,315,089	−41.0	17.6	18.4
Tennessee................	8,132	18,952	−57.1	264,483	547,240	−51.7	32.5	28.9
Alabama.................	334,239	100,609	232.2	6,288,594	1,573,796	299.6	18.8	15.6
Mississippi..............	16,933	13,997	21.0	241,601	284,791	−15.2	14.3	20.3
Arkansas................	21,962	10,192	115.5	308,676	168,608	83.1	14.1	16.5
Louisiana................	17,670	25,020	−29.4	262,888	412,037	−36.2	14.9	16.5
Oklahoma...............	13,969	1,564	793.2	297,456	31,880	833.0	21.3	20.4
Texas...................	165,407	64,327	157.1	2,731,632	1,074,998	154.1	16.5	16.7
All other states...........	1,198	816	....	30,638	17,509	....	....	......

TABLE 163.—PEANUTS—FARMS REPORTING AND VALUE, BY STATES: 1919 AND 1909.

STATE.	FARMS REPORTING.				VALUE.		AVERAGE VALUE PER BUSHEL.	
	Number.		Per cent of all farms.					
	1919	1909	1919	1909	1919	1909	1919	1909
United States........	230,380	219,003	3.6	3.4	$62,751,701	$18,271,929	$2.29	$0.94
Virginia.................	12,728	12,927	6.8	7.0	13,196,543	4,239,832	2.25	0.99
North Carolina...........	21,002	31,503	7.8	12.4	13,465,793	5,368,826	2.30	0.90
South Carolina...........	7,269	5,846	3.8	3.3	326,478	144,211	2.90	0.93
Georgia.................	37,994	32,590	12.2	11.2	9,566,301	2,440,926	2.50	0.95
Florida.................	9,165	19,219	17.0	38.4	3,344,404	2,146,862	2.45	0.93
Tennessee................	3,280	3,947	1.3	1.6	528,966	386,765	2.00	0.71
Alabama.................	58,828	37,702	23.0	14.3	13,206,050	1,490,654	2.10	0.95
Mississippi..............	19,126	23,171	7.0	8.4	543,616	317,236	2.25	1.11
Arkansas................	12,115	10,025	5.2	4.7	725,388	183,364	2.35	1.09
Louisiana................	9,999	14,492	7.4	12.0	657,231	422,232	2.50	1.02
Oklahoma...............	4,308	1,299	2.2	0.7	684,155	34,984	2.30	1.10
Texas...................	33,357	24,475	7.7	5.9	6,419,340	1,075,110	2.35	1.00
All other states...........	1,209	1,807	....	....	87,436	20,927	....	......

TABLE **164.**—FLAXSEED—ACREAGE AND PRODUCTION, BY STATES: 1919 AND 1909.

[A minus sign (−) denotes decrease.]

STATE.	ACREAGE.			PRODUCTION (BUSHELS).			AVERAGE YIELD PER ACRE (BUSHELS).	
	1919	1909	Percent of increase.	1919	1909	Percent of increase.	1919	1909
United States.....	1,260,687	2,083,142	−39.5	6,653,200	19,512,765	−65.9	5.3	9.4
Michigan.................	1,297	261	396.9	13,627	2,943	363.0	10.5	11.3
Wisconsin................	7,133	9,423	−24.3	62,579	118,793	−47.3	8.8	12.6
Minnesota...............	288,240	358,426	−19.6	2,019,464	3,277,238	−38.4	7.0	9.1
Iowa.....................	9,646	15,549	−38.0	61,007	140,906	−56.7	6.3	9.1
North Dakota...........	649,949	1,068,049	−39.1	2,972,082	10,245,684	−71.0	4.6	9.6
South Dakota...........	159,234	518,566	−69.3	1,109,303	4,759,794	−76.7	7.0	9.2
Nebraska...............	1,344	2,934	−54.2	3,757	20,647	−81.8	2.8	7.0
Kansas...................	12,368	45,014	−72.5	72,948	302,491	−75.9	5.9	6.7
Montana.................	128,851	37,647	242.3	325,838	447,484	−27.2	2.5	11.9
Wyoming................	1,212	1,110	9.2	3,136	5,983	−47.6	2.6	5.4
All other states..........	1,413	26,163	....	9,459	190,802	....	......	......

TABLE **165.**—FLAXSEED—FARMS REPORTING AND VALUE, BY STATES: 1919 AND 1909.

STATE.	FARMS REPORTING.				VALUE.		AVERAGE VALUE PER BUSHEL.	
	Number.		Per cent of all farms.					
	1919	1909	1919	1909	1919	1909	1919	1909
United States.......	53,058	77,184	0.8	1.2	$29,360,998	$28,970,554	$4.41	$1.48
Michigan..................	181	187	0.1	0.1	42,247	4,951	3.10	1.68
Wisconsin................	1,862	1,790	1.0	1.0	253,445	167,848	4.05	1.41
Minnesota................	20,458	23,010	11.5	14.7	8,885,642	4,863,328	4.40	1.48
Iowa.....................	747	1,361	0.3	0.6	262,334	182,569	4.30	1.30
North Dakota.............	19,185	30,632	24.7	41.2	13,225,765	15,488,016	4.45	1.51
South Dakota.............	6,274	14,614	8.4	18.8	4,880,931	7,001,717	4.40	1.47
Nebraska................	31	125	(1)	0.1	16,530	30,135	4.40	1.46
Kansas...................	807	2,540	0.5	1.4	291,792	327,402	4.00	1.08
Montana.................	3,244	1,208	5.6	4.6	1,449,982	676,945	4.45	1.51
Wyoming................	37	65	0.2	0.6	13,485	7,858	4.30	1.31
All other states............	232	1,652	......	......	38,845	219,785	......	......

[1] Less than one-tenth of 1 per cent.

TABLE 166.—GRASS SEED, AND CLOVER AND ALFALFA SEED—PRODUCTION

	DIVISION AND STATE.	RED CLOVER SEED.		OTHER CLOVER AND ALFALFA SEED.	
		Production (bushels).	Value.	Production (bushels).	Value.
1	United States	1,175,969	$34,768,946	868,304	$20,647,780
	GEOGRAPHIC DIVISIONS:				
2	New England	366	12,117	226	6,464
3	Middle Atlantic	31,459	1,040,873	19,292	598,032
4	East North Central	735,072	21,810,119	244,891	6,898,440
5	West North Central	270,265	7,927,511	228,491	5,152,241
6	South Atlantic	26,897	841,766	9,377	198,648
7	East South Central	16,312	484,588	60,134	1,211,294
8	West South Central	527	14,882	27,935	540,736
9	Mountain	66,680	1,797,612	219,073	4,705,764
10	Pacific	28,391	839,478	58,885	1,336,161
	NEW ENGLAND:				
11	Maine	111	3,885	43	1,290
12	New Hampshire	19	589	19	570
13	Vermont	80	2,320	88	2,464
14	Massachusetts	88	2,992	67	1,876
15	Rhode Island	19	665	7	210
16	Connecticut	49	1,666	2	54
	MIDDLE ATLANTIC:				
17	New York	5,202	174,278	17,585	545,135
18	New Jersey	114	3,876	20	600
19	Pennsylvania	26,143	862,719	1,687	52,297
	EAST NORTH CENTRAL:				
20	Ohio	89,957	2,788,791	83,967	2,351,076
21	Indiana	120,446	3,492,939	20,733	580,524
22	Illinois	172,545	5,090,103	29,318	791,586
23	Michigan	101,223	3,036,690	30,714	890,706
24	Wisconsin	250,901	7,401,596	80,159	2,284,548
	WEST NORTH CENTRAL:				
25	Minnesota	109,348	3,171,092	22,266	601,182
26	Iowa	122,268	3,668,040	19,579	518,868
27	Missouri	22,312	658,227	7,497	198,686
28	North Dakota	1,705	47,740	54,066	1,351,650
29	South Dakota	1,980	53,460	54,681	1,230,337
30	Nebraska	8,649	224,874	25,676	513,520
31	Kansas	4,003	104,078	44,726	737,998
	SOUTH ATLANTIC:				
32	Delaware	2,509	75,270	2,508	50,160
33	Maryland	7,016	224,512	1,620	34,020
34	District of Columbia				
35	Virginia	9,248	295,936	1,149	27,006
36	West Virginia	1,249	39,968	172	4,816
37	North Carolina	6,858	205,740	3,140	69,080
38	South Carolina	17	340	676	11,492
39	Georgia			112	2,074
40	Florida				
	EAST SOUTH CENTRAL:				
41	Kentucky	4,593	146,976	3,114	88,759
42	Tennessee	11,371	329,759	37,186	818,092
43	Alabama	197	4,531	2,311	41,598
44	Mississippi	151	3,322	17,523	262,845
	WEST SOUTH CENTRAL:				
45	Arkansas	411	12,330	354	9,558
46	Louisiana			20,767	415,340
47	Oklahoma			3,840	65,280
48	Texas	116	2,552	2,974	50,558
	MOUNTAIN:				
49	Montana	2,035	59,015	23,328	559,872
50	Idaho	62,862	1,697,274	44,640	1,026,720
51	Wyoming	180	4,320	15,821	300,599
52	Colorado	318	9,858	27,252	626,796
53	New Mexico	40	1,000	15,130	308,600
54	Arizona			21,322	657,762
55	Utah	1,241	26,061	61,095	1,221,900
56	Nevada	4	84	185	3,515
	PACIFIC:				
57	Washington	4,400	132,000	880	24,640
58	Oregon	23,917	705,554	16,984	450,080
59	California	74	1,924	41,021	861,441

AND VALUE OF EACH KIND OF SEED, BY DIVISIONS AND STATES: 1919.

| TIMOTHY SEED. | | MILLET SEED. | | OTHER GRASS SEED. | | |
Production (bushels).	Value.	Production (bushels).	Value.	Production (bushels).	Value.	
2,587,268	$13,673,913	1,310,953	$3,682,987	1,909,204	$8,070,206	1
1,360	9,889	98	445	446	2,785	2
33,946	217,854	7,801	23,403	327	1,962	3
431,880	2,446,018	31,810	115,187	798,999	3,329,482	4
2,102,698	10,894,683	696,338	1,423,142	328,143	1,299,121	5
3,651	21,433	1,709	6,474	80,479	403,021	6
820	5,319	49,390	185,241	345,600	1,063,276	7
136	976	83,135	166,407	294,235	1,598,806	8
12,568	76,085	440,559	1,762,236	25,835	153,085	9
209	1,656	113	452	35,140	218,668	10
288	2,118			20	130	11
22	167	2	12	127	826	12
444	3,108	45	203			13
278	2,086	51	230	194	1,164	14
203	1,472			69	449	15
125	938			36	216	16
7,974	55,422	5,474	16,422			17
130	910	125	375			18
25,842	161,522	2,202	6,606	327	1,062	19
122,470	710,328	1,671	6,270	11,899	118,694	20
30,712	181,205	10,513	42,052	19,648	137,536	21
218,668	1,202,693	6,742	23,601	765,927	3,063,708	22
4,125	24,750	7,363	29,452	1,271	8,400	23
55,905	327,042	5,521	13,812	254	1,144	24
358,962	1,866,601	54,715	136,801	300	1,200	25
1,156,531	5,898,314	35,460	70,920	23,761	95,044	26
428,730	2,250,841	21,944	43,888	137,887	434,343	27
47,355	269,924	166,475	332,950	81,039	324,156	28
65,012	341,319	111,007	277,529	1,362	8,309	29
8,838	55,242	97,005	194,010	8,785	68,523	30
37,270	212,442	209,732	367,044	75,009	367,546	31
14	89					32
728	4,259	246	984	2,345	11,725	33
						34
1,852	10,279	727	2,546	73,929	369,645	35
936	5,989	363	1,452	2,157	10,354	36
121	817	227	908	1,850	10,207	37
						38
		146	584	198	1,090	39
						40
549	3,294	961	3,605	321,533	964,599	41
256	1,922	48,334	181,256	24,067	98,677	42
15	103	95	380			43
						44
74	557	91	319	10,293	38,084	45
						46
		36,988	73,976	19,552	106,563	47
62	419	46,056	92,112	264,390	1,454,159	48
637	5,576	1,090	4,360	381	2,098	49
11,272	65,378	304	1,216	101	505	50
18	131	1,116	4,464	1,937	10,656	51
470	3,290	421,765	1,687,060	14,556	87,336	52
		16,063	64,252	6,523	35,879	53
		200	800	2,157	15,531	54
171	1,710	21	84	180	1,080	55
						56
140	1,120			5,071	32,526	57
69	536	63	252	19,210	124,869	58
		50	200	10,859	61,273	59

TABLE 167.—PRODUCTION AND VALUE OF ALL GRASS AND CLOVER SEED, AND VALUE OF FLOWER AND VEGETABLE SEEDS, BY DIVISIONS AND STATES: 1919 AND 1909.

DIVISION AND STATE.	ALL GRASS AND CLOVER SEED.				VALUE OF FLOWER AND VEGETABLE SEEDS.	
	Production (bushels).		Value.			
	1919	1909	1919	1909	1919	1909
United States	7,851,698	6,671,348	$80,843,832	$15,137,683	$8,010,128	$1,411,013
GEOGRAPHIC DIVISIONS:						
New England	2,496	5,451	31,700	10,269	47,649	45,096
Middle Atlantic	92,825	55,137	1,882,124	219,146	63,482	162,607
East North Central	2,242,652	2,157,957	34,599,246	6,320,653	294,747	357,032
West North Central	3,625,935	3,265,021	26,696,698	5,915,510	30,171	116,777
South Atlantic	122,113	78,352	1,471,342	198,638	70,676	18,839
East South Central	472,256	671,790	2,949,718	632,743	8,283	17,485
West South Central	405,968	59,624	2,321,807	223,441		34,104
Mountain	764,715	198,110	8,494,782	1,037,009	247,094	20,689
Pacific	122,738	179,906	2,396,415	580,274	7,248,026	638,384
NEW ENGLAND:						
Maine	462	527	7,423	1,544	200	950
New Hampshire	189	142	2,164	556		1,319
Vermont	657	601	8,095	1,538		2,670
Massachusetts	678	3,397	8,348	4,163	120	291
Rhode Island	298	19	2,796	39	160	2,564
Connecticut	212	765	2,874	2,429	47,169	37,302
MIDDLE ATLANTIC:						
New York	36,235	17,879	791,257	88,239	62,782	72,991
New Jersey	389	12,804	5,761	14,799		53,300
Pennsylvania	56,201	24,454	1,085,106	116,108	700	36,316
EAST NORTH CENTRAL:						
Ohio	309,964	288,605	5,975,159	1,352,136	3,601	67,303
Indiana	202,052	165,488	4,434,256	785,041	4,904	8,414
Illinois	1,193,200	1,289,996	10,171,691	1,719,420		194,626
Michigan	144,696	151,567	3,989,998	964,655	274,756	44,106
Wisconsin	392,740	262,301	10,028,142	1,499,401	11,486	42,583
WEST NORTH CENTRAL:						
Minnesota	545,591	945,666	5,776,876	1,496,438		6,645
Iowa	1,357,599	1,118,044	10,251,186	1,721,289	550	4,853
Missouri	618,370	257,872	3,585,985	756,445		17,726
North Dakota	350,640	74,162	2,326,420	99,024		1,075
South Dakota	234,042	424,623	1,910,954	594,570		25,914
Nebraska	148,953	120,423	1,056,169	451,347	16,645	39,737
Kansas	370,740	324,231	1,789,108	796,397	12,976	20,827
SOUTH ATLANTIC:						
Delaware	5,031	5,878	125,519	29,928		507
Maryland	11,955	15,080	275,500	72,785	2,550	8,792
District of Columbia						
Virginia	86,905	49,031	705,412	74,979		5,583
West Virginia	4,877	2,645	62,579	8,726		190
North Carolina	12,196	2,071	286,752	4,963		2,501
South Carolina	693	314	11,832	459		91
Georgia	456	2,197	3,748	2,508	2,894	975
Florida		1,136		4,290	65,232	200
EAST SOUTH CENTRAL:						
Kentucky	330,750	612,406	1,207,233	538,219	432	15,658
Tennessee	121,214	58,486	1,429,706	92,386	7,851	1,568
Alabama	2,618	537	46,612	1,110		240
Mississippi	17,674	361	266,167	1,028		19
WEST SOUTH CENTRAL:						
Arkansas	11,223	1,180	60,848	4,893		836
Louisiana	20,767	11,268	415,340	30,343		3,083
Oklahoma	60,380	25,825	245,819	149,070		7,253
Texas	313,598	21,351	1,599,800	39,135		22,932
MOUNTAIN:						
Montana	97,471	14,204	630,921	96,103	50,272	760
Idaho	119,179	30,463	2,791,093	172,012	762	5,398
Wyoming	19,072	17,411	320,170	85,120		275
Colorado	464,361	51,208	2,414,340	162,822	190,046	13,505
New Mexico	38,056	9,092	409,731	46,935	6,014	151
Arizona	33,679	22,598	674,093	156,840		
Utah	62,708	52,604	1,250,835	313,814		700
Nevada	189	530	3,599	3,363		10
PACIFIC:						
Washington	10,491	3,355	190,286	9,388	1,774,103	37,571
Oregon	60,243	151,016	1,281,291	364,852	1,300	6,089
California	52,004	25,535	924,838	206,034	5,472,623	594,724

TABLE **168.**—MINOR SEEDS—ACREAGE, PRODUCTION, AND VALUE, BY STATES: 1919 AND 1909.

CROP AND STATE.	ACREAGE.		PRODUCTION.			VALUE.	
	1919	1909	Unit.	1919	1909	1919	1909[1]
United States..............	124,199	80,827	......	....	....	$4,780,967	$740,431
Sorghum seed, total..............	106,963	72,497	Bu...	1,567,716	833,707	2,303,250	544,322
Nebraska......................	4,663	7,209	Bu...	61,750	83,134	101,892	46,899
Kansas........................	62,967	53,706	Bu...	936,688	656,522	1,170,877	404,329
Oklahoma......................	19,187	4,250	Bu...	237,009	30,435	402,917	23,079
Texas..........................	12,059	5,483	Bu...	205,878	38,683	339,707	50,255
Colorado.......................	3,094	704	Bu...	32,629	9,147	68,526	5,799
New Mexico....................	2,820	193	Bu...	61,445	1,021	147,469	1,248
All other states................	2,173	952	Bu...	32,317	14,765	71,862	12,713
Sugar-beet seed, total..............	7,022	....	Lbs..	3,606,947	....	2,012,142	....
Ohio...........................	44	....	Lbs..	34,867	....	17,434	....
Michigan.......................	234	....	Lbs..	96,292	....	57,775	....
Wisconsin......................	61	....	Lbs..	22,000	....	11,000	....
Montana........................	1,713	....	Lbs..	978,302	....	586,981	....
Idaho..........................	2,289	....	Lbs..	477,890	....	286,734	....
Wyoming.......................	60	....	Lbs..	90,000	....	45,000	....
Colorado.......................	1,810	....	Lbs..	1,599,285	....	799,643	....
Utah...........................	52	....	Lbs..	40,500	....	20,250	....
California......................	704	....	Lbs..	266,606	....	186,624	....
All other states................	55	....	Lbs..	1,205	....	701	....
Sunflower seed, total..............	6,614	4,731	Bu...	135,947	63,677	331,708	58,318
Illinois.........................	1,509	3,969	Bu...	29,679	49,004	74,200	44,539
Missouri........................	3,879	29	Bu...	80,161	567	192,387	405
California.......................	778	257	Bu...	19,294	6,855	48,235	6,264
All other states................	448	476	Bu...	6,813	7,251	16,886	7,110
Mustard seed, total..............	2,885	1,964	Lbs..	1,211,549	3,168,270	106,011	100,731
California.......................	2,828	1,964	Lbs..	1,182,934	3,168,270	94,635	100,731
All other states................	57		Lbs..	28,615	....	11,376	....
Broom-corn seed..................	457	1,071	Bu...	4,688	6,833	15,476	14,752
Hemp seed......................	257	563	Bu...	2,724	5,416	10,976	20,007
Tobacco seed....................	1	1	Lbs..	117	389	1,404	1,789

[1] The 1909 value includes the value of anise and golden-seal seed.

TABLE 169.—HAY AND FORAGE—ACREAGE OF THE

	DIVISION AND STATE.	All hay and forage.	HAY CROPS.				
			Total.	Timothy alone.	Timothy and clover mixed.	Clover alone.	Alfalfa.
		Acres.	*Acres.*	*Acres.*	*Acres.*	*Acres.*	*Acres.*
1	United States.........	96,121,228	72,779,888	10,941,347	19,349,405	3,160,415	8,624,811
	GEOGRAPHIC DIVISIONS:						
2	New England...........	3,573,729	3,381,095	459,570	1,812,821	24,601	5,147
3	Middle Atlantic.........	9,657,707	8,181,183	1,867,228	5,000,059	213,191	165,788
4	East North Central.....	20,374,731	14,204,086	4,501,431	6,547,231	1,399,487	389,543
5	West North Central.....	33,310,118	26,570,517	2,972,773	3,718,398	636,911	3,419,916
6	South Atlantic..........	6,558,551	3,370,687	428,208	971,978	227,043	51,410
7	East South Central......	5,024,855	3,419,269	319,741	475,087	453,349	113,364
8	West South Central.....	5,674,934	2,849,163	35,480	92,366	72,366	475,619
9	Mountain................	7,450,216	6,479,390	262,729	452,118	47,317	2,846,067
10	Pacific.................	4,496,387	4,324,498	94,187	279,347	86,150	1,157,957
	NEW ENGLAND:						
11	Maine..................	1,245,699	1,227,080	153,059	722,210	9,387	730
12	New Hampshire........	465,303	449,459	63,929	197,567	2,819	379
13	Vermont...............	991,757	926,366	113,469	626,541	5,580	1,765
14	Massachusetts.........	466,330	421,533	78,407	159,212	3,513	1,163
15	Rhode Island..........	50,490	43,984	9,360	17,242	303	110
16	Connecticut............	354,150	312,673	41,346	90,049	2,999	1,000
	MIDDLE ATLANTIC:						
17	New York..............	5,502,943	4,987,520	820,573	3,169,673	121,959	119,783
18	New Jersey............	387,642	291,739	74,714	135,998	9,497	15,232
19	Pennsylvania..........	3,767,122	2,901,924	971,941	1,694,388	81,735	30,773
	EAST NORTH CENTRAL:						
20	Ohio...................	4,917,259	3,026,527	1,436,301	1,190,646	250,010	94,418
21	Indiana................	3,303,056	2,013,983	807,501	650,045	334,974	62,351
22	Illinois................	4,013,476	3,014,762	1,021,517	837,838	507,443	88,968
23	Michigan...............	3,644,952	2,866,726	655,784	1,852,789	120,299	74,059
24	Wisconsin..............	4,495,988	3,282,088	580,328	2,015,913	186,761	69,747
	WEST NORTH CENTRAL:						
25	Minnesota..............	5,029,397	4,119,696	514,658	938,045	96,202	45,410
26	Iowa...................	4,555,824	3,582,145	808,390	1,704,997	273,912	172,043
27	Missouri...............	4,206,473	2,867,380	1,166,742	850,995	173,428	151,720
28	North Dakota..........	4,035,803	3,702,323	189,553	20,634	10,791	58,356
29	South Dakota..........	5,071,747	4,556,639	115,531	66,621	14,465	462,231
30	Nebraska..............	5,410,808	4,798,363	53,067	93,063	41,277	1,214,649
31	Kansas................	5,000,066	2,943,971	124,832	44,043	26,836	1,315,507
	SOUTH ATLANTIC:						
32	Delaware..............	201,365	70,996	9,830	31,562	12,253	1,878
33	Maryland..............	622,939	385,200	83,458	204,997	41,250	11,909
34	District of Columbia....	805	507	67	68	....	127
35	Virginia...............	1,773,650	856,257	91,147	371,396	79,956	24,348
36	West Virginia..........	910,550	701,236	229,249	314,226	16,441	4,548
37	North Carolina.........	992,374	472,421	10,976	47,373	73,355	3,240
38	South Carolina.........	668,538	333,801	1,355	496	960	2,621
39	Georgia................	1,248,814	460,332	2,106	1,860	2,828	2,725
40	Florida................	139,516	89,937	20·	....	....	14
	EAST SOUTH CENTRAL:						
41	Kentucky..............	2,084,909	1,073,222	237,568	256,158	107,266	56,211
42	Tennessee.............	1,751,123	1,382,067	78,187	213,231	239,596	16,917
43	Alabama...............	705,279	530,226	2,297	2,664	8,554	9,932
44	Mississippi............	483,544	433,754	1,689	3,034	97,933	30,304
	WEST SOUTH CENTRAL:						
45	Arkansas..............	1,002,333	759,658	23,774	85,749	32,526	61,457
46	Louisiana.............	208,631	196,521	1,489	1,376	35,463	8,289
47	Oklahoma.............	2,073,513	1,148,976	4,915	4,787	3,657	347,607
48	Texas.................	2,390,457	744,008	5,302	454	720	58,266
	MOUNTAIN:						
49	Montana...............	1,675,472	1,608,836	80,768	140,812	13,166	374,233
50	Idaho.................	1,189,220	1,169,871	82,574	102,113	20,383	651,172
51	Wyoming..............	832,482	795,610	30,429	33,716	3,847	330,094
52	Colorado...............	2,213,736	1,607,741	44,548	124,849	4,000	781,663
53	New Mexico............	436,547	223,621	6,298	2,418	1,400	116,926
54	Arizona................	197,498	152,600	309	368	193	109,633
55	Utah..................	549,967	538,295	13,343	33,164	2,849	365,190
56	Nevada................	353,300	352,786	4,460	14,678	777	117,156
	PACIFIC:						
57	Washington............	1,064,130	1,008,871	50,536	145,252	17,795	228,787
58	Oregon................	1,229,404	1,177,215	30,689	81,819	53,128	210,655
59	California.............	2,202,853	2,138,412	12,962	52,276	15,227	718,515

DIFFERENT CROPS, BY DIVISIONS AND STATES: 1919.

HAY CROPS—continued.				FORAGE CROPS.				
Other tame grasses.	Small grains cut for hay.	Annual legumes cut for hay.	Wild, salt, or prairie grasses.	Silage crops.	Kafir, sorghum, etc., for forage.	Corn cut for forage.	Root crops for forage.	
Acres. 6,055,657	*Acres.* 5,674,854	*Acres.* 1,846,914	*Acres.* 17,126,485	*Acres.* 4,003,226	*Acres.* 4,746,849	*Acres.* 14,502,932	*Acres.* 88,333	1
933,034	77,449	9,722	58,751	121,955	604	60,790	9,285	2
707,972	110,499	12,050	104,396	506,984	4,834	954,536	10,170	3
547,817	238,051	105,549	474,977	1,817,953	18,581	4,309,509	24,602	4
1,054,501	1,236,196	111,413	13,420,409	1,135,829	1,533,641	4,060,105	10,026	5
623,532	279,576	686,738	102,202	104,583	105,616	2,974,809	2,856	6
1,021,677	296,633	600,406	139,012	82,141	102,072	1,417,683	3,690	7
604,474	466,399	230,536	871,923	65,542	2,413,421	345,175	1,633	8
378,512	940,200	32,502	1,519,945	82,633	552,243	329,104	6,846	9
184,138	2,029,851	57,998	434,870	85,606	15,837	51,221	19,225	10
309,895	15,100	2,537	14,162	10,687	114	6,255	1,563	11
161,651	11,138	1,371	10,605	9,891	115	5,426	412	12
147,731	17,234	1,275	12,771	49,872	67	12,847	2,605	13
149,597	16,581	1,370	11,690	23,997	182	17,266	3,352	14
12,577	2,959	736	697	2,557	19	3,588	342	15
151,583	14,437	2,433	8,826	24,951	107	15,408	1,011	16
595,829	88,708	5,465	65,530	329,314	1,601	177,833	6,675	17
25,845	9,222	3,000	18,231	17,995	352	76,405	1,151	18
86,298	12,569	3,585	20,635	159,675	2,881	700,298	2,344	19
26,335	19,751	5,670	3,396	224,469	5,067	1,659,177	2,019	20
58,216	61,181	18,550	21,165	234,100	6,062	1,048,464	447	21
355,360	69,557	69,903	64,176	321,068	5,970	671,285	391	22
47,931	59,454	6,554	49,856	348,254	49	418,031	11,892	23
59,975	28,108	4,872	336,384	690,062	1,433	512,552	9,853	24
204,631	89,369	6,110	2,225,271	282,675	6,410	614,598	6,018	25
73,105	46,839	7,419	495,440	298,645	20,052	653,872	1,110	26
141,061	189,857	46,515	147,062	131,192	155,202	1,051,698	1,001	27
264,430	647,888	28,210	2,482,461	48,843	5,893	278,455	289	28
94,757	109,107	4,777	3,689,150	53,502	25,745	435,861	....	29
150,034	80,087	7,735	3,158,451	53,525	284,076	273,586	1,258	30
126,483	73,049	10,647	1,222,574	267,447	1,036,263	752,035	350	31
4,212	3,056	7,138	1,067	2,944	25	127,358	42	32
17,842	6,357	15,114	4,273	15,646	2,086	219,684	323	33
98	99	48	....	145	2	138	13	34
108,202	55,752	112,570	12,886	45,656	7,697	863,684	356	35
90,216	26,298	9,077	11,181	23,859	2,650	182,709	96	36
114,207	59,395	121,962	41,913	4,386	21,314	493,612	641	37
88,986	64,982	168,462	5,939	2,188	16,580	315,969	....	38
149,129	56,855	226,733	18,096	6,702	52,466	728,844	470	39
50,640	6,782	25,634	6,847	3,057	2,796	42,811	915	40
260,517	98,172	35,020	22,310	36,916	43,073	931,451	247	41
371,995	129,171	279,571	53,399	30,574	43,011	293,227	2,244	42
211,210	54,364	217,469	23,736	5,511	5,201	163,508	833	43
177,955	14,926	68,346	39,567	9,140	10,787	29,497	366	44
148,023	193,154	76,593	138,382	5,969	88,184	147,376	1,146	45
54,709	6,260	74,916	14,019	3,938	1,834	5,910	428	46
140,278	94,359	21,853	531,520	24,718	826,640	73,179	....	47
261,464	172,626	57,174	188,002	30,917	1,496,763	118,710	59	48
75,548	466,727	6,381	451,201	1,917	2,657	61,137	925	49
21,120	167,531	3,881	121,097	8,527	233	8,205	2,384	50
66,931	101,294	2,310	227,019	1,199	1,431	33,895	317	51
126,041	132,136	12,764	411,107	56,126	342,341	177,993	1,529	52
23,420	26,784	3,426	42,880	3,541	176,387	32,293	705	53
9,504	23,093	1,136	8,364	7,254	28,946	8,677	21	54
25,388	15,589	1,830	80,942	3,890	211	6,638	933	55
30,560	7,046	774	177,335	179	37	266	32	56
51,953	477,081	7,412	30,055	22,540	620	24,725	7,374	57
82,349	467,390	24,723	226,462	33,545	698	12,835	5,111	58
49,836	1,085,380	25,863	178,353	29,521	14,519	13,661	6,740	59

TABLE 170.—HAY AND FORAGE—PRODUCTION OF THE

	DIVISION AND STATE.	All hay and forage.	HAY CROPS.				
			Total.	Timothy alone.	Timothy and clover mixed.	Clover alone.	Alfalfa.
		Tons.	*Tons.*	*Tons.*	*Tons.*	*Tons.*	*Tons.*
1	United States...	146, 343, 241	90, 355, 540	12, 799, 430	25, 341, 786	4, 147, 050	18, 853, 133
	GEOGRAPHIC DIVISIONS:						
2	New England......	5, 308, 632	3, 861, 503	576, 239	2, 168, 421	37, 037	10, 993
3	Middle Atlantic....	16, 359, 065	10, 159, 859	2, 305, 751	6, 231, 216	323, 382	357, 687
4	East North Central.	37, 693, 623	17, 849, 999	5, 266, 506	8, 673, 285	1, 731, 755	778, 559
5	West North Central	48, 192, 328	30, 847, 467	3, 440, 185	5, 448, 170	961, 277	6, 465, 070
6	South Atlantic.....	5, 919, 058	3, 342, 374	431, 979	1, 050, 285	263, 998	106, 894
7	East South Central.	5, 158, 646	3, 452, 358	334, 223	549, 239	511, 631	192, 994
8	West South Central	8, 036, 383	3, 602, 104	39, 383	99, 445	90, 300	962, 860
9	Mountain..........	10, 969, 034	9, 469, 375	260, 936	604, 292	63, 015	6, 317, 186
10	Pacific.............	8, 706, 472	7, 770, 501	144, 228	517, 433	164, 655	3, 660, 890
	NEW ENGLAND:						
11	Maine.............	1, 326, 289	1, 206, 323	167, 369	727, 382	12, 221	944
12	New Hampshire...	606, 713	480, 615	77, 542	224, 332	3, 719	707
13	Vermont..........	1, 748, 358	1, 211, 240	147, 613	857, 575	9, 958	3, 914
14	Massachusetts....	871, 573	546, 011	112, 817	221, 379	5, 463	2, 604
15	Rhode Island......	90, 926	54, 522	12, 565	22, 005	526	304
16	Connecticut.......	664, 773	362, 792	58, 333	115, 748	5, 150	2, 520
	MIDDLE ATLANTIC:						
17	New York.........	9, 728, 317	6, 264, 685	1, 089, 244	3, 979, 322	196, 007	257, 785
18	New Jersey........	674, 479	394, 865	87, 983	192, 220	12, 569	35, 576
19	Pennsylvania.....	5, 956, 269	3, 500, 309	1, 128, 524	2, 059, 674	114, 806	64, 326
	EAST NORTH CENTRAL:						
20	Ohio..............	7, 661, 890	3, 716, 036	1, 702, 031	1, 467, 155	300, 680	187, 904
21	Indiana...........	5, 133, 742	2, 280, 863	910, 677	747, 656	356, 255	107, 485
22	Illinois...........	7, 063, 254	3, 637, 380	1, 135, 456	1, 189, 588	627, 868	214, 670
23	Michigan..........	6, 345, 510	3, 172, 012	718, 012	2, 044, 711	131, 517	118, 571
24	Wisconsin.........	11, 489, 227	5, 043, 708	800, 330	3, 224, 175	315, 435	149, 929
	WEST NORTH CENTRAL:						
25	Minnesota.........	9, 291, 671	5, 665, 616	656, 023	1, 543, 144	173, 853	115, 327
26	Iowa.............	9, 327, 772	5, 348, 102	1, 014, 218	2, 653, 076	427, 693	438, 338
27	Missouri..........	5, 687, 127	3, 358, 316	1, 234, 030	958, 991	232, 079	365, 036
28	North Dakota.....	3, 765, 377	2, 929, 651	172, 757	20, 957	12, 789	75, 348
29	South Dakota.....	4, 996, 846	3, 917, 259	131, 094	87, 341	19, 624	763, 316
30	Nebraska.........	6, 619, 001	5, 307, 720	69, 940	127, 578	59, 960	2, 219, 549
31	Kansas...........	8, 504, 534	4, 320, 803	162, 123	57, 083	35, 279	2, 488, 156
	SOUTH ATLANTIC:						
32	Delaware..........	223, 562	88, 857	10, 697	33, 593	20, 033	4, 780
33	Maryland.........	806, 910	444, 894	91, 981	226, 366	52, 166	25, 142
34	Dist. of Columbia..	2, 410	845	114	109		266
35	Virginia..........	1, 989, 282	944, 693	97, 791	413, 746	93, 990	50, 472
36	West Virginia.....	1, 099, 679	692, 852	217, 636	326, 147	18, 359	9, 122
37	North Carolina....	688, 843	449, 298	10, 163	47, 648	75, 579	5, 769
38	South Carolina....	400, 343	274, 816	1, 383	736	1, 009	5, 896
39	Georgia...........	608, 597	375, 010	2, 194	1, 940	2, 862	5, 412
40	Florida...........	99, 432	71, 109	20			35
	EAST SOUTH CENTRAL:						
41	Kentucky..........	2, 123, 490	1, 085, 318	243, 412	278, 634	120, 664	81, 298
42	Tennessee.........	1, 907, 345	1, 401, 646	86, 726	263, 514	258, 654	33, 237
43	Alabama..........	542, 557	443, 525	2, 376	3, 196	8, 529	13, 105
44	Mississippi........	585, 254	521, 869	1, 709	3, 895	123, 784	65, 354
	WEST SOUTH CENTRAL:						
45	Arkansas..........	989, 780	771, 853	24, 693	91, 214	36, 635	128, 147
46	Louisiana.........	278, 556	247, 999	1, 702	1, 898	48, 418	17, 224
47	Oklahoma.........	3, 038, 396	1, 582, 623	6, 190	5, 842	4, 362	680, 446
48	Texas.............	3, 729, 651	999, 629	6, 798	491	885	137, 043
	MOUNTAIN:						
49	Montana..........	1, 382, 946	1, 334, 336	62, 679	150, 433	13, 648	586, 683
50	Idaho.............	2, 330, 543	2, 247, 758	72, 682	118, 808	30, 348	1, 741, 165
51	Wyoming.........	907, 287	873, 685	20, 179	41, 864	4, 020	514, 168
52	Colorado..........	3, 580, 123	2, 762, 102	61, 865	213, 141	7, 205	1, 779, 005
53	New Mexico.......	693, 807	394, 007	7, 664	3, 418	9, 096	278, 595
54	Arizona..........	494, 686	393, 156	411	530	272	337, 622
55	Utah.............	1, 031, 609	978, 332	21, 077	53, 993	4, 043	748, 949
56	Nevada...........	548, 033	545, 639	5, 079	20, 045	1, 193	330, 999
	PACIFIC:						
57	Washington........	2, 013, 913	1, 750, 420	79, 269	306, 480	37, 108	655, 876
58	Oregon............	2, 197, 619	1, 908, 393	45, 570	135, 625	102, 953	592, 460
59	California.........	4, 494, 940	4, 111, 688	19, 389	75, 328	24, 594	2, 412, 554

DIFFERENT CROPS, BY DIVISIONS AND STATES: 1919.

HAY CROPS—continued.				FORAGE CROPS.				
Other tame grasses.	Small grains cut for hay.	Annual legumes cut for hay.	Wild, salt, or prairie grasses.	Silage crops.	Kafir, sorghum, etc., for forage.	Corn cut for forage.	Root crops for forage.	
Tons. 6,403,805	Tons. 5,462,853	Tons. 1,716,195	Tons. 15,631,288	Tons. 29,682,041	Tons. 7,912,973	Tons. 17,793,742	Tons. 598,945	1
861,379	136,826	11,914	58,694	1,210,345	1,224	189,277	46,283	2
649,380	159,357	16,940	116,146	4,905,395	9,302	1,217,133	67,376	3
493,838	234,229	100,171	571,656	13,934,969	29,387	5,750,163	129,105	4
1,409,346	1,012,353	114,855	11,996,211	7,077,333	3,005,536	7,216,080	45,912	5
553,609	233,813	596,404	105,392	802,492	75,214	1,692,109	6,869	6
963,048	246,207	529,155	125,861	476,274	173,286	1,051,480	5,248	7
783,452	450,351	228,899	947,414	329,882	3,850,121	250,492	3,784	8
388,282	574,575	37,309	1,223,780	400,450	738,187	326,889	34,133	9
301,471	2,415,142	80,548	486,134	544,901	30,716	100,119	260,235	10
258,499	24,635	2,667	12,606	87,634	244	22,817	9,271	11
141,754	20,938	1,492	10,131	104,954	272	18,755	2,117	12
144,643	32,586	1,805	13,146	475,161	177	51,850	9,930	13
156,813	32,022	2,302	12,611	256,053	345	50,668	18,496	14
12,727	4,694	1,061	640	26,341	22	8,201	1,840	15
146,943	21,951	2,587	9,560	260,202	164	36,986	4,629	16
533,595	130,133	7,711	70,888	3,157,185	4,567	255,972	45,908	17
28,474	11,719	4,289	22,035	157,872	539	115,976	5,227	18
87,311	17,505	4,940	23,223	1,590,338	4,196	845,185	16,241	19
25,011	20,875	7,974	4,406	1,906,206	7,152	2,023,982	8,514	20
53,977	65,399	18,361	21,053	1,616,509	10,074	1,222,679	3,617	21
281,281	64,247	59,930	64,340	2,325,010	8,689	1,090,178	1,997	22
50,581	44,389	6,260	57,971	2,551,806	87	566,932	54,673	23
82,988	39,319	7,646	423,886	5,535,438	3,385	846,392	60,304	24
327,089	105,859	9,826	2,734,495	2,200,973	16,675	1,375,982	32,425	25
111,967	66,004	10,619	626,187	2,334,676	57,207	1,583,457	4,330	26
141,026	205,460	43,467	178,227	658,035	339,186	1,329,157	2,433	27
324,640	387,290	22,567	1,913,303	200,624	14,041	619,970	1,091	28
115,121	75,422	4,928	2,720,413	291,599	53,274	734,714	....	29
207,725	81,537	8,714	2,532,717	264,246	596,455	446,949	3,631	30
181,778	90,781	14,734	1,290,869	1,127,180	1,928,698	1,125,851	2,002	31
5,890	3,758	8,791	1,315	15,228	63	119,206	208	32
18,001	7,746	19,162	4,330	125,417	1,950	233,779	870	33
163	138	55	....	1,351	4	145	65	34
105,517	51,415	120,171	11,591	380,855	8,350	654,444	940	35
79,328	20,767	11,351	10,142	199,980	2,967	203,400	480	36
107,769	52,714	99,243	50,413	28,931	12,607	196,848	1,159	37
77,539	49,692	133,021	5,540	10,512	12,543	102,472	....	38
114,819	42,851	189,125	15,807	27,040	33,278	172,501	768	39
44,583	4,732	15,485	6,254	13,178	3,452	9,314	2,379	40
226,792	81,645	33,281	19,592	210,049	72,571	755,054	498	41
325,183	103,093	284,942	46,297	201,406	73,682	228,033	2,578	42
206,389	45,405	143,834	20,691	27,059	13,189	57,455	1,329	43
204,684	16,064	67,098	39,281	37,760	13,844	10,938	843	44
142,435	135,971	66,705	146,053	26,162	107,371	82,852	1,542	45
70,045	6,372	83,083	19,257	21,058	4,149	3,563	1,787	46
188,265	109,524	27,252	560,742	99,901	1,264,090	91,782	....	47
382,707	198,484	51,859	221,362	182,761	2,474,511	72,295	455	48
64,179	170,960	4,655	281,099	7,769	3,300	33,482	4,059	49
25,144	139,881	3,491	116,239	55,256	514	16,622	10,393	50
59,542	49,578	1,841	173,193	6,450	966	24,748	1,438	51
131,544	125,221	17,577	364,904	238,346	440,282	191,600	7,433	52
26,571	34,282	3,620	37,511	16,609	248,540	32,996	1,655	53
15,422	29,609	1,488	7,802	42,963	44,108	14,344	115	54
33,481	17,585	4,046	95,158	31,380	360	12,623	8,914	55
32,399	7,459	591	147,874	1,677	117	474	126	56
90,913	536,868	10,727	33,179	154,832	1,334	40,740	66,587	57
143,191	581,467	39,764	267,363	182,156	4,837	34,412	67,821	58
67,367	1,296,807	30,057	185,592	207,913	24,545	24,967	125,827	59

TABLE 171.—HAY—ACREAGE, PRODUCTION, AND

[A minus sign (−)

DIVISION AND STATE.	ACREAGE.			PRODUCTION (TONS).		
	1919	1909	Per cent of increase.	1919	1909	Per cent of increase.
United States	72,779,888	68,227,310	6.7	90,355,540	87,216,351	3.6
GEOGRAPHIC DIVISIONS:						
New England	3,381,095	3,680,573	−8.1	3,861,503	3,702,132	4.3
Middle Atlantic	8,181,183	8,181,113	(¹)	10,159,859	8,936,001	13.7
East North Central	14,204,086	14,082,093	0.9	17,849,999	18,335,732	−2.6
West North Central	26,570,517	26,082,578	1.9	30,847,467	33,455,116	−7.8
South Atlantic	3,370,687	2,756,054	22.3	3,342,374	2,758,623	21.2
East South Central	3,419,269	2,388,132	43.2	3,452,358	2,448,368	41.0
West South Central	2,849,163	2,239,702	27.2	3,602,104	2,307,561	56.1
Mountain	6,479,390	4,654,302	39.2	9,469,375	8,225,417	15.1
Pacific	4,324,498	4,162,763	3.9	7,770,501	7,047,401	10.3
NEW ENGLAND:						
Maine	1,227,080	1,243,198	−1.3	1,206,323	1,030,906	17.0
New Hampshire	449,459	517,096	−13.1	480,615	473,633	1.5
Vermont	926,366	975,177	−5.0	1,211,240	1,049,454	15.4
Massachusetts	421,533	498,024	−15.4	546,011	643,823	−15.2
Rhode Island	43,984	59,602	−26.2	54,522	72,258	−24.5
Connecticut	312,673	387,476	−19.3	362,792	432,058	−16.0
MIDDLE ATLANTIC:						
New York	4,987,520	4,783,592	4.3	6,264,685	5,171,964	21.1
New Jersey	291,739	391,326	−25.4	394,865	511,338	−22.8
Pennsylvania	2,901,924	3,006,195	−3.5	3,500,309	3,252,699	7.6
EAST NORTH CENTRAL:						
Ohio	3,026,527	3,184,331	−5.0	3,716,036	4,076,609	−8.8
Indiana	2,013,983	2,098,256	−4.0	2,280,863	2,527,391	−9.8
Illinois	3,014,762	3,216,575	−6.3	3,637,380	4,061,065	−10.4
Michigan	2,866,726	2,625,193	9.2	3,172,012	3,247,282	−2.3
Wisconsin	3,282,088	2,957,738	11.0	5,043,708	4,423,385	14.0
WEST NORTH CENTRAL:						
Minnesota	4,119,696	3,823,895	7.7	5,665,616	5,631,168	0.6
Iowa	3,582,145	4,869,041	−26.4	5,348,102	7,312,591	−26.9
Missouri	2,867,380	3,463,891	−17.2	3,358,316	3,816,836	−12.0
North Dakota	3,702,323	2,820,969	31.2	2,929,651	2,902,351	0.9
South Dakota	4,556,639	3,403,206	33.9	3,917,259	3,573,286	9.6
Nebraska	4,798,363	4,397,746	9.1	5,307,720	5,545,437	−4.3
Kansas	2,943,971	3,303,830	−10.9	4,320,803	4,673,447	−7.5
SOUTH ATLANTIC:						
Delaware	70,996	79,788	−11.0	88,857	99,228	−10.5
Maryland	385,200	387,507	−0.6	444,894	440,464	1.0
District of Columbia	507	666	−23.9	845	1,485	−43.1
Virginia	856,257	750,572	14.1	944,693	780,109	21.1
West Virginia	701,236	698,016	0.5	692,852	622,768	11.3
North Carolina	472,421	359,990	31.2	449,298	353,950	26.9
South Carolina	333,801	201,672	65.5	274,816	176,891	55.4
Georgia	460,332	228,642	101.3	375,010	232,182	61.5
Florida	89,937	49,201	82.8	71,109	51,546	38.0
EAST SOUTH CENTRAL:						
Kentucky	1,073,222	924,469	16.1	1,085,318	913,747	18.8
Tennessee	1,382,067	1,023,671	35.0	1,401,646	1,038,004	35.0
Alabama	530,226	220,112	140.9	443,525	230,406	92.5
Mississippi	433,754	219,880	97.3	521,869	266,211	96.0
WEST SOUTH CENTRAL:						
Arkansas	759,658	408,867	85.8	771,853	430,817	79.2
Louisiana	196,521	179,182	9.7	247,999	242,507	2.3
Oklahoma	1,148,976	1,030,272	11.5	1,582,623	1,064,708	48.6
Texas	744,008	621,381	19.7	999,629	569,529	75.5
MOUNTAIN:						
Montana	1,608,836	1,133,975	41.9	1,334,336	1,689,763	−21.0
Idaho	1,169,871	731,688	59.9	2,247,758	1,679,514	19.3
Wyoming	790,040	581,700	35.8	870,905	817,442	3.1
Colorado	1,637,741	1,179,604	38.8	2,702,462	2,042,569	32.3
New Mexico	223,621	177,377	26.1	394,007	331,683	18.8
Arizona	152,600	97,244	56.9	393,156	235,991	66.6
Utah	538,295	402,248	33.8	978,332	977,265	0.1
Nevada	352,786	350,401	0.7	545,639	521,184	4.7
PACIFIC:						
Washington	1,008,871	730,724	38.1	1,750,420	1,349,834	29.7
Oregon	1,177,215	928,572	26.8	1,908,393	1,521,634	25.4
California	2,138,412	2,503,467	−14.6	4,111,688	4,175,933	−1.5

¹ Less than one-tenth of 1 per cent.

VALUE, BY DIVISIONS AND STATES: 1919 AND 1909.

denotes decrease.]

DIVISION AND STATE.	AVERAGE YIELD PER ACRE (TONS).		VALUE.		AVERAGE VALUE PER TON.	
	1919	1909	1919	1909	1919	1909
United States............	1.24	1.28	$1,953,149,124	$776,067,880	$21.62	$8.90
GEOGRAPHIC DIVISIONS:						
New England..............	1.14	1.01	96,309,865	54,582,556	24.94	14.74
Middle Atlantic............	1.24	1.09	249,060,888	120,562,756	24.51	13.49
East North Central.........	1.26	1.30	427,758,698	177,069,502	23.96	9.66
West North Central.........	1.16	1.28	521,108,598	200,062,426	16.89	5.98
South Atlantic.............	0.99	1.00	96,356,002	36,671,972	28.83	13.29
East South Central.........	1.01	1.03	99,847,621	28,774,256	28.92	11.75
West South Central.........	1.26	1.03	80,089,389	21,024,615	22.23	9.11
Mountain..................	1.46	1.77	208,524,482	64,068,168	22.02	7.79
Pacific...................	1.80	1.69	174,093,581	73,251,629	22.40	10.39
NEW ENGLAND:						
Maine.....................	0.98	0.83	28,321,975	14,703,218	23.48	14.26
New Hampshire............	1.07	0.92	12,388,144	7,311,629	25.78	15.44
Vermont..................	1.31	1.08	25,714,465	14,293,538	21.23	13.62
Massachusetts.............	1.30	1.29	16,942,627	10,343,734	31.03	16.07
Rhode Island.............	1.24	1.21	1,851,027	1,258,357	33.95	17.41
Connecticut..............	1.16	1.12	11,091,627	6,672,080	30.57	15.44
MIDDLE ATLANTIC:						
New York.................	1.26	1.08	143,962,495	69,408,536	22.98	13.42
New Jersey...............	1.35	1.31	11,320,102	7,377,689	28.67	14.43
Pennsylvania.............	1.21	1.08	93,778,291	43,776,531	26.79	13.46
EAST NORTH CENTRAL:						
Ohio.....................	1.23	1.28	94,431,119	40,915,967	25.41	10.04
Indiana..................	1.13	1.20	54,978,796	23,545,024	24.10	9.32
Illinois.................	1.21	1.26	87,726,056	39,262,810	24.12	9.67
Michigan.................	1.11	1.24	79,194,473	34,670,988	24.97	10.68
Wisconsin................	1.54	1.50	111,428,254	38,674,713	22.09	8.74
WEST NORTH CENTRAL:						
Minnesota................	1.38	1.47	83,335,911	25,223,041	14.71	4.48
Iowa.....................	1.49	1.50	107,990,944	56,893,892	20.19	7.78
Missouri.................	1.17	1.10	72,910,293	32,798,445	21.71	8.59
North Dakota.............	0.79	1.03	46,074,635	11,907,887	15.73	4.10
South Dakota.............	0.86	1.05	58,554,150	14,871,628	14.95	4.16
Nebraska.................	1.11	1.26	84,450,146	30,747,558	15.91	5.54
Kansas...................	1.47	1.41	67,792,519	27,619,975	15.69	5.91
SOUTH ATLANTIC:						
Delaware.................	1.25	1.24	2,539,905	1,156,759	28.58	11.66
Maryland.................	1.15	1.14	12,278,466	5,860,309	27.60	13.30
District of Columbia......	1.67	2.23	24,947	21,713	29.52	14.62
Virginia.................	1.10	1.04	27,175,207	10,032,004	28.77	12.86
West Virginia............	0.99	0.89	19,260,770	7,418,345	27.80	11.91
North Carolina...........	0.95	0.98	13,452,418	4,639,134	29.94	13.11
South Carolina...........	0.82	0.88	8,419,530	3,067,022	30.64	17.34
Georgia..................	0.81	1.02	11,177,826	3,678,007	29.81	15.84
Florida..................	0.79	1.05	2,026,933	798,679	28.50	15.49
EAST SOUTH CENTRAL:						
Kentucky.................	1.01	0.99	31,980,480	10,092,777	29.47	11.05
Tennessee................	1.01	1.01	42,261,210	12,357,011	30.15	11.90
Alabama..................	0.84	1.05	11,827,525	3,107,387	26.67	13.49
Mississippi..............	1.20	1.21	13,778,406	3,217,081	26.40	12.08
WEST SOUTH CENTRAL:						
Arkansas.................	1.02	1.05	19,221,678	4,616,431	24.90	10.72
Louisiana................	1.26	1.35	6,674,757	2,405,446	26.91	9.92
Oklahoma.................	1.38	1.03	31,003,087	7,673,945	19.59	7.21
Texas....................	1.34	0.92	23,189,867	6,328,793	23.20	11.11
MOUNTAIN:						
Montana..................	0.83	1.49	35,419,815	12,323,475	26.54	7.29
Idaho....................	1.92	2.16	49,895,421	12,063,906	22.20	7.64
Wyoming..................	1.10	1.46	20,133,534	6,035,836	23.04	7.12
Colorado.................	1.65	1.73	50,074,525	16,234,092	18.53	7.95
New Mexico...............	1.76	1.87	8,541,119	3,584,383	21.68	10.81
Arizona..................	2.58	2.43	9,428,757	2,397,761	23.98	10.16
Utah.....................	1.82	2.43	24,093,243	7,247,405	24.63	7.42
Nevada...................	1.55	1.49	10,938,068	4,181,310	20.05	8.02
PACIFIC:						
Washington...............	1.74	1.85	44,068,624	16,889,028	25.18	12.51
Oregon...................	1.62	1.64	38,672,162	14,879,496	20.26	9.78
California...............	1.92	1.67	91,352,795	41,483,105	22.22	9.93

TABLE 172.—POTATOES—ACREAGE AND PRODUCTION, BY DIVISIONS AND STATES: 1919 AND 1909.

[A minus sign (−) denotes decrease.]

DIVISION AND STATE.	ACREAGE.			PRODUCTION (BUSHELS).			AVERAGE YIELD PER ACRE (BUSHELS).	
	1919	1909	Per cent of increase.	1919	1909	Per cent of increase.	1919	1909
United States.....	3,251,703	3,668,855	−11.4	290,427,580	389,194,965	−25.4	89.3	106.1
GEOGRAPHIC DIVISIONS:								
New England........	191,901	233,095	−17.7	32,702,026	41,245,977	−20.7	170.4	176.9
Middle Atlantic......	626,917	729,323	−14.0	64,841,838	78,395,736	−17.3	103.4	107.5
East North Central..	848,455	1,106,032	−23.3	64,995,709	111,606,777	−41.8	76.6	100.9
West North Central..	777,551	783,813	−0.8	50,234,408	72,067,551	−30.3	64.6	91.9
South Atlantic.......	273,591	239,762	14.1	26,891,791	22,102,630	21.7	98.3	92.2
East South Central...	102,332	119,541	−14.4	6,659,748	9,816,160	−32.2	65.1	82.1
West South Central..	96,701	117,761	−17.9	6,368,427	7,413,887	−14.1	65.9	63.0
Mountain............	175,763	169,678	3.6	20,110,056	24,232,109	−17.0	114.4	142.8
Pacific..............	158,492	169,850	−6.7	17,623,577	22,314,138	−21.0	111.2	131.4
NEW ENGLAND:								
Maine...............	111,378	135,799	−18.0	25,531,470	28,556,837	−10.6	229.2	210.3
New Hampshire.....	13,334	17,370	−23.2	1,341,978	2,360,241	−43.1	100.6	135.9
Vermont.............	24,182	26,859	−10.0	2,277,387	4,145,630	−45.1	94.2	154.3
Massachusetts.......	21,558	24,459	−11.9	1,885,655	2,946,178	−36.0	87.5	120.5
Rhode Island........	3,149	4,649	−32.3	293,087	552,677	−47.0	93.1	118.9
Connecticut.........	18,300	23,959	−23.6	1,372,449	2,684,414	−48.9	75.0	112.0
MIDDLE ATLANTIC:								
New York...........	310,403	394,319	−21.3	32,470,847	48,597,701	−33.2	104.6	123.2
New Jersey..........	82,533	72,991	13.1	10,319,306	8,057,424	28.1	125.0	110.4
Pennsylvania........	233,981	262,013	−10.7	22,051,685	21,740,611	1.4	94.2	83.0
EAST NORTH CENTRAL:								
Ohio...............	124,917	212,808	−41.3	7,513,960	20,322,984	−63.0	60.2	95.5
Indiana.............	62,192	99,504	−37.5	2,477,034	8,905,679	−72.2	39.8	89.5
Illinois.............	86,384	138,052	−37.4	4,699,134	12,166,091	−61.4	54.4	88.1
Michigan...........	280,538	365,483	−23.2	23,929,560	38,243,828	−37.4	85.3	104.6
Wisconsin...........	294,424	290,185	1.5	26,376,021	31,968,195	−17.5	89.6	110.2
WEST NORTH CENTRAL:								
Minnesota..........	331,930	223,692	48.4	26,690,056	26,802,948	−0.4	80.4	119.8
Iowa...............	97,336	169,567	−42.6	4,438,515	14,710,247	−69.8	45.6	86.8
Missouri............	66,051	96,259	−31.4	4,057,753	7,796,410	−48.0	61.4	81.0
North Dakota.......	82,561	54,067	52.7	4,717,556	5,551,430	−15.0	57.1	102.7
South Dakota.......	58,180	50,052	16.2	2,863,186	3,441,692	−16.8	49.2	68.8
Nebraska...........	94,247	111,151	−15.2	4,452,497	8,117,775	−45.2	47.2	73.0
Kansas.............	47,246	79,025	−40.2	3,014,845	5,647,049	−46.6	63.8	71.5
SOUTH ATLANTIC:								
Delaware...........	8,255	9,703	−14.9	487,668	880,360	−44.6	59.1	90.7
Maryland...........	46,837	39,299	19.2	4,918,766	3,444,311	42.8	105.0	87.6
District of Columbia.	265	226	17.3	19,799	32,028	−38.2	74.7	141.7
Virginia............	105,789	86,927	21.7	12,263,374	8,770,778	39.8	115.9	100.9
West Virginia.......	34,526	42,621	−19.0	2,809,398	4,077,066	−31.1	81.4	95.7
North Carolina......	35,797	31,990	11.9	2,853,797	2,372,260	20.3	79.7	74.2
South Carolina......	13,402	8,610	55.7	1,077,936	782,430	37.8	80.4	90.9
Georgia............	11,195	11,877	−5.7	693,857	886,430	−21.7	62.0	74.6
Florida.............	17,525	8,509	106.0	1,767,196	856,967	106.2	100.8	100.7
EAST SOUTH CENTRAL:								
Kentucky...........	50,069	55,750	−10.2	3,131,377	5,120,141	−38.8	62.5	91.8
Tennessee..........	29,873	40,963	−27.1	1,990,951	2,922,713	−31.9	66.6	71.4
Alabama...........	13,397	14,486	−7.5	886,450	1,128,564	−21.5	66.2	77.9
Mississippi.........	8,993	8,342	7.8	650,970	644,742	1.0	72.4	77.3
WEST SOUTH CENTRAL:								
Arkansas...........	24,128	29,719	−18.8	1,765,277	2,096,893	−15.8	73.2	70.6
Louisiana..........	19,677	19,655	0.1	971,705	1,183,525	−17.9	49.4	60.2
Oklahoma..........	25,633	32,295	−20.6	1,924,194	1,897,486	1.4	75.1	58.8
Texas.............	27,263	36,092	−24.5	1,707,251	2,235,983	−23.6	62.6	62.0
MOUNTAIN:								
Montana...........	22,178	20,710	7.1	1,659,017	3,240,696	−48.8	74.8	156.5
Idaho..............	43,196	28,341	52.4	6,300,835	4,710,262	33.8	145.9	166.2
Wyoming...........	11,791	8,333	41.5	851,253	932,162	−8.7	72.2	111.9
Colorado...........	77,337	85,839	−9.9	8,874,783	11,780,674	−24.7	114.8	137.2
New Mexico........	3,070	6,230	−50.7	110,740	295,255	−62.5	36.1	47.4
Arizona............	2,505	1,151	117.6	174,301	97,141	79.4	69.6	84.4
Utah..............	12,047	14,210	−15.2	1,648,400	2,409,093	−31.6	136.8	169.5
Nevada............	3,639	4,864	−25.2	490,727	766,826	−36.0	134.9	157.7
PACIFIC:								
Washington.........	55,132	57,897	−4.8	5,866,710	7,667,171	−23.5	106.4	132.4
Oregon.............	40,055	44,265	−9.5	3,538,930	4,822,962	−26.6	88.4	109.0
California..........	63,305	67,688	−6.5	8,217,937	9,824,005	−16.3	129.8	145.1

TABLE 173.—POTATOES—FARMS REPORTING AND VALUE, BY DIVISIONS AND STATES: 1919 AND 1909.

DIVISION AND STATE.	FARMS REPORTING.				VALUE.		AVERAGE VALUE PER BUSHEL.	
	Number.		Per cent of all farms.					
	1919	1909	1919	1909	1919	1909	1919	1909
United States.......	2,887,992	3,179,907	44.8	50.0	$639,440,521	$166,423,910	$2.20	$0.43
GEOGRAPHIC DIVISIONS:								
New England..........	120,257	149,312	76.8	79.1	68,958,572	17,456,938	2.11	0.42
Middle Atlantic........	359,794	400,285	84.6	85.5	138,893,994	37,292,509	2.14	0.48
East North Central.....	711,015	865,452	65.5	77.0	144,724,922	37,427,211	2.23	0.34
West North Central....	696,565	782,450	63.5	70.5	113,474,008	30,088,015	2.26	0.42
South Atlantic.........	338,828	350,428	29.2	31.5	60,286,602	14,091,735	2.24	0.64
East South Central.....	278,875	307,436	26.5	29.5	16,108,988	5,940,784	2.42	0.61
West South Central....	234,224	189,999	23.5	20.1	14,080,043	5,439,504	2.21	0.73
Mountain..............	76,146	65,085	31.2	35.5	44,260,285	8,715,380	2.20	0.36
Pacific................	72,288	69,460	30.9	36.6	38,653,107	9,971,834	2.19	0.45
NEW ENGLAND:								
Maine.................	36,896	49,381	76.5	82.3	52,339,514	10,224,714	2.05	0.36
New Hampshire.......	16,152	21,899	78.7	80.9	2,952,351	1,204,626	2.20	0.51
Vermont..............	24,581	27,848	84.5	85.1	5,010,252	1,743,049	2.20	0.42
Massachusetts........	22,813	24,757	71.3	67.1	4,619,855	1,993,923	2.45	0.68
Rhode Island.........	2,987	3,941	73.2	74.5	674,100	408,429	2.30	0.74
Connecticut..........	16,828	21,486	74.3	80.1	3,362,500	1,882,197	2.45	0.70
MIDDLE ATLANTIC:								
New York.............	163,148	183,813	84.4	85.3	69,812,321	20,338,766	2.15	0.42
New Jersey...........	19,105	22,723	64.3	67.9	21,670,546	4,979,900	2.10	0.62
Pennsylvania.........	177,541	193,749	87.8	88.4	47,411,127	11,973,843	2.15	0.55
EAST NORTH CENTRAL:								
Ohio.................	144,203	199,410	56.2	73.3	17,657,811	9,377,955	2.35	0.46
Indiana..............	93,596	140,803	45.6	65.3	6,068,734	3,816,126	2.45	0.43
Illinois..............	151,233	189,903	63.8	75.4	11,277,926	6,401,598	2.40	0.53
Michigan.............	155,752	176,649	79.3	85.4	49,055,600	9,913,778	2.05	0.26
Wisconsin............	166,231	158,687	87.8	89.6	60,664,851	7,917,754	2.30	0.25
WEST NORTH CENTRAL:								
Minnesota............	135,611	132,492	76.0	84.9	57,383,621	7,685,259	2.15	0.29
Iowa.................	131,292	170,318	61.5	78.5	10,874,361	6,629,234	2.45	0.45
Missouri.............	159,887	185,790	60.8	67.0	10,144,410	4,470,135	2.50	0.57
North Dakota.........	54,221	51,386	69.8	69.1	10,142,747	2,079,125	2.15	0.37
South Dakota.........	43,412	44,829	58.2	57.7	7,157,983	1,967,550	2.50	0.57
Nebraska.............	79,628	90,398	64.0	69.7	10,685,998	3,785,224	2.40	0.47
Kansas...............	92,514	107,237	56.0	60.3	7,084,888	3,471,488	2.35	0.61
SOUTH ATLANTIC:								
Delaware.............	6,180	7,641	60.9	70.5	950,953	453,400	1.95	0.52
Maryland.............	32,520	34,870	67.9	71.3	9,591,592	1,782,954	1.95	0.52
District of Columbia ...	124	91	60.8	41.9	39,598	20,231	2.00	0.63
Virginia..............	91,264	106,499	49.0	57.9	26,979,423	5,667,557	2.20	0.65
West Virginia.........	70,155	81,297	80.4	84.1	6,461,619	2,278,638	2.30	0.56
North Carolina.......	79,069	77,421	29.3	30.5	6,278,351	1,755,413	2.20	0.74
South Carolina.......	21,927	13,656	11.4	7.7	3,018,221	609,424	2.80	0.78
Georgia..............	32,658	23,861	10.5	8.2	1,665,257	684,427	2.40	0.77
Florida..............	4,931	5,092	9.1	10.2	5,301,588	839,691	3.00	0.98
EAST SOUTH CENTRAL:								
Kentucky.............	101,904	130,076	37.7	50.2	7,671,876	2,724,043	2.45	0.53
Tennessee............	100,502	111,967	39.8	45.5	4,439,820	1,790,233	2.23	0.61
Alabama.............	48,010	37,374	18.7	14.2	2,304,769	884,497	2.60	0.78
Mississippi..........	28,459	28,019	10.5	10.2	1,692,523	542,011	2.60	0.84
WEST SOUTH CENTRAL:								
Arkansas.............	81,751	79,127	35.1	36.9	4,060,143	1,439,991	2.30	0.69
Louisiana............	23,382	18,230	17.3	15.1	2,137,749	924,311	2.20	0.78
Oklahoma............	66,811	45,369	34.8	23.9	4,040,810	1,250,052	2.10	0.66
Texas................	62,280	47,273	14.3	11.3	3,841,341	1,825,150	2.25	0.82
MOUNTAIN:								
Montana..............	20,490	11,248	35.5	42.9	3,898,690	1,298,830	2.35	0.40
Idaho................	16,723	14,837	39.7	48.2	13,546,798	1,583,447	2.15	0.34
Wyoming.............	6,066	5,125	38.5	46.6	2,000,443	524,489	2.35	0.56
Colorado.............	17,903	16,480	29.9	35.7	19,524,525	3,704,768	2.20	0.31
New Mexico..........	1,454	3,310	4.9	9.3	260,239	234,636	2.35	0.79
Arizona..............	791	634	7.9	6.9	435,755	98,597	2.50	1.01
Utah.................	11,453	12,199	44.6	56.3	3,494,607	873,961	2.12	0.36
Nevada..............	1,266	1,252	40.0	46.6	1,099,228	396,652	2.24	0.52
PACIFIC:								
Washington..........	36,085	31,712	54.4	56.4	12,320,093	2,993,737	2.10	0.39
Oregon..............	24,685	25,215	49.2	55.4	7,431,756	2,098,648	2.10	0.44
California...........	11,518	12,533	9.8	14.2	18,901,258	4,879,449	2.30	0.50

TABLE **174.**—SWEET POTATOES AND YAMS—ACREAGE AND PRODUCTION, BY DIVISIONS AND STATES: 1919 AND 1909.

[A minus sign (−) denotes decrease. Per cent not shown when base is less than 100. States not shown when acreage was less than 1,000 in 1919.]

DIVISION AND STATE.	ACREAGE.			PRODUCTION (BUSHELS).			AVERAGE YIELD PER ACRE (BUSHELS).	
	1919	1909	Per cent of increase.	1919	1909	Per cent of increase.	1919	1909
United States....	803,727	641,255	25.3	78,091,913	59,232,070	31.8	97.2	92.4
GEOGRAPHIC DIVISIONS:								
New England........	9	49	....	327	4,818	−93.2	36.3	98.3
Middle Atlantic......	17,867	23,923	−25.3	1,950,082	3,326,190	−41.4	109.1	139.0
East North Central...	14,018	13,300	5.4	1,089,862	1,364,256	−20.1	77.7	102.6
West North Central..	19,048	15,381	23.8	1,689,148	1,696,111	−0.4	88.7	110.3
South Atlantic.......	337,152	295,879	13.9	35,097,513	29,628,153	18.5	104.1	100.1
East South Central..	214,799	160,756	33.6	20,321,438	13,573,580	49.7	94.6	84.4
West South Central..	191,929	126,407	51.8	16,967,631	9,025,928	88.0	88.4	71.4
Mountain............	1,263	439	187.7	107,689	38,877	177.0	85.3	88.6
Pacific..............	7,642	5,121	49.2	868,223	574,157	51.2	113.6	112.1
MIDDLE ATLANTIC:								
New Jersey..........	15,427	22,504	−31.4	1,772,829	3,186,499	−44.4	114.9	141.6
Pennsylvania........	2,424	1,306	85.6	175,755	128,770	36.5	72.5	98.6
EAST NORTH CENTRAL:								
Ohio................	2,584	1,143	126.1	224,774	133,798	68.0	87.0	117.1
Indiana.............	3,409	1,561	118.4	195,515	178,300	9.7	57.4	114.2
Illinois.............	8,003	10,568	−24.3	668,845	1,050,932	−36.4	83.6	99.4
WEST NORTH CENTRAL:								
Iowa...............	3,236	2,274	42.3	216,578	232,413	−6.8	66.9	102.2
Missouri............	11,165	7,938	40.7	997,606	876,234	13.9	89.4	110.4
Kansas.............	4,366	4,883	−10.6	448,986	558,021	−19.5	102.8	114.3
SOUTH ATLANTIC:								
Delaware...........	9,813	5,229	87.7	1,505,278	733,746	105.1	153.4	140.3
Maryland...........	10,185	7,956	28.0	1,453,880	1,065,956	36.4	142.7	134.0
Virginia............	42,889	40,838	5.0	5,981,348	5,270,202	13.5	139.5	129.1
West Virginia.......	2,678	2,079	28.8	221,378	215,582	2.7	82.7	103.7
North Carolina......	74,678	84,740	−11.9	·7,959,786	8,493,283	−6.3	106.6	100.2
South Carolina......	60,325	48,878	23.4	5,369,611	4,319,926	24.3	89.0	88.4
Georgia.............	110,033	84,038	30.9	10,132,016	7,426,131	36.4	92.1	88.4
Florida.............	26,436	21,995	20.2	2,460,872	2,083,665	18.1	93.1	94.7
EAST SOUTH CENTRAL:								
Kentucky...........	14,892	11,882	25.3	1,222,651	1,326,245	−7.8	82.1	111.6
Tennessee..........	39,645	26,216	51.2	4,452,883	2,504,490	77.8	112.3	95.5
Alabama............	90,868	66,613	36.4	8,095,404	5,314,857	52.3	89.1	79.8
Mississippi.........	69,394	56,045	23.8	6,550,500	4,427,988	47.9	94.4	79.0
WEST SOUTH CENTRAL:								
Arkansas...........	39,019	22,388	74.3	3,959,870	1,685,308	135.0	101.5	75.3
Louisiana..........	68,033	56,953	19.5	5,324,419	4,251,086	25.2	78.3	74.6
Oklahoma..........	16,735	5,056	231.0	1,844,463	359,451	413.1	110.2	71.1
Texas..............	68,142	42,010	62.2	5,838,879	2,730,083	113.9	85.7	65.0
PACIFIC:								
California..........	7,632	5,111	49.3	867,300	572,814	51.4	113.6	112.1

TABLE 175.—SWEET POTATOES AND YAMS—FARMS REPORTING AND VALUE, BY DIVISIONS AND STATES: 1919 AND 1909.

[States not shown when acreage was less than 1,000 in 1919.]

DIVISION AND STATE.	FARMS REPORTING.				VALUE.		AVERAGE VALUE PER BUSHEL.	
	Number.		Per cent of all farms.					
	1919	1909	1919	1909	1919	1909	1919	1909
United States	1,406,780	1,121,900	21.8	17.6	$124,844,475	$35,429,176	$1.60	$0.60
GEOGRAPHIC DIVISIONS:								
New England	17	50	(1)	(1)	780	4,543	2.39	0.94
Middle Atlantic	19,836	18,634	4.7	4.0	4,006,904	1,638,902	2.05	0.49
East North Central	59,148	39,470	5.5	3.5	2,346,756	751,929	2.15	0.55
West North Central	74,702	47,155	6.8	4.2	3,643,524	1,095,724	2.16	0.65
South Atlantic	544,089	484,044	46.9	43.5	52,638,171	16,146,222	1.50	0.54
East South Central	433,313	368,122	41.2	35.3	30,602,493	9,116,510	1.51	0.67
West South Central	272,939	162,853	27.4	17.3	29,333,551	6,265,750	1.73	0.69
Mountain	891	420	0.4	0.2	275,384	52,596	2.56	1.35
Pacific	1,845	1,152	0.8	0.6	1,996,912	357,000	2.30	0.62
MIDDLE ATLANTIC:								
New Jersey	6,418	7,666	21.6	22.9	3,634,301	1,527,074	2.05	0.48
Pennsylvania	13,363	10,859	6.6	5.0	369,083	104,434	2.10	0.81
EAST NORTH CENTRAL:								
Ohio	12,870	8,238	5.0	3.0	528,225	104,181	2.35	0.78
Indiana	19,439	11,420	9.5	5.3	479,015	139,886	2.45	0.78
Illinois	26,745	19,675	11.3	7.8	1,337,690	506,760	2.00	0.48
WEST NORTH CENTRAL:								
Iowa	6,397	3,667	3.0	1.7	563,102	125,763	2.60	0.54
Missouri	58,242	36,258	22.1	13.1	2,094,979	567,413	2.10	0.65
Kansas	9,268	6,099	5.6	3.4	920,428	373,432	2.05	0.67
SOUTH ATLANTIC:								
Delaware	4,547	4,566	44.8	42.1	2,634,237	276,679	1.75	0.38
Maryland	11,484	11,175	24.0	22.8	2,762,373	483,751	1.90	0.45
Virginia	59,537	67,506	32.0	36.7	9,570,164	2,681,472	1.60	0.51
West Virginia	15,283	15,632	17.5	16.2	498,107	170,086	2.25	0.79
North Carolina	137,230	142,238	50.9	56.1	11,939,707	4,333,297	1.50	0.51
South Carolina	106,104	88,340	55.1	50.1	8,591,379	2,606,606	1.60	0.60
Georgia	181,987	131,458	58.6	45.2	13,171,629	4,349,806	1.30	0.59
Florida	27,847	23,076	51.6	46.1	3,445,221	1,231,238	1.40	0.59
EAST SOUTH CENTRAL:								
Kentucky	70,183	63,646	25.9	24.6	2,750,979	839,454	2.25	0.63
Tennessee	99,550	89,361	39.4	36.3	7,347,259	1,625,056	1.65	0.65
Alabama	149,639	117,522	58.4	44.7	11,333,568	3,578,710	1.40	0.67
Mississippi	113,941	97,593	41.9	35.6	9,170,687	3,073,290	1.40	0.69
WEST SOUTH CENTRAL:								
Arkansas	84,189	53,297	36.2	24.8	6,533,789	1,359,669	1.65	0.81
Louisiana	69,473	52,074	51.3	43.2	8,785,292	2,357,729	1.65	0.55
Oklahoma	36,840	9,480	19.2	5.0	3,504,490	350,553	1.90	0.98
Texas	82,437	48,002	18.9	11.5	10,509,980	2,197,799	1.80	0.81
PACIFIC:								
California	1,814	1,133	1.5	1.3	1,994,790	355,624	2.30	0.62

1Less than one-tenth of 1 per cent.

TABLE 176.—VEGETABLES RAISED FOR SALE, AND FARM GARDENS—FARMS REPORT-
ING, ACREAGE, AND VALUE, FOR THE UNITED STATES: 1919 AND 1909.

[Vegetables other than potatoes and sweet potatoes.]

ITEM.	1919			1909		
	Farms reporting.	Acreage.	Value.	Farms reporting.	Acreage.	Value.
Vegetables raised for sale, total [1]	488,254	1,475,274	$193,248,964	4,261,776	2,763,269	$216,257,068
Asparagus............................	6,728	30,244	5,102,135	5,300	25,639	2,246,631
Beans (green)........................	84,263	71,970	8,031,449	21,561	53,610	2,844,951
Beets................................	7,197	5,255	1,016,507	1,684	3,202	352,696
Brussels sprouts.....................	313	984	232,370	188	390	45,576
Cabbages............................	124,972	123,994	21,848,112	43,843	125,998	9,719,641
Cantaloupes and muskmelons......	41,093	78,436	10,766,591	16,278	52,419	3,604,636
Carrots..............................	8,968	6,522	1,563,010	2,008	3,764	473,499
Cauliflower..........................	2,403	6,513	1,328,415	1,060	3,466	602,885
Celery...............................	11,449	20,148	9,462,277	4,005	15,863	3,922,848
Corn (pop)...........................	5,914	50,778	3,158,504	2,535	12,773	326,141
Corn (sweet).........................	103,784	271,584	17,297,561	48,514	178,224	5,936,419
Cucumbers...........................	70,066	51,643	8,579,102	16,714	32,310	2,719,340
Egg plant............................	1,500	1,712	491,321	459	894	154,643
Horse radish.........................	502	922	205,767	480	1,475	233,885
Kale.................................	474	1,193	241,415	337	1,495	146,010
Lettuce..............................	20,463	21,544	8,535,092	2,178	5,489	1,595,085
Mushrooms...........................	52	....	319,911	....	....	....
Okra (gumbo)........................	1,071	986	117,175	148	347	24,969
Onions (dry).........................	76,609	64,338	21,387,221	14,989	47,625	6,709,047
Onions (green).......................	459	340	113,670	130	184	44,788
Parsley..............................	438	393	107,303	112	192	27,181
Parsnips.............................	1,575	845	244,435	436	722	102,674
Peas (green).........................	49,632	103,686	7,164,988	17,219	70,487	2,785,502
Peppers (green)......................	7,605	15,290	3,079,285	1,641	3,483	408,741
Pumpkins............................	1,674	3,056	137,626	361	1,163	29,993
Radishes.............................	1,987	2,014	437,286	895	2,269	293,062
Rhubarb.............................	2,263	2,394	673,113	1,021	2,364	338,831
Rutabagas...........................	858	837	113,741	353	631	30,970
Salsify (vegetable oyster)..........	82	41	12,386	....	....	....
Spinach..............................	2,343	10,027	1,715,869	1,152	6,668	817,069
Squashes............................	5,402	5,370	685,245	1,002	2,380	207,391
Tomatoes............................	170,693	316,399	38,675,496	64,751	207,379	13,707,929
Turnips..............................	5,088	4,056	543,071	11,732	22,324	1,169,499
Watermelons.........................	73,083	159,088	10,466,133	35,345	137,005	4,453,101
All other vegetables.................	4,544	6,333	1,241,205	....	....	....
Mixed vegetables [2].................	16,389	36,339	8,154,177	....	1,741,035	150,181,435
Farm gardens........................	5,090,293	....	344,665,728	....	....	....

[1] The 1909 totals include the farm gardens. The 1909 figures for individual vegetables represent vegetables raised in tracts of 1 acre or more of the specified vegetables.
[2] The 1909 figures represent all miscellaneous vegetables raised in tracts of less than 1 acre and include
the farm gardens.

TABLE 177.—ACREAGE AND VALUE OF VEGETABLES RAISED FOR SALE, AND VALUE OF FARM GARDENS, BY DIVISIONS AND STATES: 1919.

DIVISION AND STATE.	VEGETABLES RAISED FOR SALE.		Value of products of farm gardens.
	Acreage.	Value.	
United States	1,475,274	$193,248,964	$344,665,728
GEOGRAPHIC DIVISIONS:			
New England	54,600	12,782,232	12,602,649
Middle Atlantic	281,321	43,347,728	32,117,666
East North Central	296,271	33,432,348	58,176,993
West North Central	146,990	12,648,736	55,262,394
South Atlantic	337,379	37,736,292	69,286,220
East South Central	63,766	8,407,579	53,942,162
West South Central	91,664	10,298,457	45,924,594
Mountain	41,350	6,878,916	8,256,347
Pacific	161,933	27,716,675	9,096,703
NEW ENGLAND:			
Maine	14,073	2,161,714	3,180,673
New Hampshire	2,592	427,487	1,848,651
Vermont	1,905	260,441	2,116,561
Massachusetts	24,747	7,622,622	3,105,592
Rhode Island	2,163	394,100	412,104
Connecticut	9,120	1,915,868	1,939,068
MIDDLE ATLANTIC:			
New York	132,042	22,017,396	12,237,223
New Jersey	94,996	12,473,316	2,890,984
Pennsylvania	54,283	8,857,017	16,989,459
EAST NORTH CENTRAL:			
Ohio	62,860	9,532,727	15,646,395
Indiana	53,468	5,607,111	9,100,018
Illinois	60,705	6,330,537	12,405,254
Michigan	50,955	6,455,768	9,583,356
Wisconsin	68,283	5,506,205	11,441,970
WEST NORTH CENTRAL:			
Minnesota	14,652	2,223,305	9,305,128
Iowa	73,372	4,901,320	11,967,063
Missouri	28,838	2,962,892	15,354,668
North Dakota	964	116,857	3,465,623
South Dakota	2,397	218,687	3,323,437
Nebraska	14,823	846,063	5,444,561
Kansas	11,944	1,379,612	6,401,914
SOUTH ATLANTIC:			
Delaware	33,360	1,903,017	783,507
Maryland	119,922	9,154,530	3,910,673
District of Columbia	712	124,946	37,984
Virginia	47,307	5,921,523	12,928,987
West Virginia	8,377	1,056,184	8,699,957
North Carolina	14,710	1,718,349	15,848,541
South Carolina	15,978	1,932,911	9,832,031
Georgia	36,763	2,229,577	14,749,394
Florida	60,250	13,695,255	2,495,147
EAST SOUTH CENTRAL:			
Kentucky	16,124	1,951,375	13,789,346
Tennessee	20,877	2,101,743	14,058,428
Alabama	12,750	1,311,668	13,289,201
Mississippi	14,015	3,042,793	12,805,187
WEST SOUTH CENTRAL:			
Arkansas	18,985	1,143,487	11,898,176
Louisiana	11,668	1,421,838	6,952,241
Oklahoma	11,918	920,731	9,050,318
Texas	49,093	6,812,401	18,023,859
MOUNTAIN:			
Montana	1,273	302,823	1,780,876
Idaho	2,097	400,808	1,730,159
Wyoming	582	91,940	635,033
Colorado	18,438	3,302,158	1,965,063
New Mexico	4,071	571,959	681,959
Arizona	6,062	956,168	311,420
Utah	8,309	1,164,731	956,520
Nevada	518	88,329	195,317
PACIFIC:			
Washington	9,460	2,263,380	3,739,509
Oregon	6,231	1,341,707	2,986,909
California	146,242	24,111,588	2,370,285

TABLE 178.—TOBACCO—ACREAGE AND PRODUCTION, BY DIVISIONS AND STATES: 1919 AND 1909.

[A minus sign (−) denotes decrease. Per cent not shown when base is less than 100 or when per cent is more than 1,000. States not shown when acreage was less than 1,000 in 1919.]

DIVISION AND STATE.	ACREAGE.			PRODUCTION (POUNDS).			AVERAGE YIELD PER ACRE (POUNDS).	
	1919	1909	Per cent of increase.	1919	1909	Per cent of increase.	1919	1909
United States.....	1,864,080	1,294,911	44.0	1,372,993,261	1,055,764,806	30.0	737	815
GEOGRAPHIC DIVISIONS:								
New England........	36,225	21,745	66.6	56,732,177	37,961,893	49.4	1,566	1,746
Middle Atlantic......	45,413	45,852	−1.0	59,320,475	51,510,925	15.2	1,306	1,123
East North Central...	140,572	171,973	−18.3	136,197,872	157,959,785	−13.8	969	919
West North Central..	5,056	5,709	−11.4	4,691,739	5,704,572	−17.8	928	999
South Atlantic.......	857,155	487,411	75.9	493,732,082	334,569,496	47.6	576	686
East South Central...	777,677	560,523	38.7	621,274,971	467,348,072	32.9	799	834
West South Central..	1,279	1,683	−24.0	552,091	700,915	−21.2	432	417
Mountain............	2	11	....	1,276	3,457	−63.1	638	314
Pacific..............	701	4	....	490,578	5,691	....	700	1,423
NEW ENGLAND:								
Massachusetts........	9,109	5,521	65.0	14,282,589	9,549,306	49.6	1,568	1,730
Connecticut.........	26,930	16,042	67.9	42,193,196	28,110,453	50.1	1,567	1,752
MIDDLE ATLANTIC:								
New York............	2,613	4,109	−36.4	3,353,954	5,345,035	−37.3	1,284	1,301
Pennsylvania........	42,799	41,742	2.5	55,965,851	46,164,800	21.2	1,308	1,106
EAST NORTH CENTRAL:								
Ohio................	75,789	106,477	−28.8	64,420,472	88,603,308	−27.3	850	832
Indiana.............	22,459	23,694	−5.2	18,752,202	21,387,824	−12.3	835	903
Wisconsin...........	41,465	40,458	2.5	52,454,246	46,909,182	11.8	1,265	1,160
WEST NORTH CENTRAL:								
Missouri............	4,490	5,433	−17.4	4,074,977	5,372,738	−24.2	908	989
SOUTH ATLANTIC:								
Maryland............	28,550	26,072	9.5	17,336,859	17,845,699	−2.9	607	685
Virginia............	225,504	185,427	21.6	102,391,226	132,979,390	−23.0	454	717
West Virginia.......	11,233	17,928	−37.3	7,587,052	14,356,400	−47.2	675	801
North Carolina......	459,011	221,890	106.9	280,163,432	138,813,163	101.8	610	626
South Carolina......	103,496	30,082	244.0	71,193,072	25,583,049	178.3	688	850
Georgia.............	25,067	2,025	....	10,584,968	1,485,994	612.3	422	734
Florida.............	4,291	3,987	7.6	4,473,696	3,505,801	27.6	1,043	879
EAST SOUTH CENTRAL:								
Kentucky............	634,038	469,795	35.0	506,150,592	398,482,301	27.0	798	848
Tennessee...........	138,561	90,468	53.2	112,367,567	68,756,599	63.4	811	760
Alabama.............	3,435	211	....	2,031,235	90,572	....	591	429
Mississippi.........	1,643	49	....	725,577	18,600	....	442	380

TABLE 179.—TOBACCO—FARMS REPORTING AND VALUE, BY DIVISIONS AND STATES:
1919 AND 1909.

[States not shown when acreage was less than 1,000 in 1919.]

DIVISION AND STATE.	FARMS REPORTING.				VALUE.		AVERAGE VALUE PER POUND.	
	Number.		Per cent of all farms.					
	1919	1909	1919	1909	1919	1909	1919	1909
United States......	448,572	326,919	7.0	5.1	$444,047,481	$104,302,856	$0.32	$0.10
GEOGRAPHIC DIVISIONS:								
New England..........	4,610	3,865	2.9	2.0	19,985,748	5,670,002	0.35	0.15
Middle Atlantic........	11,857	13,032	2.8	2.8	10,878,955	4,328,854	0.18	0.08
East North Central.....	41,376	42,929	3.8	3.8	29,956,148	15,082,892	0.22	0.10
West North Central....	7,602	6,724	0.7	0.6	1,530,947	713,321	0.33	0.13
South Atlantic.........	197,014	120,731	17.0	10.9	239,022,462	32,843,156	0.48	0.10
East South Central.....	182,065	135,360	17.3	13.0	142,122,166	45,548,716	0.23	0.10
West South Central....	3,974	4,196	0.4	0.4	266,266	114,452	0.48	0.16
Mountain..............	15	53	(1)	(1)	430	778	0.34	0.23
Pacific................	59	29	(1)	(1)	284,359	685	0.58	0.12
NEW ENGLAND:								
Massachusetts..........	1,293	910	4.0	2.5	4,713,255	1,218,060	0.33	0.13
Connecticut............	3,191	2,869	14.1	10.7	15,189,551	4,415,948	0.36	0.16
MIDDLE ATLANTIC:								
New York.............	890	1,355	0.5	0.6	804,949	402,517	0.24	0.08
Pennsylvania..........	10,961	11,666	5.4	5.3	10,073,852	3,926,116	0.18	0.09
EAST NORTH CENTRAL:								
Ohio..................	20,294	23,119	7.9	8.5	13,528,302	8,998,887	0.21	0.10
Indiana...............	9,889	8,660	4.8	4.0	4,688,064	2,145,193	0.25	0.10
Wisconsin.............	9,787	9,390	5.2	5.3	11,539,932	3,855,033	0.22	0.08
WEST NORTH CENTRAL:								
Missouri...............	7,143	6,168	2.7	2.2	1,385,497	676,479	0.34	0.13
SOUTH ATLANTIC:								
Maryland.............	5,504	4,392	11.5	9.0	5,721,164	1,457,112	0.33	0.08
Virginia..............	52,409	44,472	28.1	24.2	48,123,877	12,169,086	0.47	0.09
West Virginia.........	8,610	9,299	9.9	9.6	2,731,338	1,923,180	0.36	0.13
North Carolina........	98,310	51,926	36.4	20.5	151,288,264	13,847,559	0.54	0.10
South Carolina........	25,576	8,166	13.3	4.6	23,493,714	2,123,576	0.33	0.08
Georgia...............	5,752	1,760	1.9	0.6	5,292,510	297,167	0.50	0.20
Florida...............	846	716	1.6	1.4	2,371,061	1,025,476	0.53	0.29
EAST SOUTH CENTRAL:								
Kentucky..............	143,599	108,050	53.1	41.7	116,414,639	39,868,753	0.23	0.10
Tennessee.............	35,936	25,637	14.2	10.4	24,720,869	5,661,681	0.22	0.08
Alabama..............	1,905	1,267	0.7	0.5	710,933	14,892	0.35	0.16
Mississippi...........	625	406	0.2	0.1	275,725	3,390	0.38	0.18

1 Less than one-tenth of 1 per cent.

TABLE **180.**—COTTON—ACREAGE AND PRODUCTION, BY DIVISIONS AND STATES: 1919 AND 1909.

[A minus sign (−) denotes decrease. Per cent not shown when base is less than 100 or when per cent is more than 1,000.]

DIVISION AND STATE.	ACREAGE.			PRODUCTION OF LINT COTTON (RUNNING BALES).			AVERAGE YIELD OF LINT COTTON PER ACRE (BALES).	
	1919	1909	Per cent of increase.	1919	1909	Per cent of increase.	1919	1909
United States....	33,740,106	32,043,838	5.3	11,376,130	10,649,268	6.8	0.34	0.33
GEOGRAPHIC DIVISIONS:								
West North Central..	110,027	96,563	13.9	63,808	54,508	17.1	0.58	0.56
South Atlantic........	8,883,512	9,002,776	−1.3	4,061,383	4,012,942	1.2	0.46	0.45
East South Central...	6,389,666	7,926,019	−19.4	1,985,631	2,524,714	−21.4	0.31	0.32
West South Central..	18,152,644	15,017,347	20.9	5,154,140	4,056,704	27.1	0.28	0.27
Mountain.............	116,949	809	....	64,750	217	....	0.55	0.27
Pacific...............	87,308	324	....	46,418	183	....	0.53	0.56
WEST NORTH CENTRAL:								
Missouri.............	110,027	96,527	14.0	63,808	54,498	17.1	0.58	0.56
Kansas..............	....	36	....	....	10	....	....	0.28
SOUTH ATLANTIC:								
Maryland............	....	(1)	....	....	(2)	....	....	(1)
Virginia.............	47,032	25,147	87.0	24,887	10,480	137.5	0.53	0.42
West Virginia........	....	(1)	....	....	(2)	....	....	(1)
North Carolina.......	1,373,701	1,274,404	7.8	858,406	665,132	29.1	0.62	0.52
South Carolina.......	2,631,719	2,556,467	2.9	1,476,645	1,279,866	15.4	0.56	0.50
Georgia.............	4,720,498	4,883,304	−3.3	1,681,907	1,992,408	−15.6	0.36	0.41
Florida.............	110,562	263,454	−58.0	19,538	65,056	−70.0	0.18	0.25
EAST SOUTH CENTRAL:								
Kentucky............	5,355	7,811	−31.4	2,967	3,469	−14.5	0.55	0.44
Tennessee...........	807,770	787,516	2.6	306,974	264,562	16.0	0.38	0.34
Alabama............	2,628,154	3,730,482	−29.5	718,163	1,129,527	−36.4	0.27	0.30
Mississippi..........	2,948,387	3,400,210	−13.3	957,527	1,127,156	−15.0	0.32	0.33
WEST SOUTH CENTRAL:								
Arkansas...........	2,553,811	2,153,222	18.6	869,350	776,879	11.9	0.34	0.36
Louisiana...........	1,343,334	957,011	40.4	306,791	268,909	14.1	0.23	0.28
Oklahoma...........	2,732,962	1,976,935	38.2	1,006,242	555,742	81.1	0.37	0.28
Texas..............	11,522,537	9,930,179	16.0	2,971,757	2,455,174	21.0	0.26	0.25
MOUNTAIN:								
New Mexico........	10,666	790	....	5,399	206	....	0.51	0.26
Arizona.............	106,283	19	....	59,351	11	....	0.56	0.58
PACIFIC:								
California...........	87,308	324	....	46,418	183	....	0.53	0.56

[1] Less than 1 acre reported.   [2] Less than 1 bale.

TABLE **181.**—COTTON—FARMS REPORTING AND VALUE, BY DIVISIONS AND STATES: 1919 AND 1909.

DIVISION AND STATE.	FARMS REPORTING.				VALUE (TOTAL INCLUDING COTTON SEED).		AVERAGE VALUE PER UNIT.		
	Number.		Per cent of all farms.		1919	1909	Lint cotton per bale.		Cotton seed per ton, 1919
	1919	1909	1919	1909			1919	1909	
United States....	1,905,863	1,714,149	29.6	26.9	$2,355,169,365	$824,696,287	$176.46	$66.07	$65.27
GEOGRAPHIC DIVISIONS:									
West North Central.	7,675	7,299	0.7	0.7	12,513,445	3,979,009	164.00	62.25	69.50
South Atlantic......	624,698	556,508	53.9	50.1	854,052,822	303,105,181	176.39	63.45	74.50
East South Central..	537,231	522,735	51.1	50.1	423,723,410	204,290,666	182.15	69.53	66.79
West South Central .	732,042	627,528	73.5	66.5	1,030,861,310	313,291,792	172.35	66.56	57.70
Mountain............	2,969	61	1.2	(1)	23,440,943	16,863	329.41	70.22	70.58
Pacific...............	1,248	18	0.5	(1)	10,577,435	12,776	199.00	64.17	62.50
WEST NORTH CENTRAL:									
Missouri.............	7,675	7,296	2.9	2.6	12,513,445	3,978,295	164.00	62.25	69.50
Kansas..............	....	3	......	(1)	....	714	....	60.00	......
SOUTH ATLANTIC:									
Maryland............	....	2	......	(1)	....	23	....	(2)	......
Virginia.............	9,081	5,283	4.9	2.9	5,186,943	822,267	174.00	66.39	74.50
West Virginia.......	....	2	......	(1)	....	14	....	(2)	......
North Carolina......	153,010	129,704	56.7	51.1	177,947,734	50,483,345	174.00	63.24	74.00
South Carolina......	179,979	158,167	93.4	89.6	310,392,768	96,381,067	176.00	62.77	75.50
Georgia.............	270,484	242,673	87.0	83.4	356,506,928	149,937,058	178.00	63.59	74.00
Florida.............	12,144	20,677	22.5	41.3	4,018,449	5,481,407	176.10	74.42	64.00
EAST SOUTH CENTRAL:									
Kentucky...........	420	504	0.2	0.2	574,578	246,614	159.00	64.29	75.00
Tennessee..........	76,468	67,663	30.3	27.5	58,346,576	20,682,187	159.00	67.91	65.00
Alabama............	220,990	224,871	86.3	85.5	152,440,345	87,008,432	179.00	65.70	72.00
Mississippi.........	239,353	229,697	88.0	83.7	212,361,911	96,353,433	192.00	73.77	63.50
WEST SOUTH CENTRAL:									
Arkansas............	172,632	148,311	74.2	69.1	184,684,720	63,155,683	184.00	70.23	60.00
Louisiana...........	102,498	74,373	75.7	61.7	60,187,569	20,274,747	167.00	64.43	64.00
Oklahoma...........	110,204	88,140	57.4	46.3	189,552,012	41,187,408	162.00	63.70	56.00
Texas...............	346,708	316,704	79.5	75.8	596,437,009	188,673,954	173.00	66.28	57.00
MOUNTAIN:									
New Mexico.........	337	59	1.1	0.2	1,387,842	15,996	224.00	70.43	71.50
Arizona.............	2,632	2	26.4	(1)	22,053,101	867	339.00	66.36	70.50
PACIFIC:									
California...........	1,248	18	1.1	(1)	10,577,435	12,776	199.00	64.17	62.50

¹ ¹ Less than one-tenth of 1 per cent.   ² Less than 1 bale produced in state.

TABLE **182.**—SUGAR CANE—FARMS REPORTING, ACREAGE, PRODUCTION, AND VALUE, BY STATES: 1919 AND 1909.

STATE.	FARMS REPORTING.		ACREAGE.		PRODUCTION (TONS).		VALUE.	
	1919	1909	1919	1909	1919	1909	1919	1909
United States......	271,278	278,233	372,938	476,849	3,544,679	6,240,260	$59,499,467	$26,415,952
North Carolina.............	....	596	....	294	....	1,494	....	10,697
South Carolina.............	13,600	19,857	5,537	7,053	34,947	59,865	789,592	434,634
Georgia...................	72,740	64,458	41,558	37,046	365,603	317,460	8,472,338	2,268,110
Florida...................	24,331	19,663	20,413	12,928	179,573	142,517	4,134,458	1,089,698
Alabama..................	56,604	61,226	25,302	27,211	208,342	226,634	4,228,902	1,527,166
Mississippi...............	44,795	52,860	25,256	24,861	186,283	222,600	3,923,811	1,506,887
Arkansas.................	3,686	5,286	2,406	3,330	9,695	19,868	232,399	152,298
Louisiana.................	36,421	34,487	234,049	329,684	2,435,683	4,941,996	34,600,667	17,752,537
Texas....................	19,090	19,718	18,407	34,315	124,493	307,502	3,116,162	1,669,683
All other states...........	11	82	10	127	60	324	1,138	4,242

TABLE 183.—SUGAR CANE—QUANTITY AND VALUE OF CANE SOLD, AND QUANTITY OF SIRUP MADE ON FARMS, BY STATES: 1919 AND 1909.

| STATE. | SUGAR CANE SOLD. | | | | CANE SIRUP MADE ON FARMS (GALLONS). | |
| | Quantity (tons). | | Value. | | | |
	1919	1909	1919	1909	1919	1909
United States..........	2,053,026	4,638,677	$32,880,417	$16,765,740	21,240,960	21,633,579
North Carolina............	....	11	....	103	....	21,677
South Carolina.............	3	84	59	817	563,953	881,558
Georgia..................	398	1,888	8,756	19,892	7,052,984	5,533,520
Florida.................	909	2,977	18,180	35,234	3,675,249	2,533,096
Alabama................	825	3,298	23,100	7,413	3,235,231	3,078,531
Mississippi.............	146	1,258	3,066	11,737	3,015,956	2,920,519
Arkansas..............	4	109	72	1,103	165,947	286,637
Louisiana.............	2,020,085	4,461,221	32,321,360	16,126,780	1,899,423	4,125,083
Texas.................	30,656	167,831	505,824	562,661	1,631,459	2,246,774
All other states........	....	....	....	....	758	6,184

TABLE 184.—SORGHUM GROWN FOR SIRUP—ACREAGE, PRODUCTION, AND VALUE, BY STATES: 1919 AND 1909.

| STATE. | ACREAGE. | | PRODUCTION (TONS). | | VALUE. | | SORGHUM SIRUP MADE ON FARMS (GALLONS). | |
	1919	1909	1919	1909	1919	1909	1919	1909
United States..	482,043	326,352	1,644,100	1,376,487	$24,506,228	$7,963,499	21,523,025	16,532,382
Ohio.................	5,464	4,578	24,256	28,137	435,110	177,020	290,059	354,131
Indiana..............	12,307	11,829	52,210	77,600	987,729	449,968	681,190	965,086
Illinois..............	10,654	14,846	41,767	89,421	765,578	490,569	527,981	977,238
Wisconsin...........	4,906	2,244	18,225	13,498	331,643	83,026	207,277	139,667
Minnesota...........	1,974	1,670	8,639	12,857	185,922	80,718	128,227	145,934
Iowa................	9,968	4,996	45,340	24,597	822,798	139,293	587,712	250,205
Missouri.............	33,771	37,476	115,690	176,765	1,767,792	876,970	1,414,222	1,788,391
Kansas..............	2,335	6,058	7,474	34,444	95,802	112,374	87,090	260,680
Virginia.............	13,450	8,130	47,011	40,875	658,659	217,634	598,774	441,189
West Virginia........	8,439	8,607	30,544	48,091	564,851	300,188	451,875	604,201
North Carolina.......	30,624	20,662	100,463	84,753	1,467,880	524,667	1,397,980	1,099,346
South Carolina.......	20,431	6,131	69,865	22,371	945,218	131,833	900,206	262,452
Georgia..............	37,311	14,170	142,261	60,202	2,002,189	370,773	1,820,165	740,450
Florida..............	1,485	347	6,101	2,014	101,198	8,831	101,198	22,177
Kentucky............	49,968	52,858	154,963	198,404	2,248,510	1,216,426	2,044,098	2,733,683
Tennessee...........	49,131	45,410	148,689	183,328	2,070,674	981,497	1,917,293	2,076,339
Alabama.............	52,406	16,107	172,029	67,589	2,550,769	398,934	2,429,302	809,361
Mississippi..........	38,752	16,519	139,100	50,327	1,885,140	297,044	1,795,368	622,356
Arkansas............	41,424	27,532	120,416	83,041	1,654,562	563,851	1,438,748	1,140,532
Louisiana............	1,610	1,392	6,001	4,685	77,004	21,227	70,003	47,029
Oklahoma............	15,803	12,940	53,181	35,195	774,496	252,771	704,083	514,807
Texas...............	35,589	10,175	122,170	30,902	1,773,671	214,313	1,689,205	448,185
All other states......	4,241	1,675	17,705	7,391	339,033	53,572	240,969	88,943

TABLE 185.—SUGAR BEETS—ACREAGE, PRODUCTION, AND VALUE, BY STATES: 1919 AND 1909.

STATE.	ACREAGE.		PRODUCTION (TONS).		VALUE.	
	1919	1909	1919	1909	1919	1909
United States.........	636,434	360,433	5,993,409	3,902,071	$66,051,989	$19,695,384
Ohio......................	33,561	7,009	365,415	63,546	3,836,861	318,440
Indiana................	4,119	690	44,455	6,548	444,550	37,577
Illinois................	2,830	1,170	34,654	14,916	381,194	77,335
Michigan...............	106,450	78,711	1,025,550	706,990	11,793,836	4,010,178
Wisconsin.............	12,737	12,308	136,208	126,646	1,498,288	662,243
Minnesota.............	3,509	2,197	25,507	23,756	255,070	116,472
Iowa..................	7,009	1,030	52,338	6,962	601,889	33,897
Nebraska.............	54,486	4,182	554,646	39,756	5,823,786	179,593
Montana.............	8,600	8,710	73,824	108,776	812,064	543,478
Idaho................	37,334	15,598	260,309	179,638	2,733,248	813,460
Wyoming.............	9,935	1,181	96,994	13,234	1,018,438	60,374
Colorado.............	165,840	108,005	1,658,167	1,230,718	17,410,759	6,057,529
Utah.................	93,359	27,442	930,427	413,811	10,048,611	1,857,316
Washington...........	5,363	1,270	46,386	6,556	500,969	38,007
California............	88,257	78,671	666,866	843,269	8,669,258	4,313,981
All other states.........	3,045	12,259	21,663	116,949	223,168	575,504

TABLE 186.—MAPLE SUGAR AND SIRUP—PRODUCTION AND VALUE, BY STATES: 1919 AND 1909.

STATE.	MAPLE SUGAR MADE (POUNDS).		MAPLE SIRUP MADE (GALLONS).		VALUE OF MAPLE SUGAR AND SIRUP.	
	1919	1909	1919	1909	1919	1909
United States.........	9,691,854	14,024,206	3,507,745	4,106,418	$12,381,376	$5,177,809
Maine.................	24,934	15,388	42,144	43,971	136,405	52,137
New Hampshire........	329,723	558,811	112,824	111,500	440,250	182,341
Vermont..............	6,251,734	7,726,817	631,924	409,953	3,580,369	1,086,933
Massachusetts.........	73,198	156,952	57,950	53,091	197,334	77,559
Connecticut...........	5,173	10,207	2,866	4,236	10,380	6,988
New York.............	2,012,932	3,160,300	1,080,505	993,242	3,399,434	1,240,684
Pennsylvania..........	535,954	1,188,049	273,762	391,242	888,649	471,213
Ohio.................	62,001	257,592	694,175	1,323,431	1,933,790	1,099,248
Indiana..............	14,487	33,419	167,360	273,728	448,289	300,755
Illinois..............	1,436	5,366	12,114	18,492	33,853	23,502
Michigan.............	77,178	293,301	206,795	269,093	609,519	333,791
Wisconsin............	22,430	27,199	138,627	124,117	389,746	150,038
Minnesota............	3,146	11,399	12,870	17,808	38,521	23,362
Iowa.................	3,130	6,173	4,915	8,596	14,619	11,495
Missouri.............	5,047	11,638	12,039	9,389	32,675	12,950
Maryland.............	150,957	351,908	23,155	12,172	108,407	34,386
Virginia..............	38,362	44,976	8,137	6,046	28,598	12,233
West Virginia.........	73,763	140,060	23,448	31,176	82,831	46,568
Kentucky.............	2,393	10,697	999	3,547	3,733	6,681
All other states.........	3,876	13,954	1,136	1,588	3,974	4,945

TABLE **187.**—MINOR CROPS—ACREAGE, PRODUCTION, AND VALUE, BY STATES: 1919 AND 1909.

CROP AND STATE.	ACREAGE.[1]		PRODUCTION.			VALUE.	
	1919	1909	Unit.	1919	1909	1919	1909
Broom corn, total	337,806	326,102	Lbs...	113,031,132	78,959,958	$7,945,163	$5,134,434
Pennsylvania	946	108	Lbs...	294,597	45,582	23,567	5,253
Ohio	735	170	Lbs...	346,112	92,292	24,228	9,116
Indiana	613	323	Lbs...	245,782	153,259	29,493	13,461
Illinois	16,409	38,452	Lbs...	9,244,739	19,309,425	1,109,364	1,457,172
Iowa	168	156	Lbs...	103,250	75,370	11,358	6,670
Missouri	3,072	5,339	Lbs...	700,351	1,774,536	56,026	115,243
Nebraska	506	458	Lbs...	170,886	157,146	11,963	11,116
Kansas	11,447	41,064	Lbs...	3,525,370	8,768,853	246,778	593,947
Maryland	234	19	Lbs...	80,557	18,599	5,639	2,006
Virginia	360	107	Lbs...	116,045	46,016	6,969	3,586
Kentucky	353	342	Lbs...	117,545	157,286	7,053	13,641
Tennessee	2,247	1,348	Lbs...	784,055	347,064	50,961	27,733
Mississippi	309	154	Lbs...	88,081	60,574	5,286	5,548
Arkansas	911	332	Lbs...	282,892	106,576	22,628	8,198
Louisiana	207	320	Lbs...	68,313	92,208	4,098	7,285
Oklahoma	232,733	216,350	Lbs...	71,592,015	42,741,725	5,011,446	2,559,235
Texas	39,748	9,448	Lbs...	14,285,432	2,368,490	714,286	140,533
Colorado	10,588	5,631	Lbs...	4,629,360	1,187,791	259,244	71,717
New Mexico	13,143	4,470	Lbs...	5,275,998	644,892	263,801	33,492
California	2,178	1,023	Lbs...	792,026	614,250	63,361	32,509
All other states	929	488	Lbs...	287,726	198,024	17,614	16,973
Hemp, total	7,252	7,647	Lbs...	7,148,215	7,483,295	1,175,037	412,699
Ohio	1,574	....	Lbs...	2,172,652	....	434,531	....
Indiana	289	335	Lbs...	195,600	395,467	29,340	21,755
Illinois	60	....	Lbs...	60,000	50	9,000	5
Michigan	244	....	Lbs...	255,666	....	38,350	....
Wisconsin	3,314	7	Lbs...	2,938,124	6,510	440,720	426
Minnesota	293	....	Lbs...	195,119	....	29,268	....
North Dakota	373	....	Lbs...	396,266	....	59,440	....
South Dakota	252	....	Lbs...	209,543	....	31,431	....
Kentucky	721	6,855	Lbs...	583,121	6,420,232	81,638	348,386
California	113	300	Lbs...	137,000	600,000	20,550	39,000
All other states	19	150	Lbs...	5,124	61,036	769	3,127
Hops, total	15,954	44,693	Lbs...	19,760,793	40,718,748	10,364,464	7,844,745
New York	1,024	12,023	Lbs...	723,824	8,677,138	535,629	2,597,981
Tennessee	27	....	Lbs...	12,571	220	5,028	29
Washington	1,129	2,433	Lbs...	1,615,761	3,432,504	727,092	665,493
Oregon	5,629	21,770	Lbs...	4,788,223	16,582,562	2,537,758	2,838,860
California	8,118	8,391	Lbs...	12,610,055	11,994,953	6,557,229	1,731,110
All other states	27	76	Lbs...	10,359	31,371	1,728	11,272
Cassava, total	123	....	Lbs...	783,702	....	3,918	....
California	123	....	Lbs...	783,702	....	3,918	....
Chicory, total	1,784	1,589	Lbs...	18,196,063	19,284,000	90,980	70,460
Michigan	1,784	1,584	Lbs...	18,196,063	19,204,000	90,980	70,020
California	....	5	Lbs...	....	80,000	....	440
Chufas, total	917	2,193	Bu...	16,636	44,792	64,712	90,585
Georgia	105	481	Bu...	1,625	12,531	5,689	28,194
Florida	706	1,072	Bu...	12,810	21,500	51,240	43,470
All other states	106	640	Bu...	2,201	10,761	7,783	18,921
Ginseng, total	54	23	Lbs...	18,561	....	129,927	151,888
Ohio	10	....	Lbs...	2,526	....	17,682	16,639
Illinois	2	....	Lbs...	1,700	....	11,900	770
Michigan	10	....	Lbs...	4,595	....	32,165	13,794
Wisconsin	12	16	Lbs...	5,251	....	36,757	25,977
Minnesota	7	....	Lbs...	2,048	....	14,336	7,640
All other states	13	7	Lbs...	2,441	....	17,087	87,068
Mint (mint oil), total	11,210	8,195	Lbs...	288,254	158,091	1,440,525	253,000
Indiana	7,107	1,814	Lbs...	171,085	90,021	655,425	58,110
Michigan	3,878	6,360	Lbs...	110,105	101,169	565,675	194,391
All other states	225	21	Lbs...	4,034	301	19,425	499
Teasels, total	78	162	Thou.	16,140	15,536	48,420	13,760
New York	78	110	Thou.	16,140	12,106	48,420	10,760
Oregon	....	52	Thou.	....	3,430	....	3,000
Willows, total	255	661	Tons.	476	857	30,180	44,175
New York	214	405	Tons.	439	667	26,340	19,038
All other states	41	256	Tons.	37	190	3,840	25,137

[1] Acreage not shown when reported in small fractions or when less than 1 acre.

TABLE 188.—SMALL FRUITS—ACREAGE, PRODUCTION, AND VALUE, BY DIVISIONS AND STATES: 1919 AND 1909.

DIVISION AND STATE.	ALL SMALL FRUITS.					
	Acreage.		Production (quarts).		Value.	
	1919	1909	1919	1909	1919	1909
United States	249,084	272,460	324,988,968	426,565,863	$61,732,161	$29,974,481
GEOGRAPHIC DIVISIONS:						
New England	14,385	13,777	32,265,709	37,631,006	4,133,504	2,469,094
Middle Atlantic	44,706	55,243	56,957,446	90,300,863	11,811,201	6,004,636
East North Central	57,239	56,957	63,702,944	73,745,968	12,244,568	5,813,117
West North Central	35,322	35,587	37,368,041	46,275,534	7,803,013	3,921,982
South Atlantic	25,319	45,403	28,198,785	72,300,168	5,457,777	4,122,467
East South Central	20,943	18,994	23,457,806	22,182,689	4,282,592	1,553,767
West South Central	22,713	19,417	26,666,084	23,878,888	5,413,115	1,771,332
Mountain	4,624	6,765	5,050,860	10,587,207	1,075,167	946,263
Pacific	23,833	20,317	51,321,293	49,663,540	9,511,224	3,371,823
NEW ENGLAND:						
Maine	1,573	1,260	1,561,647	2,285,415	378,714	233,124
New Hampshire	1,071	618	753,969	998,244	184,266	107,365
Vermont	694	469	749,032	826,122	187,580	92,030
Massachusetts	9,628	9,552	27,099,119	29,260,143	2,900,249	1,676,790
Rhode Island	246	281	339,064	437,560	65,666	43,033
Connecticut	1,173	1,597	1,762,878	3,823,522	417,029	316,752
MIDDLE ATLANTIC:						
New York	20,412	22,496	25,713,901	37,857,829	5,951,505	2,875,495
New Jersey	15,614	24,069	20,289,727	38,822,987	3,526,203	1,954,125
Pennsylvania	8,680	8,678	10,953,818	13,620,047	2,333,493	1,175,016
EAST NORTH CENTRAL:						
Ohio	9,447	11,591	11,963,128	15,721,023	2,359,379	1,296,343
Indiana	7,565	5,919	6,812,972	7,424,831	1,374,521	612,725
Illinois	11,215	11,723	10,591,818	13,602,676	2,064,524	1,109,747
Michigan	21,021	21,419	23,946,801	27,214,659	4,736,480	2,028,865
Wisconsin	7,991	6,305	10,388,225	9,782,779	1,709,664	765,437
WEST NORTH CENTRAL:						
Minnesota	5,008	3,738	6,165,120	4,476,575	1,316,594	493,406
Iowa	7,885	7,211	8,837,293	10,344,052	1,911,767	966,804
Missouri	16,768	17,009	17,769,936	23,696,221	3,624,941	1,761,400
North Dakota	524	399	170,771	285,696	40,979	39,641
South Dakota	412	419	224,398	401,295	52,538	47,263
Nebraska	1,147	1,411	647,321	1,594,421	143,401	159,169
Kansas	3,578	5,400	3,553,202	5,477,274	712,793	454,200
SOUTH ATLANTIC:						
Delaware	3,915	8,687	4,362,473	14,425,209	783,567	649,732
Maryland	8,360	16,595	10,278,972	26,277,054	1,848,259	1,227,548
District of Columbia	21	12	25,789	24,109	4,866	1,875
Virginia	3,518	7,295	4,439,964	11,342,980	861,680	671,843
West Virginia	3,162	2,913	2,092,376	2,336,562	400,638	191,002
North Carolina	4,099	6,701	4,776,710	12,827,427	947,714	853,076
South Carolina	498	856	269,248	1,408,099	61,440	113,254
Georgia	842	988	625,783	1,262,155	134,644	111,754
Florida	904	1,356	1,327,470	2,396,573	414,969	302,383
EAST SOUTH CENTRAL:						
Kentucky	6,163	4,387	5,323,010	4,972,702	1,007,119	357,597
Tennessee	12,544	12,539	14,620,175	13,895,493	2,552,651	923,613
Alabama	1,477	1,232	2,125,418	1,907,193	420,799	165,386
Mississippi	759	836	1,389,203	1,407,301	302,023	107,171
WEST SOUTH CENTRAL:						
Arkansas	9,873	8,032	12,538,205	8,965,572	2,584,502	601,722
Louisiana	4,052	3,587	5,342,180	6,420,207	1,227,432	486,988
Oklahoma	2,649	2,745	1,899,073	2,310,367	355,306	202,291
Texas	6,139	5,053	6,886,626	6,182,742	1,245,875	480,331
MOUNTAIN:						
Montana	386	562	338,087	766,791	75,652	86,586
Idaho	1,240	1,673	1,106,208	2,071,141	225,678	201,525
Wyoming	87	106	56,824	96,883	15,885	13,984
Colorado	1,798	2,829	2,213,619	4,294,988	482,533	398,836
New Mexico	120	66	53,750	76,532	11,998	9,335
Arizona	58	76	62,467	112,190	14,048	12,987
Utah	910	1,416	1,198,200	3,118,395	244,486	217,327
Nevada	25	37	21,705	50,287	4,887	5,683
PACIFIC:						
Washington	7,434	5,508	16,884,745	13,490,930	3,490,388	941,415
Oregon	8,463	5,122	18,977,822	9,348,490	2,927,984	641,194
California	7,936	9,687	15,458,726	26,824,120	3,092,852	1,789,214

TABLE 189.—SMALL FRUITS—PRODUCTION OF THE SEVERAL KINDS, BY DIVISIONS AND STATES: 1919.

DIVISION AND STATE.	PRODUCTION (QUARTS).					
	Strawberries.	Raspberries and loganberries.[1]	Blackberries and dewberries.	Cranberries.	Currants.	Other berries.[2]
United States	176,931,550	61,333,509	39,945,078	35,260,291	7,614,817	3,903,723
GEOGRAPHIC DIVISIONS:						
New England	6,319,419	1,374,601	790,102	23,202,683	436,729	142,175
Middle Atlantic	24,065,552	16,328,692	4,608,673	7,766,467	3,758,104	429,958
East North Central	36,133,472	14,714,507	6,721,886	3,449,056	1,516,991	1,167,032
West North Central	26,048,603	5,616,192	4,422,115	56,965	438,633	785,533
South Atlantic	23,497,227	1,694,922	2,829,944	27,018	81,085	68,589
East South Central	19,673,040	599,320	3,128,749	516	8,692	47,489
West South Central	17,690,967	191,458	8,722,827		26,149	34,683
Mountain	2,158,654	1,495,425	341,525	1,605	482,307	571,344
Pacific	21,344,616	19,318,392	8,379,257	755,981	866,127	656,920
NEW ENGLAND:						
Maine	893,740	279,254	242,478	57,637	20,429	68,109
New Hampshire	489,774	131,145	90,666	8,919	18,140	15,325
Vermont	428,335	177,575	113,210	1,572	24,437	3,903
Massachusetts	3,151,371	468,715	251,951	22,918,103	266,908	42,071
Rhode Island	116,646	47,345	6,428	152,582	13,982	2,081
Connecticut	1,239,553	270,567	85,369	63,870	92,833	10,686
MIDDLE ATLANTIC:						
New York	8,579,563	11,674,978	1,711,546	106,850	3,321,583	319,381
New Jersey	8,301,893	2,083,925	2,045,521	7,650,508	139,631	68,249
Pennsylvania	7,184,096	2,569,789	851,606	9,109	296,890	42,328
EAST NORTH CENTRAL:						
Ohio	7,165,957	2,773,819	1,481,447	1,301	431,152	109,452
Indiana	4,277,646	1,251,652	1,087,317	2,679	56,742	136,936
Illinois	6,901,199	1,945,336	1,365,223		103,471	276,589
Michigan	12,585,543	7,657,819	2,452,909	20,367	636,481	593,682
Wisconsin	5,203,127	1,085,881	334,990	3,424,709	289,145	50,373
WEST NORTH CENTRAL:						
Minnesota	4,111,969	1,516,147	181,183	54,258	208,863	92,700
Iowa	6,606,592	1,428,396	597,449	1,452	77,953	125,451
Missouri	12,861,820	1,592,556	2,958,006		17,510	340,044
North Dakota	47,157	39,173	2,485	1,255	55,134	25,567
South Dakota	141,163	30,368	1,811		32,147	18,909
Nebraska	451,798	89,672	35,433		21,436	48,982
Kansas	1,828,104	919,880	645,748		25,590	133,880
SOUTH ATLANTIC:						
Delaware	4,056,028	26,801	270,560		1,390	7,694
Maryland	8,976,057	723,738	517,525	661	43,320	17,671
District of Columbia	16,882	933	7,097		212	665
Virginia	3,803,278	280,228	313,873	25,314	7,335	9,936
West Virginia	840,273	607,495	594,833		24,387	25,388
North Carolina	3,807,598	29,073	936,251		957	2,831
South Carolina	223,745	4,111	40,187		1,205	
Georgia	505,693	19,479	96,852		2,242	1,517
Florida	1,267,673	3,064	52,766	1,043	37	2,887
EAST SOUTH CENTRAL:						
Kentucky	3,194,624	308,406	1,778,468		5,294	36,218
Tennessee	13,130,904	277,344	1,200,981		2,825	8,121
Alabama	2,024,051	9,833	87,695	516	573	2,750
Mississippi	1,323,461	3,737	61,605			400
WEST SOUTH CENTRAL:						
Arkansas	11,463,971	154,351	885,539		4,701	29,643
Louisiana	5,323,890	145	18,145			
Oklahoma	311,630	30,234	1,531,810		20,359	5,040
Texas	591,476	6,728	6,287,333		1,089	
MOUNTAIN:						
Montana	171,150	80,875	13,128		55,459	17,475
Idaho	494,818	385,510	91,056	1,187	72,000	61,637
Wyoming	27,061	10,079			15,266	3,518
Colorado	944,170	612,678	76,234		137,634	411,797
New Mexico	14,363	6,202	8,255		15,450	9,502
Arizona	17,058	677	37,040		6,856	330
Utah	484,792	364,061	115,437	418	172,201	61,291
Nevada	5,136	3,443	397		7,441	5,288
PACIFIC:						
Washington	6,377,368	5,757,456	3,691,065	585,224	254,959	218,673
Oregon	4,159,200	12,022,912	2,139,110	170,757	99,890	385,953
California	10,808,048	1,538,024	2,549,082		511,278	52,294

[1] The production of loganberries in 1919 was 12,123,062 quarts, of which 1,157,778 quarts were produced in Washington, and 10,198,011 quarts in Oregon.

[2] Mainly gooseberries.

TABLE 190.—APPLES—NUMBER OF TREES, BY DIVISIONS AND STATES: 1920 AND 1910.

DIVISION AND STATE.	TREES OF BEARING AGE.			TREES NOT OF BEARING AGE.		
	Farms reporting, 1920	Number.		Farms reporting, 1920	Number.	
		1920	1910		1920	1910
United States	2,687,685	115,309,165	151,322,840	1,034,114	36,195,085	65,791,848
GEOGRAPHIC DIVISIONS:						
New England	111,582	6,351,577	8,219,152	36,216	2,123,730	2,094,512
Middle Atlantic	339,548	17,775,068	20,302,285	111,211	6,371,590	5,849,449
East North Central	684,462	22,449,054	34,134,909	218,471	7,678,220	10,610,319
West North Central	451,980	12,506,741	31,744,757	192,527	4,166,067	9,724,993
South Atlantic	458,781	20,777,465	20,673,712	195,192	8,051,972	10,064,819
East South Central	355,506	8,238,854	12,273,277	154,976	3,093,230	5,386,555
West South Central	138,533	6,007,845	11,838,069	73,376	1,586,538	7,224,590
Mountain	52,171	6,794,915	4,614,667	17,937	723,571	6,679,166
Pacific	95,122	14,407,646	7,522,012	34,208	2,400,167	8,157,445
NEW ENGLAND:						
Maine	34,609	2,833,304	3,476,616	9,707	512,217	1,045,123
New Hampshire	14,965	721,130	1,240,885	4,328	227,933	207,289
Vermont	17,781	712,594	1,183,529	5,333	254,029	219,833
Massachusetts	24,270	1,218,870	1,367,379	10,663	791,771	355,868
Rhode Island	2,958	173,110	152,009	1,118	71,375	54,560
Connecticut	16,999	692,569	798,734	5,067	266,405	211,839
MIDDLE ATLANTIC:						
New York	148,199	9,636,698	11,248,203	38,166	2,932,281	2,828,515
New Jersey	18,517	1,149,776	1,053,626	6,738	811,256	519,749
Pennsylvania	172,832	6,988,594	8,000,456	66,307	2,628,053	2,501,185
EAST NORTH CENTRAL:						
Ohio	175,416	5,970,410	8,504,886	48,546	2,047,687	2,438,246
Indiana	126,647	3,427,816	5,764,821	34,625	929,160	1,961,974
Illinois	134,414	5,113,063	9,900,627	41,234	1,825,886	2,548,301
Michigan	133,382	5,615,905	7,534,343	38,502	2,050,229	2,253,072
Wisconsin	114,603	2,321,860	2,430,232	55,564	825,258	1,408,726
WEST NORTH CENTRAL:						
Minnesota	73,941	1,596,264	1,380,396	36,689	637,187	1,571,816
Iowa	131,732	2,996,469	5,847,034	48,522	767,351	1,914,325
Missouri	137,063	5,162,859	14,359,673	56,322	1,585,823	3,624,833
North Dakota	2,643	26,157	15,941	1,926	19,694	70,023
South Dakota	13,114	255,637	274,862	6,983	136,082	460,547
Nebraska	40,539	961,313	2,937,178	19,344	401,788	967,133
Kansas	52,948	1,508,042	6,929,673	22,741	618,142	1,116,316
SOUTH ATLANTIC:						
Delaware	6,920	816,109	429,753	2,397	308,487	263,813
Maryland	33,636	1,651,936	1,288,482	12,594	766,264	660,685
District of Columbia	62	1,036	1,654	24	1,178	29
Virginia	116,113	7,385,277	7,004,548	46,080	2,857,007	3,435,591
West Virginia	68,649	5,554,731	4,570,948	28,175	1,735,126	2,772,025
North Carolina	128,655	3,474,821	4,910,171	58,724	1,394,588	1,835,337
South Carolina	38,706	377,557	581,767	17,891	181,101	269,044
Georgia	65,854	1,515,505	1,878,209	28,944	806,731	822,327
Florida	186	493	8,180	363	1,490	5,968
EAST SOUTH CENTRAL:						
Kentucky	131,982	3,742,936	5,538,267	53,840	1,427,408	2,106,297
Tennessee	117,810	3,181,659	4,838,922	47,032	1,032,490	2,117,246
Alabama	70,360	1,044,397	1,468,436	32,625	422,646	737,689
Mississippi	35,354	269,862	427,652	21,479	210,686	425,323
WEST SOUTH CENTRAL:						
Arkansas	64,172	4,074,870	7,650,103	29,678	877,376	3,940,089
Louisiana	7,340	47,037	93,304	6,251	44,175	96,544
Oklahoma	42,159	1,417,911	2,955,810	19,759	428,502	2,060,384
Texas	24,862	468,027	1,138,852	17,688	236,485	1,127,573
MOUNTAIN:						
Montana	4,435	1,059,198	696,753	1,401	69,328	1,308,066
Idaho	18,630	2,380,523	1,005,668	5,186	144,088	1,539,896
Wyoming	1,001	50,302	27,773	803	34,197	84,024
Colorado	10,475	1,777,737	1,688,425	3,724	183,315	1,972,914
New Mexico	6,096	687,799	542,528	2,957	167,097	914,254
Arizona	1,672	70,273	62,027	1,222	35,977	53,884
Utah	9,000	726,471	517,039	2,255	80,304	789,260
Nevada	862	42,612	74,454	389	9,265	16,868
PACIFIC:						
Washington	35,535	7,964,167	3,009,337	11,401	755,898	4,862,702
Oregon	29,044	3,315,093	2,029,913	7,353	500,322	2,240,636
California	30,543	3,128,386	2,482,762	15,454	1,143,947	1,054,107

TABLE **191.**—APPLES—PRODUCTION AND VALUE, BY DIVISIONS AND STATES: 1919 AND 1909.

[A minus sign (−) denotes decrease.]

DIVISION AND STATE.	PRODUCTION (BUSHELS).			VALUE.	
	1919	1909	Per cent of increase.	1919	1909
United States............	136,560,997	145,412,318	−6.1	$241,573,577	$83,231,492
GEOGRAPHIC DIVISIONS:					
New England...............	12,070,259	10,508,457	14.9	19,562,535	6,272,726
Middle Atlantic..............	21,529,512	37,864,532	−43.1	41,733,402	19,856,752
East North Central...........	15,724,432	25,080,615	−37.3	32,712,053	14,669,289
West North Central..........	10,810,161	21,923,470	−50.7	20,837,766	11,792,016
South Atlantic...............	17,829,422	18,375,485	−3.0	29,851,290	9,461,189
East South Central...........	3,334,668	13,163,180	−74.7	5,982,316	6,073,710
West South Central..........	9,291,332	3,240,108	186.8	14,098,673	2,085,260
Mountain...................	9,639,219	5,718,372	68.6	16,473,036	5,536,183
Pacific.....................	36,331,992	9,538,099	280.9	60,322,506	7,484,367
NEW ENGLAND:					
Maine......................	4,829,346	3,636,181	32.8	6,278,151	2,121,816
New Hampshire.............	1,364,001	1,108,424	23.1	2,250,602	637,990
Vermont...................	960,252	1,459,689	−34.2	1,728,454	752,337
Massachusetts..............	3,187,211	2,550,259	25.0	6,055,701	1,780,290
Rhode Island...............	334,308	212,908	57.0	668,616	147,125
Connecticut................	1,395,141	1,540,996	−9.5	2,581,011	833,168
MIDDLE ATLANTIC:					
New York..................	14,350,317	25,409,324	−43.5	26,548,087	13,343,028
New Jersey................	1,666,400	1,406,778	18.5	3,332,800	956,108
Pennsylvania..............	5,512,795	11,048,430	−50.1	11,852,515	5,557,616
EAST NORTH CENTRAL:					
Ohio......................	2,976,436	4,663,752	−36.2	6,845,811	2,970,851
Indiana...................	925,624	2,759,134	−66.5	2,221,498	1,720,811
Illinois...................	4,673,117	3,093,321	51.1	9,346,234	2,111,866
Michigan..................	5,843,271	12,332,296	−52.6	11,686,542	5,969,080
Wisconsin.................	1,305,984	2,232,112	−41.5	2,611,968	1,896,681
WEST NORTH CENTRAL:					
Minnesota.................	1,028,478	1,044,156	−1.5	1,748,412	769,114
Iowa......................	1,810,443	6,746,668	−73.2	3,801,939	3,550,729
Missouri..................	5,132,109	9,258,977	−44.6	9,494,411	4,885,544
North Dakota..............	14,358	4,374	228.3	35,907	7,270
South Dakota..............	168,256	191,784	−12.3	353,336	158,729
Nebraska..................	907,224	3,321,073	−72.7	1,905,175	1,612,765
Kansas....................	1,749,293	1,356,438	29.0	3,498,586	807,865
SOUTH ATLANTIC:					
Delaware..................	606,286	183,094	231.1	1,091,315	115,371
Maryland..................	1,518,884	1,822,824	−16.7	2,430,217	902,077
District of Columbia..........	1,832	2,952	−37.9	3,121	2,162
Virginia...................	8,942,520	6,103,941	46.5	14,308,026	3,129,832
West Virginia..............	4,189,162	4,225,163	−0.9	7,540,491	2,461,074
North Carolina.............	1,938,038	4,775,693	−59.4	3,294,671	2,014,670
South Carolina.............	215,659	362,800	−40.6	474,448	276,410
Georgia...................	416,902	895,613	−53.5	708,735	555,744
Florida...................	139	3,405	−95.9	266	3,849
EAST SOUTH CENTRAL:					
Kentucky..................	1,280,549	7,368,499	−82.6	2,433,053	3,066,776
Tennessee.................	1,258,878	4,640,444	−72.9	2,265,979	2,172,475
Alabama..................	577,356	888,396	−35.0	923,769	620,745
Mississippi................	217,885	265,841	−18.0	359,515	213,714
WEST SOUTH CENTRAL:					
Arkansas..................	7,163,619	2,296,043	212.0	10,745,448	1,322,785
Louisiana.................	43,910	33,875	29.6	74,647	28,744
Oklahoma.................	1,596,975	742,182	115.2	2,475,309	573,076
Texas....................	486,828	168,008	189.8	803,269	160,655
MOUNTAIN:					
Montana..................	673,716	567,054	18.8	1,111,632	566,938
Idaho....................	3,645,640	659,959	452.4	6,379,873	610,504
Wyoming.................	29,999	17,606	68.?	71,997	37,580
Colorado..................	3,417,603	3,559,001	−4.0	5,639,178	3,405,442
New Mexico...............	939,102	417,143	125.1	1,502,564	420,330
Arizona...................	120,765	72,814	65.9	289,836	109,395
Utah.....................	759,696	350,023	117.0	1,367,454	319,691
Nevada...................	52,619	74,449	−29.3	110,502	66,097
PACIFIC:					
Washington................	21,568,691	2,672,100	707.2	38,823,641	2,925,761
Oregon...................	6,921,284	1,930,926	258.4	9,343,737	1,656,944
California.................	7,842,017	4,935,073	58.9	12,155,128	2,901,662

TABLE **192.**—PEACHES—NUMBER OF TREES, BY DIVISIONS AND STATES: 1920 AND 1910.

DIVISION AND STATE.	TREES OF BEARING AGE.			TREES NOT OF BEARING AGE.		
	Farms reporting, 1920	Number.		Farms reporting, 1920	Number.	
		1920	1910		1920	1910
United States..........	1,521,875	65,646,101	94,506,657	639,065	21,617,862	42,266,243
GEOGRAPHIC DIVISIONS:						
New England.........	15,999	993,003	723,810	7,808	324,117	572,237
Middle Atlantic...........	116,023	8,538,381	6,056,690	47,809	2,777,643	5,759,925
East North Central........	188,277	6,807,070	11,035,119	94,596	3,143,932	6,972,375
West North Central.......	158,999	3,430,028	13,265,526	63,495	1,097,036	2,582,028
South Atlantic.............	367,738	16,800,861	20,583,445	159,686	6,752,891	6,137,901
East South Central........	328,852	6,420,558	10,312,768	129,421	2,420,517	3,865,232
West South Central........	260,185	11,092,227	22,284,966	107,011	3,499,485	8,734,552
Mountain.................	22,242	1,444,192	1,605,285	7,486	155,135	1,696,111
Pacific...................	63,360	10,119,781	8,639,048	21,753	1,447,106	5,945,882
NEW ENGLAND:						
Maine...................	587	5,666	5,102	366	2,570	3,320
New Hampshire..........	2,398	81,287	57,571	1,019	23,200	35,213
Vermont................	201	2,915	5,492	152	3,978	2,187
Massachusetts...........	7,085	346,260	154,592	3,285	135,426	162,114
Rhode Island............	936	61,125	39,342	571	25,366	30,795
Connecticut.............	4,792	495,750	461,711	2,415	133,577	338,608
MIDDLE ATLANTIC:						
New York...............	24,554	3,038,023	2,457,187	9,392	658,868	2,216,907
New Jersey..............	8,540	1,936,632	1,216,476	4,626	884,067	1,363,632
Pennsylvania............	82,929	3,563,726	2,383,027	33,791	1,234,708	2,179,386
EAST NORTH CENTRAL:						
Ohio....................	67,402	2,924,177	3,133,368	28,801	970,183	2,092,300
Indiana.................	43,492	860,024	2,130,298	23,586	568,046	1,145,479
Illinois.................	55,968	1,011,325	2,860,120	31,090	839,712	739,358
Michigan................	21,133	2,010,022	2,907,170	10,860	764,838	2,991,090
Wisconsin...............	282	1,522	4,163	259	1,153	4,148
WEST NORTH CENTRAL:						
Minnesota...............	84	890	1,571	81	427	3,837
Iowa....................	10,596	129,939	1,090,749	5,611	61,043	283,308
Missouri................	104,249	2,358,925	6,588,034	37,585	716,325	1,404,429
North Dakota............	5	38	90	6	32	604
South Dakota............	14	109	1,815	24	177	5,259
Nebraska................	4,694	95,629	1,188,373	3,178	40,118	263,882
Kansas..................	39,357	844,498	4,394,894	17,010	278,914	620,709
SOUTH ATLANTIC:						
Delaware................	3,288	464,514	1,177,402	1,436	93,336	212,117
Maryland................	13,960	997,086	1,497,724	6,357	285,486	805,063
District of Columbia......	20	1,208	330	9	238	1
Virginia.................	61,951	1,578,253	1,585,505	28,289	783,733	780,551
West Virginia............	35,802	2,049,862	1,424,582	15,557	651,742	1,441,188
North Carolina..........	101,220	1,976,756	2,661,791	48,091	1,093,993	861,042
South Carolina..........	45,589	871,976	1,336,142	19,800	335,599	349,790
Georgia.................	92,499	8,655,051	10,609,119	33,278	3,391,851	1,531,367
Florida.................	13,409	206,155	290,850	6,869	116,913	156,782
EAST SOUTH CENTRAL:						
Kentucky................	86,756	1,671,044	2,245,402	35,746	690,483	1,110,744
Tennessee...............	100,644	2,349,656	3,163,737	33,431	690,359	1,190,727
Alabama................	86,256	1,544,700	3,177,331	33,446	546,024	838,866
Mississippi.............	55,196	855,158	1,726,298	26,798	493,651	724,895
WEST SOUTH CENTRAL:						
Arkansas................	73,325	3,342,387	6,859,962	27,599	988,966	2,884,927
Louisiana...............	23,134	408,178	903,352	13,949	231,909	316,132
Oklahoma...............	61,830	2,879,945	4,783,825	21,376	637,762	2,574,680
Texas...................	101,896	4,461,717	9,737,827	44,087	1,640,848	2,958,813
MOUNTAIN:						
Montana................	144	1,831	538	75	420	3,386
Idaho...................	5,823	178,434	73,080	1,799	26,648	212,995
Wyoming................	3	19	46	11	33	419
Colorado................	2,896	446,943	793,372	958	32,158	606,001
New Mexico.............	5,162	154,968	136,191	2,153	36,923	184,466
Arizona.................	2,441	101,855	51,415	1,304	26,681	32,562
Utah...................	5,460	554,202	544,314	1,015	28,551	651,233
Nevada.................	313	5,940	6,329	171	3,721	5,049
PACIFIC:						
Washington.............	12,846	649,085	536,875	3,464	50,254	1,028,141
Oregon.................	11,789	412,936	273,162	3,463	29,911	508,179
California..............	38,725	9,057,760	7,829,011	14,826	1,366,941	4,409,562

TABLE 193.—PEACHES—PRODUCTION AND VALUE, BY DIVISIONS AND STATES: 1919 AND 1909.

[A minus sign (−) denotes decrease. Per cent not shown when base is less than 100 or when per cent is more than 1,000.]

DIVISION AND STATE.	PRODUCTION (BUSHELS).			VALUE.	
	1919	1909	Per cent of increase.	1919	1909
United States	50,686,082	35,470,276	42.9	$95,569,868	$28,781,078
GEOGRAPHIC DIVISIONS:					
New England	479,000	406,903	17.7	1,197,192	632,411
Middle Atlantic	4,015,438	3,201,493	25.4	9,804,920	4,018,034
East North Central	1,597,933	5,120,841	−68.8	4,501,852	5,172,957
West North Central	1,490,033	1,643,257	−9.3	3,078,593	1,250,944
South Atlantic	7,985,330	5,571,628	43.3	14,913,593	4,888,459
East South Central	3,604,149	5,775,799	−37.6	6,650,294	4,098,776
West South Central	11,268,207	3,279,545	243.6	17,734,953	2,761,044
Mountain	2,227,619	940,168	136.9	4,042,350	1,071,446
Pacific	18,018,373	9,530,642	89.1	33,646,121	4,887,007
NEW ENGLAND:					
Maine	2,177	2,014	8.1	5,225	3,205
New Hampshire	39,019	23,218	68.1	91,695	37,884
Vermont	904	2,221	−59.3	2,262	4,399
Massachusetts	213,139	91,756	132.3	532,851	138,716
Rhode Island	28,771	17,704	62.5	77,682	30,609
Connecticut	194,990	269,990	−27.8	487,477	417,598
MIDDLE ATLANTIC:					
New York	1,262,480	1,736,483	−27.3	2,840,589	2,014,088
New Jersey	1,653,223	441,440	274.5	3,885,073	652,771
Pennsylvania	1,099,735	1,023,570	7.4	3,079,258	1,351,175
EAST NORTH CENTRAL:					
Ohio	617,537	1,036,340	−40.4	1,821,740	1,349,311
Indiana	82,266	1,174,389	−93.0	255,027	1,123,248
Illinois	449,601	1,222,570	−63.2	1,191,442	999,516
Michigan	448,177	1,686,586	−73.4	1,232,495	1,700,330
Wisconsin	352	956	−63.2	1,148	552
WEST NORTH CENTRAL:					
Minnesota	370	599	−38.2	944	659
Iowa	1,891	23,180	−91.8	5,766	24,950
Missouri	1,262,723	1,484,548	−14.9	2,525,446	1,110,550
North Dakota	3	35	....	9	71
South Dakota	21	148	−85.8	65	167
Nebraska	11,461	110,180	−89.6	33,813	91,129
Kansas	213,564	24,567	769.3	512,550	23,418
SOUTH ATLANTIC:					
Delaware	227,375	16,722	....	409,275	21,402
Maryland	564,111	324,609	73.8	1,071,815	361,617
District of Columbia	229	3	....	481	3
Virginia	681,528	243,446	180.0	1,363,056	227,141
West Virginia	706,411	328,901	114.8	1,518,784	368,584
North Carolina	479,218	1,344,410	−64.4	1,006,360	1,041,767
South Carolina	389,734	643,040	−39.4	837,930	557,303
Georgia	4,788,718	2,555,499	87.4	8,380,279	2,182,613
Florida	148,006	114,998	28.7	325,613	128,029
EAST SOUTH CENTRAL:					
Kentucky	459,681	1,623,379	−71.7	1,034,291	1,062,138
Tennessee	1,285,441	1,579,019	−18.6	2,378,065	1,055,379
Alabama	1,083,142	1,416,584	−23.5	1,841,344	1,055,971
Mississippi	775,885	1,156,817	−32.9	1,396,594	925,288
WEST SOUTH CENTRAL:					
Arkansas	3,340,823	1,901,647	75.7	5,178,276	1,502,996
Louisiana	381,863	290,623	31.4	630,074	228,084
Oklahoma	2,924,842	357,644	717.8	4,533,512	326,315
Texas	4,620,679	729,631	533.3	7,393,091	703,649
MOUNTAIN:					
Montana	500	198	297.7	1,656	235
Idaho	279,101	18,734	....	502,930	28,149
Wyoming	4	5	....	11	30
Colorado	721,480	692,258	4.2	1,334,741	764,561
New Mexico	198,346	32,533	509.7	426,445	37,195
Arizona	138,361	50,102	176.2	352,821	80,325
Utah	883,950	143,237	517.1	1,414,320	156,451
Nevada	5,868	3,171	85.1	9,976	4,500
PACIFIC:					
Washington	1,544,859	84,494	....	3,321,449	118,918
Oregon	504,441	179,030	181.8	781,885	194,314
California	15,969,073	9,267,118	72.3	29,542,787	4,573,775

TABLE 194.—PEARS—NUMBER OF TREES, BY DIVISIONS AND STATES: 1920 AND 1910.

DIVISION AND STATE.	TREES OF BEARING AGE.			TREES NOT OF BEARING AGE.		
	Farms reporting, 1920	Number.		Farms reporting, 1920	Number.	
		1920	1910		1920	1910
United States	1,148,610	14,647,412	15,171,524	387,878	6,052,247	8,803,885
GEOGRAPHIC DIVISIONS:						
New England	35,378	220,433	296,874	10,635	115,924	97,650
Middle Atlantic	201,921	4,012,994	3,670,094	49,077	1,282,242	2,123,242
East North Central	272,270	2,443,010	3,560,083	66,465	676,117	1,441,505
West North Central	117,377	724,393	1,154,426	47,133	249,021	589,140
South Atlantic	196,421	1,506,279	2,325,714	73,384	464,903	880,461
East South Central	136,535	651,824	831,618	55,041	252,689	506,959
West South Central	90,795	849,737	1,045,143	47,722	333,086	-936,230
Mountain	20,669	339,018	312,449	6,890	101,870	417,182
Pacific	77,244	3,899,724	1,975,123	31,531	2,576,395	1,811,516
NEW ENGLAND:						
Maine	5,504	22,525	46,683	1,637	7,120	13,013
New Hampshire	4,557	21,506	36,816	1,237	7,753	9,397
Vermont	3,281	14,352	26,315	1,063	8,484	7,726
Massachusetts	12,285	88,630	113,365	3,906	52,745	38,378
Rhode Island	1,587	13,435	16,907	463	7,955	5,405
Connecticut	8,164	59,985	56,788	2,329	31,867	23,731
MIDDLE ATLANTIC:						
New York	76,396	2,778,761	2,141,596	19,192	967,573	1,502,661
New Jersey	10,977	480,601	731,616	2,583	77,026	238,401
Pennsylvania	114,548	753,632	796,882	27,302	237,643	382,180
EAST NORTH CENTRAL:						
Ohio	82,019	616,416	899,019	18,355	147,892	333,739
Indiana	63,219	337,515	708,723	13,600	68,150	229,548
Illinois	54,858	435,707	786,349	17,614	148,810	234,037
Michigan	64,847	1,029,735	1,136,151	14,347	302,734	623,931
Wisconsin	7,327	23,637	29,841	2,549	8,531	20,250
WEST NORTH CENTRAL:						
Minnesota	205	1,626	2,792	152	882	4,135
Iowa	18,708	100,582	191,125	7,778	34,985	123,262
Missouri	58,839	376,208	606,973	20,552	101,994	272,213
North Dakota	22	486	24	11	148	327
South Dakota	64	711	1,844	68	2,044	5,087
Nebraska	7,042	36,926	59,285	5,579	29,011	51,443
Kansas	32,497	207,854	292,383	12,993	79,957	132,673
SOUTH ATLANTIC:						
Delaware	3,622	249,375	449,692	710	26,575	90,917
Maryland	18,915	305,510	540,583	3,920	48,918	138,152
District of Columbia	46	517	1,045	17	152	32
Virginia	51,485	311,199	457,177	16,589	79,561	255,083
West Virginia	20,202	116,685	154,908	7,097	43,357	102,826
North Carolina	50,420	219,725	243,367	22,715	129,104	150,368
South Carolina	19,005	78,999	105,251	8,730	33,188	54,732
Georgia	29,023	178,070	262,982	12,030	83,474	69,534
Florida	3,703	46,199	110,709	1,576	20,574	18,817
EAST SOUTH CENTRAL:						
Kentucky	45,405	238,007	337,355	17,399	76,505	131,905
Tennessee	46,661	223,556	233,407	16,848	73,679	174,675
Alabama	26,660	115,082	142,300	11,137	51,411	99,170
Mississippi	17,809	75,179	118,556	9,657	51,094	101,209
WEST SOUTH CENTRAL:						
Arkansas	17,576	145,789	221,764	9,734	49,412	196,753
Louisiana	8,036	38,796	57,630	5,989	27,336	38,242
Oklahoma	25,183	229,468	207,271	11,216	73,944	252,336
Texas	40,000	435,684	558,478	20,783	182,394	448,899
MOUNTAIN:						
Montana	664	10,278	10,297	206	1,386	12,806
Idaho	8,645	75,452	65,113	2,460	20,539	76,939
Wyoming	40	116	178	58	239	901
Colorado	2,598	136,117	99,989	879	39,979	171,367
New Mexico	2,830	49,315	37,220	1,275	19,423	100,201
Arizona	1,139	12,359	16,351	821	7,716	12,852
Utah	4,227	51,812	79,355	964	8,479	39,901
Nevada	526	3,569	3,946	227	4,109	2,215
PACIFIC:						
Washington	32,937	866,634	290,676	12,793	183,346	617,754
Oregon	20,145	727,444	273,542	4,915	214,523	795,669
California	24,162	2,305,646	1,410,905	13,823	2,178,526	398,093

TABLE 195.—PEARS—PRODUCTION AND VALUE, BY DIVISIONS AND STATES: 1919 AND 1909.

[A minus sign (−) denotes decrease. Per cent not shown when base is less than 100 or when per cent is more than 1,000.]

DIVISION AND STATE.	PRODUCTION (BUSHELS).			VALUE.	
	1919	1909	Per cent of increase.	1919	1909
United States..............	14,204,265	8,840,733	60.7	$26,439,735	$7,910,600
GEOGRAPHIC DIVISIONS:					
New England...............	194,286	233,845	−16.9	425,257	258,816
Middle Atlantic...............	2,652,903	2,185,204	21.4	5,656,591	2,029,040
East North Central............	1,060,522	1,623,176	−34.7	2,173,619	1,331,712
West North Central...........	707,359	213,678	231.0	1,331,864	239,838
South Atlantic................	1,139,048	975,162	16.8	1,938,827	680,275
East South Central...........	452,980	536,422	−15.6	820,360	450,042
West South Central...........	1,069,231	191,518	458.3	1,698,728	192,736
Mountain....................	485,191	268,205	80.9	1,036,194	371,306
Pacific......................	6,442,745	2,613,523	146.5	11,358,295	2,356,835
NEW ENGLAND:					
Maine.....................	14,291	38,964	−63.3	27,869	43,524
New Hampshire.............	17,274	24,224	−28.7	31,957	25,206
Vermont...................	10,360	20,763	−50.1	22,793	23,788
Massachusetts.............	84,486	96,071	−12.1	190,097	110,069
Rhode Island..............	10,713	12,501	−14.3	26,784	14,577
Connecticut...............	57,162	41,322	38.3	125,757	41,652
MIDDLE ATLANTIC:					
New York..................	1,830,237	1,343,089	36.3	4,026,521	1,418,218
New Jersey................	401,706	463,290	−13.3	682,902	254,582
Pennsylvania.............	420,960	378,825	11.1	947,168	356,240
EAST NORTH CENTRAL:					
Ohio......................	157,492	374,871	−58.0	393,755	332,727
Indiana...................	109,463	319,925	−65.8	218,926	243,698
Illinois...................	374,925	249,365	50.4	656,136	202,965
Michigan..................	405,189	666,023	−39.2	871,155	535,771
Wisconsin.................	13,453	12,992	3.5	33,647	16,551
WEST NORTH CENTRAL:					
Minnesota.................	265	400	−33.8	540	465
Iowa......................	30,036	44,449	−32.4	67,589	58,777
Missouri..................	430,828	142,547	202.2	753,964	148,789
North Dakota..............	83	8	....	210	15
South Dakota..............	43	162	−73.5	113	447
Nebraska..................	24,617	6,700	267.4	55,398	9,802
Kansas....................	221,487	19,412	....	454,050	21,543
SOUTH ATLANTIC:					
Delaware..................	97,703	105,357	−7.3	146,555	52,022
Maryland..................	287,199	367,359	−21.8	459,518	168,561
District of Columbia...........	919	455	102.0	1,470	412
Virginia..................	287,927	74,486	286.6	460,680	63,424
West Virginia.............	33,364	29,916	11.5	70,068	32,101
North Carolina............	111,548	84,019	32.8	211,945	81,347
South Carolina............	98,975	65,680	50.7	207,852	67,685
Georgia...................	178,181	149,667	19.1	302,916	134,604
Florida...................	43,232	98,223	−56.0	77,823	80,119
EAST SOUTH CENTRAL:					
Kentucky..................	54,764	251,536	−78.2	112,268	187,951
Tennessee.................	114,963	83,557	37.6	218,429	78,448
Alabama...................	162,509	100,041	62.4	284,399	86,866
Mississippi...............	120,744	101,288	19.2	205,264	96,777
WEST SOUTH CENTRAL:					
Arkansas..................	123,605	37,547	229.2	210,130	38,140
Louisiana.................	58,640	35,554	64.9	102,631	31,069
Oklahoma..................	249,586	7,450	....	461,735	9,248
Texas.....................	637,400	110,967	474.4	924,232	114,279
MOUNTAIN:					
Montana...................	3,960	7,543	−47.5	9,709	12,008
Idaho.....................	41,847	42,049	10.9	105,067	48,045
Wyoming...................	64	16	....	128	65
Colorado..................	269,465	132,536	103.3	592,824	210,685
New Mexico................	65,542	29,435	122.7	114,698	29,698
Arizona...................	18,201	13,289	37.0	49,144	21,331
Utah......................	76,008	38,654	96.6	155,817	44,365
Nevada....................	4,104	4,083	0.5	8,618	5,119
PACIFIC:					
Washington................	1,728,759	310,804	456.2	3,025,331	328,895
Oregon....................	761,063	374,622	103.2	1,217,703	366,977
California................	3,952,923	1,928,097	105.0	7,115,261	1,660,963

TABLE 196.—PLUMS AND PRUNES—NUMBER OF TREES, BY DIVISIONS AND STATES: 1920 AND 1910.

DIVISION AND STATE.	TREES OF BEARING AGE.			TREES NOT OF BEARING AGE.		
	Farms reporting, 1920	Number.		Farms reporting, 1920	Number.	
		1920	1910		1920	1910
United States...........	915,829	20,452,293	23,445,009	319,434	9,375,268	6,923,581
GEOGRAPHIC DIVISIONS:						
New England..............	20,990	125,988	176,038	8,348	53,570	90,498
Middle Atlantic...........	140,390	1,543,663	1,709,712	39,162	450,858	845,001
East North Central........	211,211	1,441,988	2,739,635	63,639	466,989	976,854
West North Central........	156,966	1,424,673	3,570,012	66,864	553,807	1,114,862
South Atlantic............	111,125	674,440	1,152,080	35,603	209,401	363,099
East South Central........	92,429	735,670	1,324,616	25,795	152,787	372,010
West South Central........	78,862	1,066,706	2,337,965	40,756	453,582	744,987
Mountain.................	28,741	795,886	678,268	9,588	156,293	265,810
Pacific....................	75,115	12,643,279	9,756,683	29,679	6,877,981	2,150,460
NEW ENGLAND:						
Maine....................	6,792	37,529	43,576	2,027	9,395	22,491
New Hampshire...........	3,315	18,335	23,152	1,126	6,454	12,562
Vermont.................	2,295	19,647	32,920	1,104	10,756	15,818
Massachusetts...........	5,640	32,764	41,345	2,501	16,553	23,871
Rhode Island............	387	1,964	4,836	217	1,347	2,556
Connecticut.............	2,561	15,749	30,209	1,373	9,065	13,200
MIDDLE ATLANTIC:						
New York...............	51,615	745,889	919,017	15,396	205,702	328,329
New Jersey..............	4,279	30,128	46,547	1,413	11,772	23,071
Pennsylvania............	84,496	767,646	744,148	22,353	233,384	493,601
EAST NORTH CENTRAL:						
Ohio....................	62,342	459,265	1,001,734	15,039	129,713	332,811
Indiana.................	40,487	214,202	566,988	10,037	53,178	177,931
Illinois.................	48,480	273,554	600,087	14,513	79,615	141,480
Michigan...............	40,853	377,123	464,917	12,621	142,657	253,479
Wisconsin..............	19,049	117,844	105,909	11,429	61,826	71,153
WEST NORTH CENTRAL:						
Minnesota..............	18,452	193,668	233,736	11,730	102,929	167,926
Iowa...................	38,274	313,769	1,155,041	14,135	95,356	245,281
Missouri...............	68,257	528,649	917,851	19,876	144,651	183,828
North Dakota..........	2,282	41,254	19,147	1,419	19,852	35,459
South Dakota..........	5,989	117,677	268,268	4,171	59,793	172,186
Nebraska..............	6,923	86,183	351,321	6,360	62,786	184,066
Kansas................	16,789	143,473	624,648	9,173	68,440	126,116
SOUTH ATLANTIC:						
Delaware..............	807	5,100	27,115	237	1,595	3,872
Maryland..............	9,228	41,435	69,996	2,240	11,479	29,478
District of Columbia.......	27	128	104	10	100	8
Virginia...............	26,423	118,938	171,667	8,090	35,189	59,127
West Virginia..........	20,703	180,758	234,859	6,782	58,547	125,078
North Carolina........	25,526	110,577	168,883	8,245	35,820	45,503
South Carolina........	10,179	49,736	82,212	3,421	15,488	21,657
Georgia...............	15,536	135,453	357,323	5,162	38,198	62,126
Florida...............	2,696	32,315	39,921	1,416	12,985	16,250
EAST SOUTH CENTRAL:						
Kentucky..............	39,851	282,831	355,858	9,987	57,470	128,367
Tennessee.............	33,894	281,127	499,627	8,311	47,930	108,510
Alabama..............	11,690	96,922	211,991	3,982	23,654	51,979
Mississippi...........	6,994	74,790	257,140	3,515	23,733	83,154
WEST SOUTH CENTRAL:						
Arkansas..............	20,082	292,323	731,276	7,639	70,264	179,967
Louisiana.............	5,182	87,471	149,929	3,440	36,108	41,419
Oklahoma.............	22,076	206,102	436,421	11,792	104,410	195,836
Texas.................	31,522	480,810	1,020,339	17,885	242,800	327,765
MOUNTAIN:						
Montana...............	1,536	24,501	21,140	540	4,598	15,001
Idaho.................	10,706	552,595	302,855	2,810	80,485	98,017
Wyoming..............	457	6,827	4,564	338	9,091	7,475
Colorado..............	5,243	80,027	143,921	2,318	28,055	68,525
New Mexico...........	3,587	43,766	51,257	1,572	18,042	42,351
Arizona...............	1,457	15,713	12,196	843	6,795	7,898
Utah..................	5,222	66,914	135,619	961	7,508	23,388
Nevada...............	533	5,543	6,716	206	1,719	3,155
PACIFIC:						
Washington............	25,688	875,363	823,082	6,894	309,230	122,912
Oregon................	20,145	2,999,480	1,764,896	6,112	1,331,606	427,609
California.............	29,282	8,768,436	7,168,705	16,673	5,237,145	1,599,939

TABLE 197.—PLUMS AND PRUNES—PRODUCTION AND VALUE, BY DIVISIONS AND STATES: 1919 AND 1909.

[A minus sign (—) denotes decrease.   Per cent not shown when base is less than 100.]

DIVISION AND STATE.	PRODUCTION (BUSHELS).			VALUE.	
	1919	1909	Per cent of increase.	1919	1909
United States............	19,083,942	15,480,170	23.3	$40,984,423	$10,299,495
GEOGRAPHIC DIVISIONS:					
New England............	47,838	62,733	—23.7	123,114	110,178
Middle Atlantic............	337,274	858,274	—60.7	903,862	928,673
East North Central.........	425,600	568,383	—25.1	1,074,795	674,671
West North Central.........	346,695	499,784	—30.6	736,498	535,374
South Atlantic............	274,560	257,912	6.5	562,547	236,221
East South Central.........	235,188	442,125	—46.8	440,776	314,199
West South Central.........	626,335	327,260	91.4	1,069,475	267,703
Mountain..............	651,863	366,056	78.1	1,424,973	319,651
Pacific................	16,138,589	12,097,643	33.4	34,648,383	6,912,825
NEW ENGLAND:					
Maine................	20,043	14,637	36.9	52,113	31,954
New Hampshire...........	8,429	7,542	11.8	20,230	14,039
Vermont...............	2,062	7,205	—71.4	4,843	12,927
Massachusetts...........	13,152	17,814	—26.2	36,170	28,253
Rhode Island............	465	1,872	—75.2	1,093	3,586
Connecticut............	3,687	13,663	—73.0	8,665	19,419
MIDDLE ATLANTIC:					
New York..............	244,294	553,522	—55.9	659,598	519,192
New Jersey.............	8,526	9,594	—11.1	20,461	13,476
Pennsylvania...........	84,454	295,158	—71.4	223,803	396,005
EAST NORTH CENTRAL:					
Ohio.................	84,602	215,657	—60.8	245,347	278,505
Indiana...............	33,536	77,065	—56.5	88,877	89,073
Illinois...............	83,017	78,566	5.7	182,638	80,384
Michigan..............	203,091	181,188	12.1	507,750	205,765
Wisconsin.............	21,354	15,907	34.2	50,183	20,944
WEST NORTH CENTRAL:					
Minnesota.............	24,337	19,920	22.2	51,113	27,808
Iowa................	27,929	158,036	—82.3	58,655	192,421
Missouri..............	232,025	234,872	—1.2	487,257	211,472
North Dakota...........	5,660	1,048	440.1	11,320	1,866
South Dakota...........	11,861	31,748	—62.6	24,910	36,872
Nebraska..............	11,537	41,910	—72.5	26,540	50,934
Kansas...............	33,346	12,250	172.2	76,703	14,001
SOUTH ATLANTIC:					
Delaware..............	1,613	657	145.5	2,904	540
Maryland..............	18,540	13,526	37.1	40,786	16,192
District of Columbia........	72	10	....	180	24
Virginia...............	59,561	22,597	163.6	113,168	22,772
West Virginia...........	37,099	32,948	12.6	96,462	48,522
North Carolina..........	37,415	61,406	—39.1	72,965	45,274
South Carolina..........	35,891	48,754	—26.4	69,989	37,555
Georgia...............	64,053	60,845	5.3	115,293	46,366
Florida...............	20,316	17,169	18.3	50,800	18,976
EAST SOUTH CENTRAL:					
Kentucky..............	68,317	139,346	—51.0	160,550	102,446
Tennessee.............	70,103	139,093	—49.6	122,690	86,743
Alabama..............	54,073	61,712	—12.4	89,222	45,039
Mississippi............	42,695	101,974	—58.1	68,314	79,971
WEST SOUTH CENTRAL:					
Arkansas.............	161,906	194,649	—16.8	267,146	137,003
Louisiana.............	41,683	31,473	32.4	70,863	24,641
Oklahoma.............	127,811	25,916	393.2	230,062	28,134
Texas................	294,935	75,222	292.1	501,404	77,925
MOUNTAIN:					
Montana..............	9,575	8,777	9.1	17,235	11,642
Idaho................	105,905	179,097	171.1	1,067,715	132,804
Wyoming..............	3,091	659	369.0	7,884	1,842
Colorado..............	44,944	81,539	—44.9	107,866	81,354
New Mexico............	30,047	15,528	93.5	64,601	17,054
Arizona...............	23,786	8,420	182.5	63,033	16,261
Utah................	50,677	68,249	—25.7	88,687	54,040
Nevada...............	4,418	3,857	14.5	7,952	4,654
PACIFIC:					
Washington............	785,920	1,032,077	—23.9	1,532,546	600,503
Oregon...............	2,151,864	1,747,587	23.1	4,734,103	838,783
California.............	13,200,805	9,317,979	41.7	28,381,734	5,473,539

TABLE **198.**—CHERRIES—NUMBER OF TREES, BY DIVISIONS AND STATES: 1920 AND 1910.

DIVISION AND STATE.	TREES OF BEARING AGE.			TREES NOT OF BEARING AGE.		
	Farms reporting, 1920	Number.		Farms reporting, 1920	Number.	
		1920	1910		1920	1910
United States...........	1,131,355	10,787,751	11,822,044	384,657	3,694,531	5,621,660
GEOGRAPHIC DIVISIONS:						
New England.............	14,808	70,830	68,236	7,053	42,868	32,587
Middle Atlantic............	164,344	2,080,669	1,851,144	41,536	529,524	659,953
East North Central........	372,639	3,331,857	3,853,974	102,079	980,424	1,523,247
West North Central........	230,018	1,684,272	2,768,659	101,172	834,514	1,117,533
South Atlantic.............	143,284	886,355	1,063,825	48,361	285,003	364,118
East South Central........	81,856	419,270	453,262	31,349	186,943	257,112
West South Central........	34,608	255,170	385,502	21,973	189,947	242,569
Mountain..................	27,599	677,598	390,644	9,385	135,364	581,641
Pacific....................	62,199	1,381,730	986,798	21,749	509,944	842,900
NEW ENGLAND:						
Maine.....................	2,780	12,223	14,288	1,026	4,012	6,653
New Hampshire............	2,114	11,035	9,463	963	5,928	6,326
Vermont..................	1,968	14,393	18,006	843	9,811	6,659
Massachusetts.............	4,474	18,239	13,396	2,377	13,123	6,776
Rhode Island.............	383	1,181	964	313	1,188	453
Connecticut...............	3,089	13,759	12,119	1,531	8,806	5,720
MIDDLE ATLANTIC:						
New York.................	54,546	1,027,203	673,989	15,940	279,864	342,959
New Jersey...............	7,709	101,542	102,124	2,157	32,614	36,743
Pennsylvania.............	102,089	951,924	1,075,031	23,439	217,046	280,251
EAST NORTH CENTRAL:						
Ohio.....................	101,314	805,838	1,144,271	22,408	195,187	342,328
Indiana..................	82,564	475,333	815,742	20,991	132,006	251,959
Illinois..................	87,845	536,458	843,283	29,741	217,124	239,605
Michigan.................	68,378	1,076,748	760,183	17,657	351,892	540,580
Wisconsin................	32,538	437,480	290,495	11,282	84,215	148,775
WEST NORTH CENTRAL:						
Minnesota................	7,280	38,120	25,139	6,021	27,921	38,399
Iowa.....................	65,261	391,226	908,764	23,170	130,199	229,352
Missouri.................	75,609	522,026	622,332	34,902	333,180	247,425
North Dakota.............	1,379	15,877	5,076	1,081	9,364	21,484
South Dakota.............	3,782	32,366	51,613	3,301	29,563	76,293
Nebraska.................	33,540	289,221	494,468	14,878	120,194	267,529
Kansas...................	43,167	395,436	661,267	17,819	184,093	237,051
SOUTH ATLANTIC:						
Delaware.................	1,997	12,700	16,145	656	4,006	4,598
Maryland.................	12,850	71,139	82,305	3,249	17,397	27,774
District of Columbia.......	39	197	435	15	188	4
Virginia..................	42,043	236,199	352,783	11,175	55,251	83,323
West Virginia.............	27,077	284,739	332,429	8,405	81,504	124,567
North Carolina............	32,794	158,187	168,065	13,761	71,880	74,111
South Carolina............	11,811	60,740	60,274	5,056	27,557	25,764
Georgia..................	14,657	62,415	50,723	6,031	27,156	23,479
Florida..................	16	39	666	13	64	498
EAST SOUTH CENTRAL:						
Kentucky.................	38,961	171,604	212,118	14,007	72,596	102,766
Tennessee................	34,228	220,625	201,830	12,981	98,714	128,406
Alabama.................	6,480	20,237	25,566	3,095	10,665	16,673
Mississippi...............	2,187	6,804	13,748	1,266	4,968	9,267
WEST SOUTH CENTRAL:						
Arkansas.................	10,951	82,921	60,046	6,712	65,264	47,556
Louisiana................	315	1,181	975	269	837	760
Oklahoma................	19,686	145,832	295,042	11,303	101,091	150,541
Texas....................	3,656	25,236	29,439	3,689	22,755	43,712
MOUNTAIN:						
Montana.................	1,703	65,633	19,938	540	4,073	24,237
Idaho....................	10,490	117,672	61,881	3,015	25,877	95,423
Wyoming.................	256	1,921	919	383	8,255	4,025
Colorado.................	7,301	348,832	203,806	2,694	74,799	319,624
New Mexico..............	2,791	28,173	21,925	1,217	12,544	26,818
Arizona..................	290	1,500	812	286	1,250	1,608
Utah.....................	4,526	112,695	79,775	1,105	7,646	109,119
Nevada..................	242	1,172	1,588	145	920	787
PACIFIC:						
Washington...............	29,345	329,187	241,038	8,263	72,976	229,067
Oregon..................	20,586	395,073	223,456	5,437	89,396	313,770
California................	12,268	657,470	522,304	8,049	347,572	300,063

TABLE 199.—CHERRIES—PRODUCTION AND VALUE, BY DIVISIONS AND STATES: 1919 AND 1909.

[A minus sign (−) denotes decrease. Per cent not shown when base is less than 100 or when per cent is more than 1,000.]

DIVISION AND STATE.	PRODUCTION (BUSHELS).			VALUE.	
	1919	1909	Per cent of increase.	1919	1909
United States..............	3,945,749	4,126,099	−4.4	$14,166,176	$7,231,160
GEOGRAPHIC DIVISIONS:					
New England...............	10,911	14,904	−26.8	40,910	38,424
Middle Atlantic.............	334,577	791,326	−57.7	1,367,837	1,541,708
East North Central..........	881,603	1,410,298	−37.5	3,142,892	2,362,344
West North Central.........	670,584	515,690	30.0	2,260,830	935,537
South Atlantic.............	249,087	327,706	−24.0	720,968	394,990
East South Central..........	82,014	94,873	−13.6	274,588	143,160
West South Central..........	102,522	9,954	930.0	348,644	14,401
Mountain..................	407,632	147,854	175.7	1,359,089	300,485
Pacific....................	1,206,819	813,494	48.4	4,650,418	1,500,105
NEW ENGLAND:					
Maine......................	1,846	2,403	−23.2	6,925	7,164
New Hampshire.............	2,518	1,403	79.5	9,191	4,133
Vermont...................	907	2,506	−63.8	3,628	7,651
Massachusetts.............	4,115	4,761	−13.6	15,432	10,848
Rhode Island..............	89	214	−58.4	348	464
Connecticut...............	1,436	3,617	−60.3	5,386	8,164
MIDDLE ATLANTIC:					
New York..................	166,877	271,597	−38.6	750,964	544,508
New Jersey................	34,308	44,636	−23.1	116,646	87,225
Pennsylvania..............	133,392	475,093	−71.9	500,227	909,975
EAST NORTH CENTRAL:					
Ohio......................	149,911	338,644	−55.7	584,663	657,406
Indiana...................	62,365	363,993	−82.9	215,161	508,516
Illinois..................	147,783	287,376	−48.6	465,512	453,474
Michigan..................	360,952	338,945	6.5	1,299,428	590,829
Wisconsin.................	160,592	81,340	97.4	578,128	152,119
WEST NORTH CENTRAL:					
Minnesota.................	4,592	1,526	200.9	13,776	2,973
Iowa......................	150,188	260,432	−42.3	480,598	455,022
Missouri..................	206,809	123,314	67.7	744,512	222,510
North Dakota..............	1,836	209	778.5	6,436	445
South Dakota..............	4,084	5,924	−31.1	11,843	12,981
Nebraska..................	124,872	89,876	38.9	362,133	164,872
Kansas....................	178,203	34,409	417.9	641,532	76,734
SOUTH ATLANTIC:					
Delaware..................	3,800	2,634	44.3	12,921	4,850
Maryland..................	25,111	42,315	−40.7	80,354	60,121
District of Columbia.......	112	235	−52.3	375	568
Virginia..................	117,728	132,671	−11.3	294,343	134,428
West Virginia.............	42,861	79,723	−46.2	139,305	111,043
North Carolina............	37,373	53,788	−30.5	112,119	60,453
South Carolina............	10,681	10,987	−2.8	42,724	15,880
Georgia...................	11,421	4,979	129.4	38,827	7,199
Florida...................	....	374	....	....	448
EAST SOUTH CENTRAL:					
Kentucky..................	27,288	52,163	−47.7	91,420	74,340
Tennessee.................	46,439	36,303	27.9	157,895	60,294
Alabama...................	5,538	3,588	54.3	15,786	4,783
Mississippi...............	2,749	2,819	−2.5	9,487	3,749
WEST SOUTH CENTRAL:					
Arkansas..................	33,255	5,993	454.9	99,765	8,424
Louisiana.................	602	527	14.2	1,806	921
Oklahoma..................	61,555	2,372	....	224,672	4,393
Texas.....................	7,110	1,062	569.5	22,401	663
MOUNTAIN:					
Montana...................	14,763	7,497	96.9	61,266	17,985
Idaho.....................	90,057	22,609	298.3	310,701	11,766
Wyoming...................	741	68	....	2,070	251
Colorado..................	165,087	88,937	85.6	536,537	173,895
New Mexico................	11,985	6,384	87.7	40,748	10,684
Arizona...................	969	476	103.6	4,364	840
Utah......................	123,477	21,402	476.9	401,303	54,170
Nevada....................	553	481	15.0	1,800	894
PACIFIC:					
Washington................	249,226	131,392	89.7	971,985	278,547
Oregon....................	303,893	181,089	67.8	1,063,633	269,934
California................	653,700	501,013	30.5	2,614,800	951,624

TABLE **200.**—APRICOTS—NUMBER OF TREES, 1920, PRODUCTION, 1919 AND 1909, AND VALUE, 1919, BY STATES.

STATE.	TREES OF BEARING AGE, 1920.		TREES NOT OF BEARING AGE, 1920.		PRODUCTION (BUSHELS).		Value, 1919
	Farms reporting.	Number.	Farms reporting.	Number.	1919	1909	
United States........	22,999	3,846,080	10,236	1,284,202	6,130,086	4,150,263	$12,223,052
New York...................	29	1,570	7	2,624	603	9,805	1,206
Kansas....................	630	7,957	211	1,437	2,757	374	5,514
Oklahoma..................	1,618	13,267	654	7,745	7,436	1,123	11,171
Texas.....................	1,456	7,348	833	4,024	6,490	1,839	9,764
Idaho.....................	240	4,098	99	3,009	4,349	1,108	6,958
Colorado..................	442	5,904	60	575	9,154	11,403	15,562
New Mexico...............	250	1,543	84	559	2,141	2,379	4,282
Arizona...................	823	39,464	336	4,072	60,463	6,849	126,971
Utah.....................	509	21,830	60	435	40,564	12,047	60,850
Washington...............	857	47,608	263	13,000	79,908	10,789	151,827
Oregon...................	143	3,922	45	1,560	6,807	4,616	10,214
California................	15,485	3,688,217	7,245	1,243,706	5,907,645	4,066,823	11,815,290
All other states...........	517	3,352	339	1,456	1,769	21,108	3,443

TABLE 201.—GRAPES—NUMBER OF VINES, BY DIVISIONS AND STATES: 1920 AND 1910.

DIVISION AND STATE.	VINES OF BEARING AGE.			VINES NOT OF BEARING AGE.		
	Farms reporting, 1920	Number.		Farms reporting, 1920	Number.	
		1920	1910		1920	1910
United States......	1,074,592	225,754,285	224,601,522	227,656	27,394,469	52,698,644
GEOGRAPHIC DIVISIONS:						
New England.........	20,514	432,239	207,844	4,631	132,132	92,370
Middle Atlantic.......	147,174	39,617,239	38,676,641	24,989	1,985,875	5,383,556
East North Central...	331,607	20,181,737	23,608,296	40,857	1,436,358	2,825,671
West North Central..	160,281	5,538,611	9,222,514	42,315	1,044,888	1,740,265
South Atlantic.......	208,118	2,233,953	1,903,341	51,855	427,259	543,306
East South Central...	115,019	928,072	1,308,203	29,170	253,403	265,641
West South Central...	48,301	1,954,717	3,937,376	18,821	479,345	943,918
Mountain.............	6,308	843,259	936,328	2,564	132,332	537,267
Pacific..............	37,270	154,024,458	144,800,979	12,454	21,502,877	40,366,650
NEW ENGLAND:						
Maine...............	2,006	7,339	9,731	524	1,926	1,944
New Hampshire......	2,740	12,998	15,802	553	2,843	3,016
Vermont............	1,949	7,160	9,318	439	2,441	1,845
Massachusetts.......	7,319	81,494	58,277	1,713	22,691	14,261
Rhode Island........	896	50,933	7,662	279	44,984	9,634
Connecticut.........	5,604	272,315	107,054	1,123	57,247	61,670
MIDDLE ATLANTIC:						
New York...........	37,978	30,677,555	31,802,097	6,814	1,389,042	3,801,800
New Jersey.........	8,053	1,477,617	1,603,280	1,304	194,562	558,945
Pennsylvania.......	101,143	7,462,067	5,271,264	16,871	402,271	1,022,811
EAST NORTH CENTRAL:						
Ohio...............	123,402	6,553,904	8,326,800	10,888	521,207	455,750
Indiana.............	70,861	744,043	1,049,232	8,602	100,657	149,441
Illinois.............	81,474	1,642,527	2,170,340	11,828	180,172	287,734
Michigan...........	46,090	11,097,734	11,913,576	6,617	607,149	1,869,648
Wisconsin..........	9,780	143,529	148,348	2,922	27,173	63,098
WEST NORTH CENTRAL:						
Minnesota..........	2,204	36,315	61,916	1,575	11,863	35,950
Iowa...............	53,168	1,401,613	1,983,465	14,683	304,710	446,126
Missouri............	75,437	2,444,907	3,026,526	16,254	410,604	486,044
North Dakota........	19	152	379	42	463	1,464
South Dakota.......	416	9,978	38,647	450	7,332	46,891
Nebraska...........	8,528	438,713	1,221,736	3,947	126,765	380,788
Kansas.............	20,509	1,206,933	2,889,845	5,364	183,151	343,002
SOUTH ATLANTIC:						
Delaware...........	1,877	457,162	260,963	475	19,929	98,950
Maryland...........	16,403	164,501	138,801	2,452	31,860	44,690
District of Columbia..	40	4,159	5,196	14	1,071	200
Virginia............	40,310	452,516	424,701	8,861	112,197	136,026
West Virginia........	30,799	284,435	284,074	5,264	51,391	76,465
North Carolina......	60,244	543,734	411,278	16,877	114,582	120,208
South Carolina......	19,060	87,487	79,708	6,360	27,874	19,704
Georgia............	32,112	182,119	277,658	8,420	38,588	38,233
Florida.............	7,273	57,840	20,962	3,132	29,767	8,830
EAST SOUTH CENTRAL:						
Kentucky...........	40,935	327,429	605,002	8,892	69,439	77,626
Tennessee..........	39,123	359,972	338,758	9,627	98,928	76,040
Alabama...........	24,938	183,759	287,431	7,139	60,995	77,105
Mississippi.........	10,023	56,912	77,012	3,512	24,041	34,870
WEST SOUTH CENTRAL:						
Arkansas...........	18,479	607,244	805,921	5,940	101,241	177,624
Louisiana..........	1,558	19,601	31,041	1,102	12,583	20,936
Oklahoma..........	15,853	923,609	2,388,213	5,703	200,894	447,489
Texas..............	12,411	404,263	712,201	6,076	164,627	297,869
MOUNTAIN:						
Montana...........	27	979	986	26	199	1,121
Idaho..............	1,485	73,789	68,269	624	13,432	124,806
Wyoming..........	1	2	74	16	120	1,147
Colorado...........	1,202	195,097	254,792	458	15,836	101,332
New Mexico.........	1,498	280,419	250,076	642	31,432	122,367
Arizona............	961	83,018	131,579	528	34,905	84,510
Utah...............	843	205,031	204,445	227	33,471	94,043
Nevada............	100	74,994	26,607	43	2,937	7,941
PACIFIC:						
Washington.........	4,420	467,761	322,007	1,280	78,661	371,733
Oregon............	6,537	361,484	381,302	1,756	35,570	468,598
California..........	26,313	153,195,213	144,097,670	9,418	21,388,646	39,526,319

TABLE 202.—GRAPES—PRODUCTION AND VALUE, BY DIVISIONS AND STATES: 1919 AND 1909.

[A minus sign (−) denotes decrease.]

DIVISION AND STATE.	PRODUCTION (POUNDS).			VALUE.	
	1919	1909	Per cent of increase.	1919	1909
United States	2, 516, 840, 387	2, 265, 065, 205	11. 1	$95, 586, 021	$22, 027, 961
GEOGRAPHIC DIVISIONS:					
New England	3, 935, 064	3, 413, 161	15. 3	329, 902	108, 348
Middle Atlantic	199, 521, 184	293, 527, 780	−32. 0	13, 496, 102	4, 945, 342
East North Central	175, 194, 976	194, 730, 671	−10. 0	9, 855, 816	3, 129, 363
West North Central	30, 994, 703	41, 088, 852	−24. 6	1, 943, 210	1, 156, 625
South Atlantic	26, 602, 275	32, 439, 760	−18. 0	2, 285, 296	909, 900
East South Central	5, 291, 932	8, 143, 715	−35. 0	481, 362	348, 397
West South Central	8, 656, 621	8, 265, 667	4. 7	638, 710	304, 454
Mountain	4, 195, 328	4, 858, 195	−13. 6	287, 555	128, 532
Pacific	2, 062, 448, 304	1, 678, 597, 404	22. 9	66, 268, 068	10, 997, 000
NEW ENGLAND:					
Maine	100, 789	231, 529	−56. 5	10, 080	6, 954
New Hampshire	214, 514	375, 164	−42. 8	17, 162	10, 926
Vermont	99, 422	203, 011	−51. 0	7, 955	6, 328
Massachusetts	1, 009, 479	1, 132, 838	−10. 9	80, 758	30, 858
Rhode Island	400, 975	152, 937	162. 2	24, 058	9, 759
Connecticut	2, 109, 885	1, 317, 682	60. 1	189, 889	43, 523
MIDDLE ATLANTIC:					
New York	152, 482, 698	253, 006, 361	−39. 7	10, 673, 790	3, 961, 677
New Jersey	4, 357, 396	6, 501, 221	−33. 0	261, 445	132, 957
Pennsylvania	42, 681, 090	34, 020, 198	25. 5	2, 560, 867	850, 708
EAST NORTH CENTRAL:					
Ohio	41, 722, 796	43, 933, 207	−5. 0	2, 920, 600	858, 594
Indiana	6, 612, 804	12, 817, 353	−48. 4	462, 899	287, 707
Illinois	10, 339, 018	16, 582, 785	−37. 7	620, 344	426, 468
Michigan	115, 871, 465	120, 695, 997	−4. 0	5, 793, 575	1, 531, 057
Wisconsin	648, 893	701, 329	−7. 5	58, 398	25, 537
WEST NORTH CENTRAL:					
Minnesota	141, 278	293, 805	−51. 9	14, 134	11, 021
Iowa	12, 165, 318	11, 708, 336	3. 9	729, 921	330, 078
Missouri	10, 949, 602	17, 871, 816	−38. 7	656, 971	488, 755
North Dakota	217	360	−39. 7	19	14
South Dakota	24, 209	144, 634	−83. 3	2, 178	4, 789
Nebraska	2, 404, 035	4, 752, 217	−49. 4	168, 282	137, 295
Kansas	5, 310, 044	6, 317, 684	−15. 9	371, 705	184, 673
SOUTH ATLANTIC:					
Delaware	1, 445, 121	1, 938, 267	−25. 4	115, 610	43, 967
Maryland	1, 540, 958	2, 152, 382	−28. 4	107, 865	53, 498
District of Columbia	24, 883	28, 530	−12. 8	2, 239	1, 059
Virginia	3, 970, 873	4, 108, 694	−3. 4	357, 383	156, 266
West Virginia	2, 186, 740	3, 224, 751	−32. 2	196, 809	92, 834
North Carolina	10, 679, 108	15, 116, 920	−29. 4	854, 333	336, 083
South Carolina	2, 668, 650	2, 016, 506	32. 3	266, 866	88, 620
Georgia	2, 865, 319	2, 767, 366	3. 5	286, 542	99, 216
Florida	1, 220, 623	1, 086, 344	12. 4	97, 649	38, 357
EAST SOUTH CENTRAL:					
Kentucky	1, 497, 769	3, 680, 182	−59. 3	134, 803	137, 326
Tennessee	1, 839, 450	1, 979, 480	−7. 1	165, 550	85, 423
Alabama	1, 446, 814	1, 723, 490	−16. 1	130, 213	81, 386
Mississippi	507, 899	760, 563	−33. 2	50, 796	44, 262
WEST SOUTH CENTRAL:					
Arkansas	2, 444, 598	2, 593, 727	−5. 7	195, 567	97, 985
Louisiana	67, 203	106, 595	−37. 0	6, 758	6, 099
Oklahoma	3, 888, 492	3, 762, 727	3. 3	233, 311	122, 045
Texas	2, 256, 328	1, 802, 618	25. 2	203, 074	78, 325
MOUNTAIN:					
Montana	2, 066	370	458. 4	165	17
Idaho	519, 544	604, 227	−14. 0	36, 370	18, 814
Wyoming	12	159	−92. 5	1	32
Colorado	526, 509	1, 037, 614	−49. 3	42, 122	28, 026
New Mexico	1, 003, 356	425, 415	135. 9	80, 266	16, 101
Arizona	669, 673	837, 842	−20. 1	40, 181	25, 371
Utah	1, 102, 625	1, 576, 363	−30. 1	66, 156	28, 126
Nevada	371, 543	376, 205	−1. 2	22, 294	12, 045
PACIFIC:					
Washington	3, 961, 036	1, 704, 005	132. 5	316, 882	51, 412
Oregon	2, 842, 656	3, 206, 874	−11. 4	170, 558	98, 776
California	2, 055, 644, 612	1, 673, 686, 525	22. 8	65, 780, 628	10, 846, 812

TABLE 203.—CITRUS FRUITS—NUMBER OF TREES, BY STATES: 1920 AND 1910.

CROP AND STATE.	TREES OF BEARING AGE.			TREES NOT OF BEARING AGE.		
	Farms reporting, 1920	Number.		Farms reporting, 1920	Number.	
		1920	1910		1920	1910
Total......	......	19,420,660	11,486,768	......	7,259,181	5,400,402
Oranges, total......	34,565	14,397,836	9,737,927	26,632	5,196,972	4,327,271
California......	18,540	10,297,593	6,615,805	11,069	2,598,759	2,093,410
Florida......	13,114	3,645,811	2,766,618	10,988	2,311,571	1,097,896
All other states......	2,911	454,432	355,504	4,575	286,642	1,135,965
Lemons, total......	11,045	2,921,608	956,920	7,007	813,361	396,111
California......	10,125	2,884,770	941,293	5,777	781,535	379,676
Florida......	715	34,176	11,740	664	22,756	7,329
All other states......	205	2,662	3,887	566	9,070	9,106
Grapefruit (pomeloes), total.	11,431	1,938,453	710,040	7,589	1,135,024	640,597
California......	4,249	231,136	43,424	2,239	81,873	25,589
Florida......	6,636	1,681,481	656,213	4,328	963,336	600,049
All other states......	546	25,836	10,403	1,022	89,815	14,959
Limes, total......	169	115,744	45,387	212	81,306	30,239
California......	13	120	18	12	436	151
Florida......	156	115,624	45,369	200	80,870	30,088
Tangerines, total......	809	41,310	27,271	467	30,940	3,873
California......	78	2,475	3,637	23	948	34
Florida......	728	38,516	23,234	435	29,770	3,839
All other states......	3	319	400	9	222	......
Mandarins, total......	......	......	7,227	......	......	1,923
Kumquats, total......	78	4,205	1,988	52	1,577	358
Citrons, total......	4	1,504	8	1	1	30

TABLE 204.—CITRUS FRUITS—PRODUCTION AND VALUE, BY STATES: 1919 AND 1909.

[Per cent not shown when base is less than 100.]

CROP AND STATE.	PRODUCTION (BOXES).			VALUE.	
	1919	1909	Per cent of increase.	1919	1909
Total......	38,197,060	23,502,128	62.1	$110,061,050	$22,711,448
Oranges, total......	27,757,953	19,487,481	42.4	83,398,894	17,566,464
California......	21,628,444	14,436,180	49.8	67,048,178	12,951,505
Florida......	5,930,422	4,852,967	22.2	15,715,618	4,304,987
All other states......	199,087	198,334	0.4	635,098	309,972
Lemons, total......	6,585,269	2,770,313	137.7	19,102,267	2,993,738
California......	6,551,657	2,756,221	137.7	18,999,810	2,976,571
Florida......	31,204	12,367	152.3	93,612	13,753
All other states......	2,408	1,725	39.6	8,845	3,414
Grapefruit (pomeloes), total......	3,656,437	1,189,250	207.5	7,176,703	2,060,610
California......	465,085	122,515	279.6	930,170	143,180
Florida......	3,158,431	1,061,537	197.5	6,158,941	1,907,816
All other states......	32,921	5,198	533.3	87,592	9,614
Limes, total......	97,861	11,818	146.2	97,517	12,478
California......	136	16	......	477	21
Florida......	27,725	11,302	145.3	97,040	12,457
Tangerines, total......	75,231	38,752	94.1	263,819	68,770
California......	6,658	3,581	85.9	23,306	4,188
Florida......	67,475	34,871	93.5	236,170	64,082
All other states......	1,098	300	266.0	4,343	500
Mandarins, total......	......	3,896	......	......	6,553
Kumquats, total......	2,307	1,112	107.5	13,842	2,826
Citrons, total......	2,002	6	......	8,008	9

TABLE 205.—NONCITRUS SUBTROPICAL FRUITS—NUMBER OF TREES, BY STATES: 1920 AND 1910.

CROP AND STATE.	TREES OF BEARING AGE.			TREES NOT OF BEARING AGE.		
	Farms reporting, 1920	Number.		Farms reporting, 1920	Number.	
		1920	1910		1920	1910
Figs, total	90,335	886,383	821,640	45,655	783,413	1,028,717
Alabama	14,009	44,386	52,731	5,496	24,317	33,893
California	16,561	503,973	269,001	8,085	594,736	214,527
Georgia	15,986	39,223	49,424	5,909	16,505	11,813
Louisiana	9,984	46,276	71,464	5,757	33,451	102,043
Mississippi	6,736	24,921	65,397	4,650	21,893	38,654
Texas	9,204	166,273	230,171	6,309	54,759	585,396
Other states	17,855	61,331	83,452	9,449	37,752	42,391
Pineapples, total	38	[1] 924,594	[1] 36,191,389	23	[1] 1,599,660	[1] 2,602,813
Olives, total	3,081	918,253	846,175	2,768	694,539	123,784
Arizona	22	7,363	9,353	35	7,522	1,773
California	3,059	910,890	836,347	2,733	687,017	121,659
Other states			475			352
Alligator pears, total	523	39,687	12,054	881	75,723	23,072
Bananas, total	152	14,474	23,114	106	6,970	7,515
Guavas, total	516	28,636	15,347	290	13,417	3,807
Mangoes, total	173	6,179	4,904	164	5,312	7,775
Loquats, total	296	3,296	3,791	196	462	1,011
Japanese persimmons, total	691	28,002	16,491	467	24,414	17,176
California	270	13,847	3,274	136	7,500	8,801
Other states	421	14,155	13,217	331	16,914	8,375
Pomegranates, total	399	28,169	8,933	211	28,303	9,275
California	212	24,258	1,771	160	27,321	2,745
Other states	187	3,911	7,162	51	982	6,530
Dates, total	143	18,203	4,551	180	71,592	22,269
California	122	17,299	325	153	69,896	19,552
Other states	21	904	4,226	27	1,696	2,717
Sugar apples, total	10	1,064		29	839	
Sapodillas, total	6	201		12	4,575	

[1] Number of plants.

TABLE **206.**—NONCITRUS SUBTROPICAL FRUITS—PRODUCTION AND VALUE, BY STATES: 1919 AND 1909.

[A minus sign (−) denotes decrease. Per cent not shown when more than 1,000.]

CROP AND STATE.	PRODUCTION.				VALUE.	
	Unit.	1919	1909	Per cent of increase.	1919	1909
Total					$4,807,381	$1,995,305
Figs, total	Lbs	26,876,827	35,060,395	−23.3	2,811,660	803,810
Alabama	Lbs	749,154	1,773,126	−57.7	112,372	80,960
California	Lbs	21,801,899	22,990,353	−5.2	2,180,194	260,153
Georgia	Lbs	638,509	1,183,494	−46.0	76,620	50,326
Louisiana	Lbs	1,351,060	2,025,308	−33.3	162,129	87,009
Mississippi	Lbs	296,706	1,949,301	−84.8	35,608	107,609
Texas	Lbs	949,055	2,411,876	−60.7	113,888	97,078
Other states	Lbs	1,090,444	2,726,937	−60.0	130,849	120,675
Pineapples, total	Crates	26,016	778,651	−96.7	110,569	734,090
Olives, total	Lbs	17,676,581	16,405,493	7.7	1,416,377	404,574
Arizona	Lbs	112,561	264,895	−57.5	11,256	3,073
California	Lbs	17,564,020	16,132,412	8.9	1,405,121	401,277
Other states	Lbs		8,186			224
Alligator pears, total	Crates	24,128	4,920	390.4	193,024	10,100
Bananas, total	Bunches	6,405	10,060	−36.3	8,010	5,661
Guavas, total	Lbs	295,309	354,062	−16.6	10,304	11,628
Mangoes, total	Boxes	5,263	5,278	−0.3	18,423	5,739
Loquats, total	Boxes	4,328	4,541	−4.7	17,312	5,880
Japanese persimmons, total	Bu	29,429	6,723	337.7	117,716	9,087
California	Bu	21,452	2,696	695.7	85,808	3,344
Other states	Bu	7,977	4,027	98.1	31,908	5,743
Pomegranates, total	Lbs	1,029,757	152,825	573.8	61,786	4,203
California	Lbs	953,588	30,075		57,215	968
Other states	Lbs	76,169	122,750	−37.9	4,571	3,235
Dates, total	Lbs	189,509	9,947		40,092	533
California	Lbs	144,992	3,332		28,998	418
Other states	Lbs	44,517	6,615	573.0	11,094	115
Sugar apples, total	Boxes	201			704	
Sapodillas, total	Boxes	401			1,404	

TABLE 207.—ALMONDS, PECANS, AND WALNUTS (PERSIAN OR ENGLISH)—NUMBER OF TREES, 1920 AND 1910, AND PRODUCTION AND VALUE, 1919 AND 1909, BY STATES.

CROP AND STATE.	TREES OF BEARING AGE.		TREES NOT OF BEARING AGE.		PRODUCTION (POUNDS).		VALUE.	
	1920	1910	1920	1910	1919	1909	1919	1909
Almonds, total	2,431,115	1,187,962	1,420,983	389,575	15,852,965	6,793,539	$3,963,264	$711,970
Texas	4,174	4,534	1,306	1,528	41,073	16,932	10,274	1,618
Arizona	4,699	6,639	693	845	10,335	33,759	2,583	4,193
Utah	6,477	1,408	5,515	664	48,653	10,664	12,165	1,014
Washington	2,380	695	555	8,800	12,335	770	3,085	86
Oregon	3,507	3,960	1,296	4,117	29,945	17,515	7,489	2,468
California	2,408,040	1,166,730	1,407,901	365,961	15,699,748	6,692,513	3,924,940	700,304
All other states	1,838	3,996	3,717	-7,660	10,876	21,386	2,728	2,207
Pecans, total	2,672,191	1,619,521	2,257,288	1,685,066	31,808,548	9,890,769	7,792,086	971,596
Indiana	4,590	4,883	1,755	946	18,440	19,287	5,532	1,940
Illinois	25,289	28,330	6,024	8,223	182,347	107,069	45,592	10,301
Missouri	85,434	48,822	31,891	7,214	555,184	147,420	166,561	10,467
Kansas	29,193	27,716	8,440	2,797	252,802	20,583	75,841	1,462
Virginia	12,452	868	3,897	2,337	33,927	10,568	10,184	1,356
North Carolina	17,470	6,876	37,227	20,781	145,753	74,861	43,736	8,194
South Carolina	58,025	33,366	90,025	43,639	525,783	159,823	157,734	20,442
Georgia	444,722	75,519	654,281	325,779	2,544,377	354,046	890,535	47,845
Florida	113,547	42,512	208,613	176,207	1,025,673	307,632	307,705	43,962
Kentucky	7,591	2,399	2,257	2,301	50,352	28,577	15,110	2,887
Tennessee	4,127	2,037	7,002	3,309	70,594	25,581	17,654	2,566
Alabama	176,426	44,683	257,671	125,734	1,179,735	228,341	353,924	30,540
Mississippi	129,971	60,524	254,187	148,030	1,559,245	637,293	389,823	79,936
Arkansas	19,233	13,958	26,860	13,811	348,382	249,955	87,106	17,603
Louisiana	94,513	36,527	101,285	119,547	2,242,859	723,578	672,862	70,635
Oklahoma	400,480	96,766	108,650	53,796	4,296,642	894,172	859,331	59,481
Texas	1,045,694	1,087,619	449,464	621,550	16,755,421	5,832,367	3,686,191	556,203
California	2,007	4,226	4,707	2,793	14,125	44,955	4,241	4,632
All other states	1,427	1,890	3,052	6,272	6,907	24,661	2,424	1,144
Walnuts (Persian or English), total	1,390,061	914,270	583,242	806,413	59,840,407	22,026,524	17,916,158	2,297,336
New York	1,589	456	2,238	139	10,778	9,346	2,699	858
North Carolina	1,103	2,125	982	1,731	25,576	73,303	6,396	3,686
Alabama	2,170	3,022	2,150	4,180	25,900	43,673	6,484	3,557
Mississippi	2,241	2,705	1,281	5,513	32,932	66,492	8,242	6,949
Arkansas	555	1,284	556	1,260	14,254	15,436	3,566	1,384
Louisiana	562	1,228	679	3,390	19,807	15,173	4,957	1,416
Utah	817	292	824	484	12,138	5,985	3,036	533
Washington	10,703	3,651	18,760	23,406	96,843	16,450	24,217	2,241
Oregon	88,696	9,526	93,214	177,004	461,845	79,060	115,467	8,288
California	1,274,434	853,237	455,814	546,804	59,091,390	21,432,266	17,727,417	2,247,193
All other states	7,192	36,744	6,744	42,502	48,944	269,340	13,677	21,201

TABLE **208.**—FOREST PRODUCTS OF FARMS, 1919 AND 1909, AND AREA IN MERCHANTABLE TIMBER, 1920, BY DIVISIONS AND STATES.

| DIVISION AND STATE. | VALUE OF FOREST PRODUCTS OF FARMS. | | | | | | Area in merchantable timber on farms (acres), 1920 |
| | Total. | | Products sold (or cut and held for sale). | | Products used (or cut and held for use). | | |
	1919	1909	1919	1909	1919	1909	
United States..	$394,321,828	$195,306,283	$217,716,046	$92,524,205	$176,605,782	$102,782,078	35,270,527
GEOG. DIVISIONS:							
New England...	31,352,700	17,664,763	20,611,531	11,416,425	10,741,169	6,248,338	1,895,925
Middle Atlantic .	37,118,348	19,110,765	20,795,664	9,933,362	16,322,684	9,177,403	2,298,657
E. N. Central....	57,817,314	32,161,851	25,563,930	13,977,093	32,253,384	18,184,758	3,115,283
W. N. Central...	30,460,160	19,891,878	10,532,324	6,467,404	19,927,836	13,424,474	2,916,368
South Atlantic..	113,624,917	44,010,178	65,304,549	21,554,641	48,320,368	22,455,537	10,270,191
E. S. Central....	70,410,506	29,264,946	44,183,199	13,087,601	26,227,307	16,177,345	8,133,339
W. S. Central....	34,396,936	21,026,984	18,598,546	8,208,843	15,798,390	12,818,141	4,338,422
Mountain........	4,855,047	2,580,902	2,897,320	1,614,983	1,957,727	965,919	633,288
Pacific..........	14,285,900	9,594,016	9,228,983	6,263,853	5,056,917	3,330,163	1,669,054
NEW ENGLAND:							
Maine...........	11,728,114	5,573,763	7,667,551	3,527,275	4,060,563	2,046,488	643,901
New Hampshire.	5,532,115	3,610,178	4,282,071	2,677,746	1,250,044	932,432	427,115
Vermont........	6,377,580	3,638,537	3,682,129	2,065,003	2,695,451	1,573,534	473,717
Massachusetts...	4,491,522	2,668,410	2,982,700	1,795,285	1,508,822	873,125	248,343
Rhode Island...	470,077	312,022	313,236	232,474	156,841	79,548	30,219
Connecticut.....	2,753,292	1,861,853	1,683,844	1,118,642	1,069,448	743,211	72,630
MIDDLE ATLANTIC:							
New York.......	19,311,211	10,365,651	9,020,766	4,393,220	10,290,445	5,972,431	1,027,768
New Jersey......	1,219,810	758,515	617,999	340,535	601,811	417,980	74,753
Pennsylvania....	16,587,327	7,986,599	11,156,899	5,199,607	5,430,428	2,786,992	1,196,136
E. N. CENTRAL:							
Ohio...........	11,364,709	5,761,941	6,652,306	2,757,172	4,712,403	3,004,769	860,844
Indiana.........	10,955,856	5,603,322	6,417,267	2,623,444	4,538,589	2,979,878	809,824
Illinois.........	6,259,154	3,325,259	2,644,866	1,147,156	3,614,288	2,178,103	458,464
Michigan........	12,649,621	7,911,901	4,578,940	3,531,022	8,070,681	4,380,879	442,647
Wisconsin.......	16,587,974	9,559,428	5,270,551	3,918,299	11,317,423	5,641,129	543,504
W. N. CENTRAL:							
Minnesota.......	9,067,015	5,181,508	3,113,922	2,157,747	5,953,093	3,023,761	529,392
Iowa...........	4,404,555	3,649,032	1,285,010	892,797	3,119,545	2,756,235	152,442
Missouri........	13,938,458	8,406,823	5,374,713	2,798,321	8,563,745	5,608,502	2,139,530
North Dakota...	206,317	235,386	54,057	74,557	152,260	160,829	8,759
South Dakota...	238,462	257,126	66,459	96,040	172,003	161,086	14,344
Nebraska........	933,276	795,053	194,211	138,355	739,065	656,698	30,537
Kansas..........	1,672,077	1,366,950	443,952	309,587	1,228,125	1,057,363	41,364
SOUTH ATLANTIC:							
Delaware........	777,176	346,062	383,207	166,001	393,969	180,061	46,187
Maryland.......	4,673,536	2,349,045	2,638,491	1,073,329	2,035,045	1,275,716	305,758
Dist. Columbia..	200	238	....	100	200	138	49
Virginia........	24,142,423	10,118,851	15,679,825	5,761,152	8,462,598	4,357,699	2,150,030
West Virginia...	11,346,421	4,004,484	7,524,516	2,736,980	3,821,905	1,267,504	1,134,786
North Carolina..	32,735,263	11,364,134	18,711,315	5,949,674	14,023,948	5,414,460	2,107,021
South Carolina..	14,256,764	4,513,092	5,849,318	1,420,639	8,407,446	3,092,453	1,284,162
Georgia.........	21,657,200	8,938,390	11,881,720	3,204,360	9,775,480	5,734,030	2,693,340
Florida.........	4,035,934	2,375,882	2,636,157	1,242,406	1,399,777	1,133,476	548,858
E. S. CENTRAL:							
Kentucky.......	16,606,621	7,843,142	9,569,188	4,261,898	7,037,433	3,581,244	1,821,572
Tennessee.......	20,868,262	8,510,710	13,123,124	3,951,119	7,745,138	4,559,591	2,213,221
Alabama........	18,803,353	6,308,151	12,665,474	2,480,670	6,137,879	3,827,481	2,501,297
Mississippi......	14,132,270	6,602,943	8,825,413	2,393,914	5,306,857	4,209,029	1,597,249
W. S. CENTRAL:							
Arkansas........	13,805,907	6,914,262	7,778,078	2,708,318	6,027,829	4,205,944	2,359,478
Louisiana.......	5,480,619	3,584,340	3,604,930	1,914,777	1,875,689	1,669,563	683,483
Oklahoma.......	3,508,813	1,602,720	966,520	374,814	2,542,293	1,227,906	229,472
Texas..........	11,601,597	8,925,662	6,249,018	3,210,934	5,352,579	5,714,728	1,065,989
MOUNTAIN:							
Montana........	1,253,217	541,800	665,970	328,594	587,247	213,206	149,482
Idaho..........	2,329,244	1,280,512	1,633,624	939,719	695,620	340,793	173,849
Wyoming.......	156,837	104,259	53,463	45,400	103,374	58,859	34,930
Colorado........	563,476	305,719	302,823	168,018	260,653	137,701	142,929
New Mexico.....	326,820	253,822	144,463	92,797	182,357	161,025	67,163
Arizona.........	67,754	45,312	33,028	14,011	34,726	31,301	54,512
Utah...........	120,262	6,730	50,085	921	70,177	5,809	8,408
Nevada.........	37,437	42,748	13,864	25,523	23,573	17,225	2,015
PACIFIC:							
Washington.....	4,738,116	3,754,293	2,996,915	2,698,420	1,741,201	1,055,873	337,551
Oregon..........	5,299,123	2,889,991	3,558,981	1,663,981	1,740,142	1,226,010	759,464
California.......	4,248,661	2,949,732	2,673,087	1,901,452	1,575,574	1,048,280	572,039

TABLE **209.**—NURSERIES AND GREENHOUSES, BY DIVISIONS AND STATES: 1919 AND 1909.

DIVISION AND STATE.	NURSERIES.				GREENHOUSES.			
	Acreage.		Value of products sold.		Square feet under glass.		Value of products sold.	
	1919	1909	1919	1909	1920 (Jan. 1)	1910 (Apr. 15)	1919	1909
United States..	51,453	80,618	$20,434,389	$21,050,822	162,368,593	114,655,276	$77,380,230	$34,872,329
GEOG. DIVISIONS:								
New England.....	2,532	2,647	1,255,023	989,080	20,473,847	13,896,562	9,702,750	4,677,316
Middle Atlantic...	11,399	13,675	4,398,611	4,355,340	43,938,922	37,753,770	21,981,133	11,810,076
E. North Central..	8,146	13,811	3,519,318	3,037,823	56,053,628	33,404,093	24,948,794	9,029,125
W. North Central..	7,390	16,614	2,983,215	3,841,690	15,196,378	8,212,237	7,609,294	2,642,343
South Atlantic....	8,210	9,963	2,223,545	1,851,351	7,276,675	6,962,357	3,836,612	1,932,426
E. South Central..	2,856	8,130	1,024,902	1,147,669	3,654,582	3,280,388	1,785,530	1,005,548
W. South Central..	4,765	5,734	1,237,371	1,711,284	2,629,946	1,727,192	1,677,955	846,009
Mountain..........	495	1,731	210,113	594,096	3,773,655	2,125,030	2,030,105	753,914
Pacific............	5,660	8,313	3,582,291	3,522,489	9,370,960	7,293,647	3,808,057	2,175,572
NEW ENGLAND:								
Maine.............	70	57	37,538	23,244	714,580	706,917	383,001	301,005
New Hampshire...	91	24	30,755	11,897	754,238	752,313	317,428	236,144
Vermont..........	51	37	25,725	11,014	272,876	178,199	196,897	78,726
Massachusetts.....	1,517	1,547	743,323	605,875	12,953,023	7,382,009	5,536,532	2,455,467
Rhode Island......	260	212	101,739	75,544	2,274,951	2,027,643	1,102,063	558,543
Connecticut.......	543	770	315,943	261,506	3,504,179	2,849,481	2,166,829	1,047,431
MIDDLE ATLANTIC:								
New York.........	5,288	8,680	2,310,253	2,750,957	18,289,628	15,066,587	8,689,325	5,148,949
New Jersey........	3,337	2,167	1,048,919	681,814	8,725,939	8,840,511	5,064,684	2,857,709
Pennsylvania......	2,774	2,828	1,039,439	922,569	16,923,355	13,846,672	8,227,124	3,803,418
E. NORTH CENTRAL:								
Ohio..............	2,789	4,718	1,286,947	860,351	19,397,183	7,582,562	7,052,560	2,384,830
Indiana...........	1,330	1,850	409,475	411,387	7,229,383	3,741,269	3,056,094	1,212,891
Illinois...........	1,869	3,454	780,092	822,284	19,626,091	15,950,853	9,978,606	3,694,801
Michigan..........	1,591	3,034	779,155	642,774	5,672,838	4,122,099	2,766,760	1,143,764
Wisconsin.........	567	755	263,649	301,027	4,128,133	2,007,310	2,094,774	592,839
W. NORTH CENTRAL:								
Minnesota.........	1,881	3,854	774,060	863,014	2,758,097	1,419,196	1,387,168	603,935
Iowa..............	2,158	3,430	532,399	845,912	3,663,189	2,183,182	2,059,773	657,393
Missouri..........	1,194	2,459	1,045,697	529,394	5,099,019	2,812,221	2,229,808	653,903
North Dakota.....	388	472	30,088	30,997	179,212	70,670	156,617	47,221
South Dakota.....	475	399	212,101	70,827	224,444	101,460	214,726	50,008
Nebraska..........	235	1,997	98,400	553,053	1,041,665	844,010	603,684	356,168
Kansas............	1,059	4,003	290,470	948,493	2,230,752	781,498	957,518	273,715
SOUTH ATLANTIC:								
Delaware..........	189	182	56,089	39,057	241,251	244,827	111,608	71,429
Maryland..........	3,015	4,240	392,464	456,900	2,162,958	2,175,584	931,999	597,001
Dist. of Columbia..	2	(1)	700	150	864,243	985,593	541,993	303,509
Virginia..........	425	569	100,256	159,992	1,650,354	1,413,170	720,779	362,488
West Virginia.....	188	464	38,854	79,268	467,721	296,717	210,812	78,377
North Carolina....	989	754	334,977	266,968	453,691	193,139	325,245	126,995
South Carolina....	315	21	106,871	4,409	204,913	74,318	140,178	52,094
Georgia...........	1,224	1,502	257,491	366,433	905,070	867,222	500,420	271,427
Florida...........	1,863	2,231	935,843	478,174	326,474	711,787	353,578	69,106
E. SOUTH CENTRAL:								
Kentucky..........	230	542	67,245	115,963	1,662,532	1,363,002	718,453	392,409
Tennessee.........	1,168	3,976	666,028	697,703	1,245,312	1,236,874	626,923	344,579
Alabama..........	1,311	3,079	234,670	259,057	485,952	463,575	264,625	168,239
Mississippi.......	147	533	56,959	74,946	260,786	216,937	175,529	100,321
W. SOUTH CENTRAL:								
Arkansas..........	757	528	185,860	198,579	352,904	235,134	197,829	153,421
Louisiana.........	335	502	101,097	87,643	301,004	347,473	150,323	126,212
Oklahoma.........	641	857	79,222	171,952	722,971	158,515	534,705	92,016
Texas.............	3,032	3,847	871,192	1,253,110	1,253,067	986,070	795,098	474,360
MOUNTAIN:								
Montana..........	95	341	34,582	174,427	843,902	308,939	525,128	104,601
Idaho.............	95	530	45,335	143,234	237,431	59,477	114,511	43,314
Wyoming..........	8	(1)	1,025	1,680	43,056	33,034	21,217	12,280
Colorado..........	159	241	83,062	72,090	1,982,534	1,340,824	1,062,264	468,685
New Mexico.......	22	24	2,300	9,182	158,703	87,054	76,178	31,121
Arizona...........	60	18	23,481	4,535	6,516	29,810	4,343	11,177
Utah.............	55	577	20,298	188,455	487,513	261,292	220,864	81,116
Nevada...........	1	(1)	30	493	14,000	4,600	5,600	1,620
PACIFIC:								
Washington.......	368	1,342	308,665	526,681	2,680,369	1,539,972	1,046,021	518,226
Oregon............	1,212	2,168	344,168	783,020	1,627,293	716,543	584,665	268,833
California.........	4,080	4,803	2,929,458	2,212,788	5,063,298	5,037,132	2,177,371	1,388,513

[1] Reported in small fractions.

TABLE 210.—GROSS VALUE OF FARM PRODUCTS,

DIVISION AND STATE.	GROSS VALUE OF FARM PRODUCTS.[1]		LIVE-STOCK PRODUCTS.		LIVE STOCK SOLD OR SLAUGHTERED.	
	1919	1909	1919	1909	1919 (estimated).[2]	1909 (as reported).
United States..	$21,425,623,614	$8,494,230,307	$2,667,072,273	$1,177,974,703	$3,511,050,000	$1,833,175,487
GEOG. DIVISIONS:						
New England.....	505,397,039	245,324,983	132,411,030	73,922,170	55,500,000	30,416,780
Middle Atlantic...	1,561,158,784	696,940,531	412,960,765	192,977,646	170,200,000	89,563,068
E. North Central..	4,410,240,680	1,837,378,383	721,387,462	298,143,600	784,200,000	422,925,855
W. North Central.	5,581,297,432	2,406,517,487	550,742,614	245,673,372	1,312,600,000	715,336,435
South Atlantic....	2,629,345,466	933,535,056	204,301,963	89,426,168	221,550,000	102,508,692
E. South Central..	1,795,544,716	755,030,256	159,643,789	73,815,566	256,500,000	129,996,105
W. South Central.	2,739,481,559	889,110,743	181,346,648	79,880,253	352,200,000	181,003,205
Mountain.........	921,882,633	319,880,602	121,132,969	55,917,961	230,700,000	100,115,107
Pacific............	1,281,275,305	410,512,266	183,145,033	68,217,967	127,600,000	61,310,240
NEW ENGLAND:						
Maine.............	154,076,196	61,318,188	26,075,219	13,613,815	15,700,000	8,419,921
New Hampshire..	51,771,331	28,883,566	14,681,368	8,583,337	7,700,000	4,329,750
Vermont..........	99,473,142	49,706,224	31,573,304	14,821,352	13,300,000	7,458,895
Massachusetts....	109,223,194	59,874,639	33,850,892	21,932,652	10,900,000	6,020,530
Rhode Island.....	13,682,138	8,085,786	5,367,881	3,406,278	1,300,000	746,583
Connecticut......	77,171,038	37,456,580	20,862,330	11,564,736	6,600,000	3,441,101
MIDDLE ATLANTIC:						
New York........	743,823,392	352,396,646	225,465,739	104,867,285	71,000,000	39,261,111
New Jersey.......	135,000,544	62,894,826	31,482,945	17,951,089	8,700,000	4,996,850
Pennsylvania.....	682,334,848	281,649,059	156,012,081	70,159,272	90,500,000	45,305,107
E. NORTH CENTRAL:						
Ohio.............	941,729,697	388,190,729	155,587,919	68,500,279	159,400,000	89,596,986
Indiana..........	782,101,167	341,312,962	99,350,023	44,319,539	171,100,000	92,896,132
Illinois..........	1,298,906,947	586,483,959	142,351,262	67,390,680	274,800,000	147,060,674
Michigan.........	606,886,581	253,749,286	111,076,235	48,380,551	75,600,000	43,567,427
Wisconsin........	780,616,288	267,641,447	213,022,023	69,552,551	103,300,000	49,804,636
W. NORTH CENTRAL:						
Minnesota........	734,485,441	279,063,342	113,236,965	44,645,205	104,000,000	41,064,015
Iowa.............	1,447,938,473	598,798,749	130,250,447	66,053,869	420,300,000	218,216,303
Missouri.........	952,663,253	429,669,778	105,601,436	49,839,077	270,800,000	159,239,222
North Dakota.....	368,055,889	204,914,024	30,979,932	9,832,117	34,900,000	14,456,748
South Dakota.....	411,111,307	177,513,492	35,739,209	13,660,311	63,700,000	38,359,140
Nebraska.........	784,677,206	327,145,309	54,612,075	24,961,343	208,700,000	106,077,755
Kansas...........	882,365,863	389,412,793	80,322,550	36,681,450	210,200,000	137,923,252
SOUTH ATLANTIC:						
Delaware.........	32,182,526	13,355,761	5,778,747	2,910,412	2,400,000	1,338,609
Maryland.........	158,178,779	64,171,069	25,522,172	11,967,668	16,800,000	8,469,767
Dist. of Columbia.	1,019,770	713,126	119,263	142,191	50,000	24,456
Virginia..........	425,199,212	150,872,046	46,311,494	21,473,064	61,100,000	28,982,606
West Virginia.....	169,066,516	70,770,172	26,332,970	11,984,911	34,600,000	18,456,118
North Carolina....	614,084,854	176,261,942	35,860,056	14,904,898	41,600,000	18,526,988
South Carolina....	489,979,710	156,350,420	20,354,060	7,611,077	18,000,000	6,790,617
Georgia..........	638,430,053	257,351,095	36,401,316	14,933,151	39,000,000	15,869,720
Florida..........	101,204,046	43,689,425	7,621,885	3,498,796	8,000,000	4,049,811
E. SOUTH CENTRAL:						
Kentucky.........	512,459,424	218,456,263	50,928,217	24,776,564	96,800,000	54,733,377
Tennessee........	492,407,214	192,931,905	50,960,694	22,398,336	101,000,000	49,847,367
Alabama	383,178,279	170,939,250	30,426,993	13,513,006	29,100,000	13,150,064
Mississippi.......	407,499,799	172,702,838	27,327,885	13,127,660	29,600,000	12,265,297
W. SOUTH CENTRAL:						
Arkansas..........	424,486,802	153,834,875	30,083,950	14,115,791	39,400,000	20,323,592
Louisiana........	237,628,052	90,401,857	13,613,465	7,286,958	12,100,000	5,780,166
Oklahoma........	707,895,000	214,868,112	49,887,518	20,379,510	103,800,000	61,099,694
Texas............	1,369,471,705	430,005,899	87,761,715	38,097,994	196,900,000	93,799,753
MOUNTAIN:						
Montana.........	142,597,141	64,066,171	24,809,029	12,749,555	46,000,000	21,609,099
Idaho............	181,709,556	54,963,112	22,225,355	7,749,434	30,500,000	12,865,703
Wyoming.........	68,153,818	34,480,518	14,004,109	10,234,548	23,700,000	14,224,680
Colorado.........	280,295,333	84,871,022	26,921,292	9,705,676	70,600,000	24,208,175
New Mexico......	75,172,758	24,901,620	8,447,826	5,045,808	25,700,000	10,941,885
Arizona..........	59,771,694	13,112,666	6,294,886	2,769,881	10,900,000	4,847,097
Utah.............	87,764,314	30,801,598	13,735,823	5,664,682	15,600,000	6,656,236
Nevada..........	26,418,019	12,683,895	4,694,649	1,998,377	7,700,000	4,762,232
PACIFIC:						
Washington.......	301,271,159	104,688,632	44,066,349	15,538,705	23,900,000	10,249,346
Oregon...........	209,459,266	80,842,010	35,146,671	14,401,942	36,200,000	17,433,774
California........	770,544,880	224,981,624	103,932,013	38,277,320	67,500,000	33,627,120

[1] This "gross value of farm products" corresponds approximately with the gross value of products for a manufacturing industry, and for many purposes forms a fairly satisfactory index of the relative importance of agriculture in different areas. It contains, however, a large element of duplication on account of crops fed to live stock, and some further duplication where domestic animals are sold by one farmer to another and resold within the year. The duplication is most serious in states where live-stock products are most important.

BY DIVISIONS AND STATES: 1919 AND 1909.

DIVISION AND STATE.	CROPS.		FOREST PRODUCTS.		NURSERY AND GREEN-HOUSE PRODUCTS.	
	1919	1909	1919	1909	1919	1909
United States	$14,755,364,894	$5,231,850,683	$394,321,828	$195,306,283	$97,814,619	$55,923,151
GEOGRAPHIC DIVISIONS:						
New England	275,175,536	117,654,874	31,352,700	17,664,763	10,957,773	5,666,396
Middle Atlantic	914,499,927	379,123,636	37,118,348	19,110,765	26,379,744	16,165,416
East North Central	2,818,367,792	1,072,080,129	57,817,314	32,161,851	28,468,112	12,066,948
West North Central	3,676,902,149	1,419,131,769	30,460,160	19,891,878	10,592,509	6,484,033
South Atlantic	2,083,808,429	693,806,241	113,624,917	44,010,178	6,060,157	3,783,777
East South Central	1,306,179,989	519,800,422	70,410,506	29,264,946	2,810,432	2,153,217
West South Central	2,168,622,649	604,643,008	34,396,936	21,026,984	2,915,326	2,557,293
Mountain	562,954,399	159,918,622	4,855,047	2,580,902	2,240,218	1,348,010
Pacific	948,854,024	265,691,982	14,285,900	9,594,016	7,390,348	5,698,061
NEW ENGLAND:						
Maine	100,152,324	33,386,440	11,728,114	5,573,763	420,539	324,249
New Hampshire	23,509,665	12,112,260	5,532,115	3,610,178	348,183	248,041
Vermont	47,999,600	23,697,700	6,377,580	3,638,537	222,622	89,740
Massachusetts	53,700,925	26,191,705	4,491,522	2,668,410	6,279,855	3,061,342
Rhode Island	5,340,378	2,986,816	470,077	312,022	1,203,802	634,087
Connecticut	44,472,644	19,279,953	2,753,292	1,861,853	2,482,772	1,308,937
MIDDLE ATLANTIC:						
New York	417,046,864	190,002,693	19,311,211	10,365,651	10,999,578	7,899,906
New Jersey	87,484,186	35,648,849	1,219,810	758,515	6,113,603	3,539,523
Pennsylvania	409,968,877	153,472,094	16,587,327	7,986,599	9,266,563	4,725,987
EAST NORTH CENTRAL:						
Ohio	607,037,562	221,086,342	11,364,709	5,761,941	8,339,507	3,245,181
Indiana	497,229,719	196,869,691	10,955,856	5,603,322	3,465,569	1,624,278
Illinois	864,737,833	364,190,261	6,259,154	3,325,259	10,758,609	4,517,085
Michigan	404,014,810	152,102,869	12,649,621	7,911,901	3,545,915	1,786,538
Wisconsin	445,347,868	137,830,966	16,587,974	9,559,428	2,358,423	893,866
WEST NORTH CENTRAL:						
Minnesota	506,020,233	186,705,665	9,067,015	5,181,508	2,161,228	1,466,949
Iowa	890,391,299	309,376,240	4,404,555	3,649,032	2,592,172	1,503,305
Missouri	559,047,854	211,001,359	13,938,458	8,406,823	3,275,505	1,183,297
North Dakota	301,782,935	180,311,555	206,317	235,386	186,705	78,218
South Dakota	311,006,809	125,116,080	238,462	257,126	426,827	120,835
Nebraska	519,729,771	194,401,937	933,276	795,053	702,084	909,221
Kansas	588,923,248	212,218,933	1,672,077	1,366,950	1,247,988	1,222,208
SOUTH ATLANTIC:						
Delaware	23,058,906	8,650,192	777,176	346,062	167,697	110,486
Maryland	109,858,608	40,330,688	4,673,536	2,349,045	1,324,463	1,053,901
District of Columbia	307,614	242,582	200	238	542,693	303,659
Virginia	292,824,260	89,775,045	24,142,423	10,118,851	821,035	522,480
West Virginia	96,537,459	36,167,014	11,346,421	4,004,484	249,666	157,645
North Carolina	503,229,313	131,071,959	32,735,263	11,364,134	660,222	393,963
South Carolina	437,121,837	137,379,131	14,256,764	4,513,092	247,049	56,503
Georgia	540,613,626	216,971,974	21,657,200	8,938,390	757,911	637,860
Florida	80,256,806	33,217,656	4,035,934	2,375,882	1,289,421	547,280
EAST SOUTH CENTRAL:						
Kentucky	347,338,888	130,594,808	16,606,621	7,843,142	785,698	508,372
Tennessee	318,285,307	111,133,210	20,868,262	8,510,710	1,292,951	1,042,282
Alabama	304,348,638	137,540,733	18,803,353	6,308,151	499,295	427,296
Mississippi	336,207,156	140,531,671	14,132,270	6,602,943	232,488	175 267
WEST SOUTH CENTRAL:						
Arkansas	340,813,256	112,129,230	13,805,907	6,914,262	383,689	352,000
Louisiana	206,182,548	73,536,538	5,480,619	3,584,340	251,420	213,855
Oklahoma	550,084,742	131,522,220	3,508,813	1,602,720	613,927	263,968
Texas	1,071,542,103	287,455,020	11,601,597	8,925,662	1,666,290	1,727,470
MOUNTAIN:						
Montana	69,975,185	28,886,689	1,253,217	541,800	559,710	279,028
Idaho	126,495,111	32,880,915	2,329,244	1,280,512	159,846	186,548
Wyoming	30,270,630	9,903,071	156,837	104,259	22,242	13,960
Colorado	181,065,239	50,110,677	563,476	305,719	1,145,326	540,775
New Mexico	40,619,634	8,619,802	326,820	253,822	78,478	40,303
Arizona	42,481,230	5,434,664	67,754	45,312	27,824	15,712
Utah	58,067,067	18,204,379	120,262	6,730	241,162	269,571
Nevada	13,980,303	5,878,425	37,437	42,748	5,630	2,113
PACIFIC:						
Washington	227,212,008	74,101,381	4,738,116	3,754,293	1,354,686	1,044,907
Oregon	131,884,639	45,064,450	5,299,123	2,889,991	928,833	1,051,853
California	589,757,377	146,526,151	4,248,661	2,949,732	5,106,829	3,601,301

[2] The value of domestic animals sold or slaughtered was not called for by the 1920 farm schedule. The estimated value obtained for 1919 was based on the ratio between the animals sold or slaughtered in 1909 and those on hand in 1910, and the changes in the number and average value of comparable classes of animals from 1910 to 1920.

IRRIGATION

CONTENTS.

IRRIGATION.

A census of irrigation has been taken as a part of the census of agriculture in each census from 1890 to 1920. The scope of the inquiries was considerably enlarged in 1910, particularly in the matter of sources of water supply and character of enterprises supplying water, making it possible to classify the data collected.

The tables which follow present the most important facts—acreage and cost—for the four censuses from 1890 to 1920, inclusive, and classify the data collected for 1910 and 1920 by source of water supply and by character of enterprise.

An irrigation "enterprise" is an independent irrigation establishment and includes the works for supplying water and the land to which water is supplied or is to be supplied, except that the cost or value of the land is not included in the "capital invested."

The report of crops grown on irrigated land is incomplete to some extent. Enumerators were instructed to mark on the agricultural schedule the crops that were grown on irrigated land, but it was evident from the schedules that these instructions were not always followed. So far as possible the missing information was supplied in the office, but this could not be done in all cases. Consequently, the totals given for acreage harvested, quantity produced, and value are all too small. It is believed, however, that the data given are representative and the averages of yield and value correctly represent the return from irrigated land.

TABLE 1.—SUMMARY FOR THE UNITED STATES: 1920 AND 1910.

ITEM.	CENSUS OF—		INCREASE.[1]	
	1920	1910	Amount.	Per cent.
Number of all farms	1,916,391	1,776,046	140,345	7.9
Approximate land area of states included......acres..	1,223,989,120	1,224,063,360	[2]—74,240	([3])
All land in farms in states included...........acres..	505,440,954	416,462,547	88,978,407	21.4
Improved land in farms in states included.....acres..	214,689,819	186,786,227	27,903,592	14.9
Number of farms irrigated	231,541	162,723	68,818	42.3
Area irrigated...............................acres..	19,191,716	14,433,285	4,758,431	33.0
Area enterprises were capable of irrigating.....acres..	26,020,477	20,285,403	5,735,074	28.3
Area included in enterprises...................acres..	35,890,821	32,245,464	3,645,357	11.3
Per cent irrigated:				
Number of all farms	12.1	9.2	2.9	....
Approximate land area	1.6	1.2	0.4	....
Land in farms	3.8	3.5	0.3	....
Improved land in farms	8.9	7.7	1.2	....
Excess of area enterprises were capable of irrigating over area irrigated.........................acres..	6,828,761	5,852,118	976,643	16.7
Excess of area included in enterprises over area irrigated...acres..	16,699,105	17,812,179	−1,113,074	−6.2
Area of irrigated land reported as available for settlement...acres..	2,257,981	([4])	2,257,981	....
Capital invested.................................	$697,657,328	$321,454,008	$376,203,320	117.0
Average per acre enterprises were capable of irrigating.....................................	$26.81	$15.85	$10.96	69.1
Estimated final cost of existing enterprises............	$819,778,005	$437,948,825	$381,829,180	87.2
Average per acre included in enterprises..........	$22.84	$13.58	$9.26	68.2
Average cost of operation and maintenance per acre..	$2.43	[5] $1.07	$1.36	127.1

[1] A minus sign (−) denotes decrease.
[2] Decrease due to the building of several reservoirs in connection with irrigation projects.
[3] Less than one-tenth of 1 per cent decrease.
[4] Not reported in 1910.
[5] Does not include cost of operation and maintenance for rice growing districts in Gulf states; consequently figures for 1919 and 1909 are not comparable.

TABLE 2.—NUMBER OF FARMS AND ACREAGE IRRIGATED: 1890 TO 1920.

CENSUS YEAR.	FARMS IRRIGATED.			AREA IRRIGATED.					
	Number.	Per cent of increase.	Per cent of all farms.	Acres.	Per cent of increase.	Per cent of total land area.	Per cent of land in farms.	Per cent of improved land in farms.
1920	231,541	42.3	12.1	19,191,716	33.0	1.6	3.8	8.9
1910	162,723	43.0	9.2	14,433,285	86.4	1.2	3.5	7.7
1900	113,829	110.3	8.2	7,744,467	108.4	0.7	2.2	6.2
1890	54,136	....	5.8	3,715,758	....	0.3	2.1	3.8

TABLE 3.—ACREAGE, CLASSIFIED BY SOURCE OF WATER SUPPLY: 1919 AND 1909.

CLASS.	AREA IRRIGATED (ACRES).				Area enterprises were capable of irrigating in 1920 (acres).	Area included in enterprises, 1920 (acres).
	1919	1909	Increase.[1]			
			Amount.	Per cent.		
Total	19,191,716	14,433,285	4,758,431	33.0	26,020,477	35,890,821
Streams, gravity	14,527,060	12,767,351	1,759,709	13.8	19,269,136	26,040,237
Streams, pumped	1,226,510	608,659	617,851	101.5	2,118,942	2,885,698
Streams, pumped and gravity	199,595	(2)	199,595	....	237,700	284,353
Wells, pumped	1,263,098	489,341	773,757	158.1	1,674,819	2,3o6,748
Wells, flowing	65,856	144,420	−78,564	−54.4	79,777	131,137
Wells, flowing and pumped	35,685	(2)	35,685	....	42,703	84,379
Lakes, pumped	35,730	17,826	17,904	100.4	59,760	80,564
Lakes, gravity	100,646	59,631	41,015	68.8	149,377	312,169
Springs	198,008	196,186	1,822	0.9	251,792	409,528
Stored storm water	98,873	105,792	−6,919	−6.5	223,434	319,972
City water	930	(2)	930	....	1,401	1,666
Sewage	2,578	(2)	2,578	....	3,301	5,540
Streams, gravity, and pumped wells	344,713	(2)	344,713	....	389,790	465,293
Streams, gravity, and flowing wells	82,665	(2)	82,665	....	104,569	205,121
Other mixed	996,621	44,079	952,542	....	1,398,004	2,290,850
Other and not reported	13,148	(2)	13,148	....	15,972	17,566

[1] A minus sign (−) denotes decrease.   Per cent not shown when more than 1,000.
[2] Not included in classification in 1910.

TABLE 4.—ACREAGE, CLASSIFIED BY CHARACTER OF ENTERPRISE: 1920 AND 1910.

ITEM AND CLASS.	CENSUS OF—		INCREASE.[1]	
	1920	1910	Amount.	Per cent.
ACREAGE IRRIGATED.				
Total	19,191,716	14,433,285	4,758,431	33.0
Individual and partnership	6,848,807	6,594,614	254,193	3.9
Cooperative	6,581,400	4,643,539	1,937,861	41.7
Irrigation district	1,822,887	528,642	1,294,245	244.8
Carey Act	523,929	288,553	235,376	81.6
Commercial	1,822,001	1,809,379	12,622	0.7
U. S. Reclamation Service	1,254,569	395,646	858,923	217.1
U. S. Indian Service	284,551	172,912	111,639	64.6
State	5,620	(2)	5,620	....
City	40,146	(2)	40,146	....
Other and mixed	7,236	(2)	7,236	....
Not reported	570	(2)	570	....

[1] A minus sign (−) denotes decrease.   [2] Not included in classification in 1910.

Table 4.—ACREAGE, CLASSIFIED BY CHARACTER OF ENTERPRISE: 1920 AND 1910—
Continued.

ITEM AND CLASS.	CENSUS OF—		INCREASE.[1]	
	1920	1910	Amount.	Per cent.
ACREAGE ENTERPRISES WERE CAPABLE OF IRRIGATING.				
Total	26,020,477	20,285,403	5,735,074	28.3
Individual and partnership	9,255,756	8,086,766	1,168,990	14.5
Cooperative	8,403,298	6,191,577	2,211,721	35.7
Irrigation district	2,531,425	800,451	1,730,974	216.2
Carey Act	804,298	1,089,677	—285,379	—26.2
Commercial	2,799,563	2,954,166	—154,603	—5.2
U. S. Reclamation Service	1,680,643	786,190	894,453	113.8
U. S. Indian Service	484,486	376,576	107,910	28.7
State	7,379	(2)	7,379	
City	44,458	(2)	44,458	
Other and mixed	8,546	(2)	8,546	
Not reported	625	(2)	625	
ACREAGE INCLUDED IN ENTERPRISES.				
Total	35,890,821	32,245,464	3,645,357	11.3
Individual and partnership	13,008,415	10,621,067	2,387,348	22.5
Cooperative	10,628,543	8,830,197	1,798,346	20.4
Irrigation district	3,432,109	1,581,465	1,850,644	117.0
Carey Act	1,188,937	2,573,874	—1,384,937	—53.8
Commercial	3,999,581	5,786,777	—1,787,196	—30.9
U. S. Reclamation Service	2,627,176	1,973,016	654,160	33.2
U. S. Indian Service	932,985	879,068	53,917	6.1
State	9,581	(2)	9,581	
City	49,650	(2)	49,650	
Other and mixed	13,144	(2)	13,144	
Not reported	700	(2)	700	

[1] A minus sign (—) denotes decrease.　　　　[2] Not included in classification in 1910.

Table 5.—ACREAGE IRRIGATED, 1919 AND 1902, ACREAGE ENTERPRISES WERE
CAPABLE OF IRRIGATING IN 1920, AND ACREAGE INCLUDED IN ENTERPRISES,
1920, BY PRINCIPAL DRAINAGE BASINS.

DRAINAGE BASIN.	AREA IRRIGATED (ACRES).				Area enterprises were capable of irrigating, 1920 (acres).	Area included in enterprises in 1920 (acres).
	1920	1902	Increase.			
			Amount.	Per cent.		
Total	19,191,716	8,874,408	10,317,308	116.3	26,020,477	35,890,821
Missouri River and tributaries	4,147,278	2,533,237	1,614,041	63.7	5,805,630	8,483,171
Mississippi River and tributaries other than Missouri River	958,493	393,687	564,806	143.5	1,152,261	1,543,064
Gulf streams other than Mississippi River and Rio Grande	698,077	21,833	676,244	(1)	1,157,529	1,602,169
Rio Grande and tributaries	1,293,863	496,587	797,276	160.6	1,887,433	2,594,127
Independent streams in Rio Grande drainage basin	18,992	8,355	10,637	127.3	26,852	34,026
Colorado River and tributaries	2,312,047	927,183	1,384,864	149.4	2,986,937	4,064,492
White Water Draw and tributaries	5,871	384	5,487	(1)	9,950	16,623
Great Basin	2,313,163	1,639,473	673,690	41.1	2,869,858	4,238,028
Columbia River and tributaries	3,873,245	1,297,437	2,575,808	198.5	4,968,518	6,336,801
Pacific Ocean streams other than Columbia and Colorado Rivers	3,570,687	1,556,232	2,014,455	129.4	5,155,509	6,978,320

[1] Per cent not shown when more than 1,000.

TABLE **6.**—ACREAGE IRRIGATED, 1919 AND 1909, ACREAGE ENTERPRISES WERE CAPABLE OF IRRIGATING IN 1920 AND 1910, AND ACREAGE INCLUDED IN ENTERPRISES, 1920 AND 1910, BY STATES.

STATE.	AREA IRRIGATED (ACRES).			AREA ENTERPRISES WERE CAPABLE OF IRRIGATING (ACRES).			AREA INCLUDED IN ENTERPRISES (ACRES).		
	1919	1909	Per cent of increase.[1]	1920	1910	Per cent of increase.[1]	1920	1910	Per cent of increase.[1]
Total	19,191,716	14,433,285	33.0	26,020,477	20,285,403	28.3	35,890,821	32,245,464	11.3
Arizona	467,565	320,051	46.1	627,303	387,655	61.8	813,153	944,090	−13.9
Arkansas	143,946	27,753	418.7	179,013	47,136	279.8	246,480	52,883	366.1
California	4,219,040	2,664,104	58.4	5,894,466	3,619,378	62.9	7,805,207	5,490,360	42.2
Colorado	3,348,385	2,792,032	19.9	3,855,348	3,990,166	−3.4	5,220,588	5,917,457	−11.8
Idaho	2,488,806	1,430,848	73.9	3,092,810	2,388,959	29.5	3,780,048	3,549,573	6.5
Kansas	47,312	37,479	26.2	67,853	139,995	−51.5	102,562	161,300	−36.4
Louisiana	454,882	380,200	19.6	728,742	553,220	31.7	851,211	581,965	46.3
Montana	1,681,729	1,679,084	0.2	2,753,498	2,205,155	24.9	4,329,148	3,515,602	23.1
Nebraska	442,690	255,950	73.0	562,468	429,225	31.0	766,768	680,133	12.7
Nevada	561,447	701,833	−20.0	704,708	840,962	−16.2	1,382,036	1,232,142	12.2
New Mexico	538,377	461,718	16.6	696,119	644,970	7.9	961,879	1,102,297	−12.7
North Dakota	12,072	10,248	17.8	34,235	21,917	56.2	57,476	38,173	50.6
Oklahoma	2,969	4,388	−32.3	9,672	6,397	51.2	11,742	8,528	37.7
Oregon	986,162	686,129	43.7	1,344,046	830,526	61.8	1,925,987	2,527,208	−23.8
South Dakota	100,682	63,248	59.2	150,914	128,481	17.5	188,382	201,625	−6.6
Texas	586,120	451,130	29.9	1,150,542	690,991	66.5	1,687,447	1,253,173	34.7
Utah	1,371,651	999,410	37.2	1,700,550	1,250,246	36.0	2,359,244	1,947,625	21.1
Washington	529,899	334,378	58.5	637,151	470,514	35.4	836,795	817,032	2.4
Wyoming	1,207,982	1,133,302	6.6	1,831,039	1,639,510	11.7	2,564,668	2,224,298	15.3

[1] A minus sign (−) denotes decrease.

TABLE **7.**—CAPITAL INVESTED IN IRRIGATION ENTERPRISES: 1890 TO 1920.

CENSUS YEAR.	Amount.	Per cent of increase.	AVERAGE PER ACRE.	
			Amount.	Per cent of increase.
1920	$697,657,328	117.0	$26.81	69.1
1910	321,454,008	359.2	15.85	75.3
1900	70,010,594	137.1	9.04	13.6
1890	29,533,921		7.96	

TABLE **8.**—CAPITAL INVESTED, 1920, AND COST OF OPERATION AND MAINTENANCE, 1919, CLASSIFIED BY SOURCE OF WATER SUPPLY.

[When water is pumped, cost of operation and maintenance includes cost of fuel and attendance.]

CLASS.	CAPITAL INVESTED, 1920.			OPERATION AND MAINTENANCE, 1919.	
	Amount.	Per cent of total.	Average per acre.	Area for which cost is reported (acres).	Average cost per acre.[1]
Total	$697,657,328	100.0	$26.81	16,260,750	$2.43
Streams, gravity	439,570,623	63.0	22.81	12,190,697	1.25
Streams, pumped	59,343,298	8.5	28.01	1,151,313	6.50
Streams, pumped and gravity	9,512,907	1.4	40.02	198,656	2.33
Wells, pumped	76,787,251	11.0	45.85	1,064,338	10.07
Wells, flowing	2,945,059	0.4	36.92	27,543	2.77
Wells, flowing and pumped	2,498,672	0.4	58.51	29,600	8.04
Lakes, pumped	2,274,601	0.3	38.06	45,558	5.20
Lakes, gravity	2,906,612	0.4	19.46	78,586	1.30
Springs	5,793,988	0.8	23.01	139,244	1.63
Stored storm water	15,075,592	2.2	67.47	87,666	2.39
City water	219,783	(2)	156.88	361	20.73
Sewage	174,444	(2)	52.85	1,631	9.05
Streams, gravity, and pumped wells	28,347,835	4.1	72.73	315,640	5.97
Streams, gravity, and flowing wells	2,863,194	0.4	27.38	79,354	1.36
Other mixed	48,467,251	6.9	34.67	838,622	2.71
Other and not reported	876,218	0.1	54.86	11,941	10.75

[1] Based on area irrigated in 1919.   [2] Less than one-tenth of 1 per cent.

TABLE 9.—CAPITAL INVESTED, BY PRINCIPAL DRAINAGE BASINS: 1920 AND 1902.

DRAINAGE BASIN.	1920	1902	INCREASE.		AVERAGE PER ACRE.	
			Amount.	Per cent.	1920	1902
Total..............................	$697,657,328	$82,531,665	$615,125,663	745.3	$26.81	$9.30
Missouri River and tributaries.............	131,553,106	16,176,277	115,376,829	713.2	22.66	6.39
Mississippi River and tributaries other than Missouri River............................	35,183,789	4,619,814	30,563,975	661.6	30.53	11.73
Gulf streams other than Mississippi River and Rio Grande............................	29,439,808	501,272	28,938,536	(1)	25.43	22.96
Rio Grande and tributaries.................	34,172,940	6,367,065	27,805,875	436.7	18.11	12.82
Independent streams in Rio Grande drainage basin..............................	651,171	126,550	524,621	414.6	24.25	15.15
Colorado River and tributaries...............	86,696,940	11,298,671	75,398,269	667.3	29.03	12.19
White Water Draw and tributaries..........	299,368	6,735	292,633	(1)	30.09	17.54
Great Basin................................	66,589,376	10,890,199	55,699,177	511.5	23.20	6.64
Columbia River and tributaries..............	145,672,382	10,851,415	134,820,967	(1)	29.32	8.36
Pacific Ocean streams other than Columbia and Colorado Rivers........................	167,398,448	21,693,667	145,704,781	671.6	32.47	13.94

1 Per cent not shown when more than 1,000.

TABLE 10.—CAPITAL INVESTED, 1920, AND COST OF OPERATION AND MAINTENANCE, 1919, CLASSIFIED BY CHARACTER OF ENTERPRISE.

[When water is pumped, cost of operation and maintenance includes cost of fuel and attendance.]

CLASS.	CAPITAL INVESTED, 1920.		OPERATION AND MAINTENANCE, 1919.	
	Amount.	Per cent of total.	Area for which cost was reported (acres).	Average cost per acre.[1]
Total.........................	$697,657,328	100.0	16,260,750	$2.43
Individual and partnership.................	154,634,169	22.2	5,133,421	3.02
Cooperative................................	183,041,500	26.2	5,754,232	1.67
Irrigation district..........................	88,573,514	12.7	1,701,231	2.59
Carey Act.................................	32,680,695	4.7	497,611	1.34
Commercial................................	85,735,470	12.3	1,779,595	3.48
U. S. Reclamation Service..................	129,509,819	18.6	1,098,573	2.20
U. S. Indian Service.......................	14,851,236	2.1	254,378	1.80
State......................................	344,174	(2)	1,608	4.86
City.......................................	2,936,678	0.4	33,507	3.85
Other.....................................	5,310,399	0.8	6,594	3.14
Not reported..............................	39,674	(2)	....	....

1 Based on area irrigated in 1919.   2 Less than one-tenth of 1 per cent.

TABLE 11.—CAPITAL INVESTED, BY STATES: 1890 TO 1920.

STATE.	1920	1910	1900	1890	PER CENT OF INCREASE.[1]		
					1910–1920	1900–1910	1890–1900
Total............	$697,657,328	$321,454,008	$70,010,594	$29,533,921	117.0	359.0	137.1
Arizona.............	33,498,094	17,677,966	4,438,352	465,000	89.5	298.3	854.5
Arkansas...........	7,183,322	587,834			168.5	278.4	47.5
California..........	194,886,388	72,580,030	19,181,610	13,004,817	168.5	278.4	47.5
Colorado...........	88,302,442	56,636,443	11,758,703	6,368,755	55.9	381.7	84.6
Idaho..............	91,501,009	40,977,688	5,120,399	1,029,000	123.3	700.3	397.6
Kansas.............	2,067,381	1,365,563	529,755	84,729	51.4	157.8	525.2
Louisiana..........	14,063,181	6,859,166	2,529,319		105.0	171.2	
Montana............	52,143,363	22,970,958	4,683,073	1,623,195	127.0	390.5	188.5
Nebraska...........	13,909,185	7,798,310	1,310,698	47,798	78.4	495.0	....
Nevada.............	14,754,280	6,721,924	1,537,559	1,700,975	119.5	337.2	−9.6
New Mexico.........	18,210,412	9,154,897	4,165,312	511,937	98.9	119.8	713.6
North Dakota.......	1,857,118	836,482	16,980		122.0	....	
Oklahoma...........	151,325	47,200	21,872		220.6	115.8	
Oregon.............	28,929,151	12,760,214	1,843,771	825,660	126.7	592.1	123.3
South Dakota.......	5,465,248	3,043,140	284,747	63,968	79.6	968.7	345.1
Texas..............	35,072,739	13,487,347	1,027,608		160.0	....	
Utah...............	32,037,351	14,028,717	5,865,302	2,780,000	128.4	139.2	111.0
Washington.........	29,299,011	16,219,149	1,722,369	196,660	80.6	841.7	775.8
Wyoming............	34,326,328	17,700,980	3,973,165	831,427	93.9	345.5	377.9

[1] A minus sign (−) denotes decrease.   Per cent not shown when more than 1,000.

TABLE 12.—IRRIGATION WORKS: 1920 AND 1910.

ITEM.	1920	1910	INCREASE.[1]	
			Amount.	Per cent.
Diverting dams.........................number..	23,894	(2)	23,894	......
Storage dams..........................number..	3,931	(2)	3,931	......
Main ditches:				
Number................................	51,621	46,677	4,944	10.6
Length..........................miles..	103,177	88,927	14,250	16.0
Capacity....................second-feet..	631,079	618,097	12,982	2.1
Lateral ditches:				
Number................................	57,553	36,513	21,040	57.6
Length..........................miles..	56,687	30,003	26,684	88.9
Reservoirs:				
Number................................	7,538	6,956	582	8.4
Capacity......................acre-feet..	21,246,436	12,602,924	8,643,512	68.6
Pipe lines, length....................miles..	8,878.3	(2)	8,878.3	......
Flowing wells:				
Number................................	4,606	5,071	−465	−9.2
Capacity................gallons per minute..	935,057	1,345,676	−410,619	−30.5
Pumped wells:				
Number................................	32,094	15,971	16,123	101.0
Capacity................gallons per minute..	16,396,549	7,248,699	9,147,850	126.2
Pumping plants:				
Number................................	29,458	15,803	13,655	86.4
Engine capacity..................horsepower..	748,971	361,480	387,491	107.2
Pump capacity...........gallons per minute..	36,275,005	19,355,864	16,919,141	87.4
Average lift.........................feet..	41	......	....	

[1] A minus sign (−) denotes decrease.   [2] Not included in classification in 1910.

TABLE 13.—PRINCIPAL IRRIGATION WORKS, BY STATES: 1920.

STATE.	MAIN DITCHES.			RESERVOIRS.		FLOWING WELLS.	
	Number.	Capacity (second-feet).	Length (miles).	Number.	Capacity (acre-feet).	Number.	Capacity (gallons per minute).
Total....................	51,621	631,079	103,177	7,538	21,246,436	4,606	935,057
Arizona..................	1,295	11,707	1,769	340	1,510,856	310	14,547
Arkansas.................	84	1,205	68	16	20		
California...............	6,040	115,237	14,437	3,030	1,091,394	1,415	287,187
Colorado.................	8,867	119,558	19,022	979	2,406,372	476	20,139
Idaho....................	4,553	86,273	11,144	249	3,493,511	142	15,133
Kansas...................	139	1,667	271	36	391	6	500
Louisiana................	1,298	11,889	1,584	74	7,632	9	6,255
Montana..................	8,819	94,429	16,411	468	1,571,720	41	4,608
Nebraska.................	513	11,665	1,780	59	197,890		
Nevada...................	2,032	10,554	3,123	134	504,428	123	21,942
New Mexico...............	2,228	23,432	4,469	328	2,960,718	556	376,222
North Dakota.............	32	836	58	9	1,110		
Oklahoma.................	18	344	38	8	52	1	100
Oregon...................	5,252	28,897	7,115	266	1,905,037	65	11,968
South Dakota.............	370	5,427	653	119	212,264	4	2,750
Texas....................	820	23,261	1,524	368	392,999	135	62,364
Utah.....................	2,381	29,447	6,343	476	1,600,505	1,256	96,371
Washington...............	1,873	16,242	3,851	205	477,789	60	14,925
Wyoming..................	5,007	39,009	9,517	374	2,911,748	7	46

STATE.	PUMPED WELLS.		PUMPING PLANTS.			
					Pumps.	
	Number.	Capacity (gallons per minute).	Number.	Engine capacity (horse-power).	Number.	Capacity (gallons per minute).
Total....................	32,094	16,396,549	29,458	748,971	33,804	36,275,005
Arizona..................	999	1,042,590	744	22,014	1,001	1,048,030
Arkansas.................	1,089	1,470,147	1,041	58,332	1,121	1,654,097
California...............	25,401	10,608,476	21,561	386,200	24,134	16,773,692
Colorado.................	527	210,094	406	8,635	435	299,726
Idaho....................	53	17,749	143	28,364	232	1,397,681
Kansas...................	710	266,797	198	6,946	288	297,975
Louisiana................	812	1,607,637	1,250	85,628	1,941	4,968,686
Montana..................	22	11,085	253	10,341	299	453,231
Nebraska.................	34	24,701	51	959	54	73,686
Nevada...................	129	6,798	64	409	72	35,266
New Mexico...............	461	265,618	472	8,488	491	304,789
North Dakota.............			4	2,068	10	51,250
Oklahoma.................	19	3,643	22	184	26	7,668
Oregon...................	208	47,026	573	13,769	614	600,045
South Dakota.............	1	800	25	498	25	23,320
Texas....................	901	538,565	1,369	80,511	1,641	6,825,998
Utah.....................	192	39,059	250	11,392	291	783,588
Washington...............	520	227,744	975	22,929	1,059	636,552
Wyoming..................	16	8,020	57	1,304	70	39,725

Table **14.**—ACREAGE, YIELD, AND VALUE OF PRINCIPAL CROPS GROWN ON IRRIGATED LAND IN 1919.

[Totals for the states included, used in making comparisons, are shown in the section of this abstract relating to Agriculture.]

CROP.	Area harvested (acres).	QUANTITY HARVESTED.		AVERAGE YIELD PER ACRE.			VALUE.	
		Unit.	Amount.	For states included.	On non-irrigated land.	On irrigated land.	Amount.	Average per acre.
Cereals:								
Corn...................	263,312	Bu....	7,525,354	21.9	21.8	28.6	$11,692,813	$44.41
Oats...................	325,523	Bu....	9,361,125	26.5	26.5	28.8	9,534,495	29.29
Winter wheat.........	381,127	Bu....	7,115,303	14.1	14.1	18.7	15,269,840	40.06
Spring wheat..........	877,411	Bu....	17,679,328	8.2	7.6	20.1	37,556,853	42.80
Barley.................	280,287	Bu....	7,202,430	17.9	17.3	25.7	10,775,076	38.44
Rye...................	19,014	Bu....	168,977	7.4	7.4	8.9	295,987	15.57
Kafir, milo, etc.......	152,768	Bu....	4,100,338	19.9	19.6	26.8	6,725,561	44.02
Rice (rough) [1].........	892,761	Bu....	35,032,275	39.2	4.1	39.2	96,368,090	107.94
Other grains and seeds:								
Clover and alfalfa seed [2]	39,431	Bu....	161,587	21.0	1.4	4.1	3,461,762	87.79
Dry beans, navy, etc..	177,752	Bu....	2,862,567	11.8	10.3	16.1	12,986,298	73.06
Dry peas, Canada.....	51,464	Bu....	637,560	10.8	10.0	12.4	2,042,455	39.69
Hay and forage:								
Timothy alone........	140,607	Tons..	178,112	1.12	1.09	1.27	4,582,905	32.59
Timothy and clover mixed...............	392,260	Tons..	569,591	1.48	1.50	1.45	13,782,635	35.14
Clover alone...........	40,879	Tons..	63,465	1.56	1.56	1.55	1,334,600	32.65
Alfalfa................	3,151,675	Tons..	8,430,766	2.19	1.84	2.68	186,391,209	59.14
Other tame grasses....	254,313	Tons..	316,803	1.31	1.32	1.25	6,473,377	25.45
Wild, salt, or prairie grasses..............	1,034,507	Tons..	951,345	0.83	0.82	0.92	17,954,630	17.36
Small grains cut for hay.	291,697	Tons..	372,739	0.95	0.92	1.28	8,448,901	28.96
Annual legumes cut for hay...................	19,851	Tons..	28,334	1.22	1.20	1.43	494,052	24.89
Silage crops...........	56,424	Tons..	388,830	4.75	4.54	6.89	3,831,525	67.91
Corn cut for forage....	36,689	Tons..	87,389	1.52	1.51	2.38	1,121,730	30.57
Kafir, sorghum, etc., for forage............	51,981	Tons..	106,035	1.69	1.68	2.04	1,614,325	31.06
Root crops for forage...	2,631	Tons..	19,543	10.77	11.11	7.43	340,329	129.35
Vegetables:								
Potatoes..............	154,194	Bu....	22,978,739	84.3	64.9	149.0	50,778,993	329.32
Cantaloupes and musk-melons..............	20,874	....	....	....	....	....	3,853,037	184.59
Tomatoes.............	20,649	....	....	....	....	....	2,701,968	130.85
Orchard fruits:								
Grapes................	[3] 73,675,084	Lbs...	1,131,279,429	[4] 13.2	[4] 11.3	[4] 15.4	36,304,252	....
Apples................	[5] 9,085,326	Bu....	22,406,306	[6] 2.0	[6] 1.7	[6] 2.5	24,566,584	....
Peaches...............	[5] 7,062,692	Bu....	13,224,500	[6] 1.4	[6] 1.2	[6] 1.9	24,670,264	....
Pears.................	[5] 1,849,429	Bu....	3,479,806	[6] 1.6	[6] 1.4	[6] 1.9	4,695,848	....
Plums and prunes.....	[5] 4,306,976	Bu....	7,074,240	[6] 1.2	[6] 1.0	[6] 1.6	15,188,490	....
Cherries..............	[5] 667,907	Bu....	578,354	[6] 0.7	[6] 0.6	[6] 0.9	2,139,891	....
Subtropical fruits:								
Oranges...............	[5] 8,711,152	Boxes.	18,774,366	[6] 2.1	[6] 1.8	[6] 2.2	58,244,422	....
Lemons...............	[5] 2,299,716	Boxes.	5,776,149	[6] 2.3	[6] 1.3	[6] 2.5	16,750,832	....
Miscellaneous:								
Sugar beets grown for sugar...............	377,655	Tons..	3,567,522	9.24	8.38	9.45	38,831,339	102.82
Cotton................	214,576	Bales.	113,862	0.28	0.28	0.53	30,457,881	141.94

[1] Quantity harvested and value given for irrigated land were not tabulated separately. The totals given include small amounts of rice grown without irrigation.
[2] Not including red clover seed.
[3] Number of vines of bearing age.
[4] Yield per vine.
[5] Number of trees of bearing age.
[6] Yield per tree.

DRAINAGE

CONTENTS.

(900)

DRAINAGE.

The following statistics relate to the artificial drainage of land in farms, and of other land intended to be used ultimately for agricultural purposes. Drainage was defined, for the census, as the act or process of drawing off an excess of water by underground conduits, pipe, or tile, or by open or covered trenches, for the purpose of improving the condition of the soil and crops. The drainage census divides naturally into two parts, relating to drainage on farms and to drainage enterprises, respectively. The statistics refer to conditions on January 1, 1920, except where otherwise indicated. No census of drainage has been taken heretofore.

Drainage on farms relates to land provided with artificial drainage and thereby actually benefited for growing crops, and to other land in farms that could be made suitable for growing crops by drainage or by drainage and clearing. In most cases, drainage on farms represents work done by individual farm owners, either independently or supplemental to the works of organized drainage enterprises. The statistics for drainage on farms were collected in the general census of agriculture, and are given for all states.

Drainage enterprises comprise public corporations and local improvement districts established under state laws relating to drainage, commercial enterprises draining land for sale, other organizations engaged in extensive land drainage work, and tracts of 500 acres or more drained by individual farm owners. Levee districts or other flood-protection districts are not included unless they have undertaken the construction of open ditches or tile drains. The enterprises in some states include considerable areas of timber and other unimproved land not in farms. The statistics for drainage enterprises were obtained in a special canvass of the enterprises, which did not include any of the states north or east of the Potomac River. In Alabama, Virginia, and West Virginia no enterprises of a public nature were found that had completed or had begun actual construction of drainage works, so those states are omitted entirely from this part of the drainage census. In Michigan no attempt was made to secure statistics concerning drainage done before 1897, owing to the known incompleteness of the information obtainable.

Those enterprises that on January 1, 1920, had completed or had begun actual construction of the drainage works are herein termed "operating enterprises," the others "nonoperating enterprises."

TABLE 1.—SUMMARY FOR THE UNITED STATES: 1920.

ITEM.	Amount.	Per cent of total.
DRAINAGE ON FARMS.		
Number of all farms in the United States	6,448,343	100.0
Farms reporting land having drainage	924,815	14.3
Farms reporting land needing drainage	956,095	14.8
Farms reporting both land provided with drainage and land needing drainage	402,623	6.2
All land in farms........................acres..	955,883,715	100.0
Improved land in farms..................acres..	503,073,007	52.6
Farm land reported as provided with drainage......acres..	53,024,975	5.5
Farm land reported as needing drainage...........acres..	39,169,639	4.1
DRAINAGE ENTERPRISES.		
Approximate land area of states included.........acres..	1,717,932,160	100.0
All land in operating drainage enterprises.......acres..	65,495,038	3.8
Improved land.........................acres..	44,288,235	2.6
Timber and cut-over land...............acres..	11,283,532	0.7
Other unimproved land..................acres..	9,923,271	0.6
Total capital invested in and required for completion of operating enterprises...	$434,594,979	100.0
Capital invested in these enterprises to Dec. 31, 1919	$372,273,567	85.7
Additional capital required to complete these enterprises	$62,321,412	14.3

TABLE 2.—DRAINAGE ON FARMS, BY DIVISIONS AND STATES: 1920.

DIVISION AND STATE.	NUMBER OF FARMS.				LAND IN FARMS.			
		Having drainage.			Having drainage.		Needing drainage.	
	Total.	Number.	Per cent of all farms.	Needing drainage.	Acreage.	Per cent of all land in farms.	Drainage only (acres).	Drainage and clearing (acres).
United States..	6,448,343	924,815	14.3	956,095	53,024,975	5.5	10,459,181	28,710,458
GEOGRAPHIC DIVISIONS:								
New England.....	156,564	9,083	5.8	17,571	129,799	0.8	86,991	310,276
Middle Atlantic...	425,147	61,549	14.5	69,216	1,673,638	4.1	505,910	906,128
East North Central	1,084,744	429,584	39.6	302,008	30,737,056	26.1	3,243,427	5,626,929
West North Central	1,096,951	163,714	14.9	169,593	11,758,939	4.6	4,187,385	3,073,154
South Atlantic....	1,158,976	114,983	9.9	156,780	2,865,072	2.9	696,687	6,814,543
East South Central	1,051,600	69,597	6.6	106,972	1,720,517	2.2	462,040	3,817,928
West South Central	996,088	44,835	4.5	91,595	2,365,701	1.4	734,305	6,400,267
Mountain.........	244,109	9,754	4.0	14,988	456,015	0.4	329,359	640,589
Pacific............	234,164	21,716	9.3	27,372	1,318,238	2.3	213,077	1,120,644
NEW ENGLAND:								
Maine.............	48,227	2,068	4.3	5,425	26,302	0.5	19,930	122,123
New Hampshire...	20,523	1,013	4.9	1,794	11,777	0.5	9,914	30,869
Vermont..........	29,075	1,728	5.9	3,042	35,649	0.8	19,265	49,647
Massachusetts.....	32,001	2,955	9.2	4,112	39,022	1.6	21,212	59,671
Rhode Island......	4,083	116	2.8	359	2,403	0.7	2,240	5,934
Connecticut.......	22,655	1,203	5.3	2,839	14,646	0.8	14,430	42,032
MIDDLE ATLANTIC:								
New York.........	193,195	33,896	17.5	38,523	1,180,423	5.7	318,865	460,602
New Jersey.......	29,702	4,903	16.5	3,428	174,260	7.6	29,193	48,688
Pennsylvania......	202,250	22,750	11.2	27,265	318,955	1.8	157,852	396,838
EAST NORTH CENTRAL:								
Ohio..............	256,695	130,117	50.7	85,326	7,365,532	31.3	886,557	1,128,332
Indiana...........	205,126	111,435	54.3	66,413	8,308,844	39.4	673,952	1,043,116
Illinois...........	237,181	99,246	41.8	33,731	11,247,637	35.2	641,493	587,246
Michigan..........	196,447	66,948	34.1	64,310	3,156,632	16.6	579,813	1,490,574
Wisconsin.........	189,295	21,838	11.5	52,228	658,411	3.0	461,612	1,377,661
WEST NORTH CENTRAL:								
Minnesota........	178,478	53,011	29.7	73,905	2,993,034	9.9	1,801,457	1,703,117
Iowa.............	213,439	88,865	41.6	56,083	7,334,404	21.9	1,661,744	391,198
Missouri..........	263,004	11,917	4.5	19,572	859,663	2.5	163,178	667,515
North Dakota.....	77,690	682	0.9	2,669	89,054	0.2	53,161	158,144
South Dakota.....	74,637	4,077	5.5	11,828	161,371	0.5	356,049	90,866
Nebraska..........	124,417	2,356	1.9	2,963	214,428	0.5	115,425	30,393
Kansas...........	165,286	2,806	1.7	2,573	106,985	0.2	36,371	31,921
SOUTH ATLANTIC:								
Delaware..........	10,140	4,246	41.9	2,488	185,831	19.7	7,967	61,002
Maryland.........	47,908	6,911	14.4	6,658	249,799	5.3	33,267	151,553
Dist. of Columbia..	204	21	10.3	12	197	3.5	58	57
Virginia..........	186,242	9,899	5.3	27,740	225,068	1.2	77,192	1,095,388
West Virginia.....	87,289	1,949	2.2	10,304	38,464	0.4	32,253	278,615
North Carolina....	269,763	45,246	16.8	42,247	1,066,933	5.3	189,401	1,735,942
South Carolina....	192,693	26,993	14.0	24,508	676,152	5.4	125,548	1,216,355
Georgia...........	310,732	15,121	4.9	34,337	274,688	1.1	143,187	1,676,424
Florida...........	54,005	4,597	8.5	8,486	147,940	2.4	87,814	599,207
EAST SOUTH CENTRAL:								
Kentucky..........	270,626	5,817	2.1	19,592	225,228	1.0	84,189	489,110
Tennessee.........	252,774	8,887	3.5	20,997	254,118	1.3	76,644	563,835
Alabama..........	256,099	19,967	7.8	36,511	415,293	2.1	150,028	1,460,628
Mississippi.......	272,101	34,926	12.8	29,872	825,878	4.5	151,179	1,304,355
WEST SOUTH CENTRAL:								
Arkansas..........	232,604	13,426	5.8	33,437	497,489	2.8	129,987	1,512,416
Louisiana.........	135,463	21,271	15.7	14,985	1,004,935	10.0	179,305	916,464
Oklahoma........	191,988	2,032	1.1	8,065	107,014	0.3	39,788	225,998
Texas............	436,033	8,106	1.9	35,108	756,263	0.7	385,225	3,745,389
MOUNTAIN:								
Montana..........	57,677	756	1.3	1,728	51,146	0.1	36,342	76,951
Idaho............	42,106	1,167	2.8	2,895	64,648	0.8	37,566	162,308
Wyoming.........	15,748	433	2.7	1,127	35,654	0.3	23,837	45,229
Colorado.........	59,934	2,749	4.6	4,399	127,037	0.5	80,121	190,876
New Mexico......	29,844	1,294	4.3	998	47,311	0.2	29,016	20,086
Arizona...........	9,975	241	2.4	435	9,651	0.2	9,596	32,355
Utah.............	25,662	2,729	10.6	3,085	74,316	1.5	74,786	91,140
Nevada...........	3,163	385	12.2	321	46,252	2.0	38,095	21,644
PACIFIC:								
Washington.......	66,288	10,020	15.1	14,323	274,696	2.1	45,206	530,799
Oregon...........	50,206	6,618	13.2	9,862	229,582	1.7	75,063	396,333
California.........	117,670	5,078	4.3	3,187	813,960	2.8	92,808	193,512

TABLE 3.—LAND AND CAPITAL INVESTED IN ALL ENTERPRISES, BY CHARACTER OF ENTERPRISE: 1920.

CHARACTER OF ENTERPRISE.	OPERATING ENTERPRISES.			NONOPERATING ENTERPRISES.		
	Land in enterprises (acres).[1]	Capital.		Land in enterprises (acres).[1]	Capital.	
		Invested to Dec. 31, 1919.	Additional required to complete.		Invested to Dec. 31, 1919.	Additional required to complete.
Total	65,495,038	$372,273,567	$62,321,412	3,924,821	$1,123,458	$34,937,678
Drainage districts	22,069,597	172,013,972	39,136,568	3,260,104	772,834	26,339,970
General state laws	20,239,956	147,511,259	24,593,523	2,667,056	752,830	25,073,970
Special acts	1,829,641	24,502,713	14,543,045	593,048	20,004	1,266,000
County drains	37,870,803	169,743,093	9,682,477	596,694	302,224	8,139,808
Township drains	195,133	574,963	4,500	423		2,400
State drainage projects	1,422,844	6,845,429	6,434,440			
U. S. Reclamation Service	287,899	3,912,370	2,530,243	7,000		150,000
Irrigation districts	175,200	1,459,714	2,553,829			
Commercial developments	212,421	3,279,829	1,128,000	50,000	45,000	150,000
Individual ownership	432,397	6,449,252	841,750	10,600	3,400	155,500
Not reported [2]	2,828,744	7,994,945	9,605			

[1] Before tabulation, the area in each enterprise was reduced by the amount of overlapping with enterprises organized previously.
[2] All except 35,062 acres and $218,951 invested to Dec. 31, 1919, relate to either drainage districts or county drains in Indiana.

TABLE 4.—LAND, CAPITAL INVESTED, AND COST PER ACRE FOR OPERATING ENTERPRISES, BY DATE ENTERPRISE WAS ORGANIZED: 1920.

DATE OF ORGANIZATION.	LAND.		CAPITAL.		Cost per acre (on assessed acreage).
	Area in enterprises (acres).[1]	Assessed acreage.[2]	Invested to Dec. 31, 1919.	Additional required to complete.	
Total	65,495,038	95,629,291	$372,273,567	$62,321,412	$4.54
Before 1860	97,319	98,119	182,716		1.86
1860 to 1869	783,357	932,565	1,689,852		1.81
1870 to 1879	2,077,717	3,413,277	8,126,391		2.38
1880 to 1889	5,424,294	8,843,654	23,934,330	1,840,829	2.91
1890 to 1899	6,026,937	11,575,924	24,498,861	521,310	2.16
1900 to 1904	7,606,753	12,200,468	26,706,464	709,063	2.25
1905 to 1909	14,530,397	20,228,636	76,072,320	7,612,491	4.14
1910 to 1914	17,344,098	22,245,539	120,269,596	14,455,410	6.19
1915 to 1919	11,374,619	15,828,501	87,379,002	36,771,650	7.84
Not reported	229,547	262,608	3,414,035	410,659	14.56

[1] Before tabulation, the area in each enterprise was reduced by the amount of overlapping with enterprises organized previously.
[2] These figures represent the sums of the areas in all the enterprises, without deducting for overlapping.

TABLE 5.—LAND AND CAPITAL INVESTED IN ALL ENTERPRISES,

			LAND IN DRAINAGE ENTERPRISES.				
				Operating enterprises.			
	DIVISION AND STATE.	Area of states included (acres).	All enterprises (acres).	Total area (acres).	Works completed (acres).	Works under construction (acres).	Non-operating enterprises (acres).
1	States included.	1,717,932,160	69,419,859	65,495,038	56,763,751	8,731,287	3,924,821
	GEOGRAPHIC DIVISIONS:						
2	East North Central.	157,160,960	32,073,734	31,627,176	30,475,905	1,151,271	446,558
3	West North Central	326,914,560	19,936,111	19,217,367	16,959,103	2,258,264	718,744
4	South Atlantic.....	123,405,440	3,436,887	2,385,384	861,312	1,524,072	1,051,503
5	East South Central.	82,067,200	2,796,830	2,323,595	1,732,586	591,009	473,235
6	West South Central	275,037,440	9,062,480	7,924,197	5,750,958	2,173,239	1,138,283
7	Mountain..........	549,765,760	888,809	810,076	236,872	573,204	78,733
8	Pacific............	203,580,800	1,225,008	1,207,243	747,015	460,228	17,765
	EAST NORTH CENTRAL:						
9	Ohio...............	26,073,600	8,147,546	8,107,204	8,093,994	13,210	40,342
10	Indiana...........	23,068,800	9,375,907	9,087,183	8,867,674	219,509	288,724
11	Illinois..........	35,867,520	3,982,033	3,909,049	3,430,474	478,575	72,984
12	Michigan..........	36,787,200	9,754,679	9,729,171	9,511,555	217,616	25,508
13	Wisconsin.........	35,363,840	813,569	794,569	572,208	222,361	19,000
	WEST NORTH CENTRAL:						
14	Minnesota.........	51,749,120	9,362,944	9,232,709	8,552,900	679,809	130,235
15	Iowa..............	35,575,040	5,383,012	5,224,478	4,685,080	539,398	158,534
16	Missouri..........	43,985,280	2,980,265	2,596,204	1,858,945	737,259	384,061
17	North Dakota......	44,917,120	1,248,328	1,240,328	1,100,044	140,284	8,000
18	South Dakota......	49,195,520	222,062	222,062	124,132	97,930	
19	Nebraska..........	49,157,120	633,566	607,730	565,222	42,508	25,836
20	Kansas............	52,335,360	105,934	93,856	72,780	21,076	12,078
	SOUTH ATLANTIC:						
21	North Carolina....	31,193,600	542,828	542,828	440,657	102,171	
22	South Carolina.....	19,516,800	144,237	140,031	24,864	115,167	4,206
23	Georgia...........	37,584,000	104,006	65,452	43,723	21,729	38,554
24	Florida...........	35,111,040	2,645,816	1,637,073	352,068	1,285,005	1,008,743
	EAST SOUTH CENTRAL:						
25	Kentucky..........	25,715,840	471,874	358,480	288,143	70,337	113,394
26	Tennessee.........	26,679,680	445,955	363,671	268,667	95,004	82,284
27	Mississippi.......	29,671,680	1,879,001	1,601,444	1,175,776	425,668	277,557
	WEST SOUTH CENTRAL:						
28	Arkansas..........	33,616,000	4,151,834	3,479,591	2,124,446	1,355,145	672,243
29	Louisiana.........	29,061,760	2,732,368	2,266,328	1,534,634	731,694	466,040
30	Oklahoma..........	44,424,960	12,150	12,150	11,750	400	
31	Texas.............	167,934,720	2,166,128	2,166,128	2,080,128	86,000	
	MOUNTAIN:						
32	Montana...........	93,523,840	168,682	168,682	44,682	124,000	
33	Idaho.............	53,346,560	78,732	64,642	43,892	20,750	14,090
34	Wyoming...........	62,430,720	107,041	95,474	11,740	83,734	11,567
35	Colorado..........	66,341,120	171,656	171,656	66,816	104,840	
36	New Mexico........	78,401,920	147,219	140,219	20,169	120,050	7,000
37	Arizona...........	72,838,400	64,985	39,640	9,640	30,000	25,345
38	Utah..............	52,597,760	134,554	113,823	23,993	89,830	20,731
39	Nevada............	70,285,440	15,940	15,940	15,940		
	PACIFIC:						
40	Washington........	42,775,040	99,789	94,924	90,084	4,840	4,865
41	Oregon............	61,188,480	4,000	4,000	4,000		
42	California........	99,617,280	1,121,219	1,108,319	652,931	455,388	12,900

AND IN OPERATING AND NONOPERATING ENTERPRISES: 1920.

CAPITAL INVESTED IN DRAINAGE ENTERPRISES.								
Invested to December 31, 1919.					Additional required to complete.			
All enterprises.	Operating enterprises.			Non-operating enterprises.	All enterprises.	Operating enterprises.	Non-operating enterprises.	
	Total.	Works completed.	Works under construction.					
$373,397,025	$372,273,567	$293,857,023	$78,416,544	$1,123,458	$97,259,090	$62,321,412	$34,937,678	1
134,359,233	134,269,666	119,525,193	14,744,473	89,567	13,376,507	9,452,661	3,923,846	2
121,824,200	121,562,077	102,365,306	19,196,771	262,123	23,743,744	11,632,586	12,111,158	3
19,096,139	18,847,093	6,805,285	12,041,808	249,046	17,512,611	14,476,175	3,036,436	4
11,808,449	11,523,833	9,085,234	2,438,599	284,616	7,333,076	2,306,418	5,026,658	5
29,112,366	28,946,385	20,473,933	8,472,452	165,981	21,902,834	13,411,222	8,491,612	6
7,866,066	7,839,941	3,248,713	4,591,228	26,125	6,541,844	4,668,876	1,872,968	7
49,330,572	49,284,572	32,353,359	16,931,213	46,000	6,848,474	6,373,474	475,000	8
30,707,863	30,680,145	30,636,857	43,288	27,718	397,396	91,475	305,921	9
31,201,517	31,147,682	30,154,296	993,386	53,835	2,729,055	796,176	1,932,879	10
43,595,069	43,595,069	31,424,167	12,170,902	....	9,199,841	7,798,175	1,401,666	11
24,686,729	24,683,715	24,100,929	582,786	3,014	537,645	365,265	172,380	12
4,168,055	4,163,055	3,208,944	954,111	5,000	512,570	401,570	111,000	13
42,089,304	42,017,447	36,764,850	5,252,597	71,857	5,095,002	2,166,391	2,928,611	14
49,649,775	49,627,304	44,630,537	4,996,767	22,471	6,858,477	4,542,574	2,315,903	15
20,889,328	20,723,128	13,294,035	7,429,093	166,200	10,178,401	4,026,607	6,151,794	16
2,208,049	2,208,049	1,863,788	344,261	....	77,723	53,400	24,323	17
1,461,063	1,461,063	942,757	518,306	....	271,666	271,666	....	18
4,588,578	4,588,578	4,121,486	467,092	....	821,841	298,103	523,738	19
938,103	936,508	747,853	188,655	1,595	440,634	273,845	166,789	20
3,623,518	3,623,518	3,075,018	548,500	....	902,500	902,500	....	21
583,083	582,183	198,370	383,813	900	445,845	354,331	91,514	22
828,681	794,585	614,636	179,949	34,096	1,231,176	303,654	927,522	23
14,060,857	13,846,807	2,917,261	10,929,546	214,050	14,933,090	12,915,690	2,017,400	24
1,620,027	1,521,725	1,278,701	243,024	98,302	1,825,513	299,271	1,526,242	25
2,995,515	2,925,944	2,283,589	642,355	69,571	1,447,230	522,047	925,183	26
7,192,907	7,076,164	5,522,944	1,553,220	116,743	4,060,333	1,485,100	2,575,233	27
14,217,155	14,147,174	9,385,025	4,762,149	69,981	18,637,337	11,741,425	6,895,912	28
9,117,991	9,021,991	5,956,938	3,065,053	96,000	2,564,497	968,797	1,595,700	29
76,415	76,415	76,165	250	....	1,000	1,000	....	30
5,700,805	5,700,805	5,055,805	645,000	....	700,000	700,000	....	31
664,990	664,990	393,969	271,021	....	181,476	181,476	....	32
1,678,294	1,668,569	1,237,578	430,991	9,725	250,000	120,000	130,000	33
1,182,362	1,175,962	32,231	1,143,731	6,400	901,873	491,405	410,468	34
1,081,875	1,081,875	508,663	573,212	....	203,195	203,195	....	35
1,710,796	1,710,796	361,989	1,348,807	....	1,345,500	1,195,500	150,000	36
414,925	414,425	101,425	313,000	500	1,147,000	612,000	535,000	37
1,014,973	1,005,473	495,007	510,466	9,500	2,512,800	1,865,300	647,500	38
117,851	117,851	117,851	....	....	....	....	....	39
1,442,419	1,397,419	1,376,809	20,610	45,000	114,000	39,000	75,000	40
200,000	200,000	200,000	....	....	....	....	....	41
47,688,153	47,687,153	30,776,550	16,910,603	1,000	6,734,474	6,334,474	400,000	42

TABLE 6.—LAND IN OPERATING ENTERPRISES, BY CONDITION: 1920.

DIVISION AND STATE.	OPERATING ENTERPRISES.					
	Total (acres).	Improved land (acres).	Timber and cut-over land (acres).	Other unimproved land (acres).	Swampy or subject to overflow (acres).	Suffering a loss of crops (acres).
States included.....	65,495,038	44,288,235	11,283,532	9,923,271	7,224,213	3,011,407
GEOGRAPHIC DIVISIONS:						
East North Central.....	31,627,176	25,282,065	4,457,151	1,887,960	2,012,248	1,283,296
West North Central....	19,217,367	11,630,279	2,530,012	5,057,076	2,007,511	901,857
South Atlantic..........	2,385,384	388,345	862,334	1,134,705	849,342	58,194
East South Central.....	2,323,595	1,349,791	914,404	59,400	434,602	78,809
West South Central....	7,924,197	3,877,166	2,506,431	1,540,600	1,670,037	483,495
Mountain..............	810,076	635,868	87	174,121	194,437	154,551
Pacific.................	1,207,243	1,124,721	13,113	69,409	56,036	51,205
EAST NORTH CENTRAL:						
Ohio...................	8,107,204	6,707,328	916,894	442,982	247,273	141,481
Indiana...............	9,087,183	7,605,565	942,378	539,240	386,320	210,678
Illinois...............	3,909,049	3,532,316	184,573	192,160	228,337	229,065
Michigan.............	9,729,171	7,182,352	2,195,562	351,257	1,020,207	692,224
Wisconsin............	794,569	254,504	177,744	362,321	130,111	9,848
WEST NORTH CENTRAL:						
Minnesota.............	9,232,709	3,818,490	1,370,023	4,044,196	1,193,136	471,094
Iowa..................	5,224,478	4,493,407	74,652	656,419	320,893	157,542
Missouri..............	2,596,204	1,474,302	1,074,860	47,042	454,360	242,258
North Dakota..........	1,240,328	1,026,574	....	213,754	12,332	4,819
South Dakota..........	222,062	178,540	....	43,522	6,067	481
Nebraska.............	607,730	551,517	6,342	49,871	14,019	19,575
Kansas...............	93,856	87,449	4,135	2,272	6,704	6,088
SOUTH ATLANTIC:						
North Carolina.........	542,828	204,928	244,576	93,324	77,494	12,771
South Carolina........	140,031	59,075	64,955	16,001	18,206	3,093
Georgia..............	65,452	29,753	10,155	25,544	21,951	1,832
Florida...............	1,637,073	94,589	542,648	999,836	731,691	40,498
EAST SOUTH CENTRAL:						
Kentucky.............	358,480	245,334	92,495	20,651	69,413	36,723
Tennessee............	363,671	163,218	189,945	10,508	104,063	29,879
Mississippi...........	1,601,444	941,239	631,964	28,241	261,126	12,207
WEST SOUTH CENTRAL:						
Arkansas..............	3,479,591	1,491,777	1,923,382	64,432	897,547	153,957
Louisiana.............	2,266,328	1,269,391	467,822	529,115	569,189	198,935
Oklahoma.............	12,150	8,845	3,305	....	2,250	1,838
Texas................	2,166,128	1,107,153	111,922	947,053	201,051	128,765
MOUNTAIN:						
Montana..............	168,682	141,252	....	27,430	19,630	21,964
Idaho.................	64,642	52,098	87	12,457	11,402	164
Wyoming.............	95,474	84,846	....	10,628	20,785	6,595
Colorado..............	171,656	123,031	....	48,625	26,446	15,282
New Mexico...........	140,219	92,477	....	47,742	20,572	24,420
Arizona...............	39,640	36,880	....	2,760	2,160	2,160
Utah.................	113,823	97,314	....	16,509	88,181	76,803
Nevada...............	15,940	7,970	....	7,970	5,261	7,163
PACIFIC:						
Washington...........	94,924	81,886	850	12,188	10,873	8,996
Oregon...............	4,000	4,000	....	....	....	....
California.............	1,108,319	1,038,835	12,263	57,221	45,163	42,209

TABLE 7.—LAND IN NONOPERATING ENTERPRISES, BY CONDITION: 1920.

DIVISION AND STATE.	NONOPERATING ENTERPRISES.					
	Total (acres).	Improved land (acres).	Timber and cut-over land (acres).	Other unimproved land (acres).	Swampy or subject to overflow (acres).	Suffering a loss of crops (acres).
States included	3,924,821	1,376,495	1,294,018	1,254,308	2,299,562	239,192
GEOGRAPHIC DIVISIONS:						
East North Central	446,558	270,083	77,653	98,822	144,363	61,024
West North Central	718,744	406,744	89,443	222,557	441,137	28,656
South Atlantic	1,051,503	36,800	314,640	700,063	719,579	38,280
East South Central	473,235	198,494	223,185	51,556	239,554	19,359
West South Central	1,138,283	398,471	587,147	152,665	709,355	68,150
Mountain	78,733	56,729	1,950	20,054	31,258	23,723
Pacific	17,765	9,174		8,591	14,316	
EAST NORTH CENTRAL:						
Ohio	40,342	24,375	4,363	11,604	19,776	7,603
Indiana	288,724	192,190	51,212	45,322	64,677	38,456
Illinois	72,984	44,993	3,714	24,277	29,294	13,507
Michigan	25,508	8,245	15,039	2,224	12,316	1,458
Wisconsin	19,000	280	3,325	15,395	18,300	
WEST NORTH CENTRAL:						
Minnesota	130,235	34,494	7,158	88,583	78,922	981
Iowa	158,534	84,722	4,350	69,462	68,197	5,058
Missouri	384,061	265,063	77,268	41,730	270,382	17,917
North Dakota	8,000	5,334		2,666	2,000	
South Dakota						
Nebraska	25,836	5,853	267	19,716	21,636	4,700
Kansas	12,078	11,278	400	400		
SOUTH ATLANTIC:						
North Carolina						
South Carolina	4,206	976	1,548	1,682	4,106	
Georgia	38,554	9,622	9,426	19,506	23,232	6,862
Florida	1,008,743	26,202	303,666	678,875	692,241	31,418
EAST SOUTH CENTRAL:						
Kentucky	113,394	67,526	28,539	17,329	55,339	875
Tennessee	82,284	23,116	57,150	2,018	76,004	17,536
Mississippi	277,557	107,852	137,496	32,209	108,211	948
WEST SOUTH CENTRAL:						
Arkansas	672,243	217,491	414,707	40,045	496,573	20,774
Louisiana	466,040	180,980	172,440	112,620	212,782	47,376
Oklahoma						
Texas						
MOUNTAIN:						
Montana						
Idaho	14,090	7,514	1,950	4,626	3,326	3,101
Wyoming	11,567	7,513		4,054	6,554	1,000
Colorado						
New Mexico	7,000	1,750		5,250		1,155
Arizona	25,345	22,276		3,069	1,069	1,069
Utah	20,731	17,676		3,055	20,309	17,398
Nevada						
PACIFIC:						
Washington	4,865	3,174		1,691	1,416	
Oregon						
California	12,900	6,000		6,900	12,900	

TABLE 8.—DRAINAGE WORKS OF OPERATING ENTERPRISES: 1920.

DIVISION AND STATE.	COMPLETED.			UNDER CONSTRUCTION.			PUMPING PLANTS.[1]		
	Open ditches (miles).	Tile drains (miles).	Levees [1] (miles).	Open ditches (miles).	Tile drains (miles).	Levees [1] (miles).	Engine capacity (horsepower).	Pump capacity (gallons per minute).	Area served (acres).
States included..	**107,468.2**	**42,311.7**	**3,519.8**	**4,301.8**	**2,862.1**	**810.2**	**67,189**	**15,949,166**	**1,544,010**
GEOGRAPHIC DIVISIONS:									
East North Central	64,924.3	23,325.2	866.4	408.9	369.6	112.8	20,190	2,964,014	315,879
West North Central	23,912.7	17,109.3	698.6	745.6	1,285.0	85.8	6,003	1,086,800	207,124
South Atlantic....	3,701.6	101.5	111.7	1,229.4	161.0	136.5	1,275	1,083,600	107,440
East South Central	3,256.9	325.3	49.2	436.0	55.3	47.0	250	78,000	44,000
West South Central	7,672.8	20.6	625.3	1,234.0	2.0	306.7	10,465	5,965,150	230,809
Mountain..........	827.7	1,248.2	37.5	36.1	965.5	....	480	72,560	34,312
Pacific............	3,172.2	181.6	1,131.1	211.8	23.7	121.4	28,526	4,699,042	604,446
EAST NORTH CENTRAL:									
Ohio..............	24,984.0	9,205.3	9.6	13.4	8.3	4.0	125	3,600	1,755
Indiana...........	17,470.7	8,227.6	165.8	123.4	185.7	9.2	625	55,348	5,611
Illinois...........	4,754.5	3,507.1	650.2	65.7	127.1	97.1	18,225	2,843,066	291,816
Michigan..........	16,023.8	2,173.9	33.1	118.4	8.4	....	1,065	62,000	10,100
Wisconsin.........	1,691.3	211.3	7.7	88.0	40.1	2.5	150	....	6,597
WEST NORTH CENTRAL:									
Minnesota.........	14,657.0	5,924.6	0.1	166.1	462.7	0.3	....	....	....
Iowa..............	3,998.0	10,384.9	45.2	81.1	768.6	....	3,153	530,800	134,616
Missouri..........	3,438.7	38.8	456.9	460.4	5.9	74.9	2,785	552,000	70,308
North Dakota.....	708.3	9.3	2.1	4.0	....	....	....	....	....
South Dakota.....	237.8	179.3	2.4	8.1	33.6	....	....	....	....
Nebraska..........	734.5	359.4	26.8	18.7	14.2	2.8	65	4,000	2,200
Kansas............	138.4	213.0	165.1	7.2	....	7.8	....	....	....
SOUTH ATLANTIC:									
North Carolina....	1,171.3	....	33.5	367.8	....	....	1,000	1,000,000	100,000
South Carolina....	262.7	101.5	12.0	87.7	161.0	30.0	155	44,600	2,940
Georgia...........	276.8	....	....	79.9	....	....	....	....	....
Florida...........	1,990.8	....	66.2	694.0	....	106.5	120	39,000	4,500
EAST SOUTH CENTRAL:									
Kentucky..........	664.5	86.2	0.2	77.0	1.0	....	....	....	....
Tennessee.........	777.3	0.3	42.3	135.4	0.1	10.2	....	....	....
Mississippi.......	1,815.1	238.8	6.7	223.6	54.2	36.8	250	78,000	44,000
WEST SOUTH CENTRAL:									
Arkansas..........	3,154.1	20.4	119.8	974.1	2.0	240.8	2,800	720,000	90,000
Louisiana.........	1,771.6	0.2	440.7	162.7	....	65.9	7,665	5,245,150	140,809
Oklahoma..........	18.6	....	5.0	1.6	....	....	....	....	....
Texas.............	2,728.5	....	59.8	95.6	....	....	....	....	....
MOUNTAIN:									
Montana...........	102.1	50.7	....	1.3	36.2	....	....	....	....
Idaho.............	274.5	1.8	9.5	14.7	1.8	....	285	36,200	7,912
Wyoming...........	25.1	114.2	....	1.3	71.8	....	....	....	....
Colorado..........	132.5	195.2	....	14.3	13.0	....	....	....	....
New Mexico........	124.0	282.2	....	....	65.1	....	....	....	....
Arizona...........	32.6	1.0	26.0	....	....	....	175	33,660	25,000
Utah..............	120.3	599.1	2.0	4.5	777.6	....	20	2,700	1,400
Nevada............	16.6	4.0	....	....	....	....	....	....	....
PACIFIC:									
Washington........	162.4	83.0	....	7.4	0.7	1.0	....	....	....
Oregon............	....	13.0	....	....	....	....	....	....	....
California........	3,009.8	85.6	1,131.1	204.4	23.0	120.4	28,526	4,699,042	604,446

[1] Levees and pumping plants have been included as drainage works only when they have been constructed by an enterprise that has constructed open ditches or tile drains and their cost has been assessed with the cost of the drains.

TABLE 9.—DEVELOPMENT OF LAND SINCE DRAINAGE BEGAN, AND PRINCIPAL CROPS GROWN ON DRAINED LAND, IN OPERATING ENTERPRISES: 1919.

DIVISION AND STATE.	DEVELOPMENT OF LAND.				Principal crops on drained land.[1]
	Improved land: Increase (acres).	Timber and cut-over land: Decrease (acres).	Other un-improved land: Decrease (acres).	Swampy or over-flowed land: Decrease (acres).	
States included..	19,701,999	10,470,242	9,231,757	24,472,300	Corn, wheat, cotton, hay.
GEOGRAPHIC DIVISIONS:					
East North Central.	11,771,253	8,467,450	3,303,803	11,690,363	Corn, wheat, sugar beets.
West North Central.	4,779,690	699,744	4,079,946	7,381,149	Corn, wheat, hay, cotton.
South Atlantic......	214,712	108,805	105,907	935,527	Corn, cotton, vegetables.
East South Central .	575,020	506,070	68,950	745,001	Cotton, corn.
West South Central.	1,482,530	657,729	824,801	2,681,714	Cotton, corn, sugar cane, rice.
Mountain...........	157,969	10	157,959	233,065	Hay, wheat, cotton,sugar beets.
Pacific.............	720,825	30,434	690,391	805,481	Wheat, barley, hay, potatoes.
EAST NORTH CENTRAL:					
Ohio...............	2,752,108	2,122,286	629,822	2,879,612	Corn, wheat, hay, vegetables.
Indiana.............	2,209,178	1,382,600	826,578	2,860,945	Corn, wheat, hay.
Illinois.............	1,469,795	294,925	1,174,870	1,635,801	Corn, wheat, potatoes.
Michigan...........	5,135,739	4,613,651	522,088	3,742,809	Wheat, corn, sugar beets.
Wisconsin..........	204,433	53,988	150,445	571,196	Hay, corn, oats.
WEST NORTH CENTRAL:					
Minnesota..........	2,095,615	103,797	1,991,818	3,441,505	Wheat, hay, corn, oats.
Iowa...............	1,282,911	19,342	1,263,569	1,247,067	Corn, hay.
Missouri...........	713,506	571,437	142,069	1,559,344	Corn, cotton, wheat.
North Dakota......	335,569	....	335,569	606,827	Wheat, hay.
South Dakota......	79,816	....	79,816	135,424	Corn, wheat.
Nebraska..........	258,896	2,455	256,441	381,234	Corn, wheat, sugar beets.
Kansas.............	13,377	2,713	10,664	9,748	Wheat, corn.
SOUTH ATLANTIC:					
North Carolina.....	120,214	67,050	53,164	233,616	Corn, cotton.
South Carolina.....	7,726	3,736	3,990	73,148	Cotton, corn.
Georgia............	22,524	14,926	7,598	32,141	Corn.
Florida............	64,248	23,093	41,155	596,622	Vegetables, potatoes, sugar cane.
EAST SOUTH CENTRAL:					
Kentucky..........	63,419	53,601	9,818	129,748	Corn.
Tennessee..........	77,190	72,218	4,972	248,964	Corn, cotton.
Mississippi.........	434,411	380,251	54,160	366,289	Cotton, corn.
WEST SOUTH CENTRAL:					
Arkansas..........	603,913	536,788	67,125	1,167,717	Cotton, corn.
Louisiana..........	332,489	112,596	219,893	709,806	Sugar cane, rice, cotton, corn.
Oklahoma..........	5,250	3,625	1,625	4,800	Cotton, corn, hay.
Texas..............	540,878	4,720	536,158	799,391	Corn, cotton, vegetables.
MOUNTAIN:					
Montana...........	33,607	....	33,607	35,840	Wheat, hay.
Idaho.............	27,448	10	27,438	29,040	Hay, wheat.
Wyoming..........	1,640	....	1,640	51,024	Hay, sugar beets.
Colorado..........	54,374	....	54,374	72,135	Hay, wheat, sugar beets.
New Mexico........	15,212	....	15,212	24,347	Hay, grain.
Arizona............	17,768	....	17,768	4,268	Cotton.
Utah..............	7,920	....	7,920	16,411	Hay, sugar beets.
Nevada............	....	....	....	....	Hay.
PACIFIC:					
Washington........	32,138	650	31,488	27,998	Hay, wheat.
Oregon............	....	....	....	320	Hay.
California..........	688,687	29,784	658,903	777,163	Grain, potatoes, hay, corn.

[1] All the improved land in each enterprise was tabulated under the one principal crop, as the area actually devoted to any particular crop was not determined. Those thus shown to have the greatest acreage are listed here in order. The crop designated "hay" includes alfalfa.

MANUFACTURES

(911)

CONTENTS.

75108°—23——58

MANUFACTURES.

DEFINITIONS AND EXPLANATION OF TERMS.

This chapter presents in condensed form statistics collected for the census of manufactures of 1919, and comparative figures for prior censuses. It is designed to meet the requirements of those who desire statistics for the United States as a whole, for the principal industries, and for the states, counties, and principal cities. The general report and analytical tables are presented in Volume VIII. The detailed statistics for the different industries in the states, counties, and cities are given in Volume IX, and similar details for the principal industries are contained in the special reports for such industries. The following paragraphs explain the scope of the census and the terms used in presenting the statistics:

Scope of census.—Census statistics of manufactures are compiled primarily for the purpose of showing the absolute and relative magnitude of the different branches of industry covered and their growth or decline. Incidentally, the effort is made to present data throwing light upon character of ownership, size of establishments, both by value of products and average number of wage earners and germane subjects. When use of the data is made it is imperative to note that owing to the limitations of the statistics any attempt made to derive from the figures the average wages, cost of production, or profits is not only futile but misleading.

The census did not cover establishments which were idle during the entire year or for which products were valued at less than $500, or the manufacturing done in educational, eleemosynary, and penal institutions.

Period covered.—The returns relate to the calendar year 1919, or the business year which corresponded most nearly to that calendar year, and cover a year's operations, except for establishments which began or discontinued business during the year.

The establishment.—As a rule, the term "establishment" represents a single plant or factory, but in some cases it represents two or more plants which were operated under a common ownership or for which one set of books of account was kept. If, however, the plants constituting an establishment as thus defined were not all located within the same city, county, or state, separate reports were secured in order that the figures for each plant might be included in the statistics for the city, county, or state in which it was located.

Classification by industries.—The establishments were assigned to the several classes of industries according to their products of chief value. The products reported for a given industry may thus, on the one hand, include minor products different from those covered by the class designation, and, on the other hand, may not represent the total product covered by this designation, because some of this class of product may be made in establishments in which it is not the product of chief value.

Selected industries.—The general tables at the end of this chapter give the principal facts separately for the industries and the states. A selection has been made of certain leading industries for more detailed consideration.

Comparisons with previous censuses.—Owing to changes in industrial conditions it is not always possible to classify establishments by industries in such a way as to permit accurate comparison with preceding censuses. At the census of 1909 the figures for kindred industries were combined. This practice has been followed in compiling the statistics for 1919 and 1914 when placed in comparison with those for 1909 and prior years.

Influence of increased prices.—In comparing figures for cost of materials, value of products, and value added by manufacture in 1919 with the corresponding figures for earlier censuses, account should be taken of the general increase in the prices of commodities during recent years. To the extent to which this factor has been influential the figures fail to afford an exact measure of the increase in the volume of business.

Persons engaged in the industry.—The following general classes of persons engaged in the manufacturing industries were distinguished: (1) Proprietors and firm members, (2) salaried officers of corporations, (3) superintendents and managers, (4) clerks (including other subordinate salaried employees), and (5) wage earners. In the reports for the censuses of 1904 and 1899 these five classes were shown according to the three main groups: (1) Proprietors and firm members, (2) salaried officials, clerks, etc., and (3) wage earners. In comparative tables covering the census of 1904 it is of course necessary to group the figures according to the classification that was employed at the earlier censuses.

The number of persons engaged in each industry, segregated by sex, and, in the case of wage earners, also by age (whether under 16 or 16 and over), was reported for a single representative day. The 15th of December was selected as representing for most industries normal conditions of employment, but where this date was not a representative day an earlier date was chosen.

In the case of employees other than wage earners the number thus reported for the representative date has been treated as equivalent to the average for the year, since the number of employees of this class does not ordinarily vary much from month to month. In the case of wage earners the average has been obtained in the manner explained in the next paragraph.

In addition to the more detailed report by sex and age of the number of wage earners on the representative date, a report was obtained of the number employed on the 15th of each month, by sex, without distinction of age. From these figures the average number of wage earners for the year has been calculated by dividing the sum of the numbers reported for the several months by 12. The importance of the industry as an employer of labor is believed to be more accurately measured by this average than by the number employed at any one time or on a given day.

The number of wage earners reported for the representative day, though given in certain tables for each separate industry, is not totaled for all industries combined for any state, because, in view of the variations of date, such a total is believed not to be significant. It would involve more or less duplication of persons working in different industries at different times, would not represent the total number employed in all industries at any one time, and would give an undue weight to seasonal industries as compared with industries in continual operation. This total, however, is shown for the different cities, because the limited area and greater regularity of employment largely overcame the objection incident to its publication for the separate states or the United States.

(914)

In order to determine as nearly as possible the age distribution of the average number of wage earners for a given state as a whole, the per cent distribution by age of the wage earners in each industry for December 15, or the nearest representative day, has been calculated from the actual numbers reported for that date. The percentages thus obtained have been applied to the average number of wage earners for the year in that industry to determine the average numbers 16 years and over, and under 16, employed. These calculated averages for the several industries have been added to give the average distribution for each state as a whole and for the entire country.

Salaries and wages.—Under these heads are given the total payments during the year for salaries and wages, respectively. The Census Bureau has not undertaken to calculate the average annual earnings of either salaried employees or wage earners. Such averages would possess little real value, because they would be based on the earnings of employees of both sexes, of all ages, and of widely varying degrees of skill. Furthermore, so far as wage earners are concerned, it would be impossible to calculate accurately even so simple an average as this, since the number of wage earners fluctuates from month to month in every industry, and in some cases to a very great extent. The Census Bureau's figures for wage earners, as already explained, are averages based on the number employed on the 15th of each month, and while representing the number according to the pay rolls to whom wages were paid on that date, no doubt represent a larger number than would be required to perform the work in any industry if all were continuously employed during the year.

Prevailing hours of labor.—No attempt was made to ascertain the number of wage earners working a given number of hours per week. The inquiry called merely for the prevailing practice followed in each establishment. Occasional variations in hours in an establishment from one part of the year to another were disregarded, and no attention was paid to the fact that a few wage earners might have hours differing from those of the majority. All the wage earners of each establishment are therefore counted in the class within which the establishment itself falls. In most establishments, however, practically all the wage earners work the same number of hours, so that the figures give a substantially correct representation of the hours of labor.

Capital.—The instructions on the schedule for securing data relating to capital were as follows:

"The answer should show the total amount of capital, both owned and borrowed, on the last day of the business year reported. All the items of fixed and live capital may be taken at the amounts carried on the books. If land or buildings are rented, that fact should be stated and no value given. If a part of the land or buildings is owned, the remainder being rented, that fact should be so stated and only the value of the owned property given. Do not include securities and loans representing investments in other enterprises."

These instructions were identical with those employed at the censuses of 1914 and 1909. The data compiled in respect to capital, however, at both censuses, as well as at all preceding censuses of manufacturers, have been so defective as to be of little value except as indicating very general conditions. In fact, it has been repeatedly recommended by the census authorities that this inquiry be omitted from the schedule. While there are some establishments whose accounting systems are such that an accurate return for capital could be made, this is not true of the great majority, and the figures therefore do not show the actual amount of capital invested.

Materials.—The statistics as to the cost of materials relate to the materials used during the year, which may be more or less than the materials purchased during the year. The term "materials" covers fuel, rent of power and heat, mill supplies, and containers, as well as materials which form a constituent part of the product.

Rent and taxes.—The taxes include certain Federal taxes and state, county, and local taxes. Under "Federal taxes" there are included the internal revenue tax on manufactures (tobacco, beverages, etc.), excise taxes when included in values reported for products, corporation capital stock tax, and corporation income tax, but not the income tax for individual and partnership establishments.

Value of products.—The amounts given under this heading represent the selling value or price at the factory of all products manufactured during the year, which may differ from the value of the products sold.

Value added by manufacture.—The value of products is not always a satisfactory measure of either the absolute or the relative importance of a given industry, because only a part of this value is actually created by the manufacturing processes carried on in the industry itself. Another part, and often by far the larger one, represents the value of the materials used. For many purposes, therefore, the best measure of the importance of an industry, from a manufacturing standpoint, is the value created by the manufacturing operations carried on within the industry. This value is calculated by deducting the cost of the materials used from the value of the products. The figure thus obtained is termed in the census reports "value added by manufacture."

Cost of manufacture and profits.—The census data do not show the entire cost of manufacture, and consequently can not be used for the calculation of profits. No account has been taken of depreciation or interest, rent of offices and buildings other than factory or works, insurance, ordinary repairs, advertising, and other sundry expenses.

Primary horsepower.—This item represents the total primary power generated by the manufacturing establishments plus the amount of power, principally electric, rented from other concerns. It does not cover the power of electric motors taking their current from dynamos driven by primary power machines operated by the same establishment, because the inclusion of such power would obviously result in duplication. The figures for primary horsepower represent the rated capacity of the engines, motors, etc., and not the amount of power in actual daily use.

Fuel.—Statistics of the quantity of fuel used are shown only for anthracite and bituminous coal, coke, fuel oils, gasoline and other volatile oils, and gas—natural and manufactured, and represent the quantity used during the year. As only the principal kinds of fuel are shown, comparison as to the total cost of all fuel is impracticable. A comparison, however, of the total quantities of the several kinds of fuel used in 1919 and 1914 is given.

GENERAL STATISTICS.

TABLE 1.—CONTINENTAL UNITED STATES AND NONCONTIGUOUS TERRITORY: 1919.

	MANUFACTURING INDUSTRIES.				
	Total.	Continental United States.	Alaska.	Hawaii.	Porto Rico.
Number of establishments.........	291,367	290,105	147	496	619
Persons engaged..................	10,850,250	10,812,736	7,316	11,744	18,454
Proprietors and firm members.	270,679	269,137	55	700	787
Salaried employees............	1,450,670	1,447,227	686	1,075	1,682
Wage earners (average number)	9,128,901	9,096,372	6,575	9,969	15,985
Primary horsepower..............	29,654,959	29,504,792	18,646	64,295	67,226
Capital..........................	$44,664,535,453	$44,466,593,771	$64,949,405	$48,840,967	$84,151,310
Salaries and wages...............	13,454,438,035	13,425,771,834	10,895,712	8,666,024	9,104,465
Salaries.....................	2,898,795,876	2,892,371,494	2,056,260	2,029,261	2,338,861
Wages.......................	10,555,642,159	10,533,400,340	8,839,452	6,636,763	6,765,604
Paid for contract work..........	467,044,272	464,403,700	2,447,962	34,826	157,784
Rent and taxes..................	2,305,847,617	2,291,412,446	1,577,501	10,662,930	2,194,740
Cost of materials...............	37,536,834,172	37,376,380,283	19,482,485	81,144,130	59,827,274
Value of products...............	62,678,177,262	62,418,078,773	41,495,243	133,096,412	85,506,834
Value added by manufacture [1]....	25,141,343,090	25,041,698,490	22,012,758	51,952,282	25,679,560

[1] Value of products less cost of materials.

TABLE 2.—COMPARATIVE SUMMARY: 1919, 1914, 1909, AND 1904.

	MANUFACTURING INDUSTRIES.				PER CENT OF INCREASE.[1]		
	1919	1914	1909	1904	1914–1919	1909–1914	1904–1909
Number of establishments...............	290,105	275,791	268,491	216,180	5.2	2.7	24.2
Persons engaged........	10,812,736	8,263,063	7,678,578	6,213,612	30.9	7.6	23.6
Proprietors and firm members..........	269,137	262,599	273,265	225,673	2.5	—3.9	21.1
Salaried employees...	1,447,227	964,217	790,267	519,556	50.1	22.0	52.1
Wage earners (average number)........	9,096,372	7,036,247	6,615,046	5,468,383	29.3	6.4	21.0
Primary horsepower....	29,504,792	22,437,072	18,675,376	13,487,707	31.5	20.1	38.5
Capital................	$44,466,593,771	$22,790,979,937	$18,428,269,706	$12,675,580,874	95.1	23.7	45.4
Salaries and wages......	13,425,771,834	5,354,249,384	4,365,612,851	3,184,884,275	150.7	22.6	37.1
Salaries..............	2,892,371,494	1,275,916,951	938,574,967	574,439,322	126.7	35.9	63.4
Wages................	10,533,400,340	4,078,332,433	3,427,037,884	2,610,444,953	158.3	19.0	31.3
Paid for contract work..	464,403,700	198,876,826	178,645,635	145,322,516	133.5	11.3	22.9
Rent and taxes........	2,291,412,446	582,039,665	457,883,110	[2]131,964,825	293.7	27.1	......
Cost of materials........	37,376,380,283	14,368,088,831	12,142,790,878	8,500,207,810	160.1	18.3	42.9
Value of products......	62,418,078,773	24,246,434,724	20,672,051,870	14,793,902,563	157.4	17.3	39.7
Value added by manufacture [3].............	25,041,698,490	9,878,345,893	8,529,260,992	6,293,694,753	153.5	15.8	35.5

[1] A minus sign (—) denotes decrease.   [2] Exclusive of internal revenue.
[3] Value of products less cost of materials.

TABLE 3.—SUMMARY: 1849 TO 1919.

	Number of establishments.	Wage earners (average number).	Capital.	Wages.
FACTORIES AND HAND AND NEIGHBORHOOD INDUSTRIES.				
1849 (census of 1850)	123,025	957,059	$533,245,351	$236,755,464
1859 (census of 1860)	140,433	1,311,246	$1,009,855,715	$378,878,966
Per cent of increase, 1849 to 1859	14.1	37.0	89.4	60.0
1869 (census of 1870) (gold value)	252,148	2,053,996	$1,694,567,015	$620,467,474
Per cent of increase, 1859 to 1869	79.6	56.6	67.8	63.8
1879 (census of 1880)	253,852	2,732,595	$2,790,272,606	$947,953,795
Per cent of increase, 1869 to 1879	0.7	33.0	64.7	52.8
1889 (census of 1890)	355,405	4,251,535	$6,525,050,759	$1,891,219,696
Per cent of increase, 1879 to 1889	40.0	55.6	133.8	99.5
1899 (census of 1900)	512,191	5,306,143	$9,813,834,390	$2,320,938,168
Per cent of increase, 1889 to 1899	44.1	24.8	50.4	22.7
FACTORIES, EXCLUDING HAND AND NEIGHBORHOOD INDUSTRIES.				
1899 (census of 1900)	207,514	4,712,763	$8,975,256,496	$2,008,361,119
1904 (census of 1905)	216,180	5,468,383	$12,675,580,874	$2,610,444,953
Per cent of increase, 1899 to 1904	4.2	16.0	41.2	30.0
1909 (census of 1910)	268,491	6,615,046	$18,428,269,706	$3,427,037,884
Per cent of increase, 1904 to 1909	24.2	21.0	45.4	31.3
Per cent of increase, 1899 to 1909	29.4	40.4	105.3	70.6
1914 (census of 1915)	275,791	7,036,247	$22,790,979,937	$4,078,332,433
Per cent of increase, 1909 to 1914	2.7	6.4	23.7	19.0
Per cent of increase, 1904 to 1914	27.6	28.7	79.8	56.2
1919 (census of 1920)	290,105	9,096,372	$44,466,593,771	$10,533,400,340
Per cent of increase, 1914 to 1919	5.2	29.3	95.1	158.3

	Cost of materials.	Value of products	Value added by manufacture.
FACTORIES AND HAND AND NEIGHBORHOOD INDUSTRIES.			
1849 (census of 1850)	$555,123,882	$1,019,106,616	$463,982,734
1859 (census of 1860)	$1,031,605,092	$1,885,861,676	$854,256,584
Per cent of increase, 1849 to 1859	85.8	85.0	84.1
1869 (census of 1870) (gold value)	$1,990,741,794	$3,385,860,354	$1,395,118,560
Per cent of increase, 1859 to 1869	93.0	79.5	63.3
1879 (census of 1880)	$3,396,823,549	$5,369,579,191	$1,972,755,642
Per cent of increase, 1869 to 1879	70.6	58.6	41.4
1889 (census of 1890)	$5,162,013,878	$9,372,378,843	$4,210,364,965
Per cent of increase, 1879 to 1889	52.0	74.5	113.4
1899 (census of 1900)	$7,343,627,875	$13,000,149,159	$5,656,521,284
Per cent of increase, 1889 to 1899	42.3	38.7	34.3
FACTORIES, EXCLUDING HAND AND NEIGHBORHOOD INDUSTRIES.			
1899 (census of 1900)	$6,575,851,491	$11,406,926,701	$4,831,075,210
1904 (census of 1905)	$8,500,207,810	$14,793,902,563	$6,293,694,753
Per cent of increase, 1899 to 1904	29.3	29.7	30.3
1909 (census of 1910)	$12,142,790,878	$20,672,051,870	$8,529,260,992
Per cent of increase, 1904 to 1909	42.9	39.7	35.5
Per cent of increase, 1899 to 1909	84.7	81.2	76.5
1914 (census of 1915)	$14,368,088,831	$24,246,434,724	$9,878,345,893
Per cent of increase, 1909 to 1914	18.3	17.3	15.8
Per cent of increase, 1904 to 1914	69.0	63.9	57.0
1919 (census of 1920)	$37,376,380,283	$62,418,078,773	$25,041,698,490
Per cent of increase, 1914 to 1919	160.1	157.4	153.5

TABLE 4.—PRINCIPAL INDUSTRIES, RANKED BY VALUE OF PRODUCTS: 1919.

INDUSTRY.	Number of establishments.	WAGE EARNERS. Average number.	Rank.	COST OF MATERIALS. Amount (expressed in thousands).	Rank.	VALUE OF PRODUCTS. Amount (expressed in thousands).	Rank.	VALUE ADDED BY MANUFACTURE. Amount (expressed in thousands).	Rank.
All industries..................	290,105	9,096,372	....	$37,376,380	....	$62,418,079	....	$25,041,699	....
Industries with products valued at $1,000,000,000 or over.									
Slaughtering and meat packing......	1,304	160,996	14	3,782,930	1	4,246,291	1	463,361	12
Iron and steel, steel works and rolling mills..........................	500	375,088	5	1,680,576	3	2,828,902	2	1,148,326	2
Automobiles.....................	315	210,559	9	1,578,652	4	2,387,903	3	809,251	6
Foundry and machine-shop products............................	10,934	482,767	2	948,069	7	2,289,251	4	1,341,182	1
Cotton goods....................	1,288	430,966	4	1,277,786	5	2,125,272	5	847,486	4
Flour-mill and gristmill products....	10,708	45,481	41	1,799,181	2	2,052,434	6	253,253	28
Petroleum, refining...............	320	58,889	32	1,247,908	6	1,632,533	7	384,625	19
Shipbuilding, steel...............	162	344,014	6	643,753	14	1,456,490	8	812,737	5
Lumber and timber products........	26,119	480,945	3	470,960	23	1,387,471	9	916,511	3
Cars and general shop construction and repairs by steam-railroad companies......................	1,744	484,437	1	515,803	19	1,279,235	10	763,432	7
Clothing, women's................	7,711	165,649	13	680,407	10	1,208,543	11	528,136	11
Clothing, men's..................	5,258	175,270	10	605,752	16	1,162,986	12	557,234	10
Boots and shoes, not including rubber boots and shoes................	1,449	211,049	8	715,269	8	1,155,041	13	439,772	14
Bread and other bakery products....	25,095	141,592	15	713,239	9	1,151,896	14	438,657	15
Woolen and worsted goods..........	852	166,787	12	665,595	11	1,065,434	15	399,839	17
Industries with products valued at $500,000,000 but less than $1,000,000,000.									
Electrical machinery, apparatus, and supplies.........................	1,404	212,374	7	425,098	26	997,968	16	572,870	9
Rubber tires, tubes, and rubber goods, not elsewhere specified......	437	119,848	22	525,686	18	987,088	17	461,402	13
Leather, tanned, curried, and finished............................	680	72,476	30	646,522	13	928,592	18	282,070	26
Printing and publishing, newspapers and periodicals...................	17,362	120,381	21	300,385	33	924,153	19	623,768	8
Iron and steel, blast furnaces........	195	41,660	47	621,286	15	794,467	20	173,181	34
Paper and wood pulp..............	729	113,759	23	467,483	24	788,059	21	320,576	21
Tobacco, cigars and cigarettes......	9,926	138,773	16	353,297	31	773,662	22	420,365	16
Sugar, refining, not including beet sugar...........................	20	18,202	83	662,144	12	730,987	23	68,843	73
Knit goods.......................	2,050	172,572	11	427,096	25	713,140	24	286,044	24
Automobile bodies and parts........	2,515	132,556	18	362,027	29	692,171	25	330,144	20
Silk goods.......................	1,369	126,782	19	388,469	27	688,470	26	300,001	23
Smelting and refining, copper........	34	17,345	91	584,410	17	651,102	27	66,692	78
Confectionery and ice cream.........	6,624	95,648	24	368,809	28	637,209	28	268,400	27
Food preparations, not elsewhere specified........................	1,997	30,365	60	494,597	22	631,598	29	137,001	42
Printing and publishing, book and job.............................	13,089	123,005	20	211,067	43	597,663	30	386,596	18
Butter..........................	3,738	17,641	86	514,346	20	583,163	31	68,817	74
Oil and cake, cottonseed............	711	26,766	68	495,192	21	581,245	32	86,053	62
Furniture.......................	3,154	138,331	17	261,523	37	571,356	33	309,833	22
Cars, steam-railroad, not including operations of railroad companies...	99	52,298	39	356,085	30	538,223	34	182,138	32
Lumber, planing-mill products, not including planing mills connected with sawmills.....................	5,309	86,956	25	299,266	34	500,438	35	201,172	31
Industries with products valued at $100,000,000, but less than $500,000,000.									
Brass, bronze, and copper products..	1,092	75,051	29	304,824	32	482,313	36	177,489	33
Engines, steam, gas, and water......	370	77,617	26	217,551	41	464,775	37	247,224	29
Chemicals.......................	598	55,586	35	216,301	42	438,659	38	222,358	30
Canning and preserving, fruits and vegetables......................	3,082	60,865	31	265,629	36	402,243	39	136,614	43
Liquors, malt, including cereal beverages...........................	729	34,259	52	94,793	67	379,905	40	285,112	25
Condensed milk...................	401	13,675	111	282,595	35	339,507	41	56,912	85
Gas, illuminating and heating.......	1,022	42,908	44	157,551	51	329,279	42	171,728	35
Dyeing and finishing textiles, exclusive of that done in textile mills...	628	55,985	33	174,743	47	323,968	43	149,225	39
Soap............................	348	20,436	75	238,519	39	316,740	44	78,221	67
Coke, not including gas-house coke...	278	29,319	62	224,267	40	316,516	45	92,249	57

TABLE 4.—PRINCIPAL INDUSTRIES, RANKED BY VALUE OF PRODUCTS: 1919—Con.

INDUSTRY.	Number of establishments.	WAGE EARNERS.		COST OF MATERIALS.		VALUE OF PRODUCTS.		VALUE ADDED BY MANUFACTURE.	
		Average number.	Rank.	Amount (expressed in thousands).	Rank.	Amount (expressed in thousands).	Rank.	Amount (expressed in thousands).	Rank.
Industries with products valued at $100,000,000, but less than $500,000,000—Continued.									
Agricultural implements	521	54,368	37	$144,572	52	$304,961	46	$160,389	37
Coffee and spice, roasting and grinding	794	10,540	135	243,899	38	304,792	47	60,893	82
Structural ironwork, not made in steel works or rolling mills	1,146	43,962	42	168,801	48	294,962	48	126,161	44
Fertilizers	600	26,296	70	185,041	44	281,144	49	96,103	52
Glass	371	77,520	27	90,780	69	261,884	50	171,104	36
Paints	601	17,485	88	165,604	49	256,714	51	91,110	59
Millinery and lace goods, not elsewhere specified	3,005	50,850	40	132,929	54	255,725	52	122,796	46
Tobacco, chewing and smoking, and snuff	365	18,324	82	130,270	56	239,271	53	109,001	47
Tinware, not elsewhere specified	301	34,386	51	165,171	50	233,964	54	68,793	75
Automobile repairing	15,507	55,061	36	87,649	72	224,652	55	137,003	41
Bags, other than paper, not including bags made in textile mills	216	10,756	130	176,018	46	214,059	56	38,041	107
Machine tools	403	53,111	38	59,034	92	212,400	57	153,366	38
Patent medicines and compounds	2,467	17,444	89	88,819	71	212,162	58	123,343	45
Brick and tile, terra-cotta, and fire-clay products	2,414	76,915	28	67,488	83	208,423	59	140,935	40
Boxes, paper and other, not elsewhere specified	1,201	55,862	34	101,135	65	206,419	60	105,284	48
Shirts	896	39,603	48	127,088	58	205,327	61	78,239	66
Jewelry	2,054	30,871	59	110,451	60	203,939	62	93,488	56
Smelting and refining, lead	25	6,438	173	179,374	45	196,795	63	17,421	177
Glucose and starch	56	7,795	158	130,329	55	186,256	64	55,927	87
Boxes, wooden packing, except cigar boxes	1,140	42,445	46	102,946	62	177,818	65	74,872	70
Cement	123	25,524	71	79,510	76	175,265	66	95,755	54
Iron and steel, forgings, not made in steel works or rolling mills	241	28,391	64	82,024	74	173,752	67	91,728	58
Fur goods	1,815	13,639	112	105,597	61	173,138	68	67,541	76
Shipbuilding, wooden, including boat building	913	43,432	43	66,770	85	165,872	69	99,102	49
Wire	66	19,741	78	102,814	63	162,151	70	59,337	84
Boot and shoe cut stock, exclusive of that produced in boot and shoe factories	252	9,715	141	133,887	53	161,203	71	27,316	131
Copper, tin, and sheet-iron work	4,796	27,640	67	80,899	75	160,314	72	79,415	65
Steam fittings and steam and hot-water heating apparatus	261	36,686	49	72,016	80	160,285	73	88,269	61
Phonographs and graphophones	166	28,721	63	59,740	91	158,548	74	98,808	50
Oil, not elsewhere specified	280	5,930	183	119,271	59	156,480	75	37,209	109
Locomotives, not made by railroad companies	17	26,715	69	72,376	79	156,270	76	83,894	63
Hardware	548	42,505	45	58,534	93	154,525	77	95,991	53
Sugar, beet	85	11,781	118	87,029	73	149,156	78	62,127	81
Pickles, preserves, and sauces	723	16,621	92	93,037	68	145,785	79	52,748	89
Stoves and hot-air furnaces	412	32,868	55	54,803	96	145,718	80	90,915	60
Tools, not elsewhere specified	1,125	35,585	50	45,797	114	144,202	81	98,405	51
Stamped and enameled ware, not elsewhere specified	323	34,248	53	65,457	87	143,654	82	78,197	68
Cheese	3,530	3,997	215	129,425	57	143,456	83	14,031	197
Chocolate and cocoa products	48	9,083	146	101,754	64	139,258	84	37,504	108
Ice, manufactured	2,867	30,247	61	42,878	119	137,005	85	94,127	55
Coal-tar products	183	15,663	98	63,997	90	135,482	86	71,485	72
Mineral and soda waters	5,194	17,440	90	68,600	82	135,341	87	66,741	77
Cordage and twine	120	17,622	87	89,705	70	133,366	88	43,661	96
Marble and stone work	4,240	32,768	56	49,524	107	129,165	89	79,641	64
Carpets and rugs, other than rag	75	22,933	73	67,118	84	123,254	90	56,136	86
Textile machinery and parts	432	31,823	57	45,637	115	122,089	91	76,452	69
Oil, linseed	26	2,173	259	100,578	66	120,638	92	20,060	159
Boots and shoes, rubber	25	32,875	54	50,347	104	116,917	93	66,570	79
Photographic materials	169	14,556	105	49,802	105	115,714	94	65,912	80
Druggists' preparations	524	15,568	101	55,138	95	114,593	95	59,455	83
Furnishing goods, men's	487	18,944	79	64,744	89	107,835	96	43,091	99
Paper goods, not elsewhere specified	308	14,135	108	65,295	88	107,285	97	41,990	103
Musical instruments, pianos	191	22,957	72	54,365	97	107,088	98	52,723	90
Smelting and refining, zinc	39	13,796	110	70,015	81	104,123	99	34,108	114
All other industries	51,669	1,352,090	....	3,903,058	....	7,423,144	....	3,520,086	....

TABLE 5.—RANK OF GEOGRAPHIC DIVISIONS AND STATES IN MANUFACTURING INDUSTRIES: 1919.

DIVISION AND STATE.	Number of establishments.	WAGE EARNERS.		COST OF MATERIALS.		VALUE OF PRODUCTS.		VALUE ADDED BY MANUFACTURE.	
		Average number.	Rank.	Amount.	Rank.	Amount.	Rank.	Amount.	Rank.
						Expressed in thousands.			
United States.....	290,105	9,096,372	....	$37,376,380	.....	$62,418,079	.....	$25,041,699	....
GEOGRAPHIC DIVISIONS.									
Middle Atlantic........	88,360	2,872,653	1	11,424,096	1	19,854,773	1	8,430,677	1
East North Central.....	61,332	2,396,618	2	10,621,687	2	17,737,480	2	7,115,793	2
New England..........	25,528	1,351,389	3	3,951,908	3	7,183,071	3	3,231,163	3
West North Central....	29,166	499,635	5	3,778,125	4	5,187,065	4	1,408,940	5
South Atlantic.........	29,976	817,212	4	2,596,265	5	4,455,152	5	1,858,887	4
Pacific.................	19,567	435,179	6	1,868,242	6	3,157,610	6	1,289,368	6
West South Central....	13,909	285,244	8	1,547,994	7	2,277,861	7	729,867	7
East South Central.....	14,655	329,226	7	977,824	8	1,642,391	8	664,567	8
Mountain..............	7,612	109,216	9	610,239	9	922,676	9	312,437	9
STATES.									
New York.............	49,330	1,228,130	1	4,943,214	1	8,867,005	1	3,923,791	1
Pennsylvania..........	27,973	1,135,837	2	4,210,409	2	7,315,703	2	3,105,294	2
Illinois................	18,593	653,114	5	3,488,271	3	5,425,245	3	1,936,974	4
Ohio..................	16,125	730,733	3	2,911,948	4	5,100,309	4	2,188,361	3
Massachusetts.........	11,906	713,836	4	2,260,713	6	4,011,182	5	1,750,469	5
New Jersey............	11,057	508,686	6	2,270,473	5	3,672,065	6	1,401,592	7
Michigan..............	8,305	471,242	7	1,919,243	7	3,466,188	7	1,546,945	6
California.............	11,942	243,692	11	1,218,859	8	1,981,205	8	762,346	8
Indiana...............	7,916	277,580	9	1,174,950	9	1,898,753	9	723,803	9
Wisconsin.............	10,393	263,949	10	1,127,275	10	1,846,984	10	719,709	10
Missouri..............	8,592	195,037	12	1,056,457	11	1,594,208	11	537,751	12
Connecticut...........	4,872	292,672	8	685,937	15	1,392,432	12	706,495	11
Minnesota.............	6,225	115,623	19	883,090	12	1,218,130	13	335,040	15
Texas.................	5,724	107,522	20	701,171	14	999,996	14	298,825	18
North Carolina........	5,999	157,659	13	526,906	17	943,808	15	416,902	13
Kansas...............	3,474	61,049	31	750,088	13	913,667	16	163,579	28
Maryland.............	4,937	140,342	14	549,347	16	873,945	17	324,598	17
Washington...........	4,918	132,928	16	443,178	20	809,623	18	366,445	14
Rhode Island..........	2,466	139,665	15	415,989	23	747,323	19	331,334	16
Iowa..................	5,683	80,551	27	520,241	18	745,473	20	225,232	22
Georgia...............	4,803	123,441	17	440,490	21	693,237	21	252,747	20
Louisiana.............	2,617	98,265	22	431,404	22	676,190	22	244,786	21
Virginia...............	5,603	119,352	18	371,541	24	643,512	23	271,971	19
Nebraska..............	2,884	36,521	35	480,774	19	596,042	24	115,268	33
Tennessee.............	4,589	95,167	23	344,767	25	556,253	25	211,486	23
Alabama..............	3,654	107,159	21	300,664	27	492,731	26	192,067	26
West Virginia.........	2,785	83,036	26	270,941	28	471,971	27	201,030	25
Maine................	2,995	88,651	24	254,569	29	456,822	28	202,253	24
New Hampshire.......	1,499	83,074	25	239,528	30	407,205	29	167,677	27
Oklahoma.............	2,445	29,503	38	312,606	26	401,363	30	88,757	37
Kentucky.............	3,957	69,340	30	235,715	31	395,660	31	159,945	30
South Carolina........	2,004	79,450	28	227,986	32	381,453	32	153,467	31
Oregon...............	2,707	58,559	32	206,206	33	366,783	33	160,577	29
Colorado..............	2,631	35,254	36	174,870	34	275,622	34	100,752	35
Florida...............	2,582	74,415	29	92,680	40	213,327	35	120,647	32
Arkansas..............	3,123	49,954	34	102,813	37	200,313	36	97,500	36
Mississippi...........	2,455	57,560	33	96,678	38	197,747	37	101,069	34
Vermont..............	1,790	33,491	37	95,173	39	168,108	38	72,935	39
Montana..............	1,290	17,160	41	122,162	35	166,664	39	44,512	41
Delaware.............	668	29,035	39	85,433	42	165,073	40	79,640	38
Utah.................	1,160	18,868	40	110,154	36	156,933	41	46,779	40
Arizona..............	480	8,528	44	92,645	41	120,769	42	28,124	45
Wyoming.............	576	6,634	45	42,250	46	81,445	43	39,195	42
Idaho................	922	13,917	42	43,949	44	80,511	44	36,562	44
District of Columbia....	595	10,482	43	30,940	47	68,826	45	37,886	43
South Dakota.........	1,414	6,382	46	42,986	45	62,171	46	19,185	46
North Dakota.........	894	4,472	48	44,490	43	57,374	47	12,884	47
Nevada...............	166	3,119	49	16,490	48	22,874	48	6,384	49
New Mexico...........	387	5,736	47	7,727	49	17,856	49	10,129	48

TABLE 6.—LEADING CITIES: 1919.

CITY.	Population (1920).	Number of establishments.	WAGE EARNERS. Average number.	Rank.	VALUE OF PRODUCTS. Amount.	Rank.	VALUE ADDED BY MANUFACTURE. Amount.	Rank.
New York, N. Y	5,620,048	32,590	638,775	1	$5,260,707,577	1	$2,399,231,459	1
Chicago, Ill	2,701,705	10,537	403,942	2	3,657,424,471	2	1,278,182,243	2
Philadelphia, Pa	1,823,779	9,064	281,105	3	1,996,481,074	3	840,140,755	3
Detroit, Mich	994,678	2,176	167,016	4	1,234,519,842	4	578,606,379	4
Cleveland, Ohio	796,841	2,946	157,730	5	1,091,577,490	5	478,128,046	5
St. Louis, Mo	772,897	3,205	107,919	6	871,700,438	6	330,874,091	6
Baltimore, Md	733,826	2,797	97,814	7	677,878,492	7	250,122,688	8
Buffalo, N. Y	506,775	2,093	75,899	12	634,409,733	8	233,789,004	13
Boston, Mass	748,060	3,077	88,759	8	618,921,962	9	269,316,071	7
Pittsburgh, Pa	588,343	1,875	83,290	11	614,726,978	10	247,861,681	9
Newark, N. J	414,524	2,155	86,707	9	577,608,564	11	239,646,896	11
Milwaukee, Wis	457,147	2,093	84,222	10	576,161,312	12	234,393,099	12
Akron, Ohio	208,435	304	65,054	14	558,962,067	13	244,590,473	10
Cincinnati, Ohio	401,247	2,239	69,680	13	500,040,996	14	203,760,553	14
Minneapolis, Minn	380,582	1,421	38,154	27	491,382,975	15	128,548,940	19
Kansas City, Kans	101,177	196	22,839	50	468,686,423	16	51,167,968	64
Omaha, Nebr	191,601	561	21,304	56	452,236,634	17	69,133,007	45
San Francisco, Calif	506,676	2,360	48,550	18	417,321,277	19	155,903,034	17
Indianapolis, Ind	314,194	1,004	49,977	17	398,666,553	20	131,912,215	18
Jersey City, N. J	298,103	896	36,981	30	374,182,924	21	110,761,704	25
Rochester, N. Y	295,750	1,367	63,792	15	351,416,379	22	187,133,325	16
Toledo, Ohio	243,164	671	42,090	22	293,520,900	23	120,233,281	23
Los Angeles, Calif	576,673	2,540	47,118	19	278,184,143	24	118,364,712	24
Flint, Mich	91,599	107	24,603	45	275,779,638	25	102,955,874	28
Seattle, Wash	315,312	1,229	40,843	25	274,431,239	26	124,780,864	22
Providence, R. I	237,595	1,274	53,372	16	267,629,283	27	127,302,659	20
Bayonne, N. J	76,754	152	14,994	79	260,602,109	28	63,753,208	50
Youngstown, Ohio	132,358	239	19,414	60	241,458,370	29	78,359,653	36
Perth Amboy, N. J	41,707	124	9,197	123	230,658,263	30	31,351,080	106
Camden, N. J	116,309	336	40,906	24	218,165,277	31	105,061,647	26
Paterson, N. J	135,875	1,044	37,217	28	216,659,174	32	101,697,761	30
New Bedford, Mass	121,217	267	41,630	23	210,773,312	34	88,202,554	32
Worcester, Mass	179,754	618	38,673	26	208,705,773	35	102,524,771	29
Bridgeport, Conn	143,555	443	42,862	21	208,089,797	36	125,776,942	21
Louisville, Ky	234,891	767	29,902	36	204,565,727	37	78,466,310	35
Winston-Salem, N. C	48,395	93	12,366	96	200,484,834	38	103,221,877	27
Portland, Oreg	258,288	846	26,813	40	196,380,146	39	84,993,567	33
Kansas City, Mo	324,410	997	22,137	53	192,815,052	40	68,505,148	46
Columbus, Ohio	237,031	690	26,751	41	184,021,849	41	71,302,610	40
Lawrence, Mass	94,270	194	30,319	34	183,449,096	42	72,490,486	39
New Orleans, La	87,219	873	26,641	42	182,798,561	43	69,490,062	44
Dayton, Ohio	152,559	571	31,131	31	174,990,607	44	96,530,139	31
Fall River, Mass	120,485	293	37,015	29	163,246,082	45	67,065,698	48
Lynn, Mass	99,148	442	27,355	39	160,905,792	46	75,896,446	37
Richmond, Va	171,667	550	21,759	54	156,724,322	47	67,280,390	47
Syracuse, N. Y	171,717	643	28,153	38	150,091,278	48	75,407,894	38
St. Paul, Minn	234,698	818	22,649	51	149,638,290	49	64,467,830	49
Sioux City, Iowa	71,227	251	6,749	157	146,393,134	50	21,131,710	146
Reading, Pa	107,784	527	29,122	37	141,560,831	52	58,867,003	59
Yonkers, N. Y	100,176	218	11,932	101	140,016,561	53	33,566,621	101
Lowell, Mass	112,759	291	30,111	35	137,801,538	54	60,809,030	55
Pawtucket, R. I	64,248	284	24,446	47	135,517,533	56	58,044,788	61
Oakland, Calif	216,261	593	23,347	49	134,755,470	57	70,778,506	41
Waterbury, Conn	91,715	253	30,322	33	130,193,040	58	62,881,149	52
Passaic, N. J	63,841	234	18,203	64	129,073,484	59	52,159,801	63
Cambridge, Mass	109,694	339	22,550	52	127,864,901	60	58,737,978	60
Birmingham, Ala	178,806	329	17,264	68	127,214,048	61	40,395,154	79
New Haven, Conn	162,537	769	30,874	32	125,455,547	62	70,158,742	42
Denver, Colo	256,491	1,097	16,635	70	125,411,270	63	46,071,326	70
Canton, Ohio	87,091	287	20,336	58	124,292,924	64	59,215,399	58
Trenton, N. J	119,289	389	24,547	46	122,477,987	65	62,016,537	53
Wilmington, Del	110,168	262	21,420	55	121,039,617	66	60,552,173	57
Racine, Wis	58,593	230	15,812	75	120,027,399	67	61,425,675	54
Hartford, Conn	138,036	504	26,264	43	118,002,693	68	69,683,438	43
Brockton, Mass	66,254	217	18,059	65	117,855,025	69	43,141,744	75
Memphis, Tenn	162,351	379	11,963	100	117,717,829	70	39,593,146	82
Manchester, N. H	78,384	165	25,512	44	117,493,082	71	45,705,557	71
Lorain, Ohio	37,295	55	11,677	103	116,908,616	72	50,913,851	65
Atlanta, Ga	200,616	503	15,739	77	113,991,946	73	46,121,060	69
Grand Rapids, Mich	137,634	611	23,548	48	109,135,055	74	57,973,294	62

TABLE **6.**—LEADING CITIES: 1919—Continued.

CITY.	Population (1920).	Number of establishments.	WAGE EARNERS. Average number.	Rank.	VALUE OF PRODUCTS. Amount.	Rank.	VALUE ADDED BY MANUFACTURE. Amount.	Rank.
Schenectady, N. Y	88,723	131	21,062	57	$106,531,182	75	$60,679,785	56
McKeesport, Pa	46,781	82	11,909	102	105,058,713	76	46,215,120	68
Pontiac, Mich	34,273	78	7,682	146	104,990,133	77	38,203,971	89
Lansing, Mich	57,327	147	12,349	97	104,722,115	78	39,740,775	80
Kenosha, Wis	40,472	84	13,045	91	103,725,717	79	42,327,072	76
Tacoma, Wash	96,965	348	10,714	108	103,171,756	80	29,898,339	109
Bethlehem, Pa	50,358	86	14,961	81	102,567,075	81	47,188,049	67
Somerville, Mass	93,091	140	6,111	175	99,558,513	82	12,461,172	207
Springfield, Mass	129,614	401	18,429	62	98,332,955	83	50,529,775	66
Haverhill, Mass	53,884	405	15,783	76	96,276,853	84	39,058,570	84
Chester, Pa	58,030	127	18,677	61	95,949,003	85	43,276,788	74
Dallas, Tex	158,976	457	7,913	144	93,649,654	86	28,146,461	112
Woonsocket, R. I	43,496	190	14,387	87	93,546,778	87	32,640,273	103
Holyoke, Mass	60,203	176	17,773	67	93,426,775	88	42,266,793	77
Cedar Rapids, Iowa	45,566	208	6,284	171	92,118,386	89	20,052,457	152
New Castle, Pa	44,938	87	8,014	139	91,370,618	90	26,504,347	118
Allentown, Pa	73,502	336	14,812	83	90,834,488	91	39,714,454	81
Johnstown, Pa	67,327	149	12,855	93	90,468,742	92	37,043,617	93
Chicopee, Mass	36,214	60	10,068	115	89,772,534	93	43,314,163	73
East Chicago, Ind	35,967	61	8,957	125	89,568,753	94	26,234,676	120
Niagara Falls, N. Y	50,760	186	12,238	99	89,247,170	95	38,186,804	90
Houston, Tex	138,276	383	9,860	117	86,874,480	96	29,082,240	110
Joliet, Ill	38,442	166	11,259	106	82,669,536	99	33,667,858	100
Kearny, N. J	26,724	49	14,860	82	80,832,074	100	38,132,137	91
Utica, N. Y	94,156	370	16,423	71	77,745,720	101	35,536,871	97
East St. Louis, Ill	66,767	157	8,785	127	77,292,812	102	23,389,934	133
Fort Wayne, Ind	86,549	247	16,344	72	76,713,262	103	38,804,767	87
Elizabeth, N. J	95,783	226	18,386	63	76,440,515	104	36,808,707	94
South Bend, Ind	70,983	214	14,792	84	75,339,165	105	36,633,018	95
Richmond, Calif	16,843	40	4,305	207	75,315,608	106	27,576,486	114
Duluth, Minn	98,917	226	10,472	114	75,261,387	107	32,231,933	105
Rockford, Ill	65,651	312	14,992	80	74,918,953	108	38,352,044	88
Troy, N. Y	72,013	253	15,929	74	74,837,435	109	39,041,201	85
Wheeling, W. Va	56,208	243	8,622	129	72,639,728	110	26,330,679	119
Nashville, Tenn	118,342	391	10,666	110	71,108,252	112	25,662,259	124
Durham, N. C	21,719	74	5,977	179	70,659,339	113	35,990,264	96
Erie, Pa	93,372	293	13,297	89	70,407,540	114	38,908,688	86
Hoboken, N. J	68,166	280	15,933	73	70,311,540	115	39,283,642	83
Evansville, Ind	85,264	299	12,526	95	70,230,419	116	26,081,627	122
Oklahoma City, Okla	91,295	227	4,375	206	69,970,788	118	11,326,614	212
Washington, D. C	437,571	595	10,482	113	68,826,570	119	37,886,470	92
Quincy, Mass	47,876	162	19,653	59	68,535,406	120	44,360,630	72
Springfield, Ohio	60,840	206	12,264	98	67,759,001	121	33,868,702	99
New Britain, Conn	59,316	116	17,212	69	63,621,960	123	41,455,903	78
Middletown, Ohio	23,594	56	6,442	168	62,838,289	124	27,151,077	116
Harrison, N. J	15,721	63	13,026	92	61,766,542	125	32,349,752	104
Des Moines, Iowa	126,468	379	7,085	154	59,830,954	126	26,540,392	117
York, Pa	47,512	273	13,368	88	59,588,904	127	30,214,530	108
Hammond, Ind	36,004	94	6,065	177	59,276,319	128	19,324,580	159
Fitchburg, Mass	41,029	121	9,907	116	58,164,842	129	22,109,929	138
Chattanooga, Tenn	57,895	281	10,588	111	58,021,825	130	25,507,113	125
Cicero, Ill	44,995	92	14,754	85	57,918,418	131	34,942,233	98
Macon, Ga	52,995	135	6,457	167	57,721,238	132	12,518,134	205
Peoria, Ill	76,121	253	7,977	141	57,074,893	134	21,155,975	145
Battle Creek, Mich	36,164	118	6,680	159	56,139,953	135	28,151,062	111
Muskegon, Mich	36,570	141	9,716	118	55,969,347	136	30,293,618	107
Scranton, Pa	137,783	311	14,467	86	54,629,522	137	25,683,872	123
Altoona, Pa	60,331	64	12,800	94	53,946,093	138	22,780,418	135
Peabody, Mass	19,552	91	8,013	140	52,906,722	139	21,590,914	143
Amsterdam, N. Y	33,524	117	10,713	109	52,851,242	140	22,135,378	137
Harrisburg, Pa	75,917	216	10,522	112	52,152,818	141	26,114,223	121
Knoxville, Tenn	77,818	194	11,384	104	51,694,298	142	20,959,584	147
St. Joseph, Mo	77,939	219	5,943	180	50,697,198	143	17,345,706	170
Jackson, Mich	48,374	156	9,620	119	49,517,712	144	19,529,000	156
Nashua, N. H	28,379	92	8,264	136	48,985,184	145	17,029,919	173
Fresno, Calif	45,086	223	3,903	212	48,943,823	146	11,825,605	210
Taunton, Mass	37,137	167	8,981	124	48,330,638	147	20,544,073	148
Lancaster, Pa	53,150	285	9,444	121	48,025,759	148	21,305,352	144
Norwood, Ohio	24,966	70	8,283	135	47,947,183	149	27,724,313	113
Ansonia, Conn	17,643	50	6,102	176	47,736,411	150	14,254,482	195

TABLE 6.—LEADING CITIES:.1919—Continued.

CITY.	Population (1920).	Number of establishments.	WAGE EARNERS.		VALUE OF PRODUCTS.		VALUE ADDED BY MANUFACTURE.	
			Average number.	Rank.	Amount.	Rank.	Amount.	Rank.
Watertown, Mass	21,457	25	8,420	134	$47,297,519	151	$27,563,346	115
Hamilton, Ohio	39,675	130	8,553	133	47,024,031	152	24,386,589	130
Kalamazoo, Mich	48,487	185	7,629	148	46,254,917	153	22,018,574	139
Topeka, Kans	50,022	169	5,597	186	45,707,711	154	14,474,647	192
Albany, N. Y	113,344	382	11,216	107	45,454,955	155	23,972,184	132
Ottumwa, Iowa	23,003	94	2,601	223	45,029,524	157	8,528,413	224
Moline, Ill	30,734	61	5,444	191	44,871,021	158	22,183,217	136
Butler, Pa	23,778	77	3,744	214	44,476,790	159	10,737,033	219
Superior ,Wis	39,671	94	6,162	173	44,043,214	160	16,729,268	176
Casper, Wyo	11,447	43	1,886	224	43,589,560	161	19,403,816	157
Saginaw, Mich	61,903	208	9,472	120	43,146,125	164	21,830,363	142
Charlotte, N. C	46,338	111	5,161	193	43,095,898	165	12,099,513	208
Granite City, Ill	14,757	37	5,493	190	43,039,044	166	17,279,473	171
New Brunswick, N. J	32,779	138	7,673	147	42,624,947	167	24,444,419	128
Tampa, Fla	51,608	263	13,079	90	42,461,377	168	25,188,234	126
Wilkesbarre, Pa	73,833	179	9,408	122	41,986,203	169	21,902,859	140
Terre Haute, Ind	66,083	257	6,458	166	41,967,818	170	15,064,938	186
Chicago Heights, Ill	19,653	103	5,328	192	41,788,147	171	18,686,656	164
Williamsport, Pa	36,198	145	8,566	131	41,658,834	172	18,403,536	166
Pittsfield, Mass	41,763	90	8,570	130	41,613,356	173	21,895,100	141
Auburn, N. Y	36,192	154	7,272	152	40,642,435	174	16,772,361	175
Binghamton, N. Y	66,800	228	7,477	150	40,637,625	175	18,803,663	163
Garfield, N. J	19,381	56	5,025	196	40,233,553	176	19,724,104	154
Spokane, Wash	104,437	364	4,752	198	40,149,381	177	14,497,804	191
Stamford, Conn	35,096	116	7,939	142	39,121,451	179	19,015,237	162
Anderson, Ind	29,767	99	7,928	143	38,930,509	180	16,840,340	174
Gloversville, N. Y	22,075	206	5,612	185	38,913,000	181	16,542,885	178
Kokomo, Ind	30,067	98	6,727	158	38,709,165	182	17,116,457	172
Decatur, Ill	43,818	103	5,693	183	38,683,689	183	13,995,903	196
Wichita, Kans	72,217	238	3,045	221	38,580,182	184	11,234,212	215
Fort Worth, Tex	106,482	229	4,452	204	38,160,092	185	12,502,858	206
Jamestown, N. Y	38,917	153	8,559	132	37,985,306	186	20,068,859	151
Easthampton, Mass	11,261	28	4,142	210	37,942,121	187	10,898,213	218
Huntington, W. Va	50,177	115	6,556	164	37,707,241	188	15,992,888	181
Michigan City, Ind	19,457	47	3,452	217	37,360,551	189	10,235,934	221
Augusta, Ga	52,548	93	5,156	194	37,160,571	190	12,830,836	204
Portsmouth, Ohio	33,011	60	5,914	181	36,645,736	191	16,467,980	179
West Allis, Wis	13,745	34	6,970	155	36,477,071	192	20,172,977	150
North Adams, Mass	22,282	65	6,023	178	36,203,767	193	13,917,945	198
Everett, Mass	40,120	104	4,523	202	35,775,728	194	16,716,647	177
Columbus, Ga	31,125	74	8,087	137	35,561,512	195	14,655,612	188
Waterloo, Iowa	36,230	161	4,620	201	35,481,225	196	12,088,611	209
San Antonio, Tex	161,379	318	6,614	160	35,455,578	197	13,206,975	203
Rome, N. Y	26,341	71	4,428	205	34,868,489	198	11,496,337	211
Roanoke, Va	50,842	99	7,740	145	34,864,211	199	19,314,295	161
Attleboro, Mass	19,731	144	6,763	156	34,471,577	200	15,901,897	183
Dubuque, Iowa	39,141	131	6,147	174	34,277,085	201	14,325,197	194
Meriden, Conn	29,867	162	8,794	126	34,261,304	202	18,609,902	165
Sacramento, Calif	65,908	304	6,341	170	34,198,980	203	16,388,021	180
Elmira, N. Y	45,393	142	8,024	138	33,494,164	205	19,356,661	158
Wyandotte, Mich	13,851	26	6,214	172	33,382,791	206	19,942,807	153
Salt Lake City, Utah	118,110	415	6,362	169	33,356,911	207	15,937,802	182
Muncie, Ind	36,524	121	6,559	163	33,175,525	208	14,365,274	193
Alliance, Ohio	21,603	74	5,117	195	32,871,087	209	18,081,650	167
Davenport, Iowa	56,727	219	3,928	211	32,587,229	211	11,025,434	216
Chelsea, Mass	43,184	123	6,580	162	32,536,518	212	15,833,334	184
Olean, N. Y	20,506	66	4,669	200	32,121,169	213	9,132,838	223
Mansfield, Ohio	27,824	132	4,711	199	31,877,551	214	14,518,413	190
Sheboygan, Wis	30,955	160	6,467	165	31,497,124	215	14,783,734	187
Plymouth, Mass	13,045	31	2,971	222	31,319,553	216	9,822,400	222
Jacksonville, Fla	91,558	244	7,168	153	31,212,494	217	13,612,659	200
Alton, Ill	24,682	60	3,236	219	31,036,983	218	11,261,989	214
Steubenville, Ohio	28,508	57	3,855	213	30,903,344	219	14,527,594	189
Bristol, Conn	20,620	68	7,592	149	30,689,970	220	17,702,371	168
Stockton, Calif	40,296	208	3,534	216	30,675,898	221	11,264,861	213
Berlin, N. H	16,104	25	4,236	208	30,652,522	222	13,313,638	202
Salem, Mass	42,529	153	5,672	184	30,437,957	223	13,510,464	201
Clinton, Iowa	24,151	119	3,452	217	30,321,143	224	10,976,010	217
Danville, Va	21,539	44	5,827	182	30,183,494	225	13,892,714	199
Aurora, Ill	36,397	133	6,608	161	30,038,961	226	17,355,417	169

TABLE 7.—STATISTICS OF CITIES BY POPULATION GROUPS: 1919, 1914, AND 1909.

	Census year.	Number of cities.	Population.[1]	Number of establishments.	Wage earners (average number).	Value of products.	Value added by manufacture.
						Expressed in thousands.	
Aggregate	1919		105,710,620	290,105	9,096,372	$62,418,079	$25,041,698
	1914		98,781,324	275,791	7,036,247	24,246,435	9,878,346
	1909		91,972,266	268,491	6,615,046	20,672,052	8,529,261
Total for cities having a population of 10,000 or over.	1919	747	44,723,547	166,079	6,406,335	45,291,763	18,543,531
	1914	656	38,627,333	150,844	4,701,591	16,814,653	7,058,885
	1909	593	34,021,620	135,735	4,309,431	14,281,855	5,999,238
Per cent of aggregate	1919		42.3	57.2	70.4	72.6	74.1
	1914		39.1	54.7	66.8	69.3	71.5
	1909		37.0	50.6	65.1	69.1	70.3
10,000 to 25,000	1919	460	6,953,433	22,486	977,319	6,031,095	2,476,530
	1914	401	6,092,386	20,765	741,745	2,196,432	920,361
	1909	365	5,499,015	18,949	676,289	1,958,245	804,065
Per cent of aggregate	1919		6.6	7.7	10.7	9.7	9.9
	1914		6.2	7.5	10.5	9.1	9.3
	1909		6.0	7.1	10.2	9.5	9.4
25,000 to 100,000	1919	219	10,340,788	31,285	1,639,698	10,744,903	4,475,044
	1914	194	8,834,570	28,431	1,143,968	4,125,531	1,582,171
	1909	178	8,204,960	26,989	1,118,412	3,593,829	1,423,199
Per cent of aggregate	1919		9.8	10.8	18.0	17.2	17.9
	1914		8.9	10.3	16.3	17.0	16.0
	1909		8.9	10.1	16.9	17.4	16.7
100,000 and over	1919	68	27,429,326	112,308	3,789,318	28,515,765	11,591,957
	1914	61	23,700,377	101,648	2,815,878	10,492,690	4,556,353
	1909	50	20,317,645	89,797	2,514,730	8,729,781	3,771,974
Per cent of aggregate	1919		25.9	38.7	41.7	45.7	46.3
	1914		24.0	36.9	40.0	43.2	46.1
	1909		22.1	33.4	38.0	42.2	44.2
Districts outside of cities having a population of 10,000 or over.	1919		60,987,073	124,026	2,690,037	17,126,316	6,498,167
	1914		60,153,991	124,947	2,334,656	7,431,782	2,819,461
	1909		57,950,646	132,756	2,305,615	6,390,197	2,530,023
Per cent of aggregate	1919		57.7	42.8	29.6	27.4	25.9
	1914		60.9	45.3	33.2	30.7	28.6
	1909		63.0	49.4	34.9	30.9	29.7

[1] Population of 1920, as of January 1, 1920; 1915, estimated population as of July 1, 1914 (per reports census of manufactures, 1914); 1910, as of April 15, 1910.

TABLE 8.—PERSONS ENGAGED IN MANUFACTURING INDUSTRIES: 1919, 1914, AND 1909.

CLASS.	Census year.	Total.	Male.	Female.	PER CENT OF TOTAL.	
					Male.	Fe-male.
All classes....................	1919	10,812,736	8,583,720	2,229,016	79.4	20.6
	1914	8,263,063	6,613,376	1,649,687	80.0	20.0
	1909	7,678,578	6,162,263	1,516,315	80.3	19.7
Proprietors and officials.............	1919	682,857	656,915	25,942	96.2	3.8
	1914	501,681	485,502	16,179	96.8	3.2
	1909	487,173	472,914	14,259	97.1	2.9
Proprietors and firm members....	1919	269,137	258,894	10,243	96.2	3.8
	1914	262,599	252,430	10,169	96.1	3.9
	1909	273,265	263,673	9,592	96.5	3.5
Salaried officers of corporations...	1919	132,467	127,074	5,393	95.9	4.1
	1914	92,671	89,749	2,922	96.8	3.2
	1909	80,735	78,937	1,798	97.8	2.2
Superintendents and managers...	1919	281,253	270,947	10,306	96.3	3.7
	1914	146,411	143,323	3,088	97.9	2.1
	1909	133,173	130,304	2,869	97.8	2.2
Clerks and other subordinate salaried employees.	1919	1,033,507	659,775	373,732	63.8	36.2
	1914	725,135	536,967	188,168	74.1	25.9
	1909	576,359	437,056	139,303	75.8	24.2
Wage earners (average number)......	1919	9,096,372	7,267,030	1,829,342	79.9	20.1
	1914	7,036,247	5,590,907	1,445,340	79.5	20.5
	1909	6,615,046	5,252,293	1,362,753	79.4	20.6
16 years of age and over..........	1919	8,975,453	7,202,529	1,772,924	80.2	19.8
	1914	6,914,474	5,525,108	1,389,366	79.9	20.1
	1909	6,453,553	5,163,164	1,290,389	80.0	20.0
Under 16 years of age.............	1919	120,919	64,501	56,418	53.3	46.7
	1914	121,773	65,799	55,974	54.0	46.0
	1909	161,493	89,129	72,364	55.2	44.8

TABLE 9.—SEX AND AGE DISTRIBUTION OF WAGE EARNERS IN THE 85 LEADING INDUSTRIES: 1919 AND 1914.

INDUSTRY.	Census year.	Average number.	NUMBER DEC. 15, OR NEAREST REPRESENTATIVE DAY.				PER CENT OF TOTAL.		
			Total.	16 years of age and over. Male.	16 years of age and over. Female.	Under 16 years of age.	16 years of age and over. Male.	Female.	Under 16 years of age.
All industries	1919	**9,096,372**	(1)	(1)	(1)	(1)	**79.2**	**19.5**	**1.3**
	1914	**7,036,247**	(1)	(1)	(1)	(1)	**78.5**	**19.7**	**1.7**
Agricultural implements	1919	54,368	57,592	56,547	962	83	98.2	1.7	0.1
	1914	48,459	49,608	49,019	505	84	98.8	1.0	0.2
Ammunition	1919	22,816	22,709	16,333	6,237	139	71.9	27.5	0.6
	1914	11,493	14,540	10,034	4,426	80	69.0	30.4	0.6
Automobile bodies and parts	1919	132,556	160,081	151,588	8,065	428	94.7	5.0	0.3
	1914	47,785	47,740	46,603	1,035	102	97.6	2.2	0.2
Automobiles	1919	210,559	243,128	234,916	7,921	291	96.6	3.3	0.1
	1914	79,307	81,298	79,971	1,234	93	98.4	1.5	0.1
Automobile repairing	1919	55,061	58,085	57,454	393	238	98.9	0.7	0.4
	1914	12,562	12,618	12,563	30	25	99.6	0.2	0.2
Bookbinding and blank-book making.	1919	20,361	22,946	10,694	11,564	688	46.6	50.4	3.0
	1914	21,693	21,458	11,167	9,840	451	52.0	45.9	2.1
Boots and shoes, not including rubber boots and shoes.	1919	211,049	230,457	138,497	84,641	7,319	60.1	36.7	3.2
	1914	191,555	195,347	124,148	67,549	3,650	63.6	34.6	1.9
Boots and shoes, rubber	1919	32,875	34,723	19,849	13,877	997	57.2	40.0	2.9
	1914	18,687	20,437	12,133	8,034	270	59.4	39.3	1.3
Boxes, paper and other, not elsewhere specified.	1919	55,862	61,467	24,731	33,328	3,408	40.2	54.2	5.5
	1914	45,311	45,166	17,541	25,417	2,208	38.8	56.3	4.9
Boxes, wooden packing, except cigar boxes.	1919	42,445	46,327	41,180	4,582	565	88.9	9.9	1.2
	1914	38,548	39,798	36,258	2,294	1,246	91.1	5.8	3.1
Brass, bronze, and copper products.	1919	75,051	81,720	74,669	6,799	252	91.4	8.3	0.3
	1914	40,306	39,911	37,165	2,486	260	93.1	6.2	0.7
Bread and other bakery products	1919	141,592	151,956	111,176	38,901	1,879	73.2	25.6	1.2
	1914	124,052	128,119	101,622	25,066	1,431	79.3	19.6	1.1
Brick and tile, terra-cotta, and fire-clay products.	1919	76,915	88,099	86,289	1,290	520	97.9	1.5	0.6
	1914	100,182	114,628	112,336	1,314	978	98.0	1.1	0.9
Canning and preserving, fruits and vegetables.	1919	60,865	163,346	69,847	89,306	4,193	42.8	54.7	2.6
	1914	50,325	165,109	70,646	86,306	8,157	42.8	52.3	4.9
Carpets and rugs, other than rag.	1919	22,933	27,002	16,573	9,739	690	61.4	36.1	2.6
	1914	31,309	31,448	18,143	12,654	651	57.7	40.2	2.1
Carriages and wagons, including repairs.	1919	18,173	18,955	18,621	273	61	98.2	1.4	0.3
	1914	41,304	40,458	39,889	487	82	98.6	1.2	0.2
Cars and general shop construction and repairs by electric-railroad companies.	1919	31,272	32,108	31,660	438	10	98.6	1.4	(2)
	1914	26,384	25,509	25,403	99	7	99.6	0.4	(2)
Cars and general shop construction and repairs by steam-railroad companies.	1919	484,437	510,384	506,365	3,975	44	99.2	0.8	(2)
	1914	339,518	336,316	335,805	432	79	99.8	0.1	(2)
Cars, steam-railroad, not including operations of railroad companies.	1919	52,298	50,999	50,549	429	21	99.1	0.8	(2)
	1914	54,288	57,811	57,587	208	16	99.6	0.4	(2)
Cement	1919	25,524	26,895	26,503	362	30	98.5	1.3	0.1
	1914	27,916	28,969	28,896	26	47	99.7	0.1	0.2
Chemicals	1919	55,586	58,757	53,798	4,782	177	91.6	8.1	0.3
	1914	32,311	32,496	30,585	1,621	290	94.1	5.0	0.9
Clothing, men's	1919	175,270	208,524	95,771	110,794	1,959	45.9	53.1	1.0
	1914	173,747	179,232	85,331	91,975	1,926	47.6	51.3	1.1

1 Total not given for reasons explained on page 914.
2 Less than one-tenth of 1 per cent.

TABLE 9.—SEX AND AGE DISTRIBUTION OF WAGE EARNERS IN THE 85 LEADING INDUSTRIES: 1919 AND 1914—Continued.

INDUSTRY.	Census year.	Average number.	NUMBER DEC. 15, OR NEAREST REPRESENTATIVE DAY.				PER CENT OF TOTAL.		
			Total.	16 years of age and over.		Under 16 years of age.	16 years of age and over.		Under 16 years of age.
				Male.	Female.		Male.	Female.	
Clothing, women's	1919	165,649	183,516	60,522	121,687	1,307	33.0	66.3	0.7
	1914	168,907	175,302	63,241	111,034	1,027	36.1	63.3	0.6
Coke, not including gas-house coke.	1919	29,319	30,857	30,404	8	445	98.5	(1)	1.4
	1914	21,107	19,908	19,793	3	112	99.4	(1)	0.6
Confectionery and ice cream [2]	1919	95,648	104,181	45,452	55,046	3,683	43.6	52.8	3.5
	1914	64,034	70,222	31,124	36,582	2,516	44.3	52.1	3.6
Copper, tin, and sheet-iron work	1919	27,640	31,039	30,134	711	194	97.1	2.3	0.6
	1914	28,714	29,020	28,334	514	172	97.6	1.8	0.6
Corsets	1919	18,415	21,105	3,254	17,194	657	15.4	81.5	3.1
	1914	20,496	19,418	2,528	16,300	590	13.0	83.9	3.0
Cotton goods	1919	430,966	459,845	254,380	183,810	21,655	55.3	40.0	4.7
	1914	379,366	388,297	209,186	146,061	33,050	53.9	37.6	8.5
Cutlery and edge tools	1919	19,859	22,080	17,580	4,171	329	79.6	18.9	1.5
	1914	16,561	16,697	14,515	1,942	240	86.9	11.6	1.4
Dyeing and finishing textiles, exclusive of that done in textile mills.	1919	55,985	62,462	47,132	14,098	1,232	75.5	22.6	2.0
	1914	48,467	46,776	37,853	8,175	748	80.9	17.5	1.6
Electrical machinery, apparatus, and supplies.	1919	212,374	245,324	180,152	62,920	2,252	73.4	25.6	0.9
	1914	118,078	111,251	88,411	22,167	673	79.5	19.9	0.6
Engines, steam, gas, and water	1919	77,617	85,053	83,063	1,872	118	97.7	2.2	0.1
	1914	29,657	29,371	29,274	62	35	99.7	0.2	0.1
Fertilizers	1919	26,296	30,071	29,565	428	78	98.3	1.4	0.3
	1914	22,815	25,219	25,078	108	33	99.4	0.4	0.1
Flour-mill and gristmill products.	1919	45,481	49,932	48,688	1,170	74	97.5	2.3	0.1
	1914	39,718	41,736	41,123	533	80	98.5	1.3	0.2
Food preparations, not elsewhere specified.	1919	30,365	33,829	23,810	9,707	312	70.4	28.7	0.9
	1914	20,306	22,421	16,540	5,624	257	73.8	25.1	1.1
Foundry and machine-shop products.	1919	482,767	538,308	519,425	16,655	2,228	96.5	3.1	0.4
	1914	362,471	347,364	341,088	5,069	1,207	98.2	1.5	0.3
Furnishing goods, men's	1919	18,944	20,881	3,334	16,886	661	16.0	80.9	3.2
	1914	22,459	23,220	3,898	18,760	562	16.8	80 8	2.4
Furniture	1919	138,331	156,384	141,447	12,867	2,070	90.4	8.2	1.3
	1914	127,881	126,125	120,856	3,657	1,612	95.8	2.9	1.3
Gas, illuminating and heating	1919	42,908	44,280	44,058	200	22	99.5	0.5	(1)
	1914	43,792	42,284	42,067	190	27	99.5	0.4	(1)
Glass	1919	77,520	93,320	81,214	10,410	1,696	87.0	11.2	1.8
	1914	74,502	84,158	76,909	4,999	2,250	91.4	5.9	2.7
Hardware	1919	42,505	47,585	38,360	8,283	942	80.6	17.4	2.0
	1914	41,213	39,783	34,067	4,897	819	85.6	12.3	2.1
Hats, fur-felt	1919	18,510	21,132	14,985	5,758	389	70.9	27.2	1.8
	1914	21,318	21,552	15,550	5,750	252	72.2	26.7	1.2
Ice, manufactured	1919	30,247	31,101	30,654	258	189	98.6	0.8	0.6
	1914	23,011	24,827	24,519	72	236	98.8	0.3	0.9
Iron and steel, blast furnaces	1919	41,660	46,460	46,402	54	4	99.9	0.1	(1)
	1914	29,356	29,660	29,601	6	53	99.8	(1)	0.2
Iron and steel, steel works and rolling mills.	1919	375,088	400,620	396,741	3,695	184	99.0	0.9	(1)
	1914	248,716	248,945	247,275	944	726	99.3	0.4	0.3

[1] Less than one-tenth of 1 per cent.
[2] Includes " chewing gum " in 1914.

TABLE **9.**—SEX AND AGE DISTRIBUTION OF WAGE EARNERS IN THE 85 LEADING INDUSTRIES: 1919 AND 1914—Continued.

INDUSTRY.	Census year.	Average number.	NUMBER DEC. 15, OR NEAREST REPRESENTATIVE DAY.				PER CENT OF TOTAL.		
			Total.	16 years of age and over.		Under 16 years of age.	16 years of age and over.		Under 16 years of age.
				Male.	Female.		Male.	Female.	
Iron and steel, forgings, not made in steel works or rolling mills.	1919	28,391	30,645	29,509	1,010	126	96.3	3.3	0.4
	1914	10,689	10,705	10,429	151	125	97.4	1.4	1.2
Jewelry	1919	30,871	34,656	23,372	10,270	1,014	67.4	29.6	2.9
	1914	28,289	28,523	21,458	6,397	668	75.2	22.4	2.3
Knit goods	1919	172,572	187,746	52,134	125,440	10,172	27.8	66.8	5.4
	1914	150,520	153,438	42,693	101,586	9,159	27.8	66.2	6.0
Leather, tanned, curried, and finished.	1919	72,476	79,205	72,257	6,507	441	91.2	8.2	0.6
	1914	55,936	56,371	54,345	1,863	163	96.4	3.3	0.3
Liquors, malt	1919	34,259	31,220	30,867	331	22	98.9	1.1	0.1
	1914	62,070	61,036	60,359	609	68	98.9	1.0	0.1
Locomotives, not made by railroad companies.	1919	26,715	19,877	19,734	102	41	99.3	0.5	0.2
	1914	17,391	16,548	16,539	8	1	99.9	(1)	(1)
Lumber and timber products..	1919	480,945	626,472	620,267	5,280	925	99.0	0.8	0.1
	1914	479,786	586,521	583,478	951	2,092	99.5	0.2	0.4
Lumber, planing-mill products, not including planing mills connected with sawmills.	1919	86,956	97,740	95,098	2,163	479	97.3	2.2	0.5
	1914	96,214	95,388	94,147	719	522	98.7	0.8	0.5
Machine tools [2]	1919	53,111	58,776	56,618	2,035	123	96.3	3.5	0.2
Marble and stone work	1919	32,768	36,580	36,424	90	66	99.6	0.2	0.2
	1914	54,891	56,097	55,817	99	181	99.5	0.2	0.3
Millinery and lace goods, not elsewhere specified.	1919	50,850	55,786	13,733	41,146	907	24.6	73.8	1.6
	1914	45,274	42,242	11,256	30,084	902	26.6	71.2	2.1
Musical instruments, pianos	1919	22,957	24,665	22,131	2,162	372	89.7	8.8	1.5
	1914	23,877	23,512	22,557	755	200	95.9	3.2	0.9
Oil and cake, cottonseed	1919	26,766	37,142	36,185	778	179	97.4	2.1	0.5
	1914	20,810	37,155	37,030	88	37	99.7	0.2	0.1
Paper and wood pulp	1919	113,759	122,139	111,121	10,852	166	91.0	8.9	0.1
	1914	88,457	89,005	79,508	9,391	106	89.3	10.6	0.1
Petroleum, refining	1919	58,889	62,660	61,492	1,126	42	98.1	1.8	0.1
	1914	25,366	24,938	24,742	157	39	99.2	0.6	0.2
Phonographs and graphophones.	1919	28,721	35,184	27,512	7,603	69	78.2	21.6	0.2
	1914	9,381	10,095	9,068	1,022	5	89.8	10.1	(1)
Pottery	1919	27,934	30,702	22,747	7,579	376	74.1	24.7	1.2
	1914	26,705	27,142	20,745	6,111	286	76.4	22.5	1.1
Printing and publishing, book and job.	1919	123,005	134,379	97,732	33,433	3,214	72.7	24.9	2.4
	1914	113,121	113,816	86,021	25,449	2,346	75.6	22.4	2.1
Printing and publishing, newspapers and periodicals.	1919	120,381	126,222	100,561	21,130	4,531	79.7	16.7	3.6
	1914	114,375	116,840	95,728	17,908	3,204	81.9	15.3	2.7
Rubber tires, tubes, and rubber goods, not elsewhere specified.	1919	119,848	138,081	121,006	16,330	745	87.6	11.8	0.5
	1914	50,220	49,279	42,599	6,304	376	86.4	12.8	0.8
Shipbuilding, steel	1919	344,014	309,273	308,078	972	223	99.6	0.3	0.1
	1914	33,508	31,838	31,599	63	176	99.2	0.2	0.6
Shipbuilding, wooden, including boat building.	1919	43,432	45,903	45,803	88	12	99.8	0.2	(1)
	1914	10,981	10,897	10,854	27	16	99.6	0.2	0.1
Shirts	1919	39,603	46,698	7,711	37,797	1,190	16.5	80.9	2.5
	1914	51,972	53,908	10,663	41,744	1,501	19.8	77.4	2.8
Silk goods, including throwsters.	1919	126,782	137,716	52,404	78,160	7,152	38.1	56.8	5.2
	1914	108,170	106,508	40,960	57,860	7,688	38.5	54.3	7.2

[1] Less than one-tenth of 1 per cent.
[2] Included in "foundry and machine-shop products" in 1914.

TABLE 9.—SEX AND AGE DISTRIBUTION OF WAGE EARNERS IN THE 85 LEADING INDUSTRIES: 1919 AND 1914—Continued.

INDUSTRY.	Census year.	Average number.	NUMBER DEC. 15, OR NEAREST REPRESENTATIVE DAY.				PER CENT OF TOTAL.		
			Total.	16 years of age and over.		Under 16 years of age.	16 years of age and over.		Under 16 years of age.
				Male.	Female.		Male.	Female.	
Slaughtering and meat packing.	1919	160,996	163,582	147,127	16,244	211	89.9	9.9	0.1
	1914	98,832	105,193	98,103	6,831	259	93.3	6.5	0.2
Soap	1919	20,436	20,290	14,125	5,926	239	69.6	29.2	1.2
	1914	14,172	14,053	10,429	3,398	206	74.3	24.2	1.5
Stamped and enameled ware, not elsewhere specified.	1919	34,248	37,977	29,460	7,799	718	77.6	20.5	1.9
	1914	28,731	27,731	21,641	5,326	764	78.0	19.2	2.8
Steam fittings and steam and hot-water heating apparatus.	1919	36,686	44,371	41,885	2,410	76	94.4	5.4	0.2
	1914	26,388	25,676	25,028	454	194	97.5	1.8	0.8
Stoves and hot-air furnaces	1919	32,868	36,546	35,801	411	334	98.0	1.1	0.9
	1914	29,535	29,806	29,620	70	116	99.4	0.2	0.4
Structural ironwork, not made in steel works or rolling mills.	1919	43,962	47,142	46,860	258	24	99.4	0.5	0.1
	1914	47,167	45,872	45,685	116	71	99.6	0.3	0.2
Sugar, refining, not including beet sugar.	1919	18,202	18,383	17,063	1,313	7	92.8	7.1	(1)
	1914	11,253	11,390	10,860	502	28	95.3	4.4	0.2
Textile machinery and parts [2]	1919	31,823	35,598	33,097	2,029	472	93.0	5.7	1.3
Tinware, not elsewhere specified	1919	34,386	35,221	24,846	10,163	212	70.5	28.9	0.6
	1914	22,584	21,183	16,290	4,475	418	76.9	21.1	2.0
Tobacco, chewing and smoking, and snuff.	1919	18,324	19,109	9,615	9,339	155	50.3	48.9	0.8
	1914	25,980	25,665	13,612	10,889	1,164	53.0	42.4	4.5
Tobacco, cigars and cigarettes	1919	138,773	160,463	65,099	93,341	2,023	40.6	58.2	1.3
	1914	152,892	156,443	68,666	84,067	3,710	43.9	53.7	2.4
Tools, not elsewhere specified	1919	35,585	39,697	36,155	3,176	366	91.1	8.0	0.9
	1914	16,866	16,521	15,512	812	197	93.9	4.9	1.2
Turpentine and rosin	1919	28,067	29,601	29,103	103	395	98.3	0.3	1.3
	1914	34,817	36,504	35,955	68	481	98.5	0.2	1.3
Wire	1919	19,741	21,600	20,486	1,037	77	94.8	4.8	0.4
	1914	17,600	16,764	16,082	672	10	95.9	4.0	0.1
Woolen goods	1919	62,957	72,062	47,736	23,274	1,052	66.2	32.3	1.5
	1914	49,165	52,383	34,796	16,695	892	66.4	31.9	1.7
Worsted goods	1919	103,830	122,587	57,921	57,911	6,755	47.2	47.2	5.5
	1914	109,527	111,425	53,666	52,301	5,458	48.2	46.9	4.9

[1] Less than one-tenth of 1 per cent.
[2] Included in "foundry and machine-shop products" in 1914.

75108°—23——59

TABLE 10.—WAGE EARNERS, MALES AND FEMALES,

[The month of maximum employment for each industry is indicated

	INDUSTRY.	Average number employed during year.	NUMBER EMPLOYED ON 15TH DAY OF THE MONTH OR NEAREST REPRESENTATIVE DAY.			
			January.	February.	March.	April.
1	All industries: 1919	9,096,372	8,874,477	8,679,913	8,677,006	8,666,549
2	Male	7,267,030	7,116,393	6,957,645	6,964,697	6,950,424
3	Female	1,829,342	1,758,084	1,722,268	1,712,309	1,716,125
4	1914	7,036,247	7,075,592	7,141,504	7,242,662	7,217,230
5	1909	6,615,046	6,210,063	6,297,627	6,423,517	6,437,633
6	Aeroplanes, seaplanes, and airships, and parts.	3,543	5,493	4,729	4,161	3,939
7	Male	3,255	4,827	4,243	3,799	3,637
8	Female	288	666	486	362	302
9	Agricultural implements	54,368	57,926	59,748	58,653	55,771
10	Male	53,375	56,859	58,684	57,617	54,765
11	Female	993	1,067	1,064	1,036	1,006
12	Aluminum manufactures	11,402	9,749	9,656	9,912	9,991
13	Male	10,180	8,672	8,603	8,827	8,872
14	Female	1,222	1,077	1,053	1,085	1,119
15	Ammunition	22,816	46,771	33,327	25,965	20,436
16	Male	15,635	31,553	21,844	17,622	13,717
17	Female	7,181	15,218	11,483	8,343	6,719
18	Artificial flowers	4,138	3,848	4,193	4,303	4,262
19	Male	1,174	1,089	1,158	1,210	1,182
20	Female	2,964	2,759	3,035	3,093	3,080
21	Artificial limbs	671	666	660	667	661
22	Male	621	615	609	616	609
23	Female	50	51	51	51	52
24	Artificial stone products	8,378	5,049	5,184	5,972	8,123
25	Male	8,354	5,033	5,167	5,947	8,097
26	Female	24	16	17	25	26
27	Artists' materials	926	850	859	862	877
28	Male	713	648	648	663	677
29	Female	213	202	211	199	200
30	Asbestos products, not including steam packing.	3,654	3,441	3,435	3,464	3,316
31	Male	2,834	2,754	2,712	2,665	2,572
32	Female	820	687	723	799	744
33	Automobile bodies and parts	132,556	108,857	110,025	115,005	119,577
34	Male	125,804	103,381	104,549	109,333	113,636
35	Female	6,752	5,476	5,476	5,672	5,941
36	Automobile repairing	55,061	48,702	49,343	50,738	53,137
37	Male	54,686	48,387	49,010	50,392	52,748
38	Female	375	315	333	346	389
39	Automobiles	210,559	174,634	179,147	185,578	195,198
40	Male	202,374	166,540	171,537	178,026	187,365
41	Female	8,185	8,094	7,610	7,552	7,833
42	Awnings, tents, and sails	6,028	4,881	4,890	5,287	6,390
43	Male	3,345	2,768	2,758	3,011	3,690
44	Female	2,683	2,113	2,132	2,276	2,700
45	Babbitt metal and solder	2,372	2,363	2,279	2,241	2,310
46	Male	2,171	2,161	2,084	2,043	2,113
47	Female	201	202	195	198	197
48	Bags, other than paper, not including bags made in textile mills.	10,756	10,463	9,848	9,461	9,541
49	Male	3,974	3,798	3,668	3,519	3,545
50	Female	6,782	6,665	6,180	5,942	5,996
51	Bags, paper, exclusive of those made in paper mills.	4,168	4,124	3,833	3,785	3,591
52	Male	1,964	1,933	1,757	1,779	1,742
53	Female	2,204	2,191	2,076	2,006	1,849
54	Baking powders and yeast	3,331	3,544	3,323	3,325	3,188
55	Male	2,531	2,608	2,545	2,557	2,463
56	Female	800	936	778	768	725
57	Baskets, and rattan and willow ware	4,533	3,979	4,254	4,434	4,589
58	Male	3,134	2,810	2,999	3,127	3,221
59	Female	1,399	1,169	1,255	1,307	1,368

EMPLOYED EACH MONTH, BY INDUSTRIES: 1919.

by bold-faced figures and that of minimum employment by *italic* figures.]

May.	June.	July.	August.	September.	October.	November.	December.	Per cent minimum is of maximum.	
8,718,876	8,865,621	9,120,448	9,348,600	9,507,208	9,478,439	9,556,157	**9,663,170**	89.7	1
6,986,546	7,099,576	7,289,610	7,459,389	7,565,417	7,513,311	7,595,850	**7,705,502**	90.2	2
1,732,330	1,766,045	1,830,838	1,889,211	1,941,791	**1,965,128**	1,960,307	1,957,668	87.1	3
7,148,560	7,100,278	7,018,777	7,020,593	7,086,725	7,006,241	6,736,608	*6,640,194*	91.7	4
6,457,279	6,517,469	6,486,676	6,656,933	6,898,765	6,997,090	**7,006,853**	6,990,652	88.6	5
3,397	3,168	3,109	2,944	2,840	*2,799*	2,971	2,966	51.0	6
3,162	2,959	2,898	2,747	2,639	*2,616*	2,771	2,762	54.2	7
235	209	211	197	201	*183*	200	204	27.5	8
53,994	52,817	52,900	*49,483*	51,256	51,059	52,610	56,199	82.8	9
53,043	51,925	51,950	*48,680*	50,326	49,981	51,518	55,152	83.0	10
951	892	950	*803*	930	1,078	**1,092**	1,047	73.5	11
10,696	11,002	11,984	12,027	11,715	12,444	13,543	**14,105**	68.5	12
9,539	9,783	10,662	10,704	10,477	11,154	12,180	**12,687**	67.8	13
1,157	1,219	1,322	1,323	1,238	1,290	1,363	**1,418**	74.3	14
19,113	18,869	18,768	17,285	*17,121*	17,713	18,795	19,629	36.6	15
13,283	13,325	13,396	12,032	*11,894*	12,250	13,032	13,672	37.7	16
5,830	5,544	5,372	5,253	*5,227*	5,463	5,763	5,957	34.3	17
4,054	3,868	4,041	4,138	4,146	4,185	**4,318**	4,300	89.1	18
1,133	1,102	1,128	1,170	1,194	1,223	**1,251**	1,248	87.1	19
2,921	2,766	2,913	2,968	2,952	2,962	3,067	3,052	89.2	20
665	678	664	679	674	681	**682**	675	96.8	21
614	629	615	630	626	633	633	623	96.2	22
51	49	49	49	48	48	49	52	92.3	23
9,268	9,897	10,092	10,483	**10,528**	9,805	8,609	7,526	48.0	24
9,240	9,869	10,062	10,456	**10,502**	9,781	8,587	7,507	47.9	25
28	28	30	27	26	24	22	19	53.3	26
882	919	939	958	977	972	1,001	**1,016**	83.7	27
680	710	719	732	755	760	771	**793**	81.7	28
202	209	220	226	222	212	230	223	86.5	29
3,455	3,339	3,637	3,823	3,948	4,002	3,952	**4,036**	82.2	30
2,701	*2,546*	2,768	2,931	3,025	3,095	3,091	**3,148**	80.9	31
754	793	869	892	923	907	861	888	74.4	32
122,523	125,788	133,941	140,420	147,169	153,034	156,998	**157,335**	69.2	33
116,193	119,075	126,951	133,291	139,838	145,265	148,928	**149,208**	69.3	34
6,330	6,713	6,990	7,129	7,331	7,769	8,070	**8,127**	67.4	35
55,210	56,822	58,409	**59,004**	58,719	57,813	56,539	56,296	82.5	36
54,819	56,418	58,018	**58,612**	58,332	57,431	56,158	55,907	82.6	37
391	**404**	391	392	387	382	381	389	78.0	38
194,976	206,009	217,805	224,854	231,115	236,240	239,443	**241,709**	72.2	39
186,966	198,678	210,133	216,914	222,305	226,778	229,827	**233,419**	71.3	40
8,010	*7,331*	7,672	7,940	8,810	9,462	**9,616**	8,290	76.2	41
7,051	**7,455**	7,161	6,417	5,854	5,725	5,686	5,539	65.5	42
3,998	**4,150**	3,895	3,464	3,180	3,163	3,088	2,975	66.5	43
3,053	**3,305**	3,266	2,953	2,674	2,562	2,598	2,564	63.9	44
2,266	2,398	2,576	*2,144*	2,214	2,215	2,705	**2,753**	77.9	45
2,076	2,176	2,327	*1,977*	2,051	2,065	2,473	**2,506**	78.9	46
190	222	249	167	163	*150*	232	247	60.2	47
10,155	10,495	11,013	11,531	11,499	**11,803**	11,670	11,593	80.2	48
3,775	3,888	3,943	4,141	4,256	4,409	4,331	**4,415**	79.7	49
6,380	6,607	7,070	7,390	7,243	7,394	7,339	7,178	80.4	50
3,266	3,895	4,205	4,404	4,588	4,721	4,754	**4,850**	67.3	51
1,561	1,835	1,969	2,074	2,172	2,253	2,225	**2,268**	68.8	52
1,705	2,060	2,236	2,330	2,416	2,468	2,529	**2,582**	66.0	53
3,160	3,368	3,348	3,283	3,425	3,489	3,379	*3,140*	88.6	54
2,403	2,501	2,550	2,517	2,560	2,644	2,560	2,464	90.9	55
757	867	798	766	865	845	819	*676*	72.2	56
4,623	4,686	4,683	**4,767**	4,673	4,582	4,527	4,599	83.5	57
3,254	3,252	3,174	3,244	3,210	3,112	3,069	3,136	86.4	58
1,369	1,434	1,509	1,523	1,463	1,470	1,458	1,463	76.8	59

TABLE 10.—WAGE EARNERS, MALES AND FEMALES,

[The month of maximum employment for each industry is indicated

	INDUSTRY.	Average number employed during year.	NUMBER EMPLOYED ON 15TH DAY OF THE MONTH OR NEAREST REPRESENTATIVE DAY.			
			January.	February.	March.	April.
1	Bells	237	234	227	223	215
2	Male	211	211	202	201	193
3	Female	26	23	25	22	22
4	Belting and hose, rubber	5,826	6,265	5,593	4,576	5,092
5	Male	5,122	5,378	4,868	3,952	4,464
6	Female	704	887	725	624	628
7	Belting and hose, woven, other than rubber	2,479	2,332	2,309	2,285	2,214
8	Male	1,306	1,178	1,188	1,174	1,159
9	Female	1,173	1,154	1,121	1,111	1,055
10	Belting, leather	2,765	2,830	2,684	2,683	2,586
11	Male	2,590	2,649	2,518	2,512	2,418
12	Female	175	181	166	171	168
13	Billiard tables, bowling alleys, and accessories.	2,101	1,699	1,763	1,945	2,022
14	Male	1,889	1,501	1,606	1,766	1,837
15	Female	212	198	157	179	185
16	Blacking, stains, and dressings	2,455	2,195	2,301	2,200	2,451
17	Male	1,281	1,144	1,186	1,119	1,265
18	Female	1,174	1,051	1,115	1,081	1,186
19	Bluing	360	330	337	347	332
20	Male	145	143	142	144	134
21	Female	215	187	195	203	198
22	Bone, carbon, and lamp black	675	658	687	661	669
23	Male	672	654	682	659	666
24	Female	3	4	5	2	3
25	Bookbinding and blank-book making	20,361	19,354	19,565	19,858	19,789
26	Male	10,195	9,491	9,670	9,840	9,888
27	Female	10,166	9,863	9,895	10,018	9,901
28	Boot and shoe cut stock	9,715	9,293	9,328	9,361	9,190
29	Male	7,098	6,684	6,782	6,778	6,667
30	Female	2,617	2,609	2,546	2,583	2,523
31	Boot and shoe findings	8,941	7,815	8,156	8,217	8,447
32	Male	5,763	4,974	5,174	5,208	5,359
33	Female	3,178	2,841	2,982	3,009	3,088
34	Boots and shoes, not including rubber boots and shoes.	211,049	202,905	204,440	201,295	199,025
35	Male	130,610	124,853	126,228	124,255	123,468
36	Female	80,439	78,052	78,212	77,040	75,557
37	Boots and shoes, rubber	32,875	34,591	35,339	33,977	32,455
38	Male	19,047	19,639	20,004	19,479	18,795
39	Female	13,828	14,952	15,335	14,498	13,660
40	Boxes, cigar	5,218	4,990	5,076	5,083	5,090
41	Male	2,343	2,280	2,303	2,306	2,286
42	Female	2,875	2,710	2,773	2,777	2,804
43	Boxes, paper and other, not elsewhere specified.	55,862	53,373	52,850	52,932	53,106
44	Male	23,095	22,516	21,792	21,502	21,537
45	Female	32,767	30,857	31,058	31,430	31,569
46	Boxes, wooden packing, except cigar boxes	42,445	41,849	40,707	40,751	40,682
47	Male	38,105	37,422	36,370	36,395	36,324
48	Female	4,340	4,427	4,337	4,356	4,358
49	Brass, bronze, and copper products	75,051	81,783	75,650	70,232	68,457
50	Male	68,273	72,882	67,676	63,458	62,348
51	Female	6,778	8,901	7,974	6,774	6,109
52	Bread and other bakery products	141,592	135,640	134,358	134,887	137,164
53	Male	104,515	99,569	99,288	99,830	101,601
54	Female	37,077	36,071	35,070	35,057	35,563
55	Brick and tile, terra-cotta, and fire-clay products.	76,915	56,190	55,866	60,269	70,332
56	Male	75,758	55,209	54,892	59,317	69,319
57	Female	1,157	981	974	952	1,013
58	Brooms	6,313	6,321	6,187	5,906	6,009
59	Male	5,298	5,265	5,145	4,933	5,025
60	Female	1,015	1,056	1,042	973	984

EMPLOYED EACH MONTH, BY INDUSTRIES: 1919—Continued.

by bold-faced figures and that of minimum employment by *italic* figures.]

NUMBER EMPLOYED ON 15TH DAY OF THE MONTH OR NEAREST REPRESENTATIVE DAY—continued.

May.	June.	July.	August.	September.	October.	November.	December.	Per cent minimum is of maximum.	
220	227	246	245	242	243	**262**	260	82.1	1
195	207	218	217	216	216	227	**229**	84.3	2
25	*20*	28	28	26	27	**35**	31	57.1	3
5,118	5,155	5,514	6,129	6,357	6,448	6,708	**6,957**	65.8	4
4,499	4,577	4,850	5,427	5,631	5,774	5,952	**6,092**	64.9	5
619	*578*	664	702	726	674	756	865	65.2	6
2,274	2,394	2,538	2,675	2,626	2,689	**2,722**	2,690	81.3	7
1,195	1,281	1,369	1,420	1,412	1,344	1,473	**1,479**	78.4	8
1,079	1,113	1,169	1,255	1,214	**1,345**	1,249	1,211	78.4	9
2,567	*2,566*	2,651	2,782	2,870	2,914	2,976	**3,071**	83.6	10
2,399	2,402	2,484	2,610	2,685	2,726	2,796	**2,881**	83.3	11
168	*164*	167	172	185	188	180	**190**	86.3	12
1,972	2,043	1,989	2,077	2,252	2,318	2,537	**2,595**	65.5	13
1,818	1,821	1,814	1,868	2,020	2,057	2,258	**2,302**	65.2	14
154	222	175	209	232	261	279	**293**	52.6	15
2,445	2,470	2,500	2,568	2,559	2,586	**2,625**	2,560	83.6	16
1,275	1,264	1,264	1,290	1,337	1,381	**1,429**	1,418	78.3	17
1,170	1,206	1,236	**1,278**	1,222	1,205	1,196	1,142	82.2	18
318	324	359	412	**419**	414	372	356	75.9	19
136	141	143	153	145	**157**	155	147	85.4	20
182	183	216	259	**274**	257	217	209	66.4	21
665	674	669	676	680	**698**	675	688	94.3	22
663	672	666	672	676	**695**	673	686	94.1	23
2	2	3	4	4	3	2	2	40.0	24
19,756	20,016	20,488	20,734	20,773	20,845	21,379	**21,775**	88.9	25
9,806	10,096	10,345	10,409	10,521	10,483	10,763	**11,028**	86.1	26
9,950	9,920	10,143	10,325	10,252	10,362	10,616	**10,747**	91.8	27
9,370	9,857	9,943	9,659	9,760	10,193	**10,354**	10,272	88.8	28
6,896	7,304	7,304	7,024	7,243	7,488	**7,506**	7,500	88.8	29
2,474	2,553	2,639	2,635	2,517	2,705	**2,848**	2,772	86.9	30
8,486	8,762	8,906	9,242	9,493	9,588	9,957	**10,223**	76.4	31
5,385	5,627	5,721	5,965	6,153	6,272	6,527	**6,791**	73.2	32
3,101	3,135	3,185	3,277	3,340	3,316	3,430	**3,432**	82.8	33
201,710	206,562	211,811	215,596	217,031	219,604	224,197	**228,412**	87.1	34
125,348	128,569	131,605	133,174	134,061	135,824	138,549	**141,386**	87.3	35
76,362	77,993	80,206	82,422	82,970	83,780	85,648	**87,026**	86.8	36
31,298	*30,642*	31,304	31,561	31,578	32,953	34,145	**34,657**	86.7	37
18,231	*18,098*	18,308	18,484	18,421	19,062	19,778	**20,265**	89.3	38
13,067	*12,544*	12,996	13,077	13,157	13,891	14,367	**14,392**	81.8	39
5,090	5,143	5,155	5,122	5,195	5,415	5,591	**5,666**	88.1	40
2,287	2,316	2,306	2,296	2,343	2,399	2,466	**2,528**	90.2	41
2,803	2,827	2,849	2,826	2,852	3,016	3,125	**3,138**	86.4	42
52,776	53,888	56,193	56,845	55,982	59,616	**61,455**	61,328	85.9	43
21,184	22,052	22,972	23,877	23,608	25,086	25,473	**25,541**	82.9	44
31,592	31,836	33,221	32,968	32,374	34,530	**35,982**	35,787	85.8	45
41,234	42,175	42,175	43,892	43,217	43,418	44,204	**44,881**	90.6	46
36,885	37,795	38,119	39,714	38,939	38,989	39,867	**40,441**	89.8	47
4,349	4,380	4,211	*4,178*	4,278	4,429	4,337	**4,440**	94.1	48
68,345	*67,301*	69,524	75,628	78,048	80,999	**82,382**	82,263	81.7	49
62,409	*61,358*	63,386	69,279	71,621	74,263	**75,433**	75,163	81.3	50
5,936	5,943	6,138	6,349	6,427	6,736	6,949	**7,100**	66.7	51
137,136	140,783	143,229	144,280	144,941	147,242	149,383	**150,061**	89.5	52
101,603	104,093	105,447	106,493	107,309	108,350	109,895	**110,702**	89.7	53
35,533	36,690	37,782	37,787	37,632	38,892	**39,488**	39,359	88.8	54
79,561	84,952	88,715	**90,929**	90,615	88,913	81,997	74,641	61.4	55
78,474	83,804	87,496	**89,691**	89,329	87,592	80,664	73,309	61.2	56
1,087	1,148	1,219	1,238	1,286	1,321	**1,333**	1,332	71.4	57
5,986	5,994	6,054	6,298	6,512	6,713	6,840	**6,936**	85.1	58
5,008	5,010	5,074	5,284	5,483	5,685	5,793	**5,871**	84.0	59
978	984	980	1,014	1,029	1,028	1,047	**1,065**	91.4	60

TABLE **10.**—WAGE EARNERS, MALES AND FEMALES,

[The month of maximum employment for each industry is indicated

	INDUSTRY.	Average number employed during year.	NUMBER EMPLOYED ON 15TH DAY OF THE MONTH OR NEAREST REPRESENTATIVE DAY.			
			January.	February.	March.	April.
1	Brushes	7,968	8,086	7,794	7,755	7,542
2	Male	5,389	5,496	5,205	5,280	5,081
3	Female	2,579	2,590	2,589	2,475	2,461
4	Butter	17,641	*14,796*	14,881	15,118	16,804
5	Male	15,125	*12,894*	13,031	13,214	14,456
6	Female	2,516	1,902	*1,850*	1,904	2,348
7	Butter, reworking	47	47	47	47	47
8	Male	42	42	42	42	42
9	Female	5	5	5	5	5
10	Buttons	15,577	14,839	15,051	14,878	*14,594*
11	Male	9,402	9,029	9,092	8,975	8,723
12	Female	6,175	*5,810*	5,959	5,903	5,871
13	Candles	541	500	494	*471*	479
14	Male	259	260	261	*239*	245
15	Female	282	240	233	232	234
16	Canning and preserving, fish	11,248	8,710	7,402	*6,749*	7,407
17	Male	6,844	5,350	4,657	*4,478*	4,971
18	Female	4,404	3,360	2,745	*2,271*	2,436
19	Canning and preserving, fruits and vegetables.	60,865	19,977	14,792	*14,005*	18,962
20	Male	30,573	13,610	10,747	*10,125*	12,923
21	Female	30,292	6,367	4,045	*3,880*	6,039
22	Canning and preserving, oysters	1,189	1,599	1,505	1,804	1,826
23	Male	446	606	543	673	665
24	Female	743	993	962	1,131	**1,161**
25	Card cutting and designing	1,148	*1,015*	1,053	1,117	1,092
26	Male	522	*473*	487	503	489
27	Female	626	*542*	566	614	603
28	Cardboard, not made in paper mills	1,425	*1,355*	1,405	1,403	1,370
29	Male	791	**767**	788	776	761
30	Female	634	*588*	617	627	609
31	Carpets and rugs, other than rag	22,933	*18,622*	18,681	19,374	20,792
32	Male	14,032	*11,289*	11,349	11,658	12,690
33	Female	8,901	*7,333*	*7,332*	7,716	8,102
34	Carpets, rag	2,016	*1,608*	1,640	1,723	1,933
35	Male	1,396	*1,120*	1,129	1,206	1,324
36	Female	620	*488*	511	517	609
37	Carriage and wagon materials	6,509	5,918	5,991	*5,856*	6,046
38	Male	6,281	5,710	5,779	*5,648*	5,843
39	Female	228	208	212	208	*203*
40	Carriages and sleds, children's	6,686	*5,999*	6,213	6,486	6,522
41	Male	5,617	*5,081*	5,253	5,510	5,511
42	Female	1,069	918	960	976	1,011
43	Carriages and wagons, including repairs	18,173	17,891	17,989	17,975	*17,667*
44	Male	17,899	17,655	17,735	17,705	*17,386*
45	Female	274	236	254	270	281
46	Cars and general shop construction and repairs by electric-railroad companies.	31,272	31,499	31,702	31,686	31,332
47	Male	30,773	30,905	31,119	31,112	30,766
48	Female	499	**594**	583	574	566
49	Cars and general shop construction and repairs by steam-railroad companies.	484,437	487,141	484,047	472,266	467,674
50	Male	479,959	481,015	478,558	467,371	463,128
51	Female	4,478	**6,126**	5,489	4,895	4,546
52	Cars, electric-railroad, not including operations of railroad companies.	2,920	**3,965**	3,658	3,213	2,500
53	Male	2,851	**3,889**	3,587	3,147	2,431
54	Female	69	**76**	71	66	69
55	Cars, steam-railroad, not including operations of railroad companies.	52,298	**64,974**	61,127	56,409	55,783
56	Male	51,778	**64,306**	60,579	55,884	55,303
57	Female	520	**668**	548	525	480
58	Cash registers and calculating machines	16,544	13,845	*13,778*	14,766	15,115
59	Male	13,956	*11,242*	11,285	12,326	12,716
60	Female	2,588	2,603	2,493	2,440	*2,399*

EMPLOYED EACH MONTH, BY INDUSTRIES: 1919—Continued.

by **bold-faced** figures and that of minimum employment by *italic* figures.]

NUMBER EMPLOYED ON 15TH DAY OF THE MONTH OR NEAREST REPRESENTATIVE DAY—continued.								Per cent minimum is of maximum.	
May.	June.	July.	August.	September.	October.	November.	December.		
7,489	7,501	7,716	8,005	8,045	8,368	8,567	**8,748**	85.6	1
5,073	5,097	5,205	5,405	5,439	5,635	5,796	**5,956**	85.2	2
2,416	*2,404*	2,511	2,600	2,606	2,733	2,771	**2,792**	86.1	3
18,584	**20,370**	20,322	19,829	19,024	17,861	17,394	16,709	72.6	4
15,883	17,331	**17,355**	16,847	16,136	15,151	14,873	14,329	74.3	5
2,701	**3,039**	2,967	2,982	2,888	2,710	2,521	2,380	60.9	6
47	45	46	47	*42*	46	50	53	79.2	7
42	40	42	42	*38*	42	43	47	80.9	8
5	5	4	5	4	4	7	6	57.1	9
14,659	15,049	15,663	16,238	15,886	16,333	**16,876**	16,858	86.5	10
8,692	8,966	9,248	9,761	9,612	9,927	10,297	**10,502**	82.8	11
5,967	6,083	6,415	6,477	6,274	6,406	**6,579**	6,356	88.3	12
472	490	564	561	585	611	632	**633**	74.4	13
242	251	**299**	274	265	258	255	259	79.9	14
230	237	265	320	287	353	**377**	374	61.0	15
8,394	10,667	14,288	**17,329**	17,294	16,208	11,616	8,912	38.9	16
5,990	6,655	8,404	9,739	**9,809**	9,284	7,166	5,625	45.7	17
2,404	4,012	5,884	**7,590**	7,485	6,924	4,450	3,287	29.9	18
23,402	51,029	90,986	131,963	**157,032**	122,064	55,532	30,636	8.9	19
15,344	28,707	42,288	61,113	70,318	51,820	30,416	19,465	14.4	20
8,058	22,322	48,698	70,850	**86,714**	70,244	25,116	11,171	4.5	21
894	248	*214*	619	689	1,292	1,742	**1,836**	11.7	22
364	146	*126*	196	234	453	670	676	18.6	23
530	102	*88*	423	455	839	1,072	1,160	7.6	24
1,142	1,147	1,167	1,201	1,172	1,178	1,231	**1,261**	80.5	25
508	528	537	544	535	536	552	572	82.7	26
634	619	630	657	637	642	679	689	78.7	27
1,364	1,377	1,450	1,450	1,473	1,476	**1,498**	1,479	90.5	28
747	759	810	791	802	825	830	836	89.4	29
617	618	640	659	671	651	668	643	87.6	30
22,448	23,596	24,421	25,011	24,398	25,390	25,961	**26,502**	70.3	31
13,726	14,503	14,979	15,296	14,823	15,467	16,061	**16,543**	68.2	32
8,722	9,093	9,442	9,715	9,575	9,923	9,900	**9,959**	73.6	33
2,037	2,113	2,001	2,168	2,164	2,204	2,276	**2,325**	69.2	34
1,411	1,475	1,359	1,482	1,513	1,546	1,586	**1,601**	70.0	35
626	638	642	686	651	658	690	724	67.4	36
6,208	6,397	6,646	6,902	6,964	**7,095**	7,056	7,029	82.5	37
5,986	6,156	6,400	6,665	6,723	**6,867**	6,817	6,778	82.2	38
222	241	246	237	241	228	239	251	80.9	39
6,684	6,878	6,644	6,848	6,838	6,946	6,995	**7,179**	83.6	40
5,628	5,763	5,558	5,741	5,700	5,779	5,858	**6,022**	84.4	41
1,056	1,115	1,086	1,107	1,138	**1,167**	1,137	1,157	78.7	42
17,729	17,707	18,132	18,425	18,547	18,671	**18,707**	18,636	94.4	43
17,454	17,409	17,540	18,120	18,254	18,408	**18,441**	18,381	94.3	44
275	298	292	**305**	293	263	266	255	77.4	45
30,937	*30,220*	30,896	30,796	30,960	31,568	31,774	**31,894**	94.8	46
30,413	*29,733*	30,439	30,368	30,527	31,124	31,308	**31,462**	94.5	47
524	487	457	*428*	433	444	466	432	72.1	48
466,995	*464,919*	475,570	480,705	493,057	502,119	507,617	**511,134**	91.0	49
462,623	*460,769*	471,535	476,734	489,054	498,047	503,534	**507,140**	90.9	50
4,372	4,150	4,035	*3,971*	4,003	4,072	4,083	3,994	64.8	51
2,471	2,680	2,829	2,763	2,706	2,814	2,779	2,662	62.3	52
2,404	2,616	2,758	2,694	2,637	2,742	2,710	2,597	61.8	53
67	*64*	71	69	69	72	69	65	84.2	54
54,419	51,545	50,020	48,608	46,619	*45,031*	45,159	47,882	69.3	55
53,955	51,076	49,642	48,217	46,199	44,497	*44,437*	47,241	69.1	56
464	469	*378*	391	420	534	722	641	52.4	57
16,261	16,670	17,306	17,486	18,151	18,250	18,342	**18,558**	74.2	58
13,781	14,137	14,723	14,959	15,463	15,487	15,540	**15,813**	71.1	59
2,480	2,533	2,583	2,527	2,688	2,763	**2,802**	2,745	85.6	60

TABLE **10.**—WAGE EARNERS, MALES AND FEMALES,

[The month of maximum employment for each industry is indicated

	INDUSTRY.	Average number employed during year.	January.	February.	March.	April.
1	Cement	25,524	*20,234*	20,563	21,964	23,864
2	Male	25,195	*19,945*	20,301	21,729	23,580
3	Female	329	289	262	*235*	284
4	Charcoal, not including production in the lumber and wood distillation industries.	209	244	221	210	197
5	Male	206	241	218	207	194
6	Female	3	3	3	3	3
7	Cheese	3,997	*2,843*	2,893	3,229	4,106
8	Male	3,843	*2,718*	2,765	3,084	3,948
9	Female	154	*125*	128	145	158
10	Chemicals	55,586	**60,754**	57,339	53,281	51,100
11	Male	50,834	**55,865**	52,502	48,790	*46,393*
12	Female	4,752	4,889	4,837	*4,491*	4,707
13	Chewing gum	3,190	3,106	3,178	3,228	3,351
14	Male	1,117	*1,014*	1,047	1,084	1,136
15	Female	2,073	2,092	2,131	2,154	**2,215**
16	China decorating, not including that done in potteries.	244	*204*	207	218	221
17	Male	110	94	*91*	101	99
18	Female	134	*110*	116	117	122
19	Chocolate and cocoa products	9,083	8,723	9,103	9,064	8,713
20	Male	6,555	6,101	6,397	6,442	6,276
21	Female	2,528	2,622	2,706	2,622	2,437
22	Cleansing and polishing preparations	1,955	1,880	1,806	1,811	*1,805*
23	Male	1,286	1,226	*1,179*	1,197	1,217
24	Female	669	654	627	614	*588*
25	Clocks	8,252	*7,329*	7,636	7,876	8,022
26	Male	5,618	*4,999*	5,169	5,341	5,433
27	Female	2,634	*2,330*	2,467	2,535	2,589
28	Cloth, sponging and refinishing	1,206	*991*	1,028	1,053	1,048
29	Male	1,183	*967*	1,005	1,030	1,028
30	Female	23	24	23	23	*20*
31	Clothing, horse	766	781	745	683	*677*
32	Male	342	349	336	303	*293*
33	Female	424	432	409	380	384
34	Clothing, men's	175,270	*146,278*	152,223	157,097	160,651
35	Male	80,743	*63,800*	68,322	72,581	75,240
36	Female	94,527	*82,478*	83,901	84,516	85,411
37	Clothing, men's, buttonholes	484	*413*	449	457	466
38	Male	273	*227*	256	257	261
39	Female	211	*186*	193	200	205
40	Clothing, women's	165,649	*146,080*	153,523	160,844	161,289
41	Male	53,181	47,325	52,373	54,801	51,521
42	Female	112,468	*98,755*	101,150	106,043	109,768
43	Coal-tar products	15,663	15,967	15,323	14,695	*14,311*
44	Male	15,120	15,319	14,742	14,173	*13,794*
45	Female	543	**648**	581	522	517
46	Coffee and spice, roasting and grinding	10,540	10,197	10,113	9,941	*9,937*
47	Male	5,911	5,732	5,668	5,655	*5,653*
48	Female	4,629	4,465	4,445	4,286	*4,284*
49	Coffins, burial cases, and undertakers' goods.	11,890	12,061	12,378	**12,507**	12,288
50	Male	9,654	9,706	9,955	**10,091**	9,970
51	Female	2,236	2,355	**2,423**	2,416	2,318
52	Coke, not including gas-house coke	29,319	**34,557**	32,159	30,479	28,452
53	Male	29,311	**34,549**	32,151	30,471	28,444
54	Female	8	8	8	8	8
55	Collars and cuffs, men's	11,103	*10,234*	10,326	10,620	11,032
56	Male	2,523	2,337	*2,265*	2,403	2,434
57	Female	8,580	7,897	8,061	8,217	8,598
58	Combs and hairpins, not made from metal or rubber.	2,229	2,193	2,232	**2,327**	2,249
59	Male	1,412	*1,379*	1,394	1,448	1,428
60	Female	817	814	838	*879*	821

EMPLOYED EACH MONTH, BY INDUSTRIES: 1919—Continued.

by **bold-faced** figures and that of minimum employment by *italic* figures.]

NUMBER EMPLOYED ON 15TH DAY OF THE MONTH OR NEAREST REPRESENTATIVE DAY—continued.								Per cent minimum is of maximum.	
May.	June.	July.	August.	September.	October.	November.	December.		
25,083	26,028	27,690	28,445	**29,062**	28,811	28,133	26,411	69.6	1
24,791	25,715	27,349	28,097	**28,670**	28,387	27,726	26,050	69.6	2
292	313	341	348	392	**424**	407	361	55.4	3
156	*140*	158	210	238	**258**	246	230	54.3	4
153	*137*	155	207	235	**255**	243	227	53.7	5
3	3	3	3	3	3	3	3	100.0	6
4,780	**5,026**	4,942	4,699	4,378	4,109	3,693	3,266	56.6	7
4,613	**4,853**	4,770	4,530	4,211	3,948	3,544	3,132	56.0	8
167	**173**	172	169	167	161	149	134	72.3	9
51,050	51,651	53,509	55,014	57,089	58,607	59,086	58,552	84.0	10
46,472	47,140	48,906	50,310	52,250	53,677	54,047	53,656	83.0	11
4,578	4,511	4,603	4,704	4,839	4,930	**5,039**	4,896	89.1	12
3,224	*2,995*	3,094	3,229	**3,374**	3,314	3,125	3,052	88.8	13
1,118	1,102	1,120	1,142	**1,219**	1,162	1,134	1,126	83.2	14
2,106	*1,893*	1,974	2,087	2,155	2,152	1,991	1,926	85.5	15
235	237	245	254	264	277	**285**	281	71.6	16
106	102	107	112	120	128	**132**	128	68.9	17
129	135	138	142	144	149	**153**	153	71.9	18
8,200	8,403	8,898	9,137	9,593	**10,034**	9,826	9,302	81.7	19
5,976	6,194	6,431	6,668	6,962	**7,213**	7,120	6,880	82.9	20
2,224	*2,209*	2,467	2,469	2,631	**2,821**	2,706	2,422	78.3	21
1,872	1,927	1,908	1,980	2,055	2,102	2,119	**2,195**	82.2	22
1,232	1,268	1,301	1,345	1,343	1,356	1,360	**1,408**	83.7	23
640	659	607	635	712	746	759	**787**	74.7	24
8,101	8,280	8,315	8,618	8,484	8,679	8,817	**8,867**	82.7	25
5,481	5,551	5,657	5,932	5,802	5,947	6,037	**6,067**	82.4	26
2,620	2,729	2,658	2,686	2,682	2,732	2,780	**2,800**	83.2	27
1,087	1,183	1,353	**1,378**	1,336	1,316	1,332	1,367	71.9	28
1,065	1,161	1,330	**1,354**	1,313	1,292	1,308	1,343	71.4	29
22	22	23	**24**	23	**24**	**24**	**24**	83.3	30
678	720	757	784	792	813	863	**899**	75.3	31
208	317	328	342	356	370	390	**412**	71.1	32
370	*403*	429	442	436	443	473	**487**	76.0	33
163,103	168,807	177,355	184,531	190,406	197,939	200,412	**204,438**	71.6	34
75,824	78,505	82,586	85,786	88,289	91,676	92,342	**93,965**	67.9	35
87,279	90,302	94,769	98,745	102,117	106,263	108,070	**110,473**	74.7	36
479	481	488	498	517	517	**525**	518	78.7	37
267	278	278	286	289	**293**	291	**293**	77.5	38
212	203	210	212	228	224	**234**	225	79.5	39
152,892	155,493	169,762	180,045	**184,769**	179,919	172,145	171,027	79.1	40
42,274	43,210	55,061	61,152	**61,893**	58,824	55,372	54,366	68.3	41
110,618	112,283	114,701	118,893	**122,876**	121,095	116,773	116,661	80.4	42
14,539	14,699	14,501	15,827	16,365	16,760	17,082	**17,887**	80.0	43
14,040	14,193	14,027	15,312	15,815	16,192	16,507	**17,326**	79.6	44
499	506	*474*	515	550	568	575	561	73.1	45
10,244	10,533	10,900	**11,050**	10,930	10,676	10,916	11,043	89.9	46
5,749	5,866	6,001	6,136	6,150	6,010	6,110	**6,202**	91.1	47
4,495	4,667	4,899	**4,914**	4,780	4,666	4,806	4,841	87.2	48
12,037	11,768	*11,467*	11,494	11,599	11,768	11,703	11,610	91.7	49
9,758	9,528	*9,328*	9,388	9,459	9,592	9,576	9,497	92.4	50
2,279	2,240	2,139	*2,106*	2,140	2,176	2,127	2,113	86.9	51
26,579	*26,434*	27,917	30,418	30,378	26,817	28,186	29,452	76.5	52
26,571	*26,426*	27,909	30,410	30,370	26,809	28,178	29,444	76.5	53
8	8	8	8	8	8	8	8	100.0	54
11,237	10,995	11,433	11,139	11,545	11,367	**11,661**	11,647	87.8	55
2,449	2,469	2,581	2,562	2,663	2,645	**2,739**	2,729	82.7	56
8,788	8,526	8,852	8,577	8,882	8,722	**8,922**	8,918	88.5	57
2,196	2,180	2,308	*2,172*	2,191	2,209	2,210	2,281	93.3	58
1,385	1,412	**1,465**	1,387	1,399	1,392	1,396	**1,459**	94.1	59
811	*768*	843	785	792	817	814	822	87.4	60

TABLE 10.—WAGE EARNERS, MALES AND FEMALES,

[The month of maximum employment for each industry is indicated

	INDUSTRY.	Average number employed during year.	NUMBER EMPLOYED ON 15TH DAY OF THE MONTH OR NEAREST REPRESENTATIVE DAY.			
			January.	February.	March.	April.
1	Condensed milk....................	13,675	11,383	12,276	13,028	13,961
2	Male........	11,790	9,890	10,595	11,273	12,045
3	Female........	1,885	1,493	1,681	1,755	1,916
4	Confectionery and ice cream........	95,648	86,491	89,978	91,061	90,859
5	Male........	44,732	38,564	40,015	40,619	42,041
6	Female........	50,916	47,927	49,963	50,442	48,818
7	Cooperage........	13,219	13,023	13,038	12,927	12,725
8	Male........	12,812	12,657	12,680	12,576	12,288
9	Female........	407	366	358	351	437
10	Copper, tin, and sheet-iron work........	27,640	25,479	24,602	24,787	25,451
11	Male........	27,032	24,813	24,044	24,243	24,952
12	Female........	608	666	558	544	499
13	Cordage and twine........	17,622	17,896	17,689	17,372	17,034
14	Male........	10,282	10,319	10,231	10,278	9,872
15	Female........	7,340	7,577	7,408	7,094	7,162
16	Cordials and flavoring sirups........	1,398	1,297	1,284	1,341	1,344
17	Male........	1,008	886	933	984	1,015
18	Female........	390	411	351	357	329
19	Cork, cutting........	3,545	3,706	3,613	3,533	3,495
20	Male........	2,173	2,290	2,215	2,126	2,117
21	Female........	1,372	1,416	1,398	1,407	1,378
22	Corsets........	18,415	17,052	17,188	17,222	17,481
23	Male........	2,737	2,539	2,583	2,626	2,647
24	Female........	15,678	14,513	14,605	14,596	14,834
25	Cotton goods........	430,966	432,978	417,786	415,600	414,718
26	Male........	249,749	249,452	241,750	240,757	240,037
27	Female........	181,217	183,526	176,036	174,843	174,681
28	Cotton lace........	6,490	5,941	5,975	6,003	5,961
29	Male........	3,094	2,826	2,833	2,846	2,798
30	Female........	3,396	3,115	3,142	3,157	3,163
31	Cotton small wares........	9,396	9,295	8,879	8,943	8,872
32	Male........	3,443	3,399	3,211	3,239	3,232
33	Female........	5,953	5,896	5,668	5,704	5,640
34	Crucibles........	848	954	884	850	841
35	Male........	829	937	866	832	822
36	Female........	19	17	18	18	19
37	Cutlery and edge tools........	19,859	18,960	19,565	19,644	19,272
38	Male........	15,980	15,219	15,737	15,778	15,489
39	Female........	3,879	3,741	3,828	3,866	3,783
40	Dairymen's, poultrymen's, and apiarists' supplies.	6,437	6,784	6,523	6,697	6,580
41	Male........	5,725	5,956	5,743	5,936	5,821
42	Female........	712	828	780	761	759
43	Dental goods........	5,224	4,855	4,989	5,114	5,171
44	Male........	2,789	2,578	2,635	2,686	2,735
45	Female........	2,435	2,277	2,354	2,428	2,436
46	Drug grinding........	1,347	1,372	1,399	1,335	1,220
47	Male........	1,055	1,116	1,071	1,035	935
48	Female........	292	256	328	300	285
49	Druggists' preparations........	15,568	16,275	16,359	16,159	15,484
50	Male........	7,538	7,534	7,448	7,487	7,344
51	Female........	8,030	8,741	8,911	8,672	8,140
52	Dyeing and finishing textiles, exclusive of that done in textile mills.	55,985	53,761	51,688	51,262	51,052
53	Male........	42,705	40,676	39,006	38,835	39,061
54	Female........	13,280	13,085	12,682	12,427	11,991
55	Dyestuffs and extracts—natural........	4,342	4,278	4,285	4,165	4,103
56	Male........	4,268	4,208	4,215	4,095	4,034
57	Female........	74	70	70	70	69
58	Electrical machinery, apparatus, and supplies.	212,374	209,593	205,356	201,393	198,316
59	Male........	155,937	152,763	150,069	147,042	146,084
60	Female........	56,437	56,830	55,287	54,351	52,232

EMPLOYED EACH MONTH, BY INDUSTRIES: 1919—Continued.

by bold-faced figures and that of minimum employment by *italic* figures.]

NUMBER EMPLOYED ON 15TH DAY OF THE MONTH OR NEAREST REPRESENTATIVE DAY.—continued.								Per cent minimum is of maximum.	
May.	June.	July.	August.	September.	October.	November.	December.		
14,705	15,593	15,320	14,489	13,780	13,646	13,035	12,884	73.0	1
12,647	13,430	13,149	12,447	11,865	11,733	11,232	11,174	73.6	2
2,058	2,163	2,171	2,042	1,915	1,913	1,803	1,710	68.8	3
89,453	90,449	91,900	99,382	104,608	107,004	105,212	101,379	80.8	4
43,324	46,041	47,275	49,471	50,172	48,350	46,416	44,496	76.9	5
46,129	44,408	44,625	49,911	54,436	58,654	58,796	56,883	75.5	6
12,633	13,195	13,556	13,683	13,928	13,905	13,211	12,804	90.7	7
12,181	12,757	13,144	13,266	13,497	13,504	12,792	12,402	90.2	8
452	438	412	417	431	401	419	402	77.7	9
26,192	27,399	28,374	29,175	29,434	29,818	30,483	30,486	80.7	10
25,656	26,841	27,821	28,586	28,819	29,108	29,733	29,768	80.8	11
536	558	553	589	615	710	750	718	66.5	12
17,079	17,240	17,494	17,696	17,777	17,889	18,045	18,303	93.1	13
9,855	10,091	10,145	10,404	10,359	10,494	10,574	10,762	91.6	14
7,224	7,149	7,349	7,292	7,418	7,395	7,471	7,541	93.6	15
1,446	1,457	1,604	1,486	1,370	1,295	1,325	1,527	80.0	16
1,008	1,053	1,028	1,021	1,044	984	1,013	1,127	78.6	17
438	404	576	465	326	311	312	400	54.0	18
3,494	3,482	3,501	3,517	3,511	3,493	3,587	3,608	94.0	19
2,136	2,153	2,166	2,140	2,142	2,150	2,195	2,246	92.4	20
1,358	1,329	1,335	1,377	1,369	1,343	1,392	1,362	93.9	21
17,597	17,726	18,214	18,758	19,146	19,816	20,217	20,563	82.9	22
2,666	2,689	2,753	2,811	2,841	2,872	2,877	2,940	86.4	23
14,931	15,037	15,461	15,947	16,305	16,944	17,340	17,623	82.4	24
423,295	429,213	434,345	436,312	437,375	438,711	442,252	449,007	92.4	25
245,279	248,326	251,867	253,787	254,059	254,741	256,561	260,372	92.2	26
178,016	180,887	182,478	182,525	183,316	183,970	185,691	188,635	92.6	27
6,074	6,420	6,533	6,781	6,871	7,015	7,006	7,300	81.4	28
2,900	3,064	3,109	3,227	3,304	3,335	3,350	3,536	79.1	29
3,174	3,356	3,424	3,554	3,567	3,680	3,656	3,764	82.8	30
8,884	9,180	9,634	9,646	9,622	9,774	9,921	10,102	87.8	31
3,201	3,288	3,535	3,567	3,550	3,630	3,680	3,784	84.6	32
5,683	5,892	6,099	6,079	6,072	6,144	6,241	6,318	89.3	33
839	816	805	786	800	855	875	871	82.4	34
821	800	787	767	779	835	853	849	81.9	35
18	16	18	19	21	20	22	22	72.7	36
19,666	19,453	19,497	19,097	19,903	20,842	21,087	21,322	88.9	37
15,863	15,749	15,739	15,598	15,909	16,741	16,868	17,070	89.2	38
3,803	3,704	3,758	3,499	3,994	4,101	4,219	4,252	82.3	39
6,209	6,071	6,161	6,108	6,124	6,304	6,625	7,058	86.0	40
5,524	5,469	5,533	5,436	5,451	5,618	5,901	6,312	86.1	41
685	602	628	672	673	686	724	746	72.7	42
5,140	5,211	5,371	5,339	5,299	5,280	5,433	5,486	88.5	43
2,720	2,740	2,846	2,850	2,867	2,882	2,940	2,989	86.2	44
2,420	2,471	2,525	2,489	2,432	2,398	2,493	2,497	90.2	45
1,243	1,285	1,321	1,337	1,326	1,456	1,424	1,446	83.8	46
951	979	1,005	1,008	1,034	1,163	1,159	1,204	77.7	47
292	306	316	329	292	293	265	242	73.6	48
15,219	14,941	15,138	14,961	15,221	15,547	15,709	15,803	91.3	49
7,358	7,339	7,584	7,595	7,719	7,682	7,676	7,690	95.1	50
7,861	7,602	7,554	7,366	7,502	7,865	8,033	8,113	82.7	51
53,144	55,422	57,833	58,153	57,086	58,727	61,102	62,590	81.9	52
40,779	42,617	44,376	44,472	43,351	44,824	46,606	47,857	81.1	53
12,365	12,805	13,457	13,681	13,735	13,903	14,496	14,733	81.4	54
4,214	4,336	4,511	4,472	4,454	4,360	4,488	4,438	91.0	55
4,146	4,261	4,427	4,392	4,376	4,291	4,417	4,354	91.1	56
68	75	84	80	78	69	71	84	81.0	57
196,418	198,071	204,160	212,354	218,493	227,409	235,285	241,640	81.3	58
145,070	145,752	150,865	156,269	160,140	166,730	172,299	178,161	81.4	59
51,348	52,319	53,295	56,085	58,353	60,679	62,986	63,479	80.9	60

TABLE 10.—WAGE EARNERS, MALES AND FEMALES,

[The month of maximum employment for each industry is indicated

	INDUSTRY.	Average number employed during year.	NUMBER EMPLOYED ON 15TH DAY OF THE MONTH OR NEAREST REPRESENTATIVE DAY.			
			January.	February.	March.	April.
1	Electroplating	3,024	2,623	2,616	2,735	2,844
2	Male	2,882	2,490	2,480	2,599	2,708
3	Female	142	133	136	136	136
4	Emery and other abrasive wheels	5,601	5,711	5,618	5,530	5,450
5	Male	4,775	4,819	4,774	4,714	4,676
6	Female	826	892	844	816	774
7	Enameling	694	582	567	629	637
8	Male	539	439	429	471	476
9	Female	155	143	138	158	161
10	Engines, steam, gas, and water	77,617	90,102	85,232	83,076	74,983
11	Male	75,773	87,177	83,151	81,164	73,293
12	Female	1,844	2,925	2,081	1,912	1,690
13	Engravers' materials	174	148	154	159	158
14	Male	174	148	154	159	158
15	Female					
16	Engraving and diesinking	1,878	1,628	1,694	1,711	1,727
17	Male	1,710	1,501	1,553	1,566	1,570
18	Female	168	127	141	145	157
19	Engraving, steel and copper plate, including plate printing.	7,014	6,462	6,551	6,530	6,776
20	Male	4,273	3,996	4,030	4,044	4,152
21	Female	2,741	2,466	2,521	2,486	2,624
22	Engraving, wood	235	223	227	226	238
23	Male	233	221	225	224	236
24	Female	2	2	2	2	2
25	Envelopes	8,129	7,934	7,891	7,901	7,845
26	Male	3,176	3,078	3,085	3,098	3,077
27	Female	4,953	4,856	4,806	4,803	4,768
28	Explosives	9,249	11,809	9,903	9,509	8,922
29	Male	9,059	11,362	9,654	9,239	8,776
30	Female	190	447	249	270	146
31	Fancy articles, not elsewhere specified	13,961	11,871	12,058	12,843	13,473
32	Male	6,707	5,886	5,985	6,217	6,559
33	Female	7,254	5,985	6,073	6,626	6,914
34	Feathers and plumes	3,504	3,105	3,322	3,601	3,804
35	Male	461	372	398	450	574
36	Female	3,043	2,733	2,924	3,151	3,230
37	Felt goods	5,236	5,076	5,065	4,896	4,888
38	Male	4,052	3,921	3,875	3,814	3,816
39	Female	1,184	1,155	1,190	1,082	1,072
40	Ferroalloys	2,344	2,933	2,692	2,378	2,267
41	Male	2,335	2,924	2,683	2,369	2,258
42	Female	9	9	9	9	9
43	Fertilizers	26,296	27,808	31,043	38,357	36,465
44	Male	25,888	27,289	30,530	37,881	36,038
45	Female	408	519	513	476	427
46	Files	5,767	6,251	6,025	5,728	5,573
47	Male	4,973	5,360	5,147	4,924	4,838
48	Female	794	891	878	804	735
49	Firearms	11,287	13,428	12,369	11,606	11,022
50	Male	10,171	11,806	10,966	10,362	9,878
51	Female	1,116	1,622	1,403	1,244	1,144
52	Fire extinguishers, chemical	777	981	770	834	612
53	Male	575	698	574	605	459
54	Female	202	283	196	229	153
55	Fireworks	1,222	1,141	1,188	1,260	1,283
56	Male	690	638	656	676	701
57	Female	532	503	532	584	582
58	Flags and banners	1,065	1,337	1,175	1,113	1,172
59	Male	253	313	252	249	263
60	Female	812	1,024	923	864	909
61	Flavoring extracts	2,188	1,851	1,846	1,919	1,994
62	Male	1,053	921	919	985	985
63	Female	1,135	930	927	934	1,009

EMPLOYED EACH MONTH, BY INDUSTRIES: 1919—Continued.

by bold-faced figures and that of minimum employment by *italic* figures.]

May.	June.	July.	August.	September.	October.	November.	December.	Per cent minimum is of maximum.	
2,962	2,941	3,080	3,165	3,208	3,270	3,408	**3,436**	76.1	1
2,820	2,807	2,938	3,021	3,062	3,115	3,258	**3,286**	75.5	2
142	134	142	144	146	155	150	150	85.8	3
5,293	5,280	*5,172*	5,374	5,567	5,830	6,044	**6,343**	81.5	4
4,536	4,489	*4,394*	4,573	4,766	5,002	5,114	**5,443**	80.7	5
757	791	778	801	801	828	**930**	900	81.4	6
666	677	683	750	748	781	**806**	802	70.3	7
516	528	537	589	598	615	**637**	633	67.3	8
150	149	146	161	150	166	**169**	169	81.7	9
70,193	70,452	72,749	73,265	74,811	76,852	78,240	81,449	77.9	10
68,563	68,833	71,175	71,760	73,190	75,092	76,418	79,460	78.6	11
1,630	1,619	1,574	*1,505*	1,621	1,760	1,822	1,989	51.5	12
167	168	173	185	182	192	194	**208**	71.2	13
167	168	173	185	182	192	194	**208**	71.2	14
									15
1,744	1,817	1,904	2,036	2,026	2,030	2,098	**2,121**	76.8	16
1,582	1,642	1,726	1,847	1,847	1,858	1,907	**1,921**	78.1	17
162	175	178	189	179	172	191	200	63.5	18
6,927	6,998	7,040	6,978	7,103	7,288	7,572	**7,943**	81.4	19
4,219	4,299	4,363	4,332	4,372	4,299	4,447	**4,723**	84.6	20
2,708	2,699	2,677	2,646	2,731	2,989	3,125	**3,220**	76.6	21
242	242	**246**	234	234	239	234	235	90.7	22
240	240	**244**	232	232	237	232	233	90.6	23
2	2	2	2	2	2	2	2	100.0	24
7,858	7,852	8,100	8,100	8,274	8,461	8,565	**8,767**	89.5	25
3,067	3,089	3,182	3,200	3,239	3,273	3,322	**3,402**	90.2	26
4,791	*4,763*	4,918	4,900	5,035	5,188	5,243	**5,365**	88.8	27
8,721	*8,605*	8,706	8,937	8,994	8,946	8,984	8,952	72.9	28
8,578	*8,469*	8,585	8,820	8,854	8,788	8,804	8,779	74.5	29
143	136	121	*117*	140	158	180	173	26.2	30
13,514	13,762	14,271	14,620	14,859	15,137	15,464	**15,660**	75.8	31
6,572	6,664	6,770	6,961	7,075	7,124	7,256	**7,415**	79.4	32
6,942	7,098	7,501	7,659	7,784	8,013	8,208	**8,245**	72.6	33
3,791	3,533	3,636	3,645	3,680	3,415	3,253	3,263	81.6	34
572	461	444	466	454	461	439	441	64.8	35
3,219	3,072	3,192	3,179	3,226	2,954	2,814	2,822	84.6	36
4,874	5,012	5,128	5,424	5,508	5,529	5,688	**5,744**	84.9	37
3,801	3,919	3,982	4,207	4,266	4,247	4,365	**4,411**	86.2	38
1,073	1,093	1,146	1,217	1,242	1,282	1,323	**1,333**	80.4	39
2,096	2,066	*1,879*	1,971	2,103	2,415	2,572	2,756	64.1	40
2,087	2,056	*1,870*	1,962	2,095	2,406	2,563	2,747	64.0	41
9	10	9	9	*8*	9	9	9	80.0	42
23,856	*21,071*	21,731	22,500	25,205	22,028	21,897	23,591	54.9	43
23,521	*20,791*	21,459	22,230	24,813	21,552	21,408	23,144	54.9	44
335	280	272	*270*	392	476	489	447	52.0	45
5,339	*5,298*	5,355	5,663	5,821	5,943	6,043	6,165	84.8	46
4,627	*4,606*	4,655	4,899	5,025	5,116	5,184	5,295	85.9	47
712	*692*	700	764	796	827	859	870	77.7	48
10,885	10,545	*10,194*	10,683	10,926	11,284	11,251	11,251	75.9	49
9,828	9,602	*9,239*	9,696	9,940	10,273	10,237	10,225	78.3	50
1,057	*943*	955	987	986	1,011	1,014	1,026	58.1	51
614	624	728	825	871	839	824	802	62.4	52
467	478	542	600	629	623	616	609	65.8	53
147	*146*	186	225	242	216	208	193	51.6	54
1,360	**1,383**	1,178	1,203	1,174	*1,129*	1,182	1,183	81.6	55
782	**817**	673	691	687	643	645	671	78.1	56
578	566	505	512	487	*486*	537	512	83.2	57
1,149	1,155	1,027	930	*878*	922	922	1,000	65.7	58
266	268	267	269	216	233	228	*212*	67.7	59
883	887	760	*661*	662	689	694	788	64.6	60
2,189	2,450	2,502	**2,535**	2,360	2,305	2,158	2,147	72.8	61
1,019	1,078	1,120	1,124	1,117	**1,181**	1,095	1,092	77.8	62
1,170	1,372	1,382	**1,411**	1,243	1,124	1,063	1 055	65.7	63

TABLE 10.—WAGE EARNERS, MALES AND FEMALES,

[The month of maximum employment for each industry is indicated

	INDUSTRY.	Average number employed during year.	NUMBER EMPLOYED ON 15TH DAY OF THE MONTH OR NEAREST REPRESENTATIVE DAY.			
			January.	February.	March.	April.
1	Flax and hemp, dressed................	420	*350*	364	387	391
2	Male......................	396	*339*	355	375	373
3	Female.....................	24	11	*9*	12	18
4	Flour-mill and gristmill products...........	45,481	45,123	42,837	*42,179*	43,056
5	Male........................	44,490	44,026	41,950	*41,312*	42,180
6	Female....................	991	1,097	887	867	876
7	Food preparations, not elsewhere specified.	30,365	31,006	29,592	28,346	*28,166*
8	Male........................	21,486	21,685	20,824	20,157	*20,010*
9	Female....................	8,879	9,321	8,768	8,189	*8,156*
10	Foundry and machine-shop products......	482,767	491,403	470,634	462,983	459,435
11	Male........................	466,556	473,526	454,350	447,477	443,846
12	Female....................	16,211	**17,877**	16,284	15,506	15,589
13	Foundry supplies......................	906	922	879	855	*850*
14	Male......................	882	903	858	831	*826*
15	Female....................	24	*19*	21	24	24
16	Fuel, manufactured..................	171	185	121	115	*111*
17	Male......................	165	184	121	112	*105*
18	Female....................	6	*1*	....	3	6
19	Fur goods......................:	13.639	*10 947*	11,358	12,419	12,176
20	Male......................	8,700	*6,596*	7,108	8,015	7,868
21	Female....................	4,939	4,351	*4,250*	4,404	4,308
22	Furnishing goods, men's...............	18,944	18,607	18,724	*17,636*	17,710
23	Male......................	3,256	3,227	3,219	3,120	3,123
24	Female....................	15,688	15,380	15,505	*14,516*	14,587
25	Furniture.........................	138,331	*122,680*	124,413	127,610	128,025
26	Male......................	126,471	*111,778*	113,689	116,862	117,112
27	Female....................	11,860	10,902	*10,724*	10,748	10,913
28	Furs, dressed......................	5,075	*4,012*	4,429	4,867	4,564
29	Male......................	4,282	*3,430*	3,783	4,148	3,820
30	Female....................	793	*582*	646	719	744
31	Galvanizing.......................	1,665	**1,833**	1,746	1,769	1,677
32	Male......................	1,579	**1,746**	1,659	1,681	1,595
33	Female....................	86	87	87	88	*82*
34	Gas and electric fixtures................	9,795	8,890	8,937	9,102	9,250
35	Male......................	7,578	*6,702*	6,805	6,963	7,139
36	Female....................	2,217	2,188	2,132	2,139	2,111
37	Gas, illuminating and heating............	42,908	43,793	42,220	*41,549*	41,750
38	Male......................	42,659	43,483	41,932	*41,293*	41,491
39	Female....................	249	310	288	256	259
40	Gas machines and gas and water meters...	5,589	**5,972**	5,439	5,262	5,133
41	Male......................	5,146	5,315	4,899	4,777	4,686
42	Female....................	443	**657**	540	485	447
43	Glass.........................	77,520	74,571	78,413	79,693	79,450
44	Male......................	68,140	65,438	69,132	70,234	70,003
45	Female....................	9,380	9,133	9,281	9,459	9,447
46	Glass, cutting, staining, and ornamenting..	6,480	*5,423*	5,744	5,996	6,068
47	Male......................	4,821	*3,965*	4,215	4,438	4,491
48	Female....................	1,659	*1,458*	1,529	1,558	1,577
49	Gloves and mittens, cloth, not including gloves made in textile mills.	8,986	**11,069**	10,118	9,053	7,947
50	Male......................	1,130	1,279	1,172	1,082	*980*
51	Female....................	7,856	**9,790**	8,946	7,971	6,967
52	Gloves and mittens, leather.............	10,685	10,175	10,044	*9,984*	10,046
53	Male......................	4,549	*4,151*	4,199	4,207	4,257
54	Female....................	6,136	6,024	5,845	*5,777*	5,789
55	Glucose and starch.................	7,795	8,916	8,103	6,787	6,738
56	Male......................	7,019	7,611	7,165	6,225	6,243
57	Female....................	776	1,305	938	562	*495*
58	Glue, not elsewhere specified.............	4,264	4,377	4,454	4,448	**4,478**
59	Male......................	3,798	3,899	3,971	3,976	**3,994**
60	Female....................	466	478	483	472	484
61	Gold and silver, leaf and foil.............	950	933	935	926	923
62	Male......................	444	437	431	433	433
63	Female......................	506	496	504	493	490

EMPLOYED EACH MONTH, BY INDUSTRIES: 1919—Continued.

by **bold-faced** figures and that of minimum employment by *italic* figures.]

NUMBER EMPLOYED ON 15TH DAY OF THE MONTH OR NEAREST REPRESENTATIVE DAY—continued.								Per cent minimum is of maximum.	
May.	June.	July.	August.	September.	October.	November.	December.		
397	442	387	427	453	441	487	**514**	68.1	1
371	417	359	398	426	408	451	**480**	70.6	2
26	25	28	29	27	33	**36**	34	25.0	3
43,018	42,261	43,434	46,941	48,822	49,378	49,330	**49,393**	85.4	4
42,212	41,447	42,609	45,889	47,600	48,231	48,183	**48,241**	85.6	5
806	814	825	1,052	**1,222**	1,147	1,147	1,152	66.0	6
28,716	28,969	29,935	31,105	31,516	32,243	**32,727**	32,059	86.1	7
20,203	20,387	21,313	22,053	22,488	22,968	**23,047**	22,697	86.8	8
8,513	8,582	8,622	9,052	9,028	9,275	**9,680**	9,362	84.3	9
454,222	456,529	471,149	482,050	491,802	503,709	518,850	**530,438**	85.6	10
438,843	441,299	455,248	465,996	475,375	487,138	502,020	**513,554**	85.5	11
15,379	*15,230*	15,901	16,054	16,427	16,571	16,830	16,884	85.2	12
853	880	874	898	932	958	**988**	983	86.0	13
829	852	849	871	908	934	**963**	960	85.8	14
24	**28**	25	27	24	24	25	23	67.9	15
133	133	162	149	167	207	270	**299**	37.1	16
128	124	159	139	165	201	262	**289**	36.3	17
5	9	*12*	10	2	6	8	10	....	18
12,475	13,500	14,031	14,599	15,366	15,774	**15,820**	15,203	69.2	19
8,123	8,882	9,248	9,480	9,870	**9,939**	9,855	9,416	66.4	20
4,352	4,618	4,783	5,119	5,496	5,835	**5,965**	5,787	71.2	21
17,923	18,443	18,867	19,331	19,194	19,857	**20,577**	20,459	85.7	22
3,086	3,188	3,244	3,351	3,273	3,367	**3,468**	3,406	89.0	23
14,837	15,255	15,623	15,980	15,921	16,490	**17,109**	17,053	84.8	24
131,776	134,868	140,073	145,416	145,516	149,779	153,567	**156,249**	78.5	25
120,355	123,247	128,078	133,160	133,129	136,929	140,240	**143,073**	78.1	26
11,421	11,621	11,995	12,256	12,387	12,850	**13,327**	13,176	80.5	27
5,124	5,416	5,662	**5,670**	5,594	5,350	5,283	4,929	70.8	28
4,328	4,591	**4,797**	4,763	4,708	4,487	4,394	4,135	71.5	29
796	825	865	**907**	886	863	889	794	64.2	30
1,694	1,666	1,635	1,644	1,613	*1,557*	1,563	1,583	84.9	31
1,607	1,581	1,547	1,560	1,528	*1,470*	1,474	1,500	84.2	32
87	85	88	84	85	87	**89**	83	92.1	33
9,289	9,366	9,773	10,067	10,113	10,594	10,954	**11,205**	79.3	34
7,179	7,258	7,652	7,903	7,906	8,211	8,479	**8,739**	76.7	35
2,110	*2,108*	2,121	2,164	2,207	2,383	**2,475**	2,466	85.2	36
42,122	42,338	43,237	43,231	42,554	43,754	44,068	**44,280**	93.8	37
41,879	42,114	42,967	42,972	42,298	43,543	43,860	**44,076**	93.7	38
243	224	270	259	256	211	208	*204*	65.8	39
5,051	5,606	5,718	5,809	5,737	5,688	5,747	**5,906**	84.6	40
4,635	5,167	5,282	5,377	5,348	5,323	5,395	**5,548**	83.5	41
416	439	436	432	389	365	*352*	358	53.6	42
78,191	74,719	*65,055*	68,993	78,072	83,190	**85,416**	84,477	76.2	43
68,704	65,236	*57,164*	60,731	68,575	73,194	**75,037**	74,232	76.2	44
9,487	9,483	*7,891*	8,262	9,497	9,996	**10,379**	10,245	76.0	45
6,185	6,333	6,510	6,849	6,855	7,112	7,302	**7,383**	73.5	46
4,573	4,730	4,876	5,139	5,142	5,295	5,460	**5,528**	71.7	47
1,612	1,603	1,634	1,710	1,713	1,817	1,842	**1,855**	78.6	48
7,605	7,896	8,250	8,545	8,518	8,886	9,099	10,846	68.7	49
983	1,032	1,119	1,121	1,130	1,155	1,173	**1,334**	73.5	50
6,622	6,864	7,131	7,424	7,388	7,731	7,926	9,512	67.6	51
10,190	10,515	10,887	11,125	11,042	11,286	11,303	**11,623**	85.9	52
4,374	4,534	4,670	4,780	4,700	4,879	4,842	**4,995**	83.1	53
5,816	5,981	6,217	6,345	6,342	6,407	6,461	**6,628**	87.2	54
7,055	7,603	*5,989*	7,345	**9,116**	9,089	8,690	8,109	65.7	55
6,382	6,768	*5,472*	6,702	8,137	**8,243**	7,877	7,403	66.4	56
673	835	517	643	**979**	846	813	706	37.9	57
4,323	4,181	*3,812*	4,017	4,098	4,308	4,398	4,274	85.1	58
3,863	3,736	*3,414*	3,600	3,624	3,816	3,864	3,819	85.5	59
460	445	*398*	417	474	492	**534**	455	74.5	60
920	*890*	929	935	964	989	1,021	**1,035**	86.0	61
430	*421*	433	435	447	457	481	**490**	85.9	62
490	*469*	496	500	517	532	540	**545**	86.1	63

TABLE **10.**—WAGE EARNERS, MALES AND FEMALES,

[The month of maximum employment for each industry is indicated

	INDUSTRY.	Average number employed during year.	NUMBER EMPLOYED ON 15TH DAY OF THE MONTH OR NEAREST REPRESENTATIVE DAY.			
			January.	February.	March.	April.
1	Gold and silver, reducing and refining, not from the ore.	644	628	629	*615*	633
2	Male	603	581	584	*577*	597
3	Female	41	**47**	45	38	36
4	Graphite, ground and refined	497	474	478	*454*	525
5	Male	477	454	462	439	513
6	Female	20	20	16	15	*12*
7	Grease and tallow, not including lubricating greases.	6,647	**6,815**	6,724	6,667	6,613
8	Male	6,430	**6,572**	6,503	6,440	6,386
9	Female	217	**243**	221	227	227
10	Grindstones	674	662	705	719	**775**
11	Male	670	658	701	715	**771**
12	Female	4	4	4	4	**4**
13	Haircloth	425	385	391	386	*373*
14	Male	219	203	209	195	*190*
15	Female	206	*182*	*182*	191	183
16	Hair work	1,084	*987*	1,025	1,045	1,039
17	Male	282	*255*	270	272	270
18	Female	302	*732*	755	773	769
19	Hammocks	64	56	58	66	65
20	Male	26	*21*	*21*	25	26
21	Female	38	35	37	41	39
22	Hand stamps	1,719	*1,667*	1,688	1,706	1,708
23	Male	1,432	*1,389*	1,395	1,413	1,433
24	Female	287	278	293	293	275
25	Hardware	42,505	*39,267*	39,531	39,864	40,185
26	Male	34,903	*32,106*	32,436	32,735	33,017
27	Female	7,602	7,161	7,095	7,129	7,168
28	Hardware, saddlery	3,675	3,669	3,687	3,678	*3,569*
29	Male	3,077	3,088	3,107	3,086	*2,978*
30	Female	598	581	580	592	591
31	Hat and cap materials	3,009	2,472	2,625	2,694	*2,100*
32	Male	1,875	1,594	1,705	1,742	*1,228*
33	Female	1,134	878	920	952	872
34	Hats and caps, other than felt, straw, and wool.	7,539	6,976	7,002	6,820	6,866
35	Male	4,916	4,555	4,591	4,513	4,587
36	Female	2,623	2,421	2,411	2,307	*2,279*
37	Hats, fur-felt	18,510	16,531	16,712	16,879	*16,353*
38	Male	13,478	12,014	12,211	12,305	*11,958*
39	Female	5,032	4,517	4,501	4,574	*4,395*
40	Hats, straw	7,302	8,266	**8,494**	8,471	7,891
41	Male	2,846	3,144	**3,182**	3,141	2,979
42	Female	4,456	5,122	5,312	**5,330**	4,912
43	Hats, wool-felt	1,448	*916*	1,061	1,085	1,236
44	Male	1,015	*614*	709	737	888
45	Female	433	*302*	352	348	348
46	Hones and whetstones	212	198	*197*	206	209
47	Male	189	*179*	*179*	186	186
48	Female	23	19	18	20	23
49	Horseshoes, not made in steel works or rolling mills.	744	**915**	825	758	714
50	Male	732	**895**	805	739	703
51	Female	12	**20**	**20**	19	11
52	House-furnishing goods, not elsewhere specified.	7,853	*6,576*	6,846	7,034	7,024
53	Male	3,151	*2,671*	2,795	2,873	2,870
54	Female	4,702	*3,905*	4,051	4,161	4,154
55	Ice, manufactured	30,247	*20,796*	21,408	23,275	27,310
56	Male	30,005	*20,604*	21,213	23,056	27,102
57	Female	242	*192*	195	219	208
58	Ink, printing	1,988	1,923	1,910	*1,886*	1,917
59	Male	1,921	1,852	1,839	*1,820*	1,853
60	Female	67	**71**	**71**	66	64

EMPLOYED EACH MONTH, BY INDUSTRIES: 1919—Continued.

by bold-faced figures and that of minimum employment by *italic* figures.]

NUMBER EMPLOYED ON 15TH DAY OF THE MONTH OR NEAREST REPRESENTATIVE DAY—continued.								Per cent minimum is of maximum.	
May.	June.	July.	August.	September.	October.	November.	December.		
622	·632	641	645	664	665	664	**690**	89.1	1
586	599	596	601	617	626	626	**646**	89.3	2
36	*33*	45	44	47	39	38	44	70.2	3
538	465	463	497	**575**	510	518	*467*	79.0	4
525	447	445	477	**553**	482	490	*437*	79.0	5
13	18	18	20	22	28	28	30	40.0	6
6,490	6,527	6,622	**6,853**	6,753	6,596	6,546	6,558	94.7	7
6,265	6,329	6,411	**6,640**	6,541	6,390	6,333	6,350	94.4	8
225	*198*	211	213	212	206	213	208	81.5	9
761	691	685	668	656	603	607	*556*	71.7	10
757	687	681	664	652	599	603	*552*	71.6	11
4	4	4	4	4	4	4	4	100.0	12
387	414	436	458	451	478	468	473	78.0	13
196	212	226	230	227	246	245	249	76.3	14
191	202	210	228	224	232	223	224	78.4	15
1,079	1,094	1,118	1,101	1,120	1,132	**1,144**	1,124	86.3	16
282	286	290	283	283	296	299	298	85.3	17
797	808	828	818	837	836	845	826	88.6	18
67	81	**82**	69	56	54	*53*	61	64.6	19
25	33	**34**	33	24	22	22	26	61.8	20
42	**48**	**48**	36	32	32	*31*	35	64.6	21
1,706	1,697	1,738	1,674	1,738	1,754	**1,776**	**1,776**	93.9	22
1,424	1,404	1,443	1,408	1,468	1,450	1,482	1,475	93.7	23
282	293	295	*266*	270	304	294	301	87.5	24
40,566	41,112	42,512	44,081	44,088	45,136	46,480	**47,238**	83.1	25
33,428	33,929	35,024	36,338	36,200	36,941	37,969	**38,713**	82.9	26
7,138	7,183	7,488	7,743	7,888	8,195	8,511	**8,525**	83.2	27
3,604	3,620	3,665	3,718	3,722	3,728	*3,335*	**3,605**	93.1	28
3,059	3,027	3,080	2,996	3,119	3,110	3,226	3,048	92.3	29
545	593	585	**722**	603	618	609	557	75.5	30
2,168	3,007	3,349	3,473	3,502	3,510	3,595	**3,613**	58.1	31
1,314	1,892	2,069	2,158	2,181	2,159	2,213	**2,245**	54.7	32
854	1,115	1,280	1,315	1,321	1,351	**1,382**	1,368	61.8	33
7,215	7,249	*6,789*	7,691	8,118	8,523	8,601	**8,618**	78.8	34
4,789	4,775	*4,350*	5,009	5,259	5,498	5,525	**5,541**	78.5	35
2,426	2,474	2,439	2,682	2,859	3,025	3,076	3,077	74.1	36
16,928	17,990	19,269	19,896	19,561	20,420	20,634	**20,947**	78.1	37
12,363	13,221	14,124	14,571	14,307	14,794	14,829	**15,039**	79.5	38
4,565	4,769	5,145	5,325	5,254	5,626	5,805	5,908	74.4	39
6,918	6,572	*5,808*	6,075	6,474	6,837	7,463	8,355	68.4	40
2,769	2,690	*2,457*	2,523	2,590	2,647	2,876	3,154	77.2	41
4,149	3,882	*3,351*	3,552	3,884	4,190	4,587	5,201	62.9	42
1,499	1,690	1,730	**1,923**	1,818	1,449	1,497	1,472	47.6	43
1,091	1,240	1,252	**1,394**	1,290	978	1,008	979	44.0	44
408	450	478	**529**	528	471	489	493	57.1	45
220	224	215	**225**	219	206	201	224	87.6	46
196	198	188	**200**	193	181	184	198	89.5	47
24	26	27	25	26	25	*17*	26	40.0	48
701	724	*602*	655	715	750	730	839	65.8	49
689	714	*594*	647	707	742	720	829	66.4	50
12	10	*8*	*8*	*8*	*8*	10	10	40.0	51
7,283	7,784	8,385	8,365	8,459	8,689	8,872	**8,919**	73.7	52
2,933	3,145	3,295	3,299	3,382	3,459	3,528	**3,562**	75.0	53
4,350	4,639	5,090	5,066	5,077	5,230	5,344	5,357	72.9	54
31,644	37,788	**41,078**	40,977	37,999	31,834	25,631	23,224	50.6	55
31,370	37,524	**40,773**	40,673	37,716	31,615	25,413	23,001	50.5	56
274	264	**305**	304	283	219	218	223	63.0	57
1,929	1,951	1,938	1,954	2,005	2,103	2,132	**2,188**	86.2	58
1,866	1,886	1,874	1,891	1,942	2,031	2,083	**2,115**	86.1	59
63	65	64	*63*	*63*	72	69	73	86.3	60

TABLE 10.—WAGE EARNERS, MALES AND FEMALES,

[The month of maximum employment for each industry is indicated

	INDUSTRY.	Average number employed during year.	NUMBER EMPLOYED ON 15TH DAY OF THE MONTH OR NEAREST REPRESENTATIVE DAY.			
			January.	February.	March.	April.
1	Ink, writing	702	660	*638*	695	668
2	Male	357	336	*332*	345	*332*
3	Female	345	324	*306*	350	336
4	Instruments, professional and scientific	15,931	16,230	**16,274**	15,602	*15,568*
5	Male	12,222	12,385	12,340	11,921	11,878
6	Female	3,709	3,845	**3,934**	3,681	3,690
7	Iron and steel, blast furnaces	41,660	**51,467**	47,415	44,839	40,399
8	Male	41,606	**51,409**	47,357	44,779	40,342
9	Female	54	58	58	**60**	57
10	Iron and steel, steel works and rolling mills.	375,088	**441,560**	416,541	392,803	367,514
11	Male	371,604	**437,472**	412,696	389,192	364,164
12	Female	3,484	**4,088**	3,845	3,611	3,350
13	Iron and steel, bolts, nuts, washers, and rivets, not made in rolling mills.	17,967	**19,535**	18,974	18,594	17,834
14	Male	15,430	**16,868**	16,422	16,097	15,366
15	Female	2,537	2,667	2,552	2,497	2,468
16	Iron and steel, cast-iron pipe	12,625	10,615	9,924	*9,753*	10,529
17	Male	12,573	10,569	9,883	*9,718*	10,494
18	Female	52	46	41	*35*	*35*
19	Iron and steel, doors and shutters	2,077	2,295	1,939	1,893	*1,792*
20	Male	2,047	2,265	1,910	1,862	*1,764*
21	Female	30	30	29	31	28
22	Iron and steel, forgings, not made in steel works or rolling mills.	28,391	**30,564**	29,072	28,405	27,864
23	Male	27,484	**29,528**	28,129	27,532	27,016
24	Female	907	1,036	943	873	848
25	Iron and steel, nails and spikes, cut and wrought, including wire nails, not made in steel works or rolling mills.	3,355	**3,610**	3,546	3,515	3,437
26	Male	2,414	2,567	2,532	2,492	2,468
27	Female	941	**1,043**	1,014	1,023	969
28	Iron and steel, tempering and welding	1,835	1,702	*1,625*	1,641	1,704
29	Male	1,808	1,676	*1,596*	1,613	1,677
30	Female	27	26	29	28	27
31	Iron and steel, wrought pipe	10,426	10,222	9,981	9,884	9,688
32	Male	10,325	10,131	9,883	9,788	9,573
33	Female	101	91	98	96	115
34	Ivory, shell, and bone work, not including combs and hairpins.	842	806	811	843	811
35	Male	638	606	604	630	612
36	Female	204	200	207	213	199
37	Japanning	295	*235*	241	250	271
38	Male	278	*220*	226	235	254
39	Female	17	15	15	15	17
40	Jewelry	30,871	*27,152*	28,241	29,295	30,020
41	Male	21,419	*19,152*	19,852	20,456	21,003
42	Female	9,452	*8,000*	8,389	8,839	9,017
43	Jewelry and instrument cases	2,734	*2,389*	2,446	2,532	2,602
44	Male	1,136	*1,034*	1,040	1,085	1,109
45	Female	1,598	*1,355*	1,406	1,447	1,493
46	Jute goods	7,138	6,895	6,747	6,708	*6,702*
47	Male	3,240	3,117	3,062	*3,027*	3,047
48	Female	3,898	3,778	3,685	3,681	*3,655*
49	Knit goods	172,572	168,304	163,582	*160,438*	162,956
50	Male	49,891	47,982	45,926	*45,137*	46,709
51	Female	122,681	120,322	117,656	*115,301*	116,247
52	Labels and tags	5,227	4,808	*4,769*	4,772	4,819
53	Male	3,020	*2,760*	*2,760*	2,770	2,795
54	Female	2,207	2,048	2,009	*2,002*	2,024
55	Lamps and reflectors	8,360	7,497	7,492	*7,471*	7,598
56	Male	6,292	5,681	5,666	*5,631*	5,718
57	Female	2,068	*1,816*	1,826	1,840	1,880
58	Lapidary work	1,155	*1,031*	1,067	1,133	1,125
59	Male	961	*856*	889	950	939
60	Female	194	*175*	178	183	186

EMPLOYED EACH MONTH, BY INDUSTRIES: 1919—Continued.

by **bold-faced** figures and that of minimum employment by *italic* figures.]

NUMBER EMPLOYED ON 15TH DAY OF THE MONTH OR NEAREST REPRESENTATIVE DAY—continued.								Per cent minimum is of maximum.	
May.	June.	July.	August.	September.	October.	November.	December.		
684	670	720	**753**	728	**733**	745	710	84.7	1
341	343	352	372	370	393	**402**	366	82.6	2
343	327	368	**381**	358	360	343	344	80.3	3
15,675	15,791	16,111	15,810	15,925	15,989	16,266	15,931	95.7	4
11,853	12,083	12,347	12,158	12,286	12,338	**12,567**	12,508	94.3	5
3,822	3,708	3,764	3,652	3,639	3,651	3,699	*3,423*	87.0	6
37,939	37,533	40,412	42,394	42,897	*33,628*	39,022	41,975	65.3	7
37,886	37,481	40,359	42,342	42,845	*33,578*	38,971	41,925	65.3	8
53	52	53	52	52	52	51	*50*	83.3	9
354,721	360,584	383,212	387,965	377,275	*292,469*	343,312	383,100	66.2	10
351,398	357,286	379,815	384,516	373,960	*289,458*	339,822	379,469	66.2	11
3,323	3,298	3,397	3,449	3,315	*3,011*	3,490	3,631	73.7	12
16,895	17,273	17,596	17,888	17,773	*16,624*	18,204	18,414	85.1	13
14,468	14,763	15,105	15,285	15,255	*14,216*	15,587	15,728	84.3	14
2,427	2,510	2,491	2,603	2,518	*2,408*	2,617	**2,686**	89.7	15
11,268	11,482	13,006	13,781	14,625	15,478	15,454	**15,585**	62.6	16
11,227	11,434	12,960	13,723	14,570	15,407	15,385	**15,506**	62.7	17
41	48	46	58	55	71	69	79	44.3	18
1,977	1,890	1,952	2,104	2,178	2,271	**2,337**	2,296	76.7	19
1,950	1,864	1,927	2,076	2,147	2,236	**2,302**	2,261	76.6	20
27	26	*25*	28	31	35	35	35	71.4	21
27,193	*26,650*	27,182	27,706	27,677	28,642	29,622	30,115	87.2	22
26,426	*25,901*	26,361	26,845	26,726	27,659	28,584	29,101	87.7	23
767	*749*	821	861	951	983	**1,038**	1,014	72.2	24
3,312	3,316	3,311	*2,860*	2,887	3,305	3,555	3,606	79.2	25
2,395	2,434	2,412	*2,026*	2,041	2,377	2,588	**2,636**	76.9	26
917	882	899	*834*	846	928	967	970	80.0	27
1,777	1,852	1,922	1,976	1,919	1,839	1,995	**2,068**	78.6	28
1,751	1,829	1,898	1,952	1,891	1,810	1,968	**2,035**	78.4	29
26	*23*	24	24	28	29	27	33	69.7	30
9,352	10,139	10,837	11,309	**11,805**	9,775	10,491	11,629	79.2	31
9,240	10,015	10,734	11,191	**11,721**	9,689	10,398	11,537	78.8	32
112	**124**	103	118	*84*	86	93	92	67.7	33
779	*779*	857	879	891	872	882	**894**	87.1	34
585	595	656	666	679	661	674	**688**	85.0	35
194	*184*	201	**213**	212	211	208	206	86.4	36
269	265	301	312	329	344	**367**	356	64.0	37
255	250	285	294	311	323	**346**	337	63.6	38
14	15	16	18	18	**21**	21	19	66.7	39
30,856	31,322	32,281	32,462	32,243	31,380	32,383	**32,817**	82.7	40
21,569	21,975	22,573	**22,736**	22,325	21,179	21,968	22,240	84.2	41
9,287	9,347	9,708	9,726	9,918	10,201	10,415	**10,577**	75.6	42
2,598	2,676	2,764	2,823	2,919	2,994	3,008	**3,057**	78.1	43
1,099	1,138	1,148	1,137	1,181	1,205	**1,233**	1,223	83.9	44
1,499	1,538	1,616	1,686	1,738	1,789	1,775	**1,834**	73.9	45
6,753	7,099	7,337	**7,513**	7,495	7,485	7,427	7,495	89.2	46
3,078	3,239	3,343	3,404	3,375	3,395	3,368	**3,425**	88.4	47
3,675	3,860	3,994	4,109	**4,120**	4,090	4,059	4,070	88.7	48
166,713	168,617	173,887	177,339	177,244	181,315	184,046	**186,423**	86.1	49
48,291	49,445	50,709	51,885	51,576	52,759	53,651	**54,622**	82.6	50
118,422	119,172	123,178	125,454	125,668	128,556	130,395	**131,801**	87.5	51
5,012	5,111	5,280	5,462	5,489	5,571	5,704	**5,927**	80.5	52
2,921	2,960	3,031	3,161	3,179	3,218	3,293	**3,392**	81.4	53
2,091	2,151	2,249	2,301	2,310	2,353	2,411	**2,535**	79.0	54
7,796	7,971	8,455	9,014	9,093	9,189	9,261	**9,483**	78.8	55
5,862	6,021	6,359	6,850	6,824	6,865	6,889	**7,138**	78.9	56
1,934	1,950	2,096	2,164	2,269	2,324	**2,372**	2,345	76.6	57
1,142	1,182	1,180	1,175	1,195	**1,212**	1,206	1,212	85.1	58
953	993	990	981	994	**999**	990	998	85.7	59
189	189	190	194	201	213	**216**	214	81.0	60

TABLE 10.—WAGE EARNERS, MALES AND FEMALES,

[The month of maximum employment for each industry is indicated

	INDUSTRY.	Average number employed during year.	NUMBER EMPLOYED ON 15TH DAY OF THE MONTH OR NEAREST REPRESENTATIVE DAY.			
			January.	February.	March.	April.
1	Lard, not made in slaughtering and meat-packing establishments.	13	13	13	13	13
2	Male....................................	11	11	11	11	11
3	Female.................................	2	2	2	2	2
4	Lasts....................................	2,910	2,301	2,459	2,619	2,777
5	Male....................................	2,825	2,237	2,389	2,539	2,682
6	Female.................................	85	64	70	80	95
7	Lead, bar, pipe, and sheet............	852	832	762	739	768
8	Male....................................	846	825	753	732	763
9	Female.................................	6	7	9	7	5
10	Leather goods, not elsewhere specified.....	8,945	8,019	8,082	8,097	8,314
11	Male....................................	5,568	4,937	5,039	5,038	5,205
12	Female.................................	3,377	3,082	3,043	3,059	3,109
13	Leather, tanned, curried, and finished.....	72,476	65,519	65,515	65,979	67,423
14	Male....................................	66,541	60,032	60,324	60,925	62,231
15	Female.................................	5,935	5,487	5,191	5,054	5,192
16	Lime....................................	11,405	10,442	10,370	10,844	11,515
17	Male....................................	11,393	10,432	10,359	10,833	11,506
18	Female.................................	12	10	11	11	9
19	Linen goods.............................	1,890	1,809	1,871	1,856	1,886
20	Male....................................	883	840	881	869	896
21	Female.................................	1,007	969	990	987	990
22	Liquors, distilled.......................	1,380	1,572	1,439	1,285	1,157
23	Male....................................	1,342	1,478	1,356	1,244	1,099
24	Female.................................	38	94	83	41	58
25	Liquors, malt...........................	34,259	31,991	31,712	32,291	33,605
26	Male....................................	33,901	31,628	31,346	31,898	33,212
27	Female.................................	358	363	366	393	393
28	Liquors, vinous.........................	1,011	824	840	924	831
29	Male....................................	939	757	771	849	756
30	Female.................................	72	67	69	75	75
31	Lithographing...........................	15,618	14,743	14,746	14,962	15,046
32	Male....................................	12,421	11,594	11,631	11,825	12,043
33	Female.................................	3,197	3,149	3,115	3,137	3,003
34	Locomotives, not made by railroad companies.	26,715	35,659	32,843	32,031	29,667
35	Male....................................	26,590	35,477	32,666	31,879	29,532
36	Female.................................	125	182	177	152	135
37	Looking-glass and picture frames..........	4,708	4,060	4,337	4,592	4,649
38	Male....................................	4,036	3,545	3,743	3,960	4,017
39	Female.................................	672	515	594	632	632
40	Lubricating greases......................	472	488	463	451	440
41	Male....................................	446	462	435	424	416
42	Female.................................	26	26	28	27	24
43	Lumber and timber products..............	480,945	427,802	428,806	444,868	440,965
44	Male....................................	476,543	423,406	424,410	440,470	436,565
45	Female.................................	4,402	4,396	4,396	4,398	4,400
46	Lumber, planing-mill products, not including planing mills connected with saw-mills.	86,956	74,409	74,362	75,377	78,617
47	Male....................................	84,815	72,308	72,463	73,439	76,588
48	Female.................................	2,141	2,101	1,899	1,938	2,029
49	Machine tools...........................	53,111	55,750	52,941	51,656	50,195
50	Male....................................	50,943	52,938	50,437	49,278	47,997
51	Female.................................	2,168	2,812	2,504	2,378	2,198
52	Malt....................................	1,352	1,045	1,147	1,246	1,343
53	Male....................................	1,346	1,040	1,143	1,241	1,339
54	Female.................................	6	5	4	5	4
55	Marble and stone work..................	32,768	25,308	25,604	28,177	31,447
56	Male....................................	32,671	25,207	25,504	28,068	31,340
57	Female.................................	97	101	100	109	107
58	Matches.................................	3,726	4,517	4,241	3,645	3,003
59	Male....................................	2,385	2,842	2,689	2,215	1,930
60	Female.................................	1,341	1,675	1,552	1,430	1,073

EMPLOYED EACH MONTH, BY INDUSTRIES: 1919—Continued.

by **bold-faced** figures and that of minimum employment by *italic* figures.]

NUMBER EMPLOYED ON 15TH DAY OF THE MONTH OR NEAREST REPRESENTATIVE DAY—continued.								Per cent minimum is of maximum.	
May.	June.	July.	August.	September.	October.	November.	December.		
13	13	13	13	13	13	13	13	100.0	1
11	11	11	11	11	11	11	11	100.0	2
2	2	2	2	2	2	2	2	100.0	3
2,975	3,055	3,108	3,146	2,981	3,065	3,176	**3,258**	70.6	4
2,878	2,959	3,016	3,044	2,906	2,985	3,093	**3,172**	70.5	5
97	96	92	**102**	75	80	83	86	62.7	6
794	858	883	**931**	911	905	**931**	910	79.4	7
783	851	878	**927**	907	901	**927**	905	79.0	8
11	7	5	4	4	4	4	5	36.4	9
8,458	8,575	9,012	9,240	9,328	9,973	**10,153**	10,089	79.0	10
5,276	5,344	5,588	5,770	5,801	6,227	**6,338**	6,253	77.9	11
3,182	3,231	3,424	3,470	3,527	3,746	3,815	**3,836**	79.3	12
69,655	72,725	72,902	77,202	77,586	77,855	78,341	**79,010**	82.9	13
64,104	66,821	66,995	70,678	71,008	71,291	71,703	**72,330**	82.9	14
5,551	5,904	5,907	6,524	6,578	6,564	**6,638**	6,630	76.1	15
11,572	11,306	11,445	12,034	**12,143**	11,869	11,809	11,511	85.4	16
11,562	11,295	11,435	12,024	**12,130**	11,856	11,795	11,489	85.4	17
10	11	10	10	13	13	14	22	40.9	18
1,864	*1,798*	1,908	1,863	1,855	1,911	1,980	**2,079**	86.5	19
848	828	875	877	874	892	956	960	86.2	20
1,016	970	1,033	986	981	1,019	1,024	**1,119**	86.6	21
1,121	*1,058*	1,122	1,293	1,458	1,569	1,652	**1,834**	57.7	22
1,062	990	1,115	1,286	1,451	1,560	1,644	**1,819**	54.4	23
59	68	7	7	7	9	8	15	7.4	24
34,848	38,092	**38,955**	38,756	36,025	34,478	31,168	*29,187*	74.9	25
34,458	37,712	**38,587**	38,342	35,663	34,173	30,867	*28,926*	75.0	26
390	380	368	**414**	362	305	301	*261*	63.0	27
820	759	*671*	875	1,385	**1,951**	1,380	872	34.4	28
746	686	*600*	814	1,314	**1,861**	1,308	806	32.2	29
74	73	71	*61*	71	90	72	66	67.8	30
15,141	15,420	15,844	16,000	16,121	16,179	16,364	**16,850**	87.5	31
12,122	12,373	12,720	12,858	12,863	12,768	12,897	**13,358**	86.8	32
3,019	3,047	3,124	3,142	3,258	3,411	3,467	**3,492**	86.0	33
28,094	26,011	25,707	26,322	23,778	20,376	20,255	*19,837*	55.6	34
27,969	25,894	25,595	26,228	23,674	20,274	20,157	*19,735*	55.6	35
125	117	112	*94*	104	102	98	102	51.6	36
4,686	4,676	4,831	4,761	4,806	4,949	**5,132**	5,017	79.1	37
4,060	4,013	4,148	4,041	4,051	4,188	**4,365**	4,301	81.2	38
626	663	683	720	755	761	**767**	716	67.1	39
452	447	470	490	**504**	499	486	474	87.3	40
425	423	443	461	**474**	**474**	461	454	87.8	41
27	24	27	29	**30**	25	25	*20*	66.7	42
450,884	454,835	469,977	494,725	523,450	543,075	543,298	**548,655**	78.0	43
446,483	450,433	465,575	490,322	519,046	538,669	538,890	**544,247**	77.8	44
4,401	4,402	4,402	4,403	4,404	4,406	**4,408**	**4,408**	99.7	45
83,346	87,636	91,450	93,768	94,483	96,074	**97,035**	96,915	76.6	46
81,224	85,507	89,167	91,591	92,265	93,762	**94,760**	94,706	76.3	47
2,122	2,129	2,283	2,177	2,218	**2,312**	2,275	2,209	82.1	48
49,515	50,166	51,074	52,498	52,713	55,190	56,994	**58,640**	84.4	49
47,391	48,122	49,092	50,532	50,761	53,187	54,979	**56,602**	83.7	50
2,124	2,044	1,982	1,966	*1,952*	2,003	2,015	2,038	69.4	51
1,508	1,664	1,628	**1,677**	1,387	1,266	1,215	1,098	62.3	52
1,504	1,660	1,617	**1,670**	1,380	1,258	1,209	1,091	62.3	53
4	4	**11**	7	7	8	6	7	36.4	54
33,333	34,518	35,528	35,942	**36,275**	**36,275**	35,900	34,909	69.8	55
33,229	34,419	35,426	35,856	**36,190**	36,185	35,811	34,817	69.7	56
104	99	102	86	*85*	90	89	92	78.0	57
2,921	*2,804*	3,001	3,350	3,721	4,184	4,549	**4,776**	58.7	58
1,898	*1,848*	1,987	2,135	2,316	2,660	2,952	**3,148**	58.7	59
1,023	*956*	1,014	1,215	1,405	1,524	1,597	**1,628**	57.1	60

TABLE **10.**—WAGE EARNERS, MALES AND FEMALES,

[The month of maximum employment for each industry is indicated

	INDUSTRY.	Average number employed during year.	NUMBER EMPLOYED ON 15TH DAY OF THE MONTH OR NEAREST REPRESENTATIVE DAY.			
			January.	February.	March.	April.
1	Mats and matting, from cocoa fiber, grass, and coir.	1,073	1,186	1,170	1,119	1,063
2	Male	723	764	748	731	698
3	Female	350	422	422	388	365
4	Mattresses and spring beds, not elsewhere specified.	12,637	10,767	11,144	11,447	11,809
5	Male	10,058	8,630	8,898	9,135	9,411
6	Female	2,579	2,137	2,246	2,312	2,398
7	Millinery and lace goods, not elsewhere specified.	50,850	49,849	52,521	52,083	50,787
8	Male	12,103	12,171	12,649	12,706	12,174
9	Female	38,747	37,678	39,872	39,377	38,613
10	Millstones	38	30	30	34	38
11	Male	38	30	30	34	38
12	Female					
13	Mineral and soda waters	17,440	13,650	14,067	14,848	16,233
14	Male	16,787	13,153	13,533	14,264	15,633
15	Female	653	497	534	584	600
16	Minerals and earths, ground or otherwise treated.	14,426	14,488	13,599	13,718	13,708
17	Male	14,292	14,349	13,457	13,581	13,572
18	Female	134	139	142	137	136
19	Mirrors, framed and unframed, not elsewhere specified.	2,599	2,271	2,333	2,385	2,400
20	Male	2,367	2,047	2,113	2,173	2,190
21	Female	232	224	220	212	210
22	Models and patterns, not including paper patterns.	6,949	6,148	6,237	6,382	6,446
23	Male	6,762	5,965	6,038	6,184	6,264
24	Female	187	183	199	198	182
25	Motor cycles, bicycles, and parts	10,886	11,258	10,166	10,550	10,903
26	Male	9,673	9,581	8,853	9,381	9,750
27	Female	1,213	1,677	1,313	1,169	1,153
28	Mucilage, paste, and other adhesives, not elsewhere specified.	803	773	787	761	776
29	Male	626	595	613	605	607
30	Female	177	178	174	156	169
31	Musical instruments and materials, not elsewhere specified.	4,113	3,853	3,966	3,999	4,042
32	Male	3,332	3,093	3,153	3,199	3,231
33	Female	781	760	813	800	811
34	Musical instruments, organs	1,941	1,770	1,814	1,854	1,909
35	Male	1,724	1,587	1,616	1,651	1,695
36	Female	217	183	198	203	214
37	Musical instruments, pianos	22,957	21,585	22,224	22,882	23,363
38	Male	20,978	19,687	20,319	20,963	21,401
39	Female	1,979	1,898	1,905	1,919	1,962
40	Musical instruments, piano and organ materials.	11,009	9,103	9,914	10,402	10,903
41	Male	8,147	6,795	7,344	7,704	8,182
42	Female	2,862	2,308	2,570	2,698	2,721
43	Needles, pins, and hooks and eyes	9,294	9,008	8,994	8,949	8,824
44	Male	4,499	4,301	4,230	4,241	4,244
45	Female	4,795	4,707	4,764	4,708	4,580
46	Nets and seines	859	894	918	910	878
47	Male	199	205	210	209	211
48	Female	660	689	708	701	667
49	Oakum	124	149	151	147	141
50	Male	123	149	151	147	141
51	Female	1				
52	Oil and cake, cottonseed	26,766	33,890	32,183	28,073	23,006
53	Male	26,030	32,920	31,152	27,094	22,202
54	Female	736	970	1,031	979	804
55	Oil, essential	321	299	299	295	278
56	Male	301	284	284	279	263
57	Female	20	15	15	16	15

EMPLOYED EACH MONTH, BY INDUSTRIES: 1919—Continued.

by **bold-faced** figures and that of minimum employment by *italic* figures.]

NUMBER EMPLOYED ON 15TH DAY OF THE MONTH OR NEAREST REPRESENTATIVE DAY—continued.								Per cent minimum is of maximum.	
May.	June.	July.	August.	September.	October.	November.	December.		
987	920	*893*	927	1,002	1,095	1,222	**1,292**	69.1	1
654	622	*611*	627	691	777	859	894	68.3	2
333	298	*282*	300	311	318	363	398	66.8	3
12,241	12,516	13,115	13,412	13,530	**13,957**	13,872	13,834	77.1	4
9,797	9,970	10,433	10,646	10,696	**11,084**	10,994	11,002	77.9	5
2,444	2,546	2,682	2,766	2,834	*2,873*	**2,878**	2,832	74.3	6
48,488	*47,658*	50,615	**53,748**	52,963	49,428	49,583	52,477	88.7	7
11,544	11,616	12,422	**13,018**	12,640	*10,964*	11,095	12,237	84.2	8
36,944	*36,042*	38,193	**40,730**	40,323	38,464	38,488	40,240	88.5	9
39	41	**49**	48	40	37	36	34	61.2	10
39	41	**49**	48	40	37	36	34	61.2	11
									12
17,637	20,567	**21,577**	21,385	19,991	17,914	15,953	15,458	63.3	13
16,983	19,686	**20,770**	20,643	19,244	17,244	15,391	14,900	63.3	14
654	**881**	807	742	747	670	562	558	50.4	15
13,991	14,078	14,895	**15,285**	15,227	14,665	14,832	14,626	89.0	16
13,857	13,942	14,768	**15,156**	15,103	14,536	14,697	14,486	88.8	17
134	136	127	129	*124*	129	135	140	87.3	18
2,470	2,585	2,554	2,709	2,777	2,861	2,921	**2,922**	77.7	19
2,250	2,359	2,320	2,477	2,533	2,615	**2,664**	2,663	76.8	20
220	226	234	232	244	246	257	**259**	81.1	21
6,583	6,756	6,922	7,266	7,340	7,495	7,777	**8,036**	76.5	22
6,398	6,587	6,743	7,083	7,146	7,312	7,583	**7,841**	76.1	23
185	*169*	179	183	194	183	194	195	84.9	24
10,952	10,777	10,628	10,630	10,616	11,008	11,491	**11,653**	87.2	25
9,838	9,658	9,537	9,506	9,447	9,847	10,244	**10,434**	84.8	26
1,114	1,119	*1,091*	1,124	1,169	1,161	1,247	1,219	65.1	27
783	817	789	840	819	810	839	**842**	90.4	28
601	633	629	650	631	636	**656**	**656**	90.7	29
182	184	160	**190**	188	174	183	186	82.1	30
4,006	4,025	4,136	4,117	4,170	4,302	4,363	**4,377**	88.0	31
3,230	3,259	3,344	3,374	3,424	3,527	3,567	**3,583**	86.3	32
776	766	792	*743*	746	775	796	794	91.4	33
1,941	1,951	2,000	1,961	1,937	2,005	2,039	**2,111**	83.8	34
1,716	1,722	1,770	1,747	1,723	1,776	1,808	**1,877**	84.5	35
225	229	230	214	214	229	231	**234**	78.2	36
23,461	23,954	24,202	24,508	**24,719**	*20,902*	21,201	22,483	84.6	37
21,483	21,990	22,244	22,533	**22,767**	*18,998*	19,029	20,322	83.4	38
1,978	1,964	1,958	1,975	1,952	1,904	**2,172**	2,161	87.4	39
10,984	11,045	11,816	**11,957**	11,705	11,227	11,316	11,736	76.1	40
8,205	8,254	8,742	**8,854**	8,702	8,177	8,204	8,601	76.7	41
2,779	2,791	3,074	3,103	3,003	3,050	3,112	**3,135**	73.6	42
8,823	8,925	9,314	9,587	9,525	9,692	9,835	**10,052**	87.8	43
4,256	4,381	4,429	4,581	4,702	4,769	4,875	**4,979**	85.0	44
4,567	*4,544*	4,885	5,006	4,823	4,923	4,960	**5,073**	89.6	45
836	834	841	854	827	*749*	871	**896**	81.6	46
192	192	195	193	202	*179*	195	205	84.8	47
644	642	646	661	625	*570*	676	691	80.5	48
143	115	110	98	98	*89*	124	123	58.9	49
143	112	107	98	95	*86*	124	123	57.0	50
		3	3		3	3			51
19,535	16,705	*16,333*	17,159	26,456	35,382	**36,567**	35,903	44.7	52
18,958	16,086	*15,847*	16,793	25,848	34,596	**35,715**	35,149	44.4	53
577	619	486	*366*	608	786	852	754	35.5	54
274	292	360	**396**	370	340	320	329	69.2	55
254	272	337	**373**	346	316	297	307	68.1	56
20	20	23	23	24	24	23	22	62.5	57

TABLE 10.—WAGE EARNERS, MALES AND FEMALES,

[The month of maximum employment for each industry is indicated

	INDUSTRY.	Average number employed during year.	NUMBER EMPLOYED ON 15TH DAY OF THE MONTH OR NEAREST REPRESENTATIVE DAY.			
			January.	February.	March.	April.
1	Oil, linseed	2,173	2,119	1,963	1,825	1,907
2	Male	2,130	2,052	1,905	1,762	1,874
3	Female	43	67	58	63	33
4	Oil, not elsewhere specified [1]	5,930	5,579	5,192	5,169	5,404
5	Male	5,431	4,965	4,738	4,691	4,882
6	Female	499	614	454	478	522
7	Oilcloth and linoleum, floor	5,414	4,260	4,065	4,030	4,518
8	Male	5,123	4,048	3,876	3,838	4,321
9	Female	291	212	189	192	197
10	Oilcloth, enameled	1,130	872	880	920	1,019
11	Male	1,024	790	798	836	919
12	Female	106	82	82	84	100
13	Oleomargarine and other butter substitutes.	2,851	3,389	2,783	2,678	2,812
14	Male	2,218	2,586	2,270	2,102	2,232
15	Female	633	803	513	576	580
16	Optical goods	14,723	15,208	15,230	14,359	14,622
17	Male	9,969	9,964	10,045	9,600	9,841
18	Female	4,754	5,244	5,185	4,759	4,781
19	Ordnance and accessories	11,328	19,435	15,331	15,038	13,200
20	Male	11,022	18,504	14,836	14,568	12,883
21	Female	306	931	495	470	317
22	Paints	17,485	16,094	16,070	16,262	16,625
23	Male	15,843	14,652	14,573	14,716	15,004
24	Female	1,642	1,442	1,497	1,546	1,621
25	Paper and wood pulp	113,759	113,179	109,184	108,451	107,762
26	Male	103,377	102,766	99,396	98,510	98,095
27	Female	10,382	10,413	9,788	9,941	9,667
28	Paper goods, not elsewhere specified	14,135	13,862	13,395	13,376	13,353
29	Male	8,666	8,398	8,124	8,092	8,079
30	Female	5,469	5,464	5,271	5,284	5,274
31	Paper patterns	403	381	406	421	423
32	Male	136	130	133	136	138
33	Female	267	251	273	285	285
34	Patent medicines and compounds	17,444	17,917	18,112	17,938	17,415
35	Male	8,529	8,507	8,710	8,701	8,607
36	Female	8,915	9,410	9,402	9,237	8,808
37	Paving materials	16,072	10,400	10,119	12,033	15,498
38	Male	16,067	10,396	10,115	12,029	15,494
39	Female	5	4	4	4	4
40	Peanuts, grading, roasting, cleaning, and shelling.	2,460	2,672	2,727	2,651	2,601
41	Male	896	989	975	931	902
42	Female	1,564	1,683	1,752	1,720	1,699
43	Pencils, lead	5,970	5,629	5,695	5,754	5,832
44	Male	2,700	2,524	2,524	2,538	2,578
45	Female	3,270	3,105	3,171	3,216	3,254
46	Pens, fountain and stylographic	3,207	3,008	2,973	3,127	3,237
47	Male	1,985	1,927	1,892	1,959	2,004
48	Female	1,222	1,081	1,081	1,168	1,233
49	Pens, gold	416	408	369	390	399
50	Male	372	359	328	346	356
51	Female	44	49	41	44	43
52	Pens, steel	807	825	867	876	853
53	Male	146	141	144	144	143
54	Female	661	684	723	732	710
55	Perfumery and cosmetics	5,405	4,721	4,876	5,005	5,096
56	Male	1,654	1,475	1,522	1,536	1,556
57	Female	3,751	3,246	3,354	3,469	3,540
58	Petroleum, refining	58,889	54,342	54,883	54,822	55,935
59	Male	57,702	52,750	53,499	53,620	54,823
60	Female	1,187	1,592	1,384	1,202	1,112
61	Phonographs and graphophones	28,721	23,997	25,642	26,754	27,581
62	Male	23,390	19,575	21,280	22,429	23,197
63	Female	5,331	4,422	4,362	4,325	4,384

[1] Includes "oil, castor" and "oil, lard, not made in slaughtering and meat-packing establishments."

EMPLOYED EACH MONTH, BY INDUSTRIES: 1919—Continued.

by bold-faced figures and that of minimum employment by *italic* figures.]

NUMBER EMPLOYED ON 15TH DAY OF THE MONTH OR NEAREST REPRESENTATIVE DAY—continued.								Per cent minimum is of maximum.	
May.	June.	July.	August.	September.	October.	November.	December.		
2,101	2,137	**2,465**	2,333	2,395	2,211	2,308	2,312	74.0	1
2,078	2,114	**2,434**	2,302	2,365	2,163	2,255	2,256	72.4	2
23	*23*	31	31	30	48	53	56	34.3	3
5,488	5,919	6,163	6,113	6,172	**6,691**	6,669	6,601	77.3	4
4,991	5,524	5,706	5,737	5,829	**6,187**	6,022	5,900	75.8	5
497	395	457	376	*343*	504	647	**701**	48.9	6
5,117	5,655	5,825	6,061	6,189	6,328	6,381	**6,539**	61.6	7
4,857	5,337	5,481	5,715	5,829	5,979	6,022	**6,173**	62.2	8
260	318	344	346	360	349	359	**366**	51.6	9
1,120	1,158	1,197	1,218	1,249	1,301	1,303	**1,323**	65.9	10
1,015	1,058	1,077	1,103	1,134	1,180	1,180	**1,198**	65.9	11
105	100	120	115	115	121	123	**125**	65.6	12
2,801	*2,343*	2,530	2,549	2,664	2,899	3,359	**3,405**	68.8	13
2,213	*1,801*	2,030	2,042	2,121	2,237	2,462	2,520	69.6	14
588	542	*500*	507	543	662	897	885	55.7	15
14,628	14,743	*14,189*	14,624	14,428	14,659	14,911	15,125	92.8	16
9,870	10,027	9,709	10,016	9,904	10,036	10,209	10,407	92.2	17
4,758	4,716	*4,430*	4,608	4,524	4,623	4,702	4,718	84.5	18
11,730	10,022	8,353	*7,974*	7,990	8,174	9,159	9,530	41.0	19
11,461	9,816	8,209	*7,837*	7,875	8,055	9,009	9,211	42.4	20
269	206	144	137	*115*	119	150	319	12.4	21
17,071	17,351	17,891	18,170	18,339	18,588	18,593	**18,766**	85.6	22
15,422	15,651	16,181	16,432	16,633	16,887	16,918	**17,047**	85.5	23
1,649	1,700	1,710	**1,738**	1,706	1,701	1,675	1,719	83.0	24
108,258	109,901	114,337	115,920	117,878	118,797	**120,762**	120,679	89.2	25
98,341	99,681	103,829	105,222	107,067	107,953	109,826	**103,838**	89.3	26
9,917	10,220	10,508	10,698	10,811	10,844	**10,936**	10,841	88.4	27
13,305	13,621	14,180	14,657	14,647	14,866	14,984	**15,374**	86.5	28
8,173	8,296	8,627	8,948	9,105	9,286	9,293	**9,571**	84.4	29
5,132	5,325	5,553	5,709	5,542	5,580	5,691	**5,803**	88.4	30
409	407	413	403	389	398	395	391	90.1	31
143	140	137	137	132	136	134	136	90.9	32
266	267	276	266	257	262	261	255	88.1	33
17,002	16,629	*16,607*	16,756	17,086	17,600	**18,165**	18,101	91.4	34
8,467	8,289	8,316	*8,288*	8,305	8,490	**8,846**	8,822	93.7	35
8,535	8,340	*8,291*	8,468	8,781	9,110	9,319	9,279	88.1	36
17,694	18,290	19,149	**19,912**	19,369	18,886	17,284	14,230	50.8	37
17,690	18,281	19,143	**19,907**	19,364	18,881	17,279	14,225	50.8	38
4	9	6	5	5	5	5	5	44.4	39
2,589	2,500	2,284	2,264	2,089	*1,807*	2,405	**2,931**	61.7	40
893	868	824	816	785	*775*	949	**1,045**	74.2	41
1,696	1,632	1,460	1,448	1,304	*1,032*	1,456	**1,886**	54.7	42
5,957	5,959	6,140	6,156	6,049	6,081	6,192	**6,196**	90.8	43
2,640	2,718	2,778	2,775	2,769	2,794	**2,884**	2,878	87.5	44
3,317	3,241	3,362	**3,381**	3,280	3,287	3,308	3,318	91.8	45
3,208	3,250	3,280	3,354	3,077	3,160	3,281	**3,529**	84.2	46
1,988	2,002	2,026	2,084	*1,815*	1,881	2,019	**2,223**	81.6	47
1,220	1,248	1,254	1,270	1,262	1,279	1,262	**1,306**	82.8	48
423	437	432	**468**	383	376	449	458	78.8	49
378	394	392	**418**	340	332	404	417	78.5	50
45	43	*40*	**50**	43	44	45	41	80.0	51
839	833	775	*748*	752	762	768	786	85.4	52
153	144	142	143	*141*	142	153	162	87.0	53
686	689	633	*605*	611	620	615	624	82.7	54
5,236	5,214	5,314	5,594	5,720	5,948	**6,162**	5,974	76.6	55
1,610	1,609	1,649	1,688	1,744	1,792	1,812	**1,855**	79.5	56
3,626	3,605	3,665	3,906	3,976	4,156	**4,350**	4,119	74.6	57
57,705	59,018	61,079	60,550	61,489	62,507	61,739	**62,599**	86.8	58
56,603	57,913	59,916	59,413	60,323	61,465	60,621	**61,478**	85.8	59
1,102	1,105	1,163	1,137	1,166	*1,042*	1,118	1,121	65.5	60
28,269	29,601	24,021	24,369	31,248	33,334	34,656	**35,180**	68.2	61
23,898	25,221	19,598	19,889	24,498	26,414	27,106	**27,575**	71.0	62
4,371	4,380	4,423	4,480	6,750	6,920	7,550	**7,605**	56.9	63

TABLE **10.**—WAGE EARNERS, MALES AND FEMALES,

[The month of maximum employment for each industry is indicated

	INDUSTRY.	Average number employed during year.	NUMBER EMPLOYED ON 15TH DAY OF THE MONTH OR NEAREST REPRESENTATIVE DAY.			
			January.	February.	March.	April.
1	Photographic apparatus.................	2,555	*2,141*	2,263	2,290	2,404
2	Male.................	2,072	*1,705*	1,805	1,840	1,952
3	Female..	483	*436*	458	450	452
4	Photographic materials.................	14,556	*12,626*	12,935	13,405	14,082
5	Male.................	10,126	*8,574*	8,858	9,180	9,702
6	Female..	4,430	*4,052*	4,077	4,225	4,380
7	Photo-engraving.................	6,769	*6,164*	6,261	6,409	6,588
8	Male.................	6,412	*5,844*	5,921	6,072	6,248
9	Female..	357	*320*	340	337	340
10	Pickles, preserves, and sauces.............	16,621	14,121	13,345	*13,134*	13,313
11	Male.................	8,239	7,074	6,784	*6,614*	6,794
12	Female..	8,382	7,047	6,561	6,520	*6,519*
13	Pipes, tobacco.................	2,539	2,415	2,413	2,447	2,502
14	Male.................	1,985	1,893	1,880	1,903	1,923
15	Female..	554	*522*	533	544	579
16	Plated ware.................	9,492	*7,491*	8,009	8,493	8,778
17	Male.................	7,605	*5,943*	6,398	6,799	7,001
18	Female..	1,887	*1,548*	1,611	1,694	1,777
19	Plumbers' supplies.................	13,592	12,481	11,554	11,315	*11,286*
20	Male.................	12,675	11,497	10,718	*10,504*	10,510
21	Female..	917	984	836	811	776
22	Pocketbooks.................	2,905	*2,605*	2,718	2,778	2,760
23	Male.................	1,541	*1,431*	1,477	1,490	1,465
24	Female..	1,364	*1,174*	1,241	1,288	1,295
25	Pottery.................	27,934	26,431	*26,106*	26,267	26,638
26	Male.................	20,837	19,660	*19,441*	19,557	19,837
27	Female..	7,097	6,771	*6,665*	6,710	6,801
28	Poultry, killing and dressing, not done in slaughtering and meat-packing establishments.	2,140	1,807	1,194	*1,076*	1,383
29	Male.................	1,557	1,406	973	*878*	1,032
30	Female..	583	401	221	*198*	351
31	Printing and publishing, book and job....	123,005	*119,117*	119,993	120,294	120,266
32	Male.................	91,544	*88,480*	88,916	89,080	89,518
33	Female..	31,461	30,637	31,077	31,214	30,748
34	Printing and publishing, music...........	899	*840*	863	850	890
35	Male.................	714	661	675	*658*	692
36	Female..	185	179	188	192	198
37	Printing and publishing, newspapers and periodicals.	120,381	*115,926*	116,902	118,549	118,724
38	Male.................	99,572	*95,396*	96,304	97,530	97,981
39	Female..	20,809	20,530	20,598	21,019	20,743
40	Printing materials.................	723	*620*	667	661	640
41	Male.................	678	*571*	614	617	601
42	Female..	45	49	53	44	39
43	Pulp, from fiber other than wood..........	64	57	56	62	66
44	Male.................	46	*35*	35	41	42
45	Female..	18	22	21	21	24
46	Pulp goods.................	3,041	*2,710*	2,746	2,766	2,958
47	Male.................	2,596	*2,337*	2,353	2,348	2,467
48	Female..	445	*373*	393	418	491
49	Pumps, not including power pumps.......	5,384	5,097	5,217	5,322	5,335
50	Male.................	5,135	4,847	4,975	5,066	5,080
51	Female..	249	250	242	256	255
52	Pumps, steam and other power...........	10,688	**11,463**	11,249	11,190	10,962
53	Male.................	10,383	**11,026**	10,859	10,841	10,636
54	Female..	305	**437**	390	349	326
55	Refrigerators.................	5,786	5,547	5,656	5,784	5,838
56	Male.................	5,553	5,282	5,407	5,549	5,610
57	Female..	233	**265**	249	235	228
58	Regalia, and society badges and emblems.	2,223	*2,081*	2,128	2,118	2,163
59	Male.................	871	837	862	836	*833*
60	Female..	1,352	*1,244*	1,266	1,282	1,330

EMPLOYED EACH MONTH, BY INDUSTRIES: 1919—Continued.

by **bold-faced** figures and that of minimum employment by *italic* figures.]

NUMBER EMPLOYED ON 15TH DAY OF THE MONTH OR NEAREST REPRESENTATIVE DAY— continued.								Per cent minimum is of maximum.	
May.	June.	July.	August.	September.	October.	November.	December.		
2,469	2,580	2,628	2,450	2,658	2,844	2,920	**3,013**	71.1	1
1,990	2,113	2,162	1,976	2,172	2,299	2,360	**2,490**	68.5	2
479	467	466	474	486	545	**560**	523	77.9	3
14,161	14,335	15,152	15,531	15,401	15,661	15,655	**15,728**	80.3	4
9,846	9,984	10,511	10,853	10,851	**11,084**	11,051	11,018	77.4	5
4,315	4,351	4,641	4,678	4,550	4,577	4,604	**4,710**	86.0	6
6,611	6,726	6,871	6,886	7,001	7,194	7,180	**7,337**	84.0	7
6,270	6,379	6,503	6,515	6,628	6,809	6,792	**6,963**	83.9	8
341	347	368	371	373	385	**388**	374	82.5	9
13,891	15,518	16,926	19,544	**23,032**	21,888	18,443	16,297	57.0	10
6,901	7,550	8,155	9,661	**11,385**	10,797	9,046	8,107	58.1	11
6,990	7,968	8,771	9,883	**11,647**	11,091	9,397	8,190	56.0	12
2,557	2,574	2,609	2,674	*2,201*	2,643	2,647	**2,786**	79.0	13
1,996	2,003	2,022	2,105	*1,670*	2,104	2,102	**2,219**	75.3	14
561	571	**587**	569	531	539	545	567	88.9	15
9,164	9,284	9,637	10,279	10,413	10,653	10,831	**10,872**	68.9	16
7,324	7,447	7,750	8,293	8,353	8,544	8,696	**8,712**	68.2	17
1,840	1,837	1,887	1,986	2,060	2,109	2,135	**2,160**	71.7	18
11,944	12,599	13,911	14,575	14,791	15,577	16,230	**16,841**	67.0	19
11,111	11,757	13,021	13,663	13,845	14,575	15,144	**15,755**	66.7	20
833	842	890	912	946	1,002	**1,086**	**1,086**	71.5	21
2,754	2,791	2,892	3,013	3,060	3,126	**3,194**	3,169	81.6	22
1,458	1,464	1,542	1,608	**1,656**	1,636	1,638	1,627	86.4	23
1,296	1,327	1,350	1,405	1,404	1,490	**1,556**	1,542	75.4	24
26,909	27,294	28,023	28,689	28,830	29,638	30,041	**30,342**	86.0	25
19,970	20,326	21,009	21,455	21,553	22,094	22,457	**22,685**	85.7	26
6,939	6,968	7,014	7,234	7,277	7,544	7,584	**7,657**	87.0	27
1,533	1,756	1,748	1,915	2,382	2,816	3,826	**4,244**	25.4	28
1,100	1,252	1,265	1,364	1,680	2,020	2,747	**2,967**	29.6	29
433	504	483	551	702	796	1,079	**1,277**	15.5	30
120,515	121,811	123,230	125,111	126,470	121,000	124,512	**133,741**	89.1	31
90,069	91,107	92,198	93,752	94,623	89,436	91,866	**99,483**	88.9	32
30,446	30,704	31,032	31,359	31,847	31,564	32,646	**34,258**	88.9	33
909	920	897	892	902	919	950	**956**	87.9	34
718	738	725	721	732	740	**755**	753	87.2	35
191	182	172	171	*170*	179	195	**203**	83.7	36
119,798	120,078	120,617	121,511	122,279	121,215	123,006	**125,967**	92.0	37
98,960	99,629	99,796	100,730	101,635	100,522	102,006	**104,375**	91.4	38
20,838	*20,449*	20,821	20,781	20,644	20,693	21,000	**21,592**	94.7	39
670	723	740	795	777	805	**852**	726	72.8	40
626	666	689	743	740	771	**815**	683	70.1	41
44	**57**	51	52	37	*34*	37	43	59.6	42
70	**78**	**78**	61	60	60	69	*51*	65.4	43
45	**65**	**65**	45	45	47	52	*35*	53.8	44
25	*13*	*13*	16	15	*13*	17	16	52.0	45
2,827	2,916	2,935	3,097	3,163	3,336	3,412	**3,626**	74.7	46
2,427	2,499	2,500	2,651	2,710	2,874	2,935	**3,051**	76.6	47
400	417	435	446	453	462	477	**575**	64.9	48
5,437	*4,729*	5,096	5,301	5,532	5,672	5,712	**6,158**	76.8	49
5,198	*4,512*	4,879	5,019	5,260	5,401	5,455	**5,928**	76.1	50
239	*217*	*217*	**282**	272	271	257	230	77.0	51
10,602	10,296	10,260	10,412	10,364	*10,138*	10,579	10,741	88.4	52
10,295	10,028	10,000	10,158	10,098	*9,876*	10,304	10,475	89.6	53
307	268	260	*254*	266	262	275	266	58.1	54
5,762	5,646	5,611	*5,483*	5,701	5,823	6,120	**6,461**	84.9	55
5,547	5,423	5,382	*5,279*	5,490	5,590	5,875	**6,202**	85.1	56
215	223	229	*204*	211	233	245	259	77.0	57
2,223	2,260	2,251	2,259	2,202	2,285	**2,358**	2,348	88.3	58
866	879	893	892	868	887	**902**	897	92.4	59
1,357	1,381	1,358	1,367	1,334	1,398	**1,456**	1,451	85.4	60

TABLE **10.**—WAGE EARNERS, MALES AND FEMALES,

[The month of maximum employment for each industry is indicated

	INDUSTRY.	Average number employed during year.	NUMBER EMPLOYED ON 15TH DAY OF THE MONTH OR NEAREST REPRESENTATIVE DAY.			
			January.	February.	March.	April.
1	Rice, cleaning and polishing	2,113	3,041	2,423	1,794	1,470
2	Male	2,085	3,000	2,399	1,772	1,453
3	Female	28	41	24	22	17
4	Roofing materials	8,871	7,814	7,541	7,647	7,837
5	Male	8,499	7,448	7,250	7,321	7,497
6	Female	372	366	291	326	340
7	Rubber tires, tubes, and rubber goods, not elsewhere specified.	119,848	104,075	108,422	110,130	112,712
8	Male	104,506	88,288	93,152	95,430	98,170
9	Female	15,342	15,787	15,270	14,700	14,542
10	Rules, ivory and wood	168	159	153	153	152
11	Male	120	114	102	105	103
12	Female	48	45	51	48	49
13	Saddlery and harness	10,411	10,627	10,431	10,416	10,060
14	Male	9,532	9,686	9,562	9,569	9,248
15	Female	879	941	869	847	812
16	Safes and vaults	2,949	2,786	2,755	2,827	2,682
17	Male	2,894	2,728	2,696	2,765	2,638
18	Female	55	58	59	62	44
19	Salt	6,495	6,433	6,220	6,179	6,161
20	Male	6,076	6,051	5,848	5,829	5,773
21	Female	419	382	372	350	388
22	Sand and emery paper and cloth	771	690	696	682	692
23	Male	686	613	610	612	607
24	Female	85	77	86	70	85
25	Sand-lime brick	504	314	321	343	408
26	Male	503	314	321	343	408
27	Female	1				
28	Sausage, not made in slaughtering and meat-packing establishments.	3,471	3,355	3,305	3,298	3,260
29	Male	3,056	2,978	2,932	2,929	2,880
30	Female	415	377	373	369	380
31	Saws	5,510	5,527	5,484	5,400	5,417
32	Male	5,156	5,139	5,124	5,052	5,065
33	Female	354	388	360	348	352
34	Scales and balances	5,432	4,887	5,003	4,994	5,135
35	Male	5,143	4,592	4,702	4,715	4,848
36	Female	289	295	301	279	287
37	Screws, machine	10,262	9,576	9,327	9,635	9,764
38	Male	8,738	8,063	7,938	8,170	8,297
39	Female	1,524	1,513	1,389	1,465	1,467
40	Screws, wood	4,889	5,121	5,050	4,888	4,658
41	Male	3,498	3,576	3,506	3,421	3,340
42	Female	1,391	1,545	1,544	1,467	1,318
43	Sewing-machine cases	4,171	3,792	3,933	3,950	2,715
44	Male	3,746	3,407	3,550	3,582	2,435
45	Female	425	385	383	368	280
46	Sewing machines and attachments	15,059	14,059	14,119	14,462	14,431
47	Male	12,802	11,810	11,867	12,198	12,184
48	Female	2,257	2,249	2,252	2,264	2,247
49	Shipbuilding, steel	344,014	378,842	345,596	376,102	378,623
50	Male	342,903	377,247	344,149	374,778	377,374
51	Female	1,111	1,595	1,447	1,324	1,249
52	Shipbuilding, wooden, including boat building.	43,432	65,841	60,957	56,352	50,595
53	Male	43,322	65,692	60,806	56,212	50,470
54	Female	110	149	151	140	125
55	Shirts	39,603	37,554	37,748	36,986	36,960
56	Male	6,613	6,154	6,104	6,088	6,183
57	Female	32,990	31,400	31,644	30,898	30,777
58	Show cases	1,857	1,569	1,698	1,779	1,847
59	Male	1,812	1,531	1,660	1,737	1,808
60	Female	45	38	38	42	39

EMPLOYED EACH MONTH, BY INDUSTRIES: 1919—Continued.

by **bold-faced** figures and that of minimum employment by *italic* figures.]

NUMBER EMPLOYED ON 15TH DAY OF THE MONTH OR NEAREST REPRESENTATIVE DAY—continued.								Per cent minimum is of maximum.	
May.	June.	July.	August.	September.	October.	November.	December.		
1,452	1,243	*954*	1,149	2,226	**2,840**	3,354	**3,410**	28.0	1
1,421	1,192	*922*	1,141	2,214	2,815	3,319	3,372	27.3	2
31	**51**	32	*8*	12	25	35	38	15.7	3
8,114	8,863	9,228	9,748	10,034	**10,082**	9,827	9,717	74.8	4
7,759	8,506	8,825	9,339	9,642	**9,679**	9,418	9,304	74.9	5
355	*357*	403	409	392	403	409	**413**	70.5	6
116,353	119,028	123,540	128,283	129,013	**134,423**	125,370	126,827	77.4	7
102,072	104,536	108,831	113,468	114,046	**118,624**	107,513	109,942	74.4	8
14,281	14,492	14,709	14,815	14,967	15,799	**17,857**	16,885	80.0	9
151	153	165	189	179	185	**190**	187	79.5	10
100	108	117	138	134	136	141	**142**	70.4	11
51	45	48	51	*45*	49	49	*45*	88.2	12
9,956	*9,938*	10,068	10,396	10,445	10,789	10,851	**10,955**	90.7	13
9,161	*9,120*	9,255	9,498	9,538	9,846	9,887	**10,014**	91.1	14
795	818	813	898	907	943	**964**	941	82.5	15
2,841	2,842	2,873	2,976	3,045	3,131	3,256	**3,374**	79.5	16
2,791	2,792	2,817	2,914	2,992	3,073	3,203	**3,319**	79.5	17
50	*50*	56	62	53	58	53	55	71.0	18
5,994	6,114	6,443	6,900	6,771	**7,110**	6,826	6,789	84.3	19
5,628	5,725	6,006	6,446	6,326	**6,626**	6,339	6,315	84.9	20
366	389	437	454	445	484	**487**	474	71.9	21
702	750	780	782	828	876	880	**894**	76.3	22
623	668	695	690	743	782	789	**800**	75.9	23
79	*82*	85	92	85	**94**	91	**94**	74.5	24
529	550	606	569	582	572	**633**	621	49.6	25
529	550	604	567	580	570	**631**	619	49.8	26
....	....	2	2	2	2	2	2	....	27
3,297	3,458	3,536	3,515	3,513	3,646	3,684	**3,785**	86.1	28
2,908	3,031	3,082	3,089	3,081	3,199	3,250	**3,313**	86.9	29
389	427	454	426	432	447	434	**472**	78.2	30
5,355	5,370	5,386	5,454	5,566	5,592	5,715	**5,854**	91.5	31
5,016	5,034	5,053	5,115	5,217	5,234	5,351	**5,472**	91.7	32
339	336	*333*	339	349	358	364	382	85.8	33
5,239	5,268	5,498	5,720	5,755	5,852	5,887	**5,946**	82.2	34
4,947	4,986	5,205	5,439	5,473	5,566	5,583	**5,660**	81.1	35
292	282	293	281	282	286	**304**	286	91.8	36
9,804	9,925	10,106	10,549	10,826	11,101	11,228	**11,303**	82.5	37
8,315	8,445	8,618	9,055	9,322	9,332	9,575	**9,726**	81.6	38
1,489	1,480	1,488	1,494	1,504	**1,769**	1,653	1,577	78.5	39
4,617	4,665	4,790	4,879	4,862	4,882	5,014	**5,242**	88.1	40
3,296	3,361	3,429	3,476	3,496	3,556	3,673	**3,846**	85.7	41
1,321	*1,304*	1,361	1,403	1,366	1,326	1,341	1,396	84.4	42
4,162	4,244	4,380	4,350	4,397	4,635	4,704	4,790	56.7	43
3,754	3,836	3,919	3,885	3,928	4,146	4,210	4,300	56.6	44
408	408	461	465	469	489	**494**	490	56.7	45
14,426	14,818	14,741	15,404	15,681	16,010	16,191	**16,366**	85.9	46
12,245	12,569	12,449	13,095	13,429	13,743	13,908	**14,127**	83.6	47
2,181	2,249	2,292	**2,309**	2,252	2,267	2,283	2,239	94.5	48
380,799	375,018	362,726	353,849	335,164	293,784	*273,350*	274,315	71.8	49
379,700	373,949	361,700	352,869	334,247	292,924	*272,525*	273,374	71.8	50
1,099	1,069	1,026	980	917	860	*825*	941	51.7	51
46,815	43,420	40,813	36,976	34,091	29,611	*27,822*	27,891	42.3	52
46,709	43,313	40,716	36,870	34,005	29,525	*27,735*	27,811	42.2	53
106	107	97	106	86	86	87	*80*	53.0	54
37,418	37,773	37,558	38,895	40,736	42,902	44,736	**45,970**	80.4	55
6,349	6,471	6,147	6,388	6,783	7,304	7,627	**7,758**	78.5	56
31,069	31,302	31,411	32,507	33,953	35,598	37,109	**38,212**	80.5	57
1,848	1,898	1,842	1,902	1,919	1,942	2,009	**2,031**	77.3	58
1,802	1,856	1,800	1,856	1,871	1,887	1,958	**1,978**	77.4	59
46	42	42	46	48	**55**	51	53	69.1	60

TABLE **10.**—WAGE EARNERS, MALES AND FEMALES,

[The month of maximum employment for each industry is indicated

	INDUSTRY.	Average number employed during year.	NUMBER EMPLOYED ON 15TH DAY OF THE MONTH OR NEAREST REPRESENTATIVE DAY.			
			January.	February.	March.	April.
1	Signs and advertising novelties............	10,432	8,771	8,767	9,319	9,672
2	Male..............................	6,514	*5,505*	5,550	5,948	6,156
3	Female............................	3,918	3,266	*3,217*	3,371	3,516
4	Silk goods, including throwsters..........	126,782	118,907	*118,201*	120,863	123,114
5	Male.............................	49,610	45,177	*44,644*	46,223	47,356
6	Female............................	77,172	73,730	*73,557*	74,640	75,758
7	Silversmithing and silverware............	6,453	6,167	*6,025*	6,321	6,524
8	Male.............................	5,504	5,423	*5,217*	5,448	5,552
9	Female............................	949	*744*	808	873	972
10	Slaughtering and meat packing...........	160,996	**187,609**	171,452	163,025	*150,806*
11	Male.............................	144,141	**165,028**	151,902	145,954	*135,909*
12	Female............................	16,855	**22,581**	19,550	17,071	*14,897*
13	Smelting and refining, copper............	17,345	**23,627**	20,451	18,652	17,616
14	Male.............................	17,279	**23,536**	20,378	18,580	17,547
15	Female............................	66	**91**	73	72	69
16	Smelting and refining, lead.............	6,438	**8,054**	7,551	6,441	6,402
17	Male.........·...............	6,429	**8,045**	7,542	6,432	6,393
18	Female............................	9	9	9	9	9
19	Smelting and refining, zinc.............	13,796	**16,159**	15,464	14,339	13,815
20	Male.............................	13,782	**16,145**	15,450	14,325	13,801
21	Female............................	14	14	14	14	14
22	Smelting and refining, metals, not elsewhere specified.[1]	2,041	**2,662**	2,101	1,820	*1,783*
23	Male.............................	1,842	**2,414**	1,872	*1,549*	1,591
24	Female............................	199	248	229	271	192
25	Smelting and refining, not from the ore...	2,167	**2,284**	2,196	2,119	2,073
26	Male.............................	2,152	**2,268**	2,181	2,104	2,057
27	Female............................	15	16	15	15	16
28	Soap....	20,436	20,590	18,789	18,055	*17,963*
29	Male.............................	14,490	14,578	13,266	12,880	*12,774*
30	Female............................	5,946	6,012	5,523	*5,175*	5,189
31	Soda-water apparatus....................	2,599	*1,977*	2,335	2,653	2,768
32	Male.............................	2,521	*1,904*	2,266	2,580	2,690
33	Female............................	78	*73*	*69*	73	78
34	Sporting and athletic goods.............	6,412	*5,633*	5,874	6,023	6,231
35	Male.............................	4,127	*3,632*	3,774	3,844	3,959
36	Female............................	2,285	*2,001*	2,100	2,179	2,272
37	Springs, steel, car and carriage, not made in steel works.	8,981	8,527	8,637	8,757	8,591
38	Male.............................	8,319	*7,859*	7,964	8,150	7,976
39	Female............................	662	668	673	607	615
40	Stamped and enameled ware, not elsewhere specified.	34,248	*31,374*	32,365	32,148	31,920
41	Male.............................	26,508	*23,971*	24,663	24,568	24,531
42	Female............................	7,740	7,403	7,702	7,580	7,389
43	Stationery goods, not elsewhere specified..	11,261	10,664	*10,626*	10,759	10,636
44	Male.............................	5,531	5,288	5,286	5,356	*5,250*
45	Female............................	5,730	5,376	*5,340*	5,403	5,386
46	Statuary and art goods....................	1,466	*1,245*	1,323	1,383	1,373
47	Male.............................	1,350	*1,143*	1,212	1,272	1,257
48	Female..............·............	116	*102*	111	111	116
49	Steam fittings and steam and hot-water heating apparatus.	36,686	35,881	35,522	35,224	34,119
50	Male.............................	34,568	33,648	33,380	33,166	32,116
51	Female............................	2,118	2,233	2,142	2,058	2,003
52	Steam packing.........................	6,147	6,329	6,096	5,902	5,683
53	Male.............................	5,105	5,281	5,061	4,906	4,713
54	Female............................	1,042	1,048	1,035	996	970
55	Steel barrels, drums, and tanks............	3,322	3,279	3,055	*2,727*	2,798
56	Male.............................	3,234	3,156	2,969	*2,633*	2,719
57	Female............................	88	**123**	86	94	79
58	Stencils and brands....................	417	*392*	*392*	399	402
59	Male.............................	356	339	*335*	341	348
60	Female............................	61	53	57	58	**54**

[1] Includes "smelting and refining, antimony" and "smelting and refining, tin."

EMPLOYED EACH MONTH, BY INDUSTRIES: 1919—Continued.

by bold-faced figures and that of minimum employment by *italic* figures.

NUMBER EMPLOYED ON 15TH DAY OF THE MONTH OR NEAREST REPRESENTATIVE DAY—continued.								Per cent minimum is of maximum.	
May.	June.	July.	August.	September.	October.	November.	December.		
10,020	10,353	10,778	11,130	11,269	11,628	**11,741**	11,736	74.7	1
6,335	6,515	6,763	6,923	6,990	7,119	7,229	7,135	76.2	2
3,685	3,838	4,015	4,207	4,279	4,509	4,512	**4,601**	69.9	3
125,317	125,601	127,671	128,936	129,999	130,019	135,517	**137,239**	86.1	4
48,395	49,166	50,139	50,658	51,798	52,815	54,141	**54,808**	81.5	5
76,922	76,435	77,532	78,278	78,201	77,204	81,376	**82,431**	89.2	6
6,648	6,432	6,327	6,404	6,563	6,642	6,634	**6,749**	89.3	7
5,641	5,468	5,378	5,426	5,578	5,609	5,607	**5,701**	91.5	8
1,007	964	949	978	985	1,033	1,027	**1,048**	71.0	9
151,252	157,358	157,938	156,304	154,147	155,398	158,859	167,804	80.4	10
136,320	142,224	142,895	140,957	138,676	139,110	140,480	150,237	82.4	11
14,932	15,134	15,043	15,347	15,471	16,288	18,379	17,567	66.0	12
16,426	15,742	16,505	*15,351*	15,754	15,944	16,284	15,788	65.0	13
16,363	15,679	16,445	*15,289*	15,697	15,879	16,225	15,730	65.0	14
63	63	60	62	*57*	65	59	58	62.6	15
6,353	6,001	5,988	6,011	*5,723*	6,170	6,255	6,307	71.1	16
6,344	5,992	5,979	6,002	*5,714*	6,161	6,246	6,298	71.0	17
9	9	9	9	9	9	9	9	100.0	18
13,469	*12,250*	12,691	13,572	13,807	13,095	13,034	13,857	75.8	19
13,457	*12,234*	12,676	13,556	13,794	13,081	13,021	13,844	75.8	20
12	**16**	15	**16**	13	14	13	13	75.0	21
1,904	2,117	1,977	1,991	1,979	2,054	2,108	1,996	67.0	22
1,695	1,891	1,776	1,838	1,816	1,885	1,944	1,833	64.2	23
209	226	201	*153*	163	169	164	163	56.5	24
2,070	*2,046*	2,141	2,188	2,189	2,226	2,245	2,227	89.6	25
2,055	*2,030*	2,125	2,174	2,176	2,213	2,232	2,209	89.5	26
15	16	16	14	13	13	13	**18**	72.2	27
19,223	20,932	21,759	22,567	**22,653**	22,080	21,229	19,392	79.3	28
13,753	14,856	15,434	16,091	**16,169**	15,541	14,946	13,592	79.0	29
5,470	6,076	6,325	6,476	6,484	**6,539**	6,283	5,800	79.1	30
2,847	2,759	2,721	2,650	2,586	2,591	2,623	2,678	69.4	31
2,770	2,681	2,645	2,570	2,504	2,505	2,540	2,597	68.7	32
77	78	76	80	82	**86**	83	81	80.2	33
6,263	5,956	6,340	6,506	6,612	6,859	7,139	**7,508**	75.0	34
3,994	3,910	4,053	4,168	4,249	4,442	4,628	**4,871**	74.6	35
2,269	2,046	2,287	2,338	2,363	2,417	2,511	**2,637**	75.9	36
8,504	9,052	9,046	9,224	9,389	9,239	9,295	**9,511**	89.4	37
7,904	8,400	8,343	8,521	8,719	8,564	8,615	**8,813**	89.2	38
600	652	**703**	**703**	670	675	680	698	85.3	39
32,850	32,834	33,871	35,297	35,979	36,819	37,679	**37,840**	82.9	40
25,354	25,480	26,204	27,391	27,935	28,796	29,472	**29,731**	80.6	41
7,496	*7,354*	7,667	7,906	8,044	8,023	**8,207**	8,109	89.6	42
10,861	10,711	11,081	11,240	11,593	12,124	12,309	**12,528**	84.8	43
5,319	5,257	5,479	5,469	5,622	5,907	6,009	**6,130**	85.6	44
5,542	5,454	5,602	5,771	5,971	6,217	6,300	**6,398**	83.5	45
1,425	1,445	1,461	1,498	1,550	1,618	1,633	**1,638**	76.0	46
1,310	1,330	1,346	1,376	1,426	1,502	1,509	**1,517**	75.3	47
115	115	115	122	124	116	124	121	82.3	48
33,446	32,022	*31,315*	34,041	39,505	41,728	43,162	**44,267**	70.7	49
31,485	30,082	*29,289*	32,343	37,311	39,381	40,775	**41,840**	70.0	50
1,961	1,940	2,026	*1,698*	2,194	2,347	2,387	2,427	70.0	51
5,656	5,693	5,869	6,205	6,375	6,642	6,532	6,782	83.4	52
4,673	4,739	4,832	5,184	5,311	5,530	5,371	5,659	82.6	53
983	*954*	1,037	1,021	1,064	1,112	1,161	1,123	82.2	54
2,788	3,050	3,411	3,622	3,758	3,592	3,738	4,046	67.4	55
2,716	2,977	3,328	3,540	3,665	3,504	3,646	3,955	66.6	56
72	73	83	82	93	88	92	91	58.5	57
400	398	415	416	422	433	459	**476**	82.4	58
350	345	353	358	361	363	383	396	84.6	59
50	53	62	58	61	70	76	80	62.5	60

TABLE **10.**—WAGE EARNERS, MALES AND FEMALES,

[The month of maximum employment for each industry is indicated

	INDUSTRY.	Average number employed during year.	NUMBER EMPLOYED ON 15TH DAY OF THE MONTH OR NEAREST REPRESENTATIVE DAY.			
			January.	February.	March.	April.
1	Stereotyping and electrotyping............	3,664	*3,365*	3,446	3,504	3,405
2	Male..............................	3,578	*3,288*	3,367	3,420	3,317
3	Female............................	86	*77*	79	84	88
4	Stoves and hot-air furnaces..............	32,868	*27,794*	30,109	30,513	30,717
5	Male..............................	32,511	*27,504*	29,813	30,203	30,343
6	Female............................	357	*290*	296	310	374
7	Stoves, gas and oil....................	10,565	*9,319*	9,468	9,480	9,394
8	Male..............................	9,733	*8,596*	8,740	8,758	8,644
9	Female............................	832	*723*	728	*722*	750
10	Structural ironwork, not made in steel works or rolling mills.	43,962	45,471	43,646	42,231	41,138
11	Male..............................	43,707	45,198	43,382	41,972	40,871
12	Female............................	255	273	264	259	267
13	Sugar, beet.........................	11,781	11,627	5,926	*4,661*	5,573
14	Male..............................	11,339	11,234	5,788	*4,596*	5,475
15	Female............................	442	393	138	*65*	98
16	Sugar, cane.........................	6,101	8,653	4,951	2,160	*1,514*
17	Male..............................	5,496	8,208	4,781	1,959	*1,360*
18	Female............................	605	445	170	201	154
19	Sugar refining, not including beet sugar...	18,202	*14,533*	18,692	19,311	18,904
20	Male..............................	16,904	*13,576*	17,449	17,968	17,527
21	Female............................	1,298	957	1,243	1,343	1,377
22	Sulphuric, nitric, and mixed acids........	4,961	5,529	5,301	4,690	4,438
23	Male..............................	4,935	5,487	5,265	4,670	4,422
24	Female............................	26	42	36	20	16
25	Surgical appliances...................	6,390	**7,581**	6,838	6,305	6,121
26	Male..............................	3,186	**3,599**	3,264	3,066	3,061
27	Female............................	3,204	**3,982**	3,574	3,239	3,060
28	Suspenders, garters, and elastic woven goods	10,857	9,918	*9,770*	9,854	9,915
29	Male..............................	3,650	3,330	*3,234*	3,353	3,365
30	Female............................	7,207	6,588	6,536	*6,501*	6,550
31	Textile machinery and parts............	-31,823	30,296	29,630	29,138	*28,898*
32	Male..............................	29,827	28,209	27,676	27,173	*26,967*
33	Female............................	1,996	2,087	1,954	1,965	*1,931*
34	Theatrical scenery....................	149	*108*	124	136	147
35	Male..............................	146	*105*	121	133	144
36	Female............................	3	3	3	3	3
37	Tin and other foils, not elsewhere specified.	1,908	1,996	2,076	**2,139**	2,106
38	Male..............................	1,305	1,370	1,423	**1,475**	1,454
39	Female............................	603	626	653	664	652
40	Tin plate and terneplate...............	3,122	3,487	**3,880**	3,641	2,810
41	Male..............................	2,713	3,041	**3,370**	3,166	2,445
42	Female............................	409	446	**510**	475	365
43	Tinware, not elsewhere specified........	34,386	32,644	32,644	32,201	*31,855*
44	Male..............................	23,811	22,316	22,733	22,241	*22,138*
45	Female............................	10,575	10,328	9,911	9,960	*9,717*
46	Tobacco, chewing and smoking, and snuff.	18,324	17,907	18,043	*17,252*	17,484
47	Male..............................	9,096	8,886	8,861	*8,418*	8,633
48	Female............................	9,228	9,021	9,182	8,834	8,851
49	Tobacco, cigars and cigarettes...........	138,773	142,147	142,495	142,333	138,028
50	Male..............................	55,535	57,014	56,835	56,944	54,923
51	Female............................	83,238	85,133	85,660	85,389	83,105
52	Tools, not elsewhere specified..........	35,585	35,517	34,556	34,512	33,704
53	Male..............................	32,672	32,343	31,573	31,507	30,825
54	Female............................	2,913	**3,174**	2,983	3,005	2,879
55	Toys and games......................	14,201	*10,141*	11,080	12,028	12,706
56	Male..............................	8,576	*6,341*	6,945	7,413	7,781
57	Female............................	5,625	*3,800*	4,135	4,615	4,925
58	Trunks and valises...................	11,470	*10,101*	10,471	10,711	10,785
59	Male..............................	9,677	*8,569*	8,879	9,063	9,121
60	Female............................	1,793	*1,532*	1,592	1,648	1,664
61	Turpentine and rosin..................	28,067	*25,918*	26,756	27,548	28,537
62	Male..............................	27,961	*25,806*	26,609	27,391	28,406
63	Female............................	106	112	147	**157**	131

EMPLOYED EACH MONTH, BY INDUSTRIES: 1919—Continued.

by **bold-faced** figures and that of minimum employment by *italic* figures.]

NUMBER EMPLOYED ON 15TH DAY OF THE MONTH OR NEAREST REPRESENTATIVE DAY—continued.								Per cent minimum is of maximum.	
May.	June.	July.	August.	September.	October.	November.	December.		
3,650	3,700	3,778	3,753	3,833	3,804	3,819	**3,911**	86.0	1
3,561	3,598	3,695	3,667	3,752	3,718	3,731	**3,822**	86.0	2
89	**102**	83	86	81	86	88	89	75.5	3
31,894	32,761	32,006	34,132	35,095	36,107	**36,763**	36,525	75.6	4
31,509	32,388	31,622	33,731	34,728	35,732	**36,395**	36,164	75.6	5
385	373	384	**401**	367	375	368	361	72.3	6
9,785	9,926	10,748	10,851	10,861	11,795	12,503	**12,650**	73.7	7
9,055	9,144	9,897	9,950	9,951	10,868	11,523	**11,670**	73.7	8
730	782	851	901	910	927	980	980	73.7	9
40,614	40,947	42,694	44,156	44,909	47,011	**47,680**	47,047	85.2	10
40,341	40,673	42,457	43,916	44,672	46,768	**47,439**	46,795	85.0	11
273	**274**	*237*	240	*237*	243	241	252	86.5	12
6,386	7,248	7,994	9,064	10,607	23,281	**27,064**	21,941	17.2	13
6,263	7,150	7,836	8,889	10,409	22,028	**25,515**	20,885	18.0	14
123	98	158	175	198	1,253	**1,549**	1,056	4.2	15
1,646	1,727	1,845	1,793	1,854	8,104	19,395	**19,570**	7.7	16
1,459	1,548	1,717	1,699	1,690	7,370	16,934	**17,227**	7.9	17
187	179	128	*94*	164	734	**2,461**	2,343	3.8	18
19,539	19,600	**20,501**	19,058	19,366	17,624	16,204	15,092	70.9	19
18,055	18,080	**18,875**	17,576	17,913	16,337	15,272	14,220	71.9	20
1,484	1,520	**1,626**	1,482	1,453	1,287	932	*872*	53.6	21
4,446	4,415	*4,331*	4,893	4,932	5,425	5,368	**5,764**	75.1	22
4,384	4,400	*4,314*	4,878	4,916	5,404	5,343	**5,737**	75.2	23
62	*15*	.17	*15*	16	21	25	27	24.2	24
5,994	6,124	6,013	6,222	6,327	6,317	6,404	6,434	79.1	25
3,018	3,110	3,069	3,204	3,205	3,196	3,213	3,227	83.9	26
2,976	3,014	*2,944*	3,018	3,122	3,121	3,191	3,207	73.9	27
10,275	10,472	11,326	11,431	11,530	11,885	**12,010**	11,898	81.3	28
3,521	3,541	3,883	3,885	3,905	3,923	3,914	**3,946**	82.0	29
6,754	6,931	7,443	7,546	7,625	7,962	**8,036**	7,952	80.3	30
29,503	30,706	32,456	32,904	33,981	34,361	34,577	**35,426**	81.6	31
27,552	28,759	30,495	30,933	32,020	32,338	32,473	**33,329**	80.9	32
1,951	1,947	1,961	1,971	1,961	2,023	**2,104**	2,097	91.8	33
146	161	147	**173**	155	162	172	157	62.4	34
143	158	144	**170**	152	159	169	154	61.8	35
3	3	3	3	3	3	3	3	100.0	36
2,097	1,652	*1,646*	1,653	1,666	1,909	1,940	2,016	77.0	37
1,435	*1,123*	1,149	1,152	1,164	1,279	1,287	1,349	76.1	38
662	529	*497*	501	502	630	653	**667**	74.5	39
2,606	*2,367*	3,442	3,607	3,008	2,471	2,859	3,286	61.0	40
2,285	*2,105*	3,001	3,119	2,588	2,114	2,479	2,843	62.5	41
321	*262*	441	488	420	357	380	443	51.4	42
32,878	34,513	37,312	**38,385**	36,825	35,234	34,104	34,037	83.0	43
22,707	23,855	25,573	**26,465**	25,575	24,223	23,748	24,158	83.7	44
10,171	10,658	11,739	**11,920**	11,250	11,011	10,356	9,879	81.5	45
17,536	17,519	18,219	18,810	19,392	**19,596**	19,446	18,684	88.0	46
8,677	8,709	8,996	9,370	9,646	9,728	**9,730**	9,498	86.5	47
8,859	*8,810*	9,223	9,440	9,746	**9,868**	9,716	9,186	89.3	48
137,068	133,786	124,519	*117,533*	130,455	143,071	155,729	**158,112**	74.3	49
54,855	54,846	50,180	*46,478*	52,753	57,497	61,547	**62,548**	74.3	50
82,213	78,940	74,339	*71,055*	77,702	85,574	94,182	**95,564**	74.4	51
33,739	*33,595*	34,280	35,361	36,427	37,415	38,575	**39,339**	85.4	52
30,926	*30,810*	31,570	32,601	33,587	34,513	35,523	**36,286**	84.9	53
2,813	2,785	*2,710*	2,760	2,840	2,902	3,052	3,053	85.4	54
13,564	14,348	15,574	15,942	16,283	16,471	**16,701**	15,574	60.7	55
8,246	8,669	9,411	9,610	9,758	**9,805**	9,783	9,150	64.7	56
5,318	5,679	6,163	6,332	6,525	6,666	**6,918**	6,424	54.9	57
11,065	11,353	11,678	11,942	12,178	**12,467**	12,463	12,421	81.0	58
9,385	9,607	9,864	10,078	10,256	10,453	**10,455**	10,394	82.0	59
1,680	1,751	1,814	1,864	1,922	2,014	2,008	2,027	75.6	60
28,723	**28,802**	28,664	28,692	28,319	28,617	28,296	27,932	90.0	61
28,652	**28,729**	28,569	28,602	28,227	28,515	28,184	27,842	89.8	62
71	73	95	90	92	102	112	90	45.2	63

TABLE **10.**—WAGE EARNERS, MALES AND FEMALES,

[The month of maximum employment for each industry is indicated

	INDUSTRY.	Average number employed during year.	NUMBER EMPLOYED ON 15TH DAY OF THE MONTH OR NEAREST REPRESENTATIVE DAY.			
			January.	February.	March.	April.
1	Typefounding	810	774	796	832	868
2	Male	653	634	646	665	715
3	Female	157	*140*	150	167	153
4	Typewriters and supplies	15,669	14,560	14,787	15,111	15,320
5	Male	11,897	*10,714*	10,966	11,320	11,580
6	Female	3,772	3,846	3,821	3,791	3,740
7	Umbrellas and canes	3,368	*3,016*	3,116	3,183	3,221
8	Male	1,624	*1,416*	1,496	1,561	1,540
9	Female	1,744	*1,600*	1,620	1,622	1,681
10	Upholstering materials, not elsewhere specified.	4,810	*4,268*	4,311	4,399	4,534
11	Male	3,984	3,598	*3,597*	3,645	3,732
12	Female	826	*670*	714	754	802
13	Varnishes	4,022	*3,617*	3,637	3,684	3,799
14	Male	3,641	*3,275*	3,302	3,344	3,442
15	Female	381	342	*335*	340	357
16	Vault lights and ventilators	316	274	*269*	273	275
17	Male	316	274	*269*	273	275
18	Female					
19	Vinegar and cider	1,981	1,431	1,375	1,400	1,387
20	Male	1,780	1,263	1,223	1,230	1,215
21	Female	201	168	152	170	172
22	Wall paper, not made in paper mills	4,262	4,606	4,597	4,410	4,214
23	Male	3,529	3,712	3,750	3,666	3,540
24	Female	733	894	847	744	674
25	Wall plaster and composition flooring	5,123	*3,683*	3,842	4,157	4,567
26	Male	5,054	*3,636*	3,784	4,095	4,509
27	Female	69	*47*	58	62	58
28	Washing machines and clothes wringers	5,956	*4,731*	4,947	5,196	5,112
29	Male	5,726	*4,506*	4,724	4,979	4,884
30	Female	230	225	223	217	228
31	Waste	2,686	2,565	*2,430*	2,476	2,520
32	Male	1,758	1,661	1,626	*1,587*	1,646
33	Female	928	904	*804*	889	874
34	Watch and clock materials, except watchcases.	582	513	*507*	514	540
35	Male	178	170	*166*	171	174
36	Female	404	343	*341*	343	366
37	Watchcases	3,900	*3,625*	3,759	3,767	3,797
38	Male	2,788	*2,507*	2,627	2,640	2,688
39	Female	1,112	1,118	1,132	1,127	1,109
40	Watches	15,888	*15,239*	15,326	15,490	15,689
41	Male	7,984	*7,468*	7,574	7,627	7,785
42	Female	7,904	7,771	7,752	7,863	7,904
43	Wheelbarrows	291	256	246	*242*	245
44	Male	288	250	242	*239*	242
45	Female	3	**6**	**4**	3	3
46	Whips	717	713	719	698	*688*
47	Male	502	490	500	*480*	483
48	Female	215	**223**	219	218	*205*
49	Windmills	1,932	2,001	2,017	1,979	1,946
50	Male	1,922	1,990	2,007	1,969	1,935
51	Female	10	**11**	10	10	**11**
52	Window and door screens and weather strips.	2,179	2,031	1,967	*1,955*	2,147
53	Male	1,909	1,735	1,722	*1,717*	1,903
54	Female	270	296	245	238	244
55	Window shades and fixtures	4,411	3,817	*3,789*	3,802	3,898
56	Male	3,207	*2,712*	2,733	2,760	2,853
57	Female	1,204	1,105	1,056	*1,042*	1,045
58	Wire	19,741	21,043	20,868	19,993	19,038
59	Male	18,731	19,864	19,592	18,905	18,152
60	Female	1,010	1,179	**1,276**	1,088	886

EMPLOYED EACH MONTH, BY INDUSTRIES: 1919—Continued.

by **bold-faced** figures and that of minimum employment by *italic* figures.]

NUMBER EMPLOYED ON 15TH DAY OF THE MONTH OR NEAREST REPRESENTATIVE DAY—continued.								Per cent minimum is of maximum.	
May.	June.	July.	August.	September.	October.	November.	December.		
900	884	**917**	*620*	791	763	770	805	67.6	1
734	726	**755**	*471*	637	609	608	636	62.4	2
166	158	**162**	149	154	154	162	169	82.8	3
15,436	15,464	15,534	*14,544*	14,990	16,790	17,413	**18,079**	80.4	4
11,701	11,815	11,941	11,111	11,475	12,872	13,359	**13,910**	77.0	5
3,735	3,649	3,593	*3,433*	3,515	3,918	4,054	**4,169**	82.3	6
3,253	3,279	3,268	3,443	3,477	3,624	3,748	**3,788**	79.6	7
1,556	1,607	1,527	1,682	1,703	1,739	**1,833**	1,828	77.3	8
1,697	1,672	1,741	1,761	1,774	1,885	1,915	**1,960**	81.6	9
4,666	4,789	4,879	5,041	5,132	5,168	5,203	**5,330**	80.1	10
3,798	3,911	3,979	4,143	4,235	4,305	4,402	**4,463**	80.6	11
868	878	**900**	898	897	863	801	867	74.4	12
3,834	3,960	4,081	4,259	4,340	4,339	4,324	**4,390**	82.4	13
3,469	3,581	3,692	3,860	3,912	3,917	3,915	**3,983**	82.2	14
365	379	389	399	**428**	422	409	407	78.3	15
280	300	329	350	350	**369**	362	361	72.9	16
280	300	329	350	350	**369**	362	361	72.9	17
									18
1,361	1,485	1,601	1,955	2,618	**3,468**	3,465	2,226	39.2	19
1,214	1,324	1,442	1,750	2,352	**3,168**	3,165	2,014	38.3	20
147	161	159	205	266	**300**	**300**	212	49.0	21
4,084	3,965	3,834	*3,567*	4,129	4,371	4,572	**4,795**	74.4	22
3,455	3,412	3,270	*2,996*	3,401	3,561	3,714	**3,871**	77.4	23
629	*553*	564	571	728	810	858	**924**	59.8	24
4,859	5,059	5,524	5,721	5,907	6,090	**6,103**	5,964	60.3	25
4,791	4,986	5,456	5,644	5,828	6,009	**6,020**	5,890	60.4	26
68	73	68	77	79	81	**83**	74	56.6	27
5,333	5,798	6,201	6,423	6,700	6,962	6,984	**7,085**	66.8	28
5,110	5,568	5,957	6,178	6,452	6,730	6,748	**6,876**	65.5	29
223	230	244	245	**248**	232	236	*209*	84.3	30
2,546	2,673	2,822	**2,923**	2,780	2,821	2,833	2,843	83.1	31
1,642	1,740	1,842	1,909	1,821	1,814	1,876	**1,932**	82.1	32
904	933	980	**1,014**	959	1,007	957	911	79.3	33
592	651	**665**	639	578	599	603	583	76.2	34
172	175	180	179	179	184	192	**194**	85.6	35
420	476	**485**	460	399	415	411	389	70.3	36
3,841	3,970	4,079	4,068	3,840	3,737	4,034	**4,283**	84.6	37
2,734	2,823	2,929	2,933	2,758	2,725	2,944	**3,148**	79.6	38
1,107	1,147	**1,150**	1,135	1,082	*1,012*	1,090	1,135	88.0	39
15,427	15,582	15,435	16,113	16,439	16,515	**16,713**	16,698	91.2	40
7,674	7,871	7,834	8,209	8,362	8,397	8,500	**8,507**	87.8	41
7,753	7,711	*7,601*	7,894	8,077	8,118	8,213	8,191	92.5	42
278	277	293	308	325	**348**	338	336	69.5	43
277	277	292	308	323	**342**	334	330	69.9	44
1		1		2	**6**	4	6		45
695	701	737	730	726	719	735	**743**	92.6	46
484	489	516	525	510	507	514	**526**	91.3	47
211	212	221	*205*	216	212	221	217	91.9	48
1,869	*1,588*	1,596	1,990	2,013	2,045	2,063	**2,077**	76.5	49
1,859	*1,578*	1,586	1,980	2,003	2,035	2,055	**2,067**	76.3	50
10	10	10	10	10	10	*8*	10	72.7	51
2,226	2,267	2,182	2,052	2,164	2,316	2,366	**2,475**	79.0	52
1,999	2,042	1,965	1,819	1,896	1,974	2,011	**2,125**	80.8	53
227	225	*217*	233	268	342	**355**	350	61.1	54
4,135	4,394	4,488	4,684	4,732	4,959	5,097	**5,137**	73.8	55
3,015	3,174	3,257	3,434	3,507	3,605	3,715	**3,739**	72.5	56
1,120	1,220	1,231	1,250	1,245	1,354	1,382	**1,398**	74.5	57
18,988	18,656	19,838	21,016	**21,282**	*17,335*	18,796	20,039	81.5	58
18,135	17,845	18,935	19,997	**20,281**	*16,356*	17,759	18,951	80.6	59
853	*811*	903	1,019	1,001	979	1,037	1,088	63.6	60

TABLE **10.**—WAGE EARNERS, MALES AND FEMALES,

[The month of maximum employment for each industry is indicated

	INDUSTRY.	Average number employed during year.	NUMBER EMPLOYED ON 15TH DAY OF THE MONTH OR NEAREST REPRESENTATIVE DAY.			
			January.	February.	March.	April.
1	Wirework, including wire rope and cable, not elsewhere specified.	15,224	14,996	14,964	15,048	*14,826*
2	Male	12,588	12,428	12,349	12,479	*12,316*
3	Female	2,636	2,568	2,615	2,569	*2,510*
4	Wood distillation	4,946	**5,838**	5,718	5,345	4,650
5	Male	4,918	**5,809**	5,691	5,316	4,621
6	Female	28	**29**	27	29	29
7	Wood preserving	3,978	3,465	3,472	*3,439*	3,830
8	Male	3,955	3,435	3,449	*3,406*	3,814
9	Female	23	30	23	33	*16*
10	Wood, turned and carved	10,649	*10,168*	10,234	10,454	10,478
11	Male	9,809	*9,399*	9,421	9,648	9,671
12	Female	840	*769*	813	806	807
13	Wooden goods, not elsewhere specified	6,443	6,273	6,563	6,537	6,476
14	Male	5,372	*5,211*	5,354	5,336	5,391
15	Female	1,071	1,062	**1,209**	1,201	1,085
16	Wool pulling	705	673	679	621	621
17	Male	701	670	676	618	618
18	Female	4	*3*	*3*	*3*	*3*
19	Wool scouring	2,177	1,896	1,728	*1,658*	1,757
20	Male	2,033	1,782	1,649	*1,589*	1,663
21	Female	144	114	79	*69*	94
22	Wool shoddy	2,566	2,516	*2,405*	2,444	2,585
23	Male	2,122	2,054	*1,955*	2,004	2,126
24	Female	444	**462**	450	440	459
25	Woolen goods	62,957	52,063	*47,872*	50,508	58,242
26	Male	41,993	34,043	*31,497*	33,581	39,076
27	Female	20,964	18,020	*16,375*	16,927	19,166
28	Worsted goods	103,830	88,631	*67,489*	73,916	91,796
29	Male	51,082	44,057	*32,098*	35,758	44,747
30	Female	52,748	44,574	*35,391*	38,158	47,049
31	All other industries	99	77	83	89	87
32	Male	87	*66*	71	77	73
33	Female	12	11	12	12	14

EMPLOYED EACH MONTH, BY INDUSTRIES: 1919—Continued.

by **bold-faced** figures and that of minimum employment by *italic* figures.]

NUMBER EMPLOYED ON 15TH DAY OF THE MONTH OR NEAREST REPRESENTATIVE DAY—continued.								Per cent minimum is of maximum.	
May.	June.	July.	August.	September.	October.	November.	December.		
14,903	15,108	15,468	15,045	15,435	15,331	15,623	**15,941**	93 0	1
12,318	12,522	12,792	12,401	12,757	12,611	12,916	**13,167**	93.5	2
2,585	2,586	2,676	2,644	2,678	2,720	2,707	**2,774**	90.5	3
4,503	*4,246*	4,541	4,538	4,658	4,934	5,042	5,339	72.7	4
4,476	*4,217*	4,514	4,510	4,630	4,907	5,014	5,311	72.6	5
27	**29**	*27*	28	28	*27*	28	28	93.1	6
4,139	4,086	4,213	4,164	4,160	**4,282**	4,210	4,276	89.3	7
4,122	4,069	4,193	4,144	4,142	**4,256**	4,182	4,248	80.0	8
17	17	20	20	18	26	28	28	48.5	9
10,455	10,591	10,556	10,806	10,786	10,886	11,114	**11,260**	90.3	10
9,645	9,678	9,736	9,983	9,957	10,004	10,217	**10,349**	90.8	11
810	**913**	820	823	829	882	897	911	84.2	12
6,433	6,374	*6,266*	6,319	6,299	6,297	6,530	**6,949**	90.2	13
5,335	5,346	5,351	5,370	5,284	5,280	5,429	**5,777**	90.2	14
1,098	1,028	*915*	949	1,015	1,017	1,101	1,172	75.7	15
621	*613*	693	727	754	811	816	**831**	73.8	16
618	*608*	688	722	749	806	812	**827**	73.5	17
3	5	5	**5**	5	5	4	4	60.0	18
2,132	2,363	2,512	**2,553**	2,443	2,412	2,307	2,363	64.9	19
1,957	2,148	2,288	**2,296**	2,246	2,281	2,219	2,278	69.2	20
175	215	224	**257**	197	131	88	85	26.8	21
2,664	2,650	2,580	2,592	2,637	2,530	2,520	**2,669**	90.1	22
2,206	2,200	2,130	2,154	2,207	2,109	2,089	**2,230**	87.7	23
458	450	450	438	430	*421*	431	439	91.1	24
63,086	66,442	68,638	69,131	69,571	69,428	70,129	**70,374**	68.0	25
42,240	44,523	45,922	46,236	46,584	46,419	46,732	**47,063**	66.9	26
20,846	21,919	22,716	22,895	22,987	23,009	**23,397**	23,311	70.0	27
101,375	111,621	116,593	117,664	119,097	116,646	118,637	**122,495**	55.1	28
49,501	55,457	57,968	58,664	58,616	57,306	58,319	**60,493**	53.1	29
51,874	56,164	58,625	59,000	60,481	59,340	60,318	**62,002**	57.1	30
113	101	85	94	105	121	**131**	102	58.8	31
99	89	78	82	93	110	**119**	87	55.5	32
14	12	*7*	12	12	11	12	15	46.7	33

TABLE 11.—WAGE EARNERS, BY MONTHS, GEOGRAPHIC

[The month of maximum employment for each industry is indicated by

	DIVISION AND STATE.	Average number employed during the year.	NUMBER OF WAGE EARNERS EMPLOYED ON THE 15TH DAY OF EACH MONTH OR NEAREST REPRESENTATIVE DAY.			
			January.	February.	March.	April.
1	UNITED STATES: 1919	9,096,372	8,874,477	8,679,913	8,677,006	8,666,549
2	1914	7,036,247	7,075,592	7,141,504	7,242,662	7,217,230
3	1909	6,615,046	6,210,063	6,297,627	6,423,517	6,437,633
	GEOGRAPHIC DIVISIONS: New England—					
4	1919	1,351,389	1,317,401	1,279,847	1,280,475	1,281,445
5	1914	1,140,233	1,169,928	1,173,596	1,180,259	1,170,317
6	1909	1,101,290	1,064,256	1,071,906	1,085,698	1,081,244
	Middle Atlantic—					
7	1919	2,872,653	2,845,811	2,795,876	2,771,726	2,768,454
8	1914	2,355,940	2,376,668	2,405,992	2,438,053	2,423,659
9	1909	2,207,747	2,078,441	2,109,534	2,145,651	2,155,611
	East North Central—					
10	1919	2,396,618	2,311,438	2,289,008	2,275,568	2,258,009
11	1914	1,680,281	1,696,039	1,722,595	1,747,289	1,733,258
12	1909	1,513,764	1,411,963	1,438,518	1,468,151	1,466,448
	West North Central—					
13	1919	499,635	483,424	475,396	473,710	471,343
14	1914	381,595	381,680	382,633	384,991	383,777
15	1909	374,337	345,774	352,517	360,134	361,835
	South Atlantic—					
16	1919	817,212	807,474	794,668	793,237	784,693
17	1914	685,252	688,801	694,193	707,979	704,322
18	1909	663,015	623,061	637,365	650,087	646,559
	East South Central—					
19	1919	329,226	316,135	311,057	313,855	313,415
20	1914	264,378	265,657	267,066	272,840	272,229
21	1909	261,772	250,192	252,224	255,688	252,511
	West South Central—					
22	1919	285,244	271,116	267,863	264,707	262,942
23	1914	211,940	213,921	210,806	210,944	210,670
24	1909	204,520	192,802	189,387	195,401	194,359
	Mountain—					
25	1919	109,216	106,004	101,895	99,618	101,640
26	1914	81,113	78,308	73,606	75,620	79,589
27	1909	75,435	70,754	66,672	68,698	70,359
	Pacific—					
28	1919	435,179	415,674	364,303	404,110	429,608
29	1914	235,515	204,590	211,017	224,687	239,409
30	1909	213,166	172,820	179,504	194,009	208,707
	NEW ENGLAND:					
31	Maine	88,651	84,884	79,492	78,696	78,698
32	New Hampshire	83,074	80,610	79,599	79,162	78,849
33	Vermont	33,491	31,239	31,135	31,419	31,757
34	Massachusetts	713,836	695,713	677,294	680,825	679,235
35	Rhode Island	139,665	131,724	126,903	128,044	133,559
36	Connecticut	292,672	293,231	285,424	282,329	279,347
	MIDDLE ATLANTIC:					
37	New York	1,228,130	1,179,216	1,182,279	1,187,865	1,194,824
38	New Jersey	508,686	504,994	484,983	482,240	489,806
39	Pennsylvania	1,135,837	1,161,601	1,128,614	1,101,621	1,083,824
	EAST NORTH CENTRAL:					
40	Ohio	730,733	714,195	698,911	694,564	688,040
41	Indiana	277,580	266,959	264,261	261,725	262,973
42	Illinois	653,114	650,664	643,541	636,041	620,500
43	Michigan	471,242	421,493	425,205	428,121	431,021
44	Wisconsin	263,949	258,127	257,090	255,117	250,475
	WEST NORTH CENTRAL:					
45	Minnesota	115,623	114,763	113,885	113,326	110,691
46	Iowa	80,551	75,556	75,141	75,692	76,185
47	Missouri	195,037	184,513	182,796	182,239	182,885
48	North Dakota	4,472	3,996	4,014	3,989	4,175
49	South Dakota	6,382	5,864	5,805	5,997	5,966
50	Nebraska	36,521	36,545	35,032	34,430	34,938
51	Kansas	61,049	62,187	58,723	58,037	56,503

DIVISIONS AND STATES: 1919, 1914, AND 1909.

bold-faced figures and that of minimum employment by *italic* figures.]

NUMBER OF WAGE EARNERS EMPLOYED ON THE 15TH DAY OF EACH MONTH OR NEAREST REPRESENTATIVE DAY.								Per cent minimum is of maximum.	
May.	June.	July.	August.	September.	October.	November.	December.		
8,718,876	8,865,621	9,120,448	9,348,600	9,507,208	9,478,439	9,556,157	**9,663,170**	89.7	1
7,148,560	7,100,278	7,018,777	7,020,593	7,086,725	7,006,241	6,736,608	*6,640,194*	91.7	2
6,457,279	6,517,469	6,486,676	6,656,933	6,898,765	6,997,090	**7,066,853**	6,990,652	88.6	3
1,306,223	1,332,449	1,348,448	1,367,755	1,399,266	1,414,605	1,433,947	**1,454,828**	88.0	4
1,163,457	1,146,790	1,119,838	1,107,731	1,121,361	1,122,946	1,109,694	*1,096,879*	92.9	5
1,087,333	1,088,312	1,077,016	1,093,558	1,126,756	1,141,593	1,147,951	**1,149,871**	92.6	6
2,766,820	2,800,061	2,877,600	2,933,505	2,950,608	2,930,465	2,984,517	**3,046,393**	90.8	7
2,392,603	2,368,927	2,325,574	2,319,460	2,357,792	2,347,907	2,270,109	*2,244,536*	92.1	8
2,156,236	2,169,998	2,155,844	2,195,710	2,287,845	2,338,583	*2,350,336*	2,349,165	88.4	9
2,266,743	2,329,578	2,405,965	2,477,623	2,524,065	2,500,018	2,547,170	**2,579,231**	87.4	10
1,709,904	1,699,784	1,677,985	1,678,439	1,685,138	1,660,307	1,583,747	*1,568,887*	89.8	11
1,477,079	1,497,289	1,481,802	1,518,983	1,571,342	1,600,433	1,610,588	**1,622,565**	87.0	12
478,364	489,706	498,695	514,287	522,494	527,039	529,897	**531,265**	88.7	13
383,545	386,597	387,379	**390,514**	387,276	382,463	366,188	*362,097*	92.7	14
366,543	373,610	373,496	386,710	**398,065**	394,772	392,382	386,209	86.9	15
772,392	778,369	796,265	822,535	868,064	**875,048**	850,812	862,987	88.3	16
694,804	686,455	675,459	691,353	711,615	686,137	644,970	*636,936*	89.5	17
641,772	648,032	644,252	682,609	711,296	699,110	686,416	685,630	87.6	18
310,020	*307,391*	321,186	334,381	348,081	357,071	358,103	**360,017**	85.4	19
266,539	265,712	267,030	268,677	268,386	261,419	251,333	*245,648*	90.0	20
247,286	*246,649*	250,438	263,343	276,189	282,070	**283,605**	281,068	87.0	21
269,663	267,387	280,571	293,746	299,530	308,786	317,746	**318,871**	82.5	22
207,999	209,147	**215,558**	214,843	213,191	214,659	213,013	208,529	96.5	23
190,063	195,392	200,416	203,733	210,876	223,165	**229,379**	229,260	82.6	24
104,180	108,204	112,927	113,833	111,289	117,870	**118,532**	114,600	84.0	25
82,396	85,382	**88,809**	84,242	82,922	85,504	79,835	77,143	82.9	26
72,109	75,311	77,607	77,826	79,521	**83,149**	82,673	80,542	80.2	27
444,471	452,476	478,812	**490,935**	483,811	447,537	415,433	394,978	74.2	28
247,313	251,484	261,145	**265,334**	259,044	244,899	217,719	*199,539*	75.2	29
218,858	222,876	225,805	234,461	**236,875**	234,215	223,523	206,342	73.0	30
85,289	87,769	89,503	94,092	**98,407**	97,474	95,134	94,374	80.0	31
79,972	82,221	82,600	83,325	85,663	87,070	88,593	**89,224**	88.4	32
32,638	33,184	33,385	34,272	34,649	35,621	36,003	**36,590**	85.1	33
689,490	705,382	715,599	726,537	736,391	741,911	751,909	**765,746**	88.4	34
136,656	138,544	142,223	143,452	145,556	147,108	150,175	**152,036**	83.5	35
282,178	285,349	285,117	286,077	298,600	305,421	312,133	**316,858**	88.2	36
1,186,957	1,191,679	1,228,077	**1,260,592**	1,272,811	1,260,413	1,281,760	**1,311,087**	89.9	37
496,342	503,068	510,709	516,895	519,235	528,238	530,083	**537,639**	89.7	38
1,083,521	1,105,314	1,138,814	1,156,018	1,158,562	1,141,814	1,172,674	**1,197,667**	90.5	39
687,683	710,187	740,188	768,579	773,510	740,570	761,688	**790,681**	87.0	40
267,312	272,593	278,232	285,726	**294,892**	288,486	293,484	294,317	88.8	41
618,701	628,740	638,982	658,478	681,270	681,015	**689,945**	689,491	89.7	42
442,925	461,718	480,152	497,915	507,050	515,805	**522,876**	520,623	80.6	43
250,122	256,340	268,411	266,925	267,343	274,142	279,177	**284,119**	88.0	44
109,489	112,458	114,430	116,607	118,627	120,020	120,930	**122,250**	89.6	45
77,980	79,963	81,343	83,928	85,417	84,496	**85,825**	85,086	87.6	46
187,384	190,266	194,709	202,609	206,394	**209,704**	207,586	209,359	86.9	47
4,224	4,573	4,841	4,847	4,758	**4,850**	4,731	4,666	82.2	48
6,205	6,418	6,554	6,657	6,776	6,722	6,718	**6,902**	84.1	49
34,748	36,477	36,576	37,683	37,760	37,836	38,038	**38,189**	90.2	50
58,334	59,551	60,242	61,956	62,762	63,411	**66,069**	64,813	85.5	51

TABLE 11.—WAGE EARNERS, BY MONTHS, GEOGRAPHIC

[The month of maximum employment for each industry is indicated by

DIVISION AND STATE.	Average number employed during the year.	NUMBER OF WAGE EARNERS EMPLOYED ON THE 15TH DAY OF EACH MONTH OR NEAREST REPRESENTATIVE DAY.			
		January.	February.	March.	April.
SOUTH ATLANTIC:					
1 Delaware	29,035	28,236	26,898	25,399	25,728
2 Maryland	140,342	140,053	135,797	131,774	129,128
3 District of Columbia	10,482	10,459	10,387	10,319	10,449
4 Virginia	119,352	111,943	112,177	112,455	113,802
5 West Virginia	83,036	80,721	81,101	81,170	80,719
6 North Carolina	157,659	157,470	154,933	156,407	155,349
7 South Carolina	79,450	79,274	78,606	78,828	76,361
8 Georgia	123,441	125,289	121,762	123,458	121,269
9 Florida	74,415	74,029	73,007	73,427	71,888
EAST SOUTH CENTRAL:					
10 Kentucky	69,340	66,495	66,213	66,869	66,756
11 Tennessee	95,167	90,230	88,865	89,448	90,168
12 Alabama	107,159	104,837	102,802	103,668	103,838
13 Mississippi	57,560	54,573	53,177	53,870	52,653
WEST SOUTH CENTRAL:					
14 Arkansas	49,954	44,527	44,289	44,180	43,960
15 Louisiana	98,265	93,443	91,919	89,172	89,695
16 Oklahoma	29,503	28,279	28,209	28,518	27,897
17 Texas	107,522	104,867	103,446	102,837	101,390
MOUNTAIN:					
18 Montana	17,160	17,539	16,890	16,603	16,239
19 Idaho	13,917	11,248	11,178	11,323	12,849
20 Wyoming	6,634	5,876	5,804	5,853	5,939
21 Colorado	35,254	35,173	34,208	33,333	34,361
22 New Mexico	5,736	4,992	5,164	5,337	5,181
23 Arizona	8,528	8,872	8,416	7,911	7,931
24 Utah	18,868	18,819	17,028	16,280	16,196
25 Nevada	3,119	3,485	3,207	2,978	2,944
PACIFIC:					
26 Washington	132,928	128,313	89,914	122,770	137,395
27 Oregon	58,559	55,393	54,251	57,708	59,180
28 California	243,692	231,968	220,138	223,632	233,033

DIVISIONS AND STATES: 1919, 1914, AND 1909—Continued.

bold-faced figures and that of minimum employment by *italic* figures.]

NUMBER OF WAGE EARNERS EMPLOYED ON THE 15TH DAY OF EACH MONTH OR NEAREST REPRESENTATIVE DAY.								Per cent minimum is of maximum.	
May.	June.	July.	August.	September.	October.	November.	December.		
27,117	28,806	28,124	32,821	**33,438**	32,185	29,715	29,953	76.0	1
130,161	133,609	137,456	144,217	160,313	**160,567**	141,261	139,768	80.4	2
10,463	10,559	10,522	10,578	10,332	10,375	10,618	**10,723**	96.2	3
112,572	113,536	116,759	125,148	131,680	**131,916**	125,549	124,687	84.9	4
79,617	79,901	81,129	87,105	**89,041**	84,209	84,362	87,357	89.4	5
148,683	*147,953*	150,453	152,597	159,740	167,146	168,665	**172,512**	85.8	6
74,217	*74,165*	76,281	78,550	82,889	83,136	84,268	**86,825**	85.4	7
116,548	116,940	120,406	120,221	125,305	127,806	129,266	**133,022**	87.6	8
73,014	72,900	**75,135**	*71,298*	75,326	77,708	77,108	**78,140**	91.2	9
66,268	*65,941*	67,882	69,414	72,032	74,002	74,520	**75,688**	87.1	10
90,739	90,056	94,498	97,805	100,363	102,593	103,429	**103,810**	85.6	11
99,828	*98,474*	103,013	107,229	112,526	115,740	116,331	**117,622**	83.7	12
53,185	52,920	55,793	59,933	63,160	**64,736**	63,823	62,897	81.3	13
45,308	45,543	49,206	55,605	**58,553**	58,093	55,281	54,903	75.1	14
91,541	89,800	95,429	97,890	98,868	106,465	**117,665**	117,293	75.8	15
28,236	28,020	28,648	30,096	30,810	31,482	31,582	**32,259**	86.5	16
104,578	104,024	107,288	110,155	111,299	112,746	113,218	**114,416**	88.6	17
17,062	17,719	17,554	16,906	16,973	17,421	**18,228**	16,786	89.1	18
14,020	14,637	14,555	14,568	15,552	16,252	**16,342**	14,480	68.4	19
5,996	6,409	6,885	7,216	7,127	7,509	**7,560**	7,434	76.8	20
33,974	35,019	36,749	**37,553**	*33,027*	35,877	36,636	37,138	87.9	21
5,629	5,909	6,148	**6,253**	6,170	6,025	6,019	6,005	79.8	22
8,217	8,208	8,742	8,902	8,837	**8,945**	8,772	8,583	88.4	23
16,286	17,400	19,152	19,600	20,412	**22,592**	21,740	20,911	71.7	24
2,996	2,903	3,142	*2,835*	3,191	3,249	3,235	3,263	81.3	25
141,028	141,474	141,701	146,135	**146,872**	142,083	133,821	123,630	61.2	26
61,804	61,122	61,965	**62,488**	60,261	60,641	58,396	*49,499*	79.2	27
241,639	249,880	275,146	**282,312**	276,678	244,813	223,216	221,849	78.0	28

TABLE 12.—AVERAGE NUMBER OF WAGE EARNERS CLASSIFIED ACCORDING TO PREVAILING HOURS OF LABOR PER WEEK, BY INDUSTRIES: 1919 AND 1914.

INDUSTRY.	Census year.	Total.	IN ESTABLISHMENTS WHERE THE PREVAILING HOURS OF LABOR PER WEEK WERE—							
			44 and under.	Between 44 and 48.	48.[1]	Between 48 and 54.	54.	Between 54 and 60.	60.	Over 60.
Aeroplanes, seaplanes, and airships, and parts.	1919	3,543	421	605	1,194	952	19	1	351	.....
	1914	168	(2)	(2)	2	22	51	77	16	.....
Agricultural implements	1919	54,368	169	76	2,372	27,952	6,256	15,180	2,348	15
	1914	48,459	(2)	(2)	4,461	2,632	4,559	25,258	11,539	10
Aluminum manufactures	1919	11,402	51	97	1,044	5,813	1,032	2,374	876	115
	1914	4,614	(2)	(2)	3	131	235	2,374	1,871	.....
Ammunition	1919	22,816	1,027	3,975	5,785	9,023	1,868	935	203	.....
	1914	11,493	(2)	(2)	195	287	1,879	8,613	519	.....
Artificial flowers	1919	4,138	2,655	245	658	471	43	64	2	.....
	1914	4,808	(2)	(2)	714	2,239	1,685	112	39	19
Artificial limbs	1919	671	41	15	231	217	153	12	.....	2
	1914	488	(2)	(2)	80	81	222	47	55	3
Artificial stone products	1919	8,378	605	38	1,847	536	2,099	820	2,433	.....
	1914	10,255	(2)	(2)	1,684	485	2,825	1,054	4,191	16
Artists' materials	1919	926	92	15	196	120	64	409	11	19
	1914	604	(2)	(2)	60	72	183	187	93	9
Asbestos products, not including steam packing.	1919	3,654	43	61	954	476	249	1,349	482	40
	1914	962	(2)	(2)	130	28	3	171	608	22
Automobile bodies and parts....	1919	132,556	4,808	2,761	41,857	43,340	8,433	28,935	2,399	23
	1914	47,785	(2)	(2)	1,284	8,030	7,009	25,771	5,678	13
Automobiles	1919	210,559	3,674	2,957	94,880	82,747	9,911	15,807	583	.....
	1914	79,307	(2)	(2)	13,033	19,963	10,782	28,573	6,936	20
Automobile repairing	1919	55,061	3,116	282	13,014	6,027	17,051	2,938	11,742	891
	1914	12,562	(2)	(2)	1,607	1,050	5,830	1,220	2,477	378
Awnings, tents, and sails	1919	6,028	787	328	1,538	1,297	1,286	691	98	3
	1914	5,073	(2)	(2)	943	722	2,252	489	667	.....
Babbitt metal and solder	1919	2,372	176	30	280	828	48	813	197	.....
	1914	1,035	(2)	(2)	39	117	110	553	216	.....
Bags, other than paper, not including bags made in textile mills.	1919	10,756	420	219	2,413	5,430	1,077	1,139	58	.....
	1914	9,358	(2)	(2)	101	1,478	3,520	2,730	1,529	.....
Bags, paper, exclusive of those made in paper mills.	1919	4,168	91	64	759	2,289	450	515	.....	.....
	1914	3,505	(2)	(2)	229	374	2,246	460	99	97
Baking powders and yeast	1919	3,331	187	380	1,110	739	346	467	102	.....
	1914	2,270	(2)	(2)	295	717	163	506	456	133
Baskets, and rattan and willow ware.	1919	4,533	188	233	791	1,512	685	558	523	43
	1914	4,574	(2)	(2)	475	214	937	1,487	1,458	3
Bells	1919	237	10	10	8	11	194	.....	4	.....
	1914	445	.....	.....	.....	57	33	153	202	.....
Belting and hose, rubber	1919	5,826	.....	277	4,267	587	263	432	.....	.....
	1914	5,115	.....	.....	.....	.....	1,091	2,822	1,202	.....
Belting and hose, woven, other than rubber.	1919	2,479	59	88	1,048	436	667	151	30	.....
	1914	952	(2)	(2)	91	73	476	236	76	.....
Belting, leather	1919	2,765	24	65	350	1,580	440	280	26	.....
	1914	2,951	(2)	(2)	245	528	495	1,558	122	3
Billiard tables, bowling alleys, and accessories.	1919	2,101	59	12	60	85	1,837	43	5	.....
	1914	1,453	(2)	(2)	28	279	990	120	41	.....
Blacking, stains, and dressings...	1919	2,455	187	497	552	922	74	218	4	1
	1914	1,766	(2)	(2)	318	489	531	87	341	.....
Bluing	1919	360	18	94	49	110	55	34	.....	.....
	1914	254	(2)	(2)	100	31	80	5	38	.....
Bone, carbon, and lamp black ...	1919	675	.....	.....	52	38	27	258	23	277
	1914	339	(2)	(2)	73	23	21	.....	51	171
Bookbinding and blank-book making.	1919	20,361	2,049	449	15,033	1,789	683	262	93	3
	1914	21,693	(2)	(2)	9,195	5,814	5,053	1,593	38	.....
Boot and shoe cut stock	1919	9,715	161	1,152	5,041	1,719	1,019	520	103	.....
	1914	7,819	(2)	(2)	106	1,246	2,383	3,847	211	26

[1] Includes 48 and under for 1914.   [2] Corresponding figures not available.

Table 12.—AVERAGE NUMBER OF WAGE EARNERS CLASSIFIED ACCORDING TO PREVAILING HOURS OF LABOR PER WEEK, BY INDUSTRIES: 1919 AND 1914—Continued.

INDUSTRY.	Census year.	Total.	IN ESTABLISHMENTS WHERE THE PREVAILING HOURS OF LABOR PER WEEK WERE—							
			44 and under.	Between 44 and 48.	48.[1]	Between 48 and 54.	54.	Between 54 and 60.	60.	Over 60.
Boot and shoe findings	1919	8,941	773	1,342	3,209	2,203	565	489	360	
	1914	6,714	([2])	([2])	392	646	2,257	3,252	166	1
Boots and shoes, not including rubber boots and shoes.	1919	211,049	18,511	25,580	88,406	47,431	20,898	9,466	755	2
	1914	191,555	([2])	([2])	4,966	23,263	79,699	77,854	5,773	
Boots and shoes, rubber	1919	32,875	724		26,881	1,532	5	448	3,285	
	1914	18,687				338	14,859	3,490		
Boxes, cigar	1919	5,218	85	52	900	1,419	1,441	1,289	32	
	1914	5,835	([2])	([2])	906	626	1,875	2,158	270	
Boxes, paper and other, not elsewhere specified.	1919	55,862	3,844	2,018	17,801	21,658	4,547	5,452	542	
	1914	45,311	([2])	([2])	5,451	8,585	17,771	11,186	2,139	179
Boxes, wooden packing, except cigar boxes.	1919	42,445	1,898	505	4,692	8,525	5,175	12,112	9,394	144
	1914	38,548	([2])	([2])	858	3,155	5,251	15,421	13,511	352
Brass, bronze, and copper products.	1919	75,051	2,699	3,572	11,779	23,344	3,071	29,089	1,466	31
	1914	40,306	([2])	([2])	1,851	6,680	7,545	17,401	6,669	160
Bread and other bakery products.	1919	141,592	4,121	20,778	60,062	12,425	25,338	5,247	11,085	2,536
	1914	124,052	([2])	([2])	14,556	6,887	48,579	10,334	37,365	6,331
Brick and tile, terra-cotta, and fire-clay products.	1919	76,915	1,971	500	15,676	6,971	16,342	9,275	25,392	788
	1914	100,182	([2])	([2])	10,883	4,489	18,186	13,844	51,046	1,734
Brooms	1919	6,313	1,072	276	973	1,812	545	903	728	4
	1914	5,642	([2])	([2])	820	936	1,151	1,247	1,466	22
Brushes	1919	7,968	488	384	2,463	3,241	349	950	93	
	1914	7,213	([2])	([2])	263	1,188	3,340	2,109	310	3
Butter	1919	17,641	325	51	3,013	697	2,673	2,107	5,689	3,086
	1914	14,149	([2])	([2])	1,334	243	1,859	1,131	6,106	3,476
Butter, reworking	1919	47			9			38		
	1914	304	([2])	([2])	30	10	17	6	232	9
Buttons	1919	15,577	1,901	152	4,719	3,880	1,475	2,442	1,004	4
	1914	14,511	([2])	([2])	388	2,506	5,130	4,978	1,508	1
Candles	1919	541	4	12	112	63	43	277	30	
	1914	387	([2])	([2])	.. 11	6	89	43	238	
Canning and preserving, fish	1919	11,248	759	188	4,002	1,685	1,336	387	2,633	258
	1914	9,069	([2]) .	([2])	1,826	82	2,702	196	3,937	326
Canning and preserving, fruits and vegetables.	1919	60,865	4,146	473	12,101	2,966	7,074	6,634	24,152	3,319
	1914	50,325	([2])	([2])	4,555	1,821	8,758	5,677	27,190	2,324
Canning and preserving, oysters.	1919	1,189	114		673	25	146	38	193	
	1914	2,087	([2])	([2])	615	233	192	165	872	10
Card cutting and designing	1919	1,148	119	49	471	388	121			
	1914	517	([2])	([2])	253	83	132	49		
Cardboard, not made in paper mills.	1919	1,425	568		308	286	91	93		79
	1914	1,159			593	276	175	115		
Carpets and rugs, other than rag.	1919	22,933	119		12,782	2,295	7,494	181	62	
	1914	31,309	([2])	([2])	23	2,099	23,235	5,685	267	
Carpets, rag	1919	2,016	100	72	525	537	424	309	49	
	1914	2,130	([2])	([2])	320	245	540	644	380	1
Carriage and wagon materials	1919	6,509	43	75	395	1,351	610	2,023	2,012	
	1914	11,087	([2])	([2])	471	514	1,272	5,265	3,510	55
Carriages and sleds, children's	1919	6,686	108	42	360	3,097	299	2,081	699	
	1914	5,900	([2])	([2])	88	619	1,640	1,934	1,619	
Carriages and wagons, including repairs.	1919	18,173	339	42	1,725	4,418	1,961	6,453	3,226	9
	1914	41,304	([2])	([2])	2,738	4,846	8,508	15,721	9,448	43
Cars and general shop construction and repairs by electric-railroad companies.	1919	31,272	1,278	829	5,209	8,662	7,302	3,124	2,523	2,345
	1914	26,384	([2])	([2])	1,665	1,638	6,160	6,640	6,040	4,241
Cars and general shop construction and repairs by steam-railroad companies.	1919	484,437	2,893	45,481	306,639	10,671	7,061	108,403	1,968	1,321
	1914	339,518	([2])	([2])	74,431	50,616	100,759	46,375	16,767	50,570
Cars, electric-railroad, not including operations of railroad companies.	1919	2,920	493		335	25	366	1,701		
	1914	3,840	([2])	([2])	892		403	2,103	442	

[1] Includes 48 and under for 1914.　　　[2] Corresponding figures not available.

TABLE 12.—AVERAGE NUMBER OF WAGE EARNERS CLASSIFIED ACCORDING TO PREVAILING HOURS OF LABOR PER WEEK, BY INDUSTRIES: 1919 AND 1914—Continued.

| INDUSTRY. | Census year. | Total. | IN ESTABLISHMENTS WHERE THE PREVAILING HOURS OF LABOR PER WEEK WERE— | | | | | | | |
			44 and under.	Between 44 and 48.	48.[1]	Between 48 and 54.	54.	Between 54 and 60.	60.	Over 60.
Cars, steam-railroad, not including operations of railroad companies.	1919	52,298	1,875	4,984	9,864	16,055	858	16,883	1,779	......
	1914	54,288	(2)	(2)	341	5,294	19,291	16,885	12,477	......
Cash registers and calculating machines.	1919	16,544	636	13	1,664	7,393	6,403	435	......	......
	1914	8,956	(2)	(2)	435	457	7,271	792	1	......
Cement	1919	25,524	13	......	799	......	962	7,148	6,097	10,505
	1914	27,916	(2)	(2)	24	3	73	1,536	7,790	18,490
Charcoal, not including production in the lumber and wood distillation industries.	1919	209	22	16	64	2	4	1	100	......
	1914	228	(2)	(2)	31	20	2	35	132	8
Cheese	1919	3,997	103	25	334	131	324	644	632	1,804
	1914	2,908	(2)	(2)	208	75	235	325	874	1,191
Chemicals	1919	55,586	258	2,288	18,804	8,123	2,997	15,365	5,562	2,189
	1914	32,311	(2)	(2)	947	303	1,586	12,912	5,553	11,010
Chewing gum[3]	1919	3,190	157	922	163	1,741	162	27	18	......
China decorating, not including that done in potteries.	1919	244	78	65	64	37	......	......	......	......
	1914	295	(2)	(2)	122	34	41	93	5	......
Chocolate and cocoa products	1919	9,083	8	11	3,338	859	673	3,753	248	193
	1914	4,160	(2)	(2)	21	514	644	2,102	879	......
Cleansing and polishing preparations.	1919	1,955	366	93	336	642	259	112	147	......
	1914	1,239	(2)·	(2)	286	168	380	235	170	......
Clocks	1919	8,252	10	28	1,084	2,046	97	4,987	......	......
	1914	6,754	(2)	(2)	52	1,733	2,989	1,952	28	......
Cloth, sponging and refinishing	1919	1,206	355	461	224	121	41	4	......	......
	1914	901	(2)	(2)	170	407	148	162	14	......
Clothing, horse	1919	766	4	36	56	66	192	412	......	......
	1914	1,669	(2)	(2)	136	262	266	458	547	......
Clothing, men's	1919	175,270	132,586	6,951	18,878	10,422	4,272	1,854	219	88
	1914	173,747	(2)	(2)	35,114	87,907	37,719	10,344	2,524	139
Clothing, men's, buttonholes	1919	484	348	11	84	8	32	1	......	......
	1914	672	(2)	(2)	198	328	132	9	5	......
Clothing, women's	1919	165,649	120,369	9,321	18,587	15,160	1,655	485	62	10
	1914	168,907	.(2)	(2)	11,741	123,066	28,780	4,785	508	27
Coal-tar products[4]	1919	15,663	941	182	5,205	1,589	3,805	2,171	742	1,028
Coffee and spice, roasting and grinding.	1919	10,540	1,012	1,032	2,615	3,303	1,441	341	790	6
	1914	8,549	(2)	(2)	1,297	2,125	2,491	1,959	672	5
Coffins, burial cases, and undertakers' goods.	1919	11,890	453	31	1,723	1,899	2,316	4,577	891	......
	1914	9,468	(2)	(2)	583	935	3,077	2,194	2,679	......
Coke, not including gas-house coke.	1919	29,319	342	17	9,250	112	1,854	4,307	2,010	11,427
	1914	21,107	(2)	(2)	1,582	86	6,637	1,809	4,762	6,231
Collars and cuffs, men's	1919	11,103	162	5,790	43	4,106	1,002	......	......	......
	1914	10,100	(2)	(2)	90	758	8,180	233	839	......
Combs and hairpins, not made from metal or rubber.	1919	2,229	54	......	152	1,786	65	172	......	......
	1914	2,773	(2)	(2)	53	320	587	1,638	175	......
Condensed milk	1919	13,675	24	......	497	91	2,056	1,286	5,551	4,170
	1914	6,002	(2)	(2)	58	20	433	159	2,954	2,378
Confectionery and ice cream[5]	1919	95,648	10,382	5,658	27,052	15,484	14,351	11,258	5,623	5,840
	1914	64,034	(2)	(2)	5,839	10,490	20,566	13,789	9,076	4,274
Cooperage	1919	13,219	686	367	2,619	2,545	1,627	3,161	2,201	13
	1914	17,128	(2)	(2)	2,867	1,999	2,595	3,865	5,782	20
Copper, tin, and sheet-iron work.	1919	27,640	9,994	634	6,717	4,158	2,492	1,964	1,675	6
	1914	28,714	(2)	(2)	14,308	2,500	5,840	3,624	2,441	1
Cordage and twine	1919	17,622	3	......	3,970	6,292	2,545	3,211	1,601	......
	1914	15,769	(2)	(2)	573	154	8,469	4,512	1,939	122
Cordials and flavoring sirups	1919	1,398	105	401	162	508	113	30	73	6
	1914	929	(2)	(2)	144	152	456	80	96	1

[1] Includes 48 and under for 1914.
[2] Corresponding figures not available.
[3] Included in "confectionery and ice cream" in 1914.
[4] Included in "chemicals" in 1914.
[5] Includes "chewing gum" in 1914.

TABLE 12.—AVERAGE NUMBER OF WAGE EARNERS CLASSIFIED ACCORDING TO PREVAILING HOURS OF LABOR PER WEEK, BY INDUSTRIES: 1919 AND 1914—Continued.

INDUSTRY.	Census year.	Total.	IN ESTABLISHMENTS WHERE THE PREVAILING HOURS OF LABOR PER WEEK WERE—							
			44 and under.	Between 44 and 48.	48.[1]	Between 48 and 54.	54.	Between 54 and 60.	60.	Over 60.
Cork, cutting	1919	3,545	127	14	624	1,449	399	22	910	......
	1914	3,454	(2)	(2)	25	320	2,101	431	577	......
Corsets	1919	18,415	4,394	3,290	5,702	3,666	1,363	......	......	......
	1914	20,496	(2)	(2)	992	7,409	6,169	5,909	17	......
Cotton goods	1919	430,966	1,331	373	166,825	15,721	59,437	139,777	47,035	467
	1914	379,366	(2)	(2)	1,075	1,572	149,157	68,842	157,034	1,686
Cotton lace	1919	6,490	64	......	2,513	2,263	1,103	547	......	......
	1914	7,440	(2)	(2)	1	1,039	4,591	1,809	......	......
Cotton small wares	1919	9,396	302	40	4,028	1,044	2,915	894	173	......
	1914	6,598	(2)	(2)	69	538	4,539	1,374	78	......
Crucibles	1919	848	......	95	35	371	140	207	......	......
	1914	302	......	......	......	8	7	264	23	......
Cutlery and edge tools	1919	19,859	441	36	3,335	6,667	3,114	5,133	1,133	......
	1914	16,561	(2)	(2)	1,115	2,470	1,972	6,613	4,391	......
Dairymen's, poultrymen's, and apiarists' supplies.	1919	6,437	17	5	2,437	1,616	587	1,227	537	11
	1914	5,551	(2)	(2)	142	536	1,784	1,504	1,558	27
Dental goods	1919	5,224	655	375	1,160	1,927	1,041	38	28	......
	1914	3,080	(2)	(2)	468	681	1,324	562	43	2
Drug grinding	1919	1,347	59	1	569	575	9	38	96	......
	1914	1,059	(2)	(2)	58	183	326	96	109	287
Druggists' preparations	1919	15,568	1,421	4,207	2,920	5,173	1,343	208	296	......
	1914	9,277	(2)	(2)	1,264	4,394	2,460	869	264	26
Dyeing and finishing textiles, exclusive of that done in textile mills.	1919	55,985	11,168	819	18,634	7,317	10,482	6,748	671	146
	1914	48,467	(2)	(2)	557	2,769	16,186	23,695	5,226	34
Dyestuffs and extracts, natural	1919	4,342	166	193	267	129	363	392	1,535	1,297
	1914	2,839	(2)	(2)	85	173	46	452	1,311	772
Electrical machinery, apparatus, and supplies.	1919	212,374	19,533	7,722	98,016	53,203	10,885	19,783	3,028	204
	1914	118,078	(2)	(2)	4,078	30,529	38,838	41,715	2,899	19
Electroplating	1919	3,024	447	218	989	758	132	384	96	......
	1914	2,584	(2)	(2)	307	582	665	856	172	2
Emery and other abrasive wheels	1919	5,601	44	50	347	4,783	148	139	90	......
	1914	2,387	(2)	(2)	8	37	939	1,297	106	......
Enameling	1919	694	110	166	118	100	86	109	5	......
	1914	1,314	(2)	(2)	103	239	162	533	277	......
Engines, steam, gas, and water	1919	77,617	9,289	4,619	22,899	15,410	6,662	16,949	1,786	3
	1914	29,657	(2)	(2)	1,982	1,075	8,862	14,789	2,917	32
Engravers' materials	1919	174	3	6	50	81	26	8	......	......
	1914	106	(2)	(2)	5	50	12	39	......	......
Engraving and diesinking	1919	1,878	848	78	589	251	44	60	8	......
	1914	1,536	(2)	(2)	326	385	558	261	3	3
Engraving, steel and copper plate, including plate printing.	1919	7,014	949	406	4,932	590	112	25	......	......
	1914	6,859	(2)	(2)	4,694	1,727	327	47	55	9
Engraving, wood	1919	235	172	19	31	13	......	......	......	......
	1914	302	(2)	(2)	254	24	16	8	......	......
Envelopes	1919	8,129	263	203	4,709	2,630	149	151	24	......
	1914	6,970	(2)	(2)	271	1,837	3,746	1,116	......	......
Explosives	1919	9,249	62	......	8,048	192	216	107	624	......
	1914	6,306	(2)	(2)	635	1,399	1,288	1,272	1,624	88
Fancy articles, not elsewhere specified.	1919	13,961	3,510	952	2,591	4,910	955	962	24	57
	1914	7,399	(2)	(2)	1,221	1,810	2,513	1,455	397	3
Feathers and plumes	1919	3,504	2,850	316	198		10	17	......	......
	1914	4,483	(2)	(2)	783	2,444	1,252	2	2	......
Felt goods	1919	5,236	90	38	1,121	1,663	1,067	967	290	......
	1914	4,035	(2)	(2)	5	96	1,239	1,767	917	11
Ferroalloys[3]	1919	2,344			92	......	75	224	845	1,108

[1] Includes 48 and under for 1914.
[2] Corresponding figures not available.
[3] Included in other classifications in 1914.

TABLE 12.—AVERAGE NUMBER OF WAGE EARNERS CLASSIFIED ACCORDING TO PREVAILING HOURS OF LABOR PER WEEK, BY INDUSTRIES: 1919 AND 1914—Continued.

INDUSTRY.	Census year.	Total.	IN ESTABLISHMENTS WHERE THE PREVAILING HOURS OF LABOR PER WEEK WERE—							
			44 and under.	Between 44 and 48.	48.[1]	Between 48 and 54.	54.	Between 54 and 60.	60.	Over 60.
Fertilizers	1919	26,296	574	211	1,608	921	3,624	10,238	8,395	725
	1914	22,815	(2)	(2)	281	500	2,656	3,061	14,282	2,035
Files	1919	5,767	796	26	1,314	2,501	52	1,052	26	......
	1914	4,349	(2)	(2)	92	48	2,385	1,663	161	......
Firearms	1919	11,287	282	3,080	5,576	434	932	961	22	......
	1914	7,064	......	......	......	4	2,001	4,032	1,027	......
Fire extinguishers, chemical	1919	777	477	......	54	159	9	78	......	......
	1914	256	(2)	(2)	12	11	41	175	17	......
Fireworks	1919	1,222	40	4	339	400	195	226	18	......
	1914	1,324	(2)	(2)	50	24	429	350	465	6
Flags and banners	1919	1,065	125	62	300	387	191	......	......	......
	1914	1,495	(2)	(2)	356	541	347	248	3	......
Flavoring extracts	1919	2,188	279	145	641	700	284	115	24	......
	1914	1,461	(2)	(2)	410	259	440	280	68	4
Flax and hemp, dressed	1919	420	2	......	208	......	18	......	192	......
	1914	116	(2)	(2)	24	5	42	......	45	......
Flour-mill and gristmill products.	1919	45,481	859	48	16,597	723	3,636	2,236	16,182	5,200
	1914	39,718	(2)	(2)	3,414	355	2,949	1,331	22,714	8,955
Food preparations, not elsewhere specified.	1919	30,365	1,374	931	8,306	4,430	3,727	3,745	7,114	738
	1914	20,306	(2)	(2)	2,362	1,689	4,038	2,949	6,749	2,519
Foundry and machine-shop products.	1919	482,767	42,299	10,850	126,120	115,535	71,515	90,514	24,196	1,738
	1914	362,471	(2)	(2)	25,699	45,433	110,782	129,822	49,326	1,409
Foundry supplies	1919	906	85	......	112	184	79	218	182	46
	1914	555	(2)	(2)	72	11	85	36	346	5
Fuel, manufactured	1919	171	3	......	58	......	61	14	35	......
	1914	141	(2)	(2)	48	1	14	......	50	28
Fur goods	1919	13,639	10,589	212	1,753	626	350	57	51	1
	1914	9,030	(2)	(2)	1,137	5,430	2,108	291	61	3
Furnishing goods, men's	1919	18,944	6,332	2,036	3,586	5,373	585	983	49	......
	1914	22,459	(2)	(2)	2,866	6,312	8,766	4,386	129	......
Furniture	1919	138,331	8,907	789	15,001	40,195	21,824	39,483	11,480	652
	1914	127,881	(2)	(2)	10,599	12,351	28,837	35,412	40,444	238
Furs, dressed	1919	5,075	2,975	3	230	1,589	219	36	4	19
	1914	1,525	(2)	(2)	56	131	575	681	82	......
Galvanizing	1919	1,665	11	10	74	61	852	557	100	......
	1914	1,580	(2)	(2)	73	10	55	1,071	338	33
Gas and electric fixtures	1919	9,795	1,154	295	5,114	1,644	609	974	3	2
	1914	10,913	(2)	(2)	2,248	2,758	3,133	2,488	286	......
Gas, illuminating and heating	1919	42,908	55	59	15,309	555	2,788	13,254	5,119	5,769
	1914	43,792	(2)	(2)	2,914	133	9,213	8,548	9,248	13,736
Gas machines and gas and water meters.	1919	5,589	133	26	2,446	1,761	417	339	467	......
	1914	4,972	(2)	(2)	57	830	985	3,026	74	......
Glass	1919	77,520	14,098	7,174	26,098	14,815	5,818	4,143	4,603	771
	1914	74,502	(2)	(2)	12,205	27,975	11,394	7,458	10,743	4,727
Glass, cutting, staining, and ornamenting.	1919	6,480	856	418	947	2,456	393	1,337	73	......
	1914	8,067	(2)	(2)	899	2,440	1,469	2,609	650	......
Gloves and mittens, cloth, not including gloves made in textile mills.[3]	1919	8,986	304	1,024	582	4,878	2,062	116	20	......
Gloves and mittens, leather	1919	10,685	1,190	1,111	1,295	3,357	2,108	1,461	163	......
	1914	10,668	(2)	(2)	1,030	2,229	4,063	3,044	301	1
Glucose and starch	1919	7,795	11	......	4,272	17	27	479	1,479	1510
	1914	4,509	(2)	(2)	47	......	9	16	2,903	1,534
Glue, not elsewhere specified	1919	4,264	30	4	1,530	216	836	779	815	54
	1914	3,129	(2)	(2)	24	24	156	489	1,775	661
Gold and silver, leaf and foil	1919	950	113	19	435	265	83	35	......	......
	1914	1,135	(2)	(2)	156	279	172	498	30	......

[1] Includes 48 and under for 1914.
[2] Corresponding figures not available.
[3] Included in "furnishing goods, men's" in 1914.

TABLE 12.—AVERAGE NUMBER OF WAGE EARNERS CLASSIFIED ACCORDING TO PREVAILING HOURS OF LABOR PER WEEK, BY INDUSTRIES: 1919 AND 1914—Continued.

INDUSTRY.	Census year.	Total.	IN ESTABLISHMENTS WHERE THE PREVAILING HOURS OF LABOR PER WEEK WERE—							
			44 and under.	Between 44 and 48.	48.[1]	Between 48 and 54.	54.	Between 54 and 60.	60.	Over 60.
Gold and silver, reducing and refining, not from the ore.	1919	644	68	31	98	210	77	64	36	60
	1914	456	(2)	(2)	60	101	41	225	29	......
Graphite, ground and refined....	1919	497	......	......	170	......	62	145	37	83
	1914	250	......	......	......	......	......	41	204	5
Grease and tallow, not including lubricating greases.	1919	6,647	51	3	1,451	944	1,814	340	1,693	351
	1914	5,106	(2)	(2)	257	67	605	473	3,494	210
Grindstones......................	1919	674	......	50	27	......	72	35	490	......
	1914	686	......	......	......	......	7	......	679	......
Haircloth......................	1919	425	12	13	281	57	16	46	......	......
	1914	595	(2)	(2)	1	95	499	......	......	......
Hair work......................	1919	1,084	457	76	350	161	32	8	......	......
	1914	1,193	(2)	(2)	364	303	490	24	12	......
Hammocks......................	1919	64	7	3	3	4	47	......	......	......
	1914	285	(2)	(2)	10	14	144	97	20	......
Hand stamps...................	1919	1,719	138	74	950	402	81	65	9	......
	1914	1,321	(2)	(2)	251	410	447	205	6	2
Hardware......................	1919	42,505	1,691	2,530	4,642	13,459	3,653	13,047	3,483	......
	1914	41,213	(2)	(2)	3,465	4,471	7,512	21,459	4,279	27
Hardware, saddlery.............	1919	3,675	3	......	5	1,330	593	1,734	10	......
	1914	2,511	(2)	(2)	124	249	306	1,634	198	......
Hat and cap materials..........	1919	3,009	1,083	692	164	658	9	403	......	......
	1914	1,775	(2)	(2)	80	399	316	857	123	......
Hats and caps, other than felt, straw, and wool.	1919	7,539	5,708	676	665	355	123	2	10	......
	1914	7,322	(2)	(2)	634	4,258	1,633	728	69	......
Hats, fur-felt.................	1919	18,510	7,037	5,359	3,670	2,004	103	333	4	......
	1914	21,318	(2)	(2)	3,511	12,377	3,615	1,560	255	......
Hats, straw...................	1919	7,302	2,125	335	1,626	2,124	695	394	3	......
	1914	9,483	(2)	(2)	591	1,596	1,785	4,741	770	......
Hats, wool-felt................	1919	1,448	131	......	166	202	504	390	55	......
	1914	1,249	(2)	(2)	18	257	554	219	201	......
Hones and whetstones..........	1919	212	1	......	1	40	22	132	16	......
	1914	170	(2)	(2)	4	1	16	39	110	......
Horseshoes, not made in steel works or rolling mills.	1919	744	......	......	96	198	69	378	3	......
	1914	588	(2)	(2)	106	16	179	220	67	......
House-furnishing goods, not elsewhere specified.	1919	7,853	1,010	517	2,876	2,134	378	823	93	22
	1914	6,935	(2)	(2)	654	2,284	1,222	2,343	371	61
Ice, manufactured.............	1919	30,247	215	7	4,781	362	1,720	5,880	4,177	13,105
	1914	23,011	(2)	(2)	548	58	664	2,181	3,741	15,819
Ink, printing...................	1919	1,988	56	11	1,321	442	142	16	......	......
	1914	1,391	(2)	(2)	61	405	336	497	92	......
Ink, writing...................	1919	702	375	7	182	102	36	......	......	......
	1914	512	(2)	(2)	273	51	154	4	......	......
Instruments, professional and scientific.	1919	15,931	3,242	502	6,712	3,135	1,802	420	118	......
	1914	7,107	(2)	(2)	563	1,843	2,637	1,597	467	......
Iron and steel, blast furnaces....	1919	41,660	1,471	......	1,453	......	30	2,617	8,153	27,936
	1914	29,356	(2)	(2)	11	80	1,551	13	4,474	23,227
Iron and steel, steel works and rolling mills.	1919	375,088	56,099	8,552	54,552	12,248	13,704	71,876	82,232	75,825
	1914	248,716	(2)	(2)	19,972	19,084	25,565	45,996	77,820	60,279
Iron and steel, bolts, nuts, washers, and rivets, not made in rolling mills.	1919	17,967	986	......	4,017	3,178	801	8,201	647	137
	1914	10,658	(2)	(2)	2,462	168	1,522	5,665	841	......
Iron and steel, cast-iron pipe....	1919	12,625	293	......	1,271	440	4,709	3,208	2,704	......
	1914	12,557	(2)	(2)	171	......	1,303	3,026	8,057	......

[1] Includes 48 and under for 1914.
[2] Corresponding figures not available.

TABLE 12.—AVERAGE NUMBER OF WAGE EARNERS CLASSIFIED ACCORDING TO PREVAILING HOURS OF LABOR PER WEEK, BY INDUSTRIES: 1919 AND 1914—Continued.

INDUSTRY.	Census year.	Total.	IN ESTABLISHMENTS WHERE THE PREVAILING HOURS OF LABOR PER WEEK WERE—							
			44 and under.	Between 44 and 48.	48.[1]	Between 48 and 54.	54.	Between 54 and 60.	60.	Over 60.
Iron and steel, doors and shutters.	1919	2,077	432	......	494	780	300	71	......	......
	1914	1,985	(2)	(2)	246	278	929	504	28	......
Iron and steel, forgings, not made in steel works or rolling mills.	1919	28,391	1,541	1,948	6,505	7,953	2,294	5,748	2,311	91
	1914	10,689	(2)	(2)	1,339	1,482	2,268	4,923	434	243
Iron and steel, nails and spikes, cut and wrought, including wire nails, not made in steel works or rolling mills.	1919	3,355	449	......	1,294	982	207	381	42	......
	1914	2,644	(2)	(2)	481	121	958	866	218	......
Iron and steel, tempering and welding.[3]	1919	1,835	135	16	447	448	294	389	105	1
Iron and steel, wrought pipe....	1919	10,426	2,563	336	612	1,855	46	3,298	1,716	......
	1914	8,845	(2)	(2)	33	124	608	4,469	3,611	......
Ivory, shell, and bone work, not including combs and hairpins.	1919	842	26	22	173	336	195	90	......	......
	1914	795	(2)	(2)	79	45	314	286	71	......
Japanning....................	1919	295	14	6	34	102	51	85	3	......
	1914	228	(2)	(2)	19	67	14	83	45	......
Jewelry....................	1919	30,871	9,533	596	12,635	5,730	995	1,363	16	3
	1914	28,289	(2)	(2)	3,275	5,041	9,635	9,837	465	36
Jewelry and instrument cases....	1919	2,734	515	170	926	881	146	83	13	......
	1914	2,393	(2)	(2)	111	674	1,302	259	47	......
Jute goods..................	1919	7,138	529	182	4,103	536	1,439	298	51	......
	1914	7,987	(2)	(2)	6	59	6,153	1,409	341	19
Knit goods..................	1919	172,572	7,818	4,701	54,674	46,149	30,387	23,909	4,578	356
	1914	150,520	(2)	(2)	3,673	7,860	87,549	34,260	16,515	663
Labels and tags..............	1919	5,227	308	134	3,364	1,175	111	81	54	......
	1914	2,600	(2)	(2)	474	1,038	821	249	18	......
Lamps and reflectors..........	1919	8,360	377	127	1,873	4,523	453	972	35	......
	1914	7,134	(2)	(2)	413	1,659	1,658	3,091	251	62
Lapidary work..............	1919	1,155	279	250	505	103	6	12	......	......
	1914	584	(2)	(2)	253	241	46	44	......	......
Lard, not made in slaughtering and meat-packing establishments.	1919	13	......	......	2	4	1	5	1	......
	1914	19	......	......	......	......	3	2	14	......
Lasts.......................	1919	2,910	3	59	1,043	888	429	488	......	......
	1914	2,094	(2)	(2)	8	101	1,066	804	115	......
Lead, bar, pipe, and sheet........	1919	852	......	......	58	587	120	69	18	......
	1914	585	(2)	(2)	3	85	58	356	83	......
Leather goods, not elsewhere specified.	1919	8,945	3,853	661	2,403	1,468	218	222	120	......
	1914	7,071	(2)	(2)	511	2,032	2,287	2,040	197	4
Leather, tanned, curried, and finished.	1919	72,476	2,505	2,503	28,393	21,153	7,617	5,028	4,342	935
	1914	55,936	(2)	(2)	909	3,241	10,355	22,205	19,209	17
Lime.......................	1919	11,405	27	4	1,224	211	1,456	1,149	6,357	977
	1914	12,429	(2)	(2)	220	237	1,142	1,750	7,257	1,823
Linen goods..................	1919	1,890	......	......	1,045	549	170	92	34	......
	1914	8,567	(2)	(2)	90	......	1,616	1,846	15	......
Liquors, distilled..............	1919	1,380	3	......	631	34	191	183	159	179
	1914	6,295	(2)	(2)	775	243	1,605	309	2,398	965
Liquors, malt................	1919	34,259	4,485	248	26,114	639	1,400	576	691	106
	1914	62,070	(2)	(2)	44,209	2,258	10,160	2,154	2,817	472
Liquors, vinous..............	1919	1,011	31	......	342	43	350	26	216	3
	1914	2,292	(2)	(2)	104	68	252	424	1,379	65

[1] Includes 48 and under for 1914.
[2] Corresponding figures not available.
[3] Included in "foundry and machine-shop products" in 1914.

TABLE 12.—AVERAGE NUMBER OF WAGE EARNERS CLASSIFIED ACCORDING TO PREVAILING HOURS OF LABOR PER WEEK, BY INDUSTRIES: 1919 AND 1914—Continued.

INDUSTRY.	Census year.	Total.	IN ESTABLISHMENTS WHERE THE PREVAILING HOURS OF LABOR PER WEEK WERE—							
			44 and under.	Between 44 and 48.	48.[1]	Between 48 and 54.	54.	Between 54 and 60.	60.	Over 60.
Lithographing	1919	15,618	191	481	13,644	1,259	17	16	10	----
	1914	15,171	(2)	(2)	12,622	1,910	528	20	91	----
Locomotives, not made by railroad companies.	1919	26,715			1,321	8,853	870	15,589	91	----
	1914	17,391	(2)	(2)	189	5,594	1,285	10,323	82	----
Looking-glass and picture frames.	1919	4,708	452	105	521	2,751	247	611	18	3
	1914	4,787	(2)	(2)	360	547	1,153	1,463	1,260	4
Lubricating greases	1919	472	26	11	77	157	104	97		
	1914	476	(2)	(2)	78	96	44	177	75	6
Lumber and timber products [2]	1919	480,945	11,002	2,547	101,476	18,176	26,896	36,305	272,774	11,769
	1914	479,786	(3)	(3)	12,850	10,923	21,615	24,638	355,548	54,212
Lumber, planing-mill products, not including planing mills connected with sawmills.	1919	86,956	10,551	519	16,723	12,625	17,407	15,908	12,710	513
	1914	96,214	(3)	(3)	14,173	11,349	25,402	16,605	28,213	472
Machine tools [4]	1919	53,111	239	1,024	15,313	20,749	5,407	10,259	120	
Malt	1919	1,352	74		979	43	134	95		27
	1914	1,989	(2)	(2)	763	330	353	287	140	116
Marble and stone work	1919	32,768	11,942	675	4,582	4,022	5,847	2,984	2,532	184
	1914	54,891	(3)	(3)	24,728	8,566	7,956	4,764	8,198	679
Matches	1919	3,726			345	1,846	885	624	26	
	1914	3,800	(3)	(3)	725	30	2,105	718	222	
Mats and matting, from cocoa fiber, grass, and coir.	1919	1,073	104	17		194	467	291		
	1914	869	(3)	(3)	19		225	606	19	
Mattresses and spring beds, not elsewhere specified.	1919	12,637	1,755	454	2,688	2,671	2,033	2,557	479	
	1914	11,747	(3)	(3)	2,044	1,363	2,574	3,186	2,572	8
Millinery and lace goods, not elsewhere specified.	1919	50,850	19,519	5,369	11,000	11,468	2,138	1,159	84	113
	1914	45,274	(3)	(3)	4,557	15,519	18,765	5,368	1,048	17
Millstones [5]	1919	38	8		23		3		4	
Mineral and soda waters	1919	17,440	834	149	5,554	927	4,428	1,131	4,183	234
	1914	15,506	(3)	(3)	2,468	646	3,591	1,236	7,343	222
Minerals and earths, ground or otherwise treated.	1919	14,426	30	31	1,083	931	1,653	1,513	8,465	720
	1914	4,707	(3)	(3)	91	63	309	699	3,199	346
Mirrors, framed and unframed, not elsewhere specified.	1919	2,599	327	81	335	1,180	413	186	77	
	1914	3,184	(3)	(3)	134	1,246	716	862	226	
Models and patterns, not including paper patterns.	1919	6,949	2,766	329	1,581	1,608	242	319	103	1
	1914	4,274	(3)	(3)	725	1,489	821	1,057	180	2
Motorcycles, bicycles, and parts	1919	10,886	30		3,356	2,896	959	3,518	127	
	1914	6,680	(3)	(3)	42	444	1,722	4,404	66	2
Mucilage, paste, and other adhesives, not elsewhere specified.	1919	803	188	68	112	340	33	62		
	1914	700	(3)	(3)	122	139	186	230	23	
Musical instruments and materials, not elsewhere specified.	1919	4,113	196	31	1,846	1,185	459	391	5	
	1914	1,831	(3)	(3)	87	767	411	449	117	
Musical instruments, organs	1919	1,941	11		239	651	214	506	320	
	1914	3,063	(3)	(3)	104	197	1,129	698	935	
Musical instruments, pianos	1919	22,957	2,166	208	6,437	10,063	2,248	1,355	480	
	1914	23,877	(3)	(3)	1,305	2,974	13,043	4,320	1,965	270
Musical instruments, piano and organ materials.	1919	11,009	152	103	2,361	4,648	2,835	717	193	
	1914	10,616	(3)	(3)	345	2,098	5,779	1,480	914	
Needles, pins, and hooks and eyes.	1919	9,294	837	104	1,372	2,612	324	3,992	53	
	1914	5,339	(3)	(3)	20	171	1,178	3,206	764	
Nets and seines	1919	859		8	11	251	568	21		
	1914	1,058	(3)	(3)	2	27	392	251	386	
Oakum	1919	124			5		13	106		
	1914	116	(3)	(3)	4		5	4	103	

[1] Includes 48 and under for 1914.
[2] Exclusive of "pulpwood"; not shown as a separate classification in 1919.
[3] Corresponding figures not available.
[4] Included in "foundry and machine-shop products" in 1914.
[5] Included in "all other industries" in 1914.

TABLE 12.—AVERAGE NUMBER OF WAGE EARNERS CLASSIFIED ACCORDING TO PREVAILING HOURS OF LABOR PER WEEK, BY INDUSTRIES: 1919 AND 1914—Continued.

INDUSTRY.	Census year.	Total.	IN ESTABLISHMENTS WHERE THE PREVAILING HOURS OF LABOR PER WEEK WERE—							
			44 and under.	Between 44 and 48.	48.[1]	Between 48 and 54.	54	Between 54 and 60.	60.	Over 60.
Oil and cake, cottonseed	1919	26,766	56	......	753	164	858	379	3,645	20,911
	1914	21,810	(2)	(2)	28	454	204	753	1,861	18,510
Oil, essential	1919	321	5	2	19	140	51	21	83	......
	1914	249	(2)	(2)	2	26	54	1	132	34
Oil, linseed	1919	2,173	......	......	288	25	515	......	904	441
	1914	1,488	(2)	(2)	1	......	......	78	220	1,189
Oil, not elsewhere specified [3]	1919	5,930	146	139	1,210	1,145	723	476	936	1,155
	1914	2,049	(2)	(2)	169	150	400	390	825	115
Oilcloth and linoleum, floor	1919	5,414	......	......	......	1,625	1,218	2,202	369	......
	1914	4,428	(2)	(2)	6	439	441	2,273	1,269	......
Oilcloth, enameled	1919	1,130	27	7	225	252	535	84	......	......
	1914	1,223	......	......	......	85	326	739	73	......
Oleomargarine and other butter substitutes.	1919	2,851	285	166	965	595	419	6	415	......
	1914	917	(2)	(2)	113	......	20	54	730	......
Optical goods	1919	14,723	753	405	9,907	3,013	504	123	15	3
	1914	7,919	(2)	(2)	437	2,894	3,197	1,281	109	1
Ordnance and accessories [4]	1919	11,328	1,295	......	8,077	970	......	814	......	172
Paints	1919	17,485	768	348	4,136	5,406	2,018	4,092	502	215
	1914	13,349	(2)	(2)	547	1,646	3,788	4,692	1,665	1,011
Paper and wood pulp	1919	113,759	3,994	1,228	64,979	6,998	11,332	3,801	8,011	13,416
	1914	88,457	(2)	(2)	10,624	5,581	12,702	10,427	18,993	30,130
Paper goods, not elsewhere specified.	1919	14,135	858	1,510	3,199	4,576	2,159	872	653	308
	1914	13,495	(2)	(2)	507	3,236	3,185	3,859	2,039	669
Paper patterns	1919	403	180	34	185	4	......	......	......	......
	1914	1,073	(2)	(2)	1,009	41	23	......	......	......
Patent medicines and compounds.	1919	17,444	3,075	1,664	5,860	4,581	1,262	779	200	23
	1914	13,328	(2)	(2)	4,223	4,251	2,241	1,565	1,008	40
Paving materials	1919	16,072	714	158	1,450	1,202	2,447	2,269	7,759	73
	1914	19,540	(2)	(2)	1,390	876	3,193	2,053	11,522	506
Peanuts, grading, roasting, cleaning, and shelling.	1919	2,460	37	3	21	85	496	930	852	36
	1914	2,353	(2)	(2)	43	375	382	541	1,010	2
Pencils, lead	1919	5,970	1,167	......	813	3,872	......	118	......	......
	1914	4,330	......	......	......	35	2,017	2,101	177	......
Pens, fountain and stylographic	1919	3,207	83	69	584	1,961	1	509	......	......
	1914	1,154	(2)	(2)	36	174	548	396	......	......
Pens, gold	1919	416	241	28	68	79	......	......	......	......
	1914	246	(2)	(2)	11	39	164	32	......	......
Pens, steel	1919	807	......	......	......	806	1	......	......	......
	1914	573	......	......	......	525	34	13	1	......
Perfumery and cosmetics	1919	5,405	1,627	871	1,462	1,144	263	31	7	......
	1914	2,897	(2)	(2)	886	1,249	471	256	35	......
Petroleum, refining	1919	58,889	205	701	31,059	5,444	4,907	14,251	572	1,750
	1914	25,366	(2)	(2)	1,241	848	12,621	56	2,502	8,098
Phonographs and graphophones.	1919	28,721	722	107	11,451	8,570	2,335	5,097	439	......
	1914	9,381	(2)	(2)	28	1,409	4,984	2,960	......	......
Photo-engraving	1919	6,769	1,369	543	4,563	244	42	......	8	......
	1914	6,211	(2)	(2)	5,156	794	192	60	9	......
Photographic apparatus	1919	2,555	125	2	1,427	886	111	3	1	......
	1914	2,016	(2)	(2)	595	641	351	414	15	......
Photographic materials	1919	14,556	1,670	410	10,583	1,599	50	48	196	......
	1914	6,658	(2)	(2)	117	5,670	218	604	49	......
Pickles, preserves, and sauces	1919	16,621	348	617	2,859	4,589	2,612	4,056	1,530	10
	1914	12,590	(2)	(2)	858	708	3,332	4,429	3,142	121
Pipes, tobacco	1919	2,539	1,192	111	632	156	280	168	......	......
	1914	2,354	(2)	(2)	29	1,615	217	480	13	......

[1] Includes 48 and under for 1914.
[2] Corresponding figures not available.
[3] Includes "oil, castor" and "oil, lard, not made in slaughtering and meat-packing establishments."
[4] Included in "all other industries" in 1914.

TABLE 12.—AVERAGE NUMBER OF WAGE EARNERS CLASSIFIED ACCORDING TO PREVAILING HOURS OF LABOR PER WEEK, BY INDUSTRIES: 1919 AND 1914—Continued.

INDUSTRY.	Census year.	Total.	IN ESTABLISHMENTS WHERE THE PREVAILING HOURS OF LABOR PER WEEK WERE—							
			44 and under.	Between 44 and 48.	48.[1]	Between 48 and 54.	54.	Between 54 and 60.	60.	Over 60.
Plated ware	1919	9,492	21	15	861	3,547	149	4,690	209	
Plumbers' supplies, not elsewhere specified.	1914	8,717	(²)	(²)	579	1,934	1,199	4,297	708	
	1919	13,592	1,048	78	3,113	4,264	2,831	2,098	160	
	1914	18,479	(²)	(²)	2,509	2,093	7,800	3,539	2,538	
Pocketbooks	1919	2,905	1,555	101	554	419	29	247		
	1914	1,466	(²)	(²)	212	275	702	274		
Pottery	1919	27,934	2,320	752	3,996	10,840	6,320	2,385	1,321	3
	1914	26,705	(²)	(²)	6,207	6,846	8,860	2,142	2,582	68
Poultry, killing and dressing, not done in slaughtering and meat-packing establishments.	1919	2,140	48	34	168	47	360	61	1,350	72
	1914	1,353	(²)	(²)	21	34	196	7	959	136
Printing and publishing, book and job.	1919	123,005	8,500	2,927	98,259	10,453	2,048	467	241	110
	1914	113,121	(²)	(²)	80,023	19,145	12,093	1,293	549	18
Printing and publishing, music..	1919	899	12		864	14	1	8		
	1914	873	(²)	(²)	95	676	60	39		
Printing and publishing, newspapers and periodicals.	1919	120,381	12,573	4,689	83,406	6,074	7,643	4,225	1,497	274
	1914	114,375	(²)	(²)	80,130	7,977	17,057	5,139	3,765	307
Printing materials	1919	723	73	22	194	350	4	80		
	1914	423	(²)	(²)	105	69	181	61	7	
Pulp, from fiber other than wood.[3]	1919	64	5						26	33
Pulp goods	1919	3,041	20	41	319	616	1,410	383	252	
	1914	1,654	(²)	(²)	121		380	753	187	213
Pumps, not including power pumps.	1919	5,384	619	301	396	1,133	309	2,474	152	
	1914	2,134	(²)	(²)	147	101	277	1,270	339	
Pumps, steam and other power...	1919	10,688	431	22	2,550	4,060	941	2,200	356	128
	1914	6,188	(²)	(²)	183	848	2,952	2,053	152	
Refrigerators	1919	5,786	220	39	1,268	2,070	602	1,355	232	
	1914	5,617	(²)	(²)	270	517	1,166	1,984	1,680	
Regalia, and society badges and emblems.	1919	2,223	248	147	379	1,211	16	222		
	1914	2,010	(²)	(²)	312	480	1,068	139	11	
Rice, cleaning and polishing	1919	2,113	42		101		89	74	848	959
	1914	1,253	(²)	(²)	28	18	6	7	40	1,154
Roofing materials	1919	8,871	553	17	3,265	766	116	2,089	897	1,168
	1914	4,088	(²)	(²)	561	142	921	945	1,172	347
Rubber tires, tubes, and rubber goods, not elsewhere specified.	1919	119,848	3,385	25,172	49,828	18,391	1,185	19,352	2,535	
	1914	50,220	(²)	(²)	3,216	9,621	8,019	25,427	3,548	389
Rules, ivory and wood	1919	168			6	71		91		
	1914	408				1	313	83	11	
Saddlery and harness	1919	10,411	110	140	3,050	1,693	1,932	2,138	1,333	15
	1914	12,969	(²)	(²)	464	598	4,040	4,518	3,323	26
Safes and vaults	1919	2,949	29	365	474	388	92	1,597	4	
	1914	2,972	(²)	(²)	213	295	522	1,844	98	
Salt	1919	6,495	2	12	1,291	547	1,021	1,470	1,416	736
	1914	5,089	(²)	(²)	340		772	792	2,538	647
Sand and emery paper and cloth.	1919	771			185	422	49	115		
	1914	681				165	30	117	369	
Sand-lime brick	1919	504			37	48	85	66	268	
	1914	557	(²)	(²)	81		111	10	326	29
Sausage, not made in slaughtering and meat-packing establishments.	1919	3,471	386	372	1,561	431	284	129	272	36
	1914	2,244	(²)	(²)	190	169	546	267	1,001	71

[1] Includes 48 and under for 1914.
[2] Corresponding figures not available.
[3] Included in "all other industries" in 1914

TABLE 12.—AVERAGE NUMBER OF WAGE EARNERS CLASSIFIED ACCORDING TO PREVAILING HOURS OF LABOR PER WEEK, BY INDUSTRIES: 1919 AND 1914—Continued.

INDUSTRY.	Census year.	Total.	IN ESTABLISHMENTS WHERE THE PREVAILING HOURS OF LABOR PER WEEK WERE—							
			44 and under.	Between 44 and 48.	48.[1]	Between 48 and 54.	54.	Between 54 and 60.	60.	Over 60.
Saws	1919	5,510	136	52	378	2,969	269	1,703	3	......
	1914	4,560	(2)	(2)	967	221	2,955	404	13	......
Scales and balances	1919	5,432	311	29	1,753	1,211	1,545	497	86	
	1914	4,467	(2)	(2)	48	549	2,130	1,365	375	
Screws, machine	1919	10,262	36	2,466	1,342	3,057	847	2,279	235	
	1914	3,643	(2)	(2)	1,028	80	684	1,478	373	
Screws, wood	1919	4,889			1,527	786	294	2,282		
	1914	4,446	(2)	(2)	2,168	......	1,436	839	3	
Sewing-machine cases	1919	4,171	2			78		4,091		
	1914	3,699	(2)	(2)	61			2,022	1,616	
Sewing machines and attachments.	1919	15,059	2,136	30	540	10,376	1,044	933		
	1914	14,308	(2)	(2)	499	9,232	2,087	2,467	23	
Shipbuilding, steel	1919	344,014	246,866	4,685	89,901	583	541	138	1,300	
	1914	33,508	(2)	(2)	11,928	6,861	6,900	928	6,393	498
Shipbuilding, wooden, including boat building.	1919	43,432	12,943	75	26,221	1,455	1,615	339	664	120
	1914	10,981	(2)	(2)	2,802	777	5,420	596	1,378	8
Shirts	1919	39,603	9,965	4,824	9,148	9,966	5,075	515	110	
	1914	51,972	(2)	(2)	4,051	12,562	27,222	7,363	439	335
Show cases	1919	1,857	234	......	437	488	425	202	71	
	1914	2,257	(2)	(2)	116	277	1,036	513	315	
Signs and advertising novelties	1919	10,432	1,572	352	4,366	2,640	1,158	241	98	5
	1914	9,566	(2)	(2)	2,568	3,097	2,360	1,372	149	20
Silk goods, including throwsters.	1919	126,782	31,619	2,909	26,154	47,286	14,241	3,322	774	477
	1914	108,170	(2)	(2)	1,169	4,916	56,632	43,243	2,190	20
Silversmithing and silverware	1919	6,453	1,480	(2)	406	3,646	313	608		
	1914	7,070	(2)	(2)	76	970	2,449	3,575		
Slaughtering and meat packing	1919	160,996	4,791	1,859	128,795	5,856	5,017	4,041	10,364	273
	1914	98,832	(2)	(2)	4,728	3,263	13,188	8,734	68,019	900
Smelting and refining, copper	1919	17,345			3,500	990	1,343	11,512		
	1914	17,731	(2)	(2)	336	2,225	864	11,170	2,336	800
Smelting and refining, lead	1919	6,438	1		1,002	397		4,900		138
	1914	7,385	(2)	(2)	72	......	727	5,073	108	1,405
Smelting and refining, zinc	1919	13,796	160		2,387	395		9,644	139	1,071
	1914	9,617	(2)	(2)	447	3,902		2,048	2,043	1,177
Smelting and refining, metals, not elsewhere specified.[3]	1919	2,041	......	231	340	912		513	38	7
Smelting and refining, not from the ore.	1919	2,167	24	13	263	510	101	407	518	331
	1914	2,585	(2)	(2)	42	8	176	259	618	1,482
Soap	1919	20,436	2,456	832	9,667	4,474	905	1,802	293	7
	1914	14,172	(2)	(2)	1,027	3,446	1,514	6,371	1,814	
Soda-water apparatus	1919	2,599	118	7	442	1,796	187	38		11
	1914	2,229	(2)	(2)	390	225	1,267	294	53	
Sporting and athletic goods	1919	6,412	198	24	1,857	1,427	1,296	1,505	105	
	1914	5,602	(2)	(2)	226	1,573	2,049	1,705	49	
Springs, steel, car and carriage, not made in steel works or rolling mills.	1919	8,981	694	154	2,182	2,256	394	2,392	909	
	1914	3,703	(2)	(2)	478	477	377	1,473	817	81
Stamped and enameled ware, not elsewhere specified.	1919	34,248	929	832	8,981	11,167	2,615	8,732	992	
	1914	28,731	(2)	(2)	2,627	3,864	6,077	11,623	4,028	512
Stationery goods, not elsewhere specified.	1919	11,261	675	354	5,242	3,634	837	483	36	
	1914	7,728	(2)	(2)	981	1,618	3,035	2,021	73	

1 Includes 48 and under for 1914.
2 Corresponding figures not available.
3 Included in other classifications prior to 1919 and covers "smelting and refining, antimony" and "smelting and refining, tin" which could not be shown separately in 1919.

TABLE 12.—AVERAGE NUMBER OF WAGE EARNERS CLASSIFIED ACCORDING TO PREVAILING HOURS OF LABOR PER WEEK, BY INDUSTRIES: 1919 AND 1914—Continued.

INDUSTRY.	Census year.	Total.	IN ESTABLISHMENTS WHERE THE PREVAILING HOURS OF LABOR PER WEEK WERE—							
			44 and under.	Between 44 and 48.	48.[1]	Between 48 and 54.	54.	Between 54 and 60.	60.	Over 60.
Statuary and art goods	1919	1,466	492	6	366	182	339	47	33	1
	1914	1,988	(2)	(2)	604	560	382	144	298	.....
Steam fittings and steam and hot-water heating apparatus.	1919	36,686	503	134	22,890	6,885	4,378	1,450	446	.....
	1914	26,388	(2)	(2)	3,983	1,689	3,810	7,203	9,703	.....
Steam packing	1919	6,147	175	63	868	1,304	241	1,396	1,933	167
	1914	4,213	(2)	(2)	196	1,086	756	1,558	394	223
Steel barrels, drums, and tanks [3]	1919	3,322	55	.....	362	1,808	414	614	69	.....
Stencils and brands	1919	417	90	10	143	149	18	7	.....	.....
	1914	446	(2)	(2)	53	276	72	27	18	.....
Stereotyping and electrotyping	1919	3,664	943	366	2,312	11	32	.....	.....	.....
	1914	3,457	(2)	(2)	3,045	171	222	6	13	.....
Stoves and hot-air furnaces	1919	32,868	2,606	500	11,023	5,009	8,569	3,529	1,632	.....
	1914	29,535	(2)	(2)	2,957	3,046	11,182	7,549	4,801	.....
Stoves, gas and oil	1919	10,565	152	560	5,657	2,400	785	934	77	.....
	1914	7,790	(2)	(2)	2,613	286	1,401	2,379	1,111	.....
Structural ironwork, not made in steel works or rolling mills.	1919	43,962	3,898	313	8,958	9,691	10,730	9,276	1,096	.....
	1914	47,167	(2)	(2)	1,523	8,596	13,905	19,523	3,610	.....
Sugar, beet	1919	11,781	32	.....	175	.....	107	1,742	1,213	8,512
	1914	7,997	.....	.....	.....	.....	180	108	2,558	5,151
Sugar, cane	1919	6,101	745	3	621	25	19	553	501	3,634
	1914	3,632	.....	.....	.....	2	82	14	395	3,139
Sugar, refining, not including beet sugar.	1919	18,202	.....	.....	5,022	.....	1,252	.....	6,024	5,904
	1914	11,253	(2)	(2)	614	591	.....	1,498	3,055	5,495
Sulphuric, nitric, and mixed acids	1919	4,961	.....	.....	1,635	981	.....	1,454	198	693
	1914	3,064	(2)	(2)	11	.....	229	379	490	1,955
Surgical appliances	1919	6,390	814	349	1,450	3,332	114	273	58	.....
	1914	4,282	(2)	(2)	423	536	878	2,249	196	.....
Suspenders, garters, and elastic woven goods.	1919	10,857	827	1,137	4,161	4,113	455	31	133	.....
	1914	9,646	(2)	(2)	831	1,804	2,440	4,391	180	.....
Textile machinery and parts [3]	1919	31,823	775	196	9,939	13,483	1,608	4,692	1,130	.....
Theatrical scenery	1919	149	41	.....	100	7	1	.....	.....	.....
	1914	88	(2)	(2)	80	.....	8	.....	.....	.....
Tin, and other foils, not elsewhere specified.	1919	1,908	313	.....	1,014	295	97	189	.....	.....
	1914	1,031	(2)	(2)	1	83	480	467	.....	.....
Tin plate and terneplate	1919	3,122	2,640	.....	.....	9	323	134	16	.....
	1914	5,238	(2)	(2)	2,190	7	2,657	378	6	.....
Tinware, not elsewhere specified	1919	34,386	644	529	7,044	15,250	5,814	4,635	465	5
	1914	22,584	(2)	(2)	497	2,183	8,975	8,023	2,811	95
Tobacco, chewing and smoking, and snuff.	1919	18,324	394	234	2,327	8,886	1,653	4,384	446	.....
	1914	25,980	(2)	(2)	1,275	1,677	4,952	16,478	1,582	16
Tobacco, cigars and cigarettes	1919	138,773	19,784	8,171	25,733	41,976	30,872	9,373	2,455	409
	1914	152,892	(2)	(2)	44,969	19,365	46,856	30,936	8,392	2,374
Tools, not elsewhere specified	1919	35,585	1,112	1,372	5,766	12,257	4,362	9,761	955	.....
	1914	16,866	(2)	(2)	2,202	3,455	2,519	7,936	754	.....
Toys and games	1919	14,201	1,100	869	2,342	4,984	1,497	3,102	177	130
	1914	7,887	(2)	(2)	386	1,000	2,619	3,304	578	.....
Trunks and valises	1919	11,470	790	595	3,127	3,591	1,482	1,741	139	5
	1914	9,911	(2)	(2)	466	1,589	2,498	3,566	1,756	36
Turpentine and rosin	1919	28,067	7,336	445	3,706	2,509	4,430	508	9,098	35
	1914	34,817	(2)	(2)	13,680	2,770	728	780	15,995	864

[1] Includes 48 and under for 1914.
[2] Corresponding figures not available.
[3] Included in "foundry and machine-shop products" in 1914.

TABLE 12.—AVERAGE NUMBER OF WAGE EARNERS CLASSIFIED ACCORDING TO PREVAILING HOURS OF LABOR PER WEEK, BY INDUSTRIES: 1919 AND 1914—Continued.

INDUSTRY.	Census year.	Total.	IN ESTABLISHMENTS WHERE THE PREVAILING HOURS OF LABOR PER WEEK WERE—							
			44 and under.	Between 44 and 48.	48.[1]	Between 48 and 54.	54.	Between 54 and 60.	60.	Over 60.
Type founding	1919	810	4	.....	146	612	48	.....	.....	.....
	1914	1,054	(²)	(²)	21	736	263	34	.....	.....
Typewriters and supplies	1919	15,669	294	174	1,204	7,428	3,839	2,668	62	.....
	1914	11,091	(²)	(²)	588	2,995	5,891	1,616	1	.....
Umbrellas and canes	1919	3,368	404	104	440	1,692	288	431	8	1
	1914	4,792	(²)	(²)	538	1,052	1,617	1,547	38	.....
Upholstering materials, not elsewhere specified.	1919	4,810	53	527	2,003	584	296	704	643	.....
	1914	4,426	(²)	(²)	130	346	808	1,226	1,825	91
Varnishes	1919	4,022	289	410	762	2,069	262	208	22	.....
	1914	2,734	(²)	(²)	340	1,117	272	717	278	10
Vault lights and ventilators	1919	316	136	5	9	96	2	68	.....	.....
	1914	601	(²)	(²)	205	170	91	104	31	.....
Vinegar and cider	1919	1,981	32	4	349	145	531	242	639	39
	1914	1,229	(²)	(²)	76	17	400	123	589	24
Wall paper, not made in paper mills.	1919	4,262	391	.....	306	1,531	1,287	652	95	.....
	1914	4,738	(²)	(²)	59	14	498	1,853	2,314	.....
Wall plaster and composition flooring.	1919	5,123	229	2	1,685	361	502	617	1,608	119
	1914	5,389	(²)	(²)	127	185	909	555	2,895	718
Washing machines and clothes wringers.	1919	5,956	723	.....	928	1,604	653	1,191	857	.....
	1914	2,302	(²)	(²)	107	123	436	798	838	.....
Waste	1919	2,686	210	5	536	569	168	722	476	.....
	1914	2,966	(²)	(²)	50	138	944	904	930	.....
Watch and clock materials, except watch cases.	1919	582	77	159	138	181	9	18	.....	.....
	1914	670	(²)	(²)	7	121	176	322	44	.....
Watchcases	1919	3,900	126	.....	2,574	1,126	.....	74	.....	.....
	1914	3,514	(²)	(²)	481	185	616	1,875	357	.....
Watches	1919	15,888	3,779	.....	6,272	5,147	.....	690	.....	.....
	1914	12,390	.....	.....	.....	4,212	4,054	4,124	.....	.....
Wheelbarrows	1919	291	.....	.....	8	158	.....	110	15	.....
	1914	323	(²)	(²)	1	57	32	97	136	.....
Whips	1919	717	12	6	7	374	253	65	.....	.....
	1914	1,163	(²)	(²)	17	.....	208	829	109	.....
Windmills	1919	1,932	.....	.....	59	379	493	956	45	.....
	1914	1,955	(²)	(²)	1	300	516	801	337	.....
Window and door screens and weather strips.	1919	2,179	80	55	412	801	133	572	126	.....
	1914	3,194	(²)	(²)	160	168	1,398	678	790	.....
Window shades and fixtures	1919	4,411	325	110	533	1,297	1,192	872	82	.....
	1914	4,077	(²)	(²)	946	498	1,729	326	574	4
Wire	1919	19,741	98	53	768	1,725	2,318	8,978	3,447	2,354
	1914	17,600	(²)	(²)	669	4,396	333	4,561	6,824	817
Wirework, including wire rope and cable, not elsewhere specified.	1919	15,224	537	1,221	2,365	4,237	1,222	4,355	1,187	100
	1914	12,126	(²)	(²)	410	1,389	2,107	5,244	2,976	.....
Wood distillation	1919	4,946	10	10	717	1	162	616	1,724	1,706
	1914	2,782	(²)	(²)	103	.....	8	208	1,221	1,242
Wood preserving	1919	3,978	.....	.....	738	301	462	134	1,837	506
	1914	2,830	(²)	(²)	47	51	215	173	2,180	164
Wood, turned and carved	1919	10,649	347	51	509	1,557	2,456	3,782	1,907	40
	1914	11,615	(²)	(²)	294	1,405	1,772	3,535	4,588	21

[1] Includes 48 and under for 1914.
[2] Corresponding figures not available.

TABLE **12.**—AVERAGE NUMBER OF WAGE EARNERS CLASSIFIED ACCORDING TO PREVAILING HOURS OF LABOR PER WEEK, BY INDUSTRIES: 1919 AND 1914—Continued.

INDUSTRY.	Census year.	Total.	IN ESTABLISHMENTS WHERE THE PREVAILING HOURS OF LABOR PER WEEK WERE—							
			44 and under.	Between 44 and 48.	48.[1]	Between 48 and 54.	54.	Between 54 and 60.	60.	Over 60.
Wooden goods, not elsewhere specified.	1919	6,443	88	42	708	936	1,638	1,654	1,169	208
	1914	6,418	(2)	(2)	227	387	905	2,905	1,994	......
Wool pulling	1919	705	13	......	235	59	144	220	34	......
	1914	708	(2)	(2)	125	12	151	153	267	......
Wool scouring	1919	2,177	12	......	484	121	638	775	147	......
	1914	1,059	......	......	......	......	190	516	353	......
Wool shoddy	1919	2,566	153	......	617	275	261	590	401	269
	1914	2,145	(2)	(2)	7	......	516	498	731	393
Woolen goods	1919	62,957	568	369	36,781	4,773	10,993	7,607	1,866	......
	1914	49,165	(2)	(2)	1,062	634	14,010	26,378	7,033	48
Worsted goods	1919	103,830	24	9,595	77,598	7,007	6,944	2,328	......	334
	1914	109,527	......	......	......	1,589	74,295	30,550	3,093	......
All other industries[3]	1919	99	32	......	1	......	......	66	......	......
	1914	523	(2)	(2)	323	159	......	......	5	36

[1] Includes 48 and under for 1914.
[2] Corresponding figures not available.
[3] Comprises in 1919, "straw goods, not elsewhere specified," 1 establishment; "whalebone cutting," 1; "wood carpet," 3; in 1914, "millstones," 2 establishments; "ordnance and accessories," 2; "pulp, from fiber, other than wood," 3; "whalebone cutting," 1; "wood carpet," 6.

TABLE 13.—AVERAGE NUMBER OF WAGE EARNERS CLASSIFIED ACCORDING TO PREVAILING HOURS OF LABOR PER WEEK, BY GEOGRAPHIC DIVISIONS AND STATES: 1919, 1914, AND 1909.

DIVISION AND STATE.	Census year.	Total.	IN ESTABLISHMENTS WHERE THE PREVAILING HOURS OF LABOR PER WEEK WERE—							
			44 and under.	Between 44 and 48.	48.[1]	Between 48 and 54.	54.	Between 54 and 60.	60.	Over 60.
UNITED STATES ..	1919	9,096,372	1,111,107	346,179	2,961,407	1,496,177	828,353	1,248,854	827,745	276,550
	1914	7,036,247	(2)	(2)	833,330	945,735	1,818,390	1,543,018	1,487,801	407,973
	1909	6,615,046	(2)	(2)	523,652	481,157	1,019,438	1,999,307	2,017,280	574,212
GEOG. DIVISIONS:										
New England......	1919	1,351,389	84,626	55,900	648,655	244,904	165,498	126,861	19,957	4,988
	1914	1,140,233	(2)	(2)	89,694	113,217	477,074	378,977	69,250	12,021
	1909	1,101,290	(2)	(2)	51,613	48,576	159,383	674,662	147,915	19,141
Middle Atlantic....	1919	2,872,653	582,187	117,744	874,811	496,937	258,897	301,638	153,256	87,183
	1914	2,355,940	(2)	(2)	245,925	464,095	714,601	541,442	272,012	117,865
	1909	2,207,747	(2)	(2)	180,067	245,863	325,179	766,499	533,903	156,236
East North Central.	1919	2,396,618	176,277	106,832	703,870	557,291	191,193	395,658	187,773	77,724
	1914	1,680,281	(2)	(2)	238,165	241,560	335,575	416,935	364,630	83,416
	1909	1,513,764	(2)	(2)	123,872	102,083	291,908	366,362	521,120	108,419
West North Central.	1919	499,635	28,211	23,806	185,673	63,702	67,841	55,696	56,452	18,254
	1914	381,595	(2)	(2)	66,810	35,832	91,301	49,023	114,354	24,275
	1909	374,337	(2)	(2)	44,763	23,837	72,480	61,556	145,948	25,753
South Atlantic.....	1919	817,212	85,349	18,022	131,389	87,481	57,678	232,209	176,061	29,023
	1914	685,252	(2)	(2)	62,100	53,411	66,091	84,619	350,530	68,501
	1909	663,015	(2)	(2)	46,034	32,726	56,542	78,412	319,626	129,675
East South Central.	1919	329,226	12,559	8,589	55,656	23,070	29,355	68,285	105,861	25,851
	1914	264,378	(2)	(2)	25,332	13,646	39,366	35,331	113,058	37,645
	1909	261,772	(2)	(2)	19,876	7,698	30,776	20,418	123,564	59,440
West South Central.	1919	285,244	10,666	4,045	77,907	11,458	28,157	28,206	103,789	21,016
	1914	211,940	(2)	(2)	26,264	7,780	29,733	9,250	98,749	40,164
	1909	204,520	(2)	(2)	15,137	4,889	24,743	6,130	105,470	48,151
Mountain..........	1919	109,216	3,752	3,620	50,995	3,693	7,464	26,275	6,800	6,617
	1914	81,113	(2)	(2)	17,867	5,595	11,259	17,306	19,220	9,866
	1909	75,435	(2)	(2)	10,452	3,346	11,887	15,651	21,985	12,114
Pacific.............	1919	435,179	127,480	7,621	232,451	7,641	22,270	14,026	17,796	5,894
	1914	235,515	(2)	(2)	61,173	10,599	53,390	10,135	85,998	14,220
	1909	213,166	(2)	(2)	31,838	12,139	46,540	9,617	97,749	15,283
NEW ENGLAND:										
Maine..............	1919	88,651	2,126	4,443	21,400	7,278	44,254	3,043	4,536	1,571
New Hampshire....	1919	83,074	3,650	1,160	49,726	12,579	12,287	2,324	1,130	218
Vermont...........	1919	33,491	2,926	301	9,163	3,945	9,227	4,659	2,481	789
Massachusetts.....	1919	713,836	54,454	38,904	436,806	109,036	40,902	27,012	5,655	1,067
Rhode Island.......	1919	139,665	1,794	665	61,605	30,347	37,901	6,846	406	101
Connecticut........	1919	292,672	19,676	10,427	69,955	81,719	20,927	82,977	5,749	1,242
MIDDLE ATLANTIC:										
New York..........	1919	1,228,130	317,928	52,953	420,335	208,679	102,469	65,219	41,999	18,548
New Jersey.........	1919	508,686	120,136	19,969	162,437	101,586	28,314	57,527	12,943	5,774
Pennsylvania.......	1919	1,135,837	144,123	44,822	292,039	186,672	128,114	178,892	98,314	62,861
EAST NORTH CENTRAL:										
Ohio...............	1919	730,733	48,750	48,036	198,838	156,028	51,695	136,582	59,145	31,659
Indiana............	1919	277,580	14,998	7,779	67,788	49,638	23,546	69,166	28,961	15,704
Illinois............	1919	653,114	95,221	28,194	229,427	146,879	44,746	68,615	22,881	17,151
Michigan...........	1919	471,242	8,654	8,234	148,486	166,318	48,624	51,744	33,281	5,901
Wisconsin..........	1919	263,949	8,654	14,589	59,331	38,428	22,582	69,551	43,505	7,309
WEST NORTH CENTRAL:										
Minnesota..........	1919	115,623	5,258	8,947	44,940	12,215	10,030	11,517	16,823	5,893
Iowa...............	1919	80,551	1,411	4,484	24,733	6,657	15,543	12,013	12,996	2,714
Missouri...........	1919	195,037	18,974	7,699	64,117	39,600	31,903	15,257	13,184	4,303
North Dakota......	1919	4,472	28	167	2,782	109	439	234	633	80
South Dakota......	1919	6,382	78	800	1,971	274	816	385	1,845	213
Nebraska..........	1919	36,521	812	649	15,864	2,639	3,087	5,432	5,534	2,504
Kansas............	1919	61,049	1,650	1,060	31,266	2,208	6,023	10,858	5,437	2,547

[1] Includes 48 and under for 1914 and 1909.   [2] Corresponding figures not available.

TABLE 13.—AVERAGE NUMBER OF WAGE EARNERS CLASSIFIED ACCORDING TO PREVAILING HOURS OF LABOR PER WEEK, BY GEOGRAPHIC DIVISIONS AND STATES: 1919, 1914, AND 1909—Continued.

DIVISION AND STATE.	Census year.	Total.	IN ESTABLISHMENTS WHERE THE PREVAILING HOURS OF LABOR PER WEEK WERE—							
			44 and under.	Between 44 and 48.	48.	Between 48 and 54.	54.	Between 54 and 60.	60.	Over 60.
SOUTH ATLANTIC:										
Delaware	1919	29,035	8,288	1,863	5,968	3,214	3,842	2,274	2,490	1,096
Maryland	1919	140,342	36,569	5,868	27,201	25,444	9,648	23,321	10,398	1,893
District of Columbia	1919	10,482	1,900	268	5,144	518	269	1,859	147	377
Virginia	1919	119,352	16,072	4,492	21,688	14,126	10,422	25,150	23,951	3,451
West Virginia	1919	83,036	9,105	2,222	18,493	8,040	8,277	15,127	18,226	3,546
North Carolina	1919	157,659	1,174	310	9,411	20,081	5,934	77,547	39,481	3,721
South Carolina	1919	79,450	583	379	5,099	1,914	3,562	46,076	18,748	3,089
Georgia	1919	123,441	4,948	994	18,495	8,974	7,289	36,021	38,916	7,804
Florida	1919	74,415	6,710	1,626	19,890	5,170	8,435	4,834	23,704	4,046
EAST SOUTH CENTRAL:										
Kentucky	1919	69,340	3,153	2,626	16,998	8,592	6,840	16,872	12,280	1,979
Tennessee	1919	95,167	1,750	2,511	17,046	7,880	14,344	26,103	19,490	6,043
Alabama	1919	107,159	3,316	757	17,999	4,006	5,170	22,947	38,170	14,794
Mississippi	1919	57,560	4,340	2,695	3,613	2,592	3,001	2,363	35,921	3,035
WEST SOUTH CENTRAL:										
Arkansas	1919	49,954	1,233	254	6,823	1,407	2,986	4,643	30,207	2,401
Louisiana	1919	98,265	4,811	1,918	18,151	3,881	8,493	7,496	45,742	7,773
Oklahoma	1919	29,503	917	915	11,197	717	3,342	4,913	4,326	3,176
Texas	1919	107,522	3,705	958	41,736	5,453	13,336	11,154	23,514	7,666
MOUNTAIN:										
Montana	1919	17,160	272	2,056	7,603	216	1,358	3,719	1,390	546
Idaho	1919	13,917	8	370	10,959	161	566	688	1,003	162
Wyoming	1919	6,634	24	1	851	28	524	4,195	295	716
Colorado	1919	35,254	1,684	402	18,464	1,014	3,240	5,251	1,891	3,308
New Mexico	1919	5,736	398		740	269	481	2,828	929	91
Arizona	1919	8,528	57	57	2,842	976	285	2,897	1,049	365
Utah	1919	18,868	1,302	734	7,514	1,021	896	5,879	116	1,406
Nevada	1919	3,119	7		2,022	8	114	818	127	23
PACIFIC:										
Washington	1919	132,928	41,473	3,264	80,036	730	2,835	2,612	1,679	299
Oregon	1919	58,559	11,975	477	39,915	458	1,892	1,829	1,774	239
California	1919	243,692	74,032	3,880	112,500	6,453	17,543	9,585	14,343	5,356

TABLE 14.—SIZE OF ESTABLISHMENTS, BY AVERAGE

	INDUSTRY.	TOTAL.		ESTABLISHMENTS EMPLOYING—				
				No wage earners.	1 to 5 wage earners, inclusive.		6 to 20 wage earners, inclusive.	
		Establishments.	Wage earners (average number).	Establishments.	Establishments.	Wage earners.	Establishments.	Wage earners.
1	United States	290,105	9,096,372	37,934	141,742	311,576	56,208	631,290
2	Aeroplanes, seaplanes, and airships, and parts.	31	3,543	2	10	30	5	59
3	Agricultural implements	521	54,368	40	178	393	103	1,165
4	Aluminum manufactures	83	11,402	2	17	48	15	207
5	Ammunition	42	22,816	1	2	9	8	77
6	Artificial flowers	224	4,138	29	70	214	66	772
7	Artificial limbs	177	671	46	104	227	22	225
8	Artificial stone products	2,785	8,378	352	2,093	3,326	283	2,862
9	Artists' materials	58	926	10	27	58	11	132
10	Asbestos products, not including steam packing.	46	3,654	1	9	26	15	184
11	Automobile bodies and parts	2,515	132,556	214	1,116	2,560	595	6,862
12	Automobiles	315	210,559	5	27	84	37	487
13	Automobile repairing	15,507	55,061	1,359	12,002	25,719	1,891	18,070
14	Awnings, tents, and sails	895	6,028	101	555	1,256	194	2,087
15	Babbitt metal and solder	118	2,372	9	65	146	20	235
16	Bags, other than paper, not including bags made in textile mills	216	10,756	7	68	176	62	746
17	Bags, paper, exclusive of those made in paper mills.	75	4,168	1	19	47	16	174
18	Baking powders and yeast	88	3,331	19	38	64	8	108
19	Baskets, and rattan and willow ware	375	4,533	126	118	254	70	798
20	Bells	10	237		3	7	5	46
21	Belting and hose, rubber	15	5,826				1	17
22	Belting and hose, woven, other than rubber.	41	2,479	2	3	10	8	96
23	Belting, leather	172	2,765	8	82	189	50	529
24	Billiard tables, bowling alleys, and accessories.	49	2,101	5	25	78	15	159
25	Blacking, stains, and dressings	220	2,455	36	126	291	35	345
26	Bluing	57	360	10	33	86	8	86
27	Bone, carbon, and lamp black	35	675		10	39	16	183
28	Bookbinding and blank-book making	1,113	20,361	101	449	1,217	376	3,968
29	Boot and shoe cut stock	252	9,715	11	73	208	84	949
30	Boot and shoe findings	427	8,941	30	145	357	137	1,665
31	Boots and shoes, not including rubber boots and shoes.	1,449	211,049	24	195	519	228	2,765
32	Boots and shoes, rubber	25	32,875		2	7	1	6
33	Boxes, cigar	189	5,218	9	51	148	53	664
34	Boxes, paper and other, not elsewhere specified.	1,201	55,862	10	153	456	376	4,996
35	Boxes, wooden packing, except cigar boxes.	1,140	42,445	54	332	754	264	3,236
36	Brass, bronze, and copper products	1,092	75,051	60	358	979	320	3,689
37	Bread and other bakery products	25,095	141,592	3,920	17,246	37,250	3,111	29,499
38	Brick and tile, terra-cotta, and fire-clay products.	2,414	76,915	31	638	1,792	736	9,096
39	Brooms	1,034	6,313	329	435	882	201	2,170
40	Brushes	379	7,968	45	160	417	96	1,100
41	Butter	3,738	17,641	239	2,942	5,601	403	4,362
42	Butter, reworking	5	47		3	10	1	12
43	Buttons	557	15,577	43	212	499	147	1,879
44	Candles	19	541	1	9	24	3	34
45	Canning and preserving, fish	410	11,248	11	128	331	123	1,525
46	Canning and preserving, fruits and vegetables.	3,082	60,865	199	1,241	3,313	945	11,007
47	Canning and preserving, oysters	65	1,189	5	14	39	27	309
48	Card cutting and designing	75	1,148	8	24	57	30	319
49	Cardboard, not made in paper mills	16	1,425				4	56
50	Carpets and rugs, other than rag	75	22,933	1	5	16	7	98
51	Carpets, rag	339	2,016	87	172	396	57	564
52	Carriage and wagon materials	258	6,509	27	95	223	60	727
53	Carriages and sleds, children's	103	6,686	11	25	54	16	180
54	Carriages and wagons, including repairs	2,286	18,173	458	1,366	2,788	310	3,106
55	Cars and general shop construction and repairs by electric-railroad companies.	624	31,272		229	640	174	2,069
56	Cars and general shop construction and repairs by steam-railroad companies.	1,744	484,437		125	374	206	2,617
57	Cars, electric-railroad, not including operations of railroad companies.	7	2,920				1	10

NUMBER OF WAGE EARNERS, FOR INDUSTRIES: 1919.

ESTABLISHMENTS EMPLOYING—continued.

21 to 50 wage earners, inclusive.		51 to 100 wage earners, inclusive.		101 to 250 wage earners, inclusive.		251 to 500 wage earners, inclusive.		501 to 1,000 wage earners, inclusive.		Over 1,000 wage earners.		
Establishments.	Wage earners.	Establishments	Wage earners.	Establishments.	Wage earners.	Establishments	Wage earners.	Establishments	Wage earners.	Establishments	Wage earners.	
25,379	829,301	12,405	888,344	10,068	1,581,763	3,599	1,250,875	1,749	1,205,627	1,021	2,397,596	1
4	150	2	191	2	320	4	1,656	2	1,137			2
67	2,281	43	2,961	46	7,204	21	7,494	13	10,621	10	22,249	3
17	606	9	646	12	2,207	4	1,239	6	3,750	1	2,699	4
9	289	4	281	8	1,262	3	1,084	2	1,530	5	18,284	5
40	1,299	13	923	6	930							6
4	148	1	71									7
51	1,508	4	274	2	408							8
5	159	4	259			1	318					9
6	219	5	346	5	756	4	1,198	1	925			10
275	8,841	127	9,305	92	14,740	41	14,722	34	24,164	21	51,362	11
58	2,077	42	2,926	50	8,155	44	15,215	19	12,900	33	168,715	12
203	5,939	35	2,346	14	2,082	3	905					13
28	907	13	870	2	282	2	626					14
14	477	3	265	5	711	2	538					15
28	850	16	1,232	26	4,259	6	1,724	3	1,769			16
12	447	13	914	12	1,679	2	907					17
6	201	9	590	3	494	4	1,247	1	627			18
43	1,361	9	646	8	1,201	1	273					19
1	44			1	140							20
1	43	2	157	2	309	5	1,456	2	1,426	2	2,418	21
15	460	9	585	1	109	2	604	1	615			22
19	597	7	473	6	977							23
3	92									1	1,772	24
15	425	2	142	4	722	2	530					25
6	188											26
6	173	2	124	1	156							27
101	3,203	41	2,729	35	5,145	8	2,664	2	1,435			28
42	1,362	23	1,666	13	1,771	3	1,092	2	1,368	1	1,299	29
73	2,406	25	1,736	14	1,941	3	836					30
244	8,485	233	17,374	285	46,398	153	53,010	66	45,787	21	36,711	31
						5	1,983	4	2,925	13	27,954	32
50	1,657	16	1,148	9	1,299	1	302					33
376	12,495	170	11,818	91	14,179	19	6,295	3	2,119	3	3,504	34
241	8,294	143	10,477	89	13,249	13	4,183	4	2,252			35
168	5,291	72	5,227	61	9,361	23	7,734	17	11,408	13	31,362	36
465	14,545	173	12,274	127	18,810	37	12,801	10	6,247	6	10,166	37
592	20,220	260	18,125	139	20,580	14	4,686	4	2,416			38
54	1,713	9	655	6	893							39
46	1,518	19	1,345	6	853	6	2,057	1	678			40
102	3,162	35	2,458	17	2,058							41
1	25											42
80	2,552	39	2,766	28	4,311	6	1,956	2	1,614			43
3	100	2	152	1	231							44
95	3,176	35	2,534	16	2,306	1	375			1	1,001	45
442	14,069	150	10,779	85	12,890	16	5,065	2	1,263	2	2,479	46
14	403	4	307	1	131							47
5	198	7	470	1	104							48
4	131	5	391	2	279			1	568			49
13	430	12	839	17	2,716	9	3,183	4	2,266	7	13,385	50
18	556	3	171	2	329							51
37	1,193	26	1,855	11	1,676	2	835					52
18	569	11	885	16	2,404	4	1,309	2	1,285			53
75	2,459	47	3,267	22	3,132	5	1,622	3	1,799			54
111	3,696	47	3,467	41	5,884	9	2,860	9	6,738	4	5,918	55
253	8,582	255	18,857	397	64,735	238	85,995	164	117,723	106	185,554	56
1	25			1	150	3	1,184			1	1,551	57

TABLE 14.—SIZE OF ESTABLISHMENTS, BY AVERAGE

| | | | ESTABLISHMENTS EMPLOYING— | | | | |
| | TOTAL. | | No wage earners. | 1 to 5 wage earners, inclusive. | | 6 to 20 wage earners, inclusive. | |
INDUSTRY.	Establishments.	Wage earners (average number).	Establishments.	Establishments.	Wage earners	Establishments.	Wage earners
1 Cars, steam-railroad, not including operations of railroad companies.	99	52,298	......	......	......	9	94
2 Cash registers and calculating machines.	65	16,544	7	14	42	13	166
3 Cement.	123	25,524	......	4	6	6	74
4 Charcoal, not including production in lumber and wood distillation industries.	41	209	9	21	64	9	84
5 Cheese.	3,530	3,997	628	2,846	3,072	44	440
6 Chemicals.	598	55,586	18	153	399	163	2,030
7 Chewing gum.	62	3,190	2	14	47	19	234
8 China decorating, not including that done in potteries.	43	244	5	25	49	9	93
9 Chocolate and cocoa products.	48	9,083	......	7	19	4	47
10 Cleansing and polishing preparations.	499	1,955	167	266	507	54	572
11 Clocks.	46	8,252	3	16	32	7	68
12 Cloth, sponging and refinishing.	67	1,206	6	11	33	29	434
13 Clothing, horse.	28	766	1	11	30	7	92
14 Clothing, men's.	5,258	175,270	328	1,519	4,053	1,681	20,644
15 Clothing, men's, buttonholes.	107	484	23	62	143	18	188
16 Clothing, women's.	7,711	165,649	208	1,891	5,630	3,284	40,127
17 Coal-tar products.	183	15,663	3	42	142	63	745
18 Coffee and spice, roasting and grinding.	794	10,540	76	410	959	193	2,098
19 Coffins, burial cases, and undertakers' goods.	351	11,890	27	87	235	96	1,188
20 Coke, not including gas-house coke.	278	29,319	2	48	145	64	818
21 Collars and cuffs, men's.	39	11,103	2	7	24	9	89
22 Combs and hairpins, not made from metal or rubber.	45	2,229	1	8	28	6	58
23 Condensed milk.	401	13,675	......	80	270	119	1,394
24 Confectionery and ice cream.	6,624	95,648	1,037	3,750	7,881	1,043	11,088
25 Cooperage.	1,099	13,219	92	689	1,282	180	1,902
26 Copper, tin, and sheet-iron work.	4,796	27,640	605	3,093	6,664	846	8,833
27 Cordage and twine.	120	17,622	2	7	12	21	294
28 Cordials and flavoring sirups.	149	1,398	16	91	210	30	326
29 Cork, cutting.	62	3,545	5	17	39	14	144
30 Corsets.	188	18,415	7	47	122	35	395
31 Cotton goods.	1,288	430,966	2	26	86	81	1,030
32 Cotton lace.	44	6,490	......	5	13	6	90
33 Cotton small wares.	164	9,396	......	23	78	56	722
34 Crucibles.	22	848	......	3	8	8	108
35 Cutlery and edge tools.	304	19,859	14	92	238	63	759
36 Dairymen's, poultrymen's, and apiarists' supplies.	244	6,437	25	113	258	54	572
37 Dental goods.	319	5,224	33	166	417	79	860
38 Drug grinding.	31	1,347	1	7	17	10	108
39 Druggists' preparations.	524	15,568	96	212	494	127	1,353
40 Dyeing and finishing textiles, exclusive of that done in textile mills.	628	55,985	11	106	292	178	2,186
41 Dyestuffs and extracts—natural.	144	4,342	9	59	161	29	291
42 Electrical machinery, apparatus, and supplies.	1,404	212,374	42	376	1,087	355	4,212
43 Electroplating.	515	3,024	61	291	735	133	1,413
44 Emery and other abrasive wheels.	60	5,601	2	20	47	16	203
45 Enameling.	74	694	6	41	94	18	201
46 Engines, steam, gas, and water.	370	77,617	4	62	185	74	879
47 Engravers' materials.	21	174	1	10	29	7	64
48 Engraving and diesinking.	478	1,878	195	227	486	49	541
49 Engraving, steel and copper plate, including plate printing.	421	7,014	62	150	407	146	1,699
50 Engraving, wood.	55	235	25	22	42	6	54
51 Envelopes.	106	8,129	......	7	22	26	342
52 Explosives.	118	9,249	1	38	90	15	201
53 Fancy articles, not elsewhere specified.	661	13,961	64	256	662	183	2,126
54 Feathers and plumes.	216	3,504	11	72	199	80	858
55 Felt goods.	49	5,236	1	......	......	4	44
56 Ferroalloys.	30	2,344	......	3	11	4	57
57 Fertilizers.	600	26,296	5	196	584	134	1,576
58 Files.	50	5,767	1	13	36	16	206
59 Firearms.	26	11,287	1	3	7	3	44
60 Fire extinguishers, chemical.	32	777	7	9	22	8	86
61 Fireworks.	57	1,222	9	21	53	12	134

NUMBER OF WAGE EARNERS, FOR INDUSTRIES: 1919—Continued.

ESTABLISHMENTS EMPLOYING—continued.

21 to 50 wage earners, inclusive.		51 to 100 wage earners, inclusive.		101 to 250 wage earners, inclusive.		251 to 500 wage earners, inclusive.		501 to 1,000 wage earners, inclusive.		Over 1,000 wage earners.		
Establishments.	Wage earners.	Establishments.	Wage earners.	Establishments.	Wage earners.	Establishments.	Wage earners.	Establishments.	Wage earners.	Establishments.	Wage earners.	
10	321	14	1,026	22	3,724	11	4,405	19	12,947	14	29,781	1
8	265	6	435	7	1,004	6	2,306	2	1,190	2	11,136	2
7	302	25	2,091	56	9,694	19	6,951	4	3,160	2	3,246	3
2	61											4
10	341	2	144									5
121	3,851	50	3,703	47	7,209	18	6,300	17	11,619	11	20,475	6
15	469	4	289	6	899	1	423	1	829			7
4	102											8
10	355	8	543	8	1,143	6	2,086	4	2,958	1	1,932	9
5	153	3	195	4	528							10
4	134	4	311	5	773	1	483	4	2,729	2	3,722	11
19	584	2	155									12
6	179	1	72	1	115	1	278					13
1,011	32,817	419	29,282	205	31,833	59	20,205	28	19,325	8	17,111	14
2	45	2	108									15
1,649	52,625	483	33,390	176	25,907	16	5,524	4	2,446			16
28	922	23	1,632	12	2,051	4	1,306	6	3,862	2	5,003	17
69	2,121	29	2,136	14	2,373	3	853					18
73	2,489	44	3,041	18	2,682	5	1,735	1	520			19
56	1,906	35	2,574	44	6,965	19	7,076	5	3,017	5	6,818	20
3	107	7	529	4	693	2	673	3	1,887	2	7,101	21
12	436	12	869	6	838							22
97	3,458	82	5,642	23	2,911							23
410	13,207	192	13,752	135	21,649	37	12,615	17	11,635	3	3,821	24
66	2,108	47	3,122	20	2,967	4	1,227	1	611			25
187	5,774	44	3,019	19	2,636	2	714					26
28	1,003	20	1,503	23	3,340	12	3,960	4	2,834	3	4,676	27
6	144	3	183	3	535							28
12	413	6	379	3	357	4	1,405	1	808			29
28	902	21	1,510	32	5,009	11	3,868	6	4,249	1	2,330	30
118	4,177	183	13,689	417	68,584	218	77,463	152	104,961	91	160,976	31
7	256	10	730	8	1,203	5	2,123	3	2,075			32
38	1,249	27	1,984	13	1,956	5	1,785	2	1,622			33
5	158	3	228	3	346							34
48	1,645	34	2,420	30	4,221	18	6,011	4	2,702	1	1,863	35
29	957	11	808	8	1,266	2	638	1	795	1	1,143	36
28	964	4	265	6	953	2	812	1	953			37
9	289	1	71	2	326			1	526			38
46	1,509	22	1,569	8	1,308	8	2,951	2	1,269	3	5,115	39
141	4,662	69	5,010	68	10,264	29	10,330	19	12,534	7	10,707	40
15	510	18	1,268	13	1,836	1	276					41
212	7,220	117	8,539	147	23,862	80	27,812	38	25,947	37	113,695	42
29	821	1	55									43
7	234	7	446	6	809					2	3,862	44
7	226	1	72	1	101							45
55	1,828	50	3,617	64	10,212	22	7,832	23	16,990	16	36,074	46
3	81											47
4	149	1	100	1	161	1	441					48
38	1,151	14	919	9	1,183	1	298			1	1,357	49
1	34			1	105							50
27	858	20	1,485	21	3,459	3	860	2	1,103			51
25	910	15	1,047	17	2,729	4	1,393	2	1,582	1	1,297	52
99	3,208	29	1,993	24	3,793	6	2,179					53
37	1,223	14	918	2	306							54
10	386	18	1,383	12	1,907	4	1,516					55
10	341	6	375	4	458	3	1,102					56
111	3,946	79	5,705	61	9,420	12	3,860	2	1,205			57
7	246	4	325	3	477			5	3,038	1	1,439	58
4	146	2	194	3	580	2	582	5	3,595	3	6,139	59
4	129	3	215			1	325					60
8	269	4	275	3	491							16

TABLE 14.—SIZE OF ESTABLISHMENTS, BY AVERAGE

	INDUSTRY.	TOTAL.		No wage earners.	1 to 5 wage earners, inclusive.		6 to 20 wage earners, inclusive.	
		Establishments.	Wage earners (average number).	Establishments.	Establishments.	Wage earners.	Establishments.	Wage earners.
1	Flags and banners	79	1,065	10	31	78	23	242
2	Flavoring extracts	453	2,188	145	234	509	48	463
3	Flax and hemp, dressed	20	420	1	4	11	12	150
4	Flour-mill and gristmill products	10,708	45,481	3,181	6,220	11,325	922	9,462
5	Food preparations, not elsewhere specified.	1,997	30,365	319	1,025	2,222	387	4,248
6	Foundry and machine-shop products	10,934	482,767	757	3,814	9,732	2,784	32,241
7	Foundry supplies	76	906	4	36	83	26	313
8	Fuel, manufactured	11	171		3	9	4	62
9	Fur goods	1,815	13,639	211	1,029	2,606	452	4,893
10	Furnishing goods, men's	487	18,944	39	122	346	128	1,500
11	Furniture	3,154	138,331	218	915	2,312	665	7,879
12	Furs, dressed	141	5,075	5	37	101	47	545
13	Galvanizing	52	1,665		22	72	16	184
14	Gas and electric fixtures	341	9,795	10	141	368	92	1,020
15	Gas, illuminating and heating	1,022	42,908	15	392	1,156	325	3,690
16	Gas machines and gas and water meters	105	5,589	6	35	83	23	282
17	Glass	371	77,520		8	27	21	303
18	Glass, cutting, staining, and ornamenting.	616	6,480	66	285	693	175	1,923
19	Gloves and mittens, cloth, not including gloves made in textile mills.	182	8,986	4	36	105	47	583
20	Gloves and mittens, leather	355	10,685	23	94	260	108	1,349
21	Glucose and starch	56	7,795	3	31	69	4	37
22	Glue, not elsewhere specified	62	4,264	5	22	52	6	70
23	Gold and silver, leaf and foil	87	950	4	47	121	28	320
24	Gold and silver, reducing and refining, not from the ore.	87	644	19	45	110	16	128
25	Graphite, ground and refined	24	497	1	9	31	9	100
26	Grease and tallow, not including lubricating greases.	482	6,647	50	289	642	85	936
27	Grindstones	23	674	1	3	10	4	57
28	Haircloth	18	425				12	178
29	Hair work	198	1,084	35	116	280	39	424
30	Hammocks	6	64		3	10	2	20
31	Hand stamps	298	1,719	83	143	319	54	545
32	Hardware	548	42,505	34	154	355	127	1,461
33	Hardware, saddlery	37	3,675	6	11	26	5	67
34	Hat and cap materials	133	3,009	12	63	171	39	424
35	Hats and caps, other than felt, straw, and wool.	709	7,539	87	286	749	247	2,640
36	Hats, fur-felt	176	18,510	10	53	140	25	326
37	Hats, straw	148	7,302	2	29	99	43	499
38	Hats, wool-felt	40	1,448	2	17	44	10	120
39	Hones and whetstones	11	212		6	20	2	31
40	Horseshoes, not made in steel works or rolling mills.	20	744	3	9	21		
41	House-furnishing goods, not elsewhere specified.	467	7,853	47	203	513	148	1,678
42	Ice, manufactured	2,867	30,247	51	1,538	4,236	931	10,360
43	Ink, printing	90	1,988	4	43	127	24	258
44	Ink, writing	61	702	20	28	68	7	55
45	Instruments, professional and scientific.	351	15,931	42	107	281	91	1,039
46	Iron and steel, blast furnaces	195	41,660	1	1	4	12	152
47	Iron and steel, steel works and rolling mills.	500	375,088		5	20	13	170
48	Iron and steel, bolts, nuts, washers, and rivets, not made in rolling mills.	144	17,967		31	86	25	278
49	Iron and steel, cast-iron pipe	59	12,625				2	15
50	Iron and steel, doors and shutters	57	2,077	3	11	36	24	299
51	Iron and steel, forgings, not made in steel works or rolling mills.	241	28,391	3	32	94	48	641
52	Iron and steel, nails and spikes, cut and wrought, including wire nails, not made in steel works or rolling mills.	65	3,355	2	14	42	18	223
53	Iron and steel, tempering and welding.	520	1,835	113	343	703	52	479
54	Iron and steel, wrought pipe	50	10,426		3	8	15	182
55	Ivory, shell, and bone work, not including combs and hairpins.	44	842	5	16	37	14	149
56	Japanning	36	295	1	21	56	10	111
57	Jewelry	2,054	30,871	297	898	2,258	513	5,586

NUMBER OF WAGE EARNERS, FOR INDUSTRIES: 1919—Continued.

ESTABLISHMENTS EMPLOYING—continued.

21 to 50 wage earners, inclusive.		51 to 100 wage earners, inclusive.		101 to 250 wage earners, inclusive.		251 to 500 wage earners, inclusive.		501 to 1,000 wage earners, inclusive.		Over 1,000 wage earners.		
Establishments.	Wage earners.	Establishments.	Wage earners.	Establishments.	Wage earners.	Establishments	Wage earners.	Establishments	Wage earners.	Establishments	Wage earners.	
9	267	5	346	1	132							1
19	595	5	344	2	277							2
2	55			1	204							3
251	7,613	82	5,774	42	5,852	7	2,222	1	601	2	2,632	4
148	4,723	67	4,749	35	5,184	11	4,186	3	2,247	2	2,806	5
1,636	54,264	868	62,397	703	112,855	228	78,978	107	73,145	37	59,155	6
7	207	2	167	1	136							7
4	100											8
93	3,007	23	1,491	5	810	1	270	1	562			9
113	3,756	52	3,841	23	3,267	6	2,238	2	1,273	2	2,723	10
574	19,606	431	31,204	277	41,468	49	16,370	22	14,421	3	5,071	11
27	904	12	804	11	1,758	1	267	1	696			12
7	193	4	256	2	268			1	692			13
57	1,921	25	1,780	12	2,087	2	747	1	624	1	1,248	14
151	4,918	53	3,806	54	8,011	20	7,000	6	4,241	6	10,086	15
19	648	9	708	7	1,080	4	1,486	2	1,302			16
39	1,436	86	6,362	121	19,891	65	22,137	23	14,424	8	12,940	17
70	2,308	16	1,033	4	523							18
48	1,586	26	2,007	14	2,131	6	1,982	1	592			19
73	2,587	31	2,104	22	3,183	4	1,202					20
3	105	1	60	5	1,028	5	2,031	3	2,267	1	2,198	21
9	259	8	553	7	994	3	982	2	1,354			22
5	193	2	159	1	157							23
3	72	3	186	1	148							24
2	68	2	152	1	146							25
26	879	19	1,388	11	1,542			2	1,260			26
13	477	2	130									27
5	190	1	57									28
5	163	3	217									29
1	34											30
14	426	1	64	3	365							31
94	3,004	57	4,182	47	7,490	22	7,590	6	4,024	7	14,399	32
3	113	2	113	7	1,182	1	303	1	869	1	1,002	33
8	282	4	287	4	604	2	679	1	562			34
65	1,990	18	1,291	6	869							35
26	897	24	1,665	21	3,425	11	3,996	4	2,281	2	5,780	36
30	928	25	1,857	15	2,311	3	1,031	1	577			37
5	208	2	143	2	325	2	608					38
2	71	1	90									39
1	30	6	441			1	252					40
35	1,131	19	1,372	12	1,824	2	733	1	602			41
280	8,739	48	3,186	17	2,682	1	468	1	576			42
7	214	7	524	4	567	1	298					43
2	60	1	63	3	456							44
55	1,697	26	1,883	18	3,073	8	3,007	3	2,417	1	2,534	45
13	472	46	3,496	71	10,902	31	10,313	17	11,842	3	4,479	46
32	1,133	48	3,666	97	16,763	103	38,269	102	72,797	100	242,270	47
28	962	16	1,151	24	3,894	13	4,728	6	5,566	1	1,302	48
4	165	14	961	20	3,310	14	4,772	4	2,255	1	1,147	49
9	299	3	219	6	964	1	260					50
40	1,306	34	2,456	51	7,594	23	8,644	9	5,778	1	1,878	51
15	464	8	607	5	738	2	729	1	552			52
9	243	1	62	2	348							53
7	269	8	592	8	1,505	3	1,120	3	2,251	3	4,499	54
3	95	4	303	2	258							55
4	128											56
193	6,349	102	6,891	45	7,103	5	1,587			1	1,097	57

TABLE 14.—SIZE OF ESTABLISHMENTS, BY AVERAGE

	INDUSTRY.	TOTAL. Establishments.	TOTAL. Wage earners (average number).	No wage earners. Establishments.	1 to 5 wage earners, inclusive. Establishments.	1 to 5 wage earners, inclusive. Wage earners.	6 to 20 wage earners, inclusive. Establishments.	6 to 20 wage earners, inclusive. Wage earners.
1	Jewelry and instrument cases	142	2,734	12	49	155	45	517
2	Jute goods	26	7,138	1	1	3	4	46
3	Knit goods	2,050	172,572	82	379	1,026	472	5,786
4	Labels and tags	119	5,227	5	34	90	39	478
5	Lamps and reflectors	171	8,360	10	62	155	38	432
6	Lapidary work	124	1,155	25	60	148	23	257
7	Lard, not made in slaughtering and meat-packing establishments.	6	13		6	13		
8	Lasts	64	2,910	2	9	19	19	239
9	Lead, bar, pipe, and sheet	32	852		10	32	11	138
10	Leather goods, not elsewhere specified	503	8,945	39	193	511	152	1,751
11	Leather, tanned, curried, and finished	680	72,476	23	75	190	124	1,586
12	Lime	476	11,405	28	187	342	105	1,262
13	Linen goods	10	1,890				7	78
14	Liquors, distilled	34	1,380		6	18	7	78
15	Liquors, malt	729	34,259	4	74	236	241	3,034
16	Liquors, vinous	342	1,011	97	215	243	19	191
17	Lithographing	331	15,618	41	58	172	81	1,040
18	Locomotives, not made by railroad companies.	17	26,715				1	12
19	Looking-glass and picture frames	429	4,708	100	210	464	73	841
20	Lubricating greases	53	472	4	29	53	14	156
21	Lumber and timber products	26,119	480,945	843	16,640	34,267	5,333	57,213
22	Lumber, planing-mill products, not including planing mills connected with sawmills.	5,309	86,956	357	2,405	5,795	1,510	17,824
23	Machine tools	403	53,111	8	54	157	87	1,092
24	Malt	55	1,352		9	31	23	284
25	Marble and stone work	4,240	32,768	684	2,506	5,312	697	7,493
26	Matches	21	3,726	1	1	3	3	48
27	Mats and matting, from cocoa fiber, grass, and coir.	12	1,073	1	1	2	2	31
28	Mattresses and spring beds, not elsewhere specified.	1,041	12,637	113	492	1,228	274	2,944
29	Millinery and lace goods, not elsewhere specified.	3,005	50,850	153	1,196	3,181	1,063	11,947
30	Millstones	12	38	2	8	15	2	23
31	Mineral and soda waters	5,194	17,440	731	3,692	7,751	686	6,535
32	Minerals and earths, ground or otherwise treated.	419	14,426	7	98	276	149	1,859
33	Mirrors, framed and unframed, not elsewhere specified.	186	2,599	14	71	199	62	728
34	Models and patterns, not including paper patterns.	928	6,949	98	519	1,360	246	2,552
35	Motorcycles, bicycles, and parts	51	10,886	4	9	20	3	38
36	Mucilage, paste, and other adhesives, not elsewhere specified.	127	803	26	67	158	25	256
37	Musical instruments and materials, not elsewhere specified.	240	4,113	82	82	158	36	412
38	Musical instruments, organs	68	1,941	4	24	62	11	122
39	Musical instruments, pianos	191	22,957	2	11	34	25	312
40	Musical instruments, piano and organ materials.	113	11,009	4	21	56	27	323
41	Needles, pins, and hooks and eyes	92	9,294	4	14	34	20	268
42	Nets and seines	19	859	2	4	13	6	58
43	Oakum	6	124	1	2	10	2	19
44	Oil and cake, cottonseed	711	26,766		46	174	232	3,168
45	Oil, essential	78	321	32	37	54	5	66
46	Oil, linseed	26	2,173		1	5	3	41
47	Oil, not elsewhere specified	280	5,930	13	117	293	73	802
48	Oilcloth and linoleum, floor	21	5,414				2	31
49	Oilcloth, enameled	11	1,130				2	22
50	Oleomargarine and other butter substitutes.	42	2,851		5	18	8	78
51	Optical goods	506	14,723	32	255	636	127	1,440
52	Ordnance and accessories	26	11,328					
53	Paints	601	17,485	33	256	670	151	1,706
54	Paper and wood pulp	729	113,759		24	76	87	1,179
55	Paper goods, not elsewhere specified	308	14,135	15	88	246	81	921
56	Paper patterns	19	403	1	10	25	3	42
57	Patent medicines and compounds	2,467	17,444	721	1,255	2,401	327	3,439

NUMBER OF WAGE EARNERS, FOR INDUSTRIES: 1919—Continued.

ESTABLISHMENTS EMPLOYING—continued.												
21 to 50 wage earners, inclusive.		51 to 100 wage earners, inclusive.		101 to 250 wage earners, inclusive.		251 to 500 wage earners, inclusive.		501 to 1,000 wage earners, inclusive.		Over 1,000 wage earners.		
Establishments.	Wage earners.	Establishments.	Wage earners.	Establishments.	Wage earners.	Establishments.	Wage earners.	Establishments.	Wage earners.	Establishments.	Wage earners.	
26	810	3	185	7	1,067	3	1,290	1	824	2	3,854	1
5	171	6	388	3	562							2
379	13,150	308	22,146	274	44,106	105	36,249	37	24,777	14	25,332	3
21	675	12	919	7	1,096					1	1,963	4
24	761	14	1,037	13	1,950	9	3,353	1	672			5
12	434	4	316									6
												7
14	498	11	920	9	1,234							8
8	259	1	54	2	369							9
85	2,686	18	1,335	14	2,132	2	530					10
131	4,368	140	9,978	126	19,687	37	13,003	19	12,662	5	11,002	11
87	2,994	46	3,066	19	2,601	4	1,140					12
3	107	1	92	4	771	2	920					13
10	319	9	664	2	301							14
224	7,475	113	8,059	59	8,801	10	3,555	3	1,700	1	1,399	15
7	201	3	211	1	165							16
73	2,346	40	2,885	28	4,298	6	2,095	4	2,782			17
2	68	2	133	2	331	2	766	2	1,646	6	23,759	18
24	798	10	746	12	1,859							19
4	119	2	144									20
1,547	49,909	662	48,068	698	112,573	296	100,413	85	57,936	15	20,566	21
687	21,889	217	15,280	108	16,068	21	7,432	4	2,668			22
85	2,861	65	4,693	52	8,259	25	8,810	21	14,375	6	12,864	23
16	474	6	422	1	141							24
240	7,585	70	4,848	37	5,519	5	1,500	1	511			25
3	91	4	270	3	420	3	1,028	3	1,866			26
2	57	1	64	5	919							27
107	3,275	38	2,666	16	2,207	1	317					28
376	12,586	154	10,564	48	6,998	12	3,866	3	1,708			29
												30
70	2,049	14	997	1	108							31
92	2,843	42	3,063	22	3,306	9	3,079					32
30	895	7	503	2	274							33
53	1,618	7	527	4	542	1	350					34
6	187	10	744	10	1,614	3	990	3	1,944	3	5,349	35
6	178	3	211									36
22	671	10	729	6	1,066	1	252	1	825			37
18	630	8	580	3	547							38
47	1,537	33	2,512	49	7,666	17	6,000	6	3,663	1	1,233	39
16	592	13	1,041	16	2,621	13	4,774	3	1,602			40
17	636	10	692	20	3,014	3	1,245	3	2,107	1	1,298	41
3	113			4	675							42
		1	95									43
282	9,218	110	7,370	38	5,476	2	730	1	630			44
3	115	1	86									45
6	192	8	566	7	1,031	1	338					46
40	1,243	26	1,781	9	1,183	2	628					47
3	113	3	240	6	805	3	1,162	3	1,969	1	1,004	48
2	49	2	182	4	459	1	418					49
11	417	7	491	10	1,371	1	476					50
57	1,694	18	1,237	8	1,250	7	2,320			2	6,146	51
2	81	4	276	8	1,326	7	2,680	4	2,954	1	4,011	52
71	2,264	48	3,413	32	4,942	8	2,608	1	852	1	1,030	53
158	5,140	139	10,166	204	33,732	70	24,017	38	26,340	9	13,109	54
53	1,773	29	2,022	32	4,913	8	2,822	2	1,438			55
2	52	2	143	1	141							56
109	3,501	29	2,020	21	3,387	3	990	2	1,706			57

TABLE 14.—SIZE OF ESTABLISHMENTS, BY AVERAGE

	INDUSTRY.	TOTAL.		No wage earners.	1 to 5 wage earners, inclusive.		6 to 20 wage earners, inclusive.	
		Establishments.	Wage earners (average number).	Establishments.	Establishments.	Wage earners.	Establishments.	Wage earners.
1	Paving materials	889	16,072	14	306	878	324	3,846
2	Peanuts, grading, roasting, cleaning, and shelling.	78	2,460	5	25	44	14	164
3	Pencils, lead	12	5,970				1	18
4	Pens, fountain and stylographic	56	3,207	4	12	39	13	183
5	Pens, gold	15	416		1	5	8	93
6	Pens, steel	4	807		1	1		
7	Perfumery and cosmetics	569	5,405	134	277	621	111	1,275
8	Petroleum, refining	320	58,889	2	46	152	90	1,051
9	Phonographs and graphophones	166	28,721	11	30	83	34	422
10	Photo-engraving	422	6,769	23	130	345	178	2,110
11	Photographic apparatus	68	2,555	6	31	77	13	155
12	Photographic materials	169	14,556	14	65	146	40	468
13	Pickles, preserves, and sauces	723	16,621	99	319	735	158	1,907
14	Pipes, tobacco	56	2,539	5	19	50	15	178
15	Plated ware	68	9,492	2	11	33	12	155
16	Plumbers' supplies, not elsewhere specified.	214	13,592	7	51	141	50	618
17	Pocketbooks	139	2,905	14	46	135	42	536
18	Pottery	340	27,934	32	65	112	50	615
19	Poultry, killing and dressing, not done in slaughtering and meat-packing establishments.	196	2,140	2	96	278	75	853
20	Printing and publishing, book and job	13,089	123,005	3,220	6,167	14,124	2,479	27,141
21	Printing and publishing, music	160	899	124	21	54	6	70
22	Printing and publishing, newspapers and periodicals.	17,362	120,381	5,568	9,034	19,490	1,828	19,240
23	Printing materials	82	723	7	53	162	17	205
24	Pulp, from fiber other than wood	5	64		2	9	2	29
25	Pulp goods	40	3,041		8	24	7	102
26	Pumps, not including power pumps	127	5,384	13	43	98	29	316
27	Pumps, steam and other power	112	10,688	5	24	76	24	311
28	Refrigerators	122	5,786	1	36	103	33	406
29	Regalia, and society badges and emblems.	115	2,223	18	44	115	33	368
30	Rice, cleaning and polishing	86	2,113	7	14	22	15	187
31	Roofing materials	178	8,871	11	58	141	38	412
32	Rubber tires, tubes, and rubber goods, not elsewhere specified.	437	119,848	10	76	190	91	1,141
33	Rules, ivory and wood	13	168	2	6	12	2	23
34	Saddlery and harness	1,823	10,411	453	1,135	1,740	121	1,449
35	Safes and vaults	38	2,949	1	9	24	10	136
36	Salt	86	6,495	6	15	35	10	103
37	Sand and emery paper and cloth	12	771	1			1	19
38	Sand-lime brick	32	504		5	18	18	235
39	Sausage, not made in slaughtering and meat-packing establishments.	633	3,471	82	410	899	109	1,134
40	Saws	112	5,510	12	45	120	25	265
41	Scales and balances	79	5,432	4	19	52	18	190
42	Screws, machine	143	10,262	2	30	87	46	549
43	Screws, wood	11	4,889					
44	Sewing-machine cases	5	4,171		1	2		
45	Sewing machines and attachments	40	15,059	5	6	10	6	60
46	Shipbuilding, steel	162	344,014	1	6	13	12	120
47	Shipbuilding, wooden, including boat building.	913	43,432	125	373	744	155	1,806
48	Shirts	896	39,603	34	192	613	264	3,269
49	Show cases	119	1,857	12	44	115	36	410
50	Signs and advertising novelties	779	10,432	139	401	909	150	1,646
51	Silk goods, including throwsters	1,369	126,782	9	141	396	327	4,192
52	Silversmithing and silverware	99	6,453	4	23	71	39	457
53	Slaughtering and meat packing	1,304	160,996	92	515	1,235	303	3,512
54	Smelting and refining, copper	34	17,315				1	16
55	Smelting and refining, lead	25	6,438		1	1	1	6
56	Smelting and refining, zinc	39	13,796		1	4	1	14
57	Smelting and refining, metals, not elsewhere specified.	13	2,041		2	9	3	27
58	Smelting and refining, not from the ore.	81	2,167	1	27	67	27	312
59	Soap	348	20,436	49	153	390	70	853
60	Soda-water apparatus	66	2,599	3	29	72	17	177
61	Sporting and athletic goods	188	6,412	36	54	128	42	488

NUMBER OF WAGE EARNERS, FOR INDUSTRIES: 1919—Continued.

ESTABLISHMENTS EMPLOYING—continued.

21 to 50 wage earners, inclusive.		51 to 100 wage earners, inclusive.		101 to 250 wage earners, inclusive.		251 to 500 wage earners, inclusive.		501 to 1,000 wage earners, inclusive.		Over 1,000 wage earners.		
Establishments.	Wage earners.	Establishments.	Wage earners.	Establishments.	Wage earners.	Establishments	Wage earners.	Establishments.	Wage earners.	Establishments	Wage earners.	
179	5,388	50	3,416	14	1,815	2	729					1
20	642	10	779	3	482	1	349					2
2	57	3	235	1	163			2	1,668	3	3,829	3
18	563	4	269	3	685	1	487	1	981			4
5	147			1	171							5
1	46			1	191			1	569			6
24	791	15	995	5	928	3	795					7
59	2,019	44	3,258	32	5,347	19	6,517	13	9,003	15	31,542	8
35	1,114	17	1,180	24	3,938	5	1,637	6	4,358	4	15,989	9
70	2,002	13	922	7	1,038	1	352					10
8	265	3	186	3	546	4	1,326					11
25	872	14	968	5	715	4	1,149			2	10,238	12
67	2,213	39	2,643	31	4,555	8	2,577	1	582	1	1,409	13
4	125	7	484	4	595	1	362	1	745			14
12	454	6	459	17	2,881	3	952	3	2,073	2	2,485	15
42	1,439	39	2,796	18	2,992	2	863	4	3,137	1	1,606	16
21	763	9	570	7	901							17
44	1,486	54	3,921	74	12,590	16	5,513	4	2,685	1	1,012	18
15	418	7	470	1	121							19
822	26,221	236	16,919	122	18,748	32	11,115	9	6,009	2	2,728	20
4	133	2	130	3	512							21
549	17,918	199	13,608	128	19,980	39	12,796	13	9,139	4	8,210	22
4	128			1	228							23
1	26											24
10	303	3	221	9	1,568	3	823					25
16	503	11	803	10	1,549	4	1,354	1	761			26
20	654	18	1,330	13	2,123	4	1,218	2	1,578	2	3,398	27
21	695	9	639	20	3,175	2	768					28
14	436	1	61	4	611			1	632			29
43	1,368	6	407	1	129							30
29	1,011	17	1,193	15	2,224	8	2,675	2	1,215			31
75	2,616	56	4,155	60	9,767	30	11,343	19	11,907	20	78,729	32
2	48	1	85									33
68	2,257	32	2,333	11	1,705	3	927					34
4	138	5	354	5	657	3	1,072	1	568			35
13	438	20	1,479	16	2,423	6	2,017					36
4	146	3	196	3	410							37
9	251											38
25	803	4	255	3	380							39
15	473	7	485	4	558	1	302	1	515	2	2,792	40
17	565	9	677	8	1,361	1	495	3	2,092			41
29	987	14	963	13	2,022	6	2,062	2	1,138	1	2,454	42
				8	1,148			1	564	2	3,177	43
		2	168							2	4,001	44
8	271	1	73	5	901	3	1,045	4	2,820	2	9,879	45
11	356	17	1,222	14	2,355	17	6,005	10	7,231	74	326,712	46
91	3,034	56	3,999	73	12,022	23	7,504	14	9,880	3	4,443	47
203	6,865	113	8,069	66	10,216	17	5,686	7	4,885			48
20	675	5	410	2	247							49
50	1,687	18	1,223	14	2,056	5	1,779	2	1,132			50
340	11,797	232	17,097	218	33,339	69	24,487	19	13,458	14	22,016	51
14	487	4	238	9	1,385	3	821	2	1,181	1	1,813	52
136	4,476	92	6,648	63	10,065	39	13,272	26	18,379	38	103,409	53
2	79	3	240	9	1,390	6	2,196	8	5,873	5	7,551	54
1	36	2	153	8	1,232	8	2,695	4	2,315			55
3	134	2	132	15	2,714	12	4,253	4	3,308	1	3,237	56
3	105			2	361	2	634	1	905			57
14	473	5	391	7	924							58
31	981	12	957	14	2,187	8	2,584	7	4,756	4	7,728	59
7	222	5	400	4	622					1	1,106	60
27	855	14	938	11	1,584	1	381	3	2,038			61

TABLE 14.—SIZE OF ESTABLISHMENTS, BY AVERAGE

	INDUSTRY.	TOTAL.		No wage earners.	1 to 5 wage earners, inclusive.		6 to 20 wage earners, inclusive.	
		Establishments.	Wage earners (average number).	Establishments.	Establishments.	Wage earners.	Establishments.	Wage earners.
1	Springs, steel, car and carriage, not made in steel works or rolling mills.	112	8,981	4	31	89	20	231
2	Stamped and enameled ware, not elsewhere specified.	323	34,248	4	55	152	82	971
3	Stationery goods, not elsewhere specified	223	11,261	20	56	148	53	675
4	Statuary and art goods	195	1,466	29	108	235	44	460
5	Steam fittings and steam and hot-water heating apparatus.	261	36,686	10	57	156	66	810
6	Steam packing	169	6,147	3	78	225	47	530
7	Steel barrels, drums, and tanks	33	3,322	1	3	12	6	81
8	Stencils and brands	84	417	19	46	110	17	194
9	Stereotyping and electrotyping	171	3,664	4	29	103	82	1,047
10	Stoves and hot-air furnaces	412	32,868	10	75	222	64	747
11	Stoves, gas and oil	176	10,565	11	76	200	38	426
12	Structural ironwork, not made in steel works or rolling mills.	1,146	43,962	47	416	1,139	346	4,027
13	Sugar, beet	85	11,781				1	16
14	Sugar, cane	202	6,101	5	55	86	59	758
15	Sugar, refining, not including beet sugar.	20	18,202					
16	Sulphuric, nitric, and mixed acids	39	4,961		1	1	7	97
17	Surgical appliances	268	6,390	56	133	327	45	474
18	Suspenders, garters, and elastic woven goods.	196	10,857	15	64	180	49	601
19	Textile machinery and parts	432	31,823	20	108	292	141	1,556
20	Theatrical scenery	17	149	1	5	15	10	112
21	Tin and other foils, not elsewhere specified.	15	1,908		3	5	2	37
22	Tin plate and terneplate	24	3,122	1	5	13	2	21
23	Tinware, not elsewhere specified	301	34,386	18	71	182	49	579
24	Tobacco, chewing and smoking, and snuff.	365	18,324	114	139	268	41	472
25	Tobacco, cigars and cigarettes	9,926	138,773	3,839	4,123	8,160	1,074	11,390
26	Tools, not elsewhere specified	1,125	35,585	79	438	1,144	313	3,649
27	Toys and games	541	14,201	43	178	412	162	2,024
28	Trunks and valises	597	11,470	47	276	566	154	1,829
29	Turpentine and rosin	1,191	28,067	37	179	522	551	7,171
30	Type founding	23	810	1	13	30	6	55
31	Typewriters and supplies	88	15,669	7	27	76	17	158
32	Umbrellas and canes	198	3,368	33	88	215	45	529
33	Upholstering materials, not elsewhere specified.	163	4,810	2	49	133	75	950
34	Varnishes	229	4,022	16	99	290	68	803
35	Vault lights and ventilators	41	316	3	22	65	12	139
36	Vinegar and cider	720	1,981	195	439	546	65	662
37	Wall paper, not made in paper mills	48	4,262		2	7	11	121
38	Wall plaster and composition flooring	161	5,123	3	50	130	53	578
39	Washing machines and clothes wringers	105	5,956	10	24	66	24	280
40	Waste	92	2,686		27	72	34	401
41	Watch and clock materials, except watchcases.	27	582	2	8	13	6	68
42	Watchcases	33	3,900		14	32	5	66
43	Watches	18	15,888		1	2	1	8
44	Wheelbarrows	11	291	1	1	3	5	66
45	Whips	26	717	1	10	36	10	120
46	Windmills	31	1,932	1	9	23	3	26
47	Window and door screens and weather strips.	214	2,179	34	124	300	35	395
48	Window shades and fixtures	287	4,411	59	157	350	45	523
49	Wire	66	19,741	1	5	14	9	109
50	Wirework, including wire rope and cable, not elsewhere specified.	558	15,224	68	241	572	130	1,598
51	Wood distillation	115	4,946		13	39	35	422
52	Wood preserving	73	3,978		4	11	11	163
53	Wood, turned and carved	722	10,649	92	300	730	183	2,170
54	Wooden goods, not elsewhere specified	245	6,443	27	92	207	56	670
55	Wool pulling	24	705		3	11	7	84
56	Wool scouring	33	2,177		1	1	10	121
57	Wool shoddy	78	2,566	3	21	49	21	237
58	Woolen goods	560	62,957	15	47	114	58	747
59	Worsted goods	292	103,830	2	4	8	18	277
60	All other industries	5	99		3	5		

NUMBER OF WAGE EARNERS, FOR INDUSTRIES: 1919—Continued.

ESTABLISHMENTS EMPLOYING—continued.

21 to 50 wage earners, inclusive.		51 to 100 wage earners, inclusive.		101 to 250 wage earners, inclusive.		251 to 500 wage earners, inclusive.		501 to 1,000 wage earners, inclusive.		Over 1,000 wage earners.		
Establishments.	Wage earners.	Establishments.	Wage earners.	Establishments	Wage earners.	Establishments	Wage earners.	Establishments	Wage earners.	Establishments	Wage earners.	
19	672	12	838	17	2,703	4	1,306	5	3,142			1
56	1,810	45	3,130	47	7,415	21	7,849	8	5,916	5	7,005	2
36	1,155	28	2,070	20	2,987	7	2,329	3	1,897			3
10	281	1	58	3	432							4
40	1,323	27	1,873	39	6,351	9	3,470	6	3,739	7	18,964	5
15	410	13	881	7	1,080	4	1,213	1	538	1	1,270	6
7	244	4	264	9	1,279	2	815	1	627			7
1	49	1	64									8
45	1,552	8	499	3	463							9
81	2,737	86	6,572	75	11,595	11	3,729	9	5,987	1	1,279	10
22	720	8	581	8	1,456	10	3,467	2	1,443	1	2,272	11
161	5,347	74	5,365	75	12,050	17	6,349	6	4,319	4	5,366	12
4	158	24	1,909	47	6,875	9	2,823					13
55	1,860	16	1,101	9	1,319	3	977					14
				1	180	4	1,734	7	5,228	8	11,060	15
6	206	8	521	12	1,953	4	1,371	1	812			16
13	476	12	891	5	680	1	256	2	1,568	1	1,718	17
22	742	17	1,262	20	3,123	4	1,204	4	2,446	1	1,299	18
70	2,351	39	2,749	31	4,805	10	3,444	7	5,234	6	11,392	19
1	22											20
2	76	2	172	3	538	3	1,080					21
1	44	4	306	8	1,621	3	1,117					22
40	1,319	36	2,670	38	5,968	31	10,900	15	9,581	3	3,187	23
19	615	23	1,732	12	2,115	8	3,046	4	2,459	5	7,617	24
371	11,885	227	16,459	193	31,232	64	21,401	25	16,880	10	21,366	25
158	5,280	66	4,717	50	7,824	10	3,829	10	8,018	1.	1,124	26
91	2,959	37	2,579	24	3,794	5	1,853	1	580			27
72	2,358	25	1,778	17	2,572	5	1,671	1	696			28
330	10,446	60	4,325	30	4,305	4	1,298					29
1	39	1	95					1	591			30
7	256	12	807	6	814	3	1,013	5	3,091	4	9,454	31
19	644	6	448	5	830	2	702					32
15	411	13	896	6	854	2	738	1	828			33
29	833	8	564	8	1,221	1	311					34
4	112											35
17	523	4	250									36
11	361	11	805	9	1,763	4	1,205					37
29	961	15	1,007	9	1,470	1	447	1	530			38
16	564	18	1,347	9	1,407	1	304	3	1,988			39
17	508	9	627	3	413	2	665					40
6	204	5	297									41
3	111	4	277	1	244	2	554	4	2,616			42
1	44	2	127	2	272	3	1,026	4	2,402	4	12,007	43
3	107			1	115							44
3	117			1	164	1	280					45
7	237	5	347	4	663	2	636					46
11	350	3	191	7	943							47
11	352	6	432	5	803	2	777	2	1,174			48
3	102	12	825	8	1,355	15	5,301	10	7,155	3	4,880	49
53	1,795	30	2,154	22	3,154	10	3,082	4	2,869			50
36	1,212	20	1,386	9	1,308	2	579					51
28	949	20	1,371	10	1,484							52
101	3,312	31	2,163	14	2,022	1	252					53
44	1,409	13	939	10	1,537	1	287	2	1,394			54
10	338	4	272									55
13	494	3	212	3	544	2	805					56
20	690	8	601	4	682	1	307					57
86	3,146	122	9,469	176	27,527	50	16,613	5	3,504	1	1,837	58
36	1,292	48	3,652	82	13,191	52	18,167	25	16,610	25	50,633	59
1	28	1	66									60

TABLE 15.—SIZE OF ESTABLISHMENTS, BY AVERAGE NUMBER OF WAGE

	DIVISION AND STATE.	TOTAL.		ESTABLISHMENTS EMPLOYING—				
		Establishments.	Wage earners (average number).	No wage earners. Establishments.	1 to 5 wage earners, inclusive. Establishments.	Wage earners.	6 to 20 wage earners, inclusive. Establishments.	Wage earners.
	UNITED STATES:							
1	1919	290,105	9,096,372	37,934	141,742	311,576	56,208	631,290
2	1914	275,791	7,036,247	32,856	140,971	317,216	54,379	606,609
3	1909	268,491	6,615,046	27,712	136,289	311,704	57,198	640,793
	GEOGRAPHIC DIVISIONS:							
	New England—							
4	1919	25,528	1,351,389	2,679	11,096	25,301	5,223	59,173
5	1914	25,193	1,140,233	2,527	11,282	26,531	5,359	60,312
6	1909	25,351	1,101,290	2,132	11,471	27,104	5,645	63,964
	Middle Atlantic—							
7	1919	88,360	2,872,653	12,195	38,784	88,797	19,074	218,536
8	1914	85,466	2,355,940	10,623	39,855	92,419	18,091	204,527
9	1909	81,315	2,207,747	8,918	37,917	87,637	17,847	203,741
	East North Central—							
10	1919	61,332	2,396,618	8,451	29,147	62,201	10,922	122,612
11	1914	59,896	1,680,281	7,478	30,823	66,690	10,708	119,895
12	1909	60,013	1,513,764	7,274	31,057	67,373	11,195	124,828
	West North Central—							
13	1919	29,166	499,635	4,647	16,982	34,293	4,234	46,740
14	1914	27,199	381,595	3,926	16,587	33,447	3,970	43,561
15	1909	27,171	374,337	3,667	16,739	34,200	4,048	44,009
	South Atlantic—							
16	1919	29,976	817,212	2,904	15,497	35,124	6,316	69,121
17	1914	28,925	685,252	2,024	15,113	36,146	6,854	76,533
18	1909	28,088	663,015	1,669	13,719	34,326	7,552	84,609
	East South Central—							
19	1919	14,655	329,226	1,596	7,877	17,209	2,849	31,816
20	1914	14,410	264,378	1,104	8,129	19,844	3,073	32,798
21	1909	15,381	261,772	911	8,454	21,231	3,816	41,451
	West South Central—							
22	1919	13,909	285,244	1,615	7,354	16,619	2,765	30,276
23	1914	12,417	211,940	1,464	6,928	15,423	2,391	26,718
24	1909	12,339	204,520	1,028	6,631	15,884	3,014	33,296
	Mountain—							
25	1919	7,612	109,216	1,222	4,626	9,341	1,074	11,466
26	1914	6,079	81,113	1,077	3,623	7,350	868	9,257
27	1909	5,254	75,435	677	3,174	7,059	905	9,716
	Pacific—							
28	1919	19,567	435,179	2,625	10,379	22,691	3,751	41,550
29	1914	16,206	235,515	2,633	8,631	19,366	3,065	33,008
30	1909	13,579	213,166	1,436	7,127	16,890	3,176	35,179
	NEW ENGLAND:							
31	Maine	2,995	88,651	330	1,583	3,288	527	5,684
32	New Hampshire	1,499	83,074	132	664	1,431	319	3,572
33	Vermont	1,790	33,491	186	945	1,989	363	4,097
34	Massachusetts	11,906	713,836	1,086	4,670	11,497	2,680	30,753
35	Rhode Island	2,466	139,665	280	1,027	2,296	497	5,581
36	Connecticut	4,872	292,672	665	2,207	4,800	837	9,486
	MIDDLE ATLANTIC:							
37	New York	49,330	1,228,130	6,847	21,448	49,973	11,648	134,160
38	New Jersey	11,057	508,686	1,239	4,829	11,016	2,276	25,927
39	Pennsylvania	27,973	1,135,837	4,109	12,507	27,808	5,150	58,449
	EAST NORTH CENTRAL:							
40	Ohio	16,125	730,733	2,028	7,092	16,393	3,096	34,943
41	Indiana	7,916	277,580	858	4,115	8,745	1,381	15,438
42	Illinois	18,593	653,114	2,845	8,277	18,770	3,574	40,614
43	Michigan	8,305	471,242	1,085	3,809	8,573	1,494	16,748
44	Wisconsin	10,393	263,949	1,635	5,854	9,720	1,377	14,869
	WEST NORTH CENTRAL:							
45	Minnesota	6,225	115,623	771	3,707	7,318	992	11,129
46	Iowa	5,683	80,551	781	3,490	7,101	813	8,921
47	Missouri	8,592	195,037	1,396	4,454	9,385	1,426	15,901
48	North Dakota	894	4,472	211	560	1,046	84	860
49	South Dakota	1,414	6,382	263	997	1,924	119	1,262
50	Nebraska	2,884	36,521	554	1,800	3,569	316	3,507
51	Kansas	3,474	61,049	671	1,974	3,950	484	5,160

EARNERS, FOR GEOGRAPHIC DIVISIONS AND STATES: 1919, 1914, AND 1909.

ESTABLISHMENTS EMPLOYING—continued.

21 to 50 wage earners, inclusive.		51 to 100 wage earners, inclusive.		101 to 250 wage earners, inclusive.		251 to 500 wage earners, inclusive.		501 to 1,000 wage earners, inclusive.		Over 1,000 wage earners.		
Establishments.	Wage earners.	Establishments.	Wage earners.	Establishments.	Wage earners.	Establishments.	Wage earners.	Establishments	Wage earners.	Establishments	Wage earners.	
25,379	829,301	12,405	888,344	10,068	1,581,763	3,599	1,250,875	1,749	1,205,627	1,021	2,397,596	1
22,932	742,529	11,079	791,726	8,470	1,320,972	3,108	1,075,108	1,348	926,828	648	1,255,259	2
23,544	764,408	10,964	782,298	8,116	1,258,639	2,905	1,006,457	1,223	837,473	540	1,013,274	3
2,634	85,736	1,465	105,123	1,368	216,591	547	191,987	297	203,446	219	464,032	4
2,517	81,711	1,386	99,881	1,186	188,994	502	174,774	263	182,880	171	325,150	5
2,660	87,040	1,352	96,064	1,197	188,331	502	175,508	233	163,581	159	299,698	6
9,145	299,359	4,240	301,759	3,011	470,660	1,090	382,011	503	345,968	318	765,563	7
8,472	275,117	3,971	282,283	2,821	437,703	997	346,299	423	292,001	213	425,591	8
8,508	276,954	3,919	279,053	2,691	415,309	941	327,084	396	271,396	178	346,573	9
5,475	179,913	3,045	218,832	2,568	402,430	945	329,408	508	351,448	271	729,774	10
4,920	160,176	2,661	189,634	2,047	319,129	775	266,766	333	229,914	151	328,077	11
4,895	160,205	2,516	179,996	1,974	307,856	673	232,739	314	211,593	115	229,174	12
1,663	53,835	751	53,067	541	83,665	206	69,484	91	63,816	51	94,735	13
1,440	46,581	610	43,422	413	63,376	153	54,361	72	50,729	28	46,118	14
1,425	45,785	626	44,490	417	63,676	157	54,305	63	43,390	29	44,482	15
2,450	79,839	1,160	84,085	1,078	170,391	342	116,184	155	105,978	74	156,490	16
2,414	77,546	1,099	79,794	933	144,868	315	108,262	121	80,472	52	81,631	17
2,680	86,051	1,174	83,708	839	130,198	296	101,257	126	87,099	33	55,767	18
1,073	35,485	574	41,500	466	73,074	129	45,086	63	41,630	28	43,426	19
1,105	35,954	489	34,342	335	52,186	118	40,197	43	27,574	14	21,483	20
1,201	38,351	509	36,228	339	51,959	108	37,229	34	22,882	9	12,441	21
1,154	37,293	441	31,421	378	60,113	138	47,397	44	31,438	20	30,687	22
848	26,730	348	25,184	285	45,947	106	35,214	39	26,108	8	10,616	23
937	30,045	325	23,501	281	43,478	92	30,993	22	14,010	9	13,313	24
343	11,158	129	9,315	135	21,252	51	17,378	26	18,809	6	10,497	25
245	7,642	108	7,849	97	15,434	36	12,298	21	14,570	4	6,713	26
237	7,542	123	8,690	82	13,006	37	12,982	16	11,183	3	5,257	27
1,442	46,683	600	43,242	523	83,587	151	51,940	62	43,094	34	102,392	28
971	31,072	407	29,337	353	53,335	106	36,937	33	22,580	7	9,880	29
1,001	32,435	420	30,568	296	44,826	99	34,360	19	12,339	5	6,569	30
253	8,178	127	9,310	118	18,702	28	9,898	13	8,776	16	24,815	31
151	5,006	87	6,265	90	14,307	31	11,354	12	8,576	13	32,563	32
156	4,848	65	4,560	57	8,498	9	3,253	9	6,246	......	......	33
1,410	46,214	791	56,499	689	108,715	293	102,019	169	114,094	118	244,045	34
230	7,561	155	11,144	150	24,184	74	25,314	32	22,524	21	41,061	35
434	13,929	240	17,345	264	42,185	112	40,149	62	43,230	51	121,548	36
5,227	169,598	2,107	148,875	1,309	204,318	432	151,320	206	143,650	106	226,236	37
1,200	39,535	642	46,709	495	77,538	213	74,270	93	62,366	70	171,325	38
2,718	90,226	1,491	106,175	1,207	188,804	445	156,421	204	139,952	142	368,002	39
1,615	53,388	935	66,641	799	125,932	312	110,104	168	118,061	80	205,271	40
653	21,353	378	27,240	331	51,531	110	38,386	51	36,666	39	78,221	41
1,808	59,187	921	66,033	718	110,471	236	81,846	144	98,326	70	177,867	42
747	25,050	456	33,945	414	66,285	167	57,771	78	53,182	55	209,688	43
652	20,935	355	24,973	306	48,211	120	41,301	67	45,213	27	58,727	44
383	12,234	167	11,748	127	19,300	48	15,895	18	12,633	12	25,366	45
322	10,468	135	9,470	96	15,048	25	8,650	12	8,878	9	12,015	46
623	20,390	307	21,856	224	35,394	100	34,044	44	30,549	18	27,518	47
24	765	5	380	10	1,421	......	......	......	......	......	......	48
21	644	6	356	5	875	2	652	1	669	......	......	49
109	3,454	55	3,915	30	4,531	10	3,321	5	3,028	5	11,196	50
181	5,880	76	5,342	49	7,096	21	6,922	11	8,059	7	18,640	51

TABLE 15.—SIZE OF ESTABLISHMENTS, BY AVERAGE NUMBER OF WAGE

	DIVISION AND STATE.	TOTAL.		ESTABLISHMENTS EMPLOYING—					
				No wage earners.	1 to 5 wage earners, inclusive.		6 to 20 wage earners, inclusive.		
		Establishments.	Wage earners (average number).	Establishments.	Establishments.	Wage earners.	Establishments.	Wage earners.
	SOUTH ATLANTIC:							
1	Delaware	668	29,035	67	338	776	126	1,458
2	Maryland	4,937	140,342	636	2,351	5,221	1,062	11,880
3	District of Columbia	595	10,482	134	231	589	144	1,583
4	Virginia	5,603	119,352	621	3,197	7,014	1,038	10,648
5	West Virginia	2,785	83,036	392	1,425	3,065	484	5,377
6	North Carolina	5,999	157,659	353	3,488	8,474	1,204	12,452
7	South Carolina	2,004	79,450	105	1,040	2,264	429	4,625
8	Georgia	4,803	123,441	354	2,386	5,203	1,144	12,917
9	Florida	2,582	74,415	242	1,041	2,518	685	8,181
	EAST SOUTH CENTRAL:							
10	Kentucky	3,957	69,340	498	2,353	5,270	600	6,682
11	Tennessee	4,589	95,167	668	2,390	4,988	784	8,576
12	Alabama	3,654	107,159	272	1,862	4,098	868	9,853
13	Mississippi	2,455	57,560	158	1,272	2,853	597	6,705
	WEST SOUTH CENTRAL:							
14	Arkansas	3,123	49,954	268	1,791	3,960	645	6,901
15	Louisiana	2,617	98,265	173	1,084	2,628	642	7,317
16	Oklahoma	2,445	29,503	427	1,409	2,956	374	4,009
17	Texas	5,724	107,522	747	3,070	7,075	1,104	12,049
	MOUNTAIN:							
18	Montana	1,290	17,160	203	854	1,647	139	1,526
19	Idaho	922	13,917	137	579	1,100	133	1,408
20	Wyoming	576	6,634	112	377	668	63	650
21	Colorado	2,631	35,254	461	1,495	3,130	421	4,515
22	New Mexico	387	5,736	35	272	592	47	487
23	Arizona	480	8,528	57	291	660	80	834
24	Utah	1,160	18,868	196	654	1,324	166	1,803
25	Nevada	166	3,119	21	104	220	25	243
	PACIFIC:							
26	Washington	4,918	132,928	651	2,474	5,345	959	10,924
27	Oregon	2,707	58,559	388	1,421	3,136	526	5,854
28	California	11,942	243,692	1,586	6,484	14,210	2,266	24,772

EARNERS, FOR GEOGRAPHIC DIVISIONS AND STATES: 1919, 1914, AND 1909—Continued.

ESTABLISHMENTS EMPLOYING—continued.

21 to 50 wage earners, inclusive.		51 to 100 wage earners, inclusive.		101 to 250 wage earners, inclusive.		251 to 500 wage earners, inclusive.		501 to 1,000 wage earners, inclusive.		Over 1,000 wage earners.		
Establishments.	Wage earners.	Establishments.	Wage earners.	Establishments.	Wage earners.	Establishments.	Wage earners.	Establishments	Wage earners.	Establishments	Wage earners.	
58	1,882	32	2,404	29	4,416	8	2,524	5	3,410	5	12,165	1
464	14,879	194	14,004	143	22,375	47	15,005	25	16,968	15	40,110	2
48	1,685	20	1,353	12	1,828	4	1,345	1	751	1	1,348	3
355	11,473	177	12,803	157	24,296	31	10,650	16	11,193	11	31,275	4
182	6,028	109	8,141	121	19,222	43	14,743	21	13,999	8	12,461	5
370	12,212	234	17,129	252	39,865	58	19,329	27	19,289	13	28,909	6
167	5,445	79	5,725	98	16,475	49	16,576	31	21,137	6	7,203	7
445	14,643	218	15,713	165	26,104	62	21,974	18	11,924	11	14,963	8
361	11,592	97	6,813	101	15,810	40	14,038	11	7,307	4	8,156	9
235	7,668	128	9,120	106	16,267	19	6,357	12	7,362	6	10,614	10
324	10,866	195	14,282	166	25,609	42	14,224	17	11,534	3	5,088	11
306	9,952	146	10,348	120	19,314	44	15,936	20	13,646	16	24,012	12
208	6,999	105	7,750	74	11,884	24	8,569	14	9,088	3	3,712	13
236	7,605	94	6,842	61	9,240	19	6,671	7	5,294	2	3,441	14
338	11,067	140	9,806	150	24,132	66	22,443	19	13,591	5	7,281	15
136	4,295	46	3,168	37	6,209	11	3,323	1	818	4	4,725	16
444	14,326	161	11,605	130	20,532	42	14,960	17	11,735	9	15,240	17
50	1,859	12	878	15	2,117	11	3,657	5	3,325	1	2,151	18
31	966	12	834	16	2,370	10	3,605	3	2,208	1	1,426	19
6	186	7	468	6	1,170	3	1,260	......	......	2	2,232	20
143	4,450	44	3,232	48	7,738	11	3,488	7	5,251	1	3,450	21
12	435	8	531	9	1,673	3	1,048	1	970	......	......	22
27	846	6	383	10	1,639	7	2,427	2	1,739	......	......	23
68	2,201	36	2,670	28	4,172	5	1,468	6	3,992	1	1,238	24
6	215	4	319	3	373	1	425	2	1,324	......	......	25
397	12,744	175	12,657	190	30,899	44	14,822	20	14,392	8	31,145	26
165	5,476	84	6,090	81	12,623	26	8,609	12	8,194	4	8,577	27
880	28,463	341	24,495	252	40,065	81	28,509	30	20,508	22	62,670	28

TABLE **16.**—NUMBER AND SIZE OF ESTABLISHMENTS,

[NOTE.—In some industries in order to avoid disclosing the returns of individual establishments, the cases an (x) is placed in the column from which the figures have been omitted, and the figures for the bined, each establishment is classified under its proper group.]

	INDUSTRY.	NUMBER OF ESTABLISHMENTS WITH PRODUCT OF—						WAGE EARNERS IN ESTABLISHMENTS WITH PRODUCT OF—	
		Less than $5,000.	$5,000 to $20,000.	$20,000 to $100,000.	$100,000 to $500,000.	$500,000 to $1,000,000.	$1,000,000 and over.	Less than $5,000.	$5,000 to $20,000.
1	All industries	65,485	87,440	77,911	39,647	9,208	10,414	45,813	249,722
2	Aeroplanes, seaplanes, and airships, and parts.	2	9	5	8	2	5	(x)	29
3	Agricultural implements	98	103	130	103	29	58	74	317
4	Aluminum manufactures	3	14	17	24	10	15		104
5	Ammunition		4	9	8	11	10		17
6	Artificial flowers	32	58	88	42	4		12	247
7	Artificial limbs	57	84	31	5			19	171
8	Artificial stone products	1,516	862	367	39	1		965	2,280
9	Artists' materials	16	16	14	10		2	11	35
10	Asbestos products, not including steam packing.	3	6	12	12	5	8	4	30
11	Automobile bodies and parts	392	847	742	351	61	122	233	2,248
12	Automobiles	7	12	31	82	35	148	6	38
13	Automobile repairing	5,270	7,741	2,284	200	11	1	4,561	21,745
14	Awnings, tents, and sails	217	322	257	85	10	4	130	719
15	Babbitt metal and solder	7	22	33	35	8	13	3	27
16	Bags, other than paper, not including bags made in textile mills.	9	43	61	46	12	45	10	143
17	Bags, paper, exclusive of those made in paper mills.	5	15	12	17	13	13	7	47
18	Baking powders and yeast	27	18	13	13	5	12	13	21
19	Baskets, and rattan and willow ware.	182	82	78	30	3		77	423
20	Bells		1	6	3				(x)
21	Belting and hose, rubber				2	2	11		
22	Belting and hose, woven, other than rubber.	2	4	9	15	5	6		15
23	Belting, leather	8	36	54	54	13	7	4	45
24	Blacking, stains, and dressings	39	63	67	43	2	6	17	111
25	Bluing	14	19	15	8	1		5	48
26	Bone, carbon, and lamp black	1	2	15	16		1	(x)	6
27	Bookbinding and blank-book making.	248	431	312	95	19	8	235	2,163
28	Boot and shoe cut stock	13	35	81	61	29	33	12	89
29	Boot and shoe findings	54	83	160	111	11	8	35	251
30	Boots and shoes, not including rubber boots and shoes.	57	159	279	440	186	328	58	612
31	Boots and shoes, rubber			3		1	21		
32	Boxes, cigar	25	45	81	37	1		29	213
33	Boxes, paper and other, not elsewhere specified.	50	151	543	382	47	28	84	900
34	Boxes, wooden packing, except cigar boxes.	160	193	348	363	57	19	120	657
35	Brass, bronze, and copper products.	97	203	396	264	51	81	53	509
36	Bread and other bakery products.	3,107	11,848	8,734	1,091	175	140	1,115	16,423
37	Brick and tile, terra-cotta, and fire-clay products.	301	623	874	568	39	9	568	3,804
38	Brooms	437	262	270	60	5		107	592
39	Brushes	70	114	128	50	8	9	43	329
40	Butter	90	380	2,019	1,024	129	96	38	272
41	Buttons	122	162	181	73	16	3	138	684
42	Candles	3	5	4	6		1	4	12
43	Canning and preserving, fish	38	72	132	132	28	8	60	398
44	Canning and preserving, fruits and vegetables.	739	816	858	520	77	72	1,094	4,183
45	Canning and preserving, oysters	10	18	26	11			13	141
46	Card cutting and designing	11	22	28	13		1	8	70
47	Cardboard, not made in paper mills			3	4	7	2		
48	Carpets and rugs, other than rag	2	3	7	21	15	27	(x)	10
49	Carpets, rag	179	107	43	9	1		148	505

BY VALUE OF PRODUCTS, FOR INDUSTRIES: 1919.

figures for certain groups have been consolidated with those for some one of the larger groups. In such group with which they have been consolidated are printed in *italics*. In the totals for all industries com-

| WAGE EARNERS IN ESTABLISHMENTS WITH PRODUCT OF—continued. | | | | VALUE OF PRODUCTS OF ESTABLISHMENTS WITH PRODUCT OF— | | | | | | |
| $20,000 to $100,000. | $100,000 to $500,000. | $500,000 to $1,000,000. | $1,000,000 and over. | Less than $5,000. | $5,000 to $20,000. | $20,000 to $100,000. | $100,000 to $500,000. | $500,000 to $1,000,000. | $1,000,000 and over. | |
						Expressed in thousands.				
793,528	1,719,982	1,114,615	5,172,712	$167,085	$945,603	$3,571,283	$8,965,872	$6,467,132	$42,301,104	1
70	455	(x)	*2,989*	(x)	*146*	281	1,766	(x)	*12,180*	2
1,672	5,292	4,388	42,625	241	1,137	6,618	*23,732*	20,512	252,721	3
229	1,089	1,545	8,435	8	220	777	*5,511*	*7,056*	61,706	4
215	290	1,691	20,603		33	478	1,514	8,702	77,811	5
1,159	*2,720*	(x)		76	605	4,323	*11,139*	(x)		6
271	210			150	818	1,223	1,080			7
3,518	*1,615*	(x)		3,209	8,448	15,115	*6,852*	(x)		8
137	*743*		(x)	52	170	545	*4,741*		(x)	9
118	*1,047*	(x)	2,455	9	80	561	*6,081*	(x)	17,247	10
9,267	17,737	9,369	93,702	1,102	9,112	34,002	74,514	42,218	531,223	11
291	3,402	2,609	204,213	25	175	1,675	21,084	25,033	2,339,911	12
19,827	7,128	*1,800*	(x)	15,454	79,517	83,527	36,508	9,646	(x)	13
1,798	1,921	*1,460*	(x)	632	3,294	10,678	16,735	*14,351*	(x)	14
122	557	378	1,285	19	241	1,624	8,040	5,454	43,639	15
474	1,261	523	8,345	32	478	2,905	10,720	8,479	191,445	16
111	625	1,035	2,343	15	137	510	4,278	9,368	32,956	17
53	376	230	2,638	67	179	719	3,869	3,327	38,069	18
1,489	2,113	431		361	862	3,510	5,056	2,032		19
42	195				(x)	*247*	704			20
	(x)	*216*	5,610				(x)	*1,663*	32,548	21
151	608	268	1,437	(x)	*50*	632	4,042	3,197	11,255	22
244	826	605	1,041	24	435	2,798	11,969	9,809	15,446	23
259	713	(x)	*1,355*	92	712	3,209	8,420	(x)	*12,851*	24
99	*208*	(x)		27	201	662	*1,841*	(x)		25
114	*555*		(x)	(x)	26	806	*5,354*		(x)	26
5,172	5,886	*6,905*	(x)	683	4,861	13,564	20,450	*26,463*	(x)	27
807	2,075	1,401	5,331	35	398	4,241	14,107	21,051	121,371	28
1,957	4,442	*2,256*	(x)	145	907	7,891	27,841	*26,041*	(x)	29
4,388	26,955	26,208	152,828	150	1,822	15,218	120,513	134,020	883,318	30
13		(x)	*32,862*			158		(x)	*116,759*	31
1,740	*3,236*	(x)		66	492	4,321	*8,231*	(x)		32
11,277	24,511	7,661	11,429	138	1,800	28,766	79,405	32,199	64,111	33
5,775	21,166	9,040	5,687	390	2,158	18,519	86,543	38,540	31,668	34
3,787	10,905	5,653	54,144	277	2,334	19,504	58,965	34,905	366,328	35
41,488	25,633	15,363	41,570	9,220	136,994	339,746	219,689	123,871	323,071	36
19,413	40,660	8,377	4,093	858	6,744	43,800	116,642	25,657	14,722	37
2,697	*2,917*	(x)		818	2,702	11,779	*14,906*	(x)		38
1,686	2,215	744	2,951	183	1,248	6,498	10,050	5,346	15,681	39
3,628	5,515	2,829	5,359	254	4,962	109,587	194,112	93,030	181,218	40
3,650	5,683	3,514	1,908	327	1,674	8,298	14,811	11,802	4,928	41
27	*498*		(x)	12	70	240	*3,029*		(x)	42
1,861	4,659	2,067	2,203	107	837	6,514	31,755	18,463	19,608	43
11,575	19,989	7,795	16,229	1,726	8,948	41,111	110,423	54,141	185,894	44
549	486			26	224	1,111	1,615			45
336	734		(x)	27	259	1,277	*3,760*		(x)	46
(x)	171	*1,254*	(x)			(x)	932	8,206	(x)	47
94	939	1,999	19,891	(x)	*44*	455	5,521	10,541	106,693	48
687	676	(x)		392	1,079	1,715	*2,411*	(x)		49

TABLE **16.**—NUMBER AND SIZE OF ESTABLISHMENTS,

[See note at head of this table, pp. 1002 and 1003.]

	INDUSTRY.	NUMBER OF ESTABLISHMENTS WITH PRODUCT OF—						WAGE EARNERS IN ESTABLISHMENTS WITH PRODUCT OF—	
		Less than $5,000.	$5,000 to $20,000.	$20,000 to $100,000.	$100,000 to $500,000.	$500,000 to $1,000,000.	$1,000,000 and over.	Less than $5,000.	$5,000 to $20,000.
1	Carriage and wagon materials	53	60	77	56	10	2	29	188
2	Carriages and sleds, childrens'	17	16	25	29	12	4	8	36
3	Carriages and wagons, including repairs.	968	894	289	98	23	14	590	2,613
4	Cars and general shop construction and repairs by electric-railroad companies.	73	200	227	100	9	15	117	925
5	Cars and general shop construction and repairs by steam-railroad companies.	38	130	360	618	246	352	57	686
6	Cars, steam-railroad, not including operations of railroad companies.	....	1	12	23	10	53	....	(x)
7	Cash registers and calculating machines.	5	14	20	12	6	8	9	32
8	Cement	2	1	8	22	31	59	(x)	5
9	Charcoal, not including production in the lumber and wood distillation industries.	16	19	5	1	....	....	15	108
10	Cheese	134	769	2,507	111	7	2	36	485
11	Chemicals	41	58	132	226	58	83	30	159
12	Chewing gum	5	7	11	26	3	10	9	21
13	China decorating, not including that done in potteries.	15	16	11	1	....	....	13	51
14	Chocolate and cocoa products	....	3	4	7	10	24	....	5
15	Cleansing and polishing preparations.	208	150	102	30	4	5	55	223
16	Clocks	8	8	9	12	2	7	4	25
17	Cloth, sponging and refinishing	4	16	31	16	....	....	3	60
18	Clothing, horse	3	3	13	7	....	2	8	7
19	Clothing, men's	454	1,152	1,776	1,351	306	219	682	7,712
20	Clothing, men's, buttonholes	48	51	6	2	....	....	36	237
21	Clothing, women's	505	1,487	2,862	2,368	344	145	656	8,546
22	Coal-tar products	13	12	51	60	21	26	17	52
23	Coffee and spice, roasting and grinding.	42	149	238	225	67	73	17	185
24	Coffins, burial cases, and undertakers' goods.	28	61	95	138	21	8	10	177
25	Coke, not including gas-house coke.	6	31	58	80	34	69	5	93
26	Collars and cuffs, men's	4	7	13	5	5	5	7	34
27	Combs and hairpins, not made from metal or rubber.	2	5	15	21	2	....	(x)	23
28	Condensed milk	1	10	45	136	72	137	(x)	46
29	Confectionery and ice cream	1,371	2,322	1,907	764	136	124	590	4,113
30	Cooperage	271	372	283	126	38	9	148	744
31	Copper, tin, and sheet-iron work	1,274	2,067	1,151	272	23	9	684	4,857
32	Cordage and twine	5	4	17	52	15	27	5	10
33	Cordials and flavoring sirups	23	25	52	33	4	12	7	30
34	Cork, cutting	7	11	16	21	2	5	4	23
35	Corsets	20	38	42	43	23	22	24	142
36	Cotton goods	10	17	70	343	308	540	20	101
37	Cotton lace	2	2	8	15	10	7	(x)	8
38	Cotton small wares	1	20	53	75	6	9	(x)	91
39	Crucibles	....	4	4	11	3	....	....	17
40	Cutlery and edge tools	38	69	92	77	17	11	37	250
41	Dairymen's, poultrymen's, and apiarists' supplies.	55	70	60	44	8	7	37	212
42	Dental goods	49	123	104	30	6	7	29	332
43	Drug grinding	2	3	10	9	3	4	(x)	13
44	Druggists' preparations	124	117	144	97	23	19	38	257
45	Dyeing and finishing textiles, exclusive of that done in textile mills.	28	85	180	206	64	65	71	414
46	Dyestuffs and extracts—natural	5	17	49	38	24	11	1	32
47	Electrical machinery, apparatus, and supplies.	89	271	422	331	109	182	80	982
48	Electroplating	136	239	127	11	2	....	90	858
49	Emery and other abrasive wheels	5	13	17	18	2	5	4	38
50	Enameling	20	29	20	4	1	....	18	111

BY VALUE OF PRODUCTS, FOR INDUSTRIES: 1919—Continued.

[See note at head of this table, pp. 1002 and 1003.]

WAGE EARNERS IN ESTABLISHMENTS WITH PRODUCT OF—continued.				VALUE OF PRODUCTS OF ESTABLISHMENTS WITH PRODUCT OF—continued.						
$20,000 to $100,000.	$100,000 to $500,000.	$500,000 to $1,000,000.	$1,000,000 and over.	Less than $5,000.	$5,000 to $20,000.	$20,000 to $100,000.	$100,000 to $500,000.	$500,000 to $1,000,000.	$1,000,000 and over.	
				Expressed in thousands.						
1,229	2,764	2,299	(x)	$122	$646	$3,777	$11,929	$10,291	(x)	1
448	2,014	2,166	2,014	38	159	1,262	6,862	8,382	$7,804	2
3,325	4,766	2,303	4,576	2,549	8,759	11,490	22,540	14,389	31,736	3
4,883	9,654	2,317	13,376	221	2,233	10,618	22,213	6,432	33,494	4
8,544	68,005	70,515	336,630	113	1,646	19,330	159,631	177,503	921,012	5
214	1,660	1,746	48,678	....	(x)	663	6,363	6,999	524,198	6
436	1,002	1,081	13,984	12	146	1,044	3,188	3,678	75,471	7
118	1,785	3,976	19,640	(x)	12	427	7,862	21,842	145,122	8
86	(x)	....	....	39	223	327	(x)	....		9
2,419	653	404	(x)	363	10,491	107,185	18,275	7,142	(x)	10
1,044	6,559	4,821	42,973	98	616	6,881	56,122	39,373	325,569	11
90	604	252	2,214	19	99	531	5,051	2,263	43,277	12
180	(x)			44	169	654	(x)			13
17	139	452	8,470	....	19	149	1,986	6,900	130,204	14
486	510	(x)	681	438	1,501	4,987	6,720	(x)	13,057	15
92	922	(x)	7,209	22	91	497	2,889	(x)	19,881	16
532	611	....		11	160	1,465	2,055			17
212	539			12	30	740	5,239		(x)	18
31,358	44,383	22,375	68,760	1,272	13,743	85,698	316,318	217,102	528,853	19
211	(x)			126	485	479	(x)			20
38,429	73,613	25,994	18,411	1,294	17,209	146,296	537,905	235,157	270,682	21
484	1,740	1,453	11,917	34	130	2,917	15,259	14,077	103,065	22
754	2,098	1,721	5,765	122	1,737	13,684	54,468	47,615	187,166	23
981	5,371	2,746	2,605	69	682	4,664	31,600	14,055	13,307	24
663	2,545	3,462	22,551	19	387	3,181	19,049	25,207	268,673	25
504	777	793	8,988	9	75	655	1,701	3,371	41,754	26
288	1,918	(x)		(x)	67	869	5,630	(x)	....	27
171	1,441	2,257	9,760	(x)	158	2,618	33,934	52,001	250,796	28
12,430	25,437	14,615	38,463	3,508	25,276	82,883	168,110	94,451	262,981	29
1,985	4,617	3,636	2,089	689	4,108	12,389	29,453	25,727	15,870	30
10,003	8,647	1,751	1,698	3,497	21,793	47,851	54,395	15,265	17,513	31
282	2,775	1,982	12,568	10	44	1,053	13,668	11,129	107,462	32
247	235	38	841	66	279	2,830	7,416	2,742	33,474	33
169	890	(x)	2,459	20	118	636	4,161	(x)	11,347	34
800	2,786	3,616	11,047	62	431	2,083	10,896	16,189	45,881	35
1,153	24,939	49,044	355,709	26	215	4,647	105,815	226,879	1,787,690	36
127	861	1,609	3,885	(x)	22	384	3,733	6,448	18,810	37
694	4,129	827	3,655	(x)	264	2,583	17,884	3,916	16,250	38
51	780	(x)		. 50	153	5,091	(x)	....		39
1,764	6,506	4,574	6,728	105	690	4,323	17,254	11,579	32,679	40
592	1,648	874	3,074	127	792	3,062	9,673	5,512	. 18,231	41
1,207	1,078	438	2,140	142	1,314	4,552	6,870	4,272	12,252	42
128	257	(x)	949	(x)	34	495	1,879	(x)	14,530	43
1,051	2,342	1,850	10,030	235	1,308	7,175	22,693	15,351	67,831	44
2,935	10,605	10,026	31,934	94	950	9,809	47,996	44,826	220,293	45
200	1,097	1,488	1,524	11	198	2,522	11,264	15,700	24,049	46
5,616	18,084	18,264	169,348	253	3,294	20,520	77,235	77,577	819,089	47
1,677	399	(x)		375	2,560	4,888	2,567	(x)		48
170	971	(x)	4,418	15	201	869	4,944	(x)	24,920	49
286	279	(x)	....	53	279	817	1,496	(x)	....	50

TABLE **16.**—NUMBER AND SIZE OF ESTABLISHMENTS,

[See note at head of this table, pp. 1002 and 1003.]

	INDUSTRY.	NUMBER OF ESTABLISHMENTS WITH PRODUCT OF—						WAGE EARNERS IN ESTABLISHMENTS WITH PRODUCT OF—	
		Less than $5,000.	$5,000 to $20,000.	$20,000 to $100,000.	$100,000 to $500,000.	$500,000 to $1,000,000.	$1,000,000 and over.	Less than $5,000.	$5,000 to $20,000.
1	Engines, steam, gas, and water....	22	37	88	100	46	77	21	157
2	Engravers' materials	3	6	6	5	1	......	3	21
3	Engraving and diesinking	263	165	45	3	1	1	86	464
4	Engraving, steel and copper plate, including plate printing.	90	149	139	36	5	2	36	624
5	Engraving, wood	30	17	6	1	1	......	10	37
6	Envelopes	1	11	30	40	15	9	(x)	65
7	Explosives	1	10	27	44	14	22	......	19
8	Fancy articles, not elsewhere specified.	117	168	225	125	18	8	87	613
9	Feathers and plumes	20	57	94	43	2	......	10	198
10	Felt goods	1	......	3	21	11	13	(x)	......
11	Ferroalloys	1	1	1	14	6	7	(x)	(x)
12	Fertilizers	16	59	143	202	94	86	18	172
13	Files	4	9	21	9	1	6	3	29
14	Firearms	4	......	6	7	2	7	8	......
15	Fire extinguishers, chemical	6	6	8	10	1	1	......	17
16	Fireworks	16	15	15	9	2	......	10	65
17	Flags and banners	18	19	31	9	1	1	15	74
18	Flavoring extracts	129	133	127	53	7	4	28	194
19	Flax and hemp, dressed	1	4	11	3	......	1	(x)	12
20	Flour-mill and gristmill products..	1,499	3,080	4,151	1,331	249	398	186	1,659
21	Food preparations, not elsewhere specified.	415	513	551	330	82	106	166	835
22	Foundry and machine-shop products.	1,611	2,684	3,297	2,308	522	512	1,066	9,149
23	Foundry supplies	14	14	26	16	5	1	12	37
24	Fuel, manufactured	......	2	3	4	2	......	......	(x)
25	Fur goods	211	487	700	361	35	21	95	907
26	Furnishing goods, men's	41	89	134	166	41	16	80	789
27	Furniture	387	632	864	1,017	170	84	228	1,958
28	Furs, dressed	11	27	56	36	9	2	7	106
29	Galvanizing	3	12	20	13	1	3	3	29
30	Gas and electric fixtures	22	88	139	74	13	5	16	210
31	Gas, illuminating and heating.....	74	180	455	208	48	57	64	532
32	Gas machines and gas and water meters.	11	21	32	23	12	6	6	47
33	Glass	1	12	33	186	70	69	(x)	114
34	Glass, cutting, staining, and ornamenting.	129	218	187	79	1	2	82	754
35	Gloves and mittens, cloth, not including gloves made in textile mills.	19	27	66	59	6	5	29	262
36	Gloves and mittens, leather........	29	72	130	103	17	4	16	222
37	Glucose and starch	4	18	16	3	1	14	1	24
38	Glue, not elsewhere specified	6	8	14	16	7	11	......	11
39	Gold and silver, leaf and foil	11	40	27	7	2	......	8	132
40	Gold and silver, reducing and refining, not from the ore.	12	13	23	28	3	8	4	23
41	Graphite, ground and refined	4	8	8	3	1	......	7	63
42	Grease and tallow, not including lubricating greases.	86	156	142	65	21	12	53	301
43	Grindstones	2	4	11	6	......	......	(x)	33
44	Haircloth	......	......	7	9	2	......	......	......
45	Hair work	64	74	43	16	1	......	52	261
46	Hand stamps	109	108	67	13	1	......	41	270
47	Hardware	74	102	167	138	34	33	56	315
48	Hardware, saddlery	10	8	5	7	4	3	5	31
49	Hat and cap materials	19	41	37	26	3	7	11	119
50	Hats and caps, other than felt, straw, and wool.	116	177	291	117	8	......	42	462
51	Hats, fur-felt	20	26	33	51	25	21	13	65
52	Hats, straw	5	22	42	64	10	5	3	125
53	Hats, wool-felt	5	15	5	12	1	2	6	54
54	Horseshoes, not made in steel works or rolling mills.	8	2	2	6	2	......	6	(x)
55	House-furnishing goods, not elsewhere specified.	75	112	158	99	13	10	63	304

BY VALUE OF PRODUCTS, FOR INDUSTRIES: 1919—Continued.

[See note at head of this table, pp. 1002 and 1003.]

WAGE EARNERS IN ESTABLISHMENTS WITH PRODUCT OF—continued.				VALUE OF PRODUCTS OF ESTABLISHMENTS WITH PRODUCT OF—continued.						
	$100,000 to $500,000.	$500,000 to $1,000,000.	$1,000,000 and over.	Less than $5,000.	$5,000 to $20,000.	$20,000 to $100,000.	$100,000 to $500,000.	$500,000 to $1,000,000.	$1,000,000 and over.	
				Expressed in thousands.						
1,277	5,788	6,776	63,598	$59	$460	$4,468	$25,441	$33,155	$401,192	1
38	112	(x)	----	10	73	307	1,858	(x)	----	2
531	797	(x)	(x)	683	1,518	1,717	3,433	(x)	(x)	3
2,072	1,917	2,365	(x)	251	1,655	5,772	6,994	9,537	(x)	4
188	(x)			65	138	951	(x)	(x)	----	5
528	2,486	2,316	2,734	(x)	156	1,602	10,602	11,593	15,711	6
163	1,266	1,229	6,572	(x)	155	1,411	11,608	8,972	70,329	7
3,177	5,499	2,464	2,121	284	1,905	10,768	25,391	12,283	13,423	8
1,196	2,100	(x)	----	45	625	4,646	10,062	(x)	----	9
59	1,297	966	2,914	(x)		255	7,090	7,433	24,452	10
11	452	445	1,436	(x)	(x)	70	3,771	3,891	30,852	11
957	4,816	6,237	14,096	48	748	7,987	50,761	69,281	152,319	12
354	720	(x)	4,661	12	91	908	1,911	(x)	14,695	13
154	1,924	(x)	9,201	10	----	354	3,560	(x)	26,257	14
59	701	(x)	(x)	13	66	309	5,175	(x)	(x)	15
229	918	(x)	----	37	152	824	3,617	(x)	----	16
358	618	(x)	(x)	50	216	1,380	3,700	(x)	----	17
483	866	243	374	271	1,471	5,755	11,784	4,670	6,166	18
137	271	----	(x)	(x)	31	623	1,715		(x)	19
7,380	8,062	4,042	24,152	4,025	36,393	189,254	275,539	172,691	1,374,532	20
3,040	6,476	3,496	16,352	909	5,834	25,891	75,630	57,516	465,818	21
42,951	120,799	77,104	231,698	4,344	31,119	161,428	518,045	366,630	1,207,685	22
244	327	286	(x)	39	154	1,343	3,641	4,778	(x)	23
42	129	(x)	----	----	(x)	240	1,734	(x)	----	24
3,284	5,464	1,580	2,309	632	5,557	33,502	72,841	24,223	36,383	25
2,055	5,299	4,191	6,530	110	1,007	7,048	38,645	28,044	32,981	26
11,960	60,998	27,483	35,704	969	6,977	43,412	239,753	116,347	163,898	27
801	2,036	2,125	(x)	29	326	2,954	6,937	10,139	(x)	28
211	403	(x)	1,019	12	118	990	2,588	(x)	10,768	29
1,581	3,376	1,838	2,774	59	977	7,252	14,883	8,877	10,220	30
4,160	7,732	5,122	25,298	161	2,389	21,489	46,809	35,035	223,396	31
407	938	1,403	2,788	27	254	1,716	5,438	8,950	9,882	32
874	19,999	16,723	39,810	(x)	160	1,950	51,221	49,235	159,318	33
2,581	3,063	(x)	(x)	346	2,431	8,306	17,360	(x)	(x)	34
1,510	3,992	(x)	3,193	55	346	3,279	12,532	(x)	12,008	35
1,802	5,072	2,371	1,202	76	852	6,902	22,241	11,622	5,248	36
124	122	(x)	7,524	12	200	759	1,895	(x)	183,390	37
55	492	586	3,120	11	123	703	4,183	4,535	22,579	38
368	442	(x)	----	42	457	1,179	2,784	(x)	----	39
50	181	34	352	36	132	1,261	7,389	1,672	44,993	40
110	317	(x)	----	13	100	434	1,693	(x)	----	41
862	1,606	1,346	2,479	261	1,630	7,153	14,701	14,816	28,704	42
375	266			(x)	62	578	729			43
92	333	(x)				485	2,830	(x)		44
336	435	(x)	----	169	745	1,701	4,348	(x)	----	45
703	705	(x)	----	234	1,067	3,209	3,229	(x)	----	46
2,513	8,175	6,361	25,085	185	1,143	8,758	31,993	24,388	88,058	47
109	601	834	2,095	24	88	265	2,001	2,798	8,961	48
311	529	193	1,846	49	420	1,990	5,827	2,184	16,051	49
2,508	3,631	896	----	309	1,921	13,972	22,433	5,905	----	50
258	2,291	3,057	12,826	60	285	1,436	12,286	17,095	51,583	51
432	3,571	1,387	1,784	16	287	2,154	16,140	6,914	6,676	52
40	1,348	(x)	(x)	12	164	191	6,373	(x)	(x)	53
15	723	(x)	----	24	(x)	77	3,266	(x)	----	54
1,197	2,588	1,268	2,433	208	1,304	7,750	22,258	8,840	19,852	55

TABLE **16.**—NUMBER AND SIZE OF ESTABLISHMENTS,

[See note at head of this table, pp. 1002 and 1003.]

	INDUSTRY.	NUMBER OF ESTABLISHMENTS WITH PRODUCT OF—						WAGE EARNERS IN ESTABLISHMENTS WITH PRODUCT OF—	
		Less than $5,000.	$5,000 to $20,000.	$20,000 to $100,000.	$100,000 to $500,000.	$500,000 to $1,000,000.	$1,000,000 and over.	Less than $5,000.	$5,000 to $20,000.
1	Ice, manufactured	367	1,013	1,167	306	10	4	352	3,211
2	Ink, printing	4	19	30	22	5	10	1	43
3	Ink, writing	25	16	12	5	1	2	11	38
4	Instruments, professional and scientific.	59	88	115	63	17	9	34	316
5	Iron and steel, blast furnaces			10	23	32	130		
6	Iron and steel, steel works and rolling mills.	1	6	15	83	65	330	(x)	40
7	Iron and steel, bolts, nuts, washers, and rivets, not made in rolling mills.	6	17	31	44	20	26	9	49
8	Iron and steel, cast-iron pipe			3	23	15	18		
9	Iron and steel, doors and shutters.	3	5	31	10	6	2	2	10
10	Iron and steel, forgings, not made in steel works or rolling mills.	8	27	45	67	45	49	4	117
11	Iron and steel, nails and spikes, cut and .wrought, including wire nails, not made in steel works or rolling mills.	2	7	21	25	6	4	(x)	30
12	Iron and steel, tempering and welding.	180	244	86	8		2	73	533
13	Iron and steel, wrought pipe	1	2	8	20	4	15	(x)	12
14	Ivory, shell, and bone work, not including combs and hair pins.	11	11	14	7	1		9	43
15	Japanning	10	13	13				11	57
16	Jewelry	372	576	652	378	51	25	167	1,482
17	Jewelry and instrument cases	15	45	56	26			6	170
18	Jute goods	1	1	4	10	2	8		(x)
19	Knit goods	145	251	589	717	184	164	113	1,104
20	Labels and tags	15	21	39	33	10	1	10	102
21	Lamps and reflectors	22	38	53	41	7	10	9	106
22	Lapidary work	27	45	24	13	4	11	10	124
23	Lasts	5	6	20	24	9		6	17
24	Lead, bar, pipe, and sheet		2	4	16	6	4		(x)
25	Leather goods, not elsewhere specified.	62	133	172	111	16	9	41	396
26	Leather, tanned, curried, and finished.	33	42	105	175	103	222	11	137
27	Lime	149	97	129	89	11	1	141	496
28	Linen goods			2	4	2	2		
29	Liquors, distilled		2	6	9	6	11		(x)
30	Liquors, malt	8	29	175	305	115	97	6	87
31	Liquors, vinous	140	107	67	21	6	1	35	115
32	Lithographing	41	44	95	113	24	14	7	137
33	Locomotives, not made by railroad companies.			1	4	1	11		
34	Looking-glass and picture frames.	134	144	101	45	5		48	299
35	Lubricating greases	6	16	14	12	2	3	2	23
36	Lumber and timber products	10,103	9,012	4,685	1,677	400	242	11,648	39,766
37	Lumber, planing-mill products, not including planing mills connected with sawmills.	852	1,407	1,809	1,068	119	54	574	3,729
38	Machine tools	19	47	110	134	41	52	19	226
39	Malt		4	8	17	13	13		15
40	Marble and stone work	944	1,763	1,293	224	14	2	459	3,716
41	Matches	1	1	3	7	4	5	(x)	(x)
42	Mats and matting, from cocoa fiber, grass, and coir.		2	3	3	2	2		(x)
43	Mattresses and spring beds, not elsewhere specified.	168	291	354	198	26	4	88	588
44	Millinery and lace goods, not elsewhere specified.	422	829	1,150	514	71	19	472	3,467
45	Millstones	6	5	1				4	34
46	Mineral and soda waters	1,607	2,081	1,257	231	14	4	908	4,266
47	Minerals and earths, ground or otherwise treated.	42	82	183	93	14	5	69	540
48	Mirrors, framed and unframed, not elsewhere specified.	24	39	59	58	5	1	21	102

BY VALUE OF PRODUCTS, FOR INDUSTRIES: 1919—Continued.

[See note at head of this table, pp. 1002 and 1003.]

WAGE EARNERS IN ESTABLISHMENTS WITH PRODUCT OF—continued.				VALUE OF PRODUCTS OF ESTABLISHMENTS WITH PRODUCT OF—continued.						
$20,000 to $100,000.	$100,000 to $500,000.	$500,000 to $1,000,000.	$1,000,000 and over.	Less than $5,000.	$5,000 to $20,000.	$20,000 to $100,000.	$100,000 to $500,000.	$500,000 to $1,000,000.	$1,000,000 and over.	
				Expressed in thousands.						
12,738	11,303	1,313	1,330	$1,020	$11,654	$54,632	$56,258	$6,508	$6,933	1
176	278	365	1,125	13	239	1,685	3,891	3,539	16,877	2
68	585	(x)	(x)	46	155	616	5,617	(x)	(x)	3
1,804	5,848	3,433	4,496	150	966	5,512	22,738	11,916	16,855	4
131	1,012	2,648	37,869	......	......	632	7,077	23,167	763,591	5
288	6,289	11,092	357,379	(x)	83	964	25,600	47,864	2,754,391	6
332	2,277	2,703	12,597	13	236	1,421	10,333	13,654	64,087	7
66	1,975	2,813	7,771	......	......	180	6,928	10,368	32,759	8
359	437	1,269	(x)	8	53	1,838	1,731	7,247	(x)	9
624	3,277	5,622	18,747	23	327	2,391	17,096	32,908	121,007	10
228	1,022	618	1,457	(x)	82	985	5,044	4,248	7,224	11
646	585	......	(x)	490	2,454	3,175	4,877	......	(x)	12
86	942	421	8,965	(x)	30	519	4,930	3,066	73,324	13
220	570	(x)	......	30	124	679	1,984	(x)	......	14
227			......	32	146	593				15
5,976	14,220	5,144	3,882	1,028	6,135	31,417	80,175	35,691	49,493	16
815	1,743			37	540	2,521	5,028			17
58	486	(x)	6,594	(x)	(x)	218	2,381	(x)	31,844	18
10,718	46,067	31,252	83,318	391	2,852	31,304	168,890	128,610	381,093	19
469	1,386	3,260	(x)	35	267	1,859	6,855	15,228	(x)	20
584	2,589	1,135	3,937	59	418	2,520	9,556	4,747	20,799	21
176	200	79	566	69	470	965	2,547	2,816	23,184	22
265	1,455	1,167	......	18	57	973	6,035	5,388		23
14	204	189	445	......	(x)	190	4,126	3,730	9,128	24
1,866	3,506	1,600	1,536	163	1,526	8,029	20,772	10,291	12,172	25
1,408	6,886	6,997	57,037	74	469	5,790	46,760	73,572	801,927	26
2,794	5,886	2,088	(x)	293	1,050	7,026	16,927	8,674	(x)	27
(x)	552	1,338	(x)			(x)	1,378	5,620	(x)	28
41	227	232	880	......	(x)	437	2,385	4,736	24,296	29
1,677	8,741	7,283	16,465	22	355	10,317	76,406	80,197	212,608	30
217	280	864	(x)	338	1,056	2,920	4,623	8,517	(x)	31
1,306	5,407	3,360	5,401	92	488	4,966	25,152	16,642	25,811	32
(x)	316	(x)	26,399	......	......	(x)	1,707	(x)	154,563	33
983	2,465	913		342	1,439	4,549	8,961	3,094	......	34
53	234	(x)	160	13	161	575	3,143	(x)	4,977	35
75,252	139,515	93,082	121,682	24,359	92,008	192,520	390,016	280,908	407,660	36
18,866	36,980	13,060	13,747	2,160	15,242	89,609	218,276	83,011	92,140	37
1,941	8,162	7,235	35,528	49	567	6,026	31,760	27,856	146,142	38
75	341	305	616	......	50	385	4,580	9,374	24,951	39
13,073	12,280	3,240	(x)	2,600	19,309	53,476	42,503	11,277	(x)	40
53	358	794	2,521	(x)	(x)	181	1,736	2,783	13,796	41
57	1,016	(x)	(x)	......	(x)	122	4,739	(x)	(x)	42
2,573	6,032	3,356	(x)	457	3,274	16,565	41,232	22,425	(x)	43
14,046	19,597	7,053	6,215	1,193	8,874	54,565	108,587	48,725	33,781	44
(x)	......			7	60	(x)	......		......	45
7,230	4,056	653	327	4,188	21,690	52,020	40,800	9,575	7,068	46
3,539	6,118	2,456	1,704	98	975	9,002	19,900	8,998	7,094	47
506	1,514	456	(x)	60	424	3,070	12,679	4,598	(x)	48

TABLE **16.**—NUMBER AND SIZE OF ESTABLISHMENTS,

[See note at head of this table, pp. 1002 and 1003.]

	INDUSTRY.	NUMBER OF ESTABLISHMENTS WITH PRODUCT OF—						WAGE EARNERS IN ESTABLISHMENTS WITH PRODUCT OF—	
		Less than $5,000.	$5,000 to $20,000.	$20,000 to $100,000.	$100,000 to $500,000.	$500,000 to $1,000,000.	$1,000,000 and over.	Less than $5,000.	$5,000 to $20,000.
1	Models and patterns, not including paper patterns.	209	422	260	34	2	1	129	1,427
2	Motorcycles, bicycles, and parts....	6	5	6	14	10	10	4	7
3	Mucilage, paste, and other adhesives, not elsewhere specified.	29	29	46	18	4	1	10	44
4	Musical instruments and materials, not elsewhere specified.	113	54	49	19	4	1	43	178
5	Musical instruments, organs.	7	17	23	18	3	......	4	43
6	Musical instruments, pianos.	3	13	25	78	43	29	2	60
7	Musical instruments, piano and organ materials.	8	19	26	33	18	9	6	76
8	Needles, pins, and hooks and eyes...	8	14	23	32	8	7	12	72
9	Nets and seines.	2	3	6	4	3	1		8
10	Oil and cake, cottonseed.	1	8	53	335	187	127	(x)	37
11	Oil, essential.	32	27	9	6	3	1	19	16
12	Oil, linseed.				2	2	22		
13	Oil, not elsewhere specified.	16	30	58	103	35	38	20	59
14	Oilcloth and linoleum, floor.				4	3	14		
15	Oilcloth, enameled.				4	1	6		
16	Oleomargarine and other butter substitutes.		1	4	8	8	21		(x)
17	Optical goods.	55	173	182	83	8	5	38	413
18	Ordnance and accessories.			1	5	6	14		
19	Paints.	44	88	168	185	45	71	28	155
20	Paper and wood pulp.	4	20	87	234	146	238	7	89
21	Paper goods, not elsewhere specified	18	51	91	86	37	25	13	158
22	Paper patterns.	4	4	5	6			4	7
23	Patent medicines and compounds..	942	630	551	258	44	42	330	1,047
24	Paving materials.	166	274	332	112	4	1	330	1,898
25	Peanuts, grading, roasting, cleaning and shelling.	10	12	14	21	10	11	7	26
26	Pencils, lead.			1	5	1	5		
27	Pens, fountain and stylographic....	6	7	21	16	1	5	6	23
28	Pens, gold.			10	4	1			
29	Perfumery and cosmetics.	159	154	158	73	12	13	62	243
30	Petroleum, refining.	4	6	21	65	56	168	2	20
31	Phonographs and graphophones...	11	18	49	51	13	24	7	44
32	Photo-engraving.	37	105	194	81	5		23	303
33	Photographic apparatus.	13	19	19	12	2	3	8	51
34	Photographic materials.	21	46	44	35	12	11	9	124
35	Pickles, preserves, and sauces.	146	174	193	140	33	37	66	370
36	Pipes, tobacco.	13	10	20	10	1	2	17	46
37	Plated ware.	1	13	15	21	10	8	(x)	47
38	Plumbers' supplies, not elsewhere specified.	11	30	62	87	16	8	7	84
39	Pocketbooks.	21	35	43	34	6		17	123
40	Pottery.	75	39	71	110	35	10	61	233
41	Poultry, killing and dressing, not done in slaughtering and meat-packing establishments.	1	2	98	82	7	6	(x)	3
42	Printing and publishing, book and job.	4,216	4,542	3,127	1,013	138	53	1,750	11,920
43	Printing and publishing, music.	46	41	38	29	3	3	2	32
44	Printing and publishing, newspapers and periodicals.	7,472	6,340	2,429	829	137	155	5,279	15,915
45	Printing materials.	9	22	37	13	1		7	45
46	Pulp goods.	3	3	11	8	5	10	8	9
47	Pumps, not including power pumps.	20	33	29	30	6	9	10	93
48	Pumps, steam and other power....	8	12	27	42	10	13	8	28
49	Refrigerators.	4	23	42	36	13	4	3	62
50	Regalia, and society badges and emblems.	22	41	36	12	3	1	10	133
51	Rice, cleaning and polishing.	3	7	8	9	14	45	1	4
52	Roofing materials.	23	27	49	35	18	26	16	78
53	Rubber tires, tubes, and rubber goods, not elsewhere specified.	15	58	87	129	43	105	12	210

BY VALUE OF PRODUCTS, FOR INDUSTRIES: 1919—Continued.

[See note at head of this table, pp. 1002 and 1003.]

WAGE EARNERS IN ESTABLISHMENTS WITH PRODUCT OF—continued.				VALUE OF PRODUCTS OF ESTABLISHMENTS WITH PRODUCT OF—continued. (Expressed in thousands.)						
$20,000 to $100,000.	$100,000 to $500,000.	$500,000 to $1,000,000.	$1,000,000 and over.	Less than $5,000.	$5,000 to $20,000.	$20,000 to $100,000.	$100,000 to $500,000.	$500,000 to $1,000,000.	$1,000,000 and over.	
3,125	2,268	(x)	(x)	$558	$4,683	$10,487	$9,572	(x)	(x)	1
85	954	1,329	8,507	17	40	260	4,186	$7,216	$41,387	2
247	249	253	(x)	68	299	2,495	4,200	4,168	(x)	3
781	1,550	1,561	(x)	251	598	2,465	4,487	4,705	(x)	4
357	1,537	(x)	....	24	188	1,076	4,685	(x)	....	5
437	4,564	6,374	11,520	8	165	1,585	22,199	29,550	53,581	6
413	2,322	4,036	4,156	16	194	1,362	8,711	12,843	13,664	7
541	2,671	1,596	4,402	15	152	1,221	7,852	5,492	14,573	8
44	133	674	(x)	(x)	45	278	1,210	3,581	(x)	9
372	6,769	7,619	11,969	(x)	108	3,223	96,352	130,424	351,138	10
17	112	157	(x)	90	257	320	1,415	3,616	(x)	11
....	(x)	54	2,119	....	....	....	(x)	1,908	118,730	12
182	1,604	1,100	2,965	40	339	2,894	23,839	24,764	104,604	13
....	107	258	5,049	....	....	....	1,400	1,985	49,288	14
....	202	(x)	928	....	....	....	1,969	(x)	13,468	15
18	100	288	2,445	....	(x)	206	2,298	6,276	71,036	16
1,863	3,539	1,764	7,106	159	1,932	8,140	15,731	5,527	22,229	17
(x)	357	1,324	9,647	....	....	(x)	1,100	4,957	63,439	18
732	3,136	2,194	11,240	114	987	8,735	46,284	30,591	170,003	19
1,409	10,432	16,857	84,965	10	242	5,375	60,065	106,970	615,397	20
949	2,736	3,897	6,382	46	601	4,837	22,295	27,324	52,182	21
36	356	....	....	13	36	202	1,277	....	....	22
2,854	4,503	2,067	6,643	1,978	6,499	25,475	57,084	30,735	90,391	23
6,559	6,148	1,137	(x)	442	3,017	15,425	19,738	7,119	(x)	24
65	501	(x)	1,861	27	124	626	5,766	(x)	26,811	25
(x)	473	(x)	5,497	....	....	(x)	1,845	(x)	22,289	26
359	666	(x)	2,153	18	92	1,403	3,432	(x)	11,052	27
120	296	(x)	....	....	....	567	1,234	(x)	....	28
931	1,569	632	1,968	383	1,631	7,143	15,976	8,641	25,839	29
107	680	1,640	56,440	11	65	1,383	17,462	39,504	1,574,108	30
622	2,764	1,946	23,338	25	204	2,508	11,865	8,053	135,893	31
2,389	3,300	754	....	113	1,224	10,056	14,051	3,945	....	32
203	2,293	(x)	(x)	27	194	877	8,286	(x)	(x)	33
412	1,153	1,017	11,841	57	449	2,084	8,582	7,946	96,596	34
1,370	4,079	2,794	7,942	359	1,862	9,488	29,958	23,072	81,046	35
330	2,146	(x)	(x)	40	86	960	10,468	(x)	(x)	36
262	1,836	7,347	(x)	(x)	143	774	5,750	34,968	(x)	37
789	4,457	2,406	5,849	29	356	3,180	20,448	11,172	24,870	38
571	1,605	589	....	56	372	2,210	7,883	4,029	....	39
1,954	12,003	8,522	5,161	161	408	4,021	30,473	24,530	15,326	40
376	1,083	192	486	(x)	36	5,267	21,843	4,672	9,887	41
32,640	41,821	17,137	17,737	10,360	47,715	138,463	203,567	89,454	108,104	42
82	391	392	....	110	455	1,750	6,484	5,793	(x)	43
20,774	26,201	10,233	41,979	20,024	61,499	105,596	179,021	94,186	463,827	44
177	494	(x)	....	36	260	1,558	3,065	(x)	....	45
160	389	620	1,855	7	29	558	2,062	3,499	17,453	46
339	1,350	852	2,740	48	388	1,479	5,916	4,209	19,616	47
263	2,051	1,660	6,678	25	141	1,317	10,838	7,173	34,252	48
464	2,123	1,971	1,163	11	266	2,276	8,681	8,519	6,296	49
491	454	1,135	(x)	48	450	1,817	2,070	5,010	(x)	50
9	81	255	1,763	7	82	378	2,724	10,405	76,442	51
491	982	1,206	6,098	58	318	2,324	7,321	13,418	62,456	52
1,168	5,475	5,539	107,444	39	656	4,650	29,131	30,942	921,670	53

TABLE 16.—NUMBER AND SIZE OF ESTABLISHMENTS,

[See note at head of this table, pp. 1002 and 1003.]

	INDUSTRY.	NUMBER OF ESTABLISHMENTS WITH PRODUCT OF—						WAGE EARNERS IN ESTABLISHMENTS WITH PRODUCT OF—	
		Less than $5,000.	$5,000 to $20,000.	$20,000 to $100,000.	$100,000 to $500,000.	$500,000 to $1,000,000.	$1,000,000 and over.	Less than $5,000.	$5,000 to $20,000.
1	Rules, ivory and wood	5	2	5	1			4	(x)
2	Saddlery and harness	778	691	202	111	27	14	387	976
3	Safes and vaults	3	6	9	14	3	3	4	34
4	Salt	12	9	15	29	10	11	8	34
5	Sand and emery paper and cloth	1			3	4	4		36
6	Sand-lime brick	1	6	23	2			(x)	218
7	Sausage, not made in slaughtering and meat-packing establishments	84	176	239	114	14	6	28	218
8	Saws	17	34	34	21	1	5	9	82
9	Scales and balances	9	15	20	25	3	7	11	62
10	Screws, machine	7	21	59	38	10	8	7	84
11	Screws, wood				5	3	3		22
12	Sewing machines and attachments	7	5	6	11	3	8	4	42
13	Shipbuilding, steel	3	8	12	29	10	100	3	42
14	Shipbuilding, wooden, including boat building	284	230	171	140	45	43	142	796
15	Shirts	81	207	311	192	54	51	358	2,243
16	Show cases	16	33	45	24	1		10	93
17	Signs and advertising novelties	234	268	193	71	4	9	115	746
18	Silk goods, including throwsters	52	140	341	483	175	178	67	955
19	Silversmithing and silverware	4	17	36	28	6	8		63
20	Slaughtering and meat packing	21	129	338	384	121	311	7	149
21	Smelting and refining, copper				2	2	30		
22	Smelting and refining, lead		1		1	1	22		(x)
23	Smelting and refining, zinc			2	5	3	29		
24	Smelting and refining, metals, not elsewhere specified			4	4	3	2		
25	Smelting and refining, not from the ore	2	7	20	23	16	13	(x)	19
26	Soap	69	64	78	80	21	36	32	141
27	Soda-water apparatus	5	16	23	17	3	2	2	28
28	Sporting and athletic goods	53	39	50	39	1	6	48	187
29	Springs, steel, car and carriage, not made in steel works or rolling mills	7	21	23	35	6	20	4	54
30	Stamped and enameled ware, not elsewhere specified	11	42	107	91	39	33	10	154
31	Stationery goods, not elsewhere specified	27	32	66	65	20	13	14	91
32	Statuary and art goods	65	75	48	5	2		38	246
33	Steam fittings and steam and hot-water heating apparatus	12	43	59	84	30	33	7	121
34	Steam packing	10	34	71	37	10	7	6	87
35	Steel barrels, drums, and tanks	1	2	3	12	7	8		(x)
36	Stencils and brands	29	36	16	3			16	106
37	Stereotyping and electrotyping	6	21	92	49	3		2	89
38	Stoves and hot-air furnaces	12	43	100	177	49	31	8	112
39	Stoves, gas and oil	19	42	62	32	6	15	10	95
40	Structural ironwork, not made in steel works or rolling mills	111	245	421	244	65	60	67	648
41	Sugar, beet			1	6	20	58		
42	Sugar, cane	34	17	32	81	28	10	30	36
43	Sugar, refining, not including beet sugar						20		
44	Sulphuric, nitric, and mixed acids		2	4	12	12	9		(x)
45	Surgical appliances	83	92	55	29	4	5	49	244
46	Suspenders, garters, and elastic woven goods	21	34	56	48	24	13	21	85
47	Textile machinery and parts	40	80	166	100	20	26	31	287
48	Theatrical scenery	1	3	10	3				9
49	Tin and other foils, not elsewhere specified	3		1	4	1	6	5	
50	Tin plate and terneplate	2	5	1	1		15	(x)	79
51	Tinware, not elsewhere specified	27	46	54	81	28	65	14	116
52	Tobacco, chewing and smoking, and snuff	133	74	73	43	14	28	30	127
53	Tobacco, cigars and cigarettes	5,590	2,571	1,118	451	123	73	2,098	8,098
54	Tools, not elsewhere specified	201	322	369	174	34	25	160	1,210

BY VALUE OF PRODUCTS, FOR INDUSTRIES: 1919—Continued.

[See note at head of this table, pp. 1002 and 1003.]

WAGE EARNERS IN ESTABLISHMENTS WITH PRODUCT OF—continued.				VALUE OF PRODUCTS OF ESTABLISHMENTS WITH PRODUCT OF—continued. (Expressed in thousands.)						
$20,000 to $100,000.	$100,000 to $500,000.	$500,000 to $1,000,000.	$1,000,000 and over.	Less than $5,000.	$5,000 to $20,000.	$20,000 to $100,000.	$100,000 to $500,000.	$500,000 to $1,000,000.	$1,000,000 and over.	
164	(x)	1,939	2,309	$12	(x)	$469	(x)	$18,037	$22,025	1
1,359	3,441	*1,855*	(x)	2,233	$6,402	8,828	$26,188	*10,932*	(x)	2
93	963	1,139	3,049	6	75	470	3,811	6,822	21,376	3
249	2,016	254	421	27	105	820	8,364	2,684	5,699	4
	96			(x)			921			5
468	(x)			(x)	80	1,583	(x)			6
884	1,306	648	387	214	1,965	11,095	24,928	10,056	8,352	7
462	1,160	(x)	*3,797*	45	350	1,866	5,786	(x)	*23,414*	8
244	1,451	509	3,155	30	171	892	5,071	2,511	11,966	9
880	2,150	1,766	5,375	18	260	2,907	8,794	6,455	21,581	10
	673	(x)	*4,216*				1,863	(x)	13,597	11
104	733	988	13,208	20	73	379	2,301	2,222	38,700	12
275	2,210	2,244	339,240	6	92	794	8,139	7,518	1,439,941	13
2,703	10,450	7,588	21,753	624	2,370	8,031	34,579	30,371	89,897	14
10,493	9,627	4,744	12,138	243	2,309	14,981	45,553	39,876	102,365	15
501	*1,253*	(x)		43	343	2,419	*5,489*	(x)		16
1,968	3,887	509	3,207	621	2,781	8,326	15,070	2,260	14,285	17
8,977	28,474	20,871	67,438	131	1,650	18,034	118,926	125,274	424,455	18
352	1,039	839	4,160	8	224	1,695	5,571	4,646	16,982	19
978	4,181	2,942	152,739	63	1,580	18,427	93,920	84,607	4,047,694	20
	(x)	*279*	17,066				(x)	2,024	649,078	21
(x)		(x)	*6,438*		(x)	(x)	(x)		196,795	22
(x)	*284*	478	13,034				1,448	2,186	100,489	23
28	113	(x)	*1,900*			174	875	(x)	19,026	24
78	405	776	889	(x)	*83*	1,026	5,375	11,040	32,722	25
432	1,272	1,188	17,371	130	757	3,966	17,918	13,571	280,398	26
174	667	*1,728*	(x)	14	175	1,056	4,079	*9,861*	(x)	27
740	2,432	(x)	*3,005*	129	433	2,394	8,503	(x)	*12,381*	28
207	1,654	835	6,227	18	267	964	7,960	4,197	38,074	29
1,581	5,901	6,736	19,866	34	446	5,057	22,078	27,740	88,299	30
886	3,248	2,222	4,800	75	363	3,568	14,825	13,763	25,769	31
614	*568*	(x)		164	781	1,964	*2,111*	(x)		32
675	3,828	4,521	27,534	27	493	3,313	20,528	20,598	115,326	33
537	1,102	1,229	3,186	20	433	3,470	8,448	7,001	21,153	34
29	408	679	2,206	(x)	(x)	*202*	2,863	4,638	17,240	35
163	132			62	386	675	475			36
1,215	1,895	463		14	286	4,860	8,679	2,080		37
1,262	11,399	7,669	12,418	33	433	5,253	45,734	33,174	61,091	38
549	1,752	708	7,451	51	455	3,025	8,271	4,191	39,799	39
4,310	9,648	7,463	21,826	329	2,843	21,424	58,587	46,231	165,548	40
(x)	*389*	1,873	9,519			(x)	*2,351*	15,954	130,851	41
394	2,727	*2,914*	(x)	74	144	1,992	21,730	*33,801*	(x)	42
			18,202						730,987	43
83	535	1,396	2,947		(x)	*340*	3,103	8,714	19,313	44
525	1,530	374	3,668	214	921	2,153	7,001	2,543	30,702	45
595	1,571	3,036	5,549	56	366	2,712	10,114	16,482	31,045	46
2,161	5,562	3,371	20,411	104	1,003	7,676	22,361	14,301	76,644	47
91	49			(x)	*37*	624	406			48
(x)	*285*	(x)	1,618	8		(x)	*1,808*	(x)	16,105	49
(x)	(x)		3,043	(x)	*510*	(x)	(x)		96,895	50
533	3,890	3,849	25,934	74	525	2,549	19,579	21,035	190,202	51
484	1,643	1,220	14,820	326	780	3,421	10,666	10,107	213,971	52
17,161	34,851	26,571	49,994	11,872	25,020	49,495	106,310	85,260	495,705	53
5,627	9,651	5,557	13,380	542	3,583	17,785	37,269	23,832	61,191	54

TABLE 16.—NUMBER AND SIZE OF ESTABLISHMENTS,

[See note at head of this table, pp. 1002 and 1003.]

	INDUSTRY.	NUMBER OF ESTABLISHMENTS WITH PRODUCT OF—						WAGE EARNERS IN ESTABLISHMENTS WITH PRODUCT OF—	
		Less than $5,000.	$5,000 to $20,000.	$20,000 to $100,000.	$100,000 to $500,000.	$500,000 to $1,000,000.	$1,000,000 and over.	Less than $5,000.	$5,000 to $20,000.
1	Toys and games	118	132	180	93	14	4	115	612
2	Trunks and valises	106	157	190	113	22	9	66	308
3	Turpentine and rosin	101	395	590	103	1	1	165	3,684
4	Type founding	6	11	2	3	.....	1	7	47
5	Typewriters and supplies	10	10	23	23	11	11	22	27
6	Umbrellas and canes	43	44	61	*37	9	4	20	109
7	Upholstering materials, not elsewhere specified.	15	39	69	25	7	8	28	172
8	Varnishes	9	26	62	88	23	21	6	22
9	Vault lights and ventilators	7	11	17	6	.....	.....	5	33
10	Vinegar and cider	391	156	114	51	8	.....	95	195
11	Wall paper, not made in paper mills.	.....	1	12	20	6	9	.....	(x)
12	Wall plaster and composition flooring.	8	31	60	50	10	2	5	87
13	Washing machines and clothes wringers.	12	19	21	29	15	9	12	57
14	Waste	3	10	26	40	6	7	5	19
15	Watch and clock materials, except watchcases.	6	8	8	5	.....	.....	4	50
16	Watchcases	2	6	9	7	3	6	(x)	12
17	Watches	.....	.....	5	2	5	6	.....	.....
18	Wheelbarrows	1	1	4	4	1	.....	.....	(x)
19	Whips	4	7	10	3	1	1	4	35
20	Windmills	3	5	8	9	3	3	2	12
21	Window and door screens and weather strips.	61	84	47	18	3	1	30	235
22	Window shades and fixtures	61	108	72	35	6	5	31	178
23	Wire	1	4	7	12	9	33	.....	12
24	Wirework, including wire rope and cable, not elsewhere specified.	129	146	148	90	24	21	86	422
25	Wood distillation	4	10	41	42	13	5	6	53
26	Wood preserving	1	.....	9	41	14	8	(x)	.....
27	Wood, turned and carved	195	226	210	84	6	1	121	917
28	Wooden goods, not elsewhere specified.	58	59	76	46	3	3	41	220
29	Wool pulling	.....	2	2	5	9	6	.....	(x)
30	Wool scouring	1	1	10	13	4	4	(x)	(x)
31	Wool shoddy	11	10	21	23	8	5	15	32
32	Woolen and worsted goods	36	34	78	235	196	273	30	192
33	All other industries [1]	14	29	34	20	4	8	19	86

[1] All other industries embrace: Billiard tables, bowling alleys, and accessories, 49 establishments; buttons and whetstones, 11; lard, not made in slaughtering and meat-packing establishments, 6; oakum, 6; specified, 1; whalebone cutting, 1; and wood carpet, 3.

BY VALUE OF PRODUCTS, FOR INDUSTRIES: 1919—Continued.

[See note at head of this table, pp. 1002 and 1003.]

WAGE EARNERS IN ESTABLISHMENTS WITH PRODUCT OF—continued.				VALUE OF PRODUCTS OF ESTABLISHMENTS WITH PRODUCT OF—continued.						
$20,000 to $100,000.	$100,000 to $500,000.	$500,000 to $1,000,000.	$1,000,000 and over.	Less than $5,000.	$5,000 to $20,000.	$20,000 to $100,000.	$100,000 to $500,000.	$500,000 to $1,000,000.	$1,000,000 and over.	
				Expressed in thousands.						
3,203	5,759	3,049	1,463	$269	$1,458	$9,025	$19,135	$10,271	$5,499	1
1,796	3,816	2,618	2,866	297	1,627	9,255	22,204	15,226	15,323	2
14,368	9,850	(x)	(x)	280	5,050	24,865	22,856	(x)	(x)	3
(x)	756	----	(x)	24	128	(x)	1,938	----	(x)	4
190	1,038	1,900	12,492	34	117	916	4,763	6,955	39,953	5
415	905	852	1,067	114	455	3,171	8,716	6,283	6,570	6
896	947	580	2,187	40	473	3,461	5,916	4,826	25,174	7
208	1,000	648	2,138	20	279	3,425	22,280	16,409	41,219	8
138	140	----		18	135	714	1,289			9
551	811	329	----	691	1,627	5,756	11,623	5,026		10
128	996	815	2,323		(x)	780	6,526	3,829	11,913	11
594	2,238	2,199	(x)	19	350	3,234	12,366	10,906	(x)	12
226	1,142	1,402	3,117	31	184	1,206	7,076	10,569	21,705	13
200	917	341	1,204	8	114	1,497	9,066	4,600	14,415	14
280	248	----		12	100	495	735			15
62	262	421	3,143	(x)	62	432	1,741	2,201	15,183	16
295	(x)	2,402	13,191	----	----	286	(x)	4,195	27,563	17
54	237	(x)		(x)	(x)	199	1,481	(x)	----	18
127	551	(x)	(x)	11	100	469	2,406	(x)	(x)	19
123	497	498	800	8	55	366	2,090	2,461	4,953	20
477	812	625	(x)	161	869	2,077	4,083	3,743	(x)	21
497	847	759	2,099	173	1,180	3,176	7,589	4,499	12,574	22
68	616	947	18,098	(x)	60	425	3,061	6,667	151,938	23
1,650	4,051	2,628	6,387	324	1,545	6,802	21,213	16,618	44,047	24
788	1,871	1,301	927	6	102	2,185	9,472	8,757	12,023	25
109	1,823	998	1,048	(x)	----	615	11,556	9,232	11,836	26
3,511	4,773	1,327	(x)	461	2,414	10,147	16,800	5,025	(x)	27
1,248	2,668	623	1,643	147	666	3,691	9,125	2,240	5,924	28
39	67	275	324	----	(x)	142	1,372	6,974	8,873	29
220	604	434	919	(x)	(x)	608	3,107	2,488	7,477	30
232	754	543	990	30	118	1,054	6,389	5,915	9,748	31
1,432	15,608	23,713	125,812	77	391	3,971	64,728	145,245	851,022	32
378	780	282	9,077	35	318	1,689	3,939	3,021	46,463	33

ter, reworking, 5; cars, electric-railroad, not including operations of railroad companies, 7; hammocks, 6; pens, steel, 4; pulp, from fiber other than wood, 5; sewing-machine cases, 5; straw goods, not elsewhere

TABLE 17.—GEOGRAPHIC DIVISIONS AND STATES—ESTABLISHMENTS

[NOTE.—In some states in order to avoid disclosing the returns of individual establishments, the figures have been consolidated with those for a preceding group. In such cases an (x) is shown in the column bined are printed in *italics*. At the censuses of 1914, 1909, and 1904 establishments with products valued $100,000 to $500,000, and $500,000 to $1,000,000. Separate figures for the number of establishments and combined figures for these two groups for all items for 1909 and 1904 and for average number of wage for 1919, and also for 1914 with the exception of wage earners; for 1909 and 1904 all items for $100,000 to

DIVISION AND STATE.	NUMBER OF ESTABLISHMENTS WITH PRODUCT OF—						WAGE EARNERS IN ESTABLISHMENTS WITH PRODUCT OF—		
	Less than $5,000.	$5,000 to $20,000.	$20,000 to $100,000.	$100,000 to $500,000.	$500,000 to $1,000,000.	$1,000,000 and over.	Less than $5,000.	$5,000 to $20,000.	$20,000 to $100,000.
UNITED STATES:									
1 1919	65,485	87,440	77,911	39,647	9,208	10,414	45,813	249,722	793,528
2 1914	97,060	87,931	56,814	25,847	4,320	3,819	129,623	429,037	999,510
3 1909	93,349	86,988	57,270	*27,824*	(x)	3,060	142,430	470,006	1,030,449
4 1904	71,147	72,791	48,096	*22,246*	(x)	1,900	106,353	419,466	1,027,047
GEOGRAPHIC DIVS.:									
New England—									
5 1919	4,923	7,197	6,977	3,886	1,064	1,481	3,199	21,729	79,688
6 1914	7,212	8,100	5,695	2,945	645	596	8,454	39,511	114,301
7 1909	7,353	8,187	5,835	*3,468*	(x)	518	10,085	44,128	124,229
8 1904	6,012	7,515	5,364	*3,048*	(x)	340	8,892	43,215	122,699
Middle Atlantic—									
9 1919	16,947	25,002	25,906	14,202	3,051	3,252	10,169	71,607	274,920
10 1914	26,135	28,302	19,544	8,921	1,294	1,270	31,255	144,405	363,698
11 1909	24,055	27,170	19,469	*9,557*	(x)	1,064	30,616	146,441	386,545
12 1904	19,805	23,652	15,905	*7,638*	(x)	699	28,808	140,849	354,285
East North Central—									
13 1919	12,454	17,155	17,476	9,291	2,216	2,740	7,648	42,784	153,885
14 1914	19,887	18,705	13,073	6,095	1,105	1,031	22,169	76,163	209,976
15 1909	20,805	19,069	12,868	*6,487*	(x)	784	25,720	86,503	224,375
16 1904	18,285	16,740	11,067	*5,214*	(x)	448	26,382	86,479	224,139
West North Central—									
17 1919	8,406	9,628	6,786	3,011	577	758	5,380	23,147	53,661
18 1914	11,361	8,412	5,082	1,753	312	279	11,406	30,685	62,735
19 1909	11,725	8,178	5,078	*1,949*	(x)	241	13,622	32,010	66,110
20 1904	9,015	6,667	4,128	*1,534*	(x)	148	11,647	29,190	62,125
South Atlantic—									
21 1919	8,105	9,828	7,054	3,319	860	810	8,348	37,989	89,183
22 1914	12,027	9,131	4,854	2,276	393	244	26,016	68,394	108,311
23 1909	11,387	9,248	4,917	*2,365*	(x)	171	28,998	78,935	125,795
24 1904	6,645	6,811	4,194	*1,808*	(x)	106	13,747	57,202	117,825
East South Central—									
25 1919	4,480	4,608	3,390	1,483	375	319	4,464	16,512	43,178
26 1914	6,792	3,998	2,283	1,082	167	88	15,408	26,068	47,373
27 1909	7,142	4,429	2,530	*1,210*	(x)	70	17,884	31,894	54,851
28 1904	3,511	3,452	2,350	*955*	(x)	43	6,840	23,639	54,766
West South Central—									
29 1919	3,555	4,608	3,404	1,524	432	386	2,932	13,855	37,593
30 1914	5,353	3,706	2,036	1,075	158	89	7,599	17,815	37,673
31 1909	4,979	3,996	2,215	*1,082*	(x)	67	9,247	23,661	45,203
32 1904	3,041	2,615	1,731	*861*	(x)	31	4,626	15,105	36,776
Mountain—									
33 1919	2,400	2,715	1644	589	127	137	1,457	6,384	13,918
34 1914	2,698	1,990	897	382	50	62	2,482	6,663	10,741
35 1909	2,043	1,864	936	*365*	(x)	46	2,271	7,023	12,653
36 1904	1,396	1,288	652	*239*	(x)	35	1,527	5,159	9,531
Pacific—									
37 1919	4,215	6,699	5,274	2,342	506	531	2,216	15,715	47,502
38 1914	5,595	5,587	3,350	1,318	196	160	4,834	19,333	44,702
39 1909	3,860	4,847	3,422	*1,351*	(x)	99	3,987	19,411	50,688
40 1904	3,437	4,051	2,705	*950*	(x)	49	3,884	18,628	44,901

[1] Includes 2 establishments whose value of product is $1,000,000 and over.
[2] Includes 1 establishment whose value of product is over $1,000,000.

GROUPED BY VALUE OF PRODUCTS: 1919, 1914, 1909, AND 1904.

for the groups of establishments reporting products valued at $500,000 to $1,000,000, or $1,000,000 and over from which the figures have been omitted and the figures for the group with which they have been combined at $100,000 to $1,000,000 constitute one group, but at the census of 1919 this group was subdivided into value of products have been compiled, however, from the returns for 1914. The table therefore gives earners for 1914. In the totals for the United States each establishment is classified under its proper head $500,000 and $500,000 to $1,000,000 are combined in one item, $100,000 to $1,000,000.]

WAGE EARNERS IN ESTABLISHMENTS WITH PRODUCT OF—continued.			VALUE OF PRODUCTS OF ESTABLISHMENTS WITH PRODUCT OF—						
$100,000 to $500,000.	$500,000 to $1,000,000.	$1,000,000 and over.	Less than $5,000.	$5,000 to $20,000.	$20,000 to $100,000.	$100,000 to $500,000.	$500,000 to $1,000,000.	$1,000,000 and over.	
						Expressed in thousands.			
1,719,982	1,114,615	5,172,712	$167,085	$945,603	$3,571,283	$8,965,872	$6,467,132	$42,301,104	1
3,002,071	(x)	2,476,006	233,382	905,693	2,550,229	5,742,376	3,020,694	11,794,061	2
2,896,532	(x)	2,015,629	222,464	904,646	2,544,427	7,946,935	(x)	9,053,580	3
2,515,064	(x)	1,400,453	176,128	751,048	2,129,258	6,109,013	(x)	5,628,456	4
194,011	142,981	909,781	12,439	79,070	321,945	895,483	756,525	5,117,609	5
443,341	(x)	534,626	17,884	84,133	258,906	656,594	460,285	1,448,874	6
434,177	(x)	488,671	17,960	83,216	233,824	1,060,177	(x)	1,241,889	7
432,696	(x)	333,250	15,361	77,995	238,320	911,771	(x)	782,551	8
567,027	342,648	1,606,282	42,781	273,753	1,201,135	3,196,141	2,135,404	13,005,559	9
967,986	(x)	848,596	63,192	294,327	878,194	2,011,964	892,702	3,913,204	10
945,434	(x)	698,711	58,041	288,432	865,620	2,702,739	(x)	3,226,928	11
847,830	(x)	514,793	49,165	244,273	709,195	2,113,140	(x)	2,102,493	12
410,967	275,843	1,505,491	32,029	187,840	806,804	2,108,753	1,559,780	13,042,274	13
710,480	(x)	661,493	48,692	195,282	591,833	1,345,349	778,527	3,582,578	14
689,027	(x)	488,139	50,015	197,415	577,351	1,882,826	(x)	2,504,095	15
589,262	(x)	298,266	45,496	171,086	496,156	1,445,686	(x)	1,446,945	16
103,976	59,662	253,809	21,861	102,746	315,883	648,102	405,782	3,692,691	17
154,161	(x)	122,608	27,595	84,938	223,912	381,344	219,797	1,094,606	18
1 155,245	(x)	107,350	27,373	82,793	220,926	1 565,600	(x)	907,207	19
135,903	(x)	73,496	21,308	68,276	175,847	431,857	(x)	587,158	20
175,445	120,213	386,034	19,893	104,684	312,517	767,916	607,927	2,642,215	21
325,647	(x)	156,884	27,842	92,502	218,677	495,680	273,489	574,809	22
306,447	(x)	122,840	26,455	94,530	213,327	656,709	(x)	390,165	23
1 249,371	(x)	84,466	16,298	71,594	179,556	1 469,142	(x)	237,438	24
83,708	53,669	127,695	11,150	48,119	150,334	344,732	264,560	823,496	25
133,873	(x)	41,656	14,980	40,249	100,815	246,121	116,165	182,338	26
1 126,527	(x)	30,616	15,869	44,498	111,473	1 323,868	(x)	134,781	27
2 110,177	(x)	25,807	8,750	35,550	103,307	2 234,271	(x)	82,458	28
71,808	50,562	108,494	9,314	49,308	152,718	353,080	300,126	1,413,315	29
118,529	(x)	30,324	12,687	37,050	90,830	234,084	106,777	321,111	30
103,921	(x)	22,488	11,737	40,850	100,624	284,432	(x)	187,800	31
2 75,460	(x)	11,503	7,479	26,492	79,161	2 208,952	(x)	93,148	32
3 28,087	1 13,674	45,696	6,347	28,571	72,596	3 198,690	1 84,502	531,970	33
33,024	(x)	28,203	6,428	19,401	38,201	82,466	34,454	256,618	34
4 34,706	(x)	18,782	5,079	18,676	40,490	4 115,857	(x)	183,894	35
2 22,795	(x)	13,778	3,473	13,020	28,420	2 62,794	(x)	146,956	36
89,738	55,303	224,705	11,271	71,512	237,351	522,926	348,780	1,965,770	37
115,030	(x)	51,616	14,082	57,811	148,861	288,774	138,498	419,863	38
105,791	(x)	33,289	9,935	51,236	150,792	372,666	(x)	258,882	39
76,943	(x)	19,721	8,798	42,762	119,296	239,562	(x)	141,147	40

3 Includes 10 establishments whose value of product is $500,000 to $1,000,000 and 6 of $1,000,000 and over.
4 Includes 4 establishments whose value of product is $1,000,000 and over.

TABLE **17.**—GEOGRAPHIC DIVISIONS AND STATES—ESTABLISHMENTS

[See note at head of this table, pp. 1016 and 1017.]

	DIVISION AND STATE.	NUMBER OF ESTABLISHMENTS WITH PRODUCT OF—						WAGE EARNERS IN ESTABLISHMENTS WITH PRODUCT OF—		
		Less than $5,000.	$5,000 to $20,000.	$20,000 to $100,000.	$100,000 to $500,000.	$500,000 to $1,000,000.	$1,000,000 and over.	Less than $5,000.	$5,000 to $20,000.	$20,000 to $100,000.
	NEW ENGLAND:									
1	Maine...............	880	921	698	311	84	101	645	2,920	8,364
2	New Hampshire....	322	432	405	213	51	76	236	1,459	5,044
3	Vermont............	410	558	541	207	47	27	313	1,926	6,271
4	Massachusetts.....	1,645	3,211	3,511	2,149	575	815	990	9,526	39,270
5	Rhode Island......	511	680	616	371	105	183	356	2,001	7,162
6	Connecticut........	1,155	1,395	1,206	635	202	279	659	3,897	13,577
	MIDDLE ATLANTIC:									
7	New York.........	8,743	13,378	15,621	8,467	1,664	1,457	4,797	36,330	154,569
8	New Jersey........	2,007	3,367	2,996	1,622	470	595	1,352	10,997	35,449
9	Pennsylvania......	6,197	8,257	7,289	4,113	917	1,200	4,020	24,280	84,902
	E. NORTH CENTRAL:									
10	Ohio...............	3,192	4,452	4,270	2,674	673	864	2,102	12,089	44,277
11	Indiana............	1,964	2,346	1,963	1,086	255	302	1,520	6,419	20,425
12	Illinois............	3,725	5,360	5,104	2,916	689	799	1,968	12,639	49,521
13	Michigan...........	1,539	2,278	2,361	1,341	327	459	916	5,545	20,716
14	Wisconsin..........	2,034	2,719	3,778	1,274	272	316	1,142	6,092	18,946
	W. NORTH CENTRAL:									
15	Minnesota..........	1,541	1,753	1,850	783	132	166	1,009	4,507	13,228
16	Iowa...............	1,491	1,985	1,381	642	87	97	930	4,808	10,219
17	Missouri...........	2,433	2,791	1,904	942	238	284	1,783	7,311	18,713
18	North Dakota......	357	282	175	63	5	12	202	582	892
19	South Dakota......	485	588	265	61	9	6	280	1,219	1,552
20	Nebraska...........	963	1,029	572	231	34	55	536	2,108	4,036
21	Kansas.............	1,136	1,200	639	289	72	138	640	2,612	5,021
	SOUTH ATLANTIC:									
22	Delaware...........	123	228	183	78	26	30	125	736	1,902
23	Maryland..........	1,122	1,603	1,273	675	123	141	941	5,486	14,026
24	Dist. Columbia.....	125	181	192	71	10	16	42	498	1,743
25	Virginia...........	1,826	1,874	1,149	536	118	100	1,976	6,989	12,737
26	West Virginia......	755	869	649	340	78	94	569	2,449	6,850
27	North Carolina....	1,606	2,178	1,295	584	192	144	2,024	8,478	14,465
28	South Carolina....	570	571	434	229	95	105	621	2,388	5,756
29	Georgia............	1,394	1,499	1,055	538	170	147	1,492	6,813	15,586
30	Florida............	584	825	824	268	48	33	558	4,152	16,118
	E. SOUTH CENTRAL:									
31	Kentucky..........	1,196	1,323	912	369	85	72	1,149	3,938	9,077
32	Tennessee..........	1,455	1,411	969	508	132	114	1,301	4,427	11,346
33	Alabama...........	1,070	1,125	916	349	99	95	1,145	4,736	13,580
34	Mississippi........	759	749	593	257	59	38	869	3,411	9,175
	W. SOUTH CENTRAL:									
35	Arkansas...........	930	1,105	751	240	61	36	922	3,964	10,007
36	Louisiana..........	475	719	721	441	146	115	522	2,651	9,858
37	Oklahoma..........	710	848	541	215	59	72	397	1,825	4,217
38	Texas..............	1,440	1,936	1,391	628	166	163	1,091	5,415	13,511
	MOUNTAIN:									
39	Montana...........	445	474	247	86	17	21	289	1,008	1,942
40	Idaho..............	300	314	195	74	21	18	184	760	1,371
41	Wyoming...........	195	235	108	22	10	6	103	447	660
42	Colorado...........	830	903	598	211	43	46	439	2,212	5,452
43	New Mexico........	116	169	67	28	5	2	112	474	695
44	Arizona............	110	187	126	37	8	12	80	463	1,003
45	Utah...............	367	365	263	117	20	28	231	872	2,410
46	Nevada............	37	68	40	14	3	4	19	148	385
	PACIFIC:									
47	Washington........	1,100	1,517	1,330	673	163	135	530	3,606	12,810
48	Oregon............	664	851	712	343	68	69	373	2,229	6,130
49	California..........	2,451	4,331	3,232	1,326	275	327	1,313	9,880	28,562

GROUPED BY VALUE OF PRODUCTS: 1919, 1914, 1909, AND 1904—Continued.

[See note at head of this table, pp. 1016 and 1017.]

WAGE EARNERS IN ESTABLISHMENTS WITH PRODUCT OF—continued.			VALUE OF PRODUCTS OF ESTABLISHMENTS WITH PRODUCT OF—continued.						
$100,000 to $500,000.	$500,000 to $1,000,000.	$1,000,000 and over.	Less than $5,000.	$5,000 to $20,000.	$20,000 to $100,000.	$100,000 to $500,000.	$500,000 to $1,000,000.	$1,000,000 and over.	
						Expressed in thousands.			
16,399	10,497	49,826	$2,049	$9,818	$31,875	$69,480	$59,168	$284,432	1
13,249	7,754	55,332	783	4,658	17,584	51,659	36,558	295,963	2
8,929	5,740	10,312	994	6,132	24,818	43,889	30,861	61,414	3
102,035	73,906	488,109	4,385	36,153	164,771	498,897	410,220	2,896,755	4
19,728	14,467	95,951	1,403	7,412	28,541	86,576	74,244	549,147	5
33,671	30,617	210,251	2,825	14,897	54,356	144,982	145,474	1,029,898	6
293,380	162,129	576,925	22,063	147,171	732,563	1,894,735	1,163,979	4,906,494	7
74,298	60,449	326,141	5,244	37,194	135,069	368,846	330,320	2,795,392	8
199,349	120,070	703,216	15,474	89,388	333,503	932,560	641,105	5,303,673	9
123,388	85,097	463,780	8,121	49,106	201,111	607,923	475,436	3,758,612	10
53,434	34,373	161,409	5,009	25,008	91,905	245,150	174,838	1,356,843	11
122,637	76,663	389,686	9,758	58,637	233,014	678,033	488,267	3,957,536	12
61,765	43,258	339,042	3,961	24,871	109,296	306,924	232,661	2,788,476	13
49,743	36,452	151,574	5,180	30,218	171,478	270,723	188,578	1,180,807	14
24,092	14,509	58,278	4,053	21,303	90,270	157,105	93,622	851,777	15
21,019	8,489	35,086	3,884	20,733	64,432	136,851	58,984	460,589	16
38,395	27,059	101,776	6,200	29,518	87,948	210,689	166,777	1,093,076	17
2,104	145	547	959	2,801	7,338	13,341	3,069	29,866	18
1,405	1,150	776	1,375	5,863	11,567	11,900	7,003	24,463	19
6,834	2,936	20,071	2,500	10,273	26,185	52,104	24,576	480,404	20
10,127	5,374	37,275	2,890	12,255	28,143	66,112	51,751	752,516	21
3,475	2,984	19,813	333	2,473	8,100	17,673	19,385	117,109	22
29,066	14,772	76,049	2,707	17,339	57,807	148,744	86,730	560,618	23
3,065	800	4,334	300	2,022	9,272	15,092	7,205	34,935	24
25,943	15,985	55,722	4,435	19,269	48,627	122,011	83,698	365,472	25
20,239	11,440	41,489	1,816	9,372	28,917	81,612	54,131	296,123	26
33,265	29,584	69,843	4,277	22,894	56,696	142,031	136,344	581,566	27
12,010	13,175	45,500	1,294	6,181	19,454	52,592	67,156	234,776	28
26,795	20,311	52,444	3,395	16,033	45,941	124,494	119,926	383,448	29
21,585	11,162	20,840	1,336	9,101	37,703	63,667	33,352	68,168	30
17,507	9,356	28,313	3,071	13,986	41,839	82,666	59,419	194,679	31
27,181	17,791	33,121	3,546	14,711	43,702	120,788	92,035	281,471	32
21,265	15,407	51,026	2,650	11,795	38,806	82,471	69,706	287,303	33
17,755	11,115	15,235	1,883	7,627	25,987	58,807	43,400	60,043	34
13,380	8,415	13,266	2,319	11,680	32,062	53,760	41,629	58,863	35
27,140	22,217	35,877	1,245	7,913	34,920	108,104	105,645	418,362	36
6,087	3,904	13,073	1,846	8,820	24,159	47,539	40,091	278,908	37
25,201	16,026	46,278	3,904	20,895	61,577	143,677	112,761	657,182	38
3,738	1,717	8,466	1,239	4,753	10,697	18,010	12,151	119,815	39
2,138	2,545	6,919	870	3,428	8,411	16,289	14,624	36,889	40
5,424	(x)	(x)	497	2,446	4,369	74,133	(x)	(x)	41
7,532	3,975	15,644	2,130	9,526	27,126	47,420	28,979	160,441	42
2,097	2,358	(x)	297	1,788	2,609	5,922	7,241	(x)	43
1,874	1,062	4,046	304	2,032	5,348	9,031	5,650	98,404	44
4,751	1,827	8,777	905	3,892	11,893	24,788	13,980	101,475	45
533	190	1,844	105	706	2,143	3,097	1,877	14,946	46
26,962	21,908	67,112	2,885	16,172	61,124	148,750	112,443	468,249	47
14,296	8,630	26,901	1,691	9,077	31,975	77,259	46,693	200,087	48
48,480	24,765	130,692	6,695	46,263	144,252	296,917	189,644	1,297,434	49

TABLE 18.—ESTABLISHMENTS GROUPED BY VALUE OF PRODUCTS: 1919, 1914, 1909, AND 1904.

VALUE OF PRODUCT.	ESTABLISHMENTS.		WAGE EARNERS.		VALUE OF PRODUCTS.		VALUE ADDED BY MANUFACTURE.	
	Number.	Per cent distribution.	Average number.	Per cent distribution.	Amount.	Per cent distribution.	Amount.	Per cent distribution.
All classes:								
1919.........	290,105	100.0	9,096,372	100.0	$62,418,078,773	100.0	$25,041,698,490	100.0
1914.........	275,791	100.0	7,036,247	100.0	24,246,434,724	100.0	9,878,345,893	100.0
1909.........	268,491	100.0	6,615,046	100.0	20,672,051,870	100.0	8,529,260,992	100.0
1904.........	216,180	100.0	5,468,383	100.0	14,793,902,563	100.0	6,293,694,753	100.0
Less than $5,000:								
1919.............	65,485	22.6	45,813	0.5	167,085,044	0.3	106,653,362	0.4
1914.............	97,060	35.2	129,623	1.8	233,381,081	1.0	151,739,764	1.5
1909.............	93,349	34.8	142,430	2.2	222,463,847	1.1	144,246,008	1.7
1904.............	71,147	32.9	106,353	1.9	176,128,212	1.2	114,781,124	1.8
$5,000 to $20,000:								
1919.............	87,440	30.1	249,722	2.7	945,602,857	1.5	539,698,109	2.2
1914.............	87,931	31.9	429,037	6.1	905,693,168	3.7	507,430,875	5.1
1909	86,988	32.4	470,006	7.1	904,645,664	4.4	509,907,934	6.0
1904.............	72,791	33.7	419,466	7.7	751,047,759	5.1	424,129,643	6.7
$20,000 to $100,000:								
1919.............	77,911	26.9	793,528	8.7	3,571,283,301	5.7	1,747,729,538	7.0
1914.............	56,814	20.6	999,510	14.2	2,550,229,411	10.5	1,238,879,430	12.5
1909.............	57,270	21.3	1,090,449	16.5	2,544,426,711	12.3	1,258,317,991	14.8
1904.............	48,096	22.2	1,027,047	18.8	2,129,257,883	14.4	1,090,271,887	17.3
$100,000 to $500,000:								
1919.............	39,647	13.7	1,719,982	18.9	8,965,872,131	14.4	4,152,283,862	16.6
1914.............	25,847	9.4	[1]3,002,071	42.7	5,742,376,392	23.7	[1]3,888,094,982	39.4
1909 [1]...........	27,824	10.4	2,896,532	43.8	7,946,935,255	38.4	3,572,746,038	41.9
1904 [1]...........	22,216	10.3	2,515,064	46.0	6,109,012,538	41.3	2,782,641,883	44.2
$500,000 to $1,000,000:								
1919.............	9,208	3.2	1,114,615	12.3	6,467,131,823	10.4	2,882,619,691	11.5
1914.............	4,320	1.6	([2])	....	3,020,693,743	12.5	([2])	....
$1,000,000 and over:								
1919.............	10,414	3.6	5,172,712	56.9	42,301,103.617	67.8	15,612,713,928	62.3
1914.............	3,819	1.4	2,476,006	35.2	11,794,060,929	48.6	4,092,200,842	41.4
1909.............	3,060	1.1	2,015,629	30.5	9,053,580.393	43.8	3,044,043,021	35.7
1904.............	1,900	0.9	1,400,453	25.6	5,628,456,171	38.0	1,881,870,216	29.9
Average per establishment:								
1919.............	....	....	31.4	....	215,157	....	86,319	......
1914.............	....	....	25.5	....	87,916	....	35,818	......
1909.............	....	....	24.6	....	76,993	....	31,767	......
1904.............	....	....	25.3	....	68,433	....	29,113	......

[1] Includes the group "$500,000 to $1,000,000."   [2] Included in the group "$100,000 to $500,000."

TABLE 19.—CHARACTER OF OWNERSHIP: 1919, 1914, 1909, AND 1904.

CHARACTER OF OWNERSHIP.	NUMBER.		WAGE EARNERS.		VALUE OF PRODUCTS.			VALUE ADDED BY MANUFACTURE.		
	Establishments.	Per cent distribution.	Average number.	Average per establishment.	Amount.	Average per establishment.	Per cent distribution.	Amount.	Average per establishment.	Per cent distribution.
All classes:										
1919...	290,105	100.0	9,096,372	31.0	$62,418,078,773	$215,157	100.0	$25,041,698,490	$86,319	100.0
1914...	275,791	100.0	7,036,247	26.0	24,246,434,724	87,915	100.0	9,878,345,893	35,818	100.0
1909...	268,491	100.0	6,615,046	25.0	20,672,051,870	76,393	100.0	8,529,260,992	31,767	100.0
1904...	216,180	100.0	5,468,383	25.0	14,793,902,563	68,433	100.0	6,293,694,753	29,113	100.0
Individuals:										
1919.....	138,112	47.6	623,469	4.0	3,536,321,836	25,605	5.7	1,555,136,394	11,260	6.2
1914.....	142,436	51.6	707,568	5.0	1,925,518,298	13,518	7.9	903,524,881	6,343	9.1
1909.....	140,605	52.4	804,883	6.0	2,042,061,500	14,523	9.9	968,824,072	6,890	11.4
1904.....	113,946	52.7	755,923	7.0	1,702,830,624	14,944	11.5	824,292,887	7,234	13.1
Corporations:										
1919.....	91,517	31.5	7,875,132	86.0	54,744,392,855	598,188	87.7	21,817,546,565	238,399	87.1
1914.....	78,152	28.3	5,649,891	72.0	20,183,147,103	258,255	83.2	8,092,950,040	103,554	81.9
1909.....	69,501	25.9	5,002,393	72.0	16,341,116,634	235,121	79.0	6,582,207,117	94,707	77.2
1904.....	51,097	23.6	3,862,698	76.0	10,904,069,307	213,399	73.7	4,526,055,153	88,578	71.9
All others:										
1919.....	60,476	20.8	597,771	10.0	4,137,364,082	68,413	6.6	1,669,015,531	27,598	6.7
1914.....	55,203	20.0	678,788	12.0	2,137,769,323	38,726	8.8	881,870,972	15,975	8.9
1909.....	58,385	21.7	807,770	18.0	2,288,873,736	39,203	11.1	978,229,803	16,755	11.5
1904.....	51,137	23.7	849,762	21.0	2,187,002,632	42,768	14.8	943,346,713	18,447	15.0

TABLE 20.—CHARACTER OF OWNERSHIP, BY INDUSTRIES: 1919.

[NOTE.—In some industries, in order to avoid disclosing the returns for individual establishments, the figures for certain groups (represented by only one or two establishments) have been consolidated with those for some of the larger groups. In such case an (x) is placed in the column from which the figures have been omitted, and the figures for the groups with which they have been consolidated are printed in italics. In the totals for all industries combined, each establishment is classified under its proper group; consequently the sum of the figures presented in any given column does not equal the total at the head of the column, except in number of establishments.]

INDUSTRY.	CHARACTER OF OWNERSHIP.								
	Number of establishments owned by—			Average number of wage earners in establishments owned by—			Value of products of establishments owned by—		
	Individuals.	Corporations.	All others.	Individuals.	Corporations.	All others.	Individuals.	Corporations.	All others.
							Expressed in thousands of dollars.		
All industries	138,112	91,517	60,476	623,469	7,875,132	597,771	3,536,322	54,744,393	4,137,364
Aeroplanes, seaplanes, and airships, and parts	3	26	2	*65*	3,478	(x)	*276*	14,097	(x)
Agricultural implements	139	308	74	546	53,029	793	2,392	297,302	5,267
Aluminum manufactures	8	65	10	63	11,211	128	244	74,390	644
Ammunition		38	4		22,698	118		87,895	143
Artificial flowers	134	46	44	1,595	1,627	916	6,010	6,307	3,826
Artificial limbs	102	50	25	183	408	80	878	2,007	386
Artificial stone products	1,607	533	645	2,657	4,225	1,496	10,496	17,132	6,036
Artists' materials	31	24	3	*103*	823	(x)	*566*	4,942	(x)
Asbestos products, not including steam packing	7	37	2	*38*	3,616	(x)	*179*	23,799	(x)
Automobile bodies and parts	1,101	956	458	6,098	123,685	2,773	27,383	652,229	12,559
Automobiles	14	292	9	209	210,181	169	1,299	2,384,899	1,705
Automobile repairing	8,747	2,240	4,520	22,019	21,129	11,913	85,669	87,961	51,022
Awnings, tents, and sails	551	196	138	1,609	3,730	689	9,269	30,615	5,806
Babbitt metal and solder	28	75	15	99	2,155	118	932	55,567	2,518
Bags, other than paper, not including bags made in textile mills	78	96	42	629	9,529	598	4,888	202,019	7,152
Bags, paper, exclusive of those made in paper mills	19	48	8	226	3,694	248	1,282	43,786	2,196
Baking powders and yeast	24	52	12	16	3,302	13	192	45,875	163
Baskets, and rattan and willow ware	243	65	67	840	2,734	959	2,118	7,212	2,491
Bells	2	6	2	*22*	215	(x)	*133*	818	(x)
Belting and hose, rubber		15			5,826			34,211	
Belting and hose, woven, other than rubber	6	31	4	95	2,278	106	407	18,169	600
Belting, leather	37	112	23	253	2,377	135	2,754	36,129	1,598
Billiard tables, bowling alleys, and accessories	23	17	9	82	1,962	57	419	14,985	329
Blacking, stains, and dressings	78	97	45	362	1,985	108	3,197	19,856	2,231
Bluing	26	21	10	77	229	54	464	1,809	458
Bone, carbon, and lamp black	6	26	3	*139*	536	(x)	*1,488*	4,698	(x)
Bookbinding and blank-book making	586	291	236	4,034	13,727	2,600	11,382	47,427	7,212
Boot and shoe cut stock	98	95	59	1,113	7,504	1,098	12,315	122,796	26,092
Boot and shoe findings	174	143	110	1,691	5,038	2,212	11,015	34,803	17,007
Boots and shoes, not including rubber boots and shoes	328	898	223	11,580	184,167	15,302	56,984	1,017,908	80,149
Boots and shoes, rubber	1	24		(x)	*32,875*		(x)	*116,917*	
Boxes, cigar	97	52	40	1,789	2,325	1,104	4,101	6,113	2,896
Boxes, paper and other, not elsewhere specified	318	692	191	6,259	44,757	4,846	17,259	174,406	14,754
Boxes, wooden packing, except cigar boxes	370	552	218	3,631	33,934	4,880	17,419	140,302	20,097
Brass, bronze, and copper products	362	555	175	3,216	70,151	1,684	18,442	453,076	10,795
Bread and other bakery products	19,740	1,748	3,607	51,631	76,008	13,953	431,205	596,560	124,131
Brick and tile, terra-cotta, and fire-clay products	598	1,415	401	6,757	64,857	5,301	15,621	179,095	13,707
Brooms	678	154	202	1,912	3,254	1,147	9,612	14,585	6,008
Brushes	176	135	68	844	5,367	1,757	4,104	26,395	8,507
Butter	845	1,070	1,823	1,677	11,497	4,467	50,929	348,528	183,706
Buttons	255	167	135	2,130	11,760	1,687	5,850	31,108	4,882

TABLE 20.—CHARACTER OF OWNERSHIP, BY INDUSTRIES: 1919—Continued.

[See note at head of this table, p. 1022.]

INDUSTRY.	Number of establishments owned by—			Average number of wage earners in establishments owned by—			Value of products of establishments owned by—		
	Individuals.	Corporations.	All others.	Individuals.	Corporations.	All others.	Individuals.	Corporations.	All others.
							Expressed in thousands of dollars.		
Candles	5	11	3	17	494	30	170	3,005	176
Canning and preserving, fish	94	246	70	1,223	9,214	811	5,730	68,969	2,585
Canning and preserving, fruits and vegetables	1,222	1,015	845	7,764	41,300	11,801	32,589	298,476	71,178
Canning and preserving, oysters	22	29	14	266	707	216	535	2,152	289
Card cutting and designing	37	22	16	272	758	118	1,036	3,614	673
Cardboard, not made in paper mills	2	14	......	(x)	1,425	......	(x)	9,138	......
Carpets and rugs, other than rag	11	49	15	321	20,806	1,806	2,722	107,881	12,651
Carpets, rag	242	32	65	836	612	568	2,137	1,749	1,711
Carriage and wagon materials	100	111	47	512	5,628	369	1,812	23,222	1,731
Carriages and sleds, children's	40	51	12	417	6,211	58	1,592	22,676	239
Carriages and wagons, including repairs	1,533	249	504	3,799	12,136	2,238	13,654	68,712	9,097
Cars and general shop construction and repairs by electric-railroad companies	2	619	3	(x)	31,173	99	(x)	74,864	347
Cars and general shop construction and repairs by steam-railroad companies	......	1,743	1	......	484,437	(x)	......	1,279,235	(x)
Cars, electric-railroad, not including operations of railroad companies	1	6	......	(x)	2,920	......	(x)	18,442	......
Cars, steam-railroad, not including operations of railroad companies	......	98	1	......	52,298	(x)	......	538,223	(x)
Cash registers and calculating machines	11	48	6	49	16,457	38	177	83,164	198
Cement	1	118	4	(x)	25,322	202	(x)	174,149	1,116
Charcoal, not including production in the lumber and wood distillation industries	21	16	4	86	123	......	131	451	7
Cheese	1,688	505	1,337	1,238	1,288	1,471	65,389	29,676	48,391
Chemicals	48	514	36	201	55,071	314	1,959	433,055	3,645
Chewing gum	8	47	7	91	3,007	92	550	49,943	747
China decorating, not including that done in potteries	32	5	6	159	70	15	557	255	55
Chocolate and cocoa products	3	40	5	(x)	8,770	313	(x)	131,159	8,099
Cleansing and polishing preparations	215	224	60	248	1,559	148	2,040	22,053	2,610
Clocks	7	37	2	11	8,241	(x)	47	23,333	(x)
Cloth, sponging and refinishing	17	32	18	213	755	238	601	2,342	748
Clothing, horse	8	13	7	89	584	93	448	5,116	457
Clothing, men's	2,154	1,080	2,024	29,306	98,472	47,492	157,651	635,193	370,142
Clothing, men's, buttonholes	76	4	27	207	126	151	444	353	293
Clothing, women's	2,739	1,641	3,331	40,361	62,144	63,144	283,479	398,061	527,003
Coal-tar products	9	168	6	70	15,496	97	397	133,977	1,108
Coffee and spice, roasting and grinding	218	440	136	774	8,327	1,439	12,837	239,247	52,708
Coffins, burial cases, and undertakers' goods	73	235	43	560	10,421	909	2,999	56,679	4,699
Coke, not including gas-house coke	20	251	7	507	28,664	148	6,037	309,441	1,038
Collars and cuffs, men's	8	20	11	(x)	9,389	1,714	(x)	41,987	5,578
Combs and hairpins, not made from metal or rubber	17	22	6	414	1,509	306	1,355	4,267	944
Condensed milk	11	373	17	301	13,053	321	7,840	323,255	8,412
Confectionery and ice cream	3,486	1,555	1,583	12,680	72,865	10,103	85,956	481,845	69,408
Cooperage	522	384	193	1,665	10,307	1,247	11,668	67,792	8,776
Copper, tin, and sheet-iron work	2,920	914	962	8,652	14,614	4,374	40,973	93,703	25,638
Cordage and twine	19	95	6	500	17,003	119	2,736	129,976	654
Cordials and flavoring sirups	39	95	15	77	1,257	64	1,887	43,827	1,093
Cork, cutting	17	39	6	89	3,412	44	595	15,431	256
Corsets	64	109	15	722	15,185	2,508	2,686	63,199	9,657

TABLE 20.—CHARACTER OF OWNERSHIP, BY INDUSTRIES: 1919—Continued.

[See note at head of this table, p. 1022.]

	CHARACTER OF OWNERSHIP.								
INDUSTRY.	Number of establishments owned by—			Average number of wage earners in establishments owned by—			Value of products of establishments owned by—		
	Individuals.	Corporations.	All others.	Individuals.	Corporations.	All others.	Individuals.	Corporations.	All others.
							Expressed in thousands of dollars.		
Cotton goods	67	1,164	57	2,582	424,402	3,982	11,773	2,090,733	22,766
Cotton lace	3	39	2	39	6,451	(x)	184	29,213	(x)
Cotton small wares	32	104	28	623	8,031	742	3,255	34,456	3,186
Crucibles	2	20	.....	(x)	848	.....	(x)	5,294	....
Cutlery and edge tools	86	182	36	584	18,651	624	1,748	63,339	1,543
Dairymen's, poultrymen's, and apiarists' supplies	94	119	31	358	5,921	158	2,171	33,997	1,229
Dental goods	171	80	68	768	3,843	613	3,208	20,910	5,284
Drug grinding	7	19	5	44	1,265	38	190	16,174	574
Druggists' preparations	150	323	51	901	14,229	438	5,971	104,751	3,871
Dyeing and finishing textiles, exclusive of that done in textile mills	132	400	96	1,918	48,874	5,193	11,440	268,058	44,470
Dyestuffs and extracts—natural	38	96	10	156	4,160	26	3,406	49,692	646
Electrical machinery, apparatus, and supplies	218	1,066	120	1,661	209,704	1,009	9,127	983,624	5,217
Electroplating	281	94	140	1,209	1,134	681	3,692	4,587	2,111
Emery and other abrasive wheels	14	44	2	57	5,544	(x)	236	30,713	(x)
Enameling	40	19	15	211	384	99	475	1,833	337
Engines, steam, gas, and water	47	306	17	665	76,693	259	3,263	460,334	1,178
Engravers' materials	7	11	3	18	142	14	85	2,112	51
Engraving and diesinking	377	29	72	658	1,025	195	2,329	4,216	806
Engraving, steel and copper plate, including plate printing	226	132	63	1,174	5,021	819	3,138	18,064	3,007
Engraving, wood	36	9	10	36	157	42	136	752	266
Envelopes	13	85	8	114	7,745	270	283	38,143	1,238
Explosives	2	113	3	(x)	9,230	19	(x)	92,339	136
Fancy articles, not elsewhere specified	290	231	140	2,345	9,087	2,529	9,820	40,338	15,896
Feathers and plumes	125	41	50	1,177	925	1,402	5,409	3,955	6,014
Felt goods	1	46	2	(x)	5,236	(x)	(x)	39,230	(x)
Ferroalloys	2	27	1	98	2,246	(x)	1,139	37,445	(x)
Fertilizers	55	482	63	377	25,291	628	4,413	270,173	6,558
Files	11	35	4	108	5,493	166	247	16,984	386
Firearms	4	19	3	758	10,529	(x)	1,741	28,440	(x)
Fire extinguishers, chemical	10	18	4	57	681	39	391	4,851	321
Fireworks	22	33	2	55	1,167	(x)	138	4,492	(x)
Flags and banners	44	27	8	190	722	153	867	3,709	770
Flavoring extracts	212	180	61	236	1,707	245	3,619	23,044	3,454
Flax and hemp, dressed	6	10	4	51	316	53	459	1,703	207
Flour-mill and gristmill products	4,711	2,667	3,330	5,293	34,841	5,347	152,128	1,713,800	186,506
Food preparations, not elsewhere specified	811	742	444	2,335	25,350	2,680	29,978	559,611	42,009
Foundry and machine-shop products	3,706	5,568	1,660	25,448	437,378	19,941	105,414	2,092,276	91,561
Foundry supplies	9	62	5	47	823	36	525	9,356	74
Fuel, manufactured	......	10	1	......	171	(x)	......	1,974	(x)
Fur goods	876	213	726	4,167	4,866	4,606	43,962	52,199	76,977
Furnishing goods, men's	180	169	138	2,183	12,322	4,439	16,193	62,803	28,839
Furniture	974	1,613	567	8,423	120,230	9,678	34,938	433,454	42,964
Furs, dressed	49	62	30	657	3,894	524	3,322	13,520	3,543
Galvanizing	15	31	6	91	1,551	23	781	13,524	171
Gas and electric fixtures	95	191	55	699	8,650	446	3,613	36,261	2,394
Gas, illuminating and heating	13	951	58	369	41,970	569	1,350	325,164	2,765
Gas machines and gas and water meters	13	88	4	45	5,533	11	222	25,919	126
Glass	12	342	17	618	75,468	1,434	1,795	256,643	3,446
Glass, cutting, staining, and ornamenting	278	225	113	1,457	4,195	828	6,347	18,798	3,298
Gloves and mittens, cloth, not including gloves made in textile mills	42	106	34	529	7,804	653	1,567	24,020	2,633
Gloves and mittens, leather	143	108	104	1,485	5,757	3,443	7,349	23,341	16,251

TABLE **20.**—CHARACTER OF OWNERSHIP, BY INDUSTRIES: 1919—Continued.

[See note at head of this table, p. 1022.]

	CHARACTER OF OWNERSHIP.								
	Number of establishments owned by—			Average number of wage earners in establishments owned by—			Value of products of establishments owned by—		
INDUSTRY.							Individuals.	Corporations.	All others.
	Individuals.	Corporations.	All others.	Individuals.	Corporations.	All others.	Expressed in thousands of dollars.		
Glucose and starch	17	30	9	60	7,674	61	425	185,150	681
Glue, not elsewhere specified	9	47	6	9	4,092	163	194	30,734	1,206
Gold and silver, leaf and foil	56	13	18	216	281	453	924	2,090	1,448
Gold and silver, reducing and refining, not from the ore	45	26	16	89	470	85	4,962	46,041	4,480
Graphite, ground and refined	6	16	2	*52*	445	(x)	*381*	1,859	(x)
Grease and tallow, not including lubricating greases	212	164	106	664	5,654	329	5,992	57,019	4,254
Grindstones		20	3		*674*	(x)		*1,369*	(x)
Haircloth	6	7	5	85	186	154	690	1,560	1,065
Hair work	142	24	32	495	384	205	2,571	2,337	2,055
Hand stamps	167	76	55	286	1,259	174	1,291	5,540	908
Hardware	142	329	77	1,084	40,212	1,209	4,119	145,293	5,113
Hardware, saddlery	12	21	4	162	3,497	16	394	13,696	47
Hat and cap materials	55	44	34	278	2,268	463	1,917	20,686	3,918
Hats and caps, other than felt, straw, and wool	317	137	255	1,634	3,017	2,888	9,244	16,264	19,032
Hats, fur-felt	62	78	36	778	15,194	2,538	5,025	64,013	13,707
Hats, straw	40	75	33	906	5,357	1,039	4,751	22,612	4,824
Hats, wool-felt	16	15	9	116	1,176	156	607	5,439	694
Hones and whetstones	3	7	1	*13*	199	(x)	*24*	770	(x)
Horseshoes, not made in steel works or rolling mills	7	11	2	*9*	735	(x)	*43*	3,324	(x)
House-furnishing goods, not elsewhere specified	211	169	87	1,026	5,912	915	8,623	43,470	8,119
Ice, manufactured	545	1,911	411	2,061	26,183	2,003	8,826	119,718	8,461
Ink, printing	16	62	12	128	1,822	38	1,826	23,976	442
Ink, writing	27	23	11	55	627	20	482	5,837	115
Instruments, professional and scientific	120	179	52	695	14,748	488	2,890	53,153	2,094
Iron and steel, blast furnaces	4	187	4	466	40,722	472	3,320	785,955	5,192
Iron and steel, steel works and rolling mills	10	481	9	962	373,442	684	4,794	2,820,938	3,170
Iron and steel, bolts, nuts, washers, and rivets, not made in rolling mills	20	117	7	267	17,488	212	1,288	87,720	736
Iron and steel, cast-iron pipe	2	56	1	*208*	12,417	(x)	*832*	49,403	(x)
Iron and steel, doors and shutters	7	43	7	23	1,991	63	98	10,487	292
Iron and steel, forgings, not made in steel works or rolling mills	27	200	14	248	27,918	225	1,046	171,350	1,356
Iron and steel, nails and spikes, cut and wrought, including wire nails, not made in steel works or rolling mills	16	42	7	208	3,029	118	1,081	15,669	833
Iron and steel, tempering and welding	296	101	123	515	1,103	217	2,467	7,248	1,281
Iron and steel, wrought pipe	4	42	4	128	10,265	33	527	81,161	181
Ivory, shell, and bone work, not including combs and hairpins	23	13	8	166	521	155	493	1,875	449
Japanning	21	6	9	97	118	80	260	290	221
Jewelry	935	522	597	5,031	18,184	7,656	34,727	112,946	56,266
Jewelry and instrument cases	65	39	38	521	1,766	447	1,787	4,757	1,582
Jute goods	8	15	3	*3,140*	3,998	(x)	*15,452*	18,991	(x)
Knit goods	564	1,096	390	9,986	147,052	15,534	47,201	593,140	72,799
Labels and tags	30	69	20	261	4,708	258	938	22,007	1,299
Lamps and reflectors	46	95	30	223	7,806	331	991	35,612	1,496
Lapidary work	64	25	35	195	622	338	2,209	14,989	12,853
Lasts	15	38	11	314	2,484	112	1,292	10,634	545
Lead, bar, pipe, and sheet	1	30	1	(x)	*852*	(x)	(x)	*17,174*	(x)
Leather goods, not elsewhere specified	220	165	118	1,641	5,301	2,003	8,725	33,184	11,044

TABLE 20.—CHARACTER OF OWNERSHIP, BY INDUSTRIES: 1919—Continued.

[See note at head of this table, p. 1022.]

INDUSTRY.	CHARACTER OF OWNERSHIP.								
	Number of establishments owned by—			Average number of wage earners in establishments owned by—			Value of products of establishments owned by—		
	Individuals.	Corporations.	All others.	Individuals.	Corporations.	All others.	Individuals.	Corporations.	All others.
							Expressed in thousands of dollars.		
Leather, tanned, curried, and finished	114	453	113	2,353	6x,624	5,499	22,514	828,804	77,274
Lime	194	224	58	1,034	9,623	748	2,703	29,231	2,036
Linen goods		10			1,890			6,998	
Liquors, distilled	2	32		(x)	1,380		(x)	31,854	
Liquors, malt	78	607	44	1,393	32,316	550	19,758	354,923	5,224
Liquors, vinous	250	40	52	210	709	92	3,902	12,236	1,316
Lithographing	81	225	25	595	14,399	624	2,712	68,114	2,325
Locomotives, not made by railroad companies	1	16		(x)	26,715		(x)	156,270	
Looking-glass and picture frames	255	110	64	871	3,608	229	3,810	13,159	1,416
Lubricating greases	12	38	3	17	451	4	221	8,627	21
Lumber and timber products	15,280	3,829	7,010	72,365	351,830	56,750	187,804	1,050,373	149,294
Lumber, planing-mill products, not including planing mills connected with sawmills	1,877	2,349	1,083	10,241	68,062	8,653	52,737	397,594	50,107
Machine tools	46	320	37	650	50,100	2,361	2,082	200,731	9,587
Malt	2	51	2	31	1,321	(x)	822	38,518	(x)
Marble and stone work	2,469	762	1,009	7,110	20,599	5,059	37,107	67,947	24,111
Matches	3	18		18	3,708		57	18,439	
Mats and matting, from cocoa fiber, grass, and coir	1	9	2	(x)	955	118	(x)	4,452	409
Mattresses and spring beds, not elsewhere specified	514	325	202	2,012	9,161	1,464	13,570	59,637	10,746
Millinery and lace goods, not elsewhere specified	1,514	651	840	13,658	23,456	13,736	60,717	120,016	74,992
Mineral and soda waters	2,884	1,107	1,203	5,838	8,530	3,072	35,879	74,501	24,961
Minerals and earths, ground or otherwise treated	53	317	49	486	13,166	774	1,230	42,687	2,150
Mirrors, framed and unframed, not elsewhere specified	69	81	36	547	1,640	412	4,088	13,150	3,593
Models and patterns, not including paper patterns	532	145	251	2,337	3,160	1,452	7,756	12,034	5,510
Motorcycles, bicycles, and parts	10	37	4	28	10,477	381	127	51,336	1,643
Mucilage, paste, and other adhesives, not elsewhere specified	45	61	21	88	571	144	1,046	8,384	1,800
Musical instruments and materials, not elsewhere specified	144	62	34	298	3,573	242	1,386	10,369	751
Musical instruments, organs	19	34	15	270	1,549	122	936	4,555	482
Musical instruments, pianos	18	167	6	350	22,157	450	1,757	103,157	2,174
Musical instruments, piano and organ materials	27	80	6	172	10,339	498	525	34,664	1,601
Needles, pins, and hooks and eyes	16	66	10	436	8,749	109	1,203	27,871	231
Nets and seines	5	14		40	819		412	4,702	
Oil and cake, cottonseed	28	628	55	575	24,781	1,410	11,355	546,688	23,202
Oil, essential	51	17	10	46	223	52	778	4,744	176
Oil, linseed		24	2		2,173	(x)		120,638	(x)
Oil, not elsewhere specified	47	215	18	188	5,684	58	8,172	147,111	1,197
Oilcloth and linoleum, floor	1	19	1	(x)	5,414	(x)	(x)	52,673	(x)
Oilcloth, enameled	1	9	1	(x)	1,130	(x)	(x)	15,437	(x)
Oleomargarine and other butter substitutes	1	41		(x)	2,851		(x)	79,816	
Optical goods	194	244	68	1,079	10,152	3,492	4,803	37,620	11,295
Ordnance and accessories		25	1		11,328	(x)		69,496	(x)
Paints	93	451	57	411	16,370	704	5,146	241,018	10,550
Paper and wood pulp	33	647	49	648	110,134	2,977	3,879	759,533	24,647
Paper goods, not elsewhere specified	61	223	24	370	13,255	510	2,199	101,709	3,377
Paper patterns	9	9	1		25	(x)	115	1,413	(x)
Patent medicines and compounds	990	1,214	263	1,653	14,867	924	16,438	185,370	10,354
Paving materials	274	457	158	1,952	12,406	1,714	3,975	38,105	3,661
Peanuts, grading, roasting, cleaning, and shelling	24	44	10	191	2,115	154	1,657	28,535	3,162
Pencils, lead		12			5,970			24,134	
Pens, fountain and stylographic	14	30	12	269	2,804	134	1,061	13,965	971
Pens, gold	6	6	3	71	274	71	299	1,100	402

TABLE 20.—CHARACTER OF OWNERSHIP, BY INDUSTRIES: 1919—Continued.

[See note at head of this table, p. 1022.]

INDUSTRY.	Number of establishments owned by—			Average number of wage earners in establishments owned by—			Value of products of establishments owned by—		
	Individuals.	Corporations.	All others.	Individuals.	Corporations.	All others.	Individuals.	Corporations.	All others.
							Expressed in thousands of dollars.		
Perfumery and cosmetics	218	281	70	863	4,130	412	8,339	47,497	3,777
Petroleum, refining	8	297	15	196	58,521	172	9,467	1,617,694	5,372
Phonographs and graphophones	28	132	6	277	28,363	81	1,173	156,737	638
Photo-engraving	98	255	69	524	5,691	554	2,126	24,198	3,065
Photographic apparatus	19	43	6	57	2,473	25	326	8,941	117
Photographic materials	42	112	15	205	14,285	66	1,551	113,687	476
Pickles, preserves, and sauces	296	321	106	1,666	14,335	620	11,538	129,541	4,706
Pipes, tobacco	28	17	11	402	1,592	545	1,312	7,000	3,242
Plated ware	10	51	7	101	9,178	213	351	40,337	947
Plumbers' supplies, not elsewhere specified	35	160	19	472	12,577	543	2,649	54,813	2,593
Pocketbooks	49	36	54	561	1,378	966	2,426	5,963	6,161
Pottery	88	211	41	1,044	26,175	715	2,342	71,012	1,565
Poultry, killing and dressing, not done in slaughtering and meat-packing establishments	60	90	46	318	1,539	283	5,447	30,444	5,814
Printing and publishing, book and job	7,458	3,367	2,264	20,663	90,486	11,856	92,087	445,041	60,535
Printing and publishing, music	63	76	21	133	760	6	1,187	12,101	1,304
Printing and publishing, newspapers and periodicals	9,262	4,856	3,244	20,139	90,688	9,554	93,990	768,916	61,247
Printing materials	15	56	11	38	666	19	314	4,460	145
Pulp goods	3	35	2	5	3,036	(x)	31	23,577	(x)
Pumps, not including power pumps	32	77	18	91	4,540	753	688	26,032	4,936
Pumps, steam and other power	16	86	10	261	10,096	331	1,201	50,949	1,596
Refrigerators	30	73	19	372	5,193	221	1,766	22,868	1,415
Regalia, and society badges and emblems	60	41	14	252	1,862	109	1,360	7,679	356
Rice, cleaning and polishing	15	63	8	77	1,902	134	3,970	78,957	7,111
Roofing materials	38	122	18	166	8,642	63	1,111	83,965	819
Rubber tires, tubes, and rubber goods, not elsewhere specified	46	368	23	588	119,108	152	3,694	981,863	1,531
Rules, ivory and wood	7	5	1	19	149	(x)	85	396	(x)
Saddlery and harness	1,275	253	295	1,878	7,434	1,099	13,358	61,653	8,702
Safes and vaults	9	26	3	32	2,883	34	171	15,055	68
Salt	9	67	10	50	6,180	265	109	36,605	800
Sand and emery paper and cloth	1	10	1	(x)	771	(x)	(x)	9,304	(x)
Sand-lime brick	1	30	1	(x)	504	(x)	(x)	1,663	(x)
Sausage, not made in slaughtering and meat-packing establishments	404	99	130	1,505	1,314	652	23,275	21,969	11,366
Saws	38	53	21	115	5,274	121	575	30,208	678
Scales and balances	16	53	10	187	5,088	157	543	19,576	522
Screws, machine	33	93	17	281	9,720	261	994	37,844	1,177
Screws, wood		11			4,889			15,460	
Sewing-machine cases	2	3		(x)	4,171		(x)	14,243	
Sewing machines and attachments	11	27	2	89	14,970	(x)	257	43,438	(x)
Shipbuilding, steel	8	148	6	97	343,635	282	402	1,454,961	1,127
Shipbuilding, wooden, including boat building	457	300	156	2,474	36,798	4,160	10,160	142,809	12,903
Shirts	256	359	281	4,316	25,109	10,178	16,152	123,807	65,368
Show cases	42	48	29	246	1,390	221	1,037	6,123	1,134
Signs and advertising novelties	423	265	91	1,047	9,020	365	4,641	36,917	1,785
Silk goods, including throwsters	250	811	308	6,498	108,531	11,753	38,561	581,413	68,496
Silversmithing and silverware	25	57	17	167	5,779	507	981	25,871	2,274
Slaughtering and meat packing	481	582	241	3,267	155,379	2,350	110,823	4,049,077	86,390
Smelting and refining, copper		34			17,345			651,102	
Smelting and refining, lead	1	24		(x)	6,438		(x)	196,795	
Smelting and refining, zinc		39			13,796			104,123	
Smelting and refining, metals, not elsewhere specified	1	12		(x)	2,041		(x)	20,075	

TABLE 20.—CHARACTER OF OWNERSHIP, BY INDUSTRIES: 1919—Continued.

[See note at head of this table, p. 1022.]

INDUSTRY.	Number of establishments owned by—			Average number of wage earners in establishments owned by—			Value of products of establishments owned by—		
							Individuals.	Corporations.	All others.
	Individuals.	Corporations.	All others.	Individuals.	Corporations.	All others.	Expressed in thousands of dollars.		
Smelting and refining, not from the ore	15	51	15	92	1,913	162	2,252	42,761	5,233
Soap	87	222	39	299	19,780	357	4,518	308,621	3,601
Soda-water apparatus	24	33	9	84	2,383	132	522	13,928	735
Sporting and athletic goods	83	79	26	574	5,476	362	1,668	20,565	1,607
Springs, steel, car and carriage, not made in steel works or rolling mills	25	76	11	72	8,729	180	392	50,328	760
Stamped and enameled ware, not elsewhere specified	44	251	28	552	33,138	558	2,696	138,701	2,257
Stationery goods, not elsewhere specified	61	130	32	415	9,774	1,072	1,872	51,721	4,770
Statuary and art goods	101	44	50	354	885	227	995	3,163	862
Steam fittings and steam and hot-water heating apparatus	38	207	16	398	35,968	320	2,057	155,834	2,394
Steam packing	44	113	12	222	5,859	66	1,494	38,691	340
Steel barrels, drums, and tanks	3	26	4	25	3,260	37	220	24,477	246
Stencils and brands	43	23	18	85	282	50	305	1,063	230
Stereotyping and electrotyping	37	112	22	425	2,977	262	1,842	13,051	1,026
Stoves and hot-air furnaces	53	323	36	624	31,326	918	3,269	138,155	4,294
Stoves, gas and oil	41	113	22	89	10,294	182	627	53,768	1,397
Structural ironwork, not made in steel works or rolling mills	382	612	152	2,676	38,969	2,317	13,669	266,047	15,246
Sugar, beet	1	84	......	(x)	11,781	......	(x)	149,156	......
Sugar, cane	65	102	35	1,526	4,575	(x)	12,584	45,157	(x)
Sugar, refining, not including beet sugar	......	17	3	......	16,237	1,965	......	647,850	83,137
Sulphuric, nitric, and mixed acids	......	39	......	......	4,961	......	......	31,470	......
Surgical appliances	145	92	31	471	5,725	194	2,004	40,565	965
Suspenders, garters, and elastic woven goods	87	68	41	818	9,020	1,019	4,733	48,613	7,429
Textile machinery and parts	154	202	76	1,696	28,895	1,232	6,198	111,446	4,445
Theatrical scenery	4	12	1	15	134	(x)	180	887	(x)
Tin and other foils, not elsewhere specified	3	12	......	5	1,903	......	8	17,913	......
Tin plate and terneplate	7	16	1	34	3,088	(x)	146	97,259	(x)
Tinware, not elsewhere specified	70	188	43	622	32,783	981	3,117	225,412	5,435
Tobacco, chewing and smoking, and snuff	207	105	53	704	17,180	440	6,040	230,247	2,984
Tobacco, cigars and cigarettes	8,026	796	1,104	25,749	96,849	16,175	85,637	639,487	48,538
Tools, not elsewhere specified	392	537	196	2,448	31,037	2,100	8,760	127,490	7,952
Toys and games	207	223	111	1,725	10,519	1,957	5,886	33,272	6,499
Trunks and valises	264	194	139	1,649	8,237	1,584	10,337	43,572	10,023
Turpentine and rosin	547	247	397	7,738	11,552	8,777	12,611	24,946	15,493
Type founding	7	14	2	68	742	(x)	233	1,857	(x)
Typewriters and supplies	17	62	9	87	15,493	89	909	51,105	724
Umbrellas and canes	109	37	52	505	1,689	1,174	3,674	12,111	9,524
Upholstering materials, not elsewhere specified	48	82	33	388	4,130	292	2,120	36,722	1,048
Varnishes	35	177	17	118	3,867	37	2,822	79,810	1,000
Vault lights and ventilators	12	23	6	60	222	34	319	1,502	335
Vinegar and cider	470	135	115	343	1,441	197	3,832	18,285	2,606
Wallpaper, not made in paper mills	3	45	......	128	4,134	......	941	22,107	......
Wall plaster and composition flooring	19	137	5	119	4,980	24	709	26,033	133
Washing machines and clothes wringers	20	75	10	73	5,782	101	491	39,214	1,066
Waste	24	52	16	244	2,271	171	2,603	24,725	2,372
Watch and clock materials, except watch cases	12	10	5	160	342	80	328	854	160
Watch cases	8	22	3	30	3,852	18	377	19,153	89
Watches	1	16	1	(x)	15,888	(x)	(x)	32,044	(x)
Wheelbarrows	2	7	2	32	259	(x)	78	1,602	(x)
Whips	15	6	5	114	512	91	410	2,202	374
Windmills	8	22	1	72	1,860	(x)	234	9,699	(x)

TABLE 20.—CHARACTER OF OWNERSHIP, BY INDUSTRIES: 1919—Continued.

[See note at head of this table, p. 1022.]

INDUSTRY.	CHARACTER OF OWNERSHIP.								
	Number of establishments owned by—			Average number of wage earners in establishments owned by—·			Value of products of establishments owned by—		
	Individuals.	Corporations.	All others.	Individuals.	Corporations.	All others.	Individuals.	Corporations.	All others.
							Expressed in thousands of dollars.		
Window and door screens and weather strips...............	114	63	37	293	1,766	120	1,102	9,294	537
Window shades and fixtures......	170	76	41	553	3,624	234	4,433	22,020	2,738
Wire............................	4	58	4	21	19,478	242	112	160,926	1,114
Wirework, including wire rope and cable, not elsewhere specified	229	237	92	843	13,754	627	3,871	83,847	2,831
Wood distillation................	9	99	7	164	4,690	92	483	31,888	174
Wood preserving.................	1	72	......	(x)	3,978	......	(x)	33,239	......
Wood, turned and carved........	349	224	149	1,948	7,331	1,370	5,717	24,998	4,132
Wooden goods, not elsewhere specified......................	109	111	32	631	5,417	395	2,472	18,090	1,231
Wool pulling....................	7	12	5	98	344	263	3,253	8,119	5,989
Wool scouring..................	6	26	1	549	1,628	(x)	1,594	12,086	(x)
Wool shoddy....................	26	36	16	230	2,005	331	1,022	18,207	3,125
Woolen goods...................	94	399	67	3,428	54,849	4,680	19,007	320,026	25,864
Worsted goods..................	27	229	36	2,003	96,994	4,833	14,587	649,944	36,006
All other industries.............	20	15	14	47	1,030	179	1,157	3,389	1,774

TABLE **21.**—CHARACTER OF OWNERSHIP, BY GEOGRAPHIC

| | DIVISION AND STATE. | CHARACTER OF OWNERSHIP. | | | | | |
| | | Number of establishments owned by— | | | Wage earners in establishments owned by— | | |
		Individuals.	Corporations.	All others.	Individuals.	Corporations.	All others.
	UNITED STATES:						
1	1919	138,112	91,517	60,476	623,469	7,875,132	597,771
2	1914	142,436	78,152	55,203	707,568	5,649,891	678,788
3	1909	140,605	69,501	58,385	804,883	5,002,393	807,770
4	1904	113,946	51,097	51,137	755,923	3,862,698	849,762
	GEOGRAPHIC DIVISIONS:						
	New England—						
5	1919	11,971	9,238	4,319	73,849	1,199,774	77,766
6	1914	12,767	7,953	4,473	87,274	960,685	92,274
7	1909	13,163	7,300	4,888	100,020	898,877	102,393
8	1904	11,638	5,572	5,069	103,203	708,783	128,766
	Middle Atlantic—						
9	1919	42,728	26,219	19,413	239,170	2,370,359	263,124
10	1914	46,819	21,591	17,056	297,296	1,733,012	325,632
11	1909	46,346	17,785	17,184	338,983	1,489,889	378,875
12	1904	39,640	12,460	15,599	323,858	1,160,165	402,542
	East North Central—						
13	1919	27,261	22,920	11,151	102,137	2,212,424	82,057
14	1914	28,857	19,871	11,168	114,616	1,474,227	91,438
15	1909	30,077	17,755	12,181	131,296	1,261,125	121,343
16	1904	26,024	14,093	11,637	133,720	961,109	129,699
	West North Central—						
17	1919	14,454	8,137	6,575	38,162	434,327	27,146
18	1914	14,310	7,000	5,889	38,052	316,802	26,741
19	1909	14,296	6,649	6,226	41,351	302,725	30,261
20	1904	11,103	4,816	5,573	38,668	240,815	32,878
	South Atlantic—						
21	1919	14,993	8,477	6,506	70,211	686,354	60,647
22	1914	14,909	7,532	6,484	82,518	524,116	78,618
23	1909	14,304	6,765	7,019	93,351	468,923	100,741
24	1904	9,502	4,820	5,242	74,415	[1] 358,566	89,630
	East South Central—						
25	1919	7,088	3,875	3,692	31,202	269,615	28,409
26	1914	7,315	3,673	3,422	35,220	202,511	26,647
27	1909	7,751	3,558	4,072	41,241	188,652	31,879
28	1904	4,740	2,672	2,899	31,074	161,915	28,240
	West South Central—						
29	1919	6,767	4,170	2,972	27,791	234,829	22,624
30	1914	6,486	3,533	2,398	23,510	171,491	16,939
31	1909	6,156	3,403	2,780	28,284	156,120	20,116
32	1904	4,160	2,298	1,821	21,524	105,364	16,582
	Mountain—						
33	1919	3,651	2,502	1,459	8,121	96,691	4,404
34	1914	3,108	1,969	1,002	6,640	70,999	3,474
35	1909	2,520	1,743	991	7,227	64,155	4,053
36	1904	1,834	1,114	662	5,253	[1] 44,566	2,971
	Pacific—						
37	1919	9,199	5,979	4,389	32,826	370,759	31,594
38	1914	7,865	5,030	3,311	22,442	196,048	17,025
39	1909	5,992	4,543	3,044	23,130	171,927	18,109
40	1904	5,305	3,252	2,635	24,208	121,428	18,441
	NEW ENGLAND:						
41	Maine	1,550	894	551	6,215	78,642	3,794
42	New Hampshire	713	461	325	5,762	71,774	5,538
43	Vermont	900	469	421	3,841	26,243	3,407
44	Massachusetts	5,319	4,697	1,890	41,322	621,783	50,731
45	Rhode Island	1,210	853	403	7,386	125,659	6,620
46	Connecticut	2,279	1,864	729	9,323	275,673	7,676
	MIDDLE ATLANTIC:						
47	New York	23,108	14,383	11,839	134,143	933,622	160,365
48	New Jersey	5,376	3,944	1,737	27,375	454,860	26,451
49	Pennsylvania	14,244	7,892	5,837	77,652	981,877	76,308
	EAST NORTH CENTRAL:						
50	Ohio	6,490	6,766	2,869	28,421	678,849	23,463
51	Indiana	3,539	2,963	1,414	11,998	254,627	10,955
52	Illinois	8,771	6,895	2,927	36,105	589,978	27,031
53	Michigan	3,572	3,249	1,484	14,730	444,516	11,996
54	Wisconsin	4,889	3,047	2,457	10,883	244,454	8,612

[1] Includes 3 establishments of the group "All others."

DIVISIONS AND STATES: 1919, 1914, 1909, AND 1904.

CHARACTER OF OWNERSHIP—continued.

Value of products of establishments owned by—			Value added by manufacture in establishments owned by—			
Individuals.	Corporations.	All others.	Individuals.	Corporations.	All others.	
$3,536,321,836	$54,744,392,855	$4,137,364,082	$1,555,136,394	$21,817,546,565	$1,669,015,531	1
1,925,518,298	20,183,147,103	2,137,769,323	903,524,881	8,092,950,040	881,870,972	2
2,042,061,500	16,341,116,634	2,288,873,736	968,824,072	6,582,207,117	978,229,803	3
1,702,830,624	10,904,069,307	2,187,002,632	824,292,887	4,526,055,153	943,346,713	4
371,788,438	6,370,623,061	440,659,300	170,132,752	2,868,394,514	192,635,374	5
217,020,541	2,455,017,579	254,637,272	103,477,799	1,062,551,397	102,972,234	6
232,733,537	2,173,070,560	264,261,017	112,908,952	966,012,379	114,846,905	7
219,705,940	1,509,457,541	296,834,956	105,833,468	679,504,971	124,387,096	8
1,509,459,164	16,329,608,188	2,015,705,408	662,923,155	6,925,107,175	842,646,604	9
835,065,624	6,187,127,321	1,031,451,020	386,928,960	2,547,374,814	438,347,520	10
903,266,088	5,133,389,739	1,105,105,475	424,775,302	2,078,262,639	479,225,632	11
737,324,146	3,417,242,344	1,063,699,446	353,947,341	1,438,265,811	464,057,615	12
655,570,835	16,483,878,949	598,029,815	261,656,652	6,624,335,544	229,800,314	13
361,863,793	5,845,641,117	334,755,643	163,295,078	2,444,587,165	139,339,593	14
374,810,758	4,434,329,994	402,561,412	167,870,784	1,843,830,693	165,528,692	15
317,085,630	2,913,000,832	375,281,670	151,986,538	1,250,309,920	157,534,743	16
223,513,695	4,693,649,289	269,901,782	96,010,525	1,236,308,223	76,620,792	17
133,583,366	1,746,001,245	152,607,666	61,529,877	529,029,929	43,791,713	18
143,263,021	1,513,583,331	147,052,198	62,599,219	455,459,503	43,984,725	19
118,090,743	1,044,005,587	122,349,472	51,061,709	328,521,956	42,851,485	20
281,876,983	3,899,341,957	273,932,751	133,121,539	1,609,236,069	116,529,396	21
149,542,786	1,374,488,257	158,968,056	72,811,615	533,716,371	73,402,747	22
149,029,496	1,059,302,614	172,854,100	75,439,938	434,280,550	81,461,360	23
117,077,695	1 701,534,357	155,416,363	59,960,439	1 289,831,200	74,135,005	24
117,512,367	1,400,196,233	124,682,861	58,103,133	549,384,124	57,079,687	25
60,570,451	582,699,672	57,398,003	32,303,023	255,174,065	26,180,124	26
72,168,688	494,623,131	63,696,274	40,107,574	222,304,156	31,913,112	27
55,320,418	349,227,144	59,788,249	29,859,968	154,043,519	28,275,861	28
136,511,888	2,007,929,685	133,419,720	60,818,398	617,745,588	51,303,736	29
57,861,759	690,708,525	53,967,947	27,986,939	226,827,766	20,816,680	30
62,574,834	509,339,325	53,528,886	31,434,661	188,485,184	23,392,104	31
53,313,873	315,236,430	46,681,179	25,837,178	122,510,647	20,051,424	32
44,754,332	850,838,008	27,083,752	21,482,099	278,510,406	12,444,469	33
23,287,820	401,352,064	12,928,026	12,310,269	147,120,128	5,922,577	34
22,182,329	328,459,829	13,353,440	12,493,789	115,507,479	7,302,098	35
15,545,795	1 230,401,412	8,716,057	8,771,244	1 88,139,454	4,940,219	36
195,334,134	2,708,327,485	253,948,693	90,888,141	1,108,524,922	89,955,159	37
86,722,158	900,111,323	81,055,690	42,881,321	346,568,405	31,097,784	38
82,032,749	695,018,111	66,460,934	41,193,853	278,064,534	30,575,175	39
69,366,384	423,992,759	58,206,141	37,035,002	174,940,797	27,100,143	40
29,278,873	410,003,137	17,539,773	14,065,265	180,525,294	7,662,701	41
23,505,739	358,832,142	24,867,053	11,342,333	145,211,659	11,123,325	42
19,712,681	130,015,057	18,380,334	8,990,191	56,883,625	7,061,675	43
219,327,951	3,483,117,043	308,736,538	97,330,982	1,519,657,763	133,479,751	44
33,493,110	681,416,232	32,413,516	15,192,456	300,062,750	16,078,449	45
46,470,084	1,307,239,450	38,722,086	23,211,525	666,053,423	17,229,473	46
925,821,484	6,548,076,609	1,393,106,813	414,831,676	2,918,332,722	590,626,589	47
152,512,567	3,367,501,291	152,051,129	66,359,462	1,270,813,586	64,418,660	48
431,125,113	6,414,030,288	470,547,466	181,732,017	2,735,960,867	187,601,355	49
157,660,289	4,790,633,085	152,015,354	69,084,161	2,053,180,117	66,096,579	50
64,089,047	1,774,635,258	60,029,082	27,895,287	671,500,850	24,406,682	51
225,940,504	5,004,523,563	194,780,627	97,107,048	1,754,699,526	85,167,674	52
92,181,144	3,299,255,502	74,751,837	40,010,132	1,475,524,905	31,410,203	53
115,699,851	1,614,831,541	116,452,915	27,560,024	669,430,146	22,719,176	54

TABLE 21.—CHARACTER OF OWNERSHIP, BY GEOGRAPHIC

	DIVISION AND STATE.	CHARACTER OF OWNERSHIP.					
		Number of establishments owned by—			Wage earners in establishments owned by—		
		Individuals.	Corporations.	All others.	Individuals.	Corporations.	All others.
	WEST NORTH CENTRAL:						
1	Minnesota	2,653	1,809	1,763	7,827	99,983	7,813
2	Iowa	2,767	1,540	1,376	6,912	68,089	5,550
3	Missouri	4,209	2,802	1,581	13,093	174,296	7,648
4	North Dakota	451	268	175	583	3,421	468
5	South Dakota	797	288	329	1,328	4,388	666
6	Nebraska	1,638	649	597	3,256	31,499	1,766
7	Kansas	1,939	781	754	5,163	52,651	3,235
	SOUTH ATLANTIC:						
8	Delaware	321	228	119	1,519	26,810	706
9	Maryland	2,663	1,209	1,065	14,395	110,856	15,091
10	District of Columbia	309	178	108	1,617	8,086	779
11	Virginia	2,937	1,379	1,287	10,801	101,457	7,094
12	West Virginia	1,199	1,021	565	3,578	75,883	3,575
13	North Carolina	3,065	1,608	1,326	13,084	135,350	9,225
14	South Carolina	871	728	405	4,062	72,520	2,868
15	Georgia	2,399	1,376	1,028	11,946	100,698	10,797
16	Florida	1,229	750	603	9,209	54,694	10,512
	EAST SOUTH CENTRAL:						
17	Kentucky	1,890	1,150	917	5,547	58,897	4,896
18	Tennessee	2,125	1,286	1,178	7,611	79,334	8,222
19	Alabama	1,791	941	922	9,708	89,464	7,987
20	Mississippi	1,282	498	675	8,336	41,920	7,304
	WEST SOUTH CENTRAL:						
21	Arkansas	1,553	691	879	7,352	36,567	6,035
22	Louisiana	1,103	1,118	396	6,115	86,357	5,793
23	Oklahoma	1,264	708	473	2,891	25,267	1,345
24	Texas	2,847	1,653	1,224	11,433	86,638	9,451
	MOUNTAIN:						
25	Montana	697	353	240	1,662	14,839	659
26	Idaho	447	284	191	1,051	12,084	782
27	Wyoming	296	165	115	461	6,014	159
28	Colorado	1,301	884	446	2,943	30,911	1,400
29	New Mexico	181	135	71	392	5,158	186
30	Arizona	227	161	92	618	7,660	250
31	Utah	435	453	272	886	17,096	886
32	Nevada	67	67	32	108	2,929	82
	PACIFIC:						
33	Washington	2,011	1,913	994	6,918	120,361	5,649
34	Oregon	1,146	934	627	3,415	50,860	4,284
35	California	6,042	3,132	2,768	22,493	199,538	21,661

DIVISIONS AND STATES: 1919, 1914, 1909, AND 1904—Continued.

CHARACTER OF OWNERSHIP—continued.					
Value of products of establishments owned by—			Value added by manufacture in establishments owned by—		
Individuals.	Corporations.	All others.	Individuals.	Corporations.	All others.	
$48,556,598	$1,069,259,122	$100,314,015	$19,260,597	$292,840,170	$22,939,191	1
41,052,132	644,752,520	59,668,045	17,973,926	190,437,574	16,820,390	2
69,526,094	1,480,883,324	43,798,920	31,362,664	487,843,789	18,544,721	3
5,191,635	45,548,509	6,633,478	2,036,853	9,502,872	1,344,398	4
8,397,020	48,198,970	5,574,792	4,054,313	13,026,642	2,103,957	5
21,497,462	555,935,574	18,609,462	8,982,438	100,758,225	5,527,713	6
29,292,754	849,071,270	35,303,070	12,339,734	141,898,951	9,340,422	7
9,607,487	150,957,146	4,508,376	3,136,143	74,823,774	1,680,159	8
81,391,812	707,408,302	85,144,660	32,621,368	258,834,823	33,141,204	9
8,788,904	53,176,333	6,861,333	4,335,666	29,414,529	4,136,275	10
42,956,484	560,599,658	39,955,479	19,108,309	239,253,525	13,608,954	11
19,982,517	428,213,176	23,775,184	9,013,245	184,062,230	7,954,806	12
48,846,110	853,423,735	41,538,104	26,183,197	371,801,643	18,916,928	13
13,478,065	357,107,899	10,867,020	6,997,868	141,702,301	4,766,428	14
34,535,089	622,245,546	36,456,461	18,747,064	217,151,329	16,848,646	15
22,290,515	166,210,162	24,826,134	12,978,679	92,191,912	15,475,996	16
26,994,727	338,646,978	30,018,712	11,305,235	138,048,865	10,590,691	17
36,498,083	474,208,615	45,546,464	15,301,609	177,762,690	18,422,133	18
28,455,577	437,969,430	26,305,888	16,204,105	161,039,809	14,822,691	19
25,563,980	149,371,210	22,811,797	15,292,184	72,532,760	13,244,172	20
25,845,399	149,038,772	25,428,687	13,568,895	71,507,400	12,423,586	21
30,568,791	609,292,719	36,328,260	12,241,593	220,793,463	11,750,847	22
22,749,408	367,461,271	11,152,190	8,950,774	75,646,785	4,159,481	23
57,348,290	882,136,923	60,510,583	26,057,136	249,797,940	22,969,822	24
8,372,148	153,484,858	4,807,512	4,297,066	38,298,647	1,916,881	25
5,704,034	70,230,068	4,576,647	2,701,482	31,830,993	2,029,769	26
2,899,804	77,333,678	1,211,912	1,486,849	37,047,616	660,401	27
16,054,897	250,927,940	8,639,498	7,854,672	89,001,458	3,895,930	28
2,091,542	15,001,235	763,825	893,625	8,790,961	444,533	29
3,554,146	115,651,302	1,563,664	1,563,877	25,774,143	785,655	30
5,336,254	146,593,052	5,003,765	2,303,399	42,021,437	2,453,886	31
741,507	21,615,875	516,929	381,129	5,745,151	257,414	32
38,257,362	739,639,897	31,725,725	19,580,678	329,471,376	17,393,399	33
19,399,351	322,331,966	25,051,310	9,490,384	140,118,244	10,967,958	34
137,677,421	1,646,355,622	197,171,658	61,817,079	638,935,302	61,593,802	35

TABLE **22.**—POWER USED IN MANUFACTURING INDUSTRIES: 1879 TO 1919.

POWER.	1919	1914	1909	1904	1899	1889	1879
Number of establishments..	290,105	275,791	268,491	216,180	207,514	355,405	253,852
Number of establishments reporting power..........	237,854	205,590	185,042	134,481	133,418	100,726	85,923
Primary horsepower, total..	29,504,792	22,437,072	18,675,376	13,487,707	10,097,893	5,938,635	3,410,837
Average horsepower per establishment.........	124.0	109.1	100.9	100.3	75.7	59.0	39.7
Owned................	20,062,636	18,409,941	16,802,706	12,854,805	9,778,418	5,850,064	3,410,837
Steam engines and turbines:							
Number...............	122,628	137,172	153,525	127,267	130,710	91,403	56,483
Horsepower............	17,037,973	15,591,593	¹14,228,632	¹10,917,502	¹8,189,564	¹4,586,089	2,185,458
Internal-combustion engines:							
Number...............	33,407	37,693	34,356	21,515	14,334	(²)	(²)
Horsepower............	1,259,400	991,905	751,186	289,423	134,742	8,930	(²)
Water wheels and motors:							
Number...............	14,008	18,069	21,282	20,992	23,099	39,005	55,404
Horsepower............	1,765,263	1,826,443	1,822,888	1,647,880	1,454,112	1,255,045	1,225,379
Rented...............	9,442,156	4,027,131	1,872,670	632,902	319,475	88,571	(²)
Electric:							
Motors...............	996,000	451,002	199,309	(²)	(²)	(²)	(²)
Horsepower............	9,347,556	3,897,248	1,749,031	441,589	182,562	(²)	(²)
Other horsepower...........	94,600	129,883	123,639	191,313	136,913	88,571	(²)
Electric...............	16,317,277	8,835,970	4,817,140	1,592,475	492,936	15,569	(²)
Rented:							
Motors...............	996,000	451,002	199,309	(²)	(²)	(²)	(²)
Horsepower............	9,347,556	3,897,248	1,749,031	441,589	182,562	(²)	(²)
Generated by establishment reporting:							
Motors...............	487,021	321,360	189,545	73,119	16,891	(²)	(²)
Horsepower............	6,969,721	4,938,722	3,068,109	1,150,886	310,374	(²)	(²)

¹ Includes 29,293 horsepower reported as "other" owned power in 1909; 92,154 horsepower in 1904; 49,985 horsepower in 1899; and 4,784 horsepower in 1889.
² Figures not available.

TABLE 23.—HORSEPOWER IN LEADING INDUSTRIES: 1919, 1914, 1909, AND 1904.

INDUSTRY.	Census year.	PRIMARY HORSEPOWER.						Electric horsepower owned and rented.
		Total.	Owned.			Rented.		
			Steam engines and turbines.	Water wheels and motors.	Internal-combustion engines.	Electric.	Other.	
All industries................	1919	29,504,792	17,037,973	1,765,263	1,259,400	9,347,556	94,600	16,317,277
	1914	22,437,072	15,591,593	1,826,443	991,905	3,897,248	129,883	8,835,970
	1909	18,675,376	114,228,632	1,822,888	751,186	1,749,031	123,639	4,817,140
	1904	13,487,707	110,917,502	1,647,880	289,423	441,589	191,313	1,592,475
Industries with over 18,000 wage earners in 1919:								
Agricultural implements.........	1919	128,249	69,942	6,373	4,092	47,842	....	100,263
	1914	121,428	79,688	5,691	5,113	30,764	172	83,117
	1909	100,601	71,894	8,390	4,433	15,684	200	38,905
	1904	89,738	77,175	6,300	2,360	3,828	75	20,713
Automobiles, including bodies and parts.	1919	544,242	146,212	566	12,927	379,388	5,149	490,560
	1914	173,684	60,233	411	10,075	102,156	809	135,818
	1909	75,550	39,325	287	7,000	27,641	1,297	41,829
	1904	10,109	7,376	80	1,459	1,051	143	4,229
Boots and shoes, including cut stock and findings.	1919	140,317	62,654	2,483	991	68,176	6,013	97,852
	1914	112,929	64 236	2,066	3,729	37,389	5,509	61,657
	1909	96,302	60,772	2,815	3,532	17,381	11,802	32,381
	1904	63,968	44,412	2,270	2,676	5,959	8,651	12,663
Boots and shoes, rubber.........	1919	49,400	21,220	2,462	....	25,718	....	28,320
	1914	24,621	19,885	1,275	20	3,381	60	6,607
	1909	25,903	22,293	1,883	....	1,712	15	3,407
	1904	26,084	24,145	1,300	....	39	600	1,191
Boxes, paper and other, not elsewhere specified.	1919	54,955	22,471	1,964	1,124	29,116	280	38,235
	1914	38,179	18,734	1,979	1,709	14,918	839	22,722
	1909	23,323	10,730	2,425	1,621	6,927	1,620	9,415
	1904	15,117	8,343	1,718	1,518	2,138	1,400	3,057
Brass, bronze, and copper products	1919	265,688	116,517	2,320	3,540	142,996	315	183,594
	1914	122,700	78,639	3,291	8,371	31,673	726	64,868
	1909	106,120	78,101	3,374	4,890	18,399	1,356	33,462
	1904	69,494	59,063	2,959	1,834	3,143	2,495	8,846
Bread and other bakery products.	1919	165,950	34,250	522	5,274	125,665	239	146,388
	1914	107,771	30,095	369	7,400	68,933	974	86,779
	1909	65,298	25,509	334	8,166	31,160	129	39,795
	1904	37,241	22,650	452	5,675	8,363	101	11,993
Brick, tile, pottery, and other clay products.	1919	439,194	304,094	146	18,617	115,698	639	148,061
	1914	470,758	379,626	490	21,669	68,638	335	95,080
	1909	451,186	415,486	367	14,968	20,263	102	31,773
	1904	360,280	345,879	813	8,410	4,413	765	7,720
Butter, cheese, and condensed milk.	1919	168,871	104,223	1,555	9,294	53,479	320	70,562
	1914	130,862	104,729	1,274	7,229	17,027	603	23,061
	1909	101,349	90,933	1,465	3,373	5,366	212	8,276
	1904	93,845	88,923	1,411	1,800	1,597	114	2,378
Canning and preserving.........	1919	180,812	114,140	140	9,961	56,220	351	72,674
	1914	120,004	90,778	877	8,967	18,726	656	28,438
	1909	81,179	70,392	398	4,519	5,469	401	8,728
	1904	60,831	56,122	460	1,962	1,776	511	3,150
Carpets and rugs, other than rag..	1919	38,170	28,777	2,207	85	6,524	577	24,536
	1914	43 963	29,486	4,130	19	9,159	1,169	25,251
	1909	38,553	30,680	3,305	500	2,709	1,359	10,906
	1904	33,945	29,643	2,988	55	293	966	5,587
Carriages and wagons and materials.	1919	64,666	37,786	1,441	4,762	19,999	678	32,751
	1914	112,549	66,093	3,132	10,557	32,654	113	46,384
	1909	126,032	82,928	4,667	13,120	24,969	348	39,424
	1904	106,159	82,488	3,179	9,739	8,780	1,235	16,434

[1] Figures include "other" owned power as follows: 1909, 29,293 horsepower; 1904, 92,154 horsepower.

TABLE 23.—HORSEPOWER IN LEADING INDUSTRIES: 1919, 1914, 1909, and 1904—Cont'd.

INDUSTRY.	Census year.	PRIMARY HORSEPOWER.							Electric horse-power owned and rented.
		Total.	Owned.			Rented.			
			Steam engines and turbines.	Water wheels and motors.	Internal-combustion engines.	Electric.	Other.		

Industries with over 18,000 wage earners in 1919—Continued.

INDUSTRY.	Census year.	Total.	Steam engines and turbines.	Water wheels and motors.	Internal-combustion engines.	Electric.	Other.	Electric horse-power owned and rented.
Cars and general shop construction and repairs by electric-railroad companies.	1919	53,830	5,875	....	564	47,366	25	50,016
	1914	44,989	5,997	1,010	1,121	36,861	......	44,670
	1909	35,794	4,831	....	9	30,954	......	33,024
	1904	3,154	1,355	600	40	1,159	......	10,358
Cars and general shop construction and repairs by steam-railroad companies.	1919	594,515	375,606	841	6,993	207,630	3,445	500,141
	1914	433,994	323,634	1,792	5,916	102,562	90	325,054
	1909	293,361	255,840	450	3,140	33,786	145	161,288
	1904	167,973	159,746	203	1,877	6,074	73	52,635
Cars, steam-railroad, not including operations of railroad companies.	1919	157,865	92,015	100	2,848	62,827	75	170,485
	1914	126,687	99,934	230	5,757	20,416	350	115,479
	1909	97,797	89,823	370	1,148	6,456	......	61,060
	1904	55,994	55,260	225	193	316	......	14,505
Cement..........................	1919	488,808	278,009	3,550	24,763	182,486	......	345,535
	1914	490,402	291,321	6,346	28,366	164,369	......	336,516
	1909	371,799	295,138	3,430	19,065	54,166	......	158,749
	1904	149,604	137,770	2,980	3,063	5,751	40	35,292
Chemicals.....................	1919	376,940	241,749	3,692	5,004	126,419	76	235,973
	1914	282,385	124,329	3,135	5,962	134,481	14,478	172,510
	1909	208,657	103,488	11,066	1,190	92,067	846	156,709
	1904	132,394	71,299	6,469	477	10,130	44,019	18,240
Clocks and watches, including cases and materials.	1919	18,681	12,090	511	1,551	4,529	......	12,285
	1914	15,647	11,863	198	483	3,063	40	8,844
	1909	14,957	12,593	284	425	1,612	43	7,023
	1904	10,731	9,180	449	72	892	138	3,513
Clothing, men's, including shirts.	1919	55,521	15,454	560	1,706	37,368	433	42,611
	1914	53,281	19,409	1,248	3,428	28,284	912	33,444
	1909	42,725	16,009	1,380	5,259	18,816	1,261	22,894
	1904	29,829	14,641	910	3,210	9,581	1,487	11,337
Clothing, women's..............	1919	32,622	2,283	75	529	29,534	201	29,937
	1914	28,396	2,632	88	1,125	24,029	522	24,757
	1909	22,294	4,112	206	1,958	15,175	843	16,085
	1904	14,916	4,422	309	1,593	7,494	1,098	8,027
Coke, not including gas-house coke.	1919	224,879	148,478	....	1,850	74,551	......	209,163
	1914	117,127	77,367	....	2,120	37,640	......	88,409
	1909	62,602	46,251	500	1,212	13,754	885	41,064
	1904	66,669	65,144	188	150	1,187	......	10,509
Confectionery and ice-cream [1]....	1919	179,891	52,763	50	11,800	115,069	209	138,344
	1914	98,393	45,107	63	10,781	41,836	606	62,540
Cooperage and wooden goods, not elsewhere specified.	1919	56,604	42,488	1,310	1,246	11,518	42	18,637
	1914	59,001	48,404	2,651	1,740	5,765	441	9,076
	1909	65,108	55,071	3,818	2,029	2,819	1,371	4,524
	1904	56,988	50,382	4,060	1,221	969	356	2,086
Copper, tin, and sheet-iron products.[2]	1919	106,084	34,158	106	6,422	64,961	437	84,955
	1914	75,263	35,400	224	7,431	30,644	1,564	49,473
	1909	62,366	34,655	420	8,572	17,898	821	30,771
	1904	30,229	20,824	272	2,894	5,006	1,233	7,454
Cordage and twine and jute and linen goods.	1919	104,847	58,331	18,845	778	26,806	87	51,183
	1914	93,937	65,867	14,377	2,844	10,649	200	34,098
	1909	77,091	57,581	15,768	1,270	2,353	119	14,293
	1904	65,984	52,369	12,589	98	737	191	8,271
Corsets.......................	1919	7,156	4,176	10	107	2,663	200	5,132
	1914	7,057	4,683	....	6	2,273	95	4,273
	1909	4,581	3,320	....	56	1,061	144	2,804
	1904	3,284	2,695	10	60	262	257	434

[1] Figures not available for 1909 and 1904.
[2] Includes for 1919, 1914, and 1909 some establishments manufacturing enameled stamped ware which were included under "enameling and japanning" in 1904.

TABLE 23.—HORSEPOWER IN LEADING INDUSTRIES: 1919, 1914, 1909, and 1904—Contd.

INDUSTRY.	Census year.	PRIMARY HORSEPOWER.						Electric horsepower owned and rented.
		Total.	Owned.			Rented.		
			Steam engines and turbines.	Water wheels and motors.	Internal-combustion engines.	Electric.	Other.	
Industries with over 18,000 wage earners in 1919—Continued.								
Cotton goods, including cotton small wares.	1919	1,863,542	1,025,761	307,162	2,842	523,696	4,081	874,124
	1914	1,585,953	1,011,303	314,219	4,016	252,864	3,551	512,903
	1909	1,296,517	877,201	303,024	2,812	108,512	4,968	235,902
	1904	986,604	708,333	252,923	1,786	14,095	9,467	67,139
Cutlery and tools, not elsewhere specified.	1919	107,339	30,950	9,585	7,272	58,478	1,054	74,579
	1914	73,255	36,295	9,838	8,194	17,586	1,342	34,680
	1909	68,294	38,815	13,382	6,731	8,325	1,041	17,785
	1904	54,397	34,106	11,459	4,052	3,653	1,127	8,427
Dyeing and finishing textiles, exclusive of that done in textile mills.	1919	160,430	118,197	13,543	2,124	25,993	573	85,889
	1914	130,172	111,506	9,969	690	7,162	845	51,021
	1909	107,746	92,284	10,114	1,207	2,665	1,476	24,011
	1904	84,868	70,555	10,130	711	1,087	2,385	11,724
Electrical machinery, apparatus, and supplies.	1919	438,839	193,231	1,800	7,446	235,605	757	479,366
	1914	227,731	142,085	1,065	8,694	74,476	1,411	262,119
	1909	158,768	99,897	1,114	6,753	50,045	959	164,540
	1904	105,376	77,059	1,181	2,940	21,313	2,883	61,753
Fertilizers	1919	125,939	40,482	709	4,862	79,886		93,111
	1914	114,281	60,353	337	5,786	47,450	355	65,266
	1909	64,711	49,777	365	1,825	12,579	165	19,238
	1904	47,989	44,857	353	246	2,358	175	5,275
Firearms and ammunition	1919	65,295	33,356	299	2,241	29,399		54,402
	1914	18,828	10,176	462	3,139	4,951	100	17,259
	1909	17,840	11,505	989	2,927	2,278	141	8,472
	1904	21,408	18,613	1,139	880	632	144	3,777
Flour-mill and gristmill products	1919	876,405	329,589	186,087	96,291	263,497	941	309,610
	1914	822,384	403,186	229,328	76,451	112,441	978	150,248
	1909	853,584	473,571	264,131	62,681	49,901	3,300	67,066
	1904	775,318	474,077	258,352	26,326	15,584	979	20,308
Food preparations, not elsewhere specified.[1]	1919	150,230	51,893	796	5,337	91,643	561	112,798
	1914	80,022	39,012	915	5,352	34,347	396	47,761
	1909	55,166	35,554	1,150	4,331	13,460	671	20,924
	1904	28,162	22,185	1,158	1,283	3,123	413	4,239
Foundry and machine-shop products.	1919	1,886,983	570,479	20,511	107,442	1,172,561	15,990	1,725,145
	1914	1,129,768	548,027	19,585	108,673	444,328	9,155	896,849
	1909	869,305	548,960	18,702	96,966	192,977	11,700	623,914
	1904	606,165	467,660	18,633	49,006	55,359	15,507	199,625
Furnishing goods, men's[2]	1919	19,979	9,579	785	220	9,279	116	14,482
	1914	17,300	8,946	811	569	6,374	600	10,348
	1909	12,116	7,501	480	740	2,988	407	4,860
	1904	5,421	3,514	28	597	977	305	1,586
Furniture and refrigerators	1919	275,935	173,206	4,713	4,744	91,082	2,190	143,691
	1914	251,997	185,676	5,160	7,317	48,597	5,247	88,964
	1909	221,451	185,037	6,848	5,830	20,420	3,316	43,252
	1904	169,774	149,530	6,890	4,133	4,586	4,635	9,565
Gas and electric fixtures and lamps and reflectors.	1919	22,618	6,039	227	1,169	14,843	340	18,390
	1914	18,668	7,088	197	1,722	9,206	455	11,491
	1909	15,862	6,930	244	1,544	5,896	1,248	8,788
	1904	8,444	5,126	77	1,012	1,364	865	2,213
Gas, illuminating and heating	1919	238,467	197,321	196	7,574	33,363	13	55,403
	1914	213,370	179,878	425	13,729	19,271	67	37,881
	1909	128,350	115,514	2,814	7,128	2,723	171	17,336
	1904	73,101	67,652	359	3,211	1,454	425	3,978

[1] Includes for 1919, 1914, and 1909 some establishments compounding table sirups which were included under "sugar and molasses" in 1904.

[2] Includes for 1919, 1914, and 1909 some establishments manufacturing suspenders, garters, and elastic woven goods, which were classified under "rubber goods, not elsewhere specified," or under "millinery and lace goods" in 1904.

TABLE 23.—HORSEPOWER IN LEADING INDUSTRIES: 1919, 1914, 1909, AND 1904—Contd.

INDUSTRY.	Census year.	PRIMARY HORSEPOWER.						Electric horsepower owned and rented.
		Total.	Owned.			Rented.		
			Steam engines and turbines.	Water wheels and motors.	Internal-combustion engines.	Electric.	Other.	
Industries with over 18,000 wage earners in 1919—Continued.								
Glass	1919	207,430	99,140	2,457	52,877	52,864	92	143,125
	1914	163,139	105,061	201	43,448	14,224	205	92,896
	1909	123,132	98,971	5	20,731	3,425	......	43,589
	1904	91,476	76,915	31	13,947	583	......	16,769
Hats, fur-felt	1919	20,389	15,251	120	10	4,996	12	9,631
	1914	20,851	17,936	135	48	2,655	77	8,141
	1909	19,245	16,678	20	147	2,172	228	6,186
	1904	16,630	15,871	68	48	369	274	2,434
Ice, manufactured	1919	572,970	406,942	2,542	28,003	132,438	3,045	158,552
	1914	461,988	414,685	2,727	12,535	28,991	3,050	50,546
	1909	317,789	304,685	2,262	3,264	5,414	2,164	14,253
	1904	191,660	186,549	1,075	618	1,068	2,350	4,579
Iron and steel, blast furnaces	1919	1,581,432	1,249,817	371	283,015	48,204	25	242,554
	1914	1,222,273	1,005,374	1,261	194,037	21,601	......	212,582
	1909	1,173,422	1,033,033	309	125,230	14,850	......	135,143
	1904	773,278	768,702	680	3,757	139	......	52,610
Iron and steel, steel works and rolling mills.	1919	3,820,917	2,856,556	9,041	257,473	695,097	2,750	2,350,596
	1914	2,706,553	2,435,319	12,321	73,752	182,204	2,957	1,207,715
	1909	2,100,978	1,956,846	5,829	79,391	58,797	115	716,609
	1904	1,649,299	1,618,480	4,795	11,806	6,798	7,420	254,258
Iron and steel, forgings, not made in steel works or rolling mills.	1919	101,951	24,808	848	1,602	73,738	955	90,693
	1914	38,215	16,883	780	1,832	17,048	1,672	25,076
	1909	27,803	20,011	520	2,608	4,570	94	11,493
	1904	16,069	13,918	904	672	313	262	1,945
Jewelry	1919	16,389	1,647	114	545	12,790	1,293	15,750
	1914	15,666	2,271	145	1,013	10,433	1,804	11,392
	1909	11,204	2,748	200	694	5,179	2,383	5,759
	1904	7,872	2,448	92	354	2,799	2,179	2,974
Knit goods	1919	151,601	76,003	12,941	814	59,680	2,163	91,137
	1914	125,842	80,884	14,643	1,108	26,284	2,923	46,117
	1909	103,709	74,760	12,038	1,235	13,286	2,390	25,485
	1904	78,769	57,460	13,532	668	4,648	2,461	9,724
Leather goods	1919	20,248	6,430	64	658	13,020	76	15,486
	1914	21,478	9,635	673	1,142	9,897	131	13,239
	1909	28,148	10,028	1,373	1,381	14,946	420	16,663
	1904	16,257	9,286	1,409	1,017	3,641	904	4,578
Leather, tanned, curried, and finished.	1919	218,238	150,800	2,029	6,438	58,494	477	143,935
	1914	172,712	140,299	1,868	7,997	21,570	978	73,424
	1909	148,140	131,451	1,556	7,231	6,487	1,415	35,919
	1904	117,450	107,550	1,955	5,086	2,014	845	14,539
Liquors, malt	1919	324,431	276,441	194	3,651	41,844	2,301	110,755
	1914	405,884	371,291	685	3,752	29,321	835	111,958
	1909	347,726	331,770	340	1,261	14,190	165	66,519
	1904	266,159	261,280	678	647	3,369	185	22,508
Locomotives, not made by railroad companies.	1919	97,187	34,065	......	3,355	59,084	683	118,873
	1914	50,373	35,762	450	8,380	5,781	......	76,846
	1909	35,102	28,831	200	4,520	1,551	......	40,504
	1904	29,806	26,557	1,230	545	1,474	......	13,267
Lumber and timber products [1]	1919	2,930,186	2,520,229	69,890	45,751	287,643	6,673	534,903
	1914	2,742,352	2,444,196	94,103	45,694	149,152	9,207	306,540
	1909	2,840,082	2,588,323	140,503	38,628	62,200	10,428	130,707
	1904	1,886,624	1,722,829	119,461	16,897	14,181	13,256	33,517
Marble and stone work	1919	·170,132	60,083	4,891	10,175	94,028	955	106,033
	1914	207,461	110,156	¹6,433	12,459	66,997	1,346	94,976
	1909	·187,686	132,477	9,618	10,874	32,062	2,655	53,748
	1904	102,887	82,700	6,281	5,390	6,838	1,678	11,278

[1] Includes "pulp wood" in 1914.

TABLE 23.—HORSEPOWER IN LEADING INDUSTRIES: 1919, 1914, 1909, AND 1904—Contd.

INDUSTRY.	Census year.	PRIMARY HORSEPOWER.						Electric horse-power owned and rented.
		Total.	Owned.			Rented.		
			Steam engines and turbines.	Water wheels and motors.	Internal-combustion engines.	Electric.	Other.	
Industries with over 18,000 wage earners in 1919—Continued.								
Millinery and lace goods, not elsewhere specified.[1]	1919	12,482	3,248	170	254	8,738	72	10,107
	1914	12,736	4,832	715	378	6,563	248	7,883
	1909	7,918	2,869	117	561	4,048	323	4,560
	1904	4,737	2,192	46	270	1,663	566	2,110
Musical instruments, pianos and organs and materials.	1919	47,804	30,912	436	1,280	15,030	146	28,766
	1914	44,349	32,792	643	1,592	9,046	276	21,492
	1909	41,623	33,325	1,106	1,271	5,355	566	13,226
	1904	30,134	25,706	867	741	1,932	888	5,085
Oil and cake, cottonseed.........	1919	290,636	195,356	1,512	10,857	82,256	655	93,400
	1914	249,781	218,872	1,035	6,748	23,126	......	30,893
	1909	192,342	183,629	175	1,674	6,394	470	10,855
	1904	150,246	148,914	559	115	658	....	3,079
Paint and varnish...............	1919	85,199	37,967	1,019	2,573	43,268	372	64,241
	1914	70,611	43,881	1,426	3,226	19,035	3,043	34,917
	1909	56,162	42,191	2,006	3,290	7,814	861	17,037
	1904	41,288	34,952	997	1,673	2,650	1,016	7,540
Paper and wood pulp...........	1919	1,851,014	698,983	910,863	3,191	236,662	1,315	583,586
	1914	1,621,154	597,840	876,741	9,674	127,699	9,200	325,211
	1909	1,304,265	469,364	788,146	6,675	38,610	1,470	130,120
	1904	1,093,708	370,852	717,989	1,916	2,748	203	31,604
Paper goods, not elsewhere specified.	1919	35,538	17,688	2,260	255	15,166	169	25,664
	1914	35,307	23,267	1,354	649	9,501	536	20,415
	1909	27,067	19,246	1,340	576	5,245	660	12,680
	1904	16,226	13,541	285	225	1,593	582	3,990
Patent medicines and compounds and druggists' preparations.	1919	40,571	18,713	55	951	20,556	296	29,364
	1914	28,872	15,908	179	2,000	10,422	363	17,924
	1909	25,659	16,059	264	1,712	6,882	742	11,175
	1904	17,008	12,465	173	983	2,468	919	4,894
Petroleum, refining...............	1919	238,906	144,743	131	42,647	51,385	......	108,625
	1914	128,468	94,052	1,487	18,298	14,353	278	38,614
	1909	90,268	84,085	....	5,870	28	285	8,808
	1904	46,019	43,810	....	2,059	150	......	3,468
Phonographs and graphophones.	1919	40,168	21,973	175	366	17,649	5	32,193
	1914	11,688	9,865	....	110	1,713	......	7,400
	1909	6,371	5,800	....	14	517	40	2,952
	1904	2,522	1,907	....	9	181	425	471
Printing and publishing.........	1919	362,123	46,727	864	17,132	296,401	999	331,500
	1914	329,210	57,583	1,388	27,435	240,697	2,107	277,206
	1909	297,763	59,334	2,320	32,152	197,692	6,265	229,312
	1904	166,380	54,957	3,332	24,964	75,479	7,648	93,219
Rubber tires, tubes, and rubber goods, not elsewhere specified.[1]	1919	354,188	194,459	2,534	3,367	153,214	614	304,367
	1914	151,927	121,144	3,273	1,605	25,664	241	93,998
	1909	79,062	72,010	2,455	398	3,499	700	18,848
	1904	48,381	44,726	1,984	307	1,096	268	8,596
Sewing machines, cases and attachments.	1919	32,035	27,665	382	1,222	2,748	18	23,226
	1914	24,229	21,066	291	219	2,434	219	19,378
	1909	19,426	18,131	291	62	897	45	14,063
	1904	17,162	16,301	452	66	274	69	4,694
Shipbuilding, including boat-building.	1919	553,711	121,200	71	7,019	424,981	440	476,135
	1914	115,333	79,599	94	5,336	30,085	219	66,275
	1909	88,063	75,180	86	3,503	9,264	30	35,334
	1904	78,127	73,657	87	1,785	2,367	231	17,630

[1] Includes for 1904 some establishments manufacturing suspenders, garters, and elastic woven goods, which are included with "furnishing goods, men's" in 1919, 1914, and 1909.

TABLE 23.—HORSEPOWER IN LEADING INDUSTRIES: 1919, 1914, 1909, AND 1904—Contd.

INDUSTRY.	Census year.	PRIMARY HORSEPOWER.						Electric horse-power owned and rented.
		Total.	Owned.			Rented.		
			Steam engines and turbines.	Water wheels and motors.	Internal-combustion engines.	Electric.	Other.	
Industries with over 18,000 wage earners in 1919—Continued.								
Silk goods, including throwsters.	1919	176,825	88,221	8,327	1,966	75,234	3,077	107,982
	1914	116,924	78,302	7,605	1,762	23,748	5,507	47,401
	1909	97,947	72,059	8,383	1,277	10,354	5,874	23,758
	1904	71,760	56,717	6,974	937	2,393	4,739	9,521
Slaughtering and meat packing.	1919	371,925	240,075	574	2,578	127,966	732	223,769
	1914	260,996	213,012	15	2,833	44,059	1,077	122,956
	1909	208,707	190,666	46	2,208	15,047	740	78,677
	1904	119,311	114,640	311	740	3,441	179	40,538
Soap	1919	33,710	24,787	40	201	8,672	10	30,649
	1914	35,737	29,805	166	120	4,014	1,632	16,960
	1909	28,360	24,538	255	245	1,974	1,348	12,839
	1904	20,228	18,750	53	88	517	820	4,410
Stoves and furnaces, including gas and oil stoves.	1919	60,774	24,800	104	2,292	33,502	76	45,270
	1914	49,150	27,007	124	3,418	18,506	95	30,843
	1909	45,524	32,993	259	3,060	8,966	246	18,159
	1904	32,017	26,013	555	2,241	2,831	377	6,794
Sugar, refining [1]	1919	52,541	52,181	....	....	360	....	54,668
	1914	49,666	45,407	....	69	4,190	....	24,016
	1909	38,414	37,453	....	15	946	....	14,735
Tobacco manufactures	1919	43,397	28,213	402	345	14,430	7	27,877
	1914	34,937	25,853	257	680	7,966	181	17,755
	1909	28,514	21,936	245	795	5,367	171	11,203
	1904	24,604	21,413	257	593	1,941	400	6,515
Turpentine and rosin	1919	2,303	1,343	30	884	19	27	19
	1914	2,478	1,669	20	789	....	....	2
	1909	4,129	3,877	14	231	....	7	....
	1904	1,175	1,172	3	....	....	....	....
Wire	1919	119,451	61,666	639	1,966	55,030	150	86,646
	1914	83,940	63,015	993	3,429	16,463	40	39,458
	1909	71,959	63,516	2,151	3,256	3,031	5	18,824
	1904	25,856	23,696	1,054	759	347	....	1,710
Woolen, worsted, and felt goods and wool hats.	1919	487,587	323,670	78,887	1,797	80,970	2,263	239,901
	1914	398,367	288,720	76,259	2,654	25,047	5,687	144,244
	1909	362,209	261,364	79,250	2,077	13,783	5,735	79,223
	1904	288,969	200,035	76,366	1,705	3,930	6,933	22,222
Other industries with over 26,000 horsepower in 1919.								
Aluminum manufactures [2]	1919	30,280	12,372	80	1,103	16,725	....	27,334
	1914	12,338	6,708	....	900	4,689	41	9,616
Belting and hose, rubber.	1919	26,299	10,860	618	406	14,415	....	22,723
	1914	22,995	17,518	473	66	4,938	....	14,198
	1909	17,471	12,340	470	1,963	2,698	....	5,336
	1904	12,343	10,790	950	....	603	....	665
Chocolate and cocoa products.	1919	33,440	15,273	300	1,783	16,058	26	24,552
	1914	19,736	14,410	280	2,150	2,836	60	12,875
	1909	10,593	9,047	215	....	1,316	15	7,278
	1904	5,217	4,400	120	115	460	122	2,447
Coal-tar products [3]	1919	68,342	40,698	....	265	27,376	3	53,693
Coffee and spice, roasting and grinding.	1919	29,750	4,595	100	961	24,050	44	28,079
	1914	26,634	7,468	100	1,085	17,903	78	22,278
	1909	22,334	8,825	159	992	12,205	153	22,413
	1904	15,703	9,327	188	700	5,037	451	8,160

[1] Figures not available for 1904.
[2] Figures not available for 1909 and 1904.   [3] Included in other classifications in 1914, 1909, and 1904.

TABLE 23.—HORSEPOWER IN LEADING INDUSTRIES: 1919, 1914, 1909, AND 1904—Contd.

INDUSTRY.	Census year.	Total.	Owned. Steam engines and turbines.	Owned. Water wheels and motors.	Owned. Internal-combustion engines.	Rented. Electric.	Rented. Other.	Electric horse-power owned and rented.
Other industries with over 26,000 horsepower in 1919—Continued.								
Dyestuffs and extracts—natural.	1919	34,320	31,289	113	201	2,692	25	8,341
	1914	23,290	22,032	56	455	745	2	2,750
	1909	22,213	21,685	320	15	191	2	1,664
	1904	17,671	17,424	196	4	20	27	659
Explosives	1919	51,635	33,676	1,433	40	16,486		39,305
	1914	45,778	36,304	1,518	62	7,894		25,560
	1909	28,601	25,558	2,689	221	133		14,836
	1904	29,665	22,061	7,177	427			7,889
Ferroalloys[1]	1919	37,087	32,420		88	4,579		24,035
Glucose and starch	1919	52,846	47,576	530	345	3,585	810	47,735
	1914	41,639	38,003	893	102	2,456	185	29,276
	1909	28,257	27,835	185	49	163	25	27,230
	1904	35,986	33,406	2,180	81	169	150	12,890
Iron and steel, bolts, nuts, washers, and rivets, not made in rolling mills.	1919	49,959	15,051	690	1,661	32,557		46,387
	1914	28,897	12,004	1,190	2,040	13,651	12	18,562
	1909	22,113	14,838	954	2,066	4,179	76	8,626
	1904	13,825	11,582	461	821	717	244	2,888
Lime	1919	51,735	19,946	250	2,944	28,595		32,155
	1914	39,134	25,388	316	2,122	11,253	55	12,851
	1909	27,671	24,271	441	1,418	1,497	44	2,560
	1904	18,198	16,742	243	698	475	40	1,231
Malt	1919	27,483	18,272	450		8,761		21,379
	1914	33,394	24,318	375	65	7,736	900	21,155
	1909	26,441	20,417	197	240	5,267	320	9,911
	1904	20,288	17,633	631	324	1,515	185	3,298
Mineral and soda waters	1919	41,764	12,645	97	3,277	25,148	597	27,179
	1914	25,164	7,935	319	5,466	11,001	443	11,883
	1909	19,392	8,678	375	4,580	5,504	255	6,218
	1904	12,214	7,426	414	2,370	1,760	244	1,908
Minerals and earths, ground or otherwise treated.	1919	127,074	61,367	5,712	4,456	55,529	10	61,457
	1914	44,069	25,811	7,277	1,476	9,503	2	11,378
	1909	20,920	13,029	6,283	209	1,375	24	1,664
	1904	17,325	12,061	4,414	179	290	381	305
Oil, not elsewhere specified	1919	30,075	21,749	4	674	7,640	8	10,892
	1914	10,984	8,176		807	1,506	495	2,915
	1909	6,157	4,791	240	272	669	185	788
	1904	5,707	5,236	26	280	84	81	154
Ordnance and accessories	1919	40,652	8,300	200	187	31,965		38,550
	1914	800	725		75			1,177
	1909	47			10	37		37
	1904	735	680		5	50		300
Paving materials	1919	191,543	105,581	607	4,104	81,179	72	86,730
	1914	138,026	87,852	100.	3,306	46,604	164	52,819
	1909	5,757	5,312		193	252		1,630
	1904	5,156	5,002		14	140		1,000
Photographic materials	1919	26,458	13,526		68	12,864		23,236
	1914	14,960	12,305		191	2,459	5	12,803
	1909	8,114	7,664		203	226	21	5,222
	1904	3,690	3,063	26	177	301	123	1,311
Rice, cleaning and polishing	1919	27,382	18,881		697	5,762	2,042	6,637
	1914	15,571	13,927		82	1,562		1,970
	1909	19,519	18,252	15	137	1,115		1,738
	1904	15,866	15,774			92		477

[1] Included in other classifications in 1914, 1909, and 1904.

75108°—23——66

TABLE 23.—HORSEPOWER IN LEADING INDUSTRIES: 1919, 1914, 1909, AND 1904—Contd.

INDUSTRY.	Census year.	PRIMARY HORSEPOWER.						Electric horsepower owned and rented.
		Total.	Owned.			Rented.		
			Steam engines and turbines.	Water wheels and motors.	Internal-combustion engines.	Electric.	Other.	
Other industries with over 26,000 horsepower in 1919—Continued.								
Roofing materials.............	1919	39,327	15,847	2,145	253	21,002	80	29,355
	1914	11,702	6,253	56	211	5,182	....	7,369
	1909	9,431	8,393	....	530	453	55	1,965
	1904	23,022	21,846	491	165	460	60	843
Salt.....	1919	43,187	34,309	55	981	6,706	1,136	14,771
	1914	29,007	24,900	78	779	3,250	....	7,742
	1909	27,263	25,118	108	782	1,241	14	3,425
	1904	19,434	18,556	33	439	196	210	664
Smelting and refining, copper....	1919	321,610	186,286	7,550	425	127,349	....	184,255
	1914	194,980	147,535	10,000	825	36,620	....	88,213
	1909	158,126	114,881	12,725	1,107	29,413	....	55,229
	1904	76,524	62,735	9,400	1,274	3,115	....	12,419
Smelting and refining, lead......	1919	52,565	24,905	350	84	24,329	2,897	32,535
	1914	29,734	20,387	....	145	9,202	....	19,737
	1909	26,954	23,090	....	35	3,829	....	12,166
	1904	25,667	22,440	1	100	3,126	....	10,107
Smelting and refining, zinc......	1919	73,604	56,832	....	3,264	13,508	....	52,996
	1914	36,705	33,564	300	1,751	1,090	....	24,554
	1909	21,457	19,952	192	1,313	....	....	8,448
	1904	18,404	18,356	....	48	....	....	5,048
Steam packing..................	1919	26,763	20,637	....	372	5,746	8	17,835
	1914	17,254	13,031	265	522	3,347	89	9,576
	1909	11,129	8,978	....	387	1,512	252	4,042
	1904	8,846	7,633	45	181	816	171	1,066
Sugar, beet...................	1919	127,394	117,469	35	259	9,631	....	44,871
	1914	76,705	70,507	195	928	5,075	....	17,871
	1909	57,202	54,369	200	543	2,090	....	8,868
	1904	35,490	35,016	429	40	5	....	4,702
Sugar, cane [1]................	1919	101,861	98,823	8	3,028	....	2	2,288
	1914	113,246	112,776	....	438	32	....	2,769
	1909	122,189	121,439	....	380	370	....	3,995
Sulphuric, nitric, and mixed acids.	1919	30,637	12,672	25	1,755	16,185	....	28,091
	1914	24,927	17,096	....	1,525	2,381	3,925	12,994
	1909	6,494	5,083	....	371	878	162	2,230
	1904	5,416	4,840	....	161	415	....	540
Wall plaster and composition flooring.	1919	32,356	12,457	184	1,352	18,363	....	23,856
	1914	36,626	18,730	706	2,201	14,962	27	17,684
	1909	25,892	19,095	845	1,260	4,517	175	6,167
	1904	20,054	16,161	1,580	1,084	1,059	170	1,640
Wirework, including wire rope and cable, not elsewhere specified.	1919	29,074	10,570	495	1,266	16,705	38	22,917
	1914	21,547	9,075	393	1,546	10,391	142	14,305
	1909	20,131	10,553	930	2,492	5,642	514	8,891
	1904	18,280	12,786	714	2,154	2,000	626	5,119
Wood, turned and carved........	1919	39,958	27,040	2,744	2,515	7,423	236	10,146
	1914	43,334	33,441	4,151	1,787	3,162	793	4,330
	1909	48,447	37,231	5,311	1,829	2,283	1,793	2,966
	1904	47,595	38,379	5,250	1,047	692	2,227	993
All other industries.............	1919	1,151,185	507,403	27,269	36,684	572,613	7,216	793,801
	1914	857,513	518,471	28,254	52,236	247,986	10,566	432,356
	1909	748,905	517,370	35,593	46,542	133,768	15,632	247,955
	1904	697,705	574,613	31,762	24,288	44,576	22,466	96,456

[1] Figures not available for 1904.

TABLE 24.—HORSEPOWER IN GEOGRAPHIC DIVISIONS AND STATES: 1869 TO 1919.

DIVISION AND STATE.	Census year.	PRIMARY HORSEPOWER.						Electric horsepower owned and rented.
		Total.	Owned.			Rented.		
			Steam engines and turbines.¹	Water wheels and motors.	Internal-combustion engines.	Electric.	Other.	
UNITED STATES	1919	29,504,792	17,037,973	1,765,263	1,259.400	9,347,556	94,600	16,317,277
	1914	22,437,072	15,591,593	1,826,443	991,905	3,897,248	129,883	8,835,970
	1909	18,675,376	14,228,632	1,822,888	751,186	1,749,031	123,639	4,817,140
	1904	13,487,707	10,917,502	1,647,880	289,423	441,589	191,313	1,592,475
	1899	10,097,893	8,189,564	1,454,112	134,742	182,562	136,913	492,936
	1889	5,938,635	4,586,089	1,255,045	8,930	....	88,571	15,569
	1879	3,410,837	2,185,458	1,225,379	....	....	....	....
	1869	2,346,142	1,215,711	1,130,431	....	....	....	....
GEOGRAPHIC DIVISIONS: New England	1919	3,796,846	1,867,434	747,617	34,459	1,130,308	17,028	1,926,573
	1914	3,124,329	1,872,828	757,582	49,229	419,197	25,493	1,107,677
	1909	2,715,121	1,658,966	757,332	41,801	218,642	38,380	663,143
	1904	2,125,815	1,342,503	659,071	18,068	58,745	47,428	187,194
	1899	1,792,342	1,098,885	619,209	9,978	31,613	32,657	65,951
	1889	1,156,877	634,316	497,031	545	....	24,985	3,094
	1879	743,106	320,201	422,905	....	....	....	....
	1869	514,730	152,704	362,026	....	....	....	....
Middle Atlantic	1919	8,537,660	5,250,772	396,168	410,312	2,455,360	25,048	5,068,019
	1914	6,699,576	4,730,955	454,158	372,617	1,083,618	58,228	2,924,489
	1909	5,531,502	4,163,398	470,488	274,274	568,723	54,619	1,737,236
	1904	4,255,264	3,369,872	514,951	121,567	141,588	107,286	638,209
	1899	3,139,128	2,552,354	410,173	45,751	74,256	56,594	201,201
	1889	1,939,042	1,567,822	331,964	3,044	....	36,212	5,096
	1879	1,066,409	709,719	356,690	....	....	....	....
	1869	756,420	380,350	376,070	....	....	....	....
East North Central	1919	7,735,137	4,361,731	252,829	428,493	2,659,498	32,586	4,883,500
	1914	5,421,435	3,826,501	217,164	332,269	1,016,044	29,457	2,522,465
	1909	4,382,070	3,496,184	208,441	283,450	375,876	18,119	1,297,447
	1904	3,120,369	2,716,307	194,871	90,481	95,188	23,522	432,162
	1899	2,401,808	2,127,110	171,077	45,244	30,693	27,684	124,520
	1889	1,327,784	1,153,118	155,245	2,578	....	16,843	3,839
	1879	808,033	650,386	157,647	....	....	....	....
	1869	530,810	380,984	149,826	....	....	....	....
West North Central	1919	1,594,112	801,743	92,753	102,124	596,189	1,303	920,196
	1914	1,238,988	814,714	94,957	66,970	258,506	3,841	510,553
	1909	1,101,990	839,927	86,330	57,434	115,002	3,297	266,534
	1904	753,700	628,287	63,659	25,156	32,976	3,622	80,029
	1899	605,098	515,208	51,999	17,905	14,519	5,467	31,476
	1889	410,231	345,697	60,005	832	....	3,697	1,256
	1879	220,647	149,524	71,123	....	....	....	....
	1869	126,532	89,274	37,258	....	....	....	....
South Atlantic	1919	2,795,094	1,594,200	173,108	136,579	887,201	4,006	1,388,053
	1914	2,274,785	1,599,018	176,864	72,429	417,927	8,547	716,639
	1909	1,832,001	1,436,744	183,158	36,441	171,146	4,512	343,393
	1904	1,221,040	1,034,544	137,018	16,677	28,914	3,887	100,465
	1899	851,050	705,517	124,830	6,834	5,196	8,673	24,257
	1889	468,009	319,801	145,397	778	....	2,033	708
	1879	294,186	148,618	145,568	....	....	....	....
	1869	209,814	70,085	139,729	....	....	....	....
East South Central	1919	1,415,577	1,055,152	25,007	22,893	311,138	1,387	460,143
	1914	1,157,367	975,428	23,627	16,180	141,419	713	247,815
	1909	1,036,560	955,201	29,315	12,270	38,580	1,194	108,409
	1904	753,928	716,924	24,193	3,714	8,060	1,037	28,757
	1899	513,425	480,552	25,107	2,209	3,833	1,724	9,619
	1889	304,291	268,106	34,850	299	....	1,036	260
	1879	152,907	110,085	42,822	....	....	....	....
	1869	108,772	68,154	40,618	....	....	....	....

¹ Figures include "other" owned power as follows: 1909, 29,293 horsepower; 1904, 92,154 horsepower; 1899, 49,985 horsepower; 1889, 4,784 horsepower.

TABLE 24.—HORSEPOWER IN GEOGRAPHIC DIVISIONS AND STATES: 1869 TO 1919—Con.

DIVISION AND STATE.	Census year.	PRIMARY HORSEPOWER.						Electric horsepower owned and rented.
		Total.	Owned.			Rented.		
			Steam engines and turbines.	Water wheels and motors.	Internal-combustion engines.	Electric.	Other.	
GEOG. DIVISIONS—Con.								
West South Central.....	1919	1,185,989	876,632	3,446	81,260	218,558	6,093	350,953
	1914	965,500	829,099	4,549	55,275	75,547	1,030	163,239
	1909	873,350	808,153	3,108	29,291	31,807	991	78,893
	1904	555,717	539,507	3,236	4,308	8,273	393	20,152
	1899	397,471	388,179	2,760	1,956	3,992	584	5,778
	1889	136,992	131,772	4,552	377	....	291	651
	1879	57,613	52,991	4,622				
	1869	45,756	42,239	3,517				
Mountain..............	1919	686,579	399,946	15,656	9,971	259,619	1,387	351,214
	1914	460,278	326,841	23,511	6,871	102,293	762	190,525
	1909	400,766	307,010	21,543	4,188	66,956	1,069	113,984
	1904	241,825	208,326	18,319	2,296	12,105	779	35,419
	1899	123,012	99,153	18,161	1,237	4,031	430	8,545
	1889	47,391	40,126	6,779	111	....	375	172
	1879	17,031	8,319	8,712				
	1869	16,838	9,546	7,292				
Pacific.................	1919	1,757,798	830,363	58,679	33,309	829,685	5,762	968,626
	1914	1,094,814	616,209	74,031	20,065	382,697	1,812	452,568
	1909	802,016	563,049	63,173	12,037	162,299	1,458	208,101
	1904	460,049	361,232	32,562	7,156	55,740	3,359	70,088
	1899	274,559	222,606	30,796	3,628	14,429	3,100	21,589
	1889	148,018	125,331	19,222	366	....	3,099	493
	1879	50,905	35,615	15,290				
	1869	36,470	22,375	14,095				
NEW ENGLAND:								
Maine.................	1919	547,028	173,855	274,528	4,481	92,749	1,415	164,796
	1914	487,211	176,792	258,314	4,582	46,344	1,179	107,700
	1909	459,599	168,774	258,392	3,933	27,203	1,297	54,266
	1904	343,627	127,288	203,094	3,063	8,061	2,121	26,587
	1899	259,232	89,477	158,788	2,178	7,572	1,217	9,659
	1889	150,317	42,835	104,602	10	....	2,870	191
	1879	100,476	20,759	79,717				
	1869	79,573	9,465	70,108				
New Hampshire........	1919	349,138	147,240	115,375	1,676	84,601	246	151,718
	1914	344,093	161,001	128,592	1,841	49,171	3,488	102,612
	1909	293,991	139,158	128,011	1,238	21,209	4,375	45,351
	1904	218,344	102,930	100,274	1,395	5,013	8,732	12,301
	1899	200,975	90,267	105,711	571	2,004	2,422	3,471
	1889	116,788	46,988	68,842	3	....	955	42
	1879	87,750	18,595	69,155				
	1869	77,078	8,787	68,291				
Vermont..............	1919	185,095	51,381	68,897	2,959	61,090	768	73,388
	1914	172,637	61,560	80,400	2,301	27,477	899	47,161
	1909	159,445	64,667	79,062	2,160	12,917	639	21,233
	1904	140,616	57,025	76,237	1,483	4,550	1,321	7,238
	1899	126,124	44,455	77,421	1,120	1,444	1,684	2,173
	1889	98,520	23,625	74,041	10	....	844	34
	1879	63,314	11,088	52,226				
	1869	51,322	6,425	44,897				
Massachusetts..........	1919	1,729,878	964,932	189,302	11,227	551,521	12,896	975,795
	1914	1,396,722	970,506	189,825	20,242	200,339	15,810	582,971
	1909	1,175,071	835,596	186,516	18,326	109,996	24,637	402,492
	1904	938,007	694,455	183,427	7,487	27,073	25,565	91,012
	1899	796,061	578,086	181,907	4,074	13,409	18,585	32,828
	1889	515,570	341,042	158,932	289	....	15,307	2,327
	1879	309,759	171,397	138,362				
	1869	184,356	78,502	105,854				
Rhode Island..........	1919	321,016	189,280	29,263	3,188	97,957	1,328	163,913
	1914	269,854	199,170	33,649	2,493	31,572	2,970	91,224
	1909	226,740	175,332	31,417	3,300	13,697	2,994	42,130
	1904	181,017	141,082	29,231	1,247	5,815	3,642	15,477
	1899	153,619	118,330	28,171	427	2,969	3,722	4,895
	1889	112,654	83,528	27,197	18	....	1,911	295
	1879	63,575	41,335	22,240				
	1869	42,027	23,546	18,481				

TABLE 24.—HORSEPOWER IN GEOGRAPHIC DIVISIONS AND STATES: 1869 TO 1919—Con.

| DIVISION AND STATE. | Census year. | PRIMARY HORSEPOWER. | | | | | | Electric horsepower owned and rented. |
| | | | Owned. | | | Rented. | | |
		Total.	Steam engines and turbines.	Water wheels and motors.	Internal-combustion engines.	Electric.	Other.	
NEW ENGLAND—Continued.								
Connecticut	1919	664,691	340,746	70,252	10,928	242,390	375	396,963
	1914	453,812	303,799	66,802	17,770	64,294	1,147	176,009
	1909	400,275	275,439	73,934	12,844	33,620	4,438	97,671
	1904	304,204	219,723	66,808	3,393	8,233	6,047	34,579
	1899	256,331	178,270	67,211	1,608	4,215	5,027	12,925
	1889	163,028	96,298	63,417	215	....	3,098	205
	1879	118,232	57,027	61,205	....	....	....	....
	1869	80,374	25,979	54,395	....	....	....	....
MIDDLE ATLANTIC:								
New York	1919	2,936,530	1,299,548	343,023	113,415	1,170,977	9,567	1,683,838
	1914	2,356,655	1,165,731	392,932	118,330	644,824	34,838	1,043,132
	1909	1,997,662	1,084,460	395,618	99,899	389,945	27,740	689,976
	1904	1,516,592	855,275	446,134	44,288	95,284	75,611	222,111
	1899	1,099,931	665,760	335,411	16,221	47,768	34,771	77,598
	1889	774,373	514,701	231,959	1,990	....	25,723	2,447
	1879	454,143	234,795	219,348	....	....	....	....
	1869	334,363	126,107	208,256	....	....	....	....
New Jersey	1919	1,146,744	781,434	12,528	40,830	305,762	6,190	724,153
	1914	793,063	642,608	15,901	30,592	94,605	9,357	352,206
	1909	612,293	529,848	19,676	20,867	33,157	8,745	182,475
	1904	436,274	390,095	18,197	9,070	10,603	8,309	69,301
	1899	322,503	288,956	20,161	3,284	4,126	5,976	15,857
	1889	180,042	158,802	17,543	135	....	3,562	487
	1879	99,858	72,792	27,066	....	....	....	....
	1869	58,139	32,307	25,832	....	....	....	....
Pennsylvania	1919	4,454,386	3,169,790	40,617	256,067	978,621	9,291	2,660,028
	1914	3,549,858	2,922,616	45,325	223,695	344,189	14,033	1,529,151
	1909	2,921,547	2,549,090	55,194	153,508	145,621	18,134	864,785
	1904	2,302,398	2,124,502	50,620	68,209	35,701	23,366	346,797
	1899	1,716,694	1,597,638	54,601	26,246	22,362	15,847	107,746
	1889	984,627	894,319	82,462	919	....	6,927	2,162
	1879	512,408	402,132	110,276	....	....	....	....
	1869	363,918	221,982	141,982	....	....	....	....
EAST NORTH CENTRAL:								
Ohio	1919	2,897,497	1,782,512	10,115	147,039	945,341	12,490	1,764,724
	1914	1,993,080	1,541,212	14,443	156,481	273,814	7,130	823,000
	1909	1,583,155	1,363,720	16,107	103,801	93,592	5,935	417,844
	1904	1,116,932	1,034,780	18,149	35,101	23,159	5,743	144,467
	1899	783,665	734,973	17,848	14,230	8,768	7,846	42,157
	1889	417,078	382,673	27,342	1,183	....	5,880	1,705
	1879	261,143	222,502	38,641	....	....	....	....
	1869	174,323	129,577	44,746	....	....	....	....
Indiana	1919	1,095,912	521,446	10,162	189,271	373,689	1,344	652,754
	1914	709,703	430,504	9,905	66,691	200,882	1,721	450,357
	1909	633,377	449,127	7,893	109,105	65,548	1,704	233,193
	1904	380,758	338,853	9,685	21,171	9,082	1,967	33,582
	1899	325,919	297,216	11,964	12,295	2,764	1,680	7,903
	1889	190,575	172,540	16,181	176	....	1,678	323
	1879	131,770	109,960	21,810	....	....	....	....
	1869	100,369	76,851	23,518	....	....	....	....
Illinois	1919	1,660,918	997,338	11,586	55,782	590,241	5,971	1,174,567
	1914	1,305,930	947,949	12,310	61,500	272,662	11,509	681,474
	1909	1,013,071	839,632	12,691	37,025	117,007	6,716	398,621
	1904	741,555	660,687	15,030	12,319	41,978	11,541	165,265
	1899	559,347	511,879	11,614	8,758	12,471	14,625	49,235
	1889	285,727	262,274	15,992	708	....	6,753	939
	1879	144,288	126,843	17,445	....	....	....	....
	1869	86,044	73,091	12,953	....	....	....	....
Michigan	1919	1,202,128	592,911	40,346	19,695	540,757	8,419	818,271
	1914	730,383	486,771	31,711	19,593	188,702	3,606	311,966
	1909	598,288	465,536	42,019	13,988	74,270	2,475	133,064
	1904	440,890	376,198	39,342	10,534	12,411	2,405	39,970
	1899	368,497	319,980	36,529	5,603	4,264	2,121	12,088
	1889	256,031	214,825	38,986	237	....	1,983	577
	1879	164,747	130,352	34,395	....	....	....	....
	1869	105,851	70,956	34,895	....	....	....	....

TABLE 24.—HORSEPOWER IN GEOGRAPHIC DIVISIONS AND STATES: 1869 TO 1919—Con.

DIVISION AND STATE.	Census year.	PRIMARY HORSEPOWER.						Electric horsepower owned and rented.
			Owned.			Rented.		
		Total.	Steam engines and turbines.	Water wheels and motors.	Internal-combustion engines.	Electric.	Other.	
EAST NORTH CENTRAL—Con.								
Wisconsin	1919	878,682	467,524	180,620	16,706	209,470	4,362	473,184
	1914	682,339	420,065	148,795	28,004	79,984	5,491	255,668
	1909	554,179	378,169	129,731	19,531	25,459	1,289	114,725
	1904	440,234	305,789	112,665	11,356	8,558	1,866	48,898
	1899	364,380	263,062	93,122	4,358	2,426	1,412	3,137
	1889	178,373	120,806	56,744	274	....	549	295
	1879	106,085	60,729	45,356	....	....	....	....
	1869	64,223	30,509	33,714	....	....	....	....
WEST NORTH CENTRAL:								
Minnesota	1919	473,957	198,186	73,661	33,848	167,965	297	255,119
	1914	358,737	206,144	73,341	7,454	71,224	574	121,018
	1909	297,670	199,802	59,570	7,174	30,297	827	52,212
	1904	220,934	168,115	38,245	4,710	8,594	1,270	14,427
	1899	180,124	146,826	24,932	3,624	3,769	973	6,300
	1889	112,537	83,630	27,300	126	....	1,481	280
	1879	53,880	25,191	28,689	....	....	....	....
	1869	20,139	7,085	13,054	....	....	....	....
Iowa	1919	242,946	119,442	3,862	7,030	112,486	126	166,285
	1914	190,049	125,340	5,538	8,868	50,054	249	101,827
	1909	155,384	122,029	6,411	8,025	18,463	456	40,736
	1904	118,065	101,418	6,531	4,486	5,107	523	8,663
	1899	106,664	91,570	7,315	4,524	2,613	642	6,222
	1889	77,615	64,737	12,618	70	....	190	194
	1879	54,221	33,858	20,363	....	....	....	....
	1869	39,547	25,298	14,249	....	....	....	....
Missouri	1919	477,303	269,657	3,386	22,049	181,556	655	287,572
	1914	391,385	283,490	3,203	18,321	84,362	2,009	181,981
	1909	340,467	280,494	3,738	11,159	44,056	1,020	106,941
	1904	247,861	223,879	3,727	4,960	13,965	1,330	37,671
	1899	189,117	173,802	3,113	3,279	5,624	3,299	12,725
	1889	144,567	137,758	4,755	457	....	1,597	618
	1879	80,749	72,587	8,162	....	....	....	....
	1869	55,062	48,418	6,644	....	....	....	....
North Dakota [1]	1919	17,791	10,060	260	1,981	5,490	....	6,773
	1914	14,062	9,627	299	1,198	2,856	82	3,800
	1909	13,196	10,170	530	1,304	1,164	28	1,698
	1904	9,873	8,619	322	645	281	6	477
	1899	7,351	5,932	506	759	127	27	171
	1889	3,587	3,008	540	12	....	27	2
South Dakota [1]	1919	22,191	8,360	307	3,282	10,227	15	11,130
	1914	16,324	8,972	574	2,364	4,414	....	4,632
	1909	17,666	12,257	939	2,784	1,683	3	2,084
	1904	11,154	8,497	1,069	1,397	181	10	339
	1899	11,775	9,294	1,099	1,270	100	12	234
	1889	5,552	4,468	1,052	32	....	....	3
Nebraska	1919	125,814	66,449	4,940	8,203	46,177	45	72,749
	1914	89,285	58,066	5,674	6,724	18,794	27	32,813
	1909	64,466	44,882	7,436	4,408	7,530	210	15,942
	1904	46,372	34,625	7,221	2,035	2,364	127	8,126
	1899	41,825	31,176	7,513	1,919	866	351	2,398
	1889	23,430	17,070	6,123	58	....	179	49
	1879	8,494	2,999	5,495	....	....	....	....
	1869	3,311	1,865	1,446	....	....	....	....
Kansas	1919	234,110	129,589	6,337	25,731	72,288	165	120,568
	1914	179,146	123,075	6,328	22,041	26,802	900	64,482
	1909	213,141	170,293	7,706	22,580	11,809	753	46,921
	1904	99,441	83,134	6,544	6,923	2,484	356	10,326
	1899	68,242	56,608	7,521	2,530	1,420	163	3,426
	1889	42,943	35,026	7,617	77	....	223	110
	1879	21,079	13,468	7,611	....	....	....	....
	1869	8,149	6,360	1,789	....	....	....	....

[1] The figures for Dakota Territory for the censuses preceding the separation of North Dakota and South Dakota are as follows: 1879, total primary horsepower, 2,224, steam power, 1,421, and water power, 803; 1869, total primary horsepower, 324, steam power, 248, and water power, 76.

TABLE 24.—HORSEPOWER IN GEOGRAPHIC DIVISIONS AND STATES: 1869 TO 1919—Con.

DIVISION AND STATE.	Census year.	PRIMARY HORSEPOWER.						Electric horse-power owned and rented.
		Total.	Owned.			Rented.		
			Steam engines and turbines.	Water wheels and motors.	Internal-combustion engines.	Electric.	Other.	
SOUTH ATLANTIC:								
Delaware	1919	85,150	59,743	4,448	1,607	19,307	45	44,528
	1914	64,403	48,207	4,507	1,905	9,705	79	29,544
	1909	52,779	42,266	5,195	766	4,502	50	17,910
	1904	49,490	42,542	5,280	412	1,092	164	5,764
	1899	40,134	32,898	5,399	315	605	917	1,870
	1889	26,412	21,557	4,671	80		104	104
	1879	15,428	10,643	4,785				
	1869	8,533	4,313	4,220				
Maryland	1919	406,768	177,106	9,007	65,493	155,031	131	313,811
	1914	263,753	196,199	9,935	13,822	42,243	1,554	117,707
	1909	218,244	182,395	12,074	5,736	17,108	931	44,921
	1904	165,449	145,627	10,777	4,377	3,309	1,359	18,823
	1899	132,052	116,115	10,415	3,139	733	1,650	4,174
	1889	73,335	56,548	15,633	175		979	212
	1879	51,259	33,216	18,043				
	1869	32,422	13,961	18,461				
District of Columbia	1919	33,079	10,340	666	2,103	19,960	10	21,943
	1914	24,775	15,230	540	2,568	6,407	30	9,522
	1909	16,563	12,212	775	1,073	2,433	70	4,527
	1904	12,592	10,567	710	311	996	8	1,761
	1899	10,255	8,777	369	338	100	671	348
	1889	11,374	10,422	810	91		51	70
	1879	3,143	2,263	880				
	1869	1,889	789	1,100				
Virginia	1919	419,946	256,7_ _	39,087	9,067	114,818	208	188,455
	1914	337,567	249,044	44,722	6,659	37,142		102,013
	1909	283,928	221,341	45,155	3,664	13,356	412	42,043
	1904	176,998	144,552	25,946	1,715	4,403	382	12,687
	1899	136,696	110,607	23,550	748	822	969	5,617
	1889	82,343	45,418	36,654	78		193	105
	1879	57,174	19,710	37,464				
	1869	49,612	8,410	41,202				
West Virginia	1919	328,653	217,155	9,411	38,972	62,917	198	155,224
	1914	278,504	216,976	5,554	28,537	27,152	285	66,676
	1909	217,496	184,591	10,617	16,705	5,330	253	28,543
	1904	138,578	124,735	6,404	6,569	776	94	5,199
	1899	91,894	85,139	5,425	1,045	27	298	454
	1889	55,452	44,802	10,542	33		75	5
	1879	37,910	28,456	9,454				
	1869	27,331	17,136	10,195				
North Carolina	1919	549,878	303,242	42,626	6,556	197,384	70	260,546
	1914	508,085	331,132	41,181	5,379	128,660	1,733	163,161
	1909	378,556	272,979	41,926	2,356	60,044	1,251	86,002
	1904	216,622	183,213	28,382	2,102	2,423	502	5,553
	1899	154,467	123,328	29,241	388	894	616	2,733
	1889	73,301	41,360	31,812	42		87	44
	1879	45,088	15,025	30,063				
	1869	33,152	6,941	26,211				
South Carolina	1919	395,556	214,719	40,714	2,472	137,561	90	174,148
	1914	340,224	207,480	42,413	2,063	83,754	4,514	111,988
	1909	276,378	195,452	38,497	1,264	41,130	35	67,620
	1904	197,479	157,612	31,097	239	8,451	80	32,162
	1899	112,697	81,283	27,586	323	185	3,320	6,061
	1889	45,673	29,103	16,399	97		74	8
	1879	25,868	11,995	13,873				
	1869	14,932	4,537	10,395				
Georgia	1919	436,608	243,642	26,906	5,603	157,568	2,889	194,263
	1914	357,403	245,811	27,829	7,032	76,458	273	103,140
	1909	298,241	240,800	28,748	3,380	23,890	1,423	44,264
	1904	220,419	183,721	28,304	632	6,464	1,298	15,556
	1899	136,499	111,465	22,729	365	1,668	272	2,698
	1889	84,064	55,108	28,380	119		457	157
	1879	51,169	21,102	30,067				
	1869	38,243	10,826	27,417				

TABLE 24.—HORSEPOWER IN GEOGRAPHIC DIVISIONS AND STATES: 1869 TO 1919—Con.

DIVISION AND STATE.	Census year.	PRIMARY HORSEPOWER.						Electric horse-power owned and rented.
		Total.	Owned.			Rented.		
			Steam engines and turbines.	Water wheels and motors.	Internal-com-bus-tion engines.	Elec-tric.	Other.	
SOUTH ATLANTIC—Con.								
Florida.................	1919	139,456	111,487	243	4,706	22,655	365	35,135
	1914	100,071	88,939	183	4,464	6,406	79	12,888
	1909	89,816	84,708	171	1,497	3,353	87	7,563
	1904	43,413	41,975	118	320	1,000	....	2,960
	1899	36,356	35,905	116	173	162	....	302
	1889	16,055	15,483	496	63	....	13	3
	1879	7,147	6,208	939	....	....	....	....
	1869	3,700	3,172	528	....	....	....	....
EAST SOUTH CENTRAL:								
Kentucky..............	1919	247,573	175,210	3,758	10,623	56,808	1,174	94,380
	1914	238,314	206,871	3,968	6,581	20,382	512	49,168
	1909	230,224	208,506	5,377	4,724	11,314	303	31,268
	1904	174,625	163,719	4,603	1,938	3,874	491	10,690
	1899	144,161	136,378	4,247	1,096	1,722	718	3,415
	1889	82,408	75,590	6,271	223	....	324	100
	1879	54,929	45,917	9,012	....	....	....	....
	1869	39,568	31,928	7,640	....	....	....	....
Tennessee..............	1919	338,814	227,206	7,534	5,718	98,274	82	131,411
	1914	286,857	216,156	9,395	3,435	57,858	13	83,107
	1909	242,277	215,342	9,777	1,853	14,666	639	29,586
	1904	175,780	162,044	9,995	1,084	2,230	427	6,586
	1899	130,318	116,753	11,078	593	1,370	524	2,193
	1889	84,273	68,551	15,451	54	....	217	106
	1879	51,952	33,388	18,564	....	....	....	....
	1869	37,981	18,467	19,514	....	....	....	....
Alabama..............	1919	628,376	468,746	13,534	3,595	142,412	89	199,523
	1914	445,762	375,114	9,621	4,469	56,400	158	98,189
	1909	357,837	329,007	13,923	4,616	10,104	187	39,928
	1904	293,185	281,653	9,518	472	1,448	94	10,114
	1899	173,208	162,690	9,421	376	359	362	3,421
	1889	102,282	91,603	10,382	14	....	283	51
	1879	27,576	15,779	11,797	....	....	....	....
	1869	18,751	7,740	11,011	....	....	....	....
Mississippi.............	1919	200,814	183,990	181	2,957	13,644	42	34,829
	1914	186,434	177,287	643	1,695	6,779	30	17,351
	1909	206,222	202,346	238	1,077	2,496	65	7,627
	1904	110,338	109,508	77	220	508	25	1,367
	1899	65,738	64,731	361	144	382	120	590
	1889	35,328	32,362	2,746	8	....	212	3
	1879	18,450	15,001	3,449	....	....	....	....
	1869	12,472	10,019	2,453	....	....	....	....
WEST SOUTH CENTRAL:								
Arkansas...............	1919	214,194	183,400	706	6,620	21,493	1,975	35,591
	1914	177,208	167,378	793	2,979	5,956	102	13,340
	1909	173,088	168,204	674	1,374	2,581	255	7,417
	1904	109,509	107,858	584	482	484	101	2,191
	1899	79,560	78,244	734	326	201	55	480
	1889	38,313	36,368	1,778	7	....	160	31
	1879	15,733	13,709	2,024	....	....	....	....
	1869	7,646	6,101	1,545	....	....	....	....
Louisiana.............	1919	388,605	332,154	60	13,928	41,091	1,372	84,204
	1914	355,193	328,718	1,447	3,020	16,580	428	50,006
	1909	346,652	333,771	75	3,496	9,077	233	27,139
	1904	251,963	247,885	266	961	2,778	73	6,752
	1899	190,182	187,814	313	462	1,401	192	2,069
	1889	29,730	29,444	66	213	....	7	454
	1879	11,346	11,256	90	....	....	....	....
	1869	25,066	24,924	142	....	....	....	....
Oklahoma [1]...........	1919	139,983	79,707	275	24,133	35,435	433	54,605
	1914	97,308	70,803	256	15,976	10,068	205	23,760
	1909	71,139	56,643	472	8,676	5,281	67	7,887
	1904	29,608	27,753	109	989	597	160	910
	1899	11,572	11,151	156	200	....	65	12
	1889	585	510	75	....	....	....	....

[1] Includes power for Indian Territory in 1904 and prior censuses.

TABLE **24.**—HORSEPOWER IN GEOGRAPHIC DIVISIONS AND STATES: 1869 TO 1919—Con.

DIVISION AND STATE.	Census year.	PRIMARY HORSEPOWER.						Electric horsepower owned and rented.
		Total.	Owned.			Rented.		
			Steam engines and turbines.	Water wheels and motors.	Internal-combustion engines.	Electric.	Other.	
W. SOUTH CENTRAL—Con.								
Texas	1919	443,207	281,371	2,405	36,579	120,539	2,313	176,553
	1914	335,791	262,200	2,053	28,300	42,943	295	76,133
	1909	282,471	249,535	1,887	15,745	14,868	436	36,450
	1904	164,637	156,011	2,277	1,876	4,414	59	10,299
	1899	116,157	110,970	1,557	968	2,390	272	3,217
	1889	68,364	65,450	2,633	157	....	124	166
	1879	30,534	28,026	2,508	....	....	....	....
	1869	13,044	11,214	1,830	....	....	....	....
MOUNTAIN:								
Montana	1919	153,491	42,099	7,996	1,484	101,910	2	106,207
	1914	91,671	52,918	10,135	820	27,798	....	38,109
	1909	90,402	49,654	13,646	223	26,504	375	27,301
	1904	46,736	32,441	10,315	74	3,898	8	7,979
	1899	43,679	32,618	9,717	85	1,196	63	3,184
	1889	2,805	2,105	666	17	....	17	43
	1879	1,498	544	954	....	....	....	....
	1869	1,617	822	795	....	....	....	....
Idaho	1919	73,876	53,304	1,751	578	18,207	36	29,889
	1914	50,326	38,264	1,674	431	9,928	29	16,120
	1909	42,804	35,529	2,407	242	4,606	20	8,409
	1904	16,987	15,145	1,078	127	537	100	1,702
	1899	5,649	4,010	1,605	28	6	....	6
	1889	1,999	975	1,024	....	....	....	2
	1879	1,682	546	1,136	....	....	....	....
	1869	606	311	295	....	....	....	....
Wyoming	1919	17,869	8,255	391	1,718	7,500	5	9,240
	1914	10,004	6,925	537	1,366	1,176	....	1,691
	1909	7,628	6,467	465	182	514	....	801
	1904	3,604	3,088	382	88	46	....	132
	1899	3,820	3,237	534	42	7	....	87
	1889	1,824	1,608	216	....	....	....	5
	1879	755	717	38	....	....	....	....
	1869	344	310	34	....	....	....	....
Colorado	1919	206,309	145,417	1,184	2,186	57,323	199	86,036
	1914	162,828	126,608	6,669	2,075	27,349	127	57,278
	1909	154,615	135,750	1,426	1,464	15,874	101	35,944
	1904	124,907	118,660	2,094	317	3,765	71	15,730
	1899	43,434	39,883	1,493	519	1,187	352	1,896
	1889	32,676	30,641	1,723	36	....	276	58
	1879	5,802	3,953	1,849	....	....	....	....
	1869	2,225	1,433	792	....	....	....	....
New Mexico	1919	17,260	12,595	381	920	3,364	....	5,178
	1914	12,468	10,361	23	775	1,309	....	2,617
	1909	15,465	11,781	74	365	3,245	....	4,586
	1904	5,948	5,417	149	114	203	65	233
	1899	3,658	3,433	153	64	8	....	8
	1889	1,825	1,492	323	....	....	10	....
	1879	1,359	427	932	....	....	....	....
	1869	911	252	659	....	....	....	....
Arizona	1919	103,958	77,138	200	1,773	24,847	....	44,903
	1914	54,697	44,312	70	795	8,918	602	23,118
	1909	39,140	34,212	129	1,285	3,314	200	15,100
	1904	21,412	19,338	267	1,392	165	250	4,821
	1899	8,537	7,728	400	371	38	....	534
	1889	826	457	329	....	....	40	....
	1879	530	370	160	....	....	....	....
	1869	90	80	10	....	....	....	....
Utah	1919	93,942	46,996	3,558	968	41,275	1,145	58,721
	1914	59,536	34,020	3,494	470	21,552	....	34,018
	1909	42,947	29,084	2,997	226	10,592	48	15,402
	1904	19,397	13,145	3,252	59	2,941	....	4,272
	1899	12,674	7,616	3,366	89	1,588	....	2,829
	1889	5,064	2,530	2,492	10	....	15	64
	1879	4,689	1,154	3,535	....	....	32	....
	1869	2,500	331	2,169	....	....	....	....

TABLE 24.—HORSEPOWER IN GEOGRAPHIC DIVISIONS AND STATES: 1869 TO 1919—Con.

DIVISION AND STATE.	Census year.	PRIMARY HORSEPOWER.						Electric horse-power owned and rented.
			Owned.			Rented.		
		Total.	Steam engines and turbines.	Water wheels and motors.	Internal-combustion engines.	Electric.	Other.	
MOUNTAIN—Continued.								
Nevada	1919	19,874	14,142	195	344	5,193		11,040
	1914	18,748	13,433	909	139	4,263	4	17,574
	1909	7,765	4,533	399	201	2,307	325	6,441
	1904	2,834	1,092	782	125	550	285	550
	1899	1,561	628	893	39	1		1
	1889	372	318	6	48			
	1879	716	608	108				
	1869	8,545	6,007	2,538				
PACIFIC:								
Washington	1919	687,436	453,306	7,723	6,123	215,921	4,363	278,155
	1914	389,567	291,923	9,306	3,162	84,953	223	112,485
	1909	297,897	257,249	8,065	1,494	30,951	138	43,615
	1904	168,342	150,798	4,642	493	11,650	759	15,290
	1899	87,601	77,821	6,853	189	2,562	176	3,137
	1889	42,579	37,709	4,851	3		16	63
	1879	4,395	3,210	1,185				
	1869	2,823	1,411	1,412				
Oregon	1919	304,346	165,801	43,252	2,166	92,576	551	118,187
	1914	214,222	116,591	57,275	1,289	39,010	57	48,739
	1909	175,019	112,244	47,438	428	14,811	98	20,802
	1904	81,348	55,512	20,660	371	4,727	78	5,223
	1899	60,005	37,986	19,263	195	2,243	318	2,690
	1889	32,508	22,736	9,280	2		490	37
	1879	13,589	4,334	9,255				
	1869	8,277	2,471	5,806				
California	1919	766,016	211,256	7,704	25,020	521,188	848	572,284
	1914	491,025	207,695	7,450	15,614	258,734	1,532	291,344
	1909	329,100	193,556	7,670	10,115	116,537	1,222	143,684
	1904	210,359	154,922	7,260	6,292	39,363	2,522	49,575
	1899	126,953	106,799	4,680	3,244	9,624	2,606	15,762
	1889	72,931	64,886	5,091	361		2,593	393
	1879	32,921	28,071	4,850				
	1869	25,370	18,493	6,877				

TABLE 25.—CONSUMPTION OF FUEL IN 47 LEADING FUEL-CONSUMING INDUSTRIES: 1919, 1914, AND 1909.

INDUSTRY.	Census year.	Cost of fuel and rent of power.	FUEL CONSUMED.				
			Anthracite coal (tons of 2,240 lbs.).	Bituminous coal (tons of 2,000 lbs.).	Coke (tons of 2,000 lbs.).	Oil, including gasoline (barrels).	Gas (1,000 cubic feet).
All industries.......	1919	$1,645,986,556	14,334,402	203,463,622	42,595,019	92,029,692	341,921,022
	1914	666,406,709	14,041,123	166,589,372	32,539,325	48,689,232	284,947,889
	1909	570,067,824	14,339,220	161,793,058	37,925,338	34,331,632	269,640,535
Agricultural implements..	1919	5,038,512	13,497	549,557	115,368	372,201	435,393
	1914	2,507,394	8,863	555,271	104,386	240,060	234,349
	1909	2,042,974	15,114	550,085	98,819	244,759	313,412
Automobiles, including bodies and parts.	1919	21,785,066	49,169	1,748,680	101,548	1,445,406	2,828,203
	1914	4,656,102	31,393	662,224	23,560	384,248	2,038,860
	1909	1,661,724	17,346	319,497	14,282	86,873	385,468
Boots and shoes, including cut stock and findings.	1919	6,945,277	52,455	441,447	3,127	27,873	756,801
	1914	2,310,903	80,618	302,766	3,119	4,371	201,892
	1909	1,847,885	45,089	285,545	2,134	4,324	128,314
Brass, bronze, and copper products.	1919	12,686,801	200,719	655,947	131,113	914,591	812,573
	1914	3,831,780	127,828	378,306	75,812	310,910	464,259
	1909	3,005,514	206,396	589,309	59,152	206,852	248,798
Bread and other bakery products.	1919	19,474,881	596,989	554,982	309,706	349,121	5,476,396
	1914	9,591,187	470,341	382,882	254,313	220,141	4,619,113
	1909	7,375,847	383,390	250,165	195,971	151,371	2,732,911
Brick, tile, pottery, and other clay products.	1919	39,931,963	164,410	7,526,980	35,555	1,353,055	16,654,909
	1914	26,601,525	291,366	9,170,010	66,872	1,921,256	23,821,028
	1909	25,348,623	334,684	8,799,778	45,347	1,410,740	26,368,992
Butter, cheese, and condensed milk.	1919	11,125,649	73,812	1,379,270	6,407	344,675	233,553
	1914	3,909,540	36,069	831,549	7,146	218,359	213,373
	1909	2,771,983	47,344	588,169	1,069	94,325	215,318
Canning and preserving....	1919	5,832,733	33,431	538,868	6,207	739,922	287,538
	1914	2,166,400	48,705	415,732	2,992	344,764	224,543
	1909	1,551,363	37,613	287,294	2,156	165,042	130,434
Cars and general shop construction and repairs by steam-railroad companies.	1919	31,400,634	609,078	6,964,403	260,960	3,124,953	2,530,494
	1914	12,482,370	506,696	5,486,405	79,597	2,508,703	1,829,902
	1909	8,465,983	438,349	5,255,477	54,827	982,329	1,116,127
Cars, steam-railroad, not including operations of railroad companies.	1919	6,180,615	53,644	819,988	73,638	560,469	1,108,259
	1914	2,749,760	34,978	698,097	70,886	294,826	1,221,695
	1909	2,097,659	38,895	664,638	113,013	140,725	552,803
Cement..................	1919	31,070,596	272,266	6,031,428	50,840	1,861,342	4,370,699
	1914	20,271,662	226,474	6,731,438	20,072	2,502,065	5,525,894
	1909	13,153,180	259,220	4,815,758	4,103	1,515,697	14,721,568
Chemicals................	1919	32,742,310	389,356	3,844,667	457,259	807,774	1,836,998
	1914	11,203,672	491,603	2,667,248	275,440	500,668	2,744,939
	1909	8,047,443	650,482	2,161,783	63,522	110,276	1,300,770
Coke, not including gashouse coke.	1919	200,769,464	5,808	64,245,629	560,505	107,893	658,690
	1914	64,832,328	....	50,457,474	....	....	....
	1909	60,905,891	....	59,030,005	....	....	....
Copper, tin, and sheet-iron products.	1919	5,393,671	52,872	485,762	31,339	185,328	1,439,591
	1914	2,646,518	63,454	458,576	20,400	140,330	1,529,565
	1909	2,252,642	51,448	334,754	14,917	85,096	1,337,837
Cotton goods, including cotton small wares.	1919	38,263,431	368,595	3,663,302	32,466	507,919	134,581
	1914	17,860,740	313,531	3,634,223	15,537	24,755	42,846
	1909	13,985,896	415,604	3,327,802	20,605	38,792	68,106
Dyeing and finishing textiles, exclusive of that done in textile mills.	1919	10,428,294	442,855	1,071,156	13,624	400,258	516,218
	1914	4,771,997	490,587	896,589	97	31,869	143,953
	1909	4,451,077	593,093	869,216	2,576	10,037	64,657
Electrical machinery, apparatus, and supplies.	1919	13,739,110	175,800	1,091,704	61,617	505,660	2,786,382
	1914	4,607,861	66,841	769,260	26,378	125,523	2,767,856
	1909	3,056,066	87,096	632,870	20,123	104,467	1,761,969
Flour-mill and gristmill products.	1919	15,279,876	57,034	1,582,494	5,134	730,189	1,157,455
	1914	7,780,149	56,953	1,809,968	13,941	441,693	1,627,252
	1909	6,980,675	67,459	1,880,702	3,347	424,386	3,037,008

TABLE 25.—CONSUMPTION OF FUEL IN 47 LEADING FUEL-CONSUMING INDUSTRIES:
1919, 1914, AND 1909—Continued.

INDUSTRY.	Census year.	Cost of fuel and rent of power.	Anthracite coal (tons of 2,240 lbs.).	Bituminous coal (tons of 2,000 lbs.).	Coke (tons of 2,000 lbs.).	Oil, including gasoline (barrels).	Gas (1,000 cubic feet).
				FUEL CONSUMED.			
Food preparations, not elsewhere specified.	1919	$5,563,505	65,048	456,951	10,422	113,137	976,218
	1914	2,236,975	45,276	387,200	12,987	72,664	991,297
	1909	1,333,497	31,712	272,392	9,092	35,832	368,195
Foundry and machine-shop products.	1919	82,411,421	534,185	5,957,355	2,069,855	3,225,507	26,112,351
	1914	28,880,719	519,813	4,300,909	1,473,656	965,125	12,558,076
	1909	23,750,838	624,958	4,220,640	1,919,916	677,828	13,637,341
Furniture and refrigerators.	1919	6,595,339	36,974	869,809	13,067	26,225	331,377
	1914	3,291,806	62,165	785,105	17,565	20,644	237,052
	1909	2,571,562	54,427	728,841	17,009	7,540	181,463
Gas, illuminating and heating.	1919	114,911,986	1,388,467	7,383,687	1,497,435	19,195,800	641,288
	1914	53,894,193	947,261	6,078,299	1,084,217	13,482,655	3,372,563
	1909	39,196,031	898,984	4,668,096	759,245	11,816,282	605,408
Glass	1919	24,357,862	15,268	2,653,654	131,998	910,119	38,500,857
	1914	10,934,928	41,372	2,252,268	16,770	867,836	43,336,322
	1909	7,523,937	17,906	1,859,001	17,393	468,894	43,711,519
Ice, manufactured	1919	25,606,264	205,875	3,309,636	32,327	1,633,549	6,170,964
	1914	11,340,469	213,541	3,386,275	30,493	1,292,008	7,592,003
	1909	7,780,397	244,396	2,430,454	6,872	905,952	4,348,929
Iron and steel, blast furnaces.[1]	1919	235,623,653	42,779	2,261,315	32,424,625	51,324	1,184,953
	1914	88,586,592	47,060	1,892,357	26,335,234	80,474	242,218
	1909	108,536,921	273,543	1,166,135	31,649,865	19,446	274,699
Iron and steel, steel works and rolling mills.	1919	156,964,862	598,944	25,911,098	886,062	8,490,982	90,678,288
	1914	55,447,804	558,723	20,343,767	495,214	3,011,192	81,310,122
	1909	46,136,725	765,145	19,759,678	648,637	2,063,736	86,440,031
Iron and steel, forgings, not made in steel works or rolling mills.	1919	8,737,621	26,972	717,801	65,021	1,214,040	1,043,895
	1914	1,828,462	18,068	285,573	21,737	323,875	961,363
	1909	1,087,088	27,231	241,387	29,895	165,875	612,045
Knit goods	1919	5,465,202	102,024	584,787	1,654	7,526	73,068
	1914	2,686,957	118,071	484,268	2,849	2,476	40,765
	1909	1,970,277	124,420	441,187	1,080	2,182	33,861
Leather, tanned, curried, and finished.	1919	9,823,256	89,722	1,448,166	3,740	89,232	211,404
	1914	3,757,026	89,140	1,124,444	2,489	67,252	527,657
	1909	3,292,831	98,724	1,028,215	806	46,129	598,532
Lime	1919	6,027,446	57,112	872,910	102,788	26,820	53,835
	1914	3,534,377	76,141	677,071	60,159	82,447	673,853
	1909	3,439,986	106,929	674,304	71,471	33,147	1,424,724
Liquors, malt	1919	11,568,728	346,914	1,692,067	14,527	329,849	392,964
	1914	10,470,018	571,588	2,749,600	11,198	725,672	3,314,070
	1909	8,570,892	554,029	2,424,798	11,530	527,089	3,649,380
Lumber and timber products.	1919	14,044,564	55,554	2,271,596	29,629	925,555	414,672
	1914	7,461,399	76,873	1,417,485	4,996	507,546	492,694
	1909	5,082,287	79,330	1,134,218	5,854	144,499	521,034
Oil and cake, cottonseed.	1919	8,555,622	34,763	1,172,175	10,262	394,219	1,527,974
	1914	4,010,450	5,507	1,232,031	1,762	248,806	1,519,198
	1909	3,144,795	8,583	828,357	800	376,789	372,880
Paper and wood pulp	1919	54,999,955	869,948	7,863,150	63,384	2,120,114	286,660
	1914	24,261,348	741,177	6,268,853	15,455	635,329	2,260,562
	1909	18,320,266	558,677	5,460,314	500	584,536	6,485,293
Petroleum, refining.	1919	53,505,109	1,105,503	3,619,534	319,563	23,716,521	26,919,052
	1914	13,567,284	1,367,429	2,045,485	157,621	7,455,918	10,993,746
	1909	8,376,383	1,347,519	1,264,841	99,595	3,473,758	7,519,859
Printing and publishing.	1919	13,492,954	179,403	370,398	7,048	101,954	2,567,301
	1914	8,605,057	165,903	351,395	4,830	52,849	2,270,571
	1909	7,601,152	154,932	348,698	2,895	41,265	1,633,886
Rubber tires, tubes, and rubber goods, not elsewhere specified.	1919	12,605,943	84,915	1,928,116	3,651	229,785	283,760
	1914	2,744,005	68,793	919,066	348	8,778	371,283
	1909	1,394,287	59,372	479,906	25	1,346	52,173

[1] Includes "ferroalloys" in 1914 and 1909.

TABLE 25.—CONSUMPTION OF FUEL IN 47 LEADING FUEL-CONSUMING INDUSTRIES: 1919, 1914, AND 1909—Continued.

INDUSTRY.	Census year.	Cost of fuel and rent of power.	FUEL CONSUMED.				
			Anthracite coal (tons of 2,240 lbs.).	Bituminous coal (tons of 2,000 lbs.).	Coke (tons of 2,000 lbs.).	Oil, including gasoline (barrels).	Gas (1,000 cubic feet).
Shipbuilding, including boat building.	1919	$15,604,092	50,234	868,713	97,690	1,133,851	701,461
	1914	1,418,368	13,441	251,820	10,548	122,929	404,785
	1909	1,191,654	12,080	301,501	10,725	89,916	274,071
Silk goods, including throwsters.	1919	6,201,447	306,165	269,717	1,002	46,506	44,724
	1914	2,322,684	307,607	202,514	48	2,962	148,252
	1909	1,687,981	242,771	155,256	3,601	3,072	49,673
Slaughtering and meat packing.	1919	24,619,455	227,360	3,822,531	33,831	1,915,501	1,357,411
	1914	8,584,177	226,995	2,802,845	14,340	1,203,412	2,083,407
	1909	6,700,834	193,935	2,512,864	976	1,102,550	1,091,164
Smelting and refining, copper.	1919	19,243,024	179,026	1,088,511	397,762	2,543,121	712,817
	1914	13,471,917	299,480	812,196	744,256	2,303,755	10,615
	1909	13,320,517	310,953	1,081,031	1,008,059	658,923	3,889
Smelting and refining, lead.	1919	5,676,483	7,276	292,806	321,442	202,088	20,940
	1914	3,883,589	....	358,484	389,826	186,556	90,656
	1909	3,508,126	31,958	427,479	351,968	99,157	47,393
Smelting and refining, zinc.	1919	9,446,601	835,129	1,123,590	238,432	6,646	24,343,653
	1914	4,115,854	655,766	1,066,525	92,595	145,811	22,336,089
	1909	2,218,876	432,161	634,932	52,172	41,595	11,676,995
Sugar, beet..............	1919	5,378,604	....	1,047,643	125,262	564,268	57,862
	1914	2,726,525	37,235	682,693	37,854	803,698	4,789
	1909	1,899,468	8,981	565,672	28,300	554,174	383
Sugar, refining............	1919	9,769,121	406,248	987,690	430	1,705,513	....
	1914	3,985,160	451,310	875,882	1,624	748,533	....
	1909	2,866,371	511,640	542,148	362	578,633	453
Wire.....................	1919	4,235,523	12,573	726,940	18,547	176,282	419,310
	1914	1,813,172	30,067	523,603	14,329	88,979	415,873
	1909	1,640,172	84,208	518,121	22,280	71,663	217,620
Woolen, worsted, and felt goods, and wool hats.	1919	16,128,813	233,634	1,617,424	3,581	869,068	62,269
	1914	7,525,349	257,433	1,608,872	1,524	43,207	64,577
	1909	6,489,196	277,755	1,525,988	6,985	26,611	104,746
All other industries........	1919	170,733,218	2,624,597	17,077,588	1,413,569	5,725,961	71,804,961
	1914	74,238,157	2,681,588	14,114,469	422,253	2,926,903	37,042,112
	1909	60,432,052	2,513,339	13,453,757	471,477	3,937,122	29,218,403

TABLE 26.—COMPARATIVE SUMMARY FOR 14 GENERAL GROUPS OF INDUSTRIES: 1919, 1914, 1909, AND 1904.

Group No.	GROUP.	Census year.	Number of establishments.	Wage earners (average number).	Capital.	Wages.	Cost of materials.	Value of products.	Value added by manufacture.
							Expressed in thousands.		
	All industries...	1919	290,105	9,096,372	$44,466,594	$10,533,400	$37,376,380	$62,418,079	$25,041,699
		1914	275,791	7,036,247	22,790,980	4,078,332	14,368,089	24,246,435	9,878,346
		1909	268,491	6,615,046	18,428,270	3,427,038	12,142,791	20,672,052	8,529,261
		1904	216,180	5,468,383	12,675,581	2,610,445	8,500,208	14,793,903	6,293,695
1	Food and kindred products.	1919	61,312	684,672	4,615,150	722,540	10,111,547	12,438,891	2,327,344
		1914	59,317	496,234	2,174,386	278,009	3,828,512	4,816,710	988,198
		1909	55,364	411,575	1,696,754	208,663	3,187,803	3,937,618	749,815
		1904	45,857	354,046	1,169,873	164,511	2,306,121	2,845,556	539,435
2	Textiles and their products.	1919	28,552	1,611,309	6,096,161	1,482,327	5,382,079	9,216,103	3,834,024
		1914	23,463	1,507,374	2,836,279	676,460	2,015,502	3,447,997	1,432,495
		1909	22,057	1,445,720	2,507,427	595,243	1,763,267	3,086,944	1,323,677
		1904	17,344	1,163,497	1,758,306	422,570	1,260,405	2,168,892	908,487
3	Iron and steel and their products.	1919	20,120	1,585,712	8,711,843	2,193,203	4,815,885	9,403,634	4,587,749
		1914	17,719	1,061,058	4,281,998	723,163	1,762,312	3,223,142	1,460,830
		1909	17,292	1,026,553	3,578,602	635,323	1,799,943	3,164,471	1,364,528
		1904	14,431	868,634	2,351,051	488,598	1,190,793	2,199,776	1,008,983
4	Lumber and its re-manufactures.	1919	39,955	839,008	2,580,046	847,032	1,359,999	3,070,073	1,710,074
		1914	42,036	833,529	1,723,454	440,308	762,351	1,599,712	837,361
		1909	48,539	911,593	1,570,549	424,759	717,833	1,588,274	870,441
		1904	32,501	734,136	1,009,950	335,046	517,501	1,219,749	702,248
5	Leather and its finished products.	1919	6,397	349,362	1,522,502	363,453	1,713,807	2,610,231	896,424
		1914	6,758	307,060	743,347	169,357	753,135	1,104,594	351,459
		1909	5,728	309,766	659,231	155,111	669,875	992,714	322,839
		1904	5,318	264,459	451,796	120,833	480,221	724,391	244,170
6	Paper and printing.	1919	36,403	509,875	2,382,400	564,510	1,306,718	3,012,584	1,705,866
		1914	37,196	452,900	1,433,177	296,492	580,717	1,456,047	875,330
		1909	34,828	415,990	1,133,618	242,062	451,238	1,179,285	728,047
		1904	30,803	351,640	803,663	186,422	309,012	859,814	550,802
7	Liquors and beverages.	1919	6,354	55,442	781,572	66,140	222,776	603,895	381,119
		1914	7,562	88,152	1,015,715	69,124	246,189	772,080	525,891
		1909	7,347	77,827	874,108	53,502	186,128	674,311	488,183
		1904	6,379	68,338	659,539	45,144	139,849	501,254	361,405
8	Chemicals and allied products.	1919	12,224	427,008	5,617,738	493,744	3,747,675	5,610,299	1,862,624
		1914	12,374	299,569	3,034,209	167,494	1,289,346	2,001,635	712,289
		1909	12,060	267,261	2,167,425	129,003	931,044	1,526,599	595,555
		1904	9,826	227,326	1,588,328	102,388	633,919	1,075,519	441,600
9	Stone, clay, and glass products.	1919	12,529	298,659	1,262,212	328,559	408,571	1,085,529	676,958
		1914	14,747	334,612	987,331	205,420	238,735	614,162	375,427
		1909	16,168	342,827	857,760	189,257	183,792	531,737	347,945
		1904	10,773	285,346	553,785	148,458	123,067	391,148	268,081
10	Metals and metal products, other than iron and steel.	1919	10,667	339,469	1,796,669	394,628	1,910,035	2,760,294	850,259
		1914	10,023	262,154	1,013,632	166,895	1,023,354	1,417,043	393,689
		1909	8,783	249,607	867,407	146,794	892,066	1,240,410	348,344
		1904	5,880	198,531	571,902	110,208	633,133	895,975	262,842
11	Tobacco manufactures.	1919	10,291	157,097	604,840	123,988	483,567	1,012,933	529,366
		1914	13,951	178,872	303,840	77,856	207,134	490,165	283,031
		1909	15,822	166,810	245,660	69,355	177,186	416,695	239,509
		1904	16,827	159,406	323,983	62,639	126,086	331,111	205,025
12	Vehicles for land transportation.	1919	21,152	495,939	2,423,240	689,475	2,498,225	4,058,911	1,560,686
		1914	9,909	263,076	803,496	197,077	586,670	1,034,497	447,827
		1909	6,562	202,719	521,457	121,047	306,536	561,763	255,227
		1904	6,058	136,625	287,847	72,659	177,641	320,624	142,983
13	Railroad repair shops.	1919	2,368	515,709	776,844	726,691	547,829	1,354,446	806,617
		1914	2,011	365,902	417,706	253,150	261,438	552,618	291,180
		1909	1,686	304,592	277,216	195,830	214,581	437,563	222,982
		1904	1,226	247,922	159,792	149,166	156,568	323,212	166,644
14	Miscellaneous industries.	1919	21,781	1,227,111	5,295,377	1,537,110	2,867,667	6,180,256	3,312,589
		1914	18,725	585,755	2,022,410	357,527	812,694	1,716,033	903,339
		1909	16,255	482,206	1,471,056	261,089	661,499	1,333,668	672,169
		1904	12,957	408,477	985,766	201,803	445,892	936,882	490,990

SPECIAL STATISTICS.

TABLE 27.—BUTTER, CHEESE, AND CONDENSED MILK: 1919, 1914, 1909, AND 1904.

	1919	1914	1909	1904
MATERIALS.				
Total cost	$926,366,296	$315,025,635	$235,546,064	$142,920,277
Milk:				
Pounds	10,244,874,792	8,431,426,426	9,888,727,303	12,147,304,550
Cost	$333,356,687	$114,297,630	$118,675,613	$99,729,745
Cream:				
Pounds	2,551,748,117	2,384,034,699	1,406,143,908	588,186,471
Cost	$437,267,198	$160,934,127	$95,025,507	$28,371,040
Skimmed milk:				
Pounds	1,361,188,373	525,041,086	56,974,760	36,071,335
Cost	$8,740,665	$994,201	$110,469	$59,398
Sugar:				
Pounds	636,568,407	98,836,640	78,457,978	67,810,031
Cost	$30,198,824	$4,408,053	$3,674,174	$3,315,892
All other materials, cost	$116,802,922	$34,391,624	$18,060,301	$11,444,202
PRODUCTS.				
Total value	[1] $1,066,125,489	[1] $364,285,150	[1] $274,557,718	[1] $168,182,789
Butter:				
Pounds	920,550,066	769,809,781	624,764,653	531,478,141
Value	$522,274,315	$218,021,690	$179,510,619	$113,189,453
Packed solid—				
Pounds	551,121,133	476,895,792	410,692,616	364,432,996
Value	$309,229,371	$132,259,918	$115,098,056	$74,483,306
Prints and rolls—				
Pounds	369,428,933	292,913,989	214,072,037	167,045,145
Value	$213,044,944	$85,761,772	$64,412,563	$38,706,147
Cheese:				
Pounds	473,569,199	370,278,599	311,126,317	317,144,872
Value	$136,940,464	$50,377,018	$43,239,924	$28,611,760
Full cream—				
Pounds	411,778,381	332,690,891	287,110,383	
Value	$123,731,763	$47,432,597	$40,817,073	239,652,634
Part cream—				
Pounds	9,157,736	18,318,437	10,803,392	$22,024,853
Value	$2,216,545	$1,542,280	$1,188,000	
Skimmed—				
Pounds	16,097,055	13,893,692	7,770,812	3,459,582
Value	$2,185,539	$748,586	$429,519	$148,568
Other kinds—				
Pounds	36,536,027	5,375,579	5,441,730	74,032,656
Value	$8,806,617	$653,555	$805,332	$6,438,339
Condensed and evaporated milk:				
Pounds	2,150,182,245	873,410,504	494,796,544	308,485,182
Value	$298,267,547	$58,747,252	$33,563,129	$20,149,282
Condensed, sweetened—				
Pounds	760,582,490	267,869,955	214,518,310	198,355,189
Value	$126,055,505	$21,585,139	$17,345,278	$13,478,376
Condensed, unsweetened—				
Pounds	174,004,366	331,892,914		
Value	$17,783,261	$19,928,014	280,278,234	110,129,993
Evaporated—			$16,217,851	$6,670,906
Pounds	1,215,595,389	273,647,635		
Value	$154,428,781	$17,234,099		

[1] In addition, similar products were reported by establishments engaged primarily in other industries, as follows:

	1919	1914	1909	1904
Butter:				
Pounds	17,955,316	16,193,708	2,381,212	1,971,120
Value	$11,055,867	$5,167,634	$664,171	$448,729
Cheese:				
Pounds	1,761,621	7,234,810	49,413	
Value	$340,133	$554,907	$5,745	
Condensed milk:				
Pounds	3,326,847	9,702,397	401,300	
Value	$391,490	$514,348	$24,078	
Casein and powdered milk:				
Pounds	1,878,739	2,381,445		
Value	$275,793	$166,392		
Other dairy products, value			$25,388	$71,588

TABLE 27.—BUTTER, CHEESE, AND CONDENSED MILK: 1919, 1914, 1909, AND 1904—Con.

	1919	1914	1909	1904
Cream sold:				
Pounds	120,304,163	123,511,348	81,211,374	28,131,914
Value	$26,173,920	$13,802,063	$9,828,972	$2,364,407
Skimmed milk sold:				
Value	$2,453,657	$786,050	$629,135	$1,368,738
Buttermilk sold:				
Value	$4,027,144	$1,278,700	(1)	(1)
Casein dried from skimmed milk:				
Pounds	16,615,076	18,570,220	13,018,298	11,581,874
Value	$2,188,787	$977,770	$795,544	$554,099
Whey sold:				
Value	$3,423,906	$72,979	(1)	(1)
Powdered milk:				
Pounds	48,385,548	20,454,051	(1)	(1)
Value	$11,918,105	$1,968,259	(1)	(1)
Sugar of milk:				
Pounds	10,401,416	4,051,320	(1)	(1)
Value	$2,632,776	$400,613	(1)	(1)
Other butter, cheese, or condensed milk factory products, value	$35,112,475	$11,048,820	(1)	(1)
All other products, value	$20,712,383	$6,803,936	$6,990,395	$1,945,050

¹ Not reported separately.

TABLE 28.—CANNING AND PRESERVING, FISH AND OYSTERS: 1919, 1914, 1909, AND 1904.

KIND.	1919	1914	1909	1904
Total value [1]	**$82,408,286**	**$35,267,120**	**$28,530,323**	**$23,571,499**
Canned fish and oysters, value	$53,186,286	$22,401,004	$17,592,960	$13,544,686
Salmon—				
Cases of No. 1 size cans	2,186,004	1,513,300	2,079,823	1,002,685
Value	$19,113,204	$8,712,695	$8,723,565	$4,251,387
Sardines—				
Cases of No. ¼ size cans	5,777,959	5,012,199	4,014,509	([2])
Value	$20,258,565	$6,238,933	$4,931,831	$4,380,498
Oysters—				
Cases of No. 1 size cans	717,636	944,639	([2])	([2])
Value	$3,510,119	$2,676,951	$2,443,101	$3,812,312
Shrimp—				
Cases of No. 1 size cans	322,076	459,877	171,899	([2])
Value	$1,864,793	$1,725,621	$690,021	$478,931
Tuna—				
Cases of No. ½ size cans	874,380	437,090		
Value	$5,710,188	$1,638,675		
Clams—				
Cases of No. 1 size cans	157,843	185,186	([2])	([2])
Value	$772,870	$670,363	$402,466	$274,155
All other canned sea foods—				
Cases	309,308	235,813	([2])	([2])
Value	$1,956,547	$737,766	$401,976	$347,403
Salted or pickled fish:				
Pounds	111,655,326	131,149,037	133,169,621	113,576,290
Value	$18,203,800	$8,172,477	$7,318,101	$6,409,012
Cod—				
Pounds	62,902,037	68,456,917	54,302,338	48,757,819
Value	$12,643,357	$5,123,562	$3,248,669	$3,013,320
Herring—				
Pounds	14,135,579	21,133,974	21,718,467	15,824,192
Value	$845,629	$641,603	$461,287	$409,223
Mackerel—				
Pounds	5,098,700	6,224,313	9,045,469	8,326,566
Value	$1,000,593	$519,727	$740,513	$678,326
Haddock—				
Pounds	7,691,146	4,947,286	3,065,156	4,737,975
Value	$815,180	$218,359	$148,191	$213,394
All other—				
Pounds	21,827,864	30,386,547	45,038,191	35,929,738
Value	$2,899,041	$1,669,226	$2,719,441	$2,094,749
Smoked or dried fish:				
Pounds	32,243,591	28,713,806	40,739,774	36,617,904
Value	$5,371,833	$2,759,341	$2,939,258	$2,528,240
Herring—				
Pounds	14,639,391	11,504,126	21,369,856	19,737,537
Value	$1,350,745	$719,640	$931,611	$631,352
Salmon—				
Pounds	5,574,273	4,248,896	6,836,099	6,833,560
Value	$1,681,982	$638,975	$950,540	$831,184
Finnan haddie—				
Pounds	5,696,883	4,095,693	4,513,222	3,014,160
Value	$495,404	$327,877	$304,620	$174,234
Sturgeon—				
Pounds	570,031	511,196	620,437	
Value	$435,959	$150,614	$182,786	
All other smoked or dried fish—				
Pounds	5,763,013	8,353,895	7,400,160	7,032,647
Value	$1,407,743	$922,235	$569,701	$891,470
All other products, value	$5,646,367	$1,934,298	$680,004	$1,089,561

[1] Includes for 1919, 1914, 1909, and 1904 values of similar products reported by establishments engaged primarily in other industries, as follows:

	1919	1914	1909	1904
Canned fish and oysters:				
Cases	336,388	494,372		
Value	$1,900,976	$1,409,140	$19,649	$12,900
Salted fish:				
Pounds	3,684,609	3,905,372	4,630,332	1,847,625
Value	$223,615	$388,488	$143,540	$274,403
Smoked fish:				
Pounds	102,000	1,316,575	924,785	
Value	$23,272	$120,030	$38,841	

[2] Figures not available.

TABLE 29.—CANNING AND PRESERVING, FRUITS AND VEGETABLES:[1] 1919, 1914, 1909, AND 1904.

KIND.	1919	1914	1909	1904
Total value	[2] $415,174,562	[2] $158,015,702	[2] $96,032,205	[2] $78,857,942
Canned vegetables, value	$164,573,590	$84,413,667	$53,443,001	$45,899,131
Tomatoes—				
Cases, No. 3 size cans	11,836,476	16,200,302	12,909,986	9,411,084
Value	$38,067,999	$25,532,217	$18,747,941	$14,020,846
Beans—				
Cases, No. 2 size cans	14,824,232	8,994,302	3,564,033	2,588,015
Value	$39,408,603	$16,565,021	$6,305,797	$4,133,810
Peas—				
Cases, No. 2 size cans	9,325,727	8,826,284	5,901,703	4,694,492
Value	$25,073,220	$15,089,047	$10,247,363	$7,928,791
Corn—				
Cases, No. 2 size cans	14,402,725	9,919,950	7,451,265	11,209,597
Value	$35,532,007	$13,923,057	$10,332,136	$15,952,386
Asparagus—				
Cases, No. 2 size cans	1,006,604	637,601	342,838	[3]
Value	$6,571,629	$2,790,817	$1,975,775	[3]
Kraut—				
Cases, No. 3 size cans	1,041,932	1,184,219	[3]	[3]
Value	$2,845,340	$1,567,717	[3]	[3]
Tomato pulp—				
Cases, No. 10 size cans	759,055	752,151	[3]	[3]
Value	$3,819,101	$1,454,051	[3]	[3]
Pumpkin—				
Cases, No. 3 size cans	383,211	789,368	440,303	246,557
Value	$861,436	$1,023,008	$576,043	$346,497
Sweet potatoes—				
Cases, No. 3 size cans	745,861	454,415	347,286	192,997
Value	$2,477,719	$736,759	$531,651	$284,385
Spinach—				
Cases, No. 3 size cans	676,388	391,790	149,255	[3]
Value	$2,338,497	$736,686	$294,414	[3]
Hominy—				
Cases, No. 3 size cans	587,298	686,100	[3]	[3]
Value	$1,346,044	$712,991	[3]	[3]
Beets—				
Cases, No. 3 size cans	584,309	251,632	126,422	[3]
Value	$1,951,344	$511,900	$261,398	[3]
Succotash—				
Cases, No. 2 size cans	373,977	270,077	254,365	[3]
Value	$1,142,236	$455,956	$320,141	[3]
All other canned vegetables—				
Cases	923,500	900,483	2,317,453	1,377,137
Value	$3,138,415	[4] $3,314,440	$3,850,342	$3,232,416
Canned soups:				
Cases, No. 1 size cans	5,844,821	4,886,098	853,840	....
Value	$11,857,717	$7,877,057	$2,588,834	....

[1] The figures given in this table do not agree with those in the general tables, for the reason that this table includes data for fruits and vegetables canned and preserved by establishments engaged primarily in other industries, and for the further reason that certain changes have been made in the figures for 1909 and 1904 in order to make them include the same class of data as those for 1914 and 1919.

[2] Includes the quantities and values of similar products, that can be shown without disclosing individual operations, reported by establishments engaged primarily in other industries, as follows:

	1919	1914	1909	1904
Vegetables, canned:				
Cases	3,094,824	2,599,413	769,017	140,263
Value	$8,212,268	$7,440,464	$1,714,909	$288,138
Soups, canned:				
Cases	936,333	400,466	....	....
Value	$1,390,342	$792,258	....	....
Fruit, canned:				
Cases	404,000	148,070	27,474	....
Value	$2,312,521	$441,738	$76,964	....
Dried fruit:				
Value	$266,009	$150,561	$53,159	....

[3] Included in "All other canned vegetables."
[4] Includes meat products, canned, valued at $781,291.

TABLE 29.—CANNING AND PRESERVING, FRUITS AND VEGETABLES: 1919, 1914, 1909, AND 1904—Continued.

KIND.	1919	1914	1909	1904
Canned fruits, value.........................	$127,949,357	$24,897,174	$13,015,438	$11,722,979
Peaches—				
Cases, No. 3 size cans..................	7,706,855	3,407,906	1,467,213	1,304,867
Value................................	$46,516,225	$9,585,773	$3,753,698	$3,902,441
Pears—				
Cases, No. 3 size cans..................	2,021,610	1,062,762	637,782	789,120
Value................................	$14,202,963	$3,853,700	$1,833,214	$2,192,910
Berries—				
Cases, No. 2 size cans..................	2,347,213	1,333,449	815,851	489,637
Value................................	$16,449,126	$3,102,245	$1,754,927	$1,058,659
Apricots—				
Cases, No. 3 size cans..................	3,939,768	1,051,816	630,185	539,815
Value................................	$25,167,772	$3,060,626	$1,825,311	$1,641,919
Apples—				
Cases, No. 3 size cans..................	2,447,927	1,514,939	1,205,742	490,341
Value................................	$9,081,598	$2,392,289	$1,898,720	$738,013
Cherries—				
Cases, No. 2 size cans..................	1,362,832	543,213	390,351	319,350
Value................................	$8,451,029	$1,628,975	$1,019,013	$825,522
Plums—				
Cases, No. 2 size cans..................	571,521	288,326	220,057	(1)
Value................................	$2,228,183	$438,238	$346,953	(1)
Pineapples—				
Cases, No. 3 size cans..................	156,755	94,140	78,557	(1)
Value................................	$1,365,484	$364,250	$313,647	(1)
Figs—				
Cases, No. 3 size cans..................	(1)	20,605	5,079	(1)
Value................................	(1)	$159,522	$49,970	(1)
All other canned fruits—				
Cases.................................	877,912	132,026	78,061	695,111
Value................................	$4,486,977	$311,556	$219,985	$1,363,515
Dried fruits:				
Pounds..............................	615,408,528	568,587,364	485,335,800	343,579,623
Value................................	$85,401,265	$34,771,912	$21,968,154	$15,664,784
Raisins—				
Pounds..............................	293,300,581	226,043,959	195,774,767	121,409,881
Value................................	$35,544,262	$13,938,645	$6,912,533	$6,349,381
Prunes—				
Pounds..............................	136,377,066	139,091,887	138,498,490	117,808,181
Value................................	$18,253,691	$9,004,348	$5,130,412	$3,299,628
Apricots—				
Pounds..............................	24,192,628	39,397,294	29,205,569	19,559,573
Value................................	$6,034,697	$3,615,857	$2,277,177	$1,410,838
Peaches—				
Pounds..............................	73,379,193	61,907,251	46,843,391	25,861,074
Value................................	$12,109,624	$2,915,595	$2,423,083	$1,702,205
Apples—				
Pounds..............................	46,623,499	54,957,003	44,568,244	40,737,089
Value................................	$6,772,080	$2,889,406	$3,098,095	$1,758,610
All other dried fruits—				
Pounds..............................	41,535,561	47,189,970	30,445,339	18,203.825
Value................................	$6,686,911	$2,408,061	$2,126,854	$1,144,122
All other products, value..................	$25,392,633	$6,055,892	$5,016,778	$5,571,048

[1] Included in "All other canned fruits."

TABLE 30.—FLOUR-MILL AND GRISTMILL PRODUCTS (MERCHANT MILLS): 1919, 1914, 1909, AND 1904.

	1919	1914	1909	1904
MATERIALS.				
Total cost	$1,799,180,987	$752,270,021	$767,576,479	$619,971,161
Grain ground or milled, bushels	830,026,293	818,929,321	806,247,961	754,945,729
Wheat	612,562,471	545,728,431	496,480,314	494,095,083
Corn	113,760,971	180,115,704	209,281,237	178,217,321
Rye	15,951,961	12,813,831	11,503,969	11,480,370
Buckwheat	4,764,830	5,478,045	7,156,062	6,531,305
Barley	21,151,343	20,288,396	24,509,770	18,628,552
Oats	58,579,943	50,227,050	50,241,598	45,381,009
Other	3,254,774	4,277,864	7,075,011	612,089
PRODUCTS.				
Total value	[1]$2,052,434,385	[1] $877,679,709	[2] $883,584,405	[3] $713,033,395
Wheat flour:				
Barrels	132,465,604	116,403,770	105,756,645	104,013,278
Value	$1,436,444,111	$543,839,568	$550,116,254	$480,258,514
White—				
Barrels	(4)	115,829,791	105,321,969	103,608,350
Value	(4)	$541,157,994	$548,017,654	$478,484,601
Graham and whole wheat—				
Barrels	(4)	573,979	434,676	404,928
Value	(4)	$2,681,574	$2,098,600	$1,773,913
Rye flour and rye graham:				
Barrels	2,527,752	1,937,385	1,532,139	1,503,100
Value	$21,235,808	$7,845,213	$6,383,538	$5,892,108
Buckwheat flour:				
Pounds	90,137,407	125,622,189	176,081,891	175,354,062
Value	$5,244,539	$3,754,857	$4,663,561	$4,379,359
Barley meal:				
Pounds	91,809,114	14,000,789	28,550,952	68,508,655
Value	$3,217,464	$242,343	$486,000	$922,884
Corn meal and corn flour:				
Barrels	10,682,952	16,327,993	21,552,737	23,624,693
Value	$82,059,560	$54,963,301	$66,941,095	$56,368,556
Hominy and grits:				
Pounds	288,525,592	870,364,453	827,987,702	756,861,398
Value	$9,247,224	$13,767,561	$12,509,493	$8,455,420
Bran and middlings:				
Tons	4,760,326	4,666,534	} 9,236,411	} 7,925,412
Value	$211,435,518	$104,702,735	} $230,356,342	} $152,201,659
Feed and offal:				
Tons	4,566,855	4,753,280		
Value	$262,733,518	$137,067,959		
Oatmeal:				
Pounds	28,120,649	30,451,581	} $4,720,106	(4)
Value	$1,100,875	$757,804		
Breakfast foods, rolled oats, etc.:				
Pounds	96,531,673	92,676,085		
Value	$4,349,541	$2,932,238		
All other cereal products, value	$10,033,062	$2,091,922		
Corn oil, value	(4)	$152,208	(4)	(4)
All other products, value	$5,333,165	$5,562,000	$7,408,016	$4,554,895

[1] In addition, merchant-ground products were made by establishments engaged primarily in other industries in 1919, as follows: Wheat flour, valued at $11,164,280; rye flour, $236,244; buckwheat flour, $1,715; corn meal and corn flour, $3,759,693; hominy and grits, $1,655; bran and middlings, $1,977,274; feed and offal, $29,374,409; and in 1914, as follows:
Wheat flour, valued at $2,500,937; rye flour, $125,887; buckwheat flour, $4,236; barley meal, $114,176; corn meal and corn flour, $1,065,830; hominy and grits, $1,268,612; oatmeal, $160; bran and middlings, $492,351; feed and offal, $2,810,431; corn oil, $115,891; and breakfast foods, $547,938.
[2] In addition, breakfast foods, to the value of $36,978,613 were made by establishments engaged primarily in the manufacture of food preparations; and merchant-ground products, valued at $1,637,228, were made by establishments engaged primarily in the manufacture of products other than those covered by the industry designation. The items covered by the latter amount were wheat flour, valued at $614,952; corn meal, $87,507; rye flour, $12,330; feed, $907,165; and offal, $15,274.
[3] In addition, breakfast foods to the value of $23,904,952, were made by establishments engaged primarily in the manufacture of food preparations.
[4] Not shown separately.

TABLE 31.—GLUCOSE AND STARCH: 1919, 1914, AND 1909.

	1919	1914	1909
MATERIALS.			
Total cost...............................	**$130,328,848**	**$40,207,592**	**$36,898,771**
Corn:			
Pounds......................	3,636,601,683	2,488,792,405	2,240,508,915
Cost........................	$100,161,185	$30,207,562	$26,674,779
Potatoes:			
Pounds......................	129,505,745	169,878,784	210,608,127
Cost........................	$764,247	$498,015	$541,359
Wheat:			
Pounds......................	11,162,340	....	....
Cost........................	$417,570	....	....
Wheat flour:			
Pounds......................	1,768,932	14,198,049	19,545,824
Cost........................	$88,433	$301,560	$482,263
Cornstarch:			
Pounds......................	22,860,680	9,812,659	105,299,010
Cost........................	$1,035,773	$189,296	$1,763,173
All other materials, including fuel and rent of power, cost......	$27,861,640	$9,011,159	$7,437,197
PRODUCTS.			
Total value......................	[1] **$186,256,260**	**$52,615,401**	**$48,799,311**
Starch:			
Pounds......................	783,513,087	620,764,347	677,535,647
Value.......................	$44,402,873	$15,783,781	$17,514,823
Corn—			
Pounds......................	727,962,234	574,247,697	638,825,366
Value.......................	$40,557,660	$13,784,654	$15,962,916
Potato—			
Pounds......................	16,477,186	23,540,472	24,873,415
Value.......................	$1,099,028	$718,006	$823,019
Other—			
Pounds......................	39,073,667	22,976,178	13,836,866
Value.......................	$2,746,185	$1,281,121	$728,888
Glucose (including all sirups), value..............	$80,608,100	$18,541,429	$17,922,514
Grape sugar:			
Pounds......................	157,276,442	174,368,818	159,060,478
Value.......................	$9,314,977	$3,765,515	$3,620,816
Corn oil:			
Gallons.....................	12,516,261	8,861,579	8,164,175
Value.......................	$20,333,249	$3,693,163	$2,802,768
Corn-oil cake and meal:			
Pounds......................	61,661,977	143,001,065	[2]
Value.......................	$1,842,427	$1,829,305	[2]
Dextrine:			
Pounds......................	28,757,233	[2]	[2]
Value.......................	$1,838,500	[2]	[2]
Stock feed, value.........................	$26,068,185	$6,690,412	$6,013,968
All other products, value..................	$1,847,949	$2,311,796	$924,422

[1] In addition, starches to the value of $47,830 were reported by establishments engaged primarily in other industries.
[2] Not reported separately.

TABLE 32.—RICE, CLEANING AND POLISHING: 1919, 1914, 1909, AND 1904.

	1919	1914	1909	1904
Rough rice treated, pounds..........	1,609,951,995	1,036,587,825	974,747,475	999,727,650
Domestic......................	1,608,014,880	1,025,628,075	970,873,740	990,473,625
Foreign......................	1,937,115	10,959,750	3,873,735	9,254,025
PRODUCTS.				
Total value..................	$90,038,412	$23,039,294	$22,371,457	$16,296,916
Clean rice:				
Pounds......................	1,062,813,400	674,872,108	626,089,489	623,900,245
Value......................	$83,462,235	$21,655,105	$20,685,982	$15,357,133
Polish:				
Pounds......................	36,197,025	31,053,118	29,821,813	33,290,331
Value......................	$965,655	$352,271	$362,052	$267,647
Bran:				
Pounds......................	142,984,394	99,403,200	91,208,529	120,694,130
Value......................	$2,499,788	$772,275	$736,215	$501,193
All other products, value............	$3,110,734	$259,643	$587,208	$170,943

TABLE 33.—BEET AND CANE SUGAR: 1919, 1914, AND 1909.

PRODUCT.	1919	1914	1909
Total..	$206,897,212	$84,240,583	$78,743,121
Beet products.............................	149,155,892	62,605,210	48,122,383
Cane products.............................	57,741,320	21,635,373	30,620,738
Sugar:			
Tons (2,000 pounds).............................	947,387	1,008,274	828,540
Value...	$184,758,778	$77,538,149	$72,033,302
Beet—			
Tons...	721,909	743,473	501,682
Value...	$138,099,693	$58,590,466	$45,937,629
Cane—			
Tons...	225,478	264,801	326,858
Value...	$46,659,085	$18,947,683	$26,095,673
Molasses, sirups, and all other products, value [1]............	$22,138,434	$6,702,434	$6,709,819
Beet..	$11,056,199	$4,014,744	$2,184,754
Cane..	$11,082,235	$2,687,690	$4,525,065

[1] Includes molasses, sirup, and other products of mills producing no sugar.

TABLE 34.—SLAUGHTERING AND MEAT PACKING: 1919, 1914, 1909, AND 1904.

	1919	1914	1909	1904
MATERIALS.				
Total cost..................	$3,782,929,533	$1,441,662,658	$1,191,438,076	$805,856,969
Animals slaughtered, cost.............	$3,056,387,778	$1,199,642,235	$960,587,033	$675,831,771
Beeves—				
Number........................	[1] 10,818,511	[1] 7,149,042	8,114,860	7,147,835
Cost...........................	$1,055,739,469	$490,108,203	$392,127,010	$289,040,930
Calves—				
Number........................	[1] 4,395,675	[1] 2,019,004	2,504,728	1,568,130
Cost...........................	$96,449,234	$27,623,448	$25,030,014	$12,665,557
Sheep and lambs—				
Number........................	[1] 13,497,300	[1] 15,943,743	12,255,501	10,875,339
Cost...........................	$146,775,993	$84,783,721	$59,924,931	$44,359,804
Hogs—				
Number........................	[1] 44,520,726	[1] 34,441,913	33,870,616	30,977,639
Cost...........................	$1,757,279,014	$597,097,518	$483,383,848	$329,765,480
Goats and kids—				
Number........................	[1] 23,915	[1] 8,117	33,224	[2]
Cost...........................	$144,068	$29,345	$121,230	[2]
Poultry, cost..................	$1,787,936	$2,178,144	$138,548	$61,905
Dressed meat purchased, cost..........	[3] $299,089,389	[3] $124,334,798	$93,409,286	$53,114,957
All other materials, cost.............	$425,664,430	$115,507,481	$137,303,209	$76,848,336
PRODUCTS.				
Total value..................	$4,246,290,614	$1,651,965,424	$1,355,544,431	$913,914,624
Fresh meat, value.................	$1,642,461,577	$769,383,846	$578,485,088	$398,162,589
Beef—				
Pounds....................	4,832,061,881	3,658,333,660	4,209,196,668	3,748,055,377
Value.....................	$846,794,386	$421,296,794	$327,583,456	$247,096,724
Veal—				
Pounds....................	422,978,820	194,698,880	252,997,078	154,212,652
Value.....................	$83,912,942	$26,299,446	$25,058,886	$12,856,369
Mutton and lamb—				
Pounds....................	500,360,124	629,232,690	495,457,894	460,754,244
Value.....................	$120,338,355	$74,675,627	$50,735,116	$36,880,455
Pork—				
Pounds....................	2,095,884,557	1,877,099,071	1,547,494,184	1,224,932,910
Value.....................	$532,669,835	$226,535,734	$158,714,862	$91,749,323
Edible offal and other fresh meat—				
Pounds....................	506,667,525	280,090,794	257,809,083	124,307,681
Value.....................	$56,129,725	$17,647,510	$16,392,768	$9,579,718
Poultry dressed—				
Pounds....................	7,022,695	16,575,907		
Value	$2,616,334	$2,928,735		
Cured meat, value.................	$1,245,949,819	$408,000,916	$340,289,451	$256,945,273
Beef, pickled and other cured—				
Pounds....................	129,960,004	91,571,753	126,477,662	136,896,697
Value.....................	$28,359,892	$14,395,316	$12,159,152	$8,107,952
Pork, pickled and other cured—				
Pounds....................	4,146,117,111	2,929,309,741	2,829,633,003	2,922,901,962
Value.....................	$1,217,589,927	$393,605,600	$328,130,299	$248,837,321
Canned goods:				
Pounds....................	305,955,406	160,798,955	121,376,837	[4]
Value	$96,904,341	$26,417,624	$15,345,543	$16,114,665
Sausage:				
Canned—				
Pounds....................	160,908,986	74,004,380	[5]	[5]
Value.....................	$27,965,155	$9,845,669	[5]	[5]
All other—				
Pounds....................	643,905,181	435,146,931	452,867,187	324,416,039
Value.....................	$145,622,246	$58,349,853	$44,540,912	$25,056,331
Meat puddings, scrapple, head cheese, etc:				
Pounds....................	43,182,235	42,339,926	[5]	[5]
Value.....................	$10,050,494	$4,488,461	[5]	[5]

[1] In addition 553,839 beeves, 387,692 calves, 269,128 sheep and lambs and goats and kids, and 2,290,539 hogs were slaughtered for others, in 1919, and 377,937 beeves, 243,360 calves, 795,519 sheep and lambs and goats and kids, and 2,898,994 hogs, in 1914.
[2] Not reported separately.
[3] Includes cost of animals other than those shown in detail.
[4] Comparable figures not available.
[5] Not reported separately.

TABLE 34.—SLAUGHTERING AND MEAT PACKING: 1919, 1914, 1909, AND 1904—Contd.

	1919	1914	1909	1904
PRODUCTS—continued.				
Lard:				
Pounds	1,372,869,656	1,119,188,675	1,243,567,604	1,169,086,400
Value	$415,817,212	$120,414,007	$134,396,587	$82,540,964
Lard compounds and substitutes:				
Pounds	521,121,914	396,397,950	(1)	(1)
Value	$123,724,098	$33,037,467	(1)	(1)
Oleo oil:				
Gallons	14,919,876	16,501,585	19,692,172	19,454,799
Value	$31,212,708	$11,925,832	$16,475,726	$10,201,911
Other oils:				
Gallons	6,720,822	6,715,497	11,343,186	4,893,133
Value	$9,153,123	$4,009,602	$6,350,745	$2,595,951
Tallow:				
Pounds	211,188,146	193,615,601)		
Value	$28,591,346	$12,371,206	202,844,139	(1)
Oleo stock:			$13,499,659	(1)
Pounds	29,828,070	15,998,534		
Value	$7,684,719	$1,361,550)		
Grease:				
Pounds	107,276,780	(1)	(1)	(1)
Value	$13,710,215	(1)	(1)	(1)
Soap stock:				
Pounds	39,966,722	76,003,670	(1)	(1)
Value	$2,989,878	$3,742,747	(1)	(1)
Stearin (lard, oleo, and cottonseed oil):				
Pounds	44,267,107	2 30,091,991	54,957,997	(1)
Value	$8,999,349	2 $2,752,421	$6,871,935	(1)
Oleomargarine:				
Pounds	123,538,860	60,387,881	42,912,466	(1)
Value	$36,777,815	$8,818,557	$5,963,981	(1)
Casings:				
Pounds	102,281,168	69,453,298	(1)	(1)
Value	$16,779,655	$9,077,593	(1)	(1)
Hoofs, horns, and horn tips, strips, etc.:				
Pounds	84,640,302	73,125,830	(1)	(1)
Value	$2,180,600	$944,634	(1)	(1)
Fertilizers and fertilizer materials:				
Tons (2,000 pounds)	382,132	294,388	362,136	369,074
Value	$18,314,754	$8,737,009	$8,726,818	$7,204,061
Glue:				
Pounds	36,630,195	3 40,844,650	27,936,035	17,526,456
Value	$4,489,774	3 $3,088,764	$1,944,338	$1,087,719
Hides and pelts:				
Cattle—				
Number	10,818,511	7,158,862		
Pounds	583,972,224	415,890,714		
Value	$185,020,306	$69,958,593	9,560,138	8,039,204
Calf—			504,563,930	456,443,857
Number	3,322,729	1,464,430	$68,401,515	$44,206,107
Pounds	43,549,073	18,647,761		
Value	$24,613,930	$3,512,610		
Sheep and lamb, and goat and kid—				
Number	12,188,071	15,916,618	11,724,667	4 11,344,544
Value	$33,686,165	$13,624,046	$11,425,235	4 $8,964,643
All other skins—				
Pounds	2,214,258	(1)	(1)	(1)
Value	$240,844	$389,068	(1)	(1)
Hair, hog and cattle:				
Pounds	60,343,741	(1)	(1)	(1)
Value	$4,059,096	(1)	(1)	(1)
Wool:				
Pounds	29,901,176	26,432,398	21,858,926	16,377,333
Value	$20,071,303	$7,938,212	$8,327,095	$5,229,521
All other products, including custom work, value	$89,220,092	$59,775,137	$94,499,803	$55,604,889

1 Not reported separately.
2 No cottonseed oil stearin reported in 1914.
3 Includes a very small amount of gelatine.
4 Goat and kid skins not included—figures not available. Includes some pelts purchased for wool pulling.

TABLE 35.—COTTON MANUFACTURES: 1919, 1914, AND 1909.

	1919	1914	1909
MATERIALS.			
Total cost	**$1,314,901,542**	**$443,522,515**	**$371,009,470**
Cotton (raw):[1]			
Pounds	2,731,404,436	2,523,500,837	2,335,344,906
Cost	$907,683,931	$330,315,223	$274,724,210
Domestic[1]—			
Pounds	2,612,851,431	2,431,405,884	2,259,312,974
Cost	$849,286,927	$312,586,001	$261,547,820
Foreign—			
Pounds	118,553,005	92,094,953	76,031,932
Cost	$58,397,004	$17,729,222	$13,176,390
Dyed, bleached, and other treated cotton:			
Pounds	623,047	1,052,836	191,779
Cost	$145,940	$111,423	$21,591
Cotton waste:			
Pounds	120,743,520	54,116,105	80,044,061
Cost	$14,344,834	$3,542,631	$4,225,790
All other fibers:			
Pounds	3,702,607	4,276,476	1,627,189
Cost	$4,201,302	$3,203,262	$1,176,449
Cotton yarns:			
Pounds	230,061,217	139,482,027	126,707,003
Cost	$192,018,472	$39,793,131	$34,384,791
All other yarns:			
Pounds	3,987,052	3,309,277	5,605,522
Cost	$13,963,176	$4,793,221	$8,183,206
Starch, cost	$5,579,310	$2,629,558	$2,114,756
Chemicals and dyestuffs, cost	$13,073,488	$5,769,235	$4,886,514
All other materials, cost	$163,891,089	$53,364,831	$41,292,163
PRODUCTS.			
Total value[2]	**$2,195,565,881**	**$701,300,933**	**$628,391,813**
Cotton goods	$2,125,272,193	$676,569,115	$615,217,702
Cotton lace	$29,396,853	$13,206,785	(2)
Cotton small wares	$40,896,835	$11,525,033	$13,174,111
Woven goods (over 12 inches in width):			
Square yards	6,317,397,984	6,813,540,681	6,267,561,279
Value	$1,489,610,779	$489,985,277	$447,167,319
Unbleached and bleached sheetings, shirtings, and muslins—			
Square yards	3,194,100,981	3,852,471,903	3,709,031,377
Value	$477,407,901	$196,520,984	$199,900,874
Ducks—			
Square yards	336,500,457	251,367,711	162,476,322
Value	$237,082,551	$49,179,212	$27,485,892
Ginghams—			
Square yards	368,307,601	489,661,133	537,430,463
Value	$85,070,745	$36,706,542	$37,939,040
Drills—			
Square yards	314,822,109	289,969,885	238,869,407
Value	$73,253,640	$21,256,698	$17,750,151
Twills and sateens—			
Square yards	424,478,033	392,108,735	388,314,961
Value	$101,056,691	$32,891,854	$34,274,107

[1] Not including linters.
[2] In addition, in 1919, cotton products to the value of $44,479,105, in 1914, to the value of $17,015,899, and in 1909, to the value of $10,821,250, were reported by establishments engaged primarily in other industries. Of these amounts $10,763,188, in 1919, represents the value of cotton thread and cotton yarn reported by mills engaged chiefly in the production of knit goods, silk goods, wool manufactures, and cordage and twine; $4,442,142 in 1914, and $2,067,506 in 1909, represent the value of cotton yarn reported by mills engaged chiefly in the production of knit goods, wool manufactures, and cordage and twine; and in 1919 $18,408,540, in 1914 $6,011,962, and in 1909 $6,529,649, represent the value of cotton rope and twine reported by manufactures of cordage and twine and jute and linen goods.

TABLE 35.—COTTON MANUFACTURES: 1919, 1914, AND 1909—Continued.

	1919	1914	1909
PRODUCTS—continued.			
Woven goods (over 12 inches in width)—Contd.			
Ticks and denims—			
Square yards	220,381,180	229,330,389	264,870,508
Value	$70,080,557	$24,947,983	$27,350,162
Cotton flannel—			
Square yards	268,067,853	263,862,227	305,655,864
Value	$60,152,426	$24,352,020	$25,695,367
Velvets, velveteens, corduroys, and plushes—			
Square yards	40,183,780	29,128,703	19,706,438
Value	$36,673,551	$8,540,143	$6,965,634
Toweling and terry weaves—			
Square yards	75,165,515	75,798,907	52,778,170
Value	$31,230,370	$9,805,232	$6,037,075
Tapestries—			
Square yards	21,705,586	10,137,710	10,657,385
Value	$17,295,608	$5,411,592	$4,723,907
Pillow tubing—			
Square yards	12,112,573	15,212,622	(1)
Value	$2,555,543	$1,483,847	(1)
Mosquito netting and tarlatan—			
Square yards	34,425,307	97,981,783	59,100,819
Value	$3,273,376	$2,820,524	$2,103,560
Bags and bagging [2]—			
Square yards	82,433,300	129,357,002	63,107,568
Value	$13,139,820	$9,705,616	$4,862,451
Other woven goods (over 12 inches in width)—			
Square yards	924,713,709	687,151,971	455,561,997
Value	$281,338,000	$66,363,030	$52,079,099
Lace and lace curtains—			
Value	$28,258,489	$12,521,053	$8,922,082
Tape and webbing—			
Linear yards	1,065,551,328	1,026,231,549	(3)
Value	$15,296,061	$5,030,052	$5,531,674
Twine—			
Pounds	11,860,195	13,284,875	13,715,771
Value	$5,935,245	$2,792,125	$2,417,391
Cordage and rope—			
Pounds	6,815,848	5,515,658	7,603,907
Value	$2,857,275	$891,223	$1,164,526
Thread—			
Pounds	26,441,943	26,507,023	23,700,957
Value	$55,009,176	$22,917,099	$20,516,269
Yarns for sale—			
Pounds	618,201,812	497,986,999	470,370,995
Value	$453,764,883	$127,363,952	$109,314,953
Cotton waste, for sale—			
Pounds	315,314,228	317,360,019	310,513,348
Value	$36,357,674	$14,421,929	$10,874,386
Old bagging and ties, from cotton bales	$2,507,021	$1,010,344	(1)
All other products	$105,969,278	$24,367,879	$22,483,213
EQUIPMENT.			
Producing spindles, number	34,418,869	31,645,709	27,949,519
Looms, all classes, number	697,142	676,661	638,667

[1] Not reported separately.
[2] In addition, bags to the value of $5,629,537 in 1919 were manufactured in cotton mills principally from purchased fabric. The value of such bags has been included in "all other products."
[3] Quantity in 1909 reported as 9,663,482 pounds.

TABLE 36.—KNIT GOODS: 1919, 1914, 1909, AND 1904.

	1919	1914	1909	1904
MATERIALS.				
Total cost	$427,095,570	$146,687,458	$110,241,053	$76,789,348
Cotton:				
Domestic—				
Pounds	92,446,380	86,202,432	71,986,529	48,668,643
Cost	$30,387,995	$11,083,987	$8,277,508	$5,526,396
Foreign—				
Pounds	603,938	2,187,776	3,429,494	1,918,117
Cost	$275,281	$360,919	$526,001	$342,921
Carded and other prepared—				
Pounds	838,753	1,920,124	(1)	(1)
Cost	$262,772	$235,832	(1)	(1)
Waste purchased—				
Pounds	24,832,027	24,303,514	(1)	(1)
Cost	$4,857,149	$2,190,762	(1)	(1)
Wool:				
Domestic (in condition purchased)—				
Pounds	3,706,825	5,735,395	6,596,081	16,170,183
Cost	$4,125,884	$2,436,524	$2,666,636	$5,610,440
Foreign (in condition purchased)—				
Pounds	811,243	1,212,203	472,707	1,130,433
Cost	$934,968	$530,959	$252,419	$543,418
Equivalent of above in scoured condition—				
Pounds	4,116,365	6,072,257	5,582,839	13,909,144
All other animal hair:				
Pounds	705,839	690,714	191,344	89,502
Cost	$339,577	$153,099	$62,363	$54,877
Recovered wool fiber, purchased:				
Pounds	5,367,065	3,453,682	7,482,553	7,489,358
Cost	$2,066,168	$602,392	$919,970	$923,719
Wool waste and noils, purchased:				
Pounds	5,025,522	5,946,337	8,586,261	6,020,459
Cost	$3,852,720	$1,827,122	$2,813,129	$1,711,669
Tops, purchased:				
Pounds	146,812	265,216	121,565	182,149
Cost	$240,434	$140,153	$92,995	$116,773
Raw silk, purchased:				
Pounds	1,265,568	1,590,162	(1)	(1)
Cost	$9,340,769	$6,331,413	(1)	(1)
Yarns, purchased:				
Cotton, not mercerized—				
Pounds	186,892,109	189,851,716	216,987,611	161,500,466
Cost	$120,791,157	$47,405,667	$48,165,749	$34,372,910
Mercerized cotton—				
Pounds	30,519,234	15,672,427	(1)	(1)
Cost	$49,403,099	$9,289,859	(1)	(1)
Woolen—				
Pounds	5,383,926	7,145,453	6,140,265	4,839,343
Cost	$8,866,287	$4,442,765	$3,834,094	$2,798,454
Worsted—				
Pounds	12,635,631	14,305,333	10,370,004	8,789,570
Cost	$32,148,641	$11,694,039	$10,116,325	$7,457,690
Merino—				
Pounds	6,965,256	4,333,309	4,014,609	2,568,890
Cost	$10,278,050	$2,380,702	$2,667,051	$1,118,999
Silk and spun silk—				
Pounds	5,711,110	1,913,478	982,753	320,671
Cost	$49,222,061	$7,510,872	$3,606,599	$1,200,259
Artificial silk—				
Pounds	4,153,546	1,257,243	(1)	(1)
Cost	$24,101,514	$2,337,949	(1)	(1)
Linen, jute, and other vegetable fiber—				
Pounds	288,009	70,278	241,754	62,617
Cost	$182,774	$60,839	$180,818	$56,224
Chemicals and dyestuffs, cost	$8,222,817	$2,913,027	$2,541,939	$1,677,252
All other materials, cost	$67,195,453	$32,758,577	$23,517,457	$13,277,347
Yarns made for own consumption—				
Cotton, pounds	87,063,037	75,970,761	69,171,277	39,954,890
Woolen, pounds	5,861,147	7,714,761	8,316,349	(1)
Worsted, pounds	532,694	231,752	223,404	(1)
Merino, pounds	17,239,895	24,180,036	20,856,989	(1)

[1] Not reported separately.

TABLE 36.—KNIT GOODS: 1919, 1914, 1909, AND 1904—Continued.

	1919	1914	1909	1904
PRODUCTS.				
Total value.................	[1] $713,139,689	[1] $258,912,903	[1] $200,143,527	$137,076,454
Hosiery:				
Dozen pairs.................	84,645,757	75,164,911	62,825,069	44,186,063
Value.................	$308,662,377	$98,098,590	$68,721,825	$44,113,260
Hose—				
Dozen pairs.............	51,425,340	44,186,412	[2] 34,933,976	[2] 26,041,878
Value.............	$216,651,368	$63,144,569	[2] $41,503,427	[2] $26,674,346
Cotton—				
Dozen pairs.............	36,835,602	36,952,380	32,499,104	24,169,804
Value.............	$105,647,876	$38,390,194	$34,078,622	$22,764,799
Wool—				
Dozen pairs.............	[3] 395,268	1,369,492	1,166,429	1,083,783
Value.............	[3] $2,139,960	$2,548,047	$2,358,106	$2,205,080
Merino—				
Dozen pairs.............	1,029,371	723,433	834,029	746,226
Value.............	$4,456,430	$1,414,118	$1,466,283	$1,182,164
Silk—				
Dozen pairs.............	[4] 2,589,358	2,354,648	[2] 434,414	[2] 42,065
Value.............	[4] $25,337,049	$13,851,251	[2] $3,600,416	[2] $522,303
Silk-mixed—				
Dozen pairs.............	10,575,741	2,786,459	(5)	(5)
Value.............	$79,070,053	$6,940,959	(5)	(5)
Half-hose—				
Dozen pairs.............	33,220,417	30,978,499	27,891,093	18,144,185
Value.............	$92,011,009	$34,954,021	$27,218,398	$17,438,914
Cotton—				
Dozen pairs.............	23,777,740	24,457,195	24,805,917	15,223,243
Value.............	$47,849,610	$21,241,280	$21,831,365	$11,821,830
Wool—				
Dozen pairs.............	651,782	616,341	1,061,535	1,309,876
Value.............	$3,256,910	$1,327,439	$2,087,121	$3,402,406
Merino—				
Dozen pairs.............	3,164,007	2,335,861	2,023,641	1,611,066
Value.............	$10,541,696	$3,384,831	$3,299,912	$2,214,678
Silk—				
Dozen pairs.............	[6] 1,926,995	1,305,792	(7)	(7)
Value.............	[6] $9,758,019	$4,701,969	(7)	(7)
Silk-mixed—				
Dozen pairs.............	3,699,893	2,263,310	(5)	(5)
Value.............	$20,604,774	$4,298,502	(5)	(5)
Shirts and drawers:				
Dozens.................	17,180,404	21,758,775	25,337,779	19,723,141
Value.................	$98,286,403	$57,523,051	$69,592,817	$56,643,860
Cotton—				
Dozens.................	14,655,963	19,735,898	22,567,121	17,107,958
Value.................	$72,564,633	$43,097,937	$50,007,598	$39,658,762
Wool—				
Dozens.................	315,642	373,045	178,163	485,328
Value.................	$3,055,521	$3,448,575	$1,820,521	$3,647,934
Merino—				
Dozens.................	1,848,863	1,434,504	2,536,473	2,113,810
Value.................	$19,621,964	$9,228,686	$17,055,624	$13,031,754
Silk—				
Dozens.................	85,852	69,786	[8] 56,022	[8] 16,045
Value.................	$1,404,231	$1,214,609	[8] $709,074	[8] $305,410
Silk-mixed—				
Dozens.................	[9] 274,084	43,118	(10)	(10)
Value.................	[9] $1,640,054	$313,439	(10)	(10)
All other—				
Dozens.................	(11)	102,424	(5)	(5)
Value.................	(11)	$219,805	(5)	(5)

[1] In addition, knit goods in 1919 to the value of $8,374,682, in 1914 to the value of $5,088,033, and in 1909 to the value of $2,975,749, were reported by establishments engaged primarily in other industries.
[2] Includes silk half-hose.
[3] Includes worsted.
[4] Includes 740,804 dozen pairs of artificial silk hose valued at $3,737,621.
[5] Not reported separately.
[6] Includes 846,170 dozen pairs of artificial silk half-hose valued at $2,906,113.
[7] Included in silk hose.
[8] Includes silk-mixed.
[9] Includes all other shirts and drawers to avoid disclosure of individual operations.
[10] Included in silk shirts and drawers.
[11] Included in silk-mixed shirts and drawers.

TABLE 36.—KNIT GOODS: 1919, 1914, 1909, AND 1904—Continued.

	1919	1914	1909	1904
PRODUCTS—continued.				
Union suits:				
Dozens	9,211,032	6,272,515	2,473,103	1,440,420
Value	$105,243,880	$35,596,034	$14,853,536	$6,793,947
Cotton—				
Dozens	7,518,516	5,468,730	2,047,637	1,260,301
Value	$71,122,386	$25,617,815	$9,713,597	$4,478,664
Wool—				
Dozens	76,701	147,221	50,102	68,067
Value	$2,003,011	$2,490,815	$683,289	$965,132
Merino—				
Dozens	1,133,750	486,128	364,387	105,242
Value	$21,415,647	$5,706,102	$4,217,432	$1,199,949
Silk—				
Dozens	49,388	31,714	[1] 10,977	[1] 6,810
Value	$1,313,131	$886,248	[1] $239,218	[1] $150,202
Silk-mixed—				
Dozens	432,677	29,895	[2]	[2]
Value	$9,389,705	$393,618	[2]	[2]
All other—				
Dozens		108,827	[3]	[3]
Value		$501,436	[3]	[3]
Bathing suits:				
Dozens	301,393	274,454	[3]	[3]
Value	$6,644,906	$2,033,889	[3]	[3]
Leggings:				
Dozens	4,635	74,901	65,326	122,462
Value	$62,510	$313,952	$192,242	$619,998
Gloves and mittens:				
Dozens	3,571,123	2,470,183	2,527,889	2,260,508
Value	$19,530,411	$10,519,613	$7,296,887	$5,556,260
Knitted headwear (except infants'):				
Dozens	557,732	987,178	888,223	589,315
Value	$3,996,398	$3,456,326	$3,217,985	$1,774,862
Sweaters, sweater coats, jerseys, cardigan jackets, etc.:				
Dozens	2,132,581	2,249,142	2,221,410	811,629
Value	$61,094,341	$26,195,002	$22,430,817	$8,345,369
Scarfs and shawls:				
Dozens	298,237	63,264	218,923	435,306
Value	$4,054,859	$713,545	$916,294	$1,293,348
All other fancy knit goods, value	$16,321,888	$3,196,979	$2,392,927	$2,118,842
Fleece lining (shoe and glove):				
Square yards	6,581,183	6,221,601	9,726,770	11,768,961
Value	$2,521,369	$670,095	$1,209,464	$1,249,401
Eider down:				
Square yards	941,017	1,076,995	1,298,322	4,843,939
Value	$1,174,592	$516,957	$442,431	$1,018,981
Jersey cloth and stockinette:				
Square yards	30,344,402	10,593,986	3,111,272	3,354,026
Value	$28,690,935	$4,378,544	$784,255	$1,145,127
Tricolette:				
Square yards	5,051,639	[3]	[3]	[3]
Value	$17,172,431	[3]	[3]	[3]
All other knitted cloth:				
Square yards	26,889,695	1,854,851	410,207	455,274
Value	$9,788,418	$1,251,653	$269,323	$354,316
Yarns for sale:				
Cotton—				
Pounds	17,493,355	17,052,510	7,457,412	3,304,615
Value	$9,834,118	$3,990,349	$1,568,417	$654,234
Woolen—				
Pounds	451,804	[4] 117,634	[5] 488,322	62,653
Value	$937,497	[4] $64,499	[5] $217,114	$14,268
Worsted—				
Pounds	22,833	[6]	[6]	232,869
Value	$61,262	[6]	[6]	$230,836
Merino—				
Pounds	324,638	183,147	[3]	196,037
Value	$242,767	$76,905	[3]	$100,745
Cotton waste:				
Pounds	15,452,314	12,999,218	[3]	[3]
Value	$1,490,933	$628,944	[3]	[3]
Old bagging and ties, value	$54,823	$24,452	[3]	[3]
Contract work, value	$8,771,094	$3,649,274	$1,082,485	$208,167
All other products, value	$8,501,477	$6,014,250	$4,954,708	$4,840,633

[1] Includes silk-mixed union suits.
[2] Included in silk union suits.
[3] Not reported separately.
[4] Includes worsted yarn to avoid disclosure of individual operations.
[5] Includes worsted and merino yarns.
[6] Included in woolen yarn to avoid disclosure of individual operations.

TABLE 36.—KNIT GOODS: 1919, 1914, 1909, AND 1904—Continued.

	1919	1914	1909	1904
EQUIPMENT.	*Number.*	*Number.*	*Number.*	*Number.*
Sets of cards	3,347	3,074	2,671	1,977
Woolen and shoddy	[1] 909	863	844	977
Cotton	2,438	2,211	1,827	1,000
Spindles	885,681	866,494	736,774	603,180
Producing	859,202	848,729	729,935	596,362
Woolen and shoddy	234,353	254,157	244,458	286,661
Worsted	4,458	2,585	2,360	9,664
Cotton	620,391	591,987	483,117	300,037
Doubling and twisting	26,479	17,765	6,839	6,818
Sewing machines, all classes	77,330	65,328	43,885	30,410
Knitting machines	172,363	142,240	115,019	88,374
Power	169,319	138,167	110,630	81,876
Spring-beard needle	23,789	16,138	17,308	13,564
Latch needle	145,530	122,029	93,322	68,312
Hand	3,044	4,073	4,389	6,498
Spring-beard needle	428	238	372	335
Latch needle	2,616	3,835	4,017	6,163

[1] Includes four worsted cards.

TABLE **37.**—SILK GOODS, INCLUDING THROWSTERS: 1919, 1914, 1909, AND 1904.

	1919	1914	1909	1904
MATERIALS.				
Total cost.........................	$388,469,022	$144,442,321	$107,766,916	$75,861,188
Silk:				
Raw—				
Pounds.......................	25,890,728	22,374,700	17,472,204	11,572,783
Cost.........................	$206,222,609	$86,416,857	$67,787,037	$45,318,416
Bought as such and used in manufacture—unthrown—				
Pounds.......................	10,272,040	(1)	(1)	(1)
Cost.........................	$78,853,441	(1)	(1)	(1)
Bought and thrown in mill—for consumption, not for sale—				
Pounds.......................	4,809,188	(1)	(1)	(1)
Cost.........................	$38,337,980	(1)	(1)	(1)
Bought and given out for commission throwing—				
Pounds.......................	10,809,500	(1)	(1)	(1)
Cost.........................	$89,031,188	(1)	(1)	(1)
Thrown, bought as such and used in manufacture—				
Pounds.......................	6,125,490	3,855,899	3,377,972	3,236,744
Cost.........................	$62,487,939	$16,703,096	$14,679,719	$14,552,425
Organzine—				
Pounds.......................	2,240,671	(1)	(1)	(1)
Cost.........................	$24,204,190	(1)	(1)	(1)
Tram—				
Pounds.......................	1,793,048	(1)	(1)	(1)
Cost.........................	$17,082,057	(1)	(1)	(1)
Hard-crepe twist—				
Pounds.......................	2,091,771	(1)	(1)	(1)
Cost.........................	$21,201,692	(1)	(1)	(1)
Frisons, pierced cocoons, noils, and other waste bought as such and used in manufacture—				
Pounds.......................	11,461,588	4,328,536	2,402,960	[2] 49,811
Cost.........................	$16,136,213	$3,066,297	$1,637,187	[2] $187,159
Spun silk, bought as such and used in manufacture—				
Pounds.......................	4,767,679	3,209,309	2,112,972	1,951,201
Cost.........................	$25,874,715	$8,094,427	$4,848,789	$4,310,061
Singles—				
Pounds.......................	1,868,510	(1)	(1)	(1)
Cost.........................	$10,732,794	(1)	(1)	(1)
Two or more ply—				
Pounds.......................	2,899,169	(1)	(1)	(1)
Cost.........................	$15,141,921	(1)	(1)	(1)
Artificial silk—				
Pounds.......................	3,039,257	1,902,974	914,494	466,151
Cost.........................	$15,885,564	$3,440,154	$1,926,894	$1,623,473
Singles—				
Pounds.......................	2,667,934	(1)	(1)	(1)
Cost.........................	$13,844,697	(1)	(1)	(1)
Two or more ply—				
Pounds.......................	371,323	(1)	(1)	(1)
Cost.........................	$2,040,867	(1)	(1)	(1)
Yarns, other than silk:				
Cotton (not mercerized)—				
Pounds.......................	15,131,047	16,869,511	12,617,292	8,387,048
Cost.........................	$14,151,863	$6,163,240	$4,687,173	$2,586,954
Cotton, mercerized—				
Pounds.......................	2,826,965	1,464,299	1,494,586	631,247
Cost.........................	$4,266,593	$1,078,337	$1,124,409	$471,035
Woolen and worsted—				
Pounds.......................	638,334	1,987,918	610,588	443,155
Cost.........................	$2,157,743	$2,087,804	$765,989	$409,867
Mohair—				
Pounds.......................	572,054	2,645,055	710,108	138,389
Cost.........................	$875,746	$1,604,362	$640,529	$137,097
Other—				
Pounds.......................	470,736	291,672	353,780	130,930
Cost.........................	$1,338,838	$438,944	$456,597	$108,841
All other materials, cost.....................	$39,071,199	$15,348,803	$9,212,593	$6,155,860

[1] Not reported separately.
[2] Does not include waste, noils, etc., which were included with "all other materials" in 1904.

1072   ABSTRACT OF THE CENSUS—MANUFACTURES.

Table 37.—SILK GOODS, INCLUDING THROWSTERS: 1919, 1914, 1909, AND 1904—Con.

PRODUCTS.	1919	1914	1909	1904
Total value	[1] $688,469,523	[1] $254,011,257	[1] $196,911,667	$133,288,072
Broad silks:				
Yards	310,132,060	216,033,696	185,707,316	124,871,215
Value	$391,735,902	$137,719,564	$107,881,146	$66,917,762
All-silk—				
Yards	245,860,918	142,713,359	114,876,641	97,870,717
Value	$322,502,765	$96,689,801	$74,471,291	$55,944,988
In the gray—				
Yards	86,919,172	[2]	[2]	[2]
Value	$101,976,095	[2]	[2]	[2]
Piece-dyed—				
Yards	64,771,760	59,304,041	19,693,393	21,334,584
Value	$89,458,930	$38,819,874	$11,353,242	$9,276,445
Printed—				
Yards	8,275,585	4,528,453		
Value	$11,921,575	$2,637,231		
Yarn-dyed—				
Yards	85,414,154	78,880,865	95,183,248	76,536,133
Value	$118,199,476	$55,232,696	$63,118,049	$46,668,543
Warp-printed—				
Yards	480,247			
Value	$946,689			
Mixed goods—				
Yards	64,271,142	73,320,337	70,830,675	27,000,498
Value	$69,233,137	$41,029,763	$33,409,855	$10,972,774
In the gray—				
Yards	41,869,419	[2]	[2]	[2]
Value	$35,722,740	[2]	[2]	[2]
Piece-dyed—				
Yards	8,933,396	39,559,303	40,044,433	15,603,353
Value	$12,710,941	$21,843,055	$15,728,195	$4,399,654
Printed—				
Yards	1,248,244	310,731		
Value	$1,138,154	$203,848		
Yarn-dyed—				
Yards	12,034,102	33,450,303	30,786,242	11,397,145
Value	$19,429,163	$18,982,860	$17,681,660	$6,573,120
Warp-printed—				
Yards	185,981			
Value	$232,139			
Velvets:				
Yards	16,150,689	16,318,135	10,093,583	7,262,315
Value	$20,950,239	$8,570,022	$4,767,990	$3,161,206
Plushes:				
Yards	5,860,427	9,114,992	2,759,411	2,547,367
Value	$21,601,280	$10,135,842	$2,104,768	$1,340,815
Upholstery and tapestries:				
Yards	516,281	477,699	226,717	1,766,210
Value	$2,156,617	$840,126	$382,820	$1,559,982
Ribbons, value	$66,186,609	$38,201,293	$32,744,873	$21,890,604
All silk, value	$52,047,330	[2]	[2]	[2]
Silk and other materials, value	$14,139,279	[2]	[2]	[2]
Laces, nets, veils, veiling, etc., value	$5,825,359	$1,328,933	$1,350,850	$745,489
Embroideries, value	$127,522	$33,500	$485,322	$112,362
Fringes and gimps, value	$3,026,560	$1,025,188	$824,527	$1,016,954
Braids and binding, value	$13,218,284	$3,073,648	$4,483,248	$3,493,977
Tailors' trimmings, value	$634,058	$210,741	$41,040	$700
Military trimmings, value	$682,909	$431,422	$346,963	$170,231
Machine twist:				
Pounds	773,843	659,540	1,088,780	932,998
Value	$10,644,095	$4,036,807	$6,341,719	$5,521,055
Sewing and embroidery silks:				
Pounds	515,222	902,499	747,246	811,711
Value	$7,089,813	$5,644,806	$4,179,355	$4,625,016
Fringe and floss silks:				
Pounds	38,107			
Value	$500,571			
Organzine, for sale:				
Pounds	886,014	1,492,999	1,077,931	2,025,645
Value	$9,122,457	$6,325,291	$5,330,528	$9,190,650
Tram, for sale:				
Pounds	3,611,901	2,577,402	1,662,388	
Value	$31,494,535	$9,698,637	$7,219,982	
Hard-crepe twist, for sale:				
Pounds	1,070,845	[2]	[2]	[2]
Value	$12,011,137	[2]	[2]	[2]

[1] In addition, in 1919, similar classes of silk goods to the value of $658,030, in 1914, to the value of $1,776,660, and in 1909, to the value of $1,218,101, were reported by establishments engaged primarily in other industries.
[2] Not reported separately.

TABLE 37.—SILK GOODS, INCLUDING THROWSTERS: 1919, 1914, 1909, AND 1904—Con.

	1919	1914	1909	1904
PRODUCTS—continued.				
Spun silk, for sale:				
Pounds	3,956,637	1,607,416	779,462	570,529
Value	$23,807,338	$4,577,058	$2,104,066	$1,660,647
Singles—				
Pounds	1,764,028	(1)	(1)	(1)
Value	$11,733,463	(1)	(1)	(1)
Two or more ply—				
Pounds	2,192,609	(1)	(1)	(1)
Value	$12,073,875	(1)	(1)	(1)
Artificial silk:				
Pounds	829,083	(2)	(2)	(2)
Value	$5,423,242	(2)	(2)	(2)
All other products, value	$23,895,971	$13,757,772	$7,958,120	$8,164,566
Received for contract work	$38,335,025	$8,400,607	$8,364,350	$3,716,056
WORK DONE BY THROWSTERS (MATERIALS FURNISHED BY OTHERS).				
Thrown into organzine, pounds	6,286,728	7,088,229	6,114,209	3,635,384
Thrown into tram, pounds	7,393,872	6,781,010	6,638,793	3,466,467
Crepe twist	4,795,114	(1)	(1)	(1)
EQUIPMENT.				
Spindles:				
Throwing—				
Winding (raw silk only)	923,442	710,102	624,711	624,686
Spinning and twisting	2,532,867	2,057,889	1,681,453	
Spun silk—				1,394,020
Spinning	204,955	101,382	80,305	
Looms	106,826	85,058	75,406	60,058
40-inch or under, reed space (including Jacquard looms)	17,632	26,431	28,426	
Over 40-inch reed space (including Jacquard looms)	75,268	44,549	35,214	50,449
Velvet (including Jacquard looms)	2,205	2,524	1,196	
Ribbon (including Jacquard looms)	11,721	11,554	10,570	9,609
Jacquard machines	8,846	6,826	8,985	

[1] Not reported separately.   [2] Included in "all other products."

TABLE 38.—WOOLEN AND WORSTED GOODS: 1919, 1914, 1909, AND 1904.

KIND.	1919	1914	1909	1904
MATERIALS.				
Total cost..........................	$665,594,683	$246,496,666	$273,438,570	$197,489,306
Wool:				
In condition purchased—				
Pounds.......................	443,461,904	434,728,075	474,755,366	418,703,811
Cost........................	$306,170,702	$108,087,619	$136,666,917	$105,433,451
Domestic—				
Pounds.......................	245,830,276	266,634,390	310,602,279	319,800,490
Cost........................	$170,882,888	$64,571,871	$85,018,238	$78,673,136
Foreign—				
Pounds.......................	197,631,628	168,093,685	164,153,087	98,903,321
Cost........................	$135,287,814	$43,515,748	$51,648,679	$26,760,315
Equivalent in scoured condition, pounds...	263,836,462	257,448,746	290,706,970	241,280,065
Mohair, and camel, alpaca, and vicuna hair:				
Pounds...........................	13,791,281	14,359,457	7,805,422	6,507,631
Cost.............................	$9,596,336	$4,455,354	$2,399,123	$1,957,581
All other animal hair:				
Pounds...........................	14,489,813	14,761,502	17,356,100	22,987,332
Cost.............................	$3,050,987	$1,062,810	$932,911	$1,369,776
Cotton:				
Pounds...........................	17,375,403	28,387,022	20,024,061	32,613,408
Cost.............................	$5,952,015	$3,241,352	$2,515,409	$4,072,907
Rags, clippings, etc.:				
Pounds...........................	46,453,109	59,425,149	40,402,460	79,367,290
Cost.............................	$11,772,699	$4,754,308	$2,856,966	$5,668,634
Recovered wool fiber:				
Pounds...........................	33,163,696	26,276,924	21,454,187	31,919,456
Cost.............................	$13,518,853	$3,551,217	$3,058,214	$4,472,666
Waste, and noils of wool, mohair, camel's hair, etc.:				
Pounds...........................	43,738,241	42,411,874	26,473,311	26,032,838
Cost.............................	$28,018,729	$8,906,485	$7,523,283	$6,056,227
Tops purchased:				
Pounds...........................	26,266,239	29,106,307	20,828,245	9,160,929
Cost.............................	$45,449,230	$16,679,819	$14,614,527	$5,073,078
Yarns purchased:				
Woolen—				
Pounds.......................	8,361,784	2,168,371	931,222	5,750,088
Cost........................	$12,887,478	$1,174,815	$558,270	$2,622,882
Worsted—				
Pounds.......................	42,962,105	53,626,797	59,148,771	31,047,516
Cost........................	$110,456,932	$44,660,712	$56,033,701	$24,904,511
Merino—				
Pounds.......................	1,604,553	530,863	1,971,709	2,458,085
Cost........................	$2,185,286	$168,519	$318,456	$581,107
Cotton—				
Pounds.......................	28,683,645	32,105,412	39,169,388	32,598,072
Cost........................	$21,077,436	$9,076,933	$10,492,185	$8,032,773
Silk and spun silk—				
Pounds.......................	415,790	515,950	282,536	412,307
Cost........................	$3,283,386	$2,010,885	$1,142,663	$1,679,883
All other—				
Pounds.......................	1,956,609	1,978,193	1,046,735	411,779
Cost........................	$811,128	$103,334	$40,739	$21,118
Chemicals and dyestuffs, cost..............	$22,870,502	$8,536,232	$8,820,928	$7,456,550
All other materials, cost..................	$68,492,984	$30,026,272	$25,464,278	$18,086,162
PRODUCTS.				
Total value	[1]$1,065,434,072	[1] $379,484,379	[1] $419,743,521	$307,941,710
Woven goods: [2]				
Pounds...........................	332,208,704	[3]	[3]	[3]
Square yards.....................	535,937,572	565,462,159	570,743,797	505,821,956
Value...........................	$739,279,795	$268,679,480	$296,447,594	$234,737,036
All-wool woven goods—				
Pounds.......................	211,074,296	[3]	[3]	[3]
Square yards..................	326,714,779	323,037,563	322,944,365	260,567,488
Value........................	$572,043,595	$203,390,017	$219,853,767	$158,390,336
Woolen suitings, overcoatings, and dress goods—				
Pounds.......................	117,149,070	[3]	[3]	[3]
Square yards..................	139,410,352	90,950,381	84,641,705	113,773,492
Value........................	$243,072,041	$55,660,503	$56,907,413	$66,316,381

[1] In addition, in 1919, woolen and worsted goods to the value of $12,624,758, in 1914, to the value of $2,635,889, and in 1909, to the value of $3,183,485, were made by establishments engaged primarily in other industries. Of these amounts, products to the value of $8,504,372 in 1919, $1,500,567 in 1914, and $1,902,187 in 1909 were made by carpet and rug and felt-goods mills.
[2] Does not include woven upholstery goods.
[3] Not reported.

TABLE 38.—WOOLEN AND WORSTED GOODS: 1919, 1914, 1909, AND 1904—Continued.

KIND.	1919	1914	1909	1904
PRODUCTS—continued.				
Woven goods—Continued.				
All-wool woven goods—Continued.				
Worsted suitings, overcoatings, and dress goods—				
Pounds	85,981,863	(1)	(1)	(1)
Square yards	176,506,452	222,420,785	226,110,822	127,079,304
Value	$313,679,634	$141,778,035	$156,755,217	$85,079,547
Flannels for underwear—				
Pounds	825,886	(1)	(1)	(1)
Square yards	1,733,250	2,176,264	3,856,353	8,710,131
Value	$1,860,585	$880,494	$1,257,271	$2,045,858
Blankets—				
Pounds	4,975,438	(1)	(1)	(1)
Square yards	5,916,197	6,489,689	5,137,903	7,316,179
Value	$6,897,923	$4,186,754	$3,228,797	$2,751,029
Horse blankets—				
Pounds	216,024	(1)	(1)	(1)
Square yards	387,926	102,205	247,395	740,237
Value	$648,990	$82,398	$185,430	$418,219
Carriage cloths—				
Pounds	587,041	(1)	(1)	(1)
Square yards	687,241	2 514,226	1,782,855	1,741,765
Value	$1,371,356	2 $443,223	$947,862	$964,557
Carriage robes—				
Pounds	(2)	(1)	(1)	(1)
Square yards	(2)	132,399	85,179	42,187
Value	(2)	$158,900	$17,642	$93,727
Shawls—				
Pounds	590,667	(1)	(1)	(1)
Square yards	868,971	3 124,486	704,153	895,777
Value	$854,041	3 $66,365	$404,583	$557,370
All other—				
Pounds	748,307	(1)	(1)	(1)
Square yards	1,204,390	127,128	378,000	268,416
Value	$3,659,025	$133,345	$149,552	$163,648
Cotton-warp woven goods 4—				
Pounds	79,429,188	(1)	(1)	(1)
Square yards	161,445,850	196,179,866	210,346,081	182,057,061
Value	$118,137,626	$48,816,015	$62,265,854	$50,058,293
Woolen-filling suitings, overcoatings, and dress goods—				
Pounds	23,771,643	(1)	(1)	(1)
Square yards	39,146,902	53,509,462	60,236,428	54,939,651
Value	$34,735,320	$13,598,007	$15,621,015	$16,586,520
Worsted-filling suitings, overcoatings, and dress goods—				
Pounds	21,300,561	(1)	(1)	(1)
Square yards	57,896,787	56,763,091	94,643,217	65,988,989
Value	$45,342,581	$15,563,099	$30,003,046	$19,680,956
Domett flannels and shirtings—				
Pounds	11,780,531	(1)	(1)	(1)
Square yards	22,223,880	5 16,092,266	4,571,765	4,285,838
Value	$11,600,377	5 $2,814,054	$911,967	$769,476
Linings, Italian cloths, and lastings—				
Pounds	595,222	(1)	(1)	(1)
Square yards	742,562	36,196,243	28,928,148	17,619,325
Value	$532,411	$9,804,661	$9,008,799	$4,505,927
Satinets and linseys—				
Pounds	5,863,838	(1)	(1)	(1)
Square yards	4,637,678	5 8,415,079	5,102,460	22,339,112
Value	$3,517,427	5 $1,535,291	$912,182	$4,074,800
Blankets—				
Pounds	7,603,761	(1)	(1)	(1)
Square yards	9,244,134	5 17,973,821	9,746,841	9,267,144
Value	$7,289,253	5 $3,010,070	$2,684,919	$2,218,243
Horse blankets—				
Pounds	1,448,015	(1)	(1)	(1)
Square yards	1,307,789	5,831,305	4,210,098	6,307,836
Value	$957,427	$1,539,526	$1,676,942	$1,083,154
Carriage robes—				
Pounds	1,055,935	(1)	(1)	(1)
Square yards	743,570	1,282,417	2,889,444	1,309,166
Value	$1,046,525	$936,687	$1,396,595	$1,139,217
All other—				
Pounds	6,009,682	(1)	(1)	
Square yards	25,502,548	116,182	17,680	
Value	$13,116,305	$14,620	$50,389	

1 Not reported.
2 Can not be shown separately; included in "all other" for the group.
3 Figures for 1914 apply to goods made in woolen mills only; the output of these goods by worsted mills is included in "all other all-wool woven goods."
4 Includes woolen and cotton warps with cotton filling.
5 Figures for 1914 apply to goods made in woolen mills only; the output of these goods by worsted mills is included in "all other cotton-warp woven goods.

TABLE 38.—WOOLEN AND WORSTED GOODS: 1919, 1914, 1909, and 1904—Continued.

KIND.	1919	1914	1909	1904
PRODUCTS—continued.				
Woven goods—Continued.				
Union or cotton mixed woven goods—				
Pounds	41,705,220	(1)	(1)	(1)
Square yards	47,776,943	46,244,730	37,453,351	63,197,407
Value	$49,098,574	$16,473,448	$14,327,973	$26,288,407
Cotton-mixed suitings, overcoatings, and dress goods—				
Pounds	19,497,282	(1)	(1)	(1)
Square yards	24,615,373	31,400,082	27,518,756	52,166,903
Value	$26,045,387	$11,710,610	$11,920,956	$23,331,080
Flannels for underwear—				
Pounds	2,610,419	(1)	(1)	(1)
Square yards	6,497,990	4,995,575	7,063,572	7,273,761
Value	$5,205,330	$1,089,661	$1,308,369	$1,528,928
Blankets—				
Pounds	7,459,554	(1)	(1)	(1)
Square yards	9,922,925	3,937,463	1,717,758	3,114,110
Value	$8,616,905	$2,067,934	$650,714	$1,198,706
Horse blankets—				
Pounds		(1)	(1)	(1)
Square yards		2,231,162	694,176	618,800
Value		$395,858	$186,238	$222,543
Carriage robes—				
Pounds	699,016	(1)	(1)	(1)
Square yards	553,869	354,049	459,089	23,833
Value	$861,820	$137,968	$261,696	$7,150
All other—				
Pounds	11,438,949	(1)		
Square yards	6,186,786	3,326,399		
Value	$8,369,132	$1,071,417		
Upholstery goods and sundries:				
Value	$8,481,633	$2,042,029	$1,986,330	$1,625,233
Woolen, worsted, and mohair upholstery goods—				
Pounds	2,741,232	(1)	(1)	(1)
Square yards	4,429,876	1,598,444	1,176,542	1,060,739
Value	$3,944,134	$1,809,474	$1,528,648	$908,937
All other—				
Value	$4,537,499	$232,555	$457,682	$716,296
Yarns for sale:				
Pounds	118,309,923	132,559,701	134,051,361	113,291,228
Value	$237,534,451	$85,872,215	$94,541,753	$56,297,342
Woolen—				
Pounds	28,387,039	26,125,575	28,520,493	42,878,320
Value	$32,828,522	$8,783,020	$7,505,412	$9,993,894
Worsted—				
Pounds	74,336,549	86,412,097	88,323,953	55,475,235
Value	$185,124,293	$69,801,271	$80,395,543	$40,142,077
Woolen, union or merino—				
Pounds	9,150,149	6,473,849	10,249,625	8,824,064
Value	$6,808,543	$1,689,530	$2,143,416	$2,538,018
Worsted, union or merino—				
Pounds	4,217,801	4,048,514	3,761,737	3,314,549
Value	$9,328,764	$3,173,034	$3,522,812	$2,460,558
All other—				
Pounds	2,218,385	9,499,666	3,195,553	2,799,060
Value	$3,444,329	$2,425,360	$974,570	$1,162,795
Worsted tops and slubbing:				
Pounds	9,899,257	8,985,170	11,321,279	4,772,582
Value	$14,503,006	$4,926,929	$8,027,231	$2,855,171
Noils:				
Pounds	24,054,141	23,961,100	27,479,293	15,379,600
Value	$17,809,446	$6,819,690	● $8,938,589	$4,865,976
Waste:				
Pounds	28,029,816	26,433,970	24,420,444	17,946,076
Value	$6,990,279	$3,320,447	$3,534,761	$2,448,183
All other products, value	$22,448,629	$4,386,953	$3,241,008	$3,924,232
Contract work, value	$18,386,833	$3,436,636	$3,026,255	$1,188,537
EQUIPMENT.				
Sets of woolen cards[2]	4,836	4,222	4,500	5,178
Spindles	4,976,129	4,722,032	4,287,640	3,747,934
Producing	4,205,012	3,880,583	3,553,194	3,228,423
Doubling and twisting	771,117	841,449	734,446	519,511
Looms, all classes	75,729	75,828	72,532	63,867
Wool-combing machines	2,197	2,305	1,988	1,440

[1] Not reported.　　　　　　　　　　[2] Includes shoddy cards.

TABLE 39.—FELT GOODS: 1919, 1914, 1909, AND 1904.

	1919	1914	1909	1904
MATERIALS.				
Total cost...	$22,780,775	$8,308,270	$6,967,206	$5,754,026
Wool:				
In condition purchased—				
Pounds...	11,804,373	14,969,852	12,409,826	11,868,238
Cost...	$9,359,160	$4,030,114	$3,927,393	$3,388,588
Equivalent of above in scoured condition, pounds...	9,450,913	10,476,716	9,308,172	8,131,082
Animal hair, etc.:				
Pounds...	19,663,511	11,540,635	8,144,011	6,974,634
Cost...	$1,394,810	$739,955	$239,244	$373,797
Cotton:				
Pounds...	1,442,406	3,117,272	1,375,670	1,982,624
Cost...	$437,363	$297,632	$155,815	$217,200
Recovered wool fiber:				
Pounds...	4,194,670	3,502,795	2,536,243	1,532,127
Cost...	$1,332,935	$409,518	$261,878	$157,031
Waste and noils:				
Pounds...	6,640,136	4,064,699	4,874,712	1,948,969
Cost...	$4,355,908	$1,019,687	$1,220,110	$452,509
Chemicals and dyestuffs, cost...	$604,616	$269,921	$219,891	$189,750
All other materials, cost...	$5,295,983	$1,541,443	$942,875	$975,151
PRODUCTS.				
Total value...	[1] $39,229,540	[1] $13,692,765	$11,852,626	$8,948,594
Felt cloths:				
Pounds...	3,397,378	[2]	[2]	[2]
Square yards...	2,751,497	[2]	3,764,468	3,689,610
Value...	$8,785,169	$797,048	$1,381,854	$1,830,627
Trimming and lining felts, felt skirts, table and piano covers:				
Pounds...	4,158,956	[2]	[2]	[2]
Square yards...	9,199,673	8,369,330	5,953,410	5,145,340
Value...	$3,143,678	$1,321,337	$1,329,686	$1,188,908
Polishing felts and buffing wheels:				
Pounds...	1,132,598			
Square yards...	2,185,465	[3]	[3]	[3]
Value...	$1,307,123			
Piano felts:				
Pounds...	777,558			
Square yards...	381,388	[3]	[3]	[3]
Value...	$1,945,988			
Saddle felts:				
Pounds...	812,508	2,291,662	1,650,991	[3]
Value...	$639,234	$973,353	$575,849	[3]
Endless belts:				
Pounds...	250,000	3,941,795	3,243,034	1,770,124
Value...	$478,285	$4,164,186	$3,417,822	$1,707,216
Boot and shoe linings:				
Pounds...	2,471,177	[2]	[2]	[2]
Square yards...	5,280,970	3,028,286	1,661,090	2,823,137
Value...	$2,603,724	$1,512,783	$514,456	$781,450
Hair felting:				
Pounds...	6,658,787	[2]	[2]	[2]
Square yards...	7,222,741	1,350,436	1,159,999	605,214
Value...	$2,249,653	$635,041	$531,045	$191,998
All other felts, value...	$15,369,261	$3,691,081	$3,549,876	$2,592,894
All other products, value...	$2,707,425	$597,936	$552,038	$655,501
EQUIPMENT.				
Woolen cards, sets...	416	573	472	451
Spindles...	33,258	37,492	30,353	17,817
Producing...	32,947	36,462	29,463	17,457
Doubling and twisting...	311	1,030	890	360
Looms, all classes...	510	472	408	265

[1] In addition, in 1919, felt goods to the value of $2,385,762 and in 1914, to the value of $181,640 were made by establishments engaged primarily in the manufacture of other products.
[2] Not reported.
[3] Not reported separately.

TABLE 40.—HATS, FUR-FELT: 1919, 1914, AND 1909.

	1919	1914	1909
MATERIALS.			
Total cost...................................	$40,158,019	$16,947,058	$22,109,231
Hatters' fur:			
Pounds...................................	6,205,607	5,766,904	8,645,576
Cost......................................	$20,374,170	$7,108,248	$9,278,922
Fur-felt hat bodies and hats in the rough:			
Dozens...................................	459,655	395,848	406,447
Cost......................................	$6,636,707	$2,453,503	$2,575,248
Chemicals and dyestuffs, cost.............	$820,577	$432,161	$843,587
All other materials, cost..................	$12,326,565	$6,953,146	$9,411,474
PRODUCTS.			
Total value.................................	$82,745,308	$37,349,744	$47,864,630
Fur-felt hats:			
Dozens...................................	2,100,023	2,118,634	2,989,252
Value.....................................	$71,069,038	$33,603,531	$43,442,466
Fur-felt hat bodies and hats in the rough:			
Dozens...................................	518,111	329,363	366,370
Value.....................................	$7,657,114	$2,372,937	$2,703,738
All other products, value..................	$3,995,566	$864,309	$1,164,872
Work on materials for others..............	$23,590	$508,967	$553,554

TABLE 41.—HATS, WOOL-FELT: 1919, 1914, 1909, AND 1904.

	1919	1914	1909	1904
MATERIALS.				
Total cost............................	$3,699,822	$978,339	$2,472,263	$1,369,810
Wool:				
In condition purchased:				
Pounds..........................	200,294	606,957	1,203,498	1,633,525
Cost.............................	$212,632	$298,345	$404,127	$495,594
Equivalent in scoured condition, pounds...	194,828	561,639	989,110	1,231,576
Wool waste and noils:				
Pounds..........................	711,747	454,099	1,281,764	287,363
Cost.............................	$791,900	$213,851	$661,172	$119,407
Wool-felt hat bodies and hats in the rough:				
Dozens...........................	72,213	13,449	21,864	12,089
Cost..............................	$573,925	$26,646	$83,020	$25,997
Chemicals and dyestuffs, cost.........	$172,320	$34,501	$104,503	$63,905
All other materials, cost..............	$1,949,045	$404,996	$1,219,441	$664,907
PRODUCTS.				
Total value...........................	[1] $6,739,652	[1] $1,944,484	[1] $4,382,411	$2,457,266
Wool-felt hats:				
Dozens...........................	401,893	381,044	590,957	446,121
Value............................	$5,409,505	$1,777,225	$3,646,787	$2,290,070
Wool-felt hat bodies and hats in the rough:				
Dozens...........................	104,144	5,715	53,896	18,587
Value............................	$165,469	$13,029	$309,492	$100,491
All other products, value............	$1,164,678	$154,230	$426,132	$66,705

[1] In addition, in 1919, wool-felt hats to the value of $76,404; in 1914, to the value of $305,181; and in 1909, to the value of $904,643, were made by establishments engaged primarily in other industries.

TABLE 42.—CARPETS AND RUGS, OTHER THAN RAG: 1919, 1914, 1909, AND 1904.

	1919	1914	1909	1904
MATERIALS.				
Total cost	$67,118,039	$42,280,223	$39,563,004	$37,947,954
Wool:				
In condition purchased—				
Pounds................................	36,261,904	52,552,449	64,135,020	51,320,521
Cost..................................	$13,258,069	$10,493,743	$11,752,396	$10,431,146
Equivalent of above in scoured condition, pounds.....................	21,905,916	39,218,831	51,474,353	31,551,895
Animal hair:				
Pounds................................	6,272,522	3,469,283	5,400,944	6,805,802
Cost..................................	$1,847,332	$402,225	$474,057	$593,588
Cotton:				
Pounds................................	3,864,826	3,802,789	5,147,130	1,997,369
Cost..................................	$1,426,110	$343,916	$533,302	$251,112
Waste and noils:				
Pounds................................	560,664	3,419,715	2,732,034	2,172,481
Cost..................................	$130,290	$476,610	$513,392	$341,309
Yarns, purchased:				
Woolen—				
Pounds................................	17,389,590	21,626,360	25,718,747	32,431,400
Cost..................................	$11,337,800	$5,821,848	$5,036,118	$6,648,001
Worsted—				
Pounds................................	4,164,565	9,267,278	11,292,749	11,355,993
Cost..................................	$4,479,898	$4,592,906	$5,588,915	$5,405,072
Cotton—				
Pounds................................	17,309,949	24,619,137	26,166,241	27,421,831
Cost..................................	$8,972,737	$4,637,673	$4,772,594	$4,757,850
Linen—				
Pounds................................	2,280,055	7,602,200	8,792,876	8,228,200
Cost..................................	$1,062,197	$1,414,924	$1,606,009	$1,355,892
Jute, ramie, and other vegetable fiber—				
Pounds................................	45,119,812	59,148,266	55,592,343	49,119,558
Cost..................................	$9,399,764	$6,040,186	$3,926,694	$3,404,516
Other yarns—				
Pounds................................	921,655	341,114	781,028	1,112,138
Cost..................................	$1,788,833	$658,254	$408,121	$339,285
Chemicals and dyestuffs, cost....................	$2,917,202	$1,378,509	$1,729,492	$1,467,476
All other materials, cost........................	$10,497,807	$6,019,429	$3,221,914	$2,952,707
PRODUCTS.				
Total value...............................	[1] $123,253,828	$69,128,185	[1] $71,188,152	[1] $61,586,433
Carpets and rugs:				
Pounds................................	118,071,798	[2]	[2]	[2]
Square yards...........................	52,173,092	66,340,274	81,218,881	82,670,843
Value..................................	$110,115,978	$64,683,322	$66,966,338	$56,861,775
Axminster and moquette—				
Pounds................................	36,667,823	[2]	[2]	[2]
Square yards...........................	14,700,394	15,742,835	15,691,358	8,181,606
Value..................................	$35,503,778	$18,578,693	$17,372,706	$8,476,140
Wilton—				
Pounds................................	16,464,515	[2]	[2]	[2]
Square yards...........................	4,964,321	5,616,263	5,343,616	2,395,058
Value..................................	$23,461,960	$11,929,605	$10,119,330	$4,710,444
Brussels—				
Pounds................................	2,399,118	[2]	[2]	[2]
Square yards...........................	903,127	2,698,840	4,436,457	3,024,162
Value..................................	$2,233,053	$3,995,626	$5,550,189	$3,898,675
Tapestry velvet—				
Pounds................................	22,443,519	[2]	[2]	[2]
Square yards...........................	9,865,798	13,227,819	10,660,170	8,033,288
Value..................................	$20,625,610	$12,867,635	$9,027,193	$7,754,681

[1] In addition, in 1919, carpets and rugs to the value of $40,089, in 1909 to the value of $479,161, and in 1904 to the value of $70,000 were made in establishments engaged primarily in the manufacture of products other than those covered by the industry designation.

[2] Not reported.

TABLE 42.—CARPETS AND RUGS, OTHER THAN RAG: 1919, 1914, 1909, AND 1904—Continued.

	1919	1914	1909	1904
PRODUCTS—continued.				
Carpets and rugs—Continued.				
Tapestry brussels—				
Pounds	20,205,086	(1)	(1)	(1)
Square yards	9,996,099	13,614,354	17,078,476	16,108,908
Value	$13,120,096	$9,852,647	$12,999,333	$11,464,716
Ingrain carpets—				
Pounds	1,357,793	(1)	(1)	(1)
Square yards	1,199,714	5,795,807	17,799,762	33,557,951
Value	$1,055,242	$2,241,294	$6,749,672	$13,287,302
Ingrain art squares—				
Pounds	976,122	(1)	(1)	(1)
Square yards	820,911	3,177,563	6,131,862	7,135,546
Value	$714,648	$1,165,087	$2,408,960	$2,785,457
Smyrna rugs—				
Pounds	2,658,390	(1)	(1)	(1)
Square yards	807,741	822,150	1,400,233	3,828,282
Value	$1,914,201	$870,891	$1,660,322	$4,134,500
Other carpets and rugs—				
Pounds	14,899,432	(1)	(1)	(1)
Square yards	8,914,987	5,644,643	2,676,947	406,042
Value	$11,487,390	$3,181,844	$1,078,633	$349,860
All other products, value	$13,137,850	$4,444,863	$4,221,814	$4,724,658
EQUIPMENT.				
Woolen cards	592	465	456	389
Spindles:				
Spinning mule	126,788	102,238	94,798 }	211,331
Spinning frame	72,572	110,090	116,674 }	
Doubling and twisting	33,866	34,434	40,624	44,016
Carpet and rug looms:				
Power	7,897	9,821	11,736 }	13,853
Hand	260	31	207 }	

1 Not reported.

TABLE 43.—OILCLOTH AND LINOLEUM: 1919, 1914, AND 1909.

PRODUCT.	1919	1914	1909
Total value	$68,110,081	$25,598,361	$23,339,022
Oilcloth (made on cotton back):			
Enameled—			
Square yards	8,460,738	18,357,097	17,338,440
Value	$3,421,188	$2,495,255	$2,265,146
Table, wall, shelf, and stair—			
Square yards	39,132,641	59,358,872	61,168,777
Value	$12,529,910	$6,025,348	$5,639,206
Linoleum (made on jute back):			
Linoleum, including cork carpet—			
Square yards	22,098,136	33,306,669	26,215,979
Value	$17,120,654	$10,043,436	$7,850,437
Inlaid linoleum—			
Square yards	9,834,332	8,479,202	4,460,275
Value	$10,336,391	$4,725,837	$2,994,491
Floor covering (made on felt back):			
Square yards	30,369,522	(1)	(1)
Value	$13,909,276	(1)	(1)
Artificial leather:			
Pyroxylin coated textiles—			
Square yards	3,332,085	(1)	(1)
Value	$3,922,558	(1)	(1)
All other—			
Square yards	10,300,416	(1)	(1)
Value	$4,821,190	(1)	(1)
All other products, value	$2,048,914	$2,308,485	$4,589,742

1 Not reported separately.

TABLE 44.—WOOL SHODDY: 1919, 1914, AND 1909.

	1919	1914	1909
MATERIALS.			
Total cost	$16,076,315	$5,299,903	$4,539,979
Rags, clippings, etc.:			
Pounds	63,244,868	57,367,962	43,296,261
Cost	$12,173,784	$3,103,864	$2,644,570
Wool and other noils and wool waste:			
Pounds	12,361,895	6,879,366	7,567,579
Cost	$1,607,053	$863,633	$917,976
Recovered wool fiber:			
Pounds	394,546	1,658,432	533,822
Cost	$13,164	$168,457	$48,342
Wool (in condition purchased):			
Pounds	181,052	203,868	237,097
Cost	$164,686	$81,514	$98,032
Equivalent of above in scoured condition, pounds	181,052	203,868	196,097
Chemicals and dyestuffs, cost	$489,967	$103,849	$138,241
All other materials, cost	$1,627,661	$978,586	$692,818
PRODUCTS.			
Total value	[1] $23,254,398	[1] $7,706,843	[1] $6,854,993
Recovered wool fiber:			
Pounds	58,786,504	43,156,037	38,291,465
Value	$20,644,001	$5,977,284	$5,679,283
Carbonized rags (wool extract):			
Pounds	19,786	4,627,568	3,648,662
Value	$8,092	$636,332	$593,331
All other products, value	$1,503,481	$686,527	$355,137
Amount received from contract work for others on materials or goods furnished by them	$1,098,824	$406,700	$227,242
EQUIPMENT.			
Cards, number of sets	554	574	503
Pickers, number	337	315	332
Garnett machines, number	157	178	141

[1] In addition, in 1919, similar products to the value of $1,440,480; in 1914, to the value of $151,982; and in 1909, to the value of $367,278, were reported by establishments engaged primarily in other industries.

TABLE 45.—CORDAGE AND TWINE, JUTE GOODS, AND LINEN GOODS: 1919, 1914, AND 1909.

	1919	1914	1909
MATERIALS.			
Total cost...	$111,604,303	$60,474,417	$39,536,892
Hard fibers:			
Pounds...	427,932,476	437,330,684	352,683,572
Cost...	$58,578,509	$28,576,735	$20,022,108
Manila hemp (abaca)—			
Pounds...	122,736,510	99,519,803	131,611,993
Cost...	$22,085,814	$9,395,431	$8,396,980
New Zealand hemp—			
Pounds...	28,391,553	9,672,195	2,091,217
Cost...	$4,251,960	$579,322	$415,942
Henequen—			
Pounds...	159,780,297	281,189,993	} 203,848,581
Cost...	$23,351,203	$15,736,496	$10,917,326
Sisal—			
Pounds...	30,608,827	38,982,642	
Cost...	$4,740,344	$2,471,640	
Other hard fibers—			
Pounds...	86,415,289	7,966,051	15,131,781
Cost...	$4,149,188	$393,846	$591,860
Soft fibers:			
Pounds...	205,961,862	338,345,841	307,035,404
Cost...	$23,003,914	$18,273,553	$10,838,175
Jute—			
Pounds...	126,190,459	128,312,082	121,992,427
Cost...	$11,622,610	$8,737,870	$4,134,265
Jute butts—			
Pounds...	50,612,168	114,389,155	138,364,122
Cost...	$2,991,499	$3,535,552	$2,033,176
Flax and flax tow—			
Pounds...	12,787,560	24,717,598	26,954,785
Cost...	$5,796,554	$3,205,975	$3,174,609
Hemp and hemp tow—			
Pounds...	14,939,387	22,752,353	19,724,070
Cost...	$2,433,502	$1,861,817	$1,496,125
Other soft fibers—			
Pounds...	1,432,288	48,174,653	(1)
Cost...	$159,749	$932,339	(1)
Cotton:			
Pounds...	31,685,111	32,336,685	27,624,490
Cost...	$8,536,832	$3,453,348	$2,922,933
Yarns purchased:			
Cotton—			
Pounds...	7,950,240	7,968,054	7,077,959
Cost...	$4,081,394	$1,458,159	$1,291,599
Flax, hemp, jute, and ramie—			
Pounds...	5,520,126	626,966	2,676,367
Cost...	$1,861,781	$765,444	$445,378
All other materials, cost...	$15,541,873	$7,947,178	$4,016,699
PRODUCTS.			
Total value...	2 $174,807,220	2 $83,235,068	2 $59,121,989
Rope, cable, and cordage:			
Pounds...	225,658,614	198,400,692	239,031,893
Value...	$55,369,664	$21,530,858	$19,850,635
Manila hemp—			
Pounds...	130,418,220	104,909,172	125,789,435
Value...	$32,009,929	$12,860,035	$10,719,269
Marine cordage—			
Pounds...	79,152,029	(3)	(3)
Value...	$20,538,519	(3)	(3)
Hardware rope—			
Pounds...	13,236,497	(3)	(3)
Value...	$2,906,139	(3)	(3)
Drilling cable—			
Pounds...	10,853,867	(3)	(3)
Value...	$2,640,079	(3)	(3)
Transmission rope—			
Pounds...	3,347,125	(3)	(3)
Value...	$808,987	(3)	(3)
Other commercial and bolt ropes—			
Pounds...	23,828,702	(3)	(3)
Value...	$5,116,205	(3)	(3)
Sisal—			
Pounds...	26,250,565	39,898,873	} 64,165,218
Value...	$26,250,565	$2,991,141	$4,245,723
Henequen—			
Pounds...	16,327,138	13,533,529	
Value...	$3,110,903	$1,042,457	

1 Not reported in 1909.

2 In addition, cordage and twine, jute goods, and linen goods to the value of $11,628,911 in 1919, $5,011,790 in 1914, and $4,472,546 in 1909, were reported by establishments engaged primarily in other industries. Of these amounts $8,792,520 in 1919, $3,683,348 in 1914, and $3,581,917 in 1909, represent the value of the twine and cordage and rope made by cotton mills engaged chiefly in the manufacture of yarn (see Table 35).

3 Not reported separately.

TABLE 45.—CORDAGE AND TWINE AND JUTE AND LINEN GOODS: 1919, 1914, AND 1909—Continued.

	1919	1914	1909
PRODUCTS—continued.			
Rope, cable, and cordage—Continued.			
Cotton—			
Pounds	11,947,094	13,244,198	16,760,763
Value	$6,119,785	$2,539,906	$3,011,613
Jute—			
Pounds	29,678,866		27,749,512
Value	$6,252,295	26,814,920	$1,566,160
All other—		$2,097,319	
Pounds	11,036,731		4,566,965
Value	$3,074,694		$307,870
Binder twine:			
Pounds	229,508,186	302,286,862	189,172,151
Value	$46,256,024	$24,094,565	$14,079,671
All or chiefly manila hemp (abaca)—			
Pounds	9,286,584	16,948,915	24,380,247
Value	$2,285,608	$1,637,511	$2,173,078
All or chiefly sisal—			
Pounds	197,050,557		161,591,308
Value	$38,803,930	285,337,947	$11,714,557
All other—		$22,457,054	
Pounds	23,171,045		3,200,596
Value	$5,166,486		$192,036
Twine, other than binder:			
Pounds	92,359,030	105,249,677	75,816,653
Value	$30,329,651	$13,996,522	$8,934,352
Cotton—			
Pounds	23,438,440	17,927,286	20,412,631
Value	$12,288,755	$3,472,056	$3,518,036
Jute—			
Pounds	52,398,422	55,282,159	35,516,217
Value	$10,904,168	$5,268,357	$2,557,744
Hemp—			
Pounds	7,988,085	9,318,771	8,013,349
Value	$3,864,311	$1,583,354	$1,091,291
Flax—			
Pounds	.84,415	3,953,622	2,967,053
Value	$113,836	$1,051,684	$830,969
Other, including mixed—			
Pounds	8,449,668	18,767,839	8,907,403
Value	$3,158,581	$2,621,071	$936,312
Yarns for sale:			
Pounds	60,483,739	75,875,322	68,731,258
Value	$13,288,394	$8,320,186	$5,434,037
Jute—			
Pounds	56,407,631	69,827,005	62,512,247
Value	$11,587,402	$7,357,888	$4,361,550
Other—			
Pounds	4,076,108	6,048,317	6,219,011
Value	$1,700,992	$962,298	$1,072,487
Linen thread:			
Pounds	4,279,264	5,707,668	6,530,503
Value	$6,690,440	$3,409,136	$3,407,008
Woven goods:			
Linen—			
Square yards	14,341,720	10,799,628	10,460,993
Values	$3,798,974	$1,765,798	$1,574,653
Jute—			
Carpets and rugs—			
Square yards	2,288,270	4,862,302	2,206,114
Value	$1,600,677	$1,172,257	$549,221
Bagging for baling cotton—			
Square yards	75,204,744		
Value	$11,339,670	131,827,658	69,311,288
Other bags and bagging—		$6,440,594	$3,507,482
Square yards	3,554,323		
Value	$666,887		
Webbing (not over 12 inches in width)—			
Linear yards	25,417,400	(1)	(1)
Value	$1,053,170	(1)	(1)
All other jute woven goods—			
Square yards	4,013,586	(1)	(1)
Value	$1,696,444	(1)	(1)
All other woven goods—			
Square yards	219,489	(1)	(1)
Value	$154,990	(1)	(1)
All other products, value	$2,562,235	$2,505,152	$1,784,930

1 Not reported separately.

TABLE 46.—IRON AND STEEL, BLAST FURNACES: 1919, 1914, AND 1909.

	1919	1914	1909
Number of establishments...........................	[1] 200	160	208
MATERIALS.			
Total cost..................................	[1] $626,675,640	$264,580,060	$320,637,889
Iron ore:			
Tons (2,240 pounds).........................	55,865,997	43,326,817	48,353,677
Cost...................................	$307,714,137	$150,855,740	$187,264,601
Domestic—			
Tons...................................	55,325,415	41,556,642	46,605,930
Cost...................................	$303,356,013	$141,276,713	$177,589,789
Foreign—			
Tons...................................	540,582	1,770,175	1,747,747
Cost...................................	$4,358,124	$9,579,027	$9,674,812
Crude iron ore—			
Tons...................................	54,067,079		
Cost...................................	$296,677,398		
Calcined, roasted or treated ore—			
Tons...................................	1,145,321		
Cost...................................	$7,264,016	(²)	(²)
Manganiferous ore—			
Tons...................................	364,771		
Cost...................................	$2,220,499		
Pyrite cinder—			
Tons...................................	288,826		
Cost...................................	$1,552,224		
Scrap:			
Tons (2,240 pounds).........................	1,057,908		
Cost...................................	$16,564,169	2,168,092	1,982,530
Mill cinder, scale, slag, etc.:		$6,651,055	$5,544,859
Tons (2,240 pounds).........................	2,378,943		
Cost...................................	$6,709,188		
Fluxes:			
Tons (2,000 pounds).........................	15,599,604	11,499,685	13,570,845
Cost....................................	$25,722,688	$11,184,378	$12,239,493
Fuel for smelting, cost........................	$229,201,344	$85,436,530	$105,994,112
Coke—			
Tons (2,000 pounds).........................	34,605,700	26,883,082	31,436,536
Cost...................................	$223,250,607	$83,499,448	$102,134,423
Charcoal—			
Bushels..................................	31,931,134	29,083,978	38,032,618
Cost...................................	$5,684,243	$1,683,075	$2,787,026
Anthracite—			
Tons (2,240 pounds).........................	25,153	38,874	265,401
Cost...................................	$194,280	$158,377	$904,102
Bituminous coal—			
Tons (2,000 pounds).........................	23,568	60,337	115,173
Cost...................................	$72,214	$95,630	$168,561
All other material, including fuel for generating power and rent of power................................	$40,764,114	$10,452,357	$9,594,824
PRODUCTS.			
Total value...............................	[1] $801,062,345	$317,653,983	$391,429,283
Pig iron:			
Tons (2,240 pounds)........................	30,543,167	23,269,731	25,651,798
Value..................................	$785,960,412	$312,761,617	$387,830,443
Unit value, ton...........................	$25.73	$13.44	$15.12
For consumption in works of company producing, tons..................................	21,687,376	15,495,004	15,858,203
Consumed by steel works and rolling mills during year.............................	21,170,136	15,219,696	15,252,736
Balance for foundries, etc.................	517,240	275,308	605,467
For sale, tons..............................	8,855,791	7,774,727	9,793,595
Purchased by steel works and rolling mills during year.............................	2,750,935	2,209,961	3,824,153
Balance for foundries, export, etc...........	6,104,856	5,564,766	5,969,442

[1] Includes 5 establishments with materials to the amount of $5,389,144 and pig-iron products to the value of $6,595,787, engaged primarily in the manufacture of ferroalloys. At prior censuses the industry included the blast furnace ferroalloys.
[2] Figures not available.

TABLE 46.—IRON AND STEEL, BLAST FURNACES; 1919, 1914, AND 1909—Continued.

	1919	1914	1909
PRODUCTS—continued.			
Pig iron—Continued.			
Classified according to smelting fuel—			
Coke—			
Tons	30,097,220	22,787,890	24,522,152
Value	$770,101,169	$304,356,130	$368,131,822
Unit value, ton	$25.59	$13.36	$15.01
Anthracite, and anthracite and coke mixed—			
Tons	94,465	87,919	670,991
Value	$2,975,470	$1,256,663	$10,962,150
Unit value, ton	$31.50	$14.29	$16.34
Bituminous coal and coke mixed—			
Tons	35,745	[1] 118,632	86,420
Value	$1,385,663	$2,704,134	$1,552,814
Unit value, ton	$38.77	$22.79	$17.97
Charcoal—			
Tons	315,737	[2] 275,290	372,235
Value	$11,498,110	$4,444,690	$7,183,657
Unit value, ton	$36.42	$16.15	$19.30
Classified by grade (tons, 2,240 pounds)—			
Basic	14,597,535	9,465,853	7,741,759
Bessemer	9,374,950	7,577,792	10,147,052
Low phosphorus (below 0.4 per cent)	289,726	305,738	248,720
Foundry	4,792,961	4,325,100	5,539,410
Malleable	1,090,344	730,910	934,211
Forge or mill	287,529	488,172	586,685
White, mottled, and miscellaneous	56,418	32,202	110,810
Castings direct from blast furnaces	53,704	14,384	16,181
Ferroalloys	[3]	329,580	326,970
Classified by method of delivery or casting—			
Molten to steel works, etc	18,138,453	11,936,791	12,197,686
Machine cast	7,746,656	6,007,417	5,096,797
Sand cast	3,970,309	4,681,867	7,655,568
Chill cast	634,045	629,272	685,566
Direct castings	53,704	14,384	16,181
All other products, value	$15,101,933	$4,892,366	$3,598,840
EQUIPMENT.			
(Active establishments.)			
Stacks active during the year:			
Number	385	286	370
Coke furnaces	359	252	312
Bituminous coal and coke	2	4	5
Anthracite and coke	5	4	25
Charcoal	19	26	28
Aggregate daily capacity, tons	132,114	90,172	98,973
Coke furnaces	130,291	87,846	94,499
Bituminous coal and coke	140	725	395
Anthracite and coke	438	272	2,745
Charcoal	1,245	1,329	1,334
Idle during the entire year:			
Number	27	70	24
Coke furnaces	25	62	19
Other fuels	[4] 2	[4] 8	[4] 5
Aggregate daily capacity, tons	6,433	20,004	4,027
Coke furnaces	6,343	19,547	3,750
Other fuels	90	457	277
Banked, relined, or rebuilding at end of year:			
Number	62	8	8
Coke furnaces	59	8	7
Other fuels	[5] 3		1
Aggregate daily capacity, tons	20,761	2,650	1,873
Coke furnaces	20,506	2,650	
Other fuels	255		

[1] Includes a considerable quantity of ferromanganese pig-iron.
[2] Includes a small quantity made with electricity and charcoal.
[3] Not included in the blast-furnace industry in 1919.
[4] 1919, charcoal; 1914, anthracite, 1; anthracite and coke, 3; charcoal, 4; 1909, anthracite, 1; anthracite and coke, 1; charcoal, 3.
[5] Bituminous coal and coke, 1; anthracite and coke, 1; charcoal, 1.

TABLE 46.—IRON AND STEEL, BLAST FURNACES: 1919, 1914, AND 1909—Continued.

	1919	1914	1909
EQUIPMENT—continued.			
New stacks completed since 1914 (included above), coke furnaces:			
Number	[1] 31	[1] 30	[1] 11
Aggregate daily capacity, tons	14,545	11,902	3,807
In course of construction at end of year:			
Number	[2] 5	2	10
Aggregate daily capacity, tons	1,720	850	4,100
Abandoned or dismantled since 1914:			
Number	[3] 8	[3] 12	3
Aggregate daily capacity, tons	1,560	1,865	710
Pig-casting machines	149	112	104
Heyl and Patterson	79	58	([4])
Uehling	56	49	([4])
Other	14	5	([4])
Granulated slag pits	94	85	85
Blast furnaces served	108	101	([4])
Production of granulated slag, tons	5,031,743	([4])	([4])
Gas engines using blast-furnace gas:			
Number	195	144	85
Blowing engines	115	73	42
Electric power engines	80	71	43
Less than 2,000 horsepower	18		
2,000 to 2,999 horsepower	120	([4])	([4])
3,000 to 3,999 horsepower	20		
4,000 and over horsepower	37		
Horsepower	513,470	380,820	198,040

[1] 1919, all coke; 1914, 29 coke of 11,897 tons and 1 charcoal of 5 tons; 1909, 9 coke of 3,800 tons and 2 charcoal of 7 tons.
[2] 1919, 4 coke of 1,670 tons and 1 charcoal of 50 tons.
[3] 1919, all coke; 1914, 8 coke of 1,565 tons and 4, other fuels, of 300 tons.
[4] Figures not available.

TABLE 47.—FERROALLOYS: 1919.

PRODUCT.	Tons (2,000 pounds).	Value.
Total value		$56,182,243
The classified industry		38,583,984
Ferroalloys, subsidiary products of other industries		17,598,259
Blast-furnace establishments		38,484,505
Electric-furnace establishments		17,697,738
Ferroalloys	385,806	49,326,769
Ferromanganese	185,616	25,670,127
Spiegeleisen	84,010	3,675,689
Ferrosilicon	86,022	4,821,711
Ferrophosphorus	4,757	516,231
Other ferroalloys (ferrochromium, ferromolybdenum, ferrotitanium, ferrotungsten, ferrovanadium)	25,401	14,643,011
Sand cast	148,875	
Machine cast	131,419	
Chill cast	105,299	
Delivered molten	213	
All other products		6,855,474

TABLE 48.—STEEL WORKS AND ROLLING MILLS: 1919, 1914, AND 1909.

	1919	1914	1909
Number of establishments	500	427	446
Steel works and rolling mills	145	113	89
Steel works only (no hot rolling)	112	96	99
Rolling mills only (no steel furnaces)	243	218	258
Number producing steel	257	209	188
Number doing hot rolling	388	331	347
MATERIALS.			
Total cost	$1,680,575,758	$590,825,692	$657,500,856
Iron and steel:			
For furnaces and hot rolls—			
Pig iron, including ferro-alloys—			
Tons	24,362,942	17,429,657	19,076,889
Cost	$655,002,125	$248,630,958	$297,471,122
Pig iron—			
Produced by consumer—			
Tons	21,170,136	15,111,458	15,108,244
Assigned cost	$496,313,109	$201,965,395	$224,474,026
Purchased—			
Tons	2,749,822	2,016,634	3,604,060
Cost	$85,204,226	$30,166,377	$58,189,714
Spiegeleisen and ferromanganese—			
Produced by consumer—			
Tons	123,353	108,238	144,492
Cost	$13,772,841	$3,849,738	$3,776,798
Purchased—			
Tons	223,742	193,327	220,093
Cost	$27,706,590	$12,649,448	$11,030,584
Other ferroalloys—			
Produced by consumer—			
Tons	7,215		
Cost	$1,292,822		
Purchased—		(1)	(1)
Tons	88,674		
Cost	$30,712,537		
Scrap iron or steel, including old rails not intended for rerolling—			
Total consumption, tons	16,369,210	10,656,187	9,929,710
Produced by consumer in other works—			
Tons	1,480,260	899,113	773,843
Assigned cost	$28,154,391	$11,384,960	$10,629,317
Purchased—			
Tons	5,545,822	4,171,767	4,029,774
Cost	$116,978,660	$47,996,567	$62,093,514
Made and consumed in same works, tons	9,343,128	5,585,307	5,126,093
Rails for rerolling—			
Tons	165,459	(2)	(2)
Cost	$4,154,381	(2)	(2)
Steel, crude and semi-finished (ingots, blooms, billets, slabs, and sheet and tin-plate bars)—			
Produced by consumer in other works—			
Tons	4,401,127	2,882,069	3,080,672
Assigned cost	$173,067,624	$57,587,159	$62,594,558
Purchased—			
Tons	4,545,100	3,576,330	3,427,577
Cost	$194,994,191	$74,590,904	$82,981,077
Iron ore—			
Tons	1,051,791	999,472	835,338
Domestic	1,044,907	969,617	823,306
Foreign	6,884	29,855	12,032
Cost	$8,480,622	$4,252,201	$4,292,963
Crude—			
Tons	1,014,989		
Cost	$7,185,658		
Manganiferous—			
Tons	17,709		
Cost	$234,619	(3)	(3)
Chrome—			
Tons	19,093		
Cost	$1,060,345		
Rolled forms for further manufacture—			
Iron muck and scrap bar—			
Total consumption, tons	968,512		
Produced by consumer in other works—			
Tons	106,800		
Assigned cost	$6,589,465	(2)	(2)
Purchased—			
Tons	128,203		
Cost	$7,586,489		
Made and consumed in same works, tons	733,509	(3)	(3)

[1] Included with speigeleisen and ferromanganese.
[2] Included with steel, crude and semifinished, etc.
[3] Figures not available.

TABLE 48.—STEEL WORKS AND ROLLING MILLS: 1919, 1914, AND 1909—Continued.

	1919	1914	1909
MATERIALS—continued.			
Iron and steel—Continued.			
Rolled forms for further manufacture—Continued.			
Iron and steel skelp—			
Total consumption, tons	2,425,845	1,376,313	1,578,290
Produced by consumer in other works—			
Tons	322,082	47,998	35,221
Assigned cost	$19,297,117	$1,662,917	$1,151,430
Purchased—			
Tons	437,764	144,559	141,496
Cost	$27,314,278	$3,833,933	$4,553,426
Made and consumed in same works, tons	1,665,999	1,183,756	1,401,573
Iron and steel wire rods—			
Total consumption, tons	1,375,949	1,494,761	1,465,221
Produced by consumer in other works—			
Tons	5,794	76,717	128,291
Assigned cost	$620,597	$1,864,312	$3,547,577
Purchased—			
Tons	15,528	18,978	18,134
Cost	$1,327,725	$487,715	$705,118
Made and consumed in same works, tons	1,354,627	1,399,066	1,318,796
Copper—ingots, billets, blooms, bars, and rods—			
Total consumption, tons	72,366		
Produced by consumer in other works—			
Tons	12,040		
Assigned cost	$402,305		
Purchased—			
Tons	31,318	13,335	19,545
Cost	$12,980,464	$4,069,309	$5,756,018
Made and consumed in same works, tons	29,008		
Copper scrap—			
Tons	1,714		
Cost	$524,252		
Zinc (spelter)—			
Tons	80,380	(1)	(1)
Cost	$12,283,608	(1)	(1)
Fuel and rent of power, cost	$156,964,862	$55,447,804	$46,136,725
All other materials, cost	$253,852,602	$79,016,953	$75,588,011
PRODUCTS.			
Total value	2 $2,828,902,376	2 $918,664,565	2 $985,722,534
I.—ROLLED, FORGED, AND OTHER CLASSIFIED STEEL AND IRON PRODUCTS:			
Tons	36,211,947	25,522,784	26,723,274
For sale	23,114,711	16,904,966	18,265,891
For consumption	13,097,236	8,617,818	8,457,383
Value	$2,417,012,546	$800,278,038	$863,342,711
A.—Finished rolled products and forgings—			
Tons	25,512,847	18,482,182	19,276,237
For sale	17,343,747	12,647,638	14,024,550
For consumption	8,169,100	5,834,544	5,251,687
Value	$1,859,457,051	$623,485,963	$667,393,177
Rails—			
Number of establishments	16	15	13
Tons	3 2,088,838	3 1,842,041	2,858,599
Value	$92,849,481	$54,009,918	$81,128,295
Open-hearth—			
Tons	1,893,141	1,522,684	1,215,072
Value	$82,644,646	$45,336,381	$36,400,780
Bessemer—			
Tons	195,697	319,357	1,643,527
Value	$10,204,835	$8,673,537	$44,727,515
Rerolled or renewed rails—			
Number of establishments	6	8	9
Tons	95,637	63,671	106,352
Value	$4,738,883	$1,438,237	$2,683,017
Rail joints, fastenings, etc.—			
Number of establishments	24	26	25
Tons	462,691	349,307	396,911
Value	$27,595,921	$11,526,956	$14,488,412

1 Included with all other materials.
2 In addition, steel castings and rolled steel valued at $7,143,128 were produced by 7 establishments in 1919, to the value of $2,831,964 by 13 establishments in 1914, and to the value of $6,627,639 by 29 establishments in 1909, not classified as steel works and rolling mills.
3 Includes 77,598 tons of alloy steel rails in 1919 and 27,286 tons in 1914.

TABLE **48.**—STEEL WORKS AND ROLLING MILLS: 1919, 1914, AND 1909—Continued.

	1919	1914	1909
PRODUCTS—continued.			
I.—ROLLED, FORGED, AND OTHER CLASSIFIED STEEL AND IRON PRODUCTS—Continued.			
A.— Finished rolled products and forgings—Continued.			
Structural shapes—			
Number of establishments	30	35	27
Tons	2,526,461	2,083,440	2,123,630
Value	$151,970,064	$57,475,366	$65,564,593
Bars for reinforced concrete—			
Number of establishments	34	30	25
Tons	301,453	269,966	191,358
Value	$18,428,795	$7,751,549	$5,588,963
Merchant bars, mill shafting, etc.—			
Number of establishments	140	99	
Steel—			
Tons	4,026,448	2,062,791	
Value	$326,764,260	$71,352,396	
Iron—			132
Tons	458,549	411,946	3,784,248
Value	$33,796,197	$13,057,104	$121,488,423
Bolt and nut rods, spike and chain rods, horseshoe nail rods, etc.—			
Number of establishments	29	41	
Tons	232,920	535,875	
Value	$15,333,748	$18,319,865	
Wire rods—			
Number of establishments	33	33	29
Tons	2,484,428	2,377,691	2,295,279
Value	$126,738,142	$61,578,145	$61,947,958
For sale—			
Tons	582,273	535,098	511,322
Value	$31,152,583	$14,000,752	$14,681,108
For consumption, tons	1,902,155	1,842,593	1,783,957
In works where produced	1,354,627	1,399,066	1,318,796
In other works of same company	547,528	443,527	465,161
Assigned value	$95,585,559	$47,577,393	$47,266,850
Steel rods—			
Cold-rolled, cold-drawn, cold-hammered or polished—			
Number of establishments	12		
Tons	145,697		
Value	$17,682,981		
Rolled-wire rods in coils or bars, of crucible or electric steel—		(¹)	(¹)
Number of establishments	8		
Tons	15,358		
Value	$4,767,443		
Plates or sheets, other than for tinning—			
Number of establishments	135	99	105
Tons	6,720,191	3,699,249	3,332,733
Value	$523,621,423	$129,785,963	$133,272,393
For sale—			
Tons	5,257,975	2,907,272	2,807,114
Value	$408,690,562	$96,442,998	$108,298,861
For consumption—			
Tons	1,462,216	791,977	525,619
Assigned value	$114,930,861	$33,342,965	$24,973,532
According to gauge:			
Plates No. 12 and thicker—			
Tons	4,426,998	2,183,775	² 2,392,144
Value	$295,924,025	$62,768,579	(¹)
Sheets No. 13 and thinner—			
Tons	2,293,193	1,515,474	² 940,589
Value	$227,697,398	$67,017,384	(¹)
Black plates (or sheets) for tinning—			
Number of establishments	32	30	29
Tons	1,084,175	1,011,938	631,435
Value	$94,456,189	$43,147,041	$30,955,967
For sale—			
Tons	7,107	81,583	56,275
Value	$922,391	$3,500,576	$2,736,396
For consumption—			
Tons	1,077,068	930,355	575,160
Assigned value	$93,533,798	$39,646,465	$28,219,571

¹ Figures not available.   ² Plates "16 gauge and thicker" and sheets "17 gauge and thinner."

TABLE 48.—STEEL WORKS AND ROLLING MILLS: 1919, 1914, AND 1909—Continued.

	1919	1914	1909
PRODUCTS—continued.			
I.—ROLLED, FORGED, AND OTHER CLASSIFIED STEEL AND IRON PRODUCTS—Continued.			
A.—Finished rolled products and forgings—Continued.			
Skelp:			
Number of establishments	38	38	42
Tons	2,589,064	1,960,844	2,084,286
Value	$151,557,342	$52,443,303	$64,514,728
For sale—			
Tons	379,271	506,380	580,686
Value	$21,928,860	$14,621,830	$18,415,604
For consumption—			
Tons	2,209,793	1,454,464	1,503,600
In works where produced	1,665,999	1,183,756	1,401,573
In other works of same company	543,794	270,708	102,027
Assigned value	$129,628,482	$37,821,473	$46,099,124
Hoops, bands, and cotton ties—			
Number of establishments	34	17	15
Tons	832,212	603,940	341,043
Value	$69,865,330	$19,945,078	$10,429,681
For sale—			
Tons	750,394		
Value	$63,762,389	(¹)	(¹)
For consumption—			
Tons	81,818		
Assigned value	$6,102,941		
Nail and tack plate—			
Number of establishments	7	11	12
Tons	34,579	50,302	68,557
Value	$2,548,485	$2,008,308	$2,540,022
For sale—			
Tons	18,590	19,751	25,867
Value	$1,777,166	$803,352	$960,492
For consumption—			
Tons	15,989	30,551	42,690
Assigned value	$771,319	$1,204,956	$1,579,530
Axles, rolled or forged—			
Number of establishments	7	10	8
Tons	²97,813	²89,436	102,348
Value	²$9,752,973	²$3,407,271	$3,831,344
Armor plate, gun forgings, and ordnance—			
Number of establishments	13	6	5
Tons	101,130	38,669	26,845
Value	$55,699,658	$19,947,893	$10,649,079
Car and locomotive wheels, rolled or forged—			
Tons	117,763	(¹)	(¹)
Value	$17,044,728		
All other rolled products—			
Tons	787,475	619,674	566,627
Value	$75,686,987	$37,125,670	$39,570,061
All forged or other iron and steel products not otherwise enumerated—			
Tons	309,965	411,402	365,986
Value	$38,558,021	$19,165,900	$18,740,241
B.—Semifinished rolled products (for sale or for transfer to other works of same company):			
Tons	9,265,930	6,408,030	6,799,436
Value	$389,596,293	$130,674,909	$153,493,360
Blooms, billets, and slabs, steel—			
Tons	6,024,044	3,991,873	4,887,796
Value	$249,394,083	$80,638,672	$108,514,747
For sale—			
Tons	2,039,349	1,414,619	1,841,819
Value	$90,124,414	$29,706,572	$43,021,988
For consumption in other works of producer—			
Tons	3,984,695	2,577,254	3,045,977
Assigned value	$159,269,669	$50,932,100	$65,492,759

¹ Figures not available.
² Includes for 1919, 1,566 tons of axles other than car and locomotive (automobile, carriage, etc.), valued at $317,774; and for 1914, 1,160 tons, valued at $96,069.

TABLE 48.—STEEL WORKS AND ROLLING MILLS: 1919, 1914, AND 1909—Continued.

	1919	1914	1909
PRODUCTS—continued.			
I.—ROLLED, FORGED, AND OTHER CLASSIFIED STEEL AND IRON PRODUCTS—Continued.			
B.—Semifinished rolled products—Continued.			
Rolled blooms, billets, and slabs, for forging purposes—			
Tons	186,533	65,939	84,383
Value	$10,669,833	$1,695,637	$2,247,133
Hammered charcoal blooms, billets, and slabs—			
Tons	17,785	(1)	(1)
Value	$920,704		
Sheet and tin-plate bars—			
Tons	2,864,578	2,241,735	1,652,761
Value	$117,855,738	$45,372,785	$37,745,269
For sale—			
Tons	2,555,741	2,088,769	1,625,408
Value	$104,597,932	$42,308,755	$37,105,869
For consumption in other works of producer—			
Tons	308,837	152,966	27,353
Value	$13,257,806	$3,064,030	$639,400
Muck and scrap bar—			
Tons	172,990	108,483	174,496
Value	$10,755,935	$2,967,815	$4,986,211
For sale—			
Tons	62,039	89,379	154,431
Value	$4,146,609	$2,379,056	$4,289,969
For consumption in other works of producer—			
Tons	110,951	19,104	20,065
Value	$6,609,326	$588,759	$696,242
Made and consumed in same works (tons)—			
Blooms, billets, and slabs, steel	19,344,166	13,102,896	11,375,622
Hammered charcoal blooms, billets, and slabs	33,692	35,794	
Rolled blooms and billets for forging purposes	124,321	68,856	76,614
Sheets and tin-plate bars	1,289,851	723,350	441,637
Muck and scrap bar	733,509	958,640	1,191,828
C.—Unrolled steel (for sale or transfer to other works of same company):			
Tons	1,433,170	632,572	647,601
Value	$167,959,202	$46,117,166	$42,456,174
Ingots—			
Tons	713,027	63,371	142,745
Value	$33,315,197	$1,383,468	$3,593,726
For sale—			
Tons	219,013	29,421	30,444
Value	$15,848,348	$737,382	$1,513,445
For consumption in other works of producer—			
Tons	494,014	33,950	112,301
Assigned value	$17,466,849	$646,086	$2,080,281
Direct steel castings—			
Tons	720,143	569,201	504,856
Value	$134,644,005	$44,733,698	$38,862,448
II.—SCRAP IRON OR STEEL:			
For sale—			
Tons	1,340,790	983,216	840,118
Value	$24,487,435	$11,660,297	$12,632,772
For consumption in other works of producer—			
Tons	773,855	462,948	398,436
Assigned value	$12,926,837	$4,674,546	$5,530,852
Made and consumed in same works (tons)	9,343,128	5,595,122	5,126,093
III.—ALL OTHER STEEL OR IRON PRODUCTS, NOT ROLLED, INCLUDING VALUE ADDED TO IRON AND STEEL ROLLING-MILL PRODUCTS BY FURTHER MANUFACTURE	$345,902,346	$85,238,964	$86,534,369
IV.—ALL PRODUCTS OTHER THAN STEEL OR IRON	$22,265,923	$15,103,136	$16,356,978
V.—CUSTOM WORK AND REPAIRING	$6,307,289	$1,709,584	$1,324,852

1 Figures not available.

TABLE 49.—TIN PLATE AND TERNEPLATE: 1919, 1914, AND 1909.

	1919	1914	1909
MATERIALS.			
Total cost	**$130,273,696**	**$57,906,561**	**$41,889,434**
Tin-plate and terneplate industry	$73,422,649	} $57,906,561	$41,889,434
Tin and terne dipping departments of black plate mills: plate and coating materials	$56,851,047		
Black plates, steel: [1]			
Pounds	2,630,798,873	2,107,787,589	1,321,071,691
Cost	$99,730,197	$39,803,655	$28,981,151
Produced by the establishment reporting—			
Pounds	2,593,351,524	2,084,536,669	1,291,048,109
Cost	$98,433,207	$39,335,112	$28,245,234
Purchased—			
Pounds	37,447,349	23,250,920	30,023,582
Cost	$1,296,990	$468,543	$735,917
Coating metals:			
Pig tin—			
Pounds	43,628,872	36,542,881	28,586,267
Cost	$25,350,062	$14,167,237	$8,490,794
Pig lead—			
Pounds	1,074,225	2,269,160	2,708,496
Cost	$55,054	$94,024	$117,656
Terne mixture (purchased)—			
Pounds	7,288,245	6,618,211	9,632,996
Cost	$1,439,586	$783,546	$1,061,587
Total tin and lead, including contents of terne mixture purchased, pounds	51,991,342	45,430,252	40,927,759
Tin	45,271,634	38,049,636	31,077,651
Lead	6,719,708	7,380,616	9,850,108
Plates for redipping:			
Pounds	348,565	(2)	(2)
Cost	$24,049	(2)	(2)
Fuel and rent of power	$364,189	$309,924	$289,675
All other materials	$3,310,559	$2,748,175	$2,948,571
PRODUCTS.			
Total value	**$180,325,368**	**$68,342,962**	**$47,969,645**
Tin-plate and terneplate industry	$97,404,720	} $68,342,962	$47,969,645
Dipping departments of black plate mills	$82,920,648		
Tin plate and terneplate: [3]			
Pounds	2,539,224,664	[4] 2,053,966,144	1,315,313,132
Value	$175,776,283	[4] $66,270,345	$45,815,146
Tin plate, steel—			
Pounds	2,373,253,628	1,901,331,895	1,123,968,875
Value	$164,958,677	$60,258,024	$38,259,885
Coke plate—			
Pounds	2,336,703,947	1,855,892,526	(2)
Value	$161,874,698	$58,450,853	(2)
Charcoal plate—			
Pounds	36,549,681	45,439,369	(2)
Value	$3,083,979	$1,807,171	(2)
Terneplate, including long terne, steel—			
Pounds	165,971,036	152,634,249	191,344,257
Value	$10,817,606	$6,012,321	$7,555,261
All other products, including plates redipped, tin dross, seruff, scrap, etc	$4,549,085	$2,072,617	$2,154,499
EQUIPMENT.			
Number of dipping sets at end of year	916	693	573
Usually employed on tin plate	868	615	455
Usually employed on terneplate	48	78	118
Number of building tin or terne sets at end of year	60	(2)	(2)
Daily capacity single turn, pounds	6,332,288	3,868,000	2,840,000
Tin plate	5,820,948	3,454,000	2,076,000
Terneplate	511,340	414,000	764,000
Number of establishments operating on [5]—			
Single turn	2	6	5
Double turn	3	5	10
Triple turn	30	21	16
Daily capacity as operated whether on single, double, or triple turn, pounds	18,658,000	10,726,000	7,016,000

[1] All steel in 1919; 1914 includes 6,208,969 pounds of iron plate, valued at $206,533; and 1909, 8,726,538 pounds valued at $96,914.
[2] Figures not available.
[3] In addition, 2 establishments in 1919, 1 in 1914, and 3 in 1909, engaged primarily in other lines of manufacture, made some tin plate and terneplate.
[4] Includes 6,144,890 pounds of iron plate, valued at $358,828; balance steel.
[5] Does not include 8 establishments, in 1919, engaged in retinning only.

TABLE 50.—THE WIRE INDUSTRY: 1919 AND 1914.

(Ton, 2,000 pounds.)

KIND.	TOTAL.		WIRE MILLS (WIRE RODS PURCHASED).		WIRE DEPARTMENTS OF ROLLING MILLS AND OTHER CONCERNS.	
	1919	1914	1919	1914	1919	1914
Wire drawn, tons	2,724,442	2,597,407	1,001,879	898,523	1,722,563	1,698,884
Steel and iron wire:						
Total production	2,508,890	2,435,530	920,918	821,569	1,587,972	1,613,961
For sale (plain or bare)	592,434	459,909	244,959	206,575	347,475	253,334
For consumption	1,916,456	1,975,621	675,959	614,994	1,240,497	1,360,627
Copper wire:						
Total production	184,569	138,924	78,510	72,401	106,059	66,523
For sale (plain or bare)	146,991	84,921	60,827	54,210	86,164	30,711
For consumption	37,578	54,003	17,683	18,191	19,895	35,812
Brass wire:						
Total production	23,625	19,491	1,794 }	} 4,553	21,831 }	} 18,400
Other metal:						
Total production	7,358	3,462	657 }		6,701 }	
PRODUCTS.						
Total value	$392,601,073	$172,600,546	$162,151,236	$81,841,012	$230,449,837	$90,759,534
Wire and manufactures of wire	$384,919,118	$166,999,888	$157,513,598	$78,150,487	$227,405,520	$88,849,401
Steel and iron—						
Tons	2,554,385	2,465,383	943,693	835,928	1,610,692	1,629,455
Value	$264,777,927	$116,215,503	$106,625,257	$48,809,661	$158,152,670	$67,405,842
Plain wire—						
Tons	592,434	459,909	244,959	206,575	347,475	253,334
Value	$58,756,450	$22,316,778	$28,494,089	$12,921,557	$30,262,361	$9,395,221
Galvanized wire—						
Tons	343,005 }	} 374,478	172,958 }	} 156,016	170,047 }	} 218,462
Value	$32,383,503 }	} $15,949,531	$15,812,146 }	} $7,123,026	$16,571,357 }	} $8,826,505
Other coated wire—						
Tons	49,925 }		20,598 }		29,327 }	
Value	$5,257,688 }		$2,719,707 }		$2,537,981 }	
Wire nails and spikes—						
Kegs (100 lbs.)	12,429,195	12,886,634	3,677,122	3,209,925	8,752,073	9,676,709
Value	$49,291,686	$23,368,633	$15,062,373	$6,048,598	$34,229,313	$17,320,035
Wire brads and tacks—						
Pounds	5,461,597 }	} 66,670,000	3,998,138 }	} 18,376,000	1,463,459 }	} 48,294,000
Value	$415,821 }	} $1,324,948	$248,664 }	} $386,271	$167,157 }	} $938,677
Wire staples—						
Pounds	68,221,338 }		16,084,845 }		52,136,493 }	
Value	$2,745,070 }		$617,027 }		$2,128,043 }	
Barbed wire—						
Tons	341,127	343,693	82,056	69,232	259,071	274,461
Value	$30,895,619	$13,764,367	$7,305,381	$2,823,668	$23,590,238	$10,940,699
Wire rope, cable and strand—						
Tons	103,010	52,735	55,632	43,217	47,378	9,518
Value	$29,825,513	$7,973,537	$12,187,216	$6,881,138	$17,638,297	$1,092,399
Woven-wire fence and poultry netting—						
Tons	312,146	411,460	97,064	128,379	215,082	283,081
Value	$30,526,961	$19,795,812	$10,320,876	$6,763,469	$20,206,085	$13,032,343
Other woven-wire products—						
Tons	26,614	22,721	13,417	8,614	13,197	14,107
Value	$4,274,177	$2,822,689	$2,184,987	$915,490	$2,089,190	$1,907,199
Cold-rolled flat wire—						
Tons	45,908 }		30,208 }		15,700 }	
Value	$9,751,609 }		$6,401,609 }		$3,350,000 }	
Washers—						
Tons	433 }	} 122,720	27 }	} 54,211	406 }	} 68,509
Value	$16,152 }	} $8,899,208	$7,655 }	} $4,946,444	$38,497 }	} $3,952,764
Other fabricated iron and steel wire products—						
Tons	81,482 }		32,877 }		48,605 }	
Value	$10,607,678 }		$5,263,527 }		$5,344,151 }	
Copper—						
Bare wire—						
Tons	146,991	84,921	60,827	54,210	86,164	30,711
Value	$56,647,507	$26,206,024	$26,873,030	$16,177,678	$29,774,477	$10,028,346
Insulated wire and cable[1]—						
Tons	72,607	48,386	32,687	32,410	39,920	15,976
Value	$44,465,418	$15,709,244	$21,825,439	$10,855,232	$22,639,979	$4,854,012

[1] Not including production of insulated wire and cable by establishments included in "electrical machinery, apparatus, and supplies." Total production, all establishments, 1919, 224,000 net tons, value $128,682,339.

TABLE 50.—THE WIRE INDUSTRY: 1919 AND 1914—Continued.

(Ton, 2,000 pounds.)

KIND.	TOTAL.		WIRE MILLS (WIRE RODS PURCHASED).		WIRE DEPARTMENTS OF ROLLING MILLS AND OTHER CONCERNS.	
	1919	1914	1919	1914	1919	1914
PRODUCTS—continued.						
Wire and manufactures of wire—Continued.						
Copper—Continued.						
Woven-wire products—						
Tons.....................	206		140		66	
Value.................	$223,596	2,130	$143,596	499	$80,000	1,631
Other fabricated copper-wire products—		$1,013,282		$291,380		$721,902
Tons.....................	790		....		790	
Value.................	$593,077		....		$593,077	
Brass wire—						
Pounds..................	47,249,835	39,614,500	3,588,721	4,361,148	43,661,114	35,253,352
Value.................	$11,542,020	$6,366,342	$1,040,427	$850,017	$10,501,593	$5,516,325
Other metals—						
Bronze (with phosphor-bronze and monel)—						
Pounds...............	1,342,706		163,242		1,179,464	
Value...............	$624,520		$93,820		$530,700	
Nickel, nickel silver, etc.—						
Pounds..............	1,752,952		649,000		1,103,952	
Value..............	$1,457,588	6,929,398	$714,163	5,344,730	$743,425	1,584,668
Other (includes copper-clad steel)—		$1,489,493		$1,166,519		$322,974
Pounds..............	10,671,138		501,938		10,169,200	
Value..............	$3,876,060		$197,866		$3,678,194	
Other fabricated wire products—						
Pounds..............	948,858		....		948,858	
Value..............	$711,405		....		$711,405	
Finished products, other than wire......................	$3,058,042	$2,581,000	$2,171,718	$2,088,590	$886,324	$492,410
Sulphate of iron—						
Tons..............	36,747		23,506		13,241	
Value...............	$669,871	$2,692,302	$416,342	$1,439,465	$253,529	$1,252,837
All other products............	$3,717,944		$1,813,480		$1,904,464	
Amount received for custom work and repairing.........	$236,098	$327,356	$236,098	$162,470	....	$164,886
EQUIPMENT.						
Wire-drawing blocks:						
Number.....................	62,689	51,181	26,920	33,242	35,769	17,939
Rod......................	10,530	7,503	3,165	3,005	7,365	4,498
Redrawing................	10,202	9,067	6,651	6,565	3,551	2,502
Fine wire................	41,957	34,611	17,104	23,672	24,853	10,939
Annual capacity, tons......	4,169,467	3,852,000	1,508,043	1,249,000	2,661,424	2,603,000
Wire-nail machines:						
Number....................	5,383	5,212	1,652	1,318	3,731	3,894
Annual capacity, kegs (100 pounds).................	22,049,170	23,904,000	7,451,450	5,965,000	14,597,720	17,939,000
Barbed-wire machines:						
Number....................	1,569	(1)	478	(1)	1,091	(1)
Annual capacity, tons......	855,997	(1)	252,448	(1)	603,549	(1)
Woven-wire fence machines:						
Number....................	457	583	100	161	357	422
Annual capacity, tons......	677,195	732,000	154,552	190,000	522,643	542,000
Poultry-netting machines:						
Number....................	164	(1)	84	(1)	80	(1)
Annual capacity, tons......	41,893	(1)	28,847	(1)	13,046	(1)
Stands cold-rolling machines:						
Number....................	687	(1)	380	(1)	307	(1)
Annual capacity, tons......	184,215	(1)	59,915	(1)	124,300	(1)

[1] Figures not available.

TABLE 51.—PRODUCTION OF LUMBER, LATH, AND SHINGLES: 1919, 1914, 1909, AND 1904.

PRODUCT.	1919	1914	1909	1904
Lumber (M feet B. M.)	34,552,076	37,346,023	44,509,761	34,127,165
Softwoods	27,407,130	29,406,839	33,896,959	[1] 27,345,338
Yellow pine	13,062,938	14,471,004	16,277,185	11,521,781
Douglas fir	5,902,169	4,763,693	4,856,378	2,928,409
Western yellow pine	1,755,015	1,327,365	1,499,985	1,290,526
Hemlock	1,754,998	2,165,728	3,051,399	3,268,787
White pine	1,723,642	2,632,587	3,900,034	5,332,704
Spruce	979,968	1,247,414	1,748,547	1,295,953
Cypress	656,212	1,013,013	955,635	749,592
Redwood	410,442	535,199	521,630	519,267
Larch	388,121	358,561	421,214	31,784
Cedar	332,234	499,903	346,008	222,994
White fir	223,422	112,627	89,318	[2]
Sugar pine	133,658	136,159	97,191	[2]
Balsam fir	68,030	125,212	108,702	[2]
Lodgepole pine	16,281	18,374	23,733	[2]
Hardwoods	7,144,946	7,939,184	10,612,802	6,781,827
Oak	2,708,280	3,278,908	4,414,457	2,902,855
Maple	857,489	909,763	1,106,604	587,558
Red gum	851,431	675,380	706,945	523,990
Chestnut	545,696	540,591	663,891	243,537
Birch	375,079	430,667	452,370	224,009
Beech	358,985	376,464	511,244	[3]
Yellow poplar	328,538	519,221	858,500	853,544
Elm	194,417	214,294	347,456	258,330
Basswood	183,562	264,656	399,151	228,041
Hickory	170,013	116,113	333,929	106,824
Ash	154,931	189,499	291,209	169,178
Cottonwood	144,155	195,198	265,600	321,574
Tupelo	143,730	124,480	96,676	[3]
Walnut	39,218	25,573	46,108	31,455
Sycamore	28,114	22,773	56,511	18,002
All other	61,308	55,604	62,151	312,930
Lath (thousands)	1,724,078	[2]	3,703,195	2,647,847
Shingles (thousands)	9,192,704	[2]	14,907,371	14,546,551

[1] Includes 183,541 M feet of softwoods, not reported by kinds of wood.   [2] Not reported.
[3] Included in "All other" hardwoods.

TABLE 52.—PRODUCTION OF TIGHT STAVES AND HEADING: 1919 AND 1909.

PRODUCT.	1919	1909
Staves (thousands)	353,825	379,231
Sawed	348,812	341,259
Hewed	3,269	6,321
Bucked and split	1,193	15,104
Beer and ale	551	16,547
Heading (thousand sets)	24,274	20,691
Sawed	24,265	19,736
Beer and ale	9	955

TABLE 53.—PRODUCTION OF SLACK STAVES, HEADING, AND HOOPS: 1919 AND 1909.

KIND OF WOOD.	STAVES (THOUSANDS).		HEADING (THOUSAND SETS).		HOOPS (THOUSANDS).	
	1919	1909	1919	1909	1919	1909
Total	1,121,324	2,029,548	87,381	140,234	140,772	375.793
Red gum	358,405	416,570	13,003	16,700		
Pine	327,875	306,621	42,401	38,926	(1)	
Elm	61,100	245,172	1,872	6,535	133,983	339,477
Ash	53,058	71,705	2,318	5,245	4,000	(1)
Maple	50,446	133,255	7,319	13,663	(1)	
Oak	38,920	66,675	1,986	1,963	(1)	
Beech	36,460	268,237	4,942	19,269	(1)	
Chestnut	36,303	93,290		876	(1)	
Birch	35,691	78,897	3,490	4,328	(1)	
Spruce	29,683	72,219	2,508	1,861	(1)	
All other	93,383	276,907	7,542	30,868	2,789	36,316

[1] Included with "All other."

TABLE 54.—WOOD CONSUMED IN THE MANUFACTURE OF VENEERS: 1919, 1911, AND 1909.

KIND OF WOOD.	QUANTITY OF WOOD (M FEET).		
	1919	1911	1909
Total	576,581	444,886	435,981
Domestic:			
Red gum	198,641	136,542	129,930
Yellow pine	67,071	35,400	48,143
Birch	54,079	24,208	24,643
Cottonwood	36,739	34,911	30,842
Tupelo	34,175	20,976	18,476
Yellow poplar	32,653	25,835	28,826
White oak	30,654	41,742	28,742
Maple	15,723	29,762	35,444
Walnut	14,060	4,121	2,400
Spruce	11,355	9,108	4,111
Basswood	11,134	11,602	13,715
Douglas fir	10,604	6,262	1,111
Elm	9,578	18,340	16,254
Beech	3,922	12,023	9,950
All other	13,767	22,359	18,844
Imported:			
Mahogany	27,628	4,790	16,057
All other	4,798	6,905	8,493

TABLE 55.—LEATHER, TANNED, CURRIED, AND FINISHED: 1919, 1914, 1909, AND 1904.

	1919	1914	1909	1904
MATERIALS.				
Total cost	$646,521,527	$284,245,420	$248,278,933	$191,179,073
Hides and skins, total:				
Number	[1] 123,326,726	[1] 113,841,035	[1] 116,040,986	108,206,682
Cost	$513,570,602	$229,980,036	$195,058,557	$145,467,925
Hides, total—				
Number	24,478,825	18,598,637	[2] 18,360,415	[2] 17,581,613
Cost	$317,949,025	$152,311,975	$119,410,767	$89,126,593
Cattle—				
Number	22,184,517	17,457,591	18,360,415	17,581,613
Cost	$304,994,752	$148,751,002	$119,410,767	$89,126,593
Horse—				
Number	2,294,308	1,141,046	[3]	[3]
Cost	$12,954,273	$3,560,973	[3]	[3]
Skins, total—				
Number	98,847,901	95,242,398	97,680,571	90,625,069
Cost	$195,621,577	$77,668,061	$75,647,790	$56,341,332
Calf and kip—				
Number	12,894,274	16,067,793	19,732,638	12,481,221
Cost	$74,334,355	$33,117,713	$31,790,572	$15,725,616
Goat and kid—				
Number	55,428,830	37,755,867	48,077,664	47,665,608
Cost	$82,500,845	$23,916,965	$27,833,214	$26,756,012
Sheep and lamb—				
Number	22,766,247	40,090,198	26,082,060	27,492,359
Cost	$29,415,744	$19,247,682	$12,231,618	$10,547,883
All other—				
Number	7,758,550	1,328,540	3,788,209	2,985,881
Cost	$9,370,633	$1,385,701	$3,792,386	$3,311,821
All other raw stock, cost	$8,218,990	$2,970,795		
Purchased rough leather used, cost	$16,166,339	$7,070,378	$9,556,257	$10,852,655
Tanning materials—				
Vegetable	$46,564,536			
Chemicals	$20,985,006	$44,224,211	$43,664,119	$34,858,493
Fats, oils, and other greases	$11,342,269			
All other materials, cost	$29,673,785			
PRODUCTS.				
Total value	[4] $928,591,701	[4] $367,201,705	[4] $327,874,187	[4] $252,620,986
Leather, value	$848,209,571	$341,796,436	$306,476,720	$236,765,803
Sole—				
Sides	19,715,821	18,075,482	17,805,252	17,937,938
Value	$218,829,831	$116,188,059	$88,331,713	$69,205,600
Hemlock—				
Sides	1,731,545	5,626,696	7,963,728	9,929,964
Value	$16,179,564	$31,007,435	$32,237,151	$32,676,015
Oak—				
Sides	10,086,228	5,267,936	3,805,861	3,607,963
Value	$117,522,076	$38,384,062	$26,083,793	$19,157,805
Union—				
Sides	7,314,834	6,588,799	5,756,227	4,400,011
Value	$79,917,866	$42,457,755	$28,375,815	$17,371,780
Chrome—				
Sides	583,214	592,051	279,436	[3]
Value	$5,210,325	$4,338,807	$1,634,954	[3]
Belting—				
Butts	1,483,070	647,224	521,035	429,782
Value	$32,776,994	$8,369,584	$6,995,133	$4,754,456
Harness—				
Sides	1,717,154	2,777,312	3,946,235	4,369,561
Value	$24,171,047	$20,969,169	$24,802,734	$20,274,188
Case, bag, and strap—				
Sides	1,225,577	1,004,581	[3]	[3]
Value	$11,880,766	$5,383,255	[3]	[3]

[1] Exclusive of 100,419 hides and skins in 1919, 702,894 in 1914, and 447,435 in 1909, treated by establishments engaged primarily in other industries.
[2] Cattle hides only.
[3] Not reported separately.
[4] Exclusive of leather and other products, such as hair, wool, etc., to the value of $1,193,918 for 1919, $7,311,231 for 1914, $6,231,374 for 1909, and $154,932 for 1904, reported by establishments engaged primarily in other industries.

TABLE 55.—LEATHER, TANNED, CURRIED, AND FINISHED: 1919, 1914, 1909, AND 1904—Con.

	1919	1914	1909	1904
PRODUCTS—continued.				
Leather, value—Continued.				
Upholstery leather (auto, furniture, and carriage)—				
Whole hide grains—				
Number	933,921	654,053		
Value	$18,262,372	$8,172,698	1,398,842	827,104
Whole hide splits—			$14,266,742	$7,780,804
Number	1,507,741	1,104,561		
Value	$13,962,272	$6,155,660		
Upper leather (other than patent)—				
Cattle—				
Sides	16,693,073	8,245,964	7,946,769	6,850,469
Value	$120,897,283	$32,939,139	$24,198,993	$15,487,252
Horse—				
Sides	1,720,507	406,741	(1)	(1)
Value	$10,561,999	$1,360,103	(1)	(1)
Skins—				
Number	79,663,981	66,268,840	(1)	(1)
Value	$266,547,194	$83,009,160	(1)	(1)
Patent (other than upholstery)—				
Sides	2,716,476	2,827,031	(1)	(1)
Value	$23,442,107	$9,564,110	(1)	(1)
Skins	828,870	4,871,588	(1)	(1)
Value	$3,179,650	$5,512,449	(1)	(1)
Glove—				
Skins	5,892,894	4,002,908	(1)	(1)
Value	$11,535,113	$2,901,874	(1)	(1)
Sides	5,369,969	343,949	(1)	(1)
Value	$8,893,024	$998,303	(1)	(1)
Finished splits (not elsewhere specified), value	$16,459,665	$8,547,153	(1)	(1)
Sold in the rough, value	$3,712,687	$4,494,985	$6,335,599	$10,180,949
All other, value	$63,097,567	$27,230,735	$141,545,806	$109,082,554
All other products, value	$28,619,895	$13,134,413	$8,632,689	$7,665,223
Amount received for tanning, currying, or finishing for others	$51,762,235	$12,270,856	$12,764,778	$8,189,960

[1] Not reported separately.

TABLE 56.—BOOTS, SHOES, SLIPPERS, AND OTHER FOOTWEAR, BY CLASSES:[1] 1919, 1914, AND 1904.

PRODUCT.	1919	1914	1904
Total value	[2] $1,155,041,436	[2] $501,760,458	[2] $320,107,458
Boots, shoes, and slippers:			
Number of pairs	331,224,628	292,666,468	242,110,035
Value	$1,128,286,743	$489,053,124	$315,987,387
Boots and shoes—			
Number of pairs	286,592,960	252,516,603	216,039,401
Value	$1,070,322,232	$455,398,112	$298,658,865
Men's—			
Number of pairs	95,017,356	98,031,144	83,434,322
Value	$429,740,457	$219,994,422	$142,038,632
Boys' and youths'—			
Number of pairs	26,503,432	22,895,719	21,717,236
Value	$72,883,299	$32,852,560	$24,301,298
Women's—			
Number of pairs	104,812,505	80,916,239	69,470,876
Value	$447,289,044	$148,433,738	$98,262,016
Misses' and children's—			
Number of pairs	48,538,203	48,322,395	41,416,967
Value	$102,091,213	$51,870,908	$34,056,919
Fiber—			
Number of pairs	79,391	2,351,106	(3)
Value	$166,392	$2,246,484	(3)
Athletic and sporting shoes—			
Number of pairs	585,710	(3)	(3)
Value	$2,083,402	(3)	(3)
Canvas and textile fabrics—			
Number of pairs	11,056,363	(3)	(3)
Value	$16,068,425	(3)	(3)
Slippers—			
Number of pairs	21,815,046	24,673,102	17,518,291
Value	$33,409,101	$26,082,238	$13,996,832
Men's, boys', and youths'—			
Number of pairs	3,230,086	3,666,972	4,403,097
Value	$5,308,089	$3,450,362	$3,464,561
Women's, misses', and children's—			
Number of pairs	5,264,235	14,066,717	13,115,194
Value	$12,860,767	$18,573,921	$10,532,271
Felt or other fiber—			
Number of pairs	13,320,725	6,939,413	(3)
Value	$15,240,245	$4,057,955	(3)
Infants' shoes and slippers—			
Number of pairs	16,668,912	15,476,763	(3)
Value	$18,249,791	$7,572,774	(3)
Sandals—			
Number of pairs	5,125,962	(3)	(3)
Value	$5,128,462	(3)	(3)
Moccasins—			
Number of pairs	1,021,748	(3)	(3)
Value	$1,177,157	(3)	(3)
All other kinds—			
Number of pairs			8,552,343
Value			$3,331,690
All other products, including amount received for work done for others	$26,754,693	$12,707,334	$4,120,071

[1] At the census of 1909 the value was not reported by classes and therefore statistics for 1909 are omitted from this table.
[2] Exclusive of the product of establishments primarily engaged in the manufacture of other products— 1919, 9 establishments, value $894,201; 1914, $855,582; and 1904, $89,000.
[3] Not reported separately.

TABLE 57.—LEATHER GLOVES AND MITTENS: 1919, 1914, 1909, AND 1904.

PRODUCT.	1919 [1]	1914 [1]	1909 [1]	1904 [1]
Total value........................	$46,940,511	$21,614,109	$23,630,598	$17,740,385
Gloves, mittens, and gauntlets:				
Dozen pairs.........................	3,615,703	3,082,376	3,368,655	3,370,146
Value...............................	$44,831,777	$20,296,558	$22,525,861	$17,122,772
Men's and boys'—				
Dozen pairs......................	3,040,747	2,656,875	2,888,991	2,915,415
Value............................	$34,498,656	$16,333,388	$18,135,438	$14,515,770
Unlined—				
Dozen pairs...................	1,706,795	1,623,446	1,755,229	1,598,332
Value.........................	$23,053,857	$11,486,491	$12,209,929	$8,182,689
Lined—				
Dozen pairs...................	767,801	832,695	1,133,762	1,317,083
Value.........................	$9,037,038	$4,383,271	$5,925,509	$6,333,081
Part leather and part fabric—				
Dozen pairs...................	566,151	200,734	(2)	(2)
Value.........................	$2,407,761	$463,626	(2)	(2)
Women's and children's—				
Dozen pairs......................	574,956	425,501	479,664	454,731
Value............................	$10,333,121	$3,963,170	$4,390,423	$2,607,002
Unlined—				
Dozen pairs...................	417,595	325,530	326,690	213,370
Value.........................	$8,596,567	$3,196,761	$3,375,560	$1,576,159
Lined—				
Dozen pairs...................	126,294	99,971	152,974	241,361
Value.........................	$1,568,735	$766,409	$1,014,863	$1,030,843
Part leather and part fabric—				
Dozen pairs...................	31,067	(2)	(2)	(2)
Value.........................	$167,819	(2)	(2)	(2)
All other products, value...................	$2,108,734	$1,317,551	$1,104,737	$617,613

[1] Exclusive, for 1919, of 22 establishments engaged primarily in other industries which made 534,709 dozen pairs of leather gloves, mittens, and gauntlets, valued at $3,175,014; for 1914, of 16 similar establishments which made 206,327 dozen pairs, valued at $642,462; for 1909, of 16 similar establishments which made 36,944 dozen pairs, valued at $264,961; and for 1904, of gloves, mittens, and gauntlets, to the value of $166,164.
[2] Not reported separately.

TABLE 58.—PAPER AND WOOD PULP: 1919, 1914, 1909, AND 1904.

(Ton, 2,000 pounds.)

	1919	1914	1909	1904
MATERIALS.				
Total cost..........................	**$467,482,637**	**$213,181,286**	**$165,442,341**	**$111,251,478**
Pulp wood, total:				
Cords.................................	5,477,832	4,470,763	4,001,607	3,050,717
Cost.................................	$87,386,083	$39,408,453	$34,477,540	$20,800,871
Spruce, domestic—				
Cords.................................	2,313,419	1,892,739	1,653,249	1,732,531
Cost.................................	$39,783,167	$17,893,673	(1)	$11,937,852
Spruce, imported—				
Cords.................................	873,795	768,056	768,332	538,305
Cost.................................	$18,219,970	$9,008,609	(1)	$4,570,017
Poplar, domestic—				
Cords.................................	180,160	328,513	302,876	213,058
Cost.................................	$3,214,901	$2,714,210	(1)	$1,506,971
Poplar, imported—				
Cords.................................	158,220	61,644	25,622	35,313
Cost.................................	$2,851,583	$582,924	(1)	$251,600
Hemlock—				
Cords.................................	795,154	602,754	559,657	(1)
Cost.................................	$8,760,805	$4,176,542	(1)	(1)
All other wood and waste—				
Cords.................................	1,157,084	817,057	691,871	531,510
Cost.................................	$14,555,657	$5,032,495	(1)	$2,534,431
Wood pulp purchased:				
Tons.................................	1,595,980	1,521,980	1,241,914	877,702
Cost.................................	$118,967,841	$54,207,932	$43,861,357	$27,633,164
Ground, domestic—				
Tons.................................	398,133	379,263	333,313	317,286
Cost.................................	$16,249,210	$7,540,922	$6,764,475	$5,754,259
Ground, imported—				
Tons.................................	100,440	153,463	119,536	
Cost.................................	$3,537,460	$3,148,755	$2,723,033	
Soda fiber, domestic—				
Tons.................................	153,639	155,635	145,163	120,978
Cost.................................	$13,074,318	$6,764,892	$6,464,870	$5,047,105
Soda fiber, imported—				
Tons.................................	25	5,289	9,463	
Cost.................................	$1,807	$297,838	$397,994	
Sulphite fiber, domestic—				
Tons.................................	564,776	436,196	453,636	433,160
Cost.................................	$54,389,663	$19,762,127	$19,041,329	$16,567,122
Sulphite fiber, imported—				
Tons.................................	159,307	261,172	172,393	
Cost.................................	$14,606,807	$12,128,105	$8,143,397	
Sulphate fiber, domestic—				
Tons.................................	72,440	16,414	2 8,410	2 6,278
Cost.................................	$6,350,229	$679,326	2 $326,259	2 $264,678
Sulphate fiber, imported—				
Tons.................................	108,584	88,497		
Cost.................................	$9,333,251	$3,486,540		
Screenings, mechanical—				
Tons.................................	9,488	4,806	(1)	(1)
Cost.................................	$321,006	$41,841	(1)	(1)
Screenings, chemical—				
Tons.................................	29,148	21,245	(1)	(1)
Cost.................................	$1,104,090	$357,586	(1)	(1)
Rags, including cotton and flax waste and sweepings:				
Tons.................................	277,849	361,667	357,470	294,552
Cost.................................	$24,217,978	$12,151,288	$10,721,559	$8,864,607
Paper stock: High grade shavings, including old and waste paper—				
Tons.................................	1,854,386	1,509,981	983,882	588,543
Cost.................................	$43,567,775	$19,161,400	$13,691,120	$7,430,335
Manila stock:				
Rope—				
Tons.................................	68,235	64,256	117,080	107,029
Cost.................................	$5,114,426	$2,492,094	$3,560,033	$2,502,332
Jute bagging, waste, threads, etc.—				
Tons.................................	48,759	56,914		
Cost.................................	$2,091,827	$1,553,473		
Straw:				
Tons.................................	353,399	307,839	303,137	304,585
Cost.................................	$3,594,947	$1,675,598	$1,460,282	$1,502,886

1 Not reported separately.
2 Reported as "other chemical fiber."

TABLE 58.—PAPER AND WOOD PULP: 1919, 1914, 1909, AND 1904—Continued.

(Ton, 2,000 pounds.)

	1919	1914	1909	1904
MATERIALS—continued.				
Other stock for making paper:				
Tons	106,850	97,276	29,422	(1)
Cost	$4,494,388	$1,778,669	$479,959	$1,963,066
China clay:				
Tons	258,533	(1)	(1)	(1)
Cost	$4,421,157	(1)	(1)	(1)
Bleaching powder:				
Tons	139,914	(1)	(1)	(1)
Cost	$5,647,952	(1)	(1)	(1)
Sulphur:				
Tons	187,794	136,458	(1)	130,400
Cost	$5,014,736	$3,134,699	(1)	$3,221,834
All other materials, cost	$162,963,527	$77,617,680	$57,190,491	$37,332,383
PRODUCTS.				
Total value	[2]$788,059,377	[2]$332,147,175	[2]$267,656,964	$188,715,189
News paper, in rolls and sheets:				
Tons	1,323,880	1,313,284	1,168,098	912,822
Value	$98,559,359	$52,942,774	$46,390,041	$35,906,460
Hanging papers:				
Tons	69,445	96,527	92,158	62,606
Value	$6,043,390	$4,488,910	$4,431,514	$3,013,464
Poster, novel, tablet, lining, etc.:[3]				
Tons	80,394	7,883	7,456	(1)
Value	$7,272,755	$490,766	$465,519	(1)
Book paper:				
Book, machine finished—				
Tons	532,413			
Value	$76,772,582	786,626	575,616	434,500
Book, sized and supercalendered—		$58,496,221	$42,846,674	$31,156,728
Tons	286,407			
Value	$41,498,194			
Coated—				
Tons	132,454	117,342	95,213	(1)
Value	$24,009,614	$11,605,584	$9,413,961	(1)
Plate, lithograph, map, wood cut, etc.—				
Tons	9,821	9,332	6,498	19,837
Value	$1,556,372	$588,332	$555,352	$1,458,343
Cover paper:				
Tons	22,163	21,679	17,578	22,150
Value	$5,643,191	$2,809,377	$1,982,853	$2,023,986
Fine paper:				
Ledger and highest grade—				
Tons	30,584			
Value	$12,254,967			
Pole dried—				
Tons	48,564			
Value	$19,868,978			
Air dried—				
Tons	28,786			
Value	$9,514,618	247,728	198,213	146,832
Machine dried—		$34,054,918	$29,076,638	$22,249,170
Tons	59,674			
Value	$14,665,308			
Sulphite bond—				
Tons	82,467			
Value	$17,484,179			
All other—				
Tons	75,108			
Value	$13,952,756			
Wrapping paper:				
Manila (rope, jute, etc.)—				
Tons	111,782	77,878	73,731	86,826
Value	$15,493,141	$7,070,254	$6,989,436	$6,136,080
Heavy (mill wrappers, etc.)—				
Tons	118,755	98,780	108,561	96,992
Value	$9,856,002	$3,588,357	$4,380,794	$4,035,588
Straw—				
Tons	5,895	15,606	32,988	54,232
Value	$457,606	$519,309	$870,419	$1,389,348

[1] Not reported separately.
[2] In addition, in 1919, paper to the value of $1,064,772 was produced by 5 establishments engaged primarily in the manufacture of paper boxes, roofing materials, and other products; in 1914 to the value of $2,767,407 by 9 establishments; and in 1909 to the value of $2,567,267, by 15 establishments of this character.
[3] Reported as "poster" in 1914 and 1909.

TABLE **58.**—PAPER AND WOOD PULP, 1919, 1914, 1909, AND 1904—Continued.

(Ton, 2,000 pounds.)

	1919	1914	1909	1904
PRODUCTS—continued.				
Wrapping paper—Continued.				
Bogus or wood manila, all grades—				
Tons	126,175	353,987	367,932	228,371
Value	$12,047,371	$17,975,636	$19,777,707	$10,099,772
Kraft—				
Tons	192,583	109,753	12,661	(¹)
Value	$26,575,194	$6,949,244	$936,940	(¹)
All other—				
Tons	276,182	225,795	167,194	177,870
Value	$38,639,983	$13,269,953	$9,265,095	$8,774,804
Tag stock (rope, jute, and sulphite):				
Tons	27,092	29,230	(¹)	(¹)
Value	$5,459,980	$1,935,693	(¹)	(¹)
Boards:				
Wood pulp—				
Tons	179,747	116,419	71,036	60,863
Value	$14,887,881	$4,227,493	$2,639,496	$2,347,250
Straw—				
Tons	228,248	175,244	171,789	167,278
Value	$12,229,837	$4,270,519	$3,750,851	$4,367,560
News—				
Tons	88,839	127,966	74,606	38,560
Value	$4,604,082	$3,502,134	$2,215,469	$1,174,216
Binders', trunk, and press—				
Tons	43,091	61,453	} 92,012	(¹)
Value	$3,787,860	$2,663,744	} $3,819,071	(¹)
Leather—				
Tons	28,167	26,689		
Value	$2,263,288	$1,177,189		
Cardboard, bristol board, card middles, tickets, etc.—				
Tons	84,987	83,010	51,449	39,060
Value	$11,104,105	$5,376,434	$3,352,151	$2,764,444
Chip—				
Tons	695,963	(²)	(²)	(²)
Value	$37,749,210	(²)	(²)	(²)
All other—				
Tons	518,022	700,844	422,196	253,950
Value	$37,464,380	$23,652,095	$13,720,697	$9,070,531
Tissue paper:				
High grade—				
Tons	31,025			
Value	$11,137,550	}		
White, colored, and waxing—				
Tons	36,545			
Value	$7,644,952			
Manila and No. 2 white—				
Tons	23,985	115,401	77,745	43,925
Value	$3,589,279	$11,535,720	$8,553,654	$5,056,438
Towel and napkin—				
Tons	19,266			
Value	$5,144,895			
Toilet—				
Tons	79,740			
Value	$13,178,847	}		
Blotting paper:				
Tons	13,420	14,157	9,577	8,702
Value	$3,209,137	$1,457,897	$1,186,180	$1,046,790
Building, roofing, asbestos, and sheathing paper:				
Tons	195,244	243,908	225,824	145,024
Value	$17,737,341	$9,475,733	$9,251,368	$4,845,628
All other paper:				
Tons	191,617	93,346	96,577	106,296
Value	$29,690,905	$7,464,182	$6,869,169	$6,729,820
Wood pulp made for sale or for consumption in mills other than those in which produced:				
Tons	1,100,303	912,490	910,846	780,706
Value	$80,095,047	$31,677,717	$30,177,366	$23,144,574
Ground—				
Steamed—				
Tons	61,411			
Value	$2,224,664	} 313,951	310,747	273,400
Not steamed—				
Tons	284,518	} $5,686,919	$5,649,466	$4,323,495
Value	$9,504,137			
Soda fiber—				
Tons	169,332	163,522	155,844	130,366
Value	$14,939,293	$7,213,086	$6,572,152	$5,159,615

¹ Not reported separately.   ² Included in "All other boards."

Table 58.—PAPER AND WOOD PULP: 1919, 1914, 1909, AND 1904—Continued.

(Ton, 2,000 pounds.)

	1919	1914	1909	1904
PRODUCTS—continued.				
Wood pulp made for sale or for consumption in mills other than those in which produced— Continued.				
Sulphite fiber—				
Bleached—				
Tons	288,709	214,627		
Value	$31,715,215	$10,803,787	444,255	376,940
Unbleached—			$17,955,748	$13,661,464
Tons	227,395	192,687		
Value	$17,791,975	$7,284,492		
Sulphate fiber—				
Bleached—				
Tons	4,740			
Value	$392,765	10,052	(1)	(1)
Unbleached—		$359,957	(1)	(1)
Tons	39,552			
Value	$2,743,389			
Screenings—				
Mechanical—				
Tons	2,313	2,553	(1)	(1)
Value	$33,448	$27,910	(1)	(1)
Chemical—				
Tons	22,333	15,098	(1)	(1)
Value	$750,161	$301,566	(1)	(1)
All other products, value	[2] $34,915,241	$8,880,990	$4,738,549	$1,924,195
WOOD PULP.				
Quantity produced (including that used in mills in which manufactured), total tons	3,517,952	2,893,150	2,495,523	1,921,768
Ground—				
Steamed, tons	281,635	1,293,661	1,179,266	968,976
Not steamed, tons	1,237,194			
Soda fiber—				
Bleached, tons	384,085	347,928	298,626	196,770
Unbleached, tons	27,608			
Sulphite fiber—				
Bleached, tons	509,738	385,349	1,017,631	756,022
Unbleached, tons	910,091	765,978		
Sulphate fiber—				
Bleached, tons	28,003	52,641	(1)	(1)
Unbleached, tons	92,375			
Screenings—				
Mechanical, tons	12,220	11,769	(1)	(1)
Chemical, tons	35,003	35,824	(1)	(1)

[1] Not reported separately.
[2] Includes 27,450 tons of paper bags valued at $6,469,010, made in paper mills.

TABLE 59.—PRINTING AND PUBLISHING: 1919, 1914, AND 1909.

	1919	1914	1909
Number of establishments	30,611	31,612	29,757
Book and job	13,089	12,115	10,708
Music	160	180	178
Newspapers and periodicals	17,362	19,317	18,871
PRODUCTS.			
Total value [1]	$1,536,408,283	$810,508,075	$662,591,959
Publications:			
Newspapers and periodicals	806,305,760	419,209,701	337,596,288
Subscriptions and sales	278,006,382	163,577,090	135,063,043
Advertising	528,299,378	255,632,611	202,533,245
Newspapers	566,321,409	283,588,966	232,993,094
Subscriptions and sales	192,819,519	99,541,860	84,438,702
Advertising	373,501,890	184,047,106	148,554,392
Periodicals other than newspapers	239,984,351	135,620,735	104,603,194
Subscriptions and sales	85,186,863	64,035,230	50,624,341
Advertising	154,797,488	71,585,505	53,978,853
Ready prints (patent insides and outsides)	2,010,506	1,965,214	2,293,077
Books and pamphlets:			
Published, or printed and published	132,699,383	68,587,778	62,930,394
Printed for publication by others	32,861,475	19,049,651	10,209,509
Sheet music and books of music:			
Published, or printed and published	12,509,981	6,803,491	5,510,698
Printed for publication by others	3,766,908	822,585	1,000,966
Other products for sale and in execution of orders:			
Job printing	465,419,994	249,730,932	204,154,096
Machine composition for others	12,487,551	5,682,098	(2)
Bookbinding and blank books	23,911,103	15,097,109	18,810,392
Electrotyping, engraving, lithographing, etc	11,337,829	9,698,641	8,201,398
All other products	33,097,793	13,860,875	11,885,141
Newspapers and periodicals:			
Number	20,489	22,754	22,141
Aggregate circulation per issue	222,481,983	205,594,907	164,463,040
By period of issue.			
Daily:			
Number	2,441	2,580	2,600
Aggregate circulation per issue	33,028,630	28,777,454	24,211,977
Sunday:			
Number	604	571	520
Aggregate circulation per issue	19,368,913	16,479,943	13,347,282
Triweekly:			
Number	93	84	73
Aggregate circulation per issue	492,286	549,495	335,389
Semiweekly:			
Number	452	583	635
Aggregate circulation per issue	2,020,165	2,483,629	2,312,919
Weekly:			
Number	13,375	15,172	15,097
Aggregate circulation per issue	51,902,121	50,336,963	40,822,965
Monthly:			
Number	2,647	2,822	2,491
Aggregate circulation per issue	91,681,807	79,190,838	63,280,535
Quarterly:			
Number	489	500	361
Aggregate circulation per issue	18,920,544	18,853,901	16,058,099
All other classes:			
Number	388	442	364
Aggregate circulation per issue	5,067,517	8,922,684	4,093,874
By character.			
News, politics, and family reading—			
Number	15,746	17,574	17,698
Aggregate circulation	75,830,555	69,533,556	61,074,990
Religious—			
Number	1,162	1,413	1,251
Aggregate circulation	31,348,380	34,515,249	29,523,777
Agricultural, horticultural, dairy, stock raising, etc:			
Number	334	346	316
Aggregate circulation	18,224,543	18,091,350	11,327,253
Commerce, finance, insurance, railroads, etc.—			
Number	294	323	264
Aggregate circulation	2,561,208	2,196,988	1,411,738

[1] In addition, printing and publishing to the value of $5,617,801 in 1919, $2,813,574 in 1914, and $2,942,282 in 1909, was reported by establishments assigned to other industries.
[2] Included in "Job printing."

TABLE 59.—PRINTING AND PUBLISHING: 1919, 1914, AND 1909—Continued.

	1919	1914	1909
PRODUCTS—continued.			
By character—Continued.			
Trade journals generally—			
Number	767	873	685
Aggregate circulation	4,653,164	9,284,145	3,572,441
General literature, including monthly and quarterly magazines—			
Number	252	284	340
Aggregate circulation	38,162,065	38,495,435	31,322,035
Medicine and surgery—			
Number	185	178	197
Aggregate circulation	2,493,827	910,085	931,584
Law:			
Number	59	65	56
Aggregate circulation	71,729	76,571	151,346
Science and mechanics:			
Number	214	135	139
Aggregate circulation	2,367,720	1,683,381	1,421,955
Fraternal organizations:			
Number	314	312	[1] 419
Aggregate circulation	9,147,322	7,092,592	6,982,235
Education and history :			
Number	184	231	202
Aggregate circulation	4,029,417	2,533,833	1,879,383
Society, art, music, fashions, etc.:			
Number	227	212	164
Aggregate circulation	24,441,320	14,703,958	13,445,661
College and school periodicals:			
Number	415	303	271
Aggregate circulation	638,840	353,755	330,705
Labor:			
Number	182	163	[2]
Aggregate circulation	3,634,539	1,633,700	[2]
Reform and social science:			
Number	85	179	[2]
Aggregate circulation	2,135,468	2,900,574	[2]
Miscellaneous:			
Number	69	164	139
Aggregate circulation	2,741,886	1,589,735	1,087,937
By language.			
English:			
Number	19,280	21,272	20,744
Aggregate circulation	211,501,667	193,600,407	155,432,243
Foreign (including foreign and English):			
Number	1,209	1,482	1,397
Aggregate circulation	10,980,316	11,994,500	9,030,797
French—			
Number	41	46	39
Aggregate circulation	266,046	477,436	446,739
German—			
Number	301	540	692
Aggregate circulation	2,231,312	4,095,672	4,434,146
Italian—			
Number	109	121	104
Aggregate circulation	725,710	755,367	500,475
Scandinavian—			
Number	162	167	161
Aggregate circulation	1,126,793	1,261,585	1,118,601
Letto-Slavic—			
Number	277	235	169
Aggregate circulation	2,255,451	1,655,363	917,649
All other—			
Number	319	373	232
Aggregate circulation	4,375,004	3,655,363	1,613,187

[1] Includes a number of labor publications.   [2] Not reported separately.

TABLE 60.—BOOKS AND PAMPHLETS—NUMBER: 1919, 1914, AND 1909.

CHARACTER.	NUMBER OF COPIES PRINTED.		
	1919	1914	1909
Total	252,068,816	175,166,698	161,361,844
Education	75,075,335	51,069,521	41,636,847
Fiction	24,317,643	39,598,501	46,942,399
History	6,280,483	2,458,912	2,923,187
Juvenile	24,434,912	16,399,881	10,184,030
Law	2,254,861	1,701,602	1,496,194
Medicine and hygiene	13,539,464	2,337,312	1,519,480
Philosophy	538,775	189,996	265,077
Poetry and drama	2,682,568	1,926,892	1,980,824
Religion and theology (including Bibles)	36,496,230	24,411,502	23,608,230
Scientific and similar associations	1,149,946	1,279,427	1,258,562
Works of reference	15,832,195	11,032,385	7,799,590
All others	49,466,404	22,760,767	21,747,424

TABLE 61.—CHEMICALS—DETAILED STATISTICS OF PRODUCTS, BY GROUPS: 1919, 1914, AND 1909.

(Ton, 2,000 pounds.)

	1919	1914	1909
GROUP I.—ACIDS.			
Total value	$86,194,195	$32,837,254	$26,068,617
Inorganic acids, value	$59,875,958	$25,082,873	(¹)
Arsenic and arsenious acids:			
Number of establishments	6		
Total production, pounds	2,622,389		
For sale—			
Pounds	1,076,000	(¹)	(¹)
Value	$108,233		
Made and consumed, pounds	1,546,389		
Boric (boracic) acid:			
Number of establishments	6	5	5
Pounds	13,454,100	8,584,311	5,554,914
Value	$1,754,632	$588,981	$295,776
Carbonic acid (carbon dioxide CO₂):			
Number of establishments	42	38	35
Pounds	59,771,411	50,445,779	47,953,291
Value	$6,574,250	$2,320,685	$2,345,743
Hydrochloric (muriatic) acid:			
Number of establishments	40	31	38
Total production, tons	221,749	168,584	122,367
For sale—			
Tons	150,090	85,438	101,607
Value	$4,312,253	$1,348,805	$1,758,335
Made and consumed, tons	71,659	83,146	20,760
Hydrofluoric acid:			
Number of establishments	6	9	10
Total production, pounds	5,732,198	7,209,248	8,027,290
For sale—			
Pounds	4,320,017	5,373,657	6,842,914
Value	$440,184	$325,540	$294,379
Made and consumed, pounds	1,412,181	1,835,591	1,184,376
Mixed acid (sulphuric-nitric):			
Number of establishments	42	37	14
Total production, tons	114,886	112,124	(²)
For sale—			
Tons	46,428	42,725	28,591
Value	$4,426,637	$2,204,480	$1,860,787
Made and consumed, tons	68,458	69,399	(²)
Nitric acid:			
Number of establishments	59	52	25
Total production, tons	86,992	78,589	68,717
For sale—			
Tons	19,436	14,685	13,663
Value	$2,976,095	$1,591,625	$1,357,098
Made and consumed, tons	67,556	63,904	55,054
Phosphoric acid:			
Number of establishments	9	7	9
Total production, pounds	22,109,302	(²)	(²)
For sale—			
Pounds	13,379,501	12,420,191	(²)
Value	$1,711,148	$680,239	$667,505
Made and consumed, pounds	8,729,801	(²)	(²)
Sulphuric acid:			
Number of establishments	216	194	183
Total production reduced to 50° Baumé, tons	5,552,581	4,071,566	2,764,455
For sale—			
Tons	3,331,362	2,338,284	1,479,200
Value	$35,932,605	$15,395,133	$10,103,425
Made and consumed, tons	2,221,219	1,733,282	1,285,255
Production according to strength:			
For sale—			
50° Baume—			
Tons	839,780	451,121	528,263
Value	$9,543,118	$2,709,350	$3,176,430

¹Not reported separately.   ² Figures not available.

TABLE 61.—CHEMICALS—DETAILED STATISTICS OF PRODUCTS, BY GROUPS: 1919, 1914, AND 1909—Continued.

(Ton, 2,000 pounds.)

	1919	1914	1909
GROUP I.—ACIDS—Continued.			
Production according to strength—Continued.			
For sale—Continued.			
60° Baumé—			
Tons	[1] 949,371	545,562	177,414
Value	[1] $9,498,800	$3,754,866	$1,038,358
66° Baumé—			
Tons	707,303	732,186	453,370
Value	$13,521,316	$8,042,422	$5,454,002
Oleum or fuming—			
Tons	[2] 133,655	62,354	28,594
Value	$3,369,371	$888,495	$434,635
Made and consumed, tons—			
50° Baumé	1,910,332	1,250,112	1,115,018
60° Baumé	70,681	249,927	11,970
66° Baumé	126,892	96,280	99,249
Oleum	18,149	15,404	3,743
Sulphuric acid, reclaimed:			
Number of establishments	65	14	[3]
Total production, tons	473,555	[3]	[3]
For sale—			
Tons	95,119	136,360	7,069
Value	$803,144	$518,890	$62,935
Made and consumed, tons	378,436	[3]	[3]
Organic acids, value	$26,318,237	$7,754,381	[4]
Acetic acids, value	$4,264,044		
Acetic, dilute and pyroligneous—			
Number of establishments	13		
Total production, pounds	42,248,803		
For sale—			
Pounds	33,057,776		
Value	$1,359,521		
Made and consumed, pounds	9,191,027		
Acetic, glacial—		13	13
Number of establishments	6	75,303,375	58,000,602
Total production, pounds	20,131,487	70,617,637	56,923,773
For sale—		$1,272,294	$1,336,874
Pounds	19,244,960	4,685,738	1,076,829
Value	$2,325,927		
Made and consumed, pounds	886,527		
Acetic anhydride—			
Number of establishments	7		
Total production, pounds	1,794,985		
For sale—			
Pounds	1,213,861		
Value	$578,596		
Made and consumed, pounds	581,124		
Citric acid:			
Number of establishments	6	3	5
Total production, pounds	3,260,482	2,729,943	[3]
For sale—			
Pounds	3,163,676	2,657,840	2,102,256
Value	$3,047,371	$1,516,336	$777,235
Made and consumed, pounds	96,806	72,103	[3]
Lactic acid:			
Number of establishments	4	[3]	[3]
Value	$781,828	[3]	[3]
Oleic acid:			
Number of establishments	15	7	8
Total production, pounds	44,895,453	23,187,579	[3]
For sale—			
Pounds	44,350,574	21,932,736	16,377,063
Value	$6,548,564	$1,301,353	$845,106
Made and consumed, pounds	544,879	1,254,843	[3]
Stearic acid:			
Number of establishments	9	10	11
Total production, pounds	17,048,421	14,960,109	[3]
For sale—			
Pounds	16,969,878	14,351,404	[3]
Value	$3,796,439	$1,242,492	$1,143,213
Made and consumed, pounds	78,543	608,705	[3]
Tannic acid:			
Number of establishments	4	5	[3]
Pounds	845,065	853,830	[3]
Value	$746,825	$287,142	[3]

[1] Includes a large production under a long-term, low-priced contract.
[2] Includes sulphur-trioxide, "battery acid" and "electrolyte sulphuric," 74,533 tons.
[3] Figures not available.
[4] Not reported separately.

TABLE 61.—CHEMICALS—DETAILED STATISTICS OF PRODUCTS, BY GROUPS: 1919, 1914, AND 1909—Continued.

(Ton, 2,000 pounds.)

	1919	1914	1909
GROUP I.—ACIDS—Continued.			
Tartaric acid:			
Number of establishments	4		
Pounds	5,312,965	(¹)	(¹)
Value	$4,262,376		
Other acids:			
Inorganic ²	$836,777	$108,495	$3,220,206
Organic ³	$2,870,790	$2,134,764	
GROUP II.—AMMONIUM AND CYANOGEN COMPOUNDS.			
Total value	$23,067,553	$8,064,913	(¹)
Ammonia, anhydrous: ⁴			
Number of establishments	38	14	15
Total production, pounds	27,957,000	(¹)	(¹)
For sale—			
Pounds	27,530,000	16,659,789	11,969,846
Value	$7,224,473	$3,140,848	$2,544,238
Made and consumed, pounds	427,000	(¹)	(¹)
Ammonia, aqua:			
Number of establishments	27	(¹)	(¹)
Total production, pounds	45,467,000	(¹)	(¹)
For sale—			
Pounds	30,918,000	35,544,246	20,983,476
Value	$2,241,321	$1,412,236	$839,820
Made and consumed, pounds	14,549,000	(¹)	(¹)
Ammonium chloride (sal ammoniac):			
Number of establishments	8	3	
Pounds	13,212,619	11,511,934	(¹)
Value	$1,565,340	$641,040	
Ammonium sulphate: ⁵			
Number of establishments	16	(¹)	(¹)
Total production, pounds	33,401,000	(¹)	(¹)
For sale—			
Pounds	32,873,000	8,846,616	(¹)
Value	$1,595,447	$211,314	
Made and consumed, pounds	528,000	(¹)	(¹)
Ammonium bromide and iodide:			
Number of establishments	4		
Value	$160,523		
Ammonium fluoride:		(¹)	(¹)
Number of establishments	3		
Pounds	340,156		
Value	$94,276		
Cyanogen compounds:			
Ferro and ferri cyanides of sodium, potassium (Prussian blue) and calcium—			
Number of establishments	14	(¹)	(¹)
Pounds	4,684,611		
Value	$1,467,665		
Other: Hydrocyanic (Prussic) acid, cyanides of copper, gold, mercury, nickel, potassium, silver, sodium, and zinc; cyanogen, chloride, dicyandiamine, thiocyanates of ammonium, barium, and sodium, value	$5,647,777	$2,398,674	$1,941,893
Other ammonium compounds:			
Inorganic.—Ammonium alums, ammonium chrome alums; carbonate, hypophosphate, nitrate, persulfate, phosphate, sulfide, vanadate, and miscellaneous	$2,759,616	$260,801	(¹)
Organic.—Acetate, benzoate, dimethylamine, hexamethylenetetramine, oxalate, and valerate	$311,115		

¹ Figures not available.
² Includes for 1919, chlorosulphonic, chromic, hydrobromic, hydrofluosilicic, hypophosphorous, molybdic, silicic, sulphurous, tungstic, vanadic, etc., and for 1914, sulphurous, hypophosphorous, arsenic, and hydrofluosilicic.
³ Includes for 1919, butyric, caproic, carbolic, cresylic, formic, gallic, glycerophosphoric, hydrocyanic, monochloracetic, oxalic, phthalic anhydride, propionic, pyrogallic, thymic, valerianic, etc.
⁴ Product of the chemical and manufactured gas industries. The production of anhydrous ammonia by the by-product coke ovens, as reported by the Geological Survey (mainly ammoniacal liquor and sulphate sold on pound basis of N H³) was as follows: 1919, 34 establishments, 51,646,764 pounds, value, $5,692,950; 1914, 25,370,509 pounds, value, $2,300,137.
⁵ Product of the chemical, fertilizer, and manufactured gas industries. The production of ammonium sulphate by the by-product coke ovens, as reported by the Geological Survey, was as follows: 1919, 36 establishments, 544,231,985 pounds, sales, 557,619,631 pounds, value, $21,075,718; 1914, ammonium sulphate or reduced to equivalent in sulphate, 170,763,906 pounds, value, $4,696,590.

TABLE 61.—CHEMICALS—DETAILED STATISTICS OF PRODUCTS, BY GROUPS: 1919, 1914,
AND 1909—Continued.

(Ton, 2,000 pounds.)

	1919	1914	1909
GROUP III.—SODAS, SODIUM, AND COMPOUNDS.			
Total value................	$99,689,828	[1] $32,626,335	[1] $25,048,019
Inorganic.			
Sodium:			
Borate (borax)—			
Number of establishments.............	8	7	[2]
Tons............	29,635	26,501	20,154
Value............	$4,622,286	$2,071,774	$1,756,922
Bichromate—			
Number of establishments.............	5	4	
Total production, tons.............	[3] 24,081	[2]	
For sale—			
Tons............	22,992	11,824	
Value............	$5,337,389	$1,125,398	[2]
Made and consumed, tons.............	1,089	[2]	
Bromide—			
Number of establishments.............	5		
Pounds............	1,242,443	[2]	
Value............	$511,812		
Carbonates—			
Soda ash—			
Number of establishments.............	18	10	11
Total production, tons.............	1,507,424	[2]	[2]
For sale—			
Tons............	1,033,480	935,305	646,057
Value............	$31,195,149	$10,937,945	$10,362,656
Made and consumed, tons.............	473,944	[2]	[2]
Sal soda (including monohydrate crystals)—			
Number of establishments.............	41	50	50
Tons............	82,992	106,591	86,644
Value............	$2,272,770	$1,510,449	$1,156,882
Bicarbonate—			
Number of establishments.............	10	5	7
Total production, tons.............	190,894	[2]	[2]
For sale—			
Tons............	141,556	90,169	82,800
Value............	$3,695,417	$1,439,014	$1,515,045
Made and consumed, tons.............	49,338		
Sesquicarbonate—			
Number of establishments.............	5		
Tons............	37,854	[2]	[2]
Value............	$685,500		
Fluoride—			
Number of establishments.............	4		
Pounds............	1,364,441		
Value............	$177,420		
Hydroxide (caustic soda)[4]—			
Number of establishments.............	29	25	17
Total production, tons.............	333,361	[2]	[2]
For sale—			
Tons............	322,746	291,539	131,612
Value............	$20,792,695	$9,104,920	$5,264,887
Made and consumed, tons.............	10,615		
Iodide—			
Number of establishments.............	7		
Pounds............	29,284	[2]	[2]
Value............	$103,868		
Nitrate, refined—			
Number of establishments.............	7		
Tons............	10,153		
Value............	$934,643		
Phosphate—			
Number of establishments.............	10	6	[2]
Total production, tons.............	23,867		
Monobasic (4 establishments).............	4,321	[2]	[2]
Dibasic (9 establishments).............	9,663		
Tribasic (5 establishments).............	9,883		
For sale—			
Tons............	22,351	15,397	12,290
Value............	$2,438,917	$853,528	$540,282
Made and consumed, tons.............	1,516	[2]	[2]

[1] The totals for items reported for 1914, $32,626,335, and for 1909, $25,048,019, are not comparable with total for 1919. The total for 1909 includes $3 312,117 of unclassified sodium products.
[2] Figures not available.
[3] Includes neutral chromate.
[4] Includes caustic liquor and soda lye.

TABLE 61.—CHEMICALS—DETAILED STATISTICS OF PRODUCTS, BY GROUPS: 1919, 1914, AND 1909—Continued.

(Ton, 2,000 pounds.)

	1919	1914	1909
GROUP III.—SODAS, SODIUM, AND COMPOUNDS—Con.			
Inorganic—Continued.			
Sodium—Continued.			
Silicate—			
Number of establishments	21	(1)	(1)
Total production, tons	336,093	190,648	(1)
For sale—			
Tons	286,791	169,049	34,170
Value	$6,052,318	$1,648,854	$366,621
Made and consumed, tons	49,302	21,599	(1)
Sulphates—			
Niter cake—			
Number of establishments	38	31	24
Total production, tons	97,836	46,143	(1)
For sale—			
Tons	81,170	24,129	27,546
Value	$281,476	$31,580	$53,693
Made and consumed, tons	16,666	22,014	
Salt cake—			
Number of establishments	34	29	
Total production, tons	179,003	110,263	(1)
For sale—			
Tons	122,908	90,442	
Value	$1,930,139	$841,887	
Made and consumed, tons	56,095	19,821	
Glauber's salt—			
Number of establishments	27	20	(1)
Total production, tons	42,206	(1)	(1)
For sale—			
Tons	38,330	34,537	46,471
Value	$864,264	$427,808	$512,464
Made and consumed, tons	3,876		
Refined, anhydrous—			
Number of establishments	6		
Total production, tons	2,776		
For sale—			
Tons	2,708		
Value	$221,232		
Made and consumed, tons	68	(1)	(1)
Thiosulphate (Hypo)—			
Number of establishments	9		
Total production, tons	29,818		
For sale—			
Tons	29,678		
Value	$1,541,087		
Made and consumed, tons	140		
Sulphide—			
Number of establishments	17	5	(1)
Total production, tons	39,735	(1)	(1)
For sale—			
Tons	35,178	20,263	7,673
Value	$2,316,253	$516,644	$206,450
Made and consumed, tons	4,557	(1)	(1)
Sulphite—			
Number of establishments	8	5	
Total production, tons	8,666	(1)	
For sale—			
Tons	7,209	(1)	
Value	$539,636	$66,649	
Made and consumed, tons	1,457	(1)	(1)
Washing compounds (not containing soap)—			
Number of establishments	3	7	
Tons	861	12,441	
Value	$71,021	$204,230	
Other inorganic sodium compounds [2]	$7,021,278	$1,703,535	

[1] Figures not available.

[2] Includes for 1919, sodium metal, sodium chlorate, hypophosphite, manganate, nitrite, silicofluoride, burnt chrome and sodium alums, aluminate, aluminum fluoride (refined cryolite), arsenate, arsenite, bisulphite, gold chloride, hypochlorite, perborate, peroxide, titanium sulphate, uranate, uranium nitrate, etc.

TABLE 61.—CHEMICALS—DETAILED STATISTICS OF PRODUCTS, BY GROUPS: 1919, 1914, AND 1909—Continued.

(Ton, 2,000 pounds.)

	1919	1914	1909
GROUP III.—SODAS, SODIUM, AND COMPOUNDS—Con.			
Organic.			
Sodium:			
Acetate—			
Number of establishments	12		
Total production, pounds	2,260,459		
For sale—			
Pounds	2,196,113		
Value	$165,505	(1)	(1)
Made and consumed, pounds	64,346		
Benzoate—			
Number of establishments	4		
Pounds	120,447		
Value	$68,004	$61,490	(1)
Citrate—			
Number of establishments	6		
Pounds	118,417	(1)	(1)
Value	$143,386		
Other organic sodium compounds [2]	$5,706,363	$80,630	(1)
GROUP IV.—POTASH, POTASSIUM, AND COMPOUNDS.			
Total value	$18,407,253	$7,905,744	(1)
Potash from original sources:			
Number of establishments	65		
Tons	109,737		
Value	$7,215,164	(1)	(1)
Carbonate, crude—			
Number of establishments	44		
Pounds	48,664,478		
Value	$2,300,027	$49,651	$88,940
Chloride, crude—			
Number of establishments	26		
Pounds	144,435,589		
Value	$4,169,333		
Sulphate, crude—			
Number of establishments	7		
Pounds	26,374,661		
Value	$745,804		
Acetate:			
Number of establishments	6		
Pounds	69,995		
Value	$47,473		
Bromate, bromide, chlorate, chloride (refined), and iodate:			
Number of establishments	9		
Pounds	3,324,268		
Value	$1,258,507		
Carbonate and bicarbonate, refined:			
Number of establishments	7		
Pounds	401,140	(1)	(1)
Value	$154,844		
Citrate:			
Number of establishments	6		
Pounds	64,088		
Value	$100,754		
Hydroxide (caustic):			
Number of establishments	13		
Pounds	8,358,834		
Value	$2,206,008		
Iodide:			
Number of establishments	7		
Pounds	388,678		
Value	$1,298,980		
Sulphate, refined; persulphate; sulphide; bisulphite; and metabisulphite:			
Number of establishments	11		
Pounds	877,178		
Value	$100,751		
Tartrate, Bi- (cream of tartar):			
Number of establishments	6	8	5
Pounds	4,854,550	12,646,120	15,592,937
Value	$2,620,351	$3,124,958	$2,925,883
Other potassium compounds:			
Inorganic—bichromate and chromate, refined nitrate, permanganate, phosphate, etc	$2,548,114	$4,731,135	(1)
Organic-binoxalate and oxalate, and Rochelle salts	$856,307		(1)

[1] Figures not available.

[2] Includes for 1919, sodium butyrate, formate, oxalate, propionate, sulphocarbonate, cyanide, and ferrocyanide, formaldehyde, hydrosulphite, potassium tartrate, thiocyanate, uranium acetate, etc.

TABLE 61.—CHEMICALS—DETAILED STATISTICS OF PRODUCTS, BY GROUPS: 1919, 1914, AND 1909—Continued.

(Ton, 2,000 pounds.)

	1919	1914	1909
GROUP V.—ALUMS, ALUMINUM, AND COMPOUNDS.			
Total value	$43,433,482	[1]	[1]
Alums	$17,055,891	$3,467,969	$3,022,355
Ammonium alum—			
Number of establishments	8		
Total production, tons	3,949		
For sale—			
Tons	3,797	[1]	[1]
Value	$304,018		
Made and consumed, tons	152		
Potash alum—			
Number of establishments	4	5	[1]
Tons	393	6,382	5,127
Value	$65,745	$219,968	$155,319
Sulphate (concentrated alum)—			
Number of establishments	19	11	[1]
Total production, tons	312,872	[1]	[1]
For sale—			
Tons	312,759	92,500	77,737
Value	$15,665,526	$1,728,566	$1,312,751
Made and consumed, tons	113	[1]	[1]
Other alums [2]—			
Number of establishments	12		
Total production, tons	15,337	[1]	[1]
For sale—			
Tons	15,322	57,593	55,283
Value	$1,020,602	$1,519,435	$1,554,285
Made and consumed, tons	15	[1]	[1]
Aluminous abrasives:			
Number of establishments	3		
Tons	11,306		
Value	$2,032,588		
Aluminum chloride:			
Number of establishments	7		
Total production, tons	4,411		
For sale—			
Tons	4,265	[1]	[1]
Value	$362,445		
Made and consumed, tons	146		
Aluminum hydroxide and oxide, refined:			
Number of establishments	5		
Total production, tons	6,375		
For sale—			
Tons	3,847		
Value	$514,649		
Made and consumed, tons	2,528		
All other—Aluminum and alloys, aluminum acetate, sodium aluminate, aluminum nitrate, calcined bauxite, refined cryolite, etc., value	$23,467,909		
GROUP VI.—BLEACHING COMPOUNDS.			
Total value	$12,392,806	$5,302,359	$3,215,728
Chlorine bleaches:			
Chlorine—			
Number of establishments	14	7	
Total production, pounds	91,141,000	[1]	
For sale—			
Pounds	34,392,000	12,217,000	[1]
Value	$1,425,917	$472,836	
Made and consumed, pounds	56,749,000	[1]	
Hypochlorites (calcium and sodium)—			
Number of establishments	16	14	9
Pounds	252,850,000	310,380,000	116,802,000
Value	$4,781,350	$2,916,225	$1,786,846
Peroxide bleaches:			
Barium peroxide—			
Number of establishments	3		
Pounds	3,134,000	[1]	[1]
Value	$569,483		
Hydrogen peroxide—			
Number of establishments	11	20	17
Pounds	31,515,000	32,595,000	9,926,000
Value	$2,257,282	$1,303,596	$870,541
Other peroxide bleaches, value	$612,045	[1]	[1]

[1] Figures not available.

[2] 1919—burnt, chrome and soda alums; 1914—burnt and soda alums, porous, excelsior pearl, ammonium, alum cake, etc.

TABLE 61.—CHEMICALS—DETAILED STATISTICS OF PRODUCTS, BY GROUPS: 1919, 1914, AND 1909—Continued.

(Ton, 2,000 pounds.)

	1919	1914	1909
GROUP VI.—BLEACHING COMPOUNDS—Continued.			
Sulphur bleaches:			
Bisulphite of calcium, soda, potassium, etc.,			
Number of establishments	14	14	15
Pounds	39,225,000	26,346,000	31,718,000
Value	$961,284	$243,559	$226,154
Sulphur dioxide—			
Number of establishments	3	(1)	(1)
Pounds	856,000	(1)	(1)
Value	$99,896		
Other sulphur bleaches	$1,073,464		
		$366,143	$332,187
Other bleaching compounds, not specified	$612,085		
GROUP VII.—COAL-TAR CHEMICALS.		•	
Total value	$133,499,742	$13,492,453	$7,969,672
Crudes:			
Number of establishments	56	40	42
Value	$21,148,814		
Intermediates:			
Number of establishments	100	[2] $8,065,156	[2] $4,057,591
Pounds	117,470,901		
Value	$28,250,517		
Dyes and color lakes:			
Number of establishments	106	(1)	(1)
Pounds	66,179,250	[3] 12,169,635	[3] 12,658,770
Value	$69,318,785	$4,652,947	$3,683,553
Photographic chemicals:			
Number of establishments	11		
Pounds	384,181		
Value	$1,189,995		
Medicinals:			
Number of establishments	25		
Pounds	5,724,245		
Value	$8,679,277		
Flavors and perfumes:		[4] $774,350	[4] $228,528
Number of establishments	13		
Pounds	861,143		
Value	$2,643,698		
Synthetic phenolic resins:			
Number of establishments	6		
Pounds	3,696,757		
Value	$2,268,656		
GROUP VIII.—PLASTICS.			
Total value	[5] $77,477,041	$13,895,784	$7,472,732
In form for further manufacture (rods, sheets, blocks, etc.):			
Pyroxylin (including products sold under trade names)—			
Number of establishments	4	(1)	
Total production, pounds	20,752,950	(1)	
For sale—			
Pounds	16,743,064	(1)	
Value	$20,855,988	$3,778,374	
Made and consumed, pounds	4,009,886		
Collodion and liquid solutions of pyroxylin—			
Number of establishments	10		
Total production, pounds	19,343,463		
For sale—			
Pounds	17,171,313	(1)	
Value	$3,810,187		
Made and consumed, pounds	2,172,150		(1)
Rubber substitutes—			
Number of establishments	11		
Total production, pounds	7,755,476		
For sale—			
Pounds	7,291,776		
Value	$1,309,644		
Made and consumed, pounds	463,700		
Finished articles of pyroxylin and rubber substitutes (made in the producing establishment) and nitrocellulose, value	$9,870,395	$5,526,740	
Other plastics, viscose, etc., including artificial silk, value	$41,630,827	$4,590,670	

[1] Figures not available.
[2] Reported as "Coal-tar distillery products."
[3] Coal-tar dyes and intermediates made largely from stock of foreign origin.
[4] Reported as "Chemicals or medicinal preparations from coal-tar."
[5] Not including establishments primarily engaged in the manufacture of motion-picture films (not exposed); viz., 18 establishments in 1919, with products valued at $72,152,797.

TABLE 61.—CHEMICALS—DETAILED STATISTICS OF PRODUCTS, BY GROUPS: 1919, 1914,
AND 1909—Continued.

(Ton, 2,000 pounds.)

	1919	1914	1909
GROUP IX.—COMPRESSED ANL LIQUEFIED GASES.			
(Cubic feet at atmospheric pressure.)			
Total value..	$43,263,918	$10,415,325	(1)
Acetylene: [2]			
Number of establishments.........................	49	40	
Total production, cubic feet......................	313,558,000	(1)	
For sale—			
Cubic feet.....................................	311,390,000	121,696,000	(1)
Value...	$7,140,757	$2,317,605	
Made and consumed, cubic feet.................	2,168,000	(1)	
Ammonia, anhydrous (see Group II)................	$7,224,473	$3,140,848	$2,544,238
Carbon dioxide (see Group I)......................	$6,574,250	$2,320,685	$2,345,743
Chlorine (see Group VII)..........................	$1,425,917	$472,836	
Hydrogen:			
Number of establishments.........................	40	6	
Total production, cubic feet......................	138,177,000	(1)	
For sale—			
Cubic feet.....................................	137,082,000	1,699,000	(1)
Value...	$851,397	$16,671	
Made and consumed, cubic feet.................	1,095,000		
Nitrogen:			
Number of establishments.........................	8	(1)	
Cubic feet.......................................	2,162,000		
Value...	$45,416		
Nitrous oxide (laughing gas):			
Number of establishments.........................	8	7	5
Gallons..	[3] 25,740,000	[3] 17,838,000	[4] 97,175
Value...	$515,164	$213,099	$38,589
Oxygen:			
Number of establishments.........................	94	51	20
Electrolytic.....................................	39	(1)	(1)
Other..	55	(1)	(1)
Cubic feet.......................................	1,173,414,000	104,714,000	3,814,000
Electrolytic.....................................	131,477,000	(1)	(1)
Other..	1,043,937,000	(1)	(1)
Value...	$16,577,389	$1,829,446	$177,469
Other gases.—(1) Sulphur trioxide; (2) blau gas, oil, and carbohydrogen; (3) argon; (4) sulphur dioxide; and (5) carbon monoxide, name in order of their value...	$2,909,155	$104,135	$59,756
GROUP X.—CHEMICALS, NOT ELSEWHERE SPECIFIED.			
Total value.......................................	$156,672,155	$52,898,172	$48,851,270
Organic	$72,141,542	$16,377,955	$14,039,748
Alcohols: [5]			
Amyl alcohol—			
Number of establishments.........................	5		
Total production, gallons........................	241,254		
For sale—			
Gallons.......................................	141,535		
Value...	$497,906	(6)	(6)
Made and consumed, gallons....................	99,719		
Glycerin (glycerol)—			
Crude—			
Number of establishments.........................	91		
For sale—			
Pounds..	21,402,735	16,568,920	
Value...	$2,961,583	$2,278,976	
Made and consumed in soap industry, pounds....................................	38,350,994	(1)	
Refined—			79,677,490
Number of establishments.........................	31	(1)	$11,752,580
Total production, pounds.........................	69,464,298	60,944,799	
For sale—			
Pounds..	67,342,822	59,810,405	
Value...	$20,724,033	$10,779,204	
Made and consumed, pounds...................	2,121,476	1,134,394	(1)
Other—Butyl, diacetone, limone and propyl alcohols, dextro citronellol, geraniol, guaiacol, iso-eugenol, linalool, nerol, resorcinol, rhodinol, terpineol and some ethyl alcohol ($126,299) and methyl alcohol ($5,763) produced by chemical establishments........	$553,234	(6)	(6)

[1] Figures not available.
[2] Not including acetylene distributed through mains by public service companies; in 1919, 37 establishments, 5,077,000 cubic feet, value $69,647; in 1914, 125 establishments, 14,868,000 cubic feet, value $194,019.
[3] Equivalents in cubic feet: 1919, 3,432,000; 1914, 2,378,400.
[4] Quantity reported in pounds.
[5] Not including (except as noted under "other alcohols") ethyl or grain alcohol, the product of distilleries; nor methyl or wood alcohol, for which see "Wood distillation."
[6] Figures not available; included with "Unclassified."

TABLE 61.—CHEMICALS—DETAILED STATISTICS OF PRODUCTS, BY GROUPS: 1919, 1914, AND 1909—Continued.

(Ton, 2,000 pounds.)

	1919	1914	1909
GROUP X.—CHEMICALS, NOT ELSEWHERE SPECIFIED—Con.			
Aldehydes:			
Formaldehyde—			
Number of establishments	6	3	3
Total production, pounds	25,006,815		
For sale—			
Pounds	19,663,753	8,426,247	3,794,486
Value	$3,938,322	$655,174	$363,717
Made and consumed, pounds	5,343,062	(1)	(1)
Vanillin—			
Number of establishments	4	(1)	(1)
Pounds	134,687	120,619	(1)
Value	$1,365,941	$525,219	(2)
Other, including acetic, anistic, citral, and decyl aldehydes, chloral hydrate, formaldehyde, hydrosulphite, helio-tropin and miscellaneous	$1,794,268		
Carbon and hydrocarbon compounds—			
Carbon bisulphide—			
Number of establishments	8		
Total production, pounds	15,469,567		
For sale—		(2)	(2)
Pounds	11,607,193		
Value	$640,346		
Made and consumed, pounds	3,863,374		
Other acetylene, blau gas, oil gas, calcium carbide, silicon carbide, thymene, etc	$28,362,198		
Esters:			
Amyl acetate—			
Number of establishments	8	(1)	(1)
Total production, pounds	906,764		
For sale—			
Pounds	693,383	1,300,052	1,470,568
Value	$350,573	$465,664	$442,771
Made and consumed, pounds	213,381		
Ethyl acetate—			
Number of establishments	7		
Total production, pounds	5,780,549		
For sale—			
Pounds	2,657,947		
Value	$340,011	(2)	(2)
Made and consumed, pounds	3,122,602		
Other—Amyl and ethyl butyrate, amyl valerate, butyl acetate, ethyl formate, etc	$1,007,794		
Ethers:			
Ethyl ether (sulphuric ether)—			
Number of establishments	10		
Total production, pounds	4,875,255		
For sale—			
Pounds	4,111,755	2,120,082	1,168,631
Value	$1,103,676	$278,816	$190,164
Made and consumed, pounds	763,500		
Ethyl nitrate (nitrous ether)—			
Number of establishments	5		
Pounds	43,153		
Value	$30,856		
Other—Methyl ether, etc	$22,570		
Halogen compounds:		(2)	(2)
Carbon tetrachloride—			
Number of establishments	5		
Total production, pounds	11,908,704		
For sale—			
Pounds	9,811,779		
Value	$803,648		
Made and consumed, pounds	2,096,925		
Chloroform—			
Number of establishments	6	(1)	(1)
Pounds	1,677,641	1,333,954	1,869,685
Value	$516,625	$295,317	$477,538
Ethyl chloride—			
Number of establishments	6		
Pounds	248,103		
Value	$166,235		
Other—Chlor acetyl and ehtylene chloride, ethyl bromide, ethyl iodide, iodoform, monobrom benzene, monobrom camphor, tetrachlorethane and thymol iodide	$254,248	(2)	(2)

¹ Figures not available.   ² Figures not available; included with "Unclassified."

TABLE 61.—CHEMICALS—DETAILED STATISTICS OF PRODUCTS, BY GROUPS: 1919, 1914,
AND 1909—Continued.

(Ton, 2,000 pounds.)

	1919	1914	1909
GROUP X.—CHEMICALS, NOT ELSEWHERE SPECIFIED—Con.			
Ketones:			
Acetone—			
Number of establishments	4	8	8
Pounds	6, 045, 914	10, 425, 817	7, 761, 696
Value	$767, 042	$1, 099, 585	$812, 978
Acetone oil—			
Number of establishments	3		
Gallons	99, 692		
Value	$127, 831		
Methyl ethyl ketone (methyl acetone)—			
Number of establishments	6		
Pounds	1, 158, 032		
Value	$167, 734	(¹)	(¹)
Other—Violet ketone and miscellaneous	$97, 351		
Other specified organic chemicals; amines, various coaltar products, alcogas, refined camphor, oleo resin, ossein, thymol, and sulphonal	$1, 409, 158		
Other unclassified organic chemicals	$4, 138, 359		
Inorganic	$84, 530, 613	$36, 520, 217	$34, 811, 522
Antimony:			
Chloride—			
Number of establishments	4		
Pounds	103, 466		
Value	$15, 554		
Sulphide—			
Number of establishments	5		
Pounds	2, 983, 378		
Value	$808, 433	(¹)	
Other—Oxide, oxychloride, potassium, antimonyl tartrate	$366, 040		
Arsenic:			
Arsenate of calcium—			
Number of establishments	5		
Pounds	1, 191, 868		
Value	$248, 459		
Arsenate of lead			
Number of establishments	12	11	
Total production, pounds	11, 524, 278	8, 847, 656	
For sale—			
Pounds	11, 465, 788	8, 641, 856	
Value	$2, 090, 341	$511, 688	
Made and consumed, pounds	48, 487	205, 800	
Other—Arsenous and arsenic acid, arsenical salts of copper, magnesium, sodium, and zinc, etc., some metal, and sulphide	$1, 150, 567	$134, 294	(¹)
Barium:			
Carbonate—			
Number of establishments	4		
Pounds	12, 906, 705		
Value	$359, 465		
Chloride—			
Number of establishments	9		
Total production	8, 743, 098		
For sale—			
Pounds	5, 811, 579		
Value	$229, 544	(¹)	
Made and consumed, pounds	2, 931, 519		
Nitrate—			
Number of establishments	4		
Total production	2, 025, 185		
For sale—			
Pounds	903, 377		
Value	$85, 319		
Made and consumed, pounds	1, 121, 808		
Sulphate (blanc fixe)—			
Number of establishments	10	11	
Pounds	13, 635, 789	18, 278, 000	8, 152, 000
Value	$256, 100	$257, 415	$86, 986

¹ Figures not available; included with "Unclassified."

TABLE 61.—CHEMICALS—DETAILED STATISTICS OF PRODUCTS, BY GROUPS: 1919, 1914, AND 1909—Continued.

(Ton, 2,000 pounds.)

	1919	1914	1909
GROUP X.—CHEMICALS, NOT ELSEWHERE SPECIFIED—Con.			
Barium—Continued.			
Sulphide—			
Number of establishments	7		
Total production, pounds	21,908,754		
For sale—			
Pounds	5,084,931	(¹)	
Value	$106,317		
Made and consumed, pounds	16,823,823		
Other—Barium chlorate, dioxide, fluoride, phosphate, thiocyanate, etc	$646,758	$103,204	
Bismuth:			
Subnitrate—			
Number of establishments	7		
Total production, pounds	283,286		
For sale—			
Pounds	279,786		
Value	$811,487		(¹)
Made and consumed, pounds	3,500		
Other—nitrate, oxide, subgallate, etc., and metal	$424,015		
Bromine:		(¹)	
Liquid—			
Number of establishments	5		
Pounds	211,555		
Value	$92,047		
Other—ammonium, calcium, potassium, and sodium bromides and bromates, organic bromides, etc. (see the respective groups)			
Other—Miscellaneous	$1,425,684		
Calcium:			
Acetate—			
Number of establishments	86	78	
Total production, tons	84,478	83,542	
For sale—			
Tons	76,955	81,761	70,739
Value	$2,682,232	$2,138,909	$2,118,443
Made and consumed, tons	7,523	1,781	
Chloride—			
Number of establishments	15	7	
Tons	74,699	44,753	
Value	$1,043,301	$342,271	
Phosphate—			
Number of establishments	7	3	
Pounds	44,270,166	24,192,974	
Value	$4,727,364	$1,298,566	
Other—Calcium bisulphite, bromide, carbonate, hypochlorite, sulphide and sulphate, etc., $5,172,241, carbide, citrate, ferrocyanide, lactate, lacto-phosphate, sulphocarbolate, etc., $10,436,916	$15,609,157		(¹)
Cerium compounds—Carbonate, chloride, dioxide, fluoride, nitrate, oxalate, etc	$132,283		
Chromium sulphate and chromium compounds, not elsewhere specified (see Group V)	$610,933		
Cobalt, salts and compounds	$217,689	(¹)	
Copper:			
Carbonate—			
Number of establishments	5		
Pounds	327,949		
Value	$92,230		
Sulphate (blue vitriol)—			
Number of establishments	14	14	
Pounds	35,287,881	37,152,351	36,546,553
Value	$3,164,611	$1,598,944	$1,531,574
Other copper salts and compounds	$575,537	$14,383	(¹)
Gold:			
Chloride—			
Number of establishments	4		
Ounces	7,229		
Value	$76,152	28,819	42,544
Other gold salts and compounds	$66,917	$291,658	$430,944
Iodine, resublimed and minor iodides:			
Number of establishments	7		
Pounds	10,731	(¹)	(¹)
Value	$438,002		

¹ Figures not available; included with "Unclassified."

TABLE 61.—CHEMICALS—DETAILED STATISTICS OF PRODUCTS, BY GROUPS: 1919, 1914, AND 1909—Continued.

(Ton, 2,000 pounds.)

	1919	1914	1909
GROUP X.—CHEMICALS, NOT ELSEWHERE SPECIFIED—Con.			
Iron:			
Chloride, crystals (ferric)—			
Number of establishments	7		
Pounds	917,849		
Value	$71,572	(¹)	
Chloride, liquor (ferric)—			
Number of establishments	9		
Pounds	977,133		
Value	$64,859		(¹)
Oxide—			
Number of establishments	6	6	
Tons	36,417	(²)	
Value	$574,970	$105,682	
Sulphate (copperas)—			
Number of establishments	32	29	
Tons	³ 59,383	46,239	⁴ 12,819
Value	$993,939	$352,772	$78,467
Other iron compounds—			
Inorganic—Ferroalloys, other than blast-furnace products, iron-by-hydrogen, chloride (ferrous) nitrate, sulphide, vanadate, etc	$9,274,214		
Organic.—Acetate, iron ferrocyanide, oxalate, valerate	$661,975	$3,592,793	
Lead:			
Acetate—			
Number of establishments	9		
Total production, pounds	5,131,133		
For sale—			
Pounds	4,183,621	7,290,936	
Value	$552,435	$474,430	
Made and consumed, pounds	947,512		
Arsenate (see arsenic)—			
Other lead salts	$335,906		
Lithium salts—Bromide, carbonate, chloride, etc	$502,542		(¹)
Magnesium:			
Carbonate (precipitated)—			
Number of establishments	4		
Pounds	544,022		
Value	$70,512		
Chloride—			
Number of establishments	7	(¹)	
Pounds	26,282,436		
Value	$445,087		
Oxide—			
Number of establishments	6		
Pounds	9,031,650		
Value	$1,176,858		
Sulphate (Epsom salts):			
Number of establishments	20	12	10
Total production, pounds	59,067,335		
For sale—			
Pounds	58,696,632	29,265,115	21,621,297
Value	$1,497,077	$296,999	$189,791
Made and consumed, pounds	370,703	(²)	(²)
Other magnesium salts, metal, and alloys	$376,843	(¹)	(¹)
Manganese:			
Borate—			
Number	3		
Pounds	141,828		
Value	$27,996	(¹)	(¹)
Other manganese salts and compounds ⁵	$71,399		

¹ Figures not available; included with "Unclassified."
² Figures not available.
³ Iron sulphate produced by chemical plants 12,898 tons; by rolling mills, 9,738 tons; and by wire mills, 36,747 tons.
⁴ Includes 5,845 tons of iron sulphate made and consumed.
⁵ Not including ferroalloys.

TABLE 61.—CHEMICALS—DETAILED STATISTICS OF PRODUCTS, BY GROUPS: 1919, 1914, AND 1909—Continued.

(Ton, 2,000 pounds.)

	1919	1914	1909
GROUP X.—CHEMICALS, NOT ELSEWHERE SPECIFIED—Con.			
Mercury:			
Chloride, mercuric (corrosive sublimate)—			
Number of establishments	4	(1)	
Total production, pounds	447,080	(1)	
For sale—			
Pounds	437,015		
Value	$648,774		
Made and consumed, pounds	10,065		
Chloride, mercurous (calomel)			
Number of establishments	3	605,701	
Pounds	256,388	$518,023	
Value	$414,388		
Other mercury compounds—Cyanide, oxide, and miscellaneous preparations	$711,856		(2)
Nickel compounds—Carbonate, cyanide, formate, hydrate, nitrate, sulphate, black salts, and miscellaneous	$641,645	$157,149	
Phosphorus, metal, chloride, sesquisulphide, and miscellaneous	$910,591		
Radium salts:			
Number of establishments	7		
Milligrams	27,627	(2)	
Value	$2,985,777		
Silver:			
Nitrate—			
Number of establishments	7		
Total production, ounces	3,055,903		
For sale—			
Ounces	3,017,889	2,563,238	2,030,399
Value	$2,184,051	$846,059	$727,428
Made and consumed, ounces	38,014		
Other silver salts and compounds—Chloride, collargol, cyanide, nucleinate, oxide, proteinate, and miscellaneous	$257,722		
Strontium salts—Bromide, carbonate, chloride, iodide, lactate, nitrate, salicylate, sulphate, etc	$319,373	(2)	(2)
Sulphur:			
Refined—			
Number of establishments	9	(1)	(1)
Tons	52,099	31,166	25,269
Value	$2,712,944	$1,141,100	$891,501
Chloride (red and yellow)—			
Number of establishments	8		
Total production, pounds	4,648,066		
For sale—			
Pounds	2,353,807		
Value	$124,088		
Made and consumed, pounds	2,294,259		
Other sulphur compounds	$15,926	(2)	(2)
Thorium compounds—nitrate, oxide	$664,843		
Tin:			
Chloride, stannous (crystals)—			
Number of establishments	4		
Pounds	587,963		
Value	$251,843		
Chloride, stannic (tetra and bi-)—			
Number of establishments	4		
Pounds	8,411,453		
Value	$2,735,392	8,291,239	10,293,377
Oxide—		$2,028,511	$1,535,350
Number of establishments	4		
Pounds	1,352,345		
Value	$899,525		
Titanium compounds—sodium sulphate, potassium oxalate, etc.[3]	$98,188		
Uranium compounds—acetate, sodium acetate, chloride, nitrate, nitrite, sodium, uranate, etc	$6,233	(2)	(2)
Vanadium and compounds [3]	$698,678		

[1] Figures not available.
[2] Figures not available; included with "Unclassified."
[3] Not including ferroalloys.

1122   ABSTRACT OF THE CENSUS—MANUFACTURES.

TABLE **61.**—CHEMICALS—DETAILED STATISTICS OF PRODUCTS, BY GROUPS: 1919, 1914, AND 1909—Continued.

(Ton, 2,000 pounds.)

	1919	1914	1909
GROUP X.—CHEMICALS, NOT ELSEWHERE SPECIFIED—Con.			
Zinc:			
Carbonate—			
Number of establishments	4		
Pounds	91,683		
Value	$16,645		
Chloride—			
Number of establishments	19		
Pounds	74,089,063		
Value	$4,349,096		
Oxide [1]—			
Number of establishments	5		
Total production, pounds	6,185,602		
For sale—			
Pounds	4,299,602	40,786,886	25,054,213
Value	$374,188	$1,130,959	$472,302
Made and consumed, pounds	1,886,000		
Sulphate—			
Number of establishments	12		
Total production, pounds	12,941,730		
For sale—			
Pounds	7,325,544		
Value	$267,001		
Made and consumed, pounds	5,616,186		
Other zinc compounds—Arsenite, borate, cyanide, nitrate, resinate, stearate, sulphocarbolate, valerate, etc	$442,780		
Other rare earth compounds, not elsewhere specified—Berryllium nitrate, neodymium chloride, zerconium oxide, etc	$42,171	[2]	[2]
Other rare metals, not elsewhere specified—Molybdenum, silicon, tungsten	$1,806,978	[2]	[2]
Unclassified.			
Crude, commercial, and fine chemicals not separately reported	$4,699,195	$19,184,408	$26,748,736

[1] Not including zinc oxide reported in the paint industry, 139,661 tons, value $24,082,299. Total production from all sources, 142,753 net tons.

[2] Figures not available; included with "Unclassified."

TABLE 62.—COKE: 1919, 1914, AND 1909.

(Ton, 2,000 pounds.)

	1919	1914	1909
Coal used for coking, all establishments, tons..............	65,587,918	51,623,750	59,354,937
PRODUCTS.			
The classified industry (establishments primarily engaged in the manufacture of coke)—all products..............	$316,515,838	$99,275,020	$95,696,622
Coke and coking by-products, all establishments, including subsidiary coke products of establishments in other industries.................	$322,056,708	$105,863,305	$98,078,383
Coke:			
Tons......	44,180,557	34,555,914	39,315,065
Value.......	$258,339,740	$88,334,217	$89,965,483
Made in—			
Beehive ovens—			
Tons......	19,042,936	23,335,971	33,060,421
Value......	$98,094,972	$50,254,050	$69,530,794
Retort or by-product ovens—			
Tons......	25,137,621	11,219,943	6,254,644
Value......	$160,244,768	$38,080,167	$20,434,689
By-products from retort or by-product ovens—			
Gas—			
Production, M cubic feet...........................	415,642,265	(1)	(1)
Sales, M cubic feet...........................	193,073,979	61,364,375	15,791,220
Illumination and household purposes...........	5,238,486		
Industrial purposes........................	138,179,761	(1)	(1)
To public service corporations..............	49,655,732		
Value........................	$16,685,007	$6,009,583	$2,609,211
Tar—			
Production, gallons...........................	288,898,764	(1)	(1)
Sales—			
Gallons...........................	217,780,143	109,901,315	60,126,006
Value...........................	$6,919,265	$2,867,274	$1,408,611
Ammonia (sales)—			
Sulphate—			
Pounds...........................	557,619,631	170,763,906	123,111,197
Value...........................	$21,075,718	$4,696,590	$3,227,316
Anhydrous or free ammonia [2]—			
Pounds...........................	51,646,744	(1)	(1)
Value...........................	$5,692,950	$2,958,634	$3,675,771
Benzol products (sales)...........................	$12,678,886	(1)	(1)
Other coking products...........................	$665,142	$997,007	$419,307

[1] Figures not available.   [2] Includes liquor and sulphate sold on pound basis NH[3].

TABLE 63:—DRUGGISTS' PREPARATIONS, PATENT AND PROPRIETARY MEDICINES AND COMPOUNDS, AND PERFUMERY AND COSMETICS: 1919 AND 1914.

	1919	1914
Number of establishments, total	3,839	4,092
The classified industries, establishments engaged primarily in the manufacture of—		
Druggists' preparations	524	416
Patent medicines and compounds	2,467	2,903
Perfumery and cosmetics	569	496
Other industries, establishments reporting as subsidiary products—		
Druggists' preparations	67	
Patent medicines and compounds	151	277
Perfumery and cosmetics	61	
PRODUCTS.		
Total value	$418,221,150	$176,747,080
The classified industries:		
Druggists' preparations	$114,593,486	$48,009,654
Patent medicines and compounds	$212,162,255	$102,463,374
Perfumery and cosmetics	$59,613,391	$16,899,101
Subsidiary products of other industries:		
Druggists' preparations	$21,839,202	$5,353,646
Patent medicines and compounds	$6,878,102	$3,202,057
Perfumery and cosmetics [1]	$3,134,714	$819,248
Alkaloids and derivatives	$15,416,028	$16,231,503
Quinine—		
Pounds	237,944	
Value	$3,929,606	
Morphine, pounds	38,122	
For sale—		
Pounds	37,047	
Value	$5,906,201	
Made and consumed, pounds	1,075	
Heroin—		
Pounds	6,833	(²)
Value	$1,310,883	
Codeine—		
Pounds	3,295	
Value	$473,322	
Cocaine—		
Pounds	6,781	
Value	$1,021,423	
Caffeine, pounds	40,537	
For sale—		
Pounds	18,742	
Value	$379,528	
Made and consumed, pounds	21,795	(²)
Strychnine—		
Pounds	26,029	
Value	$986,702	
Other alkaloids and alkaloids not itemized—		
Pounds	121,127	
Value	$1,408,363	
Synthetic preparations, including coal-tar medicinals	$8,899,533	$1,384,996
Biological products (serums, vaccines, toxins, etc.)	$15,876,358	$6,223,475
Other druggists' preparations (not patent or proprietary):		
Tinctures, fluid extracts, medicinal sirups, and other liquid preparations, not otherwise accounted for	$38,679,454	$13,900,402
Pills, tablets, powders, etc., not otherwise accounted for	$37,803,903	$10,903,056
Pharmaceutical metals and their salts	$420,952	$732,307
Patent and proprietary medicines:		
For sale in unbroken unit packages to the general public	$132,978,871	$83,455,264
Ethical pharmaceutical specialties	$29,494,936	
Patent and proprietary compounds	$46,351,234	$16,514,352
Perfumery, cosmetics, and toilet preparations [1]	$69,449,056	$19,160,407
Flavoring essences and extracts	$5,222,192	$8,241,318
All other products	$17,628,633	

[1] Not including perfumery and cosmetics manufactured by the soap industry to the value of $12,635,206 in 1919 and $6,804,508 in 1914.
² Figures not available.

TABLE 64.—NATURAL DYESTUFFS AND EXTRACTS: 1919, 1914, AND 1909.

[Not including tanning extracts made and consumed in establishment producing.]

	1919	1914	1909
Number of establishments	176	133	124
The classified industry—Dyestuffs and extracts—natural	144	112	107
Other industries	32	21	17
PRODUCTS.			
Total value	**$56,905,553**	[1] **$21,382,689**	[1] **$16,788,676**
The classified industry—Dyestuffs and extracts—natural	$53,744,283	$20,620,336	$15,954,574
Subsidiary products from other industries	$3,161,270	$762,353	$834,102
Dyestuffs:			
Natural dyestuffs	$4,699,111	$1,862,162	$1,135,694
Dyewood extracts—			
Logwood—			
Number of establishments	10	9	6
Pounds	32,751,757	28,989,962	22,317,248
Value	$3,292,512	$1,311,966	$991,974
Fustic—			
Number of establishments	5	5	[2]
Pounds	3,844,390	4,509,943	[2]
Value	$355,029	$222,804	[2]
Quercitron—			
Number of establishments	6	4	[2]
Pounds	6,745,979	3,844,882	[2]
Value	$303,472	$112,945	[2]
Other dyewood extracts—Brazilwood, cutch, etc.—			
Pounds	2,078,287	3,434,150	[2]
Value	$312,924	$90,934	[2]
All other, dyewoods ground or chipped, and dyestuffs not dyewoods	$435,174	$123,513	$143,720
Tanning materials	$32,616,231	$7,898,672	$7,323,971
Extracts:			
Oak and chestnut—			
Number of establishments	34	24	[2]
Pounds	507,905,777	328,197,524	266,529,514
Value	$18,663,125	$4,130,042	$4,321,637
Hemlock—			
Number of establishments	11	7	[2]
Pounds	19,705,590	18,978,013	12,588,078
Value	$879,366	$340,402	$280,487
Sumac—			
Number of establishments	5	[2]	[2]
Pounds	4,507,433	4,512,361	3,148,790
Value	$253,088	$129,631	$107,456
Other tanning extracts—Quebracho, spruce, gambier, chrome tanning, myrobalans, divi-divi, and gallnuts, in order as to value—			
Pounds	170,846,336	109,597,041	} $2,614,391
Value	$8,059,912	$2,944,906	
Other tanning materials	$4,760,740	$353,691	
Mordants:			
Tannic acid—			
Pounds	665,772	760,100	} $598,516
Value	$528,463	$234,630	
Other mordants	$690,178	$157,791	
Assistants:			
Turkey red oil—			
Pounds	2,477,874	11,681,884	1,814,506
Value	$319,050	$820,491	$108,292
Other assistants	$2,526,246	$716,510	[2]
Sizes:			
Dextrins—			
Pounds	49,328,560	18,913,641	} 16,148,431 $610,999
Value	$3,791,372	$705,584	
Gums, other than rosin—			
Pounds	8,680,048	3,832,182	
Value	$634,595	$205,282	
Rosin—			
Pounds	57,055,943	20,717,148	} $1,835,046
Value	$2,888,600	$373,218	
Other sizes	$4,264,074	$1,768,777	
All other products	$3,947,633	$6,639,572	$5,176,158

[1] Includes artificial dyestuffs, and mineral colors or dyes to the value of $5,252,693 in 1914 and $3,683,553 in 1909.
[2] Figures not available.

TABLE 65.—EXPLOSIVES: 1919, 1914, AND 1909.

(Ton, 2,000 pounds.)

	1919	1914	1909
Number of establishments	118	111	86
Number of plants represented	122	116	124
MATERIALS.			
Total cost	$45,911,049	$25,626,539	$22,811,548
Sulphur or brimstone:			
Tons	25,797	15,832	17,389
Cost	$659,219	$372,763	$367,866
Pyrites:			
Tons	6,812	25,885	36,544
Cost	$46,147	$139,496	$183,509
Nitrate of soda:			
Tons	174,742	190,960	188,889
Cost	$13,154,333	$8,979,877	$7,892,336
Glycerin:			
Tons	11,535	14,501	(1)
Cost	$5,755,319	$5,439,405	(1)
Sulphuric acid:			
Consumption, tons	2 105,256	83,605	65,056
Purchased—			
Tons	62,069	52,398	22,501
Cost	$976,295	$723,795	$406,204
Produced in works where consumed, tons	43,187	31,207	42,555
Recovered and used, tons	41,583		
Nitric acid:			
Consumption, tons	47,112	51,460	35,280
Purchased—			
Tons	1,537	4,347	3,796
Cost	$200,267	$476,404	$541,314
Produced in works where consumed, tons	45,575	47,113	31,484
Mixed acid:			
Consumption, tons	77,982	88,653	
Purchased—			
Tons	16,637	19,255	25,882
Cost	$1,567,691	$1,047,377	$1,512,626
Produced in works where consumed, tons	61,345	69,398	
All other materials, cost	$23,551,778	$8,447,422	$11,907,693
Nitrate of ammonia produced in works where consumed, pounds	43,254,887	29,891,837	10,904,319
PRODUCTS.			
Total value	3 $92,474,813	$41,432,970	$40,139,661
Explosives, total:			
Pounds	554,163,405	481,752,040	487,481,152
Value	$82,233,391	$39,645,382	$37,983,868
Dynamite—			
Number of establishments	27	26	26
Pounds	212,529,733	223,667,630	220,145,791
Value	$37,230,704	$20,553,653	$20,998,820
Permissible explosives—			
Number of establishments	15	20	13
Pounds	30,622,923	18,113,601	9,607,448
Value	$5,499,177	$1,604,072	$863,209
Nitroglycerin—			
Number of establishments	70	58	49
For sale as such	11	32	23
For consumption	67	27	26
Production, pounds	56,361,210	65,302,883	74,212,980
Sold as such—			
Pounds	714,684	3,785,474	3,923,313
Value	$301,863	$950,611	$863,360
Consumed in shooting wells, pounds	7,621,915	(4)	(4)
Consumed in works where produced, pounds	48,024,611	61,517,409	70,289,667
Blasting powder—			
Number of establishments	44	48	38
Kegs (25 pounds)	7,406,991	8,296,947	9,339,087
Value	$12,168,473	$8,459,113	$9,608,265
Gunpowder, black—			
Number of establishments	7	8	8
Pounds	11,730,094	7,685,036	12,862,700
Value	$2,096,579	$977,455	$1,736,427
Other explosives, in order named, as to value, 1919: Smokeless powder, guncotton, nitrogelatin, nitrostarch, fuse powder, trinitrotoluol, ammonium nitrate, and fulminating mercury—			
Pounds	57,744,670	21,076,624	7,464,725
Value	$24,936,595	$7,100,478	$3,913,787
Amount received for contract work, shooting wells	$3,434,835	(1)	(1)
All other products, value	$6,806,587	$1,787,588	$2,155,793

1 Figures not available.
2 Strength 66°; varying strength in prior years.
3 In addition, explosives (guncotton and fulminating mercury) to the value of $129,514 were produced by establishments not primarily engaged in the manufacture of explosives.
4 Included above with "nitroglycerin—sold as such."

TABLE 66.—FERTILIZERS: 1919, 1914, AND 1909.

(Ton, 2,000 pounds.)

	1919	1914	1909
Number of establishments	809	1,238	843
Fertilizer industry	600	784	550
Manufacturing fertilizers as subsidiary products	[1] 209	454	293
MATERIALS.			
Total cost	$193,034,389	$119,222,003	$73,165,544
The fertilizer industry	$185,040,522	$107,954,644	$69,521,920
Other industries producing fertilizers as subsidiary products	$7,993,867	$11,267,359	$3,643,624
Cottonseed meal:			
Tons	230,526	325,234	
Cost	$12,530,636	$8,419,383	842,557
Tankage and ammoniates, not elsewhere specified:			$17,200,611
Tons	689,753	887,934	
Cost	$29,949,569	$20,131,141	
Fish:			
Tons	273,252	250,110	242,045
Cost	$5,878,634	$3,111,991	$3,066,613
Ammonium sulphate:			
Tons	135,882	149,924	65,592
Cost	$12,659,056	$9,015,163	$3,732,112
Cyanamid or lime nitrogen:			
Tons	16,926	25,911	([1])
Cost	$1,329,149	$1,176,119	([1])
Nitrate of soda:			
For acid manufacture—			
Tons	21,732	15,134	
Cost	$1,692,614	$704,581	89,846
For mixed fertilizers—			$3,916,320
Tons	130,683	147,050	
Cost	$10,091,790	$6,807,228	
Phosphate rock:			
Tons	2,247,325	2,080,961	1,549,497
Cost	$17,926,097	$11,222,992	$8,828,834
Bone discard:			
Tons	12,769	3,395	([1])
Cost	$252,726	$35,007	([1])
Raw bones:			
Tons	81,304	64,590	([1])
Cost	$3,093,364	$1,603,353	([1])
Steamed bones:			
Tons	59,227	55,067	([1])
Cost	$1,815,554	$1,178,959	([1])
Ground bones, raw:			
Tons	16,471	25,139	([1])
Cost	$707,034	$593,226	([1])
Pyrites:			
Tons	398,602	613,842	456,574
Cost	$3,919,050	$3,590,235	$2,831,994
Sulphur:			
Tons	221,558	2,041	4,236
Cost	$5,669,331	$42,716	$68,924
Sulphuric acid:			
Purchased—			
Tons	636,632	728,889	620,708
Cost	$6,683,061	$4,387,317	$3,460,132
Made and consumed, tons	1,568,577	1,276,715	841,935
Superphosphate:			
Purchased—			
Tons	1,200,182	1,096,178	532,886
Cost	$18,485,969	$9,301,501	$5,175,957
Made and consumed (acid phosphate), tons	3,316,486	2,723,317	1,838,865
Basic slag or Thomas phosphate powder:			
Tons	11,394	16,190	([2])
Cost	$118,768	$144,213	([2])
Guano:			
Tons	33,053	120,128	([2])
Cost	$893,933	$445,416	([2])
Kainit:			
Tons	31,145	448,885	347,104
Cost	$920,614	$3,939,263	$3,008,183
Potash salts:			
Tons	274,992	529,973	270,459
Cost	$18,653,390	$12,774,113	$7,714,367

[1] Includes 94 cottonseed-oil mills, 32 grease and tallow rendering establishments, 51 slaughtering and meat-packing plants, and 32 establishments distributed among 13 other industries that produce wastes of fertilizer value.
[2] Figures not available.

TABLE **66.**—FERTILIZERS: 1919, 1914, AND 1909—Continued.

(Ton, 2,000 pounds.)

	1919	1914	1909
MATERIALS—continued.			
Hardwood ashes:			
Tons..	9,085	4,437	(1)
Cost..	$96,569	$54,171	(1)
All other materials..............................	$39,667,532	$20,543,915	$14,161,497
PRODUCTS.			
Total value.............................	**$306,523,899**	**$169,017,550**	**$111,871,481**
Fertilizer industry..............................	$281,143,587	$153,196,152	$103,960,213
Fertilizers, subsidiary products of other industries..........	$25,380,312	$15,821,398	$7,911,268
Fertilizers:			
Tons..	8,237,011	8,432,206	5,618,234
Value...	$284,544,523	$153,260,212	$100,089,971
Complete and ammoniated fertilizers [2]—			
Tons..	4,756,440	5,612,421	3,523,759
Value...	$200,106,419	$121,676,386	$74,109,307
Superphosphates—			
Production, tons.................................	5,712,158	4,416,022	3,062,834
For sale—			
Tons..	2,395,672	1,692,705	1,223,969
Value...	$46,221,930	$14,778,654	$13,744,831
Made and consumed, tons.....................	3,316,486	2,723,317	1,838,865
Concentrated phosphates—			
Tons..	119,609	67,585	270,128
Value...	$3,828,417	$1,367,005	$2,713,513
Other fertilizers—			
Tons..	965,290	1,059,495	600,378
Value...	$34,387,757	$15,438,167	$9,522,320
Sulphuric acid (basis of 50° Baumé)—			
Production, tons.................................	1,877,394	1,405,768	995,384
For sale—			
Tons..	308,817	129,053	153,449
Value...	$3,639,010	$768,873	$928,582
Made and consumed, tons.....................	1,568,577	1,276,715	841,935
Fish scrap:			
Tons..	47,542	62,930	78,484
Value...	$3,170,691	$1,915,530	$2,006,724
Pyrite cinder:[3]			
Tons..	116,444	245,082	291,653
Value...	$169,420	$231,869	$143,607
Oil:			
Gallons...	[4] 2,118,092	2,445,026	3,218,393
Value...	$1,831,194	$778,337	$810,938
Bone black:			
Pounds...	44,597,838	41,054,769	(1)
Value...	$2,227,113	$1,413,166	(1)
Glue..	$2,171,055	$1,131,243	(1)
Grease..	$2,015,033	$1,209,334	(1)
All other products................................	[5] $6,755,860	[5] $8,308,986	$7,891,659

[1] Figures not available.

[2] Includes fertilizers reported as ammoniated fertilizers, but containing both superphosphates and potash viz, in 1919, 1,271,215 tons; 1914, 1,519,156 tons; and 1909, 522,389 tons.

[3] Not including 116,987 tons of pyrite cinder in 1919, 155,634 tons in 1914, and 72,402 tons in 1909, of no value.

[4] Includes fish oil, 1,759,174 gallons, valued at $1,441,989; neat's-foot oil, 165,195 gallons, valued at $131,745; and cottonseed oil, 193,723 gallons, valued at $257,460.

[5] Includes chemicals (soda products, acids, etc.) to the value of $1,039,068 in 1919 and $400,597 in 1914.

TABLE 67.—GAS, ILLUMINATING AND HEATING: 1919, 1914, AND 1909.

	1919	1914	1909
MATERIALS.			
Total cost.............................	$157,550,882	$76,779,288	$52,427,844
Coal used for gas making:			
Anthracite—			
Gross tons..........................	1,307,383		
Cost.................................	$11,326,268	6,116,672	4,940,598
Bituminous—		$20,872,517	$16,304,832
Net tons............................	1 6,193,527		
Cost.................................	$32,412,349		
Coke (purchased) used for gas making:			
Net tons............................	1,335,322	964,851	591,919
Cost.................................	$11,781,932	$4,500,289	$2,667,706
Oil used for gas making:			
Gallons.............................	163,652,910		
Cost.................................	$6,183,438	715,418,623	578,309,411
Oil used for enriching gas:		$24,720,998	$17,105,981
Gallons.............................	718,020,458		
Cost.................................	$44,546,711		
Benzene or benzol:			
Gallons.............................	14,155	388,146	253,837
Cost.................................	$3,107	$54,653	$27,543
Benzine, gasoline, and naphtha:			
Gallons.............................	111,923	998,353	1,093,874
Cost.................................	$35,504	$169,020	$212,226
Calcium carbide:			
Pounds.............................	1,049,222	31,749,491	6,080,465
Cost.................................	$45,977	$887,937	$195,836
Lime, cost..............................	$26,281	(2)	(2)
Oxide or purifying material, cost.......	$1,075,748	(2)	(2)
Gas purchased (43 establishments):			
M cubic feet.......................	67,105,518		
Cost.................................	$22,612,816		
Coke oven (16 establishments)—			
M cubic feet.......................	23,995,064		
Cost.................................	$3,784,539		
Coal (5 establishments)—			
M cubic feet.......................	15,041,980		
Cost.................................	$9,343,107	28,351,074	16,769,705
Mixed coal and water (6 establishments)—		$8,883,016	$5,416,601
M cubic feet.......................	31,748		
Cost.................................	$31,524		
Carbureted water (10 establishments)—			
M cubic feet.......................	14,932,670		
Cost.................................	$7,476,894		
Natural (8 establishments)—			
M cubic feet.......................	13,104,056		
Cost.................................	$1,976,752		
Boiler fuel, cost.......................	$7,722,000	$3,784,911	$2,369,131
Retort and bench fuel, cost............	$854,754		
Water, cost.............................	$576,599	(2)	(2)
All other materials, cost...............	$7,800,498	$5,512,723	$2,590,052
Amount paid for lamps and appliances purchased for sale...	$10,546,900	$7,393,224	$5,537,936
PRODUCTS.			
Total value.........................	3 $329,278,908	3 $220,237,790	$166,814,371
Gas:			
For sale—			
M cubic feet.......................	308,440,473	203,639,260	150,835,793
Value...............................	$282,288,778	$175,065,920	$138,615,309
Plant consumption and loss, M cubic feet...........	35,679,338	1,121,108	1,730,563
Coal gas—			
M cubic feet.......................	8,029,749	10,509,946	19,985,253
Value...............................	$10,496,613	$10,726,514	$18,065,841
Carbureted water-gas—			
M cubic feet.......................	90,796,299	90,017,725	4 81,144,568
Value...............................	$83,663,451	$74,516,534	$70,802,780
Mixed coal and water-gas—			
M cubic feet.......................	179,871,832	86,281,339	40,775,283
Value...............................	$161,199,670	$72,012,021	$36,953,543

1 Includes 966 tons of cannel coal, valued at $8,818.
2 Figures not available.
3 See tabular note at end of table, p. 1131.
4 Inclndes 1,726,082 M cu. ft. of straight water-gas, valued at $1,289,031.

TABLE 67.—GAS, ILLUMINATING AND HEATING: 1919, 1914, AND 1909—Continued.

	1919	1914	1909
PRODUCTS—continued.			
Gas—Continued.			
Oil-gas—			
M cubic feet	15,421,836	16,512,274	8,688,860
Value	$18,747,496	$15,044,509	$12,111,458
Acetylene-gas—			
Distributed through mains—			
M cubic feet	5,077	14,868	
Value	$69,647	$194,019	
Delivered in containers (compressed)—			25,186
M cubic feet	(¹)	121,696	$361,348
Value	(¹)	$2,317,605	
Gasoline (cold process) gas—			
M cubic feet	20,428	181,412	216,643
Value	$41,169	$254,718	$320,339
Other (enriched natural) ²—			
M cubic feet	14,295,252		
Value	$8,070,732		
Coke:			
Production, net tons	4,278,533	3,582,565	2,631,997
For sale—			
Net tons	2,458,166	2,281,835	1,640,994
Value	$17,822,894	$8,719,920	$5,723,215
Made and consumed, net tons	1,820,367	1,300,730	991,003
Tar:			
Used in gas generators	663,265		
For retort or bench fuel	730,315	(³)	(³)
Used otherwise	426,787		
Coal-gas tar—			
Production, gallons	65,824,282		
For sale—			
Gallons	61,969,577		
Value	$2,647,813	153,311,196	109,930,058
Made and consumed, gallons	3,854,705	125,938,607	⁴ 78,339,880
Water-gas and oil-gas tar—		$3,252,765	$1,875,549
Production, gallons	105,318,339	27,372,589	31,590,178
For sale—			
Gallons	58,557,947		
Value	$2,012,723		
Made and consumed, gallons	46,760,392		
Ammonia:			
Ammonia liquors—			
Gallons	23,393,320		
Value	$1,674,449		
Anhydrous ammonia—		⁵ 50,737,762	⁵ 37,277,864
Pounds	1,846,024	$1,235,442	$725,702
Value	$150,596		
Ammonium sulphate—			
Pounds	5,073,945	6,216,618	(³)
Value	$205,101	$134,196	(³)
Hydrocarbons:			
Gallons	491,559	(³)	(³)
Value	$46,910	$35,902	$44,509
Light oil and derivatives:			
Crude light oil—			
Production, gallons	6,491,113		
For sale—			
Gallons	285,071		
Value	$34,369		
Made and consumed, gallons	6,206,042		
Secondary light oil—			
Gallons	662,897		
Value	$45,841		
Benzol—			
Crude, gallons	3,738,844		
For sale—			
Gallons	76,816	(⁶)	(⁶)
Value	$14,974		
Made and consumed, gallons	3,662,028		
Refined (pure)—			
Gallons	3,147,751		
Value	$561,732		
Toluol—			
Crude, gallons	214,270		
For sale—			
Gallons	4,146		
Value	$1,623		
Made and consumed, gallons	210,124		

¹ Included in chemicals in 1919: 311,390 M. cu. ft., valued at $7,140,757.
² Enriched natural gas not reported prior to 1919.
³ Figures not available.
⁴ In addition, 13,813,058 gallons were produced for which no value was reported.
⁵ Gallons.
⁶ Included in "All other products."

Table **67.**—GAS, ILLUMINATING AND HEATING: 1919, 1914, and 1909—Continued.

	1919	1914	1909
PRODUCTS—continued.			
Light oil and derivatives—Continued.			
Toluol—Continued.			
Refined (pure)—			
Gallons	165,612		
Value	$94,247		
Solvent naphtha—			
Gallons	187,034		
Value	$43,689		
Other refined oils—			
Gallons	567,252		
Value	$88,959		
Drip and holder oil—			
Gallons	2,659,080		
Value	$137,957		
Naphthalene:			
Crude—			
Production, pounds	1,757,317		
For sale—			
Pounds	521,459		
Value	$6,841		
Made and consumed, pounds	1,235,858		
Refined—			
Pounds	911,710		
Value	$45,585	(1)	(1)
Pitch:			
Production, pounds	13,966,731		
For sale—			
Pounds	13,834,551		
Value	$92,988		
Made and consumed, pounds	132,180		
Retort carbon:			
Production, pounds	12,145,336		
For sale—			
Pounds	1,136,575		
Value	$9,370		
Made and consumed, pounds	11,008,761		
Lampblack (gas-house):			
Production, pounds	207,944,060		
For sale—			
Pounds	34,239,800		
Value	$107,201		
Made and consumed, pounds	173,704,260		
Other by-products	$697,494		
Gas lime	$205		
Spent oxide	$32,358		
All other products	$3,055,869	$20,815,871	$12,786,697
Receipts from rents and sales of lamps and appliances:			
Rents	$1,763,187	$10,977,774	$7,043,390
Sales	$15,595,155		

NOTE.—Commercial production by 5 establishments in 1919 and 6 in 1914, engaged primarily in other lines of manufacture, not included above:

	1919		1914	
	Quantity.	Value.	Quantity.	Value.
Total value	....	$121,761	....	$158,743
Gas, M Cubic ft	64,199	112,480	56,939	131,979
Coal	17,576	29,158	41,744	45,394
Carbureted water	36,325	66,717	10,154	16,011
Oil	10,298	16,605	....	....
Acetylene (compressed)	(2)	(2)	5,041	70,574
Coke, net tons	913	6,017	2,287	9,356
Tar, gallons	23,200	1,635	35,100	2,076
Receipts from lamps and appliances	....	1,629	....	15,332

1 Included in "All other products."   2 Included in chemicals in 1919.

TABLE **68.**—PAINT AND VARNISH: 1919, 1914, AND 1909.

	1919	1914	1909
Number of establishments	886	857	863
Paint industry	601	585	588
Varnish industry	229	215	203
Subsidiary paint and varnish products, other industries	56	57	72
MATERIALS.			
Total cost	**$223,091,742**	**$88,980,635**	**$79,136,194**
Paint industry	$165,604,116	$71,588,364	$62,458,250
Varnish industry	$51,508,256	$16,877,393	$16,557,305
Other industries, producing paint and varnish as subsidiary products	$5,979,370	$514,878	$120,639
Pig lead:			
Tons (2,000 pounds)	192,558	150,762	150,163
Cost	$22,159,573	$11,488,113	$12,380,524
Grain alcohol:			
Gallons	2,985,735	1,061,324	356,225
Cost	$1,724,112	$436,509	$226,724
Wood alcohol:			
Gallons	244,561	987,451	1,325,807
Cost	$303,998	$422,122	$693,362
Linseed oil:			
Gallons	27,037,192	24,481,623	(1)
Cost	$43,721,595	$12,049,218	(1)
China wood oil:			
Gallons	6,196,134	(1)	(1)
Cost	$10,254,039	(1)	(1)
Cottonseed oil:			
Gallons	16,506	(1)	(1)
Cost	$24,028	(1)	(1)
Corn oil:			
Gallons	55,074	(1)	(1)
Cost	$76,739	(1)	(1)
Soya-bean oil:			
Gallons	2,753,173	(1)	(1)
Cost	$3,630,634	(1)	(1)
Other oils (fish oil, tar oil, kerosene, creosote, perilla, hempseed oil, etc.):			
Gallons	8,749,494	(1)	(1)
Cost	$3,373,988	(1)	(1)
Benzol:			
Gallons	1,665,605	(1)	(1)
Cost	$400,162	(1)	(1)
Turpentine:			
Gallons	6,081,902	(1)	(1)
Cost	$6,961,982	(1)	(1)
Rosin:			
Pounds	85,917,127		
Cost	$5,411,192		
Copal, damar, or kauri:			
Pounds	18,235,774		
Cost	$3,250,165	48,902,000	(1)
Shellac:		$4,797,944	(1)
Pounds	7,785,319		
Cost	$4,653,619		
Other gums:			
Pounds	17,116,381		
Cost	$1,873,210		
Fuel and rent of power	$4,122,151	$1,592,230	$1,306,297
All other materials, cost	$111,150,555	$58,194,499	$64,529,287

[1] Figures not available.

TABLE 68.—PAINT AND VARNISH: 1919, 1914, AND 1909—Continued.

PRODUCTS.	1919	1914	1909
Total value	$381,916,186	$149,173,400	$127,472,819
Paint industry	$256,714,379	$112,408,742	$94,572,005
Varnish industry	$83,632,424	$33,214,949	$30,317,417
Paint and varnish subsidiary products of other industries	$41,569,383	$3,549,709	$2,583,397
Colors (pigments)	$72,457,266	$17,450,482	$18,134,869
Paints in oil	$168,525,448	$70,582,461	$57,380,539
Water paints and kalsomine	$5,351,918	$2,202,281	$1,981,161
Varnishes and japans	$86,814,800	$36,142,256	$31,758,735
Fillers:			
Liquid—			
Gallons	2,605,285	965,636	1,166,533
Value	$1,835,573	$670,033	$828,393
Paste—			
Pounds	15,508,344	49,587,548	65,148,395
Value	$1,480,529	$1,318,720	$1,199,595
Dry—			
Pounds	1,473,164		
Value	$71,285		
Putty:			
Pounds	66,681,514	69,828,017	67,767,348
Value	$3,164,254	$1,250,421	$1,169,683
Linseed oil, raw:			
Gallons	1,693,414	2,230,988	2,098,696
Value	$2,888,623	$1,201,839	$1,106,181
Linseed oil, boiled:			
Gallons	611,126	572,561	1,379,025
Value	$1,044,814	$306,569	$806,846
Other oils:			
Gallons	3,504,333	(1)	(1)
Value	$3,115,999	$999,392	(1)
Bleached shellac:			
Pounds	8,799,191	8,654,514	3,905,593
Value	$5,955,732	$1,806,802	$772,240
Dryers:			
Gallons	408,572	1,047,140	(1)
Value	$511,485	$257,725	(1)
All other products	$28,698,460	$14,984,419	$12,334,577

[1] Figures not available.

TABLE 69.—PETROLEUM REFINING: 1919, 1914, AND 1909.

(Ton, 2,000 pounds.)

	1919	1914	1909
Number of establishments	320	176	147
MATERIALS.			
Total cost	$1,247,908,355	$325,264,509	$199,273,402
Crude petroleum used:			
Barrels (42 gallons)	365,271,803	191,262,724	120,775,439
Cost	$867,646,475	$249,727,856	$152,307,040
Average unit cost, barrel	$2.38	$1.31	$1.26
Distillates purchased and refined:			
Barrels	43,074,982	9,455,300	(1)
Cost	$151,824,598	$24,395,541	(1)
Casinghead gasoline, purchased:			
Barrels	6,952,215	(1)	(1)
Cost	$59,857,628	(1)	(1)
Casinghead gas (wet natural gas):			
Thousand cubic feet	16,671,322	(1)	(1)
Cost	$1,256,834	(1)	(1)
Sulphur:			
Tons	5,241		
Cost	$136,828		
Pyrites:			
Tons	26,275	206,053	
Cost	$224,700		$4,003,198
Sulphuric acid (purchased):			
Tons	503,920	290,455	
Cost	$10,327,060	$3,519,552	
Caustic soda:			
Pounds	45,270,896	22,216,000	
Cost	$1,736,670	$361,421	
Other chemicals	$663,660	(1)	(1)
Fuller's earth	$2,375,729	(1)	(1)
Containers, and materials therefor:			
Wooden	$34,801,732	$12,944,471	$8,937,421
Metal	$26,193,075	$7,292,207	$8,037,467
Fuel and rent of power	$53,505,109	$13,567,284	$8,376,383
All other materials	$37,358,257	$13,250,124	$17,611,893
PRODUCTS.			
Total value	$1,632,532,766	$396,361,406	$236,997,659
Naphthas and lighter products:			
Gasoline—			
Gallons	3,648,590,635	1,195,422,100	
Value	$679,867,064	$106,140,170	
Naphtha—			
Gallons	392,282,320		
Value	$65,077,854		540,327,500
Benzine—			$39,771,959
Gallons	67,491,006	264,626,100	
Value	$10,015,853	$15,779,137	
Other—			
Gallons	97,262,837		
Value	$11,045,284		
Illuminating oils:			
Gallons	2,305,489,735	1,935,274,800	1,674,789,900
Value	$235,663,055	$96,806,452	$94,547,010
Fuel oils:			
Gallons	7,767,900,556	3,734,092,050	1,701,728,850
Value	$318,124,339	$84,017,916	$36,462,883
Distillates—			
Gallons	646,652,618	457,491,650	
Value	$36,548,107	$15,999,342	
Gas oils—			
Gallons	1,393,623,486	755,558,400	
Value	$76,383,453	$22,805,340	(1)
Residual fuel oil—			
Gallons	5,727,624,452	2,521,042,000	
Value	$205,192,779	$45,213,234	
Partly refined oils, sold for rerunning:			
Gallons	428,346,637		
Above fuel oil	79,895,749		
Fuel oil	109,503,858	(1)	(1)
Below fuel oil	238,747,030		
Value	$29,268,849		

[1] Figures not available.

TABLE 69.—PETROLEUM REFINING: 1919, 1914, AND 1909—Continued.

	1919	1914	1909
PRODUCTS—continued.			
Lubricating oils:			
Gallons	821,580,400	517,838,800	537,294,250
Value	$196,242,439	$55,812,120	$38,884,236
Pale or paraffin; viscosity less than 100° Universal; or flash under 400° F.; closed cup—			
Gallons	124,372,754	93,422,100	161,961,500
Value	$28,238,302	$8,084,650	$9,473,975
Red or neutral; viscosity 100° Universal or higher; or flash 400° F. or over; closed cup (not including cylinder oils)—			
Gallons	212,357,564	116,352,500	30,744,200
Value	$44,583,095	$12,426,023	$2,255,924
Cylinder oils—			
Gallons	235,345,952	102,949,100	79,378,950
Value	$59,036,506	$13,703,772	$9,482,568
All other lubricating oils, including compounded (except cylinder) oils—			
Gallons	249,504,130	205,115,100	265,209,600
Value	$64,384,536	$21,597,675	$17,671,769
Liquid asphaltic road oils:			
Gallons	98,036,511		
Value	$4,491,388	134,844,350	89,350,400
Residuum or tar:		$4,017,858	$2,215,623
Gallons	29,163,394		
Value	$1,522,797		
Greases:			
Gallons	28,147,534	14,006,400	6,915,100
Value	$11,896,655	$3,536,491	$1,567,647
Petrolatum—			
Gallons	10,230,287	6,078,050	
Value	$3,750,028	$1,243,388	
Lubricating greases—			(1)
Gallons	12,599,628	4,980,150	
Value	$6,043,741	$1,624,949	
Axle grease—			
Gallons	5,317,619	2,948,200	(1)
Value	$2,102,886	$668,154	
Paraffin wax:			
Gallons	67,976,676	57,538,800	47,341,500
Value	$28,348,437	$8,897,106	$9,388,812
Acid oil:			
Gallons	45,600,039	(1)	(1)
Value	$992,907	(1)	(1)
Asphalt, other than liquid asphalt:			
Tons	927,151	465,157	233,328
Value	$12,500,157	$4,867,213	$2,724,752
Coke:			
Tons	798,180	213,777	(1)
Value	$3,928,345	$818,889	$507,695
Reclaimed or separated acid sold:			
Tons	136,320	89,792	133,215
Value	$687,302	$491,380	$402,295
Candles, value	$2,939,519	$1,402,945	
Other special products, value	$6,813,647	$8,507,993	$10,524,747
All other products, value	$13,106,875	$5,265,736	
EQUIPMENT.			
Stills:			
Number	6,935	3,639	2,395
Capacity (gallons)	174,295,000	(1)	(1)
Steam—			
Number	1,061	612	467
Capacity (gallons)	27,550,000	17,892,000	18,102,000
Fire—			
Number	4,394	3,027	1,928
Capacity (gallons)	130,115,000	84,882,000	69,594,000
Pressure—			
Number	1,480	(1)	(1)
Capacity (gallons)	16,630,000	(1)	(1)
Agitators:			
Number	1,083	770	529
Capacity (gallons)	52,427,181	(1)	(1)

[1] Figures not available.

TABLE 69.—PETROLEUM REFINING: 1919, 1914, AND 1909—Continued.

	1919	1914	1909
EQUIPMENT—continued.			
Chilling houses for paraffin:			
Number	105	76	79
Capacity (gallons)	4,712,000	(1)	(1)
Filter houses:			
Number	357	(1)	(1)
Capacity (gallons)	11,381,452	(1)	(1)
Hydraulic or other presses:			
Number	645	459	357
Capacity (gallons)	6,258,924	(1)	(1)
Storage tanks for:			
Crude petroleum—			
Number	2,183	1,014	678
Capacity (gallons)	1,511,889,000	580,202,000	242,591,000
Refined petroleum products—			
Number	11,380	6,967	6,476
Capacity (gallons)	2,152,820,000	1,042,836,000	1,041,627,000
Fuel oil—			
Number	1,822	807	
Capacity (gallons)	1,069,813,000	343,132,000	
Other—			
Number	5,546	4,111	(1)
Capacity (gallons)	655,346,000	646,608,000	(1)

CRUDE PETROLEUM—PRODUCTION AND REFINERY CONSUMPTION, BY FIELDS.

	1919		1914	
FIELD.	U. S. production.	Refinery consumption.	U. S. production.	Refinery consumption.
Total barrels (42 gallons)	377,719,000	326,928,292	265,762,535	185,027,479
California	101,564,000	74,200,751	99,775,327	41,901,651
Mid-Continent	196,891,000	181,039,564	97,995,400	92,462,637
Pennsylvania grade (Appalachian)	29,232,000	29,828,701	24,101,048	21,196,964
Illinois	12,436,000	10,888,115	21,919,749	17,672,279
Gulf	20,568,000	16,396,712	13,117,528	5,787,313
Lima-Indiana	3,444,000	1,737,865	5,062,543	2,564,742
Other fields—Colorado, Wyoming, etc	13,584,000	12,836,584	3,790,940	3,441,893

[1] Figures not available.

TABLE 70.—SOAP: 1919, 1914, AND 1909.

	1919	1914	1909
Number of establishments	439	513	526
The soap industry	348	371	420
Establishments manufacturing subsidiary soap products.	91	142	106
MATERIALS.[1]			
Total cost	$238,518,858	$88,866,786	$72,179,418
Animal fats, tallow, grease, etc.:			
Pounds	406,411,643		
Cost	$54,985,298		
Red oil (commercial oleic acid):			
Gallons	3,227,386	[2] 546,289,571	[2] 413,969,787
Cost	$2,598,366	$32,565,899	$23,341,905
Other, including fish oil, fatty acids, etc.:			
Gallons	4,087,087		
Cost	$3,059,407		
Vegetable oils:			
Cocoanut oil—			
Gallons	24,349,831		
Cost	$28,217,738		
Palm-kernel oil—		13,225,330	11,856,337
Gallons	606,807	$9,406,583	$5,875,294
Cost	$691,962		
Cottonseed oil—			
Gallons	7,483,977	15,903,691	24,221,712
Cost	$8,274,155	$6,700,688	$9,718,988
Other vegetable oils:			
Gallons	[3] 11,320,861		
Cost	$13,293,975	[4] 123,032,886	[4] 94,050,892
Soap stock:		$6,456,784	$2,453,609
Pounds	112,353,679		
Cost	$5,773,182		
Rosin:			
Pounds	119,529,661	185,310,786	207,296,447
Cost	$7,836,738	$4,067,992	$4,362,412
Caustic soda:			
Tons (2,000 pounds)	80,279	55,320	52,172
Cost	$5,700,421	$1,936,575	$2,212,232
Soda ash:			
Tons	92,219	140,983	121,016
Cost	$3,390,866	$1,997,575	$2,281,787
All other materials, cost	[5] $104,696,750	$25,734,690	$21,933,191
Produced in works where consumed.[1]			
Red oil, gallons	1,552,179	3,653,557	3,128,736
Tallow, pounds	67,113,763	5,331,000	16,664,000
Cottonseed oil, gallons	23,800	241,095	2,390,098
Caustic lye, gallons	28,552,086	22,777,000	15,804,000
Sodium silicate, pounds	98,603,158	43,197,255	37,466,246
Glycerine, pounds	40,472,470	2,156,591	5,879,279
Framed soap, pounds	834,198,448	618,096,000	524,775,000

[1] Not including those consumed in soap manufacture in establishments making subsidiary soap products.
[2] Reported in pounds as "tallow, grease, and other fats."
[3] Includes other vegetable oils as follows:

KIND.	Gallons.	Cost.	KIND.	Gallons.	Cost.
Castor	362,746	$463,745	Palm	2,302,463	$2,415,798
Corn	298,118	341,087	Peanut	407,359	506,490
Linseed	38,785	55,962	Soya-bean	7,786,746	8,082,380
Olive	124,644	264,896	Other vegetable oils		1,163,617

[4] Reported in pounds as "foots."
[5] Includes other materials as follows:

KIND.	Quantity.	Cost.	KIND.	Quantity.	Cost.
Hydrogenated oils, pounds	17,316,625	$1,765,895	Borax, tons	930	$129,470
Sodium silicate (ton, 2,000 lbs.)	106,087	2,041,784	Talc, etc, tons	42,708	677,215
Caustic potash, tons	1,543	605,505	Other constituent materials		564,963

TABLE **70.**—SOAP: 1919, 1914, AND 1909—Continued.

PRODUCTS.	1919	1914	1909
Total value	$337,879,913	$135,304,499	$115,455,190
Soap industry (all products)	$316,740,115	$127,942,441	$111,357,777
Subsidiary soap products from other industries	$21,139,798	$7,362,058	$4,097,413
Hard soaps:			
Quantity, pounds	2,308,612,000	2,064,228,000	1,794,249,000
Tallow, foots, and olein soaps	1,072,390,000	1,092,034,000	1,051,549,000
Toilet soap	179,350,000	169,926,000	111,571,000
Dye soap	2,455,000	(1)	(1)
Powdered soap, sold as such	472,610,000	367,744,000	301,176,000
Soap chips	181,837,000	97,746,000	} 329,953,000
All other hard soaps	399,970,000	336,778,000	
Value	$227,415,154	$104,464,542	$91,064,466
Soft soap:			
Pounds	64,463,000	57,002,000	60,037,000
Value	$3,925,060	$1,697,424	$1,269,187
Liquid soap:			
Pounds	10,033,000	(1)	(1)
Value	$1,255,213	(1)	(1)
Special soap articles:			
Pounds	30,227,719	(1)	(1)
Value	$3,204,249	$832,654	$706,177
Lye:			
Pounds	16,301,000	23,346,000	
Value	$1,789,291	$891,265	
Glycerine: [2]			
Crude, for sale—			
Pounds	18,228,447	12,745,336	
Value	$2,482,779	$1,817,536	
Refined, pounds	49,498,627	34,831,082	
For sale—			} $6,790,282
Pounds	47,377,151	32,674,491	
Value	$11,461,213	$5,775,887	
Produced and consumed, pounds	2,121,476	2,156,591	5,879,279
Stearin:			
Pounds	3,139,683		
Value	$825,402		
Candle pitch, tar or stearin pitch:			
Pounds	5,211,377		
Value	$91,336		
Red oil (commercial oleic acid):		(1)	
Produced	1,985,386		
For sale—			
Gallons	433,207		
Value	$476,146		
Made and consumed, gallons	1,552,179		
Candles:			} $15,625,078
Pounds	5,483,173	(1)	
Value	$818,676	$150,492	
Glue:			
Pounds	35,448		
Value	$2,929		
Tankage:		(1)	
Tons	14,356		
Value	$492,083		
Perfumes and toilet preparations	$12,635,206	$6,804,508	
All other products	[3] $71,005,176	$12,870,191	

[1] Figures not available.

[2] Total production of refined glycerine, all industries, in 1919—69,464,298 pounds (includes 2,121,476 pounds made and consumed): Crude glycerine made for sale, 21,402,735 pounds. See report on "Chemicals."

[3] Includes food products—lard substitutes, edible oils, etc., cottonseed products, and hardened oil—to the value of $55,705,711; patent medicines and compounds, $2,014,378; cleansing and polishing preparations, $354,521, and other miscellaneous products, $12,930,566.

TABLE 71.—BRICK, TILE, POTTERY, AND OTHER CLAY PRODUCTS: 1919, 1914, 1909 AND 1904.

PRODUCT.	1919	1914	1909	1904
Total value	$285,005,158	$179,964,016	$169,532,756	$135,652,306
Brick and tile, terra-cotta, and fire-clay products industry	208,422,920	135,921,445	168,895,365	135,352,854
Pottery industry	74,919,186	36,942,606		
Sand-lime brick industry	1,663,052	994,199		
Subsidiary products from other industries	(1)	6,105,766	637,391	299,452
Brick and tile, terra-cotta, and fire-clay products, value[2]	$210,108,677	$130,641,360	$136,387,846	$109,003,306
Brick, value	$142,793,359	$84,239,587	$97,137,844	$78,728,083
Common—				
Thousands	4,751,881	7,145,809	9,787,671	8,683,897
Value	$63,584,748	$43,763,554	$57,216,789	$51,239,871
Fire—				
Thousands	963,439	816,784	838,167	678,362
Value	$38,015,792	$16,427,547	$16,620,695	$11,752,625
Vitrified—				
Thousands	489,242	931,324	1,023,654	715,559
Value	$11,615,144	$12,500,866	$11,269,586	$7,256,088
For paving—				
Thousands	392,526	(1)	(1)	(1)
Value	$9,371,763			
Other purposes—				
Thousands	96,716			
Value	$2,243,381			
Silica brick—				
Thousands	211,420	(1)	(1)	(1)
Value	$10,914,898			
Face—				
Thousands	791,068	810,395	816,164	626,142
Value	$16,033,059	$9,289,623	$9,712,219	$7,335,511
Fancy or ornamental	$77,879	$124,459	$174,073	
Sand lime—				
Thousands	146,947	172,629	(1)	(1)
Value	$1,705,163	$1,058,512	$1,150,580	$698,003
Enameled	$846,676	$1,075,026	$993,902	$445,985
Draintile—				
Tons	1,241,168	(1)	(1)	(1)
Value	$10,945,943	$8,522,039	$9,798,978	$5,522,198
Sewer pipe—				
Tons	1,155,131	(1)	(1)	(1)
Value	$16,754,832	$14,014,767	$10,322,324	$8,416,009
Architectural terra-cotta	$3,988,182	$6,087,652	$6,251,625	$3,792,763
Fireproofing, terra-cotta lumber, and hollow building tile or blocks	$17,964,573	$8,385,337	$4,466,708	$4,317,312
Tile (not drain)—				
Value	$8,137,452	$5,705,583	$5,291,963	$2,725,717
Roofing—				
Square feet	9,414,800	(1)	(1)	(1)
Value	$1,283,901			
Floor—				
Square feet	7,790,967			
Value	$1,535,287			
Ceramic—				
Square feet	7,471,767			
Value	$1,824,372			
Faience—				
Square feet	1,550,121			
Value	$881,241			
Wall—				
Square feet	7,495,618			
Value	$2,612,651			
Stove lining	$683,844	$520,585	$423,583	(1)
Other brick and tile products	$8,840,492	$3,165,810	$2,694,821	$5,501,224

1 Figures not available.

2 The total value of products as reported by the Geological Survey for brick and tile, terra-cotta and fire-clay products, and for pottery are not comparable with the value of products for the industry as reported by the census, for the latter includes all products of the establishments, irrespective of their character, and the former includes production by establishments primarily engaged in other lines of manufacture.

TABLE 71.—BRICK, TILE, POTTERY, AND OTHER CLAY PRODUCTS: 1919, 1914, 1909, AND 1904—Continued.

PRODUCT.	1919	1914	1909	1904
Pottery, value[1]	$75,742,125	$35,398,161	$31,048,341	$25,834,513
White ware, including C. C. ware, white granite, semiporcelain ware, and semivitreous porcelain ware	29,847,261	14,968,079	13,728,316	9,195,703
Sanitary ware	14,872,364	7,874,269	5,989,295	3,932,506
Stoneware and yellow and Rockingham ware	4,603,018	3,349,301	3,993,859	3,481,521
Porcelain electrical supplies	12,614,794	4,130,270	3,047,499	1,500,283
China, bone china, delft, and belleek ware	7,708,832	2,384,686	1,766,766	3,478,627
Red earthenware	1,298,311	1,059,904	804,806	821,695
Chemical stoneware	805,321	(2)	(2)	(2)
Red and brown white-lined cooking ware	723,981	(2)	(2)	(2)
Other pottery products	[3]3,268,243	1,631,652	1,717,800	3,424,178

[1] The total value of products as reported by the Geological Survey for brick and tile, terra-cotta and fire-clay products and for pottery are not comparable with the value of products for the industry as reported by the census, for the latter includes all products of the establishments, irrespective of their character, and the former includes production by establishments primarily engaged in other lines of manufacture.
[2] Figures not available.
[3] Not including saggers, made and used, to the amount of $2,115,637.

TABLE 72.—CEMENT PRODUCTS: 1919, 1914, 1909, AND 1904.

	1919	1914	1909	1904
Total value of products	$175,264,910	$101,850,480	$63,274,715	[1] $29,873,122
The cement industry	$175,264,910	$101,756,444	$63,205,455	$29,873,122
Subsidiary cement products from other industries		$94,036	$69,260	(2)
Cement:				
Barrels	81,306,524	89,049,766	66,689,715	31,675,257
Value	$138,713,823	$82,204,096	$53,610,563	$26,031,920
Portland cement—				
Barrels	80,777,935	88,230,170	64,991,431	26,505,881
Value	$138,130,269	$81,789,368	$52,858,354	$23,355,119
Natural and puzzolan cement—				
Barrels	528,589	[3] 819,596	[3] 1,698,284	[3] 5,169,376
Value	$583,554	$414,728	$752,209	$2,676,801
All other products, value	$36,551,087	$19,646,384	$9,664,152	$3,841,202

[1] Figures for subsidiary cement products from other industries not included.
[2] Figures not available.
[3] Includes for 1914, 751,285 barrels of natural and 68,311 barrels of puzzolan; for 1909, 1,537,638 barrels of natural and 160,646 of puzzolan; and for 1904, 4,866,331 barrels of natural and 303,045 barrels of puzzolan.

TABLE 73.—GLASS PRODUCTS: 1919, 1914, 1909, AND 1904.

	1919	1914	1909	1904
Products, total value [1]	$261,884,080	$123,085,019	$92,095,203	$79,607,998
Building glass, value	$83,713,115	$36,824,069	$26,308,438	$21,697,861
Window glass—				
Square feet	368,912,209	400,998,893	346,080,550	242,615,750
Value	$41,100,724	$17,495,956	$11,742,959	$11,610,851
Obscured glass, including cathedral and skylight—				
Square feet	33,822,302	43,040,079	22,815,946	21,870,634
Value	$4,300,308	$2,417,253	$1,358,574	$972,014
Plate glass, total cast, square feet	72,849,340	75,770,261	60,105,694	34,804,986
Polished—				
Square feet	56,823,749	60,383,516	47,370,254	27,293,138
Value	$33,348,279	$14,773,787	$12,204,875	$7,978,253
Rough, made for sale as such—				
Square feet	788,742	131,492	205,690	17,784
Value	$171,118	$25,859	$37,431	$3,529
Wire glass—				
Polished—				
Square feet	1,229,077	1,707,848	(2)	(2)
Value	$635,543	$534,322	(2)	(2)
Rough, made for sale as such—				
Square feet	14,462,409	13,980,996	(2)	(2)
Value	$2,271,099	$1,056,612	(2)	(2)
All other building glass, value	$1,886,044	$520,280	$964,599	$1,133,214
Pressed and blown glass, value	$70,748,861	$30,279,290	$27,398,445	$21,956,158
Tableware, 100 pieces	2,457,938	1,554,056	1,286,056	1,283,974
Jellies, tumblers, and goblets, dozens	25,182,133	18,030,243	11,687,036	7,346,214
Lamps, dozens	917,250	580,196	322,482	487,017
Chimneys, dozens	6,615,109	6,989,624	6,652,967	7,039,756
Lantern globes, dozens	1,985,741	1,363,562	952,620	1,765,247
Shades, globes, and other gas goods, dozens	12,313,307	2,016,800	1,541,449	878,244
Blown tumblers, stem ware, and bar goods, dozens	9,668,638	11,377,310	9,182,060	6,282,606
Opal ware, dozens	2,155,972	4,636,051	3,095,666	1,091,208
Cut ware, dozens	549,170	297,957	206,336	83,736
Decorated glassware, dozens	1,052,851	1,158,077	(2)	(2)
Lenses, dozens	725,675	(2)	(2)	(2)
Electric bulbs, dozens	18,363,603	(2)	(2)	(2)
Tubing, pounds	18,147,470	(2)	(2)	(2)
Bottles and jars, value	$94,670,389	$51,958,728	$36,018,333	$33,631,063
Prescriptions, vials, and druggists' wares, gross	6,684,548	4,893,416	3,624,022	3,202,586
Beer, soda, and mineral, gross	4,178,368	4,573,610	2,345,204	2,351,852
Liquors and flasks, gross	993,030	2,689,022	1,887,344	2,157,801
Milk jars, gross	877,268	1,188,891	440,302	253,651
Fruit jars, gross	1,860,262	1,198,952	1,124,485	1,061,829
Battery jars and other electrical goods, gross	13,805	79,211	9,981	19,974
Patent and proprietary, gross	3,364,679	1,384,689	1,637,798	1,657,372
Packers and preservers, gross	4,297,076	3,271,174	1,237,175	1,237,065
Demijohns and carboys, dozens	271,119	160,796	122,570	64,450
All other products, value	$12,751,715	$4,022,932	$2,369,987	$2,322,916

[1] In addition, considerable quantities of electrical shades, globes, and bulbs, which can not be shown without disclosing the operations of individual establishments, were made in 1919 and 1914 by establishments engaged primarily in the manufacture of electrical goods. In 1909, 42,639 gross of bottles and jars, valued at $90,490, and in 1904 glassware, valued at $9,663, were made as subsidiary products by establishments engaged primarily in other lines of manufacture.
[2] Not reported separately.

TABLE 74.—AUTOMOBILES: 1919, 1914, AND 1909.

PRODUCT.	1919		1914		1909	
	Number.	Value.	Number.	Value.	Number.	Value.
Total value...............	....	¹$2,387,903,287	....	¹$503,230,137	....	¹$193,823,108
Automobiles....................	1,678,926	1,546,961,696	568,781	458,760,916	126,593	164,269,324
Gasoline and steam.............	1,675,892	1,540,737,812	564,112	448,712,320	122,767	157,009,894
Electric......................	3,034	6,223,884	4,669	10,048,596	3,826	7,259,430
Passenger vehicles (pleasure, family, and public conveyances)..........	1,555,226	1,321,137,868	543,881	414,541,820	123,296	158,935,641
Open—						
Roadsters..................	5,360	58,032,374	} 81,597	} 45,890,476	40,786	30,421,729
Runabouts..................	120,098	80,523,340				
Touring....................	1,224,347	977,410,998	451,032	345,972,679	76,114	113,403,188
Closed (limousines, cabs, etc.)..	156,328	200,015,254	11,098	22,349,767	5,205	12,729,304
All other (omnibuses, sightseeing wagons, etc.)...........	3,093	5,155,902	154	328,898	1,191	2,381,420
Government, municipal, etc. (ambulances, fire department vehicles, and patrol wagons)...............	2,786	13,619,331	728	3,941,249	42	103,660
Business vehicles (merchandise).....	120,914	212,204,497	24,172	40,277,847	3,255	5,230.023
Delivery wagons................	18,122	16,570,473	4,391	4,749,889	1,862	1,918,856
Trucks........................	101,837	193,350,933	19,519	34,741,097	1,366	3,165,512
All other......................	955	2,283,091	262	786,861	27	145,655
All other products..................	....	840,941,591	....	44,469,221	....	29,553,784

¹ In addition, 4,990 automobiles, valued at $7,919,800 in 1919; 4,258 automobiles, valued at $6,296,558 in 1914; and 694 automobiles, valued at $830,080, in 1909; were reported by establishments engaged primarily in other industries.

TABLE 75.—MOTORCYCLES, BICYCLES, AND PARTS: 1919, 1914, 1909, AND 1904.

PRODUCT.	1919	1914	1909	1904
Total value¹...........................	$53,105,895	$22,234,262	$10,698,567	$5,153,240
Motorcycles:				
Number.....................................	59,214	62,154	18,628	2,300
Value.......................................	$16,176,055	$12,161,775	$3,015,988	$354,980
Bicycles:				
Number.....................................	470,675	299,029	168,824	225,309
Value.......................................	$12,277,341	$3,757,318	$2,436,996	$3,203,505
Motorcycle parts, including side and delivery cars	$11,423,592	} $6,315,169	$5,245,583	$1,594,755
Bicycle parts................................	$4,974,668			
All other products, including repairs...........	$8,254,239			

¹ In addition, the following products were made by establishments engaged primarily in the manufacture of products other than those covered by this industry: In 1919, 8,488 bicycles, and other products, including parts, etc., valued at $2,205,748; in 1914, 639 motorcycles, valued at $144,672; 99,870 bicycles, valued at $1,603,912; and other products including parts, etc., valued at $2,089,329; in 1909, 64,883 bicycles, valued at $791,193; and other products, including parts, etc., valued at $579,927; in 1904, 25,178 bicycles, valued at $537,418; 28 motorcycles, valued at $4,200; and other products, including parts, etc., valued at $34,341.

TABLE 76.—CARRIAGES AND WAGONS, INCLUDING REPAIRS: 1919, 1914, 1909, AND 1904.

PRODUCT.	1919	1914	1909	1904
Total value [1]	$91,463,225	$106,697,437	$125,366,912	$125,332,976
Complete vehicles of all classes:				
Number	610,492	1,126,026	1,519,782	1,711,529
Value	$57,969,491	$69,899,107	$91,263,264	$97,190,693
Carriages (family and pleasure):				
Number	13,704	538,071	828,411	937,409
Value	$1,562,023	$33,329,879	$47,756,118	$55,750,276
Buggies and light pleasure vehicles:				
Number	202,105	[2]	[2]	[2]
Value	$18,114,423	[2]	[2]	[2]
Wagons:				
Number	356,837	533,601	587,685	643,755
Value	$35,183,807	$34,506,942	$39,932,910	$37,195,230
Business—				
Number	51,018	139,621	154,631	133,422
Value	$6,919,695	$13,022,860	$16,440,816	[2]
Light and package commodity, number	18,132	81,393	107,190	71,733
Heavy and bulk commodity, number	19,044	31,458	32,780	31,956
Pushcarts, number	11,593	14,937	7,330	6,089
Hearses, number	301	402	807	642
Street sprinklers, number	38	197	1,053	157
Other business wagons, number	1,910	11,234	5,471	22,845
Farm (including carts and trucks)—				
Number	303,231	384,663	429,952	505,025
Value	$27,567,838	$19,708,423	$22,615,875	[2]
Government, municipal, etc.—				
Number	2,588	9,317	3,102	5,308
Value	$696,274	$1,775,659	$876,219	[2]
Ambulances, number	1,568	346	598	245
Mail and mail carriers' wagons and carts, number	1,007	5,549	1,912	4,703
Patrol wagons (fire and police), hose wagons, and prison vans ,number	13	3,422	592	360
Public conveyances:				
Number	194	1,221	2,243	2,711
Value	$76,957	$279,656	$939,267	$1,314,952
Sleighs and sleds:				
Number	35,993	52,010	100,899	127,455
Value	$1,237,122	$1,207,705	$2,065,850	$2,694,560
Automobiles:[3]				
Number	1,659	1,123	544	199
Value	$1,795,159	$574,925	$569,119	$235,675
All other products, including parts and amount received for repair work, value	$33,493,734	$36,798,330	$34,103,648	$28,142,283

[1] In addition, in 1919, 29,057 carriages, valued at $3,005,725; 69,665 wagons, valued at $7,229,026; 83 public conveyances, valued at $28,495; 469 sleighs and sleds, valued at $31,076; and parts and repair work valued at $811,360 were made by establishments engaged primarily in the manufacture of products other than those covered by the industry designation. In 1914, this class of establishments made 12,330 carriages, valued at $863,489; 38,808 wagons, valued at $2,026,210; 63 public conveyances, valued at $45,508; 1,311 sleighs and sleds, valued at $24,309; and parts and repair work valued at $1,533,099. In 1909, this class of establishments made 14,908 carriages, valued at $1,078,935; 42,112 wagons, valued at $2,093,288; 104 public conveyances, valued at $5,615; 8,209 sleighs and sleds, valued at $165,917; and parts valued at $1,184,256, and in 1904 such establishments made carriages and wagons, valued at $612,173.

[2] Not reported separately.

[3] Manufactured in establishments devoted primarily to the manufacture of carriages and wagons.

TABLE 77.—CARS, STEAM AND ELECTRIC RAILROAD: 1919, 1914, 1909, AND 1904.

[Not including operations of railroad companies.]

PRODUCT.	1919	1914	1909	1904
Total value [1]	$556,664,807	$205,270,622	$131,539,493	$122,019,506
Steam-railroad cars:				
Number	153,288	120,101	74,945	102,782
Value	$373,945,213	$140,229,617	$75,633,245	$87,348,911
Passenger service [2]—				
Number	234	3,445	1,601	2,030
Value	$4,854,768	$44,011,882	$13,829,607	$18,140,293
Passenger—				
Number	78	1,653	957	428
Value	$1,285,630	$19,607,416	$7,209,425	$2,955,517
Baggage and express, chair, dining and buffet, parlor, sleeping, mail, and all other—				
Number	156	1,792	644	1,602
Value	$3,569,138	$24,404,466	$6,620,182	$15,184,776
Freight service—				
Number	153,054	116,656	73,344	100,752
Value	$369,090,445	$96,217,735	$61,803,638	$69,208,618
Box—				
Number	59,689	50,481	29,728	38,184
Value	$160,903,210	$40,952,538	$23,982,446	$28,508,632
Flat—				
Number	4,029	4,781	3,232	5,412
Value	$7,592,168	$3,120,084	$2,033,801	$2,893,154
Gondolas—				
Number	54,840	25,077	19,607	9,518
Value	$118,853,843	$22,808,750	$18,128,186	$5,518,084
Hopper [3]—				
Number	16,670	9,754	11,473	27,998
Value	$45,757,395	$10,708,407	$9,419,655	$21,367,218
Refrigerator [4]—				
Number	629	5,800	2,618	3,353
Value	$1,237,557	$8,077,062	$2,747,957	$3,042,835
Stock—				
Number	410	3,929	2,349	4,235
Value	$960,018	$2,587,065	$1,586,008	$2,453,123
Tank—				
Number	11,592	1,250		
Value	$26,540,682	$1,255,167		
Other varieties [5]—				
Number	5,195	15,584	4,337	12,052
Value	$7,245,572	$6,708,662	$3,905,585	$5,425,572
Electric-railroad cars:				
Number	1,898	2,542	2,525	4,384
Value	$13,502,653	$8,789,546	$6,626,357	$9,297,166
Passenger—				
Number	1,726	2,335	2,345	4,008
Value	$11,495,791	$8,075,710	$6,249,415	$8,809,261
Other varieties—				
Number	172	207	180	376
Value	$2,006,862	$713,836	$376,942	$487,905
All other products, value	$169,216,941	$56,251,459	$49,279,891	$25,373,429

[1] In addition 5,814 steam-railroad cars, valued at $14,809,729; 154 electric-railroad cars, valued at $779,947, and parts and repairs, valued at $3,290,165, were reported in 1919; 14,859 steam-railroad cars, valued at $14,566,898; 321 electric-railroad cars, valued at $1,373,604, and parts and repairs, valued at $980,074 were reported in 1914; and 23,526 steam-railroad cars, valued at $19,251,042; 247 electric-railroad cars, valued at $636,752, and parts and repairs, valued at $210,487 were reported in 1909, by establishments engaged primarily in other industries.

[2] Includes gasoline motor cars for use as passenger cars by steam railroads for 1914 and 1909.

[3] Reported as coal and coke cars in 1909 and 1904.

[4] Includes fruit cars for 1919.

[5] Includes 2,391 logging, mining, industrial, and dump cars, valued at $2,916,806 in 1919, and 9,737 cars of the same classes, valued at $1,825,693 in 1914, and 167 cars in 1914 and 136 cars in 1909 whose type was not specifically designated.

TABLE 78.— STEAM-RAILROAD REPAIR SHOPS: 1919, 1914, 1909, and 1904.

	1919	1914	1909	1904
Total value..........................	$1,279,235,393	$514,041,225	$405,600,727	$309,775,089
Motive power and machinery department, value...............................	$622,480,393	$236,723,724	$184,971,870	$149,643,953
Locomotives built—				
Number...........................	106	187	215	148
Value.............................	$5,825,096	$3,594,003	$3,289,140	$1,853,939
Repairs to locomotives, motors, etc......	$463,952,871	$169,057,932	$127,928,773	$101,326,805
Work for other corporations.............	$16,889,147	$7,053,430	$4,735,004	$5,681,307
All other products or work.............	$135,813,279	$57,018,359	$49,018,953	$40,781,902
Car department, value......................	$573,709,875	$242,976,774	$199,768,939	$149,748,820
Cars built, value.........................	$5,133,115	$11,999,983	$13,326,171	$12,990,011
Passenger—				
Number...........................	20	123	218	414
Value.............................	$191,691	$1,233,302	$1,291,354	$2,337,977
Freight—				
Number...........................	2,394	10,314	13,972	14,742
Value.............................	$4,590,482	$10,513,676	$11,767,664	$10,006,642
Other—				
Number...........................	271	308	359	2,000
Value.............................	$350,942	$253,005	$267,153	$645,392
Repairs to cars of all kinds, value	$479,229,076	$183,753,538	$147,194,065	$105,319,032
Work for other corporations, value	$31,101,248	$14,819,984	$8,784,239	$6,946,990
All other products or work, value	$58,246,436	$32,403,269	$30,464,464	$24,492,787
Bridge and building department (shopwork), value......................................	$8,535,303	$3,127,644	$2,799,898	$5,096,141
Repairs and renewals....................	$7,288,373	$2,449,821	$1,906,737	$4,351,487
Work for other corporations.............	$22,804	$37,061	$46,496	$40,581
All other products or work.............	$1,224,126	$640,762	$846,665	$704,073
All other products and work not classified, value...................................	$74,509,822	$31,213,083	$18,060,020	$5,286,175

TABLE 79.—ELECTRIC-RAILROAD REPAIR SHOPS: 1919, 1914, 1909, and 1904.

	1919	1914	1909	1904
Total value..........................	$75,210,701	$38,576,565	$31,962,561	$13,437,121
Motive power and machinery department, value.	$7,926,303	$5,380,573	$4,510,332	$510,946
Repairs to motors, etc........................	$7,081,735	$4,933,436	$4,004,336	....
Work for other corporations...................	$75,182	$56,944	$88,070	$2,626
All other products or work...................	[1] $769,386	[2] $390,193	[3] $417,926	$508,320
Car department, value........................	$64,237,805	$31,086,043	$25,835,463	$12,581,365
Cars built, value.............................	$762,293	$811,104	$626,752	$605,144
Passenger—				
Number...........................	88	235	129	288
Value.............................	$635,770	$737,926	$498,709	$580,669
Freight—				
Number...........................	46	11	63	13
Value.............................	$95,638	$21,196	$59,102	$11,366
Other—				
Number...........................	17	58	51	9
Value.............................	$30,885	$51,982	$68,941	$13,109
Repairs to cars of all kinds, value	$60,060,255	$27,628,802	$22,869,777	$11,254,505
Work for other corporations, value..........	$1,174,282	$441,323	$624,805	$36,714
All other products or work, value	$2,240,975	$2,204,814	$1,714,129	$685,002
Bridge and building department (shopwork), value..	$268,655	$434,427	$330,948	$327,855
Repairs and renewals.....................	$261,679	$199,751	$273,581	$253,133
All other products or work...................	$6,976	$234,676	$57,367	$74,722
All other products and work not classified, value.	$2,777,938	$1,675,522	$1,285,818	$16,955

[1] Includes the value of 2 electric locomotives.
[2] Includes the value of 1 locomotive.
[3] Includes the value of 3 electric locomotives.

TABLE 80.—PIANOS AND ORGANS: 1919, 1914, AND 1909.

PRODUCT.	1919	1914	1909
Total value [1]	$113,061,318	$69,072,383	$70,056,223
Pianos:			
Number	336,557	326,274	364,545
Value	$94,521,939	$56,311,863	$58,493,846
Upright—			
Without player attachment—			
Number	135,999	227,686	321,309
Value	$28,957,498	$31,431,382	$45,180,176
With player attachment—			
Number	174,729	88,078	34,495
Value	$52,515,928	$20,265,514	$9,275,001
Grand—			
Baby grand—			
Without player attachment—			
Number	17,900	9,679	8,720
Value	$8,619,054	$4,201,302	$4,009,769
With player attachment—			
Number	2,034	831	21
Value	$1,711,314	$413,665	$28,900
Parlor—			
Without player attachment—			
Number	2,172		
Value	$1,109,501		
With player attachment—			
Number	125		
Value	$119,378		
Concert—			
Number	87	(2)	(2)
Value	$54,055		
Automatic—			
Number	2,145		
Value	$896,346		
Electric—			
Number	1,366		
Value	$538,865		
Player attachments and actions made separately:			
Number	21,822	6,493	10,898
Value	$1,840,438	$854,774	$1,474,630
Organs:			
Number	28,301	42,806	65,335
Value	$6,620,616	$6,378,312	$5,309,016
Pipe—			
Number	1,151	2,273	1,224
Value	$4,185,535	$4,660,301	$2,713,587
Reed—			
Number	26,429	40,533	64,111
Value	$1,888,677	$1,718,011	$2,595,429
Orchestrions—			
Number	721		
Value	$546,494		
Perforated music rolls, value	$3,103,554	$833,357	$216,150
Parts, materials, and supplies	$1,432,797		
Pianos and organs, value	$1,258,303	$2,913,197	$2,442,611
Other musical instruments, value	$174,494		
Repairs, value	$1,252,156		
		$1,780,880	$2,119,970
All other products, value	$4,289,818		

[1] In addition, products to the value of $1,382,353 in 1919 and $754,148 in 1914 were reported by establishments engaged primarily in other industries.
[2] Not reported separately.

TABLE 81.—PHONOGRAPHS AND GRAPHOPHONES: 1919, 1914, 1909, AND 1904.

PRODUCT.	1919	1914	1909	1904
Total value [1]	$158,547,870	$27,115,916	$11,725,996	$10,237,075
Phonographs, graphophones, and talking machines: [2]				
For disc records—				
Number	2,137,596			
Value	$88,836,368			
For cylinder records—				
Number	65,957	514,154	344,681	(3)
Value	$1,315,886	$15,290,491	$5,406,684	$2,966,343
Dictating machines—				
Number	22,853			
Value	$1,416,689			
Records and blanks:				
Number	106,996,510	27,221,290	27,183,959	(3)
Value	$44,689,795	$11,111,418	$5,007,104	$4,678,547
Disc records—				
Number	101,084,961	23,314,176	8,572,805	(3)
Value	$42,930,923	$10,377,475	$2,567,717	
Cylinder records and blanks—				
Number	5,911,549	3,907,114	18,611,154	(3)
Value	$1,758,872	$733,943	$2,439,387	
Needles:				
Steel, value	$1,359,754	(4)	(4)	(4)
Other, value	$249,248			
Parts and accessories, not included in finished instruments reported:				
Cabinets, value	$3,653,418	(3)	(3)	(3)
Other parts and accessories, value	$10,515,739	$356,935	$844,631	(3)
Custom work and repairing, value	$268,803	$2,116	(5)	(5)
All other products, value	$6,242,170	$354,956	$467,577	$2,592,185

[1] In addition, in 1919, phonographs, graphophones, and parts, valued at $7,173,143, in 1914, valued at $66,531, and in 1909, valued at $31,899 were made by establishments engaged primarily in the manufacture of products other than those covered by this industry designation.
[2] Not segregated, to avoid disclosure of individual operations.
[3] Figures not available.
[4] Included in "parts and accessories."
[5] Included in "All other products."

TABLE 82.—AGRICULTURAL IMPLEMENTS: 1919, 1914, 1909, AND 1904.

	1919	1914	1909	1904
Products, total value [1]	$304,961,265	$164,086,835	$146,329,268	$112,007,344
Plows and cultivators	65,329,111	38,662,037	36,784,477	30,607,960
Planters and seeders	17,490,403	12,188,757	12,141,474	11,225,122
Harvesting implements:				
Hayrakes and hay tedders	4,772,493	3,233,630		
Mowers and reapers	40,169,591	30,974,709	34,568,131	30,862,435
Other	9,282,656	5,372,947		
Seed separators:				
Threshers	16,593,273	9,832,043	11,030,412	6,639,883
Other	5,771,670	3,264,246		
All other agricultural implements, including parts	64,105,527	27,844,180	48,690,082	30,703,648
All other products	68,500,033	31,277,021		
Amount received for repair work	12,946,508	1,437,265	3,114,692	1,968,296

Principal kinds of implements.

	Number.	Number.	Number.	Number.
Implements of cultivation:				
Cultivators—				
Beet	7,088	2,184	3,172	3,459
Hand, garden, or garden plows	419,085	238,081	469,696	239,173
One and two horse	300,122	254,158		
Wheeled—				
One row	144,259	347,329	435,429	313,088
Two rows	44,347	31,605		
Cotton scrapers	10,807	17,537	20,180	22,519
Fertilizing machines	82,554	180,854	(2)	(2)
Harrows—				
Disk	175,712	209,077	193,000	104,323
Spring-tooth	79,532	187,370	112,832	86,408
Spike-tooth	222,799	368,219	394,988	262,442
Land rollers	8,654	22,470	(2)	(2)
Land packers	19,501	(3)	(3)	(3)
Listers	31,680	37,953	44,840	23,012
Plows—				
Disk	15,431	15,708	22,132	39,146
Gang	42,240	75,839	91,686	(3)
Shovel	108,887	181,550	254,737	121,899
Engine	4,952	3,265	2,355	1,599
Sulky (single)	60,909	108,232	134,936	138,899
Tractor	98,836	(3)	(3)	(3)
Walking	720,174	870,414	1,110,006	956,898
Pulverizers	7,134	12,724	(2)	(2)
Other	29,295	80,096	(2)	(2)
Planters and seeders:				
Seeders—				
Broadcast	18,360	34,175	[4] 61,970	33,546
Wagon or endgate	16,391	16,122	(2)	(2)
Seeder attachments	34,339	10,000	(2)	(2)
Corn planters—				
Hand	28,065	101,850	96,465	86,553
Horse	93,976	114,657	122,780	90,929
Cotton planters	87,468	101,256	79,271	127,052
Potato planters	5,964	37,191	23,092	35,756
Drills—				
Corn	29,809	55,710	20,137	28,228
Grain	63,255	89,370	[5] 89,903	76,929
All other	5,870	10,688	32,507	606

[1] In addition to the amounts shown, agricultural implements to the value of $14,938,340 in 1919, $4,033,797 in 1914, $2,989,276 in 1909, and $1,349,679 in 1904 were made by establishments engaged primarily in the manufacture of products other than those covered by the industry designated.
[2] Not reported.
[3] Not reported separately.
[4] Includes 23,963 combination seeders.
[5] Includes 21,292 disk drills of all kinds.

TABLE 82.—AGRICULTURAL IMPLEMENTS: 1919, 1914, 1909, AND 1904—Continued.

	1919	1914	1909	1904
Principal kinds of implements—Continued.				
Planters and seeders—Continued.	*Number.*	*Number.*	*Number.*	*Number.*
Seed sowers, hand, field	86,763	12,608	7,847	59,910
Seed drills, hand, garden	8,971	43,113	(1)	(1)
Other planters and seeders	16,198	4,124	(1)	(1)
Harvesting implements:				
Binders—				
Grain	155,466	215,386	129,274	108,810
Corn	22,886	52,087	19,693	6,924
Grain cradles	58,239	38,728	22,635	30,056
Grain elevators for use on farm	5,995	(2)	(2)	(2)
Harvesters—				
Bean	9,528	3,401	1,409	665
Push	2,337	(2)	(2)	(2)
Harvesters and threshers combined	2,392	270	543	(2)
Other	22,887	2,758	1,707	3,161
Headers	4,187	(2)	(2)	(2)
Hay carriers	11,865	44,277	45,064	85,121
Hayforks, horse	6,323	31,976	43,675	62,801
Hay loaders	20,570	25,865	34,705	27,174
Hay rakes—				
Sulky	61,265	139,565		
Sweep	18,398	23,304	266,260	236,297
Side delivery	14,270	20,213		
Hay stackers	7,699	6,437	17,212	8,670
Hay tedders	10,282	9,796	34,396	35,745
Hay presses	7,154	(2)	(2)	(2)
Mowers	151,133	274,521	359,264	273,385
Other haying tools	130,052	37,706	(1)	(1)
Potato diggers, horse	12,484	25,758	25,632	11,703
Reapers	8,368	56,982	58,294	60,996
Stalk cutters	19,033	(2)	(2)	(2)
Other	1,096,087	13,746	(1)	(1)
Seed separators:				
Clover hullers	597	324	437	351
Corn huskers	1,194	341	318	1,327
Corn huskers and shredders	2,884	4,338	1,294	(1)
Corn pickers	3,078	(2)	(2)	(2)
Corn shellers—				
Hand	37,272	63,206	74,223	47,189
Power	8,486	11,113	9,049	6,082
Fanning mills	13,302	23,047	33,805	22,994
Feed mills	10,314	(2)	(2)	(2)
Threshers—				
Horsepower	3,766	302	822	2,237
Engine	16,162	13,246	12,957	7,950
Other	9,586	6,212	(1)	(1)
Miscellaneous:				
Dairy machinery—				
Cream separators	11,255			
Other	1,001			
Manure spreaders	80,891			
Equalizers	13,989			
Knife grinders	22,173			
Feed grinders	13,971	(2)	(2)	(2)
Ensilage cutters	18,013			
Saw trucks	328			
Pumps	21,172			
Windmills	419			
Spraying outfits	14,044			

¹ Not reported.   ² Not reported separately.

TABLE 83.—ELECTRICAL MACHINERY, APPARATUS, AND SUPPLIES: 1919, 1914, 1909, AND 1904.

	1919	1914	1909	1904
Products, total value	$1,063,526,297	$359,432,155	$240,037,479	$159,551,402
The electrical industry.—Electrical machinery, apparatus, and supplies	$997,968,119	$335,170,194	$221,308,563	$140,809,369
Subsidiary electrical products of other industries	65,558,178	24,261,961	18,728,916	18,742,033
Generating apparatus and parts, value	$86,266,114	$17,865,542	$14,077,071	$11,084,234
Generators (other than small dynamos under 10 kw.):				
Alternating current—				
Steam-turbine driven, under 2,000 kva.—				
Number	532			
Kilowatts	665,971			
Value	(1)	375		
Steam-turbine driven, 2,000 kva. or over—		600,185		
Number	144	$3,895,291	2,909	1,324
Kilowatts	1,236,827		991,728	355,832
Value	$8,262,802		$8,370,524	$4,111,104
Other, including water-wheel driven—				
Number	3,123	2,137		
Kilowatts	821,597	587,820		
Value	$4,403,290	$3,542,154		
Direct current—				
Steam-turbine driven—				
Number	2,262	264		
Kilowatts	408,866	14,916		
Value	$2,704,563	$398,379		
Other, including water-wheel driven—			13,882	13,756
Number	4,345	9,369	414,222	640,350
Kilowatts	485,266	206,305	$4,710,524	$6,975,130
Value	$3,937,080	$2,569,086		
Small dynamos (under 10 kw), starting motors, and automotive generators, not including control equipment, value	$36,662,797	$5,933,273		
Self-contained lighting outfits (as farm-lighting outfits)—				
Number	61,357	(2)	(2)	(2)
Value	$24,078,536	(2)	(2)	(2)
Parts and supplies, value	$6,217,046	$1,527,359	$996,023	(3)
Transformers and feeder potential regulators, total value	$53,495,570	$28,276,338	$14,630,715	$7,142,026
Transformers:				
Number	382,929	115,843	76,729	66,698
Kilowatts	14,484,179	2,644,794	1,635,429	728,181
Value	$25,560,901	$13,120,065	$8,801,019	$4,468,567
Under 50 kilowatts—				
Number	331,099	110,177	72,776	63,311
Value	$10,613,234	$7,316,615	$4,184,832	$3,292,207
50 to 500 kilowatts—				
Number	50,661	4,857	3,953	3,387
Value	$9,199,762	$2,625,414	$4,616,187	$1,176,360
500 kilowatts or over—				
Number	1,169	809		
Value	$5,747,905	$3,178,036		
Rheostats, resistances, controllers, motor starters, speed-controlling devices, reactances, regulators, etc., value	$23,083,265	$9,788,378	[4] $2,674,963	[4] $932,925
Converting apparatus—synchronous condensers, motor generator sets, double-current generators, dynamotors, frequency changers, and rotary-phase converters	$4,851,404	$5,367,895	$3,154,733	$1,740,534
Motors, parts, and supplies, total value	$116,893,638	$44,176,235	$32,087,482	$22,370,626
Stationary motors:				
Number	1,533,407	[5] 417,992	[5] 257,223	[5] 92,175
Horsepower	3,791,062	2,882,795	[5] 2,410,369	[5] 1,392,091
Value	$76,171,558	[5] $32,286,149	[5] $24,604,938	[5] $18,070,743
Direct current—				
Number	380,182	133,492		
Horsepower	734,691	980,820		
Value	$20,200,313	$13,316,489	257,223	92,175
Alternating current—			2,410,369	1,392,091
Under 200 horsepower—			$24,604,938	$18,070,743
Number	1,151,286	284,500		
Horsepower	2,559,526	1,901,975		
Value	$52,430,381	$18,969,660		
200 horsepower or over—				
Number	1,939			
Horsepower	496,845			
Value	$3,540,864			

1 Value included with that of generators of 2,000 kva. or over, to avoid disclosure of individual operations.
2 No segregation reported.
3 Figures not available.
4 Rheostats and resistances only.
5 Includes railway motors.

TABLE 83.—ELECTRICAL MACHINERY, APPARATUS, AND SUPPLIES: 1919, 1914, 1909, AND 1904—Continued.

	1919	1914	1909	1904
Motors, parts, and supplies—Continued.				
Marine motors:				
Number	2,630	(1)	(1)	(1)
Horsepower	8,428	(1)	(1)	(1)
Value	$816,371	(1)	(1)	(1)
For vehicles and railways:				
Number	49,256	[2] 11,880	[2] 2,796	[2] 1,819
Horsepower	351,286	[2] 36,858	[2] 12,471	[2] 19,907
Value	$6,355,102	[2] $1,351,442	[2] $294,152	[2] $152,685
For fans:				
Number	709,350	(3)	(3)	(3)
Horsepower	66,915	(3)	(3)	(3)
Value	$9,908,001	$4,835,850	$2,450,739	$1,168,254
For miscellaneous uses:				
Number	198,305	(3)	(3)	(3)
Horsepower	141,610	(3)	(3)	(3)
Value	$4,920,311	$1,190,564	$1,942,874	$2,978,944
Parts and supplies	$18,722,295	$4,512,230	$2,794,779	(1)
Electric locomotives, mining, industrial, and railway	$8,159,825	$3,720,914	(3)	(3)
Batteries, parts, and supplies, value	$92,463,195	$23,402,455	$10,612,470	$4,243,893
Storage	$60,036,152	$13,080,964	$4,678,209	$2,645,749
Value of batteries	$56,648,347	$10,615,150	$4,243,984	$1,569,371
Weight of plates, pounds	38,438,540	41,079,047	23,119,331	16,113,072
Value of parts and supplies	$3,387,805	$2,465,814	$434,225	$1,076,378
Primary	$32,427,043	$10,321,491	$5,934,261	$1,598,144
Dry—				
Number	79,300,082			
Value	$17,805,611	71,092,438	33,988,881	4,888,361
Dry, small, for flash lights—		$8,719,164	$4,583,082	$513,026
Number	94,483,894			
Value	$7,514,833			
Liquid, including testing—				
Number	2,050,946	306,351	344,650	1,734,801
Value	$3,508,624	$802,525	$729,513	$515,530
Value of parts and supplies	$3,597,975	$799,802	$621,666	$569,588
Carbons—furnace, lighting, and welding; brushes, battery and miscellaneous	$13,291,615	$3,602,741	$1,934,864	$2,710,935
Arc lamps	$606,771	$742,142	$1,706,959	$1,574,422
Searchlights, projectors, and focusing lamps	$4,342,246	$2,081,545	$935,874	$114,795
Incandescent lamps, value	$57,646,900	$17,350,385	$15,714,809	$6,953,205
Tungsten—				
Number	211,383,193	74,434,059	11,738,619	
Value	$46,628,343	$11,886,354	$6,241,133	112,711,558
Carbon filament—				$6,308,299
Number	13,330,273	14,092,055	55,038,378	
Value	$1,830,644	$1,397,572	$6,157,066	
Decorative and miniature lamps, X-ray bulbs, vacuum tubes, etc.	$5,892,211	$1,702,729	$600,619	$249,751
Gem and vacuum and vapor lamps	$2,512,435			
Other types	$783,267	$2,363,730	$2,715,991	[4] $395,155
Rectifying apparatus, including rotating commutators, electric valves, mercury rectifiers, and vibrating commutators	$1,964,876	$147,965	(3)	(3)
Telegraph apparatus	$12,816,341	$2,248,375	$1,957,432	$1,111,194
Intelligence (key, sounder, etc.), all kinds	$2,649,365	$201,956	$197,669	$187,744
Police, fire, district, and miscellaneous	$2,092,340	$1,253,954	$1,126,658	$592,070
Radio and wireless	$7,834,698	$672,575	$448,262	$114,050
Switchboards, parts, and supplies	$239,938	$119,890	$184,843	$217,330
Telephone apparatus	$46,214,342	$22,815,640	$14,259,357	$15,863,698
Central switchboards:				
Manual—				
Central battery—				
Number	1,330	(3)		
Value	$6,500,560	$10,701,764		
Magneto—				
Number	4,594	(3)		
Value	$1,344,404	$374,851		
Automatic, value	$4,327,516	$1,002,722		
Substation instruments:				
Central battery—			$10,137,534	$13,227,008
Number	642,093	641,082		
Value	$3,839,978	$3,916,869		
Magneto—				
Number	280,502	216,879		
Value	$3,276,604	$1,799,834		
Interior systems:				
Number	173,799	62,258		
Value	$1,578,778	$510,509		

[1] No segregation reported.
[2] Vehicle motors only.
[3] Figures not available.
[4] Includes vacuum and vapor, and glower lamps only.

TABLE 83.—ELECTRICAL MACHINERY, APPARATUS, AND SUPPLIES: 1919, 1914, 1909, AND 1904—Continued.

	1919	1914	1909	1904
Telephone apparatus—Continued.				
Private branch exchange switchboards—				
Number	6,880	3,693	2,252	3,917
Value	$2,287,122	$448,203	$369,915	$564,795
Parts and supplies, value	$23,059,380	$4,060,888	$3,751,908	$2,071,895
Household and industrial apparatus and devices	$54,793,195	$4,048,915	$1,954,112	$395,827
Welding apparatus (not including motor generator sets)	$2,701,378	$231,082	$83,505	(1)
Electric furnaces (for iron and steel and brass industries)	$1,040,337	(1)	(1)	(1)
Heaters (industrial heaters; air heaters, including those for cars; water heaters)	$2,889,734	$352,617	} $919,533	(1)
Stoves and ranges	$3,444,170	$671,413		
Miscellaneous cooking devices (griddles, grills, toasters, percolators, etc.)	$7,815,212	$1,327,183		
Flatirons	$5,646,421	$1,466,620	$951,074	(1)
Vacuum cleaners, vibrators, clippers, cutters, etc	$21,842,439	(1)	(1)	(1)
Other portable motor-driven devices (motor built in)	$6,985,809	(1)	(1)	(1)
Other stationary motor-driven apparatus (motor built in)	$2,427,695	(1)	(1)	(1)
Electric measuring instruments	$19,322,164	$8,786,506	$7,800,010	$5,004,763
Station meters and apparatus	$7,084,983	$1,585,500	$1,639,202	$418,998
Testing and scientific instruments	$3,336,172	$1,073,060	$546,970	$1,000,685
Meters for consumers' circuits	$8,901,009	$6,127,946	$5,613,838	$3,585,080
Magnetoignition apparatus, generators, spark plugs, and coils	$51,286,793	$22,260,847	$6,092,343	$678,077
Switchboards, panel boards, and cut-out cabinets for light and power	$17,735,780	$8,989,111	$5,971,804	$3,766,044
Railway switches, signals, and attachments	$4,466,611	[2] $6,393,551	[2] $5,377,843	[2] $1,451,337
Circuit breakers, oil	$2,733,535	(1)	(1)	(1)
Circuit breakers, air and carbon	$1,391,911	(1)	(1)	(1)
Fuses, cut-outs, and fuse plugs	$7,895,098	$1,757,430	$1,001,719	$868,079
Insulators	$6,504,147	(1)	(1)	(1)
Sockets, receptacles, bases, and attachment plugs	$15,008,365	$5,512,609	$4,521,729	$2,010,860
Wiring supplies (current carrier)	$6,857,819	(1)	(1)	(1)
Lightning arresters, choke coils, reactors, and other protective devices	$2,353,416	$1,188,773	$940,171	$587,124
Insulated wire	$67,578,732	} $69,505,573	$51,624,737	$34,519,699
Insulated cables, rubber insulation	$34,314,305			
Insulated cables, paper insulation	$26,789,302			
Pole-line hardware	$9,379,145	(1)	(1)	(1)
Circuit fittings, not elsewhere provided for	$5,052,994	$2,067,683	$1,080,287	$3,525,446
Underground conduits	$890,749	} $4,874,709	$5,098,264	$2,416,245
Interior conduits	$18,375,880			
Electric-lighting fixtures of all kinds [3]	$2,703,266	$3,383,955	$2,200,668	$3,294,606
Annunciators and push buttons	$709,941	$263,806	$235,567	$185,870
Electric clocks and time mechanisms	$1,797,909	$410,774	$352,513	$373,926
Bells, buzzers, and signal gongs	$3,616,281	(1)	(1)	(1)
Therapeutic apparatus, including X-ray tubes	$8,895,402	$2,653,098	$1,107,858	$1,036,962
All other electrical machinery, apparatus, and supplies	$95,232,300	$27,276,294	$18,995,176	} $26,267,509
All other products	$76,573,808	$17,951,652	} $17,765,645	
Amount received for custom work and repairing	$27,106,016	$5,676,592		

[1] Not reported separately.
[2] Reported as "electric switches, signals, and attachments."
[3] Not including fixtures made by establishments engaged primarily in the manufacture of "gas and electric fixtures."

TABLE 84.—ICE, MANUFACTURED: 1919, 1914, 1909, AND 1904.

	1919	1914	1909	1904
QUANTITY AND COST OF AMMONIA.				
Total cost	$2,658,658	$1,887,359	(1)	(1)
The ice industry	$2,410,100	$1,528,975	$1,021,913	$613,138
Other industries manufacturing ice as a subsidiary product	$248,558	$358,384	(1)	(1)
Anhydrous:				
Pounds	7,758,984	6,777,617	(1)	(1)
The ice industry	7,003,581	5,405,917	3,466,284	1,932,497
Other industries	755,403	1,371,700		
Used in—				
Compressor system	6,875,012	6,021,506	(1)	(1)
Absorption system	883,972	756,111		
Cost	$2,519,427	$1,777,095	(1)	(1)
The ice industry	$2,274,889	$1,421,196	$926,505	$522,275
Other industries	$244,538	$355,899	(1)	(1)
Aqua:				
Pounds	1,740,825	1,971,046	(1)	(1)
The ice industry	1,675,626	1,927,664	1,670,698	1,495,934
Other industries	65,199	43,382	(1)	(1)
Used in—				
Compressor system	94,102	(1)	(1)	(1)
Absorption system	1,646,723	1,971,046	(1)	(1)
Cost	$139,231	$110,264	(1)	(1)
The ice industry	$135,211	$107,779	$95,408	$90,863
Other industries	$4,020	$2,485	(1)	(1)
PRODUCTS.				
Total value	$149,515,630	$67,320,353	$47,202,845	$25,689,957
The ice industry	$137,004,798	$60,386,267	$42,953,055	$23,790,045
Subsidiary products from other industries	$12,510,832	$6,934,086	$4,249,790	$1,899,912
Ice:				
Tons (2,000 pounds)	27,948,463	21,043,063	14,230,208	8,014,137
The ice industry	25,292,846	18,324,691	12,647,949	7,199,448
Other industries	2,655,617	2,718,372	1,582,259	814,689
Value	$138,795,342	$62,192,413	$44,139,053	$24,350,415
The ice industry	$126,284,510	$55,258,327	$39,889,263	$22,450,503
Other industries	$12,510,832	$6,934,086	$4,249,790	$1,899,912
By kinds—				
Can ice—				
Tons	26,577,637	19,635,368	13,177,991	(1)
The ice industry	24,083,632	17,145,599	11,671,547	6,695,789
Other industries	2,494,005	2,489,769	1,506,444	(1)
Value	$133,082,307	$58,593,861	$41,123,901	(1)
The ice industry	$121,235,615	$52,150,488	$37,085,533	$21,020,547
Other industries	$11,846,692	$6,443,373	$4,038,368	(1)
Plate ice—				
Tons	1,370,826	1,407,695	1,052,217	(1)
The ice industry	1,209,214	1,179,092	976,402	503,659
Other industries	161,612	228,603	75,815	(1)
Value	$5,713,035	$3,598,552	$3,015,152	(1)
The ice industry	$5,048,895	$3,107,839	$2,803,730	$1,429,956
Other industries	$664,140	$490,713	$211,422	(1)
Cold storage receipts	$7,142,998	$5,127,940	$3,063,792	$1,339,542
All other products	$3,577,290			
EQUIPMENT.				
Machines:				
Number	5,323	4,949	(1)	(1)
Capacity, tons (per day of 24 hours)	269,179	129,998		
Storage space, cubic feet:				
For ice storage	115,313,000	100,574,000		
For cold storage	79,953,000	82,694,000		

[1] Figures not available.

TABLE 85.—RUBBER GOODS: 1919.

	Number and amount.		Number and amount.
Products, total value	[1] **$1,138,216,019**	Tires—Continued.	
		Solid—	
Boots, rubber:		Truck—	
Pairs	9,207,703	Number	1,454,807
Value	$26,066,647	Value	$43,917,152
Shoes, rubber:		All other—	
Pairs	66,145,541	Number	6,873,650
Value	$64,713,182	Value	$9,004,543
Shoes, canvas with rubber soles:		Rubberized fabrics, sold as such or on hand:	
Pairs	21,034,664	Automobile and carriage—	
Value	$25,176,684	Yards	40,750,500
Heels, sold as such and on hand:		Value	$10,696,547
Pairs	138,468,769	All other—	
Value	$16,103,501	Yards	47,162,085
Soles, including composition or fiber:		Value	$13,712,376
Pairs	9,777,085	Belting, value	$22,436,242
Value	$2,455,306	Hose, value	$26,998,292
Tires:		Packing, value	$7,316,819
Pneumatic—		Clothing, value	$8,824,430
Automobile—		Druggists' and stationers' sundries, value	$15,801,892
Casings—		Hard rubber goods, value	$34,383,231
Number	32,835,509	All other manufactures of rubber, value	$80,719,898
Value	$603,896,200	Reclaimed rubber, sold and on hand:	
Inner tubes—		Pounds	125,758,882
Number	33,255,410	Value	$20,173,040
Value	$81,312,576		
Motorcycle and bicycle—		All other products, value	$9,711,224
Casings—			
Number	4,656,121		
Value	$13,449,225		
Inner tubes—			
Number	1,125,097		
Value	$1,347,012		

[1] In addition, products to the value of $9,134,403 were reported by establishments assigned to other classifications.

TABLE 86.—NUMBER AND GROSS TONNAGE OF VESSELS LAUNCHED, AND NUMBER OF POWER BOATS: 1919, 1916, 1914, AND 1909.

CLASS.	ALL ESTABLISHMENTS.		PRIVATE ESTABLISHMENTS IN THE SHIPBUILDING INDUSTRY.		PRIVATE ESTABLISHMENTS IN OTHER INDUSTRIES.		GOVERNMENT SHIPYARDS.	
	Number.	Gross[1] tonnage.	Number.	Gross tonnage.	Number.	Gross tonnage.	Number.	Displacement tonnage.
Vessels of 5 gross tons and over:								
1919	2,202	4,662,433	2,033	4,489,809	64	51,970	105	120,654
1916	1,463	772,167	1,377	734,108			86	38,059
1914	1,255	455,567	1,113	425,060	94	13,654	48	16,853
1909	1,637	481,813	1,584	467,219	22	12,535	31	2,059
Classified by material:								
Steel—								
1919	[2]1,181	[2]3,882,894	[2]1,095	[2]3,734,201	59	47,194	27	101,499
1916	244	518,858	230	485,860			14	32,998
1914	215	268,870	126	242,959	69	9,792	20	16,119
1909	169	260,765	158	254,986	8	5,429	3	350
Wooden—								
1919	1,021	779,539	938	755,608	5	4,776	78	19,155
1916	1,219	253,309	1,147	248,248			72	5,061
1914	1,040	186,697	987	182,101	25	3,862	28	734
1909	1,468	221,048	1,426	212,233	14	7,106	28	1,709
Classified by power:								
Steam—								
1919	1,230	4,109,652	1,203	4,010,724			27	98,928
1916	206	472,597	186	442,354			20	30,243
1914	148	243,011	139	234,636			9	8,375
1909	194	235,315	181	234,633	3	429	10	253
Motor—								
1919	254	60,399	241	57,174			13	3,225
1916	434	30,316	403	29,866			31	450
1914	382	10,867	370	10,821	4	6	8	40
1909	447	9,413	445	9,389	2	24		
Sail, with auxiliary power—								
1919	28	19,242	27	17,754	1	1,488		
1916	62	30,625	62	30,625				
1914	66	6,575	58	2,799	8	3,776		
1909	68	2,652	68	2,652				
Sail, without auxiliary power—								
1919	58	64,579	57	63,091	1	1,488		
1916	62	15,456	62	15,456				
1914	40	2,224	40	2,224				
1909	51	14,807	51	14,807				
Unrigged—								
1919	632	408,561	505	341,066	62	48,994	65	18,501
1916	699	223,173	664	215,807			35	7,366
1914	619	192,890	506	174,580	82	9,872	31	8,438
1909	877	219,626	839	205,738	17	12,082	21	1,806
Power boats of less than 5 tons:								
1919	1,716		1,159		206		351	
1916	3,710		3,606				104	
1914	4,518		3,706		758		54	
1909	9,042		8,577		412		53	

[1] Includes a comparatively small amount of "displacement tonnage."
[2] Includes 14 concrete vessels, 18,034 gross tons.

Table **87.**—KIND AND VALUE OF SHIPBUILDING WORK: 1919, 1916, 1914, AND 1909.

KIND OF WORK.	All establish-ments.	Private establishments in the shipbuilding industry.	Private establish-ments in other industries.	Government shipyards.
Total:				
1919	$1,865,728,609	$1,622,361,261	$3,764,105	$239,603,243
1916	224,526,683	185,852,192	(1)	38,674,491
1914	119,423,028	88,682,071	1,523,692	29,217,265
1909	100,009,054	73,360,315	776,706	25,872,033
Work on new vessels and boats, all kinds:				
1919	1,446,789,596	1,391,688,655	3,317,305	51,783,636
1916	114,434,137	105,270,935	(1)	9,163,202
1914	52,401,805	46,334,134	1,279,630	4,788,041
1909	45,036,492	42,310,925	594,244	2,131,323
Vessels of 5 gross tons and over—				
1919	1,439,443,338	[2] 1,386,839,158	2,670,433	49,933,747
1916	110,343,073	101,531,210	(1)	8,811,863
1914	48,105,561	42,545,445	947,805	4,612,311
1909	40,145,084	37,718,018	449,089	1,977,977
Boats of less than 5 gross tons—				
1919	7,346,258	4,849,497	646,872	1,849,889
916	4,091,064	3,739,725	(1)	351,339
1914	4,296,244	3,788,689	331,825	175,730
1909	4,891,408	4,592,907	145,155	153,346
Repair work:				
1919	272,358,656	183,721,737	200,400	88,436,519
1916	71,225,368	63,508,514	(1)	7,716,854
1914	36,966,676	32,835,212	185,777	3,945,687
1909	38,304,658	26,678,643	80,461	11,545,554
All other work done:				
1919	146,580,357	[3] 46,950,869	246,400	[4] 99,383,088
1916	38,867,178	[5] 17,072,743	(1)	[6] 21,794,435
1914	30,054,547	[7] 9,512,725	58,285	20,483,537
1909	16,667,904	4,370,747	102,001	12,195,156

[1] Not reported in 1916.
[2] Includes work on concrete vessels to the value of $7,018,955.
[3] Includes work on engines to the value of $20,447,019.
[4] Includes work on engines to the value of $299,270.
[5] Includes work on engines to the value of $3,335,055.
[6] Includes work on engines to the value of $169,141.
[7] Includes work on engines to the value of $4,498,703.

GENERAL TABLES.

TABLE 88.—COMPARATIVE SUMMARY FOR THE UNITED STATES, BY INDUSTRIES: 1919 AND 1914.

NOTE.—The figures for some industries do not represent the total production, because important establishments that manufacture the same class of products may be included in other industries. (See Explanation of terms.)

Primary horsepower includes power generated in manufacturing establishments plus electric and other power rented from outside sources; it does not include electric power generated by primary units of the establishments reporting.

INDUSTRY.	Census year.	Number of establishments	Wage earners (average number).	Primary horsepower.	Capital.	Wages.	Cost of materials.	Value of products.	Value added by manufacture.
					Expressed in thousands of dollars.				
Aeroplanes, seaplanes, and airships, and parts.	1919	31	3,543	12,512	17,754	4,907	7,127	14,373	7,246
	1914	16	168	195	401	135	134	790	656
Agricultural implements......	1919	521	54,368	128,249	366,962	66,704	144,572	304,961	160,389
	1914	601	48,459	121,428	338,532	34,593	73,509	164,087	90,578
Aluminum manufactures.....	1919	83	11,402	30,280	48,490	13,327	49,272	75,278	26,006
	1914	37	4,614	12,338	11,088	2,611	14,421	19,597	5,176
Ammunition.................	1919	42	22,816	39,128	94,559	23,588	38,102	88,038	49,936
	1914	32	11,493	11,354	37,454	6,751	16,277	30,840	14,563
Artificial flowers...........	1919	224	4,138	468	6,675	3,741	7,005	16,143	9,138
	1914	217	4,808	237	3,349	1,991	3,207	7,614	4,407
Artificial limbs..............	1919	177	671	857	2,231	795	774	3,271	2,497
	1914	153	488	589	1,003	369	316	1,498	1,182
Artificial stone products......	1919	2,785	8,378	22,221	29,647	9,311	13,913	33,664	19,751
	1914	3,548	10,255	20,326	19,414	6,308	8,904	21,934	13,030
Artists' materials............	1919	58	926	3,206	4,664	896	2,687	5,508	2,821
	1914	44	604	1,977	2,947	315	2,065	3,238	1,173
Asbestos products, not including steam packing.	1919	46	3,654	9,657	16,405	3,732	12,948	23,978	11,030
	1914	32	962	2,877	3,520	484	1,360	2,814	1,454
Automobile bodies and parts..	1919	2,515	132,556	256,919	470,498	178,956	362,027	692,171	330,144
	1914	971	47,785	68,701	94,854	34,993	63,610	129,601	65,991
Automobile repairing.........	1919	15,507	55,061	82,691	141,124	71,613	87,649	224,652	137,003
	1914	3,273	12,562	16,380	17,098	10,614	9,154	29,920	20,766
Automobiles.................	1919	315	210,559	287,323	1,310,451	312,166	1,578,652	2,387,903	809,251
	1914	300	79,307	104,983	312,876	66,934	292,598	503,230	210,632
Awnings, tents, and sails.....	1919	895	6,028	4,589	26,728	5,859	26,961	45,690	18,729
	1914	888	5,073	2,610	9,958	2,954	10,155	18,138	7,983
Babbitt metal and solder....	1919	118	2,372	6,022	24,383	2,882	48,844	59,017	10,173
	1914	109	1,035	2,881	8,919	701	15,652	19,180	3,528
Bags, other than paper, not including bags made in textile mills.	1919	216	10,756	9,082	79,042	7,757	176,018	214,059	38,041
	1914	138	9,358	10,392	30,878	3,789	67,021	79,049	12,028
Bags, paper, exclusive of those made in paper mills.	1919	75	4,168	4,429	24,585	3,663	33,350	47,264	13,914
	1914	59	3,505	3,682	11,078	1,659	12,201	17,603	5,402
Baking powder and yeast....	1919	88	3,331	20,071	43,486	3,555	26,635	46,230	19,595
	1914	124	2,270	7,862	35,272	1,241	10,895	22,339	11,444
Baskets, and rattan and willow ware.	1919	375	4,533	6,319	7,195	3,369	4,904	11,821	6,917
	1914	419	4,574	7,293	4,591	1,923	2,999	6,578	3,579
Bells.....................	1919	10	237	783	1,005	205	450	951	501
	1914	12	445	787	1,040	244	438	970	532
Belting and hose, rubber.....	1919	15	5,826	26,299	45,920	6,074	18,310	34,211	15,901
	1914	18	5,115	22,995	22,437	2,902	12,967	23,561	10,594
Belting and hose, woven, other than rubber.	1919	41	2,479	5,338	17,349	2,202	11,642	19,176	7,534
	1914	31	952	2,756	4,848	460	2,869	4,441	1,572
Belting, leather.............	1919	172	2,765	7,039	27,534	3,260	28,157	40,481	12,324
	1914	151	2,951	7,411	20,139	2,070	15,480	23,036	7,556
Billiard tables, bowling alleys, and accessories.	1919	49	2,101	5,322	7,041	2,425	6,101	15,733	9,632
	1914	54	1,453	3,213	5,438	985	2,488	4,894	2,406
Blacking, stains, and dressings	1919	220	2,455	2,490	13,081	2,109	14,042	25,284	11,242
	1914	197	1,766	2,636	4,986	877	5,129	9,882	4,753
Bluing......................	1919	57	360	423	1,228	285	1,543	2,731	1,188
	1914	66	254	220	712	105	489	1,184	695
Bone, carbon, and lamp black.	1919	35	675	1,857	9,790	808	2,848	6,186	3,338
	1914	27	339	1,816	4,995	231	686	1,464	778
Bookbinding and blank-book making.	1919	1,113	20,361	11,123	43,041	18,659	23,235	66,021	42,786
	1914	1,124	21,693	11,266	29,180	11,575	13,334	38,104	24,770
Boot and shoe cut stock, exclusive of that produced in boot and shoe factories.	1919	252	9,715	9,003	61,747	9,125	133,887	161,203	27,316
	1914	236	7,819	6,829	30,455	4,052	51,450	59,965	8,515
Boot and shoe findings, exclusive of those produced in boot and shoe factories.	1919	427	8,941	10,682	28,988	8,187	40,428	62,825	22,397
	1914	369	6,714	5,868	12,563	3,226	20,304	28,303	7,999
Boots and shoes, not including rubber boots and shoes.	1919	1,449	211,049	120,632	580,625	210,735	715,269	1,155,041	430,772
	1914	1,355	191,555	100,232	254,591	105,695	310,357	501,760	191,403
Boots and shoes, rubber......	1919	25	32,875	49,400	131,513	30,883	50,347	116,917	66,570
	1914	23	18,687	24,621	46,051	9,986	23,956	53,822	29,866

TABLE 88.—COMPARATIVE SUMMARY FOR THE UNITED STATES, BY INDUSTRIES: 1919 AND 1914—Continued.

[See note at head of this table, p. 1157.]

INDUSTRY.	Census year.	Number of establishments	Wage earners (average number).	Primary horsepower.	Capital.	Wages.	Cost of materials.	Value of products.	Value added by manufacture.
									Expressed in thousands of dollars.
Boxes, cigar	1919	189	5,218	5,059	6,612	3,512	6,337	13,110	6,773
	1914	238	5,835	5,350	5,270	2,299	4,269	8,337	4,068
Boxes, paper and other, not elsewhere specified.	1919	1,201	55,862	54,955	131,391	43,326	101,135	206,419	105,284
	1914	1,043	45,311	38,179	60,027	18,705	36,268	74,711	38,443
Boxes, wooden packing, except cigar boxes.	1919	1,140	42,445	144,048	108,933	36,811	102,946	177,818	74,872
	1914	1,174	38,548	126,805	66,694	18,206	52,840	86,567	33,727
Brass, bronze, and copper products.	1919	1,092	75,051	265,688	325,300	94,132	304,824	482,313	177,489
	1914	992	40,306	122,700	116,093	25,084	115,487	162,199	46,712
Bread and other bakery products.	1919	25,095	141,592	165,950	509,266	158,237	713,239	1,151,896	438,657
	1914	25,963	124,052	107,771	271,262	76,867	274,257	491,893	217,636
Brick and tile, terra-cotta, and fire-clay products.	1919	2,414	76,915	405,746	355,848	78,256	67,488	208,423	140,935
	1914	3,239	100,182	442,813	279,860	54,907	42,723	135,921	93,198
Brooms	1919	1,034	6,313	6,062	16,708	5,709	17,365	30,205	12,840
	1914	868	5,642	4,504	8,706	2,624	7,884	14,085	6,201
Brushes	1919	379	7,968	7,384	27,208	7,113	19,598	39,006	19,408
	1914	359	7,213	6,388	14,333	3,461	9,327	17,894	8,567
Butter	1919	3,738	17,641	95,190	162,302	18,853	514,346	583,163	68,817
	1914	4,356	14,149	91,628	59,625	10,119	212,547	243,379	30,832
Butter, reworking	1919	5	47	343	603	56	2,006	2,229	223
	1914	17	304	1,349	1,397	200	5,059	5,869	810
Buttons	1919	557	15,577	16,201	29,978	13,773	16,745	41,840	25,095
	1914	517	14,511	14,398	19,075	6,424	8,702	20,712	12,010
Candles	1919	19	541	597	4,033	438	2,179	3,351	1,172
	1914	15	387	439	2,286	183	1,119	1,731	612
Canning and preserving, fish	1919	410	11,248	24,865	63,049	9,036	52,411	77,284	24,873
	1914	330	9,069	10,966	28,464	3,679	19,467	31,111	11,644
Canning and preserving, fruits and vegetables.	1919	3,082	60,865	132,422	223,692	43,593	265,629	402,243	136,614
	1914	3,153	50,325	88,303	98,738	17,306	103,293	149,176	45,883
Canning and preserving, oysters.	1919	65	1,189	1,025	2,972	469	1,583	2,976	1,393
	1914	65	2,087	1,895	2,077	424	1,225	2,238	1,013
Card cutting and designing	1919	75	1,148	743	2,298	959	2,298	5,323	3,025
	1914	58	517	449	706	265	421	1,055	634
Cardboard, not made in paper mills.	1919	16	1,425	3,276	6,493	1,337	4,954	9,138	4,184
	1914	18	1,159	2,735	5,129	580	2,962	4,350	1,388
Carpets and rugs, other than rag.	1919	75	22,933	38,170	119,196	24,216	67,118	123,254	56,136
	1914	97	31,309	43,963	85,154	14,716	42,280	69,128	26,848
Carpets, rag	1919	339	2,016	2,674	2,853	1,551	2,038	5,597	3,559
	1914	463	2,130	2,722	1,654	995	722	2,786	2,064
Carriage and wagon materials.	1919	258	6,509	23,700	17,971	5,667	14,735	26,765	12,030
	1914	456	11,087	38,215	26,845	6,059	13,546	24,850	11,304
Carriages and sleds, children's.	1919	103	6,686	6,071	15,215	6,229	11,700	24,507	12,807
	1914	92	5,900	5,652	9,380	3,181	5,682	11,752	6,070
Carriages and wagons, including repairs.	1919	2,286	18,173	40,966	78,953	19,393	48,362	91,463	43,101
	1914	4,601	41,304	74,334	150,798	26,498	52,173	106,697	54,524
Cars and general shop construction and repairs by electric-railroad companies.	1919	624	31,272	53,830	82,558	39,073	32,025	75,211	43,186
	1914	649	26,384	44,989	63,614	18,645	17,610	38,577	20,967
Cars and general shop construction and repairs by steam-railroad companies.	1919	1,744	484,437	594,515	694,286	687,617	515,803	1,279,235	763,432
	1914	1,362	339,518	433,994	354,092	234,505	243,829	514,041	270,212
Cars, electric-railroad, not including operations of railroad companies.	1919	7	2,920	9,390	17,306	4,132	12,059	18,442	6,383
	1914	14	3,840	10,014	14,752	2,467	6,350	10,495	4,145
Cars, steam-railroad, not including operations of railroad companies.	1919	99	52,298	157,865	335,207	78,285	356,085	538,223	182,138
	1914	103	54,288	126,687	157,811	41,394	132,200	194,776	62,576
Cash registers and calculating machines.	1919	65	16,544	14,650	82,798	22,537	10,890	83,539	72,649
	1914	52	8,956	10,619	41,075	6,110	3,992	30,520	26,528
Cement	1919	123	25,524	488,808	271,269	33,195	79,510	175,265	95,755
	1914	133	27,916	490,402	243,485	18,192	51,987	101,756	49,769
Charcoal, not including production in the lumber and wood-distillation industries.	1919	41	209	132	519	156	260	589	329
	1914	47	228	134	494	81	233	402	169
Cheese	1919	3,530	3,997	24,500	26,023	4,809	129,425	143,456	14,031
	1914	3,082	2,908	19,219	11,139	2,066	46,759	51,745	4,986
Chemicals	1919	598	55,586	376,940	484,488	72,848	216,301	438,659	222,358
	1914	395	32,311	282,385	224,346	22,066	89,451	158,054	68,603
Chewing gum	1919	62	3,190	6,178	23,703	2,680	25,202	51,240	26,038
	1914	74	2,048	3,030	10,625	828	7,322	17,160	9,838
China decorating, not including that done in potteries.	1919	43	244	43	470	244	311	867	556
	1914	51	295	23	463	159	340	727	397
Chocolate and cocoa products.	1919	48	9,083	33,440	60,675	9,270	101,754	139,258	37,504
	1914	36	4,160	19,736	23,685	2,036	24,483	35,713	11,230

TABLE 88.—COMPARATIVE SUMMARY FOR THE UNITED STATES, BY INDUSTRIES: 1919 AND 1914—Continued.

[See note at head of this table, p. 1157.]

INDUSTRY.	Census year.	Number of establishments	Wage earners (average number).	Primary horse-power.	Capital.	Wages.	Cost of materials.	Value of products.	Value added by manufacture.
					center: Expressed in thousands of dollars.				
Cleansing and polishing preparations.	1919	499	1,955	4,520	12,979	1,898	12,923	26,703	13,780
	1914	398	1,239	2,556	5,898	619	3,895	9,152	5,257
Clocks	1919	46	8,252	6,952	18,350	7,862	7,178	23,380	16,202
	1914	48	6,754	6,011	13,564	3,653	4,008	11,032	7,024
Cloth, sponging and refinishing.	1919	67	1,206	952	1,466	1,565	178	3,691	3,513
	1914	51	901	764	625	658	133	1,531	1,398
Clothing, horse	1919	28	766	1,577	3,705	551	3,456	6,021	2,565
	1914	37	1,669	1,903	4,482	668	3,569	5,150	1,581
Clothing, men's	1919	5,258	175,270	40,577	554,147	197,822	605,752	1,162,986	557,234
	1914	4,830	173,747	35,664	224,050	86,828	230,032	458,211	228,179
Clothing, men's, buttonholes..	1919	107	484	189	237	515	123	1,090	967
	1914	139	672	205	224	326	90	638	548
Clothing, women's	1919	7,711	165,649	32,622	390,527	195,296	680,407	1,208,543	528,136
	1914	5,564	168,907	28,396	153,549	92,574	252,345	473,888	221,543
Coal-tar products [1]	1919	183	15,663	68,342	174,992	23,402	63,997	135,482	71,485
Coffee and spice, roasting and grinding.	1919	794	10,540	29,750	127,748	9,201	243,899	304,792	60,893
	1914	696	8,549	26,634	56,596	4,508	116,520	150,749	34,229
Coffins, burial cases, and undertakers' goods.	1919	351	11,890	22,345	48,298	11,451	31,595	64,377	32,782
	1914	287	9,468	19,006	29,731	5,382	13,257	26,325	13,068
Coke, not including gas-house coke.	1919	278	29,319	224,879	365,250	42,299	224,267	316,516	92,249
	1914	231	21,107	117,127	161,561	14,289	69,138	99,275	30,137
Collars and cuffs, men's	1919	39	11,103	5,286	30,147	7,431	19,434	47,565	28,131
	1914	35	10,100	3,896	15,025	4,494	6,566	18,531	11,965
Combs and hairpins, except those made from metal or rubber.	1919	45	2,229	1,600	3,913	1,809	3,169	6,566	3,397
	1914	66	2,773	2,711	2,959	1,393	2,853	5,478	2,625
Condensed milk	1919	401	13,675	49,181	126,953	14,278	282,595	339,507	56,912
	1914	190	6,002	20,015	35,048	3,662	55,720	69,161	13,441
Confectionery and ice cream...	1919	6,624	95,648	179,991	317,044	76,160	368,809	637,209	268,400
	1914	4,754	61,986	98,393	120,545	27,489	126,465	209,668	83,203
Cooperage	1919	1,099	13,219	30,698	48,854	14,082	58,521	88,236	29,715
	1914	1,259	17,128	38,290	36,690	9,161	32,944	50,017	17,073
Copper, tin, and sheet-iron work.	1919	4,796	27,640	24,144	89,945	33,867	80,899	160,314	79,415
	1914	4,527	28,714	21,357	57,396	20,518	50,174	94,891	44,717
Cordage and twine	1919	120	17,622	66,643	100,249	14,700	89,705	133,366	43,661
	1914	105	15,769	55,377	72,472	6,996	43,605	59,761	16,156
Cordials and flavoring sirups..	1919	149	1,398	3,177	11,674	1,297	30,999	46,807	15,808
	1914	142	929	2,070	5,585	461	7,596	15,316	7,720
Cork, cutting	1919	62	3,545	8,683	14,570	3,387	9,135	16,282	7,147
	1914	52	3,454	5,814	7,602	1,582	4,751	7,875	3,124
Corsets	1919	188	18,415	7,156	43,516	13,082	38,816	75,542	36,726
	1914	167	20,496	7,057	23,893	7,977	19,587	40,551	20,964
Cotton goods	1919	1,288	430,966	1,840,201	1,853,100	355,475	1,277,786	2,125,272	847,486
	1914	1,179	379,366	1,566,757	867,044	146,130	431,603	676,569	244,966
Cotton lace	1919	44	6,490	9,078	32,260	6,087	13,076	29,397	16,321
	1914	41	7,440	9,096	20,957	3,468	5,677	13,207	7,530
Cotton small wares	1919	164	9,396	14,263	29,559	7,162	24,040	40,897	16,857
	1914	108	6,598	10,100	11,764	2,825	6,243	11,525	5,282
Crucibles	1919	22	848	2,714	8,069	923	2,233	5,294	3,061
	1914	10	302	875	1,871	171	1,270	1,886	616
Cutlery and edge tools	1919	304	19,859	38,958	68,971	20,048	19,477	66,630	47,153
	1914	252	16,561	34,781	35,666	9,076	8,186	25,541	17,355
Dairymen's, poultrymen's, and apiarists' supplies.	1919	244	6,437	11,756	36,095	7,078	18,527	37,397	18,870
	1914	236	5,551	11,639	21,281	3,363	9,248	18,950	9,702
Dental goods	1919	319	5,224	2,716	17,905	4,464	16,420	29,402	12,982
	1914	172	3,080	1,874	10,949	1,616	10,715	16,160	5,445
Drug grinding	1919	31	1,347	6,725	14,991	1,526	11,556	16,938	5,382
	1914	29	1,059	4,972	8,434	583	5,215	8,080	2,865
Druggists' preparations	1919	524	15,568	12,698	102,129	12,162	55,138	114,593	59,455
	1914	416	9,277	8,417	46,638	4,755	22,935	48,010	25,075
Dyeing and finishing textiles, exclusive of that done in textile mills.	1919	628	55,985	160,430	229,948	57,190	174,743	323,968	149,225
	1914	507	48,467	130,172	139,194	24,872	56,705	109,292	52,587
Dyestuffs and extracts—natural.	1919	144	4,342	34,320	38,689	4,735	34,593	53,744	19,151
	1914	112	2,839	23,290	21,284	1,613	13,238	20,620	7,382
Electrical machinery, apparatus, and supplies.	1919	1,404	212,374	438,839	857,855	238,189	425,098	997,968	572,870
	1914	1,030	118,078	227,731	355,725	73,806	154,728	335,170	180,442
Electroplating	1919	515	3,024	7,078	4,193	3,794	2,639	10,390	7,751
	1914	479	2,584	5,845	2,842	1,713	1,336	4,773	3,437
Emery and other abrasive wheels.	1919	60	5,601	12,963	34,803	5,879	12,228	30,949	18,721
	1914	49	2,387	4,100	8,224	1,491	3,006	7,130	4,124

[1] Included in "chemicals" in 1914.

TABLE 88.—COMPARATIVE SUMMARY FOR THE UNITED STATES, BY INDUSTRIES: 1919 AND 1914—Continued.

[See note at head of this table, p. 1157.]

INDUSTRY.	Census year.	Number of establishments	Wage earners (average number).	Primary horsepower.	Capital.	Wages.	Cost of materials.	Value of products.	Value added by manufacture.
					Expressed in thousands of dollars.				
Enameling	1919	74	694	1,183	2,083	790	950	2,645	1,695
	1914	77	1,314	1,635	2,128	649	970	2,166	1,196
Engines, steam, gas, and water	1919	370	77,617	190,021	454,125	105,435	217,551	464,775	247,224
	1914	446	29,657	63,047	131,080	21,421	31,460	72,121	40,661
Engravers' materials	1919	21	174	759	826	212	1,484	2,248	764
	1914	13	106	547	352	73	551	768	217
Engraving and diesinking	1919	478	1,878	1,760	4,696	2,392	1,927	7,351	5,424
	1914	486	1,536	1,092	1,865	1,076	596	3,134	2,538
Engraving, steel and copper plate, including plate printing.	1919	421	7,014	5,420	19,040	7,908	6,981	24,209	17,228
	1914	399	6,859	5,670	19,079	4,527	3,915	13,786	9,871
Engraving, wood	1919	55	235	67	339	407	219	1,154	935
	1914	72	302	68	246	310	96	719	623
Envelopes	1919	106	8,129	7,187	24,755	6,650	21,965	39,664	17,699
	1914	90	6,970	5,206	15,830	3,378	10,235	18,481	8,246
Explosives	1919	118	9,249	51,635	133,248	12,505	45,911	92,475	46,564
	1914	111	6,306	45,778	71,351	4,488	25,627	41,433	15,806
Fancy articles, not elsewhere specified.	1919	661	13,961	8,982	32,825	12,208	32,591	64,054	31,463
	1914	493	7,399	4,586	11,879	3,567	8,429	17,659	9,230
Feathers and plumes	1919	216	3,504	594	6,515	3,406	6,695	15,378	8,683
	1914	239	4,483	369	5,396	1,988	6,103	11,451	5,348
Felt goods	1919	49	5,236	16,411	35,024	4,873	22,781	39,230	16,449
	1914	53	4,035	14,056	20,284	2,089	8,308	13,693	5,385
Ferroalloys [1]	1919	30	2,344	37,087	42,365	3,571	28,099	38,584	10,485
Fertilizers	1919	600	26,296	125,939	311,633	25,363	185,041	281,144	96,103
	1914	784	22,815	114,281	217,065	10,532	107,955	153,196	45,241
Files	1919	50	5,767	11,905	15,693	6,192	4,228	17,617	13,389
	1914	48	4,349	8,821	11,327	2,135	1,595	5,608	4,013
Firearms	1919	26	11,287	26,167	51,918	13,333	7,614	30,181	22,567
	1914	29	7,064	7,474	15,611	5,067	2,670	10,544	7,874
Fire extinguishers, chemical	1919	32	777	855	3,780	751	2,693	5,563	2,870
	1914	27	256	391	675	200	574	1,298	724
Fireworks	1919	57	1,222	1,005	3,547	995	2,108	4,630	2,522
	1914	41	1,324	707	2,162	616	1,206	2,296	1,090
Flags and banners	1919	79	1,065	778	3,436	795	3,286	5,346	2,060
	1914	87	1,495	637	1,843	690	1,750	3,601	1,851
Flavoring extracts	1919	453	2,188	3,376	13,561	1,665	19,418	30,117	10,699
	1914	424	1,461	1,470	6,617	689	6,308	11,380	5,072
Flax and hemp, dressed	1919	20	420	1,920	2,784	447	1,709	2,369	660
	1914	16	116	832	235	45	185	283	98
Flour-mill and gristmill products.	1919	10,708	45,481	876,405	801,625	50,888	1,799,181	2,052,434	253,253
	1914	10,788	39,718	822,384	380,257	24,593	752,270	877,680	125,410
Food preparations, not elsewhere specified.	1919	1,997	30,365	150,230	245,283	29,392	494,597	631,598	137,001
	1914	1,559	20,306	80,022	91,039	10,866	153,751	219,333	65,582
Foundry and machine-shop products.	1919	10,934	482,767	1,054,840	2,104,981	622,571	948,069	2,289,251	1,341,182
	1914	10,640	362,471	770,454	1,246,043	244,146	358,122	866,545	508,423
Foundry supplies	1919	76	906	6,328	7,502	1,032	5,667	9,955	4,288
	1914	57	555	4,694	2,814	301	997	2,013	1,016
Fuel, manufactured	1919	11	171	5,180	2,908	222	1,386	1,974	588
	1914	14	141	3,444	1,771	112	609	863	254
Fur goods	1919	1,815	13,639	5,327	80,701	24,149	105,597	173,138	67,541
	1914	1,322	9,030	3,233	29,677	6,335	23,847	43,633	19,786
Furnishing goods, men's	1919	487	18,944	5,665	53,014	13,563	64,744	107,835	43,091
	1914	551	22,459	5,880	27,888	8,415	31,593	52,453	20,860
Furniture	1919	3,154	138,331	262,703	423,992	141,116	261,523	571,356	309,833
	1914	3,192	127,881	240,665	267,885	71,816	121,486	265,706	144,220
Furs, dressed	1919	141	5,075	5,621	8,867	7,098	6,339	20,385	14,046
	1914	96	1,525	2,275	2,490	923	906	2,875	1,969
Galvanizing and other coating processes.	1919	52	1,665	1,631	4,316	2,248	10,532	14,476	3,944
	1914	48	1,580	2,385	4,416	922	6,293	8,480	2,187
Gas and electric fixtures	1919	341	9,795	9,910	36,873	9,802	20,259	42,268	22,009
	1914	460	10,913	10,028	27,629	6,504	14,090	28,740	14,650
Gas, illuminating and heating.	1919	1,022	42,908	238,467	1,465,656	52,759	157,551	329,279	171,728
	1914	1,284	43,792	213,370	1,252,422	26,802	76,779	220,238	143,459
Gas machines, and gas and water meters.	1919	105	5,589	8,601	24,981	5,996	10,647	26,267	15,620
	1914	123	4,972	5,711	17,822	3,310	6,118	15,184	9,066
Glass	1919	371	77,520	207,430	215,680	87,527	90,780	261,884	171,104
	1914	348	74,502	163,139	153,926	48,656	46,017	123,085	77,068
Glass, cutting, staining, and ornamenting.	1919	616	6,480	5,110	18,089	6,155	14,358	28,443	14,085
	1914	635	8,067	5,539	11,310	4,670	7,143	16,446	9,303

[1] Included in other classifications in 1914.

TABLE 88.—COMPARATIVE SUMMARY FOR THE UNITED STATES, BY INDUSTRIES: 1919 AND 1914—Continued.

[See note at head of this table, p. 1157.]

INDUSTRY.	Census year.	Number of establishments	Wage earners (average number).	Primary horsepower.	Capital.	Wages.	Cost of materials.	Value of products.	Value added by manufacture.
							Expressed in thousands of dollars.		
Gloves and mittens, cloth [1]...	1919	182	8,986	3,364	17,688	4,855	16,092	28,220	12,128
Gloves and mittens, leather...	1919	355	10,685	3,288	29,870	8,151	26,286	46,941	20,655
	1914	352	10,668	3,357	17,080	4,558	12,171	21,614	9,443
Glucose and starch..........	1919	56	7,795	52,846	58,183	11,962	130,329	186,256	55,927
	1914	89	4,509	41,639	43,642	3,550	40,208	52,615	12,407
Glue, not elsewhere specified..	1919	62	4,264	16,979	27,237	4,777	19,280	32,134	12,854
	1914	57	3,129	13,304	17,162	1,854	9,368	13,733	4,365
Gold and silver, leaf and foil...	1919	87	950	408	1,572	984	2,655	4,462	1,807
	1914	79	1,135	360	1,174	498	1,452	2,432	980
Gold and silver, reducing and refining, not from the ore.	1919	87	644	3,279	9,757	844	49,737	55,483	5,746
	1914	78	456	2,235	4,407	391	25,709	28,588	2,879
Graphite, ground and refined.	1919	24	497	7,445	4,303	434	1,093	2,240	1,147
	1914	11	250	2,602	3,059	181	723	1,724	1,001
Grease and tallow, not including lubricating greases.	1919	482	6,647	25,584	37,360	7,954	47,756	67,265	19,509
	1914	369	5,106	17,947	18,928	3,512	17,061	24,901	7,840
Grindstones...................	1919	23	674	3,631	2,045	599	244	1,369	1,125
	1914	14	686	2,160	1,979	323	116	684	568
Haircloth..................	1919	18	425	1,153	2,999	425	2,259	3,315	1,056
	1914	19	595	1,723	2,945	290	1,654	2,395	741
Hair work.................	1919	198	1,084	119	3,581	1,065	3,829	6,963	3,134
	1914	205	1,193	68	2,543	581	1,529	3,335	1,806
Hammocks..................	1919	6	64	92	153	40	169	256	87
	1914	14	285	321	608	119	361	671	310
Hand stamps..............	1919	298	1,719	1,474	4,250	1,833	2,634	7,739	5,105
	1914	277	1,321	973	2,273	848	1,093	3,383	2,290
Hardware..................	1919	518	42,505	67,589	133,926	45,230	58,534	154,525	95,991
	1914	539	41,213	53,411	92,302	22,583	29,071	73,320	44,249
Hardware, saddlery.........	1919	37	3,675	7,161	10,992	4,044	4,282	14,137	9,855
	1914	58	2,511	4,134	5,353	1,248	1,790	4,040	2,250
Hat and cap materials.......	1919	133	3,009	4,927	19,862	3,133	16,644	26,521	9,877
	1914	98	1,775	2,954	6,417	804	5,052	6,929	1,877
Hats and caps, other than felt, straw, and wool.	1919	709	7,539	1,687	18,515	9,439	24,177	44,540	20,363
	1914	580	7,322	1,339	6,847	4,508	9,268	18,593	9,325
Hats, fur-felt............	1919	176	18,510	20,389	58,128	19,643	40,158	82,745	42,587
	1914	224	21,318	20,851	39,401	12,071	16,947	37,350	20,403
Hats, straw...............	1919	148	7,302	3,392	18,560	6,605	16,910	32,187	15,277
	1914	149	9,483	5,248	12,589	5,253	14,086	25,444	11,358
Hats, wool-felt...........	1919	40	1,448	2,696	3,831	1,388	3,700	6,740	3,040
	1914	30	1,249	3,091	2,609	600	978	1,944	966
Hones and whetstones........	1919	11	212	1,164	847	203	321	794	473
	1914	16	170	864	499	64	87	260	173
Horseshoes, not made in steel works or rolling mills.	1919	20	744	3,874	4,590	830	1,537	3,367	1,830
	1914	22	588	1,984	2,437	362	690	1,786	1,096
House-furnishing goods, not elsewhere specified.	1919	467	7,853	12,249	32,627	6,444	39,794	60,212	20,418
	1914	370	6,935	11,731	19,014	3,307	17,391	26,453	9,062
Ice, manufactured............	1919	2,867	30,247	572,970	270,726	34,002	42,878	137,005	94,127
	1914	2,543	23,011	461,988	174,309	14,841	17,755	60,386	42,631
Ink, printing................	1919	90	1,988	10,353	18,703	2,575	14,661	26,244	11,583
	1914	70	1,391	7,821	11,943	1,064	6,806	13,830	7,024
Ink, writing................	1919	61	702	610	4,803	596	3,320	6,434	3,114
	1914	54	512	612	2,464	263	1,236	2,784	1,548
Instruments, professional and scientific.	1919	351	15,931	13,020	51,570	17,500	19,495	58,137	38,642
	1914	307	7,107	6,799	16,742	4,652	5,582	17,495	11,913
Iron and steel, blast furnaces..	1919	195	41,660	1,581,432	802,417	73,769	621,286	794,467	173,181
	1914	160	29,356	1,222,273	462,282	22,781	264,580	317,654	53,074
Iron and steel, steel works and rolling mills.	1919	500	375,088	3,820,917	2,656,518	637,637	1,680,576	2,828,902	1,148,326
	1914	427	248,716	2,706,553	1,258,371	188,142	590,826	918,665	327,839
Iron and steel, bolts, nuts, washers, and rivets, not made in rolling mills.	1919	144	17,967	49,959	75,716	20,974	44,277	89,744	45,467
	1914	102	10,658	28,897	35,602	5,961	12,913	23,403	10,490
Iron and steel, cast-iron pipe.	1919	59	12,625	28,741	42,863	14,705	25,387	50,235	24,848
	1914	59	12,557	25,864	26,981	7,076	16,930	26,659	9,729
Iron and steel, doors and shutters.	1919	57	2,077	4,013	9,849	2,730	4,578	10,877	6,299
	1914	43	1,985	3,170	5,161	1,538	1,996	5,184	3,188
Iron and steel forgings, not made in steel works or rolling mills.	1919	241	28,391	101,951	135,246	39,773	82,024	173,752	91,728
	1914	191	10,689	38,215	36,320	7,487	14,611	28,961	14,350
Iron and steel, nails and spikes, cut and wrought, including wire nails, not made in steel works or rolling mills.	1919	65	3,355	8,974	13,216	3,398	8,875	17,583	8,708
	1914	64	2,644	8,235	7,883	1,508	3,594	7,199	3,605

[1] Included in "furnishing goods, men's," in 1914.

TABLE 88.—COMPARATIVE SUMMARY FOR THE UNITED STATES, BY INDUSTRIES: 1919 AND 1914—Continued.

[See note at head of this table, p. 1157.]

INDUSTRY.	Census year.	Number of establishments	Wage earners (average number).	Primary horsepower.	Capital.	Wages.	Cost of materials.	Value of products.	Value added by manufacture.
					Expressed in thousands of dollars.				
Iron and steel, tempering and welding.[1]	1919	520	1,835	8,804	7,627	2,743	3,576	10,996	7,420
Iron and steel, wrought pipe..	1919	50	10,426	23,925	72,709	14,920	51,156	81,869	30,713
	1914	36	8,845	17,542	39,408	5,750	26,296	37,655	11,359
Ivory, shell, and bone work, not including combs and hairpins.	1919	44	842	954	1,366	735	1,294	2,817	1,523
	1914	54	795	708	1,160	391	958	1,896	938
Japanning.................	1919	36	295	311	462	261	222	771	549
	1914	35	228	110	261	149	95	381	286
Jewelry.................	1919	2,054	30,871	16,389	121,070	35,864	110,451	203,939	93,488
	1914	1,914	28,289	15,666	72,404	18,302	39,116	81,006	41,890
Jewelry and instrument cases.	1919	142	2,734	1,091	3,697	2,148	3,506	8,126	4,620
	1914	125	2,393	1,059	2,187	1,094	1,450	3,621	2,171
Jute goods.................	1919	26	7,138	32,135	41,336	6,436	17,709	34,443	16,734
	1914	34	7,987	28,628	17,279	3,060	12,580	16,514	3,934
Knit goods.................	1919	2,050	172,572	151,601	516,458	125,200	427,096	713,140	286,044
	1914	1,622	150,520	125,842	215,826	59,758	146,687	258,913	112,226
Labels and tags..............	1919	119	5,227	4,061	14,119	4,550	11,275	24,244	12,969
	1914	108	2,600	2,233	5,697	1,459	2,908	6,584	3,676
Lamps and reflectors.........	1919	171	8,360	12,708	26,100	9,292	18,429	38,099	19,670
	1914	151	7,134	8,640	15,671	4,173	8,012	16,638	8,626
Lapidary work..............	1919	124	1,155	680	19,210	2,838	19,363	30,051	10,688
	1914	89	584	546	3,613	641	3,941	5,360	1,419
Lard, not made in slaughtering and meat-packing establishments.	1919	6	13	40	41	12	175	220	45
	1914	6	19	197	124	12	102	147	45
Lasts.................	1919	64	2,910	5,842	8,178	3,416	3,933	12,471	8,538
	1914	66	2,094	5,317	4,481	1,511	1,343	4,589	3,246
Lead, bar, pipe, and sheet....	1919	32	852	5,537	9,420	1,067	13,634	17,174	3,540
	1914	27	585	2,609	5,036	407	6,048	7,431	1,383
Leather goods, not elsewhere specified.	1919	503	8,945	3,902	33,341	9,415	30,036	52,953	22,917
	1914	378	7,071	3,272	10,951	3,604	10,632	19,334	8,702
Leather, tanned, curried, and finished.	1919	680	72,476	218,238	671,342	88,205	646,522	928,592	282,070
	1914	741	55,936	172,712	332,180	31,914	284,245	367,202	82,957
Lime.................	1919	476	11,405	51,735	45,845	10,869	14,297	33,970	19,673
	1914	627	12,429	39,134	34,124	6,040	7,558	18,391	10,833
Linen goods.................	1919	10	1,890	6,069	7,528	1,636	4,190	6,998	2,808
	1914	21	3,567	9,932	8,810	1,386	4,289	6,960	2,671
Liquors, distilled..............	1919	34	1,380	16,494	45,618	1,717	19,656	31,854	12,198
	1914	434	6,295	51,971	91,285	3,994	40,997	206,779	165,782
Liquors, malt.................	1919	729	34,259	324,431	583,430	45,170	94,793	379,905	285,112
	1914	1,250	62,070	405,884	792,914	53,244	129,724	442,149	312,425
Liquors, vinous..............	1919	342	1,011	5,189	14,855	1,014	8,116	17,454	9,338
	1914	318	2,292	9,356	31,516	1,194	9,489	16,618	7,129
Lithographing.................	1919	331	15,618	18,624	60,817	18,201	27,718	73,151	45,433
	1914	336	15,171	15,178	35,685	11,861	14,017	39,136	25,119
Locomotives, not made by railroad companies.	1919	17	26,715	97,187	138,276	38,799	72,376	156,270	83,894
	1914	19	17,391	50,373	86,413	11,085	23,546	43,374	19,828
Looking-glass and picture frames.	1919	429	4,708	4,689	10,080	4,775	7,227	18,385	11,158
	1914	438	4,787	4,210	8,049	2,850	4,468	11,014	6,546
Lubricating greases..........	1919	53	472	2,178	5,243	570	4,808	8,869	4,061
	1914	77	476	2,685	3,440	282	2,767	4,919	2,152
Lumber and timber products[2]	1919	26,119	480,945	2,358,937	1,357,992	489,419	470,960	1,387,471	916,511
	1914	27,249	480,207	2,192,542	917,221	240,172	282,286	715,941	433,655
Lumber, planing-mill products, not including planing mills connected with sawmills.	1919	5,309	86,956	419,671	361,848	91,977	299,266	500,438	201,172
	1914	5,841	96,214	414,817	266,805	61,949	184,227	307,672	123,445
Machine tools[1].............	1919	403	53,111	100,433	231,040	66,179	59,034	212,400	153,366
Malt.....................	1919	55	1,352	27,483	34,829	1,845	31,613	39,340	7,727
	1914	97	1,989	33,394	46,767	1,828	39,199	48,133	8,934
Marble and stone work.......	1919	4,240	32,768	170,132	112,569	38,355	49,524	129,165	79,641
	1914	4,901	54,891	207,461	118,423	37,961	37,802	107,055	69,253
Matches.................	1919	21	3,726	12,947	29,477	3,060	6,853	18,496	11,643
	1914	20	3,800	7,465	11,736	1,758	5,202	12,556	7,354
Mats and matting, from cocoa fiber, grass, and coir.	1919	12	1,073	1,670	7,191	811	2,103	4,861	2,758
	1914	12	869	1,643	5,055	455	1,170	2,236	1,066
Mattresses and spring beds, not elsewhere specified.	1919	1,041	12,637	23,469	46,213	12,805	49,209	83,953	34,744
	1914	1,000	11,747	20,767	24,922	6,723	22,399	38,717	16,318

[1] Included in "foundry and machine shops" prior to 1919.
[2] Includes "pulpwood" in 1914; not shown as a separate classification in 1919.

TABLE 88.—COMPARATIVE SUMMARY FOR THE UNITED STATES, BY INDUSTRIES: 1919 AND 1914—Continued.

[See note at head of this table, p. 1157.]

INDUSTRY.	Census year.	Number of establishments	Wage earners (average number).	Primary horsepower.	Capital.	Wages.	Cost of materials.	Value of products.	Value added by manufacture.
							Expressed in thousands of dollars.		
Millinery and lace goods, not	1919	3,005	50,850	12,482	95,539	49,849	132,929	255,725	122,796
elsewhere specified.	1914	2,079	45,274	12,736	53,101	21,545	57,676	114,160	56,484
Millstones [1]	1919	12	38	132	59	44	26	67	41
Mineral and soda waters	1919	5,194	17,440	41,764	102,839	16,393	68,600	135,341	66,741
	1914	5,463	15,506	25,164	53,233	8,864	26,779	58,401	31,622
Minerals and earths, ground	1919	419	14,426	127,074	60,209	16,310	16,270	46,067	29,797
or otherwise treated.	1914	244	4,707	44,069	27,439	2,485	4,561	10,307	5,746
Mirrors, framed and unframed,	1919	186	2,599	4,328	9,322	2,819	12,499	20,831	8,332
not elsewhere specified.	1914	182	3,184	4,673	6,517	1,968	6,014	10,189	4,175
Models and patterns, not in-	1919	928	6,949	13,869	11,754	10,318	6,396	25,300	18,904
cluding paper patterns.	1914	762	4,274	6,149	5,534	3,103	2,045	8,605	6,560
Motorcycles, bicycles, and	1919	51	10,886	14,806	35,362	12,763	25,986	53,106	27,120
parts.	1914	78	6,680	8,753	18,135	4,739	10,928	22,234	11,306
Mucilage, paste, and other ad-	1919	127	803	3,242	7,133	850	7,093	11,230	4,137
hesives, not elsewhere spec-	1914	127	700	2,456	3,550	399	3,338	5,695	2,357
ified.									
Musical instruments and ma-	1919	240	4,113	3,286	7,876	3,985	4,445	12,506	8,061
terials, not specified.	1914	241	1,831	1,865	3,858	1,161	1,023	3,625	2,602
Musical instruments, organs..	1919	68	1,941	3,251	6,771	1,979	2,217	5,973	3,756
	1914	85	3,063	3,666	8,042	1,993	2,660	6,297	3,637
Musical instruments, pianos..	1919	191	22,957	28,732	116,107	25,474	54,365	107,088	52,723
	1914	255	23,877	25,981	101,746	15,705	29,091	62,775	33,684
Musical instruments, piano	1919	113	11,009	15,821	32,324	10,467	16,693	36,790	20,097
and organ materials.	1914	138	10,616	14,702	21,201	5,655	9,502	19,876	10,374
Needles, pins, and hooks and	1919	92	9,294	8,467	26,325	8,810	10,227	29,305	19,078
eyes.	1914	49	5,339	4,813	9,424	2,507	3,242	7,891	4,649
Nets and seines	1919	19	859	959	4,156	561	3,648	5,114	1,466
	1914	15	1,058	1,940	2,678	379	2,257	3,088	831
Oakum	1919	6	124	533	978	118	576	983	407
	1914	6	116	333	495	49	235	359	124
Oil and cake, cottonseed	1919	711	26,766	290,636	203,457	20,615	495,192	581,245	86,053
	1914	882	21,810	249,781	118,073	8,490	180,976	212,127	31,151
Oil, essential	1919	78	321	1,833	6,380	391	3,903	5,698	1,795
	1914	105	249	2,309	1,617	133	1,565	2,314	749
Oil, linseed	1919	26	2,173	17,621	73,954	3,052	100,578	120,638	20,060
	1914	25	1,488	15,511	39,873	1,127	39,555	44,883	5,328
Oil, not elsewhere specified [2]..	1919	280	5,930	30,075	91,475	6,141	119,271	156,480	37,209
	1914	181	2,049	10,984	27,630	1,363	26,420	38,040	11,620
Oilcloth and linoleum, floor...	1919	21	5,414	23,509	49,804	6,518	30,369	52,673	22,304
	1914	18	4,428	18,782	20,292	2,604	11,252	17,602	6,350
Oilcloth, enameled	1919	11	1,130	4,501	10,783	1,201	11,141	15,437	4,296
	1914	13	1,223	3,490	7,749	609	6,524	7,996	1,472
Oleomargarine and other but-	1919	42	2,851	9,435	24,972	3,184	66,043	79,816	13,773
ter substitutes.	1914	17	917	3,611	2,994	584	10,257	15,080	4,823
Optical goods	1919	506	14,723	15,710	37,740	14,388	17,785	53,718	35,933
	1914	314	7,919	7,792	17,011	4,649	6,606	18,188	11,582
Ordnance and accessories [1]	1919	26	11,328	40,652	85,399	15,557	26,593	69,496	42,903
Paints	1919	601	17,485	73,702	177,315	19,550	165,604	256,714	91,110
	1914	585	13,349	62,955	99,673	8,315	71,588	112,409	40,821
Paper and wood pulp	1919	729	113,759	1,851,014	905,795	135,691	467,483	788,059	320,576
	1914	718	88,457	1,621,154	534,625	53,246	213,181	332,147	118,966
Paper goods, not elsewhere	1919	308	14,135	35,538	64,443	12,667	65,295	107,285	41,990
specified.	1914	310	13,495	27,366	37,809	6,850	28,120	48,871	20,751
Paper patterns	1919	19	403	68	1,084	374	317	1,528	1,211
	1914	25	1,073	362	2,612	577	626	3,026	2,400
Patent medicines and com-	1919	2,467	17,444	25,677	143,499	13,749	88,819	212,162	123,343
pounds.	1914	2,903	13,328	18,542	71,437	6,675	35,940	102,463	66,523
Paving materials	1919	889	16,072	191,543	67,421	17,169	16,020	45,741	29,721
	1914	609	19,540	138,026	57,432	11,184	14,163	35,678	21,515
Peanuts, grading, roasting,	1919	78	2,460	7,351	10,394	1,329	28,474	33,354	4,880
cleaning, and shelling.	1914	61	2,353	4,235	3,615	569	12,571	14,996	2,425
Pencils, lead	1919	12	5,970	8,099	29,641	5,299	9,074	24,134	15,060
	1914	14	4,330	3,738	10,670	1,944	4,564	8,328	3,764
Pens, fountain and stylo-	1919	56	3,207	1,517	9,725	2,981	5,811	15,997	10,186
graphic.	1914	55	1,154	1,157	3,270	718	1,614	6,865	5,251
Pens, gold	1919	15	416	160	398	517	962	1,801	839
	1914	12	246	138	408	174	302	642	340
Pens, steel	1919	4	807	305	1,311	679	399	1,680	1,281
	1914	5	573	244	871	243	117	513	396
Perfumery and cosmetics	1919	569	5,405	2,196	32,667	3,983	26,147	59,613	33,466
	1914	496	2,807	1,913	9,647	1,280	7,465	16,899	9,434

[1] Included in "all other industries" in 1914.
[2] Includes "oil, castor," and "oil, lard, not made in slaughtering and meat-packing establishments."

TABLE 88.—COMPARATIVE SUMMARY FOR THE UNITED STATES, BY INDUSTRIES: 1919 AND 1914—Continued.

[See note at head of this table, p. 1157.]

INDUSTRY.	Census year.	Number of establishments	Wage earners (average number).	Primary horsepower.	Capital.	Wages.	Cost of materials.	Value of products.	Value added by manufacture.
					Expressed in thousands of dollars.				
Petroleum, refining	1919	320	58,889	238,906	1,170,278	89,750	1,247,908	1,632,533	384,625
	1914	176	25,366	128,468	325,646	19,397	325,265	396,361	71,096
Phonographs and graphophones.	1919	166	28,721	40,168	105,241	33,963	59,740	158,548	98,808
	1914	18	9,381	11,688	33,771	6,341	7,048	27,116	20,068
Photographic apparatus	1919	68	2,555	2,321	7,264	2,643	3,584	9,384	5,800
	1914	87	2,016	1,522	4,397	1,289	1,535	4,273	2,738
Photographic materials	1919	169	14,556	26,458	87,205	18,966	49,802	115,714	65,912
	1914	59	6,658	14,960	31,991	4,256	10,004	34,768	24,764
Photo-engraving, not done in printing establishments.	1919	422	6,769	3,800	12,443	10,424	5,038	29,389	24,351
	1914	376	6,211	3,927	7,703	6,167	2,798	15,359	12,561
Pickles, preserves, and sauces.	1919	723	16,621	22,500	88,704	13,346	93,037	145,785	52,748
	1914	672	12,590	18,840	43,196	5,789	35,673	60,915	25,242
Pipes, tobacco	1919	56	2,539	2,001	7,635	2,555	3,497	11,554	8,057
	1914	47	2,354	1,716	3,232	1,188	2,308	4,220	1,912
Plated ware	1919	68	9,492	14,252	34,790	10,913	17,767	41,635	23,868
	1914	72	8,717	10,499	22,215	5,000	8,304	18,484	10,180
Plumbers' supplies, not elsewhere specified.	1919	214	13,592	29,762	60,981	15,963	27,797	60,055	32,258
	1914	260	18,479	28,253	48,029	11,703	18,670	43,386	24,716
Pocketbooks	1919	139	2,905	431	5,428	3,062	7,557	14,550	6,993
	1914	64	1,466	243	1,610	702	1,784	3,351	1,567
Pottery	1919	340	27,934	29,090	66,758	29,820	20,794	74,919	54,125
	1914	350	26,705	22,339	44,704	16,666	12,032	36,943	24,911
Poultry, killing and dressing, not done in slaughtering and meat-packing establishments.	1919	196	2,140	4,016	8,876	2,045	36,016	41,705	5,689
	1914	116	1,353	2,230	2,282	622	11,206	12,917	1,711
Printing and publishing, book and job.	1919	13,089	123,005	131,961	405,555	141,476	211,067	597,663	386,596
	1914	12,115	113,121	114,233	247,282	78,414	96,453	307,331	210,878
Printing and publishing, music.	1919	160	899	634	8,006	927	2,124	14,592	12,468
	1914	180	873	594	4,261	573	1,047	7,271	6,224
Printing and publishing, newspapers and periodicals.	1919	17,362	120,381	194,361	614,045	144,348	300,385	924,153	623,768
	1914	19,317	114,375	182,269	384,745	88,561	129,082	495,906	366,824
Printing materials	1919	82	723	1,357	7,245	799	1,620	4,919	3,299
	1914	94	423	671	1,771	340	763	2,111	1,348
Pulp, from fiber other than wood.[1]	1919	5	64	833	778	56	396	524	128
Pulp goods	1919	40	3,041	12,273	17,191	3,608	11,382	23,608	12,226
	1914	24	1,654	8,826	6,862	884	2,191	4,483	2,292
Pumps, not including power pumps.	1919	127	5,384	10,346	26,661	5,968	12,162	31,656	19,494
	1914	96	2,134	3,488	6,194	1,391	2,765	6,350	3,585
Pumps, steam and other power.	1919	112	10,688	22,155	54,840	13,764	23,908	53,746	29,838
	1914	87	6,188	13,723	30,656	4,164	6,693	17,864	11,171
Refrigerators	1919	122	5,786	13,232	23,601	5,809	11,949	26,049	14,100
	1914	134	5,617	11,332	14,511	3,572	7,343	15,052	7,709
Regalia, and society badges and emblems.	1919	115	2,223	1,333	6,258	1,800	4,287	9,395	5,108
	1914	138	2,010	665	4,122	980	2,205	5,025	2,820
Rice, cleaning and polishing	1919	86	2,113	27,382	23,793	1,932	76,634	90,038	13,404
	1914	59	1,253	15,571	12,627	646	20,616	23,039	2,423
Roofing materials	1919	178	8,871	39,327	57,069	10,344	52,588	85,895	33,307
	1914	170	4,088	11,702	23,645	2,642	17,605	27,978	10,373
Rubber tires, tubes, and rubber goods, not elsewhere specified.	1919	437	119,848	354,188	782,638	156,807	525,686	987,088	461,402
	1914	301	50,220	151,927	199,183	31,279	126,112	223,611	97,499
Rules, ivory and wood	1919	13	168	299	415	142	134	481	347
	1914	10	408	441	883	224	187	634	447
Saddlery and harness	1919	1,823	10,411	8,212	49,368	10,849	52,443	83,713	31,270
	1914	2,551	12,969	10,397	45,207	7,996	33,086	53,559	20,473
Safes and vaults	1919	38	2,949	5,342	13,023	3,233	6,609	15,294	8,685
	1914	39	2,972	8,406	9,360	1,860	2,646	7,257	4,611
Salt	1919	86	6,495	43,187	47,725	7,353	16,028	37,514	21,486
	1914	98	5,089	29,007	33,151	3,041	6,273	14,070	7,797
Sand and emery paper and cloth.	1919	12	771	3,977	9,058	841	5,061	9,304	4,243
	1914	12	681	3,153	5,279	359	2,687	4,328	1,641
Sand-lime brick	1919	32	504	4,358	2,230	502	575	1,663	1,088
	1914	45	557	5,606	2,185	322	350	994	644
Sausage, not made in slaughtering and meat-packing establishments.	1919	633	3,471	12,713	13,777	4,679	43,940	56,610	12,670
	1914	512	2,244	7,930	5,201	1,607	17,292	22,014	4,722
Saws	1919	112	5,510	15,098	26,665	6,281	11,792	31,461	19,669
	1914	100	4,560	11,793	15,860	3,019	4,714	12,517	7,803
Scales and balances	1919	79	5,432	7,451	22,925	6,534	6,994	20,641	13,647
	1914	83	4,467	6,201	13,895	2,934	3,174	9,734	6,560

[1] Included in "all other industries" in 1914.

TABLE 88.—COMPARATIVE SUMMARY FOR THE UNITED STATES, BY INDUSTRIES: 1919 AND 1914—Continued.

[See note at head of this table, p. 1157.]

INDUSTRY.	Census year.	Number of establishments	Wage earners (average number).	Primary horsepower.	Capital.	Wages.	Cost of materials.	Value of products.	Value added by manufacture.
					Expressed in thousands of dollars.				
Screws, machine	1919	143	10,262	23,540	53,570	12,105	14,984	40,015	25,031
	1914	66	3,643	7,988	9,762	2,310	3,058	7,248	4,190
Screws, wood	1919	11	4,889	7,764	14,633	4,865	5,552	15,460	9,908
	1914	12	4,446	8,044	10,539	1,950	2,350	6,217	3,867
Sewing-machine cases	1919	5	4,171	10,656	17,332	5,161	8,018	14,243	6,225
	1914	4	3,699	6,031	6,425	2,230	2,841	5,846	3,005
Sewing machines and attachments.	1919	40	15,059	21,379	71,364	19,333	16,384	43,695	27,311
	1914	46	14,308	18,198	34,467	8,861	7,359	21,392	14,033
Shipbuilding, steel	1919	162	344,014	475,567	1,268,640	538,373	643,753	1,456,490	812,737
	1914	79	33,508	83,706	132,712	25,166	29,270	66,217	36,947
Shipbuilding, wooden, including boat building.	1919	913	43,432	78,144	120,808	59,074	66,770	165,872	99,102
	1914	1,068	10,981	31,627	23,348	7,765	9,327	22,465	13,138
Shirts	1919	896	39,603	14,944	102,012	25,834	127,088	205,327	78,239
	1914	792	51,972	17,617	50,944	19,170	50,665	95,815	45,150
Show cases	1919	119	1,857	4,423	5,378	1,996	4,032	8,294	4,262
	1914	132	2,257	4,145	4,155	1,466	2,248	5,233	2,985
Signs and advertising novelties.	1919	779	10,432	7,730	29,249	9,715	16,072	43,343	27,271
	1914	776	9,566	7,370	21,288	5,933	9,059	24,792	15,733
Silk goods	1919	1,369	126,782	176,825	532,732	108,226	388,469	688,470	300,001
	1914	902	108,170	116,924	210,072	47,108	144,442	254,011	109,569
Silversmithing and silverware.	1919	99	6,453	6,940	34,465	7,359	13,061	29,126	16,065
	1914	108	7,070	8,239	27,942	4,795	8,276	19,786	11,510
Slaughtering and meat-packing.	1919	1,304	160,996	359,212	1,176,484	209,489	3,782,930	4,246,291	463,361
	1914	1,279	98,832	253,066	534,274	62,136	1,441,663	1,651,965	210,302
Smelting and refining, copper.	1919	34	17,345	321,610	308,680	25,723	584,410	651,102	66,692
	1914	37	17,731	194,980	171,420	16,149	379,157	444,022	64,865
Smelting and refining, lead ...	1919	25	6,438	52,565	115,677	9,180	179,374	196,795	17,421
	1914	22	7,385	29,734	143,249	6,134	154,015	171,579	17,564
Smelting and refining, zinc ...	1919	39	13,796	73,604	98,757	17,783	70,015	104,123	34,108
	1914	29	9,617	36,705	36,388	6,700	39,573	53,538	13,965
Smelting and refining, metals, not elsewhere specified.[1]	1919	13	2,041	11,700	20,228	2,963	14,957	20,075	5,118
Smelting and refining, not from the ore.	1919	81	2,167	7,921	22,157	3,093	40,676	50,246	9,570
	1914	84	2,585	10,075	21,456	1,884	31,251	39,902	8,651
Soap	1919	348	20,436	33,710	212,417	21,228	238,519	316,740	78,221
	1914	371	14,172	35,737	92,872	8,088	88,867	127,942	39,075
Soda-water apparatus	1919	66	2,599	4,146	14,712	3,232	6,627	15,185	8,558
	1914	67	2,229	3,726	10,419	1,661	3,883	8,781	4,898
Sporting and athletic goods...	1919	188	6,412	6,875	19,951	5,753	11,969	23,840	11,871
	1914	162	5,602	4,356	8,468	2,771	6,952	13,235	6,283
Springs, steel, car and carriage, not made in steel works or rolling mills.	1919	112	8,981	16,585	45,472	11,158	28,019	51,480	23,461
	1914	84	3,703	8,098	11,083	2,602	6,143	11,595	5,452
Stamped and enameled ware, not elsewhere specified.	1919	323	34,248	51,441	132,222	34,851	65,457	143,654	78,197
	1914	270	28,731	34,767	68,979	15,243	32,472	65,121	32,649
Stationery goods, not elsewhere specified.	1919	223	11,261	8,342	36,701	9,578	28,160	58,363	30,203
	1914	189	7,728	5,703	18,186	3,791	10,763	21,903	11,140
Statuary and art goods	1919	195	1,466	684	3,146	1,716	1,379	5,020	3,641
	1914	190	1,988	826	3,394	1,583	842	3,910	3,068
Steam fittings and steam and hot-water heating apparatus.	1919	261	36,686	67,504	133,097	45,743	72,016	160,285	88,269
	1914	295	26,388	38,630	85,853	16,738	26,921	63,922	37,001
Steam packing	1919	169	6,147	26,763	36,934	7,103	22,725	40,525	17,800
	1914	149	4,213	17,254	17,708	2,525	8,176	14,213	6,037
Steel barrels, drums, and tanks, portable.[2]	1919	33	3,322	10,554	18,218	4,435	15,151	24,943	9,792
Stencils and brands	1919	84	417	374	1,111	429	514	1,598	1,084
	1914	107	446	411	863	301	332	1,103	771
Stereotyping and electrotyping.	1919	171	3,664	9,613	7,860	5,003	4,234	15,919	11,685
	1914	189	3,457	6,983	4,710	3,001	2,255	8,154	5,899
Stoves and hot-air furnaces...	1919	412	32,868	49,479	122,813	41,321	54,803	145,718	90,915
	1914	438	29,535	41,196	78,524	20,777	23,802	67,941	44,139
Stoves, gas and oil	1919	176	10,565	11,295	45,734	12,579	24,472	55,792	31,320
	1914	113	7,790	7,954	16,646	5,088	10,153	21,449	11,296
Structural ironwork, not made in steel works or rolling mills.	1919	1,146	43,962	165,347	219,470	59,920	168,801	294,962	126,161
	1914	1,235	47,167	109,374	144,092	33,429	87,622	159,378	71,756
Sugar, beet	1919	85	11,781	127,394	224,585	15,908	87,029	149,156	62,127
	1914	60	7,997	76,705	142,181	6,606	41,399	62,605	21,206

[1] Included in other classifications prior to 1919 and covers "smelting and refining, antimony," and "smelting and refining, tin," which could not be shown separately in 1919.

[2] Included in "foundry and machine shops" prior to 1919.

TABLE 88.—COMPARATIVE SUMMARY FOR THE UNITED STATES, BY INDUSTRIES: 1919 AND 1914—Continued.

[See note at head of this table, p. 1157.]

INDUSTRY.	Census year.	Number of establishments.	Wage earners (average number).	Primary horsepower.	Capital.	Wages.	Cost of materials.	Value of products.	Value added by manufacture.
					Expressed in thousands of dollars.				
Sugar, cane	1919	202	6,101	101,861	55,117	4,009	44,143	57,741	13,598
	1914	181	3,632	113,246	32,997	1,561	15,958	21,635	5,677
Sugar, refining, not including beet sugar.	1919	20	18,202	52,541	193,541	22,710	662,144	730,987	68,843
	1914	18	11,253	49,666	140,500	7,823	264,085	289,399	25,314
Sulphuric, nitric, and mixed acids.	1919	39	4,961	30,637	51,160	7,917	15,857	31,470	15,613
	1914	32	3,064	24,927	35,234	2,213	6,734	15,215	8,481
Surgical appliances	1919	268	6,390	12,387	33,063	6,084	22,214	43,534	21,320
	1914	238	4,282	6,361	11,883	2,211	7,098	14,920	7,822
Suspenders, garters, and elastic woven goods.	1919	196	10,857	9,028	39,677	9,270	36,369	60,775	24,406
	1914	216	9,646	7,524	16,344	4,276	15,191	24,433	9,242
Textile machinery and parts [1]	1919	432	31,823	41,997	129,798	36,529	45,637	122,089	76,452
Theatrical scenery	1919	17	149	104	573	238	505	1,067	562
	1914	7	88	65	266	89	125	327	202
Tin and other foils, not elsewhere specified.	1919	15	1,908	6,991	11,998	1,759	13,008	17,921	4,913
	1914	14	1,031	2,458	3,349	527	3,672	5,068	1,396
Tin plate and terneplate	1919	24	3,122	18,697	34,315	5,756	73,423	97,405	23,982
	1914	31	5,238	9,355	26,847	3,924	57,907	68,343	10,436
Tinware, not elsewhere specified.	1919	301	34,386	30,499	198,387	34,493	165,171	233,964	68,793
	1914	294	22,584	19,139	118,218	12,217	53,841	81,931	28,090
Tobacco, chewing and smoking, and snuff.	1919	365	18,324	18,893	188,444	12,675	130,270	239,271	109,001
	1914	436	25,980	21,273	131,858	9,550	76,604	175,281	98,677
Tobacco, cigars and cigarettes.	1919	9,926	138,773	24,504	416,395	111,313	353,297	773,662	420,365
	1914	13,515	152,892	13,664	171,982	68,306	130,530	314,884	184,354
Tools, not elsewhere specified.	1919	1,125	35,585	68,381	134,732	43,836	45,797	144,202	98,405
	1914	661	16,866	38,474	47,618	10,217	12,235	33,893	21,658
Toys and games	1919	541	14,201	14,449	27,738	11,847	19,841	45,657	25,816
	1914	290	7,887	6,789	10,484	3,499	5,779	13,757	7,978
Trunks and valises	1919	597	11,470	7,703	34,258	12,464	33,222	63,932	30,710
	1914	561	9,911	7,566	18,571	5,540	13,625	26,472	12,847
Turpentine and rosin	1919	1,191	28,067	2,303	33,596	16,973	13,930	53,051	39,121
	1914	1,394	34,817	2,478	20,745	8,583	5,536	20,990	15,454
Type founding	1919	23	810	850	4,429	868	943	2,090	1,147
	1914	31	1,054	1,657	5,516	666	901	2,320	1,419
Typewriters and supplies	1919	88	15,669	13,066	47,794	17,009	16,144	52,738	36,594
	1914	107	11,091	10,887	30,988	6,966	5,501	24,500	18,999
Umbrellas and canes	1919	198	3,368	3,383	15,397	3,140	15,633	25,309	9,676
	1914	265	4,792	2,579	9,469	2,167	8,592	13,813	5,221
Upholstering materials, not elsewhere specified.	1919	163	4,810	19,826	32,557	4,687	25,449	39,890	14,441
	1914	179	4,426	18,753	15,879	2,144	10,796	16,492	5,696
Varnishes	1919	229	4,022	11,497	62,461	4,568	51,508	83,632	32,124
	1914	215	2,734	7,656	29,861	1,865	16,877	33,215	16,338
Vault lights and ventilators	1919	41	316	279	904	424	811	2,156	1,345
	1914	45	601	491	1,054	457	959	2,051	1,092
Vinegar and cider	1919	720	1,981	17,943	20,515	2,047	15,559	24,723	9,164
	1914	618	1,229	13,162	8,055	713	4,440	7,811	3,371
Wall paper, not made in paper mills.	1919	48	4,262	8,158	19,922	3,882	13,153	23,048	9,895
	1914	48	4,738	7,010	17,620	2,703	8,536	15,887	7,351
Wall plaster and composition flooring.	1919	161	5,123	32,356	25,307	5,834	11,821	26,875	15,054
	1914	165	5,389	36,626	29,511	3,453	7,993	16,544	8,551
Washing machines and clothes wringers.	1919	105	5,956	8,836	25,986	6,431	23,389	40,771	17,382
	1914	111	2,302	4,903	7,298	1,221	4,148	7,600	3,452
Waste	1919	92	2,686	11,391	19,472	2,107	22,144	29,700	7,556
	1914	73	2,966	8,513	10,668	1,191	15,238	17,600	2,362
Watch and clock materials, except watchcases.	1919	27	582	252	1,021	413	550	1,342	792
	1914	25	670	626	1,296	380	343	1,015	672
Watchcases	1919	33	3,900	4,275	21,791	4,001	8,206	19,619	11,413
	1914	31	3,514	2,386	20,120	1,938	4,002	7,831	3,829
Watches	1919	18	15,888	7,202	49,001	16,599	6,393	32,044	25,651
	1914	15	12,390	6,624	36,389	7,524	2,669	14,275	11,606
Wheelbarrows	1919	11	291	765	1,151	271	971	1,680	709
	1914	21	323	1,198	947	199	429	942	513
Whips	1919	26	717	853	2,461	582	1,097	2,986	1,889
	1914	40	1,163	1,076	3,050	559	1,341	3,162	1,821
Windmills	1919	31	1,932	4,761	10,005	2,145	4,960	9,933	4,973
	1914	31	1,955	3,997	6,426	1,252	2,555	5,497	2,942
Window and door screens and weather strips.	1919	214	2,179	7,530	9,749	2,047	4,897	10,933	6,036
	1914	220	3,194	8,188	9,355	1,894	4,261	9,167	4,906
Window shades and fixtures	1919	287	4,411	8,948	18,699	3,669	18,250	29,191	10,941
	1914	286	4,077	6,607	11,526	2,181	11,889	17,444	5,555
Wire	1919	66	19,741	119,451	102,017	29,290	102,814	162,151	59,337
	1914	54	17,600	83,940	64,014	11,021	56,424	81,841	25,417

[1] Included in "foundry and machine shop products" prior to 1919.

TABLE 88.—COMPARATIVE SUMMARY FOR THE UNITED STATES, BY INDUSTRIES: 1919 AND 1914—Continued.

[See note at head of this table, p. 1157.]

INDUSTRY.	Census year.	Number of establishments	Wage earners (average number).	Primary horsepower.	Capital.	Wages.	Cost of materials.	Value of products.	Value added by manufacture
					Expressed in thousands of dollars.				
Wirework, not elsewhere specified.	1919	558	15,224	29,074	65,290	15,506	50,754	90,549	39,795
	1914	552	12,126	21,547	38,509	6,719	24,114	41,789	17,675
Wood distillation..............	1919	115	4,946	15,938	42,335	5,310	20,060	32,545	12,485
	1914	95	2,782	10,045	17,563	1,565	6,496	9,883	3,387
Wood preserving.............	1919	73	3,978	16,269	28,138	4,342	23,242	33,239	9,997
	1914	68	2,830	11,801	20,155	1,785	16,060	21,055	4,995
Wood, turned and carved.....	1919	722	10,649	39,958	23,542	9,307	16,609	34,847	18,238
	1914	828	11,615	43,334	17,836	5,645	9,166	19,047	9,881
Wooden goods, not elsewhere specified.	1919	245	6,443	25,906	21,111	5,662	10,173	21,793	11,620
	1914	274	6,418	20,711	10,440	2,767	4,952	10,162	5,210
Wool pulling..................	1919	24	705	2,162	8,853	910	12,810	17,361	4,551
	1914	34	708	2,248	3,534	452	6,632	8,273	1,641
Wool scouring.................	1919	33	2,177	9,790	10,050	2,896	7,228	13,680	6,452
	1914	24	1,059	7,579	3,493	617	3,176	4,565	1,389
Wool shoddy..................	1919	78	2,566	16,694	16,991	2,653	16,076	23,254	7,178
	1914	64	2,145	12,440	6,421	1,056	5,300	7,707	2,407
Woolen and worsted goods....	1919	852	166,787	468,480	831,695	168,109	665,595	1,065,434	399,839
	1914	799	158,692	381,220	389,653	75,953	246,497	379,484	132,987
All other industries[1]........	1919	5	99	154	131	90	200	361	161
	1914	14	523	1,158	3,628	400	762	1,661	899

[1] Comprises: In 1919, "straw goods, not elsewhere specified," 1 establishment; "whalebone cutting," 1; "wood carpet," 3. In 1914, "millstones," 2 establishments; "ordnance and accessories," 2; "pulp, from fiber other than wood," 3; "whalebone cutting." 1; "wood carpet," 6.

TABLE 89.—COMPARATIVE SUMMARY, BY GEOGRAPHIC DIVISIONS AND STATES: 1919, 1914, 1909, AND 1904.

DIVISION AND STATE.	Census year.	Number of establishments.	Wage earners (average number).	Primary horsepower.	Capital.	Wages.	Cost of materials.	Value of products.
					Expressed in thousands.			
UNITED STATES....	1919	290,105	9,096,372	29,504,792	$44,466,594	$10,533,400	$37,376,380	$62,418,079
	1914	275,791	7,036,247	22,437,072	22,790,980	4,078,332	14,368,089	24,246,435
	1909	268,491	6,615,046	18,675,376	18,428,270	3,427,038	12,142,791	20,672,052
	1904	216,180	5,468,383	13,487,707	12,675,581	2,610,445	8,500,208	14,793,903
GEOGRAPHIC DIVISIONS:								
New England......	1919	25,528	1,351,389	3,796,846	·5,656,409	1,436,435	3,951,908	7,183,071
	1914	25,193	1,140,233	3,124,329	2,948,040	628,409	1,657,674	2,926,676
	1909	25,351	1,101,290	2,715,121	2,503,854	557,631	1,476,297	2,670,065
	1904	22,279	940,752	2,125,815	1,870,995	439,050	1,116,273	2,025,999
Middle Atlantic....	1919	88,360	2,872,653	8,537,660	15,005,390	3,464,931	11,424,096	19,854,773
	1914	85,466	2,355,940	6,699,576	7,836,071	1,370,131	4,680,993	8,053,644
	1909	81,315	2,207,747	5,531.502	6,505,675	1,182,568	4,159,498	7,141,761
	1904	67,699	1,886,565	4,255,264	4,742,357	926,145	2,961,995	5,218,266
East North Central	1919	61,332	2,396,618	7,735,137	12,153,594	2,992,931	10,621,687	17,737,480
	1914	59,896	1,680,281	5,421,435	5,913,681	1,072,538	3,795,039	6,542,261
	1909	60,013	1,513,764	4,382,070	4,547,225	827,152	3,034,472	5,211,702
	1904	51,754	1,224,528	3,120,369	2,895,446	615,643	2,045,537	3,605,368
West North Central	1919	29,166	499,635	1,594,112	2,679,627	546,172	3,778,125	5,187,005
	1914	27,199	381,595	1,238,988	1,424,181	235,471	1,397,841	2,032,192
	1909	27,171	374,337	1,101,990	1,171,572	204,792	1,241,855	1,803,899
	1904	21,492	312,361	753,700	857,904	157,843	862,011	1,284,446
South Atlantic.....	1919	29,976	817,212	2,795,094	3,332,334	778,027	2,596,264	4,455,152
	1914	28,925	685,252	2,274,785	1,644,539	293,063	1,003,068	1,682,999
	1909	28,088	663,015	1,832,001	1,368,475	244,378	790,005	1,381,186
	1904	19,564	522,611	1,221,040	930,420	175,461	550,102	974,028
East South Central	1919	14,655	329,226	1,415,577	1,296,448	298,711	977,825	1,642,391
	1914	14,410	264,378	1,157,367	713,357	117,987	387,011	700,668
	1909	15,381	261,772	1,036,560	586,276	102,191	336,163	630,488
	1904	10,311	221,229	753,928	405,361	83,942	252,156	464,336
West South Central	1919	13,909	285,244	1,185,989	1,463,837	293,022	1,547,994	2,277,861
	1914	12,417	211,940	965,500	687,819	116,128	526,907	802,538
	1909	12,339	204,520	873,350	547,739	97,646	382,131	625,443
	1904	8,279	143,470	555,717	328,906	67,128	246,832	415,232
Mountain..........	1919	7,612	109,216	686,579	833,985	141,902	610,239	922,676
	1914	6,079	81,113	460,278	469,971	66,358	272,215	437,568
	1909	5,254	75,435	400,766	348,977	56,870	228,692	363,996
	1904	3,610	52,790	241,825	220,569	39,046	152,813	254,663
Pacific.............	1919	19,567	435,179	1,757,798	2,044,970	581,269	1,868,242	3,157,610
	1914	16,206	235,515	1,094,814	1,153,321	178,247	647,341	1,067,889
	1909	13,579	213,166	802,016	848,477	153,810	493,678	843,512
	1904	11,192	164,077	460,049	423,623	106,187	312,489	551,565
NEW ENGLAND:								
Maine..............	1919	2,995	88,651	547,028	419,158	94,225	254,568	456,822
	1914	3,378	82,149	487,211	233,844	43,254	117,655	200,450
	1909	3,546	79,955	459,599	202,260	37,632	97,101	176,029
	1904	3,145	74,958	343,627	143,708	32,692	80,042	144,020
New Hampshire...	1919	1,499	83,074	349,138	329,167	79,326	239,528	407,205
	1914	1,736	78,993	344,093	156,749	40,642	114,993	182,844
	1909	1,961	78,658	293,991	139,990	36,200	98,157	164,581
	1904	1,618	65,366	218,344	109,495	27,693	73,216	123,611
Vermont...........	1919	1,790	33,491	185,095	134,314	34,084	95,173	168,108
	1914	1,772	32,704	172,637	79,847	18,617	42,706	76,991
	1909	1,958	33,788	159,445	73,470	17,272	34,823	68,310
	1904	1,699	33,106	140,616	62,659	15,221	32,430	63,084
Massachusetts......	1919	11,906	713,836	1,729,878	2,947,109	766,623	2,260,713	4,011,181
	1914	12,013	606,698	1,396,722	1,548,961	341,310	931,384	1,641,373
	1909	11,684	584,559	1,175,071	1,279,687	301,174	830,765	1,490,529
	1904	10,723	488,399	938,007	965,949	232,389	626,411	1,124,092
Rhode Island......	1919	2,466	139,665	321,016	594,337	137,495	415,989	747,323
	1914	2,190	113,425	269,854	308,445	59,366	162,425	279,546
	1909	1,951	113,538	226,740	290,901	55,234	158,192	280,344
	1904	1,617	97,318	181,017	215,901	43,113	112,872	202,110

TABLE 89.—COMPARATIVE SUMMARY, BY GEOGRAPHIC DIVISIONS AND STATES: 1919, 1914, 1909, AND 1904—Continued.

DIVISION AND STATE.	Census year.	Number of establishments.	Wage earners (average number).	Primary horsepower.	Capital.	Wages.	Cost of materials.	Value of products.
					Expressed in thousands.			
NEW ENGLAND—Con.								
Connecticut........	1919	4,872	292,672	664,691	$1,232,324	$324,682	$685,937	$1,392,432
	1914	4,104	226,264	453,812	620,194	125,220	288,511	545,472
	1909	4,251	210,792	400,275	517,546	110,119	257,259	490,272
	1904	3,477	181,605	304,204	373,283	87,942	191,302	369,082
MIDDLE ATLANTIC:								
New York.........	1919	49,330	1,228,130	2,936,530	6,012,083	1,458,207	4,943,214	8,867,005
	1914	48,203	1,057,857	2,356,655	3,334,278	631,042	2,108,607	3,814,661
	1909	44,935	1,003,981	1,997,062	2,779,497	557,231	1,856,904	3,369,490
	1904	37,194	856,947	1,516,592	2,031,460	430,015	1,348,603	2,488,346
New Jersey........	1919	11,057	508,686	1,146,744	2,815,577	600,658	2,270,473	3,672,065
	1914	9,742	373,605	793,063	1,352,382	211,136	883,465	1,406,633
	1909	8,817	326,223	612,293	977,172	169,710	720,034	1,145,529
	1904	7,010	266,336	436,274	715,060	128,169	470,449	774,369
Pennsylvania......	1919	27,973	1,135,837	4,454,386	6,177,730	1,406,066	4,210,409	7,315,703
	1914	27,521	924,478	3,549,858	3,149,411	527,953	1,688,921	2,832,350
	1909	27,563	877,543	2,921,547	2,749,005	455,627	1,582,560	2,626,742
	1904	23,495	763,282	2,302,398	1,995,837	367,961	1,142,943	1,955,551
EAST NORTH CENTRAL:								
Ohio...............	1919	16,125	730,733	2,897,497	3,748,744	944,652	2,911,948	5,100,309
	1914	15,658	510,435	1,993,080	1,677,552	317,924	1,020,782	1,782,808
	1909	15,138	446,934	1,583,155	1,300,733	245,450	824,202	1,437,936
	1904	13,785	364,298	1,116,932	856,989	182,429	527,637	960,812
Indiana............	1919	7,916	277,580	1,095,912	1,335,714	317,043	1,174,951	1,898,753
	1914	8,022	197,503	709,703	668,863	119,259	423,857	730,795
	1909	7,969	186,984	633,377	508,717	95,510	334,375	579,075
	1904	7,044	154,174	380,758	312,071	72,058	220,507	393,954
Illinois............	1919	18,593	653,114	1,660,918	3,366,453	801,087	3,488,270	5,425,245
	1914	18,388	506,943	1,305,930	1,943,836	340,910	1,340,184	2,247,323
	1909	18,026	465,764	1,013,071	1,548,171	273,319	1,160,927	1,919,277
	1904	14,921	379,436	741,555	975,845	208,405	840,057	1,410,342
Michigan..........	1919	8,305	471,242	1,202,128	2,340,954	639,708	1,919,243	3,466,188
	1914	8,724	271,090	730,383	869,143	182,252	592,801	1,086,163
	1909	9,159	231,499	598,288	583,947	118,968	368,612	685,109
	1904	7,446	175,229	440,890	337,894	81,279	230,081	429,120
Wisconsin.........	1919	10,393	263,949	878,682	1,361,729	290,441	1,127,275	1,846,984
	1914	9,104	194,310	682,339	754,287	112,193	417,415	695,172
	1909	9,721	182,583	554,179	605,657	93,905	346,356	590,305
	1904	8,558	151,391	440,234	412,647	71,472	227,255	411,140
WEST NORTH CENTRAL:								
Minnesota..........	1919	6,225	115,623	473,957	679,386	127,107	883,090	1,218,130
	1914	5,974	92,834	358,737	354,434	58,507	336,849	493,354
	1909	5,561	84,767	297,670	275,416	47,471	281,622	409,420
	1904	4,756	69,636	220,934	184,903	35,843	210,554	307,858
Iowa..............	1919	5,683	80,551	242,946	403,206	90,117	520,241	745,473
	1914	5,614	63,113	190,049	233,128	39,860	205,451	310,750
	1909	5,528	61,635	155,384	171,219	32,542	170,707	259,238
	1904	4,785	49,481	118,065	111,428	22,997	102,844	160,572
Missouri..........	1919	8,592	195,037	477,303	938,761	196,515	1,056,457	1,594,208
	1914	8,386	152,182	391,385	522,548	89,197	388,715	637,952
	1909	8,375	152,993	340,467	444,343	80,843	354,411	574,111
	1904	6,464	133,167	247,861	379,369	66,644	252,258	439,549
North Dakota......	1919	894	4,472	17,791	24,550	5,401	44,489	57,374
	1914	699	3,275	14,062	14,213	2,416	14,484	21,147
	1909	752	2,789	13,196	11,585	1,787	13,674	19,137
	1904	507	1,755	9,873	5,704	1,032	7,096	10,218
South Dakota......	1919	1,414	6,382	22,191	30,933	7,905	42,986	62,171
	1914	898	3,788	16,324	15,060	2,628	17,080	24,139
	1909	1,020	3,602	17,666	13,018	2,297	11,476	17,870
	1904	686	2,492	11,154	7,585	1,422	8,697	13,086
Nebraska..........	1919	2,884	36,521	125,814	245,257	46,067	480,774	596,042
	1914	2,492	25,144	89,285	121,008	16,893	174,114	221,616
	1909	2,500	24,336	64,466	99,901	13,948	151,081	199,019
	1904	1,819	20,260	46,372	80,235	11,022	124,052	154,918

TABLE 89.—COMPARATIVE SUMMARY, BY GEOGRAPHIC DIVISIONS AND STATES: 1919, 1914, 1909, AND 1904—Continued.

DIVISION AND STATE.	Census year.	Number of establishments.	Wage earners (average number).	Primary horsepower.	Capital.	Wages.	Cost of materials.	Value of products.
					Expressed in thousands.			
W. NORTH CENTRAL—								
Continued								
Kansas	1919	3,474	61,049	234,110	$357,534	$73,060	$750,088	$913,667
	1914	3,136	41,259	179,146	163,790	25,970	261,148	323,234
	1909	3,435	44,215	213,141	156,090	25,904	258,884	325,104
	1904	2,475	35,570	99,441	88,680	18,883	156,510	198,245
SOUTH ATLANTIC:								
Delaware	1919	668	29,035	85,150	148,208	37,265	85,433	165,073
	1914	808	22,155	64,403	69,324	11,382	31,649	56,035
	1909	726	21,238	52,779	60,906	10,296	30,938	52,840
	1904	631	18,475	49,490	50,926	8,158	24,884	41,160
Maryland	1919	4,937	140,342	406,768	619,607	147,867	549,347	873,945
	1914	4,797	111,585	263,753	293,211	53,792	238,972	377,749
	1909	4,837	107,921	218,244	251,227	45,436	199,049	315,669
	1904	3,852	94,174	165,449	201,878	36,144	150,024	243,376
District of Columbia	1919	595	10,482	33,079	63,008	13,189	30,940	68,826
	1914	514	8,877	24,775	40,810	6,069	12,239	28,978
	1909	518	7,707	16,563	30,553	4,989	10,247	25,289
	1904	482	6,299	12,592	20,200	3,659	7,732	18,359
Virginia	1919	5,603	119,352	419,946	463,645	120,007	371,541	643,512
	1914	5,508	102,820	337,567	261,501	44,874	155,319	264,039
	1909	5,685	105,676	283,928	216,392	38,154	125,583	219,794
	1904	3,187	80,285	176,998	147,989	27,943	83,649	148,857
West Virginia	1919	2,785	83,036	328,653	339,190	101,840	270,941	471,971
	1914	2,749	71,078	278,504	175,995	43,784	110,033	193,512
	1909	2,586	63,893	217,496	150,922	33,000	92,878	161,949
	1904	2,109	43,758	138,578	86,821	21,153	54,419	99,041
North Carolina	1919	5,999	157,659	549,878	669,144	126,680	526,906	943,808
	1914	5,507	136,844	508,085	253,842	46,039	169,942	289,412
	1909	4,931	121,473	378,556	217,185	34,355	121,861	216,656
	1904	3,272	85,339	216,622	141,001	21,375	79,268	142,521
South Carolina	1919	2,004	79,450	395,556	374,538	62,566	227,986	381,453
	1914	1,885	71,824	340,224	203,211	24,173	91,009	138,891
	1909	1,854	73,046	276,378	173,221	20,361	66,351	113,236
	1904	1,399	59,441	197,479	113,422	13,869	49,969	79,376
Georgia	1919	4,803	123,441	436,608	448,700	101,180	440,490	693,237
	1914	4,639	104,461	357,403	258,326	38,128	160,089	253,271
	1909	4,792	104,588	298,241	202,778	34,805	116,970	202,863
	1904	3,219	92,749	220,419	135,211	27,393	83,625	151,040
Florida	1919	2,582	74,415	139,456	206,294	67,433	92,680	213,327
	1914	2,518	55,608	100,071	88,319	24,822	33,816	81,112
	1909	2,159	57,473	89,816	65,291	22,982	26,128	72,890
	1904	1,413	42,091	43,413	32,972	15,767	16,532	50,298
EAST SOUTH CENTRAL:								
Kentucky	1919	3,957	69,340	247,573	276,535	67,034	235,716	395,660
	1914	4,184	64,586	238,314	193,423	31,830	114,829	230,249
	1909	4,776	65,400	230,224	172,779	27,888	111,779	223,754
	1904	3,734	59,794	174,625	147,282	24,439	86,545	159,754
Tennessee	1919	4,589	95,167	338,814	410,203	81,355	344,767	556,253
	1914	4,775	74,373	286,857	211,423	33,083	123,430	212,071
	1909	4,609	73,840	242,277	167,924	28,251	104,016	180,217
	1904	3,175	60,572	175,780	102,440	22,806	79,352	137,961
Alabama	1919	3,654	107,159	628,376	455,593	99,066	300,664	492,731
	1914	3,242	78,717	445,762	227,505	33,897	107,412	178,798
	1909	3,398	72,148	357,837	173,180	27,284	83,442	145,962
	1904	1,882	62,173	293,185	105,383	21,878	60,458	109,170
Mississippi	1919	2,455	57,560	200,814	154,117	51,256	96,678	197,747
	1914	2,209	46,702	186,434	81,006	19,177	41,340	79,550
	1909	2,598	50,384	206,222	72,393	18,768	36,926	80,555
	1904	1,520	38,690	110,338	50,256	14,819	25,801	57,451
WEST SOUTH CENTRAL:								
Arkansas	1919	3,123	49,954	214,194	138,818	47,186	102,813	200,313
	1914	2,604	41,979	177,208	77,162	20,752	44,907	83,940
	1909	2,925	44,982	173,088	70,174	19,113	34,935	74,916
	1904	1,907	33,089	109,509	46,306	14,544	21,799	53,865

TABLE 89.—COMPARATIVE SUMMARY, BY GEOGRAPHIC DIVISIONS AND STATES: 1919, 1914, 1909, AND 1904—Continued.

DIVISION AND STATE.	Census year.	Number of establishments.	Wage earners (average number).	Primary horsepower.	Capital.	Wages.	Cost of materials.	Value of products.
					Expressed in thousands.			
W. SOUTH CENTRAL—Continued.								
Louisiana	1919	2,617	98,265	388,605	$462,209	$94,406	$431,404	$676,189
	1914	2,211	77,665	355,193	261,635	39,544	157,886	255,313
	1909	2,516	76,165	346,652	221,816	33,386	134,865	223,949
	1904	2,091	55,859	251,963	150,811	25,316	117,035	186,380
Oklahoma	1919	2,445	29,503	139,983	277,034	35,026	312,606	401,363
	1914	2,518	17,443	97,308	65,478	11,011	70,970	102,006
	1909	2,310	13,143	71,139	38,873	7,240	34,153	53,682
	1904	[1] 1,123	5,456	29,608	16,124	2,799	16,394	24,459
Texas	1919	5,724	107,522	443,207	585,776	116,404	701,171	999,996
	1914	5,084	74,853	335,791	283,544	44,821	253,144	361,279
	1909	4,588	70,230	282,471	216,876	37,907	178,178	272,896
	1904	3,158	49,066	164,637	115,665	24,469	91,604	150,528
Mountain:								
Montana	1919	1,290	17,160	153,491	137,476	24,743	122,152	166,665
	1914	939	13,704	91,671	79,246	13,001	46,744	84,446
	1909	677	11,655	90,402	44,588	10,901	49,180	73,272
	1904	382	8,957	46,736	52,590	8,652	40,930	66,415
Idaho	1919	922	13,917	73,876	96,062	18,548	43,949	80,511
	1914	698	8,919	50,326	44,961	7,491	14,892	28,454
	1909	725	8,220	42,804	32,477	5,498	9,920	22,400
	1904	364	3,061	16,987	9,689	2,059	4,069	8,769
Wyoming	1919	576	6,634	17,869	82,288	11,189	42,251	81,445
	1914	337	2,989	10,004	29,270	2,312	5,560	11,224
	1909	268	2,867	7,628	6,195	2,081	2,608	6,249
	1904	169	1,834	3,604	2,696	1,261	1,301	3,523
Colorado	1919	2,631	35,254	206,309	243,827	42,975	174,870	275,622
	1914	2,126	27,278	162,828	181,776	20,200	89,756	136,839
	1909	2,034	28,067	154,615	162,668	19,912	80,491	130,044
	1904	1,606	21,813	124,907	107,664	15,100	63,114	100,144
New Mexico	1919	387	5,736	17,260	15,226	6,659	7,727	17,857
	1914	368	3,776	12,468	8,984	2,695	4,430	9,320
	1909	313	4,143	15,465	7,743	2,591	3,261	7,898
	1904	199	3,478	5,948	4,638	2,153	2,236	5,706
Arizona	1919	480	8,528	103,958	101,486	12,015	92,645	120,769
	1914	322	6,898	54,697	40,300	6,229	39,283	64,090
	1909	311	6,441	39,140	32,873	5,505	33,600	50,257
	1904	169	4,793	21,412	14,396	3,969	14,595	28,083
Utah	1919	1,160	18,868	93,942	140,785	21,455	110,154	156,933
	1914	1,109	13,894	59,536	71,843	10,852	62,233	87,112
	1909	749	11,785	42,947	52,627	8,400	41,266	61,989
	1904	606	8,052	19,397	26,004	5,158	24,940	38,927
Nevada	1919	166	3,119	19,874	16,835	4,318	16,491	22,874
	1914	180	3,655	18,748	13,591	3,578	9,317	16,083
	1909	177	2,257	7,765	9,806	1,982	8,366	11,887
	1904	115	802	2,834	2,892	694	1,628	3,096
PACIFIC:								
Washington	1919	4,918	132,928	687,436	574,235	194,968	443,178	809,623
	1914	3,829	67,205	389,567	277,715	51,703	136,609	245,326
	1909	3,674	69,120	297,897	222,261	49,766	117,888	220,746
	1904	2,751	45,199	168,342	96,953	30,087	66,166	128,822
Oregon	1919	2,707	58,559	304,346	237,255	81,094	206,206	366,782
	1914	2,320	28,829	214,222	139,500	20,931	63,258	109,762
	1909	2,246	28,750	175,019	89,082	19,902	50,552	93,005
	1904	1,602	18,523	81,348	44,023	11,443	30,597	55,525
California	1919	11,942	243,692	766,016	1,233,480	305,207	1,218,858	1,981,205
	1914	10,057	139,481	491,025	736,106	105,613	447,474	712,801
	1909	7,659	115,296	329,100	537,134	84,142	325,238	529,761
	1904	6,839	100,355	210,359	282,647	64,657	215,726	367,218

[1] Includes Indian Territory.

TABLE 90.—DETAILED STATEMENT FOR THE

[Data for this table are presented in three sections, as follows: "Financial statistics,"pp. 1172 to 1199;" Per-

	INDUSTRY.	Number of establishments.	Capital.	FINANCIAL STATISTICS. Expenses. Salaries and wages.		
				Officers.	Clerks, etc.	Wage earners.
			Dollars.	Dollars.	Dollars.	Dollars.
1	All industries..............	290,105	44,466,593,771	1,453,261,706	1,439,109.788	10,533,400,340
2	Aeroplanes, seaplanes, and airships, and parts.	31	17,753,875	825,357	1,175,333	4,906,740
3	Agricultural implements..............	521	366,962,052	9,329,013	12,596,730	66,704,434
4	Aluminum manufactures..............	83	48,490,364	1,514,373	1,792,301	13,327,306
5	Ingots, plates, and sheets..........	7	2,072,960	115,781	26,117	821,059
6	Ware.....	39	29,052,635	650,995	971,472	8,554,543
7	All other...............	37	17,364,769	747,597	794,712	3,951,104
8	Ammunition.............	42	94,558,643	4,277,331	3,329,820	23,587,692
9	Artificial flowers.............	224	6,675,418	317,405	534,394	3,740,911
10	Artificial limbs.............	177	2,231,416	296,432	241,649	794,525
11	Artificial stone products.............	2,785	29,646,743	1,637,449	653,540	9,310,899
12	Artists' materials.............	58	4,663,790	337,524	241,412	895,764
13	Crayons.............	20	1,687,280	127,840	90,462	347,488
14	All other.............	38	2,976,510	209,684	150,950	548,276
15	Asbestos products, not including steam packing.	46	16,404,739	986,232	613,501	3,731,974
16	Building materials.............	12	4,456,057	165,199	143,087	1,590,294
17	Textile-mill products.............	16	9,450,303	645,689	379,192	1,695,991
18	All other.............	18	2,498,379	175,344	91,222	445,689
19	Automobile bodies and parts.............	2,515	470,497,552	19,917,333	15,051,007	178,955,503
20	Automobile repairing.............	15,507	141,123,954	6,237,721	5,265,398	71,613,471
21	Automobiles.............	315	1,310,451,400	34,591,682	32,624,122	312,165,870
22	Awnings, tents, and sails.............	895	26,727,621	1,903,641	1,098,506	5,858,523
23	Babbitt metal and solder.............	118	24,383,342	1,091,140	1,079,550	2,882,128
24	Babbitt metal.............	54	15,498,154	530,367	663,131	1,703,690
25	White metal.............	21	3,977,918	243,831	196,643	394,900
26	Type metal.............	7	218,348	40,033	19,114	25,713
27	Solder.............	36	4,688,922	276,909	200,662	757,825
28	Bags, other than paper, not including bags made in textile mills.	216	79,042,143	2,308,815	1,784,247	7,756,582
29	Bags, paper, exclusive of those made in paper mills.	75	24,584,881	1,171,415	1,003,945	3,662,830
30	Baking powders and yeast.............	88	43,486,136	1,011,677	1,795,739	3,554,534
31	Baking powders.............	67	29,080,892	647,956	1,563,534	1,466,335
32	Yeast.............	21	14,405.244	363,721	232,205	2,088,199
33	Baskets, and rattan and willow ware..	375	7,195,394	493,082	310,564	3,369.086
34	Bells.............	10	1,004,743	48,268	10,902	205,110
35	Belting and hose, rubber.............	15	45,919,568	832,137	2,045,474	6,073,539
36	Belting.............	8	19,900,767	346,787	765,270	2,374,302
37	Hose.............	7	26,018,801	485,350	1,280,204	3,699,237
38	Belting and hose, woven, other than rubber.	41	17,348,974	738,316	803,309	2,202,188
39	Woven belting.............	24	8,843,717	395,358	395,800	1,532,805
40	All other, including woven hose....	17	8,505,257	342,958	407,509	669,383
41	Belting, leather.............	172	27,533,899	1,440,466	1,255,313	3,260,439
42	Billiard tables, bowling alleys, and accessories.	49	7,040,990	163,455	107,953	2,425,353
43	Blacking, stains, and dressings.........	220	13,080,901	1,207,158	1,412,125	2,109,103
44	Bluing.............	57	1,227,619	88,683	74,809	285,063
45	Bone, carbon, and lampblack.........	35	9,790,167	265,813	46,573	808,332
46	Bone black and lampblack.........	6	1,612,781	128,778	20,680	315,690
47	Carbon black.............	29	8,177,386	137,035	25,893	492,642

UNITED STATES, BY INDUSTRIES: 1919.

sons engaged in manufacturing industries," pp. 1200 to 1225; and " Power and fuel used," pp. 1226 to 1255.]

FINANCIAL STATISTICS—continued.

Expenses—Continued.

For contract work.	Rent and taxes.		For materials.			Value of products.	Value added by manufacture.	
	Rent of factory.	Taxes, Federal, state, county, and local.	Total.	Principal materials.	Fuel and rent of power.			
Dollars.	Dollars.	Dollars.	Dollars.	Dollars.	Dollars.	Dollars.	Dollars.	
464,403,700	212,043,089	2,079,369,357	37,376,380,283	35,730,393,727	1,645,986,556	62,418,078,773	25,041,698,490	1
13,645	64,805	622,895	7,126,965	6,858,271	268,694	14,372,643	7,245,678	2
113,421	188,432	11,986,419	144,571,943	139,533,431	5,038,512	304,961,265	160,389,322	3
10,887	96,712	3,242,394	49,271,861	47,975,756	1,296,105	75,277,948	26,006,087	4
....	2,825	229,932	4,938,378	4,820,811	117,567	6,562,220	1,623,842	5
7,800	81,488	2,400,805	33,174,047	32,470,465	703,582	50,477,473	17,303,426	6
3,087	12,399	611,657	11,159,436	10,684,480	474,956	18,238,255	7,078,819	7
146,531	9,545	6,989,609	38,101,602	36,548,160	1,553,442	88,038,223	49,936,621	8
755,978	318,802	71,405	7,004,646	6,952,595	52,051	16,143,165	9,138,519	9
3,498	133,050	49,220	774,447	748,245	26,202	3,271,406	2,496,959	10
655,316	223,376	309,026	13,913,317	13,410,496	502,821	33,664,332	19,751,015	11
139,486	40,664	180,636	2,687,226	2,601,989	85,237	5,507,656	2,820,430	12
2,837	11,388	50,909	733,779	695,859	37,920	1,741,950	1,008,171	13
136,649	29,276	129,727	1,953,447	1,906,130	47,317	3,765,706	1,812,259	14
3,228	90,596	1,015,913	12,947,702	12,570,147	377,555	23,977,557	11,029,855	15
3,228	28,010	130,650	2,646,580	2,493,348	153,232	5,635,203	2,988,623	16
....	42,899	848,844	8,672,429	8,499,001	173,428	15,456,243	6,783,814	17
....	19,687	36,419	1,628,693	1,577,798	50,895	2,886,111	1,257,418	18
1,560,201	2,903,800	19,136,223	362,027,302	353,299,208	8,728,094	692,170,692	330,143,390	19
1,409,553	7,846,451	1,808,906	87,648,853	84,013,410	3,635,443	224,652,159	137,003,306	20
198,142	1,262,023	126,893,916	1,578,651,574	1,565,694,602	12,956,972	2,387,903,287	809,251,713	21
42,931	640,702	989,698	26,961,140	26,762,652	198,488	45,690,390	18,729,250	22
2,940	108,556	460,895	48,844,269	48,336,654	507,615	59,016,983	10,172,714	23
856	31,808	241,990	27,337,026	27,044,207	292,819	33,382,900	6,045,874	24
....	49,745	78,249	10,906,867	10,816,397	90,470	12,841,442	1,934,575	25
....	3,808	7,223	445,455	439,075	6,380	624,453	178,998	26
2,084	23,19	133,433	10,154,921	10,036,975	117,946	12,168,188	2,013,267	27
63,190	332,919	7,005,541	176,017,560	175,693,964	323,596	214,059,474	38,041,914	28
2,066	141,635	1,460,724	33,350,481	33,177,718	172,763	47,263,990	13,913,509	29
713	901,886	2,349,457	26,635,429	25,352,159	1,283,270	46,230,312	19,594,883	30
613	48,373	844,083	14,879,901	14,782,145	97,756	25,950,822	11,070,921	31
100	853,513	1,505,374	11,755,528	10,570,014	1,185,514	20,279,490	8,523,962	32
67,745	99,678	402,277	4,904,241	4,805,482	98,759	11,821,167	6,916,926	33
941	1,266	18,357	450,149	433,358	16,791	950,956	500,807	34
....	4,620	1,159,836	18,310,401	17,368,748	941,653	34,210,540	15,900,139	35
....	4,620	382,669	7,316,014	6,919,303	396,711	13,148,623	5,832,609	36
....	....	777,167	10,994,387	10,449,445	544,942	21,061,917	10,067,530	37
150	37,085	555,372	11,642,011	11,462,696	179,315	19,176,277	7,534,266	38
150	15,128	298,354	6,834,438	6,726,982	107,456	11,124,065	4,289,627	39
....	21,957	257,018	4,807,573	4,735,714	71,859	8,052,212	3,244,639	40
114,526	306,764	647,706	28,156,711	27,899,058	257,653	40,480,654	12,323,943	41
1,033	44,413	568,402	6,100,852	5,963,469	137,383	15,733,047	9,632,195	42
9,884	192,101	416,916	14,041,840	13,909,136	132,704	25,284,072	11,242,232	43
775	29,360	66,312	1,542,954	1,523,745	19,209	2,731,277	1,188,323	44
4,500	3,515	173,671	2,848,059	1,461,364	1,380,695	6,186,201	3,338,145	45
....	2,220	34,102	895,333	842,540	52,793	2,251,971	1,356,638	46
4,500	1,295	139,569	1,952,726	618,824	1,333,902	3,934,233	1,981,507	47

TABLE 90.—DETAILED STATEMENT FOR THE

[See note at head of this table, pp. 1172 and 1173.]

	INDUSTRY.	Number of establishments.	Capital.	FINANCIAL STATISTICS.		
				Expenses.		
				Salaries and wages.		
				Officers.	Clerks, etc.	Wage earners.
			Dollars.	*Dollars.*	*Dollars.* ·	*Dollars.*
1	Bookbinding and blank-book making..	1,113	43,041,207	3,390,421	4,063,491	18,658,821
2	Boot and shoe cut stock	252	61,747,458	2,117,633	1,210,593	9,124,778
3	Boot and shoe findings	427	28,988,416	1,733,472	885,126	8,187,196
4	Boots and shoes, not including rubber boots and shoes.	1,449	580,625,075	26,951,705	31,173,261	210,734,610
5	Regular factory products	1,337	575,994,289	26,392,953	30,811,331	208,787,565
6	Contract work	17	125,981	15,300	2,147	266,094
7	Stitching	19	121,839	7,604	4,872	273,082
8	Crimping	3	4,563			3,560
9	Buttonholes	3	2,150	1,144		6,998
10	Overgaiters, moccasins, and leggings.	70	4,376,253	534,704	354,911	1,397,311
11	Boots and shoes, rubber	25	131,513,436	2,481,481	4,919,907	30,882,722
12	Boxes, cigar	189	6,611,944	609,822	187,703	3,512,236
13	Boxes, paper and other, not elsewhere specified.	1,201	131,390,783	9,596,145	5,976,306	43,325,554
14	Shipping containers, corrugated and fiber.	162	43,235,991	2,437,230	2,050,655	10,128,512
15	Set-up paper boxes	865	52,184,477	5,069,536	2,191,748	24,081,287
16	Cartons	127	25,712,904	1,510,153	1,423,148	6,305,476
17	Paper cans and tubes	20	6,368,291	287,381	212,560	1,453,466
18	All other	27	3,889,120	291,845	98,195	1,356,813
19	Boxes, wooden packing, except cigar boxes.	1,140	108,932,998	6,631,685	2,022,948	36,811,185
20	Brass, bronze, and copper products	1,092	325,299,738	13,560,148	10,056,528	94,132,118
21	Brass and bronze	1,007	270,637,860	12,008,636	8,702,904	79,567,785
22	Copper	47	43,659,485	1,170,698	1,042,468	12,084,924
23	All other	38	11,002,393	380,814	311,156	2,479,409
24	Bread and other bakery products	25,095	509,265,779	15,214,012	33,605,954	158,237,059
25	Biscuit and crackers	176	112,248,722	2,936,597	9,169,085	26,065,795
26	Bakery products, other than biscuit and crackers.	24,919	397,017,057	12,277,415	24,436,869	132,171,264
27	Brick and tile, terra-cotta, and fire-clay products.	2,414	355,848,355	10,989,977	4,850,930	78,256,085
28	Building brick	1,454	156,462,633	5,206,529	1,449,188	36,728,569
29	Fire brick	194	60,048,068	1,914,488	968,489	13,222,078
30	Stove lining	19	965,420	72,003	37,851	333,654
31	Sewer pipe and draintile	478	44,993,643	1,274,333	669,972	10,506,264
32	Terra-cotta products	214	56,430,447	1,676,795	1,072,484	11,648,762
33	Silicate, magnesite, and bauxite bricks and shapes.	39	28,898,031	649,766	453,005	4,562,036
34	All other	16	8,050,113	196,063	199,941	1,254,722
35	Brooms	1,034	16,707,682	994,656	951,470	5,708,885
36	From broom corn	1,000	16,382,347	970,643	944,461	5,599,564
37	All other	34	325,335	24,013	7,009	109,321
38	Brushes	379	27,208,200	1,995,872	1,652,722	7,113,201
39	Toilet	44	5,602,115	502,275	303,950	1,556,967
40	Paint and varnish	44	7,699,668	552,083	456,356	2,064,081
41	All other	291	13,906,417	941,514	892,416	3,492,153
42	Butter	3,738	162,302,108	5,247,090	4,274,999	18,852,729
43	Butter, reworking	5	602,902	14,000	8,701	56,432
44	Buttons	557	29,977,973	1,993,965 ·	1,335,363	13,772,599
45	Candles	19	4,033,426	222,284	65,548	437,581
46	Canning and preserving, fish	410	63,049,038	2,140,863	761,682	9,036,089

UNITED STATES, BY INDUSTRIES: 1919—Continued.

[See note at head of this table, pp. 1172 and 1173.]

FINANCIAL STATISTICS—continued.

Expenses—Continued.

For contract work.	Rent and taxes.		For materials.			Value of products.	Value added by manufacture.	
	Rent of factory.	Taxes, Federal, state, county, and local.	Total.	Principal materials.	Fuel and rent of power.			
Dollars.	*Dollars.*	*Dollars.*	*Dollars.*	*Dollars.*	*Dollars.*	*Dollars.*	*Dollars.*	
452,225	1,516,503	984,763	23,235,171	22,750,119	485,052	66,020,677	42,785,506	1
24,808	369,545	1,384,147	133,887,276	133,270,830	616,446	161,203,310	27,316,034	2
840,302	403,588	1,069,501	40,428,347	40,017,475	410,872	62,825,408	22,397,061	3
1,930,544	3,023,816	22,136,773	715,269,315	709,351,356	5,917,959	1,155,041,436	439,772,121	4
1,904,887	2,916,821	21,960,352	710,607,817	704,733,137	5,874,680	1,146,137,272	435,529,455	5
850	10,440	2,267	43,985	36,458	7,527	392,215	348,230	6
....	7,561	5,398	83,100	78,096	5,004	457,807	374,707	7
....	429	16	188	....	188	10,658	10,470	8
....	1,200	24	3,681	2,922	759	14,896	11.215	9
24,807	87,365	168,716	4,530,544	4,500,743	29,801	8,028,588	3,498,044	10
96,467	58,134	3,021,931	50,346,880	49,025,640	1,321,240	116,917,434	66,570,554	11
532,479	135,115	197,067	6,336,540	6,205,752	130,788	-13,110,213	6,773,673	12
357,704	2,485,396	5,506,507	101,135,292	98,932,387	2,202,905	206,419,343	105,284,051	13
102,910	439,331	2,118,426	38,741,081	37,961,040	780,041	67,585,184	28,844,103	14
209,717	1,610,877	1,911,032	39,606,724	38,635,637	971,087	93,382,066	53,775,342	15
45,017	297,954	1,105,204	16,544,331	16,227,863	316,498	33,330,163	16,785,802	16
60	91,045	264,430	3,410,823	3,346,570	64,253	6,615,949	3,205,126	17
....	46,189	107,415	2,832,303	2,761,277	71,026	5,505,981	2,673,678	18
633,898	840,668	4,177,522	102,946,235	101,905,193	1,041,042	177,818,454	74,872,219	19
419,868	851,814	13,795,301	304,823,580	292,136,779	12,686,801	482,312,790	177,489,210	20
415,772	770,487	11,797,465	234,945,137	224,374,033	10,571,104	389,550,094	154,604,957	21
2,962	62,989	1,633,904	60,192,325	58,447,508	1,744,817	78,338,948	18,146,623	22
1,134	18,338	363,932	9,686,118	9,315,238	370,880	14,423,748	4,737,630	23
711,822	11,239,480	14,597,357	713,239,411	693,764,530	19,474,881	1,151,896,318	438,656,907	24
11,857	701,037	6,104,230	103,134,410	101,336,863	1,797,547	204,020,565	100,886,155	25
699,965	10,538,443	8,493,127	610,105,001	592,427,667	17,677,334	947,875,753	337,770,752	26
528,613	425,078	4,808,971	67,488,113	33,084,160	34,403,953	208,422,920	140,934,807	27
240,461	310,133	1,988,159	27,831,794	10,226,360	17,605,434	95,160,990	67,329,196	28
74,901	27,643	1,131,399	13,361,252	8,207,925	5,153,327	36,183,815	22,822,563	29
6,657	2,437	19,765	366,090	295,933	70,157	1,094,710	728,620	30
54,040	17,141	630,668	9,608,339	4,398,086	5,210,253	27,732,324	18,123,985	31
144,424	43,607	529,027	8,209,113	4,010,094	4,199,019	29,081,405	20,872,292	32
8,130	15,700	419,079	7,207,804	5,369,870	1,837,934	15,853,257	8,645,453	33
....	8,417	90,874	903,721	575,892	327,829	3,316,419	2,412,698	34
153,414	161,705	394,132	17,365,109	17,169,441	195,668	30,205,267	12,840,158	35
148,516	149,964	391,298	17,148,308	16,956,814	191,494	29,709,839	12,561,531	36
4,898	11,741	2,834	216,801	212,627	4,174	495,428	278,627	37
118,559	290,962	1,245,749	19,598,133	19,281,639	316,494	39,005,607	19,407,474	38
27,052	46,125	485,614	3,487,494	3,417,408	70,086	7,936,001	4,448,507	39
14,922	76,147	327,173	5,942,619	5,847,849	94,770	11,171,342	5,228,723	40
76,585	168,690	432,962	10,168,020	10,016,382	151,638	19,898,264	9,730,244	41
428,799	628,124	2,786,657	514,345,739	509,928,330	4,417,409	583,163,011	68,817,272	42
....	3,637	3,929	2,005,769	1,995,699	10,070	2,229,035	223,266	43
338,209	452,104	736,456	16,745,357	16,062,931	682,426	41,840,459	25,095,102	44
3,503	5,785	67,538	2,178,528	2,140,502	38,026	3,350,806	1,172,278	45
445,746	168,200	1,410,799	52,410,951	51,539,475	871,176	77,284,412	24,873,461	46

TABLE 90.—DETAILED STATEMENT FOR THE

[See note at head of this table, pp. 1172 and 1173.]

	INDUSTRY.	Number of establishments.	Capital.	Officers.	Clerks, etc.	Wage earners.
			FINANCIAL STATISTICS.			
				Expenses.		
				Salaries and wages.		
			Dollars.	Dollars.	Dollars.	Dollars.
1	Canning and preserving, fruits and vegetables.	3,082	223,692,234	9,312,121	4,038,979	43,592,537
2	Canned vegetables	1,989	134,442,080	5,730,288	1,741,654	19,768,284
3	Canned fruits	446	68,006,910	2,929,351	1,708,627	18,563,011
4	Dried fruits	629	19,300,168	580,707	528,497	4,793,769
5	Dried vegetables	18	1,943,076	71,775	60,201	467,473
6	Canning and preserving, oysters	65	2,971,876	109,700	39,383	468,930
7	Card cutting and designing	75	2,297,970	261,022	181,880	958,877
8	Cardboard, not made in paper mills	16	6,493,032	534,639	209,084	1,337,177
9	Carpets and rugs, other than rag	75	119,196,461	2,768,222	1,981,562	24,216,121
10	Carpets, rag	339	2,853,400	159,330	224,540	1,550,501
11	Carriage and wagon materials	258	17,971,206	934,688	370,856	5,666,771
12	Carriages and sleds, children's	103	15,215,425	915,672	828,413	6,229,038
13	Carriages and wagons, including repairs.	2,286	78,952,868	2,773,967	1,757,371	19,393,395
14	Carriages and wagons	1,130	71,701,095	2,580,123	1,692,857	16,468,039
15	Repair work only	1,156	7,251,773	193,844	64,514	2,925,356
16	Cars and general shop construction and repairs by electric-railroad companies.	624	82,557,905	1,932,578	1,046,789	39,073,154
17	Cars and general shop construction and repairs by steam-railroad companies.	1,744	694,286,410	41,225,228	25,722,872	687,617,312
18	Cars, electric-railroad, not including operations of railroad companies.	7	17,306,485	475,212	377,639	4,132,090
19	Cars, steam-railroad, not including operations of railroad companies.	99	335,207,363	6,376,052	7,369,340	78,284,647
20	Cash registers and calculating machines.	65	82,798,293	1,908,421	2,074,249	22,537,265
21	Adding machines	20	45,806,563	846,967	971,512	11,824,664
22	Cash registers and parts	19	27,832,693	661,159	828,692	9,012,357
23	All other	26	9,159,037	400,295	274,045	1,700,244
24	Cement	123	271,269,259	4,031,334	5,464,467	33,194,920
25	Charcoal, not including production in the lumber and wood-distillation industries.	41	518,762	42,146	4,762	156,072
26	Cheese	3,530	26,022,734	389,924	660,119	4,808,991
27	Chemicals	598	484,488,412	12,546,127	11,794,507	72,848,324
28	Chewing gum	62	23,703,313	856,230	991,409	2,679,803
29	China decorating, not including that done in potteries.	43	470,153	38,805	42,820	244,211
30	Decalcomania work on china	9	110,642	20,000	2,702	31,816
31	All other	34	359,511	18,805	40,118	212,395
32	Chocolate and cocoa products	48	60,674,737	1,928,732	2,109,724	9,270,077
33	Cleansing and polishing preparations	499	12,979,414	1,436,604	2,261,710	1,898,447
34	Cleansing preparations	281	6,354,297	763,242	1,181,252	854,824
35	Metal polish	81	1,479,090	211,945	156,204	239,359
36	All other polishing preparations	137	5,146,027	461,417	924,254	804,264
37	Clocks	46	18,349,943	905,765	1,092,609	7,861,611
38	Cloth, sponging and refinishing	67	1,465,956	504,689	107,674	1,564,661
39	Clothing, horse	28	3,704,741	169,948	148,483	551,278
40	Clothing, men's	5,258	554,147,279	26,399,992	34,943,008	197,821,990
41	Regular factory products	2,905	542,293,058	25,524,147	34,607,616	142,774,594
42	Men's and youths'	1,768	403,200,021	18,869,566	26,581,083	108,284,289
43	Boys'	379	49,608,707	1,789,079	2,878,664	11,456,650
44	All other	758	89,484,330	4,865,502	5,147,869	23,033,655
45	Contract work	2,353	11,854,221	875,845	335,392	55,047,396
46	Men's and youths'	2,005	9,415,557	735,136	292,326	46,312,643
47	Boys'	253	1,341,740	96,460	25,118	7,358,145
48	All other	95	1,096,924	44,249	17,948	1,376,608

UNITED STATES, BY INDUSTRIES: 1919—Continued.

[See note at head of this table, pp. 1172 and 1173.]

| | Rent and taxes. | | For materials. | | | Value of products. | Value added by manufacture. | |
For contract work.	Rent of factory.	Taxes, Federal, state, county, and local.	Total.	Principal materials.	Fuel and rent of power.			
Dollars.	*Dollars.*	*Dollars.*	*Dollars.*	*Dollars.*	*Dollars.*	*Dollars.*	*Dollars.*	
328,580	1,445,342	10,426,834	265,628,525	261,910,079	3,718,446	402,242,972	136,614,447	1
198,598	445,287	4,443,930	101,836,478	100,103,219	1,733,259	162,097,699	60,261,221	2
89,991	166,803	5,277,026	89,299,975	88,115,331	1,184,644	150,474,213	61,174,238	3
39,991	827,098	658,971	72,952,712	72,264,013	688,699	87,252,343	14,299,631	4
....	6,154	46,907	1,539,360	1,427,516	111,844	2,418,717	879,357	5
56,053	12,993	30,361	1,582,838	1,526,173	56,665	2,976,011	1,393,173	6
4,519	99,705	321,777	2,298,389	2,269,678	28,711	5,323,349	3,024,960	7
3,715	24,752	284,736	4,953,915	4,802,293	151,622	9,138,415	4,184,500	8
86,716	142,850	3,841,821	67,118,039	65,390,376	1,727,663	123,253,828	56,135,789	9
39,936	105,019	34,502	2,037,874	1,947,915	89,959	5,597,057	3,559,183	10
17,448	74,002	561,082	14,734,673	14,437,114	297,559	26,765,316	12,030,643	11
9,134	75,369	522,878	11,700,158	11,492,554	207,604	24,506,596	12,806,438	12
164,591	539,453	2,282,711	48,362,456	47,210,301	1,152,155	91,463,225	43,100,769	13
117,149	210,477	2,194,956	44,912,172	43,947,489	964,683	82,013,326	37,101,154	14
47,442	228,976	87,755	3,450,284	3,262,812	187,472	9,449,899	5,999,615	15
118,335	61,576	703,887	32,025,484	30,820,218	1,205,266	75,210,701	43,185,217	16
1,389,192	192,185	2,900,993	515,803,210	484,402,576	31,400,634	1,279,235,393	763,432,183	17
....	10,879	436,110	12,058,942	11,681,416	377,526	18,441,976	6,383,034	18
39,054	158,045	30,181,196	356,084,545	349,903,930	6,180,615	538,222,831	182,138,286.	19
28,646	100,368	4,852,747	10,889,998	10,527,407	362,591	83,539,025	72,649,027	20
1,888	41,947	2,807,628	5,662,705	5,531,869	130,836	47,632,471	41,969,766	21
19,432	21,201	1,397,577	4,003,380	3,807,954	195,426	30,932,883	26,929,503	22
7,326	37,220	647,542	1,223,913	1,187,584	36,329	4,973,671	3,749,758	23
266,204	2,396,468	3,793,899	79,509,800	48,439,204	31,070,596	175,264,910	95,755,110	24
4,487	1,443	11,083	260,322	197,349	62,973	589,418	329,096	25
42,567	129,213	278,661	129,425,265	127,988,010	1,437,255	143,455,704	14,030,439	26
1,321,738	596,741	31,931,389	216,301,279	183,558,969	32,742,310	438,658,869	222,357,590	27
2,027	102,809	3,867,089	25,202,312	24,997,529	204,783	51,240,156	26,037,844	28
4,615	20,481	10,980	310,785	290,493	20,292	866,762	555,977	29
....	2,290	3,624	63,366	59,311	4,055	149,495	86,129	30
4,615	18,191	7,356	247,419	231,182	16,237	717,267	469,848	31
1,463	271,685	5,765,825	101,754,466	100,347,208	1,407,258	139,258,296	37,503,830	32
30,459	260,565	548,856	12,923,518	12,794,567	128,951	26,703,109	13,779,591	33
7,857	145,331	315,559	6,807,201	6,733,987	73,214	13,297,574	6,490,373	34
5,998	42,094	36,163	1,863,900	1,844,027	19,873	3,185,624	1,321,724	35
16,604	73,140	197,134	4,252,417	4,216,553	35,864	10,219,911	5,967,494	36
31,534	40,333	905,545	7,177,813	6,962,991	214,822	23,380,190	16,202,377	37
....	235,776	22,917	178,161	119,829	58,332	3,690,858	3,512,697	38
8,325	19,887	263,505	3,455,686	3,413,273	42,413	6,020,612	2,564,926	39
108,072,822	8,640,249	14,505,128	605,752,176	603,031,493	2,720,683	1,162,985,633	557,233,457	40
105,338,221	7,437,771	14,435,417	599,017,010	596,939,394	2,077,616	1,082,472,043	483,455,033	41
88,165,796	5,476,019	10,895,539	428,463,939	427,138,978	1,324,961	802,065,605	373,601,666	42
14,420,328	874,430	398,540	58,857,575	58,711,485	146,090	105,174,820	46,317,245	43
2,752,097	1,086,822	3,141,338	111,695,496	111,088,931	606,565	175,231,618	63,536,122	44
2,734,601	1,202,478	69,711	6,735,166	6,092,099	643,067	80,513,590	73,778,424	45
2,635,855	977,940	58,626	5,682,056	5,145,649	536,407	67,595,689	61,913,633	46
85,443	184,820	4,445	658,869	578,539	80,330	10,509,026	9,850,157	47
13,303	39,718	6,640	394,241	367,911	26,330	2,408,875	2,014,634	48

TABLE **90.**—DETAILED STATEMENT FOR THE

[See note at head of this table, pp. 1172 and 1173.]

	INDUSTRY.	Number of establishments.	FINANCIAL STATISTICS.			
			Capital.	Expenses.		
				Salaries and wages.		
				Officers.	Clerks, etc.	Wage earners.
			Dollars.	*Dollars.*	*Dollars.*	*Dollars.*
1	Clothing, men's, buttonholes...........	107	237,066	56,180	8,398	514,600
2	Clothing, women's.....................	7,711	390,526,517	26,821,938	32,214,037	195,295,834
3	Regular factory products...........	5,516	377,474,663	25,371,448	31,751,938	162,973,102
4	Suits, skirts, and cloaks........	1,820	137,634,097	8,385,135	12,707,167	67,250,369
5	Shirt waists and dresses, except house dresses.	1,873	124,494,156	9,790,711	10,821,475	58,440,997
6	Undergarments and petticoats.	637	50,667,710	3,151,401	3,860,311	15,674,749
7	Wrappers and house dresses....	238	18,065,087	954,004	1,224,739	5,058,963
8	All other.................	948	46,613,613	3,090,197	3,138,246	16,548,024
9	Contract work.....................	2,195	13,051,854	1,450,490	462,099	32,322,732
10	Suits, skirts, and cloaks......	974	5,347,676	474,244	224,285	13,809,126
11	Shirt waists and dresses, except house dresses.	888	5,997,280	804,852	222,227	14,025,785
12	Undergarments and petticoats.	76	461,890	54,559	7,392	831,898
13	Wrappers and house dresses....	47	178,434	16,633	....	447,927
14	All other.................	210	1,066,574	100,202	8,195	3,207,996
15	Coal-tar products....................	183	174,991,835	6,540,404	5,292,665	23,402,140
16	Coffee and spice, roasting and grinding.	794	127,747,535	4,829,460	11,674,557	9,201,242
17	Coffee..............................	769	120,738,665	4,528,833	11,131,461	8,170,078
18	Spice..............................	25	7,008,870	300,627	543,096	1,031,164
19	Coffins, burial cases, and undertakers' goods.	351	48,298,053	2,675,939	3,155,269	11,450,957
20	Coke, not including gas-house coke.....	278	365,249,622	3,669,708	3,936,077	42,299,292
21	Beehive ovens..................	222	137,906,875	1,298,081	1,473,650	16,238,770
22	By-product ovens.................	56	227,342,747	2,371,627	2,462,427	26,060,522
23	Collars and cuffs, men's...........	39	30,146,935	941,472	1,071,167	7,430,729
24	Combs and hairpins, not made from metal or rubber.	45	3,913,266	341,408	146,919	1,809,453
25	Condensed milk.....................	401	126,952,520	3,223,142	2,422,424	14,277,956
26	Confectionery and ice cream...........	6,624	317,043,923	19,612,246	20,183,783	76,159,866
27	Confectionery.....................	3,149	219,634,526	14,396,411	16,848,059	54,461,057
28	Ice cream...........................	3,475	97,409,397	5,215,835	3,335,724	21,698,809
29	Cooperage..........................	1,099	48,853,805	2,247,584	675,593	14,082,224
30	Hogsheads and barrels..............	995	43,780,584	1,910,880	549,560	12,344,092
31	All other.....................	104	5,073,221	336,704	126,033	1,738,132
32	Copper, tin, and sheet-iron work.......	4,796	89,944,834	7,307,177	3,702,321	33,866,823
33	Cordage and twine.................	120	100,248,987	2,673,633	1,341,868	14,700,061
34	Cordials and flavoring sirups...........	149	11,673,732	962,836	1,254,981	1,297,281
35	Cork, cutting..................	62	14,570,221	624,016	404,023	3,387,114
36	Corsets...........................	188	43,516,486	3,083,669	4,066,498	13,082,242
37	Corsets........................	142	38,733,498	2,702,687	3,414,277	11,525,956
38	Corset waists and brassieres........	46	4,782,988	380,982	652,221	1,556,286
39	Cotton goods......................	1,288	1,853,099,816	27,015,767	10,348,711	355,474,937
40	Cotton lace......................	44	32,260,216	977,540	1,046,901	6,086,557
41	Cotton small wares...............	164	29,559,474	1,679,774	695,268	7,162,218
42	Crucibles.......................	22	8,069,334	409,805	114,590	923,287
43	Graphite crucibles..................	6	2,997,527	115,634	45,105	257,119
44	Clay crucibles..................	10	4,081,174	231,965	50,860	265,461
45	Glass-house pots..................	6	990,633	62,206	18,625	400,707
46	Cutlery and edge tools..............	304	68,971,247	2,686,125	2,054,836	20,048,465
47	Table cutlery....................	24	4,889,542	270,794	160,883	2,114,878
48	Razors, plain and safety...........	33	29,028,675	677,462	901,326	3,942,711
49	Axes and hatchets.............	25	10,306,906	236,608	152,221	2,819,028
50	Scissors, shears, and clippers........	52	8,938,737	504,581	424,616	3,658,814
51	Pocketknives...................	40	9,155,131	468,832	222,303	4,456,697
52	Augers, bits, chisels, and planes...	27	2,821,826	190,627	98,233	1,296,154
53	All other....................	103	3,830,430	337,221	95,254	1,760,183

UNITED STATES, BY INDUSTRIES: 1919—Continued.

[See note at head of this table, pp. 1172 and 1173.]

FINANCIAL STATISTICS—continued.

Expenses—Continued.

For contract work.	Rent and taxes.		For materials.			Value of products.	Value added by manufacture.	
	Rent of factory.	Taxes, Federal, state, county, and local.	Total.	Principal materials.	Fuel and rent of power.			
Dollars.	Dollars.	Dollars.	Dollars.	Dollars.	Dollars.	Dollars.	Dollars.	
3,750	33,909	1,534	123,266	112,008	11,258	1,090,049	966,783	1
52,426,167	13,626,596	4,638,255	680,406,844	677,889,534	2,517,310	1,208,543,128	528,136,284	2
50,816,302	11,911,489	4,582,020	669,071,033	666,980,130	2,090,903	1,146,312,346	477,241,313	3
19,773,737	4,534,773	1,759,636	281,268,342	280,521,173	747,169	492,081,024	210,812,682	4
22,907,392	4,268,366	1,420,772	221,665,839	221,003,348	662,491	379,895,926	158,230,087	5
2,266,346	1,271,779	676,144	81,050,620	80,762,423	288,197	125,662,282	44,611,662	6
1,300,007	442,056	190,746	24,090,153	23,997,954	92,199	39,538,694	15,448,541	7
4,568,820	1,394,515	534,722	60,996,079	60,695,232	300,847	109,134,420	48,138,341	8
1,609,865	1,715,107	56,235	11,335,811	10,909,404	426,407	62,230,782	50,894,971	9
942,800	721,699	8,553	5,443,515	5,286,253	157,262	27,428,596	21,985,081	10
587,432	819,809	10,777	4,886,080	4,699,799	186,281	27,456,658	22,570,578	11
4,416	33,797	33,647	463,110	440,788	22,322	1,714,437	1,251,327	12
11,790	20,031	492	65,154	54,482	10,672	873,218	808,064	13
63,337	119,771	2,776	477,952	428,082	49,870	4,757,873	4,279,921	14
896,830	782,370	4,659,741	63,996,734	59,855,701	4,141,033	135,482,161	71,485,427	15
343,450	1,371,034	2,844,725	243,899,108	242,742,802	1,156,306	304,791,677	60,892,569	16
343,450	1,319,744	2,689,997	234,405,774	233,316,525	1,089,249	291,663,930	57,258,156	17
	51,290	154,728	9,493,334	9,426,277	67,057	13,127,747	3,634,413	18
9,359	286,448	3,244,638	31,595,287	31,061,231	534,056	64,377,133	32,781,846	19
81,127	467,217	8,835,047	224,266,674	23,497,210	200,769,464	316,515,838	92,249,164	20
6,918	318,706	2,338,836	78,155,895	7,405,378	70,750,517	112,023,466	33,867,571	21
74,209	148,511	6,496,211	146,110,779	16,091,832	130,018,947	204,492,372	58,381,593	22
977,963	62,681	1,123,784	19,434,095	19,206,564	227,531	47,564,949	28,130,854	23
24,212	22,049	78,710	3,168,818	3,082,743	86,075	6,566,365	3,397,547	24
240,609	159,842	4,861,213	282,595,292	277,324,307	5,270,985	339,506,774	56,911,482	25
1,191,586	6,233,367	27,517,170	368,809,170	360,517,580	8,291,590	637,209,168	268,399,998	26
1,071,449	4,566,590	23,837,274	252,433,691	248,264,352	4,169,339	447,726,103	195,292,412	27
120,137	1,666,777	3,679,896	116,375,479	112,253,228	4,122,251	189,483,065	73,107,586	28
25,327	284,630	1,814,476	58,520,655	58,013,251	507,404	88,236,061	29,715,406	29
24,672	233,145	1,547,567	52,041,140	51,594,720	446,420	77,986,469	25,945,329	30
655	51,485	266,909	6,479,515	6,418,531	60,984	10,249,592	3,770,077	31
474,230	1,858,459	2,081,726	80,898,528	79,924,560	973,968	160,313,945	79,415,417	32
276,617	137,376	6,098,002	89,705,282	88,324,147	1,381,135	133,366,476	43,661,194	33
4,000	234,371	2,464,125	30,998,628	30,897,129	101,499	46,806,718	15,808,090	34
23,836	133,942	439,685	9,134,950	8,734,295	400,655	16,282,239	7,147,289	35
164,587	541,364	1,920,833	38,815,803	38,556,179	259,624	75,541,959	36,726,156	36
157,785	453,783	1,584,059	34,551,453	34,316,469	234,984	66,238,860	31,687,407	37
6,802	87,581	336,774	4,264,350	4,239,710	24,640	9,303,099	5,038,749	38
3,693,742	1,647,489	118,650,637	1,277,785,597	1,240,463,758	37,321,839	2,125,272,193	847,486,596	39
258,051	26,783	1,269,592	13,075,994	12,676,005	399,989	29,396,853	16,320,859	40
211,028	184,507	1,369,101	24,039,951	23,498,348	541,603	40,896,835	16,856,884	41
9,465	26,079	225,073	2,233,072	2,093,910	139,162	5,293,688	3,060,616	42
9,465	14,153	71,978	1,045,718	1,004,711	41,007	2,146,236	1,100,518	43
	4,560	134,316	888,187	847,016	41,171	2,127,969	1,239,782	44
	7,366	18,779	299,167	242,183	56,984	1,019,483	720,316	45
12,970	142,049	5,002,122	19,477,437	18,218,583	1,258,854	66,629,570	47,152,133	46
442	14,381	107,482	1,539,808	1,401,650	138,158	4,862,906	3,323,098	47
	38,529	2,797,282	7,430,781	7,240,553	190,228	24,554,337	17,123,556	48
	4,778	787,230	3,584,013	3,252,282	331,731	9,594,334	6,010,321	49
4,464	21,123	686,351	2,216,486	2,007,925	208,561	9,965,708	7,749,222	50
	16,561	306,249	2,499,716	2,321,899	177,817	9,691,928	7,192,212	51
	10,374	163,719	825,803	736,964	88,839	3,154,407	2,328,604	52
8,064	36,303	153,808	1,380,830	1,257,310	123,520	4,805,950	3,425,120	53

TABLE 90.—DETAILED STATEMENT FOR THE

[See note at head of this table, pp. 1172 and 1173.]

	INDUSTRY.	Number of establishments.	Capital.	Expenses. Salaries and wages. Officers.	Clerks, etc.	Wage earners.
			Dollars.	*Dollars.*	*Dollars.*	*Dollars.*
1	Dairymen's poultrymen's, and apiarists' supplies.	244	36,095,331	1,797,816	1,796,590	7,078,433
2	Incubators and brooders	48	3,164,686	231,588	182,362	663,665
3	All other poultrymen's supplies	60	1,146,657	114,282	44,176	254,895
4	Cream separators	19	20,360,176	709,646	1,070,498	4,142,810
5	All other dairymen's supplies	90	8,692,776	556,055	396,160	1,571,614
6	Apiarists' supplies	27	2,731,036	96,245	103,394	445,449
7	Dental goods	319	17,904,790	1,173,863	903,820	4,463,840
8	Teeth	52	11,447,203	611,483	523,354	2,306,714
9	All other	267	6,457,587	562,380	380,466	2,157,126
10	Drug grinding	31	14,991,135	515,792	281,850	1,526,137
11	Druggists' preparations	524	102,129,257	4,899,050	8,419,436	12,161,925
12	Dyeing and finishing textiles, exclusive of that done in textile mills.	628	229,948,486	10,565,608	5,685,947	57,189,978
13	Dyestuffs and extracts—natural	144	38,689,058	1,676,984	643,930	4,734,614
14	Electrical machinery, apparatus, and supplies.	1,404	857,855,496	35,932,611	62,247,828	238,188,852
15	Electroplating	515	4,192,989	558,633	184,623	3,793,605
16	Emery and other abrasive wheels	60	34,802,542	1,197,091	1,190,379	5,878,748
17	Enameling	74	2,083,474	155,395	84,607	790,308
18	Engines, steam, gas, and water	370	454,124,733	12,895,475	18,016,564	105,435,455
19	Engravers' materials	21	826,166	121,225	44,954	212,171
20	Engraving and diesinking	478	4,695,712	271,564	220,387	2,391,504
21	Engraving, steel and copper plate, including plate printing.	421	19,040,260	1,758,996	1,120,321	7,908,109
22	Engraving, wood	55	338,908	81,705	70,457	407,215
23	Envelopes	106	24,754,818	1,455,685	1,342,626	6,649,989
24	Explosives	118	133,247,684	6,286,185	6,958,039	12,504,986
25	Fancy articles, not elsewhere specified	661	32,824,988	2,806,288	2,815,905	12,207,913
26	Beadwork	37	669,187	11,750	27,495	518,272
27	Celluloid novelties	66	6,062,190	587,234	438,246	2,685,656
28	Metal novelties	110	7,986,024	728,122	496,362	2,282,457
29	Paper novelties	63	2,580,056	242,444	282,035	819,976
30	Wood novelties	30	276,472	16,123	6,628	150,818
31	All other	355	15,251,059	1,220,615	1,565,139	5,750,734
32	Feathers and plumes	216	6,514,809	410,655	613,309	3,405,765
33	Felt goods	49	35,024,373	1,138,561	958,781	4,873,490
34	Ferroalloys	30	42,364,729	732,084	489,030	3,571,487
35	Fertilizers	600	311,633,259	5,870,938	5,700,662	25,363,132
36	Files	50	15,692,801	617,481	335,632	6,192,444
37	Firearms	26	51,917,782	856,026	1,238,157	13,333,495
38	Fire extinguishers, chemical	32	3,779,785	374,352	271,259	751,119
39	Fireworks	57	3,546,943	255,872	69,402	994,851
40	Flags and banners	79	3,436,484	244,165	236,795	795,242
41	Flavoring extracts	453	13,561,337	1,252,295	1,760,871	1,665,285
42	Flax and hemp, dressed	20	2,783,958	61,001	26,590	447,373
43	Flour-mill and gristmill products	10,708	801,624,507	17,203,661	14,809,369	50,888,383
44	Food preparations, not elsewhere specified.	1,997	245,282,687	9,555,112	12,475,482	29,392,209
45	Breadstuff preparations, such as cereals and breakfast foods.	105	69,007,129	1,890,275	3,858,538	8,508,879
46	Lard compounds and other substitutes.	27	30,254,472	428,197	805,686	2,422,741
47	Macaroni, vermicelli, and noodles	557	24,452,695	952,483	754,868	4,168,009
48	Meat products, not elsewhere specified.	86	14,832,922	559,544	1,154,512	2,133,195
49	Peanut butter	56	1,958,600	166,988	158,209	338,623
50	Sweetening sirups, other than cane.	256	22,197,874	1,133,018	1,129,407	1,849,419
51	All other preparations for human consumption.	616	38,398,438	2,361,410	2,325,007	5,489,387
52	Prepared feed for animals and fowls.	294	44,180,557	2,063,197	2,289,255	4,481,956

UNITED STATES, BY INDUSTRIES: 1919—Continued.

[See note at head of this table, pp. 1172 and 1173.]

FINANCIAL STATISTICS—continued.

Expenses—Continued.

For contract work.	Rent and taxes.		For materials.			Value of products.	Value added by manufacture.	
	Rent of factory.	Taxes, Federal, state, county, and local.	Total.	Principal materials.	Fuel and rent of power.			
Dollars.	Dollars.	Dollars.	Dollars.	Dollars.	Dollars.	Dollars.	Dollars.	
19,100	82,222	928,369	18,526,743	18,135,777	390,966	37,397,448	18,870,705	1
744	10,153	45,827	1,928,645	1,890,341	38,304	3,931,773	2,003,128	2
1,825	12,381	14,852	1,141,045	1,121,779	19,266	1,935,428	794,383	3
16,192	24,608	518,183	6,531,911	6,298,861	233,050	16,436,920	9,905,009	4
164	32,326	273,812	6,964,488	6,890,034	74,454	11,916,177	4,951,689	5
175	2,754	75,695	1,960,654	1,934,762	25,892	3,177,150	1,216,496	6
23,431	260,020	1,123,287	16,420,429	16,253,077	167,352	29,401,896	12,981,467	7
845	68,962	882,315	3,870,258	3,770,640	99,618	10,737,566	6,867,308	8
22,586	191,058	240,972	12,550,171	12,482,437	67,734	18,664,330	6,114,159	9
111,651	18,450	892,481	11,556,480	11,223,377	333,103	16,937,698	5,381,218	10
78,918	499,513	5,297,386	55,138,475	54,451,977	686,498	114,593,486	59,455,011	11
1,361,486	838,575	13,871,733	174,742,815	164,314,521	10,428,294	323,967,683	149,224,868	12
225,880	84,864	2,436,516	34,592,698	32,916,972	1,675,726	53,744,283	19,151,585	13
1,218,203	2,553,802	43,803,385	425,098,211	411,359,101	13,739,110	997,968,119	572,869,908	14
27,205	423,816	36,091	2,639,248	2,373,033	266,215	10,389,617	7,750,369	15
3,628	38,827	1,349,504	12,228,187	11,297,045	931,142	30,949,270	18,721,083	16
807	47,566	38,153	949,556	808,633	140,923	2,644,763	1,695,207	17
936,389	277,061	21,322,012	217,550,771	211,556,910	5,993,861	464,774,735	247,223,964	18
58	22,257	8,666	1,484,269	1,456,279	27,990	2,248,122	763,853	19
58,903	263,256	90,173	1,927,323	1,813,422	113,901	7,350,602	5,423,279	20
138,215	423,647	441,895	6,980,747	6,777,505	203,242	24,209,154	17,228,407	21
4,665	31,424	1,270	219,268	214,645	4,623	1,153,618	934,350	22
44,980	657,116	825,298	21,964,743	21,731,660	233,083	39,664,077	17,699,334	23
30,542	15,714	2,722,261	45,911,049	43,194,669	2,716,380	92,474,813	46,563,764	24
1,049,381	839,826	948,346	32,591,073	32,164,379	426,694	64,054,481	31,463,408	25
91,495	28,285	544	975,459	974,018	1,441	1,935,489	960,030	26
107,153	82,240	238,730	7,439,552	7,271,166	168,386	13,006,140	5,566,588	27
80,522	123,605	381,634	5,429,606	5,310,785	118,821	12,325,350	6,895,744	28
183,108	71,684	32,357	1,704,260	1,680,494	23,766	4,201,038	2,496,778	29
887	11,402	3,749	149,273	143,702	5,571	458,338	309,065	30
586,216	522,610	291,332	16,892,923	16,784,214	108,709	32,128,126	15,235,203	31
153,345	333,095	35,680	6,694,596	6,658,588	36,008	15,377,953	8,683,357	32
9,009	42,110	1,614,343	22,780,775	22,155,136	625,639	39,229,540	16,448,765	33
47,338	13,377	873,052	28,098,576	22,039,508	6,059,068	38,583,984	10,485,408	34
171,318	345,582	8,129,732	185,040,522	181,599,677	3,440,845	281,143,587	96,103,065	35
3,820	37,900	3,567,786	4,227,880	3,679,005	548,875	17,616,563	13,388,683	36
....	17,896	1,370,514	7,613,784	6,757,191	856,593	30,181,370	22,567,586	37
13,524	77,035	248,454	2,693,416	2,652,765	40,651	5,563,180	2,869,764	38
77,863	13,583	95,106	2,108,156	2,061,451	46,705	4,629,984	2,521,828	39
205,463	85,995	97,438	3,286,165	3,259,463	26,702	5,346,089	2,059,924	40
15,065	329,811	579,212	19,418,176	19,290,698	127,478	30,116,932	10,698,756	41
1,146	1,405	17,676	1,708,670	1,652,874	55,796	2,369,114	660,444	42
942,256	1,663,972	17,599,395	1,799,180,987	1,783,901,111	15,279,876	2,052,434,385	253,253,398	43
234,393	1,596,402	11,261,558	494,597,157	489,033,652	5,563,505	631,598,150	137,000,993	44
10,521	172,347	4,832,116	117,838,248	116,162,776	1,675,472	159,223,465	41,385,217	45
1,883	49,701	581,096	110,855,429	110,058,540	796,889	121,249,267	10,393,838	46
17,423	401,881	341,080	25,109,951	24,398,318	711,633	37,057,198	11,947,247	47
2,045	102,215	674,407	25,282,566	25,019,565	263,001	33,875,061	8,592,495	48
2,960	41,212	42,527	4,439,436	4,389,388	50,048	5,850,706	1,411,270	49
46,544	145,194	905,860	37,079,830	36,772,416	307,414	50,430,585	13,350,755	50
99,637	476,539	2,291,558	52,423,641	51,517,618	906,023	81,116,299	28,692,658	51
53,380	207,313	1,592,914	121,568,056	120,715,031	853,025	142,795,569	21,227,513	52

TABLE 90.—DETAILED STATEMENT FOR THE

[See note at head of this table, pp. 1172 and 1173.]

	INDUSTRY.	Number of establishments.	Capital.	FINANCIAL STATISTICS.		
				Expenses.		
				Salaries and wages.		
				Officers.	Clerks, etc.	Wage earners.
			Dollars.	*Dollars.*	*Dollars.*	*Dollars.*
1	Foundry and machine-shop products...	10,934	2,104,980,938	103,479,616	78,295,712	622,571,129
2	Boiler shops...	525	124,697,972	5,733,614	4,616,378	31,858,339
3	Foundries...	1,340	310,180,970	18,357,153	7,469,009	141,079,782
4	Machine shops...	8,110	1,312,768,602	63,249,977	53,266,219	343,378,501
5	Machine shop and foundry combined.	959	357,333,394	16,138,872	12,944,106	106,254,507
6	Foundry supplies...	76	7,501,631	549,272	338,250	1,032,029
7	Fuel, manufactured...	11	2,908,130	58,344	75,766	221,545
8	Fur goods...	1,815	80,700,925	3,369,693	4,623,453	24,149,212
9	Furnishing goods, men's...	487	53,014,066	3,058,118	5,057,190	13,562,866
10	Neckwear...	322	25,876,756	1,829,494	3,793,729	6,457,829
11	All other...	165	27,137,310	1,228,624	1,263,461	7,105,037
12	Furniture...	3,154	423,992,405	24,581,393	18,919,545	141,116,316
13	Wood, other than rattan and willow..	2,273	310,690,365	17,947,648	12,965,382	103,286,001
14	Rattan and willow...	119	9,818,705	613,150	319,496	4,091,585
15	Metal...	157	56,792,600	3,024,235	2,959,069	15,912,654
16	Store and office fixtures...	605	46,690,735	2,996,360	2,675,598	17,826,076
17	Furs, dressed...	141	8,867,403	1,153,270	351,271	7,098,286
18	Galvanizing...	52	4,316,455	432,507	169,334	2,247,953
19	Gas and electric fixtures...	341	36,872,737	2,388,748	2,100,538	9,802,380
20	Gas fixtures...	57	9,783,469	409,468	278,543	1,906,146
21	Electric fixtures...	187	13,544,453	1,467,573	1,268,481	4,710,642
22	Combination gas and electric fixtures.	71	11,511,498	387,639	479,773	2,560,085
23	All other...	26	2,033,317	124,068	73,741	625,507
24	Gas, illuminating and heating...	1,022	1,465,656,265	8,299,422	16,873,031	52,758,628
25	Gas machines and gas and water meters.	105	24,980,993	1,290,602	1,465,751	5,995,877
26	Gas and water meters...	34	15,303,711	787,128	568,736	4,003,846
27	Gas machines...	49	7,189,884	324,879	712,332	1,511,397
28	All other...	22	2,487,398	178,595	184,683	480,634
29	Glass...	371	215,680,436	8,547,791	4,816,778	87,526,625
30	Glass, cutting, staining, and ornamenting.	616	18,088,650	1,243,888	894,221	6,154,831
31	Decalcomania work on glass...	22	672,824	33,993	29,744	234,610
32	All other...	594	17,415,826	1,209,895	864,477	5,920,221
33	Gloves and mittens, cloth, not including gloves made in textile mills.	182	17,687,953	815,611	421,465	4,855,246
34	Gloves and mittens, leather...	355	29,870,277	1,740,432	1,357,614	8,150,784
35	Glucose and starch...	56	58,182,682	1,337,247	875,115	11,962,483
36	Glucose...	9	35,104,327	869,569	488,164	7,930,957
37	Starch...	47	23,078,355	467,678	386,951	4,031,526
38	Glue, not elsewhere specified...	62	27,237,123	746,128	632,508	4,776,724
39	Glue...	52	20,530,337	548,855	522,208	3,150,721
40	All other products...	10	6,706,786	197,273	110,300	1,626,003
41	Gold and silver, leaf and foil...	87	1,571,557	145,721	58,871	983,600
42	Gold and silver, reducing and refining, not from the ore.	87	9,757,415	372,857	264,836	843,608
43	Graphite, ground and refined...	24	4,302,788	132,275	144,992	434,317
44	Grease and tallow, not including lubricating greases.	482	37,360,094	1,297,070	708,014	7,954,378
45	Soap stock...	233	13,750,788	556,705	217,089	3,518,656
46	Tallow...	196	18,907,689	592,169	420,221	3,472,574
47	All other...	53	4,701,617	148,196	70,704	963,148

UNITED STATES, BY INDUSTRIES: 1919—Continued.

[See note at head of this table, pp. 1172 and 1173.]

FINANCIAL STATISTICS—continued.

For contract work.	Rent and taxes.		For materials.			Value of products.	Value added by manufacture.	
	Rent of factory.	Taxes, Federal, state, county, and local.	Total.	Principal materials.	Fuel and rent of power.			
Dollars.	Dollars.	Dollars.	Dollars.	Dollars.	Dollars.	Dollars.	Dollars.	
6,721,830	7,333,607	94,787,047	948,069,381	899,703,679	48,365,702	2,289,250,859	1,341,181,478	1
214,472	316,556	6,529,749	72,241,746	69,546,778	2,694,968	143,665,758	71,424,012	2
1,667,564	882,024	14,319,065	175,216,151	157,800,880	17,415,271	421,049,258	245,833,107	3
3,681,318	5,683,650	53,730,043	556,745,340	536,936,460	19,808,880	1,354,836,253	798,090,913	4
1,158,476	451,377	20,208,190	143,866,144	135,419,561	8,446,583	369,699,590	225,833,446	5
24,714	29,786	342,944	5,667,236	5,477,047	190,189	9,954,676	4,287,440	6
12	6,963	80,436	1,386,394	1,296,171	90,223	1,973,877	587,483	7
1,418,281	2,520,857	2,696,235	105,596,605	105,322,780	273,825	173,137,739	67,541,134	8
1,754,490	824,268	1,421,597	64,743,912	64,492,998	250,914	107,834,695	43,090,783	9
834,627	542,755	361,425	39,508,093	39,421,018	87,075	62,841,239	23,333,146	10
919,863	281,513	1,060,172	25,235,819	25,071,980	163,839	44,993,456	19,757,637	11
1,868,273	3,274,734	14,397,612	261,523,395	255,172,887	6,350,508	571,356,333	309,832,938	12
1,289,495	2,278,944	10,385,901	190,790,053	186,168,070	4,621,983	418,869,670	228,079,617	13
160,520	154,323	274,381	7,232,300	7,080,491	151,809	15,295,618	8,063,318	14
149,339	275,918	2,257,250	33,241,865	32,395,408	846,457	69,796,851	36,554,986	15
268,919	565,549	1,480,080	30,259,177	29,528,918	730,259	67,394,194	37,135,017	16
117,096	213,730	214,414	6,338,835	6,046,143	292,692	20,384,569	14,045,734	17
9,150	48,057	157,050	10,532,288	10,327,925	204,363	14,475,682	3,943,394	18
65,262	661,644	545,604	20,258,538	19,749,412	509,126	42,267,953	22,009,415	19
9,423	104,862	154,182	5,717,297	5,558,437	158,860	9,495,535	3,778,238	20
26,883	381,641	209,425	8,708,785	8,500,883	207,902	20,337,975	11,629,190	21
17,627	147,795	173,637	4,787,308	4,669,747	117,561	10,197,340	5,410,032	22
11,329	27,346	8,360	1,045,148	1,020,345	24,803	2,237,103	1,191,955	23
463,280	4,062,677	18,826,338	157,550,882	42,638,896	114,911,986	329,278,908	171,728,026	24
52,078	75,544	547,889	10,647,402	10,362,091	285,311	26,267,074	15,619,672	25
12,610	35,072	341,343	6,039,064	5,864,078	174,986	16,444,030	10,404,966	26
6,634	20,555	139,621	3,711,189	3,619,826	91,363	7,526,780	3,815,591	27
32,834	19,917	66,925	897,149	878,187	18,962	2,296,264	1,399,115	28
240,750	148,826	9,854,179	90,780,124	66,422,262	24,357,862	261,884,080	171,103,956	29
99,878	415,537	490,435	14,357,878	14,061,039	296,839	28,443,321	14,085,443	30
480	13,353	9,816	383,101	364,631	18,470	907,690	524,589	31
99,398	402,184	480,619	13,974,777	13,696,408	278,369	27,535,631	13,560,854	32
95,224	169,510	977,125	16,092,462	15,939,953	152,509	28,220,113	12,127,651	33
1,559,224	191,932	812,404	26,286,129	26,102,312	183,817	46,940,511	20,654,382	34
551	12,867	4,021,457	130,328,848	126,626,568	3,702,280	186,256,260	55,927,412	35
....	105	2,868,826	95,610,637	92,993,836	2,616,801	134,548,109	38,937,472	36
551	12,762	1,152,631	34,718,211	33,632,732	1,085,479	51,708,151	16,989,940	37
20,075	48,223	712,931	19,279,905	17,632,097	1,647,808	32,134,067	12,854,162	38
7,202	45,614	559,429	14,593,448	13,357,561	1,235,887	23,463,079	8,869,631	39
12,873	2,609	153,502	4,686,457	4,274,536	411,921	8,670,988	3,984,531	40
48,507	19,223	22,569	2,655,335	2,630,724	24,611	4,461,568	1,806,233	41
72,060	55,789	359,587	49,736,978	49,540,636	196,342	55,483,215	5,746,237	42
49,696	5,109	94,783	1,092,684	946,449	146,235	2,239,587	1,146,903	43
58,090	177,077	1,414,604	47,756,341	45,545,421	2,210,920	67,265,206	19,508,865	44
32,329	54,785	560,878	9,572,291	8,511,201	1,061,090	17,390,009	7,817,718	45
17,680	117,444	781,761	32,468,136	31,626,143	841,993	41,905,267	9,437,131	46
8,081	4,848	71,965	5,715,914	5,408,077	307,837	7,969,930	2,254,016	47

TABLE 90.—DETAILED STATEMENT FOR THE

[See note at head of this table, pp. 1172 and 1173.]

	INDUSTRY.	Number of establishments.	Capital.	Officers.	Clerks, etc.	Wage earners.
				FINANCIAL STATISTICS. Expenses. Salaries and wages.		
			Dollars.	*Dollars.*	*Dollars.*	*Dollars.*
1	Grindstones	23	2,045,469	85,149	22,961	598,631
2	Haircloth	18	2,999,150	99,646	44,264	425,149
3	Hair work	198	3,580,546	261,523	220,793	1,064,630
4	Hammocks	6	153,465	7,480	5,238	40,241
5	Hand stamps	298	4,249,546	691,983	517,630	1,832,581
6	Hardware	548	133,925,619	6,410,414	5,828,898	45,229,950
7	Locks	76	15,419,231	823,014	614,264	4,475,487
8	Builders' hardware	134	51,499,165	1,734,901	2,237,474	17,314,477
9	Piano and organ hardware	16	1,791,658	145,776	33,245	518,281
10	Vehicle hardware	53	16,794,773	998,771	644,097	7,577,363
11	All other	269	48,420,792	2,707,952	2,299,818	15,344,342
12	Hardware, saddlery	37	10,991,945	492,789	389,249	4,043,799
13	Hat and cap materials	133	19,861,835	680,168	269,959	3,132,571
14	Hats and caps, other than felt, straw, and wool.	709	18,515,472	1,407,346	1,358,343	9,438,864
15	Hats, fur-felt	176	58,127,770	2,288,891	2,342,781	19,642,531
16	Hats, straw	148	18,560,183	1,447,649	1,108,095	6,604,933
17	Hats, wool-felt	40	3,831,376	222,386	135,865	1,387,777
18	Hones and whetstones	11	847,340	54,834	30,213	203,001
19	Horseshoes, not made in steel works or rolling mills.	20	4,589,563	228,315	157,290	830,249
20	House-furnishing goods, not elsewhere specified.	467	32,626,867	1,876,560	1,893,768	6,443,915
21	Comforts and quilts	74	7,992,665	295,563	278,071	1,295,149
22	Feather pillows and beds	44	4,085,643	311,826	326,789	562,670
23	Cotton batting, not made in cotton mills.	9	889,815	52,092	27,998	156,346
24	Mops and dusters	75	1,423,270	158,509	137,538	380,916
25	All other	265	18,235,474	1,058,570	1,123,372	4,048,834
26	Ice, manufactured	2,867	270,725,786	8,109,243	2,842,888	34,001,837
27	Ink, printing	90	18,702,523	1,498,382	1,318,780	2,574,920
28	Ink, writing	61	4,803,485	371,449	585,597	596,168
29	Instruments, professional and scientific.	351	51,570,479	3,537,784	3,523,862	17,499,888
30	Medical and surgical	127	10,686,874	1,029,522	823,489	3,798,640
31	Optical	13	1,225,708	98,080	84,401	629,178
32	All other	211	39,657,897	2,410,182	2,615,972	13,072,070
33	Iron and steel, blast furnaces	195	802,416,541	6,509,884	6,925,164	73,769,395
34	Iron and steel, steel works and rolling mills.	500	2,656,518,417	43,564,408	56,316,012	637,637,430
35	Iron and steel, bolts, nuts, washers, and rivets, not made in rolling mills.	144	75,715,918	3,042,990	2,263,429	20,973,834
36	Iron and steel, cast-iron pipe	59	42,863,026	1,385,596	1,045,616	14,705,398
37	Iron and steel, doors and shutters	57	9,849,235	785,496	472,538	2,729,774
38	Iron and steel, forgings, not made in steel works or rolling mills.	241	135,246,144	6,302,301	4,023,059	39,772,553
39	Iron and steel, nails and spikes, cut and wrought, including wire nails, not made in steel works or rolling mills.	65	13,215,785	639,005	538,230	3,397,562
40	Cut nails and spikes	6	2,049,511	67,580	203,504	488,577
41	Wire nails and spikes	28	3,809,235	303,229	75,438	909,804
42	Forged nails and spikes	6	1,539,729	35,996	108,189	345,939
43	All other, including tacks	25	5,817,310	232,200	151,099	1,653,242
44	Iron and steel, tempering and welding	520	7,626,948	774,759	328,224	2,742,928
45	Treated iron and steel	35	3,715,844	345,819	152,111	768,171
46	Welding	485	3,911,104	428,940	176,113	1,974,757
47	Iron and steel, wrought pipe	50	72,709,472	1,510,064	1,344,862	14,919,676
48	Ivory, shell, and bone work, not including combs and hairpins.	44	1,365,784	118,484	99,266	734,932
49	Japanning	36	461,561	56,253	12,536	260,640

UNITED STATES, BY INDUSTRIES: 1919—Continued.

[See note at head of this table, pp. 1172 and 1173.]

FINANCIAL STATISTICS—continued.

Expenses—Continued.

For contract work.	Rent and taxes.		For materials.			Value of products.	Value added by manufacture.	
	Rent of factory.	Taxes, Federal, state, county, and local.	Total.	Principal materials.	Fuel and rent of power.			
Dollars.	*Dollars.*	*Dollars.*	*Dollars.*	*Dollars.*	*Dollars.*	*Dollars.*	*Dollars.*	
....	3,469	43,573	243,853	180,465	63,388	1,369,423	1,125,570	1
11,731	32,683	23,321	2,259,142	2,217,552	41,590	3,315,113	1,055,971	2
114,156	172,210	19,395	3,829,197	3,812,754	16,443	6,963,033	3,133,836	3
....	3,208	2,115	169,492	162,220	7,272	255,755	86,263	4
44,645	230,408	198,206	2,634,426	2,563,058	71,368	7,738,773	5,104,347	5
931,217	497,437	6,075,597	58,533,769	55,368,774	3,164,995	154,524,888	95,991,119	6
16,658	68,544	818,484	4,340,152	4,128,839	211,313	14,374,476	10,034,324	7
2,941	137,183	2,431,080	19,083,649	17,833,353	1,250,296	53,942,790	34,859,141	8
272	10,157	41,282	750,441	727,298	23,143	2,013,906	1,263,465	9
162,198	78,290	732,808	12,350,896	11,590,767	760,129	27,501,844	15,150,948	10
749,148	203,263	2,051,943	22,008,631	21,088,517	920,114	56,691,872	34,683,241	11
....	5,058	1,794,012	4,281,589	3,961,506	320,083	14,136,556	9,854,967	12
57,036	137,537	730,153	16,643,919	16,490,084	153,835	26,521,212	9,877,293	13
135,921	636,943	131,986	24,176,514	24,018,776	157,738	44,539,861	20,363,347	14
23,404	224,895	2,128,371	40,158,019	39,128,797	1,029,222	82,745,308	42,587,289	15
65,849	431,804	420,160	16,910,408	16,662,000	248,408	32,187,361	15,276,953	16
7,682	29,781	78,047	3,699,822	3,594,716	105,106	6,739,652	3,039,830	17
500	3,060	11,362	320,451	295,381	25,070	793,778	473,327	18
....	1,208	36,557	1,536,619	1,356,018	180,601	3,367,001	1,830,382	19
140,629	551,205	826,353	39,793,962	39,439,747	354,215	60,211,804	20,417,842	20
4,683	83,758	215,830	7,781,658	7,695,233	86,425	11,962,962	4,181,304	21
1,825	59,872	88,870	5,047,603	4,973,823	73,780	7,384,952	2,337,349	22
....	12,696	41,979	871,962	850,452	21,510	1,285,661	413,699	23
6,122	45,395	15,981	2,056,039	2,042,097	13,942	3,277,571	1,221,532	24
127,999	349,484	463,693	24,036,700	23,878,142	158,558	36,300,658	12,263,958	25
234,167	771,325	4,946,061	42,877,509	17,271,245	25,606,264	137,004,798	94,127,289	26
117,743	116,035	624,658	14,661,115	14,327,796	333,319	26,244,470	11,583,355	27
....	46,585	410,719	3,320,346	3,297,934	22,412	6,433,941	3,113,595	28
54,480	502,233	2,553,592	19,494,634	18,918,600	576,034	58,136,691	38,642,057	29
35,381	157,701	302,398	3,983,789	3,864,747	119,042	12,101,245	8,117,456	30
300	35,429	82,905	590,505	553,362	37,143	1,834,497	1,243,992	31
18,799	309,103	2,168,289	14,920,340	14,500,491	419,849	44,200,949	29,280,609	32
692,293	384,763	20,551,798	621,286,496	385,662,843	235,623,653	794,466,558	173,180,062	33
2,963,415	305,434	87,796,777	1,680,575,758	1,523,610,896	156,964,862	2,828,902,376	1,148,326,618	34
122,553	150,775	4,619,910	44,277,117	42,127,433	2,149,684	89,743,882	45,466,765	35
37,795	20,782	1,246,473	25,386,552	22,744,779	2,641,773	50,235,101	24,848,549	36
36,031	64,059	215,200	4,577,934	4,466,284	111,650	10,877,001	6,299,067	37
152,948	286,994	10,833,095	82,024,492	73,286,871	8,737,621	173,752,104	91,727,612	38
8,698	56,664	696,186	8,874,747	8,545,006	329,741	17,583,344	8,708,597	39
....	2,348	46,652	807,040	771,603	35,437	2,056,136	1,249,096	40
8,548	29,046	288,569	3,626,239	3,548,221	78,018	6,135,160	2,508,921	41
....	924	59,802	719,873	670,301	49,572	1,558,494	838,621	42
150	24,346	301,163	3,721,595	3,554,881	166,714	7,833,554	4,111,959	43
65,124	241,908	739,763	3,575,881	3,204,994	370,887	10,995,672	7,419,791	44
10,480	18,455	648,665	1,778,282	1,597,264	181,018	4,567,322	2,789,040	45
54,644	223,453	91,098	1,797,599	1,607,730	189,869	6,428,350	4,630,751	46
12,769	37,254	3,647,989	51,155,653	49,307,757	1,847,896	81,869,115	30,713,462	47
9,534	28,095	46,152	1,293,876	1,250,506	43,370	2,816,530	1,522,654	48
50	24,240	2,785	221,901	193,264	28,637	771,143	549,242	49

TABLE 90.—DETAILED STATEMENT FOR THE

[See note at head of this table, pp. 1172 and 1173.]

	INDUSTRY.	Number of establishments.	Capital.	Salaries and wages. Officers.	Clerks, etc.	Wage earners.
			Dollars.	Dollars.	Dollars.	Dollars.
1	Jewelry	2,054	121,070,305	7,570,795	6,617,052	35,863,718
2	Jewelry and instrument cases	142	3,697,104	470,089	199,031	2,147,648
3	Jute goods	26	41,335,845	681,074	432,941	6,436,286
4	Knit goods	2,050	516,457,991	20,165,869	12,160,713	125,199,820
5	Labels and tags	119	14,118,792	1,314,686	1,143,590	4,549,902
6	Lamps and reflectors	171	26,099,941	1,586,534	1,057,106	9,292,497
7	Automobile lamps	35	10,320,628	618,732	327,593	4,061,477
8	All other lamps	122	14,704,325	879,965	668,201	4,903,002
9	Reflectors	14	1,074,988	87,837	61,312	328,018
10	Lapidary work	124	19,209,627	569,084	129,559	2,837,811
11	Lard, not made in slaughtering and meat-packing establishments.	6	40,537		6,306	12,154
12	Lasts	64	8,177,560	758,258	352,109	3,415,950
13	Lead, bar, pipe, and sheet	32	9,419,730	264,402	290,214	1,066,941
14	Leather goods, not elsewhere specified	503	33,341,468	2,204,193	1,818,249	9,415,403
15	Leather, tanned, curried, and finished	680	671,341,553	14,382,409	5,796,563	88,205,473
16	Lime	476	45,844,532	1,366,422	629,458	10,869,196
17	Linen goods	10	7,527,596	166,926	162,399	1,635,642
18	Liquors, distilled	34	45,618,110	870,068	267,716	1,716,699
19	Alcohol, grain, including pure, neutral, or cologne spirits.	28	43,098,323	733,168	241,826	1,566,839
20	Rum, whisky, and other distilled liquors.	6	2,519,787	136,900	25,890	149,860
21	Liquors, malt	729	583,429,947	14,053,101	8,847,755	45,170,432
22	Liquors, vinous	342	14,855,481	471,564	898,524	1,013,898
23	Lithographing	331	60,817,330	4,716,652	4,396,299	18,201,089
24	Locomotives, not made by railroad companies.	17	138,275,823	1,675,164	3,103,152	38,798,641
25	Looking-glass and picture frames	429	10,079,709	946,113	779,988	4,775,227
26	Lubricating greases	53	5,242,636	376,806	787,347	569,925
27	Lumber and timber products	26,119	1,357,991,571	38,021,883	17,906,390	489,419,091
28	Lumber, planing-mill products, not including planing mills connected with sawmills.	5,309	361,848,079	18,317,441	10,218,899	91,976,526
29	Machine tools	403	231,039,843	9,491,952	8,545,904	66,178,969
30	Malt	55	34,829,495	771,496	246,005	1,845,210
31	Marble and stone work	4,240	112,568,533	5,516,733	3,244,121	38,354,822
32	Monuments and tombstones	3,256	54,949,879	2,386,661	2,006,898	17,312,451
33	Other marble and stone work, except slate.	861	50,463,102	2,749,811	1,137,227	17,957,186
34	Roofing slate	71	5,021,999	228,688	56,992	2,145,233
35	Other slate products	52	2,133,553	151,573	43,004	939,952
36	Matches	21	29,477,486	572,236	1,233,759	3,059,537
37	Mats and matting, from cocoa fiber, grass, and coir.	12	7,190,675	147,465	82,179	810,607
38	Mattresses and spring beds, not elsewhere specified.	1,041	46,212,858	3,210,459	2,347,889	12,805,351
39	Millinery and lace goods, not elsewhere specified.	3,005	95,538,769	8,673,114	7,893,021	49,848,984
40	Embroideries	1,294	26,572,232	1,976,079	1,631,294	14,387,966
41	Trimmed hats and hat frames	829	37,183,508	4,034,020	3,797,233	23,980,052
42	Dress and cloak trimmings, braids, and fringes.	156	5,243,478	411,646	311,085	1,852,582
43	Women's neckwear	150	6,830,065	808,857	1,012,238	2,766,164
44	All other	576	19,709,486	1,442,512	1,141,171	6,862,220
45	Millstones	12	58,905	10,800	1,800	43,732
46	Mineral and soda waters	5,194	102,838,582	4,897,231	3,372,987	16,393,477
47	Mineral and carbonated waters	5,025	85,805,164	4,446,752	2,794,218	15,072,293
48	Fruit beverages	84	13,026,812	306,586	397,063	901,401
49	All other	85	4,006,606	143,893	181,706	419,783

UNITED STATES, BY INDUSTRIES: 1919—Continued.

[See note at head of this table, pp. 1172 and 1173.]

	Rent and taxes.		For materials.				
For contract work.	Rent of factory.	Taxes, Federal, state, county, and local.	Total.	Principal materials.	Fuel and rent of power.	Value of products.	Value added by manufacture.	
Dollars.	Dollars.	Dollars.	Dollars.	Dollars.	Dollars.	Dollars.	Dollars.	
2,274,288	2,051,552	2,514,554	110,450,683	109,713,874	736,809	203,939,230	93,488,547	1
139,356	149,288	45,977	3,505,840	3,458,169	47,671	8,126,300	4,620,460	2
46,741	37,667	1,156,435	17,708,834	17,255,328	453,506	34,442,698	16,733,864	3
8,495,982	2,272,445	23,694,134	427,095,560	421,630,358	5,465,202	713,139,689	286,044,129	4
303,771	201,911	641,955	11,274,767	11,120,220	154,547	24,243,992	12,969,225	5
29,133	220,463	962,280	18,429,033	18,026,214	402,819	38,098,917	19,669,884	6
700	23,684	309,866	8,227,316	8,032,168	195,148	16,661,539	8,434,223	7
27,233	180,380	632,670	9,697,554	9,511,372	186,182	20,277,920	10,580,366	8
1,200	16,399	19,744	504,163	482,674	21,489	1,159,458	655,295	9
19,691	135,916	134,089	19,363,004	19,331,643	31,361	30,051,460	10,688,456	10
....	3,540	943	175,317	174,755	562	219,660	44,343	11
61,486	95,390	705,217	3,932,662	3,771,748	160,914	12,470,539	8,537,877	12
35,676	16,130	139,813	13,634,120	13,486,112	148,008	17,174,281	3,540,161	13
469,120	618,185	548,386	30,035,537	29,856,600	178,937	52,952,772	22,917,235	14
2,337,011	738,408	26,497,983	646,521,527	636,698,271	9,823,256	928,591,701	282,070,174	15
70,430	88,937	896,563	14,296,925	8,269,479	6,027,446	33,970,463	19,673,538	16
....	12,531	159,968	4,190,187	4,026,499	163,688	6,998,046	2,807,859	17
479	18,238	3,788,028	19,655,522	18,560,658	1,094,864	31,854,085	12,198,563	18
479	15,978	3,738,783	18,550,756	17,509,689	1,041,067	30,133,408	11,582,652	19
....	2,260	49,245	1,104,766	1,050,969	53,797	1,720,677	615,911	20
125,770	1,299,159	98,199,472	94,792,659	83,223,931	11,568,728	379,905,085	285,112,426	21
297,030	55,085	2,569,970	8,115,841	8,021,765	94,076	17,454,194	9,338,353	22
1,363,424	1,019,769	1,380,634	27,718,217	27,128,998	589,219	73,151,115	45,432,898	23
....	554	5,425,183	72,375,950	69,268,472	3,107,478	156,269,730	83,893,780	24
40,651	556,617	242,390	7,227,232	7,053,524	173,708	18,384,562	11,157,330	25
6,252	27,080	140,545	4,807,501	4,751,129	56,372	8,868,772	4,061,271	26
37,546,478	1,478,218	38,285,518	470,960,488	462,781,708	8,178,780	1,387,471,413	916,510,925	27
1,102,507	2,148,320	7,750,082	299,265,652	294,539,870	4,725,782	500,438,258	201,172,606	28
1,469,844	476,353	17,838,902	59,034,308	56,048,334	2,985,974	212,400,158	153,365,850	29
115	88,977	978,364	31,612,707	30,468,591	1,144,116	39,340,414	7,727,707	30
1,409,271	1,024,482	1,264,153	49,524,341	46,037,831	3,486,510	129,164,653	79,640,312	31
854,752	491,557	640,359	31,275,562	29,905,404	1,370,158	73,361,219	42,085,657	32
508,038	386,500	555,551	16,243,761	14,479,357	1,764,404	49,260,002	33,016,241	33
16,969	95,131	43,551	1,301,615	1,065,542	236,073	4,420,847	3,119,232	34
29,512	51,294	24,692	703,403	587,528	115,875	2,122,585	1,419,182	35
....	14,716	1,023,792	6,852,970	6,577,212	275,758	18,495,876	11,642,906	36
3,303	5,940	220,037	2,102,580	2,051,382	51,198	4,860,855	2,758,275	37
113,608	886,998	1,166,662	49,208,560	48,590,046	618,514	83,952,609	34,744,049	38
6,133,327	4,087,361	2,116,981	132,928,877	131,972,247	956,630	255,724,922	122,796,045	39
3,945,414	978,121	572,512	22,116,754	21,792,332	324,422	56,818,652	34,701,898	40
295,645	1,922,834	970,388	69,431,018	69,026,172	404,846	122,870,786	53,439,768	41
183,456	204,932	39,174	7,344,252	7,309,296	34,956	12,674,139	5,329,887	42
483,628	306,347	155,253	10,968,350	10,929,911	38,439	20,384,206	9,415,856	43
1,225,184	675,127	379,654	23,068,503	22,914,536	153,967	42,977,139	19,908,636	44
....	2,175	58	25,509	18,099	7,410	66,896	41,387	45
560,338	1,310,566	6,088,167	68,599,585	66,788,752	1,810,833	135,341,437	66,741,852	46
549,812	1,261,150	5,683,474	60,829,621	59,220,181	1,609,440	122,594,632	61,765,011	47
10,526	24,548	272,656	5,925,555	5,806,318	119,207	9,464,785	3,539,260	48
....	24,868	132,037	1,844,439	1,762,253	82,186	3,282,020	1,437,581	49

TABLE **90.**—DETAILED STATEMENT FOR THE

[See note at head of this table, pp. 1172 and 1173.]

	INDUSTRY.	Number of establishments.	FINANCIAL STATISTICS.			
			Capital.	Expenses.		
					Salaries and wages.	
				Officers.	Clerks, etc.	Wage earners.
			Dollars.	*Dollars.*	*Dollars.*	*Dollars.*
1	Minerals and earths, ground or otherwise treated.	419	60,208,617	2,229,424	910,389	16,309,518
2	Mirrors, framed and unframed, not elsewhere specified.	186	9,322,060	907,870	474,144	2,819,140
3	Models and patterns, not including paper patterns.	928	11,753,992	1,430,633	477,483	10,318,104
4	Motorcycles, bicycles, and parts	51	35,362,150	1,299,488	900,870	12,763,235
5	Mucilage, paste, and other adhesives, not elsewhere specified.	127	7,133,137	608,695	432,112	850,382
6	Mucilage and paste..................	48	2,915,439	213,900	133,815	364,148
7	All other......................	79	4,217,698	394,795	298,297	486,234
8	Musical instruments and materials, not elsewhere specified.	240	7,876,182	642,109	390,063	3,984,656
9	Musical instruments, organs............	68	6,770,587	339,262	184,410	1,978,518
10	Musical instruments, pianos............	191	116,106,536	3,731,656	2,666,010	25,474,200
11	Musical instruments, piano and organ materials.	113	32,323,669	1,539,948	502,476	10,467,137
12	Piano materials....................	97	31,769,045	1,456,785	488,160	10,231,122
13	Organ materials....................	16	554,624	83,163	14,316	236,015
14	Needles, pins, and hooks and eyes......	92	26,324,627	1,626,083	880,167	8,809,781
15	Nets and seines.....................	19	4,155,531	175,832	33,373	561,282
16	Oakum.............................	6	978,063	34,798	12,176	118,032
17	Oil and cake, cottonseed..............	711	203,457,371	6,247,667	3,688,050	20,615,193
18	Oil, essential.......................	78	6,379,910	151,144	77,646	391,213
19	Oil, linseed.........................	26	73,954,065	836,465	572,938	3,052,269
20	Oil, not elsewhere specified [1].........	280	91,475,009	2,768,646	2,945,722	6,141,145
21	Vegetable......................	68	38,816,696	656,433	551,256	2,440,123
22	Animal.........................	46	12,594,143	322,056	158,957	1,066,674
23	Mineral........................	39	4,697,246	226,517	165,652	227,171
24	Composite......................	127	35,366,924	1,563,640	2,069,857	2,407,177
25	Oilcloth and linoleum, floor............	21	49,803,688	922,871	856,586	6,518,089
26	Oilcloth, enameled...................	11	10,782,957	229,477	174,400	1,200,877
27	Oleomargarine and other butter substitutes.	42	24,971,947	788,001	1,195,565	3,184,118
28	Optical goods.......................	506	37,739,904	3,023,871	2,573,788	14,388,207
29	Ordnance and accessories..............	26	85,399,163	2,353,619	1,748,774	15,556,642
30	Paints..............................	601	177,314,815	7,987,233	10,282,471	19,550,371
31	Paper and wood pulp..................	729	905,794,583	18,735,837	11,216,907	135,690,642
32	Paper exclusively..................	497	363,382,919	9,550,900	5,109,600	58,324,653
33	Pulp exclusively...................	61	42,081,327	660,688	406,160	6,524,555
34	Paper and pulp....................	171	500,330,337	8,524,249	5,701,147	70,841,434
35	Paper goods, not elsewhere specified....	308	64,442,569	3,825,719	2,915,888	12,666,924
36	Playing cards.....................	8	6,149,513	421,128	216,697	1,559,638
37	All other.........................	300	58,293,056	3,404,591	2,699,191	11,107,286
38	Paper patterns......................	19	1,084,325	96,104	63,620	374,479
39	Patent medicines and compounds......	2,467	143,498,611	11,554,701	13,181,511	13,748,813
40	Patent and proprietary medicines..	1,724	114,152,017	8,855,007	10,444,554	10,713,842
41	Patent and proprietary compounds, not elsewhere specified.	743	29,346,594	2,699,694	2,736,957	3,034,971
42	Paving materials.....................	889	67,421,242	2,521,089	1,143,259	17,169,154
43	Peanuts, grading, roasting, cleaning, and shelling.	78	10,393,512	493,386	206,590	1,328,712
44	Pencils, lead........................	12	29,641,044	578,807	1,105,620	5,299,050
45	Pens fountain and stylographic........	56	9,725,362	605,475	1,126,303	2,980,663
46	Pens, gold...........................	15	397,954	47,631	9,084	517,123
47	Pens, steel..........................	4	1,311,150	67,057	64,805	679,405

[1] Includes "oil, castor" and "oil, lard" to avoid disclosing individual operations.

UNITED STATES, BY INDUSTRIES: 1919—Continued.

[See note at head of this table, pp. 1172 and 1173.]

FINANCIAL STATISTICS—continued.

For contract work.	Rent and taxes.		For materials.			Value of products.	Value added by manufacture.	
	Rent of factory.	Taxes, Federal, state, county, and local.	Total.	Principal materials.	Fuel and rent of power.			
Dollars.	Dollars.	Dollars.	Dollars.	Dollars.	Dollars.	Dollars.	Dollars.	
369,970	459,027	1,233,492	16,270,251	12,605,172	3,665,079	46,067,239	29,796,988	1
15,553	232,424	347,404	12,498,733	12,320,827	177,906	20,830,775	8,332,042	2
105,259	491,490	316,331	6,395,834	6,106,967	288,867	25,300,389	18,904,555	3
1,036	152,606	3,165,940	25,985,915	25,346,673	639,242	53,105,895	27,119,980	4
5,203	82,954	192,872	7,092,728	6,971,281	121,447	11,230,253	4,137,525	5
3,178	42,048	79,246	3,035,076	2,981,588	53,488	4,795,912	1,760,836	6
2,025	40,906	113,626	4,057,652	3,989,693	67,959	6,434,341	2,376,689	7
32,027	137,045	278,025	4,444,729	4,295,490	149,239	12,506,334	8,061,605	8
26,806	45,505	72,938	2,217,097	2,111,833	105,264	5,973,268	3,756,171	9
27,640	910,874	2,709,214	54,364,656	53,322,488	1,042,168	107,088,050	52,723,394	10
15,172	266,852	950,147	16,693,140	16,285,048	408,092	36,789,627	20,096,487	11
14,812	265,702	923,837	16,329,129	15,935,934	393,195	35,956,944	19,627,815	12
360	1,150	26,310	364,011	349,114	14,897	832,683	468,672	13
206,216	96,224	1,685,463	10,227,199	9,826,308	400,891	29,304,995	19,077,796	14
....	10,326	101,197	3,648,206	3,624,737	23,469	5,114,414	1,466,208	15
....	742	14,778	575,525	560,633	14,892	983,423	407,898	16
841,559	198,155	5,083,850	495,192,294	486,636,672	8,555,622	581,244,798	86,052,504	17
2,000	25,885	122,773	3,903,417	3,808,067	95,350	5,698,403	1,794,986	18
6,201	4,256	1,295,602	100,577,538	99,908,059	669,479	120,638,100	20,060,562	19
25,513	256,514	2,197,389	119,270,586	117,900,207	1,370,379	156,479,654	37,209,068	20
5,988	70,385	1,119,708	64,731,546	63,995,887	735,659	80,639,042	15,907,496	21
4,050	29,355	155,930	9,432,210	9,193,137	239,073	12,995,184	3,562,974	22
9,160	12,806	67,130	5,605,156	5,507,652	97,504	7,515,991	1,910,835	23
6,315	143,968	854,621	39,501,674	39,203,531	298,143	55,329,437	15,827,763	24
8,298	321	2,123,756	30,368,703	29,020,819	1,347,884	52,673,206	22,304,503	25
7,500	8,000	229,236	11,140,723	10,871,326	269,397	15,436,875	4,206,152	26
36,864	102,050	1,872,279	66,042,792	65,626,330	416,462	79,815,580	13,772,788	27
100,935	656,796	2,309,401	17,785,083	17,086,129	698,954	53,717,798	35,932,715	28
1,475	110,402	3,739,959	26,592,658	25,513,109	1,079,549	69,495,628	42,902,970	29
689,986	693,874	5,638,099	165,600,416	162,037,931	3,566,185	256,714,379	91,110,263	30
487,240	1,078,929	33,832,330	467,482,637	412,482,682	54,999,955	788,059,377	320,576,740	31
134,286	256,011	13,996,902	237,402,880	214,202,526	23,200,354	374,362,494	136,959,614	32
11,652	253,141	1,636,111	22,686,708	19,540,609	3,146,099	35,884,802	13,198,094	33
341,302	569,777	18,199,317	207,393,049	178,739,547	28,653,502	377,812,081	170,419,032	34
151,824	539,902	5,845,181	65,295,484	64,021,089	1,274,395	107,284,759	41,989,275	35
739	12,435	3,179,990	3,030,439	2,979,361	51,078	10,663,733	7,633,294	36
151,085	527,467	2,665,191	62,265,045	61,041,728	1,223,317	96,621,026	34,355,981	37
11,691	30,289	12,741	316,890	314,366	2,524	1,528,382	1,211,492	38
803,210	1,471,482	14,103,226	88,819,417	87,732,309	1,087,108	212,162,255	123,342,838	39
721,516	1,104,485	12,198,255	67,361,862	66,662,232	699,630	169,486,104	102,124,242	40
81,694	366,997	1,904,971	21,457,555	21,070,077	387,478	42,676,151	21,218,596	41
238,505	707,278	825,488	16,019,811	12,679,015	3,340,796	45,740,606	29,720,795	42
11,343	79,537	367,548	28,474,052	28,345,926	128,126	33,354,377	4,880,325	43
9,707	39,002	2,440,246	9,073,563	8,822,030	251,533	24,134,159	15,060,596	44
13,986	108,185	1,365,287	5,811,419	5,524,912	286,507	15,996,808	10,185,389	45
....	16,529	1,748	962,410	954,927	7,483	1,801,460	839,050	46
....	270	41,563	398,383	381,825	16,558	1,679,541	1,281,158	47

TABLE 90.—DETAILED STATEMENT FOR THE

[See note at head of this table, pp. 1172 and 1173.]

	INDUSTRY.	Number of establishments.	Capital.	FINANCIAL STATISTICS. Expenses. Salaries and wages. Officers.	Clerks, etc.	Wage earners.
			Dollars.	*Dollars.*	*Dollars.*	*Dollars.*
1	Perfumery and cosmetics...............	569	32,666,633	3,038,060	5,391,951	3,983,016
2	Petroleum, refining...................	320	1,170,278,189	11,315,491	15,303,533	89,749,637
3	Phonographs and graphophones........	166	105,241,359	3,374,652	5,312,916	33,963,148
4	Photo-engraving......................	422	12,442,784	2,898,198	1,964,189	10,423,541
5	Photographic apparatus...............	68	7,264,031	539,476	302,003	2,642,957
6	Cameras............................	12	1,928,765	98,790	134,054	770,541
7	Motion-picture machines............	18	2,417,233	197,639	107,494	1,076,699
8	All other apparatus and parts......	38	2,918,033	243,047	60,455	795,717
9	Photographic materials...............	169	87,204,707	3,710,389	5,490,023	18,965,941
10	Motion-picture films, not exposed..	15	44,448,942	1,367,477	1,301,240	11,119,388
11	Motion-picture projection films.....	50	37,254,232	1,742,420	3,721,243	6,708,661
12	All other..........................	104	5,501,533	600,492	467,540	1,137,892
13	Pickles, preserves, and sauces...........	723	88,703,665	3,866,049	4,499,887	13,346,467
14	Preserves..........................	195	35,941,096	1,677,713	1,518,828	5,566,890
15	Pickles and sauces.................	528	52,762,569	2,188,336	2,981,059	7,779,577
16	Pipes, tobacco........................	56	7,634,662	435,379	558,545	2,555,291
17	Plated ware..........................	68	34,789,823	1,325,398	2,111,132	10,913,091
18	Knives, forks, spoons, and other flatware.	18	23,805,824	796,625	1,476,126	7,507,867
19	Hollow ware........................	30	6,113,191	311,269	490,275	2,511,574
20	All other..........................	20	4,870,808	217,504	144,731	893,650
21	Plumbers' supplies, not elsewhere specified.	214	60,980,632	2,628,803	1,992,344	15,962,517
22	Pocketbooks..........................	139	5,427,990	565,925	559,339	3,061,903
23	Pottery...............................	340	66,757,970	3,929,097	2,074,335	29,820,278
24	Chinaware	161	53,849,247	3,198,387	1,679,609	25,673,406
25	Earthen and stone ware............	147	8,826,875	453,680	170,879	2,787,140
26	All other..........................	32	4,081,848	277,030	223,847	1,359,732
27	Poultry, killing and dressing, not done in slaughtering and meat-packing establishments.	196	8,875,942	372,129	320,479	2,045,043
28	Printing and publishing, book and job	13,089	405,554,984	35,072,491	30,648,149	141,476,243
29	Job printing.......................	11,951	312,005,583	29,024,581	17,878,359	131,316,152
30	Book publishing and printing.......	142	29,559,985	1,303,012	2,442,392	5,611,804
31	Book publishing without printing..	687	54,258,490	4,060,899	10,075,257	605,606
32	Linotype work and typesetting....	309	9,730,926	683,999	252,141	3,942,681
33	Printing and publishing, music........	160	8,006,122	1,029,874	2,017,366	926,988
34	Printing and publishing............	27	2,866,830	263,009	183,011	850,365
35	Publishing without printing........	133	5,139,292	766,865	1,834,355	76,623
36	Printing and publishing, newspapers and periodicals.	17,362	614,045,344	50,343,115	93,507,413	144,348,173
37	Printing and publishing............	1,346	285,605,477	19,195,809	45,424,796	66,045,755
38	Printing, publishing, and job printing.	12,420	266,816,289	17,979,041	24,461,786	75,055,330
39	Publishing without printing........	3,596	61,623,578	13,168,265	23,620,831	3,247,088
40	Printing materials....................	82	7,245,110	405,963	272,530	799,402
41	Pulp, from fiber other than wood.......	5	778,177	14,950	3,358	55,944
42	Pulp goods	40	17,190,849	757,717	1,161,125	3,608,314
43	Wall board........................	10	5,443,676	258,788	499,493	791,211
44	All other..........................	30	11,747,173	498,929	661,632	2,817,103
45	Pumps, not including power pumps.....	127	26,660,646	1,586,267	2,474,629	5,968,121
46	Pumps, steam and other power........	112	54,839,975	2,623,768	2,411,561	13,763,526
47	Steam.............................	62	43,192,760	1,846,803	1,659,883	11,199,533
48	Other power.......................	50	11,647,215	776,965	751,678	2,563,993

UNITED STATES, BY INDUSTRIES: 1919—Continued.

[See note at head of this table, pp. 1172 and 1173.]

FINANCIAL STATISTICS—continued.

	Rent and taxes.		For materials.				
For contract work.	Rent of factory.	Taxes, Federal, state, county, and local.	Total.	Principal materials.	Fuel and rent of power.	Value of products.	Value added by manufacture.	
Dollars.	Dollars.	Dollars.	Dollars.	Dollars.	Dollars.	Dollars.	Dollars.	
225,089	632,140	1,972,300	26,147,026	26,024,744	122,282	59,613,391	33,466,365	1
2,352,306	125,909	78,282,638	1,247,908,355	1,194,403,246	53,505,109	1,632,532,766	384,624,411	2
1,751,018	304,179	8,777,943	59,740,205	58,223,578	1,516,627	158,547,870	98,807,665	3
317,416	637,544	293,379	5,038,382	4,756,114	282,268	29,389,386	24,351,004	4
150	115,259	233,100	3,584,380	3,498,934	85,446	9,384,050	5,799,670	5
150	24,148	107,600	1,189,203	1,161,843	27,360	2,999,608	1,810,405	6
....	55,213	67,175	1,145,181	1,113,463	31,718	3,431,749	2,286,568	7
....	35,898	58,325	1,249,996	1,223,628	26,368	2,952,693	1,702,697	8
10,960	529,325	5,389,300	49,801,747	48,836,358	965,389	115,714,179	65,912,432	9
2,700	93,145	4,627,029	25,917,613	25,221,668	695,945	71,245,991	45,328,378	10
....	312,116	647,412	19,579,419	19,439,330	140,089	36,705,207	17,125,788	11
8,260	124,064	114,859	4,304,715	4,175,360	129,355	7,762,981	3,458,266	12
47,304	567,836	3,315,340	93,037,433	91,851,287	1,186,146	145,784,530	52,747,097	13
18,483	282,786	1,657,697	45,537,295	45,001,582	535,713	65,122,667	19,585,372	14
28,821	285,050	1,657,643	47,500,138	46,849,705	650,433	80,661,863	33,161,725	15
57,214	68,918	245,210	3,497,414	3,385,289	112,125	11,553,777	8,056,363.	16
12,754	79,051	1,044,632	17,766,536	17,265,899	500,637	41,634,585	23,868,049	17
936	7,703	888,455	13,764,572	13,465,868	298,704	30,962,906	17,198,334	18
11,460	33,802	132,454	2,812,978	2,657,839	155,139	7,713,976	4,900,998	19
358	37,546	23,723	1,188,986	1,142,192	46,794	2,957,703	1,768,717	20
101,699	267,884	1,957,725	27,797,007	26,346,429	1,450,578	60,055,265	32,258,258	21
167,873	177,636	104,262	7,557,155	7,524,883	32,272	14,549,659	6,992,504	22
117,384	162,132	2,677,855	20,794,076	15,400,705	5,393,371	74,919,186	54,125,110	23
102,483	135,181	2,225,215	17,559,429	13,199,917	4,359,512	63,037,078	45,477,649	24
7,580	18,460	276,631	2,041,088	1,286,987	754,101	7,994,533	5,953,445	25
7,321	8,491	176,009	1,193,559	913,801	279,758	3,887,575	2,694,016	26
3,620	88,528	274,669	36,015,817	35,850,321	165,496	41,705,079	5,689,262	27
32,243,303	11,689,552	8,163,494	211,067,174	206,081,695	4,985,479	597,663,228	386,596,054	28
7,046,956	10,268,605	6,565,665	190,145,145	185,536,351	4,608,794	487,074,733	296,929,588	29
1,668,604	306,752	393,398	10,325,818	10,106,555	219,263	29,759,696	19,433,878	30
23,441,378	881,369	1,131,328	9,615,249	9,596,995	18,254	71,974,342	62,359,093	31
86,365	232,826	73,103	980,962	841,479	139,168	8,854,457	7,873,495	32
2,713,899	296,554	345,745	2,123,781	2,097,144	26,637	14,592,177	12,468,396	33
260,547	63,692	70,563	1,086,950	1,063,481	23,469	3,814,950	2,728,000	34
2,453,352	232,862	275,182	1,036,831	1,033,663	3,168	10,777,227	9,740,396	35
50,776,049	10.038,270	20,163,412	300,385,187	293,181,862	7,203,325	924,152,878	623,767,691	36
2,895,107	3,456,968	13,510,424	168,289,962	165,284,807	3,005,155	441,418,613	273,128,651	37
3,123,207	4,486,329	4,907,519	102,446,618	98,357,295	4,089,323	315,829,398	213,382,780	38
44,757,735	2,094,973	1,745,469	29,648,607	29,539,760	108,847	166,904,867	137,256,260	39
3,184	127,594	303,014	1,619,718	1,558,852	60,866	4,918,799	3,299,081	40
....	920	5,522	395,947	374,301	21,646	524,444	128,497	41
....	15,362	952,955	11,381,972	10,742,906	639,066	23,608,403	12,226,431	42
....	6,172	148,988	4,683,897	4,587,390	96,507	7,691,330	3,007,433	43
....	9,190	803,967	6,698,075	6,155,516	542,559	15,917,073	9,218,998	44
15,133	101,213	711,383	12,161,892	11,860,966	300,926	31,656,438	19,494,546	45
24,030	122,216	2,125,916	23,907,889	23,115,714	792,175	53,745,502	29,837,613	46
5,619	70,902	1,680,188	18,148,796	17,494,246	654,550	41,068,458	22,919,662	47
18,411	51,314	445,728	5,759,093	5,621,468	137,625	12,677,044	6,917,951	48

TABLE 90.—DETAILED STATEMENT FOR THE

[See note at head of this table, pp. 1172 and 1173.]

				FINANCIAL STATISTICS.		
					Expenses.	
	INDUSTRY.	Number of establishments.	Capital.		Salaries and wages.	
				Officers.	Clerks, etc.	Wage earners.
			Dollars.	*Dollars.*	*Dollars.*	*Dollars.*
1	Refrigerators	122	23,600,628	1,110,787	1,440,535	5,809,351
2	Regalia, and society badges and emblems.	115	6,257,750	450,487	500,608	1,800,383
3	Rice, cleaning and polishing	86	23,792,509	831,034	677,906	1,932,196
4	Roofing materials	178	57,069,224	1,982,340	3,432,310	10,344,043
5	Metal shingles and ceiling	29	2,632,358	129,420	80,814	541,741
6	All other	149	54,436,866	1,852,920	3,351,496	9,802,302
7	Rubber tires, tubes, and rubber goods, not elsewhere specified.	437	782,637,722	16,249,745	58,699,712	156,806,828
8	Rules, ivory and wood	13	414,980	25,254	18,367	142,290
9	Saddlery and harness	1,823	49,368,288	2,298,662	2,091,023	10,849,066
10	Safes and vaults	38	13,023,284	611,518	538,384	3,233,318
11	Safes	21	8,255,413	425,086	419,614	2,038,762
12	Vaults	17	4,767,871	186,432	118,770	1,194,556
13	Salt	86	47,725,231	1,344,648	1,211,438	7,353,420
14	Sand and emery paper and cloth	12	9,057,698	331,613	412,669	840,766
15	Sand-lime brick	32	2,229,769	110,995	24,778	501,854
16	Sausage, not made in slaughtering and meat-packing establishments.	633	13,777,265	799,054	664,383	4,679,118
17	Sausage	547	10,255,744	643,514	501,437	3,564,169
18	Sausage casings	86	3,521,521	155,540	162,946	1,114,949
19	Saws	112	26,665,369	1,000,345	1,390,380	6,280,807
20	Scales and balances	79	22,924,843	883,536	1,382,434	6,533,978
21	Screws, machine	143	53,569,817	2,018,946	898,973	12,104,780
22	Screws, wood	11	14,632,800	446,643	523,327	4,864,613
23	Sewing-machine cases	5	17,331,959	374,702	183,326	5,161,120
24	Sewing machines and attachments	40	71,363,920	1,436,082	1,641,969	19,333,378
25	Sewing machines	29	70,293,040	1,310,154	1,626,172	18,810,196
26	Attachments	11	1,070,880	125,928	15,797	523,182
27	Shipbuilding, steel	162	1,268,640,254	27,159,274	30,102,233	538,372,576
28	New vessels	105	1,210,558,989	24,915,849	28,518,101	500,086,706
29	Concrete vessels	5	5,111,408	172,834	282,609	3,100,882
30	Repair work only	45	52,317,371	1,953,895	1,292,955	34,934,721
31	Small boats	7	652,486	116,696	8,568	250,267
32	Shipbuilding, wooden, including boat building.	913	120,807,566	5,474,326	2,378,661	59,074,072
33	New vessels	315	93,372,049	4,094,473	1,886,653	45,872,982
34	Repair work only	277	22,084,471	1,059,661	389,241	11,286,405
35	Small boats	294	4,792,460	268,349	93,851	1,750,238
36	Masts, spars, oars, and rigging	27	558,586	51,843	8,916	164,447
37	Shirts	896	102,012,047	4,646,632	5,173,723	25,833,855
38	Show cases	119	5,377,884	400,371	262,493	1,995,660
39	Signs and advertising novelties	779	29,249,133	2,648,959	3,982,511	9,715,216
40	Electric signs	65	3,968,893	315,867	244,005	1,323,074
41	Other signs	544	7,531,795	841,561	505,792	3,565,025
42	Advertising novelties	170	17,748,445	1,491,531	3,232,714	4,827,117
43	Silk goods, including throwsters	1,369	532,732,163	16,790,489	9,580,473	108,226,330
44	Finished products	1,040	447,966,397	13,962,041	8,765,826	88,571,734
45	Throwsters and winders	329	84,765,766	2,828,448	814,647	19,654,596
46	Silversmithing and silverware	99	34,465,322	1,097,374	1,232,140	7,359,409
47	Slaughtering and meat packing	1,304	1,176,483,643	19,081,909	40,603,456	209,489,263
48	Slaughtering	604	45,639,110	1,741,882	1,513,865	8,839,849
49	Meat packing	142	32,111,789	1,214,562	1,038,442	7,580,724
50	Slaughtering and meat packing	558	1,098,732,744	16,125,465	38,051,149	193,068,690

UNITED STATES, BY INDUSTRIES: 1919—Continued.

[See note at head of this table, pp. 1172 and 1173.]

FINANCIAL STATISTICS—continued.

	Rent and taxes.		For materials.				
For contract work.	Rent of factory.	Taxes, Federal, state, county, and local.	Total.	Principal materials.	Fuel and rent of power.	Value of products.	Value added by manufacture.	
Dollars.	Dollars.	Dollars.	Dollars.	Dollars.	Dollars.	Dollars.	Dollars.	
14,530	93,086	571,696	11,948,972	11,704,141	244,831	26,048,808	14,099,836	1
100,893	108,086	249,948	4,287,055	4,233,760	53,295	9,395,470	5,108,415	2
17,871	122,905	1,061,322	76,653,816	76,335,172	298,644	90,038,412	13,404,596	3
179,446	84,797	1,619,327	52,587,777	49,956,679	2,631,098	85,895,359	33,307,582	4
5,376	27,069	27,427	1,532,139	1,512,878	19,261	2,749,859	1,217,720	5
174,070	57,728	1,591,900	51,055,638	48,443,801	2,611,837	83,145,500	32,089,862	6
3,579,851	6,486,700	33,714,601	525,686,309	513,080,366	12,605,943	987,088,045	461,401,736	7
614	5,979	3,406	133,934	124,846	9,088	480,543	346,609	8
63,357	726,286	2,476,148	52,442,907	52,064,231	378,676	83,713,010	31,270,103	9
43,915	43,944	1,027,450	6,608,680	6,441,995	166,685	15,293,927	8,685,247	10
43,428	38,568	597,986	3,421,949	3,310,038	111,911	9,518,663	6,096,714	11
487	5,376	429,464	3,186,731	3,131,957	54,774	5,775,264	2,588,533	12
31,496	171,416	1,810,391	16,027,791	11,339,924	4,687,867	37,513,821	21,486,030	13
....	109,491	468,848	5,060,561	4,935,624	124,937	9,303,734	4,243,173	14
....	34,979	29,999	575,402	440,763	134,639	1,663,052	1,087,650	15
220,283	306,747	372,960	43,940,356	43,410,690	529,666	56,610,092	12,669,736	16
219,820	250,084	318,003	37,128,034	36,674,638	453,396	47,500,686	10,372,652	17
463	56,663	54,957	6,812,322	6,736,052	76,270	9,109,406	2,297,084	18
27,959	54,898	2,292,644	11,792,224	11,232,010	560,214	31,460,557	19,668,333	19
249	149,822	886,982	6,993,682	6,729,098	264,584	20,641,038	13,647,356	20
73,053	143,492	3,663,487	14,983,868	14,340,700	643,168	40,015,460	25,031,592	21
....		959,287	5,551,563	5,169,250	382,313	15,459,582	9,908,019	22
....	432	123,083	8,018,270	7,907,582	110,688	14,243,468	6,225,198	23
7,639	32,907	754,953	16,384,134	15,842,863	541,271	43,694,919	27,310,785	24
7,639	24,333	745,135	16,003,896	15,488,019	515,877	42,578,356	26,574,460	25
....	8,574	9,818	380,238	354,844	25,394	1,116,563	736,325	26
8,205,806	2,858,731	44,641,130	643,752,814	629,809,673	13,943,141	1,456,489,516	812,736,702	27
7,450,870	2,643,271	38,566,380	618,902,759	605,827,811	13,074,948	1,364,294,032	745,391,273	28
	1,800	844	3,158,032	3,115,836	42,196	6,896,280	3,738,248	29
754,936	208,040	6,059,909	21,290,717	20,474,219	816,498	84,424,665	63,133,948	30
....	5,620	13,997	401,306	391,807	9,499	874,539	473,233	31
1,901,723	647,701	3,054,424	66,769,862	65,108,911	1,660,951	165,871,745	99,101,883	32
1,660,723	423,397	2,198,311	56,898,161	55,691,733	1,206,428	133,303,335	76,405,174	33
226,290	150,590	757,242	7,293,565	6,926,237	367,328	26,549,156	19,255,591	34
12,908	63,476	82,544	2,187,418	2,105,328	82,090	5,197,682	3,010,264	35
1,802	10,238	16,327	390,718	385,613	5,105	821,572	430,854	36
10,991,206	1,302,744	2,526,017	127,087,745	126,431,922	655,823	205,327,133	78,239,388	37
6,813	106,527	102,596	4,032,123	3,930,116	102,007	8,294,308	4,262,185	38
332,853	535,031	717,958	16,071,924	15,716,571	355,353	43,343,093	27,271,169	39
21,327	70,054	27,066	2,107,883	2,077,301	30,582	4,694,802	2,586,919	40
116,478	295,658	172,640	4,368,400	4,229,845	138,555	12,909,809	8,541,409	41
195,048	169,319	518,252	9,595,641	9,409,425	186,216	25,738,482	16,142,841	42
43,146,201	2,982,226	17,612,294	388,469,022	382,267,575	6,201,447	688,469,523	300,000,501	43
40,197,415	2,561,173	14,832,847	333,435,945	329,345,649	4,090,296	590,237,835	256,801,890	44
2,948,786	421,053	2,779,447	55,033,077	52,921,926	2,111,151	98,231,688	43,198,611	45
48,806	157,722	488,559	13,060,929	12,724,302	336,627	29,126,133	16,065,204	46
1,978,648	2,054,729	17,600,117	3,782,929,533	3,758,839,744	24,089,789	4,246,290,614	463,361,081	47
212,276	489,525	991,934	212,344,204	211,085,354	1,258,850	243,061,209	30,717,005	48
320	241,224	1,412,523	74,493,632	73,554,633	938,999	92,840,368	18,346,736	49
1,766,052	1,323,980	15,195,660	3,496,091,697	3,474,199,757	21,891,940	3,910,389,037	414,297,340	50

TABLE 90.—DETAILED STATEMENT FOR THE

[See note at head of this table, pp. 1172 and 1173.]

	INDUSTRY.	Number of establishments.	Capital.	FINANCIAL STATISTICS. Expenses. Salaries and wages.		
				Officers.	Clerks, etc.	Wage earners.
			Dollars.	Dollars.	Dollars.	Dollars.
1	Smelting and refining, copper..........	34	308,680,268	2,545,376	3,350,969	25,723,371
2	Smelting...............................	21	171,825,621	1,404,443	1,838,417	12,258,730
3	Smelting and refining [1]...............	13	136,854,647	1,140,933	1,512,552	13,464,641
4	Smelting and refining, lead	25	115,676,768	1,026,786	1,075,000	9,179,615
5	Smelting...............................	18	57,992,579	620,684	796,967	6,646,469
6	Smelting and refining [2]...............	7	57,684,189	406,102	278,033	2,533,146
7	Smelting and refining, metals, not elsewhere specified.[3]	13	20,227,544	640,255	311,797	2,963,148
8	Smelting and refining, not from the ore.	81	22,156,513	993,667	577,463	3,093,140
9	Smelting and refining, zinc.............	39	98,757,355	1,265,631	1,195,838	17,783,278
10	Pigs, bars, plates, and sheets.......	33	87,770,508	1,075,593	1,081,750	16,135,100
11	All other.............................	6	10,986,847	190,038	114,088	1,648,178
12	Soap....................................	348	212,416,866	5,785,159	8,386,692	21,228,063
13	Soda-water apparatus...................	66	14,711,872	677,796	702,589	3,232,398
14	Sporting and athletic goods............	188	19,951,458	890,659	714,438	5,752,963
15	Springs, steel, car and carriage, not made in steel works or rolling mills.	112	45,472,282	2,254,501	1,290,179	11,157,874
16	Carriage and wagon.................	13	2,109,344	246,430	80,912	708,818
17	Railway.............................	6	7,387,952	387,689	158,084	743,029
18	Automobile..........................	65	26,945,406	1,154,787	715,504	6,575,230
19	Machinery and other.................	28	9,029,580	670,595	335,679	3,130,797
20	Stamped and enameled ware, not elsewhere specified.	323	132,222,094	5,379,005	4,814,136	34,851,311
21	Stamped ware.......................	279	90,098,314	4,076,459	3,679,646	23,675,506
22	Enameled ware......................	35	38,364,597	1,097,827	991,753	9,670,172
23	Bathtubs............................	5	2,209,116	102,981	104,561	903,607
24	Lavatories and sinks................	4	1,550,067	101,738	38,176	602,026
25	Stationery goods, not elsewhere specified.	223	36,700,909	2,716,468	3,865,707	9,577,867
26	Penholders..........................	5	124,429	22,580	1,548	60,174
27	All other............................	218	36,576,480	2,693,888	3,864,159	9,517,693
28	Statuary and art goods.................	195	3,145,853	245,129	109,708	1,716,067
29	Steam fittings and steam and hot-water heating apparatus.	261	133,097,464	5,416,190	7,045,518	45,742,525
30	Radiators and cast-iron heating boilers.	75	43,525,961	1,176,507	1,148,125	14,280,631
31	All other............................	186	89,571,503	4,239,683	5,897,393	31,461,894
32	Steam packing..........................	169	36,934,462	1,827,579	1,435,298	7,103,275
33	Steel barrels, drums, and tanks........	33	18,218,312	855,562	608,415	4,435,444
34	Stencils and brands....................	84	1,111,338	124,445	71,008	428,706
35	Stereotyping and electrotyping.........	171	7,860,376	1,487,627	542,279	5,002,545
36	Stoves and hot-air furnaces	412	122,813,373	6,433,427	6,863,568	41,321,133
37	Stoves and ranges...................	280	94,539,978	4,814,531	5,056,032	33,905,951
38	Hot-air furnaces....................	126	27,368,616	1,542,451	1,666,202	7,116,836
39	Fireless cookers....................	6	904,779	76,445	141,334	298,346
40	Stoves, gas and oil	176	45,734,309	1,864,785	2,435,467	12,578,830
41	Structural ironwork, not made in steel works or rolling mills.	1,146	219,470,095	10,870,315	12,239,967	59,920,132
42	Sugar, beet.............................	85	224,584,679	2,565,036	1,862,920	15,908,118
43	Sugar, cane.	202	55,117,127	1,173,706	491,742	4,009,369
44	Sugar, refining, not including beet sugar.	20	193,540,825	2,400,118	3,042,069	22,710,464

[1] Includes 4 establishments engaged exclusively in refining.
[2] Includes 2 establishments engaged exclusively in refining.

UNITED STATES, BY INDUSTRIES: 1919—Continued.

[See note at head of this table, pp. 1172 and 1173.]

FINANCIAL STATISTICS—continued.

Expenses—Continued.

For contract work.	Rent and taxes.		For materials.			Value of products.	Value added by manufacture.	
	Rent of factory.	Taxes, Federal, state, county, and local.	Total.	Principal materials.	Fuel and rent of power.			
Dollars.	Dollars.	Dollars.	Dollars.	Dollars.	Dollars.	Dollars.	Dollars.	
222,176	12,022	3,399,101	584,410,173	565,167,149	19,243,024	651,101,591	66,691,418	1
222,176	11,022	2,089,665	156,055,168	144,444,887	11,610,281	186,670,898	30,615,730	2
....	1,000	1,309,436	428,355,005	420,722,262	7,632,743	464,430,693	36,075,688	3
249,995	13,923	1,022,881	179,373,646	173,697,163	5,676,483	196,794,519	17,420,873	4
240,385	2,340	800,058	62,916,963	58,427,136	4,489,827	74,952,572	12,035,609	5
9,610	11,583	222,823	116,456,683	115,270,027	1,186,656	121,841,947	5,385,264	6
....	3,583	726,116	14,957,367	14,370,279	587,088	20,074,504	5,117,137	7
1,132	45,970	471,180	40,675,880	39,949,163	726,717	50,246,088	9,570,208	8
....	17,100	1,760,487	70,014,728	60,568,127	9,446,601	104,122,938	34,108,210	9
....	15,000	1,699,418	63,604,885	54,667,706	8,937,179	95,662,585	32,057,700	10
....	2,100	61,069	6,409,843	5,900,421	509,422	8,460,353	2,050,510	11
639,688	268,543	5,800,132	238,518,858	234,698,114	3,820,744	316,740,115	78,221,257	12
81,982	114,383	772,515	6,626,868	6,487,216	139,652	15,185,370	8,558,502	13
126,632	104,030	616,879	11,969,388	11,730,776	238,612	23,839,991	11,870,603	14
341,504	200,102	2,037,886	28,019,180	26,255,302	1,763,878	51,479,535	23,460,355	15
....	9,320	224,080	1,757,315	1,631,976	125,339	3,679,176	1,921,861	16
....	14,664	439,181	3,297,445	3,120,885	176,560	5,793,458	2,496,013	17
325,880	114,969	879,736	18,532,785	17,351,078	1,181,707	31,558,570	13,025,785	18
15,624	61,149	494,889	4,431,635	4,151,363	280,272	10,448,331	6,016,696	19
514,847	553,027	7,576,275	65,456,652	62,535,750	2,920,902	143,653,877	78,197,225	20
508,033	538,177	5,452,137	46,104,388	44,697,181	1,407,207	101,094,308	54,989,920	21
5,855	8,612	2,082,096	17,195,806	15,920,875	1,274,931	37,636,584	20,440,778	22
....	5,086	24,882	1,316,944	1,170,471	146,473	2,955,953	1,639,009	23
959	1,152	17,160	839,514	747,223	92,291	1,967,032	1,127,518	24
181,519	522,081	2,489,072	28,160,239	27,812,723	347,516	58,363,244	30,203,005	25
....	2,414	116	54,993	52,847	2,146	167,554	112,561	26
181,519	519,667	2,488,956	28,105,246	27,759,876	345,370	58,195,690	30,090,444	27
45,290	114,214	46,557	1,378,540	1,328,493	50,047	5,019,521	3,640,981	28
39,910	315,542	7,482,354	72,016,393	68,019,320	3,997,073	160,285,488	88,269,095	29
7,364	50,263	602,337	22,061,124	20,405,097	1,656,027	45,013,178	22,952,054	30
32,546	265,279	6,880,017	49,955,269	47,614,223	2,341,046	115,272,310	65,317,041	31
24,866	120,494	1,526,577	22,724,561	21,331,996	1,392,565	40,524,779	17,800,218	32
3,259	68,981	1,153,085	15,151,210	14,913,978	237,232	24,942,650	9,791,440	33
6,168	57,090	19,517	514,241	500,025	14,216	1,597,785	1,083,544	34
76,516	365,751	285,875	4,234,479	3,881,041	353,438	15,919,014	11,684,535	35
123,191	344,272	4,047,932	54,803,316	52,461,756	2,341,560	145,717,963	90,914,647	36
46,366	223,416	3,159,561	40,350,250	38,403,825	1,946,425	111,727,270	71,377,020	37
76,825	105,371	849,793	13,414,707	13,033,186	381,521	31,798,649	18,383,942	38
....	15,485	38,578	1,038,359	1,024,745	13,614	2,192,044	1,153,685	39
25,797	134,423	2,557,202	24,471,970	23,892,577	579,393	55,792,029	31,320,059	40
1,048,785	750,449	6,732,187	168,800,715	165,023,193	3,777,522	294,962,419	126,161,704	41
796,772	7,414	11,442,885	87,029,144	81,650,540	5,378,604	149,155,892	62,126,748	42
27,366	11,498	1,130,749	44,143,416	42,161,236	1,982,180	57,741,320	13,597,904	43
67,522	85,036	6,476,546	662,143,981	652,374,860	9,769,121	730,986,706	68,842,725	44

³ Includes "smelting and refining, antimony" and "smelting and refining, tin" to avoid disclosing individual operations.

TABLE 90.—DETAILED STATEMENT FOR THE

[See note at head of this table, pp. 1172 and 1173.]

	INDUSTRY.	Number of establishments.	Capital.	Officers.	Clerks, etc.	Wage earners.
					FINANCIAL STATISTICS. — Expenses. — Salaries and wages.	
			Dollars.	*Dollars.*	*Dollars.*	*Dollars.*
1	Sulphuric, nitric, and mixed acids......	39	51,160,004	1,247,633	931,884	7,916,531
2	Surgical appliances....................	268	33,063,371	1,488,430	2,611,469	6,084,143
3	Suspenders, garters, and elastic woven goods.	196	39,676,879	2,036,313	1,554,760	9,270,130
4	Textile machinery and parts...........	432	129,797,903	5,027,595	3,071,175	36,528,729
5	Theatrical scenery....................	17	572,878	106,405	31,616	237,603
6	Tin and other foils, not elsewhere specified.	15	11,998,436	440,926	158,184	1,759,320
7	Tin foil...............................	12	11,993,158	440,926	158,184	1,756,320
8	Aluminum and other..................	3	5,278	....	....	3,000
9	Tin plate and terneplate	24	34,315,066	613,072	558,914	5,756,417
10	Tinware, not elsewhere specified.......	301	198,386,695	3,668,095	4,541,793	34,493,399
11	Tobacco, chewing and smoking, and snuff.	365	188,444,100	2,400,527	4,517,964	12,674,736
12	Plug or chewing.....................	85	60,564,469	1,014,383	1,938,286	5,740,522
13	Smoking............................	199	98,539,030	1,040,213	2,148,337	5,765,259
14	Snuff..............................	34	28,664,549	328,256	420,529	1,080,052
15	All other..........................	47	676,052	17,675	10,812	88,903
16	Tobacco, cigars and cigarettes	9,926	416,395,472	10,292,242	12,100,195	111,313,348
17	Cigars.............................	9,778	220,708,832	8,412,830	6,609,553	90,418,318
18	Cigarettes.........................	135	191,173,339	1,676,149	4,951,153	19,794,550
19	Cigars and cigarettes.............	13	4,513,301	203,263	539,489	1,100,480
20	Tools, not elsewhere specified..........	1,125	134,731,947	7,438,238	5,170,558	43,836,069
21	Shovels, spades, scoops, and hoes...	42	13,830,778	405,192	252,150	2,615,842
22	Carpenters' tools, not elsewhere specified.	34	8,251,864	310,685	384,317	2,507,988
23	Machinists' tools...................	502	68,204,166	3,891,020	2,581,233	23,076,340
24	All other..........................	547	44,445,139	2,831,341	1,952,858	15,635,899
25	Toys and games.....................	541	27,738,500	2,179,342	1,383,138	11,847,277
26	Trunks and valises..................	597	34,258,034	2,723,188	2,548,589	12,463,767
27	Turpentine and rosin................	1,191	33,595,986	2,006,441	236,415	16,972,881
28	Type founding......................	23	4,428,644	48,304	28,847	867,517
29	Typewriters and supplies............	88	47,794,300	2,015,632	2,054,107	17,009,432
30	Typewriters and parts.............	37	42,524,466	1,454,037	1,327,322	16,253,876
31	Carbon paper.....................	24	3,218,350	358,640	588,750	439,487
32	Ribbon...........................	21	1,930,082	177,705	134,340	264,071
33	All other.........................	6	121,402	25,250	3,695	51,998
34	Umbrellas and canes.................	198	15,397,275	793,707	842,121	3,139,662
35	Upholstering materials, not elsewhere specified.	163	32,556,564	1,046,784	571,692	4,687,307
36	Imitation leather and leatheroid....	17	21,629,899	516,270	316,065	2,163,171
37	Excelsior..........................	95	4,685,166	265,961	60,080	1,144,503
38	Curled hair........................	15	3,164,142	98,832	53,737	736,885
39	All other..........................	36	3,077,357	165,721	141,810	642,748
40	Varnishes...........................	229	62,461,021	3,694,724	4,558,200	4,567,788
41	Vault lights and ventilators...........	41	903,670	164,668	48,676	424,197
42	Vinegar and cider...................	720	20,514,590	768,251	399,766	2,047,469
43	Vinegar............................	199	14,394,965	558,045	323,965	1,391,994
44	Cider..............................	521	6,119,625	210,206	75,801	655,475
45	Wall paper, not made in paper mills...	48	19,921,577	834,966	932,369	3,882,396
46	Wall plaster and composition flooring..	161	25,307,049	1,204,704	1,251,029	5,833,617
47	Washing machines and clothes wringers	105	25,986,355	1,255,479	1,496,604	6,431,378
48	Waste...............................	92	19,472,471	937,401	295,309	2,106,840
49	Cotton.............................	61	11,035,372	732,802	215,356	1,538,632
50	All other...........................	31	8,437,099	204,599	79,953	568,208

UNITED STATES, BY INDUSTRIES: 1919—Continued.

[See note at head of this table, pp. 1172 and 1173.]

FINANCIAL STATISTICS—continued.

For contract work.	Rent and taxes.		For materials.			Value of products.	Value added by manufacture.	
	Rent of factory.	Taxes, Federal, state, county, and local.	Total.	Principal materials.	Fuel and rent of power.			
Dollars.	*Dollars.*	*Dollars.*	*Dollars.*	*Dollars.*	*Dollars.*	*Dollars.*	*Dollars.*	
47,867	47,396	1,024,209	15,857,361	13,735,042	2,122,319	31,470,480	15,613,119	1
114,114	229,353	1,202,093	22,213,621	21,834,163	379,458	43,533,860	21,320,239	2
469,527	239,869	2,438,457	36,369,218	35,886,299	482,919	60,774,652	24,405,434	3
178,686	308,482	6,193,733	45,636,628	44,094,714	1,541,914	122,089,264	76,452,636	4
10,128	15,533	6,533	504,655	500,584	4,071	1,067,033	562,378	5
....	126,484	660,473	13,007,990	12,836,305	171,685	17,920,834	4,912,844	6
....	126,483	660,448	13,006,826	12,835,382	171,444	17,912,486	4,905,660	7
....	1	25	1,164	923	241	8,348	7,184	8
297	5,425	1,857,927	73,422,649	73,058,460	364,189	97,404,720	23,982,071	9
169,524	521,012	6,785,892	165,170,736	163,671,935	1,498,801	233,964,000	68,793,264	10
71,332	242,089	63,399,150	130,270,388	129,419,465	850,923	239,270,718	109,000,330	11
1,830	37,313	25,086,247	52,051,801	51,703,188	348,613	96,955,494	44,903,693	12
67,296	187,254	32,877,423	66,648,173	66,253,105	395,068	119,282,473	52,634,300	13
2,206	4,605	5,329,502	10,011,200	9,918,966	92,234	21,127,918	11,116,718	14
....	12,917	105,978	1,559,214	1,544,206	15,008	1,904,833	345,619	15
922,925	3,343,599	185,661,698	353,297,366	351,827,204	1,470,162	773,662,495	420,365,129	16
614,660	2,730,939	43,506,689	158,815,218	157,938,401	876,817	360,396,074	201,580,856	17
308,265	603,945	129,249,358	181,309,000	180,758,410	550,590	379,125,710	197,816,710	18
....	8,715	12,905,651	13,173,148	13,130,393	42,755	34,140,711	20,967,563	19
322,710	798,915	9,520,304	45,796,967	43,112,384	2,684,583	144,201,668	98,404,701	20
5,293	25,459	671,674	5,874,329	5,508,057	366,272	14,461,091	8,586,762	21
8,359	10,486	596,921	2,530,598	2,365,660	164,938	7,904,096	5,373,498	22
167,693	449,861	5,649,206	19,471,110	18,388,666	1,082,444	70,846,366	51,375,256	23
141,365	313,109	2,602,503	17,920,930	16,850,001	1,070,929	50,990,115	33,069,185	24
233,784	630,958	640,111	19,841,498	19,368,200	473,298	45,656,803	25,815,305	25
40,031	723,594	1,415,655	33,222,432	32,959,431	263,001	63,932,266	30,709,834	26
425,407	34,869	819,459	13,929,888	13,654,976	274,912	53,051,294	39,121,406	27
750	18,364	60,862	943,245	893,780	49,465	2,089,757	1,146,512	28
8,033	117,219	3,363,422	16,143,662	15,766,655	377,007	52,737,661	36,593,999	29
2,126	54,190	3,068,141	11,012,571	10,684,805	327,766	43,312,964	32,300,393	30
....	37,049	224,499	3,091,707	3,064,003	27,704	5,894,220	2,802,513	31
5,907	19,980	65,909	1,855,490	1,835,900	19,590	3,178,158	1,322,668	32
....	6,000	4,873	183,894	181,947	1,947	352,319	168,425	33
213,852	234,308	385,093	15,632,989	15,479,960	153,029	25,308,826	9,675,837	34
9,905	94,053	1,026,157	25,448,893	24,930,596	518,297	39,889,711	14,440,818	35
....	27,892	811,755	18,132,204	17,860,292	271,912	26,281,966	8,149,762	36
5,501	15,070	133,378	2,521,967	2,392,759	129,208	4,913,450	2,391,483	37
47	20,520	25,571	2,291,480	2,214,975	76,505	3,712,602	1,421,122	38
4,357	30,571	55,453	2,503,242	2,462,570	40,672	4,981,693	2,478,451	39
39,899	196,779	1,871,008	51,508,256	50,952,290	555,966	83,632,424	32,124,168	40
6,435	28,928	8,175	810,579	798,558	12,021	2,155,864	1,345,285	41
19,470	74,793	687,169	15,558,525	15,206,351	352,174	24,722,610	9,164,085	42
7,224	47,834	500,530	11,217,205	10,969,929	247,276	17,480,319	6,263,114	43
12,246	26,959	186,639	4,341,320	4,236,422	104,898	7,242,291	2,900,971	44
33,493	120,600	190,509	13,152,503	12,855,155	297,348	23,047,901	9,895,398	45
2,966	115,092	409,581	11,821,465	10,483,141	1,338,324	26,874,657	15,053,192	46
27,517	88,799	629,528	23,388,925	23,167,861	221,064	40,771,285	17,382,360	47
2,000	94,221	590,058	22,144,087	21,909,849	234,238	29,700,402	7,556,315	48
2,000	73,606	447,747	15,457,362	15,299,515	157,847	21,054,429	5,597,067	49
....	20,615	142,311	6,686,725	6,610,334	76,391	8,645,973	1,959,248	50

TABLE 90.—DETAILED STATEMENT FOR THE

[See note at head of this table, pp. 1172 and 1173.]

	INDUSTRY.	Number of establishments.	FINANCIAL STATISTICS.			
			Capital.	Expenses.		
				Salaries and wages.		
				Officers.	Clerks, etc.	Wage earners.
			Dollars.	*Dollars.*	*Dollars.*	*Dollars.*
1	Watch and clock materials, except watchcases.	27	1,020,628	68,565	46,436	412,820
2	Watch materials..................	21	804,614	48,182	37,237	334,801
3	Clock materials...................	6	216,014	20,383	9,199	78,019
4	Watchcases.......................	33	21,790,556	706,688	610,047	4,000,727
5	Watches..........................	18	49,000,742	1,059,499	637,531	16,598,896
6	Watches.......................	7	25,904,237	579,288	437,152	9,798,220
7	Watch movements..............	11	23,096,505	480,211	200,379	6,800,676
8	Wheelbarrows....................	11	1,151,067	89,527	51,584	271,442
9	Whips...........................	26	2,461,021	115,787	315,731	582,230
10	Windmills.......................	31	10,004,863	390,616	403,764	2,145,301
11	Window and door screens and weather strips.	214	9,749,337	554,109	271,759	2,046,768
12	Window and door screens..........	176	8,680,080	426,119	229,410	1,935,129
13	Weather strips...................	38	1,069,257	127,990	42,349	111,639
14	Window shades and fixtures.........	287	18,698,914	770,751	1,003,116	3,669,286
15	Wire............................	66	102,016,777	2,464,056	2,990,350	29,289,667
16	Wirework, not elsewhere specified......	558	65,290,309	3,537,180	2,541,377	15,505,992
17	Wire rope and cable..............	15	15,265,073	641,528	571,726	2,603,704
18	Woven-wire fencing..............	53	8,441,778	376,523	320,540	1,726,991
19	All other.......................	490	41,583,458	2,519,129	1,649,111	11,175,297
20	Wood distillation....................	115	42,334,503	950,476	372,091	5,309,689
21	Wood preserving...................	73	28,138,079	782,677	510,562	4,342,277
22	Wood, turned and carved...........	722	23,542,346	1,698,857	493,196	9,307,242
23	Wooden goods, not elsewhere specified.	245	21,110,717	779,004	432,677	5,661,674
24	Wool pulling......................	24	8,853,437	193,335	89,873	909,788
25	Wool scouring.....................	33	10,049,960	523,681	203,493	2,896,453
26	Wool shoddy......................	78	16,990,722	752,935	264,288	2,653,169
27	Woolen and worsted goods............	852	831,694,748	23,499,941	7,481,815	168,108,681
28	Woolen goods....................	560	273,973,670	10,601,093	2,540,003	66,595,826
29	Worsted goods...................	292	557,721,078	12,898,848	4,941,812	101,512,855
30	All other industries [1]...............	5	131,358	3,675	4,863	89,798

[1] Comprises the following industries with number of establishments as indicated: "Straw goods, not elsewhere specified," 1; "whalebone cutting," 1; and "wood carpet," 3.

UNITED STATES, BY INDUSTRIES: 1919—Continued.

[See note at head of this table, pp. 1172 and 1173.]

FINANCIAL STATISTICS—continued.

Expenses—Continued.

For contract work.	Rent and taxes.		For materials.			Value of products.	Value added by manufacture.	
	Rent of factory.	Taxes, Federal, state, county, and local.	Total.	Principal materials.	Fuel and rent of power.			
Dollars.	Dollars.	Dollars.	Dollars.	Dollars.	Dollars.	Dollars.	Dollars.	
11,028	14,198	38,220	549,521	531,126	18,395	1,341,697	792,176	1
10,668	12,858	35,726	471,241	460,367	10,874	1,119,951	648,710	2
360	1,340	2,494	78,280	70,759	7,521	221,746	143,466	3
27,575	28,048	1,368,396	8,205,754	8,058,887	146,867	19,618,773	11,413,019	4
225,794	13,884	2,149,732	6,392,562	6,109,014	283,548	32,044,299	25,651,737	5
9,078	4,530	1,823,020	4,316,230	4,148,301	167,929	20,088,174	15,771,944	6
216,716	9,354	326,712	2,076,332	1,960,713	115,619	11,956,125	9,879,793	7
....	12,050	59,532	971,096	954,393	16,703	1,679,538	708,442	8
13,287	19,395	51,189	1,096,642	1,063,512	33,130	2,986,285	1,889,643	9
1,312	24,080	424,861	4,960,426	4,813,861	146,565	9,932,585	4,972,159	10
6,883	78,044	567,394	4,897,389	4,798,429	98,960	10,932,857	6,035,468	11
5,083	63,526	524,487	4,302,954	4,208,538	94,416	9,592,122	5,289,168	12
1,800	14,518	42,907	594,435	589,891	4,544	1,340,735	746,300	13
10,312	191,852	853,280	18,249,540	17,892,052	357,488	29,190,649	10,941,109	14
774,423	64,543	3,531,988	102,813,591	98,578,068	4,235,523	162,151,236	59,337,645	15
126,213	419,414	4,163,770	50,754,070	49,767,178	986,892	90,549,245	39,795,175	16
1,500	27,645	1,501,171	13,059,281	12,816,537	242,744	20,969,380	7,910,099	17
1,976	17,762	461,623	13,209,818	13,109,976	99,842	17,788,705	4,578,887	18
122,737	374,007	2,200,976	24,484,971	23,840,665	644,306	51,791,160	27,306,189	19
327,473	22,638	1,237,687	20,059,651	17,772,430	2,287,221	32,545,314	12,485,663	20
93,177	25,097	719,108	23,241,858	22,458,984	782,874	33,239,313	9,997,455	21
130,340	197,926	578,908	16,609,215	16,309,563	299,652	34,847,139	18,237,924	22
24,211	75,887	503,635	10,173,353	9,980,611	192,742	21,793,261	11,619,908	23
13,636	20,941	159,663	12,809,592	12,730,810	78,782	17,361,231	4,551,639	24
4,603	59,839	449,658	7,228,350	6,789,007	439,343	13,679,584	6,451,234	25
14,695	54,760	703,499	16,076,315	15,572,310	504,005	23,254,398	7,178,083	26
9,212,822	1,072,474	52,937,307	665,594,683	650,196,615	15,398,068	1,065,434,072	399,839,389	27
1,198,862	484,512	16,306,713	217,965,333	212,189,028	5,776,305	364,896,590	146,931,257	28
8,013,960	587,962	36,630,594	447,629,350	438,007,587	9,621,763	700,537,482	252,908,132	29
2,710	7,970	220	199,589	194,813	4,776	361,431	161,842	30

	INDUSTRY.	Number of establishments.	PERSONS ENGAGED IN MANUFACTURING INDUSTRIES.					
			Total.	Proprietors and officials.				
				Total.			Proprietors and firm members.	Salaried officials of corporations.	Superintendents and managers.
				Male.	Female.			
1	All industries............	290,105	10,812,736	656,915	25,942	269,137	132,467	281,253
2	Aeroplanes, seaplanes, and airships, and parts	31	4,202	161	6	14	50	103
3	Agricultural implements.................	521	67,177	3,130	57	321	587	2,279
4	Aluminum manufactures.................	83	13,257	477	6	34	89	360
5	Ingots, plates, and sheets...............	7	744	40	......	6	5	29
6	Ware................................	39	8,907	237	5	6	46	190
7	All other.............................	37	3,606	200	1	22	38	141
8	Ammunition............................	42	27,471	1,105	15	10	103	1,007
9	Artificial flowers......................	224	4,876	340	61	234	85	82
10	Artificial limbs.......................	177	1,120	252	10	154	52	56
11	Artificial stone products................	2,785	12,879	3,857	54	3,055	396	460
12	Artists' materials.....................	58	1,205	105	11	40	43	33
13	Crayons.............................	20	508	40	4	16	16	12
14	All other.............................	38	697	65	7	24	27	21
15	Asbestos products, not including steam packing.	46	4,195	178	4	11	74	97
16	Building materials....................	12	1,324	54	1	1	31	23
17	Textile-mill products..................	16	2,264	85	3	4	27	57
18	All other.............................	18	607	39	......	6	16	17
19	Automobile bodies and parts.............	2,515	153,182	7,789	115	2,129	1,666	4,109
20	Automobile repairing..................	15,507	82,635	21,613	241	18,566	1,084	2,204
21	Automobiles..........................	315	242,922	6,392	75	36	548	5,883
22	Awnings, tents, and sails...............	895	8,413	1,367	92	871	318	270
23	Babbitt metal and solder...............	118	3,372	312	11	63	117	143
24	Babbitt metal........................	54	1,852	159	3	32	52	78
25	White metal..........................	21	497	56	......	9	18	29
26	Type metal...........................	7	58	14	2	4	11	1
27	Solder...............................	36	965	83	6	18	36	35
28	Bags, other than paper, not including bags made in textile mills.	216	12,642	551	23	166	170	238
29	Bags, paper, exclusive of those made in paper mills.	75	5,087	242	21	41	94	128
30	Baking powders and yeast...............	88	4,893	266	16	52	80	150
31	Baking powders......................	67	2,914	175	13	43	53	92
32	Yeast................................	21	1,979	91	3	9	27	58
33	Baskets, and rattan and willow ware.......	375	5,370	588	20	400	94	114
34	Bells.................................	10	275	25	2	6	16	5
35	Belting and hose, rubber................	15	7,449	137	2	....	36	103
36	Belting..............................	8	3,045	74	1	....	18	57
37	Hose................................	7	4,404	63	1	....	18	46
38	Belting and hose, woven, other than rubber.	41	3,207	166	10	19	64	93
39	Woven belting........................	24	2,149	103	8	13	36	62
40	All other, including woven hose.........	17	1,058	63	2	6	28	31
41	Belting, leather.......................	172	4,019	412	21	91	181	161
42	Billiard tables, bowling alleys, and accessories.	49	2,327	92	6	43	33	22
43	Blacking, stains, and dressings...........	220	3,765	416	27	179	139	125
44	Bluing...............................	57	515	75	8	45	16	22
45	Bone, carbon, and lamp black............	35	826	103	5	30	41	37
46	Bone black and lampblack..............	6	298	29	......	1	14	14
47	Carbon black.........................	29	528	74	5	29	27	23

[1] Totals not shown for reasons given on page 914.

UNITED STATES, BY INDUSTRIES: 1919—Continued.

[See note at head of this table, pp. 1172 and 1173.]

PERSONS ENGAGED IN MANUFACTURING INDUSTRIES—continued.

| Clerks. | | Wage earners. | | | Wage earners employed Dec. 15, or nearest representative day. | | | | | |
Male.	Female.	Average number.	Number employed 15th day of— Maximum month.	Minimum month.	Total.	16 years of age and over. Male.	Female.	Under 16 years of age. Male.	Female.	
659,775	373,732	9,096,372	De 9,663,170	Ap 8,666,549	(1)	(1)	(1)	(1)	(1)	1
312	180	3,543	Ja 5,493	Oc 2,799	3,474	3,256	212	6	......	2
7,276	2,346	54,368	Fe 59,748	Au 49,483	57,592	56,547	962	82	1	3
777	595	11,402			14,187	12,618	1,368	124	77	4
12	8	684	Oc 747	Ap 609	785	785				5
438	406	7,821	De 9,468	Ja 6,746	9,374	8,009	1,164	124	77	6
327	181	2,897	De 3,934	Fe 2,127	4,028	3,824	204			7
1,854	1,681	22,816	Se 46,771	Se 17,121	22,709	16,333	6,237	91	48	8
225	112	4,138	No 4,318	Ja 3,848	4,348	1,243	3,017	17	71	9
84	103	671	No 682	Fe 660	678	617	55	6	......	10
373	217	8,378	Se 10,528	Ja 5,049	10,987	10,947	25	15	......	11
75	88	926			1,024	777	219	22	6	12
22	28	414	De 453	Ja 372	453	318	115	17	3	13
53	60	512	De 563	Ja 478	571	459	104	5	3	14
214	145	3,654			4,038	3,125	863	28	22	15
55	31	1,183	Oc 1,346	Je 865	1,223	1,136	85	2	......	16
106	77	1,993	De 2,231	Ja 1,747	2,229	1,569	627	21	12	17
53	37	478	De 585	Ap 385	586	420	151	5	10	18
7,748	4,974	132,556	De 157,335	Ja 108,857	160,081	151,588	8,065	363	65	19
2,753	2,967	55,061	Au 59,004	Ja 48,702	58,085	57,454	393	238	......	20
16,606	9,290	210,559	De 241,709	Ja 174,634	243,128	234,916	7,921	288	3	21
538	388	6,028	Je 7,455	Ja 4,881	6,124	3,258	2,818	30	18	22
456	221	2,372			2,768	2,510	241	12	5	23
276	106	1,308	De 1,560	Au 1,051	1,576	1,468	107	1	......	24
79	45	317	De 344	Ap 281	343	340	1	2	......	25
8	7	27	Fe [2] 28	Ja [2] 26	28	26		2	......	26
93	63	720	De 822	Fe 656	821	676	133	7	5	27
774	538	10,756	Oc 11,803	Mh 9,461	11,714	4,378	7,065	73	198	28
423	233	4,168	De 4,850	My 3,266	4,790	2,210	2,468	43	69	29
841	439	3,331			3,390	2,538	835	15	2	30
739	364	1,623	Ja 1,839	De 1,420	1,648	875	756	15	2	31
102	75	1,708	Oc 1,788	My [2] 1,654	1,742	1,663	79			32
136	93	4,533	Au 4,767	Ja 3,979	5,051	3,327	1,537	99	88	33
2	9	237	No 262	Ap 215	264	232	32			34
1,078	406	5,826			6,954	6,057	829	36	32	35
488	114	2,368	Ja 2,722	Je 2,032	2,611	2,366	236	9	......	36
590	292	3,458	De 4,346	Mh 2,296	4,343	3,691	593	27	32	37
360	192	2,479			2,694	1,444	1,177	38	35	38
150	119	1,769	No 1,926	Ap 1,588	1,884	1,004	822	27	31	39
210	73	710	De 803	Ap 626	810	440	355	11	4	40
538	283	2,765	De 3,071	Je 2,566	3,066	2,803	184	76	3	41
72	56	2,101	De 2,595	Ja 1,699	2,597	2,301	293	3	......	42
597	270	2,455	No 2,625	Ja 2,195	2,613	1,377	1,141	47	48	43
49	23	360	Se 419	My 318	354	150	197	2	5	44
32	11	675			684	682	2			45
10	6	253	De 260	Jy 249	260	258	2			46
22	5	422	Oc 444	Ja 403	424	424				47

[2] Same number reported for one or more other months.

75108°—23——76

TABLE **90.**—DETAILED STATEMENT FOR THE

[See note at head of this table, pp. 1172 and 1173.]

	INDUSTRY.	Number of establishments.	PERSONS ENGAGED IN MANUFACTURING INDUSTRIES.					
			Total.	Proprietors and officials.				
				Total.		Proprietors and firm members.	Salaried officials of corporations.	Superintendents and managers.
				Male.	Female.			
1	Bookbinding and blank-book making	1,113	25,287	1,954	158	1,111	478	523
2	Boot and shoe cut stock	252	11,512	731	39	234	153	383
3	Boot and shoe findings	427	10,615	891	55	424	201	321
4	Boots and shoes, not including rubber boots and shoes.	1,449	237,107	7,961	539	883	1,747	5,870
5	Regular factory products	1,337	234,425	7,757	510	786	1,696	5,785
6	Contract work	17	298	26	2	16	1	11
7	Stitching	19	386	15	13	21		7
8	Crimping	3	6	3		3		
9	Buttonholes	3	11	2	2	3		1
10	Overgaiters, moccasins, and leggings	70	1,981	158	12	54	50	66
11	Boots and shoes, rubber	25	37,929	791	74	1	69	795
12	Boxes, cigar	189	5,761	371	20	187	78	126
13	Boxes, paper and other, not elsewhere specified.	1,201	63,408	3,308	264	767	1,232	1,573
14	Shipping containers, corrugated and fiber.	162	13,502	635	29	44	258	362
15	Set-up paper boxes	865	38,161	2,100	208	642	748	918
16	Cartons	127	7,929	396	16	52	173	187
17	Paper cans and tubes	20	1,914	86	5	10	33	48
18	All other	27	1,902	91	6	19	20	58
19	Boxes, wooden packing, except cigar boxes.	1,140	46,897	2,805	80	849	861	1,175
20	Brass, bronze, and copper products	1,092	86,106	3,998	96	751	1,099	2,244
21	Brass and bronze	1,007	73,533	3,596	93	700	991	1,998
22	Copper	47	10,219	287	2	29	65	195
23	All other	38	2,354	115	1	22	43	51
24	Bread and other bakery products	25,095	200,642	31,590	1,969	27,908	1,948	3,703
25	Biscuit and crackers	176	41,284	968	101	54	198	817
26	Bakery products, other than biscuit and crackers.	24,919	159,358	30,622	1,868	27,854	1,750	2,886
27	Brick and tile, terra-cotta, and fire-clay products.	2,414	86,503	5,871	128	1,649	1,664	2,686
28	Building brick	1,454	40,569	3,261	74	1,045	947	1,343
29	Fire brick	194	14,952	631	8	31	240	368
30	Stove lining	19	425	36	2	11	18	9
31	Sewer pipe and draintile	478	11,793	1,003	28	468	187	376
32	Terra-cotta products	214	12,588	689	14	76	212	415
33	Silicate, magnesite, and bauxite bricks and shapes.	39	4,931	175		7	37	131
34	All other	16	1,245	76	2	11	23	44
35	Brooms	1,034	8,536	1,533	28	1,162	168	231
36	From broom corn	1,000	8,369	1,490	27	1,130	161	226
37	All other	34	167	43	1	32	7	5
38	Brushes	379	9,941	778	50	330	229	269
39	Toilet	44	2,225	113	11	19	47	58
40	Paint and varnish	44	2,546	142	5	37	50	60
41	All other	291	5,170	523	34	274	132	151
42	Butter	3,738	26,339	4,342	133	2,006	746	1,723
43	Butter, reworking	5	62	7		4	1	2
44	Buttons	557	17,758	1,147	70	575	269	373
45	Candles	19	666	48	2	13	23	14
46	Canning and preserving, fish	410	12,797	909	23	275	283	374
47	Canning and preserving, fruits and vegetables.	3,082	72,744	7,944	232	3,284	1,354	3,538
48	Canned vegetables	1,989	39,854	5,497	122	2,178	1,013	2,428
49	Canned fruits	446	24,418	1,273	75	374	271	703
50	Dried fruits	629	7,844	1,135	35	729	60	381
51	Dried vegetables	18	628	39		3	10	26

[1] Same number reported throughout the year.

UNITED STATES, BY INDUSTRIES: 1919—Continued.

[See note at head of this table, pp. 1172 and 1173.]

PERSONS ENGAGED IN MANUFACTURING INDUSTRIES—continued.

Clerks.		Wage earners.			Wage earners employed Dec. 15, or nearest representative day.					
Male.	Female.	Average number.	Number employed 15th day of—		Total.	16 years of age and over.		Under 16 years of age.		
			Maximum month.	Minimum month.		Male.	Female.	Male.	Female.	
1,576	1,238	20,361	De 21,775	Ja 19,354	22,946	10,694	11,564	368	320	1
385	642	9,715	No 10,354	Ap 9,190	10,285	7,337	2,696	183	69	2
344	384	8,941	De 10,223	Ja 7,815	10,188	6,545	3,315	172	156	3
8,494	9,064	211,049	....	....	230,457	138,497	84,641	4,434	2,885	4
8,349	8,955	208,854	De 225,714	Ap 197,111	227,794	137,473	83,055	4,406	2,860	5
....	4	266	No 350	Ap 183	346	221	104	18	3	6
....	7	351	De 444	Jy 306	454	45	392	2	15	7
....	....	3	Oc 5	Fe 1	3	3	....	....	....	8
....	....	7	(1) 7	(1) 7	7	....	7	....	....	9
145	98	1,568	De 1,898	Fe 1,285	1,853	755	1,083	8	7	10
2,509	1,680	32,875	Fe 35,339	Je 30,642	34,723	19,849	13,877	411	586	11
88	64	5,218	De 5,666	Ja 4,990	5,664	2,455	3,000	73	136	12
2,126	1,848	55,862	....	....	61,467	24,731	33,328	932	2,476	13
760	492	11,586	No 12,840	My 10,484	12,796	7,356	5,192	71	177	14
711	953	34,189	De 37,443	Ja 31,373	37,609	11,124	23,951	625	1,909	15
497	291	6,729	De 7,301	My 6,241	7,258	4,513	2,596	40	109	16
90	81	1,652	No 1,852	Mh 1,370	1,880	764	789	114	213	17
68	31	1,706	Oc 2,235	Ap 1,375	1,924	974	800	82	68	18
924	643	42,445	De 44,881	Ap 40,682	46,327	41,180	4,582	493	72	19
4,470	2,491	75,051	....	....	81,720	74,669	6,799	190	62	20
3,901	2,148	63,795	Ja 70,115	Je 57,260	68,951	62,522	6,205	168	56	21
435	271	9,224	De 10,911	Jy 7,321	10,689	10,229	457	3	....	22
134	72	2,032	Mh 2,096	Je 1,924	2,080	1,918	137	19	6	23
16,660	8,831	141,592	....	....	151,956	111,176	38,901	1,281	598	24
4,521	1,353	34,341	No 37,036	Mh 32,529	36,569	17,144	18,984	113	328	25
12,139	7,478	107,251	De 113,312	Ja 101,073	115,387	94,032	19,917	1,168	270	26
2,446	1,143	76,915	....	....	88,099	86,289	1,290	505	15	27
848	402	35,984	Au 46,700	Ja 19,702	43,403	43,060	107	235	1	28
433	202	13,678	Ja 14,682	Au 13,239	13,961	13,732	56	172	1	29
21	5	361	De 395	My 337	400	396	....	4	....	30
336	163	10,263	Au 11,796	Ja 7,711	11,092	10,985	65	42	....	31
534	278	11,073	No 13,719	Fe 7,387	13,461	12,406	993	49	13	32
177	56	4,523	Ja 5,214	Je 3,876	4,611	4,545	65	1	....	33
97	37	1,033	Oc 1,260	My 897	1,171	1,165	4	2	....	34
501	161	6,313	....	....	7,103	5,899	1,052	120	32	35
496	159	6,197	De 6,821	Mh 5,782	6,948	5,781	1,019	116	32	36
5	2	116	Fe 146	Se 98	155	118	33	4	....	37
644	501	7,968	....	....	8,791	5,894	2,761	94	42	38
128	119	1,854	No 1,970	Mh 1,756	1,961	1,269	685	7	....	39
127	122	2,150	De 2,412	Ap 1,976	2,414	1,430	938	21	25	40
389	260	3,964	De 4,383	My 3,707	4,416	3,195	1,138	66	17	41
2,000	2,223	17,641	Je 20,370	Ja 14,796	17,304	14,816	2,442	40	6	42
4	4	47	De 53	Se 42	53	47	6	....	....	43
471	493	15,577	No 16,876	Ap 14,594	17,398	10,615	6,475	110	198	44
30	45	541	De 633	Mh 471	634	254	367	6	7	45
353	264	11,248	Au 17,329	Mh 6,749	18,252	10,541	7,578	68	65	46
2,124	1,579	60,865	....	....	163,346	69,847	89,306	1,534	2,659	47
908	769	32,558	Se 98,662	Fe 7,834	94,262	42,878	49,274	931	1,179	48
755	580	21,735	Au 53,799	Mh 4,115	52,514	17,884	32,728	564	1,338	49
409	212	6,053	Oc 16,315	Mh 1,776	15,647	8,727	6,739	39	142	50
52	18	519	No 784	Mh 240	923	358	565	....	....	51

TABLE 90.—DETAILED STATEMENT FOR THE

[See note at head of this table, pp. 1172 and 1173.]

INDUSTRY.	Number of establishments.	PERSONS ENGAGED IN MANUFACTURING INDUSTRIES.					
		Total.	Proprietors and officials.				
			Total.		Proprietors and firm members.	Salaried officials of corporations.	Superintendents and managers.
			Male.	Female.			
1 Canning and preserving, oysters	65	1,339	117	3	51	24	45
2 Card cutting and designing	75	1,397	130	7	69	32	36
3 Cardboard, not made in paper mills	16	1,714	100	28	2	39	87
4 Carpets and rugs, other than rag	75	24,251	486	8	50	136	308
5 Carpets, rag	339	2,716	456	30	391	34	61
6 Carriage and wagon materials	258	7,429	577	9	212	165	209
7 Carriages and sleds, children's	103	7,513	314	13	65	101	161
8 Carriages and wagons, including repairs	2,286	23,268	3,595	95	2,655	390	645
9 Carriages and wagons	1,130	19,249	2,128	67	1,265	355	575
10 Repair work only	1,156	4,019	1,467	28	1,390	35	70
11 Cars and general shop construction and repairs by electric-railroad companies	624	33,120	867	.....	1	65	801
12 Cars and general shop construction and repairs by steam-railroad companies	1,744	516,279	15,451	25	2	136	15,338
13 Cars, electric-railroad, not including operations of railroad companies	7	3,286	83	1	1	16	67
14 Cars, steam-railroad, not including operations of railroad companies	99	58,782	1,849	55	2	218	1,684
15 Cash registers and calculating machines	65	18,958	561	4	26	89	450
16 Adding machines	20	9,883	315	.....	6	26	283
17 Cash registers and parts	19	7,300	149	2	8	30	113
18 All other	26	1,775	97	2	12	33	54
19 Cement	123	30,247	853	6	9	275	575
20 Charcoal, not including production in the lumber and wood-distillation industries	41	273	54	.....	30	5	19
21 Cheese	3,530	6,993	2,707	38	2,400	157	188
22 Chemicals	598	66,947	2,946	81	122	673	2,232
23 Chewing gum	62	4,056	193	11	23	80	101
24 China decorating, not including that done in potteries	43	321	38	14	45	5	2
25 Decalcomania work on china	9	50	5	4	7	2	.....
26 All other	34	271	33	10	38	3	2
27 Chocolate and cocoa products	48	10,287	283	17	21	112	167
28 Cleansing and polishing preparations	499	4,264	744	59	356	226	221
29 Cleansing preparations	281	2,086	412	17	214	112	103
30 Metal polish	81	498	116	15	42	54	35
31 All other polishing preparations	137	1,680	216	27	100	60	83
32 Clocks	46	9,260	265	5	11	71	188
33 Cloth, sponging and refinishing	67	1,454	147	4	55	75	21
34 Clothing, horse	28	959	81	4	25	21	39
35 Clothing, men's	5,258	209,712	12,126	580	6,970	1,962	3,774
36 Regular factory products	2,905	164,092	8,422	484	3,509	1,869	3,528
37 Men's and youths'	1,768	115,163	5,731	272	2,273	1,185	2,545
38 Boys'	379	12,873	936	43	558	153	268
39 All other	758	36,056	1,755	169	678	531	715
40 Contract work	2,353	45,620	3,704	96	3,461	93	246
41 Men's and youths'	2,005	37,702	3,130	81	2,948	69	194
42 Boys'	253	6,181	431	10	394	22	25
43 All other	95	1,737	143	5	119	2	27
44 Clothing, men's, buttonholes	107	635	140	3	131	10	2
45 Clothing, women's	7,711	202,243	16,072	1,893	10,366	3,095	4,504
46 Regular factory products	5,516	171,108	12,244	1,639	7,090	2,698	4,095
47 Suits, skirts, and cloaks	1,820	53,159	4,402	156	2,556	724	1,278
48 Shirt waists and dresses, except house dresses	1,873	63,383	4,154	789	2,362	1,073	1,508
49 Undergarments and petticoats	637	22,914	1,341	249	720	354	516
50 Wrappers and house dresses	238	7,721	525	114	295	101	243
51 All other	948	23,931	1,822	331	1,157	446	550

UNITED STATES, BY INDUSTRIES: 1919—Continued.

[See note at head of this table, pp. 1172 and 1173.]

PERSONS ENGAGED IN MANUFACTURING INDUSTRIES—continued.

Clerks.		Wage earners.			Wage earners employed Dec. 15, or nearest representative day.					
		Average number.	Number employed 15th day of—		Total.	16 years of age and over.		Under 16 years of age.		
Male.	Female.		Maximum month.	Minimum month.		Male.	Female.	Male.	Female.	
19	11	1,189	De 1,836	Jy 214	2,256	842	1,409	1	4	1
60	52	1,148	De 1,261	Ja 1,015	1,248	551	665	9	23	2
84	77	1,425	No 1,498	Ja 1,355	1,475	820	622	12	21	3
566	258	22,933	De 26,502	Ja 18,622	27,002	16,573	9,739	352	338	4
115	99	2,016	De 2,325	Ja 1,608	2,367	1,591	710	36	30	5
195	139	6,509	Oc 7,095	Mh 5,856	7,157	6,885	247	25	.....	6
282	218	6,686	De 7,179	Ja 5,999	7,234	5,779	1,077	299	79	7
894	511	18,173	.....	.....	18,955	18,621	273	52	9	8
855	480	15,719	No 16,239	Je 15,207	16,414	16,106	265	34	9	9
39	31	2,454	Je 2,500	Ja 2,341	2,541	2,515	8	18	.....	10
721	260	31,272	De 31,894	Je 30,220	32,108	31,660	438	10	.....	11
12,057	4,309	484,437	De 511,134	Je 464,919	510,384	506,365	3,975	44	.....	12
184	98	2,920	Ja 3,965	My 2,471	2,709	2,641	65	3	.....	13
3,535	1,045	52,298	Ja 64,974	Oc 45,031	50,999	50,549	429	21	.....	14
1,056	793	16,544	.....	.....	18,541	15,767	2,734	20	20	15
479	449	8,640	De 10,228	Ap 7,604	10,201	8,335	1,835	14	17	16
451	284	6,414	Au 7,266	Ja 4,558	6,758	6,148	606	2	2	17
126	60	1,490	Se 1,627	Ap 1,390	1,582	1,284	293	4	1	18
2,811	1,053	25,524	Se 29,062	Ja 20,234	26,895	26,503	362	28	2	19
5	5	209	Oc 258	Je 140	254	251	3	.....	.....	20
159	92	3,997	Je 5,026	Ja 2,843	4,723	4,523	174	26	.....	21
5,460	2,874	55,586	Ja 60,754	My 51,050	58,757	53,798	4,782	88	89	22
379	283	3,190	Se 3,374	Je 2,995	3,117	1,130	1,949	7	31	23
12	13	244			285	130	150	.....	5	24
2	.....	39	De 44	Ja 36	44	9	33	.....	2	25
10	13	205	No 246	Ja 168	241	121	117	.....	3	26
611	293	9,083	Oc 10,034	My 8,200	9,313	6,838	2,383	36	56	27
934	572	1,955	.....	.....	2,212	1,410	782	13	7	28
499	266	892	De 980	Jy 839	994	686	297	8	3	29
72	53	242	De 265	Ja 221	266	169	94	2	1	30
363	253	821	De 950	Mh 707	952	555	391	3	3	31
423	315	8,252	De 8,867	Ja 7,329	8,908	5,915	2,677	178	138	32
44	53	1,206	Au 1,378	Ja 991	1,371	1,347	24	.....	.....	33
82	26	766	De 899	Ap 677	907	411	482	4	10	34
13,350	8,386	175,270	.....	.....	208,524	95,771	110,794	576	1,383	35
13,141	8,173	133,872	.....	.....	157,666	67,077	88,910	484	1,195	36
10,030	6,266	92,864	De 108,221	Ja 79,301	110,102	54,576	54,393	375	758	37
1,101	567	10,226	De 11,888	Ja 8,035	11,953	5,506	6,350	15	82	38
2,010	1,340	30,782	De 35,565	Ap 27,538	35,611	6,995	28,167	94	355	39
209	213	41,398	.....	.....	50,858	28,694	21,884	92	188	40
85	182	34,224	De 39,978	Ja 26,032	41,608	23,684	17,686	89	149	41
113	13	5,614	De 6,676	Ja 3,882	7,061	4,337	2,702	2	20	42
11	18	1,560	De 2,110	My 1,189	2,389	673	1,496	1	19	43
5	3	484	No 525	Ja 413	522	293	224	4	1	44
11,063	7,566	165,649	.....	.....	183,516	60,522	121,687	176	1,131	45
10,786	7,342	139,097	.....	.....	149,869	47,469	101,206	154	1,040	46
3,999	2,639	41,963	Se 49,056	My 32,448	46,394	30,790	15,486	65	53	47
3,433	2,831	52,176	Se 56,576	Ja 45,851	54,028	9,975	43,448	42	563	48
1,301	798	19,225	No 21,248	Mh 16,817	21,071	2,306	18,559	28	178	49
440	289	6,353	No 6,845	Fe 5,963	6,899	781	6,046	4	68	50
1,613	785	19,380	No 21,335	Ja 17,540	21,477	3,617	17,667	15	178	51

TABLE 90.—DETAILED STATEMENT FOR THE

[See note at head of this table, pp. 1172 and 1173.]

			PERSONS ENGAGED IN MANUFACTURING INDUSTRIES.					
					Proprietors and officials.			
INDUSTRY.		Number of establishments.	Total.	Total.		Proprietors and firm members.	Salaried officials of corporations.	Superintendents and managers.
				Male.	Female.			
	Clothing, women's—Continued.							
1	Contract work	2,195	31,135	3,828	254	3,276	397	409
2	Suits, skirts, and cloaks	974	10,805	1,727	24	1,516	122	113
3	Shirt waists and dresses, except house dresses.	888	14,742	1,599	153	1,297	258	197
4	Undergarments and petticoats	76	1,475	107	18	93	7	25
5	Wrappers and house dresses	47	669	68	10	64		14
6	All other	210	3,444	327	49	306	10	60
7	Coal-tar products	183	21,543	1,762	22	26	235	1,523
8	Coffee and spice, roasting and grinding	794	20,187	1,820	63	556	599	728
9	Coffee	769	18,584	1,742	62	548	564	692
10	Spice	25	1,603	78	1	8	35	36
11	Coffins, burial cases, and undertakers' goods	351	14,546	986	56	225	370	447
12	Coke, not including gas-house coke	278	32,882	1,080	5	41	165	879
13	Beehive ovens	222	15,140	436	5	41	106	294
14	By-product ovens	56	17,742	644			59	585
15	Collars and cuffs, men's	39	12,562	289	82	37	58	276
16	Combs and hairpins, not made from metal or rubber.	45	2,475	121	7	38	38	52
17	Condensed milk	401	16,533	1,022	11	46	209	778
18	Confectionery and ice cream	6,624	122,028	11,661	805	7,051	2,250	3,165
19	Confectionery	3,149	93,982	6,178	577	3,146	1,457	2,152
20	Ice cream	3,475	28,046	5,483	228	3,905	793	1,013
21	Cooperage	1,099	15,369	1,593	55	941	320	387
22	Hogsheads and barrels	995	13,286	1,393	47	857	266	317
23	All other	104	2,083	200	8	84	54	70
24	Copper, tin, and sheet-iron work	4,796	38,559	7,470	157	5,056	1,325	1,246
25	Cordage and twine	120	19,232	680	19	29	174	496
26	Cordials and flavoring sirups	149	2,588	307	16	76	135	112
27	Cork, cutting	62	4,061	194	7	30	67	104
28	Corsets	188	21,751	584	202	98	183	505
29	Corsets	142	19,143	484	182	69	141	456
30	Corset waists and brassieres	46	2,608	100	20	29	42	49
31	Cotton goods	1,288	445,423	6,928	103	239	2,453	4,339
32	Cotton lace	44	7,196	219	16	8	62	165
33	Cotton small wares	164	10,254	446	21	99	179	189
34	Crucibles	22	1,035	80		2	47	31
35	Graphite crucibles	6	289	25			16	9
36	Clay crucibles	10	343	38		2	19	17
37	Glass-house pots	6	403	17			12	5
38	Cutlery and edge tools	304	22,529	922	71	173	324	496
39	Table cutlery	24	2,336	103	8	10	29	72
40	Razors, plain and safety	33	5,229	149	37	11	44	131
41	Axes and hatchets	25	2,908	72	2	13	33	28
42	Scissors, shears, and clippers	52	3,903	181	5	32	55	99
43	Pocketknives	40	4,956	146	6	17	56	79
44	Augers, bits, chisels, and planes	27	1,298	68	4	12	30	30
45	All other	103	1,899	203	9	78	77	57
46	Dairymen's, poultrymen's, and apiarists' supplies.	244	8,614	681	22	164	184	355
47	Incubators and brooders	48	1,078	106	6	28	43	41
48	All other poultrymen's supplies	60	416	91	5	59	19	18
49	Cream separators	19	4,396	238	3	4	27	210
50	All other dairymen's supplies	90	2,063	184	7	43	81	67
51	Apiarists' supplies	27	661	62	1	30	14	19
52	Dental goods	319	6,799	580	35	316	123	176
53	Teeth	52	3,889	183	8	50	25	116
54	All other	267	2,910	397	27	266	98	60

UNITED STATES, BY INDUSTRIES: 1919—Continued.

[See note at head of this table, pp. 1172 and 1173.]

PERSONS ENGAGED IN MANUFACTURING INDUSTRIES—continued.

Clerks.		Wage earners.			Wage earners employed Dec. 15, or nearest representative day.					
			Number employed 15th day of—			16 years of age and over.		Under 16 years of age.		
Male.	Female.	Average number.	Maximum month.	Minimum month.	Total.	Male.	Female.	Male.	Female.	
277	224	26,552			33,647	13,053	20,481	22	91	1
152	85	8,817	Se 11,605	Je 4,979	11,892	8,425	3,456	9	2	2
118	127	12,745	Se 14,260	Ja 10,135	15,343	3,255	12,074	5	9	3
2	4	1,344	De 1,707	Ja 1,040	1,699	156	1,534	......	9	4
......	......	591	No 769	Jy 478	786	60	724	......	2	5
5	8	3,055	De 3,661	Ja 2,519	3,927	1,157	2,693	8	69	6
2,931	1,165	15,663	De 17,887	Ap 14,311	18,569	17,991	548	16	14	7
5,966	1,798	10,540			*11,056	6,137	4,788	65	66	8
5,724	1,721	9,335	De 9,670	Ap 8,903	9,693	5,548	4,025	64	56	9
242	77	1,205	Se 1,430	Ja 920	1,363	589	763	1	10	10
1,226	388	11,890	Mh 12,507	Jy 11,467	11,661	9,506	2,088	46	21	11
2,068	410	29,319			30,857	30,404	8	445	......	12
777	156	13,766	Ja 16,686	My 11,778	15,039	15,032	1	6	......	13
1,291	254	15,553	Ja 17,871	Oc 12,970	15,818	15,372	7	439	......	14
519	569	11,103	No 11,661	Ja 10,234	11,787	2,772	9,001	6	8	15
48	70	2,229	Mh 2,327	Au 2,172	2,411	1,453	774	96	88	16
930	895	13,675	Je 15,593	Ja 11,383	13,183	11,420	1,736	22	5	17
7,906	6,008	95,648			104,181	45,452	55,046	1,006	2,677	18
6,337	4,397	76,493	Oc 88,216	Jy 67,064	85,792	29,383	52,954	799	2,656	19
1,569	1,611	19,155	Jy 24,836	Ja 14,600	18,389	16,069	2,092	207	21	20
273	229	13,219			14,591	14,143	357	86	5	21
228	180	11,438	Se 12,181	My 10,911	12,811	12,423	329	54	5	22
45	49	1,781	Jy 1,910	De 1,695	1,780	1,720	28	32	......	23
1,849	1,443	27,640	De 30,486	Fe 24,602	31,039	30,134	711	188	6	24
575	336	17,622	De 18,303	Ap 17,034	18,899	10,907	7,504	261	227	25
615	252	1,398	Jy 1,604	Fe 1,284	1,583	1,162	421			26
159	156	3,545	Ja 3,706	Je 3,482	3,611	2,220	1,309	30	52	27
967	1,583	18,415			21,105	3,254	17,194	117	540	28
778	1,402	16,297	De 18,103	Ja 15,135	18,657	3,061	14,977	112	507	29
189	181	2,118	De 2,460	Mh 1,837	2,448	193	2,217	5	33	30
4,331	3,095	430,966	De 449,007	Ap 414,718	459,845	254,380	183,810	10,735	10,920	31
292	179	6,490	De 7,300	Ja 5,941	7,441	3,374	3,505	244	318	32
160	231	9,396	De 10,102	Ap 8,872	10,065	3,593	5,926	158	388	33
66	41	848			871	849	22			34
18	7	239	Ja 303	Je 193	258	258				35
40	28	237	Ja 264	Au 209	235	221	14			36
8	6	372	Fe 391	Au 357	378	370	8			37
973	704	19,859			22,080	17,580	4,171	251	78	38
62	48	2,115	De 2,250	Ap 1,925	2,277	1,926	254	78	19	39
513	317	4,213	De 4,739	Au 3,572	4,819	2,585	2,206	12	16	40
53	38	2,743	Oc 3,071	De 2,577	3,111	2,949	157	5		41
156	111	3,450	De 3,718	Au 3,140	3,745	3,227	444	65	9	42
125	115	4,564	De 5,125	Ja 4,032	5,191	4,235	860	67	29	43
33	27	1,166	No 1,226	Ap 1,136	1,199	1,159	27	11	2	44
31	48	1,608	De 1,731	Ap 1,522	1,738	1,499	223	13	3	45
887	587	6,437			7,282	6,481	766	28	7	46
89	95	782	De 1,086	Je 533	1,096	978	107	9	2	47
22	18	280	Ja 300	Jy 245	346	268	73	5		48
497	313	3,345	De 3,673	Au 3,112	3,694	3,365	329			49
229	98	1,545	Jy 1,644	No 1,440	1,602	1,422	161	14	5	50
50	63	485	De 531	Oc 441	544	448	96			51
461	499	5,224			5,483	2,823	2,252	170	238	52
311	253	3,134	De 3,281	Ja 2,861	3,287	1,184	1,759	110	234	53
150	246	2,090	De 2,205	Ja 1,994	2,196	1,639	493	60	4	54

TABLE **90.**—DETAILED STATEMENT FOR THE

[See note at head of this table, pp. 1172 and 1173.]

	INDUSTRY.	Number of establishments.	PERSONS ENGAGED IN MANUFACTURING INDUSTRIES.					
			Total.	Proprietors and officials.				
				Total.		Proprietors and firm members.	Salaried officials of corporations.	Superintendents and managers.
				Male.	Female.			
1	Drug grinding	31	1,661	112	1	16	46	51
2	Druggists' preparations	524	22,569	1,538	116	283	439	932
3	Dyeing and finishing textiles, exclusive of that done in textile mills.	628	62,588	2,354	84	363	757	1,318
4	Dyestuffs and extracts—natural	144	5,205	408	10	59	142	217
5	Electrical machinery, apparatus, and supplies.	1,404	271,912	10,853	321	473	1,882	8,819
6	Electroplating	515	4,032	784	28	590	133	89
7	Emery and other abrasive wheels	60	6,921	311	13	20	84	220
8	Enameling	74	880	115	1	76	20	20
9	Engines, steam, gas, and water	370	96,286	3,844	41	93	599	3,193
10	Engravers' materials	21	252	36	1	11	13	13
11	Engraving and diesinking	478	2,656	602	5	533	46	28
12	Engraving, steel and copper plate, including plate printing.	421	8,779	797	50	370	213	264
13	Engraving, wood	55	387	83	1	62	13	9
14	Envelopes	106	9,493	366	28	33	148	213
15	Explosives	118	15,429	1,521	28	28	131	1,390
16	Fancy articles, not elsewhere specified	661	17,140	1,212	164	606	372	398
17	Beadwork	37	491	55	6	54	5	2
18	Celluloid novelties	66	3,403	178	12	38	67	85
19	Metal novelties	110	3,152	214	8	78	79	65
20	Paper novelties	63	1,528	98	40	56	27	55
21	Wood novelties	30	253	33	12	27	13	5
22	All other	355	8,313	634	86	353	181	186
23	Feathers and plumes	216	4,224	337	57	239	66	89
24	Felt goods	49	5,934	200	6	8	88	110
25	Ferroalloys	30	2,750	167		8	49	110
26	Fertilizers	600	32,522	2,086	47	219	623	1,291
27	Files	50	6,343	175	1	24	60	92
28	Firearms	26	12,534	202	2	9	38	157
29	Fire extinguishers, chemical	32	1,128	117	17	19	27	88
30	Fireworks	57	1,396	102	6	26	41	41
31	Flags and banners	79	1,345	123	12	60	38	37
32	Flavoring extracts	453	4,183	738	39	356	269	152
33	Flax and hemp, dressed	20	491	49	1	26	9	15
34	Flour-mill and gristmill products	10,708	75,769	17,480	584	11,937	2,541	3,586
35	Food preparations, not elsewhere specified	1,997	44,138	4,198	177	1,908	1,074	1,393
36	Breadstuff preparations, such as cereals and breakfast foods.	105	10,919	352	18	45	109	216
37	Lard compounds and other substitutes	27	3,079	121		7	20	94
38	Macaroni, vermicelli, and noodles	557	6,226	1,004	44	687	195	166
39	Meat products, not elsewhere specified	86	3,540	196	6	77	50	75
40	Peanut butter	56	749	101	5	45	33	28
41	Sweetening sirups, other than cane	256	3,499	496	25	270	107	144
42	All other preparations for human consumption.	616	9,037	1,143	63	596	309	301
43	Prepared feed for animals and fowls	294	7,089	785	16	181	251	369
44	Foundry and machine-shop products	10,934	577,308	34,695	880	7,662	10,098	17,815
45	Boiler shops	525	27,540	1,637	49	397	565	724
46	Foundries	1,340	116,427	5,579	132	770	1,737	3,204
47	Machine shops	8,110	334,487	22,702	596	5,990	6,407	10,901
48	Machine shop and foundry combined	959	98,854	4,777	103	505	1,389	2,986
49	Foundry supplies	76	1,331	186	5	23	93	75
50	Fuel, manufactured	11	228	20		5	5	15
51	Fur goods	1,815	19,834	3,153	145	2,527	378	393
52	Furnishing goods, men's	487	22,530	1,133	148	503	277	501
53	Neckwear	322	9,069	691	85	376	172	228
54	All other	165	13,461	442	63	127	105	273

[1] Same number reported for one or more other months.

UNITED STATES, BY INDUSTRIES: 1919—Continued.

[See note at head of this table, pp. 1172 and 1173.]

PERSONS ENGAGED IN MANUFACTURING INDUSTRIES—continued.

| Clerks | | Wage earners | | | Wage earners employed Dec. 15, or nearest representative day. | | | | | |
Male.	Female.	Average number.	Maximum month.	Minimum month.	Total.	16 years of age and over — Male.	16 years of age and over — Female.	Under 16 years of age — Male.	Under 16 years of age — Female.	
126	75	1,347	Oc 1,456	Ap 1,220	1,460	1,210	236	4	10	1
3,032	2,315	15,568	Fe 16,359	Je 14,941	15,877	7,667	7,981	101	128	2
2,472	1,693	55,985	De 62,590	Ap 51,052	62,462	47,132	14,098	708	524	3
274	171	4,342	Jy 4,511	Ap 4,103	4,565	4,474	77	9	5	4
29,233	19,131	212,374	De 241,640	My 196,418	245,324	180,152	62,920	1,557	695	5
79	117	3,024	De 3,436	Fe 2,616	3,461	3,212	152	92	5	6
586	410	5,601	De 6,343	Jy 5,172	6,338	5,438	860	9	31	7
40	30	694	No 806	Fe 567	806	622	160	14	10	8
10,593	4,191	77,617	Ja 90,102	My 70,193	85,053	83,063	1,872	109	9	9
19	22	174	De 208	Ja 148	206	201		5		10
91	80	1,878	De 2,121	Ja 1,628	2,127	1,912	167	46	2	11
431	487	7,014	De 7,943	Ja 6,462	7,824	4,544	3,018	126	136	12
52	16	235	Jy 246	Ja 223	240	232	2	6		13
463	507	8,129	De 8,767	Ap 7,845	8,767	3,373	5,295	31	68	14
2,903	1,728	9,249	Ja 11,809	Je 8,605	9,020	8,845	175			15
952	851	13,961			15,863	7,222	8,007	293	341	16
19	11	400	Oc 468	Ja 331	451	40	405	2	4	17
116	156	2,941	De 3,231	Ja 2,678	3,352	1,968	1,121	141	122	18
168	195	2,567	No 2,718	Ja 2,301	2,728	1,703	937	46	42	19
83	110	1,197	De 1,641	Ap 921	1,644	318	1,169	47	110	20
4	4	200	No 240	Mh[1] 177	243	170	66	5	2	21
562	375	6,656	No 7,577	Ja 5,334	7,445	3,023	4,309	52	61	22
203	123	3,504	Ap 3,804	Ja 3,105	3,234	443	2,767	7	17	23
242	250	5,236	De 5,744	My 4,874	5,895	4,478	1,371	30	16	24
175	64	2,344	Ja 2,933	Jy 1,879	3,204	3,192	10	2		25
3,318	775	26,296	Mh 38,357	Je 21,071	30,071	29,565	428	78		26
193	207	5,767	Ja 6,251	Je 5,298	6,192	5,280	865	41	6	27
577	466	11,287	Ja 13,428	Jy 10,194	11,497	10,390	1,058	49		28
124	93	777	Ja 981	Ap 612	802	609	193			29
39	27	1,222	Je 1,383	Oc 1,129	1,268	713	527	14	14	30
68	77	1,065	Ja 1,337	Se 878	916	213	679	5	19	31
896	322	2,188	Au 2,535	Fe 1,846	2,274	1,125	1,113	17	19	32
14	7	420	De 514	Ja 350	538	493	44		1	33
8,834	3,390	45,481	De 49,393	Mh 42,179	49,932	48,688	1,170	72	2	34
6,673	2,725	30,365			33,829	23,810	9,707	177	135	35
2,219	696	7,634	Au 9,043	Mh 6,234	8,131	5,687	2,440	3	1	36
444	124	2,390	Au 2,610	Mh 1,940	2,506	2,160	339	4	3	37
442	193	4,543	Oc 4,957	Je 4,189	5,091	3,693	1,302	44	52	38
646	203	2,489	Fe 3,121	My 1,928	2,382	1,232	1,140	4	6	39
65	47	531	Au 592	Fe 483	543	242	295	3	3	40
623	167	2,188	Oc 2,788	Je 1,741	2,893	2,303	577	7	6	41
1,058	594	6,179	My 6,710	Se 5,337	7,339	3,849	3,443	23	24	42
1,176	701	4,411	De 4,858	Je 4,127	4,944	4,644	171	89	40	43
38,273	20,693	482,767			538,308	519,425	16,655	2,091	137	44
2,092	762	23,000	Ja 25,495	My 21,521	23,931	23,834	48	49		45
3,838	2,062	104,816	De 122,204	My 94,315	126,262	122,364	3,394	457		46
25,973	14,772	270,444	De 293,960	My 258,962	296,243	283,544	11,178	1,436	47	47
6,370	3,097	84,507	Ja 92,764	Je 79,233	91,872	89,683	2,035	149	5	48
141	93	906	No 988	Ap 850	972	943	22	7		49
31	6	171	De 299	Ap 111	284	274	10			50
1,753	1,144	13,639	No 15,820	Ja 10,947	15,626	9,816	5,737	42	31	51
1,505	800	18,944			20,881	3,334	16,886	103	558	52
1,053	462	6,778	No 7,523	Ja 6,143	7,545	1,949	5,542	17	37	53
452	338	12,166	No 13,054	Mh 11,044	13,336	1,385	11,344	86	521	54

TABLE 90.—DETAILED STATEMENT FOR THE

[See note at head of this table, pp. 1172 and 1173.]

	INDUSTRY.	Number of establishments.	PERSONS ENGAGED IN MANUFACTURING INDUSTRIES.						
			Total.	Proprietors and officials.					
				Total.		Proprietors and firm members.	Salaried officials of corporations.	Superintendents and managers.	
				Male.	Female.				
1	Furniture	3,154	160,289	9,336	255	2,350	2,981	4,260	
2	Wood, other than rattan and willow	2,273	120,836	6,671	180	1,644	2,166	3,041	
3	Rattan and willow	119	4,443	308	5	95	68	150	
4	Metal	157	15,998	857	29	77	267	542	
5	Store and office fixtures	605	19,012	1,500	41	534	480	527	
6	Furs, dressed	141	5,679	384	10	127	151	116	
7	Galvanizing	52	1,965	159	4	33	58	72	
8	Gas and electric fixtures	341	12,379	952	34	221	333	432	
9	Gas fixtures	57	3,046	161	13	40	55	79	
10	Electric fixtures	187	5,708	524	15	112	183	244	
11	Combination gas and electric fixtures	71	2,998	210	4	48	78	88	
12	All other	26	627	57	2	21	17	21	
13	Gas, illuminating and heating	1,022	63,328	3,417	34	27	901	2,523	
14	Gas machines and gas and water meters	105	7,076	379	9	24	133	231	
15	Gas and water meters	34	4,506	207	5	2	58	152	
16	Gas machines	49	1,936	119	3	20	46	56	
17	All other	22	634	53	1	2	29	23	
18	Glass	371	83,656	2,465	33	60	706	1,732	
19	Glass, cutting, staining, and ornamenting	616	8,248	1,001	36	531	296	210	
20	Decalcomania work on glass	22	465	32	1	17	4	12	
21	All other	594	7,783	969	35	514	292	198	
22	Gloves and mittens, cloth, not including gloves made in textile mills	182	9,746	356	37	133	104	156	
23	Gloves and mittens, leather	355	12,594	938	82	405	212	403	
24	Glucose and starch	56	8,694	432	2	37	61	336	
25	Glucose	9	5,569	262	2	1	24	239	
26	Starch	47	3,125	170	......	36	37	97	
27	Glue, not elsewhere specified	62	4,905	223	10	23	67	143	
28	Glue	52	3,543	165	10	22	55	98	
29	All other products	10	1,362	58	......	1	12	45	
30	Gold and silver, leaf and foil	87	1,146	125	18	97	22	24	
31	Gold and silver, reducing and refining, not from the ore	87	995	160	4	81	48	35	
32	Graphite, ground and refined	24	664	58	2	10	16	34	
33	Grease and tallow, not including lubricating greases	482	8,276	934	20	454	188	312	
34	Soap stock	233	3,601	422	11	202	85	146	
35	Tallow	196	3,670	404	7	195	76	140	
36	All other	53	1,005	108	2	57	27	26	
37	Grindstones	23	729	37	......	7	21	9	
38	Haircloth	18	511	41	5	19	12	15	
39	Hair work	198	1,549	231	44	210	34	31	
40	Hammocks	6	78	11	......	6	2	3	
41	Hand stamps	298	2,704	478	31	293	113	103	
42	Hardware	548	48,954	1,976	69	319	642	1,084	
43	Locks	76	5,399	252	5	42	91	124	
44	Builders' hardware	134	17,696	488	16	90	139	275	
45	Piano and organ hardware	16	606	63	1	13	8	45	
46	Vehicle hardware	53	7,686	247	8	15	93	147	
47	All other	269	17,567	926	39	159	311	495	
48	Hardware, saddlery	37	4,073	139	5	21	44	79	
49	Hat and cap materials	133	3,484	275	18	134	76	83	
50	Hats and caps, other than felt, straw, and wool	709	9,752	1,355	35	931	264	195	

1 Same number reported for one or more other months

UNITED STATES, BY INDUSTRIES: 1919—Continued.

[See note at head of this table, pp. 1172 and 1173.]

PERSONS ENGAGED IN MANUFACTURING INDUSTRIES—continued.

Clerks.		Wage earners.			Wage earners employed Dec. 15, or nearest representative day.					
		Average number.	Number employed 15th day of—		Total.	16 years of age and over.		Under 16 years of age.		
Male.	Female.		Maximum month.	Minimum month.		Male.	Female.	Male.	Female.	
7,669	4,698	138,331	De 119,424	Ja 93,512	156,384	141,447	12,867	1,751	319	1
5,082	2,946	105,957			119,342	107,594	10,143	1,374	231	2
122	116	3,892	De 4,984	Ja 3,241	5,073	3,834	1,023	149	67	3
1,335	950	12,827	De 14,444	Ap 11,477	14,429	13,666	683	74	6	4
1,130	686	15,655	De 17,397	Ja 13,910	17,540	16,353	1,018	154	15	5
137	73	5,075	Au 5,670	Ja 4,012	5,365	4,488	813	34	30	6
88	49	1,665	Ja 1,833	Oc 1,557	1,586	1,504	82			7
1,005	593	9,795			11,148	8,565	2,351	138	94	8
98	165	2,609	De 2,906	Jy 2,478	2,887	1,166	1,587	57	77	9
585	258	4,326	De 5,106	Ja 3,758	5,073	4,564	457	45	7	10
290	143	2,351	De 2,581	My 2,178	2,572	2,289	248	25	10	11
32	27	509	De 612	Ja 403	616	546	59	11		12
11,088	5,881	42,908	De 44,280	Mh 41,549	44,280	44,058	200	22		13
719	380	5,589			5,838	5,466	357	14	1	14
267	208	3,819	Ja 4,238	My 3,456	3,888	3,557	317	13	1	15
348	133	1,333	Au 1,493	My 1,155	1,450	1,426	23	1		16
104	39	437	De 497	Ja 360	500	483	17			17
2,042	1,596	77,520	No 85,416	Jy 65,055	93,320	81,214	10,410	1,415	281	18
383	348	6,480			7,445	5,502	1,799	89	55	19
7	16	409	De 476	Ja 314	481	179	294		8	20
376	332	6,071	De 6,907	Ja 5,109	6,964	5,323	1,505	89	47	21
173	194	8,986	Ja 11,069	My 7,605	10,133	1,219	8,555	76	283	22
601	288	10,685	De 11,623	Mh 9,984	11,459	4,753	6,226	201	279	23
328	137	7,795			9,737	8,796	933	7	1	24
219	77	5,009	Se 6,076	Ap 3,925	5,611	4,903	708			25
109	60	2,786	Oc 3,380	Jy 2,052	4,126	3,893	225	7	1	26
271	137	4,264			4,490	3,992	491	7		27
209	103	3,056	No 3,212	Jy 2,696	3,266	2,898	361	7		28
62	34	1,208	Fe 1,289	Jy 1,116	1,224	1,094	130			29
17	36	950	De 1,035	Je 890	1,042	480	542	13	7	30
122	65	644	De 690	Mh 615	700	655	45			31
66	41	497	Se 575	Mh 454	641	610	31			32
484	191	6,647			6,684	6,438	213	33		33
136	61	2,971	Ja 3,129	No 2,872	2,968	2,828	135	5		34
292	104	2,863	Au¹ 2,988	My 2,772	2,913	2,817	68	28		35
56	26	813	Ap 859	No 762	803	793	10			36
11	7	674	Ap 775	De 556	563	559	4			37
23	17	425	Oc 478	Ap 373	460	236	222	1	1	38
94	96	1,084	No 1,144	Ja 987	1,135	288	832	3	12	39
1	2	64	Jy 82	No 53	61	22	30	4	5	40
256	220	1,719	De¹ 1,776	Ja 1,667	1,776	1,426	290	50	10	41
2,019	2,385	42,505			47,585	38,360	8,283	646	296	42
172	254	4,716	De 4,856	Ja 4,525	4,994	3,814	1,031	84	65	43
834	851	15,507	De 17,798	Ap 14,131	17,837	14,530	3,026	219	62	44
13	21	508	De 558	Fe 431	572	456	68	38	10	45
236	198	6,997	Au 7,631	Ja 5,794	7,689	6,673	996	15	5	46
764	1,061	14,777	De 16,424	Ja 13,902	16,493	12,887	3,162	290	154	47
141	113	3,675	No 3,835	Ap 3,569	3,857	3,238	588	22	9	48
106	76	3,009	De 3,613	Ap 2,100	3,602	2,238	1,316	16	32	49
534	289	7,539	De 8,618	Jy 6,789	8,721	5,608	3,058	24	31	50

TABLE **90.**—DETAILED STATEMENT FOR THE

[See note at head of this table, pp. 1172 and 1173.]

	INDUSTRY.	Number of establishments.	PERSONS ENGAGED IN MANUFACTURING INDUSTRIES.					
			Total.	Proprietors and officials.				
				Total.		Proprietors and firm members.	Salaried officials of corporations.	Superintendents and managers.
				Male.	Female.			
1	Hats, fur-felt	176	20,318	634	46	148	210	322
2	Hats, straw	148	8,527	450	53	121	158	224
3	Hats, wool-felt	40	1,648	99	6	43	18	44
4	Hones and whetstones	11	262	21	......	6	7	8
5	Horseshoes, not made in steel works or rolling mills.	20	919	62	1	11	27	25
6	House-furnishing goods, not elsewhere specified.	467	10,010	912	76	417	236	335
7	Comforts and quilts	74	1,892	154	9	62	43	58
8	Feather pillows and beds.	44	870	98	6	39	29	36
9	Cotton batting, not made in cotton mills	9	268	26	1	8	8	11
10	Mops and dusters	75	749	107	8	55	27	33
11	All other	265	6,231	527	52	253	129	197
12	Ice, manufactured	2,867	38,605	5,260	179	1,566	1,736	2,137
13	Ink, printing	90	3,061	285	14	50	117	132
14	Ink, writing	61	1,216	129	9	55	36	47
15	Instruments, professional and scientific	351	19,787	1,121	55	248	328	600
16	Medical and surgical	127	4,857	351	25	91	114	171
17	Optical	13	732	35	......	12	8	15
18	All other	211	14,198	735	30	145	206	414
19	Iron and steel, blast furnaces	195	46,956	1,368	14	41	222	1,119
20	Iron and steel, steel works and rolling mills	500	421,861	9,673	33	35	1,150	8,521
21	Iron and steel, bolts, nuts, washers, and rivets, not made in rolling mills.	144	20,006	697	11	39	259	410
22	Iron and steel, cast-iron pipe	59	13,777	423	4	4	108	315
23	Iron and steel, doors and shutters	57	2,660	214	4	22	99	97
24	Iron and steel, forgings, not made in steel works or rolling mills.	241	32,617	1,337	11	59	428	861
25	Iron and steel, nails and spikes, cut and wrought, including wire nails, not made in steel works or rolling mills.	65	3,941	181	7	32	75	81
26	Cut nails and spikes	6	684	25	......	3	10	12
27	Wire nails and spikes	28	963	77	3	13	38	29
28	Forged nails and spikes	6	426	15	......	3	6	6
29	All other, including tacks	25	1,868	64	4	13	21	34
30	Iron and steel, tempering and welding	520	2,867	769	12	563	122	96
31	Treated iron and steel	35	695	92	......	25	39	28
32	Welding	485	2,172	677	12	538	83	68
33	Iron and steel, wrought pipe	50	11,783	331	3	13	92	229
34	Ivory, shell, and bone work, not including combs and hairpins.	44	991	73	11	45	18	21
35	Japanning	36	367	59	1	41	12	7
36	Jewelry	2,054	39,630	4,113	148	2,339	942	980
37	Jewelry and instrument cases	142	3,166	265	14	146	67	66
38	Jute goods	26	7,587	148	1	13	29	107
39	Knit goods	2,050	186,673	6,224	474	1,488	1,933	3,277
40	Labels and tags	119	6,648	417	24	73	143	225
41	Lamps and reflectors	171	9,734	570	21	116	177	298
42	Automobile lamps	35	3,586	185	2	16	46	125
43	All other lamps	122	5,760	356	17	92	118	163
44	Reflectors	14	388	29	2	8	13	10
45	Lapidary work	124	1,469	217	7	147	40	37
46	Lard, not made in slaughtering and meat-packing establishments.	6	30	7	......	7		
47	Lasts	64	3,344	221	7	43	65	120
48	Lead, bar, pipe, and sheet	32	1,124	69	3	4	21	47
49	Leather goods, not elsewhere specified	503	11,141	997	54	488	281	282

[1] Same number reported for one or more other months.

UNITED STATES, BY INDUSTRIES: 1919—Continued.

[See note at head of this table, pp. 1172 and 1173.]

PERSONS ENGAGED IN MANUFACTURING INDUSTRIES—continued.

Clerks.		Wage earners.			Wage earners employed Dec. 15, or nearest representative day.					
			Number employed 15th day of—			16 years of age and over.		Under 16 years of age.		
Male.	Fe-male.	Average number.	Maximum month.	Minimum month.	Total.	Male.	Fe-male.	Male.	Fe-male.	
714	414	18,510	De 20,947	Ap 16,353	21,132	14,985	5,758	204	185	1
519	203	7,302	Fe 8,494	Jy 5,808	8,686	3,328	5,289	29	40	2
76	19	1,448	Au 1,923	Ja 916	1,635	1,093	516	12	14	3
17	12	212	Au 225	Fe 197	223	197	26	....	....	4
71	41	744	Ja 915	Jy 602	838	803	10	25	....	5
719	450	7,853	....	....	8,998	3,523	5,247	78	150	6
74	53	1,602	Se 1,852	Fe 1,308	1,828	776	1,007	17	28	7
135	42	589	No[1] 643	Ap 536	645	435	207	2	1	8
15	8	218	No 272	Mh 166	266	152	114	....	....	9
57	49	528	Oc 597	Fe 456	600	267	304	14	15	10
438	298	4,916	De 5,602	Ja 4,072	5,659	1,893	3,615	45	106	11
1,874	1,045	30,247	Jy 41,078	Ja 20,796	31,101	30,654	258	187	2	12
503	271	1,988	De 2,188	Mh 1,886	2,189	2,104	73	12	....	13
222	154	702	Au[1] 753	Fe 638	753	376	345	11	21	14
1,502	1,178	15,931			16,324	12,482	3,610	162	70	15
389	321	3,771	My 3,842	Se 3,596	3,843	2,907	798	92	46	16
30	28	639	De 688	Ja 592	696	539	143	12	2	17
1,083	829	11,521	Ja 11,948	Ap 11,111	11,785	9,036	2,669	58	22	18
3,031	883	41,660	Ja 51,467	Oc 33,628	46,460	46,402	54	4	....	19
28,304	8,763	375,088	Ja 441,560	Oc 292,469	400,620	396,741	3,695	171	13	20
715	616	17,967	Ja 19,535	Oc 16,624	18,384	15,534	2,688	135	27	21
549	176	12,625	De 15,585	Mh 9,753	15,651	15,542	72	37	....	22
246	119	2,077	No 2,337	Ap 1,792	2,347	2,311	34	2	....	23
1,856	1,022	28,391	Ja 30,564	Je 26,650	30,645	29,509	1,010	119	7	24
259	139	3,355			3,650	2,649	946	23	32	25
117	31	511	Ja 581	No 466	486	276	179	10	21	26
32	37	814	Ja 906	Je 734	880	672	197	3	8	27
47	5	359	No 384	Jy 335	382	257	125	....	....	28
63	66	1,671	De 1,887	Au 1,224	1,902	1,444	445	10	3	29
143	108	1,835			2,075	2,047	23	5	....	30
52	23	528	De 674	Mh 427	665	654	10	1	....	31
91	85	1,307	No 1,414	Ja 1,188	1,410	1,393	13	4	....	32
681	342	10,426	Se 11,805	My 9,352	11,895	11,806	88	....	1	33
27	38	842	De 894	My[1] 779	891	671	193	18	9	34
7	5	295	No 367	Ja 235	357	334	18	5	....	35
1,965	2,533	30,871	De 32,817	Ja 27,152	34,656	23,372	10,270	573	441	36
78	75	2,734	De 3,057	Ja 2,389	3,114	1,175	1,695	81	163	37
189	111	7,138	Au 7,513	Ap 6,702	7,486	3,351	3,881	110	144	38
3,718	3,685	172,572	De 186,423	Mh 160,438	187,746	52,134	125,440	2,938	7,234	39
406	574	5,227	De 5,927	Fe 4,769	5,932	3,351	2,443	51	87	40
407	376	8,360			9,512	7,113	2,314	47	38	41
100	105	3,194	Se 3,640	Fe 2,733	3,302	2,686	614	2	....	42
282	254	4,851	De 5,846	Mh 4,239	5,865	4,100	1,689	39	37	43
25	17	315	Ja[1] 350	Au 277	345	327	11	6	1	44
49	41	1,155	Oc[1] 1,212	Ja 1,031	1,224	988	216	20	....	45
7	3	13	(2) 13	(2) 13	13	11	2	....	....	46
123	83	2,910	De 3,258	Ja 2,301	3,306	3,019	66	200	21	47
145	55	852	Au[1] 931	Mh 739	909	896	4	8	1	48
718	427	8,945	No 10,153	Ja 8,019	10,076	6,130	3,679	123	144	49

[2] Same number reported throughout the year.

	INDUSTRY.	Number of establishments.	PERSONS ENGAGED IN MANUFACTURING INDUSTRIES.					
			Total.	Proprietors and officials.				
				Total.			Proprietors and firm members.	Salaried officials of corporations.	Superintendents and managers.
				Male.	Female.			
1	Leather, tanned, curried, and finished......	680	79,292	3,187	69	398	816	2,042
2	Lime..	476	12,855	922	34	349	252	355
3	Linen goods....................................	10	2,070	42	2	....	11	33
4	Liquors, distilled..............................	34	1,741	144	1	2	52	91
5	Alcohol, grain, including pure, neutral, or cologne spirits.	28	1,588	125	1	1	44	81
6	Rum, whisky, and other distilled liquors.	6	153	19	......	1	8	10
7	Liquors, malt.................................	729	42,679	3,123	78	193	1,431	1,577
8	Liquors, vinous..............................	342	1,661	471	19	364	45	81
9	Lithographing................................	331	19,305	1,235	49	150	537	597
10	Locomotives, not made by railroad companies.	17	28,742	325	1	1	56	269
11	Looking-glass and picture frames...........	429	5,929	663	30	398	140	155
12	Lubricating greases...........................	53	1,038	118	7	19	52	54
13	Lumber and timber products...............	26,119	538,788	44,154	560	31,348	4,406	8,960
14	Lumber, planing-mill products, not including planing mills connected with sawmills.	5,309	106,481	10,933	292	4,430	3,152	3,643
15	Machine tools.................................	403	61,762	2,425	40	132	637	1,696
16	Malt...	55	1,713	180	9	8	100	81
17	Marble and stone work......................	4,240	42,214	6,825	170	4,774	1,072	1,149
18	Monuments and tombstones...........	3,256	19,637	4,747	127	3,919	446	509
19	Other marble and stone work, except slate.	861	18,574	1,780	35	758	523	534
20	Roofing slate..............................	71	2,814	201	4	59	70	76
21	Other slate products.....................	52	1,189	97	4	38	33	30
22	Matches.......................................	21	5,126	217	2	3	34	182
23	Mats and matting, from cocoa fiber, grass, and coir.	12	1,173	46	1	7	13	27
24	Mattresses and spring beds, not elsewhere specified.	1,041	16,244	1,928	91	983	510	526
25	Millinery and lace goods, not elsewhere specified.	3,005	61,999	5,023	928	3,412	1,105	1,434
26	Embroideries...........................	1,294	17,517	1,858	338	1,548	272	376
27	Trimmed hats and hat frames..........	829	27,350	1,706	354	877	512	671
28	Dress and cloak trimmings, braids, and fringes.	156	2,540	268	33	185	53	63
29	Women's neckwear.....................	150	4,305	273	82	140	89	126
30	All other................................	576	10,287	918	121	662	179	198
31	Millstones....................................	12	57	18	......	16	....	2
32	Mineral and soda waters.....................	5,194	28,351	7,725	291	5,613	1,079	1,324
33	Mineral and carbonated waters........	5,025	26,397	7,417	282	5,457	1,005	1,237
34	Fruit beverages..........................	84	1,344	170	3	54	51	68
35	All other................................	85	610	138	6	102	23	19
36	Minerals and earths, ground or otherwise treated.	419	16,110	949	30	176	333	470
37	Mirrors, framed and unframed, not elsewhere specified.	186	3,302	363	22	154	119	112
38	Models and patterns, not including paper patterns.	928	8,860	1,477	25	1,078	217	207
39	Motorcycles, bicycles, and parts...........	51	12,200	385	7	16	85	291
40	Mucilage, paste, and other adhesives, not elsewhere specified.	127	1,374	236	20	96	104	56
41	Mucilage and paste.....................	48	501	84	4	39	29	20
42	All other................................	79	873	152	16	57	75	36
43	Musical instruments and materials, not elsewhere specified.	240	4,957	410	8	223	67	128
44	Musical instruments, organs..............	68	2,285	170	7	56	60	61
45	Musical instruments, pianos.............	191	25,760	805	31	33	382	421

[1] Same number reported for one or more other months.

UNITED STATES, BY INDUSTRIES: 1919—Continued.

[See note at head of this table, pp. 1172 and 1173.]

PERSONS ENGAGED IN MANUFACTURING INDUSTRIES—continued.

Clerks.		Wage earners.			Wage earners employed Dec. 15, or nearest representative day.					
			Number employed 15th day of—			16 years of age and over.		Under 16 years of age.		
Male.	Female.	Average number.	Maximum month.	Minimum month.	Total.	Male.	Female.	Male.	Female.	
2,267	1,293	72,476	De 79,010	Fe 65,515	79,205	72,257	6,507	330	111	1
325	169	11,405	Se 12,143	Fe 10,370	12,052	11,996	26	30	....	2
73	63	1,890	De 2,079	Je 1,798	2,053	875	1,002	67	109	3
129	87	1,380			2,001	1,986	13	1	1	4
121	78	1,263	De 1,705	Je 946	1,868	1,863	3	1	1	5
8	9	117	Fe 158	Au 57	133	123	10	....		6
4,472	747	34,259	Jy 38,955	De 29,187	31,220	30,867	331	22		7
108	52	1,011	Oc 1,951	Jy 671	1,552	1,473	75	4	....	8
1,470	933	15,618	De 16,850	Ja 14,743	16,810	13,223	3,422	110	55	9
1,449	252	26,715	Ja 35,659	De 19,837	19,877	19,734	102	41		10
291	237	4,708	No 5,132	Ja 4,060	5,042	4,236	724	74	8	11
283	158	472	Se 504	Ap 440	475	452	21	2		12
9,860	3,269	480,945	De 548,655	Ja 427,802	626,472	620,267	5,280	864	61	13
5,611	2,689	86,956	No 97,035	Fe 74,362	97,740	95,098	2,163	459	20	14
3,698	2,488	53,111	De 58,640	My 49,515	58,776	56,618	2,035	121	2	15
139	33	1,352	Au 1,677	Ja 1,045	1,368	1,358	7	3	....	16
1,736	715	32,768			36,580	36,424	90	59	7	17
1,034	422	13,307	Oc 14,165	Ja 11,287	14,093	14,025	38	23	7	18
647	257	15,855	Se 18,558	Ja 11,004	18,592	18,542	34	16	....	19
31	20	2,558	Jy 2,848	Ja 2,047	2,792	2,787	....	5	....	20
24	16	1,048	De 1,120	Fe 955	1,103	1,070	18	15	....	21
1,018	163	3,726	De 4,776	Je 2,804	4,806	3,073	1,548	92	93	22
37	16	1,073	De 1,292	Jy 893	1,291	890	384	3	14	23
1,064	524	12,637	Oc 13,957	Ja 10,767	13,925	10,881	2,808	192	44	24
2,874	2,324	50,850			55,786	13,733	41,146	197	710	25
534	504	14,283	De 15,335	Ja 13,183	15,607	3,592	11,773	55	187	26
1,470	1,158	22,662	Fe 25,774	Oc 19,625	25,353	7,274	17,736	88	255	27
147	95	1,997	De 2,305	Ap 1,634	2,325	767	1,528	6	24	28
323	232	3,395	Mh 3,558	Ja 3,141	3,373	360	2,954	7	52	29
400	335	8,513	No 8,940	Mh 7,950	9,128	1,740	7,155	41	192	30
1	....	38	Jy 49	Ja¹ 30	52	52	....	....		31
1,960	935	17,440			17,481	16,411	685	380	5	32
1,723	776	16,199	Jy 20,257	Ja 12,784	16,184	15,295	505	379	5	33
167	136	868	Oc 1,445	Ja 599	904	746	158	....		34
70	23	373	Jy 480	Ja 267	393	370	22	1	....	35
428	277	14,426	Au 15,285	Fe 13,599	15,162	15,005	140	14	3	36
181	137	2,599	De 2,922	Ja 2,271	2,921	2,624	263	33	1	37
204	205	6,949	De 8,036	Ja 6,148	8,043	7,803	189	50	1	38
460	462	10,886	De 11,653	Fe 10,166	11,616	10,357	1,121	86	52	39
163	152	803			837	636	184	13	4	40
57	55	301	Au 328	Ja 271	306	251	52	3	....	41
106	97	502	De 522	Mh 475	531	385	132	10	4	42
166	260	4,113	De 4,377	Ja 3,853	4,361	3,513	774	50	24	43
84	83	1,941	De 2,111	Ja 1,770	2,132	1,850	235	41	6	44
1,168	799	22,957	Se 24,719	Oc 20,902	24,665	22,131	2,162	287	85	45

TABLE **90.**—DETAILED STATEMENT FOR THE

[See note at head of this table, pp. 1172 and 1173.]

	INDUSTRY.	Number of establishments.	PERSONS ENGAGED IN MANUFACTURING INDUSTRIES.					
			Total.	Proprietors and officials.				
				Total.		Proprietors and firm members.	Salaried officials of corporations.	Superintendents and managers.
				Male.	Female.			
1	Musical instruments, piano and organ materials.	113	11,886	372	27	38	153	208
2	Piano materials	97	11,588	339	21	25	144	191
3	Organ materials	16	298	33	6	13	9	17
4	Needles, pins, and hooks and eyes	92	10,389	422	10	39	119	274
5	Nets and seines	19	943	46	3	5	16	28
6	Oakum	6	154	19	......	8	7	4
7	Oil and cake, cottonseed	711	32,193	2,825	29	145	689	2,020
8	Oil, essential	78	493	122	1	74	15	34
9	Oil, linseed	26	2,751	116	1	4	48	65
10	Oil, not elsewhere specified¹	280	8,611	827	25	89	341	422
11	Vegetable	68	3,338	252	6	22	84	152
12	Animal	46	1,100	95	4	10	51	38
13	Mineral	39	479	99	2	22	43	36
14	Composite	127	3,694	381	13	35	163	196
15	Oilcloth and linoleum, floor	21	6,254	200	......	3	51	146
16	Oilcloth, enameled	11	1,319	60	1	4	15	42
17	Oleomargarine and other butter substitutes	42	3,868	184	5	1	59	129
18	Optical goods	506	18,807	1,336	36	494	304	574
19	Ordnance and accessories	26	13,600	440	3	3	90	350
20	Paints	601	26,645	2,097	70	226	741	1,200
21	Paper and wood pulp	729	124,935	3,901	116	171	1,312	2,534
22	Paper exclusively	497	56,796	2,261	67	143	835	1,350
23	Pulp exclusively	61	6,309	209	1	21	56	133
24	Paper and pulp	171	61,830	1,431	48	7	421	1,051
25	Paper goods, not elsewhere specified	308	17,177	960	46	124	397	485
26	Playing cards	8	2,041	54	......	2	25	27
27	All other	300	15,136	906	46	122	372	458
28	Paper patterns	19	502	30	11	11	12	18
29	Patent medicines and compounds	2,467	31,970	4,197	476	1,648	1,465	1,560
30	Patent and proprietary medicines	1,724	24,830	2,991	375	1,144	1,025	1,197
31	Patent and proprietary compounds, not elsewhere specified	743	7,140	1,206	101	504	440	363
32	Paving materials	889	18,642	1,657	31	647	418	623
33	Peanuts, grading, roasting, cleaning, and shelling	78	2,805	182	10	57	47	88
34	Pencils, lead	12	6,713	75	6	......	42	39
35	Pens, fountain and stylographic	56	3,937	187	5	40	57	95
36	Pens, gold	15	456	30	......	13	11	6
37	Pens, steel	4	894	13	1	1	8	5
38	Perfumery and cosmetics	569	9,446	949	184	373	394	366
39	Petroleum, refining	320	73,473	2,778	29	59	510	2,238
40	Phonographs and graphophones	166	33,826	881	21	43	234	625
41	Photo-engraving	422	9,198	953	42	264	454	277
42	Photographic apparatus	68	3,087	178	9	31	53	103
43	Cameras	12	1,010	30	2	6	7	19
44	Motion-picture machines	18	1,048	62	2	6	19	39
45	All other apparatus and parts	38	1,029	86	5	19	27	45
46	Photographic materials	169	19,745	935	26	76	178	707
47	Motion-picture films, not exposed	15	11,460	472	15	6	5	476
48	Motion-picture projection films	50	6,439	239	6	14	67	164
49	All other	104	1,846	224	5	56	106	67
50	Pickles, preserves, and sauces	723	21,381	1,661	113	549	449	776
51	Preserves	195	8,546	510	55	112	181	272
52	Pickles and sauces	528	12,835	1,151	58	437	268	504
53	Pipes, tobacco	56	2,902	132	16	54	24	70

¹ Includes "oil, castor" and "oil, lard," to avoid disclosing individual operations.

UNITED STATES, BY INDUSTRIES: 1919—Continued.

[See note at head of this table, pp. 1172 and 1173.]

PERSONS ENGAGED IN MANUFACTURING INDUSTRIES—continued.

Clerks.		Wage earners.			Wage earners employed Dec. 15, or nearest representative day.					
			Number employed 15th day of—			16 years of age and over.		Under 16 years of age.		
Male.	Female.	Average number.	Maximum month.	Minimum month.	Total.	Male.	Female.	Male.	Female.	
230	248	11,009	....	....	11,953	8,677	3,048	137	91	1
224	235	10,769	Au 11,717	Ja 8,862	11,693	8,501	2,970	134	88	2
6	13	240	No 261	Jy 205	260	176	78	3	3	3
299	364	9,294	De 10,052	My 8,823	9,839	4,670	4,746	119	304	4
16	19	859	Fe 918	Oc 749	857	199	612	4	42	5
8	3	124	Fe 151	Oc 89	132	130	....	2	....	6
2,112	461	26,766	No 36,567	Jy 16,333	37,142	36,185	778	179	....	7
28	21	321	Au 396	My 274	469	441	25	3	....	8
295	166	2,173	Jy 2,465	Mh 1,825	2,318	2,263	55	....	....	9
1,199	630	5,930	....	....	7,011	6,332	678	1	....	10
191	87	2,802	De 3,333	Fe 2,548	3,268	2,682	586	....	....	11
64	46	891	Oc 1,421	Ap 403	1,367	1,359	8	....	....	12
104	34	240	Au 303	Mh 174	293	292	1	....	....	13
840	463	1,997	Se 2,079	Mh 1,854	2,083	1,999	83	1	....	14
415	225	5,414	De 6,539	Mh 4,030	6,463	6,113	325	23	2	15
93	35	1,130	De 1,323	Ja 872	1,326	1,195	115	6	10	16
533	295	2,851	De 3,405	Je 2,343	3,521	2,590	923	....	8	17
1,209	1,503	14,723	Fe 15,230	Jy 14,139	15,222	10,149	4,570	327	176	18
1,249	580	11,328	Ja 19,435	Au 7,974	12,930	12,120	808	2	....	19
4,735	2,258	17,485	De 18,766	Fe 16,070	18,716	16,931	1,724	41	20	20
4,500	2,659	113,759	....	....	122,139	111,121	10,852	88	78	21
1,978	1,447	51,043	De 54,882	Ap 47,431	55,650	47,117	8,393	69	71	22
212	80	5,807	No 6,199	Mh 5,303	6,385	6,369	16	....	....	23
2,310	1,132	56,909	No 59,703	Ap 54,776	60,104	57,635	2,443	19	7	24
1,076	960	14,135	....	....	15,358	9,492	5,594	70	202	25
77	78	1,832	Mh 1,946	Se 1,747	1,906	766	1,088	9	43	26
999	882	12,303	De 13,517	Ap 11,418	13,452	8,726	4,506	61	159	27
10	48	403	Ap 423	Ja 381	391	136	252	....	3	28
5,915	3,938	17,444	....	....	18,796	9,002	9,418	137	239	29
4,540	3,136	13,788	No 14,733	Jy 13,000	14,692	6,349	7,996	124	223	30
1,375	802	3,656	Ja 4,042	Oc 3,246	4,104	2,653	1,422	13	16	31
695	187	16,072	Au 19,912	Fe 10,119	18,920	18,899	6	15	....	32
94	59	2,460	De 2,931	Oc 1,807	3,007	1,055	1,933	2	17	33
371	291	5,970	De 6,196	Ja 5,629	6,198	2,818	3,128	60	192	34
346	192	3,207	De 3,529	Fe 2,973	3,587	2,207	1,320	43	17	35
6	4	416	Au 468	Fe 369	458	416	40	2	....	36
41	32	807	Mh 876	Au 748	760	133	596	5	26	37
1,194	1,714	5,405	No 6,162	Ja 4,721	6,076	1,840	4,102	46	88	38
9,031	2,746	58,889	De 62,599	Ja 54,342	62,660	61,492	1,126	42	....	39
2,269	1,934	28,721	De 35,180	Ja 23,997	35,184	27,512	7,603	58	11	40
978	456	6,769	De 7,337	Ja 6,164	7,387	6,895	378	107	7	41
186	159	2,555	....	....	3,022	2,471	515	19	17	42
71	65	842	No 939	Ja 683	916	638	277	....	1	43
89	37	858	De 1,080	Ja 695	1,080	1,067	13	....	....	44
26	57	855	De 1,019	Ja 763	1,026	766	225	19	16	45
2,237	1,991	14,556	....	....	15,935	11,170	4,693	60	12	46
662	659	9,652	De 10,577	Ja 8,240	10,575	7,222	3,338	7	8	47
1,403	1,145	3,646	Oc 4,164	Ja 3,143	4,090	3,153	925	12	....	48
172	187	1,258	Ap 1,311	Se 1,194	1,270	795	430	41	4	49
1,990	996	16,621	....	....	19,284	9,300	9,514	159	311	50
635	307	7,039	Se 8,722	Ap 5,511	8,145	3,476	4,598	21	50	51
1,355	689	9,582	Se 14,310	Mh 7,554	11,139	5,824	4,916	138	261	52
125	90	2,539	De 2,786	Se 2,201	2,785	2,208	556	7	14	53

TABLE **90.**—DETAILED STATEMENT FOR THE

[See note at head of this table, pp. 1172 and 1173.]

	INDUSTRY.	Number of establishments.	PERSONS ENGAGED IN MANUFACTURING INDUSTRIES.					
			Total.	Proprietors and officials.				
				Total.		Proprietors and firm members.	Salaried officials of corporations.	Superintendents and managers.
				Male.	Female.			
1	Plated ware	68	11,459	393	11	24	97	283
2	Knives, forks, spoons, and other flatware.	18	7,783	227	3	1	35	194
3	Hollow ware	30	2,681	106	6	12	37	63
4	All other	20	995	60	2	11	25	26
5	Plumbers' supplies, not elsewhere specified.	214	16,162	849	18	79	276	512
6	Pocketbooks	139	3,497	282	9	168	63	60
7	Pottery	340	30,692	1,340	49	183	400	806
8	Chinaware	161	25,840	975	25	27	306	667
9	Earthen and stone ware	147	3,256	283	15	136	70	92
10	All other	32	1,596	82	9	20	24	47
11	Poultry, killing and dressing, not done in slaughtering and meat-packing establishments.	196	2,837	346	10	176	51	129
12	Printing and publishing, book and job	13,089	171,199	21,645	1,111	12,185	4,990	5,581
13	Job printing	11,951	148,632	19,385	917	11,423	4,214	4,665
14	Book publishing and printing	142	7,913	425	27	90	139	223
15	Book publishing without printing	687	11,102	1,313	144	368	531	558
16	Linotype work and typesetting	309	3,552	522	23	304	106	135
17	Printing and publishing, music	160	2,622	290	15	107	106	92
18	Printing and publishing	27	992	58	2	13	26	21
19	Publishing without printing	133	1,630	232	13	94	80	71
20	Printing and publishing, newspapers and periodicals.	17,362	228,630	28,685	2,175	14,570	5,199	11,091
21	Printing and publishing	1,346	90,244	5,037	332	689	1,089	3,591
22	Printing, publishing, and job printing	12,420	111,317	18,644	1,198	12,307	2,628	4,907
23	Publishing without printing	3,596	27,069	5,004	645	1,574	1,482	2,593
24	Printing materials	82	1,035	143	7	41	67	42
25	Pulp, from fiber other than wood	5	80	12	......	6	3	3
26	Pulp goods	40	3,984	184	7	11	60	120
27	Wall board	10	1,088	63	2	1	16	48
28	All other	30	2,896	121	5	10	44	72
29	Pumps, not including power pumps	127	7,620	555	8	78	140	345
30	Pumps, steam and other power	112	13,286	621	12	36	186	411
31	Steam	62	10,246	431	9	21	106	313
32	Other power	50	3,040	190	3	15	80	98
33	Refrigerators	122	6,994	425	9	72	147	215
34	Regalia, and society badges and emblems	115	2,919	212	24	90	61	85
35	Rice, cleaning and polishing	86	3,249	641	2	40	84	519
36	Roofing materials	178	11,805	652	11	79	182	402
37	Metal shingles and ceiling	29	604	62	2	16	27	21
38	All others	149	11,201	590	9	63	155	381
39	Rubber tires, tubes, and rubber goods, not elsewhere specified.	437	160,824	4,043	69	97	809	3,206
40	Rules, ivory and wood	13	209	20	......	9	7	4
41	Saddlery and harness	1,823	14,863	2,621	75	1,946	331	419
42	Safes and vaults	38	3,582	158	4	16	60	86
43	Safes	21	2,374	98	3	9	37	55
44	Vaults	17	1,208	60	1	7	23	31
45	Salt	86	7,682	341	16	40	109	208
46	Sand and emery paper and cloth	12	1,102	74	......	3	27	44
47	Sand-lime brick	32	600	63	1	3	25	36

[1] Same number reported for one or more other months.

UNITED STATES, BY INDUSTRIES: 1919—Continued.

[See note at head of this table, pp. 1172 and 1173.]

PERSONS ENGAGED IN MANUFACTURING INDUSTRIES—continued.

Clerks. Male.	Fe-male.	Wage earners. Average number.	Number employed 15th day of— Maximum month.	Minimum month.	Total.	16 years of age and over. Male.	Fe-male.	Under 16 years of age. Male.	Fe-male.	
783	780	9,492			10,861	8,633	2,103	73	52	1
566	621	6,366	De 7,495	Ja 4,860	7,480	5,729	1,670	38	43	2
159	113	2,297	No 2,542	Ja 1,887	2,514	2,209	271	29	5	3
58	46	829	No 894	Ja 744	867	695	162	6	4	4
1,038	665	13,592	De 16,841	Ap 11,286	16,708	15,512	1,037	147	12	5
180	121	2,905	No 3,194	Ja 2,605	3,190	1,602	1,497	33	58	6
748	621	27,934			30,702	22,747	7,579	247	129	7
594	513	23,733	De 25,983	Fe 21,899	26,181	18,960	6,885	223	113	8
85	70	2,803	Fe 2,960	Se 2,576	2,928	2,640	276	11	1	9
69	38	1,398	De 1,579	Ja 1,227	1,593	1,147	418	13	15	10
186	155	2,140	De 4,244	Mh 1,076	3,912	2,682	1,211	9	10	11
12,916	12,522	123,005			134,379	97,732	33,433	2,401	813	12
7,591	6,838	113,901	De 124,331	Ja 110,592	124,794	91,264	30,543	2,248	739	13
911	897	5,653	De 5,828	Ja 5,341	5,868	3,524	2,209	77	58	14
4,310	4,622	713	Oc 810	De 599	722	356	345	9	12	15
104	165	2,738	De 2,983	Ja 2,501	2,995	2,588	336	67	4	16
843	575	899			952	744	200	7	1	17
52	65	815	De 861	Ja 759	860	705	148	6	1	18
791	510	84	De 95	Se 67	92	39	52	1	......	19
45,102	32,287	120,381			126,219	100,559	21,129	4,244	287	20
23,291	11,931	49,653	De 51,863	Ja 47,276	51,977	45,091	5,357	1,455	74	21
13,154	9,932	68,389	De 71,699	Ja 66,327	71,863	53,846	15,077	2,743	197	22
8,657	10,424	2,339	De 2,405	Je 2,284	2,379	1,622	695	46	16	23
89	73	723	No 852	Ja 620	728	683	43	2	......	24
......	4	64	Je 1 78	De 51	70	54	16			25
417	335	3,041			3,676	3,079	566	11	20	26
247	189	587	De 716	Ja 465	722	662	60	......	......	27
170	146	2,454	De 2,910	Ja 2,245	2,954	2,417	506	11	20	28
1,193	480	5,384	De 6,158	Je 4,729	6,065	5,668	183	171	43	29
1,179	786	10,688			10,991	10,683	260	44	4	30
833	502	8,471	Ja 9,324	Oc 7,783	8,453	8,210	215	26	2	31
346	284	2,217	De 2,533	Ap 2,042	2,538	2,473	45	18	2	32
506	268	5,786	De 6,461	Au 5,483	6,438	6,142	260	34	2	33
234	226	2,223	No 2,358	Ja 2,081	2,368	887	1,446	12	23	34
438	55	2,113	De 3,410	Jy 954	3,432	3,390	39	3	......	35
1,512	759	8,871			10,137	9,709	413	9	6	36
55	30	455	Se 509	Fe 409	458	436	19	3	......	37
1,457	729	8,416	Oc 9,584	Fe 7,132	9,679	9,273	394	6	6	38
25,712	11,152	119,848	Oc 134,423	Ja 104,075	138,081	121,006	16,330	454	291	39
11	10	168	No 190	My 151	191	133	44	13	1	40
1,330	426	10,411	De 10,955	Je 9,938	11,099	10,078	960	52	9	41
309	162	2,949			3,379	3,311	53	15	......	42
223	111	1,939	De 2,241	Fe 1,727	2,242	2,206	32	4	......	43
86	51	1,010	De 1,133	Ap 881	1,137	1,105	21	11	......	44
595	235	6,495	Oc 7,110	My 5,994	7,023	6,514	481	17	11	45
178	79	771	De 894	Mh 682	896	781	95	20	......	46
20	12	504	No 633	Ja 314	691	689	2	......	......	47

TABLE 90.—DETAILED STATEMENT FOR THE

[See note at head of this table, pp. 1172 and 1173.]

	INDUSTRY.	Number of establishments.	PERSONS ENGAGED IN MANUFACTURING INDUSTRIES.					
			Total.	Proprietors and officials.				
				Total.		Proprietors and firm members.	Salaried officials of corporations.	Superintendents and managers.
				Male.	Female.			
1	Sausage, not made in slaughtering and meat-packing establishments.	633	4,994	919	31	704	128	118
2	Sausage..................	547	3,903	781	27	608	110	90
3	Sausage casings..................	86	1,091	138	4	96	18	28
4	Saws......	112	6,704	295	9	83	96	125
5	Scales and balances..................	79	6,821	296	15	38	89	184
6	Screws, machine..................	143	11,621	616	12	71	199	358
7	Screws, wood..................	11	5,439	135	2	......	35	102
8	Sewing-machine cases..................	5	4,582	233	1	2	6	226
9	Sewing machines and attachments.........	40	17,049	455	6	16	62	383
10	Sewing machines..................	29	16,420	413	.2	7	54	354
11	Attachments..................	11	629	42	4	9	8	29
12	Shipbuilding, steel..................	162	365,875	5,903	13	21	442	5,453
13	New vessels	105	342,164	5,443	8	6	348	5,097
14	Concrete vessels..................	5	2,491	43	1	......	4	40
15	Repair work only..................	45	20,966	388	3	11	79	301
16	Small boats..................	7	254	29	1	4	11	15
17	Shipbuilding, wooden, including boat building.	913	47,361	2,255	24	795	433	1,051
18	New vessels..................	315	36,672	1,265	9	210	291	773
19	Repair work only..................	277	8,554	540	7	245	88	214
20	Small boats..................	294	1,951	409	6	313	48	54
21	Masts, spars, oars, and rigging........	27	184	41	2	27	6	10
22	Shirts..................	896	45,274	2,138	278	949	401	1,066
23	Show cases..................	119	2,293	266	2	112	81	75
24	Signs and advertising novelties..........	779	14,832	1,441	54	624	382	489
25	Electric signs..................	65	1,541	161	10	41	53	77
26	Other signs..................	544	4,465	783	13	489	162	145
27	Advertising novelties..................	170	8,826	497	31	94	167	267
28	Silk goods, including throwsters...........	1,369	136,775	4,442	220	1,011	1,163	2,488
29	Finished products..................	1,040	105,660	3,437	162	807	865	1,927
30	Throwsters and winders..................	329	31,115	1,005	58	204	298	561
31	Silversmithing and silverware..................	99	7,599	309	15	58	121	145
32	Slaughtering and meat packing..................	1,304	197,392	6,665	74	1,071	1,048	4,620
33	Slaughtering..................	604	8,789	1,144	15	630	261	268
34	Meat packing..................	142	7,676	437	19	127	89	240
35	Slaughtering and meat packing........	558	180,927	5,084	40	314	698	4,112
36	Smelting and refining, copper..................	34	19,654	510	7	......	58	459
37	Smelting..................	21	9,029	242	4	......	34	212
38	Smelting and refining [1]..................	13	10,625	268	3	......	24	247
39	Smelting and refining, lead..................	25	7,354	234	1	1	29	205
40	Smelting..................	18	5,487	147	......	1	11	135
41	Smelting and refining [2]..................	7	1,867	87	1	......	18	70
42	Smelting and refining, metals, not elsewhere specified.[3]	13	2,360	170	......	1	27	142
43	Smelting and refining, not from the ore....	81	2,793	274	4	53	84	141
44	Smelting and refining, zinc..................	39	14,903	291	1	......	52	240
45	Pigs, bars, plates, and sheets..................	33	13,914	240	1	......	45	196
46	All other..................	6	989	51	......	......	7	44
47	Soap..................	348	28,919	1,426	100	183	365	978
48	Soda-water apparatus..................	66	3,448	236	4	43	69	128
49	Sporting and athletic goods..................	188	7,490	416	31	143	113	191

[1] Includes 4 establishments engaged exclusively in refining.
[2] Includes 2 establishments engaged exclusively in refining.

UNITED STATES, BY INDUSTRIES: 1919—Continued.

[See note at head of this table, pp. 1172 and 1173.]

PERSONS ENGAGED IN MANUFACTURING INDUSTRIES—continued.

Clerks.		Wage earners.			Wage earners employed Dec. 15, or nearest representative day.					
			Number employed 15th day of—			16 years of age and over.		Under 16 years of age.		
Male.	Female.	Average number.	Maximum month.	Minimum month.	Total.	Male.	Female.	Male.	Female.	
381	192	3,471	....	....	3,793	3,303	478	11	1	1
300	142	2,653	De 2,905	Ap 2,496	2,902	2,667	225	9	1	2
81	50	818	De 880	Ap 764	891	636	253	2	......	3
548	342	5,510	De 5,854	My 5,355	5,871	5,398	364	89	20	4
652	426	5,432	Do 5,946	Ja 4,887	6,105	5,777	286	42	......	5
350	381	10,262	De 11,303	Fe 9,327	11,508	9,787	1,637	78	6	6
159	254	4,889	De 5,242	My 4,617	5,240	3,781	1,369	63	27	7
103	74	4,171	De 4,790	Ap 2,715	4,790	4,293	490	7	......	8
923	606	15,059	....	....	16,368	13,790	2,193	340	45	9
917	589	14,499	De 15,761	Ja 13,525	15,763	13,414	2,059	283	7	10
6	17	560	No 613	My 514	605	376	134	57	38	11
11,610	4,335	344,014	....	....	309,273	308,078	972	223	......	12
10,798	4,128	321,787	My 358,646	De 249,724	284,710	283,600	900	210	......	13
118	52	2,277	Au 3,322	Fe 1,635	1,839	1,839	....	......	......	14
688	151	19,736	Ja 23,421	Oc 17,654	22,572	22,495	64	13	......	15
6	4	214	Ja 541	Se 68	152	144	8	....	......	16
1,146	504	43,432	....	....	45,903	45,803	88	12	......	17
904	372	34,122	Ja 56,437	De 19,601	35,953	35,884	62	7	......	18
197	80	7,730	Ap 8,681	No 6,291	8,196	8,187	8	1	......	19
39	47	1,450	Je 1,724	Ja 1,260	1,619	1,599	16	4	......	20
6	5	130	Ja 145	Je 123	135	133	2	....	......	21
1,995	1,260	39,603	De 45,970	Ap 36,960	46,698	7,711	37,797	223	967	22
106	62	1,857	De 2,031	Ja 1,569	2,048	1,989	55	4	......	23
1,790	1,115	10,432	....	....	11,868	7,146	4,448	122	152	24
240	99	1,031	De 1,227	Ja 791	1,221	1,136	84	1	......	25
261	196	3,212	Oc 3,497	Fe 2,778	3,504	2,913	535	35	21	26
1,289	820	6,189	De 7,139	Fe 5,154	7,143	3,097	3,829	86	131	27
3,027	2,304	126,782	....	....	137,716	52,404	78,160	2,368	4,784	28
2,744	1,975	97,342	De 104,154	Fe 90,659	104,516	43,224	56,862	1,469	2,961	29
283	329	29,440	De 33,085	Mh 27,501	33,200	9,180	21,298	899	1,823	30
470	352	6,453	De 6,749	Fe 6,025	6,693	5,543	995	102	53	31
23,390	6,267	160,996	....	....	163,582	147,127	16,244	184	27	32
854	220	6,556	De 7,154	Ap 6,153	7,207	7,112	87	8	......	33
663	191	6,366	Ja 8,101	My 5,631	6,042	4,433	1,604	3	2	34
21,873	5,856	148,074	Ja 172,703	Ap 138,985	150,333	135,582	14,553	173	25	35
1,518	274	17,345	....	....	16,997	16,937	60	....	......	36
761	103	7,919	Ja 10,982	Au 6,743	7,998	7,979	19	....	......	37
757	171	9,426	Ja 12,645	De 8,244	8,999	8,958	41	....	......	38
569	112	6,438	....	....	6,331	6,322	9	....	......	39
419	82	4,839	Ja 6,101	Se 4,167	4,936	4,931	5	....	......	40
150	30	1,599	Ja 1,953	De 1,354	1,395	1,391	4	....	......	41
119	30	2,041	Ja 2,662	Ap 1,783	2,187	2,024	163	....	......	42
224	124	2,167	Ja 2,284	Je 2,046	2,256	2,237	18	1	......	43
595	220	13,796	....	....	14,147	14,131	14	2	......	44
538	207	12,928	Ja 15,103	Je 11,405	13,119	13,103	14	2	......	45
57	13	868	Ja 1,056	Oc 398	1,028	1,028	....	....	......	46
3,911	3,046	20,436	Se 22,653	Ap 17,963	20,290	14,125	5,926	120	119	47
362	247	2,599	My 2,847	Ja 1,977	2,739	2,646	82	11	......	48
304	327	6,412	De 7,508	Ja 5,633	7,658	4,857	2,567	126	108	49

[3] Includes "smelting and refining, antimony" and "smelting and refining, tin," to avoid disclosing individual operations.

TABLE 90.—DETAILED STATEMENT FOR THE

[See note at head of this table, pp. 1172 and 1173.]

	INDUSTRY.	Number of establishments.	PERSONS ENGAGED IN MANUFACTURING INDUSTRIES.					
			Total.	Proprietors and officials.				
				Total.		Proprietors and firm members.	Salaried officials of corporations.	Superintendents and managers.
				Male.	Female.			
1	Springs, steel, car and carriage, not made in steel works or rolling mills.	112	10,401	493	19	55	175	282
2	Carriage and wagon	13	670	36	6	9	17	16
3	Railway	6	675	29		1	9	19
4	Automobile	65	6,036	254	7	27	97	137
5	Machinery and other	28	3,020	174	6	18	52	110
6	Stamped and enameled ware, not elsewhere specified.	323	39,453	1,386	38	101	481	842
7	Stamped ware	279	27,967	1,075	33	101	374	633
8	Enameled ware	35	10,177	264	2		83	183
9	Bathtubs	5	761	21	2		12	11
10	Lavatories and sinks	4	548	26	1		12	15
11	Stationery goods, not elsewhere specified	223	14,535	772	59	130	255	446
12	Penholders	5	119	10	3	3	5	5
13	All other	218	14,416	762	56	127	250	441
14	Statuary and art goods	195	1,906	326	21	233	61	53
15	Steam fittings and steam and hot-water heating apparatus.	261	43,864	1,367	31	73	412	913
16	Radiators and cast-iron heating boilers.	75	12,156	304	9	21	94	198
17	All other	186	31,708	1,063	22	52	318	715
18	Steam packing	169	7,761	498	20	72	187	259
19	Steel barrels, drums, and tanks	33	3,967	182	7	11	66	112
20	Stencils and brands	84	637	135	9	84	36	24
21	Stereotyping and electrotyping	171	4,623	434	13	85	190	172
22	Stoves and hot-air furnaces	412	39,153	1,887	44	139	736	1,056
23	Stoves and ranges	280	31,724	1,374	26	69	552	779
24	Hot-air furnaces	126	7,042	487	18	70	175	260
25	Fireless cookers	6	387	26			9	17
26	Stoves, gas and oil	176	12,778	564	7	99	187	285
27	Structural ironwork, not made in steel works or rolling mills.	1,146	56,205	3,571	57	721	1,221	1,686
28	Sugar, beet	85	14,190	670	2	1	113	558
29	Sugar, cane	202	7,045	621	19	165	159	316
30	Sugar, refining, not including beet sugar	20	20,921	367	4	6	47	318
31	Sulphuric, nitric, and mixed acids	39	5,860	285	9		40	254
32	Surgical appliances	268	8,953	553	61	219	140	255
33	Suspenders, garters, and elastic woven goods	196	12,466	561	60	179	130	312
34	Textile machinery and parts	432	36,126	1,525	59	354	390	840
35	Theatrical scenery	17	230	42	1	6	23	14
36	Tin and other foils, not elsewhere specified.	15	2,169	94	5	3	33	63
37	Tin foil	12	2,161	91	5		33	63
38	Aluminum and other	3	8	3		3		
39	Tin plate and terneplate	24	3,686	181	175	9	9	338
40	Tinware, not elsewhere specified	301	38,958	1,119	39	177	252	729
41	Tobacco, chewing and smoking, and snuff	365	22,468	929	28	325	195	437
42	Plug or chewing	85	10,153	386	6	48	106	238
43	Smoking	199	10,432	405	11	193	67	156
44	Snuff	34	1,711	73	7	26	19	35
45	All other	47	172	65	4	58	3	8
46	Tobacco, cigars and cigarettes	9,926	161,097	14,182	938	10,464	825	3,831
47	Cigars	9,778	132,561	13,577	856	10,352	744	3,337
48	Cigarettes	135	26,379	533	59	102	73	417
49	Cigars and cigarettes	13	2,157	72	23	10	8	77
50	Tools, not elsewhere specified	1,125	44,142	4,520	82	856	2,495	1,251
51	Shovels, spades, scoops, and hoes	42	2,861	140	6	27	48	71
52	Carpenters' tools, not elsewhere specified.	34	2,672	101	4	24	32	49
53	Machinists' tools	502	21,235	1,383	24	355	482	570
54	All other	574	17,374	2,896	48	450	1,933	561

[1] Same number reported for one or more other months.

UNITED STATES, BY INDUSTRIES: 1919—Continued.

[See note at head of this table, pp. 1172 and 1173.]

PERSONS ENGAGED IN MANUFACTURING INDUSTRIES—continued.

Clerks.		Wage earners.			Wage earners employed Dec. 15, or nearest representative day.					
			Number employed 15th day of—			16 years of age and over.		Under 16 years of age.		
Male.	Female.	Average number.	Maximum month.	Minimum month.	Total.	Male.	Female.	Male.	Female.	
537	371	8,981	....	....	9,552	8,783	718	28	23	1
31	19	578	De 601	Ja 559	602	594	7	1	....	2
75	5	566	Ja 654	Oc 495	571	567	4	....	....	3
273	223	5,279	Se 5,486	Ja 4,837	5,384	5,049	297	16	22	4
158	124	2,558	De 3,092	Ap 2,122	2,995	2,573	410	11	1	5
2,253	1,528	34,248	....	....	37,977	29,460	7,799	364	354	6
1,828	1,136	23,895	De 26,202	Ap 22,476	26,280	19,940	5,798	274	268	7
368	347	9,196	No 10,251	Ja 7,660	10,141	7,978	1,989	88	86	8
41	33	664	De 945	Mh 438	945	936	7	2	....	9
16	12	493	De 609	Ja 370	611	606	5	....	....	10
1,404	1,039	11,261	....	....	12,612	6,070	6,271	97	174	11
2	3	101	Jy 119	Ja 75	113	60	50	3	....	12
1,402	1,036	11,160	De 12,416	Ap 10,540	12,499	6,010	6,221	94	174	13
54	39	1,466	De 1,638	Ja 1,245	1,648	1,514	125	8	1	14
3,421	2,359	36,686	....	....	44,371	41,885	2,410	68	8	15
618	381	10,844	De 14,686	My 8,379	14,701	14,580	107	14	....	16
2,803	1,978	25,842	De 29,581	Jy 21,926	29,670	27,305	2,303	54	8	17
640	456	6,147	De 6,782	My 5,656	6,838	5,655	1,084	59	40	18
300	156	3,322	De 4,046	Mh 2,727	4,045	3,956	89	....	....	19
38	38	417	De 476	Ja¹ 392	478	378	81	18	1	20
337	175	3,664	De 3,911	Ja 3,365	3,892	3,768	87	37	....	21
2,975	1,379	32,868	....	....	36,546	35,801	411	332	2	22
2,179	959	27,186	No 30,227	Ja 22,542	30,028	29,363	345	319	1	23
759	373	5,405	No 6,245	Mh 4,823	6,214	6,170	31	13	....	24
37	47	277	Jy 327	Ja 210	304	268	35	....	1	25
1,112	530	10,565	De 12,650	Ja 9,319	12,704	11,620	987	90	7	26
6,699	1,916	43,962	No 47,680	My 40,614	47,142	46,860	258	24	....	27
1,266	471	11,781	No 27,064	Mh 4,661	26,489	25,275	1,213	1	....	28
281	23	6,101	De 19,570	Ap 1,514	20,586	17,910	2,504	160	12	29
1,814	534	18,202	Jy 20,501	Ja 14,533	18,383	17,063	1,313	7	....	30
407	198	4,961	De 5,764	Jy 4,331	5,890	5,862	26	2	....	31
1,083	866	6,390	Ja 7,581	My 5,994	6,437	3,203	3,109	26	99	32
549	439	10,857	No 12,010	Fe 9,770	12,175	3,866	7,699	141	469	33
1,714	1,005	31,823	De 35,426	Ap 28,898	35,598	33,097	2,029	409	63	34
20	18	149	Au 173	Ja 108	159	154	4	1	....	35
72	90	1,908	....	....	2,697	1,774	911	7	5	36
72	90	1,903	Mh 2,134	Jy 1,641	2,692	1,773	907	7	5	37
....	....	5	(²) 5	(²) 5	5	1	4	....	....	38
173	35	3,122	Fe 3,880	Je 2,367	3,567	3,077	485	5	....	39
2,204	1,210	34,386	Au 38,385	Ap 31,855	35,221	24,846	10,163	158	54	40
2,510	677	18,324	....	....	19,109	9,615	9,339	58	97	41
1,147	235	8,379	No 8,896	Mh 7,765	9,126	4,415	4,585	48	78	42
1,103	393	8,520	Oc 9,283	Ja 7,928	8,471	4,289	4,166	6	10	43
254	49	1,328	De 1,380	Au 1,265	1,397	812	572	4	9	44
6	....	97	Oc 106	Mh 89	115	99	16	....	....	45
5,284	1,920	138,773	....	....	160,463	65,099	93,341	472	1,551	46
2,768	1,061	114,299	De 131,081	Au 92,751	133,066	53,153	78,253	344	1,316	47
2,426	719	22,642	No 26,374	My 19,357	25,204	11,144	13,707	128	225	48
90	140	1,832	No 2,266	My 1,326	2,193	802	1,381	....	10	49
1,949	2,006	35,585	....	....	39,697	36,155	3,176	267	99	50
96	81	2,538	Ja 2,794	Je 2,252	2,574	2,488	67	17	2	51
162	134	2,271	De 2,420	Jy 2,175	2,437	2,113	283	28	13	52
874	1,074	17,880	De 19,865	Ap 16,687	19,914	18,455	1,286	120	53	53
817	717	12,896	De 14,349	Ap 12,211	14,772	13,099	1,540	102	31	54

² Same number reported throughout the year.

TABLE 90.—DETAILED STATEMENT FOR THE

[See note at head of this table, pp. 1172 and 1173.]

	INDUSTRY	Number of establishments.	PERSONS ENGAGED IN MANUFACTURING INDUSTRIES.					
			Total.	Proprietors and officials.			Proprietors and firm members.	Salaried officials of corporations.	Superintendents and managers.
				Total.					
				Male.	Female.			
1	Toys and games	541	16,483	1,159	79	469	326	443
2	Trunks and valises	597	14,216	1,283	59	601	360	381
3	Turpentine and rosin	1,191	31,093	2,779	28	1,460	149	1,198
4	Type founding	23	870	27	1	11	6	11
5	Typewriters and supplies	88	18,074	431	14	37	103	305
6	Typewriters and parts	37	16,659	318	9	6	54	267
7	Carbon paper	24	901	55	2	10	30	17
8	Ribbon	21	455	51	1	18	14	20
9	All other	6	59	7	2	3	5	1
10	Umbrellas and canes	198	4,173	377	18	232	85	78
11	Upholstering materials, not elsewhere specified.	163	5,620	396	7	123	112	168
12	Imitation leather and leatheroid	17	2,351	99		1	27	71
13	Excelsior	95	1,491	191	4	81	57	57
14	Curled hair	15	839	35	1	10	9	17
15	All other	36	939	71	2	31	19	23
16	Varnishes	229	7,385	774	30	72	360	372
17	Vault lights and ventilators	41	457	78	4	26	34	22
18	Vinegar and cider	720	3,333	1,000	24	724	158	142
19	Vinegar	199	1,966	353	12	153	115	97
20	Cider	521	1,367	647	12	571	43	45
21	Wall paper, not made in paper mills	48	5,098	223	6	3	120	106
22	Wall plaster and composition flooring	161	6,439	411	8	28	169	222
23	Washing machines and clothes wringers	105	7,555	418	9	40	148	239
24	Waste	92	3,177	253	8	57	113	91
25	Cotton	61	2,300	177	3	38	75	67
26	All other	31	877	76	5	19	38	24
27	Watch and clock materials, except watchcases.	27	678	46	1	24	12	11
28	Watch materials	21	565	39		22	8	9
29	Clock materials	6	113	7	1	2	4	2
30	Watchcases	33	4,587	143	10	15	52	86
31	Watches	18	16,852	292	10	3	24	275
32	Watches	7	9,437	181	2	3	13	167
33	Watch movements	11	7,415	111	8		11	108
34	Wheelbarrows	11	372	32	2	7	14	13
35	Whips	26	912	48	3	26	12	13
36	Windmills	31	2,383	140	1	10	44	87
37	Window and door screens and weather strips	214	2,782	358	7	197	93	75
38	Window and door screens	176	2,556	303	4	175	72	60
39	Weather strips	38	226	55	3	22	21	15
40	Window shades and fixtures	287	5,494	501	19	258	93	169
41	Wire	66	22,236	605	7	13	122	477
42	Wirework, not elsewhere specified	558	18,340	1,354	43	457	409	531
43	Wire rope and cable	15	2,973	133	1	3	23	108
44	Woven-wire fencing	53	1,922	151	2	25	54	74
45	All other	490	13,445	1,070	40	429	332	349
46	Wood distillation	115	5,634	392	7	28	128	243
47	Wood preserving	73	4,615	240	7	1	79	167
48	Wood, turned and carved	722	12,623	1,471	35	708	295	503
49	Wooden goods, not elsewhere specified	245	7,287	471	13	177	136	171
50	Wool pulling	24	839	78		23	22	33
51	Wool scouring	33	2,407	98	10	9	38	61
52	Wool shoddy	78	2,956	220	7	64	70	93
53	Woolen and worsted goods	852	176,392	4,667	168	387	1,236	3,212
54	Woolen goods	560	67,020	2,385	102	258	729	1,500
55	Worsted goods	292	109,372	2,282	66	129	507	1,712
56	All other industries [1]	5	109	7		5		2

[1] Same number reported for one or more other months.

UNITED STATES, BY INDUSTRIES: 1919—Continued.

[See note at head of this table, pp. 1172 and 1173.]

PERSONS ENGAGED IN MANUFACTURING INDUSTRIES—continued.

Clerks.		Wage earners.			Wage earners employed Dec. 15, or nearest representative day.					
			Number employed 15th day of—			16 years of age and over.		Under 16 years of age.		
Male.	Fe-male.	Average number.	Maximum month.	Minimum month.	Total.	Male.	Fe-male.	Male.	Fe-male.	
427	617	14,201	No 16,701	Ja 10,141	15,744	8,647	6,356	465	276	1
937	467	11,470	Oc 12,467	Ja 10,101	12,649	10,453	1,977	151	68	2
214	5	28,067	Je 28,802	Ja 25,918	29,601	29,103	103	393	2	3
18	14	810	Jy 917	Au 620	811	629	148	11	23	4
732	1,228	15,669			17,736	13,510	4,026	121	79	5
460	994	14,878	De 17,240	Au 13,769	16,864	12,957	3,739	105	63	6
218	185	441	No 477	Je 421	495	327	142	10	16	7
54	46	303	De 327	Ja¹ 289	330	201	124	5	......	8
....	3	47	My¹ 50	Ja 43	47	25	21	1	......	9
266	144	3,368	De 3,788	Ja 3,016	3,837	1,774	1,897	82	84	10
262	145	4,810			5,444	4,490	872	50	32	11
154	87	2,011	De 2,328	Fe 1,739	2,331	2,281	50	......	......	12
31	23	1,242	De 1,331	Ja 1,196	1,391	1,230	99	42	20	13
22	13	768	Au 861	Ja 590	843	561	281	1	......	14
55	22	789	Se 832	Ja 714	879	418	442	7	12	15
1,741	818	4,022	De 4,390	Ja 3,617	4,445	4,028	404	11	2	16
29	30	316	Oc 369	Fe 269	361	361	......	......	......	17
203	125	1,981			2,835	2,551	270	14	......	18
149	87	1,365	No 2,100	Mh 1,043	1,620	1,434	184	2	......	19
54	38	616	Oc 1,399	My 314	1,215	1,117	86	12	......	20
390	217	4,262	De 4,795	Au 3,567	5,100	4,071	958	57	14	21
632	265	5,123	No 6,103	Ja 3,683	6,017	5,941	74	2	......	22
759	413	5,956	De 7,085	Ja 4,731	7,356	7,126	212	18	......	23
113	117	2,686			2,857	1,920	925	5	7	24
86	83	1,951	Au 2,163	Fe 1,713	2,099	1,445	642	5	7	25
27	34	735	No 787	Ap 655	758	475	283	......	......	26
15	34	582			604	185	404	11	4	27
13	28	485	Jy 564	Mh 418	497	124	364	6	3	28
2	6	97	No¹ 107	Fe 87	107	61	40	5	1	29
221	313	3,900	De 4,283	Ja 3,625	4,300	3,094	1,079	69	58	30
218	444	15,888			16,685	8,358	8,069	165	93	31
152	293	8,809	No¹ 9,343	Jy 8,337	9,329	4,591	4,482	163	93	32
66	151	7,079	No 7,370	Ja 6,757	7,356	3,767	3,587	2	......	33
32	15	291	Oc 348	Mh 242	337	330	6	1	......	34
103	41	717	De 743	Ap 688	747	509	204	21	13	35
211	99	1,932	De 2,077	Je 1,588	2,076	2,061	10	5	......	36
134	104	2,179			2,587	2,220	354	9	4	37
108	80	2,061	De 2,335	Mh 1,852	2,445	2,082	351	8	4	38
26	24	118	De 140	Mh 103	142	138	3	1	......	39
308	255	4,411	De 5,137	Fe 3,789	5,207	3,731	1,415	44	17	40
1,295	588	19,741	Se 21,282	Oc 17,335	21,600	20,486	1,037	54	23	41
1,061	658	15,224			16,397	13,287	2,747	277	86	42
280	98	2,461	De 2,678	Au 2,177	2,692	2,554	138	......	......	43
152	116	1,501	Ap 1,619	Ja 1,319	1,591	1,583	8	......	......	44
629	444	11,262	De 11,850	Ap 10,804	12,114	9,150	2,601	277	86	45
204	85	4,946	Ja 5,838	Je 4,246	5,463	5,437	26	......	......	46
291	99	3,978	Oc 4,282	Mh 3,439	4,304	4,284	18	2	......	47
222	246	10,649	De 11,260	Ja 10,168	14,849	13,713	985	144	7	48
229	131	6,443	De 6,949	Jy 6,266	7,109	5,814	1,203	85	7	49
42	14	705	De 831	Je 613	831	827	4	......	......	50
70	52	2,177	Au 2,553	Mh 1,658	2,554	2,369	185	......	......	51
107	56	2,566	De 2,669	Fe 2,405	2,709	2,229	438	5	37	52
2,942	1,828	166,787			194,649	105,657	81,185	3,385	4,422	53
894	682	62,957	De 70,374	Fe 47,872	72,062	47,736	23,274	560	492	54
2,048	1,146	103,830	De 122,495	Fe 67,489	122,587	57,921	57,911	2,825	3,930	55
3	......	99			102	87	15	......	......	56

² Comprises the following industries with number of establishments as indicated: "Straw goods, not elsewhere specified," 1; "whalebone cutting," 1; and "wood carpet," 3.

TABLE 90.—DETAILED STATEMENT FOR THE

[See note at head of this table, pp. 1172 and 1173.]

	INDUSTRY.	Number of establishments reporting.	Total primary horse-power.	POWER AND FUEL USED. Primary power. Owned by establishments reporting. Steam engines and turbines. Number.	Horse-power.	Internal-combustion engines. Number.	Horse-power.	Water wheels and water motors. Number.	Horse-power.
1	All industries...........	237,854	29,504,792	122,628	17,037,973	33,407	1,259,400	14,008	1,765,263
2	Aeroplanes, seaplanes, and airships, and parts.	26	12,512	3	325	......	....	......	....
3	Agricultural implements...........	497	128,249	334	69,942	166	4,092	74	6,373
4	Aluminum manufactures.........	82	30,280	31	12,372	9	1,103	1	80
5	Ingots, plates, and sheets......	7	2,617	......	....	......	....	......	....
6	Ware....................	39	20,823	16	8,490	9	1,103	......	....
7	All other....................	36	6,840	15	3,882	......	....	1	80
8	Ammunition....................	39	39,128	80	19,160	11	2,241	3	141
9	Artificial flowers....................	82	468	1	50	1	5	......	....
10	Artificial limbs....................	130	857	1	25	8	71	4	143
11	Artificial stone products...........	1,854	22,221	181	4,048	1,165	5,810	24	351
12	Artists' materials....................	43	3,206	12	1,354	9	225	2	240
13	Crayons....................	13	1,132	9	554	1	4	......	....
14	All other....................	30	2,074	3	800	8	221	2	240
15	Asbestos products, not including steam packing.	44	9,657	31	4,105	2	47	1	60
16	Building materials....................	12	2,591	14	1,295	1	2	......	....
17	Textile-mill products...........	15	5,577	10	1,565	1	45	1	60
18	All other....................	17	1,489	7	1,245	......	....	......	....
19	Automobile bodies and parts......	2,271	256,919	302	41,680	179	12,066	15	566
20	Automobile repairing....................	14,825	82,691	120	1,763	2,933	17,571	28	132
21	Automobiles....................	308	287,323	194	104,532	21	861	......	....
22	Awnings, tents, and sails...........	778	4,589	7	349	9	89	......	....
23	Babbitt metal and solder...........	76	6,022	15	2,937	6	160	......	....
24	Babbitt metal....................	31	4,065	14	2,857	1	35	......	....
25	White metal....................	17	887	......	....	2	20	......	....
26	Type metal....................	3	21	......	....	......	....	......	....
27	Solder....................	25	1,049	1	80	3	105	......	....
28	Bags, other than paper, not including bags made in textile mills.	203	9,082	33	4,216	6	150	......	....
29	Bags, paper, exclusive of those made in paper mills.	64	4,429	16	1,480	5	87	1	75
30	Baking powders and yeast........	69	20,071	99	14,272	6	88	......	....
31	Baking powders....................	53	2,431	9	1,250	6	88	......	....
32	Yeast....................	16	17,640	90	13,022	......	....	......	....
33	Baskets, and rattan and willow ware.	161	6,319	96	4,157	18	183	10	370
34	Bells....................	10	783	2	132	2	135	6	402
35	Belting and hose, rubber...........	15	26,299	48	10,860	2	406	6	618
36	Belting....................	8	11,691	27	4,990	1	6	4	518
37	Hose....................	7	14,608	21	5,870	1	400	2	100
38	Belting and hose, woven, other than rubber.	40	5,338	15	1,688	3	25	3	160
39	Woven belting....................	23	3,066	6	560	......	....	......	....
40	All other, including woven hose.	17	2,272	9	1,128	3	25	3	160
41	Belting, leather....................	139	7,039	29	4,417	10	87	1	55
42	Billiard tables, bowling alleys, and accessories.	40	5,322	3	305	2	12	......	....
43	Blacking, stains, and dressings....	135	2,490	27	1,599	6	62	......	....
44	Bluing....................	34	423	......	....	2	30	......	....

UNITED STATES, BY INDUSTRIES: 1919—Continued.

[See note at head of this table, pp. 1172 and 1173.]

					POWER AND FUEL USED—continued.					
Primary power—Con.					Fuel used.					
Rented.			Electric motors run by current generated in the establishments reporting.		Coal.		Coke (tons of 2,000 lbs.).	Oil, including gasoline (barrels).	Gas (1,000 cubic feet).	
Electric.		Other.			Anthracite (tons of 2,240 lbs.).	Bituminous (tons of 2,000 lbs.).				
Motors.	Horse-power.	Horse-power.	Number.	Horse-power.						
996,000	9,347,556	94,600	487,021	6,969,721	14,334,402	203,463,622	42,595,019	92,029,692	341,921,022	1
682	12,187	....	106	600	217	22,514	13	2,405	10,028	2
4,594	47,842	....	3,399	52,421	13,497	549,557	115,368	372,201	435,393	3
945	16,725	....	625	10,609	2,457	122,142	4,415	118,049	109,095	4
92	2,617	....	....	....	....	3,636	685	8,047	16,270	5
561	11,230	....	538	6,884	1,927	97,481	2,174	16,833	56,616	6
292	2,878	....	87	3,725	530	21,025	1,556	93,169	36,209	7
1,764	17,586	....	1,877	15,973	23,112	154,863	3,146	139,853	79,424	8
258	413	....	....	....	4,112	2,807	44	13	6,460	9
221	618	....	....	....	201	384	7	406	2,771	10
1,632	11,969	43	15	98	3,354	34,921	643	8,160	24,969	11
164	1,387	....	49	567	2,363	61,114	15	1,109	5,957	12
38	574	....	34	377	89	59,384	....	1	479	13
126	813	....	15	190	2,274	1,730	15	1,108	5,478	14
337	5,445	....	124	1,966	5,443	31,817	2,325	6,623	17,633	15
67	1,294	....	35	440	3,400	12,396	2,325	3,384	....	16
225	3,907	....	37	453	1,680	12,078	....	3,233	17,611	17
45	244	....	52	1,073	363	7,343	....	6	22	18
21,773	202,458	149	1,647	17,746	32,036	628,095	19,681	430,122	713,721	19
19,537	63,057	168	147	518	34,451	127,453	2,170	30,042	449,832	20
14,283	176,930	5,000	11,419	93,426	17,133	1,120,585	81,867	1,015,284	2,114,482	21
2,621	4,133	18	14	63	2,206	8,074	82	326	11,111	22
340	2,923	2	219	2,752	4,216	46,288	4,019	64,239	44,084	23
164	1,173	....	219	2,752	1,943	29,253	2,936	53,970	20,312	24
83	865	2	....	....	1,111	4,199	942	8,202	2,338	25
4	21	....	....	....	161	719	....	....	....	26
89	864	....	....	....	1,001	12,117	141	2,067	21,434	27
1,012	4,710	6	648	3,454	3,312	23,103	344	617	4,421	28
907	2,787	....	265	624	1,034	13,708	78	275	423	29
453	5,711	....	594	5,947	2,990	219,015	598	36,046	2,608	30
197	1,093	....	109	660	2,527	6,661	....	1	2,593	31
256	4,618	....	485	5,287	463	212,354	598	36,045	15	32
228	1,609	....	5	60	909	10,767	103	691	2,420	33
14	114	....	1	20	594	762	40	454	204	34
520	14,415	....	346	8,308	32,550	84,728	274	33,651	6,699	35
298	6,177	....	47	1,055	8,300	35,521	....	23,052	1,240	36
222	8,238	....	299	7,253	24,250	49,207	274	10,599	5,459	37
362	3,428	37	51	376	3,201	12,931	70	1,412	894	38
295	2,504	2	2	13	603	9,145	....	152	240	39
67	924	35	49	363	2,598	3,786	70	1,260	654	40
433	2,453	27	111	320	15,214	15,731	22	1,642	5,380	41
553	4,944	61	3	25	731	18,938	....	9	600	42
227	785	44	66	550	5,754	6,738	69	311	11,091	43
76	393	....	5	12	259	290	3	....	1,461	44

TABLE 90.—DETAILED STATEMENT FOR THE

[See note at head of this table, pp. 1172 and 1173.]

	INDUSTRY.	Number of establishments reporting.	Total primary horsepower	POWER AND FUEL USED.					
				Primary power.					
				Owned by establishments reporting.					
				Steam engines and turbines.		Internal-combustion engines.		Water wheels and water motors.	
				Number.	Horsepower.	Number.	Horsepower.	Number.	Horsepower.
1	Bone, carbon, and lampblack	25	1,857	9	455	42	911		
2	Bone black and lampblack.....	6	1,145	5	375	5	279		
3	Carbon black...................	19	712	4	80	37	632		
4	Bookbinding and blank-book making.	922	11,123	10	555	12	133		
5	Boot and shoe cut stock...........	233	9,003	25	1,765	5	43	1	2
6	Boot and shoe findings...........	323	10,682	18	3,622	4	40	8	460
7	Boots and shoes, not including rubber boots and shoes.	1,391	120,632	371	57,267	36	908	14	2,021
8	Regular factory products......	1,286	119,594	367	57,188	34	853	14	2,021
9	Contract work...............	16	192						
10	Stitching...................	18	109						
11	Crimping...................	2	6						
12	Buttonholes................	3	7						
13	Overgaiters, moccasins, and leggings.	66	724	4	79	2	55		
14	Boots and shoes, rubber...........	23	49,400	52	21,220			11	2,462
15	Boxes, cigar....................	167	5,059	36	2,448	17	297		
16	Boxes, paper and other, not elsewhere specified.	1,144	54,955	184	22,471	65	1,124	21	1,964
17	Shipping containers, corrugated and fiber.	155	19,732	71	9,428	6	211	14	1,507
18	Set-up paper boxes...........	826	20,088	70	5,067	47	559	5	395
19	Cartons....................	123	11,239	28	6,176	10	315	2	62
20	Paper cans and tubes..........	19	2,125	9	1,200	1	4		
21	All other...................	21	1,771	6	600	1	35		
22	Boxes, wooden packing, except cigar boxes.	1,051	144,048	774	100,020	115	1,903	40	2,495
23	Brass, bronze, and copper products.	1,011	265,688	233	116,517	104	3,540	21	2,320
24	Brass and bronze...............	937	201,494	171	87,589	92	3,186	10	1,060
25	Copper.....................	42	53,157	51	26,603	7	85	6	1,000
26	All other...................	32	11,037	11	2,325	5	269	5	260
27	Bread and other bakery products..	17,151	165,950	420	34,250	869	5,274	44	522
28	Biscuit and crackers..........	161	29,273	140	18,057	2	75	16	135
29	Bakery products, other than biscuit and crackers.	16,990	136,677	280	16,193	867	5,199	28	387
30	Brick and tile, terra-cotta, and fire-clay products.	2,216	405,746	2,769	281,815	409	17,456	1	40
31	Building brick...............	1,295	222,688	1,583	152,184	239	10,976	1	40
32	Fire brick..................	188	49,363	291	35,634	27	1,146		
33	Stove lining................	17	1,021	14	610	6	74		
34	Sewer pipe and draintile.......	468	58,191	562	50,152	84	1,582		
35	Terra-cotta products..........	194	50,098	254	33,019	47	2,911		
36	Silicate, magnesite, and bauxite bricks and shapes.	38	19,338	47	7,335	5	765		
37	All other...................	16	5,047	18	2,881	1	2		
38	Brooms......................	766	6,062	29	1,467	170	987	6	36
39	From broom corn..............	744	5,907	28	1,432	164	941	6	36
40	All other...................	22	155	1	35	6	46		
41	Brushes.....................	330	7,384	34	2,694	29	445	10	221
42	Toilet.....................	41	1,395	8	433	1	20	1	75
43	Paint and varnish............	39	1,582	13	980	2	16		
44	All other...................	250	4,407	13	1,281	26	409	9	146
45	Butter......................	3,661	95,190	2,412	47,505	459	5,522	39	748
46	Butter, reworking.............	4	343	3	114	1	12		
47	Buttons.....................	413	16,201	65	6,275	71	1,047	6	267

UNITED STATES, BY INDUSTRIES: 1919—Continued.

[See note at head of this table, pp. 1172 and 1173.]

			POWER AND FUEL USED—continued.							
Primary power—Contd.			Electric motors run by current generated in the establishments reporting.		Fuel used.					
Rented.		Other.			Coal.		Coke (tons of 2,000 lbs.).	Oil, including gasoline (barrels).	Gas (1,000 cubic feet).	
Electric.					Anthracite (tons of 2,240 lbs.).	Bituminous (tons of 2,000 lbs.).				
Motors.	Horse-power.	Horse-power.	Number.	Horse-power.						
34	491	....	....	....	25	6,661	....	1,200	49,495,995	1
34	491	....	....	....	25	6,661	....	1,200	8,026	2
....	....	....	....	....	....	....	....	....	49,487,369	3
6,536	10,349	86	....	....	3,302	12,527	52	1,586	33,389	4
843	6,638	555	71	521	3,297	20,663	405	548	575,974	5
1,257	5,848	712	75	1,053	3,092	25,858	120	332	10,397	6
11,698	55,690	4,746	4,581	28,102	46,066	394,926	2,602	26,993	170,430	7
11,414	54,885	4,647	4,581	28,102	45,588	393,977	2,595	26,982	169,051	8
27	129	63	....	....	109	125	....	....	213	9
25	73	36	....	....	66	....	....	....	30	10
2	6	....	....	....	....	....	....	....	81	11
3	7	....	....	....	....	....	....	....	300	12
227	590	....	....	....	303	824	7	11	755	13
1,757	25,718	....	415	2,602	19,853	136,967	1,391	104,199	2,425	14
561	2,264	50	38	312	3,086	6,702	5	117	4,397	15
8,338	29,116	280	1,897	9,119	24,681	218,046	2,486	12,812	401,999	16
1,897	8,571	15	570	2,899	10,626	122,988	57	2,994	17,342	17
4,809	13,834	233	680	1,831	9,818	50,424	2,061	2,046	373,880	18
1,180	4,654	32	476	3,607	3,388	31,357	261	1,424	8,392	19
248	921	....	117	675	569	7,298	107	48	1,910	20
204	1,136	....	54	107	280	5,979	....	6,300	475	21
3,727	39,165	465	1,203	12,515	4,258	56,899	114	4,287	22,152	22
8,759	142,996	315	2,468	40,598	200,719	655,947	131,113	914,591	812,573	23
7,540	109,345	314	1,621	29,634	175,411	492,396	114,006	799,649	732,480	24
827	25,469	....	825	10,372	18,611	148,143	14,653	108,519	58,326	25
392	8,182	1	22	592	6,697	15,408	2,454	6,423	21,767	26
37,602	125,665	239	3,709	20,723	596,989	554,982	309,706	349,121	5,476,396	27
2,135	10,929	77	1,993	11,479	86,772	90,768	14,468	88,766	277,618	28
35,467	114,736	162	1,716	9,244	510,217	464,214	295,238	260,355	5,198,778	29
3,408	105,846	589	1,430	27,508	128,252	6,894,745	34,510	1,309,932	10,009,521	30
1,688	59,384	104	523	10,452	111,026	2,979,074	23,762	738,602	7,684,785	31
408	12,578	5	184	4,726	5,623	1,348,521	6,754	107,279	804,074	32
14	337	....	2	10	810	11,531	60	167	500	33
251	6,457	....	203	4,282	859	1,182,581	458	279,159	312,685	34
609	14,138	30	395	5,254	9,782	852,903	2,759	183,525	1,158,611	35
348	10,788	450	53	1,600	....	432,213	353	1,200	48,854	36
90	2,164	....	70	1,184	152	87,922	364	....	12	37
990	3,547	25	53	332	1,064	13,737	580	1,306	14,438	38
974	3,498	....	53	332	1,022	13,666	578	1,288	14,343	39
16	49	25	....	....	42	71	2	18	95	40
895	3,947	77	348	1,530	5,539	20,536	16	535	10,693	41
179	863	4	12	100	802	3,680	....	58	512	42
161	581	5	253	627	3,391	7,227	5	4	2,146	43
555	2,503	68	83	803	1,346	9,629	11	473	8,035	44
5,628	41,187	228	700	5,347	20,467	409,020	2,378	159,841	133,603	45
9	217	....	....	....	13	860	....	220	....	46
962	8,117	495	37	598	7,094	47,867	188	1,420	29,576	47

	INDUSTRY.	Number of establishments reporting.	Total primary horsepower.	Steam engines and turbines.		Internal-combustion engines.		Water wheels and water motors.	
				Number.	Horsepower.	Number.	Horsepower.	Number.	Horsepower.
1	Candles	14	597	11	545				
2	Canning and preserving, fish	322	24,865	309	14,119	207	2,484	1	4
3	Canning and preserving, fruits and vegetables.	2,675	132,422	2,840	86,584	702	6,162	5	81
4	Canned vegetables	1,831	95,352	2,388	71,869	359	3,583	2	26
5	Canned fruits	415	26,214	386	12,882	69	786	2	42
6	Dried fruits	414	9,447	60	1,738	265	1,414	1	13
7	Dried vegetables	15	1,409	6	95	9	379		
8	Canning and preserving, oysters	47	1,025	46	858	10	125	1	5
9	Card cutting and designing	66	743	1	60	8	53		
10	Cardboard, not made in paper mills	16	3,276	13	2,410	2	45	4	100
11	Carpets and rugs, other than rag	68	38,170	87	28,777	2	85	11	2,207
12	Carpets, rag	257	2,674	15	389	34	269		
13	Carriage and wagon materials	239	23,700	183	17,698	34	468	11	545
14	Carriages and sleds, children's	75	6,071	21	2,421	7	119	9	405
15	Carriages and wagons, including repairs.	1,888	40,966	175	20,088	537	4,294	27	896
16	Carriages and wagons	971	34,666	158	19,740	309	2,794	20	669
17	Repair work only	917	6,300	17	348	228	1,500	7	227
18	Cars and general shop construction and repairs by electric-railroad companies.	500	53,830	45	5,875	11	564		
19	Cars and general shop construction and repairs by steam-railroad companies.	1,470	594,515	2,490	375,606	158	6,993	11	841
20	Cars, electric-railroad, not including operations of railroad companies.	6	9,390	7	1,900				
21	Cars, steam-railroad, not including operations of railroad companies.	92	157,865	297	92,015	17	2,848	1	100
22	Cash registers and calculating machines.	61	14,650	23	11,265	1	15	2	250
23	Adding machines	20	7,057	12	4,765			2	250
24	Cash registers and parts	17	6,849	8	6,300				
25	All other	24	744	3	200	1	15		
26	Cement	117	488,808	477	278,009	63	24,763	8	3,550
27	Charcoal, not including production in the lumber and wood-distillation industries.	7	132			3	34		
28	Cheese	2,508	24,500	1,956	19,509	747	3,000	11	112
29	Chemicals	486	376,940	1,355	241,749	122	5,004	31	3,692
30	Chewing gum	57	6,178	16	2,589	1	10		
31	China decorating, not including that done in potteries.	13	43						
32	Decalcomania work on china	2	7						
33	All other	11	36						
34	Chocolate and cocoa products	46	33,440	52	15,273	8	1,783	14	300
35	Cleansing and polishing preparations.	243	4,520	22	1,176	23	197		
36	Cleansing preparations	159	2,918	14	813	18	131		
37	Metal polish	38	487	4	153	2	30		
38	All other polishing preparations	46	1,115	4	210	3	36		
39	Clocks	39	6,952	19	3,910	3	62	6	255
40	Cloth, sponging and refinishing	59	952	8	412	2	20		
41	Clothing, horse	25	1,577	9	1,192	1	25		

UNITED STATES, BY INDUSTRIES: 1919—Continued.

[See note at head of this table, pp. 1172 and 1173.]

POWER AND FUEL USED—continued.										
Primary power—Contd.					Fuel used.					
Rented.		Other.	Electric motors run by current generated in the establishments reporting.		Coal.		Coke (tons of 2,000 lbs.).	Oil, including gasoline (barrels).	Gas (1,000 cubic feet).	
Electric.					Anthracite (tons of 2,240 lbs.).	Bituminous (tons of 2,000 lbs.).				
Motors.	Horsepower.	Horsepower.	Number.	Horsepower.						
10	52	.....	32	174	757	4,082	....:.	1	1,776	1
1,156	8,198	60	174	1,472	5,387	36,528	4	124,318	59,340	2
5,617	39,420	175	1,242	6,663	20,238	298,336	5,901	569,343	151,031	3
2,476	19,699	175	1,088	5,938	5,199	230,011	2,293	54,9°7	43,771	4
1,929	12,504	.....	148	694	2,705	60,167	1,464	304,627	103,961	5
1,123	6,282	.....	6	31	12,334	5,079	2,136	182,171	2,899	6
89	935	.....	.....	.....	.....	3,079	8	27,558	400	7
9	37	.....	.....	.....	45	12,122	10	174	112	8
279	630	.....	.....	.....	655	115	35	61	2,245	9
101	696	25	209	1,172	19,533	5,189	.....	607	856	10
688	6,524	577	2,357	18,012	36,328	240,638	300	125	4,822	11
471	2,001	15	12	62	996	5,299	98	324	6,397	12
661	4,961	28	165	2,884	2,325	42,160	3,340	18,101	19,404	13
429	3,126	.....	29	174	1,102	17,920	83	2,377	22,777	14
3,762	15,038	650	737	9,868	6,353	138,098	5,286	25,784	126,343	15
2,306	10,828	635	727	9,839	4,522	129,677	4,979	24,801	93,541	16
1,456	4,210	15	10	29	1,831	8,421	307	983	32,802	17
3,521	47,366	25	190	2,650	15,420	80,933	1,564	34,491	30,339	18
11,636	207,630	3,445	18,549	292,511	609,078	6,964,403	260,960	3,124,953	2,530,494	19
568	7,490	.....	124	1,530	199	46,628	2,083	16,365	4,444	20
3,462	62,827	75	6,695	107,658	53,644	819,988	73,638	560,469	1,108,259	21
456	3,115	5	1,297	14,408	2,408	59,399	2,409	4,246	86,423	22
265	2,042	.....	87	6,622	1,878	15,886	122	172	65,530	23
87	549	.....	1,180	7,685	308	40,645	2,287	3,599	17,883	24
104	524	5	30	101	222	2,868	.....	475	3,010	25
4,138	182,486	.....	4,362	163,049	272,266	6,031,428	50,840	1,861,342	4,370,699	26
8	98	.....	.....	.....	.....	784	.....	591	.....	27
332	1,790	89	32	142	26,169	149,167	844	27,480	10,431	28
10,492	126,419	76	6,960	109,554	389,356	3,844,667	457,259	807,774	1,836,998	29
535	3,573	6	297	1,552	1,428	18,176	.....	327	6,317	30
26	43	.....	.....	.....	158	729	2	807	14,374	31
5	7	.....	.....	.....	44	388	.....	40	561	32
21	36	.....	.....	.....	114	341	2	767	13,813	33
1,171	16,058	26	1,059	8,494	38,562	100,744	1,966	34,381	40,021	34
456	3,137	10	45	228	2,441	8,025	2,391	1,088	14,661	35
252	1,974	.....	5	125	1,849	2,690	2,230	907	6,865	36
65	294	10	.....	.....	375	1,650	19	26	1,293	37
139	869	.....	40	103	217	3,685	142	155	6,503	38
344	2,725	.....	876	2,187	4,473	25,416	181	292	18,440	39
248	495	25	12	25	1,344	1,938	2	.....	9,161	40
90	360	.....	114	875	149	6,613	15	217	643	41

TABLE 90.—DETAILED STATEMENT FOR THE

[See note at head of this table, pp. 1172 and 1173.]

			POWER AND FUEL USED.					
			Primary power.					
			Owned by establishments reporting.					
INDUSTRY.	Number of establishments reporting.	Total primary horsepower.	Steam engines and turbines.		Internal-combustion engines.		Water wheels and water motors.	
			Number.	Horsepower.	Number.	Horsepower.	Number.	Horsepower.
1 Clothing, men's	4,640	40,577	118	8,462	126	1,068	15	258
2 Regular factory products	2,470	33,873	110	8,411	38	533	15	258
3 Men's and youths'	1,425	20,014	76	6,250	11	118	5	230
4 Boys'	325	1,857			3	21		
5 All other	720	12,002	34	2,161	24	394	10	28
6 Contract work	2,170	6,704	8	51	88	535		
7 Men's and youths'	1,827	5,148	4	27	62	356		
8 Boys'	248	1,085	4	24	21	143		
9 All other	95	471			5	36		
10 Clothing, men's, buttonholes	101	189	2	12				
11 Clothing, women's	7,414	32,622	28	2,283	43	529	3	75
12 Regular factory products	5,247	26,834	25	2,255	28	423	3	75
13 Suits, skirts, and cloaks	1,733	7,558	5	582	2	2		
14 Shirt waists and dresses, except house dresses.	1,807	8,303	5	443	2	20	1	25
15 Undergarments and petticoats.	606	4,899	10	780	11	247	2	50
16 Wrappers and house dresses	226	1,982	1	125	2	29		
17 All other	875	4,092	4	325	11	125		
18 Contract work	2,167	5,788	3	28	15	106		
19 Suits, skirts, and cloaks	964	2,090			3	21		
20 Shirt waists and dresses, except house dresses.	878	2,521			3	26		
21 Undergarments and petticoats.	75	302	1	15				
22 Wrappers and house dresses	45	151			3	14		
23 All other	205	724	2	13	6	45		
24 Coal-tar products	169	68,342	373	40,698	14	265		
25 Coffee and spice, roasting and grinding.	776	29,750	53	4,595	37	961	4	100
26 Coffee	751	26,855	42	3,728	33	583		
27 Spice	25	2,895	11	867	4	378	4	100
28 Coffins, burial cases, and undertakers' goods.	304	22,345	104	10,912	28	660	10	739
29 Coke, not including gas-house coke.	155	224,879	941	148,478	6	1,850		
30 Beehive ovens	102	39,761	204	26,569				
31 By-product ovens	53	185,118	737	121,909	6	1,850		
32 Collars and cuffs, men's	35	5,286	22	3,916	1	25	1	75
33 Combs and hairpins, not made from metal or rubber.	41	1,600	15	807	1	60	4	102
34 Condensed milk	368	49,181	726	37,209	28	772	13	695
35 Confectionery and ice cream	5,487	179,891	745	52,763	543	11,800	18	50
36 Confectionery	2,092	77,197	372	31,955	55	880	6	19
37 Ice cream	3,395	102,694	373	20,808	488	10,920	12	31
38 Cooperage	407	30,698	244	23,092	47	617	21	416
39 Hogsheads and barrels	344	26,866	191	20,153	42	586	15	221
40 All other	63	3,832	53	2,939	5	31	6	195
41 Copper, tin, and sheet-iron work	1,538	24,144	36	2,006	255	2,946	4	30
42 Cordage and twine	117	66,643	121	40,845	10	645	36	4,219
43 Cordials and flavoring sirups	92	3,177	16	2,069	1	2	2	2
44 Cork, cutting	58	8,683	26	2,099			1	25
45 Corsets	176	7,156	30	4,176	15	107	1	10
46 Corsets	132	6,667	29	4,076	13	41	1	10
47 Corset waists and brassieres	44	489	1	100	2	66		

UNITED STATES, BY INDUSTRIES: 1919—Continued.

[See note at head of this table, pp. 1172 and 1173.]

Primary power—Contd.			Electric motors run by current generated in the establishments reporting.		Fuel used.					
Rented.		Other.			Coal.		Coke (tons of 2,000 lbs.).	Oil, including gasoline (barrels).	Gas (1,000 cubic feet).	
Electric.					Anthracite (tons of 2,240 lbs.).	Bituminous (tons of 2,000 lbs.).				
Motors.	Horse-power.	Horse-power.	Number.	Horse-power.						
13,160	30,410	379	758	2,710	23,611	90,613	1,575	6,584	848,067	1
9,442	24,349	322	742	2,670	17,033	87,371	1,443	5,897	233,608	2
5,837	13,167	249	568	1,843	13,002	57,751	648	2,977	170,502	3
957	1,836	......	......	......	819	2,195	......	36	34,249	4
2,648	9,346	73	174	827	3,212	27,425	795	2,884	28,857	5
3,718	6,061	57	16	40	6,578	3,242	132	687	614,459	6
3,101	4,722	43	16	40	5,892	2,387	131	522	521,869	7
423	916	2	......	......	471	143	1	98	89,414	8
194	423	12	......	......	215	712	......	67	3,176	9
238	164	13	1	2	94	66	......	17	1,064	10
23,710	29,534	201	51	403	12,700	26,934	8,652	3,186	375,545	11
18,502	23,914	167	51	403	9,986	25,916	8,646	3,059	319,961	12
7,257	6,933	41	2	3	1,590	13,827	24	19	77,329	13
6,419	7,780	35	20	146	2,328	2,431	......	2,809	138,603	14
1,805	3,752	70	17	215	2,785	4,133	......	3	21,288	15
554	1,826	2	......	......	805	1,916	18	3	3,477	16
2,467	3,623	19	12	39	2,478	3,609	8,604	225	79,264	17
5,208	5,620	34	......	......	2,714	1,018	6	127	55,584	18
2,657	2,069	......	......	......	579	210	4	16	41,252	19
1,942	2,461	34	......	......	866	491	......	......	6,080	20
123	287	......	......	......	491	244	......	......	310	21
69	137	......	......	......	164	11	2	38	506	22
417	666	......	......	......	614	62	......	73	7,436	23
2,162	27,376	3	3,345	26,317	62,582	721,982	16,855	143,676	148,004	24
4,401	24,050	44	744	4,029	18,034	33,197	3,571	4,051	378,473	25
4,195	22,500	44	579	2,842	16,691	29,344	3,571	4,051	361,904	26
206	1,550	......	165	1,187	1,343	3,853	......	......	16,569	27
1,639	9,879	155	455	3,993	6,173	59,504	1,100	1,276	36,685	28
1,950	74,551	......	3,969	134,612	5,808	64,245,629	560,505	107,893	658,690	29
402	13,192	......	693	19,254	2,231	30,639,938	187,249	89,349	6,175	30
1,548	61,359	......	3,276	115,358	3,577	33,605,691	373,256	18,544	652,515	31
223	1,260	10	511	2,580	9,585	23,464	100	1	14,058	32
138	619	12	......	......	929	5,822	23	10	2,295	33
1,460	10,502	3	2,495	11,594	27,176	821,083	3,185	157,354	89,519	34
19,787	115,069	209	3,642	23,275	126,566	458,614	9,998	91,553	1,853,503	35
10,213	44,182	161	3,068	19,437	92,141	243,049	8,627	22,733	1,222,781	36
9,574	70,887	48	574	3,838	34,425	215,565	1,371	68,820	630,722	37
692	6,563	10	141	3,750	3,315	50,021	4,757	7,563	56,845	38
610	5,906	......	132	3,641	3,170	44,071	4,705	7,497	52,142	39
82	657	10	9	109	145	5,950	52	66	4,703	40
3,596	19,148	14	314	2,261	9,388	40,329	5,232	8,144	212,995	41
1,062	20,847	87	373	10,206	43,522	118,441	17,408	19,743	55,406	42
270	1,104	......	139	497	2,009	13,284	513	33	6,107	43
670	6,432	127	210	1,113	8,549	55,134	3,427	2,078	564,876	44
967	2,663	200	542	2,469	2,208	18,426	324	38	3,941	45
815	2,340	200	542	2,469	1,330	18,389	324	6	3,735	46
152	323	......	......	......	878	37	......	32	186	47

TABLE 90.—DETAILED STATEMENT FOR THE

[See note at head of this table, pp. 1172 and 1173.]

	INDUSTRY.	Number of establishments reporting.	Total primary horsepower.	Steam engines and turbines. Number.	Steam engines and turbines. Horsepower.	Internal-combustion engines. Number.	Internal-combustion engines. Horsepower.	Water wheels and water motors. Number.	Water wheels and water motors. Horsepower.
				POWER AND FUEL USED. Primary power. Owned by establishments reporting.					
1	Cotton goods...................	1,278	1,840,201	1,622	1,013,146	30	2,639	1,200	305,204
2	Cotton lace....................	44	9,078	66	6,708	4	77	4	175
3	Cotton small wares.............	160	14,263	37	5,907	7	126	23	1,783
4	Crucibles......................	22	2,714	14	852				
5	Graphite crucibles............	6	608	7	420				
6	Clay crucibles................	10	1,001	7	432				
7	Glass-house pots..............	6	1,105						
8	Cutlery and edge tools..........	296	38,958	85	14,106	45	1,905	70	6,286
9	Table cutlery.................	24	5,175	10	1,560	4	400	18	1,172
10	Razors, plain and safety.......	31	4,069	7	775	5	138	2	27
11	Axes and hatchets.............	24	12,414	20	6,708	5	102	18	2,861
12	Scissors, shears, and clippers...	51	4,931	16	1,793	6	99	2	42
13	Pocketknives..................	40	5,494	10	1,628	10	520	12	959
14	Augers, bits, chisels, and planes.	25	3,256	10	800	9	565	13	890
15	All other.....................	101	3,619	12	842	6	81	5	335
16	Dairymen's, poultrymen's, and apiarists' supplies.	206	11,756	50	6,039	40	487	5	52
17	Incubators and brooders.......	41	1,314	7	522	8	189		
18	All other poultrymen's supplies	46	866	8	425	17	126		
19	Cream separators.............	17	5,479	18	3,859				
20	All other dairymen's supplies.	80	2,493	11	637	6	63	2	28
21	Apiarists' supplies............	22	1,604	6	596	9	109	3	24
22	Dental goods...................	282	2,716	9	823	8	286		
23	Teeth........................	47	1,325	8	793	1	6		
24	All other.....................	235	1,391	1	30	7	280		
25	Drug grinding.................	31	6,725	52	5,445	3	50	1	12
26	Druggists' preparations.......	311	12,698	86	8,231	27	173	2	2
27	Dyeing and finishing textiles, exclusive of that done in textile mills.	580	160,430	2,042	118,197	28	2,124	80	13,543
28	Dyestuffs and extracts—natural...	117	34,320	256	31,289	9	201	3	113
29	Electrical machinery, apparatus, and supplies.	1,345	438,839	325	193,231	103	7,446	17	1,800
30	Electroplating................	484	7,078	6	152	35	601	1	15
31	Emery and other abrasive wheels..	58	12,963	21	3,131	3	12		
32	Enameling....................	55	1,183	6	377				
33	Engines, steam, gas, and water....	364	190,021	247	70,582	216	15,773	6	335
34	Engravers' materials..........	20	759	1	150	4	109		
35	Engraving and diesinking......	241	1,760	4	195	5	43		
36	Engraving, steel and copper plate, including plate printing.	268	5,420	13	799	5	40	1	5
37	Engraving, wood..............	19	67						
38	Envelopes....................	102	7,187	25	2,611	4	265	1	125
39	Explosives....................	115	51,635	324	33,676	5	40	44	1,433
40	Fancy articles, not elsewhere specified.	425	8,982	24	1,834	18	282	14	427
41	Beadwork....................	16	25						
42	Celluloid novelties...........	53	2,953	10	612			1	12
43	Metal novelties..............	85	2,980	4	432	6	84	3	119
44	Paper novelties..............	30	500	1	80	1	4		
45	Wood novelties..............	28	510	3	135	4	36	6	176
46	All other.....................	213	2,014	6	575	7	158	4	120
47	Feathers and plumes...........	96	594	2	260	2	13		
48	Felt goods....................	47	16,411	60	9,830	2	4	21	2,341
49	Ferroalloys....................	28	37,087	96	32,420	3	88		
50	Fertilizers....................	564	125,939	555	40,482	219	4,862	24	709
51	Files.........................	48	11,905	31	7,232	6	256	1	25
52	Firearms.....................	25	26,167	12	14,196			2	158

UNITED STATES, BY INDUSTRIES: 1919—Continued.

[See note at head of this table, pp. 1172 and 1173.]

POWER AND FUEL USED—continued.

Primary power—Contd.					Fuel used.					
Rented.			Electric motors run by current generated in the establishments reporting.		Coal.		Coke (tons of 2,000 lbs.).	Oil, including gasoline (barrels).	Gas (1,000 cubic feet).	
Electric.		Other.			Anthracite (tons of 2,240 lbs.).	Bituminous (tons of 2,000 lbs.).				
Motors.	Horse-power.	Horse-power.	Number.	Horse-power.						
38,152	515,309	3,903	23,303	346,300	322,668	3,610,372	32,164	460,467	59,135	1
640	2,118	......	616	2,616	36,021	28,640	....	7,981	22	2
1,151	6,269	178	369	1,512	9,906	24,290	302	39,471	75,424	3
129	1,862	......	14	195	2,769	14,709	....	3,479	44,493	4
16	188	......	6	52	1,439	3,410	....	....	....	5
38	569	......	8	143	1,315	3,285	....	....	19,336	6
75	1,105	......	......	......	15	8,014	....	3,479	25,157	7
2,115	16,258	403	403	7,827	18,238	61,182	2,104	95,745	599,031	8
113	2,043	......	10	175	1,620	6,968	10	3,926	8,604	9
660	2,929	200	99	331	3,403	6,513	186	764	13,273	10
171	2,610	133	63	2,990	4,864	19,531	828	18,107	518,580	11
366	2,989	8	2	50	1,512	11,016	616	8,852	23,994	12
433	2,387	......	190	3,841	3,606	7,266	9	2,505	22,687	13
101	1,001	......	36	413	2,189	4,876	106	60,152	4,982	14
271	2,299	62	3	27	1,044	5,012	349	1,439	6,911	15
801	5,178	......	909	5,437	3,495	36,562	1,232	5,641	49,237	16
139	603	......	15	77	59	4,242	21	40	2,086	17
57	315	......	26	150	42	1,234	....	161	5,806	18
156	1,620	......	837	4,985	3,118	24,652	1,139	5,178	30,502	19
340	1,765	......	5	61	273	4,283	72	227	9,532	20
109	875	......	26	164	3	2,151	....	35	1,311	21
1,824	1,599	8	99	471	1,366	3,063	230	14,440	29,532	22
398	526	......	86	385	969	2,400	30	14,031	10,083	23
1,426	1,073	8	13	86	397	663	200	409	19,449	24
64	1,216	2	109	326	53,151	11,151	50	45	688	25
1,229	4,264	28	1,495	4,168	15,486	78,976	29	585	46,340	26
3,506	25,993	573	5,558	59,896	442,855	1,071,156	13,624	400,258	516,218	27
294	2,692	25	245	5,649	13,585	330,092	2,325	3,796	148,848	28
42,023	235,605	757	38,472	243,761	175,800	1,091,704	61,617	505,660	2,786,382	29
1,066	6,020	290	9	25	1,963	3,624	166	493	46,493	30
694	9,820	......	108	1,992	24,339	60,189	468	2,785	5,040	31
165	801	5	47	355	2,985	8,428	44	6,527	89,060	32
10,008	103,315	16	7,488	110,412	6,399	658,919	94,940	329,761	807,064	33
50	474	26	......	......	654	682	....	6	4,779	34
462	1,512	10	......	......	1,011	1,899	25	25	67,819	35
1,884	4,509	67	154	536	3,290	6,324	39	136	10,568	36
39	67	......	......	......	5	98	....	......	72	37
2,018	4,123	63	920	1,638	2,323	16,616	52	569	5,757	38
1,058	16,486	......	1,621	22,819	40,489	440,931	4,190	181,426	65,357	39
1,370	6,114	325	52	229	8,238	14,390	1,224	3,414	28,222	40
31	24	1	......	......	20	....	....	......	113	41
285	2,287	42	12	37	2,531	8,895	5	10	3,532	42
339	2,081	264	......	......	2,909	2,387	....	2,982	9,502	43
138	413	3	......	......	363	394	....	2	2,617	44
44	152	11	......	......	161	....	....	31	600	45
533	1,157	4	40	192	2,254	2,714	1,219	389	11,858	46
168	229	92	12	165	238	353	33	244	9,868	47
411	4,236	......	500	3,690	18,447	65,588	....	17,703	5,668	48
422	4,579	......	106	19,456	2,005	83,651	815,322	1,410	4,499	49
3,758	79,886	......	777	13,225	12,749	349,612	1,306	71,375	54,397	50
210	4,384	8	41	608	16,356	41,966	730	49,621	81,475	51
846	11,813	......	548	9,030	2,174	74,415	....	12,761	29,389	52

TABLE 90.—DETAILED STATEMENT FOR THE

[See note at head of this table, pp. 1172 and 1173.]

			POWER AND FUEL USED.					
			Primary power.					
			Owned by establishments reporting.					
INDUSTRY.	Number of establishments reporting.	Total primary horse-power.	Steam engines and turbines.		Internal-combustion engines.		Water wheels and water motors.	
			Number.	Horse-power.	Number.	Horse-power.	Number.	Horse-power.
1 Fire extinguishers, chemical	22	855			3	11		
2 Fireworks	24	1,005	12	535	3	30	2	40
3 Flags and banners	64	778	3	225	2	42	1	50
4 Flavoring extracts	183	3,376	11	455	16	103	1	1
5 Flax and hemp, dressed	18	1,920	14	1,455	1	80		
6 Flour-mill and gristmill products	10,673	876,405	2,982	329,589	3,427	96,291	4,690	186,087
7 Food preparations, not elsewhere specified.	1,675	150,230	476	51,893	281	5,337	14	796
8 Breadstuff preparations, such as cereals and breakfast foods.	93	47,372	29	14,917	5	104	3	77
9 Lard compounds and other substitutes.	25	10,005	89	7,423	1	150		
10 Macaroni, vermicelli, and noodles.	538	16,709	32	3,500	169	2,566	6	270
11 Meat products, not elsewhere specified.	60	3,741	22	758	3	14		
12 Peanut butter	53	1,172	2	56	2	23		
13 Sweetening sirups, other than cane.	141	8,656	117	6,181	30	287	1	6
14 All other preparations for human consumption.	490	16,049	80	6,697	26	609	4	443
15 Prepared feed for animals and fowls.	275	46,526	105	12,361	45	1,584		
16 Foundry and machine-shop products.	10,597	1,054,840	2,570	313,066	2,158	53,717	238	13,445
17 Boiler shops	480	73,813	338	35,090	135	5,818	4	410
18 Foundries	1,322	226,533	421	53,344	145	5,494	32	1,081
19 Machine shops	7,841	558,364	1,243	160,052	1,659	33,127	159	9,731
20 Machine shop and foundry combined.	954	196,130	568	64,580	219	9,278	43	2,223
21 Foundry supplies	62	6,328	21	2,640	11	465	5	315
22 Fuel, manufactured	11	5,180	14	1,845				
23 Fur goods	1,616	5,327	6	970	2	14	1	3
24 Furnishing goods, men's	408	5,665	30	2,644	11	140	3	75
25 Neckwear	257	1,272	2	400				
26 All other	151	4,393	28	2,244	11	140	3	75
27 Furniture	2,756	262,703	1,237	165,197	210	4,279	86	4,713
28 Wood, other than rattan and willow.	1,993	208,183	1,066	138,605	136	2,713	75	4,018
29 Rattan and willow	64	3,815	7	1,624	7	119		
30 Metal	148	19,581	43	9,358	19	433	3	190
31 Store and office fixtures	551	31,124	121	15,610	48	1,014	8	505
32 Furs, dressed	124	5,621	25	1,892	5	52		
33 Galvanizing	40	1,631	7	148	6	457		
34 Gas and electric fixtures	301	9,910	34	4,172	27	588	5	162
35 Gas fixtures	49	1,769	9	911	7	110	1	2
36 Electric fixtures	168	4,520	13	1,296	10	248		
37 Combination gas and electric fixtures.	62	2,995	12	1,965	9	180	4	160
38 All other	22	626			1	50		
39 Gas, illuminating and heating	767	238,467	3,518	197,321	151	7,574	13	196
40 Gas machines and gas and water meters	97	8,601	7	575	33	1,714		
41 Gas and water meters	33	4,370	5	535	17	1,068		
42 Gas machines	44	3,496	2	40	15	638		
43 All other	20	735			1	8		
44 Glass	359	207,430	435	99,140	371	52,877	228	2,457

UNITED STATES, BY INDUSTRIES: 1919—Continued.

[See note at head of this table, pp. 1172 and 1173.]

POWER AND FUEL USED—continued.

Primary power—Contd.			Electric motors run by current generated in the establishments reporting.		Fuel used.					
Rented.					Coal.		Coke (tons of 2,000 lbs.).	Oil, including gasoline (barrels).	Gas (1,000 cubic feet).	
Electric.		Other.			Anthracite (tons of 2,240 lbs.).	Bituminous (tons of 2,000 lbs.).				
Motors.	Horse-power.	Horse-power.	Number.	Horse-power.						
87	844	......	......	......	110	867	108	8	6,604	1
65	400	......	26	40	687	6,253	230	876	625	2
180	461	......	9	15	240	780	......	120	2,427	3
715	2,817	......	40	80	1,409	7,809	30	122	21,008	4
23	385	......	1	10	55	16,781	21	......	842	5
9,667	263,497	941	1,826	46,113	57,034	1,582,494	5,134	730,189	1,157,455	6
8,798	91,643	561	2,110	21,155	65,048	456,951	10,422	113,137	976,218	7
2,082	31,894	380	1,057	11,554	9,165	121,938	1,957	5,445	33,142	8
212	2,432	......	210	2,618	29,283	119,317	2,157	61,107	8,170	9
2,203	10,357	16	327	2,043	13,563	25,530	648	2,406	110,183	10
725	2,879	90	......	......	1,702	15,333	107	1,416	46,572	11
239	1,093	......	......	......	287	1,257	150	378	308,612	12
262	2,167	15	126	1,668	3,285	42,664	260	27,460	40,617	13
1,594	8,300	......	315	1,939	5,485	67,009	3,623	5,807	371,498	14
1,481	32,521	60	75	1,333	2,278	63,903	1,520	9,118	57,424	15
63,061	660,037	14,575	25,197	293,758	302,869	3,702,807	1,377,503	2,280,310	21,833,693	16
2,388	31,529	966	2,294	32,247	17,754	289,597	38,970	61,343	189,980	17
12,793	166,229	385	2,441	37,839	45,296	1,207,086	804,283	1,007,574	6,323,554	18
37,269	342,548	12,906	13,647	150,233	164,537	1,585,414	242,772	845,049	13,073,050	19
10,611	119,731	318	6,815	73,439	75,282	620,710	291,478	366,344	2,247,109	20
201	2,907	1	31	588	1,735	17,753	6,153	761	85,755	21
154	3,335	......	8	220	7,647	4,445	675	......		22
5,785	4,340	......	......	......	4,600	3,523	14	22	14,361	23
1,737	2,800	6	339	1,242	3,892	7,651	10	4,704	8,451	24
1,185	872	......	20	177	575	768	10	......	1,702	25
552	1,928	6	319	1,065	3,317	6,883	......	4,704	6,749	26
12,962	86,527	1,987	6,584	50,194	36,346	832,562	13,000	24,015	321,982	27
9,449	61,319	1,528	4,593	32,529	26,434	635,953	3,340	5,388	163,763	28
329	2,072	......	105	400	481	13,444	35	25	3,569	29
1,088	9,571	29	1,051	11,307	5,054	98,870	9,312	17,691	105,027	30
2,096	13,565	430	835	5,958	4,377	84,295	313	911	49,623	31
544	3,477	200	50	332	4,405	14,603	142	60	3,359	32
133	966	60	106	1,048	5,033	3,616	4,298	1,179	111,332	33
908	4,734	254	385	2,682	7,039	30,617	1,044	1,948	116,873	34
133	686	60	177	595	652	12,622	58	396	76,584	35
588	2,796	180	34	237	2,096	7,563	271	508	26,001	36
108	681	9	174	1,850	4,151	9,946	715	608	12,610	37
79	571	5	......	......	140	486	......	436	1,678	38
1,413	33,363	13	1,822	22,040	1,388,467	7,383,687	1,497,435	19,195,800	641,288	39
700	6,297	15	155	1,174	5,716	8,586	1,533	2,659	69,811	40
401	2,752	15	105	862	5,524	4,941	1,330	2,251	59,796	41
232	2,818	......	50	312	146	2,993	141	408	6,226	42
67	727	......	......	......	46	652	62	......	3,789	43
3,397	52,864	92	6,323	90,261	15,268	2,653,654	131,998	910,119	38,500,857	44

TABLE 90.—DETAILED STATEMENT FOR THE

[See note at head of this table, pp. 1172 and 1173.]

	INDUSTRY.	Number of establishments reporting.	Total primary horsepower.	POWER AND FUEL USED.					
				Primary power.					
				Owned by establishments reporting.					
				Steam engines and turbines.		Internal-combustion engines.		Water wheels and water motors.	
				Number.	Horsepower.	Number.	Horsepower.	Number.	Horsepower.
1	Glass, cutting, staining, and ornamenting.	475	5,110	13	628	32	352	2	39
2	Decalcomania work on glass...	14	173	......	......	1	25	......	......
3	All other......................	461	4,937	13	628	31	327	2	39
4	Gloves and mittens, cloth, not including gloves made in textile mills.	169	3,364	10	387	14	124	......	......
5	Gloves and mittens, leather........	300	3,288	14	918	17	73	11	302
6	Glucose and starch................	52	52,846	120	47,576	13	345	8	530
7	Glucose.........................	7	34,640	45	32,206	......	......	......	......
8	Starch..........................	45	18,206	75	15,370	13	345	8	530
9	Glue, not elsewhere specified......	48	16,979	84	16,184	5	102	......	......
10	Glue............................	41	14,254	75	13,564	4	98	......	......
11	All other products.............	7	2,725	9	2,620	1	4	......	......
12	Gold and silver, leaf and foil.......	51	408	2	65	8	26	......	......
13	Gold and silver, reducing and refining, not from the ore.	72	3,279	10	1,077	10	94	......	......
14	Graphite, ground and refined......	24	7,445	17	2,468	4	233	6	475
15	Grease and tallow, not including lubricating greases.	353	25,584	385	18,243	38	339	......	......
16	Soap stock.....................	155	10,517	165	7,357	24	198	......	......
17	Tallow.........................	152	10,860	168	8,469	10	103	......	......
18	All other.......................	46	4,207	52	2,417	4	38	......	......
19	Grindstones....................	23	3,631	86	2,476	24	446	......	......
20	Haircloth.......................	15	1,153	6	620	......	......	2	206
21	Hair work......................	43	119	2	70	......	......	......	......
22	Hammocks......................	6	92	......	......	1	50	......	......
23	Hand stamps...................	211	1,474	7	517	2	12	1	4
24	Hardware......................	519	67,589	206	29,906	63	1,766	32	1,556
25	Locks..........................	71	4,390	13	2,555	8	208	......	......
26	Builders' hardware............	131	30,181	80	14,561	15	442	6	485
27	Piano and organ hardware.....	16	667	6	325	3	100	2	35
28	Vehicle hardware..............	51	9,963	25	2,050	8	247	2	32
29	All other.......................	250	22,388	82	10,415	29	769	22	1,004
30	Hardware, saddlery..............	36	7,161	21	5,306	12	209	2	80
31	Hat and cap materials...........	107	4,927	24	3,607	6	65	5	205
32	Hats and caps, other than felt, straw, and wool.	654	1,687	6	158	2	7	......	......
33	Hats, fur-felt...................	159	20,389	99	15,251	2	10	1	120
34	Hats, straw....................	137	3,392	28	1,776	3	131	2	240
35	Hats, wool-felt.................	33	2,696	15	1,874	......	......	3	365
36	Hones and whetstones..........	11	1,164	5	705	4	69	6	285
37	Horseshoes, not made in steel works or rolling mills.	16	3,874	10	2,463	5	116	2	175
38	House-furnishing goods, not elsewhere specified.	402	12,249	36	5,427	13	163	5	562
39	Comforts and quilts...........	71	3,967	13	2,230	3	40	3	487
40	Feather pillows and beds......	37	2,693	10	1,447	2	3	......	......
41	Cotton batting, not made in cotton mills.	9	905	3	175	1	10	......	......
42	Mops and dusters..............	51	403	1	20	1	5	......	......
43	All other.......................	234	4,281	9	1,555	6	105	2	75
44	Ice, manufactured...............	2,778	572,970	4,434	406,942	435	28,003	58	2,542
45	Ink, printing...................	86	10,353	28	5,335	16	681	3	29
46	Ink, writing....................	23	610	4	381	4	38	......	......

UNITED STATES, BY INDUSTRIES: 1919—Continued.

[See note at head of this table, pp. 1172 and 1173.]

POWER AND FUEL USED—continued.

Primary power—Contd.			Electric motors run by current generated in the establishments reporting.		Fuel used.					
Rented.					Coal.		Coke (tons of 2,000 lbs.).	Oil, including gasoline (barrels).	Gas (1,000 cubic feet).	
Electric.		Other.			Anthracite (tons of 2,240 lbs.).	Bituminous (tons of 2,000 lbs.).				
Motors.	Horse-power.	Horse-power.	Number.	Horse-power.						
919	4,023	68	4	70	4,710	8,428	651	2,150	92,195	1
22	148	....	....	....	66	711	....	2	12,498	2
897	3,875	68	4	70	4,644	7,717	651	2,148	79,697	3
733	2,853	....	40	192	1,056	10,557	42	59	3,666	4
749	1,995	....	18	69	2,652	10,597	128	100	8,730	5
142	3,585	810	2,856	44,150	113,141	859,133	14,822	17,546	23,335	6
60	2,434	....	1,501	22,879	112,804	561,619	10,381	17,518	23,335	7
82	1,151	810	1,355	21,271	337	297,514	4,441	28	....	8
62	693	....	818	11,201	11,420	324,287	1,092	1,490	4,699	9
58	592	....	628	9,326	5,212	258,741	592	1,288	4,670	10
4	101	....	190	1,875	6,208	65,546	500	202	29	11
87	317	....	1	5	1,177	177	141	11	754	12
388	1,970	138	18	162	430	4,280	4,168	14,678	16,751	13
114	4,269	....	6	122	5,206	7,688	....	233	115	14
408	6,962	40	339	5,796	21,133	337,311	344	82,235	266,411	15
196	2,962	....	116	1,501	13,303	150,278	152	47,629	218,405	16
153	2,268	20	186	3,592	7,418	129,381	192	31,320	48,000	17
59	1,732	20	37	703	412	57,652	....	3,286	6	18
21	709	....	5	170	....	13,610	....	65	29,089	19
10	146	181	....	....	963	2,335	....	57	....	20
45	49	....	....	....	253	832	16	2	7,608	21
7	42	....	....	....	17	608	....	120	....	22
549	941	....	105	278	1,488	4,147	19	18	20,080	23
3,265	33,866	495	846	11,200	37,933	248,791	29,368	82,688	1,222,146	24
185	1,589	38	95	1,694	4,566	7,024	797	1,097	7,292	25
893	14,628	65	364	5,134	15,637	110,747	17,631	45,431	23,416	26
25	197	10	1	5	215	1,956	2	12	3,259	27
807	7,543	91	36	746	3,646	58,666	1,049	27,589	1,125,465	28
1,355	9,909	291	350	3,621	13,869	70,398	9,889	8,559	62,714	29
82	1,551	15	113	2,365	3,563	37,662	7,108	3,515	8,932	30
352	1,050	....	132	926	8,993	9,385	542	8	2,114	31
1,705	1,522	....	16	15	988	942	28	30	34,991	32
705	4,996	12	1,084	4,635	57,297	75,038	1,130	4,050	26,649	33
493	1,235	10	155	962	4,573	20,814	62	463	8,688	34
111	455	2	53	400	788	10,297	30	17	4,507	35
7	105	....	20	261	7	2,378	....	57	225	36
68	1,120	....	14	195	4,147	19,337	50	5,033	612	37
1,335	5,705	392	198	926	6,156	21,748	113	2,120	48,966	38
194	1,210	....	21	41	1,676	5,840	3	110	465	39
160	1,243	....	75	426	2,480	6,136	74	1,625	894	40
50	718	2	....	....	60	2,138	....	12	....	41
121	373	5	5	45	76	499	....	2	1,727	42
810	2,161	385	97	414	1,864	7,135	36	371	45,880	43
5,658	132,438	3,045	2,511	26,114	205,875	3,309,636	32,327	1,633,549	6,170,964	44
284	4,184	124	199	2,725	7,059	25,177	310	6,351	19,412	45
109	191	....	60	265	1,032	1,071	3	3	870	46

TABLE **90.**—DETAILED STATEMENT FOR THE

[See note at head of this table, pp. 1172 and 1173.]

	INDUSTRY.	Number of establishments reporting.	Total primary horsepower.	Steam engines and turbines. Number.	Steam engines and turbines. Horsepower.	Internal-combustion engines. Number.	Internal-combustion engines. Horsepower.	Water wheels and water motors. Number.	Water wheels and water motors. Horsepower.
1	Instruments, professional and scientific.	320	13,020	25	3,204	29	395	1	25
2	Medical and surgical...........	113	2,628	7	1,010	12	213	1	25
3	Optical.....................	12	1,312			1	4		
4	All other...................	195	9,080	18	2,194	16	178		
5	Iron and steel, blast furnaces......	193	1,581,432	2,300	1,249,817	137	283,015	10	371
6	Iron and steel, steel works and rolling mills.	499	3,820,917	5,418	2,856,556	141	257,473	33	9,041
7	Iron and steel, bolts, nuts, washers, and rivets, not made in rolling mills.	141	49,959	84	15,051	22	1,661	10	690
8	Iron and steel, cast-iron pipe.......	58	28,741	90	11,297	1	4	1	200
9	Iron and steel, doors and shutters..	51	4,013	8	1,105	6	225	3	350
10	Iron and steel, forgings, not made in steel works or rolling mills.	239	101,951	216	24,808	35	1,602	7	848
11	Iron and steel, nails and spikes, cut and wrought, including wire nails, not made in steel works or rolling mills.	61	8,974	21	3,495	8	297	16	696
12	Cut nails and spikes...........	6	1,502	1	1,000	3	144	3	205
13	Wire nails and spikes..........	25	2,918	6	530	2	68	2	75
14	Forged nails and spikes........	5	1,177	1	175	2	35	6	200
15	All other, including tacks......	25	3,377	13	1,790	1	50	5	216
16	Iron and steel, tempering and welding.	432	8,804	14	877	45	603		
17	Treated iron and steel.........	32	5,529	5	595	3	90		
18	Welding	400	3,275	9	282	42	513		
19	Iron and steel, wrought pipe......	47	23,925	61	13,306	3	150		
20	Ivory, shell, and bone work, not including combs and hairpins.	42	954	8	407	4	53	1	25
21	Japanning....................	29	311	1	25				
22	Jewelry......................	1,809	16,389	28	1,647	31	545	3	114
23	Jewelry and instrument cases......	107	1,091	2	200	8	102		
24	Jute goods...................	26	32,135	30	14,520	1	12	9	13,046
25	Knit goods...................	1,962	151,601	589	76,003	53	814	236	12,941
26	Labels and tags...............	103	4,061	8	1,317	11	405	1	2
27	Lamps and reflectors...........	152	12,708	14	1,867	14	581	2	65
28	Automobile lamps.............	33	7,516	2	700				
29	All other lamps..............	108	4,751	12	1,167	12	531	2	65
30	Reflectors...................	11	441			2	50		
31	Lapidary work................	115	680			2	6		
32	Lard, not made in slaughtering and meat-packing establishments.	4	40	2	25				
33	Lasts........................	63	5,842	24	3,385	9	106	1	20
34	Lead, bar, pipe, and sheet.......	29	5,537	23	3,090	1	65		
35	Leather goods, not elsewhere specified.	438	3,902	17	696	17	217	5	26
36	Leather, tanned, curried, and finished.	656	218,238	1,239	150,800	69	6,438	26	2,029
37	Lime.........................	301	51,735	329	19,946	139	2,944	4	250
38	Linen goods..................	10	6,069	11	2,966	8	121	16	1,580
39	Liquors, distilled.............	29	16,494	87	7,599	3	32	1	600
40	Alcohol, grain, including pure, neutral, or cologne spirits.	24	10,296	79	6,649	2	28	1	600
41	Rum, whisky, and other distilled liquors.	5	6,198	8	950	1	4		
42	Liquors, malt................	718	324,431	3,049	276,441	34	3,651	29	194
43	Liquors, vinous..............	214	5,189	45	879	124	596	1	12
44	Lithographing................	262	18,624	50	6,442	11	575		

UNITED STATES, BY INDUSTRIES: 1919—Continued.

[See note at head of this table, pp. 1172 and 1173.]

POWER AND FUEL USED—continued.

Primary power—Contd.					Fuel used.					
Rented.		Other.	Electric motors run by current generated in the establishments reporting.		Coal.		Coke (tons of 2,000 lbs.).	Oil including gasoline (barrels).	Gas (1,000 cubic feet).	
Electric.					Anthracite (tons of 2,240 lbs.).	Bituminous (tons of 2,000 lbs.).				
Motors.	Horse-power.	Horse-power.	Number.	Horse-power.						
1,884	9,357	39	805	2,699	25,192	20,183	58	1,374	103,237	1
390	1,369	11	101	574	3,397	4,683	1	62	13,991	2
100	1,308	......	......	......	6	64	......	......	5,113	3
1,394	6,680	28	704	2,125	21,789	15,436	57	1,312	84,133	4
1,004	48,204	25	6,446	194,350	42,779	2,261,315	32,424,625	51,324	1,184,953	5
22,053	695,097	2,750	63,427	1,655,499	598,944	25,911,098	886,062	8,490,982	90,678,288	6
2,286	32,557	......	524	13,830	16,066	152,630	6,551	210,746	656,280	7
948	17,240	......	1,158	18,253	27,374	96,387	256,781	1,077	5,386	8
334	2,333	......	29	667	1,491	7,903	69	300	7,707	9
4,948	73,738	955	1,130	16,955	26,972	717,801	65,021	1,214,040	1,043,895	10
270	4,483	3	32	837	6,100	18,003	240	5,696	10,005	11
8	153	......	3	85	273	3,769	......	1,617	3,272	12
134	2,242	3	......	......	1,061	4,689	5	315	1,999	13
38	767	......	......	......	13	2,252	135	1,093	3,000	14
90	1,321	......	29	752	4,753	7,293	100	2,671	1,734	15
853	7,315	9	13	122	892	11,036	1,093	8,844	129,949	16
199	4,844	......	10	70	112	8,710	450	5,396	41,883	17
654	2,471	9	3	52	780	2,326	643	3,448	88,066	18
955	10,469	......	1,447	18,718	45,879	270,488	13,771	27,696	189,173	19
100	394	75	1	25	865	1,967	3	5	5,095	20
90	281	5	......	......	436	620	83	55	19,587	21
5,985	12,790	1,293	280	2,960	5,711	12,306	254	7,065	195,539	22
284	773	16	19	59	397	1,156	15	1,863	7,198	23
151	4,557	......	309	13,076	9,994	29,765	......	79	3,000	24
10,928	59,680	2,163	4,581	31,457	102,024	584,787	1,654	7,526	73,068	25
847	2,309	28	606	2,519	1,438	8,159	3	913	17,058	26
1,204	10,109	86	79	865	1,619	22,918	480	4,081	58,270	27
574	6,809	7	36	440	44	10,809	......	1,614	12,222	28
590	2,909	79	43	425	1,156	11,721	475	1,166	41,768	29
40	391	......	......	......	419	388	5	1,301	4,280	30
616	674	......	......	......	54	23	......	24	2,121	31
3	15	......	......	......	......	53	......	......	136	32
261	2,028	303	183	2,059	1,650	11,864	15	193	1,954	33
82	2,382	......	134	1,984	10,636	10,449	220	868	12,466	34
1,145	2,901	62	46	180	2,308	5,964	115	801	8,351	35
4,329	58,494	477	6,272	85,441	89,722	1,448,166	3,740	89,232	211,404	36
1,161	28,595	......	172	3,560	57,112	872,910	102,788	26,820	53,835	37
204	1,402	......	33	1,095	3,512	13,519	......	200	......	38
177	8,263	......	179	2,318	1,052	134,336	3,430	288,195	......	39
152	3,019	......	166	2,293	1,038	131,231	3,430	275,193	......	40
25	5,244	......	13	25	14	3,105	......	13,002	......	41
4,678	41,814	2,301	9,861	68,911	346,914	1,692,067	14,527	329,849	392,964	42
498	3,702	......	18	20	8,202	1,828	14	27,407	398	43
3,475	11,533	74	1,886	7,424	12,399	30,770	1,421	3,407	35,408	44

TABLE 90.—DETAILED STATEMENT FOR THE

[See note at head of this table, pp. 1172 and 1173.]

	INDUSTRY.	Number of establishments reporting.	Total primary horse-power.	POWER AND FUEL USED. Primary power. Owned by establishments reporting. Steam engines and turbines.		Internal-combustion engines.		Water wheels and water motors.	
				Number.	Horse-power.	Number.	Horse-power.	Number.	Horse-power.
1	Locomotives, not made by railroad companies.	17	97,187	86	34,065	5	3,355		
2	Looking-glass and picture frames..	219	4,689	17	1,434	3	19		
3	Lubricating greases................	41	2,178	11	1,162	8	293		
4	Lumber and timber products......	25,185	2,358,937	33,663	2,180,798	1,722	28,228	1,384	62,447
5	Lumber, planing-mill products, not including planing mills connected with sawmills.	5,232	419,671	2,729	234,959	741	15,283	126	4,633
6	Machine tools.....................	397	100,433	149	26,975	55	2,249	16	1,033
7	Malt............................	54	27,483	99	18,272			3	450
8	Marble and stone work..........	3,338	170,132	1,011	60,083	766	10,175	29	4,891
9	Monuments and tombstones...	2,537	51,328	121	7,171	639	6,790	18	513
10	Other marble and stone work, except slate.	684	101,220	700	43,913	122	3,331	7	4,170
11	Roofing slate..................	70	10,678	138	6,219	2	23		
12	Other slate products...........	47	6,906	52	2,780	3	31	4	208
13	Matches.......................	21	12,947	32	9,563	1	4		
14	Mats and matting, from cocoa fiber, grass, and coir.	12	1,670	7	1,255	1	70		
15	Mattresses and spring beds, not elsewhere specified.	907	23,469	41	3,847	60	1,001	10	381
16	Millinery and lace goods, not elsewhere specified.	2,244	12,482	45	3,248	21	254	8	170
17	Embroideries..................	800	3,328	4	145	7	95	1	40
18	Trimmed hats and hat frames..	706	4,843	22	1,679	2	8	1	35
19	Dress and cloak trimmings, braids, and fringes.	102	839	4	355	6	73	2	25
20	Women's neckwear............	137	523						
21	All other.....................	499	2,949	15	1,069	6	78	4	70
22	Millstones.....................	3	132	1	60	1	12		
23	Mineral and soda waters.........	4,806	41,764	411	12,645	729	3,277	52	97
24	Mineral and carbonated waters..	4,668	34,969	346	7,645	705	3,155	52	97
25	Fruit beverages...............	70	4,071	45	2,496	15	92		
26	All other.....................	68	2,724	20	2,504	9	30		
27	Minerals and earths, ground or otherwise treated.	403	127,074	807	61,367	149	4,456	52	5,712
28	Mirrors, framed and unframed, not elsewhere specified.	155	4,328	30	2,015	11	173	1	1
29	Models and patterns, not including paper patterns.	853	13,869	10	4,903	62	773	2	20
30	Motorcycles, bicycles, and parts...	48	14,806	20	3,970	4	77	2	90
31	Mucilage, paste, and other adhesives, not elsewhere specified.	90	3,242	33	1,373	5	108	2	158
32	Mucilage and paste............	33	1,028	13	413	1	10		
33	All other.....................	57	2,214	20	960	4	98	2	158
34	Musical instruments and materials, not elsewhere specified.	162	3,286	5	142	13	88	5	100
35	Musical instruments, organs.......	62	3,251	14	1,360	8	188		
36	Musical instruments, pianos.......	173	28,732	147	19,822	6	623	1	100
37	Musical instruments, piano and organ materials.	106	15,821	57	9,730	11	469	13	336
38	Piano materials...............	91	15,519	57	9,730	10	463	12	321
39	Organ materials..............	15	302			1	6	1	15
40	Needles, pins, and hooks and eyes.	91	8,467	28	4,125	1	4	14	822
41	Nets and seines...................	16	959	4	730	1	25		
42	Oakum..........................	6	533	7	410			2	50
43	Oil and cake, cottonseed...........	708	290,636	1,098	195,356	126	10,857	12	1,512

UNITED STATES, BY INDUSTRIES: 1919—Continued.

[See note at head of this table, pp. 1172 and 1173.]

POWER AND FUEL USED—continued.										
Primary power—Contd.					Fuel used.					
Rented.			Electric motors run by current generated in the establishments reporting.		Coal.		Coke (tons of 2,000 lbs.).	Oil, including gasoline (barrels).	Gas (1,000 cubic feet).	
Electric.		Other.			Anthracite (tons of 2,240 lbs.).	Bituminous (tons of 2,000 lbs.).				
Motors.	Horse-power.	Horse-power.	Number.	Horse-power.						
2,927	59,084	683	2,836	59,789	33,863	339,071	28,202	154,842	78,202	1
740	3,206	30	10	27	2,490	12,408	10	86	21,339	2
94	723	....	40	981	109	7,302	27	581	678,284	3
4,013	83,872	3,592	8,388	195,606	15,386	1,620,058	6,221	857,627	20,347	4
16,944	162,195	2,601	3,522	37,499	35,730	586,979	23,294	63,241	363,963	5
7,751	70,037	139	3,657	28,780	17,513	196,071	28,871	65,143	335,130	6
410	8,761	....	589	12,618	38,863	134,992	12,456	12,600	107	7
6,065	94,028	955	663	12,005	30,457	281,523	926	20,773	119,624	8
3,222	36,154	700	127	1,517	8,622	58,025	436	8,468	103,726	9
2,485	49,551	255	522	10,398	11,865	188,394	490	9,666	14,935	10
221	4,436	....	14	90	5,966	26,410	....	2,639	176	11
137	3,887	....	....	....	4,004	8,694	....	....	787	12
472	3,380	....	1,484	6,531	1,640	49,559	106	6,351	331	13
135	345	....	35	355	28	6,087	....	....	38	14
3,541	18,158	82	162	1,156	5,275	30,485	850	8,323	43,564	15
7,382	8,738	72	362	1,369	14,400	31,073	159	1,226	67,091	16
3,013	3,046	2	27	59	7,687	4,202	27	107	8,398	17
2,044	3,076	45	196	794	2,397	21,241	123	324	34,154	18
244	386	....	25	125	1,217	263	....	....	3,173	19
669	523	....	....	....	140	80	....	407	4,439	20
1,412	1,707	25	114	391	2,959	5,287	9	388	16,927	21
2	60	....	....	....	3	780	....	60	....	22
8,657	25,148	597	517	2,031	16,759	109,525	990	71,149	164,282	23
8,228	23,475	597	225	678	16,327	92,740	935	32,057	163,085	24
327	1,483	....	183	600	112	14,513	....	2,890	562	25
102	190	....	109	753	320	2,272	55	36,202	635	26
1,473	55,529	10	196	5,928	29,821	514,900	5,165	120,085	1,006,579	27
334	2,044	95	68	382	2,536	13,427	62	962	23,621	28
1,930	8,054	119	8	54	2,251	4,959	2,116	330	42,621	29
963	10,283	386	54	1,350	5,365	38,280	3,008	24,393	117,642	30
185	1,563	40	25	324	1,553	10,423	140	77	12,158	31
83	565	40	20	269	989	4,800	....	....	401	32
102	998	....	5	55	564	5,623	140	77	11,757	33
1,030	2,889	67	21	27	1,312	8,816	56	267	35,031	34
455	1,697	6	131	409	1,047	7,796	52	485	15,557	35
1,607	8,152	35	1,049	9,118	17,571	144,707	1,074	942	6,123	36
757	5,181	105	647	4,209	8,837	32,053	4,728	1,144	60,448	37
662	4,900	105	647	4,209	8,721	31,285	4,728	1,134	33,894	38
95	281	....	....	....	116	768	....	10	26,554	39
715	3,472	44	216	2,431	4,420	21,393	16	2,345	26,790	40
94	204	....	65	312	419	3,089	....	24	....	41
6	73	....	....	....	35	883	1,018	39	....	42
1,964	82,256	655	438	11,144	34,763	1,172,175	10,262	394,219	1,527,974	43

TABLE 90.—DETAILED STATEMENT FOR THE

[See note at head of this table, pp. 1172 and 1173.]

				POWER AND FUEL USED.					
				Primary power.					
					Owned by establishments reporting.				
	INDUSTRY.	Number of establishments reporting.	Total primary horse-power.	Steam engines and turbines.		Internal-combustion engines.		Water wheels and water motors.	
				Number.	Horse-power.	Number.	Horse-power.	Number.	Horse-power.
1	Oil, essential	33	1,833	37	1,512	13	129	2	50
2	Oil, linseed	26	17,621	33	9,175			1	250
3	Oil, not elsewhere specified [1]	224	30,075	286	21,749	38	674	1	4
4	Vegetable	63	15,250	104	9,998	12	447	1	4
5	Animal	36	9,595	92	9,086	10	61		
6	Mineral	25	1,573	16	699	9	100		
7	Composite	100	3,657	74	1,966	7	66		
8	Oilcloth and linoleum, floor	20	23,509	112	14,321	1	2		
9	Oilcloth, enameled	11	4,501	8	950				
10	Oleomargarine and other butter substitutes.	41	9,435	42	5,151	1	12	1	25
11	Optical goods	492	15,710	10	4,756	6	56	2	54
12	Ordnance and accessories	25	40,652	31	8,300	5	187	1	200
13	Paints	551	73,702	283	33,224	57	2,462	20	959
14	Paper and wood pulp	722	1,851,014	3,157	698,983	37	3,191	2,558	910,863
15	Paper exclusively	492	561,698	1,791	377,010	23	2,715	756	112,916
16	Pulp exclusively	60	143,371	148	24,473	5	87	278	108,449
17	Paper and pulp	170	1,145,945	1,218	297,500	9	389	1,524	689,498
18	Paper goods, not elsewhere specified.	284	35,538	80	17,688	17	255	12	2,260
19	Playing cards	8	2,377	9	2,045				
20	All other	276	33,161	71	15,643	17	255	12	2,260
21	Paper patterns	6	68						
22	Patent medicines and compounds.	980	25,677	136	10,187	65	744	9	53
23	Patent and proprietary medicines.	664	16,797	76	6,787	36	388	6	22
24	Patent and proprietary compounds, not elsewhere specified.	316	8,880	60	3,400	29	356	3	31
25	Paving materials	852	191,543	1,458	105,581	205	4,104	9	607
26	Peanuts, grading, roasting, cleaning, and shelling.	77	7,351	38	4,015	6	313		
27	Pencils, lead	12	8,099	16	4,615	2	48		
28	Pens, fountain and stylographic	52	1,517	3	635	8	86	2	100
29	Pens, gold	15	160			1	5		
30	Pens, steel	4	305	3	287	1	10		
31	Perfumery and cosmetics	252	2,196	10	295	4	34		
32	Petroleum, refining	257	238,906	2,460	144,743	647	42,647	20	131
33	Phonographs and graphophones	147	40,168	54	21,973	8	366	2	175
34	Photo-engraving	399	3,800	1	25	3	58	1	1
35	Photographic apparatus	61	2,321	2	375	2	28		
36	Cameras	10	652	1	125	1	3		
37	Motion-picture machines	17	1,105			1	25		
38	All other apparatus and parts.	34	564	1	250				
39	Photographic materials	124	26,458	53	13,526	5	68		
40	Motion-picture films, not exposed.	14	20,261	21	10,690				
41	Motion-picture projection films.	40	4,169	11	1,565	2	37		
42	All other	70	2,028	21	1,271	3	31		
43	Pickles, preserves, and sauces	591	22,500	211	12,579	131	1,190	1	50
44	Preserves	161	7,715	85	4,698	14	92		
45	Pickles and sauces	430	14,785	126	7,881	117	1,098	1	50
46	Pipes, tobacco	48	2,001	9	700	4	49		

[1] Includes "oil, castor" and "oil, lard," to avoid disclosing individual operations.

UNITED STATES, BY INDUSTRIES: 1919—Continued.

[See note at head of this table, pp. 1172 and 1173.]

POWER AND FUEL USED—continued.

Primary power—Contd.			Electric motors run by current generated in the establishments reporting.		Fuel used.					
Rented.					Coal.		Coke (tons of 2,000 lbs.).	Oil, including gasoline (barrels).	Gas (1,000 cubic feet).	
Electric.		Other.			Anthracite (tons of 2,240 lbs.).	Bituminous (tons of 2,000 lbs.).				
Motors.	Horsepower.	Horsepower.	Number.	Horsepower.						
18	142	......	47	350	8,943	5,384	....	4,185	7,296	1
189	8,196	......	123	2,679	31,893	73,871	85	....	757	2
600	7,640	8	186	3,252	40,578	143,153	2,633	41,496	52,139	3
170	4,801	......	103	2,347	24,278	71,524	2,272	30,607	20,760	4
76	442	6	49	637	687	30,727	....	4,721	....	5
61	774	......	6	85	193	4,330	....	1,836	19,533	6
293	1,623	2	28	183	15,420	36,572	361	4,332	11,846	7
773	9,186	......	897	8,533	36,141	181,629	2,721	7,580	....	8
438	3,301	250	60	200	3,342	16,558	52	8,675	....	9
392	4,247	......	199	2,103	5,821	41,172	11,086	6,240	1,771	10
3,728	10,783	61	....	....	2,082	19,024	31	5,805	374,421	11
1,838	31,965	......	565	6,585	36,747	66,684	3,837	59,336	2,978,491	12
2,270	36,685	372	1,282	19,168	69,766	413,309	17,047	52,050	207,610	13
6,001	236,662	1,315	11,755	346,924	869,948	7,863,150	63,384	2,120,114	286,660	14
2,409	68,682	375	4,516	108,672	279,022	3,765,545	8,472	859,874	286,660	15
182	10,112	250	577	21,881	16,752	502,075	....	10,759	....	16
3,410	157,868	690	6,662	216,371	574,174	3,595,530	54,912	1,249,481	....	17
2,669	15,166	169	1,748	10,498	30,626	108,075	228	2,417	29,117	18
73	332	......	782	2,524	....	10,725	....	28	1,919	19
2,596	14,834	169	966	7,974	30,626	97,350	228	2,389	27,198	20
37	68	......	....	....	53	....	....	....	446	21
2,784	14,425	268	851	4,621	43,033	106,045	775	11,844	102,410	22
2,044	9,491	109	800	4,172	38,096	60,259	637	2,898	72,051	23
740	4,934	159	51	449	4,937	45,786	138	8,946	30,359	24
1,708	81,179	72	160	5,551	21,939	404,013	273	90,341	4,855	25
262	3,023	......	44	555	913	12,530	18	796	15,257	26
407	3,436	......	200	2,681	15,500	9,142	511	1,736	5,014	27
351	671	25	61	545	620	2,770	....	182	4,241	28
52	140	15	....	....	33	....	....	1	717	29
4	8	......	18	87	4	2,141	2	....	3,654	30
776	1,867	......	7	19	1,732	5,354	13	5,139	18,237	31
3,576	51,385	......	3,089	57,240	1,105,503	3,619,534	319,563	23,716,521	26,919,052	32
2,392	17,649	5	1,249	14,544	42,195	127,659	16	4,124	51,448	33
2,899	3,716	......	14	13	530	1,175	8	12	329,622	34
386	1,918	......	74	274	928	3,158	16	84	950	35
154	524	......	....	....	43	1,889	10	....	189	36
138	1,080	......	5	20	539	372	....	80	12	37
94	314	......	69	254	346	897	6	4	749	38
2,285	12,864	......	2,777	10,372	5,856	127,928	68	1,176	20,378	39
1,118	9,571	......	2,383	8,916	3,586	108,342	....	817	5,093	40
833	2,567	......	236	1,031	1,274	7,870	....	24	8,482	41
334	726	......	158	425	996	11,716	68	335	6,803	42
2,292	8,565	116	1,510	8,319	7,761	191,882	292	46,087	77,055	43
747	2,845	80	324	1,367	4,126	71,021	174	22,777	36,320	44
1,545	5,720	36	1,186	6,952	3,635	120,861	118	23,310	40,735	45
188	1,252	......	116	372	1,650	2,416	19	3	1,488	46

TABLE 90.—DETAILED STATEMENT FOR THE

[See note at head of this table, pp. 1172 and 1173.]

				POWER AND FUEL USED.					
				Primary power.					
				Owned by establishments reporting.					
	INDUSTRY.	Number of establishments reporting.	Total primary horsepower.	Steam engines and turbines.		Internal-combustion engines.		Water wheels and water motors.	
				Number.	Horsepower.	Number.	Horsepower.	Number.	Horsepower.
1	Plated ware	64	14,252	38	8,018	7	200	10	512
2	Knives, forks, spoons, and other flatware.	18	10,000	18	5,488	1	32	8	355
3	Hollow ware	27	3,085	15	1,805	3	100	2	157
4	All other	19	1,167	5	725	3	68	......	....
5	Plumbers' supplies, not elsewhere specified.	199	29,762	99	16,089	22	670	5	373
6	Pocketbooks	113	431	......	....	......	....	......	....
7	Pottery	296	29,090	242	18,509	49	1,113	2	106
8	Chinaware	157	20,972	163	12,242	15	851	2	106
9	Earthen and stone ware	112	6,669	65	5,302	32	252	......	....
10	All other	27	1,449	14	965	2	10	......	....
11	Poultry, killing and dressing, not done in slaughtering and meat-packing establishments.	87	4,016	36	1,951	4	107	......	....
12	Printing and publishing, book and job.	11,875	131,961	141	13,865	400	3,095	26	75
13	Job printing	11,351	123,786	121	11,817	394	2,942	24	74
14	Book publishing and printing.	122	6,675	19	1,973	5	149	......	....
15	Book publishing without printing.	102	286	1	75	......	....	......	....
16	Linotype work and typesetting	300	1,214	......	....	1	4	2	1
17	Printing and publishing, music	26	634	......	....	2	12	......	....
18	Printing and publishing	20	573	......	....	1	10	......	....
19	Publishing without printing	6	61	......	....	1	2	......	....
20	Printing and publishing, newspapers and periodicals.	12,735	194,361	229	25,066	3,927	13,277	160	784
21	Printing and publishing	1,163	85,008	86	15,614	117	1,259	4	14
22	Printing, publishing, and job printing.	11,395	106,881	141	9,152	3,801	11,959	156	770
23	Publishing without printing	177	2,472	2	300	9	59	......	....
24	Printing materials	74	1,357	11	213	4	83	......	....
25	Pulp, from fiber other than wood	5	833	2	350	......	....	2	400
26	Pulp goods	38	12,273	53	6,752	......	....	17	2,015
27	Wall board	9	1,668	7	832	......	....	1	70
28	All other	29	10,605	46	5,920	......	....	16	1,945
29	Pumps, not including power pumps.	119	10,346	26	2,025	21	809	5	209
30	Pumps, steam and other power	106	22,155	53	10,053	17	670	2	90
31	Steam	60	17,699	47	8,535	12	601	2	90
32	Other power	46	4,456	6	1,518	5	69	......	....
33	Refrigerators	111	13,232	47	8,009	14	465	......	....
34	Regalia, and society badges and emblems.	81	1,333	2	260	4	53	......	....
35	Rice, cleaning and polishing	86	27,382	94	18,881	21	697	......	....
36	Roofing materials	133	39,327	138	15,847	8	253	12	2,145
37	Metal shingles and ceiling	22	861	1	100	3	177	......	....
38	All other	111	38,466	137	15,747	5	76	12	2,145
39	Rubber tires, tubes, and rubber goods, not elsewhere specified.	404	354,188	455	194,459	30	3,367	37	2,534
40	Rules, ivory and wood	10	299	1	150	3	56	1	5
41	Saddlery and harness	1,026	8,212	25	1,279	55	282	2	38

UNITED STATES, BY INDUSTRIES: 1919—Continued.

[See note at head of this table, pp. 1172 and 1173.]

POWER AND FUEL USED—continued.

Primary power—Contd.					Fuel used.					
Rented.			Electric motors run by current generated in the establishments reporting.		Coal.		Coke (tons of 2,000 lbs.).	Oil, including gasoline (barrels).	Gas (1,000 cubic feet).	
Electric.		Other.			Anthracite (tons of 2,240 lbs.).	Bituminous (tons of 2,000 lbs.).				
Motors.	Horse-power.	Horse-power.	Number.	Horse-power.						
594	5,482	40	624	5,386	7,973	45,675	241	10,288	47,040	1
423	4,125	......	502	4,587	5,531	30,158	111	10,026	21,790	2
128	1,023	......	98	681	1,422	11,898	50	242	14,025	3
43	334	40	24	118	1,020	3,619	80	20	11,225	4
1,110	12,563	67	736	7,565	7,391	146,178	32,999	54,895	204,429	5
370	431	......	......	......	569	559	....	1	1,355	6
1,263	9,312	50	824	4,835	34,958	610,562	1,017	41,853	6,645,388	7
1,036	7,723	50	797	4,526	33,644	484,928	975	25,461	5,337,658	8
141	1,115	......	10	127	1,155	93,362	42	14,207	928,728	9
86	474	......	17	182	159	32,272	....	2,185	379,002	10
185	1,958	......	69	253	82	19,944	10	745	14,515	11
66,733	114,441	485	2,932	9,396	38,453	126,443	1,421	8,709	766,737	12
63,476	108,468	485	2,595	8,292	31,329	118,825	1,346	7,180	516,859	13
1,778	4,553	......	334	1,103	6,073	6,848	72	1,518	6,534	14
97	211	......	......	......	736	434	....	....	3,457	15
1,382	1,209	......	3	1	315	336	3	11	239,887	16
272	622	......	......	......	160	1,103	....	50	796	17
255	563	......	......	......	3	1,054	....	50	796	18
17	59	......	......	......	157	49	....	....	....	19
48,987	154,947	287	4,609	17,743	121,799	193,231	4,115	88,066	1,720,403	20
14,379	68,113	8	2,088	10,349	48,750	66,613	2,186	61,417	906,620	21
34,083	84,723	277	2,512	7,387	72,330	121,637	1,929	26,530	755,401	22
525	2,111	2	9	7	719	4,981	....	119	58,382	23
320	1,055	6	9	18	1,722	1,916	....	2	11,653	24
6	83	......	......	......	294	3,710	....	....	....	25
263	3,506	......	201	3,022	1,835	198,142	160	618	1,477	26
57	766	......	34	326	....	13,561	....	376	....	27
206	2,740	......	167	2,696	1,835	184,581	160	242	1,477	28
978	7,303	......	133	1,211	1,453	24,580	6,936	768	91,380	29
1,067	11,282	60	262	3,624	19,551	70,101	17,823	22,254	40,376	30
675	8,413	60	158	1,427	19,092	54,091	14,053	21,819	18,430	31
392	2,869	......	104	2,197	459	16,010	3,770	435	21,946	32
581	4,555	203	418	2,415	628	37,247	67	2,210	9,395	33
364	1,008	12	54	194	268	4,113	544	107	4,694	34
188	5,762	2,042	67	875	703	10,855	....	55,066	....	35
1,133	21,002	80	536	8,353	25,400	365,026	15,384	159,785	136,830	36
63	579	5	....	....	101	1,063	122	166	2,209	37
1,070	20,423	75	536	8,353	25,299	363,963	15,262	159,619	134,621	38
7,083	153,214	614	6,533	151,153	84,915	1,928,116	3,651	229,785	283,760	39
12	88	......	......	......	13	904	....	....	1,856	40
1,890	6,606	7	35	245	1,613	20,821	126	437	22,877	41

TABLE 90.—DETAILED STATEMENT FOR THE

[See note at head of this table, pp. 1172 and 1173.]

INDUSTRY.	Number of establishments reporting.	Total primary horsepower.	POWER AND FUEL USED. Primary power. Owned by establishments reporting.					
			Steam engines and turbines.		Internal-combustion engines.		Water wheels and water motors.	
			Number.	Horsepower.	Number.	Horsepower.	Number.	Horsepower.
1 Safes and vaults	33	5,342	11	1,240	5	150	......	....
2 Safes	17	2,770	11	1,240	......	....	......	....
3 Vaults	16	2,572	......	....	5	150	......	....
4 Salt	75	43,187	370	34,309	49	981	7	55
5 Sand and emery paper and cloth	11	3,977	21	3,080	......	....	1	40
6 Sand-lime brick	31	4,358	32	3,770	8	48	......	....
7 Sausage, not made in slaughtering and meat-packing establishments.	586	12,713	72	2,058	35	560	......	....
8 Sausage	514	11,079	63	1,889	31	503	......	....
9 Sausage casings	72	1,634	9	169	4	57	......	....
10 Saws	106	15,098	17	3,655	12	335	2	45
11 Scales and balances	74	7,451	6	620	13	301	2	40
12 Screws, machine	142	23,540	16	3,379	15	519	......	....
13 Screws, wood	11	7,764	10	3,060	......	....	......	....
14 Sewing-machine cases	5	10,656	17	9,550	3	1,050	......	....
15 Sewing machines and attachments	38	21,379	28	18,115	4	172	6	382
16 Sewing machines	28	20,929	27	17,915	4	172	6	382
17 Attachments	10	450	1	200	......	....	......	....
18 Shipbuilding, steel	157	475,567	343	95,034	58	2,671	......	....
19 New vessels	102	441,056	259	88,924	49	2,488	......	....
20 Concrete vessels	5	1,985	6	280	1	4	......	....
21 Repair work only	45	32,183	76	5,780	4	79	......	....
22 Small boats	5	343	2	50	4	100	......	....
23 Shipbuilding, wooden, including boat building.	777	78,144	446	26,166	403	4,348	5	71
24 New vessels	287	59,593	305	18,807	130	1,912	1	8
25 Repair work only	242	14,675	111	6,348	149	1,531	3	51
26 Small boats	227	3,370	28	941	121	880	......	....
27 Masts, spars, oars, and rigging	21	506	2	70	3	25	1	12
28 Shirts	841	14,944	78	6,992	66	638	5	302
29 Show cases	109	4,423	10	800	7	112	......	....
30 Signs and advertising novelties	306	7,730	23	2,843	23	299	3	46
31 Electric signs	35	531	......	....	4	89	......	....
32 Other signs	159	3,016	7	1,240	10	91	2	11
33 Advertising novelties	112	4,183	16	1,603	9	119	1	35
34 Silk goods, including throwsters	1,332	176,825	504	88,221	51	1,966	69	8,327
35 Finished products	1,015	115,700	382	64,941	39	1,468	52	6,333
36 Throwsters and winders	317	61,125	122	23,280	12	498	17	1,994
37 Silversmithing and silverware	93	6,940	25	3,750	5	132	4	200
38 Slaughtering and meat packing	1,004	359,212	1,711	238,017	92	2,018	9	574
39 Slaughtering	343	28,586	223	12,645	38	299	3	21
40 Meat packing	121	11,061	58	4,205	7	262	1	8
41 Slaughtering and meat packing	540	319,565	1,430	221,167	47	1,457	5	545
42 Smelting and refining, copper	33	321,610	303	186,286	9	425	9	7,550
43 Smelting	20	173,996	145	106,590	8	375	2	1,400
44 Smelting and refining[1]	13	147,614	158	79,696	1	50	7	6,150
45 Smelting and refining, lead	25	52,565	65	24,905	3	84	1	350
46 Smelting	18	42,372	51	18,125	3	84	1	350
47 Smelting and refining[2]	7	10,193	14	6,780	......	....	......	....
48 Smelting and refining, metals, not elsewhere specified.[3]	13	11,700	22	8,287	......	....	......	....

[1] Includes 4 establishments engaged exclusively in refining.
[2] Includes 2 establishments engaged exclusively in refining.

UNITED STATES, BY INDUSTRIES: 1919—Continued.

[See note at head of this table, pp. 1172 and 1173.]

POWER AND FUEL USED—continued.

Primary power—Contd.					Fuel used.					
Rented.			Electric motors run by current generated in the establishments reporting.		Coal.		Coke (tons of 2,000 lbs.).	Oil, including gasoline (barrels).	Gas (1,000 cubic feet).	
Electric.		Other.			Anthracite (tons of 2,240 lbs.).	Bituminous (tons of 2,000 lbs.).				
Motors.	Horse-power.	Horse-power.	Number.	Horse-power.						
379	3,952	....	139	515	1,459	10,924	545	6,760	16,928	1
161	1,530	....	139	515	1,191	7,243	421	6,514	15,008	2
218	2,422	....	....	....	268	3,681	124	246	1,920	3
381	6,706	1,136	745	8,065	81,251	957,447	6,920	143,627	45.085	4
95	857	....	43	370	9,385	9,702	....	....	....	5
23	540	....	3	20	1,200	21,673	28	1,270	....	6
1,193	10,053	42	24	168	4,469	19,682	1,661	2,982	66,093	7
1,022	8,645	42	24	168	4,005	16,612	1,636	2,918	49,388	8
171	1,408	....	....	....	464	3,070	25	64	16,705	9
988	11,011	52	57	640	816	39,531	1,253	39,423	69,293	10
772	6,480	10	2	8	1,028	16,287	4,695	2,455	15,816	11
2,498	19,619	23	118	2,172	1,610	36,492	136	14,459	110,153	12
288	4,704	....	22	679	9,909	10,127	113	3,504	3,550	13
12	56	....	210	4,453	....	28,057	2,074	....	18,009	14
297	2,692	18	1,343	16,025	73,561	34,680	10,894	16,975	81,603	15
256	2,442	18	1,326	15,905	73,561	32,357	10,894	16.725	79,203	16
41	250	....	17	120	....	2,323	....	250	2,400	17
18,296	377,862	....	2,320	49,792	37,392	785,898	96,717	1,075,728	694,467	18
17,150	349,644	....	2,290	49,337	30,683	737,666	86,327	1,061,034	693,911	19
157	1,701	....	....	....	....	1,379	10	1,493	....	20
973	26,324	....	26	447	6,511	46,535	10,377	13,189	556	21
16	193	....	4	8	198	318	3	12	....	22
2,628	47,119	440	146	1,362	12,842	82,815	973	58,123	6,994	23
1,854	38,456	410	51	656	6,546	45,857	442	50,077	3,665	24
457	6,730	15	90	530	5,308	31,782	516	7,459	1,365	25
265	1,549	....	5	176	966	5,146	15	586	1,964	26
52	384	15	....	....	22	30	....	1	....	27
2,539	6,958	54	572	2,533	18,343	33,049	443	2,879	56,404	28
586	3,436	75	7	43	106	7,501	....	184	7,701	29
1,628	4,526	16	483	1,214	2,495	34,932	395	4,629	35,453	30
164	442	....	....	....	231	2,948	8	59	7,137	31
459	1,663	11	71	321	722	16,950	114	4,332	15,342	32
1,005	2,421	5	412	893	1,542	15,034	273	238	12,974	33
22,579	75,234	3,077	12,731	32,748	306,165	269,717	1,002	46,506	44,724	34
19,567	40,295	2,663	12,372	29,491	214,188	198,093	383	46,075	25,117	35
3,012	34,939	414	359	3,257	91,977	71,624	619	431	19,607	36
719	2,761	97	274	1,756	2,364	13,477	41	35,247	35,505	37
8,954	117,913	690	7,537	95,635	222,891	3,802,849	32,170	1,912,519	1,291,318	38
761	15,116	505	185	2,072	11,849	137,827	16	63,293	26,293	39
942	6,586	....	59	774	7,186	85,259	282	3,916	42,422	40
7,251	96,211	185	7,293	92,789	203,856	3,579,763	31,872	1,845,310	1,222,603	41
2,932	127,349	....	2,689	56,906	179,026	1,088,511	397,762	2,543,121	712,817	42
1,491	65,631	....	1,058	28,322	1,632	460,546	306,058	1,894,812	....	43
1,441	61,718	....	1,631	28,584	177,394	627,965	91,704	648,309	712,817	44
856	24,329	2,897	244	8,206	7,276	292,806	321,442	202,088	20,940	45
617	20,916	2,897	150	5,832	2,658	215,817	277,577	27,126	10,049	46
239	3,413	....	94	2,374	4,618	76,989	43,865	174,962	10,891	47
137	3,413	....	311	5,217	8,201	72,074	38,429	149,939	1,092	48

[3] Includes "smelting and refining, antimony" and "smelting and refining, tin," to avoid disclosing individual operations.

TABLE **90.**—DETAILED STATEMENT FOR THE

[See note at head of this table, pp. 1172 and 1173.]

				POWER AND FUEL USED.					
				Primary power.					
				Owned by establishments reporting.					
	INDUSTRY.	Number of establishments reporting.	Total primary horsepower.	Steam engines and turbines.		Internal-combustion engines.		Water wheels and water motors.	
				Number.	Horsepower.	Number.	Horsepower.	Number.	Horsepower.
1	Smelting and refining, not from the ore.	61	7,921	23	2,590	11	435	......	....
2	Smelting and refining, zinc........	39	73,604	202	56,832	46	3,264	......	....
3	Pigs, bars, plates, and sheets...	33	66,540	188	55,467	46	3,264	......	....
4	All other..................	6	7,064	14	1,365	......	....	......	....
5	Soap.....................	263	33,710	240	24,787	12	201	1	40
6	Soda-water apparatus..............	58	4,146	6	781	5	335	......	....
7	Sporting and athletic goods........	154	6,875	17	2,190	16	275	9	580
8	Springs, steel, car and carriage, not made in steel works or rolling mills.	111	16,585	32	3,417	16	1,079	6	215
9	Carriage and wagon..........	13	1,770	1	75	1	25	1	90
10	Railway..................	6	1,957	12	1,546	4	140	......	....
11	Automobile...............	65	8,628	6	1,016	7	444	5	125
12	Machinery and other..........	27	4,230	13	780	4	470	......	....
13	Stamped and enameled ware, not elsewhere specified.	315	51,441	129	20,602	48	2,498	3	64
14	Stamped ware............	271	32,402	84	11,627	35	1,043	3	64
15	Enameled ware.............	35	14,934	38	7,975	13	1,455	......	....
16	Bathtubs.................	5	2,340	4	650	......	....	......	....
17	Lavatories and sinks..........	4	1,765	3	350	......	....	......	....
18	Stationery goods, not elsewhere specified.	180	8,342	18	1,349	9	179	4	285
19	Penholders..............	5	37	1	20	......	....	......	....
20	All other..................	175	8,305	17	1,329	9	179	4	285
21	Statuary and art goods............	68	684	1	60	4	64	......	....
22	Steam fittings and steam and hot-water heating apparatus.	247	67,504	113	21,956	21	291	1	60
23	Radiators and cast-iron heating boilers	71	21,395	31	3,458	8	136	......	....
24	All other..................	176	46,109	82	18,498	13	155	1	60
25	Steam packing..............	159	26,763	100	20,637	20	372	......	....
26	Steel barrels, drums, and tanks..	30	10,554	17	1,865	6	440	......	....
27	Stencils and brands............	64	374	1	18	2	5	......	....
28	Stereotyping and electrotyping....	166	9,613	1	35	3	31	8	400
29	Stoves and hot-air furnaces........	373	49,479	162	20,490	39	1,901	4	102
30	Stoves and ranges.............	272	39,600	143	16,516	28	1,611	2	12
31	Hot-air furnaces..............	95	9,417	19	3,974	10	255	2	90
32	Fireless cookers..............	6	462	......	....	1	35	......	....
33	Stoves, gas and oil..............	147	11,295	26	4,310	23	391	1	2
34	Structural ironwork, not made in steel works or rolling mills.	1,073	165,347	282	39,790	236	10,768	3	210
35	Sugar, beet..............	85	127,394	659	117,469	19	259	1	35
36	Sugar, cane..............	186	101,861	1,103	98,823	172	3,028	1	8
37	Sugar, refining, not including beet sugar.	19	52,541	296	52,181	......	....	......	....
38	Sulphuric, nitric, and mixed acids..	37	30,637	127	12,672	15	1,755	1	25
39	Surgical appliances..............	182	12,387	27	7,710	8	151	4	435
40	Suspenders, garters, and elastic woven goods.	179	9,028	27	3,019	3	55	9	635
41	Textile machinery and parts.......	417	41,997	139	20,247	50	862	41	2,595
42	Theatrical scenery..............	12	104	......	....	......	....	......	....
43	Tin and other foils, not elsewhere specified.	15	6,991	8	1,835	3	80	......	....
44	Tin foil..................	12	6,990	8	1,835	3	80	......	....
45	Aluminum and other..........	3	1	......	....	......	....	......	....

UNITED STATES, BY INDUSTRIES: 1919—Continued.

[See note at head of this table, pp. 1172 and 1173.]

POWER AND FUEL USED—continued.										
Primary power—Contd.					Fuel used.					
Rented.			Electric motors run by current generated in the establishments reporting.		Coal.		Coke (tons of 2,000 lbs.).	Oil, including gasoline (barrels).	Gas (1,000 cubic feet).	
Electric.		Other.			Anthracite (tons of 2,240 lbs.).	Bituminous (tons of 2,000 lbs.).				
Motors.	Horse-power.	Horse-power.	Number.	Horse-power.						
494	4,896	......	11	1,951	26,839	55,353	10,203	48,832	36,532	1
639	13,508	......	1,532	39,488	835,129	1,123,590	238,432	6,646	24,343,653	2
362	7,809	......	1,519	39,098	795,904	1,020,013	236,587	6,536	22,788,806	3
277	5,699	......	13	390	39,225	103,577	1,845	110	1,554,847	4
1,097	8,672	10	3,080	21,977	107,932	606,385	1,082	96,883	12,023	5
420	3,015	15	40	555	167	12,062	2,167	231	2,351	6
651	3,735	95	186	530	2,427	18,927	10	1,904	45,870	7
1,291	11,849	25	82	1,398	3,377	54,978	1,479	236,588	1,167,812	8
87	1,555	25	....	....	1,004	139	227	19,231	76,709	9
16	271	......	32	448	....	9,013	587	18,886	236,067	10
835	7,043	......	....	....	1,491	23,511	225	142,725	783,456	11
353	2,980	......	50	950	882	22,315	440	55,746	71,580	12
2,960	28,119	158	859	8,657	19,523	330,237	24,765	163,312	823,894	13
2,332	19,510	158	432	4,315	19,438	91,375	6,653	94,923	203,615	14
479	5,504	......	403	3,942	85	224,714	9,477	54,351	398,175	15
96	1,690	......	24	400	....	3,555	5,092	13,636	146,164	16
53	1,415	......	....	....	....	10,593	3,543	402	75,940	17
2,263	6,529	......	319	975	5,431	22,169	92	346	14,362	18
7	17	......	....	....	18	302	....	....	....	19
2,256	6,512	......	319	975	5,413	21,867	92	346	14,362	20
129	558	2	31	253	1,223	1,880	100	43	41,248	21
4,154	45,187	10	799	13,045	34,490	208,393	147,474	126,134	299,975	22
1,451	17,801	......	106	1,794	2,606	69,445	96,770	8,746	72,377	23
2,703	27,386	10	693	11,251	31,884	138,948	50,704	117,388	227,598	24
625	5,746	8	893	12,089	1,225	231,581	13,789	37,380	77,040	25
692	8,249	......	155	401	444	20,960	3,333	5,318	26,340	26
140	351	......	3	9	228	125	9	3	2,214	27
3,310	9,032	115	....	....	1,404	3,558	97	461	77,717	28
2,736	26,915	71	938	9,414	13,369	161,318	121,676	7,586	104,460	29
2,244	21,396	65	766	7,095	11,959	134,811	99,929	7,124	86,827	30
449	5,092	6	172	2,319	1,320	25,705	21,747	462	16,863	31
43	427	......	....	....	90	802	....	....	770	32
941	6,587	5	335	2,354	1,058	60,685	7,138	51,567	116,614	33
9,600	114,411	168	4,618	52,049	20,990	331,698	41,174	168,580	626,774	34
457	9,631	......	1,949	35,240	....	1,047,643	125,262	564,268	57,862	35
....	....	2	108	2,288	1,233	29,823	112	1,039,666	154,277	36
3	360	......	3,920	54,308	406,248	987,690	430	1,705,513	....	37
795	16,185	......	714	11,906	52,865	259,615	6,563	179,716	196,953	38
702	4,086	5	611	4,913	823	45,764	473	2,896	20,882	39
1,487	5,219	100	538	1,381	1,538	36,661	3	460	16,190	40
1,874	18,040	253	756	9,298	14,015	91,551	27,645	43,833	52,310	41
42	104	......	....	....	20	172	....	....	659	42
266	5,076	......	89	1,937	8,545	4,287	12	70	13,916	43
265	5,075	......	89	1,937	8,542	4,284	12	70	13,916	44
1	1	......	....	....	3	3	....	....	....	45

	INDUSTRY.	Number of establishments reporting.	Total primary horsepower.	POWER AND FUEL USED.					
				Primary power.					
				Owned by establishments reporting.					
				Steam engines and turbines.		Internal-combustion engines.		Water wheels and water motors.	
				Number.	Horsepower.	Number.	Horsepower.	Number.	Horsepower.
1	Tin plate and terneplate............	23	18,697	30	17,429	1	8	......	....
2	Tinware, not elsewhere specified...	236	30,499	107	11,550	30	978	2	12
3	Tobacco, chewing and smoking, and snuff.	247	18,893	154	15,026	8	43	12	282
4	Plug or chewing................	63	6,700	52	5,637	2	9	......	......
5	Smoking......................	120	7,361	48	5,265	4	15	1	5
6	Snuff........................	28	4,068	43	3,714	2	19	10	197
7	All other.....................	36	764	11	410	......	......	1	80
8	Tobacco, cigars and cigarettes......	1,052	24,504	94	13,187	24	302	2	120
9	Cigars.......................	958	10,851	57	4,201	24	302	2	120
10	Cigarettes...................	86	12,828	32	8,756	......	......	......	......
11	Cigars and cigarettes...........	8	825	5	230	......	......	......	......
12	Tools, not elsewhere specified......	1,072	68,381	114	16,844	148	5,367	55	3,299
13	Shovels, spades, scoops, and hoes.	39	8,685	25	2,655	13	1,117	8	620
14	Carpenters' tools, not elsewhere specified.	33	4,851	21	2,867	8	143	7	342
15	Machinists' tools...............	493	27,411	29	6,872	37	1,424	11	823
16	All other.....................	507	27,434	39	4,450	90	2,683	29	1,514
17	Toys and games....................	452	14,449	44	5,520	45	691	27	692
18	Trunks and valises................	438	7,703	43	4,455	10	159	......	......
19	Turpentine and rosin..............	504	2,303	253	1,343	269	884	16	30
20	Type founding....................	20	850	4	648	2	20	......	......
21	Typewriters and supplies..........	83	13,066	40	9,388	3	41	......	......
22	Typewriters and parts..........	36	11,781	30	8,672	1	25	......	......
23	Carbon paper.................	20	533	4	140	1	10	......	......
24	Ribbon......................	21	673	6	576	1	6	......	......
25	All other....................	6	79	......	......	......	......	......	......
26	Umbrellas and canes..............	176	3,383	15	2,464	9	53	......	......
27	Upholstering materials, not elsewhere specified.	160	19,826	105	9,400	12	100	25	1,728
28	Imitation leather and leatheroid	17	4,952	17	855	......	......	1	167
29	Excelsior....................	93	10,516	61	6,585	2	5	23	1,541
30	Curled hair..................	15	1,864	5	595	......	......	......	......
31	All other....................	35	2,494	22	1,365	10	95	1	20
32	Varnishes.......................	191	11,497	69	4,743	10	111	6	60
33	Vault lights and ventilators........	29	279	......	......	2	18	......	......
34	Vinegar and cider................	673	17,943	276	7,863	295	2,806	86	2,337
35	Vinegar.....................	179	7,759	105	4,471	63	576	7	100
36	Cider.......................	494	10,184	171	3,392	232	2,230	79	2,237
37	Wall paper, not made in paper mills	48	8,158	47	5,127	2	32	......	......
38	Wall plaster and composition flooring.	137	32,356	86	12,457	23	1,352	2	184
39	Washing machines and clothes wringers.	99	8,836	16	2,929	15	248	4	82
40	Waste..........................	88	11,391	25	3,431	15	439	6	435
41	Cotton......................	59	8,869	18	2,130	6	210	5	385
42	All other....................	29	2,522	7	1,301	9	229	1	50
43	Watch and clock materials, except watchcases.	24	252	1	100	2	50	1	6
44	watch materials..............	19	181	1	100	......	......	1	6
45	Clock materials..............	5	71	......	......	2	50	......	......
46	Watchcases.....................	33	4,275	11	2,040	6	1,004	1	250
47	Watches........................	16	7,202	24	6,040	3	435	......	......
48	Watches.....................	7	4,199	12	3,740	......	......	......	......
49	Watch movements.............	9	3,003	12	2,300	3	435	......	......

UNITED STATES, BY INDUSTRIES: 1919—Continued.

[See note at head of this table, pp. 1172 and 1173.]

Motors.	Horse-power.	Horse-power.	Number.	Horse-power.	Anthracite (tons of 2,240 lbs.).	Bituminous (tons of 2,000 lbs.).	Coke (tons of 2,000 lbs.).	Oil, including gasoline (barrels).	Gas (1,000 cubic feet).	
145	1,260	......	436	7,683	122	68,728	7	3,578	114,963	1
3,002	17,694	265	2,388	9,076	23,961	115,196	1,342	13,872	402,702	2
449	3,542	......	715	6,707	6,391	156,953	723	1,739	3,207	3
143	1,054	......	404	3,209	872	72,861	287	1,678	566	4
235	2,076	......	225	2,613	2,946	63,446	300	8	1,590	5
25	138	......	85	875	2,410	19,147	136	53	821	6
46	274	......	1	10	163	1,499	....	....	230	7
2,933	10,888	7	1,127	6,740	38,325	124,335	1,042	2,830	113,324	8
2,338	6,221	7	178	834	33,532	44,520	1,000	430	101,696	9
549	4,072	......	948	5,739	2,670	78,749	42	2,400	11,628	10
46	595	......	1	167	2,123	1,066	....	....	....	11
4,584	42,220	651	580	8,274	16,242	147,690	6,324	149,157	486,551	12
438	4,293	......	23	121	3,397	21,204	1,011	24,207	154,955	13
114	1,499	......	51	522	3,500	15,550	208	2,759	7,897	14
2,069	18,140	152	292	5,098	3,642	63,394	2,010	68,004	140,764	15
1,963	18,288	499	214	2,533	5,703	47,542	3,095	54,187	182,935	16
1,695	7,520	26	174	1,388	5,700	21,902	1,297	688	60,678	17
804	3,082	7	337	2,041	2,145	25,447	109	168	15,671	18
5	19	27	....	....	515	1,415	....	4,392	....	19
85	177	5	512	968	3,884	192	....	146	3,135	20
546	3,625	12	606	6,379	17,343	32,203	1,286	15,426	63,632	21
364	3,084	......	526	6,089	14,699	31,250	784	15,366	62,195	22
87	373	10	....	....	93	953	502	2	420	23
60	89	2	80	290	2,458	....	....	58	1,017	24
35	79	......	....	....	93	....	....	....	....	25
491	840	26	28	375	9,737	5,434	50	6,640	8,521	26
667	8,394	204	28	404	5,923	53,532	130	3,204	9,351	27
195	3,930	......	14	187	5,529	28,355	130	1,953	....	28
90	2,201	184	6	102	297	10,291	....	311	9,101	29
117	1,269	......	8	115	10	12,421	....	940	....	30
265	994	20	....	....	87	2,465	....	....	250	31
898	6,583	......	240	1,805	17,359	33,828	19,272	3,984	53,681	32
54	251	10	....	....	61	234	22	3	2,203	33
656	4,937	......	107	1,527	2,785	44,964	541	5,353	5,388	34
381	2,612	......	60	1,453	1,173	37,296	432	3,154	3,613	35
275	2,325	......	47	74	1,612	7,668	109	2,199	1,775	36
333	2,964	35	174	1,723	13,672	28,174	....	10	2,600	37
800	18,363	......	224	5,493	9,151	154,116	5,167	109,535	10,855	38
625	5,557	20	76	604	1,110	19,496	9,775	1,521	27,629	39
410	6,999	87	21	905	3,278	13,542	162	2,748	15,906	40
346	6,144	......	....	....	2,905	5,695	....	2,739	590	41
64	855	87	21	905	373	7,847	162	9	15,316	42
37	96	......	....	....	618	221	....	880	1,793	43
31	75	......	....	....	600	56	....	3	1,006	44
6	21	......	....	....	18	165	....	877	787	45
169	981	......	340	2,104	1,127	22,141	180	2,553	63,711	46
174	727	......	811	3,465	5,535	34,834	....	7,959	37,515	47
128	459	......	354	2,310	50	26,122	....	6,676	36,072	48
46	268	......	457	1,155	5,485	8,712	....	1,283	1,443	49

TABLE 90.—DETAILED STATEMENT FOR THE

[See note at head of this table, pp. 1172 and 1173.]

	INDUSTRY.	Number of establishments reporting.	Total primary horsepower.	POWER AND FUEL USED.					
				Primary power.					
				Owned by establishments reporting.					
				Steam engines and turbines.		Internal-combustion engines.		Water wheels and water motors.	
				Number.	Horsepower.	Number.	Horsepower.	Number.	Horsepower.
1	Wheelbarrows........	11	765	10	490	.....	....	.....	....
2	Whips......	22	853	2	175	2	45	2	35
3	Windmills......	30	4,761	21	2,860	10	203	8	1,160
4	Window and door screens and weather strips.	187	7,530	23	4,452	30	337	4	315
5	Window and door screens......	161	7,348	23	4,452	28	320	4	315
6	Weather strips.....	26	182	.....	....	2	17	.....	....
7	Window shades and fixtures......	197	8,948	22	6,015	6	114	4	300
8	Wire......	66	119,451	129	61,666	8	1,966	10	639
9	Wirework, not elsewhere specified	433	29,074	63	10,570	77	1,266	5	495
10	Wire rope and cable.........	15	7,199	6	2,480	1	15	.....	....
11	Woven-wire fencing......	50	3,633	3	725	11	249	.....	....
12	All other......	368	18,242	54	7,365	65	1,002	5	495
13	Wood distillation......	93	15,938	209	12,736	35	810	10	109
14	Wood preserving......	68	16,269	214	15,279	8	43	.....	....
15	Wood, turned and carved........	653	39,958	387	27,040	91	2,515	85	2,744
16	Wooden goods, not elsewhere specified.	228	25,906	128	19,396	49	629	27	894
17	Wool pulling......	23	2,162	19	1,320	1	150	2	120
18	Wool scouring......	32	9,790	28	5,865	.....	....	8	875
19	Wool shoddy......	77	16,694	45	6,544	2	76	46	2,949
20	Woolen and worsted goods........	835	468,480	957	311,966	45	1,793	616	76,181
21	Woolen goods......	552	172,947	451	85,499	39	1,577	467	46,705
22	Worsted goods......	283	295,533	506	226,467	6	216	149	29,476
23	All other industries [1]......	2	154	1	150	1	4	.....	....

[1] Comprises the following industries with number of establishments as indicated: "Straw goods, not elsewhere specified," 1; "whalebone cutting," 1; and "wood carpet," 3

UNITED STATES, BY INDUSTRIES: 1919—Continued.

[See note at head of this table, pp. 1172 and 1173.]

POWER AND FUEL USED–continued.										
Primary power—Contd.			Electric motors run by current generated in the establishments reporting.		Fuel used.					
Rented.					Coal.		Coke (tons of 2,000 lbs.).	Oil, including gasoline (barrels).	Gas (1,000 cubic feet)	
Electric.		Other.			Anthracite (tons of 2,240 lbs.).	Bituminous (tons of 2,000 lbs.).				
Motors.	Horse-power.	Horse-power.	Number.	Horse-power.						
26	275	....	73	135	181	1,729	2	798	....	1
80	598	....	1	1	69	1,373	....	11	900	2
80	463	75	145	1,626	208	18,921	6,945	1,877	619	3
430	2,411	15	166	1,640	180	7,660	....	400	8,210	4
368	2,246	15	166	1,640	141	7,448	....	398	5,739	5
62	165	....	....	....	39	212	....	2	2,471	6
692	2,517	2	381	5,268	1,944	59,798	500	850	7,447	7
2,148	55,030	150	1,181	31,616	12,573	726,940	18,547	176,282	419,310	8
2,364	16,705	38	1,217	6,212	21,158	72,873	2,390	25,639	104,211	9
243	4,704	....	197	1,941	17,474	6,802	240	11,115	38,995	10
334	2,654	5	31	638	198	8,548	266	2,150	25,381	11
1,787	9,347	33	989	3,633	3,486	57,523	1,884	12,374	39,835	12
147	1,533	750	144	2,278	40,677	308,747	....	67,259	1,798,302	13
58	782	165	131	2,438	27	139,410	88	73,965	343,230	14
949	7,423	236	435	2,723	1,631	14,999	182	1,624	19,314	15
568	4,955	32	370	3,369	1,019	16,082	268	971	3,272	16
50	572	....	11	160	664	17,268	1,352	3,372	4,217	17
301	2,970	80	44	574	576	55,920	45	7,753	....	18
326	6,998	127	66	2,201	6,813	45,660	535	225	4,513	19
7,332	76,279	2,261	10,601	154,841	214,399	1,541,539	3,551	851,348	52,094	20
3,308	38,410	756	2,326	25,791	53,192	646,140	3,010	42,973	47,012	21
4,024	37,869	1,505	8,275	129,050	161,207	895,399	541	808,375	5,082	22
....	....	....	....	....	2	900	....	....	550	23

TABLE 91.—DETAILED STATEMENT, FOR THE UNITED STATES,

[This table is made up in three

	DIVISION AND STATE.	Number of establishments.	Capital.	Expenses.		
					Salaries and wages.	
				Officers.	Clerks, etc.	Wage earners.
			Dollars.	*Dollars.*	*Dollars.*	*Dollars.*
1	**United States**	290,105	44,466,593,771	1,453,261,706	1,439,109,788	10,533,400,340
	GEOGRAPHIC DIVISIONS:					
2	New England	25,528	5,656,409,560	186,152,501	148,142,507	1,436,436,587
3	Middle Atlantic	88,360	15,005,389,662	502,479,188	516,906,197	3,464,931,287
4	East North Central	61,332	12,153,594,576	411,869,358	458,150,536	2,992,930,744
5	West North Central	29,166	2,679,626,453	91,230,833	108,265,529	546,172,557
6	South Atlantic	29,976	3,332,332,432	99,234,888	70,367,854	778,026,847
7	East South Central	14,655	1,296,448,908	41,539,706	29,900,128	298,710,318
8	West South Central	13,909	1,463,837,800	41,064,456	34,676,013	293,021,663
9	Mountain	7,612	833,984,188	17,043,867	15,554,727	141,900,942
10	Pacific	19,567	2,044,970,192	62,646,909	57,146,297	581,269,395
	NEW ENGLAND:					
11	Maine	2,995	419,158,006	11,300,621	6,202,232	94,225,346
12	New Hampshire	1,499	329,166,870	7,863,707	5,348,695	79,326,341
13	Vermont	1,790	134,314,391	4,717,000	2,628,179	34,083,935
14	Massachusetts	11,906	2,947,108,527	100,235,820	83,199,585	766,623,337
15	Rhode Island	2,466	594,337,448	18,563,184	12,450,797	137,495,377
16	Connecticut	4,872	1,232,324,318	43,472,169	38,313,019	324,682,251
	MIDDLE ATLANTIC:					
17	New York	49,330	6,012,082,567	248,707,927	264,839,976	1,458,206,804
18	New Jersey	11,057	2,815,577,127	89,134,009	81,940,258	600,658,345
19	Pennsylvania	27,973	6,177,729,968	164,637,252	170,125,963	1,406,066,138
	EAST NORTH CENTRAL:					
20	Ohio	16,125	3,748,743,996	114,246,012	159,468,347	944,651,734
21	Indiana	7,916	1,335,714,103	43,304,231	41,812,215	317,042,997
22	Illinois	18,593	3,366,452,969	130,029,640	144,586,709	801,087,359
23	Michigan	8,305	2,340,954,312	79,454,081	69,580,917	639,708,093
24	Wisconsin	10,393	1,361,729,196	44,835,394	42,702,348	290,440,561
	WEST NORTH CENTRAL:					
25	Minnesota	6,225	679,386,486	20,985,065	24,374,861	127,106,505
26	Iowa	5,683	403,205,513	15,244,798	18,799,162	90,117,169
27	Missouri	8,592	938,760,773	36,636,703	42,407,947	196,515,353
28	North Dakota	894	24,549,838	858,097	575,940	5,401,330
29	South Dakota	1,414	30,933,030	970,233	1,105,966	7,905,426
30	Nebraska	2,884	245,256,684	6,462,288	9,279,649	46,066,755
31	Kansas	3,474	357,534,129	10,073,649	11,722,004	73,060,019
	SOUTH ATLANTIC:					
32	Delaware	668	148,207,598	4,448,045	3,261,023	37,265,319
33	Maryland	4,937	619,606,983	20,943,430	21,060,577	147,866,545
34	District of Columbia	595	63,008,179	2,595,491	3,071,888	13,189,031
35	Virginia	5,603	463,644,498	15,286,404	10,621,680	120,006,452
36	West Virginia	2,785	339,189,678	11,070,734	6,615,339	101,840,420
37	North Carolina	5,999	669,144,096	15,198,496	8,575,837	126,680,099
38	South Carolina	2,004	374,537,636	7,340,777	3,172,252	62,565,413
39	Georgia	4,803	448,700,194	15,390,408	10,115,015	101,180,339
40	Florida	2,582	206,293,570	6,961,103	3,874,243	67,433,229
	EAST SOUTH CENTRAL:					
41	Kentucky	3,957	276,535,395	10,787,269	8,890,382	67,033,546
42	Tennessee	4,589	410,203,443	14,381,128	10,886,831	81,355,256
43	Alabama	3,654	455,592,733	11,128,502	7,438,903	99,065,800
44	Mississippi	2,455	154,117,337	5,242,807	2,684,012	51,255,716
	WEST SOUTH CENTRAL:					
45	Arkansas	3,123	138,817,974	6,288,697	3,040,346	47,186,189
46	Louisiana	2,617	462,209,057	12,808,549	10,137,708	94,405,732
47	Oklahoma	2,445	277,034,318	6,172,107	5,789,084	35,025,942
48	Texas	5,724	585,776,451	15,795,103	15,708,875	116,403,800
	MOUNTAIN:					
49	Montana	1,290	137,476,277	2,316,014	2,425,441	24,742,562
50	Idaho	922	96,061,709	1,559,287	1,142,260	18,548,272
51	Wyoming	576	82,287,667	1,001,689	700,599	11,188,979
52	Colorado	2,631	243,826,617	6,536,451	6,509,524	42,974,879
53	New Mexico	387	15,226,253	670,609	356,732	6,658,462
54	Arizona	480	101,486,070	1,555,227	1,556,611	12,014,769
55	Utah	1,160	140,785,034	3,010,721	2,669,764	21,454,997
56	Nevada	166	16,834,561	393,869	193,796	4,318,022
	PACIFIC:					
57	Washington	4,918	574,235,319	18,564,269	11,809,497	194,968,222
58	Oregon	2,707	237,254,736	7,815,628	6,183,543	81,093,784
59	California	11,942	1,233,480,273	36,267,012	39,153,257	305,207,389

BY GEOGRAPHIC DIVISIONS AND STATES: 1919.

sections, extending over pp. 1256 to 1261.]

FINANCIAL STATISTICS—continued.

Expenses—Continued.

| For contract work. | Rent and taxes. | | For materials. | | | Value of products. | Value added by manufacture. | |
	Rent of factory.	Taxes, Federal, state, county, and local.	Total.	Principal materials.	Fuel and rent of power.			
Dollars.	*Dollars.*	*Dollars.*	*Dollars.*	*Dollars.*	*Dollars.*	*Dollars.*	*Dollars.*	
464,403,700	212,043,089	2,079,369,357	37,376,380,283	35,730,393,727	1,645,986,556	62,418,078,773	25,041,698,490	1
37,708,367	18,808,711	287,517,450	3,951,908,159	3,811,641,271	140,266,888	7,183,070,799	3,231,162,640	2
284,969,260	98,194,254	592,798,292	11,424,095,826	10,843,787,208	580,308,618	19,854,772,760	8,430,676,934	3
65,338,316	49,201,761	636,645,750	10,621,687,089	10,113,945,205	507,741,884	17,737,479,599	7,115,792,510	4
12,012,532	13,589,886	109,362,746	3,778,125,226	3,689,936,604	88,188,622	5,187,064,766	1,408,939,540	5
24,242,084	8,847,690	248,012,643	2,596,264,687	2,489,150,307	107,114,380	4,455,151,691	1,858,887,004	6
10,793,258	2,929,027	47,635,105	977,824,517	897,695,744	80,128,773	1,642,391,461	664,566,944	7
9,667,736	4,516,358	49,757,307	1,547,993,571	1,500,847,009	47,146,562	2,277,861,293	729,867,722	8
5,341,432	2,642,234	23,199,996	610,239,118	569,007,154	41,231,964	922,676,092	312,436,974	9
14,330,717	13,313,168	84,440,068	1,868,242,090	1,814,383,225	53,858,865	3,157,610,312	1,289,368,222	10
3,630,949	895,234	19,906,648	254,568,523	241,084,861	13,483,662	456,821,783	202,253,260	11
2,417,380	420,772	14,800,993	239,527,617	231,599,446	7,928,171	407,204,934	167,677,317	12
753,451	571,601	5,331,327	95,172,581	91,624,436	3,548,145	168,108,072	72,935,491	13
22,744,566	12,835,105	150,635,915	2,260,713,036	2,188,353,757	72,359,279	4,011,181,532	1,750,468,496	14
4,181,783	1,724,458	35,755,093	415,989,203	402,205,892	13,783,311	747,322,858	331,333,655	15
3,980,238	2,361,541	61,087,474	685,937,199	656,772,879	29,164,320	1,392,431,620	706,494,421	16
211,490,532	66,165,498	250,322,316	4,943,213,919	4,780,956,952	162,256,967	8,867,004,906	3,923,790,987	17
27,716,816	10,327,057	120,286,240	2,270,473,279	2,194,512,449	75,960,830	3,672,064,987	1,401,591,708	18
45,761,912	21,701,699	222,189,736	4,210,408,628	3,868,317,807	342,090,821	7,315,702,867	3,105,294,239	19
17,609,025	16,130,610	179,262,557	2,911,947,871	2,729,033,617	182,914,254	5,100,308,728	2,188,360,857	20
3,802,139	4,571,897	74,714,283	1,174,950,568	1,084,756,375	90,194,193	1,898,753,387	723,802,819	21
32,006,039	20,073,028	136,886,105	3,488,270,446	3,362,381,054	125,889,392	5,425,244,694	1,936,974,248	22
8,232,883	5,291,962	164,878,414	1,919,243,243	1,852,906,090	66,337,153	3,466,188,483	1,546,945,240	23
3,688,230	3,134,264	80,904,391	1,127,274,961	1,084,868,069	42,406,892	1,846,984,307	719,709,346	24
4,005,045	3,427,503	21,634,431	883,089,777	860,607,299	22,482,478	1,218,129,735	335,039,958	25
1,470,139	2,074,772	13,025,449	520,240,807	506,034,871	14,205,936	745,472,697	225,231,890	26
4,338,793	5,575,016	56,875,231	1,056,457,164	1,029,812,810	26,644,354	1,594,208,338	537,751,174	27
118,159	176,291	477,948	44,489,499	43,477,254	1,012,245	57,373,622	12,884,123	28
175,574	387,828	803,193	42,985,870	41,821,013	1,164,857	62,170,782	19,184,912	29
1,398,349	981,961	7,584,131	480,774,122	473,636,425	7,137,697	596,042,498	115,268,376	30
506,473	966,515	8,962,363	750,087,987	734,546,932	15,541,055	913,667,094	163,579,107	31
324,714	144,375	7,591,222	85,432,933	81,453,158	3,979,775	165,073,009	79,640,076	32
8,150,474	2,753,829	21,248,188	549,347,379	527,696,308	21,651,071	873,944,774	324,597,395	33
2,770,506	399,949	2,481,001	30,940,100	27,462,366	3,477,734	68,826,570	37,886,470	34
2,848,581	1,746,148	34,699,686	371,540,833	352,059,572	19,481,261	643,511,621	271,970,788	35
2,121,422	616,158	15,692,215	270,940,596	250,192,627	20,747,969	471,970,877	201,030,281	36
3,069,322	757,201	122,172,794	526,906,181	512,989,300	13,916,881	943,807,949	416,901,768	37
685,107	401,565	17,809,258	227,986,384	220,416,614	7,569,770	381,452,984	153,466,600	38
3,333,902	1,270,369	19,665,114	440,490,057	428,431,511	12,058,546	693,237,096	252,747,039	39
938,056	758,096	6,653,165	92,680,224	88,448,851	4,231,373	213,326,811	120,646,587	40
2,317,700	881,349	16,039,040	235,715,626	224,485,689	11,229,937	395,660,417	159,944,791	41
3,614,386	1,181,272	17,575,062	344,766,730	330,552,028	14,214,702	556,253,162	211,486,432	42
2,177,015	645,237	9,643,790	300,664,290	248,975,401	51,688,889	492,730,895	192,066,605	43
2,684,155	221,169	4,377,213	96,677,871	93,682,626	2,995,245	197,746,987	101,069,116	44
2,696,617	574,174	3,890,118	102,812,977	99,881,410	2,931,567	200,312,858	97,499,881	45
3,428,125	1,007,451	27,280,752	431,403,867	421,147,141	10,256,726	676,189,770	244,785,903	46
475,181	663,719	4,945,225	312,605,829	301,539,816	11,066,013	401,362,869	88,757,040	47
3,067,813	2,271,014	13,641,212	701,170,898	678,278,642	22,892,256	999,995,796	298,824,898	48
555,842	410,640	1,802,125	122,151,924	117,594,952	4,556,972	166,664,518	44,512,594	49
1,342,453	201,343	1,833,127	43,948,505	42,345,546	1,602,959	80,510,749	36,562,244	50
629,174	125,243	5,257,141	42,250,528	40,510,297	1,740,231	81,445,394	39,194,866	51
1,903,281	1,153,923	9,411,473	174,870,275	160,204,060	14,666,215	275,622,335	100,752,060	52
385,810	90,599	192,440	7,727,483	5,974,121	1,753,362	17,856,602	10,129,119	53
153,153	181,156	1,605,291	92,645,437	84,273,872	8,371,565	120,769,112	28,123,675	54
357,022	424,987	2,883,265	110,154,349	103,106,399	7,047,950	156,933,071	46,778,722	55
14,697	54,343	215,134	16,490,617	14,997,907	1,492,710	22,874,311	6,383,694	56
5,376,513	2,807,238	21,044,415	443,177,531	431,896,276	11,281,255	809,622,984	386,445,453	57
1,936,402	1,285,941	12,417,927	206,206,041	201,354,721	4,851,320	366,782,627	160,576,586	58
7,017,802	9,219,989	50,977,726	1,218,858,518	1,181,132,228	37,726,290	1,981,204,701	762,346,183	59

TABLE **91.**—DETAILED STATEMENT FOR THE UNITED STATES,

			PERSONS ENGAGED IN MANUFACTURING INDUSTRIES.					
				Proprietors and officials.				
	DIVISION AND STATE.	Total.	Total.			Proprietors and firm members.	Salaried officials of corporations.	Superintendents and managers.
			Male.	Female.				
1	**United States**	10,812,736	656,915	25,942	269,137	132,467	281,253
	GEOGRAPHIC DIVISIONS:						
2	New England	1,535,055	67,305	3,036	21,470	13,870	35,001
3	Middle Atlantic	3,450,593	208,481	10,527	86,266	45,220	87,522
4	East North Central	2,884,836	156,410	5,450	49,586	34,767	77,507
5	West North Central	639,323	55,357	2,041	26,859	10,406	20,133
6	South Atlantic	931,595	62,769	1,485	29,883	11,136	23,235
7	East South Central	382,595	29,748	789	15,620	5,053	9,864
8	West South Central	339,950	27,826	774	13,437	4,505	10,658
9	Mountain	133,447	12,435	456	6,829	1,553	4,509
10	Pacific	515,342	36,584	1,384	19,187	5,957	12,824
	NEW ENGLAND:						
11	Maine	99,312	5,802	173	2,745	1,029	2,201
12	New Hampshire	90,332	3,583	153	1,426	581	1,729
13	Vermont	38,845	3,133	132	1,804	574	887
14	Massachusetts	812,521	33,391	1,738	9,451	7,105	18,573
15	Rhode Island	156,012	6,312	286	2,124	1,386	3,088
16	Connecticut	338,033	15,084	554	3,920	3,195	8,523
	MIDDLE ATLANTIC:						
17	New York	1,524,761	107,118	6,564	49,484	24,832	39,366
18	New Jersey	602,170	30,282	1,141	9,349	6,547	15,527
19	Pennsylvania	1,323,662	71,081	2,822	27,433	13,841	32,629
	EAST NORTH CENTRAL:						
20	Ohio	882,918	41,863	1,225	12,823	9,825	20,440
21	Indiana	330,145	19,742	620	6,768	4,015	9,579
22	Illinois	804,805	47,499	2,061	15,282	11,024	23,254
23	Michigan	549,069	26,280	884	6,762	5,266	15,136
24	Wisconsin	317,899	21,026	660	7,951	4,637	9,098
	WEST NORTH CENTRAL:						
25	Minnesota	147,678	11,617	414	5,128	2,416	4,487
26	Iowa	105,439	10,592	373	5,393	1,883	3,689
27	Missouri	244,939	18,471	736	7,676	4,282	7,249
28	North Dakota	6,148	1,117	37	774	112	268
29	South Dakota	9,034	1,774	48	1,410	134	278
30	Nebraska	49,076	4,940	197	2,916	741	1,480
31	Kansas	77,009	6,846	236	3,562	838	2,682
	SOUTH ATLANTIC:						
32	Delaware	32,972	1,688	53	593	325	823
33	Maryland	165,875	10,478	406	5,129	1,875	3,880
34	District of Columbia	14,101	1,217	77	515	281	498
35	Virginia	139,178	11,831	208	5,900	1,766	4,373
36	West Virginia	93,688	6,004	148	2,524	997	2,631
37	North Carolina	175,423	11,669	137	6,076	2,153	3,577
38	South Carolina	86,360	4,297	99	1,754	1,034	1,608
39	Georgia	141,012	10,121	222	4,776	1,943	3,624
40	Florida	82,986	5,464	135	2,616	762	2,221
	EAST SOUTH CENTRAL:						
41	Kentucky	83,954	7,500	281	4,003	1,486	2,292
42	Tennessee	113,300	9,463	263	4,892	1,798	3,036
43	Alabama	120,889	7,891	127	3,914	1,215	2,889
44	Mississippi	64,452	4,894	118	2,811	554	1,647
	WEST SOUTH CENTRAL:						
45	Arkansas	58,202	5,860	135	3,682	692	1,621
46	Louisiana	112,523	6,385	227	2,042	1,480	3,090
47	Oklahoma	38,314	4,388	108	2,320	628	1,548
48	Texas	130,911	11,193	304	5,393	1,705	4,399
	MOUNTAIN:						
49	Montana	20,692	1,962	61	1,200	184	639
50	Idaho	16,268	1,424	41	851	145	469
51	Wyoming	8,095	887	21	567	40	301
52	Colorado	44,729	4,270	202	2,234	692	1,546
53	New Mexico	6,646	617	18	336	59	240
54	Arizona	10,347	843	26	416	134	319
55	Utah	23,107	2,152	83	1,089	266	880
56	Nevada	3,563	280	4	136	33	115
	PACIFIC:						
57	Washington	150,479	9,169	247	4,195	1,584	3,637
58	Oregon	68,005	4,810	141	2,540	917	1,494
59	California	296,858	22,605	996	12,452	3,456	7,693

BY GEOGRAPHIC DIVISIONS AND STATES: 1919—Continued.

PERSONS ENGAGED IN MANUFACTURING INDUSTRIES—continued.

| Clerks. | | Average number of wage earners. | | | | Wage earners employed 15th day of— | | |
| Male. | Female. | Total. | 16 years and over. | | Under 16 years. | Maximum month. | Minimum month. | |
			Male.	Female.				
659,775	373,732	9,096,372	7,202,529	1,772,924	120,919	Dec. 9,663,170	Apr. 8,666,549	1
59,610	53,715	1,351,389	936,926	376,922	37,541	Dec. 1,454,828	Feb. 1,279,847	2
227,564	131,368	2,872,653	2,163,658	676,679	32,316	Dec. 3,046,393	May 2,766,820	3
209,026	117,332	2,396,618	2,015,702	357,210	23,706	Dec. 2,579,231	Apr. 2,253,009	4
55,743	26,547	499,635	405,849	90,040	3,746	Dec. 531,265	Apr. 471,343	5
35,415	14,714	817,212	649,172	151,552	16,488	Oct. 875,048	May 772,392	6
16,327	6,505	329,226	284,659	41,948	2,619	Dec. 360,017	June 307,391	7
19,901	6,205	285,244	260,790	22,549	1,905	Dec. 318,871	Apr. 262,942	8
8,055	3,285	109,216	101,324	7,244	648	Nov. 118,532	Mar. 99,618	9
28,134	14,061	435,179	384,449	48,780	1,950	Aug. 490,936	Feb. 364,304	10
2,499	2,187	88,651	68,293	19,976	382	Sept. 98,407	Mar. 78,696	11
1,669	1,853	83,074	57,163	25,052	859	Dec. 89,224	Apr. 78,849	12
1,172	917	33,491	28,541	4,847	103	Dec. 36,590	Feb. 31,135	13
32,788	30,768	713,836	478,449	211,951	23,436	Dec. 765,746	Feb. 677,294	14
5,243	4,506	139,665	87,023	46,766	5,876	Dec. 152,036	Feb. 126,903	15
16,239	13,484	292,672	217,457	68,330	6,885	Dec. 316,858	Apr. 279,347	16
111,573	71,376	1,228,130	873,333	348,509	6,288	Dec. 1,311,087	Jan. 1,179,216	17
41,066	20,995	508,686	385,401	116,289	6,996	Dec. 537,639	Mar. 482,240	18
74,925	38,997	1,135,837	904,924	211,881	19,032	Dec. 1,197,667	May 1,083,521	19
71,636	37,461	730,733	622,697	104,636	3,400	Dec. 790,681	May 687,683	20
20,747	11,456	277,580	233,578	40,340	3,662	Sept. 294,892	Mar. 261,725	21
64,397	37,734	653,114	522,687	121,962	8,465	Nov. 689,945	May 618,701	22
31,258	19,405	471,242	416,616	53,134	1,492	Nov. 522,876	Jan. 421,493	23
20,988	11,276	263,949	220,124	37,138	6,687	Dec. 284,119	May 250,122	24
13,288	6,736	115,623	96,387	18,874	362	Dec. 122,250	May 109,489	25
9,312	4,611	80,551	67,641	12,179	731	Nov. 85,825	Feb. 75,141	26
20,722	9,973	195,037	146,317	46,569	2,151	Oct. 209,704	Mar. 182,239	27
325	197	4,472	4,077	330	65	Oct. 4,850	Mar. 3,989	28
461	369	6,382	5,636	659	87	Dec. 6,902	Feb. 5,805	29
5,164	2,254	36,521	31,094	5,214	213	Dec. 38,189	Mar. 34,430	30
6,471	2,407	61,049	54,697	6,215	137	Nov. 66,069	Apr. 56,503	31
1,388	808	29,035	24,626	4,155	254	Sept. 33,438	Mar. 25,399	32
10,161	4,488	140,342	103,818	34,355	2,169	Oct. 160,567	Apr. 129,128	33
1,336	989	10,482	9,157	1,273	52	Dec. 10,723	Mar. 10,319	34
5,636	2,151	119,352	98,547	19,300	1,505	Oct. 131,916	Jan. 111,943	35
3,107	1,393	83,036	74,350	8,242	444	Sept. 89,041	May 79,617	36
4,334	1,624	157,659	113,352	38,063	6,244	Dec. 172,512	June 147,953	37
1,836	678	79,450	59,011	17,124	3,315	Dec. 86,825	June 74,165	38
5,398	1,830	123,441	98,059	23,308	2,074	Dec. 133,022	May 116,548	39
2,219	753	74,415	68,252	5,732	431	Dec. 78,140	Aug. 71,298	40
4,592	2,241	69,340	58,373	10,584	383	Dec. 75,688	June 65,941	41
5,961	2,446	95,167	75,515	18,434	1,218	Dec. 103,810	Feb. 88,865	42
4,395	1,317	107,159	96,517	10,104	538	Dec. 117,622	June 98,474	43
1,379	501	57,560	54,254	2,826	480	Oct. 64,736	Apr. 52,653	44
1,660	593	49,954	47,753	2,099	102	Sept. 58,553	Apr. 43,960	45
5,937	1,709	98,265	87,776	9,341	1,148	Nov. 117,665	Mar. 89,172	46
3,100	1,215	29,503	27,508	1,839	156	Dec. 32,259	Apr. 27,897	47
9,204	2,688	107,522	97,753	9,270	499	Dec. 114,416	Apr. 101,390	48
1,096	413	17,160	16,545	551	64	Nov. 18,228	Apr. 16,239	49
614	272	13,917	13,398	469	50	Nov. 16,342	Feb. 11,178	50
355	198	6,634	6,511	88	35	Nov. 7,560	Feb. 5,804	51
3,478	1,525	35,254	31,752	3,317	185	Aug. 37,553	Sept. 33,027	52
202	73	5,736	5,571	119	46	Aug. 6,253	Jan. 4,992	53
773	177	8,528	8,360	139	29	Oct. 8,945	Mar. 7,911	54
1,432	572	18,868	16,156	2,499	213	Oct. 22,592	Apr. 16,196	55
105	55	3,119	3,031	62	26	Jan. 3,485	Aug. 2,835	56
5,405	2,730	132,928	125,202	7,453	273	Sept. 146,872	Feb. 89,914	57
2,963	1,532	58,559	53,646	4,763	150	Aug. 62,488	Dec. 49,499	58
19,766	9,799	243,692	205,601	36,564	1,527	Aug. 282,312	Feb. 220,138	59

TABLE 91.—DETAILED STATEMENT FOR THE UNITED STATES,

	DIVISION AND STATE.	Number of establishments reporting.	Total primary horsepower.	PRIMARY POWER.					
				Owned by establishments reporting.					
				Steam engines and turbines.		Internal-combustion engines.		Water wheels and water motors.	
				Number.	Horsepower.	Number.	Horsepower.	Number.	Horsepower.
1	United States...	237,854	29,504,792	122,628	17,037,973	33,407	1,259,400	14,008	1,765,263
	GEOGRAPHIC DIVISIONS:								
2	New England......	21,575	3,796,846	9,876	1,867,434	1,676	34,459	4,586	747,617
3	Middle Atlantic....	69,485	8,537,660	30,392	5,250,772	8,101	410,312	3,641	396,168
4	East North Central.	49,604	7,735,137	24,477	4,361,731	7,383	428,493	1,894	252,829
5	West North Central.	23,956	1,594,112	7,767	801,743	5,012	102,124	569	92,753
6	South Atlantic.....	25,633	2,795,094	19,525	1,594,200	3,754	136,579	2,127	173,108
7	East South Central.	12,999	1,415,577	10,816	1,055,152	1,958	22,893	532	25,007
8	West South Central.	11,727	1,135,989	9,241	876,632	2,816	81,260	86	3,446
9	Mountain...........	6,227	686,579	2,423	399,946	868	9,971	188	15,656
10	Pacific.............	16,648	1,757,798	8,111	830,363	1,839	33,309	385	58,679
	NEW ENGLAND:								
11	Maine.............	2,481	547,028	1,493	173,855	400	4,481	1,104	274,528
12	New Hampshire....	1,350	349,138	815	147,240	106	1,676	641	115,375
13	Vermont...........	1,575	185,095	630	51,381	174	2,959	652	68,897
14	Massachusetts.....	10,080	1,729,878	4,268	964,932	407	11,227	1,252	189,302
15	Rhode Island.......	2,035	321,016	893	189,280	108	3,188	266	29,263
16	Connecticut.......	4,054	664,691	1,777	340,746	481	10,928	671	70,252
	MIDDLE ATLANTIC:								
17	New York.........	38,082	2,936,530	9,265	1,299,548	3,076	113,415	1,986	343,023
18	New Jersey........	9,209	1,146,744	5,593	781,434	1,303	40,830	304	12,528
19	Pennsylvania......	22,194	4,454,386	15,534	3,169,790	3,722	256,067	1,351	40,617
	EAST NORTH CENTRAL:								
20	Ohio..............	13,624	2,897,497	7,722	1,782,512	2,797	147,039	295	10,115
21	Indiana...........	6,540	1,095,912	3,609	521,446	1,003	189,271	158	10,162
22	Illinois...........	14,223	1,660,918	5,294	997,338	1,195	55,782	149	11,586
23	Michigan..........	6,923	1,202,128	3,411	592,911	776	19,695	395	40,346
24	Wisconsin.........	8,294	878,682	4,441	467,524	1,612	16,706	897	180,620
	WEST NORTH CENTRAL:								
25	Minnesota.........	5,150	473,957	1,827	198,186	762	33,848	205	73,661
26	Iowa..............	4,740	242,946	1,239	119,442	809	7,030	94	3,862
27	Missouri..........	6,773	477,303	2,873	269,657	1,228	22,049	98	3,386
28	North Dakota......	748	17,791	114	10,060	289	1,981	6	260
29	South Dakota......	1,222	22,191	172	8,360	444	3,282	9	307
30	Nebraska..........	2,420	125,814	464	66,449	682	8,203	81	4,940
31	Kansas............	2,903	234,110	1,078	129,589	798	25,731	76	6,337
	SOUTH ATLANTIC:								
32	Delaware..........	587	85,150	609	59,743	91	1,607	108	4,448
33	Maryland.........	3,907	406,768	2,287	177,106	567	65,493	222	9,007
34	District of Columbia	427	33,079	113	10,340	54	2,103	5	666
35	Virginia..........	5,008	419,946	4,181	256,766	532	9,067	630	39,087
36	West Virginia......	2,405	328,653	1,878	217,155	779	38,972	348	9,411
37	North Carolina.....	5,581	549,878	4,502	303,242	406	6,556	548	42,626
38	South Carolina.....	1,810	395,556	1,408	214,719	257	2,472	126	40,714
39	Georgia...........	4,101	436,608	3,031	243,642	607	5,603	125	26,906
40	Florida...........	1,807	139,456	1,516	111,487	461	4,706	15	243
	EAST SOUTH CENTRAL:								
41	Kentucky.........	3,372	247,573	2,119	175,210	733	10,623	123	3,758
42	Tennessee.........	4,088	338,814	2,961	227,206	547	5,718	297	7,534
43	Alabama..........	3,264	628,376	3,349	468,746	376	3,595	100	13,534
44	Mississippi........	2,275	200,814	2,387	183,990	302	2,957	12	181
	WEST SOUTH CENTRAL:								
45	Arkansas..........	2,806	214,194	2,685	183,400	422	6,620	25	706
46	Louisiana.........	2,225	388,605	3,079	332,154	587	13,928	5	60
47	Oklahoma.........	2,022	139,983	1,080	79,707	744	24,133	22	275
48	Texas.............	4,674	443,207	2,397	281,371	1,063	36,579	34	2,405
	MOUNTAIN:								
49	Montana..........	1,076	153,491	314	42,099	224	1,484	23	7,996
50	Idaho.............	809	73,876	409	53,304	60	578	34	1,751
51	Wyoming..........	468	17,869	148	8,255	129	1,718	15	391
52	Colorado..........	2,099	206,309	792	145,417	238	2,186	37	1,184
53	New Mexico........	324	17,260	136	12,595	75	920	4	381
54	Arizona...........	400	103,958	195	77,138	68	1,773	2	200
55	Utah..............	910	93,942	368	46,996	50	968	69	3,558
56	Nevada...........	141	19,874	61	14,142	24	344	4	195
	PACIFIC:								
57	Washington.......	4,224	687,436	3,629	453,306	536	6,123	87	7,723
58	Oregon...........	2,368	304,346	1,692	165,801	250	2,166	188	43,252
59	California.........	10,056	766,016	2,790	211,256	1,053	25,020	110	7,704

BY GEOGRAPHIC DIVISIONS AND STATES: 1919—Continued.

PRIMARY POWER—con.			ELECTRIC MOTORS RUN BY CURRENT GENERATED IN THE ESTABLISHMENTS REPORTING.		FUEL USED.					
Rented.					Coal.		Coke (tons of 2,000 lbs.).	Oil, including gasoline (barrels).	Gas (1,000 cubic feet).	
Electric.		Other.			Anthracite (tons of 2,240 lbs.).	Bituminous (tons of 2,000 lbs.).				
Motors.	Horse-power.	Horse-power.	Number.	Horse-power.						
996,000	9,347,556	94,600	487,021	6,969,721	14,334,402	203,463,622	42,595,019	92,029,692	341,921,022	1
118,896	1,130,308	17,028	68,337	796,265	1,565,254	10,932,267	782,919	7,857,807	2,639,620	2
314,503	2,455,360	25,048	192,294	2,612,659	11,639,452	76,806,237	16,961,032	23,172,383	124,317,839	3
279,394	2,659,498	32,586	150,948	2,224,002	532,197	69,093,939	16,591,794	12,529,927	54,257,941	4
72,761	596,189	1,303	22,903	324,007	84,805	11,365,499	898,079	6,515,603	16,396,769	5
74,766	887,201	4,006	25,254	500,852	347,542	13,785,729	1,526,627	2,834,029	50,754,152	6
22,783	311,138	1,387	7,952	149,005	23,036	13,034,746	4,289,624	473,780	3,985,152	7
22,337	218,558	6,093	6,666	132,395	95,812	2,092,839	308,467	16,508,037	76,312,121	8
18,002	259,619	1,387	4,408	91,595	35,975	5,519,721	962,659	4,170,820	5,051,786	9
72,558	829,685	5,762	8,259	138,941	10,329	832,645	273,818	17,967,306	8,205,642	10
7,043	92,749	1,415	3,306	72,047	43,234	1,257,623	21,972	575,477	45,503	11
6,379	84,601	246	2,918	67,117	286,885	539,405	30,964	606,054	20,910	12
4,478	61,090	768	759	12,298	46,627	236,517	13,549	28,997	106,306	13
65,360	551,521	12,896	39,696	424,274	693,759	5,634,701	501,293	3,753,560	1,222,444	14
12,231	97,957	1,328	7,653	65,956	96,628	982,891	51,853	1,413,515	616,995	15
23,405	242,390	375	14,005	154,573	398,121	2,281,130	163,288	1,480,204	627,462	16
170,262	1,170,977	9,567	54,669	512,861	3,805,763	11,533,633	3,019,517	6,996,974	4,712,372	17
41,180	305,762	6,190	36,582	418,391	3,581,497	6,701,052	693,592	6,623,381	1,969,277	18
103,061	978,621	9,291	101,043	1,681,407	4,252,192	58,571,552	13,247,923	9,552,028	117,636,190	19
82,899	945,341	12,490	46,219	819,383	108,606	25,499,869	8,640,711	2,025,606	45,014,790	20
36,392	373,689	1,344	16,581	279,065	31,099	13,577,580	2,693,061	2,790,821	2,308,659	21
79,263	590,241	5,971	43,506	584,326	238,451	16,502,727	3,903,043	4,990,756	3,557,698	22
53,626	540,757	8,419	23,052	277,514	50,516	8,241,877	812,041	1,891,458	2,105,985	23
27,214	209,470	4,362	21,590	263,714	103,525	5,271,886	542,938	831,286	1,270,809	24
18,119	167,965	297	4,715	87,154	41,074	2,483,593	440,452	327,706	1,438,853	25
14,605	112,486	126	3,895	53,799	15,400	2,154,407	134,841	600,399	181,957	26
23,502	181,556	655	9,579	106,016	14,652	4,117,582	194,758	1,871,290	1,658,684	27
1,230	5,490	......	127	1,283	1,736	192,434	1,498	4,883	6,451	28
2,032	10,227	15	73	903	2,784	96,832	9,103	78,619	11,992	29
6,285	46,177	45	1,970	26,572	2,946	917,608	56,904	442,968	75,956	30
6,988	72,288	165	2,544	48,280	6,213	1,403,043	60,523	3,189,738	13,022,876	31
1,617	19,307	45	1,663	25,221	38,185	507,354	15,712	196,446	80,062	32
15,654	155,031	131	5,325	158,780	65,239	2,020,167	438,764	1,119,628	1,270,991	33
2,702	19,960	10	181	1,983	87,731	125,170	15,579	400,383	964,794	34
12,773	114,818	208	3,722	73,637	23,475	3,232,388	603,617	302,370	44,046	35
5,140	62,917	198	5,106	92,307	66,558	4,007,630	341,030	40,751	48,247,748	36
16,339	197,384	70	5,448	63,162	43,425	1,359,142	14,980	51,209	9,050	37
7,985	137,561	90	1,275	36,587	14,451	818,847	17,346	45,738	35,583	38
9,951	157,568	2,889	2,008	36,695	3,368	1,452,454	45,215	255,174	81,153	39
2,605	22,655	365	526	12,480	5,110	262,577	36,384	422,330	20,725	40
6,187	56,808	1,174	2,429	37,572	1,596	2,200,661	252,519	95,200	3,602,772	41
8,469	98,274	82	2,282	33,137	5,675	2,738,350	475,310	110,976	161,850	42
6,666	142,412	89	2,575	57,111	4,891	7,649,059	3,556,934	196,261	216,135	43
1,461	13,644	42	666	21,185	10,874	446,676	4,861	71,343	4,395	44
2,484	21,493	1,975	640	14,098	7,824	285,741	10,397	47,315	6,723,496	45
4,394	41,091	1,372	1,967	43,113	4,955	474,133	101,698	2,908,718	24,181,161	46
3,976	35,435	433	981	19,170	44,433	478,734	37,409	3,172,260	40,523,914	47
11,483	120,539	2,313	3,078	56,014	38,600	854,231	158,963	10,379,744	4,883,550	48
3,715	101,910	2	205	4,297	234	539,302	64,795	24,256	97,410	49
1,636	18,207	36	369	11,682	353	152,014	24,429	24,536	3,751	50
898	7,500	5	137	1,740	70	115,957	2,660	1,283,692	4,793,519	51
5,717	57,323	199	1,824	28,713	33,331	2,946,699	530,304	152,558	114,840	52
512	3,364	......	98	1,814	589	572,527	831	87,567	1,056	53
1,354	24,847	......	741	20,056	159	44,976	143,567	2,093,148	10,676	54
3,738	41,275	1,145	778	17,446	1,224	1,030,819	169,969	259,465	24,675	55
432	5,193	......	256	5,847	15	117,427	26,104	245,598	5,859	56
13,944	215,921	4,363	3,052	62,234	4,502	642,865	68,205	1,769,087	215,511	57
7,544	92,576	551	1,251	25,611	1,825	72,695	10,970	1,370,332	402,457	58
51,070	521,188	848	3,956	51,096	4,002	117,085	194,643	14,827,887	7,587,674	59

MINES AND QUARRIES

CONTENTS.

MINES AND QUARRIES.

DEFINITIONS AND EXPLANATION OF TERMS.

This chapter presents in condensed form statistics collected for the census of mines and quarries of 1919, and comparative figures for prior censuses. It is designed to meet the requirements of those who desire statistics for the United States as a whole, for the principal mining industries, and for states. The general report and analytical tables, and also detailed statistics for the states and selected industries are contained in the special report of mines and quarries Volume XI. An explanation of the terms used in the accompanying tables is given below.

Scope of census.—Census statistics of mines and quarries, and petroleum and natural-gas wells are compiled primarily for the purpose of showing the absolute and relative magnitude of the different branches of industry covered and their growth or decline. Incidentally, the effort is made to present data throwing light upon character of ownership, size of enterprises, and similar subjects. When use is made of the statistics it is imperative that due attention be given to their limitations, particularly in connection with any attempt to derive from them figures purporting to show average wages, cost of production, or profits.

The census did not cover enterprises which were idle, that is, in which neither productive work nor development work was done during the entire year; or enterprises the products of which were valued at less than $500, or in the case of the bituminous coal mining industry, producing less than 1,000 tons; or, if not productive, in which development work amounting to less than $5,000 was done.

Period covered.—The returns relate to the calendar year 1919, or the business year which corresponded most nearly to that calendar year, and cover a year's operations, except for enterprises which began or discontinued business during the year.

The enterprise.—The term enterprise represents one or more mines and quarries, wells or groups of wells, or natural-gas gasoline plants all under the same state operated under a common ownership or unified control, or for which only one set of books of account was kept, and for which a single report was secured. It may cover plants at several localities within the same state. If plants under unified control were not all located within the same state, separate reports were secured in order that statistics for the several enterprises thus defined might be included in statistics for the states in which they were located. The enterprise is further defined as being limited to a single industry. Separate reports were secured with very few exceptions for each industry conducted by an operator, and only where combined reports on two or more industries could not be separated does a single enterprise cover more than one industry. The number of enterprises shown in the tables is equivalent to the number of individual reports tabulated.

Number of mines, quarries, wells, and plants.—Under these designations is given the count of the number of mines, quarries, wells, and gasoline plants shown by the returns received. The unit of enumeration for mines and quarries was difficult to define. As a rule each group of workings at a given locality in which operations were conducted as a unit or were unified by common management or joint handling of some part of the mining process, has been considered as a single mine or quarry. Many individual openings, therefore, are not counted as individual mines. The total number reported comprises those in operation or in the course of development during the year 1919. For petroleum and natural-gas wells the individual wells were counted and the total number productive December 31, 1919, was reported. The number of natural-gas gasoline plants is the total number reported in operation during the year.

Classification by industries.—The enterprises reported have been grouped by industries according to the kind of products. Only a few enterprises made consolidated reports covering more than one kind of product. In such cases classification was determined by the product of chief value.

Influence of increased prices.—In comparing figures for cost of supplies and materials, and value of products, with the corresponding figures for earlier censuses, account should be taken of the general increase in the prices of commodities during recent years. To the extent to which this factor has been influential the figures fail to afford an exact measure of the increase or the decrease in the volume of business.

Persons engaged in the industries.—The following general classes of persons engaged in the mines and quarries and petroleum and natural-gas industries were distinguished: (1) Proprietors and firm members; (2) salaried officers of corporations; (3) superintendents and managers; (4) technical employees, (5) clerks (including other subordinate salaried employees); and (6) wage earners. In the reports for the census of 1909 the fourth class, technical employees, was not distinguished and was probably included with other salaried employees.

The number of persons engaged in each industry, segregated by occupation, sex, and, in the case of wage earners, also by age (whether under 16 or 16 and over), was reported for a single representative day. The 16th of December was selected as representing for most industries normal conditions of employment, but where this date was not a representative day report for another date was requested.

The number of employees other than wage earners thus reported for the representative date has been treated as equivalent to the average for the year, since the number of employees of this class does not ordinarily vary much from month to month. The average number of wage earners has been obtained in the manner explained in the next paragraph.

In addition to the more detailed report by occupation, sex, and age of the number of wage earners on the representative date, a report was obtained of the number employed on the 15th of each month, without distinction of sex or age. From these figures the average number of wage earners for the year has been calculated by dividing the sum of the numbers reported for the several months by 12. The importance of the industry as an employer of labor is believed to be more accurately measured by this average than by the number employed at any one time or on a given day.

The number of wage earners reported for the representative day is given in the table of detailed statistics for the industries, in connection with the classification of wage earners by occupation which was made for the representative day. This number is not used in any other way because, in view of the unavoidable variations of date, such a total is believed to be less significant than the average number. It would involve more or less duplication of persons working in different industries at different times, would not represent the total number employed in all industries at any one time, and would give undue weight to seasonal industries as compared with industries in continuous operation.

Salaries and wages.—Under these heads are given the total payments during the year for salaries and wages, respectively. The Census Bureau has not undertaken to calculate the average annual salaries of either salaried employees or wage earners. Such averages would possess little real value, because they would be based on the earnings of employees of both sexes, of all ages, in different occupations, and of widely varying degrees of skill. Furthermore, so far as wage earners are concerned, it would be impossible to calculate accurately even so simple an average as this, since the number of wage earners fluctuates rapidly and irregularly in every industry, and in some to a very great extent from day to day. The Census Bureau figures for wage earners, as already explained, are averages based on the number employed on the 15th of each month and while representing the number according to the pay rolls of to whom wages were paid on that date, no doubt represent a larger number than would be required to perform the work in any industry if all were continuously employed during the year.

Prevailing hours of labor.—No attempt was made to ascertain the number of wage earners working a given number of hours per week. The inquiry called merely for the prevailing practice followed in each enterprise. Occasional variations in hours in an establishment from one part of its year to another were disregarded, and no attention was paid to the fact that a few wage earners might have hours differing from those of the majority. All the wage earners of each enterprise are therefore counted in the class within which the enterprise itself falls. In most enterprises, however, practically all the wage earners work the same number of hours, so that the figures are substantially correct representation of the hours of labor.

Capital.—The instructions on the schedule for securing data relating to capital were as follows: "The answer should show the total amount of capital, owned and borrowed, invested by the operator in the enterprise on the last day of the business year reported. *Do not* include securities and loans representing investments in other enterprises." These instructions were identical with those employed at the Census of 1909. The reports received in respect to capital, however, have in so many cases been defective that the data compiled are of value only as indicating very general conditions. While there are some enterprises maintaining accounting systems such that an accurate return for capital could be made, this is not true of the great majority, and the figures therefore do not show the actual amount of capital invested.

Expenses.—The expenses reported in the Census of 1919 include salaries and wages; the cost of supplies, materials, and fuels, including the freight on these; cost of power purchased; the cost of contract work; and taxes paid or assessed. The Census of 1909 reported in addition the items of royalties and rents paid and taxes paid or assessed. The present census covered by the present census all other items of expense incident to that year's business except interest on indebtedness, dividends, and allowances for depreciation.

Supplies and materials, fuel, and power.—Statistics as to supplies and materials, fuel, and power relate to the cost of these used during the year, which may be more or less than the amount purchased during the year. The term "supplies and materials" covers mine, mill, quarry, and well supplies, and ores, coal, and natural gas purchased for treatment, resale, or distribution.

Contract work.—The amounts reported under this head include expenditures for both productive operations and those prosecuted for development only; they are in effect indirect expenditures for salaries, wages, supplies and materials, fuel, and power.

Royalties and rents.—The amounts given under this head represent the payment to fee holders of the value of share of product credited to fee holders for mineral output from leased land and also rents paid for plants, equipment, and privileges or easements.

Taxes.—The taxes include Federal capital stock; corporation income, and excess profits tax; and also state, county, and local taxes. The data compiled in respect to Federal taxes are very defective largely for the reason that many mining corporations are engaged in other business and have sources of income other than mining and do not pay Federal taxes on mining separately. For many of these corporations no data have been obtained; for others satisfactory segregation of mining could not be made.

Expenditures for development work.—The above expenses reported as defined above include costs of both productive operation and development work. In the statistics on producing enterprises that part of the expenses for salaries, wages, contract work, supplies and materials, fuel, and power which was credited by the mine operators to development work is shown as expenditures for development work. In the statistics for nonproducing enterprises the total of all these expenses is given as expenditure for development work.

Value of products.—The amounts given under this heading represent the selling value at point of production or f. o. b. point of shipment; of such other value as may represent the net value or amount received for the product mined in 1919 under the terms by which it was disposed of, and also includes the value at point of production of products used by the operating company.

Cost of mining and profits.—The census data do not show the entire cost of mining and well operations, and consequently can not be used for the calculation of profits. No account has been taken of depreciation or interest; rent of offices and buildings other than those connected with mine or quarry operation; insurance, selling, and other sundry expenses.

Lands controlled.—The inquiry on land tenure was confined to the land pertaining to the mining or well operators covered by the report. In many of these, however, land held in reserve for future development and for speculative or other purposes not pertaining to mining was included in the returns, and also a large number of more or less unsatisfactory estimates were included. Nevertheless, it is believed that the data presented reflect fairly the conditions as to land tenure in the mining industries, and show correctly the order of magnitude of land holdings pertaining to mining enterprises.

Power used.—The item, aggregate horsepower, represents the horsepower of prime movers used by the enterprises for generating power plus horsepower of motors, principally electric, and of other equipment operated by power purchased from other concerns. It does not cover the power of electric motors taking their current from generators operated by prime movers reported by the same enterprise (such equipment is reported separately), because its inclusion would obviously result in duplication. The figures on power represent the rated capacity of the engines, motors, etc., and not the amount of power in actual daily use.

Fuel.—Statistics of the quantity of fuel used are shown only for anthracite and bituminous coal, coke, wood, oil, and gas. They relate to the quantity used during the year, which may be more or less than the quantity purchased. As only the principal varieties of fuel are shown, no comparison can be made with the total cost of all fuel.

TABLE 1.—SUMMARY OF PRINCIPAL STATISTICS, ALL ENTERPRISES: 1919.

	Total.	Continental United States.	Alaska.	Hawaii.	Porto Rico.
Number of enterprises	22,361	21,997	346	5	13
Number of mines and quarries	14,802	14,417	367	5	13
Number of petroleum and natural-gas wells	257,681	257,673	8		
Number of natural-gas gasoline plants	1,115	1,115			
Persons engaged	1,088,444	1,084,796	3,267	155	226
Proprietors and firm members, total	22,769	22,155	593	4	17
Number performing manual labor	5,783	5,272	505		6
Salaried employees	75,688	75,457	199	6	26
Wage earners (average number)	989,987	987,184	2,475	145	183
Wage earners, Dec. 15, or nearest representative day	1,100,186	1,096,458	[1] 3,379	140	209
Above ground	389,523	386,932	2,242	140	209
Below ground	710,663	709,526	1,137		
Power used (aggregate horsepower)	6,816,814	6,786,475	29,979	325	35
Capital	$7,225,446,992	$7,108,623,496	$116,626,441	$112,882	$84,173
Principal expenses	2,556,682,424	2,545,925,350	10,493,020	171,850	92,204
Salaries	151,820,643	151,272,451	533,076	5,533	9,583
Wages	1,309,565,597	1,304,409,342	5,010,611	89,365	56,279
Supplies and materials	531,688,470	528,853,639	2,789,755	34,423	10,653
Cost of ore, coal, and natural gas purchased as material or for resale	35,905,352	35,905,352			
Fuel and purchased power	124,610,053	123,509,588	1,080,348	14,560	5,557
Royalties and rents	176,478,995	176,129,858	314,066	26,282	8,789
Taxes	141,878,154	141,567,734	307,390	1,687	1,343
Contract work	82,696,872	82,239,098	457,774		
Value of products	3,174,507,462	3,158,463,966	15,634,801	250,538	158,157

[1] For Alaska a report for Sept. 15 was requested.

TABLE 2.—PRINCIPAL STATISTICS, PRODUCING AND NONPRODUCING ENTERPRISES: 1919.

	All enterprises.	Producing enterprises.	NONPRODUCING ENTERPRISES.	
			Number or amount.	Per cent of total.
Number of enterprises	21,997	21,280	717	3.3
Number of mines and quarries	14,417	13,844	573	4.0
Number of petroleum and natural-gas wells	257,673	257,673		
Number of natural-gas gasoline plants	1,115	1,115		
Persons engaged	1,084,796	1,077,675	7,121	0.7
Proprietors and firm members	22,155	21,918	237	1.1
Number performing manual labor	5,272	5,245	27	0.5
Salaried employees	75,457	74,197	1,260	1.7
Wage earners (average number)	987,184	981,560	5,624	0.6
Wage earners, Dec. 15, or nearest representative day	1,096,458	1,088,189	8,269	0.8
Above ground	386,932	382,766	4,166	1.1
Below ground	709,526	705,423	4,103	0.6
Power used (aggregate horsepower)	6,786,475	6,723,786	62,689	0.9
Capital	$7,108,623,496	$6,955,466,831	$153,156,665	2.2
Principal expenses:				
Salaries	151,272,451	149,328,985	1,943,466	1.3
Wages	1,304,409,342	1,295,936,226	8,473,116	0.6
Supplies and materials	528,853,639	519,593,676	9,259,963	1.8
Cost of ore, coal, and natural gas purchased as material or for resale	35,905,352	35,905,352		
Fuel and purchased power	123,509,588	122,105,930	1,403,658	1.1
Royalties and rents	176,129,858	175,293,984	835,874	0.5
Taxes	141,567,734	140,999,626	568,108	0.4
Contract work	82,239,098	79,380,177	2,858,921	3.5
Expenditures for development (included in the above items)	334,015,265	311,276,508	22,738,757	6.8
Value of products	3,158,463,966	3,158,463,966		

TABLE 3.—COMPARATIVE SUMMARY, PRODUCING ENTERPRISES: 1919, 1909, 1902, AND 1889.

	1919	1909	1902	1889	PER CENT OF INCREASE.[1]		
					1909–1919	1902–1909	1889–1902
Number of enterprises........	21,280	21,268	46,858	(²)	0.1	−54.6	......
Number of mines and quarries......................	13,844	18,164	17,039	22,084	−23.8	6.6	−22.8
Number of petroleum and natural-gas wells...........	257,673	166,320	123,200	37,410	54.9	35.0	229.3
Number of natural-gas gasoline plants.................	1,115	....	....	....	......	......	......
Persons engaged............	1,077,675	1,041,682	....	....	3.5	......	......
Proprietors and firm members, total.........	21,918	29,922	(²)	(²)	−26.7	......	......
Number performing manual labor......	5,245	8,861	(²)	(²)	−40.8	......	......
Salaried employees.......	74,197	44,127	38,128	6,541	68.1	15.7	482.9
Wage earners (average number).............	981,560	967,633	581,728	536,043	1.4	66.3	8.5
Wage earners, Dec. 15, or nearest representative day..................	1,088,189	1,065,283	³ 581,728	³ 536,043	2.2	......	8.5
Above ground........	382,766	366,962	221,505	244,127	4.3	65.7	−9.3
Below ground........	705,423	698,321	360,223	291,916	1.0	93.9	23.4
Power used (aggregate horsepower).................	6,723,786	4,608,253	2,867,562	(⁴)	45.9	60.7	......
Capital....................	$6,955,466,831	$3,380,525,841	(²)	$1,310,535,318	105.8	......	......
Principal expenses:							
Salaries...............	149,328,985	53,393,551	$39,020,552	5,520,600	179.7	36.8	606.8
Wages................	1,295,936,226	586,774,079	369,959,960	222,041,887	103.8	58.6	66.6
Supplies and materials...	519,593,676	173,411,438	⁵ 123,814,967	86,075,925	199.6	......	43.8
Cost of ore, coal, and natural gas purchased as material or for resale...	35,905,352	29,318,316	....	....	22.5	......	......
Fuel and purchased power.................	122,105,930	45,136,550	(⁴)	(⁴)	170.5	......	......
Royalties and rents......	175,293,984	63,973,585	34,530,713	(⁴)	174.0	85.3	......
Taxes....................	140,999,626	17,796,763	(⁴)	(⁴)	692.3	......	......
Contract work..........	79,380,177	28,887,898	20,677,938	(⁴)	174.8	39.7	......
Value of products...........	3,158,463,966	1,238,410,322	796,826,417	438,111,548	155.0	55.4	81.9

[1] A minus sign (−) denotes decrease. Percentages are omitted where figures are not comparable.
[2] Not reported.
[3] Average number.
[4] Comparable figures not available.
[5] Includes cost of fuel.

TABLE 4.—COMPARISON OF VALUE OF PRODUCTS FOR THE LEADING MINING INDUSTRIES: 1919, 1909, AND 1902.

INDUSTRY.	1919	1909	1902	PER CENT OF INCREASE.[1]	
				1909–1919	1902–1909
Coal:					
Anthracite....................	$364,084,142	$149,180,471	$76,173,586	144.1	95.8
Bituminous....................	1,145,977,565	427,962,464	290,858,483	167.8	47.1
Petroleum and natural gas.........	931,793,423	185,416,684	102,265,602	402.5	71.6
Iron ore.............................	218,217,905	106,947,082	65,465,321	104.0	63.4
Copper.............................	181,258,087	134,616,987	51,178,036	34.6	163.0
Lead and zinc......................	75,579,347	31,363,094	14,600,177	141.0	114.8
Gold and silver, lode mines........	58,832,330	83,885,928	77,154,326	−29.9	8.7
Limestone.........................	52,943,924	29,832,492	30,441,801	77.5	−2.0
Granite............................	18,279,345	18,997,976	18,257,944	−3.8	4.1
Sandstone.........................	10,684,969	9,290,829	11,022,460	15.0	−15.7
Phosphate rock....................	10,300,198	10,781,192	4,922,943	−4.5	119.0
Gold, placer mines.................	9,368,561	10,237,252	5,327,726	−8.5	92.2

[1] A minus sign (−) denotes decrease.

TABLE 5.—COMPARISON OF VALUE OF PRODUCTS, BY STATES: 1919, 1909, AND 1902.

STATE.	1919	1909	1902	PER CENT OF INCREASE.[1]	
				1909–1919	1902–1909
Pennsylvania	$819,451,109	$349,059,786	$236,871,417	134.8	47.4
West Virginia	295,606,620	76,287,889	48,378,414	287.5	57.7
Oklahoma	281,927,732	25,637,892	4,508,086	999.7	468.7
Illinois	178,673,065	76,658,974	38,234,410	133.1	100.5
California	163,770,243	63,382,454	[2] 28,870,405	158.4	119.5
Texas	160,378,058	10,742,150	6,981,532	1,393.0	53.9
Ohio	134,518,505	63,767,112	57,186,922	111.0	11.5
Minnesota	130,399,254	58,664,852	25,729,545	122.3	128.0
Michigan	103,870,089	67,714,479	50,157,358	53.4	35.0
Kentucky	98,486,910	12,100,075	8,533,423	713.9	41.8
Kansas	90,338,204	18,722,634	10,700,285	382.5	75.0
Arizona	88,478,111	34,217,651	11,197,375	158.6	205.6
Alabama	59,866,040	24,350,667	17,337,992	145.8	40.2
Indiana	52,840,252	21,934,201	28,224,760	140.9	−22.3
Colorado	51,217,038	45,680,135	40,603,286	12.1	12.5
Montana	49,923,721	54,991,961	28,265,085	−9.2	94.6
Wyoming	41,928,788	10,572,188	5,684,286	296.6	86.0
Utah	41,510,802	22,083,282	12,340,350	88.0	79.0
Louisiana	[3] 40,016,535	6,547,050	279,327	511.2	2,243.9
Missouri	33,365,694	31,657,525	20,284,656	5.4	56.1
Virginia	29,363,449	8,795,646	6,607,807	233.8	33.1
New York	25,131,093	13,334,975	13,350,421	88.5	−0.1
Tennessee	23,292,114	12,692,547	9,533,782	83.5	33.1
New Mexico	18,872,560	5,587,744	2,686,473	237.7	108.0
Iowa	18,473,558	13,877,781	9,676,424	33.1	43.4
Nevada	18,053,984	23,271,597	3,518,430	−22.4	561.4
Washington	13,329,129	10,537,556	5,431,659	26.5	94.0
Idaho	11,840,301	8,649,342	8,214,671	36.9	5.3
Wisconsin	10,580,833	7,459,404	4,427,813	41.8	68.5

[1] A minus sign (−) denotes decrease.
[2] Includes 2 operators in Alaska and 1 in Hawaii.
[3] Includes Mississippi.

TABLE 6.—PRINCIPAL INDUSTRIES, PRODUCING ENTERPRISES, RANKED BY VALUE OF PRODUCTS: 1919.

INDUSTRY.	Number of enterprises.	WAGE EARNERS.		VALUE OF PRODUCTS.	
		Average number.	Per cent distribution.	Amount.	Per cent distribution.
All industries	21,280	981,560	100.0	$3,158,463,966	100.0
Coal	6,890	693,170	70.6	1,510,061,707	47.8
Anthracite	254	147,372	15.0	364,084,142	11.5
Bituminous	6,636	545,798	55.6	1,145,977,565	36.3
Petroleum and natural gas	9,814	93,205	9.5	931,793,423	29.5
Iron ore	290	45,741	4.7	218,217,905	6.9
Copper	195	43,717	4.5	181,258,087	5.7
Lead and zinc	432	21,884	2.2	75,579,347	2.4
Gold and silver, lode mines	740	15,436	1.6	58,832,330	1.9
Limestone	895	22,069	2.2	52,943,924	1.7
Granite	358	8,049	0.8	18,279,345	0.6
Sulphur	4	1,129	0.1	17,935,882	0.6
Sandstone	255	4,287	0.4	10,684,969	0.3
Phosphate rock	48	4,373	0.4	10,300,198	0.3
Clay	345	5,453	0.6	10,086,298	0.3
Basalt	163	3,336	0.3	9,657,977	0.3
Gold, placer mines	112	1,380	0.1	9,368,561	0.3
Gypsum	47	2,191	0.2	6,805,940	0.2
Slate	101	3,513	0.4	5,720,792	0.2
Marble	48	1,732	0.2	4,397,912	0.1
All other	543	10,895	1.1	26,539,369	0.8

TABLE 7.—STATISTICS FOR PRODUCING ENTERPRISES, BY GEOGRAPHIC DIVISIONS: 1919.

DIVISION.	Number of enterprises.	Number of mines and quarries.	Number of wells.	WAGE EARNERS.		VALUE OF PRODUCTS.	
				Average number.	Per cent of total.	Amount.	Per cent of total.
United States	21,280	13,844	257,673	981,560	100.0	$3,158,463,966	100.0
New England	302	334		7,213	0.7	18,723,573	0.6
Middle Atlantic	6,604	3,870	91,511	334,175	34.0	853,891,104	27.0
East North Central	2,776	2,324	54,413	190,011	19.4	480,482,744	15.2
West North Central	1,722	1,270	12,691	62,253	6.3	280,111,296	8.9
South Atlantic	2,284	1,976	27,363	129,707	13.2	352,073,775	11.1
East South Central	1,405	1,475	5,228	90,612	9.2	181,645,064	5.8
West South Central	2,821	495	56,087	60,936	6.2	490,726,862	15.5
Mountain	1,508	1,598	1,183	81,519	8.3	321,825,305	10.2
Pacific	858	502	9,197	25,134	2.6	178,984,243	5.7

TABLE 8.—STATISTICS FOR PRODUCING ENTERPRISES, BY STATES: 1919.

STATE.	Number of enterprises.	Number of mines and quarries.	Number of wells.	WAGE EARNERS.		VALUE OF PRODUCTS.	
				Average number.	Per cent of total.	Amount.	Per cent of total.
United States	21,280	13,844	257,673	981,560	100.0	$3,158,463,966	100.0
Alabama	264	348		32,579	3.3	59,866,040	1.9
Arizona	155	172		15,268	1.6	88,478,111	2.8
Arkansas	126	126	124	3,630	0.4	8,404,537	0.3
California	725	357	9,197	19,344	2.0	163,770,243	5.2
Colorado	477	523	70	16,790	1.7	51,217,038	1.6
Connecticut	41	47		543	0.1	1,649,003	0.1
Delaware	7	8		116	(1)	243,647	(1)
District of Columbia	3	3		12	(1)	15,627	(1)
Florida	36	55		3,372	0.3	8,976,413	0.3
Georgia	74	82		2,397	0.2	4,082,152	0.1
Idaho	82	83		2,455	0.3	11,840,301	0.4
Illinois	772	590	16,498	79,123	8.1	178,673,065	5.7
Indiana	503	398	2,456	26,751	2.7	52,840,252	1.7
Iowa	198	226		11,274	1.1	18,473,558	0.6
Kansas	814	238	12,690	16,136	1.6	90,338,204	2.9
Kentucky	938	864	5,214	43,563	4.4	98,486,910	3.1
Louisiana and Mississippi	137	4	2,479	5,228	0.5	40,016,535	1.3
Maine	50	51		979	0.1	1,823,442	0.1
Maryland	126	161		5,628	0.6	9,698,577	0.3
Massachusetts	74	79		1,704	0.2	4,175,699	0.1
Michigan	122	165	19	31,292	3.2	103,870,089	3.3
Minnesota	135	196		17,265	1.8	130,399,254	4.1
Missouri	468	494		14,857	1.5	33,365,694	1.1
Montana	259	269	28	16,129	1.6	49,923,721	1.6
Nebraska	9	9		162	(1)	292,766	(1)
Nevada	203	207		4,231	0.4	18,053,984	0.6
New Hampshire	30	33		682	0.1	1,568,195	(1)
New Jersey	97	102		4,576	0.5	9,308,902	0.3
New Mexico	85	103	1	7,100	0.7	18,872,560	0.6
New York	700	147	14,186	6,202	0.6	25,131,093	0.8
North Carolina	102	106		1,890	0.2	2,736,543	0.1
North Dakota	79	79		774	0.1	1,927,304	0.1
Ohio	2,283	1,064	35,440	49,298	5.0	134,518,505	4.3
Oklahoma	1,934	284	44,735	33,914	3.5	281,927,732	8.9
Oregon	50	52		740	0.1	1,884,871	0.1
Pennsylvania	5,807	3,621	77,325	323,397	32.9	819,451,109	25.9
Rhode Island	14	15		369	(1)	952,204	(1)
South Carolina	20	20		933	0.1	1,350,747	(1)
South Dakota	23	28	1	1,785	0.2	5,314,516	0.2
Tennessee	203	263	14	14,470	1.5	23,292,114	0.7
Texas	624	81	8,749	18,164	1.9	160,378,058	5.1
Utah	141	154		9,847	1.0	41,510,802	1.3
Vermont	93	109		2,936	0.3	8,555,030	0.3
Virginia	202	216		14,547	1.5	29,363,449	0.9
Washington	83	93		5,050	0.5	13,329,129	0.4
West Virginia	1,714	1,325	27,363	100,812	10.3	295,606,620	9.3
Wisconsin	92	107		3,547	0.4	10,580,833	0.3
Wyoming	106	87	1,084	9,699	1.0	41,928,788	1.3

[1] Less than one-tenth of 1 per cent.

TABLE 9.—PRINCIPAL INDUSTRIES, BY STATES, RANKED BY VALUE OF PRODUCTS, PRODUCING ENTERPRISES: 1919.

INDUSTRY AND STATE.	Number of enterprises.	WAGE EARNERS.		VALUE OF PRODUCTS.	
		Average number.	Per cent of total.	Amount.	Per cent of total.
COAL, ANTHRACITE	254	147,372	100.0	$364,084,142	100.0
Pennsylvania	254	147,372	100.0	364,084,142	100.0
COAL, BITUMINOUS	6,636	545,798	100.0	1,145,977,565	100.0
Pennsylvania	1,938	154,992	28.4	362,973,962	31.7
West Virginia	926	87,095	16.0	193,108,343	16.9
Illinois	447	73,780	13.5	138,767,835	12.1
Ohio	788	40,452	7.4	77,988,602	6.8
Kentucky	635	39,769	7.3	72,432,840	6.3
Indiana	296	27,479	5.3	29,492,726	4.0
Alabama	188	24,618	4.5	45,359,441	4.0
Colorado	191	11,252	2.1	28,342,195	2.5
Virginia	108	11,215	2.1	23,763,440	2.1
Wyoming	46	7,101	1.3	18,723,451	1.6
Iowa	167	10,584	1.9	16,903,358	1.5
Kansas	129	8,084	1.5	15,748,535	1.4
Oklahoma	94	7,040	1.3	14,477,317	1.3
Tennessee	107	6,556	1.2	14,024,432	1.2
Utah	27	3,647	0.7	12,632,035	1.1
Missouri	179	7,285	1.3	12,077,845	1.1
Washington	35	4,413	0.8	10,737,656	0.9
PETROLEUM AND NATURAL GAS	9,814	93,205	100.0	931,793,423	100.0
Oklahoma	1,669	21,180	22.7	247,497,480	26.6
Texas	533	13,699	14.6	143,337,362	15.4
California	402	12,344	13.2	139,810,663	14.9
West Virginia	751	12,302	13.2	99,518,304	10.7
Kansas	613	6,305	6.8	66,815,158	7.4
Pennsylvania	3,140	9,065	9.7	66,271,961	7.1
Ohio	1,333	5,123	5.5	45,483,526	4.9
Louisiana	133	4,371	5.2	32,016,080	3.4
Illinois	236	2,752	3.0	31,263,563	3.4
Kentucky	196	2,119	2.3	23,329,521	2.5
Wyoming	39	2,167	2.3	21,959,987	2.4
New York	361	898	0.9	9,900,894	1.1
Indiana	131	403	0.4	2,604,395	0.3
IRON ORE	290	45,741	100.0	213,217,905	100.0
Minnesota	68	16,286	35.5	128,877,174	58.8
Michigan	59	16,160	35.3	60,906,692	27.9
Alabama	39	6,485	14.2	12,291,760	5.6
New York	7	1,811	4.0	5,264,443	2.4
Wisconsin	9	1,145	2.5	3,826,872	1.8
COPPER [1]	195	43,717	100.0	181,258,087	100.0
Arizona	75	14,237	32.6	84,217,141	46.5
Michigan	22	12,235	28.0	34,476,336	19.0
LEAD AND ZINC [2]	432	21,584	100.0	75,579,347	100.0
Oklahoma	111	5,233	24.0	18,979,726	25.1
Missouri	93	4,793	21.9	18,879,177	21.0
Idaho	20	1,828	8.3	9,629,723	12.6
GOLD AND SILVER, LODE MINES [3]	740	15,436	100.0	58,832,330	100.0
Colorado	198	3,495	22.6	16,785,716	28.5
Nevada	148	2,084	13.5	9,687,431	16.5
California	99	2,881	18.7	8,773,757	14.9
LIMESTONE [4]	895	22,069	100.0	52,943,924	100.0
Pennsylvania	184	5,573	25.3	12,881,213	24.3
Ohio	90	2,262	10.2	6,742,496	12.7
Indiana	67	1,800	8.2	4,619,801	8.7
New York	55	1,739	7.9	4,597,942	8.7
Illinois	41	1,244	5.6	3,776,626	7.1
GRANITE	358	8,049	100.0	18,279,345	100.0
Vermont	27	1,062	13.2	3,563,734	19.5
Massachusetts	47	1,034	12.8	2,405,165	13.2
North Carolina	16	959	11.9	1,576,250	8.6
Wisconsin	14	753	9.4	1,484,979	8.1
New Hampshire	23	589	7.3	1,427,979	7.8
Maine	42	747	9.3	1,300,996	7.1
Minnesota	27	392	4.9	1,135,391	6.2

1 Montana and Utah, ranking 3 and 4, respectively, not shown in order to avoid disclosure of individual operations.
2 Montana, ranking 4, not shown in order to avoid disclosure of individual operations.
3 Utah, ranking 4, not shown in order to avoid disclosure of individual operations.
4 Michigan, ranking 6, not shown in order to avoid disclosure of individual operations.

TABLE **9.**—PRINCIPAL INDUSTRIES, BY STATES, RANKED BY VALUE OF PRODUCTS,
PRODUCING ENTERPRISES: 1919—Continued.

INDUSTRY AND STATE.	Number of enter-prises.	WAGE EARNERS.		VALUE OF PRODUCTS.	
		Average number.	Per cent of total.	Amount.	Per cent of total.
SANDSTONE	255	4,287	100.0	$10,684,969	100.0
Pennsylvania	100	1,673	39.0	3,534,563	33.1
Ohio	21	875	20.4	2,759,352	25.8
Illinois	15	288	6.7	1,329,389	12.4
PHOSPHATE ROCK	48	4,373	100.0	10,300,198	100.0
Florida	23	2,330	53.3	6,678,888	64.8
Tennessee	19	1,568	35.9	3,139,671	30.5
CLAY [1]	345	5,453	100.0	10,086,298	100.0
Pennsylvania	62	1,337	24.5	2,546,485	25.2
New Jersey	35	868	15.9	1,482,358	14.7
Missouri	41	622	11.4	1,420,585	14.1
BASALT	163	3,336	100.0	9,657,977	100.0
Pennsylvania	29	721	21.6	2,298,791	23.8
New Jersey	36	637	19.1	1,928,025	20.0
Massachusetts	21	547	16.4	1,548,611	16.0
Connecticut	20	363	10.9	1,262,579	13.1
GOLD, PLACER MINES	112	1,380	100.0	9,368,561	100.0
California	60	1,102	79.9	7,937,654	84.7
GYPSUM	47	2,191	100.0	6,805,940	100.0
New York	6	400	18.3	1,110,463	16.3
Iowa	5	444	20.3	1,092,920	16.1
SLATE	101	3,513	100.0	5,720,792	100.0
Pennsylvania	42	1,892	53.9	2,651,533	46.3
Vermont	38	1,039	29.6	2,057,388	36.0
MARBLE	48	1,732	100.0	4,397,912	100.0
Vermont	15	570	32.9	2,108,872	48.0
Tennessee	13	540	31.2	1,088,131	24.7

[1] Ohio, ranking 4, not shown in order to avoid disclosure of individual operations.

TABLE **10.**—PERSONS ENGAGED IN PRODUCING ENTERPRISES: 1919.

CLASS.	Total.	Male.	Female.
All classes	**1,077,675**	**1,065,051**	**12,624**
Proprietors and officials	60,409	58,330	2,079
Proprietors and firm members	21,918	20,231	1,687
Salaried officers of corporations	10,456	10,202	254
Superintendents and managers	21,704	21,648	56
Technical employees	6,331	6,249	82
Clerks and other subordinate salaried employees	35,706	25,649	10,057
Wage earners (average number)	981,560	981,072	488
Wage earners 16 years of age and over	981,361	980,873	488
Wage earners under 16 years of age	199	199	

TABLE **11.**—NUMBER OF PRODUCING ENTERPRISES AND AVERAGE NUMBER OF WAGE EARNERS, BY PREVAILING HOURS OF LABOR PER WEEK, FOR LEADING INDUSTRIES: 1919.

INDUSTRY.	TOTAL.		NUMBER WHERE THE PREVAILING HOURS OF LABOR PER WEEK WERE—			
			35 and under.		36 to 43.	
	Enterprises.	Wage earners.	Enterprises.	Wage earners.	Enterprises.	Wage earners.
All industries	[1] 17,558	981,560	1,166	17,755	732	19,856
Coal:						
Anthracite	252	147,372			1	315
Bituminous	6,574	545,798	257	15,978	425	17,163
Petroleum and natural gas	6,522	93,205	852	1,295	225	327
Iron ore	285	45,741	1	11	4	219
Copper	179	43,717			2	7
Limestone	870	22,069	3	57	8	24
Lead and zinc	391	21,884	1	115		
Gold and silver, lode mines	589	15,436			2	3
Granite	338	8,049	4	43	32	1,195
Clay	319	5,453	8	27	6	33
Phosphate rock	47	4,373	1	5	1	30
Sandstone	246	4,287			3	8
Slate	100	3,513			11	335
Basalt	161	3,336	1	20	1	3
Gypsum	47	2,191			1	1
Marble	47	1,732				
Gold, placer mines	78	1,380				
Sulphur	4	1,129				
All other	509	10,895	38	204	10	193

INDUSTRY.	NUMBER WHERE THE PREVAILING HOURS OF LABOR PER WEEK WERE—							
	44 to 53.		54 to 62.		63 to 71.		72 to 84.	
	Enterprises.	Wage earners.	Enterprises.	Wage earners.	Enterprises.	Wage earners.	Enterprises.	Wage earners.
All industries	8,862	721,899	5,262	182,126	768	26,841	768	13,083
Coal:								
Anthracite	176	145,787	71	807	3	442	1	21
Bituminous	5,546	485,574	331	25,222	12	1,841	3	20
Petroleum and natural gas	1,623	13,227	2,356	44,068	714	21,726	752	12,562
Iron ore	151	20,311	124	24,637	5	563		
Copper	79	21,150	97	21,166	1	1,394		
Limestone	187	3,774	663	17,934	9	280		
Lead and zinc	255	15,082	133	6,684			2	3
Gold and silver, lode mines	192	3,595	390	11,586	4	251	1	1
Granite	209	4,829	91	1,948	2	34		
Clay	142	2,351	161	3,033	1	4	1	5
Phosphate rock	6	309	36	3,683			3	346
Sandstone	49	483	191	3,688	3	108		
Slate	14	963	73	2,170	2	45		
Basalt	49	728	110	2,585				
Gypsum	12	830	32	1,317	2	43		
Marble	3	50	43	1,667	1	15		
Gold, placer mines	17	62	52	1,243	8	72	1	3
Sulphur			4	1,129				
All other	152	2,794	304	7,559	1	23	4	122

[1] Exclusive of 3,722 enterprises employing no wage earners in industries as follows: Abrasive materials, 5; asphalt, 2; barytes, 1; basalt, 2; clay, 26; chromite, 5; coal, anthracite, 2; coal, bituminous, 62; copper, 16; feldspar, 2; fluorspar, 4; granite, 20; gold and silver, lode mines, 151; gold, placer mines, 34; iron ore, 5; lead and zinc, 41; limestone, 25; magnesite, 1; marble, 1; mica, 6; millstones, 5; mineral pigments, 2; petroleum and natural gas, 3,292; phosphate rock, 1; sandstone, 9; slate, 1; talc and soapstone, 1.

TABLE 12.—WAGE EARNERS, BY MONTHS, ALL MINING ENTERPRISES, BY INDUS-
TRIES: 1919.

[The month of maximum employment for each industry is indicated by **bold-faced** figures and that
of minimum employment by *italic* figures.]

INDUSTRY.	Average number employed during year.	NUMBER EMPLOYED ON 15TH DAY OF THE MONTH OR NEAREST REPRESENTATIVE DAY.					
		January.	February.	March.	April.	May.	June.
All industries.........	987,184	1,030,037	989,301	973,868	956,932	963,827	970,832
Producing enterprises.....	981,560	1,025,871	985,369	969,499	952,305	958,506	965,230
FUELS:							
Coal, anthracite.............	147,372	146,241	145,985	143,437	*142,691*	144,925	145,010
Coal, bituminous............	545,798	589,864	561,861	550,126	532,682	535,110	541,647
Petroleum and natural gas..	93,205	85,225	*85,119*	87,130	88,120	90,015	91,156
METALS:							
Iron ore..................	45,741	**47,493**	47,205	46,712	44,822	45,631	44,625
Copper..................	43,717	**58,025**	49,136	43,701	40,675	38,374	*37,885*
Lead and zinc............	21,884	**25,124**	23,434	22,574	21,506	20,196	*19,949*
Gold and silver—							
Lode mines............	15,436	*14,778*	14,915	15,095	14,921	15,184	15,540
Placer mines..........	1,380	*1,274*	1,312	*1,274*	1,317	1,424	1,420
Manganese...............	909	1,202	**1,323**	1,155	1,159	1,115	767
Quicksilver.............	748	**990**	775	769	*595*	676	779
Rare metals.............	633	**921**	834	727	544	*530*	567
STONE:							
Limestone...............	22,069	18,085	*17,398*	18,847	21,476	22,992	23,667
Granite.................	8,049	*5,669*	5,844	6,504	7,771	8,620	8,945
Sandstone...............	4,287	3,471	*3,305*	3,681	4,128	4,411	4,533
Basalt..................	3,336	*2,037*	2,037	2,456	3,257	3,680	3,828
Slate...................	3,513	*2,852*	2,909	3,060	3,415	3,580	3,764
Marble..................	1,732	*1,459*	1,497	1,641	1,688	1,778	1,826
MISCELLANEOUS:							
Abrasive materials........	317	340	348	303	*255*	306	307
Asbestos.................	146	*43*	74	77	112	138	130
Asphalt.................	324	157	*156*	170	197	212	242
Barytes.................	919	773	*756*	782	826	887	938
Bauxite.................	738	755	656	636	637	612	*581*
Chromite.................	31	36	**39**	25	27	36	38
Clay....................	5,453	4,849	*4,681*	4,851	5,373	5,522	5,582
Feldspar................	349	*291*	297	342	334	347	371
Fluorspar...............	1,124	**1,377**	1,059	*957*	1,007	998	1,001
Fuller's earth..........	824	*687*	691	715	784	829	840
Graphite.................	419	432	398	*378*	454	470	447
Gypsum..................	2,191	*1,574*	1,649	1,782	1,918	2,078	2,092
Magnesite...............	448	482	*236*	342	282	245	250
Mica....................	448	414	*400*	416	430	430	431
Millstones..............	37	*26*	*26*	37	40	**42**	**42**
Mineral pigments...........	185	159	*155*	181	175	198	178
Phosphate rock.............	4,373	4,583	4,865	4,741	4,972	3,259	*2,902*
Pyrite..................	1,172	**1,651**	1,618	1,444	1,124	1,078	988
Silica..................	166	138	142	149	161	171	217
Sulphur.................	1,129	1,492	1,390	1,406	**1,545**	1,503	*814*
Talc and soapstone.........	958	902	*844*	876	885	904	931
Nonproducing enterprises.	5,624	4,166	*3,932*	4,369	4,627	5,321	5,602
FUELS:							
Coal....................	471	*211*	232	268	278	291	382
Petroleum and natural gas..	454	*260*	274	325	352	424	450
METALS:							
Iron ore..................	598	**819**	595	575	634	698	639
Gold, silver, copper, lead, or zinc..................	3,691	2,565	*2,525*	2,880	3,079	3,623	3,848
MISCELLANEOUS, all other.......	410	311	306	321	284	285	*283*

TABLE 12.—WAGE EARNERS, BY MONTHS, ALL MINING ENTERPRISES, BY INDUS-
TRIES: 1919—Continued.

[The month of maximum employment for each industry is indicated by **bold-faced** figures and that of minimum employment by *italic* figures.]

INDUSTRY.	NUMBER EMPLOYED ON 15TH DAY OF THE MONTH OR NEAREST REPRESENTATIVE DAY.						Per cent minimum is of maximum.
	July.	August.	September.	October.	November.	December.	
All industries.........	1,011,390	1,038,038	1,050,107	**1,057,820**	*765,067*	1,038,989	72.3
Producing enterprises....	1,005,219	1,031,628	1,043,719	**1,051,204**	*758,156*	1,032,014	72.1
FUELS:							
Coal, anthracite.............	148,397	149,220	149,522	150,847	150,594	**151,595**	94.1
Coal, bituminous.............	566,897	583,120	593,304	**599,550**	*308,266*	587,149	51.4
Petroleum and natural gas...	94,389	98,570	99,570	99,332	99,541	**100,293**	84.9
METALS:							
Iron ore......................	46,286	46,754	46,911	45,772	44,126	*42,555*	89.6
Copper.......................	39,919	41,386	42,595	44,395	45,246	43,267	65.3
Lead and zinc................	20,207	21,050	21,162	21,579	22,631	23,196	79.4
Gold and silver—							
Lode mines...............	16,319	**16,469**	15,349	15,536	15,456	15,670	89.7
Placer mines.............	**1,499**	1,430	1,404	1,425	1,433	1,348	85.0
Manganese...................	782	758	745	656	*622*	624	47.0
Quicksilver.................	766	758	742	708	715	703	60.1
Rare metals.................	557	569	558	646	598	545	57.5
STONE:							
Limestone...................	24,599	**25,655**	25,303	23,901	22,538	20,367	67.8
Granite.....................	9,071	**9,228**	9,024	9,101	8,741	8,070	61.4
Sandstone...................	4,667	**4,961**	4,916	4,726	4,598	4,047	66.6
Basalt......................	3,985	**4,097**	3,906	3,908	3,710	3,131	49.7
Slate.......................	3,858	3,572	3,594	3,729	3,896	**3,927**	72.6
Marble......................	1,833	1,865	1,810	**1,875**	1,759	1,753	77.8
MISCELLANEOUS:							
Abrasive materials...........	336	342	**369**	308	288	302	69.1
Asbestos....................	159	159	199	**241**	239	181	17.8
Asphalt.....................	**594**	528	401	407	399	425	26.3
Barytes.....................	980	983	**1,089**	1,065	985	964	69.4
Bauxite.....................	643	828	900	847	827	**934**	62.2
Chromite....................	31	25	35	28	33	*19*	48.7
Clay........................	5,771	5,883	**6,020**	5,853	5,538	5,513	77.8
Feldspar....................	346	**395**	**395**	352	339	379	73.7
Fluorspar...................	1,031	1,134	**1,288**	1,313	1,211	1,112	69.5
Fuller's earth..............	880	916	**923**	858	870	895	74.4
Graphite....................	398	407	**475**	415	398	*356*	74.9
Gypsum......................	2,350	2,327	2,582	2,713	**2,715**	2,512	58.0
Magnesite...................	435	534	615	629	656	**670**	35.2
Mica........................	439	464	478	490	487	**497**	80.5
Millstones..................	41	40	40	38	38	34	61.9
Mineral pigments............	**217**	193	193	193	187	191	71.4
Phosphate rock..............	3,419	3,873	4,094	4,639	5,358	**5,771**	50.3
Pyrite......................	1,076	1,065	1,118	1,017	955	*930*	56.3
Silica......................	224	220	185	144	132	*109*	48.7
Sulphur.....................	832	845	883	932	973	933	52.7
Talc and soapstone..........	986	1,005	1,022	1,036	**1,058**	1,047	79.8
Nonproducing enterprises..	6,171	6,410	6,388	6,616	6,911	**6,975**	56.4
FUELS:							
Coal........................	463	507	625	735	**833**	827	25.3
Petroleum and natural gas...	461	531	538	577	622	**634**	41.0
METALS:							
Iron ore....................	606	624	527	*452*	477	530	55.2
Gold, silver, copper, lead, or zinc........................	4,306	4,325	4,254	4,284	4,276	**4,327**	58.4
MISCELLANEOUS, all other........	335	423	444	568	**703**	657	40.3

TABLE 13.—WAGE EARNERS, BY MONTHS, ALL MINING ENTERPRISES, BY STATES: 1919.

[The month of maximum employment for each state is indicated by **bold-faced** figures and that of minimum employment by *italic* figures.]

| STATE. | Average number employed during year. | NUMBER EMPLOYED ON 15TH DAY OF THE MONTH OR NEAREST REPRESENTATIVE DAY. | | | | | |
		January.	February.	March.	April.	May.	June.
United States............	987,184	1,030,037	989,301	973,868	956,932	963,827	970,832
Producing enterprises.....	981,560	1,025,871	985,369	969,499	952,305	958,506	965,230
Alabama..................	32,579	34,594	**34,682**	34,252	32,719	31,117	31,042
Arizona..................	15,268	**19,065**	16,273	13,358	*12,808*	13,199	13,280
Arkansas.................	3,630	3,783	3,404	3,224	3,141	3,240	3,288
California...............	19,344	19,552	19,319	19,238	*18,716*	19,298	19,079
Colorado.................	16,790	18,151	17,600	17,460	16,716	15,723	15,681
Connecticut..............	543	447	*427*	491	535	590	591
Delaware.................	116	58	*51*	73	121	136	153
District of Columbia.....	12	*6*	6	8	9	14	17
Florida..................	3,372	3,848	3,903	3,861	3,934	2,202	*1,836*
Georgia..................	2,397	2,386	2,408	2,393	2,339	2,288	2,328
Idaho....................	2,455	2,773	2,733	2,067	2,056	2,391	2,517
Illinois.................	79,123	89,224	86,988	85,233	82,026	80,235	79,033
Indiana..................	26,751	29,961	28,209	26,939	25,837	27,074	26,875
Iowa.....................	11,274	**13,221**	12,926	12,592	11,194	10,868	10,622
Kansas...................	16,136	**17,448**	17,262	17,207	16,851	17,214	16,982
Kentucky.................	43,563	43,980	40,949	40,949	40,081	41,154	42,203
Louisiana................	5,221	4,913	4,706	4,943	5,047	4,864	*4,407*
Maine....................	979	461	*438*	712	968	1,236	**1,288**
Maryland.................	5,628	5,829	5,305	*5,101*	5,171	5,424	5,480
Massachusetts............	1,704	1,037	*1,017*	1,236	1,757	1,889	1,946
Michigan.................	31,292	34,436	**34,729**	34,420	30,655	29,765	*28,836*
Minnesota................	17,265	16,033	16,364	16,010	17,054	18,643	18,587
Mississippi..............	7	....	....	*5*	12	15	11
Missouri.................	14,857	**17,319**	16,479	15,406	15,014	14,501	14,401
Montana..................	16,129	**20,911**	16,661	16,017	15,329	15,104	15,324
Nebraska.................	162	*128*	134	157	174	**192**	176
Nevada...................	4,231	**5,118**	4,275	4,143	4,063	4,227	4,428
New Hampshire............	682	*344*	360	398	571	708	830
New Jersey...............	4,576	4,704	4,592	4,647	4,763	4,526	*4,162*
New Mexico...............	7,100	**8,152**	7,584	7,437	7,236	7,013	6,836
New York.................	6,202	6,180	*5,553*	5,627	6,040	6,429	6,450
North Carolina...........	1,890	*1,696*	1,728	1,846	1,849	1,852	1,878
North Dakota.............	774	1,011	878	807	636	497	*472*
Ohio.....................	49,298	51,820	48,325	48,005	47,838	50,336	52,236
Oklahoma.................	33,914	32,940	32,531	32,713	33,058	33,205	33,015
Oregon...................	740	617	565	*555*	580	695	721
Pennsylvania.............	323,397	330,698	323,086	318,975	314,592	315,610	321,150
Rhode Island.............	369	*246*	281	303	349	389	393
South Carolina...........	933	793	*784*	913	922	896	893
South Dakota.............	1,785	1,801	1,868	1,860	1,819	1,793	1,826
Tennessee................	14,470	15,364	14,322	14,114	*13,677*	14,572	14,731
Texas....................	18,164	*14,661*	15,003	15,942	16,688	17,263	17,259
Utah.....................	9,847	**11,962**	10,636	9,283	8,937	8,098	*8,072*
Vermont..................	2,936	2,725	*2,698*	2,721	2,856	3,015	**3,156**
Virginia.................	14,547	14,932	14,541	13,722	*13,308*	13,746	13,732
Washington...............	5,050	**5,956**	5,737	5,672	5,321	5,104	4,948
West Virginia............	100,812	100,187	93,274	*92,824*	93,737	97,313	99,454
Wisconsin................	3,547	3,461	3,368	3,452	3,636	**3,720**	3,676
Wyoming..................	9,699	**10,939**	10,407	10,188	9,565	9,123	8,949
Nonproducing enterprises..	5,624	4,166	*3,932*	4,369	4,627	5,321	5,602

TABLE 13.—WAGE EARNERS, BY MONTHS, ALL MINING ENTERPRISES, BY STATES: 1919—Continued.

[The month of maximum employment for each state is indicated by **bold-faced** figures and that of minimum employment by *italic* figures.]

STATE.	NUMBER EMPLOYED ON 15TH DAY OF THE MONTH OR NEAREST REPRESENTATIVE DAY.						Per cent minimum is of maximum.
	July.	August.	September.	October.	November.	December.	
United States............	1,011,390	1,038,038	1,050,107	**1,057,820**	*765,067*	1,038,989	72.3
Producing enterprises......	1,005,219	1,031,628	1,043,719	**1,051,204**	*758,156*	1,032,014	72.1
Alabama.....................	31,751	32,521	32,936	33,747	*28,781*	32,806	83.0
Arizona....................	14,366	15,588	16,036	16,441	16,484	16,318	67.2
Arkansas...................	4,062	4,542	**4,879**	4,760	*1,416*	3,821	29.0
California..................	19,266	19,176	19,182	19,555	**19,916**	19,831	94.0
Colorado...................	16,424	17,086	16,782	16,527	*15,175*	**18,155**	83.6
Connecticut................	**598**	583	558	565	578	553	71.4
Delaware...................	147	144	132	118	127	132	33.3
District of Columbia........	12	12	17	**19**	13	11	31.6
Florida....................	2,330	2,745	2,961	3,650	4,282	**4,912**	37.4
Georgia....................	2,501	**2,586**	2,510	2,479	*2,271*	2,275	87.8
Idaho.....................	2,746	2,175	*1,648*	2,008	3,078	**3,268**	50.4
Illinois...................	81,643	83,906	87,056	**89,321**	*16,782*	88,029	18.8
Indiana...................	28,145	29,434	30,907	**31,544**	*5,818*	30,269	18.4
Iowa.....................	11,012	11,811	12,524	13,052	*3,404*	12,062	25.7
Kansas....................	17,191	16,397	16,397	16,415	*8,843*	15,425	50.7
Kentucky..................	46,231	47,350	47,373	**48,834**	*35,516*	48,136	72.7
Louisiana.................	4,523	5,014	5,505	5,655	6,401	**6,674**	66.0
Maine....................	1,175	1,204	1,141	1,116	1,076	933	34.0
Maryland.................	5,743	6,119	6,157	**6,221**	5,144	5,862	82.0
Massachusetts.............	1,978	**2,032**	1,956	1,997	1,913	1,690	50.0
Michigan..................	29,599	30,303	31,365	31,780	29,202	30,414	83.0
Minnesta..................	**18,804**	18,667	18,178	17,348	16,383	*15,109*	80.3
Mississippi...............	**17**	12	6	....		6	29.4
Missouri..................	14,871	14,907	15,672	15,729	*8,965*	15,020	51.8
Montana..................	15,910	16,197	15,530	16,685	*13,922*	15,958	66.6
Nebraska.................	163	169	179	169	153	150	66.7
Nevada...................	4,381	*3,366*	3,656	4,081	4,467	4,567	65.8
New Hampshire............	839	**887**	860	871	818	698	38.8
New Jersey................	4,713	4,741	**4,780**	4,678	4,328	4,278	87.1
New Mexico...............	6,561	7,084	7,102	6,975	*6,380*	6,840	78.3
New York..................	**6,690**	6,569	6,537	6,474	6,108	5,767	83.0
North Carolina............	1,931	1,898	**2,062**	1,996	1,966	1,978	82.3
North Dakota..............	518	550	776	931	1,054	**1,158**	40.8
Ohio.....................	53,518	56,340	**56,792**	56,448	*18,793*	51,125	33.1
Oklahoma.................	34,320	35,886	36,617	**36,674**	*29,510*	36,499	80.5
Oregon...................	810	869	**934**	912	826	796	59.4
Pennsylvania..............	333,232	340,386	**341,352**	340,316	*265,170*	336,197	77.7
Rhode Island..............	427	424	**438**	395	404	379	56.2
South Carolina............	974	**1,031**	1,006	968	1,010	1,006	76.0
South Dakota..............	**1,890**	1,866	1,828	1,663	*1,574*	1,632	83.3
Tennessee.................	14,974	15,304	15,227	**15,777**	*10,406*	15,172	66.0
Texas....................	18,459	20,420	**20,975**	20,853	19,474	20,971	69.9
Utah.....................	9,184	10,069	10,319	10,315	10,577	**10,712**	67.5
Vermont..................	3,146	2,877	2,860	3,005	3,082	3,091	85.5
Virginia..................	14,821	15,096	15,224	**15,398**	14,982	15,062	86.4
Washington...............	5,195	5,455	5,659	5,567	*1,844*	4,142	31.0
West Virginia.............	104,774	106,637	107,8J1	107,778	97,245	**108,720**	85.4
Wisconsin................	3,712	3,717	3,604	3,606	3,479	*3,133*	84.2
Wyoming.................	*8,942*	9,476	9,723	9,788	9,016	10,272	81.7
Nonproducing enterprises..	6,171	6,410	6,388	6,616	6,911	**6,975**	56.4

TABLE **14.**—CHARACTER OF ORGANIZATION, PRODUCING ENTERPRISES: 1919.

INDUSTRY AND CHARACTER OF ORGANIZATION.	Number of enterprises.	Number of wage earners.	VALUE OF PRODUCTS.		PER CENT DISTRIBUTION.		
			Total.	Per enterprise.	Enterprises.	Wage earners.	Value of products.
All industries	21,280	981,560	$3,158,463,966	$148,424	100.0	100.0	100.0
Corporation............	10,879	924,421	2,954,789,792	271,605	51.1	94.2	93.6
Individual..............	4,312	24,107	71,982,739	16,694	20.3	2.5	2.3
Firm..................	5,249	28,916	103,683,684	19,753	24.7	2.9	3.3
Other.................	840	4,116	28,007,751	33,343	3.9	0.4	0.9
COAL, ANTHRACITE......	254	147,372	364,084,142	1,433,402	100.0	100.0	100.0
Corporation...........	170	143,615	355,328,907	2,090,170	66.9	97.5	97.6
Individual............	37	431	962,441	26,012	14.6	0.3	0.3
Firm.................	42	2,879	6,741,024	160,501	16.5	2.0	1.9
Other................	5	447	1,051,770	210,354	2.0	0.3	0.3
COAL, BITUMINOUS.......	6,636	545,798	1,145,977,565	172,691	100.0	100.0	100.0
Corporation...........	4,325	515,692	1,085,004,874	250,868	65.2	94.5	94.7
Individual............	1,181	13,844	28,343,965	24,000	17.8	2.5	2.5
Firm.................	1,095	14,847	30,100,087	27,489	16.5	2.7	2.6
Other................	35	1,415	2,528,639	72,247	0.5	0.3	0.2
PETROLEUM AND NATURAL GAS..............	9,814	93,205	931,793,423	94,945	100.0	100.0	100.0
Corporation...........	3,685	83,399	828,633,805	224,867	37.5	89.5	88.9
Individual............	2,063	3,242	28,759,096	13,940	21.0	3.5	3.1
Firm.................	3,296	5,002	51,758,029	15,703	33.6	5.4	5.6
Other................	770	1,562	22,642,493	29,406	7.8	1.7	2.4
IRON ORE..............	290	45,741	218,217,905	752,476	100.0	100.0	100.0
Corporation...........	267	45,152	216,718,813	811,681	92.1	98.7	99.3
Individual............	12	221	390,551	32,546	4.1	0.5	0.2
Firm [1]................	11	368	1,108,541	100,776	3.8	0.8	0.5
COPPER...............	195	43,717	181,258,087	929,529	100.0	100.0	100.0
Corporation...........	141	43,470	180,735,466	1,281,812	72.3	99.4	99.7
Individual............	24	150	310,336	12,931	12.3	0.3	0.2
Firm [1]................	30	97	212,285	7,076	15.4	0.2	0.1
LEAD AND ZINC.........	432	21,884	75,579,347	174,952	100.0	100.0	100.0
Corporation...........	287	20,508	70,551,148	245,823	66.4	93.7	93.3
Individual............	40	372	1,510,296	37,757	9.3	1.7	2.0
Firm.................	100	870	3,156,133	31,561	23.1	4.0	4.2
Other................	5	134	361,770	72,354	1.2	0.6	0.5
GOLD AND SILVER, LODE MINES..............	740	15,436	58,832,330	79,503	100.0	100.0	100.0
Corporation...........	396	14,448	55,715,104	140,695	53.5	93.6	94.7
Individual............	138	401	802,301	5,814	18.6	2.6	1.4
Firm.................	198	480	1,963,422	9,916	26.8	3.1	3.3
Other................	8	107	351,503	43,938	1.1	0.7	0.6
LIMESTONE.............	895	22,069	52,943,924	59,155	100.0	100.0	100.0
Corporation...........	462	18,324	45,890,605	99,330	51.6	83.0	86.7
Individual............	289	2,011	3,705,252	12,821	32.3	9.1	7.0
Firm.................	140	1,635	3,112,907	22,235	15.6	7.4	5.9
Other................	4	99	235,160	58,790	0.4	0.4	0.4
GRANITE..............	358	8,049	18,279,345	51,060	100.0	100.0	100.0
Corporation...........	152	6,392	14,504,529	95,425	42.5	79.4	79.3
Individual............	126	938	2,109,442	16,742	35.2	11.7	11.5
Firm [2]................	80	719	1,665,374	20,817	22.3	8.9	9.1
SULPHUR..............	4	1,129	17,935,882	4,483,971	100.0	100.0	100.0
Corporation...........	4	1,129	17,935,882	4,483,971	100.0	100.0	100.0

[1] Includes 1 "other" form of organization.   [2] Includes 2 "other" forms of organization.

TABLE **14.**—CHARACTER OF ORGANIZATION, PRODUCING ENTERPRISES: 1919—Contd.

INDUSTRY AND CHARACTER OF ORGANIZATION.	Number of enterprises.	Number of wage earners.	VALUE OF PRODUCTS.		PER CENT DISTRIBUTION.		
			Total.	Per enterprise.	Enterprises.	Wage earners.	Value of products.
SANDSTONE	255	4,287	$10,684,969	$41,902	100.0	100.0	100.0
Corporation	142	3,574	9,405,068	66,233	55.7	83.4	88.0
Individual	61	279	500,761	8,209	23.9	6.5	4.7
Firm [1]	52	434	779,140	14,983	20.4	10.1	7.3
PHOSPHATE ROCK	48	4,373	10,300,198	214,587	100.0	100.0	100.0
Corporation	39	4,058	9,546,209	244,775	81.3	92.8	92.7
Individual	4	95	187,858	46,965	.8.3	2.2	1.8
Firm	5	220	566,131	113,226	10.4	5.0	5.5
CLAY	345	5,453	10,086,298	29,236	100.0	100.0	100.0
Corporation	212	4,480	8,034,433	37,898	61.4	82.2	79.7
Individual	98	644	1,454,977	14,847	28.4	11.8	14.4
Firm [2]	35	329	596,888	17,054	10.1	6.0	5.9
BASALT	163	3,336	9,657,977	59,251	100.0	100.0	100.0
Corporation	104	2,809	8,327,873	80,076	63.8	84.2	86.2
Individual	40	356	973,250	24,331	24.5	10.7	10.1
Firm	16	149	336,073	21,005	9.8	4.5	3.5
Other	3	22	20,781	6,927	1.8	0.7	0.2
GOLD, PLACER MINES	112	1,380	9,368,561	83,648	100.0	100.0	100.0
Corporation	45	1,259	8,965,148	199,226	40.2	91.2	95.7
Individual	33	78	338,015	10,243	29.5	5.7	3.6
Firm [2]	34	43	65,398	1,923	30.4	3.1	0.7
GYPSUM	47	2,191	6,805,940	144,807	100.0	100.0	100.0
Corporation	43	2,176	6,782,826	157,740	91.5	99.3	99.7
Individual	4	15	23,114	5,779	8.5	0.7	0.3
SLATE	101	3,513	5,720,792	56,642	100.0	100.0	100.0
Corporation	71	3,007	5,021,062	70,719	70.3	85.6	87.8
Individual	8	131	187,699	23,462	7.9	3.7	3.3
Firm [1]	22	375	512,031	23,274	21.8	10.7	9.0
MARBLE	48	1,732	4,397,912	91,623	100.0	100.0	100.0
Corporation	44	1,672	4,318,737	98,153	91.7	96.5	98.2
Individual [3]	4	60	79,175	19,794	8.3	3.5	1.8

[1] Includes 1 "other" form of organization.
[2] Includes 2 "other" forms of organization.
[3] Includes 2 firms.

TABLE 15.—SIZE OF PRODUCING ENTERPRISES, BY VALUE OF PRODUCTS: 1919.

INDUSTRY AND VALUE OF PRODUCTS PER ENTERPRISE.	Number.	VALUE OF PRODUCTS. Amount.	Per cent.	INDUSTRY AND VALUE OF PRODUCTS PER ENTERPRISE.	Number.	VALUE OF PRODUCTS. Amount.	Per cent.
All industries....	21,280	$3,158,463,966	100.0	COPPER............	195	$181,258,087	100.0
Less than $5,000......	6,586	15,228,604	0.5	Less than $5,000......	60	103,183	0.1
$5,000 to $20,000......	5,539	58,745,473	1.9	$5,000 to $20,000.......	33	369,280	0.2
$20,000 to $100,000...	4,990	237,600,990	7.5	$20,000 to $100,000.....	33	1,911,892	1.1
$100,000 to $500,00....	3,005	686,788,422	21.7	$100,000 to $500,000....	28	6,799,421	3.8
$500,000 to $1,000,00...	684	472,131,636	14.9	$500,000 to $1,000,000...	9	6,350,924	3.5
$1,000,000 to $5,000,000	392	754,160,595	23.9	$1,000,000 to $5,000,000.	19	43,121,957	23.8
$5,000,000 and over...	84	933,808,246	29.6	$5,000,000 and over....	13	122,601,430	67.6
COAL..............	6,890	1,510,061,707	100.0	LEAD AND ZINC...	432	75,579,347	100.0
Less than $5,000........	855	2,801,020	0.2	Less than $5,000.......	135	261,492	0.3
$5,000 to $20,000........	1,656	18,054,536	1.2	$5,000 to $20,000.......	80	817,185	1.1
$20,000 to $100,000......	2,049	102,223,266	6.8	$20,000 to $100,000.....	85	4,494,519	5.9
$100,000 to $500,000....	1,690	396,152,362	26.2	$100,000 to $500,000....	102	25,190,455	33.3
$500,000 to $1,000,000..	409	281,472,982	18.6	$500,000 to $1,000,000..	17	11,617,808	15.4
$1,000,000 to $5,000,000..	204	372,478,693	24.7	$1,000,000 and over [2]...	13	33,197,888	43.9
$5,000,000 and over......	27	336,878,848	22.3	GOLD AND SILVER, LODE MINES.......	740	58,832,330	100.0
ANTHRACITE.......	254	364,084,142	100.0	Less than $5,000.......	381	695,409	1.2
Less than $5,000......	37	89,997	(1)	$5,000 to $20,000........	149	1,500,964	2.6
$5,000 to $20,000......	38	440,045	0.1	$20,000 to $100,000.....	113	5,149,322	8.8
$20,000 to $100,000...	43	1,843,631	0.5	$100,000 to $500,000....	67	14,986,545	25.5
$100,000 to $500,000...	39	10,076,964	2.8	$500,000 to $1,000,000...	19	13,255,565	22.5
$500,000 to $1,000,000..	32	24,276,649	6.7	$1,000,000 and over [2]...	11	23,244,525	39.5
$1,000,000 to $5,000,000	48	83,086,309	22.8	LIMESTONE.........	895	52,943,924	100.0
$5,000,000 and over...	17	244,270,547	67.1	Less than $5,000........	208	507,076	1.0
BITUMINOUS.......	6,636	1,145,977,565	100.0	$5,000 to $20,000........	259	2,915,675	5.5
Less than $5,000......	818	2,711,023	0.2	$20,000 to $100,000.....	310	14,429,913	27.3
$5,000 to $20,000......	1,618	17,614,491	1.5	$100,000 to $500,000....	103	20,834,355	39.4
$20,000 to $100,000...	2,006	100,379,635	8.8	$500,000 to $1,000,000...	10	6,904,529	13.0
$100,000 to $500,000..	1,651	386,075,398	33.7	$1,000,000 to $5,000,000.	5	7,352,376	13.9
$500,000 to $1,000,000..	377	257,196,333	22.4	GRANITE............	358	18,279,345	100.0
$1,000,000 to $5,000,000	156	289,392,384	25.3	Less than $5,000.......	90	241,093	1.3
$5,000,000 and over...	10	92,608,301	8.1	$5,000 to $20,000.......	104	1,027,383	5.6
PETROLEUM AND NATURAL GAS....	9,814	931,793,423	100.0	$20,000 to $100,000.....	110	4,786,424	26.2
Less than $5,000........	4,348	9,531,235	1.0	$100,000 to $500,000....	50	9,344,547	51.1
$5,000 to $20,000........	2,797	28,919,564	3.1	$500,000 and over [3]...	4	2,879,898	15.8
$20,000 to $100,000...	1,696	75,785,417	8.1	SANDSTONE........	255	10,684,969	100.0
$100,000 to $500,000.....	684	150,748,376	16.2	Less than $5,000.......	79	191,820	1.8
$500,000 to $5,000,000...	156	109,951,280	11.8	$5,000 to $20,000.......	78	841,052	7.9
$1,000,000 to $5,000,000..	96	204,187,367	21.9	$20,000 to $100,000.....	72	3,035,162	28.4
$5,000,000 and over.....	37	352,670,184	37.8	$100,000 and over [4]....	26	6,616,935	61.9
IRON ORE..........	290	218,217,905	100.0	PHOSPHATE ROCK..	48	10,300,198	100.0
Less than $5,000........	15	36,040	(1)				
$5,000 to $20,000........	29	392,775	0.2	Less than $20,000 [5]....	8	66,217	0.6
$20,000 to $100,000...	69	3,774,321	1.7	$20,000 to $100,000.....	16	897,741	8.7
$100,000 to $500,000.....	98	26,453,784	12.1	$100,000 to $500,000....	17	4,052,511	39.3
$500,000 to $1,000,000..	41	28,239,920	12.9	$500,000 and over [3]....	7	5,283,729	51.3
$1,000,000 to $5,000,000..	35	63,674,560	29.2				
$5,000,000 and over.....	3	95,646,505	43.8				

[1] Less than one-tenth of 1 per cent.
[2] Includes the group "$5,000,000 and over."
[3] Includes the group "$1,000,000 to $5,000,000."
[4] Includes the groups "$500,000 to $1,000,000" and "$1,000,000 to $5,000,000."
[5] Includes the group "Less than $5,000."

TABLE 15.—SIZE OF PRODUCING ENTERPRISES, BY VALUE OF PRODUCTS: 1919—Contd.

INDUSTRY AND VALUE OF PRODUCTS PER ENTERPRISE.	Number.	VALUE OF PRODUCTS.		INDUSTRY AND VALUE OF PRODUCTS PER ENTERPRISE.	Number.	VALUE OF PRODUCTS.	
		Amount.	Per cent.			Amount.	Per cent.
CLAY	345	$10,086,298	100.0	GYPSUM	47	$6,805,940	100.0
				Less than $5,000	3	5,042	0.1
Less than $5,000	82	192,739	1.9	$5,000 to $20,000	5	69,164	1.0
$5,000 to $20,000	118	1,248,365	12.4	$20,000 to $100,000	18	941,620	13.8
$20,000 to $100,000	127	5,949,044	59.0	$100,000 to $500,000	18	4,100,134	60.2
$100,000 to $500,000	18	2,696,150	26.7	$500,000 to $1,000,000	3	1,689,980	24.8
BASALT	163	9,657,977	100.0	SLATE	101	5,720,792	100.0
Less than $5,000	20	48,034	0.5	Less than $5,000	13	36,448	0.6
$5,000 to $20,000	40	490,470	5.1	$5,000 to $20,000	21	276,824	4.8
$20,000 to $100,000	77	3,850,020	39.9	$20,000 to $100,000	55	2,764,500	48.3
$100,000 and over [1]	26	5,269,453	54.6	$100,000 and over [1]	12	2,643,020	46.2
GOLD, PLACER MINES	112	9,368,561	100.0	MARBLE	48	4,397,912	100.0
				Less than $5,000	4	10,702	0.2
Less than $5,000	74	119,809	1.3	$5,000 to $20,000	8	81,157	1.8
$5,000 to $20,000	12	112,178	1.2	$20,000 to $100,000	25	1,255,344	28.5
$20,000 to $100,000	12	798,605	8.5	$100,000 and over [2]	11	3,050,709	69.4
$100,000 to $500,000	11	2,611,707	27.9				
$500,000 and over [2]	3	5,726,262	61.1				

[1] Includes the group "$500,000 to $1,000,000."
[2] Includes the group "$1,000,000 to $5,000,000."

TABLE 16.—SIZE OF PRODUCING ENTERPRISES, BY AVERAGE NUMBER OF WAGE EARNERS: 1919.

INDUSTRY AND WAGE EARNERS PER ENTERPRISE.	ENTERPRISES.		WAGE EARNERS.		INDUSTRY AND WAGE EARNERS PER ENTERPRISE.	ENTERPRISES.		WAGE EARNERS.	
	Number.	Per cent distribution.	Average number.	Per cent distribution.		Number.	Per cent distribution.	Average number.	Per cent distribution.
All industries	21,280	100.0	981,560	100.0	BITUMINOUS	6,636	100.0	545,798	100.0
No wage earners	3,722	17.5			No wage earners	62	0.9		
1 to 5	7,912	37.2	16,761	1.7	1 to 5	1,512	22.8	4,337	0.8
6 to 20	3,948	18.6	44,506	4.5	6 to 20	1,549	23.3	18,074	3.3
21 to 50	2,309	10.9	76,040	7.7	21 to 50	1,238	18.7	41,009	7.5
51 to 100	1,372	6.4	98,621	10.0	51 to 100	888	13.4	64,355	11.8
101 to 500	1,743	8.2	377,339	38.4	101 to 500	1,241	18.7	259,288	47.5
501 to 1,000	182	0.9	125,278	12.8	501 to 1,000	101	1.5	68,737	12.6
Over 1,000	92	0.4	243,015	24.8	Over 1,000	45	0.7	89,998	16.5
COAL	6,890	100.0	693,170	100.0	PETROLEUM AND NATURAL GAS	9,814	100.0	93,205	100.0
No wage earners	64	0.9			No wage earners	3,292	33.5		
1 to 5	1,574	22.8	4,476	0.6	1 to 5	4,925	50.2	8,852	9.5
6 to 20	1,588	23.0	18,543	2.7	6 to 20	1,034	10.5	11,036	11.8
21 to 50	1,258	18.3	41,638	6.0	21 to 50	296	3.0	9,874	10.6
51 to 100	901	13.1	65,336	9.4	51 to 100	133	1.4	9,592	10.3
101 to 500	1,304	18.9	277,528	40.0	101 to 500	102	1.0	21,978	23.6
501 to 1,000	134	1.9	90,541	13.1	501 to 1,000	24	0.2	17,358	18.6
Over 1,000	67	1.0	195,108	28.1	Over 1,000	8	0.1	14,515	15.6
ANTHRACITE	254	100.0	147,372	100.0	IRON ORE	290	100.0	45,741	100.0
No wage earners	2	0.8			No wage earners	5	1.7		
1 to 5	62	24.4	139	0.1	1 to 5	21	7.2	63	0.1
6 to 20	39	15.4	469	0.3	6 to 20	43	14.8	574	1.3
21 to 50	20	7.9	629	0.4	21 to 50	57	19.7	2,180	4.8
51 to 100	13	5.1	981	0.7	51 to 100	54	18.6	3,822	8.4
101 to 500	63	24.8	18,240	12.4	101 to 500	102	35.2	31,032	67.8
501 to 1,000	33	13.0	21,804	14.8	501 to 1,000	7	2.4	5,535	12.1
Over 1,000	22	8.7	105,110	71.3	Over 1,000	1	0.3	2,535	5.5

TABLE 16.—SIZE OF PRODUCING ENTERPRISES, BY AVERAGE NUMBER OF WAGE EARNERS: 1919—Continued.

INDUSTRY AND WAGE EARNERS PER ENTERPRISE.	ENTERPRISES. Number.	Per cent distribution.	WAGE EARNERS. Average number.	Per cent distribution.
COPPER	195	100.0	43,717	100.0
No wage-earners	16	8.2	....	.....
1 to 5	53	27.2	129	0.3
6 to 20	35	17.9	406	0.9
21 to 50	27	13.8	859	2.0
51 to 100	11	5.6	835	1.9
101 to 500	30	15.4	8,676	19.8
501 to 1,000	12	6.2	8,817	20.2
Over 1,000	11	5.6	23,995	54.9
LIMESTONE	895	100.0	22,069	100.0
No wage earners	25	2.8	....	.....
1 to 5	288	32.2	713	3.2
6 to 20	301	33.6	3,445	15.6
21 to 50	179	20.0	5,456	24.7
51 to 100	59	6.6	4,109	18.6
101 to 500	43	4.8	8,346	37.8
LEAD AND ZINC	432	100.0	21,884	100.0
No wage earners	41	9.5	....	.....
1 to 5	121	28.0	266	1.2
6 to 20	104	24.1	1,195	5.5
21 to 50	74	17.1	2,443	11.2
51 to 100	45	10.4	3,054	14.0
101 to 500	39	9.0	7,164	32.7
501 to 1,000	4	0.9	2,412	11.0
Over 1,000	4	0.9	5,350	24.4
GOLD AND SILVER, LODE MINES	740	100.0	15,436	100.0
No wage earners	151	20.4	....	.....
1 to 5	273	36.9	643	4.2
6 to 20	178	24.1	1,872	12.1
21 to 50	71	9.6	2,474	16.0
51 to 100	31	4.2	2,244	14.5
101 to 500	35	4.7	6,691	43.3
Over 1,000	1	0.1	1,512	9.8
GRANITE	358	100.0	8,049	100.0
No wage earners	20	5.6	....	.....
1 to 5	119	33.2	288	3.6
6 to 20	117	32.7	1,173	14.6
21 to 50	60	16.8	1,862	23.1
51 to 100	28	7.8	2,035	25.3
101 to 500	14	3.9	2,691	33.4
CLAY	345	100.0	5,453	100.0
No wage earners	26	7.5	....	.....
1 to 5	108	31.3	273	5.0
6 to 20	131	38.0	1,487	27.3
21 to 50	57	16.5	1,824	33.4
51 to 100	19	5.5	1,270	23.3
101 to 500	4	1.2	599	11.0
PHOSPHATE ROCK	48	100.0	4,373	100.0
No wage earners	1	2.1	....	.....
1 to 5	2	4.2	9	0.2
6 to 20	10	20.8	122	2.8
21 to 50	11	22.9	360	8.2
51 to 100	10	20.8	679	15.5
101 to 500	14	29.2	3,203	73.2

INDUSTRY AND WAGE EARNERS PER ENTERPRISE.	ENTERPRISES. Number.	Per cent distribution.	WAGE EARNERS. Average number.	Per cent distribution.
SANDSTONE	255	100.0	4,287	100.0
No wage earners	9	3.5	....	.....
1 to 5	105	41.2	245	5.7
6 to 20	89	34.9	1,032	24.1
21 to 50	29	11.4	942	22.0
51 to 100	17	6.7	1,249	29.1
101 to 500	6	2.4	819	19.1
SLATE	101	100.0	3,513	100.0
No wage earners	1	1.0	....	.....
1 to 5	9	8.9	32	0.9
6 to 20	32	31.7	355	10.1
21 to 50	39	38.6	1,291	36.7
51 to 100	14	13.9	1,005	28.6
101 to 500	6	5.9	830	23.6
BASALT	163	100.0	3,336	100.0
No wage earners	2	1.2	....	.....
1 to 5	36	22.1	115	3.4
6 to 20	67	41.1	782	23.4
21 to 50	47	28.8	1,502	45.0
51 to 100	6	3.7	390	11.7
101 to 500	5	3.1	547	16.4
GYPSUM	47	100.0	2,191	100.0
1 to 5	4	8.5	11	0.5
6 to 20	14	29.8	190	8.7
21 to 50	15	31.9	506	23.1
51 to 100	8	17.0	518	23.6
101 to 500	6	12.8	966	44.1
MARBLE	48	100.0	1,732	100.0
No wage earners	1	2.1	....	.....
1 to 5	4	8.3	12	0.7
6 to 20	20	41.7	250	14.4
21 to 50	16	33.3	531	30.7
51 to 100	2	4.2	147	8.5
101 to 500	5	10.4	792	45.7
GOLD, PLACER MINES	112	100.0	1,380	100.0
No wage earners	34	30.4	....	.....
1 to 5	47	42.0	112	8.1
6 to 20	17	15.2	214	15.5
21 to 50	8	7.1	250	18.1
51 to 100	4	3.6	253	18.3
101 to 500	2	1.8	551	39.9
SULPHUR	4	100.0	1,129	100.0
6 to 20	1	25.0	14	1.2
101 to 500	2	50.0	500	44.3
501 to 1,000	1	25.0	615	54.5

TABLE 17.—FUEL USED, BY PRODUCING ENTERPRISES: 1919.

INDUSTRY.	COAL.		Coke (tons, 2,000 pounds).	Wood (cords).	Fuel oils (barrels).	Gasoline and other volatile oils (barrels).	Natural gas (1,000 cubic feet).
	Anthracite (tons, 2,240 pounds).	Bituminous (tons, 2,000 pounds).					
All industries........	8,697,365	16,275,751	53,795	113,850	9,537,443	143,593	1 102,784,812
Coal:							
Anthracite.............	8,548,201	4,096	....	594	671	1,381	....
Bituminous............	....	11,124,904	14,254	....	3,235	18,963	865,907
Petroleum and natural gas.	....	67,216	....	2,852	5,898,610	45,654	99,967,358
Iron ore..................	69,753	1,499,612	24,070	912	3,807	3,550	1 89,354
Copper...................	14,889	1,364,172	9,744	5,236	1,322,100	6,932	33,456
Lead and zinc...........	33,526	503,278	272	3,570	72,517	6,261	1,390,098
Gold and silver, lode mines..................	45	191,526	369	17,755	130,269	15,821	....
Limestone................	5,409	673,989	937	4,765	33,221	11,397	5,887
Granite..................	1,723	115,250	55	4,297	13,164	2,411	....
Sulphur.................	....	308	20	....	1,087,736	740	....
Sandstone...............	2,418	128,832	1,530	160	8,621	1,423	145,943
Phosphate rock..........	28	121,273	146	39,961	657,284	10,871	....
Clay....................	345	84,065	....	1,424	51,646	1,819	9,009
Basalt...................	2,099	84,566	....	2,129	15,390	620	....
Gold, placer mines........	72	992	1	1,691	114	491	....
Gypsum.................	....	76,086	1,534	43	62,893	1,752	....
Slate....................	8,762	34,053	....	214	36	1	....
Marble..................	210	31,158	....	323	....	170	....
All other................	9,885	170,375	863	27,924	176,129	13,336	277,800

1 89,354 M cubic feet reported for the iron-ore industry was manufactured gas.

TABLE 18.—COMPARATIVE SUMMARY FOR THE UNITED STATES, BY INDUSTRIES, PRODUCING ENTERPRISES: 1919 AND 1909.

INDUSTRY AND CENSUS YEAR.	Number of enterprises.[1]	Wage earners (average number).	Power used (aggregate horsepower).	PRINCIPAL EXPENSES.					Value of products.
				Salaries and wages.	Supplies and materials.	Cost of fuel and purchased power.	Royalties and rents.	Contract work.	
						Expressed in thousands.			
All industries: [2]									
1919	21,280	981,560	6,723,786	$1,445,265	$555,499	$122,106	$175,294	$79,380	$3,158,464
1909	19,915	967,633	4,608,253	[3] 640,168	202,730	45,137	63,974	28,888	1,238,410
FUELS:									
Coal—									
Anthracite—									
1919	254	147,372	899,783	223,285	60,172	13,306	11,767	1,558	364,084
1909	192	169,367	676,753	96,901	23,505	3,193	7,981	1,702	149,180
Bituminous—									
1919	6,636	545,798	2,155,412	751,270	142,433	37,177	22,295	2,856	1,145,978
1909	3,503	511,723	1,227,401	315,997	40,499	7,510	12,082	2,210	427,962
Petroleum and natural gas—									
1919	9,814	93,205	1,821,342	167,990	223,872	20,794	106,459	68,664	931,793
1909	7,793	36,744	1,221,969	34,334	49,836	1,445	21,283	16,737	185,417
METALS:									
Iron ore—									
1919	290	45,741	370,869	82,650	27,188	10,295	24,945	1,672	218,218
1909	176	47,246	346,534	33,121	12,597	4,632	15,175	2,699	106,947
Copper—									
1919	195	43,717	523,591	74,430	35,803	14,866	537	422	181,258
1909	161	51,643	376,464	53,097	34,315	13,324	1,790	645	134,617
Gold and silver, lode mines—									
1919	740	15,436	149,680	26,823	17,709	3,959	1,016	1,237	58,832
1909	1,604	29,428	200,966	34,666	20,552	5,105	1,164	3,604	83,886
Gold, placer mines—									
1919	112	1,380	35,632	2,351	2,245	1,144	86	133	9,369
1909	678	3,084	27,278	3,100	2,194	676	142	100	10,237
Lead and zinc—									
1919	432	21,884	229,541	34,543	15,718	5,375	5,258	863	75,579
1909	977	16,807	110,559	11,570	6,783	2,401	2,302	197	31,363
Manganese—									
1919	35	909	5,800	1,220	448	98	183	149	2,188
1909	5	60	215	20	5	1	2	....	31
Quicksilver—									
1919	26	748	2,607	1,049	403	157	45	8	1,803
1909	12	544	784	486	131	55	5	10	868
Rare metals—									
1919	22	633	3,544	910	581	87	45	8	1,726
1909	26	531	3,237	485	153	126	1	41	968
STONE:									
Limestone—									
1919	895	22,069	213,717	27,653	10,968	4,176	668	666	52,944
1909	1,665	30,289	125,024	15,800	3,754	1,508	489	202	29,832
Granite—									
1919	358	8,049	55,674	9,784	2,593	1,095	139	119	18,279
1909	707	18,744	61,095	12,182	1,922	757	194	66	18,998
Sandstone—									
1919	255	4,287	33,869	5,279	1,664	848	132	54	10,685
1909	1,158	9,812	36,556	5,353	1,040	349	155	79	9,291
Basalt—									
1919	163	3,336	37,307	4,743	2,031	720	250	41	9,658
1909	196	5,256	29,211	2,886	1,018	279	283	60	5,578
Slate—									
1919	101	3,513	20,613	3,538	632	417	158	96	5,721
1909	185	8,803	29,777	4,494	522	327	271	29	6,054
Marble—									
1919	48	1,732	15,628	1,707	552	224	34	21	4,398
1909	77	6,166	21,779	3,462	544	262	48	27	6,239

[1] Operators, not enterprises in 1909.

[2] The totals for all industries include, besides those specified, statistics for the chromite industry in 1919 and for the borax, chromite, grindstone, marl, monazite, and zircon, peat, and precious stones industries in 1909, for which comparable figures could not be given. The value of products of these industries was less than one-tenth of 1 per cent of the total for all industries in 1919 and one-tenth of 1 per cent in 1909.

[3] Includes $632,000 which could not be distributed among the stone industries.

TABLE 18.—COMPARATIVE SUMMARY FOR THE UNITED STATES, BY INDUSTRIES, PRODUCING ENTERPRISES: 1919 AND 1909—Continued.

INDUSTRY AND CENSUS YEAR.	Number of enterprises.[1]	Wage earners (average number).	Power used (aggregate horsepower).	PRINCIPAL EXPENSES.					Value of products.
				Salaries and wages.	Supplies and materials.	Cost of fuel and purchased power.	Royalties and rents.	Contract work.	
				Expressed in thousands.					
MISCELLANEOUS:									
Abrasive materials—									
1919	34	317	1,748	$378	$116	$56	$26	$62	$722
1909	49	403	1,344	191	37	24	12	9	498
Asbestos—									
1919	10	146	420	121	47	5	2	....	250
1909	5	54	380	41	23	(2)	(2)	(2)	65
Asphalt—									
1919	9	324	648	431	376	25	13	6	750
1909	12	205	828	173	66	14	2	16	466
Barytes—									
1919	89	919	3,029	879	236	70	45	10	1,592
1909	23	240	262	110	22	6	14	14	225
Bauxite—									
1919	10	738	2,507	1,099	304	138	153	....	2,190
1909	10	563	1,565	231	22	34	7	....	671
Clay—									
1919	345	5,453	21,243	6,209	1,417	453	465	126	10,086
1909	261	3,262	8,868	1,587	281	108	85	48	2,946
Feldspar—									
1919	30	349	1,782	317	98	33	16	12	584
1909	22	247	993	135	41	16	9	9	271
Fluorspar—									
1919	54	1,124	7,138	1,491	634	163	101	146	3,335
1909	13	290	1,179	193	35	24	2	1	289
Fuller's earth—									
1919	9	824	2,538	635	338	300	6	9	2,019
1909	16	327	1,739	157	36	48	1	(2)	316
Graphite—									
1919	21	419	6,410	464	209	122	3	51	869
1909	19	294	2,647	186	70	36	6	4	344
Gypsum—									
1919	47	2,191	15,032	3,034	1,530	660	69	4	6,806
1909	78	3,462	17,685	2,373	987	573	75	17	5,813
Magnesite—									
1919	11	448	2,540	747	332	296	47	51	2,170
1909	6	50	126	40	6	8	(2)	....	68
Mica—									
1919	65	448	803	335	108	23	19	7	607
1909	73	272	463	139	10	12	6	6	207
Millstones—									
1919	11	37	220	60	11	7	2	....	65
1909	14	51	....	17	(2)	(2)	(2)	....	34
Mineral pigments—									
1919	23	185	1,630	215	83	30	8	1	481
1909	23		849	61	15	8	3	20	151
Phosphate rock—									
1919	48	4,373	49,639	4,662	2,162	1,819	210	164	10,300
1909	51	7,873	50,526	3,807	899	1,360	346	252	10,781
Pyrite—									
1919	17	1,172	7,338	1,570	616	222	43	87	2,409
1909	11	1,086	5,758	463	152	72	1	3	677
Silica—									
1919	24	166	2,032	199	58	22	4	2	372
1909	14	158	1,219	95	17	12	3	16	231
Sulphur—									
1919	4	1,129	15,291	2,095	1,452	2,764	....	....	17,936
1909	4	366	3,114	435	248	708	....	(2)	4,432
Talc and soapstone—									
1919	28	958	7,053	1,050	345	156	39	53	2,302
1909	39	1,256	9,433	607	196	66	31	4	1,175

[1] Operators, not enterprises, in 1909.   [2] Less than $500.

TABLE **19.**—COMPARATIVE SUMMARY FOR THE UNITED STATES, BY STATES, PRODUCING ENTERPRISES: 1919 AND 1909.

STATE AND CENSUS YEAR.	Number of enterprises.[1]	Wage earners (average number).	Power used (aggregate horsepower).	PRINCIPAL EXPENSES.					Value of products.
				Salaries and wages.	Supplies and materials.	Cost of fuel and purchased power.	Royalties and rents.	Contract work.	
				Expressed in thousands.					
United States:									
1919[2]	21,280	981,560	6,723,786	$1,445,265	$555,499	$122,106	$175,294	$79,380	$3,158,464
1909	[3]19,915	967,633	4,608,253	[4]640,168	202,730	45,127	63,974	[5]28,888	1,238,410
Alabama:									
1919	264	32,579	145,775	40,165	7,481	3,080	838	167	59,866
1909	177	28,271	91,924	15,936	2,620	1,049	334	767	24,351
Arizona:									
1919	155	15,268	166,091	29,953	16,161	5,378	439	747	88,478
1909	135	12,838	47,272	14,521	6,930	5,604	8	239	34,218
Arkansas:									
1919	126	3,630	21,365	5,175	1,402	441	387	139	8,405
1909	96	4,935	14,080	3,265	368	139	194	117	4,604
California:									
1919	725	19,344	313,213	36,890	32,692	7,047	10,911	1,377	163,770
1909	1,329	20,517	162,238	22,018	21,552	2,776	2,814	595	63,382
Colorado:									
1919	477	16,790	116,351	28,194	11,955	2,707	1,584	398	51,217
1909	672	21,483	98,777	20,576	10,390	1,956	1,017	2,996	45,680
Connecticut:									
1919	41	543	8,520	791	304	120	11	27	1,649
1909	71	1,385	6,298	812	127	72	17	14	1,376
Delaware:									
1919	7	116	660	156	34	19	5	3	244
1909	9	493	1,480	288	152	26	4	6	516
Florida:									
1919	36	3,372	44,969	3,774	1,836	1,688	141	121	8,976
1909	36	5,448	42,366	2,847	739	1,223	198	218	8,847
Georgia:									
1919	74	2,397	13,026	2,373	609	356	156	35	4,082
1909	92	3,383	10,698	1,468	254	147	59	2	2,875
Idaho:									
1919	82	2,455	31,239	4,740	2,026	514	182	194	11,840
1909	174	3,246	26,278	4,403	1,847	356	28	23	8,649
Illinois:									
1919	772	79,123	318,231	104,302	18,808	5,785	6,636	432	178,673
1909	915	72,086	225,330	49,491	8,575	1,326	3,580	2,377	76,659
Indiana:									
1919	503	26,751	129,663	34,271	6,421	2,013	940	340	52,840
1909	1,010	23,936	95,039	15,884	1,847	552	595	296	21,934
Iowa:									
1919	198	11,274	32,171	13,810	2,072	749	335	33	18,474
1909	373	16,480	23,453	11,411	1,308	222	349	41	13,878
Kansas:									
1919	814	16,136	133,984	25,249	33,396	4,306	10,712	3,998	90,338
1909	643	14,343	66,943	10,325	2,038	268	1,666	396	18,723
Kentucky:									
1919	938	43,563	148,893	56,861	15,659	2,523	5,814	3,266	98,487
1909	437	18,297	53,203	8,793	1,322	218	423	185	12,100
Louisiana and Mississippi:									
1919	137	5,228	86,135	9,003	8,502	2,813	4,312	2,043	40,016
1909[6]	33	926	8,445	1,200	867	727	496	62	6,547
Maine:									
1919	50	979	6,277	1,170	203	123	10	32	1,823
1909	97	2,144	8,141	1,452	220	85	16	7	2,056
Maryland:									
1919	126	5,628	18,660	6,941	1,178	309	138	17	9,699
1909	126	7,190	18,118	3,668	479	104	134	8	5,782
Massachusetts:									
1919	74	1,704	12,498	2,394	494	263	59	11	4,176
1909	139	3,291	15,031	2,180	364	153	55	16	3,468
Michigan:									
1919	122	31,292	337,882	54,718	15,204	8,445	6,669	29	103,870
1909	83	39,169	273,861	29,834	9,800	4,193	4,049	470	67,714
Minnesota:									
1919	135	17,265	144,199	32,431	14,192	4,682	17,643	1,513	130,399
1909	153	16,586	151,834	13,476	6,737	2,025	10,732	2,157	58,665
Missouri:									
1919	468	14,857	100,160	18,641	4,785	2,034	781	416	33,366
1909	1,021	23,420	109,672	15,669	6,202	2,221	1,954	162	31,667

[1] Operators, not enterprises, in 1909.
[2] The total for the United States includes, besides the states specified, statistics for the District of Columbia for which no statistics were reported for 1909.
[3] Exclusive of duplication, 307 operators having reported in two or more states.
[4] Includes $1,568,000 which could not be distributed among the several states.
[5] Includes $62,000 which could not be distributed among the several states.
[6] Includes statistics for Louisiana only; nothing reported for Mississippi.

TABLE **19.**—COMPARATIVE SUMMARY FOR THE UNITED STATES, BY STATES, PRODUCING ENTERPRISES: 1919 AND 1909—Continued.

STATE AND CENSUS YEAR.	Number of enterprises.[1]	Wage earners (average number).	Power used (aggregate horsepower).	PRINCIPAL EXPENSES.					Value of products.
				Salaries and wages.	Supplies and materials.	Cost of fuel and purchased power.	Royalties and rents.	Contract work.	
				Expressed in thousands.					
Montana:									
1919........	259	16,129	143,718	$28,228	$9,515	$2,980	$646	$116	$49,924
1909........	373	18,846	174,389	22,774	16,397	3,628	1,823	395	54,992
Nebraska:									
1919........	9	162	1,847	193	61	21	10	....	293
1909........	18	349	815	187	35	22	2	6	322
Nevada:									
1919........	203	4,231	50,786	8,501	5,339	1,751	144	245	18,054
1909........	266	4,642	26,862	6,801	4,986	1,312	276	197	23,272
New Hampshire:									
1919........	30	682	4,336	922	145	65	6	35	1,568
1909........	45	1,418	3,771	980	101	54	4	9	1,309
New Jersey:									
1919........	97	4,576	33,901	6,119	2,195	720	277	58	9,309
1909........	131	6,315	18,048	3,064	675	319	101	44	8,347
New Mexico:									
1919........	85	7,100	59,876	11,645	3,889	1,361	181	132	18,873
1909........	98	5,107	16,042	3,975	805	203	79	133	5,588
New York:									
1919........	700	6,202	91,339	8,928	7,417	1,402	649	789	25,131
1909........	1,351	9,305	101,759	5,425	1,953	585	466	513	13,335
North Carolina:									
1919........	102	1,890	5,039	1,689	467	221	36	6	2,737
1909........	118	2,215	6,062	986	153	103	20	37	1,359
North Dakota:									
1919........	79	774	2,037	1,189	284	38	31	31	1,927
1909........	53	562	2,025	427	95	13	11	1	565
Ohio:									
1919........	2,283	49,298	337,611	66,152	19,210	4,131	6,340	3,929	134,518
1909........	1,876	50,567	294,763	29,544	12,736	893	3,667	2,971	63,767
Oklahoma:									
1919........	1,934	33,914	448,173	59,342	65,217	4,794	30,689	18,982	281,928
1909........	864	11,658	95,074	9,118	5,028	384	2,784	2,137	25,638
Oregon:									
1919........	50	740	6,264	1,141	546	133	48	36	1,885
1909........	116	860	8,070	830	187	97	17	8	1,191
Pennsylvania:									
1919........	5,807	323,397	1,999,422	480,183	124,328	27,707	24,683	7,970	819,451
1909........	4,851	361,013	1,618,806	210,531	48,274	6,423	15,379	5,976	349,060
Rhode Island:									
1919........	14	369	3,000	482	147	55	6	1	952
1909........	21	665	2,350	468	131	27	9	....	898
South Carolina:									
1919........	20	933	4,656	820	303	150	7	....	1,351
1909........	29	1,814	7,012	709	125	118	10	7	1,253
South Dakota:									
1919........	23	1,785	11,844	2,714	1,008	284	7	12	5,314
1909........	39	3,456	15,648	3,432	1,110	421	5	(2)	6,432
Tennessee:									
1919........	203	14,470	56,685	14,626	3,892	1,260	555	174	23,292
1909........	216	16,338	34,523	8,347	1,614	645	617	54	12,692
Texas:									
1919........	624	18,164	129,063	35,988	45,402	6,190	23,912	25,774	160,378
1909........	236	6,379	32,003	4,539	1,833	256	918	152	10,742
Utah:									
1919........	141	9,847	86,131	19,114	8,043	2,019	151	491	41,511
1909........	188	10,089	47,226	10,184	4,027	1,074	72	265	22,083
Vermont:									
1919........	93	2,936	28,119	3,490	1,273	425	58	92	8,555
1909........	137	8,145	25,668	4,820	905	362	84	65	8,221
Virginia:									
1919........	202	14,547	57,880	17,798	4,760	1,217	830	341	29,363
1909........	150	15,257	34,630	5,842	1,174	485	418	119	8,796
Washington:									
1919........	83	5,050	38,198	8,128	1,729	947	177	87	13,329
1909........	93	6,904	20,742	6,236	843	246	141	14	10,538
West Virginia:									
1919........	1,714	100,812	704,279	134,532	46,612	6,909	14,846	3,890	295,607
1909........	798	73,410	416,282	39,810	12,541	1,213	7,796	4,466	76,288
Wisconsin:									
1919........	92	3,547	26,766	5,368	1,969	857	536	135	10,581
1909........	268	4,710	24,864	3,340	878	436	445	41	7,459
Wyoming:									
1919........	106	9,699	62,757	15,963	6,423	1,073	1,766	716	41,929
1909........	66	7,742	30,338	6,714	1,386	376	108	62	10,572

[1] Operators, not enterprises, in 1909.   [2] Less than $500.

TABLE 20.—DETAILED STATISTICS FOR MINES, QUARRIES, AND WELLS, PRODUCING AND NONPRODUCING ENTERPRISES, FOR THE UNITED STATES, BY INDUSTRIES: 1919.

INDUSTRY.	Number of enterprises.	Number of mines, quarries, or wells.	Number of enterprises operating beneficiating plants.	LAND CONTROLLED (ACRES).			
				Mineral land.			Timber and other lands.
				Operated.	Owned.	Leased.	
All industries	21,997	....	1,503	22,947,937	8,729,545	14,294,342	2,215,702
Producing enterprises	21,280	....	1,503	22,474,069	8,568,590	13,980,731	2,208,519
FUELS:							
Coal, anthracite	254	[1] 534	140	261,355	194,390	77,955	159,710
Coal, bituminous	6,636	8,282	134	8,261,372	5,793,651	2,528,562	751,473
Petroleum and natural gas	9,814	257,673	....	12,171,388	1,172,068	10,999,320	
METALS:							
Iron ore	290	406	74	241,508	177,296	65,280	696,140
Copper	195	226	57	392,811	378,839	14,045	255,819
Lead and zinc	432	473	262	135,262	99,338	36,118	47,053
Gold and silver, lode mines	740	799	191	142,573	113,347	29,424	46,166
Gold, placer mines	112	132	2	62,857	51,219	11,738	16,860
Manganese	35	37	8	51,574	12,463	39,111	16
Quicksilver	26	26	24	27,387	16,820	10,567	5,283
Rare metals [2]	22	22	11	18,779	17,200	1,579	30
STONE:							
Limestone	895	925	44	122,820	84,717	38,306	52,963
Granite	358	381	152	30,659	23,799	6,950	6,998
Sandstone	255	276	66	48,729	34,726	15,435	6,641
Basalt	163	174	6	15,625	7,139	8,486	1,889
Slate	101	104	61	5,440	3,673	1,767	2,805
Marble	48	62	25	28,969	11,818	17,159	6,273
MISCELLANEOUS:							
Abrasive materials [3]	34	34	14	15,885	10,334	5,551	1,433
Asbestos	10	11	3	2,371	2,200	171	
Asphalt	9	12	....	8,889	8,759	130	
Barytes	89	98	5	37,135	31,971	5,164	10,622
Bauxite	10	15	7	3,997	1,164	2,833	23,998
Chromite	15	16	1	3,389	1,034	2,355	61
Clay	345	350	45	105,706	70,498	35,263	7,040
Feldspar	30	32	4	1,480	761	719	235
Fluorspar	54	72	25	9,623	5,888	3,735	5,942
Fuller's earth	9	9	8	6,720	4,274	2,446	258
Graphite	21	24	16	8,114	7,931	183	186
Gypsum	47	48	27	41,703	36,581	5,122	490
Magnesite	11	11	7	2,931	1,375	1,556	930
Mica	65	69	9	5,188	3,225	1,963	781
Millstones	11	11	....	119	16	103	
Mineral pigments	23	23	11	2,483	1,997	486	1,836
Phosphate rock	48	69	20	160,447	156,418	4,029	81,363
Pyrite	17	18	12	9,103	5,532	3,571	8,958
Silica	24	29	8	1,989	1,263	726	439
Sulphur	4	4	1	12,946	12,946	....	7,565
Talc and soapstone	28	30	23	14,743	11,920	2,823	263
Nonproducing enterprises	717	....	....	473,868	160,955	313,611	7,183
FUELS:							
Coal	26	26	....	24,707	14,317	10,390	97
Petroleum and natural gas	156	276	....	260,131	3,645	256,486	
METALS:							
Iron ore	18	18	....	4,506	2,339	2,167	604
Gold, silver, copper, lead, or zinc	500	512	....	176,035	136,452	40,281	5,648
MISCELLANEOUS [4]	17	17	....	8,489	4,202	4,287	834

[1] Includes 79 anthracite culm washeries and 81 river dredges.
[2] Includes enterprises in industries as follows: Molybdenum, 2; titanium, 2; tungsten, 6; uranium and vanadium, 12.
[3] Includes enterprises in industries as follows: Diatomaceous earth, 9; emery, 2; garnet, 2; pebbles and lining for grinding mills, 3; pumice, 6; rotten stone, 1; stone for whetstones, 2; tripoli, 9.
[4] Includes enterprises in industries as follows: Barytes, 1; cobalt, 1; limestone, 1; manganese, 2; marble, 1; mica, 1; molybdenum, 2; phosphate rock, 1; pyrite, 1; quicksilver, 2; silica, 1; sulphur, 1; tin, 1; vanadium, 1.

TABLE 20.—DETAILED STATISTICS FOR MINES, QUARRIES, AND WELLS, PRODUCING AND NONPRODUCING ENTERPRISES, FOR THE UNITED STATES, BY INDUSTRIES: 1919—Continued.

INDUSTRY.	PERSONS ENGAGED IN INDUSTRY—continued.										
	Wage earners, Dec. 15, or nearest representative day.										
	Enginemen, hoistmen, electricians, mechanics, etc.		Miners, quarrymen, and drillmen, including their helpers.		Timbermen, trackmen, and men engaged in hauling, tramming, etc.		Muckers, loaders, and others not classified.		In mills and beneficiating plants (above ground).	Under 16 years of age (above ground).	Females (above ground).
	Above ground.	Below ground.	Above ground.	Below ground.	Above ground.	Below ground.	Above ground.	Below ground.			
All industries...	135,665	30,349	31,383	397,636	25,896	139,052	136,646	126,793	46,811	222	612
Producing enterprises.....	134,117	30,145	30,702	395,398	25,583	138,491	135,239	125,952	46,811	221	541
FUELS:											
Coal, anthracite.....	10,488	4,331	138	59,401	2,769	17,325	12,291	23,470	20,497	119	....
Coal, bituminous....	32,635	22,444	7,025	295,084	14,733	99,480	47,152	80,727	2,554	61	58
Petroleum and natural gas..........	64,230	......	......	......	......	......	36,750	......	......	......	118
METALS:											
Iron ore............	6,526	1,053	1,354	15,326	1,677	5,495	7,436	5,938	1,268	6	7
Copper............	6,167	1,254	1,185	9,455	1,005	8,115	4,352	5,743	6,589	4	74
Lead and zinc......	2,576	362	109	6,857	304	4,361	1,477	4,544	4,636	4	18
Gold and silver, lode mines............	1,713	515	208	4,980	296	2,202	1,339	3,310	1,961	....	49
Gold, placer mines..	463	......	122	60	37	4	729	7	2	1	12
Manganese..........	154	4	42	694	68	127	291	178	109	2	....
Quicksilver.........	109	7	31	151	42	114	83	91	173	....	2
Rare metals........	108	5	104	197	61	66	183	67	105	3	12
STONE:											
Limestone..........	3,278	53	8,433	204	1,930	104	8,716	409	958	9	10
Granite............	858	......	3,736	......	544	......	1,621	......	2,028	2	1
Sandstone..........	405	......	1,599	......	304	......	1,621	......	735	1	2
Basalt.............	473	......	1,120	......	192	......	1,828	......	42	......	2
Slate..............	371	3	811	488	200	54	792	150	935	4	....
Marble............	150	......	763	......	41	......	307	......	529	......	....
MISCELLANEOUS:											
Abrasive materials..	41	......	106	5	24	......	113	2	101	......	1
Asbestos...........	8	......	27	75	5	3	47	20	15	......	....
Asphalt............	35	......	75	26	8	34	229	16	......	......	....
Barytes............	74	......	318	......	53	......	629	......	49	1	....
Bauxite............	77	......	539	......	111	......	65	......	112	......	....
Chromite..........	3	......	27	9	1	2	9	3	2	......	....
Clay...............	349	25	815	1,066	426	400	2,527	207	256	1	7
Feldspar...........	27	......	228	......	51	......	66	......	44	......	2
Fluorspar..........	221	35	55	183	32	166	211	140	201	......	....
Fuller's earth......	50	......	202	......	50	......	39	......	527	......	29
Graphite...........	73	2	69	8	29	23	140	8	175	......	1
Gypsum............	105	40	159	445	25	208	239	442	816	......	11
Magnesite..........	65	2	57	56	26	14	124	109	187	......	....
Mica..............	15	4	115	87	11	19	85	28	130	......	77
Millstones.........	......	......	31	......	9	......	1	......	......	......	....
Mineral pigments...	20	......	34	21	7	13	69	10	52	......	....
Phosphate rock......	1,154	......	968	116	443	7	2,577	23	331	1	23
Pyrite.............	129	2	41	201	20	108	214	239	160	......	13
Silica.............	17	......	40	......	18	......	111	......	33	......	2
Sulphur...........	878	......	......	2	......	......	692	5	2	......	4
Talc and soapstone..	72	4	16	201	31	47	84	66	497	2	6
Nonproducing enterprises.....	1,548	204	686	2,238	313	561	1,407	841	......	1	71
FUELS:											
Coal...............	68	10	31	271	79	29	277	28	......	1	....
Petroleum and natural gas..........	520	......	......	......	......	......	242	......	......	......	5
METALS:											
Iron ore...........	151	24	46	67	58	81	150	31	......	......	1
Gold, silver, copper, lead, or zinc.......	784	162	203	1,848	156	436	607	749	......	......	59
MISCELLANEOUS.......	25	8	406	52	20	15	131	33	......	......	6

TABLE 20.—DETAILED STATISTICS FOR MINES, QUARRIES, AND WELLS, PRODUCING AND NONPRODUCING ENTERPRISES, FOR THE UNITED STATES, BY INDUSTRIES: 1919—Continued.

INDUSTRY.	Capital.	PRINCIPAL EXPENSES OF OPERATION AND DEVELOPMENT.				
			Salaries and wages.			
		Total.	Salaried officers, superintendents, managers, and technical employees.	Clerks and other subordinate salaried employees.	Wage earners.	Supplies and materials.
	Dollars.	*Dollars.*	*Dollars.*	*Dollars.*	*Dollars.*	*Dollars.*
All industries......	7,108,623,496	2,543,887,062	105,892,362	45,380,089	1,304,409,342	528,853,639
Producing enterprises........	6,955,466,831	2,518,543,956	104,235,154	45,093,831	1,295,936,226	519,593,676
FUELS:						
Coal, anthracite........	433,868,039	324,147,994	8,848,535	4,146,934	210,289,473	59,738,376
Coal, bituminous........	1,904,450,123	990,738,244	50,334,218	18,334,820	682,601,068	142,432,551
Petroleum and natural gas..................	2,421,485,942	626,468,862	21,375,372	12,092,996	134,521,247	195,058,693
METALS:						
Iron ore...............	501,396,044	177,578,869	4,198,832	2,737,828	75,713,459	27,187,832
Copper...............	853,639,017	138,286,993	5,018,974	3,020,767	66,390,194	34,275,369
Lead and zinc.........	197,223,814	65,084,781	2,714,694	1,120,246	30,708,319	15,311,548
Gold and silver, lode mines...............	280,388,711	53,070,119	2,466,693	539,068	23,817,657	13,040,897
Gold, placer mines.....	24,574,441	6,314,764	380,410	56,383	1,914,072	2,244,728
Manganese...........	7,268,426	2,159,151	104,481	29,623	1,085,899	447,833
Quicksilver...........	4,423,601	1,693,445	194,368	26,810	827,751	403,269
Rare metals...........	4,889,912	1,666,420	114,724	47,021	748,235	573,649
STONE:						
Limestone............	82,124,367	45,250,704	2,614,748	1,111,845	23,926,332	10,968,220
Granite...............	18,823,980	14,107,461	982,092	214,364	8,587,659	2,593,040
Sandstone............	18,955,321	8,173,578	630,306	200,327	4,448,811	1,664,432
Basalt...............	12,899,171	7,983,629	598,157	153,090	3,991,307	2,030,869
Slate................	6,923,172	4,914,081	341,487	67,768	3,128,249	632,459
Marble...............	9,033,522	2,661,848	191,396	62,723	1,452,440	552,439
MISCELLANEOUS:						
Abrasive materials.....	1,442,909	643,676	46,468	8,675	322,379	116,145
Asbestos.............	772,299	178,904	25,088	3,815	91,672	47,202
Asphalt..............	3,171,405	892,928	105,941	30,460	294,652	376,009
Barytes..............	2,290,455	1,259,058	82,375	27,736	768,847	218,582
Bauxite..............	1,950,173	1,795,740	103,438	53,933	941,807	303,558
Chromite.............	1,572,908	94,465	5,475	....	44,777	13,330
Clay.................	17,644,524	8,818,563	646,201	196,118	5,367,082	1,416,999
Feldspar.............	729,404	489,717	45,966	7,458	263,760	97,834
Fluorspar............	8,046,827	2,878,431	259,997	35,302	1,195,777	634,498
Fuller's earth........	1,877,233	1,406,250	85,482	8,209	541,163	338,011
Graphite.............	3,755,055	871,211	104,099	18,235	341,542	209,256
Gypsum..............	13,541,548	5,379,732	275,145	280,305	2,478,391	1,530,338
Magnesite............	2,612,605	1,488,006	78,918	16,267	652,302	300,741
Mica................	699,373	495,364	36,658	9,921	288,487	107,933
Millstones............	53,105	80,311	10,000	1,800	47,966	11,244
Mineral pigments......	815,572	341,051	31,620	8,679	174,453	83,078
Phosphate rock........	72,733,956	9,364,154	566,477	194,946	3,900,966	2,161,501
Pyrite...............	4,455,785	2,594,728	123,319	61,741	1,384,735	615,726
Silica...............	661,711	290,583	28,835	4,193	165,709	58,185
Sulphur..............	28,046,634	7,189,753	292,117	120,898	1,682,174	1,452,136
Talc and soapstone.....	6,225,747	1,690,388	172,048	42,527	835,413	345,166
Nonproducing enterprises........	153,156,665	25,343,106	1,657,208	286,258	8,473,116	9,259,963
FUELS:						
Coal.................	5,617,170	1,415,640	74,761	5,225	590,824	651,231
Petroleum and natural gas..................	24,960,853	6,655,716	305,228	105,128	875,923	3,031,107
METALS:						
Iron ore...............	10,884,660	3,212,948	76,266	31,647	985,092	654,141
Gold, silver, copper, lead, or zinc.........	105,260,998	13,256,365	1,122,291	133,419	5,636,646	4,684,728
MISCELLANEOUS..........	6,432,984	802,437	78,662	10,839	384,631	238,756

TABLE 20.—DETAILED STATISTICS FOR MINES, QUARRIES, AND WELLS, PRODUCING AND NONPRODUCING ENTERPRISES, FOR THE UNITED STATES, BY INDUSTRIES: 1919—Continued.

INDUSTRY.	PRINCIPAL EXPENSES OF OPERATION AND DEVELOPMENT—continued.					
	Cost of ore, coal, and natural gas purchased as material or for resale.	Cost of fuel.	Cost of purchased power.	Royalties and rents.	Taxes—Federal, state, county, and local.	Contract work.
	Dollars.	Dollars.	Dollars.	Dollars.	Dollars.	Dollars.
All industries.........	35, 905, 352	94, 848, 752	28, 660, 836	176, 129, 858	141, 567, 734	82, 239, 098
Producing enterprises..	35, 905, 352	93, 910, 653	28, 195, 277	175, 293, 984	140, 999, 626	79, 380, 177
FUELS:						
Coal, anthracite............	433, 318	11, 406, 117	1, 899, 835	11, 766, 598	14, 060, 963	1, 557, 845
Coal, bituminous...........	....	25, 896, 660	11, 280, 509	22, 295, 056	34, 707, 396	2, 855, 966
Petroleum and natural gas.	28, 813, 671	19, 828, 776	965, 300	106, 458, 518	38, 690, 630	68, 663, 659
METALS:						
Iron ore..................	....	8, 700, 358	1, 594, 231	24, 944, 936	30, 829, 610	1, 671, 783
Copper...................	1, 528, 056	11, 310, 485	3, 555, 530	536, 819	12, 229, 046	421, 753
Lead and zinc.............	406, 051	2, 783, 249	2, 591, 906	5, 258, 387	3, 326, 910	863, 471
Gold and silver, lode mines.	4, 668, 291	1, 623, 124	2, 336, 136	1, 015, 719	2, 325, 491	1, 237, 043
Gold, placer mines.......	....	20, 459	1, 123, 874	85, 899	356, 132	132, 807
Manganese...............	....	52, 228	46, 107	183, 087	60, 656	149, 237
Quicksilver..............	....	127, 931	29, 133	45, 194	31, 016	7, 973
Rare metals..............	7, 000	41, 416	45, 492	45, 396	35, 609	7, 878
STONE:						
Limestone...............	....	2, 897, 432	1, 278, 958	667, 751	1, 119, 861	665, 557
Granite..................	....	833, 636	261, 185	139, 202	377, 646	118, 637
Sandstone...............	....	597, 353	250, 909	131, 970	195, 309	54, 161
Basalt...................	....	562, 827	157, 161	250, 199	198, 613	41, 406
Slate....................	....	228, 954	188, 505	157, 788	73, 238	95, 633
Marble..................	....	147, 644	76, 741	34, 380	123, 503	20, 582
MISCELLANEOUS:						
Abrasive materials........	....	56, 122	....	25, 634	6, 022	62, 231
Asbestos.................	....	3, 380	2, 050	1, 740	3, 957	....
Asphalt..................	....	24, 876	....	13, 387	41, 686	5, 917
Barytes..................	17, 500	50, 389	19, 335	45, 343	18, 824	10, 127
Bauxite..................	....	137, 766	....	152, 848	102, 390	....
Chromite................	....	1, 575	....	4, 777	215	24, 316
Clay.....................	....	397, 655	54, 934	465, 184	148, 035	126, 355
Feldspar.................	....	21, 284	12, 158	16, 391	12, 793	12, 073
Fluorspar................	....	163, 239	....	101, 311	342, 391	145, 916
Fuller's earth............	....	294, 260	5, 603	5, 899	119, 067	8, 556
Graphite.................	....	81, 917	39, 697	2, 646	23, 123	50, 696
Gypsum..................	....	516, 148	144, 272	69, 403	81, 983	3, 747
Magnesite...............	31, 465	258, 411	37, 694	47, 193	14, 169	50, 846
Mica....................	....	20, 935	1, 733	18, 893	3, 479	7, 325
Millstones...............	....	3, 750	3, 360	2, 175	16	....
Mineral pigments.........	....	27, 707	2, 659	8, 499	3, 036	1, 320
Phosphate rock..........	....	1, 739, 833	79, 488	209, 687	347, 580	163, 696
Pyrite...................	....	163, 039	58, 802	43, 057	57, 248	87, 061
Silica...................	....	16, 434	5, 526	4, 060	5, 794	1, 847
Sulphur.................	....	2, 764, 194	....	....	878, 234	....
Talc and soapstone.......	....	109, 090	46, 474	38, 958	47, 955	52, 757
Nonproducing enterprises.............	....	938, 099	465, 559	835, 874	568, 108	2, 858, 921
FUELS:						
Coal....................	....	4, 548	10, 751	19, 476	46, 289	12, 535
Petroleum and natural gas.	....	242, 616	7, 727	591, 729	57, 758	1, 438, 500
METALS:						
Iron ore.................	....	170, 506	41, 343	135, 982	320, 637	797, 334
Gold, silver, copper, lead, or zinc..................	....	480, 666	404, 158	62, 848	138, 291	593, 318
MISCELLANEOUS...............	....	39, 763	1, 580	25, 839	5, 133	17, 234

TABLE 20.—DETAILED STATISTICS FOR MINES, QUARRIES, AND WELLS, PRODUCING AND NONPRODUCING ENTERPRISES, FOR THE UNITED STATES, BY INDUSTRIES: 1919—Continued.

INDUSTRY.	Expenditures for development (included in principal expenses).	Value of products.	POWER USED.					
			Aggregate.	Total horse-power.	Prime movers.			
					Steam engines (not turbines).		Steam turbines.	
					Number.	Horsepower.	Number.	Horsepower.
	Dollars.	Dollars.						
All industries..	334,015,265	3,158,463,966	6,786,475	5,147,613	46,744	3,259,076	555	474,315
Producing enterprises	311,276,508	3,158,463,966	6,723,786	5,111,531	46,433	3,238,288	553	473,985
FUELS:								
Coal, anthracite....	6,189,990	364,084,142	899,783	782,090	5,298	730,141	45	50,665
Coal, bituminous...	30,044,379	1,145,977,565	2,155,412	1,383,934	9,177	1,166,862	313	195,779
Petroleum and natural gas............	230,867,499	931,793,423	1,821,342	1,770,181	23,412	532,734		
METALS:								
Iron ore............	14,657,841	218,217,905	370,869	273,477	2,333	231,184	25	28,521
Copper.............	13,302,349	181,258,087	523,591	386,458	842	245,398	79	123,223
Lead and zinc......	4,268,914	75,579,347	229,541	117,527	411	42,821	21	35,420
Gold and silver, lode mines........	7,862,971	58,832,330	149,680	50,437	182	20,133	4	4,750
Gold, placer mines..	201,259	9,368,561	35,632	3,406	2	40		
Manganese.........	238,408	2,188,312	5,800	2,610	36	1,911		
Quicksilver.........	161,598	1,803,484	2,607	1,441	4	106		
Rare metals........	161,958	1,725,642	3,544	1,406	8	483		
STONE:								
Limestone..........	764,673	52,943,924	213,717	126,387	1,776	109,778	17	10,701
Granite.............	156,870	18,279,345	55,674	34,711	744	30,231	3	2,360
Sandstone..........	96,555	10,684,969	33,869	21,197	340	19,081		
Basalt.............	131,800	9,657,977	37,307	22,844	259	21,099	3	1,225
Slate..............	60,531	5,720,792	20,613	8,778	193	8,669		
Marble.............	30,914	4,397,912	15,628	6,021	85	5,619		
MISCELLANEOUS:								
Abrasive materials..	14,849	721,728	1,748	1,748	17	1,283		
Asbestos............	46,503	249,839	420	355	1	75		
Asphalt............	376,579	749,520	648	648	6	545		
Barytes............	20,503	1,592,245	3,029	2,049	31	1,730		
Bauxite...........	11,064	2,190,279	2,507	2,507	28	840		
Chromite..........	2,650	105,841	136	136				
Clay..............	265,009	10,086,298	21,243	16,932	263	15,653	1	100
Feldspar..........	13,197	584,296	1,782	1,227	16	1,081		
Fluorspar.........	393,465	3,334,880	7,138	7,138	121	6,036	1	50
Fuller's earth......	23,595	2,019,226	2,538	2,250	35	1,720		
Graphite..........	164,849	869,403	6,410	2,241	15	1,873		
Gypsum...........	12,050	6,805,940	15,032	7,038	47	6,132		
Magnesite.........	10,868	2,169,571	2,540	827	2	80		
Mica..............	65,024	607,025	803	763	22	700		
Millstones.........		64,631	220	60	1	60		
Mineral pigments...	5,456	480,768	1,630	1,460	18	862		
Phosphate rock.....	353,237	10,300,198	49,639	46,976	100	17,140	17	17,751
Pyrite.............	145,615	2,408,648	7,338	3,224	35	1,970	1	120
Silica.............	37,921	371,638	2,032	1,699	10	860		
Sulphur...........	56,478	17,935,882	15,291	15,291	544	11,581	23	3,320
Talc and soapstone.	59,087	2,302,393	7,053	4,057	19	1,777		
Nonproducing enterprises.....	22,738,757	....	62,689	36,082	311	20,788	2	330
FUELS:								
Coal................	1,253,604	....	2,534	1,819	13	1,785		
Petroleum and natural gas...........	5,685,921	....	5,543	5,047	103	3,695		
METALS:								
Iron ore...........	2,702,453	....	10,175	6,235	41	6,201		
Gold, silver, copper, lead, or zinc.......	12,366,117	....	42,785	21,454	142	7,997	2	330
MISCELLANEOUS......	730,662	....	1,652	1,527	12	1,110		

TABLE 20.—DETAILED STATISTICS FOR MINES, QUARRIES, AND WELLS, PRODUCING AND NONPRODUCING ENTERPRISES, FOR THE UNITED STATES, BY INDUSTRIES: 1919—Continued.

	POWER USED—continued.								
	Prime movers—Continued.				Equipment operated by purchased power.			Electric motors run by current generated by the enterprise reporting.	
INDUSTRY.	Internal-combustion engines.		Water wheels and turbines.		Electric motors.		Other.		
	Number.	Horse-power.	Number.	Horse-power.	Number.	Horse-power.	Horse-power.	Number.	Horse-power.
All industries......	57,417	1,372,698	329	41,524	41,114	1,629,580	9,282	33,039	1,260,466
Producing enterprises........	56,988	1,361,146	287	38,112	40,500	1,603,390	8,865	32,980	1,258,795
FUELS:									
Coal, anthracite.........	73	1,284	......	......	1,881	117,693	......	3,801	185,723
Coal, bituminous.......	1,246	21,219	9	74	21,186	771,131	347	21,044	707,341
Petroleum and natural gas...............	53,699	1,237,407	2	40	1,841	44,638	6,523	1,329	28,164
METALS:									
Iron ore................	45	5,397	22	8,375	1,341	97,382	10	1,112	67,595
Copper.................	129	16,327	10	1,510	3,647	135,968	1,165	3,252	161,024
Lead and zinc..........	433	35,415	30	3,871	2,389	111,874	140	625	22,884
Gold and silver, lode mines..............	370	11,149	135	14,405	2,523	98,663	580	494	18,892
Gold, placer mines......	16	719	25	2,647	624	32,226	......	22	601
Manganese.............	24	699	......	......	67	3,190	......	3	310
Quicksilver............	78	1,335	......	......	39	1,166	......	9	66
Rare metals............	22	693	2	230	60	2,138	......	28	350
STONE:									
Limestone.............	252	5,043	9	865	2,046	87,330	......	267	11,421
Granite................	84	1,343	4	777	450	20,903	60	34	1,520
Sandstone.............	71	2,116	......	......	386	12,672	......	155	4,696
Basalt.................	30	520	......	......	255	14,463	......	11	1,049
Slate..................	1	8	2	101	426	11,835	......	4	44
Marble................	2	15	3	387	408	9,607	......	19	480
MISCELLANEOUS:									
Abrasive materials.....	16	240	1	225	......	......	......	3	120
Asbestos..............	6	155	3	125	2	65	......	......	......
Asphalt...............	5	103	......	......	......	......	......	......	......
Barytes...............	16	269	1	50	28	980	......	6	225
Bauxite...............	11	1,667	......	......	......	......	......	94	2,564
Chromite..............	11	136	......	......	......	......	......	......	......
Clay..................	105	1,179	......	......	181	4,271	40	66	1,815
Feldspar..............	8	70	2	76	7	555	......	......	......
Fluorspar.............	87	1,052	......	......	......	......	......	47	729
Fuller's earth.........	9	530	......	......	10	288	......	2	18
Graphite..............	7	368	......	......	106	4,169	......	10	552
Gypsum...............	9	572	3	334	290	7,994	......	103	1,447
Magnesite.............	26	747	......	......	70	1,713	......	......	......
Mica..................	6	63	......	......	3	40	......	......	......
Millstones............	......	......	......	......	2	160	......	......	......
Mineral pigments......	6	228	5	370	8	170	......	......	......
Phosphate rock........	44	12,085	......	......	38	2,663	......	320	33,107
Pyrite................	7	84	6	1,050	98	4,114	......	27	3,696
Silica................	10	354	4	485	11	333	......	......	......
Sulphur...............	13	390	......	......	......	......	......	50	1,284
Talc and soapstone.....	11	165	9	2,115	77	2,996	......	43	1,078
Nonproducing enterprises........	429	11,552	42	3,412	614	26,190	417	59	1,671
FUELS:									
Coal..................	4	34	......	......	21	715	......	4	150
Petroleum and natural gas...............	67	1,352	......	......	8	496	......	1	2
METALS:									
Iron ore..............	2	34	......	......	44	3,940	......	6	750
Gold, silver, copper, lead, or zinc.........	344	9,715	42	3,412	540	20,914	417	48	769
MISCELLANEOUS.........	12	417	......	......	1	125	......	......	......

TABLE 21.—DETAILED STATISTICS FOR MINES, QUARRIES, AND WELLS, PRODUCING AND NONPRODUCING ENTERPRISES, FOR THE UNITED STATES, BY STATES: 1919.

STATE.	Number of enterprises.	Number of mines and quarries.	Number of wells productive Dec. 31.	LAND CONTROLLED (ACRES).			
				Mineral land.			Timber and other lands.
				Operated.	Owned.	Leased.	
United States............	21,997	14,417	257,673	22,947,937	8,729,545	14,294,342	2,215,702
Producing enterprises.....	21,280	13,844	257,673	22,474,069	8,568,590	13,980,731	2,208,519
Alabama...................	264	348	....	728,806	636,368	93,278	102,552
Arizona..................	155	172	....	70,431	56,962	13,469	17,328
Arkansas.................	126	126	124	76,416	18,181	58,315	14,912
California...............	725	357	9,197	588,517	376,108	212,429	38,003
Colorado.................	477	523	70	211,260	148,109	63,537	10,293
Connecticut..............	41	47	....	2,995	2,815	225	160
Delaware.................	7	8	....	264	250	14	9
District of Columbia.....	3	3	....	13	10	3	....
Florida..................	36	55	....	118,050	114,560	3,490	79,335
Georgia..................	74	82	....	37,736	22,095	15,651	17,862
Idaho....................	82	83	....	27,874	24,877	3,097	3,286
Illinois.................	772	590	16,498	945,362	617,833	329,448	84,502
Indiana..................	503	398	2,456	266,988	119,263	151,036	10,214
Iowa.....................	198	226	....	68,724	33,536	36,433	3,703
Kansas...................	814	238	12,690	549,300	69,621	480,629	14,161
Kentucky.................	938	864	5,214	1,093,641	506,713	587,223	101,898
Louisiana and Mississippi.......	137	4	2,479	329,869	17,196	312,673	8,565
Maine....................	50	51	....	3,562	2,602	995	3,623
Maryland.................	126	161	....	57,470	36,635	20,879	8,680
Massachusetts............	74	79	....	5,223	4,701	522	1,131
Michigan.................	122	165	19	114,356	90,683	23,799	430,773
Minnesota................	135	196	....	24,836	5,899	19,874	2?9,768
Missouri.................	468	494	....	194,732	149,345	45,492	33,124
Montana..................	259	269	28	107,541	79,300	29,653	12,132
Nebraska.................	9	9	....	1,081	821	260	....
Nevada...................	203	207	....	45,114	35,901	9,236	7,030
New Hampshire............	30	33	....	10,030	8,698	1,332	501
New Jersey...............	97	102	....	27,006	19,885	7,121	10,846
New Mexico...............	85	103	1	673,051	642,019	31,092	38,760
New York.................	700	147	14,186	365,463	79,668	285,795	119,168
North Carolina...........	102	106	....	10,015	4,284	5,731	1,068
North Dakota.............	79	79	....	17,734	9,305	8,429	824
Ohio.....................	2,283	1,064	35,440	1,914,023	413,597	1,519,201	29,889
Oklahoma.................	1,934	284	44,735	1,844,305	192,771	1,651,746	5,468
Oregon...................	50	52	....	22,963	16,472	6,591	1,580
Pennsylvania.............	5,807	1 3,621	77,325	4,352,082	1,750,822	2,615,052	359,053
Rhode Island.............	14	15	....	570	512	58	764
South Carolina...........	20	20	....	31,684	31,630	104	10
South Dakota.............	23	28	1	11,538	11,056	482	31,750
Tennessee................	203	263	14	361,660	205,832	156,856	112,318
Texas....................	624	81	8,749	1,397,678	107,867	1,289,841	88,552
Utah.....................	141	154	....	324,582	319,143	7,023	13,796
Vermont..................	93	109	....	16,048	14,417	1,631	2,121
Virginia.................	202	216	....	494,909	365,982	129,966	20,661
Washington...............	83	93	....	73,061	48,404	24,897	15,850
West Virginia............	1,714	1,325	27,363	4,578,747	1,090,320	3,514,884	82,230
Wisconsin................	92	107	....	12,064	6,938	5,126	6,986
Wyoming..................	106	87	1,084	264,695	58,584	206,113	3,280
Nonproducing enterprises 2	717	573	3 276	473,868	160,955	313,611	7,183

[1] Includes 79 anthracite culm washeries and 81 river dredges.

[2] Includes enterprises as follows: Alabama, 2; Arizona, 95; Arkansas, 2; California, 60; Colorado, 60; Connecticut, 1; Florida, 1; Georgia, 1; Idaho, 50; Illinois, 1; Iowa, 1; Kansas, 13; Kentucky, 11; Louisiana, 6; Maine, 1; Michigan, 6; Minnesota, 10; Missouri, 1; Montana, 36; Nevada, 118; New Mexico, 18; New York, 1; North Carolina, 2; Ohio, 6; Oklahoma, 30; Oregon, 6; Pennsylvania, 13; South Dakota, 5; Tennessee, 1; Texas, 65; Utah, 48; Virginia, 4; Washington, 15; West Virginia, 8; Wisconsin, 4; and Wyoming, 15.

[3] Wells on which work was done during the year, not productive and number not included in United States total.

TABLE 21.—DETAILED STATISTICS FOR MINES, QUARRIES, AND WELLS, PRODUCING AND NONPRODUCING ENTERPRISES, FOR THE UNITED STATES, BY STATES: 1919—Continued.

STATE.	Aggregate.	PERSONS ENGAGED IN INDUSTRY.							
		Proprietors and officials.						Clerks and other subordinate salaried employees.	
		Total.	Proprietors and firm members.		Salaried officers.	Superintendents and managers.	Technical employees.		
			Total.	Performing manual labor.				Male.	Female.
United States	1,084,796	61,588	22,155	5,272	10,729	22,223	6,481	25,854	10,170
Producing enterprises	1,077,675	60,409	21,918	5,245	10,456	21,704	6,331	25,649	10,057
Alabama	34,632	989	41	6	248	482	218	846	218
Arizona	16,831	892	105	68	94	300	393	581	90
Arkansas	4,073	307	109	68	59	124	15	114	22
California	22,201	1,671	442	172	393	709	127	885	301
Colorado	18,502	1,117	378	237	212	417	110	450	145
Connecticut	642	72	27	5	19	22	4	16	11
Delaware	130	10	2	1	4	4		3	1
District of Columbia	15	3	3						
Florida	3,694	197	8	2	44	91	54	99	26
Georgia	2,608	149	33	4	45	63	8	49	13
Idaho	2,759	215	83	32	27	69	36	71	18
Illinois	84,309	3,185	691	126	685	1,561	248	1,525	476
Indiana	28,738	1,338	339	164	371	535	93	485	164
Iowa	12,034	536	200	143	128	195	13	156	68
Kansas	18,689	1,656	807	123	286	412	151	588	309
Kentucky	47,893	2,640	386	115	805	1,118	331	1,326	364
Louisiana and Mississippi	6,095	403	61	2	74	223	45	345	119
Maine	1,093	95	52	36	15	24	4	9	10
Maryland	6,116	325	84	26	85	125	31	118	45
Massachusetts	1,910	140	50	10	43	40	7	44	22
Michigan	33,202	848	19	6	121	379	329	889	173
Minnesota	18,562	543	40	19	63	253	187	672	82
Missouri	16,358	1,105	497	219	198	355	55	291	105
Montana	17,345	744	293	199	68	218	165	412	60
Nebraska	186	20	5	1	2	11	2	2	2
Nevada	4,860	461	151	120	86	156	68	143	25
New Hampshire	757	63	30	17	6	25	2	6	6
New Jersey	5,029	230	40	20	53	80	57	155	68
New Mexico	7,607	302	69	29	20	108	105	176	29
New York	7,913	1,246	896	202	144	168	38	360	105
North Carolina	2,108	184	90	36	29	59	6	27	7
North Dakota	939	135	75	23	16	27	17	24	6
Ohio	56,736	5,408	3,309	509	791	1,159	149	1,279	751
Oklahoma	40,855	3,929	1,106	58	840	1,656	327	1,378	1,634
Oregon	847	91	37	20	9	36	9	12	4
Pennsylvania	350,338	18,491	8,822	2,126	2,042	6,077	1,550	6,318	2,132
Rhode Island	421	37	6		5	20	6	5	10
South Carolina	1,008	51	15	2	14	20	2	16	8
South Dakota	1,880	58	15	11	5	15	23	27	10
Tennessee	15,450	618	67	17	170	306	75	282	80
Texas	22,890	2,010	484	52	329	971	226	1,427	1,289
Utah	10,758	485	53	16	96	200	136	359	67
Vermont	3,239	209	60	18	52	86	11	49	45
Virginia	15,537	558	71	19	135	290	62	361	71
Washington	5,397	199	33	16	37	92	37	93	55
West Virginia	110,327	5,939	1,667	124	1,363	2,173	736	2,871	705
Wisconsin	3,889	215	48	19	38	105	24	93	34
Wyoming	10,273	290	19	7	87	145	39	212	72
Nonproducing enterprises	7,121	1,179	237	27	273	519	150	205	113

TABLE **21.**—DETAILED STATISTICS FOR MINES, QUARRIES, AND WELLS, PRODUCING AND NONPRODUCING ENTERPRISES, FOR THE UNITED STATES, BY STATES: 1919—Continued.

	PERSONS ENGAGED IN INDUSTRY—continued.						
	Wage earners.			Wage earners, Dec. 15, or nearest representative day.			
STATE.	Average number.	Number, 15th day of—		Total.		Foremen, shift bosses, etc.	
		Maximum month.	Minimum month.	Above ground.	Below ground.	Above ground.	Below ground.
United States...........	987,184	Oc 1,057,820	No 765,067	386,932	709,526	10,526	15,696
Producing enterprises....	981,560	Oc 1,051,204	No 758,156	382,766	705,423	10,314	15,437
Alabama.................	32,579	Fe 34,682	No 28,781	9,862	24,922	387	543
Arizona.................	15,268	Ja 19,065	Ap 12,808	7,231	9,801	261	330
Arkansas...............	3,630	Se 4,879	No 1,416	1,885	3,261	74	57
California..............	19,344	No 19,916	Ap 18,716	17,147	3,567	215	163
Colorado...............	16,790	De 18,155	No 15,175	5,703	14,090	247	388
Connecticut............	543	Jy 598	Fe 427	616	14	32	2
Delaware...............	116	Je 153	Fe 51	132	....	6	....
District of Columbia....	12	Oc 19	Ja¹ 6	11	....	1	....
Florida.................	3,372	De 4,912	Je 1,836	4,898	....	256	....
Georgia................	2,397	Au 2,586	No 2,271	2,382	273	81	14
Idaho..................	2,455	De 3,268	Se 1,648	1,516	2,229	70	80
Illinois.................	79,123	Oc 89,321	No 16,782	14,880	75,566	485	930
Indiana................	26,751	Oc 31,544	No 5,818	6,934	25,623	338	474
Iowa...................	11,274	Ja 13,221	No 3,404	1,844	11,300	100	181
Kansas.................	16,136	Ja 17,448	No 8,843	9,205	8,677	138	127
Kentucky...............	43,563	Oc 48,834	No 35,516	13,321	36,339	445	952
Louisiana and Mississippi......	5,228	De 6,680	Je 4,418	7,384	....	2	....
Maine..................	979	Je 1,288	Fe 438	1,159	51	48	5
Maryland...............	5,628	Oc 6,221	Mh 5,101	1,842	4,469	69	125
Massachusetts..........	1,704	Au 2,032	Fe 1,017	1,880	21	76	2
Michigan...............	31,292	Fe 34,729	Je 28,836	11,894	20,575	391	647
Minnesota..............	17,265	Jy 18,804	De 15,109	9,342	9,253	434	269
Missouri...............	14,857	Ja 17,319	No 8,965	7,229	10,764	247	238
Montana...............	16,129	Ja 20,911	No 13,922	4,226	13,039	197	513
Nebraska...............	162	My 192	Ja 128	159	....	9	....
Nevada................	4,231	Ja 5,118	Au 3,366	2,725	2,517	221	153
New Hampshire.........	682	Au 887	Ja 344	773	16	22	1
New Jersey.............	4,576	Se 4,780	Je 4,162	3,533	1,378	124	48
New Mexico............	7,100	Ja 8,152	No 6,380	2,812	4,678	65	124
New York..............	6,202	Jy 6,690	Fe 5,553	4,932	1,484	194	81
North Carolina.........	1,890	Se 2,062	Ja 1,696	1,903	176	79	14
North Dakota..........	774	De 1,158	Je 472	318	836	15	16
Ohio...................	49,298	Se 56,792	No 18,793	16,837	40,291	494	660
Oklahoma..............	33,914	Oc 36,674	No 29,510	26,806	11,333	197	291
Oregon................	740	Se 934	Mh 555	651	322	27	13
Pennsylvania...........	323,397	Se 341,352	No 265,170	95,748	250,822	2,063	4,803
Rhode Island...........	369	Se 438	Ja 246	420	2	20	....
South Carolina.........	933	Au 1,031	Fe 784	1,003	29	34	2
South Dakota..........	1,785	Jy 1,890	No 1,574	1,065	624	48	35
Tennessee..............	14,470	Oc 15,777	No 10,406	6,682	9,382	249	195
Texas..................	18,164	Se 20,975	Ja 14,661	18,715	2,732	131	65
Utah..................	9,847	Ja 11,962	Je 8,072	4,536	6,370	190	159
Vermont...............	2,936	Je 3,156	Fe 2,698	2,983	339	164	15
Virginia................	14,547	Oc 15,398	Ap 13,308	5,181	10,474	242	307
Washington............	5,050	Ja 5,956	No 1,844	1,982	3,971	96	135
West Virginia..........	100,812	De 108,720	Mh 92,824	34,303	75,578	889	2,114
Wisconsin..............	3,547	My 3,720	De 3,133	2,228	1,627	70	65
Wyoming..............	9,699	Ja 10,939	Jy 8,942	3,948	6,608	71	101
Nonproducing enterprises.	5,624	De 6,975	Fe 3,932	4,166	4,103	212	259

¹ Same number reported for one or more other months.

TABLE 21.—DETAILED STATISTICS FOR MINES, QUARRIES, AND WELLS, PRODUCING AND NONPRODUCING ENTERPRISES, FOR THE UNITED STATES, BY STATES: 1919—Continued.

STATE.	PERSONS ENGAGED IN INDUSTRY—continued.										
	Wage earners, Dec. 15, or nearest representive day.										
	Enginemen, hoistmen, electricians, mechanics, etc.		Miners, quarrymen, and drillmen, including their helpers.		Timbermen, trackmen, and men engaged in hauling, tramming, etc.		Muckers, loaders, and others not classified.		In mills and beneficiating plants (above ground).	Under 16 years of age (above ground).	Females (above ground).
	Above ground.	Below ground.	Above ground.	Below ground.	Above ground.	Below ground.	Above ground.	Below ground.			
United States..	135,665	30,349	31,388	397,636	25,896	139,052	136,646	126,793	46,811	222	612
Producing enterprises.....	134,117	30,145	30,702	395,398	25,583	138,491	135,239	125,952	46,811	221	541
Alabama.............	2,793	1,058	887	13,858	1,332	4,712	2,905	4,751	1,558	.....	6
Arizona.............	2,251	542	880	3,532	219	2,559	2,093	2,838	1,527	.....	8
Arkansas............	364	26	727	2,356	206	450	384	372	130	.....	:
California...........	11,554	115	417	1,586	208	575	3,933	1,128	820	1	31
Colorado............	1,507	519	428	8,375	397	2,458	2,249	2,350	875	3	44
Connecticut.........	81	....	198	12	51	....	214	....	40	.....	....
Delaware............	11	....	58	....	....	....	50	....	7	.....	....
District of Columbia..	....	....	10	....	....	....	....	....	....	.....	....
Florida.............	985	....	845	....	274	....	1,928	....	610	1	52
Georgia.............	285	3	673	157	197	44	761	55	385	.....	15
Idaho..............	296	91	136	850	32	458	394	750	588	.....	11
Illinois.............	6,667	2,207	729	43,002	924	16,822	5,298	12,605	777	.....	20
Indiana.............	2,051	881	962	14,191	586	5,584	2,363	4,493	634	2	4
Iowa...............	442	98	179	7,284	255	2,885	742	852	126	.....	1
Kansas.............	4,299	78	439	6,246	164	1,652	3,768	574	397	.....	....
Kentucky...........	3,860	1,604	1,482	19,584	1,575	6,904	5,796	7,295	163	8	....
Louisiana and Mississippi............	3,331	....	21	....	....	....	4,030	....	....	.....	5
Maine..............	127	....	341	27	147	....	78	19	418	.....	....
Maryland...........	293	131	501	3,213	163	665	768	335	48	2	....
Massachusetts.......	204	....	570	13	126	2	545	4	359	1	....
Michigan...........	4,357	653	512	10,396	587	5,773	3,788	3,106	2,259	2	58
Minnesota..........	3,267	257	1,010	5,362	775	1,493	3,335	1,872	521	2	2
Missouri...........	1,337	153	1,273	5,796	713	2,218	2,196	2,359	1,463	5	2
Montana...........	1,188	463	109	7,432	112	3,815	1,173	816	1,447	.....	4
Nebraska...........	11	....	61	....	33	....	42	....	3	.....	....
Nevada............	693	69	119	1,210	207	459	388	626	1,097	.....	21
New Hampshire......	75	....	247	15	15	....	55	....	359	1	....
New Jersey.........	545	60	429	693	130	391	1,885	186	420	1	1
New Mexico.........	840	224	117	2,718	259	793	796	819	735	4	1
New York..........	1,261	120	754	454	248	157	1,847	672	628	.....	....
North Carolina......	88	8	548	51	242	46	448	57	498	2	76
North Dakota........	42	16	35	550	35	158	191	96	....	.....	2
Ohio..............	7,352	1,507	1,707	18,163	975	7,726	5,934	12,235	375	.....	....
Oklahoma...........	13,837	124	238	6,145	297	2,771	11,053	2,002	1,184	.....	2
Oregon............	101	37	114	139	82	60	225	73	102	.....	9
Pennsylvania........	27,305	11,398	5,305	151,949	7,219	41,006	32,112	41,666	21,744	162	....
Rhode Island........	53	....	166	2	11	....	100	....	70	.....	....
South Carolina......	82	1	317	8	86	....	395	18	89	.....	5
South Dakota........	320	24	96	282	63	38	296	245	242	.....	2
Tennessee..........	973	471	1,207	5,562	872	2,099	2,798	1,055	583	3	....
Texas.............	9,839	86	232	1,863	148	509	8,166	209	199	10	35
Utah..............	1,124	494	327	2,510	943	1,516	1,014	1,691	938	.....	12
Vermont...........	338	7	1,420	175	55	23	358	119	648	.....	3
Virginia...........	1,065	1,078	820	5,280	473	2,419	1,990	1,390	591	3	31
Washington.........	492	195	257	2,344	148	998	638	299	351	3	6
West Virginia.......	13,395	4,971	2,013	37,962	3,713	16,853	14,002	13,678	291	2	....
Wisconsin..........	361	79	627	782	74	335	638	366	458	1	10
Wyoming...........	2,375	297	159	3,269	212	1,065	1,077	1,876	54	2	62
Nonproducing enterprises.....	1,548	204	686	2,238	313	561	1,407	841	....	1	71

TABLE **21.**—DETAILED STATISTICS FOR MINES, QUARRIES, AND WELLS, PRODUCING AND NONPRODUCING ENTERPRISES, FOR THE UNITED STATES, BY STATES: 1919—Continued.

STATE.	Capital.	PRINCIPAL EXPENSES OF OPERATION AND DEVELOPMENT.				Supplies and materials.
		Salaries and wages.				
		Total.	Salaried officers, superintendents, managers, and technical employees.	Clerks and other subordinate salaried employees.	Wage earners.	
	Dollars.	*Dollars.*	*Dollars.*	*Dollars.*	*Dollars.*	*Dollars.*
United States....	7,108,623,496	2,543,887,062	105,892,362	45,380,089	1,304,409,342	528,853,639
Producing enterprises.............	6,955,466,831	2,518,543,956	104,235,154	45,093,831	1,295,936,226	519,593,676
Alabama................	84,167,016	53,430,551	2,588,339	1,346,495	36,229,723	7,480,910
Arizona...............	402,419,671	60,429,191	2,465,825	1,293,504	26,193,312	14,632,835
Arkansas..............	8,688,453	7,718,693	441,616	160,211	4,573,291	1,235,726
California.............	446,782,385	98,944,077	3,646,344	1,495,206	31,748,170	31,816,525
Colorado..............	147,154,642	45,973,002	1,962,751	825,778	25,405,043	7,672,203
Connecticut...........	3,557,208	1,298,269	118,816	25,660	646,624	304,096
Delaware..............	229,023	219,429	15,974	4,505	135,502	34,214
District of Columbia.....	6,632	10,730			8,150	1,284
Florida...............	58,067,662	7,968,486	519,196	147,006	3,107,813	1,836,229
Georgia...............	6,184,470	3,582,746	281,935	73,078	2,017,460	591,266
Idaho.................	71,093,746	8,304,819	399,426	138,645	4,201,624	2,026,256
Illinois...............	231,836,571	142,852,787	7,490,424	2,633,442	94,178,504	18,716,093
Indiana...............	63,198,281	45,575,744	3,216,253	862,026	30,192,924	6,370,553
Iowa..................	16,699,094	17,187,080	1,064,602	279,095	12,466,426	2,072,308
Kansas................	255,935,807	79,933,866	2,135,884	1,164,010	21,948,799	33,097,630
Kentucky..............	201,247,725	86,728,587	5,467,309	1,843,307	49,550,588	15,618,091
Louisiana and Mississippi	97,620,406	28,412,211	937,341	560,469	7,504,657	7,761,445
Maine.................	1,692,082	1,572,661	102,200	16,079	1,051,796	203,187
Maryland..............	21,078,980	8,790,841	630,956	158,703	6,151,744	1,178,074
Massachusetts.........	4,882,574	3,304,302	252,058	72,544	2,068,844	494,249
Michigan..............	283,528,279	91,340,001	2,775,974	1,535,585	50,406,187	15,204,063
Minnesota.............	310,095,559	96,445,817	1,707,779	1,340,642	29,383,021	14,101,962
Missouri..............	47,926,850	28,728,052	1,400,938	462,686	16,777,353	4,784,079
Montana..............	209,286,955	42,502,917	1,525,799	978,502	25,723,908	9,452,659
Nebraska.............	325,788	286,512	24,180	2,957	166,202	60,996
Nevada...............	82,500,057	16,443,538	866,955	232,893	7,401,113	5,339,511
New Hampshire........	1,658,509	1,197,304	82,864	13,460	825,547	144,946
New Jersey...........	16,905,356	9,740,156	476,721	249,829	5,392,861	2,194,539
New Mexico...........	93,994,713	18,044,497	733,249	417,797	10,493,857	3,879,948
New York.............	95,446,438	19,990,461	852,046	579,555	7,496,781	4,724,500
North Carolina.........	2,250,434	2,439,802	172,569	27,043	1,489,062	467,460
North Dakota..........	1,865,347	1,591,639	120,788	38,858	1,029,126	283,633
Ohio..................	256,057,996	103,790,793	5,599,867	2,442,357	58,109,904	16,116,949
Oklahoma.............	740,757,178	189,361,709	8,170,062	4,362,390	46,809,200	55,458,900
Oregon...............	4,780,913	1,930,790	125,452	22,369	992,957	545,949
Pennsylvania..........	1,317,519,289	693,618,939	24,489,816	10,474,657	445,218,643	118,817,334
Rhode Island..........	810,066	700,075	67,693	14,988	399,648	146,637
South Carolina........	3,205,232	1,299,206	114,875	24,968	680,484	303,371
South Dakota.........	28,131,922	4,450,596	155,254	61,556	2,497,340	1,008,196
Tennessee............	51,466,345	21,115,569	1,258,804	379,591	12,987,338	3,892,397
Texas................	361,684,392	141,310,966	4,268,560	2,161,398	20,557,997	45,040,955
Utah.................	178,521,276	31,883,415	1,279,951	636,962	17,196,652	7,745,492
Vermont..............	10,710,058	5,645,298	365,479	83,254	3,041,551	1,272,796
Virginia..............	57,035,775	26,190,879	1,149,079	541,083	16,108,249	4,760,370
Washington...........	22,914,934	11,351,484	463,733	198,813	7,465,652	1,728,585
West Virginia.........	533,138,835	217,866,739	10,840,047	4,114,202	119,577,949	40,740,077
Wisconsin............	18,631,034	9,101,901	462,207	155,908	4,750,235	1,885,710
Wyoming.............	101,774,873	27,936,829	947,164	439,765	14,576,415	6,348,488
Nonproducing enterprises........	153,156,665	25,343,106	1,657,208	286,258	8,473,116	9,259,963

TABLE **21.**—DETAILED STATISTICS FOR MINES, QUARRIES, AND WELLS, PRODUCING AND NONPRODUCING ENTERPRISES, FOR THE UNITED STATES, BY STATES: 1919—Continued.

STATE.	Cost of ore, coal, and natural gas purchased as material or for resale.	Cost of fuel.	Cost of purchased power.	Royalties and rents.	Taxes—Federal, state, county, and local.	Contract work.
	Dollars.	*Dollars.*	*Dollars.*	*Dollars.*	*Dollars.*	*Dollars.*
United States........	35,905,352	94,848,752	28,660,836	176,129,858	141,567,734	82,239,098
Producing enterprises...	35,905,352	93,910,653	28,195,277	175,293,984	140,999,626	79,380,177
Alabama........		2,431,350	648,933	838,101	1,699,630	167,070
Arizona................	1,528,056	4,132,257	1,245,268	438,926	7,752,425	746,783
Arkansas...............	165,786	330,146	111,115	386,925	174,443	139,434
California..............	875,751	4,424,508	2,622,717	10,910,833	10,026,745	1,377,278
Colorado..............	4,282,353	1,253,016	1,453,464	1,583,712	1,136,752	397,930
Connecticut........		75,788	44,586	10,604	45,057	27,038
Delaware........		19,559		5,434	1,223	3,018
District of Columbia......		1,063		128	105	
Florida..............		1,613,472	74,224	140,815	408,529	121,202
Georgia..............	17,500	296,647	59,372	155,833	54,360	35,295
Idaho..............		159,294	354,484	182,364	649,069	193,657
Illinois................	91,659	4,810,013	974,466	6,636,176	6,890,455	431,555
Indiana..............	50,546	1,737,090	275,616	939,696	1,590,853	340,187
Iowa................		606,285	142,559	335,530	186,811	33,464
Kansas..............	298,353	4,067,088	238,487	10,712,223	2,273,748	3,997,644
Kentucky..............	41,104	1,937,821	584,928	5,814,424	2,605,300	3,265,715
Louisiana and Mississippi....	740,522	2,812,084	924	4,312,372	1,738,953	2,043,444
Maine................		77,561	45,231	9,986	34,253	32,368
Maryland.............		247,837	60,929	137,562	208,137	16,899
Massachusetts...........		186,694	76,651	59,067	83,009	11,186
Michigan..............		7,455,207	989,490	6,668,923	6,275,133	29,439
Minnesota..............		4,155,158	526,794	17,642,811	26,074,651	1,512,999
Missouri..............	669	1,743,747	290,666	780,604	2,071,467	415,843
Montana..............	62,210	1,267,627	1,712,301	646,125	1,018,265	115,521
Nebraska..............		11,800	9,376	9,715	1,286	
Nevada..............		1,112,427	638,839	143,708	462,663	245,429
New Hampshire..........		41,567	23,413	6,268	24,719	34,520
New Jersey..............		621,584	98,354	276,555	371,765	57,948
New Mexico.............	9,506	1,292,260	68,950	181,504	835,920	131,506
New York..............	2,692,086	967,027	435,218	649,472	804,416	789,360
North Carolina..........		213,392	7,339	36,071	21,121	5,745
North Dakota..........		32,853	4,841	30,868	19,922	30,750
Ohio..............	3,092,567	2,949,460	1,181,608	6,339,816	4,028,789	3,929,476
Oklahoma..............	9,758,073	3,826,667	966,907	30,688,890	10,338,243	18,982,377
Oregon..............		68,689	64,783	48,047	26,656	35,888
Pennsylvania.............	5,510,433	21,818,407	5,888,996	24,682,827	28,747,401	7,970,425
Rhode Island.............		45,526	9,549	5,755	9,279	1,000
South Carolina..........		122,170	28,270	7,512	17,556	
South Dakota..........		238,703	45,316	6,805	425,485	11,941
Tennessee..............		1,037,175	222,808	554,743	608,917	173,796
Texas..............	360,637	6,093,106	96,453	23,912,179	4,045,981	25,773,700
Utah..............	297,961	834,480	1,184,630	150,955	2,065,154	491,178
Vermont..............		220,276	205,122	58,506	306,564	91,750
Virginia..............		740,098	476,796	830,435	1,243,918	340,851
Washington..............		788,730	158,600	177,429	283,318	86,624
West Virginia.............	5,871,497	3,921,485	2,987,311	14,845,553	11,078,927	3,889,691
Wisconsin..............	83,802	309,187	548,078	535,600	235,881	135,293
Wyoming..............	74,281	762,272	310,515	1,765,597	1,996,372	715,960
Nonproducing enterprises................		938,099	465,559	835,874	568,108	2,858,921

TABLE **21.**—DETAILED STATISTICS FOR MINES, QUARRIES, AND WELLS, PRODUC-ING AND NONPRODUCING ENTERPRISES, FOR THE UNITED STATES, BY STATES: 1919—Continued.

			POWER USED.					
	Expenditures for development (included in principal expenses).	Value of products.			Prime movers.			
STATE.			Aggregate.	Total horsepower.	Steam engines (not turbines).		Steam turbines.	
					Number.	Horsepower.	Number.	Horsepower.
	Dollars.	*Dollars.*						
United States.	334,015,265	3,158,463,966	6,786,475	5,147,613	46,744	3,259,076	555	474,315
Producing enterprises....	311,276,508	3,158,463,966	6,723,786	5,111,531	46,433	3,238,288	553	473,985
Alabama..............	897,964	59,866,040	145,775	92,657	736	90,097	6	1,667
Arizona..............	7,233,390	88,478,111	166,091	138,529	262	52,634	21	73,037
Arkansas.............	431,908	8,404,537	21,365	15,552	174	13,003	......	......
California............	27,656,157	163,770,243	313,213	206,805	3,144	88,052	5	1,750
Colorado............	3,864,109	51,217,038	116,351	46,481	484	40,012	2	1,050
Connecticut..........	10,747	1,649,003	8,520	4,831	64	4,675	......	......
Delaware.............	....	243,647	660	660	19	632	......	......
District of Columbia...	....	15,627	97	97	......	......	......	......
Florida..............	301,881	8,976,413	44,969	42,689	83	12,428	17	17,751
Georgia.............	77,759	4,082,152	13,026	9,502	129	7,909	1	100
Idaho...............	532,077	11,840,301	31,239	2,811	23	1,103	2	930
Illinois.............	4,331,319	178,673,065	318,231	261,934	2,077	208,782	42	19,728
Indiana.............	2,111,492	52,840,252	129,663	100,632	898	92,120	16	2,052
Iowa...............	587,368	18,473,558	32,171	19,626	256	17,078	4	1,690
Kansas.............	23,448,955	90,338,204	133,984	121,477	903	36,605	......	......
Kentucky...........	12,847,964	98,486,910	148,893	102,176	716	65,827	43	23,786
Louisiana and Mississippi.............	11,001,642	40,016,535	86,135	86,101	1,389	31,009	18	720
Maine.............	10,807	1,823,442	6,277	3,562	74	3,397	......	......
Maryland............	191,878	9,698,577	18,660	14,018	172	12,302	1	750
Massachusetts........	23,813	4,175,699	12,498	7,736	194	7,406	......	......
Michigan............	2,657,899	103,870,089	337,882	274,084	1,082	208,797	28	56,770
Minnesota...........	9,953,680	130,399,254	144,199	114,354	1,293	111,508	4	1,629
Missouri............	1,141,088	33,365,694	100,160	82,967	673	51,653	20	25,560
Montana............	3,145,120	49,923,721	143,718	50,593	117	41,987	13	4,350
Nebraska............	41,582	292,766	1,847	1,317	18	1,282	......	......
Nevada.............	2,486,280	18,053,984	50,786	18,342	34	9,035	1	3,600
New Hampshire......	55,049	1,568,195	4,336	2,673	73	2,625	......	......
New Jersey..........	831,985	9,308,902	33,901	26,847	137	16,357	7	10,065
New Mexico.........	3,221,461	18,872,560	59,876	55,031	66	22,579	55	22,779
New York...........	2,232,809	25,131,093	91,339	62,426	900	30,055	8	9,720
North Carolina......	34,834	2,736,543	5,039	4,641	81	4,341	......	......
North Dakota........	93,885	1,927,304	2,037	1,783	28	1,530	......	......
Ohio...............	7,931,195	134,518,505	337,611	272,716	2,239	138,339	4	3,275
Oklahoma...........	55,218,905	281,927,732	448,173	415,781	2,649	93,792	4	700
Oregon.............	205,972	1,884,871	6,264	1,579	27	1,201	......	......
Pennsylvania........	24,930,973	819,451,109	1,999,422	1,638,599	16,841	1,274,108	146	137,213
Rhode Island........	14,200	952,204	3,000	1,844	58	1,840	......	......
South Carolina.......	111,693	1,350,747	4,656	2,572	48	2,450	......	......
South Dakota........	41,903	5,314,516	11,844	9,834	10	4,855	2	4,500
Tennessee...........	537,864	23,292,114	56,685	39,297	327	36,226	4	2,008
Texas..............	71,703,732	160,378,058	129,063	125,909	2,454	72,967	6	2,700
Utah...............	3,168,643	41,510,802	86,131	31,083	275	26,730	4	2,085
Vermont............	36,499	8,555,030	28,119	8,990	120	5,887	1	1,500
Virginia............	919,206	29,363,449	57,880	23,641	266	20,372	5	1,530
Washington..........	771,066	13,329,129	38,198	24,332	126	20,662	7	1,781
West Virginia........	17,516,298	295,606,620	704,279	485,899	4,280	216,152	40	18,969
Wisconsin...........	650,622	10,580,833	26,766	7,704	97	6,971	......	......
Wyoming............	6,060,835	41,928,788	62,757	48,817	317	22,916	16	18,240
Nonproducing enterprises.....	22,738,757	....	62,689	36,082	311	20,788	2	330

TABLE 21.—DETAILED STATISTICS FOR MINES, QUARRIES, AND WELLS, PRODUCING AND NONPRODUCING ENTERPRISES, FOR THE UNITED STATES, BY STATES: 1919—Continued.

STATE.	POWER USED—continued.								
	Prime movers—Continued.				Equipment operated by purchased power.			Electric motors run by current generated by the enterprise reporting.	
	Internal-combustion engines.		Water wheels and turbines.		Electric motors.		Other.		
	Number.	Horsepower.	Number.	Horsepower.	Number.	Horsepower.	Horsepower.	Number.	Horsepower.
United States	57,417	1,372,698	329	41,524	41,114	1,629,580	9,282	33,039	1,260,466
Producing enterprises	56,988	1,361,146	287	38,112	40,500	1,603,390	8,865	32,980	1,258,795
Alabama	34	819	9	74	1,147	53,118	......	701	30,085
Arizona	166	12,858			632	26,547	1,015	1,155	77,545
Arkansas	39	2,549			141	5,813		124	3,184
California	3,056	105,615	107	11,388	2,882	106,363	45	413	10,382
Colorado	55	1,159	21	4,260	1,802	69,680	190	342	12,525
Connecticut	7	80	2	76	46	3,689		8	44
Delaware	4	28							
District of Columbia	5	97							
Florida	52	12,510			34	2,280		272	31,710
Georgia	25	393	7	1,100	62	3,494	30	31	3,797
Idaho	18	364	16	414	545	28,248	180	19	1,120
Illinois	1,855	33,424			1,432	56,267	30	3,218	97,160
Indiana	349	6,460			785	29,031		875	43,102
Iowa	94	858			358	12,540	5	88	4,670
Kansas	3,160	84,287	7	585	499	12,507		308	8,886
Kentucky	815	12,563			1,174	46,717		1,953	53,817
Louisiana and Mississippi	1,878	54,372			2	34		53	794
Maine	14	165			57	2,715			
Maryland	24	516	3	450	139	4,642		94	3,872
Massachusetts	3	45	2	285	101	4,757	5	1	10
Michigan	15	417	16	8,100	976	63,798		1,663	107,750
Minnesota	36	1,217			578	29,845		436	13,563
Missouri	170	5,754			613	17,103	90	486	16,850
Montana	53	1,033	20	3,223	1,543	93,125		179	6,696
Nebraska	2	35			13	530			
Nevada	193	5,539	5	168	801	32,444		290	10,086
New Hampshire	5	48			49	1,663			
New Jersey	35	425			104	7,054		213	8,742
New Mexico	94	9,653	1	20	130	4,845		1,257	24,854
New York	1,533	21,726	4	925	595	28,913		139	6,321
North Carolina	10	125	1	175	14	398		19	501
North Dakota	38	253			24	254		9	100
Ohio	6,308	131,074	1	28	1,956	64,775	120	1,620	40,687
Oklahoma	9,603	314,989	2	300	695	31,492	900	207	6,161
Oregon	9	141	10	237	111	4,685		22	464
Pennsylvania	14,433	226,513	12	765	8,521	355,170	5,653	12,146	471,216
Rhode Island	1	4			29	1,156			
South Carolina	10	122			36	2,084		4	200
South Dakota	9	354	9	125	91	2,010		311	11,945
Tennessee	69	1,046	1	17	324	17,378	10	342	12,562
Texas	1,829	50,240	1	2	129	3,154		163	4,623
Utah	22	471	8	1,797	2,300	54,733	315	166	8,645
Vermont	3	32	7	1,571	696	19,109	20	26	664
Virginia	37	337	5	1,402	1,012	34,239		325	12,205
Washington	41	1,539	4	350	282	13,666	200	315	10,619
West Virginia	10,523	250,778			6,185	218,323	57	2,865	95,084
Wisconsin	16	458	6	275	500	19,062		14	1,080
Wyoming	238	7,661			355	13,940		108	4,474
Nonproducing enterprises	429	11,552	42	3,412	614	26,190	417	59	1,671